Longman Annotated English Poets

Published titles in the Annotated English Poets Series

General Editor: **F. W. Bateson**

Edmund Spenser

THE FAERIE QVEENE

Edited by A. C. Hamilton

General Editor of the Series: **F. W. Bateson**
Assisted on *The Faerie Queene* by **R. J. Manning**

Longman
London and New York

Acknowledgements

This book has been published with the help of a grant from the Humanities Research Council of Canada, using funds provided by the Canada Council.

The editor and the publishers also gratefully acknowledge the co-operation of Oxford University Press in granting permission to reproduce Spenser's 1596 text from J. C. Smith's *Faerie Queene* (Oxford English Texts edition 1909), published by the Oxford University Press and reprinted by permission of the publisher.

Longman Group Limited London

Associated companies, branches and representatives throughout the world

Published in the United States of America by Longman Inc., New York

This edition © Longman Group Limited 1977

First published 1977
First published in paperback with corrections 1980

British Library Cataloguing in Publication Data

Spenser, Edmund
  The faerie queene. – (Longman annotated English poets).

I. Title II. Hamilton, A C
821'.3   PR2358   79-41506

ISBN 0-582-49705-1

Printed in Singapore by
Singapore Offset Printing Pte. Ltd.

Contents

Dedication

To
The two women in my life
The two Marys
My mother and my wife

Preface

Since an annotator serves partly as a compiler, I am obliged and pleased to record my indebtedness to others: to the earlier critics whose studies, summarized in the Johns Hopkins Variorum Edition of Spenser's *Works*, laid the basis for the modern understanding of the poem, to the newer critics of the 1960s and to the younger critics of the 1970s. I am indebted also to those who have advised me on special problems or commented on draft annotations of a canto: Judith Anderson, Jane Aptekar, Thomas Cain, Donald Cheney, A. F. Falconer, Alastair Fowler, Kent Hieatt, Carol Kaske, Hugh MacLean, Waldo McNeir, Patrick Moore, William Nelson, Richard Neuse, James Nohrnberg, Ross Kilpatrick, Humphrey Tonkin, and the late Kathleen Williams.

The present version of annotations conflates two earlier versions. My initial problem was, and remains, the absence of any tradition of annotating the *Faerie Queene*. What Upton began so notably in his 1758 edition of the poem was only very inadequately supplemented by the spasmodic glossing in later editions and then diverted into variorum editions of general historical and critical commentary. At first I compiled the 'standard' set of annotations by glossing obsolete words, indicating major sources, and noting general scholarly background. To this end, I read nearly all the items listed in the Carpenter, Atkinson, and first edition of the McNeir bibliographies. Here I must thank the staff of the Harvard University Library who endured for several months my rifling through their collection of nineteenth-century periodicals. What I finally produced, however, was cluttered, fussy, and distracting: while that kind of annotation may serve other poets, it would not help the modern reader understand and enjoy Spenser's poem. I started afresh on a 'clean', philological set of annotations: I compiled glosses to the poem by looking up most of its words in the Oxford English Dictionary. By noting the sixteenth-century meanings of a word in the light of its context in the poem and its uses elsewhere in the poem, I became aware of Spenser's art of language. It became clear to me that the seventeenth-century Miltonic Spenser, that 'sage and serious teacher' needed to be supplemented, if not supplanted for a while, by an earlier Renaissance Spenser, that skilled craftsman in words. Since that also seemed clear to the more recent critics, I compiled a third set of annotations by investigating Spenser's art of language and noting its awareness by his modern readers. I have retained as much as I could of the earlier versions: the annotations include as much scholarly background as possible and the glosses – limited chiefly to obsolete senses – are all taken from the OED except where otherwise indicated.

Unfortunately, this final version had become bulkier than the poem. It was then that Mr Andrew MacLennan of Longman ingeniously reduced the costs of publishing by using J. C. Smith's 1909 Oxford edition of the poem. Also, he obtained the services of Mr R. J. Manning of The Queen's University of Belfast who read through what I had compiled with scrupulous care. Mr Manning's critical acumen, his thorough knowledge of the poem, and his sound judgment in proposing revisions, supplemented by my wife's suggestions, led to a much reduced and, I believe, considerably improved version.

Still, this edition would never have appeared but for the unwavering, militant support of the General Editor, F. W. Bateson, and the generous financial support of the Arts Research Committee of Queen's University and especially of the Humanities Research Council of Canada.

Since I draw upon my earlier studies on Spenser in the headnotes, I have included them in the Bibliography. In the General Introduction I use an essay on Spenser's art of language that first appeared in Kennedy and Reither (1973). In Frushell and Vondersmith (1975) I outline what I understand to be 'the philosophy of the footnote', which I seek to illustrate in the annotations.

A. C. Hamilton
Queen's University
Kingston, Canada

1552 Possibly 1553 or 1554, as conjectured from *Amor*. 60. Born in London, 'my most kyndly Nurse' (*Pro.*), perhaps East Smithfield. The family probably came from Lancashire (his father may have been a free journeyman in the Merchant Taylors' Company). S. claimed kinship with a 'house of auncient fame' (*Pro.*), the Spencers of Wormleighton in Warwickshire and of Althorp in Northamptonshire who were connected with the ancient baronial Despencers. He may have known the possible connection with William Langland whose father was *tenens domini le Spenser in comitatu Oxon* (a fifteenth-century note in a *Piers Plowman* MS, Trinity College, Dublin).

1561 Enters the newly-founded Merchant Taylors' School as a 'poor scholar', remaining for eight years. Headmaster: the classical scholar and educational propagandist Richard Mulcaster. Among fellow students: Thomas Kyd, Lancelot Andrewes and Thomas Lodge.

1569 *February.* Receives a gown and a shilling for representing the school at the funeral of Robert Nowell of Lancashire. Publishes anonymously translations of 'Visions by Petrarch' (from Marot's French version of Petrarch's 'Standomi un giorno solo a la fenestra') the first canzone translated into English, and 'Visions of Du Bellay' (from his 'Songe' in *Antiquitez de Rome*) as 'Epigrams' and 'Sonets' in *A Theatre wherein be represented as wel the miseries and calamities that follow the voluptuous Worldlings, As also the greate ioyes and plesures which the faithfull do enioy.* This apocalyptic and militantly anti-Catholic work was compiled by Jan van der Noodt, a Dutch Calvinist refugee living in London. It is the first emblem book printed in England. Later S. revised most of his translations to include them in *Complaints* (1591).
20 May. Admitted, with a grant of ten shillings, to Pembroke Hall, Cambridge, as a sizar (a poor, though not necessarily penniless, scholar given servant's duties). Friendship begins with Gabriel Harvey, Fellow of Pembroke from 1570.
18 October. Bill signed to one 'Edmonde Spencer' as bearer from Tours of letters from Sir Henry Norris, English ambassador to France, to the Queen.

1573 Graduated B.A., eleventh in a list of 120, perhaps not in order of merit.

1576 Awarded M.A., sixty-sixth in a list of seventy, surely not in order of merit. Since S. need not have remained in Cambridge during these years, he may have visited the 'Northparts', presumably the family home in Lancashire – where he had a love affair with 'Rosalind', as E.K. hints in the gloss to *S.C.* June – but returned south 'for his more preferment'.

1577 Possibly in Ireland in July. 'Irenius' (S. in *View of Ireland*) witnessed the execution of Murrogh O'Brien at Limerick in July. Otherwise nothing is known about him during these years.

1578 Secretary to John Young, Bishop of Rochester (Kent), former Master of Pembroke Hall.
20 December. With Harvey in London, presenting to him four 'foolish bookes' (*Howleglas*, *Scoggin*, *Skelton*, and *Lazarillo*) in exchange for four volumes of Lucian. Harvey describes him as a dandy ('young Italianate signor and French monsieur').

1579 Enters service of Earl of Leicester as a confidential emissary, later acknowledged that he gained from Leicester 'giftes and goodly grace' (*Pro.*).
5 October. Writes to Harvey from 'Leycester House' that he intends to devote his time 'to his Honours seruice', expecting imminently to be sent to France.
15–16 October. Writes to Harvey from Westminster that he is in 'some vse of familiarity' with Philip Sidney and Edward Dyer, discussing with them a classical reform of English metre that will bring 'a generall surceasing and silence of balde Rymers'. He alludes to an audience with the Queen. He intends to dedicate a work (presumably the *S.C.*) to Leicester but fears it may be 'too base for his excellent Lordship'.
27 October. An 'Edmounde Spenser' (probably the poet) marries Maccabaeus Chylde, aged twenty,

at St Margaret's, Westminster. Two children: Sylvanus (perhaps after Mulcaster's son) and Katherine.

Publication of *The Shepheardes Calender*. Entered Stationers' Register 5 December 1579. Prefatory Epistle by E.K. (possibly Edward Kirke of Pembroke but identification not certain) dated 10 April 1579. Signed 'Immerito' (the unworthy) and dedicated to Sidney. May have written some of *Hub.* at this time. He had started to compose the *F.Q.* (one parcel described by Harvey in April 1580 as '*Hobgoblin* runne away with the Garland from *Apollo*'). E.K. refers to some 'lost' works: *Dreames*, with commentary and illustrations, praised by Harvey for 'that singular extraordinarie veine and inuention' found in the best Greek and Italian writers, *Legendes*, *Court of Cupide* (perhaps revised in *F.Q.* III xi-xii, VI vii), a translation of Moschus's *Idyllion of Wandring Loue* (possibly from Politian's Latin version), *Pageaunts*, *The English Poete* (a critical treatise that would correspond to the second part of Sidney's *Apology for Poetry*), and *Sonnets*.

1580   Publication of correspondence with Harvey in a two-part volume: 1. *Three proper, and wittie, familiar Letters: lately passed betwene two Vniuersitie men: touching the Earthquake in April last, and our English reformed Versifying*, and 2. *Two other, very commendable Letters, of the same mens writing: both touching the foresaid Artificiall Versifying, and certain other Particulars*. The second volume contains earlier letters. S.'s two letters are dated from Leicester House, 5 October 1579 (including a letter of 15–16 October) and from Westminster, 'Quarto Nonas Aprilis 1580' (2 April, perhaps in error for 10 April). The correspondence mentions *F.Q.* for the first time and refers to a number of S.'s 'lost' works: *My Slomber*, *Dreames* (see under 1579), *Dying Pellicane* (most likely an allegory of the death of Christ), both being described by S. as 'fully finished', *Epithalamion Thamesis* ('whyche Booke I dare vndertake wil be very profitable for the knowledge, and rare for the Inuention, and manner of handling'; possibly revised in *F.Q.* IV xi), *Nine Comoedies*, named after the nine Muses (praised by Harvey for 'the finenesse of plausible Elocution' and 'the rarenesse of Poetical Inuention') and the Latin *Stemmata Dudleiana* – in praise of the Leicester family. The correspondence includes S.'s 'Iambicum Trimetrum' and two short fragments in which he applies quantitative classical metres to English versification.

Becomes a private secretary to Arthur Lord Grey de Wilton, newly appointed Lord Deputy of Ireland. Presumably arrives with him in Ireland on 12 August and lives in Dublin Castle. Salary £10 half-yearly.

November. Evidently present at the siege of Smerwick, in Munster. Grey's massacre of the invading Spanish and Italian forces contributed to his recall to England in 1582, and the end to S.'s secretaryship. Ireland now becomes his home.

1581   *The Shepheardes Calender*, second edition.

March. Appointed as registrar or clerk of Faculties in the Irish Court of Chancery, for seven years. A deputy may have carried out the duties of this post, which was to record 'faculties' (dispensations and licences) issued by the Archbishop of Dublin.

6 December. Leases the Abbey and Manor of Enniscorthy, in County Wexford; evidently forfeited almost immediately. About this time he leases New Ross, a dissolved Augustinian friary, also in County Wexford; held until 1584.

1582   Leases a house in Dublin at £3 annual rent, also the House of Friars, called New Abbey, Kilcullen (County Kildare), twenty-five miles from Dublin. S. is now accorded the rank of a landed gentleman.

1583   Appointed a commissioner for musters in County Kildare for two years.

1584   About this time becomes deputy to the Clerk of the Council of Munster, Lodowick Bryskett, who records their conversations in *A Discourse of Civill Life* (1606): see General Introduction. Other literary friends in Dublin: Geoffrey Fenton, Barnaby Googe, and Barnaby Riche.

1585   Prebendary of Effin, attached to Limerick Cathedral. Probably a benefice received without active duties.

1586   *The Shepheardes Calender*, third edition.
18 July. Sonnet to Harvey, dated from Dublin. Published in Harvey's *Foure Letters* (1592).

1588   Now, or a little later, occupies the ruined castle of Kilcolman, County Cork, with an estate of over 3,000 acres, from the forfeited lands of the Irish rebel, the Earl of Desmond. First assigned to him in 1586, the grant for possession 'for ever, in fee farm' issued on 26 October 1590, about £20 annual rent. S. established an English colony of six householders with their families.

    Abraham Fraunce, *Arcadian Rhetorike*, quotes *F.Q.* II iv 35, citing the proper Book and Canto. The first to name S. author of *S.C.* That the poem was circulating in manuscript is also shown by Marlowe's borrowings in *2 Tamburlaine* (1590, written about 1587).

1589   Visit of Raleigh, living on a large estate near Kilcolman, as S. records in *Col.*
October. Leaving a substitute deputy, journeys with Raleigh to England. He was granted an audience by the Queen who took delight in the *F.Q.* 'and it desir'd at timely houres to heare'.
1 December. Entry in Stationers' Register: 'a booke intytuled *the fayrye Queene dysposed into xii. bookes. Etc*'.

    Beginning of extended law suits with the loyal Anglo-Irish Lord Roche.

1590   Publication of *The Faerie Queene* Books I–III. S.'s appended 'Letter to Raleigh' dated 23 January 1589 (1590 N.S.). Commendatory poems by Raleigh and others. The ten dedicatory sonnets to leading noble families in England increased to seventeen in later copies. Since S. dedicates the poem to the Queen, he may have presented a copy to her.
May. May have returned briefly to Ireland to handle litigation with Lord Roche.

1591   Publication of a volume of nine poems, some written much earlier, under the title: *Complaints: containing sundrie small Poemes of the Worlds Vanitie*, 'being all complaints and meditations of the worlds vanitie, verie graue and profitable' (*The Ruines of Time, The Teares of the Muses, Virgils Gnat* (a version of the pseudo-Virgilian *Culex*), *Prosopopoia* or *Mother Hubberds Tale, The Ruines of Rome: by Bellay* (trans. from the *Antiquitez de Rome*), *Muiopotmos: or the Fate of the Butterflie* (dated 1590), *Visions of the Worlds Vanitie*, and also *The Visions of Bellay* and *The Visions of Petrarch: formerly translated* (revised from van der Noodt's *Theatre*, 1569). Satirical attack in *Hub.* apparently against William Cecil, Lord Burghley, noted by Harvey: 'Mother Hubbard in heat of choller, forgetting the pure sanguine of her sweete Faery Queene, wilfully ouer-shott her malcontented selfe'. This may have led to the volume, or some part of it, being suppressed. The publisher, Ponsonby, expressed his desire to publish other poems by S.: '*Ecclesiastes*, and *Canticum canticorum* translated, *A senights slumber* [cf. *My Slomber*, under 1580], *The hell of louers, his Purgatorie*, ... *The dying Pellican* [see under 1580], *The howers of the Lord, The sacrifice of a sinner, The seuen Psalmes* [cf. *Petrarch's seven penitentiall psalmes*, trans. Chapman 1612]'. None has survived.

    The Shepheardes Calender, fourth edition.

    Publication of *Daphnaida, An Elegie upon the death of the noble and vertuous Douglas Howard, Daughter of Lord Howard and wife of Arthure Gorges*. Dated from London 1 January 1591 (1592 N.S.). An imitation of Chaucer's *Book of the Duchess*.

25 February. Granted a life pension of £50 a year by the Queen. Returns to Ireland to resume his office as deputy clerk (or clerk?) but about this time acquires an assistant to perform his duties.

1592   Publication of the pseudo-Platonic *Axiochus. A most excellent Dialogue, written in Greeke by Plato* *the Phylosopher, trans. by Edw. Spenser.* From a Latin translation and not certainly (certainly not?) by S.

1594   *11 June, St Barnabas' Day.* Marriage to Elizabeth Boyle, kinswoman to Sir Richard Boyle, later first Earl of Cork. Their one child is named Peregrine ('Lat. Strange or outlandish', Camden [1605] 93, who includes it in a list of usual Christian names). The courtship and marriage recorded in *Amoretti* and *Epithalamion*, 1595 (entered Stationers' Register 19 November 1594, 'written not long since'). In Sonnet 80 S. writes that he has completed the six books of the *F.Q.*

Serves as Queen's Justice for County Cork.

1595   Publication of *Amoretti* together with *Epithalamion* as a single volume.

Publication of *Colin Clouts Come Home Againe*. Dated from Kilcolman, 27 December 1591 and dedicated to Raleigh: 'this simple pastorall . . . agreeing with the truth in circumstance and matter' records Raleigh's visit, their voyage to England, and stay at court. The composite volume includes *Astrophel. A Pastorall Elegie upon the death of the most Noble and valorous Knight, Sir Philip Sidney*, and six other elegies on Sidney's death by Bryskett and others.

Commendatory sonnet to William Jones's English trans. of *Nennio, or a Treatise of Nobility*.

1596   Publication of second edition of *The Faerie Queene* Books I–III together with first edition of Books IV–VI. Registered 20 January. S. may have been in England to supervise printing.

Publication of *Fowre Hymnes* (*Of Love, Of Beautie, Of Heavenly Love, Of Heavenly Beautie*), the first two written 'in the greener times of my youth'. Dedicated from the court at Greenwich, 1 September. This volume includes *Daphnaida*, second edition.

Publication of *Prothalamion*, spousal verse celebrating the betrothal of the two eldest daughters of the Earl of Worcester.

Commendatory sonnet to de La Vardin, *History of George Castriot, surnamed Scanderbeg*, trans. by Z.I. (Zachary Jones).

12 November. Complaint by King James of Scotland that his mother was slandered as Duessa in *F.Q.* V ix: 'some dishonourable effects, as the King deemeth, against himself and his mother deceased . . . he still desireth that Edmund Spenser, for his fault, may be duly tried and punished'. No action is known to have been taken despite a renewed complaint.

1597   *The Shepheardes Calender*, fifth edition.

Purchases the castle and lands of Renny in south Cork for his son Peregrine. Also about this time purchases Buttevant Abbey.

1598   *14 April.* Entry in Stationers' Register: *A viewe of the present state of Ireland. Discoursed by waye of a Dialogue betwene Eudoxus and Irenius.* Probably written in 1596; circulating in MS but not published until 1633.

Sheriff-designate of Cork, recommended as 'a gentleman dwelling in the county of Cork, who is so well known unto your lordships for his good and commendable parts (being a man endowed with good knowledge in learning and not unskilful or without experience in the service of the wars)'. *October.* The castle of Kilcolman sacked and burned by Irish rebels during Tyrone's rebellion. With his wife takes refuge in Cork.

9 December. Leaves for London and delivers despatches from the governor of Munster to the Privy Council on Christmas Eve. Also delivers his own views on behalf of the refugees: *A briefe note of Ireland*, which includes an address to the Queen and 'Certaine pointes to be considered of in the recouery of the Realme of Ireland'.

Jonson told Drummond 'that the Irish having robbed Spenser's goods and burnt his house and a little child new born [the poet's?], he and his wife escaped [to England?], and after, he died for lack of bread in King Street'.

1599   Commendatory sonnet to Gasper Contareno, *The Commonwealth and Government of Venice*, trans. L. Lewkenor.

13 January. Dies in Westminster. Jonson's assertion that he died 'for lack of bread', though supported by Camden, does not accord with the £8 he was paid on 30 December 1598 and the fact that a pension of £25 was due at Christmas. Buried in Westminster Abbey; as Camden records, 'near to Chaucer, at the charge of the Earl of Essex, his hearse being attended by poets, and mournful elegies and poems, with the pens that wrote them, thrown into the tomb'. The Queen's order that a memorial be erected was not carried out.

1609   First folio edition of *The Faerie Queene* Books I–VI, together with first edition of the 'Cantos of Mutabilitie'.

1611   First folio edition of the collected works: *The Faerie Queene: The Shepheardes Calender: Together with the other Works of England's Arch-Poet, Edm. Spenser*.

1617   Second folio edition of the collected works.

1620   Funeral memorial erected in the Abbey to 'the Prince of Poets in his tyme'. Restored in marble 1778, and still in place.

1633   Publication of *A View of the State of Ireland* ed. Sir James Ware. In the Preface, Ware refers to 'the later part' of the *F.Q.* lost by a servant.

1679   Publication of *The Works of that Famous English Poet, Mr. Edmond Spenser*.

The facts concerning S.'s life are collected in F. I. Carpenter, *Reference Guide* (Chicago 1923). The standard biography is by A. C. Judson, vol. 11 (Baltimore 1945) of the Johns Hopkins Variorum Edition of S.'s Works. The paucity of our knowledge is noted by Conyers Read: 'Outside of what Edmund Spenser himself wrote all that is positively known about his life could probably be written in a few short paragraphs. The rest is inference, surmise, and conjecture' (*American Historical Review* 51 [1946] 539).

Abbreviations

Spenser's poems

Amor. Amoretti
Col. Colin Clouts Come Home Againe
Daph. Daphnaida
Epith. Epithalamion
F.Q. *The Faerie Queene*
Gn. Virgils Gnat
H.B. An hymne in honour of beautie
H.L. An hymne in honour of love
H.H.B. An hymne of heavenly beautie
H.H.L. An hymne of heavenly love
Hub. Prosopopoia: or Mother Hubberds Tale
L.R. Letter to Raleigh
Pro. Prothalamion
S.C. The Shepheardes Calender
T.M. The Teares of the Muses
Van. Visions of the worlds vanitie

Periodicals

Camb J Cambridge Journal
CL Comparative Literature
EIC Essays in Criticism
ELH Journal of English Literary History
Eng. Misc. English Miscellany (Rome)
ELN English Language Notes
ELR English Literary Renaissance
E & S Essays and Studies
Expl Explicator
HLQ Huntington Library Quarterly
JEGP Journal of English and Germanic Philology
JWCI Journal of the Warburg & Courtauld Institutes
MLN Modern Language Notes
MLQ Modern Language Quarterly
MLR Modern Language Review
MP Modern Philology
N & Q Notes and Queries
NM Neuphilologische Mitteilungen
NS Die Neueren Sprachen
PLL Papers on Language and Literature (Illinois)
PMLA Publications of the Modern Language Association of America
PQ Philological Quarterly
Ren. N Renaissance News
Ren. Q Renaissance Quarterly
RES Review of English Studies
SB Studies in Bibliography
SEL Studies in English Literature, 1500–1900
S. News Spenser Newsletter
SP Studies in Philology
SQ Shakespeare Quarterly
S. Ren. Studies in the Renaissance
TLS Times Literary Supplement
TSE Texas Studies in English
TSLL Texas Studies in Literature and Language
UTQ University of Toronto Quarterly

THE FAERIE QVEENE

History of the text

Without either earlier drafts or manuscripts of *The Faerie Queene*, what we know of its composition is limited to a few facts. That S. intended to write a heroic poem is indicated by *The Shepheardes Calender*, 1579. In the Dedicatory Epistle, E.K. observes that 'our new Poete' follows the example of the best ancient poets, such as Virgil, in writing a pastoral poem to test his abilities 'as young birdes, that be newly crept out of the nest, by little first to proue theyr tender wyngs, before they make a greater flyght'. In the October Eclogue, Cuddie, 'the perfecte paterne of a Poete', is urged to move the wills of lawless youth by abandoning his humble pastoral disguise to 'sing of bloody Mars, of wars, of giusts', whether in praise of 'fayre *Elisa*' or her 'worthy . . . That first the white beare to the stake did bring'. As in response, the opening stanza of *The Faerie Queene* announces that the new poet has thrown off his shepherd's weeds: the sacred Muse instructs him 'To blazon broad emongst her learned throng: / Fierce warres and faithfull loues shall moralize my song'. Praise of Elizabeth as the source of virtue becomes the point of departure in each Book, and praise of her 'worthy' is treated in Arthur's heroic actions while seeking the Faerie Queene.

The poem is first mentioned by name in S.'s letter to Gabriel Harvey in April 1580, in which he says that he 'wil in hande forthwith with my *Faery Queene*, whyche I praye you hartily send me with al expedition: and your frendly Letters, and long expected Iudgement wythal'. 'Long expected' suggests that the poem was begun not later than 1579. When Harvey returned the manuscript at long last, he offered a puzzling judgment in the course of remarking that S.'s 'Eluish Queene' seeks to overgo Ariosto's *Orlando Furioso*: 'If so be the *Faerye Queene* be fairer in your eie than the *Nine Muses*, and *Hobgoblin* runne away with the Garland from *Apollo*: Marke what I saye, and yet I wil not say that I thought, but there an End for this once'. Since we do not know what parcel of the poem he read, we may only surmise that it was not Book I, for its religious argument would hardly merit this response, especially as that Book imitates the Revelation of St John which Harvey extols in the same letter as a 'Poetical Vision'. On the other hand, his judgment would be an apt response to S.'s choice of the popular legend of St George for the story of Book I, and to his use of Chaucer's absurdly comic tale of Sir Thopas for the unifying story of Arthur's love for the Faerie Queene (see I ix 13.7–9*n*).

From the dedicatory sonnet to the 1590 edition in which S. refers to his poem as 'wilde fruit, which saluage soyl hath bred', one may infer that most of the first three books were written after 1580 when he settled in Ireland. Lodowick Bryskett in his *Discourse of Civill Life* (published in 1606 but probably written, as he claims, in 1582 and later revised) purports to recount (21–2) a meeting of friends in his home near Dublin during which S. as one 'very well read in Philosophie, both morall and naturall' was called upon to speak. He declined because all there knew that 'I have already undertaken a work tending to the same effect, which is in *heroical verse*, under the title of a *Faerie Queene*, to represent all the moral vertues, assigning to every vertue, a Knight to be the patron and defender of the same: in whose actions and feates of armes and chivalry, the operations of that vertue, whereof he is the protector, are to be expressed, and the vices and unruly appetites that oppose themselves against the same, to be beaten downe and overcome'. He adds that he has 'already well entred into' the poem and intends to finish it 'according to my mind'.

Some parts of the poem were circulating in manuscript in Dublin: Bryskett remarks that his company 'shewed an extreme longing after his worke of the *Faerie Queene*, whereof some parcels had bin by some of them seene'. Some parts were also circulating in London for Abraham Fraunce cites II iv 35 in *Arcadian Rhetorike* (1588). Since he names the Book and Canto, the poem must have been organized in its final form at least to this point. There is also Marlowe's flagrant imitation of I vii 32 (see *n* and also I viii 11.5–9*n*) in *II Tamburlaine* (dated 1590 but possibly written in 1587).

For the second part of the poem, one certain evidence of the date of composition is the Burbon episode in V xi: its historical basis, the French Henry IV's recantation of Protestantism, dates it later than July 1593. The dislocation of the arguments to V xi and xii suggests that the episode was inserted after the Book was disposed into cantos. In *Amoretti* 33, S. confesses to Bryskett that he was wrong not to finish his poem, and adds that 'th'accomplishment of it / [is] sufficient worke for one mans simple head, / all were it as the rest but rudely writ'. In Sonnet 80 he refers to the poem of six books as 'halfe fordonne'; after rest, 'out of my prison I will breake anew: / and stoutly will that second worke assoyle, / with strong endeuour and attention dew'. Evidently at this time (1594; see Chronology), he planned a poem of twelve books, as the title indicates, rather than the twenty-four projected in the *L.R.*

Why this plan was not carried out is not known; possibly his increasingly troubled life leading to his death a few years later is a sufficient explanation. Some recent critics suggest that S. could not continue after completing Book VI. Berger (1961) argues that his imagination was no longer able to shape reality into the ideal images of antiquity. Neuse (1968) claims that Book VI concludes the poem because S. came to recognize that 'the potential ideal which his epic was designed to embody has been defeated by a world hopelessly antagonistic to its realization'. Craig (1972) notes S.'s increasing inability to integrate historical myth and reality. On the other hand, S. may have realized that the poem was essentially complete in its present form. Frye (1963) 70 assumes that 'the six books we have form a unified epic structure, regardless of how much might have been added that wasn't', and Fowler (1964) argues that the six books together with the *Mutabilitie Cantos* suggest a formal structure based on the sequence of planetary deities associated with the seven days of the week. Most readers find it difficult to allow that the poem could be extended beyond its concluding prayer (see headnote to the *Mutabilitie Cantos*).

The few facts cited above provide a very uncertain foundation upon which to erect hypothetical earlier versions of the poem, and all efforts to do so build castles in air upon surmise, supposition and speculation. Nevertheless, Spens (1934) claims that the seven deadly sins, rather than the twelve virtues, provided an earlier scheme of eight books each of eight cantos: the first seven books showed Arthur's triumph over the sins while the eighth book showed his reward. Walter (1941) uses internal 'inconsistencies' in the narrative as evidence of alteration and revision, and relates the books to the months of the year. Bennett (1942) seeks to reconstruct the actual process of composition episode by episode. Instead of recognizing that S. varied his allegorical method and technique according to the nature of the virtue he treats in each book, she argues that he changed his plans while writing. The dearth of evidence upon which to reconstruct an earlier version of the poem is pointed out by Owen (1953). Hough (1962) 83 observes: 'The fact is that we do not *know* anything about the order of composition, or the possible existence of an earlier scheme, and there is no means by which we can know.' The decisive reply to all speculations about construction of the poem is provided by recent critics, all of whom recognize the poem's extraordinarily unified structure. The one critical 'fact' which matters is that, the more fully we understand *The Faerie Queene*, the more clearly we see the essential rightness of each part in the present order. Failure to understand the poem we have provides no basis for reconstructing a poem we do not have.

On the other hand, seriatim composition need not be assumed, especially for an extended and comprehensive work written over more than sixteen years. By their titles – see *Chronology* under 1579, 1580, 1591 – one may surmise that some earlier 'lost' works were absorbed into the one great poem designed to be S.'s life-work. That a poem composed over a long period could absorb earlier fragments (if it did) yet remain unified (as it is) argues for some plan which would allow piecemeal construction. It is almost startling to find that, if one disregards obvious slips of the pen, there is only one narrative break in the entire poem (see VI iii 34.1–2n). In demonstrating the unity of Books III and IV, Roche (1964) 196 observes that 'in formal analysis arrangement of material is as important as the writing of it', and does not allow Bennett's (1942) hypothesizing 'any relevance to the problem of the final disposition of the poem'. Although the origins of a work may interest post-Darwinians, S.'s poem needs to be seen from the perspective of a Renaissance concern with its end and working, specifically in the light of Sidney's comment in the *Apology* 101 that 'any understanding knoweth the skill of the artificer standeth in that *Idea* or foreconceit of the work, and not in the work itself'. The presence of this 'Idea' allows Williams (1952) to claim rightly that 'from the first book to the fragmentary seventh the reader becomes increasingly aware of a clear and comprehensive vision, and of a steady purpose which impels him, through a mass of significant detail, towards a final unity' (115).

Whatever the process of composition, the first three books of *The Faerie Queene* were published in 1590 in a solid, fat quarto which is a delight even to hold, with the Letter to Raleigh appended 'for that it giueth great light to the Reader, for the better vnderstanding'. While the division of the poem is awkward because Books III and IV seem to compose a single book of twenty-four cantos, the first three books form a triad of the private moral virtues which properly stands alone. When Books IV–VI were added in the 1596 edition, the rapturously erotic concluding stanzas of Book III were cancelled to allow the story of Scudamour and Amoret to be continued, and the Letter was omitted presumably because the six books give sufficient light to the reader, or possibly because Raleigh was out of royal favour (see IV vii 36.8–9*n*). The folio edition of 1609 appended to the six books the *Mutabilitie Cantos* 'which, both for Forme and Matter, appeare to be parcell of some following Booke of the *Faerie Queene*, Vnder the Legend of *Constancie*' (see headnote). The entire poem appeared again in the first folio of the collected works in 1611, and then in 1617 and 1679. In 1715 it was edited by J. Hughes in modernized spelling with brief glosses, and in 1751 by T. Birch. In 1758 it was edited by R. Church with brief annotations, and in the same year by J. Upton 'with a glossary, and notes explanatory and critical' of some 300 pages. The first variorum edition by H. J. Todd in 1805 is useful chiefly for Upton's notes. A briefly annotated edition of the whole poem was produced by K. M. Warren in 1897–1900. Beginning in the nineteenth century, separate books were edited with notes for school-children. The most valuable are editions of Books I (1867) and II (2nd edn, 1872) by G. W. Kitchin and of Book I by H. M. Percival (1893), all with expurgated texts, and notes that tended to be heavily philological; Book V by A. B. Gough (1918), Book II by L. Winstanley (1914), and Book VI by T. A. Wolff (1959). The Oxford edition edited by J. C. Smith (1909) established a sound text by collating the first two quartos and the first folio. The same text appeared in the Oxford edition of S.'s poetical works edited by J. C. Smith and E. de Selincourt (1912) with a glossary by H. Alexander and is followed also in the present volume.

The Johns Hopkins *Variorum* edition of S.'s collected works edited by E. Greenlaw, C. G. Osgood, F. M. Padelford *et al* (10 vols, 1932–49, cited as *Var.*) sought 'to furnish an accurate text of Spenser's poetry and prose and to make accessible in convenient form the fruits of all the significant scholarship and literary criticism which have contributed to the better understanding and appreciation of this major poet'. The first six volumes established an accurate text of the *Faerie Queene* and extracted the best of the critical commentary, scholarship on sources, and general historical background. By what seems to have been deliberate editorial policy, annotation and glossing were omitted unless they involved critical cruxes or source study. Recently a number of selected editions have appeared, usually including Book I and extracts from the later books accompanied by notes and glosses, the most fully annotated being a modern spelling edition of Books I and II and the *Mutabilitie Cantos* by R. Kellogg and O. Steele (1965). What is lacking, and what the present edition seeks to supply, is a thorough annotation of the whole poem which uses the scholarship and criticism of the past twenty years. Hankins (1971) observes that 'the 1960s will be remembered as a great period of Spenser scholarship'. Along with such scholarship, but prior to it, the modern reader needs an annotated edition of the poem to help clarify his immediate response to what he reads. The assumption behind the present edition is that only by understanding precisely and fully each detail of the poem in the context of the whole poem may we understand the allegory.

Sources

The poem's full title, *The Faerie Queene. Disposed into twelue bookes, Fashioning XII Morall vertues*, directs the reader to the images of the virtues which the poem presents. These twelve virtues are said in the *L.R.* to be such 'as Aristotle hath deuised'. S.'s primary source of the virtues would seem, then, to be the

Nicomachean Ethics. Earlier efforts to use the *Ethics* as gloss on the poem are summarized in the *Variorum*. Padelford, *Var.* i 342, concludes, however, that S. would not feel himself bound 'to an unquestioning acceptance of Aristotle's exact list of virtues'. Holiness is a Christian virtue, not pagan, though 'virtue' is hardly a fit term since man's proper relationship to God requires him to recognize that he has no virtue in himself. More properly, it is the bedrock upon which all virtues may be founded. Again, Temperance is closer to Aristotle's Continence than to his Temperance, and even in the earlier cantos of Book II the virtue is more Platonic than Aristotelian. Accordingly, efforts have been made to find a gloss for the virtues in Plato, or in a Christian blend of Aristotelian and Platonic traditions in the Middle Ages. Tuve (1966) outlines the comprehensive medieval background to S.'s scheme of the virtues, specifically the traditions inherited from Aristotle, Seneca, Cicero, and Macrobius, and then transformed in the Christian Middle Ages. While Hankins (1971) has claimed that Francesco Piccolomini's *Vniversa Philosophia de Moribus* (1583) is the major source for S.'s virtues, most critics agree that S. draws his virtues from a wide background, classical and Christian, erudite and popular.

Study of the sources of the virtues helps us understand the poem because it centres our attention upon the virtues themselves. The subject of each Book is not biography, or psychological analysis, or the exploration of archetypes, but a virtue. As Tuve (1966) 369–70 notes, 'the sought virtue is the unifying factor in *every* Book': 'the unifying principle is not the *history* of a particular or an individual; the action is not a biography, a life, but an action'. Nelson (1963) 122 observes that when S. writes in the concluding canto of Book II, 'Now gins this goodly frame of Temperance / Fairely to rise', 'he is saying that he has portrayed the virtue itself, not the growth of that virtue in its champion'. Also, study of the virtues clarifies S.'s conception of them, apart from the tradition which he inherits. For one must allow his claim that the virtues and vices have been reversed since the Golden Age: 'For that which all men then did vertue call, / Is now cald vice; and that which vice was hight, / Is now hight vertue' (V Pr 4.1–3).

Study of the virtues also clarifies the relationships among the virtues established by the ordering of the Books. Frye (1963) 75 finds a Hegelian progression of thesis, antithesis, and synthesis in Books I-III and Books IV-VI. Fowler (1973) analyses various neoplatonic triads which link the three books of Part I and the three books of Part II. The nature of each virtue requires S. to vary his allegorical method. In Book I, the Red Cross Knight is the patron of Holiness, for in his person he is chosen by God and must so remain despite his sinful acts. In Book II, Temperance measures Guyon's actions as it exists apart from his person. Book III relates the first two Books as Britomart manifests the virtue of Chastity in her person and all her actions. In Part II there is a similar structuring of the virtues. Presumably the virtue of Constancy in Book VII would treat the fidelity which belongs to all the virtues and is expressed in the commitment and perseverance of the titular heroes. As such, it would be linked to the virtue of Magnificence which S. describes in the *L.R.* as 'the perfection of all the rest, and conteineth in it them all', and which the medieval tradition identified with perseverance. Such relationships among the virtues need to be explored for they determine the structure of the whole poem. S.'s chief purpose is to reveal the images of the virtues in that 'goodly golden chaine' which links man to God.

The literary tradition within which S. reveals the pattern of the virtues is outlined in the *L.R.* In showing Arthur as a knight who contains the perfection of all the virtues, S. claims to follow 'all the antique Poets historicall'. The studies summarized in the *Variorum* volumes justify his high claim. By adapting the heroic tradition to his own purposes, and going beyond it, he becomes both the English Homer and the English Virgil, and also fulfils the desire, expressed to Harvey, to outdo Ariosto. While S.'s relation to Homer has not been studied separately, his relation to Virgil is treated by Hughes (1929). Bush (1932: rev. 1963) examines his use of Homer, Virgil, and Ovid in his handling of myth; Webb (1937) shows Virgil's contribution to S.'s epic theory; and Nelson (1963) 297–302 shows how Ovid provides the literary model for the *Mutabilitie Cantos*. Tillyard (1954) treats the *Faerie Queene* in general terms as epic; Greene (1963) examines S.'s use of one epic convention, the descent of a god or angel. Lewis (1954) 380 describes

5

S.'s poem as a fusion of 'the medieval allegory and the more recent romantic epic of the Italians'. In *The Allegory of Love* (1936), he relates the poem to medieval allegory, as does Tuve (1966) more comprehensively. In addition to earlier source studies (listed in *Var.* i), the relation of the poem to Italian epic has been examined by Arthos (1956), Hough (1962), Kostić (1959), Durling (1965), Cheney (1966), and Alpers (1967). S.'s use of a romance motif, the moment of vision or revelation which transforms magic into miracle, has been examined by Giamatti (1971).

   The native tradition within which S. wrote has been neglected despite his claim in the concluding lines of *The Shepheardes Calender* that he intends to follow 'Tityrus' and 'the Pilgrim that the Ploughman playde a whyle', that is, Chaucer and Langland. Bennett (1952) 124 states that S. 'owes more to Langland and the Ploughman literature of early English Protestantism than has been generally recognized'. I examine the relation between *Piers Plowman* and the *F.Q.* in Hamilton (1958/1961), and so does J. Anderson (1976). S.'s relation to Chaucer – especially important because S. believed that his soul was inhabited by Chaucer's (see IV ii 34) – and to Milton – equally important because Milton believed that S. was his 'original' – is examined by Hieatt (1975) and Miskimin (1975). Crampton (1974) provides a study of suffering and action in S. and Chaucer. Cullen (1974) examines the flesh, the world, and the devil in S. and Milton. S.'s possible relation to the Arthurian traditions and medieval romance, particularly Malory, has not been seriously investigated except by Tuve (1966) chap. 5. His relation to Shakespeare is treated by Watkins (1950) and Potts (1958).

Criticism

Changing literary taste in the early twentieth century, which rejected Milton, did not affect S.: he was simply ignored. T. S. Eliot (1932) 443 asked, though only rhetorically: 'Who, except scholars, and except the eccentric few who are born with a sympathy for such work, or others who have deliberately studied themselves into the right appreciation, can now read through the whole of *The Faerie Queene* with delight?' Among the scholars there were such staunch defenders as W. L. Renwick, B. E. C. Davis and L. Bradner (see Bibliography). In our time the poem has enjoyed a strong champion on each side of the Atlantic. In England, C. S. Lewis treats S. in the culminating chapter of his influential *Allegory of Love* (1936), in the central chapter of his *Oxford History of English Literature in the Sixteenth Century* (1954), in *Studies in Medieval and Renaissance Literature* (1966), and in *Spenser's Images of Life* (1967). In America, Rosemond Tuve's *Elizabethan and Metaphysical Imagery* (1947) has been equally influential in upholding the poetic by which S. wrote; seven essays on S., written between 1929 and 1964, are included in her *Essays*, ed. T. P. Roche, jr (1970), and her posthumously published *Allegorical Imagery* (1966) places S. as the inheritor of medieval allegory.

   With the revival of interest by scholars that culminated in *Var.*, S. was defended in Milton's terms as 'our sage and serious Poet . . . a better teacher than *Scotus* or *Aquinas*'. *The Faerie Queene* was related to an extended background of religious and philosophical thought, Christian doctrine, and historical event. The scope and achievement of such scholarly endeavour is indicated by Woodhouse (1965) in his summary of the poem's sources:

> There is scarcely a genre that it does not involve or draw upon – epic narrative, chivalric quest, the whole range of allegorical poetry as the Middle Ages had developed it, not to mention pastoral idyll, emblem, interlude, and masque. And within its ample confines it gathers up all the principal elements of the Elizabethan cultural inheritance: the wealth of Greek and Roman philosophy, poetry, and myth, mediated through the classical Renaissance; the treasure of the Christian tradition, mediated through the Reformation; the inheritance of medieval chivalry and romance – that entrancing and impossible world of love and adventure, which forms the staple of Spenser's narrative on the literal level, but whose values he corrects by the generous Renaissance ideal of the

gentleman . . . All these things *The Faerie Queene* assembles and in measure co-ordinates. (21) When S.'s poem was first read in relation to this background, it was tempting to establish a one-to-one correspondence. The allegory was interpreted by translating the literal level into various levels of meaning, chiefly moral and historical. Characters in the poem were identified as moral abstractions, and their actions as illustrations of moral concepts or historical events. In the post-*Variorum* period of S. criticism, Berger (1957) was the first to protest against the use of non-poetic formulas to provide the meaning of a character and so justify the allegory, for 'the problem is not to make modern readers respond to the poem in one manner rather than in another; the problem is to get them to read the poem, and then to read the poem Spenser wrote rather than the poem sponsored by the editors of the *Variorum*' (201). In *Structure* (1961) I protest against any translation of the poetic image into moral concept and historical event on the grounds that such reading destroys the literal surface upon which all our response depends. My thesis is simply that we should read the literal surface in its depth in order that our delight may deepen into understanding. Others make the same point. Roche (1964) 31 writes: 'We cannot restrict ourselves to a sterile hunt for one-to-one relationships. There is no single meaning, at least no single meaning to be stated apart from the experience of the poem.' Tuve (1966) 370 argues that the reader of the poem must 'claim whole images with all their depicted feelings as the sole true statements of his [S.'s] allegorical meanings', and therefore stresses the poem's fiction: 'The notion of levels, unfortunately now a critical cliché, has served us very ill, for the connection is always open between the literal and the shadowed deeper meaning. The apprehension of both is simultaneous, and the movement should be vertically free – if we must make do with a spatial image' (413). Alpers (1967) offers the most vigorous defence of reading the poem by responding to the literal surface rather than by abstracting allegorical levels of meaning. He argues at length that in reading the poem 'one apprehends the depths only by staying on the surface' (157).

Coleridge's claim that 'no man can appreciate Spenser without some reflection on the nature of allegorical writing' is substantiated by recent critics of the *Faerie Queene*. Most have been forced to consider problems of interpretation, in particular, the problem of relating the poem's sensuous assault upon the reader to its intellectual content. From what records we have, S.'s contemporary readers responded to the morality or to the 'fancy', or to both. Thus R. Zouche, *The Dove* (1613) refers to S. as 'having . . . delivered Morall, and Heroicall matter for use and action' (*Spenser Allusions* 134), and Henry More refers to the *Faerie Queene* as 'a Poem richly fraught within divine Morality as Phansy' (ψυχωδια *Platonica* 1642, *Spenser Allusions* 210). In the nineteenth century the fancy was stressed and the morality ignored. The reading that followed was inadequate because S.'s allegory intensifies the delight and teaching, which all poetry affords, to the point at which the two seem to conflict. Hence James Russell Lowell's celebrated essay on S. as the poet of beauty and delight (1875) provoked Edward Dowden's essay, 'Spenser, the poet and teacher' (1882). Yeats (1906) xxiv, xxx remarks on the shadows of 'a joyless earnestness' in S.'s allegory, in opposition to the 'poet of the delighted senses'. Saunders (1952) 102 remarks that 'it is the *moral* purpose which becomes tedious and enervating to him [S.], and it is to his sensuous Fairyland that he clings as his real source of pleasure and inspiration'.

In recent criticism, the nature of the teaching has been clarified. Now it is generally allowed that there is no direct, one-to-one correspondence to an external reality through which the allegory acquires meaning but instead a complex allusiveness to external reality only through the poem's network of images. Roche (1964) 31 writes: 'Allegory, as I read it, is not trying to present clear and distinct speculations about philosophical niceties. There is no single object to receive the entire energy of the vehicle; there are always complexes of large and simple ideas, which are illuminated and realigned'. Cheney (1966) 7 writes: 'In speaking of Spenser's "allegory" . . . I would point to a multiplicity of meaning, not to any supposed otherness of reference'. Williams (1966) xvi–xvii claims that allegory in the *Faerie Queene* 'functions as a structural principle, working primarily towards the relating together of the various parts of the Spenserian poetic world rather than towards the attaching of that world to a series of abstract concepts outside it'. What still remains unclear is the nature of the pleasure which the poem provides, and the relation of this pleasure to its meaning.

S.'s allegory has profited from the general rehabilitation of allegory as a genre, in such works as E. Honig's *Dark Conceit: the making of allegory* (1959), A. Fletcher's *Allegory: the theory of a symbolic mode* (1964), and especially Northrop Frye's *Anatomy of Criticism* (1957). We recognize now that the poem contains many kinds of allegory. Hough (1962) 111 uses Frye's theory of symbols to argue that S.'s allegory extends 'from hieratic symbolism through naïve allegory, allegory proper and the romance of types to the freestyle allegory where thematic significance is picked up and dropped at will'. Modern criticism is beginning to realize just how right Lewis (1967) 1 was to call the *Faerie Queene* 'perhaps the most difficult poem in English'.

Modern criticism

The Faerie Queene accommodates many kinds of readers. No genuine response to the poem is ever entirely wrong, only incomplete. Giamatti (1966) 234 observes of the poem that it 'will not yield to consistent historical, or moral, or mythological, or ethical interpretation. . . . Perhaps it is a tribute to *The Faerie Queene*, and an indication of where its appeal lies, that so many differing, often contradictory or hostile approaches, can be accommodated – indeed absorbed – by the poem.' It is a fitting strength, then, of the poem's modern critics that none may be labelled, for their approaches to the poem change according to its changing demands. Nevertheless, certain characteristic approaches may be identified.

Structure   The structure of the poem concerns almost all modern critics. Among them, Berger (1957) led the way with his analysis of the dramatic structure of Book II as it turns upon Guyon's faint. Concern with structure is evident from the title of Frye's essay, 'The structure of imagery in *The Faerie Queene*' (1961), and my book on *The Structure of Allegory in 'The Faerie Queene'*. Williams (1966) analyses the internal structural relationships through which the poem achieves its 'ordered richness'. 'Such an ordered richness', she argues, 'can be achieved only through complex organization, through the allegorical narrative, the "virtues" of the several books, the structural themes which work through several of the books, and the expanding net of images, all interlocking to form the microcosm of the poem' (xvii). Since the poem's size and scope make it enormously difficult to analyse in terms of its overall structure, many critics prefer to write on a single book. Berger analyses the dramatic structure of Book II; in his study of Books III and IV, Roche writes a final chapter on 'Structure as meaning'; Dunseath (1968) 16 illustrates the 'precise ordering of Spenser's poetic vision' in Book V; and both Cheney and Tonkin (1972) show how Courtesy is defined by the structuring of episodes in Book VI.

The one exception among modern critics is Alpers: he denies the poem structure because a reader's emotional response to any episode is so immediate and intense that he cannot remember what he read in previous cantos. However, even he is prepared to allow the poem 'organization' through which 'the order in which the parts of the poem are presented to us and the emphases they are given are essential to the meaning of the poem' (1967, 113).

Rhetorical analysis   The *Faerie Queene* is being subjected increasingly to close rhetorical analysis. Cheney (1966, 7) argues that the poem must be read 'under the intensive scrutiny which has been applied in recent decades to metaphysical lyrics'. Aptekar (1969) 3 makes the same point: '*The Faerie Queene* as a whole is less an epic or a romance than, to pervert chronology, a widely expanded metaphysical lyric. Far from being enclosed within its own convention and confined to telling a pretty moral tale, it is a complex of reverberating imagery, of paradox, of logically developed sublevels, of great and various learning subtly, and often explosively, used.' Stress on irony and ambiguity has yielded such complex interpretations that it is no longer possible to summarize the allegorical significance of even a minor episode in the poem. Only a few years ago the poem had been so emptied by the Romantics that meanings had to be imported wholesale from historical background to give it some weight as epic; now it threatens to sink under its burden of meaning. While rhetorical analysis is restricted by Alpers to the reader's immediate emotional involvement in particular stanzas and lines, it is extended by other critics to stanzas in the context of the episode, of the canto, and finally of the whole poem. Rose (1975) viii notes that 'the poem creates its own world of allusion, becoming increasingly suggestive as it proceeds'.

Rhetorical criticism assumes that the poem, being addressed to the reader, is fully explicable. Necessarily, its practitioners conclude that the allegory is not enigmatic, as Kermode (1971) 7–9 notes of Alpers's surface reading of the Mammon episode. In rejecting current rhetorical analysis, Murrin (1969) substitutes the anti-rhetoric of allegorical rhetoric, arguing that S.'s allegory conceals truth by communicating only obscurely and superficially to all but an elite few in the audience. This reaction is welcome because modern rhetorical criticism of S.'s poem is bankrupt: it considers technique but ignores content. By taking the medium to be the message, it has reduced the poem's meaning to commonplace explication. Murrin 168 argues that the allegorical poet deals with two different audiences: 'the many who could never accept his revelation and the few who could. He had, therefore, simultaneously to reveal and not to reveal his truth, and for this double purpose he cloaked his truth in the veils of allegory.' S. says as much in his dedicatory sonnet to Lord Burghley:

> Vnfitly I these ydle rimes present,
> The labor of lost time, and wit vnstayd:
> Yet if their deeper sence be inly wayd,
> And the dim vele, with which from comune vew
> Their fairer parts are hid, aside be layd,
> Perhaps not vaine they may appeare to you.

Yet that veil is 'dim' and even a Burghley may lay it aside. From *L.R.* it is clear that S. writes under a veil of allegory because our minds are veiled. Reading the poem removes that veil as our minds are progressively illuminated.

Another reaction to rhetorical analysis is expressed by Evans (1970). While he approves of the rehabilitation of the poetic image by modern rhetorical critics, he emphasizes the poem's didactic content: 'Spenser would not have equated the image itself with any prose "meaning" which we may extract from it; but he would have recognized that the image began with a prose concept which the rhetorical "colours" of poetry intensify and make universally applicable' (48).

Biographical criticism A curious hang-over from earlier criticism is the concern to analyse the psychology of characters as though they were real people rather than allegorical counters, and to interpret their actions as an inner education rather than the definition of a virtue. In his study of Book V, Dunseath (1968) analyses the characters of Artegall and Britomart as though they were normal people whose biography he may trace through faults that led to their moral and spiritual downfall. Many modern critics, from Berger on, treat the poem as a *bildungsroman*, perhaps for the reason Nelson (1963) 122–3 suggests, that 'it is difficult for most modern readers to disabuse themselves of the idea that character development must be an essential feature of any extended narrative that pretends to be more than merely an entertainment'. It may be that finally there need be no divorce between a concern with the psychological development of a knight and a concern with the virtue which he expresses. Each Book of the poem treats a virtue which the patron knight may only imperfectly express. We see the virtue *through* him but also through *him*, not in abstract terms but humanized. Williams (1966) xix may be correct, then, in the middle position she adopts: 'The virtues do not define the books which they name or the knights by whom they are defended; the books and the actions of the knights define the virtues, by working them out through the narrative in human terms.' Yet the popular, and excessive, concern with the psychological development of the characters in S.'s poem only distracts the reader from the spiritual allegory which, as Tuve (1966) 55 argues, alone may restore 'the depth of a reading that does not reduce human life to a psychomachia, spiritual life to morals and images to axes and hammers'.

Archetypal criticism   The archetypal approach seeks to control and direct the multiplication of interpretations of the poem by revealing the larger framework provided by mythology. The seminal essay for its application to the *Faerie Queene* is Frye's (1961) study of its structure of imagery. The approach itself has been condemned by Gottfried (1968) in a savage attack on Frye's essay and my book. Kermode (1971) 12–32 finds the approach reductive unless the archetypes are seen in their historical context. Of Book I he writes: The achievement of Spenser . . . is not to have dived into the archetypes, but to have given them a context of Virgilian security – to have used them in the expression of an actual, unique, critical moment of a nation's culture and history.' Yet the archetypal approach has not proved reductive in Fletcher's *The Prophetic Moment* (1971), which analyses S.'s use of two contrasting archetypes, the labyrinth and the temple. His analysis of Book V needs to be extended to the other books, chiefly Books III and IV, for the reason given by Evans (1970) 90: 'Spenserean allegory consists of archetypal images'. Archetypal studies of the poem will continue for the two reasons given by Lewis (1966). First, the nature of the response that the poem awakens in readers: 'Its primary appeal is to the most naïve and innocent tastes: to that level of our consciousness which is divided only by the thinnest veil from the immemorial lights and glooms of the collective Unconscious itself' (132). Secondly, the nature of S.'s allegory:

> We now know that symbols are the natural speech of the soul, a language older and more universal than words. This truth, if not understood exactly as modern psychology would understand it, was accepted and acted upon by the ancient and medieval world, and had not yet been lost in Spenser's day. He came, in fact, just in time, just before the birth of that new outward-looking, rationalizing spirit which was going to give us victory over the inanimate while cutting us off from the depths of our own nature. . . Spenser was the last poet who could use the old language seriously and who had an audience that understood it' (137).

The surprising fact about modern Spenser studies is that there has been so little archetypal interpretation of the whole poem and of the separate Books. The first extended interpretation is by Nohrnberg (1976). On a smaller scale, the Jungian analysis of Book III by Goldberg (1976) should prove to be the first of many. So, too, should be the analysis of the mythic structures in the poem described by Hieatt (1975).

Other approaches   Many recent critics, notably Roche and Dunseath, have noted the importance of emblems, inconographical conventions, and visual images in S. to support a rhetorical analysis of the poem. The one book-length study is Aptekar's *Icons of Justice* (1969). She interprets Book V by examining its icons or visual images in relation to Renaissance iconographical traditions. There is also Bender's *Spenser and Literary Pictorialism* (1972). He ignores the conceptual basis of S.'s imagery to emphasize the perceptual, the process by which visual experience is rendered in the poem. The iconographical approach should prove most rewarding in the future because S.'s poem is central to several converging traditions: the emblem tradition, traced by R. Freeman in *English Emblem Books* (1948); the mythological tradition, treated by J. Seznec in *The Survival of the Pagan Gods* (1953) and by Douglas Bush (1963); the pagan mysteries, the subject of Edgar Wind's book of that title (rev. edn 1967); the tradition of visual epistemology, traced by F. G. Robinson in *The Shape of Things Known* (1972); symbolic images, examined by E. H. Gombrich in the book of that title (1972); and pageantry, analysed by Fowler in *Triumphal Forms* (1970). Lewis's remark, in *Spenser's Images of Life* (1967) 3, that the *Faerie Queene* is 'very often to be regarded as a verbalization of Pageant' may well be extended by interpreting the whole poem as a sequence of emblems or images for which the words serve as mottos.

The numerological patterns in the *Faerie Queene* have been revealed by Fowler, *Spenser and the Numbers of Time* (1964). The many numerical structures that he discovers allow us to see more clearly the poem's structural organization and its unity. The cosmic patterns in the poem are outlined by Heninger (1974) to support his thesis 'that the form of *The Faerie Queene* reproduces the structure of the cosmos and that its narrative reflects the fullness of the universe in all its variety and extremes' (372).

In reacting against Wordsworth's 'sweet Spenser, moving through his clouded heaven / With the moon's beauty and the moon's soft pace', modern critics have set up a Miltonic 'sage and serious poet', with the epithets listed by Lewis: 'English, Protestant, rustic, manly, churchwardenly, domestic, thrifty, honest.' Nelson (1973) argues for another epithet, 'Spenser *ludens*'. In showing S.'s seriousness, modern critics have neglected his wit, urbanity, sophistication, grace and gaiety. The combination of all these qualities gives him his defining epithet, which Lewis aptly notes in Sidney, 'joyful seriousness'. This epithet has not been applied to S. because of our preoccupation with his ideas at the expense of his language, that is, with his matter rather than his words. Once we appreciate his art of language, we may understand what Harvey meant when he said that S. was '*Hobgoblin* runne away with the Garland from *Apollo*'.

Language and style

S. is not a difficult poet to read: on the whole his verse lacks Shakespeare's dense allusiveness, Donne's crabbed complexity, and Milton's intellectual texture. In place of the verbal economy that knots the syntax of a Donne poem, the sheer abundance of words makes any line in the *Faerie Queene* clear in its context. Coleridge notes S.'s 'fluent projection' in contrast to 'the deeper and more interwoven harmonies of Shakespeare and Milton', and Walter Raleigh, *Milton* (1901), illustrates S.'s style by rendering four lines from his poem in prose:

> Beside his head there sate a faire young man,
> (*This announces the theme, as in music.*)
> Of wondrous beautie, and of freshest yeares,
> (*The fair young man was fair and young.*)
> Whose tender bud to blossome new began,
> (*The fair young man was young.*)
> And flourish faire aboue his equall peares.
> (*The fair young man was fair, fairer even than his equals, who were also his peers.*)

While these lines are cited as an example of S.'s 'diffuser style' and are not necessarily characteristic of his verse, diffuseness is always an element in a style that seeks the clarity and exactness of vision. Nor is S. a learned poet, like Milton. He does not think in poetry, even though, as Whitaker (1972) 361 observes, 'the more one studies Spenser, the more convinced one becomes that, though eclectic, he is a careful and systematic thinker who uses his language exactly'. Consequently, his poem is not immediately and directly informed and sustained by ideas and doctrine. He remains a poet of images rather than of ideas. Although his images of virtues, vices and passions have learned – often abstrusely learned – traditions behind them, their surface is simple and clear. The clarity of his verse was first noted about 1628 by Sir Kenelm Digby, in a statement which deserves to stand as preface to all interpretations of the allegory:

> Spencer in what he saith hath a way of expression peculiar to him selfe; he bringeth downe the highest and deepest misteries that are contained in human learning, to an easy and gentle forme of delivery: which sheweth he is Master of what he treateth of; he can wield it as he pleaseth: and this he hath done soe cunningly, that if one heed him not with great attention, rare and wonderful conceptions will unperceived slide by him that readeth his works, and he will thinke he hath mett

with nothing but familiar and easy discourses; but let one dwell a while upon them and he shall feele a straunge fulnesse and roundnesse in all he saith. (*Spenser Allusions* 213)

Digby's extended interpretation of II ix 32 confirmed his judgment concerning S.'s style: 'Although the beginning of his Allegory or mysticall sense, may be obscure, yet in the processe of it, he doth himself declare his own conceptions in such sort as they are obvious to any ordinary capacitie' (*Var.* ii 472). That style becomes complex partly because the *Faerie Queene* is a poem of acquired and accumulated meanings which emerge only through more careful reading of any passage in the continually expanding contexts of the canto, book and poem as a whole. The parallels, correspondences, and patterns in the poem concern most recent critics, notably Giamatti (1975). As Lewis (1967) 61 notes: 'Its characteristic thickness of texture is not a matter of local complexities (though there are plenty of those), so much as of resonances sounding at large throughout the poem.' These resonances make any stanza of the poem truly obscure through its apparent simplicity without them, for alone it may seem to invite simply a psychological and mindless response. One of the simplest kinds of resonance is found in the opening stanza of II viii:

> And is there care in heauen? and is there loue
>> In heauenly spirits to these creatures bace,
>> That may compassion of their euils moue?
>> There is: else much more wretched were the cace
>> Of men, then beasts. But O th'exceeding grace
>> Of highest God, that loues his creatures so,
>> And all his workes with mercy doth embrace,
>> That blessed Angels, he sends to and fro,
> To serue to wicked man, to serue his wicked foe.

There are few verbal obscurities to bother a reader, and, although the stanza is based on Scripture, there are no allusions to be clarified before the stanza may be understood. Only in line 9 does the repetition of 'serue' alert the reader to an allusion to the Latin and Greek root of 'angel' as a messenger, as in Heb. 1:14: 'Are they not all ministring spirits, sent forthe to minister, for their sakes which shalbe heires of salvation'? As the repetition of 'wicked' explicitly declares, Spenser extends the ministry of the angels to all men. But these are no more than the 'local complexities' to which Lewis refers.

The 'resonances' are established first with the abrupt beginning as it parallels the preceding line in the poem which ends the seventh canto: 'And all his senses were with deadly fit opprest.' By this beginning Spenser notes how God's grace follows directly on man's defeat. A larger resonance is made from the comparable stanza at the beginning of I viii, which also marks the entrance of Arthur as the instrument of heavenly grace to rescue the fallen hero. Such resonance is part of the significant paralleling between the first two books. The explicit reference to God's love for man, in contrast to Truth's love in the earlier stanza, marks the chief instance of God's direct intervention into the action of the poem, which the reader must measure against His indirect interventions at other parts of the poem in order to understand the complex relationship among the virtues, and the virtues in relation to grace, which the poem sets out to explore and define.

These resonances are realized chiefly through the poem's unity. For despite its length, vast scope and universal significance, the poem is unified through a number of devices, such as the language of allegory in which it is written, its extended, interlacing narratives, and, above all, through its patterning of the virtues. As a consequence, the meaning of any one part of the poem is the rest of the poem. As an allegory, the poem continually expands, interprets, and defines its own meanings.

S.'s style reveals him as a 'maker', that skilled craftsman of 'braue and glorious words' for which E.K. praises him in the Dedicatory Epistle to the *S.C.* His poetic language draws such attention to itself that it engages every reader. In his own day, it was both condemned and praised, as noted by Edward Guilpin, *Skialetheia* (1598):

> Some blame deep *Spencer* for his grandam words,
> Others protest that, in them he records
> His maister-peece of cunning giving praise,
> And gravity to his profound-prickt layes. (*Spenser Allusions* 58)

It was intelligently praised by Digby:

> Weight of matter was never better joyned with propriety of language and with majestey and sweetnes of verse, then by him. And if any should except his reviving some obsolete words, and using some ancient formes of speech, in my opinion he blameth that which deserveth much prayse; for Spenser doth not that out of any affection . . . but only then when they serve to expresse more lively and more concisely what he would say. (*Spenser Allusions* 212)

Later it is praised by Hazlitt (1818) but for wrong reasons: 'Spenser was the poet of our waking dreams; and he has invented not only a language, but a music of his own for them. The undulations are infinite, like those of the waves of the sea; but the effect is still the same, lulling the senses into a deep oblivion of the jarring noises of the world, from which we have no wish to be ever recalled'. What Hazlitt praises, later critics condemn, as Traversi (1954) 221 who finds a monotony in S.'s verse which reduces it 'to a flow of harmonious sound which, however skilful, is more like a decadence than the promise of a fresh beginning'. On the other hand, Yeats (1906) xxxiv refers to S.'s 'powerful and subtle language . . . which I sometimes think more full of youthful energy than even the language of the great playwrights'. A number of modern critics have examined S.'s language, particularly Renwick (1925) and McElderry (1932). Craig (1967) has analysed the secret wit of S.'s language, particularly his use of etymology and puns; she concludes that his language 'must be savored for the cunning within its gentleness and ease'. Alpers (1967) ch. 3 demonstrates S.'s ambiguous sentence structure. One would expect S.'s verbal craftsmanship to appeal to modern readers. As a craftsman of words, he is close to the fabulous artificer Joyce. He shares Yeats's faith that 'words alone are certain good'; he believes with Wallace Stevens that 'the gaiety of language is our seigneur'; and, above all, he practises the craftsmanship of words upheld by Dylan Thomas: 'I am a painstaking, conscientious, involved and devious craftsman in words . . . I use everything and anything to make my poems work and move in the directions I want them to: old tricks, new tricks, puns, portmanteau-words, paradox, allusion, paranomasia, paragram, catachresis, slang, assonantal rhymes, vowel rhymes, sprung rhythm' (quoted in Constantine FitzGibbon, *The Life of Dylan Thomas*, 1965, 371). Through his art of language, S. illustrates and justifies Sidney's daring claim that the English language is 'indeed capable of any excellent exercising of it' (*Apologie* 140).

For most words in the *Faerie Queene* one need note only the care and precision with which they are used. For example, after Guyon leaves Phædria's island and before he meets Mammon, he is compared to a mariner:

> As Pilot well expert in perilous waue,
> That to a stedfast starre his course hath bent,
> When foggy mistes, or cloudy tempests haue
> The faithfull light of that faire lampe yblent,
> And couer'd heauen with hideous dreriment,
> Vpon his card and compas firmes his eye,
> The maisters of his long experiment,
> And to them does the steddy helme apply,

Bidding his winged vessell fairely forward fly:

> So *Guyon* hauing lost his trusty guide,
>   Late left beyond that *Ydle lake*, proceedes
>   Yet on his way, of none accompanide;
>   And euermore himselfe with comfort feedes,
>   Of his owne vertues, and prayse-worthy deedes. (II vii 1–2)

These lines serve usefully enough as filler between two major episodes in Guyon's journey. The simile is too traditional to call attention to itself. Only through reading the rest of the poem may one appreciate and understand its use here and recognize, for example, its special relevance to the Knight of Temperance, whose mastery over the passions is expressed as a victory over water. The phrase 'a stedfast starre', may be taken to refer to 'the stedfast starre' (I ii 1) which, as the curious reader may note, is Arcturus, that star associated with Arthur, who guides each knight. However, the indefinite article controls any larger inference here. The balanced phrases 'faithfull light' and 'faire lampe' express the love of light and horror of darkness which extend throughout the poem, again without any special point here except as Guyon is about to enter the darkness of Mammon's house. The term 'dreriment' would strike any reader as particularly Spenserian: its general meanings, whatever they are, are felt rather than understood, and made sufficiently explicit by the re-enforcing adjective 'hideous'. The first word that needs any gloss for a modern reader is 'card', which refers to the mariner's geographical chart rather than the graduated compass card; and the first phrase that needs any explication is 'maisters of his long experiment' which means 'instruments of his long experience'. Yet even for the modern reader, the import of the two lines in which they occur is clear: as the mariner must turn from sure, heavenly guidance to his own, less reliable means, so Guyon must turn from the sure, outward guidance of the Palmer to his own inner virtue. In the ninth line the alliteration of 'f' in 'fairely forward fly' communicates a sense of speed – a dangerous speed – as it comes at the end of the stanza, but its use here as a verbal device is not obtrusive. In the next stanza the 'comfort' that Guyon finds in his own virtue has a precise sixteenth-century sense, 'aid, support' (*OED* 1). It lacks entirely the modern sense of 'moral smugness' (which it seems to arouse in Guyon's modern readers) and possesses, instead, that Renaissance sense of one's own worth that Sidney gives his ideal ruler, Evarchus, who has 'the secret assurance of his own worthiness which . . . always lives in the worthiest minds'. The entire phrase, 'with comfort feedes, / Of his owne vertues', reveals both the self-sufficiency by which Guyon may resist Mammon's temptations and also the limitations of his virtue. As he feeds upon his virtues, he confronts Mammon who 'feede[s] his eye' (st. 4) upon gold, and is led into a realm where he too 'Did feed his eyes' (st. 24) on Mammon's riches. By the end of the temptation, he has consumed his own virtues, faints through lack of food, and lies helpless before his enemies. The fuller import of the simile that opens canto vii is realized only in canto viii: heavenly powers must guide the Palmer to Guyon's side, and the Palmer, in turn, guides Arthur to uphold his side in the quarrel with Pyrochles and Cymochles. Only then does Guyon regain that sure outward guidance which will carry him successfully on his voyage to the Bower of Bliss. In that final voyage the Palmer's staff and helmsman's stiff oars comment on the 'card and compas' (notoriously unreliable means of navigation in the sixteenth century) to which his virtue may only be compared at the midpoint of his quest. Although these opening lines continually expand in significance through their context, their meaning is sufficiently clear. Here, and throughout the poem (nearly 35,000 lines) words are chosen with scrupulous care for their clarity and precision.

Scrupulous care and precision in choice of words mark any major poet. Among them S. is distinguished as a Renaissance poet by his witty use of words; and among Renaissance poets he is distinguished by his joy in words. Only Shakespeare in *Love's Labour's Lost* matches him. He was sustained to write the longest major poem in our language because words released in him enormous creative powers. He seems never to tire. Everywhere the poem displays his ceaseless curiosity about words: their etymology, history, and imagery; their clash of literal and metaphorical meanings; and the rivalry of meanings which expresses their life. Puns, quibbles, and riddles may emerge anywhere. When the usual words fail him, he invents new ones or revives obsolete senses. He labours ceaselessly to make each word contain and express its nature.

Etymology is one major poetic device by which S. forces a word to express its true meanings. The etymology of his names has been noted in a number of recent studies, and in unpublished doctoral dissertations by Martha Craig (Yale 1959), A. Blitch (Michigan State 1965) and more thoroughly by J. Belson (Columbia 1964). These studies show how a character's name reveals his nature and function in the allegory. For example, the etymology of the Red Cross Knight's name has been known since 1758 when Upton noted that the *Golden Legend* of Jacobus de Voragine was S.'s source for the life of St George. According to the *Legend*, 'George is sayd of geos / whiche is as moche to saye as erthe and orge / that is tilyenge / so george is to saye as tilyenge the erthe / that is his flesshe . . . Or George may be sayd of gera : that is holy / and of gyon that is a wrasteler / that is an holy wrasteler. For he wrasteled with the dragon'. S. frames the Knight's character and actions through an awareness of such etymologies. Thus the Knight is found in a ploughman's furrow and raised in ploughman's state by which he gains his name (x 66); he is associated with Orgoglio, his fallen form, by a shared etymology Ge-*orgos*, *Orgo*-glio (the latter also linked with a furrow, viii 8); and he is associated with Guyon, his natural form, as both are wrestlers. Like Adam, he is named after the earth (Heb. *adamah*) of which he is made: hence Contemplation names him simply 'thou man of earth' (x 52). Playing wittily on the complex etymology of names obsessed S. so entirely that, ideally, if one fully understood the poem's names, one would fully understand its allegory.

Interest in etymology may have led S. to employ etymological spelling and certainly led him to employ the etymological epithet. Hence Orgoglio may be called a 'Geant' (I vii 8) because he is the son of Gea, the earth; Duessa's breath 'abhominably smeld' (I viii 47) because she is *ab homine*, from man and hence beastly; Phædria's lake may be named the '*Ydle lake*' because the gnostic *Y* describes the paths of virtue and vice which Phædria places before man; and the feminine in opposition to the masculine is spelled 'fœminine' at II ix 22 because it is the 'foe to man'. Where spelling does not work, S. uses an epithet. As a general rule in the poem an epithet defines; rarely is it simply descriptive. The best-known example of the characterizing epithet in the poem is found in the catalogue of the rivers at IV xi, where S. labours, as he tells Harvey of the *Epithalamion Thamesis*, to give the rivers 'their righte names'. More representative of his usual practice is his description of the '*Rocke of* vile *Reproch*' which Guyon encounters on his voyage to Acrasia's Bower. Since the Rock wrecks those of 'lost credite and consumed thrift', it is a 'daungerous' place in the obsolete sense of 'to be in danger': to be in debt (*OED* 1). It is attended by 'yelling Meawes, with Seagulles hoarse and bace, / And Cormoyrants, with birds of rauenous race' (II xii 8). 'Meawes' attend because the word signifies 'prison', and they are 'yelling' because the echoic verb 'mew', which we apply to cats, was applied to sea-birds in the sixteenth century. Gulls are present because the word signifies 'trickery', and hence they are called 'bace'. 'Cormoyrant' was a term applied to usurers; and being a sea-raven, the bird is called 'rauenous'. These birds watch 'on that wastfull clift' because such a rock is a fitting punishment for the wasteful.

Often an etymological epithet expands into a brief allegory. For example, the jealous Malbecco feeds on dread 'That doth with curelesse care consume the hart' (III x 59). 'Care' is 'curelesse' because the word comes from Latin *cura*, care; it consumes the heart because of its received etymology, *cura quod cor edat*, which S.'s phrase directly translates. S.'s delight in etymology is one part of his enormous pleasure, which he expects his readers to share, in all kinds of witty word-play.

Puns spring up everywhere, most frequently in erotic episodes, but they may be found at any place where the pressure of meaning overloads a word's normal range of significance. They extend from the simplest play on double senses – 'dismall day', for example, plays on its root, *dies mali* – to the most serious conjunction of different senses. Dame Cælia greets Una with an apostrophe to the 'happie earth, / Whereon thy innocent feet doe euer tread, / . . . Yet ceasest not thy wearie soles to lead' (I x 9): 'soles' refers to men's souls as pilgrims which are in the keeping of the Church. Through extended use a pun may become part of the language of allegory. For example, 'incontinent' signifies both 'intemperate', in the literal sense of not restraining oneself, and 'immediately'. It may be, then, that both senses are present whenever the term is used. In Book I Arthur gives the Red Cross Knight a 'few drops of liquor pure . . . That any wound could heale incontinent' (ix 19). In Book II it is said that if man's body is not kept in sober government 'It growes a Monster, and incontinent / Doth loose his dignitie and natiue grace' (ix 1). In Book III Britomart laments by the seashore at the beginning of her quest: she compares her state to a storm-tossed ship and appeals for 'some gentle gale of ease' from the God of Winds 'that raignest in the seas, / That raignest also in the Continent' (iv 10), referring to those who are ruled by Love and those who are chaste. As she soon discovers, the land is ruled by the continent Marinell. When he is wounded by her, his mother comes from the ocean and throws herself 'downe on the Continent' (iv 30). Here the pun clarifies the nature of Marinell, a creature of the land and sea, and suggests why his marriage to Florimell, a creature of the land held by the sea, should resolve the action of Books III and IV. When this same word-play occurs in the following canto, it hardly constitutes a pun: the separate meanings have merged. Timias slays the lustful Foster 'Right as he entring was into the flood'; and fittingly, 'The carkas with the streame was carried downe, / But th'head fell backeward on the Continent' (v 25). Such use of puns supports the remark by Braden (1975) 26 that 'the *Faerie Queene*, even to the level of its diction, is more a collection of hovering puns than a series of discrete, stratified levels of allegory'.

The simplest kind of word-play is repetition of a word. When the 'dead' Guyon is defended by Arthur, his body is called a 'carcass' four times within a few stanzas. Such repetition enforces the literal sense of the word, 'fallen flesh', and clarifies Arthur's redemption of Guyon. When a word is repeated in different contexts, it may accumulate meanings so that it becomes a centre of our understanding, as Satterthwaite (1960) 154 observes: 'Spenser's words are heavily fraught with the meanings they acquire through their repeated use in certain contexts in his whole work. They become as "loaded" as any words a poet ever used.' Williams (1966) 142 comments similarly on Cymoent's lament for the death of her son, III iv 37. On the simple words that S. gives Cymoent, 'I feared loue: but they that loue do liue, / But they that die, doe neither loue nor hate', she writes 'any writer must recharge them if we are to be convinced that he is dealing not in paltry effects of verbal jugglery but in a felt paradox. Spenser does recharge them; they are the explosive point of an accumulated force coming from the finely structured narrative and its images.' One example of extended repetition of a word is the use of 'heart' in the Despair episode. Earlier Duessa brandishes her charmed cup: 'Death and despeyre did many thereof sup, / . . . Th'eternall bale of heauie wounded harts' (I viii 14). Though Death is defeated when the Knight is rescued from the dungeon, Despair remains. When he confronts Trevisan who flees Despair, he seeks by 'bold hartie speach' to embolden his 'bloud-frosen hart' (ix 25). He cannot do so because he and his companion were overcome by Despair when he 'felt our feeble harts / Embost with bale' (ix 29). This pun on 'heart' (a hunted hart is 'embost' when it foams with fatigue) introduces elaborate play on the word when the Knight himself confronts Despair (see I ix 48.2n). At the end, Despair's speech pierces his heart until Una's speech persuades him not to let 'vaine words bewitch [his] manly hart' (ix 53). The whole poem is composed of such significant repetition of words: being an elaborately constructed allegory, any word in it is a latent pun.

Word-play may be displayed through ambiguous syntax, as Alpers demonstrates at length. S. commonly employs the floating adjective or adverb. When Guyon confronts Mammon, he

> lightly to him leaping, stayd
> His hand, that trembled, as one terrifyde;
> And though him selfe were at the sight dismayd,
> Yet him perforce restraynd, and to him doubtfull sayd. (II vii 6)

'To him doubtfull', that is, to the fearful Mammon. Yet the term applies equally to Guyon: he is doubtful about Mammon's identity and fearful, as 'dismayd' suggests, of the temptation that confronts him. Also pronouns may be used ambiguously, as one would expect in an allegory where characters are states, and actions consist of conflict between projections of a character or aspects of his state. After the Red Cross Knight has slain the Dragon, Una approaches to praise him: 'Then God she praysd, and thankt her faithfull knight, / That had atchieu'd so great a conquest by his might' (I xi 55). 'By his might' refers both to God and to the Knight; and in so doing it resolves the action of the episode and the Book. Since God's grace is fully manifest in man's might, the Knight is seen in the lineaments of Christ, the Dragon-killer (see I xi 55.8–9*n*).

At any point in the poem a reader may be impressed by S.'s witty play upon the meanings of words and their emotive and imaginative impact. Typically Spenserian is the vaguely suggestive word, 'dreriment'. After the Red Cross Knight hears Fradubio's story, he is left 'Full of sad feare and ghastly dreriment' (I ii 44). That is, the Knight is sad. Yet S. chooses not to say that but to refer instead to the Knight's 'dreriment'. Although the word has not occurred before in the poem, and its formation – adding '-ment' to an adjective – is unusual, its general sense causes no problem. It is glossed 'dreery and heavy cheere' by E.K. when it occurs in *The Shepheardes Calender* November eclogue. 'Ghastly dreriment' functions chiefly to give weight to the simple phrase 'sad feare'. While 'ghastly' suggests explicitly the terror evoked by the sight of a ghost, here Fradubio, 'dreriment' remains purposely vague. By remaining vague, it expresses the ominous, nightmarish, and unrealized 'sad feare' from which the Knight suffers. His inner fear takes shape in outer action only later when he encounters the person of Sansjoy. 'Dreriment' belongs to a word-play extended throughout Book I. The Knight enters upon his quest 'too solemne sad' (i 2); during it he calls upon death on four occasions; and only by passing through the house of Penaunce does he learn 'Himselfe to chearish' (x 29).

Throughout his poem S. defines the meanings of his words by using them carefully and precisely in parallel but significantly differing contexts. Most often he exploits the multiple meanings of words he inherits. Adonis is slain by the boar that 'with his cruell tuske him deadly cloyd' (III vi 48). Here 'cloyd' signifies 'pierced', 'gored' (cf. *OED* v.¹ 3); also, since the boar signifies lust and his wound concupiscence, the term may include its modern sense, 'the surfeiting of desire'. Betrayed by Duessa, the Red Cross Knight is called 'dissolute' (I vii 51). This term means 'debauched', 'enfeebled', 'relaxed', and 'careless'. Also it implies 'dissolved' (*OED* 1), from the Latin *dissolutus*, loose: the Knight was betrayed when he lay 'Pourd out in loosnesse on the grassy grownd' (vii 7). Yet further, one must allow that here, as always, S. says what he means: the Knight is 'dissolute' in the precise sense of being dissolved: by drinking from the fountain, his 'chearefull bloud in faintnesse chill did melt' (vii 6), that is, his blood is corrupted into the polluted water which he drinks.

When inherited words could not be adapted to serve his needs, S. invented new ones. His 'coinages' are noted in the commentary and I cite only one of the many moments in the poem when the sheer pressure of the allegory forces S. to fashion a new word. When Una's parents may at last leave their besieged castle, they go to the field 'where that champion stout / After his foes defeasance did remaine' (I xii 12). The sense of 'defeasance', defeat, is attributed to S. by *OED*; it is used only here. S. does not use the word 'defeat', however, but fashions a new sense by adapting an earlier legal sense, from the French 'defesaunce', which means 'to render a claim null and void'. He uses 'defeasance', then, to note that the Dragon usurped Adam's kingdom: when the Dragon is defeated, his claim to the land ends. Una's parents ruled 'from East to Westerne shore' (I i 5) until they were expelled by the Dragon, and in their place Duessa's father now rules only 'the wide West' (ii 22). The prior claim of Una's parents to Eden has extended political, religious, and ecclesiastical significance which 'defeasance' is coined to clarify.

Through his art of language S. seeks to purify words by restoring them to their true, original meanings. When Adam fell, he lost that natural language in which words contain and reveal the realities they name. 17

Though corrupt, languages remain divinely given and the poet's burden is to purify the language of his own tribe. Words have been 'wrested from their true calling', and the poet attempts to wrest them back. S. 'writ no language', as Jonson noted; that is, he avoids a fallen language which would only confirm man in his state of bondage. By his language of allegory he recreates that natural language in which the word and its reality again merge. Like Adam, he gives names to his creatures which express their natures. His word-play is not an idle game but a sustained and serious effort to plant true words as seeds in the reader's imagination. In Jonson's phrase, he 'makes their minds like the thing he writes' (*Discoveries*, in *Works* viii 588). He shares Bacon's faith that the true end of knowledge is 'a restitution and reinvesting (in great part) of man to the sovereignty and power (for whensoever he shall be able to call the creatures by their true names he shall again command them) which he had in his first state of creation' (*Valerius Terminus*). Although his poem remains largely unfinished, he has restored at least those words which are capable of fashioning his reader in virtuous and gentle discipline. What is chiefly needed to understand the allegory fully is to understand all the words. That hypothesis is the basis for the annotation that follows.

The Major Characters of *The Faerie Queene*

First entrance and/or the significance of the name.

Abessa I iii 10, 18.4
Acrasia II xii 69.8
Adicia V viii 20.3
Adonis III vi 46–49
Æmylia IV vii 10, 18.9
Æsculapius I v 36
Agape IV ii 41.7–9
Agdistes II xii 48.2; see Genius
Aladine VI ii 16, 40, iii 3.9
Aldus VI iii 3.9
Alma II ix 18.1
Amauia II i 35, 55.5
Amidas V iv 9.1
Amoret III vi 28.8–9
Amyas IV vii 15, viii 50, 59.2
Anamnestes II ix 58.8–9
Angel II viii 5
Apollo IV xii 25
Archimago I i 29, 43.6
Argante III vii 37, 47.2
Artegall, or The Saluage Knight IV iv 39, V i 3.2
Arthur I vii 29–36
Astræa V i 5.4
Ate IV i 19.1
Atin II iv 37, 42.5
Beadmen, The seven I x 36.3
Belge V x 7.1–4
Bellamoure VI xii 3.4
Belphœbe II iii 21, Arg 4
Blandamour IV i 17, 32.4–5
Blandina VI iii 30, 42.6
Blatant Beast V xii 37.7
Bracidas V iv 9.6–7, 18.2
Braggadocchio II iii 4, 10.1
Bregog VII vi 40.3–6
Briana VI i 14.6
Brianor IV iv 40.8–9
Brigants VI x 39.3
Britomart III i 8.6
Burbon V xi 44, 49.1–4
Busirane III xii 31, xi 10.7
Cælia or Cœlia I x 4.1
Calepine VI iii 20, 27.1
Calidore VI i 2.2
Cambell IV ii 31.8–9
Cambina IV ii 31.8–9
Canacee IV ii 31.8–9
Care IV v 34
Charissa I x 29.7–9

Chrysogone III vi 4.1
Claribell (1) II iv 26.5; (2) IV ix 20.8; (3) VI xii 4.1
Clarin, Clarinda V iv 48.3
Colin Clout VI ix 41.6
Columbell III vii 51.6
Concord IV x 34
Contemplation I x 46.8
Corceca I iii 12, 18.4
Corflambo IV viii 38, 49.1
Coridon VI ix 10.5
Corflambo IV viii 38, 49.1
Coridon VI ix 10.5
Crudor VI i 15.1
Cupid III vi 49, xii 22, VI vii 32
Cymochles II v 26, iv 41
Cymoent, Cymodoce III iv 19.3
Cynthia VII vi 8
Despair I ix 28
Diamond IV ii 41.7–9
Diana III vi 17
Disdain (1) II vii 41.1; (2) VI vi 16, vii 27
Dolon V vi 19, 32.1
Dony III v 3, V ii 3.1
Dragon, The I xi 4
Druon IV ix 20.8
Duessa I ii 13 (disguised as Fidessa), 34.8
Dwarf. Una's I i 6; Pœana's, IV viii 38;
    Briana's VI i 29; Florimell's, see Dony
Eden, King of I xii 3
Elissa II ii 35.1
Enias VI vii 3, viii 4.3
Error I i 14.7–9
Eumnestes II ix 55, 58.8–9
Excesse II xii 55
Faerie Queene, The I ix 13
Fanchin VII vi 44.4
Faunus II ii 7.5
Ferraugh III viii 15.3–5
Ferriman II xi 4
Fidelia I x 12
Fidessa, see Duessa
Fisher III vii 27
Florimell III i 15, v 8.7
Florimell, False or Snowy III viii 5
Flourdelis V xi 49.6
Foster III i 17.2; his brothers, III v 15.5–6
Fradubio I ii 30, 33.3
Frælissa I ii 31, 37.8–9
Furor II iv 3, 10.6
Genius (1) II xii 46; (2) III vi 31
Georgos I x 66.5–6
Geryoneo V x 11.1; his Seneschall V x 30.2;
    his Monster, V xi 23–25

Thamis IV xi 24
Timias I vii 37, III i 18.9
Trevisan I ix 21, 32.5
Triamond IV ii 30, 41.7–9
Tristram VI ii 3, 28–32; Lady he defends, VI ii 4
Trompart II iii 6, 10.1
Tryphon IV xi 6

Turpine VI iii 30, 40.1–4
Una I i 4, 45.9
Venus III vi 11
Verdant II xii 72, 82.8
Villeins, Maleger's II ix 12, xi 6.1
Witch III vii 6; her son 12; her monster 22
Womanhood IV x 49

THE FAERIE QVEENE.

Difposed into twelue bookes,

Fashioning

XII. Morall vertues.

LONDON

Printed for VVilliam Ponfonbie.

1 5 9 6 .

TO
THE MOST HIGH,
MIGHTIE
And
MAGNIFICENT
EMPRESSE RENOVV-
MED FOR PIETIE, VER-
TVE, AND ALL GRATIOVS
GOVERNMENT ELIZABETH BY
THE GRACE OF GOD QVEENE
OF ENGLAND FRAVNCE AND
IRELAND AND OF VIRGI-
NIA, DEFENDOVR OF THE
FAITH, &c . HER MOST
HVMBLE SERVAVNT
EDMVND SPENSER
DOTH IN ALL HV-
MILITIE DEDI-
CATE, PRE-
SENT
AND CONSECRATE THESE
HIS LABOVRS TO LIVE
VVITH THE ETERNI-
TIE OF HER
FAME.

Title page
Disposed . . . vertues: see *L.R.* for S.'s plan to write twelve books on the twelve private moral virtues, to be followed by another twelve books on the political virtues.
Fashioning: presenting the form of, representing.

Dedication
The 1590 dedication reads simply: TO THE MOST MIGH/TIE AND MAGNIFI/CENT EMPRESSE ELI/ZABETH, BY THE / GRACE OF GOD QVEENE / OF ENGLAND, FRANCE / AND IRELAND DE/FENDER OF THE FAITH &c. Her most humble Seruant: *Ed. Spenser*.

As a Christian poet, S. begins with Holiness, that state which establishes man's right relationship to God and upon which all the virtues depend. As a Protestant poet, he shows how this virtue implies that all virtue or strength belongs to God alone. Accordingly, the Red Cross Knight turns praise from himself to God for killing the Dragon: 'His be the praise, that this atchieu'ment wrought, / Who made my hand the organ of his might; / More then goodwill to me attribute nought' (II i 33). Efforts by earlier critics to relate Holiness as a virtue to Aristotle's Highmindedness, or to Plato's *andreia*, have been unconvincing (see General Introduction under 'Sources'); Whitaker (1952) on Calvin's *Institutes* as a gloss on Holiness is more persuasive.

To display this Christian virtue, S. chose as its vehicle the legend of St George. In their analysis of his use of the legend, Padelford and O'Connor, *Var.* i 379, conclude that St George was the 'natural choice for the hero of his first book, as this patron saint of the nation would serve equally the purpose of the spiritual and of the political allegory'. In one way, it was a Hobgoblin choice; as Nelson (1963) 150 notes: 'No Renaissance humanist could have thought the legendary life of St George a respectable literary model. By the sixteenth century accretions of impossible adventure and the buffoonery of village St George plays must have rendered the story ridiculous.' For an heroic poet, however, the legend's profound appeal as a story and its contemporary meanings may have determined the choice. Of the legend, Gerard de Malynes writes:

> For wheras under the person of the noble champion Saint *George* our Saviour Christ was prefigured, delivering the Virgin (which did signifie the sinfull soules of Christians) from the dragon or divels power: So her most excellent Majesty by advancing the pure doctrine of *Christ Jesus* in all truth and sincerity, hath (as an instrument appointed by divine providence) bene used to performe the part of a valiant champion, delivering an infinite number out of the divels power, whereunto they were tied with the forcible chaines of darknesse' (*Saint George for England, allegorically described* 1601, *Spenser Allusions* 84).

Robert Salter, who claimed to be a true friend of S., saw 'this very Mysterie' in Book I, namely, the working out of the fourfold life of man in Christ (*Wonderfull Prophecies* 1626). This religious interpretation suggests why the chief source for the imagery of Book I is the Revelation of St John. Bennett (1942) 109–15 shows how the age interpreted Revelation as an allegory of the Protestant conflict with the Church of Rome. Hankins (1971) shows the relevance to this conflict of related passages from the Old Testament and concludes that together these passages 'provide Spenser's basic pattern and much of his imagery' (119).

Book I is now generally recognized as central because its Christian vision of man sustains the whole poem. Woodhouse (1965) 22 refers to Holiness as 'the one specifically religious and Christian virtue which he [S.] treats, as if to make it the foundation and guarantee of all the rest'. Williams (1966) 6 finds Book I 'essential to those succeeding stories and to the poem's imitation of nature'. Further, the point at which the Red Cross Knight completes his quest becomes the point of departure for the later knights (see II i 32.6*n*). Book I is central to a profoundly secular poem and even it does not treat Christian's 'pilgrim's progress from this world to that which is to come': the Knight's slaying the Dragon only qualifies him to enter the semi-finals as the defender of the Faerie Queene against the pagan king (I xii 18). Only after that has been accomplished may he start his climb to the New Jerusalem. Consequently, the whole poem is deeply rooted in the human condition: it treats man's life in this world more comprehensively than any other poem in our language. Lewis (1936) 358 aptly notes that 'it is like life itself, not like the products of life. It is an image of the *natura naturans*, not of the *natura naturata*. The things we read about in it are not like life, but the experience of reading it is like living.'

The traditional interpretations of Book I have been moral and historical. The first varies between extremes of psychological and spiritual readings, and the second between particular and general allusions either to contemporary or earlier events in England. There has been radical disagreement over the historical allegory: *Var.* requires some forty-six pages of summary for the conflicting historical interpretations but only twenty-six for the moral. Competing claims have tended to cancel each other and discredit the whole approach. Greenlaw (1932) 67, 96 concludes that 'historical allusions do not constitute the "continued allegory"', and what historical allegory there is 'has a general rather than a minute application'. Nevertheless, historical or ecclesiastical allegory has been revived, notably by Kermode (1971) 12–32 who argues that the apocalyptic images in Book I allude to the history of the Church from the loss of Eden to the Last Judgment (see General Introduction p. 10). Thus he interprets the Red Cross Knight's subjection to Orgoglio as the popish captivity of England from Gregory VII to Wyclif (about 300 years, the three months of viii 38). 'The *miles Christi*, disarmed, drinks of the enervating fountain of corrupt gospel and submits to Rome' (48). In similar but even narrower theological terms, Waters (1970) vii analyses Book I 'in the light of the Protestant concepts of symbolic lust and symbolic witchcraft as they merge in the Mistress-Missa tradition, which personified the Roman Mass as a whore and witch'. By this reading, Duessa personifies the Roman Mass, the fountain from which the Knight drinks symbolizes spiritual fornication of the Mass which weakens the layman, and Orgoglio 'may also function as a Mass-priest and/or the tyranny of the priest' (70), and the 'individual pride of the Mass-hearers' (78). Both Kermode and Waters provide a particular historical setting for the events of the poem, but they do so by a reductive translation that confounds the comprehensiveness of the allegory.

The main outline of the moral allegory as set down by Ruskin in one of the ten appendices to volume 3 of *The Stones of Venice* (1851) remains generally accepted. On Orgoglio's defeat of the Red Cross Knight, he writes: 'This Orgoglio is Orgueil, or Carnal Pride; not the pride of life, spiritual and subtle [which Ruskin identifies with Lucifera], but the common and vulgar pride in the power of this world: and his throwing the Redcrosse Knight into a dungeon is a type of the captivity of true religion under the temporal power of corrupt churches, more especially of the Church of Rome.' While later readers quarrel over particular identifications, they agree on this way of reading the moral allegory. According to Padelford, *Var.* i 438, 470, Orgoglio represents both 'spiritual pride' as distinct from 'carnal pride' in Lucifera, and also 'the ruthless power of Romanism, [and] in the concrete . . . he doubtless stands for Philip of Spain'. Nelson (1963) 135 denies any simple moral distinction between Orgoglio and Lucifera: 'These are inward and outward aspects of the same sin, that sin of pretended glory.'

Such efforts to identify Orgoglio raise the problem of the extent to which a 'character' may be given a label. How may we say that Orgoglio 'is' pride, whether carnal or spiritual, which defeats the Knight? When the Knight is defeated by Orgoglio, it seems reasonable to infer that he falls through pride. Most certainly he falls: one who was on horseback lies upon the ground, first to rest in the shade and then to lie with Duessa. Although he staggers to his feet, he soon falls senseless upon the ground; and finally, he is placed deep underground in the Giant's dungeon. The Giant himself is not 'identified' until after the Knight's fall; then he is not named Pride but rather Orgoglio. Though he is a proud giant, his pride is only one detail in a very complex description. In his size, descent, features, weapon, gait, and mode of fighting, he is seen as a particular giant rather than as a particular kind of Pride. To name him Pride is to select a few words – and not particularly interesting ones – such as 'arrogant' and 'presumption' out of some twenty-six lines or about two hundred words, and to weight these as pride from their significance in theology. Thus to say that the Knight falls through Pride is to ignore the poetry almost entirely. While the Knight is guilty of sloth and lust before he falls, he is not proud; in fact, he has just escaped from the House of Pride. At this point a moral reading may ignore Orgoglio altogether and find that the Knight falls through lust. Then the sin of concupiscence supplies the basis for a religious reading of the episode. Yet S. prevents any direct religious reading – he deliberately prevents it – by attributing the Knight's weakness before Orgoglio to his act of drinking, in ignorance, the enfeebling waters issuing from a nymph who, like him, rested in the middle of her quest.

Dissatisfaction with the simple, reductive meaning that follows inevitably when poetic images are translated into abstract personifications has led to more sophisticated analyses. Heninger (1959) refuses to separate the moral and historical allegories because their synthesis provides the poem's 'continued Allegory'. As an example of the 'coadunating faculty of Spenser's imagination', he argues that Orgoglio personifies an earthquake 'serving to chastise Red Crosse for his sinfulness, epitomized by his idleness and lechery beside the magic spring. And simultaneously he serves a closely related strand of allegory by representing the destruction of the world on Judgment Day, when only the elect of God will be retrieved from perdition' (178). Heninger accepts the usual historical interpretation that the Knight's defeat by Orgoglio 'reveals the incapacity of the individual soul if it succumbs to the sensuality and materialism of popish Rome' (180). Shroeder (1962) interprets the episode as an erotic allegory: since the Knight is copulating with Duessa when Orgoglio comes upon him, the fountain from which he drinks is a *fons veneris*, and Orgoglio is Lust. Cheney (1966) 34 protests that such a reading tends 'to exaggerate the sexual element in Redcross' fall'. Others seem to agree but turn a psychological reading into moral biography. Williams (1966) 20 agrees with my observation, Hamilton (1961) 75, that Orgoglio embodies 'the knight's fallen state' but places the meaning of the episode in the Knight's consciousness. The Knight is dispirited before the battle for 'now he sees where his life has been leading' and his encounter with the Giant is his 'horrified realization of the results of his turning to self, his pride'. Similarly, Evans (1970) 99–100 claims that the Knight is filled with 'the irrepressible pangs and fears of conscience' before his battle with Orgoglio: 'The triumph of the giant symbolizes that insurrection of the lower nature by which Adam fell and all his sons after.'

Dissatisfaction with the conflicting interpretations of separate episodes has led some critics to attend to overall structure, although Book I remains the only book without a full-length study of its allegory. Whitaker (1952) argues that the Book is organized logically, rather than biographically, 'according to the arrangement of Christian doctrines customary in Renaissance theological treatises and confessionals' (153). Nelson (1963) 147 claims that a paradox – Christ dead is Christ living – is the organizing theme of the Book. Fowler (1964) finds an astrological and a numerical structure: the Book may be related astrologically to Sol as both the Knight and Una are conceived in terms of the *Sol iustitiae* concept derived from Revelation, and numerically to the all-inclusive monad expressed in Una. MacIntyre (1970) finds the Book's structure coherent by grouping the Knight's adventures as Error, Sin, Regeneration, and Victory. Such studies of structure, whether concerned with logical organization or patterns of imagery or themes (such as Alpers's analysis of Book I in terms of the problem of heroism and human strength), have at least this merit, that they require us to read the poem more comprehensively so that we become more aware of the complex patterning of the episodes.

In general, recent criticism either refines Ruskin's moral reading into a close biographical/psychological reading or eschews it altogether. Anderson (1969) interprets Sansjoy's descent into hell to be cured by Aesculapius as the Knight's descent into hell. Arthos (1956) 42 sees the form of Book I as '*le roman educatif*', and Cheney (1966) 53 treats the Book as 'the hero's quest for identity'. On the other hand, Nelson (1963) 172–3 rejects any reading of the Book 'which makes of it a kind of *bildungsroman*, a story of education by experience'. While he allows that the Knight rises from sin to salvation, 'this upward progress is rather an analysis than a history'. Alpers (1967) rejects any moral reading because it involves moral judgment, and asks the reader not to judge the Knight's plight but understand it by sharing his experience: 'Orgoglio's approach [to the Knight] . . . is not a punishment that we supervise; rather, the humanity that we share with the Red Cross Knight makes us participate in the experience of terror' (150). Tuve (1966) argues that the Book shows not a moral struggle within man but the spirit's quest for its final destiny. Hence she interprets Orgoglio as pride in its universal aspect: 'the very idea of the diabolical sin, radical Pride, given a metaphorical body . . . not the Roman Church but a figure for the basic and radical ur-sin of Pride, usurping Godhead, which has taken over that once-luminous creation of God, a Church on earth' (106). These opposed readings may be reconciled if we recognize that the education takes place in the reader as he comes to possess the virtue of Holiness which S. fashions in him through the story of the

Red Cross Knight.

The complexity and comprehensiveness of the allegory give rise to many interpretations of any episode. Conflicting interpretations may lead to a more comprehensive and satisfying interpretation by forcing us to read more precisely. For example, how may it be said, as I said above, that the Knight is seen 'in the lineaments of Christ' by killing the Dragon? Or what supports the claim by Kermode (1971) 43 that the Knight 'begins . . . as *miles Christi*, to end as the knight *fidelis et verax* or Christ himself (whose bride Una is the Church)'? In opposing any Christological interpretation of Book I, Tuve (1966) maintains that the Knight is not a 'Christ figure' but 'Christ-in-man' (132), one who 'figures' Christ 'but is never equated with Him' (404). This clash of interpretation was raised to a new level of understanding by Kaske's (1969) analysis of the Knight's three-day battle against the Dragon. She shows that the battle re-enacts mankind's struggle for deliverance from the power of Satan: it begins with unregenerate man under law, progresses through Christian regenerate man, and 'culminates in Christ the perfect man, showing his swift and final victory over Satan both on his own behalf and that of others' (638).

In general, recent criticism discriminates more precisely in responding to each episode and it shows greater awareness of the careful structure of the poem in its smallest particulars.

THE FIRST
BOOKE OF THE
FAERIE QVEENE.
Contayning
THE LEGENDE OF THE
KNIGHT OF THE RED CROSSE,
OR
OF HOLINESSE.

I

LO I the man, whose Muse whilome did maske,
 As time her taught, in lowly Shepheards weeds,
 Am now enforst a far vnfitter taske,
 For trumpets sterne to chaunge mine Oaten reeds,
And sing of Knights and Ladies gentle deeds ;
Whose prayses hauing slept in silence long,
Me, all too meane, the sacred Muse areeds
To blazon broad emongst her learned throng :
Fierce warres and faithfull loues shall moralize my song.

Proem
Title
Legende: 'The word LEGEND, so called of the Latine Gerund, *Legendum*, and signifying, by the Figure *Hexoche*, things specially worthy to be read, was anciently used in an Ecclesiasticall sense, and restrained therein to things written in Prose, touching the Lives of Saints. Master EDMUND SPENSER

was the very first among us, who transferred the use of the word, LEGEND, from Prose to Verse: nor that unfortunately; the Argument of his Bookes being of a kind of sacred Nature, as comprehending in them things as well Divine as Humane. And surely, that excellent Master, knowing the weight and use of Words, did competently answere the *Decorum* of a LEGEND, in the qualitie of his Matter, and meant to give it a kind of Consecration in the Title' (Drayton, 'To the Reader', *Legends* 1619, *Works* ii 382).

Stanzas 1–4
A prologue to the whole poem rather than to Book I. The poet is like his Knight whom he describes in the *L.R.* as a 'clownish person' who assumes a quest on behalf of the Faerie Queene. Like him, he needs grace to succeed.

Stanza 1
1–5 Lines 1–4 imitate verses prefixed to the opening lines of Renaissance editions of Virgil's *Aeneid* and believed to be by him: *Ille ego, qui quondam gracili modulatus avena | carmen . . . at nunc horrentia Martis.* **5** varies the opening: *Arma virumque cano*, by way of Ariosto's imitation in *Orlando Furiosi*: *Le donne, i cavallier, l'arme, gli amori | le cortesie, l'audaci imprese io canto*. Cain (1972) 34 notes how S. turns from Virgil to Ariosto in the fifth line, the point at which his rhyme scheme (ababbcbcc) leaves Ariosto's ottave (abababcc), and returns to Ariosto in the ninth line which, as an alexandrine, overgoes Ariosto's eight.
1–2 **whilome**: some time before; strictly eleven years before the *1590* edition of the *Faerie Queene* Books I–III in *The Shepheardes Calender*, 1579. **did maske**: went in disguise, revelling as in a masque (cf. 'maske in mirth' *T.M.* 180; also *S.C.* Nov. 19) in contrast to his present high seriousness.
As time her taught: referring to the *S.C.*, either to its subject matter ('twelve Æglogues proportionable to the twelue monethes') or to its pastoral form which befitted the poet's apprenticeship to his craft. S. follows the precedent established for Renaissance poets by Virgil who wrote his pastoral *Eclogues* before attempting the *Aeneid*.
3 **enforst**: compelled by the Muse, as the Knight is 'compeld' (i 5.9) by Una.
4 **trumpets sterne**: hypallage, reversal of natural relations of the elements in a proposition (Puttenham's 'Changeling'). The trumpets of the heroic poem proclaim the stern deeds of fierce wars. **Oaten reeds**: the pastoral pipe; cf. *S.C.* Oct. 7–8.
5 **gentle**: noble; hypallage for the deeds of noble Knights and Ladies.
6 Implying the traditional exordium: 'I bring things never said before' (see Curtius, 1953, 85–6); hence the triumphant **Me** (7). In revealing what has been hidden, he assumes his role as the poet-prophet.
7 **too meane**: of low degree, in contrast to the noble Knights and Ladies. **areeds**: counsels; both 'commands' as 'enforst' (3) suggests and 'instructs' (from 'read' *OED* 12). The rhetorical figure of affected modesty, traced by Curtius 83–5, is used seriously here. Cf. VII vii 1–2.
8 **blazon broad**: make known abroad, proclaim (from 'blaze', to proclaim with a trumpet). There is a startling transformation of the lowly pastoral poet into one who throws off his disguise to thrust his work among the Muses.
9 **moralize**: the stories of fierce wars and faithful loves illustrate general moral truths rather than provide a text for a moral. Cf. 'morall laie', *Col.* 86.

2

Helpe then, O holy Virgin chiefe of nine,
   Thy weaker Nouice to performe thy will,
   Lay forth out of thine euerlasting scryne
   The antique rolles, which there lye hidden still,
   Of Faerie knights and fairest *Tanaquill*,
   Whom that most noble Briton Prince so long
   Sought through the world, and suffered so much ill,
   That I must rue his vndeserued wrong :
O helpe thou my weake wit, and sharpen my dull tong.

3

And thou most dreaded impe of highest *Ioue*,
   Faire *Venus* sonne, that with thy cruell dart
   At that good knight so cunningly didst roue,
   That glorious fire it kindled in his hart,
   Lay now thy deadly Heben bow apart,
   And with thy mother milde come to mine ayde :
   Come both, and with you bring triumphant *Mart*,
   In loues and gentle iollities arrayd,
After his murdrous spoiles and bloudy rage allayd.

4

And with them eke, O Goddesse heauenly bright,
   Mirrour of grace and Maiestie diuine,
   Great Lady of the greatest Isle, whose light
   Like *Phœbus* lampe throughout the world doth shine,
   Shed thy faire beames into my feeble eyne,
   And raise my thoughts too humble and too vile,
   To thinke of that true glorious type of thine,
   The argument of mine afflicted stile :
The which to heare, vouchsafe, O dearest dred a-while.

Stanza 2

1   **O holy Virgin**: perhaps Clio, the Muse of History:
chiefe being the 'eldest' (*T.M.* 53) of the nine Muses, called
the 'greater Muse' (VII vii 1.1). She is named 'holy Virgin' to
link her with the 'Goddesse', Elizabeth (4.1), who is the source
of the poet's inspiration. Possibly Calliope, the Muse of heroic
poetry, as Padelford argues (*Var.* i 506–14). In *T.M.* 459,
Calliope calls herself the Muse 'That lowly thoughts lift vp
to heauens hight'. S. links the two at VII vi 37.9. He may
invoke either or both (and hence does not name the goddess)

as the proper Muse of a heroic poem of praise, which is also
an 'antique history' (II Proem 1.2): see I xi 5.6–9n. The case
for Clio is argued by Spurgeon (1969) and Gregory (1974), and
that for Calliope by Starnes (1942).
2   **weaker**: too weak (the Latin absolute comparative), as
he is 'too meane' (1.7) for the Muses' task and his thoughts
'too humble and too vile' (4.6).
3   **scryne**: 'a coffer or other lyke place wherin jewels or
secreate thynges are kepte' (Cooper, 1565); also a shrine, as
Memory's 'immortall scrine' (II ix 56.6).   **euerlasting**
because it preserves deeds of everlasting fame.
5   **Tanaquill**: in Roman history, the wife of the first
Tarquin, famed as 'a very noble woman and a sad . . . her
image set up . . . as a token and a sign of chastity and labour'
(Vives, 1541, 45). At II x 76.8–9 she is named '*Glorian*', a
direct reference to Queen Elizabeth.
6–7   **that . . . Briton Prince**: Arthur, not named within the
poem until he reveals himself and is named by Una at ix 6.5.
S. follows Virgil who introduces his hero simply as the man
(*ille*).   **suffered**: i.e. for whom he suffered, extending the
parallel with Virgil's hero (*multum ille et terris iactatus et alto*)
to clarify the nature of the hero and his mission.
9   **wit**: mind, intellectual powers, which must be strengthened so that he may 'thinke' (4.7).

Stanza 3

1   **impe**: offspring.
3   **cunningly**: skilfully, craftily.   **roue**: shoot.
4   **glorious fire**: suggesting his love for Gloriana and also
his desire for glory, who appears as '*Prays-desire*' (II ix 36–39).
5–7   Cupid without his bow is the tamed divine Cupid, son
of the celestial Venus and himself a principle of order and
harmony in the universe (see II viii 6n). Mars and Venus
represent respectively war and love, the two related subjects
of the poem (1.9); their union produces the goddess Harmony.
On this ancient 'mystery' in Renaissance thought and painting,
see Wind (1967) 85f.   **Heben**: made of ebony whose blackness
suggests sinister properties, **deadly** because of its effect
upon lovers. Cf. the bow which Love's friend carries in *Le
Roman de la Rose* 914, made of the bitter-fruited tree, *plus
noirs que meure*. Heben is also 'some substance having a
poisonous juice' (*OED*); cf. '*Heben* sad' (II vii 52.2).

Stanza 4

1   **Goddesse**: a common term for princes, 'Who gods (as
God's viceregents) ar' (Countess of Pembroke's version of Ps.
82.1).
2   **Mirrour**: the earthly reflection of heavenly **grace and
Maiestie diuine**; also, as 'Goddesse' suggests, 'pattern',
'paragon'.
7   Inspired, the poet may see his sovereign, Elizabeth, in her
ideal form as the pattern of true glory. See *L.R.* on the
Faerie Queene as glory.
8   **argument**: the matter or subject, as in Milton's 'great
argument' (*Paradise Lost* i 24). Cf. 'O Queene, the matter of
my song' (III iv 3.8).   **afflicted stile**: humble pen, also a
more general reference, from the Lat. *afflictus*, 'thrown down'.
Hence the poet's need to be raised. 'Stile' may refer to the poem
itself (cf. *S.C.* Jan. 10).
9   The plea to the Queen to **heare** is renewed at II Proem
5.8; cf. IV Proem 5.1.   **dred**: as the 'Goddesse' (1) whom he
beholds with fear and reverence; cf. Isaiah 8.13: 'let him be
your dread' See vi 2.3, IV viii 17.1.

Canto I.

The Patron of true Holinesse,
Foule Errour doth defeate :
Hypocrisie him to entrapp',
Doth to his home entreate.

1

A Gentle Knight was pricking on the plaine,
Y cladd in mightie armes and siluer shielde,
Wherein old dints of deepe wounds did remaine,
The cruell markes of many' a bloudy fielde ;
Yet armes till that time did he neuer wield :
His angry steede did chide his foming bitt,
As much disdayning to the curbe to yield :
Full iolly knight he seemd, and faire did sitt,
As one for knightly giusts and fierce encounters fitt.

and here first used in English for the twelve divisions of a Book, the usual epic division from Homer (24) by way of Virgil (12). Drayton comments, 'The Italians use *Canto's*; and so our first late great Reformer, Master *Spenser*' ('To the reader', *Barons Warres*, in *Poems* 1619, *Works* ii 5).

Argument
The Argument to each Canto, in ballad metre or the common measure of the hymnbook, stands apart from the body of the poem.
1   **Patron**: protector and defender (from the Lat. *patronus*). Bryskett (1606) 22 records that S. told him that he had undertaken a work 'to represent all the moral vertues, assigning to every vertue, a Knight to be the patron and defender of the same'.
3   **Hypocrisie**: i.e. Archimago. A rare occasion in the poem in which the Argument provides information not found in the text; the word is never used later. Moral abstractions characterize the Arguments.

Stanzas 1–6
On the medieval pictorial conventions underlying the account of the Red Cross Knight with the maiden and her lamb, see Tuve (1970) 136–7. In his note to Drayton's reference to Saint George as England's patron, Selden records the story of the Knight's delivery of the King's daughter from the Dragon and adds: 'Your more neat judgements, finding no such matter in true antiquity, rather make it symbolicall then truely proper. So that some account him an allegory of our Saviour Christ; and our admired *Spencer* hath made him an emble of Religion' (*Works* iv 85). Selden may be using de Malynes, *Saint George for England* (1601): 'under the person of the noble champion Saint *George* our Saviour Christ was prefigured, delivering the Virgin (which did signifie the sinfull soules of Christians) from the dragon or divels power' (*Spenser Allusions* 84).

Stanza 1
1   **Gentle**: noble, referring to his present appearance and true nature; see VI v 1–2n. *L.R.* describes his rusticity and apparent lowliness before he dons the armour.   **pricking**: spurring.
2   **mightie armes**: 'that is the armour of a Christian man specified by Saint Paul v. Ephes.' (*L.R.*); cf. 'his godly armes' (I xi 7.9) and see Eph. 6.11–7.   **siluer shielde**: the 'shield of faith' (Eph. 6.16). The silver shield with its cross of blood was known to be St George's arms. Hardyng's *Chronicle* records that they were given to Arviragus when he was converted by Joseph of Arimathea; see *Var.* i 176.
3   **dints**: S.'s unusual spelling of 'dent', combining the blow, 'dint' (*OED* 1), with its effect. 'Those old dints have been made by the fiery darts of the wicked: and this panoply has been worn by every Christian man in every age' (Upton, 1758). His unproven role corresponds to David's when he 'girded . . . his sworde upon his rayment and began to go: for he never proved it' (1 Sam. 17.39). However, unlike David who doffs his armour to prove his God, the Knight wears his to prove himself worthy of it.
8   **iolly**: a simple, yet complex term with a wide range of meanings: gallant, brave, handsome, of proud bearing, amorous.   **seemd**: the ambiguous use of this word prepares the reader for the later clash between what is and what merely seems to be.

Canto i
Canto: Ital. 'song' taken by S. from Dante by way of Ariosto

2

But on his brest a bloudie Crosse he bore,
  The deare remembrance of his dying Lord,
  For whose sweete sake that glorious badge he wore,
  And dead as liuing euer him ador'd:
  Vpon his shield the like was also scor'd,
  For soueraine hope, which in his helpe he had:
  Right faithfull true he was in deede and word,
  But of his cheere did seeme too solemne sad;
Yet nothing did he dread, but euer was ydrad.

3

Vpon a great aduenture he was bond,
  That greatest *Gloriana* to him gaue,
  That greatest Glorious Queene of *Faerie* lond,
  To winne him worship, and her grace to haue,
  Which of all earthly things he most did craue;
  And euer as he rode, his hart did earne
  To proue his puissance in battell braue
  Vpon his foe, and his new force to learne;
Vpon his foe, a Dragon horrible and stearne.

4

A louely Ladie rode him faire beside,
  Vpon a lowly Asse more white then snow,
  Yet she much whiter, but the same did hide
  Vnder a vele, that wimpled was full low,
  And ouer all a blacke stole she did throw,
  As one that inly mournd: so was she sad,
  And heauie sat vpon her palfrey slow:
  Seemed in heart some hidden care she had,
And by her in a line a milke white lambe she lad.

---

principal subject of Book I.

5 **scor'd**: cut or painted.
6 **For soueraine hope**: i.e. to show the supreme hope. **hope** and **helpe** are linked alliteratively to indicate their causal connection. The Knight's enemy, Sansfoy, curses 'that Crosse . . . / That keepes thy body from the bitter fit' (ii 18.1–2).
7 **Right faithfull true**: cf. Rev. 19.11: 'And I sawe heaven open, and beholde a white horse, and he that sate vpon him, was called, Faithful and true'; gloss: 'He meaneth Christ.' **Right**: upright, righteous (cf. Ps. 51.10); or it may function as an adverb. 'The faithfull knight' is his common tag: as Arg. to Cantos iv, v, x.
8 **solemne sad**: grave, serious; the defining mood of Guyon, 'Still solemne sad' (II vi 37.5) when he avoids pleasure in order to pursue his quest, and of Arthur, 'somwhat sad, and solemne eke in sight' (II ix 36.8) in his desire for glory. Cf. Una who is 'sad' (4.6) in mourning. The mood marks man's settled fallen state in contrast to the sanguine temperament of unfallen man; see Klibansky *et al* (1964) 79–80, 102–3.
9 **ydrad**: dreaded.

Stanza 3
1 **bond**: obsolete form of 'bound', going; also bound by vow (cf. 54.3).
2–3 'In that Faery Queene I meane glory in my generall intention, but in my particular I conceiue the most excellent and glorious person of our soueraine the Queene' (*L.R.*). See Pr. 2.5*n*. In the poem the word 'glorious' is used for Christ's cross (2.3) before being applied to secular matters.
4 **worship**: honour, renown.
5 **earthly**: in apposition to his hope in Christ (2.6).
6 **earne**: yearn, as 7 confirms. It also carries the usual sense, seek to deserve by merit.
8 **his new force**: either the force of the armour newly given him, or his unproved power in wielding that armour. The phrasing is scriptural: e.g. Col. 3.10.

Stanza 4
Una is not named. Instead, she is associated by the **lowly Asse** (2) with Christ's humility (Matt. 21.5, from Zech. 9.9); by her whiteness with Truth (as Ripa's *Verita* is *vestita di color bianco*) and Faith (cf. x 13.1); and by her **vele** (4) with Truth which is veiled to fallen man. While her **lambe** (9) associates her with innocence and the sacrificial lamb of John 1.29, the king's daughter leading the lamb is a traditional item in the Legend of St George, as Greenlaw shows (*Var.* i 389). For the moral interpretation of Una's lamb as an attribute of innocence and truth, see Fowler (1961a) 419. Steadman (1958) 134–7, referring to the familiar Renaissance emblem subject *asinus portans mysteria*, argues that this stanza 'invests Una with both the signs, or *notae*, of the true church: (1) the ministry of the word (represented by the ass) and (2) the administration of the sacraments (symbolized by the lamb)'.
1 **louely**: also 'loving' and 'worthy of love'. **him faire beside**: as she is fair and rides becomingly by his side. **beside**: alluding to her name, Lat. *una* (together), because her 'wondrous faith' is 'firmest fixt' (ix 17.4–5) in her Knight; see 45.9*n*.
3 **the same**: i.e. her whiteness.
4 **wimpled**: lying in folds.
6 **inly**: inwardly, in her heart; 'entirely' (gloss to *S.C.* May 38).
9 **in a line**: on a rope.

Stanza 2
1. **But**] And *1590*. The change stresses the paradoxes in the Knight's appearance. **a bloudie Crosse**: the anonymous Knight is identified as the traditional Christian knight by his symbol, Christ's blood and cross, which is also the red cross of Saint George. By this badge, he symbolically 'bears' the cross; cf. *H.H.L.* 258–9 and II i 18.8–9.
2 **deare**: implying also 'dire'. **his dying Lord**: cf. 2 Cor. 4.10: 'Euerie where we beare about in our bodie the dying of the Lord Jesus, that the life of Jesus might also be made manifest in our bodies.'
4 **dead as liuing euer**: cf. Rev. 1.18: 'I was dead: and beholde, I am alive for evermore'. The pointing may be either 'dead, as liuing euer', or 'dead, as liuing, euer'. Nelson (1963) 147 notes that the paradox, Christ dead is Christ living, is the

5

So pure an innocent, as that same lambe,
  She was in life and euery vertuous lore,
  And by descent from Royall lynage came
  Of ancient Kings and Queenes, that had of yore
  Their scepters stretcht from East to Westerne shore,
  And all the world in their subiection held ;
  Till that infernall feend with foule vprore
  Forwasted all their land, and them expeld :
Whom to auenge, she had this Knight from far compeld.

6

Behind her farre away a Dwarfe did lag,
  That lasie seemd in being euer last,
  Or wearied with bearing of his bag
  Of needments at his backe.   Thus as they past,
  The day with cloudes was suddeine ouercast,
  And angry *Ioue* an hideous storme of raine
  Did poure into his Lemans lap so fast,
  That euery wight to shrowd it did constrain,
And this faire couple eke to shroud themselues were fain.

7

Enforst to seeke some couert nigh at hand,
  A shadie groue not far away they spide,
  That promist ayde the tempest to withstand:
  Whose loftie trees yclad with sommers pride,
  Did spred so broad, that heauens light did hide,
  Not perceable with power of any starre :
  And all within were pathes and alleies wide,
  With footing worne, and leading inward farre :
Faire harbour that them seemes ; so in they entred arre.

ment', which her afflicted state suggests that she suffers.
2   vertuous lore: i.e. in her knowledge of, and obedience to, moral doctrine. Her innocence is a state of perfection.
3   Royall lynage: her lineage from Adam and Eve. 'Adam was king of Eden, and universal king by parental authority; but by the prevailing power of that infernal fiend he forfeited his right. The restoration of lost Eden was reserved for the Messiah, the second Adam, imaged in this Christian knight' (Upton, 1758); see vii 43.
5   from East to Westerne shore: asserts Una's claim to be the holy Catholic Church; see ii 22.7–9n. The reformed Church of England claimed to derive its authority from the primitive Eastern Church whereas the papacy derived its authority only from Rome; see Kermode (1971) 42–3.
6   In man's original state of innocence, God 'gaue / All in his hand' (x 42.7–8) and commanded him to 'fil the earth, and subdue it' (Gen. 1.28).
7   feend: Satan.   **infernall**: from Hell; as it binds Una's parents in Hell.   **vprore**: revolt, insurrection; cf. the account of his rebellion at vii 44.
8   Forwasted: utterly laid waste.
9   compeld: called, with the stronger implication, forced to come.

Stanza 6
1   Dwarfe: variously identified by critics with the flesh, prudence, human reason, or common sense. That S. coins **needments** (4) stresses that he bears what Una 'needs', though this role is not developed.
6–7   Suggesting the myth of the marriage of the Earth and Sky, which is the beginning of creation; from Virgil, *Georg.* ii 325–6: *tum pater omnipotens fecundis imbribus Aether / coniugis in gremium laetae descendit.* The classical simile controls the Christian suggestions in the earlier stanzas and the transition from the opening allegorical pageant to the creation of fairyland. This storm initiates the action of Book I and so of the rest of the poem; hence **hideous** anticipates Error's 'hideous taile' (16.2) to which the storm leads.   **Lemans**: beloved's.
8   to shroud it: to take shelter, a usage first recorded in S. Repeated in 9, the word suggests 'concealing' or 'veiling'; cf. 8.3.
9   fain: obliged; glad.

Stanza 7
1   couert: in S., a dense thicket of woods suggests a place of peril. Cf. the entrance to Mammon's house (II vii 20.6) and to Acrasia's inner Bower (II xii 76.6).
4   pride: magnificent adornment; the most flourishing state, referring to the leaves; linked with 5, it suggests swelling pride; see 21.2n.
6   power of any starre: referring to astral influence; emanation from the stars which is both benign and malign as **any** suggests. The point is that the shade shuts out **heauens light** (5). Upton cites Statius's grove of sleep: *nulli penetrabilis astro, / lucus iners* (*Theb.* x 85–6). In Milton's *P.L.* ix 1086–7, Adam's fallen state is marked by his desire to retire into 'highest woods impenetrable / To star or sunlight'.
8   footing: footprints. The repetition of . . . *-ing* . . . *-ing in-* shows how the paths lead inward.
9   harbour: covert or place of retreat; an earlier form of 'arbour', a bower or shady retreat. As in 8, there is similar mimetic syntax, . . . *in* . . . *en-*, to note an enclosed state.

Stanza 5
1   innocent: in the religious sense, 'sinless', as the virgins who follow the lamb (Rev. 14.4); also 'undeserving of punish-

8

And foorth they passe, with pleasure forward led,
  Ioying to heare the birdes sweete harmony,
  Which therein shrouded from the tempest dred,
  Seemd in their song to scorne the cruell sky.
  Much can they prayse the trees so straight and hy,
  The sayling Pine, the Cedar proud and tall,
  The vine-prop Elme, the Poplar neuer dry,
The builder Oake, sole king of forrests all,
The Aspine good for staues, the Cypresse funerall.

9

The Laurell, meed of mightie Conquerours
  And Poets sage, the Firre that weepeth still,
  The Willow worne of forlorne Paramours,
  The Eugh obedient to the benders will,
  The Birch for shaftes, the Sallow for the mill,
  The Mirrhe sweete bleeding in the bitter wound,
  The warlike Beech, the Ash for nothing ill,
  The fruitfull Oliue, and the Platane round,
The caruer Holme, the Maple seeldom inward sound.

10

Led with delight, they thus beguile the way,
  Vntill the blustring storme is ouerblowne;
  When weening to returne, whence they did stray,
  They cannot finde that path, which first was showne,
  But wander too and fro in wayes vnknowne,
  Furthest from end then, when they neerest weene,
  That makes them doubt, their wits be not their owne :
  So many pathes, so many turnings seene,
That which of them to take, in diuerse doubt they been.

Stanza 8

1–4 The elaborate alliteration sets up its own **sweete harmony** (2) in order to convey a sense of the enclosed garden.
5 to 9.9 The list of trees displays S.'s craftsmanship as the poet of fairyland. The familiar epic catalogue announces his relation to Chaucer (*Parliament of Fowls* 176–82), Virgil (*Aen.* vi 179–82), Ovid (*Met.* x 90–105) and, through Ovid, back to Orpheus, the archetype of the poet's power to move trees and gather a forest around him as he plays upon his lyre. The characterizing of trees by their usefulness or stock associations has suggested to readers, since Upton, that the Wandering Wood, like Dante's *selva oscura*, is an emblem of man's life within society. Dixon (1597) glosses stanzas 7–9: 'worldly delighte'. The seven trees in stanza 8 are grouped by height.
5 **can**: do, did; or may: 'well may they praise'.
6 **sayling Pine**: because ships or their masts were made of pine; or itself sailing or soaring in its height; or because Chaucer writes of the 'saylynge fyr' (*Parl. Fowls* 179).
Cedar proud and tall: the biblical 'cedres of Lebanon, that are hie and exalted' (Isaiah 2.13), a symbol of pride, as also in Ezek. 31.3–10.
7 **vine-prop Elme**: because it supports the vine (as in Chaucer's 'piler elm' (*Parl. Fowls* 177); or, with a surprising reversal of the usual emblem, because it seems to be supported by the vine. The marriage of the masculine elm and feminine vine was a popular Renaissance emblem. **the Poplar neuer dry**: because 'Poplers grow by water sides' (Turner, *Herbal*

ii 98, cited *OED*); or was anciently associated with springs (Homer, *Ody.* vi 291); or because the Heliades, weeping for their brother Phaeton's death, were transformed into poplars and their tears into its oozing amber (Ovid, *Met.* ii 340–66).
8 **builder Oake**: Chaucer's 'byldere ok' (*Parl. Fowls* 176), i.e. used in building.
9 **Cypresse funerall**: Chaucer's 'cipresse, deth to playne' (*Parl. Fowls* 179), from Ovid's legend of Cyparissus who was changed into a cypress through grief for his slain hind (*Met.* x 106–42), and so was used to dress graves; cf. vi 17, II i 60.

Stanza 9

2 **weepeth still**: exudes resin continually.
3 **of forlorne Paramours**: by forsaken lovers.
4 **Eugh**: Chaucer's 'shetere ew' (*Parl. Fowls* 180), traditionally used for bows.
5 **Sallow**: 'a kind of woodde like Wyllow, fit to wreath and bynde' (E.K.'s gloss to *S.C.* Dec. 81). Placed here in contrast to the stiff birch. It is associated with stagnant water (cf. IV v 33.4–5) that would be found at a mill-pond, and may have been used to make the mill-wheel.
6 The myrrh is noted as an incense for its sweet smell (cf. Prov. 7.17, Song of Songs, *passim*), as a herb for its bitter taste (Mark 15.23), and, as the Arabian myrtle, for its medicinal gum which preserves the body. Bayley (1966) notes the density of meaning in this line: 'the myrrh is sweet-scented; bleeding because of the resinous gum; the wound from which the sweet gum comes is bitter because it painfully tore to bring forth in grief and pain the incestuous child of Myrrha'. On the birth of Adonis from the myrrh, see Ovid, *Met.* x 503–13.
7 **warlike Beech**: in Homer, *Iliad* v 838, the axle of the war chariot is made of 'the beechen tree' (Chapman's trans.).
Ash: 'hath so great vertue, that Serpentes come not in shadowe thereof' (Bartholomaeus, 1582, XVII xii). Pliny *Nat. Hist.* XVI xxiv notes its virtues and general usefulness. **for nothing ill**: in contrast to the warlike beech.
8 **Platane round**: Lat. *platanus*, f. *platea*, broad, 'none being so large as shee' (Donne, *Elegy* ix 30). The tree may have been suggested by the **Oliue**, to balance a Christian reference with a pagan one. Socrates and his friends sat by a plane tree (*Phaedrus* 230b); and see x 54.1–5.
9 **caruer Holme**: either the holly or the holm-oak, both suitable for carving; cf. Chaucer's 'holm to whippes lashe' (*Parl. Fowls* 178). Of the maple **seeldom inward sound**, Lyly asks 'Is not . . . dunge [taken] out of the Maple tree by the Scorpion?' (*Euphues*, *Works* i 242). Sinon asserted that the Trojan horse was made of maple (*Aen.* ii 112). Fair without but unsound within, it stands as a fitting climax to the delightful wood which has the monster at its centre.

Stanza 10

1 **Led with delight**: completing the description of the Wandering Wood which was introduced by the phrase, 'with pleasure forward led' (8.1). They no longer lead but are passively led.
3 **weening**: intending.
4 **was showne**: the passive tense shows how the Wood may 'beguile' (1) them.
6 **neerest weene**: think to be nearest to it.
7, 9 **doubt**: also fear.
9 **diuerse**: distracting; a usage peculiar to S., from the sense of 'divers', turned different ways. What is mentally diverse is morally distracting and dividing.

11

At last resoluing forward still to fare,
  Till that some end they finde or in or out,
  That path they take, that beaten seemd most bare,
  And like to lead the labyrinth about ;
  Which when by tract they hunted had throughout,
  At length it brought them to a hollow caue,
  Amid the thickest woods.   The Champion stout
  Eftsoones dismounted from his courser braue,
And to the Dwarfe a while his needlesse spere he gaue.

12

Be well aware, quoth then that Ladie milde,
  Least suddaine mischiefe ye too rash prouoke :
  The danger hid, the place vnknowne and wilde,
  Breedes dreadfull doubts : Oft fire is without smoke,
  And perill without show : therefore your stroke
  Sir knight with-hold, till further triall made.
  Ah Ladie (said he) shame were to reuoke
  The forward footing for an hidden shade :
Vertue giues her selfe light, through darkenesse for to wade.

13

Yea but (quoth she) the perill of this place
  I better wot then you, though now too late
  To wish you backe returne with foule disgrace,
  Yet wisedome warnes, whilest foot is in the gate,
  To stay the steppe, ere forced to retrate.
  This is the wandring wood, this *Errours den*,
  A monster vile, whom God and man does hate :
  Therefore I read beware.   Fly fly (quoth then
The fearefull Dwarfe :) this is no place for liuing men.

Stanza 11

1   **still**: in the same direction, a persistence that leads them into the centre of the labyrinth as later (28.5) it takes them out.
3   The same path leads to the house of Pride, iv 2.9.
4   **And . . . about**: i.e. would be likely to lead through the labyrinth or out of it, for they seek to go either 'in or out' (2). In a labyrinth, the way out is the way in. The Renaissance saw the labyrinth as 'an Allegorie of Mans life . . . for what liker to a Labyrinth, then the Maze of Life?' (Drayton, *Works* ii 138–9). Fletcher (1971) 24f analyses S.'s use of the image of the labyrinth. On Eden as 'an endless Maze', see Du Bartas, *Divine Weekes* II i p. 86. In Langland, *Piers Plowman* i 6, the world is a wilderness in which people are 'bisi . . . abouten the mase'.
5   **tract**: track; tracing. A hunting term used here with **hunted** because the maze leads to the Minotaur at its centre.
7   **stout**: brave, undaunted.
8   **Eftsoones**: forthwith.   **braue**: excellent, splendid.
9   **needlesse**: because the spear is used only on horseback (cf. II iii 3) except in dire need (as II viii 34).

Stanza 12

1   **aware**: watchful, on your guard. Dixon (1597) cites Eph. 5.15: 'Take hede therefore that ye walke circumspectly, not as fooles, but as wise.'   **milde**: gentle, gracious. The epithet has strong religious connotations, being commonly applied to Christ and the Virgin Mary. Cf. ix 46.6.
2   **mischiefe**: misfortune, calamity.   **rash**: functions equally as adv. and adj.
4–5   Una's proverbial expressions first establish her as Wisdom: cf. 'Yet wisedome warnes' (13.4); and cf. her moral aphorisms at 32.6–7, 33.3. Here she inverts the common proverb: 'there is no fire without smoke' (C. G. Smith, 1970, 263). Noted by Doyle (1972) as a denial of proverbial wisdom; however, Una wisely adapts the proverb to special circumstances.
7–8   For the sentiment, cf. III xi 24.5–9.   **reuoke**: draw back, from Lat. *revocare pedem*. Such usage is forced upon S. by the need to express moral states in physical terms.
9   Cf. Milton, *Comus*: 'Virtue could see to do what Virtue would / By her own radiant light' (372–3). For the proverb, see Smith 820.   **wade**: proceed, though the usual sense makes **shade** (8) a substance which impedes motion, as the biblical plague of darkness, 'even darcknes that may be felt' (Exod. 10.21).

Stanza 13

2   **wot**: know.
4   **gate**: way, applied here to the entrance of the cave.
5   **retrate**: the obsolete vb 'retrait'.
6   **wandring wood**: the wood within which one may wander or err physically, morally, and spiritually; **Errours**: from Lat. *errare*, to wander. Hankins (1971) 68 links the term to Servius's gloss on *Aen.* vi 295, with its reference to the *errorem syluarum*, the error of the woods, which leads either to vices or to virtues; see Nelson (1963) 159–60.
8–9   As later the 'wary Dwarfe' (v 45.7) counsels the Knight to flee the house of Pride.   **read**: counsel, or warn; as Una is Truth, 'wisedome warnes' (4).

14

But full of fire and greedy hardiment,
　The youthfull knight could not for ought be staide,
　But forth vnto the darksome hole he went,
　And looked in: his glistring armor made
　A litle glooming light, much like a shade,
　By which he saw the vgly monster plaine,
　Halfe like a serpent horribly displaide,
But th'other halfe did womans shape retaine,
Most lothsom, filthie, foule, and full of vile disdaine.

15

And as she lay vpon the durtie ground,
　Her huge long taile her den all ouerspred,
　Yet was in knots and many boughtes vpwound,
　Pointed with mortall sting.　Of her there bred
　A thousand yong ones, which she dayly fed,
　Sucking vpon her poisonous dugs, eachone
　Of sundry shapes, yet all ill fauored:
Soone as that vncouth light vpon them shone,
Into her mouth they crept, and suddain all were gone.

16

Their dam vpstart, out of her den effraide,
　And rushed forth, hurling her hideous taile
　About her cursed head, whose folds displaid
　Were stretcht now forth at length without entraile.
　She lookt about, and seeing one in mayle
　Armed to point, sought backe to turne againe;
　For light she hated as the deadly bale,
Ay wont in desert darknesse to remaine,
Where plaine none might her see, nor she see any plaine.

17

Which when the valiant Elfe perceiu'd, he lept
　As Lyon fierce vpon the flying pray,
　And with his trenchand blade her boldly kept
　From turning backe, and forced her to stay:
　Therewith enrag'd she loudly gan to bray,
　And turning fierce, her speckled taile aduaunst,
　Threatning her angry sting, him to dismay:
Who nought aghast, his mightie hand enhaunst:
The stroke down from her head vnto her shoulder glaunst.

7-9　As a type of Satan, Error is shown iconographically as a serpent with a woman's face. See Didron (1886) ii 139-41; cf. Langland, *Piers Plowman* xviii 335, where Satan appears 'ylyke a lusarde with a lady visage'. The classical source is Echidna in Hesiod, *Theog.* 295-305; the Christian source is the locusts in Rev. 9.7-10 who have the hair of women and the tails of scorpions. Scorpions or scourges are cited as a heavy yoke at 1 Kings 12.11. As a symbol of treachery or of fraud, see Panofsky (1962) 89-91, and cf. Dante's description of Geryon, *Inf.* xvii 10-2. In her double aspect, Error is the prototype of Duessa (see ii 40-41) and the house of Pride (see iv 5). **disdaine**: loathesomeness, exciting disdain; cf. 19.6.

Stanza 15
3　**boughtes**: coils.
4　**mortall sting**: cf. the locusts in Rev. 9.10 with 'stings in their tailes' and the gloss: 'to infect and kil with their venemous doctrine'. Error's half-woman shape represents the pleasures of the Wandering Wood; her tail, the labyrinth which entangles the Knight; and its sting, the death which comes at the end. Dixon (1597) notes: 'Hipocritie stings lyke scorpions the members of Christe.' On the connection between the labyrinth and the serpent-woman, and Error's allegorical significance, see Steadman (1961).
7　Each is distinct and separate from the others though all, being **ill fauored**, resemble their dam.
8-9　From the popular belief that an adder, when disturbed, swallows its young.

Stanza 16
1　**vpstart**: started up.　　**effraide**: alarmed (f. vb 'affray').
2　**hurling**: hurtling and whirling; cf. the violent motion of Lucifera (iv 16.3) and of Orgoglio (viii 17.9).　　**hideous**: huge; abominable; paired meanings throughout the poem: huge and therefore abominable; cf. the Dragon's tail, xi 23.1.
3　**displaid**: extended, and therefore shown to view, as 14.7.
4　**entraile**: coiling.
6　**Armed to point**: fully armed.
7　**deadly bale**: deadly injury (or by double enallage, baleful death), i.e. death; cf. John 3.20: 'For everie man that evil doeth, hateth the light, nether commeth to light, lest his dedes shulde be reproved.'
8　**Ay wont**: ever accustomed.

Stanza 17
1　**Elfe**: literally a fairy but applied generally to a knight in fairyland as distinct from a Briton knight. While the Red Cross Knight is supposed 'a Faeries sonne', he is a changeling descended 'of *Saxon* kings . . . in *Britane* land' (see x 64-65). The distinction is not always significant, for 'In th'olde dayes of the Kyng Arthour / . . . Al was this land fulfild of fayerye' (Chaucer, *Wife of Bath's Tale* 857-9).
2　**As Lyon fierce**: a deliberate opening simile which is later expanded in Una's adventures. When he abandons her and she is left without 'my Lyon, and my noble Lord' (iii 7.6), she is sustained by the lion which she makes mild (iii Arg.); but its fierceness brings its defeat by Sansloy, etc.
3　**trenchand**: sharp.
6　**speckled**: the snake's colours, signifying blots of sin; cf. the dragon's 'bespotted' tail and 'speckled brest' (xi 11.5 and 15.2).
7　**dismay**: defeat.
8　**enhaunst**: raised up.

Stanza 14
1　**hardiment**: boldness. This word describes Arthur when he begins his career, ix 12.6.
2　**ought**: anything whatever.
4　**glistring**: shining with its own light; 'Vertue giues her selfe light' (12.9), for he wears 'the armour of light' (Rom. 13.12).
5　**glooming**: gleaming; glowing (from 'gloom'); but cf. 'glooming': that appears dark (*OED* 2); hence it is **much like a shade**.

18

Much daunted with that dint, her sence was dazd,
  Yet kindling rage, her selfe she gathered round,
  And all attonce her beastly body raizd
  With doubled forces high aboue the ground :
  Tho wrapping vp her wrethed sterne arownd,
  Lept fierce vpon his shield, and her huge traine
  All suddenly about his body wound,
  That hand or foot to stirre he stroue in vaine :
God helpe the man so wrapt in *Errours* endlesse traine.

19

His Lady sad to see his sore constraint,
  Cride out, Now now Sir knight, shew what ye bee,
  Add faith vnto your force, and be not faint :
  Strangle her, else she sure will strangle thee.
  That when he heard, in great perplexitie,
  His gall did grate for griefe and high disdaine,
  And knitting all his force got one hand free,
  Wherewith he grypt her gorge with so great paine,
That soone to loose her wicked bands did her constraine.

20

Therewith she spewd out of her filthy maw
  A floud of poyson horrible and blacke,
  Full of great lumpes of flesh and gobbets raw,
  Which stunck so vildly, that it forst him slacke
  His grasping hold, and from her turne him backe :
  Her vomit full of bookes and papers was,
  With loathly frogs and toades, which eyes did lacke,
  And creeping sought way in the weedy gras :
Her filthy parbreake all the place defiled has.

Stanza 18

1 **daunted**: subdued; stupefied. **dint**: blow. **dazd**: bewildered. Throughout the episode S. wittily shows Error herself overcome by error and doubt.
2 **gathered round**: coiled.
5 She wraps her coiled tail around herself, ready to wrap it around the Knight.
6 **traine**: tail, suggesting all that follows Error.
9 The poet's prayer implies that only God may help the Knight so caught. **traine**: treachery, deceit. Duplication of the rhyme word links the literal and allegorical significances of the monster's tail, and both with the labyrinth of the Wandering Wood. Cf. the 'endlesse error' (iii 23.9) to which Abessa and Corceca condemn Una.

Stanza 19

1 **constraint**: fettered state, from Lat. *constringere*, to draw tight; also 'distress'.
2–4 Una's cry breaks the encoiling rhythm: the eight words of 2 require eight heavy stresses rising in intensity with the concluding **shew what ye bee**, and followed by the surprising and rare dactyl, **Strangle her**. Una's injunction, 'shew what ye bee', and our awareness that the Wood is the world that prevents man from undertaking his quest, suggest 1 John 5.4. 'For all that is borne of God, overcometh the worlde: and this is the victorie that overcometh the worlde, even our faith.' His **force** is his 'virtue' (*OED* 1) to which he now joins faith: 'joyne moreover vertue with your faith' (2 Pet. 1.5). This moment is repeated in the Knight's battle with Sansjoy, v 12. **faith** suggests an opposition to knowledge, with which the serpent is traditionally associated. On salvation through faith, see Article xi of the Thirty-nine Articles. **faint**: wanting in courage or strength.
5 **perplexitie**: literally, his entangled state (*OED* 3); morally, his distress and bewilderment (*OED* 1b). Later he refers to this moment as a time when Una was 'wont to comfort me affrayd' (52.9).
6 **gall**: the seat of anger. **grate**: fret. **griefe**: anger. **high disdaine**: renders the Ital. *alto sdegno*; 'high' notes approval of his state in contrast to his later 'fiery fierce disdaine' (ii 8.4).
8 **paine**: labour; also as his effort leads to her pain.

Stanza 20

3 **gobbets raw**: chunks of undigested food.
6–8 Cf. Rev. 16.13: 'And I sawe thre uncleane spirits like frogges come out of the mouth of the dragon, and out of the mouth of the beast, and out of the mouth of the false prophet.' The Geneva gloss reads: 'That is, a strong number of this great devil the Popes ambassadours which are ever crying and croking like frogs and come out of Antichrists mouth, because they shulde speake nothing but lies.' **bookes and papers** may refer to such published lies, or to learning generally in its opposition to faith.
9 **parbreake**: vomit, spewing; its etymological sense, 'breaking out or forth', shows the monster's violence – cf. 'vpstart' (16.1) – which the Knight must overcome. Error is made repulsive to each of man's senses.

21

As when old father *Nilus* gins to swell
　With timely pride aboue the *Aegyptian* vale,
　His fattie waues do fertile slime outwell,
　And ouerflow each plaine and lowly dale :
　But when his later spring gins to auale,
　Huge heapes of mud he leaues, wherein there breed
　Ten thousand kindes of creatures, partly male
　And partly female of his fruitfull seed ;
Such vgly monstrous shapes elswhere may no man reed.

22

The same so sore annoyed has the knight,
　That welnigh choked with the deadly stinke,
　His forces faile, ne can no longer fight.
　Whose corage when the feend perceiu'd to shrinke,
　She poured forth out of her hellish sinke
　Her fruitfull cursed spawne of serpents small,
　Deformed monsters, fowle, and blacke as inke,
　Which swarming all about his legs did crall,
And him encombred sore, but could not hurt at all.

23

As gentle Shepheard in sweete euen-tide,
　When ruddy *Phœbus* gins to welke in west,
　High on an hill, his flocke to vewen wide,
　Markes which do byte their hasty supper best ;
　A cloud of combrous gnattes do him molest,
　All striuing to infixe their feeble stings,
　That from their noyance he no where can rest,
　But with his clownish hands their tender wings
He brusheth oft, and oft doth mar their murmurings.

24

Thus ill bestedd, and fearefull more of shame,
　Then of the certaine perill he stood in,
　Halfe furious vnto his foe he came,
　Resolv'd in minde all suddenly to win,
　Or soone to lose, before he once would lin ;
　And strooke at her with more then manly force,
　That from her body full of filthie sin
　He raft her hatefull head without remorse ;
A streame of cole black bloud forth gushed from her corse.

Stanza 21

The comparison is suggested by the association of the Nile with the captivity of the Israelites in Egypt and hence with the fallen world, the flesh, and bondage to sin. It was a commonplace of natural history that the Nile breeds strange monsters.

2　timely pride: seasonable flooding; 'pride' is suggested by **swell** (1), being puffed up with pride, and refers to the most flourishing state, as the trees at 7.4.

3　fattie: fecund, fertilizing.　**outwell**: pour forth.

5　later spring: last spring-tide; or 'later' may function as an adverb.　**auale**: abate.

6–9　This account of spontaneous generation, abiogenesis, which popular etymology would link with Lat. *nilum*, closely follows Ovid, *Met*. i 416–37; cf. III vi 8.7–9, IV xi 20.3, also VII vii 18. Cooper (1565) writes: 'Nilus was famous for the vertue of the water thereof, whiche overflowynge the countrey of Aegypte, made the grounde woonderfull fertyle many yeres after, so that without labourynge, the earth brought foorth abundaunce of sundry graynes and plantes, delectable and profitable.'

7, 8　partly: in part, some.　**seed**: semen.

9　reed: see. A sense found only in S.: for him to read is to see; cf. III ix 2.3, V xii 39.9. The strangeness of the shapes is commonly noted, e.g. Donne: 'A thing more strange, then on Niles slime, the Sunne / E'r bred' (*Satyre* iv 18–9).

Stanza 22

1　annoyed: affected injuriously.

4　feend: applied elsewhere in Book I to the Dragon, e.g. xi 2.3.

5–6　sinke: her womb, or organs of excretion, as a cesspool. Apparently the flood of black poison (20.2) of the monster's vomit suggested the flooding of the Nile; in turn, its 'fertile slime' (21.3) suggested the **fruitfull . . . spawne of serpents** spontaneously generated by Error which she now defecates upon the Knight.

7　blacke as inke: linked with the 'bookes and papers' in Error's black vomit.

Stanza 23

The simile anticipates the Knight's victory. The gnat, or fly, is an emblem of what is merely troublesome (cf. II ix 16, 51; V xi 58; VI i 24, xi 48): the feeble stings of Error's brood contrast with her 'mortall sting' (15.4). The simile is both naturalistic and literary (S. imitates Ariosto, *Orl. Fur*. xiv 109 and Homer, *Iliad* ii 469–71). On the further significance of the fly, see 38.2n.

2　welke: wane.

5　combrous: harassing.

8　clownish: rough, belonging to a rustic, specifically to the 'clownishe younge man' described in *L.R*.

Stanza 24

1　ill bestedd: in bad plight.

3　Halfe furious: a careful qualification. Only later does he yield totally to 'furious ire' (ii 5.8) and become subject to irrational passion (cf. ii 15, v 14).

5　lin: cease, leave off.

6　manly: human. That his force is **more then** human alludes to the faith which he adds to his force. Force, by itself, has failed him, 22.3. 'Manly' force fails him before Orgoglio (vii 6) and before Despair (ix 48) because he lacks faith.

8　raft: struck off.　**remorse**: pity.

25

Her scattred brood, soone as their Parent deare
    They saw so rudely falling to the ground,
    Groning full deadly, all with troublous feare,
    Gathred themselues about her body round,
    Weening their wonted entrance to haue found
    At her wide mouth : but being there withstood
    They flocked all about her bleeding wound,
    And sucked vp their dying mothers blood,
Making her death their life, and eke her hurt their good.

26

That detestable sight him much amazde,
    To see th'vnkindly Impes of heauen accurst,
    Deuoure their dam ; on whom while so he gazd,
    Hauing all satisfide their bloudy thurst,
    Their bellies swolne he saw with fulnesse burst,
    And bowels gushing forth : well worthy end
    Of such as drunke her life, the which them nurst ;
    Now needeth him no lenger labour spend,
His foes haue slaine themselues,with whom he should contend.

27

His Ladie seeing all, that chaunst, from farre
    Approcht in hast to greet his victorie,
    And said, Faire knight, borne vnder happy starre,
    Who see your vanquisht foes before you lye :
    Well worthy be you of that Armorie,
    Wherein ye haue great glory wonne this day,
    And prou'd your strength on a strong enimie,
    Your first aduenture : many such I pray,
And henceforth euer wish, that like succeed it may.

28

Then mounted he vpon his Steede againe,
    And with the Lady backward sought to wend ;
    That path he kept, which beaten was most plaine,
    Ne euer would to any by-way bend,
    But still did follow one vnto the end,
    The which at last out of the wood them brought.
    So forward on his way (with God to frend)
    He passed forth, and new aduenture sought ;
Long way he trauelled, before he heard of ought.

29

At length they chaunst to meet vpon the way
    An aged Sire, in long blacke weedes yclad,
    His feete all bare, his beard all hoarie gray,
    And by his belt his booke he hanging had ;
    Sober he seemde, and very sagely sad,
    And to the ground his eyes were lowly bent,
    Simple in shew, and voyde of malice bad,
    And all the way he prayed, as he went,
And often knockt his brest, as one that did repent.

Stanza 25
2   rudely: violently.
4   A significant iconographical detail: earlier Error's tail surrounds her body, 18.5.
7–9   Suggests the popular legend of the pelican whose heart's

blood revives her dying brood, e.g. Whitney (1586) 87. The legend was applied to Christ who is our pelican (Dante, Parad. xxv 113). Here it is an emblem of ingratitude, as in Lear's reference to his 'pelican daughters' (Lear III iv 74), and brings death rather than life. Cf. also the popular legend of the viper in Du Bartas's praise of God for having set man's enemies at enmity with themselves: 'Thou mak'st th'ingratefull Viper (at his birth) / His dying Mothers belly to gnaw forth' (Divine Weekes I vi p. 51). S. makes much the same point.

Stanza 26
1   amazde: stunned, stupefied.
2   vnkindly Impes: unnatural offspring; 'vnkindly' includes the current sense as an ironic understatement.
5–6   The offspring of Error are revealed finally to be a type of Judas or anti-Christ. With his reward for betraying Christ, Judas purchased a field 'and when he had throwen downe him selfe head long he brast a sondre in the middes, and all his bowels gushed out' (Acts 1.18).

Stanza 27
2   greet: offer formal congratulations on; a usage found only in S.
3   happy: auspicious, propitious, referring to astral influence. Cf. her greeting when he emerges from Orgoglio's dungeon: 'what euill starre / On you hath fround, and pourd his influence bad' (viii 42.6–7).
4–8   The repetition of you and your stresses the Knight's worthiness to wear the armour of Christ (Armorie: armory, i.e. armour) and assume his role as the Knight of the Red Cross (armory as armorial bearings, OED 2). At the beginning he sought 'To proue his puissance' (3.7); now he has prou'd his strength by an adventure, which foreshadows his final defeat of the Dragon.

Stanza 28
Rose (1975) 14 observes that this central stanza divides the canto into two balancing episodes of twenty-seven stanzas each.
3   Repeating 11.3 to round out the episode.   beaten: by those entering rather than leaving; cf. the way to the House of Pride: 'All bare through peoples feet, which thither traueiled. / . . . But few returned' (iv 2.9–3.3).
4–5   To escape from the wilderness the children of Israel are exhorted to 'turne not aside to the right hand nor to the left, but walke in all the wayes which the Lord your God hath commanded you' (Deut. 5.32–3). The moral application of this injunction, given at Deut. 17.20, also applies to the Knight. The accumulation of monosyllables in 5, together with the steady rhythm, may imitate the Knight's persistence.   still: 'the same steadiness of aim that had brought the Knight face to face with Error (11.1), now leads him out of its mazes' (Percival, 1893).
7   to frend: as a friend.

Stanza 29
4   his booke: ostensibly the Bible, but see 36.8.
5   sagely sad: wise and serious, a counterpart to the sad appearance of the Knight (2.8) and Una (4.6).
7–9   The posture of the Publican who 'wolde not lift up so much as his eyes to heaven, but smote his brest' (Luke 18.13). in shew: in appearance; always in S. with the implication that the reality is different.   malice: wickedness; bad alludes to its root (Lat. malus).

30

He faire the knight saluted, louting low,
  Who faire him quited, as that courteous was :
  And after asked him, if he did know
  Of straunge aduentures, which abroad did pas.
  Ah my deare Sonne (quoth he) how should, alas,
  Silly old man, that liues in hidden cell,
  Bidding his beades all day for his trespas,
  Tydings of warre and worldly trouble tell ?
With holy father sits not with such things to mell.

31

But if of daunger which hereby doth dwell,
  And homebred euill ye desire to heare,
  Of a straunge man I can you tidings tell,
  That wasteth all this countrey farre and neare.
  Of such (said he) I chiefly do inquere,
  And shall you well reward to shew the place,
  In which that wicked wight his dayes doth weare :
  For to all knighthood it is foule disgrace,
That such a cursed creature liues so long a space.

32

Far hence (quoth he) in wastfull wildernesse
  His dwelling is, by which no liuing wight
  May euer passe, but thorough great distresse.
  Now (sayd the Lady) draweth toward night,
  And well I wote, that of your later fight
  Ye all forwearied be : for what so strong,
  But wanting rest will also want of might ?
  The Sunne that measures heauen all day long,
At night doth baite his steedes the *Ocean* waues. emong.

33

Then with the Sunne take Sir, your timely rest,
  And with new day new worke at once begin :
  Vntroubled night they say giues counsell best.
  Right well Sir knight ye haue aduised bin,
  (Quoth then that aged man ;) the way to win
  Is wisely to aduise : now day is spent ;
  Therefore with me ye may take vp your In
  For this same night.   The knight was well content :
So with that godly father to his home they went.

34

A little lowly Hermitage it was,
  Downe in a dale, hard by a forests side,
  Far from resort of people, that did pas
  In trauell to and froe : a little wyde
  There was an holy Chappell edifyde,
  Wherein the Hermite dewly wont to say
  His holy things each morne and euentyde :
  Thereby a Christall streame did gently play,
Which from a sacred fountaine welled forth alway.

Stanza 30
1   **louting** : bowing humbly.
2   **quited** : returned the salutation.
4   **straunge** : out of the country (*OED* 1b), being **abroad** ;

unusual, out of the way (*OED* 8). At the end the Knight reports to Adam of his 'perils straunge and hard' (xii 31.8).
5-9   **my deare Sonne** : more than religious formality. The Knight seeks his identity, and only when purged from the sin into which the **holy father** now leads him does he learn who he is. Finally he is addressed by Adam as 'Deare Sonne' (xii 17.2).
6   **Silly** : feeble, simple, lowly – a range of meanings to describe how he wishes to appear.   **cell** : the obsolete sense, 'a compartment of the brain', is relevant to the psychological allegory that follows when this arch image-maker infects the Knight's fancy.
7   **Bidding his beades** : saying his prayers.
9   **sits not** : is not fitting.   **mell** : mingle, concern himself.

Stanza 31
1-4   Archimago replies with characteristic equivocation : to the Knight's request for 'straunge aduentures, which abroad did pas', he tells of **daunger** and **euill** which is **homebred** yet performed by a **straunge man**, i.e. one from outside. He describes the Dragon, the intruder who has ravaged Eden, but in terms that reduce the hero to a mere chivalric knight. The false dream that he soon implants in the Knight reduces him further to a lover.
7   **weare** : spend.
8-9   The glibness of this heroic bravado may suggest an over-confident knight who has just emerged from his first test and now digresses to seek mere chivalric adventures, but the sentiment is heroic.

Stanza 32
1   **wastfull** : desolate.
4-9   Una's words to her Knight are both ironic and pro-phetic. Night brings him no rest but only the counsel to flee from her. That **might** needs rest is a dilemma throughout the poem. The state of virtue must be maintained by ceaseless vigilance and yet the frailty of the flesh requires rest.   **later** : recent.   **forwearied** : 'for' is an intensive prefix.   **baite** : give food and drink to ; rests.

Stanza 33
3   Proverbial : *Nox adfert consilium* (see C. G. Smith, 1970, 574).
6   **wisely to aduise** : heedfully take thought ; said sar-castically about Una's advice.
7   **In** : abode, as the earlier 'harbour' of the Wandering Wood where 'in they entred arre' (7.9).

Stanza 34
1-9   This false hermitage at which the Knight abandons his religious role is **Downe in a dale** because his descent into sin begins here. Cf. the true hermitage on a hill (x 46) where the Knight re-dedicates himself to his role. It is **hard by a forests side** because he flees into its wilderness, and **Far from resort of people** because he takes 'bywaies . . . / Where neuer foot of liuing wight did tread' (vii 50.3-4). The **sacred fountaine** suggests the Well of Life with its life-giving waters ; instead, however, it is the *fons sacer* of the grove in which Ovid's Muse encourages him to treat of love rather than war (*Amores* III i 3).
5   **edifyde** : built ; with the religious sense, 'strengthened in holiness', implied ironically.
7   **things** : prayers, offices.

35

Arriued there, the little house they fill,
  Ne looke for entertainment, where none was :
  Rest is their feast, and all things at their will ;
  The noblest mind the best contentment has.
  With faire discourse the euening so they pas :
  For that old man of pleasing wordes had store,
  And well could file his tongue as smooth as glas ;
  He told of Saintes and Popes, and euermore
He strowd an *Aue-Mary* after and before.

36

The drouping Night thus creepeth on them fast,
  And the sad humour loading their eye liddes,
  As messenger of *Morpheus* on them cast
  Sweet slombring deaw, the which to sleepe them biddes.
  Vnto their lodgings then his guestes he riddes,
  Where when all drownd in deadly sleepe he findes,
  He to his study goes, and there amiddes
  His Magick bookes and artes of sundry kindes,
He seekes out mighty charmes, to trouble sleepy mindes.

37

Then choosing out few wordes most horrible,
  (Let none them read) thereof did verses frame,
  With which and other spelles like terrible,
  He bad awake blacke *Plutoes* griesly Dame,
  And cursed heauen, and spake reprochfull shame
  Of highest God, the Lord of life and light ;
  A bold bad man, that dar'd to call by name
  Great *Gorgon*, Prince of darknesse and dead night,
At which *Cocytus* quakes, and *Styx* is put to flight.

38

And forth he cald out of deepe darknesse dred
  Legions of Sprights, the which like little flyes
  Fluttring about his euer damned hed,
  A-waite whereto their seruice he applyes,
  To aide his friends, or fray his enimies :
  Of those he chose out two, the falsest twoo,
  And fittest for to forge true-seeming lyes ;
  The one of them he gaue a message too,
The other by him selfe staide other worke to doo.

3   In being content, they have all that they wish in rest itself.
5   **discourse**: conversation, which Archimago turns into a Popish service by his prayers to the Virgin.
7   **file**: smooth, polish; cf. his 'faire filed tong' (II i 3.6). The derogatory implications are clear from the contrast with *Zele* 'That well could charme his tongue' (V ix 39.3). Cf. Ps. 140.3: 'Thei have sharpened their tongues like a serpent.'
9   This Protestant scorn is nicely rendered by Shakespeare in *2 Henry VI* I iii 53–4: 'all his mind is bent to holiness, / To number Ave-Maries on his beads.'

Stanza 36
2–4   **sad humour**: heavy moisture, the **deaw** of sleep. Imitating Virgil, *Aen.* v 854f where the God of Sleep shakes over Palinurus's temples a branch dripping with the dew of Lethe, the river of forgetfulness, before plunging him to his death. S. invokes his son, Morpheus, the fashioner of dreams through which the Knight will fall to his 'death'.
slombring: occasioning sleep.
5   **riddes**: despatches.
6   **deadly**: like his twin, death. With rare exceptions, sleep is perilous and never refreshing.
8   **Magick bookes**: alluding to his name, Archimago, the arch-magician.
9   **sleepy**: sleeping.

Stanza 37
4   **Plutoes griesly Dame**: i.e. Proserpina, the consort of Pluto and the goddess of the underworld, who is linked with Hecate (see 43.3) by Comes (1616) III xvi; 'griesly' because her appearance arouses horror, as at ii 2.7. She is invoked here as the patron of witches and witchcraft.
7   **call**: summon by rites; or in the sense (*OED* 23b), 'call upon the Name of the Lord' (Gen. 4.26).
8   Echoes Tasso, *Ger. Lib.* xiii 10; cf. Statius, *Thebaid* iv 514–5.   **Gorgon**: 'an inchanter, whiche was supposed to be of suche excellencie, that he had authoritie over all spirites that made men afearde' (Cooper, 1565); for Demogorgon, see v 22.5, IV ii 47.7. In Boccaccio and Cooper he is a god of the earth, his name combining demon and Gorgon. In Marlowe's *Faustus* I iii, he is one of the infernal trinity invoked with Lucifer and Beelzebub.   **dead**: not 'dread', as one might expect from 38.1 because the line answers 6.
9   **At which**: alluding to the fear aroused by uttering a god's name; cf. 43.2; cf. also Milton's 'dreaded name / Of Demogorgon' (*P.L.* ii 964–5).   **Cocytus**: the river of lamentation in Hades.   **quakes**: because even wailing ceases. **Styx**: the river of Death; even Death flees.

Stanza 38
2   **Legions**: the gloss to Matt. 26.53 interprets 'twelve legions' as an infinite number; cf. Mark 5.9.   **flyes** were regarded as the familiars of devils and spirits. On the qualities of daring, impudence, cynicism and heresy conventionally attributed to them, see Chambers (1966). The simile suggests that Archimago is Beelzebub (in Hebrew, 'Lord of the Flies'), 'chief of the devils' (Luke 11.15). In his note to *P.L.* i 81, Fowler cites Valeriano's claim that Beelzebub is so named 'because he never ceases to infest the human race in every way, and to lay now this snare, now that, for our destruction'.
3   **euer**: eternally.
5   **fray**: attack, terrify.

39

He making speedy way through spersed ayre,
  And through the world of waters wide and deepe,
  To *Morpheus* house doth hastily repaire.
  Amid the bowels of the earth full steepe,
  And low, where dawning day doth neuer peepe,
  His dwelling is; there *Tethys* his wet bed
  Doth euer wash, and *Cynthia* still doth steepe
  In siluer deaw his euer-drouping hed,
Whiles sad Night ouer him her mantle black doth spred.

40

Whose double gates he findeth locked fast,
  The one faire fram'd of burnisht Yuory,
  The other all with siluer ouercast;
  And wakefull dogges before them farre do lye,
  Watching to banish Care their enimy,
  Who oft is wont to trouble gentle Sleepe.
  By them the Sprite doth passe in quietly,
  And vnto *Morpheus* comes, whom drowned deepe
In drowsie fit he findes: of nothing he takes keepe.

41

And more, to lulle him in his slumber soft,
  A trickling streame from high rocke tumbling downe
  And euer-drizling raine vpon the loft,
  Mixt with a murmuring winde, much like the sowne
  Of swarming Bees, did cast him in a swowne:
  No other noyse, nor peoples troublous cryes,
  As still are wont t'annoy the walled towne,
  Might there be heard: but carelesse Quiet lyes,
Wrapt in eternall silence farre from enemyes.

42

The messenger approching to him spake,
  But his wast wordes returnd to him in vaine:
  So sound he slept, that nought mought him awake.
  Then rudely he him thrust, and pusht with paine,
  Whereat he gan to stretch: but he againe
  Shooke him so hard, that forced him to speake.
  As one then in a dreame, whose dryer braine
  Is tost with troubled sights and fancies weake,
He mumbled soft, but would not all his silence breake.

43

The Sprite then gan more boldly him to wake,
  And threatned vnto him the dreaded name
  Of *Hecate*: whereat he gan to quake,
  And lifting vp his lumpish head, with blame
  Halfe angry asked him, for what he came.
  Hither (quoth he) me *Archimago* sent,
  He that the stubborne Sprites can wisely tame,
  He bids thee to him send for his intent
A fit false dreame, that can delude the sleepers sent.

Stanza 39

1 **spersed**: dispersed, 'empty' (ii 32.6).
2 **world of waters**: the primal world from which land first rose.

3 to 41.9 For the details of **Morpheus house**, S. imitates the *domus et penetralia Somni* of Ovid, *Met.* xi 592–632.
6 **Tethys**: 'wyfe of Neptune, called goddesse of the sea' (Cooper, 1565); here the sea itself.
7 **Cynthia**: goddess of the moon; here the moon itself. Percival (1893) notes that S. draws from Ovid's story of Endymion and Diana. **still**: continually.
9 **sad**: dark; causing sorrow.

Stanza 40

1–3 Virgil, *Aen.* vi 893–6, describes the two gates of sleep: the one of horn from which the truth proceeds and the other of ivory from which false dreams emerge. S.'s gate of silver suggests sleep: cf. 'siluer slomber' (VI vii 19.8), 'siluer sleepe' (VI ix 22.8). **siluer** may be suggested by Virgil's description of the ivory gate, *candenti perfecta nitens elephanto*. Since both gates are locked Upton (1758) concludes that S. 'supposes the wicked Archimago not to have access to truth in any shape'. Like Aeneas, Archimago's spirit does not enter the underworld through a gate; also like him, he returns through 'the Yuorie dore' (44.6). This agrees with Servius's note: *et poetice apertus est sensus: vult autem intellegi falsa esse omnia quae dixit.*
8–9 Cheney (1966) 29 notes that Morpheus is seen like the Knight 'drownd in deadly sleepe' (36.6). Rose (1975) 21 concludes that the false dream is 'brought forth from the dark depths of the knight's soul'. **keepe**: heed.

Stanza 41

1–5 Echoes Chaucer's description of the cave of Morpheus, e.g. water 'Came rennynge fro the clyves adoun, / That made a dedly slepynge soun' (*Book of the Duchess* 161–2).
3 **vpon the loft**: in the upper region of the air (*OED* 1); or the roof (*OED* 5c) of Morpheus's house; cf. V vi 27.9.
8 **carelesse**: free from care.

Stanza 42

2 **wast**: idle, being wasted.
4 **rudely**: roughly. **paine**: effort.
7 **dryer**: too dry; 'dry' describes one of the four states in Renaissance psychology which brought troubled dreams. Phantasms in dreams were attributed to melancholy; see Galen xvi 525K, cited Robin (1911) 58.
8 **fancies**: fantasies, apparitions.
9 **all**: altogether.

Stanza 43

3 **Hecate**: an infernal deity, the female counterpart to Demogorgon. 'A name of Diana, Juno, or Proserpina' (Cooper, 1565), or of all three (Comes, 1616, III xv). As the patroness of witches and witchcraft, she is associated with magic, dreams and apparitions; see also VII vi 3.3–6.
6 **Archimago**: from Lat. *archi* + *magus*, the first or chief magician or the 'great Enchaunter' (ii Arg.) as he is frequently named; also, the architect or forger of images, of 'guilefull semblaunts, which he makes vs see' (II xii 48.6), i.e. the false Genius in man's nature. Called '*Hypocrisie*' (i Arg. 3).
7 **stubborne**: untamable. **wisely**: i.e. by his magic arts, or skilfully.
9 **fit false dreame**: as Morpheus is *artificem simulatoremque figurae* (Ovid, *Met.* xi 634), rendered by Golding, 'the feyner of mannes shape'. **delude**: deceive, in the current sense; specifically, 'impose on with false impressions' (*OED* 1). **sent**: senses.

44

The God obayde, and calling forth straight way
　A diuerse dreame out of his prison darke,
　Deliuered it to him, and downe did lay
　His heauie head, deuoide of carefull carke,
　Whose sences all were straight benumbd and starke.
　He backe returning by the Yuorie dore,
　Remounted vp as light as chearefull Larke,
　And on his litle winges the dreame he bore
In hast vnto his Lord, where he him left afore.

45

Who all this while with charmes and hidden artes,
　Had made a Lady of that other Spright,
　And fram'd of liquid ayre her tender partes
　So liuely, and so like in all mens sight,
　That weaker sence it could haue rauisht quight :
　The maker selfe for all his wondrous witt,
　Was nigh beguiled with so goodly sight :
　Her all in white he clad, and ouer it
Cast a blacke stole, most like to seeme for *Vna* fit.

46

Now when that ydle dreame was to him brought,
　Vnto that Elfin knight he bad him fly,
　Where he slept soundly void of euill thought,
　And with false shewes abuse his fantasy,
　In sort as he him schooled priuily :
　And that new creature borne without her dew,
　Full of the makers guile, with vsage sly
　He taught to imitate that Lady trew,
Whose semblance she did carrie vnder feigned hew.

47

Thus well instructed, to their worke they hast,
　And comming where the knight in slomber lay,
　The one vpon his hardy head him plast,
　And made him dreame of loues and lustfull play,
　That nigh his manly hart did melt away,
　Bathed in wanton blis and wicked ioy :
　Then seemed him his Lady by him lay,
　And to him playnd, how that false winged boy
Her chast hart had subdewd, to learne Dame pleasures toy.

5　**starke**: paralysed, unfeeling.

Stanza 45
1　**hidden**: occult.
3　**liquid**: bright. Being incorporeal, spirits must assume a
body of air to appear before men.
4　**liuely**: lifelike.　**so like**: so resembling life itself.
6–7　Possibly referring to the myth of Pygmalion, as
MacLure (1961) 7 suggests. Behind the whimsy there is recognition of the natural affinity between false dreams and man's
false Genius.
9　**Vna**: one (Lat. *una*). She is named only now when her
double appears; cf. ii 12.2*n*. S.'s common device, used throughout the poem, is to withhold the name of a character until the
image is complete. Its use here may be influenced by Genesis:
Eve is not named until after the Fall (Gen. 3.20). Una is a
common Irish name, as R. M. Smith (1935) demonstrates;
as a cult name for Elizabeth, see Millican (1939), Strong
(1958), and Yates (1947) 68. Elizabeth was declared by the
Supremacy Act to be 'the only supreme governor'. On her
motto, *semper eadem*, which was rendered in one address to
her as *semper una*, see Rosinger (1969). For the numerical
significance of Una's name, see Fowler (1964) 77–8.

Stanza 46
1　**ydle**: empty or unsubstantial (being made of air or being
a dream); or vain and frivolous (describing the nature of the
dream).
4　**abuse**: deceive.　**fantasy**: fancy or imagination, which
has the power to deceive reason. Cf. Phantastes whose role is
to deliver 'all that fained is' (II ix 51.9). In similar fashion
Milton's Satan tempts Eve with a dream, 'Assaying by his
devilish art to reach / The organs of her fancy' (*P.L.* iv 801–2)
as a prelude to the Fall. In Renaissance psychology, dreams
abuse the imagination (cf. *Romeo and Juliet* I iv 96–8) which
then, being ruled by the passions, becomes the source of
doubtful opinion. On fancy as 'the mother of all mischiefs,
confusions, disorders', see Charron, *Of Wisdom*, tr. Lennard
(1607); cited Bamborough (1952) 37.
5　**In sort as**: in the way that.
6　**borne . . . dew**: being 'miscreated' (ii 3.1), not 'from
mothers womb deriu'd by dew descent' (*Amor.* lxxiv 6).
7　**vsage sly**: her cunning behaviour by which she imitates
Una. Alpers (1967) 83 notes the structural ambiguity: the
phrase may modify **taught** (8) or **creature** (6). 'The double
grammar makes the allegorical point that the false Una is the
creature of Archimago.'
9　**hew**: shape, appearance.

Stanza 47
4–7　Although the Knight is 'void of euill thought' (46.3),
he is afflicted first by an *insomnium*, which occurs in sleep and
in which the dreamer experiences vexations similar to those
that disturb him during the day, and then by a *phantasma*
which occurs between sleep and waking in which a succubus
appears before him in the form of the false Una (see Macrobius,
Commentary on the Dream of Scipio I iii 2–8).
7　Cf. Arthur's dream, ix 13.7–8. La Primaudaye notes that
'fancie breeds the fact which it imagineth. For we see many fall
into those mishaps and inconveniences, which they imprint
in their fantasie and imagination' (*The French Academie* 415).
8　**playnd**: complained, lamented.
9　**Dame pleasure**: Venus.　**toy**: lustful play.

Stanza 44
2　**diuerse**: diverting or distracting; cf. the 'diuerse doubt'
(10.9) of the Knight in the Wandering Wood, later expressed as
Error's brood (12.4) bred in her cave, and now as the dream.
Its literal sense, 'turning different ways', is suggested when the
Knight and Una are 'diuided into double parts' (ii 9.2).
4　**carefull carke**: sorrowful anxiety, collapsing the paired
'care and cark' (see *OED* cark 3).

41

48

And she her selfe of beautie soueraigne Queene,
  Faire *Venus* seemde vnto his bed to bring
  Her, whom he waking euermore did weene
  To be the chastest flowre, that ay did spring
  On earthly braunch, the daughter of a king,
  Now a loose Leman to vile seruice bound :
  And eke the *Graces* seemed all to sing,
  Hymen iõ Hymen, dauncing all around,
Whilst freshest *Flora* her with Yuie girlond crownd.

49

In this great passion of vnwonted lust,
  Or wonted feare of doing ought amis,
  He started vp, as seeming to mistrust
  Some secret ill, or hidden foe of his :
  Lo there before his face his Lady is,
  Vnder blake stole hyding her bayted hooke,
  And as halfe blushing offred him to kis,
  With gentle blandishment and louely looke,
Most like that virgin true, which for her knight him took.

50

All cleane dismayd to see so vncouth sight,
  And halfe enraged at her shamelesse guise,
  He thought haue slaine her in his fierce despight :
  But hasty heat tempring with sufferance wise,
  He stayde his hand, and gan himselfe aduise
  To proue his sense, and tempt her faigned truth.
  Wringing her hands in wemens pitteous wise,
  Tho can she weepe, to stirre vp gentle ruth,
Both for her noble bloud, and for her tender youth.

resumed in 49.

1 **of beautie soueraigne Queene**: the phrase applies equally to 'Una' and Venus.

5 **On earthly braunch**: cf. 'borne of heauenly brood' (iii 8.7).

6 **seruice**: as the 'servant' of Love (*OED* 2c), reversing the proper role, as does Goneril in Shakespeare's *King Lear* when she says to Edmund: 'To thee a woman's services are due' (IV ii 27); cf. 54.3. Note the word-play: being **loose** she becomes **bound**.

7 **the Graces**: the handmaids of Venus.

8 **Hymen iõ Hymen**: the Roman hymeneal chant praising the god of marriage.

9 **Flora**: traditionally the flower-goddess; but also 'a notable harlotte, whiche with the abuse of hir bodie hauinge gotten exceeding great riches, at hir death lefte the people of Rome hir heire' (Cooper, 1565); cf. E.K.'s note to *S.C.* March 16. Boccaccio's stress in *De Claris Mulieribus* on her deceitful ingenuity makes her a fit figure for Archimago to use; see Tuve (1970) 98. **Yuie**: sacred to Bacchus and signifying wantonness. For the parody involved, see her later crowning with 'oliue girlond' (vi 13.9) and finally with 'girland greene' (xii 8.6).

Stanza 49

1 **passion**: *OED* credits S. with the earliest use here of the sense, 'a fit marked by abandonment to overpowering emotion'.

2 **Or**: rather than 'and' because either is sufficient to arouse the innocent Knight.

3 **mistrust**: suspect.

4 **ill**: both an internal bodily disorder and an external evil (as a foe).

5 The emphatic **is** suggests Keats's view of the working of the Imagination in his comment upon Adam's dream: 'The imagination may be compared to Adam's dream [in Milton's *P.L.*] – he awoke and found it truth' (*Letters* i 185). As the Knight dreams Una to be, so she is, first in the dream and then in the vision. When he awakens to his nightmare in which he cannot distinguish between appearance and reality, in effect he continues to dream until rescued by Arthur in Canto viii. The stages by which he yields to illusion are traced by Anderson (1969).

8 **blandishment**: flattering speech. **louely**: loving.

9 **virgin true**: Una's state is first declared now that it is doubted; cf. 46.8.

Stanza 50

1 **vncouth**: strange, unseemly; repellent.

2 **halfe enraged**: almost frantic; cf. his state 'Halfe furious' (24.3) against Error.

3 **despight**: indignation.

5–6 He seeks to test the evidence of his senses and **tempt**, i.e. test, 'Una'. Yet he is the one being tempted. His present state is illuminated by the fallen Adam's realization in Milton's *P.L.*: 'Let none henceforth seek needless cause to approve / The faith they owe; when earnestly they seek / Such proof, conclude, they then begin to fail' (ix 1140–2). At the beginning he seeks to 'proue his puissance' (3.7) by killing the Dragon; now he seeks to prove his senses. This action proves his downfall: when he forgoes faith and yields to the evidence of his senses, he proves himself false. In place of Truth in Una, he gains **faigned truth** in Duessa.

8 **Tho**: then. **can**: did.

Stanza 48
  The stanza presents 47.7 as a pageant, the action being

51

And said, Ah Sir, my liege Lord and my loue,
  Shall I accuse the hidden cruell fate,
  And mightie causes wrought in heauen aboue,
  Or the blind God, that doth me thus amate,
  For hoped loue to winne me certaine hate ?
  Yet thus perforce he bids me do, or die.
  Die is my dew : yet rew my wretched state
  You, whom my hard auenging destinie
Hath made iudge of my life or death indifferently.

52

Your owne deare sake forst me at first to leaue
  My Fathers kingdome, There she stopt with teares ;
  Her swollen hart her speach seemd to bereaue,
  And then againe begun, My weaker yeares
  Captiu'd to fortune and frayle worldly feares,
  Fly to your faith for succour and sure ayde :
  Let me not dye in languor and long teares.
  Why Dame (quoth he) what hath ye thus dismayd ?
What frayes ye, that were wont to comfort me affrayd ?

53

Loue of your selfe, she said, and deare constraint
  Lets me not sleepe, but wast the wearie night
  In secret anguish and vnpittied plaint,
  Whiles you in carelesse sleepe are drowned quight.
  Her doubtfull words made that redoubted knight
  Suspect her truth : yet since no'vntruth he knew,
  Her fawning loue with foule disdainefull spight
  He would not shend, but said, Deare dame I rew,
That for my sake vnknowne such griefe vnto you grew.

54

Assure your selfe, it fell not all to ground ;
  For all so deare as life is to my hart,
  I deeme your loue, and hold me to you bound ;
  Ne let vaine feares procure your needlesse smart,
  Where cause is none, but to your rest depart.
  Not all content, yet seemd she to appease
  Her mournefull plaintes, beguiled of her art,
  And fed with words, that could not chuse but please,
So slyding softly forth, she turnd as to her ease.

55

Long after lay he musing at her mood,
  Much grieu'd to thinke that gentle Dame so light,
  For whose defence he was to shed his blood.
  At last dull wearinesse of former fight
  Hauing yrockt a sleepe his irkesome spright,
  That troublous dreame gan freshly tosse his braine,
  With bowres, and beds, and Ladies deare delight :
  But when he saw his labour all was vaine,
With that misformed spright he backe returnd againe.

Stanza 51

1 **my liege Lord**: as the superior to whom she is in 'vile
seruice bound' (48.6). Her phrase separates his role into that of
knight and lover, subverting the former and appealing only
to the latter.

4 **amate**: dismay; but wilily suggesting 'mate'.
5 **For**: instead of.
6 **perforce**: forcibly; also implying necessity.   **do**: the
bawdy sense, 'copulate', is particularly apt to her role as the
passionate mistress.
6–8 The jangling echoes declare her falsehood.   **Die is
my dew**: i.e. I deserve to die.   **rew**: feel sorry for, as he does
(53.8) and therefore later, ii 26.8.
8 **destinie**: of the three alternatives in 2–4, she accepts
fate. The same pagan powers of fate, necessity, and destiny
are invoked by Despair to defeat the Knight at ix 42.

Stanza 52

1–2 In effect, she inverts his role as dragon-killer and
identifies him with the Dragon.
5–7 The doubling of phrases comments upon her duplicity
as Duessa. The faith which she seeks in him suggests her
assumed name, Fidessa.   **languor**: woeful plight; sorrow;
cf. Una's story to Arthur of her 'captiue langour' (vii 49.2).
9 **frayes**: frightens.

Stanza 53

1 **deare**: dire; 'dear' in the usual sense because of her
love.   **constraint**: distress; cf. the Knight in the coils of
Error (19.1).
5 **doubtfull**: fearful; also as her words arouse doubts in
him.   **redoubted**: dreaded; but he does not earn the title
'redoubted knight' until he slays the Dragon (xii 29.7). Through
her words, he is again assailed by doubt (cf. 10.7, 12.4).
6 **truth**: fidelity, as Tuve (1966) 121 argues. From testing
'her faigned truth' (50.6), he is led now to **Suspect her truth**.
7 **disdainefull spight**: indignant contempt.
8 **shend**: reproach; suggesting 'destroy', as he is tempted to
slay her (50.3).
9 **vnknowne**: unknown to her, but suggesting that he is
unknown and unproven, and hence unworthy to be Una's
lover.

Stanza 54

3 **to you bound**: correcting her address to him as her 'liege
Lord' (51.1).
4 **procure**: cause.
6 **appease**: cease, as though satisfied.
7 **beguiled of her art**: being disappointed in her intent, or
deprived of her cunning.
9 The line's serpentine movement manifests her serpentine
nature.   **turnd**: returned.

Stanza 55

1 **musing**: indicates the mental wandering which will lead
him to forsake Una; see ii 5.1n. The pattern for his fall is
suggested by Satan's temptation of Christ, as described by
Luke 4.3–13. Christ overcomes the three sins to which the
Knight, as the first Adam, becomes subject: distrust (offered
by Duessa), ambition (offered by Lucifera), and presumption
(offered by Orgoglio). Neill (1952) argues that the dream shows
the Knight's entrance into the life of sin.
2 **light**: a concealed pun. Only later does he recognize
Una as 'fairest virgin, full of heauenly light' (ix 17.3).
5 **irkesome**: tired; also troublesome. His spright cannot be
distinguished from Archimago's 'misformed' spright.
9 **misformed**: being 'miscreated' (ii 3.1), or created for evil.

Cant. II.

The guilefull great Enchaunter parts
The Redcrosse Knight from Truth:
Into whose stead faire falshood steps,
And workes him wofull ruth.

1

BY this the Northerne wagoner had set
His seuenfold teme behind the stedfast starre,
That was in Ocean waues yet neuer wet,
But firme is fixt, and sendeth light from farre
To all, that in the wide deepe wandring arre:
And chearefull Chaunticlere with his note shrill
Had warned once, that *Phœbus* fiery carre
In hast was climbing vp the Easterne hill,
Full enuious that night so long his roome did fill.

2

When those accursed messengers of hell,
That feigning dreame, and that faire-forged Spright
Came to their wicked maister, and gan tell
Their bootelesse paines, and ill succeeding night:
Who all in rage to see his skilfull might
Deluded so, gan threaten hellish paine
And sad *Proserpines* wrath, them to affright.
But when he saw his threatning was but vaine,
He cast about, and searcht his balefull bookes againe.

3

Eftsoones he tooke that miscreated faire,
And that false other Spright, on whom he spred
A seeming body of the subtile aire,
Like a young Squire, in loues and lusty-hed
His wanton dayes that euer loosely led,
Without regard of armes and dreaded fight:
Those two he tooke, and in a secret bed,
Couered with darknesse and misdeeming night,
Them both together laid, to ioy in vaine delight.

4

Forthwith he runnes with feigned faithfull hast
Vnto his guest, who after troublous sights
And dreames, gan now to take more sound repast,
Whom suddenly he wakes with fearefull frights,
As one aghast with feends or damned sprights,
And to him cals, Rise rise vnhappy Swaine,
That here wex old in sleepe, whiles wicked wights
Haue knit themselues in *Venus* shamefull chaine;
Come see, where your false Lady doth her honour staine.

Argument
2   **Truth**: Una is explicitly identified here and in iii Arg. as
'Truth'. That 'truth is one' (V ii 48.6; xi 56.8) is proverbial
(C. G. Smith, 1970, 791).
4   **ruth**: mischief, ruin.

Stanza 1
1–4   **the Northerne wagoner**: the constellation Boötes
(Gk Ploughman) viewed as the driver of the **seuenfold teme**
of Charles's Wain, the seven bright stars in Ursa Major.
the stedfast starre: the Pole Star, 'stedfast' as the centre of
the revolving stars; **yet neuer wet** because it never sets
above the 41st parallel. The brightest star of Boötes and the
second brightest star in the English sky, Arcturus, was
associated with Arthur; in Job 38.32, Arcturus is glossed 'the
North starre'. Fowler (1964) 71 notes that this *chronographia*
'places the sun in a summer sign'. For the political symbolism
of the relationship of Arthur and Arcturus in Tudor pageantry,
see Anglo (1963) 59–61.
7   **once**: i.e. once for all.   **Phœbus fiery carre**: the chariot
of the sun; cf. its progress at 29.3–6.

Stanza 2
2   **feigning**: as it causes the Knight to feign, i.e. to imagine
erroneously.   **faire-forged**: being falsely fashioned and
counterfeit in her goodly appearance; hence 'miscreated
faire' (3.1).
6   **Deluded**: frustrated in its purpose. He had asked for a
dream that would 'delude' the Knight (i 43.9).
7   **sad**: because she was carried down to the underworld to
become 'blacke *Plutoes* griesly Dame' (i 37.4); cf. iv 11.2;
also 'causing sorrow'.

Stanza 3
2   The Knight's dream, which now takes the shape of the
Squire.
3   **A seeming body**: see i 45.3n.   **subtile**: rarefied.
8   **misdeeming**: deceiving, or as it causes the Knight to
misdeem, or think evil of, Una; cf. iv 2.2.
9   **vaine**: either describing their delight, or 'useless' as their
bodies are of air. Being spirits, their only satisfaction in
fornication was to lead others into sin; see Hasker (1947) 334.

Stanza 4
2–3   **sights / And dreames**: the two stages of the earlier
temptation, the dream of love (i 47.4) and the sight of Una
(49.5). Now the two merge in the 'vision' (iii 3.6) of copulation.
repast: repose.
6   **Swaine**: youth or rustic; in contrast to the 'Squire' (3.4),
subtly reminding the Knight of his social inferiority.
7   **wex old in sleepe**: developing the false Una's suggestion,
'you in carelesse sleepe are drowned quight', while she is overcome by love (i 53.4). Upton's emendation, 'wax cold' in
contrast to Una lying warm with a bed-fellow, is not necessary;
'wex old in woe' (ix 9.9) is the lover's usual state.
8   The description of sexual intercourse extends the Knight's
horror at being bound by Error's feminine coils and his earlier
dream of Una 'to vile seruice bound' (i 48.6).

5

All in amaze he suddenly vp start
   With sword in hand, and with the old man went ;
   Who soone him brought into a secret part,
   Where that false couple were full closely ment
   In wanton lust and lewd embracement :
   Which when he saw, he burnt with gealous fire,
   The eye of reason was with rage yblent,
   And would haue slaine them in his furious ire,
But hardly was restreined of that aged sire.

6

Returning to his bed in torment great,
   And bitter anguish of his guiltie sight,
   He could not rest, but did his stout heart eat,
   And wast his inward gall with deepe despight,
   Yrkesome of life, and too long lingring night.
   At last faire *Hesperus* in highest skie
   Had spent his lampe, and brought forth dawning light,
   Then vp he rose, and clad him hastily ;
The Dwarfe him brought his steed : so both away do fly.

7

Now when the rosy-fingred Morning faire,
   Weary of aged *Tithones* saffron bed,
   Had spred her purple robe through deawy aire,
   And the high hils *Titan* discouered,
   The royall virgin shooke off drowsy-hed,
   And rising forth out of her baser bowre,
   Lookt for her knight, who far away was fled,
   And for her Dwarfe, that wont to wait each houre ;
Then gan she waile and weepe, to see that woefull stowre.

8

And after him she rode with so much speede
   As her slow beast could make ; but all in vaine :
   For him so far had borne his light-foot steede,
   Pricked with wrath and fiery fierce disdaine,
   That him to follow was but fruitlesse paine ;
   Yet she her weary limbes would neuer rest,
   But euery hill and dale, each wood and plaine
   Did search, sore grieued in her gentle brest,
He so vngently left her, whom she loued best.

9

But subtill *Archimago*, when his guests
   He saw diuided into double parts,
   And *Vna* wandring in woods and forrests,
   Th'end of his drift, he praisd his diuelish arts,
   That had such might ouer true meaning harts ;
   Yet rests not so, but other meanes doth make,
   How he may worke vnto her further smarts :
   For her he hated as the hissing snake,
And in her many troubles did most pleasure take.

Stanza 5
1   **amaze**: bewilderment, mental confusion, punning on 'maze'. First lost in the labyrinth and then caught in Error's

'endlesse traine' (i 18.9), now he wanders in a mental maze ; see i 55.1*n*.   **vp start**: the response of error ; cf. i 16.1 and esp. 49.3.
4   **ment**: joined together, 'knit' in sexual intercourse.
7   **yblent**: blinded. An inner blinding through outer sight marks a further stage of his descent into sin.
9   **hardly**: with difficulty.

Stanza 6
2   **his guiltie sight**: the guilty sight he has seen, though his own sight is also guilty ; cf. 'troublous sights' (4.2).
3   The act of jealousy : see IV vi 7.5, etc ; cf. *H.L.* 267–8 : 'that monster Gelosie, / Which eates the hart'. See C. G. Smith (1970) 203.
4   **despight**: no longer simple indignation, as i 50.3, but settled malice. The emotion is always base.
5   **Yrkesome**: tired ; cf. his earlier confident love for Una : 'so deare as life is to my hart, / I deeme your loue' (i. 54.2–3). He has begun his journey to Despair.
6   **Hesperus**: the evening and morning star, both Venus ; here named with obvious irony.

Stanza 7
1–3   **Morning** is Aurora, the goddess of the dawn, whose lover, the mortal Tithonus, was granted immortality but not eternal youth. To connect the virgin Aurora and Una, the classical and Christian day-stars, S. provides a pastiche of classical sources : **rosy-fingred** is the stock Homeric epithet, **saffron bed** is Virgil's *croceum cubile* (*Aen.* iv 585), **purple robe** is Ovid's *purpureae Aurorae* (*Met.* iii 184). Cf. xi 51.1–4. **Weary** wittily varies the set description : Morning is dissatisfied with her aged lover.
4   **discouered**: revealed.
6   **baser**: too lowly for her.
8   **wait**: attend.
9   **stowre**: time of distress or turmoil.

Stanza 8
3   **light-foot** follows from the image of Morning but in the context suggests inconstancy.
4   Referring both to the Knight and his horse, the latter being commonly associated with the passions. The horse controls him in contrast to its curbed pace at i i 1.6–7. **disdaine**: angry indignation, which was once the Knight's response to Error, i 19.6.
9   As Una is the true Church, the line invokes John's rebuke : 'thou hast left thy first love' (Rev. 2.4) ; noted Kermode (1971) 16.

Stanza 9
1   **subtill**: crafty, cunning, a strongly pejorative sense which characterizes Archimago ; cf. iii 24.6, vii 26.2.
2   **double**: two ; also 'divided'. The Knight is divided from himself, so that his mirror image appears in the false Saint George, and divided in himself so that he meets aspects of himself in Sansfoy, Sansjoy, and Orgoglio. While Una's mirror-image appears in Fidessa, she, being one, cannot be divided.
3   The broken scansion reflects her wandering state ; noted Frye (1957) 259–60. Later she is named 'the *Errant damozell*' (II i 19.8).
8   Proverbial, as *S.C.* Jan. 65. He hates her as he hates a snake and/or as a snake hates.

45

10

He then deuisde himselfe how to disguise;
  For by his mightie science he could take
  As many formes and shapes in seeming wise,
  As euer *Proteus* to himselfe could make:
  Sometime a fowle, sometime a fish in lake,
  Now like a foxe, now like a dragon fell,
  That of himselfe he oft for feare would quake,
  And oft would flie away.   O who can tell
The hidden power of herbes, and might of Magicke spell?

11

But now seemde best, the person to put on
  Of that good knight, his late beguiled guest:
  In mighty armes he was yclad anon,
  And siluer shield: vpon his coward brest
  A bloudy crosse, and on his crauen crest
  A bounch of haires discolourd diuersly:
  Full iolly knight he seemde, and well addrest,
  And when he sate vpon his courser free,
Saint George himself ye would haue deemed him to be.

12

But he the knight, whose semblaunt he did beare,
  The true *Saint George* was wandred far away,
  Still flying from his thoughts and gealous feare;
  Will was his guide, and griefe led him astray.
  At last him chaunst to meete vpon the way
  A faithlesse Sarazin all arm'd to point,
  In whose great shield was writ with letters gay
Sans foy: full large of limbe and euery ioint
He was, and cared not for God or man a point.

Stanza 10

2   mightie science: as in the biblical phrase 'mighty works', the knowledge to perform miracles (so glossed for Mark 6.2). The power to change shape is Satanic. Burton notes that devils 'can assume . . . all manner of shapes at their pleasures' (*Anat. Mel.* I ii 1.2).

3–6   Proverbial (C. G. Smith, 1970, 683). Proteus could change himself particularly into the four elements, as Comes (1616) VIII viii notes, citing Homer (*Ody.* iv 384ff), and as S. catalogues here. (The dragon suggests the fourth element of fire.) Cf. his transformations at III viii 40–41, and note the contrast to Una's oneness.

3   **seeming**: ways of seeming or appearing.

7–8   While the humour is obvious, the lines comment on the Knight who flees from himself.

Stanza 11

1–2   **the person to put on . . .**: i.e. to assume the Knight's appearance, appearance and reality now being divided in him. As the phrases borrowed from i 1 show, he assumes both the appearance of the Knight and the title that the Knight will gain after his earthly adventures when 'thou Saint *George* shalt called bee' (x 61.8).   **that good knight**: his stock epithet throughout, as 29.1, 44.3, etc.

6   **discolourd**: variously coloured. Arthur wears this badge, vii 32.1–2.

7   Cf. i 1.8.   **addrest**: armed.

8   **free**: high-spirited, willing. At this exact point in Canto i, the Red Cross Knight dismounts from his courser.

9   S. admonishes readers who might take the false Saint George for the 'true' (12.2) just as Una herself soon does; see x 65.8*n*.

Stanza 12

1   **semblaunt**: appearance.

2   **true Saint George**: named only when his double appears; see i 45.9*n*.   **wandred**: with a strong moral sense, falling into error.

4   **Will**: the emphasis stresses the stronger theological sense. The infected Will becomes subject to the passions once 'The eye of reason was with rage yblent' (5.7). Whitney (1586) 6 moralizes the emblem of *temeritas*: 'Bridle will, and reason make thy guide'.   **griefe**: anger, mental distress, with the modern sense, 'regret for what he has lost'.

6   **Sarazin**: Saracen, or pagan generally; not of the Christian faith.   **to point**: completely.

8   **Sans foy**: 'faithlesse' (6).

9   **not . . . a point**: not at all; like the unrighteous judge in Christ's parable of a loss of faith, Luke 18.2.

13

He had a faire companion of his way,
  A goodly Lady clad in scarlot red,
  Purfled with gold and pearle of rich assay,
  And like a *Persian* mitre on her hed
  She wore, with crownes and owches garnished,
  The which her lauish louers to her gaue ;
  Her wanton palfrey all was ouerspred
  With tinsell trappings, wouen like a waue,
Whose bridle rung with golden bels and bosses braue.

14

With faire disport and courting dalliaunce
  She intertainde her louer all the way :
  But when she saw the knight his speare aduaunce,
  She soone left off her mirth and wanton play,
  And bad her knight addresse him to the fray :
  His foe was nigh at hand. He prickt with pride
  And hope to winne his Ladies heart that day,
  Forth spurred fast : adowne his coursers side
The red bloud trickling staind the way, as he did ride.

15

The knight of the *Redcrosse* when him he spide,
  Spurring so hote with rage dispiteous,
  Gan fairely couch his speare, and towards ride :
  Soone meete they both, both fell and furious,
  That daunted with their forces hideous,
  Their steeds do stagger, and amazed stand,
  And eke themselues too rudely rigorous,
  Astonied with the stroke of their owne hand,
Do backe rebut, and each to other yeeldeth land.

16

As when two rams stird with ambitious pride,
  Fight for the rule of the rich fleeced flocke,
  Their horned fronts so fierce on either side
  Do meete, that with the terrour of the shocke
  Astonied both, stand sencelesse as a blocke,
  Forgetfull of the hanging victory :
  So stood these twaine, vnmoued as a rocke,
  Both staring fierce, and holding idely
The broken reliques of their former cruelty.

ing glorious show' (21.5); after Arthur appears, what seems good is good, and the term merges into 'godly'.   **scarlot**: a rich cloth associated with royalty; hence 'royall richly dight' (xii 32.4). She is the great whore of Babylon, 'araied in purple and skarlat, and guilded with golde, and precious stones, and pearles' (Rev. 17.4); as the gloss explains, 'this woman is the Antichrist, that is, the Pope with the whole bodie of his filthie creatures . . . whose beautie onely standeth in outwarde pompe and impudencie and craft like a strumpet', one 'whose crueltie and blood sheding is declared by skarlat'. Cf. Langland's Meed, daughter of Fals and wife of Falsehood, 'wortheli yclothed, / Purfiled with pelure the finest upon erthe / . . . Hire robe was ful riche, of red scarlet engreyned' (*Piers Plowman* ii 8–15); cf. also the 'richly painted' harlot in Donne's sonnet, 'Show me deare Christ'.
3   **Purfled**: embroidered.   **of rich assay**: proven of rich value.
4   **like a Persian mitre**: resembling a Persian head-dress. **Persian** suggests 'pompous pride' (iv 7.6).   **mitre**: the papal tiara.
5   **owches**: jewels. Cf. the wanton and haughty daughters of Zion (Isaiah 3.16f).
6   **lauish**: also licentious (*OED* 1b).
7   **wanton**: unruly, frisky, in contrast to Una's 'slow beast' (8.2); also 'lascivious', as the horse symbolizes her passion.
8   **tinsell**: glittering.   **wouen like a waue**: alluding to James 1.6: 'he that wavereth is like a wave of the sea.'
9   **bosses braue**: handsome studs on each side of the bit. The significance is indicated by E. K.'s gloss on the bells carried by the Fox, *S.C.* May 240: 'the reliques and ragges of popish superstition, which put no smal religion in Belles'. Cf. Chaucer's Parson: 'the synne of aorement or of apparaille is in thynges that apertenen to ridynge, as in . . . bridles covered with precious clothyng. . . . For which God seith by Zakarie the prophete, "I wol confounde the rideres of swiche horses"' (*Parson's Tale* 432–4).

Stanza 14
1   **disport**: wanton play, diversion that carries one from the right way.
7   Their courtship is interrupted before their troth is plighted, leaving the Red Cross Knight to take Sansfoy's place.

Stanza 15
1   **Redcrosse**: suggested by the 'red bloud' of the previous line. As before, the Knight is named when his double appears. 'Pricked with wrath' (8.4), as Sansfoy is 'Spurring . . . with rage' (2), he meets himself.
2   **dispiteous**: cruel, merciless.
3   **fairely couch his speare**: expertly place his spear in its rest and lower it for attack.
5   **daunted**: dazed.
7   **rigorous**: violent; also 'rigid', as they hold their spears.
8   **Astonied**: stunned.
9   **rebut**: recoil. The term suggests a literal butting of rams as described in the next stanza.

Stanza 16
1–9   The simile places the Knight upon the same brute level as Sansfoy; cf. the earlier simile, 'As Lyon fierce' (i 17.2).
6   **hanging**: i.e. in the balance.
9   **reliques**: fragments of the spears, or memorials of earlier cruelty.

Stanza 13
2   **goodly**: often, as here, 'goodly' has an ironic or scornful sense, suggesting what is good only in appearance, as in 'seem-

17

The *Sarazin* sore daunted with the buffe
  Snatcheth his sword, and fiercely to him flies ;
  Who well it wards, and quyteth cuff with cuff :
  Each others equall puissaunce enuies,
  And through their iron sides with cruell spies
  Does seeke to perce : repining courage yields
  No foote to foe.   The flashing fier flies
  As from a forge out of their burning shields,
And streames of purple bloud new dies the verdant fields.

18

Curse on that Crosse (quoth then the *Sarazin*)
  That keepes thy body from the bitter fit ;
  Dead long ygoe I wote thou haddest bin,
  Had not that charme from thee forwarned it :
  But yet I warne thee now assured sitt,
  And hide thy head.   Therewith vpon his crest
  With rigour so outrageous he smitt,
  That a large share it hewd out of the rest,
And glauncing downe his shield, from blame him fairely blest.

19

Who thereat wondrous wroth, the sleeping spark
  Of natiue vertue gan eftsoones reuiue,
  And at his haughtie helmet making mark,
  So hugely stroke, that it the steele did riue,
  And cleft his head.   He tumbling downe aliue,
  With bloudy mouth his mother earth did kis,
  Greeting his graue : his grudging ghost did striue
  With the fraile flesh ; at last it flittcd is,
Whither the soules do fly of men, that liue amis.

20

The Lady when she saw her champion fall,
  Like the old ruines of a broken towre,
  Staid not to waile his woefull funerall,
  But from him fled away with all her powre ;
  Who after her as hastily gan scowre,
  Bidding the Dwarfe with him to bring away
  The *Sarazins* shield, signe of the conqueroure.
  Her soone he ouertooke, and bad to stay,
For present cause was none of dread her to dismay.

21

She turning backe with ruefull countenaunce,
  Cride, Mercy mercy Sir vouchsafe to show
  On silly Dame, subiect to hard mischaunce,
  And to your mighty will.   Her humblesse low
  In so ritch weedes and seeming glorious show,
  Did much emmoue her stout heroïcke heart,
  And said, Deare dame, your suddein ouerthrow
  Much rueth me ; but now put feare apart,
And tell, both who ye be, and who that tooke your part.

Cf. iv 14.9.
5   **spies**: eyes; each watches cruelly where to thrust his sword through the other's armour. Since the blow follows where the eye sees, 'spies' suggests the darting thrusts of their swords.

Stanza 18
2   **bitter fit**: pangs of death.
4   **charme**: an amulet worn to avert evil; cf. 'charmed shield' (iv 50.5). The ritual of chivalric combat included an oath to abjure charms.   **forwarned**: prohibited, i.e. prevented from dying. The slightly awkward syntax allows a play on 'warne' in the next line.
5   **assured**: securely; advice given, of course, in mockery. The cross protects the Knight's body but not his head: since his 'eye of reason was with rage yblent', the 'helmet of salvation' (Eph. 6.17) may be sheared by the Knight of Faithlessness.
7   **rigour**: violence.
8   **share**: a piece cut or sheared away.
9   **blame**: injury, hurt; with the modern sense, imputation of a fault: in a judicial combat, injury was proof of fault.
fairely: entirely.   **blest**: protected. The Knight's shield of faith preserves him from harm. When he adds faith to force, the combination defeats Sansfoy as it had defeated Error (cf. i 19). Cf. the similar phrasing and sense at IV vi 13.4.

Stanza 19
2   **natiue vertue**: natural courage; cf. the 'more then manly force' with which he kills Error (i 24.6).
3   **haughtie**: also lofty, in the literal sense. The Knight's blow upon the head is the counterpart to Sansfoy's blow; however, Sansfoy cannot interpose the shield of faith and he is not protected by his helmet.
4   **hugely**: mightily.
6   **his mother earth**: indicating a kinship with Orgoglio; see II i 10.6*n*.
7   **grudging**: complaining, repining. S. imitates the closing line of Virgil's *Aeneid*: *vitaque cum gemitu fugit indignata sub umbras*. The end of Virgil's poem marks the beginning of significant action in S.'s: by killing Sansfoy, the Knight gains Duessa and stirs the wrath of Sansjoy and Sansloy; see v 10.1–6*n*.

Stanza 20
2   This image is developed and expanded at viii 23 to describe Orgoglio's fall.
3   **funerall**: death.
5   Flight from Una now becomes a flight after Duessa.

Stanza 21
1   **ruefull**: seeking to excite pity.
3–4   **silly**: helpless, and therefore subject to his **mighty will**, as she implies suggestively; cf. 22.3.   **humblesse**: humility.
5   **show**: appearance, in contrast to Archimago who had appeared 'Simple in shew' (i 29.7).
6   **emmoue**: move inwardly or strongly.
8   **Much rueth me**: greatly affects with pity (*OED* 4). He had met a similar appeal from the false dream and was led to rue her grief (i 53.8). Now wrongly placed pity will betray him further. Later he will rue this meeting with Duessa in the sense that he will regret it (*OED* 7) and suffer repentance and remorse (*OED* 9).

Stanza 17
4   **enuies**: seeks to rival, 'as each seeks to rival the other's equal force'; also in the modern sense, as 'repining' (6) suggests.

22

Melting in teares, then gan she thus lament;
  The wretched woman, whom vnhappy howre
  Hath now made thrall to your commandement,
  Before that angry heauens list to lowre,
  And fortune false betraide me to your powre,
  Was, (O what now auaileth that I was!)
  Borne the sole daughter of an Emperour,
  He that the wide West vnder his rule has,
And high hath set his throne, where *Tiberis* doth pas.

23

He in the first flowre of my freshest age,
  Betrothed me vnto the onely haire
  Of a most mighty king, most rich and sage;
  Was neuer Prince so faithfull and so faire,
  Was neuer Prince so meeke and debonaire;
  But ere my hoped day of spousall shone,
  My dearest Lord fell from high honours staire,
  Into the hands of his accursed fone,
And cruelly was slaine, that shall I euer mone.

24

His blessed body spoild of liuely breath,
  Was afterward, I know not how, conuaid
  And fro me hid: of whose most innocent death
  When tidings came to me vnhappy maid,
  O how great sorrow my sad soule assaid.
  Then forth I went his woefull corse to find,
  And many yeares throughout the world I straid,
  A virgin widow, whose deepe wounded mind
With loue, long time did languish as the striken hind.

25

At last it chaunced this proud *Sarazin*
  To meete me wandring, who perforce me led
  With him away, but yet could neuer win
  The Fort, that Ladies hold in soueraigne dread.
  There lies he now with foule dishonour dead,
  Who whiles he liu'de, was called proud *Sans foy*,
  The eldest of three brethren, all three bred
  Of one bad sire, whose youngest is *Sans ioy*,
And twixt them both was borne the bloudy bold *Sans loy*.

Stanza 22

3   **commandement**: authority.
5   Reality still enacts his dream; cf. i 51.8–9.
7–9   **sole daughter**: a challenge to Una who is Adam's 'onely daughter deare, / His onely daughter, and his onely heyre' (xii 21.2–3).   **Emperour** suggests the head of the Holy Roman Empire and the papal usurpation of imperial power. Una is repeatedly called 'the daughter of a King' (i 48.5, iii 2.5, vii 43.3); cf. the distinction in the phrase 'Renowmed kings, and sacred Emperours' (III iii 23.1) and the contest at II x 51 between the Roman Emperor and the British king.   **wide West**: in contrast to Una's parents whose 'scepters stretcht from East to Westerne shore' (i 5.5), referring to the difference between the Church of Rome and the Universal Church. Hence **has**, because the Dragon now rules the kingdom once held by Una's parents; see vii 43.3–9n. **high**: suggesting pride.   **Tiberis**: the Tiber, associated with Rome; cf. xii 26.3–4. The historical allegory implied by the conflict between Una and Duessa is freshly argued by Kermode (1971) 16–22, 39–49.

Stanza 23

4–5   Alluding to Christ, the Prince who is the bridegroom of the true Church.   **debonaire**: gentle, gracious.

Stanza 24

1   **His blessed body**: cf. Christ's 'most blessed bodie' (*H.H.L.* 148). S. associates the Church of Rome with the cult of Christ's dead body, e.g. in the Mass. Compare Mary Magdalene's lament: 'They have taken away the Lord out of the sepulchre, and we knowe not where they have laid him' (John 20.2). As the disciples were exhorted, 'Why seke ye him that liveth, among the dead?' (Luke 24.5), S.'s Protestant hero is associated with the Resurrection. Cf. *H.H.L.*: the death of Christ's 'blessed bodie' teaches man 'in thy brest his blessed image beare' (259); cf. also 'And dead as liuing euer him ador'd' (i 2.4). For a similar perspective, see Milton's comment on the inhabitants of Limbo, *P.L.* iii 476–7. **spoild of liuely breath**: robbed of the breath of life.
2   **conuaid**: carried away secretly.
3   **innocent**: being undeserved.
4   **vnhappy**: in this context 'unfortunate'; cf. 'causing trouble', 'evil' (*OED* 5).
5   **assaid**: assailed, afflicted.
9   **as the striken hind**: as the widow Dido wanders throughout the city, raging through love even as a deer struck by an arrow (Virgil, *Aen.* iv 68–9).

Stanza 25

2   **perforce**: by violence.
6–9   The names and states of the three brothers may be inferred from Gal. 5.22–3: 'But the frute of the Spirit is love, joye . . . faith . . . temperancie: against suche there is no Law.' The brothers are named in order of their appearance. In their hierarchy, Faithlessness comes first; its fruit is Joylessness; between them, as though their product, is Lawlessness. Fowler (1964) 143–4 argues that the sons are related to the themes of the first three books: Sansfoy to I, Sansloy to II, and Sansjoy to III; hence they become 'a symbolic statement of a triadic scheme implemented on a large scale throughout Books I–III'. Nelson (1963) 154 sees them as the hellish counterparts of the heavenly sisters of the House of Holiness, Speranza, Fidelia and Charissa.

49

26

In this sad plight, friendlesse, vnfortunate,
　　Now miserable I *Fidessa* dwell,
　　Crauing of you in pitty of my state,
　　To do none ill, if please ye not do well.
　　He in great passion all this while did dwell,
　　More busying his quicke eyes, her face to view,
　　Then his dull eares, to heare what she did tell;
　　And said, Faire Lady hart of flint would rew
The vndeserued woes and sorrowes, which ye shew.

27

Henceforth in safe assuraunce may ye rest,
　　Hauing both found a new friend you to aid,
　　And lost an old foe, that did you molest:
　　Better new friend then an old foe is said.
　　With chaunge of cheare the seeming simple maid
　　Let fall her eyen, as shamefast to the earth,
　　And yeelding soft, in that she nought gain-said,
　　So forth they rode, he feining seemely merth,
And she coy lookes: so dainty they say maketh derth.

28

Long time they thus together traueiled,
　　Till weary of their way, they came at last,
　　Where grew two goodly trees, that faire did spred
　　Their armes abroad, with gray mosse ouercast,
　　And their greene leaues trembling with euery blast,
　　Made a calme shadow far in compasse round:
　　The fearefull Shepheard often there aghast
　　Vnder them neuer sat, ne wont there sound
His mery oaten pipe, but shund th'vnlucky ground.

29

But this good knight soone as he them can spie,
　　For the coole shade him thither hastly got:
　　For golden *Phœbus* now ymounted hie,
　　From fiery wheeles of his faire chariot
　　Hurled his beame so scorching cruell hot,
　　That liuing creature mote it not abide;
　　And his new Lady it endured not.
　　There they alight, in hope themselues to hide
From the fierce heat, and rest their weary limbs a tide.

Stanza 26

2　miserable: wretchedly unhappy (as in Lat.).　**Fidessa**: Faithful; Lat. *fides* + *esse*, being Faith, though only seeming to be so; or 'little faith', as Whitney, *Var.* i 427, suggests. She perverts faith, which is 'the grounde of things, which are hoped for, and the evidence of things which are not sene' (Heb. 11.1). Such faith the veiled Una offers the Knight by the promise of marriage only after his quest is accomplished. Duessa fulfils hope now by exposing her beauty.

5　passion: see i 49.1*n*. Since S. rarely duplicates a rhyme word with the same sense, **dwell** may signify 'to continue in a state' (*OED* 4).

6　her face to view: in contrast to the veiled Una.

Stanza 27

1　**With these words he plights himself to her.　**assuraunce carries the secondary meaning of marriage engagement (*OED* 2); later she charges that he was 'affiaunced' (xii 27.2) to her.

2　friend: implying lover (*OED* 4).

**4　**The proverbial expression is his own (see Tilley, 1950, F686; C. G. Smith, 1970, 304). Its triteness befits a rustic who finds himself for the first time in the company of a loose lady.

6　as shamefast: as if modest.

8　feining: fashioning; dissembling (as 2.2).　**seemely**: suitable, with a play on 'seeming'.

9　**Fastidiousness or coyness makes one dear or precious (derth**: costliness) to another, so arousing desire; see Smith 145.

Stanza 28

4–6　**The **trembling leaves and the **calme shadow** are two of the conventional items of the *locus amoenus*, as Curtius (1953) 195f notes. Here **gray mosse** and the **shadow far** seem ominous. Cf. IV vii 38.6–9 and the setting of Book III: ' a forrest wyde, / Whose . . . sad trembling sound / Full griesly seem'd' (III i 14.5–7).　**far in compasse round**: as the hellish tree in the Garden of Proserpina 'shadowed all the ground' (II vii 56.2).

**7–9　**As the yew tree, 'the shadowe thereof is grievous, and slayeth such as sleepe therunder' (Bartholomaeus, 1582, XVII clxi).

Stanza 29

The sun's greatest heat at noon is associated with temptation, fall, and judgment: see vii 4.3*n*.

9　tide: while.

Stanzas 30–34

The motif of the bleeding and speaking bush is found in Dante, Ariosto, and Tasso. It derives ultimately from Virgil's story of Polydorus (*Aen.* iii 22–48); as an opening episode in Aeneas's quest, it serves as an ominous foreboding. The Fradubio episode provides a brief allegory of the Red Cross Knight's career. Its central place in the allegory of Book I is treated, e.g. by Nelson (1963) 162–4 and Cheney (1966) 36–40; see especially Kennedy (1973).

30

Faire seemely pleasaunce each to other makes,
  With goodly purposes there as they sit:
  And in his falsed fancy he her takes
  To be the fairest wight, that liued yit;
  Which to expresse, he bends his gentle wit,
  And thinking of those braunches greene to frame
  A girlond for her dainty forehead fit,
  He pluckt a bough; out of whose rift there came
Small drops of gory bloud, that trickled downe the same.

31

Therewith a piteous yelling voyce was heard,
  Crying, O spare with guilty hands to teare
  My tender sides in this rough rynd embard,
  But fly, ah fly far hence away, for feare
  Least to you hap, that happened to me heare,
  And to this wretched Lady, my deare loue,
  O too deare loue, loue bought with death too deare.
Astond he stood, and vp his haire did houe,
And with that suddein horror could no member moue.

32

At last whenas the dreadfull passion
  Was ouerpast, and manhood well awake,
  Yet musing at the straunge occasion,
  And doubting much his sence, he thus bespake;
  What voyce of damned Ghost from *Limbo* lake,
  Or guilefull spright wandring in empty aire,
  Both which fraile men do oftentimes mistake,
  Sends to my doubtfull eares these speaches rare,
And ruefull plaints, me bidding guiltlesse bloud to spare?

33

Then groning deepe, Nor damned Ghost, (quoth he,)
  Nor guilefull sprite to thee these wordes doth speake,
  But once a man *Fradubio*, now a tree,
  Wretched man, wretched tree; whose nature weake,
  A cruell witch her cursed will to wreake,
  Hath thus transformd, and plast in open plaines,
  Where *Boreas* doth blow full bitter bleake,
  And scorching Sunne does dry my secret vaines:
For though a tree I seeme, yet cold and heat me paines.

Stanza 30

1   **pleasaunce**: pleasing behaviour, courtesy; usually suggesting false or feigned, as **seemely** here indicates. See vii 4 where this moment is repeated.
2   **goodly purposes**: courteous conversation.
3   **falsed**: deceived, proved false.   **fancy**: referring to the deceiving power of the imagination; see i 46.4*n*.
5   **bends**: applies, directs; more powerfully, 'perverts from the right use' (*OED* 15).
7   The garland would crown her maiden Queen and victor (cf. 37.5), leaving him her subject and victim. Una is finally crowned with 'a girland greene' (xii 8.6) before her marriage.
8   **rift**: split, crack.
9   **gory**: clotted.

Stanza 31

3   **embard**: enclosed.
4   **for feare**: 'for feare to be induced by romish doctrin to leave the true god, and so taste of his heavie Judgment' (Dixon, 1597); cf. the Dwarf's warning at i 13.8–9.
7   Note the play on the two senses of **deare**. In the 'Morall' to Ariosto, *Orl. Fur.* vi 26–53, where Astolfo reveals that he has been transformed into a tree by the enchantress Alcina, Harington (1591) 47 notes 'how men given over to sensualitie, leese in the end the verie forme of man (which is reason) and so become beastes or stockes'; see Nelson (1963) 162. Dante's suicides (*Inf.* xiii) suffer the same transformation.
8   **Astond**: amazed; cf. the similar physical shock, 15.8.
houe: rise; transfixed, with hair on end, he assumes the posture of the tree but is unable to speak.

Stanza 32

1   **dreadfull passion**: passion of dread; cf. i 49.1, ii 26.5.
3   **musing**: marvelling.
5   **Limbo lake**: the pit (Lat. *lacus*) of hell, the place of punishment for lost souls; cf. III x 54.9. As the traditional region of hell for the unbaptized, it is a fitting place for Fradubio who must be baptized before he may be freed, 43.4.
7   **mistake**: ?mislead (not in *OED*); or, 'err as to the nature of' (*OED* 9); cf. the four alternatives posed at II xi 39.
8   **doubtfull**: full of fear; also in the current sense, as the Knight's state corresponds to Fradubio's.   **rare**: strange, as the voice of a ghost; thin-sounding (Lat. *rarus*), as the voice of an airy spirit.
9   **guiltlesse bloud**: the Knight fails to hear correctly Fradubio's plea even as he fails entirely to heed his warning.

Stanza 33

3   **Fradubio**: 'in doubt' (37.3); Ital. *fra* (in, among) + *dubbio* (doubt: one who wavers in faith). Or Brother Doubt (from *fra*, *frate*), suggesting a kinship to the Knight. He is reduced to vegetable life because loss of faith through frailty is dehumanizing.
7   **Boreas**: the north wind.
9   Though Fradubio claims not to be among the damned, he endures their punishment: cold and heat as hell's torments are expressed in Job 24.19 (Vulgate), Dante, *Inf.* iii 87, and most memorably in Shakespeare, *Measure for Measure*, III i 121–4; cf. the sufferings of the mariner, iii 31.4–6.

34

Say on *Fradubio* then, or man, or tree,
  Quoth then the knight, by whose mischieuous arts
  Art thou misshaped thus, as now I see?
  He oft finds med'cine, who his griefe imparts;
  But double griefs afflict concealing harts,
  As raging flames who striueth to suppresse.
  The author then (said he) of all my smarts,
  Is one *Duessa* a false sorceresse,
That many errant knights hath brought to wretchednesse.

35

In prime of youthly yeares, when corage hot
  The fire of loue and ioy of cheualree
  First kindled in my brest, it was my lot
  To loue this gentle Lady, whom ye see,
  Now not a Lady, but a seeming tree;
  With whom as once I rode accompanyde,
  Me chaunced of a knight encountred bee,
  That had a like faire Lady by his syde,
Like a faire Lady, but did fowle *Duessa* hyde.

36

Whose forged beauty he did take in hand,
  All other Dames to haue exceeded farre;
  I in defence of mine did likewise stand,
  Mine, that did then shine as the Morning starre:
  So both to battell fierce arraunged arre,
  In which his harder fortune was to fall
  Vnder my speare: such is the dye of warre:
  His Lady left as a prise martiall,
Did yield her comely person, to be at my call.

37

So doubly lou'd of Ladies vnlike faire,
  Th'one seeming such, the other such indeede,
  One day in doubt I cast for to compare,
  Whether in beauties glorie did exceede;
  A Rosy girlond was the victors meede:
  Both seemde to win, and both seemde won to bee,
  So hard the discord was to be agreede.
  Frælissa was as faire, as faire mote bee,
And euer false *Duessa* seemde as faire as shee.

38

The wicked witch now seeing all this while
  The doubtfull ballaunce equally to sway,
  What not by right, she cast to win by guile,
  And by her hellish science raisd streight way
  A foggy mist, that ouercast the day,
  And a dull blast, that breathing on her face,
  Dimmed her former beauties shining ray,
  And with foule vgly forme did her disgrace:
Then was she faire alone, when none was faire in place.

Stanza 34

2 **mischieuous**: harmful.
3 **as now I see**: no longer 'doubting much his sence' (32.4).
4 Proverbial (C. G. Smith, 1970, 761); cf. vii 40.6–9,
II i 46.9.
5 Hearts that conceal grief double it.

8 **Duessa**: Double Being (Ital. *due* + Lat. *esse*); two-faced,
referring to the mask of beauty which she wears. What she
seems to be, she is not; see v 26.6. **false** is her defining
word throughout the Book, always in opposition, direct or
implied, to truth and singleness in Una in whom appearance
and reality are the same; see xii 8.9. In her attractive disguise,
Duessa is 'faire falshood' (Arg. 3). On the probity assigned to
1 and the corruptiveness to 2 by Pythagorean arithmetic, see
Heninger (1974) 89. **false sorceresse** is the name given
her by Una at the end, xii 33.6. It refers to the witchcraft and
enchantments of the great whore of Rev. 18. On Duessa as an
Irish name connected with *Dubésa* and *dóibhéas*, which signify
vice, see R. M. Smith (1935).

Stanza 35

1 **corage**: nature, spirit, heart (hence the etymological
spelling).
8–9 **like**: i.e. similarly, though 9 suggests 'what was like a
fair Lady'. Punning on this word is central to the episode. The
initial stress on **Like** (9) because of the word-play brings heavy
stress on **but**.

Stanza 36

1 **forged beauty**: as the 'faire-forged Spright' (2.2), falsely
fashioned to imitate beauty. **take in hand**: not simply a
circumlocution for 'maintained': as a knight he is ready to
take spear in hand to uphold his claim.
4 **the Morning starre**: on the larger significance of this
image within Book I, see xii 21.5–9*n*.
7 **dye**: hazard; but with a pun on 'die'.
8 **prise martiall**: spoil or booty won by conflict.

Stanza 37

1 **vnlike**: diversely; the earlier sense, 'incomparably', may
be implied.
2 The clash here between **seeming such** and **such indeede**
indicates the clash between Duessa and Una, which is resolved
only when the latter, appearing as 'the morning starre' (xii
21.5), 'Did seeme such, as she was, a goodly maiden Queene'
(xii 8.9).
4 **Whether**: which of the two.
6 **won to bee**: i.e. to be overcome; with a pun, 'to be one'.
As Percival (1893) notes, the careful balancing of this line
echoes the balance of indecision in Fradubio's mind.
8–9 Similarly, the Knight takes Duessa to be one with Una,
'the fairest wight, that liued yit' (30.4). **Frælissa**: frail
nature (Ital. *frale*); in effect, 'Woman thy name is Frailty'.
Since she is reduced to her plight because she is doubted by
her lover, the description extends to 'fraile men' (32.7).

Stanza 38

5 As in the Wandering Wood and Archimago's den, 'heauens
light' (i 7.5) is hidden before enchantments begin. **mist**
signifies mental confusion: see iv 36.7*n* for its infection; here it
obscures Frælissa's heavenly beauty. Fog, raised by witches,
was associated in the Renaissance with contagion.
6 **dull**: dulling, in an active sense. **blast**: the blighting
breath of a malignant power (*OED* 6).
8 **disgrace**: mar her outward grace, with the other senses
following as a consequence.
9 **alone**: having no equal. **in place**: a rhyming tag that
suggests 'in place of her'.

39

Then cride she out, Fye, fye, deformed wight,
  Whose borrowed beautie now appeareth plaine
  To haue before bewitched all mens sight;
  O leaue her soone, or let her soone be slaine.
  Her loathly visage viewing with disdaine,
  Eftsoones I thought her such, as she me told,
  And would haue kild her; but with faigned paine,
  The false witch did my wrathfull hand with-hold;
So left her, where she now is turnd to treen mould.

40

Thens forth I tooke *Duessa* for my Dame,
  And in the witch vnweeting ioyd long time,
  Ne euer wist, but that she was the same,
  Till on a day (that day is euery Prime,
  When Witches wont do penance for their crime)
  I chaunst to see her in her proper hew,
  Bathing her selfe in origane and thyme:
  A filthy foule old woman I did vew,
That euer to haue toucht her, I did deadly rew.

41

Her neather partes misshapen, monstruous,
  Were hidd in water, that I could not see,
  But they did seeme more foule and hideous,
  Then womans shape man would beleeue to bee.
  Thens forth from her most beastly companie
  I gan refraine, in minde to slip away,
  Soone as appeard safe opportunitie:
  For danger great, if not assur'd decay
I saw before mine eyes, if I were knowne to stray.

42

The diuelish hag by chaunges of my cheare
  Perceiu'd my thought, and drownd in sleepie night,
  With wicked herbes and ointments did besmeare
  My bodie all, through charmes and magicke might,
  That all my senses were bereaued quight:
  Then brought she me into this desert waste,
  And by my wretched louers side me pight,
  Where now enclosd in wooden wals full faste,
Banisht from liuing wights, our wearie dayes we waste.

Stanza 39

1 **deformed**: marred in appearance (*OED* 1) leads to the
current sense ('marred in shape') when she is transformed into
a tree. The figurative sense, 'hateful', is also present.
6 **as she me told**: in his state of doubt he thinks as he is
told.
7–8 Cf. Archimago's similar restraint of the Knight, 5.8–9.
9 **treen mould**: the mould or form of a tree; cf. man's
nature as 'earthly mould' (V Pr.2.4) or 'Gods owne mould'
(I x 42.6) as shaped by God in his image. Apparently the
'foule vgly forme' (38.8) is her partial arborization, the
particular horror of which Ovid exploits in the *Metamorphoses*.
The tree with its roots suggests Duessa's own form with 'Her
neather partes misshapen' (41.1). Nelson (1963) 162–4 traces
the background of the human tree as a figure of man captive
to sin.

Stanza 40

2 **vnweeting**: unaware.
3 **the same**: as she appeared to be.
4–5 As penance, witches were forced to appear as beasts.
In Ariosto, *Orl. Fur*. xliii 98, the fairy Manto reveals that she
is changed into an adder every seventh day.   **Prime**: spring;
or the first appearance of the new moon when witches gather
under the aegis of Hecate; or their Sabbath.
6 **proper hew**: own shape or form.
7 **origane and thyme**: used to heal scabs (see viii 47.8–9),
as Todd (1805) notes from Gerarde's *Herball* and Langham's
Garden of Helthe; thyme was also used to treat syphilis: see
Gordon (1959) 707.
9 **toucht**: in a sexual sense.   **deadly rew**: his remorse
is greater than he realizes: 'deadly' as she brings his death.

Stanza 41

1–4 Cf. Duessa's exposure to the Knight, viii 46. Here the
erotic image of the woman waist-deep in water (cf. II xii 66)
becomes repulsive. Error (i 14) and the House of Pride (iv 5)
are seen in similar guise. What had seemed fair but was not,
now seems more ugly than a doubting mind can believe.
Since Fradubio still does not see, he becomes Duessa's victim.
What he **could not see**, the Knight sees at viii 48.
5 **companie**: sexual contact with her.
8 **decay**: death.

Stanza 42

3–5 A parody of the ointment which preserves life: see
xi 48.6–9.
7 **pight**: planted.
9 The duplicated rhyme, **waste**, intensifies the sense, 'spend
unprofitably': they consume or destroy their lives; cf. the
Knight when 'he his better dayes hath wasted all' (viii 28.8).

43

But how long time, said then the Elfin knight,
  Are you in this misformed house to dwell?
  We may not chaunge (quoth he) this euil plight,
  Till we be bathed in a liuing well;
  That is the terme prescribed by the spell.
  O how, said he, mote I that well out find,
  That may restore you to your wonted well?
  Time and suffised fates to former kynd
Shall vs restore, none else from hence may vs vnbynd.

44

The false *Duessa*, now *Fidessa* hight,
  Heard how in vaine *Fradubio* did lament,
  And knew well all was true.   But the good knight
  Full of sad feare and ghastly dreriment,
  When all this speech the liuing tree had spent,
  The bleeding bough did thrust into the ground,
  That from the bloud he might be innocent,
  And with fresh clay did close the wooden wound:
Then turning to his Lady, dead with feare her found.

45

Her seeming dead he found with feigned feare,
  As all vnweeting of that well she knew,
  And paynd himselfe with busie care to reare
  Her out of carelesse swowne.   Her eylids blew
  And dimmed sight with pale and deadly hew
  At last she vp gan lift: with trembling cheare
  Her vp he tooke, too simple and too trew,
  And oft her kist.   At length all passed feare,
He set her on her steede, and forward forth did beare.

Stanza 43

3   **may not**: also 'cannot'.
4   **liuing well**: spring of constantly flowing water (*OED* 2d).
The term refers to the biblical well of life, as John 4.14:
'Whosoever drinketh of the water that I shal giue him, shal
never be more athirst: but the water that I shal giue him, shalbe
in him a well of water, springing up into everlasting life.' More
particularly, it refers to 'the well of the water of life' proceeding
out of the throne of God in Rev. 21.6, which is glossed as 'the
livelie waters of this everlasting life'. The Knight is bathed in
'that liuing well' (xi 31.6) when he battles the Dragon. The
'liuing tree' (44.5) and the 'liuing well' juxtapose Ovidian
metamorphosis into 'death' and Christian regeneration into
new life. On such symbolic parody, see Frye (1961) 79.
A secondary sense of living well rather than badly, as they have
done, is relevant.
7   **wonted**: accustomed, with a pun on 'wanted'.   **well**:
with a pun on 'well-being'. The pun is repeated at xi 2.4.
8   **suffised**: satisfied, as 'fates all satisfide' (III iii 44.7);
cf. 'fates expired' (v 40.3). In chivalric romance, the Knight
would assume his task at this point; in S.'s poem he is helpless
without powers greater than his own.   **kynd**: human nature.
9   **restore**: the repetition of this term from 7 suggests two
senses: reinstate, free from the effects of sin.

Stanza 44

1   The Knight's companion, who caused Fradubio's fall, is
first pointedly named when his alliance with her – and his
ensuing fall – is about to be sealed with the kiss.
4   **ghastly**: terror inspired by the sight of a ghost.
dreriment: 'dreery and heauy cheere' (*S.C.* Nov. 36 gloss).
7   **bloud**: the guilt of shedding blood. Una relates to Arthur
how she found the unproved knight 'Whose manly hands
imbrew'd in guiltie blood / Had neuer bene' (vii 47.3–4).
Unwittingly, his hands now are guilty (cf. 31.2) of shedding
Fradubio's blood.

Stanza 45

4–6   Cf. Ecclus. 26.9 (Bishops'): 'The whoredome of a
woman may be knowen in the pride of her eyes and eye
liddes.' Cf. Prov. 6.25.   **carelesse**: free from care, pretending
to be unconscious; uncared for, swooning from being
unattended.   **blew**: from the veins. In Shakespeare's *Venus
and Adonis*, Venus is aroused from her faint by Adonis's care:
'Her two blue windows faintly she up-heaveth' (482), and this
leads to the kiss. In *The Tempest*, the witch Sycorax, who
imprisons Ariel in a tree, as Duessa does Fradubio, is a 'blue-
ey'd hag' (I ii 269).   **deadly hew**: death-like appearance.
6–7   **trembling cheare**: the phrase relates the Knight to the
wavering Fradubio 'trembling with euery blast' (28.5).
too simple and too trew may describe his gullibility; applied
to Duessa, the phrase is powerfully ironic: singleness (an
obsolete sense of 'simple') and truth are absolute in Una but
both are carried to excess in Duessa.

Cant. III.

Forsaken Truth long seekes her loue,
And makes the Lyon mylde,
Marres blind Deuotions mart, and fals
In band of leachour vylde.

1

NOught is there vnder heau'ns wide hollownesse,
That moues more deare compassion of mind,
Then beautie brought t'vnworthy wretchednesse
Through enuies snares or fortunes freakes vnkind:
I, whether lately through her brightnesse blind,
Or through alleageance and fast fealtie,
Which I do owe vnto all woman kind,
Feele my heart perst with so great agonie,
When such I see, that all for pittie I could die.

2

And now it is empassioned so deepe,
For fairest *Vnaes* sake, of whom I sing,
That my fraile eyes these lines with teares do steepe,
To thinke how she through guilefull handeling,
Though true as touch, though daughter of a king,
Though faire as euer liuing wight was faire,
Though nor in word nor deede ill meriting,
Is from her knight diuorced in despaire
And her due loues deriu'd to that vile witches share.

3

Yet she most faithfull Ladie all this while
Forsaken, wofull, solitarie mayd
Farre from all peoples prease, as in exile,
In wildernesse and wastfull deserts strayd,
To seeke her knight; who subtilly betrayd
Through that late vision, which th'Enchaunter wrought,
Had her abandond.   She of nought affrayd,
Through woods and wastnesse wide him daily sought;
Yet wished tydings none of him vnto her brought.

4

One day nigh wearie of the yrkesome way,
From her vnhastie beast she did alight,
And on the grasse her daintie limbes did lay
In secret shadow, farre from all mens sight:
From her faire head her fillet she vndight,
And laid her stole aside.   Her angels face
As the great eye of heauen shyned bright,
And made a sunshine in the shadie place;
Did neuer mortall eye behold such heauenly grace.

Canto iii

Argument

3   Marres blind Deuotions mart: spoils her trade, referring to Kirkrapine's trafficking of Church spoils. The blind Corceca's piety and religious zeal are named 'blind Deuotion' only here.

Stanza 1

The poet's personal lament reads oddly in context: if his subject is Una, according to the Arg., her Truth rather than her **beautie** (3) should be his theme; yet compare 6.4. His subject may be Frælissa whose beauty was brought to **wretchednesse** (3) through Duessa's envy, fortune (cf. ii 36.6), or fate (cf. ii 43.8).
3   vnworthy: undeserved.
5   her: beauty's.

Stanza 2

The heightened style imitates the Psalmist's lament for the Church, as Ps. 137.
1   empassioned: deeply moved; from Ital. *impassionare*.
5   true as touch: absolutely true; a proverbial phrase from 'touchstone' which was used to test gold by touching; see Tilley (1950) T 446. Cf. Ecclus. 6.21: Wisdom is 'as a fine touchstone' to test man. The phrase works almost as a pun: though 'true as touch', she is subject to **guilefull handeling** (4).
8   diuorced: separated, in the specific sense; their marriage contract is dissolved.
9   due loues: the love due her.   **deriu'd**: diverted, from Lat. *derivare*; also the legal sense, 'transferred'.

Stanza 3

3   prease: press, throng; cf. Chaucer's *Truth*: 'Flee fro the prees, and dwelle with sothfastnesse.'
**4   **Una is linked with the woman who fled into the wilderness (Rev. 12.6). The Geneva gloss reads: 'The Church was removed from among the Jewes to the Gentiles, which were as a baren wildernes, and so it is persecuted to and fro.'
wastfull: desolate, limitless; hence **wastnesse** (8): an uninhabited place.
9   none: no one.

Stanza 4

4   secret: secluded; concealed; or concealing; cf. ii 28 when the Knight and Duessa 'weary of their way' rest in a 'shadow'. Action in the allegory occurs at moments of inaction or relaxation. Earlier 'she her weary limbes would neuer rest' (ii 8.6).
5   fillet: the head-piece with its veil.
7   the great eye of heauen: the sun, *mundi oculus*. Una is compared to the woman in the wilderness 'clothed with the sunne' (Rev. 12.1); cf. xii 23.1–2.

55

5

It fortuned out of the thickest wood
   A ramping Lyon rushed suddainly,
   Hunting full greedie after saluage blood;
   Soone as the royall virgin he did spy,
   With gaping mouth at her ran greedily,
   To haue attonce deuour'd her tender corse:
   But to the pray when as he drew more ny,
   His bloudie rage asswaged with remorse,
And with the sight amazd, forgat his furious forse.

6

In stead thereof he kist her wearie feet,
   And lickt her lilly hands with fawning tong,
   As he her wronged innocence did weet.
   O how can beautie maister the most strong,
   And simple truth subdue auenging wrong?
   Whose yeelded pride and proud submission,
   Still dreading death, when she had marked long,
   Her hart gan melt in great compassion,
And drizling teares did shed for pure affection.

7

The Lyon Lord of euerie beast in field,
   Quoth she, his princely puissance doth abate,
   And mightie proud to humble weake does yield,
   Forgetfull of the hungry rage, which late
   Him prickt, in pittie of my sad estate:
   But he my Lyon, and my noble Lord,
   How does he find in cruell hart to hate
   Her that him lou'd, and euer most adord,
As the God of my life? why hath he me abhord?

8

Redounding teares did choke th'end of her plaint,
   Which softly ecchoed from the neighbour wood;
   And sad to see her sorrowfull constraint
   The kingly beast vpon her gazing stood;
   With pittie calmd, downe fell his angry mood.
   At last in close hart shutting vp her paine,
   Arose the virgin borne of heauenly brood,
   And to her snowy Palfrey got againe,
To seeke her strayed Champion, if she might attaine.

Stanza 5

1   **thickest wood**: as with Error's den, i 11.7.
2   **ramping**: the lion's heraldic posture, standing on its hind legs with forepaws raised in the air, is assumed here and again at its death (41.5) to suggest the symbol of royal power. On the lion as royal power, see Aptekar (1969) 61–9.
3   **saluage blood**: blood of wild animals.
6   **corse**: body.
7–9   It was popular belief that 'the lion will not touch the true prince' (Shakespeare, *1 Henry IV* II iv 262); that he protects virgins; and that he aids the faithful wearied in God's service. When Mary Magdalen wandered in the wilderness 'ne was lyoun ne leopart . . . / That ne fel to her feet and fauned with the tailles' (Langland, *Piers Plowman* xv 293–5). The story of Daniel provides the biblical text for the episode. Nelson (1963) 156 cites a sermon by Hooker on the lion that 'religiously adored the very flesh of faithful man'. The motif in English romance is traced in *Var*. i 396–8. Fowler (1964) 68 suggests that the episode 'utilizes an antique emblem of *iustitia*, in which a lion's domestication at the hand of a woman represents the power of justice over ferocious passions'. On the iconographic significance of the lion, see Marotti (1965) 69–77.
8   **remorse**: pity, as 7.5; or regret for his wrong in threatening her.

Stanza 6

2   **lilly hands**: the token of her innocent state.
4   Cf. Whitney's (1586) emblem 182, *Pulchritudo vincit*.
can: know how to.
6   A witty and playful use of oxymoron.

Stanza 7

3   The complex word-play in this line is prompted by 6.6. Though tedious to unravel, it is witty in its brevity. **mightie proud** suggests proud might; **humble weake**, weak humility; each phrase may be reversed: the Lion's strength lies in its pride, Una's humility in her weakness.
5   **estate**: state.
9   Ps. 42.8: 'In the night shal I sing of him, even a praier unto the God of my life.' Ps. 89.38: 'Thou hast rejected and abhorred, thou hast bene angrie with thine Anointed.'
abhord: cf. 27.3. There is a quibble, 'spurned as a whore', as Marotti (1965) 71 suggests, for her Knight has doubted her loyalty. She is soon accused of being a harlot (25.3).

Stanza 8

1   **Redounding**: overflowing; its further sense, 'to resound', from its confusion with 'rebound', suggests the image of 2.
2   The echo indicates Nature's sympathy for her plight.
3   **constraint**: distress; more precisely, as Percival (1893) notes, 'the idea is of being bound tight . . . in sorrow's choking grasp'.
5   The repetition from 5.8 and 7.4–5 illustrates S.'s allegorical device of using a memorable scene as a tableau.
7   **brood**: lineage.
9   **attaine**: overtake him.

9

The Lyon would not leaue her desolate,
 But with her went along, as a strong gard
 Of her chast person, and a faithfull mate
 Of her sad troubles and misfortunes hard:
 Still when she slept, he kept both watch and ward,
 And when she wakt, he waited diligent,
 With humble seruice to her will prepard:
 From her faire eyes he tooke commaundement,
And euer by her lookes conceiued her intent.

10

Long she thus traueiled through deserts wyde,
 By which she thought her wandring knight shold pas,
 Yet neuer shew of liuing wight espyde;
 Till that at length she found the troden gras,
 In which the tract of peoples footing was,
 Vnder the steepe foot of a mountaine hore;
 The same she followes, till at last she has
 A damzell spyde slow footing her before,
That on her shoulders sad a pot of water bore.

11

To whom approching she to her gan call,
 To weet, if dwelling place were nigh at hand;
 But the rude wench her answer'd nought at all,
 She could not heare, nor speake, nor vnderstand;
 Till seeing by her side the Lyon stand,
 With suddaine feare her pitcher downe she threw,
 And fled away: for neuer in that land
 Face of faire Ladie she before did vew,
And that dread Lyons looke her cast in deadly hew.

12

Full fast she fled, ne euer lookt behynd,
 As if her life vpon the wager lay,
 And home she came, whereas her mother blynd
 Sate in eternall night: nought could she say,
 But suddaine catching hold, did her dismay
 With quaking hands, and other signes of feare:
 Who full of ghastly fright and cold affray,
 Gan shut the dore. By this arriued there
Dame *Vna*, wearie Dame, and entrance did requere.

13

Which when none yeelded, her vnruly Page
 With his rude clawes the wicket open rent,
 And let her in; where of his cruell rage
 Nigh dead with feare, and faint astonishment,
 She found them both in darkesome corner pent;
 Where that old woman day and night did pray
 Vpon her beades deuoutly penitent;
 Nine hundred *Pater nosters* euery day,
And thrise nine hundred *Aues* she was wont to say.

Stanza 9

Upton (1758) first noted that the lion, as the defender of the
Faith, represents England or the English king, more particularly

Henry VIII, the first *Defensor Fidei*.
1 **desolate**: describes Una's abandoned state at vi 9.2,
vii 50.1 and x 60.4.
5 On the lion as the symbol of watchfulness, see Rowland
(1973) 118. Aristotle's belief that the lion sleeps with its eyes
open is found e.g. in Maplet (1567) 155; cf. 15.4 below. As the
lion came to express God's watchfulness over man, its image
was placed at the main church door to guard the church (see
E. P. Evans, 1896, 86–7). Here the lion is the 'faithfull gard'
(43.3) of Una, who is the true Church; but though he may
watch over her, finally he cannot defend her cause. **Still**:
always.

Stanza 10
1 **traueiled**: with the pun, as always, on 'travail'.
2 **wandring knight**: no longer the knight-errant upon a
quest but a knight wandering (cf. ii 12.2) in error; cf. 21.4.
4–5 Cf. the worn path that leads to the Wandering Wood
(i 7.8) and the beaten path that leads to Error's den (i 11.3).
6 **hore**: grey with age, or barren. The mountain suggests
that upon which Moses received the law, by which covenant
Abessa and Corceca still conduct their lives.
8 Upton's suggestion that S. modelled his description on
the woman of Samaria, John 4.7f is extended by Kellogg and
Steele (1965) who note that this woman was both an adulteress
and an idolater. When she mocks Christ by saying that 'our
fathers worshiped in this mountaine' (John 4.20), Christ
prophesies the time when she will not worship there.
9 **sad**: heavy with weight; firm.

Stanza 11
3 **rude**: 'impolite', as the line suggests; 'ignorant', as the
next line reveals.
5–9 Warton (1762) notes the awkwardness of the expression:
Abessa fears the lion but fears Una's appearance and the lion's
look equally. Actually, she fears the lion by Una's side: by
combining the two, S. symbolizes the Church supported by
royal power.
8 **Face**: appearance; presumably Una's face is veiled.

Stanza 12
2 **vpon . . . lay**: were at stake as a prize; perhaps mocking
her worthlessness.
7 **affray**: terror.
8 **Gan**: did.
9 **requere**: entreat.

Stanza 13
1 **Page**: besides filling the Knight's role, the Lion takes the
place of Una's Dwarf who has abandoned her to serve the
Knight (iv 39.2).
2 **rude**: violent, rough. **wicket**: a small door.
4 **faint astonishment**: loss of 'wits' through fainting.
6 **day and night**: cf. the true devotion in the house of
Holiness where Cælia spends her day in acts of charity,
x 3.8–9. Hence the internal rhyme.
8–9 Percival (1893) notes there are more prayers to the
Virgin than to God. He cites S.'s *View* 84: 'They are all
Papists by their profession, but in the same so blindly and
brutishly informed . . . not one amongst an hundred knoweth
any ground of religion and article of his faith, but can perhaps
say his pater noster or his Ave Maria, without any knowledge
or understanding what one word thereof meaneth.'

14

And to augment her painefull pennance more,
  Thrise euery weeke in ashes she did sit,
  And next her wrinkled skin rough sackcloth wore,
  And thrise three times did fast from any bit:
  But now for feare her beads she did forget.
  Whose needlesse dread for to remoue away,
  Faire *Vna* framed words and count'nance fit:
  Which hardly doen, at length she gan them pray,
That in their cotage small, that night she rest her may.

15

The day is spent, and commeth drowsie night,
  When euery creature shrowded is in sleepe;
  Sad *Vna* downe her laies in wearie plight,
  And at her feet the Lyon watch doth keepe:
  In stead of rest, she does lament, and weepe
  For the late losse of her deare loued knight,
  And sighes, and grones, and euermore does steepe
  Her tender brest in bitter teares all night,
All night she thinks too long, and often lookes for light.

16

Now when *Aldeboran* was mounted hie
  Aboue the shynie *Cassiopeias* chaire,
  And all in deadly sleepe did drowned lie,
  One knocked at the dore, and in would fare;
  He knocked fast, and often curst, and sware,
  That readie entrance was not at his call:
  For on his backe a heauy load he bare
  Of nightly stelths and pillage seuerall,
Which he had got abroad by purchase criminall.

17

He was to weete a stout and sturdie thiefe,
  Wont to robbe Churches of their ornaments,
  And poore mens boxes of their due reliefe,
  Which giuen was to them for good intents;
  The holy Saints of their rich vestiments
  He did disrobe, when all men carelesse slept,
  And spoild the Priests of their habiliments,
  Whiles none the holy things in safety kept;
Then he by cunning sleights in at the window crept.

18

And all that he by right or wrong could find,
  Vnto this house he brought, and did bestow
  Vpon the daughter of this woman blind,
  Abessa daughter of *Corceca* slow,
  With whom he whoredome vsd, that few did know,
  And fed her fat with feast of offerings,
  And plentie, which in all the land did grow;
  Ne spared he to giue her gold and rings:
And now he to her brought part of his stolen things.

Stanza 14

1–4 As in Dan. 9.3, where penance is expressed by 'fasting and sackecloth and ashes'; cf. the Knight's similar penance, x 26.1–7.

2 **Thrise**: indicating superstition, as at III ii 50.
4 She went without three meals of the day for the three days of the week on which she did penance. She is more righteous than the boasting Pharisee of Luke 18.12.
8 **hardly**: with difficulty.

Stanza 16
1–2 Percival (1893) notes that **Aldeboran** would be above **Cassiopeia** in the northern latitudes at midnight. Johnson (1937) 194–5 places the time at midnight and the season winter, both appropriate to Una's desperate plight. Cassiopeia is named for her blackness, as in Milton's *Il Penseroso* 17–21. Aldeboran was the principal object of the Hyades, the eye of the constellation Taurus, 'the ferste sterre . . . / The cliereste and the moste of alle' (Gower, *Conf. Aman.* vii 1310–1). Fowler (1964) 71n2 suggests that the lines describe the state of the heavens at the winter solstice when Sol is in Capricorn, and relates them to the *chronographia* at ii 1.
5 **fast**: vigorously.
8 **stelths**: thefts.   **seuerall**: diverse, from different sources.
9 **purchase criminall**: robbery.

Stanza 17
1 **stout**: fierce, arrogant.   **sturdie**: ruthless, violent.
2 **robbe Churches**: alluding to his name, which is not given until after his death, 22.3.
7 **spoild**: robbed. His crime is sacrilege: literally, 'stealing sacred objects'.   **habiliments**: holy things rather than attire, Una's 'needments' which the Dwarf was 'wearied with bearing . . . at his backe, (i 6.3–4)' and which Kirkrapine now bears.
9 **at the window**: referring to Christ's parable of those who come to steal, kill, and destroy. 'He that entreth not in by the dore into the shepefolde, but climeth up another way, he is a thefe and a robber' (John 10.1); cf. Joel's prophecy of the time of judgment when 'they shal clime up upon the houses, and enter in at the windowes like the thief' (Joel 2.9).

Stanza 18
1 The point lies in his confusion of right with wrong: see iv 27.9n.
4 **Corceca**: blind of heart; 'their foolish heart was ful of darkenes' (Rom. 1.21); the Vulgate reads: *et obscuratum est insipiens cor eorum*; cf. Ephes. 4.18: 'having their cogitation darkened, and being strangers from the life of God through the ignorance that is in them, because of the hardnes of their heart'. The Geneva gloss explains that 'the hardenes of heart is the founteine of ignorance'. Here the offspring of '*blind Deuotion*' (Arg.) is the deaf mute Abessa. As 'abbess', she suggests the abbeys and monasteries, the products of blind and ignorant superstition and the means of robbing the true Church; or, more generally, as *ab-essa*, whatever practices exist apart from, or take from, the true Church, whether abbeys or the evils of non-residency or abuse of benefices, as Falls (1953) suggests.
5–7 Cf. the sons of Eli who 'laye with the women that assembled at the doore of the Tabernacle' and made themselves 'fat of the first frutes of all the offrings of Israel' (1 Sam. 2.22, 29). Hence **whoredome** suggests the biblical sense, idolatry and unfaithfulness to God. Note the scorn shown by the excessive alliteration in 6.   **offerings**: the oblations owing to God.

19

Thus long the dore with rage and threats he bet,
  Yet of those fearefull women none durst rize,
  The Lyon frayed them, him in to let:
  He would no longer stay him to aduize,
  But open breakes the dore in furious wize,
  And entring is; when that disdainfull beast
  Encountring fierce, him suddaine doth surprize,
  And seizing cruell clawes on trembling brest,
Vnder his Lordly foot him proudly hath supprest.

20

Him booteth not resist, nor succour call,
  His bleeding hart is in the vengers hand,
  Who streight him rent in thousand peeces small,
  And quite dismembred hath: the thirstie land
  Drunke vp his life; his corse left on the strand.
  His fearefull friends weare out the wofull night,
  Ne dare to weepe, nor seeme to vnderstand
  The heauie hap, which on them is alight,
Affraid, least to themselues the like mishappen might.

21

Now when broad day the world discouered has,
  Vp *Vna* rose, vp rose the Lyon eke,
  And on their former iourney forward pas,
  In wayes vnknowne, her wandring knight to seeke,
  With paines farre passing that long wandring *Greeke*,
  That for his loue refused deitie;
  Such were the labours of this Lady meeke,
  Still seeking him, that from her still did flie,
Then furthest from her hope, when most she weened nie.

22

Soone as she parted thence, the fearefull twaine,
  That blind old woman and her daughter deare
  Came forth, and finding *Kirkrapine* there slaine,
  For anguish great they gan to rend their heare,
  And beat their brests, and naked flesh to teare.
  And when they both had wept and wayld their fill,
  Then forth they ranne like two amazed deare,
  Halfe mad through malice, and reuenging will,
To follow her, that was the causer of their ill.

23

Whom ouertaking, they gan loudly bray,
  With hollow howling, and lamenting cry,
  Shamefully at her rayling all the way,
  And her accusing of dishonesty,
  That was the flowre of faith and chastity;
  And still amidst her rayling, she did pray,
  That plagues, and mischiefs, and long misery
  Might fall on her, and follow all the way,
And that in endlesse error she might euer stray.

24

But when she saw her prayers nought preuaile,
  She backe returned with some labour lost;
  And in the way as she did weepe and waile,
  A knight her met in mighty armes embost,
  Yet knight was not for all his bragging bost,
  But subtill *Archimag*, that *Vna* sought
  By traynes into new troubles to haue tost:
  Of that old woman tydings he besought,
If that of such a Ladie she could tellen ought.

Stanza 19

3 Either the first half of the line is parenthetical or the second half suggests 'from letting him in'. The awkwardness of construction suggests a violence parallel to the lion's. 1–6 may reflect the lion's actions at 13.1–3.

6 **disdainfull**: indignant, angry.

9 **supprest**: pressed down physically.

Stanza 20

5 **strand**: ground.

7–8 **nor . . . hap**: alluding to their state of ignorance.

9 **mishappen**: happen amiss.

Stanza 21

4–6 His love of Penelope and his native land made Ulysses refuse the goddess Calypso and the immortality offered by her (*Ody.* v 203–24). Una, rather than her **wandring knight** (4), is compared to **that long wandring Greeke**. S.'s Christian poem surpasses the pagan: Ulysses refused deity because of love; Una, herself 'of heauenly brood' (8.7), seeks a love who refuses her.

8 **Still . . . still**: a play on the two senses (nevertheless; always).

Stanza 22

3 **Kirkrapine**: literally church robber, the personification of sacrilege. The primary reference to the greed of Rome, by which the English Church was pillaged, extends to any religious greed. The actions of Kirkrapine, Abessa, and Corceca are illuminated by Marprelate's attack on the bishops of the Church of England: 'Maime and deform the church no longer; sweet fathers now, make not a trade of persecuting; gentle fathers keep the people in ignoraunce no longer; good fathers now, maintain the dumbe ministerie no longer. Be the destruction of the Church no longer, good sweete babes nowe; leave your Nonresidencie, and your other sinnes, sweet Popes now: and suffer the trueth to have free passage' (*Hay any Worke for Cooper*, in *Marprelate Tracts* [*1588–89*] facs. rep. Menston, 1967, 34).

7 **amazed**: terror-stricken.

8 **reuenging will**: desire for revenge.

Stanza 23

2 **hollow**: cf. 'hollo', a loud shout; possibly suggesting 'false'.

4 **dishonesty**: unchastity; cf. 25.3. The truth of their charge is that she had dwelled in the house to which Kirkrapine brought his stolen things. Behind the charge is the debate whether the true Church could err, even though it must wander in the wilderness as John had prophesied in Rev. 12.

6 **her . . . she**: Corceca, since Abessa can only howl.
pray: in cursing she abuses prayer.

7 **mischiefs**: misfortunes.

Stanza 24

1 **preuaile**: avail, be of help. Being superstitious, she believes curses are effective.

4 **embost**: encased; adorned or decorated sumptuously (*OED* v¹.3).

5 **bost**: ostentation, pomp.

6–7 Cf. ii 9.6–7. **subtill**: crafty. **traynes**: guile.

25

Therewith she gan her passion to renew,
  And cry, and curse, and raile, and rend her heare,
  Saying, that harlot she too lately knew,
  That causd her shed so many a bitter teare,
  And so forth told the story of her feare:
  Much seemed he to mone her haplesse chaunce,
  And after for that Ladie did inquere;
  Which being taught, he forward gan aduaunce
His fair enchaunted steed, and eke his charmed launce.

26

Ere long he came, where *Vna* traueild slow,
  And that wilde Champion wayting her besyde:
  Whom seeing such, for dread he durst not show
  Himselfe too nigh at hand, but turned wyde
  Vnto an hill; from whence when she him spyde,
  By his like seeming shield, her knight by name
  She weend it was, and towards him gan ryde:
  Approching nigh, she wist it was the same,
And with faire fearefull humblesse towards him shee came.

27

And weeping said, Ah my long lacked Lord,
  Where haue ye bene thus long out of my sight?
  Much feared I to haue bene quite abhord,
  Or ought haue done, that ye displeasen might,
  That should as death vnto my deare hart light:
  For since mine eye your ioyous sight did mis,
  My chearefull day is turnd to chearelesse night,
  And eke my night of death the shadow is;
But welcome now my light, and shining lampe of blis.

28

He thereto meeting said, My dearest Dame,
  Farre be it from your thought, and fro my will,
  To thinke that knighthood I so much should shame,
  As you to leaue, that haue me loued still,
  And chose in Faery court of meere goodwill,
  Where noblest knights were to be found on earth:
  The earth shall sooner leaue her kindly skill
  To bring forth fruit, and make eternall derth,
Then I leaue you, my liefe, yborne of heauenly berth.

29

And sooth to say, why I left you so long,
  Was for to seeke aduenture in strange place,
  Where *Archimago* said a felon strong
  To many knights did daily worke disgrace;
  But knight he now shall neuer more deface:
  Good cause of mine excuse; that mote ye please
  Well to accept, and euermore embrace
  My faithfull seruice, that by land and seas
Haue vowd you to defend, now then your plaint appease.

30

His louely words her seemd due recompence
  Of all her passed paines: one louing howre
  For many yeares of sorrow can dispence:
  A dram of sweet is worth a pound of sowre:
  She has forgot, how many a wofull stowre
  For him she late endur'd; she speakes no more
  Of past: true is, that true loue hath no powre
  To looken backe; his eyes be fixt before.
60 Before her stands her knight, for whom she toyld so sore.

Stanza 25
3 **too lately**: i.e. only too lately.
9 Cf. the Knight's 'enchaunted armes' (iv 50.6).

Stanza 26
2 **that wilde Champion**: the Tudor title as defender of the faith, which he now assumes, in place of 'her strayed Champion' (8.9).   **wayting**: keeping watch, attending as a guardian servant; cf. 9.6, 15.4.
6 Una recognizes her own armour (see *L.R.*), particularly the shield of faith, which represents her role in relation to her Knight.   **by name**: own, particular; 'her true knight' (40.4).
7–8 **weend**: supposed; balanced against **wist** (knew).
9 **humblesse**: humility, in contrast to Duessa's 'humblesse low' (ii 21.4). Una submits herself to 'her' Knight: Duessa seeks his submission.

Stanza 27
1–9 Una's speech effectively counters and corrects all the false offers of love made by the false dream and Duessa.
3 **abhord**: cf. 7.9.
5 **deare**: loving; also heavy, sore.

Stanza 28
1 **thereto meeting**: responding accordingly, with similarly kind words, though his formal politeness does not meet her loving submission.
5–6 Archimago stresses her Knight's unproved state in contrast to the other knights who are known for their birth and merit. It is a lie that she chose him through **goodwill**: see vii 47.1–5.   **meere**: entire, pure, without any merit on his part.
7–9 His vow is a threat, as his continued harassment of her shows.   **kindly skill**: innate, natural art.   **derth**: famine.   **liefe**: beloved.

Stanza 29
3 **felon**: villain.
5 **deface**: discredit, defame.
6–7 **Good cause . . . accept**: this adventure is good reason to excuse my absence, which I hope you will accept graciously. He wants to trap Una into receiving as her knight one who undertakes endless adventures but never the one quest to free her captive parents.
9 **appease**: cease, by being pacified.

Stanza 30
1 **louely**: loving.
3 **dispence**: make amends or compensate for, in its literal sense (Lat. *dispendere*, to weigh out), as the next line shows.
4 Proverbial (C. G. Smith, 1970, 743).
5 **stowre**: time of distress or turmoil; terminating, so she believes, the time which began at ii 7.9.
8–9 'The interlacing of aphorism and narration and the turn on "before" are the means by which Spenser makes us both see around and participate in Una's deception' (Alpers, 1968, 437).   **her knight**: for the moment Archimago is her knight and defender; cf. 32.1.

31

Much like, as when the beaten marinere,
 That long hath wandred in the *Ocean* wide,
 Oft soust in swelling *Tethys* saltish teare,
 And long time hauing tand his tawney hide
 With blustring breath of heauen, that none can bide,
 And scorching flames of fierce *Orions* hound,
 Soone as the port from farre he has espide,
 His chearefull whistle merrily doth sound,
And *Nereus* crownes with cups; his mates him pledg around.

32

Such ioy made *Vna*, when her knight she found;
 And eke th'enchaunter ioyous seemd no lesse,
 Then the glad marchant, that does vew from ground
 His ship farre come from watrie wildernesse,
 He hurles out vowes, and *Neptune* oft doth blesse:
 So forth they past, and all the way they spent
 Discoursing of her dreadfull late distresse,
 In which she askt her, what the Lyon ment:
Who told her all that fell in iourney as she went.

33

They had not ridden farre, when they might see
 One pricking towards them with hastie heat,
 Full strongly armd, and on a courser free,
 That through his fiercenesse fomed all with sweat,
 And the sharpe yron did for anger eat,
 When his hot ryder spurd his chauffed side;
 His looke was sterne, and seemed still to threat
 Cruell reuenge, which he in hart did hyde,
And on his shield *Sans loy* in bloudie lines was dyde.

34

When nigh he drew vnto this gentle payre
 And saw the Red-crosse, which the knight did beare,
 He burnt in fire, and gan eftsoones prepare
 Himselfe to battell with his couched speare.
 Loth was that other, and did faint through feare,
 To taste th'vntryed dint of deadly steele;
 But yet his Lady did so well him cheare,
 That hope of new good hap he gan to feele;
So bent his speare, and spurnd his horse with yron heele.

35

But that proud Paynim forward came so fierce,
 And full of wrath, that with his sharp-head speare
 Through vainely crossed shield he quite did pierce,
 And had his staggering steede not shrunke for feare,
 Through shield and bodie eke he should him beare:
 Yet so great was the puissance of his push,
 That from his saddle quite he did him beare:
 He tombling rudely downe to ground did rush,
And from his gored wound a well of bloud did gush.

mariner.

6 fierce Orions hound: Sirius, the Dog Star, 'the hot *Syrian* Dog' (*Hub.* 5) whose heliacal rising marks the hottest days of the year. Cooper notes it as the star 'unto the whiche whan the sunne commeth, the ferventnesse of heate is doubled, whereby the bodies of men become sicke with heate'. More directly, it is called **scorching** from σειρος, its Greek root; Virgil calls it *Canis aestifer* (*Georg.* ii 353). The rising of Orion marks the season of storms: see Virgil, *Aen.* i 535; cf. also IV xi 13.9.

7 from farre: suggesting that the mariner is over-confident, even as Una. Although he has endured the elements of water, air, and fire, he now approaches land which has its own perils.

9 Nereus: 'th'eldest, and the best' of the children of Tethys (IV xi 18.5). **crownes with cups**: honours as a king through offering a libation to him by crowning a cup with garlands and filling it to the brim with wine. Perhaps recalling Anchises's libation upon seeing Italy, *Aen.* iii 525–6.

Stanza 32

3–5 Answering the simile, now from Archimago's perspective and pointing to his over-confidence: the **ground** from which he views with joy, he shortly lies upon (35.8) close to death. Una's quest is treated as a voyage throughout the poem – cf. particularly xii 1 – but not until the end is she seen 'As weather-beaten ship arriu'd on happie shore' (II i 2.9). See vi 1*n*.

9 her . . . fell: all that befell her. This reading is supported by the 1609 punctuation: **told, .**

Stanza 33

3–5 This description carefully modulates the Book's opening tableau in which the Red Cross Knight's 'angry steede did chide his foming bitt' (i 1.6) but was restrained by the Knight's 'curbe'. **free**: eager to charge, suggesting Sansloy's passionate nature; cf. ii 11.8. **sharpe yron**: the bit is roughened to infuriate the horse.

6 chauffed: chafed, being ripped by the spur, but also the effect of spurring: angry; cf. Sansfoy's horse, ii 14.8–9.

7 sterne: threatening; as Wrath itself, iv 33.6.

9 Sans loy: Lawlessness.

Stanza 34

4 couched: lowered ready for charging.

5 faint: lose heart.

6 taste: try by touch; cf. 39.3. **dint**: blow.

7–9 Faith, whether true or false (as v 12), always encourages man. **bent**: aimed. **spurnd**] spurd *1590*.

Stanza 35

1 Paynim: pagan, heathen; as 'Sarazin' (ii 12.6).

3 vainely crossed: bearing the cross in vain; cf. Sansfoy's curse on 'that Crosse . . . / That keepes thy body from the bitter fit' (ii 18.1–2), and Duessa's complaint that the Knight 'beares a charmed shield, / And eke enchaunted armes, that none can perce' (iv 50.5–6). In this canto S. refers only to the Enchanter's 'enchaunted steed' and 'charmed launce' (25.9), neither of which avails him now, although the steed saves him from death.

5 beare: thrust (*OED* 35), a sense different from that of 7, which allows the rhyme.

8 rudely: violently.

36

Dismounting lightly from his loftie steed,
  He to him lept, in mind to reaue his life,
  And proudly said, Lo there the worthie meed
  Of him, that slew *Sansfoy* with bloudie knife;
  Henceforth his ghost freed from repining strife,
  In peace may passen ouer *Lethe* lake,
  When morning altars purgd with enemies life,
  The blacke infernall *Furies* doen aslake:
Life from *Sansfoy* thou tookst, *Sansloy* shall from thee take.

37

Therewith in haste his helmet gan vnlace,
  Till *Vna* cride, O hold that heauie hand,
  Deare Sir, what euer that thou be in place:
  Enough is, that thy foe doth vanquisht stand
  Now at thy mercy: Mercie not withstand:
  For he is one the truest knight aliue,
  Though conquered now he lie on lowly land,
  And whilest him fortune fauour'd, faire did thriue
In bloudie field: therefore of life him not depriue.

38

Her piteous words might not abate his rage,
  But rudely rending vp his helmet, would
  Haue slaine him straight: but when he sees his age,
  And hoarie head of *Archimago* old,
  His hastie hand he doth amazed hold,
  And halfe ashamed, wondred at the sight:
  For the old man well knew he, though vntold,
  In charmes and magicke to haue wondrous might,
Ne euer wont in field, ne in round lists to fight.

39

And said, Why *Archimago*, lucklesse syre,
  What doe I see? what hard mishap is this,
  That hath thee hither brought to taste mine yre?
  Or thine the fault, or mine the error is,
  In stead of foe to wound my friend amis?
  He answered nought, but in a traunce still lay,
  And on those guilefull dazed eyes of his
  The cloud of death did sit. Which doen away,
He left him lying so, ne would no lenger stay.

40

But to the virgin comes, who all this while
  Amased stands, her selfe so mockt to see
  By him, who has the guerdon of his guile,
  For so misfeigning her true knight to bee:
  Yet is she now in more perplexitie,
  Left in the hand of that same Paynim bold,
  From whom her booteth not at all to flie;
  Who by her cleanly garment catching hold,
Her from her Palfrey pluckt, her visage to behold.

41

But her fierce seruant full of kingly awe
  And high disdaine, whenas his soueraine Dame
  So rudely handled by her foe he sawe,
  With gaping iawes full greedy at him came,
  And ramping on his shield, did weene the same
  Haue reft away with his sharpe rending clawes:
  But he was stout, and lust did now inflame
  His corage more, that from his griping pawes
62 He hath his shield redeem'd, and foorth his swerd he drawes.

Stanza 36

5 **strife**: pain, distress; cf. 'his grudging ghost' (ii 19.7).
6 **Lethe lake**: 'a lake in hell, which the Poetes call the lake of forgetfulnes. For Lethe signifieth forgetfulnes. Wherein the soules being dipped, did forget the cares of their former lyfe' (gloss to *S.C.* Mar. 23). The soul is usually said to pass into Hades over the marshy river Styx (cf. Virgil, *Aen.* vi 323) unless delayed by the want of the body's burial. At v 10.5–6 this same soul is still 'wayling by black *Stygian* lake'. S. conflates the two myths by having Sansfoy's soul delay through desire for revenge which may not be forgotten until purged by his slayer's blood; cf. iv 48.7–9. **passen ouer**: i.e. without drinking (contrast *Aen.* vi 745–51); hence not purified, for only pure souls may drink the waters of Lethe. Similarly, Milton's fallen angels 'ferry over this Lethean sound' (*P.L.* ii 604) without drinking.
7 **morning altars**: altars of mourning. **purgd**: purified, ceremonially cleansed.
8 **Furies**: 'the Authours of all euill and mischiefe' (gloss to *S.C.* Nov. 164). **aslake**: appease; a unique usage, apparently suggested by '*Lethe* lake', as though the Furies cooled or quenched their rage by its waters.

Stanza 37

3 **in place**: here; more probably, 'in rank' as 'some man of place' (IV viii 14.4).
5 **withstand**: withhold; as Una is associated with Mercy, it means 'oppose'.
6 **one the truest**: the one truest. The measure of Una's restoration is noted when she names the disguised Archimago 'The falsest man aliue' (xii 34.9).
7 **on lowly land**: low on the ground.

Stanza 38

7 **the**] that *F.E.*, referring probably to this line. **though vntold**: i.e. he knew him by sight without needing to be told; or, he knew also that he was a magician, etc. Either sense implies the instinctive kinship among evil characters.
9 **round lists**: the enclosed ground in which tournaments were held, in contrast to the chance tilting in the open field.

Stanza 39

7–8 **cloud of death**: rendering what **dazed eyes** see. **Which doen away**: i.e. when the danger of death had passed.

Stanza 40

5 **perplexitie**: trouble, distress.
8 **cleanly**: clean, pure; signifying 'morally and spiritually clean' (*OED* 1); Percival (1893) suggests 'and therefore defiled by the very touch of the Paynim'.

Stanza 41

1 **kingly awe**: the power of kings to inspire fear, but ineffectual here against lawlessness.
2 **high disdaine**: indignation; see i 19.6*n*.
5 **ramping**: the lion's heraldic posture (see 5.2*n*), appropriate to his seizing the shield, the emblem of power. **weene**: intend.
8 **corage**: here sexual inclination (*OED* 3a), referring to Sansloy's lust.
9 **redeem'd**: recovered by force.

42

O then too weake and feeble was the forse
　Of saluage beast, his puissance to withstand :
　For he was strong, and of so mightie corse,
　As euer wielded speare in warlike hand,
　And feates of armes did wisely vnderstand.
　Eftsoones he perced through his chaufed chest
　With thrilling point of deadly yron brand,
　And launcht his Lordly hart : with death opprest
He roar'd aloud, whiles life forsooke his stubborne brest.

43

Who now is left to keepe the forlorne maid
　From raging spoile of lawlesse victors will ?
　Her faithfull gard remou'd, her hope dismaid,
　Her selfe a yeelded pray to saue or spill.
　He now Lord of the field, his pride to fill,
　With foule reproches, and disdainfull spight
　Her vildly entertaines, and will or nill,
　Beares her away vpon his courser light :
Her prayers nought preuaile, his rage is more of might.

44

And all the way, with great lamenting paine,
　And piteous plaints she filleth his dull eares,
　That stony hart could riuen haue in twaine,
　And all the way she wets with flowing teares :
　But he enrag'd with rancor, nothing heares.
　Her seruile beast yet would not leaue her so,
　But followes her farre off, ne ought he feares,
　To be partaker of her wandring woe,
More mild in beastly kind, then that her beastly foe.

```
Cant. IIII.

To sinfull house of Pride, Duessa
guides the faithfull knight,
Where brothers death to wreak Sansioy
doth chalenge him to fight.
```

1

YOung knight, what euer that dost armes professe,
　And through long labours huntest after fame,
　Beware of fraud, beware of ficklenesse,
　In choice, and change of thy deare loued Dame,
　Least thou of her beleeue too lightly blame,
　And rash misweening doe thy hart remoue :
　For vnto knight there is no greater shame,
　Then lightnesse and inconstancie in loue ;
That doth this *Redcrosse* knights ensample plainly proue.

2

Who after that he had faire *Vna* lorne,
　Through light misdeeming of her loialtie,
　And false *Duessa* in her sted had borne,
　Called *Fides*', and so supposd to bee ;
　Long with her traueild, till at last they see
　A goodly building, brauely garnished,
　The house of mightie Prince it seemd to bee :
　And towards it a broad high way that led,
All bare through peoples feet, which thither traueiled.

Stanza 42
6　**chaufed** : chafed, angered.
7　**thrilling** : piercing. 　**brand** : sword ; used to express the nature of one who 'burnt in fire' (34.3).
8　**launcht** : pierced. 　**opprest** : overwhelmed.
9　**stubborne** : fierce, untamable. This final word sums up his chief characteristic. The Lion's fierceness is overcome by – that is, it leads to – lawlessness.

Stanza 43
2　'From becoming the spoil or booty of the lawless victor's raging will.' This condensed expression names him **lawlesse . . . will** ; it describes his characteristic act, **raging** ; and it shows the effect of his action, treating Una as his **spoile**.
4　**spill** : destroy.
7　**entertaines** : treats.
8　**light** : quickly.
9　Cf. 24.1. The repetition of the phrase rounds out the episode.

Stanza 44
1　**lamenting paine** : also 'painfully lamenting' ; cf. **wandring woe** (8).
2　**dull** : deaf.
9　**in beastly kind** : as a beast by nature ; or, being kind though a beast. S.'s use of antanaclasis – the repetition of 'beastly' in two different senses – is discussed by Wion (1968) 21.

Canto iv

Argument
1　**sinfull** : because the House is full of the sins.
2　**the faithfull knight** : as v Arg. and x Arg. ; cf. 'Right faithfull true' (i 2.7). He earns his title by defeating Sansfoy. Yet his relation to Duessa raises the question, 'faithful to whom ?'
3　**wreak** : avenge.

Stanza 1
3–4　**fraud** : faithlessness ; here **In choice**.
5　**blame** : evil charges, accusations ; such as made against Una at ii 4.6–9.
6　**rash misweening** : rashly mistrusting ; or rash mistrust.

Stanza 2
1　**lorne** : forsaken, leaving her 'forlorne' (iii 43.1).
2　**misdeeming** : misjudging ; thinking evil of ; cf. the 'misdeeming night' (ii 3.8) when he first mistrusts her, and her complaint to Arthur at vii 49.4–5.
3　**borne** : taken as a companion (*OED* 1e).
5　The substance of this line is repeated from ii 28.1 where it also introduces a new episode ; cf. i 28.9.
6　**goodly . . . brauely garnished** : also describes Duessa, 'A goodly Lady' who wears a crown 'garnished' with jewels, and rides a horse with 'bosses braue' (ii 13).
8　**a broad high way** : 'for it is the wide gate, and broad waye that leadeth to destruction : and manie there be which go in thereat' (Matt. 7.13) ; cf. the paths that lead to Error's den (i 11.3) and to Corceca's hovel (iii 10.4–5) in contrast to the way out, v 52.7.

3

Great troupes of people traueild thitherward
    Both day and night, of each degree and place,
    But few returned, hauing scaped hard,
    With balefull beggerie, or foule disgrace,
    Which euer after in most wretched case,
    Like loathsome lazars, by the hedges lay.
    Thither *Duessa* bad him bend his pace :
    For she is wearie of the toilesome way,
And also nigh consumed is the lingring day.

4

A stately Pallace built of squared bricke,
    Which cunningly was without morter laid,
    Whose wals were high, but nothing strong, nor thick,
    And golden foile all ouer them displaid,
    That purest skye with brightnesse they dismaid :
    High lifted vp were many loftie towres,
    And goodly galleries farre ouer laid,
    Full of faire windowes, and delightfull bowres;
And on the top a Diall told the timely howres.

5

It was a goodly heape for to behould,
    And spake the praises of the workmans wit ;
    But full great pittie, that so faire a mould
    Did on so weake foundation euer sit :
    For on a sandie hill, that still did flit,
    And fall away, it mounted was full hie,
    That euery breath of heauen shaked it :
    And all the hinder parts, that few could spie,
Were ruinous and old, but painted cunningly.

6

Arriued there they passed in forth right ;
    For still to all the gates stood open wide,
    Yet charge of them was to a Porter hight
    Cald *Maluenu*, who entrance none denide :
    Thence to the hall, which was on euery side
    With rich array and costly arras dight :
    Infinite sorts of people did abide
    There waiting long, to win the wished sight
Of her, that was the Lady of that Pallace bright.

Stanza 3

2   **place**: rank.

4   **balefull**: painful; wretched; sorrowful. Poverty, rather than sin, is stressed; cf. 'wasted wealthes decay' (v 51.4).

6   **lazars**: lepers; or (from Lazarus) those afflicted with any loathsome disease.

7   **bend his pace**: direct his steps; but also, turn from the straight way; cf. i 28.4.

Stanza 4

1   **squared bricke**: as the Tower of Babel which was built of brick (Gen. 11.3). Like the house of Pride, it was built because men 'were moved with pride and ambition, thinking to preferre their own glorie to Gods honour' (Geneva gloss). **squared**: being hewn, and hence worldly; cf. Jehovah's altar which is not built 'of hewen stones: for if thou lift up thy tole upon them, thou hast polluted them' (Exod. 20.25).

2   **without morter**: as the wall 'dawbed with untempered morter' which the Lord vows to 'bring . . . downe to the grounde, so that the fundacion thereof shal be discovered, and it shal fall' (Ezek. 13.14). Jonson, himself a bricklayer's son, notes that 'stones well squar'd . . . will rise strong a great way without mortar' (*Discoveries*, *Wks* viii 623); hence the lines may assert the castle's strength until it overreaches itself.

4   **golden foile**: suggests deception – cf. IV ii 29.4–5 and v 15.1–6 – and the hypocrisy (i Arg.) of Archimago, as that term signifies 'gilded over with gold': see Fraunce, *Lawiers logike* (1588) I xii 56v. Cf. Solomon's Temple 'overlaied . . . with golde' (1 Kings 6.22); also Dante's hypocrites, *Inf.* xxiii, for whom gilding with gold fulfils their name and state.

5   Cf. the dazzling brightness of Lucifera (8.5–9), which also seeks to outrival Nature by false, deceiving art. **purest skye**: either the empyrean, the region of purest light, or generally the sky at its brightest.

6   **loftie towres**: cf. the tower of Babel, Gen. 11.3–4.

7   **farre ouer**: high above.

9   **timely howres**: measured hours of the day. The **Diall** suggests Time's destructive power in the house where the victims 'waiting long' (6.8) 'Consumed . . . thriftlesse howres' (v 51.8); see Fowler (1964) 74n3. Cf. Heninger (1974) 354: 'By placing a clock as the copestone of his description, Spenser allows us to read Lucifera's palace as an icon for all that falls within time's jurisdiction.'

Stanza 5

1   **goodly**: as Duessa is a 'goodly Lady' (ii 13.2). **heape**: presumably 'structure', though the term emphasizes the weak foundations of a heap. The term may have been suggested by the house's heap of galleries (4.6–7), its heaps of people (16.7) and its heap of carcasses (v 49.1–2), or because Jerusalem was reduced to 'heapes of stones' (Ps. 79.1). S. avoids the synonym 'pile' which suggests strong foundations (cf. the Castle of Alma, II xi 7.2).

2   **wit**: mechanical skill.

3   **mould**: frame, structure. The reference is clearly to man, in substance and in form (see V Pr. 2.4).

5   **sandie hill**: as the 'foolish man, which hathe buylded his house upon the sand: and the raine fell, and the floods came, and the windes blewe, and beat upon that house, and it fell, and the fall thereof was great' (Matt. 7.26–7). **still did flit**: continually shifted or gave way.

8–9   See v 53. Duessa, as the 'human' form of the house of Pride, is revealed in similar terms (viii 48); cf. Error i 14. The episode fulfils the function of tragedy, which 'teacheth . . . upon how weak foundations gilden roofs are builded' (Sidney, *Apol.* 118).

Stanza 6

2   As Dante, *Inf.* xiv 87, where the threshold of hell is denied to none.

3   **Yet**: pointing up the contradiction. Everyone passes immediately through the open gates despite the porter. **hight**: committed, entrusted.

4   **Maluenù**: the opposite of Fr. *bienvenu*, welcome; hence ill-come: welcome to evil; or ill-advised (Fr. *malvenu*); or 'ominous arrival'.

6   **dight**: arrayed, furnished.

7   **sorts**: companies; or 'of each degree and place' (3.2).

8   **waiting**: suggesting both loss of time and that all who attend are servants.

7

By them they passe, all gazing on them round,
  And to the Presence mount; whose glorious vew
  Their frayle amazed senses did confound:
  In liuing Princes court none euer knew
  Such endlesse richesse, and so sumptuous shew;
  Ne *Persia* selfe, the nourse of pompous pride
  Like euer saw.   And there a noble crew
  Of Lordes and Ladies stood on euery side,
Which with their presence faire, the place much beautifide.

8

High aboue all a cloth of State was spred,
  And a rich throne, as bright as sunny day,
  On which there sate most braue embellished
  With royall robes and gorgeous array,
  A mayden Queene, that shone as *Titans* ray,
  In glistring gold, and peerelesse pretious stone:
  Yet her bright blazing beautie did assay
  To dim the brightnesse of her glorious throne,
As enuying her selfe, that too exceeding shone.

9

Exceeding shone, like *Phœbus* fairest childe,
  That did presume his fathers firie wayne,
  And flaming mouthes of steedes vnwonted wilde
  Through highest heauen with weaker hand to rayne;
  Proud of such glory and aduancement vaine,
  While flashing beames do daze his feeble eyen,
  He leaues the welkin way most beaten plaine,
  And rapt with whirling wheeles, inflames the skyen,
With fire not made to burne, but fairely for to shyne.

10

So proud she shyned in her Princely state,
  Looking to heauen; for earth she did disdayne,
  And sitting high; for lowly she did hate:
  Lo vnderneath her scornefull feete, was layne
  A dreadfull Dragon with an hideous trayne,
  And in her hand she held a mirrhour bright,
  Wherein her face she often vewed fayne,
  And in her selfe-lou'd semblance tooke delight;
For she was wondrous faire, as any liuing wight.

Stanza 7

1   **round**: on all sides. The repetition of **them** suggests a mirror and its reflection. Duessa's gorgeous attire matches the court's.

2   **Presence**: presence-chamber, where a sovereign receives guests.

6   **nourse**: nurse and nourisher.

7   **crew**: company, in a derogatory sense.

Stanza 8

Cf. the true royalty of Mercilla, V ix 29. In Book I Una alone is the 'royall virgin' (as ii 7.5, etc.). On the pictorial qualities of the stanzas that describe the Knight's approach, see Bender (1972) 124–34.

1   **cloth of State**: canopy.

5   **mayden Queene**: the 'virgine, daughter Babel' on her throne, Isaiah 47.1.   **that**: i.e. her throne.   **Titans**: the sun's; but also suggesting the proud, rebellious offspring of the earth, a symbol of pride; cf. II vii 41.6–8.

7   **bright blazing beautie**: prepares for the comparison to Phaeton in the next stanza. The throne's brightness shines, like Titan: Lucifera's brightness burns, like Phaeton.

9   The throne envied her, so the proud Queen believes, because she shines excessively.

Stanza 9

The story of Phaeton (from Ovid, *Met.* ii 19f) is treated at III xi 38 and V viii 40. Bender (1972) 131 notes that Phaeton falling epitomizes his weakness, pride, and destructiveness: the simile becomes 'an iconographically precise moral commentary' on the action.

1   **Exceeding shone**: wittily naming Phaeton (f. Gk shining) without naming him.

2   **presume**: usurp. The story of Phaeton in the *Ovide moralisé* represents Lucifer and his revolt against God, as Seznec (1953) 93 notes.   **wayne**: wagon, with the concealed pun on 'wane' anticipating Phaeton's fall. Cf. III viii 51.5.

3   **flaming mouthes**: renders Ovid's *quos [ignes] ore et naribus efflant* (*Met.* ii 85).

4   **weaker**: too weak, weaker than Titan's.

7   **welkin way**: the sun's path through the sky, Ovid's *tritum spatium* (*Met.* ii 167–8).

8   **rapt**: carried away, morally by his pride and now physically.

9   The careful pointing of this line distinguishes heavenly light from infernal fire; cf. Herrick: 'The fire of Hell this strange condition hath, / To burn, not shine (as learned *Basil* saith)' (*Poetical Works*, ed. L. C. Martin, Oxford 1956, 387).

Stanza 10

1–2   Cf. Prov. 21.4: 'A hautie loke, and a proude heart, which is the light of the wicked, is sinne.' Cf. the posture of Speranza whose eyes are fixed 'euer vp to heauen' (x 14.8) in hope of salvation.   **state**: high rank; throne.

3   **lowly**: lowliness.

5   **hideous trayne**: monstrously large and long tail; cf. the Dragon's 'huge long tayle' (xi 11.1). Later Lucifera's lengthy procession of sins assumes the shape of the dragon's tail, forming another labyrinth in which the Knight is invited to wander. Lucifera with the Dragon under her feet suggests Duessa riding the Dragon (vii 18), which is the Dragon of Rev. 12.7–9. More precisely, she is an emblem of royal power; cf. Una accompanied by the lion, and Isis with her foot 'set vppon the Crocodile' (V vii 7.1). In Frye's terms (1957) 148, she is a demonic parody of the true state shown in Mercilla ruling with a chained lion under her throne, V ix 33.

6   **mirrhour**: the common symbol of Vanitas, the chief quality of Pride.

7   **fayne**: gladly.

11

Of griesly *Pluto* she the daughter was,
  And sad *Proserpina* the Queene of hell;
  Yet did she thinke her pearelesse worth to pas
  That parentage, with pride so did she swell,
  And thundring *Ioue*, that high in heauen doth dwell,
  And wield the world, she claymed for her syre,
  Or if that any else did *Ioue* excell:
  For to the highest she did still aspyre,
Or if ought higher were then that, did it desyre.

12

And proud *Lucifera* men did her call,
  That made her selfe a Queene, and crownd to be,
  Yet rightfull kingdome she had none at all,
  Ne heritage of natiue soueraintie,
  But did vsurpe with wrong and tyrannie
  Vpon the scepter, which she now did hold:
  Ne ruld her Realmes with lawes, but pollicie,
  And strong aduizement of six wisards old,
That with their counsels bad her kingdome did vphold.

13

Soone as the Elfin knight in presence came,
  And false *Duessa* seeming Lady faire,
  A gentle Husher, *Vanitie* by name
  Made rowme, and passage for them did prepaire:
  So goodly brought them to the lowest staire
  Of her high throne, where they on humble knee
  Making obeyssance, did the cause declare,
  Why they were come, her royall state to see,
To proue the wide report of her great Maiestee.

14

With loftie eyes, halfe loth to looke so low,
  She thanked them in her disdainefull wise,
  Ne other grace vouchsafed them to show
  Of Princesse worthy, scarse them bad arise.
  Her Lordes and Ladies all this while deuise
  Themselues to setten forth to straungers sight:
  Some frounce their curled haire in courtly guise,
  Some prancke their ruffes, and others trimly dight
Their gay attire: each others greater pride does spight.

15

Goodly they all that knight do entertaine,
  Right glad with him to haue increast their crew:
  But to *Duess'* each one himselfe did paine
  All kindnesse and faire courtesie to shew;
  For in that court whylome her well they knew:
  Yet the stout Faerie mongst the middest crowd
  Thought all their glorie vaine in knightly vew,
  And that great Princesse too exceeding prowd,
That to strange knight no better countenance allowd.

Stanza 11

1   **griesly**: arousing horror. Earlier 'blacke *Plutoes* griesly Dame' (i 37.4) was summoned and her wrath (ii 2.7) invoked to betray the Knight. Appropriately, her offspring now confronts him.
3   **pas**: surpass.
5–6   **thundring Ioue**: Jupiter Tonans. In this form he overthrew Phaeton.   **wield**: rule.
8–9   She is the female counterpart of Lucifer: 'Thou saidest in thine heart, I wil ascend into heaven, and exalt my throne above beside the starres of God. . . . I wil ascend above the height of the cloudes, and I wil be like the moste high', whose downfall Isaiah prophesies: 'Thou shalt be broght downe to the grave, to the sides of the pit' (Isaiah 14.13–5).

Stanza 12

1   **Lucifera**: a name adapted from the address to the king of Babylon. 'How art thou fallen from heaven, O Lucifer, sonne of the morning' (Isaiah 14.12). According to patristic tradition, Lucifer was Satan's name in heaven. Literally, Lucifer signifies 'light-bringing', the role Lucifera wishes to fill. As the 'morning starre' (the Geneva gloss), Lucifera tries to usurp Una's role; see xii 21.5–9.
4   **natiue**: rightful, by virtue of birth.
7   **pollicie**: political cunning, expediency.
8   **wisards**: wise men; used contemptuously.
9   **vphold**: suggesting the Dragon that lies under her feet.

Stanza 13

1   **in presence**: in the special sense of attending upon royalty.
3   **Husher**: usher.
5   **goodly**: graciously.
7–9   **obeyssance**: submission.   **declare**: make clear, rather than state.   **proue**: the Knight first sought to 'proue his puissance' (i 3.7) by slaying the Dragon and was betrayed into seeking to 'proue his sense' (i 50.6); now he seeks to prove Lucifera's fame.

Stanza 14

5   **deuise**: make ready.
6   **setten forth**: exhibit (*OED* 144 j).
7   **frounce**: gather in braids.
8   **prancke**: fold, in order to display ostentatiously.
dight: arrange.
9   **gay**: usually pejorative when applied to clothes; cf. x 39.2. Each despises the greater pride of the others.

Stanza 15

4   **kindnesse**: suggesting also natural kinship for she is of their kind.
5   **whylome**: earlier.
6   **stout**: firm, as he resists their vanity; also from his present mood of injured merit, proud (*OED* 1).   **Faerie**: see i 17.1*n*. So named to indicate that he is not of their kind.   **middest**: the very middle; cf. 'the thickest woods' (i 11.7) where he encounters Error. The allegorical point is that even at the centre of Vanity Fair, he is able to resist vanity, if not entirely.
9   **strange**: foreign, not of their kind.   **countenance**: manner towards him. In her bright presence his pique reflects her vanity.

16

Suddein vpriseth from her stately place
  The royall Dame, and for her coche doth call :
  All hurtlen forth, and she with Princely pace,
  As faire *Aurora* in her purple pall,
  Out of the East the dawning day doth call :
  So forth she comes : her brightnesse brode doth blaze ;
  The heapes of people thronging in the hall,
  Do ride each other, vpon her to gaze :
Her glorious glitterand light doth all mens eyes amaze.

17

So forth she comes, and to her coche does clyme,
  Adorned all with gold, and girlonds gay,
  That seemd as fresh as *Flora* in her prime,
  And stroue to match, in royall rich array,
  Great *Iunoes* golden chaire, the which they say
  The Gods stand gazing on, when she does ride
  To *Ioues* high house through heauens bras-paued way
  Drawne of faire Pecocks, that excell in pride,
And full of *Argus* eyes their tailes dispredden wide.

Stanza 16

1 **Suddein**: 'this abrupt movement is meant to be characteristic. Pride is whimsical; so are her courtiers' (Percival, 1893).

3 **hurtlen**: rush jostlingly; 'hurlen' *1609*: rush impetuously. Both words show Pride's violence; cf. 40.1 and i 16.2*n*.
pace: movement.
4 Here she appears as Lucifera, 'light-bearing', the morning star which heralds the sun. **purple pall**: crimson robe, Ovid's *purpureae Aurorae* (*Met*. iii 184); cf. ii 7.3.
8 This image of the courtiers riding each other as the sins ride their beasts is expanded at II vii 47 to show how the ambitious oppress each other in their desire to rise. Its consequences are revealed when they are seen 'together in one heape . . . throwne, / Like carkases of beasts in butchers stall' (v 49.1–2).
9 **glitterand**: suggests light-giving, as Arthur's armour (vii 29.4), the only other use of the word in the poem.
amaze: dazzle, bewilder.

Stanza 17
On the allegorical chariot of Sin in the Renaissance, see Chew (1960).
1 **So forth she comes**: repeated from 16.6 to inflate her in her pride in order to collapse all her pretensions in the next stanza.
2–3 **gold** for Juno's chariot; **girlonds** for **Flora**, the goddess of flowers (see i 48.9*n*).
5 **chaire**: chariot.
8–9 The details are from Ovid, *Met*. ii 533f. **Pecocks**: sacred to Juno. **in pride**: in the heraldic posture with tail expanded, suggesting love of ostentatious display; noted Chew (1962) 96. **Argus eyes**: 'whose eyes it is sayd that Iuno for his eternall memory placed in her byrd the Peacocks tayle' (*S.C.* Oct. 32, gloss). **dispredden**: suggesting widely spread out.

Stanzas 18–35
Each counsellor is shown in grotesque dress appropriate to his sin, holding an object in his hand which symbolizes his inner state, suffering from a deadly disease which is a consequence of his sin, and riding a beast which symbolizes the passion associated with his sin. He is paired in a significant manner with a second sin. The six counsellors ride in three pairs, and each sin is described in three stanzas. Lucifera/Duessa as Pride makes the seventh deadly sin. Together they form the beast with seven heads as described by John, Rev. 17.3. The account of the sins is broadly traditional: each detail may be traced to the conventional iconography of the sins (see Chew, 1962, 79–113) though S. remains original in his description of the working of the sins. *Var*. i 217 notes that the sins are arranged to achieve the maximum of grotesque pictorial effect through incongruous pairing of the sins and of each sin to its beast, through contrast in dress and through increasingly grotesque description. Hughes (1715) notes that they are 'in that order in which the vices they represent naturally produce and follow each other' (*Var*. i 217). Chew (1962) 72 notes more precisely that first come the sins of the flesh (**Sloth [Idlenesse]**, **Gluttony** and **Lechery**), then the worldly sin (**Auarice**), and finally the devilish sins (**Enuie**, **Wrath** and **Pride**), the same order as the assault of the sins in *The Castle of Perseverance*. All the sins, except Lucifera or Pride, are masculine. Fittingly, Pride opens and concludes the procession. Fowler (1964) 73–4 notes that the description of the coach moving as if 'through heauens bras-paued way' (17.7) is 'a deliberate travesty of the conventional representation of Sol with his retinue of lesser planets'.

18

But this was drawne of six vnequall beasts,
    On which her six sage Counsellours did ryde,
    Taught to obay their bestiall beheasts,
    With like conditions to their kinds applyde :
    Of which the first, that all the rest did guyde,
    Was sluggish *Idlenesse* the nourse of sin ;
    Vpon a slouthfull Asse he chose to ryde,
    Arayd in habit blacke, and amis thin,
Like to an holy Monck, the seruice to begin.

19

And in his hand his Portesse still he bare,
    That much was worne, but therein little red,
    For of deuotion he had little care,
    Still drownd in sleepe, and most of his dayes ded ;
    Scarse could he once vphold his heauie hed,
    To looken, whether it were night or day :
    May seeme the wayne was very euill led,
    When such an one had guiding of the way,
That knew not, whether right he went, or else astray.

20

From worldly cares himselfe he did esloyne,
    And greatly shunned manly exercise,
    From euery worke he chalenged essoyne,
    For contemplation sake : yet otherwise,
    His life he led in lawlesse riotise ;
    By which he grew to grieuous malady ;
    For in his lustlesse limbs through euill guise
    A shaking feuer raignd continually :
Such one was *Idlenesse*, first of this company.

21

And by his side rode loathsome *Gluttony*,
    Deformed creature, on a filthie swyne,
    His belly was vp-blowne with luxury,
    And eke with fatnesse swollen were his eyne,
    And like a Crane his necke was long and fyne,
    With which he swallowd vp excessiue feast,
    For want whereof poore people oft did pyne ;
    And all the way, most like a brutish beast,
He spued vp his gorge, that all did him deteast.

22

In greene vine leaues he was right fitly clad ;
    For other clothes he could not weare for heat,
    And on his head an yuie girland had,
    From vnder which fast trickled downe the sweat :
    Still as he rode, he somewhat still did eat,
    And in his hand did beare a bouzing can,
    Of which he supt so oft, that on his seat
    His dronken corse he scarse vpholden can,
In shape and life more like a monster, then a man.

Stanza 18

1   vnequall: different, because of the different sins which they represent; cf. Chaucer's description of the sins: 'they renne in o lees, but in diverse manneres' (*Parson's Tale* 387).
3   As Anderson (1969) 478 notes, 'it is not at all clear whether the beast is obeying the counsellor, or the counsellor, obeying the beast'.
4   The bestial commands were appropriate to each beast's nature. Rider and beast are in harmony.
6   the nourse of sin: Idleness is traditionally 'the ministre and the norice unto vices' (Chaucer, *Second Nun's Prol.* 1). An 'ydle dreame' (i 46.1) first tempted the Knight to forsake Una.
8   amis: priestly vestment or monk's hood. Idleness is linked to the Roman clergy to associate the sin with the papal supremacy claimed by Lucifera.

Stanza 19

1   Portesse: a breviary carried by priests; noted as outward Popish display.
7–9   Sloth escapes the judgment upon sin by not exercising moral choice. He represents mankind's state of wandering, particularly before the coming of the law.

Stanza 20

1–3   esloyne: withdraw, remove himself from the jurisdiction of the law.   chalenged essoyne: claimed exemption. The two legal terms show that he seeks to live beyond the law in lawlessness.
5   riotise: riotous conduct; a typical S. coinage which preserves the action of the verb in the state itself.
7   lustlesse: listless; implying that lustfulness has led to this state.   guise: behaviour.

Stanzas 21–23

Nashe writes that he had intended to 'decypher' the excess of gluttony 'but that a new Laureat hath sav'd me the labor' (*Pierce Penilesse*, 1592, *Works* i 199).

Stanza 21

3   luxury: vicious indulgence (Lat. *luxuria*).
4   'Their eyes stand out for fatnes' (Ps. 73.7).
5   Crane: a common emblem for Gluttony (Lat. *glutire*, to swallow) because its long neck allows extended pleasure in swallowing.   fyne: scrawny.
9   gorge: i.e. what he had swallowed.

Stanza 22

Gluttony resembles the drunken satyr Silenus, foster-father of Bacchus.
1   right fitly: because ivy is sacred to Bacchus.
5   somewhat: something.
6   bouzing: to indicate that he drinks to excess.

23

Vnfit he was for any worldly thing,
  And eke vnhable once to stirre or go,
  Not meet to be of counsell to a king,
  Whose mind in meat and drinke was drowned so,
  That from his friend he seldome knew his fo :
  Full of diseases was his carcas blew,
  And a dry dropsie through his flesh did flow :
  Which by misdiet daily greater grew :
Such one was *Gluttony*, the second of that crew.

24

And next to him rode lustfull *Lecherie*,
  Vpon a bearded Goat, whose rugged haire,
  And whally eyes (the signe of gelosy,)
  Was like the person selfe, whom he did beare :
  Who rough, and blacke, and filthy did appeare,
  Vnseemely man to please faire Ladies eye ;
  Yet he of Ladies oft was loued deare,
  When fairer faces were bid standen by :
O who does know the bent of womens fantasy ?

25

In a greene gowne he clothed was full faire,
  Which vnderneath did hide his filthinesse,
  And in his hand a burning hart he bare,
  Full of vaine follies, and new fanglenesse :
  For he was false, and fraught with ficklenesse,
  And learned had to loue with secret lookes,
  And well could daunce, and sing with ruefulnesse,
  And fortunes tell, and read in louing bookes,
And thousand other wayes, to bait his fleshly hookes.

26

Inconstant man, that loued all he saw,
  And lusted after all, that he did loue,
  Ne would his looser life be tide to law,
  But ioyd weake wemens hearts to tempt and proue
  If from their loyall loues he might them moue ;
  Which lewdnesse fild him with reprochfull paine
  Of that fowle euill, which all men reproue,
  That rots the marrow, and consumes the braine :
Such one was *Lecherie*, the third of all this traine.

27

And greedy *Auarice* by him did ride,
  Vpon a Camell loaden all with gold ;
  Two iron coffers hong on either side,
  With precious mettall full, as they might hold,
  And in his lap an heape of coine he told ;
  For of his wicked pelfe his God he made,
  And vnto hell him selfe for money sold ;
  Accursed vsurie was all his trade,
And right and wrong ylike in equall ballaunce waide.

Stanza 23

1 **Vnfit**: like his companion Idleness, he is unfit to serve
the world.

2 **once**: ever. **go**: walk.
6 **blew**: black or livid, the colour of diseased flesh.
7 **dry dropsie**: either 'dire dropsie', as Upton (1758)
suggests (*dirus hydrops*, Horace, *Odes* II ii 13), or 'dry' because
it causes thirst. Excessive drinking causes dropsy, which, in
turn, causes insatiable thirst. Hence too his monstrous form,
particularly his swollen belly; cf. Master Adam, in Dante, *Inf.*
xxx 49, who through dropsy is shaped like a lute. It is the
disease of the covetous in Richard Rolle, *Pricke of Conscience*
2990–1.

Stanzas 24–29

After Idleness with his 'lustlesse limbs' (20.7) and Gluttony
who is unable to 'stirre or go' (23.2) follow in contrast,
Lechery, and Avarice with his 'greedy lust' (29.2).

Stanza 24

1 **next**: immediately following, because 'after Glotonye
thanne comth Lecherie, for thise two synnes been so ny cosyns
that ofte tyme they wol nat departe' (Chaucer, *Parson's Tale*
836).
2 The goat is proverbially lustful; see Rowland (1973) 85.
rugged: shaggy. **haire**: cf. Lust 'All ouergrowne with
haire' (IV vii 5.4).
3 **whally**: glaring, to indicate jealousy; or wall-eyed,
showing white as the eye rolls in jealousy.

Stanza 25

1 **greene**: 'the colour of lovers' (Shakespeare, *Love's
Labour's Lost* I ii 83); but also of fickleness (Chaucer, *Against
Women Unconstant* 7: 'In stede of blew, thus may ye were al
grene').
8 **louing bookes**: books of love.

Stanza 26

4 **tempt**: make trial of. **proue**: test.
6–8 **reprochfull**: deserving of reproach, besides being full
of reproach for his pain. **that fowle euill**: either syphilis
or leprosy. Leprosy was widely held to be transmitted venere-
ally and to be a special punishment inflicted by God; cf. III
v 14.8–9, and see Rowland (1964) 175 and Hume (1969) 242.
Syphilis rots the marrow, leaving the bones hollow: see
Shakespeare, *Measure for Measure* I ii 54 and *Venus and
Adonis* 741.

Stanza 27

1 **greedy**: as the name implies (Lat. *avarus*). **by him**:
Avarice and Lechery are paired as are Mammon and Acrasia,
the two extremes of the state of intemperance in Book II;
cf. II vii 17.
2 **Camell**: associated with the rich man through Christ's
parable, Matt. 19.24. Its hump is an emblem of the rich man's
burden (Chew, 1962, 106).
5 **told**: counted; cf. Mammon, II vii 4.7.
6 **wicked pelfe**: filthy lucre.
8 **Accursed**: usury was illegal in England, being forbidden
by Scripture.
9 The error of weighing right with wrong is exposed by
Artegall: 'For by no meanes the false will with the truth by
wayd' (V ii 45.9). Chew 108 notes that Avarice is depicted with
a pair of balances in the Lyons edition of the *Roman de la Rose*.

28

His life was nigh vnto deaths doore yplast,
   And thred-bare cote, and cobled shoes he ware,
   Ne scarse good morsell all his life did tast,
   But both from backe and belly still did spare,
   To fill his bags, and richesse to compare;
   Yet chylde ne kinsman liuing had he none
   To leaue them to; but thorough daily care
   To get, and nightly feare to lose his owne,
He led a wretched life vnto him selfe vnknowne.

29

Most wretched wight, whom nothing might suffise,
   Whose greedy lust did lacke in greatest store,
   Whose need had end, but no end couetise,
   Whose wealth was want, whose plenty made him pore,
   Who had enough, yet wished euer more;
   A vile disease, and eke in foote and hand
   A grieuous gout tormented him full sore,
   That well he could not touch, nor go, nor stand:
Such one was *Auarice*, the fourth of this faire band.

30

And next to him malicious *Enuie* rode,
   Vpon a rauenous wolfe, and still did chaw
   Betweene his cankred teeth a venemous tode,
   That all the poison ran about his chaw;
   But inwardly he chawed his owne maw
   At neighbours wealth, that made him euer sad;
   For death it was, when any good he saw,
   And wept, that cause of weeping none he had,
But when he heard of harme, he wexed wondrous glad.

31

All in a kirtle of discolourd say
   He clothed was, ypainted full of eyes;
   And in his bosome secretly there lay
   An hatefull Snake, the which his taile vptyes
   In many folds, and mortall sting implyes.
   Still as he rode, he gnasht his teeth, to see
   Those heapes of gold with griple Couetyse,
   And grudged at the great felicitie
Of proud *Lucifera*, and his owne companie.

Stanza 28

Avarice is the only sin whose age S. implies (Chew, 1962, 108). Its association with old age was proverbial (Tilley, 1950, M568); cf. Falstaff's lament: 'A man can no more separate age

and covetousness than 'a can part young limbs and lechery; but the gout galls the one, and the pox pinches the other' (*2 Henry IV* I ii 216–8).
5   **compare**: acquire.
9   **vnknowne**: i.e. he did not know how wretched he was; or he lacks knowledge of himself; or, living to himself, he was unknown to others.

Stanza 29
1–2   Proverbial: Who desires most lacks most (C. G. Smith, 1970, 175; cf. 559). Cf. Sidney: 'Wealth breeding want, more blist, more wretched grow' (*Astrophel and Stella* xxiv 4). **lacke**: want.
3   **couetise**: covetousness.
4   **Whose wealth was want**: implying that he possesses only his covetousness, as he personifies the state itself. **plenty . . . pore**: Ovid's *inopem me copia fecit* (*Met.* iii 466); proverbial (Smith 619).
5   Cf. the second beadman in the house of Holiness: 'He had enough, what need him care for more?' (x 38.8).
6–9   **disease**: his mental state is expressed as a physical disease. The pain of gout prevents him from enjoying his wealth. Its physical effect is a fitting punishment for his grasping nature.

Stanzas 30–35
Wrath and Envy are the climactic sins: the inhabitants of the house of Pride finally fall 'Prouokt with *Wrath*, and *Enuies* false surmise' (v 46.7); see 39.4–6*n*.

Stanza 30
1   Chaucer's Parson cites the two characteristics of Envy described by Augustine: 'sorwe of othere mennes wele, and joye of othere mennes harm' (*Parson's Tale* 484). S. shows Envy provoked **At neighbours wealth** (6), and **malicious**; cf. V xii 29–31.
2   **wolfe**: usually associated with avarice but its reputed paralysing glance may associate it with Envy. **still**: continually.
3   **cankred**: infected; possibly, rusted, i.e. bloody. **venemous** was a common epithet for the toad. Usually Envy chews a snake, as V xii 30.5–9, or his own heart.
5   Proverbial (C. G. Smith, 1970, 215). **maw**: guts.
6   **wealth**: well-being, welfare; or specifically the gold of his companion, Avarice (as 31.6–9).

Stanza 31
1   **kirtle**: either robes of state or a woman's gown (cf. *S.C.* Aug. 67), both appropriate to the state of Envy. **discolourd say**: a many-coloured cloth of fine texture, showing the false colours in which Envy sees everything, as the envious in Dante, *Purg.* xiii 9, appear in *livido color*. Craig (1967) 457 finds a pun on the vicious things Envy says.
2   **full of eyes**: the literal sense of Envy (Lat. *invidia*, related to *invidere*, to look maliciously upon).
4–5   **Snake**: the traditional attribute of Envy. **mortall**: death-dealing, as Error's 'mortall sting' (i 15.4). **implyes**: enfolds. Upton (1758) suggests that the snake stings Envy's bosom physically. There is also the current sense: what Envy implies wounds deepest.
7   **with griple Couetyse**: i.e. owned by grasping Avarice, implying also that he looks with covetousness.
8   **grudged**: was envious; complained.

32

He hated all good workes and vertuous deeds,
  And him no lesse, that any like did vse,
  And who with gracious bread the hungry feeds,
  His almes for want of faith he doth accuse;
  So euery good to bad he doth abuse:
  And eke the verse of famous Poets witt
  He does backebite, and spightfull poison spues
  From leprous mouth on all, that euer writt:
Such one vile *Enuie* was, that fifte in row did sitt.

33

And him beside rides fierce reuenging *Wrath*,
  Vpon a Lion, loth for to be led;
  And in his hand a burning brond he hath,
  The which he brandisheth about his hed;
  His eyes did hurle forth sparkles fiery red,
  And stared sterne on all, that him beheld,
  As ashes pale of hew and seeming ded;
  And on his dagger still his hand he held,
Trembling through hasty rage, when choler in him sweld.

34

His ruffin raiment all was staind with blood,
  Which he had spilt, and all to rags yrent,
  Through vnaduized rashnesse woxen wood;
  For of his hands he had no gouernement,
  Ne car'd for bloud in his auengement:
  But when the furious fit was ouerpast,
  His cruell facts he often would repent;
  Yet wilfull man he neuer would forecast,
How many mischieues should ensue his heedlesse hast.

35

Full many mischiefes follow cruell *Wrath*;
  Abhorred bloudshed, and tumultuous strife,
  Vnmanly murder, and vnthrifty scath,
  Bitter despight, with rancours rusty knife,
  And fretting griefe the enemy of life;
  All these, and many euils moe haunt ire,
  The swelling Splene, and Frenzy raging rife,
  The shaking Palsey, and Saint *Fraunces* fire:
Such one was *Wrath*, the last of this vngodly tire.

36

And after all, vpon the wagon beame
  Rode *Sathan*, with a smarting whip in hand,
  With which he forward lasht the laesie teme,
  So oft as *Slowth* still in the mire did stand.
  Huge routs of people did about them band,
  Showting for ioy, and still before their way
  A foggy mist had couered all the land;
  And vnderneath their feet, all scattered lay
Dead sculs and bones of men, whose life had gone astray.

Stanza 32

2 **vse**: perform.

3 **with gracious bread**: with bread graciously. S.'s phrase

identifies the deed and the doer; the gracious deed manifests his inner grace.

4 By claiming that good works reveal lack of faith, Envy contradicts the doctrine that 'of workes a man is justified, and not of faith onely' (James 2.24).

5 **abuse**: misrepresent, colour falsely.

6–8 Cf. the action of the Blatant Beast, VI xii 41.

Stanza 33

1 **him beside**: Envy's evil eyes lead to Wrath's fiery glances.

2–3 The lion is traditionally associated with wrath (Chew, 1962, 111); its well-known pride makes it an unwilling mount.

5 The stream of animal spirits emitted by Wrath's eyes infects with wrath those he looks upon with wrath.

9 **choler**: the humour that causes anger.

Stanza 34

1 **ruffin**: obsolete spelling of 'ruffian': disorderly, as befits a ruffian; suggests the ruffin, the Devil, and the colour red (Lat. *rufus*).

3 **woxen wood**: grown mad.

5 **car'd for**: i.e. cared about spilling.

7 **facts**: crimes, evil deeds. Wrath is the only sin associated with repentance (see Chew, 1962, 112–3).

9 **mischieues**: evil consequences, calamities.

Stanza 35

3 **Vnmanly**: as it destroys the man, applied both to the victim and the doer. **vnthrifty scath**: wasteful or destructive harm. vnthrifty may have the stronger sense, harmful, wicked; 'scath' is glossed as 'losse hinderaunce' for *S.C.* Dec. 100. Kitchin (1905) suggests 'mischief that never thrives'.

4 **despight**: malice. **rusty**: red with blood (for S. the term always suggests 'filthy' or 'defiled' from use, not disuse); cf. v 32.2, ix 36.8.

5 **griefe**: mental distress (*OED* 7) in a more comprehensive sense. **fretting**: gnawing, pricking. Chew (1962) 112 cites examples in which Wrath wounds himself.

7 **swelling Splene**: outburst of hot temper, scorn and ridicule, the spleen being the seat of anger and morose feeling (Robin, 1911, 67). The swelling spleen causes the decay of the entire body (see Phineas Fletcher's note to the *Purple Island* iii 19).

8 **Palsey**: associated with Wrath; cf. Richard Rolle, *Pricke of Conscience* 2996. **Saint Fraunces fire**: St Anthony's fire, erysipelas, a fever that leads to violent inflammation of the skin (Nares). Gordon (1959) 35 notes that the disease was known as St Francis's fire. As a Protestant, S. would not be concerned to get the specific saint correct.

9 **tire**: rank; procession, train.

Stanza 36

4 **Slowth**: the obsolete spelling is used here to suggest slowness. **still**: in both senses, continually, not moving.

7 **foggy mist**: associated with error and falsehood (see Chew, 1962, 113). It signifies the moral confusion that leads to sin and results from it; cf. the mist that falls upon the sorcerer as punishment for his sin, Acts 13.11. On the infection of mist, see Shakespeare, *The Tempest* II ii 1–3. Cf. the fog that envelops Guyon on his way to the Bower of Bliss, II xii 34.

37

So forth they marchen in this goodly sort,
   To take the solace of the open aire,
   And in fresh flowring fields themselues to sport;
   Emongst the rest rode that false Lady faire,
   The fowle *Duessa*, next vnto the chaire
   Of proud *Lucifera*, as one of the traine:
   But that good knight would not so nigh repaire,
   Him selfe estraunging from their ioyaunce vaine,
Whose fellowship seemd far vnfit for warlike swaine.

38

So hauing solaced themselues a space
   With pleasaunce of the breathing fields yfed,
   They backe returned to the Princely Place;
   Whereas an errant knight in armes ycled,
   And heathnish shield, wherein with letters red
   Was writ *Sans ioy*, they new arriued find:
   Enflam'd with fury and fiers hardy-hed,
   He seemd in hart to harbour thoughts vnkind,
And nourish bloudy vengeaunce in his bitter mind.

39

Who when the shamed shield of slaine *Sans foy*
   He spide with that same Faery champions page,
   Bewraying him, that did of late destroy
   His eldest brother, burning all with rage
   He to him leapt, and that same enuious gage
   Of victors glory from him snatcht away:
   But th'Elfin knight, which ought that warlike wage,
   Disdaind to loose the meed he wonne in fray,
And him rencountring fierce, reskewd the noble pray.

40

Therewith they gan to hurtlen greedily,
   Redoubted battaile ready to darrayne,
   And clash their shields, and shake their swords on hy,
   That with their sturre they troubled all the traine;
   Till that great Queene vpon eternall paine
   Of high displeasure, that ensewen might,
   Commaunded them their fury to refraine,
   And if that either to that shield had right,
In equall lists they should the morrow next it fight.

41

Ah dearest Dame, (quoth then the Paynim bold,)
   Pardon the errour of enraged wight,
   Whom great griefe made forget the raines to hold
   Of reasons rule, to see this recreant knight,
   No knight, but treachour full of false despight
   And shamefull treason, who through guile hath slayn
   The prowest knight, that euer field did fight,
   Euen stout *Sans foy* (O who can then refrayn?)
Whose shield he beares renuerst, the more to heape disdayn.

Stanza 37

1   **sort**: company.
2   **solace**: pleasure.
7   **that good knight**: his epic epithet (see ii 11.2*n*), which he deserves in this company.
8   **ioyaunce**: festivity; a coinage that emphasizes the state of joy. Blythe (1972) 346–7 argues that the presentation of the seven deadly sins as an entertainment serves to obscure the real nature of sin itself.

Stanza 38

2   **breathing**: exhaling fragrance; or (preferably) fields where they breathe to escape the stench of sin.
3   **the Princely Place**: S. reserves its final naming for the concluding phrase of Canto v.
6   **Sans ioy**: he appears here in response to the Knight's rejection of 'ioyaunce vaine' (37.8). On the state represented by the name, see ii 25.6–9*n*, v 33.1–6*n*.
7   **hardy-hed**: hardihood, over-boldness.

Stanza 39

1   **shamed**: because reversed (41.9).
3   **Bewraying**: revealing.
4–6   Sansjoy displays the two sins which cause the fall of those who inhabit the house of Pride: 'Prouokt with *Wrath*, and *Enuies* false surmise' (v 46.7).   **enuious gage**: envied pledge of victory; the 'signe of the conqueroure' (ii 20.7) which he envied or begrudged him.
7   **ought**: owned.   **warlike wage**: pledge of skill in war, or spoil of war.
9   **rencountring**: engaging in fight, suggesting (f. Fr. *rencontre*) a skirmish or accidental combat; hence Lucifera's judgment at 40.9.   **pray**: booty. Instead of seeking to free Una's parents, the Knight seeks to possess the shield of faithlessness, which he regards as his **noble pray**.

Stanza 40

1   **hurtlen**: clash violently; cf. 16.3.
2   **darrayne**: engage in order to vindicate a claim (a legal term).
3   Such details suggest a pagan encounter.
9   **equall**: impartial, just. Unlike the chance outcome of a casual encounter, a battle in the lists was an ordeal of which the outcome was considered to be a just verdict.   **the morrow next**: the breach of chivalric decorum in not allowing any waiting period is noted by McNeir (1966) 108.

Stanza 41

4   **recreant**: cowardly, a term of the greatest opprobrium; cf. the charge, 'Miscreant', against Sansjoy, v 13.1 and Sansloy vi 41.1. More precisely, one who has yielded up his faith.
5   **treachour**: traitor, an obsolete form which suggests 'treacherous'.
9   **renuerst**: turned upside down, as in the degradation of Braggadocchio at V iii 37.

42

And to augment the glorie of his guile,
　　His dearest loue the faire *Fidessa* loe
　　Is there possessed of the traytour vile,
　　Who reapes the haruest sowen by his foe,
　　Sowen in bloudy field, and bought with woe:
　　That brothers hand shall dearely well requight
　　So be, O Queene, you equall fauour showe;
　　Him litle answerd th'angry Elfin knight;
He neuer meant with words, but swords to plead his right.

43

But threw his gauntlet as a sacred pledge,
　　His cause in combat the next day to try:
　　So been they parted both, with harts on edge,
　　To be aueng'd each on his enimy.
　　That night they pas in ioy and iollity,
　　Feasting and courting both in bowre and hall;
　　For Steward was excessiue *Gluttonie*,
　　That of his plenty poured forth to all;
Which doen, the Chamberlain *Slowth* did to rest them call.

44

Now whenas darkesome night had all displayd
　　Her coleblacke curtein ouer brightest skye,
　　The warlike youthes on dayntie couches layd,
　　Did chace away sweet sleepe from sluggish eye,
　　To muse on meanes of hoped victory.
　　But whenas *Morpheus* had with leaden mace
　　Arrested all that courtly company,
　　Vp-rose *Duessa* from her resting place,
And to the Paynims lodging comes with silent pace.

45

Whom broad awake she finds, in troublous fit,
　　Forecasting, how his foe he might annoy,
　　And him amoues with speaches seeming fit:
　　Ah deare *Sans ioy*, next dearest to *Sans foy*,
　　Cause of my new griefe, cause of my new ioy,
　　Ioyous, to see his ymage in mine eye,
　　And greeu'd, to thinke how foe did him destroy,
　　That was the flowre of grace and cheualrye;
Lo his *Fidessa* to thy secret faith I flye.

46

With gentle wordes he can her fairely greet,
　　And bad say on the secret of her hart.
　　Then sighing soft, I learne that litle sweet
　　Oft tempred is (quoth she) with muchell smart:
　　For since my brest was launcht with louely dart
　　Of deare *Sansfoy*, I neuer ioyed howre,
　　But in eternall woes my weaker hart
　　Haue wasted, louing him with all my powre,
And for his sake haue felt full many an heauie stowre.

47

At last when perils all I weened past,
　　And hop'd to reape the crop of all my care,
　　Into new woes vnweeting I was cast,
　　By this false faytor, who vnworthy ware
　　His worthy shield, whom he with guilefull snare
　　Entrapped slew, and brought to shamefull graue.
　　Me silly maid away with him he bare,
　　And euer since hath kept in darksome caue,
For that I would not yeeld, that to *Sans-foy* I gaue.

Stanza 42
3　**possessed**: i.e. sexually.
4　Proverbial (C. G. Smith, 1970, 710); see also John 4.37.
5　Cf. the Dwarf's account of Fidessa 'Bought with the bloud of vanquisht Paynim bold' (vii 26.4).
6　**That**: i.e. that act.
7　**equall**: impartial, as 40.9.
8　**angry**: he is brought to the level of his wrathful opponent.
9　**words . . . swords**: S.'s frequent use of the punning device of paranomasia is discussed by Wion (1968) 20f.

Stanza 43
5　**they**: presumably the courtiers, but not excluding the two knights. Sansjoy's anger at Lucifera's charge (stanza 41) now turns to joy. That the Red Cross Knight is disgracefully compromised is shown by the two opening lines of this stanza.
5–6　Not simply a duplication of terms: they ioy in **Feasting** in the **hall**, and have **iollity** (pleasure, esp. sexual pleasure, *OED* 3) in **courting** in the **bowre**.
9　**Chamberlain**: the attendant at court in charge of the bedchambers, as the spelling indicates.

Stanza 44
1–2　**night**: personified to introduce Duessa's coming visit.
6–7　**leaden mace**: as in *Julius Caesar*: 'O murd'rous slumber! / Layest thou thy leaden mace upon my boy' (IV iii 265–6); suggested by the metal staff of office with which the sergeant tapped the person to be arrested.　**Arrested** makes a simple but effective pun. Until Book VI, sleep is usually associated with death or imprisonment.

Stanza 45
2　**annoy**: injure.
3　**amoues**: arouses, or seeks to move inwardly.　**seeming**: suitably.
9　**Lo . . . I flye**: I place myself secretly in your allegiance (playing on her name). The significance of her pledge appears at v 11.9: she perverts the pagan knight, as well as the Red Cross Knight, by making herself rather than the shield the issue of their battle. Cf. the similar moment, i 52.6.

Stanza 46
1　**can**: did.　**fairely**: courteously.
2　**secret of her hart**: not to be known of one upon whose forehead is written 'Mysterie' (Rev. 17.5). Only God 'knoweth the secrets of the heart' (Ps. 44.21); we hear a deceiving tale.
4　**muchell**: muckle, much.
5　**launcht**: pierced.　**louely**: amorous, referring to Cupid's dart of love.
7　**weaker**: too weak to resist love's dart and love's woes.
9　**stowre**: time of turmoil.

Stanza 47
1　**perils**: two have been told – her affair with the knight slain by Fradubio, and her affair with Fradubio himself.
2　Echoing Sansjoy's claim at 42.4.
4　**faytor**: impostor, because he wears Sansfoy's shield. Hence often with the epithet 'false', as xii 35.5, etc.
7　**silly**: helpless, as she claims before (ii 21.3).
9　**For that**: because. The great whore primly corrects Sansjoy's indelicate inference at 42.3–4.

73

48

But since faire Sunne hath sperst that lowring clowd,
 And to my loathed life now shewes some light,
 Vnder your beames I will me safely shrowd,
 From dreaded storme of his disdainfull spight:
 To you th'inheritance belongs by right
 Of brothers prayse, to you eke longs his loue.
 Let not his loue, let not his restlesse spright
 Be vnreueng'd, that calles to you aboue
From wandring *Stygian* shores, where it doth endlesse moue.

49

Thereto said he, Faire Dame be nought dismaid
 For sorrowes past; their griefe is with them gone:
 Ne yet of present perill be affraid;
 For needlesse feare did neuer vantage none,
 And helplesse hap it booteth not to mone.
 Dead is *Sans-foy*, his vitall paines are past,
 Though greeued ghost for vengeance deepe do grone:
 He liues, that shall him pay his dewties last,
And guiltie Elfin bloud shall sacrifice in hast.

50

O but I feare the fickle freakes (quoth shee)
 Of fortune false, and oddes of armes in field.
 Why dame (quoth he) what oddes can euer bee,
 Where both do fight alike, to win or yield?
 Yea but (quoth she) he beares a charmed shield,
 And eke enchaunted armes, that none can perce,
 Ne none can wound the man, that does them wield.
 Charmd or enchaunted (answerd he then ferce)
I no whit reck, ne you the like need to reherce.

51

But faire *Fidessa*, sithens fortunes guile,
 Or enimies powre hath now captiued you,
 Returne from whence ye came, and rest a while
 Till morrow next, that I the Elfe subdew,
 And with *Sans-foyes* dead dowry you endew.
 Ay me, that is a double death (she said)
 With proud foes sight my sorrow to renew:
 Where euer yet I be, my secrete aid
Shall follow you. So passing forth she him obaid.

Cant. V.

*The faithfull knight in equall field
subdewes his faithlesse foe,
Whom false Duessa saues, and for
his cure to hell does goe.*

1

THe noble hart, that harbours vertuous thought,
 And is with child of glorious great intent,
 Can neuer rest, vntill it forth haue brought
 Th'eternall brood of glorie excellent:
 Such restlesse passion did all night torment
 The flaming corage of that Faery knight,
 Deuizing, how that doughtie turnament
 With greatest honour he atchieuen might;
Still did he wake, and still did watch for dawning light.

74

Stanza 48

1–4 The bungled metaphor indicates her duplicity.
sperst: dispersed. **shrowd**: take shelter; also 'conceal', for she conceals herself in 'borrowed light' (viii 49.5).

6 **longs**: belongs.

7–9 **wandring Stygian shores**: wandering below on the banks of the Styx; see iii 36.6 and *n*. **Stygian** suggests blackness in contrast to the brother's light. **endlesse**: ceaselessly; forever.

Stanza 49

1–5 The tissue of proverbs befits his moral state.
vantage none: benefit anyone. **helplesse**: beyond help.

6 **vitall paines**: troubles in life, in contrast to those in death.

8 **dewties**: debts; the final obligations owed to Sansfoy: his slayer's death will 'redeeme [him] from his long wandring woe' (v 11.2).

Stanza 50

1–2 Excessive alliteration declares Duessa's duplicity.
oddes of armes: advantage through difference of armour, not of battle as he understands.

4 **alike**: as they fight 'In equall lists' (40.9) under Lucifera's 'equall fauour' (42.7).

Stanza 51

5 **dead**: qualifying Sansfoy, although it applies as well to faithlessness. **endew**: endow.

Canto v

Argument

1 See iv Arg. 2.

Stanza 1

1–4 These lines express the Renaissance faith that well-knowing leads to well-doing, as in Sidney, *Apology* 104.
vertuous implies valorous, full of manly courage rather than knowledge of the virtues. Miller (1971) 134–5 finds the praise of the Knight ironical in the light of what follows. **glorious**: eager for glory. **excellent**: supreme, rather than extremely good.

6 **corage**: mind; nature; heart. The etymological spelling (from Lat. *cor*, heart) is common throughout the poem.

7–8 Contrast Sansjoy 'Forecasting, how his foe he might annoy' (iv 45.2). See also 7.3, 6. **atchieuen**: finish, i.e. win.

2

At last the golden Orientall gate
   Of greatest heauen gan to open faire,
   And *Phœbus* fresh, as bridegrome to his mate,
   Came dauncing forth, shaking his deawie haire :
   And hurld his glistring beames through gloomy aire.
   Which when the wakeful Elfe perceiu'd, streight way
   He started vp, and did him selfe prepaire,
   In sun-bright armes, and battailous array :
For with that Pagan proud he combat will that day.

3

And forth he comes into the commune hall,
   Where earely waite him many a gazing eye,
   To weet what end to straunger knights may fall.
   There many Minstrales maken melody,
   To driue away the dull melancholy,
   And many Bardes, that to the trembling chord
   Can tune their timely voyces cunningly,
   And many Chroniclers, that can record
Old loues, and warres for Ladies doen by many a Lord.

4

Soone after comes the cruell Sarazin,
   In wouen maile all armed warily,
   And sternly lookes at him, who not a pin
   Does care for looke of liuing creatures eye,
   They bring them wines of *Greece* and *Araby*,
   And daintie spices fetcht from furthest *Ynd*,
   To kindle heat of corage priuily :
   And in the wine a solemne oth they bynd
T'obserue the sacred lawes of armes, that are assynd.

5

At last forth comes that far renowmed Queene,
   With royall pomp and Princely maiestie ;
   She is ybrought vnto a paled greene,
   And placed vnder stately canapee,
   The warlike feates of both those knights to see.
   On th'other side in all mens open vew
   Duessa placed is, and on a tree
   Sans-foy his shield is hangd with bloudy hew :
Both those the lawrell girlonds to the victor dew.

6

A shrilling trompet sownded from on hye,
   And vnto battaill bad them selues addresse :
   Their shining shieldes about their wrestes they tye,
   And burning blades about their heads do blesse,
   The instruments of wrath and heauinesse :
   With greedy force each other doth assayle,
   And strike so fiercely, that they do impresse
   Deepe dinted furrowes in the battred mayle ;
The yron walles to ward their blowes are weake and fraile.

7

The Sarazin was stout, and wondrous strong,
   And heaped blowes like yron hammers great :
   For after bloud and vengeance he did long.
   The knight was fiers, and full of youthly heat :
   And doubled strokes, like dreaded thunders threat :
   For all for prayse and honour he did fight.
   Both stricken strike, and beaten both do beat,
   That from their shields forth flyeth firie light,
And helmets hewen deepe, shew marks of eithers might.

Stanza 2

1–5   The description provides a setting for the battle between one of the 'sonnes of Day' and one of 'great *Nightes* children' (23.8, 25.7).
3–5   Cf. Ps. 19.4–5 : 'In them [the heavens] hathe he set a tabernacle for the sunne, which commeth forthe as a bridegrome out of his chambre [or vaile], and rejoyceth like a mightie man to runne his race.'   **dauncing**: a common Renaissance expression for the movement of the constellations.
8   'They that love him shal be as the sunne when he riseth in his might' (Judges 5.31).   **sun-bright**: appropriately, first recorded in S.   **battailous**: warlike.

Stanza 3

4–8   **Minstrales** compose the music, **Bardes** sing it, and **Chroniclers** set down the words.
5   Cf. 17.6–8. This line is repeated in the account of the Knight's marriage to Una, xii 38.8.
7   **Can**: knew how to.   **timely**: keeping time with the music.
8–9   Rose (1975) 64–5 notes the contrast with S.'s claim that 'Fierce warres and faithfull loues shall moralize my song'.

Stanza 4

1   **cruell**: also fierce, savage.   **Sarazin**: Saracen, or pagan generally (as Sansfoy, ii 12.6).
2   **warily**: carefully, i.e. completely ; possibly 'warly', in a warlike manner. Like his brother, he is 'all arm'd to point' (ii 12.6), in contrast to the 'enchaunted armes' (iv 50.6) which the Red Cross Knight wears.
3–4   Also imitating his brother, ii 12.9.
5–9   The oath by wine is chivalric. The laws of arms in medieval judicial combats involved an oath not to use charms. See ii 18.4*n*.   **daintie**: precious.

Stanza 5

1–2   **far renowmed**: cf. 'the wide report of her great Maiestee' (iv 13.9).   **royall pomp** indicates her pretentions to royalty : she 'made her selfe a Queene' (iv 12.2).
3   **paled greene**: the fenced grassy lists.

Stanza 6

4   **blesse**: brandish ; making the sign of the cross in the air under which they fight ; cf. viii 22.3.
5   **heauinesse**: anger, indignation. The further sense, sadness, grief (*OED* 1e), suggests that the sword is the instrument of **wrath** while the shield defends their state of **heauinesse**.

Stanza 7

The first three lines are carefully paralleled by the second three ; then the action of each set is doubled in the seventh with the repetition of striking and beating. The contrast between the two knights is developed from iv 45.2–3 and v 1.7–8.
4   **fiers**: high-spirited, brave, eager (*OED* 2, 5), or fiery (as the spelling suggests, cf. 1.6) ; cf. the 'Dragon fiers' in the next stanza.

75

8

So th'one for wrong, the other striues for right:
  As when a Gryfon seized of his pray,
  A Dragon fiers encountreth in his flight,
  Through widest ayre making his ydle way,
  That would his rightfull rauine rend away:
  With hideous horrour both together smight,
  And souce so sore, that they the heauens affray:
  The wise Southsayer seeing so sad sight,
Th'amazed vulgar tels of warres and mortall fight.

9

So th'one for wrong, the other striues for right,
  And each to deadly shame would driue his foe:
  The cruell steele so greedily doth bight
  In tender flesh, that streames of bloud down flow,
  With which the armes, that earst so bright did show,
  Into a pure vermillion now are dyde:
  Great ruth in all the gazers harts did grow,
  Seeing the gored woundes to gape so wyde,
That victory they dare not wish to either side.

10

At last the Paynim chaunst to cast his eye,
  His suddein eye, flaming with wrathfull fyre,
  Vpon his brothers shield, which hong thereby:
  Therewith redoubled was his raging yre,
  And said, Ah wretched sonne of wofull syre,
  Doest thou sit wayling by black *Stygian* lake,
  Whilest here thy shield is hangd for victors hyre,
  And sluggish german doest thy forces slake,
To after-send his foe, that him may ouertake?

11

Goe caytiue Elfe, him quickly ouertake,
  And soone redeeme from his long wandring woe;
  Goe guiltie ghost, to him my message make,
  That I his shield haue quit from dying foe.
  Therewith vpon his crest he stroke him so,
  That twise he reeled, readie twise to fall;
  End of the doubtfull battell deemed tho
  The lookers on, and lowd to him gan call
The false *Duessa*, Thine the shield, and I, and all.

12

Soone as the Faerie heard his Ladie speake,
  Out of his swowning dreame he gan awake,
  And quickning faith, that earst was woxen weake,
  The creeping deadly cold away did shake:
  Tho mou'd with wrath, and shame, and Ladies sake,
  Of all attonce he cast auengd to bee,
  And with so'exceeding furie at him strake,
  That forced him to stoupe vpon his knee;
Had he not stouped so, he should haue clouen bee.

Stanza 8
The primary allusion is to a meteorological phenomenon known as a firedrake or flying dragon, which presaged troublous times; see Heninger (1960) 95.

2 Gryfon: a lion with eagle's wings (Dan. 7.4). In Dante, *Purg.* xxix 108, a symbol for Christ in his twofold nature, human and divine; so perhaps here for the Knight and his armour. But the symbolism may be more complex. Griffins 'designe / Swiftnesse, and strength' (Jonson, *Masque of Queens* 468–9, *Works* vii 305). Its valour and magnanimity make it applicable 'unto Princes . . . and all heroick Commanders' (Browne, *Pseud. Epid.*, *Works* ii 218). On the other hand, the griffin, being associated with the guarding of gold (see Carroll, 1954, 67, 105) was an emblem of covetousness. As such, it may be associated with the Knight who fights to retain the pagan's shield.
4 ydle: if not an adverb, it refers to the air, as 'idle aire' (III xii 8.9).
5 That: i.e. the Dragon. **rauine**: spoil.
7 souce: strike, swoop down with heavy blows; a term from falconry.
8 sad: lamentable or ominous, for he interprets the conflict as a portent of disaster.

Stanza 9
2 deadly shame: also shameful death.

Stanza 10
1–6 Imitates the closing scene of Virgil, *Aen.*: inflamed by anger at the sight of Pallas's belt, Aeneas slays Turnus to atone for guilty blood. See ii 19.7*n*. Now, however, the Red Cross Knight is linked to the victim.
6 black Stygian lake: see iii 36.6, iv 48.9. In *Certain Sonnets* xvii 6, Sidney refers to 'the Stygian lake' rather than the more usual river Styx. The source is *Aen.* vi 134.
8 german: addressing himself as kinsman to Sansfoy. **slake**: diminish the fury of; **fyre** (2) and **sluggish** suggest 'quench'; cf. 'aslake' (iii 36.8 and see *n*).

Stanza 11
1 caytiue: servile, captive, a term of especial contempt for a knight.
2 Cf. iv 48.9. **redeeme**: ransom, as an expiatory sacrifice. The theme of revenge throughout the Sansfoy–Sansjoy–Sansloy episodes shows the operation of the Old Law, and counterpoints the coming of grace and the New Law when Arthur redeems the Red Cross Knight (cf. ix 1.9).
3 ghost: applied to the living knight in anticipation of his death. Upton (1758) notes the reference to Pyrrhus's address to Priam as he kills him: *referes ergo haec et nuntius ibis* (*Aen.* ii 547), another link of the Red Cross Knight's antagonist to the pagan world. **make**: i.e. deliver; or provide physically by his body; cf. 'doe' (13.2).
4 quit: recovered.
5–9 Cf. Sansfoy's stroke at ii 18.6–9. Again the Knight is saved by faith.
7 doubtfull: also dread.
8 him: referring to Sansjoy, of course, though the 'faithfull knight' (Arg. 1) assumes that he is addressed.

Stanza 12
3 quickning: life-restoring, referring to Duessa in her role as Fidessa. He responds to her cry as he did to Una's 'Add faith vnto your force' (i 19.3); earlier, however, he revived to kill his enemy.
5 sake: regard.
6 cast: resolved.

13

And to him said, Goe now proud Miscreant,
  Thy selfe thy message doe to german deare,
  Alone he wandring thee too long doth want:
  Goe say, his foe thy shield with his doth beare.
  Therewith his heauie hand he high gan reare,
  Him to haue slaine; when loe a darkesome clowd
  Vpon him fell: he no where doth appeare,
  But vanisht is.   The Elfe him cals alowd,
But answer none receiues: the darknes him does shrowd.

14

In haste *Duessa* from her place arose,
  And to him running said, O prowest knight,
  That euer Ladie to her loue did chose,
  Let now abate the terror of your might,
  And quench the flame of furious despight,
  And bloudie vengeance; lo th'infernall powres
  Couering your foe with cloud of deadly night,
  Haue borne him hence to *Plutoes* balefull bowres.
The conquest yours, I yours, the shield, and glory yours.

15

Not all so satisfide, with greedie eye
  He sought all round about, his thirstie blade
  To bath in bloud of faithlesse enemy;
  Who all that while lay hid in secret shade:
  He standes amazed, how he thence should fade.
  At last the trumpets Triumph sound on hie,
  And running Heralds humble homage made,
  Greeting him goodly with new victorie,
And to him brought the shield, the cause of enmitie.

16

Wherewith he goeth to that soueraine Queene,
  And falling her before on lowly knee,
  To her makes present of his seruice seene:
  Which she accepts, with thankes, and goodly gree,
  Greatly aduauncing his gay cheualree.
  So marcheth home, and by her takes the knight,
  Whom all the people follow with great glee,
  Shouting, and clapping all their hands on hight,
That all the aire it fils, and flyes to heauen bright.

17

Home is he brought, and laid in sumptuous bed:
  Where many skilfull leaches him abide,
  To salue his hurts, that yet still freshly bled.
  In wine and oyle they wash his woundes wide,
  And softly can embalme on euery side.
  And all the while, most heauenly melody
  About the bed sweet musicke did diuide,
  Him to beguile of griefe and agony:
And all the while *Duessa* wept full bitterly.

Stanza 13

1   **Miscreant**: misbeliever; cf. 'faithlesse' (Arg. 2, 15.3) and 'Hethen' (19.4). An appropriate term of abuse from a Knight who now renews his faith.
2   **doe**: deliver; see 11.3.
6   **clowd**: parallels in Homer, Virgil, and Tasso for the gods – here 'th'infernall powres' (14.6) – who protect their favourites from impending death by a concealing cloud are listed in *Var*. i 228. The dark cloud anticipates the coming of Night; for the cloud of death, cf. 41.8 and iii 39.8. The moment marks a change from that when the Knight's 'sun-bright armes' (2.8) could pierce the darkness of Error's cave (i 14.4–6). See xi 4.8*n*.

Stanza 14

5–6   Rightly Duessa identifies the Knight with his enemy who sought 'bloud and vengeance' (7.3).
9   **glory**: the 'glorie' (iv 15.7) of the house of Pride rather than the glory won by slaying Error, i 27.6.

Stanza 15

1–3   The Knight's present degradation becomes clear when Una tells Arthur how she found in him one 'Whose manly hands imbrew'd in guiltie blood / Had neuer bene' (vii 47.3–4).
4   Cf. the 'foggy mist' (iv 36.7) which covers the land before the procession of sins. The Knight's failure to see suggests a darkening of vision through sin.
5   **fade**: vanish.
6   **Triumph**: the official blast to salute the victor.

Stanza 16

1   **Wherewith**: with which (i.e. the shield).
2–6   His **falling** expresses his fallen state: now he becomes Lucifera's knight, riding **by her** following the sins to the house of Pride which is now his **home**.   **seene**: shown, and so proven.   **thankes**: good will, rather than expressions of gratitude. Contrast her first haughty response to him, iv 14.1–4.
goodly gree: courteous goodwill (Fr. *de bon gré*).
aduauncing: extolling.   **gay**: an appropriate epithet for the chivalry of Lucifera's knight.

Stanza 17

1   **Home**: emphatically placed here, and repeated from the preceding stanza, to expose the consequences of his victory.
2   **abide**: await, i.e. attend.
3   **salue**: anoint.
4   The medication is biblical: cf. Luke 10.34.
5   **can embalme**: did anoint. Yet the suggestion that he is being preserved in death, which is the fate of Lucifera's victims, is uncomfortably close.
7   **diuide**: in the musical sense. The melody is divided into passages of short, quick notes by separate voices singing in polyphony. In Castle Joyeous, such music is linked with the sensual '*Lydian* harmony' (III i 40.1–2). In contrast, the heavenly melody heard at the Knight's marriage to Una (xii 39) is the resolving harmony of the music of the spheres.
8   **griefe**: pain.

18

As when a wearie traueller that strayes
    By muddy shore of broad seuen-mouthed *Nile*,
    Vnweeting of the perillous wandring wayes,
    Doth meet a cruell craftie Crocodile,
    Which in false griefe hyding his harmefull guile,
    Doth weepe full sore, and sheddeth tender teares:
    The foolish man, that pitties all this while
    His mournefull plight, is swallowd vp vnwares,
Forgetfull of his owne, that mindes anothers cares.

19

So wept *Duessa* vntill euentide,
    That shyning lampes in *Ioues* high house were light:
    Then forth she rose, ne lenger would abide,
    But comes vnto the place, where th'Hethen knight
    In slombring swownd nigh voyd of vitall spright,
    Lay couer'd with inchaunted cloud all day:
    Whom when she found, as she him left in plight,
    To wayle his woefull case she would not stay,
But to the easterne coast of heauen makes speedy way.

20

Where griesly *Night*, with visage deadly sad,
    That *Phœbus* chearefull face durst neuer vew,
    And in a foule blacke pitchie mantle clad,
    She findes forth comming from her darkesome mew,
    Where she all day did hide her hated hew.
    Before the dore her yron charet stood,
    Alreadie harnessed for iourney new;
    And coleblacke steedes yborne of hellish brood,
That on their rustie bits did champ, as they were wood.

21

Who when she saw *Duessa* sunny bright,
    Adornd with gold and iewels shining cleare,
    She greatly grew amazed at the sight,
    And th'vnacquainted light began to feare:
    For neuer did such brightnesse there appeare,
    And would haue backe retyred to her caue,
    Vntill the witches speech she gan to heare,
    Saying, Yet O thou dreaded Dame, I craue
Abide, till I haue told the message, which I haue.

22

She stayd, and foorth *Duessa* gan proceede,
    O thou most auncient Grandmother of all,
    More old then *Ioue*, whom thou at first didst breede,
    Or that great house of Gods cælestiall,
    Which wast begot in *Dæmogorgons* hall,
    And sawst the secrets of the world vnmade,
    Why suffredst thou thy Nephewes deare to fall
    With Elfin sword, most shamefully betrade?
Lo where the stout *Sansioy* doth sleepe in deadly shade.

mournful crocodile / With sorrow snares relenting passengers'
(*2 Henry VI* III i 226–7). The simile relates the crocodile's
craft and guile to Duessa's. Further, it associates Duessa with
Egypt, and the Knight as a wanderer in that fallen land. Pity
for her first led him to become her knight, ii 21.
2   seuen-mouthed Nile: '*septemgemini . . . ostia Nili*'
(Virgil, *Aen.* vi 800).
8   vnwares: suddenly, being unwary.
9   of his owne: of his own care or preservation.

Stanza 19
1   euentide: the time is fixed precisely at the time of even,
the moment of balance between the opposing forces of light
and darkness.
6   inchaunted: cf. 'charmed' (29.4). These two terms
describe the Red Cross Knight's defence, his 'charmed shield'
and 'enchaunted' arms (iv 50). The dark cloud and the Knight's
'sun-bright armes' (2.8) are contrasted as the powers of night
and day.
7   in plight: i.e. in the same state in which she had left him;
or in the same perilous state. S. usually qualifies the term as
evil.

Stanza 20
The physical description of Night may be drawn from Comes
(1616) III xii, as Lotspeich (1932) suggests, or directly from
the authorities whom Comes cites, particularly Virgil. S.'s
emotive and graphic detail is original.
1   griesly: because her appearance arouses horror, as does
Proserpine's (i 37.4).   deadly sad: either sad or dismal as
death, or extremely dismal.
2   Either she does not dare to look upon Phœbus, or he
upon her.
4   mew: den; dark prison.
5   hew: both shape and colour.
9   rustie: being stained with blood.   wood: rabid.

Stanza 21
2   cleare: brightly.
3   amazed: terrified.
4–6   vnacquainted: unfamiliar, as Error's brood shun
'vncouth light' (i 15.8) and Error retreats into her cave
(16.5–9).
9   Abide: stop. Duessa brings Night to a halt as Faith may
'commaund the hastie Sunne to stay' (x 20.2).

Stanza 22
2–6   Night's genealogy is taken from Comes (1616) III xii.
breede: since Jove was fostered in a dark cave to escape being
eaten by Saturn, it may be said that darkness gave birth to him
(Upton, 1758).
5   Dæmogorgon: i.e. chaos; see i 37.8n and IV ii 47.7.
Lotspeich (1932) observes that S.'s spelling follows
Boccaccio's etymology of the name, from $\delta\alpha\iota\mu\omega\nu + \gamma\epsilon\omega\rho\gamma\delta\varsigma$,
demon of the earth. See x 66.5–6n on the etymology of the Red
Cross Knight's name, George.
6   secrets: because properly known to man only by revelation.   vnmade: i.e. before the world was formed out of
chaos; cf. Milton, *P.L.* ii 891–6: 'secrets of the hoary deep . . .
where eldest Night / And Chaos, ancestors of Nature, hold /
Eternal anarchy'.
7   Nephewes: grandsons.

Stanza 18
The crocodile of the medieval bestiaries was said to weep while
(or after) it devours a man; hence it was a symbol of hypocrisy.
It also weeps to allure man in order to devour him: 'the

23

And him before, I saw with bitter eyes
   The bold *Sansfoy* shrinke vnderneath his speare;
   And now the pray of fowles in field he lyes,
   Nor wayld of friends, nor laid on groning beare,
   That whylome was to me too dearely deare.
   O what of Gods then boots it to be borne,
   If old *Aueugles* sonnes so euill heare?
   Or who shall not great *Nightes* children scorne,
When two of three her Nephews are so fowle forlorne?

24

Vp then, vp dreary Dame, of darknesse Queene,
   Go gather vp the reliques of thy race,
   Or else goe them auenge, and let be seene,
   That dreaded *Night* in brightest day hath place,
   And can the children of faire light deface.
   Her feeling speeches some compassion moued
   In hart, and chaunge in that great mothers face:
   Yet pittie in her hart was neuer proued
Till then: for euermore she hated, neuer loued.

25

And said, Deare daughter rightly may I rew
   The fall of famous children borne of mee,
   And good successes, which their foes ensew:
   But who can turne the streame of destinee,
   Or breake the chayne of strong necessitee,
   Which fast is tyde to *Ioues* eternall seat?
   The sonnes of Day he fauoureth, I see,
   And by my ruines thinkes to make them great:
To make one great by others losse, is bad excheat.

26

Yet shall they not escape so freely all;
   For some shall pay the price of others guilt:
   And he the man that made *Sansfoy* to fall,
   Shall with his owne bloud price that he hath spilt.
   But what art thou, that telst of Nephews kilt?
   I that do seeme not I, *Duessa* am,
   (Quoth she) how euer now in garments gilt,
   And gorgeous gold arayd I to thee came;
Duessa I, the daughter of Deceipt and Shame.

27

Then bowing downe her aged backe, she kist
   The wicked witch, saying; In that faire face
   The false resemblance of Deceipt, I wist
   Did closely lurke; yet so true-seeming grace
   It carried, that I scarse in darkesome place
   Could it discerne, though I the mother bee
   Of falshood, and root of *Duessaes* race.
   O welcome child, whom I haue longd to see,
And now haue seene vnwares.   Lo now I go with thee.

Stanza 23

4   **groning**: because attended by mourners.
7   **Aueugle**: Fr. Blind. The word existed in English as a verb, to blind, hoodwink. Aueugle may be Night herself or the son/husband of Night; cf. '*Aueugles* sonne' (44.6).   **so euill heare**: such evil is reported (from Lat. *male audire*). Duessa appeals to Night's concern for the reputation of her house.
9   **so fowle forlorne**: later Arthur learns how the Red Cross Knight is 'so fowle forlore' (viii 39.4) and saves him, as Night here aids his foe.

Stanza 24

1   **dreary**: melancholy, dreadful; stronger than the modern sense; cf. vii 2.1.
4   **place**: high rank.
5   **children of faire light**: cf. 'sonnes of Day' (25.7). Later Arthur foretells that 'Dayes dearest children [The children of day *1590*] be the blessed seed, / Which darknesse shall subdew, and heauen win' (III iv 59.5–6); cf. John 12.36: 'While ye have light, beleve in the light, that ye may be the children of the light'; also Eph. 5.8, 1 Thess. 5.5.   **deface**: destroy, defame, outface, outshine by contrast.
8   **proued**: experienced.

Stanza 25

5   **chayne**: the golden chain by which Homer's Zeus controls all creation: see ix 1.1–2*n*; not here a linking in universal concord but a binding chain of necessity.
9   **excheat**: spoil, gain; or simply exchange.

Stanza 26

1   **freely**: without punishment.
2   **some**: includes one who cannot be named in this lower world, that is, Christ; but also Arthur (cf. viii 40.4–6).
4   **price**: pay for. In his struggle with Despair, the Knight invokes this concept of justice as simple revenge: 'With thine owne bloud to price his bloud' (ix 37.9); then he is overcome by Despair's argument that 'bloud must bloud repay' (43.6). Only later does the Knight escape from the covenant of the Old Law, which Night here upholds, into the new covenant of Grace.
6   Duessa's state parodies that of Una who 'Did seeme such, as she was' (xii 8.9), and of God who declared 'I am that I am' (Exod. 3.14). When Duessa is stripped, she is seen 'Such as she was' (viii 46.6).
7   **how euer**: although.   **gilt**: gilded. The rhyme with **guilt** (2) conveys its secondary meaning.
9   **Shame**: the first of the four degrees of death, the guiltiness which is the first effect of man's fall from innocence.

Stanza 27

3   **false**: even the image of Deceit is not true.
4   **closely**: secretly.
6–7   Comes (1616) III xii lists Fraud among the descendants of Night.   **falsehood**: a pun; Duessa wears a false hood.

79

28

Then to her yron wagon she betakes,
 And with her beares the fowle welfauourd witch:
 Through mirkesome aire her readie way she makes.
 Her twyfold Teme, of which two blacke as pitch,
 And two were browne, yet each to each vnlich,
 Did softly swim away, ne euer stampe,
 Vnlesse she chaunst their stubborne mouthes to twitch;
 Then foming tarre, their bridles they would champe,
And trampling the fine element, would fiercely rampe.

29

So well they sped, that they be come at length
 Vnto the place, whereas the Paynim lay,
 Deuoid of outward sense, and natiue strength,
 Couerd with charmed cloud from vew of day,
 And sight of men, since his late luckelesse fray.
 His cruell wounds with cruddy bloud congealed,
 They binden vp so wisely, as they may,
 And handle softly, till they can be healed:
So lay him in her charet, close in night concealed.

30

And all the while she stood vpon the ground,
 The wakefull dogs did neuer cease to bay,
 As giuing warning of th'vnwonted sound,
 With which her yron wheeles did them affray,
 And her darke griesly looke them much dismay;
 The messenger of death, the ghastly Owle
 With drearie shriekes did also her bewray;
 And hungry Wolues continually did howle,
At her abhorred face, so filthy and so fowle.

31

Thence turning backe in silence soft they stole,
 And brought the heauie corse with easie pace
 To yawning gulfe of deepe *Auernus* hole.
 By that same hole an entrance darke and bace
 With smoake and sulphure hiding all the place,
 Descends to hell: there creature neuer past,
 That backe returned without heauenly grace;
 But dreadfull *Furies*, which their chaines haue brast,
And damned sprights sent forth to make ill men aghast.

32

By that same way the direfull dames doe driue
 Their mournefull charet, fild with rusty blood,
 And downe to *Plutoes* house are come biliue:
 Which passing through, on euery side them stood
 The trembling ghosts with sad amazed mood,
 Chattring their yron teeth, and staring wide
 With stonie eyes; and all the hellish brood
 Of feends infernall flockt on euery side,
To gaze on earthly wight, that with the Night durst ride.

Stanza 28
2 **fowle welfauourd**: a variant of the usual 'false-fair' oxymoron.
3 **mirkesome**: more than 'murky'. This coinage suggests 'dense', 'heavy', 'polluted', so that air becomes an element in which the horses swim (6). **readie**: lying directly before her; or the adv. 'readily'.
4 **twyfold**: indicating her duplicity.
5 **browne**: dark, as a Milton's 'brown as evening' (*P.L.* ix 1088). **vnlich**: unlike. As Hecate's, Night's steeds resemble the Moon's. According to Comes (1616) III xvii, Luna's chariot is drawn *ab equis discoloribus albo et nigro*.
9 **fine element**: air, which is fine in relation to the other elements. **rampe**: rear on their hind legs.

Stanza 29
4 **charmed**: see 19.6n.
6 **cruddy**: clotted.
7 **wisely**: skilfully; carefully.
9 **in night**: S.'s allegorical technique allows him to move easily from the personification of Night to darkness itself.

Stanza 30
2–5 Upton (1758) notes the superstition that dogs are quick-sighted and quick-scented at the approach of gods or goddesses. S. seems to allude to the howling of the dogs at the coming of Hecate (Virgil, *Aen.* vi 257–8).
6–7 **Owle**: the traditional bird of ill omen, inhabiting desolation and wilderness, as Isaiah 34.11–5; an omen of death, as in Chaucer, 'of deth the bode bryngeth' (*Parl. Fowls* 343) and Ovid, *funereus bubo* (*Met.* x 453). Cf. II vii 23.3–5, xii 36.4. **ghastly**: causing terror; cf. ix 33.6–8. **bewray**: reveal.

Stanza 31
3 **Auernus**: cf. Virgil's Avernus, the dark lake in a deep cavern that leads to hell (*Aen.* vi 237–8).
4 **By**: by means of. **bace**: low in height.
6–7 In *Aen.* vi 126–31, the Sibyl tells Aeneas that those who have returned from hell have been loved by Jove or have been raised by their own merit. In contrast, **heauenly grace** alludes to Christ's descent into hell to free the imprisoned souls by his own merit. See Upton's note, *Var.* i 233–4.
8 **Furies**: the hellish spirits of discord; see iii 36.8. **chaines**: this detail may be original; yet cf. *Aen.* vi 555–8. See also ix 24.5. **brast**: burst.
9 **ill**: wicked. **aghast**: terrified (by death).

Stanza 32
The heavy alliteration in this episode, the inflated diction, and the exaggerated detail suggest a mock-heroic treatment of a set classical theme, the infernal descent.
1 **direfull dames**: suggested by the 'dreadfull *Furies*' of the last stanza (Lat. *Dirae*).
2 **fild**: defiled; also filled. **rusty**: blackened with blood; defiled; see iv 35.4n.
3 **biliue**: quickly; or a pun on being alive, as 9 may suggest.
7 **stonie**: fixed.

33

They pas the bitter waues of *Acheron*,
  Where many soules sit wailing woefully,
  And come to fiery flood of *Phlegeton*,
  Whereas the damned ghosts in torments fry,
  And with sharpe shrilling shriekes doe bootlesse cry,
  Cursing high *Ioue*, the which them thither sent.
  The house of endlesse paine is built thereby,
  In which ten thousand sorts of punishment
The cursed creatures doe eternally torment.

34

Before the threshold dreadfull *Cerberus*
  His three deformed heads did lay along,
  Curled with thousand adders venemous,
  And lilled forth his bloudie flaming tong:
  At them he gan to reare his bristles strong,
  And felly gnarre, vntill dayes enemy
  Did him appease; then downe his taile he hong
  And suffered them to passen quietly:
For she in hell and heauen had power equally.

35

There was *Ixion* turned on a wheele,
  For daring tempt the Queene of heauen to sin;
  And *Sisyphus* an huge round stone did reele
  Against an hill, ne might from labour lin;
  There thirstie *Tantalus* hong by the chin;
  And *Tityus* fed a vulture on his maw;
  Typhœus ioynts were stretched on a gin,
  Theseus condemned to endlesse slouth by law,
And fifty sisters water in leake vessels draw.

(*Aen.* vi 551); cf. II vi 50.9. S. may associate this river with the 'lake of fyre, burning with brimstone' (Rev. 19.20) into which the damned are cast. Hence the damned fry in its burning waters, for which Lotspeich (1932) cites Comes (1616) III Pr. as source; see II vi 50.8–9n. On the other hand, **Whereas** (4), paralleling **Where** (2), may imply that the souls only sit by the banks.   **bootlesse**: as the ghosts are helpless, or their crying is without avail.
7 Cf. Virgil's infernal castle (*Aen*. vi 548ff) where the dead are tortured, and the house of grief and pain in Tasso, *Ger. Lib.* ix 59. In Job 30.23, death is 'the house appointed for all the living'.

Stanza 34
1 **Cerberus**: the dog guarding the entrance to hell in Virgil, *Aen.* vi 417–23; cf. *Gn.* 345–52.
2 **along**: at full length.
4 **lilled forth**: lolled out.
6 **felly gnarre**: fiercely snarl; 'r' is the dog's letter (cf. Jonson, *English Grammar* under 'R', *Works* viii 491).
7 **appease**: Upton (1758) wonders whether by the cake, as in *Aen.* vi 420, or by a clod of earth, as in Dante, *Inf.* vi 26–7. Percival (1893) praises S. for not specifying the means. Cerberus may be appeased because Night is **dayes enemy** (6).
9 Hecate was *caeloque Ereboque potentem* (*Aen.* vi 247).

Stanza 35
The traditional sufferers in hell. Their punishments are from Seneca, Virgil, and ultimately Homer (*Ody.* xi 576f). Renaissance mythological handbooks and dictionaries made them common knowledge; for example, Watson in *Hekatompathia* (1582) writes of the 'damned soules (as the Poets faine) . . . *Tantalus* having his lippes still at the brinke of the river *Eridanus*, yet dieth for thirst. *Ixion* is tied unto a wheele; which turneth incessantly. A vulture feedeth upon the bowels of *Tityus*, which growe up againe ever as they are devoured. *Sisyphus* rowleth a great rounde stoane up a steepe hill, which being once at the top presently falleth downe amaine. *Belides* are fifty sisters, whose continuall taske is, to fill a bottomlesse tub full of water, by lading in their pitchers full at once' (Introduction to Sonnet lxii). Lotspeich (1932) notes that S. follows the order in Comes. More precisely, for **Ixion** to **Typhœus** he follows Comes's list of those who seek what cannot be obtained from the gods (VI xvi-xxii); he adds **Theseus** from Comes's list of illustrious men (VII ix), and the **fifty sisters** (Belides) from Comes IX xvii. Three are guilty of sexual assault against goddesses, three of scorning or rebelling against the gods, and the sisters of slaying their husbands. On Theseus, see II vii 63.6–9n.
4 **lin**: cease.
5 **hong by the chin**: as though suspended up to the chin in water; cf. II vii 58.
6 **maw**: liver.
7 **gin**: rack. The punishment may have been devised by S., for **Typhœus** is especially important in his mythology as the father of the lustful pair, Ollyphant and Argante (III vii 47–48) and of the Blatant Beast (VI vi 11–12). On Typhon, an alternate name, see VII vi 15.8, 29.6.
8 **Theseus**: condemned to sit forever in the chair of forgetfulness; cf. Virgil, *Aen* vi 617–8. Lotspeich cites Boccaccio's paraphrase, *Theseum perpetuo damnatum otio.*
9 **fifty sisters**: the Danaides or Belides who murdered their husbands on their wedding night; see *Gn.* 393–6.

Stanza 33
1–6 S. names two of the four rivers of Hades. 5 describes the behaviour of those on the banks of Cocytus, the river of lamentation; cf. II vii 56.8–9. The fourth, the Styx, is alluded to at 10.6. The epithet given each river suggests the Greek name. **Acheron**: ἄχος, woeful river of death.   **bitter**: being full of grief. According to Badius, *Virgilii Opera* 255ʳ (cited Nelson, 1963, 155), the name is derived from the Greek ἀ and χαρά, meaning *absque laetitia*, i.e. sans joy; cf. Servius's note to *Aen.* vi 107 for the meaning *sine gaudio*. **Phlegeton**: φλέγω, the river of fire, which Virgil describes with its waves of flames

36

They all beholding worldly wights in place,
    Leaue off their worke, vnmindfull of their smart,
    To gaze on them; who forth by them doe pace,
    Till they be come vnto the furthest part:
    Where was a Caue ywrought by wondrous art,
    Deepe, darke, vneasie, dolefull, comfortlesse,
    In which sad *Æsculapius* farre a part
    Emprisond was in chaines remedilesse,
For that *Hippolytus* rent corse he did redresse.

37

Hippolytus a iolly huntsman was,
    That wont in charet chace the foming Bore;
    He all his Peeres in beautie did surpas,
    But Ladies loue as losse of time forbore:
    His wanton stepdame loued him the more,
    But when she saw her offred sweets refused
    Her loue she turnd to hate, and him before
    His father fierce of treason false accused,
And with her gealous termes his open eares abused.

38

Who ail in rage his Sea-god syre besought,
    Some cursed vengeance on his sonne to cast:
    From surging gulf two monsters straight were brought,
    With dread whereof his chasing steedes aghast,
    Both charet swift and huntsman ouercast.
    His goodly corps on ragged cliffs yrent,
    Was quite dismembred, and his members chast
    Scattered on euery mountaine, as he went,
That of *Hippolytus* was left no moniment.

39

His cruell stepdame seeing what was donne,
    Her wicked dayes with wretched knife did end,
    In death auowing th'innocence of her sonne.
    Which hearing his rash Syre, began to rend
    His haire, and hastie tongue, that did offend:
    Tho gathering vp the relicks of his smart
    By *Dianes* meanes, who was *Hippolyts* frend,
    Them brought to *Æsculape*, that by his art
Did heale them all againe, and ioyned euery part.

40

Such wondrous science in mans wit to raine
    When *Ioue* auizd, that could the dead reuiue,
    And fates expired could renew againe,
    Of endlesse life he might him not depriue,
    But vnto hell did thrust him downe aliue,
    With flashing thunderbolt ywounded sore:
    Where long remaining, he did alwaies striue
    Himselfe with salues to health for to restore,
And slake the heauenly fire, that raged euermore.

41

There auncient Night arriuing, did alight
    From her nigh wearie waine, and in her armes
    To *Æsculapius* brought the wounded knight:
    Whom hauing softly disarayd of armes,
    Tho gan to him discouer all his harmes,
    Beseeching him with prayer, and with praise,
    If either salues, or oyles, or herbes, or charmes
    A fordonne wight from dore of death mote raise,
He would at her request prolong her nephews daies.

82

Stanza 36

1–3   From Ovid, *Met*. x 40–4: the damned pause in their toil to wonder at Orpheus's music.   **worldly**: mortal.
6   **vneasie**: entirely without ease or comfort, emphasized by its central place in a line which is itself **ywrought by wondrous art**.   **comfortlesse**: helpless, desolate.
Æsculapius (7) is not one to whom Christ's promise – 'I wil not leave you comfortles' (John 14.18) – is given; cf. vi. 6.1.
7–9   On Æsculapius as the false Christ, see Hamilton 70–1. He heals man's body, not his soul.   **remedilesse**: beyond all remedy; without hope of release. Cf. vii 51.8.   **redresse**: restore, deliver from death.

Stanzas 37–40

The story, drawn from Virgil (*Aen*. vii 761–82) or Ovid (*Met*. xv 497f), would be known to S. through Comes, Boccaccio, and Renaissance dictionaries (noted Starnes and Talbert, 1955, 68f). Cheney (1966) 52–3 argues that Hippolytus's story comments upon the Knight's condition; cf. V viii 43.

Stanza 37

1   **iolly**: gallant; brave.
9   **gealous termes**: words arousing jealousy in him.

Stanza 38

3   **two monsters**: from the sea monsters in Virgil, *Aen*. vii 780; they may suggest two sea swells, one to overturn the chariot and the other to mangle the huntsman.
7   **chast**: an implied pun. Following the chase, rather than love, proves his chastity, but his **members chast** are destroyed by his **chasing steedes** (4).
9   **moniment**: trace, identifying mark.

Stanza 39

6   **smart**: the fragments of Hippolytus's body which cause his grief.

Stanza 40

1   **science**: skill.
2   **auizd**: observed.
3   **fates expired**: the completed term of life determined by the Fates; cf. 'suffised fates' (ii 43.8).
7–9   The biblical injunction, 'Physician, heal thyself', is implicit here: Aesculapius may heal Hippolytus's wounds but not his own.

Stanza 41

2   **nigh wearie waine**: the horses of Night's chariot are exhausted either because night is far spent (for the pun on 'wane', cf. III viii 51.5) or because of their unusual journey down to earth (cf. 30.3) and then to hell.
5   **discouer**: in the literal sense, lay bare.
8   **fordonne**: the prefix serves as an intensive, 'utterly overcome'.

42

Ah Dame (quoth he) thou temptest me in vaine,
    To dare the thing, which daily yet I rew,
    And the old cause of my continued paine
    With like attempt to like end to renew.
    Is not enough, that thrust from heauen dew
    Here endlesse penance for one fault I pay,
    But that redoubled crime with vengeance new
    Thou biddest me to eeke?   Can Night defray
The wrath of thundring *Ioue*, that rules both night and day?

43

Not so (quoth she) but sith that heauens king
    From hope of heauen hath thee excluded quight,
    Why fearest thou, that canst not hope for thing,
    And fearest not, that more thee hurten might,
    Now in the powre of euerlasting Night?
    Goe to then, O thou farre renowmed sonne
    Of great *Apollo*, shew thy famous might
    In medicine, that else hath to thee wonne
Great paines, and greater praise, both neuer to be donne.

44

Her words preuaild: And then the learned leach
    His cunning hand gan to his wounds to lay,
    And all things else, the which his art did teach:
    Which hauing seene, from thence arose away
    The mother of dread darknesse, and let stay
    Aueugles sonne there in the leaches cure,
    And backe returning tooke her wonted way,
    To runne her timely race, whilst *Phœbus* pure
In westerne waues his wearie wagon did recure.

45

The false *Duessa* leauing noyous Night,
    Returnd to stately pallace of dame Pride;
    Where when she came, she found the Faery knight
    Departed thence, albe his woundes wide
    Not throughly heald, vnreadie were to ride.
    Good cause he had to hasten thence away;
    For on a day his wary Dwarfe had spide,
    Where in a dongeon deepe huge numbers lay
Of caytiue wretched thrals, that wayled night and day.

46

A ruefull sight, as could be seene with eie;
    Of whom he learned had in secret wise
    The hidden cause of their captiuitie,
    How mortgaging their liues to *Couetise*,
    Through wastfull Pride, and wanton Riotise,
    They were by law of that proud Tyrannesse
    Prouokt with *Wrath*, and *Enuies* false surmise,
    Condemned to that Dongeon mercilesse,
Where they should liue in woe, and die in wretchednesse.

Stanza 42

5   **dew**: deserved as an immortal or for his art; duly.
6   His state is mankind's before the coming of Christ.
penance: punishment.
7–8   **eeke**: augment. Possibly **redoubled** is proleptic so that
the lines read: 'you bid me to add to my crime by redoubling
it'; but it is simpler to refer **eeke** to **vengeance**.   **defray**:
settle, appease.

Stanza 43

3   **thing**: i.e. anything. She argues for despair.
4   **that**: referring to herself.
5   **euerlasting**: asserting her own immortality over that of
the gods.
6–9   Apollo 'first invented the use of phisike, and therby
deserved the name of a God' (Cooper); cf. Ovid, *Met.* i 521–2;
and cf. III iv 41.3. At IV xii 25.4 he is named 'King of
Leaches'.   **else**: already, formerly.   **donne**: ended;
surpassed.

Stanza 44

4–6   The further fortunes of Sansjoy need not be told: none
return from hell 'without heauenly grace' (31.7).   **cure**:
charge, care; combined with the current sense (as Arg.).
8   **timely race**: in the astronomical sense, the measured
course through the heavens which is fulfilled in time; 'timely'
in contrast to her journey to hell.
8–9   The reference to **Phœbus pure** concludes the episode
which began with Duessa's journey to Night 'That *Phœbus*
chearefull face durst neuer vew' (20.2). The natural cycle of
the sun's renewal contrasts with Sansjoy's infernal descent
to be renewed.   **pure**: purified and purifying light limits the
reign of foul darkness.   **recure**: restore to health, refresh.

Stanza 45

1   **noyous**: obnoxious, causing harm; as xi 50.9.
2   S. carefully withholds the simple, defining name; cf. 53.9.
4   **albe**: although.
7   **wary**: the term defines his allegorical function; cf. his
response to Error's den, i 13.8–9; cf. 'carefull' (52.1).
9   **caytiue**: captive, and therefore wretched.

Stanza 46

4   **mortgaging**: in its etymological sense, offering a death-
pledge.   **Couetise**: covetousness or Avarice (iv 27–29).
5   **wastfull**: causing desolation.   **wanton**: undisciplined.
Riotise: riotous conduct, the life of Idleness at iv 20.5.
6–7   'For the Law causeth wrath' (Rom. 4.15). Here Envy
carries the larger sense, malignant feeling, ill-will (*OED* 1);
cf. Wisdom 2.24: 'thorow envy of the devil came death into
the worlde'.   **surmise**: charge, imputation; possibly
suspicion. Envy and Wrath ride together, the third and last
pair in Lucifera's procession. If **wanton** (5) includes Gluttony
and Lechery, all the deadly sins are included in this stanza.
Tyrannesse: the female tyrant (Lucifera).
8   **mercilesse**: without hope of mercy, as Æsculapius is
imprisoned 'remedilesse' (36.8).
9   'For when we were in the flesh, the motions of sinnes,
which were by the Law, had force in our membres, to bring
forthe frute unto death' (Rom. 7.5).

47

There was that great proud king of *Babylon*,
  That would compell all nations to adore,
  And him as onely God to call vpon,
  Till through celestiall doome throwne out of dore,
  Into an Oxe he was transform'd of yore:
  There also was king *Crœsus*, that enhaunst
  His heart too high through his great riches store;
  And proud *Antiochus*, the which aduaunst
His cursed hand gainst God, and on his altars daunst.

48

And them long time before, great *Nimrod* was,
  That first the world with sword and fire warrayd;
  And after him old *Ninus* farre did pas
  In princely pompe, of all the world obayd;
  There also was that mightie Monarch layd
  Low vnder all, yet aboue all in pride,
  That name of natiue syre did fowle vpbrayd,
  And would as *Ammons* sonne be magnifide,
Till scornd of God and man a shamefull death he dide.

49

All these together in one heape were throwne,
  Like carkases of beasts in butchers stall.
  And in another corner wide were strowne
  The antique ruines of the *Romaines* fall:
  Great *Romulus* the Grandsyre of them all,
  Proud *Tarquin*, and too lordly *Lentulus*,
  Stout *Scipio*, and stubborne *Hanniball*,
  Ambitious *Sylla*, and sterne *Marius*,
High *Cæsar*, great *Pompey*, and fierce *Antonius*.

Stanzas 47–50
A catalogue of the damned, as in Chaucer, *Monk's Tale* and
Boccaccio, *De Casibus Virorum Illustrium*. It forms the
historical counterpart to the mythological figures catalogued
in 35.

Stanza 47
1–5   **king of Babylon**: Nebuchadnezzar; see Dan. 3–6.
S. assumes that the golden image which he set up to be
worshipped as God alone was his own image. He assumes
further that since 'he was driven from men, and did eat grasse
as the oxen' (Dan. 4.30), he was transformed into an ox. In
contrast, Chaucer writes that 'lyk a beest hym semed for to bee,
/ And eet hey as an oxe' (*Monk's Tale* B 3361–2).
4   **doome**: judgment.
6–7   **Crœsus**: the last king of Lydia, proverbial for his

wealth. S. assumes that he was proud because of his wealth.
Chaucer attributes his pride to his good luck, *Monk's Tale*
B 3927f.   **enhaunst**: lifted up in pride.
8–9   **Antiochus**: see 1 Macc. 1f. S. assumes that when he
caused the Temple to be defiled by fornication and the altar
to be made 'ful of suche things, as were abominable & forbiden
by the Law' (2 Macc. 6.5), he danced upon the altar.

Stanza 48
The three captives are grouped as proud conquerors of the
known world. **Nimrod** and **Ninus** are linked with the founding
of Nineveh; Nimrod and Alexander are descendants of Ham.
1–2   **Nimrod**: the first tyrant and oppressor of mankind
after the Flood; **great** as the first Giant: 'Nimrod who began
to be mighty in the earth' (Gen. 10.8). The passage was taken
to refer to the origin of giants. The founder of Babylon
(Cooper, 1565).   **warrayd**: ravaged.
3–4   **Ninus**: 'the fyrst that made warre. He conquered unto
Indie' (Cooper). Famous as the founder of Nineveh (Cooper)
but notorious for 'old Ninny's tomb'. Cf. II ix 21.5–6, 56.8.
5–9   **that mightie Monarch**: Alexander the Great.   **layd /
Low vnder all**: either through his **shamefull death** (9) from
debauchery or his shameful birth by Jupiter Ammon in the
form of a serpent. Ammon was identified with Ham (Starnes
and Talbert, 1955, 237). 'He fell into suche crueltie and pryde
(. . . commaunding him selfe to be called a god) that he became
odious to his owne people . . . At the laste whan he was in his
most glory at the citie of Babylon . . . at supper . . . [he] was
poisoned by drinkyng out of a cup' (Cooper).   **vpbrayd**:
find fault with.

Stanza 49
1–2   **in one heape**: a fitting death for the builders of towers
and cities. It is fitting, too, that Nimrod who in life hunted
men like beasts, in death lies like a beast.
4–9   These ancient Roman heroes would be well known to
any Elizabethan schoolboy: most of the material is in Cooper
(1565). Apart from **Lentulus**, they are grouped in roughly
chronological order and each is given a fitting epithet. Cheney
(1966) 54 notes that the stoic virtues are no better than syno-
nyms for pride. Williams (1966) 14 adds that Lucifera appeals
to reliance upon self 'which can masquerade as high minded
virtue'.
5   **Great Romulus**: the first king of Rome.
6   **Proud Tarquin**: the last king of Rome, 'for his proud
and sterne behaviour surnamed *Superbus*' (Cooper).   **too
lordly Lentulus**: a proud patrician family, fittingly standing
alone in this catalogue, represented by Cornelius Lentulus who
attempted to fire Rome.
7   **Stout Scipio**: Scipio Africanus, known for his martial
prowess in vanquishing Hannibal and the people of Africa.
Cooper notes his valiant courage.   **Hanniball** gains the
epithet **stubborne** for his constant warring against the
Romans: he took poison rather than become their prisoner.
8   **Ambitious Sylla**: because he was 'desirous of glorie'
(Cooper) and became dictator of Rome. He was engaged
in civil war with **Marius** who is called **sterne** for his courage.
9   'Of this man [Cæsar] and Pompei it was saide, that they
weare of so haute courages, that the one could not abyde an
equall, the other a superiour' (Cooper).   **great Pompey**:
Pompey the Great. By his war with **Cæsar**, 'al the world
almost was vexed and troubled' (Cooper).   **fierce Antonius**:
'fierce' in love and war.

84

50

Amongst these mighty men were wemen mixt,
　Proud wemen, vaine, forgetfull of their yoke:
　The bold *Semiramis*, whose sides transfixt
　With sonnes owne blade, her fowle reproches spoke;
　Faire *Sthenobœa*, that her selfe did choke
　With wilfull cord, for wanting of her will;
　High minded *Cleopatra*, that with stroke
　Of Aspes sting her selfe did stoutly kill:
And thousands moe the like, that did that dongeon fill.

51

Besides the endlesse routs of wretched thralles,
　Which thither were assembled day by day,
　From all the world after their wofull falles,
　Through wicked pride, and wasted wealthes decay.
　But most of all, which in that Dongeon lay
　Fell from high Princes courts, or Ladies bowres,
　Where they in idle pompe, or wanton play,
　Consumed had their goods, and thriftlesse howres,
And lastly throwne themselues into these heauy stowres.

52

Whose case when as the carefull Dwarfe had tould,
　And made ensample of their mournefull sight
　Vnto his maister, he no lenger would
　There dwell in perill of like painefull plight,
　But early rose, and ere that dawning light
　Discouered had the world to heauen wyde,
　He by a priuie Posterne tooke his flight,
　That of no enuious eyes he mote be spyde:
For doubtlesse death ensewd, if any him descryde.

53

Scarse could he footing find in that fowle way,
　For many corses, like a great Lay-stall
　Of murdred men which therein strowed lay,
　Without remorse, or decent funerall:
　Which all through that great Princesse pride did fall
　And came to shamefull end.   And them beside
　Forth ryding vnderneath the castell wall,
　A donghill of dead carkases he spide,
The dreadfull spectacle of that sad house of *Pride*.

Stanza 50
The three examples show why 'vertuous women wisely
vnderstand, / That they were borne to base humilitie'
(V v 25.7–8).
3–4　bold Semiramis: after her husband, King Ninus,
died, fearing that the people 'would be loth to be governed by
a woman', she disguised herself as her son and became famous
for her bravery. 'At the last falling from noblenesse to sensuall
luste, she desired the companie of hir owne sonne, and of him
was slayne' (Cooper, 1565); cf. II x 56.2. The lustful in the
second circle of Dante's *Inf.* v are led by Semiramis, followed
by Dido and Cleopatra.
5–6　Faire Sthenobœa lusted after her brother-in-law,
Bellerophon, but was refused by him.　**With wilfull cord**:
i.e. with cord wilfully. For the witty play on 'will', Allen
(1938) 118 argues that S. turned to a school text, the *Epitheta*
of Ravisius Textor. The term suggests her despair, which may
account for her death by hanging rather than by poison: see
ix 22.5–8*n*.

Stanza 51
1–2　Cf. iv 3.1–2.
4　wealthes: in the more general sense of the term, well-
being, although the particular sense is suggested by 8.
decay: downfall, from its med. Lat. root, *decadere*, to fall down.
9　stowres: afflictions.

Stanza 52
1　carefull: cf. 'wary' (45.7).
2　ensample: warning.
3　The line breaks at the end to fit the sense.
7　priuie Posterne: secret back door.
8　enuious: malicious.

Stanza 53
2　Lay-stall: a burial place, literally a place where the dead
are laid; here the lack of funeral and burial suggests a garbage-
dump or dunghill; cf. 'butchers stall' (49.2). The lowest point
of Guyon's fortunes is reached when Cymochles threatens to
'make his carkasse as the outcast dong' (II viii 28.5).
4　decent: fitting. Lacking burial, Lucifera's victims lack the
promise of resurrection; cf. the Geneva gloss to God's curse –
'thy carkeis shal be meat vnto all foules of the ayre' (Deut.
28.26) – upon those who do not follow his commandments:
'Thou shalt be cursed both in thy life and in thy death: for
the buryal is a testimonie of the resurrection, which signe for
thy wickednes you shalt lacke.' Cf. x 42 and II i 59.8–9.
9　spectacle: referring to the completed vision of the house
of Pride: its towering turrets above to the dungeon below and
the garbage-heap round about, but also to the heap itself
(iv 5.1) as an image of the House.　**that sad house of Pride**:
finally named, after two cantos of description in which the
simple name was avoided or referred to by the indefinite
article: cf. iv 2.6, 4.1, v 45.2.

Cant. VI.

*From lawlesse lust by wondrous grace
fayre Vna is releast:
Whom saluage nation does adore,
and learnes her wise beheast.*

1

AS when a ship, that flyes faire vnder saile,
    An hidden rocke escaped hath vnwares,
That lay in waite her wrack for to bewaile,
The Marriner yet halfe amazed stares
At perill past, and yet in doubt ne dares
To ioy at his foole-happie ouersight:
So doubly is distrest twixt ioy and cares
The dreadlesse courage of this *Elfin* knight,
Hauing escapt so sad ensamples in his sight.

2

Yet sad he was that his too hastie speed
    The faire *Duess'* had forst him leaue behind;
And yet more sad, that *Vna* his deare dreed
Her truth had staind with treason so vnkind;
Yet crime in her could neuer creature find,
But for his loue, and for her owne selfe sake,
She wandred had from one to other *Ynd*,
Him for to seeke, ne euer would forsake,
Till her vnwares the fierce *Sansloy* did ouertake.

3

Who after *Archimagoes* fowle defeat,
    Led her away into a forrest wilde,
And turning wrathfull fire to lustfull heat,
With beastly sin thought her to haue defilde,
And made the vassall of his pleasures vilde,
Yet first he cast by treatie, and by traynes,
Her to perswade, that stubborne fort to yilde:
For greater conquest of hard loue he gaynes,
That workes it to his will, then he that it constraines.

4

With fawning wordes he courted her a while,
    And looking louely, and oft sighing sore,
Her constant hart did tempt with diuerse guile:
But wordes, and lookes, and sighes she did abhore,
As rocke of Diamond stedfast euermore.
Yet for to feed his fyrie lustfull eye,
He snatcht the vele, that hong her face before;
Then gan her beautie shine, as brightest skye,
And burnt his beastly hart t'efforce her chastitye.

Canto vi

Argument

3   **saluage**: wild, from Ital. *selvaggio*, of the woods; see 11.3.
4   **wise beheast**: in contrast to the 'bestiall beheasts'

(iv 18.3) of Lucifera's counsellors.

Stanza 1

This mariner simile extends that used at iii 31–32; again it marks a point at which Una's perils seem past but in fact lie ahead.
3   The context suggests simply, to cause the ship's wreck. **wrack**: total destruction.   **bewaile** may be an error for 'assayle' (cf. 5.3), i.e. assault, as Church (1758) suggests. Cf. II ii 24.1–3. Or the term may derive from 'wale': choose, as Upton (1758) suggests; hence the rock chooses the ship to wreck it. It may suggest the consequences of the wreck, as *OED* suggests; hence the rock causes the ship's wreck to be bewailed. Or since Duessa is linked to the rock, her crocodile tears may be implied (cf. v 18); hence the rock may appear to be sorry for the wreck that it causes; see Tilley (1950) C831. Or a wave-washed rock may be said to be weeping; cf. Cymoent wailing so piteously 'That the hard rocks could scarse from teares refraine' (III iv 35.7).
5   **doubt**: fear.
6   **foole-happie**: plain lucky or fortunate.
8   **dreadlesse courage**: apparently he deserves this epithet even when he flees from danger.
9   **ensamples**: warnings; cf. v 52.2.

Stanza 2

1   **Yet sad**: referring to the previous line. Although he escapes the sad plight of those in the 'sad house of *Pride*' (v 53.9), the state represented by Sansjoy persists.
3   **dreed**: object of reverence and awe; cf. the address to Gloriana, Pr. 4.9.
4   **vnkind**: contrary to her nature.
5   **crime**: wrong-doing, sin.
7   **one to other Ynd**: East to the West Indies, proverbial for 'throughout the world'.

Stanza 3

2   The forest serves throughout the poem as the setting for violent, primitive, and archetypal experience. On its general symbolism, see Cirlot (1962) 107 and Calin (1966) 192. In his account of S.'s allegorical landscape, Hankins (1971) 60–73 shows how the forest serves as a place of mystery and enchantment, as the threat of formlessness, and as the den of beasts who objectify subconscious menaces within man. Fletcher (1971) 24–34 treats it as a labyrinth. It is also the setting for Arthur's vision, ix 12.7. See III i 14.5–9*n*.
6   **treatie**: entreaty.   **traynes**: guile.

Stanza 4

1   **fawning wordes**: see 12.9*n*.
2   **louely**: lovingly.
3   **diuerse**: of different kinds; also as it seeks to lead her astray; cf. i 44.2*n*.
5   **rocke of Diamond**: associated with adamant, a substance of supreme hardness; cited as a symbol of resistance (Gk unconquerable) and of constant faith. Cf. Arthur's diamond shield covered by a veil to hide its light: see vii 33.5–9*n*. Also associated with truth, as Maplet (1567) 18 records: 'Iorach calleth it an other eie: such certaintie and truth giveth it in things done in his presence.'
7   His action parallels that of Kirkrapine who disrobed the saints, iii 17.5–6.
9   **efforce**: overcome by force.

5

So when he saw his flatt'ring arts to fayle,
  And subtile engines bet from batteree,
  With greedy force he gan the fort assayle,
  Whereof he weend possessed soone to bee,
  And win rich spoile of ransackt chastetee.
  Ah heauens, that do this hideous act behold,
  And heauenly virgin thus outraged see,
How can ye vengeance iust so long withhold,
And hurle not flashing flames vpon that Paynim bold?

6

The pitteous maiden carefull comfortlesse,
  Does throw out thrilling shriekes, and shrieking cryes,
  The last vaine helpe of womens great distresse,
  And with loud plaints importuneth the skyes,
  That molten starres do drop like weeping eyes;
  And *Phœbus* flying so most shamefull sight,
  His blushing face in foggy cloud implyes,
And hides for shame.   What wit of mortall wight
Can now deuise to quit a thrall from such a plight?

7

Eternall prouidence exceeding thought,
  Where none appeares can make her selfe a way:
  A wondrous way it for this Lady wrought,
  From Lyons clawes to pluck the griped pray.
  Her shrill outcryes and shriekes so loud did bray,
  That all the woodes and forestes did resownd;
  A troupe of *Faunes* and *Satyres* far away
Within the wood were dauncing in a rownd,
Whiles old *Syluanus* slept in shady arber sownd.

8

Who when they heard that pitteous strained voice,
  In hast forsooke their rurall meriment,
  And ran towards the far rebownded noyce,
  To weet, what wight so loudly did lament.
  Vnto the place they come incontinent:
  Whom when the raging Sarazin espide,
  A rude, misshapen, monstrous rablement,
  Whose like he neuer saw, he durst not bide,
But got his ready steed, and fast away gan ride.

9

The wyld woodgods arriued in the place,
  There find the virgin dolefull desolate,
  With ruffled rayments, and faire blubbred face,
  As her outrageous foe had left her late,
  And trembling yet through feare of former hate;
  All stand amazed at so vncouth sight,
  And gin to pittie her vnhappie state,
  All stand astonied at her beautie bright,
In their rude eyes vnworthie of so wofull plight.

Stanza 5
2 **subtile engines**: cleverly designed machines of warfare –
the courtly wiles – used to assault 'that stubborne fort' (3.7).
bet from batteree: beaten from their beating.
3 One such historical moment is prophesied by Merlin: a

Norwegian King will overrun Britain 'And holy Church with
faithlesse hands deface ' (III iii 34.2).
7 **outraged**: violated.

Stanza 6
1 **carefull**: full of grief. **comfortlesse**: helpless, desolate.
The word signals the intervention of 'wondrous grace' (Arg.)
according to God's promise: 'I wil not leave you comfortles'
(John 14.18); see v 36.6*n*.
2 **thrilling**: piercing. Percival (1893) notes that the
tautology in this line is meant to indicate repetition.
5–8 Signs of the Last Judgment: 'immediatly after the
tribulations of those days, shal the sunne be darkened . . .
and the starres shal fall from heaven' (Matt. 24.29); also signs
of Nature's sympathy for her 'goddess'. **molten**: both
liquefied by heat and dissolved into tears. **implyes**:
conceals.
8–9 S. wittily alludes to his own wit. Who else would have
devised fawns and satyrs as instruments of God's grace to
rescue Holy Church in her moment of greatest peril?
9 **quit**: set free.

Stanza 7
1–2 Cf. 'the love of Christ which passeth knowledge'
(Eph. 3.19) and 'Prouidence heauenly passeth liuing thought'
(III v 27.1).
4 Cf. 2 Tim. 4.17: 'The Lord assisted me . . . and I was
delivered out of the mouth of the lion.' The immediate reference is to the Lion-Sansloy encounter: when subdued, the
lion guarded Una; but overcome by lawlessness, 'he' reverts to
his natural fierceness. Now the traditionally lustful satyrs,
subdued by Una, become her guardians.
7 **Faunes and Satyres**: the Latin and Greek woodland
deities; cf. the gloss to *S.C.* July 77–8, 'the holy *Faunes* . . .
and *Syluanes*': 'of Poetes feigned to be Gods of the Woode'.
Although they mingle here, they are distinguished by name and
nature: '*Faunes*' are the mildly benign creatures who protect
those in their territory, as Comes (1616) X 541 explains;
'*Satyres*', on the other hand, half men half goats, symbolize
concupiscence. For the ecclesiastical allegory, the significant
reference is to Isaiah 13.21: after the desolation of Palestine,
'the Satyrs shal dance there'.
8 **rownd**: either the circle into which they draw Una (13.6)
or the name of their dance.
9 **old Syluanus**: their god shares their twofold nature as
the son of Faunus, the Roman Pan, and the father of satyrs;
the epithet is from Virgil, *Georg.* ii 494, and always accompanies his name: he is aged and therefore senile, as *silva-vanus*.

Stanza 8
3 **rebownded**: re-echoed.
5 **incontinent**: headlong, intemperate in their haste to aid
another, in contrast to the incontinent Sansloy.

Stanza 9
2 **desolate**: her state when she is befriended by the Lion,
iii 9.1; cf. vii 50.1, x 60.4.
3 **blubbred**: wet with tears, lacking any suggestion of the
ludicrous.
4 **outrageous**: violent; as one who 'outraged' her, 5.7.
5 **hate**: both one who hated her, and one whom she hated.
6 **vncouth**: strange; also marvellous, as 8 suggests.
8 **astonied**: stupefied.

10

She more amaz'd, in double dread doth dwell;
  And euery tender part for feare does shake:
  As when a greedie Wolfe through hunger fell
  A seely Lambe farre from the flocke does take,
  Of whom he meanes his bloudie feast to make,
  A Lyon spyes fast running towards him,
  The innocent pray in hast he does forsake,
  Which quit from death yet quakes in euery lim
With chaunge of feare, to see the Lyon looke so grim.

11

Such fearefull fit assaid her trembling hart,
  Ne word to speake, ne ioynt to moue she had:
  The saluage nation feele her secret smart,
  And read her sorrow in her count'nance sad;
  Their frowning forheads with rough hornes yclad,
  And rusticke horror all a side doe lay,
  And gently grenning, shew a semblance glad
  To comfort her, and feare to put away,
Their backward bent knees teach her humbly to obay.

12

The doubtfull Damzell dare not yet commit
  Her single person to their barbarous truth,
  But still twixt feare and hope amazd does sit,
  Late learnd what harme to hastie trust ensu'th,
  They in compassion of her tender youth,
  And wonder of her beautie soueraine,
  Are wonne with pitty and vnwonted ruth,
  And all prostrate vpon the lowly plaine,
Do kisse her feete, and fawne on her with count'nance faine.

13

Their harts she ghesseth by their humble guise,
  And yieldes her to extremitie of time;
  So from the ground she fearelesse doth arise,
  And walketh forth without suspect of crime:
  They all as glad, as birdes of ioyous Prime,
  Thence lead her forth, about her daunsing round,
  Shouting, and singing all a shepheards ryme,
  And with greene braunches strowing all the ground,
Do worship her, as Queene, with oliue girlond cround.

14

And all the way their merry pipes they sound,
  That all the woods with doubled Eccho ring,
  And with their horned feet do weare the ground,
  Leaping like wanton kids in pleasant Spring.
  So towards old *Syluanus* they her bring;
  Who with the noyse awaked, commeth out,
  To weet the cause, his weake steps gouerning,
  And aged limbs on Cypresse stadle stout,
And with an yuie twyne his wast is girt about.

Stanza 10
1   amaz'd: terrified. Cf. her similar plight at iii 40.
3–7   The wolf and the lion are traditionally antithetical symbols of power: the former is the particular symbol of predatory power directed against the Church; cf. Jer. 5.6: 'Wherefore a lion out of the forest shal slay them, and a wolfe of the wildernes shal destroye them.'   seely: innocent, harmless.
9   chaunge of feare: i.e. from fear of the wolf to fear of the lion. The protective role of the lion, which Sansloy abused (cf. 7.4), is now assumed by the fawns.   grim: fierce, savage.

Stanza 11
1   assaid: assailed; tested.
6   horror: roughness, referring to the ruggedness of their looks with their bristling hair and horns.
9   backward bent: because they have the legs of a goat. Either their awkward efforts to kneel teach her humbly to obey their desire that she put away fear or their backward-bent knees teach them humbly to obey her, i.e. to kneel in reverence to her. Cheney (1966) 61–2 suggests that their knees symbolize their tendency to worship backwards, making Una a pastoral Queen rather than an image of divine beauty.

Stanza 12
2   single: as Truth is sole, being one, cf. 'single Truth' (*Col.* 727); but playing on various senses of the word: solitary, in contrast to their numbers as a nation, and hence weak; plain or free from duplicity in contrast to their uncivilized state; and certainly unmarried, as Holy Church relates to this ignorant nation.   truth: allegiance, expressed in their act of kneeling. Upton (1758) observes: 'how elegant truth comes in here . . . for she was Truth'. Rose (1975) 78 notes a pun on 'troth'.
9   kisse her feete: as does the lion, iii 6.1.   fawne: punning on their nature as fawns, and on their fawning worship, as the lion that licked her hands 'with fawning tong' (iii 6.2), revealed his nature in his defence of her, and as Sansloy's 'fawning wordes' (4.1) expressed his inner lawlessness.   faine: glad.

Stanza 13
1   guise: behaviour.
4   without suspect of crime: without any apprehension of guilt or without suspicion or fear of being reproached for wrong-doing; cf. her Knight who learns in the house of Holiness to frame his life in righteousness 'without rebuke or blame' (x 45.9).
9   oliue girlond: the traditional emblem of peace (as II ii 31.7, IV iii 42.5), here signifying the peace between her truth and their 'barbarous truth' (12.2). Cf. the 'girland greene' with which Una is finally crowned by the maidens so that she 'Did seeme such, as she was, a goodly maiden Queene' (xii 8.9).

Stanza 14
7–8   gouerning: i.e. guiding his steps and supporting his limbs, referring figuratively to the love for Cyparissus which firmly sustains him in his feeble age.   stadle: a tree trunk used as a staff; or a standing tree (*OED* 2), which infers that Sylvanus's life is rooted in his lost love. The Cypresse (from Virgil, *Georg.* i 20) is explained at 17.
9   yuie: sacred to Bacchus and symbol of his festivities; here it refers to his love.

15

Far off he wonders, what them makes so glad,
  Or *Bacchus* merry fruit they did inuent,
  Or *Cybeles* franticke rites haue made them mad;
  They drawing nigh, vnto their God present
  That flowre of faith and beautie excellent.
  The God himselfe vewing that mirrhour rare,
  Stood long amazd, and burnt in his intent;
  His owne faire *Dryope* now he thinkes not faire,
And *Pholoe* fowle, when her to this he doth compaire.

16

The woodborne people fall before her flat,
  And worship her as Goddesse of the wood;
  And old *Syluanus* selfe bethinkes not, what
  To thinke of wight so faire, but gazing stood,
  In doubt to deeme her borne of earthly brood;
  Sometimes Dame *Venus* selfe he seemes to see,
  But *Venus* neuer had so sober mood;
  Sometimes *Diana* he her takes to bee,
But misseth bow, and shaftes, and buskins to her knee.

17

By vew of her he ginneth to reuiue
  His ancient loue, and dearest *Cyparisse*,
  And calles to mind his pourtraiture aliue,
  How faire he was, and yet not faire to this,
  And how he slew with glauncing dart amisse
  A gentle Hynd, the which the louely boy
  Did loue as life, aboue all worldly blisse;
  For griefe whereof the lad n'ould after ioy,
But pynd away in anguish and selfe-wild annoy.

18

The wooddy Nymphes, faire *Hamadryades*
  Her to behold do thither runne apace,
  And all the troupe of light-foot *Naiades*,
  Flocke all about to see her louely face:
  But when they vewed haue her heauenly grace,
  They enuie her in their malitious mind,
  And fly away for feare of fowle disgrace:
  But all the *Satyres* scorne their woody kind,
And henceforth nothing faire, but her on earth they find.

19

Glad of such lucke, the luckelesse lucky maid,
  Did her content to please their feeble eyes,
  And long time with that saluage people staid,
  To gather breath in many miseries.
  During which time her gentle wit she plyes,
  To teach them truth, which worship her in vaine,
  And made her th'Image of Idolatryes;
  But when their bootlesse zeale she did restraine
From her own worship, they her Asse would worship fayn.

Stanza 15
2　**Bacchus merry fruit**: grapes; hence wine.　　**inuent**: find.
3　**Cybeles franticke rites**: the mad rites of the Corybantes to honour the Phrygian 'mother of the Gods' (IV xi 28.1). His second guess is close to the truth.
5　**excellent**: supreme.
6　**mirrhour**: paragon, as a mirror that reflects heavenly faith and beauty.
7　Since Una remains unveiled, her shining beauty burns Sylvanus as it 'burnt his [Sansloy's] beastly hart' (4.9). **intent**: also gaze, intense observation.
8–9　Since **Dryope** was the consort of Faunus and **Pholoe**, a nymph beloved of Pan, both may be associated with Sylvanus in his double nature.

Stanza 16
3　**bethinkes not**: cannot decide.

Stanza 17
The story of Cyparissus derives ultimately from Ovid, *Met.* x 106–42. In Ovid, the boy kills his deer and Apollo grieves for him; in Boccaccio and Comes, as in S., Silvanus kills the deer.
3　**pourtraiture aliue**: figure or likeness when alive.
8　**n'ould**: would not.
9　**pynd away**: a pun on his metamorphosis into a tree, as Rose (1975) 79 notes.　　**selfe-wild annoy**: self-imposed suffering or harm, in contrast to the accidental slaying of the deer. On the tradition of grief for the slain deer, see Allen (1960) 94–7.

Stanza 18
1　**Hamadryades**: wood-nymphs, spirits of the trees in which they live.
3　**Naiades**: freshwater-nymphs; **light-foot** because they love to dance.
5　**heauenly grace**: cf. iii 4.9.
8　**woody kind**: woodborn race.

Stanza 19
1　This word-play gains point through its context. Such **lucke** is 'wondrous grace' (Arg.) provided by 'Eternall prouidence' (7.1) to aid 'heauenly grace' (18.5).　**luckelesse** is a key term in the Knight's adventures: cf. vii 26.8, viii 2.4, ix 45.4, xii 16.4.
2　**feeble**: because they may gaze upon her unveiled beauty without being overwhelmed, or because they fail to see beyond her beauty as their 'Goddesse of the wood' (16.2).
6　**in vaine**: profanely, in the biblical sense (Exod. 20.7), for they worship her as an idol. Upton (1758) first noted that 'these Satyrs allegorized are ignorant Christians'.
7　**Image of Idolatryes**: the Idol of their worship.
9　**fayn**: gladly; or desired to worship. On the emblem of the *asinus portans mysteria*, see Steadman (1958).

20

It fortuned a noble warlike knight
  By iust occasion to that forrest came,
  To seeke his kindred, and the lignage right,
  From whence he tooke his well deserued name:
  He had in armes abroad wonne muchell fame,
  And fild far landes with glorie of his might,
  Plaine, faithfull, true, and enimy of shame,
  And euer lou'd to fight for Ladies right,
But in vaine glorious frayes he litle did delight.

21

A Satyres sonne yborne in forrest wyld,
  By straunge aduenture as it did betyde,
  And there begotten of a Lady myld,
  Faire *Thyamis* the daughter of *Labryde*,
  That was in sacred bands of wedlocke tyde
  To *Therion*, a loose vnruly swayne;
  Who had more ioy to raunge the forrest wyde,
  And chase the saluage beast with busie payne,
Then serue his Ladies loue, and wast in pleasures vayne.

22

The forlorne mayd did with loues longing burne,
  And could not lacke her louers company,
  But to the wood she goes, to serue her turne,
  And seeke her spouse, that from her still does fly,
  And followes other game and venery:
  A Satyre chaunst her wandring for to find,
  And kindling coles of lust in brutish eye,
  The loyall links of wedlocke did vnbind,
And made her person thrall vnto his beastly kind.

23

So long in secret cabin there he held
  Her captiue to his sensuall desire,
  Till that with timely fruit her belly sweld,
  And bore a boy vnto that saluage sire:
  Then home he suffred her for to retire,
  For ransome leauing him the late borne childe;
  Whom till to ryper yeares he gan aspire,
  He noursled vp in life and manners wilde,
Emongst wild beasts and woods, from lawes of men exilde.

24

For all he taught the tender ymp, was but
  To banish cowardize and bastard feare;
  His trembling hand he would him force to put
  Vpon the Lyon and the rugged Beare,
  And from the she Beares teats her whelps to teare;
  And eke wyld roring Buls he would him make
  To tame, and ryde their backes not made to beare;
  And the Robuckes in flight to ouertake,
That euery beast for feare of him did fly and quake.

25

Thereby so fearelesse, and so fell he grew,
  That his owne sire and maister of his guise
  Did often tremble at his horrid vew,
  And oft for dread of hurt would him aduise,
  The angry beasts not rashly to despise,
  Nor too much to prouoke; for he would learne
  The Lyon stoup to him in lowly wise,
  (A lesson hard) and make the Libbard sterne
Leaue roaring, when in rage he for reuenge did earne.

Stanza 20

2 **iust occasion**: in contrast to Sansloy who enters the forest to rape Una (3.2).

7 As a defender of Una, he shares the epithets **faithfull, true** given the Red Cross Knight (i 2.7).

Stanza 21

2 **aduenture**: chance.

4–6 The Greek names reveal their natures, as Percival (1893) suggests. **Thyamis**: θυμός, passion. **Labryde**: λάβρος, turbulent, greedy; possibly, as Belson (1964) suggests, Fr. *la bride*, bridle or check: 'Satyrane's behaviour shows him to be the inheritor of temperate as well as turbulent characteristics.' **Therion**: θηρίον, wild beast. Sidney chose the name for the forester in the *Lady of May* who would strike his Lady in his rages.

Stanza 22

2 **lacke**: do without.

3 **serue her turne**: answer her need, i.e. satisfy her desire.

5 **venery**: wild animals, with a pun on love-making, as Warton (1762) first suggested.

Stanza 23

1 **cabin**: ?a cave (*OED* 4); cf. Despair's cabin, ix 32.4, which is a cave (33.2).

3 **timely**: occurring in the course of time; possibly, 'ripening' (cf. *OED* 1).

5 **retire**: return.

7 **aspire**: grow up.

8 **noursled**: reared, combining 'nurse', and 'nousle', raise.

Stanza 24

1 **ymp**: child.

2 **bastard**: base-born, and therefore contemptible; his nature as a bastard. Cf. Sansloy's charge, 42.1.

4 **the Lyon and the . . . Beare**: the two animals killed by David to prove himself worthy to fight Goliath.

8 **Robuckes**: noted for their speed, as II x 7.5.

Stanza 25

2 **maister**: leader, tutor. **guise**: behaviour.

3 **horrid vew**: rough or savage appearance; cf. his 'rugged armes' (27.9); or as his actions arouse fear; cf. the 'rusticke horror' (11.6) of his race.

5 **despise**: treat with contempt.

6 **learne**: teach.

9 **earne**: yearn; he refers indifferently to Satyrane or the leopard.

26

And for to make his powre approued more,
　Wyld beasts in yron yokes he would compell;
　The spotted Panther, and the tusked Bore,
　The Pardale swift, and the Tigre cruell;
　The Antelope, and Wolfe both fierce and fell;
　And them constraine in equall teme to draw.
　Such ioy he had, their stubborne harts to quell,
　And sturdie courage tame with dreadfull aw,
That his beheast they feared, as a tyrans law.

27

His louing mother came vpon a day
　Vnto the woods, to see her little sonne;
　And chaunst vnwares to meet him in the way,
　After his sportes, and cruell pastime donne,
　When after him a Lyonesse did runne,
　That roaring all with rage, did lowd requere
　Her children deare, whom he away had wonne:
　The Lyon whelpes she saw how he did beare,
And lull in rugged armes, withouten childish feare.

28

The fearefull Dame all quaked at the sight,
　And turning backe, gan fast to fly away,
　Vntill with loue reuokt from vaine affright,
　She hardly yet perswaded was to stay,
　And then to him these womanish words gan say;
　Ah Satyrane, my dearling, and my ioy,
　For loue of me leaue off this dreadfull play;
　To dally thus with death, is no fit toy,
Go find some other play-fellowes, mine own sweet boy.

29

In these and like delights of bloudy game
　He trayned was, till ryper yeares he raught,
　And there abode, whilst any beast of name
　Walkt in that forest, whom he had not taught
　To feare his force: and then his courage haught
　Desird of forreine foemen to be knowne,
　And far abroad for straunge aduentures sought:
　In which his might was neuer ouerthrowne,
But through all Faery lond his famous worth was blown.

30

Yet euermore it was his manner faire,
　After long labours and aduentures spent,
　Vnto those natiue woods for to repaire,
　To see his sire and ofspring auncient.
　And now he thither came for like intent;
　Where he vnwares the fairest Vna found,
　Straunge Lady, in so straunge habiliment,
　Teaching the Satyres, which her sat around,
Trew sacred lore, which from her sweet lips did redound.

31

He wondred at her wisedome heauenly rare,
　Whose like in womens wit he neuer knew;
　And when her curteous deeds he did compare,
　Gan her admire, and her sad sorrowes rew,
　Blaming of Fortune, which such troubles threw,
　And ioyd to make proofe of her crueltie
　On gentle Dame, so hurtlesse, and so trew:
　Thenceforth he kept her goodly company,
And learnd her discipline of faith and veritie.

Stanza 26
1　**approued**: proved, demonstrated.
2　**compell**: drive together.
3–5　Each animal is identified by its special power. Hence **spotted Panther** because it attracts its prey by its spotted hide; cf. *Amor*. liii. **Pardale**: female leopard. 'The Pard is . . . very swift' (White, 1954, 13). **Antelope**: the Lat. *antalops*, a savage creature capable of cutting down trees with its horns.
6　**equall**: level, side by side. Satyrane's forcing wild animals to draw **in equall teme** symbolizes the governing of the passions (noted Manning); cf. the three teams of 'vnequall beasts' (iv 18.1) which draw the sins in Lucifera's procession.
9　**as a tyrans law**: cf. Lucifera's victims who suffer as beasts 'by law of that proud Tyrannesse' (v 46.6).

Stanzas 27–28
This humorous interlude (stanza 29 follows directly after 26) is borrowed from Statius's account of Thetis's fears when she sees Achilles molest wild beasts (*Achilleid* i 151f).

Stanza 27
9　**rugged**: rough with hair.

Stanza 28
3　**reuokt**: called back; restrained.
6　**Satyrane**: like a satyr; see 20.3–4 and 21.1. **dearling**: darling. As the Psalmist's cry, 'Rescue . . . my darling from the lions' (Ps. 35.17, KJ) except that **womanish words** suggests rather 'my pet'. Bridges and Weigle (1960) note that the biblical term is used to mourn an only son.

Stanza 29
2　**raught**: reached.
3　**of name**: noted, known. The twelve beasts mentioned in stanzas 24–26, counting the bear and she-bear as two, include all the traditional forest animals of strength; hence, perhaps, the full count of twelve.
5　**haught**: haughty; or high-minded, lofty.

Stanza 30
3　**repaire**: return.
4　**ofspring**: origin, 'lignage' (20.3). **auncient** refers to his race generally, or to his sire.
7　**Straunge**: as not belonging to the race of Satyrs. **habiliment**: array, referring here to the satyrs who surround her.
9　**redound**: proceed, issue (*OED* 9c); the etymological sense, from Lat. *redundare*, to flow, is implied since Una is the fount of wisdom.

Stanza 31
2　**womens wit**: alluding obliquely to the 'womanish words' (28.5) he heard from his mother.
3　**compare**: i.e. compared to those of other women; or when he compared her deeds to her words, or her deeds to her present plight.
7　**hurtlesse**: harmless, innocent, in contrast to his 'cruell pastime' (27.4) of hurting beasts; under her influence, he is emerging from his bestial state.
9　**discipline**: teaching, with the added suggestion of the ecclesiastical polity of the reformed Church.

32

But she all vowd vnto the *Redcrosse* knight,
  His wandring perill closely did lament,
  Ne in this new acquaintaunce could delight,
  But her deare heart with anguish did torment,
  And all her wit in secret counsels spent,
  How to escape.   At last in priuie wise
  To *Satyrane* she shewed her intent;
  Who glad to gain such fauour, gan deuise,
How with that pensiue Maid he best might thence arise.

33

So on a day when Satyres all were gone,
  To do their seruice to *Syluanus* old,
  The gentle virgin left behind alone
  He led away with courage stout and bold.
  Too late it was, to Satyres to be told,
  Or euer hope recouer her againe:
  In vaine he seekes that hauing cannot hold.
  So fast he carried her with carefull paine,
That they the woods are past, and come now to the plaine.

34

The better part now of the lingring day,
  They traueild had, when as they farre espide
  A wearie wight forwandring by the way,
  And towards him they gan in hast to ride,
  To weet of newes, that did abroad betide,
  Or tydings of her knight of the *Redcrosse*.
  But he them spying, gan to turne aside,
  For feare as seemd, or for some feigned losse ;
More greedy they of newes, fast towards him do crosse.

35

A silly man, in simple weedes forworne,
  And soild with dust of the long dried way ;
  His sandales were with toilesome trauell torne,
  And face all tand with scorching sunny ray,
  As he had traueild many a sommers day,
  Through boyling sands of *Arabie* and *Ynde* ;
  And in his hand a *Iacobs* staffe, to stay
  His wearie limbes vpon : and eke behind,
His scrip did hang, in which his needments he did bind.

36

The knight approching nigh, of him inquerd
  Tydings of warre, and of aduentures new ;
  But warres, nor new aduentures none he herd.
  Then *Vna* gan to aske, if ought he knew,
  Or heard abroad of that her champion trew,
  That in his armour bare a croslet red.
  Aye me, Deare dame (quoth he) well may I rew
  To tell the sad sight, which mine eies haue red :
These eyes did see that knight both liuing and eke ded.

37

That cruell word her tender hart so thrild,
  That suddein cold did runne through euery vaine,
  And stony horrour all her sences fild
  With dying fit, that downe she fell for paine.
  The knight her lightly reared vp againe,
  And comforted with curteous kind reliefe :
  Then wonne from death, she bad him tellen plaine
  The further processe of her hidden griefe ;
The lesser pangs can beare, who hath endur'd the chiefe.

Stanza 32
1   **vowd**: betrothed; cf. xii 19.9.
2   **closely**: secretly.
4   **deare**: loving.
9   **arise**: depart; the simpler sense, stand up, is implied by
the allegory. She is plucked from her palfrey by Sansloy
(iii 40.9); but with the satyrs 'from the ground she fearelesse
doth arise' (13.3). Later the satyrs 'her sat around' (30.8),
and now she is ready to 'arise' with Satyrane.

Stanza 33
9   **woods**: see 3.2*n*.   **plaine**: the allegorical setting for
chivalric encounters.

Stanzas 34–38
S.'s borrowing from the opening cantos of Ariosto's *Orl. Fur.*
for narrative details in this episode has been noted by Dodge,
Var. i 418–20.

Stanza 34
3   **forwandring**: wandering far and wide; or, as an intensive,
'utterly astray'.
8   **losse**: defeat. Or pretending to search for something
lost; cf. his similar gesture at iii 26.3–5.

Stanza 35
1   **silly**: simple, without guile, the same pose as i 30.6 when
he appeared as the hermit. Here he appears as the pilgrim, one
who comes from abroad (Lat. *peregrinus*), although he is not
named for what he seems to be until 38.1 and for what he is,
'that false *Pilgrim*', until 48.1.
7   **Iacobs staffe**: pilgrim's staff.   **stay**: support.
9   **scrip**: small bag.

Stanza 36
5   **champion**: in the specific sense, one who defends another;
cf. iii 8.9.
6   **croslet**: small cross, an heraldic term.
8   **red**: seen.

Stanza 37
1   **thrild**: pierced.
4   **dying fit**: death-like swoon.
5   **lightly**: quickly.
8   **The further processe . . .**: the rest of the tale hidden
from her that will cause her further grief.   **processe**: tale.
9   Anticipating the Dwarf's telling Una of her Knight's
apparent death, and her lament: 'Who hath endur'd the whole,
can beare each part' (vii 25.5).

38

Then gan the Pilgrim thus, I chaunst this day,
   This fatall day, that shall I euer rew,
   To see two knights in trauell on my way
   (A sory sight) arraung'd in battell new,
   Both breathing vengeaunce, both of wrathfull hew:
   My fearefull flesh did tremble at their strife,
   To see their blades so greedily imbrew,
   That drunke with bloud, yet thristed after life:
What more? the *Redcrosse* knight was slaine with Paynim knife.

39

Ah dearest Lord (quoth she) how might that bee,
   And he the stoutest knight, that euer wonne?
   Ah dearest dame (quoth he) how might I see
   The thing, that might not be, and yet was donne?
   Where is (said *Satyrane*) that Paynims sonne,
   That him of life, and vs of ioy hath reft?
   Not far away (quoth he) he hence doth wonne
   Foreby a fountaine, where I late him left
Washing his bloudy wounds, that through the steele were cleft.

40

Therewith the knight thence marched forth in hast,
   Whiles *Vna* with huge heauinesse opprest,
   Could not for sorrow follow him so fast;
   And soone he came, as he the place had ghest,
   Whereas that *Pagan* proud him selfe did rest,
   In secret shadow by a fountaine side:
   Euen he it was, that earst would haue suprest
   Faire *Vna*: whom when *Satyrane* espide,
With fowle reprochfull words he boldly him defide.

41

And said, Arise thou cursed Miscreaunt,
   That hast with knightlesse guile and trecherous train
   Faire knighthood fowly shamed, and doest vaunt
   That good knight of the *Redcrosse* to haue slain:
   Arise, and with like treason now maintain
   Thy guilty wrong, or else thee guilty yield.
   The Sarazin this hearing, rose amain,
   And catching vp in hast his three square shield,
And shining helmet, soone him buckled to the field.

42

And drawing nigh him said, Ah misborne Elfe,
   In euill houre thy foes thee hither sent,
   Anothers wrongs to wreake vpon thy selfe:
   Yet ill thou blamest me, for hauing blent
   My name with guile and traiterous intent;
   That *Redcrosse* knight, perdie, I neuer slew,
   But had he beene, where earst his armes were lent,
   Th'enchaunter vaine his errour should not rew:
But thou his errour shalt, I hope now prouen trew.

Stanza 38

1   **this day**: an emphatic lie, apparently to make his story
'plaine' (37.7).
4   **sory**: grievous, painful.   **new**: anew, after jousting with
spears. Archimago relates a second, unfought stage of his battle
with Sansloy at iii 35.
6–8   As a pilgrim and devil, he quotes Scripture: Ps. 119.
120, Jer. 46.10.   **imbrew**: soak or stain themselves in blood.

Stanza 39

1–4   **Ah dearest Lord**: presumably addressed to God: why
did He allow her knight to die? Possibly addressed to the
Knight himself: cf. her address at viii 28.7, 42.6. Presumptuously, Archimago applies it to himself by his parallel, **Ah
dearest dame**. His involved playing on **might** in 3–4 seeks to
change her appeal in 1 to what should be into an acceptance
of what he presents as fact. Percival (1893) notes that 'this
interlacing of words shows the speaker's wiliness, and is what
a musician may call a *fuga del diavolo*'.   **euer wonne**: always
conquered. Preferable to the usual sense: 'lived'.
3–4   Dixon (1597) has a puzzling comment. 'The eternall
divinitie of Jesus Christe is here plainly declared with his
manhod and victorie over death.' Hough (1964) adds that S.
would agree with Dixon's 'equating the reported death of the
Redcross knight, though he is really living, with Christ's death
and resurrection'.
7   **wonne**: stay.
8   **Foreby**: close by. Shortly the Red Cross Knight will also
be found 'foreby a fountaine side' (vii 2.7). The connection
suggests that his inner lawlessness caused her suffering at the
hands of Sansloy.

Stanza 40

7   **suprest**: violated, which is S.'s application of the general
sense, 'press down by force', to his allegorical figures.

Stanza 41

2   **knightlesse**: unknightly.   **train**: trickery.
5   **treason**: treachery; cf. the similar charge against the Red
Cross Knight, iv 41.4–7.   **maintain**: defend.
7   **amain**: at once.
8   **three square**: with three equal sides, the prevailing type
of shield in the twelfth to fourteenth centuries (*Var.* i 247).
See III i 4.4*n*.

Stanza 42

1   **misborne**: base-born, born out of wedlock; replying to
Satyrane's 'Miscreaunt'.
4   **blent**: mingled; hence, tainted, defiled.
8   **vaine**: foolish.   **his errour**: either Archimago's error in
wearing the armour to fight him, or the Red Cross Knight's
error – his slaying of Sansfoy – for which Archimago suffered.
rew: cf. 36.7, 38.2.
9   'By your death you will prove true Archimago's error in
wearing the armour to fight me.' Alternatively, 'your death in
combat will prove the Red Cross Knight's wrong-doing in
killing Sansfoy.'   **hope**: think, expect.   **prouen trew**: i.e.
through judicial combat.

93

43

Therewith they gan, both furious and fell,
  To thunder blowes, and fiersly to assaile
  Each other bent his enimy to quell,
  That with their force they perst both plate and maile,
  And made wide furrowes in their fleshes fraile,
  That it would pitty any liuing eie.
  Large floods of bloud adowne their sides did raile;
  But floods of bloud could not them satisfie:
Both hungred after death: both chose to win, or die.

44

So long they fight, and fell reuenge pursue,
  That fainting each, themselues to breathen let,
  And oft refreshed, battell oft renue:
  As when two Bores with rancling malice met,
  Their gory sides fresh bleeding fiercely fret,
  Til breathlesse both them selues aside retire,
  Where foming wrath, their cruell tuskes they whet,
  And trample th'earth, the whiles they may respire;
Then backe to fight againe, new breathed and entire.

45

So fiersly, when these knights had breathed once,
  They gan to fight returne, increasing more
  Their puissant force, and cruell rage attonce,
  With heaped strokes more hugely, then before,
  That with their drerie wounds and bloudy gore
  They both deformed, scarsely could be known.
  By this sad *Vna* fraught with anguish sore,
  Led with their noise, which through the aire was thrown,
Arriu'd, where they in erth their fruitles bloud had sown.

46

Whom all so soone as that proud Sarazin
  Espide, he gan reuiue the memory
  Of his lewd lusts, and late attempted sin,
  And left the doubtfull battell hastily,
  To catch her, newly offred to his eie:
  But *Satyrane* with strokes him turning, staid,
  And sternely bad him other businesse plie,
  Then hunt the steps of pure vnspotted Maíd:
Wherewith he all enrag'd, these bitter speaches said.

47

O foolish faeries sonne, what furie mad
  Hath thee incenst, to hast thy dolefull fate?
  Were it not better, I that Lady had,
  Then that thou hadst repented it too late?
  Most sencelesse man he, that himselfe doth hate,
  To loue another. Lo then for thine ayd
  Here take thy louers token on thy pate.
  So they to fight; the whiles the royall Mayd
Fled farre away, of that proud Paynim sore afrayd.

48

But that false *Pilgrim*, which that leasing told,
  Being in deed old *Archimage*, did stay
  In secret shadow, all this to behold,
  And much reioyced in their bloudy fray:
  But when he saw the Damsell passe away
  He left his stond, and her pursewd apace,
  In hope to bring her to her last decay.
  But for to tell her lamentable cace,
94 And eke this battels end, will need another place.

Stanzas 43–45
In these stanzas S. exhausts the conventions of chivalric combat in order to turn to a Miltonic 'argument . . . more heroic', the Red Cross Knight's spiritual conflict treated in the next canto.

Stanza 43
3 Each being determined to kill his enemy.
6 **pitty**: move to pity.
7 **Large**: copious.   **raile**: flow.

Stanza 44
5 **gory**: gored, and therefore bloody.   **fret**: gnaw, tear.
9 **entire**: fresh (after Lat. *integer*).

Stanza 45
5 **drerie**: gory, bloody, as in OE *dreorig*.
6 **deformed**: disfigured.

Stanza 46
4 **doubtfull**: dreaded; undecided.

Stanza 47
1 **faeries sonne**: curiously used of a satyr's son, perhaps because he becomes Una's champion. Elsewhere in Book I, the term is applied only to the Red Cross Knight, as ix 47.9, etc.
6–7 'As a reward for aiding Una, and in place of the lover's token worn on the helmet, take this blow on the head.'
8 **So they to fight**] two *1596*, i.e. the two go back to fighting while Una flees. The *1590* reading is weaker if taken as a preposition + substantive. Upton (1758) and Todd (1805) suggest that 'to' is an intensive. The construction is parallel to 44.1 and 45.2.

Stanza 48
1 **leasing**: falsehood.
6 **stond**: stand, place of ambush.
7 **last decay**: death.

Cant. VII.

*The Redcrosse knight is captiue made
By Gyaunt proud opprest,
Prince Arthur meets with Vna great-
ly with those newes distrest.*

1

WHat man so wise, what earthly wit so ware,
    As to descry the crafty cunning traine,
By which deceipt doth maske in visour faire,
And cast her colours dyed deepe in graine,
To seeme like Truth, whose shape she well can faine,
And fitting gestures to her purpose frame,
The guiltlesse man with guile to entertaine?
    Great maistresse of her art was that false Dame,
The false *Duessa*, cloked with *Fidessaes* name.

2

Who when returning from the drery *Night*,
    She fownd not in that perilous house of *Pryde*,
Where she had left, the noble *Redcrosse* knight,
Her hoped pray, she would no lenger bide,
But forth she went, to seeke him far and wide.
Ere long she fownd, whereas he wearie sate,
To rest him selfe, foreby a fountaine side,
    Disarmed all of yron-coted Plate,
And by his side his steed the grassy forage ate.

3

He feedes vpon the cooling shade, and bayes
    His sweatie forehead in the breathing wind,
Which through the trembling leaues full gently playes
Wherein the cherefull birds of sundry kind
Do chaunt sweet musick, to delight his mind:
The Witch approching gan him fairely greet,
And with reproch of carelesnesse vnkind
    Vpbrayd, for leauing her in place vnmeet,
With fowle words tempring faire, soure gall with hony sweet.

Canto vii

Argument

2   proud: the most explicit linking of the Giant with pride;
see 10.1–2.   **opprest**: taken by surprise; harassed; overwhelmed.

Stanza 1

1–3   Cf. Milton, *P.L.* iii 682–4: 'neither man nor angel can
discern / Hypocrisy, the only evil that walks / Invisible, except
to God alone'.   **ware**: vigilant; prudent.   **traine**: guile;
also the robe in which **deceipt doth maske**. Duessa, 'the
daughter of Deceipt', deceives even 'the mother . . . / Of
falshood' (v 27.6–7).

4   cast her colours: dispose her colours, a term in painting.
Also 'lose colour': Duessa 'clad in scarlet red' (ii 13.2) appears
in Una's **visour faire** (3). Wearing a false hood, she becomes
Falsehood, and so is named in ii Arg. etc.   **dyed deepe in
graine**: dyed thoroughly; also 'dyed scarlet', referring to
Duessa's robe.

Stanza 2

1   drery Night: see v. 24.1*n*.

7   The posture of Lawlessness – cf. vi 39.8, 40.6 – as noted
by Shroeder (1962) 144.

8   The Knight's rejection of 'the whole armour of God'
(Eph. 6.11), now dismissed as **yron-coted Plate**, reveals his
spiritual state. In Ariosto, *Orl. Fur.* vi 24, Ruggiero removes his
shield, helmet and gauntlets; in Tasso, *Ger. Lib.* xiv 59,
Rinaldo removes his helmet. By disarming **all**, S.'s knight
loses his wholeness and holiness.

9   This detail, repeated at 19.2, suggests the usual link
between the horse and the passions of the rider. As the horse
feeds on grass, the Knight 'feedes vpon the cooling shade' (3.1).

Stanza 3

1–5   The **cooling shade**, the **breathing wind**, the
trembling leaues, and the **cherefull birds** are the features
of the *locus amoenus*, e.g. Ariosto, *Orl. Fur.* vi 21, 24, where this
setting is the context for Ruggiero's enslavement to the witch
Alcina. At ii 28–29, the trembling leaves and cool shade provide
the setting for Fradubio's story of his enslavement to Duessa;
repeated here, they herald the Knight's seduction by the same
witch. Feeding upon the shade of the trees and later drinking
from the fountain parody the 'feeding' on the Tree of Life and
drinking from the Well of Life through which he finally
triumphs over the Dragon. At the beginning he seeks the shade
to escape the storm, now to escape the heat; and without Una's
faith to save him, he is thrown into the darkness of Orgoglio's
dungeon.

1   bayes: bathes; from 'embay'; cf. 'embayd' (ix 13.5).

3   Cf. Jer. 2.20: 'Like an harlot thou runnest about . . . under
all grene trees.'

4–5   Cf. 'the birdes sweete harmony' (i 8.2) which leads him
astray in the Wandering Wood. In Books I and II in particular,
the charm of birds conspires to occasion man's fall into sin;
cf. II v 31, vi 13, xii 71. Turning from the eye to the ear notes
a yielding to the inner passions.

6   fairely: courteously; with fair words. Duessa's reproach
contrasts with Una's 'faire fearefull humblesse' (iii 26.9) to
her supposed Knight; cf. viii 42.6–9.

7   carelesnesse: indifference to her plight. Ironically, her
words apply to him for he lies 'carelesse of his health' (7.3).

95

4

Vnkindnesse past, they gan of solace treat,
    And bathe in pleasaunce of the ioyous shade,
    Which shielded them against the boyling heat,
    And with greene boughes decking a gloomy glade,
    About the fountaine like a girlond made;
    Whose bubbling waue did euer freshly well,
    Ne euer would through feruent sommer fade:
    The sacred Nymph, which therein wont to dwell,
Was out of *Dianes* fauour, as it then befell.

5

The cause was this: one day when *Phœbe* fayre
    With all her band was following the chace,
    This Nymph, quite tyr'd with heat of scorching ayre
    Sat downe to rest in middest of the race:
    The goddesse wroth gan fowly her disgrace,
    And bad the waters, which from her did flow,
    Be such as she her selfe was then in place.
    Thenceforth her waters waxed dull and slow,
And all that drunke thereof, did faint and feeble grow.

6

Hereof this gentle knight vnweeting was,
    And lying downe vpon the sandie graile,
    Drunke of the streame, as cleare as cristall glas;
    Eftsoones his manly forces gan to faile,
    And mightie strong was turnd to feeble fraile.
    His chaunged powres at first them selues not felt,
    Till crudled cold his corage gan assaile,
    And chearefull bloud in faintnesse chill did melt,
Which like a feuer fit through all his body swelt.

Stanza 4

1　**solace**: pleasure, with the usual sense, alleviation of sorrow.
2　**pleasaunce**: pleasantness. This term describes the false pleasure taken by the Knight with Duessa (ii 30.1) and is used of Lucifera's crew who fed 'With pleasaunce of the breathing fields' (iv 38.2).　**ioyous shade**: in S.'s idiom, a powerful oxymoron.
3　**boyling heat**: suggests noon. Without God's Truth as his shield, the Knight is helpless before 'the plague that destroyeth at noone daye' (Ps. 91.6). On noon as the critical time of judgment, see Fowler (1964) 67, 72 and Cirillo (1962).
7　**fade**: shrink, dry up.
8　**sacred**: her title as the nymph of the fountain – cf. i 34.9; or 'accursed', referring to her disgrace.　**Nymph** denotes a follower of Diana, the *nympha nympharum*.

Stanza 5

1　**Phœbe**: Diana as goddess of the moon. The feminine of Phœbus whose heat causes the Knight to drink.
4　**in middest of the race**: see stanzas 12–13n. The weary nymph is an Ovidian counterpart to the weary Knight who also rests in the middle of his race. For the Protestant ethic implied, cf. Adam's condemnation of those who 'turn aside to tread / Paths indirect, or in the mid way faint' (Milton, *P.L.* xi 630–1).
5　**disgrace**: disfigure; bring into disgrace; literally, deprive of the graces infused into the water. Cf. the Palmer's account of the 'secret vertues' (II ii 5.6–9) in fountains. The nymph prefigures the Knight's state, 11.6. This enfeebling fountain is an emblem of idleness borrowed from Ovid's story of Hermaphroditus and Salmacis, *Met.* iv 285–386, xv 319–21: he gives up toil and she gives up Diana's chase. Edwards (1958) 80 notes that Ovid's nymph is self-centred and vain, *Met.* iv 308–12. S.'s use of the myth assumes its standard interpretation, e.g. by Golding, 'Epistle' (1567): 'that idlenesse / Is cheefest nurce and cherisher of all volupteousnesse, / And that voluptuous lyfe breedes sin: which linking all toogither / Make men too bee effeminate, unweeldy, weake and lither'.
7　**in place**: there.
9　**faint**: wanting in courage; wanting in strength; in both senses opposed to the working of faith, i 19.3.

Stanza 6

1　**vnweeting**: cf. 49.3, xi 29.2.
2　**lying downe**: a further stage of his fall. First he sits in the shade to rest and then to lie with Duessa; now he is totally prostrate.　**graile**: gravel, with a pun on 'grail' (Hamilton, 1961, 74), to note an infernal communion by which the Knight is metamorphosed into the fallen state. Yet see Tuve (1966) 124n 45. Waters (1970) 64–7 interprets this action as spiritual fornication associated with the dulling effects of the Roman mass. Shroeder (1962) 144–6 sees an overt sexual significance: the Knight's drinking signifies the act of copulation.
4　**manly**: human; see i 24.6n.
5　Playing on the supporting sense: strong might . . . frail feebleness.　**feeble fraile** defines man's fallen nature: see ix 53.1n.
7　**crudled**: congealing.　**corage**: vital powers.
8　**chearefull**: lively, living.　**did melt**: was reduced to the polluted water which he drank by losing its heat, the element of fire. There may be a precise medical sense: congealed blood is separated from the watery serum. Cf. the 'watery token' of 'corrupted blood' which declares Lucrece's polluted state (Shakespeare, *Lucrece* 1748). Shroeder 145 attributes the chill to the loss of heat in coition (citing the pseudo-Aristotelian *Problemata* 877[a]). Yet here the body suffers both chill and fever. The contrasting states anticipate the suffering of the damned: see ii 33.9n.
9　**swelt**: raged.

7

Yet goodly court he made still to his Dame,
   Pourd out in loosnesse on the grassy grownd,
   Both carelesse of his health, and of his fame:
   Till at the last he heard a dreadfull sownd,
   Which through the wood loud bellowing, did rebownd,
   That all the earth for terrour seemd to shake,
   And trees did tremble.   Th'Elfe therewith astownd,
   Vpstarted lightly from his looser make,
And his vnready weapons gan in hand to take.

8

But ere he could his armour on him dight,
   Or get his shield, his monstrous enimy
   With sturdie steps came stalking in his sight,
   An hideous Geant horrible and hye,
   That with his talnesse seemd to threat the skye,
   The ground eke groned vnder him for dreed;
   His liuing like saw neuer liuing eye,
   Ne durst behold: his stature did exceed
The hight of three the tallest sonnes of mortall seed.

9

The greatest Earth his vncouth mother was,
   And blustring *Æolus* his boasted sire,
   Who with his breath, which through the world doth pas,
   Her hollow womb did secretly inspire,
   And fild her hidden caues with stormie yre,
   That she conceiu'd; and trebling the dew time,
   In which the wombes of women do expire,
   Brought forth this monstrous masse of earthly slime,
Puft vp with emptie wind, and fild with sinfull crime.

Stanza 7

1 **his Dame**: the possessive confirms his commitment to her. 'Dame' suggests mistress or wife, as ii 40.1, xii 20.5; cf. 'his Ladie' (v 12.1).

2 **Pourd out**: the Lat. *effusus*, spread out; hence stretched out. The phrase expresses his dissipation: sexually expended and exhausted, he is like the water he drank. Water is traditionally associated with the lustful passions; cf. the biblical cry of death: 'I am like water powred out' (Ps. 22.14). **loosnesse**: licentiousness.

3 **Both**: both are careless, he is careless both, etc. **carelesse**: the state of *acedia*, the non-caring state. **health and fame** refer to the private and public virtues. **health** signifies spiritual and moral well-being, welfare, safety.

4 **at the last**: finally; evoking in this context death and the Day of Judgment.

5 **loud bellowing**: as Typhon, another offspring of the Earth (cf. III vii 47) who approaches his victims with 'the noise of a bull loud bellowing' (Hesiod, *Theog.* 832). The link may have been suggested by the name: Typhon or Typhœus signifies a great wind (Cooper, 1565).

7 **tremble**: extending the image of 'the trembling leaues' (3.3), now with apocalyptic overtones. **astownd**: confounded.

8 **lightly**: quickly, for he lacks his armour. **looser make**: too loose mate.

Stanza 8

3 **sturdie**: furious, violent; also vigorous, in contrast to the Knight's feebleness. **stalking**: lumbering with great strides, suggesting the hunter after his prey. The alliteration marks his steps; cf. 10.6.

4 **hideous**: huge, immense; also abominable. **Geant**: the etymological spelling points to his origin as son of Gea, the Earth. The giants are traditionally associated with pride and rebellion against God.

Stanza 9

Orgoglio's genealogy identifies him as an earthquake: see Heninger (1959) 172–3. Cf. Harvey's letter to S.: 'The Materiall Cause of Earthquakes . . . is no doubt great aboundance of wynde . . . emprysoned in the Caves, and Dungeons of the Earth' (*Poet. Wks S.* 616). For the earthquake as omen, see also Heninger (1960) 129–30; it is a sign of the Last Judgment in Rev. 8.5, etc.

1 **vncouth**: vile; strange, marvellous.

2 **Æolus**: here the wind. The earth was generally held to be hollow (cf. II vii 8.9) and winds caused by exhalations from its bowels. S. mocks the giant for such boasting, as Jonson mocks Vulcan: 'Sonne of the Wind! for so thy mother gone / With lust conceiv'd thee; Father thou hadst none' (*Execration upon Vulcan* 111–2).

4 **inspire**: breathe into; breathe life into (as Gen. 2.7), a parody of divine inspiration.

5 **yre**: a pun on air.

7 **expire**: give birth after full term; also 'breathing out'.

8 **earthly slime**: applied to the human body in general, as a mixture of earth and water; cf. Prometheus's creation of man out of earth and water, Ovid, *Met.* i 80–3. The Douai Bible uses slime at Gen. 2.7, instead of dust, for *de limo terrae* of the Vulgate. Cf. 'fleshly slime' (II x 50.2, III vi 3.5). The third element, air, puffs him up, and alludes to the Greek root of Orgoglio, ὀργάω, to be swollen with lust, here with wind (Upton, 1758), in parody of man's creation by the breath of life; cf. viii 24.8–9n. The fourth element, fire (associated with the soul), is necessarily missing. On the giants, formed of primeval slime, interpreted as our bodies, see Seznec (1953) 91.

9 **fild**: also 'filed': defiled, corrupted.

10

So growen great through arrogant delight
  Of th'high descent, whereof he was yborne,
  And through presumption of his matchlesse might,
  All other powres and knighthood he did scorne.
  Such now he marcheth to this man forlorne,
  And left to losse: his stalking steps are stayde
  Vpon a snaggy Oke, which he had torne
  Out of his mothers bowelles, and it made
His mortall mace, wherewith his foemen he dismayde.

11

That when the knight he spide, he gan aduance
  With huge force and insupportable mayne,
  And towardes him with dreadfull fury praunce;
  Who haplesse, and eke hopelesse, all in vaine
  Did to him pace, sad battaile to darrayne,
  Disarmd, disgrast, and inwardly dismayde,
  And eke so faint in euery ioynt and vaine,
  Through that fraile fountaine, which him feeble made,
That scarsely could he weeld his bootlesse single blade.

12

The Geaunt strooke so maynly mercilesse,
  That could haue ouerthrowne a stony towre,
  And were not heauenly grace, that him did blesse,
  He had beene pouldred all, as thin as flowre:
  But he was wary of that deadly stowre,
  And lightly lept from vnderneath the blow:
  Yet so exceeding was the villeins powre,
  That with the wind it did him ouerthrow,
And all his sences stound, that still he lay full low.

Stanza 10

1   **growen great**: interpreting his great size in terms of his pride.
5   **forlorne**: left alone; morally lost; doomed to destruction. He is abandoned by his armour, Una, and God, because he has abandoned them; cf. 'so fowle forlore' (viii 39.4). See 19.4n.
6   **losse**: perdition; destruction; death. He is 'that which was lost', one whom 'the Sonne of man is come to seke, and to save' (Luke 19.10).   **stayde**: supported, suggesting that he is maintained by power, not by right.
7   **snaggy**: knotty. The oak is cited for its strength (cf. viii 18.6). For its association with Druidism and paganism, see

Drayton, *Poly-Olbion* ix 415–20, and Selden's note (*Wks* iv 192) on the etymology Δρυς, oak; also Richard of Cirencester, *Ancient State of Britain* I iv 11, in *Six Old English Chronicles* ed. J. A. Giles (1891) 432. Virgil's Polyphemus supports his steps by a lopped pine (*Aen.* iii 659). Cf. Homer, *Ody.* ix 319–20. For the club as an attribute of the Wild Man, see Bernheimer (1952) 1, 26, Fig. 15. In Lorch's picture of the Pope as Antichrist, the Pope wields an uprooted tree; repr. in Cohn (1957) Fig 2. Shroeder (1962) 149 suggests a connection with Lust's 'tall young oake' (IV vii 7.4).
9   **mace**: used as a club it denotes a crushing blow or utter destruction (Cirlot, 1962).   **dismayde**: for the play on the word, see 11.6n.

Stanza 11

1   **That**: i.e. his mace. Emphasis falls awkwardly but strongly upon this word to emphasize the blow which is the subject of stanzas 11–14.   **aduance**: lift up.
2   **insupportable**: irresistible. The accent on the second syllable, as in Lat. idiom, stresses this key word; no human power can resist this giant. Note the three heavy accents before the caesura.   **mayne**: strength, force. It suggests the power of the sea.
3   **praunce**: strut, indicating his pride.
5   **darrayne**: engage; fight.
6   **disgrast**: put to shame, as the nymph (see 5.5n); more strongly, out of God's grace, so it would seem to the **hopelesse** (4) knight.   **dismayde**: with a pun on 'un-made'. Cf. Una's catalogue of his state: 'disauenturous' (48.7) and 'disarmed, dissolute, dismaid' (51.3). Despair adds 'defilde' (ix 46.9), alluding to this moment. Crampton (1974) 118 observes that the alliterative privatives are radical etymological puns. The negations place the Knight in the power of Dis.
8   **fraile**: i.e. causing frailness; cf. 6.5.
9   **bootlesse**: useless.   **single**: because he has the sword alone and lacks defence. Only his shield and armour are such that 'none can wound the man, that does them wield' (iv 50.7).

Stanzas 12–13

These two stanzas mark the precise midpoint of the *1590* Book I: the fall of the hero who, like the Nymph, is 'in middest of the race' (5.4). For similar midpoints, see II vii 53–55n, III vi 43n: each is found in a *locus amoenus* with its enticing retreat. See Baybak, Delany, and Hieatt (1969) 231. See also Hieatt (1973) 19–25.

Stanza 12

1   **maynly**: mightily.   **mercilesse**: both adv. and adj. (with such merciless might); contrasts with **heauenly grace** (3).
2   **That**: i.e. the stroke. The comparison is developed at viii 23 to describe Orgoglio's own fall.
3   **heauenly grace**: cf. viii 1.3. See II viii 1n. The term prepares for Arthur's entrance as the agent of God's grace. **blesse**: preserve.
4   **pouldred**: obsolete form of 'powdered': pulverized; cf. 14.3.
5   **stowre**: assault.
8   **wind**: as he is the son of Æolus. A parody of the breath of the Holy Ghost: by this wind the Knight is created as was Orgoglio and reduced to a 'slombred sencelesse corse' (15.6).
9   **stound**: stunned.

13

As when that diuelish yron Engin wrought
  In deepest Hell, and framd by *Furies* skill,
  With windy Nitre and quick Sulphur fraught,
  And ramd with bullet round, ordaind to kill,
  Conceiueth fire, the heauens it doth fill
  With thundring noyse, and all the ayre doth choke,
  That none can breath, nor see, nor heare at will,
Through smouldry cloud of duskish stincking smoke,
That th'onely breath him daunts, who hath escapt the stroke.

14

So daunted when the Geaunt saw the knight,
  His heauie hand he heaued vp on hye,
  And him to dust thought to haue battred quight,
  Vntill *Duessa* loud to him gan crye;
  O great *Orgoglio*, greatest vnder skye,
  O hold thy mortall hand for Ladies sake,
  Hold for my sake, and do him not to dye,
But vanquisht thine eternall bondslaue make,
And me thy worthy meed vnto thy Leman take.

15

He hearkned, and did stay from further harmes,
  To gayne so goodly guerdon, as she spake:
  So willingly she came into his armes,
  Who her as willingly to grace did take,
  And was possessed of his new found make.
  Then vp he tooke the slombred sencelesse corse,
  And ere he could out of his swowne awake,
Him to his castle brought with hastie forse,
And in a Dongeon deepe him threw without remorse.

16

From that day forth *Duessa* was his deare,
  And highly honourd in his haughtie eye,
  He gaue her gold and purple pall to weare,
  And triple crowne set on her head full hye,
  And her endowd with royall maiestye:
  Then for to make her dreaded more of men,
  And peoples harts with awfull terrour tye,
A monstrous beast ybred in filthy fen
He chose, which he had kept long time in darksome den.

Stanza 13

1–2 **yron Engin**: the cannon; **diuelish** because invented by the devil in deepest Hell (Ariosto, *Orl. Fur.* ix 91).
3 **windy**: producing wind. **Nitre**: potassium nitrate, the principal ingredient in gunpowder. **quick**: fiery.
4 **ordaind**: devised; also the military sense, 'drawn up in order of battle'.
5 **Conceiueth**: catches; breeds within.
8 **smouldry**: smothering.
9 The smoke or smell alone overcomes him.

Stanza 14

2 The line mimes the act of raising the weapon.
5 **Orgoglio**: Ital. 'pride, haughtines, disdaine' (Florio, 1611); cf. Eng. orgueil, orgulous. After the Knight's defeat, he is now first named; see viii 8.4–6*n*. The name contains the root of the Knight's name, George: see General Introduction.
9 **meed**: Duessa indicates her role as Lady Meed. Similarly, the Red Cross Knight wins her after his defeat of Sans Foy.

Stanza 15

1 **stay**: refrain.
4 **to grace**: into his favour.
5 In possessing her, he is possessed by her.
6 **slombred**: unconscious.

Stanzas 16–17

Based on Rev. 17.3–4: 'I sawe a woman sit upon a skarlat coloured beast, full of names of blasphemie, which had seven heads, and ten hornes. And the woman was araied in purple and skarlat, and guilded with golde, and precious stones, and pearles.' Then she is named 'great Babylon, the mother of whoredomes', as later she is named by S. 'That scarlot whore' (viii 29.2). See ii 13.2*n*, viii 14.1–5*n*. The Geneva gloss notes that 'the beast signifieth the ancient Rome; the woman that sitteth thereon, the new Rome which is the Papistrie, whose crueltie and blood sheding is declared by skarlat'. Alciati (1581) uses the image of the woman on the seven-headed beast as an emblem of False Religion.

Stanza 16

3 **purple pall**: the crimson robe of royalty.
4 **triple crowne**: the Pope's three-tiered crown, symbolizing temporal power over the world; Ovid's *triplex mundus* (land, sea, and sky) or east, south, and west (the north belongs to Satan), or the three continents (Europe, Africa and Asia). An illustration in Luther's New Testament (1522) shows the Scarlet Woman wearing the papal tiara; see Strachan (1957) 43; also Tuve (1966) 102–8.
5 Cf. Rev. 18.7: 'For she saith in her heart, I sit being a quene, and am no widowe, and shal se no mourning.' Duessa first appeared as a 'virgin widow' (ii 24.8) mourning for her slain lover.
7 **tye**: enthrall.

17

Such one it was, as that renowmed Snake
　　Which great *Alcides* in *Stremona* slew,
　　Long fostred in the filth of *Lerna* lake,
　　Whose many heads out budding euer new,
　　Did breed him endlesse labour to subdew:
　　But this same Monster much more vgly was;
　　For seuen great heads out of his body grew,
　　An yron brest, and backe of scaly bras,
And all embrewd in bloud, his eyes did shine as glas.

18

His tayle was stretched out in wondrous length,
　　That to the house of heauenly gods it raught,
　　And with extorted powre, and borrow'd strength,
　　The euer-burning lamps from thence it brought,
　　And prowdly threw to ground, as things of nought;
　　And vnderneath his filthy feet did tread
　　The sacred things, and holy heasts foretaught.
　　Vpon this dreadfull Beast with seuenfold head
He set the false *Duessa*, for more aw and dread.

19

The wofull Dwarfe, which saw his maisters fall,
　　Whiles he had keeping of his grasing steed,
　　And valiant knight become a caytiue thrall,
　　When all was past, tooke vp his forlorne weed,
　　His mightie armour, missing most at need;
　　His siluer shield, now idle maisterlesse;
　　His poynant speare, that many made to bleed,
　　The ruefull moniments of heauinesse,
And with them all departes, to tell his great distresse.

20

He had not trauaild long, when on the way
　　He wofull Ladie, wofull *Vna* met,
　　Fast flying from the Paynims greedy pray,
　　Whilest *Satyrane* him from pursuit did let:
　　Who when her eyes she on the Dwarfe had set,
　　And saw the signes, that deadly tydings spake,
　　She fell to ground for sorrowfull regret,
　　And liuely breath her sad brest did forsake,
Yet might her pitteous hart be seene to pant and quake.

Stanza 17

1–2   that renowmed Snake: the Lernean hydra slain by Hercules (**Alcides**), the second of his labours and therefore 'renowmed'. According to Ovid, *Met*. ix 68–74, the hydra had one hundred heads; later in S.'s poem it will develop a thousand. S. may invent the connection with **Stremona**, or Strymon, a river in Thrace, because that country, according to Upton (1758), was noted for its seditions. The comparison prepares for the entrance of Arthur as a second and greater Hercules.
3   filth: because 'in this lake the people . . . dyd throwe all the ordure and sweepynges of theyr streetes and houses' (Cooper, 1565). In the *Golden Legend*, the dragon slain by St George lived in 'a stagne or a ponde lyke a see' (Barclay, *Life of St George*, App. 113). In Barclay (line 501) the Dragon was bred in 'a foule infernall lake' which surrounds the castle.
5   breed: as their breeding bred his labour.
7   seuen great heads: 'And I sawe a beast rise out of the sea, having seven heads' (Rev. 13.1). The Geneva gloss reads: 'meaning Rome, because it was first governed by seven Kings or Emperours after Nero, and also is compassed about with seven mountaines'. The seven heads were related also to the seven deadly sins.
8   backe of scaly bras: cf. the Dragon's 'bras-scaly backe' (xi 11.2).
9   embrewd: stained; defiled. The shining eyes suggest the etymology of dragon (from Gk δράκων); cf. the Dragon's 'blazing eyes, like two bright shining shields' (xi 14.1); also the Leviathan whose eyes 'are like the eye lids of the morning' (Job 41.9; 18 KJ).

Stanza 18

1–7   Cf. Daniel's vision of the goat whose horn 'grewe up unto the hoste of heaven, and it cast downe some of the hoste, and of the starres to the grounde, and trode upon them . . . and the place of his [God's] Sanctuarie was cast downe' (Dan. 8.10–1; cf. 7.23); cf. also Rev. 12.3–4.
2   raught: reached.
3   extorted powre: power wrongfully obtained. Upton (1758) notes the implication that papal tyranny usurps civil power.   **borrow'd**: assumed, counterfeit; cf. Duessa's 'borrowed light' (viii 49.5) and 'borrow'd beautie' (II i 22.7). Possibly also 'loaned' by God to fulfil his purposes.
7   heasts: commands.   **foretaught**: previously taught; i.e. he treads underfoot holy doctrines that earlier had been reverenced; 'untaught' and 'mistaught' are possible readings.

Stanza 19

4   forlorne: forsaken by the Knight; cf. 'forlorne reliques' (48.1).   **weed**: armour.
5   most at need: when most needed.
7   poynant: piercing.
8   moniments of heauinesse: tokens, or reminders of grief, as 'reliques sad' (24.9) and 'heauie record' (48.8).

Stanza 20

3   greedy pray: i.e. his preying greedily on her.
4   let: hinder.
7   regret: sorrow caused by an external event. The current sense, 'sorrow due to reflection on something left undone' (not recorded by *OED* until *c*. 1641), may well be present.
8   liuely breath: the breath of life.

21

The messenger of so vnhappie newes
  Would faine haue dyde: dead was his hart within,
  Yet outwardly some little comfort shewes:
  At last recouering hart, he does begin
  To rub her temples, and to chaufe her chin,
  And euery tender part does tosse and turne:
  So hardly he the flitted life does win,
  Vnto her natiue prison to retourne:
Then gins her grieued ghost thus to lament and mourne.

22

Ye dreary instruments of dolefull sight,
  That doe this deadly spectacle behold,
  Why do ye lenger feed on loathed light,
  Or liking find to gaze on earthly mould,
  Sith cruell fates the carefull threeds vnfould,
  The which my life and loue together tyde?
  Now let the stony dart of senselesse cold
  Perce to my hart, and pas through euery side,
And let eternall night so sad sight fro me hide.

23

O lightsome day, the lampe of highest *Ioue*,
  First made by him, mens wandring wayes to guyde,
  When darknesse he in deepest dongeon droue,
  Henceforth thy hated face for euer hyde,
  And shut vp heauens windowes shyning wyde:
  For earthly sight can nought but sorrow breed,
  And late repentance, which shall long abyde.
  Mine eyes no more on vanitie shall feed,
But seeled vp with death, shall haue their deadly meed.

24

Then downe againe she fell vnto the ground;
  But he her quickly reared vp againe:
  Thrise did she sinke adowne in deadly swownd,
  And thrise he her reviu'd with busie paine:
  At last when life recouer'd had the raine,
  And ouer-wrestled his strong enemie,
  With foltring tong, and trembling euery vaine,
  Tell on (quoth she) the wofull Tragedie,
The which these reliques sad present vnto mine eie.

25

Tempestuous fortune hath spent all her spight,
  And thrilling sorrow throwne his vtmost dart;
  Thy sad tongue cannot tell more heauy plight,
  Then that I feele, and harbour in mine hart:
  Who hath endur'd the whole, can beare each part.
  If death it be, it is not the first wound,
  That launched hath my brest with bleeding smart.
  Begin, and end the bitter balefull stound;
If lesse, then that I feare, more fauour I haue found.

Stanza 21
2 **dead was his hart**: the beholder's grief is much more intense than the sufferer's; cf. 20.9.
3 Even when overcome, he provides some consolation. This line is inserted (line 4 follows 2) to point to the Dwarf's role as common sense, which begins Una's redemption.
5 **chin**: perhaps rhyme forces this synecdoche for 'face'; yet *OED* cites one use from *c*. 1340 where the word seems to signify 'cheek', as does the Greek root γένυς.
7 **So hardly**: with such difficulty. **win**: persuade.
8 **natiue prison**: her natural body which encloses her spirit (ghost) from birth; cf. Ps. 142.7.

Stanzas 22–23
The pathos of Una's lament lies in her association with light. Bajazeth's lament in Marlowe, 1 *Tamburlaine* V ii 196–241, is an overblown pastiche of these stanzas.

Stanza 22
1 Addressing her 'eyes' (20.5).
2 **deadly**: as sign of his death and cause of hers.
4 **liking**: pleasure. **earthly mould**: mortal things. **mould**: body; yet also earth (as in the phrase 'man of mould'). Her phrase emphasizes the earthliness of man's 'natiue prison'.
5 The three Fates who spin and cut the thread of life: see IV ii 47–52. **carefull**: sorrowful.
7 **senselesse cold**: the numbing cold of death.
9 Una's lament takes literally love's extravagant claim that without her Knight, who is her 'light, and shining lampe of blis', her 'chearefull day is turnd to chearelesse night' (iii 27.7, 9).

Stanza 23
2 **First made**: Gen. 1.3–4.
3 **deepest dongeon**: cf. the 'Dongeon deepe' (15.9) into which Orgoglio has cast Una's knight.
6 Una's despairing cry echoes throughout the poem; cf. Arthur's lesson: 'That blisse may not abide in state of mortall men' (viii 44.9).
7 **late**: i.e. too late.
9 **seeled vp**: closed, as the stitched eyelids of a hawk. **deadly meed**: reward of death. An appropriate image because a seeled hawk flies upward to heaven until exhausted.

Stanza 24
3–4 In any life and death struggle, three is the inevitable number.

Stanza 25
5 Cf. vi 37.9.
7 **launched**: pierced. Una refers to her earlier patrons, the 'Full many knights' (45.1) who died in their efforts to slay the dragon. In the present narrative cycle, cf. the Lion's death, iii 42.6–8.
8 **stound**: time; here, time of trial or sorrow.
9 **more**: i.e. more than I expect.

26

Then gan the Dwarfe the whole discourse declare,
  The subtill traines of *Archimago* old;
  The wanton loues of false *Fidessa* faire,
  Bought with the bloud of vanquisht Paynim bold:
  The wretched payre transform'd to treen mould;
  The house of Pride, and perils round about;
  The combat, which he with *Sansioy* did hould;
  The lucklesse conflict with the Gyant stout,
Wherein captiu'd, of life or death he stood in doubt.

27

She heard with patience all vnto the end,
  And stroue to maister sorrowfull assay,
  Which greater grew, the more she did contend,
  And almost rent her tender hart in tway;
  And loue fresh coles vnto her fire did lay:
  For greater loue, the greater is the losse.
  Was neuer Ladie loued dearer day,
  Then she did loue the knight of the *Redcrosse*;
For whose deare sake so many troubles her did tosse.

28

At last when feruent sorrow slaked was,
  She vp arose, resoluing him to find
  A liue or dead: and forward forth doth pas,
  All as the Dwarfe the way to her assynd:
  And euermore in constant carefull mind
  She fed her wound with fresh renewed bale;
  Long tost with stormes, and bet with bitter wind,
  High ouer hils, and low adowne the dale,
She wandred many a wood, and measurd many a vale.

29

At last she chaunced by good hap to meet
  A goodly knight, faire marching by the way
  Together with his Squire, arayed meet:
  His glitterand armour shined farre away,
  Like glauncing light of *Phœbus* brightest ray;
  From top to toe no place appeared bare,
  That deadly dint of steele endanger may:
  Athwart his brest a bauldrick braue he ware,
That shynd, like twinkling stars, with stons most pretious rare.

30

And in the midst thereof one pretious stone
  Of wondrous worth, and eke of wondrous mights,
  Shapt like a Ladies head, exceeding shone,
  Like *Hesperus* emongst the lesser lights,
  And stroue for to amaze the weaker sights;
  Thereby his mortall blade full comely hong
  In yuory sheath, ycaru'd with curious slights;
  Whose hilts were burnisht gold, and handle strong
Of mother pearle, and buckled with a golden tong.

Stanza 26
The semicolons divide the Knight's 'wofull Tragedie' (24.8) into five Acts. I: line 2 (Canto i and opening of Canto ii); II: lines 3–5 (the two scenes of Canto ii, the gaining of Duessa with an exemplum of the consequences told by Fradubio); III: line 6 (Canto iv); IV: line 7 (Canto v); V: lines 8–9 (Canto vii).

1   **discourse**: sequence of events.
2   **subtill traines**: crafty wiles.
4   Cf. iv 42.5.
5   **treen mould**: the form and substance of a tree; see ii 39.9*n*.
8   **stout**: also proud, haughty.

Stanza 27
2   **assay**: affliction; trial.
7   **loued dearer day**: loved life more dearly.

Stanza 28
Duessa as the 'virgin widow' (ii 24.8) who seeks in sorrow the body of her dead lover foreshadows Una's present quest.
1   **slaked**: abated, relieved; but more literally, 'quenched', for her **feruent** (burning) sorrow is caused by 'her fire' (27.5) of love.
4   **assynd**: pointed out; cf. 52.9.
5   **carefull**: sorrowful.
7   **bet**: beaten.
9   **measurd**: suggests the tedium of her travel. She continues the quest which began at ii 8.

Stanzas 29–36
One of the most extended portraits in the poem because Arthur's virtue of magnificence contains the virtues of all the knights (see *L.R.*) and his quest provides the pattern for their adventures. He is not named, except in the Arguments, until ix 6.5.

Stanza 29
2   **faire**: as an adj., pleasing to the eye; as an adv., becomingly, gently.
4–5   **glitterand**: sparkling with light; cf. II xi 17.1. Cf. his light-giving shield, 34.5; '-and', the northern form of the present participle, suggests light-giving in contrast to 'glittering' or 'light-reflecting'. Lucifera's 'glitterand light' (iv 16.9) represents Phaeton (iv 9) in contrast to the **Phœbus** image here.   **glauncing**: flashing, dazzling.
7   **dint**: stroke.
8–9   **bauldrick**: the belt worn from the right shoulder across the breast to support the sword. Its central stone (30.1) would exactly cover the heart. As a belt of **twinkling stars**, it suggests 'heauens bright-shining baudricke' (V i 11.7), the zodiac.

Stanza 30
2   **mights**: powers, virtues, referring to the magical powers possessed by certain precious stones. Here its power is gained by its shape, an effigy of the Faerie Queene. Geoffrey of Monmouth ix 4 records that Arthur's device was a picture of the Virgin Mary; cf. Drayton, *Poly-Olbion* iv 252 and Selden's note (*Works* iv 86–7).
4   **Hesperus**: Venus, to indicate the place and power of love in Arthur's quest. For the association of Venus with Astræa-Virgo-Elizabeth, see Yates (1947) 57f.
5   **amaze**: dazzle, bewilder.   **weaker sights**: eyes too weak to endure its brightness.
7   **curious slights**: elaborately wrought designs, perhaps suggesting some magical inscription. However, S. avoids the kind of magical powers given the scabbard by Merlin in Malory 54.
9   **tong**: pin.

31

His haughtie helmet, horrid all with gold,
  Both glorious brightnesse, and great terrour bred;
  For all the crest a Dragon did enfold
  With greedie pawes, and ouer all did spred
  His golden wings: his dreadfull hideous hed
  Close couched on the beuer, seem'd to throw
  From flaming mouth bright sparkles fierie red,
  That suddeine horror to faint harts did show;
And scaly tayle was stretcht adowne his backe full low.

32

Vpon the top of all his loftie crest,
  A bunch of haires discolourd diuersly,
  With sprincled pearle, and gold full richly drest,
  Did shake, and seem'd to daunce for iollity,
  Like to an Almond tree ymounted hye
  On top of greene *Selinis* all alone,
  With blossomes braue bedecked daintily;
  Whose tender locks do tremble euery one
At euery little breath, that vnder heauen is blowne.

33

His warlike shield all closely couer'd was,
  Ne might of mortall eye be euer seene;
  Not made of steele, nor of enduring bras,
  Such earthly mettals soone consumed bene:
  But all of Diamond perfect pure and cleene
  It framed was, one massie entire mould,
  Hewen out of Adamant rocke with engines keene,
  That point of speare it neuer percen could,
Ne dint of direfull sword diuide the substance would.

34

The same to wight he neuer wont disclose,
  But when as monsters huge he would dismay,
  Or daunt vnequall armies of his foes,
  Or when the flying heauens he would affray;
  For so exceeding shone his glistring ray,
  That *Phœbus* golden face it did attaint,
  As when a cloud his beames doth ouer-lay;
  And siluer *Cynthia* wexed pale and faint, ·
As when her face is staynd with magicke arts constraint.

Stanza 31

1 **haughtie**: lofty (in the literal sense); cf. ii 19.3.   **horrid**: rough, bristling; from Lat. *horridus*.

3–9 Geoffrey of Monmouth viii 14–ix 4 relates that a star 'darting forth a ray, at the end of which was a globe of fire in form of a dragon', foretold to Uther that he should have 'a most potent son'. When he carried a dragon made of gold to the wars, he became known as Uther Pendragon, the dragon's head. Consequently his son, Arthur, 'placed a golden helmet upon his head, on which was engraven the figure of a dragon'.

4 **greedie**: i.e. displaying its intense desire, as does Arthur at viii 6.9, 29.3.

6 **couched**: lying; an heraldic term.   **beuer**: the visor.

Stanza 32

1 **crest**: top of the helmet; more specifically, the attached

upright plume, a badge worn 'in tokne he was a kniht' (Gower, *Conf. Aman*. v 6044). As the symbol of knighthood, it requires an entire stanza.

2 **discolourd diuersly**: of many colours. The Red Cross Knight wears a similar crest, ii 11.6.

5–9 Aaron's rod that blossomed and bore ripe almonds was the sign that he had been chosen by God, Num. 17.5–8. The almond is connected with the miraculous in the popular legend of Phyllis, who, killed by grief at her lover's long absence, was changed into an almond tree; upon being embraced by him, the tree broke forth into fresh leaves and flowers. According to folk etymology, the name yields 'al monde', Lord of the World (H. Bayley, 1912, ii 277). The almond is also a symbol of age: 'and the almonde tre shal florish' (Eccles. 12.5) signifies white hair that crowns old age (see Geneva gloss). Cheney (1966) 70 observes that 'Arthur is already wearing that symbol of Time/ Death/Sin, as a token of his own fully attained chivalry'.

6 **Selinis**: from Virgil's *palmosa Selinus* (*Aen*. iii 705), the town of the victor's palm. In his edition of the Book (1962), R. D. Williams notes the etymological epithet: the plant σέλινον which figured on the coins of Selinus, was one of the plants used for the victor's crown in the great games of Greece, and he cites Servius on the connection of *palmosa* with equestrian victories. Marlowe imitates these lines to describe Tamburlaine's triumphant appearance, *2 Tamburlaine* IV iv 119–24.

8 **locks**: leaves (E.K.'s note to *S.C.* Nov. 125); also hairs.

Stanza 33

2 **be euer seene**: because of its brightness, as the sun.

5–9 On the diamond as the emblem of Fortitude, see Tervarent (1958) 147 citing Valeriano. 8–9 suggest the 'shield of faith' of Eph. 6.16, 'wherewith ye may quench all the fyrie dartes of the wicked'. In Phineas Fletcher, *Purple Island* xii 24, Fido's shield is 'of one pure diamond, celestiall fair'; see Allen (1937). In Tasso, *Ger. Lib*. vii 82, the diamond shield which defends God's faithful is taken by an angel to aid the Christian champion. It is said to be among the weapons used by Michael to slay the Dragon. In his 'Allegory to the Poem', Tasso identifies the shield as 'the special safeguard of the Lord God'; see Hankins (1971) 32.

5 **Diamond**: the magical properties of the stone are listed by Cooper (1565) under 'Adamas'. The three descriptive terms are not distinct in meaning.   **perfect**: functions either as adj. or adv.   **cleene**: clear; without any device or symbol engraved upon it.

6 **one . . . mould**: a shape wrought in one solid piece. **entire**: wholly of one piece (*OED* 5).

7 **Adamant rocke**: see vi 4.5*n*.   **engines**: instruments.

Stanza 34

1 **to wight**: to any creature.

3 **daunt**: vanquish; daze.   **vnequall**: disproportionate, being otherwise more than a match for him. Heb. 11.34 says of faith that it has 'turned to flight the armies of the aliantes [aliens]'.

4 **the flying heauens**: the revolving constellations are frightened by the power of the shield; such is the power of Fidelia over the heavens, x 20.2–3.

5 **glistring**: see i 14.4*n*; used of the sun's rays at v 2.5, ix 18.2.

6 **attaint**: sully, obscure by surpassing in brilliance.

8–9 On the power of witchcraft to eclipse the moon, cf. VII vi 16.5–6; Ovid, *Met*. vii 207–8.

35

No magicke arts hereof had any might,
  Nor bloudie wordes of bold Enchaunters call,
  But all that was not such, as seemd in sight,
  Before that shield did fade, and suddeine fall:
  And when him list the raskall routes appall,
  Men into stones therewith he could transmew,
  And stones to dust, and dust to nought at all;
  And when him list the prouder lookes subdew,
He would them gazing blind, or turne to other hew.

36

Ne let it seeme, that credence this exceedes,
  For he that made the same, was knowne right well
  To haue done much more admirable deedes.
  It *Merlin* was, which whylome did excell
  All liuing wightes in might of magicke spell:
  Both shield, and sword, and armour all he wrought
  For this young Prince, when first to armes he fell;
  But when he dyde, the Faerie Queene it brought
To Faerie lond, where yet it may be seene, if sought.

37

A gentle youth, his dearely loued Squire
  His speare of heben wood behind him bare,
  Whose harmefull head, thrice heated in the fire,
  Had riuen many a brest with pikehead square;
  A goodly person, and could menage faire
  His stubborne steed with curbed canon bit,
  Who vnder him did trample as the aire,
  And chauft, that any on his backe should sit;
The yron rowels into frothy fome he bit.

38

When as this knight nigh to the Ladie drew,
  With louely court he gan her entertaine;
  But when he heard her answeres loth, he knew
  Some secret sorrow did her heart distraine:
  Which to allay, and calme her storming paine,
  Faire feeling words he wisely gan display,
  And for her humour fitting purpose faine,
  To tempt the cause it selfe for to bewray;
Wherewith emmou'd, these bleeding words she gan to say.

39

What worlds delight, or ioy of liuing speach
  Can heart, so plung'd in sea of sorrowes deepe,
  And heaped with so huge misfortunes, reach?
  The carefull cold beginneth for to creepe,
  And in my heart his yron arrow steepe,
  Soone as I thinke vpon my bitter bale:
  Such helplesse harmes yts better hidden keepe,
  Then rip vp griefe, where it may not auaile,
My last left comfort is, my woes to weepe and waile.

3–4   The enchanted shield in Ariosto, *Orl. Fur.* ii 55–6, is interpreted by Harington as the power of great pomp to blind the beholders. Nelson (1963) 143 comments: 'in Spenser's version this trumpery shield becomes the divine power that destroys illusion'; see Alpers (1967) 166–79.
5   **raskall routes**: base rabble, vulgar mob.
6–7   In contrast, Orgoglio's club has the power only to batter his enemies to dust (14.3).
8   **prouder**: most proud.
9   **hew**: shape.

Stanza 36
3   **admirable**: amazing, marvellous.
8–9   Before ever Arthur acts in the poem, he is distanced from us by his death. Yet his virtue lives, as 9 suggests, potentially embodied in England. Hence the point of this line is the power of faith, and emphasis falls on **sought**. Percival (1893) comments: 'Spenser endows the shield of Arthur with the same awful mystery that surrounded the Holy Grail.' The line is very Spenserian: it seems to be whimsy – cf. III iii 8 – at the same time that it comments profoundly on the poet's aim to move the reader to virtuous action.

Stanza 37
2   **His**: Arthur's, though borne by Timias here and at II viii 17.6. The spear is not employed emblematically until wielded by Britomart, who becomes the 'Knight of the Hebene speare' (IV v 8.2, etc.). For her connection with Arthur, see III i 8.6*n*.   **heben wood**: ebony, noted for its extreme hardness. Its association with Cupid's bow (see Proem 3.5) links Arthur with love.
5   **menage**: manège, direct a horse through its paces; denoting his temperance.
6   **curbed**: fastened at the ends with a chain.   **canon bit**: a smooth round bit.
7   **trample**] amble *1590*.   **as the aire**: nimbly, as Trevisan's steed 'did tread the wind' (ix 21.8).
9   **rowels**: knobs for the chain.

Stanza 38
2   **louely**: loving, kind.   **court** signifies courteous attention or regard; cf. his 'gentle court' to Guyon (II ix 2.5) and also the Red Cross Knight's 'goodly court' (7.1) to Duessa.
4   **distraine**: afflict; tear asunder (cf. 27.4).
5–8   His 'well guided speech' (42.1) in saving Una from despair is as powerful as Despair's in Canto ix in leading the Red Cross Knight into despair.   **display**: pour forth, utter.   **purpose**: speech.
9   **emmou'd**: moved inwardly or strongly.   **bleeding words**: words expressing her wound of anguish or suffering.

Stanza 39
1–3   A curiously abrupt beginning: we do not know what Arthur has said to which she replies unless **worlds delight** refers to his 'louely court' and **ioy of liuing speach** to his 'Faire feeling words' of the last stanza.
4–5   **carefull cold**: 'for care is sayd to coole the blood' (E.K.'s note to *S.C.* Dec. 133); see Robin (1911) 127 and III x 59.6*n*; cf. Una's state at vi 37.1–2, vii 22.7–8, which culminates in her present despair, and the Knight's transformed state: 'crudled cold his corage gan assaile' (6.7).
7   **helplesse**: beyond help; preparing for Arthur's rejoinder, 40.7.

Stanza 35
1   **hereof**: concerning this, i.e. the shield.
2   **bloudie**: as they seek to shed blood.

40

Ah Ladie deare, quoth then the gentle knight,
  Well may I weene, your griefe is wondrous great;
  For wondrous great griefe groneth in my spright,
  Whiles thus I heare you of your sorrowes treat.
  But wofull Ladie let me you intreate,
  For to vnfold the anguish of your hart:
  Mishaps are maistred by aduice discrete,
  And counsell mittigates the greatest smart;
Found neuer helpe, who neuer would his hurts impart.

41

O but (quoth she) great griefe will not be tould,
  And can more easily be thought, then said.
  Right so; (quoth he) but he, that neuer would,
  Could neuer: will to might giues greatest aid.
  But griefe (quoth she) does greater grow displaid,
  If then it find not helpe, and breedes despaire.
  Despaire breedes not (quoth he) where faith is staid.
  No faith so fast (quoth she) but flesh does paire.
Flesh may empaire (quoth he) but reason can repaire.

42

His goodly reason, and well guided speach
  So deepe did settle in her gratious thought,
  That her perswaded to disclose the breach,
  Which loue and fortune in her heart had wrought,
  And said; Faire Sir, I hope good hap hath brought
  You to inquire the secrets of my griefe,
  Or that your wisedome will direct my thought,
  Or that your prowesse can me yield reliefe:
Then heare the storie sad, which I shall tell you briefe.

43

The forlorne Maiden, whom your eyes haue seene
  The laughing stocke of fortunes mockeries,
  Am th'only daughter of a King and Queene,
  Whose parents deare, whilest equall destinies
  Did runne about, and their felicities
  The fauourable heauens did not enuy,
  Did spread their rule through all the territories,
  Which Phison and Euphrates floweth by,
And Gehons golden waues doe wash continually.

Stanza 41
1   This same claim rounds out her complaint, 51.9. For the
proverb, see Tilley (1950) S664, C. G. Smith (1970) 351.
2   The first stage of rescuing her from despair: at 39.4–6
her grief was too great to 'thinke vpon'.
6   Now she allows the possibility that her state is not
'helplesse' (39.7).
7   staid: constant, sustained.
8   paire: impair; or, from 'appair': weaken.
9   reason: after his sympathetic counsel, Arthur asserts the
powers of will and faith, and now of reason.

Stanza 42
1   goodly reason: later embodied in the Palmer, II ii 5.2.
That divine grace, for which Arthur is the instrument, operates
through human reason, rather than in defiance of it, makes a
precise point in the extended controversy upon their relationship. See e.g. Hooker, Laws, V App. i (Works ii 540): 'neither
are we by inward grace carried vp into heaven, the force of
reason and will being cast into a dead sleep'.
2   gratious: probably with overtones of 'receiving grace',
which rescues her from despair. Cf. OED 6: 'endowed with
divine grace'.   thought: in the earlier, more general sense,
'mind', which allows the repetition of the rhyme word in 7.
3–6   Her hope is sound: cf. 29.1.   secrets: the plural
suggests the biblical sense in Ps. 44.21: 'Shal not God searche
this out? for he knoweth the secrets of the heart.' Cf.
Despair's parody of Arthur's actions, ix 31.5–8.
7   Or: either.

Stanza 43
1   forlorne: as iii 43.1.
3–9   th'only daughter: in opposition to Duessa who claims
to be 'the sole daughter of an Emperour' (ii 22.7 and see n).
Cf. xii 21.2–3. Her parents are Adam and Eve, the King and
Queene of Eden: see xii 26.1.   territories: at i 5.3–6 their
territories are said to cover 'all the world'. Here the world is
identified as Eden by naming three of its four rivers, from Gen.
2.11–4 (the fourth, the Tigris, is included in the Euphrates;
the Geneva Bible has a map to show how the two rivers are
one). The territories watered by the rivers may include the
whole known world: commentators took Gen. 2.5 to mean that
the whole earth was watered from Paradise (see Fowler's n
to Milton, P.L. iv 233–5).
4–5   whilest . . . about: while the impartial fates ran their
course; referring to the fixed stars which, before the Fall,
revolved justly in their orbits. For the cosmic disorder after
the Fall, see V Proem 4f.
6   fauourable: well disposed in their astral influence, and
before the Fall wholly favourable; cf. Milton, P.L. vii 374–5 on
the 'sweet influence' of the fixed stars at the Creation, and the
contrast after the Fall, x 657–64.
8   floweth by: suggesting the view that the rivers did not
take their source in Eden but only flowed through it.
9   Upton (1758) notes that the Phison, not the Gehon, is
associated with gold at Gen. 2.11–2; but the rewards of
alliteration are preferred.

44

Till that their cruell cursed enemy,
  An huge great Dragon horrible in sight,
  Bred in the loathly lakes of *Tartary*,
  With murdrous rauine, and deuouring might
  Their kingdome spoild, and countrey wasted quight:
  Themselues, for feare into his iawes to fall,
  He forst to castle strong to take their flight,
Where fast embard in mightie brasen wall,
He has them now foure yeres besiegd to make them thrall.

45

Full many knights aduenturous and stout
  Haue enterprizd that Monster to subdew;
  From euery coast that heauen walks about,
  Haue thither come the noble Martiall crew,
  That famous hard atchieuements still pursew,
  Yet neuer any could that girlond win,
  But all still shronke, and still he greater grew:
All they for want of faith, or guilt of sin,
The pitteous pray of his fierce crueltie haue bin.

46

At last yledd with farre reported praise,
  Which flying fame throughout the world had spred,
  Of doughtie knights, whom Faery land did raise,
  That noble order hight of Maidenhed,
  Forthwith to court of *Gloriane* I sped,
  Of *Gloriane* great Queene of glory bright,
  Whose kingdomes seat *Cleopolis* is red,
There to obtaine some such redoubted knight,
That Parents deare from tyrants powre deliuer might.

47

It was my chance (my chance was faire and good)
  There for to find a fresh vnproued knight,
  Whose manly hands imbrew'd in guiltie blood
  Had neuer bene, ne euer by his might
  Had throwne to ground the vnregarded right:
  Yet of his prowesse proofe he since hath made
  (I witnesse am) in many a cruell fight;
The groning ghosts of many one dismaide
Haue felt the bitter dint of his auenging blade.

48

And ye the forlorne reliques of his powre,
  His byting sword, and his deuouring speare,
  Which haue endured many a dreadfull stowre,
  Can speake his prowesse, that did earst you beare,
  And well could rule: now he hath left you heare,
  To be the record of his ruefull losse,
  And of my dolefull disauenturous deare:
  O heauie record of the good *Redcrosse*,
Where haue you left your Lord, that could so well you tosse?

Stanza 44
This stanza expands the substance of i 5.7–8.
3   **the loathly lakes . . .**: cf. 'the squalid lakes of *Tartarie*' (*Gn.* 543), from Virgil, *Culex* 333: *pallentesque lacus et squalida Tartara*. As the classical underworld, Tartarus is the region reserved for those who sin against the gods; cf. II xii 6.4–6.
4   **rauine**: violence, force; or as 'ravin': preying, voracity.
8   **embard**: imprisoned.   **brasen**: see xi 3*n*.
9   **foure yeres**: when the Dragon or Satan was cast down to the earth, he drove the woman into the wilderness where she is nourished 'for a time, and times, and halfe a time, from the presence of the serpent' (Rev. 12.14). In verse 6, the time is given as 1,260 days, which is roughly three years and six months. Upton (1758) notes that S. elegantly uses a round number. The figure may represent 4,000 years. In 'A Perfite Supputation of the Yeres and Times from Adam unto Christ', the Geneva Bible demonstrates that from Creation to the birth of Christ was 3,974 years, 6 months and 10 days. Metre, if not elegance, requires this figure to be rounded.

Stanza 45
1–2   Cf. xi 17.9.   **enterprizd**: undertaken.   **subdew**: referring to God's original commandment to man to subdue the earth (Gen. 1.28).
3   **coast**: part of the world.   **walks**: moves; the astronomy is, of course, Ptolemaic.
7   The Dragon grows greater because the knights wither or shrivel in sin and death. Later the Red Cross Knight appears with 'all his flesh shronk vp like withered flowres' (viii 41.9); cf. the description of the Dragon 'swolne with bloud of late' (viii 12.4).
8   **want of faith . . . guilt of sin**: the two key phrases in the moral allegory of Book I.

Stanza 46
4   The **order . . . of Maidenhed** is the type or pattern of the Order of the Garter whose head is the Virgin Queen, whose collar and ribbon display St George killing the Dragon, and whose star is the Red Cross (see *Enc. Brit.* xv 856, Plate I); cf. II ii 42.4–5, ix 6.6.
7   **Cleopolis**: signifying the city of Fame or Glory; see x 58.2.   **red**: named.

Stanza 47
2   **vnproued**: untried in battle; see i 3.7–8.
3   **imbrew'd . . . blood**: stained, and hence defiled, by blood shed guiltily.
8   **dismaide**: defeated.
9   **bitter**: biting, cutting (as 48.2).   **dint**: stroke.

Stanza 48
1   **forlorne**: forsaken by the knight, as 19.4.
3   **stowre**: conflict.
6, 8   **record** (6): evidence; proof; witness.   **record** (8): memorial; cf. 'ruefull moniments' (19.8).
7   **disauenturous**: unfortunate. At the beginning the Knight was 'aduenturous' (45.1); cf. ix 11.8, 45.4.   **deare**: beloved; cf. viii Arg.: 'Faire virgin to redeeme her deare'.

49

Well hoped I, and faire beginnings had,
  That he my captiue langour should redeeme,
  Till all vnweeting, an Enchaunter bad
  His sence abusd, and made him to misdeeme
  My loyalty, not such as it did seeme;
  That rather death desire, then such despight.
  Be iudge ye heauens, that all things right esteeme,
  How I him lou'd, and loue with all my might,
So thought I eke of him, and thinke I thought aright.

50

Thenceforth me desolate he quite forsooke,
  To wander, where wilde fortune would me lead,
  And other bywaies he himselfe betooke,
  Where neuer foot of liuing wight did tread,
  That brought not backe the balefull body dead;
  In which him chaunced false *Duessa* meete,
  Mine onely foe, mine onely deadly dread,
  Who with her witchcraft and misseeming sweete,
Inueigled him to follow her desires vnmeete.

51

At last by subtill sleights she him betraid
  Vnto his foe, a Gyant huge and tall,
  Who him disarmed, dissolute, dismaid,
  Vnwares surprised, and with mightie mall
  The monster mercilesse him made to fall,
  Whose fall did neuer foe before behold;
  And now in darkesome dungeon, wretched thrall,
  Remedilesse, for aie he doth him hold;
This is my cause of griefe, more great, then may be told.

52

Ere she had ended all, she gan to faint:
  But he her comforted and faire bespake,
  Certes, Madame, ye haue great cause of plaint,
  That stoutest heart, I weene, could cause to quake.
  But be of cheare, and comfort to you take:
  For till I haue acquit your captiue knight,
  Assure your selfe, I will you not forsake.
  His chearefull words reuiu'd her chearelesse spright,
So forth they went, the Dwarfe them guiding euer right.

Stanza 49

2   **captiue langour**: languishment in captivity; or their languorous (distressing) captivity. If 'captiue' is given its weaker sense from 'caitiff', she refers simply to their wretched plight (see *OED* 3). The stronger sense is preferred here because 'languor' as disease, illness (*OED* 1) was applied to Original Sin: see Augustine, *De Civ. Dei* XV vi. Cf. the false Una's complaint, i 52.7.
3   **vnweeting**: unknown to the Knight, cf. 6.1.
4   **misdeeme**: misjudge, think evil of; see iv 2.2*n*.
6   **despight**: outrage against her **loyalty** (5).
7   **esteeme**: judge. It is fitting that Una should appeal to the heavens and leave all judgment to God.

Stanza 50

3–5   He took a by-path from which no one returns alive; cf. Prov. 2.13–9 on those who have left 'the waies of righteousnes to walke in the waies of darkenes'. Wisdom must deliver them 'from the strange woman, even from the stranger, which flattereth with her wordes. . . . Surely her house tendeth to death, and her paths unto the dead. All thei that go unto her, returne not againe.'
3   **he himselfe betooke**: alternatively, he betook himself, leading himself into sin.
4   Cf. Jer. 2.6 on the land of Egypt as the wilderness, a desert and wasteland, a dry land, the shadow of death, 'a land that no man passed through, and where no man dwelt'.
5   Una refers to spiritual death in this life: 'dead in trespasses and sinnes, wherein, in time past ye walked, according to the course of this worlde' (Eph. 2.1–2); cf. man's state in hell, v 31.6–7.
7   **onely**: chief, greatest; cf. her use of the term at 43.3. The second use in the line has the adverbial sense, 'specially', 'pre-eminently'. Una first names Duessa here and indicates her duplicity by the repeated phrase.
8   **misseeming**: false appearance, unless **sweete** is a substantive.
9   **Inueigled**: beguiled; more specifically, 'blinded in judgment', from Fr. *aveugle*, alluding to Duessa's relation to Night and Aveugle, v 23.7; cf. xii 32.5.

Stanza 51

3   **dissolute**: enfeebled; relaxed, careless; debauched; and even literally 'dissolved' (*OED* 1): see 7.2*n*.   **dismaid**: see 11.6*n*.
4   **mall**: 'mace' (10.9).
8   **Remedilesse, for aie**: forever without hope of rescue since Orgoglio is **mercilesse** (5).

Stanza 52

6   **acquit**: delivered; inferring the legal sense: he will pay the ransom or debt needed to release the Knight; cf. the use of the word in viii 1.4, and the Boatman's prayer, 'God do vs well acquight' (II xii 3.3).

Cant. VIII.

Faire virgin to redeeme her deare
brings Arthur to the fight:
Who slayes the Gyant, wounds the beast,
and strips Duessa quight.

1

AY me, how many perils doe enfold
The righteous man, to make him daily fall?
Were not, that heauenly grace doth him vphold,
And stedfast truth acquite him out of all.
Her loue is firme, her care continuall,
So oft as he through his owne foolish pride,
Or weaknesse is to sinfull bands made thrall:
Else should this *Redcrosse* knight in bands haue dyde,
For whose deliuerance she this Prince doth thither guide.

2

They sadly traueild thus, vntill they came
Nigh to a castle builded strong and hie:
Then cryde the Dwarfe, lo yonder is the same,
In which my Lord my liege doth lucklesse lie,
Thrall to that Gyants hatefull tyrannie:
Therefore, deare Sir, your mightie powres assay.
The noble knight alighted by and by
From loftie steede, and bad the Ladie stay,
To see what end of fight should him befall that day.

3

So with the Squire, th'admirer of his might,
He marched forth towards that castle wall;
Whose gates he found fast shut, ne liuing wight
To ward the same, nor answere commers call.
Then tooke that Squire an horne of bugle small,
Which hong adowne his side in twisted gold,
And tassels gay.   Wyde wonders ouer all
Of that same hornes great vertues weren told,
Which had approued bene in vses manifold.

4

Was neuer wight, that heard that shrilling sound,
But trembling feare did feele in euery vaine;
Three miles it might be easie heard around,
And Ecchoes three answerd it selfe againe:
No false enchauntment, nor deceiptfull traine
Might once abide the terror of that blast,
But presently was voide and wholly vaine:
No gate so strong, no locke so firme and fast,
But with that percing noise flew open quite, or brast.

Canto viii

Argument

1–2   redeeme: not simply 'rescue' or 'save', but in the religious sense, 'deliver from sin', for Arthur acts as Redeemer. Ironically, Una chose the Red Cross Knight in the hope 'That he my captiue langour should redeeme' (vii 49.2); now she must redeem him. On Arthur's intervention in the eighth canto, as eight is the number of regeneration, see Fowler (1964) 53.

Stanza 1

This testimony to the power and working of Truth in man's life answers the power and working of Deceit as seeming Truth at vii 1. A similar testimony to the power and working of God's grace is given at the corresponding point of Book II.
3   Later Arthur as **heauenly grace** must literally **vphold** the Knight, 40.4–8.
4   acquite: cf. vii 52.6. Una, here identified with Truth, may be said to 'acquite' the Knight when she absolves him from all blame, 42.6–9, 43.3–6, 49.3–5; cf. John 8.32: 'The trueth shal make you fre.'
7   sinfull bands: bondage to sin.
9   Cf. vii 52.9.

Stanza 2

3–6   The climax to the Dwarf's role in Book I. At first he bears Una's needments (i 6.1–4) and then the Knight's armour (vii 19.4–9). Afterwards he guides Una and then Arthur (vii 28.4 and 52.9) to rescue the imprisoned Knight. His gesture marks the mid-point of an action that is completed when Una points to the castle where her parents are imprisoned (xi 3).
6   assay: put to trial; prove.
7   by and by: immediately.

Stanza 3

1   Cf. his later role as the supporter of Arthur's might in battle, 12.7–9.
4   ward: guard.
5   horne of bugle small: hunting-horn made of the horn of a wild ox (bugle).
7   ouer all: everywhere.
8   vertues: powers.
9   approued: proved.

Stanzas 4–5

As Upton (1758) notes, the enchanted horn in Italian romance, in particular the horn of justice given by Logistilla (Reason) to a good Englishman in Ariosto, *Orl. Fur*. xv 14–5, becomes the horn of salvation, the word of God whose 'sounde went out through all the earth' (Rom. 10.18); cf. the ram's horns that signal the shout that brings down the walls of Jericho (Joshua 6.3–20) and the apocalyptic trumpets of Rev. 8–9. Heninger (1959) 176 associates the horn with the trumpet that shall herald the opening of the graves at the Resurrection.

Stanza 4

5   traine: deception.
7   presently: immediately.   **voide**: ineffective, useless.
9   brast: burst open; perhaps, 'shattered'.

5

The same before the Geants gate he blew,
  That all the castle quaked from the ground,
  And euery dore of freewill open flew.
  The Gyant selfe dismaied with that sownd,
  Where he with his *Duessa* dalliance fownd,
  In hast came rushing forth from inner bowre,
  With staring countenance sterne, as one astownd,
  And staggering steps, to weet, what suddein stowre
Had wrought that horror strange, and dar'd his dreaded powre.

6

And after him the proud *Duessa* came,
  High mounted on her manyheaded beast,
  And euery head with fyrie tongue did flame,
  And euery head was crowned on his creast,
  And bloudie mouthed with late cruell feast.
  That when the knight beheld, his mightie shild
  Vpon his manly arme he soone addrest,
  And at him fiercely flew, with courage fild,
And eger greedinesse through euery member thrild.

7

Therewith the Gyant buckled him to fight,
  Inflam'd with scornefull wrath and high disdaine,
  And lifting vp his dreadfull club on hight,
  All arm'd with ragged snubbes and knottie graine,
  Him thought at first encounter to haue slaine.
  But wise and warie was that noble Pere,
  And lightly leaping from so monstrous maine,
  Did faire auoide the violence him nere;
It booted nought, to thinke, such thunderbolts to beare.

8

Ne shame he thought to shunne so hideous might:
  The idle stroke, enforcing furious way,
  Missing the marke of his misaymed sight
  Did fall to ground, and with his heauie sway
  So deepely dinted in the driuen clay,
  That three yardes deepe a furrow vp did throw:
  The sad earth wounded with so sore assay,
  Did grone full grieuous vnderneath the blow,
And trembling with strange feare, did like an earthquake show.

9

As when almightie *Ioue* in wrathfull mood,
  To wreake the guilt of mortall sins is bent,
  Hurles forth his thundring dart with deadly food,
  Enrold in flames, and smouldring dreriment,
  Through riuen cloudes and molten firmament;
  The fierce threeforked engin making way,
  Both loftie towres and highest trees hath rent,
  And all that might his angrie passage stay,
And shooting in the earth, casts vp a mount of clay.

Stanza 5

4–7 Orgoglio is surprised in the same act in which the Red Cross Knight was surprised. In effect, judgment now comes upon the Knight for his sins. **dismaied**: cf. vii 11.6, 51.3. **staring**: glaring in fury. **astownd**: cf. vii 7.7.

8 **stowre**: uproar.

Stanza 6

2–5 See vii 16–17*n*. The **fyrie tongue** (cf. 12.6) belongs to the fire-breathing dragon of folklore. The **crowned . . . creast** is from Rev. 12.3. The detail of the **bloudie mouthed** beast is transferred from the rider, 'the woman drunken with the blood of Saintes, and with the blood of the Martyrs of Jesus' (Rev. 17.6). **late**: as 12.4; apparently with some topical significance; cf. xi 13.4. Percival (1893) suggests the St Bartholomew's Day massacre, 1578, or the executions by Alva's Council of Blood in the Netherlands, 1567.

6–9 Arthur's readiness contrasts at each point with the Red Cross Knight's unpreparedness when he was confronted by Orgoglio.

7 **addrest**: made ready.

9 **eger greedinesse**: intense eagerness for battle; **eger** suggests also 'biting', 'sharp', referring to the piercing effect of the emotion. Hence **thrild**, 'penetrated', is close to the current sense, 'caught up in emotion'. The phrase defines his state of Prays-Desire: see II ix 39; cf. his 'greedie great desire' (29.3).

Stanza 7

2 **disdaine**: indignation, anger; see i 19.6*n*.

4 **snubbes**: root snags; cf. 'snaggy Oke' (vii 10.7).

7–8 The Red Cross Knight's effort ended with his **lightly leaping** away from Orgoglio's blow (cf. vii 12.6) but he could not avoid **the violence him nere**. **maine**: force. See vii 11.2 and *n*. **faire**: quite, 'clean'.

9 A thunderbolt was thought to contain a stone; see Heninger (1960) 76.

Stanza 8

1 **hideous**: immense.

4–6 Alluding to Orgoglio's name: 'orge', from tilling which is also the etymology of George, according to the *Golden Legend*: 'so george is to saye as tilyenge the erthe / that is his flesshe.' See x 66.5–6*n*. **sway**: the impetus of the blow.

7 **sad**: heavy; or as earth is associated with the humour of melancholy; or 'sad' because she is hit by her son. **assay**: attack.

Stanza 9

2 **wreake**: punish. **mortall sins**: the sins of mortals, but also sins which cause (and deserve) death.

3 **food**: feud: hatred, hostility.

4 **smouldring dreriment**: smothering gloom or darkness, in sharp contrast to the **flames**; cf. 'smouldry cloud' (vii 13.8); for 'dreriment', see ii 44.4*n*.

6 **threeforked**: Ovid's *ignes trisulci* (cf. *Met*. ii 848–9). **engin**: machine used in warfare, here a battering-ram; at vii 13 his stroke is compared to a cannon shot.

10

His boystrous club, so buried in the ground,
  He could not rearen vp againe so light,
  But that the knight him at auantage found,
  And whiles he stroue his combred clubbe to quight
  Out of the earth, with blade all burning bright
  He smote off his left arme, which like a blocke
  Did fall to ground, depriu'd of natiue might;
  Large streames of bloud out of the truncked stocke
Forth gushed, like fresh water streame from riuen rocke.

11

Dismaied with so desperate deadly wound,
  And eke impatient of vnwonted paine,
  He loudly brayd with beastly yelling sound,
  That all the fields rebellowed againe;
  As great a noyse, as when in Cymbrian plaine
  An heard of Bulles, whom kindly rage doth sting,
  Do for the milkie mothers want complaine,
  And fill the fields with troublous bellowing,
The neighbour woods arourd with hollow murmur ring.

12

That when his deare *Duessa* heard, and saw
  The euill stownd, that daungerd her estate,
  Vnto his aide she hastily did draw
  Her dreadfull beast, who swolne with bloud of late
  Came ramping forth with proud presumpteous gate,
  And threatned all his heads like flaming brands.
  But him the Squire made quickly to retrate,
  Encountring fierce with single sword in hand,
And twixt him and his Lord did like a bulwarke stand.

13

The proud *Duessa* full of wrathfull spight,
  And fierce disdaine, to be affronted so,
  Enforst her purple beast with all her might
  That stop out of the way to ouerthroe,
  Scorning the let of so vnequall foe:
  But nathemore would that courageous swayne
  To her yeeld passage, gainst his Lord to goe,
  But with outrageous strokes did him restraine,
And with his bodie bard the way atwixt them twaine.

14

Then tooke the angrie witch her golden cup,
  Which still she bore, replete with magick artes;
  Death and despeyre did many thereof sup,
  And secret poyson through their inner parts,
  Th'eternall bale of heauie wounded harts;
  Which after charmes and some enchauntments said,
  She lightly sprinkled on his weaker parts;
  Therewith his sturdie courage soone was quayd,
And all his senses were with suddeine dread dismayd.

15

So downe he fell before the cruell beast,
  Who on his necke his bloudie clawes did seize,
  That life nigh crusht out of his panting brest:
  No powre he had to stirre, nor will to rize.
  That when the carefull knight gan well auise,
  He lightly left the foe, with whom he fought,
  And to the beast gan turne his enterprise;
  For wondrous anguish in his hart it wrought,
To see his loued Squire into such thraldome brought.

110

Stanza 10

1 **boystrous**: massive.
2 **light**: quickly.
3 **at auantage**: in a favourable position.
4 **combred**: encumbered, because held fast in the ground. His mother Earth aids his downfall: as her son and the earthly Adam, he is defeated because he is earthbound.
8–9 As Moses 'lift up his hand, and with his rod he smote the rocke twise, and the water came out abundantly' (Num. 20.11). This allusion, first noted by Percival (1893), is confirmed by **fresh**. **truncked stocke**: truncated stump, referring to the trunk of his body.

Stanza 11

2 **impatient**: unable to bear the suffering (Lat. *impatiens*); cf. 17.4.
3–4 Cf. the 'bellowing' which precedes his appearance at vii 7.4–5.
5 **Cymbrian plaine**: apparently named here for the savage tribe that inhabited the land (Denmark).
6 **kindly rage**: natural lust, for Orgoglio's 'dalliance' (5.5) with Duessa was interrupted by Arthur.
7 **want**: absence. In *2 Tamb.* IV ii 114, Marlowe drably renders S.'s line as 'the females' miss'.
9 **murmur**: complaint.

Stanza 12

2 **stownd**: time of peril. **estate**: state.
4 **of late**: see 6.2–5*n*.
5 **ramping**: bounding.
8 **single sword**: i.e. sword alone, as the Red Cross Knight faced Orgoglio with 'single blade' (vii 11.9); Arthur's further power supplements the Knight's.

Stanza 13

1–2 Cf. Orgoglio's state, 7.2. **affronted**: faced in defiance.
3 **Enforst**: compelled; added (her) force to; cf. the same double meaning at II iv 32.1. The double syntax is noted by Alpers (1967) 86.
5 **let**: obstruction.
6 **nathemore**: not at all.

Stanza 14

1–5 Cf. the great whore upon her scarlet-coloured beast, who 'had a cup of golde in her hand, ful of abominations, and filthines of her fornication. . . . all nations have dronken of the wine of the wrath of her fornication' (Rev. 17.4–18.3); cf. Jer. 51.7. Cf. Fidelia's 'cup of gold' (x 13.2). **still**: always.
3 **Death** and **despeyre** are distinguished: the one is physical; the other leads to spiritual death.
5 **wounded**: i.e. by sin.
7 **weaker**: too weak.
8–9 Cf. the Red Cross Knight's drinking from the poisoned fountain, vii 6. His fall is re-enacted. **quayd**: subdued, daunted.

Stanza 15

2 **seize**: fasten.
4 **nor will**: because his will is infected.
5 **carefull**: full of care for his Squire. **auise**: observe.

16

And high aduauncing his bloud-thirstie blade,
   Stroke one of those deformed heads so sore,
   That of his puissance proud ensample made;
   His monstrous scalpe downe to his teeth it tore,
   And that misformed shape mis-shaped more:
   A sea of bloud gusht from the gaping wound,
   That her gay garments staynd with filthy gore,
   And ouerflowed all the field around;
That ouer shoes in bloud he waded on the ground.

17

Thereat he roared for exceeding paine,
   That to haue heard, great horror would haue bred,
   And scourging th'emptie ayre with his long traine,
   Through great impatience of his grieued hed
   His gorgeous ryder from her loftie sted
   Would haue cast downe, and trod in durtie myre,
   Had not the Gyant soone her succoured;
   Who all enrag'd with smart and franticke yre,
Came hurtling in full fierce, and forst the knight retyre.

18

The force, which wont in two to be disperst,
   In one alone left hand he now vnites,
   Which is through rage more strong then both were erst;
   With which his hideous club aloft he dites,
   And at his foe with furious rigour smites,
   That strongest Oake might seeme to ouerthrow:
   The stroke vpon his shield so heauie lites,
   That to the ground it doubleth him full low:
What mortall wight could euer beare so monstrous blow?

19

And in his fall his shield, that couered was,
   Did loose his vele by chaunce, and open flew:
   The light whereof, that heauens light did pas,
   Such blazing brightnesse through the aier threw,
   That eye mote not the same endure to vew.
   Which when the Gyaunt spyde with staring eye,
   He downe let fall his arme, and soft withdrew
   His weapon huge, that heaued was on hye
For to haue slaine the man, that on the ground did lye.

20

And eke the fruitfull-headed beast, amaz'd
   At flashing beames of that sunshiny shield,
   Became starke blind, and all his senses daz'd,
   That downe he tumbled on the durtie field,
   And seem'd himselfe as conquered to yield.
   Whom when his maistresse proud perceiu'd to fall,
   Whiles yet his feeble feet for faintnesse reeld,
   Vnto the Gyant loudly she gan call,
O helpe *Orgoglio*, helpe, or else we perish all.

Stanza 16
1   **aduauncing**: lifting up.
2–6   Cf. Rev. 13.3: 'And I sawe one of his heads as it were wounded to death.' This stroke is only a warning (**ensample**) of what will happen to the Dragon's **puissance proud**, for the rest of the verse in Scripture tells us that the head heals. The stroke is a token of God's promise that the seed of man 'shal breake thine [the Serpent's] head' (Gen. 3.15).
4   **scalpe**: skull.
5   **misformed**: suggesting also 'formed for evil'; cf. 'misformed spright' (i 55.9).

Stanza 17
3   **traine**: tail.
4   **impatience**: inability to endure suffering; cf. 11.2. **grieued**: afflicted with pain, injured.
5   **sted**: place.
9   **hurtling**: see iv 16.3*n*.

Stanza 18
2   **left**: i.e. remaining.
4   **hideous**: huge.   **dites**: lifts; makes ready to strike by lifting.
5   **rigour**: violence.
7   **lites**: strikes.
8   **doubleth**: suggesting a play on the giant's doubled force.
9   The question suggests its answer: no merely mortal man could.

Stanza 19
S.'s source is the enchanted shield in Ariosto, *Orl. Fur.* xxii 84–6 (cf. ii 55–6, viii 11), radically adapted to his religious allegory; see vii 33.5–9*n*, 35.3–4*n*.
2   **vele**: this term for 'covering' links the shield with the brightness of Una's face (cf. vi 4, xii 21–22) when her veil is removed; cf. the veil of the Temple which was rent at Christ's crucifixion (Matt. 27.51) to signify 'an end of all the ceremonies of the Lawe' (Geneva gloss).
3   **pas**: surpass, indicating supernatural power; cf. Lucifera's throne which shines 'as bright as sunny day' (iv 8.2). The line refers to the coming of Christ: 'then shal the wicked man be reueiled, whome the Lord shal consume with the Spirit of his mouth, and shal abolish with the brightnes of his comming' (2 Thess. 2.8). Paul's amplification, 'even him whose comming is by the working of Satan', suggests why the Giant should cause the shield to be uncovered.
4   The internal echo, **through . . . threw**, displays the light's bursting violence.
7   **soft**: after the bellowing, the stalking steps, and the violence, this word modulates the action to a close.
8–9   The precise gesture at the Red Cross Knight's defeat, vii 14.2–3.

Stanza 20
5   **seem'd . . . to yield**: by falling prostrate, he seems to submit himself to Arthur. The wounded dragon is not slain until the Red Cross Knight's apocalyptic battle in Canto xi.
9   Orgoglio is first named in her cry of triumph, vii 14.5, and now for the second time in her cry of defeat.

21

At her so pitteous cry was much amoou'd
　　Her champion stout, and for to ayde his frend,
　　Againe his wonted angry weapon proou'd:
　　But all in vaine: for he has read his end
　　In that bright shield, and all their forces spend
　　Themselues in vaine: for since that glauncing sight,
　　He hath no powre to hurt, nor to defend;
　　As where th'Almighties lightning brond does light,
It dimmes the dazed eyen, and daunts the senses quight.

22

Whom when the Prince, to battell new addrest,
　　And threatning high his dreadfull stroke did see,
　　His sparkling blade about his head he blest,
　　And smote off quite his right leg by the knee,
　　That downe he tombled; as an aged tree,
　　High growing on the top of rocky clift,
　　Whose hartstrings with keene steele nigh hewen be,
　　The mightie trunck halfe rent, with ragged rift
Doth roll adowne the rocks, and fall with fearefull drift.

23

Or as a Castle reared high and round,
　　By subtile engins and malitious slight
　　Is vndermined from the lowest ground,
　　And her foundation forst, and feebled quight,
　　At last downe falles, and with her heaped hight
　　Her hastie ruine does more heauie make,
　　And yields it selfe vnto the victours might;
　　Such was this Gyaunts fall, that seemd to shake
The stedfast globe of earth, as it for feare did quake.

24

The knight then lightly leaping to the pray,
　　With mortall steele him smot againe so sore,
　　That headlesse his vnweldy bodie lay,
　　All wallowd in his owne fowle bloudy gore,
　　Which flowed from his wounds in wondrous store.
　　But soone as breath out of his breast did pas,
　　That huge great body, which the Gyaunt bore,
　　Was vanisht quite, and of that monstrous mas
Was nothing left, but like an emptie bladder was.

25

Whose grieuous fall, when false *Duessa* spide,
　　Her golden cup she cast vnto the ground,
　　And crowned mitre rudely threw aside;
　　Such percing griefe her stubborne hart did wound,
　　That she could not endure that dolefull stound,
　　But leauing all behind her, fled away:
　　The light-foot Squire her quickly turnd around,
　　And by hard meanes enforcing her to stay,
So brought vnto his Lord, as his deserued pray.

26

The royall Virgin, which beheld from farre,
　　In pensiue plight, and sad perplexitie,
　　The whole athcieuement of this doubtfull warre,
　　Came running fast to greet his victorie,
　　With sober gladnesse, and myld modestie,
　　And with sweet ioyous cheare him thus bespake;
　　Faire braunch of noblesse, flowre of cheualrie,
　　That with your worth the world amazed make,
How shall I quite the paines, ye suffer for my sake?

Stanza 21

2　**frend**: paramour.
3　**proou'd**: tried, i.e. tried to strike (cf. 22.2).
6　**glauncing**: flashing, dazzling; cf. vii 29.5.
8–9　**Almighties**: in contrast to the pagan 'almightie *Ioue*' (9.1) to whose thunderbolt the Giant's blow is compared. **light**: descend; shine.　**dazed**: dazzled.

Stanza 22

The battle is renewed from stanza 18 to allow Arthur to triumph as though by his own power.
3　**blest**: brandished; making the sign of the cross in the air.
5–9　S. imitates the well-known simile in Virgil, *Aen*. ii 626–31, in which the fall of Troy is compared to the felling of an ancient ash.
8　**rift**: splitting.
9　**drift**: impetus.

Stanza 23

2　**subtile engins**: cleverly devised machines of warfare. **malitious slight**: clever strategy.
4　**forst**: broken open.
6　**ruine**: the action of falling (Lat. *ruina*).
8–9　A climactic assertion of the earth's terror before her son; see vii 7.6, 8.6, viii 8.7–9.

Stanza 24

8–9　Orgoglio is dismissed with an etymological play upon his name: see vii 9.8n. As Kellogg and Steele (1965) note, Chaucer's Saint Cecile dismisses her persecutor's power because 'every mortal mannes power nys / But lyk a bladdre ful of wynd, ywys' (*Second Nun's Tale* 438–9).

Stanza 25

1　**fall . . . false**: the internal echo suggests her own fall.
3　**crowned mitre**: the Papal 'triple crowne' of vii 16.4. **rudely**: violently.

Stanza 26

2　**pensiue**: anxious.　**perplexitie**: anguish.
3　**doubtfull**: also 'dreaded'.
4　**greet**: offer congratulations on; cf. i 27.2.
5　**myld**: gracious.
9　**quite**: repay.　**for my sake**: cf. ix 2.8, xi 1.8.

27

And you fresh bud of vertue springing fast,
   Whom these sad eyes saw nigh vnto deaths dore,
   What hath poore Virgin for such perill past,
   Wherewith you to reward?   Accept therefore
   My simple selfe, and seruice euermore;
   And he that high does sit, and all things see
   With equall eyes, their merites to restore,
   Behold what ye this day haue done for mee,
And what I cannot quite, requite with vsuree.

28

But sith the heauens, and your faire hándeling
   Haue made you maister of the field this day,
   Your fortune maister eke with gouerning,
   And well begun end all so well, I pray,
   Ne let that wicked woman scape away;
   For she it is, that did my Lord bethrall,
   My dearest Lord, and deepe in dongeon lay,
   Where he his better dayes hath wasted all.
O heare, how piteous he to you for ayd does call.

29

Forthwith he gaue in charge vnto his Squire,
   That scarlot whore to keepen carefully;
   Whiles he himselfe with greedie great desire
   Into the Castle entred forcibly,
   Where liuing creature none he did espye;
   Then gan he lowdly through the house to call:
   But no man car'd to answere to his crye.
   There raignd a solemne silence ouer all,
Nor voice was heard, nor wight was seene in bowre or hall.

30

At last with creeping crooked pace forth came
   An old old man, with beard as white as snow,
   That on a staffe his feeble steps did frame,
   And guide his wearie gate both too and fro:
   For his eye sight him failed long ygo,
   And on his arme a bounch of keyes he bore,
   The which vnused rust did ouergrow:
   Those were the keyes of euery inner dore,
But he could not them vse, but kept them still in store.

Stanza 27

1   She addresses the Squire who is the **bud** to the 'flowre'
(26.7).   **vertue**: manliness, valour.

3–5   **poore Virgin**: a poignant use of 'Virgin', recognizing
that the whore Duessa could easily reward her benefactors.
Una displays mature innocence in thus offering her **seruice**.

7   **equall**: impartial, just.   **restore**: make amends for,
compensate. This argument drives the Red Cross Knight to
despair, ix 47.1–2, for **merites** bears the double sense: due
reward, due punishment; cf. the theological sense: 'good
works'. Another possible reading is: 'to replace (mankind) in a
state of grace' (*OED* 4a); then 'merites' would refer to the
qualities lost by the Fall. Either way the Knight is weighed
and found wanting.

8   **Behold**: the optative, 'may He behold'; uttered, as she is
the true Church, in a tone of authority.

9   **vsuree**: interest.

Stanza 28

3   The fine distinction is worth making: the heavens and his
own skill have made him master of the field; now he alone must
master his fortune by exercising the function of government.

4   **all so**: just as.

6–7   Cf. xii 33.7–9.

8   **his better dayes**: the better part of his life. Percival
(1893) prefers the weaker sense: days 'that might have been
better spent'.   **wasted**: consumed, destroyed; see ii 42.9*n*.

Stanza 29

3   **greedie great desire**: see 6.6–9*n*.

6   **house**: the place of the dead, as Job 30.23.

8   **a solemne silence**: cf. the emptiness of Virgil's underworld where Aeneas goes *perque domos Ditis vacuas et inania
regna* (*Aen.* vi 269); cf. also III xi 53.5–7. Such awe-inspiring
silence is the precise antithetical point to the 'solemne feast'
(xii 40.2) which celebrates the Knight's marriage to Una. It is
the still point of unbearable suspense before turning from
death to life.

Stanza 30

1   The movement of this line mimics the sense.

3   **frame**: support, direct.

5   Cf. Corceca's blindness of heart, iii 18.4*n*.

6–9   The **keyes** are the 'keye of the bottomles pit' given the
fallen angel, Rev. 9.1; the Geneva gloss adds: 'This autoritie
chiefly is committed to the Pope in signe whereof he beareth
the keyes in his armes'. Cf. x 50.7.

7   **vnused rust**: rusty because unused.

8   **euery**: every one, that is, except the iron door (37.3–5)
for which he has no key.

9   **in store**: laid up for future use.

31

But very vncouth sight was to behold,
    How he did fashion his vntoward pace,
    For as he forward moou'd his footing old,
    So backward still was turnd his wrincled face,
    Vnlike to men, who euer as they trace,
    Both feet and face one way are wont to lead.
    This was the auncient keeper of that place,
    And foster father of the Gyant dead;
His name *Ignaro* did his nature right aread.

32

His reuerend haires and holy grauitie
    The knight much honord, as beseemed well,
    And gently askt, where all the people bee,
    Which in that stately building wont to dwell.
    Who answerd him full soft, he could not tell.
    Againe he askt, where that same knight was layd,
    Whom great *Orgoglio* with his puissaunce fell
    Had made his caytiue thrall; againe he sayde,
He could not tell: ne euer other answere made.

33

Then asked he, which way he in might pas:
    He could not tell, againe he answered.
    Thereat the curteous knight displeased was,
    And said, Old sire, it seemes thou hast not red
    How ill it sits with that same siluer hed
    In vaine to mocke, or mockt in vaine to bee:
    But if thou be, as thou art pourtrahed
    With natures pen, in ages graue degree,
Aread in grauer wise, what I demaund of thee.

34

His answere likewise was, he could not tell.
    Whose sencelesse speach, and doted ignorance
    When as the noble Prince had marked well,
    He ghest his nature by his countenance,
    And calmd his wrath with goodly temperance.
    Then to him stepping, from his arme did reach
    Those keyes, and made himselfe free enterance.
    Each dore he opened without any breach;
There was no barre to stop, nor foe him to empeach.

35

There all within full rich arayd he found,
    With royall arras and resplendent gold.
    And did with store of euery thing abound,
    That greatest Princes presence might behold.
    But all the floore (too filthy to be told)
    With blood of guiltlesse babes, and innocents trew,
    Which there were slaine, as sheepe out of the fold,
    Defiled was, that dreadfull was to vew,
And sacred ashes ouer it was strowed new.

Stanza 31

1   **vncouth**: strange; repellent; indecorous.
2   **vntoward**: awkward, because he comes toward while he looks back, as though going un-toward.
5–6   While we do not need to be told that men look where they go, an allegorist must tell us to clarify the nature of Ignorance; see Isaiah 44.25: God declares that he will 'turne the wise men backward, and make their knowledge foolishnes'. **trace**: walk.
8   **foster father**: i.e. nourishing father. Though born of earth and wind, Orgoglio is nourished by Ignorance.
9   **Ignaro**: Ignorance, for 'he could not tell' in replying to Arthur's queries. He is Bunyan's Ignorance after having been whisked to Hell; specifically here, ignorance of the true faith; hence his association with the papacy and pride. Comes (1616) III xii describes the ignorance and malice of man as the night of the mind, and the parents and nurse of all the plagues which afflict man. Füger (1971) traces the traditional meanings given Ignorance as a concept, as a figure in interludes, and as a porter or watchman.   **aread**: declare.

Stanza 32

3   **gently**: courteously.
8   **caytiue**: captive; also 'wretched'; cf. v 45.9.

Stanza 33

3   **curteous**: his title at ix 7.8. While he includes all the virtues in himself – see *L.R.* – he is named for the culminating virtue of Book VI.
4   **red**: perceived, learned.
5   **sits**: agrees.
7   **pourtrahed**: an etymological spelling (from Lat. *protrahere*, to draw forth).
8   **ages graue degree**: stage of life at which 'grauitie' (32.1) is befitting. Similarly, Duessa's ugliness is judged 'as in hate of honorable eld' (47.2).
9   **Aread**: declare.   **demaund**: inquire, rather than the discourteous 'ask peremptorily'.

Stanza 34

1   The implication is that he does not know himself whether he is as he appears.
2   **doted**: stupid.
4   **countenance**: behaviour.
5   **temperance**: Book II's virtue of temperance is first associated with Arthur; see ix 18.6*n*.
8–9   **breach**: breaking down, because **There was no barre to stop**; interruption, because there was no **foe him to empeach** (hinder).

Stanza 35

1–4   **arayd . . . behold**: equipped with all that the greatest prince would find worthy to behold, or that would befit a prince's court.
6   **innocents trew**: applied to all Christian martyrs but particularly to the first, Matt. 2.16; the innocents are the counterparts to the proud tyrants held in Lucifera's dungeon, v 46–51.
9   **sacred**: accursed, being used in some profane ritual to soak up 'true Christians blood' (36.3); hallowed, being the ashes of 'holy Martyrs' (36.4).

36

And there beside of marble stone was built
  An Altare, caru'd with cunning imagery,
  On which true Christians bloud was often spilt,
  And holy Martyrs often doen to dye,
  With cruell malice and strong tyranny:
  Whose blessed sprites from vnderneath the stone
  To God for vengeance cryde continually,
And with great griefe were often heard to grone,
That hardest heart would bleede, to heare their piteous mone.

37

Through euery rowme he sought, and euery bowr,
  But no where could he find that wofull thrall:
  At last he came vnto an yron doore,
  That fast was lockt, but key found not at all
  Emongst that bounch, to open it withall;
  But in the same a little grate was pight,
  Through which he sent his voyce, and lowd did call
With all his powre, to weet, if liuing wight
Were housed therewithin, whom he enlargen might.

38

Therewith an hollow, dreary, murmuring voyce
  These piteous plaints and dolours did resound;
  O who is that, which brings me happy choyce
  Of death, that here lye dying euery stound,
  Yet liue perforce in balefull darkenesse bound?
  For now three Moones haue changed thrice their hew,
  And haue beene thrice hid vnderneath the ground,
  Since I the heauens chearefull face did vew,
O welcome thou, that doest of death bring tydings trew.

39

Which when that Champion heard, with percing point
  Of pitty deare his hart was thrilled sore,
  And trembling horrour ran through euery ioynt,
  For ruth of gentle knight so fowle forlore:
  Which shaking off, he rent that yron dore,
  With furious force, and indignation fell;
  Where entred in, his foot could find no flore,
  But all a deepe descent, as darke as hell,
That breathed euer forth a filthie banefull smell.

Stanza 36
Rev. 6.9–10: 'I sawe under the altar the soules of them, that
were killed for the worde of God, and for the testimonie which
they mainteined. And they cryed with a lowde voyce, saying,
How long, Lord, holie and true! doest not thou judge and
avenge our blood on them that dwell on the earth?'

2 **imagery**: images.

Stanza 37
1 **bowr**: an inner private room.
3 **yron doore**: cf. Ps. 107.16: 'For he hathe broken the
gates of brasse, and brast the barres of yron asundre.'
6 **grate**: symbolizing the ear through which God's word
comes to free man.   **pight**: placed.
9 **enlargen**: set at large.

Stanza 38
1 **murmuring**: repining.
2 **dolours**: lamentations.
3–9 The Knight's outburst contrasts with his silence
throughout his adventures. His cry for aid is reported at 28.9.
He spoke to Sansjoy (v 13.1–4) and earlier to Fradubio
(ii 43.1–2, 6–7). He does not speak again until ix 17.
3–4 **choyce / Of death**: the chance or right to choose
death. He speaks ironically, implying 'What choice do I have:
death or a living death?'; or in despair: 'Now I may choose
death.' To be free means to him to be free to die. Since freeing
his body does not free his mind, he will meet Despair who
reminds him when he 'for death so oft did call' (ix 45.6).
At x 27.9, he is called 'The man that would not liue'. Cf. his
seeking death in the Despair episode (ix 51), in the house of
Penance (x 21–22), on the hill of Contemplation (x 63.1–5),
and in his battle against the Dragon (xi 28.4). He echoes Paul's
cry: 'O wretched man that I am, who shal deliver me from the
bodie of this death' (Rom. 7.24).
4–5 His state is that of despair (cf. ix 54.8–9) or the living
death which is hell: 'he in hell doth lie, / That liues a loathed
life, and wishing cannot die' (IV vii 11.8–9). He is among those
'that dwell in darkenes and in the shadowe of death, being
bounde in miserie and yron, because they rebelled against the
wordes of the Lord' (Ps. 107.10–1). Yet the Psalmist continues: 'Then they cryed unto the Lord in their trouble, and he
delivered them from their distres. He broght them out of
darkenes, and out of the shadowe of death, and brake their
bands asunder' (13–4).   **stound**: moment.   **balefull**: full
of evil; full of suffering.
6–7 Possibly three months but most likely nine (3×3), the
period of gestation (cf. II i 53) which leads to fulfilment (cf.
IV vi 43.9) or rebirth; cf. ix 15.9n. (The three-month period is
clearly expressed at II ii 44.1–2.)
9 Cf. his state at the beginning: 'all so deare as life is to my
hart, / I deeme your loue' (i 54.2–3).

Stanza 39
2 **deare**: heart-felt; grievous, dire.
3 **trembling horrour**: the adj. stresses the Lat. sense of
'horrour', shuddering.
4 **fowle forlore**: grievously lost, doomed to destruction;
cf. 'this man forlorne' (vii 10.5).
5 **Which shaking off, he rent . . .**: horror paralyses (cf.
ii 31.9) and by shaking it off, he may shake off the door.
Woodhouse (1965) 24 interprets the act as the irresistible
violence of grace.
7–9 **Where entred in . . .**: the bottomless pit of hell (Rev.
9.2, etc.) with its thick smoke; cf. the Dragon's mouth, xi 12.9.
breathed suggests the beast of the abyss, Rev. 11.7.
banefull: poisonous; cf. the creed, 'he descended into hell';
also Eph. 4.9: 'He had also descended first into the lowest
partes of the earth.' Stench is a traditional feature of hell.

40

But neither darkenesse fowle, nor filthy bands,
  Nor noyous smell his purpose could withhold,
  (Entire affection hateth nicer hands)
But that with constant zeale, and courage bold,
After long paines and labours manifold,
He found the meanes that Prisoner vp to reare;
  Whose feeble thighes, vnhable to vphold
His pined corse, him scarse to light could beare,
A vefull spectacle of death and ghastly drere.

41

His sad dull eyes deepe sunck in hollow pits,
  Could not endure th'vnwonted sunne to view;
His bare thin cheekes for want of better bits,
  And empty sides deceiued of their dew,
  Could make a stony hart his hap to rew;
His rawbone armes, whose mighty brawned bowrs
Were wont to riue steele plates, and helmets hew,
  Were cleane consum'd, and all his vitall powres
Decayd, and all his flesh shronk vp like withered flowres.

42

Whom when his Lady saw, to him she ran
  With hasty ioy: to see him made her glad,
And sad to view his visage pale and wan,
  Who earst in flowres of freshest youth was clad.
Tho when her well of teares she wasted had,
  She said, Ah dearest Lord, what euill starre
On you hath fround, and pourd his influence bad,
  That of your selfe ye thus berobbed arre,
And this misseeming hew your manly looks doth marre?

43

But welcome now my Lord, in wele or woe,
  Whose presence I haue lackt too long a day;
And fie on Fortune mine auowed foe,
  Whose wrathfull wreakes them selues do now alay.
And for these wrongs shall treble penaunce pay
Of treble good: good growes of euils priefe.
  The chearelesse man, whom sorrow did dismay,
Had no delight to treaten of his griefe;
His long endured famine needed more reliefe.

44

Faire Lady, then said that victorious knight,
  The things, that grieuous were to do, or beare,
Them to renew, I wote, breeds no delight;
  Best musicke breeds delight in loathing eare:
But th'onely good, that growes of passed feare,
Is to be wise, and ware of like ageín.
This dayes ensample hath this lesson deare
Deepe written in my heart with yron pen,
That blisse may not abide in state of mortall men.

Stanza 40

The fortieth stanza is chosen for the Knight's redemption
because that number marks the limit of wandering: the children
of Israel wandered forty years in the wilderness (Josh. 5.6)
and Christ wandered forty days in the wilderness (Mark 1.13).

Cf. the forty weeks of gestation. See II viii 40*n*.
1   **bands**: bonds.
2   **noyous**: noxious.
3   **Entire**: sincere; total; perfect. Cf. II ii 3.3, vi 46.2, IV
viii 22.7, V i 27.9.   **nicer**: too fastidious.
4–6   **long paines and labours manifold**: these are not
spelled out, but when Christ descended into hell he 'preached
unto the spirits that were in prison' (1 Pet. 3.19). In *Mansus* 81
Milton speaks of Arthur waging his wars even beneath the
earth: *Arturumque etiam sub terris bella mouentem.*
8   **pined corse**: wasted body; cf. ix 35.8.   **to light**: with
the secondary sense: to Una who is 'full of heauenly light'
(ix 17.3).
9   **drere**: sadness, wretchedness.

Stanza 41

3   **better bits**: proper food; more precisely, larger bites of
food to fill out his cheeks.
4   **deceiued of**: cheated out of.
6   **brawned bowrs**: brawny muscles.

Stanza 42

1   **his Lady**: see vii 7.1*n*.
3   **wan**: expressing his state of wanhope or despair; see ix
22.4–5*n*.
7   **influence**: referring to astral influence or power, the
fluid flowing from the stars which determines man's destiny.
9   **misseeming hew**: unseemly appearance.

Stanza 43

1   In welcoming him as her lord whether in his former well-
being or in his present woeful state, she renews the marriage
vow, 'in sickness or in health'.
3   In her love for the Knight, she has blamed an evil star for
his plight, rather than him; and to absolve him further, she
blames Fortune for her plight, rather than Duessa, who truly
is her **auowed foe** (cf. vii 50.7).
4   **wreakes**: acts of vengeance; also acts that vent her wrath.
5   **penaunce**: satisfaction.
6   By her counsel, she seeks to rescue him from despair.
of euils priefe: through experiencing evil.
8   **griefe**: mental pain, distress. His state is that of Sansjoy.

Stanza 44

3   **renew**: go over again.
4   **delight**: 'dislike' suggested Jortin (1734). Cf. Prov.
25.20: 'He that taketh away the garment in the colde season is
. . . like him that singeth songs to an heauie heart'. Church
(1758) reads 'no delight': 'Even *Harmony* is displeasing when
the Ear is out of tune.' Cf. Ecclus. 22.6: 'A tale out of time is
as musicke in mourning.' Grosart (1882–4) finds an antithesis
between music which soothes the mind and a relation of past
grief which does not. Possible readings are: 'music best breeds
delight, not a recital of grievous matters'; or 'only best music,
not a recital etc., may breed delight'. *Var*. editors support
'delight'.
5   **onely**: chief.
6   **ware**: wary; beware.
7   **deare**: grievous, dire; cf. 39.2.
8   **yron pen**: a biblical phrase; cf. Job 19.24.
9   Cf. vii 23.6, III i 10.7, V iii 9.1, VI xi 1.7; also the refrain,
'Nothing is sure, that growes on earthly ground' (I ix 11.5;
cf. II ix 21.9, xi 30.3–4).

45

Henceforth sir knight, take to you wonted strength,
  And maister these mishaps with patient might;
  Loe where your foe lyes stretcht in monstrous length,
  And loe that wicked woman in your sight,
  The roote of all your care, and wretched plight,
  Now in your powre, to let her liue, or dye.
  To do her dye (quoth *Vna*) were despight,
  And shame t'auenge so weake an enimy;
But spoile her of her scarlot robe, and let her fly.

46

So as she bad, that witch they disaraid,
  And robd of royall robes, and purple pall,
  And ornaments that richly were displaid;
  Ne spared they to strip her naked all.
  Then when they had despoild her tire and call,
  Such as she was, their eyes might her behold,
  That her misshaped parts did them appall,
  A loathly, wrinckled hag, ill fauoured, old,
Whose secret filth good manners biddeth not be told.

47

Her craftie head was altogether bald,
  And as in hate of honorable eld,
  Was ouergrowne with scurfe and filthy scald;
  Her teeth out of her rotten gummes were feld,
  And her sowre breath abhominably smeld;
  Her dried dugs, like bladders lacking wind,
  Hong downe, and filthy matter from them weld;
  Her wrizled skin as rough, as maple rind,
So scabby was, that would haue loathd all womankind.

48

Her neather parts, the shame of all her kind,
  My chaster Muse for shame doth blush to write;
  But at her rompe she growing had behind
  A foxes taile, with dong all fowly dight;
  And eke her feete most monstrous were in sight;
  For one of them was like an Eagles claw,
  With griping talaunts armd to greedy fight,
  The other like a Beares vneuen paw:
More vgly shape yet neuer liuing creature saw.

49

Which when the knights beheld, amazd they were,
  And wondred at so fowle deformed wight.
  Such then (said *Vna*) as she seemeth here,
  Such is the face of falshood, such the sight
  Of fowle *Duessa*, when her borrowed light
  Is laid away, and counterfesaunce knowne.
  Thus when they had the witch disrobed quight,
  And all her filthy feature open showne,
They let her goe at will, and wander wayes vnknowne.

Stanza 45
5 **care**: trouble, grief.
7–9 As Christ came to destroy 'the workes of the devil',
not the devil himself (1 John 3.8); acts of vindictiveness
(**despight**) out of desire for vengeance are the works of Duessa.

Stanzas 46–48
S.'s literary analogue is Ariosto, *Orl. Fur.* vii 72–4, which
describes the ugliness of the witch Alcina beneath her beauty.
His source is Scripture: Rev. 17.16, 18.16 tells of the time
when the great whore shall be made 'desolate [i.e. laid waste]
and naked . . . the great citie, that was clothed in fine linen and
purple, and skarlet, and guilded with golde'; cf. Isaiah 3.17–24:
'Therefore shal the Lord make the heads of the daughters of
Zion balde, and the Lord shal discover their secret partes. In
that day shal the Lord take away . . . the calles, and the round
tyres . . . And in stead of swete savour, there shalbe stinke, and
in stead of a girdle, a rent, and in stead of dressing of the
heere, baldnes . . . and burning in stead of beautie.' See
Hankins (1971) 101.

Stanza 46
1 **they**: said to be Prince Arthur alone at II i 22.6–7.
5 **tire and call**: head-dress; or attire and head-dress.

Stanza 47
2 **as in hate . . .**: i.e. such as would cause hatred for those
whose old age would otherwise claim honour, as Upton (1758)
suggests; or, in contempt of honourable age.
3 **scurfe**: scabs. **scald**: scall, a scabby disease of the
scalp.
4 The one detail taken from Ariosto; S. adds the **rotten
gummes**. **feld**: fallen.
5 **abhominably**: the spelling preserves the etymological
sense, Lat. *ab homine*, from man, and hence like a beast.
8 **wrizled**: wrinkled. **maple**: 'seeldom inward sound'
(i 9.9).
9 **scabby**: indicates God's curse, Deut. 28.27. A symptom
of syphilis in Fracastorius, *Syphilis*. **haue loathd**: i.e.
caused loathing in or of.

Stanza 48
2 **chaster**: too chaste; but not too chaste to continue with a
But.
3–9 The animal imagery is conventional: the crafty fox, the
predatory eagle, the cruel bear. She is a blazon of craftiness
from her 'craftie head' (47.1) to tail, her tail being emphasized
as she is a whore. Rowland (1973) 78 notes that the fox's outstretched tail appears to have symbolized fraud. **talaunts**:
talons. **vneuen**: rugged, rough; cf. the beast from the sea
with 'fete like a beares' (Rev. 13.2).

Stanza 49
3–4 Cf. v 26.6.
5 **borrowed light**: cf. the later description: 'of proud
ornaments / And borrow'd beautie spoyld' (II i 22.6–7).
6 **counterfesaunce**: deceit, dissimulation. Coined from Fr.
contrefaisance: literally, false face, as she is exposed in her
falshood (4); cf. Fr. *contrefaict*, 'counterfeit, deformed'
(Cotgrave, 1611).
8 **feature**: shape, body.

50

She flying fast from heauens hated face,
    And from the world that her discouered wide,
    Fled to the wastfull wildernesse apace,
    From liuing eyes her open shame to hide,
    And lurkt in rocks and caues long vnespide.
    But that faire crew of knights, and *Vna* faire
    Did in that castle afterwards abide,
    To rest them selues, and weary powres repaire,
Where store they found of all, that dainty was and rare.

Cant. IX.

His loues and lignage Arthur tells :
The knights knit friendly bands :
Sir Treuisan flies from Despayre,
Whom Redcrosse knight withstands.

1

O Goodly golden chaine, wherewith yfere
    The vertues linked are in louely wize :
    And noble minds of yore allyed were,
    In braue poursuit of cheualrous emprize,
    That none did others safety despize,
    Nor aid enuy to him, in need that stands,
    But friendly each did others prayse deuize
    How to aduaunce with fauourable hands,
As this good Prince redeemd the *Redcrosse* knight from bands.

2

Who when their powres, empaird through labour long,
    With dew repast they had recured well,
    And that weake captiue wight now wexed strong,
    Them list no lenger there at leasure dwell,
    But forward fare, as their aduentures fell,
    But ere they parted, *Vna* faire besought
    That straunger knight his name and nation tell ;
    Least so great good, as he for her had wrought,
Should die vnknown, and buried be in thanklesse thought.

3

Faire virgin (said the Prince) ye me require
    A thing without the compas of my wit :
    For both the lignage and the certain Sire,
    From which I sprong, from me are hidden yit.
    For all so soone as life did me admit
    Into this world, and shewed heauens light,
    From mothers pap I taken was vnfit :
    And streight deliuered to a Faery knight,
To be vpbrought in gentle thewes and martiall might.

Stanza 50

3   **wastfull** : desolate. The line echoes Rev. 12.6 on 'the woman fled into wildernes', which had been Una's state before it was Duessa's : see iii 3.4. Their states are now reversed.
6   **crew** : company ; used for the first time without any pejorative suggestions.
9   **dainty** : precious.

Canto ix

Argument

2   **bands**] hands *1590* (corr. *F.E.*). The uncorrected reading is supported by 1.8 and 'right hands together ioynd' (18.9) ; but **friendly bands** contrast with the 'bands' (1.9) which had bound the Knight (cf. viii 1.7, 40.1).

Stanza 1

1–2   **golden chaine** : derives ultimately from that golden chain by which Homer's Zeus threatens to draw up the entire universe into Olympus (*Iliad* viii 18–27), interpreted by commentators as a symbol of universal concord ; cf. the 'golden chaine of concord' (III i 12.8) and the works of Concord (IV x 35). See v 25.5*n*, II vii 46.2*n*. S.'s chain which links in loving manner (**in louely wize**) suggests Chaucer's 'faire cheyne of love' (*Knight's Tale* 2988) which links the elements. It symbolizes the linking of the virtues in Arthur whose virtue of magnificence 'is the perfection of all the rest, and conteineth in it them all' (*L.R.*). The linking of the virtues is shown by the relationship of the Books and the structure of the whole poem.
4   **emprize** : adventure, Ariosto's *l'audaci imprese* (*Orl. Fur.* i 2) ; chivalric undertaking that brings renown and glory.
5   **despize** : disregard, set at nought.
6   **enuy** : refuse to give.

Stanza 2

1–3   Yet see 20.4–9*n*; also x 18.1–2*n*.   **repast** : refreshment and repose.   **recured** : restored to health.
8   Arthur's rescue of the Red Cross Knight is interpreted as a service to Una rather than to the Knight ; cf. viii 26.9.

Stanza 3

1   **require** : ask.
2   **without** : beyond.
7   **vnfit** : because not weaned. In Malory 11 'sir Ectors wyf nourysshed hym with her owne pappe'.
9   **gentle thewes** : 'vertuous lore' (4.9), manners and qualities befitting one of noble birth. His education corresponds on the secular level to that given the heavenly virtues, x 4.3–4.

4

Vnto old *Timon* he me brought byliue,
  Old *Timon*, who in youthly yeares hath beene
  In warlike feates th'expertest man aliue,
  And is the wisest now on earth I weene;
  His dwelling is low in a valley greene,
  Vnder the foot of *Rauran* mossy hore,
  From whence the riuer *Dee* as siluer cleene
His tombling billowes rolls with gentle rore:
There all my dayes he traind me vp in vertuous lore.

5

Thither the great Magicien *Merlin* came,
  As was his vse, ofttimes to visit me:
  For he had charge my discipline to frame,
  And Tutours nouriture to ouersee.
  Him oft and oft I askt in priuitie,
  Of what loines and what lignage I did spring:
  Whose aunswere bad me still assured bee,
  That I was sonne and heire vnto a king,
As time in her iust terme the truth to light should bring.

6

Well worthy impe, said then the Lady gent,
  And Pupill fit for such a Tutours hand.
  But what aduenture, or what high intent
  Hath brought you hither into Faery land,
  Aread Prince *Arthur*, crowne of Martiall band?
  Full hard it is (quoth he) to read aright
  The course of heauenly cause, or vnderstand
  The secret meaning of th'eternall might,
That rules mens wayes, and rules the thoughts of liuing wight.

7

For whither he through fatall deepe foresight
  Me hither sent, for cause to me vnghest,
  Or that fresh bleeding wound, which day and night
  Whilome doth rancle in my riuen brest,
  With forced fury following his behest,
  Me hither brought by wayes yet neuer found,
  You to haue helpt I hold my selfe yet blest.
  Ah curteous knight (quoth she) what secret wound
Could euer find, to grieue the gentlest hart on ground?

on Arthur's 'long education by Timon, to whom he was by
Merlin deliuered to be brought vp, so soone as he was borne'.
The confusion may be Arthur's.   **byliue**: forthwith.
5–8   In his comment on Drayton, *Poly-Olbion* x 14 (*Wks*
iv 210), Selden cites this 'Fiction of the Muses best pupil' and
observes that 'this *Rauran-Vaur* hill is there by in *Merioneth*'.
Arthur's upbringing is associated with Wales, rather than
Cornwall, to link him with the ancestral home of the Tudors.
6   **mossy hore**: hoary with moss.
7   **Dee**: the ancient boundary between Wales and England
(see Drayton, *Poly-Olbion* viii 383–4). This reference links the
two countries and the river's divine waters (see IV xi 39.3–4*n*)
with Arthur.   **siluer cleene**: bright (and pure) as silver.
9   **vertuous lore**: knowledge of the virtues, which includes
their practice; cf. Una's purity 'in life and euery vertuous lore'
(i 5.2).

Stanza 5
3   **discipline**: instruction, education.
4   **nouriture**: upbringing, nurture. S. echoes Caxton's rubric
to 'The Tale of King Arthur' chap. iii: 'Of the byrthe of kyng
Arthur and of his nouryture.' The **Tutour** is Merlin (1).
9   **iust terme**: due course; **time** is the womb which in full
term gives birth to events. The phrasing suggests the motif,
'Truth unveiled by Time'; see Panofsky (1962) 83f; cf 14.4.
For the proverb, 'Time brings the truth to light', see C. G.
Smith (1970) 769.

Stanza 6
1   **impe**: child; scion, accepting him as the offspring of a
king.   **gent**: high-born; also 'gracious' in her response;
cf. 16.5.
3   **aduenture**: chance.
5   **Aread**: declare. Arthur does not name himself despite
Una's request (2.7); appropriately, she first names him in the
poem.
6–9   Cf. Rom. 11.33: 'How unsearcheable are his judgements,
and his wayes past finding out.' These lines introduce the
argument of the Despair episode. At 12.1–2 Arthur parallels
his plight with the Knight's; yet he maintains faith in God's
providence while the latter allows his thoughts to be ruled by
despair.
7   **cause**: used in a theological sense, e.g. as God is the first
and final cause.
8   **secret**: beyond ordinary apprehension.

Stanza 7
1   **he**: God.   **fatall**: ordained by fate; prophetic.
4   **Whilome**: 'incessantly', in this context, rather than 'at
one time'.
5   **forced fury**: force and fury; compelled fury; furious
compulsion.   **his behest**: the command of the wound or of
love; or of God: in submitting to the power of love, Arthur
obeys God's rule.
6   **by wayes**: echoing the 'bywaies' taken by the Red Cross
Knight 'Where neuer foot of liuing wight did tread' (vii 50.4).
Love leads Arthur to descend into Hell, as it led Orpheus, and
the greater Orpheus, Christ.
7   **yet**: even now; even. The term is introduced with almost
casual courtesy but its implications are profound.
8   **curteous**: see viii 33.3*n*.
9   **find**: contrive; find the means to.   **on ground**: on the
earth; cf. 16.9.

Stanza 4
1   **Timon**: Honour; from the Gk τιμή.   **he**: presumably
not the 'Faery knight' (3.8) who is Timon himself, or the 'Sire'
(3.3), but Merlin, who is named in the next stanza. Cf. *L.R.*

8

Deare Dame (quoth he) you sleeping sparkes awake,
  Which troubled once, into huge flames will grow,
  Ne euer will their feruent fury slake,
  Till liuing moysture into smoke do flow,
  And wasted life do lye in ashes low.
  Yet sithens silence lesseneth not my fire,
  But told it flames, and hidden it does glow,
  I will reuele, what ye so much desire:
Ah Loue, lay downe thy bow, the whiles I may respire.

9

It was in freshest flowre of youthly yeares,
  When courage first does creepe in manly chest,
  Then first the coale of kindly heat appeares
  To kindle loue in euery liuing brest;
  But me had warnd old *Timons* wise behest,
  Those creeping flames by reason to subdew,
  Before their rage grew to so great vnrest,
  As miserable louers vse to rew,
Which still wex old in woe, whiles woe still wexeth new.

10

That idle name of loue, and louers life,
  As losse of time, and vertues enimy
  I euer scornd, and ioyd to stirre vp strife,
  In middest of their mournfull Tragedy,
  Ay wont to laugh, when them I heard to cry,
  And blow the fire, which them to ashes brent:
  Their God himselfe, grieu'd at my libertie,
  Shot many a dart at me with fiers intent,
But I them warded all with wary gouernment.

11

But all in vaine: no fort can be so strong,
  Ne fleshly brest can armed be so sound,
  But will at last be wonne with battrie long,
  Or vnwares at disauantage found;
  Nothing is sure, that growes on earthly ground:
  And who most trustes in arme of fleshly might,
  And boasts, in beauties chaine not to be bound,
  Doth soonest fall in disauentrous fight,
And yeeldes his caytiue neck to victours most despight.

12

Ensample make of him your haplesse ioy,
  And of my selfe now mated, as ye see;
  Whose prouder vaunt that proud auenging boy
  Did soone pluck downe, and curbd my libertie.
  For on a day prickt forth with iollitie
  Of looser life, and heat of hardiment,
  Raunging the forest wide on courser free,
  The fields, the floods, the heauens with one consent
Did seeme to laugh on me, and fauour mine intent.

Stanza 8
4–5   **liuing moysture**: radical moisture, the humours that compose the body. Love's fury will endure until its heat consumes the vital juices of his body: 'as the heat consumes the water, so doth Love dry up his radical moisture' (Burton, *Anat. Mel.* III ii 3.1); or until the elements melt with the heat of the final fire (2 Pet. 3.12).   **wasted**: spent unprofitably and therefore consumed.
9   **respire**: take breath.

Stanza 9
3   **kindly heat**: natural feeling.
5   **Timons**] *Cleons 1590* (corr. *F.E.*) signifies glory (Gk κλέος).
9   By this excessive playing with the letter 'w', even beginning and ending the line with the same letter, Arthur mocks a state that soon mocks him.

Stanza 10
7   **Their God**: Cupid.
9   **gouerment**: conduct; governing his passions.

Stanza 11
1–4   The first three lines are proverbial (C. G. Smith, 1970, 281); cf. III x 10.1–2. The fourth line 'excuses' the Red Cross Knight.   **battrie**: battering.
5   Proverbial (Smith 91); see viii 44.9n.
6   Cf. Jer. 17.5: 'Cursed be the man that . . . maketh flesh his arme.'
8   **disauentrous**: unfortunate; see vii 48.7n.
9   **most despight**: greatest outrage; once conquered, he must yield to the most contemptuous treatment.

Stanza 12
1–2   This paralleling comments on the Red Cross Knight's fall: he was bound 'in beauties chaine' by yielding to Duessa and trusted 'in arme of fleshly might' by abandoning Una and his armour.   **mated**: confounded; matched; also, as a term from chess: he has been mated by a Queen; cf. *S.C.* Dec. 53: 'Loue they him called, that gaue me checkmate.'
3   **prouder**: over-proud.
5   **prickt forth**: decked out; also spurred on like his horse.
6   **looser**: too loose, being free from all bonds; too wanton. **hardiment**: boldness.
7   **forest wide**: on the significance of this forest setting, see vi 3.2n.   **free**: willing and ready to go; suggesting his youthful nature.
8–9   With this accord of natural powers which encourages the lover – in the Bower of Bliss it becomes a conspiracy – compare the laughing Venus who encourages Scudamour to seize Amoret: he saw her 'laugh at me, and fauour my pretence' (IV x 56.4).   **floods**: waters.   **intent**: frame of mind; will.

13

For-wearied with my sports, I did alight
   From loftie steed, and downe to sleepe me layd;
   The verdant gras my couch did goodly dight,
   And pillow was my helmet faire displayd:
   Whiles euery sence the humour sweet embayd,
   And slombring soft my hart did steale away,
   Me seemed, by my side a royall Mayd
   Her daintie limbes full softly down did lay:
So faire a creature yet saw neuer sunny day.

14

Most goodly glee and louely blandishment
   She to me made, and bad me loue her deare,
   For dearely sure her loue was to me bent,
   As when iust time expired should appeare.
   But whether dreames delude, or true it were,
   Was neuer hart so rauisht with delight,
   Ne liuing man like words did euer heare,
   As she to me deliuered all that night;
And at her parting said, She Queene of Faeries hight.

15

When I awoke, and found her place deuoyd,
   And nought but pressed gras, where she had lyen,
   I sorrowed all so much, as earst I ioyd,
   And washed all her place with watry eyen.
   From that day forth I lou'd that face diuine;
   From that day forth I cast in carefull mind,
   To seeke her out with labour, and long tyne,
   And neuer vow to rest, till her I find,
Nine monethes I seeke in vaine yet ni'll that vow vnbind.

16

Thus as he spake, his visage wexed pale,
   And chaunge of hew great passion did bewray;
   Yet still he stroue to cloke his inward bale,
   And hide the smoke, that did his fire display,
   Till gentle *Vna* thus to him gan say;
   O happy Queene of Faeries, that hast found
   Mongst many, one that with his prowesse may
   Defend thine honour, and thy foes confound:
True Loues are often sown, but seldom grow on ground.

Stanza 13

1   **For-wearied**: utterly wearied. The Knight sinks into the biblical 'heauie slepe' (Gen. 2.21).
3   **dight**: adorn.
5–6   Sleep is described as a yielding of the senses to love. **humour**: dew of sleep.   **embayd**: bathed, suffused.
7–9   Celtic folklore provides numerous analogues to the fairy mistress theme: see *Var*. i 267–8. S.'s immediate source is Chaucer's Sir Thopas, that gay knight who so 'wery was / For prikyng on the softe gras' that he 'leyde him in that plas'. Here he dreamed 'al this nyght' that 'An elf-queene shal my lemman be' and vows 'Alle othere wommen I forsake, / And to an elf-queene I me take / By dale and eek by downe' (*Tale of Sir Thopas* 778–96).

Stanza 14

The double obscurity of the *concubitus* is commented on by Lewis (1966) 158–9: either the experience was a dream or it took place: either the fairy rose with her virginity intact or she did not. 'We are being shown the sort of experience to which the contrast either between mere "blandishment" and full fruition or between dream and waking does not strictly apply.' That experience, Lewis concludes, is 'the soul's new-kindled raptures at its first meeting with a transcendental or at least incorporeal object of love'.
1   **glee**: entertainment; joy, describing its effect upon him. **louely blandishment**: loving flattery.
4   **iust time . . . appeare**: in due course of time. Similarly, he will learn his identity 'As time in her iust terme' (5.9) will reveal. Obviously the two moments will become one. Being projected into the future, the love of the Faerie Queene is distinguished from that offered to the 'dreaming' Red Cross Knight by the false Una: e.g. the 'gentle blandishment and louely looke' (i 49.8) which seeks immediate satisfaction.

Stanza 15

1   **deuoyd**: empty.
2   The reality of the vision is confirmed here – cf. 'Me seemed' (13.7) – but brings sorrow.
6   **cast**: resolved.
7   **tyne**: trouble, suffering (S.'s variant of 'teen').
8   **neuer vow to rest**: the construction carries two meanings: 'never vow to rest' and 'vow never to rest'.
9   **Nine monethes**: the time of fulfilment or gestation; see viii 38.6–7n; cf. III ii 11.6. One stage of his search for the Faerie Queene is fulfilled when he aids Una. At II ix 7.5–6 the elapsed time is one year, or seven years (*1590*); at II ix 38.9 it is twelve months, or three years (*1590*).

Stanza 16

3   **bale**: fire; sorrow, grief.
9   **on ground**: on earth, as 7.9; also a punning reference to Arthur's vision while lying on the grass. His love is 'earthly'.

17

Thine, O then, said the gentle *Redcrosse* knight,
　Next to that Ladies loue, shalbe the place,
　O fairest virgin, full of heauenly light,
　Whose wondrous faith, exceeding earthly race,
　Was firmest fixt in mine extremest case.
　And you, my Lord, the Patrone of my life,
　Of that great Queene may well gaine worthy grace:
　For onely worthy you through prowes priefe
Yf liuing man mote worthy be, to be her liefe.

18

So diuersly discoursing of their loues,
　The golden Sunne his glistring head gan shew,
　And sad remembraunce now the Prince amoues,
　With fresh desire his voyage to pursew:
　Als *Vna* earnd her traueill to renew.
　Then those two knights, fast friendship for to bynd,
　And loue establish each to other trew,
　Gaue goodly gifts, the signes of gratefull mynd,
And eke as pledges firme, right hands together ioynd.

19

Prince *Arthur* gaue a boxe of Diamond sure,
　Embowd with gold and gorgeous ornament,
　Wherein were closd few drops of liquor pure,
　Of wondrous worth, and vertue excellent,
　That any wound could heale incontinent:
　Which to requite, the *Redcrosse* knight him gaue
　A booke, wherein his Saueours testament
　Was writ with golden letters rich and braue;
A worke of wondrous grace, and able soules to saue.

20

Thus beene they parted, *Arthur* on his way
　To seeke his loue, and th'other for to fight
　With *Vnaes* foe, that all her realme did pray.
　But she now weighing the decayed plight,
　And shrunken synewes of her chosen knight,
　Would not a while her forward course pursew,
　Ne bring him forth in face of dreadfull fight,
　Till he recouered had his former hew:
For him to be yet weake and wearie well she knew.

21

So as they traueild, lo they gan espy
　An armed knight towards them gallop fast,
　That seemed from some feared foe to fly,
　Or other griesly thing, that him agast.
　Still as he fled, his eye was backward cast,
　As if his feare still followed him behind;
　Als flew his steed, as he his bands had brast,
　And with his winged heeles did tread the wind,
As he had beene a fole of *Pegasus* his kind.

O Una, shall be Arthur's love'; cf. i 3.5. This ambiguity may
account for the repetition of **gentle** from 16.5, and the use of
'diuersly' at 18.1.
4　**faith**: loyalty. He had left her 'Through light misdeeming
of her loialtie' (iv 2.2); cf. vii 49.4–5.
5　**case**: fortune, plight.
6　**Patrone**: protector, defender; cf. Guyon's similar tribute
to Arthur at the corresponding moment in his adventure, II
viii 55.4. Also, the model which the Knight imitates: the virtue
of Holiness is one aspect of Arthur.
7　**worthy**: excellent; fitting, deserved.
8　**onely worthy you . . .**: you alone deserve her grace by
proof of your valour.
9　**liefe**: beloved, used of a superior.

Stanza 18
5　**earnd**: yearned.
6　The virtue of Book IV is here first named; see viii 34.5*n*.
9　Their joining hands is a type of the alliance of the virtues
towards which the whole poem moves; cf. II i 34.2.

Stanza 19
The gifts are complementary. Arthur's gift heals wounds, the
Red Cross Knight's gift saves souls. The difference between
them is that between the water from the Well of Life and the
balm from the Tree of Life: see xi 46–48*n*.
1　**Diamond**: either the stone or the rock, adamant. Both
signify constant faith; see vii 33.5–9*n*.　**sure**: sound, true
(referring to **Diamond**); secure (referring to the **boxe**).
2　**Embowd**: arched, i.e. surrounded or encircled.
3–5　**liquor pure**: cf. the blood of Christ which 'clenseth
us from all sinne' (1 John 1.7).　**excellent**: pre-eminent,
supreme.　**incontinent**: straightway. The word also modifies
wound and so refers to the sin of concupiscence which the
liquor heals. Hence Arthur uses it to cure Amoret's wounds,
IV viii 20.
7–9　Since the book is the New Testament, the relation
between the two gifts may be suggested by Matt. 26.28: 'For
this is my blood of the Newe testament, that is shed for manie,
for the remission of sinnes.' Kellogg and Steele (1965) suggest
that the two gifts answer the blood and book of the old Covenant,
Exod. 24.6–8.　**his Saueours**] this Saueours *1590*. An interesting error if it is the poet's.　**braue**: splendid.

Stanza 20
3　**pray**: plunder.
4–9　Cf. 2.1–2. The substance of these lines is repeated at
x 2.1–6. The Despair episode is set apart as a prefatory interlude to the Knight's spiritual development in the second part of
the Book.　**chosen** prepares for the resolution of the episode;
but the question, 'chosen for what'?, leads the Knight into
Despair's mental maze. The dilemma that one should be saved
from death only to become subject to despair is expressed at
III v 42.7–9.

Stanza 21
1　**gan**: did.
4　**griesly** and **agast** suggest fear aroused by infernal spirits.
6　**his feare**: what he feared; or Fear itself.
9　**kind**: breed.　**Pegasus** suggests swift flight. Possibly
Pegasus's flight to the heavens suggests the knight's flight to
'Gods deare loue' (25.1) through which alone he may be saved
from despair.

Stanza 17
1–3　A deliberate ambiguity of precedence is required by the
allegory, as Upton (1758) suggests: 'O Una, the next place to
Arthur's love shall be thine'; also 'The next place to your love,

22

Nigh as he drew, they might perceiue his head
  To be vnarmd, and curld vncombed heares
  Vpstaring stiffe, dismayd with vncouth dread;
  Nor drop of bloud in all his face appeares
  Nor life in limbe: and to increase his feares,
  In fowle reproch of knighthoods faire degree,
  About his neck an hempen rope he weares,
  That with his glistring armes does ill agree;
But he of rope or armes has now no memoree.

23

The *Redcrosse* knight toward him crossed fast,
  To weet, what mister wight was so dismayd:
  There him he finds all sencelesse and aghast,
  That of him selfe he seemd to be afrayd;
  Whom hardly he from flying forward stayd,
  Till he these wordes to him deliuer might;
  Sir knight, aread who hath ye thus arayd,
  And eke from whom make ye this hasty flight:
For neuer knight I saw in such misseeming plight.

24

He answerd nought at all, but adding new
  Feare to his first amazment, staring wide
  With stony eyes, and hartlesse hollow hew,
  Astonisht stood, as one that had aspide
  Infernall furies, with their chaines vntide.
  Him yet againe, and yet againe bespake
  The gentle knight; who nought to him replide,
  But trembling euery ioynt did inly quake,
And foltring tongue at last these words seemd forth to shake.

25

For Gods deare loue, Sir knight, do me not stay;
  For loe he comes, he comes fast after mee.
  Eft looking backe would faine haue runne away;
  But he him forst to stay, and tellen free
  The secret cause of his perplexitie:
  Yet nathemore by his bold hartie speach,
  Could his bloud-frosen hart emboldned bee,
  But through his boldnesse rather feare did reach,
Yet forst, at last he made through silence suddein breach.

26

And am I now in safetie sure (quoth he)
  From him, that would haue forced me to dye?
  And is the point of death now turnd fro mee,
  That I may tell this haplesse history?
  Feare nought: (quoth he) no daunger now is nye.
  Then shall I you recount a ruefull cace,
  (Said he) the which with this vnlucky eye
  I late beheld, and had not greater grace
Me reft from it, had bene partaker of the place.

Stanza 22
Trevisan appears as did the Red Cross Knight before his fall, 'Disarmd, disgrast, and inwardly dismayde' (vii 11.6), and immediately after it, 'pale and wan' (viii 42.3).
1–2 His head is **vnarmd** because despair is an error of reason; hence his loss of memory (9). In the state of despair he lacks the helmet which is 'the hope of salvation' (1 Thess. 5.8). That S. has this text in mind is suggested by the verse that follows: 'For God hathe not appointed us unto wrath, but to obteine salvation.'
3 Vpstaring: standing on end, suggesting that his hairs stare like eyes. **vncouth**: strange, repellent; also unknown. 'The undiscover'd country from whose bourn / No traveller returns' occasions his despair or, more properly, is the result of it.
4–5 Pallidness expresses the state of wan-hope or despair.
7 hempen: indicating that he wears the hangman's halter; cf. 54.4–5. Chew (1947) 113–4 notes that the suicide of Judas Iscariot made the rope or halter the chief image of Despair; see 29.9n.

Stanza 23
2 mister: manner of.
4 The extremity both of outward fear and of inner fear produces his present traumatic shock.
7 aread: declare.
9 misseeming: cf. his own 'misseeming hew' (viii 42.9) upon emerging from Orgoglio's dungeon.

Stanza 24
2 amazment: overwhelming fear; mental stupefaction, with its literal force: Despair leads the knight into a mental maze; see 49.1.
3 stony: fixed; cf. v 32.7. **hartlesse**: lacking heart or courage; hence 'Nor drop of bloud in all his face appeares' (22.4); cf. 29.7. For the importance of the heart in the Despair episode, see 48.2n. The frozen, wounded heart contrasts with Arthur's heart 'rauisht with delight' (14.6) through love.
5 See v 31.8n.

Stanza 25
1 For Gods deare loue: a curious exclamation from one who has almost yielded to despair. Even uttered unwittingly, however, it may save him: at 26.8 he recognizes God's grace, and at 28.3 he invokes God's blessing. **do me not stay**: this inverted construction with the four heavy and rising stresses indicates the knight's terror. It balances the opening exclamation: he flees from Despair to God's love.
3 Eft: again.
5 perplexitie: trouble, distress; also mental bewilderment.
6 nathemore: not at all. **hartie**: encouraging; courageous; also literally 'full of heart' as he seeks to revive the knight's **bloud-frosen hart**.
8 reach: succeed in arousing; in Trevisan, apparently, though the loose reference in 7–8 transfers the **feare** to the Red Cross Knight.

Stanza 26
6 cace: event.
8–9 The confusing response betrays Trevisan's trepidation, as Percival (1893) notes. **greater grace**: greater than his companion enjoyed. **partaker of the place**: i.e. he would have shared his companion's fate in that place.

27

I lately chaunst (Would I had neuer chaunst)
  With a faire knight to keepen companee,
  Sir *Terwin* hight, that well himselfe aduaunst
  In all affaires, and was both bold and free,
  But not so happie as mote happie bee:
  He lou'd, as was his lot, a Ladie gent,
  That him againe lou'd in the least degree:
  For she was proud, and of too high intent,
And ioyd to see her louer languish and lament.

28

From whom returning sad and comfortlesse,
  As on the way together we did fare,
  We met that villen (God from him me blesse)
  That cursed wight, from whom I scapt whyleare,
  A man of hell, that cals himselfe *Despaire*:
  Who first vs greets, and after faire areedes
  Of tydings strange, and of aduentures rare:
  So creeping close, as Snake in hidden weedes,
Inquireth of our states, and of our knightly deedes.

29

Which when he knew, and felt our feeble harts
  Embost with bale, and bitter byting griefe,
  Which loue had launched with his deadly darts,
  With wounding words and termes of foule repriefe
  He pluckt from vs all hope of due reliefe,
  That earst vs held in loue of lingring life;
  Then hopelesse hartlesse, gan the cunning thiefe
  Perswade vs die, to stint all further strife:
To me he lent this rope, to him a rustie knife.

30

With which sad instrument of hastie death,
  That wofull louer, loathing lenger light,
  A wide way made to let forth liuing breath.
  But I more fearefull, or more luckie wight,
  Dismayd with that deformed dismall sight,
  Fled fast away, halfe dead with dying feare:
  Ne yet assur'd of life by you, Sir knight,
  Whose like infirmitie like chaunce may beare:
But God you neuer let his charmed speeches heare.

31

How may a man (said he) with idle speach
  Be wonne, to spoyle the Castle of his health?
  I wote (quoth he) whom triall late did teach,
  That like would not for all this worldes wealth:
  His subtill tongue, like dropping honny, mealt'th
  Into the hart, and searcheth euery vaine,
  That ere one be aware, by secret stealth
  His powre is reft, and weaknesse doth remaine.
O neuer Sir desire to try his guilefull traine.

Stanza 27
3 **Terwin**: cf. 'terwyn', to weary, fatigue; or coined from 'ter' + 'won': thrice-conquered. Blitch (1965) suggests an anagram of 'Winter'.
7 **againe**: in return.
8 **intent**: mind, will; suggesting 'aim', 'ambition'.

Stanza 28
1 **comfortlesse**: implying the stronger sense, 'helpless', 'desolate'.
3 **blesse**: protect by his blessing.
4 **whyleare**: a while before, 'late' (31.3).
5 While evil characters usually adopt pseudonyms in the poem, **Despaire** openly proclaims his own name.
6 **areedes**: tells.
8 **in hidden weedes**: hidden in weeds; in weeds that hide.

Stanza 29
1 **our**: Trevisan must be infected by his friend's despair.
2 **Embost with bale**: exhausted by sorrow. 'Embost' is suggested by the pun on **harts** (1), as Collier (1862) observed: a hunted hart is said to be embost when it foams with fatigue.
3 **launched**: pierced.
4 **repriefe**: insult, scorn.
5 Alluding to the etymology of despair, 'depriving of hope'.
9 For the halter and knife as attributes of despair, see Sachs (1964). The association of hanging with love may derive from the association of hanging with Cupid, as in Achilles Bocchius *Symbolicarum Quaestionum* (Bologna 1574), symb. xii.

Stanza 30
5 **deformed**: hateful; or referring to his disfigured friend. **dismall**: causing terror.
6 **dying feare**: fear of dying, which here preserves him from death.
9 **God you neuer let**: may God never let you. **charmed**: that charm; cf. 48.8.

Stanza 31
1 **idle**: foolish, in the scriptural sense: 'everie idle worde that men shal speake' (Matt. 12.36).
2 **spoyle**: despoil. **the Castle of his health**: 'our earthlie house of this tabernacle' (2 Cor. 5.1) as in Elyot, *The Castel of Helth* (1539). **health**: well-being.
4 **That like would not . . .**: that like trial would not undergo again; or **like** may refer to the act of taking one's life.
5 Cf. Prov. 5.3: 'the lippes of a strange woman drop as an honie combe'. **mealt'th**: melts.
9 **try**: make trial of. **traine**: wiles.

32

Certes (said he) hence shall I neuer rest,
  Till I that treachours art haue heard and tride;
  And you Sir knight, whose name mote I request,
  Of grace do me vnto his cabin guide.
  I that hight *Treuisan* (quoth he) will ride
  Against my liking backe, to doe you grace:
  But nor for gold nor glee will I abide
  By you, when ye arriue in that same place;
For leuer had I die, then see his deadly face.

33

Ere long they come, where that same wicked wight
  His dwelling has, low in an hollow caue,
  Farre vnderneath a craggie clift ypight,
  Darke, dolefull, drearie, like a greedie graue,
  That still for carrion carcases doth craue:
  On top whereof aye dwelt the ghastly Owle,
  Shrieking his balefull note, which euer draue
  Farre from that haunt all other chearefull fowle;
And all about it wandring ghostes did waile and howle.

34

And all about old stockes and stubs of trees,
  Whereon nor fruit, nor leafe was euer seene,
  Did hang vpon the ragged rocky knees;
  On which had many wretches hanged beene,
  Whose carcases were scattered on the greene,
  And throwne about the cliffs.   Arriued there,
  That bare-head knight for dread and dolefull teene,
  Would faine haue fled, ne durst approchen neare,
But th'other forst him stay, and comforted in feare.

35

That darkesome caue they enter, where they find
  That cursed man, low sitting on the ground,
  Musing full sadly in his sullein mind;
  His griesie lockes, long growen, and vnbound,
  Disordred hong about his shoulders round,
  And hid his face; through which his hollow eyne
  Lookt deadly dull, and stared as astound;
  His raw-bone cheekes through penurie and pine,
Were shronke into his iawes, as he did neuer dine.

36

His garment nought but many ragged clouts,
  With thornes together pind and patched was,
  The which his naked sides he wrapt abouts;
  And him beside there lay vpon the gras
  A drearie corse, whose life away did pas,
  All wallowd in his owne yet luke-warme blood,
  That from his wound yet welled fresh alas;
  In which a rustie knife fast fixed stood,
And made an open passage for the gushing flood.

Stanza 32

1 **rest**: ironic, of course, since Despair offers him rest which almost brings his death.

2 **treachours**: traitor's, an obsolete form which suggests 'treacherous'.

4, 6 **grace**: the limited sense, 'favour', clears the way for the precise religious significance at 53.6 after the Knight has **tride** (2) Despair's art and shown his need for grace. Such grace as Trevisan offers takes him into Despair's cave but not out of it.

4 **cabin**: cave.

5 **Treuisan**: Belson (1964) suggests Gk τρέω, to flee because of fear.

7 **glee**: bright colour, beauty; possibly the glitter of gold. Church (1758) suggests 'fee' as at x 43.6. Alliteration supports the text. Moreover, the whole phrase may express the two major temptations of Book II, money (Mammon) and beauty (Acrasia).

9 **leuer**: rather.

Stanza 33

3 **ypight**: pitched; suggesting that the cliff or cleft may fall upon him.

4–5 Cf. Aesculapius's cave, v 36.5–6. In contrast, Despair's cave is actively malignant.

6–8 **the ghastly Owle**: see v 30.6–7*n* on the owl as the messenger of death. Williams (1966) 26*n*17 observes: 'In medieval tradition the smaller soaring birds of day, driven from Despair's cave by the owl, connote spiritual values, the dark owl the conscious denial of these values'; see Rosenberg in Meiss (1960) i 424.

Stanza 34

1 **stockes**: stumps.

3 **knees**: cliffs, crags.

7 **teene**: grief.

Stanza 35

3 **sullein**: gloomy; morose (solein). Despair displays the outward symptoms of melancholy; see Burton, *Anat. Mel.* I iii 1.1. The term describes Saturn, III xi 43.2, who is the Lord of Melancholy; see Klibansky *et al* (1964) 127f.

4 **griesie**: grey, grizzled; horrible, hideous; filthy.

8–9 Cf. the appearance of the Red Cross Knight upon emerging from Orgoglio's dungeon, viii 41. **penurie and pine**: lack of food and the suffering that follows.

Stanza 36

1–3 His clothes display his abandoned state; cf. the 'olde rotten ragges and olde worne cloutes' put on by Jeremiah when he is taken from the dungeon, Jer. 38.11. The garment pinned with thorns belongs to the abandoned and despairing Achaemenides in Virgil, *Aen.* iii 594. Ovid, *Met.* xiv 166, selects this detail as the sign of his former state. The **thornes** signify Despair's cursed state without hope of redemption, according to God's curse, Gen. 3.18. **clouts**: rags. **abouts**: an obsolete form of 'about'.

5 **drearie**: gory, bloody.

6 **wallowd**: lying prostrate, literally rolled in his blood.

8 **rustie**: bloody.

37

Which piteous spectacle, approuing trew
  The wofull tale that *Treuisan* had told,
  When as the gentle *Redcrosse* knight did vew,
  With firie zeale he burnt in courage bold,
  Him to auenge, before his bloud were cold,
  And to the villein said, Thou damned wight,
  The author of this fact, we here behold,
What iustice can but iudge against thee right,
With thine owne bloud to price his bloud, here shed in sight?

38

What franticke fit (quoth he) hath thus distraught
  Thee, foolish man, so rash a doome to giue?
  What iustice euer other iudgement taught,
  But he should die, who merites not to liue?
  None else to death this man despayring driue,
  But his owne guiltie mind deseruing death.
  Is then vniust to each his due to giue?
Or let him die, that loatheth liuing breath?
Or let him die at ease, that liueth here vneath?

39

Who trauels by the wearie wandring way,
  To come vnto his wished home in haste,
  And meetes a flood, that doth his passage stay,
  Is not great grace to helpe him ouer past,
  Or free his feet, that in the myre sticke fast?
  Most enuious man, that grieues at neighbours good,
  And fond, that ioyest in the woe thou hast,
Why wilt not let him passe, that long hath stood
Vpon the banke, yet wilt thy selfe not passe the flood?

40

He there does now enioy eternall rest
  And happie ease, which thou doest want and craue,
  And further from it daily wanderest:
  What if some litle paine the passage haue,
  That makes fraile flesh to feare the bitter waue?
  Is not short paine well borne, that brings long ease,
  And layes the soule to sleepe in quiet graue?
Sleepe after toyle, port after stormie seas,
Ease after warre, death after life does greatly please.

41

The knight much wondred at his suddeine wit,
  And said, The terme of life is limited,
  Ne may a man prolong, nor shorten it;
  The souldier may not moue from watchfull sted,
  Nor leaue his stand, vntill his Captaine bed.
  Who life did limit by almightie doome,
  (Quoth he) knowes best the termes established;
  And he, that points the Centonell his roome,
Doth license him depart at sound of morning droome.

Stanza 37
1   **approuing**: proving, finding by experience.
4   Cf. the 'constant zeale, and courage bold' (viii 40.4) by which Arthur rescues him from the dungeon. These moral qualities now provoke the Knight's defeat.
5   **his**: Terwin's (cf. 36.6); yet applied also to the Knight

burning with **firie zeale** (4).
7   **fact**: crime.
8–9   Cf. Gen. 9.6: 'Whoso shedeth mans blood, by man shal his blood be shed.' Night uses this same argument: 'he the man that made *Sansfoy* to fall, / Shall with his owne bloud price that he hath spilt' (v 26.3–4). Her prophecy is almost fulfilled as the Knight himself invokes the justice which condemns him; cf. Rom. 2.1: 'Therefore thou art inexcusable, O man, whosoever thou art that iudgest: for in that that thou iudgest another, thou condemnest thy self.'
9   **price**: pay for; cf. Despair's use of this argument at 43.6.
in sight: not a mere rhyming tag; again the Knight is betrayed by his sight.

Stanza 38
1   **franticke**: mad with rage; also guilty of extreme folly.
2   **foolish man**: in response to the Knight's 'damned wight', noting his want of judgment and inability to argue.   **doome**: judgment.
5   **driue**: either the older form of 'drove', or the present tense, 'drives', to intensify Despair's argument.
8–9   **let him die**: i.e. is it unjust to let him die?
die at ease: i.e. die and be at ease.   **vneath**: in unease.

Stanza 39
3–5   Cf. Ps. 69.1–2: 'Save me, O God: for the waters are entred even to my soule. I sticke fast in the depe myre, where no staie is: I am come into depe waters, and the streames runne over me.'
4   **grace**: favour, in parody of God's grace which saves man.
7   **fond**: foolish.

Stanza 40
6   **well borne**: well worth bearing.
8–9   The echoing **seas** / **Ease**, rounded out with **please** characterizes the highly rhetorical nature of the commonplaces used by Despair. The pleasure of death refers to the Knight's despair in Orgoglio's dungeon, viii 38.9. Crampton (1974) 124 notes that the word 'ease' echoes through the lines, even replacing the expected 'peace' in 9.

Stanza 41
The Knight's argument against suicide is commonplace, deriving from Cicero, *De Senectute* xx 73: 'Pythagoras bids us stand like faithful sentries and not quit our post until God, our Captain, gives the word'. Cf. Sidney's *Old Arcadia* 294: 'God had appointed us captains of these our bodily forts, which without treason to that majesty were never to be delivered over till they were redemanded.'
1   **wondred**: with a pun on 'wandered': the Knight now begins to wander in a mental labyrinth like the maze of the Wandering Wood.   **suddeine wit**: quick mind.
4   **watchfull sted**: the post or station of watch assigned to him.
5   **stand**: post.   **bed**: bids.
7   **he**: Despair or the Knight; their voices blend as the Knight yields to despair.
8–9   **roome**: assigned place or station. Life is reduced to the sentinel's weary role of keeping watch; cf. Ps. 130.6: 'My soule waiteth on the Lord more then the morning watche watcheth for the morning.'   **morning droome**: with the pun on 'mourning', the Knight's argument is shifted from 'leaving when time expires' to 'leaving when mourning'.

42

Is not his deed, what euer thing is donne,
  In heauen and earth? did not he all create
  To die againe? all ends that was begonne.
  Their times in his eternall booke of fate
  Are written sure, and haue their certaine date.
  Who then can striue with strong necessitie,
  That holds the world in his still chaunging state,
  Or shunne the death ordaynd by destinie?
When houre of death is come, let none aske whence, nor why.

43

The lenger life, I wote the greater sin,
  The greater sin, the greater punishment:
  All those great battels, which thou boasts to win,
  Through strife, and bloud-shed, and auengement,
  Now praysd, hereafter deare thou shalt repent:
  For life must life, and bloud must bloud repay.
  Is not enough thy euill life forespent?
  For he, that once hath missed the right way,
The further he doth goe, the further he doth stray.

44

Then do no further goe, no further stray,
  But here lie downe, and to thy rest betake,
  Th'ill to preuent, that life ensewen may.
  For what hath life, that may it loued make,
  And giues not rather cause it to forsake?
  Feare, sicknesse, age, losse, labour, sorrow, strife,
  Paine, hunger, cold, that makes the hart to quake;
  And euer fickle fortune rageth rife,
All which, and thousands mo do make a loathsome life.

45

Thou wretched man, of death hast greatest need,
  If in true ballance thou wilt weigh thy state:
  For neuer knight, that dared warlike deede,
  More lucklesse disauentures did amate:
  Witnesse the dongeon deepe, wherein of late
  Thy life shut vp, for death so oft did call;
  And though good lucke prolonged hath thy date,
  Yet death then, would the like mishaps forestall,
Into the which hereafter thou maiest happen fall.

Stanza 42

Either Despair argues for despair – as **fate**, **necessitie**, and **destinie** render life (and death) meaningless – or the Knight argues against suicide. Alpers (1967) 355 notes that with the exception of **To die againe** all this speech could be spoken by the Knight. Yet even this phrase could be his, for all men must die: for the proverb, see C. G. Smith (1970) 12, 53.

4–5   Cf. Ps. 31.15: 'My times are in thine hand.' Such trust in God carries a threat.   **certaine date**: fixed duration.

6   The argument is Night's at v 25.5.

Stanza 43

1   **wote**: know; with the stronger sense, 'know for certain'. The necessity of sin is supported by 1 John 1.8: 'If we say that we have no sinne, we deceive our selves, and trueth is not in us.' However, the argument is answered by the next verse: 'If we acknowledge our sinnes, he is faithful and just, to forgive us our sinnes, and to clense us from all unrighteousnes.'

4   **auengement**: vengeance; the word undercuts the Knight's ambition to fight for worship and grace (cf. i 3.4).

6   See 37.8–9n. Despair invokes the Knight's concept of retributive justice to condemn him.

7   **forespent**: Despair exploits the ambiguities of this term: previously spent; entirely spent, i.e. worn out, wasted; misspent.

Stanza 44

Despair bases his present argument on Heb. 4, particularly verse 11: 'Let us studie therefore to entre into that rest, lest anie man fall after the same ensample of disobedience.'

3   **that . . . may**: that follows if you happen to live; or that results from life.

7   **makes**: the singular indicates that each of the ten listed ills is sufficient by itself to quake the heart.

Stanza 45

1   **Thou**: i.e. you especially.

4   **disauentures**: mishaps. Despair echoes Una's (Truth's) lament for her 'dolefull disauenturous deare' (vii 48.7); cf. xi 28.3.   **amate**: daunt; also match, hinting that the Knight and bad luck are inseparably linked.

6   **for . . . call**: see viii 38.3–4n.

7   Despair reduces 'heauenly grace' (viii 1.3) to mere **good lucke**, the 'good hap' of vii 29.1.   **date**: term of life, the time 'given' man. Sirluck (1950) 10 observes that 'here, if not earlier, the contemporary reader recognized the nature of Despair's fraud', which is to ignore God's mercy.

8   **then**: i.e. when you called **of late** (5); also 'consequently'. **forestall**: prevent by anticipation.

46

Why then doest thou, O man of sin, desire
    To draw thy dayes forth to their last degree?
    Is not the measure of thy sinfull hire
    High heaped vp with huge iniquitie,
    Against the day of wrath, to burden thee?
    Is not enough, that to this Ladie milde
    Thou falsed hast thy faith with periurie,
    And sold thy selfe to serue *Duessa* vilde,
With whom in all abuse thou hast thy selfe defilde?

47

Is not he iust, that all this doth behold
    From highest heauen, and beares an equall eye?
    Shall he thy sins vp in his knowledge fold,
    And guiltie be of thine impietie?
    Is not his law, Let euery sinner die:
    Die shall all flesh? what then must needs be donne,
    Is it not better to doe willinglie,
    Then linger, till the glasse be all out ronne?
Death is the end of woes: die soone, O faeries sonne.

48

The knight was much enmoued with his speach,
    That as a swords point through his hart did perse,
    And in his conscience made a secret breach,
    Well knowing true all, that he did reherse,
    And to his fresh remembrance did reuerse
    The vgly vew of his deformed crimes,
    That all his manly powres it did disperse,
    As he were charmed with inchaunted rimes,
That oftentimes he quakt, and fainted oftentimes.

49

In which amazement, when the Miscreant
    Perceiued him to wauer weake and fraile,
    Whiles trembling horror did his conscience dant,
    And hellish anguish did his soule assaile,
    To driue him to despaire, and quite to quaile,
    He shew'd him painted in a table plaine,
    The damned ghosts, that doe in torments waile,
    And thousand feends that doe them endlesse paine
With fire and brimstone, which for euer shall remaine.

Stanza 46

1   **O man of sin**: a terrible final naming, applied to the Anti-Christ at 2 Thess. 2.3. Only the Knight in despair judges himself guilty of his crimes: Una blames an evil star and Fortune (viii 42–43); Arthur blames the uncertainty of worldly bliss (viii 44.9), and the weakness of the flesh (ix 11–12); and Una's parents blame fate (xii 16.5–6).
3–5   **sinfull hire**: Yeats (1906) notes the resemblance to Rom. 6.23: 'For the wages of sinne is death.' Cf. Rom. 2.3–5: 'And thinkest thou this, O thou man, that iudgest them which do suche things, and doest the same, that thou shalt escape the judgement of God? . . . But thou . . . heapest vnto thy self wrath against the day of wrath.'   **burden**: playing on its

double sense: God's word lays a 'charge' (*OED* 2) upon the Knight and he carries its weight; cf. the extended play upon 'the burden of the Lord' in Jer. 23.33–40.
6   **this Ladie milde**: Una's presence is indicated at 52.1. Only in her presence is his sin fully manifest to him. The comparison with her 'wondrous faith, exceeding earthly race' (17.4) drives him to despair.
7   **falsed**: violated, betrayed.
8–9   Despair names the two faults which have overcome Una's earlier champions, 'want of faith, or guilt of sin' (vii 45.8).

Stanza 47

1–2   If he were not paralysed by guilt, the Knight could reply: 'The Lord is good to all, and his mercies are over all his workes' (Ps. 145.9).   **equall**: impartial, just; cf. Una's statement, viii 27.6–7.
3–4   Despair's rhetorical question suggests the solution to all these riddles: 'Christ dyed for our sinnes according to the Scriptures' (1 Cor. 15.3), answering the Old Covenant by the New; cf. 1 Pet. 3.18.
5   'The same soule that sinneth, shal dye' (Ezek. 18.20). Despair recalls only half of Scripture: 'The wages of sinne is death; but the gifte of God is eternal life through Jesus Christ our Lord' (Rom. 6.23).
6   'All flesh shal perish together' (Job 34.15).
8   **glasse**: the hour-glass.
9   Proverbial (C. G. Smith, 1970, 153).   **soone**: straightway.

Stanza 48

2   **his hart did perse**: the sign that he is overcome by despair. From Duessa's cup 'Death and despeyre did many thereof sup, / . . . Th'eternall bale of heauie wounded harts' (viii 14.3–5): although death is defeated by Arthur's descent into the dungeon, despair remains. The extended play on the wounded heart in the episode reaches a climax in these closing stanzas.
3   **conscience**: inward knowledge, consciousness, mind rather than moral sense. Once breached by Despair's arguments, it is diseased and must be cured in the house of Holiness (see x 23.8, 29.3).
4   **reherse**: say; also the current sense for Despair repeats what the Knight has done and recites Scripture.
5   **reuerse**: bring back.
8   **inchaunted rimes**: cf. his 'charmed speeches' (30.9) and Archimago's verses framed with 'mighty charmes' (i 36.9).

Stanza 49

1   **amazement**: see 24.2*n* and 41.1*n*.   **Miscreant**: misbeliever, in the literal sense.
2   **weake and fraile**: the terms define his fleshly state; cf. 53.1.
3   **trembling horror**: the adj. stresses the Lat. sense of horror, shuddering; cf. viii 39.3.   **dant**: obsolete form of 'daunt': overcome.
4   **hellish anguish**: i.e. fear of hell.
6   **table**: picture.
7–9   In his despair the Knight no longer regards death as 'the end of woes' (47.9). 'But the fearful and vnbeleving . . . shal have their parte in the lake, which burneth with fyre and brimstone, which is the seconde death' (Rev. 21.8).   **for euer**: Rev. 20.10.

50

The sight whereof so throughly him dismaid,
  That nought but death before his eyes he saw,
  And euer burning wrath before him laid,
  By righteous sentence of th'Almighties law:
  Then gan the villein him to ouercraw,
  And brought vnto him swords, ropes, poison, fire,
  And all that might him to perdition draw;
  And bad him choose, what death he would desire:
For death was due to him, that had prouokt Gods ire.

51

But when as none of them he saw him take,
  He to him raught a dagger sharpe and keene,
  And gaue it him in hand: his hand did quake,
  And tremble like a leafe of Aspin greene,
  And troubled bloud through his pale face was seene
  To come, and goe with tydings from the hart,
  As it a running messenger had beene.
  At last resolu'd to worke his finall smart,
He lifted vp his hand, that backe againe did start.

52

Which when as *Vna* saw, through euery vaine
  The crudled cold ran to her well of life,
  As in a swowne: but soone reliu'd againe,
  Out of his hand she snatcht the cursed knife,
  And threw it to the ground, enraged rife,
  And to him said, Fie, fie, faint harted knight,
  What meanest thou by this reprochfull strife?
Is this the battell, which thou vauntst to fight
With that fire-mouthed Dragon, horrible and bright?

53

Come, come away, fraile, feeble, fleshly wight,
  Ne let vaine words bewitch thy manly hart,
  Ne diuelish thoughts dismay thy constant spright.
  In heauenly mercies hast thou not a part?
  Why shouldst thou then despeire, that chosen art?
  Where iustice growes, there grows eke greater grace,
  The which doth quench the brond of hellish smart,
  And that accurst hand-writing doth deface.
Arise, Sir knight arise, and leaue this cursed place.

54

So vp he rose, and thence amounted streight.
  Which when the carle beheld, and saw his guest
  Would safe depart, for all his subtill sleight,
  He chose an halter from among the rest,
  And with it hung himselfe, vnbid vnblest.
  But death he could not worke himselfe thereby;
  For thousand times he so himselfe had drest,
  Yet nathelesse it could not doe him die,
Till he should die his last, that is eternally.

5   **ouercraw**: triumph over.
7   **perdition**: as the place of damnation of the beast (Rev. 17.8) and as eternal death.

Stanza 51
1–3   The Knight is incapable of choosing. Despair gives him the dagger, which he must accept, because his heart is already pierced (48.2).   **raught**: reached, held out.
4   Such is the doubting state of Fradubio, ii 28.5. The simile is proverbial (C. G. Smith, 1970, 29).
9   **that . . . start**: i.e. started to come down to stab himself. Alpers (1967) 357–9 argues that the Knight's hand starts back up as he revolts against suicide, and that Una intervenes because she experiences his revulsion. Yet Una despairs in horror at her Knight's intended suicide, not at any revulsion from it. Heavenly grace intervenes only when human nature is exhausted. Cf. IV i 54.9 where 'he drew it backe' means that he lowered his hand again; similarly in Book VI, Calepine interrupts the sacrifice of Serena as the priest's 'right hand adowne descends' (viii 49.2).

Stanza 52
2   **well of life**: heart.
7   **reprochfull**: deserving of reproach; also strife 'in which you reproach yourself'.

Stanza 53
After being 'enraged rife' (52.5), Una speaks more persuasively than Despair. The Knight's infected will must be moved, not simply reasoned with.
1   **fraile, feeble, fleshly**: cf. Rom. 8.1–13 on man's sinful flesh; also Matt. 26.41 on the weakness of the flesh.
2   Una echoes Paul's warning against 'entising wordes' (Col. 2.4); cf. the Knight's speech to Trevisan, 31.1–2.
3   **diuelish thoughts**: literally thoughts of devils, 49.8. **constant**: perhaps constantly, or referring to the virtue of constancy which all the heroes must uphold.
4   **heauenly mercies**: the repressed term in Despair's argument. Later despair 'Made him forget all that *Fidelia* told' (x 22.5).
5   **that chosen art**: cf. 2 Thess. 2.13: 'God hathe from the beginning chosen you to salvacion, through sanctificacion of the Spirit, and the faith of trueth'; cf. Mark 13.20 and see x 57.1–4.   **chosen** may refer to the salvation open to all though by few chosen (cf. x 10); or Una may refer to him as 'her chosen knight' (20.5); cf. i 49.9.
6   Cf. Rom. 5.20: 'The Law entred thereupon that the offence shulde abunde: nevertheles where sinne abunded, there grace abunded muche more.'
7   Cf. Eph. 6.16: 'Above all, take the shield of faith, where-with ye may quench all the fyrie dartes of the wicked.'
8   Cf. Col. 2.14: 'And putting out the hand writing of ordinances that was against us, which was contrarie to us, he even toke it out of the way, and fastened it upon the crosse.'

Stanza 54
2   **carle**: churl.
3   **for**: in spite of.
5   **vnbid vnblest**: i.e. without prayer or blessing, as given in the burial service.
7   **drest**: made ready.
9   **that is eternally**: in contrast to man: 'whosoever liveth, and believeth in him, shall not die eternally' (BCP).

Stanza 50
2–3   Meant literally and figuratively.

Cant. X.

*Her faithfull knight faire Vna brings
to house of Holinesse,
Where he is taught repentance, and
the way to heauenly blesse.*

1

WHat man is he, that boasts of fleshly might,
 And vaine assurance of mortality,
Which all so soone, as it doth come to fight,
Against spirituall foes, yeelds by and by,
Or from the field most cowardly doth fly?
Ne let the man ascribe it to his skill,
That thorough grace hath gained victory.
If any strength we haue, it is to ill,
But all the good is Gods, both power and eke will.

2

By that, which lately hapned, *Vna* saw,
 That this her knight was feeble, and too faint;
And all his sinews woxen weake and raw,
Through long enprisonment, and hard constraint,
Which he endured in his late restraint,
That yet he was vnfit for bloudie fight:
Therefore to cherish him with diets daint,
She cast to bring him, where he chearen might,
Till he recouered had his late decayed plight.

3

There was an auntient house not farre away,
 Renowmd throughout the world for sacred lore,
And pure vnspotted life: so well they say
It gouernd was, and guided euermore,
Through wisedome of a matrone graue and hore;
Whose onely ioy was to relieue the needes
Of wretched soules, and helpe the helpelesse pore:
All night she spent in bidding of her bedes,
And all the day in doing good and godly deedes.

4

Dame *Cælia* men did her call, as thought
 From heauen to come, or thither to arise,
The mother of three daughters, well vpbrought
In goodly thewes, and godly exercise:
The eldest two most sober, chast, and wise,
Fidelia and *Speranza* virgins were,
Though spousd, yet wanting wedlocks solemnize;
But faire *Charissa* to a louely fere
Was lincked, and by him had many pledges dere.

Canto x

Argument

4   blesse: bliss; also blessing, the need of which is stressed

in Trevisan's prayer, 'God from him [Despair] me blesse'
(ix 28.3).

Stanza 1

1   What man is he: implying 'how foolish is that man'.
'Cursed be the man that trusteth in man, and maketh flesh his
arme' (Jer. 17.5).

**4–5   **This comment upon the actions of Terwin and Trevisan
applies also to the Red Cross Knight: in yielding to Despair,
he forsook the battle against the Dragon, ix 52.8–9.   **by and
by**: soon.

**6–9   **'For by grace are ye saued through faith, and that not
of your selues: it is the gifte of God, not of workes, lest any
man shulde boaste himself' (Eph. 2.8–9).

**9   **Combines two texts: 'There is no power but of God'
(Rom. 13.1) and 'It is God which worketh in you, bothe the
wil and the dede' (Phil. 2.13).

Stanza 2

**1–6   **See ix 20.4–9n.

2   faint: wanting in courage; wanting in strength. Una
had once enjoined the Knight, 'Add faith . . . and be not
faint' (i 19.3); now she takes him to Fidelia to be
strengthened.

3   raw: cf. his 'rawbone armes' (viii 41.6).

4   constraint: confinement; or affliction, referring to his
long imprisonment.

**7–9   **In contrast to Duessa who brought the Knight to the
house of Pride because she was 'wearie of the toilesome way'
(iv 3.8). See 11.4–5 below.

7   cherish: foster; also cheer, gladden, as he is a victim of
despair.   **daint**: dainty, choice; cf. 18.2, 26.3.

9   recouered: got over.

Stanza 3

**1–3   **Cf. the 'spiritual house' of 1 Pet. 2.5; cf. also the
description of Una as pure 'in life and euery vertuous lore'
(i 5.2). Since the Knight is guided by Una, his experience in
the house of Holiness reverses that in the house of Pride. With
Una, the house lies **not farre away**; with Duessa, the Knight
'Long with her traueild, till at last they see / A goodly building'
(iv 2.5–6).

5   hore: hoar, venerable; cf. 5.5.

**6–7   **Cf. the works of mercy, Matt. 25.35; see 36.3n.
onely: chief.

8–9   bidding of her bedes: saying her prayers; cf. the blind
devotion of Corceca who spends both 'day and night' (iii 13.6)
saying her prayers.

Stanza 4

1   Cælia: Heavenly. Ruskin (1851) App. 2 suggests
'Heavenly Grace, the mother of the Virtues'.

**3–9   **Cf. 1 Cor. 13.13: 'And now abideth faith, hope and
love, even these thre, but the chiefest of these is love.' Charity
is the youngest, according to the doctrine, 'Faith before good
works.'

4   thewes: manners, discipline.   **godly exercise**:
'godly deedes' of the previous stanza.

7   solemnize: solemnization. Faith and Hope are not
fulfilled in this world.

8   louely fere: loving husband.

9   pledges: i.e. children regarded as tokens of their parents'
love. S., the poet of married love, fashions this sense; cf.

5

Arriued there, the dore they find fast lockt;
　　For it was warely watched night and day,
　　For feare of many foes: but when they knockt,
　　The Porter opened vnto them streight way:
　　He was an aged syre, all hory gray,
　　With lookes full lowly cast, and gate full slow,
　　Hight *Humiltá*.　They passe in stouping low;
For streight and narrow was the way, which he did show.

6

Each goodly thing is hardest to begin,
　　But entred in a spacious court they see,
　　Both plaine, and pleasant to be walked in,
　　Where them does meete a francklin faire and free,
　　And entertaines with comely courteous glee,
　　His name was *Zele*, that him right well became,
　　For in his speeches and behauiour hee
　　Did labour liuely to expresse the same,
And gladly did them guide, till to the Hall they came.

7

There fairely them receiues a gentle Squire,
　　Of milde demeanure, and rare courtesie,
　　Right cleanly clad in comely sad attire;
　　In word and deede that shew'd great modestie,
　　And knew his good to all of each degree,
　　Hight *Reuerence*.　He them with speeches meet
　　Does faire entreat; no courting nicetie,
　　But simple true, and eke vnfained sweet,
As might become a Squire so great persons to greet.

8

And afterwards them to his Dame he leades,
　　That aged Dame, the Ladie of the place:
　　Who all this while was busie at her beades:
　　Which doen, she vp arose with seemely grace,
　　And toward them full matronely did pace.
　　Where when that fairest *Vna* she beheld,
　　Whom well she knew to spring from heauenly race,
　　Her hart with ioy vnwonted inly sweld,
As feeling wondrous comfort in her weaker eld.

9

And her embracing said, O happie earth,
　　Whereon thy innocent feet doe euer tread,
　　Most vertuous virgin borne of heauenly berth,
　　That to redeeme thy woefull parents head,
　　From tyrans rage, and euer-dying dread,
　　Hast wandred through the world now long a day;
　　Yet ceasest not thy wearie soles to lead,
　　What grace hath thee now hither brought this way?
Or doen thy feeble feet vnweeting hither stray?

10

Strange thing it is an errant knight to see
　　Here in this place, or any other wight,
　　That hither turnes his steps.　So few there bee,
　　That chose the narrow path, or seeke the right:
　　All keepe the broad high way, and take delight
　　With many rather for to go astray,
　　And be partakers of their euill plight,
　　Then with a few to walke the rightest way;
O foolish men, why haste ye to your owne decay?

Bacon's 'hostages to fortune' (in 'Of marriage and single life').

Stanza 5

4　'Knocke, and it shalbe opened vnto you' (Matt. 7.7).
7　**stay**: support.
8–9　'The gate is streicte, and the way narowe that leadeth vnto life' (Matt. 7.14). These lines are interpreted in the next line; cf. 10.3–4.　**Humiltá**: Ital. *Humiltà*. He is Porter because 'except ye . . . become as litle children, ye shal not enter into the kingdome of heauen' (Matt. 18.3), which Geneva glosses as 'not vayne glorious, seking to advance them selves to worldelie honours'.

Stanza 6

1　Proverbial (C. G. Smith, 1970, 52).　**begin**: the word combines the fig. sense 'enter upon' and the literal 'enter in'.
4　**francklin**: freeholder; his zeal manifests his state of Christian liberty.　**free**: 'in the libertie wherewith Christ hathe made us fre' (Gal. 5.1).
6　**His name was**: a common formula in this canto (cf. 17.9, 23.9, etc.). In this house disguise is not needed.

Stanza 7

1　**fairely**: courteously; cf. **faire** (7). The adverb is used six times in the canto to mark the gracious formality shown by the inhabitants of the house of Holiness.
3　**sad**: sober-coloured.
5　He knew how to behave with the respect suitable to each class of society and each member in it. This virtue of civility is closely linked to courtesy: see VI ii 1.6–7n.
6　**Reuerence** is only a Squire, not venerably aged, as one might at first expect.
7　**entreat**: treat.　**courting nicetie**: affectation in paying court.
8　**simple true**: simple true behaviour; or simple truth.

Stanza 8

9　**comfort**: physical strengthening, invigoration.
weaker eld: too weak age.

Stanza 9

2　**euer**: cf. Hooker: 'this visible Church . . . is but one, continued from the first beginning of the world to the last end' (*Laws* Bk III i 3). The continuity of the Church especially concerned Protestants.
3　The claim of Una's heavenly origin is repeated from the previous stanza to distinguish the mystical Church from the visible Church on earth.
5　**euer-dying dread**: constant fear of (eternal) death.
7　**soles**: a pun on 'souls', as Una is the Church Militant.

Stanza 10

4　**chose**: in the present tense.
5　**the broad high way**: the 'broad waye that leadeth to destruction: and manie there be which go in thereat' (Matt. 7.13); it leads to the house of Pride, iv 2.8.
8　**a few**: the 'chosen' of ix 53.5.　**rightest**: the only right way (as the Lat. superlative of eminence); also the most direct way instead of going astray; cf. 'the paths of righteousnes' (Prov. 4.11).

11

Thy selfe to see, and tyred limbs to rest,
　O matrone sage (quoth she) I hither came,
　And this good knight his way with me addrest,
　Led with thy prayses and broad-blazed fame,
　That vp to heauen is blowne. The auncient Dame
Him goodly greeted in her modest guise,
　And entertaynd them both, as best became,
　With all the court'sies, that she could deuise,
Ne wanted ought, to shew her bounteous or wise.

12

Thus as they gan of sundry things deuise,
　Loe two most goodly virgins came in place,
　Ylinked arme in arme in louely wise,
　With countenance demure, and modest grace,
　They numbred euen steps and equall pace:
Of which the eldest, that *Fidelia* hight,
　Like sunny beames threw from her Christall face,
　That could haue dazd the rash beholders sight,
And round about her head did shine like heauens light.

13

She was araied all in lilly white,
　And in her right hand bore a cup of gold,
　With wine and water fild vp to the hight,
　In which a Serpent did himselfe enfold,
　That horrour made to all, that did behold;
But she no whit did chaunge her constant mood:
　And in her other hand she fast did hold
　A booke, that was both signd and seald with blood,
Wherein darke things were writ, hard to be vnderstood.

14

Her younger sister, that *Speranza* hight,
　Was clad in blew, that her beseemed well;
　Not all so chearefull seemed she of sight,
　As was her sister; whether dread did dwell,
　Or anguish in her hart, is hard to tell:
Vpon her arme a siluer anchor lay,
　Whereon she leaned euer, as befell:
　And euer vp to heauen, as she did pray,
Her stedfast eyes were bent, ne swarued other way.

15

They seeing *Vna*, towards her gan wend,
　Who them encounters with like courtesie;
　Many kind speeches they betwene them spend,
　And greatly ioy each other well to see:
　Then to the knight with shamefast modestie
They turne themselues, at *Vnaes* meeke request,
　And him salute with well beseeming glee;
　Who faire them quites, as him beseemed best,
And goodly gan discourse of many a noble gest.

Stanza 11
3 **addrest**: directed.
4–5 Cf. his reason for visiting Lucifera, iv 13.8–9.

Stanza 12
1 **deuise**: converse.
3 **louely**: loving.
5 This brief allegorical pageant contrasts with the monstrously yoked procession of the sins in the house of Pride. Faith and Hope walk in step because they go together, as the Despair episode demonstrated. On the traditional iconography of the three Christian virtues, see Chew (1962) 127–33.
6 **the eldest**: because faith precedes hope as 'the grounde of things, which are hoped for, and the evidence of things which are not sene' (Heb. 11.1).
7 **Like sunny beames**: what seemed like sunbeams; cf. Moses's face, Exod. 34.29–30; and the face of Christ, Matt. 17.2. **Christall**: clear, luminous; a pun on 'Christ'.
8 **dazd**: dazzled; as does Arthur's shield, vii 35.8–9.

Stanza 13
1 **lilly white**: 'in signe of puritie' (Geneva gloss to Rev. 7.9). **all**: Ariosto, *Orl. Fur.* xxi 1, observes that by the ancients holy Faith was always depicted in a white garment.
2–9 St John the Evangelist is usually represented with a chalice out of which issues a serpent, and with an open book in his hand (Percival, 1893). The *Golden Legend* records the familiar story of how John drank a cup of poison to prove his faith. At Mark 16.18 serpents are associated with poisoned drink.
2–5 **cup of gold**: the cup of the Holy Sacrament **wine and water**: i.e. of the Holy Communion, the healing blood and baptismal water that issued from the side of the crucified Christ; see John 19.34 and 1 John 5.6. According to the Geneva gloss, water and blood 'declare that we have our sinnes washed by him, and he hathe made ful satisfaction for the same'.
4 **Serpent**: the emblem of Aesculapius, the symbol of healing; also of the crucified Christ, the symbol of redemption. The serpent lifted up by Moses (Num. 21.9) is interpreted typologically as Christ lifted up on the cross (John 3.14). Fidelia holds the symbol of true healing, which is parodied by the healing powers of Aesculapius, v 36f. Both the wine and water and the Serpent 'answer' the death and despair which men drink from Duessa's golden cup: see viii 14.
6 'Let us kepe the profession of our hope, without wavering' (Heb. 10.23).
8 **booke**: the New Testament which is sealed with Christ's blood; cf. Mark 14.24, Rev. 5.1.
9 Cf. Peter on Paul's epistles: 'among the which some things are hard to be understand' (2 Pet. 3.16); applied here particularly to Revelation.

Stanza 14
2 **blew**: Hope's colour: 'For the hopes sake, which is layd up . . . in heaven' (Col. 1.5); for Cowley, *Davideis* i n60, 'Sacred Blew' represents 'the seat of *God*, that is, the *Heavens*'.
4–5 **dread . . . anguish**: complementary emotions which afflict those without hope, i.e. in despair; cf. ix 22.3, 49.4.
6 Cf. Heb. 6.18–9: 'to holde fast the hope that is set before s, which we have, as an ancre of the soule, both sure and stedfast'. **siluer**: for purity; 'Everie man that hathe this hope in him, purgeth himself, even as he is pure' (1 John 3.3). The *ancora spei* appears on the title-page of the 1596 edition of the poem.
7 **as befell**: as was fitting. Not a rhyming tag: stress is placed throughout the pageant of virtues on what is fitting and seemly.

16

Then *Vna* thus; But she your sister deare,
  The deare *Charissa* where is she become?
  Or wants she health, or busie is elsewhere?
  Ah no, said they, but forth she may not come:
  For she of late is lightned of her wombe,
  And hath encreast the world with one sonne more,
  That her to see should be but troublesome.
Indeede (quoth she) that should her trouble sore,
But thankt be God, and her encrease so euermore.

17

Then said the aged *Cælia*, Deare dame,
  And you good Sir, I wote that of your toyle,
  And labours long, through which ye hither came,
  Ye both forwearied be: therefore a whyle
  I read you rest, and to your bowres recoyle.
  Then called she a Groome, that forth him led
  Into a goodly lodge, and gan despoile
  Of puissant armes, and laid in easie bed;
His name was meeke *Obedience* rightfully ared.

18

Now when their wearie limbes with kindly rest,
  And bodies were refresht with due repast,
  Faire *Vna* gan *Fidelia* faire request,
  To haue her knight into her schoolehouse plaste,
  That of her heauenly learning he might taste,
  And heare the wisedome of her words diuine.
  She graunted, and that knight so much agraste,
  That she him taught celestiall discipline,
And opened his dull eyes, that light mote in them shine.

19

And that her sacred Booke, with bloud ywrit,
  That none could read, except she did them teach,
  She vnto him disclosed euery whit,
  And heauenly documents thereout did preach,
  That weaker wit of man could neuer reach,
  Of God, of grace, of iustice, of free will,
  That wonder was to heare her goodly speach:
  For she was able, with her words to kill,
And raise againe to life the hart, that she did thrill.

20

And when she list poure out her larger spright,
  She would commaund the hastie Sunne to stay,
  Or backward turne his course from heauens hight;
  Sometimes great hostes of men she could dismay,
  Dry-shod to passe, she parts the flouds in tway;
  And eke huge mountaines from their natiue seat
  She would commaund, themselues to beare away,
  And throw in raging sea with roaring threat.
Almightie God her gaue such powre, and puissance great.

Stanza 15
2   **encounters**: goes to meet (*OED* 6).
8   He returns their salutation courteously.
9   **gest**: deed.

Stanza 16
2   **deare**: stressed as she is Love.   **become**: i.e. gone to;
or, what has happened to her?
8   The visit would trouble Charissa rather than Una.
9   **her encrease**: i.e. may God give her increase.

Stanza 17
3   **through**: by means of, by reason of.
4   **forwearied**: utterly wearied, the Knight's state at
i 32.6 when his resting began his descent into Orgoglio's
dungeon.
5   **read**: counsel.   **recoyle**: retire.
9   **ared**: told; understood.

Stanza 18
1–2   Repeated from ix 2.1–2 to mark another stage in the
Knight's adventure: see ix 20.4–9*n*.   **kindly**: natural; owing
to nature, as **due** also suggests; in contrast to the 'deadly
sleepe' which overpowers the Knight in Archimago's hermitage,
i 36.6.   **repast**: refreshment on the physical level, preparing
for 'spirituall repast' (48.8).
7   **agraste**: favoured with grace.
9   As Christ sent Paul to the Gentiles 'To open their eyes,
that they may turne from darkenes to light, and from the
power of Satan unto God, that they may receive forgivenes
of sinnes, and inheritance among them, which are sanctified
by faith in me' (Acts 26.18); cf. Eph. 1.17–8.

Stanza 19
1–2   Cf. Rev. 5.1, 3: 'A Boke written within, and on the
backeside, sealed with seven seales. . . . and no man in heaven,
nor in earth, nether under the earth, was able to open the Boke
nether to loke thereon.'   **bloud**: the blood of Christ; cf.
Heb. 9.20.
2   According to the law of exegesis: *credo ut intelligam*.
4   **documents**: teachings.
8–9   2 Cor. 3.6: 'for the letter killeth, but the Spirit giveth
life.'   **thrill**: pierce.

Stanza 20
For these miracles of faith, see line **2**: Josh. 10.12–3; **3**:
2 Kings 20.10–1; **4**: Judges 7.21; **5**: Exod. 14.22 and Josh.
3.17 (and see below 53.2–5); **6–8**: Matt. 21.21. In the *1590*
and *1596* editions, which omitted line 5, the three lines given
to the miracles cited from the New Testament balance the
three from the Old Testament.
1   **larger spright**: greater power, the biblical 'spirit of the
Lord'.
4   Cf. Merlin's similar power, III iii 12.5.   **dismay**: defeat.
5   This line, added in 1609, seems unfinished: the sense
requires the expansion, 'Dry-shod that men might pass'. One
almost prefers to omit the line to keep the witty point that even
the poet's verse halts before the power of Faith. See 53.5*n*.
8   **roaring threat**: or threatening roar.

21

The faithfull knight now grew in litle space,
　By hearing her, and by her sisters lore,
　To such perfection of all heauenly grace,
　That wretched world he gan for to abhore,
　And mortall life gan loath, as thing forlore,
　Greeu'd with remembrance of his wicked wayes,
　And prickt with anguish of his sinnes so sore,
　That he desirde to end his wretched dayes:
So much the dart of sinfull guilt the soule dismayes.

22

But wise *Speranza* gaue him comfort sweet,
　And taught him how to take assured hold
　Vpon her siluer anchor, as was meet;
　Else had his sinnes so great, and manifold
　Made him forget all that *Fidelia* told.
　In this distressed doubtfull agonie,
　When him his dearest *Vna* did behold,
　Disdeining life, desiring leaue to die,
She found her selfe assayld with great perplexitie.

23

And came to *Cælia* to declare her smart,
　Who well acquainted with that commune plight,
　Which sinfull horror workes in wounded hart,
　Her wisely comforted all that she might,
　With goodly counsell and aduisement right;
　And streightway sent with carefull diligence,
　To fetch a Leach, the which had great insight
　In that disease of grieued conscience,
And well could cure the same; His name was *Patience*.

24

Who comming to that soule-diseased knight,
　Could hardly him intreat, to tell his griefe:
　Which knowne, and all that noyd his heauie spright
　Well searcht, eftsoones he gan apply reliefe
　Of salues and med'cines, which had passing priefe,
　And thereto added words of wondrous might:
　By which to ease he him recured briefe,
　And much asswag'd the passion of his plight,
That he his paine endur'd, as seeming now more light.

25

But yet the cause and root of all his ill,
　Inward corruption, and infected sin,
　Not purg'd nor heald, behind remained still,
　And festring sore did rankle yet within,
　Close creeping twixt the marrow and the skin.
　Which to extirpe, he laid him priuily
　Downe in a darkesome lowly place farre in,
　Whereas he meant his corrosiues to apply,
And with streight diet tame his stubborne malady.

the worldlie sorowe causeth death' (2 Cor. 7.10).

Stanza 22
1　**comfort sweet**: such as Una offers to save the Knight
from despair, ix 53.4–8.
6　**doubtfull**: fearful.　**agonie**: its application to Christ's
anguish in the garden of Gethsemane (*OED* 2) provides the
pattern for the Knight's experience.
9　**perplexitie**: distress; also bewilderment. Greater curative
powers than the Church may provide are needed.

Stanza 23
1　**And came to Cælia**: referring to the office of prayer.
3　**sinfull horror**: horror of sin; 'sinfull guilt' (21.9).
5　**aduisement**: advice.
7　**Leach**: surgeon.
8　**conscience**: see ix 48.3*n*; cf. 'soule-diseased' (24.1).
Percival (1893) cites Latimer on Confession: 'And those who
find themselves grieved in conscience might go to a learned
man, and there fetch of him comfort of the Word of God.'
9　**Patience**: Christian patience, continued faith in God's
mercy; cf. Rev. 14.12 which Geneva glosses as 'The faithful
are exhorted to pacience'.

Stanza 24
2　**intreat**: persuade.
3　**Which knowne**: confession is a necessary, but private,
stage in the Knight's regeneration, and S.'s treatment is brief.
He seems to agree with Hooker, *Laws* Bk VI iv.　**noyd**:
troubled.
4　**searcht**: probed, as a wound.
5　**passing priefe**: surpassing efficacy; cf. James 1.4: 'And
let pacience have her perfite worke, that ye may be perfite and
entire, lacking nothing.'
6–9　Through absolution the Knight is restored to health
(**recured**).　**briefe** suggests both 'quickly' and 'only for a
moment'. S. agrees with Hooker that the force of absolution
is not to take away sin, as the papists claim, but only to
'ascertain us of God's most gracious and merciful pardon'
(*Laws* Bk VI vi 4).
8　**passion**: suffering.
9　Alpers (1967) 50 notices the ambiguity: 'We cannot tell
whether the knight's pain has become more endurable, or
whether he has become better able to endure pain. Clearly we
are to take in both meanings, the point being that in a disease
of the soul, to endure the pain is in fact to reduce it.'

Stanza 25
1–5　'This Infection of Nature doth remain, yea in them
that are regenerated' (Article 9 of the Thirty-nine Articles of
Religion).　**infected sin**: sin that physically and morally
contaminates or is ingrained; cf. 'all loathly crime, / That is
ingenerate in fleshly slime' (III vi 3.4–5).　**rankle**: a festering, incurable wound, here original sin; cf. xi 38.9; at ix 7.4
the term describes Arthur's love for the Faerie Queene; see
VI iv 9.9*n*.
6　**extirpe**: root out, in the surgical sense (cf. 26.8), and
hence in a moral sense.
7–9　The Knight 'returns' to the dungeon of Orgoglio to
root out the sin which placed him there.　**corrosiues**: the
line requires 'corsives' (an obsolete form: cf. IV ix 14.4) or the
final phrase must be elided. The term signifies both a corrosive
drug and a caustic remedy.　**streight**: strict.　**diet**: way
of living.

Stanza 21
5　**forlore**: doomed to destruction; or, which he had
abandoned.
6–9　He yields to despair in seeking to end his life, as earlier
(ix 51); only now, guided by grace, he repents the sin itself
rather than fearing punishment for the sin: 'For godlie sorowe
causeth repentance unto salvacion, not to be repented of: but

26

In ashes and sackcloth he did array
  His daintie corse, proud humors to abate,
  And dieted with fasting euery day,
  The swelling of his wounds to mitigate,
  And made him pray both earely and eke late:
  And euer as superfluous flesh did rot
  Amendment readie still at hand did wayt,
  To pluck it out with pincers firie whot,
That soone in him was left no one corrupted iot.

27

And bitter *Penance* with an yron whip,
  Was wont him once to disple euery day:
  And sharpe *Remorse* his hart did pricke and nip,
  That drops of bloud thence like a well did play;
  And sad *Repentance* vsed to embay
  His bodie in salt water smarting sore,
  The filthy blots of sinne to wash away.
  So in short space they did to health restore
The man that would not liue, but earst lay at deathes dore.

28

In which his torment often was so great,
  That like a Lyon he would cry and rore,
  And rend his flesh, and his owne synewes eat.
  His owne deare *Vna* hearing euermore
  His ruefull shriekes and gronings, often tore
  Her guiltlesse garments, and her golden heare,
  For pitty of his paine and anguish sore;
  Yet all with patience wisely she did beare;
For well she wist, his crime could else be neuer cleare.

29

Whom thus recouer'd by wise Patience,
  And trew *Repentance* they to *Vna* brought:
  Who ioyous of his cured conscience,
  Him dearely kist, and fairely eke besought
  Himselfe to chearish, and consuming thought
  To put away out of his carefull brest.
  By this *Charissa*, late in child-bed brought,
  Was woxen strong, and left her fruitfull nest;
To her faire *Vna* brought this vnacquainted guest.

30

She was a woman in her freshest age,
  Of wondrous beauty, and of bountie rare,
  With goodly grace and comely personage,
  That was on earth not easie to compare;
  Full of great loue, but *Cupids* wanton snare
  As hell she hated, chast in worke and will;
  Her necke and breasts were euer open bare,
  That ay thereof her babes might sucke their fill;
The rest was all in yellow robes arayed still.

indulgence becomes for the Knight the means to renovate his body. Cf. Hooker's defence of fasting, *Laws* Bk V lxxii.
daintie corse: handsome body. **humors**: the bodily fluids whose proportions, according to Renaissance physiology, determine the temperament. **proud humors** signify the state of pride; in particular, the swelling of concupiscence. **abate**: put an end to.
6 **superfluous flesh**: like 'proud flesh', a term for the swelling of a wound.
7 **Amendment**: self-reformation.

Stanza 27
The formal stages of repentance begin with **Penance**, the punishment for the present state of sin; penance brings **Remorse**, the sorrow for past sins; and remorse brings **Repentance**, the resolve to sin no more.
1 **bitter**: because of his biting whip.
2 **disple**: punish or subject to penance by scourging.
3 **sharpe Remorse**: alluding to its derivation from Lat. *remorsus*, f. *remordere*, to sting, torture, from the prick of conscience.
5–7 Cf. Ps. 51.2: 'Wash me throughly from mine iniquitie, and clense me from my sinne.' The gloss adds: 'My sinnes sticke so fast in me, that I haue nede of some singular kinde of washing.' **embay**: drench, referring to the salt tears of repentance.
9 **The man that would not liue**: i.e. who otherwise would not have lived and who did not wish to live; see viii 38.3–4*n*, and cf. the repetition of this moment at xi 28.4.

Stanza 28
2 On the lion of human sin subdued by Christ, see Ruskin, *The Bible of Amiens* IV xxxiv; noted Fowler (1964) 69 *n*1.
3 Cf. Joel 2.13: 'Rent your heart'. The gloss reads: 'Mortifie your affections and serue God with purenes of heart.'
4–9 Alpers (1967) 37 observes that the Knight's shrieks and groanings are assimilated to Una's suffering. She endures with patience so that he may recover by patience.
9 **crime**: charge or accusation, Lat. *crimen*. Kitchin (1867) suggests 'be clear from the accusation of his sin'; however, 'have his sins cleansed or washed away' is a simpler reading.

Stanza 29
4 She offers him the 'kysse of love' (1 Pet. 5.14), the holy kiss of greeting in the New Testament. **fairely**: courteously, as it modifies **besought**; properly, as it modifies **chearish**.
5 **chearish**: cheer, gladden; or hold dear. The history of the Knight's adventures focuses on this word: from the moment he enters 'too solemne sad' (i 2.8), to his 'sad feare' (ii 44.4) when he hears Fradubio's story, to his meeting with Sansjoy, until, overcome by Despair, grief for his sins causes him to seek his own death.
7–9 **By this** suggests a causal connection. The reborn Knight is the child to whom Charissa has given birth. After faith, comes charity: for 'if I had all faith, so that I colde remove mountaines [cf. 20.6–8] and had not love, I were nothing' (1 Cor. 13.2). **vnacquainted**: not known to her.

Stanza 30
2 **bountie**: goodness, virtue.
3 **personage**: personal appearance.
4 **compare**: match; rival.
9 **yellow**: the colour of marriage, fertility and maternity.

Stanza 26
1–4 Cf. Corceca's penance, iii 14.2–4: her outward act of

31

A multitude of babes about her hong,
   Playing their sports, that ioyd her to behold,
   Whom still she fed, whiles they were weake and young,
   But thrust them forth still, as they wexed old :
   And on her head she wore a tyre of gold,
   Adornd with gemmes and owches wondrous faire,
   Whose passing price vneath was to be told ;
   And by her side there sate a gentle paire
Of turtle doues, she sitting in an yuorie chaire.

32

The knight and *Vna* entring, faire her greet,
   And bid her ioy of that her happie brood ;
   Who them requites with court'sies seeming meet,
   And entertaines with friendly chearefull mood.
   Then *Vna* her besought, to be so good,
   As in her vertuous rules to schoole her knight,
   Now after all his torment well withstood,
   In that sad house of *Penaunce*, where his spright
Had past the paines of hell, and long enduring night.

33

She was right ioyous of her iust request,
   And taking by the hand that Faeries sonne,
   Gan him instruct in euery good behest,
   Of loue, and righteousnesse, and well to donne,
   And wrath, and hatred warely to shonne,
   That drew on men Gods hatred, and his wrath,
   And many soules in dolours had fordonne :
   In which when him she well instructed hath,
From thence to heauen she teacheth him the ready path.

34

Wherein his weaker wandring steps to guide,
   An auncient matrone she to her does call,
   Whose sober lookes her wisedome well descride :
   Her name was *Mercie*, well knowne ouer all,
   To be both gratious, and eke liberall :
   To whom the carefull charge of him she gaue,
   To lead aright, that he should neuer fall
   In all his wayes through this wide worldes waue,
That Mercy in the end his righteous soule might saue.

35

The godly Matrone by the hand him beares
   Forth from her presence, by a narrow way,
   Scattred with bushy thornes, and ragged breares,
   Which still before him she remou'd away,
   That nothing might his ready passage stay :
   And euer when his feet encombred were,
   Or gan to shrinke, or from the right to stray,
   She held him fast, and firmely did vpbeare,
As carefull Nurse her child from falling oft does reare.

36

Eftsoones vnto an holy Hospitall,
   That was fore by the way, she did him bring,
   In which seuen Bead-men that had vowed all
   Their life to seruice of high heauens king
   Did spend their dayes in doing godly thing :
   Their gates to all were open euermore,
   That by the wearie way were traueiling,
   And one sate wayting euer them before,
To call in commers-by, that needy were and pore.

Stanza 31

2   **that ... behold**: also, whom she rejoiced to behold.
5   **tyre**: head-dress, diadem.
6   **owches**: jewels.
7   Whose surpassing worth was difficult to calculate.
8–9   **turtle doues**: the emblem here of a chaste Venus, the symbol of true love (cf. III xi 2.9) and of innocence (cf. Matt. 10.16); the **yuorie chaire** suggests Solomon's regal throne (1 Kings 10.18).

Stanza 32

3   **requites**: greets in return.   **seeming meet**: 'love doeth not boast itself: it is not puffed up: it disdaineth not' (1 Cor. 13.4–5); not a tautology for 'seemly'. The elaborate courtesy displayed in the house of Holiness contrasts with the cold disdain in the house of Pride; see 7.1*n*.
4   **entertaines**: receives.
5–6   Cf. Prov. 16.6: 'By mercie and trueth iniquitie shalbe forgiven'; noted Hankins (1971) 116.
8   **that sad house of Penaunce**: in opposition to 'that sad house of *Pride*' (v 53.9).
9   **past**: passed through, suffered.   **paines of hell**: Ps. 116.3 (BCP).

Stanza 33

2   **that Faeries sonne**: repeated at 52.3, 60.2 to prepare for the revelation of his true identity.
4   **well to donne**: well-doing.
5–7   Cf. Col. 3.6, 8.   **dolours**: sorrows.   **fordonne**: overcome, ruined.
9   **teacheth**: shows.   **ready**: direct.

Stanza 34

3   **descride**: revealed.
4   'The Lord is good to all, and his mercies are over all his workes' (Ps. 145.9).
7–9   An appropriate reference to the Public Baptismal Service: 'beyng stedfast in fayth, joyeful through hope, and rooted in charitie, may so passe the waves of this troublesome world, that finally they maye come to the lande of everlasting lyfe' (*Second Prayer Book of Edward VI*).

Stanza 35

1   Mercie is **Matrone** in the specific sense of one having knowledge of childbirth (*OED* 2); cf. line 9.
2   **a narrow way**: see 5.8–9*n*; called 'that painfull way' (46.1). It is '*the way to heauenly blesse*' (Arg.), for 'through the workes was the faith made perfite' (James 2.22).

Stanza 36

1   **Hospitall**: hostel or hospice.
2   **fore by**: close by; see 3.1–3*n*.
3   **seuen Bead-men**: literally seven men of prayer, although rather than praying they respond to the prayers of others. Their life of good works fulfils Cælia's life, 3.6–9. All seven traditional corporal works of mercy are fulfilled; the first two (feeding the hungry and giving drink to the thirsty) are combined, and one is added, the care of orphans. This last is a special chivalric theme (see III ii 14.6) enjoined by Scripture: see 43.2–3*n*. S.'s authority is Lactantius: see Mounts (1939). Chew (1947) 102–9 concludes that S.'s treatment of the theme is original.
8   **wayting**: watching.

37

The first of them that eldest was, and best,
　Of all the house had charge and gouernement,
　As Guardian and Steward of the rest :
　His office was to giue entertainement
　And lodging, vnto all that came, and went :
　Not vnto such, as could him feast againe,
　And double quite, for that he on them spent,
　But such, as want of harbour did constraine :
Those for Gods sake his dewty was to entertaine.

38

The second was as Almner of the place,
　His office was, the hungry for to feed,
　And thristy giue to drinke, a worke of grace :
　He feard not once him selfe to be in need,
　Ne car'd to hoord for those, whom he did breede :
　The grace of God he layd vp still in store,
　Which as a stocke he left vnto his seede ;
　He had enough, what need him care for more ?
And had he lesse, yet some he would giue to the pore.

39

The third had of their wardrobe custodie,
　In which were not rich tyres, nor garments gay,
　The plumes of pride, and wings of vanitie,
　But clothes meet to keepe keene could away,
　And naked nature seemely to aray ;
　With which bare wretched wights he dayly clad,
　The images of God in earthly clay ;
　And if that no spare cloths to giue he had,
His owne coate he would cut, and it distribute glad.

40

The fourth appointed by his office was,
　Poore prisoners to relieue with gratious ayd,
　And captiues to redeeme with price of bras,
　From Turkes and Sarazins, which them had stayd ;
　And though they faultie were, yet well he wayd,
　That God to vs forgiueth euery howre
　Much more then that, why they in bands were layd,
　And he that harrowd hell with heauie stowre,
The faultie soules from thence brought to his heauenly bowre.

41

The fift had charge sicke persons to attend,
　And comfort those, in point of death which lay ;
　For them most needeth comfort in the end,
　When sin, and hell, and death do most dismay
　The feeble soule departing hence away.
　All is but lost, that liuing we bestow,
　If not well ended at our dying day.
　O man haue mind of that last bitter throw ;
For as the tree does fall, so lyes it euer low.

42

The sixt had charge of them now being dead,
　In seemely sort their corses to engraue,
　And deck with dainty flowres their bridall bed,
　That to their heauenly spouse both sweet and braue
　They might appeare, when he their soules shall saue.
　The wondrous workemanship of Gods owne mould,
　Whose face he made, all beasts to feare, and gaue
　All in his hand, euen dead we honour should.
Ah dearest God me graunt, I dead be not defould.

Stanza 37

1　**best**: chiefest, as explained at 44.2.
4–5　As did Job (Job 31.32). **office**: duty. **entertaine-**
ment: provisions; provision for wants; reception. Cf. **feast**
(6) which has the general sense 'entertain hospitably'; cf. also
44.2–3: 'whose care / Was guests to welcome'.
6–8　Cf. Luke 14: 13–4. **againe**: in return. **double**
quite: repay double. **constraine**: afflict; or force to come
to him.

Stanza 38

1　**Almner**: one who distributes charitable relief among the
poor, as Christ directs: 'Sel that ye have, and give almes'
(Luke 12.33).
2–3　'For I was an hungred, and ye gave me meat: I thursted,
and ye gave me drinke' (Matt. 25.35).
7　**stocke**: fund, capital.
9　**lesse**: too little (a Latinism).

Stanza 39

4–5　**meet, seemely**: on this twofold need of clothes, cf.
Lear's eloquent argument, *King Lear* II iv 264–9.
7　Gen. 1.27.
9　Cf. Luke 3.11: 'He that hathe two coates, let him parte
with him that hathe none.' Percival (1893) cites the story of
St Martin of Tours who divided his coat with a beggar.

Stanza 40

3　**price of bras**: payment of money.
4　**stayd**: imprisoned.
5　**they**: the prisoners; but also **captiues** (3), as Upton
(1758) suggests. On the topicality of this work, see Chew
(1937) 385–6. Bryan (1968) argues that many Turkish captives
were guilty of giving up their faith.
7　**why**: for which.
8–9　After his crucifixion Christ descended into hell to
release those who had been held in Satan's power; cf. *Amor.*
lxviii 1–4. **harrowd**: robbed. **stowre**: assault, referring
to the gates and bars of Hell broken by Christ in his descent
(Ps. 107.16); 'conflict with death' (*OED* 2) is a relevant sense
in this context. **faultie**: guilty.

Stanza 41

6　**bestow**: store up.
8　**throw**: throe, the agony of death; also overthrow.
9　Eccles. 11.3: 'In the place that the tre falleth, there it
shalbe.'

Stanza 42

2　**engraue**: put in a grave; cf. Tobit 12.12.
3–5　Cf. Rev. 21.2 on the redeemed who are prepared to
meet Christ the bridegroom 'as a bride trimmed for her
housband'. **sweet and braue** is typically Spenserian.
6　Gen. 1.27. **mould**: image (as 39.7); the term suggests
'moulding'.
7–8　Cf. Gen. 9.2: 'Also the feare of you, and the dread
of you shalbe upon everie beast of the earth . . . into your hand
are thei delivered.'
9　**defould**: defiled; cf. Ps. 16.10: 'Nether wilt thou suffer
thine holie one to se corruption.'

43

The seuenth now after death and buriall done,
    Had charge the tender Orphans of the dead
    And widowes ayd, least they should be vndone:
    In face of iudgement he their right would plead,
    Ne ought the powre of mighty men did dread
    In their defence, nor would for gold or fee
    Be wonne their rightfull causes downe to tread:
    And when they stood in most necessitee,
He did supply their want, and gaue them euer free.

44

There when the Elfin knight arriued was,
    The first and chiefest of the seuen, whose care
    Was guests to welcome, towardes him did pas:
    Where seeing *Mercie*, that his steps vp bare,
    And alwayes led, to her with reuerence rare
    He humbly louted in meeke lowlinesse,
    And seemely welcome for her did prepare:
    For of their order she was Patronesse,
Albe *Charissa* were their chiefest founderesse.

45

There she awhile him stayes, him selfe to rest,
    That to the rest more able he might bee:
    During which time, in euery good behest
    And godly worke of Almes and charitee
    She him instructed with great industree;
    Shortly therein so perfect he became,
    That from the first vnto the last degree,
    His mortall life he learned had to frame
In holy righteousnesse, without rebuke or blame.

46

Thence forward by that painfull way they pas,
    Forth to an hill, that was both steepe and hy;
    On top whereof a sacred chappell was,
    And eke a litle Hermitage thereby,
    Wherein an aged holy man did lye,
    That day and night said his deuotion,
    Ne other worldly busines did apply;
    His name was heauenly *Contemplation*;
Of God and goodnesse was his meditation.

47

Great grace that old man to him giuen had;
    For God he often saw from heauens hight,
    All were his earthly eyen both blunt and bad,
    And through great age had lost their kindly sight,
    Yet wondrous quick and persant was his spright,
    As Eagles eye, that can behold the Sunne:
    That hill they scale with all their powre and might,
    That his frayle thighes nigh wearie and fordonne
Gan faile, but by her helpe the top at last he wonne.

48

There they do finde that godly aged Sire,
    With snowy lockes adowne his shoulders shed,
    As hoarie frost with spangles doth attire
    The mossy braunches of an Oke halfe ded.
    Each bone might through his body well be red,
    And euery sinew seene through his long fast:
    For nought he car'd his carcas long vnfed;
    His mind was full of spirituall repast,
And pyn'd his flesh, to keepe his body low and chast.

Stanza 43

2–3   As Isaiah 1.17: 'Seke judgement, relieve the oppressed: judge the fatherles and defend the widowe.' Cf. James 1.27. Such is Guyon's task, II i 61.6–8, and Artegall's, III ii 14.6.
4   **In . . . iudgement**: in court.
6   **fee**: bribe.
7   **wonne**: persuaded, i.e. bribed.

Stanza 44

8–9   **Patronesse**: protector (Lat. *patronus*); founder of a religious order, as **chiefest** suggests; defender before a court of justice, as she pleads for man before God (51.7–9).

Stanza 45

3–4   **good behest** and **godly worke** are distinguished, the latter referring to acts of charity; see 3.9, 4.4, 36.5.
9   **In holy righteousnesse**: for the first and only time the Knight is linked directly with the virtue of Holiness, which is not an inner moral state but an active virtue displayed in acts of charity.   **without**: beyond.

Stanza 46

3–4   Cf. Archimago's hermitage 'Downe in a dale' with its chapel 'a little wyde' (i 34).
7   **Ne other worldly busines . . .**: i.e. he did not attend to any worldly concern.
8   **Contemplation**: the state of vision (from Lat. *contemplare*, to see) which goes beyond the active life in the holy Hospital.

Stanza 47

3   **All**: although.
4   **kindly**: natural.
5   **persant**: piercing.
6   As the eagle was thought to strengthen its sight by gazing at the sun; cf. Milton: 'As an eagle . . . kindling her undazl'd eyes at the full midday beam' (*Yale prose works* ii 558); cf. *H.H.B.* 138–40.
8   **fordonne**: exhausted.

Stanza 48

5   **red**: seen.
7   **car'd**: took care of.   **carcas**: retains the etymological sense, 'dead flesh'; his body is dead to sin.
9   **pyn'd**: starved; cf. Rom. 8.13: 'if ye mortifie the dedes of the bodie by the Spirit, ye shal live.'   **low**: weak, and therefore humble.

49

Who when these two approching he aspide,
  At their first presence grew agrieued sore,
  That forst him lay his heauenly thoughts aside;
  And had he not that Dame respected more,
  Whom highly he did reuerence and adore,
  He would not once haue moued for the knight.
  They him saluted standing far afore;
  Who well them greeting, humbly did requight,
And asked, to what end they clomb that tedious height.

50

What end (quoth she) should cause vs take such paine,
  But that same end, which euery liuing wight
  Should make his marke, high heauen to attaine?
  Is not from hence the way, that leadeth right
  To that most glorious house, that glistreth bright
  With burning starres, and euerliuing fire,
  Whereof the keyes are to thy hand behight
  By wise *Fidelia*? she doth thee require,
To shew it to this knight, according his desire.

51

Thrise happy man, said then the father graue,
  Whose staggering steps thy steady hand doth lead,
  And shewes the way, his sinfull soule to saue.
  Who better can the way to heauen aread,
  Then thou thy selfe, that was both borne and bred
  In heauenly throne, where thousand Angels shine?
  Thou doest the prayers of the righteous sead
  Present before the maiestie diuine,
And his auenging wrath to clemencie incline.

52

Yet since thou bidst, thy pleasure shalbe donne.
  Then come thou man of earth, and see the way,
  That neuer yet was seene of Faeries sonne,
  That neuer leads the traueiler astray,
  But after labours long, and sad delay,
  Brings them to ioyous rest and endlesse blis.
  But first thou must a season fast and pray,
  Till from her bands the spright assoiled is,
And haue her strength recur'd from fraile infirmitis.

53

That done, he leads him to the highest Mount;
  Such one, as that same mighty man of God,
  That bloud-red billowes like a walled front
  On either side disparted with his rod,
  Till that his army dry-foot through them yod,
  Dwelt fortie dayes vpon; where writ in stone
  With bloudy letters by the hand of God,
  The bitter doome of death and balefull mone
He did receiue, whiles flashing fire about him shone.

Stanza 49

4   **more**: also greatly.
7   **far afore**: in order not to disturb his privacy, so Percival (1893) suggests; or as a token of respect (cf. xii 5.6).

Stanza 50

7   **keyes**: 'the keyes of the kingdome of heaven' (Matt. 16.19) given Peter for his great faith.   **behight**: delivered. Cf. the keys carried by Ignaro, viii 30.6–9.
8   **require**: request.
9   **according**: consenting to, granting.

Stanza 51

1   **happy**: blessed.
4   **aread**: make known; show (cf. 50.9).
6   See Rev. 5.11.
7   **righteous sead**: the redeemed.

Stanza 52

2   **thou man of earth**: as man is of the dust of the ground (Gen. 2.7); also referring to the Knight's name, George, from Gk *georgos*, ploughman; see 66.5–6n.
7   **a season**: for a time.
8   The bonds from which the Knight's spirit must be delivered are those of the flesh, the old Adam: 'the first man is of the earth, earthlie' (1 Cor. 15.47).   **assoiled**: released, in the etymological sense (Lat. *absolvere*, to loose).
9   **recur'd**: restored to health.

Stanzas 53–54

An example of S.'s syncretic imagery; see Phillips (1969) 121–2. All four mounts are places where 'after similarly arduous spiritual trials, men have been given a revelation of ultimate truth'. The examples are chosen from Jewish, Christian and pagan history. Cf. *S.C.* July 45–52, 73.

Stanza 53

1   **the highest Mount**: the very top of the mountain, with the inference that the revelation it provides is higher than that which 'that pleasaunt Mount' (54.6) provided for classical poets. It is the 'great and an hie mountaine' from which John is shown the New Jerusalem, Rev. 21.10.
2–9   Mount Sinai upon which Moses spent forty days (Exod. 24.18) and received the tablets of the law. Apart from the detail of the **bloud-red billowes** (3), S.'s account remains close to Exod. 14.21–2.
2   **man of God**: Deut. 33.1; here in apposition to 'man of earth' (52.2).
4   **disparted**: parted asunder.
5   **yod**: went; cf. 20.5. The reference here may explain the omission of the earlier line.
7   **bloudy**: 'the blood of the covenant' (Exod. 24.8).
8   **doome of death**: 'the ministration of death written with letters and ingraven in stones' (2 Cor. 3.7).
9   Cf. Deut. 4.11, 'and the mountaine burnt with fire'.

54

Or like that sacred hill, whose head full hie,
    Adornd with fruitfull Oliues all arownd,
    Is, as it were for endlesse memory
    Of that deare Lord, who oft thereon was fownd,
    For euer with a flowring girlond crownd:
    Or like that pleasaunt Mount, that is for ay
    Through famous Poets verse each where renownd,
    On which the thrise three learned Ladies play
Their heauenly notes, and make full many a louely lay.

55

From thence, far off he vnto him did shew
    A litle path, that was both steepe and long,
    Which to a goodly Citie led his vew;
    Whose wals and towres were builded high and strong
    Of perle and precious stone, that earthly tong
    Cannot describe, nor wit of man can tell;
    Too high a ditty for my simple song;
    The Citie of the great king hight it well,
Wherein eternall peace and happinesse doth dwell.

56

As he thereon stood gazing, he might see
    The blessed Angels to and fro descend
    From highest heauen, in gladsome companee,
    And with great ioy into that Citie wend,
    As commonly as friend does with his frend.
    Whereat he wondred much, and gan enquere,
    What stately building durst so high extend
    Her loftie towres vnto the starry sphere,
And what vnknowen nation there empeopled were.

57

Faire knight (quoth he) *Hierusalem* that is,
    The new *Hierusalem*, that God has built
    For those to dwell in, that are chosen his,
    His chosen people purg'd from sinfull guilt,
    With pretious bloud, which cruelly was spilt
    On cursed tree, of that vnspotted lam,
    That for the sinnes of all the world was kilt:
    Now are they Saints all in that Citie sam,
More deare vnto their God, then younglings to their dam.

Stanza 54

By associating the Mount of Olives of Matt. 24.3 with Parnassus, S. links Christ with the Muses, and through them with poetry. The **heauenly notes** and songs of love (**louely lay**) (9) contrast with the 'balefull mone' which results from Moses's sojourn on Mount Sinai.

3   **memory**: probably 'memorial' rather than 'remembrance'.
4   **oft** is supported by Scripture (Luke 21.37, 22.39) but the detail in 5 is not.
7   **each where**: everywhere.

Stanza 55

3–5   Rev. 21.10–21: 'And he shewed me the great citie, holie Jerusalem . . . her shining was like unto a stone most precious . . . And had a great wall and hie . . . And the fundacions of the wall of the citie were garnished with all maner of precious stones. . . . And the twelve gates were twelve pearles.'
7   **ditty**: subject.
8   Ps. 48.2: 'Mount Zion . . . is the ioye of the whole earth, and the citie of the great King.'

Stanza 56

2–5   Cf. Jacob's vision of the ladder stretching from earth to heaven 'and lo, the Angels of God went up and downe by it' (Gen. 28.12). The vision moved him to accept the Lord, as it moves the Knight here. Christ's prophecy of the time when 'ye se heaven open, and the Angels of God ascending, and descending upon the Sonne of man' (John 1.51) is applied to God's elect ascending to Heaven to be greeted by the descending angels. Cf. Heb. 12.22.
5   **commonly**: familiarly; cf. Exod. 33.11.

Stanza 57

1–4   **Hierusalem**: so spelt in the Bishops' Bible, 1582; cf. Rev. 21.2: 'And I John sawe the holie citie newe Jerusalem come downe from God out of heaven.' The Geneva gloss adds: 'the holie companie of the elect.'
4   **chosen people**: cf. 1 Pet. 2.9: 'Ye are a chosen generacion, a royal Priesthode, an holie nacion, a peculiar people.' Cf. Rev. 17.14 and Una's reminder to the Knight that he is chosen, ix 53.5.   **purg'd . . . guilt**: cf. Heb. 1.3.
4–7   Cf. 1 Pet. 1.19: 'the precious blood of Christ, as of a Lambe undefiled, and without spot'; cf. 1 Pet. 2.24: 'Who his owne self bare our sinnes in his bodie on the tre, that we being delivered from sinne shulde live in righteousnes.' John 1.29: 'Beholde the lambe of God, which taketh away the sinne of the worlde'; cf. 1 John 2.2.   **cursed tree**: cf. Gal. 3.13: 'Christ hathe redemed us from the curse of the Law, when he was made a curse for us (for it is written, Cursed is everie one that hangeth on tre).'
8   **sam**: together; enforcing the sense of 'commonly' (56.5); cf. Eph. 2.19: 'Ye are no more strangers and foreners: but citizens with the Saintes, and of the housholde of God.'

58

Till now, said then the knight, I weened well,
 That great *Cleopolis*, where I haue beene,
 In which that fairest *Faerie Queene* doth dwell,
 The fairest Citie was, that might be seene;
 And that bright towre all built of christall cleene,
Panthea, seemd the brightest thing, that was:
 But now by proofe all otherwise I weene;
 For this great Citie that does far surpas,
And this bright Angels towre quite dims that towre of glas.

59

Most trew, then said the holy aged man;
 Yet is *Cleopolis* for earthly frame,
 The fairest peece, that eye beholden can:
 And well beseemes all knights of noble name,
 That couet in th'immortall booke of fame
 To be eternized, that same to haunt,
 And doen their seruice to that soueraigne Dame,
 That glorie does to them for guerdon graunt:
For she is heauenly borne, and heauen may iustly vaunt.

60

And thou faire ymp, sprong out from English race,
 How euer now accompted Elfins sonne,
 Well worthy doest thy seruice for her grace,
 To aide a virgin desolate foredonne.
 But when thou famous victorie hast wonne,
 And high emongst all knights hast hong thy shield,
 Thenceforth the suit of earthly conquest shonne,
 And wash thy hands from guilt of bloudy field:
For bloud can nought but sin, and wars but sorrowes yield.

61

Then seeke this path, that I to thee presage,
 Which after all to heauen shall thee send;
 Then peaceably thy painefull pilgrimage
 To yonder same *Hierusalem* do bend,
 Where is for thee ordaind a blessed end:
 For thou emongst those Saints, whom thou doest see,
 Shalt be a Saint, and thine owne nations frend
 And Patrone: thou Saint *George* shalt called bee,
Saint *George* of mery England, the signe of victoree.

62

Vnworthy wretch (quoth he) of so great grace,
 How dare I thinke such glory to attaine?
 These that haue it attaind, were in like cace
 (Quoth he) as wretched, and liu'd in like paine.
 But deeds of armes must I at last be faine,
 And Ladies loue to leaue so dearely bought?
 What need of armes, where peace doth ay remaine,
 (Said he) and battailes none are to be fought?
As for loose loues are vaine, and vanish into nought.

Stanza 58

2–6 **Cleopolis**: the city of Fame or Glory (cf. vii 46.7); historically, London; or, as Hankins (1971) 201 suggests, Westminster. See III ix 51.5 where Troynovant or London is distinguished from Cleopolis. **Panthea**, from παν, all + θεα, sight: i.e. the best of sights. Historically, this faery tower may be Westminster Abbey and its Royal Chapel with the tombs of Elizabeth's ancestors, from θεά, referring to her divine ancestors in an English Pantheon (see II x 73.3–4*n*); or Windsor Castle where the Queen resided; or the Queen's Palace at Richmond, known as Shene (= bright), so Quekett, *Var.* i 291, suggests. If the Abbey is alluded to, there is a nice distinction, observed by Percival (1893), between the living city and the place of the dead, or between secular and religious houses.

5 **cleene**: clear, pure.

Stanza 59

2 **for earthly frame**: considered as an earthly structure.

3 **peece**: structure; masterpiece.

9 **vaunt**: i.e. boast of as her home; cf. Una 'borne of heauenly brood' (iii 8.7).

Stanza 60

2 **accompted**: obsolete form of 'accounted'.

3 **grace**: favour; cf. i 3.4. The term blends with the search for heavenly grace, 62.1.

5–9 Ellrodt (1960) 209 concludes that only the medieval duality of action and contemplation may explain 'the otherwise incoherent pronouncements of the Hermit'. Anderson (1970) 29 interprets the exchange between Contemplation and the Knight as a process of self-debate and self-resolution.

6 **high**: inferring that the Knight will have the honoured position; cf. xi 2.9.

7 **suit**: pursuit.

Stanza 61

1 **presage**: show prophetically (cf. 55.1); predict, i.e. that it will take you to heaven.

3 On his role as pilgrim, see 66.5–6*n*.

6–8 Cf. II i 32.3–5.

8 **Patrone**: guardian saint. **shalt called bee**: referring to Rev. 3.12: 'Him that overcometh . . . I wil write upon him my new Name.'

9 **signe**: mark or token (Lat. *signum*); signal or battle cry: 'our ancient word of courage, fair Saint George' (*Richard III* V iii 349). On the legend of St George, see *Var.* i 379–90.

Stanza 62

The Knight's first question (1–2) is answered by Contemplation (3–4); his second question (5–6) has two parts: the first is parried by a double question (7–8) and the second dismissed with reproof (9). The revisions show S.'s difficulties with this structure: 4 As wretched men, and liued in like paine. *1590*; 8 and bitter battailes all are fought? *1590*.

5 **faine**: content to leave.

6 Cf. vii 26.4.

9 **vaine . . . vanish**: suggests that loves vanish because they are vain.

63

O let me not (quoth he) then turne againe
  Backe to the world, whose ioyes so fruitlesse are ;
  But let me here for aye in peace remaine,
  Or streight way on that last long voyage fare,
  That nothing may my present hope empare.
  That may not be (said he) ne maist thou yit
  Forgo that royall maides bequeathed care,
  Who did her cause into thy hand commit,
Till from her cursed foe thou haue her freely quit.

64

Then shall I soone, (quoth he) so God me grace,
  Abet that virgins cause disconsolate,
  And shortly backe returne vnto this place,
  To walke this way in Pilgrims poore estate.
  But now aread, old father, why of late
  Didst thou behight me borne of English blood,
  Whom all a Faeries sonne doen nominate ?
  That word shall I (said he) auouchen good,
Sith to thee is vnknowne the cradle of thy brood.

65

For well I wote, thou springst from ancient race
  Of *Saxon* kings, that haue with mightie hand
  And many bloudie battailes fought in place
  High reard their royall throne in *Britane* land,
  And vanquisht them, vnable to withstand:
  From thence a Faerie thee vnweeting reft,
  There as thou slepst in tender swadling band,
  And her base Elfin brood there for thee left.
Such men do Chaungelings call, so chaungd by Faeries theft.

66

Thence she thee brought into this Faerie lond,
  And in an heaped furrow did thee hyde,
  Where thee a Ploughman all vnweeting fond,
  As he his toylesome teme that way did guyde,
  And brought thee vp in ploughmans state to byde,
  Whereof *Georgos* he thee gaue to name;
  Till prickt with courage, and thy forces pryde,
  To Faery court thou cam'st to seeke for fame,
And proue thy puissaunt armes, as seemes thee best became.

Stanza 63

7 **bequeathed care**: the **cause** (8) entrusted to him; or her distress which he has undertaken to relieve. What faith has revealed to him and he holds in **present hope** (5) must now be perfected in charity.
9 The conditions for entry into his pilgrimage are expanded at xii 18. **freely quit**: entirely freed; or delivered to make her free; or released by the Knight's free will.

Stanza 64

2 **Abet**: maintain.
5 **aread**: tell.
6 **behight**: name.
7 **nominate**: call.
8 **auouchen**: prove.
9 **cradle of thy brood**: place from which his race derives; probably used with the literal sense, for he was taken from his cradle; cf. III iii 26.6–7.

Stanza 65

Craig (1972) 528 notes that 'here, where allegory gives way to vision, . . . Spenser briefly discards the fashionable notion that he and his countrymen were the descendants of Geoffrey's legendary Britons'.
3 **in place**: there.
5 **them**: the Britons.
6 **vnweeting**: modifying **thee** (i.e. without your knowing) or **reft** (without the knowledge of anyone); cf. 66.3.
7 **tender**: infant.
8 The line may explain why S. says that when Archimago disguised himself as the Knight, '*Saint George* himself ye would haue deemed him to be' (ii 11.9). The Knight whom we know as Saint George is only of **base Elfin brood**.
9 The popular superstition, noted in *Enc. Brit.*, that change-lings could be made only before christening explains why the Knight must be baptized. **chaungd**: exchanged.

Stanza 66

3 **vnweeting**: inadvertently; or, as at 65.6, referring to the Knight who does not remember.
5–6 According to the *Golden Legend*, 'George is sayd of *geos* / whiche is as moche to saye as *erthe* and *orge* / that is tilyenge / so george is to saye as tilyenge the erthe / that is his flesshe. . . . Or George may be sayd of *gera*: that is holy / and of *gyon* that is a wrasteler / that is an holy wrasteler. For he wrasteled with the dragon. or it is sayd of george that is a pylgrym / and *geyr* that is cut or detrenched out and *us* that is a counseyllour. He was a pylgryme in the syght of the worlde / and he was cut and detrenched by the crowne of martyrdome / and he was a good counseyllour in prechynge' (Appx. Barclay, 1515, 112). See Padelford and O'Connor (1926) 156. S. has framed his character through an awareness of such etymologies (see viii 8.4–6*n*) and the accepted etymology of Adam from Heb. 'red', after the red earth of which he was made. The plowman destined to walk 'in Pilgrims poore estate' (64.4) alludes to Langland's *Piers Plowman*. Tristram White, *The Martyrdome of Saint George* (1614), cites the stanza to show S.'s 'playing upon the Etymologie of this Name [George]' and notes the allusion to 'Tilth'; cited *Spenser Allusions* 139.
6 **Whereof**: wherefore. **to name**: as a name.
7 **forces pryde**: natural powers in their prime.
9 **thee best became**: as best suited you.

67

O holy Sire (quoth he) how shall I quight
　The many fauours I with thee haue found,
　That hast my name and nation red aright,
　And taught the way that does to heauen bound?
　This said, adowne he looked to the ground,
　To haue returnd, but dazed were his eyne,
　Through passing brightnesse, which did quite confound
His feeble sence, and too exceeding shyne.
So darke are earthly things compard to things diuine.

68

At last whenas himselfe he gan to find,
　To *Vna* back he cast him to retire;
　Who him awaited still with pensiue mind.
　Great thankes and goodly meed to that good syre,
　He thence departing gaue for his paines hyre;
　So came to *Vna*, who him ioyd to see,
　And after litle rest, gan him desire,
　Of her aduenture mindfull for to bee.
So leaue they take of *Cælia*, and her daughters three.

Cant. XI.

The knight with that old Dragon fights
two dayes incessantly:
The third him ouerthrowes, and gayns
most glorious victory.

1

HIgh time now gan it wex for *Vna* faire,
　To thinke of those her captiue Parents deare,
　And their forwasted kingdome to repaire:
　Whereto whenas they now approched neare,
　With hartie words her knight she gan to cheare,
　And in her modest manner thus bespake;
　Deare knight, as deare, as euer knight was deare,
　That all these sorrowes suffer for my sake,
High heauen behold the tedious toyle, ye for me take.

2

Now are we come vnto my natiue soyle,
　And to the place, where all our perils dwell;
　Here haunts that feend, and does his dayly spoyle,
　Therefore henceforth be at your keeping well,
　And euer ready for your foeman fell.
　The sparke of noble courage now awake,
　And striue your excellent selfe to excell;
　That shall ye euermore renowmed make,
Aboue all knights on earth, that batteill vndertake.

3

And pointing forth, lo yonder is (said she)
　The brasen towre in which my parents deare
　For dread of that huge feend emprisond be,
　Whom I from far see on the walles appeare,
　Whose sight my feeble soule doth greatly cheare:
　And on the top of all I do espye
　The watchman wayting tydings glad to heare,
　That O my parents might I happily
Vnto you bring, to ease you of your misery.

Stanza 67

1　**quight**: repay.
4　**bound**: lead. The context suggests 'destined'.
6–9　The surpassing brightness of heavenly revelation is emphasized by the inverted construction of 6–8, and is further enforced by the inversion of 9. S. may imply a distinction between the eyes dazzled by brightness and the senses confounded by **shyne** (brilliance or source of shining). Cf. the dazzling of Orgoglio's senses (another man of earth) by the brightness of Arthur's shield, viii 19.

Stanza 68

1　**to find**: to recover from his bright vision. All the Knight's adventures lead to this point at which he finds himself: in the past, his name and nation; in the present, his commitment to Una's cause; in the future, after serving the Faerie Queene, his pilgrimage to the heavenly Jerusalem; and thereafter his role as St George of England.
3　**pensiue**: anxious.
4–5　**Great thankes** would be the only **goodly meed** that Contemplation would accept as payment for his efforts.
hyre: reward.

Canto xi

Argument

1　**that old Dragon**: first named with the indefinite article (i 3.9) and later called 'that fire-mouthed Dragon' (ix 52.9); but now named as in Rev. 20.2, 'the dragon that olde serpent, which is the devil and Satan'.

Stanza 1

3　**forwasted**: utterly laid waste; cf. i 5.8 and vii 44.5.
repaire: restore; heal.
5　**hartie**: bold, full of courage, to arouse his heart, the seat of courage; cf. ix 25.6–7.

Stanza 2

1　**natiue**: applies properly only to Eden.
3　**feend**: the devil (*OED* 2).
4　**be . . . well**: be well on your guard; with the implied pun: the keeping well is the Well of Life which alone may keep man well; cf. ii 43.7. More of a benediction than a caution.
7　**excellent**: pre-eminent, excelling, as the word-play and accent indicate.
8　**That**: referring to his coming battle.

Stanza 3

Omitted *1590*, for no apparent reason. Some description of the **brasen towre** (2), which imprisons Una's parents, is needed to establish the allegorical connection with the brazen Dragon. Cf. vii 44.8 and xii 3.6. Perhaps a **watchman** who waits to **heare** (7) bothered S.; cf. xii 2.4–6.
2–3　As Kaske (1969) 635 notes, the Knight returns to the active life to perform one of the seven corporal works of mercy, release of prisoners (x 40), which is analogous to Christ's harrowing of hell.

143

4

With that they heard a roaring hideous sound,
    That all the ayre with terrour filled wide,
    And seemd vneath to shake the stedfast ground.
    Eftsoones that dreadfull Dragon they espide,
    Where stretcht he lay vpon the sunny side
    Of a great hill, himselfe like a great hill.
    But all so soone, as he from far descride
    Those glistring armes, that heauen with light did fill,
He rousd himselfe full blith, and hastned them vntill.

5

Then bad the knight his Lady yede aloofe,
    And to an hill her selfe with draw aside,
    From whence she might behold that battailles proof
    And eke be safe from daunger far descryde:
    She him obayd, and turnd a little wyde.
    Now O thou sacred Muse, most learned Dame,
    Faire ympe of *Phœbus*, and his aged bride,
    The Nourse of time, and euerlasting fame,
That warlike hands ennoblest with immortall name;

6

O gently come into my feeble brest,
    Come gently, but not with that mighty rage,
    Wherewith the martiall troupes thou doest infest,
    And harts of great Heroës doest enrage,
    That nought their kindled courage may aswage,
    Soone as thy dreadfull trompe begins to sownd;
    The God of warre with his fiers equipage
    Thou doest awake, sleepe neuer he so sownd,
And scared nations doest with horrour sterne astownd.

7

Faire Goddesse lay that furious fit aside,
    Till I of warres and bloudy *Mars* do sing,
    And Briton fields with Sarazin bloud bedyde,
    Twixt that great faery Queene and Paynim king,
    That with their horrour heauen and earth did ring,
    A worke of labour long, and endlesse prayse:
    But now a while let downe that haughtie string,
    And to my tunes thy second tenor rayse,
That I this man of God his godly armes may blaze.

8

By this the dreadfull Beast drew nigh to hand,
    Halfe flying, and halfe footing in his hast,
    That with his largenesse measured much land,
    And made wide shadow vnder his huge wast;
    As mountaine doth the valley ouercast.
    Approching nigh, he reared high afore
    His body monstrous, horrible, and vast,
    Which to increase his wondrous greatnesse more,
Was swolne with wrath, and poyson, and with bloudy gore.

the earth shakes 'uneasily'; cf. Orgoglio's bellowing 'That all the earth for terrour seemd to shake' (vii 7.6).
6   The striking effect of the two spondees in **great hill**, each preceded by a pyrrhic foot, is noted by Percival (1893). Traditionally, Eden is a great hill, as Ezekiel's 'holy mountaine of God' (Ezek. 28.14).
7   The Dragon's vigilance is traditional.
8   The Knight has travelled far from that first moment when 'his glistring armor made / A litle glooming light, much like a shade' (i 14.4–5) in Error's cave.
9   **blith**: joyfully; perhaps with the earlier sense, 'kindly'. The Dragon appears as a courteous host coming to greet his guest; cf. 15.4.   **vntill**: towards.

Stanza 5
The stanza is divided into two parts as both the Knight and poet prepare for battle; **warlike hands** (9) applies to them both. The analogy extends into the next stanza.
1   **yede aloofe**: go aside.
3   **proof**: issue.
6–9   **sacred Muse**: Clio, the muse of History, offspring of Phœbus or Apollo and Mnemosyne or Memory; cf. IV xi 10.1–2. She is the **Nourse of time, and . . . fame** because she cherishes the memory of famous deeds. See III iii 4. Or she may be Calliope: see Proem 1.7, 2.1n. Apollo is named **Phœbus** because the contest is between light and darkness.

Stanza 6
3   **infest**: attack, Lat. *infestare*, in the sense 'make fierce' or 'inspire'. Often confused with 'infect', according to *OED*, as may be implied here: the rage so infects the heroes that they fight.
7   **equipage**: equipment; 'order' (E.K.'s gloss to *S.C.* Oct. 114).

Stanza 7
1   **that furious fit**: strain of music, as 7 suggests. It parallels for the poet 'that mighty rage' (6.2) in the hero.
2–6   Later the Knight reveals his promise to serve the Faerie Queene 'Gainst that proud Paynim king, that workes her teene' (xii 18.8). In the historical allegory, that pagan king would be the Catholic Philip II of Spain. In a dedicatory sonnet to Essex, S. promises to write a poem in which his Muse 'shall dare alofte to sty / To the last praises of this Faery Queene'. Presumably this subject would have been treated in the projected Book XII.
7   **let downe**: by loosening the string to lower the pitch. **haughtie**: high; hence high-pitched.
8   **second tenor**: either lower strain or pitch; or supporting tenor.
9   S. adapts the Virgilian formula, *arma virumque cano*: his man is **of God** and his arms **godly**; moreover, he sings of arms rather than the man, as the contest reveals. Cf. the earlier distinction between the Knight as 'man of earth' and Moses as 'man of God' (x 52.2, 53.2).   **blaze**: proclaim.

Stanza 8
3   The indefinite size creates the horror; cf. 11.7. Cf. Milton's Satan who lay floating 'many a rood' (*P.L.* i 196) and Virgil's Tityos who covers nine acres (*Aen.* vi 596).
4   **wast**: waist, referring to its vast body; also to the devastation to which the land has been reduced under his shadow; cf. vii 44.5.

Stanza 4
3   **vneath**: not scarcely, hardly, or almost (as *OED* suggests). The term may be a contraction of 'underneath', or indicate that

9

And ouer, all with brasen scales was armd,
 Like plated coate of steele, so couched neare,
 That nought mote perce, ne might his corse be harmd
 With dint of sword, nor push of pointed speare;
 Which as an Eagle, seeing pray appeare,
 His aery plumes doth rouze, full rudely dight,
 So shaked he, that horrour was to heare,
 For as the clashing of an Armour bright,
Such noyse his rouzed scales did send vnto the knight.

10

His flaggy wings when forth he did display,
 Were like two sayles, in which the hollow wynd
 Is gathered full, and worketh speedy way:
 And eke the pennes, that did his pineons bynd,
 Were like mayne-yards, with flying canuas lynd,
 With which whenas him list the ayre to beat,
 And there by force vnwonted passage find,
 The cloudes before him fled for terrour great,
And all the heauens stood still amazed with his threat.

11

His huge long tayle wound vp in hundred foldes,
 Does ouerspred his long bras-scaly backe,
 Whose wreathed boughts when euer he vnfoldes,
 And thicke entangled knots adown does slacke,
 Bespotted as with shields of red and blacke,
 It sweepeth all the land behind him farre,
 And of three furlongs does but litle lacke;
 And at the point two stings in-fixed arre,
Both deadly sharpe, that sharpest steele exceeden farre.

12

But stings and sharpest steele did far exceed
 The sharpnesse of his cruell rending clawes;
 Dead was it sure, as sure as death in deed,
 What euer thing does touch his rauenous pawes,
 Or what within his reach he euer drawes.
 But his most hideous head my toung to tell
 Does tremble: for his deepe deuouring iawes
 Wide gaped, like the griesly mouth of hell,
Through which into his darke abisse all rauin fell.

13

And that more wondrous was, in either iaw
 Three rancks of yron teeth enraunged were,
 In which yet trickling bloud and gobbets raw
 Of late deuoured bodies did appeare,
 That sight thereof bred cold congealed feare:
 Which to increase, and all atonce to kill,
 A cloud of smoothering smoke and sulphur seare
 Out of his stinking gorge forth steemed still,
That all the ayre about with smoke and stench did fill.

2–4 As the Leviathan in Job 41.6–8: 'The majestie of his scales is like strong shields, and are sure sealed. One is set to another, that no winde can come betwene them. One is joyned to another; they sticke together, that they can not be sondred.' See Hankins (1971) 110. **so couched neare**: placed so closely. **dint**: blow.
6 **rouze**: ruffle in anger. **rudely dight**: ruggedly arrayed.
8–9 Cf. Rev. 9.9. The detail is repeated at 15.7–8 in order to make the Dragon appal all the senses.

Stanza 10
1 **flaggy**: drooping.
2 **hollow wynd**: as wind makes the sails hollow.
4 **pennes**: the ribs of his wings.
7 **vnwonted**: as the air is unaccustomed to such beating.
9 With the spondee the line stands still at its centre.
threat: thrust or pressure (from Lat. *trudo*) from the beating wings.

Stanza 11
1 **long**: for 'his taile drue the third parte of the starres of heaven, and cast them to the earth' (Rev. 12.4); cf. vii 18.1–5.
3 **boughts**: coils; cf. Error, i 15.3.
5 **shields**: scales, as the Leviathan (Job 41.6 quoted 9.2–4*n*). Cf. Error's speckled tail (i 17.6), and the Dragon's 'speckled brest' (15.2), associated with the serpent's colouring and generally with sin; cf. the red Dragon, Rev. 12.3. **Bespotted** suggests defilement, the spots of sin.
8–9 Cf. the locusts of Rev. 9.10. The **two stings** may be the 'want of faith, or guilt of sin' (vii 45.8) through which the Dragon has always triumphed over Una's champions, or 'Death and despeyre' (viii 14.3) which Duessa carries in her cup; or Sin and Death. Holbein's title-page to Coverdale's Bible of 1535 displays the transfigured Christ triumphing over sin and death (rep. in Strachan, 1957, Fig. 111); or simply duplicity which symbolizes evil.

Stanza 12
1–2 **sharpnesse** is the subject of the sentence.
3 The repetition of a pair of words in inverted order (*antimetabole*) relates the Dragon to death. S.'s use of such figures is analysed by Morgan (1966). **in deed**: in its effect.
8 'Therefore hel hathe inlarged it self ['gapeth' in Elizabethan versions other than the Genevan], and hathe opened his mouth, without measure' (Isaiah 5.14). For hell-mouth as the gaping mouth of the Dragon, see Hughes (1968) 175–201. **griesly**: horrible.
9 **abisse**: used in the sixteenth century for hell, the bowels of the earth, and chaos; cf. IV ii 47.6–7; also cf. *T.M.* 260 and the 'bottomles pit' of Rev. 20.3. See viii 39.7–9*n*. **rauin**: plunder, prey.

Stanza 13
2 The description is traditional; cf. the dragon slain by Cadmus: *triplici stant ordine dentes* (Ovid, *Met.* iii 34). Cf. also the 'great yron teeth' of the beast in Dan. 7.7, and the Leviathan whose 'teeth are fearful round about' (Job 41.5). **enraunged**: placed in a row.
3 **gobbets raw**: chunks of undigested food; as Error, i 20.3.
4 **late**: see viii 6.2–5*n*.
7 **smoke** and **sulphur** suggest hell-fire, as v. 31.5. **seare**: searing; see 26.7, 50.6.
9 **fill**: also 'file': pollute.

Stanza 9
1 **And ouer, all**: and over his body, all . . .; or the pointing may be: 'And, ouer all', i.e. 'and everywhere his body', etc. **brasen**: proverbial for hardness and indestructibility.

14

His blazing eyes, like two bright shining shields,
  Did burne with wrath, and sparkled liuing fyre;
  As two broad Beacons, set in open fields,
  Send forth their flames farre off to euery shyre,
  And warning giue, that enemies conspyre,
  With fire and sword the region to inuade;
  So flam'd his eyne with rage and rancorous yre:
  But farre within, as in a hollow glade,
Those glaring lampes were set, that made a dreadfull shade.

15

So dreadfully he towards him did pas,
  Forelifting vp aloft his speckled brest,
  And often bounding on the brused gras,
  As for great ioyance of his newcome guest.
  Eftsoones he gan aduance his haughtie crest,
  As chauffed Bore his bristles doth vpreare,
  And shoke his scales to battell readie drest;
  That made the *Redcrosse* knight nigh quake for feare,
As bidding bold defiance to his foeman neare.

16

The knight gan fairely couch his steadie speare,
  And fiercely ran at him with rigorous might:
  The pointed steele arriuing rudely theare,
  His harder hide would neither perce, nor bight,
  But glauncing by forth passed forward right;
  Yet sore amoued with so puissant push,
  The wrathfull beast about him turned light,
  And him so rudely passing by, did brush
With his long tayle, that horse and man to ground did rush.

17

Both horse and man vp lightly rose againe,
  And fresh encounter towards him addrest:
  But th'idle stroke yet backe recoyld in vaine,
  And found no place his deadly point to rest.
  Exceeding rage enflam'd the furious beast,
  To be auenged of so great despight;
  For neuer felt his imperceable brest
  So wondrous force, from hand of liuing wight;
Yet had he prou'd the powre of many a puissant knight.

18

Then with his wauing wings displayed wyde,
  Himselfe vp high he lifted from the ground,
  And with strong flight did forcibly diuide
  The yielding aire, which nigh too feeble found
  Her flitting partes, and element vnsound,
  To beare so great a weight: he cutting way
  With his broad sayles, about him soared round:
  At last low stouping with vnweldie sway,
Snatcht vp both horse and man, to beare them quite away.

19

Long he them bore aboue the subiect plaine,
  So farre as Ewghen bow a shaft may send,
  Till struggling strong did him at last constraine,
  To let them downe before his flightes end:
  As hagard hauke presuming to contend
  With hardie fowle, aboue his hable might,
  His wearie pounces all in vaine doth spend,
  To trusse the pray too heauie for his flight;
Which comming downe to ground, does free it selfe by fight.

Stanza 14
1 **His blazing eyes**: alluding to the etymology of dragon, from Gk δράκων, to see clearly, to stare; see vii 17.9*n*.
3–6 The simile links the danger and the warning against it. The same simile describes the vigilant eyes of the Castle of Alma, II ix 46.3–4, and of Disdain, VI vii 42.2.
8–9 Cf. the chiaroscuro effect of the Knight's armour which made 'A litle glooming light, much like a shade' (i 14.5) in Error's den.

Stanza 15
1 **pas**: pace.
4 **ioyance**: joy; coined to emphasize the state of joy; it suggests the Dragon's long, unchallenged supremacy.
guest: not simply a humorous use. The Knight is a guest throughout his adventures, e.g. of Archimago, Despair, the house of Penance, and finally of Adam.
5 **haughtie**: lofty; also proud.
7 **readie drest**: made ready.
8 **That**: that shaking, which is the formal defiance before battle.

Stanza 16
2 **rigorous**: violent; also stiff, referring to the **steadie speare**.
3, 8 **rudely**: violently.
4 **harder**: too hard; also, harder than the spear; cf. 24.4–6.
7 **light**: quickly.
8–9 In this opening contest between the Knight's spear and the Dragon's tail, S. distinguishes between the spear that idly passes **forward right** (5) and the tail **passing by** (*en passant*). **to ground**: see 11.1*n* for the quotation from Rev. 12.4.

Stanza 17
6 **despight**: outrage, insulting action.
9 Cf. vii 45. **prou'd**: tested.

Stanza 18
The Dragon's flight relates him to 'the prince that ruleth in the aire' (Eph. 2.2).
5 **flitting**: moving, unstable; or yielding, as II viii 2.4.
vnsound: lacking solidity.
7–8 **sayles**: cf. 10.2. As a term for the wings of a hawk, it leads to **stouping**: descending swiftly, as a hawk swoops down on its prey. **vnweldie**: implying also that the Knight cannot wield his force against the Dragon's. **sway**: force.

Stanza 19
1 **subiect**: as lying below.
5 **hagard hauke**: the untamed, adult hawk noted for its powerful flight, in contrast to the young 'Eyas hauke' (34.6) to which the Knight is compared.
6 **hable might**: proper or sufficient strength; the sixteenth-century spelling preserves the Lat. *habilis*. **hable** may carry the sense, 'strong', 'powerful'.
7 **pounces**: anterior claws.
8 **trusse**: seize and carry off.

20

He so disseized of his gryping grosse,
  The knight his thrillant speare againe assayd
  In his bras-plated body to embosse,
  And three mens strength vnto the stroke he layd;
  Wherewith the stiffe beame quaked, as affrayd,
  And glauncing from his scaly necke, did glyde
  Close vnder his left wing, then broad displayd.
The percing steele there wrought a wound full wyde,
That with the vncouth smart the Monster lowdly cryde.

21

He cryde, as raging seas are wont to rore,
  When wintry storme his wrathfull wreck does threat,
  The rolling billowes beat the ragged shore,
  As they the earth would shoulder from her seat,
  And greedie gulfe does gape, as he would eat
  His neighbour element in his reuenge:
  Then gin the blustring brethren boldly threat,
  To moue the world from off his stedfast henge,
And boystrous battell make, each other to auenge.

22

The steely head stucke fast still in his flesh,
  Till with his cruell clawes he snatcht the wood,
  And quite a sunder broke. Forth flowed fresh
  A gushing riuer of blacke goarie blood,
  That drowned all the land, whereon he stood;
  The streame thereof would driue a water-mill.
  Trebly augmented was his furious mood
  With bitter sense of his deepe rooted ill,
That flames of fire he threw forth from his large nosethrill.

23

His hideous tayle then hurled he about,
  And therewith all enwrapt the nimble thyes
  Of his froth-fomy steed, whose courage stout
  Striuing to loose the knot, that fast him tyes,
  Himselfe in streighter bandes too rash implyes,
  That to the ground he is perforce constraynd
  To throw his rider: who can quickly ryse
  From off the earth, with durty bloud distaynd,
For that reprochfull fall right fowly he disdaynd.

Stanza 20

1   **disseized of his gryping grosse**: dispossessed of his
heavy grasping.   **disseized** is a legal term; Collier (1862)
notes that **grosse** is a large prey in falconry.
2   **thrillant**: piercing.
3   **embosse**: plunge; a S. coinage used to convey the literal
sense of encasing or sheathing the spear in the Dragon's body.
4   **three mens strength**: signifying the greatest human
strength, as in the threefold Orgoglio, and the spear's third
thrust (cf. 16.3–5, 17.3–4). Cf. the Dragon's 'hable might'
(19.6). Both exert full strength in equal battle; then the Knight
triumphs through supernatural power.
5   **beame**: the spear's wooden shaft. Since the Knight's
armour fills heaven with light, 'beam of light' is implied.
7–9   Since the wing had been 'displayed wyde' (18.1) in
flight, the Knight triumphs over the powers of the air. From
36.8–9 it is clear that the Dragon's body is not wounded.

Stanza 21

The Dragon is linked here with the elements of water, earth,
and air, and in the next stanza with the fourth element, fire.
2   **wreck**: ruin, adding the comic (and apocalyptic) note that
the raging seas themselves should fear wreck.
4–8   Images of chaos are common in Renaissance cosmology.
It was feared that chaos, though tamed in creation, would
return if ever established order were violated in any particular.
5   **greedie gulfe**: the eddies made by the waves after they
break, or the yawning chasm of the oncoming wave.
6   **His neighbour element**: the earth.
8   **henge**: axle.
9   **boystrous**: violently fierce, savage.

Stanza 22

1–4   The alliteration of 's' and 'f' in each half of 1, divided
by the strong caesura, shows how fast the head stuck. The
breaking of the spear in 3 is indicated by the break in the line,
appropriately after **broke**. The flowing of the blood is rendered
by the alliteration in **Forth flowed fresh**.   **goarie**: clotted.
5–6   Clearly comic details, expressing the poet's joy in his
craftsmanship.
8   **sense**: feeling.   **ill**: injury, wound; perhaps also his own
evil nature.

Stanza 23

1   **hideous**: huge.   **hurled**: apparently identified with
hurtled and whirled (*OED*); cf. Error 'hurling her hideous
taile' (i 16.2).
5   **streighter**: tighter.   **too rash**: all too quickly; or too
hasty, referring to the horse. Either way he co-operates in his
fall.   **implyes**: entangles, as the serpent enfolds (*implicat*)
the bodies of Laocoon and his sons (Virgil, *Aen.* ii 215).
6–7   The Knight's passions, represented by the horse,
occasion his fall, re-enacting his fall into sin through Duessa.
can: did.
8   **durty bloud**: i.e. with dirt and blood. Later such defilement illustrates the intemperance of Pyrocles, II v 22.4, vi
41.6–7.   **distaynd**: deeply stained or defiled.
9   **disdaynd**: was indignant about.

24

And fiercely tooke his trenchand blade in hand,
  With which he stroke so furious and so fell,
  That nothing seemd the puissance could withstand:
  Vpon his crest the hardned yron fell,
  But his more hardned crest was armd so well,
  That deeper dint therein it would not make;
  Yet so extremely did the buffe him quell,
  That from thenceforth he shund the like to take,
But when he saw them come, he did them still forsake.

25

The knight was wrath to see his stroke beguyld,
  And smote againe with more outrageous might;
  But backe againe the sparckling steele recoyld,
  And left not any marke, where it did light;
  As if in Adamant rocke it had bene pight.
  The beast impatient of his smarting wound,
  And of so fierce and forcible despight,
  Thought with his wings to stye aboue the ground;
But his late wounded wing vnseruiceable found.

26

Then full of griefe and anguish vehement,
  He lowdly brayd, that like was neuer heard,
  And from his wide deuouring ouen sent
  A flake of fire, that flashing in his beard,
  Him all amazd, and almost made affeard:
  The scorching flame sore swinged all his face,
  And through his armour all his bodie seard,
  That he could not endure so cruell cace,
But thought his armes to leaue, and helmet to vnlace.

27

Not that great Champion of the antique world,
  Whom famous Poetes verse so much doth vaunt,
  And hath for twelue huge labours high extold,
  So many furies and sharpe fits did haunt,
  When him the poysoned garment did enchaunt
  With *Centaures* bloud, and bloudie verses charm'd,
  As did this knight twelue thousand dolours daunt,
  Whom fyrie steele now burnt, that earst him arm'd,
That erst him goodly arm'd, now most of all him harm'd.

and spear, the Knight fights on foot with his sword, and since the Dragon is deprived of its power of flight, both fight on equal terms on the ground. Unlike the traditional St George who slays the Dragon while on horseback, the Red Cross Knight fights on foot, as the Archangel Michael in medieval art when he slays the Dragon.
6   **deeper**: i.e. no deep wound at all; cf. 25.4.
7   **buffe**: blow.
9   **still forsake**: ever shun.

Stanza 25
1   **beguyld**: foiled.
5   **in . . . pight**: thrust at.   **Adamant rocke**: see vii 33.5–9n.
6   **impatient**: unable to bear the suffering.
7   **forcible despight**: powerful injury. The term combines the injury and its cause in the Knight's contemptuous defiance of the Dragon.
8   **stye**: mount.

Stanza 26
1   **griefe**: pain.
3–7   **flake**: flame. The Dragon's fire expresses God's 'euer burning wrath' (ix 50.3, cf. 53.7) against sinful man; cf. the punishment of man by the vials of God's wrath in Rev. 16.8–9: the fourth angel torments man 'with heat of fyre, and men boyled in great heat'.   **flashing in his beard**: Kaske (1969) 610–2 links this curious detail to the metaphor of sin as fire and the beard to the *fomes peccati*, the corruption of man's nature. When the flake is not subdued, it scorches **all his face** and finally sears **all his bodie**. Crawford (1970) argues that the fire symbolizes both the difficulties encountered by a Christian and the purging of sin.   **almost**: perhaps the intensive, 'indeed' (*OED* 4); cf. 15.8.   **swinged**: singed, scorched; also whipped, as the lash of a tail.
7–9   **seard**: literally, 'burned by hot iron'.   **cace**: plight; with a pun on the armour which encloses him. The witty word play points to the paradox: putting off the armour had brought his fall; now put on, it causes his fall.   **armes** are linked with his battle against Orgoglio; **helmet**, which is 'the hope of salvation' (1 Thess. 5.8), with his battle against Despair.   **thought**: intended. Kaske 619 notes here the second of the traditional stages of sin in which mental confusion leads to consent.

Stanza 27
1–6   **that great Champion**: Hercules. When he put on the garment soaked in the Centaur's poisoned blood, his flesh burned and he died in great agony. The garment was given him by his wife as a love-charm, hence it was **With . . . bloudie verses charm'd**; see Ovid, *Met.* ix 134–272. The comparison is apt because the Knight's armour is also 'charmed' (cf. iv 50.5–6), but chiefly because Hercules's fiery death was interpreted as punishment for concupiscence, e.g. by Comes (1616) VII i.
3   **extold**: the context suggests the obsolete sense, 'made too much of'.
7   **twelue thousand**: an allusion to the labours of Hercules. The Christian Knight endures his twelve labours all at once while the pain is multiplied a thousandfold.   **dolours**: pains.
8, 9   **arm'd, harm'd**: the jingle, which Percival (1893) notes as 'a perfectly serious euphuistic pun', enforces the paradox mentioned at 26.7–9n.

Stanza 24
1   **trenchand**: sharp; cf. i 17.3. This romance term introduces the next stage of the encounter. Being deprived of horse

28

Faint, wearie, sore, emboyled, grieued, brent
  With heat, toyle, wounds, armes, smart, and inward fire
  That neuer man such mischiefes did torment;
  Death better were, death did he oft desire,
  But death will neuer come, when needes require.
  Whom so dismayd when that his foe beheld,
  He cast to suffer him no more respire,
  But gan his sturdie sterne about to weld,
And him so strongly stroke, that to the ground him feld.

29

It fortuned (as faire it then befell)
  Behind his backe vnweeting, where he stood,
  Of auncient time there was a springing well,
  From which fast trickled forth a siluer flood,
  Full of great vertues, and for med'cine good.
  Whylome, before that cursed Dragon got
  That happie land, and all with innocent blood
  Defyld those sacred waues, it rightly hot
The well of life, ne yet his vertues had forgot.

30

For vnto life the dead it could restore,
  And guilt of sinfull crimes cleane wash away,
  Those that with sicknesse were infected sore,
  It could recure, and aged long decay
  Renew, as one were borne that very day.
  Both *Silo* this, and *Iordan* did excell,
  And th'English *Bath*, and eke the german *Spau*,
  Ne can *Cephise*, nor *Hebrus* match this well:
Into the same the knight backe ouerthrowen, fell.

31

Now gan the golden *Phœbus* for to steepe
  His fierie face in billowes of the west,
  And his faint steedes watred in Ocean deepe,
  Whiles from their iournall labours they did rest,
  When that infernall Monster, hauing kest
  His wearie foe into that liuing well,
  Can high aduance his broad discoloured brest,
  Aboue his wonted pitch, with countenance fell,
And clapt his yron wings, as victor he did dwell.

7 **suffer**: answering the Knight's sufferings because of which he desires death.   **respire**: live.
8 **weld**: wield.

Stanza 29

1 **faire**: auspiciously.
2 **vnweeting**: i.e. not known to him. Grace does not come by his own powers or even awareness.
4 **fast, flood**: suggest Protestant baptism by immersion in running water; cf. 'drenched lay' (34.2), which suggests total immersion.
5 **vertues**: powers.
8 **hot**: was called.
9 Cf. John 4.14: 'The water that I shal giue him, shalbe in him a well of water, springing vp into euerlasting life.' The Geneva gloss adds, 'of the spiritual grace'. Cf. Rev. 22.1.

Stanza 30

1 'Even when we were dead by sinnes, [God] hathe quickened us together in Christ, by whose grace ye are saved' (Eph. 2.5).
2 'Arise, and be baptized, and washe away thy sinnes' (Acts 22.16).   **cleane**: as adj.; and as adv., 'entirely'. The Knight is purged of that 'guilt of sin' (vii 45.8) which had caused all of Una's previous champions to be defeated.
3–4 The *Golden Legend* 114 (see x 66.5–6n) records that, after the Dragon was bound, the people were baptized and a church built 'in the whiche yet sourdeth a fountayne of lyvynge [i.e. running] water whiche heleth the seke people that drynken therof'; noted Snyder (1961) 250.
4–5 Cf. John 3.5: 'Except that a man be borne of water and of the Spirit, he can not enter into the kingdome of God.'
6–8 These waters are famous either for their healing powers or their purity. The man born blind was cured by washing in the pool of Siloam 'which is by interpretation, Sent' (John 9.7); the Geneva gloss adds: 'Hereby was prefigured the Messias, who shulde be sent vnto them.' S. prefers the Vulgate form *Silo*. In the **Iordan**, Naaman was cured of his leprosy (2 Kings 5.14); but its waters are associated chiefly with John's baptism of Christ, Matt. 3.16. After the two spiritual waters, the two contemporary European waters are given precedence over the classical. The waters of **Bath** are described at II x 26. **Cephise**: its purifying waters were used to sprinkle Deucalion and Pyrrha before they entered the temple, *Met.* i 369–70. Sandys (1632) 69 refers to its 'holywater'.   **Hebrus**: its healing powers are noted by Servius in his gloss to Virgil, *Eclogue* x 65.

Stanza 31

1–4 **faint**: lacking in strength; as the Knight, 28.1. **iournall**: daily; cf. 33.2. The Dragon's victory over the Knight is the victory of the West over the sun. Yet **iournall** suggests that dawn will follow, and **steepe** implies both cleansing and renewal. The sun and the Knight are bathed, as they rest for renewed labours. Their relation is extended throughout the battle until it achieves its climactic expression in stanza 52. On the Knight's role as *Sol iustitiæ*, see Fowler (1964) 69.
5 **infernall Monster**: cf. his title at i 5.7.
6 **liuing**: constantly flowing; alluding to its name.
7 **Can**: did.   **discoloured**: variously coloured; 'speckled' (15.2); also stained.
8 **pitch**: height; also blackness.
9 **dwell**: remain.

Stanza 28

1–2 **Faint . . . fire**: faint with heat, weary with toil, etc. **emboyled**: literally boiled in his armour. Some editors prefer a more elegant reading: agitated, panting, full of boils.
3 **mischiefes**: misfortunes; cf. ix 45.3–4: now he is beyond despair.
4 He sought death when he suffered imprisonment in Orgoglio's dungeon, despair in Despair's cave, guilty anguish in the house of Penaunce, and world-weariness on the mount of Contemplation. His present desire for death sums up all his earlier plight, as the opening catalogue indicates, and is now fulfilled by the Dragon's blow. Kaske (1969) 625 argues that the Knight's spiritual death comes with his consent.
6 **dismayd**: he relives his earlier plight; see vii 11.6n.

32

Which when his pensiue Ladie saw from farre,
  Great woe and sorrow did her soule assay,
  As weening that the sad end of the warre,
  And gan to highest God entirely pray,
  That feared chance from her to turne away;
  With folded hands and knees full lowly bent
  All night she watcht, ne once adowne would lay
  Her daintie limbs in her sad dreriment,
But praying still did wake, and waking did lament.

33

The morrow next gan early to appeare,
  That *Titan* rose to runne his daily race;
  But early ere the morrow next gan reare
  Out of the sea faire *Titans* deawy face,
  Vp rose the gentle virgin from her place,
  And looked all about, if she might spy
  Her loued knight to moue his manly pace:
  For she had great doubt of his safety,
Since late she saw him fall before his enemy.

34

At last she saw, where he vpstarted braue
  Out of the well, wherein he drenched lay;
  As Eagle fresh out of the Ocean waue,
  Where he hath left his plumes all hoary gray,
  And deckt himselfe with feathers youthly gay,
  Like Eyas hauke vp mounts vnto the skies,
  His newly budded pineons to assay,
  And marueiles at himselfe, still as he flies:
So new this new-borne knight to battell new did rise.

35

Whom when the damned feend so fresh did spy,
  No wonder if he wondred at the sight,
  And doubted, whether his late enemy
  It were, or other new supplied knight.
  He, now to proue his late renewed might,
  High brandishing his bright deaw-burning blade,
  Vpon his crested scalpe so sore did smite,
  That to the scull a yawning wound it made:
The deadly dint his dulled senses all dismaid.

Stanza 32
1 **pensiue**: anxious, as x 68.3.
2 **assay**: assail; also test, as an attack tests or proves
endurance.
4 **entirely**: earnestly, whole-heartedly.
7–9 Matt. 26.41: 'watch, and pray'.   **dreriment**: dismal
plight.

Stanza 33
1–5 A prolepsis to relate Una to the new dawn (cf. 51) or to
the morning star (cf. xii 21) which precedes the sun's rising.
The lines prepare for the Knight's resurrection: as the sun
rears **Out of the sea**, the renewed eagle rises 'out of the
Ocean waue' (34.3) and the Knight 'Out of the well' (34.2).
race: the sun's daily course.
7 **moue his manly pace**: the formality of the phrase
suggests the ordered movement of the sun.   **manly** is the
key word. The Knight's manly heart had melted with Archimago's dream (i 47.5), his manly force failed him before
Orgoglio (vii 6.4), his manly looks were marred by imprisonment (viii 42.9), Despair's arguments dispersed his manly
powers and bewitched his manly heart (ix 48.7, 53.2). Now he
becomes fully man, and more than man.

Stanza 34
Cf. Zech. 6.12: *Ecce vir Oriens nomen eius.*
1 **braue**: courageous; also splendidly dressed, as the eagle.
2 **drenched**: submerged, referring to his baptism; see
29.4*n.*
3–9 The eagle was said to renew its youth every ten years
by plunging into the ocean: see *Physiologus* by Theobald, ed.
A. W. Rendell (1928) 8–12. It became a type of the crucifixion
and resurrection of Christ and the baptism of Christians; see
Cirlot (1962) 87–9, Tervarent (1958) 6–7. The comparison of
the Dragon to the eagle at 9.5–7 now serves to place the old
Dragon and old eagle (and the old Adam) in contrast to the
renewed eagle and the **new-borne knight** (9). Cf. Isaiah 40.31:
'they that waite upon the Lord shal renue their strength: they
shal lift up the wings as the egles', and Ps. 103.4–5: '[God]
redemeth thy life from the grave, and crowneth thee with
mercie and compassions . . . and thy youth is renued like the
egles.' Cf. Malachi 4.2 on the day when 'the Sunne of righteousnes [shall] arise, and health shalbe under his wings';
noted Fowler (1964) 69.
6 **Eyas hauke**: a young untamed hawk. As a symbol of
victory, see Tervarent 162; called 'King of fowles in maiesty
and powre' (VI x 6.9).
9 **to battell new**: here 'new' also modifies **knight**, as the
word-play suggests. Cf. Edward VI's *First Prayer Book* on
private Baptism: 'Graunte that the olde Adam, in them that
shalbe baptized in this fountayne, maye so be buried, that the
newe man may be raised up agayne.'

Stanza 35
1 **damned**: in contrast to the Knight who has been released
from damnation.
6 **deaw-burning**: shining with 'that holy water dew' (36.2);
cf. '*Titans* deawy face' (33.4).
7–9 Cf. Arthur's similar blow at viii 16; now the Knight
goes on to kill 'that old Dragon'.

36

I wote not, whether the reuenging steele
    Were hardned with that holy water dew,
    Wherein he fell, or sharper edge did feele,
    Or his baptized hands now greater grew;
    Or other secret vertue did ensew;
    Else neuer could the force of fleshly arme,
    Ne molten mettall in his bloud embrew;
    For till that stownd could neuer wight him harme,
By subtilty, nor slight, nor might, nor mighty charme.

37

The cruell wound enraged him so sore,
    That loud he yelded for exceeding paine;
    As hundred ramping Lyons seem'd to rore,
    Whom rauenous hunger did thereto constraine:
    Then gan he tosse aloft his stretched traine,
    And therewith scourge the buxome aire so sore,
    That to his force to yeelden it was faine;
    Ne ought his sturdie strokes might stand afore,
That high trees ouerthrew, and rocks in peeces tore.

38

The same aduauncing high aboue his head,
    With sharpe intended sting so rude him smot,
    That to the earth him droue, as stricken dead,
    Ne liuing wight would haue him life behot:
    The mortall sting his angry needle shot
    Quite through his shield, and in his shoulder seasd,
    Where fast it stucke, ne would there out be got:
    The griefe thereof him wondrous sore diseasd,
Ne might his ranckling paine with patience be appeasd.

39

But yet more mindfull of his honour deare,
    Then of the grieuous smart, which him did wring,
    From loathed soile he can him lightly reare,
    And stroue to loose the farre infixed sting:
    Which when in vaine he tryde with struggeling,
    Inflam'd with wrath, his raging blade he heft,
    And strooke so strongly, that the knotty string
    Of his huge taile he quite a sunder cleft,
Fiue ioynts thereof he hewd, and but the stump him left.

Stanza 36

1–5   Four possible explanations are given. 1. the sword is tempered by **holy water dew** (2), referring to the drops of holy water on the sword; through the miracle of manna, dew was associated with God's providential care for man; at 48.5 the balm from the Tree of Life is also linked with dew. 2. the

sword is sharpened by the dew, as 'deaw-burning blade' (35.6) suggests. Percival (1893) cites Heb. 4.12: 'The worde of God is . . . sharper then anie two edged sword.' 3. The Knight's hands are baptized in the literal sense of the Lat. and Gk root, 'to drench', 'bathe', which is also the spiritual sense of baptism. 4. some other secret power follows as the result of the Knight's fall into the Well. Tuve (1966) 110 rejects any suggestion of baptism at the font despite the phrase **baptized hands**, and suggests instead 'added fortitude received through grace in extremity', agreeing with Kitchin's note (1867) that the water is 'simply allegorical of spiritual comfort and help in the struggle'. However, any literal-minded reading must also account for the phrase **now greater grew**. In all earlier battles against Una's knights, the Dragon 'still . . . greater grew' (vii 45.7), where 'greater' suggests proud, arrogant (*OED* 4). Now applied to the Knight, it signifies 'stronger', or more 'full-grown' (*OED* 7).

7   **molten mettall**: the forging of weapons from melted metal is contrasted to the tempering (or sharpening) of the Knight's sword in the Well of Life.   **embrew**: steep; suggesting the baptism of his sword.

8–9   See 20.7–9*n*.   **stownd**: moment.   **slight**: deception.

Stanza 37

Rose (1975) 141 observes that the Knight's blow is prologue to a battle in which the Dragon employs each of his three weapons in turn – tail, claws, and mouth.

3–4   See x 28.2*n*.
5   **traine**: tail.
6   **buxome**: unresisting.
7   **faine**: obliged.
8   **sturdie**: violent.

Stanza 38

2   **intended**: extended (from Lat. *intendere*, to stretch out); also 'designed'. The fully extended tail displays the Dragon's full physical power.   **rude**: violently.
3   The Knight's fall to the ground, as in the first day's battle (23.6–7), symbolizes his earlier fall into sin.
4   **behot**: promised.
5   **mortall sting**: cf. Phedon's 'mortall sting' (II iv 33.5). Kaske (1969) 612–4 cites the Geneva gloss on Paul's 'thorn in the flesh': 'He meaneth concupiscence, that sticketh fast in us, as it were a pricke.'
6   **seasd**: penetrated. The wound in the (left) shoulder which bears the shield alludes to powers of defence.
8   **griefe**: pain.   **diseasd**: tormented.
9   In contrast to his earlier disease which could be cured by patience, x 23.8–9.   **ranckling**: from med. Lat. *dranculus*, from *draco*, dragon.

Stanza 39

2   **wring**: vex; or afflict with pain.
3   **loathed**: because defeat brings dishonour which he loathes; cf. 23.9.   **soile** suggests 'defiling'.
6   **heft**: heaved.
8   This stage of the battle may be marked by the question: 'O death, where is thy sting?' (1 Cor. 15.55).
9   **Fiue**: Percival (1893) cites Rev. 17.10 concerning the heads of the red Dragon: 'Five are fallen, and one is, and another is not yet come.' Kaske (1969) 615 suggests man's five senses, his contacts with sin, which the Knight now prevents from reigning over him.

40

Hart cannot thinke, what outrage, and what cryes,
  With foule enfouldred smoake and flashing fire,
  The hell-bred beast threw forth vnto the skyes,
  That all was couered with darknesse dire:
  Then fraught with rancour, and engorged ire,
  He cast at once him to auenge for all,
  And gathering vp himselfe out of the mire,
  With his vneuen wings did fiercely fall
Vpon his sunne-bright shield, and gript it fast withall.

41

Much was the man encombred with his hold,
  In feare to lose his weapon in his paw,
  Ne wist yet, how his talants to vnfold;
  Nor harder was from *Cerberus* greedie iaw
  To plucke a bone, then from his cruell claw
  To reaue by strength the griped gage away:
  Thrise he assayd it from his foot to draw,
  And thrise in vaine to draw it did assay,
It booted nought to thinke, to robbe him of his pray.

42

Tho when he saw no power might preuaile,
  His trustie sword he cald to his last aid,
  Wherewith he fiercely did his foe assaile,
  And double blowes about him stoutly laid,
  That glauncing fire out of the yron plaid;
  As sparckles from the Anduile vse to fly,
  When heauie hammers on the wedge are swaid;
  Therewith at last he forst him to vnty
One of his grasping feete, him to defend thereby.

43

The other foot, fast fixed on his shield,
  Whenas no strength, nor stroks mote him constraine
  To loose, ne yet the warlike pledge to yield,
  He smot thereat with all his might and maine,
  That nought so wondrous puissance might sustaine;
  Vpon the ioynt the lucky steele did light,
  And made such way, that hewd it quite in twaine;
  The paw yet missed not his minisht might,
But hong still on the shield, as it at first was pight.

44

For griefe thereof, and diuelish despight,
  From his infernall fournace forth he threw
  Huge flames, that dimmed all the heauens light,
  Enrold in duskish smoke and brimstone blew;
  As burning *Aetna* from his boyling stew
  Doth belch out flames, and rockes in peeces broke,
  And ragged ribs of mountaines molten new,
  Enwrapt in coleblacke clouds and filthy smoke,
That all the land with stench, and heauen with horror choke.

45

The heate whereof, and harmefull pestilence
  So sore him noyd, that forst him to retire
  A little backward for his best defence,
  To saue his bodie from the scorching fire,
  Which he from hellish entrailes did expire.
  It chaunst (eternall God that chaunce did guide)
  As he recoyled backward, in the mire
  His nigh forwearied feeble feet did slide,
And downe he fell, with dread of shame sore terrifide.

Stanza 40
1 **outrage**: violent clamour.
2 **enfouldred**: charged with thunderbolts, black as a
thunder cloud. The word enwraps its epithet, **foule**.
5 **engorged**: swallowed, and hence swollen; the same sense
as **fraught**.
8 **vneuen wings**. because one is wounded.
9 **withall**: as well. The Dragon first attacks the Knight with
fire, and almost defeats him because of his armour; then he
attacks the Knight by piercing his shield; now he attacks the
shield of faith itself.

Stanza 41
4–5 **Cerberus**: the hound that guards the entrance to hell
(see v 34). The Dragon is a 'hell-bred beast' (40.3) whose
throat gapes like the mouth of hell (12.8–9). The simile suggests
that the Knight will triumph over the Dragon even as Hercules
defeated Cerberus. Hercules's victory over Cerberus was
interpreted as a victory over hell and death: see VI xii 35n.
6 **gage**: the pawn for which they fight: 'warlike pledge'
(43.3).
7–8 'The inversion of the order of the words in the sentence
is meant to represent the tugging to and fro' (Percival, 1893).

Stanza 42
1–2 With his own power – cf. 'strength' (41.6) – exhausted,
the Knight finds his last aid in the power of his arms. Kaske
(1969) 616 cites Heb. 4.12: 'For the worde of God is livelie,
and mightie in operation, and sharper then anie two edged
sworde, and entreth through, even unto the dividing asonder
of the soule and the spirit, and of the joynts, and the marie
[marrow].' See 36.1–5n.
5 **yron**: the Dragon's iron claws, rather than the Knight's
sword.
7 **wedge**: metal ingot. **swaid**: swung.
8 **vnty**: relax his hold. The grasping talons (cf. the tail's
'knotty string', 39.7) suggest a knot which must be undone.

Stanza 43
8 **minisht**: diminished.
9 **pight**: fixed.

Stanza 44
1 **griefe**: pain.
2–4 Cf. the end of the first day's battle, 26.3–7 and see
n. **blew**: the colour of burning brimstone or sulphur,
symbolically the colour of **diuelish** (1) flame. Finally the
Dragon will be cast into the lake of fire 'burning with brimstone' (Rev. 19.20).
5–9 The Monster's infernal nature is shown by comparing
this simile with its source, *Aen.* iii 571–7. To Virgil's horrific
details, S. adds the defilement expressed in 9. **stew**:
cauldron.

Stanza 45
1–2 **pestilence**: cf. Ps. 91.3: 'Surely he wil deliver thee . . .
from the noisome pestilence.' **noyd**: harmed.
5 **expire**: breathe out, from Lat. *expirare*; suggesting 'to
breathe one's last in death'.
7 Cf. the first day when the Dragon 'to the ground him feld'
(28.9); now the Knight co-operates with saving grace. Precisely
because of his backsliding, grace comes to his aid: not to
support him, however, but to cause his fall.

46

There grew a goodly tree him faire beside,
  Loaden with fruit and apples rosie red,
  As they in pure vermilion had beene dide,
  Whereof great vertues ouer all were red:
  For happie life to all, which thereon fed,
  And life eke euerlasting did befall:
  Great God it planted in that blessed sted
  With his almightie hand, and did it call
The tree of life, the crime of our first fathers fall.

47

In all the world like was not to be found,
  Saue in that soile, where all good things did grow,
  And freely sprong out of the fruitfull ground,
  As incorrupted Nature did them sow,
  Till that dread Dragon all did ouerthrow.
  Another like faire tree eke grew thereby,
  Whereof who so did eat, eftsoones did know
  Both good and ill: O mornefull memory:
That tree through one mans fault hath doen vs all to dy.

48

From that first tree forth flowd, as from a well,
  A trickling streame of Balme, most soueraine
  And daintie deare, which on the ground still fell,
  And ouerflowed all the fertill plaine,
  As it had deawed bene with timely raine:
  Life and long health that gratious ointment gaue,
  And deadly woundes could heale, and reare againe
  The senselesse corse appointed for the graue.
Into that same he fell: which did from death him saue.

49

For nigh thereto the euer damned beast
  Durst not approch, for he was deadly made,
  And all that life preserued, did detest:
  Yet he it oft aduentur'd to inuade.
  By this the drouping day-light gan to fade,
  And yeeld his roome to sad succeeding night,
  Who with her sable mantle gan to shade
  The face of earth, and wayes of liuing wight,
And high her burning torch set vp in heauen bright.

Stanzas 46–48
The distinctions between the Well and the Tree are observed by Kaske (1969) 637. The Well bestows 'life' (30.1); the Tree, 'happie life . . . / And life eke euerlasting' (46.5–6; cf. 48.6). The Well cures chronic disabilities, 'sicknesse' and 'aged long decay' (30.3–4); the Tree, 'deadly woundes' (48.7). For similar distinctions between the gifts exchanged by Arthur and the Red Cross Knight, see ix 19*n*.

Stanza 46
The Knight's 'feeding' upon the Tree is usually interpreted as Holy Communion. Tuve (1966) 110–2 argues to the contrary.
1   Cf. Rev. 2.7: 'To him that overcometh wil I give to eate of the tree of life which is in the middes of the Paradise of God.'   **faire beside**: close by, or auspiciously; cf. 29.1–2.
2   Rev. 22.2: 'The tre of life, which bare twelve maner of frutes.'
4   **ouer . . . red**: everywhere were told.
7   **sted**: place.
9   **the crime . . . fall**: i.e. the cause of reproach, or accusation (Lat. *crimen*), against Adam. Because he ate from the Tree of Knowledge, he and his posterity are denied the Tree of Life. More directly, since God expelled Adam from Eden so that he would not eat from the Tree of Life (Gen. 3.22), the Tree 'caused' his expulsion from Eden. On Renaissance interpretations of the Tree of Life, see Steadman (1968) 82–9. Cornelius (1971) suggests that the Tree is 'both the tree of life of Genesis and Revelation, and also the tree of everlasting life – the Cross of Calvary. As the latter, it is both the criminal consequence of the Fall and the divine response to that event.'

Stanza 47
6   **thereby**: Gen. 2.9 notes only the presence of the two trees but S. must note their close relationship.
8   **memory**: memorial, memento; also a witty play on the usual sense: **mornefull memory** indicates man's knowledge of **good and ill**.
9   Cf. Rom. 5.12.

Stanza 48
The Knight, refreshed by the water from the Well of Life and by the fruit from the Tree of Life, is the second Adam who regains the Paradise that the first Adam lost. Major (1967) 470 points to the suggestive analogy in Milton's *Paradise Regained* iv 589–90: the triumphant Christ is given 'fruits fetched from the tree of life, / And from the fount of life ambrosial drink'.
2–8   Cf. Rev. 22.2: 'The leaves of the tre [of life] served to heale the nations with.' Dixon (1597) comments on this stanza: 'a fiction of the incarnation of Christe'. Hankins (1971) 118–9 associates the **Balme** with the healing oil of the sacrament of Extreme Unction administered to those in peril of death.
2   **soueraine**: applied to a remedy of supreme healing powers.
3   **daintie deare**: exceedingly precious.
6   **health**: spiritual and moral well-being.   **gratious**: endowed with God's grace.   **ointment**: cf. 2 Esdras 2.12: 'They shal have at wil the tre of life, smelling of ointement: they shal nether labour nor be weary.'
8   **appointed**: made ready.

Stanza 49
2   **deadly made**: i.e. being made for death, belonging to it.
4   **aduentur'd**: dared, attempted.

50

When gentle *Vna* saw the second fall
  Of her deare knight, who wearie of long fight,
  And faint through losse of bloud, mou'd not at all,
  But lay as in a dreame of deepe delight,
  Besmeard with pretious Balme, whose vertuous might
  Did heale his wounds, and scorching heat alay,
  Againe she stricken was with sore affright,
  And for his safetie gan deuoutly pray;
And watch the noyous night, and wait for ioyous day.

51

The ioyous day gan early to appeare,
  And faire *Aurora* from the deawy bed
  Of aged *Tithone* gan her selfe to reare,
  With rosie cheekes, for shame as blushing red;
  Her golden lockes for haste were loosely shed
  About her eares, when *Vna* her did marke
  Clymbe to her charet, all with flowers spred,
  From heauen high to chase the chearelesse darke;
With merry note her loud salutes the mounting larke.

52

Then freshly vp arose the doughtie knight,
  All healed of his hurts and woundes wide,
  And did himselfe to battell readie dight;
  Whose early foe awaiting him beside
  To haue deuourd, so soone as day he spyde,
  When now he saw himselfe so freshly reare,
  As if late fight had nought him damnifyde,
  He woxe dismayd, and gan his fate to feare;
Nathlesse with wonted rage he him aduaunced neare.

53

And in his first encounter, gaping wide,
  He thought attonce him to haue swallowd quight,
  And rusht vpon him with outragious pride;
  Who him r'encountring fierce, as hauke in flight,
  Perforce rebutted backe. The weapon bright
  Taking aduantage of his open iaw,
  Ran through his mouth with so importune might,
  That deepe emperst his darksome hollow maw,
And back retyrd, his life bloud forth with all did draw.

54

So downe he fell, and forth his life did breath,
  That vanisht into smoke and cloudes swift;
  So downe he fell, that th'earth him vnderneath
  Did grone, as feeble so great load to lift;
  So downe he fell, as an huge rockie clift,
  Whose false foundation waues haue washt away,
  With dreadfull poyse is from the mayneland rift,
  And rolling downe, great *Neptune* doth dismay;
So downe he fell, and like an heaped mountaine lay.

55

The knight himselfe euen trembled at his fall,
  So huge and horrible a masse it seem'd;
  And his deare Ladie, that beheld it all,
  Durst not approch for dread, which she misdeem'd,
  But yet at last, when as the direfull feend
  She saw not stirre, off-shaking vaine affright,
  She nigher drew, and saw that ioyous end:
  Then God she praysd, and thankt her faithfull knight,
That had atchieu'd so great a conquest by his might.

Stanza 50

Cf. Rev. 2.11: 'He that overcometh shal not be hurt of the seconde death.' The Geneva gloss notes that 'the first death is the natural death of the bodie, the seconde is the eternal death'. From this second death of the soul, the Knight is saved by the Tree which gives 'life eke euerlasting' (46.6).
5–6 Cf. Duessa's ointment, ii 42.3–5. **vertuous**: efficacious in healing.
9 **noyous**: irksome.

Stanza 51

1 Cf. 33.1.
2 **Aurora**: cf. ii 7.1–4 on the dawning of a different day, which the present stanza answers.
9 The topos of the lark's salutation to the dawn is traced by Bawcutt (1972).

Stanza 52

2 'The third day I shalbe perfited' (Luke 13.32).
4 **awaiting**: keeping watch.
5 **as day he spyde**: to remind us at this crucial moment that the Knight is one of 'the children of faire light' (v 24.5).
7 **damnifyde**: injured; implying the theological sense.

Stanza 53

4 **as hauke in flight**: see 34.3–9n.
5–9 This personification of the weapon shows that spiritual armour, not the man, kills the Dragon, as the Knight himself explains: 'His [God's] be the praise, that this atchieu'ment wrought, / Who made my hand the organ of his might' (II i 33.2–3); see 55.8–9n.
7 **importune**: grievous, violent. On the Dragon's mouth as an emblem of hell, see 12.8n. Symbolically, the Knight enters Hell and leaves triumphant.
9 **back retyrd**: i.e. on being drawn back.

Stanza 54

1 **So downe he fell**: cf. 'It is fallen, it is fallen, Babylon the great citie' (Rev. 14.8). S. uses the iterative device of *anaphora* to suggest the fall of Babylon, 'of which this dragon is a type' (Upton, 1758). The repetition connects the Dragon's fall with air, earth, and sea. **Neptune** (8) is dismayed because the victory heralds the Last Judgment when there shall be no sea (Rev. 21.1).
6 **false**: treacherous, having been made such by the waves.
7 **poyse**: weight; force. **rift**: split.

Stanza 55

4 **which she misdeem'd**: she misjudged, or was mistaken in fearing either for her Knight's safety or that the Dragon was not dead. While she hastens to congratulate him on his first victory over Error (i 27.2) and also Arthur on his victory over Orgoglio (viii 26.4), this present victory is greater than Faith itself may believe.
8–9 There is careful, deliberate ambiguity in **his**: it refers to both God and the Knight. Man's might and God's grace merge as the Knight is revealed in the lineaments of Christ, the Dragon-killer, even as Michael, the Dragon-killer of Rev. 12.7, is identified by the Geneva gloss with Christ.

Cant. XII.

*Faire Vna to the Redcrosse knight
betrouthed is with ioy :
Though false Duessa it to barre
her false sleights doe imploy.*

1

BEhold I see the hauen nigh at hand,
To which I meane my wearie course to bend;
Vere the maine shete, and beare vp with the land,
The which afore is fairely to be kend,
And seemeth safe from stormes, that may offend;
There this faire virgin wearie of her way
Must landed be, now at her iourneyes end:
There eke my feeble barke a while may stay,
Till merry wind and weather call her thence away.

2

Scarsely had *Phœbus* in the glooming East
Yet harnessed his firie-footed teeme,
Ne reard aboue the earth his flaming creast,
When the last deadly smoke aloft did steeme,
That signe of last outbreathed life did seeme
Vnto the watchman on the castle wall;
Who thereby dead that balefull Beast did deeme,
And to his Lord and Ladie lowd gan call,
To tell, how he had seene the Dragons fatall fall.

3

Vprose with hastie ioy, and feeble speed
That aged Sire, the Lord of all that land,
And looked forth, to weet, if true indeede
Those tydings were, as he did vnderstand,
Which whenas true by tryall he out fond,
He bad to open wyde his brazen gate,
Which long time had bene shut, and out of hond
Proclaymed ioy and peace through all his state;
For dead now was their foe, which them forrayed late.

4

Then gan triumphant Trompets sound on hie,
That sent to heauen the ecchoed report
Of their new ioy, and happie victorie
Gainst him, that had them long opprest with tort,
And fast imprisoned in sieged fort.
Then all the people, as in solemne feast,
To him assembled with one full consort,
Reioycing at the fall of that great beast,
From whose eternall bondage now they were releast.

5

Forth came that auncient Lord and aged Queene,
Arayd in antique robes downe to the ground,
And sad habiliments right well beseene;
A noble crew about them waited round
Of sage and sober Peres, all grauely gownd;
Whom farre before did march a goodly band
Of tall young men, all hable armes to sownd,
But now they laurell braunches bore in hand;
Glad signe of victorie and peace in all their land.

Canto xii

Argument

Dixon (1597) glosses the historical allegory: 'A fiction of our Queene Eliz: the maintainer of the gospell of Christe, to be by god himselfe betrouthed unto Christe, though by k[ing] p[hilip] and r[oman] c[atholics] for 6 yeares it was debared.' As Hough (1964) notes, he refers to the six years of Mary's reign and the Spanish Catholic domination in England.

4   sleights: wiles.

Stanza 1

Curtius (1953) 128–30 describes the tradition in which the poet compares his poem to a voyage. S. makes the nautical metaphor personal by comparing himself to Una **wearie of her way** (6); cf. 17.7–8 and the concluding stanza.
3   To **Vere** the sail is to let it out so that it holds less wind (cf. V xii 18.8); to **beare vp** 'is to bring the ship to goe large or before the wind' (John Smith, *A Sea Grammar*, 1627, 44). S. will no longer tack but run before the wind, steering directly towards the land.
5   **offend**: harm, strike.
9   **merry**: favourable.

Stanza 2

1–4   This is the dawn which appears at xi 51 to herald the Knight's defeat of the Dragon.   **glooming**: gleaming, glowing.   **deadly**: glossed in the next line.
9   **fatall**: also 'ordained by fate', i.e. by prophecy.

Stanza 3

5   **tryall**: investigation.   **out fond**: found out.
7   **out of hond**: immediately.
8   Cf. the 'eternall peace and happinesse' (x 55.9) of the New Jerusalem, which is the type of Adam's state; cf. Lev. 25.10 which announces the Jubilee: 'proclaime libertie in the land to all the inhabitants thereof.'

Stanza 4

4   **tort**: wrong, injustice.
6   **solemne feast**: sacred or holy festival.
7   **consort**: accord; also the musical sense, 'concert'.
9   **eternall**: they are released for ever, as Percival (1893) suggests; cf. the eternal bondage of the devil in hell (Rev. 20.10). The term may apply also to mankind whose bondage lasts throughout time.

Stanza 5

3   **sad habiliments . . .**: sober-coloured attire very attractive to be seen.   **beseene** may signify 'appointed'; or as 'beseem', appropriate to their state (cf. 8.8).
6   **farre before**: cf. x 49.7.
7   **all hable armes to sownd**: all able to strike arms in battle, to fight, as knights 'clash their shields' (iv 40.3); cf. xi 9.8.   **tall**: also comely, handsome; good at arms.

155

6

Vnto that doughtie Conquerour they came,
    And him before themselues prostrating low,
    Their Lord and Patrone loud did him proclaime,
    And at his feet their laurell boughes did throw.
    Soone after them all dauncing on a row
    The comely virgins came, with girlands dight,
    As fresh as flowres in medow greene do grow,
    When morning deaw vpon their leaues doth light:
And in their hands sweet Timbrels all vpheld on hight.

7

And them before, the fry of children young
    Their wanton sports and childish mirth did play,
    And to the Maydens sounding tymbrels sung
    In well attuned notes, a ioyous lay,
    And made delightfull musicke all the way,
    Vntill they came, where that faire virgin stood;
    As faire *Diana* in fresh sommers day
    Beholds her Nymphes, enraung'd in shadie wood,
Some wrestle, some do run, some bathe in christall flood.

8

So she beheld those maydens meriment
    With chearefull vew; who when to her they came,
    Themselues to ground with gratious humblesse bent,
    And her ador'd by honorable name,
    Lifting to heauen her euerlasting fame:
    Then on her head they set a girland greene,
    And crowned her twixt earnest and twixt game;
    Who in her selfe-resemblance well beseene,
Did seeme such, as she was, a goodly maiden Queene.

9

And after, all the raskall many ran,
    Heaped together in rude rablement,
    To see the face of that victorious man:
    Whom all admired, as from heauen sent,
    And gazd vpon with gaping wonderment.
    But when they came, where that dead Dragon lay,
    Stretcht on the ground in monstrous large extent,
    The sight with idle feare did them dismay,
Ne durst approch him nigh, to touch, or once assay.

10

Some feard, and fled; some feard and well it faynd;
    One that would wiser seeme, then all the rest,
    Warnd him not touch, for yet perhaps remaynd
    Some lingring life within his hollow brest,
    Or in his wombe might lurke some hidden nest
    Of many Dragonets, his fruitfull seed;
    Another said, that in his eyes did rest
    Yet sparckling fire, and bad thereof take heed;
Another said, he saw him moue his eyes indeed.

11

One mother, when as her foolehardie chyld
    Did come too neare, and with his talants play,
    Halfe dead through feare, her litle babe reuyld,
    And to her gossips gan in counsell say;
    How can I tell, but that his talants may
    Yet scratch my sonne, or rend his tender hand?
    So diuersly themselues in vaine they fray;
    Whiles some more bold, to measure him nigh stand,
To proue how many acres he did spread of land.

Stanza 6
3–4   Cf. Christ's entry into Jerusalem, John 12.13. See
13.4*n*.   **Patrone**: protector, defender; as the Knight
addressed Arthur, 'my Lord, the Patrone of my life' (ix 17.6).
8   **light**: in two senses, 'settle', 'shine'.
9   **Timbrels**: tambourines. Associated with giving thanks
to God for victory: cf. Exod. 15.20, Ps. 68.25. At 1 Sam. 18.6
the women come out 'singing and dansing to mete King Saul,
with timbrels, with instruments of joye'.

Stanzas 7–11
A humorous interlude before the entrance of Una's parents.

Stanza 7
2   **wanton**: playful.
4–5   On the significance of this linking of vocal and
instrumental music, see 38.6 to 39.9*n*.
8   **enraung'd**: ranging.

Stanza 8
3   **humblesse**: humility.
4   **by honorable name**: with titles of honour.
6   Cf. the earlier mock crowning with 'Yuie girlond' (i 48.9)
and 'oliue girlond' (vi 13.9).
8   **her selfe-resemblance**: i.e. resembling her true self.
well beseene: see 5.3*n*.
9   Her state contrasts with Duessa's: 'I that do seeme not I'
(v 26.6). Crowned in the pastoral game, she appears as she is,
a Queene.

Stanza 9
1   **raskall many**: rabble throng.
2   **rablement**: confusion; rabble.
3   Dixon (1597) glosses simply: 'Christe'.
4   **admired**: viewed with wonder.
8   **idle**: baseless.
9   **once assay**: i.e. even venture to touch.

Stanza 10
1   **faynd**: concealed.
6   **Dragonets**: young dragons.

Stanza 11
4   **gossips**: cronies.   **in counsell**: privately.
7   **fray**: frighten.

12

Thus flocked all the folke him round about,
  The whiles that hoarie king, with all his traine,
  Being arriued, where that champion stout
  After his foes defeasance did remaine,
  Him goodly greetes, and faire does entertaine,
  With princely gifts of yuorie and gold,
  And thousand thankes him yeelds for all his paine.
Then when his daughter deare he does behold,
Her dearely doth imbrace, and kisseth manifold.

13

And after to his Pallace he them brings,
  With shaumes, and trompets, and with Clarions sweet;
  And all the way the ioyous people sings,
  And with their garments strowes the paued street:
  Whence mounting vp, they find purueyance meet
  Of all, that royall Princes court became,
  And all the floore was vnderneath their feet
  Bespred with costly scarlot of great name,
On which they lowly sit, and fitting purpose frame.

14

What needs me tell their feast and goodly guize,
  In which was nothing riotous nor vaine?
  What needs of daintie dishes to deuize,
  Of comely seruices, or courtly trayne?
  My narrow leaues cannot in them containe
  The large discourse of royall Princes state,
  Yet was their manner then but bare and plaine:
  For th'antique world excesse and pride did hate;
Such proud luxurious pompe is swollen vp but late.

15

Then when with meates and drinkes of euery kinde
  Their feruent appetites they quenched had,
  That auncient Lord gan fit occasion finde,
  Of straunge aduentures, and of perils sad,
  Which in his trauell him befallen had,
  For to demaund of his renowned guest:
  Who then with vtt'rance graue, and count'nance sad,
  From point to point, as is before exprest,
Discourst his voyage long, according his request.

16

Great pleasure mixt with pittifull regard,
  That godly King and Queene did passionate,
  Whiles they his pittifull aduentures heard,
  That oft they did lament his lucklesse state,
  And often blame the too importune fate,
  That heapd on him so many wrathfull wreakes:
  For neuer gentle knight, as he of late,
  So tossed was in fortunes cruell freakes;
And all the while salt teares bedeawd the hearers cheaks.

17

Then said that royall Pere in sober wise;
  Deare Sonne, great beene the euils, which ye bore
  From first to last in your late enterprise,
  That I note, whether prayse, or pitty more:
  For neuer liuing man, I weene, so sore
  In sea of deadly daungers was distrest;
  But since now safe ye seised haue the shore,
  And well arriued are, (high God be blest)
Let vs deuize of ease and euerlasting rest.

Stanza 12

4   **defeasance**: defeat. S. adapts an earlier legal sense,
'to render a claim null and void', to emphasize the end of the
Dragon's usurpation of Adam's kingdom.
6   **yuorie and gold**: traditional gifts, as 1 Kings 10.22,
Virgil, *Aen.* iii 464.
9   **manifold**: many times.

Stanza 13

2–3   See 38.6 to 39.9*n*.   **shaumes**: a kind of oboe; cf.
Ps. 98.6: 'With shalmes and sounde of trumpets sing loude
before the Lord the King.'
4   Cf. Luke 19.36: 'And as he [Christ] went, they spred their
clothes in the way.' Dixon (1597) cites Rev. 19.4, 5.
5   **purueyance**: provisions.
8   **scarlot**: a rich cloth.   **of great name**: well-known,
of great value.
9   **fitting purpose**: seemly conversation.

Stanza 14

1   **guize**: behaviour.
3   **deuize**: tell.
4   **seruices**: courses.
6   **large discourse**: lengthy account.
9   **luxurious**: extravagant; suggesting vicious indulgence,
as Lat. *luxuria*; also *luxurio*, to swell.

Stanza 15

Following the epic convention that a meal is shared before
stories are told.
7   **sad**: grave, serious, in keeping with his tale of **perils sad** (4)
(i.e. distressing, heavy).
8   Evidently not: see 31.8*n*.
9   **according**: granting.

Stanza 16

2   **passionate**: express with passion; possibly, fill with
compassion.
5   **importune**: grievous; Lat. *fata importuna*.
6   **wrathfull wreakes**: injuries or vengeful acts that express
Fate's wrath; cf. viii 43.3. Only Despair allows that the Knight
suffers through his own faults.

Stanza 17

2   **euils**: misfortunes.
4   **note**: know not.
5–6   Cf. Despair's interpretation, ix 45.3–4.
7–9   **safe**: also saved in the theological sense, 'delivered from
sin'.   **seised**: reached.   **deuize**: talk.   **euerlasting rest**:
man's state in heaven; cf. x 62.7.

18

Ah dearest Lord, said then that doughty knight,
    Of ease or rest I may not yet deuize;
    For by the faith, which I to armes haue plight,
    I bounden am streight after this emprize,
    As that your daughter can ye well aduize,
    Backe to returne to that great Faerie Queene,
    And her to serue six yeares in warlike wize,
    Gainst that proud Paynim king, that workes her teene:
Therefore I ought craue pardon, till I there haue beene.

19

Vnhappie falles that hard necessitie,
    (Quoth he) the troubler of my happie peace,
    And vowed foe of my felicitie;
    Ne I against the same can iustly preace:
    But since that band ye cannot now release,
    Nor doen vndo; (for vowes may not be vaine)
    Soone as the terme of those six yeares shall cease,
    Ye then shall hither backe returne againe,
The marriage to accomplish vowd betwixt you twain.

20

Which for my part I couet to performe,
    In sort as through the world I did proclame,
    That who so kild that monster most deforme,
    And him in hardy battaile ouercame,
    Should haue mine onely daughter to his Dame,
    And of my kingdome heire apparaunt bee:
    Therefore since now to thee perteines the same,
    By dew desert of noble cheualree,
Both daughter and eke kingdome, lo I yield to thee.

21

Then forth he called that his daughter faire,
    The fairest *Vn'* his onely daughter deare,
    His onely daughter, and his onely heyre;
    Who forth proceeding with sad sober cheare,
    As bright as doth the morning starre appeare
    Out of the East, with flaming lockes bedight,
    To tell that dawning day is drawing neare,
    And to the world does bring long wish'ed light;
So faire and fresh that Lady shewd her selfe in sight.

22

So faire and fresh, as freshest flowre in May;
    For she had layd her mournefull stole aside,
    And widow-like sad wimple throwne away,
    Wherewith her heauenly beautie she did hide,
    Whiles on her wearie iourney she did ride;
    And on her now a garment she did weare,
    All lilly white, withoutten spot, or pride,
    That seemd like silke and siluer wouen neare,
But neither silke nor siluer therein did appeare.

Stanza 18
4   **streight**: with close bonds; immediately.   **emprize**: enterprise; see ix 1.4*n.*
7   **six**: corresponds to the six days of the creation before the seventh day of 'euerlasting rest'; see Heb. 4.1–9. Dixon (1597) refers the six years to the reign of Philip and Mary: see Arg. *n.*
8   **teene**: harm, injury.

Stanza 19
4   **preace**: press, contend.
6   **not be vaine**: i.e. not be made vain; cf. Num. 30.3: 'Whosoever . . . sweareth an othe to binde him selfe by a bonde, he shal not breake his promes.' Stress on the Knight's vow prepares for the revelation of his 'bloudy vowes' (30.1) to Duessa.
9   **accomplish**: the term distinguishes between wedlock which is contracted or performed (as the next line indicates; cf. 'betrouthed', Arg. 2) and completed, i.e. consummated; cf. III ix 42.6–7. See 40.4–5*n.* Cf. the Geneva gloss to Rev. 19.7: 'God made Christ the bridgrome of his Church at the beginning, and at the last day it shalbe fully accomplished when we shal be joyned with our head.' Upton (1758) first noted the allusion to the mystical union of Christ and his Church described in Revelation and the Song of Solomon.

Stanza 20
2   **In sort as**: in the way that; even as.
5   **to his Dame**: as his wife.
9   Dixon (1597) glosses: 'the true Church and heaven'.

Stanza 21
1–5   Cf. the praise of the bride in Song of Sol. 6.8–9: 'my doove is alone, and my undefiled, she is the onelie daughter of her mother, and she is deare to her that bare her. . . . Who is she that loketh forthe as the morning, faire as the moone, pure as the sunne'; cf. 'th'only daughter of a King and Queene' (vii 43.3). The emphasis derives from the Creed, 'his only Son our Lord'. Further, **onely** gives Una her name and suggests also 'incomparable', 'peerless' (*OED* 5).   **sad sober cheare** expresses her womanhood: see IV x 49.5–9.   **sad**: steadfast, constant.
5–9   Cf. Rev. 22.16: 'I Jesus . . . am . . . the bright morning starre'; cf. 2.28: 'so wil I give him the morning starre'. In associating Una with the dawn (see xi 33, 51) and with the morning star, S. may have been influenced by the theme, *veritas filia temporis*; see Panofsky (1962) 83f. In *View* 84, S. refers to man 'lightened with the morning star of truth'.

Stanza 22
Cf. Rev. 19.7–8: 'the mariage of the Lambe is come, and his wife hathe made her self readie. And to her was granted, that she shulde be araied with pure fyne linen and shining.'
7   **All lilly white**: as Fidelia appears; see x 13.1*n.* **withoutten**: a form used by S. for emphasis.   **spot, or pride**: blemish or ostentatious ornament in contrast to Duessa, ii 13; hence without sin or pride; cf. Song of Sol. 4.7: 'Thou art all faire, my love, and there is no spot in thee.' At III iv 59.8, Truth is called 'Most sacred virgin, without spot of sin'.
8   **neare**: closely.

23

The blazing brightnesse of her beauties beame,
  And glorious light of her sunshyny face
  To tell, were as to striue against the streame.
  My ragged rimes are all too rude and bace,
  Her heauenly lineaments for to enchace.
  Ne wonder; for her owne deare loued knight,
  All were she dayly with himselfe in place,
  Did wonder much at her celestiall sight:
Oft had he seene her faire, but neuer so faire dight.

24

So fairely dight, when she in presence came,
  She to her Sire made humble reuerence,
  And bowed low, that her right well became,
  And added grace vnto her excellence:
  Who with great wisedome, and graue eloquence
  Thus gan to say.   But eare he thus had said,
  With flying speede, and seeming great pretence,
  Came running in, much like a man dismaid,
A Messenger with letters, which his message said.

25

All in the open hall amazed stood,
  At suddeinnesse of that vnwarie sight,
  And wondred at his breathlesse hastie mood.
  But he for nought would stay his passage right,
  Till fast before the king he did alight;
  Where falling flat, great humblesse he did make,
  And kist the ground, whereon his foot was pight;
  Then to his hands that writ he did betake,
Which he disclosing, red thus, as the paper spake.

26

To thee, most mighty king of *Eden* faire,
  Her greeting sends in these sad lines addrest,
  The wofull daughter, and forsaken heire
  Of that great Emperour of all the West;
  And bids thee be aduized for the best,
  Ere thou thy daughter linck in holy band
  Of wedlocke to that new vnknowen guest:
  For he already plighted his right hand
Vnto another loue, and to another land.

27

To me sad mayd, or rather widow sad,
  He was affiaunced long time before,
  And sacred pledges he both gaue, and had,
  False erraunt knight, infamous, and forswore:
  Witnesse the burning Altars, which he swore,
  And guiltie heauens of his bold periury,
  Which though he hath polluted oft of yore,
  Yet I to them for iudgement iust do fly,
And them coniure t'auenge this shamefull iniury.

28

Therefore since mine he is, or free or bond,
  Or false or trew, or liuing or else dead,
  Withhold, O soueraine Prince, your hasty hond
  From knitting league with him, I you aread;
  Ne weene my right with strength adowne to tread,
  Through weakenesse of my widowhed, or woe:
  For truth is strong, her rightfull cause to plead,
  And shall find friends, if need requireth soe,
So bids thee well to fare, Thy neither friend, nor foe,

Stanza 23

1–3   Cf. *H.H.B.* 170: the light from eternal Truth 'Is many thousand times more bright, more cleare', than that of the sun. At last Una is seen by her Knight as she is, 'clothed with the sunne' (Rev. 12.1).
4   **ragged**: rough to the ear; cf. III ii 3.6.
5   **for to enchace**: to serve as a setting for; a fig. sense from the jeweller's art of setting gems. Upon the simplest level it means 'portray', 'display', 'adorn': the poet's words both reveal and enclose her heavenly image.

Stanza 24

1   **in presence**: in the sense of attending upon royalty.
5–6   He is about to bid the banns, as 36.6–7 makes clear, when Archimago enters as in response.
7   **pretence**: purpose; claim to importance.

Stanza 25

2   **vnwarie**: unexpected. A unique usage adapted from the current sense, 'unguarded', 'incautious', which applies to the spectators.
4   **right**: direct, straightforward.
5   **alight**: arrive, stop. Another unique usage, either forced by the rhyme or doggedly literal: he descends from his 'flying speede' (24.7).
8   **betake**: deliver.
9   **disclosing**: unfolding.

Stanza 26

Dixon (1597) glosses as a fiction of the challenge by Mary Queen of Scots 'that the religion by hir maintained [was] the truth'.
3–4   Cf. ii 22.7–9.

Stanza 27

1   **widow**: cf. her role as a 'virgin widow' (ii 24.8).
4   **forswore**: forsworn.
5   **which**: by which (a Latinism). The altars burn with sacrifices that confirm the marriage vows.
6   **guiltie heauens . . . periury**: and witness also the heavens by which he swore and so made guilty, etc., implying that the heavens will punish his guilt; cf. Despair's charge: 'Thou falsed hast thy faith with periurie' (ix 46.7).
9   **coniure**: implore; also invoke by supernatural power, as she is a witch.   **iniury**: also offensive speech, specifically perjury.

Stanza 28

1   **bond**: bound.
4   **aread**: counsel.
7   Proverbial (C. G. Smith, 1970, 792); cf. III i 29.8.
9   **well to fare**: farewell.

159

29

When he these bitter byting words had red,
  The tydings straunge did him abashed make,
  That still he sate long time astonished
  As in great muse, ne word to creature spake.
  At last his solemne silence thus he brake,
  With doubtfull eyes fast fixed on his guest;
  Redoubted knight, that for mine onely sake
  Thy life and honour late aduenturest,
Let nought be hid from me, that ought to be exprest.

30

What meane these bloudy vowes, and idle threats,
  Throwne out from womanish impatient mind?
  What heauens? what altars? what enraged heates
  Here heaped vp with termes of loue vnkind,
  My conscience cleare with guilty bands would bind?
  High God be witnesse, that I guiltlesse ame.
  But if your selfe, Sir knight, ye faultie find,
  Or wrapped be in loues of former Dame,
With crime do not it couer, but disclose the same.

31

To whom the *Redcrosse* knight this answere sent,
  My Lord, my King, be nought hereat dismayd,
  Till well ye wote by graue intendiment,
  What woman, and wherefore doth me vpbrayd
  With breach of loue, and loyalty betrayd.
  It was in my mishaps, as hitherward
  I lately traueild, that vnwares I strayd
  Out of my way, through perils straunge and hard;
That day should faile me, ere I had them all declard.

32

There did I find, or rather I was found
  Of this false woman, that *Fidessa* hight,
  Fidessa hight the falsest Dame on ground,
  Most false *Duessa*, royall richly dight,
  That easie was t' inuegle weaker sight:
  Who by her wicked arts, and wylie skill,
  Too false and strong for earthly skill or might,
  Vnwares me wrought vnto her wicked will,
And to my foe betrayd, when least I feared ill.

33

Then stepped forth the goodly royall Mayd,
  And on the ground her selfe prostrating low,
  With sober countenaunce thus to him sayd;
  O pardon me, my soueraigne Lord, to show
  The secret treasons, which of late I know
  To haue bene wrought by that false sorceresse.
  She onely she it is, that earst did throw
  This gentle knight into so great distresse,
That death him did awaite in dayly wretchednesse.

34

And now it seemes, that she suborned hath
  This craftie messenger with letters vaine,
  To worke new woe and improuided scath,
  By breaking of the band betwixt vs twaine;
  Wherein she vsed hath the practicke paine
  Of this false footman, clokt with simplenesse,
  Whom if ye please for to discouer plaine,
  Ye shall him *Archimago* find, I ghesse,
The falsest man aliue; who tries shall find no lesse.

Stanza 29

4   **muse**: astonishment.
5   **solemne silence**: cf. the 'solemne silence' (viii 29.8) in Orgoglio's Castle, which also marks a turning-point in the Knight's progress.
7   **Redoubted**: dread, with a pun on 'being doubted'; as i 53.5.   **for mine onely sake**: for my sake alone.

Stanza 30

4   **vnkind**: ungrateful; unnaturally wicked; applied to Duessa and to the Knight.
6   Adam calls upon **High God**, not pagan **heauens** (3).
7   **faultie**: guilty.
8   **former Dame**: Duessa is 'his Dame' at vii 7.1; as Una is now, 20.5.
9   **crime**: i.e. the crime of perjury.

Stanza 31

1   **answere**: in the legal sense, a reply made to a charge.
2   These titles renounce Duessa's claim that he is plighted 'to another land' (26.9).
3   **intendiment**: careful consideration.
7   **vnwares**: without his knowledge; or 'suddenly', referring to his hasty flight from Una; cf. 32.8.
8   The omission of any reference to Duessa in his 'point to point' account of his 'straunge aduentures, and of perils sad' (15.4, 8) indicates that the Knight is not yet wedded to Truth. Even the memory of his sin seems to have been purged in the house of Holiness until he is now reminded. At 32.9, he recalls the precise moment when he lay with Duessa, vii 7.

Stanza 32

4   **royall richly dight**: royally and richly dressed, dressed with royal richness. A compound that turns several ways: e.g. it suggests that she usurps royalty that belongs only to Adam and 'the goodly royall Mayd' (33.1).
5   **inuegle**: beguile; blind; cf. vii 50.9.   **weaker**: too weak.
6–7   **wicked arts, and wylie skill**: her arts were too strong for earthly might, her skill too false for earthly skill. The love is not denied but instead its cause (witchcraft), its means (working on man's weakness), and its effect (betraying him, 31.5) are stressed.

Stanza 33

1   The intervention of Una as the **royall Mayd**, in contrast to Duessa who is only dressed as such, proclaims her the one to whom the Knight rightly owes his allegiance.
4   **pardon me**: give me leave; her humble posture contrasts with Duessa's proud presumption in counselling Adam (26.5).
7–9   Cf. viii 28.6–7.

Stanza 34

In a suit of law, an appellant was required to abjure the use of enchantments and to rely only on the justness of his cause. Duessa's case is exposed by revealing her messenger's disguise. As she is 'the falsest Dame on ground' (32.3), he is **The falsest man aliue** (9). Una's perception of Archimago contrasts with her earlier deception, as Miller (1971) 140–1 notes.
2   **vaine**: either 'in vain' or, as the adj., 'idle', i.e. false.
3   **improuided**: unforeseen, after Lat. *improvidus*.
scath: harm.
5   **practicke paine**: crafty pains.
7   **discouer**: literally, remove the cover from.

35

The king was greatly moued at her speach,
  And all with suddein indignation fraight,
  Bad on that Messenger rude hands to reach.
  Eftsoones the Gard, which on his state did wait,
  Attacht that faitor false, and bound him strait:
  Who seeming sorely chauffed at his band,
  As chained Beare, whom cruell dogs do bait,
  With idle force did faine them to withstand,
And often semblaunce made to scape out of their hand.

36

But they him layd full low in dungeon deepe,
  And bound him hand and foote with yron chains.
  And with continuall watch did warely keepe;
  Who then would thinke, that by his subtile trains
  He could escape fowle death or deadly paines?
  Thus when that Princes wrath was pacifide,
  He gan renew the late forbidden banes,
  And to the knight his daughter deare he tyde,
With sacred rites and vowes for euer to abyde.

37

His owne two hands the holy knots did knit,
  That none but death for euer can deuide;
  His owne two hands, for such a turne most fit,
  The housling fire did kindle and prouide,
  And holy water thereon sprinckled wide;
  At which the bushy Teade a groome did light,
  And sacred lampe in secret chamber hide,
  Where it should not be quenched day nor night,
For feare of euill fates, but burnen euer bright.

38

Then gan they sprinckle all the posts with wine,
  And made great feast to solemnize that day;
  They all perfumde with frankincense diuine,
  And precious odours fetcht from far away,
  That all the house did sweat with great aray:
  And all the while sweete Musicke did apply
  Her curious skill, the warbling notes to play,
  To driue away the dull Melancholy;
The whiles one sung a song of loue and iollity.

39

During the which there was an heauenly noise
  Heard sound through all the Pallace pleasantly,
  Like as it had bene many an Angels voice,
  Singing before th'eternall maiesty,
  In their trinall triplicities on hye;
  Yet wist no creature, whence that heauenly sweet
  Proceeded, yet eachone felt secretly
  Himselfe thereby reft of his sences meet,
And rauished with rare impression in his sprite.

Stanza 35
5 **Attacht**: seized. **faitor**: impostor.
8 **idle force**: force used idly. In his falseness, he only
pretended (**did faine**) to be unable to escape, as he only
seeming (6) chafed at his bonds. Alternatively, he appeared
to be angered and wished to withstand the guard but his force
was unavailing.

Stanza 36
1–5 Rev. 20.1–3: 'And I sawe an Angel come downe from
heaven, having . . . a great chaine in his hand. And he toke
the dragon that olde serpent, which is the devil and Satan, and
he bounde him a thousand yeres, And cast him into the bottomles pit, and he shut him up, and sealed the dore upon him . . .
till the thousand yeres were fulfilled: for after that he must be
losed for a litle season.'
3 **warely**: watchfully.
7 **renew**: repeat. **banes**: banns of marriage.

Stanza 37
3 **turne**: act; task.
4–5 The fire and water of the Roman marriage rites are
adapted for a Christian marriage. **housling**: of the Eucharist
or Holy Communion, suggesting 'sacramental', in contrast to
Duessa's 'burning Altars' (27.5). The holy water sprinkled
on the fire suggests baptism, the sanctification of wedded love.
S. writes obliquely because of the controversy over marriage.
According to Article XXV of the Church of England, marriage
is not allowed to be one of the sacraments of the Gospels
although, in one of the Homilies, it is compared to the sacrament of baptism. See Welsford (1967) 141.
6 **Teade**: the nuptial torch.
7–9 Upton (1758) cites Lev. 6.13: 'The fire shal ever burne
upon the altar, and never go out', and sees an allusion to the
mystical meaning of the lamps of the wise virgins.

Stanza 38
1–5 The language is close to the *Epithalamion*: 'sprinkle all
the postes and wals with wine, / That they may sweat, and
drunken be withall' (253–4). The Roman custom, in which the
bride anoints the doorposts of her new home, here becomes a
festive celebration by the wedding guests of the bridal bed,
suggesting joy and fertility.
3 **all**: if not taken absolutely, as 'all being perfumed', but
objectively, 'everything', then **sweat** (5) refers to the sprinkled
perfumes of the marriage preparations. **diuine**: the epithet
is deserved since the gift was given to the Christ child, Matt.
2.11.
6 to 39.9 Hollander (1971) 227–8 notes the progression from
the music of timbrels (7.3–5) attuned to human voices, to the
wind instruments orchestrated with voices (13.2–3), to
personified **sweete Musicke**, and finally to the heavenly
harmonies. 'We are being shown almost literally the relation
of the two sorts of music, one actual, the other transcendent,
whose signature only is to be glimpsed in actual **sweete** (in
the sense of "well-tuned") human music'. See II xii 71*n*.
7 **curious**: elaborate, intricate.
8 This line describes the festivities at the house of Pride,
v 3.5.
9 The song is the epithalamium.

Stanza 39
Upton notes the allusion to the song sung at the marriage
of the Lamb (Rev. 19.6–7), with Christ typified in the Knight
and the Church in Una. The music of the spheres in its nine-
fold harmony has not been audible to man since the Fall.
1 **noise**: melodious sound.
5 **trinall triplicities**: triple triad, the nine orders of angels
divided into three threefold hierarchies.
6 **sweet**: sweet sound.

40

Great ioy was made that day of young and old,
  And solemne feast proclaimd throughout the land,
  That their exceeding merth may not be told:
  Suffice it heare by signes to vnderstand
  The vsuall ioyes at knitting of loues band.
  Thrise happy man the knight himselfe did hold,
  Possessed of his Ladies hart and hand,
  And euer, when his eye did her behold,
His heart did seeme to melt in pleasures manifold.

41

Her ioyous presence and sweet company
  In full content he there did long enioy,
  Ne wicked enuie, ne vile gealosy
  His deare delights were able to annoy:
  Yet swimming in that sea of blisfull ioy,
  He nought forgot, how he whilome had sworne,
  In case he could that monstrous beast destroy,
  Vnto his Farie Queene backe to returne:
The which he shortly did, and *Vna* left to mourne.

42

Now strike your sailes ye iolly Mariners,
  For we be come vnto a quiet rode,
  Where we must land some of our passengers,
  And light this wearie vessell of her lode.
  Here she a while may make her safe abode,
  Till she repaired haue her tackles spent,
  And wants supplide.   And then againe abroad
  On the long voyage whereto she is bent:
Well may she speede and fairely finish her intent.

Stanza 40

2   **solemne feast**: sacred festival, as 4.6.
4–5   **signes**: tokens; but more specifically, indications of a
coming event: the consummation of the marriage, which seems
to be celebrated now, is only a token of that future event.
Here the betrothal is celebrated: the **knitting of loues band**
follows only after all other bonds that imprison the Knight
have been undone; cf. 26.6–7, the false 'bond' of 28.1, 30.5,
34.4 and 37.1–2.
6   So held by Contemplation, x 51.1.

Stanza 41

5   Cf. the 'sea of deadly daungers' (17.6) which had
distressed him.
8   The line repeats the vow made at 18.6.

Stanza 42

This stanza rounds out the canto by developing the opening
nautical metaphor: the vered sails are now struck. Cf. particularly the use of **safe** (5) and compare 17.7–9*n.*

   2   **rode**: roadstead, place of safe anchorage.

As Holiness is the bedrock on which the virtues are founded, Temperance is the basis of the virtues themselves. As a consequence, Books I and II are central in the whole poem and their relationship is crucial to the interpretation of its allegory. Woodhouse (1949) 204 argued that Book I moves with reference to the order of grace and Book II to the order of nature: 'Whereas what touches the Redcross Knight bears primarily upon revealed religion, or belongs to the order of grace, whatever touches Guyon bears upon natural ethics, or belongs to the order of nature.' Later critics have replied that the two orders of grace and nature merge when Guyon is reconciled to the Red Cross Knight in the opening episode and proceeds on his adventure with the Palmer's blessing, 'God guide thee, *Guyon*', and that the two orders are not sharply distinguished because S. views Temperance in Christian terms, as shown when heavenly love in the form of an angel befriends Guyon in his faint. Fowler (1964) 85 argues that 'each book after the first is built upon the preceding book, and takes for granted the spiritual territory already conquered'. Cheney (1966) 66 writes: 'Once we have recognized the existence of this basic contrast between Nature and Grace, it becomes apparent that Spenser has provided so intricate a contrapuntal pattern in his presentation of the two stories as to deny any simple contrast of the Christian and pagan contexts.' I have argued elsewhere (Hamilton, 1958a) that it is the pattern of inner meaning expressed by the parallel structure of the first two books, rather than reducible historical background provided by the two orders of nature and grace, which reveals the perspective for an understanding of the two Books and the unity of the whole poem.

Earlier critics, summarized in the *Variorum*, found in Aristotle's *Ethics* a gloss for S.'s concept of the virtue of Temperance and for his treatment of the virtue as a mean between extremes of excess and deficiency. Sirluck (1952) 100 concludes that Book II is a 'poetic version' of the *Ethics*; DeMoss, *Var.* ii 420, argues that 'not only did Spenser derive his moral virtues from Aristotle, as he himself asserted, but like Aristotle he developed or defined each virtue by presenting it as the mean between two contrasted extremes, and by contrasting it with its opposite'. Padelford, *Var.* ii 420–2, supports his argument by analysing the episodes of Book II in the light of Aristotle's discussion of Continence.

Later critics do not find Aristotle alone a sufficient gloss on S.'s image of Temperance. In Hamilton (1961) 49–50, I argue that even in the Medina episode, which offers the simplest analysis of Temperance, S. goes far beyond Aristotle. While the opening tableau of Medina and her sisters represents the Aristotelian concept of temperance as the mean between the two extremes of excess and defect, the confused battle between Guyon and the suitors that follows represents the Platonic concept of temperance as the struggle between the rational part of the soul (Guyon) and the irrational, the latter being divided into the irascible (Huddibras) and the concupiscent (Sansloy). Their reconciliation when they join the three sisters at a feast suggests a Christian humanist concept of the virtue, such as that implicit in Milton's remark: 'Wherefore did he [God] create passions within us, pleasures round about us, but that these rightly tempered are the very ingredients of virtue?' Nelson (1963) 194–5 notes that 'what interests Aristotle in the *Nicomachean Ethics* does not, for the most part, concern Spenser. . . . The chosen spirits of the *Ethics* and the *Republic* are capable of learning to subordinate their passions and so to become their own guardians. Neither Guyon nor Prince Arthur is always able to do so.' Tuve (1966) 76 disposes of the debate over sources by showing how the classical virtues 'were changed and vivified and made all the more congenial by developments during Christian times' so that they were 'no longer separable from the resulting amalgamations'.

Not sources, then, but ends is the proper concern of any reader of Book II. Once the reader grasps its structure he will understand why S. may claim in the final canto, 'Now gins this goodly frame of Temperance / Fairely to rise'. Just how the frame of temperance emerges through the structuring of the episodes in the Book has been the subject of fruitful debate.

While the Book of Holiness reveals man's spiritual life through his right relationship to God in the vertical perspective of heaven and hell, the Book of Temperance analyses man's natural life through his right relationship to his own nature in a horizontal perspective of the world in which he lives. Through temperance man so controls his own nature that he may control external nature. Self-control requires that reason control the hard and soft emotions, anger and desire. Accordingly, Guyon, directed by the Palmer who functions as his reason, confronts and subdues the irascible Furor and finally Pyrochles. When he confronts the concupiscent Cymochles in his ireful aspect, however, he has yielded to Phædria's frivolous pleasures, and must yield to a truce. According to Greenlaw, *Var.* ii 427, the first six cantos examine man's rational control over the irascible emotions, the second six over the concupiscent: 'The seemingly unrelated Episodes in the first six cantos of Book II are *exempla* illustrating the evil effects of anger, or spirit in the unfavorable sense. Amavia, Pyrochles and Cymochles, Furor, etc., illustrate this method admirably. . . . In the last six cantos the stories of Maleger, Acrasia, etc., illustrate the evils of sensuality.' In the terms given above, the first six cantos show the power of temperance over man's internal nature, the second six show this power over external nature. As with man's internal nature, external nature may be divided into hard and soft forces. Of the forces which assault the highest sense in the temperate body, 'two then all more huge and violent, / Beautie, and money, they that Bulwarke sorely rent' (II xi 9). The one is imaged in Mammon and the other in Acrasia; accordingly they tempt Guyon at the climactic mid and final points of his quest.

A different basis for a division of the Book into a first and second half is suggested by Berger (1957). He finds a shift from classical to Christian cosmology marked by the entrance of the angel to succour the fallen Guyon:

> The first six cantos are dominated by a hero whose temperance is Aristotelian – a natural, aristocratic virtue rendering its possessor immune to inner struggle and temptation. . . . Canto vii dramatizes the insufficiency of Aristotelian temperance, the innocence and limited wisdom resulting from reflexes so easy, so assured. Cantos viii-xi disclose the workings of a different kind of temperance: the Christian virtue, supernaturally infused, accessible to all, but gained and retained by each with difficulty. Canto xii . . . recapitulates the contrast. (62–3)

However, our interpretation of the Book need not be changed by this argument but rather clarified. Through natural virtue man may control his irascible emotions although only to a point of exhaustion. Only by supernatural assistance may he conquer his own nature and finally assert the virtue of temperance over external nature.

Another pairing is suggested by Nelson (1963) who claims that the dichotomy of the passions into 'forward' and 'froward' is one of the principal motifs of the Book: 'As the froward passion ranges in its manifestations from modesty and inactivity to grief, wrath, and suicide, so the forward passion takes such various forms as hunger for money, power, and glory; desire for ease, beauty, and sexual satisfaction' (185). Fowler (1964) argues that Book II is structured in terms of the dyad, noting, for example, that 'so regular is the arrangement of characters in complementary pairs, in this book, that one might almost think it a direct translation of the number symbolism into purely formal terms – a kind of Pythagorean literary ballet' (11-2). On the thematic pairing throughout the Book, see Hieatt (1975) 209.

Recent criticism of Book II has focused on the four episodes in which temperance is tested to the point at which one becomes aware both of its power and its limitations: the washing of Ruddymane's hands, Guyon's temptation by Mammon, the defeat of Maleger, and the destruction of the Bower of Bliss.

Amazement temporarily overcomes reason in two related episodes that are turning-points in the action. When Guyon out of pity seeks to cleanse the bloody-handed Babe in the waters of a fountain, the water contrary to its nature fails to cleanse the Babe: 'The which him into great amaz'ment droue, / And into diuerse doubt his wauering wonder cloue.' He continues in this state until the Palmer offers him 'goodly reason' by relating a mythological tale about the pure waters. Then Guyon assumes his mission to avenge the Babe's parents by destroying the power of Acrasia. The related episode is that in which Arthur out of
164 anger seeks to slay the ghost-like Maleger. When his sword, contrary to its nature, fails to kill him, 'His

wonder farre exceeded reasons reach, / That he began to doubt his dazeled sight, / And oft of error did himselfe appeach'. He continues in this state until he recalls the mythological tale of Hercules slaying Antaeus. Then he is able to slay Maleger by casting him into 'a standing lake'. Since Maleger is associated with the original sin of concupiscence – symbolized by the Babe's bloody hands – the final cleansing of this sin by water allows Guyon to overcome the powers of concupiscence and go on to defeat Acrasia.

The other paired episodes provide the climactic moments at the middle and end of Guyon's adventures. Guyon triumphs over all Mammon's temptations but then faints and lies helpless before his enemies. Only when his enemies are slain may he continue his mission. At the end he triumphs over all the temptations of the Bower of Bliss, and then fulfils his mission by binding Acrasia and destroying her Bower in 'the tempest of his wrathfulnesse'. On the limitations of his virtue, which are implied by the paired episodes, see the Headnote to Book III.

Ruddymane

In *L.R.*, S. explains that the occasion of Guyon's adventure, the Palmer's story of the bloody-handed Babe whose parents were slain by Acrasia, is 'the beginning of the second booke and the whole subiect thereof'. By 'subject' he means 'invention', that is, the discovery of the matter which he labours to express in the poem. Earlier critics, distracted by the apparent disagreement between a formal analysis of the subject of Book II and its narrative vehicle in the poem, failed to realize the significance of the episode even though Winstanley (1914) 243 had suggested that the Babe's stained hands 'typify the sin of the flesh which is inherent and cannot be removed by any earthly means'. Bowers (1951) proposes that the stained hands refer to the 'doctrine of retribution' and that the waters which refuse to cleanse the hands bear a 'sacramental reference'. In Hamilton (1958b) I suggest that the stained hands refer to mankind infected by Original Sin; as such, they may not be cleansed because even baptism may not remove such sin. Fowler (1961b) 100–1 argues that S.'s subject is 'baptismal regeneration': 'Ablution is performed by Guyon to portray the intimate relation between baptism and temperance; for Spenser conceives temperance theologically as the destruction, by repeated mortifications, of the "body of sin", the relic of the old man buried with Christ at baptism.' Kaske (1976) notes S.'s model in the ineffectual washing of the bloody babe in Ezekiel 16.

Since the waters in this episode are not cleansing, unlike the waters from the Well of Life in Book I, some readers query the theological allegory and others reject it entirely. Miller (1966) 157 prefers a secular reading: 'the Palmer's mythic analysis (a blend of the Daphne and Arethusa tales) replaces any theological notions we or Guyon may have entertained. For Miller, the Babe's blood-stained hands serve only 'to remind us and Guyon of a crime which remains unavenged'. Evans (1970) 119 also rejects baptismal regeneration although he finds in the bloody hands a possible allusion 'to the Christ child who, through the Fall of Adam, takes on human corruption and, bearing on his hands the stigmata of sin, carries thereby the promise of redemption which his Incarnation makes possible'.

The clash of these views – and there seems to be no consensus – indicates the complexity of S.'s poetry, the difficulty of interpreting allegory, and the need for more careful, controlled reading (see II ii 4*n*).

Mammon episode

In his three-day passage underground, Guyon is tempted by Mammon, triumphs, but then faints so that he lies helpless when his enemies arrive to despoil his 'dead' body. In Berger's (1957) dramatic reading of Guyon as a fictional character, Guyon is led into temptation because of his 'idle curiosity', he is tempted because he seeks 'to understand Temperance by example and experience', and he faints in order to learn his human limitations: 'he has ignored his common humanity – the needs of his body – and we know when he faints that he must learn to confront this condition which he shares with Everyman if he is to actualize his unique powers' (29). In contrast to this psychological reading, Kermode (1971) 60–83 presents an archetypal reading which follows Upton's (1758) suggestion that Guyon undergoes an initiation comparable to that of the Eleusinian mysteries and takes account of the clear analogies, also first pointed out by Upton, to the temptation of Christ in the wilderness. He argues that Guyon undergoes an initiation to perfect his virtue by overcoming a total temptation parallel to Christ's threefold temptation. Guyon progresses 'through a purgatorial process from human to semi-divine virtue, from a human to a divine *phronesis*' (82–3; see II vii 9–63*n*). By this reading, Guyon is tempted because he represents human nature and he faints because initiation leads to a rebirth which leaves the initiate in need of external aid. Alpers (1967) 235–75 rejects both readings. He does not grant Berger's assumption that Guyon is a fictional character with psychological traits: the confrontation with Mammon concerns 'issues about the human use of wealth', not 'the dramatic interplay of personalities'. He rejects Kermode's initiation ritual pattern because he prefers a 'simple, even simple-minded understanding' that conveys only those meanings accessible to the common reader. Alpers's quarrel with Berger is over the nature of allegory: is the narrative to be read as narrative? His quarrel with Kermode is over the kind of reader the poem demands: a 'common' reader who responds only emotionally or the 'curious' reader who is willing to contemplate the enigmatic images in S.'s 'darke conceit'.

Guyon's faint may be explained, and explained away, simply: he is hungry and over-tired. Three days without food or rest – and there is no record that he had water to drink – would leave anyone exhausted. It is a fact well known to nutritionists that after even six hours without food a body begins to feed upon muscle fat. Or his faint may have allegorical significance. S. allows both responses: careful reading of the episode indicates that Guyon has simply fainted and also that he appears to be dead. One would expect as much of an allegory in which the narrative is the means through which the 'darke conceit' is expressed. For this reason, most readers understand Guyon's faint for reasons other than physical. Sonn (1961) 26, 30 sees the unconscious Guyon as an image of 'the spiritual death of self-reliance': 'If the argument of these cantos [vii and viii] is the inadequacy of natural man, their truth is the infinite mercy of God.' Miller (1964) 42 argues that 'Guyon faints not only because he has ignored his bodily needs, but also because he has assumed a psychological stance which abhors the body and any pleasures which may be derived from it'. Tuve (1966) 416 observes that 'faints are standard behavior for heroes of romances', particularly if they have been in contact with the supernatural world: 'if evil is intimated, exhaustion and shock are the usual reactions displayed to crossing that threshhold'. Cullen (1970) 168 argues that Guyon faints 'not because he has sinned, but because Adam sinned and because he has reached the limitations of his own virtue' and must develop as '*microchristus*' in order to defeat Acrasia.

If these readings have merit, Guyon's temptation by Mammon, which culminates in his faint, needs more than a common-sense explanation. Any adequate explanation must take account of Guyon's psychology and Adam's psychology, stock romance behaviour and ritual rebirth, and especially the capacities and limitations of temperance in relation to the irrational soul. Further, the temptation and faint must be related to the Red Cross Knight's similar crisis at the corresponding point in Book I. Even more revealing is the moment when Britomart at the beginning of her quest, rather than at the middle, passes over the gold, pearls, and precious stones of the Rich Strond. She is not tempted; she does not faint or even pause 'But them despised all; for all was in her powre' (III iv 18).

Our understanding of the Mammon episode as a whole needs to arise from a more precise awareness of S.'s craftsmanship. It needs to be noted, for example, that the temptations are carefully structured, those in the dark glade relating precisely to those in Mammon's house (see II vii 9–63*n*). Only recently has it been observed that Guyon's stay in Mammon's house extends through precisely forty stanzas in accord with Guyon's *imitatio Christi* (see vii 26.5*n*). No critic has investigated the significance of Guyon's progress from the house of Riches to the temple of Philotime, to the garden of Proserpina, and beyond its walls to lower hell. Thus there is no agreement as to why Tantalus and Pilate should be seen together, although their pairing may well provide the device upon which our entire understanding of the episode hinges.

Maleger

Since Temperance must be exercised against both the internal enemy, man's fallen nature, and the external enemy, the fallen world in which man lives, Arthur must intervene twice at those two crucial points at which the virtue needs to be aided by grace. When he slays the two elements of the irrational soul, Pyrochles and Cymochles, Guyon revives and the renewed temperate body may be displayed in the Castle of Alma. Then Arthur must slay the captain of the enemies that besiege the Castle in order that Guyon may defeat Acrasia's power.

Earlier critics interpret Maleger in general terms: 'Captain of the Lusts of the Flesh' (Ruskin, *Works* x 383), the passions, sensuality, deadly sin, physical disease which results from sin or simply disease as it attacks the physical body, or death. S. defines him as that body so 'Distempred through misrule and passions bace: / It growes a Monster, and incontinent / Doth loose his dignitie and natiue grace' (II ix 1). As such, his appearance parodies the temperate body seen in the Castle of Alma: 'His bodie leane and meagre as a rake, / And skin all withered like a dryed rooke' (xi 22). Woodhouse (1949) 221 interprets Maleger in specific terms as 'original sin or human depravity, the result of the fall' and suggests that 'the marks of physical disease and death are the symbols of the inherited taint, the moral and spiritual malady, which man is powerless to remove'. In Woodhouse (1950), he interprets Maleger's death by water as baptismal regeneration. In Hamilton (1961) 102–4 I support this reading through analysing the relationship between Books I and II.

Maleger's nature may be clarified by attending to the symbolic details of Arthur's struggle against him. Against Maleger's fierce attack in full flight, which indicates his intemperate and paradoxical state, Arthur must learn first to 'keepe his standing' (II xi 27); this is the stance of the Castle of Alma (xi 15). At the next stage of the battle, he assumes Guyon's stance, which is that of the wrestler, for he fights on his behalf. Like him, he falls unconscious at the crucial moment of his testing. From this state he is able to rouse himself 'As one awakt out of long slombring shade, / Reuiuing thought of glorie and of fame' (xi 31): that is, he is awakened out of intemperance, which is the Cymochlean state of sleeping in the shade (v 32), by the memory of himself, which is his '*Prays-desire*' (ix 39). When Maleger dismounts to attack him, he is caught, as Arthur was, and fills Arthur's place on the ground. The struggle that follows points to the mystery of Maleger's nature:

> Flesh without bloud, a person without spright,
> Wounds without hurt, a bodie without might,
> That could doe harme, yet could not harmed bee,
> That could not die, yet seem'd a mortall wight,
> That was most strong in most infirmitee. (xi 40.4–8)

These riddles, which defeat 'reasons reach', suggest that Maleger is the old Adam in us, against whom Paul laments: 'O wretched man that I am, who shal deliver me from the bodie of this death?' (Rom. 7.24). That Arthur's struggle is internal, that he battles himself, is suggested by the unamended *1590* text: he 'thought his labour lost and trauell vaine, / Against his lifelesse shadow so to fight'. Since such a foe is 'of the earth, earthlie' (1 Cor. 15.47), he is sustained by the earth.

To defeat Maleger, Arthur must go beyond what all other knights have done and throw away his armour. He subdues him by crushing his body, as Hercules overcomes Antaeus. This classical parallel was first noted by Upton (1758) who cites Fulgentius's interpretation of the myth as reason's conquest over the lusts of the flesh. Yet this action is not sufficient. While Hercules may prevent Antaeus from reviving by holding his crushed body off the ground, Arthur must also cast Maleger's crushed body into a standing lake. The significant parallel within the poem is the story of another son of the earth, Georgos, the Red Cross Knight, who also is sustained when he falls to the ground during his battle with the Dragon. When he is 'cast' into the living water of the Well of Life, and later into the mire formed by the balm from the Tree of Life, he rises renewed. While Maleger does not rise from the lake – its waters are stagnant rather than flowing – Arthur is left near death, needing to be sustained by his Squire and nursed back to life in the Castle of Alma. His 'infirmity' (xi 49) suggests Maleger's (xi 40). Although baptism may slay the Old Adam in us and allow lapsed powers to be renewed, the infection of original sin remains. On the third day, as II xii 2 indicates, the final struggle against the lusts of the flesh, following baptism, is shown in Guyon's triumph over Acrasia and her Bower of Bliss.

Guyon and the Bower

The beauty of the wanton Bower of Bliss which Guyon destroys so wantonly, its intemperance of sensuality being countered, apparently, by his intemperance of irascibility, suggests a clash in S. between the poet and the moralist. Grierson (1929) 54 writes: 'the moralist must convince us that the sacrifice [of the Bower] is required in the interest of what is a higher and more enduring good, that the sensuous yields place to the spiritual. It is this Spenser fails to do imaginatively, whatever doctrine one may extract intellectually from the allegory.' Lewis (1936) 326 replies that the Bower only seems to be a natural garden of joyous sensuality; actually it is art not nature, and not a place of love but rather lust turned into *skeptophilia*. In reply to Lewis, Brooke (1949) 434 notes that art is not bad in itself but only as it wars with nature. Guth (1961) shows that the artifice in the Bower, and elsewhere in the poem, does not have clear or consistent evil connotations (see II xii 61*n*). Nevo (1962) replies in similar terms: an improper rivalry between art and nature corrupts the proper ends of both. Yet as Hough (1962) 164 rightly observes, 'the obstinate beauty of the scene remains unchanged'. Alpers (1967) 305 finds that S.'s description 'in no way denies the hold the Bower of Bliss has had on us as readers or could have on us as men'.

As a consequence, Guyon's destruction of the Bower remains deeply disturbing. Berger (1957) 218 refers to Guyon's 'Puritan frenzy'; Hough 164 writes that 'the Bower with all its mazy loveliness is suddenly and abruptly defaced; and we are shocked'; and Alpers 306 is perturbed by Guyon's 'vindictive hostility'. The response of S.'s readers is that of Acrasia's victims when they are changed from beasts to men. No one is happy: 'they did vnmanly looke, / And stared ghastly, some for inward shame, / And some for wrath, to see their captiue Dame'. Grill in preferring to remain a beast is only 'aboue the rest', not different from them.

One may reasonably assume that S. expected some of his readers, if not all, to respond to the Bower of Bliss as Acrasia's victims had done. Okerlund (1973) 64 claims that 'the psychological impact of the poetry compels a self-recognition and admission of our own intemperate desires'. In a rejoinder, Hawkins (1973) 1186 attempts to justify such a response by calling Guyon 'a self-righteous prig' for denying the appeal to his senses, a response which goes a stage beyond what S. allows Grill. Since S. seeks to fashion the reader in virtuous discipline, he would allow that a virtue not fully manifest even in the heroic figure of Guyon would be less manifest in others. Miller (1971) 146 concludes that he means us to be offended because we are betrayed into a human or Grillish response to the Bower's beauty while Guyon 'has become something more than human; he has assumed the role of an abstract concept, the ideal for which he has striven; he has become Temperance'. It is clear that S. manipulates the reader's response in order to reach that final moment of full awakening to the realization that the Bower is 'nam'd amis' (xii 69) when it is named the Bower of Bliss. As a moment of birth and initiation into the state of virtue, it is painful. Yet the moment remains painful only for readers who regard the end of the Book as the end of the poem. After only a few stanzas of Book III, it would seem that Guyon's response to the Bower has initiated an action that requires the rest of the poem to resolve, namely, how to release the feminine from masculine tyranny. See Headnote to Book III.

THE SECOND

BOOKE OF THE
FAERIE QVEENE.
Contayning,
THE LEGEND OF SIR GVYON.
OR
Of Temperaunce.

1

Ight well I wote most mighty Soueraine,
That all this famous antique history,
Of some th'aboundance of an idle braine
Will iudged be, and painted forgery,
Rather then matter of iust memory,
Sith none, that breatheth liuing aire, does know,
Where is that happy land of Faery,
Which I so much do vaunt, yet no where show,
But vouch antiquities, which no body can know.

2

But let that man with better sence aduize,
That of the world least part to vs is red:
And dayly how through hardy enterprize,
Many great Regions are discouered,
Which to late age were neuer mentioned.
Who euer heard of th'Indian *Peru*?
Or who in venturous vessell measured
The *Amazons* huge riuer now found trew?
Or fruitfullest *Virginia* who did euer vew?

3

Yet all these were, when no man did them know;
Yet haue from wisest ages hidden beene:
And later times things more vnknowne shall show.
Why then should witlesse man so much misweene
That nothing is, but that which he hath seene?
What if within the Moones faire shining spheare?
What if in euery other starre vnseene
Of other worldes he happily should heare?
He wonder would much more: yet such to some appeare.

4

Of Faerie lond yet if he more inquire,
By certaine signes here set in sundry place
He may it find; ne let him then admire,
But yield his sence to be too blunt and bace,
That no'te without an hound fine footing trace.
And thou, O fairest Princesse vnder sky,
In this faire mirrhour maist behold thy face,
And thine owne realmes in lond of Faery,
And in this antique Image thy great auncestry.

Proem
Stanza 1
4   **painted forgery**: deceiving invention.
5   **iust memory**: true, accurate record or history. Browne praises S. as one of the 'sons of Memory' (*Britannia's Pastorals* II i 1027).
8   **vaunt**: display; praise.
9   **antiquities**: from the 'antique rolles' mentioned at I Proem 2.4; cf. IV xi 10.1–5. The whimsy is clarified by the later claim that no one can find the strange ways in Faeryland 'but who was taught them by the Muse' (VI Proem 2.9).

Stanza 2
1   **aduize**: consider, reflect.
2   **red**: told, and therefore made known.
6   **th'Indian Peru**: Peru was believed to be India.
7   **measured**: travelled; also, determined its length.
8   **now found trew**: in 1541 when Orellana first sailed down the river.
9   This reference to the state, and the addition, 'and of Virginia', to the titles of Elizabeth in the 1596 dedication are among the first references in literature.   **fruitfullest**: for the glowing account given by the early explorers, see, e.g., Barlowe's report to Raleigh in 1586, in Wright (1965) 104–5.

Stanza 3
4   **witlesse**: perhaps a sly allusion to the paradise of fools found on the Moon (Ariosto, *Orl. Fur.* xxxiv).   **misweene**: wrongly judge; cf. Chaucer, Prol. to *Legend of Good Women* 12–5: 'Men shal not wenen every thing a lye / But yf himself yt seeth, or elles dooth; / For, God wot, thing is never the lasse sooth, / Thogh every wight ne may it nat ysee.'
6–9   On the Renaissance literature concerning an inhabited moon and the plurality of worlds, see Nicolson (1936). This is one of the earliest references, according to Kocher (1953) 86. Cf. Dante's use of the heavens: **within** may render the sensation, recorded in *Parad.* ii 31–45, of entering into the moon's body.   **vnseene**: i.e. worlds at present unseen by man. **happily**: by chance.

Stanza 4
1   **inquire**: seek after.
2   **By certaine signes**: reminds us that the allegory shadows forth a type.   **in sundry place**: in different places.
3   **admire**: i.e. wonder at what his own senses have revealed.
5   **note . . . trace**: does not know how to track faint or cunning footsteps without a hound.
6–9   The reality in Faeryland is reflected in England. 7 refers to Belphœbe in Canto iii, the image of fruitful virginity who represents the Virgin Queen (*L.R.*); 8 refers to '*Briton moniments*' (ix 59.6) read by Arthur (x 5–68); and 9 refers to '*Antiquitie* of *Faerie* lond' (ix 60.2) read by Guyon (x 70–76); cf. x 1.7–9. On the relation between Britain and Faeryland, see Roche (1964) 46. Murrin (1974) 73 argues that the ideal (Faeryland) mirrors the real (Britain) to 'move us from wonder at his [S.'s] art to wonder at ourselves'.

5

The which O pardon me thus to enfold
  In couert vele, and wrap in shadowes light,
  That feeble eyes your glory may behold,
  Which else could not endure those beames bright,
  But would be dazled with exceeding light.
  O pardon, and vouchsafe with patient eare
  The braue aduentures of this Faery knight
  The good Sir *Guyon* gratiously to heare,
In whom great rule of Temp'raunce goodly doth appeare.

Cant. I.

Guyon by Archimage abusd,
* The Redcrosse knight awaytes,*
Findes Mordant and Amauia slaine
* With pleasures poisoned baytes.*

1

THat cunning Architect of cancred guile,
  Whom Princes late displeasure left in bands,
  For falsed letters and suborned wile,
  Soone as the *Redcrosse* knight he vnderstands
  To beene departed out of *Eden* lands,
  To serue againe his soueraine Elfin Queene,
  His artes he moues, and out of caytiues hands
  Himselfe he frees by secret meanes vnseene;
His shackles emptie left, him selfe escaped cleene.

2

And forth he fares full of malicious mind,
  To worken mischiefe and auenging woe,
  Where euer he that godly knight may find,
  His onely hart sore, and his onely foe,
  Sith *Vna* now he algates must forgoe,
  Whom his victorious hands did earst restore
  To natiue crowne and kingdome late ygoe:
  Where she enioyes sure peace for euermore,
As weather-beaten ship arriu'd on happie shore.

Stanza 5

1–2 **O pardon me**: give me leave; as Una addresses the King of Eden, I xii 33.4. The **vele** may be compared to the covering that Moses put upon his face because it 'shone bright' after God had talked with him: the children of Israel 'were afraide to come nere him' (Exod. 34.30). For the common Renaissance view that poetry 'veils truth in a fair and fitting garment of fiction' (Boccaccio, *Gen. Deor.* XIV vii), see Osgood (1956) 157. This usual view is inverted here: the poet veils the light in order that his readers may see. **couert**: concealing. **light**: with a pun, for the shadow gives light.
7 **this Faery knight**: contrasts with the emphasis on Britain in Book I.
8 **Guyon**: the name belongs to a romance hero, such as Guy of Warwick or Guy of Burgundy who in *Sir Firumbras* (ed. O'Sullivan, 1935) 465 is called 'the good Gyoun'. Also it is chosen for its etymology: the name signifies 'wrestler' according to the *Golden Legend*; see I x 66.5–6*n*. Snyder (1961) observes that wrestling is an important motif in Book II. Camden, *Remains* (1605) 82, derives 'Guy' from Lat. *guido* and Fr. *guide*: 'A guide, leader or director to others'. Guyon, however, is himself guided both by the Palmer (cf. i 34.4) and by God (cf. i 32.8). Fowler (1960a) argues that the name is derived from Gihon, the second of the four rivers of Eden (Gen. 2.13), which was interpreted allegorically by Ambrose as the virtue of temperance because 'it cleanses the worthless body, and quenches the fire of vile flesh'.

Canto i

Argument

1 **abusd**: deceived; misused.
2 **awaytes**: waylays, ambushes.
3 **Mordant**: at 49.9 named *Mordtant, 1590, 1596*; **Amauia** is not named until the end of their story, ii. 45.8. On the names, see 55.4*n*, 5*n*.
4 **pleasures**: i.e. Acrasia's; cf. ii 45.4. Acrasia is also named Pleasure at xii 1.8, 48.8; cf. iii 41.8.

Stanza 1

1 **That cunning Architect**: alluding to his name, Archimago; see I i 43.6*n*. The phrase introduces the new world of Book II. On his escape, see Rev. 20.1–3 (cited I xii 36.1–5*n*). **cancred**: venomous; infectious.
3 Duessa 'suborned' Archimago to break the bond between Una and the Red Cross Knight 'with letters vaine' (I xii 34). These are **falsed**, then, as they seek to break loyalty, and Archimago's wile is **suborned** as he is secretly bribed to give false testimony.
7 **moues**: applies. **caytiues hands**: either the hands of those who held him captive or the hands of menials; cf. 'rude hands' (I xii 35.3).

Stanza 2

4 **onely**: chief, special.
5 **algates**: altogether.
7 **late ygoe**: lately; suggesting that Book II follows Book I in time. See 32.6*n*.
9 Cf. I xii 42; also 32.9 below.

3

Him therefore now the obiect of his spight
    And deadly food he makes: him to offend
    By forged treason, or by open fight
    He seekes, of all his drift the aymed end:
    Thereto his subtile engins he does bend,
    His practick wit, and his faire filed tong,
    With thousand other sleights: for well he kend,
    His credit now in doubtfull ballaunce hong;
For hardly could be hurt, who was already stong.

4

Still as he went, he craftie stales did lay,
    With cunning traines him to entrap vnwares,
    And priuie spials plast in all his way,
    To weete what course he takes, and how he fares;
    To ketch him at a vantage in his snares.
    But now so wise and warie was the knight
    By triall of his former harmes and cares,
    That he descride, and shonned still his slight:
The fish that once was caught, new bait will hardly bite.

5

Nath'lesse th'Enchaunter would not spare his paine,
    In hope to win occasion to his will;
    Which when he long awaited had in vaine,
    He chaungd his minde from one to other ill:
    For to all good he enimy was still.
    Vpon the way him fortuned to meet,
    Faire marching vnderneath a shady hill,
    A goodly knight, all armd in harnesse meete,
That from his head no place appeared to his feete.

6

His carriage was full comely and vpright,
    His countenaunce demure and temperate,
    But yet so sterne and terrible in sight,
    That cheard his friends, and did his foes amate:
    He was an Elfin borne of noble state,
    And mickle worship in his natiue land;
    Well could he tourney and in lists debate,
    And knighthood tooke of good Sir *Huons* hand,
When with king *Oberon* he came to Faerie land.

7

Him als accompanyd vpon the way
    A comely Palmer, clad in blacke attire,
    Of ripest yeares, and haires all hoarie gray,
    That with a staffe his feeble steps did stire,
    Least his long way his aged limbes should tire:
    And if by lookes one may the mind aread,
    He seemd to be a sage and sober sire,
    And euer with slow pace the knight did lead,
Who taught his trampling steed with equall steps to tread.

Stanza 3

2   **food**: feud: hatred, hostility. The sixteenth-century spelling suggests 'food for death'; cf. 'pleasures poisoned baytes' (Arg. 4).   **offend**: injure, harm.

3   **forged**: made up, invented by the 'cunning Architect' (1.1).

4   **drift**: plot, purpose; as I ii 9.4 where 'Th'end of his drift' is Una.

5   **subtile engins**: cunning wiles; also machines of warfare, extending the metaphor of **aymed end** (4).

6   **practick**: crafty; cf. his 'practicke paine', I xii 34.5.
faire filed: smooth, as I i 35.7.

8   **credit**: credibility.

Stanza 4

1   **stales**: baits, decoys; soon he uses the Red Cross Knight as a decoy to trap Guyon.

2   **traines**: stratagems.

3   **priuie spials**: hidden spies.

5   **at a vantage**: i.e. at his advantage and the Knight's disadvantage.

Stanza 5

7   **vnderneath a shady hill**: cf. the Wandering Wood which encloses the Red Cross Knight before he begins his quest.

8   **A goodly knight**: in contrast to 'that godly knight' (2.3) and pointing to the difference between the spiritual allegory of Book I and the moral allegory of Book II.   **all armd**: armed cap-à-pie, as Arthur at I vii 29.6.   **harnesse meete**: fitting armour, i.e. appropriate; also close-fitting.

Stanza 6

2   **demure**: serious or grave, suggesting modesty or Shamefastnesse (ix 43.9), corresponding to the Red Cross Knight's sadness. The term describes Fidelia and Speranza (I x 12.4), its only other use in the poem.   **temperate**: referring to the proper mingling of the humours as it expresses the 'great rule of Temp'raunce' (Pr. 5.9) in the Knight.

4   **amate**: daunt; cf. Artegall whose 'manly face . . . did his foes agrize' (III ii 24.4).

5   **Elfin**: elf, to distinguish Guyon's race from the Red Cross Knight's; see I x 65.

6   **mickle worship**: much honour.

7   **debate**: fight.

8–9   **Sir Huon**: the hero of the medieval romance, *Sir Huon of Bordeaux*, favoured by Oberon, whom S. names King of Faeryland and father of Tanaquill or Gloriana, x 75, 76.

Stanza 7

2   **comely**: decent, decorous, as also applied to Guyon above; or, adverbially, 'suitably clad'.   **Palmer**: a pilgrim (cf. 52.8); or more specifically, one who has returned from the Holy Land. His presence indicates the Christian sanction of right reason.   **blacke**: his identifying epithet, 34.4, etc.

4   **stire**: steer, guide.

6   **aread**: know or guess.

7   **He seemd to be**: i.e. he was.

9   A Platonic emblem of the temperate man who controls his passions; cf. iv 2.1–2.   **with equall steps**: once he quickens his pace, he becomes intemperate; cf. 13.1–2.

8

Such whenas *Archimago* them did view,
    He weened well to worke some vncouth wile,
    Eftsoones vntwisting his deceiptfull clew,
    He gan to weaue a web of wicked guile,
    And with faire countenance and flattring stile,
    To them approching, thus the knight bespake:
    Faire sonne of *Mars*, that seeke with warlike spoile,
    And great atchieu'ments great your selfe to make,
Vouchsafe to stay your steed for humble misers sake.

9

He stayd his steed for humble misers sake,
    And bad tell on the tenor of his plaint;
    Who feigning then in euery limbe to quake,
    Through inward feare, and seeming pale and faint
    With piteous mone his percing speach gan paint;
    Deare Lady how shall I declare thy cace,
    Whom late I left in langourous constraint?
    Would God thy selfe now present were in place,
To tell this ruefull tale; thy sight could win thee grace.

10

Or rather would, O would it so had chaunst,
    That you, most noble Sir, had present beene,
    When that lewd ribauld with vile lust aduaunst
    Layd first his filthy hands on virgin cleene,
    To spoile her daintie corse so faire and sheene,
    As on the earth, great mother of vs all,
    With liuing eye more faire was neuer seene,
    Of chastitie and honour virginall:
Witnesse ye heauens, whom she in vaine to helpe did call.

11

How may it be, (said then the knight halfe wroth,)
    That knight should knighthood euer so haue shent?
    None but that saw (quoth he) would weene for troth,
    How shamefully that Maid he did torment.
    Her looser golden lockes he rudely rent,
    And drew her on the ground, and his sharpe sword
    Against her snowy brest he fiercely bent,
    And threatned death with many a bloudie word;
Toung hates to tell the rest, that eye to see abhord.

12

Therewith amoued from his sober mood,
    And liues he yet (said he) that wrought this act,
    And doen the heauens afford him vitall food?
    He liues, (quoth he) and boasteth of the fact,
    Ne yet hath any knight his courage crackt,
    Where may that treachour then (said he) be found,
    Or by what meanes may I his footing tract?
    That shall I shew (said he) as sure, as hound
The stricken Deare doth chalenge by the bleeding wound.

13

He staid not lenger talke, but with fierce ire
    And zealous hast away is quickly gone
    To seeke that knight, where him that craftie Squire
    Supposd to be. They do arriue anone,
    Where sate a gentle Lady all alone,
    With garments rent, and haire discheueled,
    Wringing her hands, and making piteous mone;
    Her swollen eyes were much disfigured,
And her faire face with teares was fowly blubbered.

Stanza 8

3–4   **clew**: ball of thread. Perhaps an allusion to the ball of thread which led Theseus out of the labyrinth. Instead of a guide through a maze, Archimago's untwisted **clew** forms a web to enclose the knight. The web is an emblem of Mammon's house (vii 28.7–9) and describes the allure of Acrasia's dress (xii 77.7–9).

7–8   This appeal to Guyon as the traditional heroic (and classical) warrior is echoed by the mermaids, xii 32.3–5.

9   **misers**: wretch's.

Stanza 9

5   **paint**: depict vividly but also falsely.

7   **langourous constraint**: sorrowful distress; also referring to her rape, as ii 8.3. It suggests an erotic analogue to the Red Cross Knight's adventure to redeem Una's parents from 'captiue langour' (I vii 49.2).

Stanza 10

3–5   Archimago refers to the stripping of Duessa by the Red Cross Knight and Arthur, I viii 46. **ribauld**: a wicked, licentious person. **aduaunst**: incited, pricked, in contrast to the temperate knight's restraint. Guyon is particularly sensitive to the charge of rape. **cleene**: pure. **sheene**: beautiful.

6   **great mother**: this stock title for the earth, *omniparens*, reveals Archimago's nature. The earth is the mother, e.g. of the Giants and Titans, of Sansfoy (I ii 19.6), Orgoglio (I vii 9.1), Maleger (II xi 45.2), Argante (III vii 47.8) and Grantorto (V xii 23.7). In Book II the earth is associated with man's fall into intemperance; see vii 17.1–4.

Stanza 11

1   **halfe wroth**: cf. 13.1–2. When he is not guided by the Palmer he becomes 'inflam'd with wrathfulnesse' (25.8).

2   **shent**: disgraced.

5   **looser**: loose, 'discheueled' (13.6). Contrast Medina's braided locks, ii 15.7–9. Occasion wears her hair 'loosely hong vnrold' (iv 4.6).

7   **bent**: levelled.

Stanza 12

4   **fact**: crime.

6   **treachour**: obsolete form of 'traitor', which suggests 'treacherous'.

7   **tract**: trace.

9   **chalenge**: follow the scent of. The trail which should lead to the accused Red Cross Knight leads instead to Duessa. The change may indicate Archimago's duplicity. Fosso (1965) 104 notes that the wounded Amavia is compared to the stricken deer at 38.6–7.

Stanza 13

3   **Squire**: see 21.8–9.

14

The knight approching nigh, thus to her said,
  Faire Ladie, through foule sorrow ill bedight,
  Great pittie is to see you thus dismaid,
  And marre the blossome of your beautie bright:
  For thy appease your griefe and heauie plight,
  And tell the cause of your conceiued paine.
  For if he liue, that hath you doen despight,
  He shall you doe due recompence againe,
Or else his wrong with greater puissance maintaine.

15

Which when she heard, as in despightfull wise,
  She wilfully her sorrow did augment,
  And offred hope of comfort did despise:
  Her golden lockes most cruelly she rent,
  And scratcht her face with ghastly dreriment,
  Ne would she speake, ne see, ne yet be seene,
  But hid her visage, and her head downe bent,
  Either for grieuous shame, or for great teene,
As if her hart with sorrow had transfixed beene.

16

Till her that Squire bespake, Madame my liefe,
  For Gods deare loue be not so wilfull bent,
  But doe vouchsafe now to receiue reliefe,
  The which good fortune doth to you present.
  For what bootes it to weepe and to wayment,
  When ill is chaunst, but doth the ill increase,
  And the weake mind with double woe torment?
  When she her Squire heard speake, she gan appease
Her voluntarie paine, and feele some secret ease.

17

Eftsoone she said, Ah gentle trustie Squire,
  What comfort can I wofull wretch conceaue,
  Or why should euer I henceforth desire
  To see faire heauens face, and life not leaue,
  Sith that false Traytour did my honour reaue?
  False traytour certes (said the Faerie knight)
  I read the man, that euer would deceaue
  A gentle Ladie, or her wrong through might:
Death were too little paine for such a foule despight.

18

But now, faire Ladie, comfort to you make,
  And read, who hath ye wrought this shamefull plight;
  That short reuenge the man may ouertake,
  Where so he be, and soone vpon him light.
  Certes (saide she) I wote not how he hight,
  But vnder him a gray steede did he wield,
  Whose sides with dapled circles weren dight;
  Vpright he rode, and in his siluer shield
He bore a bloudie Crosse, that quartred all the field.

19

Now by my head (said *Guyon*) much I muse,
  How that same knight should do so foule amis,
  Or euer gentle Damzell so abuse:
  For may I boldly say, he surely is
  A right good knight, and true of word ywis:
  I present was, and can it witnesse well,
  When armes he swore, and streight did enterpris
  Th'aduenture of the *Errant damozell*,
In which he hath great glorie wonne, as I heare tell.

Stanza 14
2   **ill bedight**: ill-arrayed, referring to her disfiguring tears.
3   **pittie**: the chief emotion which confounds Guyon
throughout his quest.   **dismaid**: if there is a pun on
'dis-maid', it is the poet's.
5   **For thy**: therefore.
6   **conceiued**: although the cause of her grief is openly
apparent, temperance is concerned with the inner state;
cf. 17.2.
7   **despight**: injury, outrage.

Stanza 15
5   **dreriment**: grief.
8   **teene**: woe.

Stanza 16
1   **liefe**: dear; corresponding to 'Sir' as an address to a
superior.
5-7   A confusing construction because Archimago answers
his question as he asks it.   **wayment**: lament.
9   **voluntarie**: self-inflicted.

Stanza 17
7   **read**: consider.

Stanza 18
2   **read**: tell.
3   **short**: speedy.
6   **gray**: since the lustful Argante rides a grey horse (III
vii 37.3), the colour may represent the lust with which the
Red Cross Knight is charged.   **wield**: manage.
8-9   The description is heraldic: the red cross divides the
whole **field** or surface of the shield into quarters.   **Vpright**:
as Guyon, 6.1.

Stanza 19
1   **by my head**: this classical oath – cf. Virgil's *per caput hoc
iuro* (*Aen.* ix 300) – indicates Guyon's dependence upon his
own powers. Apart from the Proem (the Argument does not
count) Guyon is first named when he has abandoned the
Palmer who represents his reason. Cf. the naming of the Red
Cross Knight, I ii 12.2*n*.   **muse**: wonder.
2   **amis**: evil deed.
3   **abuse**: violate.
5   **ywis**: indeed; I know.
7   **enterpris**: undertake.
8   **Errant damozell**: used in two senses: like a Knight
errant she undertakes an adventure to release her parents;
also, she wanders in search of her Knight; cf. III i 24.7.

20

Nathlesse he shortly shall againe be tryde,
  And fairely quite him of th'imputed blame,
  Else be ye sure he dearely shall abyde,
  Or make you good amendment for the same:
  All wrongs haue mends, but no amends of shame.
  Now therefore Ladie, rise out of your paine,
  And see the saluing of your blotted name.
  Full loth she seemd thereto, but yet did faine;
For she was inly glad her purpose so to gaine.

21

Her purpose was not such, as she did faine,
  Ne yet her person such, as it was seene,
  But vnder simple shew and semblant plaine
  Lurckt false *Duessa* secretly vnseene,
  As a chast Virgin, that had wronged beene:
  So had false *Archimago* her disguisd,
  To cloke her guile with sorrow and sad teene;
  And eke himselfe had craftily deuisd
To be her Squire, and do her seruice well aguisd.

22

Her late forlorne and naked he had found,
  Where she did wander in waste wildernesse,
  Lurking in rockes and caues farre vnder ground,
  And with greene mosse cou'ring her nakednesse,
  To hide her shame and loathly filthinesse;
  Sith her Prince *Arthur* of proud ornaments
  And borrow'd beautie spoyld. Her nathelesse
  Th'enchaunter finding fit for his intents,
Did thus reuest, and deckt with due habiliments.

23

For all he did, was to deceiue good knights,
  And draw them from pursuit of praise and fame,
  To slug in slouth and sensuall delights,
  And end their daies with irrenowmed shame.
  And now exceeding griefe him ouercame,
  To see the *Redcrosse* thus aduaunced hye;
  Therefore this craftie engine he did frame,
  Against his praise to stirre vp enmitye
Of such, as vertues like mote vnto him allye.

24

So now he *Guyon* guides an vncouth way
  Through woods and mountaines, till they came at last
  Into a pleasant dale, that lowly lay
  Betwixt two hils, whose high heads ouerplast,
  The valley did with coole shade ouercast,
  Through midst thereof a little riuer rold,
  By which there sate a knight with helme vnlast,
  Himselfe refreshing with the liquid cold,
After his trauell long, and labours manifold.

25

Loe yonder he, cryde *Archimage* alowd,
  That wrought the shamefull fact, which I did shew;
  And now he doth himselfe in secret shrowd,
  To flie the vengeance for his outrage dew;
  But vaine: for ye shall dearely do him rew,
  So God ye speed, and send you good successe;
  Which we farre off will here abide to vew.
  So they him left, inflam'd with wrathfulnesse,
174 That streight against that knight his speare he did addresse.

Stanza 20
2 **fairely quite him**: fully prove himself innocent.
blame: charge.
3 **abyde**: suffer; pay the penalty.
4 **amendment**: reparation.
5 **mends**: recompense. Wrong may be amended by punishing the wrong-doer; yet the one wronged still suffers shame.
Or **shame** may be imputed to the wrong-doer: while wrongful acts may be amended by the wrong-doer, shameful ones may never be.
7 **saluing**: vindication, clearing.

Stanza 21
3 **semblant plaine**: honest appearance.
9 **aguisd**: arrayed, i.e. disguised.

Stanza 22
Cf. I viii 50.
7 **borrow'd beautie**: in Book I where the central conflict is between powers of light and darkness, the phrase is 'borrowed light' (viii 49.5); in Book II, 'beautie' is the key term once Duessa's role is assumed by Acrasia.
9 **reuest**: clothe again.   **due habiliments**: fitting attire.

Stanza 23
3 **delights**: suggests the plural of 'delice', sensual pleasure. Also a key term in Book II: cf. v 27.2, 33.1, xii 1.8, etc.
4 **irrenowmed**: adds to 'unrenowned' an intensive sense to note a negation of all praise.
6 Here, the Protestant faith; cf. 31.8.   **aduaunced**: raised, extolled.
7 **engine**: plot, snare to deceive the mind (Lat. *ingenium*).
9 **as vertues like**: those of similarly virtuous nature, referring to the relation between the virtues and their ultimate merging in magnanimity.

Stanza 24
1 **So now he Guyon guides**: the verbal echo and heavy stress indicate the change; now Archimago, not the Palmer, guides the knight. See Proem 5.8*n*.   **vncouth**: strange, wild, expressing the state of intemperance into which Guyon is led. Hence the way leads back to a wood. Cf. the similar setting at 5.7.
4 **ouerplast**: overhanging.

Stanza 25
2 **fact**: crime.
5 **But vaine**: i.e. he hides in vain.   **do**: cause.
6 Note the equivocation: not God prosper you but God hasten you into intemperate speed. Cf. the Palmer's benediction, 'God guide thee' (32.8). Church (1758) reads this line as parenthetical.
8–9 **So . . . / That**: i.e. so angry that.   **addresse**: aim.

26

Who seeing him from farre so fierce to pricke,
　His warlike armes about him gan embrace,
　And in the rest his readie speare did sticke;
　Tho when as still he saw him towards pace,
　He gan rencounter him in equall race.
　They bene ymet, both readie to affrap,
　When suddenly that warriour gan abace
His threatned speare, as if some new mishap
Had him betidde, or hidden daunger did entrap.

27

And cryde, Mercie Sir knight, and mercie Lord,
　For mine offence and heedlesse hardiment,
　That had almost committed crime abhord,
　And with reprochfull shame mine honour shent,
　Whiles cursed steele against that badge I bent,
　The sacred badge of my Redeemers death,
　Which on your shield is set for ornament:
But his fierce foe his steede could stay vneath,
Who prickt with courage kene, did cruell battell breath.

28

But when he heard him speake, streight way he knew
　His error, and himselfe inclyning sayd;
　Ah deare Sir *Guyon*, well becommeth you,
　But me behoueth rather to vpbrayd,
　Whose hastie hand so farre from reason strayd,
　That almost it did haynous violence
　On that faire image of that heauenly Mayd,
　That decks and armes your shield with faire defence:
Your court'sie takes on you anothers due offence.

29

So bene they both attone, and doen vpreare
　Their beuers bright, each other for to greete;
　Goodly comportance each to other beare,
　And entertaine themselues with court'sies meet.
　Then said the *Redcrosse* knight, Now mote I weet,
　Sir *Guyon*, why with so fierce saliaunce,
　And fell intent ye did at earst me meet;
　For sith I know your goodly gouernaunce,
Great cause, I weene, you guided, or some vncouth chaunce.

30

Certes (said he) well mote I shame to tell
　The fond encheason, that me hither led.
　A false infamous faitour late befell
　Me for to meet, that seemed ill bested,
　And playnd of grieuous outrage, which he red
　A knight had wrought against a Ladie gent;
　Which to auenge, he to this place me led,
　Where you he made the marke of his intent,
And now is fled; foule shame him follow, where he went.

Stanza 26

2　**embrace**: put on, buckle.
3　**rest**: a support for the spear when levelled for charging.
5　**rencounter**: charge in return.　**race**: charge.
6　**affrap**: strike.
7　**that warriour**: purposefully vague although we soon realize that Guyon is meant. A fitting term for this 'sonne of *Mars*' (8.7); cf. 39.1, vii 32.6, etc.; it could never apply to the gentle Knight.　**abace**: lower, implying the moral sense.
9　**betidde**: befallen.

Stanza 27

1　Guyon utters a twofold prayer, to the Knight and to God (upon seeing the Red Cross): 'pardon me Sir knight' and 'grant mercy to me Lord'. The different meanings of **mercie** are indicated by the different stresses. S.'s chivalric code does not encourage unprovoked aggression; cf. IV vi 4.1–3.
2　**offence**: attack; transgression; also 'occasion of doubt', here referring to his misjudging the Red Cross Knight. **hardiment**: boldness, rashness; later manifest in Huddibras's 'foole-hardize' (ii 17.7).
4　While defending a lady who claimed that a knight 'did my honour reaue' (17.5), Guyon almost loses his own.
shent: disgraced. The charge that he made against the Red Cross Knight (11.2), he now takes upon himself.
6　**my Redeemers death**: the possessive indicates that the classical virtue of temperance is placed within a Christian framework.
8–9　Since the **steede** embodies the knight's aroused passion, **Who** may refer to either.　**vneath**: only with difficulty.
kene: fierce.

Stanza 28

2　**inclyning**: turning his spear aside (from Guyon).
5　**reason**: an important key term fittingly introduced by the knight of Holiness.
7　**that heauenly Mayd**: the Faerie Queene; cf. v 11.7–8.
8　**decks**: ornaments, as does the Cross on his own shield (27.7).　**armes**: protects, as shown at viii 43.1–6.

Stanza 29

1　**attone**: at one, reconciled.
3　**comportance**: behaviour; coined to emphasize the mutual response.
6　**saliaunce**: assault, onslaught; coined to stress the hasty violence of Guyon's attack made without the formal challenge. See v 3.2, and Arthur's rebuke against Pyrocles's similar attack, viii 31.6–9. Cf. 'salied' (vi 38.5, xii 38.4).
8　**gouernaunce**: self-control, wise behaviour. A term used only in this Book to indicate the control which temperance must exercise over the passions. It defines the Palmer's role: see esp. 54.6, iv 7.2, 36.4.

Stanza 30

2　**fond encheason**: foolish occasion.
3　**faitour**: so named at I xii 35.5.
4　**ill bested**: in bad plight.
5　**red**: declared.
8　**intent**: Archimago's intent became his (29.7).

175

31

So can he turne his earnest vnto game,
    Through goodly handling and wise temperance.
    By this his aged guide in presence came;
    Who soone as on that knight his eye did glance,
    Eft soones of him had perfect cognizance,
    Sith him in Faerie court he late auizd;
    And said, Faire sonne, God giue you happie chance,
    And that deare Crosse vpon your shield deuizd,
Wherewith aboue all knights ye goodly seeme aguizd.

32

Ioy may you haue, and euerlasting fame,
    Of late most hard atchieu'ment by you donne,
    For which enrolled is your glorious name
    In heauenly Registers aboue the Sunne,
    Where you a Saint with Saints your seat haue wonne:
    But wretched we, where ye haue left your marke,
    Must now anew begin, like race to runne;
    God guide thee, *Guyon*, well to end thy warke,
And to the wished hauen bring thy weary barke.

33

Palmer, (him answered the *Redcrosse* knight)
    His be the praise, that this atchieu'ment wrought,
    Who made my hand the organ of his might;
    More then goodwill to me attribute nought:
    For all I did, I did but as I ought.
    But you, faire Sir, whose pageant next ensewes,
    Well mote yee thee, as well can wish your thought,
    That home ye may report thrise happie newes;
For well ye worthie bene for worth and gentle thewes.

34

So courteous conge both did giue and take,
    With right hands plighted, pledges of good will.
    Then *Guyon* forward gan his voyage make,
    With his blacke Palmer, that him guided still.
    Still he him guided ouer dale and hill,
    And with his steedie staffe did point his way:
    His race with reason, and with words his will,
    From foule intemperance he oft did stay,
And suffred not in wrath his hastie steps to stray.

35

In this faire wize they traueild long yfere,
    Through many hard assayes, which did betide;
    Of which he honour still away did beare,
    And spred his glorie through all countries wide.
    At last as chaunst them by a forest side
    To passe, for succour from the scorching ray,
    They heard a ruefull voice, that dearnly cride
    With percing shriekes, and many a dolefull lay;
Which to attend, a while their forward steps they stay.

Stanza 31
1   can he: does he; or knows he how to.

3   By this: an allegorical pointer which collapses 'by this time' into 'by this means'. When temperance is restored, reason follows.
5–6   cognizance: recognition and understanding; in heraldry, the device by which a person is known. The Palmer instantly knows the Knight by his Red Cross and confirms Guyon's belated recognition, 27.5–7.   auizd: observed.
8   deuizd: drawn or painted as a device.
9   aguizd: arrayed, i.e. armed. The Palmer places the Crosse (8) above the image of Gloriana.

Stanza 32
4   heauenly Registers: the Book of Life, Rev. 3.5. Cf. Luke 10.20: 'rejoyce, because your names are written in heaven.'
6   Fowler (1964) 85 notes the implication: 'Each book after the first is built upon the preceding book, and takes for granted the spiritual territory already conquered.' Woodhouse (1949) 205 n17, however, argues that Guyon sets out from the point at which the Red Cross Knight started, not the point which he reached.
7   race: course in a tournament. Also in the biblical sense; cf. Heb. 12.1: 'Let us runne with pacience the race that is set before us.' The Palmer translates 'race' into moral terms at 34.7.
8   Alludes to one etymological association of Guyon's name, from 'guide': see Proem 5.8n; cf. 34.4; and cf. the Boatman's appeal, xii 3.3.

Stanza 33
3   organ: in the double sense, instrument and a part of the body.
6   Sir: in opposition to 'Saint' (32.5).   pageant: Guyon's 'race' is regarded as an allegorical procession.   next: on the second day of the Faerie Queene's annual feast, according to *L.R.*
7   thee: prosper.
8   report: bring, carry back.
9   gentle thewes: virtuous habits befitting one of noble birth; see I ix 3.9n.

Stanza 34
1   conge: a ceremonious farewell.
2   Cf. the plighting between the Red Cross Knight and Arthur, I ix 18.9. Later the Knight is said to be 'with *Guyon* knit in one consent' (iii 11.8).
4   still: always.
6–9   The distinctions here depend upon differences between the irascible and concupiscible appetites. The former concerns his forward path (race) from which he will stray with hastie steps unless controlled by reason. The latter concerns his will: he will be led into foule intemperance unless words support him.

Stanza 35
1   yfere: together. The echo shows why their union is called faire.
2   assayes: trials.
5–6   The setting for Fradubio's warning tale, I ii 29, is abbreviated here.   succour: shelter.
7   dearnly: dismally, both sorrowfully and earnestly; cf. its use at III xii 34.4.
8   lay: strain.

36

But if that carelesse heaue..s (quoth she) despise
  The doome of iust reuenge, and take delight
  To see sad pageants of mens miseries,
  As bound by them to liue in liues despight,
  Yet can they not warne death from wretched wight.
  Come then, come soone, come sweetest death to mee,
  And take away this long lent loathed light:
  Sharpe be thy wounds, but sweet the medicines bee,
That long captiued soules from wearie thraldome free.

37

But thou, sweet Babe, whom frowning froward fate
  Hath made sad witnesse of thy fathers fall,
  Sith heauen thee deignes to hold in liuing state,
  Long maist thou liue, and better thriue withall,
  Then to thy lucklesse parents did befall:
  Liue thou, and to thy mother dead attest,
  That cleare she dide from blemish criminall;
  Thy litle hands embrewd in bleeding brest
Loe I for pledges leaue.   So giue me leaue to rest.

38

With that a deadly shrieke she forth did throw,
  That through the wood reecchoed againe,
  And after gaue a grone so deepe and low,
  That seemd her tender heart was rent in twaine,
  Or thrild with point of thorough piercing paine;
  As gentle Hynd, whose sides with cruell steele
  Through launched, forth her bleeding life does raine,
  Whiles the sad pang approching she does feele,
Brayes out her latest breath, and vp her eyes doth seele.

39

Which when that warriour heard, dismounting straict
  From his tall steed, he rusht into the thicke,
  And soone arriued, where that sad pourtraict
  Of death and dolour lay, halfe dead, halfe quicke,
  In whose white alabaster brest did sticke
  A cruell knife, that made a griesly wound,
  From which forth gusht a streme of gorebloud thick,
  That all her goodly garments staind around,
And into a deepe sanguine dide the grassie ground.

40

Pittifull spectacle of deadly smart,
  Beside a bubbling fountaine low she lay,
  Which she increased with her bleeding hart,
  And the cleane waues with purple gore did ray;
  Als in her lap a louely babe did play
  His cruell sport, in stead of sorrow dew;
  For in her streaming blood he did embay
  His litle hands, and tender ioynts embrew;
Pitifull spectacle, as euer eye did view.

Stanza 36

1–2   Her words outline Guyon's quest: see 61.5–8.
doome: judging, execution.
3   pageants: a tableau shown on the stage, a 'spectacle'
(40.1); see 33.6*n*.
4   bound: obliged.   in liues despight: either men must
live though they scorn life or their state scorns life in its
miseries. Amavia reverses the state revealed in her name:
'love to live' or 'live to love'. See 55.5*n*. Here she lovingly
woos death.
5   warne: forbid.

Stanza 37

1   froward: adverse, unfavourable.
3   thee: the heavy stress excludes her.
6   attest: bear witness to; a legal term, suggested by
witnesse (2), to emphasize her oath.
7   Her suicide is not regarded as sinful: cf. the Palmer's
judgment, 58.6–7.
8–9   In the legal sense, the babe's bloody hands are sureties
to be forfeited if he does not attest that his mother died free
from criminal blemish. It is a witty paradox that bloody hands
should be held up as a token of innocence. That guilt is a
stain points to an earlier unstained state, as man's present guilt
is evidence of a previous innocence.   embrewd: plunged;
stained; implying also infected, 'defild' (50.9). Upton (1758)
suggests that she stabs herself at this moment, comparing
Dido in Virgil, *Aen.* iv 660.

Stanza 38

5   thrild: pierced.
8   the sad pang: i.e. death.
9   Brayes: breathes out with a cry.   latest: last.   seele:
close, as the stitched eyelids of a hawk; see I vii 23.9*n*.

Stanza 39

2   the thicke: the thickest part; here the centre.
4   dolour] labour *1596* may have been suggested by her
search for her husband and efforts to release him from
Acrasia's power, or her labour in child-birth.   quicke: alive.
6   griesly: arousing horror.
7   gorebloud: clotted blood.
9   sanguine: blood red.

Stanza 40

1   spectacle: also in the dramatic sense; cf. 'pageants' (36.3).
In the moral allegory, the term signifies 'model' or 'pattern':
the dead father, the dying mother, and the living, yet stained,
offspring present a brief allegory of the human condition.
4   ray: defile. Since these waters may not 'with any filth
be dyde' (ii 9.8), the term may signify 'streaked with rays of
blood' without mingling, a mixture rather than a solution.
Perhaps the water accepts Amavia's blood but not Mortdant's;
cf. the dying Lucrece's two bloods (Shakespeare, *Lucrece*
1737f).
7–9   The simile of the 'gentle Hynd' (38.6–7) extended in
bleeding hart (3) suggests the ritual act in which hunters
wash their hands in the blood of the slain deer. Cf. Marvell,
'Nymph complaining for the death of her faun' 18–22.
embay: bathe.   embrew: see 37.8–9*n*.

41

Besides them both, vpon the soiled gras
  The dead corse of an armed knight was spred,
  Whose armour all with bloud besprinckled was;
  His ruddie lips did smile, and rosy red
  Did paint his chearefull cheekes, yet being ded:
  Seemd to haue beene a goodly personage,
  Now in his freshest flowre of lustie hed,
  Fit to inflame faire Lady with loues rage,
But that fiers fate did crop the blossome of his age.

42

Whom when the good Sir *Guyon* did behold,
  His hart gan wexe as starke, as marble stone,
  And his fresh bloud did frieze with fearefull cold,
  That all his senses seemd bereft attone:
  At last his mightie ghost gan deepe to grone,
  As Lyon grudging in his great disdaine,
  Mournes inwardly, and makes to himselfe mone;
  Till ruth and fraile affection did constraine
His stout courage to stoupe, and shew his inward paine.

43

Out of her gored wound the cruell steele
  He lightly snatcht, and did the floudgate stop
  With his faire garment: then gan softly feele
  Her feeble pulse, to proue if any drop
  Of liuing bloud yet in her veynes did hop;
  Which when he felt to moue, he hoped faire
  To call backe life to her forsaken shop;
  So well he did her deadly wounds repaire,
That at the last she gan to breath out liuing aire.

44

Which he perceiuing greatly gan reioice,
  And goodly counsell, that for wounded hart
  Is meetest med'cine, tempred with sweet voice;
  Ay me, deare Lady, which the image art
  Of ruefull pitie, and impatient smart,
  What direfull chance, armd with reuenging fate,
  Or cursed hand hath plaid this cruell part,
  Thus fowle to hasten your vntimely date;
Speake, O deare Lady speake: help neuer comes too late.

45

Therewith her dim eie-lids she vp gan reare,
  On which the drery death did sit, as sad
  As lump of lead, and made darke clouds appeare;
  But when as him all in bright armour clad
  Before her standing she espied had,
  As one out of a deadly dreame affright,
  She weakely started, yet she nothing drad:
  Streight downe againe her selfe in great despight
She groueling threw to ground, as hating life and light.

46

The gentle knight her soone with carefull paine
  Vplifted light, and softly did vphold:
  Thrise he her reard, and thrise she sunke againe,
  Till he his armes about her sides gan fold,
  And to her said; Yet if the stony cold
  Haue not all seized on your frozen hart,
  Let one word fall that may your griefe vnfold,
  And tell the secret of your mortall smart;
He oft finds present helpe, who does his griefe impart.

178

Stanza 41

1   **soiled**: stained, suggesting 'defiled'; cf. the soiled arms of Phedon (iv 16.4), Atin (iv 37.7), and Pyrochles (v 4.9, see 22.4*n*, vi 41.6–8*n*).
5   **yet being ded**: having just died.
7   **lustie hed**: youthful vigour; also 'lustfulness' of which Verdant (xii 79) is the type.

Stanza 42

2–4   **starke**: hard.   **fearefull cold**: i.e. cold caused by fear. Fear and pity are the fitting responses to Amavia's tragedy. Through sympathy caused by his own **fraile affection** (8), he almost dies himself (cf. 48.9). Pity balances the anger he felt in the encounter with Duessa.   **attone**: together; at once.
6–7   The lion was noted as the most merciful (see Carroll, 1954, 32, 109) and the most compassionate of beasts.
grudging: growling.   **disdaine**: indignation.
9   **courage**: spirit, nature.

Stanza 43

5   **hop**: leap. Beyond the demands of rhyme, this term is apt.
7   **shop**: body; the place where the heart operates (*OED* 3c). Upton (1758) finds the expression mean but the thought elegant, as the body is the house or tabernacle for the soul.

Stanza 44

2–3   Proverbial (C. G. Smith, 1970, 123), although allegory's bones stick through.
4–5   **image**: emblem; pattern; embodiment. As a 'pourtraict' (39.3) or 'spectacle' (40.1), Amavia is interpreted in moral terms; later the Palmer calls her 'the image of mortalitie' (57.2).   **impatient smart**: unendurable pain.
8   **date**: end of life.

Stanza 45

The stanza echoes Virgil's description of the death of Dido: seeking to lift her heavy eyes, she swoons again (*Aen*. iv 688). Yet Dido seeks the light; Amavia, the dark.
2   **sad**: heavy.
8   **despight**: contempt of life.
9   **groueling**: prostrate, face down.

Stanza 46

3–4   As Una thrice falls down in a swoon and is thrice revived by the Dwarf, I vii 24.1–4. Amavia's name suggests that she may revive only when Guyon embraces her; see 55.5*n*.
9   Proverbial: as the Red Cross Knight to Fradubio, I ii 34.4, an analogue to the present encounter.

47

Then casting vp a deadly looke, full low
  Shee sight from bottome of her wounded brest,
  And after, many bitter throbs did throw
  With lips full pale and foltring tongue opprest,
  These words she breathed forth from riuen chest;
  Leaue, ah leaue off, what euer wight thou bee,
  To let a wearie wretch from her dew rest,
  And trouble dying soules tranquilitee.
Take not away now got, which none would giue to me.

48

Ah farre be it (said he) Deare dame fro mee,
  To hinder soule from her desired rest,
  Or hold sad life in long captiuitee:
  For all I seeke, is but to haue redrest
  The bitter pangs, that doth your heart infest.
  Tell then, O Lady tell, what fatall priefe
  Hath with so huge misfortune you opprest?
  That I may cast to compasse your reliefe,
Or die with you in sorrow, and partake your griefe.

49

With feeble hands then stretched forth on hye,
  As heauen accusing guiltie of her death,
  And with dry drops congealed in her eye,
  In these sad words she spent her vtmost breath:
  Heare then, O man, the sorrowes that vneath
  My tongue can tell, so farre all sense they pas:
  Loe this dead corpse, that lies here vnderneath,
  The gentlest knight, that euer on greene gras
Gay steed with spurs did pricke, the good Sir *Mordant* was.

50

Was, (ay the while, that he is not so now)
  My Lord my loue; my deare Lord, my deare loue,
  So long as heauens iust with equall brow
  Vouchsafed to behold vs from aboue,
  One day when him high courage did emmoue,
  As wont ye knights to seeke aduentures wilde,
  He pricked forth, his puissant force to proue,
  Me then he left enwombed of this child,
This lucklesse child, whom thus ye see with bloud defild.

51

Him fortuned (hard fortune ye may ghesse)
  To come, where vile *Acrasia* does wonne,
  Acrasia a false enchaunteresse,
  That many errant knights hath foule fordonne:
  Within a wandring Island, that doth ronne
  And stray in perilous gulfe, her dwelling is;
  Faire Sir, if euer there ye trauell, shonne
  The cursed land where many wend amis,
And know it by the name; it hight the *Bowre of blis*.

52

Her blisse is all in pleasure and delight,
  Wherewith she makes her louers drunken mad,
  And then with words and weedes of wondrous might,
  On them she workes her will to vses bad:
  My lifest Lord she thus beguiled had;
  For he was flesh: (all flesh doth frailtie breed.)
  Whom when I heard to beene so ill bestad,
  Weake wretch I wrapt my selfe in Palmers weed,
And cast to seeke him forth through daunger and great dreed.

Stanza 47
7 **let**: prevent.
9 **now got**: i.e. the peace of death.

Stanza 48
4 **redrest**: remedied, by exacting revenge; cf. 61.7.
5 **infest**: assail; infect.
6 **priefe**: experience, trial.
8 **cast to compasse**: plan to accomplish.

Stanza 49
3 She is now beyond life's griefs.
4 **vtmost**: last.
5 **vneath**: scarcely.
9 **Mordant**: see 55.4*n*.

Stanza 50
2 The repetition reveals Amavia's loving nature. That her love leads to death relates her to Fradubio: cf. his lament, 'O too deare loue, loue bought with death too deare' (I ii 31.7).
3 **equall**: impartial, just.

Stanza 51
2–4 **Acrasia**: Gk Incontinence; see xii 69.8*n*. As the **false enchaunteresse**, she combines the roles of the false Duessa and the enchanter Archimago.   **false**: refers to the vanity of her delights. 4 indicates that her role corresponds to that of the Dragon in Book I.   **fordonne**: killed (cf. ii 44.9); ruined.
5–6 On this **wandring Island**, see xii 11–12.
9 **know it by the name**: i.e. the name reveals its nature.

Stanza 52
1–2 Cf. Aristotle, *Ethics VII* iii 1147[a]: 'Incontinent people must be said to be in a similar condition to men asleep, mad, or drunk.'
3 **weedes**: herbs, 'drugs' (54.8); cf. v 34.9. Cf. Circe's powerful weeds in Virgil, *Aen.* vii 19, and the Whore's wine in Rev. 14.8. Cf. also the description of Duessa's cup, I viii 14.1–5. Later Acrasia's **words and weedes** are called 'charme and venim' (ii 4.6).
5 **lifest**: dearest. The spelling points to the irony: he is Mordant, one who gives death.
6 Matt. 26.41: 'the flesh is weake.'
7 **so ill bestad**: in such bad plight.

53

Now had faire *Cynthia* by euen tournes
　Full measured three quarters of her yeare,
　And thrise three times had fild her crooked hornes,
　Whenas my wombe her burdein would forbeare,
　And bad me call *Lucina* to me neare.
　Lucina came : a manchild forth I brought:
　The woods, the Nymphes, my bowres, my midwiues weare,
　Hard helpe at need.　So deare thee babe I bought,
Yet nought too deare I deemd, while so my dear I sought.

54

Him so I sought, and so at last I found,
　Where him that witch had thralled to her will,
　In chaines of lust and lewd desires ybound,
　And so transformed from his former skill,
　That me he knew not, neither his owne ill;
　Till through wise handling and faire gouernance,
　I him recured to a better will,
　Purged from drugs of foule intemperance:
Then meanes I gan deuise for his deliuerance.

55

Which when the vile Enchaunteresse perceiu'd,
　How that my Lord from her I would repriue,
　With cup thus charmd, him parting she deceiu'd;
　Sad verse, giue death to him that death does giue,
　And losse of loue, to her that loues to liue,
　So soone as Bacchus with the Nymphe does lincke:
　So parted we and on our iourney driue,
　Till comming to this well, he stoupt to drincke:
The charme fulfild, dead suddenly he downe did sincke.

56

Which when I wretch, Not one word more she sayd
　But breaking off the end for want of breath,
　And slyding soft, as downe to sleepe her layd,
　And ended all her woe in quiet death.
　That seeing good Sir *Guyon*, could vneath
　From teares abstaine, for griefe his hart did grate,
　And from so heauie sight his head did wreath,
　Accusing fortune, and too cruell fate,
Which plunged had faire Ladie in so wretched state.

Stanza 53

4　**burdein**: the child borne in the womb (*OED* 4).
forbeare: give up; ill-beare any longer.
5　**Lucina**: as Diana is patron of women in labour; cf. 'of wemens labours thou hast charge, / And generation goodly dost enlarge' (*Epith.* 383–4). The setting alludes to the etymology of her name, from Lat. *lucus*, a grove. Juno, the goddess of marriage, is not invoked because this marriage is suspect. For the allusion to the birth of Bacchus, see Kaske (1976) 197–9.

Stanza 54

4　**skill**: reason, power of discernment; in a wider sense, 'knowledge', particularly of what is right, which is the means by which temperance is maintained.
6　**gouernance**: either his temperate behaviour (cf. 29.8) or, preferably, her governing. She plays the Palmer's role: cf. 52.8. Cf. 31.2.
7　**recured**: restored.
8　**drugs**: 'weedes' (52.3); cf. Cymochles 'Made drunke with drugs of deare voluptuous receipt' (v 34.9).

Stanza 55

2　**repriue**: take back; rescue.
4　**Sad verse**: a strong or powerful incantation or charm, 'words . . . of wondrous might' (52.3); also Lat. *tristis*, ill-omened: hence a fatal charm. Cf. Busirane's 'sad verse' (III xii 36.4); cf. also I xi 27.6.　**that death does giue**: the etymology of Mortdant. As a warrior, he brings death to his foes: 'mordant' (biting) is often applied to the sword to signify martial prowess. As Amavia's husband, he brings her death. As a father, he brings spiritual death to his descendants, even as Adam 'Brought death into the world' (Milton, *P.L.* i 3). Also as 'he was flesh' (52.6), he is given to death. Allen (1958) suggests that the name means 'the bitter self-destroyer', in accord with Aquinas's claim that lechery leads directly to self-destruction. As one overcome by Acrasia, he is the counterpart to Verdant: cf. 41.7 and xii 79.7–9.
5　**that loues to liue**: the etymology of her name, *Ama-via*, *ama-vita*, one who loves in order to live or who lives to love, loving and living being one in her. Nelson (1963) 189 suggests an allusion to Virgil's Amata, the suicide mother of Lavinia. Her name is given at ii 45.8.
6　**Bacchus** signifies wine and the **Nymphe** water. Upton (1758) cites Heliodorus as source: 'I drink to you the nymphs that are pure and unlinked with Bacchus.' Nelson 190 notes that Acrasia's name signifies 'bad mixture' (see xii 69.8*n*) and cites Erasmus's 'Profane Banquet' in the *Colloquies*: 'Bacchus . . . is made more temperate being united with the nymphs.' As he observes, S. inverts Erasmus's meaning. The mixing of wine and water is a traditional emblem of temperance: see the sources cited by Fowler (1960b). In Comes (1616) X p. 541, Bacchus is the male generative virtue of the sun and the nymph is the female principle or the water in which generation arises. Lemmi, *Var.* ii 193–4, interprets the linking of Bacchus and the nymph as sexual intercourse between Mortdant and Amavia. Mortdant's drinking from Acrasia's poisoned cup corresponds to the Red Cross Knight's drinking from the enfeebling fountain. Both acts parody the mingling of wine and water in the Communion chalice. Here the pure water will not be corrupted by wine even as it will not cleanse the Babe's bloody hands, ii 3. The next canto presents a parallel and contrasting event in the story of the watery nymph who refuses to be linked to a woodland Bacchus; see ii 7–9.
8　At ii 4.6 it is assumed that both parents drank from the cup, as **lincke** (6) here suggests.

Stanza 56

1　The witty point is that, in the narration, his death brings hers.
6　**grate**: fret.
7　**wreath**: turn, twist.

57

Then turning to his Palmer said, Old syre
  Behold the image of mortalitie,
  And feeble nature cloth'd with fleshly tyre,
  When raging passion with fierce tyrannie
  Robs reason of her due regalitie,
  And makes it seruant to her basest part:
  The strong it weakens with infirmitie,
  And with bold furie armes the weakest hart;   [smart.
The strong through pleasure soonest falles, the weake through

58

But temperance (said he) with golden squire
  Betwixt them both can measure out a meane,
  Neither to melt in pleasures whot desire,
  Nor fry in hartlesse griefe and dolefull teene.
  Thrise happie man, who fares them both atweene:
  But sith this wretched woman ouercome
  Of anguish, rather then of crime hath beene,
  Reserue her cause to her eternall doome,
And in the meane vouchsafe her honorable toombe.

59

Palmer (quoth he) death is an equall doome
  To good and bad, the common Inne of rest;
  But after death the tryall is to come,
  When best shall be to them, that liued best:
  But both alike, when death hath both supprest,
  Religious reuerence doth buriall teene,
  Which who so wants, wants so much of his rest:
  For all so great shame after death I weene,
As selfe to dyen bad, vnburied bad to beene.

60

So both agree their bodies to engraue;
  The great earthes wombe they open to the sky,
  And with sad Cypresse seemely it embraue,
  Then couering with a clod their closed eye,
  They lay therein those corses tenderly,
  And bid them sleepe in euerlasting peace.
  But ere they did their vtmost obsequy,
  Sir *Guyon* more affection to increace,
Bynempt a sacred vow, which none should aye releace.

61

The dead knights sword out of his sheath he drew,
  With which he cut a locke of all their heare,
  Which medling with their bloud and earth, he threw
  Into the graue, and gan deuoutly sweare;
  Such and such euill God on *Guyon* reare,
  And worse and worse young Orphane be thy paine,
  If I or thou dew vengeance doe forbeare,
  Till guiltie bloud her guerdon doe obtaine:
So shedding many teares, they closd the earth againe.

Stanza 57
On the antitheses, see iv 2.6–9n.
3   **tyre**: attire, vesture.
6   **basest**: lowest, referring to the passions. Reason should exercise royal authority over her subjects, the passions.
7–9   The distinction is that between two kinds of intemperance, the irascible and the concupiscent, later expressed in Pyrochles and Cymochles.

Stanza 58
1   **golden squire**: referring to the golden set-square, *norma temperantiae*, a common emblem of temperance.
4   **fry**: burn; 'fryze', sugg. Church (1758), would provide a fitting antithesis to **melt** (3), and describe the effects of excessive grief, as in 'his fresh bloud did frieze with fearefull cold' (42.3); cf. Amavia's 'frozen hart' (46.6).   **hartlesse griefe**: i.e. grief that lacks the courage to endure.   **teene**: suffering, anguish.
9   **in the meane**: in the meantime. Suggesting also the mean between judging her case (**cause** 8) and reserving judgment to God, which is to bury her. The Palmer excludes Mortdant because he was overcome by **crime** (7). If the debate concerns Amavia, **crime** refers to her suicide.

Stanza 59
In this one matter Guyon refuses to submit to the Palmer's judgment: burial customs are too deeply felt to yield to reason.
6   **teene**: grant, afford, or require; so the context implies. If Guyon alludes to the Palmer's use of the term at 58.4, the line suggests that grief leads him to grant them burial.
7–9   Guyon's judgment prepares for the later irony when he is not afforded burial; see viii 12–17.
9   **selfe to dyen bad**: possibly a reference to the sin of self-slaughter; yet see 37.7, 58.7. For the importance of burial, see I v 53.4n.

Stanza 60
1   **engraue**: place in a grave.
3   **Cypresse**: 'vsed of the old Paynims in the furnishing of their funerall Pompe. And properly the signe of all sorow and heauinesse' (E.K., gloss to *S.C.* Nov. 145). These rituals are classical in contrast to the Christian burial provided by the sixth bead-man, I x 42.   **embraue**: adorn.
8   **affection**: deep feeling, piety.
9   **Bynempt**: swore. This obsolete form makes the occasion more solemn.   **releace**: revoke.

Stanza 61
2   **all**: of both the dead, or possibly including the Palmer and himself.
3   **medling**: mingling.
5–8   The heightened language is biblical, as 1 Sam. 3.17: 'God do so to thee, and more also, if thou hide anie thing from me.'
7   **dew vengeance**: cf. the 'iust reuenge' (36.2) against Acrasia which Amavia believes the heavens will not provide. Guyon assumes the chivalric role of 'Defending . . . Orphans right' (III ii 14.6). See I x 43.2–3n.
8   **guiltie bloud**: blood shed guiltily, though the blood itself is guilty; see ii 4.5.

181

Cant. II.

Babes bloudie hands may not be clensd:
the face of golden Meane.
Her sisters two Extremities
striue her to banish cleane.

1

THus when Sir *Guyon* with his faithfull guide
  Had with due rites and dolorous lament
The end of their sad *Tragedie* vptyde,
  The litle babe vp in his armes he hent;
  Who with sweet pleasance and bold blandishment
Gan smyle on them, that rather ought to weepe,
  As carelesse of his woe, or innocent
  Of that was doen, that ruth emperced deepe
In that knights heart, and wordes with bitter teares did steepe.

2

Ah lucklesse babe, borne vnder cruell starre,
  And in dead parents balefull ashes bred,
Full litle weenest thou, what sorrowes are
  Left thee for portion of thy liuelihed,
  Poore Orphane in the wide world scattered,
As budding braunch rent from the natiue tree,
  And thrown forth, till it be withered:
  Such is the state of men: thus enter wee
Into this life with woe, and end with miseree.

3

Then soft himselfe inclyning on his knee
  Downe to that well, did in the water weene
(So loue does loath disdainfull nicitee)
  His guiltie hands from bloudie gore to cleene.
  He washt them oft and oft, yet nought they beene
For all his washing cleaner. Still he stroue,
  Yet still the litle hands were bloudie seene;
  The which him into great amaz'ment droue,
And into diuerse doubt his wauering wonder cloue.

Canto ii

Argument

2–4 **face**: outward appearance or form; in the architectural sense, the front of the castle (see 12.6) flanked by opposing bastions, the **Extremities**. **golden Meane**: *aurea mediocritas* (as Horace, *Odes* II x 5). Hence **Extremities**: extremes as opposed to the mean (cf. 38.4); figuratively, hands and feet in relation to **face**. Cf. the architectural image at xii 1.

Stanza 1

1 **faithfull**: the defining adjective for the Red Cross Knight in Book I; see I i 2.7*n*.
7 **innocent**: referring to the Babe's state of innocence (cf. 4.3) until the syntax restricts the meaning in the next line.

Stanza 2

1 **cruell starre**: evil astral influence; cf. I viii 42.6–7.
2 Alluding to the phoenix who, after immolating itself, emerges from its ashes with renewed youth. The suggestion of renewal is qualified by **balefull** and by recognition of the babe's inheritance of his parents' sin. **balefull**: full of evil; also with reference to the phoenix legend, from 'bale': funeral pyre.
5 **scattered**: cast down, dropped at random.
8–9 'Man that is borne of woman hath but a short time to live, and is ful of miserie' (Job 14.1, Bishops').

Stanza 3

Fowler (1961b) 97 interprets the well, or 'bubbling fountaine' (i 40.2) as a symbol of repentance and baptismal regeneration. The Babe has **guiltie hands** (4) because stained hands and the attempt to wash them are traditional symbols of guilt; cf. vii 61. Guyon's vain efforts to wash the Babe's hands amaze him partly because of the Babe's innocence. The explanation may lie in the limits of baptism: while man, born in sin, may be 'borne anewe of water' (baptismal service), the inner corruption of original sin remains; see Burnet (1699) 135–6. **bloudie gore** (4) may indicate the blood's corruption; cf. i 40.4; cf. also I viii 16.7, 24.4.
3 **nicitee**: fastidiousness; cf. I viii 40.3.
9 **diuerse**: distracting. **cloue**: divided.

4

He wist not whether blot of foule offence
    Might not be purgd with water nor with bath;
    Or that high God, in lieu of innocence,
    Imprinted had that token of his wrath,
    To shew how sore bloudguiltinesse he hat'th;
    Or that the charme and venim, which they druncke,
    Their bloud with secret filth infected hath,
    Being diffused through the senselesse truncke,
That through the great contagion direfull deadly stunck,

5

Whom thus at gaze, the Palmer gan to bord
    With goodly reason, and thus faire bespake;
    Ye bene right hard amated, gratious Lord,
    And of your ignorance great maruell make,
    Whiles cause not well conceiued ye mistake.
    But know, that secret vertues are infusd
    In euery fountaine, and in euery lake,
    Which who hath skill them rightly to haue chusd,
To proofe of passing wonders hath full often vsd.

6

Of those some were so from their sourse indewd
    By great Dame Nature, from whose fruitfull pap
    Their welheads spring, and are with moisture deawd;
    Which feedes each liuing plant with liquid sap,
    And filles with flowres faire *Floraes* painted lap:
    But other some by gift of later grace,
    Or by good prayers, or by other hap,
    Had vertue pourd into their waters bace,
And thenceforth were renowmd, and sought from place to place.

7

Such is this well, wrought by occasion straunge,
    Which to her Nymph befell. Vpon a day,
    As she the woods with bow and shafts did raunge,
    The hartlesse Hind and Robucke to dismay,
    Dan Faunus chaunst to meet her by the way,
    And kindling fire at her faire burning eye,
    Inflamed was to follow beauties chace,
    And chaced her, that fast from him did fly;
As Hind from her, so she fled from her enimy.

Stanza 4
Guyon's efforts to understand the nature of the stain define original sin. Two explanations are given as to why the hands may not be cleansed, one supernatural and the other natural: (*a*) not **with water** because God has imprinted the stain, and (*b*) not **with bath** because the infection has spread throughout the parents' bodies. Fowler (1961b) 99–100 finds two theories of original sin present: the *reatus* theory by which the blood taint is a token that signifies God's wrath which extends to Adam's descendants, and the *vitium* theory by which human nature itself is regarded as damaged. See also Fowler (1960b)

145.
3   **Or**: either.   **in lieu of innocence**: in place of innocence; see i 37.8–9*n*. 'loue', sugg. Church (1758), is supported by III viii 29.5: 'So much high God doth innocence embrace.'
5   **bloudguiltinesse**: 'guiltie bloud' (i 61.8) rather than the sin of bloodshed (its sense at 30.3); cf. vii 19.5. The term occurs only in Book II. It describes the fleshliness through which Mortdant and Amavia die: concupiscence in the one, and love's rage that leads to suicide in the other. Also it refers to original sin which their child inherits. Cf. Ps. 51.14: 'Deliver me from bloodgiltinesse O God' (Bishops'). In this Psalm, David recognizes original sin in himself – 'I was borne in iniquitie, and in sinne hathe my mother conceived me' – and pleads for baptism to 'clense me from my sinne'.
6   **charme and venim**: Acrasia's 'words and weedes' (i 52.3).   **venim** may suggest venereal disease; **they** suggests that Mortdant's drinking is to be interpreted as sexual: see i 55.6*n*.
7–9   The stench from bodies recently dead confirms the natural explanation but implies a supernatural working. Although Renaissance writers did not know about the circulation of the blood, they knew that poison 'will disperse itself through all the veins' (*Romeo and Juliet* V i 61). As Fowler 100 notes, Burnet (1699) 131–41 variously explains original sin as an alteration of the blood, a contagion, and a slow-acting poison.

Stanza 5
While Guyon speculates on the nature of the stain, the practical Palmer explains why it cannot be removed.
1   **at gaze**: standing in bewilderment.   **bord**: address.
3   **amated**: dismayed; confounded.
6   **secret vertues**: hidden powers; held to be in all things, especially water. Cf. the Well of Life, 'Full of great vertues, and for med'cine good', which can 'guilt of sinfull crimes cleane wash away' (I xi 29.5, 30.2). The point for Book II is either the absence of such purifying waters or the lack of **skill** (8) in using them.
9   **To proofe of**: to the effecting of, and hence proving, their powers.   **passing**: surpassing.

Stanza 6
The Palmer posits two kinds of waters: virtuous liquid from Nature's breast to which water is added (1–5) and **waters bace** (8), i.e. ordinary, to which virtue is added.
1   **indewd**: also in the literal sense, moisture added to the well.
5   **Flora**: the goddess of flowers.
6   **other some**: some others.   **later**: either at some later date or later in its course.

Stanza 7
4   **hartlesse**: timid, lacking heart; a repressed pun. **Robucke**: noted for its swift flight (as x 7.5).
5   **Dan Faunus**: the Wood God; linked with Bacchus and hence with Acrasia's charm, i 55.6. From his proclivity for chasing nymphs (Horace, *Odes* III xviii 1), he was called *Luxuria* by the emblem writers, e.g. by Ripa (1603) 295.
7   **chace**: 'pray' (i.e. prey) sugg. Collier (1862), from Drayton's note in the 1611 Folio, preserves the 'b' rhyme but sacrifices the play on the word in the next line.   **beauties chace** describes Guyon's quest of Acrasia and is a central theme in Books III and IV.

8

At last when fayling breath began to faint,
  And saw no meanes to scape, of shame affrayd,
She set her downe to weepe for sore constraint,
  And to *Diana* calling lowd for ayde,
  Her deare besought, to let her dye a mayd.
The goddesse heard, and suddeine where she sate,
  Welling out streames of teares, and quite dismayd
  With stony feare of that rude rustick mate,
Transformd her to a stone from stedfast virgins state.

9

Lo now she is that stone, from whose two heads,
  As from two weeping eyes, fresh streames do flow,
Yet cold through feare, and old conceiued dreads;
  And yet the stone her semblance seemes to show,
  Shapt like a maid, that such ye may her know;
And yet her vertues in her water byde:
  For it is chast and pure, as purest snow,
  Ne lets her waues with any filth be dyde,
But euer like her selfe vnstained hath beene tryde.

10

From thence it comes, that this babes bloudy hand
  May not be clensd with water of this well:
Ne certes Sir striue you it to withstand,
  But let them still be bloudy, as befell,
  That they his mothers innocence may tell,
As she bequeathd in her last testament;
  That as a sacred Symbole it may dwell
  In her sonnes flesh, to minde reuengement,
And be for all chast Dames an endlesse moniment.

11

He hearkned to his reason, and the childe
  Vptaking, to the Palmer gaue to beare;
But his sad fathers armes with bloud defilde,
  An heauie load himselfe did lightly reare,
  And turning to that place, in which whyleare
He left his loftie steed with golden sell,
  And goodly gorgeous barbes, him found not theare.
  By other accident that earst befell,
He is conuaide, but how or where, here fits not tell.

Stanza 8
3 **constraint**: distress; also compulsion, alluding to the rape which she fears.
5 **deare**: earnestly.
7–9 **Welling**: as she becomes a well. **dismayd**: overwhelmed with fear; perhaps punning on 'dis-made' and 'dis-maid'. Through **stony feare** she is changed to stone: her emotional state becomes physical; the pun extends to **stedfast**. This Ovidian metamorphosis is paralleled by Daphne's (Ovid, *Met.* i 474f; cf. esp. her prayer, 486–7) and Arethusa's (*Met.* v 601f).

Stanza 9
Edwards (1958) 83 notes that 'the stone now shows her **semblance** (4) just as she in her virginity had previously reflected the quality of the stone'.
3–4 **Yet**: still.
6 **vertues**: these powers are present, then, 'by gift of later grace' (6.6) from Diana, or 'by good prayers' (6.7) of the nymph. On the other hand, they come from 'their sourse' (6.1), the transformed Nymph.
9 **tryde**: proven, found to be.

Stanza 10
5–6 At i 37.6–9 the dying Amavia prays that the Babe's bloody hands be seen as pledges 'That cleare she dide from blemish criminall'. Fowler (1961b) 105–6 interprets her innocence as Nature's before man sinned.
7–8 **Symbole**: sign or token. **sacred** may suggest 'accursed' as the blood is 'filth' (9.8) and the 'token of his [God's] wrath' (4.4). **dwell**: in the biblical sense, 'the sinne that dwelleth in me' (Rom. 7.17). **In**: possibly the obsolete sense 'on', but probably refers to man's indwelling sin, diffused through the babe's body as through his father's (4.7–9).
9 **moniment**: token of remembrance; warning.

Stanza 11
2 According to *L.R.*, 'a Palmer bearing an Infant with bloody hands' marks the beginning of Guyon's adventures. As dramatized in the poem, the beginning comes when Guyon proceeds on foot to avenge the Babe.
3–4 An allegorical tableau: Guyon has exchanged his horse for the burden of Mortdant's defiled arms. Fowler (1961b) 104 notes the ambiguity: Guyon accepts 'the burden of his own flesh with its unavoidable sin and decay'. **with bloud defilde**: as the Babe is 'with bloud defild' (i 50.9).
6 **sell**: saddle, the seat of authority. **golden**: associated with the golden mean, the emblem of the rule of temperance over the passions. The horse's name, 'Brigadore', Golden Bridle (Span. *briglia d'oro*), given at V iii 34.3, carries similar significance.
7 **barbes**: protective coverings, as Guyon in complete armour (i 5.8–9).
8 **accident**: change; event.
9 **conuaide**: stolen.

12

Which when Sir *Guyon* saw, all were he wroth,
  Yet algates mote he soft himselfe appease,
  And fairely fare on foot, how euer loth;
  His double burden did him sore disease.
  So long they traueiled with litle ease,
  Till that at last they to a Castle came,
  Built on a rocke adioyning to the seas;
  It was an auncient worke of antique fame,
And wondrous strong by nature, and by skilfull frame.

13

Therein three sisters dwelt of sundry sort,
  The children of one sire by mothers three;
  Who dying whylome did diuide this fort
  To them by equall shares in equall fee:
  But strifull minde, and diuerse qualitee
  Drew them in parts, and each made others foe:
  Still did they striue, and dayly disagree;
  The eldest did against the youngest goe,
And both against the middest meant to worken woe.

14

Where when the knight arriu'd, he was right well
  Receiu'd, as knight of so much worth became,
  Of second sister, who did far excell
  The other two; *Medina* was her name,
  A sober sad, and comely curteous Dame;
  Who rich arayd, and yet in modest guize,
  In goodly garments, that her well became,
  Faire marching forth in honorable wize,
Him at the threshold met, and well did enterprize.

15

She led him vp into a goodly bowre,
  And comely courted with meet modestie,
  Ne in her speach, ne in her hauiour,
  Was lightnesse seene, or looser vanitie,
  But gratious womanhood, and grauitie,
  Aboue the reason of her youthly yeares:
  Her golden lockes she roundly did vptye
  In breaded tramels, that no looser heares
Did out of order stray about her daintie eares.

Stanza 12

2   **algates**: nevertheless.

3   Lewis (1936) 338 notes that temperance is a pedestrian
virtue. Also S. places his knight outside the chivalric tradition:
'What is a knyght but whan he is on horsebacke? For I sette
nat by a knyght when he is on foote' (Malory 667).

4   **disease**: trouble; with the current sense, for the arms are
'defilde' (11.3).

7   Its situation suggests the control of temperance over the
temptations of land and sea; cf. the Castle of Alma 'plast/
Foreby a riuer in a pleasant dale' (ix 10. 3–4).   **on a rocke**:
as the 'wise man, which hathe buylded his house on a rocke'
(Matt. 7.24).

9   Its strength **by nature** is shown by its foundations, which
suggests the body; its strength by . . . **frame** refers to the
'goodly gouernaunce' (i 29.8) of temperance; cf. xii 1.

Stanza 13

1–2   According to Platonic and Aristotelian theory, the **sire**
would be reason or mind; the **mothers three**, the three souls:
rational, sensible and vegetable; or the three faculties of the
soul: rational, irascible and concupiscible. For a popular
account, see *Batman on Bartolome*, cited Bamborough (1952) 31.
sundry: different, individually distinct.

4   **in equall fee**: in equal possession as a heritable right.
Hence the ideal temperate state is not a victory of the mean over
the two extremes but a shared governing held in harmony by
the mean.

6   **parts**: factions.

7–9   Cf. Aristotle, *Ethics* II vii 1108[b]: 'There are three
kinds of disposition, then, two of them vices, involving
excess and deficiency respectively, and one a virtue, viz. the
mean, and all are in a sense opposed to all; for the extreme
states are contrary both to the intermediate state and to each
other, and the intermediate to the extremes. . . . the greatest
contrariety is that of the extremes to each other, rather than to
the intermediate.' Padelford (1911) 10 argues that Medina
represents the *via media* of the Church of England between the
barren Puritan (Elissa) and the sensuous Church of Rome
(Perissa). One detail which supports this allegory is the
description of Medina's dress (14.6–7; see *n*).

Stanza 14

4   **Medina**: from Lat. *medium*, the mean; not simply the
Aristotelian mean between the two extremes but their union.
Nelson (1963) 194 suggests the root: Lat. *medens*, healer.

5   **sober sad**: severely grave, balanced (as she is the mean)
by **comely curteous**; cf. Una's 'sad sober cheare' (I xii 21.4).

6–7   Magill (1970) 174 suggests that Medina's apparel
reflects the Church of England's approval of canonical dress.

9   **enterprize**: take in hand.

Stanza 15

4   **looser**: loose, illustrated in 8.

6   **Aboue the reason**: Lat. *ultra rationem*, beyond the
proportion to be expected.

7   **roundly**: in a circle.

8   **breaded tramels**: braids rather than nets (cf. III ix
20.4–6), though either contrasts with Duessa's 'discheueled'
hair (i 13.6) and with Medina's 'tresses torne' (27.2) when the
knights fight.

16

Whilest she her selfe thus busily did frame,
    Seemely to entertaine her new-come guest,
    Newes hereof to her other sisters came,
    Who all this while were at their wanton rest,
    Accourting each her friend with lauish fest:
    They were two knights of perelesse puissance,
    And famous far abroad for warlike gest,
    Which to these Ladies loue did countenaunce,
And to his mistresse each himselfe stroue to aduaunce.

17

He that made loue vnto the eldest Dame,
    Was hight Sir *Huddibras*, an hardy man;
    Yet not so good of deedes, as great of name,
    Which he by many rash aduentures wan,
    Since errant armes to sew he first began;
    More huge in strength, then wise in workes he was,
    And reason with foole-hardize ouer ran;
    Sterne melancholy did his courage pas,
And was for terrour more, all armd in shyning bras.

18

But he that lou'd the youngest, was *Sans-loy*,
    He that faire *Vna* late fowle outraged,
    The most vnruly, and the boldest boy,
    That euer warlike weapons menaged,
    And to all lawlesse lust encouraged,
    Through strong opinion of his matchlesse might:
    Ne ought he car'd, whom he endamaged
    By tortious wrong, or whom bereau'd of right.
He now this Ladies champion chose for loue to fight.

19

These two gay knights, vowd to so diuerse loues,
    Each other does enuie with deadly hate,
    And dayly warre against his foeman moues,
    In hope to win more fauour with his mate,
    And th'others pleasing seruice to abate,
    To magnifie his owne. But when they heard,
    How in that place straunge knight arriued late,
    Both knights and Ladies forth right angry far'd,
And fiercely vnto battell sterne themselues prepar'd.

20

But ere they could proceede vnto the place,
    Where he abode, themselues at discord fell,
    And cruell combat ioynd in middle space:
    With horrible assault, and furie fell,
    They heapt huge strokes, the scorned life to quell,
    That all on vprore from her settled seat
    The house was raysd, and all that in did dwell;
    Seemd that lowde thunder with amazement great
Did rend the ratling skyes with flames of fouldring heat.

21

The noyse thereof cald forth that straunger knight,
    To weet, what dreadfull thing was there in hand;
    Where when as two braue knights in bloudy fight
    With deadly rancour he enraunged fond,
    His sunbroad shield about his wrest he bond,
    And shyning blade vnsheathd, with which he ran
    Vnto that stead, their strife to vnderstond;
    And at his first arriuall, them began
With goodly meanes to pacifie, well as he can.

Stanza 16
1   **frame**: apply.
5   **Accourting**: courting, stressing their affectation in contrast to Medina who 'comely courted' (15.2); as also **fest**: festivity, or literally a feast, in contrast to Medina's 'with meet modestie' (15.2); cf. her feast at 39.1.
7   **gest**: deeds.
8   **countenaunce**: make a show of; possibly 'pretend', though Medina appeals to their love at 27.6.

Stanza 17
Sir Huddibras (2) is **great of name** (3) as he bears the name of a British king; see x 25.4. His name suggests 'hardi-bras', foolhardiness. The **shyning bras** (9) which he wears – the only knight so armed – signifies endurance or hardness. Blitch (1965) 63 links the name with the Age of Brass in contrast to the Golden Age of Medina.
8   **melancholy**: also irascibility, anger.

Stanza 18
2   See I vi 5.7.
4   **menaged**: wielded.
8   **tortious**: injurious, illegal.

Stanza 19
1   **gay**: excellent, fine; used ironically.
2–3 See 13.7–9n. **enuie**: regard with hatred.
5   **abate**: bring down in estimation.

Stanza 20
3   **middle space**: relates their contest to the temperate mean. Extremes meet at the middle or mean where they may be reconciled; cf. iv 32.4. Used in the same sense in Book V of the balance of justice (e.g. x 32.1).
5   **quell**: kill. The other's life is scorned; also their rage is suicidal.
8   **with amazement great**: i.e. to the great consternation of the inhabitants.
9   **fouldring**: thundering, flashing; see I xi 40.2n.

Stanza 21
4   **enraunged**: standing in battle order.
5   **sunbroad shield**: cf. the Red Cross Knight's 'sunne-bright shield' (I xi 40.9). Here size seems the point of reference.
7   **stead**: place. **vnderstond**: also 'come between'.
9   **meanes**: with a pun on 'mean'.

22

But they him spying, both with greedy forse
    Attonce vpon him ran, and him beset
    With strokes of mortall steele without remorse,
    And on his shield like yron sledges bet:
    As when a Beare and Tygre being met
    In cruell fight on lybicke Ocean wide,
    Espye a traueiler with feet surbet,
    Whom they in equall pray hope to deuide,
They stint their strife, and him assaile on euery side.

23

But he, not like a wearie traueilere,
    Their sharpe assault right boldly did rebut,
    And suffred not their blowes to byte him nere,
    But with redoubled buffes them backe did put:
    Whose grieued mindes, which choler did englut,
    Against themselues turning their wrathfull spight,
    Gan with new rage their shields to hew and cut;
    But still when *Guyon* came to part their fight,
With heauie load on him they freshly gan to smight.

24

As a tall ship tossed in troublous seas,
    Whom raging windes threatning to make the pray
    Of the rough rockes, do diuersly disease,
    Meetes two contrary billowes by the way,
    That her on either side do sore assay,
    And boast to swallow her in greedy graue;
    She scorning both their spights, does make wide way,
    And with her brest breaking the fomy waue,
Does ride on both their backs, and faire her selfe doth saue.

25

So boldly he him beares, and rusheth forth
    Betweene them both, by conduct of his blade.
    Wondrous great prowesse and heroick worth
    He shewd that day, and rare ensample made,
    When two so mighty warriours he dismade:
    Attonce he wards and strikes, he takes and payes,
    Now forst to yield, now forcing to inuade,
    Before, behind, and round about him layes:
So double was his paines, so double be his prayse.

26

Straunge sort of fight, three valiaunt knights to see
    Three combats ioyne in one, and to darraine
    A triple warre with triple enmitee,
    All for their Ladies froward loue to gaine,
    Which gotten was but hate. So loue does raine
    In stoutest minds, and maketh monstrous warre;
    He maketh warre, he maketh peace againe,
    And yet his peace is but continuall iarre:
O miserable men, that to him subiect arre.

27

Whilst thus they mingled were in furious armes,
    The faire *Medina* with her tresses torne,
    And naked brest, in pitty of their harmes,
    Emongst them ran, and falling them beforne,
    Besought them by the womb, which them had borne,
    And by the loues, which were to them most deare,
    And by the knighthood, which they sure had sworne,
    Their deadly cruell discord to forbeare,
And to her iust conditions of faire peace to heare.

Stanza 22

3   **remorse**: also intermission.
5–9   **lybicke Ocean**: the African desert. Aeneas wandered 'emongst the Lybicke sands' (III ix 41.6). Starnes and Talbert (1955) 73 trace S.'s phrase to Stephanus's *Dictionary*. Topsell (1607) i 28 lists 'Lybican' as an epithet of the bear. Bears and tigers are associated with violence, especially sexual; hence 'Beres and Tygres, that maken fiers warre' decorate the mazer in *S.C.* Aug. 26–8. Their traditional association with the concupiscible and irascible emotions (see Rowland, 1973, 33, 151) relates them to Huddibras and Sansloy respectively. Further, they are known enemies, the one from the forest and the other from the desert (see IV vii 2.6–7); cf. IV viii 4.9, V v 40.6.
7   **surbet**: sore.

Stanza 23

5   **choler**: one of the four humours. Its excess causes anger: see Anderson (1927) 34.   **englut**: fill; devour.

Stanza 24

The handling of alliteration in this stanza is especially remarkable.
3   **disease**: distress.
5   **assay**: assail; put to the test.
6   **boast**: threaten.
8   To imitate the sense, the line breaks in the middle and the accent falls on **breaking**.

Stanza 25

2   **conduct**: skilful handling, displaying virtue in battle.
5   **dismade**: defeated.
7   **forcing to inuade**: i.e. exerting force in order to attack.

Stanza 26

1–5   Each knight, Guyon included, fights for his lady's love. **triple warre**: because each knight fights an inner conflict. **darraine**: wage. Also in the legal sense, 'to vindicate a claim by wager of battle'.
4   **froward**: perverse, ungovernable. Such love is described in 5–9.
5–9   Cf. the denunciation of love at iv 35, v 16.
9   **miserable**: wretchedly unhappy.

Stanza 27

2   **tresses torne**: in contrast to her coiffured hair at 15.7–9.
9   **heare**: the judicial sense, listen to in a court of law. Her plea establishes a new law of harmony; cf. 32.8.

28

But her two other sisters standing by,
  Her lowd gainsaid, and both their champions bad
  Pursew the end of their strong enmity,
  As euer of their loues they would be glad.
  Yet she with pitthy words and counsell sad,
  Still stroue their stubborne rages to reuoke,
  That at the last suppressing fury mad,
They gan abstaine from dint of direfull stroke,
And hearken to the sober speaches, which she spoke.

29

Ah puissaunt Lords, what cursed euill Spright,
  Or fell *Erinnys*, in your noble harts
  Her hellish brond hath kindled with despight,
  And stird you vp to worke your wilfull smarts?
  Is this the ioy of armes? be these the parts
  Of glorious knighthood, after bloud to thrust,
  And not regard dew right and iust desarts?
Vaine is the vaunt, and victory vniust,
That more to mighty hands, then rightfull cause doth trust.

30

And were there rightfull cause of difference,
  Yet were not better, faire it to accord,
  Then with bloud guiltinesse to heape offence,
  And mortall vengeaunce ioyne to crime abhord?
  O fly from wrath, fly, O my liefest Lord:
  Sad be the sights, and bitter fruits of warre,
  And thousand furies wait on wrathfull sword;
Ne ought the prayse of prowesse more doth marre,
Then fowle reuenging rage, and base contentious iarre.

31

But louely concord, and most sacred peace
  Doth nourish vertue, and fast friendship breeds;
  Weake she makes strong, and strong thing does increace,
  Till it the pitch of highest prayse exceeds:
  Braue be her warres, and honorable deeds,
  By which she triumphes ouer ire and pride,
  And winnes an Oliue girlond for her meeds:
Be therefore, O my deare Lords, pacifide,
And this misseeming discord meekely lay aside.

32

Her gracious wordes their rancour did appall,
  And suncke so deepe into their boyling brests,
  That downe they let their cruell weapons fall,
  And lowly did abase their loftie crests
  To her faire presence, and discrete behests.
  Then she began a treatie to procure,
  And stablish termes betwixt both their requests,
That as a law for euer should endure;
Which to obserue in word of knights they did assure.

33

Which to confirme, and fast to bind their league,
  After their wearie sweat and bloudy toile,
  She them besought, during their quiet treague,
  Into her lodging to repaire a while,
  To rest themselues, and grace to reconcile.
  They soone consent: so forth with her they fare,
  Where they are well receiu'd, and made to spoile
  Themselues of soiled armes, and to prepare
188 Their minds to pleasure, and their mouthes to dainty fare.

Stanza 28
4 **As euer**: i.e. even as, with the threat, 'if ever'.
5 **sad**: grave, serious.
6 **stubborne**: fierce. **reuoke**: check, restrain.

Stanza 29
2–9 **Erinnys**: the Furies, spirits of fury and discord;
'nothinge but the wringinges, tourmentes, and gnawinges of yll
consciences that vexed naughty men' (Cooper, 1565). There are
traditionally three of them, as here there are the three knights
provoked by 'fury mad' (28.7). The Furies are the traditional
instruments of retribution which Medina seeks to replace by
dew right, **iust desarts** and **rightfull cause**. Cf. 30.7.
6 **thrust**: both 'thrust' and 'thirst', as the latter leads to
conflict.

Stanza 30
3 **bloud guiltinesse**: invokes God's curse against those who
seek revenge. The concupiscible appetite causes
'bloudguiltinesse' at 4.5; the irascible appetite causes it here;
both cause it in the story of Phedon, iv 17–33.
5 She addresses the three lords as one, or each alone; cf.
31.8.

Stanza 31
1–2 **concord, and ... peace ...**: concord nourishes virtue
in the individual and peace breeds friendship with others. This
role of Concord is described at IV x 34–35. In place of rage,
Medina seeks concord to 'prepare/Their minds to pleasure'
(33.8–9); this argument is perverted by Phædria and Acrasia.
louely: loving.
3–4 Her role expands from the Aristotelian mean between
two vices to 'a moderator of the passions and a peacemaker'
(Nelson, 1963, 194).
7 **meeds**: reward.

Stanza 32
1 **appall**: quell.
6 **procure**: endeavour to arrange.
8 The limit of her law is revealed by Rom. 7.23: 'I se another
law in my membres, rebelling against the law of my minde,
and leading me captive unto the law of sinne, which is in my
membres.'

Stanza 33
3 **treague**: truce; combining 'league' and 'truce', from Ital.
tregua, 'a truce, a league, an atonement' (Florio).
5 **grace to reconcile**: to regain each other's favour; Lat.
gratiam reconciliare.

34

And those two froward sisters, their faire loues
    Came with them eke, all were they wondrous loth,
    And fained cheare, as for the time behoues,
    But could not colour yet so well the troth,
    But that their natures bad appeard in both:
    For both did at their second sister grutch,
    And inly grieue, as doth an hidden moth
    The inner garment fret, not th'vtter touch;
One thought their cheare too litle, th'other thought too mutch.

35

Elissa (so the eldest hight) did deeme
    Such entertainment base, ne ought would eat,
    Ne ought would speake, but euermore did seeme
    As discontent for want of merth or meat;
    No solace could her Paramour intreat
    Her once to show, ne court, nor dalliance,
    But with bent lowring browes, as she would threat,
    She scould, and frownd with froward countenaunce,
Vnworthy of faire Ladies comely gouernaunce.

36

But young *Perissa* was of other mind,
    Full of disport, still laughing, loosely light,
    And quite contrary to her sisters kind;
    No measure in her mood, no rule of right,
    But poured out in pleasure and delight;
    In wine and meats she flowd aboue the bancke,
    And in excesse exceeded her owne might;
    In sumptuous tire she ioyd her selfe to prancke,
But of her loue too lauish (litle haue she thancke.)

37

Fast by her side did sit the bold *Sans-loy*,
    Fit mate for such a mincing mineon,
    Who in her loosenesse tooke exceeding ioy;
    Might not be found a franker franion,
    Of her lewd parts to make companion:
    But *Huddibras*, more like a Malecontent,
    Did see and grieue at his bold fashion;
    Hardly could he endure his hardiment,
Yet still he sat, and inly did him selfe torment.

38

Betwixt them both the faire *Medina* sate
    With sober grace, and goodly carriage:
    With equall measure she did moderate
    The strong extremities of their outrage;
    That forward paire she euer would asswage,
    When they would striue dew reason to exceed;
    But that same froward twaine would accourage,
    And of her plenty adde vnto their need:
So kept she them in order, and her selfe in heed.

Stanza 34
1   **froward**: perverse, ungovernable (as 26.4) because they turn away from the mean; see 38.5–8*n*.
6   **grutch**: grumble.
7–8   **fret**: consume; cf. Ps. 39.12 (BCP): when man is rebuked for sin, 'he waxeth woe and wan: as doth a cloth that mothes haue fret'. The sisters are eaten inwardly by their emotions while remaining outwardly unchanged.
9   **One** should be the excessive Perissa and **th'other** the deficient Elissa.

Stanza 35
1   **Elissa**: from ελάσσων, too little; the personification of moral deficiency, the Aristotelian ελλειψις, inadequacy (Upton, 1758).
2   **entertainment**: provisions; more broadly, 'hospitality'.
5   **solace**: pleasure.   **intreat**: persuade.
6   **court**: courtesy.
9   **gouernaunce**: behaviour.

Stanza 36
1   **Perissa**: Excess, from περρισός, too much, excessive; Aristotle's Hyperbole: going beyond the mean, overflowing. **of other mind**: literally so; see 13.7–9*n*.
2   **disport**: merriment that carries one from the mean. **still**: ever. Her **laughing** anticipates Phædria's: see vi 3.4.
3   **kind**: disposition.
5   **poured out**: for the sexual sense, see I vii 7.2*n*; cf. Cymochles in the Bower, v 28.5.

Stanza 37
2   **Fit mate**: he also personifies 'no rule of right' (36.4). **mincing**: excessively dainty; used ironically for the humorous alliterative description.   **mineon**: mistress.
4   **franker franion**: looser paramour.
5   **parts**: attributes; also in the obscene sense.
6   **Malecontent**: a type of melancholic humour. See G. B. Harrison's essay on Elizabethan melancholy in his edition of Breton's *Melancholike Humours* (1929). The malcontent was associated with Puritanism, as is **Huddibras**.
8   **hardiment**: boldness in love; in contrast to his own boldness in war; cf. 17.7.

Stanza 38
On Medina (1) as peacemaker, see 14.4*n*, 31.3–4*n*. Her role as hostess at a banquet is Platonic rather than Aristotelian as she seeks harmony rather than the mean.
3   **equall**: also 'just'.
4   **extremities**: violent outbursts; also the extreme positions in relation to the mean, as Arg. 3.   **outrage**: excesses, want of moderation.
5–8   The **forward paire** is Perissa-Sansloy; the **froward twaine**, Elissa-Huddibras; as at 34.1, **froward** means 'from-ward' in addition to 'perverse'.   **accourage**: encourage; the heavy stress suggests 'urge to take heart'.
9   **in heed**: heeded, respected; it also suggests 'takes care of herself', for the mean exists only in relation to the extremes.

39

Thus fairely she attempered her feast,
    And pleasd them all with meete satietie,
    At last when lust of meat and drinke was ceast,
    She *Guyon* deare besought of curtesie,
    To tell from whence he came through ieopardie,
    And whither now on new aduenture bound.
    Who with bold grace, and comely grauitie,
    Drawing to him the eyes of all around,
From lofty siege began these words aloud to sound.

40

This thy demaund, O Lady, doth reuiue
    Fresh memory in me of that great Queene,
    Great and most glorious virgin Queene aliue,
    That with her soueraigne powre, and scepter shene
    All Faery lond does peaceably sustene.
    In widest Ocean she her throne does reare,
    That ouer all the earth it may be seene;
    As morning Sunne her beames dispredden cleare,
And in her face faire peace, and mercy doth appeare.

41

In her the richesse of all heauenly grace
    In chiefe degree are heaped vp on hye:
    And all that else this worlds enclosure bace
    Hath great or glorious in mortall eye,
    Adornes the person of her Maiestie;
    That men beholding so great excellence,
    And rare perfection in mortalitie,
    Do her adore with sacred reuerence,
As th'Idole of her makers great magnificence.

42

To her I homage and my seruice owe,
    In number of the noblest knights on ground,
    Mongst whom on me she deigned to bestowe
    Order of *Maydenhead*, the most renownd,
    That may this day in all the world be found:
    An yearely solemne feast she wontes to make
    The day that first doth lead the yeare around;
    To which all knights of worth and courage bold
Resort, to heare of straunge aduentures to be told.

43

There this old Palmer shewed himselfe that day,
    And to that mighty Princesse did complaine
    Of grieuous mischiefes, which a wicked Fay
    Had wrought, and many whelmd in deadly paine,
    Whereof he crau'd redresse. My Soueraine,
    Whose glory is in gracious deeds, and ioyes
    Throughout the world her mercy to maintaine,
    Eftsoones deuisd redresse for such annoyes;
Me all vnfit for so great purpose she employes.

Stanza 39

1   **attempered**: controlled, alluding to the tempering of
temperance; cf. Alma's banquet 'Attempred goodly well for
health and for delight' (xi 2.9).
2, 3   **meete, meat**: the pun indicates the allegorical nature
of the feast.
3–4   On this epic convention, see I xii 15.1–6*n*.   **lust**:
desire.
8–9   Cf. Virgil, *Aen*. i 753–6: Dido asks Aeneas to tell his
story and he begins (ii 1–2) with solemn formality. Here such
formality prepares for the identification of the Faerie Queene,
more closely than elsewhere in the poem, with Elizabeth.
siege: seat.

Stanza 40

4   **shene**: bright.
8   **dispredden**: spread abroad or far.
9   **peace and mercy**: two of the four daughters of God.
They seek forgiveness for man against the claims of Truth and
Justice for satisfaction; see Chew (1947) ch. ii. Cf. Mercilla
attended by Eirene (Peace), V ix 31–32.

Stanza 41

1   **richesse**: wealth. Cf. Lucifera's 'endlesse richesse'
(I iv 7.5) and 'the house of Richesse' (II vii 24.9). Cf. also
Belphœbe: 'So glorious mirrhour of celestiall grace' (iii 25.6).
3   **bace**: low, being of the earth.
9   **Idole**: image; an earthly embodiment of the divine; one
made in the image of God; cf. IV vi 17.5.   **magnificence**:
sovereign bounty, glory, splendour, grandeur, imposing beauty.
Significantly, it describes Arthur's virtue in *L.R.* Its only other
use in the poem is to describe Radigund, V v 4.2, who parodies
Gloriana's rule.

Stanza 42

4–5   See I vii 46.4*n*.
6–7   Cf. the Faerie Queene's 'Annuall feaste' in *L.R.* The
day may be 17 November, the Coronation (Accession) day
of Elizabeth's reign; or 25 March, the vernal equinox: 'For it
is wel known . . . that the yeare beginneth in March' (E.K.,
Arg. to *S.C.*).   **make**: 'hold' sugg. edd. for the rhyme.

Stanza 43

3   **Fay**: fairy.
4   **whelmd**: destroyed; also drowned, buried.   **deadly
paine**: refers not to Acrasia's victims who enjoy their captivity but to those, such as Mortdant, who seek to escape
(cf. 45.7).
6   Alluding to her name, Gloriana.
8   **annoyes**: injuries.

44

Now hath faire *Phœbe* with her siluer face
    Thrise seene the shadowes of the neather world,
Sith last I left that honorable place,
    In which her royall presence is introld;
    Ne euer shall I rest in house nor hold,
Till I that false *Acrasia* haue wonne;
    Of whose fowle deedes, too hideous to be told,
    I witnesse am, and this their wretched sonne,
Whose wofull parents she hath wickedly fordonne.

45

Tell on, faire Sir, said she, that dolefull tale,
    From which sad ruth does seeme you to restraine,
That we may pitty such vnhappy bale,
    And learne from pleasures poyson to abstaine:
    Ill by ensample good doth often gayne.
Then forward he his purpose gan pursew,
    And told the storie of the mortall payne,
    Which *Mordant* and *Amauia* did rew;
As with lamenting eyes him selfe did lately vew.

46

Night was far spent, and now in *Ocean* deepe
    Orion, flying fast from hissing snake,
His flaming head did hasten for to steepe,
    When of his pitteous tale he end did make;
    Whilest with delight of that he wisely spake,
Those guestes beguiled, did beguile their eyes
    Of kindly sleepe, that did them ouertake.
    At last when they had markt the chaunged skyes,
They wist their houre was spent; then each to rest him hyes.

Cant. III.

*Vaine Braggadocchio getting Guyons
    horse is made the scorne
Of knighthood trew, and is of fayre
    Belphœbe fowle forlorne.*

1

SOone as the morrow faire with purple beames
    Disperst the shadowes of the mistie night,
And *Titan* playing on the eastern streames,
    Gan cleare the deawy ayre with springing light,
    Sir *Guyon* mindfull of his vow yplight,
Vprose from drowsie couch, and him addrest
    Vnto the iourney which he had behight:
    His puissaunt armes about his noble brest,
And many-folded shield he bound about his wrest.

Stanza 44

1–4   This elaborate paraphrase for 'three months have passed' is cited by Warton (1762) i 114 as an example of the poem's 'trifling and tedious circumlocutions'. Yet the language suits the formal taking of a vow. If the year begins in March, the time is June: the time of the false summer of the Bower of Bliss where Verdant (Spring) is held a prisoner. Yet see 46.1–3*n*. On the significance of the moon, see I viii 38.6–7*n*. Here the three-month period may indicate the incompleteness of the quest. See ix 7.5*n*.
4   **introld**: either enrolled, i.e. celebrated (cf. i 32.3) or 'encircled', continuing the image of the Queen surrounded by her knights.
5   **hold**: place of refuge; fort.
6   **wonne**: subdued.
9   **fordonne**: killed.

Stanza 45

4   The pleasure is inferred from the name *Acrasia* (44.6). Cf. 'pleasures poisoned baytes' (i Arg.).
6   **purpose**: discourse.
8   **Amauia**: here first named; see i 55.5*n*.   **rew**: 'suffer' is the required sense; i.e. the suffering which they regretted (*OED* 7) or lamented (*OED* 11).

Stanza 46

1–3   As Scorpion rises in the east, Orion sets in the west pursued by his slayer (see VII vii 39.6–8); they are never together in the same hemisphere.   **Orion**: the 'starre [which] bringeth in winter' (Geneva gloss to Job 38.31). It rises at midnight and sets at dawn. By this computation, the present time is winter and the day at 42.7 would be 17 November, Elizabeth's Accession Day, the festival at which each Knight begins his quest. See Fowler (1964) 170 *n*1.
8   **the chaunged skyes**: i.e. the changed position of the stars.

Canto iii

Argument

1   **Vaine**: foolish; his stock epithet: see 4.5*n*.
4   **Belphœbe**: Lat. *bella*, handsome + Gk φοιβη, pure, radiant. 'faire *Phœbe*' (ii 44.1) suggests her name; see 22.1–4*n*. She is not named in Book II. On her name, see III v 27.9*n*. At III vi 28.5, Dame *Phœbe* (Diana) 'of her selfe her name *Belphœbe* red'.   **fayre**: her stock epithet.   **fowle forlorne**: disgracefully put to shame; deserted: see 43.7–9.

Stanza 1

1   **purple beames**: the stock classical description of dawn; see I ii 7.1–3. Cf. the Virgilian *lumine vestit / purpureo* (*Aen.* vi 640–1).
4   **springing**: dawning.
7   **behight**: vowed.
9   **many-folded**: 'seuenfolded' (v 6.3; cf. viii 32.5); the classical shield (see v 6.3*n*).

191

2

Then taking *Congé* of that virgin pure,
  The bloudy-handed babe vnto her truth
  Did earnestly commit, and her coniure,
  In vertuous lore to traine his tender youth,
  And all that gentle noriture ensu'th:
  And that so soone as ryper yeares he raught,
  He might for memorie of that dayes ruth,
  Be called *Ruddymane*, and thereby taught,
T'auenge his Parents death on them, that had it wrought.

3

So forth he far'd, as now befell, on foot,
  Sith his good steed is lately from him gone;
  Patience perforce; helpelesse what may it boot
  To fret for anger, or for griefe to mone?
  His Palmer now shall foot no more alone:
  So fortune wrought, as vnder greene woods syde
  He lately heard that dying Lady grone,
  He left his steed without, and speare besyde,
And rushed in on foot to ayd her, ere she dyde.

4

The whiles a losell wandring by the way,
  One that to bountie neuer cast his mind,
  Ne thought of honour euer did assay
  His baser brest, but in his kestrell kind
  A pleasing vaine of glory vaine did find,
  To which his flowing toung, and troublous spright
  Gaue him great ayd, and made him more inclind:
  He that braue steed there finding ready dight,
Purloynd both steed and speare, and ran away full light.

5

Now gan his hart all swell in iollitie,
  And of him selfe great hope and helpe conceiu'd,
  That puffed vp with smoke of vanitie,
  And with selfe-loued personage deceiu'd,
  He gan to hope, of men to be receiu'd
  For such, as he him thought, or faine would bee:
  But for in court gay portaunce he perceiu'd,
  And gallant shew to be in greatest gree,
Eftsoones to court he cast t'auaunce his first degree.

6

And by the way he chaunced to espy
  One sitting idle on a sunny bancke,
  To whom auaunting in great brauery,
  As Peacocke, that his painted plumes doth prancke,
  He smote his courser in the trembling flancke,
  And to him threatned his hart-thrilling speare:
  The seely man seeing him ryde so rancke,
  And ayme at him, fell flat to ground for feare,
And crying Mercy lowd, his pitious hands gan reare.

Stanza 2
1 **Congé**: ceremonious farewell, as i 34.1. **virgin pure**: as temperance is virginal; cf. Alma, ix 18.1. The female figures in Book II are either virgin or violated.
2 **truth**: trust; virtue.
3 **coniure**: solemnly entreat; charge; literally, 'to swear together'.
4 **vertuous lore**: moral doctrine. Moral education must counter weakness inherited from both parents.
5 **gentle noriture**: noble upbringing.
8 **Ruddymane**: i.e. **bloudy-handed** (2), 'with bloud defild' (i 50.9); 'bloody-hand' in Forest law is a sign of guilt (see *OED*).

Stanza 3
3 **Patience perforce**: proverbial (C. G. Smith, 1970, 598). **perforce**: upon compulsion; through necessity.
4 **anger** and **griefe** unrestrained by temperance are illustrated in the Phedon episode: see iv 33.4*n*.

Stanza 4
1 **losell**: scoundrel. Its etymological sense, 'one who is lost', is given in this line; its moral sense is given in 2.
2 **bountie**: valour. **cast**: applied.
4 **baser**: most base (the Lat. absol. comp.). **kestrell kind**: a small hawk of poor breed and base nature; a term of contempt for one who preys on others; cf. 36. Cf. his 'Capons courage' (III viii 15.6) which is associated, like **kestrell**, with 'eunuch'.
5 **glory**: boasting, vainglory; in contrast to the 'most glorious virgin Queene' (ii 40.3). J. C. Smith (1909) ii 506 defends **glory vaine** against 'glory he' *1590* because the play on words is Spenserian.

Stanza 5
2–4 Cf. Guyon who 'euermore himselfe with comfort feedes, / Of his owne vertues, and prayse-worthy deedes' (vii 2.4–5). **selfe-loued personage**: love of his own image or impersonation.
7 **portaunce**: bearing, demeanour. Soon he is confronted by Belphœbe's 'stately portance' (21.9).
8 **gree**: favour, goodwill.
9 **his first degree**: the first stage in attaining knighthood or promotion; later symbolized by Philotime's chain in which each link is 'a step of dignity' (vii 46.9).

Stanza 6
3 **auaunting**: advancing; boasting; hence, 'advancing boastfully'. **brauery**: bravado, 'splendour', referring to the armour, mere outward show without inner worth. It is the final description of him at V iii 39.7. The only two uses of the term in the poem refer to him.
4 **prancke**: proudly display.
7 **seely**: mean, miserable, helpless. **rancke**: fiercely, proudly.
9 **Mercy lowd**: 'Mercy Lord', sugg. Upton (1758), would echo Guyon's appeal to the Red Cross Knight at i 27.1 and indicate an alliance of vices; yet cf. 8.2. **his pitious hands**: a witty play upon hands appealing for pity.

7

Thereat the Scarcrow wexed wondrous prowd,
　　Through fortune of his first aduenture faire,
　　And with big thundring voyce reuyld him lowd;
　　Vile Caytiue, vassall of dread and despaire,
　　Vnworthie of the commune breathed aire,
　　Why liuest thou, dead dog, a lenger day,
　　And doest not vnto death thy selfe prepare.
　　Dye, or thy selfe my captiue yield for ay;
Great fauour I thee graunt, for aunswere thus to stay.

8

Hold, O deare Lord, hold your dead-doing hand,
　　Then loud he cryde, I am your humble thrall.
　　Ah wretch (quoth he) thy destinies withstand
　　My wrathfull will, and do for mercy call.
　　I giue thee life: therefore prostrated fall,
　　And kisse my stirrup; that thy homage bee.
　　The Miser threw him selfe, as an Offall,
　　Streight at his foot in base humilitee,
And cleeped him his liege, to hold of him in fee.

9

So happy peace they made and faire accord:
　　Eftsoones this liege-man gan to wexe more bold,
　　And when he felt the folly of his Lord,
　　In his owne kind he gan him selfe vnfold:
　　For he was wylie witted, and growne old
　　In cunning sleights and practick knauery,
　　From that day forth he cast for to vphold
　　His idle humour with fine flattery,
And blow the bellowes to his swelling vanity.

10

Trompart fit man for Braggadocchio,
　　To serue at court in view of vaunting eye;
　　Vaine-glorious man, when fluttring wind does blow
　　In his light wings, is lifted vp to skye:
　　The scorne of knighthood and trew cheualrye,
　　To thinke without desert of gentle deed,
　　And noble worth to be aduaunced hye:
　　Such prayse is shame; but honour vertues meed
Doth beare the fairest flowre in honorable seed.

11

So forth they pas, a well consorted paire,
　　Till that at length with Archimage they meet:
　　Who seeing one that shone in armour faire,
　　On goodly courser thundring with his feet,
　　Eftsoones supposed him a person meet,
　　Of his reuenge to make the instrument:
　　For since the Redcrosse knight he earst did weet,
　　To beene with Guyon knit in one consent,
The ill, which earst to him, he now to Guyon ment.

12

And comming close to Trompart gan inquere
　　Of him, what mighty warriour that mote bee,
　　That rode in golden sell with single spere,
　　But wanted sword to wreake his enmitee:
　　He is a great aduenturer, (said he)
　　That hath his sword through hard assay forgone,
　　And now hath vowd, till he auenged bee,
　　Of that despight, neuer to wearen none;
That speare is him enough to doen a thousand grone.

13

Th'enchaunter greatly ioyed in the vaunt,
　　And weened well ere long his will to win,
　　And both his foen with equall foyle to daunt.
　　Tho to him louting lowly, did begin
　　To plaine of wrongs, which had committed bin
　　By Guyon, and by that false Redcrosse knight,
　　Which two through treason and deceiptfull gin,
　　Had slaine Sir Mordant, and his Lady bright:
That mote him honour win, to wreake so foule despight.

Stanza 7
1　**Scarcrow**: as one dressed in another's clothes, and fit only to scare crows.
4–9　His vaunting comments upon the chivalric tradition. **Caytiue**: wretch; captive.

Stanza 8
7　**Miser**: wretch.　**Offall**: refuse, something thrown down; from 'off fall' as the stress shows. Perhaps a play on 'oaf', an elf's child, hence 'misbegotten'.
9　**in fee**: in absolute possession, i.e. to be his **thrall** (2).

Stanza 9
4　**kind**: nature.
6　**practick**: crafty.
9　**blow the bellowes**: alluding to his name and Braggadocchio's puffed-up state; cf. 5.3, 10.3–4.

Stanza 10
1　**Trompart**: the Deceiver (cf. 'trompant': cheating, deceiving, and 'trump': to deceive); the Flatterer, from his role as a trumpet to 'blow the bellowes' (9.9) to Braggadocchio's vanity. **Braggadocchio**: Brag, Vainglory, from brag + occhio, the Italian augmentative; 'Brag' also signifies 'show', 'pomp'; see 18.8n.
8–9　**honour . . . in honorable seed**: honour, the reward of valour, flourishes best among the nobility.

Stanza 11
8　**in one consent**: in mutual accord; in one fellowship.
9　**ment**: directed.

Stanza 12
3　**golden sell**: as ii 11.6.　**single spere**: i.e. spear alone.
6　**assay**: encounter.　**forgone**: forfeited; at 17.6–9 the Boaster offers a more flattering explanation.

Stanza 13
3　**equall foyle**: i.e. the defeat of both, referring to the wrestler's throw; or equal weapon, referring to the sword which he will supply.
7　**gin**: device, craft.
9　**wreake**: punish.

14

Therewith all suddeinly he seemd enraged,
  And threatned death with dreadfull countenaunce,
  As if their liues had in his hand beene gaged;
  And with stiffe force shaking his mortall launce,
  To let him weet his doughtie valiaunce,
  Thus said; Old man, great sure shalbe thy meed,
  If where those knights for feare of dew vengeaunce
  Do lurke, thou certainly to me areed,
That I may wreake on them their hainous hatefull deed.

15

Certes, my Lord, (said he) that shall I soone,
  And giue you eke good helpe to their decay,
  But mote I wisely you aduise to doon;
  Giue no ods to your foes, but do puruay
  Your selfe of sword before that bloudy day:
  For they be two the prowest knights on ground,
  And oft approu'd in many hard assay,
  And eke of surest steele, that may be found,
Do arme your selfe against that day, them to confound.

16

Dotard (said he) let be thy deepe aduise;
  Seemes that through many yeares thy wits thee faile,
  And that weake eld hath left thee nothing wise,
  Else neuer should thy iudgement be so fraile,
  To measure manhood by the sword or maile.
  Is not enough foure quarters of a man,
  Withouten sword or shield, an host to quaile?
  Thou little wotest, what this right hand can:
Speake they, which haue beheld the battailes, which it wan.

17

The man was much abashed at his boast;
  Yet well he wist, that who so would contend
  With either of those knights on euen coast,
  Should need of all his armes, him to defend;
  Yet feared least his boldnesse should offend,
  When Braggadocchio said, Once I did sweare,
  When with one sword seuen knights I brought to end,
  Thence forth in battell neuer sword to beare,
But it were that, which noblest knight on earth doth weare.

18

Perdie Sir knight, said then th'enchaunter bliue,
  That shall I shortly purchase to your hond:
  For now the best and noblest knight aliue
  Prince Arthur is, that wonnes in Faerie lond;
  He hath a sword, that flames like burning brond.
  The same by my deuice I vndertake
  Shall by to morrow by thy side be fond.
  At which bold word that boaster gan to quake,
And wondred in his mind, what mote that monster make.

19

He stayd not for more bidding, but away
  Was suddein vanished out of his sight:
  The Northerne wind his wings did broad display
  At his commaund, and reared him vp light
  From off the earth to take his aerie flight.
  They lookt about, but no where could espie
  Tract of his foot: then dead through great affright
  They both nigh were, and each bad other flie:
194 Both fled attonce, ne euer backe returned eie.

20

Till that they come vnto a forrest greene,
  In which they shrowd themselues from causelesse feare;
  Yet feare them followes still, where so they beene,
  Each trembling leafe, and whistling wind they heare,
  As ghastly bug their haire on end does reare:
  Yet both doe striue their fearfulnesse to faine.
  At last they heard a horne, that shrilled cleare
  Throughout the wood, that ecchoed againe,
And made the forrest ring, as it would riue in twaine.

Stanza 14
1   all suddeinly: marks his intemperate rashness; cf.
Guyon's response to a similar tale at i 11–12.
3   gaged: i.e. given as pledges.
5   valiaunce: valour.
8   areed: tell.

Stanza 15
2   decay: death.
3   wisely: referring to his advice, or how Braggadocchio
should act.
4   puruay: supply.
7   approu'd: tested.

Stanza 16
6   The traditional four parts of the body, each with a limb,
specifying one complete man.

Stanza 17
3   euen coast: i.e. equal ground; or, as 'cost': equal terms;
cf. IV iii 24.8.
6   Once: once for all.

Stanza 18
1   Perdie: assuredly; or an oath to confirm Braggadocchio's
vow.   bliue: quickly.
2   purchase: procure.
3   noblest knight: as xi 30.7.
6   deuice: devising.
8   boaster: Braggadocchio's title throughout the poem.
9   what mote that monster make: how that marvel (Lat.
monstrum) could be accomplished.

Stanza 19
3–5   As Satan, he is 'the prince that ruleth in the aire'
(Eph. 2.2) and associated with the North (cf. Isaiah 14.13).

Stanza 20
2–5   Cf. Ps. 53.5: 'They were afraied for feare, where no
feare was'; Lev. 26.36: 'The sounde of a leafe shaken shal chase
them'; and Wisd. Sol. 17.14, 17 where the wicked are said to be
'troubled with monstrous visions' and bound with terror by
'an hyssing winde'.   ghastly bug: terrifying apparition.
6   faine: conceal.

21

Eft through the thicke they heard one rudely rush;
  With noyse whereof he from his loftie steed
  Downe fell to ground, and crept into a bush,
  To hide his coward head from dying dreed.
  But *Trompart* stoutly stayd to taken heed
  Of what might hap.   Eftsoone there stepped forth
  A goodly Ladie clad in hunters weed,
  That seemd to be a woman of great worth,
And by her stately portance, borne of heauenly birth.

22

Her face so faire as flesh it seemed not,
  But heauenly pourtraict of bright Angels hew,
  Cleare as the skie, withouten blame or blot,
  Through goodly mixture of complexions dew;
  And in her cheekes the vermeill red did shew
  Like roses in a bed of lillies shed,
  The which ambrosiall odours from them threw,
  And gazers sense with double pleasure fed,
Hable to heale the sicke, and to reuiue the ded.

23

In her faire eyes two liuing lamps did flame,
  Kindled aboue at th'heauenly makers light,
  And darted fyrie beames out of the same,
  So passing persant, and so wondrous bright,
  That quite bereau'd the rash beholders sight:
  In them the blinded god his lustfull fire
  To kindle oft assayd, but had no might;
  For with dredd Maiestie, and awfull ire,
She broke his wanton darts, and quenched base desire.

24

Her iuorie forhead, full of bountie braue,
  Like a broad table did it selfe dispred,
  For Loue his loftie triumphes to engraue,
  And write the battels of his great godhed:
  All good and honour might therein be red:
  For there their dwelling was. And when she spake,
  Sweet words, like dropping honny she did shed,
  And twixt the perles and rubins softly brake
A siluer sound, that heauenly musicke seemd to make.

Stanzas 21–31
The most extended portrait in the poem (cf. Arthur's at I vii
29–36). Belphœbe mirrors the person of Elizabeth, 'a most
vertuous and beautifull Lady' (*L.R.*). The vision of innocence
and beauty in her sustains the reader against the assault of
Acrasia. The pictorial conventions of the Amazon used here are
treated by Tuve (1970) 120–7. Cf. the description of Radigund,
V v 2–3. S.'s use of imagery from the Song of Solomon is
noted below.

Stanza 21
1   **Eft**: afterwards; or **Eftsoone** (6): forthwith.   **thicke**:
thicket.   **rudely**: violently.
4   **dying dreed**: fear of dying. Cf. Sidney's Dametas who
thrusts himself into a bush when wild beasts appear, 'resolved
not to see his owne death' (*Works* i 123).
8   **worth**: rank, dignity.
9   **stately portance**: majestic bearing. The next ten stanzas
define this term.

Stanza 22
1–3   Wittily alluding to the etymology of Belphœbe's name
without naming her: see Arg. 4*n*.   **Cleare**: brightly shining,
Lat. *clarus*.   **withouten**: used for emphasis.   **blame**:
fault.   **blot**: as Una, I xii 22.7; cf. Song of Sol. 4.7: 'Thou
art all faire, my love, and there is no spot in thee.'
4–5   **complexions dew**: the proper combination of colour
in her face; or the temperate combination of the four humours
in her body which produces her beauty.   **vermeill red**:
indicates her sanguine nature as one unaffected by passion, and
manifests her shamefastness; cf. ix 41.3–7.
7   **ambrosiall**: divinely fragrant; cf. Diana's locks sprinkled
'with sweet *Ambrosia*' (III vi 18.9); from Venus's *ambrosiae
comae* (*Aen.* i 403).
9   Combines the powers of the Well of Life and the Tree of
Life (I xi 30, 48).

Stanza 23
Belphœbe's eyes have the blinding power of the sun given to
Arthur's shield (I vii 35.9) and Fidelia's face 'That could haue
dazd the rash beholders sight' (I x 12.8). Here **rash** (5) signifies
lustful. The power of virginity over lust is signified by Medusa's
head on Minerva's shield (Comes, 1616, IV v). See Alciati's
(1581) emblem *Custodiendas virgines*, and Aptekar (1969) 102–3.
Hence Cupid is referred to as **the blinded god** (6). Cf.
Acrasia's eyes whose 'fierie beames . . . thrild / Fraile harts,
yet quenched not' (xii 78.7–8).
4   **passing persant**: exceedingly piercing.

Stanza 24
1   **bountie braue**: excellent goodness.
2   **table**: surface for painting.
4–5   Not the 'blinded god' of the previous stanza but a love
whose wars record **All good and honour**.
7   Cf. Song of Sol. 4.11: 'Thy lippes, my spouse, droppe as
honie combes.'
8   **rubins**: rubies, her lips.

25

Vpon her eyelids many Graces sate,
Vnder the shadow of her euen browes,
Working belgards, and amorous retrate,
And euery one her with a grace endowes:
And euery one with meekenesse to her bowes.
So glorious mirrhour of celestiall grace,
And soueraine moniment of mortall vowes,
How shall fraile pen descriue her heauenly face,
For feare through want of skill her beautie to disgrace?

26

So faire, and thousand thousand times more faire
She seemd, when she presented was to sight,
And was yclad, for heat of scorching aire,
All in a silken Camus lylly whight,
Purfled vpon with many a folded plight,
Which all aboue besprinckled was throughout
With golden aygulets, that glistred bright,
Like twinckling starres, and all the skirt about
Was hemd with golden fringe

27

Below her ham her weed did somewhat traine,
And her streight legs most brauely were embayld
In gilden buskins of costly Cordwaine,
All bard with golden bendes, which were entayld
With curious antickes, and full faire aumayld:
Before they fastned were vnder her knee
In a rich Iewell, and therein entrayld
The ends of all their knots, that none might see,
How they within their fouldings close enwrapped bee.

28

Like two faire marble pillours they were seene,
Which doe the temple of the Gods support,
Whom all the people decke with girlands greene,
And honour in their festiuall resort;
Those same with stately grace, and princely port
She taught to tread, when she her selfe would grace,
But with the wooddie Nymphes when she did play,
Or when the flying Libbard she did chace,
She could them nimbly moue, and after fly apace.

29

And in her hand a sharpe bore-speare she held,
And at her backe a bow and quiuer gay,
Stuft with steele-headed darts, wherewith she queld
The saluage beastes in her victorious play,
Knit with a golden bauldricke, which forelay
Athwart her snowy brest, and did diuide
Her daintie paps; which like young fruit in May
Now little gan to swell, and being tide,
Through her thin weed their places only signifide.

P. Fletcher, *Piscatory Eclogues* vii 17: 'Her eyebrow black,
like to an ebon bow'.
3   Fashioning loving looks and amorous countenance.
belgards: from Ital. *bel guardo*, but suggesting also beauty's
guard against love; cf. III ix 52.9.   **retrate**: from Ital.
ritratto, picture, portrait (cf. ix 4.2), referring to her looks
which arouse love; but suggesting also the lover's retreat (see
OED 'retrait').
6   Cf. the praise of Elizabeth, I Proem iv 2.
8   **descriue**: describe, in the special sense, 'represent',
'picture'.

Stanza 26

4   **Camus**: a light loose dress.   **lylly whight**: denoting her
virginity; cf. Alma, ix 19.1.
5   **Purfled**: embroidered.   **plight**: pleat. The pleats express
her modesty; cf. Shamefastnesse's attire, ix 40.6.
7, 9   One may expect Diana's colour, silver (cf. III vi 18.3);
yet **golden** declares her kinship with Apollo, her father.
aygulets: tags or sequins.
9   The only half-line in the poem for which there is not an
apparent reason: see viii 55.9n, III iv 39.7n, ix 37.5n. It stands
at the centre of the ten stanzas that describe Belphœbe.

Stanza 27

1   **Below . . . did . . . traine**: i.e. her skirt extends below her
thigh; or **ham** may refer to the back of the knee.   **traine**:
hang down.
2   **embayld**: enclosed; from 'bail', a ring, or 'embay',
enclose.
3   **gilden**: gilded.   **Cordwaine**: cordovan, a Spanish
leather.
4   **bendes**: bars or straps, an heraldic term.   **entayld**:
engraved.
5   **curious antickes**: elaborate, grotesque figures. These
charms suggest the magical power that protects her virginity.
aumayld: enamelled.
6–9   The hidden ends suggest that her armour cannot be
undone, being a virgin's knot, in contrast to Venus's girdle
which may be loosened.   **Before**: i.e. in front, to declare her
virginity.   **entrayld**: entwined.

Stanza 28

1–2   Cf. Song Sol. 5.15: 'His legs are as pillers of marble.'
The Pauline doctrine of the body as the 'temple of the holie
Gost' (1 Cor. 6.19) suggests this simile; cf. VI viii 42.7–9.
5–6   She graced herself when she walked **with stately
grace**, as Venus reveals herself to be a goddess by her step
(Virgil, *Aen.* i 405).
7   **play**: 'sport' sugg. Church (1758) for the rhyme; cf.
VI x 9.5.
8   **Libbard**: leopard. The emblem of incontinence in Dante,
Inf. i 32, which virginity seeks to destroy.

Stanza 29

1   **bore-speare**: for slaying the boar of lust.
3   **queld**: killed.
5   **Knit**: fastened. The Amazon warrior, Penthesilea, wears a
golden girdle below her bare breast in Virgil, *Aen.* i 492; cf.
31.5–9.
7–8   The month of May in the Old Style extends into our
June.   **young fruit**: cf. the *pome acerbe* of Ariosto's Alcina,
Orl. Fur. vii 14.

Stanza 25

1–2   Cf. *Amor.* xl 3–4: 'on each eyelid sweetly doe appeare
/ an hundred Graces as in shade to sit', and E.K.'s gloss to
S.C. June 25.   **euen**: 'ebon' is a possible reading; cf.

30

Her yellow lockes crisped, like golden wyre,
  About her shoulders weren loosely shed,
  And when the winde emongst them did inspyre,
  They waued like a penon wide dispred,
  And low behinde her backe were scattered:
  And whether art it were, or heedlesse hap,
  As through the flouring forrest rash she fled,
  In her rude haires sweet flowres themselues did lap,
And flourishing fresh leaues and blossomes did enwrap.

31

Such as *Diana* by the sandie shore
  Of swift *Eurotas*, or on *Cynthus* greene,
  Where all the Nymphes haue her vnwares forlore,
  Wandreth alone with bow and arrowes keene,
  To seeke her game: Or as that famous Queene
  Of *Amazons*, whom *Pyrrhus* did destroy,
  The day that first of *Priame* she was seene,
  Did shew her selfe in great triumphant ioy,
To succour the weake state of sad afflicted *Troy*.

32

Such when as hartlesse *Trompart* her did vew,
  He was dismayed in his coward mind,
  And doubted, whether he himselfe should shew,
  Or fly away, or bide alone behind:
  Both feare and hope he in her face did find,
  When she at last him spying thus bespake;
  Hayle Groome; didst not thou see a bleeding Hind,
  Whose right haunch earst my stedfast arrow strake?
If thou didst, tell me, that I may her ouertake.

33

Wherewith reviu'd, this answere forth he threw;
  O Goddesse, (for such I thee take to bee)
  For neither doth thy face terrestriall shew,
  Nor voyce sound mortall; I auow to thee,
  Such wounded beast, as that, I did not see,
  Sith earst into this forrest wild I came.
  But mote thy goodlyhed forgiue it mee,
  To weet, which of the Gods I shall thee name,
That vnto thee due worship I may rightly frame.

34

To whom she thus; but ere her words ensewed,
  Vnto the bush her eye did suddein glaunce,
  In which vaine *Braggadocchio* was mewed,
  And saw it stirre: she left her percing launce,
  And towards gan a deadly shaft aduaunce,
  In mind to marke the beast. At which sad stowre,
  Trompart forth stept, to stay the mortall chaunce,
  Out crying, O what euer heauenly powre,
Or earthly wight thou be, withhold this deadly howre.

35

O stay thy hand, for yonder is no game
  For thy fierce arrowes, them to exercize,
  But loe my Lord, my liege, whose warlike name
  Is farre renowmd through many bold emprize;
  And now in shade he shrowded yonder lies.
  She staid: with that he crauld out of his nest,
  Forth creeping on his caitiue hands and thies,
  And standing stoutly vp, his loftie crest
Did fiercely shake, and rowze, as comming late from rest.

Stanza 30

1 **crisped**: curled.
3 **inspyre**: breathe. Perhaps from Virgil's description of
Venus who allowed her hair to be scattered by the winds, *Aen.*
i 319.
7–9 Botticelli's *Primavera* seems the closest analogue to this
startling image; see Wind (1967) 113f. **flouring**: flourishing
and flowering, which mean the same in her. **rash**: quickly.
rude: disordered, being loosely flowing.

Stanza 31

Suggested by Virgil, *Aen.* i 498–9: Dido approaches Aeneas
'even as on the banks of Eurotas or on the heights of Cynthus
Diana guides her bands', while he gazes upon the picture which
shows Penthesilea defending Troy (490–3).
2 **swift Eurotas**: swift from εὐροέω, to flow well.
3 **forlore**: left.
6 The story of Penthesilea's death by **Pyrrhus** follows
popular legend.

Stanza 32

7–9 Imitating Venus's address to Aeneas and Achates,
Aen. i 321–4, as Trompart's reply shows. Although no
analogy is intended between Trompart and Aeneas, there is an
analogy between Belphœbe and Venus-Virgo (see Wind, 1967,
77–80) as an emblem of the active life.
8 **stedfast**: steady.

Stanza 33

2–4 Echoes Aeneas's reply to Venus, *Aen.* i 327–8.
7 **thy goodlyhed**: a form of address.

Stanza 34

3 **vaine**: foolish; as Arg. 1. **mewed**: shut up as a hawk in
a cage; preparing for 'nest' (35.6) and the extended simile, 36.
4 **left**: lifted.
5 **towards**: in his direction.
6 **marke**: strike as a target. **stowre**: peril.

Stanza 35

2 **exercize**: use; or 'harass', if **them** refers to **game**.
4 **emprize**: chivalric enterprise.
9 **rowze**: combines several senses. Applied to a bird:
'ruffle the feathers' (of his crest); to a man: 'awaken from sleep';
to game: 'rise from cover'.

36

As fearefull fowle, that long in secret caue
    For dread of soaring hauke her selfe hath hid,
    Not caring how, her silly life to saue,
    She her gay painted plumes disorderid,
    Seeing at last her selfe from daunger rid,
    Peepes foorth, and soone renewes her natiue pride;
    She gins her feathers foule disfigured
Proudly to prune, and set on euery side,
So shakes off shame, ne thinks how erst she did her hide.

37

So when her goodly visage he beheld,
    He gan himselfe to vaunt: but when he vewed
    Those deadly tooles, which in her hand she held,
    Soone into other fits he was transmewed,
    Till she to him her gratious speach renewed;
    All haile, Sir knight, and well may thee befall,
    As all the like, which honour haue pursewed
Through deedes of armes and prowesse martiall;
All vertue merits praise, but such the most of all.

38

To whom he thus; O fairest vnder skie,
    True be thy words, and worthy of thy praise,
    That warlike feats doest highest glorifie.
    Therein haue I spent all my youthly daies,
    And many battailes fought, and many fraies
    Throughout the world, wher so they might be found,
    Endeuouring my dreadded name to raise
Aboue the Moone, that fame may it resound
In her eternall trompe, with laurell girland cround.

39

But what art thou, O Ladie, which doest raunge
    In this wilde forrest, where no pleasure is,
    And doest not it for ioyous court exchaunge,
    Emongst thine equall peres, where happie blis
    And all delight does raigne, much more then this?
    There thou maist loue, and dearely loued bee,
    And swim in pleasure, which thou here doest mis;
    There maist thou best be seene, and best maist see:
The wood is fit for beasts, the court is fit for thee.

40

Who so in pompe of proud estate (quoth she)
    Does swim, and bathes himselfe in courtly blis,
    Does waste his dayes in darke obscuritee,
    And in obliuion euer buried is:
    Where ease abounds, yt's eath to doe amis;
    But who his limbs with labours, and his mind
    Behaues with cares, cannot so easie mis.
Abroad in armes, at home in studious kind
Who seekes with painfull toile, shall honor soonest find.

41

In woods, in waues, in warres she wonts to dwell,
    And will be found with perill and with paine;
    Ne can the man, that moulds in idle cell,
    Vnto her happie mansion attaine:
    Before her gate high God did Sweat ordaine,
    And wakefull watches euer to abide:
    But easie is the way, and passage plaine
To pleasures pallace; it may soone be spide,
And day and night her dores to all stand open wide.

42

In Princes court, The rest she would haue said,
    But that the foolish man, fild with delight
    Of her sweet words, that all his sence dismaid,
    And with her wondrous beautie rauisht quight,
    Gan burne in filthy lust, and leaping light,
    Thought in his bastard armes her to embrace.
    With that she swaruing backe, her Iauelin bright
Against him bent, and fiercely did menace:
So turned her about, and fled away apace.

Stanza 36
3   **silly**: helpless.
7   **foule**: as the 'Peacocke' (6.4), 'Scarcrow' (7.1), and now
fearefull fowle (1), Braggadocchio deserves this pun.
8   **prune**: preen.

Stanza 37
2   **vaunt**: bear proudly.
3   **tooles**: weapons.
4   **transmewed**: changed; perhaps echoing 'mewed' (34.3),
noting his present transformation.

Stanza 38
2   **thy praise**: your own praiseworthiness; or, as Upton
(1758) suggests, 'he is worthy of your praise who, etc.',
including himself.
5   **fraies**: conflicts.
8   **Aboue the Moone**: asserting his superiority over the
Diana figure **vnder skie** (1); cf. Aeneas's boast to Venus:
fama super aethera notus (Virgil, *Aen.* i 379).

Stanza 39
7   **mis**: lack.

Stanza 40
The argument extends the familiar defence of the active life as
superior to the contemplative to include the life of the scholar-
poet. Ease results in true obscurity but **labours**, whether by the
active knight or contemplative scholar-poet, yield honour.
7   **Behaues**: regulates, governs.   **cares**: study, thought;
from Lat. *cura*, 'care, thought, studie' (Cooper, 1565).   **mis**:
err; or, referring to Braggadocchio's use of the term, 'lack
honour'.
8   **kind**: fashion, manner, referring to the life of the scholar.

Stanza 41
4   **mansion**: dwelling-place.
5   Gen. 3.19: 'In the sweat of thy face shalt thou eat bread,
til thou returne to the earth.'

Stanza 42
1   A diplomatic interruption: Belphœbe is about to identify
the **Princes court** with 'pleasures pallace' (41.8).
2–3   Not the sense of her words but only the sound; cf.
24.6–9. He understands honour only in the bawdy sense.
6   **bastard**: mean, base; as he is a spurious knight, a
'Peasant' (43.1).
7   **swaruing backe**: retreating.

43

Which when the Peasant saw, amazd he stood,
 And grieued at her flight; yet durst he not
 Pursew her steps, through wild vnknowen wood;
 Besides he feard her wrath, and threatned shot
 Whiles in the bush he lay, not yet forgot:
 Ne car'd he greatly for her presence vaine,
 But turning said to *Trompart*, What foule blot
 Is this to knight, that Ladie should againe
Depart to woods vntoucht, and leaue so proud disdaine?

44

Perdie (said *Trompart*) let her passe at will,
 Least by her presence daunger mote befall.
 For who càn tell (and sure I feare it ill)
 But that she is some powre celestiall?
 For whiles she spake, her great words did apall
 My feeble courage, and my hart oppresse,
 That yet I quake and tremble ouer all.
 And I (said *Braggadocchio*) thought no lesse,
When first I heard her horne sound with such ghastlinesse.

45

For from my mothers wombe this grace I haue
 Me giuen by eternall destinie,
 That earthly thing may not my courage braue
 Dismay with feare, or cause one foot to flie,
 But either hellish feends, or powres on hie:
 Which was the cause, when earst that horne I heard,
 Weening it had beene thunder in the skie,
 I hid my selfe from it, as one affeard;
But when I other knew, my selfe I boldly reard.

46

But now for feare of worse, that may betide,
 Let vs soone hence depart.   They soone agree;
 So to his steed he got, and gan to ride,
 As one vnfit therefore, that all might see
 He had not trayned bene in cheualree.
 Which well that valiant courser did discerne;
 For he despysd to tread in dew degree,
 But chaufd and fom'd, with courage fierce and sterne,
And to be easd of that base burden still did erne.

Cant. IIII.

Guyon does Furor bind in chaines,
and stops Occasion:
Deliuers Phedon, and therefore
by Strife is rayld vpon.

I

IN braue pursuit of honorable deed,
 There is I know not what great difference
 Betweene the vulgar and the noble seed,
 Which vnto things of valorous pretence
 Seemes to be borne by natiue influence;
 As feates of armes, and loue to entertaine,
 But chiefly skill to ride, seemes a science
 Proper to gentle bloud; some others faine
To menage steeds, as did this vaunter; but in vaine.

2

But he the rightfull owner of that steed,
 Who well could menage and subdew his pride,
 The whiles on foot was forced for to yeed,
 With that blacke Palmer, his most trusty guide;
 Who suffred not his wandring feet to slide.
 But when strong passion, or weake fleshlinesse
 Would from the right way seeke to draw him wide,
 He would through temperance and stedfastnesse,
Teach him the weake to strengthen, and the strong suppresse.

Stanza 43
1   **Peasant**: knave; a term of abuse.
6   **vaine**: i.e. useless to him because she rejects his assault,
or because he is unable, being base, 'loue to entertaine' (iv 1.6).
9   **vntoucht**: in the sexual sense, *intacta*; cf. IV vii 18.8.
His presumption is broadly humorous.

Stanza 44
9   **ghastlinesse**: terror induced by a spirit.

Stanza 45
Braggadocchio is a coward on instinct.
4   **one**] on *1590, 1596.*
5   **But**: i.e. unless it be.
9   **other**: otherwise.

Stanza 46
2   **soone**: without delay. Later S. wryly recalls how
Belphœbe 'made him fast out of the forrest runne' (III v 27.8).
4   **therefore**: for that.
5   **cheualree**: horsemanship.
7   **in dew degree**: 'with equall steps' (i 7.9).
9   **erne**: yearn.

Canto iv

Argument
3   **Phedon**] *Phaon 1590.* See 36.7*n*.

Stanza 1
On the inherent superiority of the well-born, see VI v 1–2*n*.
4   **pretence**: design; what may rightly claim to be valorous.
5   **natiue influence**: influence of the stars which presided
at birth.
6   **entertaine**: engage in.
9   **menage**: manège, direct a horse through its paces.

Stanza 2
3   **yeed**: go.
5   **slide**: slip; err morally.
6–9   The Mortdant-Amavia episode reveals the extremes of
strong passion and **weake fleshlinesse** in mortal nature; see
i 57. The latter refers to the weakness of the flesh generally:
'all flesh doth frailtie breed' (i 52.6). The extremes are controlled by **temperance** and **stedfastnesse** or fortitude, as
Hankins (1971) 15 notes, citing Francesco Piccolomini:
temperance controls the lusts of the concupiscible faculty of
the soul, fortitude the passions of the irascible faculty. See also
v 1.1–2, xii 29.6. Cf. the distinction between grief and fury in
the Phedon episode: see 33.4*n*.

3

It fortuned forth faring on his way,
  He saw from farre, or seemed for to see
  Some troublous vprore or contentious fray,
  Whereto he drew in haste it to agree.
  A mad man, or that feigned mad to bee,
  Drew by the haire along vpon the ground,
  A handsome stripling with great crueltee,
That cheekes with teares, and sides with bloud did all abound.

4

And him behind, a wicked Hag did stalke,
  In ragged robes, and filthy disaray,
  Her other leg was lame, that she no'te walke,
  But on a staffe her feeble steps did stay;
  Her lockes, that loathly were and hoarie gray,
  Grew all afore, and loosely hong vnrold,
  But all behind was bald, and worne away,
And eke her face ill fauourd, full of wrinckles old.

5

And euer as she went, her tongue did walke
  In foule reproch, and termes of vile despight,
  Prouoking him by her outrageous talke,
  To heape more vengeance on that wretched wight;
  Sometimes she raught him stones, wherwith to smite,
  Sometimes her staffe, though it her one leg were,
  Withouten which she could not go vpright;
Ne any euill meanes she did forbeare,
That might him moue to wrath, and indignation reare.

6

The noble *Guyon* mou'd with great remorse,
  Approching, first the Hag did thrust away,
  And after adding more impetuous forse,
  His mightie hands did on the madman lay,
  And pluckt him backe; who all on fire streight way,
  Against him turning all his fell intent,
  With beastly brutish rage gan him assay,
  And smot, and bit, and kickt, and scratcht, and rent,
And did he wist not what in his auengement.

7

And sure he was a man of mickle might,
  Had he had gouernance, it well to guide:
  But when the franticke fit inflamd his spright,
  His force was vaine, and strooke more often wide,
  Then at the aymed marke, which he had eide:
  And oft himselfe he chaunst to hurt vnwares,
  Whilst reason blent through passion, nought descride,
  But as a blindfold Bull at randon fares,   [nought cares.
And where he hits, nought knowes, and whom he hurts,

Stanza 3
2   **seemed for to see** indicates the allegorical nature of the encounter which projects mental and moral forces within Guyon.
4   **agree**: conciliate; a more active role than at ii 21.

Stanza 4
As always, S. allows the reader to recreate the image before divulging the name. Even though this minor classical deity had accumulated stock iconographical description, S.'s presentation remains highly individual. Traditionally she embodies the proverb, 'Take time (Occasion) by the forelock' (C. G. Smith, 1970, 777). Her hair hangs before her face so that she may not be recognized until she has passed; she is bald behind so that she cannot be grasped once she has passed. Here she is the occasion for wrath, providing both the cause and the opportunity for wrath to divert knights from achieving their quests. On the relation of S.'s figure to the traditional iconography, see McManaway (1934) and Alpers (1967) 209–14.
1   **stalke**: walk with stiff steps, as her lameness suggests; but also walk stealthily after game; cf. Orgoglio's stride, I vii 8.3.
3   **other leg**: one of her legs; or possibly the left or unlucky leg; cf. Impotence, xi 23.6.   **no'te**: could not.
4   **stay**: support.
5   See i 11.5n.

Stanza 5
1   **walke**: move briskly, in contrast to her feet.
5   **raught**: reached.
9   Wrong done to another is one occasion when wrath seems to be justified. Here **indignation** links Furor and Guyon. Cf. Guyon's 'fierce ire' and 'wrathfulnesse' (i 13.1 and 25.8) when he learns of Duessa's rape.   **reare**: arouse.

Stanza 6
1   **mou'd**: repeated from the previous line. In effect, Occasion has moved him to wrath and indignation.
remorse: pity, compassion.
4   **His mightie hands**: the psychological and physical nature of temperance is expressed through the power of the hand in contrast to holiness which depends upon spiritual armour. The encounter that follows connects Guyon with 'wrestler', one etymological significance of his name. See Proem 5.8n.
7   **assay**: attack.
9   **auengement**: vengeance; almost literally, 'vengeance that he meant to inflict'.

Stanza 7
2   **gouernance**: self-control; see i 29.8n.
5   **eide**: aimed at.
7   **blent**: blinded; cf. 'The eye of reason was with rage yblent' (I ii 5.7).
8   **at randon**: heedlessly; suggesting speed and violence.

8

His rude assault and rugged handeling
  Straunge seemed to the knight, that aye with foe
  In faire defence and goodly menaging
  Of armes was wont to fight, yet nathemoe
  Was he abashed now not fighting so,
  But more enfierced through his currish play,
  Him sternely grypt, and haling to and fro,
  To ouerthrow him strongly did assay,
But ouerthrew himselfe vnwares, and lower lay.

9

And being downe the villein sore did beat,
  And bruze with clownish fistes his manly face:
  And eke the Hag with many a bitter threat,
  Still cald vpon to kill him in the place.
  With whose reproch and odious menace
  The knight emboyling in his haughtie hart,
  Knit all his forces, and gan soone vnbrace
  His grasping hold: so lightly did vpstart,
And drew his deadly weapon, to maintaine his part.

10

Which when the Palmer saw, he loudly cryde,
  Not so, O *Guyon*, neuer thinke that so
  That Monster can be maistred or destroyd:
  He is not, ah, he is not such a foe,
  As steele can wound, or strength can ouerthroe.
  That same is *Furor*, cursed cruell wight,
  That vnto knighthood workes much shame and woe;
  And that same Hag, his aged mother, hight
Occasion, the root of all wrath and despight.

11

With her, who so will raging *Furor* tame,
  Must first begin, and well her amenage:
  First her restraine from her reprochfull blame,
  And euill meanes, with which she doth enrage
  Her franticke sonne, and kindles his courage,
  Then when she is withdrawen, or strong withstood,
  It's eath his idle furie to asswage,
  And calme the tempest of his passion wood;
The bankes are ouerflowen, when stopped is the flood.

12

Therewith Sir *Guyon* left his first emprise,
  And turning to that woman, fast her hent
  By the hoare lockes, that hong before her eyes,
  And to the ground her threw: yet n'ould she stent
  Her bitter rayling and foule reuilement,
  But still prouokt her sonne to wreake her wrong;
  But nathelesse he did her still torment,
  And catching hold of her vngratious tong,
Thereon an yron lock did fasten firme and strong.

13

Then when as vse of speach was from her reft,
  With her two crooked handes she signes did make,
  And beckned him, the last helpe she had left:
  But he that last left helpe away did take,
  And both her hands fast bound vnto a stake,
  That she note stirre. Then gan her sonne to flie
  Full fast away, and did her quite forsake;
  But *Guyon* after him in haste did hie,
And soone him ouertooke in sad perplexitie.

14

In his strong armes he stiffely him embraste,
  Who him gainstriuing, nought at all preuaild:
  For all his power was vtterly defaste,
  And furious fits at earst quite weren quaild:
  Oft he re'nforst, and oft his forces fayld,
  Yet yield he would not, nor his rancour slacke.
  Then him to ground he cast, and rudely hayld,
  And both his hands fast bound behind his backe,
And both his feet in fetters to an yron racke.

Stanza 8
3 **goodly menaging**: fighting according to rule, or with arms.
4 **nathemoe**: not at all.
6 **more enfierced**: made more fierce, thus sharing Furor's wrath.
9 In this *psychomachia*, Guyon overthrows himself, as Furor who 'oft himselfe . . . chaunst to hurt vnwares' (7.6).

Stanza 9
2 **clownish**: coarse, rustic, as opposed to **manly**.
4 **in the place**: on the spot, at once.
6 **emboyling**: boiling with rage. Later Guyon advises Pyrochles to 'quench thy whot emboyling wrath' (v 18.5).

Stanza 10
6 **Furor**: personifying **wrath and despight** (9) or any emotion whose unchecked raging is a kind of madness.

Stanza 11
Cf. 2 Cor. 11.12: 'Cut away occasion from them which desire occasion.'
2 **amenage**: control; from manège, controlling a horse through its paces. See 1.9, 2.2.
5 **courage**: anger.
8 **passion wood**: mad outburst of anger.
9 **The bankes are ouerflowen . . .**: i.e. to stop Furor only increases his fury, as a river overflows when it is dammed. He may be controlled only when the 'root' (10.9) or source of his wrath is stopped.

Stanza 12
1 **emprise**: undertaking.
2–3 Guyon obeys the proverb 'to take time by the forelock'.
4 **n'ould**: would not.
8 **vngratious**: rude, both wicked in itself and denying grace in others. She wears the scold's bridle; see Isaiah 37.29.

Stanza 13
6 **note**: could not; knew not how to.
9 **perplexitie**: distress.

Stanza 14
2 **gainstriuing**: striving against.
3 **defaste**: destroyed.
4 **at earst**: at once.   **quaild**: subdued.
5 **re'nforst**: renewed his force.

201

15

With hundred yron chaines he did him bind,
　And hundred knots that did him sore constraine:
　Yet his great yron teeth he still did grind,
　And grimly gnash, threatning reuenge in vaine;
　His burning eyen, whom bloudie strakes did staine,
Stared full wide, and threw forth sparkes of fire,
　And more for ranck despight, then for great paine,
　Shakt his long lockes, coloured like copper-wire,
And bit his tawny beard to shew his raging ire.

16

Thus when as *Guyon Furor* had captiu'd,
　Turning about he saw that wretched Squire,
　Whom that mad man of life nigh late depriu'd,
　Lying on ground, all soild with bloud and mire:
　Whom when as he perceiued to respire,
He gan to comfort, and his wounds to dresse.
　Being at last recured, he gan inquire,
　What hard mishap him brought to such distresse,
And made that caitiues thral, the thral of wretchednesse.

17

With hart then throbbing, and with watry eyes,
　Faire Sir (quoth he) what man can shun the hap,
　That hidden lyes vnwares him to surpryse?
　Misfortune waites aduantage to entrap
　The man most warie in her whelming lap.
So me weake wretch, of many weakest one,
　Vnweeting, and vnware of such mishap,
　She brought to mischiefe through occasion,
Where this same wicked villein did me light vpon.

18

It was a faithlesse Squire, that was the sourse
　Of all my sorrow, and of these sad teares,
　With whom from tender dug of commune nourse,
　Attonce I was vpbrought, and eft when yeares
　More rype vs reason lent to chose our Peares,
Our selues in league of vowed loue we knit:
　In which we long time without gealous feares,
　Or faultie thoughts continewd, as was fit;
And for my part I vow, dissembled not a whit.

19

It was my fortune commune to that age,
　To loue a Ladie faire of great degree,
　The which was borne of noble parentage,
　And set in highest seat of dignitee,
　Yet seemd no lesse to loue, then loued to bee:
Long I her seru'd, and found her faithfull still,
　Ne euer thing could cause vs disagree:
　Loue that two harts makes one, makes eke one will:
Each stroue to please, and others pleasure to fulfill.

20

My friend, hight *Philemon*, I did partake
　Of all my loue and all my priuitie;
　Who greatly ioyous seemed for my sake,
　And gratious to that Ladie, as to mee,
　Ne euer wight, that mote so welcome bee,
As he to her, withouten blot or blame,
　Ne euer thing, that she could thinke or see,
　But vnto him she would impart the same:
O wretched man, that would abuse so gentle Dame.

Stanza 15

1–2　As Furor is bound in Virgil, *Aen.* i 294–6, by a
hundred knots.
6　**Stared**: opened wide in fury; shone: cf. Mammon's
fiends, vii 37.6, and the lustful Argante: 'Her firie eyes with
furious sparkes did stare' (III vii 39.8). The eyes reveal an
inner burning that may not be quenched.
7　**ranck**: excessive.
8–9　Red hair is commonly associated with anger; cf.
Pyrochles's steed, v 2.8.

Stanza 16

4　**soild**: see i 41.1*n*.

Stanza 17

4　**waites aduantage**: watches for the opportunity or
occasion.
5　**whelming lap**: cf. the common phrase, 'fall into the lap
of'.　lap may carry the common bawdy sense, as v 36.3.
8　**mischiefe**: misfortune, evil plight.

Stanzas 18–36

The source is the story of Ariodante and Ginevra in Ariosto,
Orl. Fur. v 5–74. Bullough (1958) ii 533 lists almost a dozen
adaptations of the story up to 1590. S. uses the story to explore
the effects of intemperate passions. For a comparison with the
source, see Alpers (1967) 54–69. The story parallels the
opening episode of the Book, the false tale of the 'violated'
Duessa, which led Guyon into intemperance.

Stanza 18

4　**eft**: afterwards.

Stanza 20

1　**My friend . . . Philemon**: i.e. φιλη + ὲ μου.　**partake**:
inform, make partaker.
2　**priuitie**: personal affairs.
9　**abuse**: malign, revile, suggested by Occasion's 'foule
reuilement' (12.5; cf. 5.2); but also 'violate': cf. 24.9, 27.9. The
theme of the violated body, introduced by Archimago's lying
tale (cf. i 19.3) is central to the virtue of temperance which
establishes the unviolated and inviolable body.

21

At last such grace I found, and meanes I wrought,
  That I that Ladie to my spouse had wonne;
  Accord of friends, consent of parents sought,
  Affiance made, my happinesse begonne,
  There wanted nought but few rites to be donne,
  Which mariage make; that day too farre did seeme:
  Most ioyous man, on whom the shining Sunne
  Did shew his face, my selfe I did esteeme,
And that my falser friend did no lesse ioyous deeme.

22

But ere that wished day his beame disclosd,
  He either enuying my toward good,
  Or of himselfe to treason ill disposd,
  One day vnto me came in friendly mood,
  And told for secret how he vnderstood
  That Ladie whom I had to me assynd,
  Had both distaind her honorable blood,
  And eke the faith, which she to me did bynd;
And therfore wisht me stay, till I more truth should fynd.

23

The gnawing anguish and sharpe gelosy,
  Which his sad speech infixed in my brest,
  Ranckled so sore, and festred inwardly,
  That my engreeued mind could find no rest,
  Till that the truth thereof I did outwrest,
  And him besought by that same sacred band
  Betwixt vs both, to counsell me the best.
  He then with solemne oath and plighted hand
Assur'd, ere long the truth to let me vnderstand.

24

Ere long with like againe he boorded mee,
  Saying, he now had boulted all the floure,
  And that it was a groome of base degree,
  Which of my loue was partner Paramoure:
  Who vsed in a darkesome inner bowre
  Her oft to meet: which better to approue,
  He promised to bring me at that howre,
  When I should see, that would me nearer moue,
And driue me to withdraw my blind abused loue.

25

This gracelesse man for furtherance of his guile,
  Did court the handmayd of my Lady deare,
  Who glad t'embosome his affection vile,
  Did all she might, more pleasing to appeare.
  One day to worke her to his will more neare,
  He woo'd her thus: *Pryene* (so she hight)
  What great despight doth fortune to thee beare,
  Thus lowly to abase thy beautie bright,
That it should not deface all others lesser light?

26

But if she had her least helpe to thee lent,
  T'adorne thy forme according thy desart,
  Their blazing pride thou wouldest soone haue blent,
  And staynd their prayses with thy least good part;
  Ne should faire *Claribell* with all her art,
  Though she thy Lady be, approch thee neare:
  For proofe thereof, this euening, as thou art,
  Aray thy selfe in her most gorgeous geare,
That I may more delight in thy embracement deare.

27

The Maiden proud through prayse, and mad through loue
  Him hearkned to, and soone her selfe arayd,
  The whiles to me the treachour did remoue
  His craftie engin, and as he had sayd,
  Me leading, in a secret corner layd,
  The sad spectatour of my Tragedie;
  Where left, he went, and his owne false part playd,
  Disguised like that groome of base degree,
Whom he had feignd th'abuser of my loue to bee.

Stanza 21
1   grace: favour.
4   Affiance: betrothal.
5–6   **Which mariage make**: cf. *Epith.* 216–7: 'The sacred ceremonies . . . which do endlesse matrimony make.' make: be the essential criterion of (*OED* 24). Wickert (1968) 138 notes that S. 'thinks of the Rite of Matrimony as somehow essentially constituting the Estate and Perpetuity of Marriage'.
9   that: i.e. the marriage day.   falser: most false.

Stanza 22
2   toward: coming.
6   assynd: appointed, chosen (for marriage); a legal sense.
7   distaind: defiled.

Stanza 23
5   outwrest: draw out.
8   plighted hand: pledge sworn by the clasping of hands; friendship takes the place of marriage.
9   Assur'd: pledged.

Stanza 24
1   boorded: accosted, addressed.
2   Proverbial.   boulted: sifted.
3   Class distinctions are important here. Phedon is a 'Squire' (33.8); a **groome of base degree** is linked with a lady 'of great degree' (19.2).
6   approue: show to be true.
8   nearer moue: affect more deeply.

Stanza 25
3   embosome: cherish; literally, 'fix in the bosom'.
6   Pryene: suggesting fire (Gk πυρ) as she is 'mad through loue' (27.1) and the cause of wrathful fire in Phedon.
9   deface: outshine, and therefore disfigure; alluding to the etymology of Claribell.

Stanza 26
3   blent: blinded; blemished.
4   staynd: eclipsed; defaced; continuing the image of 25.9.
5   Claribell: famous or bright in beauty (Lat. *clara+bella*); cf. her namesake, VI xii 3.9.
7   as thou art: as you truly are.

Stanza 27
3   treachour: traitor, suggesting 'treacherous'.   **did remoue**: moved again; cf. 24.1.
4   engin: plot.

28

Eftsoones he came vnto th'appointed place,
  And with him brought *Pryene*, rich arayd,
  In *Claribellaes* clothes. Her proper face
  I not descerned in that darkesome shade,
  But weend it was my loue, with whom he playd.
  Ah God, what horrour and tormenting griefe
  My hart, my hands, mine eyes, and all assayd?
  Me liefer were ten thousand deathes priefe,
Then wound of gealous worme, and shame of such repriefe.

29

I home returning, fraught with fowle despight,
  And chawing vengeance all the way I went,
  Soone as my loathed loue appeard in sight,
  With wrathfull hand I slew her innocent;
  That after soone I dearely did lament:
  For when the cause of that outrageous deede
  Demaunded, I made plaine and euident,
  Her faultie Handmayd, which that bale did breede,
Confest, how *Philemon* her wrought to chaunge her weede.

30

Which when I heard, with horrible affright
  And hellish fury all enragd, I sought
  Vpon my selfe that vengeable despight
  To punish: yet it better first I thought,
  To wreake my wrath on him, that first it wrought.
  To *Philemon*, false faytour *Philemon*
  I cast to pay, that I so dearely bought;
  Of deadly drugs I gaue him drinke anon,
And washt away his guilt with guiltie potion.

31

Thus heaping crime on crime, and griefe on griefe,
  To losse of loue adioyning losse of frend,
  I meant to purge both with a third mischiefe,
  And in my woes beginner it to end:
  That was *Pryene*; she did first offend,
  She last should smart: with which cruell intent,
  When I at her my murdrous blade did bend,
  She fled away with ghastly dreriment,
And I pursewing my fell purpose, after went.

32

Feare gaue her wings, and rage enforst my flight;
  Through woods and plaines so long I did her chace,
  Till this mad man, whom your victorious might
  Hath now fast bound, me met in middle space,
  As I her, so he me pursewd apace,
  And shortly ouertooke: I, breathing yre,
  Sore chauffed at my stay in such a cace,
  And with my heat kindled his cruell fyre;
Which kindled once, his mother did more rage inspyre.

33

Betwixt them both, they haue me doen to dye,
  Through wounds, and strokes, and stubborne handeling,
  That death were better, then such agony,
  As griefe and furie vnto me did bring;
  Of which in me yet stickes the mortall sting,
  That during life will neuer be appeasd.
  When he thus ended had his sorrowing,
  Said *Guyon*, Squire, sore haue ye beene diseasd;
But all your hurts may soone through temperance be easd.

34

Then gan the Palmer thus, Most wretched man,
  That to affections does the bridle lend;
  In their beginning they are weake and wan,
  But soone through suffrance grow to fearefull end;
  Whiles they are weake betimes with them contend:
  For when they once to perfect strength do grow,
  Strong warres they make, and cruell battry bend
  Gainst fort of Reason, it to ouerthrow:
Wrath, gelosie, griefe, loue this Squire haue layd thus low.

Stanza 28

3   **proper**: own.
7   **assayd**: assailed.
8   **priefe**: proof, experience.
9   **gealous worme**: the serpent of jealousy; hence 'sharpe gelosy' (23.1).   **repriefe**: disgrace.

Stanza 29

2   **chawing**: meditating, the fig. sense, is secondary to the physical sense; cf. jealousy in Envy (I iv 30.2–3), Malbecco (III x 18.1), and Britomart (V vi 19.2).
5   **That**: i.e. that action.
8   **faultie**: guilty of wrong-doing.

Stanza 30

1   **affright**: terror.
3   **vengeable despight**: cruel outrage (cf. 46.2) or outrage that demands vengeance.
6   **faytour**: impostor.

Stanza 31

2   **adioyning**: adding.
8   **ghastly dreriment**: fearful horror.

Stanza 32

1   **enforst**: gave fresh vigour to; compelled.
4   **in middle space**: where the temperate mean may be asserted; see ii 20.3*n*.
7   **stay**: hindrance.
9   **inspyre**: blow into.

Stanza 33

2   **stubborne**: fierce.
4   **griefe and furie**: cf. the grief and anger which Guyon restrains at the loss of his horse (iii 3.4); see also i 57–58, vi 1.6–7, and viii 33.1–2.
5   **mortall**: deadly, belonging to man; cf. the Dragon's 'mortall sting' (I xi 38.5 and see *n*).
8   **diseasd**: tormented.
9   Guyon may dress his wounds (see 16.6) but not cure them; cf. Amavia's vain efforts to cure concupiscence in Mortdant by 'faire gouernance' (i 54.6).

Stanza 34

2   **affections**: passions, violent emotions.   **bridle**: a traditional emblem of temperance; cf. xii 53.5.
4   **suffrance**: being permitted; also passivity.
5   **betimes**: speedily.
7–8   Cf. xi 1.1–4.

35

Wrath, gealosie, griefe, loue do thus expell:
  Wrath is a fire, and gealosie a weede,
  Griefe is a flood, and loue a monster fell;
  The fire of sparkes, the weede of little seede,
  The flood of drops, the Monster filth did breede:
  But sparks, seed, drops, and filth do thus delay;
  The sparks soone quench, the springing seed outweed,
  The drops dry vp, and filth wipe cleane away:
So shall wrath, gealosie, griefe, loue dye and decay.

36

Vnlucky Squire (said *Guyon*) sith thou hast
  Falne into mischiefe through intemperaunce,
  Henceforth take heede of that thou now hast past,
  And guide thy wayes with warie gouernaunce,
  Least worse betide thee by some later chaunce.
  But read how art thou nam'd, and of what kin.
  Phedon I hight (quoth he) and do aduaunce
  Mine auncestry from famous *Coradin*,
Who first to rayse our house to honour did begin.

37

Thus as he spake, lo far away they spyde
  A varlet running towards hastily,
  Whose flying feet so fast their way applyde,
  That round about a cloud of dust did fly,
  Which mingled all with sweate, did dim his eye.
  He soone approched, panting, breathlesse, whot,
  And all so soyld, that none could him descry;
  His countenaunce was bold, and bashed not
For *Guyons* lookes, but scornefull eyglaunce at him shot.

38

Behind his backe he bore a brasen shield,
  On which was drawen faire, in colours fit,
  A flaming fire in midst of bloudy field,
  And round about the wreath this word was writ,
  Burnt I do burne. Right well beseemed it,
  To be the shield of some redoubted knight;
  And in his hand two darts exceeding flit,
  And deadly sharpe he held, whose heads were dight
In poyson and in bloud, of malice and despight.

39

When he in presence came, to *Guyon* first
  He boldly spake, Sir knight, if knight thou bee,
  Abandon this forestalled place at erst,
  For feare of further harme, I counsell thee,
  Or bide the chaunce at thine owne ieoperdie.
  The knight at his great boldnesse wondered,
  And though he scornd his idle vanitie,
  Yet mildly him to purpose answered;
For not to grow of nought he it coniectured.

Stanza 35
Quoted by Fraunce, *Arcadian Rhetorike* (1588) to illustrate
'conceited verses'. Specifically, it is correlative verse arranged
as follows: I (1) the four passions ordered to be expelled, (2–3)
their naming by comparisons, (4–5) their sources; II (6) the
four sources ordered to be expelled, (7–8) the means
catalogued; III (9) resolution with the concluding declaration.
The four passions form interlocked pairs. On **wrath and
griefe**, see 33.4*n*.
3 On love as a **monster**, see III xi 51.7–9.
5 Cf. the 'monstrous shapes' bred from the mud of the Nile,
I i 21.6–9; cf. also the Dragon, I vii 17.3.
6 **delay**: allay; remove.

Stanza 36
2 **mischiefe**: misfortune; evil plight, as 17.8.
4 **gouernaunce**: self-control, wise behaviour, as i 29.8.
5 John 5.14: 'Sinne no more, lest a worse thing come unto
thee.' **chaunce** refers to Occasion.
6 **read**: tell.
7 **Phedon**] *Phaon* 1590, 'the name of a fayre yonge man'
(Cooper, 1565); hence 'A handsome stripling' (3.7). It is the
name of the boatman of Mitylene to whom Aphrodite gave
youth and beauty. Cf. the temperate boatman at xii 21. Belson
(1964) suggests the root φαος, fire, alluding to the wrathful fire
which overcomes him. For **Phedon**, Blitch (1965) 73 suggests
an ironic reference to Lat. *fido*. Alpers (1967) 69 notes that he is
named after he has been restored to humanity. **aduaunce**:
claim; boast.
8 **Coradin**: Lat. *cor*, heart + Gk αδυναμια, want of power;
hence uncontrollable or turbulent spirit, the source of
Phedon's intemperate nature (Belson).

Stanza 37
2 **varlet**: an attendant upon a knight; a Squire.
5 **his eye**: his countenance or the sight of him, as 7.
Perhaps an oblique allusion to Homer's Ate (see 42.5*n*) who
blinds men as she moves swiftly above their heads.
7 **soyld**: see i 41.1*n*.
8 **bashed**: daunted; literally, he did not lower his eyes.

Stanza 38
1 **brasen**: noting its indestructibility, as the unquenchable
fire which it bears. In Cupid's masque, III xii 12.8, Fear bears a
brazen shield.
3–4 **field**: in heraldry, the shield's surface. **wreath**: an
ornamental band bearing the motto of the *impresa*. **word**:
motto. It is literally fulfilled at vi 44.
7–9 Each dart is double-pronged; cf. 'forckhead' (46.8).
flit: swift. **dight**: prepared, i.e. dipped. **poyson and
bloud** refer to man's infected will which leads to the irascible
passions.

Stanza 39
3–6 Atin tests Guyon's advice to Phedon (36.3–5).
forestalled: taken beforehand, the 'middle space' (32.4)
claimed by Furor and now by Pyrochles, but which Guyon
must claim for temperance; cf. 'this fearefull stead' (42.8).
at erst: at once.
7 **idle**: empty, related to the etymology of **vanitie** (Lat.
vanus).
8 **mildly**: demonstrating his control over Furor. **to
purpose**: to the point at issue.

40

Varlet, this place most dew to me I deeme,
　Yielded by him, that held it forcibly.
　But whence should come that harme, which thou doest seeme
　To threat to him, that minds his chaunce t'abye?
　Perdy (said he) here comes, and is hard by
　A knight of wondrous powre, and great assay,
　That neuer yet encountred enemy,
　But did him deadly daunt, or fowle dismay;
Ne thou for better hope, if thou his presence stay.

41

How hight he then (said *Guyon*) and from whence?
　Pyrochles is his name, renowmed farre
　For his bold feats and hardy confidence,
　Full oft approu'd in many a cruell warre,
　The brother of *Cymochles*, both which arre
　The sonnes of old *Acrates* and *Despight*,
　Acrates sonne of *Phlegeton* and *Iarre*;
　But *Phlegeton* is sonne of *Herebus* and *Night*;
But *Herebus* sonne of *Aeternitie* is hight.

42

So from immortall race he does proceede,
　That mortall hands may not withstand his might,
　Drad for his derring do, and bloudy deed;
　For all in bloud and spoile is his delight.
　His am I *Atin*, his in wrong and right,
　That matter make for him to worke vpon,
　And stirre him vp to strife and cruell fight.
　Fly therefore, fly this fearefull stead anon,
Least thy foolhardize worke thy sad confusion.

43

His be that care, whom most it doth concerne,
　(Said he) but whither with such hasty flight
　Art thou now bound? for well mote I discerne
　Great cause, that carries thee so swift and light.
　My Lord (quoth he) me sent, and streight behight
　To seeke *Occasion*, where so she bee:
　For he is all disposd to bloudy fight,
　And breathes out wrath and hainous crueltie;
Hard is his hap, that first fals in his ieopardie.

Stanza 40
4　that minds . . . t'abye: i.e. who intends to 'bide the
chaunce' (39.5).
6　assay: proven worth.
8　deadly daunt: vanquish by death.
9　stay: await.

Stanza 41
The nature of each character is revealed by name and
genealogy. The relation of **Pyrochles** to **Cymochles** is
suggested by a Latin poem addressed to Harvey in which S.
refers to the safe middle road between the two extremes where
'here the wave would overwhelm, there the fire consume you'
(*Poet. Wks* 637; see *Var. Prose Wks* 257). **Pyrochles**: πυρ,
fire + ὀχλεω, to disturb, cause annoyance, or κλεος, fame,
glory. He represents anger; or the fiery temper, troubled
himself and troubling others; or the fiery temper that seeks
fame. In this latter role he parodies '*Prays-desire*' in Arthur,
ix 39.8. 'Pyrrhochles' is the spelling in both the *1590* and *1596*
editions. **Cymochles**: κυμα, wave, indicates his unstable
nature: he moves between wrath and lust; cf. Chapman's
'moist man . . . / That's ever flitting, ever ravishing' (*Ody*. vi
311–2), derived from Spondanus's mistranslation *humidus
homo*: see Lord (1956) 93–4. Gilbert, *Var*. ii 231, noting
that Cymochles is often associated with fire, derives his name
from καυμα, burning, glow. Similarly, Pyrochles is first
described in terms of light 'Vpon the trembling waue' (v 2.5).
But S.'s allusions are as popular as they are learned: cf. the
proverb 'as false as water, as rash as fire' (cf. Tilley, 1950, W 86).
Together the brothers embody the two median and warring
elements, fire and water, and represent the irascible and concupiscent parts of the soul. See Hieatt (1975) 176, 184–5. On the
brothers as humours, see Berger (1957) 59–61. Fowler (1964) 11
notes that 'the fact that Guyon's double enemies are dualities
resident in fallen human nature itself makes it difficult to
describe them adequately as Aristotelian moral extremes'. On
their relation, see James 4.1: 'From whence are warres and
contentions among you? are they not hence, even of your
lustes, that fight in your members?' Their lack of control
over their elements is inherited from **Acrates**, Gk
Intemperance: see i 51.2–4n. The elements themselves are
derived from **Phlegeton**, the infernal river of burning fire
(see I v 33.1–6n).
3　**confidence**: fearlessness; overboldness.
4　**approu'd**: tested.
6　**Despight**: Ital. *dispetto*, malice or anger; cf. 38.9, etc.
7　**Iarre**: discord, dissent.
8–9　**Herebus**: the lowest region of hell or the god of
darkness. At III iv 55.7–8 he is addressed as the husband of
Night and 'the foe / Of all the Gods'. Among their offspring
are the Fates; see Starnes and Talbert (1955) 356. The double
alexandrine emphasizes the genealogy.

Stanza 42
3　**derring do**: daring deeds, 'manhoode and cheualrie'
(E. K.'s gloss to *S.C.* Oct. 65).
5　**Atin**: Gk Ἀτη, Strife (as Arg.), the goddess of mischief in
Homer, *Iliad* xix 91–3; cf. the account of Ate at IV i 19.1–4.
Hieatt (1957) derives the name from O. F. *atine*: provocation,
defiance. The name is linked also with 'tine', trouble, suffering,
a variant of 'teen', as at I ix 15.7, and with 'tynd', inflamed; see
viii 11.4–5n. Steinberg (1971) 750 derives the name from the
anglicized Irish *athainne*, embers, or Irish *aithinne*, firebrand.
5–7　The role of Occasion: see 5.3–9.
8　**stead**: place.
9　**foolhardize**: foolhardiness, as ii 17.7.　**confusion**: ruin.

Stanza 43
5　**behight**: commanded.

44

Madman (said then the Palmer) that does seeke
   Occasion to wrath, and cause of strife;
   She comes vnsought, and shonned followes eke.
   Happy, who can abstaine, when Rancour rife
   Kindles Reuenge, and threats his rusty knife;
   Woe neuer wants, where euery cause is caught,
   And rash *Occasion* makes vnquiet life.
   Then loe, where bound she sits, whom thou hast sought,
(Said *Guyon*,) let that message to thy Lord be brought.

45

That when the varlet heard and saw, streight way
   He wexed wondrous wroth, and said, Vile knight,
   That knights and knighthood doest with shame vpbray,
   And shewst th'ensample of thy childish might,
   With silly weake old woman thus to fight.
   Great glory and gay spoile sure hast thou got,
   And stoutly prou'd thy puissaunce here in sight;
   That shall *Pyrochles* well requite, I wot,
And with thy bloud abolish so reprochfull blot.

46

With that one of his thrillant darts he threw,
   Headed with ire and vengeable despight;
   The quiuering steele his aymed end well knew,
   And to his brest it selfe intended right:
   But he was warie, and ere it empight
   In the meant marke, aduaunst his shield atweene,
   On which it seizing, no way enter might,
   But backe rebounding, left the forckhead keene;
Eftsoones he fled away, and might no where be seene.

Cant. V.

Pyrochles does with Guyon fight,
   And Furors chayne vnbinds:
Of whom sore hurt, for his reuenge
   Atin Cymochles finds.

1

WHo euer doth to temperaunce apply
   His stedfast life, and all his actions frame,
   Trust me, shall find no greater enimy,
   Then stubborne perturbation, to the same;
   To which right well the wise do giue that name,
   For it the goodly peace of stayed mindes
   Does ouerthrow, and troublous warre proclame:
   His owne woes authour, who so bound it findes,
As did *Pyrochles*, and it wilfully vnbinds.

2

After that varlets flight, it was not long,
   Ere on the plaine fast pricking *Guyon* spide
   One in bright armes embatteiled full strong,
   That as the Sunny beames do glaunce and glide
   Vpon the trembling waue, so shined bright,
   And round about him threw forth sparkling fire,
   That seemd him to enflame on euery side:
   His steed was bloudy red, and fomed ire,
When with the maistring spur he did him roughly stire.

Stanza 44
5   **rusty**: rusty with blood.
6   'A fine transmutation of the traditional moral of Occasion and her forelock' (Alpers, 1967, 232).

Stanza 45
2–7   Modelled on Juno's mockery of Venus and Aeneas for subduing Dido, *Aen.* iv 93–5. Atin's mockery is well-directed and extends to Guyon's quest to capture Acrasia; cf. Pyrochles's reproach, v 5.3–7.
3   **vpbray**: upbraid, bring reproach on.
5   **silly**: helpless.

Stanza 46
1   **thrillant**: piercing.
2   Cf. 38.8–9.
4   **intended**: made its way.
5   **empight**: implanted itself.
6   Cf. Eph. 6.16: 'Above all, take the shield of faith, wherewith ye may quench all the fyrie dartes of the wicked.'
8   The shaft rebounds while the head remains stuck on the shield.

Canto v

Argument
2–4   **vnbinds . . . Cymochles finds]** *vntyes | Who him sore wounds, whiles Atin to | Cymochles for ayd flyes 1590.* See 19.1, 25.8–9. The revision extends the action beyond stanza 25 to the discovery of Cymochles in the Bower of Bliss; **reuenge** better defines the aid which Atin seeks: see stanza 36.

Stanza 1
1–2   On the distinction between temperance and steadfastness, see iv 2.6–9*n*.
4   **stubborne**: fierce, implacable.
5   The **wise** include Cicero: in *De Fin.* III x, he names four kinds of perturbations, which Upton (1758) distributes among characters in Book II: sorrow in Amavia, fearfulness in Braggadocchio, lasciviousness in Cymochles, and idle pleasure in Phædria.
6–7   For it . . . / Does ouerthrow: alluding to the etymology of **perturbation** (4): Lat. *turbare*, to trouble, confuse.
stayed: staid, steadfast.

Stanza 2
3   **embatteiled**: armed for battle.
4–7   Pyrochles's nature is expressed through this image of fire in motion. To describe his perturbation in 4–5, S. wittily adapts a pun in Scripture: 'He that wavereth is like a wave of the sea' (James 1.6).
9   **stire**: incite.

3

Approching nigh, he neuer stayd to greete,
　Ne chaffar words, prowd courage to prouoke,
　But prickt so fiers, that vnderneath his feete
　The smouldring dust did round about him smoke,
　Both horse and man nigh able for to choke;
　And fairly couching his steele-headed speare,
　Him first saluted with a sturdy stroke;
　It booted nought Sir *Guyon* comming neare
To thinke, such hideous puissaunce on foot to beare.

4

But lightly shunned it, and passing by,
　With his bright blade did smite at him so fell,
　That the sharpe steele arriuing forcibly
　On his broad shield, bit not, but glauncing fell
　On his horse necke before the quilted sell,
　And from the head the body sundred quight.
　So him dismounted low, he did compell
　On foot with him to matchen equall fight;
The truncked beast fast bleeding, did him fowly dight.

5

Sore bruzed with the fall, he slow vprose,
　And all enraged, thus him loudly shent;
　Disleall knight, whose coward courage chose
　To wreake it selfe on beast all innocent,
　And shund the marke, at which it should be ment,
　Thereby thine armes seeme strong, but manhood fraile;
　So hast thou oft with guile thine honour blent;
　But litle may such guile thee now auaile,
If wonted force and fortune do not much me faile.

6

With that he drew his flaming sword, and strooke
　At him so fiercely, that the vpper marge
　Of his seuenfolded shield away it tooke,
　And glauncing on his helmet, made a large
　And open gash therein: were not his targe,
　That broke the violence of his intent,
　The weary soule from thence it would discharge;
　Nathelesse so sore a buff to him it lent,
That made him reele, and to his brest his beuer bent.

7

Exceeding wroth was *Guyon* at that blow,
　And much ashamd, that stroke of liuing arme
　Should him dismay, and make him stoup so low,
　Though otherwise it did him litle harme:
　Tho hurling high his yron braced arme,
　He smote so manly on his shoulder plate,
　That all his left side it did quite disarme;
　Yet there the steele stayd not, but inly bate
Deepe in his flesh, and opened wide a red floodgate.

8

Deadly dismayd, with horrour of that dint
　Pyrochles was, and grieued eke entyre;
　Yet nathemore did it his fury stint,
　But added flame vnto his former fire,
　That welnigh molt his hart in raging yre,
　Ne thenceforth his approued skill, to ward,
　Or strike, or hurtle round in warlike gyre,
　Remembred he, ne car'd for his saufgard,
But rudely rag'd, and like a cruell Tygre far'd.

Stanza 3
2　chaffar: exchange. On Guyon's failure to offer the usual challenge before an encounter, see i 29.6*n*. In similar fashion, Pyrochles does not defy Arthur; see viii 30.5–7, 31.6–9.
4　smouldring: suffocating. The line develops iv 37.3–5 which describes Atin's approach: Pyrochles follows in his steps.
7　sturdy: violent.

Stanza 4
6　An obvious but necessary symbolic act in a book of Temperance; cf. IV vi 13.6–9.
9　truncked: truncated.　**him**: Pyrochles, but possibly Guyon.　**dight**: soil, defile.

Stanza 5
2　shent: reproached; (verbally) defiled; cf. i 11.2.
3–7　Galahad was shamed when he smote off the head of Palomydes's horse by accident (Malory 656); cf. Atin's charge against Guyon's knighthood, iv 45.
5　ment: aimed.
7　blent: mingled; defiled.

Stanza 6
1–2　Displays dramatically the charge on Pyrochles's shield: 'A flaming fire in midst of bloudy field' (iv 38.3); cf. 8.4–5, 9.5, etc.
3　seuenfolded shield: the classical shield of Ajax (Homer, *Iliad* vii 220) and Turnus (Virgil, *Aen*. xii 925) although, in the Book of Temperance, seven folds suggests the protection given by the seven virtues – the three intellectual and the four moral virtues of classical ethics or the three Christian and the four classical virtues – against the assault of the seven deadly sins; cf. viii 32.5. Cf. iii 1.9. For similar associations, cf. Artegall's shield, III ii 25.7, and Arthur's sword, II viii 20.7–9.
5　targe: shield.
9　beuer: visor of the helmet.

Stanza 7
5　hurling: the term renders the violence of whirling and hurtling as the blow begins to descend.
8–9　Cf. Arthur's wound which is received on Guyon's behalf at viii 38.9, and see *n*. S. may have in mind some similar difference between the wounded left side and the right. For the left as the side of the appetitive faculties of the soul, see Freccero (1959) 253f.　**inly bate**: cut inward.

Stanza 8
1　Deadly dismayd: going beyond Guyon's state at 7.3.
dint: blow.
2　entyre: entirely; inwardly; exceedingly, as the context suggests.
7　gyre: the action of closely wheeling around a foe (Lat. *gyrus*) in an effort to strike him.
8　saufgard: safeguard, the guard in fencing.
9　far'd: acted.

9

He hewd, and lasht, and foynd, and thundred blowes,
And euery way did seeke into his life,
Ne plate, ne male could ward so mighty throwes,
But yielded passage to his cruell knife.
But *Guyon*, in the heat of all his strife,
Was warie wise, and closely did awayt
Auauntage, whilest his foe did rage most rife;
Sometimes a thwart, sometimes he strooke him strayt,
And falsed oft his blowes, t'illude him with such bayt.

10

Like as a Lyon, whose imperiall powre
A prowd rebellious Vnicorne defies,
T'auoide the rash assault and wrathfull stowre
Of his fiers foe, him to a tree applies,
And when him running in full course he spies,
He slips aside; the whiles that furious beast
His precious horne, sought of his enimies,
Strikes in the stocke, ne thence can be releast,
But to the mighty victour yields a bounteous feast.

11

With such faire slight him *Guyon* often faild,
Till at the last all breathlesse, wearie, faint
Him spying, with fresh onset he assaild,
And kindling new his courage seeming queint,
Strooke him so hugely, that through great constraint
He made him stoup perforce vnto his knee,
And do vnwilling worship to the Saint,
That on his shield depainted he did see;
Such homage till that instant neuer learned hee.

12

Whom *Guyon* seeing stoup, pursewed fast
The present offer of faire victory,
And soone his dreadfull blade about he cast,
Wherewith he smote his haughty crest so hye,
That streight on ground made him full low to lye;
Then on his brest his victour foote he thrust,
With that he cryde, Mercy, do me not dye,
Ne deeme thy force by fortunes doome vniust,
That hath (maugre her spight) thus low me laid in dust.

13

Eftsoones his cruell hand Sir *Guyon* stayd,
Tempring the passion with aduizement slow,
And maistring might on enimy dismayd:
For th'equall dye of warre he well did know;
Then to him said, Liue and allegaunce owe,
To him that giues thee life and libertie,
And henceforth by this dayes ensample trow,
That hasty wroth, and heedlesse hazardrie
Do breede repentaunce late, and lasting infamie.

Stanza 9
1 **foynd**: lunged.
3 **throwes**: thrusts; blows; attacks (an earlier form of 'throe').
6 **closely**: secretly.
9 **falsed**: feinted. **illude**: deceive.

Stanza 10
Cf. Shakespeare's *Timon of Athens* IV iii 330–1: 'Wert thou the unicorn, pride and wrath would confound thee, and make thine own self the conquest of thy fury.' The unicorn is cited in Job 39.12–5 as a beast that may not be tamed; cf. Topsell (1607) i 557.
3 **stowre**: encounter.
4 **applies**: makes his way.
7 **precious**: being full of marvellous medicinal virtues.

Stanza 11
1 **faild**: deceived; caused to fail.
4 **queint**: quenched; referring to Pyrochles's fiery nature.
7 **Saint**: 'image of that heauenly Mayd' (i 28.7), Gloriana. See also viii 43.3.
8 **depainted**: depicted.

Stanza 12
4–5 **so hye**: with such extreme force, so the context suggests; or the phrase may modify the **haughty** (high) crest in order to stress Pyrochles's fall **full low**; 5 measures the knight's length upon the ground.
8–9 Pyrochles's point is clear: fortune, not Guyon's force, has defeated him; but the word-play, **deeme . . . doome**, and the sense of **maugre**, cause confusion. The simplest reading is: 'Do not judge your force according to the unjust judgment of Fortune: for it is fortune (damn her spite!) which has defeated me.' Cf. his earlier confidence in his 'force and fortune' (5.9). **maugre** remains a crux: the sense 'curse on' is not found elsewhere; cf. III v 7.5. Kermode (1952) 161 amends **deeme** to 'mete', takes **That** to refer to **force** and **maugre** in its usual sense, 'in spite of', to read: 'Do not measure your force by the injustice of fortune; after all, it prevailed only in defiance of fortune.' Cf. Pyrochles's claim when Arthur defeats him: 'And say, that I not ouercome do dye, / But in despight of life, for death do call' (viii 52.3–4).

Stanza 13
2 **aduizement**: deliberation.
3 **maistring might**: Guyon masters his might by knowing when not to use it; cf. xii 53.5. His dilemma as a warrior is that he must often refrain from using force. **dismayd**: defeated.
4 **equall dye**: equal hazard or chance; a gaming metaphor: honest dice allow equal chance; cf. 'ods of armes' (14.6). **dye** is used here with a scarcely repressed pun. In effect, Guyon allows Pyrochles's claim in the previous stanza.
8 **hazardrie**: risk; the same gaming metaphor, playing at hazard or dicing. The risk is to seek '*Occasion* to wrath, and cause of strife' (iv 44.2).
9 **late**: i.e. too late.

14

So vp he let him rise, who with grim looke
    And count'naunce sterne vpstanding, gan to grind
    His grated teeth for great disdeigne, and shooke
    His sandy lockes, long hanging downe behind,
    Knotted in bloud and dust, for griefe of mind,
    That he in ods of armes was conquered;
    Yet in himselfe some comfort he did find,
    That him so noble knight had maistered,
Whose bounty more then might, yet both he wondered.

15

Which *Guyon* marking said, Be nought agrieu'd,
    Sir knight, that thus ye now subdewed arre:
    Was neuer man, who most conquestes atchieu'd,
    But sometimes had the worse, and lost by warre,
    Yet shortly gaynd, that losse exceeded farre:
    Losse is no shame, nor to be lesse then foe,
    But to be lesser, then himselfe, doth marre
    Both loosers lot, and victours prayse alsoe.
Vaine others ouerthrowes, who selfe doth ouerthrowe.

16

Fly, O *Pyrochles*, fly the dreadfull warre,
    That in thy selfe thy lesser parts do moue,
    Outrageous anger, and woe-working iarre,
    Direfull impatience, and hart murdring loue;
    Those, those thy foes, those warriours far remoue,
    Which thee to endlesse bale captiued lead.
    But sith in might thou didst my mercy proue,
    Of curtesie to me the cause aread,
That thee against me drew with so impetuous dread.

17

Dreadlesse (said he) that shall I soone declare:
    It was complaind, that thou hadst done great tort
    Vnto an aged woman, poore and bare,
    And thralled her in chaines with strong effort,
    Voide of all succour and needfull comfort:
    That ill beseemes thee, such as I thee see,
    To worke such shame.   Therefore I thee exhort,
    To chaunge thy will, and set *Occasion* free,
And to her captiue sonne yield his first libertee.

18

Thereat Sir *Guyon* smilde, And is that all
    (Said he) that thee so sore displeased hath?
    Great mercy sure, for to enlarge a thrall,
    Whose freedome shall thee turne to greatest scath.
    Nath'lesse now quench thy whot emboyling wrath:
    Loe there they be; to thee I yield them free.
    Thereat he wondrous glad, out of the path
    Did lightly leape, where he them bound did see,
And gan to breake the bands of their captiuitee.

19

Soone as *Occasion* felt her selfe vntyde,
    Before her sonne could well assoyled bee,
    She to her vse returnd, and streight defyde
    Both *Guyon* and *Pyrochles*: th'one (said shee)
    Bycause he wonne; the other because hee
    Was wonne: So matter did she make of nought,
    To stirre vp strife, and do them disagree:
    But soone as *Furor* was enlargd, she sought
To kindle his quencht fire, and thousand causes wrought.

210

Stanza 14
3   **grated**: clenched, as a grate; or gnashing; cf. Furor, iv 15. 3–4.
4   Cf. Furor's 'long lockes, coloured like copper-wire' (iv 15.8).
9   **wondered**: wondered at.

Stanza 15
3   **most**: also greatest.
7–8   If the loser or the victor becomes intemperate, the one's lot and the other's praise are marred.
9   **Vaine . . . ouerthrowes**: he who overthrows himself, overthrows others in vain.

Stanza 16
2   **lesser parts**: the body's inner parts which produce the passions.
3–4   Extends Medina's exhortation to fly from 'rage, and . . . iarre' (ii 30.9) and parallels the Palmer's exhortation to Phedon to expel 'Wrath, gealosie, griefe, loue' (iv 35.1).   **iarre**: discord; an ancestor of Pyrochles, iv 41.7.   **impatience**: the Lat. sense of *impatiens*, inability to bear grief or suffering; as applied to Amavia's grief, see i 58.4. Later personified as Maleger's hag, xi 23.9.   **hart murdring loue** applies especially to Amavia.
8   **aread**: declare.
9   **dread**: dreadfulness; as one to be dreaded; or the whole phrase may signify 'so impetuously as to arouse dread'.

Stanza 17
1   **Dreadlesse**: fearless one; a term of address in response to Guyon's closing word.
2   **tort**: wrong; a legal term which suggests a breach of knightly code.
3–4   Commenting obliquely on Guyon's 'heroic' quest to chain Acrasia; see iv 45.2–7n.   **bare**: defenceless; see iv 45.5.
5   **comfort**: aid.
9   **first**: i.e. as he was at first.

Stanza 18
3–4   **Great mercy**: great favour it is! (Fr. *grandmerci*). Guyon's irony proves double-edged: freeing Pyrochles turns to **greatest scath** (harm) against himself.
7   **out of the path**: i.e. from the path of temperance.

Stanza 19
2   **assoyled**: set free, in the etymological sense (Lat. *absolvere*, to loose).
3   **vse**: customary behaviour.
6   **wonne**: defeated.
7   **do**] garre *1590*; i.e. cause (cf. E.K.'s gloss to *S.C.* Apr. 1).

20

It was not long, ere she inflam'd him so,
  That he would algates with *Pyrochles* fight,
And his redeemer chalengd for his foe,
Because he had not well mainteind his right,
But yielded had to that same straunger knight:
Now gan *Pyrochles* wex as wood, as hee,
And him affronted with impatient might:
So both together fiers engrasped bee,
Whiles *Guyon* standing by, their vncouth strife does see.

21

Him all that while *Occasion* did prouoke
  Against *Pyrochles*, and new matter framed
Vpon the old, him stirring to be wroke
Of his late wrongs, in which she oft him blamed
For suffering such abuse, as knighthood shamed,
And him dishabled quite.   But he was wise
Ne would with vaine occasions be inflamed;
Yet others she more vrgent did deuise:
Yet nothing could him to impatience entise.

22

Their fell contention still increased more,
  And more thereby increased *Furors* might,
That he his foe has hurt, and wounded sore,
And him in bloud and durt deformed quight.
His mother eke, more to augment his spight,
Now brought to him a flaming fire brond,
Which she in *Stygian* lake, ay burning bright,
Had kindled: that she gaue into his hond,
That armd with fire, more hardly he mote him withstond.

23

Tho gan that villein wex so fiers and strong,
  That nothing might sustaine his furious forse;
He cast him downe to ground, and all along
Drew him through durt and myre without remorse,
And fowly battered his comely corse,
That *Guyon* much disdeignd so loathly sight.
At last he was compeld to cry perforse,
Helpe, O Sir *Guyon*, helpe most noble knight,
To rid a wretched man from hands of hellish wight.

24

The knight was greatly moued at his plaint,
  And gan him dight to succour his distresse,
Till that the Palmer, by his graue restraint,
Him stayd from yielding pitifull redresse;
And said, Deare sonne, thy causelesse ruth represse,
Ne let thy stout hart melt in pitty vayne:
He that his sorrow sought through wilfulnesse,
And his foe fettred would release agayne,
Deserues to tast his follies fruit, repented payne.

25

Guyon obayd; So him away he drew
  From needlesse trouble of renewing fight
Already fought, his voyage to pursew.
But rash *Pyrochles* varlet, *Atin* hight,
When late he saw his Lord in heauy plight,
Vnder Sir *Guyons* puissant stroke to fall,
Him deeming dead, as then he seemd in sight,
Fled fast away, to tell his funerall
Vnto his brother, whom *Cymochles* men did call.

Stanza 20
2 **algates**: at all costs.
3 See viii 22.5–9*n*.
6 **wood**: frantic.
7 **affronted**: attacked.   **impatient**: unable to be endured or contained.
9 **vncouth**: strange; marvellous; unseemly.

Stanza 21
3 **wroke**: wreaked, revenged.
6 **dishabled**: dishonoured.
6–7 The use of the term, **vaine occasions**, resolves the theme of the opening episode in which Archimago 'In hope to win occasion to his will' (i 5.2) deceives Guyon into wrathful action. After defeating Occasion, Guyon is no longer the errant knight subject to every passing incident and may proceed upon his quest.
9 **entise**: provoke.

Stanza 22
4 **bloud and durt**: Pyrochles becomes increasingly defiled. He enters in a cloud of dust (3.4), becomes soiled with blood (4.9), falls to the ground to rise with his hair 'Knotted in bloud and dust' (14.5), and finally is deformed in blood and dirt. Cf. 23.4 and see vi 41.6–8*n*.
5–9 Illustrating James 3.6: 'And the tongue is fyre, yea, a worlde of wickednes: so is the tongue set among our members, that it defileth the whole bodie, and setteth on fyre the course of nature, and it is set on fyre of hel.'
7 **Stygian lake**: the fiery river Phlegeton would be correct mythology (cf. 'Firebrand of hell first tynd in Phlegeton', IV ii 1.1) but the true origin of the fire of dissentious anger is the cold, dark, sluggish water of the 'black *Stygian* lake' (I v 10.6). S. is preparing for Pyrochles's vain efforts to quench these flames in the sluggish waters of the Idle Lake (vi 46–50). Cf. Milton's etymological description of 'Abhorred Styx the flood of deadly hate' (*P.L.* ii 577).
9 **hardly**: hardily; vigorously.

Stanza 23
4 **remorse**: pity.
6 **disdeignd**: was indignant at.

Stanza 24
4 **pitifull redresse**: aid given out of pity. The vain occasion to anger is now succeeded by the vain occasion to pity. Both occasions were illustrated in the opening action when Guyon was moved to anger by pity for the 'violated' Duessa, his opening words to her being 'Great pittie is to see you thus dismaid' (i 14.3).
9 **repented payne**: i.e. pain which he repents, indicated by his plea to Guyon to rid him 'from hands of hellish wight' (23.9).

Stanza 25
8 **funerall**: death (Lat. *funus*).

26

He was a man of rare redoubted might,
　Famous throughout the world for warlike prayse,
　And glorious spoiles, purchast in perilous fight:
　Full many doughtie knights he in his dayes
　Had doen to death, subdewde in equall frayes,
　Whose carkases, for terrour of his name,
　Of fowles and beastes he made the piteous prayes,
　And hong their conquered armes for more defame
On gallow trees, in honour of his dearest Dame.

27

His dearest Dame is that Enchaunteresse,
　The vile *Acrasia*, that with vaine delightes,
　And idle pleasures in her *Bowre* of *Blisse*,
　Does charme her louers, and the feeble sprightes
　Can call out of the bodies of fraile wightes:
　Whom then she does transforme to monstrous hewes,
　And horribly misshapes with vgly sightes,
　Captiu'd eternally in yron mewes,
And darksom dens, where *Titan* his face neuer shewes.

28

There *Atin* found *Cymochles* soiourning,
　To serue his Lemans loue: for he, by kind,
　Was giuen all to lust and loose liuing,
　When euer his fiers hands he free mote find:
　And now he has pourd out his idle mind
　In daintie delices, and lauish ioyes,
　Hauing his warlike weapons cast behind,
　And flowes in pleasures, and vaine pleasing toyes,
Mingled emongst loose Ladies and lasciuious boyes.

29

And ouer him, art striuing to compaire
　With nature, did an Arber greene dispred,
　Framed of wanton Yuie, flouring faire,
　Through which the fragrant Eglantine did spred
　His pricking armes, entrayld with roses red,
　Which daintie odours round about them threw,
　And all within with flowres was garnished,
　That when myld *Zephyrus* emongst them blew,
Did breath out bounteous smels, and painted colors shew.

30

And fast beside, there trickled softly downe
　A gentle streame, whose murmuring waue did play
　Emongst the pumy stones, and made a sowne,
　To lull him soft a sleepe, that by it lay;
　The wearie Traueiler, wandring that way,
　Therein did often quench his thristy heat,
　And then by it his wearie limbes display,
　Whiles creeping slomber made him to forget
His former paine, and wypt away his toylsom sweat.

31

And on the other side a pleasaunt groue
　Was shot vp high, full of the stately tree,
　That dedicated is t'*Olympicke Ioue*,
　And to his sonne *Alcides*, whenas hee
　Gaynd in *Nemea* goodly victoree;
　Therein the mery birds of euery sort
　Chaunted alowd their chearefull harmonie:
　And made emongst them selues a sweet consort,
That quickned the dull spright with musicall comfort.

Stanza 26

1–5　Cf. the description of Pyrochles, iv 41.2–4. **glorious spoiles**: conquests that bring him glory. **purchast**: got by conquest in war.

6–7　See vi 28.7–9.

8　**defame**: disgrace.

Stanza 27

6–9　Acrasia is worse than Homer's Circe who transforms her lovers' bodies but not their minds (*Ody.* x 238–41). See xii 85.5*n*. **monstrous hewes**: the shapes of monsters. **sightes**: appearances. **mewes**: prisons.

Stanza 28

2　**by kind**: by his nature.

6　**delices**: delights, sensual pleasures; cf. xii 85.7.

8–9　**flowes . . . / Mingled**: indicating his watery nature. See iv 41*n*. Cf. the Red Cross Knight with Duessa 'Pourd out in loosnesse on the grassy grownd' (I vii 7.2). **toyes**: amorous dallyings; cf. xii 72.9.

Stanza 29

1–2　On the rivalry between art and nature in the Bower, see xii 59. **compaire**: vie.

3–5　**wanton**: as ivy is luxuriant in growth, wanders and clings, and is sacred to Bacchus; cf. xii 61.2. **flouring**: flourishing. **Yuie and Eglantine** (sweet-briar) also flourish on Venus's mount in the Garden of Adonis, III vi 44.5–6. For the **roses**, see xii 77.1. **pricking**: from the etymology of Eglantine, Lat. *aculentus*, prickly. Since Cymochles has cast away his warlike arms, there is a pun, as Williams (1966) 53 notes. Cf. Phædria's preference for love's arms over those of war, vi 34.

8　**Zephyrus**: the west wind, 'the frolic wind that breathes the spring' (Milton, *L'Allegro* 18); see xii 33.5*n*.

Stanza 30

3　**pumy stones**: pumice. **sowne**: the obsolete spelling avoids the harsh dental of 'sound'.

7　**display**: extend.

Stanza 31

1–5　**the stately tree**: either the oak dedicated to Jove (as Homer, *Ody.* xix 296–7) or the poplar most dear to **Alcides**, i.e. Hercules (as Virgil, *Ecl.* vii 61). Here associated first with victories at the Olympic games and then with Hercules's victories, the first over the Nemean lion, and (by inference) the last, his victory over hell symbolized by the crown of poplar leaves which he wore on his return. These references emphasize Cymochles's rejection of the active, heroic life. The tree **shot vp high** comments upon his fallen state. Further, the reference to **Olympicke Ioue** suggests the free state of the gods on Olympus in contrast to the knight's bound state in the Bower. Hence the grove is **on the other side**, set apart from the slothful knight.

8　**consort**: company; accord.

9　**comfort**: the term cancels the effect of **quickned**. Instead of that awakening call which hurries Chaucer's pilgrims on their way, the birds, like the waters, lull the traveller.

32

There he him found all carelesly displayd,
    In secret shadow from the sunny ray,
    On a sweet bed of lillies softly layd,
    Amidst a flocke of Damzels fresh and gay,
    That round about him dissolute did play
    Their wanton follies, and light meriment;
    Euery of which did loosely disaray
    Her vpper parts of meet habiliments,
And shewd them naked, deckt with many ornaments.

33

And euery of them stroue, with most delights,
    Him to aggrate, and greatest pleasures shew;
    Some framd faire lookes, glancing like euening lights,
    Others sweet words, dropping like honny dew;
    Some bathed kisses, and did soft embrew
    The sugred licour through his melting lips:
    One boastes her beautie, and does yeeld to vew
    Her daintie limbes aboue her tender hips;
Another her out boastes, and all for tryall strips.

34

He, like an Adder, lurking in the weeds,
    His wandring thought in deepe desire does steepe,
    And his fraile eye with spoyle of beautie feedes;
    Sometimes he falsely faines himselfe to sleepe,
    Whiles through their lids his wanton eies do peepe,
    To steale a snatch of amorous conceipt,
    Whereby close fire into his heart does creepe:
    So, them deceiues, deceiu'd in his deceipt,
Made drunke with drugs of deare voluptuous receipt.

35

Atin arriuing there, when him he spide,
    Thus in still waues of deepe delight to wade,
    Fiercely approching, to him lowdly cride,
    Cymochles; oh no, but *Cymochles* shade,
    In which that manly person late did fade,
    What is become of great *Acrates* sonne?
    Or where hath he hong vp his mortall blade,
    That hath so many haughtie conquests wonne?
Is all his force forlorne, and all his glory donne?

36

Then pricking him with his sharpe-pointed dart,
    He said; Vp, vp, thou womanish weake knight,
    That here in Ladies lap entombed art,
    Vnmindfull of thy praise and prowest might,
    And weetlesse eke of lately wrought despight,
    Whiles sad *Pyrochles* lies on senselesse ground,
    And groneth out his vtmost grudging spright,
    Through many a stroke, and many a streaming wound,
Calling thy helpe in vaine, that here in ioyes art dround.

37

Suddeinly out of his delightfull dreame
    The man awoke, and would haue questiond more;
    But he would not endure that wofull theame
    For to dilate at large, but vrged sore
    With percing words, and pittifull implore,
    Him hastie to arise. As one affright
    With hellish feends, or *Furies* mad vprore,
    He then vprose, inflam'd with fell despight,
And called for his armes; for he would algates fight.

Stanza 32
2 A prelude to the hell in which Acrasia finally places her lovers, 27.9.
6 follies: lewd actions.
9 ornaments: possibly jewellery, such as Duessa wears, rather than natural blessings. Cf. Amoret's naked breast 'Without adorne of gold or siluer bright' (III xii 20.2).

Stanza 33
1 most: greatest.   delights: sensual pleasures, as 'delices' (28.6).
2 aggrate: please, gratify; from Ital. *aggratare* (Florio, 1611); or from Lat. *adgratus*, to make agreeable.   shew: cf. xii 68.9.
4 Cf. Prov. 5.3: 'For the lippes of a strange woman drop as an honie combe.'
5 embrew: pour, cause to drink, is the primary sense; but also with the senses, 'steep', 'thrust', 'stain', 'infect'.
7–9 Repeated with embellishments at xii 66.   tryall: examination; with a pun on her challenge to 'try all'.

Stanza 34
3 spoyle of beautie: the despoiling or stripping of the damsels; also, the spoiling of their beauty by their naked wantonness.
6 snatch: quick grab, hasty glimpse; trap, entanglement (*OED* 2).   conceipt: thought, image.
7 close: secret.
9 Cf. Acrasia's lovers 'drunken mad' and her 'drugs of foule intemperance' (i 52.2, 54.8).   deare: dire, grievous; possibly, 'precious'.   receipt: recipe; referring primarily to what he receives, the sight of the voluptuous maidens.

Stanza 35
2 Alluding to the etymology of his name: see iv 41*n*.
4 to 36.9 Atin's reproof parallels earlier admonitions to warriors who have yielded to sensuality: Mercury to Aeneas in Libya serving Dido (Virgil, *Aen*. iv 265–76), Melissa to Ruggiero on Alcina's island (Ariosto, *Orl. Fur*. vii 57–64), and Ubaldo to Rinaldo in Armida's bower (Tasso, *Ger. Lib*. xvi 32–3).
4 shade: image or ghost.
5 fade: vanish.
6 The epithet shows what he has become: Acrasia's son.
9 forlorne: lost.

Stanza 36
3 lap: with the bawdy sense.
7 his vtmost grudging spright: his last complaining (or tormented) breath.

Stanza 37
4 dilate: relate at length.
5 pittifull implore: appeal for pity.
8 The dart (36.1) is poisoned by 'despight' (iv 38.9).

38

They bene ybrought; he quickly does him dight,
   And lightly mounted, passeth on his way,
   Ne Ladies loues, ne sweete entreaties might
   Appease his heat, or hastie passage stay;
   For he has vowd, to beene aueng'd that day,
   (That day it selfe him seemed all too long:)
   On him, that did *Pyrochles* deare dismay:
   So proudly pricketh on his courser strong,
And *Atin* aie him pricks with spurs of shame and wrong.

Cant. VI.

Guyon is of immodest Merth
led into loose desire,
Fights with Cymochles, whiles his bro-
ther burnes in furious fire.

1

A Harder lesson, to learne Continence
   In ioyous pleasure, then in grieuous paine:
   For sweetnesse doth allure the weaker sence
   So strongly, that vneathes it can refraine
   From that, which feeble nature couets faine;
   But griefe and wrath, that be her enemies,
   And foes of life, she better can restraine;
   Yet vertue vaunts in both their victories,
And *Guyon* in them all shewes goodly maisteries.

2

Whom bold *Cymochles* trauelling to find,
   With cruell purpose bent to wreake on him
   The wrath, which *Atin* kindled in his mind,
   Came to a riuer, by whose vtmost brim
   Wayting to passe, he saw whereas did swim
   A long the shore, as swift as glaunce of eye,
   A litle Gondelay, bedecked trim
   With boughes and arbours wouen cunningly,
That like a litle forrest seemed outwardly.

3

And therein sate a Ladie fresh and faire,
   Making sweet solace to her selfe alone;
   Sometimes she sung, as loud as larke in aire,
   Sometimes she laught, that nigh her breth was gone,
   Yet was there not with her else any one,
   That might to her moue cause of meriment:
   Matter of merth enough, though there were none,
   She could deuise, and thousand waies inuent,
To feede her foolish humour, and vaine iolliment.

Stanza 38
2   **lightly**: quickly.
7   **deare dismay**: grievously vanquish.
8–9   A fresh rendering of the stock figure of the rider ridden.

Canto vi

Argument
1   **immodest**: improper, lewd; but also the Lat. sense of *immodestus*, intemperate, excessive; cf. 37.4, its only other use.

Stanza 1
1–2   Cf. Aristotle, *Ethics* II iii 1105[a]: 'It is harder to fight with pleasure than with anger.'   **Continence**: 'a vertue whiche kepeth the pleasaunt appetite of man under the yoke of reason' (Elyot, *Governour* III xvii).
3   **weaker**: too weak.
4   **vneathes**: hardly.
5   **faine**: willingly.
6–7   **griefe and wrath**: see iv 33.4*n*. The terms apply to all the episodes in Book II up to this point except those that involve Acrasia.
7   **restraine**] abstaine *1590* has the obsolete sense 'keep back'.

Stanza 2
4   **vtmost brim**: extreme edge; perhaps the mouth of the river which flows into the Idle Lake and thence to the Bower of Bliss; cf. 'that deepe ford' (4.4).
6   Cf. 5.2. The contrast throughout the canto between the swift boat and sluggish waves applies generally to the contrast between the nimble mind and the gross body, and more particularly to the contrast between the active, ranging fancy and the passive flesh.
7   **Gondelay**: Craig (1967) 464 suggests an etymological play on Ital. *gongolare*, 'to laugh till ones heart be sore' (Florio, 1611). Cf. 'frigot' (7.9). Phædria's humour depends upon the obscene significance of her boat and its use. The Renaissance association of the **Gondelay** with sexual licence is noted by Crossley and Edwards (1973) 315–6.
8–9   Cf. the description of the Bower of Bliss, v 29.1–3. **arbours**: vines or trailing shrubs.

Stanza 3
2   **solace**: amusement.
3   The lark as an amorous symbol in the Renaissance is noted by Bawcutt (1972).
4   **that ... gone**] as merry as Pope Ione *1590*, alluding to the legendary female Pope. For the proverb, see C. G. Smith (1970) 529.
7–9   As Occasion 'matter [of anger] did . . . make of nought' (v 19.6; cf. 21.2). Loud laughter characterizes Phædria, and her island, 24.6; cf. xii 15.4 and her title 'immodest Merth' (Arg.). Her frivolity distinguishes her from Acrasia. Cf. Perissa 'still laughing' (ii 36.2). **foolish humour**: her disposition of wanton idleness or obsessive frivolity.

4

Which when farre off *Cymochles* heard, and saw,
    He loudly cald to such, as were a bord,
    The little barke vnto the shore to draw,
    And him to ferrie ouer that deepe ford:
    The merry marriner vnto his word
    Soone hearkned, and her painted bote streightway
    Turnd to the shore, where that same warlike Lord
    She in receiu'd; but *Atin* by no way
She would admit, albe the knight her much did pray.

5

Eftsoones her shallow ship away did slide,
    More swift, then swallow sheres the liquid skie,
    Withouten oare or Pilot it to guide,
    Or winged canuas with the wind to flie,
    Only she turn'd a pin, and by and by
    It cut away vpon the yielding waue,
    Ne cared she her course for to apply:
    For it was taught the way, which she would haue,
And both from rocks and flats it selfe could wisely saue.

6

And all the way, the wanton Damzell found
    New merth, her passenger to entertaine:
    For she in pleasant purpose did abound,
    And greatly ioyed merry tales to faine,
    Of which a store-house did with her remaine,
    Yet seemed, nothing well they her became;
    For all her words she drownd with laughter vaine,
    And wanted grace in vtt'ring of the same,
That turned all her pleasance to a scoffing game.

7

And other whiles vaine toyes she would deuize
    As her fantasticke wit did most delight,
    Sometimes her head she fondly would aguize
    With gaudie girlonds, or fresh flowrets dight
    About her necke, or rings of rushes plight;
    Sometimes to doe him laugh, she would assay
    To laugh at shaking of the leaues light,
    Or to behold the water worke, and play
About her litle frigot, therein making way.

8

Her light behauiour, and loose dalliaunce
    Gaue wondrous great contentment to the knight,
    That of his way he had no souenaunce,
    Nor care of vow'd reuenge, and cruell fight,
    But to weake wench did yeeld his martiall might.
    So easie was to quench his flamed mind
    With one sweet drop of sensuall delight,
    So easie is, t'appease the stormie wind
Of malice in the calme of pleasant womankind.

9

Diuerse discourses in their way they spent,
    Mongst which *Cymochles* of her questioned,
    Both what she was, and what that vsage ment,
    Which in her cot she daily practised.
    Vaine man (said she) that wouldest be reckoned
    A strariger in thy home, and ignoraunt
    Of *Phædria* (for so my name is red)
    Of *Phædria*, thine owne fellow seruaunt;
For thou to serue *Acrasia* thy selfe doest vaunt.

Stanza 5
2   **liquid**: clear, bright; a Virgilian phrase (cf. *Aen*. v 217) to
note the mingling of water and sky.
5   **pin**: cf. the throttle on the brass steed in Chaucer,
Squire's Tale 127. There are similar boats in Homer, *Ody*.
viii 557–63, Ariosto, *Orl. Fur*. xxx 11, and Tasso, *Ger. Lib*.
xv 6–8.   **by and by**: immediately.
6   The 1611 reading, 'a way', provides characteristic
Spenserian word-play on **waue**.   **waue**: water, as 18.7,
47.1. There are no waves on this lake; cf. 'still waues' (v 35.2).
7   **apply**: steer.
9   **wisely**: skilfully.

Stanza 6
1   **wanton**: undisciplined, frivolous, gay, carefree, in addition
to the usual sense, 'lascivious'. It is her usual appellation: 40.8,
viii 3.3, xii 17.1. Cf. Acrasia, 'That wanton Ladie' (xii 76.8).
3   **purpose**: speech. With a pun: in her frivolity she lacks
purpose, and changes Cymochles's 'wrathfull purpose' (13.9).
6–9   Cf. Aristotle's admonition against buffoons who aim
'rather at raising a laugh than at saying what is becoming'
(*Ethics* IV viii 1128ᵃ). The lines suggest that she tells off-colour
stories.   **the same**: i.e. her words; but possibly her
unbecoming laughter.   **pleasance**: pleasing behaviour.

Stanza 7
1   **other whiles**: at times.   **toyes**: amorous sports, tricks.
2   **fantasticke wit**: fantasy; or imaginative wit.
3   **fondly**: foolishly.   **aguize**: array.
4   **gaudie**: showy or festive (not necessarily disparaging).
9   **frigot**: Craig (1967) 464 suggests an etymological reference
to Ital. *frigotare*, to chuckle, citing Florio; see 2.7n.

Stanza 8
3   **souenaunce**: memory.
6–7   These lines prepare for Pyrochles's vain efforts to
quench his inner fire in the Idle Lake, stanzas 49–50.

Stanza 9
1   **Diuerse**: various; distracting; hence diverting him from
his way.
4   **cot**: a small boat used in Ireland; 'shelter' (*OED* sb.¹ 2) is
preferable: decked 'like a litle forrest' (2.9), it is like
Cymochles's **home** (6), the Bower of Bliss.
5   **Vaine**: foolish.
7   **Phædria**: glittering, cheerful (Gk φαιδρός), referring to
her superficial pleasure and superfluous frivolity.   **red**: called.
8   Implying, 'since you serve Acrasia, I serve you'. Preferable
to the weaker, 'I am a servant of Acrasia even as you are'.

10

In this wide Inland sea, that hight by name
  The *Idle lake*, my wandring ship I row,
  That knowes her port, and thither sailes by ayme,
  Ne care, ne feare I, how the wind do blow,
  Or whether swift I wend, or whether slow:
  Both slow and swift a like do serue my tourne,
  Ne swelling *Neptune*, ne loud thundring *Ioue*
  Can chaunge my cheare, or make me euer mourne;
My litle boat can safely passe this perilous bourne.

11

Whiles thus she talked, and whiles thus she toyd,
  They were farre past the passage, which he spake,
  And come vnto an Island, waste and voyd,
  That floted in the midst of that great lake,
  There her small Gondelay her port did make,
  And that gay paire issuing on the shore
  Disburdned her.   Their way they forward take
  Into the land, that lay them faire before,
Whose pleasaunce she him shew'd, and plentifull great store.

12

It was a chosen plot of fertile land,
  Emongst wide waues set, like a litle nest,
  As if it had by Natures cunning hand
  Bene choisely picked out from all the rest,
  And laid forth for ensample of the best:
  No daintie flowre or herbe, that growes on ground,
  No arboret with painted blossomes drest,
  And smelling sweet, but there it might be found
To bud out faire, and her sweet smels throw all around.

13

No tree, whose braunches did not brauely spring;
  No braunch, whereon a fine bird did not sit:
  No bird, but did her shrill notes sweetly sing;
  No song but did containe a louely dit:
  Trees, braunches, birds, and songs were framed fit,
  For to allure fraile mind to carelesse ease.
  Carelesse the man soone woxe, and his weake wit
  Was ouercome of thing, that did him please;
So pleased, did his wrathfull purpose faire appease.

14

Thus when she had his eyes and senses fed
  With false delights, and fild with pleasures vaine,
  Into a shadie dale she soft him led,
  And laid him downe vpon a grassie plaine;
  And her sweet selfe without dread, or disdaine,
  She set beside, laying his head disarm'd
  In her loose lap, it softly to sustaine,
  Where soone he slumbred, fearing not be harm'd,
The whiles with a loud lay she thus him sweetly charm'd.

15

Behold, O man, that toilesome paines doest take,
  The flowres, the fields, and all that pleasant growes,
  How they themselues doe thine ensample make,
  Whiles nothing enuious nature them forth throwes
  Out of her fruitfull lap; how, no man knowes,
  They spring, they bud, they blossome fresh and faire,
  And deck the world with their rich pompous showes;
  Yet no man for them taketh paines or care,
216 Yet no man to them can his carefull paines compare.

Stanza 10
1 **Inland sea**: suggests the Mediterranean, an appropriate reference in the classical scheme of Book II. For the association with the Dead Sea, or what J. Wybarne, *The New Age of Old Names* (1609), calls Phædria's 'dead sea of pleasure' (*Spenser Allusions*, 120), see 46.6–9n.
9 **perilous bourne**: referring to the 'riuer' (2.4) or 'that deepe ford' (4.4), though the term suggests 'boundary' or 'limit', particularly of life itself. Cf. 'perlous foord' (19.9) and 'perlous shard' (38.9).

Stanza 11
3–4 As Acrasia's 'wandring Island . . . in perilous gulfe' (i 51.5–6). **waste and voyd**: uninhabited.
9 **pleasaunce**: pleasantness (as 6.9, 21.6), or with reference to a secluded garden.

Stanza 12
3–5 Cf. the Bower of Bliss, which is the best choice of Nature that art could imitate, xii 42.3–4.
6–9 As an earthly Paradise, it contains all plant life; cf. Gen. 2.5. See IV x 22.1–5n. **arboret**: shrub.

Stanza 13
4 **dit**: ditty, as subject matter, theme.
6 **carelesse**: free from care.

Stanza 14
2 **fild**: also defiled (from 'file'); cf. vii 24.4.
7 He resumes his earlier posture, v 36.3.
9 **loud**] loue 1590. At 3.3 she sings 'as loud as larke'; yet cf. xii 74.1: 'louely lay', i.e. lay of love. **charm'd**: from Lat. *carmen*, song.

Stanzas 15–17
Imitates the song to Rinaldo on Armida's enchanted island, which urges him to follow nature (Tasso, *Ger. Lib.* xiv 62–4). Its argument parodies Christ's sermon on the mount, Matt. 6.25–34, particularly verses 28–9: 'Learne, how the lilies of the field do growe: they labour not, nether spinne: yet I say unto you, that even Solomon in all his glorie was not arayed like one of these.' Upton (1758) comments: 'This mock representation of tranquillity [shows] how the best of sayings may be perverted to the worst of meanings.' Cf. the Song of the Rose in Acrasia's Bower, xii 74–75.

Stanza 15
4 **nothing enuious**: in no way grudging; a Latinism for 'all-bountiful'.
5 The contrast is clear between her 'loose lap' (14.7) and Nature's **fruitfull lap**.

16

The lilly, Ladie of the flowring field,
    The Flowre-deluce, her louely Paramoure,
    Bid thee to them thy fruitlesse labours yield,
    And soone leaue off this toylesome wearie stoure;
    Loe loe how braue she decks her bounteous boure,
    With silken curtens and gold couerlets,
    Therein to shrowd her sumptuous Belamoure,
    Yet neither spinnes nor cardes, ne cares nor frets,
But to her mother Nature all her care she lets.

17

Why then dost thou, O man, that of them all
    Art Lord, and eke of nature Soueraine,
    Wilfully make thy selfe a wretched thrall,
    And wast thy ioyous houres in needlesse paine,
    Seeking for daunger and aduentures vaine?
    What bootes it all to haue, and nothing vse?
    Who shall him rew, that swimming in the maine,
    Will die for thirst, and water doth refuse?
Refuse such fruitlesse toile, and present pleasures chuse.

18

By this she had him lulled fast a sleepe,
    That of no worldly thing he care did take;
    Then she with liquors strong his eyes did steepe,
    That nothing should him hastily awake:
    So she him left, and did her selfe betake
    Vnto her boat againe, with which she cleft
    The slouthfull waue of that great griesly lake;
    Soone she that Island farre behind her left,
And now is come to that same place, where first she weft.

19

By this time was the worthy *Guyon* brought
    Vnto the other side of that wide strond,
    Where she was rowing, and for passage sought:
    Him needed not long call, she soone to hond
    Her ferry brought, where him she byding fond,
    With his sad guide; himselfe she tooke a boord,
    But the *Blacke Palmer* suffred still to stond,
    Ne would for price, or prayers once affoord,
To ferry that old man ouer the perlous foord.

20

Guyon was loath to leaue his guide behind,
    Yet being entred, might not backe retyre;
    For the flit barke, obaying to her mind,
    Forth launched quickly, as she did desire,
    Ne gaue him leaue to bid that aged sire
    Adieu, but nimbly ran her wonted course
    Through the dull billowes thicke as troubled mire,
    Whom neither wind out of their seat could forse,
Nor timely tides did driue out of their sluggish sourse.

21

And by the way, as was her wonted guize,
    Her merry fit she freshly gan to reare,
    And did of ioy and iollitie deuize,
    Her selfe to cherish, and her guest to cheare:
    The knight was courteous, and did not forbeare
    Her honest merth and pleasance to partake;
    But when he saw her toy, and gibe, and geare,
    And passe the bonds of modest merimake,
Her dalliance he despisd, and follies did forsake.

1–2   The **lilly** is called 'mistress of the field' in Shakespeare,
Henry VIII III i 152; the **Flowre-deluce** is the fleur de lis,
the flowering-lily. The two are associated in *The Winter's Tale*
IV iv 126–7. By its etymology, the latter was taken to be the
flos deliciae, the iris, a flower of chastity; cf. E.K.'s gloss to
S.C. Apr. 144: 'Flowre delice, that which they vse to misterme,
Flowre de luce, being in Latine called Flos delitiarum'.
Hieatt (1975a) 106 sees the fleur-de-lis as a phallic image and
the mating of the flowers as Cymochles's 'obscene picture
which disguises itself as natural and hides among the manifestations of Nature herself, thus profaned'.   **louely**: loving.
3   **to them**: before them; in the face of their ease.
4   **stoure**: time of turmoil, struggle.
7   **Belamoure**: fair lover; from Fr. *bel+amour*. A flower in
Amor. lxiv 7.
9   **lets**: leaves.

1–2   Cf. Ps. 8.6–8.
9   Note the artful reiteration: 'toilesome paines' (15.1),
'carefull paines' (15.9), 'fruitlesse labours' (16.3), 'toylesome
wearie stoure' (16.4), 'needlesse paine' (17.4), ending with
fruitlesse toile.

7   **griesly**: arousing horror. At 46.7 these waters 'did them
[Pyrochles and Atin] foule agrise'.   **griesly**] griesy *1590*:
horrible; also 'sluggish', as the waters are 'thicke as troubled
mire' (20.7) and 'Engrost with mud' (46.7). It represents that
mixture of earth and water to which Phædria reduces man's
nature. Cf. the description at 20.7, 38.3, 46.6.
9   **weft**: sailed; its association with 'weft' (as III x 36.3)
suggests 'wandering'.

2   **the other side**: Cymochles travels from the Bower and
Guyon to it.   **strond**: sea; or shore.
6   **sad**: grave; in contrast to 'immodest Merth' (Arg. 1)
which now guides Guyon.   **tooke a boord**: a flirtatious use
of the bawdy sense; cf. III x 6.4 and 38.1 below.
8–9   Cf. her treatment of Atin at 4.8–9.   **affoord**: grant.

3–4   As the Phaiacian ships in Homer, *Ody.* viii 559, need
not be steered for they understand men's thoughts and
purposes.   **as she did desire**: points to the allegorical
significance.   **flit**: swift.
9   **timely**: i.e. obedient to time; see 26.9n.

1   **wonted guize**: customary manner.
2   **reare**: commence.
3   **iollitie**: pleasure, esp. sexual pleasure.
4   **Her selfe to cherish**: to make herself cherished; or to
cheer herself.
7   **gibe, and geare**: jest and joke (or jeer); cf. V iii 39.4.
8   **bonds**: bounds.   **modest**: moderate; as she is
'immodest Merth' (Arg. 1).
9   **follies**: lewd desires or actions.   **forsake**: decline, shun.   217

22

Yet she still followed her former stile,
   And said, and did all that mote him delight,
   Till they arriued in that pleasant Ile,
   Where sleeping late she left her other knight.
   But when as *Guyon* of that land had sight,
   He wist himselfe amisse, and angry said;
   Ah Dame, perdie ye haue not doen me right,
Thus to mislead me, whiles I you obaid:
Me litle needed from my right way to haue straid.

23

Faire Sir (quoth she) be not displeasd at all;
   Who fares on sea, may not commaund his way,
   Ne wind and weather at his pleasure call:
   The sea is wide, and easie for to stray;
   The wind vnstable, and doth neuer stay.
   But here a while ye may in safety rest,
   Till season serue new passage to assay;
Better safe port, then be in seas distrest.
Therewith she laught, and did her earnest end in iest.

24

But he halfe discontent, mote nathelesse
   Himselfe appease, and issewd forth on shore:
   The ioyes whereof, and happie fruitfulnesse,
   Such as he saw, she gan him lay before,
   And all though pleasant, yet she made much more:
   The fields did laugh, the flowres did freshly spring,
   The trees did bud, and earely blossomes bore,
   And all the quire of birds did sweetly sing,
And told that gardins pleasures in their caroling.

25

And she more sweet, then any bird on bough,
   Would oftentimes emongst them beare a part,
   And striue to passe (as she could well enough)
   Their natiue musicke by her skilfull art:
   So did she all, that might his constant hart
   Withdraw from thought of warlike enterprize,
   And drowne in dissolute delights apart,
   Where noyse of armes, or vew of martiall guize
Might not reuiue desire of knightly exercize.

26

But he was wise, and warie of her will,
   And euer held his hand vpon his hart:
   Yet would not seeme so rude, and thewed ill,
   As to despise so courteous seeming part,
   That gentle Ladie did to him impart,
   But fairely tempring fond desire subdewd,
   And euer her desired to depart.
   She list not heare, but her disports poursewd,
And euer bad him stay, till time the tide renewd.

27

And now by this, *Cymochles* howre was spent,
   That he awoke out of his idle dreme,
   And shaking off his drowzie dreriment,
   Gan him auize, how ill did him beseeme,
   In slouthfull sleepe his molten hart to steme,
   And quench the brond of his conceiued ire.
   Tho vp he started, stird with shame extreme,
   Ne staied for his Damzell to inquire,
But marched to the strond, there passage to require.

Stanza 22
8   **whiles I you obaid**: as the boat 'obaying to her mind' does 'as she did desire' (20.3, 4). Guyon has given up the guidance of reason to follow the fancies of relaxed will.

Stanza 24
1–2   Cf. his response at ii 12.2.
4   **gan him lay before**: bring to his sight, describe to him.
6   A biblical expression, Ps. 65.13.

Stanza 25
1–4   On the morally unwholesome blending of sound categories, see xii 71*n*.
8   **martiall guize**: knightly armour.

Stanza 26
1–2   Against the passion of anger, he was 'wise' (v 21.6–9); against desire's corrupt **will**, he is also **warie**. His posture declares his control over his will.
3–5   Cf. 21.5–6.   **thewed ill**: ill-mannered.   **part**: referring to her treatment of him, or to the feigning role she plays (cf. 25.2).
6   **fairely tempring . . . subdewd**: properly governing himself, he subdued foolish desire.
7   **to depart**: i.e. to let him depart, as 36.8.
8   **disports**: merriment, sports; suggesting its etymological sense (Lat. *dis*, away + *portare*, to carry) for her diversions have led him from the right way.
9   **tide**: i.e. the right moment (so she would have him believe), but in fact never as her world is tideless (20.9) and timeless.

Stanza 27
3   **dreriment**: heaviness, replacing his earlier merriment.
5   **steme**: ?steep (sugg. by the context); or noting that the heat of anger dissipates in steam.

28

And in the way he with Sir *Guyon* met,
    Accompanyde with *Phædria* the faire,
    Eftsoones he gan to rage, and inly fret,
    Crying, Let be that Ladie debonaire,
    Thou recreant knight, and soone thy selfe prepaire
    To battell, if thou meane her loue to gaine:
    Loe, loe alreadie, how the fowles in aire
    Doe flocke, awaiting shortly to obtaine
Thy carcasse for their pray, the guerdon of thy paine.

29

And therewithall he fiercely at him flew,
    And with importune outrage him assayld;
    Who soone prepard to field, his sword forth drew,
    And him with equall value counteruayld:
    Their mightie strokes their haberieons dismayld,
    And naked made each others manly spalles;
    The mortall steele despiteously entayld
Deepe in their flesh, quite through the yron walles,
That a large purple streme adown their giambeux falles.

30

Cymochles, that had neuer met before
    So puissant foe, with enuious despight
    His proud presumed force increased more,
    Disdeigning to be held so long in fight;
    Sir *Guyon* grudging not so much his might,
    As those vnknightly raylings, which he spoke,
    With wrathfull fire his courage kindled bright,
    Thereof deuising shortly to be wroke,
And doubling all his powres, redoubled euery stroke.

31

Both of them high attonce their hands enhaunst,
    And both attonce their huge blowes downe did sway;
    Cymochles sword on *Guyons* shield yglaunst,
    And thereof nigh one quarter sheard away;
    But *Guyons* angry blade so fierce did play
    On th'others helmet, which as *Titan* shone,
    That quite it cloue his plumed crest in tway,
    And bared all his head vnto the bone;
Wherewith astonisht, still he stood, as senselesse stone.

32

Still as he stood, faire *Phædria*, that beheld
    That deadly daunger, soone atweene them ran;
    And at their feet her selfe most humbly feld,
    Crying with pitteous voice, and count'nance wan;
    Ah well away, most noble Lords, how can
    Your cruell eyes endure so pitteous sight,
    To shed your liues on ground? wo worth the man,
    That first did teach the cursed steele to bight
In his owne flesh, and make way to the liuing spright.

33

If euer loue of Ladie did empierce
    Your yron brestes, or pittie could find place,
    Withhold your bloudie hands from battell fierce,
    And sith for me ye fight, to me this grace
    Both yeeld, to stay your deadly strife a space.
    They stayd a while: and forth she gan proceed:
    Most wretched woman, and of wicked race,
    That am the author of this hainous deed,
And cause of death betweene two doughtie knights doe breed.

Stanza 28
4   **debonaire**: of pleasing disposition.
5   **recreant**: cowardly, a term of the greatest opprobrium; literally, one who has given up the cause (of knighthood). **soone**: immediately.
7–9   **Loe, loe**: Look! look! Cf. the Philistine's threat to David, 1 Sam. 17.44, and God's curse upon those who do not obey his laws: 'thy carkeis shal be meat unto all foules of the ayre' (Deut. 28.26). Cymochles's threat befits his obsession with the flesh; cf. v 26.6–7. Despoiling the dead body is associated with Mammon's house (vii 30.9), and provides the climax to Guyon's adventures in the first half of the Book: see viii 28.5. Since the body's wholeness is the goal of temperance, its despoiling becomes a central theme. **carcasse**: with its etymological significance, Lat. *caro+casa*, fallen flesh; see viii 12.5*n*.

Stanza 29
1   **therewithall**: that being said.
2   **importune outrage**: violent fury.
3   **to field**: to fight.
4   **value**: valour.   **counteruayld**: resisted, counter-attacked; from Lat. *contra valere*, to be of worth against.
5   **haberieons**: a sleeveless coat of mail.   **dismayld**: stripped the mail off.
6   **spalles**: shoulders; from Ital. *spalla*, or Eng. 'spell', splinter, referring to the bones.
7   **entayld**: cut into, carved.
9   **giambeux**: jambeux, leg-armour.

Stanza 30
2   **enuious despight**: malicious anger.
3   **presumed force**: i.e. force upon which he relies presumptuously.
5   **grudging**: being vexed at.

Stanza 31
1   **enhaunst**: raised.
2   **sway**: swing.
9   **astonisht**: stunned.

Stanza 32
Parodies Medina's intercession at ii 27: she seeks to end conflict caused by intemperate love; see ii 31.1–2*n*, and 36.2*n* below.
7–9   Cf. vii 17.1–2.   **wo worth**: may evil befall.   **In his owne flesh**: i.e. in human flesh, but emphasizing the *psychomachia*.

Stanza 33
4   **grace**: favour.

34

But if for me ye fight, or me will serue,
  Not this rude kind of battell, nor these armes
  Are meet, the which doe men in bale to sterue,
  And dolefull sorrow heape with deadly harmes:
  Such cruell game my scarmoges disarmes:
  Another warre, and other weapons I
  Doe loue, where loue does giue his sweet alarmes,
  Without bloudshed, and where the enemy
Does yeeld vnto his foe a pleasant victory.

35

Debatefull strife, and cruell enmitie
  The famous name of knighthood fowly shend;
  But louely peace, and gentle amitie,
  And in Amours the passing houres to spend,
  The mightie martiall hands doe most commend;
  Of loue they euer greater glory bore,
  Then of their armes: Mars is Cupidoes frend,
  And is for Venus loues renowmed more,
Then all his wars and spoiles, the which he did of yore.

36

Therewith she sweetly smyld.   They though full bent
  To proue extremities of bloudie fight,
  Yet at her speach their rages gan relent,
  And calme the sea of their tempestuous spight,
  Such powre haue pleasing words: such is the might
  Of courteous clemencie in gentle hart.
  Now after all was ceast, the Faery knight
  Besought that Damzell suffer him depart,
And yield him readie passage to that other part.

37

She no lesse glad, then he desirous was
  Of his departure thence; for of her ioy
  And vaine delight she saw he light did pas,
  A foe of folly and immodest toy,
  Still solemne sad, or still disdainfull coy,
  Delighting all in armes and cruell warre,
  That her sweet peace and pleasures did annoy,
  Troubled with terrour and vnquiet iarre,
That she well pleased was thence to amoue him farre.

38

Tho him she brought abord, and her swift bote
  Forthwith directed to that further strand;
  The which on the dull waues did lightly flote
  And soone arriued on the shallow sand,
  Where gladsome Guyon salied forth to land,
  And to that Damzell thankes gaue for reward.
  Vpon that shore he spied Atin stand,
  There by his maister left, when late he far'd
In Phædrias flit barke ouer that perlous shard.

39

Well could he him remember, sith of late
  He with Pyrochles sharp debatement made;
  Streight gan he him reuile, and bitter rate,
  As shepheards curre, that in darke euenings shade
  Hath tracted forth some saluage beastes trade;
  Vile Miscreant (said he) whither doest thou flie
  The shame and death, which will thee soone inuade?
  What coward hand shall doe thee next to die,
That art thus foully fled from famous enemie?

Stanza 34
3   doe men in bale to sterue: cause men to die in pain.
5   Either 'your war prevents my war of love' or 'my war stops yours' as Venus disarms Mars (cf. next stanza).   scarmoges: skirmishes.
7   alarmes: assaults.

Stanza 35
1   Debatefull: contentious.
2   shend: disgrace.
3   louely: loving.
4   Amours: love-making.
7–9   Cf. III vi 24.2–3, xi 36.4–5, 44.1–4. Cf. the poet's appeal to Mars 'In loues and gentle iollities arrayd' (I Proem 3.8). Concord within the soul is the goal of Temperance but here it is parodied by immodest mirth.

Stanza 36
2   To proue extremities: to fight to the death. extremities: the extreme degree, in contrast to the mean. While Medina 'did moderate / The strong extremities of their outrage' (ii 38.3–4) to include the warring states in the temperate mean, Phædria seeks to reduce them to the calme (4) of her Idle Lake.
5   Prov. 15.1. C. G. Smith (1970) 23 notes S.'s frequent use of the proverb. The power of words is balanced by the might of courtesy. Kellogg and Steele (1965) suggest that Cymochles yields because of Phædria's words, Guyon out of courtesy.

Stanza 37
Alpers (1967) 317 comments on the comedy: 'Most of the lines mean one thing to Phædria and another to Guyon and us.'
3   light did pas: easily disregarded; made light of.
4   folly: wantonness.   immodest: see Arg. 1n.   toy: amorous sport.
5   Still: ever.   solemne sad: grave, serious; applied to the Red Cross Knight (I i 2.8 and see n) and to Arthur (II ix 36.8).   coy: distant; similar in sense to disdainfull.
6   Cf. vii 10.
8   iarre: discord.

Stanza 38
2   Cf. 19.2. Explicit directions are given throughout the Book. The way to the Bower lies beyond the Idle Lake.
5   gladsome: gladly.   salied: leaped (from Lat. salio) rather than 'issued forth'; cf. xii 38.4 and see i 29.6n.
9   shard: dividing water (sugg. OED); cf. 'perilous bourne' (10.9). Another sense, 'dung', suggests the water's filth: cf. 46.6–7. The sense of 'boundary' or 'division' supports the concept of temperance as a voyage between boundaries or extremities. Its usual sense, 'cleft' or 'gap', applies to the channel of water across which Guyon must be ferried to the Bower of Bliss. Cf. 'ford' (4.4, 19.9, 47.8).

Stanza 39
2   debatement: strife.
5   trade: track, tread.
6–9   Ironically, Atin's curse is almost fulfilled by his master's hand; cf. viii 13.4.   Miscreant: wretch.   inuade: attack.

40

With that he stiffely shooke his steelehead dart:
  But sober *Guyon,* hearing him so raile,
  Though somewhat moued in his mightie hart,
  Yet with strong reason maistred passion fraile,
  And passed fairely forth.   He turning taile,
  Backe to the strond retyrd, and there still stayd,
  Awaiting passage, which him late did faile;
  The whiles *Cymochles* with that wanton mayd
The hastie heat of his auowd reuenge delayd.

41

Whylest there the varlet stood, he saw from farre
  An armed knight, that towards him fast ran,
  He ran on foot, as if in lucklesse warre
  His forlorne steed from him the victour wan;
  He seemed breathlesse, hartlesse, faint, and wan,
  And all his armour sprinckled was with bloud,
  And soyld with durtie gore, that no man can
  Discerne the hew thereof.   He neuer stood,
But bent his hastie course towards the idle flood.

42

The varlet saw, when to the flood he came,
  How without stop or stay he fiercely lept,
  And deepe him selfe beducked in the same,
  That in the lake his loftie crest was steept,
  Ne of his safetie seemed care he kept,
  But with his raging armes he rudely flasht
  The waues about, and all his armour swept,
  That all the bloud and filth away was washt,
Yet still he bet the water, and the billowes dasht.

43

Atin drew nigh, to weet what it mote bee;
  For much he wondred at that vncouth sight;
  Whom should he, but his owne deare Lord, there see,
  His owne deare Lord *Pyrochles,* in sad plight,
  Readie to drowne himselfe for fell despight,
  Harrow now out, and well away, he cryde,
  What dismall day hath lent this cursed light,
  To see my Lord so deadly damnifyde?
Pyrochles, O *Pyrochles,* what is thee betyde?

44

I burne, I burne, I burne, then loud he cryde,
  O how I burne with implacable fire,
  Yet nought can quench mine inly flaming syde,
  Nor sea of licour cold, nor lake of mire,
  Nothing but death can doe me to respire.
  Ah be it (said he) from *Pyrochles* farre
  After pursewing death once to require,
  Or think, that ought those puissant hands may marre:
Death is for wretches borne vnder vnhappie starre.

45

Perdie, then is it fit for me (said he)
  That am, I weene, most wretched man aliue,
  Burning in flames, yet no flames can I see,
  And dying daily, daily yet reuiue:
  O *Atin,* helpe to me last death to giue,
  The varlet at his plaint was grieued so sore,
  That his deepe wounded hart in two did riue,
  And his owne health remembring now no more,
Did follow that ensample, which he blam'd afore.

Stanza 40
5   Marks the end of Guyon's subjection to Atin's fury. Now he controls the irascible passions without the Palmer's guidance. **fairely**: peaceably.
8–9   Cymochles remains unchanged; cf. 8.4–5.   **delayd**: allayed, quenched; 'postponed' may be implied: anger is allayed only for the moment.

Stanza 41
4   **forlorne**: lost.
5   The last two adjectives duplicate the first two.
6–8   A climax to his staining; see v 22.4*n.* The stained armour expresses the body's defilement; cf. i 41.3. Cf. Pyrochles's brilliant first appearance, v 2.   **stood**: stopped.

Stanza 42
6   **flasht**: splashed; also referring to his burning.

Stanza 43
6   **Harrow . . . and well away**: a cry of alarm followed by a cry of grief.
7   **dismall day**: one of the evil or cursed days – a pun on *dies mali;* hence often the day of death; cf. vii 26.7, viii 51.5.
8   **damnifyde**: injured; suggesting also 'damned'.
9   **what is thee betyde?**: what has happened to you?

Stanza 44
1–3   The motto on his shield, '*Burnt I do burne*' (iv 38.5), is now confirmed: outer fire manifests his inner burning. **implacable**: that cannot be assuaged.
5   The paradox is indicated by **respire**: only through death may he breathe again. Cf. Phedon's lament, iv 33.5–6.
7   **After . . . require**: i.e. that he should seek death which pursues him.   **require**: call upon, seek after.
9   **vnhappie**: inauspicious.

Stanza 45
8   **health**: safety.

46

Into the lake he lept, his Lord to ayd,
  (So Loue the dread of daunger doth despise)
And of him catching hold him strongly stayd
From drowning.   But more happie he, then wise
Of that seas nature did him not auise.
The waues thereof so slow and sluggish were,
Engrost with mud, which did them foule agrise,
That euery weightie thing they did vpbeare,
Ne ought mote euer sinke downe to the bottome there.

47

Whiles thus they strugled in that idle waue,
  And stroue in vaine, the one himselfe to drowne,
The other both from drowning for to saue,
Lo, to that shore one in an auncient gowne,
Whose hoarie locks great grauitie did crowne,
Holding in hand a goodly arming sword,
By fortune came, led with the troublous sowne:
Where drenched deepe he found in that dull ford
The carefull seruant, striuing with his raging Lord.

48

Him *Atin* spying, knew right well of yore,
  And loudly cald, Helpe helpe, O *Archimage*;
To saue my Lord, in wretched plight forlore;
Helpe with thy hand, or with thy counsell sage:
Weake hands, but counsell is most strong in age.
Him when the old man saw, he wondred sore,
To see *Pyrochles* there so rudely rage:
Yet sithens helpe, he saw, he needed more
Then pittie, he in hast approched to the shore.

49

And cald, *Pyrochles*, what is this, I see?
  What hellish furie hath at earst thee hent?
Furious euer I thee knew to bee,
Yet neuer in this straunge astonishment.
These flames, these flames (he cryde) do me torment.
What flames (quoth he) when I thee present see,
In daunger rather to be drent, then brent?
Harrow, the flames, which me consume (said hee)
Ne can be quencht, within my secret bowels bee.

50

That cursed man, that cruell feend of hell,
  Furor, oh *Furor* hath me thus bedight:
His deadly wounds within my liuers swell,
And his whot fire burnes in mine entrails bright,
Kindled through his infernall brond of spight,
Sith late with him I batteil vaine would boste;
That now I weene *Ioues* dreaded thunder light
Does scorch not halfe so sore, nor damned ghoste
In flaming *Phlegeton* does not so felly roste.

51

Which when as *Archimago* heard, his griefe
  He knew right well, and him attonce disarmd:
Then searcht his secret wounds, and made a priefe
Of euery place, that was with brusing harmd,
Or with the hidden fire too inly warmd.
Which done, he balmes and herbes thereto applyde,
And euermore with mighty spels them charmd,
That in short space he has them qualifyde,
And him restor'd to health, that would haue algates dyde.

222

Stanza 46

4–5   But . . . auise: i.e. in not knowing that the sea would not drown Pyrochles, Atin was more lucky than wise in so leaping in.

6–9   Significant analogues to Phædria's 'lake of mire' (44.4) are found in Tasso, *Ger. Lib.* x 62 (nothing sinks in the lake which contains the enchantress's island), Dante, *Inf.* vii 108f (the black mire of the sluggish marsh of the Styx covers those overcome by anger) and the biblical Salt or Dead Sea, 'the Sea of the wildernes' (Josh. 3.16) whose 'heavie waters [are] hardly to be moved by the winds' (George Sandys, *Relation of a Journey*, 1615, 142). Cf. also Virgil's Cocytus whose muddy waters confine the damned souls in hell (*Aen.* vi 132, 323, 438–9).

7   Engrost: made thick.   **which . . . agrise**: which rendered them foully horrible; or 'which terrified them', taking **foule** as an adj.   **them**: referring to the waves or to Pyrochles and Atin.

Stanza 47

6   arming: i.e. forming part of knightly arms. Presumably the sword is Arthur's, which Archimago has procured as he had promised, iii 18. He parodies the role of the Palmer–Arthur in relation to Guyon in Canto viii.

8   drenched: submerged.

9   carefull: full of care.

Stanza 48

3   forlore: ruined.

5   Weake hands: i.e. hands are weak.

Stanza 49

2   A literal expression of v 23.   **at earst**: now.   **hent**: seized.

4   straunge astonishment: extreme dismay or loss of wits.

7   drent: drenched, drowned.

8–9   As Shakespeare's Venus 'bathes in water, yet her fire must burn' (*Venus and Adonis* 94). Cf. Hell-fire: 'the fyre that never shal be quenched' (Mark 9.43).

Stanza 50

2   bedight: treated, i.e. maltreated.

3   The liver is the seat of violent passion. The plural may be an error (cf. 'liuer' *1609*) or used because the liver is divided into five lobes. The liver rules the lower regions of the body (Burton, *Anatomy* I i 2.4); from it is drawn a poisonous liquor 'like fire, / All flaming hot, red, furious, and fell, / The spring of dire debate, and civile ire' (P. Fletcher, *Purple Island* iii 15).

4   Refined by fire, his body becomes translucent.

5   Cf. v 22.6–9.

7   thunder light: lightning.

8–9   Phlegeton: the infernal river of fire (see I v 33.1–6n) from which Pyrochles derives, iv 41.7. In Dante, *Inf.* xii, it is a river of boiling blood in which tyrants are submerged.
felly: fiercely.

Stanza 51

3   searcht: probed.   **priefe**: examination.

8   qualifyde: moderated, assuaged.

9   algates: otherwise.

Cant. VII.

Guyon findes Mammon in a delue,
Sunning his threasure hore:
Is by him tempted, and led downe,
To see his secret store.

1

AS Pilot well expert in perilous waue,
  That to a stedfast starre his course hath bent,
When foggy mistes, or cloudy tempests haue
The faithfull light of that faire lampe yblent,
And couer'd heauen with hideous dreriment,
Vpon his card and compas firmes his eye,
The maisters of his long experiment,
And to them does the steddy helme apply,
Bidding his winged vessell fairely forward fly:

2

So *Guyon* hauing lost his trusty guide,
  Late left beyond that *Ydle lake*, proceedes
Yet on his way, of none accompanide;
And euermore himselfe with comfort feedes,
Of his owne vertues, and prayse-worthy deedes.
So long he yode, yet no aduenture found,
Which fame of her shrill trompet worthy reedes:
For still he traueild through wide wastfull ground,
That nought but desert wildernesse shew'd all around.

3

At last he came vnto a gloomy glade,
  Couer'd with boughes and shrubs from heauens light,
Whereas he sitting found in secret shade
An vncouth, saluage, and vnciuile wight,
Of griesly hew, and fowle ill fauour'd sight;
His face with smoke was tand, and eyes were bleard,
His head and beard with sout were ill bedight,
His cole-blacke hands did seeme to haue beene seard
In smithes fire-spitting forge, and nayles like clawes appeard.

Canto vii

Argument

1   **Mammon**: see 8.1–4*n*.   **delue**: i.e. 'glade' (3.1);
cf. 20.6, viii 4.6.
2   Lewis (1964) 106 suggests that Mammon's hoard is grey
because it is not gold; he suns it that it may become gold.

Cf. Chapman's note on *Hero and Leander* iii 24: 'He cals
Phœbus the God of Gold, since the vertue of his beams creates
it.' Yet **hore** may signify simply grey with age, or with 'rust'
(4.1) like his coat, and hence the hoard needs to be 'turned
vpsidowne' (4.8) to show its beauty. In his ode on temperance
(II ii), Horace observes that metal loses its lustre when hidden
in the earth; hence Guyon argues, as does Horace, that wealth
should receive its 'right vsaunce' (7.4). The confrontation
suggests folk-tales of gnomes who are surprised by unwary
strangers as they sun their treasures. The substance of the line
is repeated at viii 4.7.

Stanza 1

2   **a stedfast starre**: 'the stedfast starre' of I ii 1.2 as 4
suggests; yet called 'some star' in *Amor.* xxxiv 1–4.
6   **card**: prob. the mariner's geographical chart rather than
the graduated compass card although either sense may apply.
See Falconer (1964) 89. The danger of sailing 'withouten
starres' is noted at III iv 9.8; cf. III ii 7.7.   **firmes**: firmly
fixes.
7   **maisters**: instruments; instructors.   **experiment**:
experience, referring to his art of navigation.
8   **apply**: steer.

Stanza 2

1–5   Suggests a parallel with Christ's temptation in the
wilderness. As Christ put aside godhead to be tested in the
flesh, Guyon leaves the Palmer behind to be tested in himself.
See Kermode (1971) 77–9.
2   **Ydle**: if not a printer's convention, the capital suggests the
Pythagorean letter Y whose two shafts represent the paths of
virtue and vice; see Servius's gloss on Virgil, *Aen.* vi 136, and
Chapman, 'Vergil's Epigram of this letter Y', in *Poems* 234–5.
4   **comfort**: aid, support, not necessarily implying compla-
cency. Like the mariner, Guyon turns from sure, heavenly
guidance to his own means. His inner assurance is parodied by
Braggadocchio, iii 5.2–4. Cf. Britomart's state, III ii 49.2–3,
and Arthur's, III iv 53.3–4.   **feedes**: indicates the strength
and limitations of his self-sufficiency. See Headnote. On the
image of feeding, cf. 4.8, 9.3, 24.4, and his final faint through
lack of food, 65.3.
6   **So long**] Long so *1590* (corr. in some copies), as the
Var. notes, makes better sense but lacks authority.   **yode**:
went.
7   **reedes**: considers.
8–9   **traueild**: with the play on 'travail'.   **wastfull**:
desolate. Limitless expanse suggests the absence of the bounds
of temperance. Cf. xii 35.3.   **desert wildernesse**: suggests
the wilderness in which Christ was tempted, Matt. 4.1.

Stanza 3

4   **vncouth**: strange, repellent, clumsy.   **saluage**: wild,
as a woodland creature; the Renaissance Wild or Salvage Man
covered with gold rather than green.   **vnciuile**: barbarous.
5   **griesly hew**: shape that arouses horror.
6–9   Mammon appears as a blacksmith; cf. the description
of the blacksmith Care, IV v 34.4–9.   **bleard**: inflamed; as
Leah is 'bleare eied' (Gen. 29.17, gloss); here induced by smoke
or by lack of sleep from watching his wealth, or with reference
to his moral nature. Cf. Langland's Avarice 'with two blered
eyghen' (*Piers Plowman* v 191).   **ill bedight**: ill-arrayed,
disfigured.   **seard**: scorched. On the claws of Avarice, see
Chew (1962) 105.

4

His yron coate all ouergrowne with rust,
  Was vnderneath enueloped with gold,
  Whose glistring glosse darkned with filthy dust,
  Well yet appeared, to haue beene of old
  A worke of rich entayle, and curious mould,
  Wouen with antickes and wild Imagery:
  And in his lap a masse of coyne he told,
  And turned vpsidowne, to feede his eye
And couetous desire with his huge threasury.

5

And round about him lay on euery side
  Great heapes of gold, that neuer could be spent:
  Of which some were rude owre, not purifide
  Of *Mulcibers* deuouring element;
  Some others were new driuen, and distent
  Into great Ingoes, and to wedges square;
  Some in round plates withouten moniment;
  But most were stampt, and in their metall bare
The antique shapes of kings and kesars straunge and rare.

6

Soone as he *Guyon* saw, in great affright
  And hast he rose, for to remoue aside
  Those pretious hils from straungers enuious sight,
  And downe them poured through an hole full wide,
  Into the hollow earth, them there to hide.
  But *Guyon* lightly to him leaping, stayd
  His hand, that trembled, as one terrifyde;
  And though him selfe were at the sight dismayd,
Yet him perforce restraynd, and to him doubtfull sayd.

7

What art thou man, (if man at all thou art)
  That here in desert hast thine habitaunce,
  And these rich heapes of wealth doest hide apart
  From the worldes eye, and from her right vsaunce?
  Thereat with staring eyes fixed askaunce,
  In great disdaine, he answerd; Hardy Elfe,
  That darest vew my direfull countenaunce,
  I read thee rash, and heedlesse of thy selfe,
To trouble my still seate, and heapes of pretious pelfe.

Stanza 4

4 **yet]** it *1596*. yet suggests 'even though it was darkened'.
5–6 The patterned figures suggest that Mammon is protected by charms. **entayle**: carving, engraving. In medieval romance 'of rich entail' means 'of rich quality'. **curious mould**: elaborately wrought pattern or design. **antickes**: fantastic figures; cf. Belphœbe's buskins 'entayld / With curious antickes' (iii 27.4–5). **Imagery**: images; hence **wild** suggests fantastic or grotesque; cf. Acrasia's fountain wrought 'with curious imageree' (xii 60.5).
7 As Avarice, I iv 27.5. **told**: counted.
8 **vpsidowne**: the more archaic form, as J. C. Smith (1909) ii 507 notes.
9 **threasury**: treasure.

Stanza 5

2 Mammon's coins are not common currency; cf. 7.4. Chaucer's Parson defines Avarice as the desire to keep things 'withoute rightful nede' (*Parson's Tale* 744).
4 **deuouring element**: fire, the element whose deity is Mulciber (signifying the purifier of metals) or Vulcan.
5 **driuen, and distent**: beaten out and extended, although 3–4 suggest 'smelted and beaten'.
6 **Ingoes**: a S. variant of 'ingot'. **wedges**: ingots of gold.
7 **moniment**: identifying mark, superscription.
9 **kings and kesars**: terms that are always paired; **kesar**, Caesar, signifies the absolute monarch; cf. III xi 29.9, IV vii 1.4, etc. The allusion to Matt. 22.20–1 indicates to whom this wealth is owing.

Stanza 6

3 **hils**: Upton (1758) prefers 'heapes' (5.2, 7.3); however, the term is a mid-stage from 'heapes' to 'mountaines' (9.2).
5 **hollow earth**: cf. 8.9, 20.8.
6–9 Guyon's fearful response to wealth prepares for his temptation: soon he is almost dismayed (37.7) and finally he lies dismayed (cf. viii 7.5). **perforce**: forcibly. **to him doubtfull**: i.e. to the fearful Mammon, although the term applies also to Guyon who is doubtful about Mammon's identity and fearful of the temptation that confronts him.

Stanza 7

3 **heapes]** hils *1590*.
4 **her**: referring to **world**. **right vsaunce**: proper use. The term may imply usury, alluding to the parable of the talents, Matt. 25.14f. Phædria asks Guyon: 'What bootes it all to haue, and nothing vse?' (vi 17.6), but she omits the key term 'right'.
5 **Thereat**: because of that. **staring**: glaring.
askaunce: sideways, suggesting disdain, distrust and guile; cf. the glance of Malbecco, III ix 27.3; Suspect, III xii 15.2; Envy, V xii 29.2; and Disdain, VI vii 42.3–4. In Malecasta, this detail suggests wanton guile, III i 41.6. Mammon, as an infernal creature, has the full staring eyes of the Dragon (I xi 14) and Despair (I ix 35.7).
6–9 In reply, Mammon asserts that he is no man at all but a god whose face may not be looked upon with impunity; hence **Hardy**: rashly bold or foolhardy, as applied to Huddibras, ii 17.2; cf. 27.1 below. **Elfe**: knight. Since Mammon is evidently a gnome, he claims kinship with Guyon; cf. his use of 'Sonne' (18.1). **read**: consider. **seate**: throne, rather than abode. Sitting upon the earth establishes him as 'God of the world'.

8

God of the world and worldlings I me call,
　Great *Mammon*, greatest god below the skye,
　That of my plenty poure out vnto all,
　And vnto none my graces do enuye:
　Riches, renowme, and principality,
　Honour, estate, and all this worldes good,
　For which men swinck and sweat incessantly,
Fro me do flow into an ample flood,
And in the hollow earth haue their eternall brood.

9

Wherefore if me thou deigne to serue and sew,
　At thy commaund lo all these mountaines bee;
　Or if to thy great mind, or greedy vew
　All these may not suffise, there shall to thee
　Ten times so much be numbred francke and free.
　Mammon (said he) thy godheades vaunt is vaine,
　And idle offers of thy golden fee;
　To them, that couet such eye-glutting gaine,
Proffer thy giftes, and fitter seruaunts entertaine.

10

Me ill besits, that in der-doing armes,
　And honours suit my vowed dayes do spend,
　Vnto thy bounteous baytes, and pleasing charmes,
　With which weake men thou witchest, to attend:
　Regard of worldly mucke doth fowly blend,
　And low abase the high heroicke spright,
　That ioyes for crownes and kingdomes to contend;
Faire shields, gay steedes, bright armes be my delight:
Those be the riches fit for an aduent'rous knight.

Stanza 8

1–4　**Mammon**: signifying **Riches** (5; cf. 'Richesse' 24.9), the 'Money God' (39.1). In Matt. 6.24 and Luke 16.9–13, the Geneva Bible renders Mammon as 'riches'. He is named God of the world in 2 Cor. 4.4 and 'prince of this worlde' in John 12.31. As Satan, the rival and parody of God, his **grace** is gold. The classical god of riches, Plutus, was often confused with Pluto, god of the underworld. Cf. Milton's reference to 'the den of *Plutus*, or the cave of *Mammon*' (*Animadversions, Prose Wks* i 719).　**enuye**: refuse.
5–6　**renowme** is linked with **Honour, principality** (exalted rank or dignity) with **estate**, and **Riches** with **all this worldes good**. Mammon's daughter rewards her followers with 'Honour and dignitie . . . and all this worldes blis' (48.7–8). 'Guyon undergoes . . . a *total* temptation parallel to that of Christ in the wilderness' (Kermode, 1971, 68).
7　**swinck**: labour.
9　**brood**: birth or breeding-place.

Stanzas 9–63

The entire temptation is carefully structured. First, Mammon offers wealth which Guyon rejects for the pursuit of glory. In the debate that follows, wealth is offered as the means to glory but rejected as the source of evil. Then Mammon renews his offer, allowing Guyon to choose from the wealth that he sees. Guyon rejects it with reservations: he will not accept wealth until he knows how and where it was obtained. From this debate follow three temptations: wealth, glory, and physical hunger. (1) At the house of Richesse, Mammon tempts him with wealth as the 'worldes blis' (32.7). Guyon rejects it for another bliss, the life of chivalry. He rejects also the source of wealth, 'the fountaine of the worldes good' (38.6) because he is content with what he can use. (2) Mammon tempts him with worldly advancement through marriage to Philotime. Guyon chooses not to accept. (3) When Mammon invites him to eat the golden fruit and sit on the silver stool, he refuses. Kermode (1971) 69f interprets the three temptations as lust, pride, and curiosity, citing parallel temptations in Augustine and Marvell. Cullen (1974) xxv–xxxvi applies instead the Gregorian triad of vices: gluttony (or *concupiscentia carnis*), vainglory, and avarice. He argues further (68–76) that there is a triple temptation outside the cave to parallel and complement the events within the cave. Alpers (1967) 269 concludes that 'the canto is perhaps the most extraordinary rendering in world literature of the experience of saying No to an evil'.

Stanza 9

1　**serue and sew**: give suit and service. The attendance owing from **seruaunts** (9) to the feudal lord is used here of a worshipper to his god. Mammon tempts Guyon as Satan tempted Christ: 'All these wil I give thee, if thou wilt fall downe, and worship me' (Matt. 4.9). The final temptation in Matthew is a preliminary temptation here.
3　**great mind**: i.e. 'huge desire' (17.6) or ambition, perverting Aristotle's concept of magnanimity or great-mindedness.
5　**francke and free**: i.e. as a gift rather than an obligation.
6　**godheades vaunt**: boast of divinity.
7　**fee**: money, bribe.
9　**entertaine**: keep, retain; used of Guyon's service to the Faerie Queene, ix 6.5.

Stanza 10

Bolton (1967) 21–2 claims that eight words in this stanza 'have made their first appearance in the sixteenth century, or at any rate their first appearance in this meaning or form'. **der-doing** (1), **heroicke** (6), and **contend** (7) are new words; **contend**: compete, vie (*OED* 4) is not recorded before 1589; new meanings are **suit** (2): pursuit of honour (*OED* 6); **witch** (4): charm, entice (*OED* 3).
1–2　**Me . . . spend**: it ill suits me who, in arms, doing daring deeds and in the pursuit of honour have vowed to spend my days. This answer leads to his second temptation for he may seem to be 'Vaine glorious' (11.1) and akin to Braggadocchio (cf. iii 10.3).
3　**bounteous baytes**: temptations of bounty; displayed in Phædria, Mammon, and Acrasia to tempt man to intemperance, in contrast to God's 'soueraigne bountie' (16.4) offered to unfallen man.
5　**mucke**: manure; cf. 'mucky pelfe' (III ix 4.1).　**blend**: blind; defile.
8　Cf. vi 37.6.

11

Vaine glorious Elfe (said he) doest not thou weet,
    That money can thy wantes at will supply?
    Sheilds, steeds, and armes, and all things for thee meet
    It can puruay in twinckling of an eye;
    And crownes and kingdomes to thee multiply.
    Do not I kings create, and throw the crowne
    Sometimes to him, that low in dust doth ly?
    And him that raignd, into his rowme thrust downe,
And whom I lust, do heape with glory and renowne?

12

All otherwise (said he) I riches read,
    And deeme them roote of all disquietnesse;
    First got with guile, and then preseru'd with dread,
    And after spent with pride and lauishnesse,
    Leauing behind them griefe and heauinesse.
    Infinite mischiefes of them do arize,
    Strife, and debate, bloudshed, and bitternesse,
    Outrageous wrong, and hellish couetize,
That noble heart as great dishonour doth despize.

13

Ne thine be kingdomes, ne the scepters thine;
    But realmes and rulers thou doest both confound,
    And loyall truth to treason doest incline;
    Witnesse the guiltlesse bloud pourd oft on ground,
    The crowned often slaine, the slayer cround,
    The sacred Diademe in peeces rent,
    And purple robe gored with many a wound;
    Castles surprizd, great cities sackt and brent:
So mak'st thou kings, and gaynest wrongfull gouernement.

14

Long were to tell the troublous stormes, that tosse
    The priuate state, and make the life vnsweet:
    Who swelling sayles in Caspian sea doth crosse,
    And in frayle wood on *Adrian* gulfe doth fleet,
    Doth not, I weene, so many euils meet.
    Then *Mammon* wexing wroth, And why then, said,
    Are mortall men so fond and vndiscreet,
    So euill thing to seeke vnto their ayd,
And hauing not complaine, and hauing it vpbraid?

15

Indeede (quoth he) through fowle intemperaunce,
    Frayle men are oft captiu'd to couetise:
    But would they thinke, with how small allowaunce
    Vntroubled Nature doth her selfe suffise,
    Such superfluities they would despise,
    Which with sad cares empeach our natiue ioyes:
    At the well head the purest streames arise,
    But mucky filth his braunching armes annoyes,
And with vncomely weedes the gentle waue accloyes.

16

The antique world, in his first flowring youth,
    Found no defect in his Creatours grace,
    But with glad thankes, and vnreproued truth,
    The gifts of soueraigne bountie did embrace:
    Like Angels life was then mens happy cace;
    But later ages pride, like corn-fed steed,
    Abusd her plenty, and fat swolne encreace
    To all licentious lust, and gan exceed
The measure of her meane, and naturall first need.

Stanza 11

4   **puruay**: provide; cf. Luke 4.5: 'The devil . . . shewed him all the kingdomes of the worlde in the twinkeling of an eye.'

6   He arrogates to himself God's role: 'By me, Kings reigne' (Prov. 8.15), which declares 'that honors, dignitie or riches come not of mans wisdome or industrie, but by the providence of God' (Geneva gloss).

8   **rowme**: a particular place to which he properly belongs.

9   **lust**: choose.

Stanza 12

1–2   Cf. Tim. 6.10: 'The desire of money is the roote of all evil.'   **read**: consider.

8   **couetize**: covetousness.

9   **That**: that which.

Stanza 13

Mammon's godhead is denied on grounds that he fails to exercise providence over the kingdoms which he claims as his right.

2   **confound**: overthrow.

3   **incline**: bend.

9   **So**: in this manner (strongly contemptuous).

Stanza 14

2   **priuate state**: the private life in contrast to public office described above.

3–5   The Caspian and the Adriatic were proverbial for their violence.   **fleet**: sail.

9   **vpbraid**: i.e. speak reproachfully against riches; or be reproached for riches.

Stanza 15

3–9   Cf. Boethius, *Consol. Phil.* II Prosa v: 'For with ful fewe thynges and with ful litel thynges nature halt hir apayed; and yif thow wolt achoken the fulfillynge of nature with superfluytees, certes thilke thynges that thow wolt thresten or powren into nature schulle ben unjoyeful to the, or elles anoyous' (trans. Chaucer).

6–9   The metaphor was probably suggested by Chaucer's 'achoken'.   **empeach**: impair.   **braunching armes**: the mouths of the river rather than its tributaries.   **annoyes**: harms.

Stanza 16

For praise of the **antique world**, see Levin (1969).

3   **vnreproued**: i.e. without condemning or reproaching the giver; answering Mammon's charge at 14.9.   **truth**: sincerity; faith, trust.

5   **cace**: state.

6   **corn-fed steed**: proverbial (C. G. Smith, 1970, 121).

9   **measure of her meane**: i.e. the temperate mean.

17

Then gan a cursed hand the quiet wombe
  Of his great Grandmother with steele to wound,
  And the hid treasures in her sacred tombe,
  With Sacriledge to dig.   Therein he found
  Fountaines of gold and siluer to abound,
  Of which the matter of his huge desire
  And pompous pride eftsoones he did compound;
  Then auarice gan through his veines inspire
His greedy flames, and kindled life-deuouring fire.

18

Sonne (said he then) let be thy bitter scorne,
  And leaue the rudenesse of that antique age
  To them, that liu'd therein in state forlorne;
  Thou that doest liue in later times, must wage
  Thy workes for wealth, and life for gold engage.
  If then thee list my offred grace to vse,
  Take what thou please of all this surplusage;
  If thee list not, leaue haue thou to refuse:
But thing refused, do not afterward accuse.

19

Me list not (said the Elfin knight) receaue
  Thing offred, till I know it well be got,
  Ne wote I, but thou didst these goods bereaue
  From rightfull owner by vnrighteous lot,
  Or that bloud guiltinesse or guile them blot.
  Perdy (quoth he) yet neuer eye did vew,
  Ne toung did tell, ne hand these handled not,
  But safe I haue them kept in secret mew,
From heauens sight, and powre of all which them pursew.

20

What secret place (quoth he) can safely hold
  So huge a masse, and hide from heauens eye?
  Or where hast thou thy wonne, that so much gold
  Thou canst preserue from wrong and robbery?
  Come thou (quoth he) and see.   So by and by
  Through that thicke couert he him led, and found
  A darkesome way, which no man could descry,
  That deepe descended through the hollow ground,
And was with dread and horrour compassed around.

II metre v: 'Allas! what was he that first dalf up . . . the
weyghtes of gold covered undir erthe' (trans. Chaucer; cf.
Chaucer, 'The Former Age' 27–32). Cf. also the contrast
between Abel, the keeper of sheep, and Cain, the tiller of the
ground, the one a type of faith and the other an example of one
who distrusts God's providence.
2   **great Grandmother**: i.e. female ancestor; cf. 'the earth,
great mother of vs all' (i 10.6).
4   **Sacriledge**: in the etymological sense, 'to take away
sacred objects', here from **her sacred tombe** (3).
8   As man searches the veins of his mother earth for wealth,
he opens his own veins to infection.   **inspire**: breathe.

Stanza 18
3   Mammon rejects the concept of the golden age which
Harvey, *Works* i 46, claims S. strongly upheld.
4   **wage**: put out to hire.
5   **engage**: pledge.
7   **surplusage**: superabundance. The offer now allows a
measure of choice.

Stanza 19
Guyon's qualified refusal exposes him to the ensuing
temptation. In the name of temperance, he must render
unto Mammon the things which are Mammon's without
becoming his victim.
1–2   The argument is Aristotle's: the liberal man will not
accept money from a tainted source (*Ethics* IV i).
3   **bereaue**: take away by violence.
4   **lot**: share of plunder acquired either by slaying the rightful
owner or by cheating him.
5   **bloud guiltinesse**: the sin of bloodshed; see ii 4.5*n*.
6   Repeated at 31.5, 37.4–5, 38.2.
7   **tell**: count.   **ne . . . not**: the double negative remains
doubly negative.
8   **mew**: place of concealment.

Stanza 20
3–4   **wonne**: dwelling place; or 'riches' (*OED* sb.^{3} 5), for
Guyon's second question concerns the source of Mammon's
wealth; see 38.3–5.
5   **Come thou . . . and see**: adding lust of the eye to
Guyon's desire to 'know' (19.2). Cf. Milton's comment that S.
'describing true temperance under the person of *Guion*, brings
him in with his palmer through the cave of Mammon, and the
bowr of earthly blisse that he might see and know, and yet
abstain' (*Prose Wks* ii 516). Kellogg and Steele (1965)
hear an ironic echo of Christ's answer to the two disciples who
ask 'where dwellest thou?': 'He said unto them, Come, and se'
(John 1.38–9).   **by and by**: immediately.
6   **he him led**: the three words get equal stress: Mammon,
not the Palmer, now guides Guyon. Variations on the phrase
mark further stages of temptation: 35.1, 39.9, 51.2.

Stanzas 21–23
Similar allegorical personages are described by Boccaccio,
Gen Deor. VIII vi. Boccaccio interprets Virgil's Dis (*Aen.* vi
541) as a house of riches and associates it with Dante's Dis (*Inf.*
viii); noted Lotspeich (1932) 65–6. Cf. also the figures at the
entrance to Pluto's realm in *Aen.* vi 273–81, and those in
imitations such as Sackville's 'Induction' to *A Mirror for
Magistrates* (1563). The figures serve to illustrate the evils
catalogued by Guyon, stanzas 12–13.

Stanza 17
In Ovid, *Met.* i 135–40, mining marks the iron age; his *viscera
terrae* suggests S.'s **wombe** (1). Cf. Boethius, *Consol. Phil.*

21

At length they came into a larger space,
  That stretcht it selfe into an ample plaine,
  Through which a beaten broad high way did trace,
  That streight did lead to *Plutoes* griesly raine:
  By that wayes side, there sate infernall Payne,
  And fast beside him sat tumultuous Strife:
  The one in hand an yron whip did straine,
  The other brandished a bloudy knife,
And both did gnash their teeth, and both did threaten life.

22

On thother side in one consort there sate,
  Cruell Reuenge, and rancorous Despight,
  Disloyall Treason, and hart-burning Hate,
  But gnawing Gealosie out of their sight
  Sitting alone, his bitter lips did bight,
  And trembling Feare still to and fro did fly,
  And found no place, where safe he shroud him might,
  Lamenting Sorrow did in darknesse lye,
And Shame his vgly face did hide from liuing eye.

23

And ouer them sad Horrour with grim hew,
  Did alwayes sore, beating his yron wings;
  And after him Owles and Night-rauens flew,
  The hatefull messengers of heauy things,
  Of death and dolour telling sad tidings;
  Whiles sad *Celeno*, sitting on a clift,
  A song of bale and bitter sorrow sings,
  That hart of flint a sunder could haue rift:
Which hauing ended, after him she flyeth swift.

24

All these before the gates of *Pluto* lay,
  By whom they passing, spake vnto them nought.
  But th'Elfin knight with wonder all the way
  Did feed his eyes, and fild his inner thought.
  At last him to a litle dore he brought,
  That to the gate of Hell, which gaped wide,
  Was next adioyning, ne them parted ought:
  Betwixt them both was but a litle stride,
That did the house of Richesse from hell-mouth diuide.

25

Before the dore sat selfe-consuming Care,
  Day and night keeping wary watch and ward,
  For feare least Force or Fraud should vnaware
  Breake in, and spoile the treasure there in gard:
  Ne would he suffer Sleepe once thither-ward
  Approch, albe his drowsie den were next;
  For next to death is Sleepe to be compard:
  Therefore his house is vnto his annext;
Here Sleep, there Richesse, and Hel-gate them both betwext.

Stanza 21

3 **broad high way**: cf. the 'broad high way' (I iv 2.8) that
leads to the house of Pride. Contrast the 'litle dore' (24.5) that
leads out, and the 'narrow strait' (40.1) that leads to a further
temptation.
4 **Plutoes griesly raine**: hell, the horrifying kingdom or
realm under the rule of Pluto; called '*Plutoes* balefull bowres'
(I v 14.8) and 'Plutoes griesly land' (IV iii 13.3).
5 **infernall Payne**: i.e. Punishment; as the goddess Poena.
'internall' *1590* applies to pain as suffering, seen in Pyrochles;
but **infernall** describes punishment in hell.
7 **straine**: grasp tightly and hold extended; cf. the fiend at
27.5–6.

Stanza 22

1 **On thother side**: in Virgil, *Aen*. vi 278–81, War and
Strife are on the opposite side of the threshold from the
horrors of their actions. **consort**: company.
7 **shroud**: conceal.

Stanza 23

1 **ouer them**: i.e. the fiends, but equally Mammon and
Guyon. Cf. **after him** (9): i.e. Horror, but equally Guyon.
hew: appearance.
3–5 Both birds, traditionally birds of evil omen, assault
Guyon and the Palmer at xii 36.4–5. On the owl as the
messenger of death, see I v 30.6–7*n*.
5 **dolour**: pain rather than grief. The physical suffering in
this line is balanced by the mental suffering in 7.
6–9 **Celeno**: chief of the harpies, 'prophets of sad destiny'
(xii 36.9), and associated here with defiling greed. Her presence
implies that Guyon may not eat. In Virgil, *Aen*. iii 245–6, she
perches on a rock and cries out. Boccaccio, *Gen. Deor*. X lxi,
associates her with avarice (Lotspeich, 1932). The pathos of her
song is a strange detail, as Lewis (1967) 72–3 notes. It may
relate to Guyon's misplaced pity at i 14.3 and xii 28.3. **rift**:
riven.

Stanza 24

2 Guyon's silence (cf. 31.1) is associated with his temptation:
to ask would be to desire, and so become Mammon's victim;
cf. Ovid, *Met*. iv 432–3, where the way to the infernal realm
leads *per muta silentia*.
6 **gaped wide**: as the gates of hell, Virgil, *Aen*. vi 127; cf.
the dwelling of Ate 'Hard by the gates of hell' (IV i 20.1).
7 **ne . . . ought**: i.e. nothing separated them. **ought]**
nought *1590* would duplicate the rhyme.
9 **house**: critics have consistently misnamed Mammon's
dwelling a cave; it is explicitly named a house (cf. 29.5 and
viii 3.2), and is only 'Like an huge caue' (28.2). As a house, it is
the infernal counterpart to the house of Alma. **Richesse**:
Wealth, as Mammon is named in the Geneva Bible.

Stanza 25

Cullen (1970) 158 notes that the picture of Care resembles the
opening description of Mammon.
4 **spoile**: plunder. **gard**: keeping.
5–6 Guyon's **selfe-consuming Care** (1), which does not
suffer him to sleep, is the second of two privations he must
experience; see 27.4, 65.3. **next**: i.e. 'next adioyning' (24.7).
7–8 Death and Sleep are commonly associated by S. In
Virgil, *Aen*. vi 278, Sleep is Death's brother.

26

So soone as *Mammon* there arriu'd, the dore
   To him did open, and affoorded way;
   Him followed eke Sir *Guyon* euermore,
   Ne darkenesse him, ne daunger might dismay.
   Soone as he entred was, the dore streight way
   Did shut, and from behind it forth there lept
   An vgly feend, more fowle then dismall day,
   The which with monstrous stalke behind him stept,
And euer as he went, dew watch vpon him kept.

27

Well hoped he, ere long that hardy guest,
   If euer couetous hand, or lustfull eye,
   Or lips he layd on thing, that likt him best,
   Or euer sleepe his eye-strings did vntye,
   Should be his pray.   And therefore still on hye
   He ouer him did hold his cruell clawes,
   Threatning with greedy gripe to do him dye
   And rend in peeces with his rauenous pawes,
If euer he transgrest the fatall *Stygian* lawes.

28

That houses forme within was rude and strong,
   Like an huge caue, hewne out of rocky clift,
   From whose rough vaut the ragged breaches hong,
   Embost with massy gold of glorious gift,
   And with rich metall loaded euery rift,
   That heauy ruine they did seeme to threat;
   And ouer them *Arachne* high did lift
   Her cunning web, and spred her subtile net,
Enwrapped in fowle smoke and clouds more blacke then let.

29

Both roofe, and floore, and wals were all of gold,
   But ouergrowne with dust and old decay,
   And hid in darkenesse, that none could behold
   The hew thereof: for vew of chearefull day
   Did neuer in that house it selfe display,
   But a faint shadow of vncertain light;
   Such as a lamp, whose life does fade away:
   Or as the Moone cloathed with clowdy night,
Does shew to him, that walkes in feare and sad affright.

30

In all that rowme was nothing to be seene,
   But huge great yron chests and coffers strong,
   All bard with double bends, that none could weene
   Them to efforce by violence or wrong;
   On euery side they placed were along.
   But all the ground with sculs was scattered,
   And dead mens bones, which round about were flong,
   Whose liues, it seemed, whilome there were shed,
And their vile carcases now left vnburied.

31

They forward passe, ne *Guyon* yet spoke word,
   Till that they came vnto an yron dore,
   Which to them opened of his owne accord,
   And shewd of richesse such exceeding store,
   As eye of man did neuer see before;
   Ne euer could within one place be found,
   Though all the wealth, which is, or was of yore,
   Could gathered be through all the world around,
And that aboue were added to that vnder ground.

Stanza 26
5   Hieatt (1975) 196 notes that at this point Guyon enters Mammon's house and remains until 66.4: the forty stanzas of his temptation suggests the forty days of Christ's temptation.
6–9   Upton (1758) claims that Guyon undergoes an initiation comparable to that of the Eleusinian mysteries. This **vgly feend** is akin to the fury who follows the initiate to ensure that he does not transgress 'the fatall *Stygian* lawes' (27.9). See Kermode (1971) 76.   **feend**: applied earlier to the Dragon (I i 5.7) and to Error (I i 22.4).   **dismall day**: day of death; see vi 43.7*n*.

Stanza 27
3   **likt**: pleased.
9   **Stygian lawes**: laws of the infernal kingdom, named from the river Styx over which souls pass into hell; **fatall** because they control man's destiny.

Stanza 28
3   **vaut**: vault.   **breaches**: projecting arches of rock rather than fissures.
4   **Embost**: adorned; raised.   **glorious gift**: rich or brilliant quality.
5   **rift**: also a projecting fragment or vein of ore rather than fissure, as xii 4.5; or possibly the gap between protruding rocks. Cf. Keats's remark to Shelley that the artist 'must serve Mammon . . . and "load every rift" of your subject with ore' (*Letters* ii 322–3).
6   **ruine**: downfall.
7–9   Arachne's web is a trap; cf. Acrasia's covering veil, xii 77.7.   **high did lift** suggests that the web is an emblem of ambitious envy, from Arachne's challenge to Minerva. S. relates the story in *Muiopotmos* 257–352. Cf. the story of the Sirens, xii 31, and of ambitious Tantalus below, 59. **subtile**: artfully contrived.

Stanza 29
6–9   Cf. the use of chiaroscuro at 37.1–7, 42.2, 45.2–3. S. imitates Virgil's simile, *Aen.* vi 270–2.

Stanza 30
3   **bends**: bands.
6–9   As the land over which the deadly sins ride 'all scattered lay / Dead sculs and bones of men, whose life had gone astray' (I iv 36.8–9); see vi 28.7–9*n*.

Stanza 31
1   On Guyon's silence, see 24.2*n*.
3   Doors open spontaneously – cf. 26.1–6 and 35.3 – to lead the prisoner deeper into the dungeon; perhaps in contrast to Acts 12.10: the iron gate opened of its own accord to allow Peter, guided by the Angel, to escape from prison.

32

The charge thereof vnto a couetous Spright
   Commaunded was, who thereby did attend,
   And warily awaited day and night,
   From other couetous feends it to defend,
   Who it to rob and ransacke did intend.
   Then *Mammon* turning to that warriour, said;
   Loe here the worldes blis, loe here the end,
   To which all men do ayme, rich to be made:
Such grace now to be happy, is before thee laid.

33

Certes (said he) I n'ill thine offred grace,
   Ne to be made so happy do intend:
   Another blis before mine eyes I place,
   Another happinesse, another end.
   To them, that list, these base regardes I lend:
   But I in armes, and in atchieuements braue,
   Do rather choose my flitting houres to spend,
   And to be Lord of those, that riches haue,
Then them to haue my selfe, and be their seruile sclaue.

34

Thereat the feend his gnashing teeth did grate,
   And grieu'd, so long to lacke his greedy pray;
   For well he weened, that so glorious bayte
   Would tempt his guest, to take thereof assay:
   Had he so doen, he had him snatcht away,
   More light then Culuer in the Faulcons fist.
   Eternall God thee saue from such decay.
   But whenas *Mammon* saw his purpose mist,
Him to entrap vnwares another way he wist.

35

Thence forward he him led, and shortly brought
   Vnto another rowme, whose dore forthright,
   To him did open, as it had beene taught:
   Therein an hundred raunges weren pight,
   And hundred fornaces all burning bright;
   By euery fornace many feends did bide,
   Deformed creatures, horrible in sight,
   And euery feend his busie paines applide,
To melt the golden metall, ready to be tride.

36

One with great bellowes gathered filling aire,
   And with forst wind the fewell did inflame;
   Another did the dying bronds repaire
   With yron toungs, and sprinckled oft the same
   With liquid waues, fiers *Vulcans* rage to tame,
   Who maistring them, renewd his former heat;
   Some scumd the drosse, that from the metall came;
   Some stird the molten owre with ladles great;
And euery one did swincke, and euery one did sweat.

37

But when as earthly wight they present saw,
   Glistring in armes and battailous aray,
   From their whot worke they did themselues withdraw
   To wonder at the sight: for till that day,
   They neuer creature saw, that camethat way.
   Their staring eyes sparckling with feruent fire,
   And vgly shapes did nigh the man dismay,
   That were it not for shame, he would retire,
Till that him thus bespake their soueraigne Lord and sire.

Stanza 32

2   **Commaunded**: committed.

3   **awaited**: kept watch.

7–8   Cf. the similar claim at 48.8–9.

Stanza 33

1–4   Guyon answers with the opening argument of Aristotle's *Ethics* that happiness is the chief good desired for its own sake, and the end of all we do. Mammon offers the bliss now that men strive for in the future – to be rich. Guyon replies that he does not want now to be **so happy**, i.e. prosperous, because **Another blis** (chivalric honour?) is his goal for the future.

5   **base regardes**: heed for low matters; cf. 47.4.

8–9   Cicero, *de Senect.* xvi 56, tells the familiar story of Manius Curius who returned a gift of gold because he would rather command those who had gold than have it himself. Williams (1966) 58 cites the apocryphal Acts of John: those who love the world serve their master, the devil Mammon; they 'do not possess riches, but are possessed by them' (*Apoc. N. T.*, ed. M. R. James, Oxford 1924, 259–60). **sclaue**: obsolete form of 'slave'.

Stanza 34

1   **feend**: the 'vgly feend' (26.7) who follows him rather than Mammon, although no distinction is needed for lines 1–4.

2   **his greedy pray**: i.e. the prey for which he is greedy.

4   **assay**: trial by touching, as suggested at 27.2–3; but also testing of metals to determine their quality.

6   **light**: quickly.   **Culuer**: a dove.

7   Cf. the poet's cry at the Red Cross Knight's predicament, I i 18.9.   **decay**: death.

8   **purpose**: with a pun on the sense, 'speech'. Guyon is tempted both by the eye and by the ear.

9   **vnwares**: unexpectedly; or as an adj., 'unwary', to stress Guyon's need for vigilance.

Stanza 35

1   **he him led**: marks the second stage of the temptation (see 20.6*n*). Control of the source of riches would make Guyon 'Lord of those, that riches haue' (33.8). The two stages differ as the mine and the furnace, or the pioneer and the smith.

2–3   See 31.3*n*.

4   **pight**: placed.

9   **tride**: purified.

Stanza 36

Cf. Virgil's Cyclopean furnaces (*Aen.* viii 416–22, 449–51).

3   **bronds**: embers.

7   **scumd**: skimmed off.

Stanza 37

2   **Glistring** suggests that the arms outshine the furnace. **battailous**: warlike.

6   **staring**: also shining; see iv 15.6*n*; cf. Mammon's 'staring eyes' (7.5).   **feruent** suggests Lat. *fervere*, to glow.

38

Behold, thou Faeries sonne, with mortall eye,
    That liuing eye before did neuer see:
    The thing, that thou didst craue so earnestly,
    To weet, whence all the wealth late shewd by mee,
    Proceeded, lo now is reueald to thee.
    Here is the fountaine of the worldes good:
    Now therefore, if thou wilt enriched bee,
    Auise thee well, and chaunge thy wilfull mood,
Least thou perhaps hereafter wish, and be withstood.

39

Suffise it then, thou Money God (quoth hee)
    That all thine idle offers I refuse.
    All that I need I haue; what needeth mee
    To couet more, then I haue cause to vse?
    With such vaine shewes thy worldlings vile abuse:
    But giue me leaue to follow mine emprise.
    Mammon was much displeasd, yet no'te he chuse,
    But beare the rigour of his bold mesprise,
And thence him forward led, him further to entise.

40

He brought him through a darksome narrow strait,
    To a broad gate, all built of beaten gold:
    The gate was open, but therein did wait
    A sturdy villein, striding stiffe and bold,
    As if that highest God defie he would;
    In his right hand an yron club he held,
    But he himselfe was all of golden mould,
    Yet had both life and sence, and well could weld
That cursed weapon, when his cruell foes he queld.

41

Disdayne he called was, and did disdaine
    To be so cald, and who so did him call:
    Sterne was his looke, and full of stomacke vaine,
    His portaunce terrible, and stature tall,
    Far passing th'hight of men terrestriall;
    Like an huge Gyant of the *Titans* race,
    That made him scorne all creatures great and small,
    And with his pride all others powre deface:
More fit amongst blacke fiendes, then men to haue his place.

42

Soone as those glitterand armes he did espye,
    That with their brightnesse made that darknesse light,
    His harmefull club he gan to hurtle hye,
    And threaten batteill to the Faery knight;
    Who likewise gan himselfe to batteill dight,
    Till *Mammon* did his hasty hand withhold,
    And counseld him abstaine from perilous fight:
    For nothing might abash the villein bold,
Ne mortall steele emperce his miscreated mould.

43

So hauing him with reason pacifide,
    And the fiers Carle commaunding to forbeare,
    He brought him in. The rowme was large and wide,
    As it some Gyeld or solemne Temple weare:
    Many great golden pillours did vpbeare
    The massy roofe, and riches huge sustayne,
    And euery pillour decked was full deare
    With crownes and Diademes, and titles vaine,
Which mortall Princes wore, whiles they on earth did rayne.

Stanza 38

3–5   Mammon refers to Guyon's question at 20.3–4 but adds **earnestly** to suggest that Guyon is intemperate.
6   **worldes good**: as 'worldes blis' (32.7), the *summum bonum*.
8   **Auise thee**: consider.
9   Cf. 18.9.

Stanza 39

1   **Money God**: an ironic address since God is 'the fountaine of the worldes good' (38.6).
2   **idle**: vain; worthless.
5   **abuse**: deceive.
6   **emprise**: adventure.
7   **no'te**: could not.
8   **mesprise**: scorn.

Stanza 40

1–2   **strait**: confined passage; it leads out of the house of Richesse as the 'litle dore' (24.5) leads in. The **broad gate** suggests 'the gate of Hell, which gaped wide' (24.6).
4   **sturdy**: ruthless, violent.   **villein**: villain; also a serf, a bondsman to his disdain of others.
7   **golden**] yron *1590*.
8   The allegorist insists that his most allegorical figure is not merely allegorical.
9   **when . . . queld**: i.e. when he cruelly killed his foes.

Stanza 41

1   **Disdayne** appears in response to Guyon's 'bold mesprise' (39.8). A fitting porter of the court of Philotime: see Aristotle on the pride which the goods of fortune arouse in those without virtue: 'Disdainful and insolent, however, even those who have such goods become. . . . being unable to bear them, and thinking themselves superior to others, they despise others' (*Ethics* IV iii 1124ᵇ; cited Kellogg and Steele, 1965). Cf. Mammon's 'great disdaine' (7.6).
3   **stomacke**: pride, haughtiness.
4   **portaunce**: bearing.
6   **Titans race**: the proud, rebellious offspring of the Earth 'which did make / Warre against heauen . . . [to] put *Ioue* from his right' (III vii 47.3–5). On the war of the Giants against Jove, see Ovid, *Met.* i 151–3, Hesiod, *Theog.* 617–735. Starnes and Talbert (1955) 74 cite Stephanus as source. S. links this battle with the battle of the Titans against Saturn and Jove (Lotspeich, 1932, 63, 112). References to these battles figure prominently throughout the poem, e.g. x 3.3–4, III ix 22, xi 22.8–9, V i 9.5–9, vii 10.4–5, VI vii 41.5–7, VII vi 27, 33.
8   **deface**: abash (cf. 42.8).

Stanza 42

1   **glitterand**: shining; cf. xi 17.1 and see I vii 29.4*n*.
3   **hurtle**: violently brandish.
6–9   Mammon plays the Palmer's role, iv 10.2–5, in order to save Guyon for greater temptations; cf. 43.1. Nothing can **abash**, i.e. confound, Disdain: to disdain Disdain, i.e. to become angry with him, only increases his power.   **miscreated mould**: unnaturally created body, being made of gold.

Stanza 43

2   **Carle**: churl.
4   **Gyeld**: guildhall.   **solemne**: grand, sumptuous.
7   **deare**: richly.

44

A route of people there assembled were,
　Of euery sort and nation vnder skye,
　Which with great vprore preaced to draw nere
　To th'vpper part, where was aduaunced hye
　A stately siege of soueraigne maiestye;
　And thereon sat a woman gorgeous gay,
　And richly clad in robes of royaltye,
That neuer earthly Prince in such aray
His glory did enhaunce, and pompous pride display.

45

Her face right wondrous faire did seeme to bee,
　That her broad beauties beam great brightnes threw
　Through the dim shade, that all men might it see:
　Yet was not that same her owne natiue hew,
　But wrought by art and counterfetted shew,
　Thereby more louers vnto her to call;
　Nath'lesse most heauenly faire in deed and vew
　She by creation was, till she did fall;
Thenceforth she sought for helps, to cloke her crime withall.

46

There, as in glistring glory she did sit,
　She held a great gold chaine ylincked well,
　Whose vpper end to highest heauen was knit,
　And lower part did reach to lowest Hell;
　And all that preace did round about her swell,
　To catchen hold of that long chaine, thereby
　To clime aloft, and others to excell:
　That was *Ambition*, rash desire to sty,
And euery lincke thereof a step of dignity.

47

Some thought to raise themselues to high degree,
　By riches and vnrighteous reward,
　Some by close shouldring, some by flatteree;
　Others through friends, others for base regard;
　And all by wrong wayes for themselues prepard.
　Those that were vp themselues, kept others low,
　Those that were low themselues, held others hard,
　Ne suffred them to rise or greater grow,
But euery one did striue his fellow downe to throw.

48

Which whenas *Guyon* saw, he gan inquire,
　What meant that preace about that Ladies throne,
　And what she was that did so high aspire.
　Him *Mammon* answered; That goodly one,
　Whom all that folke with such contention,
　Do flocke about, my deare, my daughter is;
　Honour and dignitie from her alone
　Deriued are, and all this worldes blis
For which ye men do striue: few get, but many mis.

49

And faire *Philotime* she rightly hight,
　The fairest wight that wonneth vnder skye,
　But that this darksome neather world her light
　Doth dim with horrour and deformitie,
　Worthy of heauen and hye felicitie,
　From whence the gods haue her for enuy thrust:
　But sith thou hast found fauour in mine eye,
　Thy spouse I will her make, if that thou lust,
232　That she may thee aduance for workes and merites iust.

Stanza 44

4–9　Cf. Lucifera's court (I iv 7.4–7) and attire (8.3–4).
Each vision of glory is a prelude to a vision of the damned.
siege: throne; suggested by the siege of suitors.

Stanza 45

2–3　**threw / Through**: the juxtaposition emphasizes her
attraction.
8–9　Her brightness and fall associate her with Satan: 'How
art thou fallen from heaven, O Lucifer, sonne of the morning'
(Isaiah 14.12). Her **crime** is clearly ambition.

Stanza 46

2　**a great gold chaine**: cf. the golden chain by which
Homer's Zeus controls all creation (*Iliad* viii 18–27). See I v
25.5n, ix 1.1–2n. Comes (1616) II iv interprets it as ambition
which draws many, but not the good man, from the true faith.
Cf. Chapman, 'Shadow of Night' (*Hymnus in noctem*) 159–60:
'The golden chaine of Homers high deuice / Ambition is, or
cursed auarice.' As a symbol of cosmic concord, see IV i
30.8–9.
5　The suitors act out the etymological sense of 'ambition': to
go around. **preace**: throng. **swell**: also behave proudly;
here, ambitiously.
8　**sty**: mount up.
9　**step of dignity**: also a rank in society; see iii 5.9n.

Stanza 47

4　**regard**: payment, i.e. bribes, **vnrighteous reward** (2).
Perhaps 'attention to ambition', the 'base regardes' (33.5) which
Guyon leaves to Mammon's worldlings.

Stanza 48

7–9　Parallel to the temptation of riches (32.7–8) is the
temptation of fame to which all S.'s knights are open.

Stanza 49

1　**Philotime**: Gk love of honour, indicating an intemperate
devotion to honour for its own sake. To her suit Guyon had
vowed himself at 10.2.
8　**lust**: wish; also implying its modern sense.
9　Mammon offers grace; his daughter offers salvation by
good works contrary to the Protestant emphasis on faith rather
than works. The nature of these works is revealed in the various
'wrong wayes' catalogued at 47.2–5. **merites**: also 'good
works viewed as entitling reward from God' (*OED* 5); see I viii
27.7n. Such merit must be renounced even though **iust**. Cf. the
Faerie Queene's freely offered grace to advance her servants, ix
5.4–5, and Arthur's free act, viii 56.1–6.

50

Gramercy *Mammon* (said the gentle knight)
  For so great grace and offred high estate;
  But I, that am fraile flesh and earthly wight,
  Vnworthy match for such immortall mate
  My selfe well wote, and mine vnequall fate;
  And were I not, yet is my trouth yplight,
  And loue auowd to other Lady late,
That to remoue the same I haue no might:
To chaunge loue causelesse is reproch to warlike knight.

51

Mammon emmoued was with inward wrath;
  Yet forcing it to faine, him forth thence led
  Through griesly shadowes by a beaten path,
  Into a gardin goodly garnished
  With hearbs and fruits, whose kinds mote not be red:
  Not such, as earth out of her fruitfull woomb
  Throwes forth to men, sweet and well sauoured,
But direfull deadly blacke both leafe and bloom,
Fit to adorne the dead, and decke the drery toombe.

52

There mournfull *Cypresse* grew in greatest store,
  And trees of bitter *Gall*, and *Heben* sad,
  Dead sleeping *Poppy*, and blacke *Hellebore*,
  Cold *Coloquintida*, and *Tetra* mad,
  Mortall *Samnitis*, and *Cicuta* bad,
  With which th'vniust *Atheniens* made to dy
  Wise *Socrates*, who thereof quaffing glad
Pourd out his life, and last Philosophy
To the faire *Critias* his dearest Belamy.

53

The *Gardin of Proserpina* this hight;
  And in the midst thereof a siluer seat,
  With a thicke Arber goodly ouer dight,
  In which she often vsd from open heat
  Her selfe to shroud, and pleasures to entreat;
  Next thereunto did grow a goodly tree,
  With braunches broad dispred and body great,
Clothed with leaues, that none the wood mote see
And loaden all with fruit as thicke as it might bee.

Stanza 50
Guyon speaks ironically but not disdainfully. His answer shows
how he 'did beguile the Guyler of the pray' (64.9). Mammon
tempts him as a worldling; as a worldling, Guyon rejects an
offer to marry an **immortall mate**.
1   **Gramercy**: thanks; also with reference to the
etymological sense of Fr. *merci*, reward: 'Great reward that
would be!'
5   **vnequall**: i.e. not being an equal match for her.

7   The **Lady** is unnamed but presumably she is the honour
which Philotime parodies.
9   **causelesse**: without good cause; cf. I iv 1.

Stanza 51
2   **him . . . led**: announcing the final temptation; see 20.6n.
5   **red**: told.

Stanza 52
1–5   **Cypresse**: the traditional funereal tree (cf. I i 8.9, II i
60.3).   **Gall**: the oak whose fruit is called oak-gall; **Gall**,
therefore **bitter**.   **Heben**: either the ebony-tree or the
Hebenon which Gower calls 'that slepi Tree' (*Conf. Aman.* iv
3017) and Cooper (1565) 'a tree wherof the wodde is blacke
as jette within, and beareth nor leaues nor fruite'.
Hellebore: its name suggests 'hell-born', and therefore **blacke**.
Coloquintida: the poisonous wild gourd of 2 Kings 4.39–40;
the Geneva gloss reads: 'which the Apoticaries call colloquin-
tida, and is moste vehement and dangerous in purging'.
Cold: perhaps suggested by the name.   **Tetra mad**: the
deadly nightshade which causes madness.   **Samnitis**: a
unique usage. Since the Samnites were neighbours of the
Sabines, Upton (1758) conjectures that it is the savine tree,
arbor Sabina; called **Mortall** because it procures abortion.
Cicuta: hemlock.
6–9   If S. meant **Critias** and knew that he became Socrates's
enemy, **dearest Belamy** must be taken as ironical, or **dearest**
read in the sense of 'direst', most grievous. It is simpler to
allow a mistake for Crito, the friend present at Socrates's
death; or a simple confusion because of the parallel story of
Theramenes: according to Xenophon, (*Hell.* II iii 56, Loeb
edn), it was Theramenes who drank hemlock to the health of
his beloved Critias. See IV Proem 3.6–8n.   **Belamy**: sweet
friend (Fr. *bel ami*) used in the sense of belamour (cf. vi 16.7).

Stanzas 53–55
Baybak, Delany and Hieatt (1969) 231 note that these three
stanzas are the numerical midpoint of the *1590* edition (not
counting the Proems): hence the phrase 'in the midst' (53.2).
The middle stanza, 54, describes the apples which constitute
the culminating temptation. On the centres of Books I and III,
each a *locus amoenus* which is here reversed, see I vii 12–13n,
III vi 43n.

Stanza 53
This **Gardin** is a counterpart to Phædria's island paradise
(vi 12–13) and the Bower of Bliss (v 29–31). The grove of
Proserpina, found at the entrance to the lower world in Homer
(*Ody.* x 509–10), contains 'Tall firs, and sallows that their
fruits soon lose' (trans. Chapman). Some details may be
drawn from Claudian, *Rape of Proserpine*. Proserpina's consort,
Plutus, is associated with Mammon: see 8.1–4n. In Virgil,
Georg. iv 468, the grove at the gates of Dis is darkened with
black terror. Here the blackness of the trees expresses their
deadly effect; cf. the black, funereal hue of the Tree of
Knowledge in the O. E. *Genesis B*.
2   **siluer seat**: see 63.6–9n.
3   **ouer dight**: overspread.
5   **entreat**: occupy herself in; entice others to indulge in.
6–9   Cf. the tree with golden fruit consecrated to Proserpina
in Claudian, *Rape of Proserpine* ii 290–2. The tree
bears the golden-haired fruit which Aeneas must pluck in order
to descend into Hell, *Aen.* vi 136–43. See 63.6–9n.

233

54

Their fruit were golden apples glistring bright,
　That goodly was their glory to behold,
　On earth like neuer grew, ne liuing wight
　Like euer saw, but they from hence were sold;
　For those, which *Hercules* with conquest bold
　Got from great *Atlas* daughters, hence began,
　And planted there, did bring forth fruit of goid:
　And those with which th'*Eubæan* young man wan
Swift *Atalanta*, when through craft he her out ran.

55

Here also sprong that goodly golden fruit,
　With which *Acontius* got his louer trew,
　Whom he had long time sought with fruitlesse suit:
　Here eke that famous golden Apple grew,
　The which emongst the gods false *Ate* threw;
　For which th'*Idæan* Ladies disagreed,
　Till partiall *Paris* dempt it *Venus* dew,
　And had of her, faire *Helen* for his meed,
That many noble *Greekes* and *Troians* made to bleed.

56

The warlike Elfe much wondred at this tree,
　So faire and great, that shadowed all the ground,
　And his broad braunches, laden with rich fee,
　Did stretch themselues without the vtmost bound
　Of this great gardin, compast with a mound,
　Which ouer-hanging, they themselues did steepe,
　In a blacke flood which flow'd about it round;
　That is the riuer of *Cocytus* deepe,
In which full many soules do endlesse waile and weepe.

57

Which to behold, he clomb vp to the banke,
　And looking downe, saw many damned wights,
　In those sad waues, which direfull deadly stanke,
　Plonged continually of cruell Sprights,
　That with their pitteous cryes, and yelling shrights,
　They made the further shore resounden wide:
　Emongst the rest of those same ruefull sights,
　One cursed creature he by chaunce espide,
That drenched lay full deepe, vnder the Garden side.

58

Deepe was he drenched to the vpmost chin,
　Yet gaped still, as coueting to drinke
　Of the cold liquor, which he waded in,
　And stretching forth his hand, did often thinke
　To reach the fruit, which grew vpon the brincke:
　But both the fruit from hand, and floud from mouth
　Did flie abacke, and made him vainely swinke:
　The whiles he steru'd with hunger and with drouth
He daily dyde, yet neuer throughly dyen couth.

Stanza 54
1–2　Cf. Philotime who sits 'in glistring glory' (46.1). The **apples** suggest *malum*, the forbidden fruit of evil. Though **golden**, the fruit is 'deadly blacke' (51.8); cf. the Dead Sea fruit eaten by the fallen angels in Milton, *P.L.* x 560–6.
4　**sold**: procured; stolen.
5–9　The **conquest bold** in which **Hercules** slew the dragon that guarded the apples of the garden of the Hesperides, **great Atlas daughters**, is balanced against the **craft** by which Hippomenes, from Eubœa, outran **Atalanta** by throwing down golden apples which she paused to pick up (Ovid, *Met.* x 560–680). The two stories are linked by Comes (1616) VII vii. S. links them again in *Amor.* lxxvii 7–8. As Lemmi notes, Comes interprets the apples from the Garden as symbols of wealth which test men's souls (*Var.* ii 264). Williams (1966) 60 cites Alexander Ross's interpretation of the fruit as 'the golden apples of wordly pleasure and profit, which Hippomenes the Devil flings in our way'.

Stanza 55
1–3　**Acontius** tricked Cydippe into repeating an ambiguous and binding marriage vow written on the rind of a golden fruit (Ovid, *Heroides* xx). **fruitlesse**: the pun cannot be resisted.
4–9　that famous golden **Apple** was inscribed 'to the fairest', and thrown by Eris or Ate, goddess of discord, among the guests at the marriage of Peleus and Thetis. When Venus, Minerva, and Juno quarrelled over its possession, Paris awarded it to Venus on Mount Ida; his reward, Helen, led to the Trojan war. Cf. III ix 34, IV i 22.3–6, xi 19.3–7. On **Ate**, see IV i 19.1–4. On the importance within the poem of this marriage, see VI x 22*n*, VII vii 12*n*. We are aware of Eve's apple by its deliberate omission.
7　**dempt**: judged.

Stanza 56
3　**fee**: wealth.
4　**without**: beyond.
5　**mound**: embankment; here a ditch.
6–9　The overhanging branches suggest that the damned may have eaten the fruit of this tree; but see 58.4–8.
Cocytus: one of the four rivers of hell; see I v 33.1–6*n*. Cf. III iv 55.4–6. It is 'named of lamentation loud' (Milton, *P.L.* ii 579), being associated with the wailing of damned souls. In Dante, *Inf.* vii 109–30, the wrathful are immersed in the muddy marsh of the Styx.

Stanza 57
3　**sad**: alluding to the etymology of Cocytus but suggesting also 'dark', 'deep'. **waues**: waters. **direfull deadly stanke**: describing the waters or the damned wights; cf. the bodies of Amavia and Mortdant which 'direfull deadly stunck' (ii 4.9) through their sin, and Pyrochles and Atin in the Idle Lake 'Engrost with mud, which did them foule agrise' (vi 46.7).
4　**of**: by.
5　**shrights**: shrieks.
9　**drenched**: submerged.

Stanza 58
3　**liquor**: liquid.
8　**drouth**: thirst.
9　Cf. Despair, I ix 54.8. **couth**: could.

59

The knight him seeing labour so in vaine,
  Askt who he was, and what he ment thereby:
  Who groning deepe, thus answerd him againe;
  Most cursed of all creatures vnder skye,
  Lo *Tantalus*, I here tormented lye:
  Of whom high *Ioue* wont whylome feasted bee,
  Lo here I now for want of food doe dye:
  But if that thou be such, as I thee see,
Of grace I pray thee, giue to eat and drinke to mee.

60

Nay, nay, thou greedie *Tantalus* (quoth he)
  Abide the fortune of thy present fate,
  And vnto all that liue in high degree,
  Ensample be.of mind intemperate,
  To teach them how to vse their present state.
  Then gan the cursed wretch aloud to cry,
  Accusing highest *Ioue* and gods ingrate,
  And eke blaspheming heauen bitterly,
As authour of vniustice, there to let him dye.

61

He lookt a little further, and espyde
  Another wretch, whose carkasse deepe was drent
  Within the riuer, which the same did hyde:
  But both his hands most filthy feculent,
  Aboue the water were on high extent,
  And faynd to wash themselues incessantly;
  Yet nothing cleaner were for such intent,
  But rather fowler seemed to the eye;
So lost his labour vaine and idle industry.

62

The knight him calling, asked who he was,
  Who lifting vp his head, him answerd thus:
  I *Pilate* am the falsest Iudge, alas,
  And most vniust, that by vnrighteous
  And wicked doome, to Iewes despiteous
  Deliuered vp the Lord of life to die,
  And did acquite a murdrer felonous;
  The whiles my hands I washt in puritie,
The whiles my soule was soyld with foule iniquitie.

powers; or because he was invited by the gods to their banquet and either betrayed their secrets (so Cooper, 1565; cf. *Gn.* 386) or grew ambitious not knowing 'how to vse [his] present state' (60.5). Cf. I v 35.5.

6 Of whom: following Comes VI xviii who observes that Jove was entertained by Tantalus; hence supporting Tantalus's charge that the gods are ungrateful (60.7). Upton (1758) suggests 'Who of' to agree with the usual version that Jove was the host.

Stanza 60

2 Abide: suffer.
6–9 That punishment does not cause him to repent reveals that he is confirmed in his sin, as the stubborn sinners of Rev. 16.9 'blasphemed the Name of God'. **ingrate**: ungrateful, applied to Tantalus; yet see 59.6*n*. **let him dye**: i.e. suffer eternally, or until he dies.

Stanza 61

It is not known why S. links Tantalus and Pilate (named in 62). Some connection is indicated by their similar posture: while the hands of both are extended above the water, one is submerged to the chin and the other totally. Kermode (1971) 73 sees Tantalus as 'a type of blasphemous or intemperate knowledge' because he sought to test the immortality of the gods, and associates Pilate with the sin of *curiositas* because he asked 'what is truth?' Alpers (1967) 272 argues that the pair 'combine the intense experience of knowing an evil with a severe testing of our valuation of heroism'. Cullen (1970) 166 claims that they share 'a presumptuous pride which is manifested in a distrust of God and a profanation by parody of the two sacraments whereby man is renewed in grace and in faith, the Eucharist and Holy Baptism'. Tonkin (1973) 11 calls them 'representatives of a general self-indulgence of horrific proportions' and emblems of the episode because the one questioned the divinity of the gods and the other denied God Himself. Hieatt (1973) 35 argues that they share 'man's infringement upon, and arrogation of, the divine – Satanic and intemperate pride'.

2 drent: submerged, drowned.
4–9 'Pilate . . . toke water and wasshed his hands before the multitude, saying, I am innocent of the blood of this just man' (Matt. 27.24). That his hands remain **feculent**, i.e. covered with faeces, filthy, shows how futile his washing is and how defiled he remains inwardly (62.8–9); cf. Isaiah 1.15: 'And when you shal stretch out your hands, I wil hide mine eyes from you . . . for your hands are ful of blood.'
5 extent: extended.
6 faynd: desired; or pretended, as they are held out of the water, to indicate his contradictory state. On the motif of outstretched hands, cf. Philotime's suitors (46.6) and Guyon's fiend (27.5–6).

Stanza 62

Cf. the legend (recorded in *Enc. Brit.*) that Pilate, after his suicide, was plunged in a gulf near Lucerne from which his body is raised every Good Friday so he may wash his hands in vain.
5 despiteous: spiteful, cruel.
6–7 Cf. Acts 3.14–5, Mark 15.8–15. **felonous**: wicked.
8 in puritie: the ceremonial cleansing, as Ps. 26.6: 'I wil wash my hands in innocencie.'
9 soyld: on the defiling by blood, see i 41.1*n*.

Stanza 59

3 againe: in reply.
5 From Homer, *Ody*. xi 582–92, Tantalus became a traditional type of avarice and greed. He is also a type of blasphemous or intemperate knowledge in Comes (1616) VI xviii; cited Kermode (1971) 73. He was **cursed** either because he invited the gods to a banquet of his son's flesh to test their

63

Infinite moe, tormented in like paine
  He there beheld, too long here to be told:
  Ne *Mammon* would there let him long remaine,
  For terrour of the tortures manifold,
  In which the damned soules he did behold,
  But roughly him bespake. Thou fearefull foole,
  Why takest not of that same fruit of gold,
  Ne sittest downe on that same siluer stoole,
To rest thy wearie person, in the shadow coole.

64

All which he did, to doe him deadly fall
  In frayle intemperance through sinfull bayt;
  To which if he inclined had at all,
  That dreadfull feend, which did behind him wayt,
  Would him haue rent in thousand peeces strayt:
  But he was warie wise in all his way,
  And well perceiued his deceiptfull sleight,
  Ne suffred lust his safetie to betray;
So goodly did beguile the Guyler of the pray.

65

And now he has so long remained there,
  That vitall powres gan wexe both weake and wan,
  For want of food, and sleepe, which two vpbeare,
  Like mightie pillours, this fraile life of man,
  That none without the same enduren can.
  For now three dayes of men were full outwrought,
  Since he this hardie enterprize began:
  For thy great *Mammon* fairely he besought,
Into the world to guide him backe, as he him brought.

66

The God, though loth, yet was constrain t'obay,
  For lenger time, then that, no liuing wight
  Below the earth, might suffred be to stay:
  So backe againe, him brought to liuing light.
  But all so soone as his enfeebled spright
  Gan sucke this vitall aire into his brest,
  As ouercome with too exceeding might,
  The life did flit away out of her nest,
And all his senses were with deadly fit opprest.

Stanza 63
2 **too . . . told**: because S. is reaching the end of the forty stanzas on Guyon's underground passage; see 26.5*n*.
6–9 **foole**: 'Whosoever shal say, Foole, shalbe worthie to be punished with hel fyre' (Matt. 5.22). The **fruit of gold** is traditionally the forbidden fruit. Eating the pomegranate condemned Proserpina to hell. The **siluer stoole** suggests the temptation to idleness or sloth. Thus Theseus is 'condemned to endlesse slouth by law' (I v 35.8) by sitting on this same chair of forgetfulness to which his flesh grew (cf. Virgil, *Aen.* vi 617–8). Yet this stool suggests some magical significance. Upton (1758) interprets it as the forbidden seat of the goddess Ceres in the Eleusinian mysteries; supported by Kermode (1971) 74–5. The first temptation relates to Tantalus who seeks to eat the fruit; the second, less clearly, to Pilate who cannot rest. Alpers (1967) 240–8 interprets both temptations as an appeal to the lust of the flesh, as S. says explicitly at 64.8. Less persuasively, Kermode interprets both as an appeal to blasphemous curiosity.

Stanza 64
2 **frayle**: alluding to the frailty of the flesh (cf. 50.3) through which he needs food and rest. **bayt**: temptation (cf. 34.3); food; rest.
3 **inclined**: both literally and metaphorically.
5 On the threat of despoiling, see vi 28.7–9*n*.
8 **lust**: both desire and appetite.
9 **Guyler**: beguiler.

Stanza 65
3–5 Cf. 'for what so strong, / But wanting rest will also want of might?' (I i 32.6–7); cf. III vii 3.5. The implied metaphor of the body as 'our earthlie house' (2 Cor. 5.1) is developed in the account of the Castle of Alma.
6 **outwrought**: completed.
8 **For thy**: therefore. **fairely**: courteously. Guyon must submit to trial and not yield even to disdain.

Stanza 66
1 The limitations on Mammon, even though he is the **God**, are stated earlier: 18.8, 39.7.
2–3 'For as Jonas was thre dayes, and thre nights in the whales bellie: so shal the Sonne of man be thre dayes and thre nights in the heart of the earth' (Matt. 12.40).
5–9 The paradox is noted by Alpers (1967) 275: **vitall aire** (6) brings loss of life.
9 **deadly fit**: the trance of death.

Cant. VIII.

Sir Guyon laid in swowne is by
Acrates sonnes despoyld,
Whom Arthur soone hath reskewed
And Paynim brethren foyld.

1

ANd is there care in heauen? and is there loue
In heauenly spirits to these creatures bace,
That may compassion of their euils moue?
There is: else much more wretched were the cace
Of men, then beasts.   But O th'exceeding grace
Of highest God, that loues his creatures so,
And all his workes with mercy doth embrace,
That blessed Angels, he sends to and fro,
To serue to wicked man, to serue his wicked foe.

2

How oft do they, their siluer bowers leaue,
To come to succour vs, that succour want?
How oft do they with golden pineons, cleaue
The flitting skyes, like flying Pursuiuant,
Against foule feends to aide vs millitant?
They for vs fight, they watch and dewly ward,
And their bright Squadrons round about vs plant,
And all for loue, and nothing for reward:
O why should heauenly God to men haue such regard?

3

During the while, that *Guyon* did abide
In *Mammons* house, the Palmer, whom whyleare
That wanton Mayd of passage had denide,
By further search had passage found elsewhere,
And being on his way, approched neare,
Where *Guyon* lay in traunce, when suddenly
He heard a voice, that called loud and cleare,
Come hither, come hither, O come hastily;
That all the fields resounded with the ruefull cry.

4

The Palmer lent his eare vnto the noyce,
To weet, who called so importunely:
Againe he heard a more efforced voyce,
That bad him come in haste.   He by and by
His feeble feet directed to the cry;
Which to that shadie delue him brought at last,
Where *Mammon* earst did sunne his threasury:
There the good *Guyon* he found slumbring fast
In senselesse dreame; which sight at first him sore aghast.

Canto viii

Argument

2   **Acrates sonnes**: see 10n. Since Guyon is not **despoyld**, **soone** may mean 'without delay', 'straightway'. Cf. 12.4. The implication that he is despoiled shows his need for God's grace.
4   **Paynim**: see 10n.

Stanza 1

As I viii 1 marks the entrance of Arthur as the instrument of heavenly grace to rescue the fallen hero; see also I vii 12.3. The present stanza notes the chief instance of God's direct intervention into the action of the poem; cf. V vi 34.6. Cf. His indirect intervention to save Una (I vi 7), Timias (III v 27), Florimell (III viii 29), and Amoret (IV vii 23).
1   **And**: parallels the previous line (vii 66.9), 'And all his senses . . .' Man's defeat is answered by God's grace. He is assured of God's care in 1 Pet. 5.7. Hieatt (1973b) 25 compares *Amor.* 61, 66.
2   **creatures bace**: 'low', but implying the moral sense. Mammon's worldlings (vii 8.1) are now claimed by God as His **workes** (7).
3   **euils**: misfortunes.
5   **exceeding**: glorious, of surpassing excellence.
7   Ps. 145.9: 'His mercies are over all his workes.'
8–9   Alluding to the Lat. and Gk root of angel, a messenger; cf. Heb. 1.14: 'Are they not all ministring spirits, sent forthe to minister, for their sakes which shalbe heires of salvation?' S. extends the ministry of angels to all men. Cf. I ix 53.5; cf. also *H.H.L.* 64–8.   **serue**: the biblical 'minister to'.

Stanza 2

Cf. Matt. 4.11: 'The devil left him [Christ]: and beholde, the Angels came, and ministred unto him.'
1–5   In contrast to the upward striving in Mammon's golden kingdom with its betraying silver seat, there is the contrary motion from God to man: angels from **siluer bowers** fly down on **golden** wings.
2   **succour**: supply, aid, in the military sense. On this word, cf. 8.5, 25.7, ix 9.3.   **want**: lack; desire.
4   **flitting**: yielding, shifting.   **Pursuiuant**: a royal messenger, here from God the King.
5   **millitant**: warring; referring to the angels who fight on our behalf but also to man's warfare on earth. Giles Fletcher refers to Christ 'looking downe on his weake Militants' (*Christ's Triumph after Death* xxx 3).
6–7   Cf. Ps. 34.7: 'The Angel of the Lord pitcheth rounde about them, that feare him, and delivereth them.'
Squadrons: the square military formation, the usual formation of angelic troops (Du Bartas, *Divine Weekes* I i p. 6), taken up to guard the four sides or four quarters of man. On the square as symbol of virtue, see Fowler (1964) 278.
9   Ps. 144.3: 'Lord, what is man that thou regardest him?'

Stanza 3

2   **whyleare**: some time ago.
3   **That wanton Mayd**: Phædria; see vi 6.1n.
8   The urgency of the call is conveyed by the stress.

Stanza 4

2   **importunely**: persistently.
3   **more efforced**: uttered with more effort.
4   **by and by**: immediately.
6–7   Repeating vii Proem 1–2.

5

Beside his head there sate a faire young man,
  Of wondrous beautie, and of freshest yeares,
  Whose tender bud to blossome new began,
  And flourish faire aboue his equall peares;
  His snowy front curled with golden heares,
  Like *Phœbus* face adornd with sunny rayes,
  Diuinely shone, and two sharpe winged sheares,
  Decked with diuerse plumes, like painted Iayes,
Were fixed at his backe, to cut his ayerie wayes.

6

Like as *Cupido* on *Idæan* hill,
  When hauing laid his cruell bow away,
  And mortall arrowes, wherewith he doth fill
  The world with murdrous spoiles and bloudie pray,
  With his faire mother he him dights to play,
  And with his goodly sisters, *Graces* three;
  The Goddesse pleased with his wanton play,
  Suffers her selfe through sleepe beguild to bee,
The whiles the other Ladies mind their merry glee.

7

Whom when the Palmer saw, abasht he was
  Through fear and wonder, that he nought could say,
  Till him the child bespoke, Long lackt, alas,
  Hath bene thy faithfull aide in hard assay,
  Whiles deadly fit thy pupill doth dismay;
  Behold this heauie sight, thou reuerend Sire,
  But dread of death and dolour doe away;
  For life ere long shall to her home retire,
And he that breathlesse seemes, shal corage bold respire.

8

The charge, which God doth vnto me arret,
  Of his deare safetie, I to thee commend;
  Yet will I not forgoe, ne yet forget
  The care thereof my selfe vnto the end,
  But euermore him succour, and defend
  Against his foe and mine: watch thou I pray;
  For euill is at hand him to offend.
  So hauing said, eftsoones he gan display
His painted nimble wings, and vanisht quite away.

9

The Palmer seeing his left empty place,
  And his slow eyes beguiled of their sight,
  Woxe sore affraid, and standing still a space,
  Gaz'd after him, as fowle escapt by flight;
  At last him turning to his charge behight,
  With trembling hand his troubled pulse gan try;
  Where finding life not yet dislodged quight,
  He much reioyst, and courd it tenderly,
As chicken newly hatcht, from dreaded destiny.

Stanza 5
On the pictorial conventions of the angel as Cupid, see Tuve
(1970) 127–9. The angel who waits sitting by the right side of
Christ's tomb is described as a young man, Mark 16.5; cf.
Matt. 28.3: 'And his countenance was like lightning, and his
raiment white as snowe.'
4   equall peares: companions of the same age or rank.
7–9   Wings denote the cherubs, the second of the nine orders
of angels: 'those bright *Cherubins*, / Which all with golden
wings are ouerdight' (*H.H.B*. 92–3). The brightness of angel
wings is traditional; cf. Chaucer, *Parl. Fowls* 356: 'the pekok,
with his aungels fetheres bryghte'. Cf. Gabriel in Tasso, *Ger.
Lib.* i 13–4. A cherub brings the Palmer, or Reason, to aid
Guyon because the order was reputed to excel in knowledge,
particularly in the knowledge of God; see Bartholomaeus
(1582) II ix.   **sheares**: wings.   **diuerse**: variously
coloured. The jay is noted for its beautiful feathers.

Stanza 6
On Mount Ida Paris awarded the apple of beauty to the goddess
of love: see vii 55.4–9. The comparison with Cupid reminds
us that God 'loues his creatures' (1.6). **Cupido** is the divine
Cupid, son of the celestial Venus, invoked at I Proem 3.1–5,
or the tamed and unarmed Cupid who is allowed into the
Castle of Alma (ix 34.6–9) and the Garden of Adonis (III vi
49.3–9). On the triad of the **Graces** and the circle of divine
love, see Wind (1967) 36f. In making the Graces sisters of
Cupid, S. follows Boccaccio, *Gen. Deor.* III xxii, and Comes
(1616) IV xiii. Cf. their parentage at VI x 22 and *T.M.* 401–6.
Cupid appears 'With spotted winges like Peacocks trayne' in
S.C. March 80. For the iconographical traits that link Cupid
with Mercury, see Cummings (1970).

Stanza 7
2   fear and wonder: the proper response of reason to the
divine. The Palmer is **abasht** (1) even as Guyon lies in **dismay**
(5). Soon, however, reason responds to divine prompting.
3   child: youth of gentle birth; see 56.1–3*n*.
4   assay: affliction; trial.
5   dismay: defeat.
6   reuerend: the Palmer is worthy to be revered even by
God's messenger.
8   retire: return.
9   corage: spirit, life; hence, 'he shall regain the breath of
life'. Throughout the episode Guyon is regarded as both alive
and dead.

Stanza 8
1–2   'For he shal give his Angels charge over thee to kepe
thee in all thy waies' (Ps. 91.11).   **arret**: entrust, lay to the
charge of.
3–6   The Angel prepares the Palmer for the intercession of
Arthur whose **succour** is sought at 25.7, offered, and then
renewed (ix 9.3).
6   Cf. Mark 13.33: 'Take hede: watche, and pray.'
7   offend: attack, harm.

Stanza 9
5   his charge behight: the charge committed (cf. 'commend',
8.2) or 'assynd' (11.7) to him.
8   courd: protected, covered literally, as the simile suggests.
it: i.e. his charge.
9   A biblical simile, Matt. 23.37, for God's care.

10

At last he spide, where towards him did pace
　　Two Paynim knights, all armd as bright as skie,
　　And them beside an aged Sire did trace,
　　And farre before a light-foot Page did flie,
　　That breathed strife and troublous enmitie;
　　Those were the two sonnes of *Acrates* old,
　　Who meeting earst with *Archimago* slie,
　　Foreby that idle strond, of him were told,
That he, which earst them combatted, was *Guyon* bold.

11

Which to auenge on him they dearely vowd,
　　Where euer that on ground they mote him fynd;
　　False *Archimage* prouokt their courage prowd,
　　And stryfull *Atin* in their stubborne mynd
　　Coles of contention and whot vengeance tynd.
　　Now bene they come, whereas the Palmer sate,
　　Keeping that slombred corse to him assynd;
　　Well knew they both his person, sith of late
With him in bloudie armes they rashly did debate.

12

Whom when *Pyrochles* saw, inflam'd with rage,
　　That sire he foule bespake, Thou dotard vile,
　　That with thy brutenesse shendst thy comely age,
　　Abandone soone, I read, the caitiue spoile
　　Of that same outcast carkasse, that erewhile
　　Made it selfe famous through false trechery,
　　And crownd his coward crest with knightly stile;
　　Loe where he now inglorious doth lye,
To proue he liued ill, that did thus foully dye.

13

To whom the Palmer fearelesse answered;
　　Certes, Sir knight, ye bene too much to blame,
　　Thus for to blot the honour of the dead,
　　And with foule cowardize his carkasse shame,
　　Whose liuing hands immortalizd his name.
　　Vile is the vengeance on the ashes cold,
　　And enuie base, to barke at sleeping fame:
　　Was neuer wight, that treason of him told;
Your selfe his prowesse prou'd and found him fiers and bold.

14

Then said *Cymochles*; Palmer, thou doest dote,
　　Ne canst of prowesse, ne of knighthood deeme,
　　Saue as thou seest or hearst.　But well I wote,
　　That of his puissance tryall made extreeme;
　　Yet gold all is not, that doth golden seeme,
　　Ne all good knights, that shake well speare and shield:
　　The worth of all men by their end esteeme,
　　And then due praise, or due reproch them yield;
Bad therefore I him deeme, that thus lies dead on field.

15

Good or bad (gan his brother fierce reply)
　　What doe I recke, sith that he dyde entire?
　　Or what doth his bad death now satisfy
　　The greedy hunger of reuenging ire,
　　Sith wrathfull hand wrought not her owne desire?
　　Yet since no way is left to wreake my spight,
　　I will him reaue of armes, the victors hire,
　　And of that shield, more worthy of good knight;
For why should a dead dog be deckt in armour bright?

Stanza 10

The four figures merge as an image of intemperance. Atin, the
spirit of discord, flies ahead to seek occasion for enmity.
Archimago is called **an aged Sire** as he parodies the Palmer
who is so addressed at vi 20.5, ix 60.8, and called 'reuerend
Sire' (7.6). He is seen to **trace**: i.e. walk, but also 'stalk',
'pursue', referring to his designs against Guyon. Pyrochles
and Cymochles are called **Paynim** (pagan) knights, a term used
in Book I to describe the enemies of the Red Cross Knight –
and used only in this canto in Book II – to note that Guyon's
enemies are God's, as the angel has declared, 8.6. They are
named **sonnes of Acrates** (cf. Arg. 2) as they oppose the
knight of Temperance; cf. iv 41.6. They **pace** because the
irascible and concupiscible emotions move steadily together to
destroy Guyon.
9　**bold**: with pejorative connotations since Archimago is
being quoted, but also pathetic in this context; cf. 13.9.

Stanza 11

1　**dearely**: earnestly; direly.
2　**on ground**: with a pun, for they find him on the ground.
4-5　Cf. Prov. 26.21: 'As the cole maketh burning coles, and
wood a fyre, so the contentious man is apt to kindle strife.'
stubborne: implacable, ruthless.　**tynd**: inflamed (alluding
to the etymology of **Atin**).
7　**slombred**: unconscious.
9　**debate**: fight.

Stanza 12

3　**brutenesse**: stupidity, in believing that he can protect
Guyon.　**shendst**: disgrace.　**comely**: what is comely for.
4　**soone**: without delay.　**read**: advise.　**caitiue**:
wretched; 'captive', as he claims possession of Guyon.
5　**carkasse**: in its etymological sense, 'fallen flesh'.
6-7　He refers to the binding of Occasion (iv 45, v 17) and
the killing of his horse (v 4-5).　**stile**: title; outward appearance (cf. IV ii 29.7).
8-9　Cf. 14.7-9.

Stanza 13

1　**fearelesse**: contrast his response to the Angel, 7.2, 9.3.

Stanza 14

5　Proverbial (C. G. Smith, 1970, 336).
6　**shake**: wield.

Stanza 15

1　**gan**: did.
2　**entire**: wholly, completely. Alternatively, Pyrochles is
angered because Guyon died a natural death: he died unbroken
(Lat. *integer*) rather than wounded to death in revenge.
7-9　The Palmer condemns the classical custom that the
victor may claim the arms of a defeated knight; yet cf. IV iv
31.2-3 and esp. VI ii 39.1-2. According to chivalric code, it
was an offence for another to reave the dead. Arthur seems
ready to allow the claim as a 'right' (27.7). See 16.4-5n.
dead dog: a biblical term of ignomiy, as I Sam. 24.15;
mouthed by Braggadocchio at iii 7.6.

239

16

Faire Sir, said then the Palmer suppliaunt,
  For knighthoods loue, do not so foule a deed,
  Ne blame your honour with so shamefull vaunt
  Of vile reuenge.   To spoile the dead of weed
  Is sacrilege, and doth all sinnes exceed;
  But leaue these relicks of his liuing might,
  To decke his herce, and trap his tomb-blacke steed.
What herce or steed (said he) should he haue dight,
But be entombed in the rauen or the kight?

17

With that, rude hand vpon his shield he laid,
  And th'other brother gan his helme vnlace,
  Both fiercely bent to haue him disaraid;
  Till that they spide, where towards them did pace
  An armed knight, of bold and bounteous grace,
  Whose squire bore after him an heben launce,
  And couerd shield.   Well kend him so farre space
Th'enchaunter by his armes and amenaunce,
When vnder him he saw his Lybian steed to praunce.

18

And to those brethren said, Rise rise by liue,
  And vnto battell doe your selues addresse;
  For yonder comes the prowest knight aliue,
  Prince *Arthur*, flowre of grace and nobilesse,
  That hath to Paynim knights wrought great distresse,
  And thousand Sar'zins foully donne to dye.
  That word so deepe did in their harts impresse,
That both eftsoones vpstarted furiously,
And gan themselues prepare to battell greedily.

19

But fierce *Pyrochles*, lacking his owne sword,
  The want thereof now greatly gan to plaine,
  And *Archimage* besought, him that afford,
  Which he had brought for *Braggadocchio* vaine.
  So would I (said th'enchaunter) glad and faine
  Beteeme to you this sword, you to defend,
  Or ought that else your honour might maintaine,
But that this weapons powre I well haue kend,
To be contrarie to the worke, which ye intend.

20

For that same knights owne sword this is of yore,
  Which *Merlin* made by his almightie art
  For that his noursling, when he knighthood swore,
  Therewith to doen his foes eternall smart.
  The metall first he mixt with *Medæwart*,
  That no enchauntment from his dint might saue;
  Then it in flames of *Aetna* wrought apart,
And seuen times dipped in the bitter waue
Of hellish *Styx*, which hidden vertue to it gaue.

21

The vertue is, that neither steele, nor stone
  The stroke thereof from entrance may defend;
  Ne euer may be vsed by his fone,
  Ne forst his rightfull owner to offend,
  Ne euer will it breake, ne euer bend.
  Wherefore *Morddure* it rightfully is hight.
  In vaine therefore, *Pyrochles*, should I lend
The same to thee, against his lord to fight,
For sure it would deceiue thy labour, and thy might.

240

Stanza 16
3   **blame**: bring into disrepute.
4   **vile reuenge**: associated with Guyon's antagonists throughout, in contrast to his 'dew vengeance' (i 61.7).
4–5   It is odd that reaving the dead of arms should be held to exceed all sins. Perhaps it is that they seek to despoil his dead body. Later the Palmer calls their intent 'Vnworthy vsage' (25.4), and Arthur calls it 'rude' (26.1). Cf. Langland, *Piers Plowman* xviii 96–7: 'Cursed caytyve! kniȝthod was it nevere / To mysdo a ded body by day or by nyȝte.'
7–9   **herce**: corpse. **trap**: adorn. **tomb-blacke**: referring to the funereal black trappings of the horse. On this threat, see vi 28.7–9*n*. **dight**: i.e. dressed for him.

Stanza 17
4   The line 'answers' 10.1: God's grace responds to evil.
5   **bold and bounteous grace**: this short phrase (contrast the description at I vii 29–36) suggests 'th'exceeding grace / Of highest God' (1.5–6) to his creatures.
6–7   The lance and shield, described fully at I vii 37, 33–34, serve as identifying insignia.
8   **amenaunce**: noble bearing.
9   Arthur's horse is not mentioned in Book I: it is mentioned here because the rider on his horse signifies the control of the passions by reason, a type of temperance. See xi 19.6–9.
Lybian: Arabian; evidently a type of excellence.

Stanza 18
1   An address appropriate to the fallen Guyon.   **by liue**: at once.
6   **Sar'zins**: Saracens.

Stanza 19
1   Presumably Pyrochles's wrath led to his abandoning his sword, vi 41; cf. vi 51.2.
2   **plaine**: lament.
3–4   Cf. iii 18.1–7, vi 47.6.   **vaine**: foolish, as iii 34.3.
5   **faine**: willingly.
6   **Beteeme**: grant.
8   **kend**: found out.

Stanza 20
2   On **Merlin** as craftsman, see I vii 36.2–7. The sword is mentioned only in passing in Book I.
5–6   Herbs were thought to possess particular powers against enchantments. **Medæwart**: mede-wart or meadow-plant. In Book I the shield (vii 35.1–4) and horn (viii 4.5–6) are given this power. **dint**: blow.
7–9   The flames of **Aetna** are associated with Vulcan's forge where Aeneas's arms were made. Turnus's sword, made by Vulcan for his father, is dipped into the Stygian lake, *Aen.* xii 90–1.
8   **seuen times**: therefore proof against the seven deadly sins; see note on 'seuenfolded shield' (v 6.3).
9   **vertue**: power.

Stanza 21
3   **fone**: foes.
4   **offend**: injure.
6   **Morddure**: i.e. hard-biter (Ital. *mordere*+*duro*). On its biting power, see 38.4, 44.8.

22

Foolish old man, said then the Pagan wroth,
  That weenest words or charmes may force withstond:
  Soone shalt thou see, and then beleeue for troth,
  That I can carue with this inchaunted brond
  His Lords owne flesh.   Therewith out of his hond
  That vertuous steele he rudely snatcht away,
  And *Guyons* shield about his wrest he bond;
  So readie dight, fierce battaile to assay,
And match his brother proud in battailous array.

23

By this that straunger knight in presence came,
  And goodly salued them; who nought againe
  Him answered, as courtesie became,
  But with sterne lookes, and stomachous disdaine,
  Gaue signes of grudge and discontentment vaine:
  Then turning to the Palmer, he gan spy
  Where at his feete, with sorrowfull demaine
  And deadly hew, an armed corse did lye,
In whose dead face he red great magnanimity.

24

Said he then to the Palmer, Reuerend syre,
  What great misfortune hath betidd this knight?
  Or did his life her fatall date expyre,
  Or did he fall by treason, or by fight?
  How euer, sure I rew his pitteous plight.
  Not one, nor other, (said the Palmer graue)
  Hath him befalne, but cloudes of deadly night
  A while his heauie eylids couer'd haue,
And all his senses drowned in deepe senselesse waue.

25

Which, those his cruell foes, that stand hereby,
  Making aduantage, to reuenge their spight,
  Would him disarme, and treaten shamefully,
  Vnworthy vsage of redoubted knight.
  But you, faire Sir, whose honorable sight
  Doth promise hope of helpe, and timely grace,
  Mote I beseech to succour his sad plight,
  And by your powre protect his feeble cace.
First praise of knighthood is, foule outrage to deface.

26

Palmer, (said he) no knight so rude, I weene,
  As to doen outrage to a sleeping ghost:
  Ne was there euer noble courage seene,
  That in aduauntage would his puissance bost:
  Honour is least, where oddes appeareth most.
  May be, that better reason will asswage
  The rash reuengers heat.   Words well dispost
  Haue secret powre, t'appease inflamed rage:
If not, leaue vnto me thy knights last patronage.

27

Tho turning to those brethren, thus bespoke,
  Ye warlike payre, whose valorous great might
  It seemes, iust wrongs to vengeance doe prouoke,
  To wreake your wrath on this dead seeming knight,
  Mote ought allay the storme of your despight,
  And settle patience in so furious heat?
  Not to debate the chalenge of your right,
  But for this carkasse pardon I entreat,
Whom fortune hath alreadie laid in lowest seat.

Stanza 22
2   **words**: perhaps referring to the sword's name, which possesses magical power.
4   **inchaunted brond**: also as it overcomes all enchantments.
5–9   That Arthur is opposed by his own sword and Guyon's shield in his effort to save Guyon shows how man's powers, both active and passive, oppose his redemption. 'The spirit in dede is readie, but the flesh is weake' (Matt. 26.41). Earlier Pyrochles 'his redeemer chalengd for his foe' (v 20.3).
vertuous: possessing certain virtues or powers; cf. the balm from the Tree of Life (I xi 50.5) and the power of the Palmer's staff (II xii 26.6, 86.1).

Stanza 23
2   **goodly salued**: courteously saluted.
4   **stomachous**: resentful.
7   **demaine**: demeanour; also behaviour.
9   **great magnanimity**: its outward expression is 'magnificence', which the *L.R.* calls 'the perfection of all the rest [of the virtues], and conteineth in it them all.' In its only other use in the poem, Scudamour praises Britomart's 'huge heroicke magnanimity' (III xi 19.2) when she vows to rescue Amoret. It applies to Arthur in its literal sense, 'doing great deeds'; cf. the praise of his 'great mind' (51.1). On the term, see Greaves (1964).

Stanza 24
1   **Reuerend syre**: echoing the Angel, 7.6.
3   **fatall date**: i.e. the term of life given (Lat. *datus*) by fate; cf. I ix 42.4–5.
5   **How euer**: in either case.
9   Describes the extremes of intemperance: both the irascible state of Pyrochles 'Readie to drowne himselfe for fell despight' (vi 43.5) and the concupiscence of Cymochles 'in ioyes . . . drownd' (v 36.9).

Stanza 25
3   **disarme . . . shamefully**: i.e. by disarming, treat shamefully.
5   **sight**: appearance.
7   **succour**: see 8.3–6*n*.
8   **cace**: condition; with a punning reference to Guyon's body or armour.
9   **deface**: destroy; prevent (sugg. by the context).

Stanza 26
2   **ghost**: person, spirit.
5   **most**: i.e. most in one's favour.
7–8   Proverbial: see vi 36.5*n*.
9   **patronage**: defence; more specifically, guardianship: the 'charge' and 'care' (8.1, 4) over Guyon assumed by the Angel; cf. 55.4.

Stanza 27
3   To allay the passions by reason, Arthur allows that the brothers may be justly angry for wrongs done them. Yet **iust wrongs** suggests that **wrongs** done to them are **iust**.
7   **debate the challenge**: contest the claim.

241

28

To whom *Cymochles* said; For what art thou,
  That mak'st thy selfe his dayes-man, to prolong
  The vengeance prest? Or who shall let me now,
  On this vile bodie from to wreake my wrong,
  And make his carkasse as the outcast dong?
  Why should not that dead carrion satisfie
  The guilt, which if he liued had thus long,
  His life for due reuenge should deare abie?
The trespasse still doth liue, albe the person die.

29

Indeed (then said the Prince) the euill donne
  Dyes not, when breath the bodie first doth leaue,
  But from the grandsyre to the Nephewes sonne,
  And all his seed the curse doth often cleaue,
  Till vengeance vtterly the guilt bereaue:
  So streightly God doth iudge. But gentle knight,
  That doth against the dead his hand vpreare,
  His honour staines with rancour and despight,
And great disparagment makes to his former might.

30

Pyrochles gan reply the second time,
  And to him said, Now felon sure I read,
  How that thou art partaker of his crime:
  Therefore by *Termagaunt* thou shalt be dead.
  With that his hand, more sad then lomp of lead,
  Vplifting high, he weened with *Morddure*,
  His owne good sword *Morddure*, to cleaue his head.
  The faithfull steele such treason no'uld endure,
But swaruing from the marke, his Lords life did assure.

31

Yet was the force so furious and so fell,
  That horse and man it made to reele aside;
  Nath'lesse the Prince would not forsake his sell:
  For well of yore he learned had to ride,
  But full of anger fiercely to him cride;
  False traitour miscreant, thou broken hast
  The law of armes, to strike foe vndefide.
  But thou thy treasons fruit, I hope, shalt taste
Right sowre, and feele the law, the which thou hast defast.

32

With that his balefull speare he fiercely bent
  Against the Pagans brest, and therewith thought
  His cursed life out of her lodge haue rent:
  But ere the point arriued, where it ought,
  That seuen-fold shield, which he from *Guyon* brought
  He cast betwene to ward the bitter stound:
  Through all those foldes the steelehead passage wrought
  And through his shoulder pierst; wherwith to ground
He groueling fell, all gored in his gushing wound.

---

see 30.3*n*. **prolong**: delay.
3 **prest**: at hand. **let**: hinder.
6 **dead carrion**: rejecting Arthur's 'dead seeming' (27.4).
8 **abie**: pay for.

Stanza 29

1–6   20.5: 'I am the Lord thy God, a jelouse God, visiting the iniquitie of the fathers upon the children, upon the third generacion and upon the fourth of them that hate me.'
3 **Nephewes**: grandson's.
5–6 By claiming that vengance belongs to God, Arthur resolves this theme in Book II; cf. Guyon's vow to seek 'dew vengeance . . . / Till guiltie bloud her guerdon doe obtaine' (i 61.7–8). His enemies seek revenge: 11.5, 13.6, 27.3, 28.3. **streightly**: rigorously.
7 **vpreare**: 'vpheaue' is suggested by the rhyme.

Stanza 30

1 **gan . . . time**: i.e. offer a second reply to Arthur.
2 **felon**: villain; accusing him of committing a felony in defending Guyon. **read**: discern.
3 **partaker of his crime**: cf. Arthur's role as Guyon's 'dayes-man' (28.2). Christ is the archetype of Arthur's role in Book II. The role of the 'dayes-man' for whom Job pleaded in vain was assumed by Christ when he became the partaker of man's crime. Hence Arthur's wound in his right side, 39.1–2.
4 **Termagaunt**: the 'thrice-great' Saracen god. His brother adds 'Mahoune', 33.3. This pair of gods is invoked again at VI vii 47.9. Their names alone are intimidating, as Joseph Hall observes: 'Nor fright the Reader with the Pagan vaunt / Of mightie Mahound, or great Termagaunt' (*Virgidemiarum* I i 3–4).
5 **sad**: heavy.
8 **no'uld**: would not.
9 **assure**: render secure.

Stanzas 31–39

Each stroke has precise allegorical significance. Of particular importance is the nature of each wound. Five strokes are highlighted: (1) Pyrochles strikes Arthur with his own sword (31.1–3); though he misses his head, he causes him and his horse to reel. (2) In response, Arthur wounds him in the shoulder and unhorses him (32.7–9). (3) Cymochles strikes Arthur on the head with his sword, unhorsing him (33.5–7). (4) In response, Arthur wounds him in the thigh (36.5) and presumably unhorses him. (5) Both brothers strike together: Pyrochles strikes the shield without effect, Cymochles cuts through the spear that had wounded him and pierces Arthur's right side (38–39). The number five may be chosen to suggest the five senses.

Stanza 31

3 **sell**: saddle.
6–9 The laws of chivalry require that a challenge be given and accepted before a blow is struck. Cf. the charge of unknightly conduct made by Pyrochles against Guyon, v 5.3–7. See i 29.6*n*, v 3.2*n*. **miscreant**: misbeliever; cf. 'Paynim' (10.2 and see *n*). **defast**: defamed, discredited.

Stanza 32

5 **seuen-fold shield**: see v 6.3*n*.
6 **stound**: attack.
9 **groueling**: face down.

Stanza 28

2 **dayes-man**: mediator; cf. Job's appeal for a 'dayes man'
to intervene between him and God's wrath (Job 9.33, Bishops');

33

Which when his brother saw, fraught with great griefe
  And wrath, he to him leaped furiously,
  And fowly said, By *Mahoune*, cursed thiefe,
  That direfull stroke thou dearely shalt aby.
  Then hurling vp his harmefull blade on hye,
  Smote him so hugely on his haughtie crest,
  That from his saddle forced him to fly:
  Else mote it needes downe to his manly brest
Haue cleft his head in twaine, and life thence dispossest.

34

Now was the Prince in daungerous distresse,
  Wanting his sword, when he on foot should fight:
  His single speare could doe him small redresse,
  Against two foes of so exceeding might,
  The least of which was match for any knight.
  And now the other, whom he earst did daunt,
  Had reard himselfe againe to cruell fight,
  Three times more furious, and more puissaunt,
Vnmindfull of his wound, of his fate ignoraunt.

35

So both attonce him charge on either side,
  With hideous strokes, and importable powre,
  That forced him his ground to trauerse wide,
  And wisely watch to ward that deadly stowre:
  For in his shield, as thicke as stormie showre,
  Their strokes did raine, yet did he neuer quaile,
  Ne backward shrinke, but as a stedfast towre,
  Whom foe with double battry doth assaile,
Them on her bulwarke beares, and bids them nought auaile.

36

So stoutly he withstood their strong assay,
  Till that at last, when he aduantage spyde,
  His poinant speare he thrust with puissant sway
  At proud *Cymochles*, whiles his shield was wyde,
  That through his thigh the mortall steele did gryde:
  He swaruing with the force, within his flesh
  Did breake the launce, and let the head abyde:
  Out of the wound the red blood flowed fresh,
That vnderneath his feet soone made a purple plesh.

37

Horribly then he gan to rage, and rayle,
  Cursing his Gods, and himselfe damning deepe:
  Als when his brother saw the red bloud rayle
  Adowne so fast, and all his armour steepe,
  For very felnesse lowd he gan to weepe,
  And said, Caytiue, cursse on thy cruell hond,
  That twise hath sped; yet shall it not thee keepe
  From the third brunt of this my fatall brond:
Loe where the dreadfull Death behind thy backe doth stond.

38

With that he strooke, and th'other strooke withall,
  That nothing seem'd mote beare so monstrous might:
  The one vpon his couered shield did fall,
  And glauncing downe would not his owner byte:
  But th'other did vpon his troncheon smyte,
  Which hewing quite a sunder, further way
  It made, and on his hacqueton did lyte,
  The which diuiding with importune sway,
It seizd in his right side, and there the dint did stay.

Stanza 33
1–2 **griefe / And wrath**: see iv 33.4*n*.
3 **Mahoune**: Mohammed; see 30.4*n*. **thiefe**: a general term of reproach (*OED* 2) though it may be taken as an epithet of his god.
4 **aby**: pay for.
5 **hurling**: renders the violence of whirling and hurtling as the blow descends; cf. v 7.5.
6–7 The blow at 31.3 repeated with Cymochles's sword has its full effect. That the concupiscible Cymochles's blow is the more effective follows from Arthur's love for Gloriana. The *psychomachia* is Arthur's as well as Guyon's. From this point all are assumed to fight on foot.

Stanza 34
1–4 In contrast to Guyon who also fought on foot but had a sword and fought against Pyrochles alone at v 4.
3 **single speare**: i.e. spear alone. **redresse**: aid.
6 **daunt**: subdue.
9 **ignoraunt**: ignoring, not caring.

Stanza 35
2 **importable**: too heavy to be borne.
3 **his ground to trauerse**: i.e. to shift his ground; dodge without retreating.
4 **stowre**: assault.
8 **double battry**: i.e. two battering rams; possibly two cannon.
9 **bids**: ?allows.

Stanza 36
1 **assay**: attack; also testing.
3–5 **poinant**: piercing. **sway**: force. **wyde**: not close to his body, or to one side. It is appropriate that the lustful Cymochles be wounded in the thigh and that he should cause the head to be embedded. **proud**: suggests lascivious; yet cf. 11.3, 22.9. **gryde**: pierce; so glossed by E.K. to *S.C.* Feb. 4.
9 **plesh**: pool.

Stanza 37
3 **rayle**: flow. This sense allows the duplicate rhyme with 1.
5 **felnesse**: fury.
7 **sped**: attained its purpose.
8 **brunt**: blow.

Stanza 38
1 **withall**: as well; at the same time.
3–4 Cf. Orgoglio's blow which uncovers Arthur's shield (I viii 19). Although the shield again saves Arthur, he must continue to fight.
5 **troncheon**: the broken spear shaft.
7 **hacqueton**: jacket plated with mail.
8–9 Cymochles fulfils Pyrochles's boast at 22.4–5.
importune sway: grievous, violent force. **seizd**: penetrated. For the significance of the wound in Christ's right side, see Gurewich (1957, 1963). The biblical support, Ezek. 47.1–2, was interpreted as baptism; noted Barb (1971).

243

39

Wyde was the wound, and a large lukewarme flood,
  Red as the Rose, thence gushed grieuously;
  That when the Paynim spyde the streaming blood,
  Gaue him great hart, and hope of victory.
  On th'other side, in huge perplexity,
  The Prince now stood, hauing his weapon broke;
  Nought could he hurt, but still at ward did ly:
  Yet with his troncheon he so rudely stroke
Cymochles twise, that twise him forst his foot reuoke.

40

Whom when the Palmer saw in such distresse,
  Sir *Guyons* sword he lightly to him raught,
  And said; Faire Son, great God thy right hand blesse,
  To vse that sword so wisely as it ought.
  Glad was the knight, and with fresh courage fraught,
  When as againe he armed felt his hond;
  Then like a Lion, which hath long time saught
  His robbed whelpes, and at the last them fond
Emongst the shepheard swaynes, then wexeth wood and yond.

41

So fierce he laid about him, and dealt blowes
  On either side, that neither mayle could hold,
  Ne shield defend the thunder of his throwes:
  Now to *Pyrochles* many strokes he told;
  Eft to *Cymochles* twise so many fold:
  Then backe againe turning his busie hond,
  Them both attonce compeld with courage bold,
  To yield wide way to his hart-thrilling brond;
And though they both stood stiffe, yet could not both withstand.

42

As saluage Bull, whom two fierce mastiues bayt,
  When rancour doth with rage him once engore,
  Forgets with warie ward them to awayt,
  But with his dreadfull hornes them driues afore,
  Or flings aloft, or treads downe in the flore,
  Breathing out wrath, and bellowing disdaine,
  That all the forrest quakes to heare him rore:
  So rag'd Prince *Arthur* twixt his foemen twaine,
That neither could his mightie puissance sustaine.

43

But euer at *Pyrochles* when he smit,
  Who *Guyons* shield cast euer him before,
  Whereon the Faery Queenes pourtract was writ,
  His hand relented, and the stroke forbore,
  And his deare hart the picture gan adore,
  Which oft the Paynim sau'd from deadly stowre.
  But him henceforth the same can saue no more;
  For now arriued is his fatall howre,
That no'te auoyded be by earthly skill or powre.

44

For when *Cymochles* saw the fowle reproch,
  Which them appeached, prickt with guilty shame,
  And inward griefe, he fiercely gan approch,
  Resolu'd to put away that loathly blame,
  Or dye with honour and desert of fame;
  And on the hauberk stroke the Prince so sore,
  That quite disparted all the linked frame,
  And pierced to the skin, but bit no more,
Yet made him twise to reele, that neuer moou'd afore.

244

Stanza 39
5 **perplexity**: distress.
7 **at ward**: on guard; a defensive posture.
9 **reuoke**: withdraw.

Stanza 40
The turning-point in the battle, when the Palmer blesses Arthur and in God's name gives him Guyon's sword, becomes the 'redemptive' stanza: see I viii 40*n*.
2 **raught**: handed.
3 Cf. the blessing of the Red Cross Knight: 'Faire sonne, God giue you happie chance' (i 31.7) and then of Guyon (32.8).
4 **wisely as it ought**] well, as he it ought *1590*, i.e. as he who owns it. The 1590 reading makes better sense: the essential point is that the sword is Guyon's.
7–9 Cf. Hosea 13.8: 'I wil mete thee, as a beare that is robbed of her whelpes . . . and there wil I deuoure them like a lyon.' This passage refers to God's destruction of the fallen Israel, and applies here to the fallen, intemperate body.
9 **wood**: mad. **yond**: fierce, savage; 'beyond, or perhaps more than **wood**', as Collier (1862) suggests.

Stanza 41
3 **throwes**: thrusts, blows.
4 **told**: counted.
5 **twise . . . fold**: twofold, in return for Cymochles's two wounding strokes; cf. 39.8–9.
8 **thrilling**: piercing.

Stanza 42
2 **engore**: **rancour** and **rage**, which **engore** him, cause him to engore his enemies.

Stanza 43
1–5 The sacred nature of the royal portrait in Elizabethan England is examined by Strong (1963) ch. vi. **writ**: drawn; cf. 'decks' (i 28.8), and 'depainted' (v 11.8). **deare**: loving.
6 **deadly stowre**: death.
9 **no'te**: may not.

Stanza 44
One expects Pyrochles's death to follow immediately. However, he must be overcome by his own irascibility, which is provoked by his brother's death. Before he dies, Arthur's failure to strike 'his' shield because it bears his love's image provides occasion for his wounding by the concupiscible Cymochles.
2 **appeached**: brought as a charge against them. Defeat would dishonour them, as it did Guyon, 14.7–9. Cymochles is sensitive to shame: cf. v 38.9, vi 27.7.
6 **hauberk**: chain-mail that covers the neck.
8 **no more**] not thore *1590*, i.e. not there, or not through. In either case, it is a token wound.
9 **twise**: as 39.9, the prelude to a third and final effort. Cymochles retires twice and then approaches to make a final stroke which occasions his death. Similarly, Arthur reels twice and then delivers the stroke that kills Cymochles.

45

Whereat renfierst with wrath and sharpe regret,
  He stroke so hugely with his borrowd blade,
  That it empierst the Pagans burganet,
  And cleauing the hard steele, did deepe inuade
  Into his head, and cruell passage made
  Quite through his braine. He tombling downe on ground,
  Breathd out his ghost, which to th'infernall shade
  Fast flying, there eternall torment found,
For all the sinnes, wherewith his lewd life did abound.

46

Which when his german saw, the stony feare
  Ran to his hart, and all his sence dismayd,
  Ne thenceforth life ne courage did appeare,
  But as a man, whom hellish feends haue frayd,
  Long trembling still he stood: at last thus sayd;
  Traytour what hast thou doen? how euer may
  Thy cursed hand so cruelly haue swayd
  Against that knight: Harrow and well away,
After so wicked deed why liu'st thou lenger day?

47

With that all desperate as loathing light,
  And with reuenge desiring soone to dye,
  Assembling all his force and vtmost might,
  With his owne sword he fierce at him did flye,
  And strooke, and foynd, and lasht outrageously,
  Withouten reason or regard. Well knew
  The Prince, with patience and sufferaunce sly
  So hasty heat soone cooled to subdew:
Tho when this breathlesse woxe, that batteil gan renew.

48

As when a windy tempest bloweth hye,
  That nothing may withstand his stormy stowre,
  The cloudes, as things affrayd, before him flye;
  But all so soone as his outrageous powre
  Is layd, they fiercely then begin to shoure,
  And as in scorne of his spent stormy spight,
  Now all attonce their malice forth do poure;
  So did Prince *Arthur* beare himselfe in fight,
And suffred rash *Pyrochles* wast his idle might.

49

At last when as the Sarazin perceiu'd,
  How that straunge sword refusd, to serue his need,
  But when he stroke most strong, the dint deceiu'd,
  He flong it from him, and deuoyd of dreed,
  Vpon him lightly leaping without heed,
  Twixt his two mighty armes engrasped fast,
  Thinking to ouerthrow and downe him tred:
  But him in strength and skill the Prince surpast,
And through his nimble sleight did vnder him down cast.

50

Nought booted it the Paynim then to striue;
  For as a Bittur in the Eagles claw,
  That may not hope by flight to scape aliue,
  Still waites for death with dread and trembling aw;
  So he now subiect to the victours law,
  Did not once moue, nor vpward cast his eye,
  For vile disdaine and rancour, which did gnaw
  His hart in twaine with sad melancholy,
As one that loathed life, and yet despisd to dye.

Stanza 45
1 **renfierst**: re-enforced; rendered more fierce. **regret**: pain; sorrow.
3 **burganet**: helmet.
6 **through**: answering his blow which 'bit not thore' (44.8, *1590*).
7 The soul was said to leave by the mouth; see Didron (1886) ii 173–4.

Stanza 46
1 **german**: full brother.
2–5 He shares his brother's death and punishment.
4 **frayd**: terrified.
7 **swayd**: swung.
8 **Harrow and well away**: a cry of alarm followed by a cry of grief, as vi 43.6.
9 **lenger day**: i.e. a day longer; or longer life.

Stanza 47
1 **light**: i.e. life. As earlier (vi 42–50), he seeks to end his own life; cf. 52.3–4.
4 **his owne**: Arthur's.
5 **foynd**: thrust.
7 **sufferaunce sly**: wise forbearance.
9 **this**: Pyrochles. **that**: Arthur.

Stanza 48
2 **stowre**: tumult.
5 **layd**: subsided.
7 **malice**: power to harm.
8 **Prince Arthur**] Sir *Guyon 1590, 1596*; corr. *1609*. The error may be due to the fact that Arthur fights on Guyon's behalf the same battle fought earlier against the same foes. At v 9.1, Pyrochles 'hewd, and lasht, and foynd, and thundred blowes' while Guyon waited for his intemperate wrath to spend itself. Here Pyrochles 'strooke, and foynd, and lasht outrageously' (47.5) while Arthur waits.

Stanza 49
2 **straunge**: belonging to another.
3 **deceiu'd**: as Archimago had warned him, 21.9. The sword did not bite hard as its name promised.
5–9 Again there is a significant reversal of Guyon's previous battle: cf. iv 8.6–9. **sleight**: dexterity.

Stanza 50
2 **Bittur**: the bittern, 'a cruell bird and full of revenge' (Topsell, 1607). Arthur is compared to the eagle with its prey at xi 43.
4 **aw**: terror.
8 **melancholy**: irascibility, anger.

51

But full of Princely bounty and great mind,
　The Conquerour nought cared him to slay,
　But casting wrongs and all reuenge behind,
　More glory thought to giue life, then decay,
　And said, Paynim, this is thy dismall day;
　Yet if thou wilt renounce thy miscreaunce,
　And my trew liegeman yield thy selfe for ay,
And all thy wrongs will wipe out of my souenaunce.

52

Foole (said the Pagan) I thy gift defye,
　But vse thy fortune, as it doth befall,
　And say, that I not ouercome do dye,
　But in despight of life, for death do call.
　Wroth was the Prince, and sory yet withall,
　That he so wilfully refused grace;
　Yet sith his fate so cruelly did fall,
　His shining Helmet he gan soone vnlace,
And left his headlesse body bleeding all the place.

53

By this Sir *Guyon* from his traunce awakt,
　Life hauing maistered her sencelesse foe;
　And looking vp, when as his shield he lakt,
　And sword saw not, he wexed wondrous woe:
　But when the Palmer, whom he long ygoe
　Had lost, he by him spide, right glad he grew,
　And said, Deare sir, whom wandring to and fro
　I long haue lackt, I ioy thy face to vew;
Firme is thy faith, whom daunger neuer fro me drew.

54

But read what wicked hand hath robbed mee
　Of my good sword and shield? The Palmer glad,
　With so fresh hew vprising him to see,
　Him answered; Faire sonne, be no whit sad
　For want of weapons, they shall soone be had.
　So gan he to discourse the whole debate,
　Which that straunge knight for him sustained had,
　And those two Sarazins confounded late,
Whose carcases on ground were horribly prostrate.

55

Which when he heard, and saw the tokens trew,
　His hart with great affection was embayd,
　And to the Prince bowing with reuerence dew,
　As to the Patrone of his life, thus sayd;
　My Lord, my liege, by whose most gratious ayd
　I liue this day, and see my foes subdewd,
　What may suffise, to be for meede repayd
　Of so great graces, as ye haue me shewd,
But to be euer bound

56

To whom the Infant thus, Faire Sir, what need
　Good turnes be counted, as a seruile bond,
　To bind their doers, to receiue their meede?
　Are not all knights by oath bound, to withstond
　Oppressours powre by armes and puissant hond?
　Suffise, that I haue done my dew in place.
　So goodly purpose they together fond,
　Of kindnesse and of curteous aggrace;
The whiles false *Archimage* and *Atin* fled apace.

Stanza 51

1　**bounty**: virtue, goodness.　　**great mind**: Aristotle's
high-mindedness, Guyon's 'great magnanimity' (23.9).
4　**decay**: death.
5　**dismall day**: i.e. day of death; see vi 43.7*n*.
6　**miscreaunce**: false faith; cf. 'miscreant' (31.6).
8　**valiaunce**: valour.
9　**souenaunce**: memory.

Stanza 52

1–2　**Foole**: he calls the Palmer 'dotard vile' (12.2) and
Archimago 'Foolish old man' (22.1). Now he invokes the
biblical injunction: 'whosoever shal say, Foole, shalbe worthie
to be punished with hel fyre' (Matt. 5.22). He echoes Turnus's
words before his death (Virgil, *Aen.* xii 931–2); hence Arthur's
wrath suggests Aeneas's.
3–4　Cf. his equivocation at v 12.7–9; but then he pleads not
to die.　**despight**: scorn.
8–9　The gesture completes the action begun when Cymochles 'gan his [Guyon's] helme vnlace' (17.2).　**shining
Helmet**: cf. vi 31.6.

Stanza 53

1–2　An allegorical statement of the slaying of Guyon's
enemies.
4　**woe**: woeful.
7–8　Cf. 7.3–4.
9　Cf. the Red Cross Knight's tribute to Una, I ix 17.4–5.

Stanza 54

1　**read**: declare.
4　**Faire sonne**: as he addresses Arthur, 40.3.
6　**debate**: fight.
8　**confounded**: defeated.

Stanza 55

2　**embayd**: suffused; literally, bathed.
4　**the Patrone of his life**: i.e. protector, as Arthur had
vowed, 26.9. The Red Cross Knight also addresses Arthur as
'the Patron of my life' (I ix 17.6) and so later does Alma
(xi 16.9).
5　**my liege**: offering the submission just refused by
Pyrochles.
9　Church (1758) suggests that 'the speech of Sir Guyon is
plainly unfinished; the Prince breaks in upon him.'

Stanza 56

1–3　Arthur stresses his grace as an absolute gift; reward
would be a **seruile bond**.　**Infant**: youth of noble birth
(*OED* 3), from Span. *infante*, prince; applied to Arthur
again at xi 25.7. On Arthur as 'child', see IV viii 44.8*n*. Cf. the
Angel as 'the child' (7.3).　**Faire Sir** illustrates the courtesy
of temperance. Guyon addresses the Palmer as 'Deare sir'
(53.7) and is addressed by him as 'Faire sonne' (54.4).
6　**dew**: duty.　**in place**: here.
7　**purpose**: conversation.　**fond**: devised.
8　**aggrace**: favour.

Cant. IX.

The house of Temperance, in which
doth sober Alma dwell,
Besiegd of many foes, whom straunger
knightes to flight compell.

1

OF all Gods workes, which do this world adorne,
　There is no one more faire and excellent,
　Then is mans body both for powre and forme,
　Whiles it is kept in sober gouernment;
　But none then it, more fowle and indecent,
　Distempred through misrule and passions bace:
　It growes a Monster, and incontinent
　Doth loose his dignitie and natiue grace.
Behold, who list, both one and other in this place.

2

After the Paynim brethren conquer'd were,
　The *Briton* Prince recou'ring his stolne sword,
　And *Guyon* his lost shield, they both yfere
　Forth passed on their way in faire accord,
　Till him the Prince with gentle court did bord;
　Sir knight, mote I of you this curt'sie read,
　To weet why on your shield so goodly scord
Beare ye the picture of that Ladies head?
Full liuely is the semblaunt, though the substance dead.

3

Faire Sir (said he) if in that picture dead
　Such life ye read, and vertue in vaine shew,
　What mote ye weene, if the trew liuely-head
　Of that most glorious visage ye did vew?
　But if the beautie of her mind ye knew,
　That is her bountie, and imperiall powre,
　Thousand times fairer then her mortall hew,
　O how great wonder would your thoughts deuoure,
And infinite desire into your spirite poure!

4

She is the mighty Queene of *Faerie*,
　Whose faire retrait I in my shield do beare;
　She is the flowre of grace and chastitie,
　Throughout the world renowmed far and neare,
　My liefe, my liege, my Soueraigne, my deare,
　Whose glory shineth as the morning starre,
　And with her light the earth enlumines cleare;
　Far reach her mercies, and her prayses farre,
As well in state of peace, as puissaunce in warre.

5

Thrise happy man, (said then the *Briton* knight)
　Whom gracious lot, and thy great valiaunce
　Haue made thee souldier of that Princesse bright,
　Which with her bounty and glad countenance
　Doth blesse her seruaunts, and them high aduaunce.
　How may straunge knight hope euer to aspire,
　By faithfull seruice, and meet amenance,
　Vnto such blisse? sufficient were that hire
For losse of thousand liues, to dye at her desire.

Canto ix

Argument
2　**sober**: as Medina, ii 14.5.

Stanza 1
The previous canto shows God's care over 'all his workes'
(viii 1.7); now temperance exercises care over the body, the
most excellent **Of all Gods workes** (1); cf. 21.8, 23.3, 41.6,
46.9, 47.2. The text of the canto is 'The wondrous workemanship of Gods owne mould' (I x 42.6).
3　**powre and forme**: the two divisions of the house of
Temperance, its structure (21–46) and its faculties (47–58).
4　**sober gouernment**: sober behaviour or conduct under
the rule of '*sober Alma*' (Arg.); cf. Guyon's 'goodly gouernaunce' (i 29.8). In the temperate body, 'the soule [Alma] doth
rule the earthly masse, / And all the seruice of the bodie frame'
(IV ix 2.6–7).
5　**indecent**: uncomely; in the etymological sense, 'not
fitting'.
6　**Distempred**: disordered, disturbing the proper temper of
the bodily humours.
7　**incontinent**: immediately; being concupiscent.
8　**loose**: also, do away with, violate. When reason does not
rule, the soul 'loseth hir dignite, and becommith ministre
unto the sences. . . . And so Man . . . is become equalle or
rather inferior to brute beastes' (Elyot, *Of the Knowledge which
maketh a Wise Man*, 119–20).
9　**one and other**: i.e. Alma's house of temperance and
Maleger.

Stanza 2
3　**yfere**: together.
5　**gentle court**: courteous regard; cf. 20.3.
6　**read**: ?ask; perhaps used loosely in the sense, 'to reveal
meaning' (*OED* 2): 'by your courtesy would you expound'.
7　**scord**: produced by cutting; or painted, as I i 2.5.
9　**liuely**: lifelike.　**semblaunt**: image.

Stanza 3
1　**Faire Sir**: answering Arthur's address, viii 56.1.
2　**vertue**: power.
3　**liuely-head**: living original; literally, the living head
rather than its picture.
6　**bountie**: goodness.
7　**hew**: shape.

Stanza 4
2　**retrait**: portrait.
5　**liefe**: beloved.　**liege**: cf. viii 55.5.
6　See I xii 21.5–9n.

Stanza 5
2　**valiaunce**: valour; praised by Arthur in Pyrochles, viii
51.8.
4–5　Cf. Philotime whose suitors advance through their own
'workes and merites iust' (vii 49.9).　**glad**: bright, shining;
as in Guyon's praise, 3.4.
7　**meet amenance**: proper conduct. It marks Arthur's
bearing at viii 17.8.
9　**dye**: with the sexual sense.

6

Said *Guyon*, Noble Lord, what meed so great,
  Or grace of earthly Prince so soueraine,
  But by your wondrous worth and warlike feat
  Ye well may hope, and easely attaine?
  But were your will, her sold to entertaine,
  And numbred be mongst knights of *Maydenhed*,
  Great guerdon, well I wote, should you remaine,
  And in her fauour high be reckoned,
As *Arthegall*, and *Sophy* now beene honored.

7

Certes (then said the Prince) I God auow,
  That sith I armes and knighthood first did plight,
  My whole desire hath beene, and yet is now,
  To serue that Queene with all my powre and might.
  Now hath the Sunne with his lamp-burning light,
  Walkt round about the world, and I no lesse,
  Sith of that Goddesse I haue sought the sight,
  Yet no where can her find: such happinesse
Heauen doth to me enuy, and fortune fauourlesse.

8

Fortune, the foe of famous cheuisaunce
  Seldome (said *Guyon*) yields to vertue aide,
  But in her way throwes mischiefe and mischaunce,
  Whereby her course is stopt, and passage staid.
  But you, faire Sir, be not herewith dismaid,
  But constant keepe the way, in which ye stand;
  Which were it not, that I am else delaid
  With hard aduenture, which I haue in hand,
I labour would to guide you through all Faery land.

9

Gramercy Sir (said he) but mote I weete,
  What straunge aduenture do ye now pursew?
  Perhaps my succour, or aduizement meete
  Mote stead you much your purpose to subdew.
  Then gan Sir *Guyon* all the story shew
  Of false *Acrasia*, and her wicked wiles,
  Which to auenge, the Palmer him forth drew
  From Faery court.   So talked they, the whiles
They wasted had much way, and measurd many miles.

10

And now faire *Phœbus* gan decline in hast
  His weary wagon to the Westerne vale,
  Whenas they spide a goodly castle, plast
  Foreby a riuer in a pleasaunt dale,
  Which choosing for that euenings hospitale,
  They thither marcht: but when they came in sight,
  And from their sweaty Coursers did auale,
  They found the gates fast barred long ere night,
And euery loup fast lockt, as fearing foes despight.

11

Which when they saw, they weened fowle reproch
  Was to them doen, their entrance to forstall,
  Till that the Squire gan nigher to approch;
  And wind his horne vnder the castle wall,
  That with the noise it shooke, as it would fall:
  Eftsoones forth looked from the highest spire
  The watch, and lowd vnto the knights did call,
  To weete, what they so rudely did require.
Who gently answered, They entrance did desire.

Stanza 6

5   **sold**: pay, as a soldier or servant.   **entertaine**: receive.
6   **knights of Maydenhed**: cf. I vii 46.4, II ii 42.4.
7   **remaine**: await.
9   Presumably **Sophy** would be the hero of a projected Book,
as **Arthegall** is of Book V. A holy Welsh king of this name is
recorded in Drayton, *Poly-Olbion* Song xxiv 219.
Sophia, Gk Wisdom, is linked with Artegall because Wisdom
and Justice form a natural pair of virtues.

Stanza 7

5   **Now hath**] Seuen times *1590*. Similarly at 38.9: 'twelue
moneths' where *1590* reads 'three years'; cf. the nine months
referred to at I ix 15.9 (see *n*). One, seven (see 12.8–9*n*), and
nine, suggest completed cycles of time. Cf. Guyon's three-
month search for Acrasia, ii 44.1–4.
9   **enuy**: begrudge.

Stanza 8

1–2   Fortune's opposition to virtue is proverbial.
cheuisaunce: chivalric enterprise or achievement; 'sometime
of Chaucer vsed for gaine: sometime of other for spoyle, or
bootie, or enterprise, and sometime for chiefdome' (E.K.'s
gloss to *S.C.* May 92).

Stanza 9

3   **succour**: see viii 8.3–6*n*.   **aduizement**: counsel.
4   **stead**: help; i.e. stand you in good stead. If Arthur's words
apply to his slaying of Maleger, **stead** refers to his part in
firmly establishing the temperate body of the Castle of Alma;
see xii 1.4–5.   **subdew**: attain; suggests 'to achieve your end
by struggle'.
5–8   Cf. ii 43 and the account in *L.R.*

Stanza 10

3–4   Cf. the Castle of Medina 'Built on a rocke adioyning to
the seas' (ii 12.7). The river leads to the Bower of Bliss.
5   **hospitale**: place of lodging.
7   **auale**: dismount.
9   **loup**: loop-hole.

Stanza 11

5   See I viii 4.8–9 for the power of the Squire's horn.
9   **gently**: courteously.

12

Fly fly, good knights, (said he) fly fast away
  If that your liues ye loue, as meete ye should;
  Fly fast, and saue your selues from neare decay,
  Here may ye not haue entraunce, though we would:
  We would and would againe, if that we could;
  But thousand enemies about vs raue,
  And with long siege vs in this castle hould:
  Seuen yeares this wize they vs besieged haue,
And many good knights slaine, that haue vs sought to saue.

13

Thus as he spoke, loe with outragious cry
  A thousand villeins round about them swarmd
  Out of the rockes and caues adioyning nye,
  Vile caytiue wretches, ragged, rude, deformd,
  All threatning death, all in straunge manner armd,
  Some with vnweldy clubs, some with long speares,
  Some rusty kniues, some staues in fire warmd.
  Sterne was their looke, like wild amazed steares,
Staring with hollow eyes, and stiffe vpstanding heares.

14

Fiersly at first those knights they did assaile,
  And droue them to recoile: but when againe
  They gaue fresh charge, their forces gan to faile,
  Vnhable their encounter to sustaine;
  For with such puissaunce and impetuous maine
  Those Champions broke on them, that forst them fly,
  Like scattered Sheepe, whenas the Shepheards swaine
  A Lyon and a Tigre doth espye,
With greedy pace forth rushing from the forest nye.

15

A while they fled, but soone returnd againe
  With greater fury, then before was found;
  And euermore their cruell Capitaine
  Sought with his raskall routs t'enclose them round,
  And ouerrun to tread them to the ground.
  But soone the knights with their bright-burning blades
  Broke their rude troupes, and orders did confound,
  Hewing and slashing at their idle shades;
For though they bodies seeme, yet substance from them fades.

16

As when a swarme of Gnats at euentide
  Out of the fennes of Allan do arise,
  Their murmuring small trompets sounden wide,
  Whiles in the aire their clustring army flies,
  That as a cloud doth seeme to dim the skies;
  Ne man nor beast may rest, or take repast,
  For their sharpe wounds, and noyous iniuries,
  Till the fierce Northerne wind with blustring blast
Doth blow them quite away, and in the *Ocean* cast.

17

Thus when they had that troublous rout disperst,
  Vnto the castle gate they come againe,
  And entraunce crau'd, which was denied erst.
  Now when report of that their perilous paine,
  And combrous conflict, which they did sustaine,
  Came to the Ladies eare, which there did dwell,
  She forth issewed with a goodly traine
  Of Squires and Ladies equipaged well,
And entertained them right fairely, as befell.

Stanza 12

3 **decay**: death.
4–5 'The spirit in dede is readie, but the flesh is weake' (Matt. 26.41).
6 **raue**: rage.
8–9 Cf. the many knights who sought to kill the Dragon which besieged Una's parents for four years, I vii 44–45. **Seuen yeares** may refer to the seven ages of man (see Chew, 1962, 163–9); the seven ages of the world (as catalogued in an Appendix to the Geneva Bible); or generally to seven as the ruling number of man's life: 'seven is the number by which man is conceived, developed in the womb, is born, lives and is sustained, and passing through all the stages of life attains old age; his whole life is regulated by it' (Macrobius, *Commentary on the Dream of Scipio* 112).

Stanza 13

2 **villeins**: serfs, bond-slaves, indicating 'passions bace' (1.6). Their significance is suggested by Ariosto, *Orl. Fur.* vi 60–70: a monstrous rabble, representing the passions, attacks Ruggiero as he makes his way to the realm of Logistilla and tries to force him into the city of the witch, Alcina.
7 **warmd**: and therefore hardened.

Stanza 14

5 **maine**: force.

Stanza 15

3 **Capitaine**: the spelling serves the metre and stresses Maleger's role as head of the troops that assault the head of the temperate body; see also xi 14.6.
4 **raskall routs**: base rabble. In Book I Arthur's shield overthrows 'the raskall routes' (vii 35.5); now he is seen **Hewing and slashing** (8) at shades which cannot be injured. Virgil saves Aeneas this effort, *Aen.* vi 290–4.
7 **orders**: ranks.
8 **idle**: empty.

Stanza 16

2 **the fennes of Allan**: the bogs of central Ireland.
7 **noyous**: annoying. Gnats 'do more annoy the naked rebels . . . and do more sharply wound them than all their enemies' swords or spears' (*View* 52).
9 Anticipates Arthur's defeat of Maleger.

Stanza 17

5 **combrous**: harassing; suggested by the gnats: cf. the 'cloud of combrous gnattes' (I i 23.5).
8 **equipaged**: arrayed; or furnished with the **goodly traine**.
9 **entertained**: received. **as befell**: as was fitting.

18

Alma she called was, a virgin bright;
　That had not yet felt *Cupides* wanton rage,
　Yet was she woo'd of many a gentle knight,
　And many a Lord of noble parentage,
　That sought with her to lincke in marriage:
　For she was faire, as faire mote euer bee,
　And in the flowre now of her freshest age;
　Yet full of grace and goodly modestee,
That euen heauen reioyced her sweete face to see.

19

In robe of lilly white she was arayd,
　That from her shoulder to her heele downe raught,
　The traine whereof loose far behind her strayd,
　Braunched with gold and pearle, most richly wrought,
　And borne of two faire Damsels, which were taught
　That seruice well.　Her yellow golden heare
　Was trimly wouen, and in tresses wrought,
　Ne other tyre she on her head did weare,
But crowned with a garland of sweete Rosiere.

20

Goodly she entertaind those noble knights,
　And brought them vp into her castle hall;
　Where gentle court and gracious delight
　She to them made, with mildnesse virginall,
　Shewing her selfe both wise and liberall:
　There when they rested had a season dew,
　They her besought of fauour speciall,
　Of that faire Castle to affoord them vew;
She graunted, and them leading forth, the same did shew.

21

First she them led vp to the Castle wall,
　That was so high, as foe might not it clime,
　And all so faire, and fensible withall,
　Not built of bricke, ne yet of stone and lime,
　But of thing like to that *Ægyptian* slime,
　Whereof king *Nine* whilome built *Babell* towre;
　But O great pitty, that no lenger time
　So goodly workemanship should not endure:
Soone it must turne to earth; no earthly thing is sure.

Stanza 18

1　Alma signifies 'the soule of man' (Florio, 1611), as xi 1.4;
anima, or reason (suggested Fowler, 1964, 86) and
hence the rational soul or Mind, as xi 26.1–7, which controls the
body; cf. Langland's Castle of Anima, *Piers Plowman* ix 1–63.
The term also signifies virgin: '*Hebraeis significat adolescentulam
puellam, sed virginem: sic appellatam, quod esset occulta viro.
A mayden*' (Cooper, 1565). The adj. 'alma' signifies 'gracious';
hence Alma is 'full of grace' (18.8); also 'that norisheth; fayre;
beautifull' (Cooper), as 18.6–7.

Stanza 19

1　Denoting her virginity: cf. Una's robe 'All lilly white'
(I xii 22.7) and Belphœbe's 'Camus' (II iii 26.4).
4　**Braunched**: embroidered, referring to branch-like figured
patterns.
5　Presumably the irascible and concupiscible faculties which
attend the temperate soul.
6–7　Cf. Medina's braided golden locks, ii 15.7–9.
8　**tyre**: head-dress.
9　**Rosiere**: roses, or rose bush, sacred to Venus;
significantly, in a bush and not gathered; cf. Acrasia lying on a
bed of roses, xii 77.1.

Stanza 20

4　**mildnesse virginall**: i.e. graciousness befitting a virgin.
5　**liberall**: free in bestowing bounty (*OED* 2); cf. Mercy
'both gratious, and eke liberall' (I x 34.5).

Stanza 21

1–2　Suggests man's erect, unfallen stature.
3　**fensible**: able to be defended.
4–6　**Babell towre** was built of brick and slime (Gen. 11.3);
slime: because man's body was made *de limo terrae* (Gen. 2.7
Vulg.); see I vii 9.8*n*.　**Ægyptian**: because Babylon was a
name for Cairo; see Tuve (1970) 99–100.　**Nine**: Ninus, the
eponymous founder of Nineveh; see I v 48.3–4*n*. Linked with
Nimrod who founded Babylon and **Babell towre**: see I v
48.1–2*n*. A parody of the nine from which the temperate body
is constructed, 22.8.
9　Cf. I ix 11.5.

22

The frame thereof seemd partly circulare,
  And part triangulare, O worke diuine;
  Those two the first and last proportions are,
  The one imperfect, mortall, fœminine;
  Th'other immortall, perfect, masculine,
  And twixt them both a quadrate was the base,
  Proportioned equally by seuen and nine;
  Nine was the circle set in heauens place,
All which compacted made a goodly diapase.

23

Therein two gates were placed seemly well:
  The one before, by which all in did pas,
  Did th'other far in workmanship excell;
  For not of wood, nor of enduring bras,
  But of more worthy substance fram'd it was;
  Doubly disparted, it did locke and close,
  That when it locked, none might thorough pas,
  And when it opened, no man might it close,
Still open to their friends, and closed to their foes.

24

Of hewen stone the porch was fairely wrought,
  Stone more of valew, and more smooth and fine,
  Then Iet or Marble far from Ireland brought;
  Ouer the which was cast a wandring vine,
  Enchaced with a wanton yuie twine.
  And ouer it a faire Portcullis hong,
  Which to the gate directly did incline,
  With comely compasse, and compacture strong,
Neither vnseemely short, nor yet exceeding long.

25

Within the Barbican a Porter sate,
  Day and night duely keeping watch and ward,
  Nor wight, nor word mote passe out of the gate,
  But in good order, and with dew regard;
  Vtterers of secrets he from thence debard,
  Bablers of folly, and blazers of crime.
  His larumbell might lowd and wide be hard,
  When cause requird, but neuer out of time;
Early and late it rong, at euening and at prime.

Stanza 22
This stanza demands more commentary than a short note can
provide. Extended significance lies behind each term, as
Kenelm Digby's lengthy commentary in 1644 first suggested.
See *Var*. ii 472–85 for the earlier commentary by Digby, Upton,
and Robin; for recent commentary, see Fowler (1964) 260–88.
See also Cummings (1967). Mills (1967) notes that 22, the
number of the stanza, is associated with moderation or
temperance.
  The simplest physical explanation is that **circulare** refers
to the head, the **quadrate** to the body, and **triangulare** to the
lower body with legs astride. As a primary figure
(**Proportioned**) without beginning or end, the circle is **perfect**,

and **immortall** as it refers to God and eternity. Being less
simple and stable, the triangle is **imperfect**, and by contrast
mortall. As creation imposes form upon matter, the one is
masculine and the other **fœminine**. (Here the spelling
suggests that the feminine is 'foe to man', i.e. opposed to the
masculine.) Their union illustrates the hermaphroditic state.
Further, the circle and triangle refer to spirit and matter, or
soul and body. The **quadrate**, a rectangle or square, is the
trunk of the body. Symbolically, these three figures refer to the
three souls in man: the circle to the rational soul (see 47.6–9*n*),
the quadrate to the sensible, and the triangle to the vegetable.
(These figures are used in Bartholomaeus, *De Prop. Rer.* 14ᵛ,
cited Bamborough, 1952, 31, to describe the threefold division
of the soul in Aristotle, *De anima* II iii.) The quadrate contains
the four bodily humours which connect soul to body.
  For **seuen** as the number of the body, see 12.8–9*n*. Also it is
the number of the planets, each of which governs a part of the
body. **Nine** is the number of mind or soul because there are
nine spheres in the Ptolemaic system and nine orders of angels
which govern the soul. Seven and nine have architectural
significance as female and male proportions: see Vitruvius,
De Arch. IV i 7–8. Their product, the number **Proportioned
equally by seuen and nine**, is 63, the climacteric year of
man's life. The **quadrate** 4 is connected with 7 and 9 because
its square is their sum.
  The **circle set in heauens place** is the ninth sphere of the
fixed stars which encloses the universe. Though body and soul
are opposed, they are held in harmony even as the octave, 8, is
the arithmetic mean between 7 and 9. Being so joined or
compacted, there is **a goodly diapase** or complete harmony.
Mills (1973) suggests a persuasively simple description from
the Mortalist controversy over the relation between the soul and
the body which Bryskett claimed to have discussed with S. (see
General Introduction: History of the text). The triangle
represents the vegetative soul and part of the sensitive, the
circle expresses the perfection of the *mens*, or spiritual faculty of
the mind, and the quadrate is to be taken as the four virtues and
the square of reason. Line 9 suggests that the triangle is within
the square which is, in turn, within the circle.

Stanza 23
2   **The one before**: the mouth.
3   **th'other**: the anus, the 'back-gate' (32.7).
6   **Doubly disparted**: referring to the upper and lower jaws.
7–9 Cf. Ps. 141.3: 'Set a watch, O Lord, before my mouth,
and kepe the dore of my lippes.'

Stanza 24
The **porch** is the jaw or chin; the **vine**, the beard; the
yuie twine, the moustache; and the **Portcullis** (a grating that
closes the gateway of a castle), the nose, whose length observes
the golden mean (not unreasonably resembling S.'s own in the
Pembroke College portrait).
1   **fairely**: beautifully.
5   **Enchaced**: adorned.   **wanton**: luxuriant in growth.
8   **compasse**: proportion.   **compacture**: compact
structure.

Stanza 25
The **Barbican** is a castle's outer defences; here, the oral cavity.
The **Porter** in charge of the **larumbell** (7) is the tongue.
6   **blazers**: proclaimers.
8   **out of time**: i.e. at an inappropriate time.

251

26

And round about the porch on euery side
   Twise sixteen warders sat, all armed bright
   In glistring steele, and strongly fortifide:
   Tall yeomen seemed they, and of great might,
   And were enraunged ready, still for fight.
   By them as *Alma* passed with her guestes,
   They did obeysaunce, as beseemed right,
   And then againe returned to their restes:
The Porter eke to her did lout with humble gestes.

27

Thence she them brought into a stately Hall,
   Wherein were many tables faire dispred,
   And ready dight with drapets festiuall,
   Against the viaundes should be ministred.
   At th'upper end there sate, yclad in red
   Downe to the ground, a comely personage,
   That in his hand a white rod menaged,
   He Steward was hight *Diet*; rype of age,
And in demeanure sober, and in counsell sage.

28

And through the Hall there walked to and fro
   A iolly yeoman, Marshall of the same,
   Whose name was *Appetite*; he did bestow
   Both guestes and meate, when euer in they came,
   And knew them how to order without blame,
   As him the Steward bad.   They both attone
   Did dewty to their Lady, as became;
   Who passing by, forth led her guestes anone
Into the kitchin rowme, ne spard for nicenesse none.

29

It was a vaut ybuilt for great dispence,
   With many raunges reard along the wall;
   And one great chimney, whose long tonnell thence
   The smoke forth threw.   And in the midst of all
   There placed was a caudron wide and tall,
   Vpon a mighty furnace, burning whot,
   More whot, then *Aetn'*, or flaming *Mongiball*:
   For day and night it brent, ne ceased not,
So long as any thing it in the caudron got.

30

But to delay the heat, least by mischaunce
   It might breake out, and set the whole on fire,
   There added was by goodly ordinaunce,
   An huge great paire of bellowes, which did styre
   Continually, and cooling breath inspyre.
   About the Caudron many Cookes accoyld,
   With hookes and ladles, as need did require;
   The whiles the viandes in the vessell boyld
They did about their businesse sweat, and sorely toyld.

used as a place of debate (*OED* 3).
2   warders: the teeth.   **Twise sixteen**: the one factual
detail in this allegorical pageant, to prepare for the teeth coming
forward to bow. On the teeth as guardians, cf. Jonson,
Discoveries: 'It was excellently said of that Philosopher
[Plutarch]; that there was a Wall, or Parapet of teeth set in our
mouth, to restraine the petulancy of our words' (*Wks* viii 573).
4   Tall: comely; bold, valiant.
7   as beseemed right: as was rightly fitting.
9   lout: obeisance.   **gestes**: gestures.

Stanza 27
The **Hall** is the passage to the gullet; the **comely personage**
(6), the back of the throat; his **white rod** (7) – the symbol of royal
power (see III iii 49.6–9*n*) – the uvula. As **Steward** (8), Alma's
minister is in charge of the stew or cauldron (*OED* 1), here the
stomach. **Diet** also personifies the temperate course of life
(*OED* 1); and also the parliamentary body, as Alma signifies
the ordered commonwealth (noted Nelson, 1963, 198).
2   dispred: spread out.
3   drapets: cloths.
4   Against: for the time when.
7   menaged: wielded.
8–9   Witty praise of the poet's own name, which signifies
'steward'.

Stanza 28
2   yeoman: an assistant to an official.
3   bestow: place.
5   order: arrange.
7   their Lady: as the soul maintains the nutritive part of
man, functioning as the vegetative soul whose seat is the
stomach.
8   anone: straightway.
9   nicenesse: fastidiousness.

Stanza 29
In their Cook's tour Guyon and Arthur visit the three vital
organs: the stomach or liver, the seat of the passions; the heart,
of the affections; and the brain, of reason. These are linked
with the natural, vital, and animal spirits; or with the three
souls: vegetative, sensible, and rational (see 22*n*). The tour
avoids the sexual organs. On the Renaissance physiology of
digestion, Robin (1911) 76–7 cites Galen, *On the natural
faculties* III vii, who describes the stomach as a cauldron which
digests food by boiling.
1   vaut: vault.   **dispence**: expenditure, consumption.
3   chimney: fireplace and flue; also a psychological term for
'a vent for humour' or 'fumosities' of the body (*OED* 6b).
7   Mongiball: another name for Aetna.

Stanza 30
1   delay: allay, moderate. Robin (1911) 62 cites Galen, *Hipp.
et Platon.* VII ix, on the use of the lungs to cool the native
heat of the stomach; cf. Du Bartas, *Divine Weekes* I vi, p. 55:
'the Lungs, whose motions light / Our inward heat doo temper
day and night.'
3   ordinaunce: planning, management.
4   bellowes: the lungs serve as a cooling rather than a
kindling implement; the ME form, *beli*, is the same word as
'belly'.   **styre**: stir, move to and fro.
5   inspyre: breathe in.
6   accoyld: gathered together.

Stanza 26
1–5   A witty play on the porch as a double-pillared colonnade

31

The maister Cooke was cald *Concoction*,
　A carefull man, and full of comely guise:
　The kitchin Clerke, that hight *Digestion*,
　Did order all th'Achates in seemely wise,
　And set them forth, as well he could deuise.
　The rest had seuerall offices assind,
　Some to remoue the scum, as it did rise;
　Others to beare the same away did mind;
And others it to vse according to his kind.

32

But all the liquour, which was fowle and wast,
　Not good nor seruiceable else for ought,
　They in another great round vessell plast,
　Till by a conduit pipe it thence were brought:
　And all the rest, that noyous was, and nought,
　By secret wayes, that none might it espy,
　Was close conuaid, and to the back-gate brought,
　That cleped was *Port Esquiline*, whereby
It was auoided quite, and throwne out priuily.

33

Which goodly order, and great workmans skill
　Whenas those knights beheld, with rare delight,
　And gazing wonder they their minds did fill;
　For neuer had they seene so straunge a sight.
　Thence backe againe faire *Alma* led them right,
　And soone into a goodly Parlour brought,
　That was with royall arras richly dight,
　In which was nothing pourtrahed, nor wrought,
Not wrought, nor pourtrahed, but easie to be thought.

34

And in the midst thereof vpon the floure,
　A louely beuy of faire Ladies sate,
　Courted of many a iolly Paramoure,
　The which them did in modest wise amate,
　And eachone sought his Lady to aggrate:
　And eke emongst them litle *Cupid* playd
　His wanton sports, being returned late
　From his fierce warres, and hauing from him layd
His cruell bow, wherewith he thousands hath dismayd.

Stanza 31
S. follows the old physiology which recognized three processes involved in digestion. The first, in which food is turned into chylus, he names **Cocoction**, the **maister Cooke**, from Lat. *coquere*, to cook. The second, by which the chylus is turned into blood and distributed to the body, he names **Digestion**, from Lat. *digerere*, to distribute. The third is elimination which he processes in the next stanza.
2　guise: behaviour.
4　order: arrange, as 28.5.　**Achates**: provisions; used for organs which receive nourishment from the stomach.
6　seuerall offices: particular duties.
7–8　Robin (1911) 78, 82 notes that in concoction the liver produced a sort of fermentation which escaped as yellow bile (choler) and was strained off from the blood to be lodged in the gall bladder.

Stanza 32
1–4　S. avoids naming the attendant in charge of tasting the liquor – he is the Sewer – in order to turn to more fundamental matters.　**vessell**: the bladder.　**conduit pipe**: urinary canal or penis.
5　noyous: noxious.　**nought**: useless; bad in condition.
7　close: covertly.
8　Port Esquiline: a gate in ancient Rome, its anus as it gave passage to the common dump.
9　auoided: also excreted.　**priuily**: with a pun on 'privy'.

Stanza 33
1–4　These lines counter Mammon's repeated claim that he would show **so straunge a sight** to Guyon (vii 19.6–7, etc.). Cf. the journey to Mammon's house: 'th'Elfin knight with wonder all the way / Did feed his eyes, and fild his inner thought' (vii 24.3–4). Cf. also Guyon's progress through the Bower of Bliss.
6–9　goodly Parlour: the heart, the seat of the affections and of the sensible soul; its **royall arras** (appropriately red) notes that Alma, the soul, resides here, as the heart is the seat of the various faculties. The absence of mythological representations usual in tapestry may be intended to stress the simple clarity of innate ideas, the simplicity of the heart's affections. Berger (1957) 77*n* suggests that the arras contains preconceptual phantasms awaiting activation by the Imagination.　**but** (9) may signify 'except', as Mills (1970) 568–9 suggests: the arras is not bare but contains 'the simplest of perceived sensory forms awaiting conceptualization and transmission to the higher soul through the secondary stage symbolized by Phantastes'.

Stanza 34
3　iolly: amorous; also splendid, handsome, gay, lively, etc.
4　amate: keep company.
5　aggrate: please, gratify.
8–9　On this unarmed Cupid, see I Proem 3.5–7*n*.

253

35

Diuerse delights they found them selues to please;
  Some song in sweet consort, some laught for ioy,
  Some plaid with strawes, some idly sat at ease;
  But other some could not abide to toy,
  All pleasaunce was to them griefe and annoy:
  This fround, that faund, the third for shame did blush,
  Another seemed enuious, or coy,
  Another in her teeth did gnaw a rush:
But at these straungers presence euery one did hush.

36

Soone as the gracious *Alma* came in place,
  They all attonce out of their seates arose,
  And to her homage made, with humble grace:
  Whom when the knights beheld, they gan dispose
  Themselues to court, and each a Damsell chose:
  The Prince by chaunce did on a Lady light,
  That was right faire and fresh as morning rose,
  But somwhat sad, and solemne eke in sight,
As if some pensiue thought constraind her gentle spright.

37

In a long purple pall, whose skirt with gold
  Was fretted all about, she was arayd;
  And in her hand a Poplar braunch did hold:
  To whom the Prince in curteous manner said;
  Gentle Madame, why beene ye thus dismaid,
  And your faire beautie do with sadnesse spill?
  Liues any, that you hath thus ill apaid?
  Or doen you loue, or doen you lacke your will?
What euer be the cause, it sure beseemes you ill.

38

Faire Sir, (said she halfe in disdainefull wise,)
  How is it, that this mood in me ye blame,
  And in your selfe do not the same aduise?
  Him ill beseemes, anothers fault to name,
  That may vnwares be blotted with the same:
  Pensiue I yeeld I am, and sad in mind,
  Through great desire of glory and of fame;
  Ne ought I weene are ye therein behind,   (find.
That haue twelue moneths sought one, yet no where can her

39

The Prince was inly moued at her speach,
  Well weeting trew, what she had rashly told;
  Yet with faire semblaunt sought to hide the breach,
  Which chaunge of colour did perforce vnfold,
  Now seeming flaming whot, now stony cold.
  Tho turning soft aside, he did inquire,
  What wight she was, that Poplar braunch did hold:
  It answered was, her name was *Prays-desire*,
That by well doing sought to honour to aspire.

Stanza 35
Nine affections or moods are displayed emblematically in this stanza: four forward or concupiscible passions, earlier associated with Perissa, are shown together in groups; five froward or irascible passions, earlier associated with Elissa, are seen alone. On the forward-froward distinction, see Nelson (1963) 182–3. They are carefully ordered according to degrees of inwardness. Later both knights choose from the second group.
2 **consort**: harmony; concert.
3–8 Presumably playing with straws signifies trifling amusement and moroseness.
5 **pleasaunce**: pleasing behaviour.
6 **faund**: cringed; not in servility but in refusing to accept pleasure.
7 **enuious**: full of ill-will. **coy**: disdainful.

Stanza 36
1 **gracious**: full of grace; cf. 'natiue grace' (1.8).
8 **sad, and solemne**: the heroic mood of the Red Cross Knight 'too solemne sad' (I i 2.8) and Guyon 'Still [always] solemne sad' (II vi 37.5).
9 **constraind**: distressed.

Stanza 37
1–3 The purple and gold robe indicates her sovereignty (as I vii 16.3) among Arthur's passions; alternatively, the colours suggest Aurora and awakening desire. In Ripa (1603), Temperance is dressed in purple. As that colour balances red and blue, temperance balances desire and reason. Her emblem, the **Poplar braunch**, which is Hercules's tree, associates her with heroic striving and the desire for glory; see v 31.1–5n.
  fretted: adorned.
6 **spill**: spoil.
7 **ill apaid**: ill-requited.

Stanza 38
2 **mood**: sugg. Collier (1862). 'word' *1590, 1596* may stand: she accuses him of being too ready **anothers fault to name** (4), i.e. 'sadnesse' (37.6), and defends her word or name.
3 **aduise**: perceive.
4–5 Proverbial (C. G. Smith, 1970, 244).
7 **desire of glory**: Arthur's love of Gloriana.
9 **twelue moneths**] three years *1590*; see 7.5n.

Stanza 39
3 **semblaunt**: appearance, demeanour.
8 **Prays-desire**: the desire for praise or fame; cf. 'Due praise that is the spur of dooing well' (*T.M.* 454), 'thought of glorie and of fame' (II xi 31.8), 'thoughts aspyring to eternall fame' (IV ix 2.5), etc.

40

The whiles, the *Faerie* knight did entertaine
   Another Damsell of that gentle crew,
   That was right faire, and modest of demaine,
   But that too oft she chaung'd her natiue hew:
   Straunge was her tyre, and all her garment blew,
   Close round about her tuckt with many a plight:
   Vpon her fist the bird, which shonneth vew,
And keepes in couerts close from liuing wight,
Did sit, as yet ashamd, how rude *Pan* did her dight.

41

So long as *Guyon* with her commoned,
   Vnto the ground she cast her modest eye,
   And euer and anone with rosie red
   The bashfull bloud her snowy cheekes did dye,
   That her became, as polisht yuory,
   Which cunning Craftesmans hand hath ouerlayd
   With faire vermilion or pure Castory.
   Great wonder had the knight, to see the mayd
So straungely passioned, and to her gently sayd,

42

Faire Damzell, seemeth, by your troubled cheare,
   That either me too bold ye weene, this wise
   You to molest, or other ill to feare
   That in the secret of your hart close lyes,
   From whence it doth, as cloud from sea arise.
   If it be I, of pardon I you pray;
   But if ought else that I mote not deuise,
   I will, if please you it discure, assay,
To ease you of that ill, so wisely as I may.

43

She answerd nought, but more abasht for shame,
   Held downe her head, the whiles her louely face
   The flashing bloud with blushing did inflame,
   And the strong passion mard her modest grace,
   That *Guyon* meruayld at her vncouth cace:
   Till *Alma* him bespake, Why wonder yee
   Faire Sir at that, which ye so much embrace?
   She is the fountaine of your modestee;
You shamefast are, but *Shamefastnesse* it selfe is shee.

44

Thereat the Elfe did blush in priuitee,
   And turnd his face away; but she the same
   Dissembled faire, and faynd to ouersee.
   Thus they awhile with court and goodly game,
   Themselues did solace each one with his Dame,
   Till that great Ladie thence away them sought,
   To vew her castles other wondrous frame,
   Vp to a stately Turret she them brought,
Ascending by ten steps of Alablaster wrought.

Stanza 40

The two ladies are associated in Elyot, *Governour* I ix, as
shamefastness and the desire for praise, two of the most
necessary qualities in a youth: 'By shamfastnes, as it were with
a bridell, they rule as well theyr dedes as their appetites. And
desire of prayse addeth to a sharpe spurre to their disposition
towarde lernyng and vertue.' (The bridle and spur indicate
contrary states.) Elyot's source is Aristotle, *Ethics* III vii
1116[a], on the balance between fear of shame and the desire for
honour in courageous men.

3   **demaine**: demeanour.

5–6   Her strange attire coloured blue may signify her
withdrawal from the world; cf. Belphœbe's similarly pleated
dress, iii 26.5.

7–9   The **bird** has been variously identified as the owl,
cuckoo, and wryneck; but Fowler (1961c) 235–6 argues
persuasively that it is the turtle-dove. He cites Valeriano who
observes that this bird 'spends its life in secret places far from
the multitude, seeking out lonely mountains or coverts removed
from the meeting-place of the other birds'. **dight**: abuse
sexually. The myth may be S.'s. **ashamd** refers equally to
the bird and the damsel.

Stanza 41

1   **commoned**: conversed.

2   She keeps this posture at IV x 50.2.

3–7   Blushing is a sign of innocence but also shows an
awareness of guilt; cf. Donne's comment on the creation of
Adam from red earth: 'a rednesse that amounts to a
shamefastnesse, to a blushing at our own infirmities, is
imprinted in us by Gods hand' (*Sermons* ix 64).

7   **Castory**: apparently a red dye.

Stanza 42

6–9   The piling-up of monosyllables betrays an awkwardness
in Guyon. **deuise**: guess. **discure**: discover.

Stanza 43

5   **vncouth**: strange; unseemly.

7   **embrace**: cultivate; cherish.

8   **modestee**: also moderation, keeping due measure (Lat.
modestus).

9   **shamefast**: restrained by shame. Cf. his horror of shame
at i 27.4, 30.1, etc. **Shamefastnesse**: as Lat. *verecundia* or
pudicitia; Venus's attendant at IV x 50.

Stanza 44

1   **in priuitee**: privately.

3   **ouersee**: overlook.

5   **solace**: take enjoyment.

6   **sought**: entreated.

8–9   **stately Turret**: the head, the seat of the rational soul.
The **ten steps of Alablaster** (or alabaster) refer to the spinal
vertebrae: though there are only seven cervical vertebrae, the
three thoracic vertebrae are needed to move from the heart to
the brain. At issue is the easy and natural ascent from the
feminine part of the body to the masculine (22.4–5).

45

That Turrets frame most admirable was,
　　Like highest heauen compassed around,
　　And lifted high aboue this earthly masse,
　　Which it suruew'd, as hils doen lower ground;
　　But not on ground mote like to this be found,
　　Not that, which antique *Cadmus* whylome built
　　In *Thebes*, which *Alexander* did confound;
　　Nor that proud towre of *Troy*, though richly guilt,
From which young *Hectors* bloud by cruell *Greekes* was spilt.

46

The roofe hereof was arched ouer head,
　　And deckt with flowers and herbars daintily;
　　Two goodly Beacons, set in watches stead,
　　Therein gaue light, and flam'd continually:
　　For they of liuing fire most subtilly
　　Were made, and set in siluer sockets bright,
　　Couer'd with lids deuiz'd of substance sly,
　　That readily they shut and open might.
O who can tell the prayses of that makers might!

47

Ne can I tell, ne can I stay to tell
　　This parts great workmanship, and wondrous powre,
　　That all this other worlds worke doth excell,
　　And likest is vnto that heauenly towre,
　　That God hath built for his owne blessed bowre.
　　Therein were diuerse roomes, and diuerse stages,
　　But three the chiefest, and of greatest powre,
　　In which there dwelt three honorable sages,
The wisest men, I weene, that liued in their ages.

48

Not he, whom *Greece*, the Nourse of all good arts,
　　By *Phœbus* doome, the wisest thought aliue,
　　Might be compar'd to these by many parts:
　　Nor that sage *Pylian* syre, which did suruiue
　　Three ages, such as mortall men contriue,
　　By whose aduise old *Priams* cittie fell,
　　With these in praise of pollicies mote striue.
　　These three in these three roomes did sundry dwell,
And counselled faire *Alma*, how to gouerne well.

49

The first of them could things to come foresee:
　　The next could of things present best aduize;
　　The third things past could keepe in memoree,
　　So that no time, nor reason could arize,
　　But that the same could one of these comprize.
　　For thy the first did in the forepart sit,
　　That nought mote hinder his quicke preiudize:
　　He had a sharpe foresight, and working wit,
That neuer idle was, ne once could rest a whit.

Stanza 45

1　**admirable**: marvellous, evoking wonder.
4　**suruew'd**: surveyed.
6–7　Ovid, *Met.* iii 1–130. Cooper (1565) notes that the city was subverted by Alexander.　**confound**: demolish.
8–9　Ovid, *Met.* xiii 415–7. Cooper notes that 'the Greekes cruelly threwe [Astyanax] downe from a towre, so that his braynes cleaved to the walles'.　**guilt**: gilded; but with the pun which may allude to man's intellectual powers.

Stanza 46

1　**ouer head**: a heady pun but unavoidable.
2　**herbars**: a garden of herbs.
3–5　**in watches stead**: i.e. in place of watchmen.
subtilly: ingeniously.
7　**sly**: cleverly or finely made.

Stanza 47

2　On the distinction between **workmanship** and **powre**, see 1.3 and *n*.
4–5　**that heauenly towre**: the New Jerusalem seen by the Red Cross Knight, I x 55–57, seen now by Guyon and Arthur in its human form.
6–9　The three rooms with the three sages relate to the three parts of the brain which contain the three interior senses of the mind or higher faculties of the sensitive soul. Cf., for example, Bacon's Imagination, Reason, and Memory (*Adv. Learning*). On the threefold division in general, see R. L. Anderson (1927) 15–6. Panofsky (1962) 149, in his iconographic analysis of Titian's 'Allegory of Prudence', shows that the three stages of human life (youth, maturity and old age) were connected with the three psychological faculties (foresight, intelligence and memory). S. names only the first and third, imagination and memory.

Stanza 48

1–2　'Apollo beynge demaunded who was the wysest man lyvynge, aunswered, Socrates' (Cooper, 1565).　**doome**: judgment.
3　**parts**: times.
4–6　Nestor, whom Homer praises as the Pylian orator who had ruled over three ages or generations of men, *Iliad* i 247–52. Largely through his counsel, Troy fell.　**contriue**: wear away, spend (time).
7　**in praise of pollicies**: i.e. in whatever is praiseworthy in statecraft.
8　**sundry**: separately.

Stanza 49

5　**comprize**: comprehend.
6　**For thy**: therefore.
7　**preiudize**: prejudgment, forethought.
8　**working**: active.

50

His chamber was dispainted all within,
　With sundry colours, in the which were writ
Infinite shapes of things dispersed thin;
Some such as in the world were neuer yit,
Ne can deuized be of mortall wit;
Some daily seene, and knowen by their names,
Such as in idle fantasies doe flit:
Infernall Hags, *Centaurs*, feendes, *Hippodames*,
Apes, Lions, Ægles, Owles, fooles, louers, children, Dames.

51

And all the chamber filled was with flyes,
Which buzzed all about, and made such sound,
That they encombred all mens eares and eyes,
Like many swarmes of Bees assembled round,
After their hiues with honny do abound:
All those were idle thoughts and fantasies,
Deuices, dreames, opinions vnsound,
Shewes, visions, sooth-sayes, and prophesies;
And all that fained is, as leasings, tales, and lies.

52

Emongst them all sate he, which wonned there,
That hight *Phantastes* by his nature trew;
A man of yeares yet fresh, as mote appere,
Of swarth complexion, and of crabbed hew,
That him full of melancholy did shew;
Bent hollow beetle browes, sharpe staring eyes,
That mad or foolish seemd: one by his vew
Mote deeme him borne with ill disposed skyes,
When oblique *Saturne* sate in the house of agonyes.

53

Whom *Alma* hauing shewed to her guestes,
Thence brought them to the second roome, whose wals
Were painted faire with memorable gestes,
Of famous Wisards, and with picturals
Of Magistrates, of courts, of tribunals,
Of commen wealthes, of states, of pollicy,
Of lawes, of iudgements, and of decretals;
All artes, all science, all Philosophy,
And all that in the world was aye thought wittily.

54

Of those that roome was full, and them among
There sate a man of ripe and perfect age,
Who did them meditate all his life long,
That through continuall practise and vsage,
He now was growne right wise, and wondrous sage.
Great pleasure had those stranger knights, to see
His goodly reason, and graue personage,
That his disciples both desir'd to bee;
But *Alma* thence them led to th'hindmost roome of three.

Stanza 50

1　dispainted: diversely painted.
7–9　At first reading, all seem lumped together: four fantastical creatures, four animals, and four of inferior humankind reaching a climax in the contemptuous reference to **Dames**. At second reading, however, it is clear that shapes such as **Infernall Hags . . . Owles** are found in the **idle fantasies** of **fooles . . . Dames**. This list of fantasies suggests the deformed creatures who assault the Castle; cf. xi 8f.
8　**Hippodames**: perhaps a humorous variant of 'hippotame', the sixteenth-century spelling of hippopotamus. **Lions** and **Ægles** are juxtaposed as they combine in the gryphon.

Stanza 51

1–5　Cf. 'A head full of bees', a proverbial expression for one full of whims and idle fantasies.　**flyes**: a symbol of persistence.
7　**Deuices**: conceits.
8　**sooth-sayes**: predictions.
9　**leasings**: falsehoods.

Stanza 52

Phantastes is the shaper of fancies or fantasies in the imaginative faculty. The Renaissance view of the imagination is traced by Rossky (1958). He shows the grudging acceptance yet strong distrust of the faculty. The relationship between the imaginative man devoted to intellectual pursuits and melancholy is examined by Klibansky *et al* (1964). Fowler (1964) 104 concludes that 'a melancholic is located in Alma's turret, the intellectual part of her castle, because this condition is specifically associated with man's Saturn-influenced aspiration above the merely sensual to the rational and contemplative'.
6　'The beetled browes signifieth malice, cruelty, letchery, and envy' (*Shepherdes Kalender* sig. P2; cited Skeat, ed. Langland, *Piers Plowman* ii 81).
8–9　**oblique Saturne**: the planet's oblique ascension; or its perverse influence upon men's lives. In Chaucer, *Knight's Tale* 2456–69, Saturn lists his baleful effects upon mankind 'Whil I dwelle in the signe of the leoun'. At that time his influence is most malignant. Kitchin (1872) argues that **house** is the district of the heavens in which a planet rises, and that **agonyes** refers to the belief that under Saturn strife and contention (αγωνες) largely prevail. Fowler (1964) 289–91 notes C. H. Josten's suggestion that **house of agonyes** may not refer to a zodiacal House at all but to a House of the horoscope, namely the twelfth House which was associated with adversity. The point is developed by Thomson (1966).

Stanza 53

3　gestes: deeds.
4　picturals: pictures.
7　decretals: decrees.
8　science: knowledge.
9　aye thought wittily: ever wisely thought, using 'wit' in its older sense of 'intellectual power'.

Stanza 54

2　perfect age: full age.
7　personage: appearance.

55

That chamber seemed ruinous and old,
    And therefore was remoued farre behind,
    Yet were the wals, that did the same vphold,
    Right firme and strong, though somewhat they declind;
    And therein sate an old oldman, halfe blind,
    And all decrepit in his feeble corse,
    Yet liuely vigour rested in his mind,
    And recompenst him with a better scorse:
Weake body well is chang'd for minds redoubled forse.

56

This man of infinite remembrance was,
    And things foregone through many ages held,
    Which he recorded still, as they did pas,
    Ne suffred them to perish through long eld,
    As all things else, the which this world doth weld,
    But laid them vp in his immortall scrine,
    Where they for euer incorrupted dweld:
    The warres he well remembred of king *Nine*,
Of old *Assaracus*, and *Inachus* diuine.

57

The yeares of *Nestor* nothing were to his,
    Ne yet *Mathusalem*, though longest liu'd;
    For he remembred both their infancies:
    Ne wonder then, if that he were depriu'd
    Of natiue strength now, that he them suruiu'd.
    His chamber all was hangd about with rolles,
    And old records from auncient times deriu'd,
    Some made in books, some in long parchment scrolles,
That were all worme-eaten, and full of canker holes.

58

Amidst them all he in a chaire was set,
    Tossing and turning them withouten end;
    But for he was vnhable them to fet,
    A litle boy did on him still attend,
    To reach, when euer he for ought did send;
    And oft when things were lost, or laid amis,
    That boy them sought, and vnto him did lend.
    Therefore he *Anamnestes* cleped is,
And that old man *Eumnestes*, by their propertis.

59

The knights there entring, did him reuerence dew
    And wondred at his endlesse exercise,
    Then as they gan his Librarie to vew,
    And antique Registers for to auise,
    There chaunced to the Princes hand to rize,
    An auncient booke, hight *Briton moniments*,
    That of this lands first conquest did deuize,
    And old diuision into Regiments,
Till it reduced was to one mans gouernments.

60

Sir *Guyon* chaunst eke on another booke,
    That hight *Antiquitie* of *Faerie* lond,
    In which when as he greedily did looke,
    Th'off-spring of Elues and Faries there he fond,
    As it deliuered was from hond to hond:
    Whereat they burning both with feruent fire,
    Their countries auncestry to vnderstond,
    Crau'd leaue of *Alma*, and that aged sire,
To read those bookes; who gladly graunted their desire.

Stanza 55
2–4   Memory is popularly associated with the back of the mind, with what is farthest away. The chamber fits its inhabitant: though both appear physically decrepit, one is strongly founded and the other mentally vigorous.   **declind**: i.e. inclined.
8   **scorse**: exchange.

Stanza 56
5   **weld**: have to do with; rule over.
6   **scrine**: chest; see I Proem 2.3.
8–9   **Nine**: Ninus of Babylon, 'the fyrst that made warre' (Cooper, 1565); see 21.4–6*n*.   **Assaracus**: son of the founder of Troy, the great-grandfather of Aeneas; cf. x 9.7.   **Inachus diuine**: a river god, first King of Argos. Eumnestes's memory extends to the beginnings of biblical, classical, and mythical military history.

Stanza 57
2   Mathusalem lived 969 years, according to Gen. 5.27. Cooper (1565) says that Nestor was almost 300 years old when he went to Troy.

Stanza 58
3   **fet**: fetch.
7   **lend**: give.
8–9   **Anamnestes**: the Reminder.   **Eumnestes**: Good Memory. See Yates (1966) ch. 2 on memory as one of the three powers of the soul.   **laid amis** (6) points to memory as recollection, a distinction found in Plato, *Phaedrus* 275[a].

Stanza 59
4   **auise**: look at.
5   **rize**: happen; come to hand.
6   **Briton moniments**: records or chronicles of Britain, such as Geoffrey of Monmouth, *Historia Regum Britanniae*.
7   **deuize**: recount.
8   **Regiments**: independent kingdoms.
9   **one mans**: i.e. Arthur's.

Stanza 60
4   **off-spring**: origin.

Cant. X.

A chronicle of Briton kings,
from Brute to Vthers rayne.
And rolles of Elfin Emperours,
till time of Gloriane.

1

WHo now shall giue vnto me words and sound,
　Equall vnto this haughtie enterprise?
Or who shall lend me wings, with which from ground
My lowly verse may loftily arise,
And lift it selfe vnto the highest·skies?
More ample spirit, then hitherto was wount,
Here needes me, whiles the famous auncestries
Of my most dreaded Soueraigne I recount,
By which all earthly Princes she doth farre surmount.

2

Ne vnder Sunne, that shines so wide and faire,
　Whence all that liues, does borrow life and light,
Liues ought, that to her linage may compaire,
Which though from earth it be deriued right,
Yet doth it selfe stretch forth to heauens hight,
And all the world with wonder ouerspred;
A labour huge, exceeding farre my might:
How shall fraile pen, with feare disparaged,
Conceiue such soueraine glory, and great bountihed?

3

Argument worthy of *Mæonian* quill,
　Or rather worthy of great *Phœbus* rote,
Whereon the ruines of great *Ossa* hill,
And triumphes of *Phlegræan Ioue* he wrote,
That all the Gods admird his loftie note.
But if some relish of that heauenly lay
His learned daughters would to me report,
To decke my song withall, I would assay,
Thy name, O soueraine Queene, to blazon farre away.

4

Thy name O soueraine Queene, thy realme and race,
　From this renowmed Prince deriued arre,
Who mightily vpheld that royall mace,
Which now thou bear'st, to thee descended farre
From mightie kings and conquerours in warre,
Thy fathers and great Grandfathers of old,
Whose noble deedes aboue the Northerne starre
Immortall fame for euer hath enrold;
As in that old mans booke they were in order told.

5

The land, which warlike Britons now possesse,
　And therein haue their mightie empire raysd,
In antique times was saluage wildernesse,
Vnpeopled, vnmanurd, vnprou'd, vnpraysd,
Ne was it Island then, ne was it paysd
Amid the *Ocean* waues, ne was it sought
Of marchants farre, for profits therein praysd,
But was all desolate, and of some thought
By sea to haue bene from the *Celticke* mayn-land brought.

Canto x

Argument

1–2　Harper (1910), abstracted in *Var*. ii, analyses S.'s use of
the standard chronicles, chiefly Geoffrey of Monmouth,
Historia Regum Britanniae, Holinshed, *Chronicles*, Hardyng,
Chronicle, and Stow, *Annales*. I cite them below only where S.'s
use, or departure from them, is noteworthy.
1, 3　On the distinction between **kings** and **Emperours**, see
I ii 22.7–9*n*.　**rolles**: records, as a register or catalogue;
distinct from a **chronicle**.

Stanza 1

S.'s translation – the most literal in the poem – of Ariosto, *Orl.
Fur*. iii 1, that begins: *Chi mi darà la voce e le parole | convenienti
e sì nobil suggetto?* Since Ariosto wrote an eight-line stanza, the
ninth line is S.'s.

Stanza 2

1　Still translating Ariosto iii 2.3: *o Febo, che'l gran mondo
lustri*.
2　**borrow**: S.'s addition to Ariosto to remind us that life is
not given or derived.
4　**right**: to assert Elizabeth's claim to rightful succession.
5　Cf. III iii 22 where the substance of this line is expanded
to introduce the second part of the history.
8　**disparaged**: cast down, degraded.
9　**bountihed**: names Elizabeth the head or the fountain of
goodness.

Stanza 3

1　**Mæonian**: Homer's surname was Mæonides.　**quill**:
perhaps the plectrum, pipe, or pen.
2–5　**Phœbus rote**: the lyre or harp of Apollo, the god of
music and poetry. In their assault upon heaven, the Giants
tried to pile **Ossa** on Pelion and top it with Olympus (Virgil,
Georg. i 281–3).　**ruines** implies the defeat of the giants; cf.
Ovid, *Met*. i 151–5.　**Phlegræan Ioue**: because the battle
took place 'in the Phlegrean plaine' (V vii 10.5). Starnes and
Talbert (1955) 75 note that Stephanus's *Dictionarium* contains
this information.　**wrote**: i.e. on which he composed and set
to music. S. still follows Ariosto iii 3.　**admird**: wondered at.
6　**relish**: trace.
7　**His learned daughters**: the Muses; see I xi 5.6–9*n*.
report: bring back.
9　**blazon**: proclaim by trumpet (and thus with a louder note
than that given by Homer's quill or Apollo's rote).

Stanza 4

2　**this renowmed Prince**: Arthur.
3　**royall mace**: the sceptre of sovereignty.
6　**Grandfathers**: forefathers.
7　**the Northerne starre**: cited for its constancy. 'Of whose
true-fix'd and resting quality / There is no fellow in the
firmament' (Shakespeare, *Julius Caesar* III i 61–2).

Stanza 5

1　**possesse**: inhabit.
4　**vnmanurd**: uncultivated.　**vnprou'd**: untried as a
place to live.
5　**paysd**: poised.
7　**praysd**: appraised.
8–9　**of some thought**: referring to the chroniclers.

6

Ne did it then deserue a name to haue,
  Till that the venturous Mariner that way
  Learning his ship from those white rocks to saue,
  Which all along the Southerne sea-coast lay,
  Threatning vnheedie wrecke and rash decay,
  For safeties sake that same his sea-marke made,
  And namd it *Albion*.   But later day
  Finding in it fit ports for fishers trade,
Gan more the same frequent, and further to inuade.

7

But farre in land a saluage nation dwelt,
  Of hideous Giants, and halfe beastly men,
  That neuer tasted grace, nor goodnesse felt,
  But like wild beasts lurking in loathsome den,
  And flying fast as Roebucke through the fen,
  All naked without shame, or care of cold,
  By hunting and by spoiling liued then;
  Of stature huge, and eke of courage bold,
That sonnes of men amazd their sternnesse to behold.

8

But whence they sprong, or how they were begot,
  Vneath is to assure; vneath to wene
  That monstrous error, which doth some assot,
  That *Dioclesians* fiftie daughters shene
  Into this land by chaunce haue driuen bene,
  Where companing with feends and filthy Sprights,
  Through vaine illusion of their lust vnclene,
  They brought forth Giants and such dreadfull wights,
As farre exceeded men in their immeasurd mights.

9

They held this land, and with their filthinesse
  Polluted this same gentle soyle long time:
  That their owne mother loathd their beastlinesse,
  And gan abhorre her broods vnkindly crime,
  All were they borne of her owne natiue slime,
  Vntill that *Brutus* anciently deriu'd
  From royall stocke of old *Assaracs* line,
  Driuen by fatall error, here arriu'd,
And them of their vniust possession depriu'd.

10

But ere he had established his throne,
  And spred his empire to the vtmost shore,
  He fought great battels with his saluage fone;
  In which he them defeated euermore,
  And many Giants left on groning flore;
  That well can witnesse yet vnto this day
  The westerne Hogh, besprincled with the gore
  Of mightie *Goëmot*, whom in stout fray
Corineus conquered, and cruelly did slay.

Stanza 6

1–7 Cf. Cooper (1565): 'It was named *Albion*, *ab albis rupibus*, of white rockes, because that vnto them, that come by sea, from the east or southe, the bankes and rockes of this Ile doe appeare whyte.' He cites also the explanation that Greek adventurers 'rejoysinge at their good and fortunate arriuall, named this yle in greeke *Olbion*, which in englishe signifieth happy, in latine *Faelix*'.
5 **Threatning . . . decay**: i.e. threatening **wrecke** if he should be **vnheedie**, and destruction if **rash**.
9 **inuade**: enter.

Stanza 7

1–2 Cf. III ix 49.8–9.   **hideous**: huge.
6 **naked without shame**: as Adam and Eve (Gen. 2.25) before they sinned.
9 **sternnesse**: fierceness; formidableness.

Stanza 8

Dioclesians . . . daughters, like the Danaides, killed their husbands on their wedding-night, all except Albine, from whom Albion was derived. S.'s interest in classical myth led him to keep **fiftie** from Danao instead of the thirty or thirty-three belonging to Dioclesian. Cooper (1565) relates the fable but adds that it is one in which 'is neither similitude of trouth, reasone, nor honestie'.
2 **Vneath . . . wene**: it is difficult to affirm, difficult to believe.
3 **That monstrous error**: with the added sense, the daughters' error by which monsters were conceived.   **assot**: befool.
4 **shene**: beautiful.
6 **companing**: copulating.
7 **Through vaine illusion . . .**: i.e. they were deceived by their lust.
9 **immeasurd**: immeasurable.

Stanza 9

3–5 **their owne mother**: the **soyle** (2) of Albion; see i 10.6*n*. Holinshed, *Chronicles* i 432, notes that these giants 'tooke their name of the soile where they were borne: for *Gigantes* signifieth the sons of the earth'.   **vnkindly**: unnatural.
7 **Assarac**: the founder of Troy and great-grandfather of Aeneas (see ix 56.9) who was great-grandfather of Brutus.
8 **fatall error**: wandering ordained by fate. He was directed to England by a vision after his error of accidentally killing his father; cf. III ix 48.4–5 and the phrase, 'by fatall course' (49.1). His story is told by Geoffrey of Monmouth I iii-xv.

Stanza 10

Cf. the similar account at III ix 50.
3 **fone**: foes.
7–9 Described by Geoffrey I xvi; the place of the battle, Plymouth Hoe, agrees with local tradition preserved in Richard Carew, *Survey of Cornwall*, 1602.

11

And eke that ample Pit, yet farre renownd,
　For the large leape, which *Debon* did compell
　Coulin to make, being eight lugs of grownd;
　Into the which returning backe, he fell,
　But those three monstrous stones doe most excell
　Which that huge sonne of hideous *Albion*,
　Whose father *Hercules* in Fraunce did quell,
　Great *Godmer* threw, in fierce contention,
At bold *Canutus*; but of him was slaine anon.

12

In meed of these great conquests by them got,
　Corineus had that Prouince vtmost west,
　To him assigned for his worthy lot,
　Which of his name and memorable gest
　He called *Cornewaile*, yet so called best:
　And *Debons* shayre was, that is *Deuonshyre*:
　But *Canute* had his portion from the rest,
　The which he cald *Canutium*, for his hyre;
Now *Cantium*, which Kent we commenly inquire.

13

Thus *Brute* this Realme vnto his rule subdewd,
　And raigned long in great felicitie,
　Lou'd of his friends, and of his foes eschewd,
　He left three sonnes, his famous progeny,
　Borne of faire *Inogene* of Italy;
　Mongst whom he parted his imperiall state,
　And *Locrine* left chiefe Lord of *Britany*.
　At last ripe age bad him surrender late
His life, and long good fortune vnto finall fate.

14

Locrine was left the soueraine Lord of all;
　But *Albanact* had all the Northrene part,
　Which of himselfe *Albania* he did call;
　And *Camber* did possesse the Westerne quart,
　Which *Seuerne* now from *Logris* doth depart:
　And each his portion peaceably enioyd,
　Ne was there outward breach, nor grudge in hart,
　That once their quiet gouernment annoyd,
But each his paines to others profit still employd.

15

Vntill a nation straung, with visage swart,
　And courage fierce, that all men did affray,
　Which through the world then swarmd in euery part,
　And ouerflow'd all countries farre away,
　Like *Noyes* great flood, with their importune sway,
　This land inuaded with like violence,
　And did themselues through all the North display:
　Vntill that *Locrine* for his Realmes defence,
Did head against them make, and strong munifience.

16

He them encountred, a confused rout,
　Foreby the Riuer, that whylome was hight
　The auncient *Abus*, where with courage stout
　He them defeated in victorious fight,
　And chaste so fiercely after fearfull flight,
　That forst their Chieftaine, for his safeties sake,
　(Their Chieftaine *Humber* named was aright)
　Vnto the mightie streame him to betake,
Where he an end of battell, and of life did make.

Stanza 11
A confusing stanza. Its construction is: **that ample Pit** also
bears witness to the battle against the giants; but **the three . . .
stones** best bear witness. **Albion**, a legendary giant, was killed
in France by **Hercules**; his son, **Godmer**, threw the stones
at **Canutus**. **Debon**'s defeat of **Coulin** is referred to briefly
at III ix 50.4–5 where again it follows the story of Goemot
or Gogmagog. It seems to be S.'s invention, as also is Godmer's
defeat.
7　**quell**: kill.

Stanza 12
Geoffrey suggests that **Corineus** was the eponymous founder
of Cornwall; S. invents the rest.
5　**so called best**: referring to the preferred spelling,
Cornewaile.
6　S. etymologizes rather than puns.
7　**from the rest**: apart from the others.
9　**inquire**: call (sugg. by the context).

Stanza 13
3　**eschewd**: avoided.
5　**of Italy**: traditionally of Greece. S.'s authority may be
alliteration and rhyme, as Harper (1910) 53 suggests.
7　**Britany**: Britain.

Stanza 14
3　**Albania**: Scotland.
4　**possesse**: inhabit.　**quart**: region, quarter, referring to
Cambria or Wales.
5　**Logris**: England.　**depart**: separate.

Stanza 15
1　**straung**: foreign; referring here to the Huns.
5　**importune sway**: heavy force. The simile befits a nation
whose leader, Humber, gave his name to a river associated with
tidal flood (e.g. in Drayton, *Poly-Olbion* xxviii 480–3).
7　**display**: spread out.
9　**munifience**: fortification; from 'munify', to fortify.
Upton (1758) prefers 'munificence' *1590*: subsidies, aids.
Warton (1762) glosses 'defence', from Lat. *munio+facio*;
Church (1758) suggests 'munitience', from Lat. *munitio*,
fortification.

Stanza 16
7　Humber **named was aright** because the river was named
after him; cf. IV xi 38.5–7.

261

17

The king returned proud of victorie,
  And insolent wox through vnwonted ease,
  That shortly he forgot the ieopardie,
  Which in his land he lately did appease,
  And fell to vaine voluptuous disease:
  He lou'd faire Ladie *Estrild*, lewdly lou'd,
  Whose wanton pleasures him too much did please,
  That quite his hart from *Guendolene* remou'd,
From *Guendolene* his wife, though alwaies faithfull prou'd.

18

The noble daughter of *Corineus*
  Would not endure to be so vile disdaind,
  But gathering force, and courage valorous,
  Encountred him in battell well ordaind,
  In which him vanquisht she to fly constraind:
  But she so fast pursewd, that him she tooke,
  And threw in bands, where he till death remaind;
  Als his faire Leman, flying through a brooke,
She ouerhent, nought moued with her piteous looke.

19

But both her selfe, and eke her daughter deare,
  Begotten by her kingly Paramoure,
  The faire *Sabrina* almost dead with feare,
  She there attached, farre from all succoure;
  The one she slew in that impatient stoure,
  But the sad virgin innocent of all,
  Adowne the rolling riuer she did poure,
  Which of her name now *Seuerne* men do call:
Such was the end, that to disloyall loue did fall.

20

Then for her sonne, which she to *Locrin* bore,
  Madan was young, vnmeet the rule to sway,
  In her owne hand the crowne she kept in store,
  Till ryper yeares he raught, and stronger stay:
  During which time her powre she did display
  Through all this realme, the glorie of her sex,
  And first taught men a woman to obay:
  But when her sonne to mans estate did wex,
She it surrendred, ne her selfe would lenger vex.

21

Tho *Madan* raignd, vnworthie of his race:
  For with all shame that sacred throne he fild:
  Next *Memprise*, as vnworthy of that place,
  In which being consorted with *Manild*,
  For thirst of single kingdome him he kild.
  But *Ebranck* salued both their infamies
  With noble deedes, and warreyd on *Brunchild*
  In *Henault*, where yet of his victories
Braue moniments remaine, which yet that land enuies.

22

An happie man in his first dayes he was,
  And happie father of faire progeny:
  For all so many weekes as the yeare has,
  So many children he did multiply;
  Of which were twentie sonnes, which did apply
  Their minds to praise, and cheualrous desire:
  Those germans did subdew all Germany,
  Of whom it hight; but in the end their Sire
With foule repulse from Fraunce was forced to retire.

23

Which blot his sonne succeeding in his seat,
  The second *Brute*, the second both in name,
  And eke in semblance of his puissance great,
  Right well recur'd, and did away that blame
  With recompence of euerlasting fame.
  He with his victour sword first opened
  The bowels of wide Fraunce, a forlorne Dame,
  And taught her first how to be conquered;
Since which, with sundrie spoiles she hath beene ransacked.

Stanza 17

2 **insolent**: intemperate; proud.
4 **appease**: settle; pacify.
5 **disease**: disturbed state; or referring to his voluptuousness as an affliction.

Stanza 18

4 **ordaind**: drawn up, set in order.
6–7 Invented by S.
9 **ouerhent**: overtook.

Stanza 19

4 **attached**: seized.
5 **in that impatient stoure**] vpon the present floure *1590*, i.e. upon the very spot. Perhaps revised because traditionally Estreldis was ordered to be thrown into the river. **stoure**: emotional tumult.
6–9 S. departs from his authorities to provide an historical example of a British river that 'Had vertue pourd into [its] waters bace' (ii 6.8). Cf. Bladud's act of infusing virtue into the waters at Bath, stanza 26. **poure**: a nonce use for sending down the stream; it identifies **Sabrina** (3) with her waters.

Stanza 20

1 **for**: because.
2 **sway**: wield.
4 **stay**: strength.
5 **display**: extend.

Stanza 21

2 **fild**: also defiled.
5 **single**: undivided, i.e. desiring to rule alone.
6 **salued**: made amends for.
7 **warreyd**: made war.
8 **Henault**: Hainaut, a province in Belgium.
9 **enuies**: regards with dislike.

Stanza 22

3–8 Adds two children to Ebranck's reputed fifty; etymology requires Germany to be named from the twenty **germans** (7), brothers.

Stanza 23

4 **recur'd**: remedied.
6–7 The facts are Stow's; the brutal expression and granting of **euerlasting fame** for disembowelling are the poet's.
9 **spoiles**: plunderings.

24

Let *Scaldis* tell, and let tell *Hania*,
  And let the marsh of *Estham bruges* tell,
What colour were their waters that same day,
  And all the moore twixt *Eluersham* and *Dell*,
  With bloud of *Henalois*, which therein fell.
How oft that day did sad *Brunchildis* see
  The greene shield dyde in dolorous vermell?
That not *Scuith guiridh* it mote seeme to bee,
But rather *y Scuith gogh*, signe of sad crueltee.

25

His sonne king *Leill* by fathers labour long,
  Enioyd an heritage of lasting peace,
And built *Cairleill*, and built *Cairleon* strong.
  Next *Huddibras* his realme did not encrease,
  But taught the land from wearie warres to cease.
Whose footsteps *Bladud* following, in arts
  Exceld at *Athens* all the learned preace,
From whence he brought them to these saluage parts,
And with sweet science mollifide their stubborne harts.

26

Ensample of his wondrous faculty,
  Behold the boyling Bathes at *Cairbadon*,
Which seeth with secret fire eternally,
  And in their entrails, full of quicke Brimston,
  Nourish the flames, which they are warm'd vpon,
That to their people wealth they forth do well,
  And health to euery forreine nation:
Yet he at last contending to excell
The reach of men, through flight into fond mischief fell.

27

Next him king *Leyr* in happie peace long raind,
  But had no issue male him to succeed,
But three faire daughters, which were well vptraind,
  In all that seemed fit for kingly seed:
  Mongst whom his realme he equally decreed
To haue diuided.   Tho when feeble age
  Nigh to his vtmost date he saw proceed,
He cald his daughters; and with speeches sage
Inquyrd, which of them most did loue her parentage.

28

The eldest *Gonorill* gan to protest,
  That she much more then her owne life him lou'd:
And *Regan* greater loue to him profest,
  Then all the world, when euer it were proou'd;
  But *Cordeill* said she lou'd him, as behoou'd:
Whose simple answere, wanting colours faire
  To paint it forth, him to displeasance moou'd,
That in his crowne he counted her no haire,
But twixt the other twaine his kingdome whole did shaire.

29

So wedded th'one to *Maglan* king of Scots,
  And th'other to the king of *Cambria*,
And twixt them shayrd his realme by equall lots:
  But without dowre the wise *Cordelia*
  Was sent to *Aganip* of *Celtica*.
Their aged Syre, thus eased of his crowne,
  A priuate life led in *Albania*,
With *Gonorill*, long had in great renowne,
That nought him grieu'd to bene from rule deposed downe.

30

But true it is, that when the oyle is spent,
  The light goes out, and weeke is throwne away;
So when he had resigned his regiment,
  His daughter gan despise his drouping day,
  And wearie waxe of his continuall stay.
Tho to his daughter *Regan* he repayrd,
  Who him at first well vsed euery way;
But when of his departure she despayrd,
Her bountie she abated, and his cheare empayrd.

Stanza 24

1–4   Referring to the rivers Scheldt (**Scaldis**) and **Hania** (from the province of Hainaut) and the marshes of the town of Bruges (named **Estham bruges**, the camp of Brutus). **Eluersham** and **Dell** seem to be S.'s addition.

5   **Henalois**: men of 'Henault' (21.8).

7   **vermell**: vermilion.

8–9   **not Scuith guiridh . . . / But . . . y Scuith gogh**: not 'the green shield' (Brutus's surname) but 'the red shield'. These Welsh words stress the Welsh descent of the Tudors.

Stanza 25

1–3   Since Stow writes that **Leill** repaired **Cairleon**, the *Var.* editors suggest that **built . . . strong** could mean 'made it strong'; **strong** may comment on the etymology, 'city of the lion'.

5   **wearie warres**: wars of aggression, as Harper (1910) 71 suggests.

7   **preace**: throng.

9   **science**: knowledge, learning.   **mollifide**: softened.

Stanza 26

1   **wondrous faculty**: referring to his magical 'arts' (25.6).

2   **Cairbadon**: the city of Bath.

4   **quicke Brimston**: fiery sulphur.

6   **wealth**: well-being.

8–9   In attempting to fly with artificial wings, as did Icarus, he broke his neck.   **fond mischief**: foolish death.

Stanza 27

9   **parentage**: parents; here, parent.

Stanza 28

4   **proou'd**: put to the test.

5   **as behoou'd**: as was fitting (to a father).

7   **displeasance**: displeasure.

8   **crowne** and **haire** suggest a pun.

Stanza 29

Cambria: Wales; **Celtica**: France; **Albania**: Scotland.

4   **wise**: from Stow; noted Harper (1910) 79.

Stanza 30

2   **weeke**: wick; with a pun on 'weak', referring to Lear's 'feeble age' (27.6).

3   **regiment**: office.

9   **cheare**: kindly reception.

31

The wretched man gan then auise too late,
    That loue is not, where most it is profest,
    Too truely tryde in his extreamest state;
    At last resolu'd likewise to proue the rest,
    He to *Cordelia* him selfe addrest,
    Who with entire affection him receau'd,
    As for her Syre and king her seemed best;
    And after all an army strong she leau'd,
To war on those, which him had of his realme bereau'd.

32

So to his crowne she him restor'd againe,
    In which he dyde, made ripe for death by eld,
    And after wild, it should to her remaine:
    Who peaceably the same long time did weld:
    And all mens harts in dew obedience held:
    Till that her sisters children, woxen strong
    Through proud ambition, against her rebeld,
    And ouercommen kept in prison long,
Till wearie of that wretched life, her selfe she hong.

33

Then gan the bloudie brethren both to raine:
    But fierce *Cundah* gan shortly to enuie
    His brother *Morgan*, prickt with proud disdaine,
    To haue a pere in part of soueraintie,
    And kindling coles of cruell enmitie,
    Raisd warre, and him in battell ouerthrew:
    Whence as he to those woodie hils did flie,
    Which hight of him *Glamorgan*, there him slew:
Then did he raigne alone, when he none equall knew.

34

His sonne *Riuallo* his dead roome did supply,
    In whose sad time bloud did from heauen raine:
    Next great *Gurgustus*, then faire *Cæcily*
    In constant peace their kingdomes did containe,
    After whom *Lago*, and *Kinmarke* did raine,
    And *Gorbogud*, till farre in yeares he grew:
    Then his ambitious sonnes vnto them twaine
    Arraught the rule, and from their father drew,
Stout *Ferrex* and sterne *Porrex* him in prison threw.

35

But O, the greedy thirst of royall crowne,
    That knowes no kinred, nor regardes no right,
    Stird *Porrex* vp to put his brother downe;
    Who vnto him assembling forreine might,
    Made warre on him, and fell him selfe in fight:
    Whose death t'auenge, his mother mercilesse,
    Most mercilesse of women, *Wyden* hight,
    Her other sonne fast sleeping did oppresse,
And with most cruell hand him murdred pittilesse.

36

Here ended *Brutus* sacred progenie,
    Which had seuen hundred yeares this scepter borne,
    With high renowme, and great felicitie;
    The noble braunch from th'antique stocke was torne
    Through discord, and the royall throne forlorne:
    Thenceforth this Realme was into factions rent,
    Whilest each of *Brutus* boasted to be borne,
    That in the end was left no moniment
Of *Brutus*, nor of Britons glory auncient.

264

Stanza 31
1   **auise**: reflect.
3   **tryde**: proven.
6–7   **with . . . affection / . . . seemed best**: i.e. she 'lou'd him, as behoou'd' (28.5). **entire**: sincere; perfect.
8   **after all**: afterwards. **leau'd**: levied.

Stanza 32
3   **after wild**: willed that afterwards.
4   **weld**: wield.
9   S.'s major departure from Geoffrey of Monmouth. Hanging is his emblem for death in despair; see I ix 22.5–8*n*.

Stanza 33
4   **pere**: peer, equal.

Stanza 34
1   **Riuallo]** *Rivall'* *1590*. **his dead roome**: his office after he died.
3   **faire**: because S. takes Sisillius or Cycilly to be a woman.
4   **containe**: keep.
6   **Gorbogud**: Gorboduc.
8   **Arraught**: seized by force. **drew**: withdrew.
9   Harper (1910) 89 notes that the father's imprisonment is not found in the chronicles. **Stout**: proud; fierce; rebellious. **sterne**: cruel.

Stanza 35
8   **oppresse**: take by surprise.

Stanza 36
S. departs from the chronicles in order to draw upon the *Tragedy of Gorboduc*, specifically the concluding lament by Eubulus; see Harper (1910) 91. Norton and Sackville stress the dangers of faction; S., contrary to the evidence he himself has compiled, upholds the glory of the past.
1   **sacred**: because descended from the Trojan kings who claimed kinship with the gods.
2   **seuen hundred yeares**: see 74.3*n*.
5   **forlorne**: abandoned.
8   **moniment**: record.

37

Then vp arose a man of matchlesse might,
    And wondrous wit to menage high affaires,
    Who stird with pitty of the stressed plight
    Of this sad Realme, cut into sundry shaires
    By such, as claymd themselues *Brutes* rightfull haires,
    Gathered the Princes of the people loose,
    To taken counsell of their common cares;
    Who with his wisedom won, him streight did choose
Their king, and swore him fealty to win or loose.

38

Then made he head against his enimies,
    And *Ymner* slew, of *Logris* miscreate;
    Then *Ruddoc* and proud *Stater*, both allyes,
    This of *Albanie* newly nominate,
    And that of *Cambry* king confirmed late,
    He ouerthrew through his owne valiaunce;
    Whose countreis he redus'd to quiet state,
    And shortly brought to ciuill gouernaunce,
Now one, which earst were many, made through variaunce.

39

Then made he sacred lawes, which some men say
    Were vnto him reueald in vision,
    By which he freed the Traueilers high way,
    The Churches part, and Ploughmans portion,
    Restraining stealth, and strong extortion;
    The gracious *Numa* of great *Britanie*:
    For till his dayes, the chiefe dominion
    By strength was wielded without pollicie;
Therefore he first wore crowne of gold for dignitie.

40

Donwallo dyde (for what may liue for ay?)
    And left two sonnes, of pearelesse prowesse both;
    That sacked *Rome* too dearely did assay,
    The recompence of their periured oth,
    And ransackt *Greece* well tryde, when they were wroth;
    Besides subiected *Fraunce*, and *Germany*,
    Which yet their prayses speake, all be they loth,
    And inly tremble at the memory
Of *Brennus* and *Bellinus*, kings of Britany.

41

Next them did *Gurgunt*, great *Bellinus* sonne
    In rule succeede, and eke in fathers prayse;
    He Easterland subdewd, and *Danmarke* wonne,
    And of them both did foy and tribute raise,
    The which was dew in his dead fathers dayes:
    He also gaue to fugitiues of *Spayne*,
    Whom he at sea found wandring from their wayes,
    A seate in *Ireland* safely to remayne,
Which they should hold of him, as subiect to *Britayne*.

42

After him raigned *Guitheline* his hayre,
    The iustest man and trewest in his dayes,
    Who had to wife Dame *Mertia* the fayre,
    A woman worthy of immortall prayse,
    Which for this Realme found many goodly layes,
    And wholesome Statutes to her husband brought;
    Her many deemd to haue beene of the *Fayes*,
    As was *Aegerie*, that *Numa* tought;
Those yet of her be *Mertian* lawes both nam'd and thought.

Stanza 37
1 Upton (1758) notes S.'s art in not naming the **man** until after his achievements are recorded. Such art directs our attention to the new age which begins with Donwallo, the first British king (39.9).
3 **stressed**: afflicted.
4 **sundry shaires**: cf. 'old diuision into Regiments' (ix 59.8).
6 **loose**: disunited.
8–9 This detail, not found in the chronicles, is suggested by the legend of Numa (see 39.6). Numa 'was chosen by the people and Senate of Rome . . . for his excellent vertues and learning' (Cooper, 1565). He ruled after Romulus, as Donwallo succeeded Brutus.

Stanza 38
2 **miscreate**: unlawfully made king, or created unnaturally (being illegitimate); hence applied to England (**Logris**); or an abusive epithet applied to **Ymner**.
4, 5 **Albanie** is Scotland; **Cambry**, Wales. Thus he achieves the earlier union established under Brute (stanza 14), the union of 'great *Britanie*' (39.6).
8 **gouernaunce**: order.
9 **variaunce**: dissension.

Stanza 39
5 **stealth**: theft.
6 **Numa**: 'by his policie and ceremonies, brought the Romaines . . . in . . . a wonderfull quietnesse and honest fourme of lyving' (Cooper, 1565). The reference is made more apt by adding the claim that Donwallo's laws were divinely revealed, as Numa claimed: 'that the people myght have in more estimation, he feigned that he devised them [the laws] by the instruction of the goddesse or nymph *Aegeria*' (Cooper). Cf. 42.8. Starnes and Talbert (1955) 66 cite Stephanus as a source for this information.
8 **pollicie**: polity, civil order.

Stanza 40
3 **sacked Rome too dearely did assay**: i.e. Rome, which they sacked, too dearly learned of their prowess by experience.
4 **periured**: falsely sworn, referring to an oath of allegiance.
5 **ransackt Greece well tryde**: i.e. Greece, which they ransacked, well proved their prowess.

Stanza 41
3 **Easterland**: 'vaguely, the country to the east' (Dodge, 1908); cf. 63.2.
4 **foy**: fealty; or specifically the tribute paid as a sign of allegiance.
9 Kitchin (1872), noting how carefully S. follows Holinshed III v, concludes: 'this is a manifesto, to shew the right of England over Ireland in the days of Queen Elizabeth.' Harper (1910) 98 notes that S.'s claim that Ireland should be **subiect to Britayne** is based on Holinshed; cf. *View* 9–10.

Stanza 42
5 **found**: established. **layes**: laws; perhaps the specific sense, 'religious law', is suggested by **goodly**.
7–9 See 39.6n. Starnes and Talbert (1955) 66 suggest that Stephanus's description of Numa as *rex iustitia & pietate insignis* suggests S.'s description of **Guitheline** in 1–2.
Fayes: fairies. **thought**: i.e. conceived by her.

265

43

Her sonne *Sisillus* after her did rayne,
  And then *Kimarus*, and then *Danius*;
  Next whom *Morindus* did the crowne sustaine,
  Who, had he not with wrath outrageous,
  And cruell rancour dim'd his valorous
  And mightie deeds, should matched haue the best:
  As well in that same field victorious
  Against the forreine *Morands* he exprest;
Yet liues his memorie, though carcas sleepe in rest.

44

Fiue sonnes he left begotten of one wife,
  All which successiuely by turnes did raine;
  First *Gorboman* a man of vertuous life;
  Next *Archigald*, who for his proud disdaine,
  Deposed was from Princedome soueraine,
  And pitteous *Elidure* put in his sted;
  Who shortly it to him restord againe,
  Till by his death he it recouered;
But *Peridure* and *Vigent* him disthronized.

45

In wretched prison long he did remaine,
  Till they outraigned had their vtmost date,
  And then therein reseized was againe,
  And ruled long with honorable state,
  Till he surrendred Realme and life to fate.
  Then all the sonnes of these fiue brethren raynd
  By dew successe, and all their Nephewes late,
  Euen thrise eleuen descents the crowne retaynd,
Till aged *Hely* by dew heritage it gaynd.

46

He had two sonnes, whose eldest called *Lud*
  Left of his life most famous memory,
  And endlesse moniments of his great good:
  The ruin'd wals he did reædifye
  Of *Troynouant*, gainst force of enimy,
  And built that gate, which of his name is hight,
  By which he lyes entombed solemnly.
  He left two sonnes, too young to rule aright,
Androgeus and *Tenantius*, pictures of his might.

47

Whilst they were young, *Cassibalane* their Eme
  Was by the people chosen in their sted,
  Who on him tooke the royall Diademe,
  And goodly well long time it gouerned,
  Till the prowd *Romanes* him disquieted,
  And warlike *Cæsar*, tempted with the name
  Of this sweet Island, neuer conquered,
  And enuying the Britons blazed fame,
(O hideous hunger of dominion) hither came.

48

Yet twise they were repulsed backe againe,
  And twise renforst, backe to their ships to fly,
  The whiles with bloud they all the shore did staine,
  And the gray *Ocean* into purple dy:
  Ne had they footing found at last perdie,
  Had not *Androgeus*, false to natiue soyle,
  And enuious of Vncles soueraintie,
  Betrayd his contrey vnto forreine spoyle:
266 Nought else, but treason, from the first this land did foyle.

Stanza 43

3   sustaine: bear.
9   S. departs from his sources: the chroniclers record that in the midst of his tyranny, **Morindus** (3) was swallowed by a sea-monster. Perhaps S. was confused by the name: Morindus was also named Morvidus, and his enemies, **the forreine Morands**, were the Morini, a nation of Gaul; cf. Virgil, *extremi hominum Morini* (*Aen.* viii 727).

Stanza 44

4-5   **Archigald**: Arthgallo in Geoffrey III xvii, Archigallus (or Artogaill) in Holinshed III vii, Arthegall in Hardyng xxxvii. A prototype of Artegall; see V i 3.2*n.*
6   **pitteous**: pious, because he was surnamed Pius; full of pity, because of his pity for his brother; exciting pity, because he was dethroned (**disthronized**, 9).

Stanza 45

3   **reseized**: reinstated, in the legal sense of 'seise', put in legal possession.
7   **By dew successe**: by rightful succession.   **Nephewes**: descendants.
8   **descents**: generations.

Stanza 46

4-5   **Troynouant**: New Troy or London; founded by Brutus, III ix 46. S. follows Geoffrey's *renovavit muros* (Harper, 1910, 106).
6   **that gate**: Ludgate.
7   **solemnly**: sumptuously.

Stanza 47

1   **Eme**: uncle.
8   **blazed**: published.
9   **of dominion**: for power to rule.

Stanza 48

2   **renforst**: forced again; or reinforced.
3-4   Geoffrey IV iii notes only that the ground was drenched with blood as though it had been washed by the tide.
5   **perdie**: assuredly. Geoffrey claims that the Britons repulsed the Romans through the blessing of God.
9   **foyle**: overthrow, defeat; defile, pollute; in this latter sense corresponding to original sin, anticipating 50.4.

49

So by him *Cæsar* got the victory,
Through great bloudshed, and many a sad assay,
In which him selfe was charged heauily
Of hardy *Nennius*, whom he yet did slay,
But lost his sword, yet to be seene this day.
Thenceforth this land was tributarie made
T'ambitious *Rome*, and did their rule obay,
Till *Arthur* all that reckoning defrayd;
Yet oft the Briton kings against them strongly swayd.

50

Next him *Tenantius* raigned, then *Kimbeline*,
What time th'eternall Lord in fleshly slime.
Enwombed was, from wretched *Adams* line
To purge away the guilt of sinfull crime:
O ioyous memorie of happy time,
That heauenly grace so plenteously displayd;
(O too high ditty for my simple rime.)
Soone after this the *Romanes* him warrayd;
For that their tribute he refusd to let be payd.

51

Good *Claudius*, that next was Emperour,
An army brought, and with him battell fought,
In which the king was by a Treachetour
Disguised slaine, ere any thereof thought:
Yet ceased not the bloudy fight for ought;
For *Aruirage* his brothers place supplide,
Both in his armes, and crowne, and by that draught
Did driue the *Romanes* to the weaker side,
That they to peace agreed. So all was pacifide.

52

Was neuer king more highly magnifide,
Nor dred of *Romanes*, then was *Aruirage*,
For which the Emperour to him allide
His daughter *Genuiss'* in marriage:
Yet shortly he renounst the vassalage
Of *Rome* againe, who hither hastly sent
Vespasian, that with great spoile and rage
Forwasted all, till *Genuissa* gent
Perswaded him to ceasse, and her Lord to relent.

53

He dyde; and him succeeded *Marius*,
Who ioyd his dayes in great tranquillity,
Then *Coyll*, and after him good *Lucius*,
That first receiued Christianitie,
The sacred pledge of Christes Euangely;
Yet true it is, that long before that day
Hither came *Ioseph* of *Arimathy*,
Who brought with him the holy grayle, (they say)
And preacht the truth, but since it greatly did decay.

54

This good king shortly without issew dide,
Whereof great trouble in the kingdome grew,
That did her selfe in sundry parts diuide,
And with her powre her owne selfe ouerthrew,
Whilest *Romanes* dayly did the weake subdew:
Which seeing stout *Bunduca*, vp arose,
And taking armes, the *Britons* to her drew;
With whom she marched streight against her foes,
And them vnwares besides the *Seuerne* did enclose.

Stanza 49

2 **sad assay**: heavy attack.
5 Geoffrey IV iv records that Caesar's sword was buried with *Nennius* at the north gate of Troynovant.
8 This addition is S.'s. **all ... defrayd**: evened the account either by getting revenge or by withholding 'tribute' (50.9). Arthur's freeing of England is associated with Christ's purging man of sin (see the next stanza).
9 **swayd**: moved hostilely.

Stanza 50

2–4 Cf. Rom. 8.3: 'God sending his owne Sonne, in the similitude of sinful flesh, and for sinne, condemned sinne in the flesh.' **fleshly slime**: the human body; see I vii 9.8*n*; cf. III vi 3.4–5.
7 Said of the vision of the New Jerusalem, I x 55.7.
8 **warrayd**: made war upon.

Stanza 51

1 **Good**: Geoffrey IV xiv records that he chose to reconcile the Britons by wisdom and policy. **next**: after 'warlike *Cæsar*' (47.6).
3 **Treachetour**: traitor. *OED* suggests an error for 'treacherour', a treacher or traitor; cf. i 12.6, etc. Yet the word appears again at VI viii 7.4. Ward, in *F.Q. II*, ed. Bayley (1965) 36, suggests a blending of 'treachour' and M.E. *tregetour*.
7 **draught**: device, stratagem; also image or representation, from wearing his brother's armour.

Stanza 52

1 **magnifide**: extolled.
2 **dred**: dreaded.
8 **Forwasted**: utterly wasted. **gent**: noble.

Stanza 53

5 **sacred pledge**: baptism. **Euangely**: Gospel.
7–9 **Ioseph of Arimathy**: the disciple who buried Jesus, Matt. 27.57–60. Holinshed, *Chronicles* i 486, records that Joseph of Arimathea first taught the gospel in England; legend and medieval romance associate him with the holy grail.

Stanzas 54–56

Harper (1910) 117–20 observes that the story of **Bunduca** or Boadicea, although not in Geoffrey, was accepted by the best chroniclers. S. transfers her story to the time after Lucius's death. He has no known authority for her defeats in stanzas 54–55; 56, which follows the chroniclers in praising Bunduca's victories, 'in part contradicts and in part repeats the narrative in the preceding stanzas'.

Stanza 54

6 **stout**: valiant.
9 **besides**: by the side of.

267

55

There she with them a cruell battell tride,
  Not with so good successe, as she deseru'd ;
  By reason that the Captaines on her side,
  Corrupted by *Paulinus*, from her sweru'd :
  Yet such, as were through former flight preseru'd,
  Gathering againe, her Host she did renew,
  And with fresh courage on the victour seru'd :
  But being all defeated, saue a few,
Rather then fly, or be captiu'd her selfe she slew.

56

O famous moniment of womens prayse,
  Matchable either to *Semiramis*,
  Whom antique history so high doth raise,
  Or to *Hypsiphil'* or to *Thomiris* :
  Her Host two hundred thousand numbred is ;
  Who whiles good fortune fauoured her might,
  Triumphed oft against her enimis ;
  And yet though ouercome in haplesse fight,
She triumphed on death, in enemies despight.

57

Her reliques *Fulgent* hauing gathered,
  Fought with *Seuerus*, and him ouerthrew ;
  Yet in the chace was slaine of them, that fled :
  So made them victours, whom he did subdew.
  Then gan *Carausius* tirannize anew,
  And gainst the *Romanes* bent their proper powre,
  But him *Allectus* treacherously slew,
  And took on him the robe of Emperoure :
Nath'lesse the same enioyed but short happy howre :

58

For *Asclepiodate* him ouercame,
  And left inglorious on the vanquisht playne,
  Without or robe, or rag, to hide his shame.
  Then afterwards he in his stead did rayne ;
  But shortly was by *Coyll* in battell slaine :
  Who after long debate, since *Lucies* time,
  Was of the *Britons* first crownd Soueraine :
  Then gan this Realme renewe her passed prime :
He of his name *Coylchester* built of stone and lime.

59

Which when the *Romanes* heard, they hither sent
  Constantius, a man of mickle might,
  With whom king *Coyll* made an agreement,
  And to him gaue for wife his daughter bright,
  Faire *Helena*, the fairest liuing wight ;
  Who in all godly thewes, and goodly prayse
  Did far excell, but was most famous hight
  For skill in Musicke of all in her dayes,
Aswell in curious instruments, as cunning layes.

60

Of whom he did great *Constantine* beget,
  Who afterward was Emperour of *Rome* ;
  To which whiles absent he his mind did set,
  Octauius here lept into his roome,
  And it vsurped by vnrighteous doome :
  But he his title iustifide by might,
  Slaying *Traherne*, and hauing ouercome
  The *Romane* legion in dreadfull fight :
So settled he his kingdome, and confirmd his right.

61

But wanting issew male, his daughter deare
  He gaue in wedlocke to *Maximian*,
  And him with her made of his kingdome heyre,
  Who soone by meanes thereof the Empire wan,
  Till murdred by the friends of *Gratian* ;
  Then gan the Hunnes and Picts inuade this land,
  During the raigne of *Maximinian* ;
  Who dying left none heire them to withstand,
But that they ouerran all parts with easie hand.

Stanza 55
4 sweru'd: deserted.
6 Host: army.
7 seru'd: brought action.

Stanza 56
Cf. the praise at III iii 54.7–8.
1 prayse: virtue, excellence.
2–5 Semiramis: the famous queen who, disguised as her
son, performed 'many noble enterprices and valiaunt actes'
(Cooper, 1565). For her ambition she is placed in the dungeon
of the house of Pride (I v 50.3–4).   Hypsiphil': the queen of
Lemnos who preserved her father when her female subjects
killed their male relatives.   Thomiris: the savage Queen of
Scythia who killed Cyrus. She was aided by 200,000 Persians
(Cooper); Holinshed says 230,000. Bunduca's ambiguous reputation may explain S.'s conflicting comparisons.

Stanza 57
1 reliques: the residue of her army, the 'few' (55.8).
6 proper: own.

Stanza 58
5 Coyll: Coyll II; not the merry old soul of 53.3.
7 Harper (1910) 126 notes that no authority for S.'s
assertion has been discovered.

Stanza 59
4 bright: beautiful.
6 thewes: manners, qualities.   goodly prayse: i.e. what
deserves goodly praise; cf. 56.1.
7 hight: named.
9 curious: requiring skill.

Stanza 60
1 great Constantine: Constantine the Great.
3 whiles absent: i.e. during his absence while he was
applying himself to the duties of his office.
4 roome: office.
5 doome: law or act.

Stanza 61
7 Maximinian: a variant of Maximian (2) to avoid dupli-
cating the rhyme.

62

The weary *Britons*, whose war-hable youth
  Was by *Maximian* lately led away,
  With wretched miseries, and woefull ruth,
  Were to those Pagans made an open pray,
  And dayly spectacle of sad decay :
  Whom *Romane* warres, which now foure hundred yeares,
  And more had wasted, could no whit dismay ;
  Till by consent of Commons and of Peares,
They crownd the second *Constantine* with ioyous teares,

63

Who hauing oft in battell vanquished
  Those spoilefull Picts, and swarming Easterlings,
  Long time in peace his Realme established,
  Yet oft annoyd with sundry bordragings
  Of neighbour Scots, and forrein Scatterlings,
  With which the world did in those dayes abound :
  Which to outbarre, with painefull pyonings
  From sea to sea he heapt a mightie mound,
Which from *Alcluid* to *Panwelt* did that border bound.

64

Three sonnes he dying left, all vnder age ;
  By meanes whereof, their vncle *Vortigere*
  Vsurpt the crowne, during their pupillage ;
  Which th'Infants tutors gathering to feare,
  Them closely into *Armorick* did beare :
  For dread of whom, and for those Picts annoyes,
  He sent to *Germanie*, straunge aid to reare,
  From whence eftsoones arriued here three hoyes
Of *Saxons*, whom he for his safetie imployes.

65

Two brethren were their Capitans, which hight
  Hengist and *Horsus*, well approu'd in warre,
  And both of them men of renowmed might ;
  Who making vantage of their ciuill iarre,
  And of those forreiners, which came from farre,
  Grew great, and got large portions of land,
  That in the Realme ere long they stronger arre,
  Then they which sought at first their helping hand,
And *Vortiger* enforst the kingdome to aband.

66

But by the helpe of *Vortimere* his sonne,
  He is againe vnto his rule restord,
  And *Hengist* seeming sad, for that was donne,
  Receiued is to grace and new accord,
  Through his faire daughters face, and flattring word ;
  Soone after which, three hundred Lordes he slew
  Of British bloud, all sitting at his bord ;
  Whose dolefull moniments who list to rew,
Th'eternall markes of treason may at *Stonheng* vew.

67

By this the sonnes of *Constantine*, which fled,
  Ambrose and *Vther* did ripe years attaine,
  And here arriuing, strongly challenged
  The crowne, which *Vortiger* did long detaine :
  Who flying from his guilt, by them was slaine,
  And *Hengist* eke soone brought to shamefull death.
  Thenceforth *Aurelius* peaceably did rayne,
  Till that through poyson stopped was his breath ;
So now entombed lyes at Stoneheng by the heath.

Stanza 62

The utter desolation of England prepares for the coming of Arthur.

1 **war-hable**: fit for war.
3 **ruth**: sorrow; ruin.
5 **decay**: death.
8 S. substitutes the **Commons** and **Peares** for the military.

Stanza 63

2 **spoilefull**: plundering. **Easterlings**: evidently pirates from Denmark and Norway; cf. 41.3.
4 **bordragings**: raids; specifically border raids; a variant of 'bodrage'.
5 **Scatterlings**: vagrants; presumably the **Easterlings**, as they live scattered or scatter before English power.
7–9 On the Picts' Wall, see IV xi 36.1–5. **pyonings**: excavations, the work of pioneers.

Stanza 64

3 **pupillage**: minority.
4 **gathering to feare**: gathering cause to fear, coming to fear; or **to feare**: tofere, together.
5 **closely**: secretly.
7 **He**: Vortigern. **straunge**: foreign.
8 **hoyes**: small boats.

Stanza 65

2 **well approu'd**: well-tried.
9 **aband**: abandon.

Stanza 66

5 Usually S.'s chronicle is independent of its sources; however, **flattring word** may allude to Rowen's address to Vortigern as 'Lord king' (Geoffrey VI xii).
9 **markes**: stone standing as a memorial (*OED* sb.[1] 5).

Stanza 67

3 **challenged**: laid claim to.
9 **the heath**: Salisbury Plain.

269

68

After him *Vther*, which *Pendragon* hight,
  Succeding There abruptly it did end,
  Without full point, or other Cesure right,
  As if the rest some wicked hand did rend,
  Or th'Authour selfe could not at least attend
  To finish it: that so vntimely breach
  The Prince him selfe halfe seemeth to offend,
  Yet secret pleasure did offence empeach,
And wonder of antiquitie long stopt his speach.

69

At last quite rauisht with delight, to heare
  The royall Ofspring of his natiue land,
  Cryde out, Deare countrey, O how dearely deare
  Ought thy remembraunce, and perpetuall band
  Be to thy foster Childe, that from thy hand
  Did commun breath and nouriture receaue?
  How brutish is it not to vnderstand,
  How much to her we owe, that all vs gaue,
That gaue vnto vs all, what euer good we haue.

70

But *Guyon* all this while his booke did read,
  Ne yet has ended: for it was a great
  And ample volume, that doth far excead
  My leasure, so long leaues here to repeat:
  It told, how first *Prometheus* did create
  A man, of many partes from beasts deriued,
  And then stole fire from heauen, to animate
  His worke, for which he was by *Ioue* depriued
Of life him selfe, and hart-strings of an Ægle riued.

71

That man so made, he called *Elfe*, to weet
  Quick, the first authour of all Elfin kind:
  Who wandring through the world with wearie feet,
  Did in the gardins of *Adonis* find
  A goodly creature, whom he deemd in mind
  To be no earthly wight, but either Spright,
  Or Angell, th'authour of all woman kind;
  Therefore a *Fay* he her according hight,
Of whom all *Faeryes* spring, and fetch their lignage right

Stanza 68

1-2   The chronicle breaks here because Uther Pendragon is
the father of Arthur, and Arthur remains ignorant of his
parentage, I ix 3.3–4. It continues with Arthur's half-brother,

Artegall, at III iii 27.
2   **abruptly**: a new word in 1590, from Lat. *abruptus*,
broken off.
3   **Without . . . right**: without full stop or proper formal
break.
5   **th'Authour selfe**: a possible pun since the account ends
with the coming of Arthur.   **at least**: at the last.
6   **breach**: break, interruption of the history.
7   **to offend**: i.e. to be offended.
8   **empeach**: prevent.

Stanza 69
2   **royall Ofspring**: ancestry or descent of the kings.
5   **foster Childe**: because nurtured by the land as though
her own, in contrast to her own, such as the giants at 9.1–5.

Stanzas 70–71
Though parallel to the Genesis story, the Promethean creation
belongs to a late medieval tradition which interprets it as the
beginning of human civilization; noted Roche (1964) 34–6.
This second creation leads men to a society centred around
the city. For the background, see Raggio (1958).

Stanza 70
2   He has not ended because the '*Antiquitie* of *Faerie* lond'
(ix 60.2) extends to the reign of Elizabeth.
5–9   Horace's claim that Prometheus took some part from
every animal to add to the clay of which he made man
(*Odes* I xvi 13–6) is extended by Comes (1616) IV vi in a full
account of those **many partes** animated by the theft of fire
from heaven.
8–9   **depriued / Of life**: as he was deprived of happiness, or
separated from heaven by being bound upon a rock.
hart-strings: the tendons that were considered to sustain the
heart. Cooper (1565) has the heart in place of the liver, the
organ usually cited.

Stanza 71
1–2   The etymology of Elfe, **Quick** (i.e. a living thing), is
S.'s. Since the term was applied to supernatural and infernal
creatures, the **Elfe** finds its own kind in a **Fay** (8) who is no
earthly wight.   **authour**: ancestor.
4   **the gardins of Adonis** are revealed at III vi 29f as the
source of all life; here the place serves as an analogue to Eden,
to which it is linked by etymology.
8   **Fay**: fairy.   **according**: fittingly.

Stanzas 72–76
The 'rolles of Elfin Emperours' roughly parallel the 'chronicle
of Briton kings' (Arg.). Yates, *TLS* 3 July 1948, 373, notes
the double genealogy: first, the British story, the descent of
Trojan Brutus until the ancient British blood is returned to
power with the Tudors; and second, in its elfin form, a
religious story, with the ancient British imperial legends being
used to sanction the Tudor imperial reform. Berger (1957) 110
notes that the two chronicles present two different worlds, for
in the second 'all difficulties are left out, and the good works
are made much better'. Identification of the Elfin emperors
remains confused. Rathborne (1937) 65–128 suggested figures
from the history of Rome, but modified her claims in an
exchange with Kendrick and Yates in *TLS* (1948), 7 Feb., 79;
24 Apr., 233; 15 May, 275; 3 July, 373. Roche (1964) 37f argues
against any particular identifications.

72

Of these a mightie people shortly grew,
    And puissaunt kings, which all the world warrayd,
    And to them selues all Nations did subdew:
    The first and eldest, which that scepter swayd,
    Was *Elfin*; him all *India* obayd,
    And all that now *America* men call:
    Next him was noble *Elfinan*, who layd
Cleopolis foundation first of all:
But *Elfiline* enclosd it with a golden wall.

73

His sonne was *Elfinell*, who ouercame
    The wicked *Gobbelines* in bloudy field:
    But *Elfant* was of most renowmed fame,
    Who all of Christall did *Panthea* build:
    Then *Elfar*, who two brethren gyants kild,
    The one of which had two heads, th'other three:
    Then *Elfinor*, who was in Magick skild;
    He built by art vpon the glassy See
A bridge of bras, whose sound heauens thunder seem'd to bee.

74

He left three sonnes, the which in order raynd,
    And all their Ofspring, in their dew descents,
    Euen seuen hundred Princes, which maintaynd
    With mightie deedes their sundry gouernments;
    That were too long their infinite contents
    Here to record, ne much materiall:
    Yet should they be most famous moniments,
    And braue ensample, both of martiall,
And ciuill rule to kings and states imperiall.

75

After all these *Elficleos* did rayne,
    The wise *Elficleos* in great Maiestie,
    Who mightily that scepter did sustayne,
    And with rich spoiles and famous victorie,
    Did high aduaunce the crowne of *Faery*:
    He left two sonnes, of which faire *Elferon*
    The eldest brother did vntimely dy;
    Whose emptie place the mightie *Oberon*
Doubly supplide, in spousall, and dominion.

Stanzas 72–74
Berger (1957) 110 notes that stanzas 72–74 'alternate examples

of martial with examples of civil success'.

Stanza 72
2   **warrayd**: ravaged by war.
4–6   **Elfin**: identified with Osiris-Bacchus by Rathborne
(1937) 108–11. Bacchus-Hercules would be a possible identification: the pair conquered the East and West (see V i 2).
7–8   **Next**: i.e. next in importance in the Elfin line.
Elfinan: identified by Kendrick (*TLS*) with Brutus, the
founder of London.   **Cleopolis**: see I vii 46.7, x 58.2.
9   **Elfiline**: identified by Rathborne (*TLS*) with Lud who
built the wall of London. If so, he is displaced in the
chronology.

Stanza 73
1–2   **His sonne**: i.e. Elfinan's son. Rathborne (*TLS*) identifies **Elfinell** with Locrine, son of Brutus. The **Gobbelines**, as
enemies of the Elfs – after the analogy of the Italian Guelfs and
Ghibellines, are the Huns whom Locrine overthrew, stanza
15. See E.K.'s gloss to *S.C.* June 25.
3–4   **Elfant**: identified with Lucius, the first British King
(53.3–5), by Kendrick (*TLS*), and supported by Yates
(*TLS*). British history begins with Lucius in Foxe's *Acts and
Monuments* (1570). If so, **Panthea** may be identified with
Westminster Abbey, which was built by Lucius (Holinshed IV
xix), or Windsor Castle; but see I x 58.2–6n.
5–6   **Elfar**: identified by Rathborne (*TLS*) with Constantine
I. Since he conquered Rome, the two-headed giant would
signify his victories over Maxentius and Licinius, and the
three-headed giant his victory over pagan religion.
7–9   **Elfinor**: identified by Rathborne with Constantine II.
The **bridge of bras** upon **the glassy See**, which suggests an
idealized (and allegorical) London Bridge over the Thames, is
interpreted by Yates as Constantine's defence against paganism.
Her interpretation is supported by the parallel between Elfinor's
easy art and Constantine's labours. On this distinction, see
Berger (1957) 110. The 'glassie sea' of Rev. 15.2 is interpreted
by the Geneva gloss as 'this brittel and inconstant worlde'.
Cf. Rev. 4.6: 'And before the throne there was a sea of glasse
like unto cristal.' The **thunder** refers to the roar of tidal water;
see III ix 45.

Stanza 74
1   **three sonnes**: associated with the three sons of Constantine II (see 64.1).
3   **seuen hundred Princes**: Harrison, in Holinshed i 49–51,
claims that the changes in the government and in the religion of
Britain occurred in cycles, and that the number of years in each
cycle was a multiple of seven or nine. Cf. the seven kings listed
in 72–73; cf. also 36 where the rule of Brutus's progeny for
seven hundred years is interpreted as a cycle. Fowler (1964)
92n cites Bongo, *Mysticae numerorum*, on seven hundred as
signifying the reign of a just king. See also Mills (1977).
6   **ne much materiall**: nor of much consequence. 'The
evolution of the ideal city was complete before their reigns'
(Roche, 1964, 38).

Stanza 75
The historical analogues are transparent: **Elficleos** is Henry
VII; his two sons are **Elferon** or Prince Arthur who died
young, and **Oberon** or Henry VIII who **Doubly supplide**
his brother's place by assuming his rule and marrying his
widow.

76

Great was his power and glorie ouer all,
　Which him before, that sacred seate did fill,
　That yet remaines his wide memoriall:
　He dying left the fairest *Tanaquill*,
　Him to succeede therein, by his last will:
　Fairer and nobler liueth none this howre,
　Ne like in grace, ne like in learned skill;
　Therefore they *Glorian* call that glorious flowre,
Long mayst thou *Glorian* liue, in glory and great powre.

77

Beguild thus with delight of nouelties,
　And naturall desire of countreys state,
　So long they red in those antiquities,
　That how the time was fled, they quite forgate,
　Till gentle *Alma* seeing it so late,
　Perforce their studies broke, and them besought
　To thinke, how supper did them long awaite.
　So halfe vnwilling from their bookes them brought,
And fairely feasted, as so noble knights she ought.

Cant. XI.

*The enimies of Temperaunce
besiege her dwelling place:
Prince Arthur them repelles, and fowle
Maleger doth deface.*

1

WHat warre so cruell, or what siege so sore,
　As that, which strong affections do apply
Against the fort of reason euermore
To bring the soule into captiuitie:
Their force is fiercer through infirmitie
Of the fraile flesh, relenting to their rage,
And exercise most bitter tyranny
Vpon the parts, brought into their bondage:
No wretchednesse is like to sinfull vellenage.

2

But in a body, which doth freely yeeld
His partes to reasons rule obedient,
And letteth her that ought the scepter weeld,
All happy peace and goodly gouernment
Is setled there in sure establishment;
There *Alma* like a virgin Queene most bright,
Doth florish in all beautie excellent:
And to her guestes doth bounteous banket dight,
Attempred goodly well for health and for delight.

3

Early before the Morne with cremosin ray,
The windowes of bright heauen opened had,
Through which into the world the dawning day
Might looke, that maketh euery creature glad,
Vprose Sir *Guyon*, in bright armour clad,
And to his purposd iourney him prepar'd:
With him the Palmer eke in habit sad,
Him selfe addrest to that aduenture hard:
So to the riuers side they both together far'd.

Stanza 76
3　**memoriall**: memory.
4　**Tanaquill**: Elizabeth. See I Proem 2.5*n*.
5　**by his last will**: Henry's final will in which he declared that 'the said imperyall crowne . . . shall wholely remaine and come to our said daughter Elizabeth'; cited Kitchin (1872).

Stanza 77
1–2　The same motive led them to read the chronicles: 'burning both with feruent fire, / Their countries auncestry to vnderstond' (ix 60.6–7). **desire**: desire to understand; or the object of their desire, their love.

Canto xi

Argument
4　**deface**: destroy.

Stanza 1
1–4　On the siege of the temperate body, cf. ix 12.7, xi 5.5, 9.2, 14.2; also iv 34.7–8. **affections**: passions, violent emotions.
5–6　Cf. Paul on 'the infirmities of [the] flesh' (Rom. 6.19); cf. particularly 7.23: 'I se another law in my membres, rebelling against the law of my minde, and leading me captive vnto the law of sinne, which is in my membres.' **relenting**: yielding.
9　**sinfull vellenage**: bondage to sin through the will (Lat. *velle*). Maleger is called a 'villein' (26.6, 29.4, 35.3) to indicate his state of bondage.

Stanza 2
5　**establishment**: established condition.
6　**a virgin Queene**: the term applies equally to the body politic, as does the whole stanza.
8　**bounteous banket**: cf. the feast at the house of Medina, ii 39.1–2. The 'firme foundation' of Temperance is 'true bountihed' (xii 1.5). **dight**: prepare.
9　**Attempred**: controlled, as ii 39.1, suggesting the exercise of temperance. **health**: spiritual and moral well-being.

Stanza 3
Cf. iii 1 which marks the beginning of Guyon's journey to the Bower; repeated here, it notes his renewed effort.
2　The language (but not the meaning) of Gen. 7.11.
7　**sad**: grave, in contrast to Guyon's **bright armour** (5).

4

Where them awaited ready at the ford
　　The *Ferriman*, as *Alma* had behight,
　　With his well rigged boate: They go abord,
　　And he eftsoones gan launch his barke forthright.
　　Ere long they rowed were quite out of sight,
　　And fast the land behind them fled away.
　　But let them pas, whiles wind and weather right
　　Do serue their turnes: here I a while must stay,
To see a cruell fight doen by the Prince this day.

5

For all so soone, as *Guyon* thence was gon
　　Vpon his voyage with his trustie guide,
　　That wicked band of villeins fresh begon
　　That castle to assaile on euery side,
　　And lay strong siege about it far and wide.
　　So huge and infinite their numbers were,
　　That all the land they vnder them did hide;
　　So fowle and vgly, that exceeding feare
Their visages imprest, when they approched neare.

6

Them in twelue troupes their Captain did dispart
　　And round about in fittest steades did place,
　　Where each might best offend his proper part,
　　And his contrary obiect most deface,
　　As euery one seem'd meetest in that cace.
　　Seuen of the same against the Castle gate,
　　In strong entrenchments he did closely place,
　　Which with incessaunt force and endlesse hate,
They battred day and night, and entraunce did awate.

7

The other fiue, fiue sundry wayes he set,
　　Against the fiue great Bulwarkes of that pile,
　　And vnto each a Bulwarke did arret,
　　T'assayle with open force or hidden guile,
　　In hope thereof to win victorious spoile.
　　They all that charge did feruently apply,
　　With greedie malice and importune toyle,
　　And planted there their huge artillery,
With which they dayly made most dreadfull battery.

8

The first troupe was a monstrous rablement
　　Of fowle misshapen wights, of which some were
　　Headed like Owles, with beckes vncomely bent,
　　Others like Dogs, others like Gryphons dreare,
　　And some had wings, and some had clawes to teare,
　　And euery one of them had Lynces eyes,
　　And euery one did bow and arrowes beare:
　　All those were lawlesse lustes, corrupt enuies,
And couetous aspectes, all cruell enimies.

Stanza 4
2　behight: commanded.

Stanza 5
3　That wicked band: the 'thousand villeins' at ix 13.2.
villeins: serfs; see 1.9n.
8–9　So fowle and vgly: from the poet's perspective in the castle, 4.8–9.

Stanza 6
1　Of the twelue, seven are the deadly sins which batter the body and five are the vices which assault the five senses.
dispart: divide.
2　steades: positions.
3　offend: attack.
6　Castle gate: the mouth (see ix 23) as it provides an entrance to the heart.
7　closely: secretly.

Stanza 7
2　great Bulwarkes: the five senses as fortifications or powers of defence; cf. 'breaches' (14.7).　pile: castle.
3　arret: commit in charge.
6　apply: attend.
7　importune: ceaseless; grievous.

Stanzas 8–13
On the association of the deadly sins with animals, see Bloomfield (1952) 245–9. Chew (1962) 192–4 notes a contemporary mural in which the senses are associated with animals, as in S.: smell is a vulture, touch a spider, and hearing a boar. See also Janson (1952) ch. viii. Ripa (1603) links the boar with hearing, the lynx with sight, the ape with taste, the vulture with smell, and the spider with touch. S.'s literary source is Alcina's animal-headed crew in Ariosto, *Orl. Fur.* vi 61–4, although no animals correspond. Cf. the 'rout of monsters, headed like sundry sorts of wild beasts, but otherwise like men and women' in Milton, *Comus* S.D. 92, and their description, 69–72. Three animals are associated with each of the five senses and then with three (or three groups) of moral faults.

Stanza 8
1　monstrous rablement: also rabble of monsters.
2　fowle: hardly a pun in this context.
3–4　Owles: generally a bird of ill-omen; see I v 30.6–7n, and cf. the 'ill-faste Owle' (xii 36.4).　beckes: beaks.
Gryphons: a composite beast (half eagle, half lion) usually associated with covetousness and traditionally sharp-sighted. See I v 8.2n.　dreare: dreadful.
6–7　The keen sight of the lynx was proverbial (C. G. Smith, 1970, 510).
8　lawlesse lustes: 'fleshlie lustes, which fight against the soule' (I Pet. 2.11).　enuies: used in the etymological sense, 'to look upon (with malice)'.
9　aspectes: looks, gazes.

9

Those same against the bulwarke of the *Sight*
  Did lay strong siege, and battailous assault,
  Ne once did yield it respit day nor night,
  But soone as *Titan* gan his head exault,
  And soone againe as he his light with hault,
  Their wicked engins they against it bent:
  That is each thing, by which the eyes may fault,
  But two then all more huge and violent,
Beautie, and money, they that Bulwarke sorely rent.

10

The second Bulwarke was the *Hearing* sence,
  Gainst which the second troupe dessignment makes;
  Deformed creatures, in straunge difference,
  Some hauing heads like Harts, some like to Snakes,
  Some like wild Bores late rouzd out of the brakes;
  Slaunderous reproches, and fowle infamies,
  Leasings, backbytings, and vaine-glorious crakes,
  Bad counsels, prayses, and false flatteries.
All those against that fort did bend their batteries.

11

Likewise that same third Fort, that is the *Smell*
  Of that third troupe was cruelly assayd:
  Whose hideous shapes were like to feends of hell,
  Some like to hounds, some like to Apes, dismayd,
  Some like to Puttockes, all in plumes arayd:
  All shap't according their conditions,
  For by those vgly formes weren pourtrayd,
  Foolish delights and fond abusions,
Which do that sence besiege with light illusions.

12

And that fourth band, which cruell battry bent,
  Against the fourth Bulwarke, that is the *Tast*,
  Was as the rest, a grysie rablement,
  Some mouth'd like greedy Oystriges, some fast
  Like loathly Toades, some fashioned in the wast
  Like swine; for so deformd is luxury,
  Surfeat, misdiet, and vnthriftie wast,
  Vaine feasts, and idle superfluity:
All those this sences Fort assayle incessantly.

13

But the fift troupe most horrible of hew,
  And fierce of force, was dreadfull to report:
  For some like Snailes, some did like spyders shew,
  And some like vgly Vrchins thicke and short:
  Cruelly they assayled that fift Fort,
  Armed with darts of sensuall delight,
  With stings of carnall lust, and strong effort
  Of feeling pleasures, with which day and night
Against that same fift bulwarke they continued fight.

'idle fantasies' at ix 50.7.   **with hault**: withheld.
6   **engins**: both machines used in warfare and snares which deceive the mind (Lat. *ingenium*); cf. 'open force or hidden guile' (7.4).
7   The attack from without is interpreted as an attack from within.   **fault**: sin.
9   **Beautie, and money**: Guyon's chief foes, Acrasia and Mammon, the powers of Cupid and cupidity.
they ... rent] they against that Bulwarke lent *1590*.   'lent', i.e. 'pressed against' is too weak a term; **rent** applies to 'breaches' (14.7).

Stanza 10
2   **dessignment**: design, plan of attack; as a military term, preferable to 'assignment' *1590*.
3–5   **in straunge difference**: i.e. different from each other. The hart is opposed to the boar and both to the snake. Harvey refers to the 'Hartes hearing' in a letter to S. (S., *Poetical Wks* 626). Actaeon wearing the stag's head is usually an emblem of man transformed by desire; here, perhaps, the victim of (sexual?) slander.   **brakes**: bushes.
6–8   Three kinds of vices are listed: **infamies**, slanders (Lat. *infamia*) which lead to evil fame; **Leasings**, lies; and **crakes**, braggings.

Stanza 11
2   **assayd**: assaulted.
3–5   **dismayd**: applied by Upton (1758) to the Apes only, as they are frightened; as 'dis-made', i.e. 'mis-made', the term applies to the third troop, as the first is 'misshapen' (8.2) and the second 'Deformed' (10.3). Possibly some creatures are half hounds, half apes, while the puttocks wear false feathers.
hounds and **Puttockes** (kites or buzzards) have acute smell; the ape is usually associated with taste (see Janson, 1952, 239–41, 255n9).   **in plumes arayd**: perhaps because smell is associated with the air.
6   **according their conditions**: suitable to their natures, i.e. to their allegorical functions.
8   **fond abusions**: foolish deceptions.

Stanza 12
3   **grysie**: terrible, fearful; or, as 'grisly': horrible to see, hideous.
4–6   This troop is deformed in mouth, face, and body; cf. 10.3.   **Oystriges**: ostriches.   **greedy** because they eat anything, even iron, as in Du Bartas, *Divine Weekes* I v p. 46.
fast: faced.   **Toades**: generally symbolizing what is **loathly** but cited here because they have wide mouths.
6–8   **luxury**: vicious indulgence, illustrated by 7.
misdiet: improper feeding.   **Vaine feasts** describes **Surfeat** and **misdiet**.   **vnthriftie wast**: this last term is a pun because the vice is embodied in the waistless swine.

Stanza 13
The only sense not directly named, perhaps because it is treated in the Bower of Bliss.
1   **hew**: appearance, shape.
3–4   Harvey cites the 'spiders touching' in a letter to S. (S., *Poetical Wks* 626).   **Vrchins**: the hedgehog; cited here for its bristling spines.
7   **effort**: power.
8   **feeling**: tactile, sentient.

Stanza 9
3–5   Cf. Burton on the operation of the fancy: 'In time of sleep this faculty [Phantasy] is free, and many times conceives strange, stupend, absurd shapes' (*Anat. Mel.* I i 2.7). Cf. the

14

Thus these twelue troupes with dreadfull puissance
  Against that Castle restlesse siege did lay,
  And euermore their hideous Ordinance
  Vpon the Bulwarkes cruelly did play,
  That now it gan to threaten neare decay:
  And euermore their wicked Capitaine
  Prouoked them the breaches to assay,
  Somtimes with threats, somtimes with hope of gaine,
Which by the ransack of that peece they should attaine.

15

On th'other side, th'assieged Castles ward
  Their stedfast stonds did mightily maintaine,
  And many bold repulse, and many hard
  Atchieuement wrought with perill and with paine,
  That goodly frame from ruine to sustaine:
  And those two brethren Giants did defend
  The walles so stoutly with their sturdie maine,
  That neuer entrance any durst pretend,
But they to direfull death their groning ghosts did send.

16

The noble virgin, Ladie of the place,
  Was much dismayed with that dreadfull sight:
  For neuer was she in so euill cace,
  Till that the Prince seeing her wofull plight,
  Gan her recomfort from so sad affright,
  Offring his seruice, and his dearest life
  For her defence, against that Carle to fight,
  Which was their chiefe and th'author of that strife:
She him remercied as the Patrone of her life.

17

Eftsoones himselfe in glitterand armes he dight,
  And his well proued weapons to him hent;
  So taking courteous conge he behight,
  Those gates to be vnbar'd, and forth he went.
  Faire mote he thee, the prowest and most gent,
  That euer brandished bright steele on hye:
  Whom soone as that vnruly rablement,
  With his gay Squire issuing did espy,
They reard a most outrageous dreadfull yelling cry.

18

And therewith all attonce at him let fly
  Their fluttring arrowes, thicke as flakes of snow,
  And round about him flocke impetuously,
  Like a great water flood, that tombling low
  From the high mountaines, threats to ouerflow
  With suddein fury all the fertile plaine,
  And the sad husbandmans long hope doth throw
  A downe the streame, and all his vowes make vaine,
Nor bounds nor banks his headlong ruine may sustaine.

19

Vpon his shield their heaped hayle he bore,
  And with his sword disperst the raskall flockes,
  Which fled a sunder, and him fell before,
  As withered leaues drop from their dried stockes,
  When the wroth Western wind does reaue their locks;
  And vnder neath him his courageous steed,
  The fierce *Spumador* trode them downe like docks,
  The fierce *Spumador* borne of heauenly seed:
Such as *Laomedon* of *Phœbus* race did breed.

Stanza 14

3–4   **Ordinance**: applied to a cannon or battering ram.
play: fire; batter.
5   **decay**: destruction.
6   **Capitaine**: see ix 15.3*n*.
7   **assay**: assail.
9   **peece**: fortress or castle; masterpiece.

Stanza 15

1   **assieged**: besieged.   **ward**: garrison.
2   **stonds**: posts.
6–9   The **two brethren Giants** are the hands; noted
Gilbert (1955) 93–4. Perhaps with a pun on **maine**: hand
(Fr. *main*). Hands are 'the kepers of the house' (Eccles. 12.3),
which the gloss spells out as 'the hands, which kepe the bodie'.
See iv 6.4*n*.   **pretend**: attempt.

Stanza 16

1–3   At the lowest point of Alma's fortunes, Arthur comes
to her aid.   **place**: fortress.
5   **affright**: terror.
6   **his dearest life**: i.e. life most precious to him, life itself.
7   **Carle**: villain.
9   **remercied**: thanked (for his mercy).   **Patrone**:
protector; see viii 55.4*n*.

Stanza 17

1   **glitterand**: sparkling with light; cf. 'Glistring in armes'
(24.2). Cf. vii 42.1 and see I vii 29.4*n*.
2   **hent**: seized.
3   **conge**: leave.   **behight**: commanded.
5   **Faire . . . thee**: i.e. auspiciously may he thrive; cf. the
Red Cross Knight's blessing on Guyon (i 33.7). This rare
intrusion by the poet into his poem indicates the universal
significance of Arthur's defeat of Maleger. Cf. the personal
address at 30.6–9.   **gent**: valiant; courteous; noble.

Stanza 18

The arrows **thicke as flakes of snow** (2) translates the hurling
of darts *crebra nivis ritu* which opens the last battle in Virgil,
Aen. xi 611. The simile in 4–9 combines that used by Aeneas
to describe his first impression of Troy's fall and that used to
describe the bursting of Troy's gate (*Aen.* ii 305–8, 496–9).
8   **vowes**: prayers for a good harvest.
9   **ruine**: fall (Lat. *ruina*), applied both to the water and to
the farm's destruction.

Stanza 19

3   **before**: in the causal sense, they fell by his hand.
5   After the harvest in England, 'the Westerne wynde
beareth most swaye' (E.K.'s gloss to *S.C.* Sept. 49).
6–9   See viii 17.9*n*.   **Spumador**: the Foaming One (Lat.
spuma). Suggested by the simile imitated in 18: *spumeus amnis*
(*Aen.* ii 496), although *spumosus* is commonly linked with a
horse (as *Aen.* vi 881). His spirit displays his fiery, and therefore
heavenly, nature.   **docks**: weeds.
9   **Laomedon**: grandfather of Aeneas. His grandfather, Tros,
gained Jupiter's heavenly horses, linked by analogy with the
horses of the sun. Cf. the horses given Aeneas, *Aen.* vii 280–3.

20

Which suddeine horrour and confused cry,
    When as their Captaine heard, in haste he yode,
    The cause to weet, and fault to remedy;
    Vpon a Tygre swift and fierce he rode,
    That as the winde ran vnderneath his lode,
    Whiles his long legs nigh raught vnto the ground;
    Full large he was of limbe, and shoulders brode,
    But of such subtile substance and vnsound,
That like a ghost he seem'd, whose graue-clothes were vnbound.

21

And in his hand a bended bow was seene,
    And many arrowes vnder his right side,
    All deadly daungerous, all cruell keene,
    Headed with flint, and feathers bloudie dide,
    Such as the *Indians* in their quiuers hide;
    Those could he well direct and streight as line,
    And bid them strike the marke, which he had eyde,
    Ne was their salue, ne was their medicine,
That mote recure their wounds: so inly they did tine.

22

As pale and wan as ashes was his looke,
    His bodie leane and meagre as a rake,
    And skin all withered like a dryed rooke,
    Thereto as cold and drery as a Snake,
    That seem'd to tremble euermore, and quake:
    All in a canuas thin he was bedight,
    And girded with a belt of twisted brake,
    Vpon his head he wore an Helmet light,
Made of a dead mans skull, that seem'd a ghastly sight.

23

Maleger was his name, and after him,
    There follow'd fast at hand two wicked Hags,
    With hoarie lockes all loose, and visage grim;
    Their feet vnshod, their bodies wrapt in rags,
    And both as swift on foot, as chased Stags;
    And yet the one her other legge had lame,
    Which with a staffe, all full of litle snags
    She did support, and *Impotence* her name:
But th'other was *Impatience*, arm'd with raging flame.

24

Soone as the Carle from farre the Prince espyde,
    Glistring in armes and warlike ornament,
    His Beast he felly prickt on either syde,
    And his mischieuous bow full readie bent,
    With which at him a cruell shaft he sent:
    But he was warie, and it warded well
    Vpon his shield, that it no further went,
    But to the ground the idle quarrell fell:
Then he another and another did expell.

Stanza 20

2   **yode**: went.
4–5   **a Tygre swift**: 'the Tiger gets his name from his speedy pace; for the Persians, Greeks and Medes used to call an arrow "tygris" ' (White, 1954, 12). Cf. Maplet (1567) 175. See 26.1–2. An emblem of cruelty, wrath and lust, generally signifying the most inhuman state, as Marotti (1965) 77 notes.
8–9   Cf. ix 15.8–9.   **subtile**: rarefied; in contrast to the firm substance of the Castle of Alma.   **vnsound**: i.e. as man's life, 30.3.

Stanza 21

The arrow is a common emblem of sin which assaults the body, e.g. *Romance of the Rose* 957–84; cf. Ephes. 6.16: 'all the fyrie dartes of the wicked'.
8   **their**: there (the Elizabethan spelling).
9   **tine**: hurt, give pain.

Stanza 22

1   **pale and wan as ashes**: as Fear, III xii 12.6. More directly, it applies to death: cf. VI vii 17.8.
2   **leane and meagre**: alluding to his name, and suggesting that he is worn out by evil.   **meagre**: emaciated; fleshless like the skeleton Death. The comparison to a **rake** is proverbial (C. G. Smith, 1970, 451).
3–4   His bodily humour is cold and dry, the worst of all humours.   **rooke**: a stack of hay or a stook. With his clothes tied by bracken, he appears as a harvest figure; cf. the image of Arthur as the Western wind, 19.4–5.   **Thereto**: moreover. **drery**: horrid.

Stanza 23

1   **Maleger**: Lat. *mal*, evil + *aeger*, 'sicke, sorowfull, pensiffe, or heauie' (Cooper, 1565), i.e. desperately diseased. Associated with Antaeus, who was interpreted by Renaissance mythographers as lust. Woodhouse (1949) 221 suggests that Maleger is 'original sin'; see headnote.
6   **other legge**: simply one of her legs, or her left (the unlucky) leg; cf. Occasion, iv 4.3.
8   **Impotence**: unruliness, intemperance (Lat. *impotentia*); also feebleness (Lat. *im-potens*, unable to do), earlier manifest in Mortdant (i 58.3, 52.6) and in Cymochles (v 28.2–4). Defined by Cooper as the condition of one 'that can not bridle his lustes and affections . . . vnhable to rule himselfe'; see xii 69.8*n*. The two senses, 'unruliness' and 'feebleness', suggest that Maleger's strength is his weakness, and his weakness his strength. Hence he is 'most strong in most infirmitee' (40.8) as the force of 'strong affections . . . is fiercer through infirmitie / Of the fraile flesh' (1.2–6).
9   **Impatience**: from Lat. *impatiens*, 'that cannot suffer or abide' (Cooper), earlier manifest in Amavia (i 44.4–5) and in Pyrochles (v 16.4).

Stanza 24

3   **felly**: fiercely.
4   **mischieuous**: capable of inflicting injury.
8   **quarrell**: a square-headed arrow shot from a cross-bow; noted for its speed and accuracy. Also the current sense: the shot is an occasion to wrath which Arthur resists.   **idle**: because shot in vain.
9   **expell**: shoot.

25

Which to preuent, the Prince his mortall speare
  Soone to him raught, and fierce at him did ride,
  To be auenged of that shot whyleare:
  But he was not so hardie to abide
  That bitter stownd, but turning quicke aside
  His light-foot beast, fled fast away for feare:
  Whom to pursue, the Infant after hide,
  So fast as his good Courser could him beare,
But labour lost it was, to weene approch him neare.

26

For as the winged wind his Tigre fled,
  That vew of eye could scarse him ouertake,
  Ne scarse his feet on ground were seene to tred;
  Through hils and dales he speedie way did make,
  Ne hedge ne ditch his readie passage brake,
  And in his flight the villein turn'd his face,
  (As wonts the *Tartar* by the *Caspian* lake,
  When as the *Russian* him in fight does chace)
Vnto his Tygres taile, and shot at him apace.

27

Apace he shot, and yet he fled apace,
  Still as the greedy knight nigh to him drew,
  And oftentimes he would relent his pace,
  That him his foe more fiercely should pursew:
  Who when his vncouth manner he did vew,
  He gan auize to follow him no more,
  But keepe his standing, and his shaftes eschew,
  Vntill he quite had spent his perlous store,
And then assayle him fresh, ere he could shift for more.

28

But that lame Hag, still as abroad he strew
  His wicked arrowes, gathered them againe,
  And to him brought, fresh battell to renew·
  Which he espying, cast her to restraine
  From yielding succour to that cursed Swaine,
  And her attaching, thought her hands to tye;
  But soone as him dismounted on the plaine,
  That other Hag did farre away espy
Binding her sister, she to him ran hastily.

29

And catching hold of him, as downe he lent,
  Him backward ouerthrew, and downe him stayd
  With their rude hands and griesly graplement,
  Till that the villein comming to their ayd,
  Vpon him fell, and lode vpon him layd;
  Full litle wanted, but he had him slaine,
  And of the battell balefull end had made,
  Had not his gentle Squire beheld his paine,
And commen to his reskew, ere his bitter bane.

30

So greatest and most glorious thing on ground
  May often need the helpe of weaker hand;
  So feeble is mans state, and life vnsound,
  That in assurance it may neuer stand,
  Till it dissolued be from earthly band.
  Proofe be thou Prince, the prowest man aliue,
  And noblest borne of all in *Britayne* land;
  Yet thee fierce Fortune did so nearely driue,
That had not grace thee blest, thou shouldest not suruiue.

Stanza 25
5 **stownd**: encounter; moment of peril.
7 **Infant**: Prince; see viii 56.1–3*n*.

Stanza 26
2 This expression is based on the Renaissance theory that one sees by emission from the eyes.
5 **readie**: straight. **brake**: stopped.
6–9 By this Parthian strategy (befitting his paradoxical state noted in stanza 40), Maleger overcomes his foe by flight.

Stanza 27
3 **relent**: slacken.
6 **gan auize**: determined.
7 **keepe his standing**: as the Castle of Alma maintains its 'stedfast stonds' (15.2); cf. his standing 'as a stedfast towre' (viii 35.7).
8 **perlous**: perilous.

Stanza 28
4 **cast**: resolved.
6 **attaching**: seizing.

Stanza 29
3 **their rude hands**: indicates that Arthur must triumph by 'his puissant hands' (46.1). For the hand in relation to temperance, see iv 6.4*n*. **griesly graplement**: horrible grappling.
6 **wanted**: was lacking.
9 **bane**: death.

Stanza 30
Cf. the Squire's role in Book I when he encounters the Dragon and 'twixt him and his Lord did like a bulwarke stand' (I viii 12.9).
1 **on ground**: on earth; with a pun on Arthur's present position.
4 **assurance**: security.
5 Cf. gloss to 2 Cor. 5.1: 'After this bodie shalbe dissolued, it shalbe made incorruptible and immortal.'
8 **so nearely driue**: press so hard.
9 **blest**: saved.

31

The Squire arriuing, fiercely in his armes
　　Snatcht first the one, and then the other Iade,
　　His chiefest lets and authors of his harmes,
　　And them perforce withheld with threatned blade,
　　Least that his Lord they should behind inuade;
　　The whiles the Prince prickt with reprochfull shame,
　　As one awakt out of long slombring shade,
　　Reuiuing thought of glorie and of fame,
Vnited all his powres to purge himselfe from blame.

32

Like as a fire, the which in hollow caue
　　Hath long bene vnderkept, and downe supprest,
　　With murmurous disdaine doth inly raue,
　　And grudge, in so streight prison to be prest,
　　At last breakes forth with furious vnrest,
　　And striues to mount vnto his natiue seat;
　　All that did earst it hinder and molest,
　　It now deuoures with flames and scorching heat,
And carries into smoake with rage and horror great.

33

So mightily the *Briton* Prince him rouzd
　　Out of his hold, and broke his caitiue bands,
　　And as a Beare whom angry curres haue touzd,
　　Hauing off-shakt them, and escapt their hands,
　　Becomes more fell, and all that him withstands
　　Treads downe and ouerthrowes.　Now had the Carle
　　Alighted from his Tigre, and his hands
　　Discharged of his bow and deadly quar'le,
To seize vpon his foe flat lying on the marle.

34

Which now him turnd to disauantage deare;
　　For neither can he fly, nor other harme,
　　But trust vnto his strength and manhood meare,
　　Sith now he is farre from his monstrous swarme,
　　And of his weapons did himselfe disarme.
　　The knight yet wrothfull for his late disgrace,
　　Fiercely aduaunst his valorous right arme,
　　And him so sore smote with his yron mace,
That groueling to the ground he fell, and fild his place.

35

Well weened he, that field was then his owne,
　　And all his labour brought to happie end,
　　When suddein vp the villein ouerthrowne,
　　Out of his swowne arose, fresh to contend,
　　And gan himselfe to second battell bend,
　　As hurt he had not bene.　Thereby there lay
　　An huge great stone, which stood vpon one end,
　　And had not bene remoued many a day;
Some land-marke seem'd to be, or signe of sundry way.

36

The same he snatcht, and with exceeding sway
　　Threw at his foe, who was right well aware
　　To shunne the engin of his meant decay;
　　It booted not to thinke that throw to beare,
　　But ground he gaue, and lightly leapt areare:
　　Eft fierce returning, as a Faulcon faire
　　That once hath failed of her souse full neare,
　　Remounts againe into the open aire,
And vnto better fortune doth her selfe prepaire.

Stanza 31
3　His: refers to Arthur but also to the Squire and Maleger.
lets: hindrances.
4　perforce: forcibly.
6–9　The simile contrasts Arthur's state with that of Acrasia's victims who remain asleep in the shade; cf. Cymochles, v 32.2, pricked with shame by Atin at 38.9. Arthur recovers from a faint akin to Guyon's. In **Reuiuing thought of glorie and of fame**, he remembers the 'great desire of glory and of fame' (ix 38.7), which is named his '*Prays-desire*' (39.8).

Stanza 32
3　disdaine: indignation.
4　grudge: grumble.　　streight: narrow; confining.
5　vnrest] infest *1590*: ? hostility (the adj. signifying 'hostile' used as a substantive).
6　natiue seat: above earth, water, and air. In the Renaissance, volcanic eruption was explained as the result of fire imprisoned underground seeking its natural place next to the moon.

Stanza 33
2　his hold: i.e. the bonds that held him.　　caitiue bands: captive (or vile) bonds; the 'chaines and bands' (47.4) carried by Impatience.
3　touzd: worried.
6–7　Maleger is caught in Arthur's posture when he dismounted from his horse.
8　Discharged: rid; literally having discharged his arrows.
9　marle: earth. It suggests 'defiling'; cf. Langland: 'lond overe-layde with marle and with donge' (*Piers Plowman* C xiii 231).

Stanza 34
1　deare: grievous, dire.
2　other harme: i.e. harm the other (Arthur); do other harm; or otherwise harm.
3　meare: solely.
8　The **yron mace** is cited to show that force cannot defeat Maleger.
9　groueling: prostrate, face downward; the posture in which he gains sustenance from his mother earth.　　fild his place: unless a rhyming tag, he filled Arthur's place; or it may refer to each man's place in the ground.

Stanza 35
5　bend: apply.
6–9　S. alludes to the stone that Turnus hurls at Aeneas before his death, Virgil, *Aen.* xii 896–8. He alludes to the same episode at viii 52.1–2.
8　not bene remoued: implying that Maleger goes beyond all bounds. In Virgil, the stone marks the boundary of fields; in S., it marks the choice of paths.

Stanza 36
1　sway: force.
2　aware: watchful.
7　souse: swoop.　　full neare: only by a very little.

37

So braue returning, with his brandisht blade,
  He to the Carle himselfe againe addrest,
  And strooke at him so sternely, that he made
  An open passage through his riuen brest,
  That halfe the steele behind his back did rest;
  Which drawing backe, he looked euermore
  When the hart bloud should gush out of his chest,
  Or his dead corse should fall vpon the flore;
But his dead corse vpon the flore fell nathemore.

38

Ne drop of bloud appeared shed to bee,
  All were the wounde so wide and wonderous,
  That through his carkasse one might plainely see:
  Halfe in a maze with horror hideous,
  And halfe in rage, to be deluded thus,
  Againe through both the sides he strooke him quight,
  That made his spright to grone full piteous:
  Yet nathemore forth fled his groning spright,
But freshly as at first, prepard himselfe to fight.

39

Thereat he smitten was with great affright,
  And trembling terror did his hart apall,
  Ne wist he, what to thinke of that same sight,
  Ne what to say, ne what to doe at all;
  He doubted, least it were some magicall
  Illusion, that did beguile his sense,
  Or wandring ghost, that wanted funerall,
  Or aerie spirit vnder false pretence,
Or hellish feend raysd vp through diuelish science.

40

His wonder farre exceeded reasons reach,
  That he began to doubt his dazeled sight,
  And oft of error did himselfe appeach:
  Flesh without bloud, a person without spright,
  Wounds without hurt, a bodie without might,
  That could doe harme, yet could not harmed bee,
  That could not die, yet seem'd a mortall wight,
  That was most strong in most infirmitee;
Like did he neuer heare, like did he neuer see.

41

A while he stood in this astonishment,
  Yet would he not for all his great dismay
  Giue ouer to effect his first intent,
  And th'vtmost meanes of victorie assay,
  Or th'vtmost issew of his owne decay.
  His owne good sword *Morddure*, that neuer fayld
  At need, till now, he lightly threw away,
  And his bright shield, that nought him now auayld,
And with his naked hands him forcibly assayld.

42

Twixt his two mightie armes him vp he snatcht,
  And crusht his carkasse so against his brest,
  That the disdainfull soule he thence dispatcht,
  And th'idle breath all vtterly exprest:
  Tho when he felt him dead, a downe he kest
  The lumpish corse vnto the senselesse grownd;
  Adowne he kest it with so puissant wrest,
  That backe againe it did aloft rebownd,
And gaue against his mother earth a gronefull sownd.

Stanza 37
3 **sternely**: fiercely.

Stanza 38
2 **All**: although.
4 **in a maze**: in amazement; suggesting 'being in a maze';
cf. 44.1.
7–9 On a demon's pain when his substance is cut, followed
by quick and thorough healing, West (1955) 146–7 cites
Ficino's trans. of Psellus, *de Daemonibus* (Lyons 1577): 'the
body of the demon when it is cut soon is recreated in itself
again. . . . Yet meanwhile it suffers while divided.'

Stanza 39
5–6 The rare run-on line draws attention to the four possible
explanations of the riddle.   **doubted**: feared.
7 **ghost, that wanted funerall**: hence unable to enter
Hades, being graveless; as Virgil, *Aen.* vi 325–6.   **wanted**:
lacked.
8 **aerie**: belonging to the air, or having assumed a body of
air; see I i 45.3*n*.   **pretence**: appearance.

Stanza 40
The seven riddles are carefully posed to challenge and defeat
our **reasons reach**. Arthur's dilemma is man's: 'O wretched
man that I am, who shal deliver me from the bodie of this
death' (Rom. 7.24); cf. 'lifelesse shadow' (44.3), 'dead-liuing
swaine' (44.7), and Furor as not one whom 'steele can wound,
or strength can ouerthroe' (iv 10.5).
3 **appeach**: accuse.
7 **mortall**: and therefore subject to death.
8 **most strong . . . infirmitee**: i.e. sin gains its strength
from man's weakness; cf. Milton: 'All wickedness is weakness'
(*Samson Agonistes* 834).

Stanza 41
3 **Giue ouer**: give up trying.
6–9 In abandoning his armour, Arthur uses the most
extreme means to gain victory.

Stanza 42
4 **exprest**: squeezed out.
6 **lumpish**: heavy.   **senselesse**: modifying **corse**.
7 **wrest**: throw.
9 **his mother earth**: as the old Adam, he is 'of the earth,
earthlie' (1 Cor. 15.47).

43

As when *Ioues* harnesse-bearing Bird from hie
  Stoupes at a flying heron with proud disdaine,
  The stone-dead quarrey fals so forciblie,
  That it rebounds against the lowly plaine,
  A second fall redoubling backe againe.
  Then thought the Prince all perill sure was past,
  And that he victor onely did remaine;
  No sooner thought, then that the Carle as fast
Gan heap huge strokes on him, as ere he downe was cast.

44

Nigh his wits end then woxe th'amazed knight,
  And thought his labour lost and trauell vaine,
  Against this lifelesse shadow so to fight:
  Yet life he saw, and felt his mightie maine,
  That whiles he marueild still, did still him paine:
  For thy he gan some other wayes aduize,
  How to take life from that dead-liuing swaine,
  Whom still he marked freshly to arize
From th'earth, and from her wombe new spirits to reprize.

45

He then remembred well, that had bene sayd,
  How th'Earth his mother was, and first him bore;
  She eke so often, as his life decayd,
  Did life with vsury to him restore,
  And raysd him vp much stronger then before,
  So soone as he vnto her wombe did fall;
  Therefore to ground he would him cast no more,
  Ne him commit to graue terrestriall,
But beare him farre from hope of succour vsuall.

46

Tho vp he caught him twixt his puissant hands,
  And hauing scruzd out of his carrion corse
  The lothfull life, now loosd from sinfull bands,
  Vpon his shoulders carried him perforse
  Aboue three furlongs, taking his full course,
  Vntill he came vnto a standing lake;
  Him thereinto he threw without remorse,
  Ne stird, till hope of life did him forsake;
So end of that Carles dayes, and his owne paines did make.

47

Which when those wicked Hags from farre did spy,
  Like two mad dogs they ran about the lands,
  And th'one of them with dreadfull yelling cry,
  Throwing away her broken chaines and bands,
  And hauing quencht her burning fier brands,
  Hedlong her selfe did cast into that lake;
  But *Impotence* with her owne wilfull hands,
  One of *Malegers* cursed darts did take,
So riu'd her trembling hart, and wicked end did make.

48

Thus now alone he conquerour remaines;
  Tho comming to his Squire, that kept his steed,
  Thought to haue mounted, but his feeble vaines
  Him faild thereto, and serued not his need,
  Through losse of bloud, which from his wounds did bleed,
  That he began to faint, and life decay:
  But his good Squire him helping vp with speed,
  With stedfast hand vpon his horse did stay,
And led him to the Castle by the beaten way.

Stanza 43

1 **Ioues . . . Bird**: the eagle which bears Jove's armour (his thunderbolts) in its claws.
2 **Stoupes**: swoops; a term in falconry.
3 **quarrey**: a bird flown at and killed by a hawk.
4–5 **rebounds . . .**: apparently factual; a shot bird often bounces when it hits the ground.

Stanza 44

3 **this**] his *1590* (corr. *F.E.*) notes the *psychomachia*; see headnote.
6 **For thy**: therefore.   **aduize**: consider.
9 **reprize**: take anew.

Stanzas 45–46

Arthur's wrestling with Maleger parallels Hercules's contest with Antaeus, which was one of his most difficult labours, according to Lucan, *Pharsalia* iv 593f. As interpreted in the Renaissance, Hercules's victory shows how reason or spirit conquers the lusts of the flesh. Boccaccio interpreted the contest as the defeat of the lusts which are born of the body; noted Lotspeich (1932) 37. Hercules slays Antaeus by holding his crushed body off the ground but Arthur must also cast Maleger into the lake. This further act suggests baptism; see 46.6n.

Stanza 45

4 **vsury**: interest.

Stanza 46

1 **his puissant hands**: see iv 6.4n.
2 **scruzd**: screwed and squeezed.
3 **lothfull**: loathsome; reluctant to die. **sinfull bands**: i.e. bondage to sin. Freeing Maleger from bondage to sin corresponds to the death of the old Adam in man.
5 **Aboue three furlongs**: Arthur paces out the length of the Dragon's tail and beyond, I xi 11.7. **taking his full course**: measuring the full distance.
6 **a standing lake**: one whose waters neither ebb nor flow; hence not renewing. Cf. the 'liuing well' of I ii 43.4, xi 31.6, which refers to the flowing waters of baptism. Woodhouse (1950) 222 argues that the casting of Maleger into the lake 'invokes the power of grace, symbolized by water, to destroy evil'.

Stanza 47

4 **chaines and bands**: perhaps those used by Arthur to bind Impotence, 28.6, and by which he was bound, 33.2.
6 Hankins (1971) 86–7 suggests that the source of the standing lake is Luke 8.33: when the Gadarene swine are invaded by the devils whom Christ had cast out of the man, 'the herd was caryed with violence from a stepe downe place into the lake, and was choked'. Milton also associates the story of the Gadarene swine with the Hercules-Antaeus myth, *Paradise Regained* iv 563–75, 630.

Stanza 48

7–9 The Squire ministers to Arthur as the Angel does to Guyon after his struggle against Mammon. **stay**: support.

49

Where many Groomes and Squiers readie were,
  To take him from his steed full tenderly,
  And eke the fairest *Alma* met him there
  With balme and wine and costly spicery,
  To comfort him in his infirmity;
  Eftsoones she causd him vp to be conuayd,
  And of his armes despoyled easily,
In sumptuous bed she made him to be layd,
And all the while his wounds were dressing, by him stayd.

Cant. XII.

Guyon, by Palmers gouernance,
  passing through perils great,
Doth ouerthrow the Bowre of blisse,
  and Acrasie defeat.

1

NOw gins this goodly frame of Temperance
  Fairely to rise, and her adorned hed
  To pricke of highest praise forth to aduance,
  Formerly grounded, and fast setteled
  On firme foundation of true bountihed;
  And this braue knight, that for that vertue fights,
  Now comes to point of that same perilous sted,
  Where Pleasure dwelles in sensuall delights,
Mongst thousand dangers, and ten thousand magick mights.

2

Two dayes now in that sea he sayled has,
  Ne euer land beheld, ne liuing wight,
  Ne ought saue perill, still as he did pas:
  Tho when appeared the third *Morrow* bright,
  Vpon the waues to spred her trembling light,
  An hideous roaring farre away they heard,
  That all their senses filled with affright,
  And streight they saw the raging surges reard
Vp to the skyes, that them of drowning made affeard.

3

Said then the Boteman, Palmer stere aright,
  And keepe an euen course; for yonder way
  We needes must passe (God do vs well acquight,)
  That is the *Gulfe of Greedinesse*, they say,
  That deepe engorgeth all this worldes pray:
  Which hauing swallowd vp excessiuely,
  He soone in vomit vp againe doth lay,
  And belcheth forth his superfluity,
That all the seas for feare do seeme away to fly.

Stanza 49
Arthur's weakened state parallels that of Acrasia's victims
whom Guyon will now cure by overthrowing the power of
Intemperance. **infirmity** (5) glances back at Maleger 40.8.

While baptism may destroy the old Adam in us, and allow
lapsed powers to be renewed, the infection of original sin,
expressed in concupiscence, remains.
4   spicery: spices.

Canto xii

Argument
1–2   by . . . passing through] through . . . through passing
1590 suggests that Guyon overthrows the Bower because he
passes through it, resisting its temptations.

Stanza 1
1   frame: structure; cf. particularly ix 22.1, 44.7, xi 15.5.
Also the structuring of the body by temperance: see ii 12.9*n*.
2   Fairely: handsomely.
3   To pricke of highest praise: to the highest point of
praise.
4   Formerly: first of all.
5   bountihed: goodness, virtue.
7   point: the same metaphor is behind **pricke** (3): the mark
aimed at in shooting, the bull's eye. Temperance is achieved
only when it is tested fully.
8   Pleasure: Acrasia, as 48.8; see i Arg. 4*n*.

Stanzas 2–38
The chief classical precedents for Guyon's voyage are the voyage
of Ulysses in Homer, *Ody*. xii, and of Aeneas in Virgil, *Aen*.
ii–iii. The allegorical interpretation of these voyages is summarized by Lotspeich (1932) 21–2. The Christian conventions of
the voyage are examined by Nellist (1963). Crampton (1974)
135f interprets the voyage as a threefold assault upon the three
interior senses, memory, imagination, and common sense. The
forty stanzas that treat the dangers – the traditional number in a
full temptation (see vii 26.5*n*) – thirty-six at sea and four on
land (39–41), divide into groups of four (except that the Quicksand and Whirlpool have two each), alternating between peril
and pleasure. The first four dangers (Gulf and Rock, Wandering Islands and Phædria) lead to a second inserted four (see
stanzas 18–29*n*) and culminate in four which comprise all the
dangers of sea (Mermaids), air (fog and fowls), and land
(beasts).

Stanza 3
3   Cf. the Palmer's injunction at i 32.8.   **acquight**:
deliver. In Book I, this role is given to Arthur (vii 52.6) and to
Truth (viii 1.4).
4 to 4.9   The **Gulfe of Greedinesse** (3.4) and the **hideous
Rocke** (4.1) derive from Homer's Charybdis and Scylla (*Ody*.
xii 73–110, 234–59) by way of Virgil (*Aen*. iii 420–32, 555–67).
Lotspeich (1932) 106 argues for the direct influence of Comes
(1616) VIII xii, but S. would not need Comes for this proverbial
description of the twin perils of the sea. More relevant to his
theme is Comes's interpretation of the passage as virtue's
mean between two extremes, both of which must be avoided:
'Life is most full of hardships and perils, like a voyage between
two terrible rocks; and unless this is most wisely guided, men
are caught by voluptuous desire and fall into the most wretched
miseries' (456–7).
6–8   excessiuely: also greedily.   **lay**: throw; cf. Gluttony,
I iv 21.8–9.
9   Cf. Ps. 114.3: 'The sea sawe it and fled.'   281

4

On th'other side an hideous Rocke is pight,
   Of mightie *Magnes* stone, whose craggie clift
   Depending from on high, dreadfull to sight,
   Ouer the waues his rugged armes doth lift,
   And threatneth downe to throw his ragged rift
   On who so commeth nigh; yet nigh it drawes
   All passengers, that none from it can shift:
   For whiles they fly that Gulfes deuouring iawes,
They on this rock are rent, and sunck in helplesse wawes.

5

Forward they passe, and strongly he them rowes,
   Vntill they nigh vnto that Gulfe arriue,
   Where streame more violent and greedy growes:
   Then he with all his puissance doth striue
   To strike his oares, and mightily doth driue
   The hollow vessell through the threatfull waue,
   Which gaping wide, to swallow them aliue,
   In th'huge abysse of his engulfing graue,
Doth rore at them in vaine, and with great terror raue.

6

They passing by, that griesly mouth did see,
   Sucking the seas into his entralles deepe,
   That seem'd more horrible then hell to bee,
   Or that darke dreadfull hole of *Tartare* steepe,
   Through which the damned ghosts doen often creepe
   Backe to the world, bad liuers to torment:
   But nought that falles into this direfull deepe,
   Ne that approcheth nigh the wide descent,
May backe returne, but is condemned to be drent.

7

On th'other side, they saw that perilous Rocke,
   Threatning it selfe on them to ruinate,
   On whose sharpe clifts the ribs of vessels broke,
   And shiuered ships, which had bene wrecked late,
   Yet stuck, with carkasses exanimate
   Of such, as hauing all their substance spent
   In wanton ioyes, and lustes intemperate,
   Did afterwards make shipwracke violent,
Both of their life, and fame for euer fowly blent.

8

For thy, this hight *The Rocke of* vile *Reproch*,
   A daungerous and detestable place,
   To which nor fish nor fowle did once approch,
   But yelling Meawes, with Seagulles hoarse and bace,
   And Cormoyrants, with birds of rauenous race,
   Which still sate waiting on that wastfull clift,
   For spoyle of wretches, whose vnhappie cace,
   After lost credite and consumed thrift,
At last them driuen hath to this despairefull drift.

9

The Palmer seeing them in safetie past,
   Thus said; Behold th'ensamples in our sights,
   Of lustfull luxurie and thriftlesse wast:
   What now is left of miserable wights,
   Which spent their looser daies in lewd delights,
   But shame and sad reproch, here to be red,
   By these rent reliques, speaking their ill plights?
   Let all that liue, hereby be counselled,
To shunne *Rocke of Reproch*, and it as death to dred.

Stanza 4

1–2 Homer's Scylla is transformed into a magnet. For a parallel, see *Huon of Burdeux* (*Var.* ii 353).   **hideous**: immense.   **pight**: placed.   **Magnes stone**: the magnet or loadstone (Lat. *magnes*), which was said to attract ships by their nails.
3 **Depending**: hanging down.
5 **rift**: projecting fragments rather than fissures (cf. vii 28.5).
6–7 **it drawes / All passengers**: cf. *et navis in saxa trahentem* (*Aen*. iii 425).   **passengers**: passers by.
8–9 Cooper (1565) cites the proverb: *Decidit in Scyllam cupiens vitare Charybdim*.   **wawes**: waves; suggesting 'woes'.

Stanza 5

7–8 Cf. Prov. 1.12: 'We wil swallowe them up alive like a grave even whole, as those that go downe into the pit.'

Stanza 6

4 **Tartare**: Tartarus, the infernal regions and place of punishment; see I vii 44.3*n*.
9 **drent**: drenched; drowned.

Stanza 7

2 **ruinate**: fall down and bring ruin.
3–5 These details are from Comes (1616).   **broke**: made bankrupt, on the allegorical level.   **exanimate**: deprived of the soul.
6–9 Cf. 1 Tim. 6.9: 'For they that wil be riche, fall into temptation and snares, and into many foolish and noysome lustes, which drowne men in perdition and destruction.' Comes VIII xii p. 457 interprets the fable of Scylla as a warning against running into debt.   **blent**: despoiled.

Stanza 8

Craig (1967) 465 notes some of the puns in this stanza.
1 **For thy**: therefore.
2 **daungerous**: suggests the obsolete sense, 'being in debt' (*OED* 1).
4 **Meawes**: the common gull.   **Seagulles**: a symbol of greed and trickery; hence the epithet **bace**.
5 **Cormoyrants**: a large, voracious sea-bird, the sea-raven (*corvus marinus*), a symbol of greed applied to usurers and those guilty of rapaciousness.   **rauenous**: with a pun on 'raven'.
6 **waiting**: watching.   **wastfull**: desolate; causing devastation. A fitting punishment for the wasteful. Cf. 35.3, 80.7.
7 **spoyle**: ruin; booty.
8 **thrift**: savings.
9 **drift**: course; with the sense of 'driving' victims to their desperate end.

Stanza 9

The Palmer's lesson directed against the **Rocke** (9) includes the 'Gulfe of Greedinesse': one becomes victim of the former by fleeing the latter, as the antithesis to Mammon's greedy labour for riches is the sensual sloth of Acrasia's Bower.
3 **luxurie**: vicious indulgence (Lat. *luxuria*).   **thriftlesse wast**: cf. the 'vnthriftie wast' which assaults the Castle of Alma, xi 12.7.
4 **miserable**: poverty-stricken; wretchedly unhappy.
5 **looser**: too loose.
6 **red**: seen; interpreted.

10

So forth they rowed, and that *Ferryman*
   With his stiffe oares did brush the sea so strong,
   That the hoare waters from his frigot ran,
   And the light bubbles daunced all along,
   Whiles the salt brine out of the billowes sprong.
   At last farre off they many Islands spy,
   On euery side floting the floods emong:
   Then said the knight, Loe I the land descry,
Therefore old Syre thy course do thereunto apply.

11

That may not be, said then the *Ferryman*
   Least we vnweeting hap to be fordonne:
   For those same Islands, seeming now and than,
   Are not firme lande, nor any certein wonne,
   But straggling plots, which to and fro do ronne
   In the wide waters: therefore are they hight
   The *wandring Islands*.   Therefore doe them shonne;
   For they haue oft drawne many a wandring wight
Into most deadly daunger and distressed plight.

12

Yet well they seeme to him, that farre doth vew,
   Both faire and fruitfull, and the ground dispred
   With grassie greene of delectable hew,
   And the tall trees with leaues apparelled,
   Are deckt with blossomes dyde in white and red,
   That mote the passengers thereto allure;
   But whosoeuer once hath fastened
   His foot thereon, may neuer it recure,
But wandreth euer more vncertein and vnsure.

13

As th'Isle of *Delos* whylome men report
   Amid th' *Ægæan* sea long time did stray,
   Ne made for shipping any certaine port,
   Till that *Latona* traueiling that way,
   Flying from *Iunoes* wrath and hard assay,
   Of her faire twins she there deliuered,
   Which afterwards did rule the night and day;
   Thenceforth it firmely was established,
And for *Apolloes* honor highly herried.

14

They to him hearken, as beseemeth meete,
   And passe on forward: so their way does ly,
   That one of those same Islands, which doe fleet
   In the wide sea, they needes must passen by,
   Which seemd so sweet and pleasant to the eye,
   That it would tempt a man to touchen there:
   Vpon the banck they sitting did espy
   A daintie damzell, dressing of her heare,
By whom a litle skippet floting did appeare.

15

She them espying, loud to them can call,
   Bidding them nigher draw vnto the shore;
   For she had cause to busie them withall;
   And therewith loudly laught: But nathemore
   Would they once turne, but kept on as afore:
   Which when she saw, she left her lockes vndight,
   And running to her boat withouten ore
   From the departing land it launched light,
And after them did driue with all her power and might.

283

16

Whom ouertaking, she in merry sort
　Them gan to bord, and purpose diuersly,
　Now faining dalliance and wanton sport,
　Now throwing forth lewd words immodestly;
　Till that the Palmer gan full bitterly
　Her to rebuke, for being loose and light:
　Which not abiding, but more scornefully
　Scoffing at him, that did her iustly wite,
She turnd her bote about, and from them rowed quite.

17

That was the wanton *Phædria*, which late
　Did ferry him ouer the *Idle lake*:
　Whom nought regarding, they kept on their gate,
　And all her vaine allurements did forsake,
　When them the wary Boateman thus bespake;
　Here now behoueth vs well to auyse,
　And of our safetie good heede to take;
　For here before a perlous passage lyes,
Where many Mermayds haunt, making false melodies.

18

But by the way, there is a great Quicksand,
　And a whirlepoole of hidden ieopardy,
　Therefore, Sir Palmer, keepe an euen hand;
　For twixt them both the narrow way doth ly.
　Scarse had he said, when hard at hand they spy
　That quicksand nigh with water couered;
　But by the checked waue they did descry
　It plaine, and by the sea discoloured:
It called was the quicksand of *Vnthriftyhed*.

19

They passing by, a goodly Ship did see,
　Laden from far with precious merchandize,
　And brauely furnished, as ship might bee,
　Which through great disauenture, or mesprize,
　Her selfe had runne into that hazardize;
　Whose mariners and merchants with much toyle,
　Labour'd in vaine, to haue recur'd their prize,
　And the rich wares to saue from pitteous spoyle,
But neither toyle nor trauell might her backe recoyle.

20

On th'other side they see that perilous Poole,
　That called was the *Whirlepoole of decay*,
　In which full many had with haplesse doole
　Beene suncke, of whom no memorie did stay:
　Whose circled waters rapt with whirling sway,
　Like to a restlesse wheele, still running round,
　Did couet, as they passed by that way,
　To draw their boate within the vtmost bound
Of his wide *Labyrinth*, and then to haue them dround.

21

But th'heedfull Boateman strongly forth did stretch
　His brawnie armes, and all his body straine,
　That th'vtmost sandy breach they shortly fetch,
　Whiles the dred daunger does behind remaine.
　Suddeine they see from midst of all the Maine,
　The surging waters like a mountaine rise,
　And the great sea puft vp with proud disdaine,
　To swell aboue the measure of his guise,
As threatning to deuoure all, that his powre despise.

Stanza 16

1　**sort**: manner.
2　**bord**: accost; also the nautical sense, 'come alongside to attack'; also 'jest'.　**purpose diuersly**: talk of various matters; engage in small talk.
8　**wite**: blame.
9　**rowed**: not to be taken literally, as Collier (1862) warns. Perhaps the Palmer has defeated her power. Perhaps a witty metaphor; cf. 37.2.

Stanza 17

3　**gate**: way, journey.
6　**auyse**: take thought; cf. 69.6.

Stanzas 18–29

As the previous lines announce, the 'perlous passage' lies 'here before' the calm bay of the mermaids (30). These inserted stanzas describe four dangers which clarify and extend the significance of the earlier ones. S.'s disciple, Ralph Aylett, seems to have grasped the connection: 'Besides the Rocks, that threat this Boat to rive; / Are many Gulphes and Whirl-pooles of decay / Which wait th'Affections and the Senses five / By force and sweet Allurements to assay' (*Divine and Moral Speculations* [1654], *Spenser Allusions* 170).

Stanza 18

3　**euen**: straight, direct; referring to the path, or a mean between extremes.
7　**checked**: restrained by the sand and therefore 'checkered'.
9　**Vnthriftyhed**: thriftlessness, extravagance; cf. the 'thriftlesse wast' (9.3) which brings ships to ruin upon the '*Rocke of* vile *Reproch*' (8.1). Cf. 'unthrift': dissolute conduct (*OED* 2).

Stanza 19

4　**disauenture**: mishap.　**mesprize**: mistake; from 'misprize', to commit an offence; but also from 'mis-prize', to fail to value, here referring to the middle way.
5　**hazardize**: hazardous situation.
7　**prize**: used of a stranded vessel whose cargo may be claimed as booty.
9　**backe recoyle**: draw back.

Stanza 20

3　**doole**: grief, suffering, guile, fraud.
5　**circled**: circling.　**sway**: motion in a circle.

Stanza 21

1　**heedfull**] earnest *1590*. The change agrees with his own advice: 'of our safetie good heede to take' (17.7).
3　**sandy breach**: where the waves break upon the sand; presumably the extreme edge of the quicksand, the channel between it and the whirlpool.　**fetch**: reach, in the nautical sense.
8　**guise**: custom, usual manner.

22

The waues come rolling, and the billowes rore
  Outragiously, as they enraged were,
  Or wrathfull *Neptune* did them driue before
  His whirling charet, for exceeding feare:
  For not one puffe of wind there did appeare,
  That all the three thereat woxe much afrayd,
  Vnweeting, what such horrour straunge did reare.
  Eftsoones they saw an hideous hoast arrayd,
Of huge Sea monsters, such as liuing sence dismayd.

23

Most vgly shapes, and horrible aspects,
  Such as Dame Nature selfe mote feare to see,
  Or shame, that euer should so fowle defects
  From her most cunning hand escaped bee;
  All dreadfull pourtraicts of deformitee:
  Spring-headed *Hydraes*, and sea-shouldring Whales,
  Great whirlpooles, which all fishes make to flee,
  Bright Scolopendraes, arm'd with siluer scales,
Mighty *Monoceroses*, with immeasured tayles.

24

The dreadfull Fish, that hath deseru'd the name
  Of Death, and like him lookes in dreadfull hew,
  The griesly Wasserman, that makes his game
  The flying ships with swiftnesse to pursew,
  The horrible Sea-satyre, that doth shew
  His fearefull face in time of greatest storme,
  Huge *Ziffius*, whom Mariners eschew
  No lesse, then rockes, (as trauellers informe,)
And greedy *Rosmarines* with visages deforme.

25

All these, and thousand thousands many more,
  And more deformed Monsters thousand fold,
  With dreadfull noise, and hollow rombling rore,
  Came rushing in the fomy waues enrold,
  Which seem'd to fly for feare, them to behold:
  Ne wonder, if these did the knight appall;
  For all that here on earth we dreadfull hold,
  Be but as bugs to fearen babes withall,
Compared to the creatures in the seas entrall.

26

Feare nought, (then said the Palmer well auiz'd;)
  For these same Monsters are not these in deed,
  But are into these fearefull shapes disguiz'd
  By that same wicked witch, to worke vs dreed,
  And draw from on this iourney to proceede.
  Tho lifting vp his vertuous staffe on hye,
  He smote the sea, which calmed was with speed,
  And all that dreadfull Armie fast gan flye
Into great *Tethys* bosome, where they hidden lye.

Stanza 22

1–4   **billowes rore . . . feare**: i.e. the waves roared in great fear as though Neptune drove them before his chariot.
2   **Outragiously**: intemperately; from the obsolete sense of 'outrage', violence that goes beyond all bounds; cf. 39.2.
6   **all the three**: 'the knight' at 25.6.
7   **horreur**: the roughness or ruffling of the water and its effect upon the beholders. **reare**: bring about.

Stanza 23

4   The **cunning hand** belongs rather to the compilers of animal lore, such as Pliny, *Historia Naturalis*, Conrad Gesner, *Historia Animalium*, and Olaus Wormius, *History of the Northern Nations*. On these sources, see Robin (1932) 119f.
6   **Spring-headed Hydraes**: spouting whales, as Lemmi conjectures (*Var*. ii 359), adapted from the 'many heads out budding euer new' (I vii 17.4) of the Lernean hydra slain by Hercules. See VI xii 32. **sea-shouldring Whales**: i.e. lifting the sea before them; identified with the Leviathan by the Geneva gloss to Job 40.20.
7   **whirlpooles**: the spouting whale.
8   **Scolopendraes**: apparently S.'s own fabulous sea-fish and not the bait-vomiting annelid worm that fascinated the natural historians.
9   **Monoceroses**] *Monoceros 1590, 1596*: a one-horned fish, such as the narwhal. Jortin (1734) suggested **Monoceroses** which editors since Child have generally adopted. But S.'s form is already in the plural. Upton (1758) observed the witty point: 'The verse is **immeasured**', i.e. immeasurable.

Stanza 24

These fish are drawn chiefly from the depths of Gesner.
Death: the walrus or morse, from *mors* (Lat. death).
Wasserman: *homo marinus*, a merman. **Sea-satyre**: Pan or *satyrus marinus*, a sea-monster partly in the form of a satyr.
Ziffius: the Xiphias or sword-fish, a kind of whale.
Rosmarines: the sea-horse; **greedy** because it climbs on rocks to feed on grass, or on dew (Lat. *ros*).

Stanza 25

7–9   S. goes beyond the common notion that the sea contains every kind of creature found on land or in the air, as in Du Bartas, *Divine Weekes* I v: 'In the Waters one may see all Creatures, / And all that in this All is to be found; / As if the World within the Deeps were drown'd'. Cf. R. Lynche, *Fountaine of Ancient Fiction* (1599): 'There are many most ouglie monsters and strange-formed creatures in the sea (thought indeed to bee much more then on the land)'; cited Crampton (1974) 138.
8   **bugs**: bugbears.

Stanza 26

1   **well auiz'd**: very wary; also keen-sighted.
3   **disguiz'd**: transformed.
6–7   Suggests Moses dividing the Red Sea: 'Lift thou up thy rod, and stretch out thine hand upon the Sea and devide it' (Exod. 14.16), and Christ calming the sea: 'He arose, and rebuked the windes and the sea: and so there was a great calme' (Matt. 8.26). **vertuous**: possessing magical powers; cf. 40.3.
9   **Tethys**: 'the wyfe of Neptune, called goddesse of the sea' (Cooper, 1565).

27

Quit from that daunger, forth their course they kept,
  And as they went, they heard a ruefull cry
Of one, that wayld and pittifully wept,
  That through the sea the resounding plaints did fly:
  At last they in an Island did espy
A seemely Maiden, sitting by the shore,
  That with great sorrow and sad agony,
  Seemed some great misfortune to deplore,
And lowd to them for succour called euermore.

28

Which *Guyon* hearing, streight his Palmer bad,
  To stere the boate towards that dolefull Mayd,
That he might know, and ease her sorrow sad:
  Who him auizing better, to him sayd;
  Faire Sir, be not displeasd, if disobayd:
For ill it were to hearken to her cry;
  For she is inly nothing ill apayd,
  But onely womanish fine forgery,
Your stubborne hart t'affect with fraile infirmity.

29

To which when she your courage hath inclind
  Through foolish pitty, then her guilefull bayt
She will embosome deeper in your mind,
  And for your ruine at the last awayt.
  The knight was ruled, and the Boateman strayt
Held on his course with stayed stedfastnesse,
  Ne euer shruncke, ne euer sought to bayt
  His tyred armes for toylesome wearinesse,
But with his oares did sweepe the watry wildernesse.

30

And now they nigh approched to the sted,
  Where as those Mermayds dwelt: it was a still
And calmy bay, on th'one side sheltered
  With the brode shadow of an hoarie hill,
  On th'other side an high rocke toured still,
That twixt them both a pleasant port they made,
  And did like an halfe Theatre fulfill:
  There those fiue sisters had continuall trade,
And vsd to bath themselues in that deceiptfull shade.

31

They were faire Ladies, till they fondly striu'd
  With th'*Heliconian* maides for maistery;
Of whom they ouer-comen, were depriu'd
  Of their proud beautie, and th'one moyity
  Transform'd to fish, for their bold surquedry,
But th'vpper halfe their hew retained still,
  And their sweet skill in wonted melody;
  Which euer after they abusd to ill,
T'allure weake trauellers, whom gotten they did kill.

32

So now to *Guyon*, as he passed by,
  Their pleasaunt tunes they sweetly thus applide;
O thou faire sonne of gentle Faery,
  That art in mighty armes most magnifide
  Aboue all knights, that euer battell tride,
O turne thy rudder hither-ward a while:
  Here may thy storme-bet vessell safely ride;
  This is the Port of rest from troublous toyle,
The worlds sweet In, from paine and wearisome turmoyle.

Stanza 27
Guyon must relive his first error when the tale of the weeping
Maid so aroused his pity that he almost struck the Red Cross
Knight. Now he is warned against 'foolish pitty' (29.2).
4   The added syllable in **the** gives added stress on
resounding.
6   **seemely**: fair, pleasing to see; but with a play on
'seeming'.

Stanza 28
4   **him auizing better**: taking better thought himself; or
better counselling Guyon.
7   **ill apayd**: distressed.
8   **fine forgery**: cunning deception.

Stanza 29
1   **courage**: heart, mind.
3   **embosome**: infix; perhaps suggested by 26.9.
6   **stayed**: staid, constant.
7   **bayt**: rest.

Stanza 30
1–2   Referring back to 17.8–9.   **sted**: place.   **those
Mermayds**: the Sirens (from Homer, *Ody*. xii 39–54,
165–200) 'whom poets feigned to be mermaydens' (Cooper,
1565). They are **fiue** (8) in number, instead of the usual three,
because they tempt the five senses. Comes (1616) VII xiii p. 398
interprets the sirens as all voluptuous desire. In Dante, *Purg*.
xix, the siren displays the sins of the flesh. Robertson (1962)
142–4 supplies the background.
2–9   S. imitates details from the bay of nymphs which Aeneas
and his followers reach after their voyage, and which leads them
to the lustful Dido; see *Aen*. i 157–68.
3   **bay**: suggesting a retreat from the active life and also a
place of last extremity.
7   **like an halfe Theatre**: i.e. the hill and rock occupied, or
formed, what seemed like a half-theatre, a semicircle rather
than an amphitheatre.   **fulfill**: fill full, in the etymological
sense.
8   **trade**: referring to their manner of life or resort; hence,
where they always lived.
9   **deceiptfull**: because here they practise their deceit.

Stanza 31
1–5   **th'Heliconian maides**: the Muses on Mount Helicon.
Comes (1616) VII xiii p. 395 records a contest in which the three
sirens who dared to challenge the Muses in song were defeated
and punished by having their wings plucked; noted Cutts
(1968).   **fondly**: foolishly.   **moyity**: half.   **surquedry**:
presumption. Cf. 'Might wanting measure moueth surquedry'
(III x 2.5). Boccaccio, *Gen. Deor*. VII xx, interprets the fishlike
nature of mermaids as the libidinousness and concupiscence of
women; cited Lotspeich (1932) 81. Starnes and Talbert (1955)
109–10 note the same reading in Renaissance dictionaries.
6   **hew**: shape.

Stanza 32
2   **applide**: addressed.
4   **magnifide**: extolled.

33

With that the rolling sea resounding soft,
    In his big base them fitly answered,
    And on the rocke the waues breaking aloft,
    A solemne Meane vnto them measured,
    The whiles sweet *Zephirus* lowd whisteled
    His treble, a straunge kinde of harmony;
    Which *Guyons* senses softly tickeled,
That he the boateman bad row easily,
And let him heare some part of their rare melody.

34

But him the Palmer from that vanity,
    With temperate aduice discounselled,
    That they it past, and shortly gan descry
    The land, to which their course they leueled;
    When suddeinly a grosse fog ouer spred
    With his dull vapour all that desert has,
    And heauens chearefull face enueloped,
    That all things one, and one as nothing was,
And this great Vniuerse seemd one confused mas.

35

Thereat they greatly were dismayd, ne wist
    How to direct their way in darkenesse wide,
    But feard to wander in that wastfull mist,
    For tombling into mischiefe vnespide.
    Worse is the daunger hidden, then descride.
    Suddeinly an innumerable flight
    Of harmefull fowles about them fluttering, cride,
    And with their wicked wings them oft did smight,
And sore annoyed, groping in that griesly night.

36

Euen all the nation of vnfortunate
    And fatall birds about them flocked were,
    Such as by nature men abhorre and hate,
    The ill-faste Owle, deaths dreadfull messengere,
    The hoars Night-rauen, trump of dolefull drere,
    The lether-winged Bat, dayes enimy,
    The ruefull Strich, still waiting on the bere,
    The Whistler shrill, that who so heares, doth dy,
The hellish Harpies, prophets of sad destiny.

37

All those, and all that else does horrour breed,
    About them flew, and fild their sayles with feare:
    Yet stayd they not, but forward did proceed,
    Whiles th'one did row, and th'other stifly steare;
    Till that at last the weather gan to cleare,
    And the faire land it selfe did plainly show.
    Said then the Palmer, Lo where does appeare
    The sacred soile, where all our perils grow;
Therefore, Sir knight, your ready armes about you throw.

Stanza 33
2   **big**: loud.
4   **solemne Meane**: middle part or tenor of the waves which is proportioned between the bass (the sea) and the alto (the Sirens). Four-part harmony is gained by the treble of the West Wind.   **measured**: proportioned.
5   **Zephirus**: associated with sexual desire by Comes (1616) IV xiii; hence it blows through the Bower of Bliss, v 29.8–9.

Stanza 34
1–3   In contrast to Ulysses who needed to be bound hand and foot and then bound more (*Ody.* xii 178–96).
temperate aduice: advice counselling temperance.
5   **fog**: cf. the 'foggy mist' that covers all the land before the procession of the deadly sins (I iv 36.7). S.'s source is the smoke which Ulysses encounters after passing the Sirens (*Ody.* xii 202).
6   **has**: i.e. has overspread.
8–9   As the repetition of **one** suggests, these lines play upon the etymological sense of **Vniuerse**, 'one-turning', 'turning into one', to indicate the return of creation to chaos.

Stanza 35
3   **wastfull**: desolate; causing desolation. Limitless expanse suggests the lack of bounds in intemperance; cf. vii 2.8.
4   **For**: for fear of.

Stanza 36
1–2   **nation**: class, kind.   **vnfortunate**: ill-omened, inauspicious.   **fatall**: ominous.
4–5   The **Owle** and the **Night-rauen** guard the entrance to Mammon's house, vii 23.3–5. They occur together in *S.C.* June 23–4, to which E.K. adds the gloss: 'By such hatefull byrdes, hee meaneth all misfortunes (Whereof they be tokens) flying euery where.'   **ill-faste**: evil-faced; cf. xi 8.3. On the Owle, see I v 30.6–7n; on the **Night-rauen**, cf. *Epith.* 346: 'the night Rauen that still deadly yels.'   **trump**: trumpet. **drere**: sadness.
7   **Strich**: the lich-owl, so called because its cry portends death ('lich': corpse). The name suggests its screech.
waiting on: lingering near, in expectation of imminent death. See Harrison (1956) 64–5.
8   **Whistler**: known only by this description. The name was applied to a curlew; see Harrison 65. The Seven Whistlers are well known in folklore as birds of death.
9   **Harpies**: see vii 23.6–9n. Virgil calls them *obscenae volucres* (*Aen.* iii 262) and places them in hell (vi 289).

Stanza 37
4   **stifly**: resolutely, steadily.
8   **sacred**: accursed (*OED* 6); cf. 'cursed land' (i 51.8). Also the more usual sense, 'consecrated to a deity', here the goddess Pleasure; perhaps even 'holy' as the Bower is a perverted Eden. Cf. Una's statement to the Red Cross Knight, I xi 2.1–2, with the distinction between 'where all our perils dwell' and **where all our perils grow**. In *View* 92, S. refers to the ancient name of Ireland as '*Banno* or *Sacra Insula*, taking *sacra* for *accursed*'.   **soile** suggests a pun on 'defiling'.

287

38

He hearkned, and his armes about him tooke,
  The whiles the nimble boate so well her sped,
  That with her crooked keele the land she strooke,
  Then forth the noble *Guyon* sallied,
  And his sage Palmer, that him gouerned;
  But th'other by his boate behind did stay.
  They marched fairly forth, of nought ydred,
  Both firmely armd for euery hard assay,
With constancy and care, gainst daunger and dismay.

39

Ere long they heard an hideous bellowing
  Of many beasts, that roard outrageously,
  As if that hungers point, or *Venus* sting
  Had them enraged with fell surquedry;
  Yet nought they feard, but past on hardily,
  Vntill they came in vew of those wild beasts:
  Who all attonce, gaping full greedily,
  And rearing fiercely their vpstarting crests,
Ran towards, to deuoure those vnexpected guests.

40

But soone as they approcht with deadly threat,
  The Palmer ouer them his staffe vpheld,
  His mighty staffe, that could all charmes defeat:
  Eftsoones their stubborne courages were queld,
  And high aduaunced crests downe meekely feld,
  In stead of fraying, they them selues did feare,
  And trembled, as them passing they beheld:
  Such wondrous powre did in that staffe appeare,
All monsters to subdew to him, that did it beare.

41

Of that same wood it fram'd was cunningly,
  Of which *Caduceus* whilome was made,
  Caduceus the rod of *Mercury*,
  With which he wonts the *Stygian* realmes inuade,
  Through ghastly horrour, and eternall shade;
  Th' infernall feends with it he can asswage,
  And *Orcus* tame, whom nothing can perswade,
  And rule the *Furyes*, when they most do rage:
Such vertue in his staffe had eke this Palmer sage.

42

Thence passing forth, they shortly do arriue,
  Whereas the Bowre of *Blisse* was situate;
  A place pickt out by choice of best aliue,
  That natures worke by art can imitate:
  In which what euer in this worldly state
  Is sweet, and pleasing vnto liuing sense,
  Or that may dayntiest fantasie aggrate,
  Was poured forth with plentifull dispence,
And made there to abound with lauish affluence.

Stanza 38
3   **crooked**: curved at the prow.
4   **sallied**: leaped (sally, *OED* v.¹); or issued forth (*OED*
v.²1: 'of a warlike force, to issue suddenly to make an attack').
Cf. vi 38.5, and see i 29.6*n*.
5   **gouerned**: guided.
8   **firmely armd**: armed with inward firmness, as the next
line indicates.   **assay**: attack, trial.

Stanza 39
1–5   The assault on Guyon's hearing by the beasts of the sea,
birds of the air, and now the beasts on the land prepares for
the assault upon his sight in the Bower. In Homer, *Ody*. x 210–
9, Circe's beasts fawn upon the visitors; in Virgil, *Aen*. vii
15–20, they are heard to rage in the distance; and in Ovid, *Met*.
xiv 254–9, their rage suddenly collapses into fawning. S. differs
in order to show the power of the Palmer's staff.
2   **outrageously**: cf. 22.2.
3   **Venus sting**: *Veneris stimuli* or sexual desire; cf. III
viii 25.2, IV ii 5.5.
4   **fell surquedry**: fierce arrogance; suggesting sexual
indulgence, as III x 2.5.
9   **towards**: in their direction.

Stanza 40
6   **fraying**: frightening (others).
8–9   Comes (1616) VI vi p. 309 interprets Circe's wild beasts
as the depraved appetites which may be controlled only by
reason. Cf. the function of Cambina's 'rod of peace' (IV iii 42).

Stanza 41
1   **cunningly**: skilfully.
2–8   Cf. Virgil's account of the power of the **Caduceus**,
Aen. iv 242–4. He gives the rod power over the living and the
dead; S. uses only his claim that it calls the pale spirits up from
Orcus.
3   **Mercury**: the god of wisdom and reason; on his role as
the *psychopompos* or guide of souls, see Wind (1967) 121f.
7   **Orcus**: Pluto, god of hell.

Stanza 42
1–4   **of best aliue**: i.e. the best artisans alive picked out
the place; in contrast to Phædria's island 'by Natures cunning
hand . . . picked out from all the rest' (vi 12.3–4). Or 'from the
best of any that exists', which still points to art, rather than
nature, as the agent that chooses. For the poet, **art** is the
literary tradition of the *locus amoenus* which he picks out by
choice of best aliue, chiefly Alcina's isle (Ariosto, *Orl. Fur*.
vi 19–25) and Armida's isle (Tasso, *Ger. Lib*., xv 53f) with its
enclosed garden (xvi 1–26). The classical antecedents are traced
by Curtius (1953) 195–200; for the antecedents in Italian
romance, see Giamatti (1966).
7   **aggrate**: please; cf. v 33.2.
8   **dispence**: liberality. This praise of nature's abundance
reminds us that nature herself is good, though abused by art:
'For the earth is the Lords, and all that therein is' (1 Cor.
10.26).

43

Goodly it was enclosed round about,
   Aswell their entred guestes to keepe within,
   As those vnruly beasts to hold without;
   Yet was the fence thereof but weake and thin;
   Nought feard their force, that fortilage to win,
   But wisedomes powre, and temperaunces might,
   By which the mightiest things efforced bin:
   And eke the gate was wrought of substaunce light,
Rather for pleasure, then for battery or fight.

44

Yt framed was of precious yuory,
   That seemd a worke of admirable wit;
   And therein all the famous history
   Of *Iason* and *Medæa* was ywrit;
   Her mighty charmes, her furious louing fit,
   His goodly conquest of the golden fleece,
   His falsed faith, and loue too lightly flit,
   The wondred *Argo*, which in venturous peece
First through the *Euxine* seas bore all the flowr of *Greece*.

45

Ye might haue seene the frothy billowes fry
   Vnder the ship, as thorough them she went,
   That seemd the waues were into yuory,
   Or yuory into the waues were sent;
   And other where the snowy substaunce sprent
   With vermell, like the boyes bloud therein shed,
   A piteous spectacle did represent,
   And otherwhiles with gold besprinkeled;
Yt seemd th'enchaunted flame, which did *Creüsa* wed.

46

All this, and more might in that goodly gate
   Be red; that euer open stood to all,
   Which thither came: but in the Porch there sate
   A comely personage of stature tall,
   And semblaunce pleasing, more then naturall,
   That trauellers to him seemd to entize;
   His looser garment to the ground did fall,
   And flew about his heeles in wanton wize,
Not fit for speedy pace, or manly exercize.

Stanza 43

1   **enclosed**: introduces the theme of the *hortus conclusus*, the 'garden inclosed' of the Song of Solomon 4.12. On the medieval treatment, see Robertson (1962) 386–8. See also Stewart (1966).

5–6   **Nought feard**: it was not at all feared that the physical force of the beasts without could win that fortress; what was feared was wisdom's power, etc.   **their**: 'they', sugg. Church (1758), clarifies this reading. On the distinction between **force** and **wisedom**, see I vii 42.7–8; force plays the role in Book I that wisdom does in Book II.   **fortilage**: fortress.

Stanza 44

Cf. the gate of ivory through which Archimago's spright brings the false lustful dream to delude the Red Cross Knight; see I i 40.1–3n. Tuve (1970) 107–11 suggests that S. may have seen the story of Jason and Medea carved in ivory.

2   **admirable wit**: marvellous skill.

3 to 45.9   **the famous history / Of Iason and Medæa**: together with the choice Grecian warriors, Jason sailed in the Argo to Colchis to obtain the Golden Fleece belonging to King Aeetes. He was aided by the magical powers of Medea, the King's daughter, who passionately loved him. After he obtained the fleece and fled with her, they escaped capture when she threw pieces of her brother's body into the sea for her father to retrieve. When she was abandoned by Jason, she sent his new bride, Creüsa, an enchanted garment which burned her to death. In this sense Creüsa **wed** the flame. Cf. V viii 47.3–4. Comes (1616) VI vii p. 314 notes that Jason gave himself up to voluptuous desire. Medea inherits her magic and sensuality from her aunt Circe with whom Acrasia is associated; see 85.5n. Hieatt (1973) 48 argues that the verbal links between this **piteous spectacle** (45.7) and the 'Pittifull spectacle' (i 40.1) of Amavia reveal the similarity between Medea and Acrasia, two enchantresses who use their magic arts to destroy their rivals.

7   **falsed**: violated.   **flit**: altering.

8   **venturous peece**: adventurous ship.

9   **First**: the **Argo** was the first ocean-going ship. This initial conquest of the perils of the sea failed when Jason yielded to a sorceress's love. It contrasts with the present voyage in which Guyon triumphs over concupiscence.

Stanza 45

Bender (1972) 179–80 notes that this stanza 'represents the sensuous impression of an illusion, and through its diction reminds us that the illusion is a product of craft'.

1   **fry**: foam.

5   **other where**: elsewhere.   **sprent**: sprinkled.

Stanza 46

7–9   His dress identifies him with Idleness, the porter of the garden in the *Romance of the Rose* 582; cf. Chaucer, *Second Nun's Tale* Prol. 1–3: 'The ministre and the norice unto vices, / Which that men clepe in Englissh ydelnesse, / That porter of the gate is of delices.'   **looser**: too loose.

47

They in that place him *Genius* did call:
  Not that celestiall powre, to whom the care
  Of life, and generation of all
  That liues, pertaines in charge particulare,
  Who wondrous things concerning our welfare,
  And straunge phantomes doth let vs oft forsee,
  And oft of secret ill bids vs beware:
  That is our Selfe, whom though we do not see,
Yet each doth in him selfe it well perceiue to bee.

48

Therefore a God him sage Antiquity
  Did wisely make, and good *Agdistes* call:
  But this same was to that quite contrary,
  The foe of life, that good enuyes to all,
  That secretly doth vs procure to fall,
  Through guilefull semblaunts, which he makes vs see.
  He of this Gardin had the gouernall,
  And Pleasures porter was deuizd to bee,
Holding a staffe in hand for more formalitee.

49

With diuerse flowres he daintily was deckt,
  And strowed round about, and by his side
  A mighty Mazer bowle of wine was set,
  As if it had to him bene sacrifide;
  Wherewith all new-come guests he gratifide:
  So did he eke Sir *Guyon* passing by:
  But he his idle curtesie defide,
  And ouerthrew his bowle disdainfully;
And broke his staffe, with which he charmed semblants sly.

50

Thus being entred, they behold around
  A large and spacious plaine, on euery side
  Strowed with pleasauns, whose faire grassy ground
  Mantled with greene, and goodly beautifide
  With all the ornaments of *Floraes* pride,
  Wherewith her mother Art, as halfe in scorne
  Of niggard Nature, like a pompous bride
  Did decke her, and too lauishly adorne,
When forth from virgin bowre she comes in th'early morne.

Stanzas 47–48
S. follows Comes (1616) IV iii closely, as Lotspeich (1932) 62 notes. Any distinction between **Genius** and the **good Agdistes** involves awkward syntax, however the text is read. Warton (1762) i 81–3 treats 47.2 to 48.2 as a parenthetical account of the good genius, our second self, whom the ancients named Agdistes. Lewis (1966) 169–74 argues that this parenthesis is too extended and also fails to distinguish between the god of generation (47.2–4) and the good genius in each man (47.5 to 48.2). He proposes that 47.2–4 be read as a parenthetical account of the god of generation. Yet his distinction is more confusing than the extended parenthesis required by Warton's reading. In Lewis (1936) 361–3, he notes the different meanings of 'Genius' in earlier literature.

Stanza 47
1–4   This role of the good **Genius** – or the god of generation, if Lewis's distinction is allowed – is taken by the porter of the 'corresponding' garden, the Garden of Adonis, III vi 31–33. Comes (1616) IV iii p. 154 notes that genius is so called either because it is born with us or because it is believed to be entrusted with the care of generation. He describes the power of this genius to show us *spectra et imagines*.

Stanza 48
2   **Agdistes**: Genius is so named by Comes.
3–6   The distinction between the good and evil genius given by Comes IV iii p. 153 is still made: we speak of our good and bad angel, or our better self, the guardian spirit which preserves us, and our worser self which leads us astray.   **enuyes**: begrudges.   **procure**: cause.   **which he makes vs see**: the key phrase. The Bower forces man to see and be over-whelmed by its sight. Cf. the power of Archimago in Book I.
7–8   **gouernall**: management. As each place has its genius, he is the tutelary or guardian spirit of the Bower.   **Pleasures porter**: because the evil Genius leads man into lust, according to Comes; or because the *Geruli* (porters) were associated with Genii and genial gods in Renaissance dictionaries: see Starnes (1964).   **deuizd**: appointed; contrived, referring to his artful appearance.
9   **for more formalitee**: in contrast to the Palmer's staff whose power to subdue the passions is exercised over the beasts, 40.1–7.

Stanza 49
1–4   S. follows Comes, who follows Horace, in associating the worship of Agdistes with flowers and the offering of wine in bowls.   **Mazer bowle**: a drinking-cup made of maple; in *S.C.* Aug. 26–30 its trail of 'wanton Yuie' associates it with intemperance.   **Mazer**: associated with 'maze', bewilder, and with 'mazer', to knock on the head, referring to the wine's potency. At i 55, Mortdant dies after drinking from such a cup. Cf. Duessa's cup at I viii 14.1–5. The **bowle** (8) and **staffe** (9) or wand are Circe's attributes and carry the same sexual significance.   **sacrifide**: offered as a sacrifice, consecrated.
5   **gratifide**: welcomed; also gave pleasure to.
9   **charmed semblants sly**: i.e. conjured up the 'guilefull semblaunts, which he makes vs see' (48.6).   **sly**: as an adv., in a cunning manner; as an adj., cleverly or finely made. Hieatt (1969) 316 notes the implied contrast with the Palmer's staff, 40.3.

Stanza 50
3   **pleasauns**: pleasure-grounds or small parks.
5   **Floraes pride**: the goddess of flowers at her most flourishing; see I i 48.9*n*.
6–8   Art's scorn of Nature is one aspect of the Fall according to Guyon: the golden age was lost when man 'gan exceed / The measure of her [Nature's] meane, and naturall first need' (vii 16.8–9).

51

Thereto the Heauens alwayes Iouiall,
　Lookt on them louely, still in stedfast state,
　Ne suffred storme nor frost on them to fall,
　Their tender buds or leaues to violate,
　Nor scorching heat, nor cold intemperate
　T'afflict the creatures, which therein did dwell,
　But the milde aire with season moderate
Gently attempred, and disposd so well,
That still it breathed forth sweet spirit and holesome smell.

52

More sweet and holesome, then the pleasant hill
　Of *Rhodope*, on which the Nimphe, that bore
　A gyaunt babe, her selfe for griefe did kill;
　Or the Thessalian *Tempe*, where of yore
　Faire *Daphne Phœbus* hart with loue did gore;
　Or *Ida*, where the Gods lou'd to repaire,
　When euer they their heauenly bowres forlore;
Or sweet *Parnasse*, the haunt of Muses faire;
Or *Eden* selfe, if ought with *Eden* mote compaire.

53

Much wondred *Guyon* at the faire aspect
　Of that sweet place, yet suffred no delight
　To sincke into his sence, nor mind affect,
　But passed forth, and lookt still forward right,
　Bridling his will, and maistering his might:
　Till that he came vnto another gate;
　No gate, but like one, being goodly dight
With boughes and braunches, which did broad dilate
Their clasping armes, in wanton wreathings intricate.

54

So fashioned a Porch with rare deuice,
　Archt ouer head with an embracing vine,
　Whose bounches hanging downe, seemed to entice
　All passers by, to tast their lushious wine,
　And did themselues into their hands incline,
　As freely offering to be gathered:
　Some deepe empurpled as the *Hyacint*,
　Some as the Rubine, laughing sweetly red,
Some like faire *Emeraudes*, not yet well ripened.

the same in both versions).　**Iouiall**: joyous, serene, being
under the influence of Jove. Since the rule of Jove brought
seasonal change (Ovid, *Met.* i 113–8), **always** notes that
the Bower enjoys eternal summer without the renewal of
spring or fruition of autumn. Hence **still**: always; implying a
static, sterile state.　**louely**: lovingly.
4　violate: damage by violence.
5–9　Imitating Chaucer, *Parl. Fowls* 204–6, 210: 'Th'air of
that place so attempre was / That nevere was ther grevaunce
of hot ne cold; / There wex ek every holsom spice and géas;
. . . But ay cler day.'
8　attempred: modified its temperature. Climate is
temperate in the Bower but leads man into intemperance. Cf.
the birds' song, 71.2.　**disposd**: regulated.
9　spirit: breath. Nevo (1962) 21 notes that the terms are
startlingly attuned to the kind of values or sensibility associated
with Temperance itself.

Stanza 52
The five comparisons evoke varying scenes of natural beauty
which, except for **Parnasse**, are marred by sin and death. Two
legends of **Rhodope** become one: that she was transformed
into the mountain because she and her brother dared to assume
the names of the gods (Ovid, *Met.* vi 87–9) and that, after she
gave birth to a **gyaunt babe** by Neptune, she presumptuously
assumed the name of Juno (Regius's note; cited Lotspeich,
1932, 105). Rhodope is the **pleasaunt hill** where Orpheus
sang (*Met.* x 86f) and where he was torn to pieces (*Met.*
xi 39f). Phœbus's love for **Daphne** (*Met.* i 452f), his first
love, led to her metamorphosis, a type of all that follow in
Ovid. **Ida** is the mountain where the three goddesses appeared
before Paris in a judgment that led to the war of Troy and
where the gods assembled to watch that war. **Eden** signifies
'pleasure', the *paradisum voluptatis* of Gen. 2.8 (Vulgate) and
place of the Fall. Henry Reynolds, *Mythomystes* (1632) etymologizes Eden from the Greek ἡδονή, and Lat. *voluptas*,
the garden of delight (Spingarn, 1908, i 176).
7　forlore: left.
9　compaire: be compared.

Stanza 53
4　forward right: straight ahead; cf. Prov. 4.25: 'Let thine
eyes beholde the right, and let thine eyeliddes direct thy way
before thee.'　**forward** is a key word in this canto: cf. 5.1,
14.2, 37.3, 57.9, 69.3; its climax comes in the phrase: 'kept
their forward way' (76.5).
5　Bridling: see iv 34.2n.　**maistering his might**:
paradoxically, Guyon exercises his might by restraining its use
(cf. v 13.3) until the moment when he destroys the Bower.
8　dilate: extend.
**9　The line conveys the twisting it describes.

Stanza 54
1　deuice: design.
7　Hyacint: hyacinth or jacinth, a sapphire-coloured stone.
Hyacine (1611) provides the rhyme. Either S. did not want an
internal echo with **Rubine** or he holds up the rhyme to
surprise us with that word.
8　Rubine: ruby.
9　Emeraudes: emeralds. Perhaps climactic; cf. Drayton:
'The Emerauld then, most deepely greene, / For beauty most
excelling' (*Muses Elizium*, Ninth Nimphall 107–8).

Stanza 51
1–2　Thereto] Therewith *1590*: added to that (the sense is

55

And them amongst, some were of burnisht gold,
  So made by art, to beautifie the rest,
  Which did themselues amongst the leaues enfold,
  As lurking from the vew of couetous guest,
  That the weake bowes, with so rich load opprest,
  Did bow adowne, as ouer-burdened.'
  Vnder that Porch a comely dame did rest,
  Clad in faire weedes, but fowle disordered,
And garments loose, that seemd vnmeet for womanhed.

56

In her left hand a Cup of gold she held,
  And with her right the riper fruit did reach,
  Whose sappy liquor, that with fulnesse sweld,
  Into her cup she scruzd, with daintie breach
  Of her fine fingers, without fowle empeach,
  That so faire wine-presse made the wine more sweet :
  Thereof she vsd to giue to drinke to each,
  Whom passing by she happened to meet :
It was her guise, all Straungers goodly so to greet.

57

So she to *Guyon* offred it to tast ;
  Who taking it out of her tender hond,
  The cup to ground did violently cast,
  That all in peeces it was broken fond,
  And with the liquor stained all the lond :
  Whereat *Excesse* exceedingly was wroth,
  Yet no'te the same amend, ne yet withstond,
  But suffered him to passe, all were she loth ;
Who nought regarding her displeasure forward goth.

58

There the most daintie Paradise on ground,
  It selfe doth offer to his sober eye,
  In which all pleasures plenteously abound,
  And none does others happinesse enuye :
  The painted flowres, the trees vpshooting hye,
  The dales for shade, the hilles for breathing space,
  The trembling groues, the Christall running by ;
  And that, which all faire workes doth most aggrace,
The art, which all that wrought, appeared in no place.

59

One would haue thought, (so cunningly, the rude,
  And scorned parts were mingled with the fine,)
  That nature had for wantonesse ensude
  Art, and that Art at nature did repine ;
  So striuing each th'other to vndermine,
  Each did the others worke more beautifie ;
  So diff'ring both in willes, agreed in fine :
  So all agreed through sweete diuersitie,
This Gardin to adorne with all varietie.

60

And in the midst of all, a fountaine stood,
  Of richest substaunce, that on earth might bee,
  So pure and shiny, that the siluer flood
  Through euery channell running one might see ;
  Most goodly it with curious imageree
  Was ouer-wrought, and shapes of naked boyes,
  Of which some seemd with liuely iollitee,
  To fly about, playing their wanton toyes,
Whilest others did them selues embay in liquid ioyes.

Stanza 55

1–4   Giamatti (1966) 272 observes that 'the artificial . . . infects all around it with its artificiality'.
5–6   **bowes**: the spelling suggests the etymology.
9   As Genius wears a loose garment not fit for 'manly exercize' (46.9).

Stanza 56

1   **left**: from its association with the left, or heart, side ; indicating the temptation of sensual indulgence.
4   **scruzd**: screwed and squeezed.   **breach**: crushing.
5   **without fowle empeach**: without injury to the grapes; or without foul injury to her appearance by soiling her fingers. The context suggests 'hindrance'.
9   **guise**: custom.   **all**: as Genius offers wine to 'all newcome guests' (49.5); and as the bathing maidens display their beauty to the eyes of all (63.9).

Stanza 57

2–3   Guyon must expose himself to temptation and reject it. Cf. his act at 49.8–9 where he rejects a similar offer of courtesy. The religious basis of his act is given by Paul, Eph. 5.18: 'Be not drunke with wine, wherein is excesse but be fulfilled with the Spirit.'
3   In distinction to 49.8. His mood develops from 'disdainfully' to **violently** to 'rigour pittilesse' (83.2).
7   **no'te**: could not.

Stanza 58

Based on Tasso, *Ger. Lib.* xvi 9, the last two lines being a direct translation.
1–2   **daintie**: choice, excellent.   **on ground**: implying an earthly paradise. 2 notes how actively the paradise tempts man.
7   **Christall**: crystal streams.
8   **aggrace**: add grace to; a S. intensification that renders Tasso's *accresce*.

Stanza 59

Developing and extending Tasso, xvi 10.1–4. In imitating his sources throughout this episode, S.'s art is as subtle, various, and diverse as the art he treats. The proper relation of art to nature is expressed by Cowley: 'Wise *Natures* use *Art* strove not to outgo' (*Davideis* Bk I, *Poems* 259). Cf. v 29.1–2. Cf. the harmony of art and nature on the island of the Temple of Venus, IV x 21.6–9.
3   **wantonesse**: playfulness, unruliness, the literal sense of intemperance; also arrogance.   **ensude**: imitated.
4   **repine**: fret.
7   **in fine**: in the end.

Stanza 60

The **fountaine** is S.'s addition – of phallic significance according to Lemmi, *Var.* ii 383 – to Tasso's pool with its bathing virgins, xv 58–66. See 62*n* below.
3   **pure**: clear, transparent; cf. the altar in the Temple of Venus, IV x 39.7–9.
6   **ouer-wrought**: wrought all over and excessively wrought.
8   **toyes**: amorous sports.
9   **embay**: bathe.

61

And ouer all, of purest gold was spred,
  A trayle of yuie in his natiue hew:
  For the rich mettall was so coloured,
  That wight, who did not well auis'd it vew,
  Would surely deeme it to be yuie trew:
  Low his lasciuious armes adown did creepe,
  That themselues dipping in the siluer dew,
  Their fleecy flowres they tenderly did steepe,
Which drops of Christall seemd for wantones to weepe.

62

Infinit streames continually did well
  Out of this fountaine, sweet and faire to see,
  The which into an ample lauer fell,
  And shortly grew to so great quantitie,
  That like a little lake it seemd to bee;
  Whose depth exceeded not three cubits hight,
  That through the waues one might the bottom see,
  All pau'd beneath with Iaspar shining bright,
That seemd the fountaine in that sea did sayle vpright.

63

And all the margent round about was set,
  With shady Laurell trees, thence to defend
  The sunny beames, which on the billowes bet,
  And those which therein bathed, mote offend.
  As *Guyon* hapned by the same to wend,
  Two naked Damzelles he therein espyde,
  Which therein,bathing, seemed to contend,
  And wrestle wantonly, ne car'd to hyde,
Their dainty parts from vew of any, which them eyde.

64

Sometimes the one would lift the other quight
  Aboue the waters, and then downe againe
  Her plong, as ouer maistered by might,
  Where both awhile would couered remaine,
  And each the other from to rise restraine;
  The whiles their snowy limbes, as through a vele,
  So through the Christall waues appeared plaine:
  Then suddeinly both would themselues vnhele,
And th'amarous sweet spoiles to greedy eyes reuele.

65

As that faire Starre, the messenger of morne,
  His deawy face out of the sea doth reare:
  Or as the *Cyprian* goddesse, newly borne
  Of th'Oceans fruitfull froth, did first appeare:
  Such seemed they, and so their yellow heare
  Christalline humour dropped downe apace.
  Whom such when *Guyon* saw, he drew him neare,
  And somewhat gan relent his earnest pace,
His stubborne brest gan secret pleasaunce to embrace.

66

The wanton Maidens him espying, stood
  Gazing a while at his vnwonted guise;
  Then th'one her selfe low ducked in the flood,
  Abasht, that her a straunger did a vise:
  But th'other rather higher did arise,
  And her two lilly paps aloft displayd,
  And all, that might his melting hart entise
  To her delights, she vnto him bewrayd:
The rest hid vnderneath, him more desirous made.

Stanza 61
2 **trayle of yuie**: trailing ornament of ivy. A symbol of lust: see v 29.3–5*n*.
4 **well auis'd**: carefully.
8 **tenderly**] fearefully *1590*.

Stanza 62
This fountain is linked with the heart by Brooke (1949) 430. Fowler (1960b) 149 adds that the passionate heart is traditionally the fountain of the will, and notes (145) that its streams are **Infinit** because concupiscence may never be eradicated by baptism. Cf. Calvin: 'this perversity never ceases in us, but continually bears new fruits . . . just as . . . a spring ceaselessly gives forth water' (*Inst*. IV xv 11). In the *Romance of the Rose* 1536, the Fountain of Narcissus never ceases to flow.
3 **lauer**: the basin of the fountain.
6 **three cubits**: less than five feet; about breast-high, as we soon see.
9 **sayle**: 'project' is a relevant sense.

Stanza 63
1 **margent**: margin.
2 **defend**: ward off.
4 **offend**: harm.
6 **Two naked Damzelles**: borrowed from Tasso, *Ger. Lib.* xv 58–66, where they perform before another upright pair.

Stanza 64
8 **vnhele**: expose to view.
9 **amarous**: lovely; arousing desire.   **spoiles**: cf. Cymochles who 'his fraile eye with spoyle of beautie feedes' (v 34.3).

Stanza 65
1–4 Cf. the Red Cross Knight's full vision of Una as the morning star (I xii 21.5–9). Only barely titillated, Guyon must turn aside from his vision.   **the Cyprian goddesse**: '*Venus* of the fomy sea' (IV xii 2.2).
6 **humour**: moisture.
8 **relent**: slacken; cf. 68.4.

Stanza 66
2 **guise**: behaviour; with a pun on 'gaze'.
4 **a vise**: view.
8 **bewrayd**: exposed.

293

67

With that, the other likewise vp arose,
  And her faire lockes, which formerly were bownd
  Vp in one knot, she low adowne did lose:
  Which flowing long and thick, her cloth'd arownd,
  And th'yuorie in golden mantle gownd:
  So that faire spectacle from him was reft,
  Yet that, which reft it, no lesse faire was fownd:
  So hid in lockes and waues from lookers theft,
Nought but her louely face she for his looking left.

68

Withall she laughed, and she blusht withall,
  That blushing to her laughter gaue more grace,
  And laughter to her blushing, as did fall:
  Now when they spide the knight to slacke his pace,
  Them to behold, and in his sparkling face
  The secret signes of kindled lust appeare,
  Their wanton meriments they did encreace,
  And to him beckned, to approch more neare,
And shewd him many sights, that courage cold could reare.

69

On which when gazing him the Palmer saw,
  He much rebukt those wandring eyes of his,
  And counseld well, him forward thence did draw.
  Now are they come nigh to the *Bowre of blis*
  Of her fond fauorites so nam'd amis:
  When thus the Palmer; Now Sir, well auise;
  For here the end of all our trauell is:
  Here wonnes *Acrasia*, whom we must surprise,
Else she will slip away, and all our drift despise.

70

Eftsoones they heard a most melodious sound,
  Of all that mote delight a daintie eare,
  Such as attonce might not on liuing ground,
  Saue in this Paradise, be heard elswhere:
  Right hard it was, for wight, which did it heare,
  To read, what manner musicke that mote bee:
  For all that pleasing is to liuing eare,
  Was there consorted in one harmonee,
Birdes, voyces, instruments, windes, waters, all agree.

71

The ioyous birdes shrouded in chearefull shade,
  Their notes vnto the voyce attempred sweet;
  Th'Angelicall soft trembling voyces made
  To th'instruments diuine respondence meet:
  The siluer sounding instruments did meet
  With the base murmure of the waters fall:
  The waters fall with difference discreet,
  Now soft, now loud, vnto the wind did call:
The gentle warbling wind low answered to all.

72

There, whence that Musick seemed heard to bee,
  Was the faire Witch her selfe now solacing,
  With a new Louer, whom through sorceree
  And witchcraft, she from farre did thither bring:
  There she had him now layd a slombering,
  In secret shade, after long wanton ioyes:
  Whilst round about them pleasauntly did sing
  Many faire Ladies, and lasciuious boyes,
294 That euer mixt their song with light licentious toyes.

Stanza 68

1 **Withall . . . withall**: with that . . . because of that.
9 **courage**: sexual desire.   **reare**: arouse; or in the explicitly erotic sense, 'cause to stand up'.

Stanza 69

3 Cf. the similar transition at 29.5, 34.1–3.
6 **auise**: consider.
7 **trauell**: also travail.
8 **Acrasia**: from med. Lat. *acrasia*, which combines Gk ἀκρᾱσῐᾱ, ill-temperature, badly mixed quality and ἀκρασια, impotence, want of self-command (*OED*). Hence Acrasia, as the personification of incontinence or intemperate pleasure, combines the bad mixture of the humours and the figure Impotence who attends Maleger. For the link with Acrates, and hence with Impatience who also attends Maleger, see iv 41*n*. The cognate form 'acraze', to weaken, enfeeble, is relevant.
9 **drift**: purpose; plot.   **despise**: set at nought.

Stanza 70

Following the temptation of sight comes the temptation of hearing.
3 **attonce**: together, at one time.
6 **read**: discern.
8 **consorted**: harmoniously combined; cf. v 31.8. The five tones together form the complete pentatonic scale, appealing to all five senses.

Stanza 71

The harmony is revealed by the harmony of the stanza: the interlocking repetition and skilful variation of each sound, and the final harmony of **meet** rhymed with **meet** at the centre. With this quintet, cf. the trio at 33. Hollander (1971) shows how this music is marked by a morally unwholesome blending of its musical categories. He concludes that the mingled measure of the Bower, which transcends all music, represents 'the total undermining of modes of recognition, of the travesties of variety, through which the Bower's ultimately deadly attractiveness is manifested' (238).
1 **chearefull shade**: for S., an oxymoron; cf. 'ioyous shade' (I vii 4.2).
2 **attempred**: attuned; cf. 76.2.
4 **respondence meet**: fitting response.
5 **meet**: blend.
6 **base**: with a pun.
7 **difference discreet**: distinct variation.

Stanza 72

9 **toyes**: amorous play; 'free musical compositions', according to Hollander (1971) 235.

73

And all that while, right ouer him she hong,
　With her false eyes fast fixed in his sight,
　As seeking medicine, whence she was stong,
　Or greedily depasturing delight:
　And oft inclining downe with kisses light,
　For feare of waking him, his lips bedewd,
　And through his humid eyes did sucke his spright,
　Quite molten into lust and pleasure lewd;
Wherewith she sighed soft, as if his case she rewd.

74

The whiles some one did chaunt this louely lay;
　Ah see, who so faire thing doest faine to see,
　In springing flowre the image of thy day;
　Ah see the Virgin Rose, how sweetly shee
　Doth first peepe forth with bashfull modestee,
　That fairer seemes, the lesse ye see her may;
　Lo see soone after, how more bold and free
　Her bared bosome she doth broad display;
Loe see soone after, how she fades, and falles away.

75

So passeth, in the passing of a day,
　Of mortall life the leafe, the bud, the flowre,
　Ne more doth flourish after first decay,
　That earst was sought to decke both bed and bowre,
　Of many a Ladie, and many a Paramowre:
　Gather therefore the Rose, whilest yet is prime,
　For soone comes age, that will her pride deflowre:
　Gather the Rose of loue, whilest yet is time,
Whilest louing thou mayst loued be with equall crime.

76

He ceast, and then gan all the quire of birdes
　Their diuerse notes t'attune vnto his lay,
　As in approuance of his pleasing words.
　The constant paire heard all, that he did say,
　Yet swarued not, but kept their forward way,
　Through many couert groues, and thickets close,
　In which they creeping did at last display
　That wanton Ladie, with her louer lose,
Whose sleepie head she in her lap did soft dispose.

Lib. xvi 19, which this stanza imitates. She literally feeds upon him: he becomes her pasture; cf. 'her louers, which her lusts did feed' (85.3). Cf. Venus who 'reape[s] sweet pleasure' of Adonis, III vi 46.3.

6–7　Upton (1758) reads: 'his eyes bedewd . . . through his humid lips'. In kissing his eyes, however, she could hardly suck his spirit through his lips. By her eyes **fast fixed in his sight** (2), she literally draws his spirit through his closed eyes. Cf. Venus's similar posture over the sleeping Adonis: 'with ambrosiall kisses bathe his eyes' while her eyes search his body (III i 36.4–6). Giamatti (1966) 279 comments upon this 'image of death – a love which is almost necrophilia, a woman whose kiss brings death'.

8　**pleasure**: sensual gratification.

9　Her apparent pity for his lustful state sharpens the moral disapproval expressed by the poet at 80.9.

Stanzas 74–75

A brilliant imitation of the bird's song in Tasso, *Ger. Lib.* xvi 14–5. While it follows Tasso closely, it is wholly original. It is the definitive expression of a commonplace, *carpe florem*. On the commonplace, see Leishman (1961) 66–9 and Quinones (1972) 256–7. The answer to it is given by the *Faerie Queene's* single speech in the poem, reported by Arthur: 'dearely sure her loue was to me bent, / As when just time expired should appeare' (I ix 14.3–4; see *n*).

Stanza 74

1　**louely lay**: lay of love.
2　**faine**: delight.
4–8　The rose imitates the coyness and then the bare display of the two bathing damsels at 66.

Stanza 75

6　**prime**: the flower's most flourishing state; the 'springtime' of human life.
7　**pride**: as prime.
9　**with equall crime**: the phrase places the pagan tradition in a Christian perspective. Tasso's song concludes: *amiamo or quando | esser si puote riamato amando*, which Fairfax renders as 'Loving, be lov'd; embracing, be embrast.' Cheney (1966) 100–1 suggests that the phrase 'conveys the sense less of "mutual enjoyment (and hence no crime at all)" than that of "a reprobate guilt to be shared by all"'. Or it may suggest the joy in sinning, the special mark of sin, as Augustine records in *Conf.* II iv. Durling (1954) 342 cites Aquinas (*Summa theol.* II, ii, Q.155, Art. 4): 'The intemperate man rejoices in having sinned.' Cf. Acrasia's invitation to 'pleasant sin' (77.2). Hence **crime** suggests both the sin and the judgment upon it.

Stanza 76

4　**constant**: steadfast, resolute; but also in the etymological sense, 'standing' and 'standing together', in contrast to the posture of Acrasia's victims.
7　While only by **creeping** may they get through the **couert groues** (6), their posture is unheroic: Ignaro creeps (I viii 30.1) and so do Braggadocchio (II iii 35.7), Malbecco (III x 44.1) and Defetto (VI v 20.5). Guyon becomes a peeping Tom. **display**: discover; cited by *OED* as an erroneous use of the term as if 'to unfold to one's own view'. Yet the active form, used with passive significance, conveys the assault that beauty makes upon the eyes when it is uncovered.
9　**dispose**: lay down, in the etymological sense.

Stanza 73

3　**medicine**: cure.
4　**depasturing**: consuming, from Lat. *depascere*. More powerful than the traditional image of feeding in Tasso, *Ger.*

77

Vpon a bed of Roses she was layd,
  As faint through heat, or dight to pleasant sin,
  And was arayd, or rather disarayd,
  All in a vele of silke and siluer thin,
  That hid no whit her alablaster skin,
  But rather shewd more white, if more might bee:
  More subtile web *Arachne* cannot spin,
  Nor the fine nets, which oft we wouen see
Of scorched deaw, do not in th'aire more lightly flee.

78

Her snowy brest was bare to readie spoyle
  Of hungry eies, which n'ote therewith be fild,
  And yet through languour of her late sweet toyle,
  Few drops, more cleare then Nectar, forth distild,
  That like pure Orient perles adowne it trild,
  And her faire eyes sweet smyling in delight,
  Moystened their fierie beames, with which she thrild
Fraile harts, yet quenched not; like starry light
Which sparckling on the silent waues, does seeme more bright.

79

The young man sleeping by her, seemd to bee
  Some goodly swayne of honorable place,
  That certes it great pittie was to see
  Him his nobilitie so foule deface;
  A sweet regard, and amiable grace,
  Mixed with manly sternnesse did appeare
  Yet sleeping, in his well proportiond face,
And on his tender lips the downy heare
Did now but freshly spring, and silken blossomes beare.

80

His warlike armes, the idle instruments
  Of sleeping praise, were hong vpon a tree,
  And his braue shield, full of old moniments,
  Was fowly ra'st, that none the signes might see;
  Ne for them, ne for honour cared hee,
  Ne ought, that did to his aduauncement tend,
  But in lewd loues, and wastfull luxuree,
  His dayes, his goods, his bodie he did spend:
O horrible enchantment, that him so did blend.

81

The noble Elfe, and carefull Palmer drew
  So nigh them, minding nought, but lustfull game,
  That suddein forth they on them rusht, and threw
  A subtile net, which onely for the same
  The skilfull Palmer formally did frame.
  So held them vnder fast, the whiles the rest
  Fled all away for feare of fowler shame.
  The faire Enchauntresse, so vnwares opprest,
Tryde all her arts, and all her sleights, thence out to wrest.

4–7 Bender (1972) 43 notes the ambiguity – **vele** or **skin** may be the subject of **shewd** – and observes that the function of the veil is ambiguous because it both reveals and heightens to conceal. Cf. Arachne's 'subtile net' (vii 28.7–9) suspended over Mammon's gold. The spider is an emblem of touch; Acrasia is seen as the spider in the web. Cf. Dante's Geryon, the personification of Fraud, who appears in colours that are compared to Arachne's web, *Inf.* xvii 18.

8–9 **the fine nets**: gossamer on which the dew has dried.

Stanza 78
2 **n'ote**: could not.
3–5 **languour**: weariness. Her lover sleeps 'after long wanton ioyes' (72.6). The term may have been suggested by Tasso's *langue per vezzo* (xvi 18) in a passage that goes on to describe her sweat. **sweet toyle**: a nicely chosen phrase for love's sports. **Orient**: lustrous, sparkling; applied to the brilliant pearls of the East; **pure** stresses this detail. **trild**: trickled.
6–8 **fierie beames**: the emission of spirits from the eyes, particularly from the eyes of lovers. As **toyle** (3) implies the corporal sense and **eyes** the spiritual sense, the inference is that neither serves to unite lovers' souls. See IV viii 39.1–6. Cf. the 'fyrie beames' from Belphœbe's eyes which quench desire (iii 23.3–9). **thrild**: pierced. **quenched**: killed. Since the Bower is described in terms of earth and air, and Acrasia is linked with fire and water, all four elements oppose Guyon's temperance.

Stanza 79
2 **place**: rank.
4 **deface**: disgrace.
5 **regard**: demeanour.
7 **Yet sleeping**: even as he slept.
8–9 Alluding to his name, Verdant.

Stanza 80
1–2 Arms are the means to gain praise; since they are left **idle**, praise now sleeps with him. The detail points to the analogies in classical mythology of warriors who lay their arms aside to lie with their mistresses: as Mars with Venus, Hercules with Omphale, Bacchus with Ariadne, Antony with Cleopatra, etc.
3 **moniments**: identifying marks, the records of heroic deeds.
4 **ra'st**: erased by scraping; used again, 83.8, to describe Guyon's fitting revenge for this disgrace.
7 **luxuree**: licentiousness.
9 **blend**: blind (shown by his sleeping); defile.

Stanza 81
3–5 In contrast, Ulysses rushes against Circe with drawn sword as though to kill her (*Ody.* x 321–2). The net Vulcan used to catch Venus with her lover (*Ody.* viii 276f), which is also compared to a spider's web, is analogous to the Palmer's net. Cf. Ovid, *Met.* iv 178–9. **subtile**: finely woven and skilfully devised, covering her in place of the 'subtile web' to which her veil is compared (77.7). **for the same**: i.e. for that purpose. **formally**: expressly, i.e. just for that purpose; or describing how it was framed: skilfully, in good form.
7 **fowler**: referring also to the fowler's net; cf. V ix 13–14.
8 **opprest**: taken by surprise. Its other relevant sense, 'violate', 'ravish', suggests a reversal of roles.

Stanza 77
2 **dight to**: made ready for.

82

And eke her louer stroue: but all in vaine;
  For that same net so cunningly was wound,
  That neither guile, nor force might it distraine.
  They tooke them both, and both them strongly bound
  In captiue bandes, which there they readie found:
  But her in chaines of adamant he tyde;
  For nothing else might keepe her safe and sound;
  But *Verdant* (so he hight) he soone vntyde,
And counsell sage in steed thereof to him applyde.

83

But all those pleasant bowres and Pallace braue,
  Guyon broke downe, with rigour pittilesse;
  Ne ought their goodly workmanship might saue
  Them from the tempest of his wrathfulnesse,
  But that their blisse he turn'd to balefulnesse:
  Their groues he feld, their gardins did deface,
  Their arbers spoyle, their Cabinets suppresse,
  Their banket houses burne, their buildings race,
And of the fairest late, now made the fowlest place.

84

Then led they her away, and eke that knight
  They with them led, both sorrowfull and sad:
  The way they came, the same retourn'd they right,
  Till they arriued, where they lately had
  Charm'd those wild-beasts, that rag'd with furie mad.
  Which now awaking, fierce at them gan fly,
  As in their mistresse reskew, whom they lad;
  But them the Palmer soone did pacify.
Then *Guyon* askt, what meant those beastes, which there did ly.

85

Said he, These seeming beasts are men indeed,
  Whom this Enchauntresse hath transformed thus,
  Whylome her louers, which her lusts did feed,
  Now turned into figures hideous,
  According to their mindes like monstruous.
  Sad end (quoth he) of life intemperate,
  And mournefull meed of ioyes delicious:
  But Palmer, if it mote thee so aggrate,
Let them returned be vnto their former state.

86

Streight way he with his vertuous staffe them strooke,
  And streight of beasts they comely men became;
  Yet being men they did vnmanly looke,
  And stared ghastly, some for inward shame,
  And some for wrath, to see their captiue Dame:
  But one aboue the rest in speciall,
  That had an hog beene late, hight *Grille* by name,
  Repined greatly, and did him miscall,
That had from hoggish forme him brought to naturall.

Stanza 82
2   **wound**: woven.
3   **distraine**: tear asunder.
6   **adamant**: steel or some substance of surpassing hardness.
7   Evans (1970) viii believes that the reader is left 'genuinely uncertain whether she is kept safely locked up or safely preserved in her fetters of reason'.
8   **Verdant**: literally one who gives vegetation or life; Spring. Cf. Acrasia's other lover, Mortdant, one who gives death: see i 55.4*n*.

Stanza 83
Cf. the destruction wrought by Josiah: 'The King defiled the hie places . . . which Salomon the King of Israel had buylt for Ashtoreth . . . and he brake the images in pieces, and cut downe the groves' (2 Kings 23:13–4); cf. Isaiah 13.9.
1   **braue**: splendid, showy.
2   **rigour**: violence.   **pittilesse**: reveals that Guyon has mastered the pity to which he was once subject.
4   **tempest**: suggests that the Bower is destroyed by a natural force. The only other use of the term in Book II describes Furor, 'the tempest of his passion wood' (iv 11.8). S. would be aware of its etymological connection with temperance.
5   **balefulnesse**: distress; full of grief.
6   **deface**: destroy. Guyon's counter-action to Acrasia's destruction of her lover: 'his nobilitie so foule deface' (79.4); as Arthur 'fowle Maleger doth deface' (xi Arg.) in response to his attempt to 'deface' the Castle of Alma (xi 6.4).
7   **spoyle**: ravage; the term describes the Dragon's plundering of Eden, I vii 44.5.   **Cabinets**: garden bowers.
suppresse: put down.
8   **race**: raze; literally, 'root out'.

Stanza 85
3   **which**: suggesting also 'upon which'.
5   Even as their minds were similarly monstrous. In Homer, *Ody.* x 238–41, Circe's victims retain the minds of men. S. follows Comes (1616) VI vi p. 308 who notes that each of Circe's victims took the shape to which he was inclined: the libidinous into swine, the wrathful into lions or bears, etc.
7   **delicious**: voluptuous.
8   **aggrate**: please.

Stanza 86
1   **vertuous**: possessing 'wondrous powre' (40.8); cf. 26.6.
7   **Grille**: the companion of Ulysses who was transformed by Circe into a hog (hence his name γρυλλος, hog, a type of lechery) and refused to be changed back to human shape. The story derives from a dialogue by Plutarch popularly titled *Gryllus*. In English the name signifies 'fierce', 'cruel'.
8   **miscall**: revile.
9   **naturall**: i.e. human.

87

Said *Guyon*, See the mind of beastly man,
　　That hath so soone forgot the excellence
　　Of his creation, when he life began,
　　That now he chooseth, with vile difference,
　　To be a beast, and lacke intelligence.
　　To whom the Palmer thus, The donghill kind
　　Delights in filth and foule incontinence:
　　Let *Grill* be *Grill*, and haue his hoggish mind,
But let vs hence depart, whilest wether serues and wind.

Stanza 87

1–5　　The reference is general in its application: 'See the
mind of man which is beastly.' Since none of Acrasia's victims
is happy in his renewed state, 2–3 would seem to allude to the
briefness of man's unfallen state.
4　　**vile difference**: vile discrimination or preference.
8　　**Let Grill be Grill**: let Grill be himself, i.e. a hog. Cf.
Rev. 22.11: 'he which is filthie, let him be filthie stil.' 2 Pet.
2:22: 'It is come unto them, according to the true proverbe ...
the sowe that was washed [is returned] to the wallowing in the
myer.' S. may have been influenced by the homely moral, 'as
swine are to gardens, etc.' It is used, e.g., on the title-page of
Sidney's *Arcadia* 1593. On animalitarianism in the Renaissance,
see Levin (1969) 80–3.

The virtue of Chastity is related to Holiness and Temperance in the opening canto. After Britomart unhorses Guyon and his 'wrathfull will' is mollified by the Palmer and Arthur, they are reconciled 'Through goodly temperance, and affection chaste'. When Arthur joins their 'golden chaine of concord', 'goodly all agreed'. Afterwards Britomart aids the Red Cross Knight against the enemies of chastity who sorely besiege him – for failure to love chastely causes his downfall in Book I – and later she is closely aided by him against these same enemies, 'ioyning foot to foot, and side to side'. As the unifying virtue, Chastity deserves the opening praise given to it as 'That fairest vertue, farre aboue the rest'. Even in the simplest sense of virtue as strength or power it provides the climax to the first three Books. The Knight of Holiness knows that he is only the willing instrument of God's might. The Knight of Temperance exercises his virtue most often by not acting, and until the end his only actions, not later shown as undone, are to bind the tongue and hands of an old lady, capture a naked lady, and destroy her bower. In contrast, the Knight of Chastity possesses an inner strength through which she triumphs over all her enemies, for in her 'loue does always bring forth bounteous deeds' (i 49).

In what may be seen as the adolescent state of temperance, the feminine appears only as the virgin Belphœbe or the whore Acrasia, that is, the rejection of sexual love or its abuse. Though Guyon is the servant of the 'heauenly Mayd', he never sees the one and only spies on the other as a peeping Tom. He may respond to Acrasia only by binding her. Such repressive action cannot be Britomart's. As Nelson (1963) 228 observes, 'Not the subjection of the passionate to the rational soul but the yoking together of affection and chastity is the central task of her legend.' In the allegory of love in the poem, the binding of Acrasia occasions the flight of Florimell. A central theme in Books III to V is the effort to free the feminine from masculine tyranny. Hence Book III concludes with the freeing of Amoret and Book IV with the freeing of Florimell. A central concern of the allegory in Books III and IV is to establish the conditions under which Acrasia may be released. S.'s pattern for this larger movement may be Tasso, *Ger. Lib.* xx: the enchantress, Armida, is finally accepted by her former victim, Rinaldo, when she submits herself to him. At the centre of Book V Britomart frees a womanized Artegall from his male chauvinism and, in so doing, frees herself from the jealous fears that infect her love for him.

Yet Guyon also destroys the Bower where perpetual summer expresses its sterility and so frees Verdant whose name suggests spring with its regeneration. The temperate body, seen in the Castle of Alma, 'had not yet felt *Cupides* wanton rage'. With the renewal of the cycle of the seasons, however, love enters the world: 'all liuing wights, soone as they see / The spring breake forth out of his lusty bowres, / They all doe learne to play the Paramours' (IV x 45). In Book III the temperate body has now felt '*Cupides* wanton rage': knights lie wounded or helpless and their ladies are seen either in flight or imprisoned. All except Britomart: though wounded, she is armed with chastity as she follows 'the guidaunce of her blinded guest' (iv 6.8), the love for Artegall, which she nourishes within her.

Chastity is viewed in Christian terms by Renwick (1925) 167 as 'nothing other than truth and honour in the question of sex, sanctified by the spirit of God, Who is Love, and serving the world as His agent', and by Tuve (1966) 368 who defines the virtue 'with its traditional Christian overtones of total fidelity, love purified of idolatry, lust and self-indulgence'. Yet Woodhouse's (1949) objection remains: there is no religious motivation or sanction for Britomart's love and no reason to regard it as specifically Christian. Lewis (1936) 340 defines the virtue in historical terms as married love opposed to courtly love: 'Courtly Love is in Spenser's view the chief opponent of Chastity. But Chastity for him means Britomart, married love.' Roche (1964) 110–6 replies that virginity remains the human ideal in the Book and that virginity and marriage represented in the twin sisters, Belphœbe and Amoret, resolve the opposition between them. Rose (1968) 112 expands his argument to conclude that S.'s story 'is not, then, the struggle between two opposed forms of love, but rather the transformation of passionate love into matrimonial love'. While chastity may belong to the state of virginity, it may be defined simply and fully as faithful love; and in treating the virtue, S. emphasizes faithful love in marriage.

Book III provides an anatomy of love. Its motto is given in the opening lines of Canto v: 'Wonder it is to see, in diuerse minds, / How diuersly loue doth his pageants play, / And shewes his powre in variable kinds.' Lewis (1967) ch. i distinguishes a false Cupid from one who represents true love; my own view (Hamilton, 1961, 155) is that there is only one Cupid in the poem even as there is only one Venus. Love's pageants vary according to man's inner moral state. Donno (1974) 47 argues that Book III does not distinguish a kind of Cupid or a kind of Love but rather love's compelling power manifested in diverse characters: 'The Legend of Chastity illustrates the triumph of Cupid in human affairs, depicted in a wide spectrum of possible responses, but it is a Cupid who functions within the providential scheme.' In a poem dedicated to the Virgin Queen, virginity is accorded 'the highest staire / Of th'honorable stage of womanhead' (v 54.7–8). Its central 'stage' is occupied by Britomart, the virgin in love who seeks to lose her virginity to a stranger whose face she has seen in a looking-glass. Since she loves chastely, her goal is marriage, in which she may lose her virginity but keep her chastity. While S.'s stress on the fulfilment of sexual love leads Evans (1970) 152 to describe it as 'the book of sex', and Brill (1971) to describe Chastity as 'ideal sexuality', his anatomy of love extends downward to the natural order, outward to the cosmos, and also includes the political order in which the 'Most famous fruits of matrimoniall bowre' (iii 3.7) are the progeny of English kings.

The virtues fashioned in the first two books permit S. to use the structural motif of the quest. Each Knight pursues his goal directly and during his course engages in chivalric action in the open field. Being led, he proceeds directly to his goal. In Book III, in contrast, the anatomy of love involves a number of related stories of knights and ladies, some on a quest and others the object of a quest. Led by 'blind loue' (IV v 29), the Knight of Chastity wanders aimlessly not knowing where to find her unknown paramour. The sexual theme removes the action from the open field to the forest and the sea. Hankins (1971) 72 explains this archetypal setting: 'In so far as the body obeys, protects, and nourishes the soul, it is a castle. In so far as its weakness clogs, annoys, and imperils the soul, it is a forest. The beasts which inhabit the forest are themselves passions of the soul; the body provides the setting, but the warfare is within the soul.' The second landscape of the Book is the sea, which is seen by Murtaugh (1973) 326 as 'the negation of all life'. Accordingly, the conjunction of these two settings, the seashore, may be seen to provide the turning-point of the action in the Book.

S.'s subject in Book III determines his literary model, Italian romance, in which the interwoven themes of love and war contrast arms and the man. S. stresses the arms in Book I and the man in Book II. In turn, that model determines S.'s manner of imitation. In Book I he imitates Scripture: by deriving his structure of imagery chiefly from Revelation, he makes his Book central within the Christian vision of man. In Book II he imitates classical epic: as a Christian poet he is able to transcend his model. In Book III he seeks to 'overgo' Ariosto, as he told Harvey. As a consequence, Lewis (1936) 305 may refer to the *Faerie Queene* as 'primarily an English branch of that excellent Italian *genre* the romantic epic'. After analysing S.'s imitation of Ariosto, Alpers (1967) 198 concludes that S. had the whole of the *Orlando Furioso* at his fingertips.

S.'s literary model provides him with his method of polyphonic narrative or *entrelacement*, that is, the interlocking of separate stories into a pattern of relationships. As Tuve (1966) 363 explains: 'Events connected by entrelacement are not juxtaposed; they are interlaced, and when we get back to our first character he is not where we left him as we finished his episode, but in the place of psychological state or condition of meaningfulness to which he has been pulled by the events occurring in following episodes written about some one else.'

The interlaced stories in Book III centre on Britomart, the female warrior and virgin in love who contains both Diana and Venus. As she is a virgin, her love for Artegall is treated in the Belphœbe–Timias story. As she is in love and seeks to fulfil her love in marriage, her relationship to Artegall is treated in the Scudamour–Amoret story. As that marriage has the apocalyptic import prophesied by Merlin, its significance in relation to Nature is treated in the Marinell–Florimell story. Like Florimell, Britomart loves a knight faithfully; but he does not love her in return, not knowing of her love. Yet Florimell knows her lover while Britomart has seen only the image of hers. In contrast to both, Amoret loves faithfully, and is loved faithfully in return. And in contrast to all, Belphœbe does not know that she is loved by Timias and does not love him. The pattern of the polyphonic narrative made up by these stories provides the allegory of Book III.

In *L.R.*, S. refers to Britomart as 'a Lady knight, in whome I picture Chastity', but S.'s critics, attending only to his opening phrase, treat her as though she were no more than a dramatic and human character. Since Roche (1964) 51 finds her 'a more dramatic characterization than any other in the poem', he refers to her despair upon leaving the house of Malecasta as 'occasioned by the young girl's first encounter with love and her reaction against it' (71). Mother Mary Parker (1960) 176 is assured that 'beneath the armour of the Saxon Queen there beats a very tender heart', and Rose (1968) 103 concludes that the opening cantos witness 'the growth of Britomart from a young girl, as ignorant of herself as of the world around her, into a great lady of considerable wisdom and knowledge'. A fitting title for much of the criticism of Book III is 'The Girlhood of Spenser's Heroines'. Yet there are exceptions. Lanham (1967) 444 protests that Britomart is not a credible personality but instead 'a literal embodiment of the violence of the man-woman relationship'. Berger (1969a) 234 rejects the usual character study of Britomart, arguing that the problems of Book III are generic and archetypal 'in the sense that they arise from one's being a masculine or feminine creature rather than a unique individual like Arthur or Britomart. The feminine fears and fantasies . . . are the products of tendencies inherent in the female psyche.'

Britomart may be related to the virtue of chastity, rather than treated as a character in fiction, by relating her story to the stories of Belphœbe, Amoret, and Florimell. I suggest (Hamilton, 1961, 144) that 'as the titular heroes are aspects of Arthur, these women are different revelations of this female Arthur's complex role in the allegory. Roughly speaking, Belphœbe represents the power of her chastity; Amoret's story embodies the fortunes of her love for Artegall; and Florimell symbolizes its cosmic significances.' To Berger (1968a) 17 they personify aspects of human nature: 'Belphoebe, Florimell, and Amoret come by a process of allegorical assimilation to represent conflicting aspects of the feminine psyche in general and of Britomart's psyche in particular'. Roche (1964) 102–3 adds an archetypal dimension to his usual character-centred study: 'Belphoebe is the Heavenly Venus, eschewing earthly love; Amoret is the Earthly Venus, beset by all the dangers love is heir to. Britomart is the human embodiment of both types, passing from the virginity of youth to the chaste married love of maturity.'

The stories of Belphœbe, Amoret, and Florimell may be examined separately, as they are by Roche, since each constitutes 'a fictional line' (195). Belphœbe's exemplary nature as the ideal of virginity makes her the simplest of the three, and, for modern critics, the least attractive. Cheney (1966) 102 finds that 'a certain narcissistic obtuseness to the concerns of others is the price which she pays for her immunity to lust'. Alpers (1967) 390 believes that S. 'limits her as an exemplary image of the human individual', and even Miss Williams (1966) 102 concludes that 'when the ideal [of virginity] is thought of as embodied in a lady of remote but demanding purity pitfalls begin to open before the admirer's feet'. So much for 'the highest staire / Of th'honorable stage of womanhead'.

Florimell's story is the most hauntingly evocative of all. Its meanings are as elusive as she is in her flight and subject to as many transformations. To consider briefly the moment in her long flight when she passes from the land to the sea. Upton cannot bring himself to say that she is Mary Queen of Scots, and that the spotted monster that pursues her refers to the motley dress of her subjects from whom she seeks to escape. Instead, he cites Camden who tells how Mary escaped from prison and 'was so terrified, that she rode that day above sixty miles; and then chose rather to commit herself to the miseries of the sea, than to the falsed fidelity of her people'. I suggest (Hamilton, 1961, 150) that the loss and tearing of her girdle as she leaps into the sea, which S. later says 'would loose, or else a sunder teare' (IV v 3) from one who is unchaste, 'is the loss of her maidenhead'. Other readers strongly differ. Nelson (1963) 135 calls her an 'unhappy girl [who] is here made to lose her girdle only in order that Satyrane may have it to bind the spotted beast', as though her handkerchief or scarf might do. Roche (1964) 157 concludes that Florimell's loss of the girdle of chastity and the devouring of her horse by the Hyena that 'feeds on womens flesh' (III vii 22) does not mean that she lost her chastity. Evans (1970) 170 claims that 'this is not the physical rape of Florimell, however, as it has often been interpreted, but the destruction of beauty, so that the virgin girdle is no longer a thing of such value: it is devouring time that has ravished her'.

These efforts to interpret the mysterious events involved in Florimell's descent into the sea, or, alternatively, to find meanings at odds with the text, make a mythical reading the most satisfactory. Spens (1934) 84 regards her as Proserpine. Frye (1957) 153 refers to Florimell and Marinell as 'spirits of flowers and water, a Proserpine and an Adonis'. His interpretation is supported by Blissett (1965) 101 who refers to the myth of Florimell as 'an independent myth in allusion to the established myth of Proserpine. It presents a springtime coming to life in man and the world but not the recurring cycle of the seasons.' Lewis (1967) 126 suggests an allegory at only one point of Florimell's story, the moment when Proteus imprisons her under the sea: 'Florimell may (at least at this point) be the *anima semplicetta* come from the sweet golden clime into the sea of matter and the power of Proteus. Her imprisonment seems very like an allegory of the descent of the soul into material embodiment.' Williams (1966) 138 writes that the narrative of Florimell and Marinell 'enacts the union of elemental cosmic opposites, the destructive and the gentle aspects of the natural creation'. Such efforts at mythic interpretation may seem as desperate as the others, and as radically incomplete. Cain (1972) 24 notes that 'no poet of the Renaissance is more attuned to mythopoeic creation than is Spenser'. Until his mythopoeic powers are better understood, however, what alone is clearly seen is that Florimell's movement from land to sea is the opposite to that of '*Venus* of the fomy sea' (IV xii 2): see headnote to Book IV.

Since S. uses polyphonic narrative in Book III, he cannot structure his image of the virtue as he had in the first two books. He solves the problem brilliantly in the simplest manner by balancing the opening and concluding cantos against the middle canto. Canto vi is the centre of the Book as it treats the centre or source of all life. Symmetrically placed in relation to it are the two balancing accounts of Britain's historical destiny, Merlin's prophecy to Britomart concerning her famous British progeny in canto iii and the account of her ancestry in canto ix. In both these accounts, as Murtaugh (1973), 325 observes, 'we see how the good but merely natural generative power, whose subjects move in circles in and out of Genius's two gates, becomes humanized, fostering kingly generations which march in a straight line to history's goal in God'. The houses of Malecasta and Busirane reveal the forces opposed to chastity – love is perverted in the one and bound in the other – and at the centre the natural forces that sustain love are revealed in the Garden where Amoret (Love) was 'vpbrought in goodly womanhed' (vi 28).

The simplest of the three cantos is the first. Both Malecasta and Britomart are infected by love through an evil casting (mala-casta?) of their eyes upon a passing stranger (see III i 41.7–9n). Malecasta is evilly chaste (mala-casta; see III i 57.4n), that is, not chaste at all, for she loves every passing stranger while Britomart loves one alone. Brill (1975) 210 finds the canto morally complex by judging that Britomart ought to have known better than to enter Malecasta's Castle. The unnecessary conflicts into which she is led illustrate the canto's 'diversely realized theme of spuriousness and meretriciousness which leads to multiple or ambiguous moral signification'.

For any reader the Garden of Adonis episode is a mysterious, but central and initiatory moment to his possessing the whole poem. Here he enters into the creative source of Nature, of 'great creating Nature', *natura naturans*. Later he will enter into the corresponding 'sacred noursery / Of vertue' (VI Pr. 3) in the Dance of the Graces in VI x. Perhaps because the moment is largely inexpressible by the usual critical vocabulary, the reader may expect little help from critics beyond Lewis's (1936) argument that the corrupt artifice of the Bower of Bliss is answered by the natural Garden: 'the one is artifice, sterility, death: the other, nature, fecundity, life' (326). Generally critics have been content to try to identify some philosophical source or sources of the Garden. If one grants that the episode may be read as philosophical statement rather than as part of a poem, and that the language is logically consistent, what are its sources? In support of this concern with sources, there is Digby's judgment that S. 'bringeth down the highest and deepest mysteries that are contained in human learning to an easy and gentle form of delivery'. On the scope and complexity of this 'human learning', Nelson (1963) 209 notes that the interpretation of the philosophy of the Garden is 'one of the principal cruxes' of the poem. His list of analogues proposed by earlier scholars is daunting: 'an allegorized Ovid, the *Zodiacus Vitae* of Palingenius, the poems of the twelfth-century Alain de Lille and Bernard Sylvestris, St Augustine's literal commentary on Genesis, the writings of Ficino, Leone Ebreo, Louis Le Roy, Boethius, Claudian, Lucretius, Empedocles, Plotinus, and Plato'. Hankins fills some fifty pages with possible sources of the episode.

Kermode (1965) 208 all but rejects such source study: 'The sources matter only in so far as Spenser's myth is unintelligible without such information; and in fact only a very little is needed to make it self-explanatory.' Hough (1962) 177 rejects source study outright on the grounds that S. 'works by vision, image and action; for him the formal notions of philosophy are only a species of metaphor, and take their place in a series of imaginative tableaux, not in a logical structure'. If the views of Kermode and Hough prevail, readers may hope that critical interest will turn from the Garden's philosophical sources to its poetic function.

In his interpretation of the allegory of chastity in Book III, Padelford, *Var*. iii 329, explains the Busirane episode in a single sentence: 'It is chastity alone that can liberate and unite these lovers [Scudamour and Amoret], and chastity performs its supreme office when it teaches those united in marriage that the body must be subordinate to the spirit.' He explains Amoret's imprisonment as a fault in her education in the Garden of Adonis: she was not prepared 'to place the spiritual values of matrimony uppermost' and 'could not refrain from surrendering herself to physical delight when once it enjoyed the conventional sanction of marriage'. It is curious and salutary to recognize that this interpretation, authoritative in its day, has been totally undone.

From the poem it is clear that Amoret is bound because she refuses to yield her body to Busirane; and once she is freed, she freely yields herself to Scudamour – in the *1590* text – in an ecstasy of physical delight. Further, as the poem makes clear, after she is 'lessoned / In all the lore of loue' in the Garden, she serves in the Temple of Venus. The virtues which accompany her in the Temple are such as no man, except a victim of Acrasia or Radigund, would allow to be faulty education for marriage: in climactic order, Shamefulness, Cheerfulness, Modesty, Courtesy, Silence and Obedience. Accordingly, recent critics seek other reasons for Amoret's imprisonment. Lewis, as noted above, identifies Busirane as Courtly Love which tries to pervert love into lust. Since we learn later that Busirane abducted Amoret during her wedding feast, Roche (1964) 80–3 argues that he objectifies her fears of sexual love. He binds her because he abuses marriage with fears of adulterous love, and Britomart may free her because 'as a woman she understands Amoret's attitude toward the physical side of love, and as the exemplar of chastity she is able to make the moral distinction between marriage and adulterous love'. Gilde (1971a) interprets Amoret's 'problem' as a failure to reconcile sexuality with love. In Hamilton (1961) 182, I argue that Amoret was bound by womanly fears of masculine 'maisterie': see headnote to Book IV. Fowler (1970) 47–58 argues that Amoret fears the physical surrender of marriage, specifically sexual penetration. Berger (1971) 100 returns to Lewis's reading by interpreting the episode as the war between the sexes, with Busirane 'the male imagination trying busily (because unsuccessfully) to dominate and possess woman's will by art, by magic, by sensory illusions and threats – by all the instruments of culture except the normal means of persuasion'.

THE THIRD

BOOKE OF THE

FAERIE QVEENE.

Contayning,

THE LEGEND OF BRITOMARTIS.

OR

Of Chastitie.

1

IT falls me here to write of Chastity,
That fairest vertue, farre aboue the rest;
For which what needs me fetch from *Faery*
Forreine ensamples, it to haue exprest?
Sith it is shrined in my Soueraines brest,
And form'd so liuely in each perfect part,
That to all Ladies, which haue it profest,
Need but behold the pourtraict of her hart,
If pourtrayd it might be by any liuing art.

2

But liuing art may not least part expresse,
Nor life-resembling pencill it can paint,
All were it *Zeuxis* or *Praxiteles*:
His dædale hand would faile, and greatly faint,
And her perfections with his error taint:
Ne Poets wit, that passeth Painter farre
In picturing the parts of beautie daint,
So hard a workmanship aduenture darre,
For fear through want of words her excellence to marre.

3

How then shall I, Apprentice of the skill,
That whylome in diuinest wits did raine,
Presume so high to stretch mine humble quill?
Yet now my lucklesse lot doth me constraine
Hereto perforce. But O dred Soueraine
Thus farre forth pardon, sith that choicest wit
Cannot your glorious pourtraict figure plaine
That I in colour showes may shadow it,
And antique praises vnto present persons fit.

4

But if in liuing colours, and right hew,
Your selfe you couet to see pictured,
Who can it doe more liuely, or more trew,
Then that sweet verse, with *Nectar* sprinckeled,
In which a gracious seruant pictured
His *Cynthia*, his heauens fairest light?
That with his melting sweetnesse rauished,
And with the wonder of her beames bright,
My senses lulled are in slomber of delight.

304

Proem

Stanza 1

2   **farre**: 'fayre' sugg. Upton (1758), to avoid the claim that chastity is far above all the virtues.   **the rest** may refer to Holiness and Temperance, which Chastity unifies, as Britomart's relation to the Red Cross Knight and Guyon makes clear. Cf. Milton's ordering of Faith, Hope, and Chastity, *Comus* 212–4, in which Chastity is the Love or Charity of 1 Cor. 13.13.

6   **form'd**: bodied forth.   **liuely**: lifelike.

Stanza 2

1   **expresse**: portray, depict; referring to painting and sculpture.

2   **life-resembling**: life-representing.

3   **Zeuxis** and **Praxiteles** are respectively the painter and sculptor of antiquity famed for rendering female beauty.

4   **dædale**: skilful, as though belonging to Daedalus, the great artificer.

7   **daint**: choice, excellent.

Stanza 3

4–5   Cf. the opening phrase of stanza 1, 'It falls me'; both passages suggest the ordering of the virtues in the first three Books.

8   **shadow**: portray; represent by an imperfect image. Also in the Platonic sense: the shadow is related to reality as the phenomenal world to the heavenly world of Ideas; and in the Christian sense: 'foreshadowing', for the Faerie Queene is the shadow of Elizabeth, as 'the Lawe [is] the shadowe of good things to come, and not the very image of the things' (Heb. 10.1). The Geneva gloss explains: 'which was as it were the first draught and purtrait of the liuelie paterne to come'.
colourd showes: in *L.R.*, S. says that his poem is 'coloured with an historicall fiction'.

Stanza 4

3–9   The **gracious seruant** (5) is Sir Walter Raleigh whose 'song was all a lamentable lay, / Of great vnkindnesse, and of vsage hard, / Of *Cynthia* the Ladie of the sea' (*Col.* 164–6). The surviving fragment of the poem is entitled 'The 11th and last book of the Ocean to Cynthia'.

5

But let that same delitious Poet lend
A little leaue vnto a rusticke Muse
To sing his mistresse prayse, and let him mend,
If ought amis her liking may abuse:
Ne let his fairest *Cynthia* refuse,
In mirrours more then one her selfe to see,
But either *Gloriana* let her chuse,
Or in *Belphœbe* fashioned to bee:
In th'one her rule, in th'other her rare chastitee.

Cant. I.

*Guyon encountreth Britomart,
faire Florimell is chaced:
Duessaes traines and Malecastaes
champions are defaced.*

1

THe famous Briton Prince and Faerie knight,
After long wayes and perilous paines endured,
Hauing their wearie limbes to perfect plight
Restord, and sory wounds right well recured,
Of the faire *Alma* greatly were procured,
To make there lenger soiourne and abode;
But when thereto they might not be allured,
From seeking praise, and deeds of armes abrode,
They courteous conge tooke, and forth together yode.

2

But the captiu'd *Acrasia* he sent,
Because of trauell long, a nigher way,
With a strong gard, all reskew to preuent,
And her to Faerie court safe to conuay,
That her for witnesse of his hard assay,
Vnto his *Faerie* Queene he might present:
But he him selfe betooke another way,
To make more triall of his hardiment,
And seeke aduentures, as he with Prince *Arthur* went.

3

Long so they trauelled through wastefull wayes,
Where daungers dwelt, and perils most did wonne,
To hunt for glorie and renowmed praise;
Full many Countries they did ouerronne,
From the vprising to the setting Sunne,
And many hard aduentures did atchieue;
Of all the which they honour euer wonne,
Seeking the weake oppressed to relieue,
And to recouer right for such, as wrong did grieue.

4

At last as through an open plaine they yode,
They spide a knight, that towards pricked faire,
And him beside an aged Squire there rode,
That seem'd to couch vnder his shield three-square,
As if that age bad him that burden spare,
And yield it those, that stouter could it wield:
He them espying, gan himselfe prepare,
And on his arme addresse his goodly shield
That bore a Lion passant in a golden field.

Stanza 5
In a dedicatory sonnet to Raleigh, S. offers his 'rusticke
Madrigale' as a stop-gap: 'till that thou thy Poeme wilt make
knowne, / Let thy faire Cinthias praises bee thus rudely
showne.'
7–9 Cf. *L.R.*: 'In that Faery Queene . . . in my particular
[intention] I conceiue the most excellent and glorious person
of our soueraine the Queene . . . And yet in some places els,
I doe otherwise shadow her. For considering she beareth two
persons, the one of a most royall Queene or Empresse, the
other of a most vertuous and beautifull Lady, this latter part
in some places I doe expresse in Belphœbe, fashioning her
name according to your owne excellent conceipt of Cynthia,
(Phœbe and Cynthia being both names of Diana).' The
medieval concept of the king's 'body politic' and 'body natural'
is analysed by Kantorowicz (1957).

Canto i

Argument
3 **Duessaes traines**: in Book II, Duessa is the instrument
of Archimago's 'traines' (i 4.2) to deceive Guyon. In Book III,
her similar intention to deceive Britomart is announced
although she does not appear. Apparently her role is assumed
by Malecasta. **Malecasta**: see 57.4*n*.
4 **defaced**: defeated.

Stanza 1
4 **sory**: painful. **recured**: healed.
5 **procured**: urged.
7–9 Alluding to the destruction of the Bower of Bliss.
conge: farewell. **yode**: went.

Stanza 2
5 **assay**: endeavour.

Stanza 3
1 **wastefull**: desolate.

Stanza 4
1 **an open plaine**: cf. 'equall plaine' (8.5). In Books I and
II it is the setting for chivalric encounters. After this episode,
the forest becomes the dominant setting for Books III and IV.
See 14.5–9*n*, 20.5–7*n*.
2 **towards**: in their direction.
4 **couch**: stoop. **three-square**: with three equal sides;
see I vi 41.8*n*. Upton (1758) notes: 'like the shield of our
English kings: for Britomart is a British princess.' Cf.
Marinell's 'threesquare scuchin' (iv 16.3).
8 **addresse**: make ready.
9 **a Lion passant**: the heraldic description of a lion walking,
looking toward the dexter side, with the dexter fore-paw raised,
against a golden background. Church (1758) notes that the arms
of Brutus (from whom Britomart is descended) was a lion
passant gules, in a field *or*. Cf. the description, 'Upon the
Frontispice', Drayton, *Poly-Olbion*: 'In Golden field the Lion
passant red.'

5

Which seeing good Sir *Guyon*, deare besought
  The Prince of grace, to let him runne that turne.
  He graunted: then the Faery quickly raught
  His poinant speare, and sharpely gan to spurne
  His fomy steed, whose fierie feete did burne
  The verdant grasse, as he thereon did tread;
  Ne did the other backe his foot returne,
  But fiercely forward came withouten dread,
And bent his dreadfull speare against the others head.

6

They bene ymet, and both their points arriued,
  But *Guyon* droue so furious and fell,
  That seem'd both shield and plate it would haue riued;
  Nathelesse it bore his foe not from his sell,
  But made him stagger, as he were not well:
  But *Guyon* selfe, ere well he was aware,
  Nigh a speares length behind his crouper fell,
  Yet in his fall so well him selfe he bare,
That mischieuous mischance his life and limbes did spare.

7

Great shame and sorrow of that fall he tooke;
  For neuer yet, sith warlike armes he bore,
  And shiuering speare in bloudie field first shooke,
  He found himselfe dishonored so sore.
  Ah gentlest knight, that euer armour bore,
  Let not thee grieue dismounted to haue beene,
  And brought to ground, that neuer wast before;
  For not thy fault, but secret powre vnseene,
That speare enchaunted was, which layd thee on the greene.

8

But weenedst thou what wight thee ouerthrew,
  Much greater griefe and shamefuller regret
  For thy hard fortune then thou wouldst renew,
  That of a single damzell thou wert met
  On equall plaine, and there so hard beset;
  Euen the famous *Britomart* it was,
  Whom straunge aduenture did from *Britaine* fet,
  To seeke her louer (loue farre sought alas,)
Whose image she had seene in *Venus* looking glas.

9

Full of disdainefull wrath, he fierce vprose,
  For to reuenge that foule reprochfull shame,
  And snatching his bright sword began to close
  With her on foot, and stoutly forward came;
  Die rather would he, then endure that same.
  Which when his Palmer saw, he gan to feare
  His toward perill and vntoward blame,
  Which by that new rencounter he should reare:
For death sate on the point of that enchaunted speare.

10

And hasting towards him gan faire perswade,
  Not to prouoke misfortune, nor to weene
  His speares default to mend with cruell blade;
  For by his mightie Science he had seene
  The secret vertue of that weapon keene,
  That mortall puissance mote not withstond:
  Nothing on earth mote alwaies happie beene.
  Great hazard were it, and aduenture fond,
306 To loose long gotten honour with one euill hond.

Stanza 5
1 **good Sir Guyon**: his title in the opening episode of Book II (see Proem 5.8, i 42.1, etc.).
2 **of grace**: as a matter of favour; with a pun on Arthur's identity.
3 **raught**: seized.
4 **poinant**: sharp.   **spurne**: spur.
9 **bent**: aimed.

Stanza 6
1 **They bene ymet**: repeated from the encounter between the Red Cross Knight and Guyon, II i 26.6. The reconciliation which relates the virtues of Books I and II parallels the subsequent reconciliation here, which relates the virtues of II and III. See 12.7–9n.
7 The **speares length** measures chastity's power; cf. her blow at iv 16.7.   **crouper**: crupper, the back of the saddle.

Stanza 7
3 **shiuering speare**: capable of splitting; quivering while poised to strike. The weapon of the classical warrior; the *tremibunda hasta* in Virgil (*Aen*. x 522) or Turnus's quivering (*trementem*) spear (*Aen*. xii 94).   **shooke**: wielded, brandished.
9 Britomart becomes known as the 'Knight of the Hebene speare' (see IV v 8.2n), as it manifests the power of her chastity. Fowler (1964) 125 compares the sharp spear carried by Minerva, which was interpreted as the power of wisdom: see Tervarent (1958) 230. Cf. Guyon's loss of his spear at II iii 3.8.

Stanza 8
6 **the famous Britomart**: echoing 'The famous Briton Prince' (1.1), to suggest that she is a female Arthur. Her name suggests Brito-Mart (Mars), the martial Britoness. Hence she is called 'the Britonesse' (58.5), 'Briton Mayd' (ii 4.5) and 'martiall Mayd' (ii 9.4). One source of her name is from Virgil, *Ciris* 295–305, where Britomartis – cf. 67.2, iii 19.5 – is associated with Diana; hence the name befits a knight of chastity. Lotspeich (1932) 43 cites Boccaccio, *Gen. Deor*. IX xxxv: *Britona, Martis filia, quae cum virgo adhaesisset Dianae*. S. regards her as a Diana–Venus figure, or Venus *armata*. On the latter, see Wind (1967) 91f.
7 **aduenture**: chance.   **fet**: fetch.
9 **Venus looking glas**: see ii 18.8n.

Stanza 9
1 **disdainefull**: indignant.
4 **on foot**: the state in which he establishes his virtue in Book II.
7 **toward**: approaching; playing against **vntoward** because his unlucky shame is imminent.   **blame**: injury; shame (as 7.1, 9.2).
8 **rencounter**: encounter between two knights; also re-encounter.   **reare**: bring about.

Stanza 10
1 **perswade**: urge.
3 **default**: fault.
5 **vertue**: the spear's power is its virtue.
7–9 The Palmer as reason fittingly expresses himself here in proverbs. **happie**: fortunate.   **aduenture fond**: foolish risk.   **hond**: action.

11

By such good meanes he him discounselled,
  From prosecuting his reuenging rage;
  And eke the Prince like treaty handeled,
  His wrathfull will with reason to asswage,
  And laid the blame, not to his carriage,
  But to his starting steed, that swaru'd asyde,
  And to the ill purueyance of his page,
  That had his furnitures not firmely tyde:
So is his angry courage fairely pacifyde.

12

Thus reconcilement was betweene them knit,
  Through goodly temperance, and affection chaste,
  And either vowd with all their power and wit,
  To let not others honour be defaste,
  Of friend or foe, who euer it embaste,
  Ne armes to beare against the others syde:
  In which accord the Prince was also plaste,
  And with that golden chaine of concord tyde.
So goodly all agreed, they forth yfere did ryde.

13

O goodly vsage of those antique times,
  In which the sword was seruant vnto right;
  When not for malice and contentious crimes,
  But all for praise, and proofe of manly might,
  The martiall brood accustomed to fight:
  Then honour was the meed of victorie,
  And yet the vanquished had no despight,
  Let later age that noble vse enuie,
Vile rancour to auoid, and cruell surquedrie.

14

Long they thus trauelled in friendly wise,
  Through countries waste, and eke well edifyde,
  Seeking aduentures hard, to exercise
  Their puissance, whylome full dernely tryde:
  At length they came into a forrest wyde,
  Whose hideous horror and sad trembling sound
  Full griesly seem'd: Therein they long did ryde,
  Yet tract of liuing creatures none they found,
Saue Beares, Lions, and Buls, which romed them around.

15

All suddenly out of the thickest brush,
  Vpon a milk-white Palfrey all alone,
  A goodly Ladie did foreby them rush,
  Whose face did seeme as cleare as Christall stone,
  And eke through feare as white as whales bone:
  Her garments all were wrought of beaten gold,
  And all her steed with tinsell trappings shone,
  Which fled so fast, that nothing mote him hold,
And scarse them leasure gaue, her passing to behold.

Stanza 11
1 **discounselled**: dissuaded.
3 **treaty**: entreaty.
5 **carriage**: conduct or action.
6–8 While being tactful, Arthur tells the truth: Guyon is defeated because he failed to control his steed, i.e. his passions. **purueyance**: preparation. **furnitures**: harness, such as the bridle and bit, which should govern the passions.
9 **courage**: spirit. **fairely**: entirely.

Stanza 12
2 Expressing the moral states of the two knights; cf. the 'friendly league of loue perpetuall' which binds Britomart and the Red Cross Knight (iv 4.4–5); cf. also iii 62.7–8.
3 **wit**: skill.
5 **embaste**: degraded.
7–9 Cf. the 'Goodly golden chaine, wherewith yfere / The vertues linked are in louely wize' (I ix 1.1–2). The present linking of Arthur, Guyon, and Britomart is extended to include the Red Cross Knight when Britomart comes to his aid (28–30) and he comes to hers (66.7–9). Fowler (1964) 22 notes the use of the triad of Fidius, Veritas–Virtus–Amor, as the basic structural device of the first three Books. Rose (1968) 84 argues that this episode introduces the theme of 'the reconciliation of temperance and passionate love in the chaste affection of marriage'.

Stanza 13
8 **enuie**: seek to rival.
9 **rancour** applies to the defeated; cf. II viii 50.7. **surquedrie** is the arrogance of the victor; cf. iii 46.9.

Stanza 14
2 **edifyde**: built up.
4 **whylome**: at times. **dernely**: grievously (sugg. by the context).
5–9 On the significance of the forest setting, see 20.5–7n, I vi 3.2n. As a symbol of the unconscious, see Cirlot (1962) 107. The forest is contrasted with the plain where knights on horse-back may assert their virtues. The beasts are cited for their extreme violence: see II ii 22.5–9n. **griesly**: horrible. **tract**: track.

Stanza 15
2 As Una rides a 'snowy Palfrey' (I iii 8.8).
3 **foreby**: close by.
4–5 The description is courtly and traditional: cf. 'your throte as clere as crystall stone . . . and your neke as whyte as whalles bone' (Robbins, no. 130, 25–7). **cleare**: brightly shining. The simile in 5 is proverbial (C. G. Smith, 1970, 842) and associates Florimell with the sea.
6 Here gay garments do not imply evil as they do at I v 26.7; cf. the description of the Church in Ps. 45.14 (Sternhold-Hopkins): 'all deckt in beaten gold'.
7 **tinsell**: glittering.

307

16

Still as she fled, her eye she backward threw,
  As fearing euill, that pursewd her fast;
  And her faire yellow locks behind her flew,
  Loosely disperst with puffe of euery blast:
  All as a blazing starre doth farre outcast
  His hearie beames, and flaming lockes dispred,
  At sight whereof the people stand aghast:
  But the sage wisard telles, as he has red,
That it importunes death and dolefull drerihed.

17

So as they gazed after her a while,
  Lo where a griesly Foster forth did rush,
  Breathing out beastly lust her to defile:
  His tyreling iade he fiercely forth did push,
  Through thicke and thin, both ouer banke and bush
  In hope her to attaine by hooke or crooke,
  That from his gorie sides the bloud did gush:
  Large were his limbes, and terrible his looke,
And in his clownish hand a sharp bore speare he shooke.

18

Which outrage when those gentle knights did see,
  Full of great enuie and fell gealosy,
  They stayd not to auise, who first should bee,
  But all spurd after fast, as they mote fly,
  To reskew her from shamefull villany.
  The Prince and *Guyon* equally byliue
  Her selfe pursewd, in hope to win thereby
  Most goodly meede, the fairest Dame aliue:
But after the foule foster *Timias* did striue.

19

The whiles faire *Britomart*, whose constant mind,
  Would not so lightly follow beauties chace,
  Ne reckt of Ladies Loue, did stay behind,
  And them awayted there a certaine space,
  To weet if they would turne backe to that place:
  But when she saw them gone, she forward went,
  As lay her iourney, through that perlous Pace,
  With stedfast courage and stout hardiment;
Ne euill thing she fear'd, ne euill thing she ment.

suggests the wonder aroused by Florimell's beauty. The superstition about comets was common. **red**: predicted; interpreted. **importunes**: portends; suggesting the etymological sense, 'troublesome' (Lat. *importunus*). Hence 'portend what will prove to be grievous'. **drerihed**: disaster.

Stanza 17

1 **So as**: the comet's raging heat arouses the fire of love in Guyon and Arthur so that they join the Foster in pursuit of Florimell.
2 **Foster**: forester, a personification of the forest's violence; hence the repetition of **griesly** from 14.7. A parody of the Zephyrs in Botticelli's 'Birth of Venus' who blow the goddess from the sea towards the land: Florimell flees from the land towards the sea.
4 **tyreling**: tired.
7 **gorie**: pierced, and therefore bloody.
9 **clownish**: rough, belonging to a rustic. **bore speare**: associated with the wound of lust, from the story of Adonis wounded by the Boar; cf. II iii 29.1.

Stanza 18

1 Pointedly omitting the Palmer from the emotional tumult that follows.
2 **enuie**: hostility; also with the current sense.
gealosy: indignation; also with the current sense.
3 **auise**: consider.
5 **villany**: ill-usage.
6–8 This pursuit is 'beauties chace' (19.2) and the 'chace of beautie excellent' (iv 45.5). **byliue**: eagerly. **the fairest Dame aliue**: the stock description of Florimell, inherited from Una and Gloriana. Her literary analogue is Angelica, in Ariosto, *Orl. Fur.* i, whom Harington (1591) 63 identifies with Beauty. At viii 36.2, Florimell is named 'beautie'. See v 8.7*n*. The same description is applied to Britomart at ix 21.9.
9 **Timias**: Arthur's Squire, here first named. The name signifies 'honoured', 'dear'. His pursuit of the Foster rather than the Lady is explained later: he 'That Ladies loue [i.e. the love of Florimell] vnto his Lord forlent' (iv 47.2).

Stanza 19

2 The non-metaphorical use of **beauties chace** is acted out in Book II when Faunus sees the nymph: he 'Inflamed was to follow beauties chace, / And chaced her' (II ii 7.7–8); but, by Diana's intervention, the nymph remains 'chast' (9.7). Since Florimell is Beauty itself, the phrase is applied literally. There is the implied pun: one who is chaste is not chased.
3 **Ladies Loue**: the capital letters may point to the significance of Florimell's dramatic entrance: love is aroused by the sight of beauty. Those who pursue Florimell seek her love; cf. iv 47.2.
7 **perlous Pace**: perilous passage; cf. 'Pace Perelus' in Malory 308.
8 **stedfast** defines chaste love. It is applied to Florimell, v 8.5; Belphœbe, v 55.1; Amoret, vi 53.8; Psyche, vi 50.6; and Britomart, xii 2.9, 37.5. In Book IV it is used once to describe the eyes of Womanhood (x 49.7).
9 **ment**: 'intended' is a possible, but weak, sense. 'She did not intend to fear evil' is a possible reading. The contrast with Florimell is clear: Britomart is pure in thought while Florimell fears even Arthur who 'ment / To her no euill thought, nor euill deed' (iv 50.2–3).

Stanza 16

5 **a blazing starre**: a comet; its etymology, 'long-haired', is referred to in the next line. With the awakening to 'beauties chace' and 'Ladies Loue' (19.2–3) consequent to Florimell's appearance as a comet, cf. *S.C.* Dec. 55–60: Colin relates how the fire of love is stirred up by a comet.

7–9 Heninger (1960) 89 notes that the rarity of comets

20

At last as nigh out of the wood she came,
  A stately Castle farre away she spyde,
  To which her steps directly she did frame.
  That Castle was most goodly edifyde,
  And plaste for pleasure nigh that forrest syde:
  But faire before the gate a spatious plaine,
  Mantled with greene, it selfe did spredden wyde,
  On which she saw sixe knights, that did darraine
Fierce battell against one, with cruell might and maine.

21

Mainly they all attonce vpon him laid,
  And sore beset on euery side around,
  That nigh he breathlesse grew, yet nought dismaid,
  Ne euer to them yielded foot of ground
  All had he lost much bloud through many a wound,
  But stoutly dealt his blowes, and euery way
  To which he turned in his wrathfull stound,
  Made them recoile, and fly from dred decay,
That none of all the sixe before, him durst assay.

22

Like dastard Curres, that hauing at a bay
  The saluage beast embost in wearie chace,
  Dare not aduenture on the stubborne pray,
  Ne byte before, but rome from place to place,
  To get a snatch, when turned is his face.
  In such distresse and doubtfull ieopardy,
  When *Britomart* him saw, she ran a pace
  Vnto his reskew, and with earnest cry,
Bad those same sixe forbeare that single enimy.

23

But to her cry they list not lenden eare,
  Ne ought the more their mightie strokes surceasse,
  But gathering him round about more neare,
  Their direfull rancour rather did encreasse;
  Till that she rushing through the thickest preasse,
  Perforce disparted their compacted gyre,
  And soone compeld to hearken vnto peace:
  Tho gan she myldly of them to inquyre
The cause of their dissention and outrageous yre.

24

Whereto that single knight did answere frame;
  These sixe would me enforce by oddes of might,
  To chaunge my liefe, and loue another Dame,
  That death me liefer were, then such despight,
  So vnto wrong to yield my wrested right,
  For I loue one, the truest one on ground,
  Ne list me chaunge; she th'*Errant Damzell* hight,
  For whose deare sake full many a bitter stownd,
I haue endur'd, and tasted many a bloudy wound.

25

Certes (said she) then bene ye sixe to blame,
  To weene your wrong by force to iustifie:
  For knight to leaue his Ladie were great shame,
  That faithfull is, and better were to die.
  All losse is lesse, and lesse the infamie,
  Then losse of loue to him, that loues but one;
  Ne may loue be compeld by maisterie;
  For soone as maisterie comes, sweet loue anone
Taketh his nimble wings, and soone away is gone.

Stanza 20

3 **frame**: direct.
4 **edifyde**: built.
5–7 Explains the allegorical setting. The **spatious plaine,** / **Mantled with greene** is related to the 'spacious plaine . . . / Mantled with greene' of the Bower of Bliss (II xii 50.2–4).
8 **darraine**: wage.

Stanza 21

1 **Mainly**: mightily; with main.
7 **stound**: storm, referring here to his wrathful mood; cf. 24.8.
8 **decay**: death.
9 **before**: i.e. in front of him; cf. 22.4.   **assay**: assail.

Stanza 22

1 **at a bay**: at bay, the close quarters at which a hunted animal turns to face its pursuers.
2 **embost**: driven to extremity; exhausted.
3 **stubborne**: fierce.
6 **doubtfull**: dread.
7 **a pace**: quickly.
9 **forbeare**: leave alone.

Stanza 23

2 **surceasse**: stop.
6 **Perforce**: forcibly.   **compacted gyre**: the action of wheeling around a foe.

Stanza 24

2 **oddes**: advantage.
3 **liefe**: beloved.
4 **liefer**: preferable. The Red Cross Knight's stand anticipates Amoret's suffering in the house of Busirane because she will not forsake Scudamour.
6–7 **one** names Una; **truest one** names her Truth. She is called 'the *Errant damozell*' at II i 19.8. Britomart imitates Una who wandered to seek her knight.
8 **stownd**: time of peril.

Stanza 25

7 **maisterie**: superior force. Cf. Duessa's parody of this claim at IV i 46.8–9 and Arthur's application of it at IV ix 37.6–8. S. imitates Chaucer, *Franklin's Tale*: 'Love wol nat been constreyned by maistrye. / Whan maistrie comth, the God of Love anon / Beteth his wynges, and farewel, he is gon!' (764–6); see Tilley (1950) L 499. The theme of 'maisterie' in the marriage group of the *Canterbury Tales* unifies Books III and IV and extends into Book V; see Hamilton (1961) 180–6. There is the dramatic irony here that the lines are spoken by one in whom love holds the **maisterie**.

309

26

Then spake one of those sixe, There dwelleth here
　Within this castle wall a Ladie faire,
　Whose soueraine beautie hath no liuing pere,
　Thereto so bounteous and so debonaire,
　That neuer any mote with her compaire.
　She hath ordaind this law, which we approue,
　That euery knight, which doth this way repaire,
　In case he haue no Ladie, nor no loue,
Shall doe vnto her seruice neuer to remoue.

27

But if he haue a Ladie or a Loue,
　Then must he her forgoe with foule defame,
　Or else with vs by dint of sword approue,
　That she is fairer, then our fairest Dame,
　As did this knight, before ye hither came.
　Perdie (said *Britomart*) the choise is hard:
　But what reward had he, that ouercame?
　He should aduaunced be to high regard,
(Said they) and haue our Ladies loue for his reward.

28

Therefore a read Sir, if thou haue a loue.
　Loue haue I sure, (quoth she) but Lady none;
　Yet will I not fro mine owne loue remoue,
　Ne to your Lady will I seruice done,
　But wreake your wrongs wrought to this knight alone,
　And proue his cause.　With that her mortall speare
　She mightily auentred towards one,
　And downe him smot, ere well aware he weare,
Then to the next she rode, and downe the next did beare.

29

Ne did she stay, till three on ground she layd,
　That none of them himselfe could reare againe;
　The fourth was by that other knight dismayd,
　All were he wearie of his former paine,
　That now there do but two of sixe remaine;
　Which two did yield, before she did them smight.
　Ah (said she then) now may ye all see plaine,
　That truth is strong, and trew loue most of might,
That for his trusty seruaunts doth so strongly fight.

30

Too well we see, (said they) and proue too well
　Our faulty weaknesse, and your matchlesse might:
　For thy, faire Sir, yours be the Damozell,
　Which by her owne law to your lot doth light,
　And we your liege men faith vnto you plight.
　So vnderneath her feet their swords they mard,
　And after her besought, well as they might,
　To enter in, and reape the dew reward:
She graunted, and then in they all together far'd.

31

Long were it to describe the goodly frame,
　And stately port of *Castle Ioyeous*,
　(For so that Castle hight by commune name)
　Where they were entertaind with curteous
　And comely glee of many gracious
　Faire Ladies, and of many a gentle knight,
　Who through a Chamber long and spacious,
　Eftsoones them brought vnto their Ladies sight,
That of them cleeped was the *Lady of delight*.

Stanza 26
4　**debonaire**: affable, generous in her favours, as **bounteous** suggests.
6　**approue**: make good, uphold.

Stanza 27
2　**defame**: infamy, which follows whether he yields or not.
3　**approue**: prove, confirm; close to the legal sense at 26.6. The same legal imagery as in 'proue' (28.6, 30.1).
5　Apparently the Red Cross Knight seeks to prove by force of arms that Una is the fairest; if he should win, however, he gains Malecasta's love. Cf. his defeat of Sansfoy by which he gains Duessa's love, I ii 20f.
9　Through Malecasta's lust, the law of Castle Joyeous enforces infidelity.

Stanza 28
1　**a read**: tell.
2　Britomart turns their terms (27.1–2) into a riddle.
5　**alone**: i.e. 'single' (22.9).
7　**auentred**: aimed by setting in its rest (sugg. by the context); or a variant of 'afeutre', to set in the rest (sugg. by *OED*); 'thrust forward' is suggested by its use at IV iii 9.1; cf. Ital. *aventare*: 'to dart or cast with violence' (Florio).
8　**aware**: on his guard; cf. 6.6.

Stanza 29
3　**dismayd**: defeated.
8　**truth**: playing on 'troth'.　**truth is strong**: proverbial (C. G. Smith, 1970, 792); cf. I xii 28.7.

Stanza 30
2　**faulty weaknesse**: i.e. weakness because they are at fault, as Britomart infers.
3　**For thy**: therefore.
6　**mard**: damaged, spoiled, although the sense is strained. They debased (the honour of) their swords by placing them under her feet, in a vow of loyalty which they do not mean to keep; cf. the action at V iv 16.7–8.

Stanza 31
1　**frame**: structure.
2　**port**: appearance; or style of living within the Castle. **Castle Ioyeous**: cf. the *Palazzo Gioioso* in Boiardo, *Orlando Innamorato* (1495) I viii 1–14 (cited Blanchard, *Var*. iii 208). The theme of adultery suggests Launcelot's 'Joyous Gard' in Malory.
4–6　A rare example of double run-on lines; perhaps to emphasize the excessive courtliness.　**glee**: entertainment.
9　**the Lady of delight**: later called Malecasta; see 57.4*n*.

32

But for to tell the sumptuous aray
  Of that great chamber, should be labour lost:
  For liuing wit, I weene, cannot display
  The royall riches and exceeding cost,
  Of euery pillour and of euery post;
  Which all of purest bullion framed were,
  And with great pearles and pretious stones embost,
That the bright glister of their beames cleare
Did sparckle forth great light, and glorious did appeare.

33

These straunger knights through passing, forth were led
  Into an inner rowme, whose royaltee
  And rich purueyance might vneath be red;
  Mote Princes place beseeme so deckt to bee.
  Which stately manner when as they did see,
  The image of superfluous riotize,
  Exceeding much the state of meane degree,
They greatly wondred, whence so sumptuous guize
Might be maintaynd, and each gan diuersely deuize.

34

The wals were round about apparelled
  With costly clothes of *Arras* and of *Toure*,
  In which with cunning hand was pourtrahed
  The loue of *Venus* and her Paramoure
  The faire *Adonis*, turned to a flowre,
  A worke of rare deuice, and wondrous wit.
  First did it shew the bitter balefull stowre,
Which her assayd with many a feruent fit,
When first her tender hart was with his beautie smit.

35

Then with what sleights and sweet allurements she
  Entyst the Boy, as well that art she knew,
  And wooed him her Paramoure to be;
  Now making girlonds of each flowre that grew,
  To crowne his golden lockes with honour dew;
  Now leading him into a secret shade
  From his Beauperes, and from bright heauens vew,
Where him to sleepe she gently would perswade,
Or bathe him in a fountaine by some couert glade.

36

And whilst he slept, she ouer him would spred
  Her mantle, colour'd like the starry skyes,
  And her soft arme lay vnderneath his hed,
  And with ambrosiall kisses bathe his eyes;
  And whilest he bath'd, with her two crafty spyes,
  She secretly would search each daintie lim,
  And throw into the well sweet Rosemaryes,
And fragrant violets, and Pances trim,
And euer with sweet Nectar she did sprinkle him.

3   **purueyance**: furnishings; cf. the 'rich purueyance' of
the house of Busirane (xi 53.9).   **vneath be red**: hardly
be told.
6   **superfluous**: immoderate, intemperate.   **riotize**:
extravagance. Cf. the 'wanton Riotise' (I v 46.5) in the house
of Pride and esp. the 'Consuming *Riotise*' in Cupid's masque
(xii 25.7).
7   **meane**: moderate.
8   **guize**: conduct; fashion.
9   **deuize**: guess.

Stanzas 34–38
The myth of Venus and Adonis was known chiefly from Ovid,
Met. x 519–739, and Comes V xvi. On its interpretation, see
vi 46–49*n*. Particularly relevant is the association of the boar
with lust. The four panels of the tapestry are carefully balanced:
(*a*) 34.7–9: the meeting of Venus and Adonis. (*b*) 35–37: three
stanzas on her art of love. (His sleep and bathing, 35.8–9, are
described separately, 36.1–4, 5–8, and then together, 36.9.)
(*c*) 38.1–6: his wounding and death. (*d*) 38.7–9: his transformation. The myth provides the pattern for the love stories
that follow in Book III. It is acted out in Malecasta's wooing of
Britomart; see Edwards (1958) 225f. Thompson (1972)
examines the rhetorical devices by which S. seeks to arouse
wonder in the reader.

Stanza 34
2   Cf. the 'goodly arras' in the house of Busirane, xi 28f.
3   **pourtrahed**: the etymological spelling gives the extra
syllable and rhyme.
6   Commenting upon the mysteries concealed in the myth.
deuice: design.   **wit**: skill.
7   **stowre**: time of turmoil.
8   **assayd**: assailed.

Stanza 35
1–2   The stress on **she** / **Entyst** suggests Venus's aggressive
wooing.   **sleights and sweet allurements** suggest a
reluctant Adonis.
4–9   Cf. the use of **girlonds, shade, bathe**, and **fountaine**
in Duessa's seduction of the Red Cross Knight (I vii 3–4)
and Acrasia's triumph over Verdant (II xii 72–73).   **shade**:
from Ovid, *Met*. x 555.
7   Note the careful balance in this line.   **Beauperes**:
companions; literally those who equal him in beauty or
hunting.
8   Edwards (1958) 243 notes that S. adds this detail to Ovid.

Stanza 36
2   Venus's garment hides Adonis from 'bright heauens vew'
(35.7) by covering him with the night sky. Cf. 'Venus' mantle
lined with stars' (*View* 50).
4   The antique custom of kissing the eyelids, still followed
by some.
5–6   and 35.9 suggest Salmacis and Hermaphroditus in Ovid,
Met. iv 285f, esp. 344–5. Cf. also Acrasia, II xii 73.1–2.
spyes: i.e. her eyes.
7–8   **Rosemaryes**: associated with remembrance.
fragrant violets: the *viola adorata*, the white violet; praised
by Bacon, *Of Gardens*, as the flower of sweetest smell;
associated with Venus, it has erotic connotations, perhaps of
languor.   **Pances**: the pansy, hearts-ease or love-in-idleness.

Stanza 32
6   **bullion**: solid gold or silver.

Stanza 33
2   **royaltee**: magnificence.

311

37

So did she steale his heedelesse hart away,
　　And ioyd his loue in secret vnespyde.
　　But for she saw him bent to cruell play,
　　To hunt the saluage beast in forrest wyde,
　　Dreadfull of daunger, that mote him betyde,
　　She oft and oft aduiz'd him to refraine
　　From chase of greater beasts, whose brutish pryde
Mote breede him scath vnwares: but all in vaine;
For who can shun the chaunce, that dest'ny doth ordaine?

38

Lo, where beyond he lyeth languishing,
　　Deadly engored of a great wild Bore,
　　And by his side the Goddesse groueling
　　Makes for him endlesse mone, and euermore
　　With her soft garment wipes away the gore,
　　Which staines his snowy skin with hatefull hew:
　　But when she saw no helpe might him restore,
　　Him to a dainty flowre she did transmew,
Which in that cloth was wrought, as if it liuely grew.

39

So was that chamber clad in goodly wize,
　　And round about it many beds were dight,
　　As whilome was the antique worldes guize,
　　Some for vntimely ease, some for delight,
　　As pleased them to vse, that vse it might:
　　And all was full of Damzels, and of Squires,
　　Dauncing and reueling both day and night,
　　And swimming deepe in sensuall desires,
And *Cupid* still emongst them kindled lustfull fires.

40

And all the while sweet Musicke did diuide
　　Her looser notes with *Lydian* harmony;
　　And all the while sweet birdes thereto applide
　　Their daintie layes and dulcet melody,
　　Ay caroling of loue and iollity,
　　That wonder was to heare their trim consort,
　　Which when those knights beheld, with scornefull eye,
　　They sdeigned such lasciuious disport,
And loath'd the loose demeanure of that wanton sort.

41

Thence they were brought to that great Ladies vew,
　　Whom they found sitting on a sumptuous bed,
　　That glistred all with gold and glorious shew,
　　As the proud *Persian* Queenes accustomed:
　　She seemd a woman of great bountihed,
　　And of rare beautie, sauing that askaunce
　　Her wanton eyes, ill signes of womanhed,
　　Did roll too lightly, and too often glaunce,
Without regard of grace, or comely amenaunce.

Stanza 37
2　Refutes Lewis (1936) 332 that this Venus, in contrast to
the Venus in the Garden of Adonis (vi 46.9), is a picture of lust
suspended, mere *skeptophilia*. See Alpers (1967) 374–7. There
is only one Venus in the poem: her appearance depends upon
the eye of the beholder.

5　**Dreadfull**: fearful.
8　**scath**: harm.

Stanza 38
The image of the wounded Adonis is the prototype of the
masculine figures in Book III; cf. Marinell (iv 16.9) and
Timias (v 26.5).
1　**beyond**: i.e. in a farther tapestry.　**languishing**:
growing faint; wasting away through desire.
2　**Deadly**: fatally.
3　**groueling**: lying prostrate.
8　**dainty flowre**: the anemone.　**transmew**: transform;
suggesting confinement in a mew or prison.
9　**liuely**: as a living thing.

Stanza 39
The pleasures associated with Venus: 'my delight is all in
ioyfulnesse, / In beds, in bowres, in banckets, and in feasts'
(vi 22.3–4).
2　**beds**: couches, chiefly for love-making.　**dight**:
arranged.
3　**guize**: custom.
4　**vntimely**: prob. referring to the daytime.
7–9　Alpers (1967) 47–8 concludes that S. uses commonplace
formulas which the reader does not seek to analyse. Yet note
the deliberate progression from narrative action to moral
comment, and finally to mythological description which wittily
'fixes' the courtiers in relation to the tapestries.

Stanza 40
1–2　**diuide**: execute divisions, i.e. to break a plain theme
into a number of melodic passages.　**looser notes**: too free
from restriction to the theme; too wanton; cf. the music in the
house of Pride, I v 17.7 and see *n*.　**Lydian harmony**: a
mode of Greek music condemned by Plato (*Rep.* iii 398e) and
so by the Renaissance, e.g. Guilpin, *Skialetheia* (1598) Satyre
Preludium 1–2: 'Fie on these *Lydian* tunes which blunt our
sprights / And turne our gallants to *Hermaphrodites*.'
6　**trim consort**: pleasing harmony; a well-balanced
instrumental ensemble, according to Hollander (1961) 112,
who notes the evil implicit in the union of natural singers and
artificial music-makers.
7　**Which** refers to all that they see and hear.
8　**sdeigned**: disdained (Ital. *sdegnare*).　**disport**:
entertainment.
9　**sort**: company.

Stanza 41
4　**Persian**: as Duessa (I ii 13.4) and Lucifera (I iv 7.6).
5　**bountihed**: generosity, liberal in bestowing her favours;
cf. 26.4. On the difference between lust's bounty and love's,
see 49.4, 8.
6　**askaunce**: sidelong; suggesting wanton guile; cf.
Mammon's glance, II vii 7.5 and see *n*.
7–9　Alluding to her name, Malecasta: casting lewd love-
glances; see 50.6–7, 57.4*n*. Upton (1758) cites 2 Pet. 2.14:
'Having eyes ful of adulterie, and that can not cease to sinne,
beguiling unstable soules.'
8　**lightly**] lightly *1609*; highly *1590, 1596*. Perhaps S.
followed his description of Lucifera: see I iv 7.2–7, 14.1.
9　**amenaunce**: noble bearing. Cf. Womanhood, IV x
49.5–9, and the bride in *Epith.* 236–7, 'That suffers not one
looke to glaunce awry'.

42

Long worke it were, and needlesse to deuize
   Their goodly entertainement and great glee:
   She caused them be led in curteous wize
   Into a bowre, disarmed for to bee,
   And cheared well with wine and spiceree:
   The *Redcrosse* Knight was soone disarmed there,
   But the braue Mayd would not disarmed bee,
   But onely vented vp her vmbriere,
And so did let her goodly visage to appere.

43

As when faire *Cynthia*, in darkesome night,
   Is in a noyous cloud enueloped,
   Where she may find the substaunce thin and light,
   Breakes forth her siluer beames, and her bright hed
   Discouers to the world discomfited;
   Of the poore traueller, that went astray,
   With thousand blessings she is heried;
   Such was the beautie and the shining ray,
With which faire *Britomart* gaue light vnto the day.

44

And eke those six, which lately with her fought,
   Now were disarmd, and did them selues present
   Vnto her vew, and company vnsoght;
   For they all seemed curteous and gent,
   And all sixe brethren, borne of one parent,
   Which had them traynd in all ciuilitee,
   And goodly taught to tilt and turnament;
   Now were they liegemen to this Lady free,
And her knights seruice ought, to hold of her in fee.

45

The first of them by name *Gardante* hight,
   A iolly person, and of comely vew;
   The second was *Parlante*, a bold knight,
   And next to him *Iocante* did ensew;
   Basciante did him selfe most curteous shew;
   But fierce *Bacchante* seemd too fell and keene;
   And yet in armes *Noctante* greater grew:
   All were faire knights, and goodly well beseene,
But to faire *Britomart* they all but shadowes beene.

46

For she was full of amiable grace,
   And manly terrour mixed therewithall,
   That as the one stird vp affections bace,
   So th'other did mens rash desires apall,
   And hold them backe, that would in errour fall;
   As he, that hath espide a vermeill Rose,
   To which sharpe thornes and breres the way forstall,
   Dare not for dread his hardy hand expose,
But wishing it far off, his idle wish doth lose.

Stanza 42
1   **deuize**: describe.
5   **wine and spiceree**: i.e. with spiced wine.
8   **vented vp her vmbriere**: lifted up her visor for air.

Stanza 43
Cf. the comet to which Florimell's hair is compared, 16.5–9.
Cf. ix 20.6–9. Britomart's relation to chastity makes the
comparison to the moon especially apt. Her lover's light is
compared to the sun, ii 24.6–7. This paired imagery continues
throughout their story. This is the first of four occasions on
which gazers are startled by the revelation of her beauty: cf.
ix 23, IV i 14, vi 19–20. Giamatti (1971) 17–31 analyses S.'s
use of this motif.
2   **noyous**: troublesome.
5   **discomfited**: disconcerted by the loss of light.
7   **heried**: praised.

Stanza 44
4   **gent**: noble.
6   **ciuilitee**: proper behaviour, politeness.
7   The two kinds of contest: the **tilt** between two mounted
knights with spears and the **turnament** among many knights
with spears and swords.
8–9   **liegemen**: stresses the feudal nature of Castle Joyeous
(cf. 30.5).   **free**: the stock epithet for a lady of noble birth
suggests both her liberality in offering her favours and the
bondage of her knights.   **ought**: did owe.   **to . . . fee**:
referring to her feudal possession of them and their obligation
to serve her.

Stanza 45
The names of these knights denote the rungs of the ladder of
lechery: gazing, conversing, courtly playing, formal kissing,
drunken revelling, and night's consummation of love. S.
reinterprets the traditional five stages (sight, conversation,
touching, kissing and copulating) and adds a sixth. See Fowler
(1959) and Friedman (1966). Since **Gardante** signifies loving
glances upon beauty, he himself is handsome (**iolly**). Glances
lead to boldness of seductive speech (Ital. **Parlante**), to
Iocante's 'courtly play' (56.9; from Ital. *giocare*, *giocante*), to
kissing (**Basciante**; see 56.8*n*) and finally to the intoxication of
desire by which lovers become fierce votaries of Bacchus.
Bacchante is **keene** as he is bold or fierce and sexually
excited; see Partridge (1947). The six stages of love are acted
out in Malecasta's courtship of Britomart.
8   **goodly well beseene**: of good appearance.
9   **shadowes**: ironic, since she loves a shadow, ii 44.3, 9.

Stanza 46
1–5   **amiable**: pleasing, as she arouses love (3); worthy to
be loved. Her **amiable grace** complements Artegall's
'Heroicke grace' (ii 24.9). Though Britomart arouses love in
others, her chastity prevents the pursuit which leads Florimell's
lovers into **errour**, i.e. wandering. Cf. the power of
Belphœbe's eyes, II iii 23.
7   **forstall**: obstruct.

47

Whom when the Lady saw so faire a wight,
  All ignoraunt of her contrary sex,
  (For she her weend a fresh and lusty knight)
  She greatly gan enamoured to wex,
  And with vaine thoughts her falsed fancy vex:
  Her fickle hart conceiued hasty fire,
  Like sparkes of fire, which fall in sclender flex,
  That shortly brent into extreme desire,
And ransackt all her veines with passion entire.

48

Eftsoones she grew to great impatience
  And into termes of open outrage brust,
  That plaine discouered her incontinence,
  Ne reckt she, who her meaning did mistrust;
  For she was giuen all to fleshly lust,
  And poured forth in sensuall delight,
  That all regard of shame she had discust,
  And meet respect of honour put to flight:
So shamelesse beauty soone becomes a loathly sight.

49

Faire Ladies, that to loue captiued arre,
  And chaste desires do nourish in your mind,
  Let not her fault your sweet affections marre,
  Ne blot the bounty of all womankind;
  'Mongst thousands good one wanton Dame to find:
  Emongst the Roses grow some wicked weeds;
  For this was not to loue, but lust inclind;
  For loue does alwayes bring forth bounteous deeds,
And in each gentle hart desire of honour breeds.

50

Nought so of loue this looser Dame did skill,
  But as a coale to kindle fleshly flame,
  Giuing the bridle to her wanton will,
  And treading vnder foote her honest name:
  Such loue is hate, and such desire is shame.
  Still did she roue at her with crafty glaunce
  Of her false eyes, that at her hart did ayme,
  And told her meaning in her countenaunce;
But Britomart dissembled it with ignoraunce.

51

Supper was shortly dight and downe they sat,
  Where they were serued with all sumptuous fare,
  Whiles fruitfull Ceres, and Lyæus fat
  Pourd out their plenty, without spight or spare:
  Nought wanted there, that dainty was and rare;
  And aye the cups their bancks did ouerflow,
  And aye betweene the cups, she did prepare
  Way to her loue, and secret darts did throw;
But Britomart would not such guilfull message know.

52

So when they slaked had the feruent heat
  Of appetite with meates of euery sort,
  The Lady did faire Britomart entreat,
  Her to disarme, and with delightfull sport
  To loose her warlike limbs and strong effort,
  But when she mote not thereunto be wonne,
  (For she her sexe vnder that straunge purport
  Did vse to hide, and plaine apparaunce shonne:)
In plainer wise to tell her grieuaunce she begonne.

Stanza 47
3   lusty: vigorous; but also (she hopes) lustful.
5   fancy: the deceiving power of the imagination which here produces deceiving images of love. See I ii 30.3.
9   entire: inward, as an 'in burning fire' (53.3); or as her passion entirely possesses her.

Stanza 48
Elaborating her state as Malecasta, 'evilly chaste'.
2   termes: state, condition.   outrage: intemperance, the 'strong extremitie' (53.9) of passion.
4   mistrust: suspect.
6   poured forth: in the sexual sense; see I vii 7.2n.
7   discust: shaken off.

Stanza 49
This apology also prefaces the story of Hellenore, ix 1–2.
4   bounty: goodness.
8–9   S.'s distinction between love and lust is based upon the kind of action to which love leads; cf. ii 7.1–5. The same definition is found at iii 1.7–9, v 1.8–9; cf. IV Pr. 2.6–9.
bounteous: full of goodness, virtuous.

Stanza 50
1   looser: too loose.   skill: i.e. have knowledge.
2   fleshly flame defines Pyrochles's intemperance in Book II; applied to sexual lust in Book III.
6–7   Alluding to her name; cf. 41.7–9 and see 57.4n.
roue: the sense, 'shoot an arrow at a mark selected at pleasure', fits the amatory situation.   crafty glaunce: cf. Venus's 'crafty spyes' (36.5). Malecasta acts out Venus's role as the female wooer.

Stanza 51
1   dight: prepared.
3   Ceres signifies food, Lyæus wine. Upton (1758) cites the proverb: sine Cerere et Baccho friget Venus; see Tilley (1950) C 211. S. may borrow from Virgil, Ciris 229–30.
4   spight or spare: grudging or frugality.
5   dainty: precious.

Stanza 52
1–5   Malecasta's double request confuses the syntax, befitting her confused state: she asks Britomart to unloose her warlike limbs by disarming and to relax her strong effort, or power, by turning to delightfull sport.   loose suggests moral laxity.
7   purport: i.e. her appearance as it expresses her intent.

53

And all attonce discouered her desire
 With sighes, and sobs, and plaints, and piteous griefe,
 The outward sparkes of her in burning fire;
 Which spent in vaine, at last she told her briefe,
 That but if she did lend her short reliefe,
 And do her comfort, she mote algates dye.
 But the chaste damzell, that had neuer priefe
 Of such malengine and fine forgerie,
Did easily beleeue her strong extremitie.

54

Full easie was for her to haue beliefe,
 Who by self-feeling of her feeble sexe,
 And by long triall of the inward griefe,
 Wherewith imperious loue her hart did vexe,
 Could iudge what paines do louing harts perplexe.
 Who meanes no guile, be guiled soonest shall,
 And to faire semblaunce doth light faith annexe;
 The bird, that knowes not the false fowlers call,
Into his hidden net full easily doth fall.

55

For thy she would not in discourteise wise,
 Scorne the faire offer of good will profest;
 For great rebuke it is, loue to despise,
 Or rudely sdeigne a gentle harts request;
 But with faire countenaunce, as beseemed best,
 Her entertaynd; nath'lesse she inly deemd
 Her loue too light, to wooe a wandring guest:
 Which she misconstruing, thereby esteemd
That from like inward fire that outward smoke had steemd.

56

Therewith a while she her flit fancy fed,
 Till she mote winne fit time for her desire,
 But yet her wound still inward freshly bled,
 And through her bones the false instilled fire
 Did spred it selfe, and venime close inspire.
 Tho were the tables taken all away,
 And euery knight, and euery gentle Squire
 Gan choose his dame with *Basciomani* gay,
With whom he meant to make his sport and courtly play.

57

Some fell to daunce, some fell to hazardry,
 Some to make loue, some to make meriment,
 As diuerse wits to diuers things apply;
 And all the while faire *Malecasta* bent
 Her crafty engins to her close intent.
 By this th'eternall lampes, wherewith high *Ioue*
 Doth light the lower world, were halfe yspent,
 And the moist daughters of huge *Atlas* stroue
Into the *Ocean* deepe to driue their weary droue.

58

High time it seemed then for euery wight
 Them to betake vnto their kindly rest;
 Eftsoones long waxen torches weren light,
 Vnto their bowres to guiden euery guest:
 Tho when the Britonesse saw all the rest
 Auoided quite, she gan her selfe despoile,
 And safe commit to her soft fethered nest,
 Where through long watch, and late dayes weary toile,
She soundly slept, and carefull thoughts did quite assoile.

Stanza 53

1 **discouered**: revealed, exhibited.
5 **but if**: unless.
6 **algates**: otherwise.
7 **priefe**: experience.
8 **malengine**: deceit. Personified at V ix 5. **fine forgerie**: consummate deception. Cf. Britomart's 'inward griefe' (54.3) and her love, ii 5. Her innocence leads to her deception.

Stanza 54

4 **vexe**: trouble, afflict.
5 **perplexe**: torment.
7 **light**: also ready. **annexe**: join; i.e. one who believes in appearances too readily is soonest beguiled, as she has fallen in love with Artegall's 'semblant' (ii 38.1–5).

Stanza 55

1 **For thy**: accordingly.
3–4 On chastity and courtesy, see v 55. **rebuke**: shame. **sdeigne**: disdain.
5 **faire countenaunce**: courteous behaviour.

Stanza 56

1 **flit**: changing.
4–5 Cf. Cupid's 'poysned arrow, / That wounds the life, and wastes the inmost marrow' (*H.B.* 62–3). **close**: secretly.
8 **Basciomani**: from the phrase, *bascio le mani*.
9 **sport**: amorous dalliance or intercourse.

Stanza 57

1 **hazardry**: dicing.
4 **Malecasta**: now named when her nature is fully revealed. She is evilly unchaste: Lat. *malus* (wicked, lewd) + *castus* (chaste). Her name refers also to the lewd casting of her love on any stranger, and to her lewd loving glances; see 41.7–9*n*. 'cast': artifice, trick (*OED* 24) is relevant to her nature. Britomart also loves a stranger, but she is constant to him.
5 **engins**: wiles. **close intent**: secret purpose.
6–9 **the moist daughters**: the Hyades or rainy ones. 'They . . . rayse stormes and wyndes. They goe downe the fourtenthe Calendes of Maye. Poetes name them the daughters of Atlas' (Cooper, 1565). Fowler (1964) 145–6 uses this *chronographia* to fix the date of the present episode. Since the Hyades set at midnight on or about the vernal equinox in the latitudes of Northern Europe around the date 1590, one zodiacal house is Pisces which is associated with Venus: 'The moist sign Pisces and the rain-bearing constellation Hyades . . . fitly usher in a book which deals with the generative power of Venus.' It is midnight, the time when Britomart is tested again in the house of Busirane: see xii 2.7*n*.

Stanza 58

2 **kindly**: natural, owing to nature.
6 **Auoided**: retired. **despoile**: undress. Despoiling of herself leads to her wounding.
7 Contrasts with her invincible masculine role when armed.
9 **assoile**: dispel, set herself free. Loosening her armour leads to a loosening of thoughts for her care.

59

Now whenas all the world in silence deepe
   Yshrowded was, and euery mortall wight
   Was drowned in the depth of deadly sleepe,
   Faire *Malecasta*, whose engrieued spright
   Could find no rest in such perplexed plight,
   Lightly arose out of her wearie bed,
   And vnder the blacke vele of guilty Night,
   Her with a scarlot mantle couered,
That was with gold and Ermines faire enueloped.

60

Then panting soft, and trembling euerie ioynt,
   Her fearfull feete towards the bowre she moued;
   Where she for secret purpose did appoynt
   To lodge the warlike mayd vnwisely loued,
   And to her bed approching, first she prooued,
   Whether she slept or wakt, with her soft hand
   She softly felt, if any member mooued,
   And lent her wary eare to vnderstand,
If any puffe of breath, or signe of sence she fond.

61

Which whenas none she fond, with easie shift,
   For feare least her vnwares she should abrayd,
   Th'embroderd quilt she lightly vp did lift,
   And by her side her selfe she softly layd,
   Of euery finest fingers touch affrayd;
   Ne any noise she made, ne word she spake,
   But inly sigh'd. At last the royall Mayd
   Out of her quiet slomber did awake,
And chaungd her weary side, the better ease to take.

62

Where feeling one close couched by her side,
   She lightly lept out of her filed bed,
   And to her weapon ran, in minde to gride
   The loathed leachour. But the Dame halfe ded
   Through suddein feare and ghastly drerihed,
   Did shrieke alowd, that through the house it rong,
   And the whole family therewith adred,
   Rashly out of their rouzed couches sprong,
And to the troubled chamber all in armes did throng.

63

And those six Knights that Ladies Champions,
   And eke the *Redcrosse* knight ran to the stownd,
   Halfe armd and halfe vnarmd, with them attons:
   Where when confusedly they came, they fownd
   Their Lady lying on the sencelesse grownd;
   On th'other side, they saw the warlike Mayd
   All in her snow-white smocke, with locks vnbownd,
   Threatning the point of her auenging blade,
That with so troublous terrour they were all dismayde.

64

About their Lady first they flockt arownd,
   Whom hauing laid in comfortable couch,
   Shortly they reard out of her frosen swownd;
   And afterwards they gan with fowle reproch
   To stirre vp strife, and troublous contecke broch:
   But by ensample of the last dayes losse,
   None of them rashly durst to her approch,
   Ne in so glorious spoile themselues embosse;
Her succourd eke the Champion of the bloudy Crosse.

65

But one of those six knights, *Gardante* hight,
   Drew out a deadly bow and arrow keene,
   Which forth he sent with felonous despight,
   And fell intent against the virgin sheene:
   The mortall steele stayd not, till it was seene
   To gore her side, yet was the wound not deepe,
   But lightly rased her soft silken skin,
   That drops of purple bloud thereout did weepe,
Which did her lilly smock with staines of vermeil steepe.

Stanza 59
6   **Lightly**: quickly; also unchastely; cf. the opposing act at 62.2.
7–9   Malecasta's association with covering **Night** 'answers' Britomart's association with light in darkness, 43. The ermine, a traditional emblem of chastity, was also associated with lust; see Alciati (1581) Emblem 79 and *n* on 'Ermilin' (ii 25.7–9). In *S.C.* Apr. 57–8, the virgin Eliza is clad 'in Scarlot like a mayden Queene, / And Ermines white'.

Stanza 60
5   **prooued**: tested.
7   **softly**: also describes Venus (36.3, 38.5); cf. Britomart's 'soft silken skin' (65.7).
8   **wary**] weary *1590*, *1596* is supported by Collier (1862): she would be weary of listening.

Stanza 61
1   **shift**: change of position; movement.
2   **abrayd**: arouse, startle.

Stanza 62
2   Cf. 59.6 and ii 30.3. **lightly**: swiftly. **filed**: defiled.
3–4   **gride**: pierce through; cf. love's wound at ii 37.8–9. Britomart is as deceived as Malecasta.
5   **ghastly drerihed**: fearful terror.
8   **Rashly**: hastily.

Stanza 63
2   **stownd**: uproar; place.
3   **attons**: together.

Stanza 64
5   **contecke**: discord.
8   **embosse**: cover, decorate; i.e. none tries to possess her as his spoil or booty.
9   Distinguishes him from 'that Ladies Champions' (63.1).

Stanza 65
3   **felonous**: fierce, cruel.
4   **sheene**: beautiful, shining; cf. 43.8.
5–9   This token wound manifests her inner wounding (cf. ii 39.1–6) by the sight of Artegall, mentioned earlier (8.9). Hence **Gardante** (1) wounds her; see V vii 5.8–9*n*. The gored side is a sexual wound; cf. the gore which stains Adonis's snowy skin (38.5–6) and Britomart's wounding by Busirane, xii 33.4–5. **rased**: cut, scratched.

66

Wherewith enrag'd she fiercely at them flew,
　And with her flaming sword about her layd,
　That none of them foule mischiefe could eschew,
　But with her dreadfull strokes were all dismayd:
　Here, there, and euery where about her swayd
　Her wrathfull steele, that none mote it abide;
　And eke the *Redcrosse* knight gaue her good aid,
　Ay ioyning foot to foot, and side to side,
That in short space their foes they haue quite terrifide.

67

Tho whenas all were put to shamefull flight,
　The noble *Britomartis* her arayd,
　And her bright armes about her body dight:
　For nothing would she lenger there be stayd,
　Where so loose life, and so vngentle trade
　Was vsd of Knights and Ladies seeming gent:
　So earely ere the grosse Earthes gryesy shade
　Was all disperst out of the firmament,
They tooke their steeds, and forth vpon their iourney went.

Cant. II.

The *Redcrosse* knight to *Britomart*
describeth *Artegall*:
The wondrous myrrhour, by which she
in loue with him did fall.

1

HEre haue I cause, in men iust blame to find,
　That in their proper prayse too partiall bee,
And not indifferent to woman kind,
To whom no share in armes and cheualrie
They do impart, ne maken memorie
Of their braue gestes and prowesse martiall;
Scarse do they spare to one or two or three,
Rowme in their writs; yet the same writing small
Does all their deeds deface, and dims their glories all.

2

But by record of antique times I find,
　That women wont in warres to beare most sway,
And to all great exploits them selues inclind:
Of which they still the girlond bore away,
Till enuious Men fearing their rules decay,
Gan coyne streight lawes to curb their liberty;
Yet sith they warlike armes haue layd away,
They haue exceld in artes and pollicy,
That now we foolish men that prayse gin eke t'enuy.

3

Of warlike puissaunce in ages spent,
　Be thou faire *Britomart*, whose prayse I write,
But of all wisedome be thou precedent,
O soueraigne Queene, whose prayse I would endite,
Endite I would as dewtie doth excite;
But ah my rimes too rude and rugged arre,
When in so high an obiect they do lite,
And striuing, fit to make, I feare do marre:
Thy selfe thy prayses tell, and make them knowen farre.

4

She trauelling with *Guyon* by the way,
　Of sundry things faire purpose gan to find,
　T'abridg their iourney long, and lingring day;
　Mongst which it fell into that Faeries mind,
　To aske this Briton Mayd, what vncouth wind,
　Brought her into those parts, and what inquest
　Made her dissemble her disguised kind:
　Faire Lady she him seemd, like Lady drest,
But fairest knight aliue, when armed was her brest.

Stanza 66

3　**mischiefe**: harm, evil.　**eschew**: escape.
5　**swayd**: swung.

Stanza 67

5　**vngentle trade**: discourteous conduct, not befitting those
of gentle birth.
7　**gryesy**: grey; horrible, being grey.

Canto ii

Stanza 1

2　**proper**: own.
3　**indifferent**: just.
8　**the same writing small**: i.e. the deeds of a few women
although briefly recorded.
9　**deface**: outshine by contrast.

Stanza 2

4　**still**: always.
6　**streight**: strict.
8　**pollicy**: administration of public affairs; culture,
civilization.

Stanza 3

1–3　**Of warlike puissaunce ... precedent**: i.e. Britomart,
be thou **precedent of warlike puissaunce**.　**precedent**:
pattern, model; president.
8　**fit to make**: i.e. to compose fitting verses.

Stanza 4

1　**Guyon**: an error for Red Cross; given correctly at 16.8.
Faeries mind (4) fits Guyon but applies also to the Red Cross
Knight who is known as 'a Faeries sonne' (I x 64.7).
2　**purpose**: conversation.
5–6　Proverbial (C. G. Smith, 1970, 852) but applies to her
passion-driven state; cf. iv 10.
6　**inquest**: quest. The form suggests an inner quest,
referring to her love and her inner questioning.
7　**kind**: sex.

5

Thereat she sighing softly, had no powre
    To speake a while, ne ready answere make,
    But with hart-thrilling throbs and bitter stowre,
    As if she had a feuer fit, did quake,
    And euery daintie limbe with horrour shake;
    And euer and anone the rosy red,
    Flasht through her face, as it had been a flake
    Of lightning, through bright heauen fulmined;
At last the passion past she thus him answered.

6

Faire Sir, I let you weete, that from the howre
    I taken was from nourses tender pap,
    I haue beene trained vp in warlike stowre,
    To tossen speare and shield, and to affrap
    The warlike ryder to his most mishap;
    Sithence I loathed haue my life to lead,
    As Ladies wont, in pleasures wanton lap,
    To finger the fine needle and nyce thread;
Me leuer were with point of foemans speare be dead.

7

All my delight on deedes of armes is set,
    To hunt out perils and aduentures hard,
    By sea, by land, where so they may be met,
    Onely for honour and for high regard,
    Without respect of richesse or reward.
    For such intent into these parts I came,
    Withouten compasse, or withouten card,
    Far fro my natiue soyle, that is by name
The greater *Britaine*, here to seeke for prayse and fame.

8

Fame blazed hath, that here in Faery lond
    Do many famous Knightes and Ladies wonne,
    And many straunge aduentures to be fond,
    Of which great worth and worship may be wonne;
    Which I to proue, this voyage haue begonne.
    But mote I weet of you, right curteous knight,
    Tydings of one, that hath vnto me donne
    Late foule dishonour and reprochfull spight,
The which I seeke to wreake, and *Arthegall* he hight.

9

The word gone out, she backe againe would call,
    As her repenting so to haue missayd,
    But that he it vp-taking ere the fall,
    Her shortly answered; Faire martiall Mayd
    Certes ye misauised beene, t'vpbrayd
    A gentle knight with so vnknightly blame:
    For weet ye well of all, that euer playd
    At tilt or tourney, or like warlike game,
The noble *Arthegall* hath euer borne the name.

10

For thy great wonder were it, if such shame
    Should euer enter in his bounteous thought,
    Or euer do, that mote deseruen blame:
    The noble courage neuer weeneth ought,
    That may vnworthy of it selfe be thought.
    Therefore, faire Damzell, be ye well aware,
    Least that too farre ye haue your sorrow sought:
    You and your countrey both I wish welfare,
And honour both; for each of other worthy are.

Stanza 5
Cf. Malecasta's confession of love, i 53.
3 **stowre**: convulsion; inner emotional struggle, in contrast
to her outward 'warlike stowre' (6.3) before she fell in love;
cf. Venus's 'bitter balefull stowre' (i 34.7).
7 **flake**: flash.
8 **fulmined**: sent forth, flashed out.

Stanza 6
4 **tossen**: brandish.   **affrap**: strike down.
5 **mishap**: misfortune.
6 **Sithence**: ever since.
8 Cf. Tasso's Amazon, Clorinda: 'Her lofty hand would of
itself refuse / To touch the dainty needle, or nice thread'
(*Ger. Lib.* ii 39, trans. Fairfax) and Virgil's Camilla, *Aen.* vii
805–7.   **nyce**: thin.
9 **Me leuer were**: I had rather.

Stanza 7
7 When Guyon encounters Mammon, he is compared to a
mariner sailing with card and compass (II vii 1–2). Britomart is
not so complete within herself; cf. iv 9.6–9.
9 **greater Britaine**: Wales rather than England; cf. 'your
countrey' (10.8).

Stanza 8
2 **wonne**: dwell.
4 **worth and worship**: paralleling 'honour and . . . high
regard' (7.4).   **worth** signifies what is truly valuable,
'honour'; **worship**: renown.
6–9 At 12.6–9 the accusation of rape is more overt. Her
story is as false and slanderous as Duessa's which deceives
Guyon at II i; yet with respect to her earlier inviolate state,
what she says is true. On **Arthegall**, see iii 26.2*n*.

Stanza 9
2 **missayd**: spoken abusively.
3 **ere the fall**: before the lowering of her voice at the end of
her speech; or before she had finished speaking.
4 **martiall Mayd**: see i 8.6*n*. The term combines the roles
of Diana (or Venus) and Mars.
5 **misauised**: wrongly informed.
8 **tilt or tourney**: see i 44.7*n*.
9 **borne the name**: had a reputation (presumably of
honour); or has always been worthy of his name.

Stanza 10
1 **For thy**: therefore.
2 **bounteous thought**: valiant, virtuous mind.
4–5 **courage**: nature, mind.   **weeneth**: thinks (as applied
to Artegall); suspects (in rebuke of Britomart).
6–9 Cf. his benediction to Guyon, II i 33.6–9. He speaks
as patron saint of England.   **aware**: vigilant. Advice lost on
Britomart who has no defence against her love for Artegall.
welfare: to fare well.

11

The royall Mayd woxe inly wondrous glad,
  To heare her Loue so highly magnifide,
  And ioyd that euer she affixed had,
  Her hart on knight so goodly glorifide,
  How euer finely she it faind to hide:
  The louing mother, that nine monethes did beare,
  In the deare closet of her painefull side,
  Her tender babe, it seeing safe appeare,
Doth not so much reioyce, as she reioyced theare.

12

But to occasion him to further talke,
  To feed her humour with his pleasing stile,
  Her list in strifull termes with him to balke,
  And thus replide, How euer, Sir, ye file
  Your curteous tongue, his prayses to compile,
  It ill beseemes a knight of gentle sort,
  Such as ye haue him boasted, to beguile
  A simple mayd, and worke so haynous tort,
In shame of knighthood, as I largely can report.

13

Let be therefore my vengeaunce to disswade,
  And read, where I that faytour false may find.
  Ah, but if reason faire might you perswade,
  To slake your wrath, and mollifie your mind,
  (Said he) perhaps ye should it better find:
  For hardy thing it is, to weene by might,
  That man to hard conditions to bind,
  Or euer hope to match in equall fight,
Whose prowesse paragon saw neuer liuing wight.

14

Ne soothlich is it easie for to read,
  Where now on earth, or how he may be found;
  For he ne wonneth in one certaine stead,
  But restlesse walketh all the world around,
  Ay doing things, that to his fame redound,
  Defending Ladies cause, and Orphans right,
  Where so he heares, that any doth confound
  Them comfortlesse, through tyranny or might;
So is his soueraine honour raisde to heauens hight.

15

His feeling words her feeble sence much pleased,
  And softly sunck into her molten hart;
  Hart that is inly hurt, is greatly eased
  With hope of thing, that may allegge his smart;
  For pleasing words are like to Magick art,
  That doth the charmed Snake in slomber lay:
  Such secret ease felt gentle *Britomart*,
  Yet list the same efforce with faind gainesay;
So dischord oft in Musick makes the sweeter lay.

16

And said, Sir knight, these idle termes forbeare,
  And sith it is vneath to find his haunt,
  Tell me some markes, by which he may appeare,
  If chaunce I him encounter parauaunt;
  For perdie one shall other slay, or daunt:
  What shape, what shield, what armes, what steed, what sted,
  And what so else his person most may vaunt?
  All which the *Redcrosse* knight to point ared,
And him in euery part before her fashioned.

Stanza 11
2 magnifide: extolled.
5 finely: cunningly.
6–9 Cf. John 16.21.   theare: i.e. on that occasion.

Stanza 12
3 balke: bandy words.
5 compile: heap up.
8 so haynous tort: such wicked harm or torment.

Stanza 13
2 read: tell.   faytour: deceiver.
4 mollifie: allay the anger of.
6–7 At V iv 49, Artegall is bound by Radigund's **hard conditions**.
9 **Whose prowesse . . . :** i.e. no one has seen the match or rival of his prowess.

Stanza 14
1 soothlich: truly.
3–4 Dixon (1597) glosses: 'Justice not tyed to one place.' stead: place.
5–9 See I x 43.2–3n.   confound: overthrow. comfortlesse: helpless.

Stanza 15
1 feeling: i.e. affecting her with emotion.
4 allegge: allay; bring forward as a legal ground.
5–6 Cf. Ps. 58.4–5, Jer. 8.17.
8 efforce: force or struggle against; i.e. for her greater gratification, she chose to struggle against the ease she felt.
9 Cf. *S.C.* Epistle Ded.: 'So oftentimes a dischorde in Musick maketh a comely concordaunce.'

Stanza 16
2 vneath: difficult.
4 parauaunt: before, i.e. openly, publicly; cf. their meeting at IV vi 19, 26. Perhaps a shortened form of 'paraventure': by chance.
5 daunt: subdue.
6 shape: as her first concern, cf. iv 5.5.   sted: mark or imprint, presumably birthmark or scar, as **some markes** (3) suggests. The expanding reference – person to arms to steed – suggests 'place'; cf. 'one certaine stead' (14.3).
7 vaunt: proudly display.
8 to point ared: exactly declared.

17

Yet him in euery part before she knew,
  How euer list her now her knowledge faine,
  Sith him whilome in *Britaine* she did vew,
  To her reuealed in a mirrhour plaine,
  Whereof did grow her first engraffed paine;
  Whose root and stalke so bitter yet did tast,
  That but the fruit more sweetnesse did containe,
  Her wretched dayes in dolour she mote wast,
And yield the pray of loue to lothsome death at last.

18

By strange occasion she did him behold,
  And much more strangely gan to loue his sight,
  As it in bookes hath written bene of old.
  In *Deheubarth* that now South-wales is hight,
  What time king *Ryence* raign'd, and dealed right,
  The great Magitian *Merlin* had deuiz'd,
  By his deepe science, and hell-dreaded might,
  A looking glasse, right wondrously aguiz'd,
Whose vertues through the wyde world soone were solemniz'd.

19

It vertue had, to shew in perfect sight,
  What euer thing was in the world contaynd,
  Betwixt the lowest earth and heauens hight,
  So that it to the looker appertaynd;
  What euer foe had wrought, or frend had faynd,
  Therein discouered was, ne ought mote pas,
  Ne ought in secret from the same remaynd;
  For thy it round and hollow shaped was,
Like to the world it selfe, and seem'd a world of glas.

20

Who wonders not, that reades so wonderous worke?
  But who does wonder, that has red the Towre,
  Wherein th'Ægyptian *Phao* long did lurke
  From all mens vew, that none might her discoure,
  Yet she might all men vew out of her bowre?
  Great *Ptolomæe* it for his lemans sake
  Ybuilded all of glasse, by Magicke powre,
  And also it impregnable did make;
Yet when his loue was false, he with a peaze it brake.

21

Such was the glassie globe that *Merlin* made,
  And gaue vnto king *Ryence* for his gard,
  That neuer foes his kingdome might inuade,
  But he it knew at home before he hard
  Tydings thereof, and so them still debar'd.
  It was a famous Present for a Prince,
  And worthy worke of infinite reward,
  That treasons could bewray, and foes conuince;
Happie this Realme, had it remained euer since.

22

One day it fortuned, faire *Britomart*
  Into her fathers closet to repayre;
  For nothing he from her reseru'd apart,
  Being his onely daughter and his hayre:
  Where when she had espyde that mirrhour fayre,
  Her selfe a while therein she vewd in vaine;
  Tho her auizing of the vertues rare,
  Which thereof spoken were, she gan againe
320 Her to bethinke of, that mote to her selfe pertaine.

Stanza 17

2 **faine**: conceal.
5 **engraffed**: engrafted; suggests the image of a tree growing out of her body; see iii 22.2–4.

Stanza 18

3 **bookes**: romances rather than chronicles.
4 **Deheubarth**: Holinshed, *Chronicles* i 26, refers to 'Dehenbarth' as a name for what is commonly called South Wales.
5 In Malory 38–41, a King of North Wales who was an enemy of Arthur.   **dealed**: governed.
8 The **looking glasse**, earlier called '*Venus* looking glas' (i 8.9), is not a mirror (a traditional attribute of Venus) but a 'glassie globe' (21.1), which signifies fragile marital harmony in Renaissance iconography (Panofsky, 1962, 162).   **aguiz'd**: equipped.
9 **solemniz'd**: celebrated.

Stanza 19

The glass mirror in Chaucer, *Squire's Tale* 132–41, reveals any adversity that will befall its owner. It shows 'openly who is youre freend or foo' and reveals to a lady any deception by her lover. Cf. Genius who reveals 'wondrous things concerning our welfare' (II xii 47.5).
4 **So that**: provided that; cf. 22.9.

Stanza 20

In Chaucer, some 'wondred on the mirour, / That born was up into the maister-tour' and one cites various magical mirrors 'As knowen they that han hir bookes herd' (225–35).   **Phao**: φάος, light, signifies erotic gazing upon **all men**.
1 **reades**: sees (a sense unique to S.).
4 **discoure**: discover.
9 **peaze**: heavy blow.

Stanza 21

3 Britomart sees Artegall in the mirror for he invades her kingdom.
8 **bewray**: reveal.   **conuince**: expose or convict, hence conquer.

Stanza 22

4 As Una, I xii 21.3.
5–6 In Plato, *Phaedrus* 255d, the lover is said to be a mirror in which he beholds himself; cf. the fountain of Narcissus in the *Romance of the Rose* 1571–602. Britomart's inward-looking gaze projects an image of beauty which arouses love for Artegall; hence the vision of him follows. It leads also to a self-division; hence she compares herself to Narcissus at 44.6–9.
7 **auizing**: remembering.
9 As 19.4.

23

But as it falleth, in the gentlest harts
 Imperious Loue hath highest set his throne,
 And tyrannizeth in the bitter smarts
 Of them, that to him buxome are and prone:
 So thought this Mayd (as maydens vse to done)
 Whom fortune for her husband would allot,
 Not that she lusted after any one;
 For she was pure from blame of sinfull blot,
Yet wist her life at last must lincke in that same knot.

24

Eftsoones there was presented to her eye
 A comely knight, all arm'd in complete wize,
 Through whose bright ventayle lifted vp on hye
 His manly face, that did his foes agrize,
 And friends to termes of gentle truce entize,
 Lookt foorth, as *Phœbus* face out of the east,
 Betwixt two shadie mountaines doth arize;
 Portly his person was, and much increast
Through his Heroicke grace, and honorable gest.

25

His crest was couered with a couchant Hound,
 And all his armour seem'd of antique mould,
 But wondrous massie and assured sound,
 And round about yfretted all with gold,
 In which there written was with cyphers old,
 Achilles armes, which Arthegall did win.
 And on his shield enueloped seuenfold
 He bore a crowned litle Ermilin,
That deckt the azure field with her faire pouldred skin.

26

The Damzell well did vew his personage,
 And liked well, ne further fastned not,
 But went her way; ne her vnguilty age
 Did weene, vnwares, that her vnlucky lot
 Lay hidden in the bottome of the pot;
 Of hurt vnwist most daunger doth redound:
 But the false Archer, which that arrow shot
 So slyly, that she did not feele the wound,
Did smyle full smoothly at her weetlesse wofull stound.

mour against her will and the active Florimell who pursues the man she has singled out to love.

Stanza 24
Through this vision of Artegall, Britomart imitates Arthur who seeks his beloved after a similar vision: 'From that day forth I lou'd that face diuine' (I ix 15.5). She sees an imagined, idealized beauty, more attractive than the Salvage Knight proves to be in fact. On this neoplatonic commonplace, see Castiglione (1561) 317: 'through the vertue of imagination, hee shall fashion with himselfe that beautie much more faire than it is in deede.'
2   **arm'd in complete wize**: i.e. he is armed cap-à-pie, as Arthur (I vii 29.6) and Guyon (II i 5.8).
4–5   Cf. the description of Guyon, II i 6.3–4.   **agrize**: terrify.   **friends**: used generally of those who become allies; cf. 19.5.
6–7   As Britomart's face is compared to the moon, i 43 (see *n*); cf. V vii 4.7–8.
8   **Portly**: handsome, dignified.
9   **gest**: bearing.

Stanza 25
1   **couchant**: lying with the body resting on the legs and the head lifted up (an heraldic term); hence ready to spring. The **Hound** may herald the victory over the 'pagan hound' (V viii 42.5) who is Philip II of Spain.
4   **yfretted**: adorned; in heraldry, interlaced.
5   **cyphers**: characters.
6   In Boiardo, *Orl. Inn.* III i 23f, Mandricardo wins the arms of Hector; cf. Ariosto, *Orl. Fur.* xiv 31. Williams (1966) 133 comments: 'The near identification with Achilles works to establish Artegall as a supreme warrior and hero, worthy to bear the armour of the greatest of the Greeks, a trophy his survivors had competed for.' The reference is the first of many to connect Artegall with Achilles. On the relation of Achilles to Hercules, and both to Artegall, see Dunseath (1968) 52–9.
7–9   The classical shield worn by Guyon: see II v 6.3*n*. **Ermilin**: ermine, an heraldic term for white marked with black spots, here in the shape of an ermine, a traditional emblem of chastity. The crowned ermine is associated with British royalty, specifically with the Virgin Queen; the 'Ermine' portrait of Queen Elizabeth (in Strong, 1963) is analysed by F. A. Yates, Hatfield House Booklet, no. 1. In *S.C.* Apr. 57–8, Elissa appears 'like a mayden Queene' in 'Ermines white'.
azure: symbolizing the heavenly nature of justice. Dunseath 58 cites the shield of justice with its field blue in Legh, *Accendence of Armorie* (1591).   **pouldred**: powdered, spotted.

Stanza 26
1   **personage**: image.
2   **ne further fastned not**: i.e. she gave no further thought to him. She is in that second stage of loving: 'I saw and liked, I liked but loved not' (Sidney, *Astrophel and Stella* ii 5).
4   **vnwares**: immediately; or as she was unwary.
5   Since the lucky lot would be drawn off first, her **vnlucky** lot remains hidden until revealed by Merlin's magic.
6   **redound**: proceed, arise.
7   **false Archer**: not meant to characterize the god but to note the perspective of the victim, as Donno (1974) 44 observes. Since Britomart's union with Artegall is destined, Cupid is controlled by Providence. Cf. x 4.3, xi 51.8.
9   **stound**: time of trial.

Stanza 23
4   **buxome**: yielding.
7   **any one**: i.e. any particular person. Britomart forms the mean between the passive Amoret who is claimed by Scuda-

27

Thenceforth the feather in her loftie crest,
  Ruffed of loue, gan lowly to auaile,
  And her proud portance, and her princely gest,
  With which she earst tryumphed, now did quaile:
  Sad, solemne, sowre, and full of fancies fraile
  She woxe; yet wist she neither how, nor why,
  She wist not, silly Mayd, what she did aile,
  Yet wist, she was not well at ease perdy,
Yet thought it was not loue, but some melancholy.

28

So soone as Night had with her pallid hew
  Defast the beautie of the shining sky,
  And reft from men the worlds desired vew,
  She with her Nourse adowne to sleepe did lye;
  But sleepe full farre away from her did fly:
  In stead thereof sad sighes, and sorrowes deepe
  Kept watch and ward about her warily,
  That nought she did but wayle, and often steepe
Her daintie couch with teares, which closely she did weepe.

29

And if that any drop of slombring rest
  Did chaunce to still into her wearie spright,
  When feeble nature felt her selfe opprest,
  Streight way with dreames, and with fantasticke sight
  Of dreadfull things the same was put to flight,
  That oft out of her bed she did astart,
  As one with vew of ghastly feends affright:
  Tho gan she to renew her former smart,
And thinke of that faire visage, written in her hart.

30

One night, when she was tost with such vnrest,
  Her aged Nurse, whose name was *Glauce* hight,
  Feeling her leape out of her loathed nest,
  Betwixt her feeble armes her quickly keight,
  And downe againe in her warme bed her dight;
  Ah my deare daughter, ah my dearest dread,
  What vncouth fit (said she) what euill plight
  Hath thee opprest, and with sad drearyhead
Chaunged thy liuely cheare, and liuing made thee dead?

31

For not of nought these suddeine ghastly feares
  All night afflict thy naturall repose,
  And all the day, when as thine equall peares
  Their fit disports with faire delight doe chose,
  Thou in dull corners doest thy selfe inclose,
  Ne tastest Princes pleasures, ne doest spred
  Abroad thy fresh youthes fairest flowre, but lose
  Both leafe and fruit, both too vntimely shed,
As one in wilfull bale for euer buried.

32

The time, that mortall men their weary cares
  Do lay away, and all wilde beastes do rest,
  And euery riuer eke his course forbeares,
  Then doth this wicked euill thee infest,
  And riue with thousand throbs thy thrilled brest;
  Like an huge *Aetn'* of deepe engulfed griefe,
  Sorrow is heaped in thy hollow chest,
  Whence forth it breakes in sighes and anguish rife,
322 As smoke and sulphure mingled with confused strife.

Stanza 27
1–4   **loftie crest**: the symbol of knightly prowess; cf.
iv 7.3, ix 20.3 and see I vii 32.1*n*.   **Ruffed**: ruffled; suggesting
'made rough'.   **auaile**: fall, drop down (applied to the
helmet).   **portance**: demeanour.   **quaile**: decline. She is
crest-fallen:
5   **Sad, solemne**: the dominant mood of the male knight;
see I i 2.8*n*.   **sowre** applies to those in love, 17.6.   **full of
fancies fraile**: Amoret's state in the house of Busirane.
7   **silly**: innocent.

Stanza 28
1   **pallid**: from Lat. *pallidus*, pale; or 'palled': covered with a
pall (sugg. Collier, 1862).
8–9   Cf. Ps. 6.6: 'I cause my bed every night to swimme, and
watter my couche with my teares.'   **closely**: secretly.

Stanza 29
2   **still**: distil; also as the dew of sleep makes her still.
4   **fantasticke**: i.e. produced by her fancy; cf. the
'phantasies / In wauering wemens wit' (xii 26.3–4).
6   **astart**: start up.

Stanzas 30–51
A close imitation of Virgil, *Ciris* 220f, which tells how the aged
Carme aids the love-stricken Scylla. In place of the lust-crazed
Scylla who destroys her own city, S. substitutes Carme's
virgin daughter, Britomartis, for his figure of one whose love
establishes a royal line. Nelson (1963) 142–3 cites the episode
as an example of perverse imitation.

Stanza 30
Cf. *Ciris* 220–8.
2   **Glauce**: the mother of Diana (Cicero, *De natura deorum*
III lviii). As Britomart is associated with Minerva, her nurse is
associated with the traditional companion of that Goddess, the
owl (Gk Γλαυκη); noted Aptekar (1969) 189. As Fowler (1964)
126 *n*4 observes, the name 'may fitly denote the attendant either
of Britomart *qua* Diana or of Britomart *qua* Minerva'. The
name may derive from γλαυκή, grey, referring to her age: her
common epithet is 'aged' or 'old'.
3   Cf. i 62.2 and V vi 24.5 to 27.9.
5   **dight**: placed.
8   **drearyhead**: sorrow.

Stanza 31
6–9   Expanded at v 51.

Stanza 32
1–3   Translating *Ciris* 232–3.
4   **infest**: assail; infect; swarm about.
5   **thrilled**: pierced; affected with emotion.

33

Aye me, how much I feare, least loue it bee;
But if that loue it be, as sure I read
By knowen signes and passions, which I see,
Be it worthy of thy race and royall sead,
Then I auow by this most sacred head
Of my deare foster child, to ease thy griefe,
And win thy will: Therefore away doe dread;
For death nor daunger from thy dew reliefe
Shall me debarre, tell me therefore my liefest liefe.

34

So hauing said, her twixt her armes twaine
She straightly straynd, and colled tenderly,
And euery trembling ioynt, and euery vaine
She softly felt, and rubbed busily,
To doe the frosen cold away to fly;
And her faire deawy eies with kisses deare
She oft did bath, and oft againe did dry;
And euer her importund, not to feare
To let the secret of her hart to her appeare.

35

The Damzell pauzd, and then thus fearefully;
Ah Nurse, what needeth thee to eke my paine?
Is not enough, that I alone doe dye,
But it must doubled be with death of twaine?
For nought for me but death there doth remaine.
O daughter deare (said she) despaire no whit;
For neuer sore, but might a salue obtaine:
That blinded God, which hath ye blindly smit,
Another arrow hath your louers hart to hit.

36

But mine is not (quoth she) like others wound;
For which no reason can find remedy.
Was neuer such, but mote the like be found,
(Said she) and though no reason may apply
Salue to your sore, yet loue can higher stye,
Then reasons reach, and oft hath wonders donne.
But neither God of loue, nor God of sky
Can doe (said she) that, which cannot be donne.
Things oft impossible (quoth she) seeme, ere begonne.

37

These idle words (said she) doe nought asswage
My stubborne smart, but more annoyance breed,
For no no vsuall fire, no vsuall rage
It is, O Nurse, which on my life doth feed,
And suckes the bloud, which from my hart doth bleed.
But since thy faithfull zeale lets me not hyde
My crime, (if crime it be) I will it reed.
Nor Prince, nor pere it is, whose loue hath gryde
My feeble brest of late, and launched this wound wyde.

38

Nor man it is, nor other liuing wight;
For then some hope I might vnto me draw,
But th'only shade and semblant of a knight,
Whose shape or person yet I neuer saw,
Hath me subiected to loues cruell law:
The same one day, as me misfortune led,
I in my fathers wondrous mirrhour saw,
And pleased with that seeming goodly-hed,
Vnwares the hidden hooke with baite I swallowed.

39

Sithens it hath infixed faster hold
Within my bleeding bowels, and so sore
Nowranckleth in this same fraile fleshly mould,
That all mine entrailes flow with poysnous gore,
And th'vlcer groweth daily more and more;
Ne can my running sore find remedie,
Other then my hard fortune to deplore,
And languish as the leafe falne from the tree,
Till death make one end of my dayes and miserie.

Stanza 33

Imitating *Ciris* 237–49.

2   **read**: discern.

7–9   Excessive alliteration mocks the Nurse's mock heroics
(*Ciris* 247–8).   **liefest liefe**: dearest love.

Stanza 34

Cf. *Ciris* 250–6.

2   **straightly straynd**: tightly clasped.   **colled**: embraced.

Stanzas 35–36

Cf. *Ciris* 257–64.

Stanza 35

2   **eke**: increase.

7   Proverbial (C. G. Smith, 1970, 672).

Stanza 36

2   **For which**: i.e. mine is such for which.

4–6   **reason**: refers to the power of temperance; cf. II iv 34.
Cf. 46.1–5. The power greater than temperance that controls
love is chastity.   **stye**: ascend.

7   **God of sky**: 'sky-ruling Ioue' (VI x 22.1).

Stanza 37

3   Cf. *Ciris* 259.   **For no**: 'For know' sugg. Upton (1758).

7   **reed**: tell.

8   **gryde**: pierced.

9   **launched**: cut.

Stanza 38

3   **But th'only shade and semblant**: but only the illusion
and image.

8   **goodly-hed**: goodly appearance.

Stanza 39

1   **Sithens**: since that time.

2–5   Apart from one humorous reference, the Castle of Alma
treats the body from the waist up, in accord with Temperance's
control over the passions. Book III treats the body's lower half,
here the bowels as the seat of love and compassion.

2   **bleeding bowels**: cf. 'troubled bowels' (iv 8.9).

3   **ranckleth**: describes the incurable wound of love in
Arthur (I ix 7.4) and in Marinell (IV xii 22.7).   **fleshly
mould**: the body.

40

Daughter (said she) what need ye be dismayd,
　Or why make ye such Monster of your mind?
　Of much more vncouth thing I was affrayd;
　Of filthy lust, contrarie vnto kind:
　But this affection nothing straunge I find;
　For who with reason can you aye reproue,
　To loue the semblant pleasing most your mind,
　And yield your heart, whence ye cannot remoue?
No guilt in you, but in the tyranny of loue.

41

Not so th'*Arabian Myrrhe* did set her mind;
　Nor so did *Biblis* spend her pining hart,
　But lou'd their natiue flesh against all kind,
　And to their purpose vsed wicked art:
　Yet playd *Pasiphaë* a more monstrous part,
　That lou'd a Bull, and learnd a beast to bee;
　Such shamefull lusts who loaths not, which depart
　From course of nature and of modestie?
Sweet loue such lewdnes bands from his faire companie.

42

But thine my Deare (welfare thy heart my deare)
　Though strange beginning had, yet fixed is
　On one, that worthy may perhaps appeare;
　And certes seemes bestowed not amis:
　Ioy thereof haue thou and eternall blis.
　With that vpleaning on her elbow weake,
　Her alablaster brest she soft did kis,
　Which all that while she felt to pant and quake,
As it an Earth-quake were; at last she thus bespake.

43

Beldame, your words doe worke me litle ease;
　For though my loue be not so lewdly bent,
　As those ye blame, yet may it nought appease
　My raging smart, ne ought my flame relent,
　But rather doth my helpelesse griefe augment.
　For they, how euer shamefull and vnkind,
　Yet did possesse their horrible intent:
　Short end of sorrowes they thereby did find;
So was their fortune good, though wicked were their mind.

44

But wicked fortune mine, though mind be good,
　Can haue no end, nor hope of my desire,
　But feed on shadowes, whiles I die for food,
　And like a shadow wexe, whiles with entire
　Affection, I doe languish and expire.
　I fonder, then *Cephisus* foolish child,
　Who hauing vewed in a fountaine shere
　His face, was with the loue thereof beguild;
I fonder loue a shade, the bodie farre exild.

45

Nought like (quoth she) for that same wretched boy
　Was of himselfe the idle Paramoure;
　Both loue and louer, without hope of ioy,
　For which he faded to a watry flowre.
　But better fortune thine, and better howre,
　Which lou'st the shadow of a warlike knight;
　No shadow, but a bodie hath in powre:
　That bodie, wheresoeuer that it light,
May learned be by cyphers, or by Magicke might.

Stanza 40
The Nurse implies that Britomart loves the ideal image of her
desire, that is, what she wants to see in her lover. Cf. iv 5.7–9.
The **Monster** is embodied in the 'monstrous formes' (xi 51.7)
of love displayed in the house of Busirane.

Stanza 41
1–4　th'**Arabian Myrrhe** tricked her father into committing
incest with her (Ovid, *Met*. x 311f). The reference, taken from
Ciris 238–40, leads to other traditional examples of unnatural
love.　　**Biblis** lusted after her brother (Ovid, *Met*. ix 454f).
5　**Pasiphaë** enjoyed a bull by rigging herself inside a model
of a cow (Ovid, *Met*. ix 735–40).
9　**bands**: bans; banishes (sugg. by the context).

Stanza 42
1　Cf. the Red Cross Knight's benediction, 10.8.
8–9　Continuing the image at 32.6–9. The derangement of
the earth's body in an earthquake was related to the derangement of the human body by violent emotion; see Heninger
(1960) 130–1.

Stanza 43
1　**Beldame**: good mother (a respectful form of address).
4　**relent**: abate.
6　**vnkind**: contrary to nature, 'against all kind' (41.3).
7　**possesse**: gain.

Stanza 44
1　**mind**: echoing **mine** and answering 40.2; cf. 41.1.
4　**entire**: sincere; complete; blameless (in contrast to
Myrrha and the others).
6–9　**Cephisus foolish child**: Narcissus; see Ovid, *Met*.
iii 402f. Lotspeich (1932) 87 notes that, for S., 'Narcissus was
not so much one who loved himself as one who was deluded
and starved by shadows'.　　**fonder**: more foolish (Ovid's
credule); more foolish. Narcissus loved the shadow thinking
it substance (*Met*. iii 417) but Britomart loves the shadow
knowing that it is not substance. Edwards (1958) 165f analyses
S.'s use of the Narcissus myth.　　**shere**: clear.

Stanza 45
2　**idle**: vain; unable to act (in contrast to action open to
Britomart).
4　**watry flowre**: the narcissus 'that likes the watry shore'
(vi 45.5).
6　**shadow**: reflected image; playing on 'shadowes' (44.3).
7　**in powre**: i.e. controlling it.
9　**cyphers**: astrological signs or geomantic figures.

46

But if thou may with reason yet represse
   The growing euill, ere it strength haue got,
   And thee abandond wholly doe possesse,
   Against it strongly striue, and yield thee not,
   Till thou in open field adowne be smot.
   But if the passion mayster thy fraile might,
   So that needs loue or death must be thy lot,
   Then I auow to thee, by wrong or right
To compasse thy desire, and find that loued knight.

47

Her chearefull words much cheard the feeble spright
   Of the sicke virgin, that her downe she layd
   In her warme bed to sleepe, if that she might;
   And the old-woman carefully displayd
   The clothes about her round with busie ayd;
   So that at last a little creeping sleepe
   Surprisd her sense: She therewith well apayd,
   The drunken lampe downe in the oyle did steepe,
And set her by to watch, and set her by to weepe.

48

Earely the morrow next, before that day
   His ioyous face did to the world reueale,
   They both vprose and tooke their readie way
   Vnto the Church, their prayers to appeale,
   With great deuotion, and with litle zeale:
   For the faire Damzell from the holy herse
   Her loue-sicke hart to other thoughts did steale;
   And that old Dame said many an idle verse,
Out of her daughters hart fond fancies to reuerse.

49

Returned home, the royall Infant fell
   Into her former fit; for why, no powre
   Nor guidance of her selfe in her did dwell.
   But th'aged Nurse her calling to her bowre,
   Had gathered Rew, and Sauine, and the flowre
   Of *Camphora*, and Calamint, and Dill,
   All which she in a earthen Pot did poure,
   And to the brim with Colt wood did it fill,
And many drops of milke and bloud through it did spill.

50

Then taking thrise three haires from off her head,
   Them trebly breaded in a threefold lace,
   And round about the pots mouth, bound the thread,
   And after hauing whispered a space
   Certaine sad words, with hollow voice and bace,
   She to the virgin said, thrise said she it;
   Come daughter come, come; spit vpon my face,
   Spit thrise vpon me, thrise vpon me spit;
Th'vneuen number for this businesse is most fit.

51

That sayd, her round about she from her turnd,
   She turned her contrarie to the Sunne,
   Thrise she her turnd contrary, and returnd,
   All contrary, for she the right did shunne,
   And euer what she did, was streight vndonne.
   So thought she to vndoe her daughters loue:
   But loue, that is in gentle brest begonne,
   No idle charmes so lightly may remoue,
That well can witnesse, who by triall it does proue.

Stanza 46

3   **possesse**: suggesting demonic possession by the God of
Love; cf. 36.4–6.
5   Later expanded into the battle between Britomart and
Artegall, IV vi 19f.

Stanza 47

Combining *Ciris* 250–1 and 340–8.
7   **apayd**: satisfied.
8   **drunken lampe**: because it drinks oil; translating
bibulum lumen (*Ciris* 344). The Nurse would believe the superstition, recorded by Upton (1758), that blowing out a lamp
brings bad luck.

Stanza 48

1–2   Cf. *Ciris* 349.
3   **readie**: direct.
4   **appeale**: offer (Lat. *appellare*); address (to God); or
offer prayers in appeal to God.
6   **herse**: ceremony.
8   **verse**: incantation or charm; cf. Busirane's 'sad verse'
(xii 36.4).
9   **reuerse**: turn away, in the etymological sense.

Stanza 49

1   **Infant**: Princess; used elsewhere only for Arthur; cf.
II viii 56.1.
2   **for why**: because.
3   She is guided by Cupid: see iv 9.6–8*n*, IV v 29.5.
5–9   Upton (1758) notes the various herbs used to abate
sexual desire and procure barrenness. Both uses are to be condemned because Britomart's love yields her famous progeny.
In *Ciris* 369–70, Carme mixes various savoury herbs; Glauce
substitutes English equivalents. Maplet (1567) notes that **Rew**
is 'the Medicinable Herbe'; **Sauine** is used 'to remedie and
help all griefs in the inward partes and bowels'; **Calamint** or
Mint 'stoppeth and stencheth all kinde of swellings'; and **Dill**
is 'a hinderance to issue'. Drayton notes 'the wonder-working
Dill / . . . Which curious women use in many a nice disease'
(*Poly-Olbion* xiii 207–8). The **milke and bloud** are added to
propitiate Hecate.

Stanza 50

Imitating *Ciris* 371–3 but with much more humour. Carme's
ter in gremium mecum despue becomes **spit vpon my face** (7),
which sounds like a schoolboy's joke.
5   **sad**: serious, solemn.

Stanza 51

7–9   Cf. Amoret's resistance to Busirane's charms, xi 16.6 to
17.4.

52

Ne ought it mote the noble Mayd auayle,
　Ne slake the furie of her cruell flame,
　But that she still did waste, and still did wayle,
　That through long languour, and hart-burning brame
　She shortly like a pyned ghost became,
　Which long hath waited by the Stygian strond.
　That when old *Glauce* saw, for feare least blame
　Of her miscarriage should in her be fond,
She wist not how t'amend, nor how it to withstond.

Cant. III.

Merlin bewrayes to Britomart,
　the state of Artegall.
And shewes the famous Progeny
　which from them springen shall.

1

Ost sacred fire, that burnest mightily
　In liuing brests, ykindled first aboue,
Emongst th'eternall spheres and lamping sky,
And thence pourd into men, which men call Loue;
Not that same, which doth base affections moue
In brutish minds, and filthy lust inflame,
But that sweet fit, that doth true beautie loue,
And choseth vertue for his dearest Dame,
Whence spring all noble deeds and neuer dying fame:

2

Well did Antiquitie a God thee deeme,
　That ouer mortall minds hast so great might,
　To order them, as best to thee doth seeme,
　And all their actions to direct aright;
　The fatall purpose of diuine foresight,
　Thou doest effect in destined descents,
　Through deepe impression of thy secret might,
　And stirredst vp th'Heroes high intents,
Which the late world admyres for wondrous moniments.

3

But thy dread darts in none doe triumph more,
　Ne brauer proofe in any, of thy powre
　Shew'dst thou, then in this royall Maid of yore,
　Making her seeke an vnknowne Paramoure,
　From the worlds end, through many a bitter stowre:
　From whose two loynes thou afterwards did rayse
　Most famous fruits of matrimoniall bowre,
　Which through the earth haue spred their liuing prayse,
That fame in trompe of gold eternally displayes.

4

Begin then, O my dearest sacred Dame,
　Daughter of *Phœbus* and of *Memorie*,
　That doest ennoble with immortall name
　The warlike Worthies, from antiquitie,
　In thy great volume of Eternitie:
　Begin, O *Clio*, and recount from hence
　My glorious Soueraines goodly auncestrie,
　Till that by dew degrees and long protense,
Thou haue it lastly brought vnto her Excellence.

Stanza 52

4 **languuour**: affliction. **brame**: desire.
5-6 Dunseath (1968) 24 notes that 'Britomart has become a shade just like her lover in the magic glass'. **long hath waited**: because it is unable to cross the Styx until its body has been buried or its death avenged.
8 **miscarriage**: failure in managing.

Canto iii

Argument
1 **bewrayes**: reveals.

Stanza 1
S. uses the familiar neoplatonic distinctions between heavenly love, human love, and bestial love, and the twin neoplatonic doctrines that love is the desire for beauty and that virtue manifests itself in beauty. The distinction implicit in 7-8, between the love of beauty and the love of virtue, leads to the stories of Florimell and the False Florimell. Britomart and Amoret occupy the mean between the love of beauty and the love of virtue. Ellrodt (1960) 34 argues that the concluding lines reject neoplatonic love: 'It appears that the higher love is conceived as a spur to virtuous action on earth rather than an invitation to fly back to heaven.' See i 49.8-9*n*.
3 **lamping**: shining, full of lamps.
5 **affections**: passions.

Stanza 2
1-4 As Phaedrus in the opening of Plato, *Symposium* 178a, claims that Love is a great god.
5 **fatall**: ordained by fate; cf. the 'fatall deepe foresight' of 'th'eternall might' (I ix 6.8 to 7.1); cf. also 24.3-4.
6 **destined descents**: lines of descent fixed by fate.

Stanza 3
Upton (1758) notes the mixture of tenses to bring the past (**of yore**) into the present (**liuing**). Britomart and Artegall belong to two historical periods: the time of the chronicle told by Merlin and a thousand years later, the time of Elizabeth and her defenders.
2 **brauer**: more glorious.
4 **Paramoure**: lover.
5 **stowre**: struggle; time of turmoil.
7 **matrimoniall bowre**: contrasts with the Bower of Bliss.

Stanza 4
Cf. the invocation at I xi 5.6-9 (and see *n*).
4 **Worthies**: perhaps the Nine Worthies. Later S. claims that the British Worthies 'all the antique Worthies merits far did passe' (ix 50.9).
8 **dew degrees**: as 'destined descents' (2.6). **protense**: extension in time (from Lat. *protendere*, to stretch forth); or a shortened form of 'protension'. **protense**] pretence *1596* is an unfortunate (and dangerous) slip.
9 **lastly**: at the end, ultimately.

5

Full many wayes within her troubled mind,
　Old *Glauce* cast, to cure this Ladies griefe:
　Full many waies she sought, but none could find,
　Nor herbes, nor charmes, nor counsell, that is chiefe
　And choisest med'cine for sicke harts reliefe:
　For thy great care she tooke, and greater feare,
　Least that it should her turne to foule repriefe,
　And sore reproch, when so her father deare
Should of his dearest daughters hard misfortune heare.

6

At last she her auisd, that he, which made
　That mirrhour, wherein the sicke Damosell
　So straungely vewed her straunge louers shade,
　To weet, the learned *Merlin*, well could tell,
　Vnder what coast of heauen the man did dwell,
　And by what meanes his loue might best be wrought:
　For though beyond the *Africk Ismaell*,
　Or th'Indian *Peru* he were, she thought
Him forth through infinite endeuour to haue sought.

7

Forthwith themselues disguising both in straunge
　And base attyre, that none might them bewray,
　To *Maridunum*, that is now by chaunge
　Of name *Cayr-Merdin* cald, they tooke their way:
　There the wise *Merlin* whylome wont (they say)
　To make his wonne, low vnderneath the ground,
　In a deepe delue, farre from the vew of day,
　That of no liuing wight he mote be found,
When so he counseld with his sprights encompast round.

8

And if thou euer happen that same way
　To trauell, goe to see that dreadfull place:
　It is an hideous hollow caue (they say)
　Vnder a rocke that lyes a little space
　From the swift *Barry*, tombling downe apace,
　Emongst the woodie hilles of *Dyneuowre*:
　But dare thou not, I charge, in any cace,
　To enter into that same balefull Bowre,
For fear the cruell Feends should thee vnwares deuowre.

9

But standing high aloft, low lay thine eare,
　And there such ghastly noise of yron chaines,
　And brasen Caudrons thou shalt rombling heare,
　Which thousand sprights with long enduring paines
　Doe tosse, that it will stonne thy feeble braines,
　And oftentimes great grones, and grieuous stounds,
　When too huge toile and labour them constraines:
　And oftentimes loud strokes, and ringing sounds
From vnder that deepe Rocke most horribly rebounds.

10

The cause some say is this: A litle while
　Before that *Merlin* dyde, he did intend,
　A brasen wall in compas to compile
　About *Cairmardin*, and did it commend
　Vnto these Sprights, to bring to perfect end.
　During which worke the Ladie of the Lake,
　Whom long he lou'd, for him in hast did send,
　Who thereby forst his workemen to forsake,
Them bound till his returne, their labour not to slake.

Stanza 5
2　cast: considered.
4–5　Cf. II i 44.2–3.
6–9　Cf. ii 52.7–9. Such repetition invariably points to an
inset episode or digression.
6　For thy: therefore.　care: concern; grief.
7　repriefe: reproof.

Stanza 6
1　her auisd: recalled.
5　coast: region.
7–8　the Africk Ismaell: Northern Africa, so called because
the Mohammedans were regarded as descendants of Ishmael.
th'Indian Peru: held to be India. Named as the extreme
boundaries of south and west.

Stanza 7
2　bewray: discover; betray.
3–6　Cayr-Merdin: Carmarthen, in Wales.　they say: i.e.
the chroniclers, here Geoffrey of Monmouth, *Historia Regum
Britanniae* VI xvii. Camden notes that the Britons called the
town Maridunum (cited *Var*. iii 225); so does Selden in his note
to Drayton, *Poly-Olbion* iv 331.
7　deepe delue: Ariosto's *grotta* (*Orl. Fur*. iii 10). S. borrows
his story of the heroine who visits Merlin to learn about her
royal progeny.
9　counseld: took counsel.

Stanzas 8–11
A playful interlude; hence the repetition of the tag **they say**
(7.5, 8.3) and **some say** (10.1); cf. 'men say' (13.1). Merlin's
story is told by Drayton, *Poly-Olbion* iv 331–48.

Stanza 8
4–6　a little space: more than fifty miles according to
Osgood (*Var*. iii 224–5). Perhaps S. was misled by Harrison's
account (in Holinshed) of the English rivers.

Stanza 9
6　stounds: roars; suggesting roars provoked by pain.
7　constraines: afflicts.

Stanza 10
3　in compas: in a circle.　compile: build.
4　commend: commit to their charge.
9　slake: slacken.

11

In the meane time through that false Ladies traine,
   He was surprisd, and buried vnder beare,
   Ne euer to his worke returnd againe:
   Nath'lesse those feends may not their worke forbeare,
   So greatly his commaundement they feare,
   But there doe toyle and trauell day and night,
   Vntill that brasen wall they vp doe reare:
   For *Merlin* had in Magicke more insight,
Then euer him before or after liuing wight.

12

For he by words could call out of the sky
   Both Sunne and Moone, and make them him obay:
   The land to sea, and sea to maineland dry,
   And darkesome night he eke could turne to day:
   Huge hostes of men he could alone dismay,
   And hostes of men of meanest things could frame,
   When so him list his enimies to fray:
   That to this day for terror of his fame,
The feends do quake, when any him to them does name.

13

And sooth, men say that he was not the sonne
   Of mortall Syre, or other liuing wight,
   But wondrously begotten, and begonne
   By false illusion of a guilefull Spright,
   On a faire Ladie Nonne, that whilome hight
   Matilda, daughter to *Pubidius*,
   Who was the Lord of *Mathrauall* by right,
   And coosen vnto king *Ambrosius*:
Whence he indued was with skill so maruellous.

14

They here ariuing, staid a while without,
   Ne durst aduenture rashly in to wend,
   But of their first intent gan make new dout
   For dread of daunger, which it might portend:
   Vntill the hardie Mayd (with loue to frend)
   First entering, the dreadfull Mage there found
   Deepe busied bout worke of wondrous end,
   And writing strange characters in the ground,
With which the stubborn feends he to his seruice bound.

15

He nought was moued at their entrance bold:
   For of their comming well he wist afore,
   Yet list them bid their businesse to vnfold,
   As if ought in this world in secret store
   Were from him hidden, or vnknowne of yore.
   Then *Glauce* thus, Let not it thee offend,
   That we thus rashly through thy darkesome dore,
   Vnwares haue prest: for either fatall end,
Or other mightie cause vs two did hither send.

16

He bad tell on; And then she thus began.
   Now haue three Moones with borrow'd brothers light,
   Thrice shined faire, and thrice seem'd dim and wan,
   Sith a sore euill, which this virgin bright
   Tormenteth, and doth plonge in dolefull plight,
   First rooting tooke; but what thing it mote bee,
   Or whence it sprong, I cannot read aright:
   But this I read, that but if remedee
Thou her afford, full shortly I her dead shall see.

17

Therewith th'Enchaunter softly gan to smyle
   At her smooth speeches, weeting inly well,
   That she to him dissembled womanish guyle,
   And to her said, Beldame, by that ye tell,
   More need of leach-craft hath your Damozell,
   Then of my skill: who helpe may haue elsewhere,
   In vaine seekes wonders out of Magicke spell.
   Th'old woman wox half blanck, those words to heare;
And yet was loth to let her purpose plaine appeare.

Stanza 11

1   **traine**: treachery; 'hir subtyle worchyng' (Malory 126).
2   **vnder beare**: in a sepulchre. Malory says 'undir a grete stone'.

Stanza 12

A secular analogue to the powers of Fidelia (I x 20). Similarly, Arthur's shield defeats armies of men, terrifies the heavens, and changes men into stones, dust, and to nothing at all (I vii 34–35). In Virgil, *Ecl.* viii 69, songs are said to have the power to draw the moon from heaven.
5   **dismay**: defeat.
7   **fray**: terrify; attack.

Stanza 13

Geoffrey of Monmouth VI xviii records that Merlin never had a father: an incubus in the shape of a young man lay with his mother. He records only that she lived among nuns. S. names her **Matilda**, which signifies 'noble or honourable Lady of Maids' (Camden, 1605, 105). See VI iv 29.3*n*.   **Mathrauall**: one of the three divisions of Wales.   **Ambrosius**: the brother of Uther, cited at II x 67.2.
8   **coosen**: kinsman.

Stanza 14

5   **to frend**: as a friend; cf. the Red Cross Knight who goes forward 'with God to frend' (I i 28.7).
6   **Mage**: magician.
8   Britomart surprises Busirane 'Figuring straunge characters of his art' (xii 31.2). Cf. Christ's action when he confronted the accusers of the woman taken in adultery: he 'stouped downe, and with his finger wrote on the grounde' (John 8.6).
9   **stubborn**: untamable, fierce; cf. Archimago, I i 43.7.

Stanza 15

8   **fatall end**: 'fatall purpose' (2.5); cf. 19.7, 21.6.

Stanza 16

2–3   Nine months, the period of gestation; see I viii 38.6–7*n*.
7   **read**: guess.
8   **read**: predict.   **but if**: unless.

Stanza 17

1   **Enchaunter**: applied to Busirane in Canto xii; he inherits the role from Archimago.
5   **leach-craft**: medical healing.

18

And to him said, If any leaches skill,
　Or other learned meanes could haue redrest
　This my deare daughters deepe engraffed ill,
　Certes I should be loth thee to molest:
　But this sad euill, which doth her infest,
　Doth course of naturall cause farre exceed,
　And housed is within her hollow brest,
　That either seemes some cursed witches deed,
Or euill spright, that in her doth such torment breed.

19

The wisard could no lenger beare her bord,
　But brusting forth in laughter, to her sayd;
　Glauce, what needs this colourable word,
　To cloke the cause, that hath it selfe bewrayd?
　Ne ye faire *Britomartis*, thus arayd,
　More hidden are, then Sunne in cloudy vele;
　Whom thy good fortune, hauing fate obayd,
　Hath hither brought, for succour to appele:
The which the powres to thee are pleased to reuele.

20

The doubtfull Mayd, seeing her selfe descryde,
　Was all abasht, and her pure yuory
　Into a cleare Carnation suddeine dyde;
　As faire *Aurora* rising hastily,
　Doth by her blushing tell, that she did lye
　All night in old *Tithonus* frosen bed,
　Whereof she seemes ashamed inwardly.
　But her old Nourse was nought dishartened,
But vauntage made of that, which *Merlin* had ared.

21

And sayd, Sith then thou knowest all our griefe,
　(For what doest not thou know?) of grace I pray,
　Pitty our plaint, and yield vs meet reliefe.
　With that the Prophet still awhile did stay,
　And then his spirite thus gan forth display;
　Most noble Virgin, that by fatall lore
　Hast learn'd to loue, let no whit thee dismay
　The hard begin, that meets thee in the dore,
And with sharpe fits thy tender hart oppresseth sore.

22

For so must all things excellent begin,
　And eke enrooted deepe must be that Tree,
　Whose big embodied braunches shall not lin,
　Till they to heauens hight forth stretched bee.
　For from thy wombe a famous Progenie
　Shall spring, out of the auncient *Troian* blood,
　Which shall reuiue the sleeping memorie
　Of those same antique Peres, the heauens brood,
Which *Greeke* and *Asian* riuers stained with their blood.

23

Renowmed kings, and sacred Emperours,
　Thy fruitfull Ofspring, shall from thee descend;
　Braue Captaines, and most mighty warriours,
　That shall their conquests through all lands extend
　And their decayed kingdomes shall amend:
　The feeble Britons, broken with long warre,
　They shall vpreare, and mightily defend
　Against their forrein foe, that comes from farre,
Till vniuersall peace compound all ciuill iarre.

Stanza 18

2　**redrest**: healed.
3　**engraffed ill**: cf. 'engraffed paine' (ii 17.5). Guyon's enemies are internal, having a **naturall cause** (6) in the passions. Love attacks Britomart from without but becomes natural through grafting.
5　**infest**: assail; infect. Cf. ii 32.4.

Stanza 19

1　**bord**: idle tale; deception.
3　**colourable**: deceiving.

Stanza 20

1　**doubtfull**: apprehensive.　**descryde**: revealed.
4–6　Cf. I xi 51.2–6. The myth is particularly appropriate to the virgin's hidden desires and fears.
9　**vauntage**: opportunity.　**ared**: divined.

Stanza 21

2　**of grace**: as a favour.
4　**still**: a solemn state, in contrast to the Sibyl's frenzy in Virgil, *Aen.* vi 78–80.
5　**display**: pour forth.
6　**fatall lore**: the teaching of fate; cf. 2.5.
7–9　**let no whit . . .**: i.e. let not the hard beginning in any way dismay you. He refers to the flames which she will meet at the door to the house of Busirane where her **tender hart** is displayed as Amoret's wounded heart.

Stanza 22

1–4　**enrooted**: extends the image of Britomart's grief since love 'First rooting tooke' (16.6).　**embodied**: a tree composed of human bodies, as in adaptations of the Tree of Jesse (cf. Isaiah 11.1, Dan. 4.7–8) in medieval and Renaissance genealogical tables. Cf. iv 3.6–9.　**lin**: cease.
4　Repeated from II x 2.5 where the first half of the story is told. The story is told again at ix 38–51.
5–6　As announced by the Argument.
8　**heauens brood**: referring to the divine origin of the Trojans; cf. 'sacred progenie' (II x 36.1).
9　**their**: i.e. the Greek and Asian enemies.

Stanza 23

Summarizing Merlin's history up to the 'sacred Peace' of Elizabeth's reign, 49.1–5.
1　On the distinction, see I ii 22.7–9*n*.
5　**amend**: restore.
9　**compound**: settle.

329

24

It was not, *Britomart,* thy wandring eye,
　Glauncing vnwares in charmed looking glas,
　But the streight course of heauenly destiny,
　Led with eternall prouidence, that has
　Guided thy glaunce, to bring his will to pas:
　Ne is thy fate, ne is thy fortune ill,
　To loue the prowest knight, that euer was.
Therefore submit thy wayes vnto his will,
And do by all dew meanes thy destiny fulfill.

25

But read (said *Glauce*) thou Magitian
　What meanes shall she out seeke, or what wayes take
　How shall she know, how shall she find the man?
　Or what needs her to toyle, sith fates can make
　Way for themselues, their purpose to partake?
　Then *Merlin* thus; Indeed the fates are firme,
　And may not shrinck, though all the world do shake:
　Yet ought mens good endeuours them confirme,
And guide the heauenly causes to their constant terme.

26

The man whom heauens haue ordaynd to bee
　The spouse of *Britomart,* is *Arthegall*:
　He wonneth in the land of *Fayeree,*
　Yet is no *Fary* borne, ne sib at all
　To Elfes, but sprong of seed terrestriall,
　And whilome by false *Faries* stolne away,
　Whiles yet in infant cradle he did crall;
　Ne other to himselfe is knowne this day,
But that he by an Elfe was gotten of a *Fay.*

27

But sooth he is the sonne of *Gorlois,*
　And brother vnto *Cador* Cornish king,
　And for his warlike feates renowmed is,
　From where the day out of the sea doth spring,
　Vntill the closure of the Euening.
　From thence, him firmely bound with faithfull band,
　To this his natiue soyle thou backe shalt bring,
　Strongly to aide his countrey, to withstand
The powre of forrein Paynims, which inuade thy land.

Stanza 24

The emphasis on God's providence indicates that God's
grace is exercised throughout Britomart's adventures rather
than at the mid-point as in the first two Books. The 'fates'
(25.6) refer to divine order. Thus Golding (1567) Epistle
326–7 speaks of fate even in pagan writers as 'the order which
is set and stablished in things / By Gods eternall will and word'.
Cf. Ps. 37.5: 'Commit thy waye vnto the Lord . . . and he shal
bring it to passe.'

3　**streight**: strict; straight; as Luke 3.4: 'Prepare ye the way
of the Lord: make his paths straight.' In contrast to **wandring**
(1).
8　**his will**: i.e. both the will of **heauenly destiny** (3) and
Artegall's will.

Stanza 25
1　**read**: declare.
4–5　*Fata viam invenient* (Virgil, *Aen.* iii 395), a classical tag
which Merlin answers.　**partake**: fulfil (sugg. by the context).
8–9　The argument that man should cooperate to fulfil his
destiny has an extended background in religious controversy
over predestination. S. stresses man's cooperation with God's
will.　**constant terme**: fixed goal or end.

Stanza 26
2　**Arthegall**: Arthgal of Cargueit or Warguit (Warwick) is
included in a list of consuls by Geoffrey of Monmouth IX xii;
he is cited by Hardyng as a knight of the Round Table. For
further on his name, see V i 3.2*n.*
4　**sib**: kin.
6–7　A similar story is told of the Red Cross Knight,
I x 65.6–7.

Stanzas 27–50
Merlin's chronicle begins with the historical Artegall and
concludes with his rapturous vision of the coming of
Elizabeth. The first cycle of sixteen stanzas, 27–42, pits the
Britons against the Saxons and ends with the triumph of the
Saxons. The second cycle of eight stanzas, 43–50, covers 800
years from the end of the Britons' rule to their return in the
Tudors. The time is divided into two hundred years of Saxon
rule, followed two hundred years later by the coming of the
Normans, and ending with a period of four hundred years that
leads to the coming of the Tudors. Berger (1969c) argues for a
series of three cycles each of eight stanzas (26–34, 35–42,
43–50). However, there is no historical break at 34, as there is
at 42: Gormund is succeeded by Ethelred and the Saxon
triumph continues.
　This chronicle forms the concluding section of the three-part
history of the Tudors. In II x 5–68 their story is told from the
coming of Brutus to the birth of Arthur. In III ix 41–51 the
beginning is told, from the fall of Troy to Brutus's building of
Troynovant.

Stanza 27
The chronicle at II x 5–68 ends with the succession of Uther
Pendragon. Geoffrey of Monmouth VIII xix tells how he
lusted after Igerna – called 'the Lady Igrayne' in *L.R.* – wife
of Gorlois, Duke of Cornwall. When he was transformed by
Merlin into the likeness of her husband he lay with her and
begot Arthur. See also Malory 7–9. Since Artegall is the son of
Gorlois, he is half-brother to Arthur. Hence he is 'Art-egall'
or 'equal to Arthur'. Harper (1910) 144 notes that Artegall
takes Arthur's place in the chronicle. The parallel story in
myth is Jove's similar deception of Alcmena which resulted in
the birth of Hercules.
2　In Geoffrey of Monmouth and Holinshed (1577), the
Duke of Cornwall aids Arthur. S. may have used Hardyng, as
Harper 144 suggests; or have made the identification because
Arthur left the crown to Cador's son, Constantine (Geoffrey of
Monmouth XI ii).
6　**From thence**: from Faeryland.

28

Great aid thereto his mighty puissaunce,
   And dreaded name shall giue in that sad day:
   Where also proofe of thy prow valiaunce
   Thou then shalt make, t'increase thy louers pray.
   Long time ye both in armes shall beare great sway,
   Till thy wombes burden thee from them do call,
   And his last fate him from thee take away,
   Too rathe cut off by practise criminall
Of secret foes, that him shall make in mischiefe fall.

29

With thee yet shall he leaue for memory
   Of his late puissaunce, his Image dead,
   That liuing him in all actiuity
   To thee shall represent.   He from the head
   Of his coosin *Constantius* without dread
   Shall take the crowne, that was his fathers right,
   And therewith crowne himselfe in th'others stead:
   Then shall he issew forth with dreadfull might,
Against his Saxon foes in bloudy field to fight.

30

Like as a Lyon, that in drowsie caue
   Hath long time slept, himselfe so shall he shake,
   And comming forth, shall spred his banner braue
   Ouer the troubled South, that it shall make
   The warlike *Mertians* for feare to quake:
   Thrise shall he fight with them, and twise shall win,
   But the third time shall faire accordaunce make:
   And if he then with victorie can lin,
He shall his dayes with peace bring to his earthly In.

31

His sonne, hight *Vortipore*, shall him succeede
   In kingdome, but not in felicity;
   Yet shall he long time warre with happy speed,
   And with great honour many battels try:
   But at the last to th'importunity
   Of froward fortune shall be forst to yield.
   But his sonne *Malgo* shall full mightily
   Auenge his fathers losse, with speare and shield,
And his proud foes discomfit in victorious field.

32

Behold the man, and tell me *Britomart*,
   If ay more goodly creature thou didst see;
   How like a Gyaunt in each manly part
   Beares he himselfe with portly maiestee,
   That one of th'old *Heroes* seemes to bee:
   He the six Islands, comprouinciall
   In auncient times vnto great Britainee,
   Shall to the same reduce, and to him call
Their sundry kings to do their homage seuerall.

33

All which his sonne *Careticus* awhile
   Shall well defend, and *Saxons* powre suppresse,
   Vntill a straunger king from vnknowne soyle
   Arriuing, him with multitude oppresse;
   Great *Gormond*, hauing with huge mightinesse
   Ireland subdewd, and therein fixt his throne,
   Like a swift Otter, fell through emptinesse,
   Shall ouerswim the sea with many one
Of his Norueyses, to assist the Britons fone.

Stanza 28
Cf. the prophecy by the priest of Isis, V vii 23.
3   **prow valiaunce**: brave valour.
4   **pray**: prey, spoils.
6   **burden**: the child borne in the womb.
8   **rathe**: soon.   **practise**: treachery.
9   **mischiefe**: evil plight.

Stanza 29
Artegall's son is not named though Geoffrey of Monmouth
XI iv–v records that Conanus killed his uncle, Constantine,
who had succeeded Arthur as king. S. is deliberately vague.
2   **his Image dead**: the image of him (Artegall) when he
is dead.
3   **in all actiuity**: i.e. as he really was, as shown in his
actions.

Stanza 30
1–2   Holinshed V xv quotes Gildas's comparison of Conan
to a lion's whelp. The simile is biblical: Gen. 49.9. Cf. V vii
23.7–9.
4–9   S. invents Conan's wars against the **Mertians** who are
warlike because of their name.   **lin**: leave off.

Stanza 31
3   **speed**: success.
4   **try**: undergo, experience.
5   **importunity**: cruelty; grievous demands.
7–9   Not in the chronicles.   **discomfit**: entirely defeat.

Stanza 32
Geoffrey of Monmouth XI vii says that Malgo was the most
handsome of men and of great strength.
6   **comprouinciall**: belonging to the same province.
Harper (1910) 150 suggests that this word may be taken from
Geoffrey's *sex comprovinciales Oceani insulas*.
8   **reduce**: make subject.
9   **seuerall**: particular; or (as adv.) separately.

Stanza 33
1–2   S. improves upon history by claiming genealogical
succession and by making **Careticus** triumphant before he is
overthrown.
3–9   The simile is the poet's, playing upon **Gormond**:
gourmand, glutton.   **oppresse**: overwhelm.   **Norueyses**:
Norwegians.

34

He in his furie all shall ouerrunne,
  And holy Church with faithlesse hands deface,
  That thy sad people vtterly fordonne,
  Shall to the vtmost mountaines fly apace :
  Was neuer so great wast in any place,
  Nor so fowle outrage doen by liuing men :
  For all thy Cities they shall sacke and race,
  And the greene grasse, that groweth, they shall bren,
That euen the wild beast shall dy in starued den.

35

Whiles thus thy Britons do in languour pine,
  Proud *Etheldred* shall from the North arise,
  Seruing th'ambitious will of *Augustine*,
  And passing *Dee* with hardy enterprise,
  Shall backe repulse the valiaunt *Brockwell* twise,
  And *Bangor* with massacred Martyrs fill ;
  But the third time shall rew his foolhardise :
  For *Cadwan* pittying his peoples ill,
Shall stoutly him defeat, and thousand *Saxons* kill.

36

But after him, *Cadwallin* mightily
  On his sonne *Edwin* all those wrongs shall wreake ;
  Ne shall auaile the wicked sorcery
  Of false *Pellite*, his purposes to breake,
  But him shall slay, and on a gallowes bleake
  Shall giue th'enchaunter his vnhappy hire ;
  Then shall the Britons, late dismayd and weake,
  From their long vassalage gin to respire,
And on their Paynim foes auenge their ranckled ire.

37

Ne shall he yet his wrath so mitigate,
  Till both the sonnes of *Edwin* he haue slaine,
  Offricke and *Osricke*, twinnes vnfortunate,
  Both slaine in battell vpon Layburne plaine,
  Together with the king of *Louthiane*,
  Hight *Adin*, and the king of *Orkeny*,
  Both ioynt partakers of their fatall paine :
  But *Penda*, fearefull of like desteny,
Shall yield him selfe his liegeman, and sweare fealty.

38

Him shall he make his fatall Instrument,
  T'afflict the other *Saxons* vnsubdewd ;
  He marching forth with fury insolent
  Against the good king *Oswald*, who indewd
  With heauenly powre, and by Angels reskewd,
  All holding crosses in their hands on hye,
  Shall him defeate withouten bloud imbrewd :
  Of which, that field for endlesse memory,
Shall *Heuenfield* be cald to all posterity.

39

Where at *Cadwallin* wroth, shall forth issew,
  And an huge hoste into Northumber lead,
  With which he godly *Oswald* shall subdew,
  And crowne with martyrdome his sacred head.
  Whose brother *Oswin*, daunted with like dread,
  With price of siluer shall his kingdome buy,
  And *Penda*, seeking him adowne to tread,
  Shall tread adowne, and do him fowly dye,
But shall with gifts his Lord *Cadwallin* pacify.

40

Then shall *Cadwallin* dye, and then the raine
  Of *Britons* eke with him attonce shall dye ;
  Ne shall the good *Cadwallader* with paine,
  Or powre, be hable it to remedy,
  When the full time prefixt by destiny,
  Shalbe expird of *Britons* regiment.
  For heauen it selfe shall their successe enuy,
  And them with plagues and murrins pestilent
Consume, till all their warlike puissaunce be spent.

Stanza 34
2   Geoffrey of Monmouth XI viii notes only that the clergy were destroyed.   **deface**: ruin, lay waste.
7   **race**: raze.
9   **in starued den**: i.e. starved in its den.

Stanza 35
Harper (1910) 154–8 shows that there is authority for S.'s variations from Geoffrey of Monmouth in Grafton, *Abridgement*; the *Description of Cambria*; the *Breviary of Britayne*; Hardyng, *Chronicle*; and Stow, *Annales*.
1   **languour**: woeful plight; or 'long vassalage' (36.8).
7   **foolhardise**: foolhardiness.

Stanza 36
5–6   S. substitutes hanging for Geoffrey of Monmouth's stabbing.   **hire**: reward.
7   **dismayd**: defeated; discouraged.
8   **respire**: recover courage.

Stanza 37
7   **fatall paine**: i.e. the pain of death; or endeavours which brought death.

Stanza 38
3   **insolent**: proud, arrogant.
4   **indewd**: invested.
6   **All holding crosses**: history records only that the cross was set up in the field.
7   **imbrewd**: i.e. being spilled, or staining their hands.

Stanza 39
5   **like dread**: dread of suffering the like.
7–8   **And Penda . . . dye**: Oswin shall tread down and slay Penda who sought to tread him down.

Stanza 40
1–2   S. ignores Cadwallader's twelve-year reign; noted Harper (1910) 164.
6   **regiment**: rule.
7   **enuy**: begrudge.
8   **murrins**: pestilences.

41

Yet after all these sorrowes, and huge hills
   Of dying people, during eight yeares space,
   Cadwallader not yielding to his ills,
   From *Armoricke*, where long in wretched cace
   He liu'd, returning to his natiue place,
   Shalbe by vision staid from his intent:
   For th'heauens haue decreed, to displace
   The *Britons*, for their sinnes dew punishment,
And to the *Saxons* ouer-giue their gouernment.

42

Then woe, and woe, and euerlasting woe,
   Be to the Briton babe, that shalbe borne,
   To liue in thraldome of his fathers foe;
   Late King, now captiue, late Lord, now forlorne,
   The worlds reproch, the cruell victors scorne,
   Banisht from Princely bowre to wastfull wood:
   O who shall helpe me to lament, and mourne
   The royall seed, the antique *Troian* blood,
Whose Empire lenger here, then euer any stood.

43

The Damzell was full deepe empassioned,
   Both for his griefe, and for her peoples sake,
   Whose future woes so plaine he fashioned,
   And sighing sore, at length him thus bespake;
   Ah but will heauens fury neuer slake,
   Nor vengeaunce huge relent it selfe at last?
   Will not long misery late mercy make,
   But shall their name for euer be defast,
And quite from of the earth their memory be rast?

44

Nay but the terme (said he) is limited,
   That in this thraldome *Britons* shall abide,
   And the iust reuolution measured,
   That they as Straungers shalbe notifide.
   For twise foure hundreth yeares shalbe supplide,
   Ere they to former rule restor'd shalbee,
   And their importune fates all satisfide:
   Yet during this their most obscuritee,
Their beames shall oft breake forth, that men them faire may see.

45

For *Rhodoricke*, whose surname shalbe Great,
   Shall of him selfe a braue ensample shew,
   That Saxon kings his friendship shall intreat;
   And *Howell Dha* shall goodly well indew
   The saluage minds with skill of iust and trew;
   Then *Griffyth Conan* also shall vp reare
   His dreaded head, and the old sparkes renew
   Of natiue courage, that his foes shall feare,
Least backe againe the kingdome he from them should beare.

46

Ne shall the Saxons selues all peaceably
   Enioy the crowne, which they from Britons wonne
   First ill, and after ruled wickedly:
   For ere two hundred yeares be full outronne,
   There shall a Rauen far from rising Sunne,
   With his wide wings vpon them fiercely fly,
   And bid his faithlesse chickens ouerronne
   The fruitfull plaines, and with fell cruelty,
In their auenge, tread downe the victours surquedry.

Stanza 41
4   **Armoricke**: Brittany.
5   **returning**: intending to return, as Geoffrey of Monmouth
XII xvii records.
9   **ouer-giue**: give over.

Stanza 42
1   The language of Rev. 8.13: 'Wo, wo, wo, to the
inhabitants of the earth.'
6   **wastfull**: desolate.
9   Over 1,800 years, according to Church's (1758) estimate.
The longest of the seven ages into which the Geneva Bible
divides human history is 1,656 years.

Stanza 43
2   In Geoffrey of Monmouth VII iii, Merlin bursts into
tears when his prophetical spirit reveals the disasters that will
befall the British nation.
9   **of**: off.   **rast**: erased.

Stanza 44
3   **iust**: full, complete; exact; proper; cf. 48.1.
4   **notifide**: denoted, known.
5   The interval between Cadwallader's death and the
accession of Henry VII is almost 800 years.   **supplide**:
completed.
7   **importune**: grievous; cruel.

Stanza 45
S. selects three Welsh kings whose reigns cover almost three
hundred years before the middle of the interregnum of British
rule.
5   **skill**: knowledge.

Stanza 46
4   The period corresponds roughly to that of Rhodoricke
the Great.
5–9   The **Rauen** of the arms of Denmark; **his faithlesse
chickens**: the heathen brood of Danes.
9   **auenge**: vengeance.   **surquedry**: arrogance.

333

47

Yet shall a third both these, and thine subdew;
    There shall a Lyon from the sea-bord wood
    Of *Neustria* come roring, with a crew
    Of hungry whelpes, his battailous bold brood,
    Whose clawes were newly dipt in cruddy blood,
    That from the Daniske Tyrants head shall rend
    Th'vsurped crowne, as if that he were wood,
    And the spoile of the countrey conquered
Emongst his young ones shall diuide with bountyhed.

48

Tho when the terme is full accomplishid,
    There shall a sparke of fire, which hath long-while
    Bene in his ashes raked vp, and hid,
    Be freshly kindled in the fruitfull Ile
    Of *Mona*, where it lurked in exile;
    Which shall breake forth into bright burning flame,
    And reach into the house, that beares the stile
    Of royall maiesty and soueraigne name;
So shall the Briton bloud their crowne againe reclame.

49

Thenceforth eternall vnion shall be made
    Betweene the nations different afore,
    And sacred Peace shall louingly perswade
    The warlike minds, to learne her goodly lore,
    And ciuile armes to exercise no more:
    Then shall a royall virgin raine, which shall
    Stretch her white rod ouer the *Belgicke* shore,
    And the great Castle smite so sore with all,
That it shall make him shake, and shortly learne to fall.

50

But yet the end is not.   There *Merlin* stayd,
    As ouercomen of the spirites powre,
    Or other ghastly spectacle dismayd,
    That secretly he saw, yet note discoure:
    Which suddein fit, and halfe extatick stoure
    When the two fearefull women saw, they grew
    Greatly confused in behauioure;
    At last the fury past, to former hew
Hee turnd againe, and chearefull looks ⟨as earst⟩ did shew.

51

Then, when them selues they well instructed had
    Of all, that needed them to be inquird,
    They both conceiuing hope of comfort glad,
    With lighter hearts vnto their home retird;
    Where they in secret counsell close conspird,
    How to effect so hard an enterprize,
    And to possesse the purpose they desird:
    Now this, now that twixt them they did deuise,
And diuerse plots did frame, to maske in strange disguise.

52

At last the Nourse in her foolhardy wit
    Conceiu'd a bold deuise, and thus bespake;
    Daughter, I deeme that counsell aye most fit,
    That of the time doth dew aduauntage take;
    Ye see that good king *Vther* now doth make
    Strong warre vpon the Paynim brethren, hight
    Octa and *Oza*, whom he lately brake
    Beside *Cayr Verolame*, in victorious fight,
334 That now all *Britanie* doth burne in armes bright.

Stanza 47
2–4   The **Lyon of Neustria** is William I of Normandy.
S. imitates Merlin's speech in Geoffrey of Monmouth VII iii:
'Woe to thee, Neustria, because the lion's brain shall be
poured upon thee. . . . The roaring whelps shall watch, and,
leaving the woods, shall hunt within the walls of cities.'
sea-bord: bordering on the sea.
5   **cruddy**: clotted.
7   **wood**: insane.
9   **bountyhed**: liberality.

Stanza 48
Henry of Richmond, the future Henry VII, was born in the
Isle of Anglesey (**Mona**), the last stronghold of the Britons.
Burkhart (1975) 18 comments rightly: 'surely it is the Tudor
line which Spenser has in mind as reclaiming the Briton
crown.'
7   **stile**: title.

Stanza 49
2   **different**: differing.
5   **ciuile armes**: referring to civil dissension between
England and Wales, or within England; cf. 'ciuill iarre' (23.9).
6–9   The **royall virgin** is Elizabeth who brought peace to
the Netherlands and defeated Philip II of Spain. The **white
rod** is her symbol of power; see *Shakespeare's England*
(1916–7) i 84 and Fletcher (1971) 277. As King of Castile,
Philip's arms contained a castle. In the Dedicatory Sonnet to
Lord Howard, S. refers to the Spanish Armada as 'those huge
castles of Castilian king'. This prophecy is fulfilled when
Mercilla sends Arthur to aid Belge, V x 16f. For the **great
Castle**, see V x 26f.

Stanza 50
1   The language of prophecy: 'but the end is not yet'
(Matt. 24.6).
4   **note discoure**: could not reveal; or did not know how to
reveal since S. is not a prophet.
5   **halfe extatick stoure**: Merlin's ecstatic trance after the
quiet beginning (see 21.4–5) and the grief of his lament at 42
suggest a vision of England's domination over Europe.
9   **as earst**] added *1609*.

Stanza 51
2   **Of all . . . to be inquird**: of all they needed to ask.
7   **possesse**: achieve.
9   Britomart assumes 'straunge / And base attyre' (7.1–2)
to learn about her love. Cf. V vii 21.1. Love masks in strange
disguise throughout Books III and IV: Florimell 'in so
straunge disguizement there did maske' (vii 14.3); Jove appears
'In straunge disguize' (xi 30.4); Amoret takes part in a masque
(xii 19–21; cf. IV i 14.8); and Artegall appears 'In quyent
disguise' (IV iv 39.3).

Stanza 52
5–9   These events surround the story of Arthur: **lately**
refers to the events recorded by Geoffrey of Monmouth VIII
xviii, **now** to those in xxii–xxiv. Arthur's birth is told in xix–xx.
brake: defeated.

53

That therefore nought our passage may empeach,
 Let vs in feigned armes our selues disguize,
 And our weake hands (whom need new strength shall teach)
 The dreadfull speare and shield to exercize:
 Ne certes daughter that same warlike wize
 I weene, would you misseeme; for ye bene tall,
 And large of limbe, t'atchieue an hard emprize,
 Ne ought ye want, but skill, which practize small
Will bring, and shortly make you a mayd Martiall.

54

And sooth, it ought your courage much inflame,
 To heare so often, in that royall hous,
 From whence to none inferiour ye came,
 Bards tell of many women valorous
 Which haue full many feats aduenturous
 Performd, in paragone of proudest men:
 The bold *Bunduca*, whose victorious
 Exploits made *Rome* to quake, stout *Guendolen*,
Renowmed *Martia*, and redoubted *Emmilen*.

55

And that, which more then all the rest may sway,
 Late dayes ensample, which these eyes beheld,
 In the last field before *Meneuia*
 Which *Vther* with those forrein Pagans held,
 I saw a *Saxon* Virgin, the which feld
 Great *Vlfin* thrise vpon the bloudy plaine,
 And had not *Carados* her hand withheld
 From rash reuenge, she had him surely slaine,
Yet *Carados* himselfe from her escapt with paine.

56

Ah read, (quoth *Britomart*) how is she hight?
 Faire *Angela* (quoth she) men do her call,
 No whit lesse faire, then terrible in fight:
 She hath the leading of a Martiall
 And mighty people, dreaded more then all
 The other *Saxons*, which do for her sake
 And loue, themselues of her name *Angles* call.
 Therefore faire Infant her ensample make
Vnto thy selfe, and equall courage to thee take.

57

Her harty words so deepe into the mynd
 Of the young Damzell sunke, that great desire
 Of warlike armes in her forthwith they tynd,
 And generous stout courage did inspire,
 That she resolu'd, vnweeting to her Sire,
 Aduent'rous knighthood on her selfe to don,
 And counseld with her Nourse, her Maides attire
 To turne into a massy habergeon,
And bad her all things put in readinesse anon.

58

Th'old woman nought, that needed, did omit;
 But all things did conueniently puruay:
 It fortuned (so time their turne did fit)
 A band of Britons ryding on forray
 Few dayes before, had gotten a great pray
 Of Saxon goods, emongst the which was seene
 A goodly Armour, and full rich aray,
 Which long'd to *Angela*, the Saxon Queene,
All fretted round with gold, and goodly well beseene.

Stanza 53

1   **empeach**: hinder.
2   **feigned**: i.e. serving to disguise.
3   **(whom . . . teach)**] (need makes good schollers) teach
1590. The revision improves the line but confuses the syntax.
4   **exercize**: use.
6   **misseeme**: misbecome.
7   **emprize**: enterprise.
9   **a mayd Martiall**: at this point Britomart forsakes one
etymology of her name for a more comprehensive one; see
i 8.6*n*.

Stanza 54

6   **paragone**: emulation.
7–9   **Bunduca**: see II x 54–56.   **Guendolen**: see II x
18–20.   **Martia**: see II x 42.   **Emmilen**: perhaps the
Queen of Cornwall and mother of Tristram, VI ii 29.

Stanza 55

3   **last field**: after the battle against the Saxons at **Meneuia**,
news arrives of Aurelius's death (Geoffrey of Monmouth
VIII xvi).
5   **a Saxon Virgin**: Harper (1910) 165–8 notes that the
chronicles provide barely more than the name, Angela.
6   **Great Vlfin** helped Arthur seduce Igerna and for that
reason may be singled out for punishment.
9   **paine**: difficulty.

Stanza 56

1   **read**: tell.
7   This naming of England is discussed by the chroniclers.

Stanza 57

1   **harty**: bold (cf. 52.1); also as they give her heart or
courage.
3   **tynd**: kindled.
4   **generous**: high-born (cf. 54.1–3); high-spirited.
8   **habergeon**: a sleeveless coat of mail; it is associated with
virtue and especially with chastity. Thus it is worn by Guyon
and Cymochles when they fight on Phædria's Isle (II vi 29.5);
and also by Timias when he is wounded by the lustful Foster
(III v 19.3): when it is removed (31.8), he is wounded by love
for Belphœbe. It is worn also by Scudamour (III xi 7.5) and
by Radigund (V v 2.9).

Stanza 58

2   **conueniently**: fittingly.   **puruay**: furnish.
5   **pray**: plunder.
9   **fretted**: adorned.   **goodly well beseene**: of good
appearance.

59

The same, with all the other ornaments,
King *Ryence* caused to be hanged hy
In his chiefe Church, for endlesse moniments
Of his successe and gladfull victory:
Of which her selfe auising readily,
In th'euening late old *Glauce* thither led
Faire *Britomart*, and that same Armory
Downe taking, her therein appareled,
Well as she might, and with braue bauldrick garnished.

60

Beside those armes there stood a mighty speare,
Which *Bladud* made by Magick art of yore,
And vsd the same in battell aye to beare;
Sith which it had bin here preseru'd in store,
For his great vertues proued long afore:
For neuer wight so fast in sell could sit,
But him perforce vnto the ground it bore:
Both speare she tooke, and shield, which hong by it:
Both speare and shield of great powre, for her purpose fit.

61

Thus when she had the virgin all arayd,
Another harnesse, which did hang thereby,
About her selfe she dight, that the young Mayd
She might in equall armes accompany,
And as her Squire attend her carefully:
Tho to their ready Steeds they clombe full light,
And through back wayes, that none might them espy,
Couered with secret cloud of silent night,
Themselues they forth conuayd, and passed forward right.

62

Ne rested they, till that to Faery lond
They came, as *Merlin* them directed late:
Where meeting with this *Redcrosse* knight, she fond
Of diuerse things discourses to dilate,
But most of *Arthegall*, and his estate.
At last their wayes so fell, that they mote part:
Then each to other well affectionate,
Friendship professed with vnfained hart,
The *Redcrosse* knight diuerst, but forth rode *Britomart*.

Cant. IIII.

Bold Marinell of Britomart,
Is throwne on the Rich strond:
Faire Florimell of Arthur is
Long followed, but not fond.

1

WHere is the Antique glory now become,
That whilome wont in women to appeare?
Where be the braue atchieuements doen by some?
Where be the battels, where the shield and speare,
And all the conquests, which them high did reare,
That matter made for famous Poets verse,
And boastfull men so oft abasht to heare?
Bene they all dead, and laid in dolefull herse?
Or doen they onely sleepe, and shall againe reuerse?

2

If they be dead, then woe is me therefore:
But if they sleepe, O let them soone awake:
For all too long I burne with enuy sore,
To heare the warlike feates, which *Homere* spake
Of bold *Penthesilee*, which made a lake
Of *Greekish* bloud so oft in *Troian* plaine;
But when I read, how stout *Debora* strake
Proud *Sisera*, and how *Camill'* hath slaine
The huge *Orsilochus*, I swell with great disdaine.

Stanza 59

5   **auising readily**: seeing ready at hand.
7   **Armory**: armour.
9   **bauldrick**: a belt worn from the shoulder to support the sword.

Stanza 60

2   **Bladud**: a Briton king whose magical powers are told at II x 25–26. The powers of the Saxons and the Britons are brought together in Britomart's armour.
7   **perforce**: forcibly.

Stanza 61

2   **harnesse**: suit of armour.
6   **clombe**: see iv 61.6*n*.
9   **conuayd**: stole away.   **forward right**: applied to Guyon at the end of his quest (II xii 53.4) but characteristic of Britomart; see iv 18.1–3*n*.

Stanza 62

5   **estate**: state, fortune.
7–8   Stressing the bond between Chastity and Holiness.
9   **diuerst**: turned aside (from Lat. *diversus*). A final turning aside for the Knight; he does not appear again. Cf. iv 4.6–9.
forth: 'forward right' (61.9). It signals the renewed beginning of her quest; cf. iv 5.1.

Canto iv

Stanza 1
Cf. ii 1.
1   **become**: gone.
9   **reuerse**: return.

Stanza 2
4–9   Homer does not in fact speak of **Penthesilee** although Virgil describes her (*Aen.* i 490–3; see II iii 31.5–9) and also tells how **Camilla** slew **Orsilochus** (*Aen.* xi 690–8). For **Debora**, see Judges 4; through her the Lord delivered Sisera into the hands of Jael who drove the tent-pin into his temple. For the cult of Elizabeth as Deborah, see Wilson (1939) ch. ii.
9   **disdaine**: i.e. pride for women or contempt for men; or indignation that he does not have such matter for his song.

3

Yet these, and all that else had puissaunce,
　Cannot with noble *Britomart* compare,
　Aswell for glory of great valiaunce,
　As for pure chastitie and vertue rare,
　That all her goodly deeds do well declare.
　Well worthy stock, from which the branches sprong,
　That in late yeares so faire a blossome bare,
　As thee, O Queene, the matter of my song,
Whose lignage from this Lady I deriue along.

4

Who when through speaches with the *Redcrosse* knight,
　She learned had th'estate of *Arthegall*,
　And in each point her selfe informd aright,
　A friendly league of loue perpetuall
　She with him bound, and *Congé* tooke withall.
　Then he forth on his iourney did proceede,
　To seeke aduentures, which mote him befall,
　And win him worship through his warlike deed,
Which alwayes of his paines he made the chiefest meed.

5

But *Britomart* kept on her former course,
　Ne euer dofte her armes, but all the way
　Grew pensiue through that amorous discourse,
　By which the *Redcrosse* knight did earst display
　Her louers shape, and cheualrous aray;
　A thousand thoughts she fashioned in her mind,
　And in her feigning fancie did pourtray
　Him such, as fittest she for loue could find,
Wise, warlike, personable, curteous, and kind.

6

With such selfe-pleasing thoughts her wound she fed,
　And thought so to beguile her grieuous smart;
　But so her smart was much more grieuous bred,
　And the deepe wound more deepe engord her hart,
　That nought but death her dolour mote depart.
　So forth she rode without repose or rest,
　Searching all lands and each remotest part,
　Following the guidaunce of her blinded guest,
Till that to the sea-coast at length she her addrest.

7

There she alighted from her light-foot beast,
　And sitting downe vpon the rocky shore,
　Bad her old Squire vnlace her lofty creast;
　Tho hauing vewd a while the surges hore,
　That gainst the craggy clifts did loudly rore,
　And in their raging surquedry disdaynd,
　That the fast earth affronted them so sore,
　And their deuouring couetize restraynd,
Thereat she sighed deepe, and after thus complaynd.

8

Huge sea of sorrow, and tempestuous griefe,
　Wherein my feeble barke is tossed long,
　Far from the hoped hauen of reliefe,
　Why do thy cruell billowes beat so strong,
　And thy moyst mountaines each on others throng,
　Threatning to swallow vp my fearefull life?
　O do thy cruell wrath and spightfull wrong
　At length allay, and stint thy stormy strife,
Which in these troubled bowels raignes, and rageth rife.

Stanza 3
4　The first reference to Britomart's chastity, made explicit now that her love for Artegall is known.　pure is strongly assertive, perhaps because chastity may be queried in one who seeks to lose her virginity to an unknown paramour.
5　As virtue is always manifest in virtuous action.
6–9　See iii 22.2–9.　**along**: continuously or directly.

Stanza 4
4–5　Repeating the gist of iii 62.7–8. See i 12.7–9*n*.
8–9　**worship**: honour. Honour was the chief reward of his endeavours.

Stanza 5
7–9　Britomart's **feigning fancie**, portraying what she desires, leads her to virtuous action; in contrast, Amoret's 'phantasies' (xii 26.3), portraying what she fears, imprison her in the house of Busirane. Britomart's catalogue proceeds from the private virtue in **Wise** to the public virtue in **warlike**, to handsome appearance and courteous bearing, and finally to **kind**, which means 'well-born', 'courteous', and (above all) 'loving'.

Stanza 6
2　**beguile**: divert attention from.
4　The metaphor is acted out in Amoret's heart 'transfixed with a deadly dart' (xii 21.3).
5　Arthur claims as much, I ix 8.3–5; but Britomart's love expresses the marriage vow, 'to love . . . til death us departe'.
dolour: physical pain; grief.　**depart**: remove.
8　**her blinded guest**: Cupid; cf. 'making blind loue her guide' (IV v 29.5).

Stanza 7
4　**surges hore**: white waves.
5–8　Cf. Job 38.8–11.　**surquedry**: arrogance.
disdaynd: angered.　**fast**: firmly fixed.　**affronted**: confronted; suggesting the etymological sense, 'to strike in the face'.　**couetize**: covetousness.

Stanzas 8–10
Britomart's complaint is termed an allegory by Alexander Gil, *Logonomia Anglica* (1619) 99. When she projects her inner emotional disorder into nature's disorder, the literal and allegorical senses merge. The correspondence is enforced by the change in 8.9 from 'thy' *1590* to **these**. Cf. her complaint, ii 39, and Florimell's complaint against the sea, IV xii 9. The topos used here is from Ps. 69.15: 'Let not the waterflood drowne me, nether let the depe swallowe me up.' Cf. *Amor*. xxxiv and its source in Petrarch, *Rime* 189. The motif of the storm-tossed ship also describes temperance, II ii 24. On the motif itself, see Williams (1970–1). Weld (1951) shows how the word-play relates her mental and moral states; Alpers (1967) 383 notes how her turbulent feelings of love are expressed in martial wrath; Brill (1971) 19 describes her conversion of sexual energies as sublimation.

Stanza 8
8　**stint**: stop.

337

9

For else my feeble vessell crazd, and crackt
  Through thy strong buffets and outrageous blowes,
  Cannot endure, but needs it must be wrackt
  On the rough rocks, or on the sandy shallowes,
  The whiles that loue it steres, and fortune rowes;
  Loue my lewd Pilot hath a restlesse mind
  And fortune Boteswaine no assuraunce knowes,
  But saile withouten starres gainst tide and wind:
How can they other do, sith both are bold and blind?

10

Thou God of winds, that raignest in the seas,
  That raignest also in the Continent,
  At last blow vp some gentle gale of ease,
  The which may bring my ship, ere it be rent,
  Vnto the gladsome port of her intent:
  Then when I shall my selfe in safety see,
  A table for eternall moniment
  Of thy great grace, and my great ieopardee,
Great *Neptune*, I auow to hallow vnto thee.

11

Then sighing softly sore, and inly deepe,
  She shut vp all her plaint in priuy griefe;
  For her great courage would not let her weepe,
  Till that old *Glauce* gan with sharpe repriefe,
  Her to restraine, and giue her good reliefe,
  Through hope of those, which *Merlin* had her told
  Should of her name and nation be chiefe,
  And fetch their being from the sacred mould
Of her immortall wombe, to be in heauen enrold.

12

Thus as she her recomforted, she spyde,
  Where farre away one all in armour bright,
  With hastie gallop towards her did ryde;
  Her dolour soone she ceast, and on her dight
  Her Helmet, to her Courser mounting light:
  Her former sorrow into suddein wrath,
  Both coosen passions of distroubled spright,
  Conuerting, forth she beates the dustie path;
Loue and despight attonce her courage kindled hath.

13

As when a foggy mist hath ouercast
  The face of heauen, and the cleare aire engrost,
  The world in darkenesse dwels, till that at last
  The watry Southwinde from the seabord cost
  Vpblowing, doth disperse the vapour lo'st,
  And poures it selfe forth in a stormy showre;
  So the faire *Britomart* hauing disclo'st
  Her clowdy care into a wrathfull stowre,
The mist of griefe dissolu'd, did into vengeance powre.

14

Eftsoones her goodly shield addressing faire,
  That mortall speare she in her hand did take,
  And vnto battell did her selfe prepaire.
  The knight approching, sternely her bespake;
  Sir knight, that doest thy voyage rashly make
  By this forbidden way in my despight,
  Ne doest by others death ensample take,
  I read thee soone retyre, whiles thou hast might,
Least afterwards it be too late to take thy flight.

Stanza 9

1 **crazd**: battered.
4 The wrecked metre enforces the meaning.
6–8 The metaphor clarifies the earlier statement that
Britomart is 'Following the guidaunce of her blinded guest'
(6.8) for 'no powre / Nor guidance of her selfe in her did dwell'
(ii 49.2–3). Cf. iii 14.5. Merlin reveals that her love is guided by
God's providence, iii 24. Cf. the Red Cross Knight guided by
Una, and Guyon by the Palmer and the Boatswain.
6 **lewd**: ignorant, unskilful; wicked; unchaste.
7 **assuraunce**: steadiness.
8 Cf. ii 7.7, and Arthur at 53.3–4.

Stanza 10

1–2 **Continent**: land, with the obvious pun; cf. 30.5.
Weld (1951) 550 observes that she prays to Aeolus who represents reason (according to Comes) so that, ruled by reason, she
may be continent. The sea and the land are the realms of
Marinell and Florimell.
7–9 **table**: votive tablet to the god, or picture of her suffering (perhaps from Horace, *Odes* I v). Neptune, to whom Britomart pleads for release from her 'Huge sea of sorrow' later
releases Florimell from her imprisonment under the sea, IV
xii 32. **hallow**: consecrate.

Stanza 11

4 **repriefe**: reproof.

Stanza 12

4 **dolour**: lamentation.
5 The **Helmet** is the token of her prowess; and the
Courser, the emblem of her control over the weaker passions.
6–7 Wrath and grief are the two extremes which denote
Phedon's intemperance, II iv 34–35; cf. Amavia's grief, II i
57–58. **distroubled**: greatly troubled.

Stanza 13

1–6 Personal observation is supported by Ovid, *Met.* i
264–9. For the meteorological theory, see Svendsen (1956) 97.
engrost: thickened.   **lo'st**: lossed, i.e. dissolved by dispers-
ing or precipitation; cf. II viii 48.
7 **disclo'st**: set free, converted; cf. 12.8.
8 **care**: grief.   **stowre**: fury, storm.
9 **dissolu'd**: turned into a liquid; dissolved in tears, referring to grief.   **powre**: the gathering strength of the line forces
the pun.

Stanza 14

1 **addressing faire**: arranging properly.
6 **in my despight**: in contemptuous defiance of me. Upton
(1758) notes the custom in medieval romance of passage being
forbidden a knight until he proved his manhood by combat.
7 **ensample**: warning.
8 **read**: advise.   **soone**: straightway.

15

Ythrild with deepe disdaine of his proud threat,
　She shortly thus; Fly they, that need to fly;
　Words fearen babes.　I meane not thee entreat
　To passe; but maugre thee will passe or dy.
　Ne lenger stayd for th'other to reply,
　But with sharpe speare the rest made dearly knowne.
　Strongly the straunge knight ran, and sturdily
　Strooke her full on the brest, that made her downe
Decline her head, and touch her crouper with her crowne.

16

But she againe him in the shield did smite
　With so fierce furie and great puissaunce,
　That through his threesquare scuchin percing quite,
　And through his mayled hauberque, by mischaunce
　The wicked steele through his left side did glaunce;
　Him so transfixed she before her bore
　Beyond his croupe, the length of all her launce,
　Till sadly soucing on the sandie shore,
He tombled on an heape, and wallowd in his gore.

17

Like as the sacred Oxe, that carelesse stands,
　With gilden hornes, and flowry girlonds crownd,
　Proud of his dying honor and deare bands,
　Whiles th'altars fume with frankincense arownd,
　All suddenly with mortall stroke astownd,
　Doth groueling fall, and with his streaming gore
　Distaines the pillours, and the holy grownd,
　And the faire flowres, that decked him afore;
So fell proud *Marinell* vpon the pretious shore.

18

The martiall Mayd stayd not him to lament,
　But forward rode, and kept her readie way
　Along the strond, which as she ouer-went,
　She saw bestrowed all with rich aray
　Of pearles and pretious stones of great assay,
　And all the grauell mixt with golden owre;
　Whereat she wondred much, but would not stay
　For gold, or perles, or pretious stones an howre,
But them despised all; for all was in her powre.

19

Whiles thus he lay in deadly stonishment,
　Tydings hereof came to his mothers eare;
　His mother was the blacke-browd *Cymoent*,
　The daughter of great *Nereus*, which did beare
　This warlike sonne vnto an earthly peare,
　The famous *Dumarin*; who on a day
　Finding the Nymph a sleepe in secret wheare,
　As he by chaunce did wander that same way,
Was taken with her loue, and by her closely lay.

Stanza 15
3　**fearen**: frighten.
7　**sturdily**: violently.
8　The blow on the breast is appropriate to Book III, as the wound in the head is to Book II; the distinction is that between love and reason. Cf. her 'thrilled brest' (ii 32.5; cf. 37.9) and Amoret's 'bleeding brest' (xii 38.4).
9　**crouper**: crupper, the back of the saddle or horse; cf. her blow at i 6.7.

Stanza 16
1　**againe**: in return.
3　**threesquare scuchin**: triangular shield; see i 4.4*n*.
4　**mayled hauberque**: long coat of chain mail.　**mischaunce**: evil fate.
5　The wound in the left or heart side indicates a love-wound; cf. v 20. See II v 7.8–9*n*. Not the thigh because Marinell is not wounded by lust.　**glaunce**: stronger than 'grazing', although the blow's full effect is muted.
7　**Beyond the crupper** indicates that her blow is stronger than his (15.9).　**the length of all her launce**: he is measured by chastity, as was Guyon (i 6.7).
8　**sadly soucing**: heavily falling.
9　**on**: in.

Stanza 17
Sacrifice of the castrated male animal provides a fitting simile for the male figure overcome by a woman.
1　**sacred**: appointed for sacrifice.　**carelesse**: free from care or unattended, to indicate a willing sacrifice.
3　**dying honor**: i.e. honour gained by dying.　**deare**: precious; grievous.
5　**astownd**: stunned.
7　**Distaines**: deeply stains.

Stanza 18
1–3　**readie**: direct; cf. 5.1, 44.9, iii 61.9, 62.9. Like Guyon she keeps the straight path; unlike him she is not tempted by wealth. See 21.5*n*. In Ripa (1603) 66, Chastity stands on coins to signify the defeat of avarice. Cf. the Red Cross Knight dazzled by Duessa's 'ritch weedes' (I ii 21.5).
5　**assay**: value.
8　**an howre**: i.e. a moment.
9　**for**: because. As Una's parents before their imprisonment 'all the world in their subiection held' (I i 5.6). Horace, *Odes* II ii, praises the temperate who may pass great heaps of treasure without glancing back.

Stanza 19
1　**deadly stonishment**: death-like numbness.
3　**Cymoent**: as also 33.2; *Cymodoce* at IV xi 53.7, xii 3.6. Cymodoce is a daughter of **Nereus** who comforts Achilles (Homer, *Iliad* xviii 39); cf. Virgil, *Aen*. v 826. Her name suggests 'flowing', or a 'wave' (κυμα); more explicitly, 'wave-tamer': see IV xi 53.7*n*. Her story parallels that of Thetis whom Peleus caught sleeping in a secret cave (Ovid, *Met*. xi 217–65) and who sought in vain to protect her child, Achilles, from the harm she was told would happen to him (*Met*. xiii 162–4). As with Marinell, that harm came from a woman; see Comes (1616) IX xii. On the relation between Marinell and Achilles, see Williams (1966) 118–9 and Roche (1964) 184–9.
4　**great**: as he is Homer's Old Man of the Sea. Virgil calls him *grandaevus* (*Georg*. iv 392). See IV xi 18.5 to 19.9.
5　**peare**: mate.
6　**Dumarin**: i.e. of the sea.
7　**wheare**: place.
9　**closely**: secretly.

20

There he this knight of her begot, whom borne
  She of his father *Marinell* did name,
  And in a rocky caue as wight forlorne,
  Long time she fostred vp, till he became
  A mightie man at armes, and mickle fame
  Did get through great aduentures by him donne:
  For neuer man he suffred by that same
  Rich strond to trauell, whereas he did wonne,
But that he must do battell with the Sea-nymphes sonne.

21

An hundred knights of honorable name
  He had subdew'd, and them his vassals made,
  That through all Farie lond his noble fame
  Now blazed was, and feare did all inuade,
  That none durst passen through that perilous glade.
  And to aduance his name and glorie more,
  Her Sea-god syre she dearely did perswade,
  T'endow her sonne with threasure and rich store,
Boue all the sonnes, that were of earthly wombes ybore.

22

The God did graunt his daughters deare demaund,
  To doen his Nephew in all riches flow;
  Eftsoones his heaped waues he did commaund,
  Out of their hollow bosome forth to throw
  All the huge threasure, which the sea below
  Had in his greedie gulfe deuoured deepe,
  And him enriched through the ouerthrow
  And wreckes of many wretches, which did weepe,
And often waile their wealth, which he from them did keepe.

23

Shortly vpon that shore there heaped was,
  Exceeding riches and all pretious things,
  The spoyle of all the world, that it did pas
  The wealth of th'East, and pompe of *Persian* kings;
  Gold, amber, yuorie, perles, owches, rings,
  And all that else was pretious and deare,
  The sea vnto him voluntary brings,
  That shortly he a great Lord did appeare,
As was in all the lond of Faery, or elsewheare.

24

Thereto he was a doughtie dreaded knight,
  Tryde often to the scath of many deare,
  That none in equall armes him matchen might,
  The which his mother seeing, gan to feare
  Least his too haughtie hardines might reare
  Some hard mishap, in hazard of his life:
  For thy she oft him counseld to forbeare
  The bloudie battell, and to stirre vp strife,
But after all his warre, to rest his wearie knife.

25

And for his more assurance, she inquir'd
  One day of *Proteus* by his mightie spell,
  (For *Proteus* was with prophecie inspir'd)
  Her deare sonnes destinie to her to tell,
  And the sad end of her sweet *Marinell*.
  Who through foresight of his eternall skill,
  Bad her from womankind to keepe him well:
  For of a woman he should haue much ill,
340 A virgin strange and stout him should dismay, or kill.

26

For thy she gaue him warning euery day,
  The loue of women not to entertaine;
  A lesson too too hard for liuing clay,
  From loue in course of nature to refraine:
  Yet he his mothers lore did well retaine,
  And euer from faire Ladies loue did fly;
  Yet many Ladies faire did oft complaine,
  That they for loue of him would algates dy:
Dy, who so list for him, he was loues enimy.

Stanza 20
2   **Marinell**: links the sea (from his father Dumarin) and
the land (from his association with Florimell). His **Rich
strond** (8) is tideland which belongs to both the sea and land.
The name also suggests 'Mars' and 'martial prowess'.
Sea-nymphes sonne (9) declares his mother-dominated state.
3   **rocky caue**: see viii 37*n*, IV xii 7.3*n*.

Stanza 21
1   **hundred**: an absolute or full number, as at IV iv 31.6, etc.
4   **inuade**: take possession of.
5   **perilous glade**: although inappropriate for the sea coast,
it is connected with Mammon's 'gloomy glade' (II vii 3.1)
where Guyon is tempted by wealth. Britomart triumphs over
Guyon's two major temptations, Beauty (Florimell) and Money,
before she begins her adventure.
7   **dearely**: earnestly. **perswade**: urge.

Stanza 22
1   **deare**: earnest; expensive.
2   **Nephew**: grandson.
4   **hollow bosome**: the troughs between the waves.

Stanza 23
5   **amber**: an alloy of gold and silver, from the biblical use,
as Ezek. 1.4. **owches**: jewels.

Stanza 24
1   **Thereto**: in addition to that.
2   **Tryde often . . . deare**: grievously proven to the harm of
many.
5   **hardines**: boldness.
7   **For thy**: therefore.

Stanza 25
1   **assurance**: security.
2–9   The prophetic powers of **Proteus** were widely known
(e.g. Virgil, *Georg.* iv 387–93) and parallel Merlin's. His
prophecy applies also to Florimell.
6   **eternall skill**: art of knowing eternal matters.
9   **strange**: foreign; cf. v 9.8. **dismay**: overthrow.

Stanza 26
5   **lore**: teaching.
6   Cf. v 9.5–7, and esp. IV xi 5.3–4: 'wemens loue [he] did
from his hart expell, / And all those ioyes that weake mankind
entyse.' Male chastity is Britomart's first threat in her effort
to conquer the love-despising Artegall (see IV vi 28.7–9).
8   **algates**: by all means; otherwise.

27

But ah, who can deceiue his destiny,
   Or weene by warning to auoyd his fate?
   That when he sleepes in most security,
   And safest seemes, him soonest doth amate,
   And findeth dew effect or soone or late.
   So feeble is the powre of fleshly arme.
   His mother bad him womens loue to hate,
   For she of womans force did feare no harme;
So weening to haue arm'd him, she did quite disarme.

28

This was that woman, this that deadly wound,
   That *Proteus* prophecide should him dismay,
   The which his mother vainely did expound,
   To be hart-wounding loue, which should assay
   To bring her sonne vnto his last decay.
   So tickle be the termes of mortall state,
   And full of subtile sophismes, which do play
   With double senses, and with false debate,
T'approue the vnknowen purpose of eternall fate.

29

Too true the famous *Marinell* it fownd,
   Who through late triall, on that wealthy Strond
   Inglorious now lies in senselesse swownd,
   Through heauy stroke of *Britomartis* hond.
   Which when his mother deare did vnderstond,
   And heauy tydings heard, whereas she playd
   Amongst her watry sisters by a pond,
   Gathering sweet daffadillyes, to haue made
Gay girlonds, from the Sun their forheads faire to shade;

30

Eftsoones both flowres and girlonds farre away
   She flong, and her faire deawy lockes yrent,
   To sorrow huge she turnd her former play,
   And gamesom merth to grieuous dreriment:
   She threw her selfe downe on the Continent,
   Ne word did speake, but lay as in a swowne,
   Whiles all her sisters did for her lament,
   With yelling outcries, and with shrieking sowne;
And euery one did teare her girlond from her crowne.

31

Soone as she vp out of her deadly fit
   Arose, she bad her charet to be brought,
   And all her sisters, that with her did sit,
   Bad eke attonce their charets to be sought;
   Tho full of bitter griefe and pensiue thought,
   She to her wagon clombe; clombe all the rest,
   And forth together went, with sorrow fraught.
   The waues obedient to their beheast,
Them yielded readie passage, and their rage surceast.

32

Great *Neptune* stood amazed at their sight,
   Whiles on his broad round backe they softly slid
   And eke himselfe mournd at their mournfull plight,
   Yet wist not what their wailing ment, yet did
   For great compassion of their sorrow, bid
   His mightie waters to them buxome bee:
   Eftsoones the roaring billowes still abid,
   And all the griesly Monsters of the See
Stood gaping at their gate, and wondred them to see.

33

A teme of Dolphins raunged in aray,
   Drew the smooth charet of sad *Cymoent*;
   They were all taught by *Triton*, to obay
   To the long raynes, at her commaundement:
   As swift as swallowes, on the waues they went,
   That their broad flaggie finnes no fome did reare,
   Ne bubbling roundell they behind them sent;
   The rest of other fishes drawen weare,
Which with their finny oars the swelling sea did sheare.

34

Soone as they bene arriu'd vpon the brim
   Of the *Rich strond*, their charets they forlore,
   And let their temed fishes softly swim
   Along the margent of the fomy shore,
   Least they their finnes should bruze, and surbate sore
   Their tender feet vpon the stony ground:
   And comming to the place, where all in gore
   And cruddy bloud enwallowed they found
The lucklesse *Marinell*, lying in deadly swound;

Stanza 27

1   **deceiue**: frustrate, cheat; parallels auoyd (2); cf. 36.9.
3   **That**: i.e. his fate.   **security**: culpable carelessness; see IV viii 31.1–5*n*.
4   **amate**: cast down.
5   **effect**: accomplishment, fulfilment.

Stanza 28

3   **vainely**: foolishly, for she was wrong.
5   **last decay**: death.
6   **tickle**: uncertain.
8   **debate**: wrangling, fallacious arguments 'that palter with us in a double sense' (*Macbeth* V viii 20).
9   **approue**: make good.

Stanza 30

4   **dreriment**: sorrow.
5   **Continent**: shore. See 10.1–2*n*. The shore belongs to the continent Marinell.

Stanza 31

5   **pensiue**: sorrowful.

Stanza 32

A mythological explanation of the two previous lines.
6   **buxome**: yielding.
7   **still abid**: remained (or became) still.
9   **their gate**: the manner in which they proceed.

Stanza 33

3–4   Comes (1616) VIII iii associates Triton with control over dolphins.
5   The swallow also skims the water.
7   **bubbling roundell**: circles or swirls of bubbles.

Stanza 34

2   **forlore**: left.
5   **surbate**: batter.
8   **cruddy**: clotted.

35

His mother swowned thrise, and the third time
    Could scarce recouered be out of her paine ;
    Had she not bene deuoyd of mortall slime,
    She should not then haue bene reliu'd againe,
    But soone as life recouered had the raine,
    She made so piteous mone and deare wayment,
    That the hard rocks could scarse from teares refraine,
    And all her sister Nymphes with one consent
Supplide her sobbing breaches with sad complement.

36

Deare image of my selfe (she said) that is,
    The wretched sonne of wretched mother borne,
    Is this thine high aduauncement, O is this
    Th'immortall name, with which thee yet vnborne
    Thy Gransire Nereus promist to adorne?
    Now lyest thou of life and honor reft ;
    Now lyest thou a lumpe of earth forlorne,
    Ne of thy late life memory is left,
Ne can thy irreuocable destiny be weft ?

37

Fond Proteus, father of false prophecis,
    And they more fond, that credit to thee giue,
    Not this the worke of womans hand ywis,
    That so deepe wound through these deare members driue.
    I feared loue : but they that loue do liue,
    But they that die, doe neither loue nor hate.
    Nath'lesse to thee thy folly I forgiue,
    And to my selfe, and to accursed fate
The guilt I doe ascribe : deare wisedome bought too late.

38

O what auailes it of immortall seed
    To beene ybred and neuer borne to die?
    Farre better I it deeme to die with speed,
    Then waste in woe and wailefull miserie.
    Who dyes the vtmost dolour doth abye,
    But who that liues, is left to waile his losse :
    So life is losse, and death felicitie.
    Sad life worse then glad death : and greater crosse
To see friends graue, then dead the graue selfe to engrosse.

39

But if the heauens did his dayes enuie,
    And my short blisse maligne, yet mote they well
    Thus much afford me, ere that he did die
    That the dim eyes of my deare Marinell
    I mote haue closed, and him bed farewell,
    Sith other offices for mother meet
    They would not graunt ;
    Yet maulgre them farewell, my sweetest sweet ;
Farewell my sweetest sonne, sith we no more shall meet.

40

Thus when they all had sorrowed their fill,
    They softly gan to search his griesly wound :
    And that they might him handle more at will,
    They him disarm'd, and spredding on the ground
    Their watchet mantles frindgd with siluer round,
    They softly wipt away the gelly blood
    From th'orifice ; which hauing well vpbound,
    They pourd in soueraine balme, and Nectar good,
342 Good both for earthly med'cine, and for heauenly food.

Stanza 35
3   **mortall slime**: cf. 'liuing clay' (26.3).
4   **reliu'd**: restored to life.
6   **deare wayment**: grievous lamentation.
8   **consent**: accord, in full harmony.
9   Their cries supplement hers by filling up the intervals between her sobs.

Stanza 36
7   **lumpe of earth**: in contrast to 'liuing clay' (26.3).
9   **weft**: avoided.

Stanza 37
1   **Fond**: foolish ; ignorant.
3   **ywis**: certainly ; or 'I know', in contrast to Proteus's ignorance.
4   **members**: limbs.

Stanza 38
2   In contrast to mortal seed which is **borne to die**.
5   **abye**: endure.
9   To see the grave of a friend rather than, dead oneself, to fill the grave.

Stanza 39
1   **enuie**: regard with dislike.
2   **maligne**: begrudge, or regard with envy.
4–5   In Virgil, *Aen*. ix 486–7, Euryalus's mother claims this office to the dead.
7   An incomplete line, perhaps left to show the mother's grief. She stops cursing the heavens to bid her dead son farewell.
8   **maulgre**: in spite of. Although the gods would not allow her to bid him farewell when he died, she may bid him farewell now.
9   **sith we no more shall meet**] till we againe may meet *1590*. The emendation increases the pathos.

Stanza 40
2   **search**: probe.
5   **watchet**: light blue, the colour of water, as IV xi 27.2.
8–9   As Venus washes Aeneas's wound, *Aen*. xii 418–9, and Thetis preserves Patroclus's body, *Iliad* xix 38–9. Nymphs are often associated with the art of healing.

41

Tho when the lilly handed *Liagore,*
  (This *Liagore* whylome had learned skill
  In leaches craft, by great *Appolloes* lore,
  Sith her whylome vpon high *Pindus* hill,
  He loued, and at last her wombe did fill
  With heauenly seed, whereof wise *Pæon* sprong)
  Did feele his pulse, she knew their staied still
  Some litle life his feeble sprites emong;
Which to his mother told, despeire she from her flong.

42

Tho vp him taking in their tender hands,
  They easily vnto her charet beare:
  Her teme at her commaundement quiet stands,
  Whiles they the corse into her wagon reare,
  And strow with flowres the lamentable beare:
  Then all the rest into their coches clim,
  And through the brackish waues their passage sheare;
  Vpon great *Neptunes* necke they softly swim,
And to her watry chamber swiftly carry him.

43

Deepe in the bottome of the sea, her bowre
  Is built of hollow billowes heaped hye,
  Like to thicke cloudes, that threat a stormy showre,
  And vauted all within, like to the sky,
  In which the Gods do dwell eternally:
  There they him laid in easie couch well dight;
  And sent in haste for *Tryphon,* to apply
  Salues to his wounds, and medicines of might:
For *Tryphon* of sea gods the soueraine leach is hight.

44

The whiles the *Nymphes* sit all about him round,
  Lamenting his mishap and heauy plight;
  And oft his mother vewing his wide wound,
  Cursed the hand, that did so deadly smight
  Her dearest sonne, her dearest harts delight.
  But none of all those curses ouertooke
  The warlike Maid, th'ensample of that might,
  But fairely well she thriu'd, and well did brooke
Her noble deeds, ne her right course for ought forsooke.

45

Yet did false *Archimage* her still pursew,
  To bring to passe his mischieuous intent,
  Now that he had her singled from the crew
  Of courteous knights, the Prince, and Faery gent,
  Whom late in chace of beautie excellent
  She left, pursewing that same foster strong;
  Of whose foule outrage they impatient,
  And full of fiery zeale, him followed long,
To reskew her from shame, and to reuenge her wrong.

46

Through thick and thin, through mountaines and through
  Those two great champions did attonce pursew   (plains,
  The fearefull damzell, with incessant paines:
  Who from them fled, as light-foot hare from vew
  Of hunter swift, and sent of houndes trew.
  At last they came vnto a double way,
  Where, doubtfull which to take, her to reskew,
  Themselues they did dispart, each to assay,
Whether more happie were, to win so goodly pray.

Stanza 41
S. adapts the story of Apollo who ravishes Oenone and then teaches her the secrets of medicine. Finally Apollo himself must cure Marinell, IV xii 25.
1 **Liagore**: a nereid in Hesiod, *Theog.* 257.
3 **lore**: teaching.
6 **Pæon**: the healer; 'an excellent phisition' (Cooper, 1565); physician to the gods in Homer, *Iliad* v 401.

Stanza 42
2 **easily**: gently.
5 **lamentable**: attended by lamenting nymphs.

Stanza 43
1–5 In Virgil, *Georg.* iv 359–73, as the nymph Cyrene brings her mortal son to her bower beneath the water, the arching waves stand as mountains to allow them to enter.
vauted: vaulted.
7–9 **Tryphon**: a brother of Aesculapius, according to Boccaccio, *Gen. Deor.* VII xxxvi; noted Lotspeich (1932) 113. Selden supports S.'s mythologizing in his note to Drayton, *Poly-Olbion* xi 64: 'justifiable . . . as wel as to make *Tryphon* their Surgeon, which our excellent *Spenser* hath done' (*Works* iv 233).

Stanza 44
7 **ensample of that might**: example of 'womans force' (27.8) that overcame Marinell.
8 **fairely**: fully. **brooke**: bear up, ply.

Stanza 45
1–6 **Archimage**: he appears for the last time, serving to link the first three books. Cf. II i 5.1–5 and see i Arg. 3*n*.
His role as evil magician is assumed by Busirane.
4 **gent**: noble, valiant.
5 Cf. i 19.2.
8 **zeale**: ardour in pursuit; ardent love for Florimell.

Stanza 46
2 **attonce**: together.
4 **hare**: a prized animal of the chase and associated with the traditional hunt of Venus.
5 **trew**: sure, applied to scent; trusty or reliable, applied to the hounds.
8 **dispart**: separate.
9 **Whether more happie were**: which of the two would be more fortunate.

343

47

But *Timias*, the Princes gentle Squire,
　That Ladies loue vnto his Lord forlent,
　And with proud enuy, and indignant ire,
　After that wicked foster fiercely went.
　So beene they three three sundry wayes ybent.
　But fairest fortune to the Prince befell,
　Whose chaunce it was, that soone he did repent,
　To take that way, in which that Damozell
Was fled afore, affraid of him, as feend of hell.

48

At last of her farre off he gained vew:
　Then gan he freshly pricke his fomy steed,
　And euer as he nigher to her drew,
　So euermore he did increase his speed,
　And of each turning still kept warie heed:
　Aloud to her he oftentimes did call,
　To doe away vaine doubt, and needlesse dreed:
　Full myld to her he spake, and oft let fall
Many meeke wordes, to stay and comfort her withall.

49

But nothing might relent her hastie flight;
　So deepe the deadly feare of that foule swaine
　Was earst impressed in her gentle spright:
　Like as a fearefull Doue, which through the raine,
　Of the wide aire her way does cut amaine,
　Hauing farre off espyde a Tassell gent,
　Which after her his nimble wings doth straine,
　Doubleth her haste for feare to be for-hent,
And with her pineons cleaues the liquid firmament.

50

With no lesse haste, and eke with no lesse dreed,
　That fearefull Ladie fled from him, that ment
　To her no euill thought, nor euill deed;
　Yet former feare of being fowly shent,
　Carried her forward with her first intent:
　And though oft looking backward, well she vewd,
　Her selfe freed from that foster insolent,
　And that it was a knight, which now her sewd,
Yet she no lesse the knight feard, then that villein rude.

51

His vncouth shield and straunge armes her dismayd,
　Whose like in Faery lond were seldome seene,
　That fast she from him fled, no lesse affrayd,
　Then of wilde beastes if she had chased beene:
　Yet her he her followd still with courage keene,
　So long that now the golden *Hesperus*
　Was mounted high in top of heauen sheene,
　And warnd his other brethren ioyeous,
To light their blessed lamps in *Ioues* eternall hous.

52

All suddenly dim woxe the dampish ayre,
　And griesly shadowes couered heauen bright,
　That now with thousand starres was decked fayre;
　Which when the Prince beheld, a lothfull sight,
　And that perforce, for want of lenger light,
　He mote surcease his suit, and lose the hope
　Of his long labour, he gan fowly wyte
　His wicked fortune, that had turnd aslope,
And cursed night, that reft from him so goodly scope.

53

Tho when her wayes he could no more descry,
　But to and fro at disauenture strayd;
　Like as a ship, whose Lodestarre suddenly
　Couered with cloudes, her Pilot hath dismayd;
　His wearisome pursuit perforce he stayd,
　And from his loftie steed dismounting low,
　Did let him forage.　Downe himselfe he layd
　Vpon the grassie ground, to sleepe a throw;
The cold earth was his couch, the hard steele his pillow.

Stanza 47

2　forlent: gave up; i.e. he left the love of Florimell to Arthur. Her rescue is described as 'beauties chace' and interpreted as the search for 'Ladies Loue' (i 19.2–3); cf. 45.5.
3　enuy: desire, longing; here to perform a deed of chivalry.
5　ybent: bent, directed.
6　fairest fortune falls to Arthur because he follows the fairest, the Faerie Queene.
9　him: from Florimell's perspective, referring both to the Foster and to Arthur.

Stanza 48

7　vaine doubt: 'idle feare' (vi 54.9). The apprehensions of women in love are described in the masque of Cupid, xii 7–26.

Stanza 49

1　relent: slacken.
4–9　In the antique age, 'the Doue sate by the Faulcons side' (IV viii 31.2); their opposition marks the fallen world of Book III. Cf. the opposition of the eagle and dove in Donne, 'Canonization' 22. raine: region. amaine: with all her might; at full speed. Tassell gent: the tercel-gentle, a male falcon. for-hent: overtaken and seized. liquid: clear, bright.

Stanza 50

4　shent: defiled.
7　insolent: lustful.
8　sewd: pursued.

Stanza 51

1　vncouth: strange, being covered with a veil.
5　courage keene: the erotic implications explain her fear.
6–9　Hesperus: the evening star, the planet Venus, the goddess of Love; her place in mid-heaven marks her ascendancy over Arthur's thoughts.

Stanza 52

6　He must abandon his pursuit/courtship.
7　wyte: blame.
9　scope: sight; target.

Stanza 53

2　at disauenture: aimlessly, implying misfortune.
3–4　Cf. 9.6–8.
8　a throw: a while.

54

But gentle Sleepe enuyde him any rest ;
  In stead thereof sad sorrow, and disdaine
  Of his hard hap did vexe his noble brest,
  And thousand fancies bet his idle braine
  With their light wings, the sights of semblants vaine:
  Oft did he wish, that Lady faire mote bee
  His Faery Queene, for whom he did complaine:
  Or that his Faery Queene were such, as shee:
And euer hastie Night he blamed bitterlie.

55

Night thou foule Mother of annoyance sad,
  Sister of heauie death, and nourse of woe,
  Which wast begot in heauen, but for thy bad
  And brutish shape thrust downe to hell below,
  Where by the grim floud of *Cocytus* slow
  Thy dwelling is, in *Herebus* blacke hous,
  (Blacke *Herebus* thy husband is the foe
  Of all the Gods) where thou vngratious,
Halfe of thy dayes doest lead in horrour hideous.

56

What had th'eternall Maker need of thee,
  The world in his continuall course to keepe,
  That doest all things deface, ne lettest see
  The beautie of his worke ? Indeed in sleepe
  The slouthfull bodie, that doth loue to steepe
  His lustlesse limbes, and drowne his baser mind,
  Doth praise thee oft, and oft from *Stygian* deepe
  Calles thee, his goddesse in his error blind,
And great Dame Natures handmaide, chearing euery kind.

57

But well I wote, that to an heauy hart
  Thou art the root and nurse of bitter cares,
  Breeder of new, renewer of old smarts:
  In stead of rest thou lendest rayling teares,
  In stead of sleepe thou sendest troublous feares,
  And dreadfull visions, in the which aliue
  The drearie image of sad death appeares:
  So from the wearie spirit thou doest driue
Desired rest, and men of happinesse depriue.

58

Vnder thy mantle blacke there hidden lye,
  Light-shonning theft, and traiterous intent,
  Abhorred bloudshed, and vile felony,
  Shamefull deceipt, and daunger imminent;
  Foule horror, and eke hellish dreriment:
  All these I wote in thy protection bee,
  And light doe shonne, for feare of being shent:
  For light ylike is loth'd of them and thee,
And all that lewdnesse loue, doe hate the light to see.

59

For day discouers all dishonest wayes,
  And sheweth each thing, as it is indeed:
  The prayses of high God he faire displayes,
  And his large bountie rightly doth areed.
  Dayes dearest children be the blessed seed,
  Which darknesse shall subdew, and heauen win:
  Truth is his daughter; he her first did breed,
  Most sacred virgin, without spot of sin.
Our life is day, but death with darknesse doth begin.

Stanza 54
1 **enuyde**: refused.
2 **disdaine**: vexation, indignation.
5 **semblants**: appearances.
6–8 Cf. his response to Gloriana: 'So faire a creature yet saw neuer sunny day' (I ix 13.9). While Gloriana is fair, Florimell is fairness itself. Cf. IV ii 23.2–4. Lewis (1967) 132–5 sees a Platonic significance: the desire to find in an earthly image satisfaction for the spiritual eros leads man to seek divine glory. **complaine**: lament.

Stanzas 55–60
Arthur's complaint belongs to the moral tradition of the medieval complaint. As an aubade, it inverts the usual complaint on the brevity of night, e.g. Chaucer, *Troilus and Criseyde* iii 1429–42, 1450–6. Cf. the common praise of night, e.g. Du Bartas, *Divine Weekes* (1633) I i pp. 5–6.

Stanza 55
3–7 Cf. I v 22.3–6. On **Herebus** (6) and **Night** (1), see II iv 41.8–9*n*.
8 **vngratious**: wicked, devoid of spiritual grace.

Stanza 56
6 **lustlesse**: listless. **baser**: too base.
7–9 Desiring to sleep, man summons Night from hell, praising her as his goddess and Nature's handmaid.

Stanza 57
4 **rayling**: gushing; also the tears of those who rail.
7 **drearie**: horrid.

Stanza 58
Comes (1616) III xii lists the offspring of Night (cited Lotspeich, 1932, 91) and so does Hesiod, *Theog.* 211–25, but the correspondence with S. is not close.
3 **felony**: treachery.
4 **daunger**: mischief, harm or the power to harm.
7–9 'For everie man that evil doeth, hateth the light, nether commeth to light, lest his dedes shulde be reproved' (John 3.20). **shent**: put to shame. **lewdnesse**: wickedness.

Stanza 59
1–2 Cf. 1 Cor. 3.13.
4 **areed**: make known.
5–6 See I v 24.5*n*. **Dayes dearest children**] The children of day *1590*.

345

60

O when will day then turne to me againe,
　And bring with him his long expected light?
　O *Titan*, haste to reare thy ioyous waine:
Speed thee to spred abroad thy beames bright,
And chase away this too long lingring night,
Chase her away, from whence she came, to hell.
She, she it is, that hath me done despight:
There let her with the damned spirits dwell,
And yeeld her roome to day, that can it gouerne well.

61

Thus did the Prince that wearie night outweare,
　In restlesse anguish and vnquiet paine:
　And earely, ere the morrow did vpreare
His deawy head out of the *Ocean* maine,
He vp arose, as halfe in great disdaine,
And clombe vnto his steed.　So forth he went,
With heauie looke and lumpish pace, that plaine
In him bewraid great grudge and maltalent:
His steed eke seem'd t'apply his steps to his intent.

Cant. V.

*Prince Arthur heares of Florimell:
three fosters Timias wound,
Belphebe finds him almost dead,
and reareth out of sownd.*

1

Wonder it is to see, in diuerse minds,
　How diuersly loue doth his pageants play,
　And shewes his powre in variable kinds:
The baser wit, whose idle thoughts alway
Are wont to cleaue vnto the lowly clay,
It stirreth vp to sensuall desire,
And in lewd slouth to wast his carelesse day:
But in braue sprite it kindles goodly fire,
That to all high desert and honour doth aspire.

2

Ne suffereth it vncomely idlenesse,
　In his free thought to build her sluggish nest:
　Ne suffereth it thought of vngentlenesse,
Euer to creepe into his noble brest,
But to the highest and the worthiest
Lifteth it vp, that else would lowly fall:
It lets not fall, it lets it not to rest:
It lets not scarse this Prince to breath at all,
But to his first poursuit him forward still doth call.

3

Who long time wandred through the forrest wyde,
　To finde some issue thence, till that at last
　He met a Dwarfe, that seemed terrifyde
With some late perill, which he hardly past,
Or other accident, which him aghast;
Of whom he asked, whence he lately came,
And whither now he trauelled so fast:
For sore he swat, and running through that same
Thicke forest, was bescratcht, and both his feet nigh lame.

4

Panting for breath, and almost out of hart,
　The Dwarfe him answerd, Sir, ill mote I stay
　To tell the same.　I lately did depart
From Faery court, where I haue many a day
Serued a gentle Lady of great sway,
And high accompt through out all Elfin land,
Who lately left the same, and tooke this way:
Her now I seeke, and if ye vnderstand
Which way she fared hath, good Sir tell out of hand.

Stanza 60

3　**waine**: chariot.

Stanza 61

5　**disdaine**: vexation, indignation; cf. 54.2.
6　**clombe**: indicating the labour of mounting, perhaps humorously. Cf. IV v 46.1 and the contrast at iii 61.6.
8　**bewraid**: revealed.　**grudge**: resentment.　**maltalent**: ill-temper.
9　**apply**: adapt.　**intent**: frame of mind.

Canto v

Argument

4　**sownd**: swoon.

Stanza 1
Cf. iii 1.
2　**doth . . . play**: acts his parts; cf. Love's pageants in cantos xi and xii.
3　**variable kinds**: diverse natures.
4–9　Timias illustrates the **baser wit**: his pursuit of the lustful Foster associates him with lust. Lust leads him to forsake Arthur and retire into the forest. The **braue sprite** (8) is Arthur, but also Britomart. The contrast is not between two kinds of love but between the effects of love upon two different natures.
8–9　For the doctrine that love leads to virtuous action, see i 49.8–9*n*.

Stanza 2
1–4　These lines apply to Timias, specifically to his treatment of Amoret at IV vii 35.
3　**vngentlenesse**: discourtesy, boorishness; cf. Paridell's 'vngentlenesse' (x 6.9).
9　**his first poursuit**: i.e. of the Faerie Queene, I ix 15, who is **the highest and the worthiest** (5). By 12.1 he has turned back to aid Florimell, from which one infers that the two pursuits are one.

Stanza 3
2　Indicates that he has given up his pursuit of Florimell; cf. 12.1.
4　**hardly**: with difficulty.
5　**aghast**: terrified.

Stanza 4
6　**accompt**: account, estimation.

5
What mister wight (said he) and how arayd?
  Royally clad (quoth he) in cloth of gold,
  As meetest may beseeme a noble mayd;
  Her faire lockes in rich circlet be enrold,
  A fairer wight did neuer Sunne behold,
  And on a Palfrey rides more white then snow,
  Yet she her selfe is whiter manifold:
  The surest signe, whereby ye may her know,
Is, that she is the fairest wight aliue, I trow.

6
Now certes swaine (said he) such one I weene,
  Fast flying through this forest from her fo,
  A foule ill fauoured foster, I haue seene;
  Her selfe, well as I might, I reskewd tho,
  But could not stay; so fast she did foregoe,
  Carried away with wings of speedy feare.
  Ah dearest God (quoth he) that is great woe,
  And wondrous ruth to all, that shall it heare.
But can ye read Sir, how I may her find, or where?

7
Perdy me leuer were to weeten that,
  (Said he) then ransome of the richest knight,
  Or all the good that euer yet I gat:
  But froward fortune, and too forward Night
  Such happinesse did, maulgre, to me spight,
  And fro me reft both life and light attone.
  But Dwarfe aread, what is that Lady bright,
  That through this forest wandreth thus alone;
For of her errour straunge I haue great ruth and mone.

8
That Lady is (quoth he) where so she bee,
  The bountiest virgin, and most debonaire,
  That euer liuing eye I weene did see;
  Liues none this day, that may with her compare
  In stedfast chastitie and vertue rare,
  The goodly ornaments of beautie bright;
  And is ycleped *Florimell* the faire,
  Faire *Florimell* belou'd of many a knight,
Yet she loues none but one, that *Marinell* is hight.

9
A Sea-nymphes sonne, that *Marinell* is hight,
  Of my deare Dame is loued dearely well;
  In other none, but him, she sets delight,
  All her delight is set on *Marinell*;
  But he sets nought at all by *Florimell*:
  For Ladies loue his mother long ygoe
  Did him, they say, forwarne through sacred spell.
  But fame now flies, that of a forreine foe
He is yslaine, which is the ground of all our woe.

10
Fiue dayes there be, since he (they say) was slaine,
  And foure, since *Florimell* the Court for-went,
  And vowed neuer to returne againe,
  Till him aliue or dead she did inuent:
  Therefore, faire Sir, for loue of knighthood gent,
  And honour of trew Ladies, if ye may
  By your good counsell, or bold hardiment,
  Or succour her, or me direct the way;
Do one, or other good, I you most humbly pray.

Stanza 5
1   **mister wight**: kind of person.
4   **rich circlet**: the circle into which her locks are coiled. The description links her with the sun; cf. vii 11.3, 'With golden wreath and gorgeous ornament'.
8–9   See i 18.6–8*n*.

Stanza 6
5   **foregoe**: go on before.
8   **ruth**: occasion for sorrow.
9   **read**: tell.

Stanza 7
1   **Perdy . . . weeten that**: Truly I would rather know that.
4   **froward**: perverse; with a play on **forward**: fortune leaves the Knight, Night comes on him too fast.
5   **maulgre**: a general imprecation; cf. II v 12.9.
7   **aread**: declare.
9   **errour**: wandering.

Stanza 8
2   **bountiest**: most virtuous; noting also liberality in love that is parodied by Malecasta (i 26.4); cf. vi 3.8.
debonaire: gracious.
4–6   Florimell's virtue links her with Britomart for whom beauty is the ornament of her chastity. Cf. the praise of Britomart 'for pure chastitie and vertue rare' (iv 3.4). Belphœbe's chastity is such that 'none liuing may compaire' (54.4). Cf. 53.6–7.
7   **Florimell**: the name suggests 'sweet flowers', with which she is continually associated, and Flora, the goddess of flowers. From Lat. *floreo*, to have flowers+*mel*, honey; or *flos*, flower+*mel*, sweetness. Her role associates her with Proserpina, who is also associated with flowers.

Stanza 9
6   **For**: against.
8   **fame**: rumour.

Stanza 10
1–2   Contradicts the earlier account that her flight from the Foster preceded Marinell's wounding; cf. viii 46.5–6. Her pursuit by lust both precedes and follows the defeat of male chastity by woman's force. Blissett (1965) 95 notes: 'At the cost of discrepancy in the narrative, Spenser has linked Florimell's flight and Marinell's wound.'   **for-went**: left.
4   **inuent**: discover.

11

So may ye gaine to you full great renowme,
  Of all good Ladies through the world so wide,
  And haply in her hart find highest rowme,
  Of whom ye seeke to be most magnifide:
  At least eternall meede shall you abide.
  To whom the Prince; Dwarfe, comfort to thee take,
  For till thou tidings learne, what her betide,
  I here auow thee neuer to forsake.
Ill weares he armes, that nill them vse for Ladies sake.

12

So with the Dwarfe he backe return'd againe,
  To seeke his Lady, where he mote her find;
  But by the way he greatly gan complaine
  The want of his good Squire late left behind,
  For whom he wondrous pensiue grew in mind,
  For doubt of daunger, which mote him betide;
  For him he loued aboue all mankind,
  Hauing him trew and faithfull euer tride,
And bold, as euer Squire that waited by knights side.

13

Who all this while full hardly was assayd
  Of deadly daunger, which to him betid;
  For whiles his Lord pursewd that noble Mayd,
  After that foster fowle he fiercely rid,
  To bene auenged of the shame, he did
  To that faire Damzell: Him he chaced long
  Through the thicke woods, wherein he would haue hid
  His shamefull head from his auengement strong,
And oft him threatned death for his outrageous wrong.

14

Nathlesse the villen sped him selfe so well,
  Whether through swiftnesse of his speedy beast,
  Or knowledge of those woods, where he did dwell,
  That shortly he from daunger was releast,
  And out of sight escaped at the least;
  Yet not escaped from the dew reward
  Of his bad deeds, which dayly he increast,
  Ne ceased not, till him oppressed hard
The heauy plague, that for such leachours is prepard.

15

For soone as he was vanisht out of sight,
  His coward courage gan emboldned bee,
  And cast t'auenge him of that fowle despight,
  Which he had borne of his bold enimee.
  Tho to his brethren came: for they were three
  Vngratious children of one gracelesse sire,
  And vnto them complained, how that he
  Had vsed bene of that foolehardy Squire;
So them with bitter words he stird to bloudy ire.

16

Forthwith themselues with their sad instruments
  Of spoyle and murder they gan arme byliue,
  And with him forth into the forest went,
  To wreake the wrath, which he did earst reuiue
  In their sterne brests, on him which late did driue
  Their brother to reproch and shamefull flight:
  For they had vow'd, that neuer he aliue
  Out of that forest should escape their might;
Vile rancour their rude harts had fild with such despight.

17

Within that wood there was a couert glade,
  Foreby a narrow foord, to them well knowne,
  Through which it was vneath for wight to wade;
  And now by fortune it was ouerflowne:
  By that same way they knew that Squire vnknowne
  Mote algates passe; for thy themselues they set
  There in await, with thicke woods ouer growne,
  And all the while their malice they did whet
With cruell threats, his passage through the ford to let.

Stanza 11
3 rowme: place.
5 At least . . . abide: if not renown in this world, reward in heaven awaits you.
8 Cf. his promise to rescue the Red Cross Knight, I vii 52.7, and to save Guyon, II viii 26.9.
9 nill: will not, is unwilling.

Stanza 12
6 doubt: fear.
8 tride: proven.

Stanza 13
1 assayd: assailed.

Stanza 14
5 at the least: at last.
9 heauy plague: mortal blow or wound (OED 1), the punishment that follows his over-boldness, administered at 23.4–7; possibly implying syphilis or leprosy, 'that fowle euill' (I iv 26.7 and see n).

Stanza 15
3 cast: determined.
5–6 The three brothers represent 'the luste of the flesh, the luste of the eyes, and the pride of life' (1 John 2.16). On these three lusts, see Bloomfield (1952) 165. Presumably the Foster who pursues Florimell is the lust of the eye. Once she is out of sight, he is, too; but then the other lusts have been aroused. Vngratious: wicked, devoid of spiritual grace.

Stanza 16
1 sad: causing sorrow; heavy.
2 byliue: immediately.
5 sterne: cruel.

Stanza 17
3 vneath: difficult.
5 vnknowne: i.e. unknown to him.
6 algates: in any case.   for thy: therefore.
7 await: ambush.
9 let: prevent.

18

It fortuned, as they deuized had,
  The gentle Squire came ryding that same way,
  Vnweeting of their wile and treason bad,
  And through the ford to passen did assay;
  But that fierce foster, which late fled away,
  Stoutly forth stepping on the further shore,
  Him boldly bad his passage there to stay,
  Till he had made amends, and full restore
For all the damage, which he had him doen afore.

19

With that at him a quiu'ring dart he threw,
  With so fell force and villeinous despighte,
  That through his haberieon the forkehead flew,
  And through the linked mayles empierced quite,
  But had no powre in his soft flesh to bite:
  That stroke the hardy Squire did sore displease,
  But more that him he could not come to smite;
  For by no meanes the high banke he could sease,
But labour'd long in that deepe ford with vaine disease.

20

And still the foster with his long bore-speare
  Him kept from landing at his wished will;
  Anone one sent out of the thicket neare
  A cruell shaft, headed with deadly ill,
  And fethered with an vnlucky quill;
  The wicked steele stayd not, till it did light
  In his left thigh, and deepely did it thrill:
  Exceeding griefe that wound in him empight,
But more that with his foes he could not come to fight.

21

At last through wrath and vengeaunce making way,
  He on the bancke arriu'd with mickle paine,
  Where the third brother him did sore assay,
  And droue at him with all his might and maine
  A forrest bill, which both his hands did straine;
  But warily he did auoide the blow,
  And with his speare requited him againe,
  That both his sides were thrilled with the throw,
And a large streame of bloud out of the wound did flow.

22

He tombling downe, with gnashing teeth did bite
  The bitter earth, and bad to let him in
  Into the balefull house of endlesse night,
  Where wicked ghosts do waile their former sin.
  Tho gan the battell freshly to begin;
  For nathemore for that spectacle bad,
  Did th'other two their cruell vengeaunce blin,
  But both attonce on both sides him bestad,
And load vpon him layd, his life for to haue had.

23

Tho when that villain he auiz'd, which late
  Affrighted had the fairest *Florimell*,
  Full of fiers fury, and indignant hate,
  To him he turned, and with rigour fell
  Smote him so rudely on the Pannikell,
  That to the chin he cleft his head in twaine:
  Downe on the ground his carkas groueling fell;
  His sinfull soule with desperate disdaine,
Out of her fleshly ferme fled to the place of paine.

24

That seeing now the onely last of three,
  Who with that wicked shaft him wounded had,
  Trembling with horrour, as that did foresee
  The fearefull end of his auengement sad,
  Through which he follow should his brethren bad,
  His bootelesse bow in feeble hand vpcaught,
  And therewith shot an arrow at the lad;
  Which faintly fluttring, scarce his helmet raught,
And glauncing fell to ground, but him annoyed naught.

Stanza 18
1   **deuized**: schemed.
8   **restore**: restitution.

Stanza 19
3–5   The failure to wound him indicates his chaste heart and breast. **haberieon**: see iii 57.8*n*. **forkehead**: the barbed head.
6   **displease**: deeply annoy or grieve.
8   **sease**: reach.
9   **disease**: distress.

Stanza 20
2   **at his wished will**: as he desired.
3   **one**: presumably lust of the flesh.
5   **vnlucky**: causing harm.
7   Timias's wound in the left thigh suggests the wound of lust. That he is not wounded by the **bore-speare** (1) suggests why he may be cured by Belphœbe and then wounded by love's dart (42.3–6). **thrill**: pierce.
8   **griefe**: pain. **empight**: implanted.

Stanza 21
3   **assay**: assail.
5   **forrest bill**: long-bladed axe or sickle. **straine**: grasp tightly.

Stanza 22
7   **blin**: stop.
8   **bestad**: beset.

Stanza 23
1   **auiz'd**: observed.
4   **rigour**: violence.
5   **Pannikell**: skull, brain-pan; properly, membranes of the brain.
9   **ferme**: enclosure (sugg. by the context); from farm, or Fr. *fermer*, to lock up, and hence 'prison' (cf. 'natiue prison', I vii 21.8); possibly a farm held on lease, as the body holds the soul on lease. At 31.4 the body is called the seat of the soul; cf. 'shop' (II i 43.7).

Stanza 24
1–3   Upton (1758) compares Virgil's description of the feeble dart flung by Priam, *Aen.* ii 544–6. Lust of the flesh weakens after the other lusts are defeated.

25

With that he would haue fled into the wood;
  But *Timias* him lightly ouerhent,
  Right as he entring was into the flood,
  And strooke at him with force so violent,
  That headlesse him into the foord he sent:
  The carkas with the streame was carried downe,
  But th'head fell backeward on the Continent.
So mischief fel vpon the meaners crowne;
They three be dead with shame, the Squire liues with renowne.

26

He liues, but takes small ioy of his renowne;
  For of that cruell wound he bled so sore,
  That from his steed he fell in deadly swowne;
  Yet still the bloud forth gusht in so great store,
  That he lay wallowd all in his owne gore.
  Now God thee keepe, thou gentlest Squire aliue,
  Else shall thy louing Lord thee see no more,
  But both of comfort him thou shalt depriue,
And eke thy selfe of honour, which thou didst atchiue.

27

Prouidence heauenly passeth liuing thought,
  And doth for wretched mens reliefe make way;
  For loe great grace or fortune thither brought
  Comfort to him, that comfortlesse now lay.
  In those same woods, ye well remember may,
  How that a noble hunteresse did wonne,
  She, that base *Braggadochio* did affray,
  And made him fast out of the forrest runne;
Belphœbe was her name, as faire as *Phœbus* sunne.

28

She on a day, as she pursewd the chace
  Of some wild beast, which with her arrowes keene
  She wounded had, the same along did trace
  By tract of bloud, which she had freshly seene,
  To haue besprinckled all the grassy greene;
  By the great persue, which she there perceau'd,
  Well hoped she the beast engor'd had beene,
  And made more hast, the life to haue bereau'd:
But ah, her expectation greatly was deceau'd.

29

Shortly she came, whereas that woefull Squire
  With bloud deformed, lay in deadly swownd:
  In whose faire eyes, like lamps of quenched fire,
  The Christall humour stood congealed rownd;
  His locks, like faded leaues fallen to grownd,
  Knotted with bloud, in bounches rudely ran,
  And his sweete lips, on which before that stownd
  The bud of youth to blossome faire began,
Spoild of their rosie red, were woxen pale and wan.

30

Saw neuer liuing eye more heauy sight,
  That could haue made a rocke of stone to rew,
  Or riue in twaine: which when that Lady bright
  Besides all hope with melting eyes did vew,
  All suddeinly abasht she chaunged hew,
  And with sterne horrour backward gan to start:
  But when she better him beheld, she grew
  Full of soft passion and vnwonted smart:
350 The point of pitty perced through her tender hart.

Stanza 25
2 **lightly ouerhent**: swiftly or easily overtook.
7 **Continent**: see iv 10.2 and *n*.
8 **meaners crowne**: head of one who meant mischief.

Stanza 26
5 Cf. the wounded Marinell, iv 16.9, 34.7–9.
9 Since his name signifies honour (see i 18.9*n*), loss of honour would mean loss of name and identity. At this moment of exhaustion, grace intervenes.

Stanza 27
1 'The love of Christ which passeth knowledge' (Eph. 3.19). Cf. I vi 7.1.
4 **Comfort**: aid, succour; hence **comfortlesse**: helpless.
5 Referring to II iii 21f.
9 **Phœbus sunne**: Phœbus Apollo; providing one etymology of Belphœbe's name. For other etymological significances, see II iii Arg. 4*n*. Cf. Florimell at 5.4–5.

Stanza 28
The **tract** (track) of blood **freshly seene** associates Timias with the beast Belphœbe has wounded. The connection is stressed at 37.1–6. Cf. II iii 34 where Belphœbe takes Braggadocchio to be the hind she has wounded. She comes to kill the beast: later through love of her, caused by her 'vnwary dart' (42.5), Timias is 'destroyed quight' (41.9).
6 **persue**: the track of blood left by a wounded beast.

Stanza 29
2 **deformed**: disfigured.
7 **stownd**: hard time; cf. 38.5.

Stanza 30
3 **that Lady bright**: alluding to her name; see 27.9*n*.
4–9 **Besides all hope**: beyond or contrary to hope, i.e. having no hope that he was alive. She pities him and then retreats in horror because 'pity melts the mind to love' (see C. G. Smith, 1970, 611). Hence Marinell 'learne[s] to loue, by learning louers paines to rew' (IV xii 13.9). In effect, Diana becomes Venus who nurses a dying Adonis. **abasht**: checked with shame. **sterne**: merciless; threatening. **passion**: affection aroused through pity.

31

Meekely she bowed downe, to weete if life
   Yet in his frosen members did remaine,
   And feeling by his pulses beating rife,
   That the weake soule her seat did yet retaine,
   She cast to comfort him with busie paine:
   His double folded necke she reard vpright,
   And rubd his temples, and each trembling vaine;
   His mayled haberieon she did vndight,
And from his head his heauy burganet did light.

32

Into the woods thenceforth in hast she went,
   To seeke for hearbes, that mote him remedy;
   For she of hearbes had great intendiment,
   Taught of the Nymphe, which from her infancy
   Her nourced had in trew Nobility:
   There, whether it diuine *Tobacco* were,
   Or *Panachæa*, or *Polygony*,
She found, and brought it to her patient deare
Who al this while lay bleeding out his hart-bloud neare.

33

The soueraigne weede betwixt two marbles plaine
   She pownded small, and did in peeces bruze,
   And then atweene her lilly handes twaine,
   Into his wound the iuyce thereof did scruze,
   And round about, as she could well it vze,
   The flesh therewith she suppled and did steepe,
   T'abate all spasme, and soke the swelling bruze,
   And after hauing searcht the intuse deepe,
She with her scarfe did bind the wound from cold to keepe.

34

By this he had sweete life recur'd againe,
   And groning inly deepe, at last his eyes,
   His watry eyes, drizling like deawy raine,
   He vp gan lift toward the azure skies,
   From whence descend all hopelesse remedies:
   Therewith he sigh'd, and turning him aside,
   The goodly Mayd full of diuinities,
   And gifts of heauenly grace he by him spide,
Her bow and gilden quiuer lying him beside.

35

Mercy deare Lord (said he) what grace is this,
   That thou hast shewed to me sinfull wight,
   To send thine Angell from her bowre of blis,
   To comfort me in my distressed plight?
   Angell, or Goddesse do I call thee right?
   What seruice may I do vnto thee meete,
   That hast from darkenesse me returnd to light,
   And with thy heauenly salues and med'cines sweete,
Hast drest my sinfull wounds? I kisse thy blessed feete.

36

Thereat she blushing said, Ah gentle Squire,
   Nor Goddesse I, nor Angell, but the Mayd,
   And daughter of a woody Nymphe, desire
   No seruice, but thy safety and ayd;
   Which if thou gaine, I shalbe well apayd.
   We mortall wights, whose liues and fortunes bee
   To commun accidents still open layd,
   Are bound with commun bond of frailtee,
To succour wretched wights, whom we captiued see.

Stanza 31

3 **rife**: frequently; strongly.
4 **her seat**: see 23.9*n*.
5 **cast**: sought. **paine**: trouble. By her pain she seeks to cure his, only to cause him fresh pain; hence her 'vnfruitfull paine' (42.1). Cf. 50.1.

Stanza 32

3 **intendiment**: understanding.
4–5 By this nymph, she is 'vpbrought in perfect Maydenhed' (vi 28.4). Cf. vi 3.7–8. Nymphs are associated with healing, as at iv 41.
6–7 Herbs held to possess medicinal properties. S. is guilty of being the first English poet to praise **Tobacco**; **diuine** refers to its magical curative properties for which it was called *sana sanata*, the holy herb. **Panachæa**: 'cure for all'; given by Venus to cure Aeneas (Virgil, *Aen.* xii 419) and by Angelica to cure Medoro (Ariosto, *Orl. Fur.* xix 22f). **Polygony** stanches blood (Pliny, *Nat. Hist.* XXVII xci). S. does not reveal the herb used by Belphœbe; it may be moly which cures concupiscence, according to Golding (1567) Epistle 278–9.

Stanza 33

1–4 From *Orl. Fur.* xix 24, omitting such Ariostan details as sprinkling the breast and belly. **soueraigne**: supremely efficacious. **plaine**: flat or smooth. **bruze**: crush. **scruze**: squeeze.
6 **suppled**: softened, massaged.
8 **searcht**: probed. **intuse**: bruise.

Stanza 34

1 **recur'd**: recovered.
3 **His watry eyes**: tears denote restored life; cf. 29.3–4.
5 **hopelesse**: unhoped for; for the hopeless.
6–9 He looks to heaven for God's grace but finds it by **turning him aside** and seeing the maiden full of **heauenly grace**. **diuinities**: divine qualities; cf. Britomart, ix 24.4. **gilden**: golden. See II iii 26.7–9*n*.

Stanza 35

5–6 Cf. Trompart's address, II iii 33.2–4.
7 The language is appropriately biblical: 'that hathe called you out of darkenes into his marveilous light' (1 Pet. 2.9).
9 **sinfull**: because they signify the wound of concupiscence inflicted by the lustful foster; cf. 'foule sore' (41.8).

Stanza 36

2 The definite article stresses her virginity.
3 **woody**: woodland. She refers to the nymph who raised her (see 32.4–5), not to her mother who 'A Faerie was, yborne of high degree' (vi 4.3).
5 **apayd**: requited.

37

By this her Damzels, which the former chace
  Had vndertaken after her, arriu'd,
  As did *Belphœbe*, in the bloudy place,
  And thereby deemd the beast had bene depriu'd
  Of life, whom late their Ladies arrow ryu'd:
  For thy the bloudy tract they follow fast,
  And euery one to runne the swiftest stryu'd;
  But two of them the rest far ouerpast,
And where their Lady was, arriued at the last.

38

Where when they saw that goodly boy, with blood
  Defowled, and their Lady dresse his wownd,
  They wondred much, and shortly vnderstood,
  How him in deadly case their Lady fownd,
  And reskewed out of the heauy stownd.
  Eftsoones his warlike courser, which was strayd
  Farre in the woods, whiles that he lay in swownd,
  She made those Damzels search, which being stayd,
They did him set thereon, and forth with them conuayd.

39

Into that forest farre they thence him led,
  Where was their dwelling, in a pleasant glade,
  With mountaines round about enuironed,
  And mighty woods, which did the valley shade,
  And like a stately Theatre it made,
  Spreading it selfe into a spatious plaine.
  And in the midst a little riuer plaide
  Emongst the pumy stones, which seemd to plaine
With gentle murmure, that his course they did restraine.

40

Beside the same a dainty place there lay,
  Planted with mirtle trees and laurels greene,
  In which the birds song many a louely lay
  Of gods high prayse, and of their loues sweet teene,
  As it an earthly Paradize had beene:
  In whose enclosed shadow there was pight
  A faire Pauilion, scarcely to be seene,
  The which was all within most richly dight,
That greatest Princes liuing it mote well delight.

41

Thither they brought that wounded Squire, and layd
  In easie couch his feeble limbes to rest,
  He rested him a while, and then the Mayd
  His ready wound with better salues new drest;
  Dayly she dressed him, and did the best
  His grieuous hurt to garish, that she might,
  That shortly she his dolour hath redrest,
  And his foule sore reduced to faire plight:
It she reduced, but himselfe destroyed quight.

42

O foolish Physick, and vnfruitfull paine,
  That heales vp one and makes another wound:
  She his hurt thigh to him recur'd againe,
  But hurt his hart, the which before was sound,
  Through an vnwary dart, which did rebound
  From her faire eyes and gracious countenaunce.
  What bootes it him from death to be vnbound,
  To be captiued in endlesse duraunce
352 Of sorrow and despaire without aleggeaunce?

Stanza 37
5 **ryu'd**: pierced.
8 **two of them**: a puzzling detail unless three nymphs are meant in opposition to the three fosters.

Stanza 39
5–6 Cf. Milton's description of Paradise: 'a woody theatre / Of stateliest view' (*P.L.* iv 141–2). Todd (1805) cites the description of Ceylon in Purchas's *Pilgrimage*: 'Sense and Sensuality have here stymbled on a paradise. There woodie hils (a natural ampitheatre) doe encompasse a large plain.' Cf. the dwelling of the mermaids, II xii 30.7.
8–9 **pumy stones**: pumice-stones. **plaine**: complain. Hence **murmure**, an expression of discontent. A cunning variation of the same detail in the Bower of Bliss where the sound of water falling over pumice lulls the traveller to sleep, II v 30.1–4.

Stanza 40
1 **dainty**: delightful, excellent.
2 **mirtle trees**: sacred to Venus (Virgil, *Ecl.* vii 62); an emblem of her virtue, for she hid behind this tree when she was surprised bathing (Ovid, *Fasti* iv 139–44). See Panofsky (1962) 161. **laurels**: 'meed of mightie Conquerours' (I i 9.1). Together they give sweet fragrance (Virgil, *Ecl.* ii 54–5). Here they are emblems of Venus and Mars, love and renown, the passive and the active lives, represented together in the martial maid, Belphœbe. In contrast, only the mirtle is found on Venus's mount, vi 43.3.
3–4 **louely lay**: song of love; the god may be God or Cupid. **teene**: grief.

Stanza 41
4 **ready**: properly dressed.
6 **garish**: heal.
7 **dolour**: pain. **redrest**: relieved.
8 **reduced**: restored.

Stanza 42
1–2 Cf. Donne: 'this medicine, love, which cures all sorrow / With more' ('Love's Growth' 7–8). **paine**: labour.
4–6 In contrast to the ineffectual dart hurled by the first foster; presumably the lust of the eye (19.1–5). **vnwary**: unexpected. **rebound**: proceed.
7–9 An erotic analogue to the Red Cross Knight's state on being released from Orgoglio's dungeon. **duraunce**: constraint, imprisonment. **aleggeaunce**: relief; cf. the legal sense, 'allegation': Timias is unable to plead his love. Cf. ii 15.4.

43

Still as his wound did gather, and grow hole,
  So still his hart woxe sore, and health decayd:
  Madnesse to saue a part, and lose the whole.
  Still whenas he beheld the heauenly Mayd,
  Whiles dayly plaisters to his wound she layd,
  So still his Malady the more increast,
  The whiles her matchlesse beautie him dismayd.
  Ah God, what other could he do at least,
But loue so faire a Lady, that his life release?

44

Long while he stroue in his courageous brest,
  With reason dew the passion to subdew,
  And loue for to dislodge out of his nest:
  Still when her excellencies he did vew,
  Her soueraigne bounty, and celestiall hew,
  The same to loue he strongly was constraind:
  But when his meane estate he did reuew,
  He from such hardy boldnesse was restraind,
And of his lucklesse lot and cruell loue thus plaind.

45

Vnthankfull wretch (said he) is this the meed,
  With which her soueraigne mercy thou doest quight?
  Thy life she saued by her gracious deed,
  But thou doest weene with villeinous despight,
  To blot her honour, and her heauenly light.
  Dye rather, dye, then so disloyally
  Deeme of her high desert, or seeme so light:
  Faire death it is to shonne more shame, to dy:
Dye rather, dy, then euer loue disloyally.

46

But if to loue disloyalty it bee,
  Shall I then hate her, that from deathes dore
  Me brought? ah farre be such reproch fro mee.
  What can I lesse do, then her loue therefore,
  Sith I her dew reward cannot restore?
  Dye rather, dye, and dying do her serue,
  Dying her serue, and liuing her adore;
  Thy life she gaue, thy life she doth deserue:
Dye rather, dye, then euer from her seruice swerue.

47

But foolish boy, what bootes thy seruice bace
  To her, to whom the heauens do serue and sew?
  Thou a meane Squire, of meeke and lowly place,
  She heauenly borne, and of celestiall hew.
  How then? of all loue taketh equall vew:
  And doth not highest God vouchsafe to take
  The loue and seruice of the basest crew?
  If she will not, dye meekly for her sake;
Dye rather, dye, then euer so faire loue forsake.

48

Thus warreid he long time against his will,
  Till that through weaknesse he was forst at last,
  To yield himselfe vnto the mighty ill:
  Which as a victour proud, gan ransack fast
  His inward parts, and all his entrayles wast,
  That neither bloud in face, nor life in hart
  It left, but both did quite drye vp, and blast;
  As percing leuin, which the inner part
Of euery thing consumes, and calcineth by art.

49

Which seeing faire *Belphœbe*, gan to feare,
  Least that his wound were inly well not healed,
  Or that the wicked steele empoysned were:
  Litle she weend, that loue he close concealed;
  Yet still he wasted, as the snow congealed,
  When the bright sunne his beams thereon doth beat;
  Yet neuer he his hart to her reuealed,
  But rather chose to dye for sorrow great,
Then with dishonorable termes her to entreat.

Stanza 43

1 A curious, but relevant, ambiguity: a wound is said to **gather** when it becomes infected; **hole** suggests an open wound.

9 **release**: i.e. delivered from death, 'saued' (45.3).

Stanza 44

2 **dew**: fitting, proper; with a play on **subdew**: 'it is fitting for reason to subdue passion.'

5 **bounty**: goodness; liberality. See 8.2n.   **hew**: appearance.

Stanza 45

2 **quight**: requite.

8 It is a fair death to die in order to shun more shame.

Stanza 47

2 **sew**: do homage. Upton (1758) notes the appropriateness to Elizabeth.

Stanza 48

1 **warreid**: made war.   **will**: also lust.

4–7 Cf. love's effect in Britomart, ii 39. Instead of bleeding, Timias lies lifeless.   **blast**: wither.

8–9 **percing leuin**: piercing lightning. Its intense heat caused death by disintegrating the body's internal parts (Heninger, 1960, 79).   **calcineth by art**: reduces to powder by its skill; possibly referring to alchemical art which reduced metals from their oxides by burning.   **by art** has been variously explained: by its nature or quality; after its manner; naturally as its custom is; in a wonderful or mysterious way (all unsupported by *OED*).

Stanza 49

5–6 S. continues to imitate Ariosto (see 32.6–7n): Angelica cures Medoro but falls in love with him and wastes away as snow melted by the sun (*Orl. Fur.* xix 29). That she allows him to gather the first rose gives point to S.'s imitation.

50

She gracious Lady, yet no paines did spare,
  To do him ease, or do him remedy :
  Many Restoratiues of vertues rare,
  And costly Cordialles she did apply,
  To mitigate his stubborne mallady :
  But that sweet Cordiall, which can restore
  A loue-sick hart, she did to him enuy ;
  To him, and to all th'vnworthy world forlore
She did enuy that soueraigne salue, in secret store.

51

That dainty Rose, the daughter of her Morne,
  More deare then life she tendered, whose flowre
  The girlond of her honour did adorne :
  Ne suffred she the Middayes scorching powre,
  Ne the sharp Northerne wind thereon to showre,
  But lapped vp her silken leaues most chaire,
  When so the froward skye began to lowre :
  But soone as calmed was the Christall aire,
She did it faire dispred, and let to florish faire.

52

Eternall God in his almighty powre,
  To make ensample of his heauenly grace,
  In Paradize whilome did plant this flowre,
  Whence he it fetcht out of her natiue place,
  And did in stocke of earthly flesh enrace,
  That mortall men her glory should admire :
  In gentle Ladies brest, and bounteous race
  Of woman kind it fairest flowre doth spire,
And beareth fruit of honour and all chast desire.

53

Faire ympes of beautie, whose bright shining beames
  Adorne the world with like to heauenly light,
  And to your willes both royalties and Realmes
  Subdew, through conquest of your wondrous might,
  With this faire flowre your goodly girlonds dight,
  Of chastity and vertue virginall,
  That shall embellish more your beautie bright,
  And crowne your heades with heauenly coronall,
Such as the Angels weare before Gods tribunall.

54

To youre faire selues a faire ensample frame,
  Of this faire virgin, this *Belphœbe* faire,
  To whom in perfect loue, and spotlesse fame
  Of chastitie, none liuing may compaire :
  Ne poysnous Enuy iustly can empaire
  The prayse of her fresh flowring Maidenhead ;
  For thy she standeth on the highest staire
  Of th'honorable stage of womanhead,
That Ladies all may follow her ensample dead.

55

In so great prayse of stedfast chastity,
  Nathlesse she was so curteous and kind,
  Tempred with grace, and goodly modesty,
  That seemed those two vertues stroue to find
  The higher place in her Heroick mind :
  So striuing each did other more augment,
  And both encrease the prayse of woman kind,
  And both encrease her beautie excellent ;
So all did make in her a perfect complement.

Stanza 50
4   **Cordialles**: medicine that invigorates the heart (Lat. *cor*).
6–7   Cf. the Paracelsian doctrine that 'love for the patient . . . should be the physician's first virtue' (Paracelsus, ed. Jacobi, 143). **enuy**: refuse.
8   **forlore**: wretched, forsaken (by her).

Stanza 51
1   The **Rose** suggests her virginity but is not equated with it.
2   **tendered**: cherished.
4–5   Perhaps alluding to her own conception when her mother displayed her naked body to the generative powers of the sun, vi 7. Hesiod, *Geor.* 518–21, notes that the north wind 'cannot blast / The tender and the delicately-grac't / Flesh of the virgin' kept indoors by her mother (trans. Chapman). The allusion includes the generative power of the wind : see E.K.'s gloss to *S.C.* Apr. 122 on the story of Zephyrus's love for Chloris. See Wind (1967) 113–7. Cf. Venus's mount where 'nether *Phœbus* beams could through them throng, / Nor *Aeolus* sharp blast could worke them [the flowers] any wrong' (vi 44.8–9).
6   **chaire**: carefully.
7   **froward**: adverse.
8–9   Cf. the Nurse's injunction to Britomart to 'spred / Abroad thy fresh youthes fairest flowre' (ii 31.6–7). The difference distinguishes virginity from chastity.

Stanza 52
5   **enrace**: implant.
8   **spire**: shoot forth.

Stanza 53
1   **ympes**: offspring ; here, literally, shoots or slips.
5–7   Cf. 8.5–6 and 55.8. Outward beauty manifests inner virtue.
8–9   Cf. 1 Peter 1.4, 5.4.

Stanza 54
Cf. the praise of Florimell at 8.4–5, viii 43. It is extended here as a compliment to Elizabeth. As S. explains in *L.R.*, the Queen as 'a most vertuous and beautifull Lady . . . I doe expresse in Belphœbe'.
1–3   Cf. this exhortation to virgins with that to lovers, xi 2.6–9.
7   **staire**: position ; step, degree.
9   **dead**: i.e. when she is dead.

Stanza 55
1–5   **prayse**: excellence, praiseworthiness. **Tempred**: mingled in proper balance. Her second virtue is Courtesy, the subject of the third book of the second half of the poem. On the relation of the two virtues, see IV x 50–51*n* and VI x 27.5–6.
8   As 53.7. **excellent**: supreme.
9   **complement**: completeness, fulfilment.

Cant. VI.

*The birth of faire Belphœbe and
Of Amoret is told.
The Gardins of Adonis fraught
With pleasures manifold.*

1

WEll may I weene, faire Ladies, all this while
　Ye wonder, how this noble Damozell
So great perfections did in her compile,
Sith that in saluage forests she did dwell,
So farre from court and royall Citadell,
The great schoolmistresse of all curtesy:
Seemeth that such wild woods should far expell
All ciuill vsage and gentility,
And gentle sprite deforme with rude rusticity.

2

But to this faire *Belphœbe* in her berth
　The heauens so fauourable were and free,
Looking with myld aspect vpon the earth,
In th'*Horoscope* of her natiuitee,
That all the gifts of grace and chastitee
On her they poured forth of plenteous horne;
Ioue laught on *Venus* from his soueraigne see,
And *Phœbus* with faire beames did her adorne,
And all the *Graces* rockt her cradle being borne.

3

Her berth was of the wombe of Morning dew,
　And her conception of the ioyous Prime,
And all her whole creation did her shew
Pure and vnspotted from all loathly crime,
That is ingenerate in fleshly slime.
So was this virgin borne, so was she bred,
So was she trayned vp from time to time,
In all chast vertue, and true bounti-hed
Till to her dew perfection she was ripened.

4

Her mother was the faire *Chrysogonee*,
　The daughter of *Amphisa*, who by race
A Faerie was, yborne of high degree,
She bore *Belphœbe*, she bore in like cace
Faire *Amoretta* in the second place:
These two were twinnes, and twixt them two did share
The heritage of all celestiall grace.
That all the rest it seem'd they robbed bare
Of bountie, and of beautie, and all vertues rare.

Canto vi

Stanza 1
3 **compile**: gather together, compose, forming 'a perfect

complement' (v 55.9). Like Arthur's, her virtue 'is the perfection of all the rest [of the virtues], and conteineth in it them
all' (*L.R.*).
4 **saluage: wild** (7).

Stanzas 2–3
From these nativity stanzas Berleth (1973) constructs
Belphœbe's horoscope to account for her manifold significances
and her association with Elizabeth.

Stanza 2
2 **free**: generous.
3 **myld aspect**: referring to the favourable relationship of
the planets at the moment of her birth.
6 **plenteous horne**: the cornucopia, Amalthea's horn of
plenty.
7–8 Fowler (1964) 83 notes that 'in Neoplatonic mythology
Jupiter, Venus and Sol were regarded as corresponding to the
three Graces'. **from** suggests that Venus and Jove are in a
trine aspect, the most felicitous aspect of all; noted Delacy
(1934) 537. **laught on**: cf. IV x 56.4. Berleth (1973) notes
that the sign is used in astrological works to indicate perfect
harmony and friendship between planets. **see**: throne;
Berleth 489 notes that **soueraigne see** 'confirms that Jove is
dominant to Venus, for as lord of the physical universe it is he
who laughs upon her'.

Stanza 3
1–2 Cf. Ps. 110.3 (BCP): 'Thy birthes dew is the dew that
doth from wombe of morning fall.' Roche (1964) 105–6 notes
that the verse was taken to refer to the begetting of Christ,
and concludes that the miraculous birth here is an analogue
to the Incarnation. See 27.1–3*n*.
5 **ingenerate**: inborn, innate; referring to original sin.
fleshly slime: see I vii 9.8*n*.
6 **bred**: referring to her immaculate conception. S. distinguishes conception, nourishment in the womb, and birth.
7 **from time to time**: at all times.
8 **bounti-hed**: goodness; as the Castle of Alma is established
'On firme foundation of true bountihed' (II xii 1.5).
9 **dew perfection**: the pun stresses her perfection from her
original innocence at birth, in implied contrast to the perfection
which a woman was said to put on in marriage.

Stanza 4
1 **Chrysogonee**: golden-born (sugg. Draper, 1932),
alluding to the myth of Danae who conceived when Jove came
down upon her in a golden shower; see xi 31. Or 'gold-produc-
ing', from Lat. *Chrysogonum*: 'that bryngeth foorth golde'
(Cooper, 1565); also Cotgrave (1611), s.v. Chrysogone. Belson
(1964) 126 finds an allusion to Chrysogone, the wife of Amphi-
cles, noted for her virginity, in Theocritus, *Epig.* xiii. See
Hankins (1971) 278*n*2.
2 **Amphisa**: of double nature (Draper), either as she is
both mortal and immortal, or as her daughter gives birth to the
differing qualities of Amoret and Belphœbe. Lewis (1966) 158
suggests 'Both Equal' or 'Equally Both', as her descendants
are the two archetypes, the Terrible Huntress and the Yielding
Bride. However, Belphœbe is the first-born – see also 51.2–
which suggests either that she is superior, or that virginity
precedes love. At v 54.7–8 Belphœbe's virginity places her
'on the highest staire / Of th'honorable stage of womanhead'.
Cf. Rose (1968) 111.

5

It were a goodly storie, to declare,
    By what straunge accident faire *Chrysogone*
    Conceiu'd these infants, and how them she bare,
    In this wild forrest wandring all alone,
    After she had nine moneths fulfild and gone:
    For not as other wemens commune brood,
    They were enwombed in the sacred throne
    Of her chaste bodie, nor with commune food,
As other wemens babes, they sucked vitall blood.

6

But wondrously they were begot, and bred
    Through influence of th'heauens fruitfull ray,
    As it in antique bookes is mentioned.
    It was vpon a Sommers shynie day,
    When *Titan* faire his beames did display,
    In a fresh fountaine, farre from all mens vew,
    She bath'd her brest, the boyling heat t'allay;
    She bath'd with roses red, and violets blew,
And all the sweetest flowres, that in the forrest grew.

7

Till faint through irkesome wearinesse, adowne
    Vpon the grassie ground her selfe she layd
    To sleepe, the whiles a gentle slombring swowne
    Vpon her fell all naked bare displayd;
    The sunne-beames bright vpon her body playd,
    Being through former bathing mollifide,
    And pierst into her wombe, where they embayd
    With so sweet sence and secret power vnspide,
That in her pregnant flesh they shortly fructifide.

8

Miraculous may seeme to him, that reades
    So straunge ensample of conception;
    But reason teacheth that the fruitfull seades
    Of all things liuing, through impression
    Of the sunbeames in moyst complexion,
    Doe life conceiue and quickned are by kynd:
    So after *Nilus* invndation,
    Infinite shapes of creatures men do fynd,
Informed in the mud, on which the Sunne hath shynd.

9

Great father he of generation
    Is rightly cald, th'author of life and light;
    And his faire sister for creation
    Ministreth matter fit, which tempred right
    With heate and humour, breedes the liuing wight.
    So sprong these twinnes in wombe of *Chrysogone*,
    Yet wist she nought thereof, but sore affright,
    Wondred to see her belly so vpblone,
Which still increast, till she her terme had full outgone.

10

Whereof conceiuing shame and foule disgrace,
    Albe her guiltlesse conscience her cleard,
    She fled into the wildernesse a space,
    Till that vnweeldy burden she had reard,
    And shund dishonor, which as death she feard:
    Where wearie of long trauell, downe to rest
    Her selfe she set, and comfortably cheard;
    There a sad cloud of sleepe her ouerkest,
And seized euery sense with sorrow sore opprest.

Stanza 5
2   **accident**: event.

Stanza 6
2   **influence**: the infusion of ethereal fluid, the emanation from the heavens as they 'poured forth' (2.6) their gifts.
8–9   **roses** and **violets** are singled out from **all** the flowers for their association with love and virginity, Venus and Diana, and so with Amoret and Belphœbe.

Stanza 7
3   **swowne**: deep sleep.
5   **playd**: suggesting the erotic sense; cf. Danae's conception, xi 31.1–4.
6   **mollifide**: made tender; as seed, softened by moisture, is germinated by the sun.
7   **embayd**: steeped.
8   **sence**: sensation.

Stanza 8
S. follows Ovid's account of the abiogenetic origin of life (*Met.* i 416–37).
3–4   **fruitfull seades / Of all things**: Ovid's *fecunda semina rerum*.
5   **moyst complexion**: i.e. when the body's humour is predominantly moist; cf. 'moysture mixt with equall heate all living things createth' (*Met.* i 516, tr. Golding).
6   **by kynd**: naturally; according to their species.
7–9   See I i 21.6–9 and *n*.   **Infinite shapes**: Ovid's *innumeras species*.   **Informed**: formed within; Upton (1758) suggests Lat. *informatus*, imperfectly formed, from Ovid's *inperfecta*.

Stanza 9
1–5   The moon provides matter because it controls mortal bodies, particularly woman's body and her womb. Hankins (1971) 244 suggests that the moon provides the moisture by the menses which fit the matter for generation. On the tempering of matter by heat and moisture, see *Met.* i 430–1.
2   **rightly cald**: by Comes (1616) V xvi–xvii, who identifies Adonis with the sun because he nourishes all things and is the author of germination. Lewis (1967) 48 cites Aristotle, *Met.* 1071ᵃ, *hominem generat homo et sol*. On the relationship between this myth of Titan and **Chrysogone** and the later myth of Venus and Adonis in the Garden, see Fowler (1964) 141.
4   **Ministreth**: provides.

Stanza 10
1   **conceiuing**: with the pun.
4   **burden**: the child borne in the womb (*OED* 4).   **reard**: brought into existence.
6   **trauell**: also 'travail', the labour of child-birth.
7   **comfortably**: consolingly.

11

It fortuned, faire *Venus* hauing lost
    Her little sonne, the winged god of loue,
    Who for some light displeasure, which him crost,
    Was from her fled, as flit as ayerie Doue,
    And left her blisfull bowre of ioy aboue,
    (So from her often he had fled away,
    When she for ought him sharpely did reproue,
    And wandred in the world in strange aray,
Disguiz'd in thousand shapes, that none might him bewray.)

12

Him for to seeke, she left her heauenly hous,
    The house of goodly formes and faire aspects,
    Whence all the world deriues the glorious
    Features of beautie, and all shapes select,
    With which high God his workmanship hath deckt;
    And searched euery way, through which his wings
    Had borne him, or his tract she mote detect:
    She promist kisses sweet, and sweeter things
Vnto the man, that of him tydings to her brings.

13

First she him sought in Court, where most he vsed
    Whylome to haunt, but there she found him not;
    But many there she found, which sore accused
    His falsehood, and with foule infamous blot
    His cruell deedes and wicked wyles did spot:
    Ladies and Lords she euery where mote heare
    Complayning, how with his empoysned shot
    Their wofull harts he wounded had whyleare,
And so had left them languishing twixt hope and feare.

14

She then the Citties sought from gate to gate,
    And euery one did aske, did he him see;
    And euery one her answerd, that too late
    He had him seene, and felt the crueltie
    Of his sharpe darts and whot artillerie;
    And euery one threw forth reproches rife
    Of his mischieuous deedes, and said, That hee
    Was the disturber of all ciuill life,
The enimy of peace, and author of all strife.

15

Then in the countrey she abroad him sought,
    And in the rurall cottages inquired,
    Where also many plaints to her were brought,
    How he their heedlesse harts with loue had fyred,
    And his false venim through their veines inspyred;
    And eke the gentle shepheard swaynes, which sat
    Keeping their fleecie flockes, as they were hyred,
    She sweetly heard complaine, both how and what
Her sonne had to them doen; yet she did smile thereat.

16

But when in none of all these she him got,
    She gan auize, where else he mote him hyde:
    At last she her bethought, that she had not
    Yet sought the saluage woods and forrests wyde,
    In which full many louely Nymphes abyde,
    Mongst whom might be, that he did closely lye,
    Or that the loue of some of them him tyde:
    For thy she thither cast her course t'apply,
To search the secret haunts of *Dianes* company.

Stanzas 11–26
Venus's search for the runaway Cupid is the subject of an idyll by Moschus, 'The Fugitive Love', which E.K. notes in his gloss to *S.C.* March 79 was translated into Latin by Politianus and 'translated also into English Rymes' by S. The poem was expanded by Tasso in the Prologue to *Aminta*, and now is expanded from both. It prepares for Cupid's pageant in Canto xi. On the ensuing debate between Venus and Diana, Lewis (1936) 342–3 notes that the Venus who takes part is a Venus severed from Cupid who is associated with courtly love. He notes also that the *débat* ends with a reconciliation. In Lewis (1967) 51, he calls her *Venus naturalis*, the source of the power by which all things are generated, in contrast to *Venus coelestis*, the heavenly Venus. Roche (1964) 109 notes that this is the only occasion at which an Olympian deity takes part in the narrative.

Stanza 11
4   **Doue**: cited as **Venus's** bird.
8–9   Cf. Jove's wandering urged by love, xi 30.3–4.
bewray: reveal.

Stanza 12
1–5   Venus's **heauenly hous** is her planetary house or orb; hence **aspects** is used in the astrological sense, as at 2.3. Lewis (1967) 49 notes that the lines seem 'to fuse Venus-as-Paradigma with Venus-as-planetary-deity'.   **select**: choice.
7   **tract**: track.
8–9   In Moschus, a less liberal Venus offers a kiss for tidings of Cupid and better guerdon only for his capture and return.

Stanza 13
5   **spot**: vilify.
8   **whyleare**: a while before.

Stanza 14
5   **artillerie**: shot.
8   **ciuill life**: also in the sense, 'ciuill vsage' (1.8).

Stanza 15
5   **inspyred**: breathed.
9   Venus smiles with pleasure at the sweet verse in their complaints; or at the affectation of mere shepherds complaining of love; or with pride in her son's exploits.

Stanza 16
2   **auize**: consider.
6   **closely**: secretly.
8   **For thy**: therefore.

357

17

Shortly vnto the wastefull woods she came,
　Whereas she found the Goddesse with her crew,
　After late chace of their embrewed game,
　Sitting beside a fountaine in a rew,
　Some of them washing with the liquid dew
　From off their dainty limbes the dustie sweat,
　And soyle which did deforme their liuely hew;
　Others lay shaded from the scorching heat;
The rest vpon her person gaue attendance great.

18

She hauing hong vpon a bough on high
　Her bow and painted quiuer, had vnlaste
　Her siluer buskins from her nimble thigh,
　And her lancke loynes vngirt, and brests vnbraste,
　After her heat the breathing cold to taste;
　Her golden lockes, that late in tresses bright
　Embreaded were for hindring of her haste,
　Now loose about her shoulders hong vndight,
And were with sweet *Ambrosia* all besprinckled light.

19

Soone as she *Venus* saw behind her backe,
　She was asham'd to be so loose surprized,
　And woxe halfe wroth against her damzels slacke,
　That had not her thereof before auized,
　But suffred her so carelesly disguized
　Be ouertaken.　Soone her garments loose
　Vpgath'ring, in her bosome she comprized,
　Well as she might, and to the Goddesse rose,
Whiles all her Nymphes did like a girlond her enclose.

20

Goodly she gan faire *Cytherea* greet,
　And shortly asked her, what cause her brought
　Into that wildernesse for her vnmeet,
　From her sweete bowres, and beds with pleasures fraught :
　That suddein change she strange aduenture thought.
　To whom halfe weeping, she thus answered,
　That she her dearest sonne *Cupido* sought,
　Who in his frowardnesse from her was fled ;
That she repented sore, to haue him angered.

21

Thereat *Diana* gan to smile, in scorne
　Of her vaine plaint, and to her scoffing sayd ;
　Great pittie sure, that ye be so forlorne
　Of your gay sonne, that giues ye so good ayd
　To your disports : ill mote ye bene apayd.
　But she was more engrieued, and replide ;
　Faire sister, ill beseemes it to vpbrayd
　A dolefull heart with so disdainfull pride ;
The like that mine, may be your paine another tide.

22

As you in woods and wanton wildernesse
　Your glory set, to chace the saluage beasts,
　So my delight is all in ioyfulnesse,
　In beds, in bowres, in banckets, and in feasts :
　And ill becomes you with your loftie creasts,
　To scorne the ioy, that *Ioue* is glad to seeke ;
　We both are bound to follow heauens beheasts,
　And tend our charges with obeisance meeke :
358　Spare, gentle sister, with reproch my paine to eeke.

Stanzas 17–19
S. imitates Ovid, *Met*. iii 173–90, which describes the grotto in which Actaeon surprises Diana and her train bathing. He borrows from the same source his account of the nymphs gathering about Diana to hide her body. See Friedmann (1966).

Stanza 17
1　**wastefull**: desolate.
3　**embrewed**: blood-stained.

Stanza 18
3　**siluer**: Diana's colour as goddess of the moon.
4　**lancke loynes**: slender waist.
7　**Embreaded**: braided.　**for hindring**: lest they should hinder.
9　**Ambrosia**: anoints the gods to signify their immortality; in Virgil, *Aen*. i 403, Venus's 'ambrosial tresses breathed celestial fragrance'; cf. the 'ambrosiall odours' (II iii 22.7) from Belphœbe's cheeks.

Stanza 19
3　**slacke**: remiss; loose. As her garments are 'loose' about her, so too are her nymphs; when she gathers her clothes about her, her nymphs enclose her. The governing image, taken from v 51, is of the rose of maidenhead whose leaves spread out at a time of safety.
5　**disguized**: undressed.
7　**comprized**: gathered together.

Stanza 20
1–5　The implied answer is love of Adonis; see Ovid, *Met*. x 532–6.　**Goodly**: courteously, with a sarcastic edge as **shortly** (quickly or curtly) suggests.　**Cytherea**: so named because she arose from the sea off this island (see 29.4); so named here to note that she does not belong to the woods. **sweet bowres**: the Garden of Adonis rather than Venus's 'blisfull bowre of ioy aboue' (11.5).
5　**aduenture**: chance.
8　**frowardnesse**: being ungovernable.

Stanza 21
3　**forlorne**: bereft.
5　**disports**: sports; suggesting 'mis-sports'.　**ill . . . apayd**: either sarcastic, 'you must be really suffering', or a curse, 'may you be ill-rewarded'.
9　**tide**: time.

Stanza 22
1　**wanton**: luxuriant or wild.
4　**banckets**: carousals.　**feasts**: suggests the banquet of the senses.
9　**eeke**: increase.

23

And tell me, if that ye my sonne haue heard,
  To lurke emongst your Nymphes in secret wize;
  Or keepe their cabins: much I am affeard,
  Least he like one of them him selfe disguize,
  And turne his arrowes to their exercize:
  So may he long himselfe full easie hide:
  For he is faire and fresh in face and guize,
  As any Nymph (let not it be enuyde.)
So saying euery Nymph full narrowly she eyde.

24

But *Phœbe* therewith sore was angered,
  And sharply said; Goe Dame, goe seeke your boy,
  Where you him lately left, in *Mars* his bed;
  He comes not here, we scorne his foolish ioy,
  Ne lend we leisure to his idle toy:
  But if I catch him in this company,
  By *Stygian* lake I vow, whose sad annoy
  The Gods doe dread, he dearely shall abye:
Ile clip his wanton wings, that he no more shall fly.

25

Whom when as *Venus* saw so sore displeased,
  She inly sory was, and gan relent,
  What she had said: so her she soone appeased,
  With sugred words and gentle blandishment,
  Which as a fountaine from her sweet lips went,.
  And welled goodly forth, that in short space
  She was well pleasd, and forth her damzels sent,
  Through all the woods, to search from place to place,
If any tract of him or tydings they mote trace.

26

To search the God of loue, her Nymphes she sent
  Throughout the wandring forrest euery where:
  And after them her selfe eke with her went
  To seeke the fugitiue, both farre and nere,
  So long they sought, till they arriued were
  In that same shadie couert, whereas lay
  Faire *Crysogone* in slombry traunce whilere:
  Who in her sleepe (a wondrous thing to say)
Vnwares had borne two babes, as faire as springing day.

27

Vnwares she them conceiu'd, vnwares she bore:
  She bore withouten paine, that she conceiued
  Withouten pleasure: ne her need implore
  Lucinaes aide: which when they both perceiued,
  They were through wonder nigh of sense bereaued,
  And gazing each on other, nought bespake:
  At last they both agreed, her seeming grieued
  Out of her heauy swowne not to awake,
But from her louing side the tender babes to take.

28

Vp they them tooke, each one a babe vptooke,
  And with them carried, to be fostered;
  Dame *Phœbe* to a Nymph her babe betooke,
  To be vpbrought in perfect Maydenhed,
  And of her selfe her name *Belphœbe* red:
  But *Venus* hers thence farre away conuayd,
  To be vpbrought in goodly womanhed,
  And in her litle loues stead, which was strayd,
Her *Amoretta* cald, to comfort her dismayd.

Stanza 23

5 **exercize**: customary practice; suggesting that he may cause Diana's nymphs to fall in love.
8 **let not it be enuyde**: i.e. do not begrudge him such praise.

Stanza 24

1 **Phœbe**: Diana.
3 Referring to Venus's affair with Mars.
5 **toy**: game.
7–8 **By Stygian lake**: Virgil, *Aen.* vi 324, refers to the Stygian marsh by the power of which the gods fear to swear falsely; cf. 46.7. **abye**: suffer, pay the penalty.

Stanza 25

2 **relent**: soften in temper, qualify.
3–7 Venus acts as Concord, her traditional role.

Stanza 26

1 **search**: try to find.
7 **whilere**: a while before.
9 **springing**: dawning.

Stanza 27

1–3 Upton (1758) notes that goddesses and heroines often bear children painlessly, as Latona gave birth to Diana and as Mary gave birth to Christ; see 3.1–2*n*. Hankins (1971) 137 notes the tradition that Mary did not suffer Eve's curse.
4 **Lucina**: Juno as the patron of women in labour; see II i 53.5*n*. **which**: refers to Chrysogone lying unconscious after child-birth. Or it may refer to the miraculous birth itself, as Alpers (1967) 41 argues; or to the painless, unattended birth.
9 Noting that they take part in the birth.

Stanza 28

3–4 Cf. v 32.4–5, vi 3.7–8. **betooke**: gave in charge.
5 For further on the etymology, see II iii Arg. 4*n*. **red**: named.
8–9 Since she takes the place of Cupid (Amor), she is named Amoretta, a little love (Ital. *amoretto*), and serves as 'th'ensample of true loue alone' (52.4). Hence the search for Cupid at 26.5–6 leads directly to her.

359

29

She brought her to her ioyous Paradize,
    Where most she wonnes, when she on earth does dwel.
    So faire a place, as Nature can deuize:
    Whether in *Paphos*, or *Cytheron* hill,
    Or it in *Gnidus* be, I wote not well;
    But well I wote by tryall, that this same
    All other pleasant places doth excell,
    And called is by her lost louers name,
The *Gardin* of *Adonis*, farre renowmd by fame.

30

In that same Gardin all the goodly flowres,
    Wherewith dame Nature doth her beautifie,
    And decks the girlonds of her paramoures,
    Are fetcht: there is the first seminarie
    Of all things, that are borne to liue and die,
    According to their kindes. Long worke it were,
    Here to account the endlesse progenie
    Of all the weedes, that bud and blossome there;
But so much as doth need, must needs be counted here.

31

It sited was in fruitfull soyle of old,
    And girt in with two walles on either side;
    The one of yron, the other of bright gold,
    That none might thorough breake, nor ouer-stride:
    And double gates it had, which opened wide,
    By which both in and out men moten pas;
    Th'one faire and fresh, the other old and dride:
    Old *Genius* the porter of them was,
Old *Genius*, the which a double nature has.

Stanza 29

3   **deuize**: fashion.

4–5   **Paphos, or Cytheron**: well-known haunts of Venus; for Cytheron, see VI x 9.

6–7   **by tryall**: as a poet, referring to his experience of the Bower of Bliss, etc.; as a person, to his experience of the delights of love on earth, as Lewis (1966) 155 suggests.

Stanzas 30–50

Originally the Garden of Adonis was a name for a forcing-bed of quick-growing herbs (e.g. Plato, *Phaedrus* 276b) and served

as an example of ephemerality. By a later etymological confusion of Adonis with Eden, it became a 'ioyous Paradize' (29.1). Comes (1616) V xvi lists places associated with the worship of Adonis in which seeds were sown and where there were many fruit-yielding trees: 'Such places are called *hortos Adonios* because here Adonis took delight.' Such a paradise preserves the permanence of the species despite individual ephemerality. Critics of S.'s Garden have tried to deduce a philosophical account of creation that may be traced to a specific source, classical or Christian, erudite or popular. *Var.* iii 340–52 summarizes earlier views. Ellrodt (1960) 70–90 argues that S. uses the Augustinian tradition according to which the Garden is the storehouse of seeds in which all living beings were preformed from the first day of Creation. Nelson (1963) 210–20 claims that the Plotinian tradition supplies the gloss which most clearly illuminates the philosophical meaning of the Garden. Milne (1973) uses the Aristotelian doctrine of act and potency to interpret the metaphysical basis of the Garden. The controversy is by no means settled (see, e.g. Hankins, 1971, 234–86) because 'this passage is a myth after the manner of Plato – an appeal to the imagination in treating of matters beyond the grasp of reason' (Renwick, 1923, 197).

Recently some efforts have been made to analyse the Garden as a poetic image. Cheney (1966) 126–40 argues that there are three distinct gardens: a kind of conservatory (30–38), an image of the natural world itself (39–42), and the 'stately Mount' (43–50) which represents Nature on a higher level. Ramsay (1966) 192–3 argues that the garden of immutable forms which displays Venus's 'heauenly hous' (12.1) is set apart from the mutable garden. Yet S. insists throughout these stanzas that the Garden is one and that it exists 'on earth' (29.2). Murrin (1969) 143–6 argues that S. offers three differing perspectives on the Garden in order to treat certain intellectual problems of mutability.

Stanza 30

4–5   Gen. 2.5 implies that the Garden of Eden contained every plant and herb before it grew. Ellrodt (1960) 76–9 cites the Augustinian tradition that creation was instantaneous and involved an everlasting store of preformed beings or seminal reasons that would come into existence in orderly succession. Since these seminal reasons cannot exist apart from matter, as can the 'naked babes' (32.3), Milne (1973) 281 identifies S.'s forms with Aristotle's substantial forms which exist prior to matter, and through which matter comes to exist.
seminarie: seed-plot.

6   **According to their kindes**: the language of Gen. 1.24–5.

7   **account**: relate.

8   **weedes**: plants.

9   **counted**: recounted.

Stanza 31

1   **sited**: placed.   **fruitfull soyle**: cf. the 'fruitfull ground' of Eden, I xi 47.2–4.

2–7   Either there is one double wall, an outer wall of iron which may not be broken and a separate inner wall of gold which may not be surmounted, or **on either side** suggests that there are two end walls, the golden wall contains the fair and fresh gate and the iron wall contains the old and dried gate. The gate is a natural image of birth: cf. 'the dores of my mothers wombe' (Job 3.10); and also of death: cf. Marvell's 'Iron gates of Life'. Double gates of life and death appear in Plato's myth of Er, *Rep.* x 614.

32

He letteth in, he letteth out to wend,
  All that to come into the world desire;
  A thousand thousand naked babes attend
  About him day and night, which doe require,
  That he with fleshly weedes would them attire:
  Such as him list, such as eternall fate
  Ordained hath, he clothes with sinfull mire,
  And sendeth forth to liue in mortall state,
Till they againe returne backe by the hinder gate.

33

After that they againe returned beene,
  They in that Gardin planted be againe;
  And grow afresh, as they had neuer seene
  Fleshly corruption, nor mortall paine.
  Some thousand yeares so doen they there remaine;
  And then of him are clad with other hew,
  Or sent into the chaungefull world againe,
  Till thither they returne, where first they grew:
So like a wheele around they runne from old to new.

34

Ne needs there Gardiner to set, or sow,
  To plant or prune: for of their owne accord
  All things, as they created were, doe grow,
  And yet remember well the mightie word,
  Which first was spoken by th'Almightie lord,
  That bad them to increase and multiply:
  Ne doe they need with water of the ford,
  Or of the clouds to moysten their roots dry;
For in themselues eternall moisture they imply.

35

Infinite shapes of creatures there are bred,
  And vncouth formes, which none yet euer knew,
  And euery sort is in a sundry bed
  Set by it selfe, andranckt in comely rew:
  Some fit for reasonable soules t'indew,
  Some made for beasts, some made for birds to weare,
  And all the fruitfull spawne of fishes hew
  In endlesse rancks along enraunged were,
That seem'd the *Ocean* could not containe them there.

36

Daily they grow, and daily forth are sent
  Into the world, it to replenish more;
  Yet is the stocke not lessened, nor spent,
  But still remaines in euerlasting store,
  As it at first created was of yore.
  For in the wide wombe of the world there lyes,
  In hatefull darkenesse and in deepe horrore,
  An huge eternall *Chaos*, which supplyes
The substances of natures fruitfull progenyes.

deliberately not called souls) divested of body. Upton (1758) cites Virgil, *Aen*. vi 679–81. Ellrodt (1960) 82 calls them 'seeds' of human bodies or the pre-existent vegetative souls of men. Lewis (1966) 154 claims that they are rational, human souls.
4   **require**: ask, request.
5   **fleshly weedes**: the flesh, **sinfull mire** (7); cf. Job 10.11: 'Thou hast clothed me with skinne and flesh.'

Stanza 33
5   Following Virgil, *Aen*. vi 743–51: the souls dwell in Elysium for a thousand years in order to be purified; then they return to new bodies. Cf. *H.B.* 201–3 on the soul's pre-existence.
6   **hew**: form.
7   **Or**: a puzzling term; one expects 'and'. In Virgil, some souls are exempt from rebirth: they remain in the Happy Fields where, presumably, they are purified, i.e. **clad with other hew**. Nelson (1963) 216 suggests that S. may be thinking of 'two modes of re-entry into the mundane, from time to time in "new substances" or every cosmic year in the identical substance'. Lewis (1966) 154 cites the Orphic doctrine in Plutarch, *De Facie* 943–5, as set out in Henry More, *Immortality of the Soul* (1659) III i 16: all human souls become aerial daemons after death; at some later stage, however, some gain aetherial bodies while others suffer reincarnation in terrestrial bodies.
9   Upton (1758) cites Ovid, *Met*. xv 249, and Plato, *Timaeus* 79, on the image of the wheel.

Stanza 34
1–3   In contrast, the Garden of Eden needed man to subdue it, Gen. 1.28.
4–6   Gen. 1.22.
7–9   As in Eden before the creation of man: 'the Lord God had not caused it to raine upon the earth. . . . but a myst went up from the earth, and watred all the earth' (Gen. 2.5–6). Contrast the material generation by the sun, moisture and seeds as described at 8.3–9.   **eternall moisture** suggests the 'radical moisture' which is inherent in all plants and animals, its presence being a necessary condition of their vitality (*OED*). **ford**: stream.   **imply**: contain.

Stanza 35
2   Ellrodt (1960) 79 compares Augustine's concept of the pre-existent seminal seeds which include creatures not yet born. **vncouth**: strange.
3–7   'All flesh is not the same flesh, but there is one flesh of men, and another flesh of beastes, and another of fishes, and another of birdes' (1 Cor. 15.39).   **sundry**: separate, different. **reasonable soules**: i.e. human beings.   **indew**: assume, put on (as a garment).   **hew**: shape.

Stanza 36
3–9   **stocke**: the matter (cf. **substances**) which supplies material existence to the forms in the Garden; or the pure forms themselves before becoming matter; or both, as Hankins (1971) 259–63 argues. The Ovidian primeval chaos (*Met*. i 5–20) was reconciled to Genesis (see, e.g. Golding, 1567, Epistle 346–71) except for its being **eternall** (see, e.g. Sandys, 1632, 49). Cf. Milton's description of Chaos as 'the womb of nature and perhaps her grave' (*P.L.* ii 911). In *Ruines of Rome* xxii, S. says that 'The seedes, of which all things at first were bred,/ Shall in great *Chaos* wombe againe be hid'.

Stanza 32
3   **naked babes**: the souls in their pre-existent state (although

37

All things from thence doe their first being fetch,
  And borrow matter, whereof they are made,
  Which when as forme and feature it does ketch,
Becomes a bodie, and doth then inuade
The state of life, out of the griesly shade.
That substance is eterne, and bideth so,
Ne when the life decayes, and forme does fade,
Doth it consume, and into nothing go,
But chaunged is, and often altred to and fro.

38

The substance is not chaunged, nor altered,
  But th'only forme and outward fashion;
  For euery substance is conditioned
To change her hew, and sundry formes to don,
Meet for her temper and complexion:
For formes are variable and decay,
By course of kind, and by occasion;
And that faire flowre of beautie fades away,
As doth the lilly fresh before the sunny ray.

39

Great enimy to it, and to all the rest,
  That in the *Gardin* of *Adonis* springs,
  Is wicked *Time*, who with his scyth addrest,
Does mow the flowring herbes and goodly things,
And all their glory to the ground downe flings,
Where they doe wither, and are fowly mard:
He flyes about, and with his flaggy wings
Beates downe both leaues and buds without regard,
Ne euer pittie may relent his malice hard.

40

Yet pittie often did the gods relent,
  To see so faire things mard, and spoyled quight:
  And their great mother *Venus* did lament
The losse of her deare brood, her deare delight:
Her hart was pierst with pittie at the sight,
When walking through the Gardin, them she spyde,
Yet no'te she find redresse for such despight.
For all that liues, is subiect to that law:
All things decay in time, and to their end do draw.

41

But were it not, that *Time* their troubler is,
  All that in this delightfull Gardin growes,
  Should happie be, and haue immortall blis:
For here all plentie, and all pleasure flowes,
And sweet loue gentle fits emongst them throwes,
Without fell rancor, or fond gealosie;
Franckly each paramour his leman knowes,
Each bird his mate, ne any does enuie
Their goodly meriment, and gay felicitie.

Stanza 37

3   **feature**: shape, 'outward fashion' (38.2).   **ketch**: take, assume; seize.
4   **inuade**: enter (a Latinism); implying the stronger sense, 'make a hostile incursion into'.
6   **substance**: used here, and at 38.1,3, for matter. The etymological sense suggests that which lies under being, the pre-existing matter before the imposition of form.
7–9   Ellrodt (1960) 72 cites Bartholomaeus VIII i: the first matter 'remains unaltered as to the substance, though changing continually as to the transmutable qualities . . . all material things arise out of it and revert to it as to the womb'.   **Doth it consume**: i.e. is it consumed.

Stanza 38

2   **But th'only**: except only the.   **fashion**: appearance.
3   **conditioned**: has the capacity or nature; possibly 'required', 'bound'.
5   Fitting its temperament and nature, referring to the combination of humours in the body.
7   **kind**: nature.   **occasion**: necessity.

Stanza 39

The gardens of Adonis were recognized to be subject to time in their brief flourishing. On Time and his scythe, see Panofsky (1962) 69–93. Whether Time works within or without the Garden has been debated. Ellrodt (1960) 81 claims that Time cuts down the corporeal creatures in the world and not the pre-existent seeds in the garden. Lewis (1966) 153–4 agrees but asks: 'is it conceivable that he [Time] mows and is their "troubler" (41.1) because he brings the inexorable hour that sends them "forth to liue in mortall state" (32.8)? For their birth is of course the beginning of their death.' Yet the next stanza places the destruction within the garden. Tonkin (1973b) 411 argues that Time is not in the Garden but represents the effect of mutability on the forms when they go out into the world.
3   **addrest**: armed.
7   **flaggy**: drooping.
9   **relent**: cause to relent.

Stanza 40

Only at the end of the poem are we reassured that **All things decay in time** in order that they may be fulfilled; then Nature interprets **end** (9) as the completion to which all things move (VII vii 58.7).
3   **great mother Venus**: *Venus genetrix*.
6   **spyde**: saw, sugg. Church (1758) for the rhyme.
7   **no'te**: could not; knew not how to.

Stanza 41

5   **fits**: surges of passion.
6   **fond**: foolish.
7   **leman**: mistress.   **knowes**: in the sexual sense.

42

There is continuall spring, and haruest there
  Continuall, both meeting at one time:
  For both the boughes doe laughing blossomes beare,
  And with fresh colours decke the wanton Prime,
  And eke attonce the heauy trees they clime,
  Which seeme to labour vnder their fruits lode:
  The whiles the ioyous birdes make their pastime
  Emongst the shadie leaues, their sweet abode,
And their true loues without suspition tell abrode.

43

Right in the middest of that Paradise,
  There stood a stately Mount, on whose round top
  A gloomy groue of mirtle trees did rise,
  Whose shadie boughes sharpe steele did neuer lop,
  Nor wicked beasts their tender buds did crop,
  But like a girlond compassed the hight,
  And from their fruitfull sides sweet gum did drop,
  That all the ground with precious deaw bedight,
Threw forth most dainty odours, and most sweet delight.

44

And in the thickest couert of that shade,
  There was a pleasant arbour, not by art,
  But of the trees owne inclination made,
  Which knitting their rancke braunches part to part,
  With wanton yuie twyne entrayld athwart,
  And Eglantine, and Caprifole emong,
  Fashiond aboue within their inmost part,
  That nether *Phœbus* beams could through them throng,
Nor *Aeolus* sharp blast could worke them any wrong.

45

And all about grew euery sort of flowre,
  To which sad louers were transformd of yore;
  Fresh *Hyacinthus*, *Phœbus* paramoure,
  And dearest loue,
  Foolish *Narcisse*, that likes the watry shore,
  Sad *Amaranthus*, made a flowre but late,
  Sad *Amaranthus*, in whose purple gore
  Me seemes I see *Amintas* wretched fate,
To whom sweet Poets verse hath giuen endlesse date.

Stanza 42

1–6 **continuall spring** and the bearing of buds and fruit at the same time are traditional features of the *locus amoenus*, both in the classical tradition, from Homer's garden of Alcinous (*Ody.* vii 112–9), and in the biblical, from God's command in Gen. 1.12 that the earth produce at the same time the bud of the herb and the fruit of the tree. Cf. Ovid's golden age (*Met.* i 107–10), Ariosto's earthly paradise (*Orl. Fur.* xxxiv 49), and

Tasso's garden of Armida (*Ger. Lib.* xvi 10). Cf. also S.'s Mount Acidale, VI x 6.5.
1 **haruest**: autumn.
4 **Prime**: spring.
5 **heauy] heauenly** *1590*.

Stanza 43

Baybak *et al* (1969) 228 observe that this stanza with its opening phrase **Right in the middest** occupies the exact midpoint of Book III in the *1590* edition, the 340th of 679 stanzas (excluding the proems and the arguments to the cantos). See I vii 12–13*n* and II vii 53–55*n*. Also it is the centre of the Garden; as such, it treats Venus's concealment of Adonis who represents the Garden's generative principle. The beginning and end of the Book – the houses of Malecasta and Busirane – show the perversion of the sexual love displayed here. **middest** is carefully placed as the middle word of its line.
2–9 An anatomical interpretation of Venus's mount as the *mons veneris* is endorsed by recent critics, following Ellrodt (1960) 88 *n*165. Fowler (1964) 137 cites Valeriano: 'It should not be disguised that the myrtle signifies the female pudendum.' On the **mirtle tree** as sacred to Venus, see v 40.2*n*.

Stanza 44

2 **not by art**: this natural garden is the counter to the artificial Bower of Bliss; cf. 29.3, 30.1–4.
3 **inclination**: i.e. their leaning position; also their natural disposition.
4 **rancke**: dense.
5–6 **yuie** and **Eglantine** are found in the Bower of Bliss; see II v 29.3–5*n*. **wanton**: luxuriant in growth. **entrayld**: entwined. **Caprifole**: the honeysuckle or woodbine.
8–9 See v 51.4–5*n*. **throng**: press. **Aeolus**: the wind.

Stanza 45

1 **euery sort**: cf. 30.1; now the emphasis is that every kind or species endures even though the individual flower dies.
3–4 When his quoit, blown out of its course by the wind's jealousy, killed **Hyacinthus, Phœbus** caused the hyacinth to spring from his lost love's blood (Ovid, *Met.* x 162–219). The death illustrates the dangers of the sun and wind named at 44.8–9. **dearest loue**: as Ovid's *ante omnes* (167). Line 4 was added in 1609; Smith (1909) I xix argues that to add a broken line seems a touch beyond an editor. There may be a witty point: the poet's verse is cut short even as lovers' lives have been cut short both **of yore** and **but late**.
5 **Narcisse** died through love of his own reflection in the water; see ii 44.6–9*n*. The flower to which he gives his name grows near water.
6–9 **Amaranthus**: Gk, unfading; hence a symbol of **endlesse date** and associated with the 'incorruptible crowne of glorie,' (1 Peter 5.4). **Amintas** has been taken to refer to Sidney whose death **but late** (in 1586) had been marked with elegies by most poets of the time including S. In *Astrophel* 152, he shows Sidney as Adonis 'With crudled blood and filthie gore deformed'. Ringler (1954) argues that the lines refer to Thomas Watson's Latin *Amyntas* (1585), or its English paraphrase by Abraham Fraunce (1587) in which Amintas, having died through grief for Phillis, was transformed into the Amaranthus. **purple gore**: the entire plant is purple; hence the reference to 'Red *Amaranthus*' (Gn. 677). Its common name was Love-lies-a-bleeding.

46

There wont faire *Venus* often to enioy
　　Her deare *Adonis* ioyous company,
　　And reape sweet pleasure of the wanton boy;
　　There yet, some say, in secret he does ly,
　　Lapped in flowres and pretious spycery,
　　By her hid from the world, and from the skill
　　Of *Stygian* Gods, which doe her loue enuy;
　　But she her selfe, when euer that she will,
Possesseth him, and of his sweetnesse takes her fill.

47

And sooth it seemes they say: for he may not
　　For euer die, and euer buried bee
　　In balefull night, where all things are forgot;
　　All be he subiect to mortalitie,
　　Yet is eterne in mutabilitie,
　　And by succession made perpetuall,
　　Transformed oft, and chaunged diuerslie:
　　For him the Father of all formes they call;
Therefore needs mote he liue, that liuing giues to all.

48

There now he liueth in eternall blis,
　　Ioying his goddesse, and of her enioyd:
　　Ne feareth he henceforth that foe of his,
　　Which with his cruell tuske him deadly cloyd:
　　For that wilde Bore, the which him once annoyd,
　　She firmely hath emprisoned for ay,
　　That her sweet loue his malice mote auoyd,
　　In a strong rocky Caue, which is they say,
Hewen vnderneath that Mount, that none him losen may.

49

There now he liues in euerlasting ioy,
　　With many of the Gods in company,
　　Which thither haunt, and with the winged boy
　　Sporting himselfe in safe felicity:
　　Who when he hath with spoiles and cruelty
　　Ransackt the world, and in the wofull harts
　　Of many wretches set his triumphes hye,
　　Thither resorts, and laying his sad darts
Aside, with faire *Adonis* playes his wanton parts.

Stanzas 46–49
The reference to lovers transformed into flowers leads directly to **Adonis** who is not yet transformed although he lies 'Lapped in flowres' (46.5). At 29.8 he is announced as Venus's 'lost louer': he lives here where 'he may not / For euer die' (47.1–2). According to one standard interpretation, he is the Sun, the boar winter, and Venus the earth during his absence. See e.g. Sandys (1632) 493 and Comes (1616) V xvi p. 287. Since Adonis does not remain buried 'In balefull night' (47.3) and the boar is imprisoned, the Garden enjoys 'continuall spring' (42.1). The repeated 'some say' (46.4), 'they call' (47.8), 'they say' (48.8), after the confident 'I see' (45.8), separates the myth from S.'s use of it. See Alpers (1967) 328. Finding Adonis 'obstinately un-solar', Lewis (1966) 157 accepts an anatomical significance: 'Adonis is male; yet the Form-giver, approaching his dim bower, is descending to the womb.' Kermode (1967) 78 calls Adonis 'the entire biological cycle, conceived as subsisting in the *aevum*. This is what defeats the boar, for the boar is death.'

Stanza 46
2　**company**: as sexual companion (*OED* 2).
3　**reape**: cf. Acrasia 'greedily depasturing delight' upon Verdant, II xii 73.4.
5　His state suggests (sexual) death; cf. Donne: 'Wee kill our selves to propagate our kinde' ('First Anniversary' 110).
spycery: spices. On the association of Adonis with myrrh, see I i 9.6n.
6　**skill**: knowledge.
7　**Stygian Gods**: the infernal gods; from Styx, a river of hell.
9　**sweetnesse**: refers to the etymology of Adonis, ἡδονη.
takes her fill: in the erotic sense of being impregnated.

Stanza 47
1　**And sooth . . . say**: And it seems true what they say.
5–6　Cf. the distinction in Boethius, *Consol. Phil.* v Pr. 6: 'yif we wollen putten worthi names to thinges and folwen Plato, lat us seyen thanne sothly that God is "eterne", and that the world is "perpetuel"' (trans. Chaucer).
8–9　Lewis (1966) 155 suggests that Form is embodied in the feminine image, and Matter in the masculine 'in defiance of all tradition'. Hough (1962) 178, not allowing that S. would be so untraditional, takes 'form' in the popular sense as 'shapes'. Tonkin (1973b) 412 argues that Adonis is the father of forms 'because he gives forms their substance, brings creatures into being, not because he himself is form'.

Stanza 48
2　**Ioying**: enjoying.
4　**cloyd**: gored (from 'accloy', to pierce or stab); 'surfeited' through the over-gratification of desire (interpreting the boar as lust). See i 34–38n.
5　**annoyd**: injured.

Stanza 49
8–9　On the tamed Cupid, see I Proem 3.5–7n, II viii 6n.

50

And his true loue faire *Psyche* with him playes,
  Faire *Psyche* to him lately reconcyld,
After long troubles and vnmeet vpbrayes,
With which his mother *Venus* her reuyld,
And eke himselfe her cruelly exyld:
But now in stedfast loue and happy state
She with him liues, and hath him borne a chyld,
Pleasure, that doth both gods and men aggrate,
Pleasure, the daughter of *Cupid* and *Psyche* late.

51

Hither great *Venus* brought this infant faire,
  The younger daughter of *Chrysogonee*,
And vnto *Psyche* with great trust and care
Committed her, yfostered to bee,
And trained vp in true feminitee:
Who no lesse carefully her tendered,
Then her owne daughter *Pleasure*, to whom shee
Made her companion, and her lessoned
In all the lore of loue, and goodly womanhead.

52

In which when she to perfect ripenesse grew,
  Of grace and beautie noble Paragone,
She brought her forth into the worldes vew,
To be th'ensample of true loue alone,
And Lodestarre of all chaste affectione,
To all faire Ladies, that doe liue on ground.
To Faery court she came, where many one
Admyrd her goodly haueour, and found
His feeble hart wide launched with loues cruell wound.

53

But she to none of them her loue did cast,
  Saue to the noble knight Sir *Scudamore*,
To whom her louing hart she linked fast
In faithfull loue, t'abide for euermore,
And for his dearest sake endured sore,
Sore trouble of an hainous enimy;
Who her would forced haue to haue forlore
Her former loue, and stedfast loialty,
As ye may elsewhere read that ruefull history.

54

But well I weene, ye first desire to learne,
  What end vnto that fearefull Damozell,
Which fled so fast from that same foster stearne,
Whom with his brethren *Timias* slew, befell:
That was to weet, the goodly *Florimell*;
Who wandring for to seeke her louer deare,
Her louer deare, her dearest *Marinell*,
Into misfortune fell, as ye did heare,
And from Prince *Arthur* fled with wings of idle feare.

Stanza 50
The tale of **Cupid** and **Psyche** is told by Apuleius, *Golden Ass*
v. When Psyche attempted to see her nightly lover, Cupid, she
was abandoned and not reunited with him in heaven until she
endured severe trials imposed by Venus. When she became
immortal and married Cupid, she bore his child, Voluptas. For
the Renaissance interpretation of the tale as an allegory of the
sufferings of the human soul, see Allen (1960) 26–31. Roche
(1964) 126 argues that as Venus and Adonis 'figure forth the
union of form and matter . . . Cupid and Psyche represent the
next, more specific stage in generation – the creation of the
soul through the action of Love'. On S.'s use of the myth, see
Hamilton (1961) 138–48.
1   **playes**: suggests sexual pleasures corresponding to the
continual sexual activity between Venus and Adonis which
sustains creation.
3   **vpbrayes**: upbraidings.
8   **aggrate**: please.

Stanza 51
2   **younger daughter**: as 4.5.
5   **feminitee**: femininity, womanliness.
6   **tendered**: cared for.
9   **lore**: doctrine. Expanded in Scudamour's vision of
Amoret in the lap of Womanhood surrounded by the feminine
virtues, IV x 49–52. Cf. 28.6–7.   **womanhead**: cf.
Belphœbe's 'Maidenhead . . . the highest staire / Of
th'honorable stage of womanhead' (v 54.6–8).

Stanza 52
2   Cf. IV x 52.9: 'Shyning with beauties light, and heauenly
vertues grace.'
5   **Lodestarre**: the guiding star as a centre of attraction.
7–9   These lines prepare for the concluding cantos of the
Book where she suffers in retribution the pain she inflicts upon
her lovers; see xi 10.7n.   **haueour**: behaviour.   **launched**:
pierced.

Stanza 53
7   **haue forlore**: forsake.

Stanza 54
3   **stearne**: cruel.
9   Cf. iv 49.

Cant. VII.

*The witches sonne loues Florimell:
she flyes, he faines to die.
Satyrane saues the Squire of Dames
from Gyants tyrannie.*

1

Like as an Hynd forth singled from the heard,
That hath escaped from a rauenous beast,
Yet flyes away of her owne feet affeard,
And euery leafe, that shaketh with the least
Murmure of winde, her terror hath encreast;
So fled faire *Florimell* from her vaine feare,
Long after she from perill was releast:
Each shade she saw, and each noyse she did heare,
Did seeme to be the same, which she escapt whyleare.

2

All that same euening she in flying spent,
And all that night her course continewed:
Ne did she let dull sleepe once to relent,
Nor wearinesse to slacke her hast, but fled
Euer alike, as if her former dred
Were hard behind, her readie to arrest:
And her white Palfrey hauing conquered
The maistring raines out of her weary wrest,
Perforce her carried, where euer he thought best.

3

So long as breath, and hable puissance
Did natiue courage vnto him supply,
His pace he freshly forward did aduaunce,
And carried her beyond all ieopardy,
But nought that wanteth rest, can long aby.
He hauing through incessant trauell spent
His force, at last perforce a downe did ly,
Ne foot could further moue: The Lady gent
Thereat was suddein strooke with great astonishment.

4

And forst t'alight, on foot mote algates fare,
A traueller vnwonted to such way:
Need teacheth her this lesson hard and rare,
That fortune all in equall launce doth sway,
And mortall miseries doth make her play.
So long she trauelled, till at length she came
To an hilles side, which did to her bewray
A little valley, subiect to the same,
All couerd with thick woods, that quite it ouercame.

5

Through the tops of the high trees she did descry
A litle smoke, whose vapour thin and light,
Reeking aloft, vprolled to the sky:
Which, chearefull signe did send vnto her sight,
That in the same did wonne some liuing wight.
Eftsoones her steps she thereunto applyde,
And came at last in weary wretched plight
Vnto the place, to which her hope did guyde,
To find some refuge there, and rest her weary syde.

6

There in a gloomy hollow glen she found
A little cottage, built of stickes and reedes
In homely wize, and wald with sods around,
In which a witch did dwell, in loathly weedes,
And wilfull want, all carelesse of her needes;
So choosing solitarie to abide,
Far from all neighbours, that her deuilish deedes
And hellish arts from people she might hide,
And hurt far off vnknowne, whom euer she enuide.

Canto vii

Argument
2   faines: desires.

Stanzas 1–2
Repeating the substance of iv 49–50.

Stanza 2
1–2   The night which Arthur endures, iv 52–60.
3   relent: slacken, as iv 49.1.
6   arrest: seize.
7–9   The traditional emblem of passion overpowering reason;
cf. 18.9. It marks the beginning of her metamorphosis.

Stanza 3
1   hable puissance: able or sufficient strength. The
sixteenth-century spelling combines the Lat. *habilis* with the
active sense, 'strong', 'powerful'. See I xi 19.6n.
5   Proverbial (C. G. Smith, 1970, 652). Cf. I i 32.6–7.
aby: abide.
8   gent: noble; beautiful.
9   astonishment: dismay; also (anticipating her later plight)
numbness, deadness; cf. viii 35.6.

Stanza 4
1   algates: necessarily, at all events.
3   rare: unusual in its severity.
4   sway: rule; move to and fro; move or press down, as the
metaphor of the scales indicates. Suggesting that Fortune
weighs all equally, and implying that her scales are weighted
against man's happiness.
5   Fortune makes sport of human miseries.
7   bewray: reveal.
8   subiect to: lying below.
9   ouercame: overspread.

Stanza 5
1   the tops] th'tops *1609*, as the metre requires.
3   Reeking: rising.
6   applyde: directed.

Stanza 6
1   E. K. glosses glen in *S.C.* Apr. 26 as 'a country Hamlet
or borough'; but here a valley.
4–9   'The most complete witch in the regular English
tradition' (Briggs, 1962, 75). She is accompanied by a loutish
son, as is usual.
9   enuide: bore a grudge against.

7

The Damzell there arriuing entred in;
    Where sitting on the flore the Hag she found,
    Busie (as seem'd) about some wicked gin:
    Who soone as she beheld that suddein stound,
    Lightly vpstarted from the dustie ground,
    And with fell looke and hollow deadly gaze
    Stared on her awhile, as one astound,
    Ne had one word to speake, for great amaze,
But shewd by outward signes, that dread her sence did daze.

8

At last turning her feare to foolish wrath,
    She askt, what deuill had her thither brought,
    And who she was, and what vnwonted path
    Had guided her, vnwelcomed, vnsought?
    To which the Damzell full of doubtfull thought,
    Her mildly answer'd; Beldame be not wroth
    With silly Virgin by aduenture brought
    Vnto your dwelling, ignorant and loth,
That craue but rowme to rest, while tempest ouerblo'th.

9

With that adowne out of her Christall eyne
    Few trickling teares she softly forth let fall,
    That like two Orient pearles, did purely shyne
    Vpon her snowy cheeke; and therewithall
    She sighed soft, that none so bestiall,
    Nor saluage hart, but ruth of her sad plight
    Would make to melt, or pitteously appall;
    And that vile Hag, all were her whole delight
In mischiefe, was much moued at so pitteous sight.

10

And gan recomfort her in her rude wyse,
    With womanish compassion of her plaint,
    Wiping the teares from her suffused eyes,
    And bidding her sit downe, to rest her faint
    And wearie limbs a while.   She nothing quaint
    Nor s'deignfull of so homely fashion,
    Sith brought she was now to so hard constraint,
    Sate downe vpon the dusty ground anon,
As glad of that small rest, as Bird of tempest gon.

11

Tho gan she gather vp her garments rent,
    And her loose lockes to dight in order dew,
    With golden wreath and gorgeous ornament;
    Whom such whenas the wicked Hag did vew,
    She was astonisht at her heauenly hew,
    And doubted her to deeme an earthly wight,
    But or some Goddesse, or of *Dianes* crew,
    And thought her to adore with humble spright;
T'adore thing so diuine as beauty, were but right.

12

This wicked woman had a wicked sonne,
    The comfort of her age and weary dayes,
    A laesie loord, for nothing good to donne,
    But stretched forth in idlenesse alwayes,
    Ne euer cast his mind to couet prayse,
    Or ply him selfe to any honest trade,
    But all the day before the sunny rayes
    He vs'd to slug, or sleepe in slothfull shade:
Such laesinesse both lewd and poore attonce him made.

13

He comming home at vndertime, there found
    The fairest creature, that he euer saw,
    Sitting beside his mother on the ground;
    The sight whereof did greatly him adaw,
    And his base thought with terrour and with aw
    So inly smot, that as one, which had gazed
    On the bright Sunne vnwares, doth soone withdraw
    His feeble eyne, with too much brightnesse dazed,
So stared he on her, and stood long while amazed.

Stanza 7
3   **gin**: device, stratagem.
4   **stound**: startling appearance. Despite her evil nature, she, too, is overwhelmed by the appearance of Beauty.
7   **astound**: stunned.

Stanza 8
5   **doubtfull**: fearful.
6   **Beldame**: good mother.
7   **silly**: helpless.   **by aduenture**: by chance.
9   **while**: until.

Stanza 9
3   **two**: 'to' sugg. Hughes (1715).
4   **snowy cheeke**: anticipating her alter ego, the snowy Florimell. Cf. Shamefastnesse's 'snowy cheekes' (II ix 41.4).
7   **pitteously appall**: quell with pity.

Stanza 10
3   **suffused**: suffused with tears, rendering Virgil's description of Venus *lacrimis oculos suffusa* (*Aen.* i 228).
5   **quaint**: fastidious.
6   **s'deignfull**: disdainful.
7   **constraint**: distress; compulsion.
8   **dusty ground**: repeated from 7.5 to mark this stage of Florimell's descent.

Stanza 11
1   In the next stage of her flight, she leaves these garments behind; see viii 9.1–2.
2   **dight**: arrange.
3   Cf. v 5.4.

Stanza 12
3   A lazy lout good for nothing. Cf. E. K.'s etymology of **loord** in his gloss to *S.C.* July 33.
6   **ply**: apply.
8   Cf. Acrasia's knights who 'slug in slouth and sensuall delights' (II i 23.3).
9   **lewd**: ignorant; implying also the sexual sense; cf. 20.1.

Stanza 13
1   **vndertime**: variously identified as morning, noon, afternoon, evening, and meal-time. Since Florimell has ridden all night, morning would be appropriate. The imagery suggests noon: one who loves to lie 'before the sunny rayes' (12.7) now gazes on one who dazzles his eyes as does the brightest sun.
4   **adaw**: daunt; confound; cf. E. K.'s note to *S.C.* Feb. 141.

14

Softly at last he gan his mother aske,
  What mister wight that was, and whence deriued,
  That in so straunge disguizement there did maske,
  And by what accident she there arriued:
  But she, as one nigh of her wits depriued,
  With nought but ghastly lookes him answered,
  Like to a ghost, that lately is reuiued
From *Stygian* shores, where late it wandered;
So both at her, and each at other wondered.

15

But the faire Virgin was so meeke and mild,
  That she to them vouchsafed to embace
  Her goodly port, and to their senses vild,
  Her gentle speach applide, that in short space
  She grew familiare in that desert place.
  During which time, the Chorle through her so kind
  And curteise vse conceiu'd affection bace,
  And cast to loue her in his brutish mind;
No loue, but brutish lust, that was so beastly tind.

16

Closely the wicked flame his bowels brent,
  And shortly grew into outrageous fire;
  Yet had he not the hart, nor hardiment,
  As vnto her to vtter his desire;
  His caytiue thought durst not so high aspire,
  But with soft sighes, and louely semblaunces,
  He ween'd that his affection entire
She should aread; many resemblaunces
To her he made, and many kind remembraunces.

17

Oft from the forrest wildings he did bring,
  Whose sides empurpled were with smiling red,
  And oft young birds, which he had taught to sing
  His mistresse prayses, sweetly caroled,
  Girlonds of flowres sometimes for her faire hed
  He fine would dight; sometimes the squirell wild
  He brought to her in bands, as conquered
To be her thrall, his fellow seruant vild;
All which, she of him tooke with countenance meeke and mild.

18

But past awhile, when she fit season saw
  To leaue that desert mansion, she cast
  In secret wize her selfe thence to withdraw,
  For feare of mischiefe, which she did forecast
  Might be by the witch or that her sonne compast:
  Her wearie Palfrey closely, as she might,
  Now well recouered after long repast,
  In his proud furnitures she freshly dight,
His late miswandred wayes now to remeasure right.

19

And earely ere the dawning day appeard,
  She forth issewed, and on her iourney went;
  She went in perill, of each noyse affeard,
  And of each shade, that did it selfe present;
  For still she feared to be ouerhent,
  Of that vile hag, or her vnciuile sonne,
  Who when too late awaking, well they kent,
  That their faire guest was gone, they both begonne
368 To make exceeding mone, as they had bene vndonne.

Stanza 14
2   **mister wight**: kind of creature.
3   The language suggests the masque of Cupid in the house of Busirane. See iii 51.9*n*.

Stanza 15
2   **embace**: make base, humble; another stage in her descent.
3   **vild**: vile.
5   **familiare**: i.e. on a family footing.
6–7   **so kind / And curteise vse**: cf. Belphœbe 'so curteous and kind', v 55.2.   **vse**: habit, behaviour.
8   **cast**: determined.
9   **tind**: inflamed.

Stanza 16
1   **Closely**: secretly.
3–5   Cf. Timias's dilemma in loving Belphœbe, v 44–47. **caytiue**: vile.
6   **louely semblaunces**: shows of love.
7   **entire**: inward; sincere.
8   **aread**: guess.   **resemblaunces**: demonstrations of affection.

Stanza 17
1   **wildings**: wild fruit.
6   **dight**: prepare.   **squirell**: on its association with lechery, see VI ix 40.2–3*n*.

Stanza 18
1   After some time had passed.
2   **mansion**: lodging.
5   **Might be by the witch or that her sonne compast**]
Might by the witch or by her sonne compast *1590*: 'be' is understood. The emended reading requires the slurring of by the. Osgood, *Var*. iii 424, suggests that **Might be** is a milder adverbial 'maybe'.
6   **closely**: secretly.
7   **repast**: repose.
8   **furnitures**: harness.
9   **miswandred**: in which he had gone astray.   **remeasure**: retrace.

Stanza 19
3–4   Cf. her state at 1.4–9. Her fear of all things soon appears as Proteus who assumes 'euery shape' (viii 40.2).
5   **still**: always.   **ouerhent**: overtaken.
6   **vnciuile**: barbarous, uncouth.
7   **kent**: kenned, knew.

20

But that lewd louer did the most lament
  For her depart, that euer man did heare;
  He knockt his brest with desperate intent,
  And scratcht his face, and with his teeth did teare
  His rugged flesh, and rent his ragged heare:
  That his sad mother seeing his sore plight,
  Was greatly woe begon, and gan to feare,
  Least his fraile senses were emperisht quight,
And loue to frenzy turnd, sith loue is franticke hight.

21

All wayes she sought, him to restore to plight,
  With herbs, with charms, with counsell, and with teares,
  But tears, nor charms, nor herbs, nor counsell might
  Asswage the fury, which his entrails teares:
  So strong is passion, that no reason heares.
  Tho when all other helpes she saw to faile,
  She turnd her selfe backe to her wicked leares
  And by her deuilish arts thought to preuaile,
To bring her backe againe, or worke her finall bale.

22

Eftsoones out of her hidden caue she cald
  An hideous beast, of horrible aspect,
  That could the stoutest courage haue appald;
  Monstrous mishapt, and all his backe was spect
  With thousand spots of colours queint elect,
  Thereto so swift, that it all beasts did pas:
  Like neuer yet did liuing eye detect;
  But likest it to an *Hyena* was,
That feeds on womens flesh, as others feede on gras.

23

It forth she cald, and gaue it streight in charge,
  Through thicke and thin her to pursew apace,
  Ne once to stay to rest, or breath at large,
  Till her he had attaind, and brought in place,
  Or quite deuourd her beauties scornefull grace.
  The Monster swift as word, that from her went,
  Went forth in hast, and did her footing trace
  So sure and swiftly, through his perfect sent,
And passing speede, that shortly he her ouerhent.

24

Whom when the fearefull Damzell nigh espide,
  No need to bid her fast away to flie;
  That vgly shape so sore her terrifide,
  That it she shund no lesse, then dread to die,
  And her flit Palfrey did so well apply
  His nimble feet to her conceiued feare,
  That whilest his breath did strength to him supply,
  From perill free he her away did beare:
But when his force gan faile, his pace gan wex areare.

25

Which whenas she perceiu'd, she was dismayd
  At that same last extremitie full sore,
  And of her safetie greatly grew afrayd;
  And now she gan approch to the sea shore,
  As it befell, that she could flie no more,
  But yield her selfe to spoile of greedinesse.
  Lightly she leaped, as a wight forlore,
  From her dull horse, in desperate distresse,
And to her feet betooke her doubtfull sickernesse.

Stanza 20

2   **depart**: departure.
8   **emperisht**: enfeebled.
9   Cf. C. G. Smith (1970) 486. Love and lunacy are also linked in Shakespeare, *Midsummer Night's Dream* V i 7.

Stanza 21

1   **plight**: health.
7   **leares**: lore, magic.
9   **her finall bale**: her death.

Stanza 22

5   **queint elect**: strangely or cleverly chosen either for disguise or to arouse fear. The **spots** signify spots of sin or 'corrupted flesh' (32.6), specifically concupiscence which Florimell fears most.
6   **Thereto**: in addition.   **pas**: surpass.
8–9 In medieval lore, the **Hyena** dug up graves to eat the carcasses, and was used by witches. The Geneva gloss to Ecclus. 13.19 cites it as a beast that lures men to devour them. Rowland (1973) 113 notes that it could typify sexual perversion. S. associates the beast with lust in women and towards women; cf. Lust that 'fed on fleshly gore' (IV vii 5.8).

Stanza 23

1   **streight**: strictly; immediately.
4   **in place**: here, in her presence.
7   **footing**: footprints.
9   **passing**: surpassing all, including Florimell.

Stanza 24

5   **flit**: swift.   **apply**: accommodate, adapt; see iv 61.9n.
9   **wex areare**: grow backward, i.e. fall behind.

Stanza 25

1   **dismayd**: a pun may be implicit.
4   When guarded by Marinell, the **sea shore** was the preserve of male chastity; with his defeat, the monster 'That feeds on womens flesh' (22.9) prowls there.
7   **forlore**: doomed to destruction; lost.
9   **sickernesse**: security. She committed her safety, which was doubtful, to the care of her feet.

26

Not halfe so fast the wicked *Myrrha* fled
  From dread of her reuenging fathers hond:
  Nor halfe so fast to saue her maidenhed,
  Fled fearefull *Daphne* on th'*Ægæan* strond,
  As *Florimell* fled from that Monster yond,
  To reach the sea, ere she of him were raught:
  For in the sea to drowne her selfe she fond,
  Rather then of the tyrant to be caught:
Thereto feare gaue her wings, and neede her courage taught

27

It fortuned (high God did so ordaine)
  As she arriued on the roring shore,
  In minde to leape into the mighty maine,
  A little boate lay houing her before,
  In which there slept a fisher old and pore,
  The whiles his nets were drying on the sand:
  Into the same she leapt, and with the ore
  Did thrust the shallop from the floting strand:
So safetie found at sea, which she found not at land.

28

The Monster ready on the pray to sease,
  Was of his forward hope deceiued quight;
  Ne durst assay to wade the perlous seas,
  But greedily long gaping at the sight,
  At last in vaine was forst to turne his flight,
  And tell the idle tidings to his Dame:
  Yet to auenge his deuilish despight,
  He set vpon her Palfrey tired lame,
And slew him cruelly, ere any reskew came.

29

And after hauing him embowelled,
  To fill his hellish gorge, it chaunst a knight
  To passe that way, as forth he trauelled;
  It was a goodly Swaine, and of great might,
  As euer man that bloudy field did fight;
  But in vaine sheows, that wont yong knights bewitch,
  And courtly seruices tooke no delight,
  But rather ioyd to be, then seemen sich:
For both to be and seeme to him was labour lich.

30

It was to weete the good Sir *Satyrane*,
  That raungd abroad to seeke aduentures wilde,
  As was his wont in forrest, and in plaine;
  He was all armd in rugged steele vnfilde,
  As in the smoky forge it was compilde,
  And in his Scutchin bore a Satyres hed:
  He comming present, where the Monster vilde
  Vpon that milke-white Palfreyes carkas fed,
Vnto his reskew ran, and greedily him sped.

31

There well perceiu'd he, that it was the horse,
  Whereon faire *Florimell* was wont to ride,
  That of that feend was rent without remorse:
  Much feared he, least ought did ill betide
  To that faire Mayd, the flowre of womens pride;
  For her he dearely loued, and in all
  His famous conquests highly magnifide:
  Besides her golden girdle, which did fall
370 From her in flight, he found, that did him sore apall.

Stanza 26

1–4 **Myrrha** and **Daphne** represent extremes of guilt and innocence in flight from lust, the one associated with prostitution and incest and the other with virginity. See Ovid, *Met.* x 311–476, i 452–530. **Myrrha**'s flight from her father parallels Florimell's rejection of the Fisherman, whom she calls 'father' (viii 23.7). Incest is implied by the old man's lust after the young girl. **Daphne** is saved by the waters of Peneus, her father (*Met.* i 543–52), as Florimell is saved by the sea. These same classical comparisons describe Amoret's flight from Lust, IV vii 22.8–9.
5 **yond**: furious: see II viii 40.9*n*; or 'yonder', as Collier (1862) suggests.
7 **fond**: would try; 'In minde to' (27.3).

Stanza 27

1 On fortune and God's providence, see v 27.1–3.
4 **houing**: hovering, floating.
7–9 This event is borrowed from the legend of Britomartis: loved by Minos, she fled to find safety by leaping into the sea from which she was saved by fishermen with their nets (Diodorus Siculus, *Biblio. Hist.*, v 76.3–4).
floting strand: the shore off which the boat was floating.

Stanza 28

2 **forward**: chief; well advanced, on the point of being gratified.

Stanza 29

1 The bowels are the seat of the passions; repeated at viii 49.4.
8–9 It was as difficult for him to pretend to be a good knight as to be one. For the proverb, see C. G. Smith (1970) 43. Cf. Guazzo, *Civile Conversation* (1581) i 147–8: 'Socrates . . . beeing demaunded which was the readiest way for a man to winne honour and renowne: answered, To indevour, to bee such a one in deede, as hee desireth to seeme to bee in shewe.'

Stanza 30

1 **to weete**: namely. **Satyrane** gains the epithet **good** from his defence of Una (I vi). He defeats the beast because he is 'Plaine, faithfull, true, and enimy of shame' (I vi 20.7).
4 **vnfilde**: unpolished.
5 **compilde**: fashioned.
6 **Scutchin**: shield. The **Satyres hed** announces his name and nation as a satyr's son, I vi 21.1.
8 **milke-white Palfrey**: reverts to the opening description, i 15.2.

Stanza 31

5 **the flowre . . . pride**: one etymology of Florimell's name; cf. IV v 5.7 and see III v 8.7*n*.
7 **magnifide**: glorified by fighting in her name.
8–9 The loss of the **golden girdle** suggests loss of maidenhead: see IV v 3, V iii 28. Cf. Persephone who loses her girdle when she is raped by Pluto (Ovid, *Met.* v 468–70). Cf. Homer, *Ody.* xi 245.

32

Full of sad feare, and doubtfull agony,
    Fiercely he flew vpon that wicked feend,
    And with huge strokes, and cruell battery
    Him forst to leaue his pray, for to attend
    Him selfe from deadly daunger to defend :
    Full many wounds in his corrupted flesh
    He did engraue, and muchell bloud did spend,
    Yet might not do him dye, but aye more fresh
And fierce he still appeard, the more he did him thresh.

33

He wist not, how him to despoile of life,
    Ne how to win the wished victory,
    Sith him he saw still stronger grow through strife,
    And him selfe weaker through infirmity ;
    Greatly he grew enrag'd, and furiously
    Hurling his sword away, he lightly lept
    Vpon the beast, that with great cruelty
    Rored, and raged to be vnder-kept :
Yet he perforce him held, and strokes vpon him hept.

34

As he that striues to stop a suddein flood,
    And in strong banckes his violence enclose,
    Forceth it swell aboue his wonted mood,
    And largely ouerflow the fruitfull plaine,
    That all the countrey seemes to be a Maine,
    And the rich furrowes flote, all quite fordonne :
    The wofull husbandman doth lowd complaine,
    To see his whole yeares labour lost so soone,
For which to God he made so many an idle boone.

35

So him he held, and did through might amate :
    So long he held him, and him bet so long,
    That at the last his fiercenesse gan abate,
    And meekely stoup vnto the victour strong :
    Who to auenge the implacable wrong,
    Which he supposed donne to *Florimell*,
    Sought by all meanes his dolour to prolong,
    Sith dint of steele his carcas could not quell :
His maker with her charmes had framed him so well.

36

The golden ribband, which that virgin wore
    About her sclender wast, he tooke in hand,
    And with it bound the beast, that lowd did rore
    For great despight of that vnwonted band,
    Yet dared not his victour to withstand,
    But trembled like a lambe, fled from the pray,
    And all the way him followd on the strand,
    As he had long bene learned to obay ;
Yet neuer learned he such seruice, till that day.

37

Thus as he led the Beast along the way,
    He spide far off a mighty Giauntesse,
    Fast flying on a Courser dapled gray,
    From a bold knight, that with great hardinesse
    Her hard pursewd, and sought for to suppresse ;
    She bore before her lap a dolefull Squire,
    Lying athwart her horse in great distresse,
    Fast bounden hand and foote with cords of wire,
Whom she did meane to make the thrall of her desire.

38

Which whenas *Satyrane* beheld, in hast
    He left his captiue Beast at liberty,
    And crost the nearest way, by which he cast
    Her to encounter, ere she passed by :
    But she the way shund nathemore for thy,
    But forward gallopt fast ; which when he spyde,
    His mighty speare he couched warily,
    And at her ran : she hauing him descryde,
Her selfe to fight addrest, and threw her lode aside.

Stanza 32

6–9   As a symbol of concupiscence, the monster, whose
corrupted flesh is strengthened by being wounded, may be
compared to Maleger (II xi 38). Satyrane imitates Arthur in
throwing away his sword to grapple with his opponent.
7   **engraue**: cut deeply.

Stanza 33

7   **cruelty**: suffering ; also in the usual sense, as viii 21.2.

Stanza 34

The burden of the simile, that restraint only produces greater
violence, is suggested by Satyrane's efforts to subdue the
monster (32.8–9). Its terms are pertinent to the flight of
Florimell, who may be compared to the **fruitfull plaine** (4)
overwhelmed by the sea. Also the simile relates to the tideland
where the present action takes place.
2   **enclose]** containe, MS. corr. in Malone 615 (J. C. Smith),
used in the obsolete sense, 'confine' ; cf. V xii 1.4.
5   **Maine**: sea.
6   **flote**: are flooded.   **fordonne**: laid waste.
9   **boone**: prayer.

Stanza 35

1   **amate**: subdue.
2   **bet**: beat with his fists.
5   **implacable**: not to be assuaged, irremediable ; cf. II vi
44.2.
7   **dolour**: pain.
8   **quell**: kill.

Stanza 36

In Jacobus de Voragine's *Golden Legend*, St George subdues the
dragon and binds him with his lady's girdle.
6   **pray**: one who preys ; or preying.

Stanza 37

3   **gray**: see II i 18.6*n*.

Stanza 38

3   **cast**: determined, planned.

39

Like as a Goshauke, that in foote doth beare
  A trembling Culuer, hauing spide on hight
  An Egle, that with plumy wings doth sheare
  The subtile ayre, stouping with all his might,
  The quarrey throwes to ground with fell despight,
  And to the battell doth her selfe prepare:
  So ran the Geauntesse vnto the fight;
  Her firie eyes with furious sparkes did stare,
And with blasphemous bannes high God in peeces tare.

40

She caught in hand an huge great yron mace,
  Wherewith she many had of life depriued,
  But ere the stroke could seize his aymed place,
  His speare amids her sun-broad shield arriued;
  Yet nathemore the steele a sunder riued,
  All were the beame in bignesse like a mast,
  Ne her out of the stedfast sadle driued,
  But glauncing on the tempred mettall, brast
In thousand shiuers, and so forth beside her past.

41

Her Steed did stagger with that puissaunt strooke;
  But she no more was moued with that might,
  Then it had lighted on an aged Oke;
  Or on the marble Pillour, that is pight
  Vpon the top of Mount *Olympus* hight,
  For the braue youthly Champions to assay,
  With burning charet wheeles it nigh to smite:
  But who that smites it, mars his ioyous play,
And is the spectacle of ruinous decay.

42

Yet therewith sore enrag'd, with sterne regard
  Her dreadfull weapon she to him addrest,
  Which on his helmet martelled so hard,
  That made him low incline his lofty crest,
  And bowd his battred visour to his brest:
  Wherewith he was so stund, that he n'ote ryde,
  But reeled to and fro from East to West:
  Which when his cruell enimy espyde,
She lightly vnto him adioyned side to syde;

43

And on his collar laying puissant hand,
  Out of his wauering seat him pluckt perforse,
  Perforse him pluckt, vnable to withstand,
  Or helpe himselfe, and laying thwart her horse,
  In loathly wise like to a carion corse,
  She bore him fast away. Which when the knight,
  That her pursewed, saw, with great remorse
  He neare was touched in his noble spright,
And gan encrease his speed, as she encreast her flight.

44

Whom when as nigh approching she espyde,
  She threw away her burden angrily;
  For she list not the battell to abide,
  But made her selfe more light, away to fly:
  Yet her the hardy knight pursewd so nye,
  That almost in the backe he oft her strake:
  But still when him at hand she did espy,
  She turnd, and semblaunce of faire fight did make;
But when he stayd, to flight againe she did her take.

Stanza 39
The eagle is a symbol of masculine strength; the goshawk of feminine aggressiveness; cf. V iv 42.
2 **Culuer**: dove.
4 **subtile**: rarefied. **stouping**: descending swiftly on its prey.
5 **quarrey**: prey.
8 Her eyes infect the beholder, as do Corflambo's eyes at IV viii 39. **stare**: shine.
9 **bannes**: curses, specifically using parts of God's body. As the rioters in Chaucer, *Pardoner's Tale* 474, 'Oure blissed Lordes body . . . totere'.

Stanza 40
1 The 'mortall mace' (I vii 10.9) borne by the giant Orgoglio and the 'massie yron mace' (IV viii 43.6) by Corflambo have similar phallic significance.
3 **seize**: reach; penetrate.
6 In Homer, *Ody.* ix 322, the comparison describes the club of Polyphemus. In Tasso, *Ger. Lib.* vi 40, Tancredi and Argante carry masts instead of spears; cf. Goliath's spear 'like a weavers beame' (1 Sam. 17.7).

Stanza 41
4–9 This error is found in a number of Renaissance writers, e.g. Cooper (1565): '*olympicum certamen*, Was a game or pryce kept on the hyll of *Olympus*.' Milton's fallen angels indulge in this game, the classical equivalent to the grand slalom, which requires one to 'shun the goal / With rapid wheels' (*P.L.* ii 531–2).
9 **decay**: destruction.

Stanza 42
1 **sterne regard**: terrible and threatening aspect.
2 **addrest**: aimed.
3 **martelled**: hammered.
6 **n'ote**: could not.
9 **adioyned**: joined herself to him by approaching alongside, suggesting sexual intimacy. Such *double entendre* is used throughout this episode.

Stanza 43
1–4 **Perforse**: forcibly. The inversion in 3 is for comic effect. His position in 4 is that of Argante's previous victim, 37.7.
7 **remorse**: compassion.

45

By this the good Sir *Satyrane* gan wake
  Out of his dreame, that did him long entraunce,
  And seeing none in place, he gan to make
  Exceeding mone, and curst that cruell chaunce,
  Which reft from him so faire a cheuisaunce:
  At length he spide, whereas that wofull Squire,
  Whom he had reskewed from captiuaunce
  Of his strong foe, lay tombled in the myre,
Vnable to arise, or foot or hand to styre.

46

To whom approching, well he mote perceiue
  In that foule plight a comely personage,
  And louely face, made fit for to deceiue
  Fraile Ladies hart with loues consuming rage,
  Now in the blossome of his freshest age:
  He reard him vp, and loosd his yron bands,
  And after gan inquire his parentage,
  And how he fell into that Gyaunts hands,
And who that was, which chaced her along the lands.

47

Then trembling yet through feare, the Squire bespake,
  That Geauntesse *Argante* is behight,
  A daughter of the *Titans* which did make
  Warre against heauen, and heaped hils on hight,
  To scale the skyes, and put *Ioue* from his right:
  Her sire *Typhœus* was, who mad through merth,
  And drunke with bloud of men, slaine by his might,
  Through incest, her of his owne mother Earth
Whilome begot, being but halfe twin of that berth.

48

For at that berth another Babe she bore,
  To weet the mighty *Ollyphant*, that wrought
  Great wreake to many errant knights of yore,
  And many hath to foule confusion brought.
  These twinnes, men say, (a thing far passing thought)
  Whiles in their mothers wombe enclosd they were,
  Ere they into the lightsome world were brought,
  In fleshly lust were mingled both yfere,
And in that monstrous wise did to the world appere.

49

So liu'd they euer after in like sin,
  Gainst natures law, and good behauioure:
  But greatest shame was to that maiden twin,
  Who not content so fowly to deuoure
  Her natiue flesh, and staine her brothers bowre,
  Did wallow in all other fleshly myre,
  And suffred beasts her body to deflowre:
  So whot she burned in that lustfull fyre,
Yet all that might not slake her sensuall desyre.

50

But ouer all the countrey she did raunge,
  To seeke young men, to quench her flaming thrust,
  And feed her fancy with delightfull chaunge:
  Whom so she fittest finds to serue her lust,
  Through her maine strength, in which she most doth trust,
  She with her brings into a secret Ile,
  Where in eternall bondage dye he must,
  Or be the vassall of her pleasures vile,
And in all shamefull sort him selfe with her defile.

51

Me seely wretch she so at vauntage caught,
  After she long in waite for me did lye,
  And meant vnto her prison to haue brought,
  Her lothsome pleasure there to satisfye;
  That thousand deathes me leuer were to dye,
  Then breake the vow, that to faire *Columbell*
  I plighted haue, and yet keepe stedfastly:
  As for my name, it mistreth not to tell;
Call me the *Squyre of Dames*, that me beseemeth well.

Stanza 45
5 **cheuisaunce**: chivalric enterprise; see II ix 8.1–2*n*.
7 **captiuaunce**: captivity.
9 **styre**: stir.

Stanza 47
2 **Argante** inherits her nature from **Typhœus**: see I v 35.7*n*. Belson (1964) 35 suggests that her name is coined from αργός, bright, shining (i.e. with lust); also swift. He notes her 'sun-broad shield' (40.4) and her swift flight (37.3). The spelling **Geauntesse** indicates her earth-born nature, from Gea, the earth.
3–5 On the war of the Giants against Jove, see II vii 41.6*n*.
8 **incest**: in fact and etymology incest is the extreme degree of unchastity (Lat. *incestus*).

Stanza 48
2 **Ollyphant**: from Chaucer, *Tale of Sir Thopas* vii 807–9: 'a greet geaunt . . . A perilous man of dede'. As the Renaissance spelling of 'elephant', the name may suggest this creature's size. The story of these twins is told again at xi 3.4 to 4.4.
3 **wreake**: harm.
4 **And . . . foule**] Till him Chylde *Thopas* to *1590*. The change was made because Chaucer's tale breaks off before Ollyphant was slain. **confusion**: ruin.
8 **yfere**: together.

Stanza 49
4 **deuoure**: make a prey of, in the sexual sense.

Stanza 50
2 **thrust**: thirst, though 'thrust' applies to a nymphomaniac's desire.
6 Corresponding to Proteus's bower, viii 37–42.

Stanza 51
1 **seely**: miserable, pitiable.
5 **me leuer were**: I would rather.
6 **Columbell**: Fr. *colombelle*, little dove (Venus's bird); or Lat. *columba*, dove + *bella*, pretty; or *bell* may be eulogistic: among ladies she bears the bell. For the dove's association with lechery, see Chew (1962) 105 and Bloomfield (1952) 249.
8 **it mistreth not**: it is not necessary.
9 **Squyre of Dames**: one who devotes himself to the service of ladies. The full title of his office indicates the nature of his service: Squire of the Dame's body. Cf. II i 21.8–9.

373

52

But that bold knight, whom ye pursuing saw
  That Geauntesse, is not such, as she seemed,
  But a faire virgin, that in martiall law,
  And deedes of armes aboue all Dames is deemed,
  And aboue many knights is eke esteemed,
  For her great worth; She *Palladine* is hight:
  She you from death, you me from dread redeemed.
But she, or such as she, that is so chaste a wight.

53

Her well beseemes that Quest (quoth *Satyrane*)
  But read, thou *Squyre of Dames*, what vow is this,
  Which thou vpon thy selfe hast lately ta'ne?
  That shall I you recount (quoth he) ywis,
  So be ye pleasd to pardon all amis.
  That gentle Lady, whom I loue and serue,
  Did aske me, how I could her loue deserue,
And how she might be sure, that I would neuer swerue.

54

I glad by any meanes her grace to gaine,
  Bad her commaund my life to saue, or spill.
  Eftsoones she bad me, with incessaunt paine
  To wander through the world abroad at will,
  And euery where, where with my power or skill
  I might do seruice vnto gentle Dames,
  That I the same should faithfully fulfill,
  And at the twelue monethes end should bring their names
And pledges; as the spoiles of my victorious games.

55

So well I to faire Ladies seruice did,
  And found such fauour in their louing hartes,
  That ere the yeare his course had compassid,
  Three hundred pledges for my good desartes,
  And thrise three hundred thanks for my good partes
  I with me brought, and did to her present:
  Which when she saw, more bent to eke my smartes,
  Then to reward my trusty true intent,
She gan for me deuise a grieuous punishment.

56

To weet, that I my trauell should resume,
  And with like labour walke the world around,
  Ne euer to her presence should presume,
  Till I so many other Dames had found,
  The which, for all the suit I could propound,
  Would me refuse their pledges to afford,
  But did abide for euer chast and sound.
  Ah gentle Squire (quoth he) tell at one word,
How many foundst thou such to put in thy record?

57

In deed Sir knight (said he) one word may tell
  All, that I euer found so wisely stayd;
  For onely three they were disposd so well,
  And yet three yeares I now abroad haue strayd,
  To find them out. Mote I (then laughing sayd
  The knight) inquire of thee, what were those three,
  The which thy proffred curtesie denayd?
  Or ill they seemed sure auizd to bee,
Or brutishly brought vp, that neu'r did fashions see.

58

The first which then refused me (said hee)
  Certes was but a common Courtisane,
  Yet flat refusd to haue a do with mee,
  Because I could not giue her many a Iane.
  (Thereat full hartely laughed *Satyrane*)
  The second was an holy Nunne to chose,
  Which would not let me be her Chappellane,
  Because she knew, she said, I would disclose
Her counsell, if she should her trust in me repose.

Stanza 52
6 **Palladine**: from 'paladin', a knightly hero. The name is
linked with Pallas and hence with Minerva, the classical
goddess of Chastity. Britomart is compared to Minerva at
ix 22. See Fowler (1964) 127.

Stanza 53
2 **read**: declare.
4–5 As Ariosto apologizes for the host's tale, *Orl. Fur.*
xxviii 1, an episode of which – a journey to test chastity in
women – S. now imitates. Harington (1591) 373 comments:
'The hosts tale . . . is a bad one: *M. Spencers* tale . . . is to the
like effect, sharpe and well conceyted.' **ywis**: assuredly.
8–9 The demands are contradictory: he must show that he
deserves her love by serving other ladies and yet remain
faithful to her.

Stanza 54
1 **grace**: favour.
2 **spill**: destroy.
6 **seruice**: i.e. become their lover.

Stanza 55
5 **partes**: suggesting privy parts.

Stanza 57
2 **stayd**: resolute.
7 **denayd**: refused.
8 **auizd**: counselled.

Stanza 58
2 **Courtisane**: suggesting one who responds to 'proffred
curtesie' (57.7).
3 **haue a do**: in the bawdy sense.
4 **Iane**: a small silver coin, mentioned in Chaucer, *Sir Thopas.*
6 **to chose**: if you please (Dodge, 1908).
7–9 With the Protestant innuendo on women in their
relation to priestly confessors.

59

The third a Damzell was of low degree,
Whom I in countrey cottage found by chaunce;
Full little weened I, that chastitee
Had lodging in so meane a maintenaunce,
Yet was she faire, and in her countenance
Dwelt simple truth in seemely fashion.
Long thus I woo'd her with dew obseruance,
In hope vnto my pleasure to haue won;
But was as farre at last, as when I first begon.

60

Safe her, I neuer any woman found,
That chastity did for it selfe embrace,
But were for other causes firme and sound;
Either for want of handsome time and place,
Or else for feare of shame and fowle disgrace.
Thus am I hopelesse euer to attaine
My Ladies loue, in such a desperate case,
But all my dayes am like to wast in vaine,
Seeking to match the chaste with th'vnchaste Ladies traine.

61

Perdy, (said *Satyrane*) thou *Squire of Dames*,
Great labour fondly hast thou hent in hand,
To get small thankes, and therewith many blames,
That may emongst *Alcides* labours stand.
Thence backe returning to the former land,
Where late he left the Beast, he ouercame,
He found him not; for he had broke his band,
And was return'd againe vnto his Dame,
To tell what tydings of faire *Florimell* became.

Cant. VIII.

*The Witch creates a snowy Lady,
like to Florimell,
Who wronged by Carle ·by Proteus sau'd,
is sought by Paridell.*

1

SO oft as I this history record,
My hart doth melt with meere compassion,
To thinke, how causelesse of her owne accord
This gentle Damzell, whom I write vpon,
Should plonged be in such affliction,
Without all hope of comfort or reliefe,
That sure I weene, the hardest hart of stone,
Would hardly find to aggrauate her griefe;
For misery craues rather mercie, then repriefe.

2

But that accursed Hag, her hostesse late,
Had so enranckled her malitious hart,
That she desyrd th'abridgement of her fate,
Or long enlargement of her painefull smart.
Now when the Beast, which by her wicked art
Late forth she sent, she backe returning spyde,
Tyde with her broken girdle, it a part
Of her rich spoyles, whom he had earst destroyd,
She weend, and wondrous gladnesse to her hart applyde.

3

And with it running hast'ly to her sonne,
Thought with that sight him much to haue reliued;
Who thereby deeming sure the thing as donne,
His former griefe with furie fresh reuiued,
Much more then earst, and would haue algates riued
The hart out of his brest: for sith her ded
He surely dempt, himselfe he thought depriued
Quite of all hope, wherewith he long had fed
His foolish maladie, and long time had misled.

Stanza 59
4 **maintenaunce**: state or means of subsistence.

Stanza 60
1 **Safe**: save.
4 **handsome**: suitable.

Stanza 61
2 **fondly**: foolishly.   **hent**: taken.
4 As a prelude to his first labour, Hercules served the fifty virgin daughters of Thespius in one night.
7 Satyrane's defeat by Argante frees the beast, as Dunseath (1968) 31 suggests. Or perhaps his loose laughter does.

Canto viii

Argument
3 **Carle**: a churl.

Stanza 1
2 **meere**: entire.
3 **causelesse of her owne accord**: i.e. not through her own assent (hence not deserving reproof); or through no blame of her own act (sugg. *Var.*). She cannot avoid love nor avoid arousing love in others.
5 **affliction**: in the etymological sense, 'thrown down'. Finally she is thrown under the sea.
7 **hardest hart of stone**: as the walls of stone that imprison her under the sea until Marinell's 'stony heart' (IV xii 13.1) softens with love for her.
8 **find**: find the means to; be hard-hearted enough; also devise, invent.   **aggrauate**: in the literal sense, add weight to, increase.
9 **repriefe**: reproof.

Stanza 2
2 **enranckled**: embittered.
3 **fate**: the length of life allotted by the fates.
7 **broken**] golden *1590*, apparently to agree with the claim that the beast 'had broke his band' (vii 61.7); yet cf. vii 36.1, viii 49.8, IV ii 27.2, etc.

Stanza 3
2 **reliued**: revived.
5 Cf. vii 20.3–5.   **algates**: altogether.
7 **dempt**: deemed.

4

With thought whereof, exceeding mad he grew,
  And in his rage his mother would haue slaine,
  Had she not fled into a secret mew,
  Where she was wont her Sprights to entertaine
  The maisters of her art: there was she faine
  To call them all in order to her ayde,
  And them coniure vpon eternall paine,
  To counsell her so carefully dismayd,
How she might heale her sonne, whose senses were decayd.

5

By their aduise, and her owne wicked wit,
  She there deuiz'd a wondrous worke to frame,
  Whose like on earth was neuer framed yit,
  That euen Nature selfe enuide the same,
  And grudg'd to see the counterfet should shame
  The thing it selfe.   In hand she boldly tooke
  To make another like the former Dame,
  Another *Florimell*, in shape and looke
So liuely and so like, that many it mistooke.

6

The substance, whereof she the bodie made,
  Was purest snow in massie mould congeald,
  Which she had gathered in a shadie glade
  Of the *Riphœan* hils, to her reueald
  By errant Sprights, but from all men conceald:
  The same she tempred with fine Mercury,
  And virgin wex, that neuer yet was seald,
  And mingled them with perfect vermily,
That like a liuely sanguine it seem'd to the eye.

7

In stead of eyes two burning lampes she set
  In siluer sockets, shyning like the skyes,
  And a quicke mouing Spirit did arret
  To stirre and roll them, like a womans eyes;
  In stead of yellow lockes she did deuise,
  With golden wyre to weaue her curled head;
  Yet golden wyre was not so yellow thrise
  As *Florimells* faire haire: and in the stead
Of life, she put a Spright to rule the carkasse dead.

8

A wicked Spright yfraught with fawning guile,
  And faire resemblance aboue all the rest,
  Which with the Prince of Darknesse fell somewhile,
  From heauens blisse and euerlasting rest;
  Him needed not instruct, which way were best
  Himselfe to fashion likest *Florimell*,
  Ne how to speake, ne how to vse his gest,
  For he in counterfeisance did excell,
And all the wyles of wemens wits knew passing well.

9

Him shaped thus, she deckt in garments gay,
  Which *Florimell* had left behind her late,
  That who so then her saw, would surely say,
  It was her selfe, whom it did imitate,
  Or fairer then her selfe, if ought algate
  Might fairer be.   And then she forth her brought
  Vnto her sonne, that lay in feeble state;
  Who seeing her gan streight vpstart, and thought
She was the Lady selfe, whom he so long had sought.

Stanza 4

3 **mew**: hiding-place.
5 **maisters**: instruments.   **faine**: accustomed.
7 **coniure**: charge, adjure.
8 **carefully**: with care or grief.

Stanza 5

1 **aduise**] deuice *1590*; probably a printer's error suggested
by **deuiz'd** (2). She asks only for their counsel.
5–6 This statement is acted out at V iii 23–24.
9 **So liuely and so like**: so lifelike and so resembling life
itself. As the dream fashioned by Morpheus at Archimago's
bidding to deceive the Red Cross Knight, I i 45.4.

Stanza 6

2 **massie**: solid.
4 **the Riphœan hils**: 'mountaines in Scythia, where as is
continuall wynter, and snow with huge wyndes' (Cooper,
1565). Its snow expresses Florimell's frigidity, 34.7. Gough
(1921) 197, citing Euripides, *Helena*, compares the false Helen,
the phantom made of clouds and sunbeams which Paris carried
off instead of Helen. Cf. Plato, *Rep.* 586c, *Phaedrus* 243a.
Roche (1964) 152–4 argues that this myth provides the
archetype for Florimell's story.
6 **Mercury**: one of the three basic substances of man; see
Paracelsus (ed. Jacobi, 1951) 329.   **fine** suggests the
philosophical mercury or *prima materia*.
7 **virgin wex ... seald**: cf. Sidney's blason, 'What toong
can her perfections tell': 'A daintie seale of virgin-waxe, /
Where nothing but impression lackes' (75–6).
8 **vermily**: vermilion.
9 **sanguine**: a blood-red colour, suggesting one of the four
complexions in the body whose predominance brings an
amorous disposition.

Stanza 7

3 **quicke**: living.   **arret**: place in charge.
7 **thrise**: i.e. by many times.

Stanza 8

1–4 Cf. ix 2.6–9. The masculine spirit inhabiting the
female body parodies the hermaphroditic Venus.
somewhile: at one time.
5 **instruct**: i.e. to be instructed.
7 **gest**: bearing.
8 **counterfeisance**: counterfeiting; from Fr.
contrefaisance, suggesting the false face assumed by the
sprite; cf. I viii 49.6.
9 **passing**: exceedingly.

Stanza 9

1 **garments gay**: as 26.9; cf. i 15.6.
5 **algate**: by any means.

10

Tho fast her clipping twixt his armes twaine,
    Extremely ioyed in so happie sight,
    And soone forgot his former sickly paine;
    But she, the more to seeme such as she hight,
    Coyly rebutted his embracement light;
    Yet still with gentle countenaunce retained,
    Enough to hold a foole in vaine delight:
    Him long she so with shadowes entertained,
As her Creatresse had in charge to her ordained.

11

Till on a day, as he disposed was
    To walke the woods with that his Idole faire,
    Her to disport, and idle time to pas,
    In th'open freshnesse of the gentle aire,
    A knight that way there chaunced to repaire;
    Yet knight he was not, but a boastfull swaine,
    That deedes of armes had euer in despaire,
    Proud *Braggadocchio*, that in vaunting vaine
His glory did repose, and credit did maintaine.

12

He seeing with that Chorle so faire a wight,
    Decked with many a costly ornament,
    Much merueiled thereat, as well he might,
    And thought that match a fowle disparagement:
    His bloudie speare eftsoones he boldly bent
    Against the silly clowne, who dead through feare,
    Fell streight to ground in great astonishment;
    Villein (said he) this Ladie is my deare,
Dy, if thou it gainesay: I will away her beare.

13

The fearefull Chorle durst not gainesay, nor dooe,
    But trembling stood, and yielded him the pray;
    Who finding litle leasure her to wooe,
    On *Tromparts* steed her mounted without stay,
    And without reskew led her quite away.
    Proud man himselfe then *Braggadocchio* deemed,
    And next to none, after that happie day,
    Being possessed of that spoyle, which seemed
The fairest wight on ground, and most of men esteemed.

14

But when he saw himselfe free from poursute,
    He gan make gentle purpose to his Dame,
    With termes of loue and lewdnesse dissolute;
    For he could well his glozing speaches frame
    To such vaine vses, that him best became:
    But she thereto would lend but light regard,
    As seeming sory, that she euer came
    Into his powre, that vsed her so hard,
To reaue her honor, which she more then life prefard.

15

Thus as they two of kindnesse treated long,
    There them by chaunce encountred on the way
    An armed knight, vpon a courser strong,
    Whose trampling feet vpon the hollow lay
    Seemed to thunder, and did nigh affray
    That Capons courage: yet he looked grim,
    And fain'd to cheare his Ladie in dismay;
    Who seem'd for feare to quake in euery lim,
And her to saue from outrage, meekely prayed him.

16

Fiercely that stranger forward came, and nigh
    Approching, with bold words and bitter threat,
    Bad that same boaster, as he mote, on high
    To leaue to him that Lady for excheat,
    Or bide him battell without further treat.
    That challenge did too peremptory seeme,
    And fild his senses with abashment great;
    Yet seeing nigh him ieopardy extreme,
He it dissembled well, and light seem'd to esteeme.

Stanza 10
5   rebutted: repelled.   light: nimbly; or as adj. 'wanton'.
8   with shadowes: as she is unreal and an image of
Florimell.

Stanza 11
2   Idole: as she is the god whom he worships; also magic
counterfeit. Upton (1758) compares the phantom or *imago* of
Aeneas in Virgil, *Aen.* x 643, translating Homer's εἰδωλον
(*Iliad* v 449). The counterfeit woman leads directly to the
counterfeit knight, Braggadocchio.
3   disport: entertain.
7   He despaired ever to perform deeds of arms; or one
despaired of such deeds from him.

Stanza 12
4   disparagement: the disgrace of marriage to one of
inferior rank.
5   bloudie speare: ironic, as Church (1758) observes; cf.
18.7.   bent: aimed.
8   Villein: serf.

Stanza 13
4   stay: delay; hindrance.
7   next to none: i.e. second to none.
8–9   The False Florimell assumes Florimell's title, 'the
fairest Dame aliue' (i 18.8), though she only seemed such.

Stanza 14
2   gentle purpose: polite conversation.
9   reaue: take away by force.

Stanza 15
1   kindnesse: affection.
3–5   Later explicitly named Sir Ferraugh but announced
here by his warlike entrance: see 16.2–3*n*, IV ii 4.5–9*n*.
lay: ground.
6   Capon: a term of reproach; its sense, 'eunuch', befits
Braggadocchio.

Stanza 16
2–3   with bold words: alluding to his name, Ferraugh,
which S., *View* 54–5, notes was an Irish battle-cry. Hence on
high: as loudly as he could.
4   excheat: forfeit, what belongs by right to the lord of the
manor.
5   bide him battell: challenge him to fight; endure battle
with him.   treat: parley.

377

17

Saying, Thou foolish knight, that weenst with words
  To steale away, that I with blowes haue wonne,
  And brought throgh points of many perilous swords:
  But if thee list to see thy Courser ronne,
  Or proue thy selfe, this sad encounter shonne,
  And seeke else without hazard of thy hed.
  At those proud words that other knight begonne
  To wexe exceeding wroth, and him ared
To turne his steede about, or sure he should be ded.

18

Sith then (said *Braggadocchio*) needes thou wilt
  Thy dayes abridge, through proofe of puissance,
  Turne we our steedes, that both in equall tilt
  May meet againe, and each take happie chance.
  This said, they both a furlongs mountenance
  Retyrd their steeds, to ronne in euen race:
  But *Braggadocchio* with his bloudie lance
  Once hauing turnd, no more returnd his face,
But left his loue to losse, and fled himselfe apace.

19

The knight him seeing fly, had no regard
  Him to poursew, but to the Ladie rode,
  And hauing her from *Trompart* lightly reard,
  Vpon his Courser set the louely lode,
  And with her fled away without abode.
  Well weened he, that fairest *Florimell*
  It was, with whom in company he yode,
  And so her selfe did alwaies to him tell;
So made him thinke him selfe in heauen, that was in hell.

20

But *Florimell* her selfe was farre away,
  Driuen to great distresse by Fortune straunge,
  And taught the carefull Mariner to play,
  Sith late mischaunce had her compeld to chaunge
  The land for sea, at randon there to raunge:
  Yet there that cruell Queene auengeresse,
  Not satisfide so farre her to estraunge
  From courtly blisse and wonted happinesse,
Did heape on her new waues of weary wretchednesse.

21

For being fled into the fishers bote,
  For refuge from the Monsters crueltie,
  Long so she on the mightie maine did flote,
  And with the tide droue forward careleslie;
  For th'aire was milde, and cleared was the skie,
  And all his windes *Dan Aeolus* did keepe,
  From stirring vp their stormy enmitie,
  As pittying to see her waile and weepe;
But all the while the fisher did securely sleepe.

22

At last when droncke with drowsinesse, he woke,
  And saw his drouer driue along the streame,
  He was dismayd, and thrise his breast he stroke,
  For maruell of that accident extreame;
  But when he saw that blazing beauties beame,
  Which with rare light his bote did beautifie,
  He marueild more, and thought he yet did dreame
  Not well awakt, or that some extasie
Assotted had his sense, or dazed was his eie.

Stanza 17
6 **else**: elsewhere.
8 **ared**: advised.

Stanza 18
4 **happie chance**: the chance of fortune.
5 **mountenance**: distance.
8 **returnd**: turned back.

Stanza 19
1 **regard**: interest.
3 **lightly**: easily; indicating the transfer of her affections.
The true Florimell prefers death to the charge that 'she lightly
did remoue' (42.5).
5 **abode**: delay.
7 **yode**: went.
9 Cf. the similar expression, IV ii 9.8–9.

Stanza 20
3 **taught . . . to play**: Fortune taught her to act the part of
a mariner. The further sense of **play**, to sport amorously,
anticipates her next distress. Cf. ix 4.8.   **carefull**: full of
care.
6 Referring to **Fortune** (2). With a pun on 'quean', strumpet
(cf. IV viii 28.8).
9 **waues**: referring to her woes, but anticipating her descent
under water; cf. IV xi 3.

Stanza 21
6 **Aeolus**: god of the winds.   **Dan**: form of address.
9 **securely**: free from care (the Lat. sense), as Florimell
rides **careleslie** (4), i.e. without apprehension.

Stanza 22
1 **droncke with drowsinesse**: i.e. having slept his fill.
2 **drouer**: a fishing boat.   **streame**: the tide.
5–6 Cf. 'The blazing brightnesse of her beauties beame'
(I xii 23.1) when Una is unveiled; cf. also i 16.5.
8 **extasie**: madness which produces a 'fantasticke sight'
(23.2).
9 **Assotted**: infatuated.

23

But when her well auizing, he perceiued
  To be no vision, nor fantasticke sight,
  Great comfort of her presence he conceiued,
  And felt in his old courage new delight
  To gin awake, and stirre his frozen spright:
  Tho rudely askt her, how she thither came.
  Ah (said she) father, I note read aright,
  What hard misfortune brought me to the same;
Yet am I glad that here I now in safety am.

24

But thou good man, sith farre in sea we bee,
  And the great waters gin apace to swell,
  That now no more we can the maine-land see,
  Haue care, I pray, to guide the cock-bote well,
  Least worse on sea then vs on land befell.
  Thereat th'old man did nought but fondly grin,
  And said, his boat the way could wisely tell:
  But his deceiptfull eyes did neuer lin,
To looke on her faire face, and marke her snowy skin.

25

The sight whereof in his congealed flesh,
  Infixt such secret sting of greedy lust,
  That the drie withered stocke it gan refresh,
  And kindled heat, that soone in flame forth brust:
  The driest wood is soonest burnt to dust.
  Rudely to her he lept, and his rough hand
  Where ill became him, rashly would haue thrust,
  But she with angry scorne him did withstond,
And shamefully reproued for his rudenesse fond.

26

But he, that neuer good nor maners knew,
  Her sharpe rebuke full litle did esteeme;
  Hard is to teach an old horse amble trew.
  The inward smoke, that did before but steeme,
  Broke into open fire and rage extreme,
  And now he strength gan adde vnto his will,
  Forcing to doe, that did him fowle misseeme:
  Beastly he threw her downe, ne car'd to spill
Her garments gay with scales of fish, that all did fill.

27

The silly virgin stroue him to withstand,
  All that she might, and him in vaine reuild:
  She struggled strongly both with foot and hand,
  To saue her honor from that villaine vild,
  And cride to heauen, from humane helpe exild.
  O ye braue knights, that boast this Ladies loue,
  Where be ye now, when she is nigh defild
  Of filthy wretch? well may shee you reproue
Of falshood or of slouth, when most it may behoue.

28

But if that thou, Sir *Satyran*, didst weete,
  Or thou, Sir *Peridure*, her sorie state,
  How soone would yee assemble many a fleete,
  To fetch from sea, that ye at land lost late;
  Towres, Cities, Kingdomes ye would ruinate,
  In your auengement and dispiteous rage,
  Ne ought your burning fury mote abate;
  But if Sir *Calidore* could it presage,
No liuing creature could his cruelty asswage.

Stanza 23
1 **auizing**: observing.
2 **fantasticke sight**: imaginary sight or phantasm.
3–5 Imitating Ariosto, *Orl. Fur.* ii 13, viii 31: the frozen
marrow of the old Hermit blazes with lust at the sight of
Angelica. **comfort**: physical strengthening or invigoration.
courage: spirit; also in the bawdy sense, 'sexual vigour';
cf. the naked maidens 'that courage cold could reare' (II xii
68.9).
7–9 As Angelica appeals to the Hermit, *Orl. Fur.* viii 46.
note read: cannot tell.

Stanza 24
4, 7 **cock-bote**: a small ship's boat too dangerous for use at
sea (Falconer, 1964, 98); perhaps used as a euphemism, for
more than the seas **gin apace to swell** (2). Strong comic
irony runs through the episode.
6 **fondly**: foolishly; lovingly. **grin**: associated with lust;
cf. Lust's 'grenning laughter' (IV vii 24.9).
7 **wisely**: cunningly.
8 **lin**: cease.

Stanza 25
S. seeks to outdo Ariosto's bawdy play on the Hermit's fallen
steed (*Orl. Fur.* viii 48–50).
9 **fond**: doting.

Stanza 26
5 **rage**: sexual passion.
7 Using force to do what foully misbecame him.
8 **Beastly**: like a beast. **ne . . . spill**: nor cared if he
defiled.
9 Suggesting that Florimell is being transformed into a
mermaid. **fill**: also defile (cf. 32.2), referring to her garments.

Stanza 27
1 **silly**: helpless.
9 **when most it may behoue**: when it is most fitting to
aid her.

Stanza 28
2 **Sir Peridure**: cited in the chronicle of British kings at
II x 44.9, and as one of Arthur's knights in Geoffrey of
Monmouth IX xii. His name signifies 'one who endures', from
Lat. *perdure*.
5 **ruinate**: lay waste.
6 **dispiteous**: merciless.
8–9 **Sir Calidore**, the knight of courtesy in Book VI.
cruelty: as one etymology of his name is Lat. *calidus*, fierce,
rash. **presage**: have a presentiment of.

29

But sith that none of all her knights is nye,
  See how the heauens of voluntary grace,
  And soueraine fauour towards chastity,
  Doe succour send to her distressed cace:
  So much high God doth innocence embrace.
  It fortuned, whilest thus she stifly stroue,
  And the wide sea importuned long space
  With shrilling shriekes, *Proteus* abroad did roue,
Along the fomy waues driuing his finny droue.

30

Proteus is Shepheard of the seas of yore,
  And hath the charge of *Neptunes* mightie heard;
  An aged sire with head all frory hore,
  And sprinckled frost vpon his deawy beard:
  Who when those pittifull outcries he heard,
  Through all the seas so ruefully resound,
  His charet swift in haste he thither steard,
  Which with a teeme of scaly *Phocas* bound
Was drawne vpon the waues, that fomed him around.

31

And comming to that Fishers wandring bote,
  That went at will, withouten carde or sayle,
  He therein saw that yrkesome sight, which smote
  Deepe indignation and compassion frayle
  Into his hart attonce: streight did he hayle
  The greedy villein from his hoped pray,
  Of which he now did very litle fayle,
  And with his staffe, that driues his Heard astray,
Him bet so sore, that life and sense did much dismay.

32

The whiles the pitteous Ladie vp did ryse,
  Ruffled and fowly raid with filthy soyle,
  And blubbred face with teares of her faire eyes:
  Her heart nigh broken was with weary toyle,
  To saue her selfe from that outrageous spoyle,
  But when she looked vp, to weet, what wight
  Had her from so infamous fact assoyld,
  For shame, but more for feare of his grim sight,
Downe in her lap she hid her face, and loudly shright.

33

Her selfe not saued yet from daunger dred
  She thought, but chaung'd from one to other feare;
  Like as a fearefull Partridge, that is fled
  From the sharpe Hauke, which her attached neare,
  And fals to ground, to seeke for succour theare,
  Whereas the hungry Spaniels she does spy,
  With greedy iawes her readie for to teare;
  In such distresse and sad perplexity
Was *Florimell*, when *Proteus* she did see thereby.

Arthur as the power of grace (see I viii Arg.*n*), except in this book in which the heavens send aid through Proteus. See IV viii 18*n*. Grace intercedes on three occasions: when Belphœbe succours Timias (v 27), when Proteus rescues Florimell, and when Britomart frees Amoret (xi 14, 16). Cf. the reference to God's grace aiding Florimell, vii 27.1. Giamatti (1975) 121 argues that Arthur's displacement by the embodiments of falsity and chaos, the False Florimell and Proteus, 'underscores the centrality of these forces of dispersal and decay'.
2–5   Cf. Milton, *Comus* 215–9, 1021–2.   **voluntary**: as God's grace is freely offered man. Here it answers Florimell's prayer at 27.5.   **embrace**: accept; protect. Cf. the boatman's attempt to embrace Florimell.

Stanza 30
1–4   A parenthetical footnote. **Proteus** is 'the god of the sea, whom Homere nameth to be the heardman of the fyshes called *Phocae*, and also a prophete [see iv 25.2–9*n*] . . . He also tourned himselfe into sundry fygures' (Cooper, 1565). Boccaccio, *Gen. Deor.* VII ix, says that his many shapes indicate passions; noted Lotspeich (1932) 104. His imprisonment of Florimell suggests, then, the passions to which she is subject through love of Marinell. Proteus also signifies mutable nature, specifically the cycle of the seasons, in particular winter which overwhelms beauty; see Roche (1964) 159–60. Lewis (1967) 126 interprets Proteus as a personification of matter, and Florimell as 'the *anima semplicetta* come from the sweet golden clime into the sea of matter and the power of Proteus'. He concludes that 'her imprisonment seems very like an allegory of the descent of the soul into material embodiment'.
3   **frory hore**: frosty with foam.
8   **Phocas**: seals.   **scaly**: perhaps because his chariot is usually drawn by fishes, as Virgil, *Georg.* iv 388–9.

Stanza 31
1–2   Cf. Phædria's 'wandring ship' (II vi 10.2) which goes without pilot or wind.   **will**: associated with the fisherman's lust. Cf. 24.7; now his lust cannot be restrained.   **carde**: chart or compass card.
3   **yrkesome**: loathsome.
4   **frayle**: tender.
8   **astray**: on their way.
9   **dismay**: overwhelm.

Stanza 32
1–3   **raid**: defiled; arrayed.   **soyle**: stain or filth, alluding to the fish scales which cover her; in contrast to the virgin's state, 'without stain or spot'.   **blubbred**: disfigured from weeping. Cf. Una's 'ruffled rayments, and faire blubbred face' (I vi 9.3) when she is almost raped by Sansloy.
5   **spoyle**: rape; or becoming his spoil.
7   **fact**: evil deed.   **assoyld**: set free.
9   **shright**: shrieked.

Stanza 33
3–7   Turberville, *Booke of Faulconrie* (1575), notes that one device of the falconer is 'a conspiracye (as it were) betwixt the dogges and Hawkes'; cited Harrison (1956) 70. The simile illustrates the dangers of Florimell's flight from one element to another.
4   **sharpe**: eager for prey.   **attached neare**: nearly seized.

Stanza 29
The eighth canto of each book is marked by the intercession of

34

But he endeuoured with speeches milde
　Her to recomfort, and accourage bold,
　Bidding her feare no more her foeman vilde,
　Nor doubt himselfe; and who he was, her told.
　Yet all that could not from affright her hold,
　Ne to recomfort her at all preuayld;
　For her faint heart was with the frozen cold
　Benumbd so inly, that her wits nigh fayld,
And all her senses with abashment quite were quayld.

35

Her vp betwixt his rugged hands he reard,
　And with his frory lips full softly kist,
　Whiles the cold ysickles from his rough beard,
　Dropped adowne vpon her yuorie brest:
　Yet he himselfe so busily addrest,
　That her out of astonishment he wrought,
　And out of that same fishers filthy nest
　Remouing her, into his charet brought,
And there with many gentle termes her faire besought.

36

But that old leachour, which with bold assault
　That beautie durst presume to violate,
　He cast to punish for his hainous fault;
　Then tooke he him yet trembling sith of late,
　And tyde behind his charet, to aggrate
　The virgin, whom he had abusde so sore:
　So drag'd him through the waues in scornefull state,
　And after cast him vp, vpon the shore;
But *Florimell* with him vnto his bowre he bore.

37

His bowre is in the bottome of the maine,
　Vnder a mightie rocke, gainst which do raue
　The roaring billowes in their proud disdaine,
　That with the angry working of the waue,
　Therein is eaten out an hollow caue,
　That seemes rough Masons hand with engines keene
　Had long while laboured it to engraue:
　There was his wonne, ne liuing wight was seene,
Saue one old *Nymph*, hight *Panope* to keepe it cleane.

38

Thither he brought the sory *Florimell*,
　And entertained her the best he might
　And *Panope* her entertaind eke well,
　As an immortall mote a mortall wight,
　To winne her liking vnto his delight:
　With flattering words he sweetly wooed her,
　And offered faire gifts t'allure her sight,
　But she both offers and the offerer
Despysde, and all the fawning of the flatterer.

39

Daily he tempted her with this or that,
　And neuer suffred her to be at rest:
　But euermore she him refused flat,
　And all his fained kindnesse did detest,
　So firmely she had sealed vp her brest.
　Sometimes he boasted, that a God he hight:
　But she a mortall creature loued best:
　Then he would make himselfe a mortall wight;
But then she said she lou'd none, but a Faerie knight.

40

Then like a Faerie knight himselfe he drest;
　For euery shape on him he could endew:
　Then like a king he was to her exprest,
　And offred kingdomes vnto her in vew,
　To be his Leman and his Ladie trew:
　But when all this he nothing saw preuaile,
　With harder meanes he cast her to subdew,
　And with sharpe threates her often did assaile,
So thinking for to make her stubborne courage quaile.

Stanza 34

2　**accourage**: encourage; 'take heart'.
4　**doubt**: also fear.
9　**quayld**: overpowered.

Stanza 35

2　**frory**: frozen; cf. 30.3.
5–8　Her change from 34.9 allows her removal, as the repetition of **out of** indicates. **addrest**: applied. **astonishment**: dismay; numbness.

Stanza 36

3　**cast**: resolved.
5　**aggrate**: please.

Stanza 37

In Virgil, *Georg.* iv 418–22, Proteus shelters himself on the sea-shore behind a huge rock in a cave which has been hollowed out of the mountain side; cf. Cymoent's bower, iv 43.
7　**engraue**: cut.
9　**Panope**: a Nereid at IV xi 49.8; her name means 'all-seeing'.

Stanza 39

4　**kindnesse**: affection.　　**fained**: because devised to win her.
5　Her **sealed** breast explains why she is imprisoned; cf. Amoret's breast with its wide wound, xii 20.5.
7　Guyon offers this same excuse to reject Philotime, II vii 50.3–5.

Stanzas 40–41.4

In his traditional role, he changes into all shapes to escape capture; now he does so in order to capture. Proteus as lover derives from Ariosto, *Orl. Fur.* viii 52f. Edwards (1958) 85 notes that Ovid, *Ars Amat.* i 759–62, advises the lover to be like the nimble Proteus in adapting himself to the variable disposition of his mistress. Starnes and Talbert (1955) 72–3 note that Stephanus relates Proteus to Vertumnus (Ovid, *Met.* xiv 641–55) who changes his shape to gain Pomona's love. On Proteus as courtier, see Perry (1954). In his transformation, he first appears as the God of the Sea (39.6) and ends as the storming sea itself. On Proteus's role in the canto, see Giamatti (1975) 121f.

Stanza 40

2　**endew**: assume, put on.
3　**exprest**: revealed.
6　**preuaile**: avail.

381

41

To dreadfull shapes he did himselfe transforme,
   Now like a Gyant, now like to a feend,
   Then like a Centaure, then like to a storme,
   Raging within the waues: thereby he weend
   Her will to win vnto his wished end.
   But when with feare, nor fauour, nor with all
   He else could doe, he saw himselfe esteemd,
   Downe in a Dongeon deepe he let her fall,
And threatned there to make her his eternall thrall.

42

Eternall thraldome was to her more liefe,
   Then losse of chastitie, or chaunge of loue:
   Die had she rather in tormenting griefe,
   Then any should of falsenesse her reproue,
   Or loosenesse, that she lightly did remoue.
   Most vertuous virgin, glory be thy meed,
   And crowne of heauenly praise with Saints aboue,
   Where most sweet hymmes of this thy famous deed
Are still emongst them song, that far my rymes exceed.

43

Fit song of Angels caroled to bee;
   But yet what so my feeble Muse can frame,
   Shall be t'aduance thy goodly chastitee,
   And to enroll thy memorable name,
   In th'heart of euery honourable Dame,
   That they thy vertuous deedes may imitate,
   And be partakers of thy endlesse fame.
   It yrkes me, leaue thee in this wofull state,
To tell of *Satyrane*, where I him left of late.

44

Who hauing ended with that *Squire of Dames*
   A long discourse of his aduentures vaine,
   The which himselfe, then Ladies more defames,
   And finding not th' *Hyena* to be slaine,
   With that same *Squire*, returned backe againe
   To his first way. And as they forward went,
   They spyde a knight faire pricking on the plaine,
   As if he were on some aduenture bent,
And in his port appeared manly hardiment.

45

Sir *Satyrane* him towards did addresse,
   To weet, what wight he was, and what his quest:
   And comming nigh, eftsoones he gan to gesse
   Both by the burning hart, which on his brest
   He bare, and by the colours in his crest,
   That *Paridell* it was. Tho to him yode,
   And him saluting, as beseemed best,
   Gan first inquire of tydings farre abrode;
And afterwardes, on what aduenture now he rode.

46

Who thereto answering, said; The tydings bad,
   Which now in Faerie court all men do tell,
   Which turned hath great mirth, to mourning sad,
   Is the late ruine of proud *Marinell*,
   And suddein parture of faire *Florimell*,
   To find him forth: and after her are gone
   All the braue knights, that doen in armes excell,
   To sauegard her, ywandred all alone;
Emongst the rest my lot (vnworthy) is to be one.

47

Ah gentle knight (said then Sir *Satyrane*)
   Thy labour all is lost, I greatly dread,
   That hast a thanklesse seruice on thee ta'ne,
   And offrest sacrifice vnto the dead:
   For dead, I surely doubt, thou maist aread
   Henceforth for euer *Florimell* to be,
   That all the noble knights of *Maydenhead*,
   Which her ador'd, may sore repent with me,
And all faire Ladies may for euer sory be.

48

Which words when *Paridell* had heard, his hew
   Gan greatly chaunge, and seem'd dismayd to bee;
   Then said, Faire Sir, how may I weene it trew,
   That ye doe tell in such vncertaintee?
   Or speake ye of report, or did ye see
   Iust cause of dread, that makes ye doubt so sore?
   For perdie else how mote it euer bee,
   That euer hand should dare for to engore
Her noble bloud? the heauens such crueltie abhore.

Stanza 41

3   **Centaure**: a symbol of lust; see Cirlot (1962) 39.
8   Called 'lowest hell' at IV xii 6.7.

Stanza 42

1   **more liefe**: preferable.

Stanza 43

1   **of**: by.
3   **aduance**: extol.
4–7   Cf. the praise of Belphœbe, v 54.7–9.

Stanza 45

1   **addresse**: direct his course.
4–6   Cf. the 'burning hart' (I iv 25.3) in the hand of Lechery, and Florimell's frozen heart, 34.7. Paridell's name denotes his descent from the Trojan Paris (see ix 36–37). Fowler (1959) 585*n*3 suggests 'Paris-idell'.   **yode**: went.

Stanza 46

4   **ruine**: fall.
5–6   See v 10.1–2*n*.   **parture**: departure.

Stanza 47

5   **doubt**: fear.   **surely**: Upton (1758) suggests 'sorely' from Paridell's response, 48.6; cf. 'Right sore I feare' (ix 1.3). **aread**: deem.
8   **repent**: referring to their reproof because of her 'death'; cf. 27.8–9.

Stanza 48

5   **report**: rumour.
8   **engore**: stain itself in; shed.

49

These eyes did see, that they will euer rew
  T'haue seene, (quoth he) when as a monstrous beast
  The Palfrey, whereon she did trauell, slew,
  And of his bowels made his bloudie feast:
  Which speaking token sheweth at the least
  Her certaine losse, if not her sure decay:
  Besides, that more suspition encreast,
  I found her golden girdle cast astray,
Distaynd with durt and bloud, as relique of the pray.

50

Aye me, (said *Paridell*) the signes be sad,
  And but God turne the same to good soothsay,
  That Ladies safetie is sore to be drad:
  Yet will I not forsake my forward way,
  Till triall doe more certaine truth bewray.
  Faire Sir (quoth he) well may it you succeed,
  Ne long shall *Satyrane* behind you stay,
  But to the rest, which in this Quest proceed
My labour adde, and be partaker of their speed.

51

Ye noble knights (said then the *Squire of Dames*)
  Well may ye speed in so praiseworthy paine:
  But sith the Sunne now ginnes to slake his beames,
  In deawy vapours of the westerne maine,
  And lose the teme out of his weary waine,
  Mote not mislike you also to abate
  Your zealous hast, till morrow next againe
  Both light of heauen, and strength of men relate:
Which if ye please, to yonder castle turne your gate.

52

That counsell pleased well; so all yfere
  Forth marched to a Castle them before,
  Where soone arriuing, they restrained were
  Of readie entrance, which ought euermore
  To errant knights be commun: wondrous sore
  Thereat displeasd they were, till that young Squire
  Gan them informe the cause, why that same dore
  Was shut to all, which lodging did desire:
The which to let you weet, will further time require.

Cant. IX.

Malbecco will no straunge knights host,
* For peeuish gealosie:*
Paridell giusts with Britomart:
* Both shew their auncestrie.*

1

REdoubted knights, and honorable Dames,
  To whom I leuell all my labours end,
  Right sore I feare, least with vnworthy blames
  This odious argument my rimes should shend,
  Or ought your goodly patience offend,
  Whiles of a wanton Lady I do write,
  Which with her loose incontinence doth blend
  The shyning glory of your soueraigne light,
And knighthood fowle defaced by a faithlesse knight.

2

But neuer let th'ensample of the bad
  Offend the good: for good by paragone
  Of euill, may more notably be rad,
  As white seemes fairer, macht with blacke attone;
  Ne all are shamed by the fault of one:
  For lo in heauen, whereas all goodnesse is,
  Emongst the Angels, a whole legione
  Of wicked Sprights did fall from happy blis;
What wonder then, if one of women all did mis?

Stanza 49
6 **decay**: death.
9 **Distaynd**: deeply stained, defiled.

Stanza 50
2 **but**: unless.   **soothsay**: omen.
5 **bewray**: reveal.
9 **speed**: success; also the usual sense: cf. 51.7.

Stanza 51
2 **speed**: succeed.   **paine**: effort.
5 **lose**: loosen.   **waine**: wagon; but also a pun on 'wane',
decrease; cf. I v 41.2.
6 May it not displease you.
8 **relate**: restore. The usual sense also applies: man's
strength relates to day as both abate and need to be restored.

Canto ix

Argument
2 **peeuish**: perverse, obstinate.

Stanzas 1–3.4
Cf. the apology for the story of Malecasta, i 49. It comes rather
weakly after what the Squire of Dames has disclosed about
honorable Dames at vii 57–60. The address to the readers in
3.1–4 is particularly awkward: **Lordings** (3.1) seems to
exclude Dames who, presumably, decide to skip the story.
Fortunately S. allows the Squire to take over at 3.5.

Stanza 1
4 **argument**: subject.   **shend**: disgrace.
7 **blend**: defile; dim.

Stanza 2
2 **paragone**: comparison.
3 **rad**: discerned.
4 **attone**: together.
6–9 Cf. Rev. 12.3–4, 7–9. Cf. viii 8.3–4. The analogy
associates the fall of the angels, and hence Eve's fall, with
Hellenore's fall.   **legione**: vast host of angels or spirits
(*OED* 3); an infinite number in the Geneva gloss to Matt.
26.53.   **mis**: err.

3

Then listen Lordings, if ye list to weet
   The cause, why *Satyrane* and *Paridell*
   Mote not be entertaynd, as seemed meet,
   Into that Castle (as that Squire does tell.)
   Therein a cancred crabbed Carle does dwell,
   That has no skill of Court nor courtesie,
   Ne cares, what men say of him ill or well;
   For all his dayes he drownes in priuitie,
Yet has full large to liue, and spend at libertie.

4

But all his mind is set on mucky pelfe,
   To hoord vp heapes of euill gotten masse,
   For which he others wrongs, and wreckes himselfe;
   Yet is he lincked to a louely lasse,
   Whose beauty doth her bounty far surpasse,
   The which to him both far vnequall yeares,
   And also far vnlike conditions has;
   For she does ioy to play emongst her peares,
And to be free from hard restraint and gealous feares.

5

But he is old, and withered like hay,
   Vnfit faire Ladies seruice to supply;
   The priuie guilt whereof makes him alway
   Suspect her truth, and keepe continuall spy
   Vpon her with his other blincked eye;
   Ne suffreth he resort of liuing wight
   Approch to her, ne keepe her company,
   But in close bowre her mewes from all mens sight,
Depriu'd of kindly ioy and naturall delight.

6

Malbecco he, and *Hellenore* she hight,
   Vnfitly yokt together in one teeme,
   That is the cause, why neuer any knight
   Is suffred here to enter, but he seeme
   Such, as no doubt of him he neede misdeeme.
   Thereat Sir *Satyrane* gan smile, and say;
   Extremely mad the man I surely deeme,
   That weenes with watch and hard restraint to stay
A womans will, which is disposd to go astray.

7

In vaine he feares that, which he cannot shonne:
   For who wotes not, that womans subtiltyes
   Can guilen *Argus*, when she list misdonne?
   It is not yron bandes, nor hundred eyes,
   Nor brasen walls, nor many wakefull spyes,
   That can withhold her wilfull wandring feet;
   But fast good will with gentle curtesyes,
   And timely seruice to her pleasures meet
May her perhaps containe, that else would algates fleet.

8

Then is he not more mad (said *Paridell*)
   That hath himselfe vnto such seruice sold,
   In dolefull thraldome all his dayes to dwell?
   For sure a foole I do him firmely hold,
   That loues his fetters, though they were of gold.
   But why do we deuise of others ill,
   Whiles thus we suffer this same dotard old,
   To keepe vs out, in scorne of his owne will,
And rather do not ransack all, and him selfe kill?

Stanza 3
3   **entertaynd**: received as guests.
5   **cancred**: ill-tempered.   **Carle**: churl; also with the sense, 'miser'; repeated at 12.9, 17.8.
6   **skill**: knowledge.
8   **priuitie**: seclusion.
9   **large**: largesse, which brings freedom; cf. 'bounty' (4.5).

Stanza 4
1   **mucky pelfe**: 'filthy lucre'.
2   **masse**: treasure.
5   **bounty**: virtue. The proper balance is seen in Cambina: 'with her beautie bountie did compare [vie]' (IV iii 39.8).
7   **conditions**: manners.
8   **play**: sport amorously.

Stanza 5
1   **withered like hay**: cf. the fisherman's 'drie withered stocke' (viii 25.3).
2   **seruice**: cf. the Squire of Dames's service, vii 54.6.
3   **priuie**: secret; punning on privy parts.
5   **his other blincked eye**: i.e. with his one, or left, eye which is affected with a blink or dim with age; his other eye is blind. See 27.6–7. Nelson (1963) 131 sees his blindness 'as a metaphor for the watchful blindness of jealousy'. Also it expresses his state as a miser: cf. 'misers blind' (x 15.9).
8   **mewes**: hides.
9   **kindly**: natural.

Stanza 6
1   **Malbecco**: Lat. *malus*, wicked + Ital. *becco*, he-goat, cuckold.   **Hellenore**: 'This second *Hellene*' (x 13.1), named after Helen of Troy. See note on Paridell, viii 45.4–6*n*. Nelson (1953) 228 suggests that the name combines Helen and Elinor, the wife of Suspicion in George Gascoigne's *Adventures of Master F. J.* (1573). Fowler (1959) 585*n*3 suggests 'Helenwhore'. To her husband, she is the cuckolding wife; to Paridell, she is Helen, making him a modern, trivialized Paris.
5   **misdeeme**: suspect.

Stanza 7
1   Proverbial (C. G. Smith, 1970, 250).
3   **guilen**: beguile.   **Argus**: the monster with a hundred eyes set to guard Io by the jealous Juno (Ovid, *Met.* i 622–7). The proverb, 'As full of eyes as Argus' (Smith 25), suggests the helplessness of the one-eyed Malbecco.
9   **containe**: keep under control; keep chaste.   **algates**: otherwise.

Stanza 8
4–5   Proverbial (C. G. Smith, 1970, 258); cf. *Amor.* xxxvii 13–4.
6   **deuise**: talk.
8   **in scorne of his owne will**: i.e. in his scornful will; or scornfully and wilfully.

9

Nay let vs first (said *Satyrane*) entreat
 The man by gentle meanes, to let vs in,
 And afterwardes affray with cruell threat,
 Ere that we to efforce it do begin:
 Then if all fayle, we will by force it win,
 And eke reward the wretch for his mesprise,
 As may be worthy of his haynous sin.
That counsell pleasd: then *Paridell* did rise,
And to the Castle gate approcht in quiet wise.

10

Whereat soft knocking, entrance he desyrd.
 The good man selfe, which then the Porter playd,
 Him answered, that all were now retyrd
 Vnto their rest, and all the keyes conuayd
 Vnto their maister, who in bed was layd,
 That none him durst awake out of his dreme;
 And therefore them of patience gently prayd.
Then *Paridell* began to chaunge his theme,
And threatned him with force and punishment extreme.

11

But all in vaine; for nought mote him relent,
 And now so long before the wicket fast
 They wayted, that the night was forward spent,
 And the faire welkin fowly ouercast,
 Gan blowen vp a bitter stormy blast,
 With shoure and hayle so horrible and dred,
 That this faire many were compeld at last,
To fly for succour to a little shed,
The which beside the gate for swine was ordered.

12

It fortuned, soone after they were gone,
 Another knight, whom tempest thither brought,
 Came to that Castle, and with earnest mone,
 Like as the rest, late entrance deare besought;
 But like so as the rest he prayd for nought,
 For flatly he of entrance was refusd,
 Sorely thereat he was displeasd, and thought
How to auenge himselfe so sore abusd,
And euermore the Carle of curtesie accusd.

13

But to auoyde th'intollerable stowre,
 He was compeld to seeke some refuge neare,
 And to that shed, to shrowd him from the showre,
 He came, which full of guests he found whyleare,
 So as he was not let to enter there:
 Whereat he gan to wex exceeding wroth,
 And swore, that he would lodge with them yfere,
Or them dislodge, all were they liefe or loth;
And so defide them each, and so defide them both.

14

Both were full loth to leaue that needfull tent,
 And both full loth in darkenesse to debate;
 Yet both full liefe him lodging to haue lent,
 And both full liefe his boasting to abate;
 But chiefly *Paridell* his hart did grate,
 To heare him threaten so despightfully,
 As if he did a dogge to kenell rate,
That durst not barke; and rather had he dy,
Then when he was defide, in coward corner ly.

15

Tho hastily remounting to his steed,
 He forth issew'd; like as a boistrous wind,
 Which in th'earthes hollow caues hath long bin hid,
 And shut vp fast within her prisons blind,
 Makes the huge element against her kind
 To moue, and tremble as it were agast,
 Vntill that it an issew forth may find;
Then forth it breakes, and with his furious blast
Confounds both land and seas, and skyes doth ouercast.

Stanza 9
4 **efforce**: gain by force.
6 **mesprise**: contempt.

Stanza 11
2 **wicket fast**: locked gate.
7 **many**: company.
8 **succour**: refuge.
9 **ordered**: prepared.

Stanza 12
3 **mone**: complaint, i.e. plea.
4 **deare**: earnestly.
9 **of curtesie accusd**: i.e. accused him in the name of
courtesy.

Stanza 13
The repeated **he, him**, here and in the preceding stanza,
prepare for the surprise of 'his' identity.
1 **stowre**: storm.
4 **whyleare**: a while before.
8 **liefe or loth**: willing or not.
9 **both**: Paridell and the Squire of Dames, as 14.1.

Stanza 14
2 **debate**: fight.
5 **grate**: fret.
6 **despightfully**: contemptuously.

Stanza 15
2–9   The simile links Britomart's victory over Paridell with
her victory over the storm which drives her to seek refuge, and
prepares for her resistance to the whirlwind in the house of
Busirane, xii 3. Cf. the inner storm which she overcomes before
she meets Marinell, iv 8–10, 13. Berger (1969d) 141 suggests
that the simile shows that Paridell embodies ancient elemental
forces which express themselves only in destructive violence.
5 **kind**: nature.

16

Their steel-hed speares they strongly coucht, and met
　Together with impetuous rage and forse,
　That with the terrour of their fierce affret,
　They rudely droue to ground both man and horse,
　That each awhile lay like a sencelesse corse.
　But *Paridell* sore brused with the blow,
　Could not arise, the counterchaunge to scorse,
　Till that young Squire him reared from below;
Then drew he his bright sword, and gan about him throw.

17

But *Satyrane* forth stepping, did them stay
　And with faire treatie pacifide their ire,
　Then when they were accorded from the fray,
　Against that Castles Lord they gan conspire,
　To heape on him dew vengeaunce for his hire.
　They bene agreed, and to the gates they goe
　To burne the same with vnquenchable fire,
　And that vncurteous Carle their commune foe
To do fowle death to dye, or wrap in grieuous woe.

18

Malbecco seeing them resolu'd in deed
　To flame the gates, and hearing them to call
　For fire in earnest, ran with fearefull speed,
　And to them calling from the castle wall,
　Besought them humbly, him to beare with all,
　As ignoraunt of seruants bad abuse,
　And slacke attendaunce vnto straungers call.
　The knights were willing all things to excuse,
Though nought beleu'd, and entraunce late did not refuse.

19

They bene ybrought into a comely bowre,
　And seru'd of all things that mote needfull bee;
　Yet secretly their hoste did on them lowre,
　And welcomde more for feare, then charitee;
　But they dissembled, what they did not see,
　And welcomed themselues.　Each gan vndight
　Their garments wet, and weary armour free,
　To dry them selues by *Vulcanes* flaming light,
And eke their lately bruzed parts to bring in plight.

20

And eke that straunger knight emongst the rest
　Was for like need enforst to disaray:
　Tho whenas vailed was her loftie crest,
　Her golden locks, that were in tramels gay
　Vpbounden, did them selues adowne display,
　And raught vnto her heeles; like sunny beames,
　That in a cloud their light did long time stay,
　Their vapour vaded, shew their golden gleames,
And through the persant aire shoote forth their azure streames.

21

She also dofte her heauy haberieon,
　Which the faire feature of her limbs did hyde,
　And her well plighted frock, which she did won
　To tucke about her short, when she did ryde,
　She low let fall, that flowd from her lanck syde
　Downe to her foot, with carelesse modestee,
　Then of them all she plainly was espyde,
　To be a woman wight, vnwist to bee,
386 The fairest woman wight, that euer eye did see.

Stanza 16
3　**affret**: onslaught. From Ital. *affretare*, to hasten, or from 'fret': a sudden disturbance; hence a hasty encounter.
4　**rudely**: violently.
5　In contrast to earlier encounters in which she triumphs by her enchanted spear; hence **steel-hed** spear (1). Perhaps for this reason she is not named here. Within the Castle, as *Brito*-mart, she converses on equal terms with Paridell about their common ancestry.
7　**the counterchaunge to scorse**: the requital to exchange; trade return blows.
8　**from below**: either from the ground, or (preferably, because of the symbolism) from below his horse.
9　**throw**: brandish.

Stanza 17
2　**treatie**: entreaty.
5　**hire**: reward.

Stanza 18
5　**him to beare**: to bear with him.

Stanza 19
5　They pretended not to notice Malbecco's want of hospitality.
9　**in plight**: to good condition, i.e. to heal.

Stanza 20
Cf. IV i 13. Gottfried (1963) suggests that Britomart's revelation of her sex in 20–25 is a later addition; hence Malbecco is jealous of her at 27.3–4 and Paridell refers to her as a man at IV i 35.1.
3　**vailed**: taken off.
4–6　**tramels**: braids. By this detail S. distinguishes between Temperance, Chastity, and Beauty: cf. Medina's golden locks tied up in 'breaded tramels' (II ii 15.8), Britomart's braided hair which falls loosely when she takes off her helmet, and Florimell's yellow locks 'Loosely disperst' (III i 16.4). Praise of long hair in a woman is biblical, e.g. 1 Cor. 11.15. The length is noted again at IV i 13.3.
8　**vaded**: vanished, dispersed.
9　**persant** and **azure** may have changed places in the printing, as Collier (1862) suggests; otherwise the **persant aire** means 'piercing through the air'.

Stanza 21
2　**feature**: shape.
3　**plighted**: pleated. On this detail, see II iii 26.5*n*.　　**did won**: was accustomed.
5　**lanck**: slender.
6　**carelesse**: artless; carefree.
8　**vnwist to bee**: without it having been known.
9　Cf. Florimell, 'the fairest Dame aliue' (i 18.8).

22

Like as *Minerua*, being late returnd
  From slaughter of the Giaunts conquered;
  Where proud *Encelade*, whose wide nosethrils burnd
  With breathed flames, like to a furnace red,
  Transfixed with the speare, downe tombled ded
  From top of *Hemus*, by him heaped hye;
  Hath loosd her helmet from her lofty hed,
  And her *Gorgonian* shield gins to vntye
From her left arme, to rest in glorious victorye.

23

Which whenas they beheld, they smitten were
  With great amazement of so wondrous sight,
  And each on other, and they all on her
  Stood gazing, as if suddein great affright
  Had them surprised.   At last auizing right,
  Her goodly personage and glorious hew,
  Which they so much mistooke, they tooke delight
  In their first errour, and yet still anew
With wonder of her beauty fed their hungry vew.

24

Yet note their hungry vew be satisfide,
  But seeing still the more desir'd to see,
  And euer firmely fixed did abide
  In contemplation of diuinitie:
  But most they meruaild at her cheualree,
  And noble prowesse, which they had approued,
  That much they faynd to know, who she mote bee;
  Yet none of all them her thereof amoued,
Yet euery one her likte, and euery one her loued.

25

And *Paridell* though partly discontent
  With his late fall, and fowle indignity,
  Yet was soone wonne his malice to relent,
  Through gracious regard of her faire eye,
  And knightly worth, which he too late did try,
  Yet tried did adore.   Supper was dight;
  Then they *Malbecco* prayd of curtesy,
  That of his Lady they might haue the sight,
And company at meat, to do them more delight.

26

But he to shift their curious request,
  Gan causen, why she could not come in place;
  Her crased health, her late recourse to rest,
  And humid euening ill for sicke folkes cace:
  But none of those excuses could take place;
  Ne would they eate, till she in presence came.
  She came in presence with right comely grace,
  And fairely them saluted, as became,
And shewd her selfe in all a gentle curteous Dame.

27

They sate to meat, and *Satyrane* his chaunce
  Was her before, and *Paridell* besyde;
  But he him selfe sate looking still askaunce,
  Gainst *Britomart*, and euer closely eyde
  Sir *Satyrane*, that glaunces might not glyde:
  But his blind eye, that syded *Paridell*,
  All his demeasnure from his sight did hyde:
  On her faire face so did he feede his fill,
And sent close messages of loue to her at will.

Stanza 22

1 **Minerua**] *Bellona 1590*; both are names of the Roman
goddess of war. The comparison to Bellona is made at IV i
14.6–7 when Britomart again unveils herself. The change may
have been suggested by the serpent-headed Medusa depicted
on Minerva's shield which turned those who looked at it to
stone, as the sight of Britomart's hair amazes the knights. Since
Minerva is associated with wisdom, her name is preferable to
Bellona's which is associated with aggressive violence (see VII
vi 3, 32). In Petrarch, *Triumph of Chastity*, Laura, as the
goddess of Chastity, bears Medusa's shield; in Comes (1616) IV
v, the shield is said to symbolize power over lustful eyes. Cf.
Epith. 185–90. On Britomart as Minerva, see Fowler (1964)
124–32. On Bellona as a name for Elizabeth, see Wilson (1939)
88.

3–6 **Encelade**: probably S. follows Comes VI xxi in having
Minerva, rather than Jove, battle Enceladus. There is no
authority for his placing the battle on Mount Haemus where
Jove killed Typhoeus. S. associates the mountain with the
marriage of Peleus and Thetis: see VII vii 12.3. The simile
prepares for Britomart's victory over Busirane's flames with
her sword and shield, xi 25.

Stanza 23

5 **auizing**: observing.
6 **personage**: personal appearance. **hew**: also shape.

Stanza 24

1 **note**: could not.
4 Cf. Belphœbe 'full of diuinities' (v 34.7).
6 **approued**: tested by experience.
7 **faynd**: desired.
8–9 None questioned who she was even though they liked
and loved her. Or, she was not moved inwardly to love any of
them even though they liked and loved her.

Stanza 25

2 **indignity**: because defeated by a woman; cf. i 8.1–5.
3 **relent**: soften, qualify.
4 **gracious**: modifies Britomart's eye and her knightly worth.
6 **dight**: set out.

Stanza 26

1 **shift**: evade.
2 **Gan causen**: gave causes or reasons. **come in place**:
appear. The expression leads to the verbal play: **came** . . .
comely . . . **became**.
3 **crased**: broken. **late recourse**: recent retiring;
recently betaking herself.
5 **take place**: find acceptance.
8 **fairely**: courteously. **saluted**: kissed, as a salutation.
as became: as was fitting.

Stanza 27

2 **Was her before**: i.e. opposite her. **Paridell** sits on
Malbecco's left (and blind) side between him and Hellenore.
3–5 **he him selfe**: Malbecco, the 'good man selfe' (10.2).
askaunce: the glance of Suspect, xii 15.2. Either he does not
know she is a woman (see 20*n*) or his jealousy extends even to
a woman.
7 **demeasnure**: demeanour, behaviour.
8 **so**: by that means.
9 **close**: secret.

387

28

And euer and anone, when none was ware,
  With speaking lookes, that close embassage bore,
  He rou'd at her, and told his secret care:
  For all that art he learned had of yore.
  Ne was she ignoraunt of that lewd lore,
  But in his eye his meaning wisely red,
  And with the like him answerd euermore:
  She sent at him one firie dart, whose hed
Empoisned was with priuy lust, and gealous dred.

29

He from that deadly throw made no defence,
  But to the wound his weake hart opened wyde;
  The wicked engine through false influence,
  Past through his eyes, and secretly did glyde
  Into his hart, which it did sorely gryde.
  But nothing new to him was that same paine,
  Ne paine at all; for he so oft had tryde
  The powre thereof, and lou'd so oft in vaine,
That thing of course he counted, loue to entertaine.

30

Thenceforth to her he sought to intimate
  His inward griefe, by meanes to him well knowne,
  Now *Bacchus* fruit out of the siluer plate
  He on the table dasht, as ouerthrowne,
  Or of the fruitfull liquor ouerflowne,
  And by the dauncing bubbles did diuine,
  Or therein write to let his loue be showne;
  Which well she red out of the learned line,
A sacrament prophane in mistery of wine.

31

And when so of his hand the pledge she raught,
  The guilty cup she fained to mistake,
  And in her lap did shed her idle draught,
  Shewing desire her inward flame to slake:
  By such close signes they secret way did make
  Vnto their wils, and one eyes watch escape;
  Two eyes him needeth, for to watch and wake,
  Who louers will deceiue. Thus was the ape,
By their faire handling, put into *Malbeccoes* cape.

32

Now when of meats and drinks they had their fill,
  Purpose was moued by that gentle Dame,
  Vnto those knights aduenturous, to tell
  Of deeds of armes, which vnto them became,
  And euery one his kindred, and his name.
  Then *Paridell*, in whom a kindly pryde
  Of gracious speach, and skill his words to frame
  Abounded, being glad of so fit tyde
Him to commend to her, thus spake, of all well eyde.

33

Troy, that art now nought, but an idle name,
  And in thine ashes buried low dost lie,
  Though whilome far much greater then thy fame,
  Before that angry Gods, and cruell skye
  Vpon thee heapt a direfull destinie,
  What boots it boast thy glorious descent,
  And fetch from heauen thy great Genealogie,
  Sith all thy worthy prayses being blent,
Their of-spring hath embaste, and later glory shent.

Stanza 28
1 **ware**: watchful.
2 **embassage**: message.
3 **rou'd**: shot glances; cf. i 50.6.   **care**: also passion (Lat. *cura*).
5 **lewd lore**: doctrine of love; specifically courtly love.

Stanza 29
Cf. Amoret's wounded heart, xii 20.
1 **throw**: thrust.
3 **false**: deceiving.   **influence**: influx, infusion.
5 **gryde**: pierce gratingly.
9 **of course**: to be expected, as a matter of course.

Stanzas 30–31
The game, as Upton (1758) notes, was called 'cottabus': spilt wine was used to guess the name of one's love or to write messages of love (as in Ovid, *Amores* II v 17–8, and *Heroides* xvii 75–90, where Helen recalls that she and Paris played the game). An antique game, according to Harington (1591) Preface, 'he that should make love so now, his love would mocke him for his labour, and count him but a slovenly sutor'. Since wine in the sacrament of Holy Communion is a symbol that contains a divine mystery, S. suggests that the wine is used profanely as a symbol of unlawful love (Upton). See Tuve (1947) 221.

Stanza 30
3 **plate**: cup.

Stanza 31
1 Cf. Vives (1541) 47: 'Worse becometh a good woman to taste a cup of drink in a feast or a banket, reached unto her by another man.'
2 **mistake**: take wrongly, and hence cause to spill.
7 **wake**: guard.
8–9 A proverb which means 'to dupe' (*OED* 4). On the ape as a type of female lasciviousness, see Janson (1952) 261–86.

Stanza 32
2 **Purpose was moued**: a proposal was made.
4 **became**: befell.
6 **kindly**: native.
8 **tyde**: opportunity.

Stanzas 33–51
This account completes the history of Britain. In II x 5–68, the story extends from the arrival of the Trojans to the succession of Uther Pendragon, Arthur's father; and at III iii 27–50, from after Arthur's reign to the coming of Elizabeth. Now the beginning is told, from the fall of Troy to the arrival of the Trojans in Britain.

Stanza 33
7 **from heauen**: because the original founder, Dardanos, was a son of Jove; cf. Homer, *Iliad* xx 215.
8 **blent**: obscured; blemished.
9 **embaste**: made base.   **shent**: disgraced, confounded.

34

Most famous Worthy of the world, by whome
  That warre was kindled, which did *Troy* inflame,
  And stately towres of *Ilion* whilome
  Brought vnto balefull ruine, was by name
  Sir *Paris* far renowmd through noble fame,
  Who through great prowesse and bold hardinesse,
  From *Lacedæmon* fetcht the fairest Dame,
  That euer *Greece* did boast, or knight possesse,
Whom *Venus* to him gaue for meed of worthinesse.

35

Faire *Helene*, flowre of beautie excellent,
  And girlond of the mighty Conquerours,
  That madest many Ladies deare lament
  The heauie losse of their braue Paramours,
  Which they far off beheld from *Troian* toures,
  And saw the fieldes of faire *Scamander* strowne
  With carcases of noble warriours,
  Whose fruitlesse liues were vnder furrow sowne,
And *Xanthus* sandy bankes with bloud all ouerflowne.

36

From him my linage I deriue aright,
  Who long before the ten yeares siege of *Troy*,
  Whiles yet on *Ida* he a shepheard hight,
  On faire *Oenone* got a louely boy,
  Whom for remembraunce of her passed ioy,
  She of his Father *Parius* did name;
  Who, after *Greekes* did *Priams* realme destroy,
  Gathred the *Troian* reliques sau'd from flame,
And with them sayling thence, to th'Isle of *Paros* came.

37

That was by him cald *Paros*, which before
  Hight *Nausa*, there he many yeares did raine,
  And built *Nausicle* by the *Pontick* shore,
  The which he dying left next in remaine
  To *Paridas* his sonne.
  From whom I *Paridell* by kin descend;
  But for faire Ladies loue, and glories gaine,
  My natiue soile haue left, my dayes to spend
In sewing deeds of armes, my liues and labours end.

38

Whenas the noble *Britomart* heard tell
  Of *Troian* warres, and *Priams* Citie sackt,
  The ruefull story of Sir *Paridell*,
  She was empassiond at that piteous act,
  With zelous enuy of *Greekes* cruell fact,
  Against that nation, from whose race of old
  She heard, that she was lineally extract:
  For noble *Britons* sprong from *Troians* bold,
And *Troynouant* was built of old *Troyes* ashes cold.

39

Then sighing soft awhile, at last she thus:
  O lamentable fall of famous towne,
  Which raignd so many yeares victorious,
  And of all *Asie* bore the soueraigne crowne,
  In one sad night consumd, and throwen downe:
  What stony hart, that heares thy haplesse fate,
  Is not empierst with deepe compassiowne,
  And makes ensample of mans wretched state,
That floures so fresh at morne, and fades at euening late?

40

Behold, Sir, how your pitifull complaint
  Hath found another partner of your payne:
  For nothing may impresse so deare constraint,
  As countries cause, and commune foes disdayne.
  But if it should not grieue you, backe agayne
  To turne your course, I would to heare desyre,
  What to *Aeneas* fell; sith that men sayne
  He was not in the Cities wofull fyre
Consum'd, but did him selfe to safetie retyre.

Stanza 34

1   Paris is not included among the Nine Worthies; his
worthinesse (9) lay in choosing Venus's bribe over those
offered by the other goddesses: see II vii 55. His rape of Helen
is the archetypal story of adultery which Paridell seeks to
imitate. The story of how he **fetcht** Helen is told again at IV
xi 19.3–7.

Stanza 35

1   **excellent**: supreme.
3   **deare**: dearly.
6, 9   **Scamander** and **Xanthus** name the same river though
S. treats the former as a plain.
8   **fruitlesse** clashes with **sowne** to stress horror of the war.

Stanza 36

1   **aright**: directly; but also commenting ironically on his
bastardy.

Stanza 37

2   **Nausa**: no authority is known for the name. Roche (1964)
63 suggests that this Greek word for ship fits the Trojan story.
3   The shift from Troy to an island in the Aegean sea and
then to the shore of the Black Sea suggests that the journey is
in the opposite direction to that taken by Aeneas.
4   **next in remaine**: as the next remaining representative.
5   The short line may indicate the break in the chronology.
9   **sewing**: pursuing.

Stanza 38

4   **empassiond**: deeply moved.
5   **enuy**: hostile feeling.   **fact**: evil deed.
7   **extract**: descended.
9   **Troynouant**: New Troy or London; see II x 46.5. The
line suggests the phoenix arising from its ashes.

Stanza 39

9   Cf. Ps. 90.6: 'In the morning it [man's life] florisheth and
groweth, in the evening it is cut downe and withereth.'

Stanza 40

1   **complaint**: the term designates the literary form, one
favourite topic of which was the fall of Troy.
3   **so deare constraint**: such grievous distress.

41

Anchyses sonne begot of *Venus* faire,
  (Said he,) out of the flames for safegard fled,
  And with a remnant did to sea repaire,
  Where he through fatall errour long was led
  Full many yeares, and weetlesse wandered
  From shore to shore, emongst the *Lybicke* sands,
  Ere rest he found.   Much there he suffered,
  And many perils past in forreine lands,
To saue his people sad from victours vengefull hands.

42

At last in *Latium* he did arriue,
  Where he with cruell warre was entertaind
  Of th'inland folke, which sought him backe to driue,
  Till he with old *Latinus* was constraind,
  To contract wedlock: (so the fates ordaind.)
  Wedlock contract in bloud, and eke in blood
  Accomplished, that many deare complaind:
  The riuall slaine, the victour through the flood
Escaped hardly, hardly praisd his wedlock good.

43

Yet after all, he victour did suruiue,
  And with *Latinus* did the kingdome part.
  But after, when both nations gan to striue,
  Into their names the title to conuart,
  His sonne *Iülus* did from thence depart,
  With all the warlike youth of *Troians* bloud,
  And in long *Alba* plast his throne apart,
  Where faire it florished, and long time stoud,
Till *Romulus* renewing it, to *Rome* remoud.

44

There there (said *Britomart*) a fresh appeard
  The glory of the later world to spring,
  And *Troy* againe out of her dust was reard,
  To sit in second seat of soueraigne king,
  Of all the world vnder her gouerning.
  But a third kingdome yet is to arise,
  Out of the *Troians* scattered of-spring,
  That in all glory and great enterprise,
Both first and second *Troy* shall dare to equalise.

45

It *Troynouant* is hight, that with the waues
  Of wealthy *Thamis* washed is along,
  Vpon whose stubborne neck, whereat he raues
  With roring rage, and sore him selfe does throng,
  That all men feare to tempt his billowes strong,
  She fastned hath her foot, which standes so hy,
  That it a wonder of the world is song
  In forreine landes, and all which passen by,
Beholding it from far, do thinke it threates the skye.

46

The *Troian Brute* did first that Citie found,
  And *Hygate* made the meare thereof by West,
  And *Ouert* gate by North: that is the bound
  Toward the land; two riuers bound the rest.
  So huge a scope at first him seemed best,
  To be the compasse of his kingdomes seat:
  So huge a mind could not in lesser rest,
  Ne in small meares containe his glory great,
That *Albion* had conquered first by warlike feat.

Stanza 41
Paridell draws details of Aeneas's story from Virgil, at times translating, e.g. **a remnant**: *reliquias* (*Aen.* i 30); **Much there he suffered**: *multum ille . . . multa quoque et bello passus* (3,5). He follows Virgil in introducing the story at a banquet; noted Lotspeich (1932) 33.
2 **safegard**: safety.
4 **fatall errour**: wandering ordained by fate; cf. *Aen.* i 2.
5 **weetlesse**: in ignorance.
6 **emongst the Lybicke sands**: i.e. on the shores of Africa.

Stanza 42
2 **entertaind**: received.
5–6 Cf. *Aen.* vii 318–9.
7 **deare**: grievously.
8–9 The **riuall** is Turnus; **flood** refers to their final battle. That Aeneas regretted his marriage is added by Paridell.
hardly: with difficulty.

Stanza 43
Based on the prophecy in *Aen.* i 267–77.
2 **part**: divide into parts.
4 **conuart**: convert; each tried to gain the title of sovereignty.
7–8 **long Alba**: Alba Longa, in Latium. S. interprets **long** as time rather than distance.   **long time** is three hundred years.
9 **remoud**: the old spelling is used for the rhyme.

Stanza 44
1 **There there**: suggests prophetic vision. The source is the vision given Brutus of the second Troy, Troia Nova (Geoffrey of Monmouth, I xi, xvii).
4 **To sit in second seat . . .**: i.e. for a second time to be ruler of the world.
9 **equalise**: equal.

Stanza 45
3–5 **whereat . . . strong** is parenthetical. The piers of London Bridge produce dangerous currents when the tide is running. Frobisher refers to 'the waterfall of London Bridge' (Hakluyt, 1904 edn, vii 334). See II x 73.7–9.   **throng**: press.   **tempt**: try; venture upon.

Stanza 46
2 **meare**: boundary.
3 **Ouert**: open.   **bound**: boundary.
4 Stow (1598) 10 names two rivers: the Thames to the south and the 'river of the *wels*' to the west. What he refers to as the 'walbrooke' through the middle, must be S.'s second river.
8 **containe**: confine.
9 **Albion**: Britain, rather than the giant of that name.
first: i.e. was the first to conquer. Cf. II x 9–11.

47

Ah fairest Lady knight, (said *Paridell*)
    Pardon I pray my heedlesse ouersight,
    Who had forgot, that whilome I heard tell
    From aged *Mnemon*; for my wits bene light.
    Indeed he said (if I remember right,)
    That of the antique *Troian* stocke, there grew
    Another plant, that raught to wondrous hight,
And far abroad his mighty branches threw,
Into the vtmost Angle of the world he knew.

48

For that same *Brute*, whom much he did aduaunce
    In all his speach, was *Syluius* his sonne,
    Whom hauing slaine, through luckles arrowes glaunce
    He fled for feare of that he had misdonne,
    Or else for shame, so fowle reproch to shonne,
    And with him led to sea an youthly trayne,
    Where wearie wandring they long time did wonne,
And many fortunes prou'd in th'*Ocean* mayne,
And great aduentures found, that now were long to sayne.

49

At last by fatall course they driuen were
    Into an Island spatious and brode,
    The furthest North, that did to them appeare:
    Which after rest they seeking far abrode,
    Found it the fittest soyle for their abode,
    Fruitfull of all things fit for liuing foode,
    But wholy wast, and void of peoples trode,
Saue an huge nation of the Geaunts broode,
That fed on liuing flesh, and druncke mens vitall blood.

50

Whom he through wearie wars and labours long,
    Subdewd with losse of many *Britons* bold:
    In which the great *Goemagot* of strong
    Corineus, and *Coulin* of *Debon* old
    Were ouerthrowne, and layd on th'earth full cold,
    Which quaked vnder their so hideous masse,
    A famous history to be enrold
In euerlasting moniments of brasse,
That all the antique Worthies merits far did passe.

51

His worke great *Troynouant*, his worke is eke
    Faire *Lincolne*, both renowmed far away,
    That who from East to West will endlong seeke,
    Cannot two fairer Cities find this day,
    Except *Cleopolis*: so heard I say
    Old *Mnemon*. Therefore Sir, I greet you well
    Your countrey kin, and you entirely pray
Of pardon for the strife, which late befell
Betwixt vs both vnknowne. So ended *Paridell*.

52

But all the while, that he these speaches spent,
    Vpon his lips hong faire Dame *Hellenore*,
    With vigilant regard, and dew attent,
    Fashioning worlds of fancies euermore
    In her fraile wit, that now her quite forlore:
    The whiles vnwares away her wondring eye,
    And greedy eares her weake hart from her bore:
    Which he perceiuing, euer priuily
In speaking, many false belgardes at her let fly.

53

So long these knights discoursed diuersly,
    Of straunge affaires, and noble hardiment,
    Which they had past with mickle ieopardy,
    That now the humid night was farforth spent,
    And heauenly lampes were halfendeale ybrent:
    Which th'old man seeing well, who too long thought
    Euery discourse and euery argument,
Which by the houres he measured, besought
Them go to rest. So all vnto their bowres were brought.

Stanza 47
4   **Mnemon**: Remembrancer.
7   **raught**: reached.
9   **the vtmost Angle**: corner, outlying place; as Ariosto's
l'ultima Inghilterra (*Orl. Fur.* x 72); cf. the derivation '*ab
Angulo*, as from a corner of the world', cited Holinshed i 9.

Stanzas 48–51
Outlined at II x 9.6 to 10.9; based chiefly on Geoffrey of
Monmouth I iii-xv.

Stanza 48
1   **aduaunce**: extol.
7   **wonne**: remain.
8   **prou'd**: suffered.

Stanza 49
1   **fatall**: destined; cf. 41.4.
7   **wast**: uninhabited.   **trode**: tread.

Stanza 50
6   **hideous**: huge.
9   **the antique Worthies**: probably the Nine Worthies; see
iii 4.4*n*.

Stanza 51
1–2   Geoffrey of Monmouth I xvii claims that Brutus
founded New Troy. There is no authority for S.'s claim that
he also founded Lincoln.
3   **endlong**: from end to end.
5   **Cleopolis**: see I x 58.2–6*n*.
7   **countrey kin**: countryman, kinsman.   **entirely**:
earnestly.

Stanza 52
Hellenore responds to Paridell's speech as Dido does to
Aeneas's (cf. *Aen.* iv 1–5). Her **worlds of fancies** parody
Amoret's suffering in the house of Busirane; cf. xii 26.3–5.
3   **attent**: attention.
5   **forlore**: forsook.
9   **belgardes**: loving looks (Ital. *bel guardo*), a term of
courtly love; cf. II iii 25.3.

Stanza 53
2   **hardiment**: bold exploits.
4   **humid night**: as the dewy night is speeding from the sky
when Aeneas tells his story (*Aen.* ii 8).   **farforth**: far.
5   **halfendeale**: half; cf. II ii 46.

Cant. X.

Paridell rapeth Hellenore:
Malbecco her pursewes:
Findes emongst Satyres, whence with him
To turne she doth refuse.

1

THe morow next, so soone as *Phœbus* Lamp
  Bewrayed had the world with early light,
  And fresh *Aurora* had the shady damp
  Out of the goodly heauen amoued quight,
  Faire *Britomart* and that same *Faerie* knight
  Vprose, forth on their iourney for to wend:
  But *Paridell* complaynd, that his late fight
  With *Britomart*, so sore did him offend,
That ryde he could not, till his hurts he did amend.

2

So forth they far'd, but he behind them stayd,
  Maulgre his host, who grudged grieuously,
  To house a guest, that would be needes obayd,
  And of his owne him left not liberty:
  Might wanting measure moueth surquedry.
  Two things he feared, but the third was death;
  That fierce youngmans vnruly maistery;
  His money, which he lou'd as liuing breath;
And his faire wife, whom honest long he kept vneath.

3

But patience perforce he must abie,
  What fortune and his fate on him will lay,
  Fond is the feare, that findes no remedie;
  Yet warily he watcheth euery way,
  By which he feareth euill happen may:
  So th'euill thinkes by watching to preuent;
  Ne doth he suffer her, nor night, nor day,
  Out of his sight her selfe once to absent.
So doth he punish her and eke himselfe torment.

4

But *Paridell* kept better watch, then hee,
  A fit occasion for his turne to find:
  False loue, why do men say, thou canst not see,
  And in their foolish fancie feigne thee blind,
  That with thy charmes the sharpest sight doest bind,
  And to thy will abuse? Thou walkest free,
  And seest euery secret of the mind;
  Thou seest all, yet none at all sees thee;
All that is by the working of thy Deitee.

5

So perfect in that art was *Paridell*,
  That he *Malbeccoes* halfen eye did wyle,
  His halfen eye he wiled wondrous well,
  And *Hellenors* both eyes did eke beguyle,
  Both eyes and hart attonce, during the whyle
  That he there soiourned his wounds to heale;
  That *Cupid* selfe it seeing, close did smyle,
  To weet how he her loue away did steale,
And bad, that none their ioyous treason should reueale.

6

The learned louer lost no time nor tyde,
  That least auantage mote to him afford,
  Yet bore so faire a saile, that none espyde
  His secret drift, till he her layd abord.
  When so in open place, and commune bord,
  He fortun'd her to meet, with commune speach
  He courted her, yet bayted euery word,
  That his vngentle hoste n'ote him appeach
Of vile vngentlenesse, or hospitages breach.

Canto x

Argument

1   **rapeth**: carries off; cf. 13.8–9.
4   **turne**: return.

Stanza 1

1–4   The awkwardness in having sunrise before the dawn –
in contrast to the set description, e.g. in Virgil, *Aen.* iv 6–8 –
may have been caused by the concealed pun in **Bewrayed**:
revealed, but referring also to the sun's rays.   **damp**: fog
(cf. 47.5 when night returns); also the noxious vapours associated with night.
8   **offend**: hurt.

Stanza 2

2   **Maulgre**: in spite of.   **grudged**: complained.
5   With proverbial force: unlimited power leads to arrogance;
surquedry also signifies sexual indulgence.
6   **the third** is loss of **his faire wife** (9), which would be as
death to him. Later he changes his mind, 14–15.
7   **maistery**: superior power, specifically sexual prowess.
9   **honest**: chaste.   **vneath**: with difficulty.

Stanza 3

1   **patience perforce**: proverbial (C. G. Smith, 1970, 598).
perforce: upon compulsion, through necessity.   **abie**:
endure.
3   Proverbial (Smith 250).   **Fond**: foolish.
4–6   Cf. Smith 826: 'Good watch prevents misfortune.'

Stanza 5

2   **halfen eye**: his one 'blincked eye' (ix 5.5); half his eye-
sight.   **wyle**: beguile.
7   **close**: secretly.

Stanza 6

4   **drift**: purpose; also drifting, suggested by the image of
sailing.   **layd abord**: the nautical sense, run alongside to
board; applied with bawdy innuendo.
7   **bayted**: bated, moderated; or baited. Either he spoke
mildly or he used the everyday language of courtesy with
double entendre.
8   **n'ote him appeach**: could not accuse him.
9   **vngentlenesse**: discourtesy.   **hospitages breach**:
breach of hospitality by a guest.

7

But when apart (if euer her apart)
  He found, then his false engins fast he plyde,
  And all the sleights vnbosomd in his hart ;
  He sigh'd, he sobd, he swownd, he perdy dyde,
  And cast himselfe on ground her fast besyde :
  Tho when againe he him bethought to liue,
  He wept, and wayld, and false laments belyde,
  Saying, but if she Mercie would him giue
That he mote algates dye, yet did his death forgiue.

8

And otherwhiles with amorous delights,
  And pleasing toyes he would her entertaine,
  Now singing sweetly, to surprise her sprights,
  Now making layes of loue and louers paine,
  Bransles, Ballads, virelayes, and verses vaine ;
  Oft purposes, oft riddles he deuysd,
  And thousands like, which flowed in his braine,
  With which he fed her fancie, and entysd
To take to his new loue, and leaue her old despysd.

9

And euery where he might, and euery while
  He did her seruice dewtifull, and sewed
  At hand with humble pride, and pleasing guile,
  So closely yet, that none but she it vewed,
  Who well perceiued all, and all indewed.
  Thus finely did he his false nets dispred,
  With which he many weake harts had subdewed
  Of yore, and many had ylike misled :
What wonder then, if she were likewise carried ?

10

No fort so fensible, no wals so strong,
  But that continuall battery will riue,
  Or daily siege through dispuruayance long,
  And lacke of reskewes will to parley driue ;
  And Peece, that vnto parley eare will giue,
  Will shortly yeeld it selfe, and will be made
  The vassall of the victors will byliue :
  That stratageme had oftentimes assayd
This crafty Paramoure, and now it plaine displayd.

11

For through his traines he her intrapped hath,
  That she her loue and hart hath wholy sold
  To him, without regard of gaine, or scath,
  Or care of credite, or of husband old,
  Whom she hath vow'd to dub a faire Cucquold.
  Nought wants but time and place, which shortly shee
  Deuized hath, and to her louer told.
  It pleased well.   So well they both agree ;
So readie rype to ill, ill wemens counsels bee.

12

Darke was the Euening, fit for louers stealth,
  When chaunst *Malbecco* busie be elsewhere,
  She to his closet went, where all his wealth
  Lay hid : thereof she countlesse summes did reare,
  The which she meant away with her to beare ;
  The rest she fyr'd for sport, or for despight ;
  As *Hellene*, when she saw aloft appeare
  The *Troiane* flames, and reach to heauens hight
Did clap her hands, and ioyed at that dolefull sight.

Stanza 7

2 **engins** : wiles.
3 **sleights** : cunning tricks.
4 **perdy dyde** : assuredly would die.
7 **belyde** : counterfeited.
8 **but if** : unless.
9 **algates** : altogether ; otherwise. Yet he would pardon her for causing his death.

Stanza 8

1 **otherwhiles** : at other times.
2 **toyes** : amorous sports.
3 **surprise** : overcome ; ambush.
5 **Bransles** : a song for dance music ; the French brawl, associated with love.   **Ballads** : a dance tune.   **virelayes** : a song or short poem.
6 **purposes** : a game consisting of questions and answers, also associated with love.   **riddles** : as Slender needs a 'Book of Riddles' to woo Ann Page (Shakespeare, *Merry Wives* I i 183).
9 **to**] with *1590*. Both convey the sense, to accept his new love.

Stanza 9

2 **sewed** : did homage.
5 **indewed** : took in, 'inwardly digested'.
6 **finely** : cunningly.

Stanza 10

1–2 Proverbial (C. G. Smith, 1970, 281).   **fensible** : well-fortified, able to defend itself.
3 **dispuruayance** : lack of provisions.
5 **Peece** : fortress ; with a pun on 'peace'.
7 **byliue** : quickly.
8 **assayd** : tried, proven.

Stanza 11

1 **traines** : guile ; literally, snares to trap an animal.
3 **scath** : harm.
4 **credite** : with a secondary sense suggested by the money image.

Stanza 12

4 **reare** : collect.
7–9 Perhaps suggested by Helen's bacchic dance on the night of Troy's fall (Virgil, *Aen*. vi 517–9).

13

This second *Hellene*, faire Dame *Hellenore*,
    The whiles her husband ranne with sory haste,
    To quench the flames, which she had tyn'd before,
    Laught at his foolish labour spent in waste;
    And ranne into her louers armes right fast;
    Where streight embraced, she to him did cry,
    And call aloud for helpe, ere helpe were past;
    For loe that Guest would beare her forcibly,
And meant to rauish her, that rather had to dy.

14

The wretched man hearing her call for ayd,
    And readie seeing him with her to fly,
    In his disquiet mind was much dismayd:
    But when againe he backward cast his eye,
    And saw the wicked fire so furiously
    Consume his hart, and scorch his Idoles face,
    He was therewith distressed diuersly,
    Ne wist he how to turne, nor to what place;
Was neuer wretched man in such a wofull cace.

15

Ay when to him she cryde, to her he turnd,
    And left the fire; loue money ouercame:
    But when he marked, how his money burnd,
    He left his wife; money did loue disclame:
    Both was he loth to loose his loued Dame,
    And loth to leaue his liefest pelfe behind,
    Yet sith he n'ote saue both, he sau'd that same,
    Which was the dearest to his donghill mind,
The God of his desire, the ioy of misers blind.

16

Thus whilest all things in troublous vprore were,
    And all men busie to suppresse the flame,
    The louing couple need no reskew feare,
    But leasure had, and libertie to frame
    Their purpost flight, free from all mens reclame;
    And Night, the patronesse of loue-stealth faire,
    Gaue them safe conduct, till to end they came:
    So bene they gone yfeare, a wanton paire
Of louers loosely knit, where list them to repaire.

17

Soone as the cruell flames yslaked were,
    Malbecco seeing, how his losse did lye,
    Out of the flames, which he had quencht whylere
    Into huge waues of griefe and gealosye
    Full deepe emplonged was, and drowned nye,
    Twixt inward doole and felonous despight;
    He rau'd, he wept, he stampt, he lowd did cry,
    And all the passions, that in man may light,
Did him attonce oppresse, and vex his caytiue spright.

18

Long thus he chawd the cud of inward griefe,
    And did consume his gall with anguish sore,
    Still when he mused on his late mischiefe,
    Then still the smart thereof increased more,
    And seem'd more grieuous, then it was before:
    At last when sorrow he saw booted nought,
    Ne griefe might not his loue to him restore,
    He gan deuise, how her he reskew mought,
Ten thousand wayes he cast in his confused thought.

19

At last resoluing, like a pilgrim pore,
    To search her forth, where so she might be fond,
    And bearing with him treasure in close store,
    The rest he leaues in ground: So takes in hond
    To seeke her endlong, both by sea and lond.
    Long he her sought, he sought her farre and nere,
    And euery where that he mote vnderstond,
    Of knights and ladies any meetings were,
And of eachone he met, he tydings did inquere.

Stanza 13
1   **second Hellene** suggests 'Helen-o'er'.
3   **tyn'd**: kindled.
4   **in waste**: in vain.

Stanza 14
6   **Consume his hart**: since his heart lies in his possessions, it is literally consumed; cf. 21.9, 26.6, 45.4, 48.6, and 59.6.

Stanza 15
Malbecco stands between beauty and money, the forces of Cupid and cupidity. Cf. the assault of beauty and money on the bulwark of the sight in the castle of Alma, II xi 9.9. In Book II these temptations, displayed in Acrasia and Mammon, confront the Knight of Temperance. See II iv 18.1–3*n*, 21.5*n*.
1   **Ay**: ever.
5   **loose**: lose; allow to become loose. Cf. 16.9, 36.1.
6   **liefest pelfe**: most beloved wealth; more dear to him than his loued Dame.
7   **n'ote**: might not; knew not how to.

Stanza 16
4   **frame**: set out upon.
5   **reclame**: recall.
6   A more formal statement of 12.1.
8   **yfeare**: together.
9   **loosely**: with a pun on 'immorally'.

Stanza 17
6   **doole**: grief.   **felonous**: fierce, cruel.
7   Cf. 7.4.
8–9   Malbecco's state is the masculine counterpart of Amoret's in the house of Busirane: overwhelmed by the passions, but lacking her constancy, he is further transformed.

Stanza 18
2   **gall**: the seat of anger; cf. 59.7.
3   **mischiefe**: misfortune.
9   **cast**: pondered.

Stanza 19
1   A parody of the pilgrim who, as lover, seeks the beloved as his saint; cf. 25.6–7.
5   **endlong**: from end to end of the country.

20

But all in vaine, his woman was too wise,
   Euer to come into his clouch againe,
And he too simple euer to surprise
   The iolly *Paridell*, for all his paine.
One day, as he forpassed by the plaine
   With weary pace, he farre away espide
A couple, seeming well to be his twaine,
   Which houed close vnder a forrest side,
As if they lay in wait, or else themselues did hide.

21

Well weened he, that those the same mote bee,
   And as he better did their shape auize,
Him seemed more their manner did agree;
   For th'one was armed all in warlike wize,
Whom, to be *Paridell* he did deuize;
   And th'other all yclad in garments light,
Discolour'd like to womanish disguise,
   He did resemble to his Ladie bright;
And euer his faint hart much earned at the sight.

22

And euer faine he towards them would goe,
   But yet durst not for dread approchen nie,
But stood aloofe, vnweeting what to doe;
   Till that prickt forth with loues extremitie,
That is the father of foule gealosy,
   He closely nearer crept, the truth to weet:
But, as he nigher drew, he easily
   Might scerne, that it was not his sweetest sweet,
Ne yet her Belamour, the partner of his sheet.

23

But it was scornefull *Braggadocchio*,
   That with his seruant *Trompart* houerd there,
Sith late he fled from his too earnest foe:
   Whom such when as *Malbecco* spyed clere,
He turned backe, and would haue fled arere;
   Till *Trompart* ronning hastily, him did stay,
And bad before his soueraine Lord appere:
   That was him loth, yet durst he not gainesay,
And comming him before, low louted on the lay.

24

The Boaster at him sternely bent his browe,
   As if he could haue kild him with his looke,
That to the ground him meekely made to bowe,
   And awfull terror deepe into him strooke,
That euery member of his bodie quooke,
   Said he, Thou man of nought, what doest thou here,
Vnfitly furnisht with thy bag and booke,
   Where I expected one with shield and spere,
To proue some deedes of armes vpon an equall pere.

25

The wretched man at his imperious speach,
   Was all abasht, and low prostrating, said;
Good Sir, let not my rudenesse be no breach
   Vnto your patience, ne be ill ypaid;
For I vnwares this way by fortune straid,
   A silly Pilgrim driuen to distresse,
That seeke a Lady, There he suddein staid,
   And did the rest with grieuous sighes suppresse,
While teares stood in his eies, few drops of bitternesse.

26

What Ladie, man? (said *Trompart*) take good hart,
   And tell thy griefe, if any hidden lye;
Was neuer better time to shew thy smart,
   Then now, that noble succour is thee by,
That is the whole worlds commune remedy.
   That chearefull word his weake hart much did cheare,
And with vaine hope his spirits faint supply,
   That bold he said; O most redoubted Pere,
Vouchsafe with mild regard a wretches cace to heare.

27

Then sighing sore, It is not long (said hee)
   Sith I enioyd the gentlest Dame aliue;
Of whom a knight, no knight at all perdee,
   But shame of all, that doe for honor striue,
By treacherous deceipt did me depriue;
   Through open outrage he her bore away,
And with fowle force vnto his will did driue,
   Which all good knights, that armes do beare this day,
Are bound for to reuenge, and punish if they may.

Stanza 20
4   **iolly**: amorous; lively.
5   **forpassed**: passed along.
8   **houed**: waited; cf. 'houerd' (23.2). Suggesting the falcon
waiting to seize its prey; developed from **clouch** (2). Cf.
30.5–6.

Stanza 21
2   **auize**: observe.
5   **deuize**: guess.
6–8   Suggests transvestism.   **Discolour'd**: variously
coloured.   **resemble**: liken.
9   **earned**: yearned; grieved.

Stanza 22
1   **faine**: desirous.
5   **foule gealosy**: anticipates the transformation at the end
of the canto.
8   **scerne**: discern.
9   **Belamour**: sweetheart.

Stanza 23
9   **louted**: bowed.   **lay**: ground.

Stanza 25
3   Two negatives strengthen the negation.
4   **ill ypaid**: displeased.
6   **silly**: humble.

Stanza 27
2   **gentlest**: noblest; cf. 36.1, ix 26.9; in opposition to her
later bestiality.

28

And you most noble Lord, that can and dare
    Redresse the wrong of miserable wight,
    Cannot employ your most victorious speare
    In better quarrell, then defence of right,
    And for a Ladie gainst a faithlesse knight;
    So shall your glory be aduaunced much,
    And all faire Ladies magnifie your might,
    And eke my selfe, albe I simple such,
Your worthy paine shall well reward with guerdon rich.

29

With that out of his bouget forth he drew
    Great store of treasure, therewith him to tempt;
    But he on it lookt scornefully askew,
    As much disdeigning to be so misdempt,
    Or a war-monger to be basely nempt;
    And said; Thy offers base I greatly loth,
    And eke thy words vncourteous and vnkempt;
    I tread in dust thee and thy money both,
That, were it not for shame, So turned from him wroth.

30

But *Trompart*, that his maisters humor knew,
    In lofty lookes to hide an humble mind,
    Was inly tickled with that golden vew,
    And in his eare him rounded close behind:
    Yet stoupt he not, but lay still in the wind,
    Waiting aduauntage on the pray to sease;
    Till *Trompart* lowly to the ground inclind,
    Besought him his great courage to appease,
And pardon simple man, that rash did him displease.

31

Bigge looking like a doughtie Doucepere,
    At last he thus; Thou clod of vilest clay,
    I pardon yield, and with thy rudenesse beare;
    But weete henceforth, that all that golden pray,
    And all that else the vaine world vaunten may,
    I loath as doung, ne deeme my dew reward:
    Fame is my meed, and glory vertues pray.
    But minds of mortall men are muchell mard,
And mou'd amisse with massie mucks vnmeet regard.

32

And more, I graunt to thy great miserie
    Gratious respect, thy wife shall backe be sent,
    And that vile knight, who euer that he bee,
    Which hath thy Lady reft, and knighthood shent,
    By *Sanglamort* my sword, whose deadly dent
    The bloud hath of so many thousands shed,
    I sweare, ere long shall dearely it repent;
    Ne he twixt heauen and earth shall hide his hed,
But soone he shall be found, and shortly doen be ded.

33

The foolish man thereat woxe wondrous blith,
    As if the word so spoken, were halfe donne,
    And humbly thanked him a thousand sith,
    That had from death to life him newly wonne.
    Tho forth the Boaster marching, braue begonne
    His stolen steed to thunder furiously,
    As if he heauen and hell would ouerronne,
    And all the world confound with cruelty,
That much *Malbecco* ioyed in his iollity.

34

Thus long they three together traueiled,
    Through many a wood, and many an vncouth way,
    To seeke his wife, that was farre wandered:
    But those two sought nought, but the present pray,
    To weete the treasure, which he did bewray,
    On which their eies and harts were wholly set,
    With purpose, how they might it best betray;
    For sith the houre, that first he did them let
The same behold, therewith their keene desires were whet.

Stanza 28
6   **aduaunced**: praised.
7   **magnifie**: extol.
8   **albe I simple such**: although I am so humble/poor.

Stanza 29
1   **bouget**: pouch.
3   **askew**: sidelong, expressing contempt.
4   **misdempt**: misjudged; thought evil of.
5   **war-monger**: mercenary soldier.   **nempt**: called.
7   **vnkempt**: rude.
8-9   He threatens to slay him, except that it would be
shameful for a knight to slay a peasant.

Stanza 30
2   **humble**: base, low.
4   **rounded**: whispered.
5   **stoupt**: swooped, a term from falconry. Braggadocchio
did not swoop upon his prey but hovered above it.
8   **courage**: anger.

Stanza 31
1   **Doucepere**: as an illustrious knight, one of the twelve
peers (*le douze pairs*) of France.
4   **pray**: booty.
7-9   The sentiment is worthy of Guyon (cf. II vii 10) but
excessive alliteration exposes the vain boasting; cf. Britomart's
claim, ii 7.1-5.   **pray**] pay *1609*.   **vertues pray** balances
golden pray but duplicates the rhyme; the emendation may be
correct.   **muchell mard**: much corrupted.

Stanza 32
2   **Gratious**: implying the benevolent response of a ruler to
his inferior.   **respect**: regard, consideration.
4   **shent**: disgraced.
5   **Sanglamort**: Bloody Death. He has forgotten that he has
vowed not to use his sword; see II iii 12.   **dent**: stroke.

Stanza 33
3   **sith**: times.
8   **confound**: overthrow.
9   **iollity**: magnificent appearance (cf. 'braue', 35.4);
gallantry; presumption.

Stanza 34
5   **bewray**: reveal.
7   **betray**: deliver (Lat. *tradere*) it out of his possession.

35

It fortuned as they together far'd,
    They spide, where *Paridell* came pricking fast
    Vpon the plaine, the which himselfe prepar'd
    To giust with that braue straunger knight a cast,
    As on aduenture by the way he past :
    Alone he rode without his Paragone;
    For hauing filcht her bels, her vp he cast
    To the wide world, and let her fly alone,
He nould be clogd. So had he serued many one.

36

The gentle Lady, loose at randon left,
    The greene-wood long did walke, and wander wide
    At wilde aduenture, like a forlorne weft,
    Till on a day the *Satyres* her espide
    Straying alone withouten groome or guide;
    Her vp they tooke, and with them home her led,
    With them as housewife euer to abide,
    To milk their gotes, and make them cheese and bred,
And euery one as commune good her handeled.

37

That shortly she *Malbecco* has forgot,
    And eke Sir *Paridell*, all were he deare;
    Who from her went to seeke another lot,
    And now by fortune was arriued here,
    Where those two guilers with *Malbecco* were :
    Soone as the oldman saw Sir *Paridell*,
    He fainted, and was almost dead with feare,
    Ne word he had to speake, his griefe to tell,
But to him louted low, and greeted goodly well.

38

And after asked him for *Hellenore*,
    I take no keepe of her (said *Paridell*)
    She wonneth in the forrest there before.
    So forth he rode, as his aduenture fell;
    The whiles the Boaster from his loftie sell
    Faynd to alight, something amisse to mend;
    But the fresh Swayne would not his leasure dwell,
    But went his way; whom when he passed kend,
He vp remounted light, and after faind to wend.

39

Perdy nay (said *Malbecco*) shall ye not :
    But let him passe as lightly, as he came :
    For litle good of him is to be got,
    And mickle perill to be put to shame.
    But let vs go to seeke my dearest Dame,
    Whom he hath left in yonder forrest wyld:
    For of her safety in great doubt I am,
    Least saluage beastes her person haue despoyld:
Then all the world is lost, and we in vaine haue toyld.

40

They all agree, and forward them addrest:
    Ah but (said craftie *Trompart*) weete ye well,
    That yonder in that wastefull wildernesse
    Huge monsters haunt, and many dangers dwell;
    Dragons, and Minotaures, and feendes of hell,
    And many wilde woodmen, which robbe and rend
    All trauellers; therefore aduise ye well,
    Before ye enterprise that way to wend:
One may his iourney bring too soone to euill end.

Stanza 35
4   **braue**: referring to his outward show; cf. 33.5.   **cast**: throw, bout.
6   **Paragone**: companion; consort.
7   **filcht her bels**: a metaphor from hawking. The bells and jesses confine the hawk (cf. VI iv 19.7–9) as the marriage bond restrains Hellenore until she elopes.   **filcht** suggests that he took from her what he wanted and let her go, as the falconer takes the bells from the hawk to let it go. Orange (1972) 546 suggests the bawdy sense, 'rifle her *belle chose*'. The sense, 'to steal things of small value', is entirely fitting : her bells were not worth much. S. rings further changes upon the term at 48.9.
9   **nould**: would not.

Stanza 36
1   **at randon**: at liberty, free from restraint; a hawking term for prey that fails to rise for the hawk.
3   **At wilde aduenture**: at hazard in the wilderness.
weft: waif; in the legal sense, 'property left ownerless'.
9   **good**: property.

Stanza 37
3   **lot**: prize.
5   **guilers**: deceivers.

Stanza 38
5   **Boaster**: repeated from 24.1, 33.5. Here he is exposed to be merely that.
7   **fresh Swayne**: lusty lover, in contrast to 'oldman' (37.6).
dwell: abide.
8   **But went his way**: the repetition from 4 suggests that Paridell may have expected to joust with Braggadocchio.

Stanza 39
2   **lightly**: quickly; comments on Paridell's fickleness.
8–9   Florimell's knights fear the same for her (viii 47–49) but Malbecco's fears are comically confirmed: the **saluage beastes** turn out to be the satyrs whose despoiling Hellenore enjoys.

Stanza 40
1   **them addrest**: made their way.
6   **woodmen**: savages.
7   **aduise**: consider.
8   **enterprise**: attempt.

41

Malbecco stopt in great astonishment,
   And with pale eyes fast fixed on the rest,
   Their counsell crau'd, in daunger imminent.
   Said Trompart, You that are the most opprest
   With burden of great treasure, I thinke best
   Here for to stay in safetie behind;
   My Lord and I will search the wide forrest.
That counsell pleased not Malbeccoes mind;
For he was much affraid, himselfe alone to find.

42

Then is it best (said he) that ye doe leaue
   Your treasure here in some securitie,
   Either fast closed in some hollow greaue,
   Or buried in the ground from ieopardie,
   Till we returne againe in safetie:
   As for vs two, least doubt of vs ye haue,
   Hence farre away we will blindfolded lie,
   Ne priuie be vnto your treasures graue.
It pleased: so he did.   Then they march forward braue.

43

Now when amid the thickest woods they were,
   They heard a noyse of many bagpipes shrill,
   And shrieking Hububs them approching nere,
   Which all the forrest did with horror fill:
   That dreadfull sound the boasters hart did thrill,
   With such amazement, that in haste he fled,
   Ne euer looked backe for good or ill,
   And after him eke fearefull Trompart sped;
The old man could not fly, but fell to ground halfe ded.

44

Yet afterwards close creeping, as he might,
   He in a bush did hide his fearefull hed,
   The iolly Satyres full of fresh delight,
   Came dauncing forth, and with them nimbly led
   Faire Hellenore, with girlonds all bespred,
   Whom their May-lady they had newly made:
   She proud of that new honour, which they red,
   And of their louely fellowship full glade,
Daunst liuely, and her face did with a Lawrell shade.

45

The silly man that in the thicket lay
   Saw all this goodly sport, and grieued sore,
   Yet durst he not against it doe or say,
   But did his hart with bitter thoughts engore,
   To see th'vnkindnesse of his Hellenore.
   All day they daunced with great lustihed,
   And with their horned feet the greene grasse wore,
   The whiles their Gotes vpon the brouzes fed,
Till drouping Phœbus gan to hide his golden hed.

46

Tho vp they gan their merry pypes to trusse,
   And all their goodly heards did gather round,
   But euery Satyre first did giue a busse
   To Hellenore: so busses did abound.
   Now gan the humid vapour shed the ground
   With perly deaw, and th'Earthes gloomy shade
   Did dim the brightnesse of the welkin round,
   That euery bird and beast awarned made,
To shrowd themselues, whiles sleepe their senses did inuade.

47

Which when Malbecco saw, out of his bush
   Vpon his hands and feete he crept full light,
   And like a Gote emongst the Gotes did rush,
   That through the helpe of his faire hornes on hight,
   And misty dampe of misconceiuing night,
   And eke through likenesse of his gotish beard,
   He did the better counterfeite aright:
   So home he marcht emongst the horned heard,
That none of all the Satyres him espyde or heard.

Stanza 41
1 astonishment: dismay, dread.
2 pale eyes: signifying despair; cf. 54.8.

Stanza 42
3 greaue: grove; here, tree.

Stanza 43
2 On the bagpipes as a folk instrument that symbolizes lechery, see Block (1954).
6 amazement: overwhelming fear.

Stanza 44
1 close creeping, as he might: i.e. creeping as secretly as possible.
3 iolly: also amorous, as Paridell, 20.4.
7 red: declared, in making her their May-lady.
8 louely: loving.
9 Lawrell: crowning her their Queen.

Stanza 45
5 vnkindnesse: unnatural conduct.
6 lustihed: lustiness; lustfulness.
7 Cf. the satyrs dancing around Una, I vi 14.3.
8 brouzes: young shoots.

Stanza 46
3 busse: kiss; with the distinction noted in Herrick's line: 'We busse our Wantons, but our Wives we kisse' (Poetical Works 189).

Stanza 47
3 Goats, being proverbially lustful, are associated with the lustful, goatlike Satyrs.
4 Malbecco now earns his name – see ix 6.1n. The horns are the horns of the cuckold. Upton (1758) notes: 'His imaginary horns . . . now become real horns.'
5 misconceiuing: causing misconception.

48

At night, when all they went to sleepe, he vewd,
Whereas his louely wife emongst them lay,
Embraced of a *Satyre* rough and rude,
Who all the night did minde his ioyous play:
Nine times he heard him come aloft ere day,
That all his hart with gealosie did swell;
But yet that nights ensample did bewray,
That not for nought his wife them loued so well,
When one so oft a night did ring his matins bell.

49

So closely as he could, he to them crept,
When wearie of their sport to sleepe they fell,
And to his wife, that now full soundly slept,
He whispered in her eare, and did her tell,
That it was he, which by her side did dwell,
And therefore prayd her wake, to heare him plaine.
As one out of a dreame not waked well,
She turned her, and returned backe againe:
Yet her for to awake he did the more constraine.

50

At last with irkesome trouble she abrayd;
And then perceiuing, that it was indeed
Her old *Malbecco*, which did her vpbrayd,
With loosenesse of her loue, and loathly deed,
She was astonisht with exceeding dreed,
And would haue wakt the *Satyre* by her syde;
But he her prayd, for mercy, or for meed,
To saue his life, ne let him be descryde,
But hearken to his lore, and all his counsell hyde.

51

Tho gan he her perswade, to leaue that lewd
And loathsome life, of God and man abhord,
And home returne, where all should be renewd
With perfect peace, and bandes of fresh accord,
And she receiu'd againe to bed and bord,
As if no trespasse euer had bene donne:
But she it all refused at one word,
And by no meanes would to his will be wonne,
But chose emongst the iolly *Satyres* still to wonne.

52

He wooed her, till day spring he espyde;
But all in vaine: and then turnd to the heard,
Who butted him with hornes on euery syde,
And trode downe in the durt, where his hore beard
Was fowly dight, and he of death afeard.
Early before the heauens fairest light
Out of the ruddy East was fully reard,
The heardes out of their foldes were loosed quight,
And he emongst the rest crept forth in sory plight.

53

So soone as he the Prison dore did pas,
He ran as fast, as both his feete could beare,
And neuer looked, who behind him was,
Ne scarsely who before: like as a Beare
That creeping close, amongst the hiues to reare
An hony combe, the wakefull dogs espy,
And him assayling, sore his carkasse teare,
That hardly he with life away does fly,
Ne stayes, till safe himselfe he see from ieopardy.

54

Ne stayd he, till he came vnto the place,
Where late his treasure he entombed had,
Where when he found it not (for *Trompart* bace
Had it purloyned for his maister bad :)
With extreme fury he became quite mad,
And ran away, ran with himselfe away:
That who so straungely had him seene bestad,
With vpstart haire, and staring eyes dismay,
From Limbo lake him late escaped sure would say.

Stanza 48
An analogy to the loves of the gods depicted in the house of
Busirane where Jove appears 'like a Ram, faire *Helle* to peruart'
(xi 30.5).
2   louely: loving.
3–5   According to Pliny, the satyr gets his name – here he
earns it – from the *membrum virile*; cf. Sandys (1632) 289. The
satyr imitates Ovid who took Corinna nine times in one short
night (*Amores* III vii 25–6).

Stanza 49
6   plaine: complain.
9   constraine: exert himself.

Stanza 50
1   abrayd: awoke.

Stanza 51
1   perswade: urge.
5   to bed and bord: as wife and mistress of the household.
7   at one word: at once.
9   Hellenore is the female counterpart of Grill. For her,
however, sexual satisfaction means fulfilment rather than a fall.
still: always.

Stanza 52
2   turnd: returned.
5   dight: soiled.

Stanza 53
5   reare: take away.
6   hony combe: honey as the sweets of sexual pleasure
underlies this simile.

Stanza 54
The loss of his wealth is the final and greatest blow: 'For the
desire of money is the roote of all evil, which while some
lusted after, thei . . . perced them selves through with many
sorowes' (1 Tim. 6.10).
6   The addition points to the disintegration of his person;
cf. 55.7.
7   so straungely . . . bestad: i.e. so strangely disposed.
8   dismay: dismayed; or staring in dismay.
9   From Limbo lake . . . escaped: i.e. as a lost soul; see
I ii 32.5.

399

55

High ouer hilles and ouer dales he fled,
  As if the wind him on his winges had borne,
  Ne banck nor bush could stay him, when he sped
  His nimble feet, as treading still on thorne:
  Griefe, and despight, and gealosie, and scorne
  Did all the way him follow hard behind,
  And he himselfe himselfe loath'd so forlorne,
  So shamefully forlorne of womankind;
That as a Snake, still lurked in his wounded mind.

56

Still fled he forward, looking backward still,
  Ne stayd his flight, nor fearefull agony,
  Till that he came vnto a rockie hill,
  Ouer the sea, suspended dreadfully,
  That liuing creature it would terrify,
  To looke adowne, or vpward to the hight:
  From thence he threw himselfe dispiteously,
  All desperate of his fore-damned spright,
That seem'd no helpe for him was left in liuing sight.

57

But through long anguish, and selfe-murdring thought
  He was so wasted and forpined quight,
  That all his substance was consum'd to nought,
  And nothing left, but like an aery Spright,
  That on the rockes he fell so flit and light,
  That he thereby receiu'd no hurt at all,
  But chaunced on a craggy cliff to light;
  Whence he with crooked clawes so long did crall,
That at the last he found a caue with entrance small.

58

Into the same he creepes, and thenceforth there
  Resolu'd to build his balefull mansion,
  In drery darkenesse, and continuall feare
  Of that rockes fall, which euer and anon
  Threates with huge ruine him to fall vpon,
  That he dare neuer sleepe, but that one eye
  Still ope he keepes for that occasion;
  Ne euer rests he in tranquillity,
The roring billowes beat his bowre so boystrously.

59

Ne euer is he wont on ought to feed,
  But toades and frogs, his pasture poysonous,
  Which in his cold complexion do breed
  A filthy bloud, or humour rancorous,
  Matter of doubt and dread suspitious,
  That doth with curelesse care consume the hart,
  Corrupts the stomacke with gall vitious,
  Croscuts the liuer with internall smart,
And doth transfixe the soule with deathes eternall dart.

Stanza 55

4, 9   Jealousy is associated with the **thorne**, e.g. Sidney, *Astrophel and Stella* 78 where the jealous husband is described with 'nimble feet as stirre still, though on thornes'. Cf. Doubt in Cupid's pageant, xii 10.6, and the jealous Scudamour, IV v 31.3. Also with the **Snake**: e.g. Ariosto's Jealousy, *Orl. Fur.* xlii 47.

5   Upton (1758) notes that these figures were intended by the poet as persons. More directly, they suggest the fragmenting of Malbecco's person. At first his jealousy pursues him; then he embodies it; and finally, he becomes its embodiment.

9   **That**: i.e. the thought that Hellenore preferred the Satyrs to him.

Stanza 56

7   **dispiteously**: mercilessly. As he expects no mercy in his despair, he shows no mercy to himself.

8   **desperate**: despairing.   **fore-damned**: previously or utterly damned by attempted suicide.   **spright**: soul.

Stanza 57

2   **forpined**: wasted away.

5   **flit**: unsubstantial.

8   When Daedalion threw himself from a cliff, he was transformed into an eagle with curved claws (Ovid, *Met.* xi 342); the source is noted by Nelson (1963) 324–5.

Stanza 58

2   **mansion**: dwelling-place.

3–5   Cf. Despair whose cave is placed 'vnderneath a craggie clift' (I ix 33.3).

5   **ruine**: fall. Alpers (1967) 220–1 compares the punishment of Tantalus, 'overhanging dread', which is described as a rock hanging over him (Cicero, *Tusc. Disp.* IV xvi). However, that rock may be the cliff itself which seems to overhang. McNeir (1959) 36 notes that Ariosto's Sospetto lives on a cliff high above the sea, and it is the cliff itself that threatens to fall (*Cinque Canti* ii 18). Cf. the house of Care, 'Vnder a steepe hilles side' (IV v 33.1). Or the rock may be simply the roof of the cave.

Stanza 59

Alpers (1967) 222–4 analyses the medical background.

2   **pasture**: food.

3   **complexion**: temperament.

4   **filthy bloud**: excess or corrupt humour in the blood which causes illness.   **humour rancorous**: associated with despite, II vii 22.2, VI vi 43.8.

5   **Matter**: also blood, or excrement from it.

6   **curelesse care**: puns on the etymology of 'cure' (from Lat. *cura*). The rest of the line refers to the well-known etymology of care: *cura quod cor edat.*

7   **vitious**: noxious.

8   Jealous love is centred in the liver, which is the centre of the lower affections; cf. II vi 50.3.

60

Yet can he neuer dye, but dying liues,
  And doth himselfe with sorrow new sustaine,
  That death and life attonce vnto him giues.
  And painefull pleasure turnes to pleasing paine.
  There dwels he euer, miserable swaine,
  Hatefull both to him selfe, and euery wight;
  Where he through priuy griefe, and horrour vaine,
  Is woxen so deform'd, that he has quight
Forgot he was a man, and *Gealosie* is hight.

Cant. XI.

Britomart chaceth Ollyphant,
findes Scudamour distrest:
Assayes the house of Busyrane,
where Loues spoyles are exprest.

1

O Hatefull hellish Snake, what furie furst
  Brought thee from balefull house of *Proserpine*,
  Where in her bosome she thee long had nurst,
  And fostred vp with bitter milke of tine,
  Fowle Gealosie, that turnest loue diuine
  To ioylesse dread, and mak'st the louing hart
  With hatefull thoughts to languish and to pine,
  And feed it selfe with selfe-consuming smart?
Of all the passions in the mind thou vilest art.

2

O let him far be banished away,
  And in his stead let Loue for euer dwell,
  Sweet Loue, that doth his golden wings embay
  In blessed Nectar, and pure Pleasures well,
  Vntroubled of vile feare, or bitter fell,
  And ye faire Ladies, that your kingdomes make
  In th'harts of men, them gouerne wisely well,
  And of faire *Britomart* ensample take,
That was as trew in loue, as Turtle to her make.

3

Who with Sir *Satyrane*, as earst ye red,
  Forth ryding from *Malbeccoes* hostlesse hous,
  Far off aspyde a young man, the which fled
  From an huge Geaunt, that with hideous
  And hatefull outrage long him chaced thus;
  It was that *Ollyphant*, the brother deare
  Of that *Argante* vile and vitious,
  From whom the *Squire of Dames* was reft whylere;
This all as bad as she, and worse, if worse ought were.

4

For as the sister did in feminine
  And filthy lust exceed all woman kind,
  So he surpassed his sex masculine,
  In beastly vse that I did euer find;
  Whom when as *Britomart* beheld behind
  The fearefull boy so greedily pursew,
  She was emmoued in her noble mind,
  T'employ her puissance to his reskew,
And pricked fiercely forward, where she him did vew.

Stanza 60
Malbecco shares the immortality of Despair, I ix 54.8–9, and of Adonis, III vi 47.
7   priuy griefe: the secret suffering of jealousy which began in his 'priuie guilt' (ix 5.3).
9   Upton (1758) remarks that 'no metamorphosis in Ovid is worked up, from beginning to end, with finer imagery, or with a better moral allusion'.   Forgot: as Grill 'forgot the excellence / Of his creation' (II xii 87.2–3). Gilde (1971b) 239 notes that 'the revolting monster he becomes is only the visual image of the monster with whom Hellenore lived'. S.'s witty point is that Malbecco is transformed into himself. Berger (1969d) 148–50 argues that S. discards Malbecco as an 'antiquated form' to be replaced by 'boundary figures' such as Scudamour and Amoret.

Canto xi

Argument
3   Assayes: assails; cf. 22.3, 25.4, 26.2.
4   Loues spoyles: generally, Cupid's booty gained by preying upon mankind (cf. 45.7); specifically, Amoret, his 'proud spoyle' (xii 22.7). At IV x Scudamour reveals how Amoret became his spoil. Later she becomes Lust's spoil, IV vii 25.5. Cf. xii 47.2 (*1590*).   exprest: portrayed, set forth.

Stanza 1
1–4   Usually snakes compose the hair of the Furies (e.g. Virgil, *Aen.* vii 346); cf. x 55.9.   house of Proserpine: Hell, the classical Underworld.   tine: affliction.
5   Fowle Gealosie: punning on Malbecco's transformation into 'an aery Spright' (x 57.4) with crooked claws.

Stanza 2
3   embay: steep.
4   blessed Nectar: the drink of the gods; its sweetness contrasts with the 'bitter milke' drunk by Jealousy.
5   fell: rancour (Lat. *fel*, gall).
6–9   Cf. the exhortation to virgins to imitate Belphœbe, v 54.1–2.
9   Turtle: the turtle-dove.   make: mate.

Stanza 3
2   hostlesse: inhospitable.
4 to 4.4   Cf. vii 47–49. On Ollyphant, see vii 48.2*n*.
8   reft: taken away.

Stanza 4
4   that I did euer] all, that I euer *1590*. Church (1758) suggests 'all I did euer', and Upton (1758), 'all that I e'er did'. The personal attestation seems provoked by Ollyphant, masculine lust.

5

Ne was Sir *Satyrane* her far behinde,
　But with like fiercenesse did ensew the chace:
　Whom when the Gyaunt saw, he soone resinde
　His former suit, and from them fled apace;
　They after both, and boldly bad him bace,
　And each did striue the other to out-goe,
　But he them both outran a wondrous space,
　For he was long, and swift as any Roe,
And now made better speed, t'escape his feared foe.

6

It was not *Satyrane*, whom he did feare,
　But *Britomart* the flowre of chastity;
　For he the powre of chast hands might not beare,
　But alwayes did their dread encounter fly:
　And now so fast his feet he did apply,
　That he has gotten to a forrest neare,
　Where he is shrowded in security.
　The wood they enter, and search euery where,
They searched diuersely, so both diuided were.

7

Faire *Britomart* so long him followed,
　That she at last came to a fountaine sheare,
　By which there lay a knight all wallowed
　Vpon the grassy ground, and by him neare
　His haberieon, his helmet, and his speare;
　A little off, his shield was rudely throwne,
　On which the winged boy in colours cleare
　Depeincted was, full easie to be knowne,
And he thereby, where euer it in field was showne.

8

His face vpon the ground did groueling ly,
　As if he had bene slombring in the shade,
　That the braue Mayd would not for courtesy,
　Out of his quiet slomber him abrade,
　Nor seeme too suddeinly him to inuade:
　Still as she stood, she heard with grieuous throb
　Him grone, as if his hart were peeces made,
　And with most painefull pangs to sigh and sob,
That pitty did the Virgins hart of patience rob.

9

At last forth breaking into bitter plaintes
　He said; O soueraigne Lord that sit'st on hye,
　And raignst in blis emongst thy blessed Saintes,
　How suffrest thou such shamefull cruelty,
　So long vnwreaked of thine enimy?
　Or hast thou, Lord, of good mens cause no heed?
　Or doth thy iustice sleepe, and silent ly?
　What booteth then the good and righteous deed,
If goodnesse find no grace, nor righteousnesse no meed?

Stanza 5

2　**ensew**: pursue.
4　**suit**: pursuit.
5　**bad him bace**: challenged him, alluding to the children's game, prisoners' base, in which two sides take turns chasing each other; cf. V viii 5.4–5, VI x 8.4. The pursuer becomes the pursued, as in the game of love.
8　**swift as any Roe**: as 2 Sam. 2.18.

Stanza 6

9　**diuersely**: in different directions.

Stanzas 7–25

In Tasso, *Rinaldo* v, the hero finds the despairing lover and, after listening to his lament, enters a cave of love, the entrance to which is barred by enchanted fire. To this story S. adds details from Ariosto, *Orl. Fur.* ii 34–43: the chaste heroine Bradamante finds the lover Pinabello by a fountain despairing because his mistress is imprisoned in an enchanted castle, and later frees her. Analogues to the fire-barrier are found in popular romance and court of love allegories. Cf. Tasso, *Ger. Lib.* xiii 33–6. The matter was well-known: Milton, *Prolusion* vi, refers to the champions of King Arthur who 'ever more easily subdue and scatter the enchantments of a fire- and flame-girdled castle' (ed. Hughes 618).

Stanza 7

1–2　The relation between **so long** and **at last** is clarified by the allegorical nature of the meeting: the Giant of masculine lust is Scudamour as he appears to Amoret's tortured fancy. The **fountaine** is associated with love and the lover throughout the poem. **sheare**: clear, pure.
3　**wallowed**: lying prostrate; the posture of the wounded Adonis (cf. i 38.1).
6–9　Hence the knight's name, Scudamour: Fr. *écu* (or *éscu*), shield + *d'amour*, of love; cf. Ital. *scudo* + *amore*. Cf. IV i 39.1–3, x 55.3–4. **Depeincted**: depicted; suggesting 'painted'. **field**: referring to tilt or tournament; with the heraldic sense: Cupid's man is known wherever the surface of the shield displays **the winged boy**.

Stanza 8

4　**abrade**: arouse.
5　**inuade**: intrude upon.
9　As 12.8 and 14.2.

Stanza 9

5　**vnwreaked**: unavenged.
9　**righteousnesse**: just deeds.

10

If good find grace, and righteousnesse reward,
  Why then is *Amoret* in caytiue band,
  Sith that more bounteous creature neuer far'd
  On foot, vpon the face of liuing land?
  Or if that heauenly iustice may withstand
  The wrongfull outrage of vnrighteous men,
  Why then is *Busirane* with wicked hand
  Suffred, these seuen monethes day in secret den
My Lady and my loue so cruelly to pen?

11

My Lady and my loue is cruelly pend
  In dolefull darkenesse from the vew of day,
  Whilest deadly torments do her chast brest rend,
  And the sharpe steele doth riue her hart in tway,
  All for she *Scudamore* will not denay.
  Yet thou vile man, vile *Scudamore* art sound,
  Ne canst her ayde, ne canst her foe dismay;
  Vnworthy wretch to tread vpon the ground,
For whom so faire a Lady feeles so sore a wound.

12

There an huge heape of singultes did oppresse
  His strugling soule, and swelling throbs empeach
  His foltring toung with pangs of drerinesse,
  Choking the remnant of his plaintife speach,
  As if his dayes were come to their last reach.
  Which when she heard, and saw the ghastly fit,
  Threatning into his life to make a breach,
  Both with great ruth and terrour she was smit,
Fearing least from her cage the wearie soule would flit.

13

Tho stooping downe she him amoued light;
  Who therewith somewhat starting, vp gan looke,
  And seeing him behind a straunger knight,
  Whereas no liuing creature he mistooke,
  With great indignaunce he that sight forsooke,
  And downe againe himselfe disdainefully
  Abiecting, th'earth with his faire forhead strooke:
  Which the bold Virgin seeing, gan apply
Fit medcine to his griefe, and spake thus courteously.

Since he defiled his temples with strangers' blood (Ovid, *Met.*
ix 182–3), Fowler (1964) 20 deduces that he was 'a ready-made
symbol for adultery'. On the medieval Busire pictured as a
wizard who watches murder, see Tuve (1970) 133–4. As the
owner of man-eating horses (cf. Chaucer, *Monk's T.* VII
2103–4), he was an apt symbol for flesh-devouring lust.
Williams (1966) 109–10 connects him with the Busiris in Ovid,
Ars Amat. i 658: his story illustrates the moral that a woman
should 'feel the wound that first she inflicted'. Earlier Amoret
wounded her lovers (vi 52.7–9); now she suffers for this act.
Comes (1616) VII vii p. 385 relates that Busiris 'infatuated
with the beauty of the Atlantides, the daughters of Atlas, sent
robbers and pirates to seize them'; cf. Diodorus Siculus
Biblio. Hist. IV xxvii 1–5. Britomart's defeat of Busirane
completes a first stage of her quest which began when 'the
moist daughters of huge *Atlas* stroue / Into the *Ocean* deepe
to driue their weary droue' (i 57.8–9). Roche (1964) 82 suggests
that the name indicates 'abuse' in the sixteenth-century sense:
imposture, ill-usage, delusion. His name occurs only here in the
entire Book. On the link with Osyris, see V vii 2–4*n*. See also
48.6–9*n* below.
8 seuen monethes day: a period of seven months, as IV
i 4.1. It is the length of Florimell's imprisonment, IV xi 4.6,
and associated with the reign of winter. Fowler (1964) 139
notes that Adonis returns in the seventh month; see
Macrobius, *Saturnalia* I xxi. Cf. the seven-year siege of the
Castle of Alma, II ix 12.8, and see *n*. This period of time leads
to renewal: see Macrobius, *In Somn. Scip.* I vi 45–7.

Stanza 11
3–5 Amoret's physical and psychological states are
juxtaposed, as the one expresses the other. Constancy in love is
upheld by the Knight of Holiness, i 24, and later by Florimell,
viii 42. **for**: because.
6 vile: cf. xii 31.1, etc. The lover and tormentor later
merge: see xii 31.7*n*.
7 dismay: defeat.

Stanza 12
1 singultes: sobs, from Lat. *singultus*.
2 empeach: hinder; also 'accuse of treason' (as he is
guilty of her suffering).
3 drerinesse: anguish.
4 plaintife: sad; also as he is a plaintiff in his suit.
8 Cf. Belphœbe's pity and horror when she comes upon the
wounded Timias, v 30.5–9. **ruth** or pity leads to love.
terrour follows because she encounters Cupid's man and to
his lord she is victim. Cf. her earlier response to Malecasta, i
62; now she is prepared to aid love. Cf. IV x 55.5.

Stanza 13
1 amoued: aroused; touched.
3–5 He does not take her to be a living creature but a
goddess. He turns away because in his despair he rejects the
heavenly aid which she represents; cf. Timias's response to
Belphœbe, v 35. That he sees and rejects the Knight of
Chastity suggests his moral failure and the reason for Amoret's
suffering. **mistooke**: supposed wrongly to be.
indignaunce: indignation, from Lat. *indignans*; or
unworthiness, from Lat. *indignus*; cf. IV i 30.5.
7 Abiecting: throwing, suggesting self-debasement. The
posture indicates that he is inwardly downcast; cf. the moment
of greater grief at 27.6.

Stanza 10
3 bounteous: virtuous.
7 Busirane: from Busiris, a king of Egypt famous for his
cruelty, identified with the Pharaoh of Exodus, e.g. by
Sandys (1632) 428; hence a symbol of tyranny. Fraunce,
Lamentations of Amyntas (1587) iv 33, refers to Cupid as a
tyrant whose cruelty surpasses 'Busiris beastlie behauiour'.

14

Ah gentle knight, whose deepe conceiued griefe
  Well seemes t'exceede the powre of patience,
  Yet if that heauenly grace some good reliefe
  You send, submit you to high prouidence,
  And euer in your noble hart prepense,
  That all the sorrow in the world is lesse,
  Then vertues might, and values confidence,
  For who nill bide the burden of distresse,
Must not here thinke to liue: for life is wretchednesse.

15

Therefore, faire Sir, do comfort to you take,
  And freely read, what wicked felon so
  Hath outrag'd you, and thrald your gentle make.
  Perhaps this hand may helpe to ease your woe,
  And wreake your sorrow on your cruell foe,
  At least it faire endeuour will apply.
  Those feeling wordes so neare the quicke did goe,
  That vp his head he reared easily,
And leaning on his elbow, these few wordes let fly.

16

What boots it plaine, that cannot be redrest,
  And sow vaine sorrow in a fruitlesse eare,
  Sith powre of hand, nor skill of learned brest,
  Ne worldly price cannot redeeme my deare,
  Out of her thraldome and continuall feare?
  For he the tyraunt, which her hath in ward
  By strong enchauntments and blacke Magicke leare,
  Hath in a dungeon deepe her close embard,
And many dreadfull feends hath pointed to her gard.

17

There he tormenteth her most terribly,
  And day and night afflicts with mortall paine,
  Because to yield him loue she doth deny,
  Once to me yold, not to be yold againe:
  But yet by torture he would her constraine
  Loue to conceiue in her disdainfull brest;
  Till so she do, she must in doole remaine,
  Ne may by liuing meanes be thence relest:
What boots it then to plaine, that cannot be redrest?

18

With this sad hersall of his heauy stresse,
  The warlike Damzell was empassiond sore,
  And said; Sir knight, your cause is nothing lesse,
  Then is your sorrow, certes if not more;
  For nothing so much pitty doth implore,
  As gentle Ladies helplesse misery.
  But yet, if please ye listen to my lore,
  I will with proofe of last extremity,
Deliuer her fro thence, or with her for you dy.

Stanza 14

2   Referring also to her own loss of patience, 8.9.
3–4   She regards herself as the instrument of God's grace and persuades him to submit to her, 20.1–3. Cf. Arthur's role in relation to Una, I vii 40–52.
5   **prepense**: consider beforehand.
7   **values confidence**: confidence in valour.
8   **nill**: will not.

Stanza 15

2   **read**: tell.
3   **make**: companion; beloved.
8   **easily**: calmly; readily.

Stanza 16

1   This proverb (C. G. Smith, 1970, 14) concludes his complaint, 17.9.   **plaine**: to complain.
3–5   The lines define Britomart's heroism. In Book I the Dragon cannot be wounded 'By subtilty, nor slight, nor might, nor mighty charme' (I xi 36.9) and the Red Cross Knight triumphs through the **powre of hand** supported by grace. In Book II Guyon triumphs over Acrasia by **skill of learned brest**, specifically, the power of reason represented by the Palmer. Britomart may triumph over her antagonist only by substituting herself as his victim. She offers what is beyond **worldly price**, namely herself, to ransom Amoret. First she must pass through the fire which cannot be quenched 'by any wit or might' (23.7). Line 5 indicates that Amoret's **thraldome** is her **continuall feare**.
6   **in ward**: under guard as a prisoner.
7   **leare**: lore; art. Amoret's resistance (cf. xii 31) recapitulates Britomart's: 'loue, that is in gentle brest begonne, / No idle charmes so lightly may remoue' (ii 51.7–8). Cf. vii 21.1–5.
9   **pointed**: appointed.

Stanza 17

1–3   Cf. *L.R.*: 'Busirane had in hand a most faire Lady called Amoretta, whom he kept in most grieuous torment, because she would not yield him the pleasure of her body.' Cf. xii 31.6 and IV i 4.2.
4   **yold**: yielded. Repeated to stress their betrothal or marriage.
7   **doole**: physical pain; grief or mental distress.
8   **liuing meanes**: any living person; anything short of death.

Stanza 18

1   **hersall**: rehearsal.   **stresse**: affliction.
2   As the 'Virgin' she pities him (cf. 8.9); as 'the bold Virgin' (13.8) she seeks the cause of his suffering; as the **warlike Damzell** she offers herself in battle.
3–4   **your cause is nothing lesse, / . . . more**: your cause is as worthy as your sorrow is great, even more so.
7   **lore**: opposes Busirane's 'Magicke leare' (16.7).
8   **with proofe of last extremity**: i.e. at the extreme peril of my life, the utmost point of suffering.

19

Ah gentlest knight aliue, (said *Scudamore*)
  What huge heroicke magnanimity
  Dwels in thy bounteous brest? what couldst thou more,
  If she were thine, and thou as now am I?
  O spare thy happy dayes, and them apply
  To better boot, but let me dye, that ought;
  More is more losse: one is enough to dy.
  Life is not lost, (said she) for which is bought
Endlesse renowm, that more then death is to be sought.

20

Thus she at length perswaded him to rise,
  And with her wend, to see what new successe
  Mote him befall vpon new enterprise;
  His armes, which he had vowed to disprofesse,
  She gathered vp and did about him dresse,
  And his forwandred steed vnto him got:
  So forth they both yfere make their progresse,
  And march not past the mountenaunce of a shot,
Till they arriu'd, whereas their purpose they did plot.

21

There they dismounting, drew their weapons bold
  And stoutly came vnto the Castle gate;
  Whereas no gate they found, them to withhold,
  Nor ward to wait at morne and euening late,
  But in the Porch, that did them sore amate,
  A flaming fire, ymixt with smouldry smoke,
  And stinking Sulphure, that with griesly hate
  And dreadfull horrour did all entraunce choke,
Enforced them their forward footing to reuoke.

22

Greatly thereat was *Britomart* dismayd,
  Ne in that stownd wist, how her selfe to beare;
  For daunger vaine it were, to haue assayd
  That cruell element, which all things feare,
  Ne none can suffer to approchen neare:
  And turning backe to *Scudamour*, thus sayd;
  What monstrous enmity prouoke we heare,
  Foolhardy as th'Earthes children, the which made
Battell against the Gods? so we a God inuade.

23

Daunger without discretion to attempt,
  Inglorious and beastlike is: therefore Sir knight,
  Aread what course of you is safest dempt,
  And how we with our foe may come to fight.
  This is (quoth he) the dolorous despight,
  Which earst to you I playnd: for neither may
  This fire be quencht by any wit or might,
  Ne yet by any meanes remou'd away,
So mighty be th'enchauntments, which the same do stay.

24

What is there else, but cease these fruitlesse paines,
  And leaue me to my former languishing?
  Faire *Amoret* must dwell in wicked chaines,
  And *Scudamore* here dye with sorrowing.
  Perdy not so, (said she) for shamefull thing
  It were t'abandon noble cheuisaunce,
  For shew of perill, without venturing:
  Rather let try extremities of chaunce,
Then enterprised prayse for dread to disauaunce.

Stanza 19

1 **gentlest**: noblest, most generous.
2 **magnanimity**: lofty courage; literally, doing great deeds.
See II viii 23.9*n*. The virtue that appears in Guyon's face
dwells in Britomart's breast.
6 **boot**: advantage.
9 **death**: 'life', sugg. Jortin (1734). Yet the text may stand:
'**Endlesse renowm** and not **death** should be the principal
object of every brave man's thoughts' (Church, 1758).

Stanza 20

2 **successe**: fortune.
4 **disprofesse**: renounce.
5–6 She anticipates her maternal aid to Artegall, V vii 41.
dresse: array. **forwandred**: wandered away.
7 **progresse**: journey.
8 **not past the mountenaunce of a shot**: i.e. a distance not
greater than a bow-shot, a measuring unit appropriate for a
'tilt' directed against Cupid's house.

Stanza 21

4 Nor guard to keep watch.
5 **amate**: daunt.
6–8 The smoke and burning sulphur suggest hell-fire, as
I v 31.5. **smouldry**: smothering. **hate**: implying active
malignancy, the effect of which is to arouse **horrour**.
choke: also as it chokes all who seek to enter.
9 **reuoke**: draw back; see I i 12.7–8*n*.

Stanza 22

1 **dismayd**: a pun may be suggested by the context.
2 **stownd**: time of sudden peril.
7 **prouoke**: challenge, defy; also the usual sense, for
Scudamour's approach stirs up the flames.
8–9 She refers to the Titans' war against the Gods, and
compares the fire to Jove's thunderbolts, which struck them
down. The **God** is Mulciber, the God of fire (26.5), or Cupid
who arouses the flames of love.

Stanza 23

3 **Aread**: declare. **dempt**: deemed.
7 **wit or might**: see 16.3–5.
9 **stay**: support.

Stanza 24

6 **cheuisaunce**: chivalric enterprise; see II ix 8.1–2*n*.
9 Than retreat through dread from praiseworthy action
already begun. She repeats the substance of lines 5–7 and
confirms her vow, 18.8–9.

405

25

Therewith resolu'd to proue her vtmost might,
  Her ample shield she threw before her face,
  And her swords point directing forward right,
  Assayld the flame, the which eftsoones gaue place,
  And did it selfe diuide with equall space,
  That through she passed; as a thunder bolt
  Perceth the yielding ayre, and doth displace
  The soring clouds into sad showres ymolt;
So to her yold the flames, and did their force reuolt.

26

Whom whenas *Scudamour* saw past the fire,
  Safe and vntoucht, he likewise gan assay,
  With greedy will, and enuious desire,
  And bad the stubborne flames to yield him way:
  But cruell *Mulciber* would not obay
  His threatfull pride, but did the more augment
  His mighty rage, and with imperious sway
  Him forst (maulgre) his fiercenesse to relent,
And backe retire, all scorcht and pitifully brent.

27

With huge impatience he inly swelt,
  More for great sorrow, that he could not pas,
  Then for the burning torment, which he felt,
  That with fell woodnesse he effierced was,
  And wilfully him throwing on the gras,
  Did beat and bounse his head and brest full sore;
  The whiles the Championesse now entred has
  The vtmost rowme, and past the formest dore,
The vtmost rowme, abounding with all precious store.

28

For round about, the wals yclothed were
  With goodly arras of great maiesty,
  Wouen with gold and silke so close and nere,
  That the rich metall lurked priuily,
  As faining to be hid from enuious eye;
  Yet here, and there, and euery where vnwares
  It shewd it selfe, and shone vnwillingly;
  Like a discolourd Snake, whose hidden snares
Through the greene gras his long bright burnisht backe declares.

love has aroused in her, ii 37. With Scudamour's state cf. her despair that nothing could 'my flame relent' (ii 43.4). For the iconography of the fire of love, see Praz (1939–47) under 'fire', 'flame'. A significant analogue is Dante's passage through the wall of fire in order to purge the sin of lust, *Purg*. xxvii. The sexual symbolism of S.'s episode places the fire at the gate of the house.

3 Since Britomart is on foot, her sword substitutes for her 'enchaunted speare' (i 9.9) whose virtue manifests the magical power of chastity. There are the Christian overtones of the shield of faith that quenches 'all the fyrie dartes of the wicked' (Eph. 6.16).
5 **with equall space**: i.e. equally on both sides.
8 **sad**: heavy; as they are weeping. **showres**: heavy downpour. **ymolt**: melted.
9 **reuolt**: turn back.

Stanza 26
3 He fails because his **will** and **desire** cause the flames. **enuious desire**: also desire to emulate Britomart.
5–9 Fowler (1964) 128 notes that Britomart's encounter with **cruell Mulciber** is 'a re-enactment of the archetypal myth; for the lustful Vulcan (alias Mulciber) was Minerva's traditional opponent'. He is named as the symbol of jealous love. **maulgre**: in spite of himself, or of his fierceness.

Stanza 27 to Canto xii 29.
After passing through the fire, Britomart progresses through three rooms. The foremost door leads into a room which contains tapestries depicting the loves of the gods and a statue of Cupid. Behind the statue (see 50.1–4*n*) is a door inscribed, **Be bold**; through it, she enters a room overlaid with gold, decorated with monstrous forms of love, and adorned with the spoils of captains and conquerors. The door is inscribed on the inside with the same motto repeated many times. Over an iron door leading to the third and inmost room is inscribed, **Be not too bold**. From this room the masque issues. She enters this room at midnight of the second night, that is, at the beginning of the third day, and sees Busirane and Amoret. Berger (1971) analyses Britomart's experience in the house of Busirane in phases represented by her experience in each room.

Stanza 27
1 **inly swelt**: inwardly burned, corresponding to being outwardly burned; the two merge in **burning torment** (3).
4 **fell woodnesse**: fierce fury. **effierced**: maddened, made more fierce.
6 **bounse**: thump; cf. 13.7.
7 **entred**] decked *1590*; defended by Collier (1862) on the ground that in her beauty Britomart adorned the room.
8 **vtmost**: outermost. **formest**: foremost.

Stanza 28
2 **of great maiesty**: i.e. befitting a sovereign.
3 **nere**: presumably tightly-woven.
4–7 In contrast to Medua's dress in which the silver metal was hidden yet 'Bewrayd it selfe, to let men plainely wot, / It was no mortall worke, that seem'd and yet was not' (IV xi 45. 8–9); cf. the false art of the Bower of Bliss, II xii 58.9. **vnwares**: unexpectedly.
8 **discolourd**: variously coloured.
9 The line's movement measures the snake's length. Lewis (1936) 329 notes its sinister suggestion.

Stanza 25
On the numerous analogues to the hero who penetrates the enchanted fire-barring entrance into a forbidden castle, see note to stanzas 7–25. Here Britomart overcomes the flames that

29

And in those Tapets weren fashioned
   Many faire pourtraicts, and many a faire feate,
   And all of loue, and all of lusty-hed,
   As seemed by their semblaunt did entreat;
   And eke all *Cupids* warres they did repeate,
   And cruell battels, which he whilome fought
   Gainst all the Gods, to make his empire great;
   Besides the huge massacres, which he wrought
On mighty kings and kesars, into thraldome brought.

30

Therein was writ, how often thundring *Ioue*
   Had felt the point of his hart-percing dart,
   And leauing heauens kingdome, here did roue
   In straunge disguize, to slake his scalding smart;
   Now like a Ram, faire *Helle* to peruart,
   Now like a Bull, *Europa* to withdraw:
   Ah, how the fearefull Ladies tender hart
   Did liuely seeme to tremble, when she saw
The huge seas vnder her t'obay her seruaunts law.

31

Soone after that into a golden showre
   Him selfe he chaung'd faire *Danaë* to vew,
   And through the roofe of her strong brasen towre
   Did raine into her lap an hony dew,
   The whiles her foolish garde, that little knew
   Of such deceipt, kept th'yron dore fast bard,
   And watcht, that none should enter nor issew;
   Vaine was the watch, and bootlesse all the ward,
Whenas the God to golden hew him selfe transfard.

32

Then was he turnd into a snowy Swan,
   To win faire *Leda* to his louely trade:
   O wondrous skill, and sweet wit of the man,
   That her in daffadillies sleeping made,
   From scorching heat her daintie limbes to shade:
   Whiles the proud Bird ruffing his fethers wyde,
   And brushing his faire brest, did her inuade;
   She slept, yet twixt her eyelids closely spyde,
How towards her he rusht, and smiled at his pryde.

Stanzas 29–46
These tapestries copy the embroidered web that Arachne wove when she challenged Minerva in the art of weaving (Ovid, *Met*. vi 103–28). Further examples are supplied from mythological handbooks and dictionaries, and possibly contemporary tapestries. Fowler (1964) 150–3 discovers a numerological pattern similar to that in the masque of Cupid (see xii 7–25n) in the total of thirty-three gods and lovers: Jupiter or **Ioue** and his twelve loves (30–35); **Cupid** with **Phœbus** and his five loves (36–39); and various gods and their loves numbering thirteen (41–45). In Ovid, the order of the gods and the number of stories is: Jove (9), Neptune (6), Phœbus (4), Bacchus (1) and Saturn (1). S. varies and extends this order, but keeps much the same emphasis: Jove (12), Phœbus (8), Neptune (5), Saturn (1), Bacchus (1), Mars (1), and unnamed nymphs. Thompson (1972) analyses the rhetorical devices by which S. seeks to move the reader to share his response to the artistry of the tapestries.

Stanza 29
1 **Tapets**: tapestries.
2 **pourtraicts**: pictures, designs.
4 **entreat**: treat.
5–7 In his war against the gods, **Cupid** acts as another Titan; cf. 22.8–9. **repeate**: celebrate; recount.

Stanza 30
1 **writ**: drawn, i.e. woven.
5 Lotspeich (1932) 68 explains this version of the myth by noting that Ovid identifies the ram which bore **Helle** across the Hellespont with the constellation Aries (*Fasti* iii 851–76), and that Boccaccio associates the influence of Aries with Jove as a lover (*Gen. Deor.* IV lxviii). **peruart**: turn away, both literally and morally.
6 The **Bull** is the zodiacal sign that follows the **Ram**; see V Proem 5.6–9, VII vii 32–33; hence the paralleling of 5 and 6.
8 **liuely**: lifelike.
9 **seruaunts**: lover's.

Stanza 31
Ovid, *Met.* vi 113, notes simply that Jupiter *aureus ut Danaen . . . luserit*. The details of S.'s expansion may be drawn from Comes (1616) VII xviii p. 422, as Lotspeich (1932) 52 claims; or from Stephanus, as Starnes and Talbert (1955) 85 claim.
1 **Soone after**: i.e. in another part of the tapestry.
3 **brasen**: leads to **yron dore** (6) and **golden hew** (9).
4 **hony dew**: 'an ideally sweet or luscious substance; often like dew, represented as falling' (*OED* 2).
9 **hew**: shape. **transfard**: i.e. transformed; or transferred into another body; cf. 'transmoue' (43.5).

Stanza 32
2 **louely trade**: amorous dealings.
3 **wit**: ingenuity. The **sweet wit** is S.'s as he expands Ovid's six words (*Met.* vi 109) into six lines.
6–7 **ruffing**: ruffling; bristling in desire, as **pryde** suggests. **brushing**: preening itself in (sexual) pride. **inuade**: in the Lat. sense, 'enter'.
9 The smile conveys her **pryde** at his. The term itself alludes to a bird preening itself, here in desire. Cf. the passive Cymochles, II v 34.4–9.

33

Then shewd it, how the *Thebane Semelee*
　　Deceiu'd of gealous *Iuno*, did require
　　To see him in his soueraigne maiestee,
　　Armd with his thunderbolts and lightning fire,
　　Whence dearely she with death bought her desire.
　　But faire *Alcmena* better match did make,
　　Ioying his loue in likenesse more entire;
　　Three nights in one, they say, that for her sake
He then did put, her pleasures lenger to partake.

34

Twise was he seene in soaring Eagles shape,
　　And with wide wings to beat the buxome ayre,
　　Once, when he with *Asterie* did scape,
　　Againe, when as the *Troiane* boy so faire
　　He snatcht from *Ida* hill, and with him bare;
　　Wondrous delight it was, there to behould,
　　How the rude Shepheards after him did stare,
　　Trembling through feare, least down he fallen should,
And often to him calling, to take surer hould.

35

In *Satyres* shape *Antiopa* he snatcht:
　　And like a fire, when he *Aegin'* assayd:
　　A shepheard, when *Mnemosyne* he catcht:
　　And like a Serpent to the *Thracian* mayd.
　　Whiles thus on earth great *Ioue* these pageaunts playd,
　　The winged boy did thrust into his throne,
　　And scoffing, thus vnto his mother sayd,
　　Lo now the heauens obey to me alone,
And take me for their *Ioue*, whiles *Ioue* to earth is gone.

36

And thou, faire *Phœbus*, in thy colours bright
　　Wast there enwouen, and the sad distresse,
　　In which that boy thee plonged, for despight,
　　That thou bewray'dst his mothers wantonnesse,
　　When she with *Mars* was meynt in ioyfulnesse:
　　For thy he thrild thee with a leaden dart,
　　To loue faire *Daphne*, which thee loued lesse:
　　Lesse she thee lou'd, then was thy iust desart,
Yet was thy loue her death, and her death was thy smart.

37

So louedst thou the lusty *Hyacinct*,
　　So louedst thou the faire *Coronis* deare:
　　Yet both are of thy haplesse hand extinct,
　　Yet both in flowres do liue, and loue thee beare,
　　The one a *Paunce*, the other a sweet breare:
　　For griefe whereof, ye mote haue liuely seene
　　The God himselfe rending his golden heare,
　　And breaking quite his gyrlond euer greene,
With other signes of sorrow and impatient teene.

38

Both for those two, and for his owne deare sonne,
　　The sonne of *Climene* he did repent,
　　Who bold to guide the charet of the Sunne,
　　Himselfe in thousand peeces fondly rent,
　　And all the world with flashing fier brent;
　　So like, that all the walles did seeme to flame.
　　Yet cruell *Cupid*, not herewith content,
　　Forst him eftsoones to follow other game,
And loue a Shepheards daughter for his dearest Dame.

Stanza 33
1–5　Ovid, *Met*. iii 253–309; Comes (1616) V xiii.
require: request.
6–9　Ovid, *Met*. vi 112; Comes VI i.　**entire**: perfect,
containing all that is desirable. He appeared to Alcmena in the
likeness of her husband and to Semele in his own likeness as a
god. Comes allows him the extra night.

Stanza 34
2　**buxome**: yielding, unresisting.
3　Cf. Ovid, *Met*. vi 108.
4–9　Virgil, *Aen*. v 252–7, places Jove's rape of Ganymede
on Mount Ida, and includes details of the guardians pleading
with outstretched hands. Comes (1616) IX xiii relates that Jove
himself in the form of an eagle stole Ganymede.

Stanza 35
1–4　Follows Ovid's order, *Met*. vi 110–4, omitting Alcmena
and Danae because they are cited earlier.
5　**pageaunts**: cf. v 1.2.

Stanza 36
4–9　According to Ovid, *Met*. iv 171–97, Apollo was
punished for revealing Venus's adultery to Vulcan by being
made to dote upon Leucothoe. For her, S. substitutes his first
love, Daphne (*Met*. i 452–76). In Ovid, Apollo is struck by
Cupid's golden dart; S. substitutes the **leaden dart** which
signifies unhappy love. See 48.4.　**meynt**: joined in sexual
intercourse.　**For thy**: therefore.　**thrild**: pierced.
lesse: too little; a Latinism.
9　Yet . . . **smart**: stands as a motto to Cupid's wars.

Stanza 37
1　Ovid, *Met*. x 162–219. Cf. vi 45.3–4.　**lusty**: beautiful.
2　Ovid, *Met*. ii 542–632. In Ovid, the laurel garland falls
from his head when he learns of her unchastity.
5　**Paunce**: the pansy. A purple flower, like the hyacinth;
see *Met*. xiii 394–8.　**sweet breare**: not in Ovid.
6　**liuely**: lifelike.

Stanza 38
2　**sonne of Climene**: Phaethon; see I iv 9 *n*.
4　**fondly rent**: i.e. was torn because he foolishly wished to
guide the sun's chariot.
6　**like**: lifelike.

39

He loued *Isse* for his dearest Dame,
  And for her sake her cattell fed a while,
  And for her sake a cowheard vile became,
  The seruant of *Admetus* cowheard vile,
  Whiles that from heauen he suffered exile.
  Long were to tell each other louely fit,
  Now like a Lyon, hunting after spoile,
  Now like a Stag, now like a faulcon flit:
All which in that faire arras was most liuely writ.

40

Next vnto him was *Neptune* pictured,
  In his diuine resemblance wondrous lyke:
  His face was rugged, and his hoarie hed
  Dropped with brackish deaw; his three-forkt Pyke
  He stearnly shooke, and therewith fierce did stryke
  The raging billowes, that on euery syde
  They trembling stood, and made a long broad dyke,
  That his swift charet might haue passage wyde,
Which foure great *Hippodames* did draw in temewise tyde.

41

His sea-horses did seeme to snort amayne,
  And from their nosethrilles blow the brynie streame,
  That made the sparckling waues to smoke agayne,
  And flame with gold, but the white fomy creame,
  Did shine with siluer, and shoot forth his beame.
  The God himselfe did pensiue seeme and sad,
  And hong adowne his head, as he did dreame:
  For priuy loue his brest empierced had,
Ne ought but deare *Bisaltis* ay could make him glad.

42

He loued eke *Iphimedia* deare,
  And *Aeolus* faire daughter *Arne* hight,
  For whom he turnd him selfe into a Steare,
  And fed on fodder, to beguile her sight.
  Also to win *Deucalions* daughter bright,
  He turnd him selfe into a Dolphin fayre;
  And like a winged horse he tooke his flight,
  To snaky-locke *Medusa* to repayre,
On whom he got faire *Pegasus*, that flitteth in the ayre.

43

Next *Saturne* was, (but who would euer weene,
  That sullein *Saturne* euer weend to loue?
  Yet loue is sullein, and *Saturnlike* seene,
  As he did for *Erigone* it proue,)
  That to a *Centaure* did him selfe transmoue.
  So prou'd it eke that gracious God of wine,
  When for to compasse *Philliras* hard loue,
  He turnd himselfe into a fruitfull vine,
And into her faire bosome made his grapes decline.

44

Long were to tell the amorous assayes,
  And gentle pangues, with which he maked meeke
  The mighty *Mars*, to learne his wanton playes:
  How oft for *Venus*, and how often eek
  For many other Nymphes he sore did shreek,
  With womanish teares, and with vnwarlike smarts,
  Priuily moystening his horrid cheek,
  There was he painted full of burning darts,
And many wide woundes launched through his inner parts.

Stanza 39

1–5 Two stories about Apollo are combined: (*a*) his disguise as a shepherd to trick **Isse**, daughter of Macareus (*Met*. vi 124); and (*b*) 'Apollo, being exiled out of heaven by Jupiter, came for reliefe [to **Admetus**] and kept his cattel' (Cooper, 1565). Chaucer, *Troilus and Criseyde* i 663–4, refers to his love for 'the doughter of the kynge Amete'. **Admetus** is a shepherd in Comes (1616) IV x; or he may be called **cowheard vile** because he allowed his wife to descend into hell in his place.
6 **louely fit**: amorous passion.
7–8 Ovid, *Met*. vi 123, mentions Phœbus's transformations into a hawk and a lion.
Stag] sugg. Jortin (1734), in place of 'Hag' *1590, 1596*, is supported by Comes IV x; applied to any male animal in its prime.

Stanzas 40–41
The sketch for this picture of **Neptune** is found in Homer, *Iliad* xiii 23–31, and Virgil, *Aen*. i 145–56, v 817–24. In Homer, the god wears gold; Virgil avoids description to comment on the effect of his appearance; in S., the god appears like the water he rules.

Stanza 40
9 **Hippodames**: the hippocamp or hippopotamus. Perhaps a humorous variation of 'hippotame', the sixteenth-century spelling. **in temewise**: as a team.

Stanza 41
1 **amayne**: with all their might.
9 Cf. Ovid, *Met*. vi 117.

Stanza 42
S. expands Ovid, *Met*. vi 115–20, perhaps by consulting Regius's commentary, as Lotspeich (1932) 80 suggests.
7–9 **snaky-locke**: indicates **Medusa**'s punishment for defiling Minerva's temple when she was ravished there by Neptune, *Met*. iv 798–803.

Stanza 43
Upton (1758) suggests that Erigone and Philyra have reversed their proper places through the fault of the printer. Their stories are juxtaposed in *Met*. vi 125–6.
1 **weene**: suppose.
2 **sullein**: a characterizing epithet; see II ix 52.8–9*n*.
weend: was minded.
5 **Centaure**: a type of lust (being half horse). **transmoue**: transform, literally move into another; cf. 31.9.
6 **gracious**: attractive.

Stanza 44
1 **assayes**: assaults.
7 **horrid**: rough, bristling.

45

Ne did he spare (so cruell was the Elfe)
   His owne deare mother, (ah why should he so?)
   Ne did he spare sometime to pricke himselfe,
   That he might tast the sweet consuming woe,
   Which he had wrought to many others moe.
   But to declare the mournfull Tragedyes,
   And spoiles, wherewith he all the ground did strow,
   More eath to number, with how many eyes
High heauen beholds sad louers nightly theeuereyes.

46

Kings Queenes, Lords Ladies, Knights and Damzels gent
   Were heap'd together with the vulgar sort,
   And mingled with the raskall rablement,
   Without respect of person or of port,
   To shew Dan *Cupids* powre and great effort:
   And round about a border was entrayld,
   Of broken bowes and arrowes shiuered short,
   And a long bloudy riuer through them rayld,
So liuely and so like, that liuing sence it fayld.

47

And at the vpper end of that faire rowme,
   There was an Altar built of pretious stone,
   Of passing valew, and of great renowme,
   On which there stood an Image all alone,
   Of massy gold, which with his owne light shone;
   And wings it had with sundry colours dight,
   More sundry colours, then the proud *Pauone*
   Beares in his boasted fan, or *Iris* bright,
When her discolourd bow she spreds through heauen bright.

48

Blindfold he was, and in his cruell fist
   A mortall bow and arrowes keene did hold,
   With which he shot at randon, when him list,
   Some headed with sad lead, some with pure gold;
   (Ah man beware, how thou those darts behold)
   A wounded Dragon vnder him did ly,
   Whose hideous tayle his left foot did enfold,
   And with a shaft was shot through either eye,
That no man forth might draw, ne no man remedye.

Stanza 45

1   **Elfe**: a supernatural being or spirit, more malignant than playful.
7   **ground**: earth; also the tapestry.
8–9   A close rendering of Ariosto, *Orl. Fur.* xiv 99.7–8. See IV xi 53.1–2*n*.   **eath**: easy.

Stanza 46

1   **gent**: noble, gentle.
2   **sort**: company.
4   **port**: social position.
5   **effort**: strength.
6   **entrayld**: entwined; describes work that is fretted or carved, here woven.
7   Evidently tokens of broken love; see 52.6*n*. As the weapons of Diana, *virginis arma*, see Wind (1967) 78.
8   **bloudy riuer**: associated with the death of Adonis, e.g. in Lucian, *The Goddesse of Surrye* 8 (Loeb edn iv 347).   **rayld**: flowed.
9   **like**: lifelike.   **fayld**: deceived; caused to fail.

Stanza 47

5   **massy**: solid.
6   **dight**: adorned.
7–9   Both comparisons suggest that Cupid's wings are spread wide, as on Scudamour's shield (IV i 39.3). Cf. Cupid in *S.C.* March 80, 'With spotted winges like Peacocks trayne'. **Pauone**: Ital. peacock.   **discolourd**: many-coloured. **heauen bright**: 'heauens hight', sugg. Church (1758) as 'more suitable to the phenomenon of the rainbow'. Also it avoids the duplicated rhyme.

Stanza 48

On the blindfold Cupid, see Panofsky (1962) 95f.
4   As Ovid, *Met.* i 470–1. These arrows are interpreted by E.K. in his gloss to *S.C.* March 79 as 'both pleasure for the gracious and loued, and sorow for the louer that is disdayned or forsaken'.   **sad**: heavy; causing sorrow.
6–9   The **Dragon** guardian of chastity protects the golden fruit of the Hesperian tree. It accompanies the virgin goddess Minerva; see Alciati's emblem, *Custodiendas virgines*, reproduced in Aptekar (1969) 102. As a symbol of vigilance, see Tervarent (1958) 149. For a general discussion, see Lewis (1967) 22–4, and Aptekar 102–3. Here the dragon is blinded and so unable to guard chastity against the arrows of love which shoot **at randon** (3). Its tail placed over Cupid's left foot suggests their alliance. MacIntyre (1966) suggests that the triumphant Cupid is the prisoner of his victim, held by the weaker foot: 'This detail, absent in Alciati, suggests the inextricability of blind love and want of wisdom.' Cupid and the **Dragon** are associated, as they are in the story of Cupid and Psyche: see Apuleius, *The Golden Ass* (trans. Adlington 1566) 106–8. That the dragon's wound is incurable suggests that Amoret's later healing will not last long.

49

And vnderneath his feet was written thus,
Vnto the Victor of the Gods this bee:
And all the people in that ample hous
Did to that image bow their humble knee,
And oft committed fowle Idolatree.
That wondrous sight faire *Britomart* amazed,
Ne seeing could her wonder satisfie,
But euermore and more vpon it gazed,
The whiles the passing brightnes her fraile sences dazed.

50

Tho as she backward cast her busie eye,
To search each secret of that goodly sted,
Ouer the dore thus written she did spye
Be bold: she oft and oft it ouer-red,
Yet could not find what sence it figured:
But what so euer therein or writ or ment,
She was no whit thereby discouraged
From prosecuting of her first intent,
But forward with bold steps into the next roome went.

51

Much fairer, then the former, was that roome,
And richlier by many partes arayd:
For not with arras made in painefull loome,
But with pure gold it all was ouerlayd,
Wrought with wilde Antickes, which their follies playd,
In the rich metall, as they liuing were:
A thousand monstrous formes therein were made,
Such as false loue doth oft vpon him weare,
For loue in thousand monstrous formes doth oft appeare.

52

And all about, the glistring walles were hong
With warlike spoiles, and with victorious prayes,
Of mighty Conquerours and Captaines strong,
Which were whilome captiued in their dayes
To cruell loue, and wrought their owne decayes:
Their swerds and speres were broke, and hauberques rent;
And their proud girlonds of tryumphant bayes
Troden in dust with fury insolent,
To shew the victors might and mercilesse intent.

53

The warlike Mayde beholding earnestly
The goodly ordinance of this rich place,
Did greatly wonder, ne could satisfie
Her greedy eyes with gazing a long space,
But more she meruaild that no footings trace,
Nor wight appear'd, but wastefull emptinesse,
And solemne silence ouer all that place:
Straunge thing it seem'd, that none was to possesse
So rich purueyance, ne them keepe with carefulnesse.

Stanza 49

6–9 Britomart re-experiences the emotion she felt when she saw Artegall in the mirror, but now she is at a further stage in her progress from virginity to married chastity. The archetype of this moment is Psyche's first vision of Cupid: 'shee greatly feared, and amazed in mind, with a pale countenance all trembling fel on her knees' (Apuleius 108). Cf. Britomart's wonder at the decorations in the second room, 53.3–5.

Stanza 50

1–4 **backward**: i.e. behind the statue rather than back to the door through which she entered the room; 'that same dore' (54.2) indicates that this door leads into the next room.
sted: place.

9 At the outset of her quest, Britomart's love which guides her is called 'bold and blind' (iv 9.9). She meets such love in the blindfold Cupid, who is a victor over the gods. At the beginning of the episode, she is called 'the bold Virgin' (13.8); now she obeys the motto on the door as she enters the second room **with bold steps**. For Scudamour's corresponding boldness, which requires her present boldness, see IV x 4.6n, 54.2n.

Stanzas 51–53

The first two rooms are complementary, as Fowler (1970) 48–9 argues: 'They treat the same subjects differently, the second room being conceived on a more human and personal scale. . . . The first room was populous [cf. 49.3], but this is appropriately deserted, the scene of the ritual of a private, inner tragedy.' Further, there is a change from bestial lust, which busily seeks to satisfy desire, to cruel and despairing love that ends in suicide. The first shows love's strength, the second its weakness. In contrast to the tapestries, the bas-relief seems both more outwardly realistic and inwardly psychological.

Stanza 51

2 **by many partes**: i.e. by many times.
3 **made in painefull loome**: made painstakingly.
4–6 These figures seem to be embossed or in bas-relief. **Antickes**: fantastic figures, the product of fancy. **playd**: acted out.
7–9 Lewis (1967) 27 suggests that these lines further clarify the significance of the metamorphoses in the tapestries. The **monstrous formes** refer to Love's 'strange aray, / Disguiz'd in thousand shapes' (vi 11.8–9) when he wanders in the world. Cf. 'loue [is] a monster fell' (II iv 35.3).

Stanza 52

2 **prayes**: booty.
5 **decayes**: downfall; implying suicide. Moral responsibility is their own, as in the house of Pride (I v 51.9).
6 Corresponding to the bows and arrows in the tapestries, 46.7.

Stanza 53

1 **warlike Mayde**: links her with the warriors just mentioned; cf. 18.2.
2 **ordinance**: warlike equipment.
6 **wastefull**: uninhabited.
7 Cf. the house of Orgoglio: 'There raignd a solemne silence ouer all' (I viii 29.8).
9 **purueyance**: array, furnishings.

54

And as she lookt about, she did behold,
How ouer that same dore was likewise writ,
Be bold, be bold, and euery where *Be bold*,
That much she muz'd, yet could not construe it
By any ridling skill, or commune wit,
At last she spyde at that roomes vpper end,
Another yron dore, on which was writ,
Be not too bold; whereto though she did bend
Her earnest mind, yet wist not what it might intend.

55

Thus she there waited vntill euentyde,
Yet liuing creature none she saw appeare :
And now sad shadowes gan the world to hyde,
From mortall vew, and wrap in darkenesse dreare;
Yet nould she d'off her weary armes, for feare
Of secret daunger, ne let sleepe oppresse
Her heauy eyes with natures burdein deare,
But drew her selfe aside in sickernesse,
And her welpointed weapons did about her dresse.

Cant. XII.

*The maske of Cupid, and th'enchaunted
Chamber are displayd.
Whence Britomart redeemes faire
Amoret, through charmes decayd.*

1

THo when as chearelesse Night ycouered had
Faire heauen with an vniuersall cloud,
That euery wight dismayd with darknesse sad,
In silence and in sleepe themselues did shroud,
She heard a shrilling Trompet sound aloud,
Signe of nigh battell, or got victory ;
Nought therewith daunted was her courage proud,
But rather stird to cruell enmity,
Expecting euer, when some foe she might descry.

2

With that, an hideous storme of winde arose,
With dreadfull thunder and lightning atwixt,
And an earth-quake, as if it streight would lose
The worlds foundations from his centre fixt;
A direfull stench of smoke and sulphure mixt
Ensewd, whose noyance fild the fearefull sted,
From the fourth houre of night vntill the sixt;
Yet the bold *Britonesse* was nought ydred,
Though much emmou'd, but stedfast still perseuered.

Stanza 54
Shakespeare's reference in *Much Ado* I i 186 to a line in the
'old tale' of Bluebeard establishes its provenance in the
Renaissance. According to the English nursery tale version, the
Lady Mary visited the home of her suitor, the mysterious Mr
Fox, and saw written over the portal of the hall, 'Be bold, be
bold – but not too bold, lest that your heart's blood should run
cold.' When she opened the door, she found the room filled
with skeletons and tubs of blood of his former brides. Earlier
editors, such as Collier, note S.'s use of the story. See E. B.
Fowler (1921) 56 and Briggs (1964) 171. The sexual significance
of the yron dore (7) gives **bold** the sense of 'immodest'. More
relevant, however, are the wider significances of the symbolic
threshold over which the hero must pass in order to be
initiated into his role. Britomart obeys Merlin's injunction at
the beginning of her quest: 'let no whit thee dismay / The hard
begin, that meets thee in the dore, / And with sharpe fits thy
tender hart oppresseth sore' (iii 21.7–9). That she will ignore the
injunction, **Be not too bold**, is shown by her resolution to
'try extremities of chaunce' (24.8). Hill (1971) interprets the
inscriptions in the light of Ovid's myth of Venus and Adonis
(*Met.* x 614–31). Venus warns Adonis to 'bee bold' in hunting
small game but warns him to 'forbeare too bold to bee' in
hunting the boar (trans. Golding).
5   **commune wit**: common sense.
9   **intend**: mean.

Stanza 55
5   **nould**: would not.
8   **sickernesse**: security.
9   **welpointed**: ready at hand; sharp, as 25.3.   **dresse**:
make ready.

Canto xii

Argument
1   **maske**: the form of masque in which emblematic figures
remain mute, as in a dumb show; see 7–25*n*. Cf. 'that mask of
loue' (IV i 3.6).
4   **decayd**: physically wasted away.

Stanza 1
8   **cruell**: fierce.
9   **Expecting euer**: waiting always.

Stanza 2
1–6   These details herald the appearance of the god of love,
as in 1 Kings 19.11–2, the appearance of God is accompanied
by strong wind, earthquake and fire, and in Exod. 19.16–8
by thunder, lightning, thick cloud, 'the sound of the trumpet
exceding loude', and smoke. Cf. 37.1–2. The smoke and
sulphur suggest hell-fire; cf. xi 21.6–7.
2   **atwixt**: i.e. accompanying the wind.
4   **centre fixt**: fixed centre.
6   **noyance**: annoyance.   **fild**: also defiled.   **sted**: place.
7   Night was divided into four watches, each of three hours,
beginning at 6 p.m. See, e.g. Geneva gloss to Matt. 14.25,
and the four divisions at Mark 13.35. Hence the masque begins
at midnight; cf. 29.6. In the Castle of Malecasta, Britomart
is tested at midnight: see i 57.6–9.
8   **bold**: as the inscription (xi 54.3) demands; cf. 29.8 and
see xi 50.9*n*.
9   **perseuered**: remained.

3

All suddenly a stormy whirlwind blew
  Throughout the house, that clapped euery dore,
  With which that yron wicket open flew,
  As it with mightie leuers had bene tore :
  And forth issewd, as on the ready flore
  Of some Theatre, a graue personage,
  That in his hand a branch of laurell bore,
  With comely haueour and count'nance sage,
Yclad in costly garments, fit for tragicke Stage.

4

Proceeding to the midst, he still did stand,
  As if in mind he somewhat had to say,
  And to the vulgar beckning with his hand,
  In signe of silence, as to heare a play,
  By liuely actions he gan bewray
  Some argument of matter passioned ;
  Which doen, he backe retyred soft away,
  And passing by, his name discouered,
Ease, on his robe in golden letters cyphered.

5

The noble Mayd, still standing all this vewd,
  And merueild at his strange intendiment ;
  With that a ioyous fellowship issewd
  Of Minstrals, making goodly meriment,
  With wanton Bardes, and Rymers impudent,
  All which together sung full chearefully
  A lay of loues delight, with sweet concent :
  After whom marcht a iolly company,
In manner of a maske, enranged orderly.

6

The whiles a most delitious harmony,
  In full straunge notes was sweetly heard to sound,
  That the rare sweetnesse of the melody
  The feeble senses wholly did confound,
  And the fraile soule in deepe delight nigh dround :
  And when it ceast, shrill trompets loud did bray,
  That their report did farre away rebound,
  And when they ceast, it gan againe to play,
The whiles the maskers marched forth in trim aray.

Stanza 3
Fowler (1970) 53 links this whirlwind that penetrates
Throughout the house and opens **that yron wicket** with
Amoret's wound (stanza 20) to suggest that her horror is
occasioned by sexual penetration.
2 **clapped** : slammed.
3 **that yron wicket** : 'yron dore' (xi 54.7).
5 **ready** : i.e. awaiting the performance, applied to the stage
and to the audience, here Britomart, who is 'Expecting euer'

(1.9).
8 **haueour** : bearing.

Stanza 4
2 **somewhat** : something.
3 **vulgar** : the groundlings.
4 **as to heare a play** : he uses the gesture, instead of
speech, to invoke silence.
6 **argument** : subject or theme of the dumb show which he
introduces. **passioned** : expressing passion.
9 **Ease** presents the spectacle as Idleness leads the pageant
of the sins in the house of Pride (I iv 18–20). In the
Romance of the Rose 531f, Idleness admits the lover into the
garden of mirth. **cyphered** : written.

Stanza 5
2 **intendiment** : purpose, intent.
3 **fellowship** : company.
5 **impudent** : shameless.
7 **concent**] consent *1596* : harmony ; also yielding to love as
'consent' indicates.
9 **enranged** : arranged.

Stanza 6
7 **rebound** : re-echo.

Stanzas 7–25
E. B. Fowler (1921) 108–31 shows that the masque combines
the medieval processional form of the Court of Love with his
followers and victims and the Renaissance Triumph in which
Cupid displays his spoils. Walton (1960) relates the masque
to Renaissance theatrical practices. Twelve was the favourite
number of masquers, as E. B. Fowler 124 notes. Arranged in
six couples, they provide an anatomy of love in the progression
of love's effects. Each masquer bears an emblem and (except
for the final pair) wears appropriate clothing. Together they
present the stages of Britomart's love for Artegall. Grellner
(1968) 40 claims that 'the Mask is to Britomart not only a
summation of her psychological development thus far, but also
a foreshadowing and cautionary prefiguration of emotional
upsets yet to come'. Roche (1964) 78 notes that 'the first six
couples present the progress of an allegorical courtship in terms
of medieval and Renaissance love psychology'. He sees the first
hint of any ambiguity in **Daunger** (11.1) after whom the
descriptions are 'both sonnet conventions and visions of the
horrors of love, depending on whether we read them from the
man's or woman's point of view'. Fowler (1964) 148–50 notes
the contrast between the orderly grouping of characters that
precede Cupid and the hurried confusion that follows him as a
contrast between 'earlier and later stages of a sexual relationship ;
the later stages showing the cruel and chaotic effects of Cupid
at his most despotic'. On the numerical pattern, Fowler
observes that Cupid is at the centre of the masquers, as he
should be in a triumph, and also at the centre of his own party.
Cf. xi 29–46*n*. Ease (4.9) and the twelve named masquers
(excluding the unnamed 'Minstrals . . . Bardes, and Rymers'
[5.4–5] who lead the masque) form a party of thirteen described
in thirteen stanzas (4, 7–18). Amoret is the thirteenth in a
group of three, described in three stanzas (19–21), followed by
Cupid (22–23), three figures who are described (24) and thirteen
who are catalogued (25). On the numerical significance of this
13/3/Cupid/3/13 grouping, see Fowler (1970) 52. He notes that
the total, 33, symbolizes false chastity.

413

7

The first was *Fancy*, like a louely boy,
  Of rare aspect, and beautie without peare;
  Matchable either to that ympe of *Troy*,
  Whom *Ioue* did loue, and chose his cup to beare,
  Or that same daintie lad, which was so deare
  To great *Alcides*, that when as he dyde,
  He wailed womanlike with many a teare,
  And euery wood, and euery valley wyde
He fild with *Hylas* name; the Nymphes eke *Hylas* cryde.

8

His garment neither was of silke nor say,
  But painted plumes, in goodly order dight,
  Like as the sunburnt *Indians* do aray
  Their tawney bodies, in their proudest plight:
  As those same plumes, so seemd he vaine and light,
  That by his gate might easily appeare;
  For still he far'd as dauncing in delight,
  And in his hand a windy fan did beare,
That in the idle aire he mou'd still here and there.

9

And him beside marcht amorous *Desyre*,
  Who seemd of riper yeares, then th'other Swaine,
  Yet was that other swayne this elders syre,
  And gaue him being, commune to them twaine:
  His garment was disguised very vaine,
  And his embrodered Bonet sat awry;
  Twixt both his hands few sparkes he close did straine,
  Which still he blew, and kindled busily,
That soone they life conceiu'd, and forth in flames did fly.

10

Next after him went *Doubt*, who was yclad
  In a discolour'd cote, of straunge disguyse,
  That at his backe a brode *Capuccio* had,
  And sleeues dependant *Albanese*-wyse:
  He lookt askew with his mistrustfull eyes,
  And nicely trode, as thornes lay in his way,
  Or that the flore to shrinke he did auyse,
  And on a broken reed he still did stay
His feeble steps, which shrunke, when hard theron he lay.

11

With him went *Daunger*, cloth'd in ragged weed,
  Made of Beares skin, that him more dreadfull made,
  Yet his owne face was dreadfull, ne did need
  Straunge horrour, to deforme his griesly shade;
  A net in th'one hand, and a rustie blade
  In th'other was, this Mischiefe, that Mishap;
  With th'one his foes he threatned to inuade,
  With th'other he his friends ment to enwrap:
For whom he could not kill, he practizd to entrap.

12

Next him was *Feare*, all arm'd from top to toe,
  Yet thought himselfe not safe enough thereby,
  But feard each shadow mouing to and fro,
  And his owne armes when glittering he did spy,
  Or clashing heard, he fast away did fly,
  As ashes pale of hew, and wingyheeld;
  And euermore on daunger fixt his eye,
  Gainst whom he alwaies bent a brasen shield,
Which his right hand vnarmed fearefully did wield.

Stanza 7

1 **Fancy**: the power of the imagination to deceive with false images of love; hence 'falsed fancy' (I ii 30.3) leads the Red Cross Knight to prefer Duessa to Una. Also it signifies love of a capricious, casual and wanton nature. When Britomart first sees Artegall, she is left 'full of fancies fraile' (ii 27.5; cf. 48.8–9, iv 5.7–9).
3 **that ympe of Troy**: Ganymede; see xi 34.4–9.
5–9 **that same daintie lad**: Hylas loved by Hercules. When he was drowned, Hercules 'lefte the Argonautes, and went over all Mysia seekyng and criyng for Hylas' (Cooper, 1565).

Stanza 8

1 **say**: a cloth of fine texture; worn by Envy, I iv 31.1.
3 **the sunburnt Indians**: of North America.
4 **plight**: attire.
7 **far'd**: conducted himself.
8–9 The fan gives **Fancy** his attribute by means of a pun. **windy**: causing wind; suggesting vain.   **idle**: empty; or the adv. idly.

Stanza 9

1–3 **Desyre** seems older than Fancy, although Fancy is his father.
5 **disguised very vaine**: fantastically or foolishly designed.
7 **straine**: clasp.

Stanzas 10–11

Doubt and **Daunger** oppose Scudamour in his courtship of Amoret, IV x 12, 16–17.

Stanza 10

2 **discolour'd**: many-coloured.   **disguyse**: fashion.
3 **Capuccio**: Ital. hood; an emblem of Fraud (see Chew, 1962, 341). Perhaps suggested by **disguyse**.
4 **dependant Albanese-wyse**: hanging down in Albanian fashion (?). The reference may be to the alb, a tunic of white cloth hanging down to the feet. S. has a note on the 'manche' or hanging sleeve in *View* 61.
6 **nicely**: cautiously.
7 **shrinke**: give way.   **auyse**: perceive.
8–9 'Lo, thou trustest now in this broken staffe of rede . . . on which if a man leane, it wil go into his hand' (2 Kings 18.21). **stay**: support.   **shrunke**: collapsed.

Stanza 11

1 **Daunger**: power to hurt, expressed through his offensive weapons of force and fraud.
2 On the bear's sexual significance, see Rowland (1973) 32–3.
4 **Straunge**: added from outside.   **shade**: image or appearance.
5–9 **Mischiefe**: evil-doing; presumably the knife.   **rustie**: red with blood.   **inuade**: attack.   **practizd**: plotted.

Stanza 12

8 Cf. the brazen shield borne by Atin, II iv 38.1.   **bent**: turned.
9 He carries his shield on his sword arm to defend himself.

13

With him went *Hope* in rancke, a handsome Mayd,
  Of chearefull looke and louely to behold;
  In silken samite she was light arayd,
  And her faire lockes were wouen vp in gold;
  She alway smyld, and in her hand did hold
  An holy water Sprinckle, dipt in deowe,
  With which she sprinckled fauours manifold,
  On whom she list, and did great liking sheowe,
Great liking vnto many, but true loue to feowe.

14

And after them *Dissemblance*, and *Suspect*
  Marcht in one rancke, yet an vnequall paire:
  For she was gentle, and of milde aspect,
  Courteous to all, and seeming debonaire,
  Goodly adorned, and exceeding faire:
  Yet was that all but painted, and purloynd,
  And her bright browes were deckt with borrowed haire:
  Her deedes were forged, and her words false coynd,
And alwaies in her hand two clewes of silke she twynd.

15

But he was foule, ill fauoured, and grim,
  Vnder his eyebrowes looking still askaunce;
  And euer as *Dissemblance* laught on him,
  He lowrd on her with daungerous eyeglaunce;
  Shewing his nature in his countenance;
  His rolling eyes did neuer rest in place,
  But walkt each where, for feare of hid mischaunce,
  Holding a lattice still before his face,
Through which he still did peepe, as forward he did pace.

16

Next him went *Griefe*, and *Fury* matcht yfere;
  Griefe all in sable sorrowfully clad,
  Downe hanging his dull head, with heauy chere,
  Yet inly being more, then seeming sad:
  A paire of Pincers in his hand he had,
  With which he pinched people to the hart,
  That from thenceforth a wretched life they lad,
  In wilfull languor and consuming smart,
Dying each day with inward wounds of dolours dart.

17

But *Fury* was full ill appareiled
  In rags, that naked nigh she did appeare,
  With ghastly lookes and dreadfull drerihed;
  For from her backe her garments she did teare,
  And from her head oft rent her snarled heare:
  In her right hand a firebrand she did tosse
  About her head, still roming here and there;
  As a dismayed Deare in chace embost,
Forgetfull of his safety, hath his right way lost.

18

After them went *Displeasure* and *Pleasance*,
  He looking lompish and full sullein sad,
  And hanging downe his heauy countenance;
  She chearefull fresh and full of ioyance glad,
  As if no sorrow she ne felt ne drad;
  That euill matched paire they seemd to bee:
  An angry Waspe th'one in a viall had
  Th'other in hers an hony-lady Bee;
Thus marched these six couples forth in faire degree.

Stanza 13
Cf. Hope, I x 14. Cf. Joy in the *Romance of the Rose* 831–64
who gives the gift of love: she is beautiful, her hair is laced
with a golden thread, and her dress is samite worked in gold.
1   **in rancke**: by his side.
3   **samite**: a rich fabric.
6–9   **Sprinckle**: an aspergillum, a brush to sprinkle holy
water.   **deowe**: traditionally associated with God's
providence.

Stanza 14
1   **Dissemblance, and Suspect**: Dissimulation and
Suspicion.
4   **debonaire**: gracious.
7   'Here, as too often in this great poem, that which is
and may be known, but cannot *appear* from the given point
of view, is confounded with the visible. It is no longer a mask-
figure, but the character, of a Dissembler' (Coleridge,
Miscellaneous Criticism, ed. Raysor, 1936, 39).
9   **clewes**: balls of thread. Cf. the clew that Archimago
unwinds to weave his web of guile (II i 8.3–4). It suggests
holding one within a maze.

Stanza 15
2   Cf. Milton's 'squint suspicion' (*Comus* 412).
3   **laught on**: i.e. in encouragement.
4   **daungerous**: severe, threatening harm.
7   **walkt each where**: moved everywhere.
8–9   Alluding to the Ital. *gelosia*, 'false window' (Florio);
or lattices through which the jealous may see without being
seen (sugg. Upton, 1758).

Stanza 16
1   **yfere**: together.
8   **languor**: woeful plight; possibly illness.

Stanza 17
Cf. Wrath, I iv 33–34, and Furor, II iv 7.
3   **drerihed**: utter wretchedness.
6   **she did tosse**: 'she tost' sugg. Church (1758) for the
rhyme. Cf. Furor's fire-brand, II v 22.5–9.   **tosse**: brandish.
8   **embost**: driven to extremity, or into the woods.

Stanza 18
2   **lompish**: dejected, low-spirited.   **sullein**: gloomy;
morose. See I ix 35.3*n*.
8   **hony-lady Bee**: either a honey-bee or honey-laden bee.
9   **faire degree**: fair order or manner; 'euill ordered' (23.4).

19

After all these there marcht a most faire Dame,
　Led of two grysie villeins, th'one *Despight*,
　The other cleped *Cruelty* by name :
　She dolefull Lady, like a dreary Spright,
　Cald by strong charmes out of eternall night,
　Had deathes owne image figurd in her face,
　Full of sad signes, fearefull to liuing sight ;
　Yet in that horror shewd a seemely grace,
And with her feeble feet did moue a comely pace.

20

Her brest all naked, as net iuory,
　Without adorne of gold or siluer bright,
　Wherewith the Craftesman wonts it beautify,
　Of her dew honour was despoyled quight,
　And a wide wound therein (O ruefull sight)
　Entrenched deepe with knife accursed keene,
　Yet freshly bleeding forth her fainting spright,
　(The worke of cruell hand) was to be seene,
That dyde in sanguine red her skin all snowy cleene.

21

At that wide orifice her trembling hart
　Was drawne forth, and in siluer basin layd,
　Quite through transfixed with a deadly dart,
　And in her bloud yet steeming fresh embayd:
　And those two villeins, which her steps vpstayd,
　When her weake feete could scarcely her sustaine,
　And fading vitall powers gan to fade,
　Her forward still with torture did constraine,
And euermore encreased her consuming paine.

22

Next after her the winged God himselfe
　Came riding on a Lion rauenous,
　Taught to obay the menage of that Elfe,
　That man and beast with powre imperious
　Subdeweth to his kingdome tyrannous :
　His blindfold eyes he bad a while vnbind,
　That his proud spoyle of that same dolorous
　Faire Dame he might behold in perfect kind;
Which seene, he much reioyced in his cruell mind.

23

Of which full proud, himselfe vp rearing hye,
　He looked round about with sterne disdaine;
　And did suruay his goodly company :
　And marshalling the euill ordered traine,
　With that the darts which his right hand did straine,
　Full dreadfully he shooke that all did quake,
　And clapt on hie his coulourd winges twaine,
　That all his many it affraide did make:
Tho blinding him againe, his way he forth did take.

Stanza 19
Roche (1964) 75 interprets **Cruelty** as 'a personification of the metaphor of the cruel mistress or cruel love so common in the sonnets' and **Despight** as derived from the medieval 'despitous' lady.
2　**grysie**: horrible, grim.
5　Referring both to the **Lady** and to the **Spright**, as Alpers (1967) 82 notes.
9　**comely**: pleasing.

Stanza 20
1　**net**: clear, pure.
2　**adorne**: adornment.
4　**dew honour**: adornment befitting her honour or chastity; its absence defines Amoret's helpless virginity. Cf. Florimell: 'In stedfast chastitie and vertue rare, / The goodly ornaments of beautie bright' (v 8.5–6).
6　**accursed**: i.e. through enchantments.

Stanza 21
Lechery bears in his hand 'a burning hart' (I iv 25.3), as Busirane forces Amoret to bear/bare her heart, for he 'ioyd weake wemens hearts to tempt and proue / If from their loyall loues he might them moue' (26.4–5); cf. 31.6–9. Gilde (1971a) 71 sees Amoret's gesture of holding out her heart as an emblem of the painful failure to reconcile chaste love and sexual passion, in contrast to the later moment when her body, joined to her lover's, becomes 'the sweet lodge of loue and deare delight' (45.4 [*1590*]).
4　**embayd**: steeped.

Stanza 22
1　**the winged God**: Cupid; cf. xi 47.6–9.
2　**riding on a Lion**: cf. Wrath (I iv 33.1–2); here noting love's rage. *S.C.* Dec. 57–8 refers to 'the raging fyre' of love in summer, 'For loue then in the Lyons house did dwell'. Cf. *H.L.* 43–9. On the emblem, see Marotti (1965) 74. Rowland (1973) 121 notes that Cupid's claim in Lucan, *Dialogue of the Gods*, that he is not afraid to climb upon the backs of lions, was used to illustrate the motto *amor vincit omnia*.
3　**menage**: manège, horsemanship.　**Elfe**: as xi 45.1.
7　**his proud spoyle**: as xi Arg. 4.
8　**in perfect kind**: in perfect manner, i.e. clearly; or, in perfect condition being wounded by him; possibly referring to the belief that woman puts on perfection in marriage.

Stanza 23
2　**sterne**: cruel, threatening.
5　**With that**: either 'whereupon' or 'with'. The syntax is confusing.　**straine**: clasp.
6　**shooke**: brandished.
8　**many**: company.

24

Behinde him was *Reproch*, *Repentance*, *Shame*;
  Reproch the first, *Shame* next, *Repent* behind:
  Repentance feeble, sorrowfull, and lame:
  Reproch despightfull, carelesse, and vnkind;
  Shame most ill fauourd, bestiall, and blind:
  Shame lowrd, *Repentance* sigh'd, *Reproch* did scould;
  Reproch sharpe stings, *Repentance* whips entwind,
  Shame burning brond-yrons in her hand did hold:
All three to each vnlike, yet all made in one mould.

25

And after them a rude confused rout
  Of persons flockt, whose names is hard to read:
  Emongst them was sterne *Strife*, and *Anger* stout,
  Vnquiet *Care*, and fond *Vnthriftihead*,
  Lewd *Losse of Time*, and *Sorrow* seeming dead,
  Inconstant *Chaunge*, and false *Disloyaltie*,
  Consuming *Riotise*, and guilty *Dread*
  Of heauenly vengeance, faint *Infirmitie*,
Vile *Pouertie*, and lastly *Death* with infamie.

26

There were full many moe like maladies,
  Whose names and natures I note readen well;
  So many moe, as there be phantasies
  In wauering wemens wit, that none can tell,
  Or paines in loue, or punishments in hell;
  All which disguized marcht in masking wise,
  About the chamber with that Damozell,
  And then returned, hauing marched thrise,
Into the inner roome, from whence they first did rise.

27

So soone as they were in, the dore streight way
  Fast locked, driuen with that stormy blast,
  Which first it opened; and bore all away.
  Then the braue Maid, which all this while was plast
  In secret shade, and saw both first and last,
  Issewed forth, and went vnto the dore,
  To enter in, but found it locked fast:
  It vaine she thought with rigorous vprore
For to efforce, when charmes had closed it afore.

28

Where force might not auaile, there sleights and art
  She cast to vse, both fit for hard emprize;
  For thy from that same roome not to depart
  Till morrow next, she did her selfe auize,
  When that same Maske againe should forth arize.
  The morrow next appeard with ioyous cheare,
  Calling men to their daily exercize,
  Then she, as morrow fresh, her selfe did reare
Out of her secret stand, that day for to out weare.

29

All that day she outwore in wandering,
    And gazing on that Chambers ornament,
    Till that againe the second euening
    Her couered with her sable vestiment,
    Wherewith the worlds faire beautie she hath blent:
    Then when the second watch was almost past,
    That brasen dore flew open, and in went
    Bold *Britomart*, as she had late forecast,
Neither of idle shewes, nor of false charmes aghast.

30

So soone as she was entred, round about
    She cast her eies, to see what was become
    Of all those persons, which she saw without:
    But lo, they streight were vanisht all and some,
    Ne liuing wight she saw in all that roome,
    Saue that same woefull Ladie, both whose hands
    Were bounden fast, that did her ill become,
    And her small wast girt round with yron bands,
Vnto a brasen pillour, by the which she stands.

31

And her before the vile Enchaunter sate,
    Figuring straunge characters of his art,
    With liuing bloud he those characters wrate,
    Dreadfully dropping from her dying hart,
    Seeming transfixed with a cruell dart,
    And all perforce to make her him to loue.
    Ah who can loue the worker of her smart?
    A thousand charmes he formerly did proue;
Yet thousand charmes could not her stedfast heart remoue.

32

Soone as that virgin knight he saw in place,
    His wicked bookes in hast he ouerthrew,
    Not caring his long labours to deface,
    And fiercely ronning to that Lady trew,
    A murdrous knife out of his pocket drew,
    The which he thought, for villeinous despight,
    In her tormented bodie to embrew:
    But the stout Damzell to him leaping light,
His cursed hand withheld, and maistered his might.

33

From her, to whom his fury first he ment,
    The wicked weapon rashly he did wrest,
    And turning to her selfe his fell intent,
    Vnwares it strooke into her snowie chest,
    That little drops empurpled her faire brest.
    Exceeding wroth therewith the virgin grew,
    Albe the wound were nothing deepe imprest,
    And fiercely forth her mortall blade she drew,
To giue him the reward for such vile outrage dew.

Stanza 29

4   **Her**: ambiguous, for it applies also to Britomart who plays a role in Cupid's pageant.

5   **blent**: obscured; confounded.

6   **the second watch**: from 9 p.m. to 12 midnight; cf. 2.7.

7   **That brasen dore**: the 'yron wicket' (3.3) or 'yron dore' (xi 54.7).

8   **forecast**: planned.

9   Cf. Milton, *Comus* 204–10: although the Lady is oppressed by 'a thousand fantasies . . . / Of calling shapes, and beckoning shadows dire', she declares that 'These thoughts may startle well, but not astound / The virtuous mind'.

Stanza 30

4   **all and some**: every one of them.

8–9   **yron bands**: cf. Florimell's golden girdle which binds her waist; cf. also '*Venus* shamefull chaine' (I ii 4.8) which binds lovers. Here it becomes the symbol of the marriage bond, whose permanence is suggested by **brasen**.   **pillour**: a phallic symbol. Amoret is bound by what she fears to what she fears.

Stanza 31

Magic could be used to secure love; its use was not condemned by Parliament until 1604. See Shakespeare, *Othello* I iii 76n in *Furness Var*.

1   **the vile Enchaunter**: so called in *L.R.*

2   Cf. Merlin 'writing strange characters in the ground' (iii 14.8). The **characters** are also linked with the tapestry in the first room, the bas-relief in the second room, and the characters in the masque.

5   **Seeming**: a key word; cf. 'Quite through transfixed' (21.3).

6   **perforce**: by force.

7   The **worker of her smart** is as much Scudamour as Busirane. Cf. *H.L.* 31–2: 'And ye faire Nimphs, which often-times haue loued / The cruell worker of your kindly smarts'. At VI x 31.6–7, love compels Calidore 'to returne againe / To his wounds worker'.

8   **charmes**: verses with magical powers.   **thousand**: cf. the 'thousand monstrous formes' (xi 51.7) of false love, and the 'thousand thoughts' of love which Britomart fashions at the first sight of her lover (iv 5.6).   **proue**: try.

Stanza 32

1   **in place**: present.

3   He does not care if he destroys **his long labours**, the charms in his books (cf. 43.9) and/or Amoret whose love he labours to win.

7   **embrew**: plunge.

Stanza 33

1   **ment**: directed.

2   **rashly**: suddenly; in a slashing manner.   **wrest**: twist.

4–7   Cf. her wounding by Gardante, i 65.5–9. She submits to Amoret's torture. Hence **imprest** also signifies 'imprinted': Busirane marks in her flesh characters that charm Amoret.

4   **Vnwares**: her state when she first sees Artegall (ii 26.4; cf. 38.9, iii 24.2).

34

So mightily she smote him, that to ground
  He fell halfe dead; next stroke him should haue slaine,
  Had not the Lady, which by him stood bound,
  Dernely vnto her called to abstaine,
  From doing him to dy. For else her paine
  Should be remedilesse, sith none but hee,
  Which wrought it, could the same recure againe.
  Therewith she stayd her hand, loth stayd to bee;
For life she him enuyde, and long'd reuenge to see.

35

And to him said, Thou wicked man, whose meed
  For so huge mischiefe, and vile villany
  Is death, or if that ought do death exceed,
  Be sure, that nought may saue thee from to dy,
  But if that thou this Dame doe presently
  Restore vnto her health, and former state;
  This doe and liue, else die vndoubtedly.
  He glad of life, that lookt for death but late,
Did yield himselfe right willing to prolong his date.

36

And rising vp, gan streight to ouerlooke
  Those cursed leaues, his charmes backe to reuerse;
  Full dreadfull things out of that balefull booke
  He red, and measur'd many a sad verse,
  That horror gan the virgins hart to perse,
  And her faire locks vp stared stiffe on end,
  Hearing him those same bloudy lines reherse;
  And all the while he red, she did extend
Her sword high ouer him, if ought he did offend.

37

Anon she gan perceiue the house to quake,
  And all the dores to rattle round about;
  Yet all that did not her dismaied make,
  Nor slacke her threatfull hand for daungers dout,
  But still with stedfast eye and courage stout
  Abode, to weet what end would come of all.
  At last that mightie chaine, which round about
  Her tender waste was wound, adowne gan fall,
And that great brasen pillour broke in peeces small.

38

The cruell steele, which thrild her dying hart,
  Fell softly forth, as of his owne accord,
  And the wyde wound, which lately did dispart
  Her bleeding brest, and riuen bowels gor'd,
  Was closed vp, as it had not bene bor'd,
  And euery part to safety full sound,
  As she were neuer hurt, was soone restor'd:
  Tho when she felt her selfe to be vnbound,
And perfect hole, prostrate she fell vnto the ground.

39

Before faire *Britomart*, she fell prostrate,
  Saying, Ah noble knight, what worthy meed
  Can wretched Lady, quit from wofull state,
  Yield you in lieu of this your gratious deed?
  Your vertue selfe her owne reward shall breed,
  Euen immortall praise, and glory wyde,
  Which I your vassall, by your prowesse freed,
  Shall through the world make to be notifyde,
And goodly well aduance, that goodly well was tryde.

Stanza 34

Britomart's restraint contrasts with Guyon's wrathful destruction of the Bower of Bliss (II xii 83). Here the feminine is freed rather than bound. See 42.3*n*.

4 Dernely: ?earnestly, ?dismally, as the dying Amavia 'dearnly cride' (II i 35.7); possibly 'secretly' so that Busirane would not hear: if he did hear, Britomart's threat at 35.4–7 would be in vain.

6 remedilesse: see I vii 51.8*n*.

7 recure: heal.

9 enuyde: begrudged.

Stanza 35

1–6 The syntax is confusing. One possible reading: 'Since you deserve worse than death, if there is anything worse, you may be sure that you are going to die unless you free Amoret.' **But if**: unless. **presently**: immediately.

9 date: term of life.

Stanza 36

1 ouerlooke: look over.

2 In Ovid, *Met.* xiv 300–1, Circe strikes her beasts with her reversed rod and retracts her charms to restore them to manhood. Sandys (1632) 654 comments: 'As *Circes* rod, waved over their heads from the right side to the left presents those false and sinister perswasions of pleasure, which so much deformes them: so the reversion thereof, by discipline, and a view of their owne deformity, restores them to their former beauties.'

4 measur'd: read through; implying also 'according to its correct metre'. **verse**: incantation or charm. **sad**: powerful; calamitous (cf. II i 55.4); ill-omened.

5–7 Now Britomart undergoes Amoret's torture by having her heart pierced with horror through hearing Busirane's charms. **vp stared**: stood up. **reherse**: say over again what he said previously to charm Amoret. In Milton, *Comus* 816, the Enchanter's 'backward mutters of dissevering power' partly free the bound Lady.

Stanza 37

1–2 See 2.1–6*n*.

3 See xi 22.1*n*; cf. 42.5 below.

4 Nor relax her threatening hand through fear of danger.

6 Abode: waited.

8 Her: the reference is deliberately ambiguous.

Stanza 38

1 thrild: pierced.

3 dispart: divide.

4 riuen bowels gor'd: cf. Britomart's 'bleeding bowels' pierced by Love's dart, ii 39.2.

7 soone: immediately.

8 Tho: then; though (as it introduces a paradox).

Stanza 39

4 in liew of: as reward for.

5 Your vertue selfe: your virtue itself, or your virtuous self; cf. 'Virtue is its own reward' (C. G. Smith, 1970, 818); cf. also V xi 17.9.

7 vassall: in effect, she submits herself to the bondage of chastity; cf. IV ix 18.7.

9 aduance: extol. **that**: that which, referring to Britomart's virtue.

419

40

But *Britomart* vprearing her from ground,
  Said, Gentle Dame, reward enough I weene
For many labours more, then I haue found,
This, that in safety now I haue you seene,
And meane of your deliuerance haue beene:
Henceforth faire Lady comfort to you take,
And put away remembrance of late teene;
  In stead thereof know, that your louing Make,
Hath no lesse griefe endured for your gentle sake.

41

She much was cheard to heare him mentiond,
  Whom of all liuing wights she loued best.
Then laid the noble Championesse strong hond
Vpon th'enchaunter, which had her distrest
So sore, and with foule outrages opprest:
With that great chaine, wherewith not long ygo
He bound that pitteous Lady prisoner, now relest,
  Himselfe she bound, more worthy to be so,
And captiue with her led to wretchednesse and wo.

42

Returning backe, those goodly roomes, which erst
  She saw so rich and royally arayd,
Now vanisht vtterly, and cleane subuerst
She found, and all their glory quite decayd,
That sight of such a chaunge her much dismayd,
Thence forth descending to that perlous Porch,
Those dreadfull flames she also found delayd,
  And quenched quite, like a consumed torch,
That erst all entrers wont so cruelly to scorch.

43

More easie issew now, then entrance late
  She found: for now that fained dreadfull flame,
Which chokt the porch of that enchaunted gate,
And passage bard to all, that thither came,
Was vanisht quite, as it were not the same,
And gaue her leaue at pleasure forth to passe.
Th'Enchaunter selfe, which all that fraud did frame,
  To haue efforst the loue of that faire lasse,
Seeing his worke now wasted deepe engrieued was.

44

But when the victoresse arriued there,
  Where late she left the pensife *Scudamore*,
With her owne trusty Squire, both full of feare,
Neither of them she found where she them lore:
Thereat her noble hart was stonisht sore;
But most faire *Amoret*, whose gentle spright
Now gan to feede on hope, which she before
  Conceiued had, to see her owne deare knight,
Being thereof beguyld was fild with new affright.

45

But he sad man, when he had long in drede
  Awayted there for *Britomarts* returne,
Yet saw her not nor signe of her good speed,
His expectation to despaire did turne,
Misdeeming sure that her those flames did burne;
And therefore gan aduize with her old Squire,
Who her deare nourslings losse no lesse did mourne,
  Thence to depart for further aide t'enquire:
Where let them wend at will, whilest here I doe respire.

Stanza 40

5 meane: instrument; intercessor as she has received the wound intended for Amoret.
6 She offers the same advice to Scudamour, xi 15.1.
7 teene: injury, affliction.

Stanza 41

7 Unless the six feet measure the chain, a word needs to be omitted: pitteous, Lady or prisoner. As the line stands, however, it emphasizes Amoret's plight.

Stanza 42

3 subuerst: razed. Cf. Guyon's deliberate razing of the 'goodly workmanship' of the Bower of Bliss, II xii 83.3. Upton (1758) notes the similar vanishing of the enchanted palace and gardens in Italian romance, e.g. Ariosto, *Orl. Fur.* iv 38, xxii 23.
4 decayd: destroyed; as before Amoret was 'through charmes decayd' (Arg. 4).
7 delayd: quenched.

Stanzas 43–45

These three stanzas first appeared in the *1596* edition, displacing 43–47 (*1590*). It seems reasonable to assume that they were written for that edition rather than being themselves displaced to provide an 'ending' for the first three Books. 43.1–6 repeat the substance of the previous three lines, as though S. were picking up his subject again.

Stanza 43

2 fained: being imaginary; or only imagined to be dreadful.
8 efforst: compelled.

Stanza 44

2 pensife: apprehensive; sad.
4 lore: left.

Stanza 45

3 speed: success.
5 Misdeeming: mistakenly supposing.
6 aduize: consult.

Stanzas 43–47 (*1590 Edition*)

43

At last she came vnto the place, where late
  She left Sir *Scudamour* in great distresse,
  Twixt dolour and despight halfe desperate,
  Of his loues succour, of his owne redresse,
  And of the hardie *Britomarts* successe:
  There on the cold earth him now thrown she found,
  In wilfull anguish, and dead heauinesse,
  And to him cald; whose voices knowen sound
Soone as he heard, himself he reared light from ground.

44

There did he see, that most on earth him ioyd,
  His dearest loue, the comfort of his dayes,
  Whose too long absence him had sore annoyd,
  And wearied his life with dull delayes:
  Straight he vpstarted from the loathed layes,
  And to her ran with hasty egernesse,
  Like as a Deare, that greedily embayes
  In the coole soile, after long thirstinesse,
Which he in chace endured hath, now nigh breathlesse.

45

Lightly he clipt her twixt his armes twaine,
  And streightly did embrace her body bright,
  Her body, late the prison of sad paine,
  Now the sweet lodge of loue and deare delight:
  But she faire Lady ouercommen quight
  Of huge affection, did in pleasure melt,
  And in sweete rauishment pourd out her spright:
  No word they spake, nor earthly thing they felt,
But like two senceles stocks in long embracement dwelt.

46

Had ye them seene, ye would haue surely thought,
  That they had beene that faire *Hermaphrodite*,
  Which that rich *Romane* of white marble wrought,
  And in his costly Bath causd to bee site:
  So seemd those two, as growne together quite,
  That *Britomart* halfe enuying their blesse,
  Was much empassiond in her gentle sprite,
  And to her selfe oft wisht like happinesse,
In vaine she wisht, that fate n'ould let her yet possesse.

47

Thus doe those louers with sweet counteruayle,
  Each other of loues bitter fruit despoile.
  But now my teme begins to faint and fayle,
  All woxen weary of their iournall toyle:
  Therefore I will their sweatie yokes assoyle
  At this same furrowes end, till a new day:
  And ye faire Swayns, after your long turmoyle,
  Now cease your worke, and at your pleasure play;
Now cease your worke; to morrow is an holy day.

Stanza 43 (*1590*)
3–5   Cf. Malbecco 'Twixt inward doole and felonous despight' (x 17.6); cf. Scudamour's 'great despight' (IV i 52.1) in his jealousy when he has cause again to envy Britomart's **successe**.   **redresse**: aid.
6   Cf. his posture at xi 7.3–4, 13.6–7 when first found by Britomart; cf. Amoret's posture at xii 38.9.
7   **heauinesse**: torpor; grief.

Stanza 44 (*1590*)
5   **layes**: ground.
7–9   Proverbial for the point of last extremity; cf. Gervase Markham, *The English Arcadia* (1607): 'The poor hunted beast . . . by taking soil in a great lake . . . showed how near he was come to the last point of his utter ruin.' It signifies also escape and relief; cf. Walsingham to Sir Henry Sidney: 'no less a refreshing unto me . . . than the soil is to the chafed stag.' **soile**: a pool of water. Anticipates the use of the myth of Salmacis in the next stanza. Cf. the same simile at IV x 55.8–9 to describe their first union.

Stanza 45 (*1590*)
Cf. Castiglione's description of the kiss: 'That bonde is the opening of an entrie to the soules, which drawne with a coveting the one of the other, poure them selves by turne the one into the others bodie, and bee so mingled together, that each of them hath two soules' (*Courtier* 315).
2   **streightly**: tightly.
3–4   Amoret fulfils her name and nature in a transformation as complete for the moment as Malbecco's.
6   **melt**: suggests orgasm, but goes beyond it.
9   Borrowed from Ovid, *Met.* iv 375–7, which describes the union of Salmacis and Hermaphroditus.

Stanza 46 (*1590*)
Ovid tells how Hermaphroditus became male and female in one body, *Met.* iv 285–388. S.'s primary allusion is to marriage in which man 'shal cleave to his wife, and they shalbe one flesh' (Gen. 2.24). Lewis (1967) 38 comments: 'of true marriage in this Biblical sense, of *henosis*, Spenser's image is obviously a visual emblem.' He links this emblem with the hermaphroditic Venus (IV x 41) and Nature (VII vii 5) as 'images of the *natura unialis*, the ultimate unity that underlies all being' (42); cf. Roche (1964) 134–6. Cirillo (1969) shows the use of the hermaphrodite as an image of the mystical union of souls in the Renaissance. See Cheney (1972).
1–4   Cheney 194 notes that all efforts to identify this apparent allusion with a specific statue have been unsuccessful.
9   **n'ould**: would not.

Stanza 47 (*1590*)
1   **counteruayle**: reciprocation.
4   **iournall**: daily, in opposition to **holy day** (9).
5   **assoyle**: set free; referring back to 44.8 (1590).
7   **ye faire Swayns**: Scudamour and Amoret; cf. 45.9. The stanza links the lovers and S.'s **teme** (3) or his Muses. At VI ix 1.1, he refers to his Muse as a 'iolly swayne' who drives his team. Cf. 'ye iolly Mariners' (I xii 42.1).

Book IV seems to many readers the least interesting. Usually it is considered an extension of Book III as it continues and resolves the stories of Belphœbe and Timias, Florimell and Marinell, and apparently of Scudamour and Amoret (see ix 38*n*), and advances the story of Britomart and Artegall to their pledging of love. The virtue of friendship seems limited to several *exempla* of true and false friendship in the opening cantos. No recent critic has chosen to write on the allegory of friendship. Lewis (1936) 338 treats Books III and IV as 'a single book on the subject of love'. In the one major study of the two books, Roche (1964) 198–200 sees their relationship as the hinge on which the structural patterns of the whole poem depend. Yet S. published Book IV as a separate book on the legend of friendship and included it in the second half of the poem (Books IV–VI) that may be seen to treat the public, rather than the private, virtues. Clearly it ought to be examined on its own terms. By continuing the stories of love, S. shows how the virtue of friendship is displayed in the power of concord to heal the wounds of love. The natural and cosmic harmony achieved under the aegis of friendship gains increasingly strong apocalyptic overtones as the Book progresses. One reason for the neglect of the Book is cited by Murrin (1969) 95–6 in observing that the modern critic, as a formalist, wants to analyse a 'poem-as-object': 'He worries about Spenser's messy plot . . . forgetting that Spenser may not have cared particularly about his story as an end in itself.' S.'s rhetorical purpose is 'to create a moral change within a man's soul. If Book IV of *The Faerie Queene* succeeds in this purpose, it is a good poem, whether the story hangs together or not.' Anderson (1976) 113–23 defends the content and form of the Book by demonstrating the central importance of the poet's role.

The background of the virtue of friendship has been traced to a number of sources in classical, medieval and Renaissance literature, both learned and commonplace. The index of sources and analogues in the *Variorum* edition fills five pages compared to three for Book III. Jones (1930) 240 concludes that 'we have no difficulty in tracing in Aristotle and Cicero most of Spenser's ideas on friendship'. Yet C. G. Smith, *Var.* iv 333–4, traces parallels in Alain's *Complaint of Nature* and also writes an essay on S.'s theory of friendship as an Elizabethan commonplace. For more recent critics, 'friendship' is a less useful critical term than 'concord'. Roche hardly uses the term in his extended analysis of Book IV. Instead, he stresses the theme of *discordia concors*, the emergence of harmony out of discord which he traces throughout the Book and, in a particularly illuminating manner, in such central emblems as Cambina in her chariot and Concord holding Love and Hate in union. Berger (1968a) 4 develops the view of concord as 'the emergence of order from chaos and of friendship from enmity' by showing its active and dynamic stage: 'Concord is not founded on the desire of absolute union but on the discipline of tempered *com*munion.'

The structure of Book IV has been analysed as a change from discord to concord by Notcutt (1926). In Hamilton (1961) 159f I argue that the theme of Book IV is the contest between love and discord. Ate, the personification of strife, seeks to preserve the chaos to which Guyon's sword reduces nature, art, and human nature by destroying the Bower, while out of that chaos love creates a new order which will redeem them all. Nelson (1963) 236 writes: 'The Legend of Chastitie has for its subject the power of love; the Legend of Friendship is an anatomy of the relationship which love creates.' Roche (1964) argues that Books III and IV form one continuous legend in which there are correspondences between each half. He traces four movements of six cantos each, moving from the inception of love to marriage:

> The first movement is initiated by Britomart's quest and ends with the vision of the Garden of Adonis. Its subject, if we must name one, is love. The second movement begins with the adventures of Florimell and ends with the triumph of Britomart over Busyrane. Its subject is beauty and the lust inspired by it. The third movement progresses from the inception of Ate's power to the confrontation of Britomart and Arthegall, where the destructive forces of discord run rampant. The fourth movement begins with the capture of Amoret by Lust and ends with the union of Florimell and Marinell. Its subject is the emergence of concord from discord, personal, social, and cosmic. Each movement is either initiated or concluded by the next development in Britomart's quest. (202)

According to Roche, Britomart's parallelism to Arthur makes his intervention in Book III unnecessary and explains why he does not rescue the titular hero in Book IV. Yet Arthur's role is more structurally prominent than this statement suggests. While Arthur need not intervene in Book III because Britomart is a female Arthur and, being wounded by love, cannot intervene for he is involved equally with the others in the action, in all other Books he intervenes as many times as the number of the Book. In Book IV he emerges as the chief force to achieve concord. He aids Amoret and Æmylia, restoring the latter to her lover; he slays Corflambo who is the source of all lust of the eye; he resolves the anatomy of love expressed by the combat of the six knights; and finally, one must assume, he resolves the theme of 'maisterie' in Books III and IV by presenting Amoret to the assembled company at the end of Canto ix so that she may freely choose, and, of course, choose Scudamour.

The interlacing of the four stories of Book III provides the narrative structure of Book IV until each may be resolved in the five concluding Cantos. Belphœbe and Timias are reconciled (Canto viii); Britomart's relation to love is resolved, and hence her relation to Artegall, when Arthur stints all strife in love (Canto ix); the Scudamour-Amoret story is rounded out by the account of its beginning (Canto x); and the Florimell-Marinell story is concluded (Cantos xi and xii), and will be sealed by their marriage in Book V.

For the Belphœbe-Timias story, critical attention has centred on the historical allegory, or, more correctly, on the application of the moral allegory to a contemporary scandal, namely, Raleigh's banishment from Elizabeth's presence for dishonouring one of her maids of honour. Upton (1758) first suggested this topical reference and it has been generally supported. Nelson (1963) 254 finds the reference unmistakable and most readers seem to agree. Nothing but the distracting pressure of contemporary allusion may explain the drabness of the verse in the episode.

Britomart's relation to Artegall is treated in two central episodes of the Book as a complex allegory of courtship. In the Tournament in Canto iv Britomart, in defence of maidenhead, defeats Artegall's manhood. As a consequence, in their personal combat in Canto vi, he falls in love when he sees her beauty. He falls literally when he kneels to offer her the 'maisterie'. Her yielding to love, which arouses the fear of being overcome by lust, is treated in the account of Amoret's abduction by Lust and her wounding by Timias.

Scudamour's story of his rape of Amoret from the Temple of Venus provides the climax to the relation between the sexes displayed in Books III and IV. Roche (1964) 129 interprets it as 'a vision of the relation of the sexes (as well as other hierarchical relationships) in which man *by nature* is the aggressor and must win the woman'. In Hamilton (1961) 166, 182, I treat the episode in terms of 'maisterie' and note that Scudamour's actions are patterned after Britomart's through the injunction 'Be bold' found in the house of Busirane. Hieatt (1962) 510 develops independently the same argument: 'He [Scudamour] has overstepped the bounds of love in asserting a passionate mastery incompatible with what he really wants, which is happy marriage, to be gained in Spenser's estimate only by the superimposition of a freely yielded and mutually willed spiritual friendship upon the equally important facts of Nature.' The larger meaning of the episode has been defined as 'cosmic harmony' (Hough, 1962, 189), or a vision of 'the reality and unity of love' (Roche, 1964, 133), or the 'final state of lovers' bliss' (Hamilton, 1961, 156). Berger (1969b) 12 finds instead 'a brilliantly articulated state of fragmentation in which all parties work at cross-purposes' by seeking that final bliss too prematurely.

The role of Florimell in the allegory of love in Books III and IV is indicated by S.'s lament when Slander attempts to undo Arthur's rescue of Amoret. He contrasts the innocence of the antique world to its present decline:

> Then beautie, which was made to represent
>   The great Creatours owne resemblance bright,
>   Vnto abuse of lawlesse lust was lent,
>   And made the baite of bestiall delight:

Then faire grew foule, and foule grew faire in sight,
And that which wont to vanquish God and man,
Was made the vassall of the victors might;
Then did her glorious flowre wex dead and wan,
Despisd and troden downe of all that ouerran. (viii 32)

This stanza traces the progress of Florimell more accurately than that of Amoret, specifically, her flight from the lustfull Foster and her replacement by the False Florimell. When the flower of her beauty is 'dead and wan' and her place taken by the snowy Florimell, the renewal of spring and the fruitfulness of autumn that is found in the Garden of Adonis (III vi 42) yields to winter. As Frye (1961) 83 observes, 'Florimell is imprisoned under the sea during a kind of symbolic winter in which a "snowy" Florimell takes her place'. This state endures until the marriage of the Thames and the Medway, which all the rivers attend, establishes the renewed harmony of nature. In this marriage with its procession of the rivers, Roche (1964) 181 sees revealed 'the unity underlying the multiplicity of life'; Berger (1969b) 15 finds a return to the natural origins of life by the 'interchange between geography and history, between the eternally recurrent flow-through of water and the continually changing organization of society'; and Giamatti (1975) 132 claims that S. 'has finally married his powers of invention to the natural world, giving a pageant of concord about the attainment of harmony'. Florimell returns from the sea to the land as '*Venus* of the fomy sea' (IV xii 2) to restore the dying Marinell. In the sunshine of her presence he revives 'As withered weed through cruell winters tine, / That feeles the warmth of sunny beames reflection, / Liftes vp his head, that did before decline / And gins to spread his leafe before the faire sunshine'. With this powerful image of Marinell that suggests a reviving Adonis or, more exactly, a restored Verdant, the larger patterns of Books III and IV would seem to be resolved.

THE FOVRTH

BOOKE OF THE
FAERIE QVEENE.

Containing

The Legend of CAMBEL and TELAMOND,

OR

OF FRIENDSHIP.

1

THe rugged forhead that with graue foresight
Welds kingdomes causes, and affaires of state,
My looser rimes (I wote) doth sharply wite,
For praising loue, as I haue done of late,
And magnifying louers deare debate;
By which fraile youth is oft to follie led,
Through false allurement of that pleasing baite,
That better were in vertues discipled,
Then with vaine poemes weeds to haue their fancies fed.

2

Such ones ill iudge of loue, that cannot loue,
Ne in their frosen hearts feele kindly flame:
For thy they ought not thing vnknowne reproue,
Ne naturall affection faultlesse blame,
For fault of few that haue abusd the same.
For it of honor and all vertue is
The roote, and brings forth glorious flowres of fame,
That crowne true louers with immortall blis,
The meed of them that loue, and do not liue amisse.

3

Which who so list looke backe to former ages,
And call to count the things that then were donne,
Shall find, that all the workes of those wise sages,
And braue exploits which great Heroes wonne,
In loue were either ended or begunne:
Witnesse the father of Philosophie,
Which to his *Critias*, shaded oft from sunne,
Of loue full manie lessons did apply,
The which these Stoicke censors cannot well deny.

4

To such therefore I do not sing at all,
But to that sacred Saint my soueraigne Queene,
In whose chast breast all bountie naturall,
And treasures of true loue enlocked beene,
Boue all her sexe that euer yet was seene;
To her I sing of loue, that loueth best,
And best is lou'd of all aliue I weene:
To her this song most fitly is addrest,
The Queene of loue, and Prince of peace from heauen blest.

Title

Telamond: Triamond at ii 31.8, etc. Defended by Roche (1964) 16–7 because its etymology, 'perfect world' (Gk τελεος + Lat. *mundus*), is consonant with the Book's metaphysics of friendship.

Proem

Stanza 1

1 Apparently alluding to William Cecil, Lord Burleigh, Elizabeth's chief minister. In a dedicatory sonnet he is referred to as one 'whose carefull brest / To menage of most graue affaires is bent'. Cf. the reference in the final stanza of Book VI to 'a mighty Peres displeasure'. **rugged**: furrowed, frowning; perhaps 'burly'. **forhead**: associated with **foresight**, II ix 49.1.
2 **Welds**: wields; governs.
3 **looser**: too loose. **wite**: blame.
4 **of late**: in *H.H.L.* 8–11, S. confesses that he had written 'Many lewd layes . . . / In praise of that mad fit, which fooles call loue, / . . . That in light wits did loose affection moue.'
5 **magnifying**: extolling; treating at length. **deare debate**: grievous or loving strife.
6 **follie**: lewdness.
8–9 Cf. *L.R.*: 'To some I know this Methode will seeme displeasaunt, which had rather haue good discipline deliuered plainly in way of precepts, or sermoned at large, as they vse, then thus clowdily enwrapped in Allegoricall deuises.' **discipled**: taught; made subject to discipline. **weeds**: the garment of poetry; or noxious growth. In answer, S. claims that love (and his poem) produce 'glorious flowres of fame' (2.7).

Stanza 2

2 **kindly flame**: natural affection.
3 **For thy**: therefore.
6–9 Cf. his defence of love at III i 49.8–9, iii 1–2, v 1.8–9. S. defends his poem by adding to the 1596 dedication the claim that it will 'liue with the eternitie of her [Elizabeth's] fame'.

Stanza 3

4–5 Cooper (1565) connects **Heroes** and Lat. *eros*, love: '*Heros*, he that for the love of vertue susteineth great labours.'
6–8 Socrates discoursed on love to Phaedrus in the shade of the plane tree (Plato, *Phaedrus* 229b–30b). See II vii 52.6–9n. Unless S. errs, there is no simple explanation why he should name **Critias**, a disciple of Socrates in several of Plato's dialogues. **father of Philosophie**: *parens philosophiae* (Cicero, *de Fin.* II i 1).

Stanza 4

2 In all other Proems, S. addresses the Queen directly.
3 **bountie**: goodness.

5

Which that she may the better deigne to heare,
　Do thou dred infant, *Venus* dearling doue,
　From her high spirit chase imperious feare,
　And vse of awfull Maiestie remoue:
　In sted thereof with drops of melting loue,
　Deawd with ambrosiall kisses, by thee gotten
　From thy sweete smyling mother from aboue,
　Sprinckle her heart, and haughtie courage soften,
That she may hearke to loue, and read this lesson often.

Cant. I.

Fayre Britomart saues Amoret,
Duessa discord breedes
Twixt Scudamour and Blandamour:
Their fight and warlike deedes.

1

OF louers sad calamities of old,
　Full many piteous stories doe remaine,
　But none more piteous euer was ytold,
　Then that of *Amorets* hart-binding chaine,
　And this of *Florimels* vnworthie paine:
　The deare compassion of whose bitter fit
　My softened heart so sorely doth constraine,
　That I with teares full oft doe pittie it,
And oftentimes doe wish it neuer had bene writ.

2

For from the time that *Scudamour* her bought
　In perilous fight, she neuer ioyed day,
　A perilous fight when he with force her brought
　From twentie Knights, that did him all assay:
　Yet fairely well he did them all dismay:
　And with great glorie both the shield of loue,
　And eke the Ladie selfe he brought away,
　Whom hauing wedded as did him behoue,
A new vnknowen mischiefe did from him remoue.

3

For that same vile Enchauntour *Busyran*,
　The very selfe same day that she was wedded,
　Amidst the bridale feast, whilest euery man
　Surcharg'd with wine, were heedlesse and ill hedded,
　All bent to mirth before the bride was bedded,
　Brought in that mask of loue which late was showen:
　And there the Ladie ill of friends bestedded,
　By way of sport, as oft in maskes is knowen,
Conueyed quite away to liuing wight vnknowen.

4

Seuen moneths he so her kept in bitter smart,
　Because his sinfull lust she would not serue,
　Vntill such time as noble *Britomart*
　Released her, that else was like to sterue,
　Through cruell knife that her deare heart did kerue.
　And now she is with her vpon the way,
　Marching in louely wise, that could deserue
　No spot of blame, though spite did oft assay
To blot her with dishonor of so faire a pray.

Stanza 5
2　**dearling**: darling.
3　**imperious feare**: majesty which arouses fear in others; suggesting also that the Virgin Queen fears love.
7　**smyling mother**: Venus, 'Mother of laughter' (x 47.8); cf. x 44.4.
9　**this lesson**: Cupid's lesson, not to fear love.

Canto i

Stanza 1
4　**hart-binding chaine**: combines the iron bands that bind her body with her wounded heart; see III xii 30.8–9 and 31.1–5.
5　**vnworthie**: undeserved.
6　**of**: for.　**bitter fit**: pangs of extreme grief.
7　**constraine**: afflict.

Stanza 2
For the fight, see x 7–10; for his seizure of Amoret, see x 53–57.
1　**bought**: set free by paying a price; cf. 'redeemed' (8.4).
4　**twentie**: see x 7.6*n*.　**assay**: assail.
5　**fairely**: fully.　**dismay**: defeat.

Stanza 3
Only one example of feminine rhyme occurs in the first three books; now it becomes frequent.
1　**vile Enchauntour**: his title at III xii 31.1.
7　That Amoret's abduction results from a failure in friendship links her story with the virtue of Book IV; noted Alpers (1967) 110.　**bestedded**: attended.
8　**sport**: refers to the anti-masque which parodies the masque, as Amoret's bondage parodies marriage. See E. B. Fowler (1921) 121–2.
9　Two senses are noted by Fowler (1970) 51: (*a*) she is carried off without anyone noticing; (*b*) she experiences Busirane's captivity inwardly, without anyone knowing.

Stanza 4
1　**Seuen moneths**: see III xi 10.8*n*.
2　Cf. the less direct statement at III xi 17.3, xii 31.6.
4　**sterue**: die.
5　**kerue**: cut; pierce.
7　**louely**: affectionate.
9　**her**: i.e. Britomart. Being supposed a man, she may be slandered for travelling with Amoret; cf. viii 29.

427

5

Yet should it be a pleasant tale, to tell
  The diuerse vsage and demeanure daint,
  That each to other made, as oft befell.
  For *Amoret* right fearefull was and faint,
  Lest she with blame her honor should attaint,
  That euerie word did tremble as she spake,
  And euerie looke was coy, and wondrous quaint,
  And euerie limbe that touched her did quake:
Yet could she not but curteous countenance to her make.

6

For well she wist, as true it was indeed,
  That her liues Lord and patrone of her health
  Right well deserued as his duefull meed,
  Her loue, her seruice, and her vtmost wealth.
  All is his iustly, that all freely dealth:
  Nathlesse her honor dearer then her life,
  She sought to saue, as thing reseru'd from stealth;
  Die had she leuer with Enchanters knife,
Then to be false in loue, profest a virgine wife.

7

Thereto her feare was made so much the greater
  Through fine abusion of that Briton mayd:
  Who for to hide her fained sex the better,
  And maske her wounded mind, both did and sayd
  Full many things so doubtfull to be wayd,
  That well she wist not what by them to gesse,
  For other whiles to her she purpos made
  Of loue, and otherwhiles of lustfulnesse,
That much she feard his mind would grow to some excesse.

8

His will she feard; for him she surely thought
  To be a man, such as indeed he seemed,
  And much the more, by that he lately wrought,
  When her from deadly thraldome he redeemed,
  For which no seruice she too much esteemed,
  Yet dread of shame, and doubt of fowle dishonor
  Made her not yeeld so much, as due she deemed.
  Yet *Britomart* attended duly on her,
As well became a knight, and did to her all honor.

9

It so befell one euening, that they came
  Vnto a Castell, lodged there to bee,
  Where many a knight, and many a louely Dame
  Was then assembled, deeds of armes to see:
  Amongst all which was none more faire then shee,
  That many of them mou'd to eye her sore.
  The custome of that place was such, that hee
  Which had no loue nor lemman there in store,
Should either winne him one, or lye without the dore.

10

Amongst the rest there was a iolly knight
  Who being asked for his loue, auow'd
  That fairest *Amoret* was his by right,
  And offred that to iustifie alowd.
  The warlike virgine seeing his so prowd
  And boastfull chalenge, wexed inlie wroth,
  But for the present did her anger shrowd;
  And sayd, her loue to lose she was full loth,
428 But either he should neither of them haue, or both.

Stanza 5
2 **diuerse vsage**: different, or diverting, conduct.
5 **attaint**: taint; convict.
7 **quaint**: prim.
9 **countenance**: demeanour.

Stanza 6
2 Cf. Arthur's relationship to the Red Cross Knight (I ix 17.6) and to Guyon (II viii 55.4). **patrone of her health**: defender of her well-being but referring also to the healing of her wounded body; cf. III xii 35.6.
3 **duefull**: due; emphasizing what is fully due.
5 **dealth**: dealeth, bestows.
7 **stealth**: plundering.
9 **a virgine wife**: defines her role in the poem.

Stanza 7
1 **Thereto**: moreover.
2 **fine abusion**: cunning deception.
4 The 'mask of loue' (3.6) is not concluded: Britomart appears as a male knight; at 14.8 she appears as a woman in what is called 'a maske of strange disguise', and at 17.7 Duessa and Ate appear 'vnder maske of beautie and good grace'.
7-8 **For other whiles . . . / . . . and otherwhiles**: for at one time . . . and at another time. **purpos**: conversation.

Stanza 8
1 **will**: sexual desire, lust.
5 **seruice**: implying sexual service which she fears she owes. Woman as the prize or booty of chivalric prowess is a central theme in the Book. It is rendered fully in Scudamour's account of gaining Amoret as his spoil (Canto x). At 33.4 Amoret is called Britomart's 'conquests part'.
6 **doubt**: fear.

Stanza 10
1 **iolly**: handsome; gallant; amorous (cf. 11.3-4).
3 **by right**: see 12.4*n*, 39.6*n*.
4 **alowd**: loudly; publicly.
8-9 Britomart must quibble: if he gains her love, Amoret, he would also gain her.

11

So foorth they went, and both together giusted;
 But that same younker soone was ouerthrowne,
 And made repent, that he had rashly lusted
 For thing vnlawfull, that was not his owne:
 Yet since he seemed valiant, though vnknowne,
 She that no lesse was courteous then stout,
 Cast how to salue, that both the custome showne
 Were kept, and yet that Knight not locked out,
That seem'd full hard t'accord two things so far in dout.

12

The Seneschall was cal'd to deeme the right,
 Whom she requir'd, that first fayre *Amoret*
 Might be to her allow'd, as to a Knight,
 That did her win and free from chalenge set:
 Which straight to her was yeelded without let.
 Then since that strange Knights loue from him was quitted,
 She claim'd that to her selfe, as Ladies det,
 He as a Knight might iustly be admitted;
So none should be out shut, sith all of loues were fitted.

13

With that her glistring helmet she vnlaced;
 Which doft, her golden lockes, that were vp bound
 Still in a knot, vnto her heeles downe traced,
 And like a silken veile in compasse round
 About her backe and all her bodie wound:
 Like as the shining skie in summers night,
 What time the dayes with scorching heat abound,
 Is creasted all with lines of firie light,
That it prodigious seemes in common peoples sight.

14

Such when those Knights and Ladies all about
 Beheld her, all were with amazement smit,
 And euery one gan grow in secret dout
 Of this and that, according to each wit:
 Some thought that some enchantment faygned it;
 Some, that *Bellona* in that warlike wise
 To them appear'd, with shield and armour fit;
 Some, that it was a maske of strange disguise:
So diuersely each one did sundrie doubts deuise.

15

But that young Knight, which through her gentle deed
 Was to that goodly fellowship restor'd,
 Ten thousand thankes did yeeld her for her meed,
 And doubly ouercommen, her ador'd:
 So did they all their former strife accord;
 And eke fayre *Amoret* now freed from feare,
 More franke affection did to her afford,
 And to her bed, which she was wont forbeare,
Now freely drew, and found right safe assurance theare.

16

Where all that night they of their loues did treat,
 And hard aduentures twixt themselues alone,
 That each the other gan with passion great,
 And griefull pittie priuately bemone.
 The morow next so soone as *Titan* shone,
 They both vprose, and to their waies them dight:
 Long wandred they, yet neuer met with none,
 That to their willes could them direct aright,
Or to them tydings tell, that mote their harts delight.

Stanza 11
2 younker: 'young Knight' (15.1).
6 On the conjunction of courtesy and chivalry, see iii
2.6–9, VI i 2.7–9n.   stout: brave.
7 **Cast how to salue . . .**: i.e. she considered how to
reconcile the conflict.   salue suggests healing.   showne:
decreed.
9 accord: reconcile.   so far in dout: difficult in not
being consistent.

Stanza 12
1 **Seneschall**: the household official who administers
justice.   deeme: judge.
2 **Whom she requir'd**: of whom she asked.
4 **free from chalenge set**: freed from any claim, referring
to ownership gained through knightly combat. Britomart wins
Amoret in combat as Scudamour had done: see 39.6.
5 let: hindrance.
7–9 Britomart claims him as he would have claimed her if
she had lost, 10.9.

Stanza 13
Cf. III ix 20.3–9. Of her four 'appearances' in the poem (see
III i 43n) this is the most erotic. Bender (1972) 60–1 comments
on S.'s representation of complex visual phenomena in his
imagery.
4 **in compasse**: encompassing.
6–9 Fulgetrum, a kind of lightning, which, according to
William Fulke (*A Goodly Gallery*, 1571), 'is seen on sommer
nights and eveninges, after a whote daie . . . terrible to beholde,
not hurtful to any thing'; cited Heninger (1960) 75.
prodigious: ominous; cf. Florimell's hair which, like a comet,
inspires people with fear (III i 16.5–9).

Stanza 14
6 **Bellona**: the goddess of war; see III ix 22.1n.

Stanza 15
4 **doubly**: by her prowess and courtesy as a knight and by
her beauty as a Lady.
6 Britomart frees Amoret for a second time.
8 forbeare: avoid, shun.

Stanza 16
6 **dight**: went.

429

17

Lo thus they rode, till at the last they spide
Two armed Knights, that toward them did pace,
And ech of them had ryding by his side
A Ladie, seeming in so farre a space,
But Ladies none they were, albee in face
And outward shew faire semblance they did beare;
For vnder maske of beautie and good grace,
Vile treason and fowle falshood hidden were,
That mote to none but to the warie wise appeare.

18

The one of them the false *Duessa* hight,
That now had chang'd her former wonted hew:
For she could d'on so manie shapes in sight,
As euer could Cameleon colours new;
So could she forge all colours, saue the trew.
The other no whit better was then shee,
But that such as she was, she plaine did shew;
Yet otherwise much worse, if worse might bee,
And dayly more offensiue vnto each degree.

19

Her name was *Ate*, mother of debate,
And all dissention, which doth dayly grow
Amongst fraile men, that many a publike state
And many a priuate oft doth ouerthrow.
Her false *Duessa* who full well did know,
To be most fit to trouble noble knights,
Which hunt for honor, raised from below,
Out of the dwellings of the damned sprights,
Where she in darknes wastes her cursed daies and nights.

20

Hard by the gates of hell her dwelling is,
There whereas all the plagues and harmes abound,
Which punish wicked men, that walke amisse:
It is a darksome delue farre vnder ground,
With thornes and barren brakes enuirond round,
That none the same may easily out win;
Yet many waies to enter may be found,
But none to issue forth when one is in:
For discord harder is to end then to begin.

21

And all within the riuen walls were hung
With ragged monuments of times forepast,
All which the sad effects of discord sung:
There were rent robes, and broken scepters plast,
Altars defyl'd, and holy things defast,
Disshiuered speares, and shields ytorne in twaine,
Great cities ransackt, and strong castles rast,
Nations captiued, and huge armies slaine:
Of all which ruines there some relicks did remaine.

22

There was the signe of antique Babylon,
Of fatall Thebes, of Rome that raigned long,
Of sacred Salem, and sad Ilion,
For memorie of which on high there hong
The golden Apple, cause of all their wrong,
For which the three faire Goddesses did striue:
There also was the name of *Nimrod* strong,
Of *Alexander*, and his Princes fiue,
430 Which shar'd to them the spoiles that he had got aliue.

Stanza 17

1 **Lo thus**: 'Long thus' sugg. Church (1758), comparing 16.7.
4 **seeming in so farre a space**: i.e. appearing at that distance to be a lady. Ate's appearance changes from an attractive Lady to an ugly Hag according to the eye of the beholder. See 48.1*n*.

Stanza 18

4–5 Proverbial (C. G. Smith, 1970, 92).
9 **vnto each degree**: to people of all classes.

Stanza 19

1 **Ate**: Homer's Goddess of Discord (*Iliad* xix 91–4, 126–31). Cf. Virgil's *Discordia demens* (*Aen.* vi 280).
debate: strife. Ate plays her role in relation to 'louers deare debate' (Proem 1.5).
3 **publike state**: the emphasis on the social effects of Discord indicates the change from the private virtues of Books I–III to the public virtues of Books IV–VI.
7–9 In Homer, Ate is thrown from heaven down to earth; cf. 26.7–8, ii 1.1–3. At V ix 47.3 she is 'that old hag of hellish hew'.

Stanza 20

4 **delue**: pit.
5 **barren brakes**: either bracken growing in barren ground (cf. 25.2) or barren of fruit.
6 **out win**: get out of.
8 **none**: 'few' sugg. Church (1758), to agree with 6 and 9.

Stanza 21

3 **effects**: also signs, outward manifestations. **sung**: proclaimed, suggesting the musical sense.
6 **Disshiuered**: shattered.
7 **rast**: razed.

Stanza 22

1–3 **Thebes** and **Ilion** are the subject of classical drama and epic; **Babylon** and **Salem** are biblical cities. **signe**: emblem, token, monument, as 21.2, 24.8. **fatall**: refers to the curse upon Thebes through Oedipus. **Salem**: Jerusalem, and therefore **sacred**.
4–6 Cf. II vii 55.4–9.
7 **Nimrod**: see I v 48.1–2*n*.
8–9 Cf. 1 Macc. 1.7. **fiue**: not mentioned in the Bible. It may be inferred from the Geneva gloss to Daniel's vision, Dan. 8.8–9: after the horn of the goat was broken, 'it came up foure that appeared towarde the foure winds of the heaven. And out of one of them came forthe a litle horne.' The gloss lists the four: Cassander, Seleucus, Antigonus, and Ptolomeus, the fifth being Antiochus. **to them**: i.e. among themselves.

23

And there the relicks of the drunken fray,
　The which amongst the *Lapithees* befell,
　And of the bloodie feast, which sent away
　So many *Centaures* drunken soules to hell,
　That vnder great *Alcides* furie fell :
　And of the dreadfull discord, which did driue
　The noble *Argonauts* to outrage fell,
　That each of life sought others to depriue,
All mindlesse of the Golden fleece, which made them striue.

24

And eke of priuate persons many moe,
　That were too long a worke to count them all;
　Some of sworne friends, that did their faith forgoe;
　Some of borne brethren, prov'd vnnaturall;
　Some of deare louers, foes perpetuall :
　Witnesse their broken bandes there to be seene,
　Their girlonds rent, their bowres despoyled all;
　The moniments whereof there byding beene,
As plaine as at the first, when they were fresh and greene.

25

Such was her house within; but all without,
　The barren ground was full of wicked weedes,
　Which she her selfe had sowen all about,
　Now growen great, at first of little seedes,
　The seedes of euill wordes, and factious deedes;
　Which when to ripenesse due they growen arre,
　Bring foorth an infinite increase, that breedes
　Tumultuous trouble and contentious iarre,
The which most often end in bloudshed and in warre.

26

And those same cursed seedes doe also serue
　To her for bread, and yeeld her liuing food :
　For life it is to her, when others sterue
　Through mischieuous debate, and deadly feood,
　That she may sucke their life, and drinke their blood,
　With which she from her childhood had bene fed.
　For she at first was borne of hellish brood,
　And by infernall furies nourished,
That by her monstrous shape might easily be red.

27

Her face most fowle and filthy was to see,
　With squinted eyes contrarie wayes intended,
　And loathly mouth, vnmeete a mouth to bee,
　That nought but gall and venim comprehended,
　And wicked wordes that God and man offended :
　Her lying tongue was in two parts diuided,
　And both the parts did speake, and both contended;
　And as her tongue, so was her hart discided,
That neuer thoght one thing, but doubly stil was guided.

28

Als as she double spake, so heard she double,
　With matchlesse eares deformed and distort,
　Fild with false rumors and seditious trouble,
　Bred in assemblies of the vulgar sort,
　That still are led with euery light report.
　And as her eares so eke her feet were odde,
　And much vnlike, th'one long, the other short,
　And both misplast; that when th'one forward yode,
The other backe retired, and contrarie trode.

29

Likewise vnequall were her handes twaine,
　That one did reach, the other pusht away,
　That one did make, the other mard againe,
　And sought to bring all things vnto decay;
　Whereby great riches gathered manie a day,
　She in short space did often bring to nought,
　And their possessours often did dismay.
　For all her studie was and all her thought,
How she might ouerthrow the things that Concord wrought.

Stanza 23

1–5　S. conflates the battle between the Lapithae and the Centaurs at the marriage of Pirithous (Ovid, *Met*. xii 210–535) and Hercules's fight with the Centaurs (536–41). The connection between them is implicit in Ovid but explicit in Boccaccio, *Gen. Deor*. XIII i (as Lotspeich, 1932, 68 notes) and in Cooper and Stephanus (as Starnes and Talbert, 1955, 114, 424 note). See VI x 13*n*.
6–9　The strife was quelled by Orpheus with his music; see ii 1.7–9.　**which made them striue**: apparently invented by S. to link the classical stories of discord with the contest over the golden girdle; cf. *Amor*. xliv 1–4.

Stanza 24

6–7　**bandes** signifies friendship; **girlonds**, kinship; and **bowres**, lovers. The three kinds of love are listed at ix 1.5–7.
8　**byding beene**: remain.

Stanza 26

1–2　Cf. Christ whose body is 'the living bread' (John 6. 51) upon which men may feed and not die.　**liuing food**: food that nourishes life.
4　**mischieuous debate**: injurious conflict.　**feood** (feud): hatred, hostility.
7–9　See 19.7–9*n*.　**red**: seen.

Stanza 27

2　**intended**: directed.
4　**comprehended**: contained.
8　**discided**: cut asunder; playing on the etymology of discord: Lat. *dis*, asunder+*cor*, *cord*, heart.

Stanza 28

2　**matchlesse**: unmatched.
5　**still**: always.
6　**odde**: unequal.
8　**yode**: went.

Stanza 29

2　**That**: that which.

30

So much her malice did her might surpas,
   That euen th'Almightie selfe she did maligne,
   Because to man so mercifull he was,
   And vnto all his creatures so benigne,
   Sith she her selfe was of his grace indigne:
   For all this worlds faire workmanship she tride,
   Vnto his last confusion to bring,
   And that great golden chaine quite to diuide,
With which it blessed Concord hath together tide.

31

Such was that hag, which with *Duessa* roade,
   And seruing her in her malitious vse,
   To hurt good knights, was as it were her baude,
   To sell her borrowed beautie to abuse.
   For though like withered tree, that wanteth iuyce,
   She old and crooked were, yet now of late,
   As fresh and fragrant as the floure deluce
   She was become, by chaunge of her estate,
And made full goodly ioyance to her new found mate.

32

Her mate he was a iollie youthfull knight,
   That bore great sway in armes and chiualrie,
   And was indeed a man of mickle might:
   His name was *Blandamour*, that did descrie
   His fickle mind full of inconstancie.
   And now himselfe he fitted had right well,
   With two companions of like qualitie,
   Faithlesse *Duessa*, and false *Paridell*,
That whether were more false, full hard it is to tell.

33

Now when this gallant with his goodly crew,
   From farre espide the famous *Britomart*,
   Like knight aduenturous in outward vew,
   With his faire paragon, his conquests part,
   Approching nigh, eftsoones his wanton hart
   Was tickled with delight, and iesting sayd;
   Lo there Sir *Paridel*, for your desart,
   Good lucke presents you with yond louely mayd,
For pitie that ye want a fellow for your ayd.

34

By that the louely paire drew nigh to hond:
   Whom when as *Paridel* more plaine beheld,
   Albee in heart he like affection fond,
   Yet mindfull how he late by one was feld,
   That did those armes and that same scutchion weld,
   He had small lust to buy his loue so deare,
   But answerd, Sir him wise I neuer held,
   That hauing once escaped perill neare,
Would afterwards afresh the sleeping euill reare.

35

This knight too late his manhood and his might,
   I did assay, that me right dearely cost,
   Ne list I for reuenge prouoke new fight,
   Ne for light Ladies loue, that soone is lost.
   The hot-spurre youth so scorning to be crost,
   Take then to you this Dame of mine (quoth hee)
   And I without your perill or your cost,
   Will chalenge yond same other for my fee:
So forth he fiercely prickt, that one him scarce could see.

36

The warlike Britonesse her soone addrest,
   And with such vncouth welcome did receaue
   Her fayned Paramour, her forced guest,
   That being forst his saddle soone to leaue,
   Him selfe he did of his new loue deceaue:
   And made him selfe thensample of his follie.
   Which done, she passed forth not taking leaue,
   And left him now as sad, as whilome iollie,
Well warned to beware with whom he dar'd to dallie.

Stanza 30
2   **maligne**: regard with hatred.
3–4   Cf. II viii 1.5–7.
5   **indigne**: unworthy.
7   **confusion**: overthrow.
8–9   **that great golden chaine**: see I v 25.5, ix 1.1–2 and
II vii 46.2. Here it serves as a symbol of cosmic concord as in
Chaucer, *Knight's Tale* 2987–93.

Stanza 31
4   **her borrowed beautie**: cf. I viii 49.5, II i 22.7.   **to
abuse**: to be defiled.
7–8   Cf. 48.1.

Stanza 32
4–5   **Blandamour**: flattering lover, from Lat. *blandus*,
flattering, smooth tongue; cf. ii 10.3–5. The name may have
been taken from Chaucer's Pleyndamour (spelt Blayndamour in
Thynne's 1532 edition) in the *Tale of Sir Thopas* 900. He seeks
love by flattery or slander rather than by conquest; see 39.6 and
iv 4.1–5. He is noted for his fickleness: ii 5.1–3, ix 21.5–6. Cf.
his role at V ix 41. Draper (1932) suggests Lat. *blandus*,
merry + *amour*, love, on the basis of 33.6; cf. 36.8.
Blandamour represents 'fayned blandishment' which is
absent from the Temple of Venus (x 26.7), and may be
compared to Blandina: see VI iii 42.6*n*.   **descrie**: disclose;
describe.
9   **whether**: which of the two.

Stanza 33
4   **paragon**: companion.   **conquests part**: booty, reward
of conquest.
9   **ayd**: sexual, rather than military.

Stanza 34
1   **louely**: affectionate.
5   **scutchion**: shield, or device on the shield.

Stanza 35
5   **hot-spurre**: because he fiercely prickt (9).
8   **chalenge**: claim.   **fee**: prize; rightful possession.

Stanza 36
1   **addrest**: made ready.
2   **vncouth**: unpleasing; rude.
3–5   Seeking to be Amoret's lover, he is forced back by
Britomart.   **Her**: refers either to Britomart or to Amoret; in
effect, Blandamour seeks Britomart's love. As **dallie** (9) –
'flirt', 'wanton' – suggests, the encounter is to be read as a
courtship.   **deceaue**: cheat out of.

37

Which when his other companie beheld,
  They to his succour ran with readie ayd:
  And finding him vnable once to weld,
  They reared him on horsebacke, and vpstayd,
  Till on his way they had him forth conuayd:
  And all the way with wondrous griefe of mynd,
  And shame, he shewd him selfe to be dismayd,
More for the loue which he had left behynd,
Then that which he had to Sir *Paridel* resynd.

38

Nathlesse he forth did march well as he might,
  And made good semblance to his companie,
  Dissembling his disease and euill plight;
  Till that ere long they chaunced to espie
  Two other knights, that towards them did ply
  With speedie course, as bent to charge them new.
  Whom when as *Blandamour* approching nie,
Perceiu'd to be such as they seemd in vew,
He was full wo, and gan his former griefe renew.

39

For th'one of them he perfectly descride,
  To be Sir *Scudamour*, by that he bore
  The God of loue, with wings displayed wide,
  Whom mortally he hated euermore,
  Both for his worth, that all men did adore,
  And eke because his loue he wonne by right:
  Which when he thought, it grieued him full sore,
That through the bruses of his former fight,
He now vnable was to wreake his old despight.

40

For thy he thus to *Paridel* bespake,
  Faire Sir, of friendship let me now you pray,
  That as I late aduentured for your sake,
  The hurts whereof me now from battell stay,
  Ye will me now with like good turne repay,
  And iustifie my cause on yonder knight.
  Ah Sir (said *Paridel*) do not dismay
Your selfe for this, my selfe will for you fight,
As ye haue done for me: the left hand rubs the right.

41

With that he put his spurres vnto his steed,
  With speare in rest, and toward him did fare,
  Like shaft out of a bow preuenting speed.
  But *Scudamour* was shortly well aware
  Of his approch, and gan him selfe prepare
  Him to receiue with entertainment meete.
  So furiously they met, that either bare
The other downe vnder their horses feete,
That what of them became, themselues did scarsly weete.

42

As when two billowes in the Irish sowndes,
  Forcibly driuen with contrarie tydes
  Do meete together, each abacke rebowndes
  With roaring rage; and dashing on all sides,
  That filleth all the sea with fome, diuydes
  The doubtfull current into diuers wayes:
  So fell those two in spight of both their prydes,
But *Scudamour* himselfe did soone vprayse,
And mounting light his foe for lying long vpbrayes.

43

Who rolled on an heape lay still in swound,
  All carelesse of his taunt and bitter rayle,
  Till that the rest him seeing lie on ground,
  Ran hastily, to weete what did him ayle,
  Where finding that the breath gan him to fayle,
  With busie care they stroue him to awake,
  And doft his helmet, and vndid his mayle:
So much they did, that at the last they brake
His slomber, yet so mazed, that he nothing spake.

44

Which when as *Blandamour* beheld, he sayd,
  False faitour *Scudamour*, that hast by slight
  And foule aduantage this good Knight dismayd,
  A Knight much better then thy selfe behight,
  Well falles it thee that I am not in plight
  This day, to wreake the dammage by thee donne:
  Such is thy wont, that still when any Knight
Is weakned, then thou doest him ouerronne:
So hast thou to thy selfe false honour often wonne.

Stanza 37
1   **other companie**: companions.
3   **once to weld**: even to move.

Stanza 38
2   **made good semblance**: put on a fair demeanour.
3   **disease**: distress.
5   **ply**: move.

Stanza 39
1–3   Cf. III xi 7.6–9.   **descride**: perceived.
6   Scudamour possesses Amoret **by right** of conquest;
cf. ix 38.8 and the story of his conquest in Canto x. His claim
is challenged by the unnamed knight, 10.3, and is denied by
Blandamour and Duessa, 51.2, 7.

Stanza 40
The aphorism, 'To beg a thing at a friend's hand is to buy it',
is cited by Mills (1937) 432 to note the absence of friendship.
1   **For thy**: therefore.
9   Proverbial (C. G. Smith, 1970, 355).

Stanza 41
3   **preuenting speed**: passing speed itself, being swifter.

Stanza 42
1   **sowndes**: with the pun, as **roaring** (4) suggests,
appropriate to the narrow waters of a strait.
9   **vpbrayes**: upbraids; suggesting 'brays': loud calling.

Stanza 43
1   **on**: in.
2   **rayle**: railing.

Stanza 44
2   **faitour**: villain; impostor.   **slight**: trickery.
4   **behight**: called; esteemed.
5   **plight**: good condition.

45

He little answer'd, but in manly heart
　His mightie indignation did forbeare,
　Which was not yet so secret, but some part
　Thereof did in his frouning face appeare:
　Like as a gloomie cloud, the which doth beare
　An hideous storme, is by the Northerne blast
　Quite ouerblowne, yet doth not passe so cleare,
　But that it all the skie doth ouercast
With darknes dred, and threatens all the world to wast.

46

Ah gentle knight, then false *Duessa* sayd,
　Why do ye striue for Ladies loue so sore,
　Whose chiefe desire is loue and friendly aid
　Mongst gentle Knights to nourish euermore?
　Ne be ye wroth Sir *Scudamour* therefore,
　That she your loue list loue another knight,
　Ne do your selfe dislike a whit the more;
　For Loue is free, and led with selfe delight,
Ne will enforced be with maisterdome or might.

47

So false *Duessa*, but vile *Ate* thus;
　Both foolish knights, I can but laugh at both,
　That striue and storme with stirre outrageous,
　For her that each of you alike doth loth,
　And loues another, with whom now she goth
　In louely wise, and sleepes, and sports, and playes;
　Whilest both you here with many a cursed oth,
　Sweare she is yours, and stirre vp bloudie frayes,
To win a willow bough, whilest other weares the bayes.

48

Vile hag (sayd *Scudamour*) why dost thou lye?
　And falsly seekst a vertuous wight to shame?
　Fond knight (sayd she) the thing that with this eye
　I saw, why should I doubt to tell the same?
　Then tell (quoth *Blandamour*) and feare no blame,
　Tell what thou saw'st, maulgre who so it heares.
　I saw (quoth she) a stranger knight, whose name
　I wote not well, but in his shield he beares
(That well I wote) the heads of many broken speares.

49

I saw him haue your *Amoret* at will,
　I saw him kisse, I saw him her embrace,
　I saw him sleepe with her all night his fill,
　All manie nights, and manie by in place,
　That present were to testifie the case.
　Which when as *Scudamour* did heare, his heart
　Was thrild with inward griefe, as when in chace
　The Parthian strikes a stag with shiuering dart,
The beast astonisht stands in middest of his smart.

50

So stood Sir *Scudamour*, when this he heard,
　Ne word he had to speake for great dismay,
　But lookt on *Glauce* grim, who woxe afeard
　Of outrage for the words, which she heard say,
　Albee vntrue she wist them by assay.
　But *Blandamour*, whenas he did espie
　His chaunge of cheere, that anguish did bewray,
　He woxe full blithe, as he had got thereby,
And gan thereat to triumph without victorie.

51

Lo recreant (sayd he) the fruitlesse end
　Of thy vaine boast, and spoile of loue misgotten,
　Whereby the name of knight-hood thou dost shend,
　And all true louers with dishonor blotten,
　All things not rooted well, will soone be rotten.
　Fy fy false knight (then false *Duessa* cryde)
　Vnworthy life that loue with guile hast gotten,
　Be thou, where euer thou do go or ryde,
Loathed of ladies all, and of all knights defyde.

Stanza 45
2　**forbeare**: control.

Stanza 46
1　**Ah gentle knight**: addressing Blandamour.
8–9　Duessa parodies Britomart's claim, 'Ne may loue be compeld by maisterie' (III i 25.7); cf. IV ix 37. 6–9. The false claim is asserted through a true one, that love may not be enforced by might.　**maisterdome**: masterful behaviour.

Stanza 47
4　Ate interprets the encounter between Scudamour and Paridell as a struggle for Amoret.
6　**louely**: amorous.　**sleepes**, **sports** and **playes** suggest mounting sexual pleasures.
9　**willow bough**: 'worne of forlorne Paramours' (I i 9.3). **bayes**: the laurel, 'meed of mightie Conquerours' (I i 9.1).

Stanza 48
1　**Vile hag**: her change in appearance expresses the discord she arouses; noted Dallett (1960).
3　**Fond**: foolish.
4　**doubt**: fear.
6　**maulgre**: notwithstanding.
9　The sign of many conquests; cf. III xi 52.6.

Stanza 49
4　**in place**: there.
7–9　Perhaps suggested by Virgil, *Aen*. xii 856–9: the Parthian arrow is armed with an incurable poison; here the wound of slander. The stag suggests cuckold's horns. Cf. Prov. 25.18: 'A man that beareth false witnes against his neighbour is like . . . a sharpe arrowe.' At the next news of his love, he is compared to 'a mazed steare' (vi 37.4–5). **shiuering**: quivering; or capable of splitting.

Stanza 50
5　**assay**: trial, i.e. knowledge.
8　**got**: profited; gained, i.e. gained the victory.

Stanza 51
1　**recreant**: coward, a term of the greatest opprobrium, used here because Amoret's infidelity infers Scudamour's lack of knighthood/manhood.
2　**misgotten**: wrongly obtained by **guile** (7); contrast 39.6. Scudamour 'boasts' of his gaining Amoret as his **spoile** at x 3.3, 58.3.

52

But *Scudamour* for passing great despight
    Staid not to answer, scarcely did refraine,
    But that in all those knights and ladies sight,
    He for reuenge had guiltlesse *Glauce* slaine:
    But being past, he thus began amaine;
    False traitour squire, false squire, of falsest knight,
    Why doth mine hand from thine auenge abstaine,
    Whose Lord hath done my loue this foule despight?
Why do I not it wreake, on thee now in my might?

53

Discourteous, disloyall *Britomart*,
    Vntrue to God, and vnto man vniust,
    What vengeance due can equall thy desart,
    That hast with shamefull spot of sinfull lust
    Defil'd the pledge committed to thy trust?
    Let vgly shame and endlesse infamy
    Colour thy name with foule reproaches rust.
    Yet thou false Squire his fault shalt deare aby,
And with thy punishment his penance shalt supply.

54

The aged Dame him seeing so enraged,
    Was dead with feare, nathlesse as neede required,
    His flaming furie sought to haue assuaged
    With sober words, that sufferance desired,
    Till time the tryall of her truth expyred:
    And euermore sought *Britomart* to cleare.
    But he the more with furious rage was fyred,
    And thrise his hand to kill her did vpreare,
And thrise he drew it backe: so did at last forbeare.

Cant. II.

*Blandamour winnes false Florimell,
Paridell for her striues,
They are accorded: Agape
doth lengthen her sonnes liues.*

1

Firebrand of hell first tynd in Phlegeton,
    By thousand furies, and from thence out throwen
    Into this world, to worke confusion,
    And set it all on fire by force vnknowen,
    Is wicked discord, whose small sparkes once blowen
    None but a God or godlike man can slake;
    Such as was *Orpheus*, that when strife was growen
    Amongst those famous ympes of Greece, did take
His siluer Harpe in hand, and shortly friends them make.

2

Or such as that celestiall Psalmist was,
    That when the wicked feend his Lord tormented,
    With heauenly notes, that did all other pas,
    The outrage of his furious fit relented.
    Such Musicke is wise words with time concented,
    To moderate stiffe minds, disposd to striue:
    Such as that prudent Romane well inuented,
    What time his people into partes did riue,
Them reconcyld againe, and to their homes did driue.

3

Such vs'd wise *Glauce* to that wrathfull knight,
    To calme the tempest of his troubled thought:
    Yet *Blandamour* with termes of foule despight,
    And *Paridell* her scornd, and set at nought,
    As old and crooked and not good for ought.
    Both they vnwise, and wareless of the euill,
    That by themselues vnto themselues is wrought,
    Through that false witch, and that foule aged dreuill,
The one a feend, the other an incarnate deuill.

Stanza 52
1 **passing**: exceeding.
5 **But being past**: i.e. getting over the anger through which he would have slain Glauce; or having passed from the sight of the others; yet see ii 3.   **amaine**: vehemently.
7 **thine auenge**: i.e. revenge upon you.

Stanza 53
1 **disloyall**: unfaithful; as later he dreams, v 43.8. Cf. his praise of Britomart as 'gentlest knight aliue' (III xi 19.1).
6–7 He transfers to Britomart the charges made against him, 51.3–9.
8 **aby**: pay the penalty for.

Stanza 54
4 **sufferance**: forbearance.
5 **Till time . . . expyred**: i.e. until the passing of time brought proof of Britomart's loyalty by revealing the truth. Scudamour must see for himself that Britomart is loyal. See vi 28.1–5.

Canto ii
Argument
3 **accorded**: reconciled.

Stanza 1
1–3 Cf. Furor's firebrand kindled in the Stygian lake, II v 22.6–8.   **tynd**: kindled.   **Phlegeton**: the infernal river of fire; see I v 33.3.   **confusion**: destruction, ruin.
7–9 See i 23.6–9n. The **famous ympes** (youths) of Greece are the Argonauts. For the role of Orpheus, see Apollonius, *Argonautica* i 492f.

Stanza 2
1–4 'When the evil spirit of God came upon Saul, David toke an harpe and plaied with his hand, and Saul was refreshed, and was eased: for the evil spirit departed from him' (1 Sam. 16.23).
5–6 **with time concented**: harmonized; fitting for the time. **stiffe**: obstinate.
7–9 When his countrymen were divided into factions, Menenius Agrippa reconciled them with his fable of the belly. Sidney, *Apol.* 115, cites the well-known tale to demonstrate the persuasive power of fiction.

Stanza 3
6 **wareless**: unaware; unwary.
8 **dreuill**: a dirty person.

435

4

With whom as they thus rode accompanide,
　They were encountred of a lustie Knight,
　That had a goodly Ladie by his side,
　To whom he made great dalliance and delight.
　It was to weete the bold Sir *Ferraugh* hight,
　He that from *Braggadocchio* whilome reft
　The snowy *Florimell*, whose beautie bright
Made him seeme happie for so glorious theft;
Yet was it in due triall but a wandring weft.

5

Which when as *Blandamour*, whose fancie light
　Was alwaies flitting as the wauering wind,
　After each beautie, that appeard in sight,
　Beheld, eftsoones it prickt his wanton mind
　With sting of lust, that reasons eye did blind,
　That to Sir *Paridell* these words he sent;
　Sir knight why ride ye dumpish thus behind,
Since so good fortune doth to you present
So fayre a spoyle, to make you ioyous meriment?

6

But *Paridell* that had too late a tryall
　Of the bad issue of his counsell vaine,
　List not to hearke, but made this faire denyall;
　Last turne was mine, well proued to my paine,
　This now be yours, God send you better gaine.
　Whose scoffed words he taking halfe in scorne,
　Fiercely forth prickt his steed as in disdaine,
　Against that Knight, ere he him well could torne:
By meanes whereof he hath him lightly ouerborne.

7

Who with the sudden stroke astonisht sore,
　Vpon the ground a while in slomber lay;
　The whiles his loue away the other bore,
　And shewing her, did *Paridell* vpbray;
　Lo sluggish Knight the victors happie pray:
　So fortune friends the bold: whom *Paridell*
　Seeing so faire indeede, as he did say,
　His hart with secret enuie gan to swell,
And inly grudge at him, that he had sped so well.

8

Nathlesse proud man himselfe the other deemed,
　Hauing so peerelesse paragon ygot:
　For sure the fayrest *Florimell* him seemed,
　To him was fallen for his happie lot,
　Whose like aliue on earth he weened not:
　Therefore he her did court, did serue, did wooe,
　With humblest suit that he imagine mot,
　And all things did deuise, and all things dooe,
That might her loue prepare, and liking win theretoo.

9

She in regard thereof him recompenst
　With golden words, and goodly countenance,
　And such fond fauours sparingly dispenst:
　Sometimes him blessing with a light eye-glance,
　And coy lookes tempring with loose dalliance;
　Sometimes estranging him in sterner wise,
　That hauing cast him in a foolish trance,
　He seemed brought to bed in Paradise,
436 And prou'd himselfe most foole, in what he seem'd most wise.

10

So great a mistresse of her art she was,
　And perfectly practiz'd in womans craft,
　That though therein himselfe he thought to pas,
　And by his false allurements wylie draft
　Had thousand women of their loue beraft,
　Yet now he was surpriz'd: for that false spright,
　Which that same witch had in this forme engraft,
　Was so expert in euery subtile slight,
That it could ouerreach the wisest earthly wight.

11

Yet he to her did dayly seruice more,
　And dayly more deceiued was thereby;
　Yet *Paridell* him enuied therefore,
　As seeming plast in sole felicity:
　So blind is lust, false colours to descry.
　But *Ate* soone discouering his desire,
　And finding now fit opportunity
　To stirre vp strife, twixt loue and spight and ire,
Did priuily put coles vnto his secret fire.

Stanza 4
2　**lustie**: young; vigorous.
5–9　**Ferraugh**: or '*Ferrau*' (iv 8.2), a pagan knight who loves Angelica, in Ariosto, *Orl. Fur.* i 14–20. The name suggests 'ferray', an obsolete form of 'foray'. See III viii 15.3–5*n*, 16.2–3*n*. His **so glorious theft** anticipates Scudamour's theft of Amoret told in Canto x.　**in due triall**: when duly tried. **wandring weft**: in its legal sense, property left ownerless (as III x 36.3); it suggests something not worth claiming. The true waif is **Florimell**; cf. xii 31.3.

Stanza 5
1–3　His fickleness is stressed by the repetition of his response from i 33.5–9.

Stanza 6
6　**scoffed**: spoken in scoff.
8–9　Blandamour attacks without formal challenge. **lightly**: easily.

Stanza 7
2　**in slomber**: unconscious.
4　**vpbray**: upbraid; as 'bray', spoke loudly to.

Stanza 8
2　**paragon**: companion.
7　**mot**: might, could.

Stanza 9
8　Cf. her effect on Ferraugh: 'So made him thinke him selfe in heauen, that was in hell' (III viii 19.9).

Stanza 10
3　**pas**: excel.
4　**draft**: power of attraction.
6　**surpriz'd**: overcome.
6–9　Cf. III viii 8.　**slight**: sleight; cunning trick.

12

By sundry meanes thereto she prickt him forth,
  Now with remembrance of those spightfull speaches,
  Now with opinion of his owne more worth,
  Now with recounting of like former breaches
  Made in their friendship, as that Hag him teaches:
  And euer when his passion is allayd,
  She it reuiues and new occasion reaches:
  That on a time as they together way'd,
He made him open chalenge, and thus boldly sayd.

13

Too boastfull *Blandamour*, too long I beare
  The open wrongs, thou doest me day by day;
  Well know'st thou, when we friendship first did sweare,
  The couenant was, that euery spoyle or pray
  Should equally be shard betwixt vs tway:
  Where is my part then of this Ladie bright,
  Whom to thy selfe thou takest quite away?
  Render therefore therein to me my right,
Or answere for thy wrong, as shall fall out in fight.

14

Exceeding wroth thereat was *Blandamour*,
  And gan this bitter answere to him make;
  Too foolish *Paridell*, that fayrest floure
  Wouldst gather faine, and yet no paines wouldst take:
  But not so easie will I her forsake;
  This hand her wonne, this hand shall her defend.
  With that they gan their shiuering speares to shake,
  And deadly points at eithers breast to bend,
Forgetfull each to haue bene euer others frend.

15

Their firie Steedes with so vntamed forse
  Did beare them both to fell auenges end,
  That both their speares with pitilesse remorse,
  Through shield and mayle, and haberieon did wend,
  And in their flesh a griesly passage rend,
  That with the furie of their owne affret,
  Each other horse and man to ground did send;
  Where lying still a while, both did forget
The perilous present stownd, in which their liues were set.

16

As when two warlike Brigandines at sea,
  With murdrous weapons arm'd to cruell fight,
  Doe meete together on the watry lea,
  They stemme ech other with so fell despight,
  That with the shocke of their owne heedlesse might,
  Their wooden ribs are shaken nigh a sonder;
  They which from shore behold the dreadfull sight
  Of flashing fire, and heare the ordenance thonder,
Do greatly stand amaz'd at such vnwonted wonder.

17

At length they both vpstarted in amaze,
  As men awaked rashly out of dreme;
  And round about themselues a while did gaze,
  Till seeing her, that *Florimell* did seme,
  In doubt to whom she victorie should deeme,
  Therewith their dulled sprights they edgd anew,
  And drawing both their swords with rage extreme,
  Like two mad mastiffes each on other flew,
And shields did share, and mailes did rash, and helmes did hew.

18

So furiously each other did assayle,
  As if their soules they would attonce haue rent
  Out of their brests, that streames of bloud did rayle
  Adowne, as if their springs of life were spent;
  That all the ground with purple bloud was sprent,
  And all their armours staynd with bloudie gore,
  Yet scarcely once to breath would they relent,
  So mortall was their malice and so sore,
Become of fayned friendship which they vow'd afore.

Stanza 12
3   opinion: favourable estimate.
7   reaches: gives.
8   way'd: journeyed; made their way.

Stanza 13
3–5   The proverbial idea that friends' goods are held in common is used only by false friends; noted C. G. Smith (1935) 50.

Stanza 14
4   faine: gladly.
7   shiuering: quivering; capable of splitting.
8   bend: aim.

Stanza 15
2   to fell auenges end: to cruel revenge.
3   remorse: cutting force.
6   affret: furious onslaught.
9   stownd: moment of peril.

Stanza 16
1   Brigandines: brigantines; also body armour.   warlike: equipped for war.
4   stemme: ram.

Stanza 17
1   amaze: bewilderment.
2   rashly: suddenly.
6–7   their dulled sprights . . . their swords: since their dulled spirits are newly edged or sharpened, they fight with swords.
9   share: cut.   rash: slash.

Stanza 18
3   rayle: flow.
5   sprent: besprinkled.
7   relent: slacken.
9   Become: their malice is fierce because their friendship is only feigned; cf. ix 27.8–9.

437

19

And that which is for Ladies most besitting,
  To stint all strife, and foster friendly peace,
  Was from those Dames so farre and so vnfitting,
  As that in stead of praying them surcease,
  They did much more their cruelty encrease;
  Bidding them fight for honour of their loue,
  And rather die then Ladies cause release.
With which vaine termes so much they did them moue,
That both resolu'd the last extremities to proue.

20

There they I weene would fight vntill this day,
  Had not a Squire, euen he the Squire of Dames,
  By great aduenture trauelled that way;
  Who seeing both bent to so bloudy games,
  And both of old well knowing by their names,
  Drew nigh, to weete the cause of their debate:
  And first laide on those Ladies thousand blames,
That did not seeke t'appease their deadly hate,
But gazed on their harmes, not pittying their estate.

21

And then those Knights he humbly did beseech,
  To stay their hands, till he a while had spoken:
  Who lookt a little vp at that his speech,
  Yet would not let their battell so be broken,
  Both greedie fiers on other to be wroken.
  Yet he to them so earnestly did call,
  And them coniur'd by some well knowen token,
That they at last their wrothfull hands let fall,
Content to heare him speake, and glad to rest withall.

22

First he desir'd their cause of strife to see:
  They said, it was for loue of *Florimell*.
  Ah gentle knights (quoth he) how may that bee,
  And she so farre astray, as none can tell.
  Fond Squire, full angry then sayd *Paridell*,
  Seest not the Ladie there before thy face?
  He looked backe, and her aduizing well,
Weend as he said, by that her outward grace,
That fayrest *Florimell* was present there in place.

23

Glad man was he to see that ioyous sight,
  For none aliue but ioy'd in *Florimell*,
  And lowly to her lowting thus behight;
  Fayrest of faire, that fairenesse doest excell,
  This happie day I haue to greete you well,
  In which you safe I see, whom thousand late
  Misdoubted lost through mischiefe that befell;
Long may you liue in health and happie state.
She litle answer'd him, but lightly did aggrate.

24

Then turning to those Knights, he gan a new;
  And you Sir *Blandamour* and *Paridell*,
  That for this Ladie present in your vew,
  Haue rays'd this cruell warre and outrage fell,
  Certes me seemes bene not aduised well,
  But rather ought in friendship for her sake
  To ioyne your force, their forces to repell,
That seeke perforce her from you both to take,
And of your gotten spoyle their owne triumph to make.

25

Thereat Sir *Blandamour* with countenance sterne,
  All full of wrath, thus fiercely him bespake;
  A read thou Squire, that I the man may learne,
  That dare fro me thinke *Florimell* to take.
  Not one (quoth he) but many doe partake
  Herein, as thus.   It lately so befell,
  That *Satyran* a girdle did vptake,
Well knowne to appertaine to *Florimell*,
Which for her sake he wore, as him beseemed well.

26

But when as she her selfe was lost and gone,
  Full many knights, that loued her like deare,
  Thereat did greatly grudge, that he alone
  That lost faire Ladies ornament should weare,
  And gan therefore close spight to him to beare:
  Which he to shun, and stop vile enuies sting,
  Hath lately caus'd to be proclaim'd each where
A solemne feast, with publike turneying,
To which all knights with them their Ladies are to bring.

Stanza 19

1 **besitting**: befitting.
3 **vnfitting**: i.e. to their natures.
4 **surcease**: stop.
9 **the last extremities to proue**: to suffer death.

Stanza 20

1 Not poetical whimsy: the discord aroused by feigned friendship may never end.
3 **aduenture**: chance.
6 **debate**: also strife.
9 **estate**: state.

Stanza 21

5 **wroken**: wreaked, avenged.
7 The **token**, which is not specified, anticipates Cambina's 'rod of peace' (iii 42.1).   **coniur'd** suggests magical power.

Stanza 22

5 **Fond**: foolish.
7 **aduizing**: looking upon.

Stanza 23

3 **lowting**: bowing.   **behight**: addressed.
7 **Misdoubted**: feared.
9 **She . . . lightly did aggrate**: she thanked him in slighting fashion.

Stanza 24

5 The irony is that he has not **aduised well**; cf. 22.7.

Stanza 25

1 **sterne**: threatening.
3 **A read**: tell.
6–8 See III viii 49.8.

Stanza 26

5 **close**: secret.

27

And of them all she that is fayrest found,
  Shall haue that golden girdle for reward,
  And of those Knights who is most stout on ground,
  Shall to that fairest Ladie be prefard.
  Since therefore she her selfe is now your ward,
  To you that ornament of hers pertaines,
  Against all those, that chalenge it to gard,
  And saue her honour with your ventrous paines;
That shall you win more glory, then ye here find gaines.

28

When they the reason of his words had hard,
  They gan abate the rancour of their rage,
  And with their honours and their loues regard,
  The furious flames of malice to asswage.
  Tho each to other did his faith engage,
  Like faithfull friends thenceforth to ioyne in one
  With all their force, and battell strong to wage
  Gainst all those knights, as their professed fone,
That chaleng'd ought in *Florimell*, saue they alone.

29

So well accorded forth they rode together
  In friendly sort, that lasted but a while;
  And of all old dislikes they made faire weather,
  Yet all was forg'd and spred with golden foyle,
  That vnder it hidde hate and hollow guyle.
  Ne certes can that friendship long endure,
  How euer gay and goodly be the style,
  That doth ill cause or euill end enure:
For vertue is the band, that bindeth harts most sure.

30

Thus as they marched all in close disguise
  Of fayned loue, they chaunst to ouertake
  Two knights, that lincked rode in louely wise,
  As if they secret counsels did partake;
  And each not farre behinde him had his make,
  To weete, two Ladies of most goodly hew,
  That twixt themselues did gentle purpose make,
  Vnmindfull both of that discordfull crew,
The which with speedie pace did after them pursew.

31

Who as they now approched nigh at hand,
  Deeming them doughtie as they did appeare,
  They sent that Squire afore, to vnderstand,
  What mote they be: who viewing them more neare
  Returned readie newes, that those same weare
  Two of the prowest Knights in Faery lond;
  And those two Ladies their two louers deare,
  Couragious *Cambell*, and stout *Triamond*,
With *Canacee* and *Cambine* linckt in louely bond.

32

Whylome as antique stories tellen vs,
  Those two were foes the fellonest on ground,
  And battell made the dreddest daungerous,
  That euer shrilling trumpet did resound;
  Though now their acts be no where to be found,
  As that renowmed Poet them compyled,
  With warlike numbers and Heroicke sound,
  Dan *Chaucer*, well of English vndefyled,
On Fames eternall beadroll worthie to be fyled.

Stanza 27
4 **be prefard**: be offered or given in preference; or be preferred by her, as happens at v 26.8–9. Also 'be settled in marriage'.
6–8 **To you ... paines**: it concerns you to guard her ornament against all who lay claim to it. The girdle is associated with Florimell's honour; see v 3–5*n*.

Stanza 28
9 **saue they alone**: evidently they agree that she 'equally be shard' (13.5).

Stanza 29
1 **accorded**: reconciled; as Arg. 3.
3 **made faire weather**: made a show of friendliness.
4–5 Cf. v 15.1–6; see I iv 4.4*n*.
7 **style**: outward demeanour; mere appearance.
8 **enure**: put into practice. Friendship is a legal covenant which comes into existence both through a good cause and as it seeks a good end.
9 Proverbial (C. G. Smith, 1970, 311). Cf. Aristotle, *Ethics* VIII iv 1157a: 'Clearly only good men can be friends; for bad men do not delight in each other unless some advantage come of the relation.'

Stanza 30
In the **discordfull crew**, each knight has a lady riding by his side (i 17.3); in contrast, the true friends ride together with **their ladies not far behind**; cf. iv 2.6–9, 14.9. The false friends are unevenly linked – Paridell is linked with Duessa and Ate, and shares the False Florimell with Blandamour – while the true friends are evenly paired.
3 **louely**: loving.
7 **gentle purpose**: polite gossip.

Stanza 31
8–9 **Cambell** is taken from Camballo in Chaucer, *Squire's Tale* (ed. Thynne), adapted to link with Lat. *bellum*, to suggest his warlike nature. **Canacee** is unchanged from Chaucer (Canace in Thynne). For **Triamond**, see 41.7–9*n*. **Cambine**: from Ital. *cambiare*, 'to exchange, to change' (Florio, 1611) because she changes hatred to love; or from 'combine' because she joins the others in love (sugg. Belson, 1964). **louely**: loving.

Stanza 32
S.'s continuation of Chaucer's *Squire's Tale* begins by imitating the first line of the first of the *Canterbury Tales*: 'Whilom, as olde stories tellen us'. He begins where the *Squire's Tale* ends: 'And after wol I speke of Cambalo, / That faught in lystes with the brethren two / For Canacee er that he myghte hire wynne.'
2 **fellonest**: fiercest.
8–9 **Dan**: Master. **well ... vndefyled**: cf. 'That old *Dan Geffrey* (in whose gentle spright / The pure well head of Poesie did dwell)' (VII vii 9.3–4); cf. Holinshed's (1577) praise of Chaucer: 'For reducing our English toong to a perfect conformitie, he hath excelled therein all other' (iii 58). **beadroll**: catalogue. **fyled**: placed for preservation.

439

33

But wicked Time that all good thoughts doth waste,
  And workes of noblest wits to nought out weare,
  That famous moniment hath quite defaste,
  And robd the world of threasure endlesse deare,
  The which mote haue enriched all vs heare.
  O cursed Eld the cankerworme of writs,
  How may these rimes, so rude as doth appeare,
  Hope to endure, sith workes of heauenly wits
Are quite deuourd, and brought to nought by little bits?

34

Then pardon, O most sacred happie spirit,
  That I thy labours lost may thus reuiue,
  And steale from thee the meede of thy due merit,
  That none durst euer whilest thou wast aliue,
  And being dead in vaine yet many striue:
  Ne dare I like, but through infusion sweete
  Of thine owne spirit, which doth in me suruiue,
  I follow here the footing of thy feete,
That with thy meaning so I may the rather meete.

35

Cambelloes sister was fayre Canacee,
  That was the learnedst Ladie in her dayes,
  Well seene in euerie science that mote bee,
  And euery secret worke of natures wayes,
  In wittie riddles, and in wise soothsayes,
  In power of herbes, and tunes of beasts and burds;
  And, that augmented all her other prayse,
  She modest was in all her deedes and words,
And wondrous chast of life, yet lou'd of Knights and Lords.

36

Full many Lords, and many Knights her loued,
  Yet she to none of them her liking lent,
  Ne euer was with fond affection moued,
  But rul'd her thoughts with goodly gouernement,
  For dread of blame and honours blemishment;
  And eke vnto her lookes a law she made,
  That none of them once out of order went,
  But like to warie Centonels well stayd,
Still watcht on euery side, of secret foes affrayd.

37

So much the more as she refusd to loue,
  So much the more she loued was and sought,
  That oftentimes vnquiet strife did moue
  Amongst her louers, and great quarrels wrought,
  That oft for her in bloudie armes they fought.
  Which whenas Cambell, that was stout and wise,
  Perceiu'd would breede great mischiefe, he bethought
  How to preuent the perill that mote rise,
And turne both him and her to honour in this wise.

38

One day, when all that troupe of warlike wooers
  Assembled were, to weet whose she should bee,
  All mightie men and dreadfull derring dooers,
  (The harder it to make them well agree)
  Amongst them all this end he did decree;
  That of them all, which loue to her did make,
  They by consent should chose the stoutest three,
  That with himselfe should combat for her sake,
440 And of them all the victour should his sister take.

39

Bold was the chalenge, as himselfe was bold,
  And courage full of haughtie hardiment,
  Approued oft in perils manifold,
  Which he atchieu'd to his great ornament:
  But yet his sisters skill vnto him lent
  Most confidence and hope of happie speed,
  Conceiued by a ring, which she him sent,
  That mongst the manie vertues, which we reed,
Had power to staunch al wounds, that mortally did bleed.

Stanza 33
Cf. Milton's view in *Il Penseroso* 109 that Chaucer's tale was 'left half-told'. Speght, *Chaucer's Works* (1598) Ciiii ˘, allows that much of the tale 'is either lost, or els never finished'. S. applies Chaucer's own image of transitory Fame: in the *House of Fame* 1144–7, on the rock of ice 'of the lettres oon or two / Was molte away of every name, / So unfamous was woxe hir fame. / But men seyn "What may ever laste?"'
6–9 S. imitates Chaucer's complaint: 'This olde storie, in Latyn which I fynde, / . . . That elde, which that al can frete and bite, / As hit hath freten mony a noble storie, / Hath nygh devoured out of oure memorie' (*Anelida and Arcite* 10–4).

Stanza 34
1 **happie**: blessed.
6–9 Speght, *Chaucer's Works* (1598) C iii, notes that in this episode 'for his like naturall disposition that Chaucer had, hee [S.] sheweth that none that lived with him, nor none that came after him, durst presume to revive Chaucers lost labours in that unperfite tale of the Squire, but only himselfe'.
6 **Ne dare I like**: nor would I dare to strive. **infusion**: pouring in; cf. the use of the concept of traduction in the story that follows, iii 13.6.
8 **feete**: also metrical divisions.
9 **That . . . I may the rather meete**: That I may accord with your meaning.

Stanza 35
3 **seene**: skilled.
6 The enchanted ring gives Chaucer's Canacee the power to understand birds and the knowledge of herbs; S. adds the other powers.
7 **that**: that which.

Stanza 36
4 **gouernement**: temperance; see II i 29.8*n*, ix 1.4*n*.

Stanza 38
3 **derring dooers**: daring doers.

Stanza 39
2 **courage**: heart, spirit. **hardiment**: boldness.
8–9 As the ring gave Canacee the knowledge of medicinal herbs, which 'it wol do boote, / Al be his woundes never so depe and wyde' (*Squire's Tale* 154–5).

40

Well was that rings great vertue knowen to all,
    That dread thereof, and his redoubted might
Did all that youthly rout so much appall,
    That none of them durst vndertake the fight;
    More wise they weend to make of loue delight,
Then life to hazard for faire Ladies looke,
    And yet vncertaine by such outward sight,
    Though for her sake they all that perill tooke,
Whether she would them loue, or in her liking brooke.

41

Amongst those knights there were three brethren bold,
    Three bolder brethren neuer were yborne,
Borne of one mother in one happie mold,
    Borne at one burden in one happie morne,
    Thrise happie mother, and thrise happie morne,
That bore three such, three such not to be fond;
    Her name was *Agape* whose children werne
    All three as one, the first hight *Priamond*,
The second *Dyamond*, the youngest *Triamond*.

42

Stout *Priamond*, but not so strong to strike,
    Strong *Diamond*, but not so stout a knight,
But *Triamond* was stout and strong alike:
    On horsebacke vsed *Triamond* to fight,
    And *Priamond* on foote had more delight,
But horse and foote knew *Diamond* to wield:
    With curtaxe vsed *Diamond* to smite,
    And *Triamond* to handle speare and shield,
But speare and curtaxe both vsd *Priamond* in field.

43

These three did loue each other dearely well,
    And with so firme affection were allyde,
As if but one soule in them all did dwell,
    Which did her powre into three parts diuyde;
    Like three faire branches budding farre and wide,
That from one roote deriu'd their vitall sap:
    And like that roote that doth her life diuide,
    Their mother was, and had full blessed hap,
These three so noble babes to bring forth at one clap.

44

Their mother was a Fay, and had the skill
    Of secret things, and all the powres of nature,
Which she by art could vse vnto her will,
    And to her seruice bind each liuing creature,
    Through secret vnderstanding of their feature.
Thereto she was right faire, when so her face
    She list discouer, and of goodly stature;
    But she as Fayes are wont, in priuie place
Did spend her dayes, and lov'd in forests wyld to space.

45

There on a day a noble youthly knight
    Seeking aduentures in the saluage wood,
Did by great fortune get of her the sight,
    As she sate carelesse by a cristall flood,
    Combing her golden lockes, as seemd her good:
And vnawares vpon her laying hold,
    That stroue in vaine him long to haue withstood,
    Oppressed her, and there (as it is told)
Got these three louely babes, that prov'd three champions bold.

Stanza 40
7   **by such outward sight**: by what they could see.
9   **brooke**: remain.

Stanzas 41–43
Wind (1967) 210 discusses the 'unfolding' of Agape into her
sons. Fowler (1973) 56–7 comments on the mystical unfolding
of the triad in stanza 42.

Stanza 41
4   **burden**: applied to child-birth.
7–9   **Agape**: Gk charity or love; specifically, brotherly love.
Priamond: Lat. *prima*+*mundus*: first-born; or as he has one
life in contrast to his brothers (sugg. Belson, 1964).
Dyamond: *duo*+*mundus*: the second born; or two lives: the
life of the dead Priamond joins his, and he loses both at the
same time.   **Triamond**: *tres*+*mundus*, the third born who
enjoys three lives at iii 22.

Stanza 42
Correlative verse with the pattern 1–2–3, 3–1–2, 2–3–1. It
circles back on itself to form three pairs: 3,3;2,2;1,1.
1   **Stout**: brave, courageous; cf. *Cambell*, 'stout and wise'
(37.6).
7   **curtaxe**: curtal-axe, a shortened battle-axe.

Stanza 43
3–6   The lines explain the basis of traduction and
friendship. Friendship as 'one soul in bodies twain' is
proverbial (C. G. Smith, 1970, 306); one soul in three bodies
also suggests the three souls in man.
9   **at one clap**: at once.

Stanzas 44–52
Upton (1758) notes Agape's similarity to Virgil's Feronia; cf.
44.9 and *Aen.* vii 800. Feronia procured three souls for her son
Erulus so that he needed to be slain three times before he was
killed (viii 564–7). Fowler (1964) 28 notes that, according to
Servius, Erulus's three lives symbolize man's multiplicity of
souls.

Stanza 44
1–5   Cf. Canacee's knowledge of nature, 35.3–4. Agape's
powers are referred to again at iii 40.1–5.   **Fay**: fairy.
skill: understanding.   **feature**: form.
9   **space**: roam.

Stanza 45
2   **saluage**: wild.
8   **Oppressed**: raped.

441

46

Which she with her long fostred in that wood,
　Till that to ripenesse of mans state they grew:
　Then shewing forth signes of their fathers blood,
　They loued armes, and knighthood did ensew,
　Seeking aduentures, where they anie knew.
　Which when their mother saw, she gan to dout
　Their safetie, least by searching daungers new,
　And rash prouoking perils all about,
Their days mote be abridged through their corage stout.

47

Therefore desirous th'end of all their dayes
　To know, and them t'enlarge with long extent,
　By wondrous skill, and many hidden wayes,
　To the three fatall sisters house she went.
　Farre vnder ground from tract of liuing went,
　Downe in the bottome of the deepe *Abysse*,
　Where *Demogorgon* in dull darknesse pent,
　Farre from the view of Gods and heauens blis,
The hideous *Chaos* keepes, their dreadfull dwelling is.

48

There she them found, all sitting round about
　The direfull distaffe standing in the mid,
　And with vnwearied fingers drawing out
　The lines of life, from liuing knowledge hid.
　Sad *Clotho* held the rocke, the whiles the thrid
　By griesly *Lachesis* was spun with paine,
　That cruell *Atropos* eftsoones vndid,
　With cursed knife cutting the twist in twaine:
Most wretched men, whose dayes depend on thrids so vaine.

49

She them saluting, there by them sate still,
　Beholding how the thrids of life they span:
　And when at last she had beheld her fill,
　Trembling in heart, and looking pale and wan,
　Her cause of comming she to tell began.
　To whom fierce *Atropos*, Bold Fay, that durst
　Come see the secret of the life of man,
　Well worthie thou to be of *Ioue* accurst,
And eke thy childrens thrids to be a sunder burst.

50

Whereat she sore affrayd, yet her besought
　To graunt her boone, and rigour to abate,
　That she might see her childrens thrids forth brought,
　And know the measure of their vtmost date,
　To them ordained by eternall fate.
　Which *Clotho* graunting, shewed her the same:
　That when she saw, it did her much amate,
　To see their thrids so thin, as spiders frame,
And eke so short, that seemd their ends out shortly came.

51

She then began them humbly to intreate,
　To draw them longer out, and better twine,
　That so their liues might be prolonged late.
　But *Lachesis* thereat gan to repine,
　And sayd, Fond dame that deem'st of things diuine
　As of humane, that they may altred bee,
　And chaung'd at pleasure for those impes of thine.
　Not so; for what the Fates do once decree,
442 Not all the gods can chaunge, nor *Ioue* him self can free.

52

Then since (quoth she) the terme of each mans life
　For nought may lessened nor enlarged bee,
　Graunt this, that when ye shred with fatall knife
　His line, which is the eldest of the three,
　Which is of them the shortest, as I see,
　Eftsoones his life may passe into the next;
　And when the next shall likewise ended bee,
　That both their liues may likewise be annext
Vnto the third, that his may so be trebly wext.

Stanza 46
4　ensew: follow.
6　dout: fear.

Stanza 47
4–9　Cf. the house of the Fates in Ovid, *Met*. xv 808–9.
Boccaccio, *Gen. Deor*. I v, notes that the Fates, as the daughters
of Demogorgon, were coeval with the beginnings of things
(Lotspeich, 1932, 58–9).
5　tract . . . went: track of any living creature's path.
7　Demogorgon: an infernal deity; see I i 37.8*n*.

Stanza 48
Cf. Cooper (1565) on the Parcae: 'Ladies of destenie. The
names of them be *Clotho, Lachesis*, and *Atropos*. The first of
them is devised to beare the distaffe, the seconde to spynne
out the threade of mans lyfe so longe as it doth continue, the
third breaketh of the thread, and endeth the mans life.' Cf. also
E.K.'s note to *S.C.* Nov. 148.
2　direfull: perhaps alluding to the 'Dirae', the Furies.
5　Sad: steadfast; grave.　rocke: distaff.
9　vaine: useless, being frail.

Stanza 49
6　Atropos replies because she is the unchangeable one.

Stanza 50
2　boone: request.
4　date: term of life; cf. 52.1.
7　amate: dismay.

Stanza 51
7　impes: children.
8–9　Cf. III iii 25.6–7. For the unchangeableness of the
gods' decrees, see Ovid, *Met*. xv 780–1.　free: get rid of.

Stanza 52
3　shred: cut in two.

53

They graunted it; and then that carefull Fay
 Departed thence with full contented mynd;
 And comming home, in warlike fresh aray
 Them found all three according to their kynd:
 But vnto them what destinie was assynd,
 Or how their liues were eekt, she did not tell;
 But euermore, when she fit time could fynd,
 She warned them to tend their safeties well,
And loue each other deare, what euer them befell.

54

So did they surely during all their dayes,
 And neuer discord did amongst them fall;
 Which much augmented all their other praise.
 And now t'increase affection naturall,
 In loue of *Canacee* they ioyned all:
 Vpon which ground this same great battell grew,
 Great matter growing of beginning small;
 The which for length I will not here pursew,
But rather will reserue it for a Canto new.

Cant. III.

*The battell twixt three brethren with
Cambell for Canacee:
Cambina with true friendships bond
doth their long strife agree.*

1

O Why doe wretched men so much desire,
 To draw their dayes vnto the vtmost date,
 And doe not rather wish them soone expire,
 Knowing the miserie of their estate,
 And thousand perills which them still awate,
 Tossing them like a boate amid the mayne,
 That euery houre they knocke at deathes gate?
 And he that happie seemes and least in payne,
Yet is as nigh his end, as he that most doth playne.

2

Therefore this Fay I hold but fond and vaine,
 The which in seeking for her children three
 Long life, thereby did more prolong their paine.
 Yet whilest they liued none did euer see
 More happie creatures, then they seem'd to bee,
 Nor more ennobled for their courtesie,
 That made them dearely lou'd of each degree;
 Ne more renowmed for their cheualrie,
That made them dreaded much of all men farre and nie.

3

These three that hardie chalenge tooke in hand,
 For *Canacee* with *Cambell* for to fight:
 The day was set, that all might vnderstand,
 And pledges pawnd the same to keepe a right,
 That day, the dreddest day that liuing wight
 Did euer see vpon this world to shine,
 So soone as heauens window shewed light,
 These warlike Champions all in armour shine,
Assembled were in field, the chalenge to define.

Stanza 53
1   **carefull**: full of care.
3–4   **in . . . aray . . . / . . . according to their kynd**:
i.e. each was arrayed according to his ability, Diamond with a
curtaxe, etc., as described at 42.7–9.
6   **eekt**: lengthened.

Stanza 54
4–5   Contrasts with the usual clash between friendship and
love, as in Chaucer's *Knight's Tale*.
8–9   The poet intrudes himself again at the conclusion to
Cantos iv–vii, ix–xii.

Canto iii

Argument
4   **agree**: conciliate.

Stanza 1
2   **vtmost date**: term of life, as ii 50.4.
3   **expire**: brought to an end.
9   **playne**: lament.

Stanza 2
1   **fond**: foolish.   **vaine**: thoughtless.
6–9   Cf. the conjunction of courtesy and chivalry in
Britomart, i 11.6, and in Calidore: see VI i 2.7–9n.
7   **of each degree**: by all social classes.

Stanzas 3–35
The battle shows the passage of life from the first brother to the
second and then to the third, as the Fates had promised (ii 52).
When Priamond is slain, his soul enters Diamond (13); when
Diamond is beheaded, both souls enter Triamond (22).
Triamond loses one soul from a throat-wound (30) and a
second from a wound in the arm-pit (34). Although he falls
dead, he starts up 'breathing now another spright' (35.8),
which is his own. The three battles are carefully varied in the
weapons used (spear, axe, sword), in the precise nature and
number of the wounds, in stanza length (8,8,16), etc.

Stanza 3
8   **shine**: shining; or 'sheen': bright.
9   **define**: decide.

443

4

The field with listes was all about enclos'd,
　To barre the prease of people farre away;
　And at th'one side sixe iudges were dispos'd,
　To view and deeme the deedes of armes that day;
　And on the other side in fresh aray,
　Fayre *Canacee* vpon a stately stage
　Was set, to see the fortune of that fray,
　And to be seene, as his most worthie wage,
That could her purchase with his liues aduentur'd gage.

5

Then entred *Cambell* first into the list,
　With stately steps, and fearelesse countenance,
　As if the conquest his he surely wist.
　Soone after did the brethren three aduance,
　In braue aray and goodly amenance,
　With scutchins gilt and banners broad displayd:
　And marching thrise in warlike ordinance,
　Thrise lowted lowly to the noble Mayd,
The whiles shril trompets and loud clarions sweetly playd.

6

Which doen the doughty chalenger came forth,
　All arm'd to point his chalenge to abet:
　Gainst whom Sir *Priamond* with equall worth,
　And equall armes himselfe did forward set.
　A trompet blew; they both together met,
　With dreadfull force, and furious intent,
　Carelesse of perill in their fiers affret,
　As if that life to losse they had forelent,
And cared not to spare, that should be shortly spent.

7

Right practicke was Sir *Priamond* in fight,
　And throughly skild in vse of shield and speare;
　Ne lesse approued was *Cambelloes* might,
　Ne lesse his skill in weapons did appeare,
　That hard it was to weene which harder were.
　Full many mightie strokes on either side
　Were sent, that seemed death in them to beare,
　But they were both so watchfull and well eyde,
That they auoyded were, and vainely by did slyde.

8

Yet one of many was so strongly bent
　By *Priamond,* that with vnluckie glaunce
　Through *Cambels* shoulder it vnwarely went,
　That forced him his shield to disaduaunce:
　Much was he grieued with that gracelesse chaunce,
　Yet from the wound no drop of bloud there fell,
　But wondrous paine, that did the more enhaunce
　His haughtie courage to aduengement fell:
Smart daunts not mighty harts, but makes them more to swell.

9

With that his poynant speare he fierce auentred,
　With doubled force close vnderneath his shield,
　That through the mayles into his thigh it entred,
　And there arresting, readie way did yield,
　For bloud to gush forth on the grassie field;
　That he for paine himselfe n'ote right vpreare,
　But too and fro in great amazement reel'd,
　Like an old Oke whose pith and sap is seare,
444 At puffe of euery storme doth stagger here and theare.

10

Whom so dismayd when *Cambell* had espide,
　Againe he droue at him with double might,
　That nought mote stay the steele, till in his side
　The mortall point most cruelly empight:
　Where fast infixed, whilest he sought by slight
　It forth to wrest, the staffe a sunder brake,
　And left the head behind: with which despight
　He all enrag'd, his shiuering speare did shake,
And charging him a fresh thus felly him bespake.

Stanza 4
1　listes: barriers; cf. 'raile' 46.2.
4　deeme: judge.
8　wage: reward.
9　with his liues aduentur'd gage: i.e. by offering his life as a pledge.

Stanza 5
5　amenance: bearing; more particularly, noble bearing.
6　scutchins: shields.
7　ordinance: array.

Stanza 6
2　to point: completely.　abet: maintain.
7　affret: furious onslaught; see III ix 16.3*n*.
8　forelent: given up beforehand.

Stanza 7
1　practicke: skilled.
2　Cf. ii 42.7–9. The line notes his powers of defence and attack. This first stage of the battle is fought with spear (cf. 9.1, 10.8) as though the knights were on horseback.
5　harder: capable of greater exertion; or, 'hardier': stronger.

Stanza 8
1　bent: aimed.
3　vnwarely: unexpectedly; as he was unwary.
5　gracelesse: cruel.
8　aduengement: the sixteenth-century spelling here links with disaduaunce (4). Since he may not defend himself, he is forced to attack.

Stanza 9
1　poynant: piercing.　auentred: thrust forward (sugg. by the context). At III i 28.7, the term suggests a spear aimed by setting it in its rest. Cf. IV vi 11.3.
4　arresting: stopping.
6　n'ote] not *1596*; both forms signify 'knew not (how to)'.
7　amazement: loss of self-possession; overwhelming fear.
9　stagger: sway.

Stanza 10
4　empight: implanted itself.
5　slight: skilful handling.
8　shiuering: capable of splitting; quivering.

11

Lo faitour there thy meede vnto thee take,
  The meede of thy mischalenge and abet :
  Not for thine owne, but for thy sisters sake,
  Haue I thus long thy life vnto thee let :
  But to forbeare doth not forgiue the det.
  The wicked weapon heard his wrathfull vow,
  And passing forth with furious affret,
  Pierst through his beuer quite into his brow,
That with the force it backward forced him to bow.

12

Therewith a sunder in the midst it brast,
  And in his hand nought but the troncheon left,
  The other halfe behind yet sticking fast,
  Out of his headpeece *Cambell* fiercely reft,
  And with such furie backe at him it heft,
  That making way vnto his dearest life,
  His weasand pipe it through his gorget cleft :
  Thence streames of purple bloud issuing rife,
Let forth his wearie ghost and made an end of strife.

13

His wearie ghost assoyld from fleshly band,
  Did not as others wont, directly fly
  Vnto her rest in Plutoes griesly land,
  Ne into ayre did vanish presently,
  Ne chaunged was into a starre in sky :
  But through traduction was eftsoones deriued,
  Like as his mother prayd the Destinie,
  Into his other brethren, that suruiued,
In whom he liu'd a new, of former life depriued.

14

Whom when on ground his brother next beheld,
  Though sad and sorie for so heauy sight,
  Yet leaue vnto his sorrow did not yeeld,
  But rather stird to vengeance and despight,
  Through secret feeling of his generous spright,
  Rusht fiercely forth, the battell to renew,
  As in reuersion of his brothers right ;
  And chalenging the Virgin as his dew.
His foe was soone addrest : the trompets freshly blew.

15

With that they both together fiercely met,
  As if that each ment other to deuoure ;
  And with their axes both so sorely bet,
  That neither plate nor mayle, whereas their powre
  They felt, could once sustaine the hideous stowre,
  But riued were like rotten wood a sunder,
  Whilest through their rifts the ruddie bloud did showre
  And fire did flash, like lightning after thunder,
That fild the lookers on attonce with ruth and wonder.

Stanza 11

1 **faitour**: villain. At last used without its intensive, 'false'.
2 **The meede ... abet**: The reward for your wrongful challenge and for your maintaining it. **abet**: encouragement of an offence; also trickery, wiles; cf. 6.2. The description of the challenge as 'Bold' (ii 39.1) glosses over its incestuous implications, inferred in the conclusion to Chaucer's *Squire's Tale* and in the Man of Law's reference to Canacee 'That loved hir owene brother synfully' (II B^1 79).
4 **let**: granted possession; allowed.
5 Proverbial (C. G. Smith, 1970, 279). In keeping with the money imagery in 1–4, **to forbeare** means to abstain from enforcing payment after it has become due; also, **forgiue**: give up the claim to.

Stanza 12

2 **troncheon**: broken spear shaft.
5 **heft**: heaved, hurled.
7–9 The soul usually leaves the body through the mouth; see Didron (1886) ii 173f. **weasand pipe**: windpipe or throat. **gorget**: armour for the throat.

Stanza 13

1 **assoyld**: set free.
2–6 Four choices are allowed the soul separated from the body: to descend into hell, rise into the air, ascend to the heavens, or remain on earth by entering another body. It is not clear which of the four is its 'natiue home' (30.9). Each involves a different state: unchanged in hell, evaporating into the air, stellified in the heavens, and united with another soul in a body. For the first three, the classical analogues are revealing: the death of Turnus (Virgil, *Aen.* xii 952), of Dido (*Aen.* iv 705), and of Caesar (Ovid, *Met.* xv 845–6). The fourth illustrates Pythagorean metempsychosis, as Upton (1758) notes.
4 **presently**: at once.
6 **traduction**: transmission, a metempsychosis or transmigration of the soul; cf. 'infusion' (ii 34.6). **deriued**: conveyed; transferred.
8 **his other brethren**: or 'the next' (ii 52.6). S. refers to its double flight.

Stanza 14

1 **his brother next**: his second brother, Diamond.
5 **his**: his brother's or his own (as the two are joined). **generous**: high-spirited; vigorous; courageous (cf. 'Stout' ii 42.1); or in the usual sense, as it freely offers itself to him.
7 **in reuersion of**: in the legal sense, the right of succession to an office after the death of the holder.
9 **addrest**: prepared.

Stanza 15

4 **whereas**: where.
5 **stowre**: conflict.
8 Thunder precedes lightning, for it was believed to be caused by clouds clashing together.
9 **ruth and wonder**: the emotions aroused by tragedy; cf. III xi 12.8.

16

As when two Tygers prickt with hungers rage,
  Haue by good fortune found some beasts fresh spoyle,
  On which they weene their famine to asswage,
  And gaine a feastfull guerdon of their toyle,
  Both falling out doe stirre vp strifefull broyle,
  And cruell battell twixt themselues doe make,
  Whiles neither lets the other touch the soyle,
  But either sdeignes with other to partake:
So cruelly these Knights stroue for that Ladies sake.

17

Full many strokes, that mortally were ment,
  The whiles were enterchaunged twixt them two;
  Yet they were all with so good wariment
  Or warded, or auoyded and let goe,
  That still the life stood fearelesse of her foe:
  Till *Diamond* disdeigning long delay
  Of doubtfull fortune wauering to and fro,
  Resolu'd to end it one or other way;
And heau'd his murdrous axe at him with mighty sway.

18

The dreadfull stroke in case it had arriued,
  Where it was ment, (so deadly it was ment)
  The soule had sure out of his bodie riued,
  And stinted all the strife incontinent.
  But *Cambels* fate that fortune did preuent:
  For seeing it at hand, he swaru'd asyde,
  And so gaue way vnto his fell intent:
  Who missing of the marke which he had eyde,
Was with the force nigh feld whilst his right foot did slyde.

19

As when a Vulture greedie of his pray,
  Through hunger long, that hart to him doth lend,
  Strikes at an Heron with all his bodies sway,
  That from his force seemes nought may it defend;
  The warie fowle that spies him toward bend
  His dreadfull souse, auoydes it shunning light,
  And maketh him his wing in vaine to spend;
  That with the weight of his owne weeldlesse might,
He falleth nigh to ground, and scarse recouereth flight.

20

Which faire aduenture when *Cambello* spide,
  Full lightly, ere himselfe he could recower,
  From daungers dread to ward his naked side,
  He can let driue at him with all his power,
  And with his axe him smote in euill hower,
  That from his shoulders quite his head he reft:
  The headlesse tronke, as heedlesse of that stower,
  Stood still a while, and his fast footing kept,
Till feeling life to fayle, it fell, and deadly slept.

21

They which that piteous spectacle beheld,
  Were much amaz'd the headlesse tronke to see
  Stand vp so long, and weapon vaine to weld,
  Vnweeting of the Fates diuine decree,
  For lifes succession in those brethren three.
  For notwithstanding that one soule was reft,
  Yet, had the bodie not dismembred bee,
  It would haue liued, and reuiued eft;
But finding no fit seat, the lifelesse corse it left.

22

It left; but that same soule, which therein dwelt,
  Streight entring into *Triamond*, him fild
  With double life, and griefe, which when he felt,
  As one whose inner parts had bene ythrild
  With point of steele, that close his hartbloud spild,
  He lightly lept out of his place of rest,
  And rushing forth into the emptie field,
  Against *Cambello* fiercely him addrest;
Who him affronting soone to fight was readie prest.

Stanza 16
2 **spoyle**: prey. Canacee is the spoil over whom the earlier suitors, and now these two knights, fought.
7 **soyle**: either an error for **spoyle** (2) or suggesting 'prey', being the ground where the prey lies or the place where a hunted deer takes final refuge (cf. esp. x 55.8–9).

Stanza 17
3 **wariment**: wariness.
5 **her foe**: Death.
9 **axe**: his 'curtaxe' (ii 42.7). **sway**: impetus, force.

Stanza 18
1 **in case**: if.
4 **incontinent**: immediately; also as an adj., 'intemperate'.

Stanza 19
Since the vulture feeds only on carrion, as Harrison (1956) 76–7 notes, the point may be that it is driven by hunger to excessive fierceness.
5 **bend**: aim.
6 **souse**: swoop. **light**: quickly; nimbly.
8 **weeldlesse**: unwieldy.

Stanza 20
1 **aduenture**: chance, i.e. opportunity; cf. 'aduantage' 30.1.
4 **can**: began.
7 **stower**: blow.
9 **deadly**: i.e. in death.

Stanza 21
8 **eft**: again.

Stanza 22
1–3 **It**: i.e. the second soul; or referring to both Priamond and Diamond, for they were allied 'As if but one soule in them all did dwell' (ii 43.3); cf. 13.8. **double life**: refers to Priamond's and Diamond's soul(s).
5 **close**: secretly; completely.
9 **affronting**: confronting. **prest**: prepared.

23

Well mote ye wonder how that noble Knight,
　　After he had so often wounded beene,
　　Could stand on foot, now to renew the fight.
　　But had ye then him forth aduauncing seene,
　　Some newborne wight ye would him surely weene:
　　So fresh he seemed and so fierce in sight;
　　Like as a Snake, whom wearie winters teene
　　Hath worne to nought, now feeling sommers might,
Casts off his ragged skin and freshly doth him dight.

24

All was through vertue of the ring he wore,
　　The which not onely did not from him let
　　One drop of bloud to fall, but did restore
　　His weakned powers, and dulled spirits whet,
　　Through working of the stone therein yset.
　　Else how could one of equall might with most,
　　Against so many no lesse mightie met,
　　Once thinke to match three such on equall cost,
Three such as able were to match a puissant host.

25

Yet nought thereof was *Triamond* adredde,
　　Ne desperate of glorious victorie,
　　But sharpely him assayld, and sore bestedde,
　　With heapes of strokes, which he at him let flie,
　　As thicke as hayle forth poured from the skie:
　　He stroke, he soust, he foynd, he hewd, he lasht,
　　And did his yron brond so fast applie,
　　That from the same the fierie sparkles flasht,
As fast as water-sprinkles gainst a rocke are dasht.

26

Much was *Cambello* daunted with his blowes.
　　So thicke they fell, and forcibly were sent,
　　That he was forst from daunger of the throwes
　　Backe to retire, and somewhat to relent,
　　Till th'heat of his fierce furie he had spent:
　　Which when for want of breath gan to abate,
　　He then afresh with new encouragement
　　Did him assayle, and mightily amate,
As fast as forward erst, now backward to retrate.

27

Like as the tide that comes fro th'Ocean mayne,
　　Flowes vp the Shenan with contrarie forse,
　　And ouerruling him in his owne rayne,
　　Driues backe the current of his kindly course,
　　And makes it seeme to haue some other sourse:
　　But when the floud is spent, then backe againe
　　His borrowed waters forst to redisbourse,
　　He sends the sea his owne with double gaine,
And tribute eke withall, as to his Soueraine.

28

Thus did the battell varie to and fro,
　　With diuerse fortune doubtfull to be deemed:
　　Now this the better had, now had his fo;
　　Then he halfe vanquisht, then the other seemed,
　　Yet victors both them selues always esteemed.
　　And all the while the disentrayled blood
　　Adowne their sides like litle riuers stremed,
　　That with the wasting of his vitall flood,
Sir *Triamond* at last full faint and feeble stood.

29

But *Cambell* still more strong and greater grew,
　　Ne felt his blood to wast, ne powres emperisht,
　　Through that rings vertue, that with vigour new,
　　Still when as he enfeebled was, him cherisht,
　　And all his wounds, and all his bruses guarisht,
　　Like as a withered tree through husbands toyle
　　Is often seene full freshly to haue florisht,
　　And fruitfull apples to haue borne awhile,
As fresh as when it first was planted in the soyle.

Stanza 23
6–9　　Cf. 29.6–9 for the emphasis on **freshly**.　　**teene**:
affliction.

Stanza 24
1–5　　The ring stanches bleeding (cf. ii 39.7–9); its stone
renews strength and courage.
6　　**of equall might with most**: of no more than average
strength.
8　　**equall cost**: either 'coast', i.e. on fair ground, or 'on
even terms'; cf. II iii 17.3.

Stanza 25
1　　**adredde**: terrified.
2　　**desperate**: despairing.
3　　**bestedde**: beset.
6　　**soust**: dealt heavy blows.　　**foynd**: lunged.
7　　**yron brond**: sword.

Stanza 26
3　　**throwes**: thrusts, blows.
4　　**relent**: yield.
8　　**amate**: dismay.

Stanza 27
2　　**Shenan**: the Shannon; see xi 41.3.
3　　**rayne**: realm.
4　　**kindly**: natural.
7　　**redisbourse**: pay back again; suggested by the metaphor
of lending money in 6–9.
8–9　　Cf. VI Proem 7.4–5.

Stanza 28
6　　**disentrayled**: drawn from the entrails; also interlacing
streams.

Stanza 29
2　　**emperisht**: impaired.
5　　**guarisht**: healed.
6　　**husbands**: farmer's.

30

Through which aduantage, in his strength he rose,
  And smote the other with so wondrous might,
  That through the seame, which did his hauberk close,
  Into his throate and life it pierced quight,
  That downe he fell as dead in all mens sight:
  Yet dead he was not, yet he sure did die,
  As all men do, that lose the liuing spright:
  So did one soule out of his bodie flie
Vnto her natiue home from mortall miserie.

31

But nathelesse whilst all the lookers on
  Him dead behight, as he to all appeard,
  All vnawares he started vp anon,
  As one that had out of a dreame bene reard,
  And fresh assayld his foe, who halfe affeard
  Of th'vncouth sight, as he some ghost had seene,
  Stood still amaz'd, holding his idle sweard;
  Till hauing often by him stricken beene,
He forced was to strike, and saue him selfe from teene.

32

Yet from thenceforth more warily he fought,
  As one in feare the Stygian gods t'offend,
  Ne followd on so fast, but rather sought
  Him selfe to saue, and daunger to defend,
  Then life and labour both in vaine to spend.
  Which *Triamond* perceiuing, weened sure
  He gan to faint, toward the battels end,
  And that he should not long on foote endure,
A signe which did to him the victorie assure.

33

Whereof full blith, eftsoones his mightie hand
  He heav'd on high, in mind with that same blow
  To make an end of all that did withstand:
  Which *Cambell* seeing come, was nothing slow
  Him selfe to saue from that so deadly throw;
  And at that instant reaching forth his sweard
  Close vnderneath his shield, that scarce did show,
  Stroke him, as he his hand to strike vpreard,
In th'arm-pit full, that through both sides the wound appeard.

34

Yet still that direfull stroke kept on his way,
  And falling heauie on *Cambelloes* crest,
  Strooke him so hugely, that in swowne he lay,
  And in his head an hideous wound imprest:
  And sure had it not happily found rest
  Vpon the brim of his brode plated shield,
  It would haue cleft his braine downe to his brest.
  So both at once fell dead vpon the field,
And each to other seemd the victorie to yield.

35

Which when as all the lookers on beheld,
  They weened sure the warre was at an end,
  And Iudges rose, and Marshals of the field
  Broke vp the listes, their armes away to rend;
  And *Canacee* gan wayle her dearest frend.
  All suddenly they both vpstarted light,
  The one out of the swownd, which him did blend,
  The other breathing now another spright,
448 And fiercely each assayling, gan afresh to fight.

36

Long while they then continued in that wize,
  As if but then the battell had begonne:
  Strokes, wounds, wards, weapons, all they did despise,
  Ne either car'd to ward, or perill shonne,
  Desirous both to haue the battell donne;
  Ne either cared life to saue or spill,
  Ne which of them did winne, ne which were wonne.
  So wearie both of fighting had their fill,
That life it selfe seemd loathsome, and long safetie ill.

Stanza 30
3 **hauberk**: chain-mail that covers the neck.
5 **sight**: judgment.

Stanza 31
2 **behight**: esteemed.
6 **vncouth**: marvellous.
9 **teene**: injury.

Stanza 32
2 **the Stygian gods**: the infernal gods; from Styx, a river of hell.
4 **defend**: keep off.

Stanza 33
5 **throw**: blow.
6 **reaching**: thrusting.

Stanza 34
4 **imprest**: imprinted; pressed in; cf. III xii 33.7.

Stanza 35
3–4 McNeir (1966) 103, 108 notes that the officials are eager to collect the fees allowed them according to Thomas of Woodstock's rules for judicial combat: the Marshall gets the **listes** and the Constable gets the **armes**.
7 **blend**: blind; confound.

Stanza 36
3 **wards**: 'swords', sugg. Church (1758), would avoid the tautology in 4 but introduce one in 3, as Collier (1862) notes. **wards** balances **Strokes**: the knights give up both offensive and defensive postures.
6 **spill**: destroy.

37

Whilst thus the case in doubtfull ballance hong,
　Vnsure to whether side it would incline,
　And all mens eyes and hearts, which there among
　Stood gazing, filled were with rufull tine,
　And secret feare, to see their fatall fine,
　All suddenly they heard a troublous noyes,
　That seemd some perilous tumult to desine,
　Confusd with womens cries, and shouts of boyes,
Such as the troubled Theaters oftimes annoyes.

38

Thereat the Champions both stood still a space,
　To weeten what that sudden clamour ment;
　Lo where they spyde with speedie whirling pace,
　One in a charet of straunge furniment,
　Towards them driuing like a storme out sent.
　The charet decked was in wondrous wize,
　With gold and many a gorgeous ornament,
　After the Persian Monarks antique guize,
Such as the maker selfe could best by art deuize.

39

And drawne it was (that wonder is to tell)
　Of two grim lyons, taken from the wood,
　In which their powre all others did excell;
　Now made forget their former cruell mood,
　T'obey their riders hest, as seemed good.
　And therein sate a Ladie passing faire
　And bright, that seemed borne of Angels brood,
　And with her beautie bountie did compare,
Whether of them in her should haue the greater share.

40

Thereto she learned was in Magicke leare,
　And all the artes, that subtill wits discouer,
　Hauing therein bene trained many a yeare,
　And well instructed by the Fay her mother,
　That in the same she farre exceld all other.
　Who vnderstanding by her mightie art,
　Of th'euill plight, in which her dearest brother
　Now stood, came forth in hast to take his part,
And pacifie the strife, which causd so deadly smart.

41

And as she passed through th'vnruly preace
　Of people, thronging thicke her to behold,
　Her angrie teame breaking their bonds of peace,
　Great heapes of them, like sheepe in narrow fold,
　For hast did ouer-runne, in dust enrould,
　That thorough rude confusion of the rout,
　Some fearing shriekt, some being harmed hould,
　Some laught for sport, some did for wonder shout,
And some that would seeme wise, their wonder turnd to dout.

42

In her right hand a rod of peace shee bore,
　About the which two Serpents weren wound,
　Entrayled mutually in louely lore,
　And by the tailes together firmely bound,
　And both were with one oliue garland crownd,
　Like to the rod which *Maias* sonne doth wield,
　Wherewith the hellish fiends he doth confound.
　And in her other hand a cup she hild,
The which was with Nepenthe to the brim vpfild.

Stanza 37

2　**whether**: which.
4　**rufull tine**: pitiful sorrow.
5　**fatall fine**: destined death; or fatal end.
7　**desine**: indicate.

Stanza 38

4　**furniment**: fittings.
8　**Persian Monarks**: traditionally associated with wealth; cf. I iv 7.5–6.

Stanza 39

1–5　For the iconography of Cambina and her lions, see Roche (1964) 23–8. On the lion as an emblem of power, see Aptekar (1969) 61–9. Cf. the lion that Una tamed, I iii 5, and the chained lion under Mercilla's feet, V ix 33.
5　**hest**: command.
8　Cf. Hellenore, III ix 4.5.　**bountie**: goodness.
compare: vie.

Stanza 40

1–5　Cf. ii 44.1–5.　**Thereto**: also; but perhaps suggesting that she has magical power because of her beauty and goodness.　**leare**: lore.

Stanza 41

4–5　In her haste, the team tramples great heaps of the people, enfolding them in dust; or, the people who outran each other in their haste to see her were enfolded in dust. Cambina makes no attempt to bring harmony to the vulgar.
7　**hould**: howled.
9　**dout**: fear.

Stanza 42

On the Renaissance interpretation of the caduceus as a rod of peace, see Fowler (1964) 157–62. He suggests that **louely lore** (3) recalls Valeriano's interpretation of the caduceus as a *doctrinae virga*. The knot binding the tails of the serpents was interpreted by Valeriano and Macrobius as the power of Fate, which suggests Agape's appeal to the Fates. The Palmer carries a wand made of the same wood as Mercury's caduceus (II xii 41).
3　**Entrayled**: entwined; or because the serpents represent the entrails, as in Valeriano, *Hieroglyphica*; cited Fowler 164 *n*3.　**in louely lore**: in amorous fashion (sugg. by the context); or as in loving instruction, i.e. instructing others to love, as in Cambina's 'reasons' (47.7) to the knights to restrain their enmity.
6–7　On Mercury's caduceus, see II xii 41.2–8*n*; cf. VII vi 18.2–3. In *Hub.* 1293–4 this wand is described as that 'With which the damned ghosts he gouerneth, / And furies rules, and Tartare tempereth'. Cooper (1565) notes that the caduceus is a white rod used when 'goyng to intreate of peace'.

449

43

Nepenthe is a drinck of souerayne grace,
   Deuized by the Gods, for to asswage
   Harts grief, and bitter gall away to chace,
   Which stirs vp anguish and contentious rage:
   In stead thereof sweet peace and quiet age
   It doth establish in the troubled mynd.
   Few men, but such as sober are and sage,
Are by the Gods to drinck thereof assynd;
But such as drinck, eternall happinesse do fynd.

44

Such famous men, such worthies of the earth,
   As *Ioue* will haue aduaunced to the skie,
   And there made gods, though borne of mortall berth,
   For their high merits and great dignitie,
   Are wont, before they may to heauen flie,
   To drincke hereof, whereby all cares forepast
   Are washt away quite from their memorie.
   So did those olde Heroes hereof taste,
Before that they in blisse amongst the Gods were plaste.

45

Much more of price and of more gratious powre
   Is this, then that same water of Ardenne,
   The which *Rinaldo* drunck in happie howre,
   Described by that famous Tuscane penne:
   For that had might to change the hearts of men
   Fro loue to hate, a change of euill choise:
   But this doth hatred make in loue to brenne,
   And heauy heart with comfort doth reioyce.
Who would not to this vertue rather yeeld his voice?

46

At last arriuing by the listes side,
   Shee with her rod did softly smite the raile,
   Which straight flew ope, and gaue her way to ride.
   Eftsoones out of her Coch she gan auaile,
   And pacing fairely forth, did bid all haile,
   First to her brother, whom she loued deare,
   That so to see him made her heart to quaile:
   And next to *Cambell*, whose sad ruefull cheare
Made her to change her hew, and hidden loue t'appeare.

47

They lightly her requit (for small delight
   They had as then her long to entertaine,)
   And eft them turned both againe to fight,
   Which when she saw, downe on the bloudy plaine
   Her selfe she threw, and teares gan shed amaine;
   Amongst her teares immixing prayers meeke,
   And with her prayers reasons to restraine
   From blouddy strife, and blessed peace to seeke,
By all that vnto them was deare, did them beseeke.

48

But when as all might nought with them preuaile,
   Shee smote them lightly with her powrefull wand.
   Then suddenly as if their hearts did faile,
   Their wrathfull blades downe fell out of their hand,
   And they like men astonisht still did stand.
   Thus whilest their minds were doubtfully distraught,
   And mighty spirites bound with mightier band,
   Her golden cup to them for drinke she raught,
450 Whereof full glad for thirst, ech drunk an harty draught.

49

Of which so soone as they once tasted had,
   Wonder it is that sudden change to see:
   Instead of strokes, each other kissed glad,
   And louely haulst from feare of treason free,
   And plighted hands for euer friends to be.
   When all men saw this sudden change of things,
   So mortall foes so friendly to agree,
   For passing ioy, which so great maruaile brings,
They all gan shout aloud, that all the heauen rings.

Stanza 43
This explanatory note is after the manner of Virgil's explanation of Mercury's use of the caduceus (*Aen.* iv 242–4).
1   **Nepenthe**: signifying 'dispelling grief'.
5   **quiet age**: quietude.

Stanza 44
4   **dignitie**: desert, merit.

Stanza 45
1   **price**: worth.   **gratious powre**: power to bestow grace and favour.
2–6   The fountain of love in the Ardennes, in Boiardo, *Orl. Inn.* I iii 35; cf. Ariosto, *Orl. Fur.* i 78, xlii 63.
7   **brenne**: burn.

Stanza 46
4   **auaile**: descend.
5   Her salutation expresses her health-giving role.

Stanza 47
1   **requit**: saluted in return.
4–9   Church (1758) notes the just gradation of her appeal: she begs in tears to arouse their pity, urges with reason, and lastly beseeches in the name of **blessed peace** (8). Her actions suggest the means to achieve concord.
5   **amaine**: vehemently.
6   **immixing**: mingling.
9   **beseeke**: beseech.

Stanza 48
4–5   Cf. Britomart's effect upon the wrathful Artegall, vi 21.
6   **distraught**: distracted; 'drawn apart' so their spirits may be bound in friendship.

Stanza 49
4   **louely haulst**: lovingly embraced.

50

All which, when gentle *Canacee* beheld,
  In hast she from her lofty chaire descended,
  To weet what sudden tidings was befeld:
  Where when she saw that cruell war so ended,
  And deadly foes so faithfully affrended,
  In louely wise she gan that Lady greet,
  Which had so great dismay so well amended,
  And entertaining her with curt'sies meet,
Profest to her true friendship and affection sweet.

51

Thus when they all accorded goodly were,
  The trumpets sounded, and they all arose,
  Thence to depart with glee and gladsome chere.
  Those warlike champions both together chose,
  Homeward to march, themselues there to repose,
  And wise *Cambina* taking by her side
  Faire *Canacee*, as fresh as morning rose,
  Vnto her Coch remounting, home did ride,
Admir'd of all the people, and much glorifide.

52

Where making ioyous feast theire daies they spent
  In perfect loue, deuoide of hatefull strife,
  Allide with bands of mutuall couplement;
  For *Triamond* had *Canacee* to wife,
  With whom he ledd a long and happie life;
  And *Cambel* tooke *Cambina* to his fere,
  The which as life were each to other liefe.
  So all alike did loue, and loued were,
That since their days such louers were not found elswhere.

Cant. IIII.

Satyrane makes a Turneyment
For loue of Florimell:
Britomart winnes the prize from all,
And Artegall doth quell.

1

IT often fals, (as here it earst befell)
That mortall foes doe turne to faithfull frends,
  And friends profest are chaungd to foemen fell:
  The cause of both, of both their minds depends,
  And th'end of both likewise of both their ends.
  For enmitie, that of no ill proceeds,
  But of occasion, with th'occasion ends;
  And friendship, which a faint affection breeds
Without regard of good, dyes like ill grounded seeds.

2

That well (me seemes) appeares, by that of late
  Twixt *Cambell* and Sir *Triamond* befell,
  As als by this, that now a new debate
  Stird vp twixt *Scudamour* and *Paridell*,
  The which by course befals me here to tell:
  Who hauing those two other Knights espide
  Marching afore, as ye remember well,
  Sent forth their Squire to haue them both descride,
And eke those masked Ladies riding them beside.

Stanza 50
Earlier Ate and Duessa actively stir up discord, and Canacee,
who is the cause of discord, stands aside; now Cambina resolves
discord into concord.
5   **affrended**: made friends, suggesting compulsion.
6   **greet**: congratulate upon her victory.
7   **so great dismay**: the term combines the event with its
effect upon the beholders.

Stanza 51
1   **accorded**: reconciled. Cf. the false friends at ii 29.1; now
that reconciliation is **goodly**.
6–7   The alliance of **wise** and **Faire** points to the inclusive-
ness of true friendship.

Stanza 52
A complex interlocking relationship is established. Each is
linked with the other three by the three kinds of love listed at
ix 1: kinship, sexual love, and friendship.

Cambell ———— Cambina

Triamond ———— Canacee

Cambell and **Triamond** change from hate to love while
Canacee adds to her friendship for **Cambell** (35.5) love which
earlier she rejected (ii 37.1). Fowler (1964) 28 observes a
correspondence with the tetrad at the Temple of Venus: Love–
Friendship–Peace–Hate. See x 32.4–5n.
3   **couplement**: union of pairs.
6   **to his fere**: as his wife.
7   **liefe**: dear.

Canto iv

Stanza 1
3   **profest**: i.e. merely pretended.
4   **of both their minds depends**: depends on the minds of
both.

Stanza 2
1–3   **As als**] As els *1596* is defended by Smith against the
later emendation because the proposition in the previous stanza
is twofold, concerning enmity and friendship: 'Reading *As als*
we have two illustrations of this twofold proposition. Reading
As els we have an independent illustration of each of its parts.'
Yet **That well** may be taken to refer to 'enmitie, that of no ill
proceeds', namely, that between **Cambell** and **Triamond**;
and **As als** to 'friendship, which a faint affection breeds',
namely, that between Blandamour and **Paridell**.
4   **Scudamour**: clearly an error for Blandamour.
7, 9   **Marching afore . . . them beside**: see ii 30.3–8.
beside: close by.

3

Who backe returning, told as he had seene,
  That they were doughtie knights of dreaded name;
  And those two Ladies, their two loues vnseene;
  And therefore wisht them without blot or blame,
  To let them passe at will, for dread of shame.
  But *Blandamour* full of vainglorious spright,
  And rather stird by his discordfull Dame,
  Vpon them gladly would haue prov'd his might,
But that he yet was sore of his late lucklesse fight.

4

Yet nigh approching, he them fowle bespake,
  Disgracing them, him selfe thereby to grace,
  As was his wont, so weening way to make
  To Ladies loue, where so he came in place,
  And with lewd termes their louers to deface.
  Whose sharpe prouokement them incenst so sore,
  That both were bent t'auenge his vsage base,
  And gan their shields addresse them selues afore:
For euill deedes may better then bad words be bore.

5

But faire *Cambina* with perswasions myld,
  Did mitigate the fiercenesse of their mode,
  That for the present they were reconcyld,
  And gan to treate of deeds of armes abrode,
  And strange aduentures, all the way they rode:
  Amongst the which they told, as then befell,
  Of that great turney, which was blazed brode,
  For that rich girdle of faire *Florimell*,
The prize of her, which did in beautie most excell.

6

To which folke-mote they all with one consent,
  Sith each of them his Ladie had him by,
  Whose beautie each of them thought excellent,
  Agreed to trauell, and their fortunes try.
  So as they passed forth, they did espy
  One in bright armes, with ready speare in rest,
  That toward them his course seem'd to apply,
  Gainst whom Sir *Paridell* himselfe addrest,
Him weening, ere he nigh approcht to haue represt.

7

Which th'other seeing, gan his course relent,
  And vaunted speare eftsoones to disaduaunce,
  As if he naught but peace and pleasure ment,
  Now falne into their fellowship by chance,
  Whereat they shewed curteous countenaunce.
  So as he rode with them accompanide,
  His rouing eie did on the Lady glaunce,
  Which *Blandamour* had riding by his side:
Whom sure he weend, that he some wher tofore had eide.

8

It was to weete that snowy *Florimell*,
  Which *Ferrau* late from *Braggadochio* wonne,
  Whom he now seeing, her remembred well,
  How hauing reft her from the witches sonne,
  He soone her lost: wherefore he now begunne
  To challenge her anew, as his owne prize,
  Whom formerly he had in battell wonne,
  And proffer made by force her to reprize,
Which scornefull offer, *Blandamour* gan soone despize.

9

And said, Sir Knight, sith ye this Lady clame,
  Whom he that hath, were loth to lose so light,
  (For so to lose a Lady, were great shame)
  Yee shall her winne, as I haue done in fight:
  And lo shee shall be placed here in sight,
  Together with this Hag beside her set,
  That who so winnes her, may her haue by right:
  But he shall haue the Hag that is ybet,
And with her alwaies ride, till he another get.

Stanza 3
3 **vnseene**: unknown because 'masked' (2.9).
7–9 **discordfull Dame**: Ate, as i 32. **late lucklesse
fight**: his fight with Paridell at ii 14–20 or with Britomart at
i 36.

Stanza 4
1–5 His flattering speech – cf. ii 10.4–5, i 32.4–5*n* – now
changes to slander. **Disgracing**: reviling, literally seeking
to mar their grace. **deface**: defame.
6 **prouokement**: provocation.
9 **bore**: borne.

Stanza 5
2 **mode**: mood: anger.
7 **blazed brode**: proclaimed widely.

Stanza 6
1 **folk-mote**: 'a place for people to meet or talk of anything
that concerned any difference between parties' (*View* 77).
3 **excellent**: supreme.

Stanza 7
1 **relent**: slacken.
2 **vaunted**: thrust forward boastfully. **disaduaunce**:
lower.
9 **tofore**: before.

Stanza 8
6 **challenge**: claim. **prize**: booty.
8 **proffer**: offer; attempt. **reprize**: take back again,
literally as his prize.
9 **soone**: immediately. **despize**: treat with contempt.

Stanza 9
8 **ybet**: beaten.

10

That offer pleased all the company,
    So *Florimell* with *Ate* forth was brought,
    At which they all gan laugh full merrily:
    But *Braggadochio* said, he neuer thought
    For such an Hag, that seemed worse then nought,
    His person to emperill so in fight.
    But if to match that Lady they had sought
    Another like, that were like faire and bright,
His life he then would spend to iustifie his right.

11

At which his vaine excuse they all gan smile,
    As scorning his vnmanly cowardize:
    And *Florimell* him fowly gan reuile,
    That for her sake refus'd to enterprize
    The battell, offred in so knightly wize.
    And *Ate* eke prouokt him priuily,
    With loue of her, and shame of such mesprize.
    But naught he car'd for friend or enemy,
For in base mind nor friendship dwels nor enmity.

12

But *Cambell* thus did shut vp all in iest,
    Braue Knights and Ladies, certes ye doe wrong
    To stirre vp strife, when most vs needeth rest,
    That we may vs reserue both fresh and strong,
    Against the Turneiment which is not long.
    When who so list to fight, may fight his fill,
    Till then your challenges ye may prolong;
    And then it shall be tried, if ye will,
Whether shall haue the Hag, or hold the Lady still.

13

They all agreed, so turning all to game,
    And pleasaunt bord, they past forth on their way,
    And all that while, where so they rode or came,
    That masked Mock-knight was their sport and play.
    Till that at length vpon th'appointed day,
    Vnto the place of turneyment they came;
    Where they before them found in fresh aray
    Manie a braue knight, and manie a daintie dame
Assembled, for to get the honour of that game.

14

There this faire crewe arriuing, did diuide
    Them selues asunder: *Blandamour* with those
    Of his, on th'one; the rest on th'other side.
    But boastfull *Braggadocchio* rather chose,
    For glorie vaine their fellowship to lose,
    That men on him the more might gaze alone.
    The rest them selues in troupes did else dispose,
    Like as it seemed best to euery one:
The knights in couples marcht, with ladies linckt attone.

15

Then first of all forth came Sir *Satyrane*,
    Bearing that precious relicke in an arke
    Of gold, that bad eyes might it not prophane:
    Which drawing softly forth out of the darke,
    He open shewd, that all men it mote marke.
    A gorgeous girdle, curiously embost
    With pearle and precious stone, worth many a marke;
    Yet did the workmanship farre passe the cost:
It was the same, which lately *Florimel* had lost.

16

That same aloft he hong in open vew,
    To be the prize of beautie and of might;
    The which eftsoones discouered, to it drew
    The eyes of all, allur'd with close delight,
    And hearts quite robbed with so glorious sight,
    That all men threw out vowes and wishes vaine.
    Thrise happie Ladie, and thrise happie knight,
    Them seemd that could so goodly riches gaine,
So worthie of the perill, worthy of the paine.

Stanza 10
7–9   The offer suits a loser, but as Florimell has no equal,
it is entirely safe.

Stanza 11
4   **enterprize**: undertake.
7   **mesprize**: scorn.

Stanza 12
7   **prolong**: postpone.
9   **Whether**: which.

Stanza 13
2   **bord**: jesting.
4   **masked**: as he is a **Mock-knight**.

Stanza 14
6   **alone**: being alone he will be gazed on **the more**.
9   **attone**: together.

Stanza 15
2   **arke**: chest.
6–8   Alluding to the etymology of Lat. *cestus*, embroidered.
curiously embost: elaborately ornamented.

Stanza 16
2   Referring to the two contests: the tournament to decide
the strongest knight and the beauty contest among their
ladies. In both, masculine strength and feminine beauty are
simply physical: the former is not concerned with force as the
instrument of right nor the latter with beauty as the expression
of virtue. Ideally, the noblest knight should triumph and be
chosen by the most virtuous lady as her defender. Cf. VI vii
29.9: 'noblest she, that serued is of noblest knight'. Their
union would show concord in war and love. Instead, the outcome is discord in both.   **prize**: used in this canto and
throughout the Book for (*a*) reward or symbol of superiority,
(*b*) booty or plunder gained by force.
4   **close**: secret, inner.
5   **robbed**: ravished.

453

17

Then tooke the bold Sir *Satyrane* in hand
  An huge great speare, such as he wont to wield,
  And vauncing forth from all the other band
  Of knights, addrest his maiden-headed shield,
  Shewing him selfe all ready for the field.
  Gainst whom there singled from the other side
  A Painim knight, that well in armes was skild,
  And had in many a battell oft bene tride,
Hight *Bruncheual* the bold, who fiersly forth did ride.

18

So furiously they both together met,
  That neither could the others force sustaine;
  As two fierce Buls, that striue the rule to get
  Of all the heard, meete with so hideous maine,
  That both rebutted, tumble on the plaine:
  So these two champions to the ground were feld,
  Where in a maze they both did long remaine,
  And in their hands their idle troncheons held,
Which neither able were to wag, or once to weld.

19

Which when the noble *Ferramont* espide,
  He pricked forth in ayd of *Satyran*;
  And him against Sir *Blandamour* did ride
  With all the strength and stifnesse that he can.
  But the more strong and stiffely that he ran,
  So much more sorely to the ground he fell,
  That on an heape were tumbled horse and man.
  Vnto whose rescue forth rode *Paridell*;
But him likewise with that same speare he eke did quell.

20

Which *Braggadocchio* seeing, had no will
  To hasten greatly to his parties ayd,
  Albee his turne were next; but stood there still,
  As one that seemed doubtfull or dismayd.
  But *Triamond* halfe wroth to see him staid,
  Sternly stept forth, and raught away his speare,
  With which so sore he *Ferramont* assaid,
  That horse and man to ground he quite did beare,
That neither could in hast themselues againe vpreare.

21

Which to auenge, Sir *Deuon* him did dight,
  But with no better fortune then the rest:
  For him likewise he quickly downe did smight,
  And after him Sir *Douglas* him addrest,
  And after him Sir *Paliumord* forth prest,
  But none of them against his strokes could stand,
  But all the more, the more his praise increst.
  For either they were left vppon the land,
Or went away sore wounded of his haplesse hand.

(1964) 175–80 for a chart and analysis of the pattern in names and encounters. He concludes that the tournament is 'a poetic imitation of a *balletic* tournament, of a kind which actually took place in the sixteenth century'. See 17–25*n*, 26–36*n*, 37–48*n*.

Stanzas 17–25
In the first day of the Tournament, **Satyrane**'s encounter with **Bruncheual** ends in a draw. On his behalf, i.e. on behalf of the knights of Maidenhead, **Ferramont** overcomes three knights, **Blandamour**, **Paridell** and **Braggadocchio** (who declines to fight), only to be defeated by the fourth, **Triamond** who fights with Braggadocchio's spear. Then Triamond, in turn, overcomes three knights only to be overcome by the fourth, who is Satyrane. Masculine aggressiveness on this day is expressed by the 'huge great speare' (17.2; cf. 24.1). Although there may be a witty point in having the phallic spear defend maidenhead, the weapon is linked with chastity in Books III and IV; see III i 7.9*n*.

Stanza 17
3 **vauncing**: advancing.
4 **addrest**: i.e. put on his arm. **maiden-headed shield**: as he is the champion of the knights of Maidenhead. Cf. the 'Satyres hed' on his shield at III vii 30.6; cf. Guyon's shield (II i 28.7).
7 **Painim**: pagan, as he opposes the religion of love.
9 **Bruncheual**: dark knight (Fr. *brun*+*chevalier*). Hankins (1971) 146 interprets the name as 'dark horse' and sees the knight as the concupiscible faculty, from Plato's dark horse, *Phaedrus* 246.

Stanza 18
3–5 The first of the animal images that define the masculine encounter: the knights are compared to boars (29.8–9), lions (32.5, 41.5) and wolves (35.6–9). The animal imagery extends to the names of the knights: see 17.9*n*, 40.3*n*, 9*n*. See Dunseath (1968) 33–6. **maine**: force. **rebutted**: driven back; literally butted back.
8 **troncheons**: the broken spear shafts.
9 **wag**: brandish.

Stanza 19
1 **Ferramont**: suggests Lat. *ferramenta*, implements of iron, indicating masculine aggressiveness; or Iron Mountain, indicating steadfastness (Hankins, 1971, 146).
4 **stifnesse**: force, referring to the firmness with which he holds his spear.

Stanza 20
5 **staid**: standing still.
6 **raught**: snatched.
7 **assaid**: assailed.

Stanza 21
The names are puzzling. Possibly for the three parts of Gloriana's kingdom: **Deuon**, for England (cf. Debon who gave his name to Devonshire, II x 12.6); **Douglas** for Albania or Scotland; and **Paliumord** (?*Palinmord*; *Dabumord* in some *1596* copies) for Wales.
1 **dight**: make ready.
7 **But all the more**: i.e. the more there were.
9 **haplesse**: dealing mishap.

Stanzas 17–48
The three-day tournament is elaborately patterned. See Fowler

22

And now by this, Sir *Satyrane* abraid,
　Out of the swowne, in which too long he lay ;
　And looking round about, like one dismaid,
　When as he saw the mercilesse affray,
　Which doughty *Triamond* had wrought that day,
　Vnto the noble Knights of Maidenhead,
　His mighty heart did almost rend in tway,
For very gall, that rather wholly dead
Himselfe he wisht haue beene, then in so bad a stead.

23

Eftsoones he gan to gather vp around
　His weapons, which lay scattered all abrode,
　And as it fell, his steed he ready found.
　On whom remounting, fiercely forth he rode,
　Like sparke of fire that from the anduile glode,
　There where he saw the valiant *Triamond*
　Chasing, and laying on them heauy lode.
That none his force were able to withstond,
So dreadfull were his strokes, so deadly was his hond.

24

With that at him his beamlike speare he aimed,
　And thereto all his power and might applide :
　The wicked steele for mischiefe first ordained,
　And hauing now misfortune got for guide,
　Staid not, till it arriued in his side,
　And therein made a very griesly wound,
　That streames of bloud his armour all bedide.
Much was he daunted with that direfull stound,
That scarse he him vpheld from falling in a sound.

25

Yet as he might, himselfe he soft withdrew
　Out of the field, that none perceiu'd it plaine,
　Then gan the part of Chalengers anew
　To range the field, and victorlike to raine,
　That none against them battell durst maintaine.
　By that the gloomy euening on them fell,
　That forced them from fighting to refraine,
　And trumpets sound to cease did them compell,
So *Satyrane* that day was iudg'd to beare the bell.

26

The morrow next the Turney gan anew,
　And with the first the hardy *Satyrane*
　Appear'd in place, with all his noble crew,
　On th'other side, full many a warlike swaine,
　Assembled were, that glorious prize to gaine.
　But mongst them all, was not Sir *Triamond*,
　Vnable he new battell to darraine,
　Through grieuaunce of his late receiued wound,
That doubly did him grieue, when so himselfe he found.

27

Which *Cambell* seeing, though he could not salue,
　Ne done vndoe, yet for to salue his name,
　And purchase honour in his friends behalue,
　This goodly counterfesaunce he did frame.
　The shield and armes well knowne to be the same,
　Which *Triamond* had worne, vnwares to wight,
　And to his friend vnwist, for doubt of blame,
　If he misdid, he on himselfe did dight,
That none could him discerne, and so went forth to fight.

28

There *Satyrane* Lord of the field he found,
　Triumphing in great ioy and iolity ;
　Gainst whom none able was to stand on ground ;
　That much he gan his glorie to enuy,
　And cast t'auenge his friends indignity.
　A mightie speare eftsoones at him he bent ;
　Who seeing him come on so furiously,
　Met him mid-way with equall hardiment,
That forcibly to ground they both together went.

Stanza 22
1　**abraid**: awoke.
4　**affray**: attack ; or the panic that follows.
9　**stead**: position.

Stanza 23
4–5　Cf. Chaucer, *Tale of Sir Thopas*: 'His goode steede al
he bistrood, / And forth upon his wey he glood / As sparcle
out of the bronde' (903–5).　**glode**: glided.

Stanza 24
8　**stound**: attack ; stunning blow.
9　**sound**: swoon.

Stanza 25
3　**part**: faction.

Stanzas 26–36
Day 2 reverses Day 1 : Friendship defeats Maidenhead. In
Triamond's armour, **Cambell** defeats **Satyrane** ; and when
he is captured by Satyrane's rescuers, he is saved by Triamond
in his armour. After the initial encounter with the spear, the
sword is used.

Stanza 26
7　**darraine**: engage in.
8　**grieuaunce**: pain.

Stanza 27
1–2　**salue**: heal. The first use may suggest 'remedy what
had been done', and the second 'preserve'.
3　**behalue**: name.
4　**counterfesaunce**: deception ; literally putting on a false
front (hence the qualification **goodly**).
7　**doubt**: fear.

Stanza 28
5　**cast**: resolved.
6　This **mightie speare** is Braggadocchio's : see 6.6, 20.6.
bent: aimed.

455

29

They vp againe them selues can lightly reare,
  And to their tryed swords them selues betake;
  With which they wrought such wondrous maruels there,
  That all the rest it did amazed make,
  Ne any dar'd their perill to partake;
  Now cuffling close, now chacing to and fro,
  Now hurtling round aduantage for to take:
  As two wild Boares together grapling go,
Chaufing and foming choler each against his fo.

30

So as they courst, and turneyd here and theare,
  It chaunst Sir *Satyrane* his steed at last,
  Whether through foundring or through sodein feare
  To stumble, that his rider nigh he cast;
  Which vauntage *Cambell* did pursue so fast,
  That ere him selfe he had recouered well,
  So sore he sowst him on the compast creast,
  That forced him to leaue his loftie sell,
And rudely tumbling downe vnder his horse feete fell.

31

Lightly *Cambello* leapt downe from his steed,
  For to haue rent his shield and armes away,
  That whylome wont to be the victors meed;
  When all vnwares he felt an hideous sway
  Of many swords, that lode on him did lay.
  An hundred knights had him enclosed round,
  To rescue *Satyrane* out of his pray;
  All which at once huge strokes on him did pound,
In hope to take him prisoner, where he stood on ground.

32

He with their multitude was nought dismayd,
  But with stout courage turnd vpon them all,
  And with his brondiron round about him layd;
  Of which he dealt large almes, as did befall:
  Like as a Lion that by chaunce doth fall
  Into the hunters toile, doth rage and rore,
  In royall heart disdaining to be thrall.
  But all in vaine: for what might one do more?
They haue him taken captiue, though it grieue him sore.

33

Whereof when newes to *Triamond* was brought,
  There as he lay, his wound he soone forgot,
  And starting vp, streight for his armour sought:
  In vaine he sought; for there he found it not;
  Cambello it away before had got:
  Cambelloes armes therefore he on him threw,
  And lightly issewd forth to take his lot.
  There he in troupe found all that warlike crew,
Leading his friend away, full sorie to his vew.

34

Into the thickest of that knightly preasse
  He thrust, and smote downe all that was betweene,
  Caried with feruent zeale, ne did he ceasse,
  Till that he came, where he had *Cambell* seene,
  Like captive thral two other Knights atweene,
  There he amongst them cruell hauocke makes,
  That they which lead him, soone enforced beene
  To let him loose, to saue their proper stakes,
Who being freed, from one a weapon fiercely takes.

35

With that he driues at them with dreadfull might,
  Both in remembrance of his friends late harme,
  And in reuengement of his owne despight,
  So both together giue a new allarme,
  As if but now the battell wexed warme.
  As when two greedy Wolues doe breake by force
  Into an heard, farre from the husband farme,
  They spoile and rauine without all remorse,
So did these two through all the field their foes enforce.

Stanza 29
1 **can**: did.
6 **cuffling**: scuffling or fighting at close quarters; cf. I ii 17.3.
7 **hurtling**: dashing or skirmishing.

Stanza 30
Upton (1758) suggests that S. had the ending of Chaucer's *Knight's Tale* in view: after defeating Palamon, Arcite falls headlong to his death when his horse at the sight of a fury 'for fere gan to turne' (2686). See 32.8–9n.
1 **courst**: ran their courses.
3 **foundring**: falling through lameness.
7 **sowst**: struck.   **compast creast**: round helmet.

Stanza 31
2–3 On reaving the dead, see II viii 15.7–9n.
4 **sway**: force, referring to downward blows.
6 **hundred**: an absolute number, as at III iv 21.1.
7 **out of his pray**: i.e. from his preying.

Stanza 32
3 **brondiron**: sword.
4 **Of which he dealt large almes**: with which he freely gave out blows; suggested by the knights who surround him as petitioners.
6 **toile**: net or trap.
8–9 Upton (1758) suggests a connection with Palamon's capture in Chaucer's *Knight's Tale* 2648–9.

Stanza 34
8 **their proper stakes**: their own lives placed at hazard in the battle.

Stanza 35
4 **allarme**: assault.
7 **husband farme**: farmer's house; possibly the tilled land.
8 **all**: any.
9 **enforce**: drive by force.

36

Fiercely they followd on their bolde emprize,
  Till trumpets sound did warne them all to rest;
  Then all with one consent did yeeld the prize
  To *Triamond* and *Cambell* as the best.
  But *Triamond* to *Cambell* it relest.
  And *Cambell* it to *Triamond* transferd;
  Each labouring t'aduance the others gest,
  And make his praise before his owne preferd:
So that the doome was to another day differd.

37

The last day came, when all those knightes againe
  Assembled were their deedes of armes to shew.
  Full many deedes that day were shewed plaine:
  But *Satyrane* boue all the other crew,
  His wondrous worth declared in all mens view.
  For from the first he to the last endured,
  And though some while Fortune from him withdrew,
  Yet euermore his honour he recured,
And with vnwearied powre his party still assured.

38

Ne was there Knight that euer thought of armes,
  But that his vtmost prowesse there made knowen,
  That by their many wounds, and carelesse harmes,
  By shiuered speares, and swords all vnder strowen,
  By scattered shields was easie to be shewen.
  There might ye see loose steeds at randon ronne,
  Whose luckelesse riders late were ouerthrowen;
  And squiers make hast to helpe their Lords fordonne,
But still the Knights of Maidenhead the better wonne.

39

Till that there entred on the other side,
  A straunger knight, from whence no man could reed,
  In quyent disguise, full hard to be descride.
  For all his armour was like saluage weed,
  With woody mosse bedight, and all his steed
  With oaken leaues attrapt, that seemed fit
  For saluage wight, and thereto well agreed
  His word, which on his ragged shield was writ,
Saluagesse sans finesse, shewing secret wit.

40

He at his first incomming, charg'd his spere
  At him, that first appeared in his sight:
  That was to weet, the stout Sir *Sangliere*,
  Who well was knowen to be a valiant Knight,
  Approued oft in many a perlous fight.
  Him at the first encounter downe he smote,
  And ouerbore beyond his crouper quight,
  And after him another Knight, that hote
Sir *Brianor*, so sore, that none him life behote.

41

Then ere his hand he reard, he ouerthrew
  Seuen Knights one after other as they came:
  And when his speare was brust, his sword he drew,
  The instrument of wrath, and with the same
  Far'd like a lyon in his bloodie game,
  Hewing, and slashing shields, and helmets bright,
  And beating downe, what euer nigh him came,
  That euery one gan shun his dreadfull sight,
No lesse then death it selfe, in daungerous affright.

Stanza 36
1 **emprize**: enterprise.
7 **gest**: exploit.
9 **doome**: judgment. **differd**: deferred.

Stanzas 37–48
On the third and final day, **Satyrane** and the Knights of
Maidenhead triumph until they encounter **Artegall**, the
example of 'sole manhood' (43.2), who defeats them in three
encounters (against **Sangliere**, **Brianor**, and a group of seven
knights) only to be defeated in the fourth by **Britomart**. She
triumphs in four encounters, a total achieved for the first time
and one which makes her victory complete (against **Artegall**,
Cambell, **Triamond**, and **Blandamour**) to which she adds
'Full many others' (46.1). She triumphs, then, over the forces
of manhood, friendship and false friendship.

Stanza 37
7 **some while**: at one time.
8 **recured**: recovered.
9 **assured**: rendered secure.

Stanza 38
3 **carelesse harmes**: untended injuries.
8 **fordonne**: overcome, i.e. overthrown.

Stanza 39
2 **reed**: guess.
3 **quyent disguise**: strange disguise; cf. 42.5, v 29.9. Cf.
Britomart 'in strange disguise' (III iii 51.9), and 'queint
disguise' (V vii 21.1). **describe**: described; 'made out';
interpreted.
4 **saluage weed**: the dress of the salvage man.
6 The **oaken leaues** symbolize Artegall's salvage state. The
oak is associated with lust (see vii 7*n*) and with physical force
(see Tervarent, 1958, 91). **attrapt**: furnished as trappings.
8 **word**: motto.
9 **Saluagesse sans finesse**: wildness without refinement or
artfulness. **wit**: meaning.

Stanza 40
1 **charg'd**: aimed.
3 **Sangliere**: Fr. wild boar; appropriately the Salvage
Knight's first foe. Cf. the savage Sanglier (V i 17–20), Artegall's
first foe on his quest.
7–9 An intentional pun: Artegall overbore the boar. It
triggers the jingle, **Brianor, so sore**. **hote**: was called.
Brianor: Bear (Bruin). **behote**: promised.

Stanza 41
1 **ere his hand he reard**: i.e. while he levelled his spear and
before he raised the sword.
3 **brust**: burst, shivered.
4 Williams (1966) 134 associates his **wrath** with the wrath
of Achilles. Like Achilles, he sulks (v 9) when he is not properly
rewarded.
5 **Far'd**: raged.

42

Much wondred all men, what, or whence he came,
  That did amongst the troupes so tyrannize;
  And each of other gan inquire his name.
  But when they could not learne it by no wize,
  Most answerable to his wyld disguize
  It seemed, him to terme the saluage knight.
  But certes his right name was otherwize,
  Though knowne to few, that *Arthegall* he hight,
The doughtiest knight that liv'd that day, and most of might.

43

Thus was Sir *Satyrane* with all his band
  By his sole manhood and atchieuement stout
  Dismayd, that none of them in field durst stand,
  But beaten were, and chased all about.
  So he continued all that day throughout,
  Till euening, that the Sunne gan downward bend.
  Then rushed forth out of the thickest rout
  A stranger knight, that did his glorie shend:
So nought may be esteemed happie till the end.

44

He at his entrance charg'd his powrefull speare
  At *Artegall*, in middest of his pryde,
  And therewith smote him on his Vmbriere
  So sore, that tombling backe, he downe did slyde
  Ouer his horses taile aboue a stryde;
  Whence litle lust he had to rise againe.
  Which *Cambell* seeing, much the same enuyde,
  And ran at him with all his might and maine;
But shortly was likewise seene lying on the plaine.

45

Whereat full inly wroth was *Triamond*,
  And cast t'auenge the shame doen to his freend:
  But by his friend himselfe eke soone he fond,
  In no lesse neede of helpe, then him he weend.
  All which when *Blandamour* from end to end
  Beheld, he woxe therewith displeased sore,
  And thought in mind it shortly to amend:
  His speare he feutred, and at him it bore;
But with no better fortune, then the rest afore.

46

Full many others at him likewise ran:
  But all of them likewise dismounted were,
  Ne certes wonder; for no powre of man
  Could bide the force of that enchaunted speare,
  The which this famous *Britomart* did beare;
  With which she wondrous deeds of arms atchieued,
  And ouerthrew, what euer came her neare,
  That all those stranger knights full sore agrieued,
And that late weaker band of chalengers relieued.

47

Like as in sommers day when raging heat
  Doth burne the earth, and boyled riuers drie,
  That all brute beasts forst to refraine fro meat,
  Doe hunt for shade, where shrowded they may lie,
  And missing it, faine from themselues to flie;
  All trauellers tormented are with paine:
  A watry cloud doth ouercast the skie,
  And poureth forth a sudden shoure of raine,
458 That all the wretched world recomforteth againe.

48

So did the warlike *Britomart* restore
  The prize, to knights of Maydenhead that day,
  Which else was like to haue bene lost, and bore
  The prayse of prowesse from them all away.
  Then shrilling trompets loudly gan to bray,
  And bad them leaue their labours and long toyle,
  To ioyous feast and other gentle play,
  Where beauties prize shold win that pretious spoyle:
Where I with sound of trompe will also rest a whyle.

Stanza 43
2   **manhood**: manliness, the 'powre of man' (46.3), which defeats the forces of maidenhead, is defeated in turn by the lady knight whose disguise displays 'manhood and . . . might' (i 35.1).   **sole**: unrivalled; standing alone.
3   **Dismayd**: overthrown; referring to maidenhead whose force has been defeated.
5–6   The masculine power of the sun is about to be replaced by the feminine power of the moon; cf. 47.
7   While Artegall intrudes from the outside, Britomart emerges from the centre of the forces of maidenhead.
8   **shend**: destroy; put to shame.

Stanza 44
1–5   Britomart's entrance parallels Artegall's at 40.1–7. **pryde**: most flourishing state; cf. his excuse at vi 6.8.
3   **Vmbriere**: the visor of his helmet. She strikes him here because later she overcomes him by the sight of her beauty, vi 19–22.
6   **lust**: desire; playing on **pryde** (2) as sexual prowess.
7   **enuyde**: was indignant at.

Stanza 45
4   **weend**: i.e. thought in need of help.
8   **feutred**: put in its rest.

Stanza 46
4   **that enchaunted speare**: see III i 7.9*n*.

Stanza 47
This simile comments on the resolution of the tournament: it draws on the association of Artegall with the sun in 43.5–6. The beasts flee the sun's power, as the knights flee from Artegall, 41.8–9. Britomart is compared to 'a stormy showre' (III iv 13.6) when she defeats Marinell.

Stanza 48
8   **beauties prize**: i.e. the most beautiful lady, 'beauties soueraine grace' (v 2.3).

Cant. V.

The Ladies for the girdle striue
of famous Florimell:
Scudamour comming to Cares house,
doth sleepe from him expell.

1

IT hath bene through all ages euer seene,
   That with the praise of armes and cheualrie,
   The prize of beautie still hath ioyned beene;
   And that for reasons speciall priuitie:
   For either doth on other much relie.
   For he me seemes most fit the faire to serue,
   That can her best defend from villenie;
   And she most fit his seruice doth deserue,
That fairest is and from her faith will neuer swerue.

2

So fitly now here commeth next in place,
   After the proofe of prowesse ended well,
   The controuerse of beauties soueraine grace;
   In which to her that doth the most excell,
   Shall fall the girdle of faire *Florimell*:
   That many wish to win for glorie vaine,
   And not for vertuous vse, which some doe tell
   That glorious belt did in it selfe containe,
Which Ladies ought to loue, and seeke for to obtaine.

3

That girdle gaue the vertue of chast loue,
   And wiuehood true, to all that did it beare;
   But whosoeuer contrarie doth proue,
   Might not the same about her middle weare,
   But it would loose, or else a sunder teare.
   Whilome it was (as Faeries wont report)
   Dame *Venus* girdle, by her steemed deare,
   What time she vsd to liue in wiuely sort;
But layd aside, when so she vsd her looser sport.

4

Her husband *Vulcan* whylome for her sake,
   When first he loued her with heart entire,
   This pretious ornament they say did make,
   And wrought in *Lemno* with vnquenched fire:
   And afterwards did for her loues first hire,
   Giue it to her, for euer to remaine,
   Therewith to bind lasciuious desire,
   And loose affections streightly to restraine;
Which vertue it for euer after did retaine.

5

The same one day, when she her selfe disposd
   To visite her beloued Paramoure,
   The God of warre, she from her middle loosd,
   And left behind her in her secret bowre,
   On *Acidalian* mount, where many an howre
   She with the pleasant *Graces* wont to play.
   There *Florimell* in her first ages flowre
   Was fostered by those *Graces*, (as they say)
And brought with her from thence that goodly belt away.

Canto v

Stanza 1
Comments on the 'prayse of prowesse' and 'beauties prize' in the previous stanza. The connection between chivalry and beauty is not supported by what follows: the **fairest**, the False Florimell, chooses not the strongest but Braggadocchio. Cf. ii 27.3–4.

Stanza 2
3   **controuerse**: controversy: suggesting 'converse'.

Stanzas 3–5
In Homer, *Iliad* xiv 214–21, Venus's girdle arouses loose desire and is worn when the goddess **vsd her looser sport** (3.9). Similarly, in Tasso, *Ger. Lib.* xvi 24–5, Armida wears her girdle when she wants to be loved. In S., the girdle binds lust and inconstancy (4.7–9). Lotspeich (1932) 115 compares Boccaccio, *Gen. Deor.* III xxii, IV xlvii. On the cestus as a chastity belt, see 6.1–2n. See also III vii 31.8–9n, IV ii 27.6–8n.

Stanza 3
1–5   Cf. V iii 28.6–9.
7   **steemed**: esteemed.
9   **vsd**: engaged in.   **sport**: amorous dalliance.

Stanza 4
Apparently S. invents the legend that **Vulcan** fashioned the Cestus. Sawtelle (1896) 124 suggests a connection with the net that Vulcan fashioned to trap Venus in adultery.
4   **vnquenched**: unquenchable; cf. the fire at the gate to Busirane's house, III xi 23.7.
5–8   **first hire**: referring to Vulcan's consummation of their love.   **lasciuious desire**, which is loosened in marriage, is bound by the cestus.   **affections**: passions; lust. **streightly**: strictly.

Stanza 5
1–3   Their love is notorious: cf. I Proem 3.7–9, II vi 35.7–9, III vi 24.2–3, etc.
4–6   On the **Acidalian mount**, see VI x 6–9n.

6

That goodly belt was *Cestus* hight by name,
　　And as her life by her esteemed deare.
　　No wonder then, if that to winne the same
　　So many Ladies sought, as shall appeare;
　　For pearelesse she was thought, that did it beare.
　　And now by this their feast all being ended,
　　The iudges which thereto selected were,
　　Into the Martian field adowne descended,
To deeme this doutfull case, for which they all contended.

7

But first was question made, which of those Knights
　　That lately turneyd, had the wager wonne:
　　There was it iudged by those worthie wights,
　　That *Satyrane* the first day best had donne:
　　For he last ended, hauing first begonne.
　　The second was to *Triamond* behight,
　　For that he sau'd the victour from fordonne:
　　For *Cambell* victour was in all mens sight,
Till by mishap he in his foemens hand did light.

8

The third dayes prize vnto that straunger Knight,
　　Whom all men term'd Knight of the Hebene speare,
　　To *Britomart* was giuen by good right;
　　For that with puissant stroke she downe did beare
　　The *Saluage* Knight, that victour was whileare,
　　And all the rest, which had the best afore,
　　And to the last vnconquer'd did appeare;
　　For last is deemed best. To her therefore
The fayrest Ladie was adiudgd for Paramore.

9

But thereat greatly grudged *Arthegall*,
　　And much repynd, that both of victors meede,
　　And eke of honour she did him forestall.
　　Yet mote he not withstand, what was decreede;
　　But inly thought of that despightfull deede
　　Fit time t'awaite auenged for to bee.
　　This being ended thus, and all agreed,
　　Then next ensew'd the Paragon to see
Of beauties praise, and yeeld the fayrest her due fee.

10

Then first *Cambello* brought vnto their view
　　His faire *Cambina*, couered with a veale;
　　Which being once withdrawne, most perfect hew
　　And passing beautie did eftsoones reueale,
　　That able was weake harts away to steale.
　　Next did Sir *Triamond* vnto their sight
　　The face of his deare *Canacee* vnheale;
　　Whose beauties beame eftsoones did shine so bright,
That daz'd the eyes of all, as with exceeding light.

11

And after her did *Paridell* produce
　　His false *Duessa*, that she might be seene,
　　Who with her forged beautie did seduce
　　The hearts of some, that fairest her did weene;
　　As diuerse wits affected diuers beene.
　　Then did Sir *Ferramont* vnto them shew
　　His *Lucida*, that was full faire and sheene,
　　And after these an hundred Ladies moe

460 Appear'd in place, the which each other did outgoe.

12

All which who so dare thinke for to enchace,
　　Him needeth sure a golden pen I weene,
　　To tell the feature of each goodly face.
　　For since the day that they created beene,
　　So many heauenly faces were not seene
　　Assembled in one place: ne he that thought
　　For *Chian* folke to pourtraict beauties Queene,
　　By view of all the fairest to him brought,
So many faire did see, as here he might haue sought.

Stanza 6
1–2　As a marriage-girdle, the **Cestus** was worn by the bride
and unloosed by her husband to release her from virginity:
'a gyrdell or corse, whiche the husbande dydde putte aboute his
wyfe, whan he was maried, and at nyght dydde plucke it of.'
8　**the Martian field**: relates the contests of prowess and
beauty to their titular deities, Mars and Venus.

Stanza 7
6　**behight**: granted; adjudged.
7　**fordonne**: i.e. being overcome.

Stanza 8
2　Associates **Britomart** with Hebe, the goddess of youth
and fertility, and with Cupid who bears a 'deadly Heben bow'
(I Proem 3.5). See III i 7.9*n*. Cf. 20.5, vi 6.4.
6　**which had the best afore**: which had been the best.

Stanza 9
1　**grudged**: complained.
3　**forestall**: deprive.
8　**Paragon**: pattern, model; also competition: cf. 'that
Turneyment for beauties prise' (vii 3.2).

Stanzas 10–13
There are six couples, the same number as in the masque of
Cupid (III xii 18.9): the first four followed by an unnamed
one hundred ladies, then **Britomart** and **Amoret** followed by
Blandamour and the False **Florimell**.

Stanza 10
4　**passing**: surpassing.
7　**vnheale**: expose to view.

Stanza 11
3　**forged beautie**: counterfeit, being made by art, as
I ii 36.1. Cf. 15.9.
5　**As . . . beene**: As different minds are affected differently.
7　**Lucida**: signifying **faire and sheene** (bright).

Stanza 12
1　**enchace**: portray; describe.
6–9　S. refers to this popular story of Apelles and his Venus
of Cos in his dedicatory sonnet, 'To all the gratious and
beautifull Ladies in the Court'.

13

At last the most redoubted *Britonesse*,
　Her louely *Amoret* did open shew;
　Whose face discouered, plainely did expresse
　The heauenly pourtraict of bright Angels hew.
　Well weened all, which her that time did vew,
　That she should surely beare the bell away,
　Till *Blandamour*, who thought he had the trew
　And very *Florimell*, did her display:
The sight of whom once seene did all the rest dismay.

14

For all afore that seemed fayre and bright,
　Now base and contemptible did appeare,
　Compar'd to her, that shone as Phebes light,
　Amongst the lesser starres in euening cleare.
　All that her saw with wonder rauisht weare,
　And weend no mortall creature she should bee,
　But some celestiall shape, that flesh did beare:
　Yet all were glad there *Florimell* to see;
Yet thought that *Florimell* was not so faire as shee.

15

As guilefull Goldsmith that by secret skill,
　With golden foyle doth finely ouer spred
　Some baser metall, which commend he will
　Vnto the vulgar for good gold insted,
　He much more goodly glosse thereon doth shed,
　To hide his falshood, then if it were trew:
　So hard, this Idole was to be ared,
　That *Florimell* her selfe in all mens vew
She seem'd to passe: so forged things do fairest shew.

16

Then was that golden belt by doome of all
　Graunted to her, as to the fayrest Dame.
　Which being brought, about her middle small
　They thought to gird, as best it her became;
　But by no meanes they could it thereto frame.
　For euer as they fastned it, it loos'd
　And fell away, as feeling secret blame.
　Full oft about her wast she it enclos'd;
And it as oft was from about her wast disclos'd.

17

That all men wondred at the vncouth sight,
　And each one thought, as to their fancies came.
　But she her selfe did thinke it doen for spight,
　And touched was with secret wrath and shame
　Therewith, as thing deuiz'd her to defame.
　Then many other Ladies likewise tride,
　About their tender loynes to knit the same;
　But it would not on none of them abide,
But when they thought it fast, eftsoones it was vntide.

18

Which when that scornefull *Squire of Dames* did vew,
　He lowdly gan to laugh, and thus to iest;
　Alas for pittie that so faire a crew,
　As like can not be seene from East to West,
　Cannot find one this girdle to inuest.
　Fie on the man, that did it first inuent,
　To shame vs all with this, *Vngirt vnblest*.
　Let neuer Ladie to his loue assent,
That hath this day so many so vnmanly shent.

19

Thereat all Knights gan laugh, and Ladies lowre:
　Till that at last the gentle *Amoret*
　Likewise assayd, to proue that girdles powre;
　And hauing it about her middle set,
　Did find it fit, withouten breach or let.
　Whereat the rest gan greatly to enuie:
　But *Florimell* exceedingly did fret,
　And snatching from her hand halfe angrily
The belt againe, about her bodie gan it tie.

Stanza 13
4　As Belphœbe is described, II iii 22.2.

Stanza 15
1–6　An apt simile because **Florimell**'s clothes are 'wrought of beaten gold' (III i 15.6) and her hair bound 'With golden wreath' (III vii 11.3).
7　**Idole**: image; imitation.　**ared**: made known; i.e. as a counterfeit.

Stanza 16
4　**best** is seen as beauty for its own sake, not as it manifests virtue.
7　**blame**: fault; blameworthiness in her: she does not possess 'the vertue of chast loue, / And wiuehood true' (3.1–2).
9　**disclos'd**: unfastened.

Stanza 17
6–9　At V iii 28 it is said that the ladies prove themselves to be not 'continent and chast'.

Stanza 18
1–2　Cf. Satyrane's loud laughter at the Squire of Dames's predicament arising from woman's lack of chastity (III vii 57.5, 58.5).
5　**inuest**: put on.
7　**Vngirt vnblest**: proverbial (Tilley, 1950, U10).
9　**shent**: disgraced.　**vnmanly**: because seen by men.

Stanza 19
5　**withouten breach or let**: without any break in it, in contrast to the 'broken girdle' (III viii 2.7); or without any impediment to her keeping it on.
6　**enuie**: grudge.

461

20

Yet nathemore would it her bodie fit;
　Yet nathelesse to her, as her dew right,
　It yeelded was by them, that iudged it:
　And she her selfe adiudged to the Knight,
　That bore the Hebene speare, as wonne in fight.
　But *Britomart* would not thereto assent,
　Ne her owne *Amoret* forgoe so light
For that strange Dame, whose beauties wonderment
She lesse esteem'd, then th'others vertuous gouernment.

21

Whom when the rest did see her to refuse,
　They were full glad, in hope themselues to get her:
　Yet at her choice they all did greatly muse.
　But after that the Iudges did arret her
　Vnto the second best, that lou'd her better;
　That was the *Saluage* Knight: but he was gone
　In great displeasure, that he could not get her.
　Then was she iudged *Triamond* his one;
But *Triamond* lou'd *Canacee*, and other none.

22

Tho vnto *Satyran* she was adiudged,
　Who was right glad to gaine so goodly meed:
　But *Blandamour* thereat full greatly grudged,
　And litle prays'd his labours euill speed,
　That for to winne the saddle, lost the steed.
　Ne lesse thereat did *Paridell* complaine,
　And thought t'appeale from that, which was decreed,
　To single combat with Sir *Satyrane*.
Thereto him *Ate* stird, new discord to maintaine.

23

And eke with these, full many other Knights
　She through her wicked working did incense,
　Her to demaund, and chalenge as their rights,
　Deserued for their perils recompense.
　Amongst the rest with boastfull vaine pretense
　Stept *Braggadochio* forth, and as his thrall
　Her claym'd, by him in battell wonne long sens:
　Whereto her selfe he did to witnesse call;
Who being askt, accordingly confessed all.

24

Thereat exceeding wroth was *Satyran*;
　And wroth with *Satyran* was *Blandamour*;
　And wroth with *Blandamour* was *Eriuan*;
　And at them both Sir *Paridell* did loure.
　So all together stird vp strifull stoure,
　And readie were new battell to darraine.
　Each one profest to be her paramoure,
　And vow'd with speare and shield it to maintaine;
Ne Iudges powre, ne reasons rule mote them restraine.

25

Which troublous stirre when *Satyrane* auiz'd,
　He gan to cast how to appease the same,
　And to accord them all, this meanes deuiz'd:
　First in the midst to set that fayrest Dame,
　To whom each one his chalenge should disclame,
　And he himselfe his right would eke releasse:
　Then looke to whom she voluntarie came,
　He should without disturbance her possesse:
Sweete is the loue that comes alone with willingnesse.

26

They all agreed, and then that snowy Mayd
　Was in the middest plast among them all;
　All on her gazing wisht, and vowd, and prayd,
　And to the Queene of beautie close did call,
　That she vnto their portion might befall.
　Then when she long had lookt vpon each one,
　As though she wished to haue pleasd them all,
　At last to *Braggadochio* selfe alone
She came of her accord, in spight of all his fone.

Stanza 20

1　nathemore: never the more.
9　gouernment: behaviour; shown by the girdle which fits her.

Stanza 21

3　muse: wonder.
4　arret her: commit her to the charge.
8　his one: his own; his only.

Stanza 22

4　euill speed: ill success.
5　Proverbial (C. G. Smith, 1970, 401).

Stanza 23

3　chalenge: claim.
5　pretense: false claim.
6　as his thrall: as woman is the prize or booty of prowess, denying her right to freely choose her love (cf. III i 25.7–9).

Stanza 24

3　Eriuan: Vain Strife; sugg. Fowler (1964) 178. Named at the end of the tournament to note the final discord.
5　stoure: tumult.
6　darraine: wage.

Stanza 25

1　auiz'd: perceived.
9　alone: voluntarie (7), 'of her accord' (26.9). Cf. Scudamour's choice of Amoret against her will, x 57.

Stanza 26

4　close: secretly.

27

Which when they all beheld they chaft and rag'd,
    And woxe nigh mad for very harts despight,
    That from reuenge their willes they scarse asswag'd:
    Some thought from him her to haue reft by might;
    Some proffer made with him for her to fight.
    But he nought car'd for all that they could say:
    For he their words as wind esteemed light.
    Yet not fit place he thought it there to stay,
But secretly from thence that night her bore away.

28

They which remaynd, so soone as they perceiu'd,
    That she was gone, departed thence with speed,
    And follow'd them, in mind her to haue reau'd
    From wight vnworthie of so noble meed.
    In which poursuit how each one did succeede,
    Shall else be told in order, as it fell.
    But now of *Britomart* it here doth neede,
    The hard aduentures and strange haps to tell;
Since with the rest she went not after *Florimell*.

29

For soone as she them saw to discord set,
    Her list no longer in that place abide;
    But taking with her louely *Amoret*,
    Vpon her first aduenture forth did ride,
    To seeke her lou'd, making blind loue her guide.
    Vnluckie Mayd to seeke her enemie,
    Vnluckie Mayd to seeke him farre and wide,
    Whom, when he was vnto her selfe most nie,
She through his late disguizement could him not descrie.

30

So much the more her griefe, the more her toyle:
    Yet neither toyle nor griefe she once did spare,
    In seeking him, that should her paine assoyle;
    Whereto great comfort in her sad misfare
    Was *Amoret*, companion of her care:
    Who likewise sought her louer long miswent,
    The gentle *Scudamour*, whose hart whileare
    That stryfull hag with gealous discontent
Had fild, that he to fell reueng was fully bent.

31

Bent to reuenge on blamelesse *Britomart*
    The crime, which cursed *Ate* kindled earst,
    The which like thornes did pricke his gealous hart,
    And through his soule like poysned arrow perst,
    That by no reason it might be reuerst,
    For ought that *Glauce* could or doe or say.
    For aye the more that she the same reherst,
    The more it gauld, and grieu'd him night and day,
That nought but dire reuenge his anger mote defray.

32

So as they trauelled, the drouping night
    Couered with cloudie storme and bitter showre,
    That dreadfull seem'd to euery liuing wight,
    Vpon them fell, before her timely howre;
    That forced them to seeke some couert bowre,
    Where they might hide their heads in quiet rest,
    And shrowd their persons from that stormie stowre.
    Not farre away, not meete for any guest
They spide a little cottage, like some poore mans nest.

33

Vnder a steepe hilles side it placed was,
    There where the mouldred earth had cav'd the banke;
    And fast beside a little brooke did pas
    Of muddie water, that like puddle stanke,
    By which few crooked sallowes grew in ranke:
    Whereto approaching nigh, they heard the sound
    Of many yron hammers beating ranke,
    And answering their wearie turnes around,
That seemed some blacksmith dwelt in that desert ground.

Stanza 27
Cf. Plato, *Rep. IX* 586c, on the incontinent multitude: 'Are not the pleasures with which they dwell inevitably commingled with pains, phantoms of true pleasure, illusions of scene painting, so colored by contrary juxtaposition as to seem intense in either kind, and to beget mad loves of themselves in senseless souls, and to be fought for, as Stesichorus says the wraith of Helen was fought for at Troy through ignorance of the truth?'

Stanza 28
5–6   This promise is fulfilled at ix 20f where **each one** appears **in order**.   **else**: at another time; elsewhere.
7–9   The brief episode inserted here parallels the opening of Book III where **Britomart** remained behind while the other knights sought **Florimell**. Now she renews her quest accompanied by Amoret.

Stanza 29
5   Cf. III iv 6.8: 'Following the guidaunce of her blinded guest'.

Stanza 30
3   **assoyle**: dispel; i.e. deliver her from pain; cf. vii 3.9.
4   **misfare**: misfortune; literally, going astray.
6   **miswent**: gone astray.

Stanza 31
3   **his gealous hart**: the subject of the ensuing episode; cf. vi 7.5. When Amoret becomes Britomart's 'care' (30.5), he becomes Care's victim.
5   **reuerst**: removed.
7   **reherst**: related.

Stanza 32
7   **stowre**: time of turmoil.

Stanza 33
1–2   Cf. Malbecco's cave in the cliff, III x 58.1–5. Bender (1972) 102 notes that the sense of spatial closure and constriction 'symbolizes the almost psychotic introversion of the knight's jealousy'.
4–5   The lover's willow growing crooked in stagnant water becomes an emblem of the jealous lover's state.   **puddle**: polluted water.   **ranke**: a pun is forced by the rhyme.
7   **ranke**: violently.
8   **wearie turnes**: referring to the ceaseless echoes.

463

34

There entring in, they found the goodman selfe,
  Full busily vnto his worke ybent;
  Who was to weet a wretched wearish elfe,
  With hollow eyes and rawbone cheekes forspent,
  As if he had in prison long bene pent:
  Full blacke and griesly did his face appeare,
  Besmeard with smoke that nigh his eye-sight blent;
  With rugged beard, and hoarie shagged heare,
The which he neuer wont to combe, or comely sheare.

35

Rude was his garment, and to rags all rent,
  Ne better had he, ne for better cared:
  With blistred hands emongst the cinders brent,
  And fingers filthie, with long nayles vnpared,
  Right fit to rend the food, on which he fared.
  His name was *Care*; a blacksmith by his trade,
  That neither day nor night from working spared,
  But to small purpose yron wedges made;
Those be vnquiet thoughts, that carefull minds inuade.

36

In which his worke he had sixe seruants prest,
  About the Andvile standing euermore,
  With huge great hammers, that did neuer rest
  From heaping stroakes, which thereon soused sore:
  All sixe strong groomes, but one then other more;
  For by degrees they all were disagreed;
  So likewise did the hammers which they bore,
  Like belles in greatnesse orderly succeed,
That he which was the last, the first did farre exceede.

37

He like a monstrous Gyant seem'd in sight,
  Farre passing *Bronteus*, or *Pyracmon* great,
  The which in *Lipari* doe day and night
  Frame thunderbolts for *Ioues* auengefull threate.
  So dreadfully he did the anduile beat,
  That seem'd to dust he shortly would it driue:
  So huge his hammer and so fierce his heat,
  That seem'd a rocke of Diamond it could riue,
And rend a sunder quite, if he thereto list striue.

38

Sir *Scudamour* there entring, much admired
  The manner of their worke and wearie paine;
  And hauing long beheld, at last enquired
  The cause and end thereof: but all in vaine;
  For they for nought would from their worke refraine,
  Ne let his speeches come vnto their eare.
  And eke the breathfull bellowes blew amaine,
  Like to the Northren winde, that none could heare:
Those *Pensifenesse* did moue; and *Sighes* the bellows weare.

39

Which when that warriour saw, he said no more,
  But in his armour layd him downe to rest:
  To rest he layd him downe vpon the flore,
  (Whylome for ventrous Knights the bedding best)
  And thought his wearie limbs to haue redrest.
  And that old aged Dame, his faithfull Squire,
  Her feeble ioynts layd eke a downe to rest;
  That needed much her weake age to desire,
After so long a trauell, which them both did tire.

Stanza 34
1 **the goodman selfe**: i.e. the master blacksmith; cf. 44.1.
3 **wearish**: wizened; suggesting weary (like the sound of his hammers, 33.8); worn away, as he causes others to become. **elfe**: a malignant being.
4 As Despair, I ix 35.6–9. Scudamour is subject to love's despair, as is Terwin (I ix 29). **forspent**: wasted away.

Stanzas 35–36
Steadman (1964) 665 notes the relationship between Care, Vulcan, and Tubalcain, and the etymological relationship between Lat. *cura* and *aemulatio*.

Stanza 35
2 **cared**: with the pun implied.

Stanza 36
1 **sixe seruants**: Nelson (1963) 250 suggests that S. alludes to the discovery of the relationship of numerical proportion to musical harmony. Upon hearing blacksmiths beating on their anvils, Pythagoras discovered that six combinations of weights produced harmony. See Macrobius, *In Somn. Scip.* II i 9–12. Steadman (1964) 665 notes that an image traditionally associated with concord becomes an *exemplum* of discord. **prest**: at hand.
3 **hammers**: suggested by Ital. *martello*, 'a hammer. Also jealousie in love, panting or throbbing of the heart' (Florio, 1611); noted Steadman (1960) 208.
4 **soused**: fell heavily.
6 They were unlike, each differing from the next by a fixed quantity; hence the play on **degrees . . . disagreed**.

Stanza 37
2–4 Drawn from the Cyclopes on Lipare, Virgil, *Aen.* viii 424–8. **Bronteus**: 'interpreted thunder' (Cooper, 1565). **Pyracmon**: Gk fire + anvil.

Stanza 38
1 **admired**: wondered at.
9 **Pensifenesse**: also 'full of thought', i.e. anxious thought, apprehensiveness; cf. 'thoughts vnkind', vi 1.3.

Stanza 39
2 **in his armour . . . to rest**: infers apprehension and care.
5 **redrest**: restored, i.e. refreshed.
8 **That**: i.e. rest.
9 **trauell**: travel and travail.

40

There lay Sir *Scudamour* long while expecting,
  When gentle sleepe his heauie eyes would close;
  Oft chaunging sides, and oft new place electing,
  Where better seem'd he mote himselfe repose;
  And oft in wrath he thence againe vprose;
  And oft in wrath he layd him downe againe.
  But wheresoeuer he did himselfe dispose,
  He by no meanes could wished ease obtaine:
So euery place seem'd painefull, and ech changing vaine.

41

And euermore, when he to sleepe did thinke,
  The hammers sound his senses did molest;
  And euermore, when he began to winke,
  The bellowes noyse disturb'd his quiet rest,
  Ne suffred sleepe to settle in his brest.
  And all the night the dogs did barke and howle
  About the house, at sent of stranger guest:
  And now the crowing Cocke, and now the Owle
Lowde shriking him afflicted to the very sowle.

42

And if by fortune any litle nap
  Vpon his heauie eye-lids chaunst to fall,
  Eftsoones one of those villeins him did rap
  Vpon his headpeece with his yron mall;
  That he was soone awaked therewithall,
  And lightly started vp as one affrayd;
  Or as if one him suddenly did call.
  So oftentimes he out of sleepe abrayd,
And then lay musing long, on that him ill apayd.

43

So long he muzed, and so long he lay,
  That at the last his wearie sprite opprest
  With fleshly weaknesse, which no creature may
  Long time resist, gaue place to kindly rest,
  That all his senses did full soone arrest:
  Yet in his soundest sleepe, his dayly feare
  His ydle braine gan busily molest,
  And made him dreame those two disloyall were:
The things that day most minds, at night doe most appeare.

44

With that, the wicked carle the maister Smith
  A paire of redwhot yron tongs did take
  Out of the burning cinders, and therewith
  Vnder his side him nipt, that forst to wake,
  He felt his hart for very paine to quake,
  And started vp auenged for to be
  On him, the which his quiet slomber brake:
  Yet looking round about him none could see;
Yet did the smart remaine, though he himselfe did flee

45

In such disquiet and hartfretting payne,
  He all that night, that too long night did passe.
  And now the day out of the Ocean mayne
  Began to peepe aboue this earthly masse,
  With pearly dew sprinkling the morning grasse:
  Then vp he rose like heauie lumpe of lead,
  That in his face, as in a looking glasse,
  The signes of anguish one mote plainely read,
And ghesse the man to be dismayd with gealous dread.

46

Vnto his lofty steede he clombe anone,
  And forth vpon his former voiage fared,
  And with him eke that aged Squire attone;
  Who whatsoeuer perill was prepared,
  Both equall paines and equall perill shared:
  The end whereof and daungerous euent
  Shall for another canticle be spared.
  But here my wearie teeme nigh ouer spent
Shall breath it selfe awhile, after so long a went.

Stanza 40
1 **expecting**: waiting.

Stanza 41
3 **winke**: close his eyes; sleep.

Stanza 42
4 Since Scudamour's jealousy has been aroused by Ate's false witness, S. may allude to Prov. 25.18: 'A man that beareth fals witness against his neighbor is a maul' (K. J. ['hammer', Geneva]).
8 **abrayd**: awoke with a start.
9 **on that him ill apayd**: on what ill-pleased him.

Stanza 43
4 **kindly**: natural, owing to nature.
5 **arrest**: seize.
6 **dayly feare**: the fears of the day.
9 Traditional dream psychology: cf. Nashe, *Terrors of the Night* (*Works* i 356): 'A Dreame is nothing els but the Eccho of our conceipts in the day.'

Stanza 44
Coleridge offers an interesting reading: 'At night, and in sleep, cares are not only doubly burdensome, but some matters, that then seem to us sources of great anxiety, are not so in fact; and when we are thoroughly awake, and in possession of all our faculties, they really seem nothing, and we wonder at the influence they have had over us.' In defence of his reading of line 9, he adds: 'What Spenser meant was, that sleep much enhanced and exaggerated that suffering; yet when Scudamour awoke, the cause of the increase was nowhere to be found' (cited *Var.* iv 198).

Stanza 45
1 **hartfretting payne**: on the etymology of care as that which corrodes the heart, see III x 59.6*n*; cf. 31.3 above.

Stanza 46
1 **clombe**: indicating the labour of mounting; cf. III iv 61.6.
3 **attone**: together.
6 **euent**: outcome.
7 **canticle**: canto.
8–9 The poet shares his subject's weariness. **went**: journey.

465

Cant. VI.

Both Scudamour and Arthegall
Doe fight with Britomart,
He sees her face; doth fall in loue,
and soone from her depart.

1

WHat equall torment to the griefe of mind,
   And pyning anguish hid in gentle hart,
That inly feeds it selfe with thoughts vnkind,
And nourisheth her owne consuming smart?
What medicine can any Leaches art
Yeeld such a sore, that doth her grieuance hide,
And will to none her maladie impart?
Such was the wound that *Scudamour* did gride;
For which *Dan Phebus* selfe cannot a salue prouide.

2

Who hauing left that restlesse house of *Care*,
   The next day, as he on his way did ride,
Full of melancholie and sad misfare,
Through misconceipt; all vnawares espide
An armed Knight vnder a forrest side,
Sitting in shade beside his grazing steede;
Who soone as them approaching he descride,
Gan towards them to pricke with eger speede,
That seem'd he was full bent to some mischieuous deede.

3

Which *Scudamour* perceiuing, forth issewed
   To haue rencountred him in equall race;
But soone as th'other nigh approaching, vewed
The armes he bore, his speare he gan abase,
And voide his course: at which so suddain case
He wondred much. But th'other thus can say;
Ah gentle *Scudamour*, vnto your grace
I me submit, and you of pardon pray,
That almost had against you trespassed this day.

4

Whereto thus *Scudamour*, Small harme it were
   For any knight, vpon a ventrous knight
Without displeasance for to proue his spere.
But reade you Sir, sith ye my name haue hight,
What is your owne, that I mote you requite.
Certes (sayd he) ye mote as now excuse
Me from discouering you my name aright:
For time yet serues that I the same refuse,
But call ye me the *Saluage Knight*, as others vse.

5

Then this, Sir *Saluage Knight* (quoth he) areede;
   Or doe you here within this forrest wonne,
That seemeth well to answere to your weede?
Or haue ye it for some occasion donne?
That rather seemes, sith knowen armes ye shonne.
This other day (sayd he) a stranger knight
Shame and dishonour hath vnto me donne;
On whom I waite to wreake that foule despight,
When euer he this way shall passe by day or night.

Canto vi

Stanza 1
3   **vnkind**: unnatural, because self-destroying.
5   **Leaches**: physician's.
8   **gride**: pierce gratingly.
9   **Dan Phebus**: '*Apollo* King of Leaches' (xii 25.4). Cf.
Ovid, *Met*. i 521–4: Phœbus declares that love cannot be cured
by herbs. On the incurable wound of jealousy, see Ariosto,
Orl. Fur. xxxi 5–6.

Stanza 2
3   **sad misfare**: grief caused by misfortune or going astray.
Cf. Britomart's 'sad misfare' (v 30.4); yet she is comforted by
love, Amoret.
4   **misconceipt**: misconception, for he assumes Britomart
to be a man.
6   **Sitting, shade**, and **grazing steede** recall the moment of
the Red Cross Knight's fall, I vii 2–3; cf. 22.2–3.

Stanza 3
2   **rencountred**: counter-engaged in battle.   **race**: a
technical term for the chivalric encounter.
4   **abase**: lower.
5   **voide**: turn aside.
6   **can**: did.
7–9   The first stage of his submission to love; cf. his
apology at 22.6–7.

Stanza 4
1–3   The chivalric code allowed unprovoked aggression when
both parties were willing.   **displeasance**: cause of grievance.
proue: test.
4   **reade**: tell.
5   **requite**: salute in return.
7   **discouering**: revealing.

Stanza 5
5   **seemes . . . shonne**: i.e. it seems that you have come into
the forest for some particular reason since you do not wear
known arms.
8–9   Nursing a grudge and seeking revenge show Artegall's
virtue of Justice at its most primitive level. Cf. v 9.1–6. His
ambush of Britomart contrasts with her search for him. As
Dunseath (1968) 38 notes, he echoes Britomart's slander,
III ii 8.7–9.

6

Shame be his meede (quoth he) that meaneth shame.
  But what is he, by whom ye shamed were?
  A stranger knight, sayd he, vnknowne by name,
  But knowne by fame, and by an Hebene speare,
  With which he all that met him, downe did beare.
  He in an open Turney lately held,
  Fro me the honour of that game did reare;
  And hauing me all wearie earst, downe feld,
The fayrest Ladie reft, and euer since withheld.

7

When *Scudamour* heard mention of that speare,
  He wist right well, that it was *Britomart*,
  The which from him his fairest loue did beare.
  Tho gan he swell in euery inner part,
  For fell despight, and gnaw his gealous hart,
  That thus he sharply sayd; Now by my head,
  Yet is not this the first vnknightly part,
  Which that same knight, whom by his launce I read,
Hath doen to noble knights, that many makes him dread.

8

For lately he my loue hath fro me reft,
  And eke defiled with foule villanie
  The sacred pledge, which in his faith was left,
  In shame of knighthood and fidelitie;
  The which ere long full deare he shall abie.
  And if to that auenge by you decreed
  This hand may helpe, or succour ought supplie,
  It shall not fayle, when so ye shall it need.
So both to wreake their wrathes on *Britomart* agreed.

9

Whiles thus they communed, lo farre away
  A Knight soft ryding towards them they spyde,
  Attyr'd in forraine armes and straunge aray:
  Whom when they nigh approcht, they plaine descryde
  To be the same, for whom they did abyde.
  Sayd then Sir *Scudamour*, Sir *Saluage* knight
  Let me this craue, sith first I was defyde,
  That first I may that wrong to him requite:
And if I hap to fayle, you shall recure my right.

10

Which being yeelded, he his threatfull speare
  Gan fewter, and against her fiercely ran.
  Who soone as she him saw approching neare
  With so fell rage, her selfe she lightly gan
  To dight, to welcome him, well as she can:
  But entertaind him in so rude a wise,
  That to the ground she smote both horse and man;
  Whence neither greatly hasted to arise,
But on their common harmes together did deuise.

11

But *Artegall* beholding his mischaunce,
  New matter added to his former fire;
  And eft auentring his steeleheaded launce,
  Against her rode, full of despiteous ire,
  That nought but spoyle and vengeance did require.
  But to himselfe his felonous intent
  Returning, disappointed his desire,
  Whiles vnawares his saddle he forwent,
And found himselfe on ground in great amazement.

Stanza 6

1   **Shame be his meede . . .**: *Honi soit qui mal y pense*, the
motto of the Knights of the Garter; see *Enc. Brit*. xv 856 Pl. 1.
The motto judges Artegall.   **meaneth**: intends.
7   **reare**: take away.

Stanza 7

3   **his fairest loue**: distinguishes Amoret from the 'fayrest
Ladie' (6.9), Florimell.
5   **gnaw . . . hart**: cf. v 31.3. Refers to his jealousy: see
III x 59.6*n*.
6   **by my head**: a classical oath; perhaps to suggest his
abandonment of the head, reason; see II i 19.1*n*.
8   **read**: make out, know.
9   **many makes**: i.e. makes many.

Stanza 8

2   Refers back to **my loue** before it extends forward to
sacred pledge.
5   **abie**: make amends for.
6   **auenge**: vengeance.   **decreed**: determined, with the
legal sense, 'decided judicially'.

Stanza 9

1   **communed**: consulted.
2   **soft**: at a slow pace; cf. Artegall's 'eger speede' (2.8) and
Scudamour's 'equall race' (3.2).
4   **when they**: 'when he' sugg. Dodge (1908). **they** would
include Amoret; yet see 34f.
9   **recure**: recover.

Stanza 10

2   **fewter**: put into its rest.
4   **lightly**: quickly.
5   **dight**: make ready.
6   **entertaind**: received.
9   **deuise**: confer. The male knight with spear in rest bearing
down upon a woman knight suggests courtship, the comic and
bawdy implications of which are presented in all Britomart's
chivalric encounters, but particularly here.

Stanza 11

3   **eft**: again, i.e. in return.   **auentring**: aiming by setting
in its rest; or thrusting forward: see III i 28.7*n*, IV iii 9.1.
steeleheaded launce: in opposition to 'Hebene speare' (6.4).
5   **require**: seek.
6   **felonous**: fierce, cruel.
8   **forwent**: left.

12

Lightly he started vp out of that stound,
   And snatching forth his direfull deadly blade,
   Did leape to her, as doth an eger hound
   Thrust to an Hynd within some couert glade,
   Whom without perill he cannot inuade.
   With such fell greedines he her assayled,
   That though she mounted were, yet he her made
   To giue him ground, (so much his force preuayled)
And shun his mightie strokes, gainst which no armes auayled.

13

So as they coursed here and there, it chaunst
   That in her wheeling round, behind her crest
   So sorely he her strooke, that thence it glaunst
   Adowne her backe, the which it fairely blest
   From foule mischance; ne did it euer rest,
   Till on her horses hinder parts it fell;
   Where byting deepe, so deadly it imprest,
   That quite it chynd his backe behind the sell,
And to alight on foote her algates did compell.

14

Like as the lightning brond from riuen skie,
   Throwne out by angry *Ioue* in his vengeance,
   With dreadfull force falles on some steeple hie;
   Which battring, downe it on the church doth glance,
   And teares it all with terrible mischance.
   Yet she no whit dismayd, her steed forsooke,
   And casting from her that enchaunted lance,
   Vnto her sword and shield her soone betooke;
And therewithall at him right furiously she strooke.

15

So furiously she strooke in her first heat,
   Whiles with long fight on foot he breathlesse was,
   That she him forced backward to retreat,
   And yeeld vnto her weapon way to pas:
   Whose raging rigour neither steele nor bras
   Could stay, but to the tender flesh it went,
   And pour'd the purple bloud forth on the gras;
   That all his mayle yriv'd, and plates yrent,
Shew'd all his bodie bare vnto the cruell dent.

16

At length when as he saw her hastie heat
   Abate, and panting breath begin to fayle,
   He through long sufferance growing now more great,
   Rose in his strength, and gan her fresh assayle,
   Heaping huge strokes, as thicke as showre of hayle,
   And lashing dreadfully at euery part,
   As if he thought her soule to disentrayle.
   Ah cruell hand, and thrise more cruell hart,
That workst such wrecke on her, to whom thou dearest art.

17

What yron courage euer could endure,
   To worke such outrage on so faire a creature?
   And in his madnesse thinke with hands impure
   To spoyle so goodly workmanship of nature,
   The maker selfe resembling in her feature?
   Certes some hellish furie, or some feend
   This mischiefe framd, for their first loues defeature,
   To bath their hands in bloud of dearest freend,
Thereby to make their loues beginning, their liues end.

18

Thus long they trac'd, and trauerst to and fro,
   Sometimes pursewing, and sometimes pursewed,
   Still as aduantage they espyde thereto:
   But toward th'end Sir *Arthegall* renewed
   His strength still more, but she still more decrewed.
   At last his lucklesse hand he heau'd on hie,
   Hauing his forces all in one accrewed,
   And therewith stroke at her so hideouslie,
That seemed nought but death mote be her destinie.

Stanza 12

1   **stound**: state of amazement.
3   **eger**: fierce, savage.
4   **Thrust to**: lunge towards.
6   **assayled**: wooed (*OED* 10) suggests the allegory of courtship; cf. 16.4.

Stanza 13

3   **it**: the stroke of the sword.   **glaunst**: perhaps a play on the 'glaunce' in the mirror (cf. III iii 24.5) which wounds Britomart with love of Artegall.
4   **fairely blest**: entirely protected; in glancing down her back, the stroke protected her from serious injury; cf. I ii 18.9. His second stroke, 19.1–4, glances down her front; together they show that her chaste body is inviolate.
8   **chynd his backe**: split or broke the back (chine).
9   **algates**: altogether.

Stanza 14

The simile extends the significance of Artegall's stroke.
6–9   Cf. Merlin's warning: 'yield thee not [to love], / Till thou in open field adowne be smot' (III ii 46.4–5). The wounding of the horse's hind quarters has a sexual significance. Being on foot, Britomart is deprived of her lance, the symbol of chastity.

Stanza 15

5   **rigour**: hardness; violence.
8   **mayle**: the pun on 'male' is implicit.
9   **dent**: blow.

Stanza 16

7   **disentrayle**: draw forth from the inward parts.
9   **wrecke**: vengeance, cf. 11.5; also 'wrack' (as 21.2), injury or outrage. The term collapses 'wreak' (revenge) and 'wreck' (ruin).

Stanza 17

4–5   Cf. 24.5–6.
7   **defeature**: undoing, in contrast to God's **workmanship** (4).
8   **freend**: lover.

Stanza 18

1   **trac'd, and trauerst**: pursued, and then turned aside, as 2 explains.
5–7   **decrewed**: decreased; the opposite of **accrewed**, gathered up.

19

The wicked stroke vpon her helmet chaunst,
    And with the force, which in it selfe it bore,
    Her ventayle shard away, and thence forth glaunst
    A downe in vaine, ne harm'd her any more.
    With that her angels face, vnseene afore,
    Like to the ruddie morne appeard in sight,
    Deawed with siluer drops, through sweating sore,
    But somewhat redder, then beseem'd aright,
Through toylesome heate and labour of her weary fight.

20

And round about the same, her yellow heare
    Hauing through stirring loosd their wonted band,
    Like to a golden border did appeare,
    Framed in goldsmithes forge with cunning hand:
    Yet goldsmithes cunning could not vnderstand
    To frame such subtile wire, so shinie cleare.
    For it did glister like the golden sand,
    The which *Pactolus* with his waters shere,
Throwes forth vpon the riuage round about him nere.

21

And as his hand he vp againe did reare,
    Thinking to worke on her his vtmost wracke,
    His powrelesse arme benumbd with secret feare
    From his reuengefull purpose shronke abacke,
    And cruell sword out of his fingers slacke
    Fell downe to ground, as if the steele had sence,
    And felt some ruth, or sence his hand did lacke,
    Or both of them did thinke, obedience
To doe to so diuine a beauties excellence.

22

And he himselfe long gazing thereupon,
    At last fell humbly downe vpon his knee,
    And of his wonder made religion,
    Weening some heauenly goddesse he did see,
    Or else vnweeting, what it else might bee;
    And pardon her besought his errour frayle,
    That had done outrage in so high degree:
    Whilest trembling horrour did his sense assayle,
And made ech member quake, and manly hart to quayle.

23

Nathelesse she full of wrath for that late stroke,
    All that long while vpheld her wrathfull hand,
    With fell intent, on him to bene ywroke,
    And looking sterne, still ouer him did stand,
    Threatning to strike, vnlesse he would withstand:
    And bad him rise, or surely he should die.
    But die or liue for nought he would vpstand
    But her of pardon prayd more earnestlie,
Or wreake on him her will for so great iniurie.

24

Which when as *Scudamour*, who now abrayd,
    Beheld, whereas he stood not farre aside,
    He was therewith right wondrously dismayd,
    And drawing nigh, when as he plaine descride
    That peerelesse paterne of Dame natures pride,
    And heauenly image of perfection,
    He blest himselfe, as one sore terrified,
    And turning his feare to faint deuotion,
Did worship her as some celestiall vision.

25

But *Glauce*, seeing all that chaunced there,
    Well weeting how their errour to assoyle,
    Full glad of so good end, to them drew nere,
    And her salewd with seemely belaccoyle,
    Ioyous to see her safe after long toyle.
    Then her besought, as she to her was deare,
    To graunt vnto those warriours truce a whyle;
    Which yeelded, they their beuers vp did reare,
And shew'd themselues to her, such as indeed they were.

Stanza 19

3   **ventayle**: the movable front of the helmet.   **shard**: cut.

Stanza 20

5–6   As Florimell's hair surpasses imitation, III viii 7.5–8. **vnderstand**: know how.   **subtile**: fine.
7–9   **Pactolus**: 'a ryver in Lydia, havyng golden gravel' (Cooper, 1565).   **shere**: clear.   **riuage**: bank.

Stanza 21

2   **his vtmost wracke**: the greatest destruction he could inflict; see 16.9*n*.
3–9   As Dunseath (1968) 42 observes, Artegall does not abandon his sword wilfully; cf. his action at V v 13.3–4.
7   **sence**: capacity to feel.

Stanza 22

A variant of Marinell's defeat. Artegall does not fear woman's force but should have feared her love; Marinell feared woman's love but should have feared her force.
3   **religion**: devotion; i.e. his wonder was turned to religious adoration; cf. 24.8–9.
8   **trembling**: stressing the Lat. sense of **horrour**, shuddering.

Stanza 23

3   **ywroke**: avenged.
4   **sterne**: threatening.

Stanza 24

1   **abrayd**: awoke, i.e. revived after his fall.
8   **faint**: because he is **dismayd** (3) and **terrifide** (7).

Stanza 25

2   **assoyle**: purge; absolve from sin.
4   **And her ... belaccoyle**: And saluted her with fitting kind greeting. Dunseath (1968) 43 observes that in the *Romance of the Rose* 2787f, 'it is *Belacoil*, as an aspect of the lady, who first extends a welcome to the lover'. Here the nurse addresses the lady, rather than her lover, although on his behalf.

469

26

When *Britomart* with sharpe auizefull eye
    Beheld the louely face of *Artegall*,
    Tempred with sternesse and stout maiestie,
    She gan eftsoones it to her mind to call,
    To be the same which in her fathers hall
    Long since in that enchaunted glasse she saw.
    Therewith her wrathfull courage gan appall,
    And haughtie spirits meekely to adaw,
That her enhaunced hand she downe can soft withdraw.

27

Yet she it forst to haue againe vpheld,
    As fayning choler, which was turn'd to cold:
    But euer when his visage she beheld,
    Her hand fell downe, and would no longer hold
    The wrathfull weapon gainst his countnance bold:
    But when in vaine to fight she oft assayd,
    She arm'd her tongue, and thought at him to scold;
    Nathlesse her tongue not to her will obayd,   (sayd.
But brought forth speeches myld, when she would haue mis-

28

But *Scudamour* now woxen inly glad,
    That all his gealous feare he false had found,
    And how that Hag his loue abused had
    With breach of faith and loyaltie vnsound,
    The which long time his grieued hart did wound,
    He thus bespake; Certes Sir *Artegall*,
    I ioy to see you lout so low on ground,
    And now become to liue a Ladies thrall,
That whylome in your minde wont to despise them all.

29

Soone as she heard the name of *Artegall*,
    Her hart did leape, and all her hart-strings tremble,
    For sudden ioy, and secret feare withall,
    And all her vitall powres with motion nimble,
    To succour it, themselues gan there assemble,
    That by the swift recourse of flushing blood
    Right plaine appeard, though she it would dissemble,
    And fayned still her former angry mood,
Thinking to hide the depth by troubling of the flood.

30

When *Glauce* thus gan wisely all vpknit;
    Ye gentle Knights, whom fortune here hath brought,
    To be spectators of this vncouth fit,
    Which secret fate hath in this Ladie wrought,
    Against the course of kind, ne meruaile nought,
    Ne thenceforth feare the thing that hethertoo
    Hath troubled both your mindes with idle thought,
    Fearing least she your loues away should woo,
Feared in vaine, sith meanes ye see there wants theretoo.

31

And you Sir *Artegall*, the saluage knight,
    Henceforth may not disdaine, that womans hand
    Hath conquered you anew in second fight:
    For whylome they haue conquerd sea and land,
    And heauen it selfe, that nought may them withstand.
    Ne henceforth be rebellious vnto loue,
    That is the crowne of knighthood, and the band
    Of noble minds deriued from aboue,
Which being knit with vertue, neuer will remoue.

32

And you faire Ladie knight, my dearest Dame,
    Relent the rigour of your wrathfull will,
    Whose fire were better turn'd to other flame;
    And wiping out remembrance of all ill,
    Graunt him your grace, but so that he fulfill
    The penance, which ye shall to him empart:
    For louers heauen must passe by sorrowes hell.
    Thereat full inly blushed *Britomart*;
But *Artegall* close smyling ioy'd in secret hart.

Stanza 26

1   **auizefull**: attentive.
2   **louely**: loving.
7   **appall**: fail, wax faint.
8   **adaw**: become subdued.
9   **enhaunced**: uplifted.   **soft**: as the encounter began
when she entered 'soft ryding' (9.2); cf. 'softly' (41.5).

Stanza 27

2   **choler**: associated with heat.
5   **bold**: applied to the lover rather than the warrior.
9   Cf. her slander of Artegall which she repented 'so to haue
missayd' (III ii 9.2).   **missayd**: spoken abusively.

Stanza 28

6   **He**] Her *1596*; 'Him' sugg. Upton (1758) and Church
(1758) who compares 34.5.
7–9   Later Artegall becomes Radigund's **thrall**. Since
Britomart seeks his love, not his servitude, she must free him
from the implications of his present action. See 41.8*n*.

Stanza 29

6   **recourse**: flow.   **flushing**: rushing.

Stanza 30

3   **vncouth fit**: strange, painful experience.
5   **kind**: nature.
7–9   Artegall is included because he has suffered jealousy;
see v 9.2, 21.6–7, vi 6.9.

Stanza 31

4–5   A compliment to Elizabeth, as Upton (1758) notes,
although 5 suggests Cupid's assaults against the gods, III
xi 29f.
8   **deriued from aboue**: cf. III iii 1.1–4.

Stanza 32

5   **grace**: favour.
6   **empart**: impose.
7   **by**: through.
9   **close**: secretly.

33

Yet durst he not make loue so suddenly,
　Ne thinke th'affection of her hart to draw
　From one to other so quite contrary:
　Besides her modest countenance he saw
　So goodly graue, and full of princely aw,
　That it his ranging fancie did refraine,
　And looser thoughts to lawfull bounds withdraw;
　Whereby the passion grew more fierce and faine,
Like to a stubborne steede whom strong hand would restraine.

34

But *Scudamour* whose hart twixt doubtfull feare
　And feeble hope hung all this while suspence,
　Desiring of his *Amoret* to heare
　Some gladfull newes and sure intelligence,
　Her thus bespake; But Sir without offence
　Mote I request you tydings of my loue,
　My *Amoret*, sith you her freed fro thence,
　Where she captiued long, great woes did proue;
That where ye left, I may her seeke, as doth behoue.

35

To whom thus *Britomart*, Certes Sir knight,
　What is of her become, or whether reft,
　I can not vnto you aread a right.
　For from that time I from enchaunters theft
　Her freed, in which ye her all hopelesse left,
　I her preseru'd from perill and from feare,
　And euermore from villenie her kept;
　Ne euer was there wight to me more deare
Then she, ne vnto whom I more true loue did beare.

36

Till on a day as through a desert wyld
　We trauelled, both wearie of the way
　We did alight, and sate in shadow myld;
　Where fearelesse I to sleepe me downe did lay.
　But when as I did out of sleepe abray,
　I found her not, where I her left whyleare,
　But thought she wandred was, or gone astray.
　I cal'd her loud, I sought her farre and neare;
But no where could her find, nor tydings of her heare.

37

When *Scudamour* those heauie tydings heard,
　His hart was thrild with point of deadly feare;
　Ne in his face or bloud or life appeard,
　But senselesse stood, like to a mazed steare,
　That yet of mortall stroke the stound doth beare.
　Till *Glauce* thus; Faire Sir, be nought dismayd
　With needelesse dread, till certaintie ye heare:
　For yet she may be safe though somewhat strayd;
Its best to hope the best, though of the worst affrayd.

38

Nathlesse he hardly of her chearefull speech
　Did comfort take, or in his troubled sight
　Shew'd change of better cheare: so sore a breach
　That sudden newes had made into his spright;
　Till *Britomart* him fairely thus behight;
　Great cause of sorrow certes Sir ye haue:
　But comfort take: for by this heauens light
　I vow, you dead or liuing not to leaue,
Till I her find, and wreake on him that her did reaue.

39

Therewith he rested, and well pleased was.
　So peace being confirm'd amongst them all,
　They tooke their steeds, and forward thence did pas
　Vnto some resting place, which mote befall,
　All being guided by Sir *Artegall*.
　Where goodly solace was vnto them made,
　And dayly feasting both in bowre and hall,
　Vntill that they their wounds well healed had,
And wearie limmes recur'd after late vsage bad.

Stanza 33
8–9　**faine**: eager.　**stubborne**: untamable, fierce.
steede: the traditional emblem of sexual desire.

Stanza 34
2　**suspence**: i.e. in suspense; literally suspended.
8　**proue**: suffer, endure.

Stanza 35
2　**whether**: whither.
3　**aread**: declare.
5　**all hopelesse**: refers to Scudamour (cf. III xi 16.1–5,
xii 45.4) and therefore to Amoret.
7　**villenie**: ill-usage; dishonour.
8–9　Since Amoret is **true loue**, Britomart plays upon her
name and reveals her commitment to love.

Stanza 36
4　**fearelesse**: cf. Amoret before she is raped by Lust, vii 4.1.
Without Britomart's virtue, she lapses into fear; cf. i 5.4, vii
21.1. Allegorically, her fear is related to Britomart's 'secret
feare' (29.3) on seeing Artegall.
5　**abray**: awake.

Stanza 37
4–5　The **steare** suggests impotence. At i 49.7–9, he is
compared to a struck stag. Marinell is compared to a 'sacred
Oxe' (III iv 17) when he is struck down by Britomart.
stound: shock.
7　**certaintie**: that which is certain.
9　Proverbial (C. G. Smith, 1970, 399).

Stanza 38
2　**sight**: appearance.
5–9　**behight**: vowed; 'addressed' better fits the context.
She extends her earlier vow, III xi 18.7–9: now she will
accompany him instead of leaving him behind. She accompanies
Cupid's man since she has accepted Artegall's love.

Stanza 39
5　Artegall has replaced Cupid; cf. III iv 6.8, IV v 29.5.
6　**solace**: pleasure, entertainment.
9　**recur'd**: restored.

40

In all which time, Sir *Artegall* made way
   Vnto the loue of noble *Britomart*,
   And with meeke seruice and much suit did lay
   Continuall siege vnto her gentle hart,
   Which being whylome launcht with louely dart,
   More eath was new impression to receiue,
   How euer she her paynd with womanish art
   To hide her wound, that none might it perceiue:
Vaine is the art that seekes it selfe for to deceiue.

41

So well he woo'd her, and so well he wrought her,
   With faire entreatie and sweet blandishment,
   That at the length vnto a bay he brought her,
   So as she to his speeches was content
   To lend an eare, and softly to relent.
   At last through many vowes which forth he pour'd,
   And many othes, she yeelded her consent
   To be his loue, and take him for her Lord,
Till they with mariage meet might finish that accord.

42

Tho when they had long time there taken rest,
   Sir *Artegall*, who all this while was bound
   Vpon an hard aduenture yet in quest,
   Fit time for him thence to depart it found,
   To follow that, which he did long propound;
   And vnto her his congee came to take.
   But her therewith full sore displeasd he found,
   And loth to leaue her late betrothed make,
Her dearest loue full loth so shortly to forsake.

43

Yet he with strong perswasions her asswaged,
   And wonne her will to suffer him depart;
   For which his faith with her he fast engaged,
   And thousand vowes from bottome of his hart,
   That all so soone as he by wit or art
   Could that atchieue, whereto he did aspire,
   He vnto her would speedily reuert:
   No longer space thereto he did desire,
But till the horned moone three courses did expire.

44

With which she for the present was appeased,
   And yeelded leaue, how euer malcontent
   She inly were, and in her mind displeased.
   So early in the morrow next he went
   Forth on his way, to which he was ybent.
   Ne wight him to attend, or way to guide,
   As whylome was the custome ancient
   Mongst Knights, when on aduentures they did ride,
Saue that she algates him a while accompanide.

45

And by the way she sundry purpose found
   Of this or that, the time for to delay,
   And of the perils whereto he was bound,
   The feare whereof seem'd much her to affray:
   But all she did was but to weare out day.
   Full oftentimes she leaue of him did take;
   And eft againe deuiz'd some what to say,
   Which she forgot, whereby excuse to make:
So loth she was his companie for to forsake.

46

At last when all her speeches she had spent,
   And new occasion fayld her more to find,
   She left him to his fortunes gouernment,
   And backe returned with right heauie mind,
   To *Scudamour*, who she had left behind,
   With whom she went to seeke faire *Amoret*,
   Her second care, though in another kind;
   For vertues onely sake, which doth beget
True loue and faithfull friendship, she by her did set

47

Backe to that desert forrest they retyred,
   Where sorie *Britomart* had lost her late;
   There they her sought, and euery where inquired,
   Where they might tydings get of her estate;
   Yet found they none.   But by what haplesse fate,
   Or hard misfortune she was thence conuayd,
   And stolne away from her beloued mate,
   Were long to tell; therefore I here will stay
Vntill another tyde, that I it finish may.

Stanza 40

5   **launcht with louely dart**: pierced with the dart of love.
6   **eath**: easy.
7   **How euer**: however much.   **paynd**: strived.

Stanza 41

1   **wrought**: prevailed upon; persuaded.
3   **vnto a bay**: to the last extremity, as a hunted animal when forced to face its pursuer. The phrase continues the image of his 'siege vnto her gentle hart' (40.4), punning on 'hart'.
8   A key line in the battle for 'maisterie' (III i 25.7–9). Artegall submits to her as her 'thrall' (28.8); she submits to him as **his loue** and **her Lord**. When she frees him from thraldom to Radigund, he becomes simply 'her noble Lord sir *Artegall*' (V vii 45.6).

Stanza 42

3   **in quest**: i.e. uncompleted.
5   **propound**: purpose or intend.
6   **congee**: farewell; suggesting 'leave to depart': cf. 44.2.

Stanza 43

7   **reuert**: return.
9   **three** suggests fulfilment; cf. III iii 16.2–3.

Stanza 45

1   **sundry purpose**: various subjects of conversation.

Stanza 46

7–9   She esteemed Amoret only for the sake of virtue.

Stanza 47

4   **estate**: state.
9   **tyde**: suitable opportunity.

Cant. VII.

Amoret rapt by greedie lust
Belphebe saues from dread,
The Squire her loues, and being blam'd
his dayes in dole doth lead.

1

GReat God of loue, that with thy cruell dart
Doest conquer greatest conquerors on ground,
And setst thy kingdome in the captiue harts
Of Kings and Keasars, to thy seruice bound,
What glorie, or what guerdon hast thou found
In feeble Ladies tyranning so sore;
And adding anguish to the bitter wound,
With which their liues thou lanchedst long afore,
By heaping stormes of trouble on them daily more?

2

So whylome didst thou to faire *Florimell*;
And so and so to noble *Britomart*:
So doest thou now to her, of whom I tell,
The louely *Amoret*, whose gentle hart
Thou martyrest with sorow and with smart,
In saluage forrests, and in deserts wide,
With Beares and Tygers taking heauie part,
Withouten comfort, and withouten guide,
That pittie is to heare the perils, which she tride.

3

So soone as she with that braue Britonesse
Had left that Turneyment for beauties prise,
They trauel'd long, that now for wearinesse,
Both of the way, and warlike exercise,
Both through a forest ryding did deuise
T'alight, and rest their wearie limbs awhile.
There heauie sleepe the eye-lids did surprise
Of *Britomart* after long tedious toyle,
That did her passed paines in quiet rest assoyle.

4

The whiles faire *Amoret*, of nought affeard,
Walkt through the wood, for pleasure, or for need;
When suddenly behind her backe she heard
One rushing forth out of the thickest weed,
That ere she backe could turne to taken heed,
Had vnawares her snatched vp from ground.
Feebly she shriekt, but so feebly indeed,
That *Britomart* heard not the shrilling sound,
There where through weary trauel she lay sleeping sound.

5

It was to weet a wilde and saluage man,
Yet was no man, but onely like in shape,
And eke in stature higher by a span,
All ouergrowne with haire, that could awhape
An hardy hart, and his wide mouth did gape
With huge great teeth, like to a tusked Bore:
For he liu'd all on rauin and on rape
Of men and beasts; and fed on fleshly gore,
The signe whereof yet stain'd his bloudy lips afore.

Canto vii

Argument
1   **rapt**: carried off.
4   **dole**: grief, sorrow.

Stanza 1
6   **tyranning**: playing the tyrant.
8   **lanchedst**: wounded.

Stanza 2
1–4   **faire, noble,** and **louely** carefully distinguish their natures.   **so and so**: in like manner; or perhaps, 'thus and thus again'.
7   **Beares and Tygers**: symbolizing sexual violence; cf. III i 14.5–9. See II ii 22.5–9*n*; cf. IV viii 4.9.   **taking heauie part**: i.e. contributing to her fear.
8   **Withouten**: used for emphasis.   **comfort**: aid, succour.
9   **tride**: underwent.

Stanza 3
9   **assoyle**: dispel.

Stanza 4
1   **of nought affeard**: see vi 36.4*n*.
2   **need**: a euphemism; but suggests that **Amoret** exposes herself to rape under some inner compulsion.
4   **weed**: undergrowth.
7   **Feebly**: suggests that she does not want to, or cannot, arouse **Britomart**'s virtue. Cf. Una's 'thrilling shriekes, and shrieking cryes' (I vi 6.2).

Stanza 5
1   **saluage man**: the wodwo of Elizabethan pageantry: naked or dressed in ivy, he carried an oak club; see Bernheimer (1952) 71. Cf. Artegall's disguise as the Salvage Knight.
4   Cf. the 'rugged haire' of Lechery's goat (I iv 24.2). **awhape**: terrify; utterly confound.
6   **Bore**: a symbol of lust.
7   **rauin**: plunder.

473

6

His neather lip was not like man nor beast,
　But like a wide deepe poke, downe hanging low,
　In which he wont the relickes of his feast,
　And cruell spoyle, which he had spard, to stow:
　And ouer it his huge great nose did grow,
　Full dreadfully empurpled all with bloud;
　And downe both sides two wide long eares did glow,
　And raught downe to his waste, when vp he stood,
More great then th'eares of Elephants by *Indus* flood.

7

His wast was with a wreath of yuie greene
　Engirt about, ne other garment wore:
　For all his haire was like a garment seene;
　And in his hand a tall young oake he bore,
　Whose knottie snags were sharpned all afore,
　And beath'd in fire for steele to be in sted.
　But whence he was, or of what wombe ybore,
　Of beasts, or of the earth, I haue not red:
But certes was with milke of Wolues and Tygres fed.

8

This vgly creature in his armes her snatcht,
　And through the forrest bore her quite away,
　With briers and bushes all to rent and scratcht;
　Ne care he had, ne pittie of the pray,
　Which many a knight had sought so many a day.
　He stayed not, but in his armes her bearing
　Ran, till he came to th'end of all his way,
　Vnto his caue farre from all peoples hearing,
And there he threw her in, nought feeling, ne nought fearing.

9

For she deare Ladie all the way was dead,
　Whilest he in armes her bore; but when she felt
　Her selfe downe soust, she waked out of dread
　Streight into griefe, that her deare hart nigh swelt,
　And eft gan into tender teares to melt.
　Then when she lookt about, and nothing found
　But darknesse and dread horrour, where she dwelt,
　She almost fell againe into a swound,
Ne wist whether aboue she were, or vnder ground.

10

With that she heard some one close by her side
　Sighing and sobbing sore, as if the paine
　Her tender hart in peeces would diuide:
　Which she long listning, softly askt againe
　What mister wight it was that so did plaine?
　To whom thus aunswer'd was: Ah wretched wight
　That seekes to know anothers griefe in vaine,
　Vnweeting of thine owne like haplesse plight:
Selfe to forget to mind another, is ouersight.

11

Aye me (said she) where am I, or with whom?
　Emong the liuing, or emong the dead?
　What shall of me vnhappy maid become?
　Shall death be th'end, or ought else worse, aread.
　Vnhappy mayd (then answerd she) whose dread
　Vntride, is lesse then when thou shalt it try:
　Death is to him, that wretched life doth lead,
　Both grace and gaine; but he in hell doth lie,
474 That liues a loathed life, and wishing cannot die.

12

This dismall day hath thee a caytiue made,
　And vassall to the vilest wretch aliue,
　Whose cursed vsage and vngodly trade
　The heauens abhorre, and into darkenesse driue.
　For on the spoile of women he doth liue,
　Whose bodies chast, when euer in his powre
　He may them catch, vnable to gainestriue,
　He with his shamefull lust doth first deflowre,
And afterwards themselues doth cruelly deuoure.

Stanza 6
2　**poke**: bag.
4　**spard**: saved.
5–9　A description of the male genitals. The Indian elephant is the strongest (Topsell, 1607, 150).　**by Indus flood**: apparently alluding to the elephants' favourite habitation; they copulate in water. The Indian elephant was reputed the largest. See III vii 48.2*n*. Freeman (1970) 238 cites a description of lust in a medieval trans. of the French *Yvain*: 'Unto his belt hang his hare – and / He had eres als ane olyfant.' For monsters with large ears and lips in travel literature, see *Var*. iv 204.

Stanza 7
The ivy wreath and the oak weapon are attributes of the savage man. The ivy is a common symbol of lust; cf. Sylvanus, I vi 14.9. Cf. Orgoglio's oak, I vii 10.7. Shroeder (1962) 149 claims that the club looks like a penis.
6　**beath'd in fire . . . in sted**: heated in fire to be hardened and serve in place of steel.

Stanza 8
3　**all to**: entirely.
9　Before she was seized by Lust, she was 'of nought affeard' (4.1).

Stanza 9
3　**soust**: thrown.
4　**swelt**: swooned.
8　**swound**: swoon.

Stanza 10
4　**againe**: in response.
5　**What mister**: what kind of.　**plaine**: lament.
7　**in vaine**: foolishly.

Stanza 11
4　**aread**: tell.
6　**try**: undergo, experience.
7–9　The answer to Amoret's two double questions: 'Am I among the living or among the dead in hell? Shall I suffer death or worse?' is that she suffers hell in life.

Stanza 12
1　**dismall day**: an unlucky day, *dies mali*.　**caytiue**: captive.
3　**trade**: practice.
7　**gainestriue**: oppose.

13

Now twenty daies, by which the sonnes of men
 Diuide their works, haue past through heuen sheene,
 Since I was brought into this dolefull den;
 During which space these sory eies haue seen
 Seauen women by him slaine, and eaten clene.
 And now no more for him but I alone,
 And this old woman here remaining beene;
 Till thou cam'st hither to augment our mone,
And of vs three to morrow he will sure eate one.

14

Ah dreadfull tidings which thou doest declare,
 (Quoth she) of all that euer hath bene knowen:
 Full many great calamities and rare
 This feeble brest endured hath, but none
 Equall to this, where euer I haue gone.
 But what are you, whom like vnlucky lot
 Hath linckt with me in the same chaine attone?
 To tell (quoth she) that which ye see, needs not;
A wofull wretched maid, of God and man forgot.

15

But what I was, it irkes me to reherse;
 Daughter vnto a Lord of high degree;
 That ioyd in happy peace, till fates peruerse
 With guilefull loue did secretly agree,
 To ouerthrow my state and dignitie.
 It was my lot to loue a gentle swaine,
 Yet was he but a Squire of low degree;
 Yet was he meet, vnlesse mine eye did faine,
By any Ladies side for Leman to haue laine.

16

But for his meannesse and disparagement,
 My Sire, who me too dearely well did loue,
 Vnto my choise by no meanes would assent,
 But often did my folly fowle reproue.
 Yet nothing could my fixed mind remoue,
 But whether willed or nilled friend or foe,
 I me resolu'd the vtmost end to proue,
 And rather then my loue abandon so,
Both sire, and friends, and all for euer to forgo.

17

Thenceforth I sought by secret meanes to worke
 Time to my will, and from his wrathfull sight
 To hide th'intent, which in my heart did lurke,
 Till I thereto had all things ready dight.
 So on a day vnweeting vnto wight,
 I with that Squire agreede away to flit,
 And in a priuy place, betwixt vs hight,
 Within a groue appointed him to meete;
To which I boldly came vpon my feeble feete.

18

But ah vnhappy houre me thither brought:
 For in that place where I him thought to find,
 There was I found, contrary to my thought,
 Of this accursed Carle of hellish kind,
 The shame of men, and plague of womankind,
 Who trussing me, as Eagle doth his pray,
 Me hether brought with him, as swift as wind,
 Where yet vntouched till this present day,
I rest his wretched thrall, the sad *Æmylia*.

19

Ah sad *Æmylia* (then sayd *Amoret,*)
 Thy ruefull plight I pitty as mine owne.
 But read to me, by what deuise or wit,
 Hast thou in all this time, from him vnknowne
 Thine honor sau'd, though into thraldome throwne.
 Through helpe (quoth she) of this old woman here
 I haue so done, as she to me hath showne.
 For euer when he burnt in lustfull fire,
She in my stead supplide his bestiall desire.

Stanza 13
1 The **twenty** corresponds to the twenty knights whom
Scudamour overcomes to gain Amoret; see x 7.6*n*. The
number symbolizes the obstacles to their union.
8 **mone**: state of grief.

Stanza 15
1 **irkes**: troubles; grieves. **reherse**: relate.
5 **dignitie**: honour, **high degree** (2).
8 **faine**: mistake.

Stanza 16
Cf. viii 50.
1 **meannesse**: humble rank. **disparagement**: the
disgrace of marriage to an inferior.
4 **fowle**: grievously; as an adj., referring to her father's (or
the poet's) judgment.
5 **fixed**: stubborn rather than constant.
6 **willed or nilled**: agreeing or not.
7 Cf. Amoret at 21.2.

Stanza 17
2 **will**: purpose; carnal desire; wilfulness. Lust destroys the
bonds of family, friendship, and class.
4 **dight**: prepared.
7 **hight**: named.

Stanza 18
4 **of hellish kind**: in contrast to Love 'deriued from aboue'
(vi 31.8).
6 **trussing**: seizing as quarry and carrying off; a hawking
term.
8 **vntouched**: not sexually violated; cf. 19.4.
9 **sad Æmylia**: a vaguely romantic name and epithet; cf.
34.1, viii 63.1.

Stanza 19
3 **read**: relate.
9 **supplide**: satisfied.

20

Thus of their euils as they did discourse,
  And each did other much bewaile and mone;
  Loe where the villaine selfe, their sorrowes sourse,
  Came to the caue, and rolling thence the stone,
  Which wont to stop the mouth thereof, that none
  Might issue forth, came rudely rushing in,
  And spredding ouer all the flore alone,
  Gan dight him selfe vnto his wonted sinne;
Which ended, then his bloudy banket should beginne.

21

Which when as fearefull *Amoret* perceiued,
  She staid not the vtmost end thereof to try,
  But like a ghastly Gelt, whose wits are reaued,
  Ran forth in hast with hideous outcry,
  For horrour of his shamefull villany.
  But after her full lightly he vprose,
  And her pursu'd as fast as she did flie:
  Full fast she flies, and farre afore him goes,
Ne feeles the thorns and thickets pricke her tender toes.

22

Nor hedge, nor ditch, nor hill, nor dale she staies,
  But ouerleapes them all, like Robucke light,
  And through the thickest makes her nighest waies;
  And euermore when with regardfull sight
  She looking backe, espies that griesly wight
  Approching nigh, she gins to mend her pace,
  And makes her feare a spur to hast her flight:
  More swift then *Myrrh'* or *Daphne* in her race,
Or any of the Thracian Nimphes in saluage chase.

23

Long so she fled, and so he follow'd long;
  Ne liuing aide for her on earth appeares,
  But if the heauens helpe to redresse her wrong,
  Moued with pity of her plenteous teares.
  It fortuned *Belphebe* with her peares
  The woody Nimphs, and with that louely boy,
  Was hunting then the Libbards and the Beares,
  In these wild woods, as was her wonted ioy,
To banish sloth, that oft doth noble mindes annoy.

24

It so befell, as oft it fals in chace,
  That each of them from other sundred were,
  And that same gentle Squire arriu'd in place,
  Where this same cursed caytiue did appeare,
  Pursuing that faire Lady full of feare,
  And now he her quite ouertaken had;
  And now he her away with him did beare
  Vnder his arme, as seeming wondrous glad,
That by his grenning laughter mote farre off be rad.

25

Which drery sight the gentle Squire espying,
  Doth hast to crosse him by the nearest way,
  Led with that wofull Ladies piteous crying,
  And him assailes with all the might he may,
  Yet will not he the louely spoile downe lay,
  But with his craggy club in his right hand,
  Defends him selfe, and saues his gotten pray.
  Yet had it bene right hard him to withstand,
But that he was full light and nimble on the land.

26

Thereto the villaine vsed craft in fight;
  For euer when the Squire his iauelin shooke,
  He held the Lady forth before him right,
  And with her body, as a buckler, broke
  The puissance of his intended stroke.
  And if it chaunst, (as needs it must in fight)
  Whilest he on him was greedy to be wroke,
  That any little blow on her did light,
Then would he laugh aloud, and gather great delight.

Stanza 20
7–9   **his wonted sinne** is to deflower maidens and then eat them (12.8–9); yet this act suggests masturbation, which illustrates lust's self-centredness. For all his lust, the two virgins remain unknown to him.

Stanza 21
2   **the vtmost end**: with the implied bawdy reference; cf. 16.7. The comedy extends throughout the stanza.
3   **ghastly Gelt**: fearful lunatic. Perhaps suggesting 'gelding', a creature who would display a similar horror of sex.

Stanza 22
1   **she staies**: she stays for; or stops her.
8–9   The similar flight of Florimell is compared to that of **Myrrha and Daphne**, III vii 26.1–4. Both comparisons fit Æmylia: she flees from her father's wrath, as does Myrrha, and from her lover's lust, as does Daphne.   **the Thracian Nimphes**: presumably the Amazons of Thrace; cf. Virgil, *Aen.* xi 659–60.

Stanza 23
3–4   Her need for grace prepares for Belphœbe's intervention. **But if**: unless.
5   **peares**: companions.
6   **that louely boy**: Timias, now seen as Cupid in the service of a chaste Venus.   **louely**: loving.
7   **Libbards**: leopards; cf. II iii 28.8.

Stanza 24
3   **gentle**: makes his lapse into brutishness untypical and worthy of forgiveness.
9   **grenning laughter**: a mark of lust; cf. III viii 24.6.
rad: perceived.

Stanza 25
1   **drery**: grievous.
5   **the louely spoile**: cf. Love's 'proud spoyle' (III xii 22.7) and 'beauties spoile' (IV x 3.3).
9   **on the land**: on the ground, i.e. on his feet.

Stanza 26
2   **shooke**: brandished in order to strike.
4   **buckler**: used to catch the blow of an adversary.
7   **wroke**: avenged.

27

Which subtill sleight did him encumber much,
    And made him oft, when he would strike, forbeare;
    For hardly could he come the carle to touch,
    But that he her must hurt, or hazard neare:
    Yet he his hand so carefully did beare,
    That at the last he did himselfe attaine,
    And therein left the pike head of his speare.
A streame of coleblacke bloud thence gusht amaine,
That all her silken garments did with bloud bestaine.

28

With that he threw her rudely on the flore,
    And laying both his hands vpon his glaue,
    With dreadfull strokes let driue at him so sore,
    That forst him flie abacke, himselfe to saue:
    Yet he therewith so felly still did raue,
    That scarse the Squire his hand could once vpreare,
    But for aduantage ground vnto him gaue,
    Tracing and trauersing, now here, now there;
For bootlesse thing it was to think such blowes to beare.

29

Whilest thus in battell they embusied were,
    Belphebe raunging in that forrest wide,
    The hideous noise of their huge strokes did heare,
    And drew thereto, making her eare her guide.
    Whom when that theefe approching nigh espide,
    With bow in hand, and arrowes ready bent,
    He by his former combate would not bide,
    But fled away with ghastly dreriment,
Well knowing her to be his deaths sole instrument.

30

Whom seeing flie, she speedily poursewed
    With winged feete, as nimble as the winde,
    And euer in her bow she ready shewed
    The arrow, to his deadly marke desynde.
    As when *Latonaes* daughter cruell kynde,
    In vengement of her mothers great disgrace,
    With fell despight her cruell arrowes tynde
    Gainst wofull *Niobes* vnhappy race,
That all the gods did mone her miserable case.

31

So well she sped her and so far she ventred,
    That ere vnto his hellish den he raught,
    Euen as he ready was there to haue entred,
    She sent an arrow forth with mighty draught,
    That in the very dore him ouercaught,
    And in his nape arriuing, through it thrild
    His greedy throte, therewith in two distraught,
    That all his vitall spirites thereby spild,
And all his hairy brest with gory bloud was fild.

32

Whom when on ground she groueling saw to rowle,
    She ran in hast his life to haue bereft:
    But ere she could him reach, the sinfull sowle
    Hauing his carrion corse quite sencelesse left,
    Was fled to hell, surcharg'd with spoile and theft,
    Yet ouer him she there long gazing stood,
    And oft admir'd his monstrous shape, and oft
    His mighty limbs, whilest all with filthy bloud
The place there ouerflowne, seemd like a sodaine flood.

33

Thence forth she past into his dreadfull den,
    Where nought but darkesome drerinesse she found,
    Ne creature saw, but hearkned now and then
    Some litle whispering, and soft groning sound.
    With that she askt, what ghosts there vnder ground
    Lay hid in horrour of eternall night?
    And bad them, if so be they were not bound,
    To come and shew themselues before the light,
Now freed from feare and danger of that dismall wight.

Stanza 27

1   **sleight**: cunning trick.
4   **hazard**: endanger.
5–9   Implies an allegory of sexual intercourse. Later
interpreted as a wounding of Amoret: 'Als of his owne rash
hand one wound was to be seene' (35.9). Cf. the thrust of the
fisherman's hand when he attacks Florimell, III viii 25.6–9.
S.'s source may be the lover's assault upon the lady's shrine
with his staff in the *Romance of the Rose*.
6   **did himselfe attaine**: i.e. overtook and struck Lust.

Stanza 28
2   **glaue**: halbert; here his club (25.6).
8   **Tracing and trauersing**: pursuing and then turning
aside; see vi 18.1.

Stanza 29
6   **bent**: aimed (cf. 30.3–4).

Stanza 30
2   She equals Lust's speed at 18.7.
4   **desynde**: destined; or aimed.
5–9   **Latonaes daughter**: Diana; see II xii 13. Niobe
'brought foorth seven sonnes, and as many daughters of
excellent beautie: whereof she vaunted and preferred hir selfe
before Latona, mother of Apollo and Diana. Wherefore Latona
beynge angry, commaunded Apollo to slea all the sonnes, and
Diana al the daughters' (Cooper, 1565). Cf. V x 7.8–9.
cruell kynde: of cruel nature; or cruel to Niobe, kind to her
mother.   **tynde**: kindled, expressing rage; or pointed, from
the tines of the arrows.

Stanza 31
1   **ventred**: ventured, alluding to the peril of pursuing Lust
to his den.
4   **draught**: drawing of the bow.
7   **distraught**: pulled asunder, i.e. split.
9   **fild**: defiled.

Stanza 32
5   **surcharg'd**: weighed down.
7   **admir'd**: wondered at.

Stanza 33
1   **Thence forth**: from that place onward.
9   **dismall**: terrible; causing terror.

477

34

Then forth the sad *Æmylia* issewed,
  Yet trembling euery ioynt through former feare;
  And after her the Hag, there with her mewed,
  A foule and lothsome creature did appeare;
  A leman fit for such a louer deare.
  That mou'd *Belphebe* her no lesse to hate,
  Then for to rue the others heauy cheare;
  Of whom she gan enquire of her estate.
Who all to her at large, as hapned, did relate.

35

Thence she them brought toward the place, where late
  She left the gentle Squire with *Amoret*:
  There she him found by that new louely mate,
  Who lay the whiles in swoune, full sadly set,
  From her faire eyes wiping the deawy wet,
  Which softly stild, and kissing them atweene,
  And handling soft the hurts, which she did get.
  For of that Carle she sorely bruz'd had beene,
Als of his owne rash hand one wound was to be seene.

36

Which when she saw, with sodaine glauncing eye,
  Her noble heart with sight thereof was fild
  With deepe disdaine, and great indignity,
  That in her wrath she thought them both haue thrild,
  With that selfe arrow, which the Carle had kild:
  Yet held her wrathfull hand from vengeance sore,
  But drawing nigh, ere he her well beheld;
  Is this the faith, she said, and said no more,
But turnd her face, and fled away for euermore.

37

He seeing her depart, arose vp light,
  Right sore agrieued at her sharpe reproofe,
  And follow'd fast: but when he came in sight,
  He durst not nigh approch, but kept aloofe,
  For dread of her displeasures vtmost proofe.
  And euermore, when he did grace entreat,
  And framed speaches fit for his behoofe,
  Her mortall arrowes she at him did threat,
And forst him backe with fowle dishonor to retreat.

38

At last when long he follow'd had in vaine,
  Yet found no ease of griefe, nor hope of grace,
  Vnto those woods he turned backe againe,
  Full of sad anguish, and in heauy case:
  And finding there fit solitary place
  For wofull wight, chose out a gloomy glade,
  Where hardly eye mote see bright heauens face,
  For mossy trees, which couered all with shade
And sad melancholy: there he his cabin made.

39

His wonted warlike weapons all he broke,
  And threw away, with vow to vse no more,
  Ne thenceforth euer strike in battell stroke,
  Ne euer word to speake to woman more;
  But in that wildernesse, of men forlore,
  And of the wicked world forgotten quight,
  His hard mishap in dolor to deplore,
  And wast his wretched daies in wofull plight;
So on him selfe to wreake his follies owne despight.

Stanza 35
3   **mate**: lover, paramour.   **louely**: loving.
5–9   Cf. Arg.: 'The Squire her loues'. On the wound, see
27.5–9, viii 19.7–9.   **stild**: trickled down.   **atweene**: i.e.
between wiping her eyes and handling her hurts.

Stanza 36
1   **sodaine**: quick.
3   **indignity**: indignation, anger provoked by a shameful act.
5   **With that selfe arrow**: because the Squire is guilty of
lust, and so is Amoret.
8–9   The historical reference, first noted by Upton (1758), is
to the Queen's banishment of Raleigh for debauching one of her
maids of honour. Aikin (1802) notes that the wound inflicted
on Amoret by Timias while she is in the grasp of sensual passion
alludes to Raleigh's seduction of Elizabeth Throckmorton. S.
alludes to an occasion of Raleigh's banishment in *Col.* 164–71.
Oakeshott (1960) 93–8 reviews the matter, and in a later
article (1971) cites pertinent annotations and markings by
Lady Raleigh and her son in their copy of the poem. Milton,
Comus 443–5, writes of Diana as one who 'set at nought / The
frivolous bolt of Cupid, gods and men / Feared her stern
frown'.

Stanza 37
1   **light**: quickly; unchaste.
6   **grace**: favour. Perhaps suggesting Raleigh's suit for the
Queen's favour.
7   **behoofe**: advantage.
9   Since Timias's name signifies honour, **dishonor** brings
death; hence he is seen as a ghost, 41.4, viii 12.7. See III v
26.9*n*. Roche (1964) 143–7 argues that, since Timias's honour
resides in Belphœbe's judgment of him, 'his rejection becomes
a shameful, living death'.

Stanza 38
9   **cabin**: rude dwelling; also cell of an anchorite.

Stanza 39
1   **wonted**: customary.
5   **forlore**: abandoned.
9   **follies**: lewdness, wantonness.

40

And eke his garment, to be thereto meet,
  He wilfully did cut and shape anew;
  And his faire lockes, that wont with ointment sweet
  To be embaulm'd, and sweat out dainty dew,
  He let to grow and griesly to concrew,
  Vncomb'd, vncurl'd, and carelesly vnshed;
  That in short time his face they ouergrew,
  And ouer all his shoulders did dispred,
That who he whilome was, vneath was to be red.

41

There he continued in this carefull plight,
  Wretchedly wearing out his youthly yeares,
  Through wilfull penury consumed quight,
  That like a pined ghost he soone appeares.
  For other food then that wilde forrest beares,
  Ne other drinke there did he euer tast,
  Then running water, tempred with his teares,
  The more his weakened body so to wast:
That out of all mens knowledge he was worne at last.

42

For on a day, by fortune as it fell,
  His owne deare Lord Prince *Arthure* came that way,
  Seeking aduentures, where he mote heare tell;
  And as he through the wandring wood did stray,
  Hauing espide this Cabin far away,
  He to it drew, to weet who there did wonne;
  Weening therein some holy Hermit lay,
  That did resort of sinfull people shonne;
Or else some woodman shrowded there from scorching sunne.

43

Arriuing there, he found this wretched man,
  Spending his daies in dolour and despaire,
  And through long fasting woxen pale and wan,
  All ouergrowen with rude and rugged haire;
  That albeit his owne deare Squire he were,
  Yet he him knew not, ne auiz'd at all,
  But like strange wight, whom he had seene no where,
  Saluting him, gan into speach to fall,
And pitty much his plight, that liu'd like outcast thrall.

44

But to his speach he aunswered no whit,
  But stood still mute, as if he had beene dum,
  Ne signe of sence did shew, ne common wit,
  As one with griefe and anguishe ouercum,
  And vnto euery thing did aunswere mum:
  And euer when the Prince vnto him spake,
  He louted lowly, as did him becum,
  And humble homage did vnto him make,
Midst sorrow shewing ioyous semblance for his sake.

45

At which his vncouth guise and vsage quaint
  The Prince did wonder much, yet could not ghesse
  The cause of that his sorrowfull constraint;
  Yet weend by secret signes of manlinesse,
  Which close appeard in that rude brutishnesse,
  That he whilome some gentle swaine had beene,
  Traind vp in feats of armes and knightlinesse;
  Which he obseru'd, by that he him had seene
To weld his naked sword, and try the edges keene.

Stanza 40
Timias assumes the traditional guise of the love-melancholic.
4   **embaulm'd**: anointed.
5   **concrew**: mat together.
6   **vnshed**: unparted; cf. 43.4. Timias assumes the
appearance of Lust, 7.3. Now repentant, he appears as the
anchorite upon whom heaven bestows a protecting coat of hair.
9   **vneath was to be red**: with difficulty was to be known.

Stanza 41
1   **carefull**: sorrowful.
3   **penury**: lack of food, 'long fasting' (43.3).
4   As Britomart in her love-longing, III ii 52. 5–6.
7   Cf. Raleigh, 'Like to a Hermite poore' (*Poems* 11),
lamenting his estrangement from the Queen: 'My drink
nought else but teares falne from mine eies.' See Oakeshott
(1960) 169–70.

Stanzas 42–47
Arthur appears before his usual entrance in the eighth
canto (see viii 18*n*) to indicate that even he is unable to rescue
Timias. Only time may 'him restore to former grace againe'
(47.7).

Stanza 42
4   **through the wandring wood did stray**: cf. 'through the
endlesse world did wander wide' (viii 18.8).

Stanza 43
6   **auiz'd**: recognized.

Stanza 44
Except for the outburst to Belphœbe at viii 16–17, Timias's
silent shame extends for the rest of the poem: cf. VI v 24. 2–5,
viii 5. 1–7, 27.3. From now on his name and state suggest Ital.
timidezza, bashfulness.
5   **mum**: not a word.
9   **semblance**: demeanour.

Stanza 45
1   **vsage quaint**: odd behaviour.
3   **constraint**: distress.
8–9   With intent to commit suicide; see viii 16.9.

479

46

And eke by that he saw on euery tree,
  How he the name of one engrauen had,
  Which likly was his liefest loue to be,
  For whom he now so sorely was bestad;
  Which was by him *BELPHEBE* rightly rad.
  Yet who was that *Belphebe*, he ne wist;
  Yet saw he often how he wexed glad,
  When he it heard, and how the ground he kist,
Wherein it written was, and how himselfe he blist:

47

Tho when he long had marked his demeanor,
  And saw that all he said and did, was vaine,
  Ne ought mote make him change his wonted tenor,
  Ne ought mote ease or mitigate his paine,
  He left him there in languor to remaine,
  Till time for him should remedy prouide,
  And him restore to former grace againe.
  Which for it is too long here to abide,
I will deferre the end vntill another tide.

Cant. VIII.

The gentle Squire recouers grace,
Sclaunder her guests doth staine:
Corflambo chaseth Placidas,
And is by Arthure slaine.

1

WEll said the wiseman, now prou'd true by this,
  Which to this gentle Squire did happen late,
  That the displeasure of the mighty is
  Then death it selfe more dread and desperate.
  For naught the same may calme ne mitigate,
  Till time the tempest doe thereof delay
  With sufferaunce soft, which rigour can abate,
  And haue the sterne remembrance wypt away
Of bitter thoughts, which deepe therein infixed lay.

2

Like as it fell to this vnhappy boy,
  Whose tender heart the faire *Belphebe* had
  With one sterne looke so daunted, that no ioy
  In all his life, which afterwards he lad,
  He euer tasted, but with penaunce sad
  And pensiue sorrow pind and wore away,
  Ne euer laught, ne once shew'd countenance glad;
  But alwaies wept and wailed night and day,
As blasted bloosme through heat doth languish and decay;

3

Till on a day, as in his wonted wise
  His doole he made, there chaunst a turtle Doue
  To come, where he his dolors did deuise,
  That likewise late had lost her dearest loue,
  Which losse her made like passion also proue.
  Who seeing his sad plight, her tender heart
  With deare compassion deeply did emmoue,
  That she gan mone his vndeserued smart,
And with her dolefull accent beare with him a part.

480

4

Shee sitting by him as on ground he lay,
  Her mournefull notes full piteously did frame,
  And thereof made a lamentable lay,
  So sensibly compyld, that in the same
  Him seemed oft he heard his owne right name.
  With that he forth would poure so plenteous teares,
  And beat his breast vnworthy of such blame,
  And knocke his head, and rend his rugged heares,
That could haue perst the hearts of Tigres and of Beares.

Stanza 46
In his *Book of the Ocean to Cynthia* 269–72, 327, Raleigh refers to the Queen as Belphœbe and laments his banishment from her.
3 **liefest**: dearest.
4 **bestad**: beset.
6 Cf. viii 22.1–6.
9 **blist**: either blessed, by crossing himself at that holy name, or 'blasted', i.e. cursed.

Stanza 47
5 **languor**: sorrow.

Canto viii

Stanza 1
1–4 Alludes to Prov. 16.14: 'The wrath of a King is as messengers of death'; but 5–9 contradicts the second half of the proverb: 'but a wise man wil pacifie it'.
6 Cf. vii 47.6. **delay**: allay.
7 **sufferaunce**: patient endurance.

Stanza 2
9 **bloosme**: blossom.

Stanza 3
Roche (1964) 146 notes that the dove symbolizes Timias's emotional state: he is 'like the dove a mourner, chaste, sorrowful, and faithful'.
2 **doole**: dole, lamentation.
3 **his dolors did deuise**: recounted his griefs.
5 **passion**: suffering. **proue**: experience.
9 **beare with him a part**: i.e. she sustains the burden of his song.

Stanza 4
3 **lamentable**: mournful.
4 **sensibly compyld**: feelingly composed.
5 Possibly an allusion to Raleigh's nickname, Water, which, pronounced with a burr, might sound to a demented mind like a dove's cooing. He responds, appropriately, with water; cf. 13.3–4.
9 **Tigres and of Beares**: see vii 2.7*n*.

5

Thus long this gentle bird to him did vse,
  Withouten dread of perill to repaire
  Vnto his wonne, and with her mournefull muse
  Him to recomfort in his greatest care,
  That much did ease his mourning and misfare:
  And euery day for guerdon of her song,
  He part of his small feast to her would share;
  That at the last of all his woe and wrong
Companion she became, and so continued long.

6

Vpon a day as she him sate beside,
  By chance he certaine miniments forth drew,
  Which yet with him as relickes did abide
  Of all the bounty, which *Belphebe* threw
  On him, whilst goodly grace she did him shew:
  Amongst the rest a iewell rich he found,
  That was a Ruby of right perfect hew,
  Shap'd like a heart, yet bleeding of the wound,
And with a litle golden chaine about it bound.

7

The same he tooke, and with a riband new,
  In which his Ladies colours were, did bind
  About the turtles necke, that with the vew
  Did greatly solace his engrieued mind.
  All vnawares the bird, when she did find
  Her selfe so deckt, her nimble wings displaid,
  And flew away, as lightly as the wind:
  Which sodaine accident him much dismaid,
And looking after long, did marke which way she straid.

8

But when as long he looked had in vaine,
  Yet saw her forward still to make her flight,
  His weary eie returnd to him againe,
  Full of discomfort and disquiet plight,
  That both his iuell he had lost so light,
  And eke his deare companion of his care.
  But that sweet bird departing, flew forth right
  Through the wide region of the wastfull aire,
Vntill she came where wonned his *Belphebe* faire.

9

There found she her (as then it did betide)
  Sitting in couert shade of arbors sweet,
  After late weary toile, which she had tride
  In saluage chase, to rest as seem'd her meet.
  There she alighting, fell before her feet,
  And gan to her her mournfull plaint to make,
  As was her wont, thinking to let her weet
  The great tormenting griefe, that for her sake
Her gentle Squire through her displeasure did pertake.

10

She her beholding with attentiue eye,
  At length did marke about her purple brest
  That precious iuell, which she formerly
  Had knowne right well with colour ribbands drest:
  Therewith she rose in hast, and her addrest
  With ready hand it to haue reft away.
  But the swift bird obayd not her behest,
  But swaru'd aside, and there againe did stay;
She follow'd her, and thought againe it to assay.

11

And euer when she nigh approcht, the Doue
  Would flit a litle forward, and then stay,
  Till she drew neare, and then againe remoue;
  So tempting her still to pursue the pray,
  And still from her escaping soft away:
  Till that at length into that forrest wide,
  She drew her far, and led with slow delay.
  In th'end she her vnto that place did guide,
Whereas that wofull man in languor did abide.

Stanza 5
4 **care**: sorrow.
5 **misfare**: misfortune.

Stanza 6
2 **miniments**: articles; in the specific legal sense: evidences or proofs of Belphœbe's bounty and his former right to it.
6–9 The **Ruby** was believed to control amorous desires of the wearer. It was returned to Belphœbe by the dove because it produces concord: its red colour removes anger. See Kunz (1913) 101–3, 370. Brink (1972) notes that a heart-shaped ruby was presented to Elizabeth by Arthur Throckmorton to soften her displeasure over his sister's marriage to Raleigh.

Stanza 7
2 **colours**: her insignia or device.

Stanza 8
4 **discomfort**: distress.
5 **light**: easily; carelessly.

Stanza 9
3 **tride**: undergone.
9 **pertake**: partake: endure.

Stanza 10
2 **purple**: the colour of mourning.
9 **assay**: touch; try.

Stanza 11
1, 7 **the Doue / . . . led**: cf. Virgil, *Aen*. vi 190–204: doves, sacred to Venus, guide Aeneas to the golden bough. On the dove as the emblem of concord, see Tervarent (1958) 106.

12

Eftsoones she flew vnto his fearelesse hand,
   And there a piteous ditty new deuiz'd,
   As if she would haue made him vnderstand,
   His sorrowes cause to be of her despis'd.
   Whom when she saw in wretched weedes disguiz'd,
   With heary glib deform'd, and meiger face,
   Like ghost late risen from his graue agryz'd,
   She knew him not, but pittied much his case,
And wisht it were in her to doe him any grace.

13

He her beholding, at her feet downe fell,
   And kist the ground on which her sole did tread,
   And washt the same with water, which did well
   From his moist eies, and like two streames procead,
   Yet spake no word, whereby she might aread
   What mister wight he was, or what he ment,
   But as one daunted with her presence dread,
   Onely few ruefull lookes vnto her sent,
As messengers of his true meaning and intent.

14

Yet nathemore his meaning she ared,
   But wondred much at his so selcouth case,
   And by his persons secret seemlyhed
   Well weend, that he had beene some man of place,
   Before misfortune did his hew deface:
   That being mou'd with ruth she thus bespake.
   Ah wofull man, what heauens hard disgrace,
   Or wrath of cruell wight on thee ywrake?
Or selfe disliked life doth thee thus wretched make?

15

If heauen, then none may it redresse or blame,
   Sith to his powre we all are subiect borne:
   If wrathfull wight, then fowle rebuke and shame
   Be theirs, that haue so cruell thee forlorne;
   But if through inward griefe or wilfull scorne
   Of life it be, then better doe aduise.
   For he whose daies in wilfull woe are worne,
   The grace of his Creator doth despise,
That will not vse his gifts for thanklesse nigardise.

16

When so he heard her say, eftsoones he brake
   His sodaine silence, which he long had pent,
   And sighing inly deepe, her thus bespake;
   Then haue they all themselues against me bent:
   For heauen, first author of my languishment,
   Enuying my too great felicity,
   Did closely with a cruell one consent,
   To cloud my daies in dolefull misery,
And make me loath this life, still longing for to die.

17

Ne any but your selfe, O dearest dred,
   Hath done this wrong, to wreake on worthlesse wight
   Your high displesure, through misdeeming bred:
   That when your pleasure is to deeme aright,
   Ye may redresse, and me restore to light.
   Which sory words her mightie hart did mate
   With mild regard, to see his ruefull plight,
   That her inburning wrath she gan abate,
482 And him receiu'd againe to former fauours state.

Stanza 12
1   **fearelesse**: referring to the dove.
3   **him**: 'her' sugg. Church (1758).
6   **glib**: as worn by the Irish, 'a thick curled bush of hair hanging down over their eyes, and monstrously disguising them' (*View* 50). Here it is related to the large-brimmed hat of the love-melancholic.
7   **agryz'd**: horrified; and of horrible appearance.

Stanza 13
5   **aread**: guess.
6   **mister**: kind of.

Stanza 14
2   **selcouth**: seldom known; strange.
3–5   Cf. Arthur's insight, vii 45.4–9.   **secret seemlyhed**: disguised seemliness or pleasing appearance. **of place**: of rank. **hew**: form.
8   **ywrake**: wreaked.

Stanza 15
3   **rebuke**: disgrace.
4   **forlorne**: brought to ruin.
7–9   **he whose daies . . . vse his gifts**: he who spends his days in woe, not using God's gifts, despises His grace.
nigardise: niggardliness.

Stanza 16
1–2   **eftsoones he brake . . . silence**: he suddenly broke his silence. 'This sudden abruptness is plainly shewn in his speech' (Upton, 1758).
4   **they**: alluding to heaven, some cruel wight (Belphœbe), and himself.
5   **languishment**: suffering.
7   **closely**: secretly.

Stanza 17
1   **O dearest dred**: cf. the address to Elizabeth, I Proem 4.9.
5   **restore to light**: also literally, for he lives in darkness (vii 38.6–9).
6   **mate**: join; overcome.

18

In which he long time afterwards did lead
    An happie life with grace and good accord,
    Fearlesse of fortunes chaunge or enuies dread,
    And eke all mindlesse of his owne deare Lord
    The noble Prince, who neuer heard one word
    Of tydings, what did vnto him betide,
    Or what good fortune did to him afford,
    But through the endlesse world did wander wide,
Him seeking euermore, yet no where him descride.

19

Till on a day as through that wood he rode,
    He chaunst to come where those two Ladies late,
    Æmylia and Amoret abode,
    Both in full sad and sorrowfull estate;
    The one right feeble through the euill rate
    Of food, which in her duresse she had found:
    The other almost dead and desperate
    Through her late hurts, and through that haplesse wound,
With which the Squire in her defence her sore astound.

20

Whom when the Prince beheld, he gan to rew
    The euill case in which those Ladies lay;
    But most was moued at the piteous vew
    Of Amoret, so neare vnto decay,
    That her great daunger did him much dismay.
    Eftsoones that pretious liquour forth he drew,
    Which he in store about him kept alway,
    And with few drops thereof did softly dew
Her wounds, that vnto strength restor'd her soone anew.

21

Tho when they both recouered were right well,
    He gan of them inquire, what euill guide
    Them thether brought, and how their harmes befell.
    To whom they told all, that did them betide,
    And how from thraldome vile they were vntide
    Of that same wicked Carle, by Virgins hond;
    Whose bloudie corse they shew'd him there beside,
    And eke his caue, in which they both were bond:
At which he wondred much, when all those signes he fond.

22

And euermore he greatly did desire
    To know, what Virgin did them thence vnbind;
    And oft of them did earnestly inquire,
    Where was her won, and how he mote her find.
    But when as nought according to his mind
    He could outlearne, he them from ground did reare:
    No seruice lothsome to a gentle kind;
    And on his warlike beast them both did beare,
Himselfe by them on foot, to succour them from feare.

23

So when that forrest they had passed well,
    A litle cotage farre away they spide,
    To which they drew, ere night vpon them fell;
    And entring in, found none therein abide,
    But one old woman sitting there beside,
    Vpon the ground in ragged rude attyre,
    With filthy lockes about her scattered wide,
    Gnawing her nayles for felnesse and for yre,
And there out sucking venime to her parts entyre.

24

A foule and loathly creature sure in sight,
    And in conditions to be loath'd no lesse:
    For she was stuft with rancour and despight
    Vp to the throat, that oft with bitternesse
    It forth would breake, and gush in great excesse,
    Pouring out streames of poyson and of gall
    Gainst all, that truth or vertue doe professe,
    Whom she with leasings lewdly did miscall,
And wickedly backbite: Her name men Sclaunder call.

Stanza 18

Arthur appears in his usual canto in a book (but see III viii 29n). He intervenes once in Book I, twice in Book II, and four times in Book IV. He rescues Æmylia and Amoret, and saves them from Sclaunder; he slays Corflambo and unites the two friends with Æmylia and Pœana; he resolves the discord created at the Tournament by pacifying the six knights; and, presumably, he restores Amoret to Scudamour at the end of canto ix.

Stanza 19
5   euill rate: poor, unsatisfactory allowance.
6   duresse: imprisonment.
9   astound: i.e. stunned with his stroke.

Stanza 20
4   decay: death.
6   that pretious liquour: the 'liquor pure . . . That any wound could heale incontinent' (I ix 19. 3–5), i.e. immediately, referring to the wound of concupiscence.
8   dew: associated with God's grace; cf. 33.3–5.

Stanza 22
1–4   Arthur's desire to know Belphœbe (cf. vii 46.6) follows from her 'identification' with Elizabeth in the Timias-Belphœbe episode; see also L.R. In Book III he sought Florimell: cf. III i 18.6–8, iv 54.6–8, v 11–12. He enters Book IV in search of Timias: see 18.8–9 above. By finding Amoret, he may renew his former quest: see ix 17.   won: dwelling-place.
6   outlearne: find out.
7   Cf. I viii 40.3.   kind: nature.
8   warlike: equipped for war.

Stanza 23
1   The action leaves the forest which has been the setting since the pursuit of Florimell, III i. The transition indicates the approaching resolution of the two books; significantly it occurs under the guidance of Arthur.
8   felnesse: malignity.
9   parts entyre: 'inward parts' (26.4).

Stanza 24
2   conditions: characteristics.
8   with leasings lewdly did miscall: with lies wickedly reviled.
9   Sclaunder: Slander. The sixteenth-century spelling suggests scandal.

25

Her nature is all goodnesse to abuse,
  And causelesse crimes continually to frame,
  With which shé guiltlesse persons may accuse,
  And steale away the crowne of their good name;
  Ne euer Knight so bold, ne euer Dame
  So chast and loyall liu'd, but she would striue
  With forged cause them falsely to defame;
  Ne euer thing so well was doen aliue,
But she with blame would blot, and of due praise depriue.

26

Her words were not, as common words are ment,
  T'expresse the meaning of the inward mind,
  But noysome breath, and poysnous spirit sent
  From inward parts, with cancred malice lind,
  And breathed forth with blast of bitter wind;
  Which passing through the eares, would pierce the hart,
  And wound the soule it selfe with griefe vnkind:
  For like the stings of Aspes, that kill with smart,
Her spightfull words did pricke, and wound the inner part.

27

Such was that Hag, vnmeet to host such guests,
  Whom greatest Princes court would welcome fayne,
  But neede, that answers not to all requests,
  Bad them not looke for better entertayne;
  And eke that age despysed nicenesse vaine,
  Enur'd to hardnesse and to homely fare,
  Which them to warlike discipline did trayne,
  And manly limbs endur'd with litle care
Against all hard mishaps and fortunelesse misfare.

28

Then all that euening welcommed with cold,
  And chearelesse hunger, they together spent;
  Yet found no fault, but that the Hag did scold
  And rayle at them with grudgefull discontent,
  For lodging there without her owne consent:
  Yet they endured all with patience milde,
  And vnto rest themselues all onely lent,
  Regardlesse of that queane so base and vilde,
To be vniustly blamd, and bitterly reuilde.

29

Here well I weene, when as these rimes be red
  With misregard, that some rash witted wight,
  Whose looser thought will lightly be misled,
  These gentle Ladies will misdeeme too light,
  For thus conuersing with this noble Knight;
  Sith now of dayes such temperance is rare
  And hard to finde, that heat of youthfull spright
  For ought will from his greedie pleasure spare,
More hard for hungry steed t'abstaine from pleasant lare.

30

But antique age yet in the infancie
  Of time, did liue then like an innocent,
  In simple truth and blamelesse chastitie,
  Ne then of guile had made experiment,
  But voide of vile and treacherous intent,
  Held vertue for it selfe in soueraine awe:
  Then loyall loue had royall regiment,
  And each vnto his lust did make a lawe,
From all forbidden things his liking to withdraw.

Stanza 25

2 **causelesse**: not having any basis in fact, as **forged cause** (7).
4 Cf. Thomas Wilson, *Arte of Rhetorique* (1560) 124: 'A slaunderer is worse then any Theefe, because a good name is better then all the goodes in the world.'

Stanza 26

Slander wounds through the ears by her breath as Corflambo wounds through the eyes by his eyes, stanza 39. Traditionally, hearing may infect the soul.
3 **noysome**: ill-smelling; suggesting also its noxious effects.
8–9 Cf. V xii 36.3–4.

Stanza 27

2 **fayne**: gladly.
4 **entertayne**: reception.
5 Cf. the praise of the antique age, 30–31. **nicenesse**: luxury.
8 **endur'd**: sustained; hardened, playing on Latin *durus*, hard, as suggested by 6.
9 **fortunelesse misfare**: unfortunate mischance.

Stanza 28

8 **queane**: harlot.

Stanza 29

2 **misregard**: lack of care; misconstruction.
3 **looser**: too loose.
5 **conuersing**: associating; but Sclaunder infers 'cohabiting with'.
6 **temperance**: restraint of sensual impulses, or chastity.
7–9 It is harder for youth to abstain from pleasure than for a hungry steed, etc. **lare**: pasture; cf. 51.5.

Stanza 30

7 **regiment**: self-control. **royall**: implies rule by a sovereign.
8–9 S.'s formulation relates to a Renaissance debate upon the legitimacy of pleasure, e.g. Tasso's account of the golden age, *Aminta* I ii Chorus: *S'ei piace, ei lice*, 'whatever pleases is lawful', countered by Guarini's claim, *Il Pastor Fido* IV ix Chorus: *Piaccia, se lice*, 'man should delight only in what is lawful'.

31

The Lyon there did with the Lambe consort,
  And eke the Doue sate by the Faulcons side,
  Ne each of other feared fraud or tort,
  But did in safe securitie abide,
  Withouten perill of the stronger pride:
  But when the world woxe old, it woxe warre old
  (Whereof it hight) and hauing shortly tride
  The traines of wit, in wickednesse woxe bold,
And dared of all sinnes the secrets to vnfold.

32

Then beautie, which was made to represent
  The great Creatours owne resemblance bright,
  Vnto abuse of lawlesse lust was lent,
  And made the baite of bestiall delight:
  Then faire grew foule, and foule grew faire in sight,
  And that which wont to vanquish God and man,
  Was made the vassall of the victors might;
  Then did her glorious flowre wex dead and wan,
Despisd and troden downe of all that ouerran.

33

And now it is so vtterly decayd,
  That any bud thereof doth scarse remaine,
  But if few plants preseru'd through heauenly ayd,
  In Princes Court doe hap to sprout againe,
  Dew'd with her drops of bountie Soueraine,
  Which from that goodly glorious flowre proceed,
  Sprung of the auncient stocke of Princes straine,
  Now th'onely remnant of that royall breed,
Whose noble kind at first was sure of heauenly seed.

34

Tho soone as day discouered heauens face
  To sinfull men with darknes ouerdight,
  This gentle crew gan from their eye-lids chace
  The drowzie humour of the dampish night,
  And did themselues vnto their iourney dight,
  So forth they yode, and forward softly paced,
  That them to view had bene an vncouth sight;
  How all the way the Prince on footpace traced,
The Ladies both on horse, together fast embraced.

35

Soone as they thence departed were afore,
  That shamefull Hag, the slaunder of her sexe,
  Them follow'd fast, and them reuiled sore,
  Him calling theefe, them whores; that much did vexe
  His noble hart; thereto she did annexe
  False crimes and facts, such as they neuer ment,
  That those two Ladies much asham'd did wexe:
  The more did she pursue her lewd intent,
And rayl'd and rag'd, till she had all her poyson spent.

36

At last when they were passed out of sight,
  Yet she did not her spightfull speach forbeare,
  But after them did barke, and still backbite,
  Though there were none her hatefull words to heare:
  Like as a curre doth felly bite and teare
  The stone, which passed straunger at him threw;
  So she them seeing past the reach of eare,
  Against the stones and trees did rayle anew,
Till she had duld the sting, which in her tongs end grew.

Stanza 31

1–5 Cf. Isaiah 11.6: 'The wolfe also shal dwell with the
lambe, and the leoparde shal lye with the kid, and the calfe, and
the lyon, and the fat beast together.' S.'s animals are traditional
emblems of strength and gentleness. The dove's flight from the
falcon is a common image in the poem, as III iv 49.4–9.
1 **there**: then, as 30.2, 32.1,5,8.
3 **tort**: wrong, injustice.
4 **safe securitie**: suggests over-confident carelessness;
cf. III iv 27.3.
5 **stronger pride**: pride or tyranny of the stronger.
6 It grew worse being old, or grew worse the older it got (as
V Proem 1.9). **warre old**: the popular etymology of world.
Cf. Ps. 102, 25–6: '. . . the fundation of the earth, and the
heauens . . . shal waxe olde as doeth a garment.'
8 **traines**: wiles.

Stanza 32

This stanza outlines Florimell's predicament: Beauty was
abused by lust when she was pursued by the Foster, and made
the bait of bestial delight by the Witch's son and the fisherman.
It grew foul and foul grew fair when her place was taken by the
False Florimell and she became the vassal of Proteus. Florimell
is compared to a **glorious flowre** (8) throughout Books III and
IV.
1 **represent**: make visible or manifest.
6 Cf. VII vi 31.4 where the beauty of Mutabilitie holds sway
in heaven.
9 **of all that ouerran**: i.e. of all who trampled down the
flower of beauty. The flower of beauty is Chastity; cf.
Belphœbe's rose, III v 51–52.

Stanza 33

3 **But if**: unless.
6 **flowre**: Elizabeth; cf. 'Therefore they *Glorian* call that
glorious flowre' (II x 76.8).
7 **straine**: lineage.

Stanza 34

2 **sinfull men**: caps the claim of the previous stanzas.
ouerdight: covered over.
6 **yode**: went. **softly**: slowly; gently; cf. 37.2.
7 **vncouth**: strange.
8 **on footpace traced**: on foot, and at a footpace, walked.

Stanza 35

2 **slaunder of her sexe**: wittily turning her condition
against herself.
4 The basis of her charge against Arthur is that he found the
two and did not gain them by right of conquest.
5 **annexe**: join, add.
6 **facts**: evil deeds.
8 **lewd**: evil.

Stanza 36

3 **backbite**: literally bite behind their backs.
5–6 Proverbial (C. G. Smith, 1970, 190).

485

37

They passing forth kept on their readie way,
  With easie steps so soft as foot could stryde,
  Both for great feeblesse, which did oft assay
  Faire *Amoret*, that scarcely she could ryde,
  And eke through heauie armes, which sore annoyd
  The Prince on foot, not wonted so to fare;
  Whose steadie hand was faine his steede to guyde,
  And all the way from trotting hard to spare,
So was his toyle the more, the more that was his care.

38

At length they spide, where towards them with speed
  A Squire came galloping, as he would flie;
  Bearing a litle Dwarfe before his steed,
  That all the way full loud for aide did crie,
  That seem'd his shrikes would rend the brasen skie:
  Whom after did a mightie man pursew,
  Ryding vpon a Dromedare on hie,
  Of stature huge, and horrible of hew,
That would haue maz'd a man his dreadfull face to vew.

39

For from his fearefull eyes two fierie beames,
  More sharpe then points of needles did proceede,
  Shooting forth farre away two flaming streames,
  Full of sad powre, that poysonous bale did breede
  To all, that on him lookt without good heed,
  And secretly his enemies did slay:
  Like as the Basiliske of serpents seede,
  From powrefull eyes close venim doth conuay
Into the lookers hart, and killeth farre away.

40

He all the way did rage at that same Squire,
  And after him full many threatnings threw,
  With curses vaine in his auengefull ire:
  But none of them (so fast away he flew)
  Him ouertooke, before he came in vew.
  Where when he saw the Prince in armour bright,
  He cald to him aloud, his case to rew,
  And rescue him through succour of his might,
From that his cruell foe, that him pursewd in sight.

41

Eftsoones the Prince tooke downe those Ladies twaine
  From loftie steede, and mounting in their stead
  Came to that Squire, yet trembling euery vaine:
  Of whom he gan enquire his cause of dread;
  Who as he gan the same to him aread,
  Loe hard behind his backe his foe was prest,
  With dreadfull weapon aymed at his head,
  That vnto death had doen him vnredrest,
Had not the noble Prince his readie stroke represt.

42

Who thrusting boldly twixt him and the blow,
  The burden of the deadly brunt did beare
  Vpon his shield, which lightly he did throw
  Ouer his head, before the harme came neare.
  Nathlesse it fell with so despiteous dreare
  And heauie sway, that hard vnto his crowne
  The shield it droue, and did the couering reare,
  Therewith both Squire and dwarfe did tomble downe
Vnto the earth, and lay long while in senselesse swowne.

486

Stanza 37

3–4 At 20.9 the wound is cured, but not its infection from slander, from which she now suffers.   **assay**: afflict.

7   **faine**: wont; obliged.

8   **spare**: refrain; restrain.

Stanza 38

1–2 In contrast to Arthur's slow pace.

7   The dromedary is noted for its speed, from its etymology, δρομάς, running. It is a symbol of sin: cf. Jeremiah's denunciation of the children of Israel for playing the harlot: 'Thou art like a swift dromedarie, that runneth by his wayes' (Jer. 2.23).

Stanza 39

1–6 Corflambo's power is related to the concept that lovers emit spirits by means of beams from their eyes. Cf. Burton, *Anatomy* III ii 2.2: 'The rays . . . sent from the eyes, carry certain spiritual vapours with them, and so infect the other party, and that in a moment.' He adds an analogy to the Basilisk 'that kills afar off by sight'. Cf. Acrasia's eyes: 'their fierie beames, with which she thrild / Fraile harts' (II xii 78.7–8).   **sad**: heavy, causing sorrow.

7–9 Proverbial (Tilley, 1950, B 99).   **close**: secret.

Stanza 40

4–5 The Squire was out of hearing.

7   **to rew**: to succour.

9   **in sight**: relates to the nature of the antagonist.

Stanza 41

5   **aread**: tell.

6   **prest**: at hand.

7   **at his head**: because Corflambo attacks through the eyes. Hence he must be decapitated.

8   **vnredrest**: i.e. without hope of remedy.

9   **represt**: forced back.

Stanza 42

2   **brunt**: stroke.

5–6 **dreare**: direfulness; dire, as it describes **sway** or force.

6–9 The meaning is not clear.   **couering** may refer to the Squire's helmet: Arthur's shield, bashing down upon his head, knocks his helmet off. Or the blow may raise his beaver, also causing him to be struck by the beams from Corflambo's eyes. Or **couering** may refer to Arthur's shield: the covering is raised, causing the Squire and the dwarf to be struck by its beams, as Orgoglio is struck at I viii 19. This second reading is the simpler, and suggests that lovers are wounded by those who aid them, as Timias by Belphœbe.

43

Whereat the Prince full wrath, his strong right hand
  In full auengement heaued vp on hie,
  And stroke the Pagan with his steely brand
  So sore, that to his saddle bow thereby
  He bowed low, and so a while did lie:
  And sure had not his massie yron mace
  Betwixt him and his hurt bene happily,
  It would haue cleft him to the girding place,
Yet as it was, it did astonish him long space.

44

But when he to himselfe returnd againe,
  All full of rage he gan to curse and sweare,
  And vow by *Mahoune* that he should be slaine.
  With that his murdrous mace he vp did reare,
  That seemed nought the souse thereof could beare,
  And therewith smote at him with all his might.
  But ere that it to him approched neare,
  The royall child with readie quicke foresight,
Did shun the proofe thereof and it auoyded light.

45

But ere his hand he could recure againe,
  To ward his bodie from the balefull stound,
  He smote at him with all his might and maine,
  So furiously, that ere he wist, he found
  His head before him tombling on the ground.
  The whiles his babling tongue did yet blaspheme
  And curse his God, that did him so confound;
  The whiles his life ran foorth in bloudie streame,
His soule descended downe into the Stygian reame.

46

Which when that Squire beheld, he woxe full glad
  To see his foe breath out his spright in vaine:
  But that same dwarfe right sorie seem'd and sad,
  And howld aloud to see his Lord there slaine,
  And rent his haire and scratcht his face for paine.
  Then gan the Prince at leasure to inquire
  Of all the accident, there hapned plaine,
  And what he was, whose eyes did flame with fire;
All which was thus to him declared by that Squire.

47

This mightie man (quoth he) whom you haue slaine,
  Of an huge Geauntesse whylome was bred;
  And by his strength rule to himselfe did gaine
  Of many Nations into thraldome led,
  And mightie kingdomes of his force adred;
  Whom yet he conquer'd not by bloudie fight,
  Ne hostes of men with banners brode dispred,
  But by the powre of his infectious sight,
With which he killed all, that came within his might.

48

Ne was he euer vanquished afore,
  But euer vanquisht all, with whom he fought;
  Ne was there man so strong, but he downe bore,
  Ne woman yet so faire, but he her brought
  Vnto his bay, and captiued her thought.
  For most of strength and beautie his desire
  Was spoyle to make, and wast them vnto nought,
  By casting secret flakes of lustfull fire
From his false eyes, into their harts and parts entire.

49

Therefore *Corflambo* was he cald aright,
  Though namelesse there his bodie now doth lie,
  Yet hath he left one daughter that is hight
  The faire *Pœana*; who seemes outwardly
  So faire, as euer yet saw liuing eie:
  And were her vertue like her beautie bright,
  She were as faire as any vnder skie,
  But ah she giuen is to vaine delight,
And eke too loose of life, and eke of loue too light.

Stanza 43
8   **girding place**: the waist.
9   **astonish**: stun.

Stanza 44
3   **Mahoune**: Mohammed, god of the Saracens or pagans generally; see II viii 30.4*n*.
5   **souse**: downward blow.
8   **royall child**: applied to a youth of noble birth or to a knight in the prime of manhood, but by S. only to Arthur. Cf. V viii 32.1, xi 8.8, etc. Cf. 'Infant' (II viii 56.1).
9   **proofe**: issue.

Stanza 45
1   **recure**: recover.
2   **stound**: attack.
4–7   Cf. Homer, *Iliad* x 457, and Ariosto, *Orl. Fur.* xxix 26. In Ovid, *Met.* v 104–6, the severed head speaks.
9   **reame**: realm.

Stanza 46
7   **accident**: event.

Stanza 47
4   **Nations into thraldome led**: i.e. nations enthralled by lust are ruled by Corflambo.

Stanza 48
5   **Vnto his bay**: to close quarters before him, used of a hunter's quarry surrounded by the hounds.   **captiued**: enthralled.
6   **strength and beautie**: cf. the contests of 'beautie and . . . might' (iv 16.2) in the Tournaments in Cantos iv and v. Corflambo triumphs over both.
9   **parts entire**: inward parts; cf. 23.9.

Stanza 49
1   **Corflambo**: Lat. *cor*, heart + Fr. *flambeau*, flaming torch. The significance of his name is revealed in the two previous lines; cf. 39.7–9.
2   Referring to the anonymity of death, which Virgil applies even to Priam when he lies headless, *Aen.* ii 558.
4–7   **Pœana**: from Lat. *poena*, 'paine; punishment; tourment' (Cooper, 1565); from pæan, the 'ioyous glee' of 52.2 (cf. 59.6–7). See also ix 6.2*n*. Both pain and joy characterize her: her grief turns to joy at ix 13–16. Cf. Scudamour's lament at x 1. She only **seemes** beautiful: if she were virtuous, she would be so.

50

So as it fell there was a gentle Squire,
　That lou'd a Ladie of high parentage,
　But for his meane degree might not aspire
　To match so high, her friends with counsell sage,
　Dissuaded her from such a disparage.
　But she, whose hart to loue was wholly lent,
　Out of his hands could not redeeme her gage,
　But firmely following her first intent,
Resolu'd with him to wend, gainst all her friends consent.

51

So twixt themselues they pointed time and place,
　To which when he according did repaire,
　An hard mishap and disauentrous case
　Him chaunst; in stead of his *Æmylia* faire
　This Gyants sonne, that lies there on the laire
　An headlesse heape, him vnawares there caught,
　And all dismayd through mercilesse despaire,
　Him wretched thrall vnto his dongeon brought,
Where he remaines, of all vnsuccour'd and vnsought.

52

This Gyants daughter came vpon a day
　Vnto the prison in her ioyous glee,
　To view the thrals, which there in bondage lay:
　Amongst the rest she chaunced there to see
　This louely swaine the Squire of low degree;
　To whom she did her liking lightly cast,
　And wooed him her paramour to bee:
　From day to day she woo'd and prayd him fast,
And for his loue him promist libertie at last.

53

He though affide vnto a former loue,
　To whom his faith he firmely ment to hold,
　Yet seeing not how thence he mote remoue,
　But by that meanes, which fortune did vnfold,
　Her graunted loue, but with affection cold
　To win her grace his libertie to get.
　Yet she him still detaines in captiue hold,
　Fearing least if she should him freely set,
He would her shortly leaue, and former loue forget.

54

Yet so much fauour she to him hath hight,
　Aboue the rest, that he sometimes may space
　And walke about her gardens of delight,
　Hauing a keeper still with him in place,
　Which keeper is this Dwarfe, her dearling base,
　To whom the keyes of euery prison dore
　By her committed be, of speciall grace,
　And at his will may whom he list restore,
And whom he list reserue, to be afflicted more.

55

Whereof when tydings came vnto mine eare,
　Full inly sorie for the feruent zeale,
　Which I to him as to my soule did beare;
　I thether went where I did long conceale
　My selfe, till that the Dwarfe did me reueale,
　And told his Dame, her Squire of low degree
　Did secretly out of her prison steale;
　For me he did mistake that Squire to bee;
For neuer two so like did liuing creature see.

56

Then was I taken and before her brought,
　Who through the likenesse of my outward hew,
　Being likewise beguiled in her thought,
　Gan blame me much for being so vntrew,
　To seeke by flight her fellowship t'eschew,
　That lou'd me deare, as dearest thing aliue.
　Thence she commaunded me to prison new;
　Whereof I glad did not gainesay nor striue,
But suffred that same Dwarfe me to her dongeon driue.

Stanzas 50–51
Cf. Æmylia's version of this story at vii 15–18. Placidas tells of the friends' opposition to the marriage, rather than the father's.

Stanza 50
5　**disparage**: unequal match: cf. 'disparagement' (vii 16.1).

Stanza 51
1　**pointed**: appointed.
2　**according**: accordingly; or, as they had agreed.
3　**disauentrous case**: unfortunate event.
5　**laire**: ground; cf. 29.9.
7　**mercilesse**: without hope of mercy, as 64.5; cf. Æmylia's state, vii 11.7–9.

Stanza 52
8　**fast**: earnestly.

Stanza 53
1　**affide**: betrothed.
8　**freely set**: set free.
9　**former loue**: parallels the phrase in 1 in order to relate Æmylia and Pœana. When Æmylia and Amyas elope, each is imprisoned by the other's lust. See ix Arg. 2n.

Stanza 54
1　**hight**: granted.
2　**space**: roam.
3　**her gardens of delight**: with erotic overtones of the woman's body as the garden which her lover enjoys.
5　**dearling**: favourite.
8–9　**restore**: i.e. to liberty; in contrast to **reserue**: keep in his possession.

Stanza 55
2　**zeale**: ardent love; as ix 1.7.
3　Cf. Deut. 13.6: 'thy frende, which is as thy owne soule'.
8　**did mistake**: supposed in error.
9　Since true friendship involves 'one soul in bodies twain', ideally friends are identical in appearance.

Stanza 56
2　**hew**: shape.

57

There did I finde mine onely faithfull frend
  In heauy plight and sad perplexitie;
  Whereof I sorie, yet my selfe did bend,
  Him to recomfort with my companie.
  But him the more agreeu'd I found thereby:
  For all his ioy, he said, in that distresse
  Was mine and his *Æmylias* libertie.
  Æmylia well he lou'd, as I mote ghesse;
Yet greater loue to me then her he did professe.

58

But I with better reason him auiz'd,
  And shew'd him how through error and mis-thought
  Of our like persons eath to be disguiz'd,
  Or his exchange, or freedome might be wrought.
  Whereto full loth was he, ne would for ought
  Consent, that I who stood all fearelesse free,
  Should wilfully be into thraldome brought,
  Till fortune did perforce it so decree.
Yet ouerrul'd at last, he did to me agree.

59

The morrow next about the wonted howre,
  The Dwarfe cald at the doore of *Amyas*,
  To come forthwith vnto his Ladies bowre.
  In steed of whom forth came I *Placidas*,
  And vndiscerned, forth with him did pas.
  There with great ioyance and with gladsome glee,
  Of faire *Pœana* I receiued was,
  And oft imbrast, as if that I were hee,
And with kind words accoyd, vowing great loue to mee.

60

Which I, that was not bent to former loue,
  As was my friend, that had her long refusd,
  Did well accept, as well it did behoue,
  And to the present neede it wisely vsd.
  My former hardnesse first I faire excusd;
  And after promist large amends to make.
  With such smooth termes her error I abusd,
  To my friends good, more then for mine owne sake,
For whose sole libertie I loue and life did stake.

61

Thenceforth I found more fauour at her hand,
  That to her Dwarfe, which had me in his charge,
  She bad to lighten my too heauie band,
  And graunt more scope to me to walke at large.
  So on a day as by the flowrie marge
  Of a fresh streame I with that Elfe did play,
  Finding no meanes how I might vs enlarge,
  But if that Dwarfe I could with me conuay,
I lightly snatcht him vp, and with me bore away.

62

Thereat he shriekt aloud, that with his cry
  The Tyrant selfe came forth with yelling bray,
  And me pursew'd; but nathemore would I
  Forgoe the purchase of my gotten pray,
  But haue perforce him hether brought away.
  Thus as they talked, loe where nigh at hand
  Those Ladies two yet doubtfull through dismay
  In presence came, desirous t'vnderstand
Tydings of all, which there had hapned on the land.

63

Where soone as sad *Æmylia* did espie
  Her captiue louers friend, young *Placidas*;
  All mindlesse of her wonted modestie,
  She to him ran, and him with streight embras
  Enfolding said, And liues yet *Amyas*?
  He liues (quoth he) and his *Æmylia* loues.
  Then lesse (said she) by all the woe I pas,
  With which my weaker patience fortune proues.
But what mishap thus long him fro my selfe remoues?

Stanza 57

1   **onely**: one, above all others.
2   **perplexitie**: distress; also 'bewilderment', as he must choose between the two women, and between them and his friend.
8–9   Within the conventions of friendship, he makes the correct choice.

Stanza 58

2   **mis-thought**: mistaken opinion.
3   **eath**: easy.
9   **agree**: accede to my proposal.

Stanza 59

2   **Amyas**: Lat. *amo*+Fr. *ami*, as he combines love and friendship. Ayres, *Var*. iv 322–4, notes the parallels with the romance *Amis and Amiloun* which treats the conflicting claims of love and friendship.
4   **Placidas**: Lat. *placidus*, peaceful, friendly; 'gentill, meeke' (Cooper, 1565).
9   **accoyd**: appeased, soothed, for having been placed in the dungeon.

Stanza 60

9   **sole libertie**: liberty alone.

Stanza 61

5   **marge**: margin.
8   **But if**: unless.

Stanza 62

4   **purchase**: acquisition.
7   **doubtfull**: fearful.

Stanza 63

4   **streight**: close.
7   **Then lesse . . . the woe I pas**: i.e. since he lives, I mind less the woes I suffer.
8   **weaker**: too weak.

64

Then gan he all this storie to renew,
  And tell the course of his captiuitie;
  That her deare hart full deepely made to rew,
  And sigh full sore, to heare the miserie,
  In which so long he mercilesse did lie.
  Then after many teares and sorrowes spent,
  She deare besought the Prince of remedie:
  Who thereto did with readie will consent,
And well perform'd, as shall appeare by his euent.

Cant. IX.

*The Squire of low degree releast
Pœana takes to wife:
Britomart fightes with many Knights,
Prince Arthur stints their strife.*

1

HArd is the doubt, and difficult to deeme,
  When all three kinds of loue together meet,
  And doe dispart the hart with powre extreme,
  Whether shall weigh the balance downe; to weet
  The deare affection vnto kindred sweet,
  Or raging fire of loue to woman kind,
  Or zeale of friends combynd with vertues meet.
  But of them all the band of vertuous mind
Me seemes the gentle hart should most assured bind.

2

For naturall affection soone doth cesse,
  And quenched is with *Cupids* greater flame:
  But faithfull friendship doth them both suppresse,
  And them with maystring discipline doth tame,
  Through thoughts aspyring to eternall fame.
  For as the soule doth rule the earthly masse,
  And all the seruice of the bodie frame,
  So loue of soule doth loue of bodie passe,
No lesse then perfect gold surmounts the meanest brasse.

3

All which who list by tryall to assay,
  Shall in this storie find approued plaine;
  In which these Squires true friendship more did sway,
  Then either care of parents could refraine,
  Or loue of fairest Ladie could constraine.
  For though *Pœana* were as faire as morne,
  Yet did this trustie Squire with proud disdaine
  For his friends sake her offred fauours scorne,
And she her selfe her syre, of whom she was yborne.

4

Now after that Prince *Arthur* graunted had,
  To yeeld strong succour to that gentle swayne,
  Who now long time had lyen in prison sad,
  He gan aduise how best he mote darrayne
  That enterprize, for greatest glories gayne.
  That headlesse tyrants tronke he reard from ground,
  And hauing ympt the head to it agayne,
  Vpon his vsuall beast it firmely bound,
And made it so to ride, as it aliue was found.

5

Then did he take that chaced Squire, and layd
  Before the ryder, as he captiue were,
  And made his Dwarfe, though with vnwilling ayd,
  To guide the beast, that did his maister beare,
  Till to his castle they approched neare.
  Whom when the watch, that kept continuall ward
  Saw comming home; all voide of doubtfull feare,
  He running downe, the gate to him vnbard;
Whom straight the Prince ensuing, in together far'd.

Stanza 64

1 **renew**: repeat. Presumably not **all**: not that Amyas loved him more than her.

5 **mercilesse**: without hope of mercy; cf. 51.7 which points to the need for Arthur's grace.

9 **by his euent**: by what happened to him.

Canto ix

Argument

2 **Pœana**: Æmylia sugg. Church (1758). Dodge (1908) notes that the only marriage specifically mentioned is Pœana's to the trusty Squire, Placidas (15.3–9). 15.1 and 17.2 suggest a double marriage. Though Amyas is the **Squire of low degree**, Placidas may share his station, for they cannot be distinguished (11). The confusion may follow from the connection between the two ladies: see viii 53.9*n*. The matter is examined by Staton (1965) 108–11.

4 **stints**: stops.

Stanza 1

1 **deeme**: judge; decide.

3 **dispart**: divide.

4 **Whether**: which.

7 **zeale**: ardent love; cf. viii 55.2. A mean between **deare affection** and **raging . . . loue**, applies particularly to friendship; cf. iv 34.3, x 26.8.

8–9 The heart split asunder by the three kinds of love may be bound by the **vertuous mind** of friendship.

Stanza 2

3–4 Friendship subdues natural affection and sexual love by its **maystring discipline**.

9 **surmounts**: excels.

Stanza 3

2 **approued**: both proved and commended.

4 **refraine**: restrain.

6–9 Placidas flees from **Pœana**, even though he enjoys her favours, in order to find means to free his friend (see viii 61.7). Pœana scorns her sire by releasing her lover from his prison (viii 54.1–3; cf. 61.1–4).

Stanza 4

4 **aduise**: consider. **darrayne**: arrange.

7 **ympt**: fixed.

Stanza 5

9 **ensuing**: following.

6

There he did find in her delitious boure
  The faire *Pæana* playing on a Rote,
  Complayning of her cruell Paramoure,
  And singing all her sorrow to the note,
  As she had learned readily by rote.
  That with the sweetnesse of her rare delight,
  The Prince halfe rapt, began on her to dote:
  Till better him bethinking of the right,
He her vnwares attacht, and captiue held by might.

7

Whence being forth produc'd, when she perceiued
  Her owne deare sire, she cald to him for aide.
  But when of him no aunswere she receiued,
  But saw him sencelesse by the Squire vpstaide,
  She weened well, that then she was betraide:
  Then gan she loudly cry, and weepe, and waile,
  And that same Squire of treason to vpbraide.
  But all in vaine, her plaints might not preuaile,
Ne none there was to reskue her, ne none to baile.

8

Then tooke he that same Dwarfe, and him compeld
  To open vnto him the prison dore,
  And forth to bring those thrals, which there he held.
  Thence forth were brought to him aboue a score
  Of Knights and Squires to him vnknowne afore:
  All which he did from bitter bondage free,
  And vnto former liberty restore.
  Amongst the rest, that Squire of low degree
Came forth full weake and wan, not like him selfe to bee.

9

Whom soone as faire *Æmylia* beheld,
  And *Placidas*, they both vnto him ran,
  And him embracing fast betwixt them held,
  Striuing to comfort him all that they can,
  And kissing oft his visage pale and wan.
  That faire *Pæana* them beholding both,
  Gan both enuy, and bitterly to ban;
  Through iealous passion weeping inly wroth,
To see the sight perforce, that both her eyes were loth.

10

But when a while they had together beene,
  And diuersly conferred of their case,
  She, though full oft she both of them had seene
  A sunder, yet not euer in one place,
  Began to doubt, when she them saw embrace,
  Which was the captiue Squire she lou'd so deare,
  Deceiued through great likenesse of their face,
  For they so like in person did appeare,
That she vneath discerned, whether whether weare.

11

And eke the Prince, when as he them auized,
  Their like resemblaunce much admired there,
  And mazd how nature had so well disguized
  Her worke, and counterfet her selfe so nere,
  As if that by one patterne seene somewhere,
  She had them made a paragone to be,
  Or whether it through skill, or errour were.
  Thus gazing long, at them much wondred he,
So did the other knights and Squires, which him did see.

12

Then gan they ransacke that same Castle strong,
  In which he found great store of hoorded threasure,
  The which that tyrant gathered had by wrong
  And tortious powre, without respect or measure.
  Vpon all which the Briton Prince made seasure,
  And afterwards continu'd there a while,
  To rest him selfe, and solace in soft pleasure
  Those weaker Ladies after weary toile;
To whom he did diuide part of his purchast spoile.

Stanza 6
1 **her delitious boure**: 'her gardens of delight' (viii 54.3).
2 **Rote**: lyre, lute, or harp; see II x 3.2. Upton (1758) relates her name to her singing: *laetumque choro paeana canentis* (*Aen*. vi 657). See viii 49.4–7*n*.
6–7 She enchants hearing as her father infected sight. As Corflambo's daughter, she has the power also to arouse desire by beauty's glance.
9 **attacht**: seized.

Stanza 7
8 **preuaile**: avail, be of use.
9 **ne none to baile**: cf. Amyas whose friend was ready to bail him.

Stanza 9
6 **Pœana**] *Pæana 1596*. The changed spelling prepares for her changed state: see viii 49.4–7*n*.
7 **ban**: curse.

Stanza 10
9 **whether whether weare**: which was which.

Stanza 11
1 **auized**: observed.
2 **admired**: wondered at.
3 **mazd**: marvelled.   **disguized**: decked out (cf. *OED* 1).
6 **paragone**: match.
9 **him**: 'them' sugg. Hughes (1715); however, the two are one although divided.

Stanza 12
4 **tortious**: wrongful, i.e. wrongfully used.
without respect: without discrimination; cf. viii 48.3–5.
8 **weaker**: too weak.
9 **purchast**: procured; obtained by conquest.

13

And for more ioy, that captiue Lady faire
  The faire *Pœana* he enlarged free;
  And by the rest did set in sumptuous chaire,
  To feast and frollicke; nathemore would she
  Shew gladsome countenaunce nor pleasaunt glee:
  But grieued was for losse both of her sire,
  And eke of Lordship, with both land and fee:
  But most she touched was with griefe entire,
For losse of her new loue, the hope of her desire.

14

But her the Prince through his well wonted grace,
  To better termes of myldnesse did entreat,
  From that fowle rudenesse, which did her deface;
  And that same bitter corsiue, which did eat
  Her tender heart, and made refraine from meat,
  He with good thewes and speaches well applyde,
  Did mollifie, and calme her raging heat.
  For though she were most faire, and goodly dyde,
Yet she it all did mar with cruelty and pride.

15

And for to shut vp all in friendly loue,
  Sith loue was first the ground of all her griefe,
  That trusty Squire he wisely well did moue
  Not to despise that dame, which lou'd him liefe,
  Till he had made of her some better priefe,
  But to accept her to his wedded wife.
  Thereto he offred for to make him chiefe
  Of all her land and lordship during life:
He yeelded, and her tooke; so stinted all their strife.

16

From that day forth in peace and ioyous blis,
  They liu'd together long without debate,
  Ne priuate iarre, ne spite of enemis
  Could shake the safe assuraunce of their state.
  And she whom Nature did so faire create,
  That she mote match the fairest of her daies,
  Yet with lewd loues and lust intemperate
  Had it defaste; thenceforth reformd her waies,
That all men much admyrde her change, and spake her praise.

17

Thus when the Prince had perfectly compylde
  These paires of friends in peace and setled rest,
  Him selfe, whose minde did trauell as with chylde,
  Of his old loue, conceau'd in secret brest,
  Resolued to pursue his former quest;
  And taking leaue of all, with him did beare
  Faire *Amoret*, whom Fortune by bequest
  Had left in his protection whileare,
Exchanged out of one into an other feare.

18

Feare of her safety did her not constraine,
  For well she wist now in a mighty hond,
  Her person late in perill, did remaine,
  Who able was all daungers to withstond.
  But now in feare of shame she more did stond,
  Seeing her selfe all soly succourlesse,
  Left in the victors powre, like vassall bond;
  Whose will her weakenesse could no way represse,
In case his burning lust should breake into excesse.

19

But cause of feare sure had she none at all
  Of him, who goodly learned had of yore
  The course of loose affection to forstall,
  And lawlesse lust to rule with reasons lore;
  That all the while he by his side her bore,
  She was as safe as in a Sanctuary;
  Thus many miles they two together wore,
  To seeke their loues dispersed diuersly,
Yet neither shewed to other their hearts priuity.

Stanza 13
7 **fee**: possessions; wealth.
8 **entire**: sincere; total; inward.
9 **new loue**: presumably Placidas who has replaced Amyas.

Stanza 14
4 **corsiue**: corrosive; 'cor' links the word to the heart. Here the devouring emotion is jealousy: see I ii 6.3*n*.
6 **thewes**: behaviour.
7 **raging heat**: cf. 'raging fire of loue' (1.6).
8 **dyde**: coloured; hence of fine complexion.

Stanza 15
4 **liefe**: dearly.
5 **priefe**: proof.
9 **stinted . . . strife**: cf. also Arg. 3–4, which refers to the following episode. Arthur reconciles opposing factions in love and war to achieve friendship in love.

Stanza 16
2 **debate**: strife.

Stanza 17
1 **compylde**: composed.
3 **trauell**: travail; labour in birth.

Stanza 18
Cf. her 'dread of shame' (i 8.6) when attended by Britomart. Now she is held by a knight overcome by 'his old loue' (17.4).

Stanza 19
3 **affection**: passion, lust.   **forstall**: obstruct, subdue.
9 **priuity**: private thought.

20

At length they came, whereas a troupe of Knights
  They saw together skirmishing, as seemed:
  Sixe they were all, all full of fell despight,
  But foure of them the battell best beseemed,
  That which of them was best, mote not be deemed.
  Those foure were they, from whom false *Florimell*
  By *Braggadochio* lately was redeemed.
    To weet, sterne *Druon*, and lewd *Claribell*,
Loue-lauish *Blandamour*, and lustfull *Paridell*.

21

Druons delight was all in single life,
  And vnto Ladies loue would lend no leasure:
  The more was *Claribell* enraged rife
  With feruent flames, and loued out of measure:
  So eke lou'd *Blandamour*, but yet at pleasure
  Would change his liking, and new Lemans proue.
  But *Paridell* of loue did make no threasure,
    But lusted after all, that him did moue.
So diuersly these foure disposed were to loue.

22

But those two other which beside them stoode,
  Were *Britomart*, and gentle *Scudamour*,
  Who all the while beheld their wrathfull moode,
  And wondred at their impacable stoure,
  Whose like they neuer saw till that same houre:
  So dreadfull strokes each did at other driue,
  As if that euery dint the ghost would riue
    Out of their wretched corses, and their liues depriue.

23

As when *Dan Æolus* in great displeasure,
  For losse of his deare loue by *Neptune* hent,
  Sends forth the winds out of his hidden threasure,
  Vpon the sea to wreake his fell intent;
  They breaking forth with rude vnruliment,
  From all foure parts of heauen doe rage full sore,
  And tosse the deepes, and teare the firmament,
    And all the world confound with wide vprore,
As If in stead thereof they *Chaos* would restore.

24

Cause of their discord, and so fell debate,
  Was for the loue of that same snowy maid,
  Whome they had lost in Turneyment of late,
  And seeking long, to weet which way she straid,
  Met here together, where through lewd vpbraide
  Of *Ate* and *Duessa* they fell out,
  And each one taking part in others aide,
    This cruell conflict raised thereabout,
Whose dangerous successe depended yet in dout.

25

For sometimes *Paridell* and *Blandamour*
  The better had, and bet the others backe,
  Eftsoones the others did the field recoure,
  And on their foes did worke full cruell wracke:
  Yet neither would their fiendlike fury slacke,
  But euermore their malice did augment;
  Till that vneath they forced were for lacke
    Of breath, their raging rigour to relent,
And rest themselues for to recouer spirits spent.

Stanza 20
4 **the battell best beseemed**: seemed best fit for battle, as they embody love that leads to discord.
8 **Druon**: i.e. cruel, from Lat. *durus*, hard; or O.F. *dru*, violent (sugg. Belson, 1964); or δρυς, oak, to link him with the savage Artegall (iv 39.6) and Lust (vii 7.4).   **Claribell**: Lat. *clarus+bellum*, famous in war. Or suggesting a lady's man as he bears a woman's name. Or famous in beauty, referring to the 'famous prize of beauty' (28.9) for which he fights.
9 **Loue-lauish**: flattering love, as the name Blandamour suggests; see i 32.4–5*n*.

Stanzas 21–27
Druon rejects love through constancy to single life; **Claribell** loves excessively; **Blandamour** loves excessively but inconstantly; **Paridell** rejects love through inconstant lust. At the beginning, the first and second pairs are opposed in a battle of constancy against inconstancy. Then the two who reject love fight those who accept it. See Fowler (1964) 31–2.

Stanza 21
1–2 As Marinell was 'loues enimy' (III iv 26.9); cf. Artegall, IV vi 28.6–9.
3–4 **The more**: greatly; or Claribell's womanizing is a function of Druon's male chastity. As much as the one rejected love, the other accepted it.
6 **proue**: try.

Stanza 22
4 **impacable**: that cannot be pacified. Only Arthur may reconcile them.
8 **dint**: blow.

Stanza 23
The conflict of the four winds symbolizes the chaos of human passions and expresses the four conflicting types of love. For Neptune's love for Æolus's daughter Arne, see III xi 42.2–4.
2 **hent**: taken away.
3 **threasure**: store; cf. Ps. 135.7: 'He draweth forthe the winde out of his treasures.' Cf. also Virgil, *Aen*. i 52–9, 84–9.
5 **vnruliment**: unruliness.

Stanza 24
5 **vpbraide**: reproach.
9 **successe**: outcome.   **depended**: hung.

Stanza 25
3 **recoure**: recover.
7 **vneath**: only with difficulty.
8 **rigour**: violence.

493

26

There gan they change their sides, and new parts take;
　For *Paridell* did take to *Druons* side,
　For old despight, which now forth newly brake
　Gainst *Blandamour*, whom alwaies he enuide:
　And *Blandamour* to *Claribell* relide.
　So all afresh gan former fight renew.
　As when two Barkes, this caried with the tide,
　That with the wind, contrary courses sew,
If wind and tide doe change, their courses change anew.

27

Thenceforth they much more furiously gan fare,
　As if but then the battell had begonne,
　Ne helmets bright, ne hawberks strong did spare,
　That through the clifts the vermeil bloud out sponne,
　And all adowne their riuen sides did ronne.
　Such mortall malice, wonder was to see
　In friends profest, and so great outrage donne:
　But sooth is said, and tride in each degree,
Faint friends when they fall out, most cruell fomen bee.

28

Thus they long while continued in fight,
　Till *Scudamour*, and that same Briton maide,
　By fortune in that place did chance to light:
　Whom soone as they with wrathfull eie bewraide,
　They gan remember of the fowle vpbraide,
　The which that Britonesse had to them donne,
　In that late Turney for the snowy maide:
　Where she had them both shamefully fordonne,
And eke the famous prize of beauty from them wonne.

29

Eftsoones all burning with a fresh desire
　Of fell reuenge, in their malicious mood
　They from them selues gan turne their furious ire,
　And cruell blades yet steeming with whot bloud,
　Against those two let driue, as they were wood:
　Who wondring much at that so sodaine fit,
　Yet nought dismayd, them stoutly well withstood;
　Ne yeelded foote, ne once abacke did flit,
But being doubly smitten likewise doubly smit.

30

The warlike Dame was on her part assaid,
　Of *Claribell* and *Blandamour* attone;
　And *Paridell* and *Druon* fiercely laid
　At *Scudamour*, both his professed fone.
　Foure charged two, and two surcharged one;
　Yet did those two them selues so brauely beare,
　That the other litle gained by the lone,
　But with their owne repayed duely weare,
And vsury withall: such gaine was gotten deare.

31

Full oftentimes did *Britomart* assay
　To speake to them, and some emparlance moue;
　But they for nought their cruell hands would stay,
　Ne lend an eare to ought, that might behoue,
　As when an eager mastiffe once doth proue
　The tast of bloud of some engored beast,
　No words may rate, nor rigour him remoue
　From greedy hold of that his blouddy feast:
So litle did they hearken to her sweet beheast.

494

32

Whom when the Briton Prince a farre beheld
　With ods of so vnequall match opprest,
　His mighty heart with indignation sweld,
　And inward grudge fild his heroicke brest:
　Eftsoones him selfe he to their aide addrest,
　And thrusting fierce into the thickest preace,
　Diuided them, how euer loth to rest,
　And would them faine from battell to surceasse,
With gentle words perswading them to friendly peace.

Stanza 26
5　**relide**: rallied.
8　**sew**: follow.

Stanza 27
4　**clifts**: clefts, or chinks.　　**sponne**: spurted.
8–9　Proverbial (C. G. Smith, 1970, 303).

Stanza 28
4　**bewraide**: discovered.
8　**fordonne**: overcome.

Stanza 29
5　**wood**: mad.

Stanza 30
1–4　Britomart's two foes reject virtuous love – one is
excessive in love and the other is excessive and inconstant –
while Scudamour's foes reject love itself.　**assaid**: attacked.
attone: together, at the same time.　**laid**: struck.
5–9　For the elaborate word-play, see Orange (1958).
charged: attacked, made a pecuniary charge;　**surcharged**:
made an overwhelming attack, overcharged;　**beare**: endure
the attack, endure the financial burden;　**gained by the
lone**: gained by their blows, gained by lending money;
repayed: with blows, with money;　**duely**: fittingly,
legally due;　**vsury**: more blows than were received, interest;
gaine: additional blows received, financial gain;　**deare**:
physically and financially costly.

Stanza 31
2　**emparlance**: parleying.
5–8　Suggested by an obsolete meaning of **assay** (1): test by
tasting.　**eager**: fierce, savage.　**proue**: find out.

Stanza 32
4　**grudge**: resentment.
8　**would them ... surceasse**: desired them to desist from
battle.

33

But they so farre from peace or patience were,
　That all at once at him gan fiercely flie,
　And lay on load, as they him downe would beare;
　Like to a storme, which houers vnder skie
　Long here and there, and round about doth stie,
　At length breakes downe in raine, and haile, and sleet,
　First from one coast, till nought thereof be drie;
　And then another, till that likewise fleet;
And so from side to side till all the world it weet.

34

But now their forces greatly were decayd,
　The Prince yet being fresh vntoucht afore;
　Who them with speaches milde gan first disswade
　From such foule outrage, and them long forbore:
　Till seeing them through suffrance hartned more,
　Him selfe he bent their furies to abate,
　And layd at them so sharpely and so sore,
　That shortly them compelled to retrate,
And being brought in daunger, to relent too late.

35

But now his courage being throughly fired,
　He ment to make them know their follies prise,
　Had not those two him instantly desired
　T'asswage his wrath, and pardon their mesprise.
　At whose request he gan him selfe aduise
　To stay his hand, and of a truce to treat
　In milder tearmes, as list them to deuise:
　Mongst which the cause of their so cruell heat
He did them aske, who all that passed gan repeat.

36

And told at large how that same errant Knight,
　To weet faire *Britomart*, them late had foyled
　In open turney, and by wrongfull fight
　Both of their publicke praise had them despoyled,
　And also of their priuate loues beguyled,
　Of two full hard to read the harder theft.
　But she that wrongfull challenge soone assoyled,
　And shew'd that she had not that Lady reft,
(As they supposd) but her had to her liking left.

37

To whom the Prince thus goodly well replied;
　Certes sir Knight, ye seemen much to blame,
　To rip vp wrong, that battell once hath tried;
　Wherein the honor both of Armes ye shame,
　And eke the loue of Ladies foule defame;
　To whom the world this franchise euer yeelded,
　That of their loues choise they might freedom clame,
　And in that right should by all knights be shielded:
Gainst which me seemes this war ye wrongfully haue wielded.

38

And yet (quoth she) a greater wrong remaines:
　For I thereby my former loue haue lost,
　Whom seeking euer since with endlesse paines,
　Hath me much sorrow and much trauell cost;
　Aye me to see that gentle maide so tost.
　But *Scudamour* then sighing deepe, thus saide,
　Certes her losse ought me to sorrow most,
　Whose right she is, where euer she be straide,
Through many perils wonne, and many fortunes waide.

39

For from the first that I her loue profest,
　Vnto this houre, this present lucklesse howre,
　I neuer ioyed happinesse nor rest,
　But thus turmoild from one to other stowre,
　I wast my life, and doe my daies deuowre
　In wretched anguishe and incessant woe,
　Passing the measure of my feeble powre,
　That liuing thus, a wretch and louing so,
I neither can my loue, ne yet my life forgo.

Stanza 33
1–3　Presumably **they** excludes Britomart and Scudamour who seek pardon for the others at 35.4.
5　**stie**: rise.
7　**coast**: place, quarter.
8　**fleet**: floats, i.e. covered with water.
9　**weet**: wets.

Stanza 34
5　**suffrance**: forbearance.
9　**relent**: give way; slacken.

Stanza 35
3　**instantly**: urgently.
4　**mesprise**: scorn (of him).

Stanza 36
6　**read**: guess.
7　**that wrongfull challenge . . . assoyled**: acquitted herself of that wrongful accusation.
8–9　It is not clear on the narrative level why Britomart is accused of taking the False Florimell from them: she refused to accept her, v 20.6–9.

Stanza 37
2　**Knight**: 'Knights', sugg. Upton (1758), arguing that blame should be distributed.
6–9　Cf. i 46.8–9 where Duessa parodies Britomart's similar claim, 'Ne may loue be compeld by maisterie' (III i 25.7). Arthur's statement prepares for Scudamour's account in the next canto of how he gained Amoret. Cf. particularly x 57.5.

Stanza 38
Though Amoret is with Arthur, she is not present until he chooses to present her, as apparently S. may have intended him to do between stanzas 39 and 40.
2　**thereby**: in addition to that, i.e. to the wrong described at 37.3.　**former loue** associates Amoret with Britomart's love; **former** functions as an adverb.
8　**right**: insists upon his masculine prerogative over Amoret's 'right' (37.8).
9　**waide**: weighed or valued, and so counted dear; cf. x 1.3; or 'made way', as ii 12.8.

Stanza 39
4　**turmoild**: driven, tossed; as Amoret, 38.5.　**stowre**: disturbance.

495

40

Then good sir *Claribell* him thus bespake,
 Now were it not sir *Scudamour* to you
Dislikefull paine, so sad a taske to take,
Mote we entreat you, sith this gentle crew
Is now so well accorded all anew;
That as we ride together on our way,
Ye will recount to vs in order dew
All that aduenture, which ye did assay
For that faire Ladies loue: past perils well apay.

41

So gan the rest him likewise to require,
 But *Britomart* did him importune hard,
To take on him that paine: whose great desire
He glad to satisfie, him selfe prepar'd
To tell through what misfortune he had far'd,
In that atchieuement, as to him befell.
And all those daungers vnto them declar'd,
Which sith they cannot in this Canto well
Comprised be, I will them in another tell.

Cant. X.

*Scudamour doth his conquest tell,
 Of vertuous Amoret:
Great Venus Temple is describ'd,
 And louers life forth set.*

1

TRue he it said, what euer man it sayd,
 That loue with gall and hony doth abound,
But if the one be with the other wayd,
For euery dram of hony therein found,
A pound of gall doth ouer it redound.
That I too true by triall haue approued:
For since the day that first with deadly wound
My heart was launcht, and learned to haue loued,
I neuer ioyed howre, but still with care was moued.

2

And yet such grace is giuen them from aboue,
 That all the cares and euill which they meet,
May nought at all their setled mindes remoue,
But seeme gainst common sence to them most sweet;
As bosting in their martyrdome vnmeet.
So all that euer yet I haue endured,
I count as naught, and tread downe vnder feet
Since of my loue at length I rest assured,
That to disloyalty she will not be allured.

3

Long were to tell the trauell and long toile,
 Through which this shield of loue I late haue wonne,
And purchased this peerelesse beauties spoile,
That harder may be ended, then begonne.
But since ye so desire, your will be donne.
Then hearke ye gentle knights and Ladies free,
My hard mishaps, that ye may learne to shonne;
For though sweet loue to conquer glorious bee,
Yet is the paine thereof much greater then the fee.

4

What time the fame of this renowmed prise
 Flew first abroad, and all mens eares possest,
I hauing armes then taken, gan auise
To winne me honour by some noble gest,
And purchase me some place amongst the best.
I boldly thought (so young mens thoughts are bold)
That this same braue emprize for me did rest,
And that both shield and she whom I behold,
Might be my lucky lot; sith all by lot we hold.

Stanza 40

1   **good sir Claribell**: the 'lewd *Claribell*' (20.8) is reformed by Arthur's presence, as the others are **so well accorded** (5).
9   **past perils well apay**: perils when past please in their telling.

Stanza 41

1   **require**: request.

Canto x

Stanza 1

1–5   Cf. Thomalin's emblem to *S.C.* March: 'Of Hony and of Gaule in loue there is store: / The Honye is much, but the Gaule is more.' By VI xi 1, the odds, 1 to 96 (troy measure), have increased 1 to 1,000.   **redound**: preponderate.
6   **approued**: shown to be true.
7–9   Repeating ix 39.1–4. Cf. Amoret's state: 'from the time that *Scudamour* her bought / In perilous fight, she neuer ioyed day' (i 2.1–2).   **launcht**: pierced.   **still**: always.

Stanza 2

1–3   As Amoret proves in the house of Busirane: 'thousand charmes could not her stedfast heart remoue' (III xii 31.9).   **them**: i.e. lovers.

Stanza 3

1   **trauell**: travail.
3   He refers to Amoret who stands beside him; cf. 4.8. She is the spoil or plunder which he acquires when he pillages the Temple of Venus.   **spoile** suggests 'rape'; cf. 55.9, 58.3.
4   **That**: i.e. the **trauell**.
6   **free**: of gentle birth; also, not captive as Amoret was.
9   **fee**: reward.

Stanza 4

4   **gest**: deed.
6   **boldly . . . bold**: links Scudamour's actions to Amoret's imprisonment in the house of Busirane whose inner doors are inscribed, '*Be bold*', '*Be not too bold*' (III xi 50.4, 54.3, 8).
7   **emprize**: chivalric enterprise; see I ix 1.4*n*.

5

So on that hard aduenture forth I went,
  And to the place of perill shortly came.
  That was a temple faire and auncient,
  Which of great mother *Venus* bare the name,
  And farre renowmed through exceeding fame;
  Much more then that, which was in *Paphos* built,
  Or that in *Cyprus*, both long since this same,
  Though all the pillours of the one were guilt,
And all the others pauement were with yuory spilt.

6

And it was seated in an Island strong,
  Abounding all with delices most rare,
  And wall'd by nature gainst inuaders wrong,
  That none mote haue accesse, nor inward fare,
  But by one way, that passage did prepare.
  It was a bridge ybuilt in goodly wize,
  With curious Corbes and pendants grauen faire,
  And arched all with porches, did arize
On stately pillours, fram'd after the Doricke guize.

7

And for defence thereof, on th'other end
  There reared was a castle faire and strong,
  That warded all which in or out did wend,
  And flancked both the bridges sides along,
  Gainst all that would it faine to force or wrong.
  And therein wonned twenty valiant Knights;
  All twenty tride in warres experience long;
  Whose office was, against all manner wights
By all meanes to maintaine that castels ancient rights.

8

Before that Castle was an open plaine,
  And in the midst thereof a piller placed;
  On which this shield, of many sought in vaine,
  The shield of Loue, whose guerdon me hath graced,
  Was hangd on high with golden ribbands laced;
  And in the marble stone was written this,
  With golden letters goodly well enchaced,
  Blessed the man that well can vse his blis:
Whose euer be the shield, faire Amoret be his.

9

Which when I red, my heart did inly earne,
  And pant with hope of that aduentures hap:
  Ne stayed further newes thereof to learne,
  But with my speare vpon the shield did rap,
  That all the castle ringed with the clap.
  Streight forth issewd a Knight all arm'd to proofe,
  And brauely mounted to his most mishap:
  Who staying nought to question from aloofe,
Ran fierce at me, that fire glaunst from his horses hoofe.

10

Whom boldly I encountred (as I could)
  And by good fortune shortly him vnseated.
  Eftsoones out sprung two more of equall mould;
  But I them both with equall hap defeated:
  So all the twenty I likewise entreated,
  And left them groning there vpon the plaine.
  Then preacing to the pillour I repeated
  The read thereof for guerdon of my paine,
And taking downe the shield, with me did it retaine.

Stanza 5

2 **the place of perill**: cf. the Dragon's lair 'where all our perils dwell' (I xi 2.2) and Acrasia's bower 'where all our perils grow' (II xii 37.8).
4 **great mother Venus**: *Venus genetrix*, as III vi 40.3.
6–9 Both were well-known temples dedicated to Venus; cf. 29.8–30.9. **spilt**: covered or overlaid in mosaic.

Stanza 6

2 **delices**: delights; delicacies.
4 **fare**: passage.
5 **prepare**: provide.
7–9 **curious Corbes**: skilfully wrought corbels, i.e. projecting supports. **pendants**: supporting shafts on which the corbels rest, or which rest on the corbels. **the Doricke guize**: suggests manlike appearance (Vitruvius, *De Architecture* IV i 6), being based on the proportions of a man's body.

Stanza 7

1–5 Cf. the Bower of Bliss whose fence 'Aswell their entred guestes to keepe within, / As those vnruly beasts to hold without', is 'but weake and thin' (II xii 43.2–4). **th'other end**: i.e. across from the island. **warded**: protected. **flancked**: in the military sense, fortified to protect the sides. **faine**: desire.
6 **twenty**: as i 2.4, may allude to the number of years that Ulysses struggled to reach Penelope – cf. V vii 39 – and hence symbolize the obstacles between Scudamour and his love. Cf. Æmylia's twenty days in Lust's cave, vii 13.1.

Stanza 8

8–9 Cited by Collier (1862) as a general axiom. It is more of a threat than a blessing. To have bliss is not enough: one must know how to use it. Hieatt (1962) 509 argues that Scudamour understands the second line but in his overboldness fails to comprehend the first. Cf. Una's comment to Arthur: 'sith the heauens, and your faire handeling / Haue made you maister of the field this day, / Your fortune maister eke with gouerning' (I viii 28.1–3).

Stanza 9

1 **earne**: yearn.
2 **hap**: good fortune, success; cf. 'lot' (4.9) and 'fortune' (10.2, esp. 17.5).
6 **arm'd to proofe**: fully armed; with armour of tested power.
7 **most mishap**: greatest misfortune.

Stanza 10

1 **as I could**: as I knew how to do; or as boldly as I could.
3 **equall mould**: similar stature.
5 **entreated**: dealt with.
7–8 **repeated / The read . . . paine**: recited aloud the saying or counsel concerning the reward for my labour. He interprets **paine** as the effort to gain the shield rather than the difficulty of using it well. Cf. Britomart who ponders the mystery in mottos, III xi 50.4–6 and 54.4–5.

497

11

So forth without impediment I past,
    Till to the Bridges vtter gate I came:
    The which I found sure lockt and chained fast.
    I knockt, but no man aunswred me by name;
    I cald, but no man answerd to my clame.
    Yet I perseuer'd still to knocke and call,
    Till at the last I spide within the same,
    Where one stood peeping through a creuis small,
To whom I cald aloud, halfe angry herewithall.

12

That was to weet the Porter of the place,
    Vnto whose trust the charge thereof was lent:
    His name was *Doubt*, that had a double face,
    Th'one forward looking, th'other backeward bent,
    Therein resembling *Ianus* auncient,
    Which hath in charge the ingate of the yeare:
    And euermore his eyes about him went,
    As if some proued perill he did feare,
Or did misdoubt some ill, whose cause did not appeare.

13

On th'one side he, on th'other sate *Delay*,
    Behinde the gate, that none her might espy;
    Whose manner was all passengers to stay,
    And entertaine with her occasions sly,
    Through which some lost great hope vnheedily,
    Which neuer they recouer might againe;
    And others quite excluded forth, did ly
    Long languishing there in vnpittied paine,
And seeking often entraunce, afterwards in vaine.

14

Me when as he had priuily espide,
    Bearing the shield which I had conquerd late,
    He kend it streight, and to me opened wide.
    So in I past, and streight he closd the gate.
    But being in, *Delay* in close awaite
    Caught hold on me, and thought my steps to stay,
    Feigning full many a fond excuse to prate,
    And time to steale, the threasure of mans day,
Whose smallest minute lost, no riches render may.

15

But by no meanes my way I would forslow,
    For ought that euer she could doe or say,
    But from my lofty steede dismounting low,
    Past forth on foote, beholding all the way
    The goodly workes, and stones of rich assay,
    Cast into sundry shapes by wondrous skill,
    That like on earth no where I recken may:
    And vnderneath, the riuer rolling still
With murmure soft, that seem'd to serue the workmans will.

16

Thence forth I passed to the second gate,
    The *Gate of good desert*, whose goodly pride
    And costly frame, were long here to relate.
    The same to all stoode alwaies open wide:
    But in the Porch did euermore abide
    An hideous Giant, dreadfull to behold,
    That stopt the entraunce with his spacious stride,
    And with the terrour of his countenance bold
498 Full many did affray, that else faine enter would.

Stanza 11
2   vtter: outer.
5   clame: call. Or he announces his claim to Amoret.

Stanza 12
3   Doubt's **double face** derives from his etymology: Lat. *dubius*, moving two ways.
5–6   **Ianus . . . the ingate of the yeare**: cf. Argument to *S.C.*: 'Ianuarie . . . so called tanquam Ianua anni the gate and entraunce of the yere, or of the name of the god Ianus.'
9   **misdoubt**: suspect; playing on his name.

Stanza 13
1   On **Delay** and '*Daunger*' (17) as traditional barriers between the courtly lover and his lady, see E. B. Fowler (1921) 95–6. Cf. 43.3.
3   **manner**: custom.   **passengers**: passers-by.
4   **occasions**: pretexts.
5   **vnheedily**: heedlessly.
7   **forth**: from going forward, being shut out.
8   'The poet has made the flow of the . . . verse *languishing*, like the excluded lover' (Upton, 1758).

Stanza 14
1   **priuily**: stealthily.
3   **kend**: recognized.
5   **close awaite**: secret ambush.
9   **minute**: the smallest measure of time to the Elizabethan.

Stanza 15
1   **forslow**: delay.
5   **of rich assay**: proven of rich quality.
7   **recken**: allege.
8–9   The river obeys the bridge's architect, being tamed by his design.

Stanza 16
1   **Thence forth**: from that place onwards, rather than 'afterwards'.
6   **hideous**: huge.
7   **spacious stride**: the straddle of his legs.

17

His name was *Daunger* dreaded ouer all,
  Who day and night did watch and duely ward,
  From fearefull cowards, entrance to forstall,
  And faint-heart-fooles, whom shew of perill hard
  Could terrifie from Fortunes faire adward:
  For oftentimes faint hearts at first espiall
  Of his grim face, were from approaching scard;
  Vnworthy they of grace, whom one deniall
Excludes from fairest hope, withouten further triall.

18

Yet many doughty warriors, often tride
  In greater perils to be stout and bold,
  Durst not the sternnesse of his looke abide,
  But soone as they his countenance did behold,
  Began to faint, and feele their corage cold.
  Againe some other, that in hard assaies
  Were cowards knowne, and litle count did hold,
  Either through gifts, or guile, or such like waies,
Crept in by stouping low, or stealing of the kaies.

19

But I though meanest man of many moe,
  Yet much disdaining vnto him to lout,
  Or creepe betweene his legs, so in to goe,
  Resolu'd him to assault with manhood stout,
  And either beat him in, or driue him out.
  Eftsoones aduauncing that enchaunted shield,
  With all my might I gan to lay about:
  Which when he saw, the glaiue which he did wield
He gan forthwith t'auale, and way vnto me yield.

20

So as I entred, I did backeward looke,
  For feare of harme, that might lie hidden there;
  And loe his hindparts, whereof heed I tooke,
  Much more deformed fearefull vgly were,
  Then all his former parts did earst appere.
  For hatred, murther, treason, and despight,
  With many moe lay in ambushment there,
  Awayting to entrap the warelesse wight,
Which did not them preuent with vigilant foresight.

21

Thus hauing past all perill, I was come
  Within the compasse of that Islands space;
  The which did seeme vnto my simple doome,
  The onely pleasant and delightfull place,
  That euer troden was of footings trace.
  For all that nature by her mother wit
  Could frame in earth, and forme of substance base,
  Was there, and all that nature did omit,
Art playing second natures part, supplyed it.

22

No tree, that is of count, in greenewood growes,
  From lowest Iuniper to Ceder tall,
  No flowre in field, that daintie odour throwes,
  And deckes his branch with blossomes ouer all,
  But there was planted, or grew naturall:
  Nor sense of man so coy and curious nice,
  But there mote find to please it selfe withall;
  Nor hart could wish for any queint deuice,
But there it present was, and did fraile sense entice.

Stanza 17
1   **Daunger**: refusal, or difficult granting, of love, as **deniall** (8) indicates. In the *Romance of the Rose* 2824–3158, he is a large churl with a hideous face who stands in the path to guard the rose with his club and causes the lover to flee. Cf. Danger at III xii 11.   **ouer all**: everywhere; especially.
3   **forstall**: bar.
5   **adward**: award.

Stanza 18
1   **tride**: proven.
6   **assaies**: endeavours.
7   **litle count did hold**: held in low esteem.

Stanza 19
2   **lout**: bow.
6–9   Cf. Britomart who uses her shield and sword to pass into the house of Busirane, III xi 25.   **glaiue**: bill or halberd. **auale**: lower.

Stanza 20
8   **warelesse**: unwary.
9   Since Scudamour sees these dangers only by looking back, **vigilant foresight** seems a humorous point, as R. O. Evans (1959) 298 notes. Cf. 'true loue hath no powre / To looken backe; his eyes be fixt before' (I iii 30.7–8).   Cf. Doubt, 12.4. **preuent**: anticipate.

Stanza 21
1   **all perill**: i.e. of the second gate. Now he faces the peril of the island; cf. 36.9.
3   **doome**: judgment.
4   **onely**: one alone, 'none other' (28.3).
6–9   Nature and art are in harmony; cf. their rivalry in the Bower of Bliss, II xii 59.   **mother wit**: natural powers.

Stanza 22
1–5   The Garden of Eden contains 'everie tre pleasant to the sight, and good for meat' (Gen. 2.9); Mount Acidale, 'all trees of honour' (VI x 6.4); and the Garden of Adonis, 'euery sort of flowre' (III vi 45.1). In contrast, the Bower of Bliss contains only 'trees vpshooting hye' (II xii 58.5). Cf. Phædria's island, II vi 12.6–9.   **count**: note.   **growes**: groves or growths.
6   **so coy and curious nice**: however reserved and over-fastidious. The garden satisfies man's senses, instead of merely arousing them as does the Bower.
8   **queint**: skilfully designed, and thus beautiful.

23

In such luxurious plentie of all pleasure,
  It seem'd a second paradise to ghesse,
  So lauishly enrich with natures threasure,
  That if the happie soules, which doe possesse
  Th'Elysian fields, and liue in lasting blesse,
  Should happen this with liuing eye to see,
  They soone would loath their lesser happinesse,
  And wish to life return'd againe to bee,
That in this ioyous place they mote haue ioyance free.

24

Fresh shadowes, fit to shroud from sunny ray;
  Faire lawnds, to take the sunne in season dew;
  Sweet springs, in which a thousand Nymphs did play;
  Soft rombling brookes, that gentle slomber drew;
  High reared mounts, the lands about to vew;
  Low looking dales, disloignd from common gaze;
  Delightfull bowres, to solace louers trew;
  False Labyrinthes, fond runners eyes to daze;
All which by nature made did nature selfe amaze.

25

And all without were walkes and alleyes dight
  With diuers trees, enrang'd in euen rankes;
  And here and there were pleasant arbors pight,
  And shadie seates, and sundry flowring bankes,
  To sit and rest the walkers wearie shankes,
  And therein thousand payres of louers walkt,
  Praysing their god, and yeelding him great thankes,
  Ne euer ought but of their true loues talkt,
Ne euer for rebuke or blame of any balkt.

26

All these together by themselues did sport
  Their spotlesse pleasures, and sweet loues content.
  But farre away from these, another sort
  Of louers lincked in true harts consent;
  Which loued not as these, for like intent,
  But on chast vertue grounded their desire,
  Farre from all fraud, or fayned blandishment;
  Which in their spirits kindling zealous fire,
Braue thoughts and noble deedes did euermore aspire.

Stanza 23
1   **luxurious**: extravagant; cf. Eden's 'enormous bliss',
Milton, *P.L.* v 297.
2   **to ghesse**: i.e. one might suppose it to be.
4–9   **Elysian fields**: 'deuised of Poetes to be a place of
pleasure like Paradise, where the happye soules doe rest in
peace and eternal happynesse' (E.K.'s gloss to *S.C.* Nov. 179).
A common piece of mythological lore: Cooper (1565) describes
the *Elysii campi* as 'a place of pleasure, where poetes did
suppose the soules of good men to dwell'.
4   **happie**: blessed.
9   **ioyance**: delight.

Stanza 24
1   **Fresh**: cool, refreshing.
2   **lawnds**: launds, open spaces between woods.
6   **disloignd**: remote.
7   **solace**: delight, please.
8   **Labyrinthes**: in landscape gardening a maze formed by
paths bordered by high hedges.   **False**: deceiving. Cf.
Du Bartas's account of Adam's walk through Eden: 'Musing,
anon through crooked Walks he wanders, / Round-winding
rings, and intricate Meanders, / False-guiding paths, doubtfull
beguiling strays, / And right-wrong errors of an end-less Maze'
(*Divine Weekes*, II i 1 p. 86).   **fond**: both foolish and loving.

Stanza 25
1   **dight**: adorned.
4   **sundry**: 'sunny', sugg. Upton (1758), 'which the opposition and sense requires'; cf. 24.1–2.
6–9   The *locus amoenus* was considered by Servius as the
place of love-making; see Curtius (1953) 192.
9   **balkt**: stopped or ceased talking. The lovers talked freely
of their loues, never quibbling for fear of rebuke or blame. Cf.
their 'spotlesse' pleasures (26.2) enjoyed 'free from feare and
gealosye' (28.5). The absence of shame marks the golden age in
Tasso, *Aminta*; see viii 30.8–9n.

Stanza 26
1   **by themselues**: i.e. apart from the others.
3   **sort**: company; kind.
4   **consent**: harmony.
8   **Which**: i.e. their desire.
9   On love as the source of all virtuous action, see III i
49.8–9n.   **aspire**: inspire.

27

Such were great *Hercules,* and *Hylas* deare;
  Trew *Ionathan,* and *Dauid* trustie tryde;
  Stout *Theseus,* and *Pirithous* his feare;
  Pylades and *Orestes* by his syde;
  Myld *Titus* and *Gesippus* without pryde;
  Damon and *Pythias* whom death could not seuer:
  All these and all that euer had bene tyde
  In bands of friendship, there did liue for euer,
Whose liues although decay'd, yet loues decayed neuer.

28

Which when as I, that neuer tasted blis,
  Nor happie howre, beheld with gazefull eye,
  I thought there was none other heauen then this;
  And gan their endlesse happinesse enuye,
  That being free from feare and gealosye,
  Might frankely there their loues desire possesse;
  Whilest I through paines and perlous ieopardie,
  Was forst to seeke my lifes deare patronesse:
Much dearer be the things,which come through hard distresse.

29

Yet all those sights, and all that else I saw,
  Might not my steps withhold, but that forthright
  Vnto that purposd place I did me draw,
  Where as my loue was lodged day and night:
  The temple of great *Venus,* that is hight
  The Queene of beautie, and of loue the mother,
  There worshipped of euery liuing wight;
  Whose goodly workmanship farre past all other
That euer were on earth, all were they set together.

30

Not that same famous Temple of *Diane,*
  Whose hight all *Ephesus* did ouersee,
  And which all *Asia* sought with vowes prophane,
  One of the worlds seuen wonders sayd to bee,
  Might match with this by many a degree:
  Nor that, which that wise King of *Iurie* framed,
  With endlesse cost, to be th'Almighties see;
  Nor all that else through all the world is named
To all the heathen Gods, might like to this be clamed.

31

I much admyring that so goodly frame,
  Vnto the porch approcht, which open stood;
  But therein sate an amiable Dame,
  That seem'd to be of very sober mood,
  And in her semblant shewed great womanhood:
  Strange was her tyre; for on her head a crowne
  She wore much like vnto a Danisk hood,
  Poudred with pearle and stone, and all her gowne
Enwouen was with gold, that raught full low a downe.

Stanza 27

This list and the description of male lovers are broadly traditional except for the epithets applied to **Titus and Gesippus.**

Four of the five pairs of friends are found in Lyly, *Euphues*
(*Works* i 198). S. differs from the usual catalogues by adding
the biblical pair. The last three couples are stressed because
they were willing to die for each other.
1   See III xii 7.5–9.   **Hylas**] *Hyllus 1596,* who is Hercules's
son. Their names are easily confused, especially when they
appear together, as in Cooper's (1565) account of Hylas; see
Starnes and Talbert (1955) 59–60.
2   See 1 Sam. 18.3f.   **trustie**: faithfully.
3   **Theseus** aided **Pirithous** in his battle against the
Centaurs and later descended into hell to help him carry off
Persephone.   **feare**: companion.
4   **Pylades**: 'A gentillman of Phocæa, whiche was so faithful
a friend to Orestes (with whom he kept companie whyles he
was madde) that he would never forsake him, but folowed him
into the countrey called *Taurica,* where strangers were sacrificed
vnto Diana, where Orestes beyng apprehended, when he shuld
be slaine, Pylades would needes die for hym, that he might
escape' (Cooper).
5   **Gesippus** gave **Titus** his betrothed when he learned that
his friend loved her. Later when he was under penalty of
death, he was saved by Titus who offered his own life as a
substitute.   **Myld**: kind, gracious.
6   'When Dionyse . . . had condemned the one of them to
death . . . the other became suertie for him on this condition,
that if his frinde retourned not he would be content to suffer
death for him' (Cooper). When the friend returned on the
appointed day, both were pardoned.
9   Cf. xi 16.8–9.

Stanza 28

4–6   Cf. the love in the Garden of Adonis: 'Without fell
rancor, or fond gealosie, / Franckly each paramour his leman
knowes' (III vi 41.6–7). There '*Time* their troubler is'; here
lovers enjoy **endlesse happinesse.** Later **feare** possesses
Amoret, **gealosye** Scudamour.
8   Amoret as patron of life suggests Arthur's relationship to
the Red Cross Knight (I ix 17.6) and to Guyon (II viii 55.4).
9   **dearer**: more precious.

Stanza 29

5–6   **Venus . . . / The Queene of beautie**: cf. I i 48.1,
IV v 26.4.

Stanza 30

1–4   'Ephesus, a noble auncient citie in Asia the lesse. . . . In
this citie was the famous temple of Diana, numbred among the
vii wonders of the worlde, edified by all Asia' (Cooper, 1565);
cf. Acts 19.27 on 'the temple of the great goddesse Diana'
whose magnificence 'all Asia and the worlde worshippeth'.
6–7   The Temple of Jerusalem built by Solomon, King of
the Jews, at great cost; see 1 Kings 6.   **see**: dwelling-place.
9   **clamed**: called; proclaimed.

Stanza 31

3   **amiable**: friendly (Fr. *amiable*); also, as *aimable,* worthy
to be loved, 'loveable' (Cotgrave, 1611).
5   **semblant**: demeanour.
6   **tyre**: head-dress.
7   **Danisk**: Danish, combining 'Dansk' and 'Danish'.
Osgood's suggestion, *Var.* iv 226, that the costume resembles
the Queen's is supported by a number of portraits in Strong
(1963): see plates 28, 33 in which the crown descends in a hood.

32

On either side of her, two young men stood,
　　Both strongly arm'd, as fearing one another;
　　Yet were they brethren both of halfe the blood,
　　Begotten by two fathers of one mother,
　　Though of contrarie natures each to other:
　　The one of them hight *Loue*, the other *Hate*,
　　Hate was the elder, *Loue* the younger brother;
　　Yet was the younger stronger in his state
Then th'elder, and him maystred still in all debate.

33

Nathlesse that Dame so well them tempred both,
　　That she them forced hand to ioyne in hand,
　　Albe that *Hatred* was thereto full loth,
　　And turn'd his face away, as he did stand,
　　Vnwilling to behold that louely band.
　　Yet she was of such grace and vertuous might,
　　That her commaundment he could not withstand,
　　But bit his lip for felonous despight,
And gnasht his yron tuskes at that displeasing sight.

34

Concord she cleeped was in common reed,
　　Mother of blessed *Peace*, and *Friendship* trew;
　　They both her twins, both borne of heauenly seed,
　　And she her selfe likewise diuinely grew;
　　The which right well her workes diuine did shew:
　　For strength, and wealth, and happinesse she lends,
　　And strife, and warre, and anger does subdew:
　　Of litle much, of foes she maketh frends,
And to afflicted minds sweet rest and quiet sends.

35

By her the heauen is in his course contained,
　　And all the world in state vnmoued stands,
　　As their Almightie maker first ordained,
　　And bound them with inuiolable bands;
　　Else would the waters ouerflow the lands,
　　And fire deuoure the ayre, and hell them quight,
　　But that she holds them with her blessed hands.
　　She is the nourse of pleasure and delight,
And vnto *Venus* grace the gate doth open right.

36

By her I entring halfe dismayed was,
　　But she in gentle wise me entertayned,
　　And twixt her selfe and *Loue* did let me pas;
　　But *Hatred* would my entrance haue restrayned,
　　And with his club me threatned to haue brayned,
　　Had not the Ladie with her powrefull speach
　　Him from his wicked will vneath refrayned;
　　And th'other eke his malice did empeach,
Till I was throughly past the perill of his reach.

37

Into the inmost Temple thus I came,
　　Which fuming all with frankensence I found,
　　And odours rising from the altars flame.
　　Vpon an hundred marble pillors round
　　The roofe vp high was reared from the ground,
　　All deckt with crownes, and chaynes, and girlands gay,
　　And thousand pretious gifts worth many a pound,
　　The which sad louers for their vowes did pay;
And all the ground was strow'd with flowres, as fresh as May.

Stanza 32
4–5　Wind (1967) 211 interprets the allegory as the 'infolding' of opposites into one. Fowler (1964) 27 *n*1 adds that the one is itself 'unfolded' into two, Peace and Friendship (34.2). On *discordia concors*, see Roche (1964) 17, 23 *et passim*; see also Berger (1968a).
7–9　In *H.L.* 57–91, S. relates how Love at his birth reduced chaos to cosmos: 'Ayre hated earth, and water hated fyre, / Till Loue relented their rebellious yre.'　**still**: always.

Stanza 33
1　**tempred**: governed.
5　**louely band**: loving bond. Their hands join where Concord sits.
7　**commaundment**: authority.
8　**felonous**: fierce; cruel.

Stanza 34
1–2　At II ii 31.1–2, Medina extols 'louely concord, and most sacred peace / [which] Doth nourish vertue, and fast friendship breeds'.　**reed**: speech.
6　**wealth**: well-being.

Stanza 35
On the cosmological theory behind Concord's role in reconciling the warring elements, see Tuve (1970) 49–63. In the medieval tradition, Concord's role is usually given to Nature. Upton (1758) notes that S. imitates Chaucer's rendering of Boethius (*De Consol. Phil.* II metre 8) in *Knight's Tale* 2987–93 and *Troilus and Criseyde* iii 1751–64.
2　**vnmoued**: steadfast.
6　**. . . and hell them quight**: and hell requite or retaliate against the waters and fire by overcoming them in turn, so reducing all to original chaos. Alternatively, **hell** may be an obsolete form of 'hele', to conceal, cover; hence, 'water and fire would entirely cover land and air'. Cf. 'vnhele' (II xii 64.8, IV v 10.7). The *Var.* editors, following Warton, suggest that, if we understand **deuoure** after **hell**, **hell** is a substantive; hence, 'and hell devour them (land, air and water) entirely'. Rowlands (1605) 193 explains 'helled over' as 'hidden or covered in low obscuritie'.
7　Berger (1968a) 3 notes the ambiguous syntax that shifts power from the Almighty's **inuiolable bands** (4), which suggests determinism, to Concord's **blessed hands**, which suggests 'a more precarious and ongoing effort of control'.
9　**Venus grace**: those to whom Venus offers the grace of true love.

Stanza 36
2　**entertayned**: received.
7–8　Concord restrains his power to act, Love his desire. **vneath refrayned**: restrained with difficulty.　**empeach**: prevent.

Stanza 37
8　**sad**: also steadfast, constant; cf. III xi 45.9.

38

An hundred Altars round about were set,
   All flaming with their sacrifices fire,
   That with the steme thereof the Temple swet,
   Which rould in clouds to heauen did aspire,
   And in them bore true louers vowes entire:
   And eke an hundred brasen caudrons bright,
   To bath in ioy and amorous desire,
   Euery of which was to a damzell hight;
For all the Priests were damzels, in soft linnen dight.

39

Right in the midst the Goddesse selfe did stand
   Vpon an altar of some costly masse,
   Whose substance was vneath to vnderstand:
   For neither pretious stone, nor durefull brasse,
   Nor shining gold, nor mouldring clay it was;
   But much more rare and pretious to esteeme,
   Pure in aspect, and like to christall glasse,
   Yet glasse was not, if one did rightly deeme,
But being faire and brickle, likest glasse did seeme.

40

But it in shape and beautie did excell
   All other Idoles, which the heathen adore,
   Farre passing that, which by surpassing skill
   Phidias did make in *Paphos* Isle of yore,
   With which that wretched Greeke, that life forlore,
   Did fall in loue: yet this much fairer shined,
   But couered with a slender veile afore;
   And both her feete and legs together twyned
Were with a snake, whose head and tail were fast combyned.

41

The cause why she was couered with a vele,
   Was hard to know, for that her Priests the same
   From peoples knowledge labour'd to concele.
   But sooth it was not sure for womanish shame,
   Nor any blemish, which the worke mote blame;
   But for, they say, she hath both kinds in one,
   Both male and female, both vnder one name:
   She syre and mother is her selfe alone,
Begets and eke conceiues, ne needeth other none.

42

And all about her necke and shoulders flew
   A flocke of litle loues, and sports, and ioyes,
   With nimble wings of gold and purple hew;
   Whose shapes seem'd not like to terrestriall boyes,
   But like to Angels playing heauenly toyes;
   The whilest their eldest brother was away,
   Cupid their eldest brother; he enioyes
   The wide kingdome of loue with Lordly sway,
And to his law compels all creatures to obay.

Stanza 38

1–4   Cf. the Temple of Venus in Virgil, *Aen.* i 416–7, with its hundred altars which steam with Sabaean incense and are fragrant with garlands ever fresh.

5   **entire**: unbroken; earnest.

6   **caudrons**: cauldrons, baths; cf. the ten cauldrons and

the hundred basins in the Temple of Solomon (2 Chron. 4.6, 8).

8   **Euery**: each.   **hight**: assigned.

Stanza 39

3–9   **Whose substance**: i.e. mass, referring to the altar or possibly to the statue.   **vneath to vnderstand**: difficult to be comprehended; in addition, **vnderstand** may involve the etymological sense, 'stand under'. Hence, 'it was difficult to know how the sub-stance could prop up the statue'. Lewis (1967) 41 suggests that the substance may be symbolic of beauty. In a note to Lewis's suggestion, Fowler relates the glass-like substance to Merlin's 'glassie globe' which is compared to the magic tower of glass built by Ptolemy for his love but destroyed by him when she was false, III ii 20. 'In each case the glass symbolizes the conditional durability and complete-ness of the marriage bond. . . . In other words, the sexual love of the Temple of Venus is based upon a faithful personal relation.' Yet S. is careful to observe that the substance is not glass. See II x 73.7–9n. It may be crystal, as the ancient statues described by Lynche (1599) Ciᵛ.

4   **durefull**: durable, enduring.

6   **to esteeme**: to be valued.

7   **Pure**: clear, transparent. S. seems to associate rich substance with transparency; cf. II xii 60.2–4.

Stanza 40

Our vision of the Idol moves upward from the altar to the feet and legs.

2   **Idoles**: images, statues; suggesting objects of idolatry.

3–6   A similar story is told by Pliny, *Nat. Hist.* xxxvi 21, of a statue of Venus by Praxiteles.   **Phidias**: 'an excellent woorkeman in makyng great ymages of golde or Ivorie' (Cooper, 1565). His statues of Venus are mentioned by Pliny xxxvi 15–6.

7–9   Fowler (1964) 164 sees an allusion to the image of Janus in Macrobius, *Saturnalia* I ix 11, which symbolizes the annual cycle of generation: 'A serpent coiled and swallowing its own tail [is] a visible image of the universe which feeds on itself and returns to itself again.' Fowler relates this serpent to the combined serpents of the caduceus (see iii 42.2–4) as they suggest the union of the male and female genitals. Cf. Scudamour and Amoret embracing as 'that faire *Hermaphrodite*' (III xii 46.2, *1590*).   **slender**: thin, to allow the statue to shine; long, to cover her completely.

Stanza 41

4   **not sure**: to be sure not.

6–9   **kinds**: sexes. As she is 'Great God of men and women' (47.7). As *Venus Hermaphroditus*, she includes both male (Hermes) and female (Aphrodite) in one name: see Wind (1967) 211f. Cf. Nature, VII vii 5.5–9. Cf. *Col.* 801–2: 'For *Venus* selfe doth soly couples seeme, / Both male and female, through commixture ioynd.' She is veiled to indicate that her state is a mystery veiled from profane eyes. See III xii 46 (*1590*)n.

Stanza 42

1–5   **litle loues**: suggests Amor-etta; see III vi 28.8–9. **sports**: amorous play; personified as *amorini* who attend Venus. **gold and purple**: the colours of sovereignty, as I vii 16.3. Cf. Cupid's wings 'of purple and blewe' (*S.C.* Mar. 33). **purple**: Ovid's *purpurea*, shining, crimson.   **toyes**: sports, games.

43

And all about her altar scattered lay
  Great sorts of louers piteously complayning,
  Some of their losse, some of their loues delay,
  Some of their pride, some paragons disdayning,
  Some fearing fraud, some fraudulently fayning,
  As euery one had cause of good or ill.
  Amongst the rest some one through loues constrayning,
  Tormented sore, could not containe it still,
But thus brake forth, that all the temple it did fill.

44

Great *Venus*, Queene of beautie and of grace,
  The ioy of Gods and men, that vnder skie
  Doest fayrest shine, and most adorne thy place,
  That with thy smyling looke doest pacifie
  The raging seas, and makst the stormes to flie;
  Thee goddesse, thee the winds, the clouds doe feare,
  And when thou spredst thy mantle forth on hie,
  The waters play and pleasant lands appeare,
And heauens laugh, and al the world shews ioyous cheare.

45

Then doth the dædale earth throw forth to thee
  Out of her fruitfull lap aboundant flowres,
  And then all liuing wights, soone as they see
  The spring breake forth out of his lusty bowres,
  They all doe learne to play the Paramours;
  First doe the merry birds, thy prety pages
  Priuily pricked with thy lustfull powres,
  Chirpe loud to thee out of their leauy cages,
And thee their mother call to coole their kindly rages.

46

Then doe the saluage beasts begin to play
  Their pleasant friskes, and loath their wonted food;
  The Lyons rore, the Tygres loudly bray,
  The raging Buls rebellow through the wood,
  And breaking forth, dare tempt the deepest flood,
  To come where thou doest draw them with desire:
  So all things else, that nourish vitall blood,
  Soone as with fury thou doest them inspire,
In generation seeke to quench their inward fire.

47

So all the world by thee at first was made,
  And dayly yet thou doest the same repayre:
  Ne ought on earth that merry is and glad,
  Ne ought on earth that louely is and fayre,
  But thou the same for pleasure didst prepayre.
  Thou art the root of all that ioyous is,
  Great God of men and women, queene of th'ayre,
  Mother of laughter, and welspring of blisse,
O graunt that of my loue at last I may not misse.

48

So did he say: but I with murmure soft,
  That none might heare the sorrow of my hart,
  Yet inly groning deepe and sighing oft,
  Besought her to graunt ease vnto my smart,
  And to my wound her gratious help impart.
  Whilest thus I spake, behold with happy eye
  I spyde, where at the Idoles feet apart
  A beuie of fayre damzels close did lye,
Wayting when as the Antheme should be sung on hye.

504

Stanza 43

2   **sorts**: companies.
4   **of their pride . . .**: of their mistresses' pride and of their disdain.

Stanzas 44–47

A paraphrase of Lucretius's invocation to Venus at the beginning of *De Rerum Natura*. Some details are influenced by Virgil's account of spring in *Georg*. ii 323–38, and of the power of love, iii 242–54.

Stanza 44

2   **vnder skie**: beneath the highest heaven, within the universe.
4   Cf. 'thy sweete smyling mother from aboue' (Proem 5.7).

Stanza 45

1   **dædale**: fruitful, fertile, Lucretius's *daedala tellus*. From Daedalus, the artificer, the term suggests 'skilful in invention or creation'; see III Proem 2.4.
4   **breake forth**: such bursting energy is expressed by the complaining lover (43.9) and the animals (46.5).   **lusty**: joyful; delightful; lustful; vigorous.
5   **play**: sport amorously; cf. 46.1.
7   **Priuily pricked**: secretly urged or driven; as Chaucer's singing birds, 'so priketh hem nature'.
9   **kindly rages**: natural desire or lust.

Stanza 46

5   **tempt**: risk the perils of.

Stanza 47

1–2   Not Lucretius but Comes (1616) IV xiii p. 212: *Venerem mundum procreasse et conseruare*; noted Lotspeich (1932) 116. Cf. the Garden of Adonis from which creatures enter the world 'it to replenish more' (III vi 36.2). Lewis (1967) 43–4 notes the two aspects of Venus: in 2, the planetary deity who arouses the amorousness which replenishes the world, and in 1, the 'Paradigma' of creation, the eternal pattern of beauty, described by Plato, *Timaeus* xxix.
7–8   **queene of th'ayre, / Mother of laughter**: from Comes.

Stanza 48

1   **murmure**: complaint.
2   Cf. the complaints that fill the temple, 43.9.
7–8   **apart**: i.e. to one side, although still close to her; or **close** may suggest close together; or hidden, being under her protection.

49

The first of them did seeme of ryper yeares,
  And grauer countenance then all the rest;
  Yet all the rest were eke her equall peares,
  Yet vnto her obayed all the best.
  Her name was *Womanhood*, that she exprest
  By her sad semblant and demeanure wyse:
  For stedfast still her eyes did fixed rest,
  Ne rov'd at randon after gazers guyse,
Whose luring baytes oftimes doe heedlesse harts entyse.

50

And next to her sate goodly *Shamefastnesse*,
  Ne euer durst her eyes from ground vpreare,
  Ne euer once did looke vp from her desse,
  As if some blame of euill she did feare,
  That in her cheekes made roses oft appeare:
  And her against sweet *Cherefulnesse* was placed,
  Whose eyes like twinkling stars in euening cleare,
  Were deckt with smyles, that all sad humors chaced,
And darted forth delights, the which her goodly graced.

51

And next to her sate sober *Modestie*,
  Holding her hand vpon her gentle hart;
  And her against sate comely *Curtesie*,
  That vnto euery person knew her part;
  And her before was seated ouerthwart
  Soft *Silence*, and submisse *Obedience*,
  Both linckt together neuer to dispart,
  Both gifts of God not gotten but from thence,
Both girlonds of his Saints against their foes offence.

Stanza 49
4   **her obayed all the best**: gave her the best obedience.
6   **sad semblant**: grave countenance.
8   **guyse**: fashion.

Stanzas 50–51
The seating arrangement is carefully spelled out but confusing because of ambiguous reference. **And next to her** (50.1) places **Shamefastnesse** beside **Womanhood** (49.5); **her against** (6): i.e. directly opposite *Shamefastnesse* is **Cherefulnesse**, the contrary and balancing state. **And next to her** (51.1): i.e. next to *Shamefastnesse* comes **Modestie** who shares her sobriety. **And her against** (3): as *Curtesie* is *Modestie's* balancing virtue. **Silence** and **Obedience** are seated **ouerthwart** (5): i.e. across from *Curtesie* but to the side. As virtues essential to marriage, the climax is **Obedience**, as in the marriage vow.

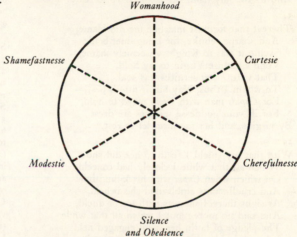

This seating places **Silence** and **Obedience** beside **Modestie** and across from **Womanhood**, and **Curtesie** next to **Cherefulnesse**. **Womanhood** appears between **Shamefastnesse** and **Curtesie**; cf. the striving of courtesy and modesty in Belphœbe's chastity, III v 55.

Stanza 50
1–5   **Shamefastnesse** appears in the Castle of Alma to express the essential characteristic of the Knight of Temperance, II ix 40–43.   **desse**: dais.

Stanza 51
4   **knew her part**: knew how to behave with the respect due each person, which is the virtue of Civility; see VI ii 1.6–7n. Cf. Reverence who 'knew his good to all of each degree' (I x 7.5).
6   **submisse**: submissive.
7   **dispart**: separate.
9   **girlonds**: 'Gardians', sugg. Church (1758); 'guerdons', sugg. Collier (1862), from **gifts** (8). Yet **girlonds** keeps the sense of crowning: these virtues are the means – and the token – of victory, against the attack of foes.

52

Thus sate they all a round in seemely rate:
  And in the midst of them a goodly mayd,
  Euen in the lap of *Womanhood* there sate,
  The which was all in lilly white arayd,
  With siluer streames amongst the linnen stray'd;
  Like to the Morne, when first her shyning face
  Hath to the gloomy world it selfe bewray'd,
  That same was fayrest *Amoret* in place,
Shyning with beauties light, and heauenly vertues grace.

53

Whom soone as I beheld, my hart gan throb,
  And wade in doubt, what best were to be donne:
  For sacrilege me seem'd the Church to rob,
  And folly seem'd to leaue the thing vndonne,
  Which with so strong attempt I had begonne.
  Tho shaking off all doubt and shamefast feare,
  Which Ladies loue I heard had neuer wonne
  Mongst men of worth, I to her stepped neare,
And by the lilly hand her labour'd vp to reare.

54

Thereat that formost matrone me did blame,
  And sharpe rebuke, for being ouer bold;
  Saying it was to Knight vnseemely shame,
  Vpon a recluse Virgin to lay hold,
  That vnto *Venus* seruices was sold.
  To whom I thus, Nay but it fitteth best,
  For *Cupids* man with *Venus* mayd to hold,
  For ill your goddesse seruices are drest
By virgins, and her sacrifices let to rest.

55

With that my shield I forth to her did show,
  Which all that while I closely had conceld;
  On which when *Cupid* with his killing bow
  And cruell shafts emblazond she beheld,
  At sight thereof she was with terror queld,
  And said no more: but I which all that while
  The pledge of faith, her hand engaged held,
  Like warie Hynd within the weedie soyle,
For no intreatie would forgoe so glorious spoyle.

56

And euermore vpon the Goddesse face
  Mine eye was fixt, for feare of her offence,
  Whom when I saw with amiable grace
  To laugh at me, and fauour my pretence,
  I was emboldned with more confidence,
  And nought for nicenesse nor for enuy sparing,
  In presence of them all forth led her thence,
  All looking on, and like astonisht staring,
Yet to lay hand on her, not one of all them daring.

Stanza 52

1 **sate they . . . rate**: they sat in a circle in fitting manner. Surrounded by these virtues, **Amoret** is 'vertuous Amoret' (Arg.).
4–5 **lilly white**: denoting her virginity, as also 53.9.
linnen declares that she is one of Venus's 'Priests' (38.9).
7 **bewray'd**: revealed, with a pun on 'ray'.
8 **in place**: no mere rhyming tag, as the disastrous sequel shows.
9 Cf. Venus as 'Queene of beautie and of grace' (44.1). Amoret shines as does the statue, 40.6.

Stanza 53

3 **sacrilege**: the purloining of sacred objects.
6–8 Records his earlier victory over Doubt, Delay and Daunger, and over Amoret's guardian virtues. **shamefast**: bashful; perhaps 'shameful'. He acts out the proverb: 'Faint heart never won fair lady' (C. G. Smith, 1970, 233).
9 As Orpheus rescues Eurydice; see 58.4–5*n*.

Stanza 54

1 **Thereat**: because of that.
2 Cf. the motto over the door to the inmost room of the house of Busirane: '*Be not too bold*' (III xi 54.8). Britomart must ignore that motto in order to release Amoret because Scudamour is **ouer bold** in first seizing her.
5 **sold**: given; dedicated.
6–9 His argument is that Amoret should become a sacrifice to love rather than remain one who tends the 'sacrifices fire' (38.2). As Warton first observed, his claim parallels Leander's in Musaeus, *Hero and Leander*. Leander seizes Hero's hand and embraces her, and when she protests that she is a priest of Venus, he replies: 'As Priest of Venus, practice Venus' rites. / Come, and instruct me in her bed's-delights. / It fits not you, a virgin, to vow aids / To Venus' service; Venus Loves no maids' (trans. Chapman, 1616). **drest**: ordered, performed.
let to rest: allowed to cease.

Stanza 55

5 **with terror queld**: hence Amoret's paralysing fear under Busirane's power.
6–7 Indicates the pledging of his hand in marriage.
8–9 **warie**: 'wearie', sugg. Upton (1758); i.e. 'her hand was held in mine as firmly as a weary hind keeps to its refuge'. Amoret is the **spoyle** whom the hunter, Scudamour, has ambushed. Cf. *Amor.* lxvii. Yet he is also the ambushed deer for she is his refuge. **soyle**: a pool of water in which the hunted animal seeks refuge. The same comparison is used at their reunion, III xii 44.7–8 (*1590*).

Stanza 56

2 **offence**: displeasure.
3 **amiable**: see 31.3*n*.
4 Cf. her 'smyling looke' (44.4); cf. Nature's encouragement of Arthur, I ix 12.8–9. **at me**: i.e. on me; as I ix 12.9.
pretence: claim; asserting a right.
6 **nought . . . enuy**: i.e. neither for modesty in Amoret nor for envy in the others.
8 **like**: equally; all alike.

57

She often prayd, and often me besought,
  Sometime with tender teares to let her goe,
  Sometime with witching smyles: but yet for nought,
  That euer she to me could say or doe,
  Could she her wished freedome fro me wooe;
  But forth I led her through the Temple gate,
  By which I hardly past with much adoe:
  But that same Ladie which me friended late
In entrance, did me also friend in my retrate.

58

No lesse did *Daunger* threaten me with dread,
  When as he saw me, maugre all his powre,
  That glorious spoyle of beautie with me lead,
  Then *Cerberus*, when *Orpheus* did recoure
  His Leman from the Stygian Princes boure.
  But euermore my shield did me defend,
  Against the storme of euery dreadfull stoure:
  Thus safely with my loue I thence did wend.
So ended he his tale, where I this Canto end.

Cant. XI.

Marinells former wound is heald,
he comes to Proteus hall,
Where Thames doth the Medway wedd,
and feasts the Sea-gods all.

1

BVt ah for pittie that I haue thus long
  Left a fayre Ladie languishing in payne:
  Now well away, that I haue doen such wrong,
  To let faire *Florimell* in bands remayne,
  In bands of loue, and in sad thraldomes chayne;
  From which vnlesse some heauenly powre her free
  By miracle, not yet appearing playne,
  She lenger yet is like captiu'd to bee:
That euen to thinke thereof, it inly pitties mee.

2

Here neede you to remember, how erewhile
  Vnlouely *Proteus*, missing to his mind
  That Virgins loue to win by wit or wile,
  Her threw into a dongeon deepe and blind,
  And there in chaynes her cruelly did bind,
  In hope thereby her to his bent to draw:
  For when as neither gifts nor graces kind
  Her constant mind could moue at all he saw,
He thought her to compell by crueltie and awe.

3

Deepe in the bottome of an huge great rocke
  The dongeon was, in which her bound he left,
  That neither yron barres, nor brasen locke
  Did neede to gard from force, or secret theft
  Of all her louers, which would her haue reft.
  For wall'd it was with waues, which rag'd and ror'd
  As they the cliffe in peeces would haue cleft;
  Besides ten thousand monsters foule abhor'd
Did waite about it, gaping griesly all begor'd.

Stanza 57
5   **freedome**: see ix 37.6–9*n*.
7–9   **By which I hardly past . . .**: i.e. by which I would
have passed only with much difficulty had not that same Lady,
etc.

Stanza 58
3   Cf. 'this peerelesse beauties spoile' (3.3); the phrase is
repeated here to round out his story.
4–5   When **Orpheus** descended into hell to recover
Eurydice, he was opposed by **Cerberus**, the guardian of hell.
S. may refer to the less common version of the story in which
Orpheus recovered Eurydice; but the subsequent history of the
courtship parallels the tragic version. Orpheus lost Eurydice
immediately, as Scudamour loses Amoret, because he was
overcome by desire. On S.'s use of the Orpheus myth, see
Cain (1972) 36–7. The myth relates also to Amoret who is
wounded by love. Eurydice died on her wedding-day by a
wound in her heel, as Amoret was stolen on her wedding-day.
'By wounding in the hele is meant lustfull loue' (E.K.'s gloss
to *S.C.* March 97).   **recoure**: recover.
7   **stoure**: assault.

Canto xi

Stanza 1
S. continues from his last words about her imprisonment: 'It
yrkes me, leaue thee in this wofull state' (III viii 43.8).
5   **bands of loue**: bonds of love for Marinell.   **chayne**:
Proteus's love for her.
8   **like**: likely.

Stanza 2
2   **Vnlouely**: ugly; cf. 'his grim sight' (III viii 32.8);
possibly, 'unloved'.   **missing**: failing.
4   **blind**: dark.
6   **bent**: purpose; with the sense from archery (suggested by
draw): bending.
9   **awe**: behaviour that inspires fear.

Stanza 3
9   **begor'd**: stained with gore.

507

4

And in the midst thereof did horror dwell,
   And darkenesse dredd, that neuer viewed day,
   Like to the balefull house of lowest hell,
   In which old *Styx* her aged bones alway,
   Old *Styx* the Grandame of the Gods, doth lay.
   There did this lucklesse mayd seuen months abide,
   Ne euer euening saw, ne mornings ray,
   Ne euer from the day the night descride,
But thought it all one night, that did no houres diuide.

5

And all this was for loue of *Marinell*,
   Who her despysd (ah who would her despyse?)
   And wemens loue did from his hart expell,
   And all those ioyes that weake mankind entyse.
   Nathlesse his pride full dearely he did pryse;
   For of a womans hand it was ywroke,
   That of the wound he yet in languor lyes,
   Ne can be cured of that cruell stroke
Which *Britomart* him gaue, when he did her prouoke.

6

Yet farre and neare the Nymph his mother sought,
   And many salues did to his sore applie,
   And many herbes did vse.   But when as nought
   She saw could ease his rankling maladie,
   At last to *Tryphon* she for helpe did hie,
   (This *Tryphon* is the seagods surgeon hight)
   Whom she besought to find some remedie:
   And for his paines a whistle him behight
That of a fishes shell was wrought with rare delight.

7

So well that Leach did hearke to her request,
   And did so well employ his carefull paine,
   That in short space his hurts he had redrest,
   And him restor'd to healthfull state againe:
   In which he long time after did remaine
   There with the Nymph his mother, like her thrall;
   Who sore against his will did him retaine,
   For feare of perill, which to him mote fall,
Through his too ventrous prowesse proued ouer all.

8

It fortun'd then, a solemne feast was there
   To all the Sea-gods and their fruitfull seede,
   In honour of the spousalls, which then were
   Betwixt the *Medway* and the *Thames* agreed.
   Long had the *Thames* (as we in records reed)
   Before that day her wooed to his bed;
   But the proud Nymph would for no worldly meed,
   Nor no entreatie to his loue be led;
Till now at last relenting, she to him was wed.

Busirane. As the passage of time that leads to renewal, see III xi 10.8*n*. Cf. Arthur's sword dipped into the Styx seven times: see II viii 20.7–9*n*. J. C. Smith notes that some *1596* copies read 'three', and cites the change as a correction at press. The *Var.* editors note that all their copies with 'seuen' have corrected a faulty reading at x 23.2, 8, so 'seuen' seems to be the poet's second thought.
8 **descride**: distinguished.

Stanza 5
5 **pryse**: pay for.
6 **ywroke**: inflicted.
7 **languor**: illness; woeful plight.

Stanza 6
4 **rankling**: used by S. for a festering, incurable wound; see I x 25.1–5*n*. **maladie**: used by S. chiefly for love-sickness.
5–7 On Tryphon as sea-surgeon, see III iv 43.7–9*n*.
8 **behight**: promised.

Stanza 7
6–9 Cf. xii 18.6. Like Florimell (see xii 9.3), he is kept a prisoner. **ouer all**: everywhere.

Stanzas 8–53
The marriage of the Thames and the Medway may relate to the subject of S.'s projected – or unpublished – *Epithalamion Thamesis*, discussed in a letter to Harvey in *1580* as a work 'very profitable for the knowledge, and rare for the Inuention, and manner of handling'. His intent in this work, to give all the English rivers 'their righte names, and right passage', is here fulfilled. Their names are clarified by an etymological epithet and they are placed in order. For his matter, he turns to Holinshed, *Chronicles* (*1577*) and Harrison, 'Description of Britain' in Holinshed; also he draws upon his extensive knowledge of Irish rivers: see Joyce (*1911*) and Judson (*1933*). For his poetic form, he employs the genre of the river-marriage poem, established for him by Camden, *De Connubio Tamae et Isis*; see Oruch (*1967*) and Roche (*1964*) 167–84. The genre is derived from the epic catalogue, e.g. in Homer, *Iliad* ii 484–877.

   In the *S.C.* July 81–4, S. refers to 'The salt Medway, that trickling stremis / adowne the dales of Kent: / Till with his elder brother Themis / his brackish waues be meynt.' That he should change the sex of the Medway, and celebrate its mingling with the Thames in the Thames estuary as a marriage, has been variously explained. Upton (*1758*) saw the choice as a compliment to the Sidney family because the Medway flows by Sidney's home at Penshurst; cf. Buchan (*1944*) 245.

   Fowler (*1964*) 172–5 associates the river-marriage with the marriage of England to Elizabeth. Since the Medway was the centre of naval operations, he interprets the event as 'a festival piece, celebrating a visionary England – and Ireland – united in friendly alliance, and married to a sovereign whose policy promises a strong and prosperous peace'. Roche 181 claims that 'the essential purpose of this procession is to show the unity underlying the multiplicity of life, as symbolized by the world of the sea'.

Stanza 8
6 **bed**: the pun follows naturally from the marriage of the two rivers.

Stanza 4
4–5 **Styx**: river goddess of the lower world; probably cited here as the river of death.

6 **seuen months**: the period Amoret spends in the house of

9

So both agreed, that this their bridale feast
    Should for the Gods in *Proteus* house be made;
    To which they all repayr'd, both most and least,
    Aswell which in the mightie Ocean trade,
    As that in riuers swim, or brookes doe wade.
    All which not if an hundred tongues to tell,
    And hundred mouthes, and voice of brasse I had,
    And endlesse memorie, that mote excell,
In order as they came, could I recount them well.

10

Helpe therefore, O thou sacred imp of *Ioue*,
    The noursling of Dame *Memorie* his deare,
    To whom those rolles, layd vp in heauen aboue,
    And records of antiquitie appeare,
    To which no wit of man may comen neare;
    Helpe me to tell the names of all those floods,
    And all those Nymphes, which then assembled were
    To that great banquet of the watry Gods,
And all their sundry kinds, and all their hid abodes.

11

First came great *Neptune* with his threeforkt mace,
    That rules the Seas, and makes them rise or fall;
    His dewy lockes did drop with brine apace,
    Vnder his Diademe imperiall:
    And by his side his Queene with coronall,
    Faire *Amphitrite*, most diuinely faire,
    Whose yuorie shoulders weren couered all,
    As with a robe, with her owne siluer haire,
And deckt with pearles, which th'Indian seas for her prepaire.

12

These marched farre afore the other crew;
    And all the way before them as they went,
    Triton his trompet shrill before them blew,
    For goodly triumph and great iollyment,
    That made the rockes to roare, as they were rent.
    And after them the royall issue came,
    Which of them sprung by lineall descent:
    First the Sea-gods, which to themselues doe clame
The powre to rule the billowes, and the waues to tame.

6–7 Translates Virgil, *Georg.* ii 43–4 (cf. *Aen.* vi 623–6) except that the voice of iron (*ferrea vox*) becomes the **voice of brasse**.
8 **endlesse memorie** is S.'s addition, serving to introduce the Muses as daughters of Memory.

Stanza 10
1–2 Clio, the Muse of History, offspring of Jove and Mnemosyne; yet see I xi 5.6–9*n*.
4–5 Cf. II Proem 1.9.

Stanzas 11–53
S.'s promise to describe the sea-gods and their seed 'In order as they came' (9.9) is amply fulfilled, as Fowler's (1964, 182–91) numerological analysis shows. The reference at xii 2.6–7 to the 'count / Of Gods, of Nymphs, of riuers' outlines the three main divisions. First come **Neptune** and his seed, the sea-gods and the founders of nations; then the source of this seed in Ocean and his seed, the rivers and the nymphs.

I. **Neptune and his seed** (11–16). Following **Neptune** and **Amphitrite** (11) led by **Triton**, come the Gods: 17 sea-gods (13–14) who rule the waves, and 9 Founders of Nations (15–16) who possess the world.
II. **Ocean and his seed** (18–52). **Ocean** and **Tethys** followed by **Nereus** (18–19), and
    i. rivers: 1. eighteen famous rivers (20–21)
         2. English and Irish rivers (24–47) led by **Arion** (23)
              (a) Bridegroom's party:
                   parents and two pages (24–26)
                   Bridegroom (27–28)
                   6 pages (29)
                   34 neighbour floods (30–39)
                   18 Irish rivers (40–44)
              (b) Bride and party of four (45–47)
    ii. nymphs: 50 (48–52).
Fowler notes many examples of the symmetry of arrangement, e.g. the eighteen famous rivers and the eighteen Irish rivers, and the eighteen sons of **Neptune** (including Triton), and concludes that the high degree of formal organization is such that 'there would literally be no room for a single additional stanza or an extra river'.

Stanza 11
1–2 **threeforkt mace**: trident, by which he is known as *Tridentifer*, alluding to his power to raise and calm storms (Comes, 1616, II viii p. 88). Usually he does not govern the tides.
5–9 **Amphitrite**: 'daughter to Nereus, and wyfe to Neptunus, God of the sea. And some tyme it is taken for the sea' (Cooper, 1565). At 49.2 she appears among the Nereids as 'goodly *Amphitrite*'. The description here shows her as the sea.

Stanza 12
8–9 They assume this power from Neptune, 11.2.

Stanzas 13–14
The catalogue of the Sea-gods is drawn from Comes (1616) II viii, as Jortin (1734) first observed. Although the correspondence is close, S. has selected his names, telling 'Only what needeth' (17.7). He chooses those with a wider reference than simply being the offspring of Amphitrite, and he adds **Glaucus**.

Stanza 9
2–3 **in Proteus house**: because all rivers return to the sea.
most and least: the highest and lowest in rank.
4 **trade**: go.
6–9 This disclaimer introduces Homer's catalogue, *Iliad* ii 488–93.

13

Phorcys, the father of that fatall brood,
  By whom those old Heroes wonne such fame;
And *Glaucus*, that wise southsayes vnderstood;
  And tragicke *Inoes* sonne, the which became
  A God of seas through his mad mothers blame,
Now hight *Palemon*, and is saylers frend;
  Great *Brontes*, and *Astræus*, that did shame
  Himselfe with incest of his kin vnkend;
And huge *Orion*, that doth tempests still portend.

14

The rich *Cteatus*, and *Eurytus* long;
  Neleus and *Pelias* louely brethren both;
Mightie *Chrysaor*, and *Caïcus* strong;
  Eurypulus, that calmes the waters wroth;
  And faire *Euphœmus*, that vpon them goth
As on the ground, without dismay or dread:
  Fierce *Eryx*, and *Alebius* that know'th
  The waters depth, and doth their bottome tread;
And sad *Asopus*, comely with his hoarie head.

15

There also some most famous founders were
  Of puissant Nations, which the world possest;
Yet sonnes of *Neptune*, now assembled here:
  Ancient *Ogyges*, euen th'auncientest,
  And *Inachus* renowmd aboue the rest;
Phœnix, and *Aon*, and *Pelasgus* old,
  Great *Belus*, *Phœax*, and *Agenor* best;
  And mightie *Albion*, father of the bold
And warlike people, which the *Britaine* Islands hold.

16

For *Albion* the sonne of *Neptune* was,
  Who for the proofe of his great puissance,
Out of his *Albion* did on dry-foot pas
  Into old *Gall*, that now is cleeped *France*,
  To fight with *Hercules*, that did aduance
To vanquish all the world with matchlesse might,
  And there his mortall part by great mischance
  Was slaine: but that which is th'immortall spright
Liues still: and to this feast with *Neptunes* seed was dight.

Stanza 13

1–2 **Phorcys**: introduces a sub-catalogue of his **fatall brood** and the **old Heroes**. He was father of Medusa slain by Perseus, and of the Dragon of the Hesperides slain by Hercules, etc. Virgil, *Aen.* v 822–4 (cf. 239–40), lists Neptune's train as whales, Glaucus, Palaemon, the Tritons, and the band of Phorcus.
3 Cf. Milton's 'old soothsaying Glaucus' (*Comus* 873).
4–6 Ovid, *Met.* iv 416–542. **mad mother**: Ovid's *concita mater* (519). **Now hight Palemon**: Ovid's climax, *Palaemona dixit.* Comes (1616) VIII iv p. 434 notes that
510 Palaemon presides over sailors. Ino's story is mentioned again

at V viii 47.1–2. **blame**: fault.
7–8 **Great Brontes**: *maxime Brontes* (Comes IX viii p. 511), one of the Cyclopes, who are sons of Neptune. **Astræus**: *qui per inscitiam congressus cum Alcipa sorore* (Comes II viii p. 86).
9 **huge Orion**: a large and conspicuous constellation. In Virgil, *nimbosus Orion* (*Aen.* i 535); see I iii 31.6n.

Stanza 14

1 **Cteatus and Eurytus** are linked by Comes. **rich**: from κτεανον, possessions, wealth. **Eurytus**: from εὐρυ, long; cf. εὐρυτος, full-flowing.
2 **Neleus and Pelias**: listed together by Comes. **louely**: added by S.
3 **Chrysaor**: **Mightie** as the father of Geryon; or because Chrysaoreus is a surname of Jupiter: see V i 9.5–9n. **Caïcus** may be **strong** because a Trojan of that name defended Troy (*Aen.* ix 35–8).
4–6 **Eurypulus . . . Euphœmus**: listed together by Comes, who does not mention the power given the first, but of the second declares: *cui munus dedit ut super undis tanquam super terra proficisceretur.*
7 **Fierce Eryx**: Virgil's *acer Eryx* (*Aen.* v 402) but refers to his ancestor, the son of Neptune and Venus (Cooper, 1565). **Alebius**: simply named by Comes. His powers counter those of **Euphœmus**.
9 **Asopus**: **sad** because his daughter Aegina was raped by Jove in a flame, III xi 35.2.

Stanzas 15–16

This catalogue of the founders of nations is also drawn from Comes II viii. S. adds **Inachus** and the account of **Albion**. The selection and groupings are his own, as are the characterizing descriptions.

Stanza 15

4 **Ogyges**: founder of Thebes (Cooper, 1565), reputed the oldest city in the world. Upton (1758) notes that things ancient were called 'Ogygia'.
5 In the Castle of Alma, Eumnestes's memory goes back to '*Inachus diuine*' (II ix 56.9), the first King of Argos. Comes (1616) VIII xxii calls him *celeberrimum*; in Horace, *Odes* II iii 21–4, the name seems synonymous with wealthy descent.
6–7 **Phœnix**: the founder of Phoenicia; named third as he is third in line from Neptune and son of **Agenor** who rounds out this two-line grouping. **Aon**: founder of Aonia.
Pelasgus: **old** because the Pelasgi, named after him, are 'people whiche came out of Greece' (Cooper), i.e. they were its earliest inhabitants. **Belus**: **Great** because he was 'an auncient kynge of Assyria, to whom the fyrst ymage or ydole to be honoured, was made' (Cooper); or because he was reputed to be the founder of Babylon. **Phœax**: founder of Phaeacia. **Agenor**: **best** either as founder of Carthage (*Aen.* i 338) or as father of Europa, and of Cadmus who built Thebes (Cooper). Chosen to balance **Great**.

Stanza 16

Albion's defeat by Hercules is described by Holinshed (1577) i 432–3 and Cooper (1565); cf. II x 11.6–7.
3 **on dry-foot**: see II x 5.5–9.
4 **Gall**: Lat. form of Gaul.
5 **aduance**: go forward; propose; boast.
9 **was dight**: i.e. made its way.

17

But what doe I their names seeke to reherse,
　　Which all the world haue with their issue fild?
　　How can they all in this so narrow verse
　　Contayned be, and in small compasse hild?
　　Let them record them, that are better skild,
　　And know the moniments of passed times:
　　Onely what needeth, shall be here fulfild,
　　T'expresse some part of that great equipage,
Which from great *Neptune* do deriue their parentage.

18

Next came the aged *Ocean*, and his Dame,
　　Old *Tethys*, th'oldest two of all the rest,
　　For all the rest of those two parents came,
　　Which afterward both sea and land possest:
　　Of all which *Nereus* th'eldest, and the best,
　　Did first proceed, then which none more vpright,
　　Ne more sincere in word and deed profest;
　　Most voide of guile, most free from fowle despight,
Doing him selfe, and teaching others to doe right.

19

Thereto he was expert in prophecies,
　　And could the ledden of the Gods vnfold,
　　Through which, when *Paris* brought his famous prise
　　The faire Tindarid lasse, he him fortold,
　　That her all *Greece* with many a champion bold
　　Should fetch againe, and finally destroy
　　Proud *Priams* towne.　So wise is *Nereus* old,
　　And so well skild; nathlesse he takes great ioy
Oft-times amongst the wanton Nymphs to sport and toy.

20

And after him the famous riuers came,
　　Which doe the earth enrich and beautifie:
　　The fertile Nile, which creatures new doth frame;
　　Long Rhodanus, whose sourse springs from the skie;
　　Faire Ister, flowing from the mountaines hie;
　　Diuine Scamander, purpled yet with blood
　　Of Greekes and Troians, which therein did die;
　　Pactolus glistring with his golden flood,
And Tygris fierce, whose streames of none may be withstood.

Stanza 17

This stanza of authorial comment divides the catalogue of
Neptune's seed from that of Ocean's seed. For its significance
in the numerical composition of the canto, see Fowler (1964)
182–3.

1　**reherse**: recount in order.
6　**times**: 'age', sugg. Church (1758) for the rhyme.
8　**equipage**: following.

Stanza 18

1–4　Comes (1616) VIII i–ii claims that the **Ocean** and
Tethys are the source of all waters and living things. 4 refers
back to the gods who govern the sea (12.8–9) and the Founders
of Nations who possess the world (15.2), and forward to the
rivers which possess the land in being possessed by it. The
ambiguity is noted by Berger (1969b) 17.
5 to 19.9　This praise of **Nereus** derives from Hesiod, as
cited by Comes VIII vi, but is much expanded with hints from
Comes himself: cf. 19.8–9 and Comes's *delectari choris puellarum*.
Lotspeich (1932) 90 concludes that S. does not include anything
not in Comes.

Stanza 19

2　**ledden**: speech.
3–7　From Horace, *Odes* I xv 1–8, by way of Comes, and also
freely embellished.　**Tindarid lasse**: Virgil's *Tyndaridis*
(*Aen*. ii 601).　On the **Paris** story, see III ix 34.　**fortold**:
warned beforehand.
7　**Nereus old**: *grandaevus Nereus* (Virgil, *Georg*. iv 392).

Stanza 20

3　On the **Nile**, see I i 21.6–9n.
4　**Rhodanus**: the Rhone; its source lies in the high Alps.
5　**Ister**: 'While it is in Germany, it is called Danubius, and
whan it commeth into a parte of Thracia called Istria, where it
is broadest, it is than called Ister' (Cooper, 1565).
6–7　**Scamander**: cf. III ix 35.6–9 where it is also called
the Xanthus.　**Diuine** because the gods call it Xanthus
(*Iliad* xx 74).　**purpled** yet balances golden Pactolus. The
description may follow from the gathering of the Greeks and
Trojans by the Scamander.
8　**Pactolus**: see vi 20.7–9n.
9　**Tygris fierce**: the epithet derives from the name and
popular etymology. Cf. White (1954) 12: 'From him [the tiger]
the River Tigris is named, because it is the most rapid of all
rivers.'

511

21

Great Ganges, and immortall Euphrates,
  Deepe Indus, and Mæander intricate,
  Slow Peneus, and tempestuous Phasides,
  Swift Rhene, and Alpheus still immaculate:
  Ooraxes, feared for great *Cyrus* fate;
  Tybris, renowmed for the Romaines fame,
  Rich Oranochy, though but knowen late;
  And that huge Riuer, which doth beare his name
Of warlike Amazons, which doe possesse the same.

22

Ioy on those warlike women, which so long
  Can from all men so rich a kingdome hold;
  And shame on you, O men, which boast your strong
  And valiant hearts, in thoughts lesse hard and bold,
  Yet quaile in conquest of that land of gold.
  But this to you, O Britons, most pertaines,
  To whom the right hereof it selfe hath sold;
  The which for sparing litle cost or paines,
Loose so immortall glory, and so endlesse gaines.

23

Then was there heard a most celestiall sound,
  Of dainty musicke, which did next ensew
  Before the spouse: that was *Arion* crownd;
  Who playing on his harpe, vnto him drew
  The eares and hearts of all that goodly crew,
  That euen yet the Dolphin, which him bore
  Through the Ægæan seas from Pirates vew,
  Stood still by him astonisht at his lore,
And all the raging seas for ioy forgot to rore.

24

So went he playing on the watery plaine.
  Soone after whom the louely Bridegroome came,
  The noble Thamis, with all his goodly traine,
  But him before there went, as best became,
  His auncient parents, namely th'auncient Thame.
  But much more aged was his wife then he,
  The Ouze, whom men doe Isis rightly name;
  Full weake and crooked creature seemed shee,
And almost blind through eld, that scarce her way could see.

Stanza 21

1   **Ganges**: 'a great ryver . . . called in holy scripture
Phison, one of the fowre ryvers whiche come out of Paradise'
(Cooper, 1565). Hence it follows the naming of the Tigris.

Euphrates: another river of Paradise, Gen. 2.14 (gloss), and
hence **immortall**. Named with the Phison and Gehon at
I vii 43.8–9.
2   **Indus**: 'A noble ryver, that . . . incloseth Indie on the
west . . . in breadth . . . twelve myles and an halfe' (Cooper).
Mæander: the epithet provides the etymology of the name;
'hereof all crooked and subtylle tournyng wayes, meanes and
divises be called Mæandri' (Cooper).
3   **Peneus**: 'a ryver in Greece' (Cooper). Called *Peneus
senex* in Ovid, *Met*. ii 243.   **Phasides**: Ovid, *Met*. vii 6,
speaks of its swift waters.
4   **Rhene**: the Rhine; Perhaps **Swift** because 'renish'
signifies fierce, wild.   **Alpheus**: **immaculate** because the
river flows from Arcadia to Sicily under the sea without being
mingled with salt water; see *Aen*. iii 694–6.   **still**: always.
5   Cyrus's decision to cross the **Ooraxes** led to his death.
See Herodotus, *History* i 201–14.
7–9   **Oranochy**: mentioned by Raleigh in his *Discovery of
Guiana*, 1595. In the same work he describes the Amazons who
live in the region between the Orinoco and the Amazon.

Stanza 22

5   **that land of gold** is Guiana with the empire of the
Amazons on its southern border. In the *Discovery of Guiana*,
Raleigh urges its conquest. S.'s exhortation to his countrymen
to plunder the land was topical; cf. Chapman, *De Guiana*
(1596).

Stanza 23

3   **spouse**: bridegroom.
3–9   The story of **Arion** carried from pirates upon a dolphin's
back is told by Ovid, *Fasti* ii 79–118. See *Amor*. xxxviii. The
story is interpreted by Comes (1616) VIII xiv. S. adds the
dolphin's astonishment and the calmed seas.   **Arion crownd**
is a hieroglyphic of love and in this role he introduces the
bridegroom.
8   **lore**: song; learning or skill.

Stanzas 24–47

These twenty-four stanzas catalogue the English and Irish
rivers as the parties of the bridegroom and of the bride. The
Bridegroom is preceded by his two parents with their two
pages (24–26) and followed by his six pages (29), the neighbour
floods (30–39), and Irish rivers (40–44). The bride (45–46)
is followed by her two handmaids and preceded by two pages
(47). Roche (1964) 180 observes that S. names the tributaries
of the Thames, and then follows a counter-clockwise order,
beginning with the Severne and ending with the Lindus.
S.'s chief sources for his English rivers (24–39) are Harrison,
'Description of Britain' chaps. xi–xvi (in Holinshed, *Chronicles*,
1577), and Camden, *Britannia* (1586), cited below in Holland's
1610 trans. Osgood (1920) 65–108 analyses these sources.
My notes are indebted to his work.

Stanza 24

3–7   **Thamis . . . Thame . . . Ouze . . . Isis**: Harrison
(1577) 79 notes that the river is called the Isis or Ouze at its
source but later joins the Thame to receive the composite name,
Thamesis or Thames. Camden (1610) 384 refers to the meeting
of the Tame and Isis in one stream as their being joined in
wedlock. Saxton's map of England (1579) shows the crooked
course of the Isis.
7   Camden refers to the '*Isis* vulgo *Ouze*'.

25

Therefore on either side she was sustained
  Of two smal grooms, which by their names were hight
  The *Churne*, and *Charwell*, two small streames, which pained
  Them selues her footing to direct aright,
  Which fayled oft through faint and feeble plight:
  But *Thame* was stronger, and of better stay;
  Yet seem'd full aged by his outward sight,
  With head all hoary, and his beard all gray,
Deawed with siluer drops, that trickled downe alway.

26

And eke he somewhat seem'd to stoupe afore
  With bowed backe, by reason of the lode,
  And auncient heauy burden, which he bore
  Of that faire City, wherein make abode
  So many learned impes, that shoote abrode,
  And with their braunches spred all Britany,
  No lesse then do her elder sisters broode.
  Ioy to you both, ye double noursery
Of Arts, but Oxford thine doth *Thame* most glorify.

27

But he their sonne full fresh and iolly was,
  All decked in a robe of watchet hew,
  On which the waues, glittering like Christall glas,
  So cunningly enwouen were, that few
  Could weenen, whether they were false or trew.
  And on his head like to a Coronet
  He wore, that seemed strange to common vew,
  In which were many towres and castels set,
That it encompast round as with a golden fret.

28

Like as the mother of the Gods, they say,
  In her great iron charet wonts to ride,
  When to *Ioues* pallace she doth take her way:
  Old *Cybele*, arayd with pompous pride,
  Wearing a Diademe embattild wide
  With hundred turrets, like a Turribant.
  With such an one was Thamis beautifide;
  That was to weet the famous Troynouant,
In which her kingdomes throne is chiefly resiant.

29

And round about him many a pretty Page
  Attended duely, ready to obay;
  All little Riuers, which owe vassallage
  To him, as to their Lord, and tribute pay:
  The chaulky Kenet, and the Thetis gray,
  The morish Cole, and the soft sliding Breane,
  The wanton Lee, that oft doth loose his way,
  And the still Darent, in whose waters cleane
Ten thousand fishes play, and decke his pleasant streame.

Stanza 25
3   **The Churne, and Charwell**: the Ouze 'runneth directlie toward the east . . . and meeteth with the Cirne or Churne. . . . it passeth at length by Oxford . . . where it meeteth with Charwell' (Harrison 79). He notes that the Chirne enters into the Isis 'on the left side' (which would be west) and that the Charwell enters by the east and south bridge of Oxford (79, 82, 84).
6   **stay**: strength.

Stanza 26
1–4   Referring to the dip in the Isis (rather than the Thames) at **Oxford** (9), which appears on the map as though the river were borne down by the weight of the city.
5   **impes**: offshoots; scions or descendants.
7   **her elder sister**: Cambridge, founded earlier than Oxford; so S., a Cantabrigian, prefers to believe.

Stanza 27
1–5   Edwards (1958) 193 notes how S. 'makes us see at once the person in the river and the river in the person'.
2   **watchet**: light blue.
6–9   **like to a Coronet**: Saxton's (1579) map shows London on the Thames as a crowded cluster of towers arranged coronet-wise; cf. Milton's 'royal towered Thame' (*Vacation Exercise* 100). **fret**: an ornamental border of intersecting lines; here the streets. Fowler (1970) 67*n* observes that the bridegroom occupies the central stanza of the canto.

Stanza 28
1–6   **Cybele**: 'named of Paynims the mother of the goddes' (Cooper, 1565). She appears with towered crown because she first taught men to fortify cities. The crown marks the chief city on Elizabethan maps. In Virgil, *Aen.* vi 784–7, the simile heralds famed Rome (*incluta Roma*); used here, the simile shows that **famous Troynouant** (8) or London replaces Rome; cf. *Ruines of Rome* vi 1–4. **pompous**: stately, ceremonious. **embattild**: having its sides shaped like battlements. **hundred turrets**: as the hundred gods held by Cybele, *Aen.* vi 786.   **Turribant**: turban; literally, a band of turrets.
9   **her**: 'his', referring to the Thames (sugg. Church, 1758); or **her**, referring to **Troynouant** or obliquely to the Faerie Queene. Berger (1969b) 19 takes Cybele to be the likely antecedent in order to develop Roche's (1964) 182 comment that 'Cybele is a symbol of ancient civilization and fertility, of which Troynouant is the latest example'.   **resiant**: resident.

Stanza 29
1–2   As Cybele in Virgil rides in her car clasping her offspring.
4   These six rivers **tribute pay** to the Thames because they are its tributaries. They are named in order of their occurrence as the Thames flows to the sea.
5–9   The **Kenet** is **chaulky** because it rises near Marleborow (from 'marl', chalk) and as it receives the Chalkburne (Holinshed i 85). Camden (1610) 255 notes that 'it lieth neere a chaulkey hill, which our Ancestours . . . named *Marle*.' The **Thetis** may be called **gray** to make it a fitting companion to the Kenet. The **Cole** is **morish**, i.e. moorish or marshy, in contrast to the **Breane**. The **Lee** is called **wanton** from its devious route.   **Darent**: this form is derived from Lat. *dare*, to give; hence its fruitfulness.

30

Then came his neighbour flouds, which nigh him dwell,
  And water all the English soile throughout;
  They all on him this day attended well;
  And with meet seruice waited him about;
  Ne none disdained low to him to lout:
  No not the stately Seuerne grudg'd at all,
  Ne storming Humber, though he looked stout;
  But both him honor'd as their principall,
And let their swelling waters low before him fall.

31

There was the speedy Tamar, which deuides
  The Cornish and the Deuonish confines;
  Through both whose borders swiftly downe it glides,
  And meeting Plim, to Plimmouth thence declines:
  And Dart, nigh chockt with sands of tinny mines.
  But Auon marched in more stately path,
  Proud of his Adamants, with which he shines
  And glisters wide, as als' of wondrous Bath,
And Bristow faire, which on his waues he builded hath.

32

And there came Stoure with terrible aspect,
  Bearing his sixe deformed heads on hye,
  That doth his course through Blandford plains direct,
  And washeth Winborne meades in season drye.
  Next him went Wylibourne with passage slye,
  That of his wylinesse his name doth take,
  And of him selfe doth name the shire thereby:
  And Mole, that like a nousling Mole doth make
His way still vnder ground, till Thamis he ouertake.

33

Then came the Rother, decked all with woods
  Like a wood God, and flowing fast to Rhy:
  And Sture, that parteth with his pleasant floods
  The Easterne Saxons from the Southerne ny,
  And Clare, and Harwitch both doth beautify:
  Him follow'd Yar, soft washing Norwitch wall,
  And with him brought a present ioyfully
  Of his owne fish vnto their festiuall,
Whose like none else could shew, the which they Ruffins call.

34

Next these the plenteous Ouse came far from land,
  By many a city, and by many a towne,
  And many riuers taking vnder hand
  Into his waters, as he passeth downe,
  The Cle, the Were, the Grant, the Sture, the Rowne.
  Thence doth by Huntingdon and Cambridge flit,
  My mother Cambridge, whom as with a Crowne
  He doth adorne, and is adorn'd of it
With many a gentle Muse, and many a learned wit.

Stanzas 30–39
The thirty-four **neighbour flouds** catalogued here plus the six
tributaries of the Thames make up forty English rivers. The
generative and harmonic properties of this number are noted
by Fowler (1964) 189.

Stanza 30
6 The **Seuerne** is **stately** because 'severane' is an obsolete
form of sovereign.
7 **storming Humber**: from Gk ὄμβρος, storm; see 37.8–
38.9. **stout**: arrogant; fierce.

Stanza 31
1–4 Camden (1610) 196 notes that the **Tamar**, which forms
the boundary between Devonshire and Cornwall, 'taketh his
course with a swift running streame'.
5 Harrison (Holinshed i 103) notes that the sand from the
tin mines 'choketh the depth' of the **Dart**.
6–9 The **Auon** is 'growne to be verie famous' (Holinshed i
115). Its **stately path** contrasts with the swift and the sluggish
courses of the other two. **Adamants**: Bristol-diamonds,
rock crystal or quartz.

Stanza 32
1–4 After the Avon, Harrison (Holinshed i 98) treats the
Stoure which 'riseth of six heads' but he does not single out the
other facts stressed here. It has a **terrible aspect** because the
name signifies 'tumult', 'uproar'.
8–9 The **Mole** 'maketh him selfe a way under the ground in
manner of mouldwarp, . . . whereof it may seeme it tooke
name, seeing that creature living within the ground, is called
also in English a *Mole*' (Camden, 1610, 296).

Stanza 33
1–2 Camden (1610) 306 notes that the region of the
Ashdown forest where the **Rother** takes its rise 'by reason of
the woods was hardly passable'.
3–5 **Sture . . . Clare, and Harwitch**: 'The Sture or
Stoure parteth Essex from Suffolke' (Holinshed i 177). Both
Harrison and Camden mention Clare and Harwich on the river.
6–9 **Yar** signifies also a fishgarth, an inclosure extending
into a river, for catching fish (*OED*). On Saxton's (1579) map,
the Yar seems to touch the city. Camden 476 observes that the
river teems with ruff.

Stanza 34
1 **Ouse**: the river in the East Midlands, not that named the
Isis (24.7).
5 **Cle . . . Were . . . Grant . . . Sture . . . Rowne**: these
five tributaries are named generally in order as the Ouse flows
to the sea. **Grant**: the Granta or Cam. **Rowne**: 'Downe',
sugg. Osgood (1920) 81, or the Little Ouse.
6 **Thence**: applies to the river system since the two towns
are not on the same river.

35

And after him the fatall Welland went,
  That if old sawes proue true (which God forbid)
  Shall drowne all Holland with his excrement,
  And shall see Stamford, though now homely hid,
  Then shine in learning, more then euer did
  Cambridge or Oxford, Englands goodly beames.
  And next to him the Nene downe softly slid;
  And bounteous Trent, that in him selfe enseames
Both thirty sorts of fish, and thirty sundry streames.

36

Next these came Tyne, along whose stony bancke
  That Romaine Monarch built a brasen wall,
  Which mote the feebled Britons strongly flancke
  Against the Picts, that swarmed ouer all,
  Which yet thereof Gualseuer they doe call:
  And Twede the limit betwixt Logris land
  And Albany: And Eden though but small,
  Yet often stainde with bloud of many a band
Of Scots and English both, that tyned on his strand.

37

Then came those sixe sad brethren, like forlorne,
  That whilome were (as antique fathers tell)
  Sixe valiant Knights, of one faire Nymphe yborne,
  Which did in noble deedes of armes excell,
  And wonned there, where now Yorke people dwell;
  Still Vre, swift Werfe, and Oze the most of might,
  High Swale, vnquiet Nide, and troublous Skell;
  All whom a Scythian king, that Humber hight,
Slew cruelly, and in the riuer drowned quight.

38

But past not long, ere *Brutus* warlicke sonne
  Locrinus them aueng'd, and the same date,
  Which the proud Humber vnto them had donne,
  By equall dome repayd on his owne pate:
  For in the selfe same riuer, where he late
  Had drenched them, he drowned him againe;
  And nam'd the riuer of his wretched fate;
  Whose bad condition yet it doth retaine,
Oft tossed with his stormes, which therein still remaine.

39

These after, came the stony shallow Lone,
  That to old Loncaster his name doth lend;
  And following Dee, which Britons long ygone
  Did call diuine, that doth by Chester tend;
  And Conway which out of his streame doth send
  Plenty of pearles to decke his dames withall,
  And Lindus that his pikes doth most commend,
  Of which the auncient Lincolne men doe call;
All these together marched toward *Proteus* hall.

Stanza 35

1–6   The prophecy that the **Welland** – **fatall** also as it is
deadly – would drown that part of Norfolk called **Holland** has

not been found in any earlier writer. Drayton, *Poly-Olbion*
xxiv 5, records the prophecy 'from Ages past'. See Tilley (1950)
W 266. The name, signifying 'pouring forth', suggests its
flooding. The pun on **Holland**, hole-land, suggests
excrement. Selden, in Drayton's *Works* iv 154, records
'that suppos'd prophesie of *Merlin*' that the University
of Stamford would rival Oxford, 'which you shall have
Englished in that solemnized marriage of *Thames* and *Medway*,
by a most admired Muse of our nation'.
7   The **Nene** or Avon **softly slid** because 'it divideth it selfe
into sundrie armes, and those into severall branches and
draines, among the fennes and medowes, not possible almost to
be numbred' (Holinshed i 172).
8–9   **Trent** means thirty; cf. Milton, *Vacation Exercise*
93–4.   **enseames**: brings together; perhaps from 'seam', fat
+ 'en' to signify 'fattens', 'breeds'.

Stanza 36

1–5   Cf. II x 63.7–9.   **brasen**: as strong as brass.
flancke: defend on the flank.   **Gualseuer**: i.e. the wall of
Severus.
6–7   **the limit betwixt Logris land / And Albany**: the
boundary between England and Scotland; see II x 14.
7–9   Camden (1610) 776 records the drowning in the **Eden** of
border-raiders.   **tyned**: perished; suggested by the **Tyne** (1)

Stanza 37

No source for this story is known. It prepares for **Humber**'s
punishment and explains why the tributaries of the Humber
are literally **drowned** in it.
6–7   Not in any geographical order, as Osgood (1920) 87
notes; but there is a climactic order of adjectives in each line,
mixing geographical and etymological detail. Camden (1610)
701, 696 records that the **Vre** flows with a gentle stream; the
Werfe is called swift from its etymology: 'from the word *Guer*,
which in British signifieth *swift* and *violent*'. The **Oze** is **most of
might** because it is the union of the others. The **Swale** is
High because it was so, and because the name is an obsolete
form of 'swell'; the **Nide** is **vnquiet** because the name is an
obsolete form of 'need', i.e. disturbance; and the **Skell** is
troublous because 'skellum' means rascal.

Stanza 38

The source is Geoffrey of Monmouth and William Harrison;
see Harper (1910) 58. Cf. II x 15–16.
2   **date**: thing given or done (from Lat. *datum*); or perhaps
limit to the term of life.
4   Cf. Ps. 7.16: 'His crueltie shal fall upon his owne pate.'
dome: punishment or death.
6   **drenched**: drowned.
8–9   See 30.7n.   **condition**: nature.

Stanza 39

2   **Loncaster**: as from 'loan' ('lone' in sixteenth-century
spelling)+Lat. *castra*, camp.
3–4   **Dee** . . . / . . . **diuine**: from Lat. *divus*; cf. 'where Deva
spreads her wizard stream' (Milton, *Lycidas* 55). See I ix
4.5–8n. The river was held to possess magical power of
divination: its change of course prophesied victory to the
English or the Welsh.   **tend**: make its way.
7   Harrison (Holinshed i 169) notes that Lindis is an old
name of Witham, and records the proverb: 'Ancolme ele, and
Witham pike, / Search all England and find not the like.'

515

40

Ne thence the Irishe Riuers absent were,
　　Sith no lesse famous then the rest they bee,
　　And ioyne in neighbourhood of kingdome nere,
　　Why should they not likewise in loue agree,
　　And ioy likewise this solemne day to see?
　　They saw it all, and present were in place;
　　Though I them all according their degree,
　　Cannot recount, nor tell their hidden race,
Nor read the saluage cuntreis, thorough which they pace.

41

There was the Liffy rolling downe the lea,
　　The sandy Slane, the stony Aubrian,
　　The spacious Shenan spreading like a sea,
　　The pleasant Boyne, the fishy fruitfull Ban,
　　Swift Awniduff, which of the English man
　　Is cal'de Blacke water, and the Liffar deep,
　　Sad Trowis, that once his people ouerran,
　　Strong Allo tombling from Slewlogher steep,
And Mulla mine, whose waues I whilom taught to weep.

42

And there the three renowmed brethren were,
　　Which that great Gyant *Blomius* begot,
　　Of the faire Nimph *Rheusa* wandring there.
　　One day, as she to shunne the season whot,
　　Vnder Slewbloome in shady groue was got,
　　This Gyant found her, and by force deflowr'd,
　　Whereof conceiuing, she in time forth brought
　　These three faire sons, which being thence forth powrd
In three great riuers ran, and many countreis scowrd.

43

The first, the gentle Shure that making way
　　By sweet Clonmell, adornes rich Waterford;
　　The next, the stubborne Newre, whose waters gray
　　By faire Kilkenny and Rosseponte boord,
　　The third, the goodly Barow, which doth hoord
　　Great heapes of Salmons in his deepe bosome:
　　All which long sundred, doe at last accord
　　To ioyne in one, ere to the sea they come,
So flowing all from one, all one at last become.

44

There also was the wide embayed Mayre,
　　The pleasant Bandon crownd with many a wood,
　　The spreading Lee, that like an Island fayre
　　Encloseth Corke with his deuided flood;
　　And balefull Oure, late staind with English blood:
　　With many more, whose names no tongue can tell.
　　All which that day in order seemly good
　　Did on the Thamis attend, and waited well
To doe their duefull seruice, as to them befell.

45

Then came the Bride, the louely *Medua* came,
　　Clad in a vesture of vnknowen geare,
　　And vncouth fashion, yet her well became;
　　That seem'd like siluer, sprinckled here and theare
　　With glittering spangs, that did like starres appeare,
　　And wau'd vpon, like water Chamelot,
　　To hide the metall, which yet euery where
　　Bewrayd it selfe, to let men plainely wot,
It was no mortall worke, that seem'd and yet was not.

Stanzas 40–44
S.'s personal experience is his chief authority for the description of the Irish rivers; see Joyce (1911) 72–94. The parallel between the eighteen Irish rivers and the eighteen famous rivers named in stanzas 20–21 is indicated by 'famous' (20.1, 40.2).

Stanza 40
7　　**according**: fitting.
8　　**race**: also rush of water.
9　　**saluage**: wild.

Stanza 41
Joyce (1911) 83–6 notes the exact order in which the Irish rivers are named.
2　　**the stony Aubrian**: the one river not identified by Joyce. R. M. Smith (1944) identifies it as the Arlo.
7　　**Sad Trowis**: from Irish *truaghas*, sadness (Joyce 79). The legend is recorded by earlier Irish writers.
9　　In *Col.* 100–155, S. celebrates the **Mulla** – his name for the Awbeg – which flowed through his estate at Kilcolman. See also VII vi 40.3–6.

Stanza 42
2, 5　　**Blomius . . . Slewbloome**: the Slieve Bloom mountains from which the three rivers are said to take their source. **Rheusa** is named from Gk $\rho\epsilon\omega$, to flow (Joyce, 1911, 87); the image is extended in 43.9. The story is S.'s. In Camden, as Upton (1758) notes, the Three rivers are called the Three Sisters. Joyce (1911) 86 notes that S. departs from fact: only the Barrow flows from Slieve Bloom.

Stanza 43
1　　**the gentle Shure**: cf. 'the faire *Shure*, in which are thousand Salmons bred' (VII vi 54.9).
2　　**sweet Clonmell**: alluding to the ending, Lat. *mel*, honey.
3　　**stubborne**: fierce, untamable.
4　　**boord**: border upon; flows', according to Joyce (1911) 87.
5–6　　**Barow**: barrow, a mountain or hill, suggests **Great heapes**.

Stanza 44
1　　**embayed**: formed into bays.
2　　**pleasaunt Bandon**: suggested by 'bandon', at one's pleasure.
5　　The **Oure** is balefull from its full name: 'Glen malure' (so named in *View* 117); or alluding to the defeat of Lord Gray on the banks of the Avonbeg in 1580.

Stanza 45
1　　**Medua**: 'the Midwaie water . . . called in Latine Medeuia (as some write) bicause the course therof is midwaie in a manner betweene London and . . . Canturburie' (Holinshed i 90).
2　　**geare**: material.
5　　**spangs**: spangles.
6　　**wau'd vpon, like water Chamelot**: i.e. with an undulating design shimmering in the light like camlet, a fabric with a moiré or wavy finish.
7–9　　Cf. the arras in the House of Busirane, III xi 28.4–7. **Bewrayd**: revealed.

46

Her goodly lockes adowne her backe did flow
  Vnto her waste, with flowres bescattered,
  The which ambrosiall odours forth did throw
  To all about, and all her shoulders spred
  As a new spring; and likewise on her hed
  A Chapelet of sundry flowers she wore,
  From vnder which the deawy humour shed,
  Did tricle downe her haire, like to the hore
Congealed litle drops, which doe the morne adore.

47

On her two pretty handmaides did attend,
  One cald the *Theise*, the other cald the *Crane*;
  Which on her waited, things amisse to mend,
  And both behind vpheld her spredding traine;
  Vnder the which, her feet appeared plaine,
  Her siluer feet, faire washt against this day:
  And her before there paced Pages twaine,
  Both clad in colours like, and like array,
The *Doune* and eke the *Frith*, both which prepard her way.

48

And after these the Sea Nymphs marched all,
  All goodly damzels, deckt with long greene haire,
  Whom of their sire *Nereides* men call,
  All which the Oceans daughter to him bare
  The gray eyde *Doris*: all which fifty are;
  All which she there on her attending had.
  Swift *Proto*, milde *Eucrate*, *Thetis* faire,
  Soft *Spio*, sweete *Eudore*, *Sao* sad,
Light *Doto*, wanton *Glauce*, and *Galene* glad.

49

White hand *Eunica*, proud *Dynamene*,
  Ioyous *Thalia*, goodly *Amphitrite*,
  Louely *Pasithee*, kinde *Eulimene*,
  Light foote *Cymothoe*, and sweete *Melite*,
  Fairest *Pherusa*, *Phao* lilly white,
  Wondred *Agaue*, *Poris*, and *Nesæa*,
  With *Erato* that doth in loue delite,
  And *Panopæ*, and wise *Protomedæa*,
And snowy neckd *Doris*, and milkewhite *Galathæa*.

Stanza 47

1–4 Osgood (1920) 91 notes that on a map the Medway 'seems to the fanciful eye to be curiously trailing that part of her course from her source to Yalding, where she stands more erect towards the north. These two handmaids attend her just at this point, and seem to help uphold her train.' The office given the **Crane** is fitting: the bird is an emblem of diligence (Ripa, 1603, 502–3). It is fortuitous that **Theise**, θείς signifies 'honoured'.

6 Wittily adapts the ceremonial feet-washing at marriage.

Stanzas 48–51

The chief sources for names of the **Nereides** were Homer, *Iliad* xviii 39–49, Virgil, *Aen.* v 825–6, and chiefly Hesiod, *Theog.* 240–64 in Mombritius's Latin trans. in which epithets were added. See Bennett, *Var.* iv 274. S. follows the bare catalogue of names in Comes (1616) VIII vi more closely than he does Hesiod. He goes far beyond his predecessors in using a significant epithet. Lotspeich (1932) 89 notes that S. adds **Phao** and **Poris** to make the full fifty; he also lists examples of S.'s etymologizing independent of his sources; Starnes and Talbert (1955) 106–7 note similar etymologizing in contemporary dictionaries. The complexity of S.'s epithets makes any short commentary inadequate. Some of his descriptions simply translate Mombritius; some unfold directly the Greek root of the name; and some depend upon other associations of the name. Only examples of kinds of etymologizing will be noted below. Braden (1975) 31–3 reviews these etymologies and proposes new ones. The fifty nymphs are named in thirty lines of the four stanzas: 9+18+12+11, carefully interlinked in numbers per line: 3×3, 5×2, 1×3, 1×1, 5×2, 2×0, 2×2, 7×1, 1×3, 1×0, 1×2, 1×1. By such rhythmic gathering S. seeks to produce the effect of waves. Lewis (1967) 131 notes that the nymphs have 'true mythological presence; for they unfold the separate qualities of womanhood we may suppose to be gathered in the bride they follow'.

Stanza 48

7 **Proto** heads the list as her name suggests πρῶτος, first; she is **Swift** from προωθέω, rush on. **Eucrate**: **milde** because her name signifies good temperament.

Stanza 49

2 **Thalia**: **Ioyous** from her namesake, the muse of comedy; cf. '*Thalia* merry' (VI x 22.8).

3 **Pasithee**: **Louely** because she is one of the graces; see Homer, *Iliad* xiv 269.

4 **Cymothoe**: **Light foote** as her name signifies 'wave-swift'.

5–6 Braden (1975) 34 notes the etymological epithet for **Phao**, φάω root of φαίνω to shine. **Poris**, one of the seven nereides without an epithet, may be derived from πορίζω to carry, as he suggests, or πόρις a young maiden. Braden concludes that S.'s 'invention of two names that possess in some intricacy the genre features of the other forty-eight is home-made history, an act of the conscious mind to assert its own potency in the midst of "real" history's apparently impersonal flow'.

9 **milkewhite Galathæa**: translating her name, as in Theocritus, *Idyll* xi.

Stanza 46

8 **like to the hore**: i.e. to hoar-frost.

50

Speedy *Hippothoe*, and chaste *Actea*,
   Large *Lisianassa*, and *Pronæa* sage,
   Euagore, and light *Pontoporea*,
   And she, that with her least word can asswage
   The surging seas, when they do sorest rage,
   Cymodoce, and stout *Autonoe*,
   And *Neso*, and *Eione* well in age,
   And seeming still to smile, *Glauconome*,
And she that hight of many heastes *Polynome*.

51

Fresh *Alimeda*, deckt with girlond greene;
   Hyponeo, with salt bedewed wrests:
   Laomedia, like the christall sheene;
   Liagore, much praisd for wise behests;
   And *Psamathe*, for her brode snowy brests;
   Cymo, *Eupompe*, and *Themiste* iust;
   And she that vertue loues and vice detests
   Euarna, and *Menippe* true in trust,
And *Nemertea* learned well to rule her lust.

52

All these the daughters of old *Nereus* were,
   Which haue the sea in charge to them assinde,
   To rule his tides, and surges to vprere,
   To bring forth stormes, or fast them to vpbinde,
   And sailers saue from wreckes of wrathfull winde.
   And yet besides three thousand more there were
   Of th'Oceans seede, but *Ioues* and *Phœbus* kinde;
   The which in floods and fountaines doe appere,
And all mankinde do nourish with their waters clere.

53

The which, more eath it were for mortall wight,
   To tell the sands, or count the starres on hye,
   Or ought more hard, then thinke to reckon right.
   But well I wote, that these which I descry,
   Were present at this great solemnity:
   And there amongst the rest, the mother was
   Of luckelesse *Marinell Cymodoce*.
   Which, for my Muse her selfe now tyred has,
Vnto an other Canto I will ouerpas.

Cant. XII.

Marin for loue of Florimell,
In languor wastes his life:
The Nymph his mother getteth her,
And giues to him for wife.

1

O What an endlesse worke haue I in hand,
   To count the seas abundant progeny,
   Whose fruitfull seede farre passeth those in land,
   And also those which wonne in th'azure sky?
   For much more eath to tell the starres on hy,
   Albe they endlesse seeme in estimation,
   Then to recount the Seas posterity:
   So fertile be the flouds in generation,
So huge their numbers, and so numberlesse their nation.

Stanza 50

4–6   Following Hesiod, *Theog.* 252–4: **Cymodoce** easily calms the waves (κυματα) upon the misty sea, and the blasts of the raging winds.

9   **hight of many heastes Polynome**: i.e. so called because of her many names.

Stanza 51

9   **lust**: desire.

Stanza 52

3   **surges**: waves.

7   **but**: 'both' sugg. Upton (1758), i.e. of the kindred both of Jupiter and Apollo. Dodge (1908) reads: the **floods and fountaines** (8) 'are indeed born of the ocean, but through the agency of sun and air'. If **but** is retained, the sense is that these nymphs belong rather to the race of **Ioue** and **Phœbus** as spirits of air whose father is the sun.

Stanza 53

1–2   **eath**: easy.   **tell**: number. The task belongs to God: 'He counteth the number of the starres, and calleth them all by their names' (Ps. 147.4); cf. Gen. 22.17. Cf. III xi 45.8–9. On counting the sands, see Ps.139.18. Both expressions are proverbial: see Tilley (1950) S91, C. G. Smith (1970) 720. Drayton notes that the rivers 'first, by *Spenser* numbred were' (*Poly-Olbion* xviii 108).

4   **descry**: describe.

7   **Cymodoce**: Cymoent at III iv 19.3. The change of name prepares for her change of role in relation to her son. The change is suggested by the power given the nereid, Cymodoce: 'that with her least word can asswage / The surging seas, when they do sorest rage' (50.4–5). She overcomes Proteus's power over Florimell and soothes the storm of passion that has continued unabated since Britomart began her quest, III iv 8–10.

Canto xii

Argument

2   **languor**: woeful plight.

Stanza 1

Upton (1758) defends the repetition of the preceding stanza because it allows the reader's mind to dwell on the poet's endless work. The stanza justifies itself by its triumphant energy, all the more astonishing after the poet's complaint of being tired.

3   Behind this claim is the commonplace of Renaissance natural philosophy that the sea contains replicas of all the creatures to be found on land.

6   **seeme**: not 'is' because the universe is not infinite.

2

Therefore the antique wisards well inuented,
　That *Venus* of the fomy sea was bred;
　For that the seas by her are most augmented,
　Witnesse th'exceeding fry, which there are fed,
　And wondrous sholes, which may of none be red.
　Then blame me not, if I haue err'd in count
　Of Gods, of Nymphs, of riuers yet vnred:
　For though their numbers do much more surmount,
Yet all those same were there, which erst I did recount.

3

All those were there, and many other more,
　Whose names and nations were too long to tell,
　That *Proteus* house they fild euen to the dore;
　Yet were they all in order, as befell,
　According their degrees disposed well.
　Amongst the rest, was faire *Cymodoce*,
　The mother of vnlucky *Marinell*,
　Who thither with her came, to learne and see
The manner of the Gods when they at banquet be.

4

But for he was halfe mortall, being bred
　Of mortall sire, though of immortall wombe,
　He might not with immortall food be fed,
　Ne with th'eternall Gods to bancket come;
　But walkt abrode, and round about did rome,
　To view the building of that vncouth place,
　That seem'd vnlike vnto his earthly home:
　Where, as he to and fro by chaunce did trace,
There vnto him betid a disauentrous case.

5

Vnder the hanging of an hideous clieffe,
　He heard the lamentable voice of one,
　That piteously complaind her carefull griefe,
　Which neuer she before disclosd to none,
　But to her selfe her sorrow did bemone.
　So feelingly her case she did complaine,
　That ruth it moued in the rocky stone,
　And made it seeme to feele her grieuous paine,
And oft to grone with billowes beating from the maine.

6

Though vaine I see my sorrowes to vnfold,
　And count my cares, when none is nigh to heare,
　Yet hoping griefe may lessen being told,
　I will them tell though vnto no man neare:
　For heauen that vnto all lends equall eare,
　Is farre from hearing of my heauy plight;
　And lowest hell, to which I lie most neare,
　Cares not what euils hap to wretched wight;
And greedy seas doe in the spoile of life delight.

7

Yet loe the seas I see by often beating,
　Doe pearce the rockes, and hardest marble weares;
　But his hard rocky hart for no entreating
　Will yeeld, but when my piteous plaints he heares,
　Is hardned more with my aboundant teares.
　Yet though he neuer list to me relent,
　But let me waste in woe my wretched yeares,
　Yet will I neuer of my loue repent,
But ioy that for his sake I suffer prisonment.

8

And when my weary ghost with griefe outworne,
　By timely death shall winne her wished rest,
　Let then this plaint vnto his eares be borne,
　That blame it is to him, that armes profest,
　To let her die, whom he might haue redrest.
　There did she pause, inforced to giue place,
　Vnto the passion, that her heart opprest,
　And after she had wept and wail'd a space,
She gan afresh thus to renew her wretched case.

Stanza 2
1　**antique wisards**: ancient wisemen.
2–3　**Venus of the fomy sea**: links the Temple of Venus and the marriage of the rivers as sources of love and life. The expression prepares for Florimell's restoration to her lover; see 33.3*n*.
5　**sholes**: schools.　**red**: counted.
7　**vnred**: unseen; uncounted.
8　**surmount**: exceed.

Stanza 3
2　**nations**: classes; kinds.
5　**According . . . disposed**: i.e. arranged in order by rank.

Stanza 4
1–2　See III iv 19.3–9.
8　**trace**: go.
9　**disauentrous case**: unfortunate event.

Stanza 5
1　Indicating Florimell's despair; cf. I ix 33.3.
2　**lamentable**: lamenting.
3　**carefull**: full of care.

Stanza 6
2　**count**: recount; number.
3　Proverbial (C. G. Smith, 1970, 761).
5　**equall**: impartial; or, to all equally.
9　**spoile**: plundering. She is the sea's spoil as Amoret is the 'spoyle of beautie' (x 58.3). Her state is Una's 'plung'd in sea of sorrowes deepe' (I vii 39.2).

Stanza 7
3　**his hard rocky hart**: cf. 'his stony heart' (13.1). The expression 'identifies' Marinell with the 'rocky stone' (5.7) which imprisons her.
5　**aboundant**: punning on the etymology, 'flowing in waves': like the seas, her tears will wear down his marble heart.

Stanza 8
1　**ghost**: spirit.
2　**timely**: early; hence untimely.
5　**redrest**: delivered from death.
9　**renew**: go over again.

519

9

Ye Gods of seas, if any Gods at all
    Haue care of right, or ruth of wretches wrong,
    By one or other way me woefull thrall,
    Deliuer hence out of this dungeon strong,
    In which I daily dying am too long.
    And if ye deeme me death for louing one,
    That loues not me, then doe it not prolong,
    But let me die and end my daies attone,
And let him liue vnlou'd, or loue him selfe alone.

10

But if that life ye vnto me decree,
    Then let mee liue, as louers ought to do,
    And of my lifes deare loue beloued be:
    And if he shall through pride your doome vndo,
    Do you by duresse him compell thereto,
    And in this prison put him here with me:
    One prison fittest is to hold vs two:
    So had I rather to be thrall, then free;
Such thraldome or such freedome let it surely be.

11

But O vaine iudgement, and conditions vaine,
    The which the prisoner points vnto the free,
    The whiles I him condemne, and deeme his paine,
    He where he list goes loose, and laughes at me.
    So euer loose, so euer happy be.
    But where so loose or happy that thou art,
    Know *Marinell* that all this is for thee.
    With that she wept and wail'd, as if her hart
Would quite haue burst through great abundance of her smart.

12

All which complaint when *Marinell* had heard,
    And vnderstood the cause of all her care
    To come of him, for vsing her so hard,
    His stubborne heart, that neuer felt misfare
    Was toucht with soft remorse and pitty rare;
    That euen for griefe of minde he oft did grone,
    And inly wish, that in his powre it weare
    Her to redresse: but since he meanes found none
He could no more but her great misery bemone.

13

Thus whilst his stony heart with tender ruth
    Was toucht, and mighty courage mollifide,
    Dame *Venus* sonne that tameth stubborne youth
    With iron bit, and maketh him abide,
    Till like a victor on his backe he ride,
    Into his mouth his maystring bridle threw,
    That made him stoupe, till he did him bestride:
    Then gan he make him tread his steps anew,
And learne to loue, by learning louers paines to rew.

14

Now gan he in his grieued minde deuise,
    How from that dungeon he might her enlarge:
    Some while he thought, by faire and humble wise
    To *Proteus* selfe to sue for her discharge:
    But then he fear'd his mothers former charge
    Gainst womens loue, long giuen him in vaine.
    Then gan he thinke, perforce with sword and targe
    Her forth to fetch, and *Proteus* to constraine:
520 But soone he gan such folly to forthinke againe.

15

Then did he cast to steale her thence away,
    And with him beare, where none of her might know.
    But all in vaine: for why he found no way
    To enter in, or issue forth below:
    For all about that rocke the sea did flow.
    And though vnto his will she giuen were,
    Yet without ship or bote her thence to row,
    He wist not how her thence away to bere;
And daunger well he wist long to continue there.

16

At last when as no meanes he could inuent,
    Backe to him selfe he gan returne the blame,
    That was the author of her punishment;
    And with vile curses, and reprochfull shame
    To damne him selfe by euery euill name;
    And deeme vnworthy or of loue or life,
    That had despisde so chast and faire a dame,
    Which him had sought through trouble and long strife;
Yet had refusde a God that her had sought to wife.

Stanza 9

8   **attone**: i.e. all days together, once for all, instead of
daily dying (5).
9   **vnlou'd**: not loving another.

Stanza 11

2   **points**: appoints, ordains.
3   **deeme his paine**: decree his punishment.

Stanza 12

2   **care**: grief.
4   **misfare**: mishap. Only his body was wounded by
Britomart; cf. 19.6.

Stanza 13

While the figure of Love riding the lover is Petrarchan (e.g.
Rime clxi 9–11), the application is S.'s. Love is aroused not
by beauty but by pity. See III v 30.4–9*n*.
2   **courage**: spirit, heart.   **mollifide**: softened; made less
obdurate.

Stanza 14

5–6   Cf. III iv 26.1–2.
7   **perforce**: forcibly.
9   **forthinke**: unthink.

Stanza 15

1   **cast**: resolve.
3   **for why**: because.

Stanza 16

1   **inuent**: discover.

17

In this sad plight he walked here and there,
  And romed round about the rocke in vaine,
  As he had lost him selfe, he wist not where;
  Oft listening if he mote her heare againe;
  And still bemoning her vnworthy paine.
  Like as an Hynde whose calfe is falne vnwares
  Into some pit, where she him heares complaine,
  An hundred times about the pit side fares,
Right sorrowfully mourning her bereaued cares.

18

And now by this the feast was throughly ended,
  And euery one gan homeward to resort.
  Which seeing *Marinell*, was sore offended,
  That his departure thence should be so short,
  And leaue his loue in that sea-walled fort.
  Yet durst he not his mother disobay,
  But her attending in full seemly sort,
  Did march amongst the many all the way:
And all the way did inly mourne, like one astray.

19

Being returned to his mothers bowre,
  In solitary silence far from wight,
  He gan record the lamentable stowre,
  In which his wretched loue lay day and night,
  For his deare sake, that ill deseru'd that plight:
  The thought whereof empierst his hart so deepe,
  That of no worldly thing he tooke delight;
  Ne dayly food did take, ne nightly sleepe,
But pyn'd, and mourn'd, and languisht, and alone did weepe.

20

That in short space his wonted chearefull hew
  Gan fade, and liuely spirits deaded quight:
  His cheeke bones raw, and eie-pits hollow grew,
  And brawney armes had lost their knowen might,
  That nothing like himselfe he seem'd in sight.
  Ere long so weake of limbe, and sicke of loue
  He woxe, that lenger he note stand vpright,
  But to his bed was brought, and layd aboue,
Like ruefull ghost, vnable once to stirre or moue.

21

Which when his mother saw, she in her mind
  Was troubled sore, ne wist well what to weene,
  Ne could by search nor any meanes out find
  The secret cause and nature of his teene,
  Whereby she might apply some medicine;
  But weeping day and night, did him attend,
  And mourn'd to see her losse before her eyne,
  Which grieu'd her more, that she it could not mend:
To see an helpelesse euill, double griefe doth lend.

22

Nought could she read the roote of his disease,
  Ne weene what mister maladie it is,
  Whereby to seeke some meanes it to appease.
  Most did she thinke, but most she thought amis,
  That that same former fatall wound of his
  Whyleare by *Tryphon* was not throughly healed,
  But closely rankled vnder th'orifis:
  Least did she thinke, that which he most concealed,
That loue it was, which in his hart lay vnreuealed.

23

Therefore to *Tryphon* she againe doth hast,
  And him doth chyde as false and fraudulent,
  That fayld the trust, which she in him had plast,
  To cure her sonne, as he his faith had lent:
  Who now was falne into new languishment
  Of his old hurt, which was not throughly cured.
  So backe he came vnto her patient,
  Where searching euery part, her well assured,
That it was no old sore, which his new paine procured.

24

But that it was some other maladie,
  Or griefe vnknowne, which he could not discerne:
  So left he her withouten remedie.
  Then gan her heart to faint, and quake, and earne,
  And inly troubled was, the truth to learne.
  Vnto himselfe she came, and him besought,
  Now with faire speches, now with threatnings sterne,
  If ought lay hidden in his grieued thought,
It to reueale: who still her answered, there was nought.

Stanza 17
5 **vnworthy**: undeserved; cf. i 1.5.
9 **her bereaued cares**: i.e. the object of her cares of which she has been deprived.

Stanza 18
4 **short**: near at hand.
8 **many**: company.

Stanza 19
3 **record**: i.e. go over in his mind. **stowre**: distress.

Stanza 20
1–5 Cf. the Red Cross Knight's appearance on emerging from Orgoglio's dungeon, I viii 41. Marinell's appearance manifests love's despair.
2 **liuely spirits deaded quight**: vital spirits entirely died.
3 **raw**: i.e. raw-boned.
7 **note**: could not.

Stanza 21
9 **helpelesse**: beyond help.

Stanza 22
1 **read**: discover.
2 **what mister**: what kind of.
3 **appease**: relieve.

Stanza 23
5 **languishment**: illness.
9 **procured**: caused.

Stanza 24
4 **earne**: grieve.

25

Nathlesse she rested not so satisfide,
  But leauing watry gods, as booting nought,
  Vnto the shinie heauen in haste she hide,
  And thence *Apollo* King of Leaches brought.
  Apollo came; who soone as he had sought
  Through his disease, did by and by out find,
  That he did languish of some inward thought,
  The which afflicted his engrieued mind;
Which loue he red to be, that leads each liuing kind.

26

Which when he had vnto his mother told,
  She gan thereat to fret, and greatly grieue.
  And comming to her sonne, gan first to scold,
  And chyde at him, that made her misbelieue:
  But afterwards she gan him soft to shrieue,
  And wooe with faire intreatie, to disclose,
  Which of the Nymphes his heart so sore did mieue.
  For sure she weend it was some one of those,
Which he had lately seene, that for his loue he chose.

27

Now lesse she feared that same fatall read,
  That warned him of womens loue beware:
  Which being ment of mortall creatures sead,
  For loue of Nymphes she thought she need not care,
  But promist him, what euer wight he weare,
  That she her loue to him would shortly gaine:
  So he her told: but soone as she did heare
  That *Florimell* it was, which wrought his paine,
She gan a fresh to chafe, and grieue in euery vaine.

28

Yet since she saw the streight extremitie,
  In which his life vnluckily was layd,
  It was no time to scan the prophecie,
  Whether old *Proteus* true or false had sayd,
  That his decay should happen by a mayd.
  It's late in death of daunger to aduize,
  Or loue forbid him, that is life denayd:
  But rather gan in troubled mind deuize,
How she that Ladies libertie might enterprize.

29

To *Proteus* selfe to sew she thought it vaine,
  Who was the root and worker of her woe:
  Nor vnto any meaner to complaine,
  But vnto great king *Neptune* selfe did goe,
  And on her knee before him falling lowe,
  Made humble suit vnto his Maiestie,
  To graunt to her, her sonnes life, which his foe
  A cruell Tyrant had presumpteouslie
By wicked doome condemn'd, a wretched death to die.

30

To whom God *Neptune* softly smyling, thus;
  Daughter me seemes of double wrong ye plaine,
  Gainst one that hath both wronged you, and vs:
  For death t'adward I ween'd did appertaine
  To none, but to the seas sole Soueraine.
  Read therefore who it is, which this hath wrought,
  And for what cause; the truth discouer plaine.
  For neuer wight so euill did or thought,
522 But would some rightfull cause pretend, though rightly nought.

31

To whom she answerd, Then it is by name
  Proteus, that hath ordayn'd my sonne to die;
  For that a waift, the which by fortune came
  Vpon your seas, he claym'd as propertie:
  And yet nor his, nor his in equitie,
  But yours the waift by high prerogatiue.
  Therefore I humbly craue your Maiestie,
  It to repleuie, and my sonne repriue:
So shall you by one gift saue all vs three aliue.

Stanza 25
4   On Apollo as god of medicine, see I v 43.6–9*n*. When he
was first wounded, Marinell was treated by the nymph who had
learned her skill from Apollo (III iv 41); now the god himself
appears. The union of sea and land in the marriage of Marinell
and Florimell is accomplished under the aegis of the lord of the
heavens.
9   Marinell confirms Venus's power, x 44–47.   **red**:
interpreted.

Stanza 26
5   **shrieue**: question; also, hear him confess his sin.
7   **mieue**: obsolete form of 'move'.

Stanza 27
1   **fatall read**: prophetic or foreboding counsel.
5   Cymoent uses **wight** in its restricted sense, a non-earthly
being, but Marinell takes advantage of its extended sense as a
mortall creature (3).

Stanza 28
1   **streight**: severe.
5   **decay**: downfall. The prophecy that 'A virgin strange and
stout him should dismay, or kill' (III iv 25.9) had applied to
Britomart and applies now to Florimell.
6   **aduize**: take thought.
9   **enterprize**: attempt to gain.

Stanza 30
2   **plaine**: complain.
6   **Read**: tell.

Stanza 31
3–6   **waift**: waif, in the legal sense of property left ownerless
(cf. III x 36.3) and hence no longer **propertie**; also the
obsolete sense of 'wafted': carried over water.
Knight (1970) 269 notes that Neptune, as god of the sea, may
claim all property lost in it.
8   **repleuie**: recover, or command to be restored, by bailing
from prison. The term plays against **repriue** (reprieve):
'rescue from death', because Florimell's release from prison
determines her own and Marinell's release from death.

32

He graunted it: and streight his warrant made,
  Vnder the Sea-gods seale autenticall,
  Commaunding *Proteus* straight t'enlarge the mayd,
  Which wandring on his seas imperiall,
  He lately tooke, and sithence kept as thrall.
  Which she receiuing with meete thankefulnesse,
  Departed straight to *Proteus* therewithall:
  Who reading it with inward loathfulnesse,
Was grieued to restore the pledge, he did possesse.

33

Yet durst he not the warrant to withstand,
  But vnto her deliuered *Florimell*.
  Whom she receiuing by the lilly hand,
  Admyr'd her beautie much, as she mote well:
  For she all liuing creatures did excell;
  And was right ioyous, that she gotten had
  So faire a wife for her sonne *Marinell*.
  So home with her she streight the virgin lad,
And shewed her to him, then being sore bestad.

34

Who soone as he beheld that angels face,
  Adorn'd with all diuine perfection,
  His cheared heart eftsoones away gan chace
  Sad death, reuiued with her sweet inspection,
  And feeble spirit inly felt refection;
  As withered weed through cruell winters tine,
  That feeles the warmth of sunny beames reflection,
  Liftes vp his head, that did before decline
And gins to spread his leafe before the faire sunshine.

35

Right so himselfe did *Marinell* vpreare,
  When he in place his dearest loue did spy;
  And though his limbs could not his bodie beare,
  Ne former strength returne so suddenly,
  Yet chearefull signes he shewed outwardly.
  Ne lesse was she in secret hart affected,
  But that she masked it with modestie,
  For feare she should of lightnesse be detected:
Which to another place I leaue to be perfected.

Stanza 32
2   **autenticall**: authentic: having legal force.
8   **loathfulnesse**: reluctance.

Stanza 33
3   By just this gesture Scudamour seizes Amoret, x 53.9.
When Amoret is taken from the Temple, she is compared to
the lost Eurydice (x 58.4–5), while **Florimell** emerges from the
sea as does Venus.

Stanza 34
1–2   A climax to the vision of Amoret's 'bright Angels hew'
(v 13.4) and of Britomart's 'angels face' (vi 19.5).
4   **her . . . inspection**: i.e. his sight of her, but also her sight
of him as she is **faire sunshine** (9).
5   **refection**: refreshment; restoration.
6   **tine**: affliction.

Stanza 35
8   **detected**: accused.

While Book IV arouses the least interest, Book V has been judged the simplest and remains the least liked. Only very recently has our understanding of it been radically revised and its allegorical complexity appreciated.

Earlier critics found the 'darke conceit' only too transparent. Warren (1898) V vii writes:

> The allegorical matter . . . is, on the whole, quite easy to follow. It is chiefly historical, and the historical meaning, in its main outline, stands clearly forth. Much of the narrative in this Book will bear nothing beyond an interpretation by history: it is impossible to find in it any moral or spiritual meaning. . . . In the greater part of the poem there is no double allegory, and where any other meaning does appear it is often of the simplest.

Her claims are supported by Jones (1930) 249f. Of the three sections of the Book, he calls the first (Cantos i, ii, and the first half of iv) 'a set of *exempla*' in which S. 'follows the main lines of Aristotle's analysis of the virtue in Book V of the *Nicomachean Ethics*'. The second section (Cantos iii, v-vii), which concludes earlier narratives, he ignores, except for the political allegory: Dolon's plot against Britomart in Canto vi 'clearly reflects Catholic attempts against the life of the Queen', and the Radigund–Britomart duel in Canto vii 'is obviously to be interpreted as the conflict between Mary Queen of Scots and Elizabeth'. The final section is seen to consist of scarcely concealed historical allegory. Canto viii first 'glances at' Elizabeth's diplomacy and details of the Pagan's battle with Arthur may be 'referred to the Spanish Armada'; Canto ix 'points so clearly' to the trial of Mary, Queen of Scots; Canto x 'deals with' the conflict in the Netherlands ('no allegory could be more transparent than this'); the Burbon episode in Canto xi is 'almost self-explanatory'; and the characters in Canto xii are identified with historical persons, Grantorto with the Pope and Artegall with Lord Gray. It is allowed at best that in this final section S. distorts history. Gough (1921) 289 notes that in the historical matter in Canto x the part played by England is 'entirely misrepresented' and suggests that S. describes 'what he hoped and believed would be done'. Of S.'s justification of the actions of Lord Gray in Ireland, which provides the historical matter of Canto xii, Gough 317 notes in a fine understatement, 'It was not easy for Spenser to make the petty military operations of Gray, with their accompaniment of ceaseless hangings, massacres, burnings, and harryings the crowning achievement of the heroic Knight of Justice.'

Most earlier critics were restrained in their personal response to Book V. Jones writes at length without expressing approval or condemnation. Warren V xiv allows only a question mark to escape: 'The Book . . . is not the presentation of the universal principle of Justice, but of Justice (?) as displayed in the British Islands in the sixteenth century.' Not so later critics. For Lewis (1936) 349, 'Spenser was the instrument of a detestable policy in Ireland, and in his fifth book the wickedness he had shared begins to corrupt his imagination'. On Talus's tumbling of the giant, Hough (1962) 195 comments: 'It is the willingness to settle what is after all a real debate by these brutal and summary methods that casts a faintly malodorous cloud over this and some other parts of Book V.' Of the same episode, Alpers (1967) 300 complains: 'Spenser seems to expect us to relish the violence and fearfulness of Talus' power.'

Unlike the earlier critics who saw the matter of Book V as chiefly historical, modern critics stress the moral meaning. Dunseath (1968) 7 claims that 'by emphasizing history as such, we often lose sight of the poem and Spenser's artistic purpose'. He expounds the moral allegory through an extended psychological analysis of Britomart and Artegall, tracing the successive stages of their moral and spiritual downfall until they redeem themselves in Canto vii. Through such character-study he demonstrates the progress in the Book from justice absolute to equity and finally to mercy. Also he shows the artistry by which this allegory is conveyed by demonstrating, for example, how the myth of the labours of Hercules determines the structure and controls the imagery.

Aptekar (1969) 8 also chooses not to stress historical reference and political allegory in the Book on the grounds that S. 'was writing a philosophical not a political poem'. She treats the moral allegory by examining the iconographical sources of three major themes: the images which show justice in terms of orthodox

Elizabethan concepts, those which show the foes of justice in terms of force and fraud, and the Hercules myth. Justice emerges from her study as an ambiguous virtue: although godly, it is dependent on guile and violence, and subject, like Hercules, to excessive strength and weakness.

Later readings further refine our understanding of the moral allegory by revealing its complexity. Bieman (1968) stresses the central role of Britomart in the book. Davidson (1969) shows how the figure of Isis in her Temple provides a focus for our understanding the allegory of Justice. Anderson (1970b) 65 sees a split in Artegall between Knight and Justicer: 'Artegall's limitations and those of his Legend prove inseparable from the virtue which he champions, for this virtue, taken as an absolute ideal, makes demands which neither human history nor individual human beings can satisfy'. Phillips (1970) argues that principles of logical analysis by which Renaissance theorists on justice arranged and developed their points provide the structure of Book V. Justice Absolute is illustrated in the six narrative episodes in the opening four cantos, Equity in the central cantos, and Mercy in the six narrative episodes in the final section of the Book. Knight (1970) claims that Equity provides the narrative unity of Book V. Now that Kermode (1971) 50–9 and Fletcher (1971) 276–87 have explained the Elizabethan concept of Equity, the moral allegory of Book V becomes increasingly clear.

It is far otherwise with the historical allegory. Its claims have been strongly urged by Kermode (1971) 4 as S.'s means of applying archetypal images to the human condition in his age: '*The Faerie Queene* is, among other things, a very topical poem about events that were always seen as given meaning by reference to those great myths of religious and national history which provided structures for all time and the whole world.' When Kermode applies this fresh concept of historical allegory to Book V, he interprets the Temple of Isis episode as an allegory of the Elizabethan debate on Equity. S. says only that Isis is Equity, but Kermode interprets her as the source of law: her one foot on the crocodile and the other on the ground 'reflect the criminal equity of Star Chamber'; her wand 'stands for the power of Chancery in civil cases'; her crocodile is 'purely human law', and its tail 'suggests an impotent enmity towards imperial Equity'. Clearly this fresh concept takes us back to the older one-to-one allegorizing that made the *Variorum* reading an over-simplification. Yet the problem may lie not in the concept itself but rather in the Book, for the reason offered by Craig (1972) 540: 'in the closing cantos of Book V archetype and history are so irreconcilable, so antithetical, as to drive one another out'. In the Belgae, Burbon and Irena episodes it is hardly possible to allow that there is anything beyond the painfully obvious topical allusion.

The application of certain episodes in Book V to events in Elizabethan history remains painfully obvious, despite the unsatisfactory interpretation offered by critics. Earlier critics allowed topical allusion to determine their understanding of Book V as though the whole book was written only to justify Elizabeth's foreign policy in the Netherlands, France, Spain, and Ireland. The discrepancies between the allegory and historical reality led Gough to reject Cantos x and xi as an idealized version of history and suggest that S. described what should be rather than what was. Northrop (1969) 291 has argued that S. departs from history because his defence of Elizabeth 'is included within and co-ordinated to his general conception of justice'.

The historical allegory of Book V is treated more comprehensively by Fletcher (1971). Like Kermode, he relates the archetypes to an historical context; yet for him the two merge: 'Allusions to current happenings tend to go *through* their historical particularity, till they reach a level of transcendent meaning' (42). When he applies this concept of historical allegory, he combines historical matters with the mythical and psychological in a manner that revitalizes the whole approach. On the Temple of Isis episode, for example, he observes that it 'shows Britomart passing through three stages of a female mystery: her initiation, her coronation, and her marriage' (277). Since she becomes identified with Isis or Equity, she may defeat 'the masculine, violent, inequitable aspect of her own Amazonian nature' (279) seen in Radigund.

THE FIFTH
BOOKE OF THE
FAERIE QVEENE.
Contayning,
THE LEGEND OF ARTEGALL
.OR
OF IVSTICE.

1

SO oft as I with state of present time,
The image of the antique world compare,
When as mans age was in his freshest prime,
And the first blossome of faire vertue bare,
Such oddes I finde twixt those, and these which are,
As that, through long continuance of his course,
Me seemes the world is runne quite out of square,
From the first point of his appointed sourse,
And being once amisse growes daily wourse and wourse.

2

For from the golden age, that first was named,
It's now at earst become a stonie one;
And men themselues, the which at first were framed
Of earthly mould, and form'd of flesh and bone,
Are now transformed into hardest stone:
Such as behind their backs (so backward bred)
Were throwne by *Pyrrha* and *Deucalione*:
And if then those may any worse be red,
They into that ere long will be degendered.

3

Let none then blame me, if in discipline
Of vertue and of ciuill vses lore,
I doe not forme them to the common line
Of present dayes, which are corrupted sore,
But to the antique vse, which was of yore,
When good was onely for it selfe desyred,
And all men sought their owne, and none no more;
When Iustice was not for most meed outhyred,
But simple Truth did rayne, and was of all admyred.

4

For that which all men then did vertue call,
Is now cald vice; and that which vice was hight,
Is now hight vertue, and so vs'd of all:
Right now is wrong, and wrong that was is right,
As all things else in time are chaunged quight.
Ne wonder; for the heauens reuolution
Is wandred farre from where it first was pight,
And so doe make contrarie constitution
Of all this lower world, toward his dissolution.

Proem

Stanzas 1–9
The decay of the world is alluded to throughout the poem – see esp. I xii 14.8–9, II vii 16–17, III i 13, IV viii 29–33 – but is treated fully here because justice confronts the fallen world directly. The increasing degeneration of mankind is seen as a prelude to the Apocalypse. Belief in the world's decay was strongly held by S. Harvey writes to him: 'You suppose the first age was the goulde age. . . . You suppose it a foolish madd worlde, wherein all thinges ar overrulid by fansye' (*Letter-Book* 86). Harris (1949) 119 claims that S. is 'the earliest of the English poets of this period to make much use of the concept that the world grows old and weary'.

Stanza 1
5 **oddes**: difference.
7–9 The determinism in these lines is commented upon by Berger (1968) 153: the 'premise of irreversible decline . . . encourages the violent repressiveness of iron-age justice'.
out of square: into disorder, referring to the set square as the emblem of justice. Cf. *S.C.* Feb. 11–4.

Stanza 2
2 **at earst**: at length. **stonie**: adding a sixth and final degenerate age to Hesiod's fifth or iron age.
4 **mould**: form; earth, enforcing **earthly**.
6–7 Ovid, *Met.* i 395–415. S. follows Comes (1616) VIII xvii p. 466 who explains man's stoniness by the stones; noted Lotspeich (1932) 53. The parenthesis suggests that man degenerates rather than evolves. On the implied analogy to Noah, see Allen (1963) 188.
8 **red**: supposed.
9 **degendered**: degenerated; downward bred; also suggesting 'made sterile'.

Stanza 3
1–2 The terms distinguish between the private and public virtues, as in *L.R.* **discipline**: instruction; art. **ciuill vses lore**: art of political wisdom.
3 **line**: standard of practice.
8 **for most meed outhyred**: let out to hire for the largest bribe.

Stanza 4
6–9 S. sees a causal relationship between moral and political degeneration and the progressive physical disorder of the universe. The wandering of the **heauens reuolution** refers to the effect of the precession of the equinoxes: the signs of the zodiac no longer correspond to the constellations after which they were originally named, that is, as they were, presumably, at the time of creation. Hence the principal star of the constellation of the Ram, which in the time of Ptolemy was in the zodiacal sign of the Ram, by the Elizabethan period had wandered to the sign of the Bull. See *Shakespeare's England* i 450. Cf. Mutabilitie's use of this doctrine, VII vii 55.6–7. A further effect is implied: instead of working towards perfection, the elements now move towards dissolution.

5

For who so list into the heauens looke,
　And search the courses of the rowling spheares,
　Shall find that from the point, where they first tooke
　Their setting forth, in these few thousand yeares
　They all are wandred much; that plaine appeares.
　For that same golden fleecy Ram, which bore
　Phrixus and *Helle* from their stepdames feares,
　Hath now forgot, where he was plast of yore,
And shouldred hath the Bull, which fayre *Europa* bore.

6

And eke the Bull hath with his bow-bent horne
　So hardly butted those two twinnes of *Ioue*,
　That they haue crusht the Crab, and quite him borne
　Into the great *Nemæan* lions groue.
　So now all range, and doe at randon roue
　Out of their proper places farre away,
　And all this world with them amisse doe moue,
　And all his creatures from their course astray,
Till they arriue at their last ruinous decay.

7

Ne is that same great glorious lampe of light,
　That doth enlumine all these lesser fyres,
　In better case, ne keepes his course more right,
　But is miscaried with the other Spheres.
　For since the terme of fourteene hundred yeres,
　That learned *Ptolomæe* his hight did take,
　He is declyned from that marke of theirs,
　Nigh thirtie minutes to the Southerne lake;
That makes me feare in time he will vs quite forsake.

8

And if to those Ægyptian wisards old,
　Which in Star-read were wont haue best insight,
　Faith may be giuen, it is by them told,
　That since the time they first tooke the Sunnes hight,
　Foure times his place he shifted hath in sight,
　And twice hath risen, where he now doth West,
　And wested twice, where he ought rise aright.
　But most is *Mars* amisse of all the rest,
And next to him old *Saturne*, that was wont be best.

9

For during *Saturnes* ancient raigne it's sayd,
　That all the world with goodnesse did abound:
　All loued vertue, no man was affrayd
　Of force, ne fraud in wight was to be found:
　No warre was knowne, no dreadfull trompets sound,
　Peace vniuersall rayn'd mongst men and beasts,
　And all things freely grew out of the ground:
　Iustice sate high ador'd with solemne feasts,
And to all people did diuide her dred beheasts.

Stanza 5
2　**the rowling spheares**: the transparent hollow concentric
spheres in which, according to ancient and medieval astronomy,
the heavenly bodies were fixed (Gough, 1921).

4　Less than six thousand according to the calendar in the
Geneva Bible.
6 to 6.4　As Gough notes, S. mentions the first five signs of
the zodiac: Aries, Taurus, Gemini, Cancer, and Leo. The sixth
is Virgo or Astræa who appears later in 'euerlasting place'
(i 11.5). In arguing that Jupiter is the patron deity of Book V,
Fowler (1964) 204 notes that the god constitutes the mythological focus for the imagery in these lines. At III xi 30.5–6
the tapestries in the house of Busirane show how Joue bore
Helle as a **Ram** and **Europa** as a **Bull**. Castor and Pollux are the
'two twynnes begotten on Leda by Jupiter' (Cooper, 1565).
Fowler 204 notes that the descriptions of the remaining
constellations allude to Jupiter through his son Hercules: Leo
is the **great Nemœan lion** (6.4) killed by Hercules. The **Crab**
is **crusht**, 'a reference to the slaying of its mythological fore-
runner by Hercules'. Aptekar (1969) 160–2 argues that
Hercules, the representative hero of justice, was connected with
all the signs of the zodiac: he put **Phrixus** on the ram, was with
the Argonauts who sought the golden fleece, captured the
Cretan bull (which was often identified with Europa's bull)
and was associated with the twins.

Stanza 6
2　**hardly**: violently; perhaps closely.

Stanza 7
2　**these lesser fyres**: the stars and planets whose source of
light was believed to be the sun.
4　**miscaried**: gone astray.
5–9　By 1592 the obliquity of the ecliptic had declined
$21\frac{1}{2}$ minutes from the time of its measurement by Ptolemy, as
Gough (1921) notes. Fowler (1964) 194 observes that widely
different readings were given by Renaissance authorities.
Selden, in Drayton, *Works* iv 300–1, estimates 23 degrees $31\frac{1}{2}$
minutes.
7　**theirs**: referring to the ancient astronomers.
8　**the Southerne lake**: the southern hemisphere of water.

Stanza 8
1–7　According to **those Ægyptian wisards**, 'these strange
alterations were marked in the Sunne at four sundry times.
Two sundry times it was seene to rise from that place where it
is now wont to fall, and in like manner to set in those regions
from whence it now ariseth, which also came to passe two
seuerall times' (Herodotus, *The Faymous Hystory*, trans. B.R.
1584; cited *Var*. v 159).　**Star-read**: star-lore, astronomy.
8–9　The assumption that the planets had circular orbits
caused problems with their apparent eccentricity until Kepler's
De Motibus Stellae Martis (1609) established the law of elliptical
orbits. The eccentricity of Mars and Saturn is discussed at
VII vii 52. The special problem of Mars is noted by
Shakespeare, *1 Henry VI* I ii 1–2.

Stanza 9
1　**Saturnes ancient raigne**: Ovid, *Met*. i 89–112, describes
the Age of Saturn as the time when all men kept faith and did
what was right: there was no fear of punishment and no alarm
of trumpets, for men lived secure from war, and the earth of
herself freely gave all things needful.
9　**diuide**: dispense. Unlike Ovid's golden age in which all
freely did right without law (*Met*. i 89–90), S.'s age exists
sub lege. See Aptekar (1969) 230 *n*1. Cf. Astræa's 'stedfast
doome' executed by Talus, i 12.3.

10

Most sacred vertue she of all the rest,
  Resembling God in his imperiall might;
  Whose soueraine powre is herein most exprest,
  That both to good and bad he dealeth right,
  And all his workes with Iustice hath bedight.
  That powre he also doth to Princes lend,
  And makes them like himselfe in glorious sight,
  To sit in his owne seate, his cause to end,
And rule his people right, as he doth recommend.

11

Dread Souerayne Goddesse, that doest highest sit
  In seate of iudgement, in th'Almighties stead,
  And with magnificke might and wondrous wit
  Doest to thy people righteous doome aread,
  That furthest Nations filles with awfull dread,
  Pardon the boldnesse of thy basest thrall,
  That dare discourse of so diuine a read,
  As thy great iustice praysed ouer all:
The instrument whereof loe here thy *Artegall*.

Cant. I.

Artegall trayn'd in Iustice lore
Irenaes quest pursewed,
He doeth auenge on Sanglier
his Ladies bloud embrewed.

1

THough vertue then were held in highest price,
  In those old times, of which I doe intreat,
  Yet then likewise the wicked seede of vice
  Began to spring which shortly grew full great,
  And with their boughes the gentle plants did beat.
  But euermore some of the vertuous race
  Rose vp, inspired with heroicke heat,
  That cropt the branches of the sient base,
And with strong hand their fruitfull rancknes did deface.

2

Such first was *Bacchus*, that with furious might
  All th'East before vntam'd did ouerronne,
  And wrong repressed, and establisht right,
  Which lawlesse men had formerly fordonne.
  There Iustice first her princely rule begonne.
  Next *Hercules* his like ensample shewed,
  Who all the West with equall conquest wonne,
  And monstrous tyrants with his club subdewed;
The club of Iustice dread, with kingly powre endewed.

Stanza 10

1–2 Cf. Hooker, *Works* iii 623f, on the theme: 'in God there is this divine virtue called Justice'. Cf. vii 1.

4 Matt. 5.45: 'He maketh his sunne to arise on the evil, and the good, and sendeth raine on the juste, and unjuste.'

5 **bedight**: adorned; ordered (sugg. by context). For S., what is fitly ordered adorns.

6–9 Cf. Proverbs 8.15: 'By me [God's Wisdom], Kings reigne, and princes decree justice.' Also 2 Chron. 9.8: '. . . to set thee on his throne as King, in the stead of the Lord thy God.' Hence in the Dedication to Elizabeth: 'by the grace of God Queene'. **end**: fulfil.

Stanza 11

1 Cf. the address to Elizabeth at I Proem 4.1. On Elizabeth as Astræa, see i 5.4*n*.

2 **stead**] place *1596*, the obvious rhyming word, is supported by the reference to 10.6–9.

3 **magnificke**: renowned.

4 **aread**: declare.

7 **read**: subject; matter, sugg. by the context.

9 **Artegall**: see i 3.2*n*.

Canto i

Argument

1 **Iustice lore**: the doctrine of Justice, 'the rules of iustice' (5.9).

4 **embrewed**: shed.

Stanza 1

1 **price**: esteem, regard.

2 **intreat**: treat.

8 **sient base**: base shoots.

9 The metaphor suggests Guyon's destruction of the Bower of Bliss. **fruitfull** and **rancknes** suggest luxuriant growth and whatever is proud, rebellious, coarse. **deface**: lay waste; cf. II xii 83.6.

Stanza 2

Bacchus and his son **Hercules** are commonly linked by the mythographers, as Upton first noticed; the one established justice in the east, the other in the west. Cf. Comes (1616) V xiii p.263: *a Baccho in Oriente, ut in Occidente ab Hercule*. See *T.M.* 461. Bacchus 'went a great part of the world, destroiying monsters and tyrannes, and conquered the countrey of India' (Cooper, 1565).

4 **fordonne**: destroyed.

8–9 **The club of Iustice**: the club wielded by Orgoglio, Disdain, Lust, and Hatred is an instrument of oppression and brute power. As Hercules's weapon, it is the instrument of Justice. Cf. Talus's flail. In place of divine justice under which 'no man was affrayd/Of force' (Proem 9.3–4), justice now is strictly executed: all fear to disobey.

3

And such was he, of whom I haue to tell,
   The Champion of true Iustice *Artegall*,
   Whom (as ye lately mote remember well)
   An hard aduenture, which did then befall,
   Into redoubted perill forth did call;
   That was to succour a distressed Dame,
   Whom a strong tyrant did vniustly thrall,
   And from the heritage, which she did clame,
Did with strong hand withhold: *Grantorto* was his name.

4

Wherefore the Lady, which *Irena* hight,
   Did to the Faery Queene her way addresse,
   To whom complayning her afflicted plight,
   She her besought of gratious redresse.
   That soueraine Queene, that mightie Emperesse,
   Whose glorie is to aide all suppliants pore,
   And of weake Princes to be Patronesse,
   Chose *Artegall* to right her to restore;
For that to her he seem'd best skild in righteous lore.

5

For *Artegall* in iustice was vpbrought
   Euen from the cradle of his infancie,
   And all the depth of rightfull doome was taught
   By faire *Astræa*, with great industrie,
   Whilest here on earth she liued mortallie.
   For till the world from his perfection fell
   Into all filth and foule iniquitie,
   Astræa here mongst earthly men did dwell,
And in the rules of iustice them instructed well.

6

Whiles through the world she walked in this sort,
   Vpon a day she found this gentle childe,
   Amongst his peres playing his childish sport:
   Whom seeing fit, and with no crime defilde,
   She did allure with gifts and speaches milde,
   To wend with her.   So thence him farre she brought
   Into a caue from companie exilde,
   In which she noursled him, till yeares he raught,
And all the discipline of iustice there him taught.

Stanza 3

1   The association of **Artegall** and Hercules extends
throughout the Book. See Dunseath (1968) 49 and Cheney
(1966) 173–4. Aptekar (1969) 153–200 traces the two views of
Hercules – the lustful hero enslaved to Omphale and the stoic
hero who chooses *virtus* rather than *voluptas* – and shows how
they are illustrated in the relation of Artegall to Radigund and
Britomart.
2   Historically, as Artgallo, the brother of Cador, son of
Gorlois, he is half-brother to Arthur. Harper (1910) 144 notes
that he takes Arthur's place in the chronicle. See III iii 27n. In
Geoffrey of Monmouth III xvii, his namesake Artgallo is an
unjust king until, having been deposed and restored, he begins
'exercising strict iustice towards all men'; see II x 44.4–7.
Art-egall signifies 'equal to Arthur' and 'iudge of equity'
(iii 36.7); cf. 'best skild in righteous lore' (4.9; cf. 7.1–3). In
Book III and the first part of Book IV, the spelling 'Arthegall'
suggests the relationship to Arthur. A thousand years, from the
sixth to the sixteenth century, separate the historical Artegall
and Gloriana's knight; see Hankins (1971) 150.
3–5   The 'hard aduenture' mentioned at IV vi 42.3.
7–9   Cf. the restatement at 13.3–5.   **Grantorto**: Ital. *gran
torto*, great wrong; suggesting the etymology 'twisted',
'wrested'. Knight (1970) 273 notes the legal meaning in the
name: 'To do something by tort is not merely to commit a
wrong, but to possess something illegally.' As 'great tort' he
epitomizes all the other tyrants in the poem who extort
property.

Stanza 4

1   **Irena**] *Eirena 1596*, an anagram of Ierne, the classical
name of Erin or Ireland. As Gk εἰρήνη, her name signifies
'peace'; cf. 'myld *Eirene*' (ix 32.6) who attends Mercilla, as
ideally a peaceful Ireland should pay homage to Elizabeth.
Dunseath (1968) 63 cites Isaiah 32.17: 'And the worke of iustice
shalbe peace, even the worke of iustice and quietnes, and
assurance for ever.' Artegall's quest becomes an effort to
restore the Golden Age when 'Peace vniuersall rayn'd mongst
men and beasts' (Proem 9.6).
4   **redresse**: aid.

Stanza 5

4   **Astræa**: 'the daughter of . . . Iupiter and Themis. It is
taken for iustice, as the woorde doth signifie. She detesting the
naughtie and unjust livinge of men, flewe to heaven' (Cooper,
1565). She is identified with the constellation Virgo and seen as
the righteous Virgin next to Libra, the scales of iustice (11.4–9).
Her return is celebrated in Virgil's fourth Eclogue: *iam redit et
Virgo, redeunt Saturnia regna*. The cult of Elizabeth as Astræa
is traced by Yates (1947). As Williams (1966) 155 notes,
however, 'she is not so to Spenser although the compliment is
one that asks to be made'. Cf. Cheney (1966) 159–60. See ix
37.8–9n.
5   **mortallie**: as a mortal.

Stanza 6

1   **sort**: manner.
3   **peres**: companions.
5–6   The education of worldly iustice commences with
bribery. See 9.2n.
8   **noursled**: trained.   **yeares**: mature age; cf. 8.3.

7

There she him taught to weigh both right and wrong
  In equall ballance with due recompence,
  And equitie to measure out along,
  According to the line of conscience,
  When so it needs with rigour to dispence.
  Of all the which, for want there of mankind,
  She caused him to make experience
  Vpon wyld beasts, which she in woods did find,
With wrongfull powre oppressing others of their kind.

8

Thus she him trayned, and thus she him taught,
  In all the skill of deeming wrong and right,
  Vntill the ripenesse of mans yeares he raught;
  That euen wilde beasts did feare his awfull sight,
  And men admyr'd his ouerruling might;
  Ne any liu'd on ground, that durst withstand
  His dreadfull heast, much lesse him match in fight,
  Or bide the horror of his wreakfull hand,
When so he list in wrath lift vp his steely brand.

9

Which steely brand, to make him dreaded more,
  She gaue vnto him, gotten by her slight
  And earnest search, where it was kept in store
  In *Ioues* eternall house, vnwist of wight,
  Since he himselfe it vs'd in that great fight
  Against the *Titans*, that whylome rebelled
  Gainst highest heauen; *Chrysaor* it was hight;
  Chrysaor that all other swords excelled,
Well prou'd in that same day, when *Ioue* those Gyants quelled.

10

For of most perfect metall it was made,
  Tempred with Adamant amongst the same,
  And garnisht all with gold vpon the blade
  In goodly wise, whereof it tooke his name,
  And was of no lesse vertue, then of fame.
  For there no substance was so firme and hard,
  But it would pierce or cleaue, where so it came;
  Ne any armour could his dint out ward,
But wheresoeuer it did light, it throughly shard.

11

Now when the world with sinne gan to abound,
  Astræa loathing lenger here to space
  Mongst wicked men, in whom no truth she found,
  Return'd to heauen, whence she deriu'd her race;
  Where she hath now an euerlasting place,
  Mongst those twelue signes, which nightly we doe see
  The heauens bright-shining baudricke to enchace;
  And is the *Virgin*, sixt in her degree,
And next her selfe her righteous ballance hanging bee.

included here. **along**: i.e. along with justice. The weighing of justice and measuring of equity are a single activity, as God 'with righteousnes shal . . . judge the worlde, and the people with equitie' (Ps. 98.9). **equitie** is traditionally the conscience of the law. On the relation of justice to equity, see Fletcher (1971) 280–7 and Kermode (1971) 50–6. **dispence**: either 'administer' (applying the letter of the law) or 'dispense with' **rigour** by easing punishment.
7–9   The classical analogue is Chiron's instruction of Achilles in the precepts of divine justice and Achilles's practice upon beasts; see Statius, *Achilleid* ii 96–167.

Stanza 8
2   **deeming**: distinguishing.
5   **admyr'd**: marvelled at.
7   **heast**: command.
8   **bide**: endure. **wreakfull**: avenging.
9   **steely brand**: sword.

Stanza 9
2   **slight**: craft. That justice should be administered by a pilfered sword need not have ironical overtones. Fowler (1964) 201 suggests that the sword is so taken 'because mortals – even mortals such as Astræa and Arthegall – can have no title to virtue'.
5–9   On the battles of the Titans and Giants against the Olympians, see II vii 41.6*n*.
7   **Chrysaor**: Gk golden sword. Appropriately an epithet for Apollo, as Homer, *Iliad* v 509; less appropriately, the father of Geryon, the enemy of Justice, as Nelson (1963) 335 observes. The sword takes the place of Jove's traditional thunderbolt. Cf. 2 Macc. 15. 15–6: '*Ieremias* . . . gave unto Judas a sworde of golde: and as he gave it, he spake thus: Take this holie sworde, a gifte from God, wherewith thou shalt wounde the adversaries.' Accordingly, **Ioues eternall house** suggests God's armoury, as in Jer. 50.25: 'The Lord hathe opened his treasure, and hathe broght forthe the weapons of his wrath'.

Stanza 10
1–5   **gold** is the most perfect of the metals. **Adamant**: a metal of surpassing hardness, suggesting αδαμας, unconquerable. Fowler (1964) 201 notes the etymological pun: since *Chrysos aor*, in addition to being an epithet of Jupiter, means 'golden sword', **his** (4) refers both to the sword and to Jove. **vertue**: power, efficacy.
8   **dint**: blow.
9   **shard**: cut.

Stanza 11
1–4   Cf. VII vii 37. 6–9, *Hub*. 1–4. The classical source is Ovid, *Met*. i 149–50; see 5.4*n* **space**: walk.
6   **those twelue signes**: the signs of the zodiac. After the twelfth stanza, the story of **Astræa**'s substitute properly begins.
7   The zodiac or the Milky Way, which runs diagonally across the heavens and in which most of the constellations are set, is likened to the richly ornamented sword-belt which a knight wore diagonally across his shoulder; cf. Arthur's belt, I vii 29.8–9. **enchace**: adorn.
8–9   **sixt in her degree**: as Virgo, the sign of August, the sixth month after March which begins the year. **her righteous ballance**: the constellation Libra, the sign of September. See VII vii 38. 7–9. Cheney (1966) 157 notes that 'Artegall is at no point associated with this image'.

Stanza 7
1–5   She expounds the significance of 'her righteous ballance' (11.9). S. names two aspects of justice: justice absolute and equity. Phillips (1970) 106 finds mercy also

12

But when she parted hence, she left her groome
   An yron man, which did on her attend
   Alwayes, to execute her stedfast doome,
   And willed him with *Artegall* to wend,
   And doe what euer thing he did intend.
   His name was *Talus*, made of yron mould,
   Immoueable, resistlesse, without end.
   Who in his hand an yron flale did hould,
With which he thresht out falshood, and did truth vnfould.

13

He now went with him in this new inquest,
   Him for to aide, if aide he chaunst to neede,
   Against that cruell Tyrant, which opprest
   The faire *Irena* with his foule misdeede,
   And kept the crowne in which she should succeed.
   And now together on their way they bin,
   When as they saw a Squire in squallid weed,
   Lamenting sore his sorowfull sad tyne,
With many bitter teares shed from his blubbred eyne.

14

To whom as they approched, they espide
   A sorie sight, as euer seene with eye;
   An headlesse Ladie lying him beside,
   In her owne blood all wallow'd wofully,
   That her gay clothes did in discolour die.
   Much was he moued at that ruefull sight;
   And flam'd with zeale of vengeance inwardly,
   He askt, who had that Dame so fouly dight;
Or whether his owne hand, or whether other wight?

15

Ah woe is me, and well away (quoth hee)
   Bursting forth teares, like springs out of a banke,
   That euer I this dismall day did see:
   Full farre was I from thinking such a pranke;
   Yet litle losse it were, and mickle thanke,
   If I should graunt that I haue doen the same,
   That I mote drinke the cup, whereof she dranke:
   But that I should die guiltie of the blame,
The which another did, who now is fled with shame.

16

Who was it then (sayd *Artegall*) that wrought?
   And why? doe it declare vnto me trew.
   A knight (said he) if knight he may be thought,
   That did his hand in Ladies bloud embrew,
   And for no cause, but as I shall you shew.
   This day as I in solace sate hereby
   With a fayre loue, whose losse I now do rew,
   There came this knight, hauing in companie
This lucklesse Ladie, which now here doth headlesse lie.

17

He, whether mine seem'd fayrer in his eye,
   Or that he wexed weary of his owne,
   Would change with me; but I did it denye;
   So did the Ladies both, as may be knowne,
   But he, whose spirit was with pride vpblowne,
   Would not so rest contented with his right,
   But hauing from his courser her downe throwne,
   Fro me reft mine away by lawlesse might,
And on his steed her set, to beare her out of sight.

Stanza 12

S. fashions **Talus** from Plato's Talos, one who upheld the laws inscribed in brazen tablets, and thus was named 'brazen' (*Minos* 320 C); or, from the man of bronze, in Apollodorus, *Argonautica* iv 1638–48, made by Vulcan and given to the wife of Minos, King of Crete and famous law-giver, to guard the island. Upton (1758) sees S.'s figure as executioner rather than judge. Most simply, he is executive power, 'the right hand of Iustice truely hight' (iv 1.9). Lotspeich (1932) 109 notes that in Comes (1616) II ii Astræa left behind her a 'testamentum' of laws. Accordingly, Talus may be regarded as the law itself; see Padelford, *Var.* v 276–80. Cf. *View* 33: 'The laws ought to be like to stony tables, plain, steadfast, and unmovable'. The name suggests 'talion', retaliation or simple retributive justice, from Lat. *talio*: 'an equall or like payne in recompence of an hurte' (Cooper, 1565).
4   Earlier **Artegall** goes on his way 'Ne wight him to attend' (IV vi 44.6); cf. iv 3.8–9, viii 3.8–9. Apparently **Talus** is not to be regarded as separate from the exercise of Artegall's virtue.
6   **yron mould**: because he belongs to the iron age. See Aptekar (1969) 110-5. Fletcher (1971) 141 notes the connection with the giant made of gold, silver, bronze, iron, and clay in Nebuchadnezzar's dream (Dan. 2.32–3).
7   The line declares **Talus**'s iron nature, according to the etymology of his name, $\tau\lambda\alpha\omega$, to endure steadfastly.   **without end**: immortal, unlike Talos who was vulnerable in the ankle.
8–9   **yron flale**: a military weapon in the Renaissance, adapted from the wooden flail or thresher (cf. vi 29.7). Yet see iv 44.2 and *n*. Since Astræa is associated with the harvest (cf. VII vii 37), her instrument, Talus, is associated with threshing: see Aptekar 49–51. It is an instrument of punishment (cf. vii 35.7–9) but its end is to unfold truth. Aptekar 47 notes that Talus's weapon recalls the flail of Mars, the club of Hercules, and the scourge of God's wrath.

Stanza 13
1   **inquest**: quest, suggesting also a judicial inquiry.
7   **squallid**: from Lat. *squalidus*, dirty. It indicates extreme degradation: cf. iv 34.6, xii 12.2.
8   **tyne**: trouble.

Stanza 14
7   Artegall's characteristic response; see IV vi 5.8–9*n*.
8   **dight**: abused.

Stanza 15
3   **dismall day**: unlucky or evil day.
4   **pranke**: malicious deed.
5   **mickle thanke**: much favour or occasion for thanks.

Stanza 16
4   **embrew**: imbrue, stain; cf. Arg. 4.

18

Which when his Ladie saw, she follow'd fast,
　And on him catching hold, gan loud to crie
　Not so to leaue her, nor away to cast,
　But rather of his hand besought to die.
　With that his sword he drew all wrathfully,
　And at one stroke cropt off her head with scorne,
　In that same place, whereas it now doth lie.
So he my loue away with him hath borne,
And left me here, both his and mine owne loue to morne.

19

Aread (sayd he) which way then did he make?
　And by what markes may he be knowne againe?
　To hope (quoth he) him soone to ouertake,
　That hence so long departed, is but vaine:
　But yet he pricked ouer yonder plaine,
　And as I marked, bore vpon his shield,
　By which it's easie him to know againe,
A broken sword within a bloodie field;
Expressing well his nature, which the same did wield.

20

No sooner sayd, but streight he after sent
　His yron page, who him pursew'd so light,
　As that it seem'd aboue the ground he went:
　For he was swift as swallow in her flight,
　And strong as Lyon in his Lordly might.
　It was not long, before he ouertooke
　Sir *Sanglier*; (so cleeped was that Knight)
Whom at the first he ghessed by his looke,
And by the other markes, which of his shield he tooke.

21

He bad him stay, and backe with him retire;
　Who full of scorne to be commaunded so,
　The Lady to alight did eft require,
　Whilest he reformed that vnciuill fo:
　And streight at him with all his force did go.
　Who mou'd no more therewith, then when a rocke
　Is lightly stricken with some stones throw;
But to him leaping, lent him such a knocke,
That on the ground he layd him like a sencelesse blocke.

22

But ere he could him selfe recure againe,
　Him in his iron paw he seized had;
　That when he wak't out of his warelesse paine,
　He found him selfe, vnwist, so ill bestad,
　That lim he could not wag.　Thence he him lad,
　Bound like a beast appointed to the stall:
　The sight whereof the Lady sore adrad,
And fain'd to fly for feare of being thrall;
But he her quickly stayd, and forst to wend withall.

23

When to the place they came, where *Artegall*
　By that same carefull Squire did then abide,
　He gently gan him to demaund of all,
　That did betwixt him and that Squire betide.
　Who with sterne countenance and indignant pride
　Did aunswere, that of all he guiltlesse stood,
　And his accuser thereuppon defide:
For neither he did shed that Ladies bloud,
Nor tooke away his loue, but his owne proper good.

24

Well did the Squire perceiue him selfe too weake,
　To aunswere his defiaunce in the field,
　And rather chose his challenge off to breake,
　Then to approue his right with speare and shield.
　And rather guilty chose him selfe to yield.
　But *Artegall* by signes perceiuing plaine,
　That he it was not, which that Lady kild,
But that strange Knight, the fairer loue to gaine,
Did cast about by sleight the truth thereout to straine.

Stanza 19
1　**Aread**: declare.
8–9　The **broken sword** is a sign of disgrace: see iii 37.9 and v 21.8. The **bloodie field** refers to the surface of the shield and also the field of battle; it suggests his name, Sanglier, from Fr. *sang*, blood.

Stanza 20
2　**light**: quickly.
7　**Sanglier**: Fr. wild boar. He is Artegall's first opponent in the Tournament, IV iv 40.3, and marks the change from the 'wyld beasts' (7.8) upon which Artegall has practised his justice. Dunseath (1968) 73 links the episode with Hercules's labour to capture the Erymanthean Boar.

Stanza 21
3　**eft**: in turn; then.　**require**: ask.
4　**reformed**: punished.　**vnciuill**: barbarous, uncouth.

Stanza 22
1　**recure**: recover.
3　**warelesse paine**: his painful plight of which, being unconscious, he was unaware, or against which he could not guard himself.
4　**vnwist**: not knowing how.
8　**fain'd**: sought.

Stanza 23
2　**carefull**: sorrowful.
3　**gently**: courteously.　**demaund**: ask.
7　**defide**: challenged to judicial combat.
9　**proper good**: private property.

Stanza 24
3　**challenge**: claim.
4　**approue**: show to be true (by his victory).
5　**yield**: acknowledge, admit.

533

25

And sayd, Now sure this doubtfull causes right
  Can hardly but by Sacrament be tride,
  Or else by ordele, or by blooddy fight;
  That ill perhaps mote fall to either side.
  But if ye please, that I your cause decide,
  Perhaps I may all further quarrell end,
  So ye will sweare my iudgement to abide.
Thereto they both did franckly condiscend,
And to his doome with listfull eares did both attend.

26

Sith then (sayd he) ye both the dead deny,
  And both the liuing Lady claime your right,
  Let both the dead and liuing equally
  Deuided be betwixt you here in sight,
  And each of either take his share aright.
  But looke who does dissent from this my read,
  He for a twelue moneths day shall in despight
  Beare for his penaunce that same Ladies head;
To witnesse to the world, that she by him is dead.

27

Well pleased with that doome was *Sangliere*,
  And offred streight the Lady to be slaine.
  But that same Squire, to whom she was more dere,
  When as he saw she should be cut in twaine,
  Did yield, she rather should with him remaine
  Aliue, then to him selfe be shared dead;
  And rather then his loue should suffer paine,
  He chose with shame to beare that Ladies head.
True loue despiseth shame, when life is cald in dread.

28

Whom when so willing *Artegall* perceaued;
  Not so thou Squire, (he sayd) but thine I deeme
  The liuing Lady, which from thee he reaued:
  For worthy thou of her doest rightly seeme.
  And you, Sir Knight, that loue so light esteeme,
  As that ye would for little leaue the same,
  Take here your owne, that doth you best beseeme,
  And with it beare the burden of defame;
Your owne dead Ladies head, to tell abrode your shame.

29

But *Sangliere* disdained much his doome,
  And sternly gan repine at his beheast;
  Ne would for ought obay, as did become,
  To beare that Ladies head before his breast.
  Vntill that *Talus* had his pride represt,
  And forced him, maulgre, it vp to reare.
  Who when he saw it bootelesse to resist,
  He tooke it vp, and thence with him did beare,
As rated Spaniell takes his burden vp for feare.

30

Much did that Squire Sir *Artegall* adore,
  For his great iustice, held in high regard;
  And as his Squire him offred euermore
  To serue, for want of other meete reward,
  And wend with him on his aduenture hard.
  But he thereto would by no meanes consent;
  But leauing him forth on his iourney far'd:
  Ne wight with him but onely *Talus* went.
They two enough t'encounter an whole Regiment.

Stanza 25

1–4   The customary means to determine the right in a
dispute.   **Sacrament**: the oath of purgation by which the
accused sought to clear himself.   **ordele**: the trial by fire or
water.   **blooddy fight**: the challenge to decide guilt or
innocence by single combat. Artegall warns that these trials
may be determined by fortune and advises them to submit to
his just and wise judgment.

8   **condiscend**: consent.

9   **listfull**: attentive.

Stanza 26

Jortin (1734) first noticed that Artegall's 'doome' is taken from
the Judgment of Solomon, 1 Kings 3. 16–27. Dunseath (1968)
81–2 notes that Solomon's first judgment is also Artegall's.

3–5   Artegall may indulge in legal quibbling: to divide both
ladies equally could mean that one (the living lady) would be
awarded to the victor and the other (the dead lady) to the
defeated party. Instead, the Knight and Squire assume that he
means that each would be awarded half of each lady.

6–9   When the Squire dissents from this counsel, he reveals
his innocence and is excused; but Sanglier, who does not dissent, must carry the lady's head. The form of punishment
occurs in Malory 284–5. Aptekar (1969) 123 finds it 'hard to
imagine a more guileful and dishonorable – and effective – process of law'. Yet Artegall upholds justice by his **read** and
distributes equity by his 'doome' (29.1). The Squire's dissent
proves him both innocent of murdering the dead lady and
worthy to have the living one.   **day**: space of time.   **in
despight**: i.e. to his own scorn.

Stanza 27

9   **cald in dread**: put in danger.

Stanza 28

2–5   **thou** and **Sir** note the difference in rank between a
Squire and a Knight.

8   **defame**: disgrace.

Stanza 29

4   **before his breast**: i.e. allegorically, 'on his conscience'.

6   **maulgre**: in spite of himself.

Stanza 30

1   **adore**: praise.

Cant. II.

Artegall beares of Florimell,
Does with the Pagan fight:
Him slaies, drownes Lady Munera,
Does race her castle quight.

1

NOught is more honorable to a knight,
Ne better doth beseeme braue cheualry,
Then to defend the feeble in their right,
And wrong redresse in such as wend awry.
Whilome those great Heroes got thereby
Their greatest glory, for their rightfull deedes,
And place deserued with the Gods on hy.
Herein the noblesse of this knight exceedes,
Who now to perils great for iustice sake proceedes.

2

To which as he now was vppon the way,
He chaunst to meet a Dwarfe in hasty course;
Whom he requir'd his forward hast to stay,
Till he of tidings mote with him discourse.
Loth was the Dwarfe, yet did he stay perforse,
And gan of sundry newes his store to tell,
As to his memory they had recourse:
But chiefely of the fairest *Florimell*,
How she was found againe, and spousde to *Marinell*.

3

For this was *Dony*, *Florimels* owne Dwarfe,
Whom hauing lost (as ye haue heard whyleare)
And finding in the way the scattred scarfe,
The fortune of her life long time did feare.
But of her health when *Artegall* did heare,
And safe returne, he was full inly glad,
And askt him where, and when her bridale cheare
Should be solemniz'd: for if time he had,
He would be there, and honor to her spousall ad.

4

Within three daies (quoth hee) as I do here,
It will be at the Castle of the strond;
What time if naught me let, I will be there
To doe her seruice, so as I am bond.
But in my way a little here beyond
A cursed cruell Sarazin doth wonne,
That keepes a Bridges passage by strong hond,
And many errant Knights hath there fordonne;
That makes all men for feare that passage for to shonne.

5

What mister wight (quoth he) and how far hence
Is he, that doth to trauellers such harmes?
He is (said he) a man of great defence;
Expert in battell and in deedes of armes;
And more emboldned by the wicked charmes,
With which his daughter doth him still support;
Hauing great Lordships got and goodly farmes,
Through strong oppression of his powre extort;
By which he stil them holds, and keepes with strong effort.

Canto ii

Argument

Omits the subject of the second half of the canto (29–54), the
Giant with the Scales. S's theme of distributive justice
determines a careful distribution of the stanzas: nine of
preparation (2–10), nine on the Pagan (11–19), and nine on
Munera (20–28). Guizor, as a base groom, is allowed only nine
lines, 6.6–9, 11.5–9.

4 **race**: raze.

Stanza 1

5–9 **those great Heroes**: particularly Bacchus and
Hercules (see i 2). **noblesse**: used twice of Arthur (I viii
26.7, II viii 18.4). It suggests the exercise of nobility.

Stanza 2

3 **requir'd**: requested.
7 **had recourse**: recurred; cf. vii 20.3.
9 **spousde**: betrothed.

Stanza 3

1 **Dony**: from donzel, Ital. *donzello*, a page, squire.
2 **Whom hauing lost**: i.e. **Florimell** whom the Dwarf lost.
whyleare: III v 3–5.
3 **the scattred scarfe**: the broken girdle dropped when
Florimell fled from the hyena, III vii 31.8–9, and found by
Satyrane. Cf. iii 27.4–7.
5 **health**: safety.
7 **cheare**: reception.

Stanza 4

2 **the Castle of the strond**: cf. the '*Rich strond*' (III iv
20.8) guarded by Marinell.
3 **let**: prevent.
6 **Sarazin**: Saracen or pagan (12.1).
8 **fordonne**: ruined.

Stanza 5

1 **mister wight**: kind of person.
3 **defence**: ability to defend himself.
5–6 She supports him by magic and he supports her by
spoil (9.1–2). Their unnatural relationship is expressed in their
unnatural public actions.
7 **Lordships**: estates belonging to lords. **farmes**:
possibly the collecting of taxes.
8 **extort**: wrongly obtained.

6

And dayly he his wrongs encreaseth more,
  For neuer wight he lets to passe that way,
  Ouer his Bridge, albee he rich or poore,
  But he him makes his passage-penny pay:
  Else he doth hold him backe or beat away.
  Thereto he hath a groome of euill guize,
  Whose scalp is bare, that bondage doth bewray,
  Which pols and pils the poore in piteous wize;
But he him selfe vppon the rich doth tyrannize.

7

His name is hight *Pollente*, rightly so
  For that he is so puissant and strong,
  That with his powre he all doth ouergo,
  And makes them subiect to his mighty wrong;
  And some by sleight he eke doth vnderfong.
  For on a Bridge he custometh to fight,
  Which is but narrow, but exceeding long;
  And in the same are many trap fals pight,
Through which the rider downe doth fall through ouersight.

8

And vnderneath the same a riuer flowes,
  That is both swift and dangerous deepe withall;
  Into the which whom so he ouerthrowes,
  All destitute of helpe doth headlong fall,
  But he him selfe, through practise vsuall,
  Leapes forth into the floud, and there assaies
  His foe confused through his sodaine fall,
  That horse and man he equally dismaies,
And either both them drownes, or trayterously slaies.

9

Then doth he take the spoile of them at will,
  And to his daughter brings, that dwels thereby:
  Who all that comes doth take, and therewith fill
  The coffers of her wicked threasury;
  Which she with wrongs hath heaped vp so hy,
  That many Princes she in wealth exceedes,
  And purchast all the countrey lying ny
  With the reuenue of her plenteous meedes,
Her name is *Munera*, agreeing with her deedes.

10

Thereto she is full faire, and rich attired,
  With golden hands and siluer feete beside,
  That many Lords haue her to wife desired:
  But she them all despiseth for great pride.
  Now by my life (sayd he) and God to guide,
  None other way will I this day betake,
  But by that Bridge, whereas he doth abide:
  Therefore me thither lead.   No more he spake,
But thitherward forthright his ready way did make.

11

Vnto the place he came within a while,
  Where on the Bridge he ready armed saw
  The Sarazin, awayting for some spoile.
  Who as they to the passage gan to draw,
  A villaine to them came with scull all raw,
  That passage money did of them require,
  According to the custome of their law,
  To whom he aunswerd wroth, Loe there thy hire;
And with that word him strooke, that streight he did expire.

12

Which when the Pagan saw, he wexed wroth,
  And streight him selfe vnto the fight addrest,
  Ne was Sir *Artegall* behinde: so both
  Together ran with ready speares in rest.
  Right in the midst, whereas they brest to brest
  Should meete, a trap was letten downe to fall
  Into the floud: streight leapt the Carle vnblest,
  Well weening that his foe was falne withall:
But he was well aware, and leapt before his fall.

Stanza 6

3 **his Bridge**: the possessive suggests that laws of private property and public right-of-way are in conflict, as Knight (1970) 275 notes. Neff, *Var.* v 170–1, suggests that abuse of toll bridges illustrates the danger of oppressive private monopolies and cites contemporary examples. In *Areopagitica*, Milton refers to 'a narrow bridge of licencing where the challenger should passe' (*Prose Wks* ii 562).
albee: whether.
6 **guize**: behaviour; alluding to his name, Guizor (vi 33.6).
7 **bewray**: reveal.
8 **pols and pils**: plunders and pillages by cutting off the hair and skin; alluding to his master's name, Pollente.

Stanza 7

1 **Pollente**: strong (Lat. *pollens*).
5 **vnderfong**: entrap, alluding to the trap in the bridge.
8 **trap fals**: trapdoors (that fall); cf. 12.6. Aptekar (1969) 126 suggests a pun on 'false'.
9 **ouersight**: i.e. seeing over but not under.

Stanza 8

5 **practise vsuall**: habitual practice or treachery; cf. 13.5–7.
6 **assaies**: assails.
8 **dismaies**: defeats.

Stanza 9

8 **meedes**: corrupt gain.
9 **Munera**: Lat. rewards, gifts. Cf. Langland's Lady Meed, *Piers Plowman* ii 8–17.

Stanza 11

4 **Who**: 'When' sugg. Drayton, according to Collier (1862); 'Tho' sugg. Church (1758). Yet 'who to them' is common in older English for 'to whom', as Gough (1921) notes. The same expression is used at vi 37.2 when Britomart comes to this bridge.

Stanza 12

1–2 He does not submit his case to be judged: see i 25.1–4n.
7 **vnblest**: unblessed, because he is a pagan; hence accursed. Cf. 18.8.
8 **withall**: as well, i.e. with the trap.
9 **aware**: wary.

13

There being both together in the floud,
  They each at other tyrannously flew;
  Ne ought the water cooled their whot bloud,
  But rather in them kindled choler new.
  But there the Paynim, who that vse well knew
  To fight in water, great aduantage had,
  That oftentimes him nigh he ouerthrew:
  And eke the courser, whereuppon he rad,
Could swim like to a fish, whiles he his backe bestrad.

14

Which oddes when as Sir *Artegall* espide,
  He saw no way, but close with him in hast;
  And to him driuing strongly downe the tide,
  Vppon his iron coller griped fast,
  That with the straint his wesand nigh he brast.
  There they together stroue and struggled long,
  Either the other from his steede to cast;
  Ne euer *Artegall* his griple strong
For any thing wold slacke, but still vppon him hong.

15

As when a Dolphin and a Sele are met,
  In the wide champian of the Ocean plaine:
  With cruell chaufe their courages they whet,
  The maysterdome of each by force to gaine,
  And dreadfull battaile twixt them do darraine:
  They snuf, they snort, they bounce, they rage, they rore,
  That all the sea disturbed with their traine,
  Doth frie with fome aboue the surges hore.
Such was betwixt these two the troublesome vprore.

16

So *Artegall* at length him forst forsake
  His horses backe, for dread of being drownd,
  And to his handy swimming him betake.
  Eftsoones him selfe he from his hold vnbownd,
  And then no ods at all in him he fownd:
  For *Artegall* in swimming skilfull was,
  And durst the depth of any water sownd.
  So ought each Knight, that vse of perill has,
In swimming be expert through waters force to pas.

17

Then very doubtfull was the warres euent,
  Vncertaine whether had the better side:
  For both were skild in that experiment,
  And both in armes well traind and throughly tride.
  But *Artegall* was better breath'd beside,
  And towards th'end, grew greater in his might,
  That his faint foe no longer could abide
  His puissance, ne beare him selfe vpright,
But from the water to the land betooke his flight.

18

But *Artegall* pursewd him still so neare,
  With bright Chrysaor in his cruell hand,
  That as his head he gan a litle reare
  Aboue the brincke, to tread vpon the land,
  He smote it off, that tumbling on the strand
  It bit the earth for very fell despight,
  And gnashed with his teeth, as if he band
  High God, whose goodnesse he despaired quight,
Or curst the hand, which did that vengeance on him dight.

Stanza 14
5 **straint**: strain, pressure. **wesand**: windpipe.
8 **griple**: grasp.

Stanza 15
1 **Dolphin**: the dolphin signifies guile, particularly that
which the good man uses to overcome a guileful opponent;
Aptekar (1969) 127 cites Ripa's icon '*Stratagemma
Militare*'. **Sele**: 'stinking Seales' (*Col.* 249) suggests why that animal is
compared to Pollente.
2 **champian**: open stretches.
5 **darraine**: wage.
6 **bounce**: thump, as 21.6.
7 **traine**: the track made by their bodies.
8 **frie**: boil.

Stanza 16
3 **handy**: with his hands; or in which he was handy.
4-5 **from his hold vnbownd,/. . . no ods at all in him**:
i.e. even when he released himself from Artegall's hold,
Pollente had no advantage over him.
6-9 West (1973) cites Renaissance lore on the art
(generally scorned) of knights swimming in full armour.
vse: frequent experience.

Stanza 17
1 **euent**: outcome.
2 **whether**: which of the two.
3 **experiment**: experience, i.e. of swimming.

Stanza 18
1-5 The sword delivers the coup de grâce. Talus's flail
enforces justice throughout the Book until the sword is used
against Grantorto.
2 **cruell**: a surprising epithet; yet cf. iii 22.1, v 13.1, and
Osyris's 'cruell doomes' (vii 22.9). It signifies 'severe', 'strict',
'rigorous'; cf. Jove's 'cruell vengeance' (ix 31.9). Cf. Isaiah
13.9.
6 More than a classical detail, as in Virgil, *Aen.* xi 418: the
curse upon the serpent is that it shall eat dust (Gen. 3.14).
Repeated at the fall of Gereoneo (xi 14.7) and Grantorto
(xii 23.7).
7-9 The cursing acknowledges that punishment for injustice
comes from God. The conjunction of **God** and **Artegall**
points to the latter as His avenging minister. **band**: cursed.
dight: execute.

537

19

His corps was carried downe along the Lee,
   Whose waters with his filthy bloud it stayned:
   But his blasphemous head, that all might see,
   He pitcht vpon a pole on high ordayned;
   Where many years it afterwards remayned,
   To be a mirrour to all mighty men,
   In whose right hands great power is contayned,
   That none of them the feeble ouerren,
But alwaies doe their powre within iust compasse pen.

20

That done, vnto the Castle he did wend,
   In which the Paynims daughter did abide,
   Guarded of many which did her defend:
   Of whom he entrance sought, but was denide,
   And with reprochfull blasphemy defide,
   Beaten with stones downe from the battilment,
   That he was forced to withdraw aside;
   And bad his seruant Talus to inuent
Which way he enter might, without endangerment.

21

Eftsoones his Page drew to the Castle gate,
   And with his iron flaile at it let flie,
   That all the warders it did sore amate,
   The which erewhile spake so reprochfully,
   And made them stoupe, that looked earst so hie.
   Yet still he bet, and bounst vppon the dore,
   And thundred strokes thereon so hideouslie,
   That all the peece he shaked from the flore,
And filled all the house with feare and great vprore.

22

With noise whereof the Lady forth appeared
   Vppon the Castle wall, and when she saw
   The daungerous state, in which she stood, she feared
   The sad effect of her neare ouerthrow;
   And gan entreat that iron man below,
   To cease his outrage, and him faire besought,
   Sith neither force of stones which they did throw,
   Nor powr of charms, which she against him wrought,
Might otherwise preuaile, or make him cease for ought.

23

But when as yet she saw him to proceede,
   Vnmou'd with praiers, or with piteous thought,
   She ment him to corrupt with goodly meede;
   And causde great sackes with endlesse riches fraught,
   Vnto the battilment to be vpbrought,
   And powred forth ouer the Castle wall,
   That she might win some time, though dearly bought
   Whilest he to gathering of the gold did fall.
But he was nothing mou'd, nor tempted therewithall.

24

But still continu'd his assault the more,
   And layd on load with his huge yron flaile,
   That at the length he has yrent the dore,
   And made way for his maister to assaile.
   Who being entred, nought did then auaile
   For wight, against his powre them selues to reare:
   Each one did flie; their hearts began to faile,
   And hid them selues in corners here and there;
And eke their dame halfe dead did hide her self for feare.

25

Long they her sought, yet no where could they finde her,
   That sure they ween'd she was escapt away:
   But Talus, that could like a limehound winde her,
   And all things secrete wisely could bewray,
   At length found out, whereas she hidden lay
   Vnder an heape of gold. Thence he her drew
   By the faire lockes, and fowly did array,
   Withouten pitty of her goodly hew,
That Artegall him selfe her seemelesse plight did rew.

26

Yet for no pitty would he change the course
   Of Iustice, which in Talus hand did lye;
   Who rudely hayld her forth without remorse,
   Still holding vp her suppliant hands on hye,
   And kneeling at his feete submissiuely.
   But he her suppliant hands, those hands of gold,
   And eke her feete, those feete of siluer trye,
   Which sought vnrighteousnesse, and iustice sold,
Chopt off, and nayld on high, that all might them behold.

Stanza 19

1–2   **Lee**: river; cf. 'watry lea' (IV ii 16.3), referring to the river as open ground; cf. also 15.2. The river which was the means of his injustice becomes the means of his just punishment, and is punished itself. Cf. 27.4–5, 9.

4   **vpon a pole**: the punishment fits his name.

6   **mirrour**: warning.

7   **right**: the pun suggests why power is symbolized by the right hand.

Stanza 20

5   **blasphemy**: slander, specifically against God's minister.

8   **inuent**: find out.

Stanza 21

3   **amate**: dismay.

4   **reprochfully**: abusively.

6   **bounst**: thumped.

8   **peece**: fortress.

Stanza 22

4   **effect**: accomplishment.

Stanza 25

3   **like a limehound winde her**: like a bloodhound get the wind of her.

7   **array**: afflict.

8   **hew**: appearance; also colour, here of gold and silver.

9   **seemelesse**: unseemly.

Stanza 26

6–8   Possibly the terms are to be distributed: he chopped off her silver feet which **sought vnrighteousnesse** and her golden hands which **iustice sold**.   **trye**: for tried: refined.

27

Her selfe then tooke he by the sclender wast,
  In vaine loud crying, and into the flood
  Ouer the Castle wall adowne her cast,
  And there her drowned in the durty mud:
  But the streame washt away her guilty blood.
  Thereafter all that mucky pelfe he tooke,
  The spoile of peoples euill gotten good,
  The which her sire had scrap't by hooke and crooke,
And burning all to ashes, powr'd it downe the brooke.

28

And lastly all that Castle quite he raced,
  Euen from the sole of his foundation,
  And all the hewen stones thereof defaced,
  That there mote be no hope of reparation,
  Nor memory thereof to any nation.
  All which when *Talus* throughly had perfourmed,
  Sir *Artegall* vndid the euill fashion,
  And wicked customes of that Bridge refourmed.
Which done, vnto his former iourney he retourned.

29

In which they measur'd mickle weary way,
  Till that at length nigh to the sea they drew;
  By which as they did trauell on a day,
  They saw before them, far as they could vew,
  Full many people gathered in a crew;
  Whose great assembly they did much admire.
  For neuer there the like resort they knew.
  So towardes them they coasted, to enquire
What thing so many nations met, did there desire.

30

There they beheld a mighty Gyant stand
  Vpon a rocke, and holding forth on hie
  An huge great paire of ballance in his hand,
  With which he boasted in his surquedrie,
  That all the world he would weigh equallie,
  If ought he had the same to counterpoys.
  For want whereof he weighed vanity,
  And fild his ballaunce full of idle toys:
Yet was admired much of fooles, women, and boys.

31

He sayd that he would all the earth vptake,
  And all the sea, deuided each from either:
  So would he of the fire one ballaunce make,
  And one of th'ayre, without or wind, or wether:
  Then would he ballaunce heauen and hell together,
  And all that did within them all containe;
  Of all whose weight, he would not misse a fether.
  And looke what surplus did of each remaine,
He would to his owne part restore the same againe.

Stanza 27

2–4   The punishment fits her attempted bribery, 23.4–6.
6   **mucky pelfe**: 'filthy lucre', used here for pilfered property.
9   He imitates Moses who burned the golden calf and cast its dust into the river, Deut. 9.21.

Stanza 28

1   **raced**: razed, as Arg. 4. Cf. Job 15.34: 'Fyre shal devoure the houses of bribes.' The Geneva gloss identifies such houses as those 'which were buylt or mainteined by powling, and briberie'. See Dunseath (1968) 94.
3   **defaced**: destroyed.
4   **reparation**: repair.

Stanza 29

1   **measur'd**: travelled.
6   **admire**: wonder at.
8   **coasted**: approached; 'travelled along the coast' fits the context, and their destination which is 'the Castle of the strond' (4.2). Apparently Marinell's rich strond becomes the setting for the Giant's argument for the redistribution of all material things.

Stanza 30

1   The giants of Gen. 6.4 are glossed as tyrants in the Geneva Bible. Cf. Fraunce, *Third Part of Yvychurch* (1592) sig 9: 'These allegorically are seditious and rebellious subjects in a common wealth, or schismaticall and hæreticall seducers in the Church . . . the Giants, rebells or heretikes: the hills, their aspiring deseignes and accursed stratagems.'
3   The **Gyant** has usurped Astræa's 'righteous ballance' (i 11.9) and God's balance: see 35*n*. Dunseath (1968) 98 cites the apocalyptic figure in Rev. 6.5, the rider on a black horse who 'had balances in his hand'.
4   **surquedrie**: arrogance, presumption.
5–6   He echoes Archimedes's famous boast: 'Give me a place to stand and I will move the earth.'
7–9   Cf. Ps. 62.9: 'Yet the children of men are vanitie, the chief men are lies: to lay them upon a balance thei are altogether lighter then vanitie.' Weighing vanity plays on the etymology, from Lat. *vanus*, empty. If **fooles** and **women** were inverted, 9 would be more regular (proposed by Warton, 1762), but would lose its witty emphasis.

Stanza 31

By reweighing the four elements, the Giant threatens to undo creation and restore the universe to its original state of chaos, when 'the earth was without forme and voyde' (Gen. 1.2).
2   On the third day of creation God divided the earth from the sea.
3–4   He claims that he can weigh air, regardless of its state, against fire.   **wether**: tempest.
5–6   Dunseath (1968) 102 cites Jer. 31.37: 'Thus saith the Lord, If the heavens can be measured, or the fundacions of the earth be searched out beneth, then wil I cast of all the sede of Israel.'

539

32

For why, he sayd they all vnequall were,
   And had encroched vppon others share,
   Like as the sea (which plaine he shewed there)
   Had worne the earth, so did the fire the aire,
   So all the rest did others parts empaire.
   And so were realmes and nations run awry.
   All which he vndertooke for to repaire,
   In sort as they were formed aunciently;
And all things would reduce vnto equality.

33

Therefore the vulgar did about him flocke,
   And cluster thicke vnto his leasings vaine,
   Like foolish flies about an hony crocke,
   In hope by him great benefite to gaine,
   And vncontrolled freedome to obtaine.
   All which when *Artegall* did see, and heare,
   How he mis-led the simple peoples traine,
   In sdeignfull wize he drew vnto him neare,
And thus vnto him spake, without regard or feare.

34

Thou that presum'st to weigh the world anew,
   And all things to an equall to restore,
   In stead of right me seemes great wrong dost shew,
   And far aboue thy forces pitch to sore.
   For ere thou limit what is lesse or more
   In euery thing, thou oughtest first to know,
   What was the poyse of euery part of yore:
   And looke then how much it doth ouerflow,
Or faile thereof, so much is more then iust to trow.

35

For at the first they all created were
   In goodly measure, by their Makers might,
   And weighed out in ballaunces so nere,
   That not a dram was missing of their right,
   The earth was in the middle centre pight,
   In which it doth immoueable abide,
   Hemd in with waters like a wall in sight;
   And they with aire, that not a drop can slide:
Al which the heauens containe, and in their courses guide.

36

Such heauenly iustice doth among them raine,
   That euery one doe know their certaine bound,
   In which they doe these many yeares remaine,
   And mongst them al no change hath yet beene found.
   But if thou now shouldst weigh them new in pound,
   We are not sure they would so long remaine:
   All change is perillous, and all chaunce vnsound.
   Therefore leaue off to weigh them all againe,
Till we may be assur'd they shall their course retaine.

37

Thou foolishe Elfe (said then the Gyant wroth)
   Seest not, how badly all things present bee,
   And each estate quite out of order goth?
   The sea it selfe doest thou not plainely see
   Encroch vppon the land there vnder thee;
   And th'earth it selfe how daily its increast,
   By all that dying to it turned be?
   Were it not good that wrong were then surceast,
And from the most, that some were giuen to the least?

Stanza 32
1   **For why**: because.
3–4   Cf. *H.L.* 78–91 and VII vii 25.4–9.
8   **In sort as**: in the manner.
9   **reduce**: bring back, restore.

Stanza 33
2   **leasings**: lies.
3   The simile implies more than attraction: the flies are foolish because once stuck they die, as do the people.

Stanza 34
1–4   The Giant's argument depends upon the sense of Lat. *aequus*, fair, equitable, just, to which Artegall replies that simple equality need not be just. Properly used, Astræa's scales 'equall gaue to each as Iustice duly scann'd' (VII vii 38.9), where 'equall' signifies what Justice regards as equitable. **an equall**: a state of equality.
4   **pitch**: the height to which a falcon soars before swooping upon its prey.
5   **lesse or more**: too little or too much.
7   **poyse**: weight.
9   The general thought is clear: only by knowing the original weight of all things may one know what is more or less than just or right.   **to trow**: to be believed.

Stanza 35
In answer to the Giant who seeks to reduce all things to what he supposes to have been their original equality, Artegall argues that God created each thing in its proper place by measurement and weighing in balances. For the concept of the balance, see 2 Esdras 4.36 and especially Job 28.23–5, 38.4–6.
1   **at the first**: referring to the creation. Artegall ignores the physical effects of the Fall.
5–9   S. retains Ptolemy's geocentric theory in which the earth, as the centre of the universe, is surrounded by successive concentric spheres of water, air, and fire.

Stanza 36
4   Since the Proem recognizes change in the universe, Gough (1921) suggests that Artegall claims that the elements have not varied in quantity since the creation.
5   **new in pound**: anew in the balance.
7   As *View* 94: 'All innovation is perilous.'

Stanza 37
3   **estate**: state.
4   His atrocious pun determines his punishment, 49.9.
8   **surceast**: entirely stopped.
9   **most**: greatest.

38

Therefore I will throw downe these mountaines hie,
  And make them leuell with the lowly plaine:
  These towring rocks, which reach vnto the skie,
  I will thrust downe into the deepest maine,
  And as they were, them equalize againe.
  Tyrants that make men subiect to their law,
  I will suppresse, that they no more may raine;
  And Lordings curbe, that commons ouer-aw;
And all the wealth of rich men to the poore will draw.

39

Of things vnseene how canst thou deeme aright,
  Then answered the righteous *Artegall*,
  Sith thou misdeem'st so much of things in sight?
  What though the sea with waues continuall
  Doe eate the earth, it is no more at all:
  Ne is the earth the lesse, or loseth ought,
  For whatsoeuer from one place doth fall,
  Is with the tide vnto an other brought:
For there is nothing lost, that may be found, if sought.

40

Likewise the earth is not augmented more,
  By all that dying into it doe fade.
  For of the earth they formed were of yore,
  How euer gay their blossome or their blade
  Doe flourish now, they into dust shall vade.
  What wrong then is it, if that when they die,
  They turne to that, whereof they first were made?
  All in the powre of their great Maker lie:
All creatures must obey the voice of the most hie.

41

They liue, they die, like as he doth ordaine,
  Ne euer any asketh reason why.
  The hils doe not the lowly dales disdaine;
  The dales doe not the lofty hils enuy.
  He maketh Kings to sit in souerainty;
  He maketh subiects to their powre obay;
  He pulleth downe, he setteth vp on hy;
  He giues to this, from that he takes away.
For all we haue is his: what he list doe, he may.

42

What euer thing is done, by him is donne,
  Ne any may his mighty will withstand;
  Ne any may his soueraine power shonne,
  Ne loose that he hath bound with stedfast band.
  In vaine therefore doest thou now take in hand,
  To call to count, or weigh his workes anew,
  Whose counsels depth thou canst not vnderstand,
  Sith of things subiect to thy daily vew
Thou doest not know the causes, nor their courses dew.

43

For take thy ballaunce, if thou be so wise,
  And weigh the winde, that vnder heauen doth blow;
  Or weigh the light, that in the East doth rise;
  Or weigh the thought, that from mans mind doth flow.
  But if the weight of these thou canst not show,
  Weigh but one word which from thy lips doth fall,
  For how canst thou those greater secrets know,
  That doest not know the least thing of them all?
Ill can he rule the great, that cannot reach the small.

Stanza 38
1–5 The Giant assumes an apocalyptic role: 'Everie valley shalbe filled, and everie mountaine, and hil shalbe broght lowe' (Luke 3.5). Allen (1946) comments on the medieval view that in the beginning the world was level. See also Nicolson (1959) ch. 2.
8–9 The Giant acts as did Artegall's historical namesake, Artgallo; see i 3.2*n*. Fletcher (1971) 157 calls the episode 'Artegall learning to be just, in dialogue with himself.'
Lordings: petty lords. The Giant's argument has expanded from 'some' (37.9) to **all**.

Stanza 39
4–9 This argument determines Artegall's judgment on the quarrel between Bracidas and Amidas; cf. iv 19.

Stanza 40
4–5 The imagery is scriptural; cf. James 1.10: 'As the flower of the grasse shal he vanish away.' **vade**: vanish.

Stanzas 41–42
Artegall rounds on the Giant as does the angel on the prophet in 2 Esdras 4, and Jehovah on Job – see Job 28. Artegall's eloquence links him with Hercules who enchained men by the power of his words.

Stanza 41
1–2 Cf. Dan. 4.32: 'According to his wil he worketh . . . and none can stay his hand, nor say unto him, What doest thou?'
5–6 Cf. Proem 10.6–9. Cf. Rom. 13.1–2, Prov. 8.15.
maketh shifts meaning from 'appoints' to 'compels'.
7–8 Cf. 1 Sam. 2.7: 'The Lord maketh poore and maketh riche: bringeth lowe, and exalteth.' Ps. 75.7: 'God is the judge: he maketh low and he maketh hie.' Job 1.21: 'The Lord hathe given, and the Lord hathe taken it.'
9 Cf. Job. 42.2: 'I knowe that thou canst do all things.'
may: can; but carrying the threat that he will.

Stanza 42
2 Cf. 2 Chron. 20.6: 'In thine hand is power and might, and none is able to withstand thee.'
5–9 Cf. Uriel's rebuke of Esdras: 'Thine owne things . . . canst thou not knowe: how shulde thy vessel then be able to comprehend the wayes of the Hiest?' (2 Esdras 4.10–1). Cf. Rom. 11.33–4. Cf. I ix 6.6–9.
6 **count**: account.

Stanza 43
1–2 Cf. 2 Esdras 4.5: 'Weigh me the weight of the fyre, or measure me the blast of the winde.' Cf. Job 28.25.
7 **secrets**: the hidden workings of God, known only through revelation.

541

44

Therewith the Gyant much abashed sayd;
　That he of little things made reckoning light,
　Yet the least word that euer could be layd
　Within his ballaunce, he could way aright.
　Which is (sayd he) more heauy then in weight,
　The right or wrong, the false or else the trew?
　He answered, that he would try it streight,
　So he the words into his ballaunce threw,
But streight the winged words out of his ballaunce flew.

45

Wroth wext he then, and sayd, that words were light,
　Ne would within his ballaunce well abide.
　But he could iustly weigh the wrong or right.
　Well then, sayd *Artegall*, let it be tride.
　First in one ballance set the true aside.
　He did so first; and then the false he layd
　In th'other scale; but still it downe did slide,
　And by no meane could in the weight be stayd.
For by no meanes the false will with the truth be wayd.

46

Now take the right likewise, sayd *Artegale*,
　And counterpeise the same with so much wrong.
　So first the right he put into one scale;
　And then the Gyant stroue with puissance strong
　To fill the other scale with so much wrong.
　But all the wrongs that he therein could lay,
　Might not it peise; yet did he labour long,
　And swat, and chauf'd, and proued euery way:
Yet all the wrongs could not a litle right downe way.

47

Which when he saw, he greatly grew in rage,
　And almost would his balances haue broken:
　But *Artegall* him fairely gan asswage,
　And said; Be not vpon thy balance wroken:
　For they doe nought but right or wrong betoken;
　But in the mind the doome of right must bee;
　And so likewise of words, the which be spoken,
　The eare must be the ballance, to decree
And iudge, whether with truth or falshood they agree.

48

But set the truth and set the right aside,
　For they with wrong or falshood will not fare;
　And put two wrongs together to be tride,
　Or else two falses, of each equall share;
　And then together doe them both compare.
　For truth is one, and right is euer one.
　So did he, and then plaine it did appeare,
　Whether of them the greater were attone.
But right sate in the middest of the beame alone.

49

But he the right from thence did thrust away,
　For it was not the right, which he did seeke;
　But rather stroue extremities to way,
　Th'one to diminish, th'other for to eeke.
　For of the meane he greatly did misleeke.
　Whom when so lewdly minded *Talus* found,
　Approching nigh vnto him cheeke by cheeke,
　He shouldered him from off the higher ground,
And down the rock him throwing, in the sea him dround.

542

Stanza 45
1　**light**: implying also 'of no consequence.'
8–9　**by no meane**: the repetition invokes Aristotle's
doctrine that virtue is the mean between the two extremes:
there is no mean between the true and the false; see 48–49*n*.
weight: scales; cf. Avarice who 'right and wrong ylike in
equall ballaunce waide' (I iv 27.9).

Stanza 46
7　**peise**: counterbalance.
8　**proued**: tried.

Stanza 47
3　**fairely**: courteously.
4　**wroken**: avenged.
6–9　In effect, Artegall tells the Giant that only the mind
and ear can weigh opposites; scales weigh only like things.

Stanzas 48–49
Gough (1921) notes that these stanzas allude to the Aristotelian
theory of virtue as a mean between two extremes.

Stanza 48
4　**falses**: falsehoods.
6　Proverbial (C. G. Smith, 1970, 791). Cf. 'truth is one in
all' (xi 56.8).
8　**Whether**: which.　**attone**: i.e. when brought together.

Stanza 49
4　**eeke**: increase.
6　**lewdly**: ignorantly, evilly.
8 to 50.9　His punishment recalls the death of Antiochus:
'All the membres of his bodie were bruised with the great fall.
And thus he that a litle afore thoght he might . . . weigh the hie
mountaines in ye balance, was now cast on the ground . . .
declaring vnto all the manifest power of God' (2 Macc. 9.7–8).
Talus's gesture recalls the image of Aries who 'shouldred hath
the Bull' (Proem 5.9). In effect, Talus tips the scales against
the giant, making him lose his balance. Death by drowning
fulfils his argument that the sea encroaches upon the land,
32.3–4, 37.4–5. One who wished to thrust down the towering
rocks into the sea (38.3–9) is himself thrown from his rock into
the sea. Fletcher (1971) 139 notes that the death of the Giant
resembles that of Talos in the *Argonautica*. Dunseath (1968)
108 compares the death by drowning of the Old Testament
giants who lived before the Flood.

50

Like as a ship, whom cruell tempest driues
   Vpon a rocke with horrible dismay,
   Her shattered ribs in thousand peeces riues,
   And spoyling all her geares and goodly ray,
   Does make her selfe misfortunes piteous pray.
   So downe the cliffe the wretched Gyant tumbled;
   His battred ballances in peeces lay,
   His timbered bones all broken rudely rumbled,
So was the high aspyring with huge ruine humbled.

51

That when the people, which had there about
   Long wayted, saw his sudden desolation,
   They gan to gather in tumultuous rout,
   And mutining, to stirre vp ciuill faction,
   For certaine losse of so great expectation.
   For well they hoped to haue got great good,
   And wondrous riches by his innouation.
   Therefore resoluing to reuenge his blood,
They rose in armes, and all in battell order stood.

52

Which lawlesse multitude him comming too
   In warlike wise, when *Artegall* did vew,
   He much was troubled, ne wist what to doo.
   For loth he was his noble hands t'embrew
   In the base blood of such a rascall crew;
   And otherwise, if that he should retire,
   He fear'd least they with shame would him pursew.
   Therefore he *Talus* to them sent, t'inquire
The cause of their array, and truce for to desire.

53

But soone as they him nigh approching spide,
   They gan with all their weapons him assay,
   And rudely stroke at him on euery side:
   Yet nought they could him hurt, ne ought dismay.
   But when at them he with his flaile gan lay,
   He like a swarme of flyes them ouerthrew;
   Ne any of them durst come in his way,
   But here and there before his presence flew,
And hid themselues in holes and bushes from his vew.

54

As when a Faulcon hath with nimble flight
   Flowne at a flush of Ducks, foreby the brooke,
   The trembling foule dismayd with dreadfull sight
   Of death, the which them almost ouertooke,
   Doe hide themselues from her astonying looke,
   Amongst the flags and couert round about.
   When *Talus* saw they all the field forsooke
   And none appear'd of all that raskall rout,
To *Artegall* he turn'd, and went with him throughout.

Cant. III.

The spousals of faire Florimell,
where turney many knights:
There Braggadochio is vncas'd
in all the Ladies sights.

1

AFter long stormes and tempests ouerblowne,
   The sunne at length his ioyous face doth cleare:
   So when as fortune all her spight hath showne,
   Some blisfull houres at last must needes appeare;
   Else should afflicted wights oftimes despeire.
   So comes it now to *Florimell* by tourne,
   After long sorrowes suffered whyleare,
   In which captiu'd she many moneths did mourne,
To tast of ioy, and to wont pleasures to retourne.

Stanza 50
2   **dismay**: referring to the effect upon her crew.
4   **geares**: rigging.   **ray**: array.
8   **timbered**: massive, being structured like a ship or his own balances.
9   Cf. Matt. 23.12: 'Whosoever wil exalt himself, shalbe broght low.'   **ruine**: downfall.

Stanza 52
4–5   A knight was forbidden by chivalric code to fight with his social inferiors; and a knight of justice cannot control a mob.   **embrew**: stain.   **rascall**: knavish, villainous, belonging to the rabble.

Stanza 53
The resort to martial law may link the episode to the Peasants' Revolt but the application remains general.
2   **assay**: assail.

Stanza 54
2   **flush**: flight of birds suddenly started up.
5   **astonying**: paralysing.
6   **flags**: reeds.
9   **turn'd**: returned.

Canto iii

Argument
3   **vncas'd**: exposed literally when stripped of his armour (37.8) and figuratively when his 'counterfeits were thus vncased' (39.1).

Stanza 1
1–2   Extends the simile at IV xii 34.6–9 which associates Florimell with the sun. See 19*n*.
9   **wont**: wonted, accustomed.

2

Who being freed from *Proteus* cruell band
　By *Marinell*, was vnto him affide,
　And by him brought againe to Faerie land;
　Where he her spous'd, and made his ioyous bride.
　The time and place was blazed farre and wide;
　And solemne feasts and giusts ordain'd therefore.
　To which there did resort from euery side
　Of Lords and Ladies infinite great store;
Ne any Knight was absent, that braue courage bore.

3

To tell the glorie of the feast that day,
　The goodly seruice, the deuicefull sights,
　The bridegromes state, the brides most rich aray,
　The pride of Ladies, and the worth of knights,
　The royall banquets, and the rare delights
　Were worke fit for an Herauld, not for me:
　But for so much as to my lot here lights,
　That with this present treatise doth agree,
True vertue to aduance, shall here recounted bee.

4

When all men had with full satietie
　Of meates and drinkes their appetites suffiz'd,
　To deedes of armes and proofe of cheualrie
　They gan themselues addresse, full rich aguiz'd,
　As each one had his furnitures deuiz'd.
　And first of all issu'd Sir *Marinell*,
　And with him six knights more, which enterpriz'd
　To chalenge all in right of *Florimell*,
And to maintaine, that she all others did excell.

5

The first of them was hight Sir *Orimont*,
　A noble Knight, and tride in hard assayes:
　The second had to name Sir *Bellisont*,
　But second vnto none in prowesse prayse;
　The third was *Brunell*, famous in his dayes;
　The fourth *Ecastor*, of exceeding might;
　The fift *Armeddan*, skild in louely layes;
　The sixt was *Lansack*, a redoubted Knight:
All sixe well seene in armes, and prou'd in many a fight.

6

And them against came all that list to giust,
　From euery coast and countrie vnder sunne:
　None was debard, but all had leaue that lust.
　The trompets sound; then all together ronne.
　Full many deedes of armes that day were donne,
　And many knights vnhorst, and many wounded,
　As fortune fell; yet litle lost or wonne:
　But all that day the greatest prayse redounded
To *Marinell*, whose name the Heralds loud resounded.

7

The second day, so soone as morrow light
　Appear'd in heauen, into the field they came,
　And there all day continew'd cruell fight,
　With diuers fortune fit for such a game,
　In which all stroue with perill to winne fame.
　Yet whether side was victor, note be ghest:
　But at the last the trompets did proclame
　That *Marinell* that day deserued best.
So they disparted were, and all men went to rest.

8

The third day came, that should due tryall lend
　Of all the rest, and then this warlike crew
　Together met, of all to make an end.
　There *Marinell* great deeds of armes did shew;
　And through the thickest like a Lyon flew,
　Rashing off helmes, and ryuing plates a sonder,
　That euery one his daunger did eschew,
　So terribly his dreadfull strokes did thonder,
That all men stood amaz'd, and at his might did wonder.

Stanza 2
2　**affide**: betrothed.
6　**solemne**: ceremonial.

Stanza 3
2　**deuicefull sights**: ingenious spectacles, masques, and triumphs.
8　**treatise**: story; story that treats virtue.

Stanza 4
4　**aguiz'd**: arrayed.
5　**furnitures**: equipment or suit of armour.
7　**enterpriz'd**: undertook.

Stanza 5
In addition to their etymological significances, the names may convey veiled compliments to living knights, e.g. *Orimont*, the Earl of Ormond.　**Bellisont**: wager of war (Draper, 1921).　**Brunell**: Ital. *brunello*, little brown man (Gough, 1921).　**Ecastor**: from Castor, breaker of horses (Homer, *Ody.* xi 300) and a giver of gowns (Malory 823); Cooper (1565) notes that the name is a Roman oath used only by women; hence it befits a tournament of love.　**Armeddan**: from Span. *armada, armade*, 'fighting noble' (Dunseath, 1968, 113); or, armed one.　**Lansack**: despoiler of land, from land + sack (Belson, 1964).
2　**tride in hard assayes**: proven in hard assaults.
7　**louely layes**: lays of love.
9　**seene**: skilled.

Stanza 6
2　**coast**: region.
3　**lust**: chose.

Stanza 7
1　**morrow**: morning.
6　**whether**: which.　**note**: could not.
9　**disparted**: parted asunder.

Stanza 8
6　**Rashing**: shearing.
7　**daunger**: power to inflict injury; the reach of his weapons.

9

But what on earth can alwayes happie stand?
 The greater prowesse greater perils find.
 So farre he past amongst his enemies band,
 That they haue him enclosed so behind,
 As by no meanes he can himselfe outwind.
 And now perforce they haue him prisoner taken;
 And now they doe with captiue bands him bind;
 And now they lead him thence, of all forsaken,
Vnlesse some succour had in time him ouertaken.

10

It fortun'd whylest they were thus ill beset,
 Sir *Artegall* into the Tilt-yard came,
 With *Braggadochio*, whom he lately met
 Vpon the way, with that his snowy Dame.
 Where when he vnderstood by common fame,
 What euill hap to *Marinell* betid,
 He much was mou'd at so vnworthie shame,
 And streight that boaster prayd, with whom he rid,
To change his shield with him, to be the better hid.

11

So forth he went, and soone them ouer hent,
 Where they were leading *Marinell* away,
 Whom he assayld with dreadlesse hardiment,
 And forst the burden of their prize to stay.
 They were an hundred knights of that array;
 Of which th'one halfe vpon himselfe did set,
 The other stayd behind to gard the pray.
 But he ere long the former fiftie bet;
And from the other fiftie soone the prisoner fet.

12

So backe he brought Sir *Marinell* againe;
 Whom hauing quickly arm'd againe anew,
 They both together ioyned might and maine,
 To set afresh on all the other crew.
 Whom with sore hauocke soone they ouerthrew,
 And chaced quite out of the field, that none
 Against them durst his head to perill shew.
 So were they left Lords of the field alone:
So *Marinell* by him was rescu'd from his fone.

13

Which when he had perform'd, then backe againe
 To *Braggadochio* did his shield restore:
 Who all this while behind him did remaine,
 Keeping there close with him in pretious store
 That his false Ladie, as ye heard afore.
 Then did the trompets sound, and Iudges rose,
 And all these knights, which that day armour bore,
 Came to the open hall, to listen whose
The honour of the prize should be adiudg'd by those.

14

And thether also came in open sight
 Fayre *Florimell*, into the common hall,
 To greet his guerdon vnto euery knight,
 And best to him, to whom the best should fall.
 Then for that stranger knight they loud did call,
 To whom that day they should the girlond yield.
 Who came not forth, but for Sir *Artegall*
 Came *Braggadochio*, and did shew his shield,
Which bore the Sunne brode blazed in a golden field.

15

The sight whereof did all with gladnesse fill:
 So vnto him they did addeeme the prise
 Of all that Tryumph.   Then the trompets shrill
 Don *Braggadochios* name resounded thrise:
 So courage lent a cloke to cowardise.
 And then to him came fayrest *Florimell*,
 And goodly gan to greet his braue emprise,
 And thousand thankes him yeeld, that had so well
Approu'd that day, that she all others did excell.

Stanza 9
5   **outwind**: extricate; suggesting a labyrinth.

Stanza 10
5   **fame**: report.
9   As Triamond seizes Braggadocchio's spear to attack the forces of Maidenhead, IV iv 20.6.

Stanza 11
1   **ouer hent**: overtook.
3   **hardiment**: courage.
5   **hundred**: corresponds to the number of knights defeated by Marinell in defence of his Rich Strond, III iv 21.1, and the number who uphold the force of maidenhead at the previous tournament, IV iv 31.6; cf. viii 50.6.   **array**: a military force.
9   **fet**: fetched.

Stanza 13
4   **Keeping . . . in pretious store**: secretly in his keeping as a precious thing.

Stanza 14
3   To congratulate each knight upon his reward.
8–9   **his**: ambiguous, as Aptekar (1969) 77 notes: 'In fact the shield is Braggadocchio's property. But it more properly belongs to Artegall.' She notes that the device is appropriate to the representative of justice. Cf. Arthur's 'sunlike shield' (viii 41.2). Upton (1758) notes the heraldic impossibility of the device, befitting a false knight. Metal cannot be laid upon metal, as the golden sun upon a gold field would require. **blazed**: blazoned, described heraldically.

Stanza 15
2   **addeeme**: adjudge.
5   **So courage lent a cloke . . .:** the reputation of being the best knight disguises his true cowardice.
7   **emprise**: enterprise.
9   **Approu'd**: shown to be true.

16

To whom the boaster, that all knights did blot,
  With proud disdaine did scornefull answere make;
  That what he did that day, he did it not
  For her, but for his owne deare Ladies sake,
  Whom on his perill he did vndertake,
  Both her and eke all others to excell:
  And further did vncomely speaches crake.
Much did his words the gentle Ladie quell,
And turn'd aside for shame to heare, what he did tell.

17

Then forth he brought his snowy *Florimele*,
  Whom *Trompart* had in keeping there beside,
  Couered from peoples gazement with a vele.
  Whom when discouered they had throughly eide,
  With great amazement they were stupefide;
  And said, that surely *Florimell* it was,
  Or if it were not *Florimell* so tride,
  That *Florimell* her selfe she then did pas.
So feeble skill of perfect things the vulgar has.

18

Which when as *Marinell* beheld likewise,
  He was therewith exceedingly dismayd;
  Ne wist he what to thinke, or to deuise,
  But like as one, whom feends had made affrayd,
  He long astonisht stood, ne ought he sayd,
  Ne ought he did, but with fast fixed eies
  He gazed still vpon that snowy mayd;
  Whom euer as he did the more auize,
The more to be true *Florimell* he did surmize.

19

As when two sunnes appeare in the azure skye,
  Mounted in *Phœbus* charet fierie bright,
  Both darting forth faire beames to each mans eye,
  And both adorn'd with lampes of flaming light,
  All that behold so strange prodigious sight,
  Not knowing natures worke, nor what to weene,
  Are rapt with wonder, and with rare affright.
So stood Sir *Marinell*, when he had seene
The semblant of this false by his faire beauties Queene.

20

All which when *Artegall*, who all this while
  Stood in the preasse close couered, well aduewed,
  And saw that boasters pride and gracelesse guile,
  He could no longer beare, but forth issewed,
  And vnto all himselfe there open shewed,
  And to the boaster said; Thou losell base,
  That hast with borrowed plumes thy selfe endewed,
  And others worth with leasings doest deface,
When they are all restor'd, thou shalt rest in disgrace.

21

That shield, which thou doest beare, was it indeed,
  Which this dayes honour sau'd to *Marinell*;
  But not that arme, nor thou the man I reed,
  Which didst that seruice vnto *Florimell*.
  For proofe shew forth thy sword, and let it tell,
  What strokes, what dreadfull stoure it stird this day:
  Or shew the wounds, which vnto thee befell;
  Or shew the sweat, with which thou diddest sway
So sharpe a battell, that so many did dismay.

22

But this the sword, which wrought those cruell stounds,
  And this the arme, the which that shield did beare,
  And these the signes, (so shewed forth his wounds)
  By which that glorie gotten doth appeare.
  As for this Ladie, which he sheweth here,
  Is not (I wager) *Florimell* at all;
  But some fayre Franion, fit for such a fere,
  That by misfortune in his hand did fall.
For proofe whereof, he bad them *Florimell* forth call.

Stanza 16
1   Cf. 38.6.
7   **crake**: utter boastfully.
8   **quell**: cause to quail, disconcert.

Stanza 17
7–9   Cf. III viii 5.   **so tride**: i.e. when examined.
skill: power of discrimination.

Stanza 18
8   **auize**: regard.

Stanza 19
A just simile, as Upton (1758) observes: the false Florimell is the mock sun, or parhelion, while Florimell is the true sun to which she is frequently compared, e.g. IV xii 34.6–9. It suggests wonder: 'When two suns do appear / Some say it doth betoken wonders near' (Sidney, *Old Arcadia* 213).
5   **prodigious**: ominous.
9   **semblant**: appearance; suggesting false appearance, mere resemblance.

Stanza 20
2   **aduewed**: the obsolete form suggests the formal inspection made by the knight of justice before he intervenes. Also, it indicates a penetrating sight/insight which the others lack.
3   **gracelesse**: wicked.
5   He exposes himself before he exposes Braggadocchio.
6   **losell**: scoundrel. The word first defined him (II iii 4.1) and has been reserved for this moment when he is exposed. Cf. 35.5.
7   **borrowed plumes**: from Aesop's fable of the jackdaw who clothed himself with peacock feathers.

Stanza 21
3   **reed**: consider; declare.
6   **stoure**: turmoil of battle.
9   **dismay**: defeat.

Stanza 22
1   **stounds**: times of trial; fierce attacks.
6   **wager**: a formal oath to challenge anyone who denies his claim.
7   The excessive alliteration shows Artegall's contempt.
Franion: loose woman.

23

So forth the noble Ladie was ybrought,
　Adorn'd with honor and all comely grace:
　Whereto her bashfull shamefastnesse ywrought
　A great increase in her faire blushing face;
　As roses did with lillies interlace.
　For of those words, the which that boaster threw,
　She inly yet conceiued great disgrace.
　Whom when as all the people such did vew,
They shouted loud, and signes of gladnesse all did shew.

24

Then did he set her by that snowy one,
　Like the true saint beside the image set,
　Of both their beauties to make paragone,
　And triall, whether should the honor get.
　Streight way so soone as both together met,
　Th'enchaunted Damzell vanisht into nought:
　Her snowy substance melted as with heat,
　Ne of that goodly hew remayned ought,
But th'emptie girdle, which about her wast was wrought.

25

As when the daughter of *Thaumantes* faire,
　Hath in a watry cloud displayed wide
　Her goodly bow, which paints the liquid ayre;
　That all men wonder at her colours pride;
　All suddenly, ere one can looke aside,
　The glorious picture vanisheth away,
　Ne any token doth thereof abide:
　So did this Ladies goodly forme decay,
And into nothing goe, ere one could it bewray.

26

Which when as all that present were, beheld,
　They stricken were with great astonishment,
　And their faint harts with senselesse horrour queld,
　To see the thing, that seem'd so excellent,
　So stolen from their fancies wonderment;
　That what of it became, none vnderstood.
　And *Braggadochio* selfe with dreriment
　So daunted was in his despeyring mood,
That like a lifelesse corse immoueable he stood.

27

But *Artegall* that golden belt vptooke,
　The which of all her spoyle was onely left;
　Which was not hers, as many it mistooke,
　But *Florimells* owne girdle, from her reft,
　While she was flying, like a weary weft,
　From that foule monster, which did her compell
　To perils great; which he vnbuckling eft,
　Presented to the fayrest *Florimell*;
Who round about her tender wast it fitted well.

28

Full many Ladies often had assayd,
　About their middles that faire belt to knit;
　And many a one suppos'd to be a mayd:
　Yet it to none of all their loynes would fit,
　Till *Florimell* about her fastned it.
　Such power it had, that to no womans wast
　By any skill or labour it would sit,
　Vnlesse that she were continent and chast,
But it would lose or breake, that many had disgrast.

29

Whilest thus they busied were bout *Florimell*,
　And boastfull *Braggadochio* to defame,
　Sir *Guyon* as by fortune then befell,
　Forth from the thickest preasse of people came,
　His owne good steed, which he had stolne, to clame;
　And th'one hand seizing on his golden bit,
　With th'other drew his sword: for with the same
　He ment the thiefe there deadly to haue smit:
And had he not bene held, he nought had fayld of it.

Stanza 24

The two Florimells are weighed in the scales of justice and the result confirms that 'by no meanes the false will with the truth be wayd' (ii 45.9).

3　**paragone**: comparison.

4　**whether**: which of the two.

6　**enchaunted**: i.e. made by enchantment; see III viii 5–8.

9　As Braggadocchio's shield proclaims his bravery, the girdle displays the False Florimell's virginity, until both are uncased by justice.

Stanza 25

1　**the daughter of Thaumantes**: Iris, called Thaumantias by Cooper (1565).

3　**liquid ayre**: clear, bright air; see I i 45.3n.

4　Alluding to θαυμα, a wonder.

9　**bewray**: reveal, point to.

Stanza 26

2　**astonishment**: numbness.

3　**senselesse**: as it takes away their senses.

5　Imagination deceives them; cf. the Red Cross Knight's 'falsed fancy' (I ii 30.3) in preferring Duessa.

Stanza 27

5　**weft**: waif; cf. IV xii 31.3.

7　**eft**: afterwards. The bridegroom's undoing the bride's girdle is performed symbolically by the knight of justice. The action represents the merging of chastity and justice realized in the marriage of Britomart and Artegall.

Stanza 28

3　**mayd**: virgin, as 8 makes explicit.

6–9　On the power of the girdle, see IV v 3, 16–17. Since they are not **continent**, they cannot be contained; not being **chast**, the cestus (Lat. *chaste*) cannot gird them.

Stanza 29

3　**Guyon** emerges from anonymity as does Artegall at
20.1–2.

30

Thereof great hurly burly moued was
  Throughout the hall, for that same warlike horse.
  For *Braggadochio* would not let him pas;
  And *Guyon* would him algates haue perforse,
  Or it approue vpon his carrion corse.
  Which troublous stirre when *Artegall* perceiued,
  He nigh them drew to stay th'auengers forse,
  And gan inquire, how was that steed bereaued,
Whether by might extort, or else by slight deceaued.

31

Who all that piteous storie, which befell
  About that wofull couple, which were slaine,
  And their young bloodie babe to him gan tell;
  With whom whiles he did in the wood remaine,
  His horse purloyned was by subtill traine:
  For which he chalenged the thiefe to fight.
  But he for nought could him thereto constraine.
  For as the death he hated such despight,
And rather had to lose, then trie in armes his right.

32

Which *Artegall* well hearing, though no more
  By law of armes there neede ones right to trie,
  As was the wont of warlike knights of yore,
  Then that his foe should him the field denie,
  Yet further right by tokens to descrie,
  He askt, what priuie tokens he did beare.
  If that (said *Guyon*) may you satisfie,
  Within his mouth a blacke spot doth appeare,
Shapt like a horses shoe, who list to seeke it there.

33

Whereof to make due tryall, one did take
  The horse in hand, within his mouth to looke:
  But with his heeles so sorely he him strake,
  That all his ribs he quite in peeces broke,
  That neuer word from that day forth he spoke.
  Another that would seeme to haue more wit,
  Him by the bright embrodered hedstall tooke:
  But by the shoulder him so sore he bit,
That he him maymed quite, and all his shoulder split.

34

Ne he his mouth would open vnto wight,
  Vntill that *Guyon* selfe vnto him spake,
  And called *Brigadore* (so was he hight)
  Whose voice so soone as he did vndertake,
  Eftsoones he stood as still as any stake,
  And suffred all his secret marke to see:
  And when as he him nam'd, for ioy he brake
  His bands, and follow'd him with gladfull glee,
And friskt, and flong aloft, and louted low on knee.

35

Thereby Sir *Artegall* did plaine areed,
  That vnto him the horse belong'd, and sayd;
  Lo there Sir *Guyon*, take to you the steed,
  As he with golden saddle is arayd;
  And let that losell, plainely now displayd,
  Hence fare on foot, till he an horse haue gayned.
  But the proud boaster gan his doome vpbrayd,
  And him reuil'd, and rated, and disdayned,
That iudgement so vniust against him had ordayned.

548

36

Much was the knight incenst with his lewd word,
  To haue reuenged that his villeny;
  And thrise did lay his hand vpon his sword,
  To haue him slaine, or dearely doen aby.
  But *Guyon* did his choler pacify,
  Saying, Sir knight, it would dishonour bee
  To you, that are our iudge of equity,
  To wreake your wrath on such a carle as hee:
It's punishment enough, that all his shame doe see.

Stanza 30
4   algates: nevertheless.
5   approue: prove.
8   bereaued: carried off.
9   by slight deceaued: taken by trickery.

Stanza 31
1–5   For the story see II i 35f; for the theft see II ii 11 and
iii 4.   traine: guile.
8   despight: defiance.

Stanza 34
3   Brigadore: from Brigliadoro, the name of Orlando's horse
in Boiardo and Ariosto. As 'bridle of gold', it indicates the
rule of temperance, the golden mean, over the wilful passions
symbolized by the horse; cf. its 'golden bit' (29.6) and golden
saddle (II ii 11.6 and 35.4 below).
4   vndertake: hear.

Stanza 35
1   areed: decide.

Stanza 36
1   lewd: evil, wicked.
4   aby: i.e. suffer for it.
7   iudge of equity: reminding him of one significance of
his name, 'Art-egall'.

37

So did he mitigate Sir *Artegall*,
But *Talus* by the backe the boaster hent,
And drawing him out of the open hall,
Vpon him did inflict this punishment.
First he his beard did shaue, and fowly shent:
Then from him reft his shield, and it renuerst,
And blotted out his armes with falshood blent,
And himselfe baffuld, and his armes vnherst,
And broke his sword in twaine, and all his armour sperst.

38

The whiles his guilefull groome was fled away:
But vaine it was to thinke from him to flie.
Who ouertaking him did disaray,
And all his face deform'd with infamie,
And out of court him scourged openly.
So ought all faytours, that true knighthood shame,
And armes dishonour with base villanie,
From all braue knights be banisht with defame:
For oft their lewdnes blotteth good deserts with blame.

39

Now when these counterfeits were thus vncased
Out of the foreside of their forgerie,
And in the sight of all men cleane disgraced,
All gan to iest and gibe full merilie
At the remembrance of their knauerie.
Ladies can laugh at Ladies, Knights at Knights,
To thinke with how great vaunt of brauerie
He them abused, through his subtill slights,
And what a glorious shew he made in all their sights.

40

There leaue we them in pleasure and repast,
Spending their ioyous dayes and gladfull nights,
And taking vsurie of time forepast,
With all deare delices and rare delights,
Fit for such Ladies and such louely knights:
And turne we here to this faire furrowes end
Our wearie yokes, to gather fresher sprights,
That when as time to *Artegall* shall tend,
We on his first aduenture may him forward send.

Cant. IIII.

*Artegall dealeth right betwixt
two brethren that doe striue,
Saues Terpine from the gallow tree,
and doth from death repriue.*

1

WHo so vpon him selfe will take the skill
True Iustice vnto people to diuide,
Had neede haue mightie hands, for to fulfill
That, which he doth with righteous doome decide,
And for to maister wrong and puissant pride.
For vaine it is to deeme of things aright,
And makes wrong doers iustice to deride,
Vnlesse it be perform'd with dreadlesse might.
For powre is the right hand of Iustice truely hight.

Stanza 37

1   **mitigate**: mollify, literally 'make mild'.
2   **hent**: seized.
5–9   The public infamy of a knight is an elaborate ritual; shaving the beard is a sign of disgrace, as 2 Sam. 10.4–5. **shent**: disfigured, soiled; or perhaps cut in the middle, as were the clothes of David's servants.   **renuerst**: turned upside down 'to heape disdayn' (I iv 41.9).   **blent**: stained. **baffuld**: disgraced; cf. VI vii 27.2–3.   **vnherst**: removed piece by piece. Gough (1921) suggests that the meaning of the term derives from 'hearse', a monument upon which armour was hung. Upton (1758) notes that cowards in the lists were punished by having their armour first taken from them, beginning at the heels, and then flung piece by piece over the barriers.   **sperst**: scattered.

Stanza 38

1   **guilefull**: implies the etymology of his name: 'trompart', cheating, as Church (1758) notices.
4   **face**: external appearance.
6   **faytours**: impostors.
8   **defame**: dishonour.
9   **lewdnes**: evil behaviour.

Stanza 39

2   **foreside**: outward appearance; façade.
6–9   Bieman (1968) 161 notes that the cleansing laughter differs from the ribaldry that followed the tournament, IV v 18–19.
6   **can**: began to; did.   **at**: with.
9   **glorious**: also boastful, vainglorious; cf. II iii 4.5.

Stanza 40

1   **repast**: repose.
3   **vsurie**: interest, gain; hence, taking reward for their former labour.
4   **delices**: pleasures.
5   **louely**: loving.
7   **sprights**: vigour of mind.
8   **tend**: attend, serve.

Canto iv

Argument

4   **repriue**: reprieve.

Stanza 1

1–2   **skill**: the art of discrimination by which the ruler may diuide, i.e. dispense, justice; cf. Proem 9.9, vii 1.9.

2

Therefore whylome to knights of great emprise
  The charge of Iustice giuen was in trust,
  That they might execute her iudgements wise,
  And with their might beat downe licentious lust,
  Which proudly did impugne her sentence iust.
  Whereof no brauer president this day
  Remaines on earth, preseru'd from yron rust
  Of rude obliuion, and long times decay,
Then this of *Artegall*, which here we haue to say.

3

Who hauing lately left that louely payre,
  Enlincked fast in wedlockes loyall bond,
  Bold *Marinell* with *Florimell* the fayre,
  With whom great feast and goodly glee he fond,
  Departed from the Castle of the strond,
  To follow his aduentures first intent,
  Which long agoe he taken had in hond:
  Ne wight with him for his assistance went,
But that great yron groome, his gard and gouernment.

4

With whom as he did passe by the sea shore,
  He chaunst to come, whereas two comely Squires,
  Both brethren, whom one wombe together bore,
  But stirred vp with different desires,
  Together stroue, and kindled wrathfull fires:
  And them beside two seemely damzels stood,
  By all meanes seeking to asswage their ires,
  Now with faire words; but words did little good, (mood.
Now with sharpe threats; but threats the more increast their

5

And there before them stood a Coffer strong,
  Fast bound on euery side with iron bands,
  But seeming to haue suffred mickle wrong,
  Either by being wreckt vppon the sands,
  Or being carried farre from forraine lands.
  Seem'd that for it these Squires at ods did fall,
  And bent against them selues their cruell hands.
  But euermore, those Damzels did forestall
Their furious encounter, and their fiercenesse pall.

6

But firmely fixt they were, with dint of sword,
  And battailes doubtfull proofe their rights to try,
  Ne other end their fury would afford,
  But what to them Fortune would iustify.
  So stood they both in readinesse thereby,
  To ioyne the combate with cruell intent;
  When *Artegall* arriuing happily,
  Did stay a while their greedy bickerment,
Till he had questioned the cause of their dissent.

7

To whom the elder did this aunswere frame;
  Then weete ye Sir, that we two brethren be,
  To whom our sire, *Milesio* by name,
  Did equally bequeath his lands in fee,
  Two Ilands, which ye there before you see
  Not farre in sea; of which the one appeares
  But like a little Mount of small degree;
  Yet was as great and wide ere many yeares,
550 As that same other Isle, that greater bredth now beares.

Stanza 2
1 **whylome**: in time past. **emprise**: martial prowess.
5 **impugne**: oppose.
6 **brauer**: more glorious. **president**: precedent: pattern,
model.

Stanza 3
1 **louely**: loving.
3 Their names are coupled as at the first, III iv Arg.
Bold has changed its meaning from male arrogance that
rejects love to bravery in defending it.
9 **gouernment**: i.e. means of governing, his executive
power; cf. viii 3.9. Used of temperance (see II i 29.8*n*), the
term now extends that private virtue to public exercise.

Stanza 4
Marinell's **sea shore**, the setting for the Giant's desire to
redistribute wealth, is the setting for the problem of alluvion
(the formation of new land by the action of water).
6 **seemely**: fair.
9 **mood**: anger.

Stanza 5
4 **wreckt**: cast ashore.
7 **them selues**: not simply 'each other': each injures
himself in the quarrel.
8 **forestall**: seek to hinder.
9 **pall**: abate.

Stanza 6
1 **dint of sword**: force of arms.
2 **doubtfull**: because ordeal by combat allows Fortune
rather than Justice to determine right. Cf. i 25.4. Fortune has
bestowed their possessions; now Justice decides their right to
them.
5 **thereby**: by that means.

Stanza 7
The story of the sons of Milesio has been linked with Irish
legend and Irish legal tradition: see Gough (1921) and R. M.
Smith (1942). H. B. Nelson (1940) discusses the story in relation to maritime law. Fowler (1964) 207 notes that **Milesio**
is one of Jupiter's surnames in Comes and argues that the
episode treats Jupiter as the divider: 'The disputed possessions
are not possessions at all, but divine gifts.'
4 **in fee**: in fee-simple, as an absolute and rightful possession
for ever.
8 **ere many yeares**: not long ago.

8

But tract of time, that all things doth decay,
  And this deuouring Sea, that naught doth spare,
  The most part of my land hath washt away,
  And throwne it vp vnto my brothers share:
  So his encreased, but mine did empaire.
  Before which time I lou'd, as was my lot,
  That further mayd, hight *Philtera* the faire,
  With whom a goodly doure I should haue got,
And should haue ioyned bene to her in wedlocks knot.

9

Then did my younger brother *Amidas*
  Loue that same other Damzell, *Lucy* bright,
  To whom but little dowre allotted was;
  Her vertue was the dowre, that did delight.
  What better dowre can to a dame be hight?
  But now when *Philtra* saw my lands decay,
  And former liuelod fayle, she left me quight,
  And to my brother did ellope streight way:
Who taking her from me, his owne loue left astray.

10

She seeing then her selfe forsaken so,
  Through dolorous despaire, which she conceyued,
  Into the Sea her selfe did headlong throw,
  Thinking to haue her griefe by death bereaued.
  But see how much her purpose was deceaued.
  Whilest thus amidst the billowes beating of her
  Twixt life and death, long to and fro she weaued,
  She chaunst vnwares to light vppon this coffer,
Which to her in that daunger hope of life did offer.

11

The wretched mayd that earst desir'd to die,
  When as the paine of death she tasted had,
  And but halfe seene his vgly visnomie,
  Gan to repent, that she had beene so mad,
  For any death to chaunge life though most bad:
  And catching hold of this Sea-beaten chest,
  The lucky Pylot of her passage sad,
  After long tossing in the seas distrest,
Her weary barke at last vppon mine Isle did rest.

12

Where I by chaunce then wandring on the shore,
  Did her espy, and through my good endeuour
  From dreadfull mouth of death, which threatned sore
  Her to haue swallow'd vp, did helpe to saue her.
  She then in recompence of that great fauour,
  Which I on her bestowed, bestowed on me
  The portion of that good, which Fortune gaue her,
  Together with her selfe in dowry free;
Both goodly portions, but of both the better she.

13

Yet in this coffer, which she with her brought,
  Great threasure sithence we did finde contained;
  Which as our owne we tooke, and so it thought.
  But this same other Damzell since hath fained,
  That to her selfe that threasure appertained;
  And that she did transport the same by sea,
  To bring it to her husband new ordained,
  But suffred cruell shipwracke by the way.
But whether it be so or no, I can not say.

14

But whether it indeede be so or no,
  This doe I say, that what so good or ill
  Or God or Fortune vnto me did throw,
  Not wronging any other by my will,
  I hold mine owne, and so will hold it still.
  And though my land he first did winne away,
  And then my loue (though now it little skill,)
  Yet my good lucke he shall not likewise pray;
But I will it defend, whilest euer that I may.

Stanza 8

1   tract: passing; lapse.
5   empaire: 'decay' (9.6); become less.
7   Philtera: Love of Land, as 9.6–7 reveals. Bracidas mistakes her for φιλτέρα, dearer.

Stanza 9

1   Amidas: Lat. *am*+ Gk ἰδία, fond of possessions; sugg. Osgood, *Var.* v 195.
2   Lucy bright: the epithet gives the meaning of the name.
5   hight: committed, assigned.
6–7   Hence his name, Bracidas: narrow means; see 18.2n.
decay: decrease.   liuelod: livelihood; property, inheritance.

Stanza 10

7   weaued: wandered, tossed by the waves; cf. 'weft' to describe Florimell, iii 27.5. Now justice decides the ownership of such a waif.
8   light: a punning reference to her name.

Stanza 11

3   visnomie: physiognomy, face.
7–9   As the Pylot guides a ship to harbour.

Stanza 12

3–4   The 'deuouring Sea' (8.2) which had seized his land now threatens his new bride.

Stanza 13

7   ordained: chosen.

Stanza 14

7   little skill: i.e. matters little.
8   pray: prey upon, take as booty.

15

So hauing sayd, the younger did ensew;
　　Full true it is, what so about our land
　　My brother here declared hath to you:
　　But not for it this ods twixt vs doth stand,
　　But for this threasure throwne vppon his strand;
　　Which well I proue, as shall appeare by triall,
　　To be this maides, with whom I fastned hand,
　　Known by good markes, and perfect good espiall,
Therefore it ought be rendred her without deniall.

16

When they thus ended had, the Knight began;
　　Certes your strife were easie to accord,
　　Would ye remit it to some righteous man.
　　Vnto your selfe, said they, we giue our word,
　　To bide what iudgement ye shall vs afford.
　　Then for assuraunce to my doome to stand,
　　Vnder my foote let each lay downe his sword,
　　And then you shall my sentence vnderstand.
So each of them layd downe his sword out of his hand.

17

Then *Artegall* thus to the younger sayd;
　　Now tell me *Amidas*, if that ye may,
　　Your brothers land the which the sea hath layd
　　Vnto your part, and pluckt from his away,
　　By what good right doe you withhold this day?
　　What other right (quoth he) should you esteeme,
　　But that the sea it to my share did lay?
　　Your right is good (sayd he) and so I deeme,
That what the sea vnto you sent, your own should seeme.

18

Then turning to the elder thus he sayd;
　　Now *Bracidas* let this likewise be showne.
　　Your brothers threasure, which from him is strayd,
　　Being the dowry of his wife well knowne,
　　By what right doe you claime to be your owne?
　　What other right (quoth he) should you esteeme,
　　But that the sea hath it vnto me throwne?
　　Your right is good (sayd he) and so I deeme,
That what the sea vnto you sent, your own should seeme.

19

For equall right in equall things doth stand,
　　For what the mighty Sea hath once possest,
　　And plucked quite from all possessors hand,
　　Whether by rage of waues, that neuer rest,
　　Or else by wracke, that wretches hath distrest,
　　He may dispose by his imperiall might,
　　As thing at randon left, to whom he list.
　　So *Amidas*, the land was yours first hight,
And so the threasure yours is *Bracidas* by right.

20

When he his sentence thus pronounced had,
　　Both *Amidas* and *Philtra* were displeased:
　　But *Bracidas* and *Lucy* were right glad,
　　And on the threasure by that iudgement seased.
　　So was their discord by this doome appeased,
　　And each one had his right. Then *Artegall*
　　When as their sharpe contention he had ceased,
　　Departed on his way, as did befall,
To follow his old quest, the which him forth did call.

Stanza 15

1　ensew: follow.
4　ods: strife.
7　fastned hand: handfasted, i.e. betrothed myself.
8　espiall: close observation that leads to identification.

Stanza 16

3　some righteous man: Artegall's title, ii 39.2, vii 22.4.
8　A ponderous pun, yet vnderstand implies 'cause his doome (6) to stand'.

Stanzas 17–18

The stanzas declare Artegall's impartiality by being as similar as circumstances and rhyme allow.

Stanza 17

8–9　Gough (1921) notes that the legal business involved here concerns alluvion (see stanza 4*n*). **Artegall** applies the principle which he had spelled out to the Giant, ii 39.4–9.

Stanza 18

2　**Bracidas**: few possessions, from βραχυς + ιδια; see 9.6–7*n*. Or possessions thrown up (by the sea), βρασσω + ιδια (*Var*. v 195). Evidently a proverbial figure for boldness, e.g. Gosson: 'in boldenesse a Brasidas' (*Ephemerides of Phialo*, 1579), as he shows at 14.

Stanza 19

The law of wreck covers whatever is thrown up on land by the sea. According to Elizabethan law, **Bracidas** had no legal right to the treasure or to damages for his lost land. The usual view, that the case at hand involves a clash between law and equity (see Osgood, *Var*. v 195), is challenged by Phillips (1970) 109 who claims that Artegall applies the letter of the law of God and Nature as he had expounded it at ii 39; cf. Dunseath (1968) 125. Behind Artegall's judgment is another law of nature which declares that the grosser element must sustain the higher, as here the earth feeds the sea. Cf. Milton's statement: 'of elements / The grosser feeds the purer, earth the sea' (*P.L.* v 415–6).

1　in equall things: recognizing the rule of equity in justice.
6　S. may allude to English law according to which all wreck is the property of the sovereign.

Stanza 20

3　right glad: because they are judged right.
4　seased: took possession.
7　ceased: put a stop to.

21

So as he trauelled vppon the way,
  He chaunst to come, where happily he spide
  A rout of many people farre away;
  To whom his course he hastily applide,
  To weete the cause of their assemblaunce wide.
  To whom when he approched neare in sight,
  (An vncouth sight) he plainely then descride
  To be a troupe of women warlike dight,
With weapons in their hands, as ready for to fight.

22

And in the midst of them he saw a Knight,
  With both his hands behinde him pinnoed hard,
  And round about his necke an halter tight,
  As ready for the gallow tree prepard:
  His face was couered, and his head was bar'd,
  That who he was, vneath was to descry;
  And with full heauy heart with them he far'd,
  Grieu'd to the soule, and groning inwardly,
That he of womens hands so base a death should dy.

23

But they like tyrants, mercilesse the more,
  Reioyced at his miserable case,
  And him reuiled, and reproched sore
  With bitter taunts, and termes of vile disgrace.
  Now when as *Artegall* arriu'd in place,
  Did aske, what cause brought that man to decay,
  They round about him gan to swarme apace,
  Meaning on him their cruell hands to lay,
And to haue wrought vnwares some villanous assay.

24

But he was soone aware of their ill minde,
  And drawing backe deceiued their intent;
  Yet though him selfe did shame on womankinde
  His mighty hand to shend, he *Talus* sent
  To wrecke on them their follies hardyment:
  Who with few sowces of his yron flaile,
  Dispersed all their troupe incontinent,
  And sent them home to tell a piteous tale,
Of their vaine prowesse, turned to their proper bale.

25

But that same wretched man, ordaynd to die,
  They left behind them, glad to be so quit:
  Him *Talus* tooke out of perplexitie,
  And horrour of fowle death for Knight vnfit,
  Who more then losse of life ydreaded it;
  And him restoring vnto liuing light,
  So brought vnto his Lord, where he did sit,
  Beholding all that womanish weake fight;
Whom soone as he beheld, he knew, and thus behight.

26

Sir *Terpine*, haplesse man, what make you here?
  Or haue you lost your selfe, and your discretion,
  That euer in this wretched case ye were?
  Or haue ye yeelded you to proude oppression
  Of womens powre, that boast of mens subiection?
  Or else what other deadly dismall day
  Is falne on you, by heauens hard direction,
  That ye were runne so fondly far astray,
As for to lead your selfe vnto your owne decay?

27

Much was the man confounded in his mind,
  Partly with shame, and partly with dismay,
  That all astonisht he him selfe did find,
  And little had for his excuse to say,
  But onely thus; Most haplesse well ye may
  Me iustly terme, that to this shame am brought,
  And made the scorne of Knighthod this same day.
  But who can scape, what his owne fate hath wrought?
The worke of heauens will surpasseth humaine thought.

Stanza 21

2 **happily**: by chance.
4 **applide**: directed.
5 **assemblaunce**: assembly.

Stanza 22

2 **pinnoed**: pinned and pinioned.
6 **vneath**: difficult.
9 As Abimelech feared that men would say of him, a woman slew him (Judges 9.54). Hanging is the most shameful death; cf. 25.4–5.

Stanza 23

6 **decay**: ruin.
9 **assay**: assault.

Stanza 24

3–4 **did shame on womankinde / . . . to shend**: i.e. he would be shamed if he disgraced his might by attacking women. By stanza 41, however, he is swimming in his slaughter of them.
5 **wrecke**: wreak; suggesting also the effect of his action, the wreck or ruin to which they are reduced.   **hardyment**: boldness.
6 **sowces**: blows.
7 **incontinent**: at once; with a pun on 'intemperate'.
9 **proper bale**: own harm.

Stanza 25

3 **perplexitie**: physical and mental distress.
6 **liuing light**: cf. 'the light of the living' (Ps. 56.13) which the Geneva Bible glosses: 'in this life and light of the sunne'.
9 **behight**: addressed.

Stanza 26

1 **Terpine**: thrice-wretched, as Cheney (1966) 203 suggests, noting that Artegall offers three possible explanations for his unhappy fate. *Turpine 1596*, from Lat. *turpis*, shameful, is reserved for the antagonist of courtesy in Book VI; see VI iii 40.1–4*n*.
4–5 Recalling his subjection to Britomart and preparing for his subjection to Radigund; see v 17.1–2.
6 **dismall day**: unlucky day.
8 **fondly**: foolishly; also 'amorously', as subjection to women implies.

28

Right true: but faulty men vse oftentimes
  To attribute their folly vnto fate,
  And lay on heauen the guilt of their owne crimes.
  But tell, Sir *Terpin*, ne let you amate
  Your misery, how fell ye in this state.
  Then sith ye needs (quoth he) will know my shame,
  And all the ill, which chaunst to me of late,
  I shortly will to you rehearse the same,
In hope ye will not turne misfortune to my blame.

29

Being desirous (as all Knights are woont)
  Through hard aduentures deedes of armes to try,
  And after fame and honour for to hunt,
  I heard report that farre abrode did fly,
  That a proud Amazon did late defy
  All the braue Knights, that hold of Maidenhead,
  And vnto them wrought all the villany,
  That she could forge in her malicious head,
Which some hath put to shame, and many done be dead.

30

The cause, they say, of this her cruell hate,
  Is for the sake of *Bellodant* the bold,
  To whom she bore most feruent loue of late,
  And wooed him by all the waies she could:
  But when she saw at last, that he ne would
  For ought or nought be wonne vnto her will,
  She turn'd her loue to hatred manifold,
  And for his sake vow'd to doe all the ill
Which she could doe to Knights, which now she doth fulfill.

31

For all those Knights, the which by force or guile
  She doth subdue, she fowly doth entreate.
  First she doth them of warlike armes despoile,
  And cloth in womens weedes: And then with threat
  Doth them compell to worke, to earne their meat,
  To spin, to card, to sew, to wash, to wring;
  Ne doth she giue them other thing to eat,
  But bread and water, or like feeble thing,
Them to disable from reuenge aduenturing.

32

But if through stout disdaine of manly mind,
  Any her proud obseruaunce will withstand,
  Vppon that gibbet, which is there behind,
  She causeth them be hang'd vp out of hand;
  In which condition I right now did stand.
  For being ouercome by her in fight,
  And put to that base seruice of her band,
  I rather chose to die in liues despight,
Then lead that shamefull life, vnworthy of a Knight.

Stanza 28

1–3 As Artegall lays the guilt of his own crime on heaven, xi 41.6–9. Cf. VI ix 29.1–2 and *View* 1–2: 'It is the manner of men that when they are fallen into any absurdity, or their actions succeed not as they would, they are ready always to impute the blame thereof unto the heavens, so to excuse their own follies and imperfections.' **faulty**: guilty.
4–5 **ne let you amate / Your misery**: do not let your misery overwhelm you.
8 **rehearse**: relate.

Stanza 29

5–6 For the **Amazon** in sixteenth-century literature, see Wright (1940). For a contemporary account, see William Painter, *The Palace of Pleasure* II i. On the Order of **Maidenhead**, see I vii 46.4*n*. Amazons are enemies of Maidenhead in their sexual aggressiveness. **hold of**: maintain allegiance to.
9 **done be dead**: put to death.

Stanza 30

1 **cruell hate**: the Amazons' cruelty is traditional; cf. 23.8, v 47.1. As in Ariosto, *Orl. Fur.* xx 22f, their cruelty derives from sexual frustration.
2 **Bellodant**: given to war (Lat. *bellum+dare*) rather than to love; or giving war (*bellum+dant*), as he does when he rejects her.
7 Cf. the change from concupiscence to wrath in Cymochles, II v 36–38.

Stanza 31

1 **force or guile**: see vii 7.1–4*n*. Tonkin (1973b) 415 notes that Radigund parodies Isis, for she exploits the powers Isis controls.
2 **entreate**: treat.
3–9 S. combines traditional accounts of male slavery practised by the Amazons (as in Ariosto, *Orl. Fur.* xix 57–8) and the subjection of Hercules to Omphale (see v 24*n*).
8 **feeble**: mean, scanty; enfeebling.

Stanza 32

1 **manly**: noting the war between the sexes. The term describes Artegall at III ii 24.4, IV vi 22.9, V vii 40.3, 7.
2 **obseruaunce**: rule.
7 **band**: bond.
8–9 **liues despight**: scorn of life. His choice of death before dishonour has proverbial force (C. G. Smith, 1970, 157). It measures Artegall's decision to choose his plighted troth over both death and dishonour.

33

How hight that Amazon (sayd *Artegall*)?
  And where, and how far hence does she abide?
  Her name (quoth he) they *Radigund* doe call,
  A Princesse of great powre, and greater pride,
  And Queene of Amazons, in armes well tride,
  And sundry battels, which she hath atchieued
  With great success, that her hath glorifide,
  And made her famous, more then is belieued;
Ne would I it haue ween'd, had I not late it prieued.

34

Now sure (said he) and by the faith that I
  To Maydenhead and noble knighthood owe,
  I will not rest, till I her might doe trie,
  And venge the shame, that she to Knights doth show.
  Therefore Sir *Terpin* from you lightly throw
  This squalid weede, the patterne of dispaire,
  And wend with me, that ye may see and know,
  How Fortune will your ruin'd name repaire,
And knights of Maidenhead, whose praise she would empaire.

35

With that, like one that hopelesse was repryu'd
  From deathes dore, at which he lately lay,
  Those yron fetters, wherewith he was gyu'd,
  The badges of reproch, he threw away,
  And nimbly did him dight to guide the way
  Vnto the dwelling of that Amazone.
  Which was from thence not past a mile or tway:
  A goodly citty and a mighty one,
The which of her owne name she called *Radegone*.

36

Where they arriuing, by the watchmen were
  Descried streight, who all the citty warned,
  How that three warlike persons did appeare,
  Of which the one him seem'd a Knight all armed,
  And th'other two well likely to haue harmed.
  Eftsoones the people all to harnesse ran,
  And like a sort of Bees in clusters swarmed:
  Ere long their Queene her selfe, halfe like a man
Came forth into the rout, and them t'array began.

37

And now the Knights being arriued neare,
  Did beat vppon the gates to enter in,
  And at the Porter, skorning them so few,
  Threw many threats, if they the towne did win,
  To teare his flesh in peeces for his sin.
  Which when as *Radigund* there comming heard,
  Her heart for rage did grate, and teeth did grin:
  She bad that streight the gates should be vnbard,
And to them way to make, with weapons well prepard.

38

Soone as the gates were open to them set,
  They pressed forward, entraunce to haue made.
  But in the middle way they were ymet
  With a sharpe showre of arrowes, which them staid,
  And better bad aduise, ere they assaid
  Vnknowen perill of bold womens pride.
  Then all that rout vppon them rudely laid,
  And heaped strokes so fast on euery side,
And arrowes haild so thicke, that they could not abide.

Stanza 33

3 **Radigund**: may allude to the legend of St Radigund's refusal to consummate her marriage; see Walter (1941) 51. S. would have known her story through Jesus College, Cambridge, the College of St Rhadegund; see Hankins (1971) 153. In *Hub.* 497 she is called 'Saintlike'. The name may derive from the valorous Persian princess, Rhodogune, in Plutarch, *Artaxerxes*, of whom Philostratus, *Imagines* ii 5, said that 'she prays to conquer men, even as she has now conquered them'; see Allen (1952) 122. Both figures serve as exemplars of unjust female dominance, the direct opposite of Amoret's helpless state. Cooper (1565) records that a certain Rhodogune killed her nurse who tried to persuade her to marry again. From its etymology, $\rho\alpha\delta\iota\alpha + \gamma\upsilon\nu\eta$, the name suggests 'reckless woman' (Draper, 1932). Camden, *Remains* 106, offers the suggestive etymology, 'favourable counsel'; her counsel defeats knights: cf. 49.1–5, vii 28.2–4.

9 **prieued**: proved (an obsolete form).

Stanza 34

1–2 Cf. his defeat of the Knights of Maidenhead by his manhood, IV iv 39–43.

6 **This squalid weede**: apparently the halter (22.3) which is **the patterne of dispaire** for Despair himself at I ix 54; or 'yron fetters' (35.3), rather than 'womens weedes' (31.4) which he refused to wear. Yet cf. the Squire's 'squallid weed' (i 13.7).

Stanza 35

1 **repryu'd**: reprieved.

5 **dight**: make ready.

Stanza 36

6 **harnesse**: arms.

7 **sort**: company, swarm.

8 **halfe like a man**: as she is an Amazon or virago.

Stanza 37

1–3 **neare**: 'newe', sugg. Church (1758). **so few**: 'to feare', sugg. Collier (1862). The first conjecture gains the rhyme; the second accounts for the fierce revenge threatened by the knights.

7 **grate**: fret. **teeth did grin**: she bares her teeth in rage; or grin may signify grind; as the tiger threatens at VI xii 27.6.

39

But *Radigund* her selfe, when she espide
  Sir *Terpin*, from her direfull doome acquit,
  So cruell doale amongst her maides diuide,
  T'auenge that shame, they did on him commit,
  All sodainely enflam'd with furious fit,
  Like a fell Lionesse at him she flew,
  And on his head-peece him so fiercely smit,
  That to the ground him quite she ouerthrew,
Dismayd so with the stroke, that he no colours knew.

40

Soone as she saw him on the ground to grouell,
  She lightly to him leapt, and in his necke
  Her proud foote setting, at his head did leuell,
  Weening at once her wrath on him to wreake,
  And his contempt, that did her iudg'ment breake.
  As when a Beare hath seiz'd her cruell clawes
  Vppon the carkasse of some beast too weake,
  Proudly stands ouer, and a while doth pause,
To heare the piteous beast pleading her plaintiffe cause.

41

Whom when as *Artegall* in that distresse
  By chaunce beheld, he left the bloudy slaughter,
  In which he swam, and ranne to his redresse.
  There her assayling fiercely fresh, he raught her
  Such an huge stroke, that it of sence distraught her:
  And had she not it warded warily,
  It had depriu'd her mother of a daughter.
  Nathlesse for all the powre she did apply,
It made her stagger oft, and stare with ghastly eye.

42

Like to an Eagle in his kingly pride,
  Soring through his wide Empire of the aire,
  To weather his brode sailes, by chaunce hath spide
  A Goshauke, which hath seized for her share
  Vppon some fowle, that should her feast prepare;
  With dreadfull force he flies at her byliue,
  That with his souce, which none enduren dare,
  Her from the quarrey he away doth driue,
And from her griping pounce the greedy prey doth riue.

43

But soone as she her sence recouer'd had,
  She fiercely towards him her selfe gan dight,
  Through vengeful wrath and sdeignfull pride half mad:
  For neuer had she suffred such despight.
  But ere she could ioyne hand with him to fight,
  Her warlike maides about her flockt so fast,
  That they disparted them, maugre their might,
  And with their troupes did far a sunder cast:
But mongst the rest the fight did vntill euening last.

44

And euery while that mighty yron man,
  With his strange weapon, neuer wont in warre,
  Them sorely vext, and courst, and ouerran,
  And broke their bowes, and did their shooting marre,
  That none of all the many once did darre
  Him to assault, nor once approach him nie,
  But like a sort of sheepe dispersed farre
  For dread of their deuouring enemie,
Through all the fields and vallies did before him flie.

Stanza 39
2 **doome**: sentence of punishment. She usurps Artegall's role; cf. 'her iudg'ment' (40.5) and 'My law' (49.3). **acquit**: released.
3 **So . . . diuide**: i.e. dealing out such cruel blows among her maids. **doale** combines the dealing of blows and the grief and pain that follow them.

Stanza 40
4–5 **her wrath . . . / And his contempt**: i.e. to vent her wrath on him and avenge his contempt for her.
9 **plaintiffe**: being the plaintiff in her suit, and being plaintive.

Stanza 41
2 **slaughter**: occurs eight times in Book V but only three times in the rest of the poem, as Aptekar (1969) 117–8 notes.
3 **redresse**: aid, extending the legal imagery of the previous stanza.
5 **distraught**: distracted; deprived.

Stanza 42
1–4 Cf. III vii 39. The **Eagle** is an emblem of masculine strength (cf. xii 5.9); the **Goshauke**, a bird of prey, of feminine aggressiveness.
3 **weather**: air, a term in falconry.
6 **byliue**: with speed.
7 **souce**: the downward swoop of a bird of prey.
8 **quarrey**: the bird flown at by a bird of prey.
9 **pounce**: the talons of a bird of prey. **greedy prey**: i.e. the prey greedily seized.

Stanza 43
2 **gan dight**: made way.
7 **disparted**: separated.

Stanza 44
1 **euery while**: always, all the while.
2 **wont**: used. Or they were not accustomed to such a military weapon: see i 12.8–9*n*.
3 **courst**: thrashed. **ouerran**: trampled down.
5 **many**: both 'meanie' (i.e. many) and 'meinie' (mob).
darre: dare (an obsolete form).
7–9 The simile stops short of naming Talus as the wolf.
sort: flock. Cf. vi 30.4–6, xii 38.5–6. Aptekar (1969) 45–7 comments on the wolf-imagery in Book V.

45

But when as daies faire shinie-beame, yclowded
  With fearefull shadowes of deformed night,
  Warn'd man and beast in quiet rest be shrowded,
  Bold *Radigund* with sound of trumpe on hight,
  Causd all her people to surcease from fight,
  And gathering them vnto her citties gate,
  Made them all enter in before her sight,
  And all the wounded, and the weake in state,
To be conuayed in, ere she would once retrate.

46

When thus the field was voided all away,
  And all things quieted, the Elfin Knight
  Weary of toile and trauell of that day,
  Causd his pauilion to be richly pight
  Before the city gate, in open sight;
  Where he him selfe did rest in safety,
  Together with sir *Terpin* all that night:
  But *Talus* vsde in times of ieopardy
To keepe a nightly watch, for dread of treachery.

47

But *Radigund* full of heart-gnawing griefe,
  For the rebuke, which she sustain'd that day,
  Could take no rest, ne would receiue reliefe,
  But tossed in her troublous minde, what way
  She mote reuenge that blot, which on her lay.
  There she resolu'd her selfe in single fight
  To try her Fortune, and his force assay,
  Rather then see her people spoiled quight,
As she had seene that day a disauenterous sight.

48

She called forth to her a trusty mayd,
  Whom she thought fittest for that businesse,
  Her name was *Clarin*, and thus to her sayd;
  Goe damzell quickly, doe thy selfe addresse,
  To doe the message, which I shall expresse.
  Goe thou vnto that stranger Faery Knight,
  Who yesterday droue vs to such distresse,
  Tell, that to morrow I with him wil fight,
And try in equall field, whether hath greater might.

49

But these conditions doe to him propound.
  That if I vanquishe him, he shall obay
  My law, and euer to my lore be bound,
  And so will I, if me he vanquish may;
  What euer he shall like to doe or say:
  Goe streight, and take with thee, to witnesse it,
  Sixe of thy fellowes of the best array,
  And beare with you both wine and iuncates fit,
And bid him eate, henceforth he oft shall hungry sit.

50

The Damzell streight obayd, and putting all
  In readinesse, forth to the Towne-gate went,
  Where sounding loud a Trumpet from the wall,
  Vnto those warlike Knights she warning sent.
  Then *Talus* forth issuing from the tent,
  Vnto the wall his way did fearelesse take,
  To weeten what that trumpets sounding ment:
  Where that same Damzell lowdly him bespake,
And shew'd, that with his Lord she would emparlaunce make.

51

So he them streight conducted to his Lord,
  Who, as he could, them goodly well did greete,
  Till they had told their message word by word:
  Which he accepting well, as he could weete,
  Them fairely entertaynd with curt'sies meete,
  And gaue them gifts and things of deare delight.
  So backe againe they homeward turnd their feete.
  But *Artegall* him selfe to rest did dight,
That he mote fresher be against the next daies fight.

Stanza 45
Artegall's prowess endures until the coming of night, according to the pattern established in his battle against Britomart: see IV iv 43.5–6*n*.
4 **on hight**: on high; hence loud.
5 **surcease**: entirely cease.

Stanza 46
1 **voided**: cleared.
2 **the Elfin Knight**: see III iii 26.4–5.
3 **trauell**: travail.

Stanza 47
1 **griefe**: anger; bitterness.
2 **rebuke**: disgrace; the 'huge stroke' (41.5) – see *OED* 3b – which brings disgrace.
9 **disauenterous**: unfortunate, disastrous.

Stanza 48
3 **Clarin**: short for Clarinda (v 29.3), after Clorinda, an Amazon in Tasso, *Ger. Lib.* ii 38. Belson (1964) notes that the etymology of the name, from 'clarion', refers to her role as spokesman.
5 **doe**: deliver.
9 **whether**: which.

Stanza 49
2–5 A heads-I-win, tails-you-lose proposition: either way she becomes his mistress in place of his betrothed.
8 **iuncates**: delicacies, sweet dishes.
9 **bid him eate**: suggests Eve bidding Adam to eat the forbidden fruit.

Stanza 50
9 **emparlaunce**: parleying.

Stanza 51
2 **as he could**: as he knew well how to do; or, as well as he knew how.
4 Artegall accepts the ordeal by battle which earlier (i 25.4) he rejected. Cf. v 5.9. **as he could weete**: as he knew how. His relaxed affability bodes ill.
5 **fairely**: courteously.

Cant. V.

Artegall fights with Radigund
And is subdewd by guile:
He is by her emprisoned,
But wrought by Clarins wile.

1

SO soone as day forth dawning from the East,
Nights humid curtaine from the heauens withdrew,
And earely calling forth both man and beast,
Comaunded them their daily workes renew,
These noble warriors, mindefull to pursew
The last daies purpose of their vowed fight,
Them selues thereto preparde in order dew;
The Knight, as best was seeming for a Knight,
And th'Amazon, as best it likt her selfe to dight.

2

All in a Camis light of purple silke
Wouen vppon with siluer, subtly wrought,
And quilted vppon sattin white as milke,
Trayled with ribbands diuersly distraught
Like as the workeman had their courses taught;
Which was short tucked for light motion
Vp to her ham, but when she list, it raught
Downe to her lowest heele, and thereuppon
She wore for her defence a mayled habergeon.

3

And on her legs she painted buskins wore,
Basted with bends of gold on euery side,
And mailes betweene, and laced close afore:
Vppon her thigh her Cemitare was tide,
With an embrodered belt of mickell pride;
And on her shoulder hung her shield, bedeckt
Vppon the bosse with stones, that shined wide,
As the faire Moone in her most full aspect,
That to the Moone it mote be like in each respect.

4

So forth she came out of the citty gate,
With stately port and proud magnificence,
Guarded with many damzels, that did waite
Vppon her person for her sure defence,
Playing on shaumes and trumpets, that from hence
Their sound did reach vnto the heauens hight.
So forth into the field she marched thence,
Where was a rich Pauilion ready pight,
Her to receiue, till time they should begin the fight.

5

Then forth came *Artegall* out of his tent,
All arm'd to point, and first the Lists did enter:
Soone after eke came she, with fell intent,
And countenaunce fierce, as hauing fully bent her,
That battels vtmost triall to aduenter.
The Lists were closed fast, to barre the rout
From rudely pressing to the middle center;
Which in great heapes them circled all about,
Wayting, how Fortune would resolue that daungerous dout.

Canto v

Argument

2 **guile**: not 'force' (iv 31.1).
4 **wrought**: practised on.

Stanza 1

6 **vowed fight**: referring to the conditions of the fight.
8–9 A nice distinction between the male who arms himself according to his role and the female who arms herself according to her desire.

Stanzas 2–3

The pictorial tradition behind S.'s Amazon is described by Tuve (1970) 120–7. Radigund's attire resembles Belphœbe's at II iii 26–27. Radigund's **Camis** is **purple** (2.1) to indicate her aspirations to sovereignty (cf. I vii 16.3); Belphœbe's is lily-white to indicate her virginity.

Stanza 2

1 **Camis**: light, loose dress. **purple**: Lat. *purpurea*, crimson; cf. Dido who wears a *purpuream vestem* (Virgil, *Aen.* iv 139) to meet Aeneas.
4 Decorated with a trailing ornament of ribbons drawn in different directions.
7 Cf. Belphœbe's camis which goes modestly 'Below her ham' (II iii 27.1).

Stanza 3

2 **Basted with bends**: sewn with bands.
3 **mailes**: lace-holes.
4 **Cemitare**: scimitar, a weapon associated with pagans, curved like the moon. In Ripa (1603) 232 the weapon of Injustice, signifying twisted justice.
5 Cf. the cestus worn by Hippolyta, Queen of the Amazons, which Hercules took from her. His act was interpreted by Renaissance commentators as the triumph of virtue over lust; see Aptekar (1969) 176.
6–9 The repetition stresses Radigund's association with the moon; cf. 12.8. In *Aen.* i 490, the Amazons carry crescent-shaped shields; Radigund's is compared to the full moon. The **stones** suggest Amazonian richness.

Stanza 4

2 **magnificence**: display of splendour.
5 **shaumes and trumpets**: these instruments herald her victory; cf. I xii 13.2.
7–9 **a rich Pauilion ready pight**: perhaps pitched by Artegall; yet see vii 26.1–3.

Stanza 5

2 **to point**: completely.
4 **countenaunce**: bearing.
5 **aduenter**: venture herself.
9 **Fortune**, rather than justice, decides the outcome; cf. iv 34.8, 47.7.

6

The Trumpets sounded, and the field began;
    With bitter strokes it both began, and ended.
    She at the first encounter on him ran
    With furious rage, as if she had intended
    Out of his breast the very heart haue rended:
    But he that had like tempests often tride,
    From that first flaw him selfe right well defended.
    The more she rag'd, the more he did abide;
She hewd, she foynd, she lasht, she laid on euery side.

7

Yet still her blowes he bore, and her forbore,
    Weening at last to win aduantage new;
    Yet still her crueltie increased more,
    And though powre faild, her courage did accrew,
    Which fayling he gan fiercely her pursew.
    Like as a Smith that to his cunning feat
    The stubborne mettall seeketh to subdew,
    Soone as he feeles it mollifide with heat,
With his great yron sledge doth strongly on it beat.

8

So did Sir *Artegall* vpon her lay,
    As if she had an yron anduile beene,
    That flakes of fire, bright as the sunny ray,
    Out of her steely armes were flashing seene,
    That all on fire ye would her surely weene.
    But with her shield so well her selfe she warded,
    From the dread daunger of his weapon keene,
    That all that while her life she safely garded:
But he that helpe from her against her will discarded.

9

For with his trenchant blade at the next blow
    Halfe of her shield he shared quite away,
    That halfe her side it selfe did naked show,
    And thenceforth vnto daunger opened way.
    Much was she moued with the mightie sway
    Of that sad stroke, that halfe enrag'd she grew,
    And like a greedie Beare vnto her pray,
    With her sharpe Cemitare at him she flew,
That glauncing downe his thigh, the purple bloud forth drew.

10

Thereat she gan to triumph with great boast,
    And to vpbrayd that chaunce, which him misfell,
    As if the prize she gotten had almost,
    With spightfull speaches, fitting with her well;
    That his great hart gan inwardly to swell
    With indignation, at her vaunting vaine,
    And at her strooke with puissance fearefull fell;
    Yet with her shield she warded it againe,
That shattered all to peeces round about the plaine.

11

Hauing her thus disarmed of her shield,
    Vpon her helmet he againe her strooke,
    That downe she fell vpon the grassie field,
    In sencelesse swoune, as if her life forsooke,
    And pangs of death her spirit ouertooke.
    Whom when he saw before his foote prostrated,
    He to her lept with deadly dreadfull looke,
    And her sunshynie helmet soone vnlaced,
Thinking at once both head and helmet to haue raced.

Stanza 6
1   **field**: battle.
5   Suggests the sexual significance of the battle.
7   **flaw**: sudden squall of wind.
9   **foynd**: lunged.

Stanza 7
1   **forbore**: spared.
4   **accrew**: gather, i.e. remain.
5   **Which**: i.e. her powre.
6   **feat**: art.

Stanza 8
9   **discarded**: forced away.

Stanza 9
1   **trenchant**: cutting.
2   **shared**: cut.
3   **naked**: unarmed, bare; hence she fights like a **Beare** (7).
5   **sway**: force.
6   **sad**: heavy.
7   The image is extended from iv 40.6–9.
9   A sexual wound, as at III v 20.7.

Stanza 10
8   **it**: the stroke. Upton (1758) observes that the substantive is included in the verb.
9   **That**: her shield.

Stanza 11
7   **deadly**: preparing for the **looke** that proves deadly to him in the next stanza.
8   Her masculine armour is associated with the sun, her feminine beauty in the next stanza with the moon.
9   **raced**: cut off.

12

But when as he discouered had her face,
  He saw his senses straunge astonishment,
  A miracle of natures goodly grace,
  In her faire visage voide of ornament,
  But bath'd in bloud and sweat together ment;
  Which in the rudenesse of that euill plight,
  Bewrayd the signes of feature excellent:
  Like as the Moone in foggie winters night,
Doth seeme to be her selfe, though darkned be her light.

13

At sight thereof his cruell minded hart
  Empierced was with pittifull regard,
  That his sharpe sword he threw from him apart,
  Cursing his hand that had that visage mard:
  No hand so cruell, nor no hart so hard,
  But ruth of beautie will it mollifie.
  By this vpstarting from her swoune, she star'd
  A while about her with confused eye;
Like one that from his dreame is waked suddenlye.

14

Soone as the knight she there by her did spy,
  Standing with emptie hands all weaponlesse,
  With fresh assault vpon him she did fly,
  And gan renew her former cruelnesse:
  And though he still retyr'd, yet nathelesse
  With huge redoubled strokes she on him layd;
  And more increast her outrage mercilesse,
  The more that he with meeke intreatie prayd,
Her wrathful hand from greedy vengeance to haue stayd.

15

Like as a Puttocke hauing spyde in sight
  A gentle Faulcon sitting on an hill,
  Whose other wing, now made vnmeete for flight,
  Was lately broken by some fortune ill;
  The foolish Kyte, led with licentious will,
  Doth beat vpon the gentle bird in vaine,
  With many idle stoups her troubling still:
  Euen so did *Radigund* with bootlesse paine
Annoy this noble Knight, and sorely him constraine.

16

Nought could he do, but shun the dred despight
  Of her fierce wrath, and backward still retyre,
  And with his single shield, well as he might,
  Beare off the burden of her raging yre;
  And euermore he gently did desyre,
  To stay her stroks, and he himselfe would yield:
  Yet nould she hearke, ne let him once respyre,
  Till he to her deliuered had his shield,
And to her mercie him submitted in plaine field.

17

So was he ouercome, not ouercome,
  But to her yeelded of his owne accord;
  Yet was he iustly damned by the doome
  Of his owne mouth, that spake so warelesse word,
  To be her thrall, and seruice her afford.
  For though that he first victorie obtayned,
  Yet after by abandoning his sword,
  He wilfull lost, that he before attayned.
No fayrer conquest, then that with goodwill is gayned.

Stanza 12
In Tasso, *Ger. Lib*. iii 21–2, Tancred knocks the helmet off the Amazon, Clorinda, only to be overcome by her beauty.
Behind both incidents lies the story of how Achilles vanquished Penthesilea, the Amazon Queen, only to be overcome by her beauty.
2   **He saw . . . astonishment**: i.e. what he saw strangely astonished his senses. But also he saw his senses' astonishment; cf. the beauty that astonished him when he first saw Britomart, IV vi 19–22.
3   Cf. the double address to Britomart as 'That peerelesse paterne of Dame natures pride,/ And heauenly image of perfection' (IV vi 24.5–6).
5   **ment**: mingled.
7   **Bewrayd**: revealed.
8–9   **the Moone . . . / . . . though darkned be her light**: cf. Britomart's face 'Like to the ruddie morne' (IV vi 19.6). Radigund is compared to the darkened moon, Britomart to the full moon in its brightness (III i 43). Cf. III ix 20.6–9, IV i 13.6–9.

Stanza 13
1–2   Jones (1930) 257 notes that cruelty and pity are the vices of justice and mercy respectively.
3   When he sees Britomart's beauty, his 'cruell sword out of his fingers slacke/Fell downe to ground' (IV vi 21.5–6). In throwing his sword away, he wilfully cooperates in his own fall.
5–6   Earlier Artegall was compared to the smith who 'mollifide' (7.8) the hard metal.

Stanza 15
1–2   The Amazon is compared to a bird of prey, the kite; the noble but effeminate Artegall to the falcon-gentle, the female of the peregrine falcon.
3   **Whose other**: i.e. one of whose.
7   **stoups**: the swoops of a bird of prey upon its quarry.
8   **bootlesse**: to no purpose (because he has already yielded).
9   **constraine**: distress.

Stanza 16
3   **single shield**: i.e. shield alone.
7   **nould**: would not.
9   **in plaine field**: in open (full) battle. She claims to win by her force rather than by his yielding.

Stanza 17
1–2   He conquers himself instead of being conquered by her, yielding to her by his own **goodwill** (9); cf. 20.2, 32.2–3, vi 16.4–5. The significant analogy is Adam's submission to Eve. See S.'s comment, vi 1.
3   **damned**: condemned, with obvious religious overtones.
4   **warelesse**: imprudent.
8   **wilfull**: voluntarily, of free will, following his lustful desire; cf. 20.2.

18

Tho with her sword on him she flatling strooke,
    In signe of true subiection to her powre,
    And as her vassall him to thraldome tooke.
    But *Terpine* borne to'a more vnhappy howre,
    As he, on whom the lucklesse starres did lowre,
    She causd to be attacht, and forthwith led
    Vnto the crooke t'abide the balefull stowre,
    From which he lately had through reskew fled :
Where he full shamefully was hanged by the hed.

19

But when they thought on *Talus* hands to lay,
    He with his yron flaile amongst them thondred,
    That they were fayne to let him scape away,
    Glad from his companie to be so sondred ;
    Whose presence all their troups so much encombred
    That th'heapes of those, which he did wound and slay,
    Besides the rest dismayd, might not be nombred :
    Yet all that while he would not once assay,
To reskew his owne Lord, but thought it iust t'obay.

20

Then tooke the Amazon this noble knight,
    Left to her will by his owne wilfull blame,
    And caused him to be disarmed quight,
    Of all the ornaments of knightly name,
    With which whylome he gotten had great fame :
    In stead whereof she made him to be dight
    In womans weedes, that is to manhood shame,
    And put before his lap a napron white,
In stead of Curiets and bases fit for fight.

21

So being clad, she brought him from the field,
    In which he had bene trayned many a day,
    Into a long large chamber, which was sield
    With moniments of many knights decay,
    By her subdewed in victorious fray ;
    Amongst the which she causd his warlike armes
    Be hang'd on high, that mote his shame bewray ;
    And broke his sword, for feare of further harmes,
With which he wont to stirre vp battailous alarmes.

22

There entred in, he round about him saw
    Many braue knights, whose names right well he knew,
    There bound t'obay that Amazons proud law,
    Spinning and carding all in comely rew,
    That his bigge hart loth'd so vncomely vew.
    But they were forst through penurie and pyne,
    To doe those workes, to them appointed dew :
    For nought was giuen them to sup or dyne,
But what their hands could earne by twisting linnen twyne.

23

Amongst them all she placed him most low,
    And in his hand a distaffe to him gaue,
    That he thereon should spin both flax and tow ;
    A sordid office for a mind so braue.
    So hard it is to be a womans slaue.
    Yet he it tooke in his owne selfes despight,
    And thereto did himselfe right well behaue,
    Her to obay, sith he his faith had plight,
Her vassall to become, if she him wonne in fight.

Stanza 18

1–2   She dubs him her knight.   **flatling** : with the flat side.

5   **lucklesse** : referring to malign astral influence, which makes him unlucky.

6   **attacht** : seized, legally arrested. She assumes Artegall's role as the knight of justice.

7   **crooke** : gibbet.   **balefull stowre** : pain of death.

Stanza 19

3   **fayne** : glad.

7   **dismayd** : routed.

8–9   **iust** according to the law of arms : Artegall had promised to obey her if defeated (iv 49.2–3).

Stanza 20

2   **her will** includes her sexual desire.   **wilfull blame** doubly stresses his fault : he suffers blame through his own blameful will.

8   **before his lap** : suggesting impotence.   **napron** : apron ; a token of his fall. After sinning, Adam and Eve 'made themselves aprons' (Gen. 3.7, 1611).

9   **Curiets** : cuirasses, the knight's breastplate and backplate.
bases : the skirt of mail worn by knights on horseback.

Stanza 21

3–4   Cf. the house of Busirane, III xi 52.   **sield** : lined on the walls and ceiling.   **decay** : overthrow.

7   **bewray** : reveal.

8   As Braggadocchio is disgraced, iii 37.9.

9   **battailous** : warlike.

Stanza 22

4–5   Gough (1921) notes that the pleasing orderliness of the scene is contrasted with its moral repulsiveness.   **bigge** : stout.

6   **penurie and pyne** : probably a stock phrase ; cf. I ix 35.8. Literally, lack of food and the suffering that follows.

Stanza 23

4   **sordid** : menial ; debasing ; foul.

6   Cf. Terpine who 'rather chose to die in liues despight' (iv 32.8) than suffer such shame ; cf. 26.5.

7   **behaue** : conduct, manage.

24

Who had him seene, imagine mote thereby,
  That whylome hath of *Hercules* bene told,
  How for *Iolas* sake he did apply
  His mightie hands, the distaffe vile to hold,
  For his huge club, which had subdew'd of old
  So many monsters, which the world annoyed;
  His Lyons skin chaungd to a pall of gold,
  In which forgetting warres, he onely ioyed
In combats of sweet loue, and with his mistresse toyed.

25

Such is the crueltie of womenkynd,
  When they haue shaken off the shamefast band,
  With which wise Nature did them strongly bynd,
  T'obay the heasts of mans well ruling hand,
  That then all rule and reason they withstand,
  To purchase a licentious libertie.
  But vertuous women wisely vnderstand,
  That they were borne to base humilitie,
Vnlesse the heauens them lift to lawfull soueraintie.

26

Thus there long while continu'd *Artegall*,
  Seruing proud *Radigund* with true subiection;
  How euer it his noble heart did gall,
  T'obay a womans tyrannous direction,
  That might haue had of life or death election:
  But hauing chosen, now he might not chaunge.
  During which time, the warlike Amazon,
  Whose wandring fancie after lust did raunge,
Gan cast a secret liking to this captiue straunge.

27

Which long concealing in her couert brest,
  She chaw'd the cud of louers carefull plight;
  Yet could it not so thoroughly digest,
  Being fast fixed in her wounded spright,
  But it tormented her both day and night:
  Yet would she not thereto yeeld free accord,
  To serue the lowly vassall of her might,
  And of her seruant make her souerayne Lord:
So great her pride, that she such basenesse much abhord.

28

So much the greater still her anguish grew,
  Through stubborne handling of her loue-sicke hart;
  And still the more she stroue it to subdew,
  The more she still augmented her owne smart,
  And wyder made the wound of th'hidden dart.
  At last when long she struggled had in vaine,
  She gan to stoupe, and her proud mind conuert
  To meeke obeysance of loues mightie raine,
And him entreat for grace, that had procur'd her paine.

29

Vnto her selfe in secret she did call
  Her nearest handmayd, whom she most did trust,
  And to her said; *Clarinda* whom of all
  I trust a liue, sith I thee fostred first;
  Now is the time, that I vntimely must
  Thereof make tryall, in my greatest need:
  It is so hapned, that the heauens vniust,
  Spighting my happie freedome, haue agreed,
562 To thrall my looser life, or my last bale to breed.

Stanza 24

S. may confuse Iole with Omphale, as did his contemporaries,
e.g. Cooper, who writes of Iole: 'whome Hercules loved so
much, that he served hir in a womans apparaile, and spanne on
a distaffe'. (Of Omphale he writes, 'whom Hercules dyd serve,
and she caused him to spinne on a rocke'.) Or he may deliberately conflate the stories of the two in relation to Hercules in
order to parallel Britomart and Radigund in relation to Artegall.
In one version, Hercules won Iole but was refused her;
thereupon he killed Iphitus, and to expiate his offence underwent a three-year penance during which he served Omphale.
See Aptekar (1969) 179. Tuve (1970) 83–96 compares Boccaccio's *De Claris Mulieribus*: Iole appears as the subtlest
temptation encountered by Hercules acting as the instrument
of Justice.
7 For the first of his labours, Hercules killed the Nemean
lion and wore its skin as a sign of victory. See viii 2.4–5.
pall: robe.

Stanza 25

2 **shamefast band**: bond of modesty, i.e. bonds that
restrain from shame.
4 **heasts**: behests.
7–9 S. agrees with the moderate Puritans; noted Phillips
(1942) 5–32, 211–34. **base**: low, humble; not necessarily
mean or servile. Yet the word so disturbed the author of *Hic
Mulier* (1620) that he substituted 'milde'; see Wells (1972) 157.
9 The line makes the obvious, and necessary, exception of
Elizabeth. **lawfull** emphasizes her claim to the crown.

Stanza 26

3 **How euer**: however much.
5–6 He might have chosen death, as did Terpine (iv 32.8);
once having chosen to live by her mercy, however, he has no
choice.
7–9 Cf. Raleigh's account of the Amazons in the *Discovery of
Guiana*: 'If in the wars they took any prisoners, . . . they used
to accompany [cohabit] with those also at what time soever, but
in the end for certain they put them to death' (*Selected prose*
122). **straunge**: foreign.

Stanza 27

2 **carefull**: sorrowful.

Stanza 28

2 **stubborne**: fierce, harsh.
7 **conuert**: change.
9 **procur'd**: caused.

Stanza 29

6 **Thereof**: i.e. of my trust in you.
8 **Spighting**: regarding with ill-will.
9 **looser**: too loose. **last bale**: death.

30

With that she turn'd her head, as halfe abashed,
  To hide the blush which in her visage rose,
  And through her eyes like sudden lightning flashed,
  Decking her cheeke with a vermilion rose:
  But soone she did her countenance compose,
  And to her turning, thus began againe;
  This griefes deepe wound I would to thee disclose,
  Thereto compelled through hart-murdring paine,
But dread of shame my doubtfull lips doth still restraine.

31

Ah my deare dread (said then the faithfull Mayd)
  Can dread of ought your dreadlesse hart withhold,
  That many hath with dread of death dismayd,
  And dare euen deathes most dreadfull face behold?
  Say on my souerayne Ladie, and be bold;
  Doth not your handmayds life at your foot lie?
  Therewith much comforted, she gan vnfold
  The cause of her conceiued maladie,
As one that would confesse, yet faine would it denie.

32

Clarin (sayd she) thou seest yond Fayry Knight,
  Whom not my valour, but his owne braue mind
  Subiected hath to my vnequall might;
  What right is it, that he should thraldome find,
  For lending life to me a wretch vnkind;
  That for such good him recompence with ill?
  Therefore I cast, how I may him vnbind,
  And by his freedome get his free goodwill;
Yet so, as bound to me he may continue still.

33

Bound vnto me, but not with such hard bands
  Of strong compulsion, and streight violence,
  As now in miserable state he stands;
  But with sweet loue and sure beneuolence,
  Voide of malitious mind, or foule offence.
  To which if thou canst win him any way,
  Without discouerie of my thoughts pretence,
  Both goodly meede of him it purchase may,
And eke with gratefull seruice me right well apay.

34

Which that thou mayst the better bring to pas,
  Loe here this ring, which shall thy warrant bee,
  And token true to old Eumenias,
  From time to time, when thou it best shalt see,
  That in and out thou mayst haue passage free.
  Goe now, Clarinda, well thy wits aduise,
  And all thy forces gather vnto thee;
  Armies of louely lookes, and speeches wise,
With which thou canst euen Ioue himselfe to loue entise.

35

The trustie Mayd, conceiuing her intent,
  Did with sure promise of her good indeuour,
  Giue her great comfort, and some harts content.
  So from her parting, she thenceforth did labour
  By all the meanes she might, to curry fauour
  With th'Elfin Knight, her Ladies best beloued;
  With daily shew of courteous kind behauiour,
  Euen at the markewhite of his hart she roued,
And with wide glauncing words, one day she thus him proued.

36

Vnhappie Knight, vpon whose hopelesse state
  Fortune enuying good, hath felly frowned,
  And cruell heauens haue heapt an heauy fate;
  I rew that thus thy better dayes are drowned
  In sad despaire, and all thy senses swowned
  In stupid sorow, sith thy iuster merit
  Might else haue with felicitie bene crowned:
  Looke vp at last, and wake thy dulled spirit,
To thinke how this long death thou mightest disinherit.

Stanza 30
9 doubtfull: fearful.

Stanza 31
1–4 Upton (1758) observes that the maid rings changes on dread like a professed punster.

Stanza 32
2 braue mind: so she says because he was too weak to kill her in battle; cf. 23.4.
7 cast: consider.
8–9 She has his goodwill at 17.9 though not free.

Stanza 33
2 streight: severe.
4 beneuolence: affection.
7 pretence: intent, as 35.1.
9 Extended to Artegall, seruice implies sexual activity; cf. 17.5. Hence gratefull implies his being thankful and pleasing to her. apay: requite.

Stanza 34
3 Eumenias: Kindly One, referring to the 'goodwill' (32.8) which is the means of access to Artegall's love.
8 louely: loving.

Stanza 35
1 conceiuing: apprehending; also suggesting that she conceives the same desire for Artegall as her mistress; cf. 43.8.
8 markewhite: white bull's eye of a target. roued: shot.
9 wide glauncing: indirect, as a roving arrow is shot at an elevation rather than directly to a target. proued: tested.

Stanza 36
Echoes Una's lament that the Red Cross Knight 'his better dayes hath wasted all' (I viii 28.8) in Orgoglio's dungeon. Like him, Artegall endures a long death (9), and must be redeemed by grace. He is imprisoned by 'his owne doome, that none can now vndoo' (vi 16.5).
6 stupid: that which stuns. iuster: most just.

563

37

Much did he maruell at her vncouth speach,
  Whose hidden drift he could not well perceiue;
  And gan to doubt, least she him sought t'appeach
  Of treason, or some guilefull traine did weaue,
  Through which she might his wretched life bereaue.
  Both which to barre, he with this answere met her;
  Faire Damzell, that with ruth (as I perceaue)
  Of my mishaps, art mou'd to wish me better,
For such your kind regard, I can but rest your detter.

38

Yet weet ye well, that to a courage great
  It is no lesse beseeming well, to beare
  The storme of fortunes frowne, or heauens threat,
  Then in the sunshine of her countenance cleare
  Timely to ioy, and carrie comely cheare.
  For though this cloud haue now me ouercast,
  Yet doe I not of better times despeyre;
  And, though (vnlike) they should for euer last,
Yet in my truthes assurance I rest fixed fast.

39

But what so stonie mind (she then replyde)
  But if in his owne powre occasion lay,
  Would to his hope a windowe open wyde,
  And to his fortunes helpe make readie way?
  Vnworthy sure (quoth he) of better day,
  That will not take the offer of good hope,
  And eke pursew, if he attaine it may.
  Which speaches she applying to the scope
Of her intent, this further purpose to him shope.

40

Then why doest not, thou ill aduized man,
  Make meanes to win thy libertie forlorne,
  And try if thou by faire entreatie, can
  Moue *Radigund*? who though she still haue worne
  Her dayes in warre, yet (weet thou) was not borne
  Of Beares and Tygres, nor so saluage mynded,
  As that, albe all loue of men she scorne,
  She yet forgets, that she of men was kynded: (blynded.
And sooth oft seene, that proudest harts base loue hath

41

Certes *Clarinda*, not of cancred will,
  (Sayd he) nor obstinate disdainefull mind,
  I haue forbore this duetie to fulfill:
  For well I may this weene, by that I fynd,
  That she a Queene, and come of Princely kynd,
  Both worthie is for to be sewd vnto,
  Chiefely by him, whose life her law doth bynd,
  And eke of powre her owne doome to vndo,
And als' of princely grace to be inclyn'd thereto.

42

But want of meanes hath bene mine onely let,
  From seeking fauour, where it doth abound;
  Which if I might by your good office get,
  I to your selfe should rest for euer bound,
  And readie to deserue, what grace I found.
  She feeling him thus bite vpon the bayt,
  Yet doubting least his hold was but vnsound,
  And not well fastened, would not strike him strayt,
564 But drew him on with hope, fit leasure to awayt.

43

But foolish Mayd, whyles heedlesse of the hooke,
  She thus oft times was beating off and on,
  Through slipperie footing, fell into the brooke,
  And there was caught to her confusion.
  For seeking thus to salue the Amazon,
  She wounded was with her deceipts owne dart,
  And gan thenceforth to cast affection,
  Conceiued close in her beguiled hart,
To *Artegall*, throung pittie of his causelesse smart.

Stanza 37
1 **vncouth**: strange.
3 **doubt**: fear. **appeach**: accuse.
4 **traine**: treachery.

Stanza 38
8 **though (vnlike)**] though vnlike, 1596 requires a usage,
'And = if', unique in S.'s poem. **vnlike**: i.e. it is unlikely.
they: referring to **fortunes frowne** or **heauens threat** (3)
that produce **this cloud** (6).

Stanza 39
9 **purpose**: proposal. **shope**: shaped, addressed.

Stanza 40
2 **forlorne**: lost.
6 **Beares and Tygres**: see II ii 22.5–9n.
8 **kynded**: begotten; made kind, being made of human kind.
9 **base**: low, humble; also debasing.

Stanza 42
Artegall responds as does Amyas who loves Æmylia faithfully
yet uses the means provided by Fortune when the giant's
daughter woos him: 'Her graunted loue, but with affection cold/
To win her grace his libertie to get' (IV viii 53.5–6). Cf. his
promise that would break his oath to Radigund, 55.8–9.
1 **let**: hindrance.
8 **strike**: i.e. jerk the line to fix the hook.

Stanza 43
2 **beating off and on**: obviously an angling term though
OED offers no support. It suggests short strikes to test the hold
upon the bait.
5 **salue**: heal.

44

Yet durst she not disclose her fancies wound,
  Ne to himselfe, for doubt of being sdayned,
  Ne yet to any other wight on ground,
  For feare her mistresse shold haue knowledge gayned,
  But to her selfe it secretly retayned,
  Within the closet of her couert brest:
  The more thereby her tender hart was payned.
  Yet to awayt fit time she weened best,
And fairely did dissemble her sad thoughts vnrest.

45

One day her Ladie, calling her apart,
  Gan to demaund of her some tydings good,
  Touching her loues successe, her lingring smart.
  Therewith she gan at first to change her mood,
  As one adaw'd, and halfe confused stood;
  But quickly she it ouerpast, so soone
  As she her face had wypt, to fresh her blood:
  Tho gan she tell her all, that she had donne,
And all the wayes she sought, his loue for to haue wonne.

46

But sayd, that he was obstinate and sterne,
  Scorning her offers and conditions vaine;
  Ne would be taught with any termes, to lerne
  So fond a lesson, as to loue againe.
  Die rather would he in penurious paine,
  And his abridged dayes in dolour wast,
  Then his foes loue or liking entertaine:
  His resolution was both first and last,
His bodie was her thrall, his hart was freely plast.

47

Which when the cruell Amazon perceiued,
  She gan to storme, and rage, and rend her gall,
  For very fell despight, which she conceiued,
  To be so scorned of a base borne thrall,
  Whose life did lie in her least eye-lids fall;
  Of which she vow'd with many a cursed threat,
  That she therefore would him ere long forstall.
  Nathlesse when calmed was her furious heat,
She chang'd that threatfull mood, and mildly gan entreat.

48

What now is left *Clarinda*? what remaines,
  That we may compasse this our enterprize?
  Great shame to lose so long employed paines,
  And greater shame t'abide so great misprize,
  With which he dares our offers thus despize.
  Yet that his guilt the greater may appeare,
  And more my gratious mercie by this wize,
  I will a while with his first folly beare,
Till thou haue tride againe, and tempted him more neare.

49

Say, and do all, that may thereto preuaile;
  Leaue nought vnpromist, that may him perswade,
  Life, freedome, grace, and gifts of great auaile,
  With which the Gods themselues are mylder made:
  Thereto adde art, euen womens witty trade,
  The art of mightie words, that men can charme;
  With which in case thou canst him not inuade,
  Let him feele hardnesse of thy heauie arme: (harme.
Who will not stoupe with good, shall be made stoupe with

50

Some of his diet doe from him withdraw;
  For I him find to be too proudly fed.
  Giue him more labour, and with streighter law,
  That he with worke may be forwearied.
  Let him lodge hard, and lie in strawen bed,
  That may pull downe the courage of his pride;
  And lay vpon him, for his greater dread,
  Cold yron chaines, with which let him be tide;
And let, what euer he desires, be him denide.

Stanza 44
1 **fancies wound**: wound by love, as Radigund 'Whose wandring fancie after lust did raunge' (26.8).
2 **doubt**: fear. **sdayned**: disdained.

Stanza 45
5 **adaw'd**: daunted.
7 A 'realistic' detail almost without precedent in the poem.

Stanza 46
What one might have expected Artegall to say instead of compromising as he does.
4 **fond**: foolish; amorous. **againe**: in return.
5 **penurious paine**: pain of starvation (cf. 22.6).

Stanza 47
2 **gall**: the source of anger and malice.
7 **forstall**: deprive.

Stanza 48
4 **misprize**: scorn.

Stanza 49
Cf. her earlier wooing of Bellodant 'by all the waies she could' (iv 30.4); see 51.5*n*.
3 **auaile**: benefit.
4 Proverbial (C. G. Smith, 1970, 321).
5 **witty**: cunning, clever.

Stanza 50
3 **streighter**: more strict.
4 **forwearied**: utterly wearied.

51

When thou hast all this doen, then bring me newes
  Of his demeane: thenceforth not like a louer,
  But like a rebell stout I will him vse.
  For I resolue this siege not to giue ouer,
  Till I the conquest of my will recouer.
  So she departed, full of griefe and sdaine,
  Which inly did to great impatience moue her.
  But the false mayden shortly turn'd againe
Vnto the prison, where her hart did thrall remaine.

52

There all her subtill nets she did vnfold,
  And all the engins of her wit display;.
  In which she meant him warelesse to enfold,
  And of his innocence to make her pray.
  So cunningly she wrought her crafts assay,
  That both her Ladie, and her selfe withail,
  And eke the knight attonce she did betray:
  But most the knight, whom she with guilefull call
Did cast for to allure, into her trap to fall.

53

As a bad Nurse, which fayning to receiue
  In her owne mouth the food, ment for her chyld,
  Withholdes it to her selfe, and doeth deceiue
  The infant, so for want of nourture spoyld:
  Euen so *Clarinda* her owne Dame beguyld,
  And turn'd the trust, which was in her affyde,
  To feeding of her priuate fire, which boyld
  Her inward brest, and in her entrayles fryde,
The more that she it sought to couer and to hyde.

54

For comming to this knight, she purpose fayned,
  How earnest suit she earst for him had made
  Vnto her Queene, his freedome to haue gayned;
  But by no meanes could her thereto perswade:
  But that in stead thereof, she sternely bade
  His miserie to be augmented more,
  And many yron bands on him to lade.
  All which nathlesse she for his loue forbore:
So praying him t'accept her seruice euermore.

55

And more then that, she promist that she would,
  In case she might finde fauour in his eye,
  Deuize how to enlarge him out of hould.
  The Fayrie glad to gaine his libertie,
  Can yeeld great thankes for such her curtesie,
  And with faire words, fit for the time and place,
  To feede the humour of her maladie,
  Promist, if she would free him from that case,
He wold by all good means he might, deserue such grace.

56

So daily he faire semblant did her shew,
  Yet neuer meant he in his noble mind,
  To his owne absent loue to be vntrew:
  Ne euer did deceiptfull *Clarin* find
  In her false hart, his bondage to vnbind;
  But rather how she mote him faster tye.
  Therefore vnto her mistresse most vnkind
  She daily told, her loue he did defye,
And him she told, her Dame his freedome did denye.

57

Yet thus much friendship she to him did show,
  That his scarse diet somewhat was amended,
  And his worke lessened, that his loue mote grow:
  Yet to her Dame him still she discommended,
  That she with him mote be the more offended.
  Thus he long while in thraldome there remayned,
  Of both beloued well, but litle frended;
  Vntill his owne true loue his freedome gayned,
Which in an other Canto will be best contayned.

Stanza 51
2 **demeane**: behaviour.
5 She resumes the aggressive masculine role which she first assumed when she could not win Bellodant 'vnto her will' (iv 30.6).
6 **sdaine**: disdain.

Stanza 52
1 **subtill**: finely woven; skilfully devised; crafty.
2 **engins**: snares.
3 **warelesse**: unwary.
5–9 Radigund is betrayed by Clarinda, Clarinda by love, and Artegall by violating his oath to Radigund 'To be her thrall, and seruice her afford' (17.5). **assay**: endeavour; best effort.
8–9 The image of the fowler who nets birds by making imitative calls. **cast**: scheme.

Stanza 53
6 **affyde**: confided.

Stanza 54
1 **purpose**: discourse; a story.
7 **lade**: load.

Stanza 55
3 **hould**: confinement.
5 **Can**: did.

Stanza 56
1 **faire semblant**: favourable countenance.
8 **defye**: reject.

Cant. VI.

Talus brings newes to Britomart,
of Artegals mishap,
She goes to seeke him, Dolon meetes,
who seekes her to entrap.

1

SOme men, I wote, will deeme in *Artegall*
Great weaknesse, and report of him much ill,
For yeelding so himselfe a wretched thrall,
To th'insolent commaund of womens will;
That all his former praise doth fowly spill.
But he the man, that say or doe so dare,
Be well aduiz'd, that he stand stedfast still:
For neuer yet was wight so well aware,
But he at first or last was trapt in womens snare.

2

Yet in the streightnesse of that captiue state,
This gentle knight himselfe so well behaued,
That notwithstanding all the subtill bait,
With which those Amazons his loue still craued,
To his owne loue his loialtie he saued:
Whose character in th'Adamantine mould
Of his true hart so firmely was engraued,
That no new loues impression euer could
Bereaue it thence: such blot his honour blemish should.

3

Yet his owne loue, the noble *Britomart*,
Scarse so conceiued in her iealous thought,
What time sad tydings of his balefull smart
In womans bondage, *Talus* to her brought;
Brought in vntimely houre, ere it was sought:
For after that the vtmost date, assynde
For his returne, she waited had for nought,
She gan to cast in her misdoubtfull mynde
A thousand feares, that loue-sicke fancies faine to fynde.

4

Sometime she feared, least some hard mishap
Had him misfalne in his aduenturous quest;
Sometime least his false foe did him entrap
In traytrous traine, or had vnwares opprest:
But most she did her troubled mynd molest,
And secretly afflict with iealous feare,
Least some new loue had him from her possest;
Yet loth she was, since she no ill did heare,
To thinke of him so ill: yet could she not forbeare.

5

One while she blam'd her selfe; another whyle
She him condemn'd, as trustlesse and vntrew:
And then, her griefe with errour to beguyle,
She fayn'd to count the time againe anew,
As if before she had not counted trew.
For houres but dayes; for weekes, that passed were,
She told but moneths, to make them seeme more few:
Yet when she reckned them, still drawing neare,
Each hour did seeme a moneth, and euery moneth a yeare.

Canto vi

Stanza 1

4 **insolent**: proud, overbearing.

5 **spill**: destroy.

7 Cf. 1 Cor. 10. 12: 'Let him that thinketh he standeth, take hede lest he fall.'

8 **aware**: vigilant.

Stanza 2

1 **streightnesse**: strictness, hardship.

2 As v 23.7.

6 **character**: figure or **impression** (8), the Lat. sense.
Adamantine: suggesting also 'loving', from the popular etymology, Lat. *ad-amantem*.

9 **Bereaue**: remove.

Stanzas 3–18

In Ariosto, *Orl. Fur*. xxx 76 to xxxi 7, xxxii 10–49, the jealous Bradamante, watching from a window, counts the time until her lover's return. Hearing that Ruggiero is betrothed to the warrior maiden Marfisa, she throws herself upon her bed in a jealous rage and later arms herself to search for him.

Stanza 3

Artegall's constancy and Britomart's lack of faith illustrate the Homily 'Of the state of matrimonie': 'For the woman is a weak creature, not endued with like strength and constancy of mind: therefore they be the sooner disquieted, and they be the more prone to all weak affections and dispositions of mind, more than men be, and lighter they be and more vain in their fantasies and opinions'. *Second Book of Homilies* (1563) 503.

8 **cast**: contrive. **misdoubtfull**: suspicious.

9 **faine**: wont.

Stanza 4

2 **aduenturous**: perilous.

4 **traine**: snare. **opprest**: taken by surprise.

7 **possest**: taken.

Stanza 5

4 **fayn'd**: sought; desired; also, in so doing, feigned.

6–9 **For houres but dayes . . .**: i.e. she reckoned the time in days rather than hours, and months rather than weeks, to make the estimate seem shorter. Macaulay (1910) 374 notes that the opposite result follows: her mind exaggerates each period so that hours seem as long as months, and months as years.
neare: i.e. to an end.

6

But when as yet she saw him not returne,
　She thought to send some one to seeke him out;
　But none she found so fit to serue that turne,
　As her owne selfe, to ease her selfe of dout.
　Now she deuiz'd amongst the warlike rout
　Of errant Knights, to seeke her errant Knight;
　And then againe resolu'd to hunt him out
　Amongst loose Ladies, lapped in delight:
And then both Knights enuide, and Ladies eke did spight.

7

One day, when as she long had sought for ease
　In euery place, and euery place thought best,
　Yet found no place, that could her liking please,
　She to a window came, that opened West,
　Towards which coast her loue his way addrest.
　There looking forth, shee in her heart did find
　Many vaine fancies, working her vnrest;
　And sent her winged thoughts, more swift then wind,
To beare vnto her loue the message of her mind.

8

There as she looked long, at last she spide
　One comming towards her with hasty speede:
　Well weend she then, ere him she plaine descride,
　That it was one sent from her loue indeede.
　Who when he nigh approcht, shee mote arede
　That it was *Talus, Artegall* his groome;
　Whereat her heart was fild with hope and drede;
　Ne would she stay, till he in place could come,
But ran to meete him forth, to know his tidings somme.

9

Euen in the dore him meeting, she begun;
　And where is he thy Lord, and how far hence?
　Declare at once; and hath he lost or wun?
　The yron man, albe he wanted sence
　And sorrowes feeling, yet with conscience
　Of his ill newes, did inly chill and quake,
　And stood still mute, as one in great suspence,
　As if that by his silence he would make
Her rather reade his meaning, then him selfe it spake.

10

Till she againe thus sayd; *Talus* be bold,
　And tell what euer it be, good or bad,
　That from thy tongue thy hearts intent doth hold.
　To whom he thus at length. The tidings sad,
　That I would hide, will needs, I see, be rad.
　My Lord, your loue, by hard mishap doth lie
　In wretched bondage, wofully bestad.
　Ay me (quoth she) what wicked destinie?
And is he vanquisht by his tyrant enemy?

11

Not by that Tyrant, his intended foe;
　But by a Tyrannesse (he then replide,)
　That him captiued hath in haplesse woe.
　Cease thou bad newes-man, badly doest thou hide
　Thy maisters shame, in harlots bondage tide.
　The rest my selfe too readily can spell.
　With that in rage she turn'd from him aside,
　Forcing in vaine the rest to her to tell,
And to her chamber went like solitary cell.

12

There she began to make her monefull plaint
　Against her Knight, for being so vntrew;
　And him to touch with falshoods fowle attaint,
　That all his other honour ouerthrew.
　Oft did she blame her selfe, and often rew,
　For yeelding to a straungers loue so light,
　Whose life and manners straunge she neuer knew;
　And euermore she did him sharpely twight
For breach of faith to her, which he had firmely plight.

13

And then she in her wrathfull will did cast,
　How to reuenge that blot of honour blent;
　To fight with him, and goodly die her last:
　And then againe she did her selfe torment,
　Inflicting on her selfe his punishment.
　A while she walkt, and chauft; a while she threw
　Her selfe vppon her bed, and did lament:
　Yet did she not lament with loude alew,
As women wont, but with deepe sighes, and singults few.

Stanza 6
6　**errant**: suggesting also morally erring.
8　**lapped**: i.e. enjoying their laps in the sexual sense;
enveloped; noted Orange (1972) 545.
9　**spight**: regard with spite.

Stanza 7
4　**West**: the direction of the setting sun; in the political
allegory, the direction of Ireland: cf. 22.4; also, the westward
movement of Empire from Troy to Rome to Britain.
5　**coast**: direction.

Stanza 8
5　**arede**: perceive.

Stanza 9
5　**conscience**: knowledge, consciousness.

Stanza 10
2–3　**tell . . . / . . . thy hearts intent**: i.e. say what is in your
heart.　**intent**: meaning.
5　**rad**: discovered.
7　**bestad**: placed.

Stanza 11
1　**that Tyrant**: Grantorto.
2　**Tyrannesse**: links Radigund with the tyrants, Geryoneo
and Grantorto.
8　**Forcing**: striving.

Stanza 12
6　**light**: as adv., applied to her; as adj., applied to him.
8　**twight**: twit, reproach.

Stanza 13
2　**that blot of honour blent**: i.e. his honour (and hers)
stained by falsehood.
8　**alew**: halloo.
9　**singults**: sobs; see III xi 12.1*n*.

14

Like as a wayward childe, whose sounder sleepe
　　Is broken with some fearefull dreames affright,
　　With froward will doth set him selfe to weepe;
　　Ne can be stild for all his nurses might,
　　But kicks, and squals, and shriekes for fell despight:
　　Now scratching her, and her loose locks misusing;
　　Now seeking darkenesse, and now seeking light;
　　Then crauing sucke, and then the sucke refusing.
Such was this Ladies fit, in her loues fond accusing.

15

But when she had with such vnquiet fits
　　Her selfe there close afflicted long in vaine,
　　Yet found no easement in her troubled wits,
　　She vnto *Talus* forth return'd againe,
　　By change of place seeking to ease her paine;
　　And gan enquire of him, with mylder mood,
　　The certaine cause of *Artegals* detaine;
　　And what he did, and in what state he stood,
And whether he did woo, or whether he were woo'd.

16

Ah wellaway (sayd then the yron man,)
　　That he is not the while in state to woo;
　　But lies in wretched thraldome, weake and wan,
　　Not by strong hand compelled thereunto,
　　But his owne doome, that none can now vndoo.
　　Sayd I not then (quoth shee) erwhile aright,
　　That this is things compacte betwixt you two,
　　Me to deceiue of faith vnto me plight,
Since that he was not forst, nor ouercome in fight?

17

With that he gan at large to her dilate
　　The whole discourse of his captiuance sad,
　　In sort as ye haue heard the same of late.
　　All which when she with hard enduraunce had
　　Heard to the end, she was right sore bestad,
　　With sodaine stounds of wrath and griefe attone:
　　Ne would abide, till she had aunswere made,
　　But streight her selfe did dight, and armor don;
And mounting to her steede, bad *Talus* guide her on.

18

So forth she rode vppon her ready way,
　　To seeke her Knight, as *Talus* her did guide:
　　Sadly she rode, and neuer word did say,
　　Nor good nor bad, ne euer lookt aside,
　　But still right downe, and in her thought did hide
　　The felnesse of her heart, right fully bent
　　To fierce auengement of that womans pride,
　　Which had her Lord in her base prison pent,
And so great honour with so fowle reproch had blent.

19

So as she thus melancholicke did ride,
　　Chawing the cud of griefe and inward paine,
　　She chaunst to meete toward the euen-tide
　　A Knight, that softly paced on the plaine,
　　As if him selfe to solace he were faine.
　　Well shot in yeares he seem'd, and rather bent
　　To peace, then needlesse trouble to constraine.
　　As well by view of that his vestiment,
As by his modest semblant, that no euill ment.

20

He comming neare, gan gently her salute,
　　With curteous words, in the most comely wize;
　　Who though desirous rather to rest mute,
　　Then termes to entertaine of common guize,
　　Yet rather then she kindnesse would despize,
　　She would her selfe displease, so him requite.
　　Then gan the other further to deuize
　　Of things abrode, as next to hand did light,
And many things demaund, to which she answer'd light.

21

For little lust had she to talke of ought,
　　Or ought to heare, that mote delightfull bee;
　　Her minde was whole possessed of one thought,
　　That gaue none other place. Which when as hee
　　By outward signes, (as well he might) did see,
　　He list no lenger to vse lothfull speach,
　　But her besought to take it well in gree,
　　Sith shady dampe had dimd the heauens reach,
To lodge with him that night, vnles good cause empeach.

Stanza 15
7　**detaine**: detention.

Stanza 16
5　See v 36*n*.
7　**compacte**: compacted.

Stanza 17
1　**dilate**: relate fully.
2　**discourse**: account.　**captiuance**: captivity.
6　**stounds**: pangs.　**wrath and griefe**: companion
emotions; see II iv 33.4*n*.　**attone**: at the same time.

Stanza 18
9　**blent**: stained; cf. 13.2.

Stanza 19
2　Cf. Radigund at v 27.2.
6　**shot**: advanced.
8　**vestiment**: garb.
9　**semblant**: outward appearance.

Stanza 20
1　**gently**: courteously.
4　**guize**: fashion; hence 'small talk'.
5　Dolon's trap is his **kindnesse**: his kind of nature is
treachery.
6　**requite**: i.e. requited, saluted in return.
7　**deuize**: converse.
9　**light**: lightly, or little.

Stanza 21
1　**lust**: desire.
7　**well in gree**: in good part, with good will.
8　**dampe**: fog.
9　**empeach**: prevent.

22

The Championesse, now seeing night at dore,
  Was glad to yeeld vnto his good request:
  And with him went without gaine-saying more.
  Not farre away, but little wide by West,
  His dwelling was, to which he him addrest;
  Where soone arriuing they receiued were
  In seemely wise, as them beseemed best:
For he their host them goodly well did cheare,
And talk't of pleasant things, the night away to weare.

23

Thus passing th'euening well, till time of rest,
  Then *Britomart* vnto a bowre was brought;
  Where groomes awayted her to haue vndrest.
  But she ne would vndressed be for ought,
  Ne doffe her armes, though he her much besought.
  For she had vow'd, she sayd, not to forgo
  Those warlike weedes, till she reuenge had wrought
Of a late wrong vppon a mortall foe;
Which she would sure performe, betide her wele or wo.

24

Which when their Host perceiu'd, right discontent
  In minde he grew, for feare least by that art
  He should his purpose misse, which close he ment:
  Yet taking leaue of her, he did depart.
  There all that night remained *Britomart*,
  Restlesse, recomfortlesse, with heart deepe grieued,
  Not suffering the least twinckling sleepe to start
Into her eye, which th'heart mote haue relieued,
But if the least appear'd, her eyes she streight reprieued.

25

Ye guilty eyes (sayd she) the which with guyle
  My heart at first betrayd, will ye betray
  My life now to, for which a little whyle
  Ye will not watch? false watches, wellaway,
  I wote when ye did watch both night and day
  Vnto your losse: and now needes will ye sleepe?
  Now ye haue made my heart to wake alway,
  Now will ye sleepe? ah wake, and rather weepe,
To thinke of your nights want, that should yee waking keepe.

26

Thus did she watch, and weare the weary night
  In wayfull plaints, that none was to appease;
  Now walking soft, now sitting still vpright,
  As sundry chaunge her seemed best to ease.
  Ne lesse did *Talus* suffer sleepe to seaze
  His eye-lids sad, but watcht continually,
  Lying without her dore in great disease;
Like to a Spaniell wayting carefully
Least any should betray his Lady treacherously.

27

What time the natiue Belman of the night,
  The bird, that warned *Peter* of his fall,
  First rings his siluer Bell t'each sleepy wight,
  That should their mindes vp to deuotion call,
  She heard a wondrous noise below the hall.
  All sodainely the bed, where she should lie,
  By a false trap was let adowne to fall
Into a lower roome, and by and by
570 The loft was raysd againe, that no man could it spie.

Stanza 22

4   little wide by West: i.e. a little to the west; cf. 7.4. She is taken from her direct way to Artegall.

5   addrest: made his way.

Stanza 23

3   awayted: attended.

Stanza 24

2   art: device, means.

3   close: secretly.

6   recomfortlesse: without comfort; not to be comforted.

9   streight: severely.   **reprieued**: reproved.

Stanza 25

Christ's three visits to his sleeping disciples with the injunction, 'slepest thou? coldest not thou watch one houre? Watch ye, and pray, that ye entre not into temptacion' (Mark 14. 37–8), supply the pattern for Britomart's thrice-repeated question and lead to the allusion to Peter's fall in 27.

3   for which: because.

9   your nights want: i.e. the need I have of you tonight. Church's (1758) suggestion, 'Knights want', is possible as a play on words rather than an emendation.

Stanza 26

2   that none was to appease: i.e. that no one could pacify, for she is 'recomfortlesse' (24.6).

5   Ne lesse: the context requires 'No more'.

6   sad: heavy.

7   disease: disquiet.

Stanza 27

1–5   Britomart has responded to the call to devotion in her love for Artegall and so she escapes the trap. Unlike Peter, she remains faithful.   **natiue Belman**: Nature's night-watchman, the cock; see Mark 14.68, 72.

6–9   Graziani (1964a) 387–9 sees a political reference to the attempt by Leonard des Trappes to blow up Elizabeth in bed. However, the bed trick refers primarily to the allegory of marriage: love led Britomart to 'leape out of her loathed nest' (III ii 30.3) and declare her love for Artegall. At Malecasta's Castle, she 'lightly lept out of her filed bed' (III i 62.2) and so distinguished her love from Malecasta's lust.   **false . . . fall**: a deliberate echo; cf. the trap in the bridge (ii 7.8), which is Artegall's test.   **loft**: floor of the room.

28

With sight whereof she was dismayd right sore,
　Perceiuing well the treason, which was ment:
　Yet stirred not at all for doubt of more,
　But kept her place with courage confident,
　Wayting what would ensue of that euent.
　It was not long, before she heard the sound
　Of armed men, comming with close intent
　Towards her chamber; at which dreadfull stound
She quickly caught her sword, and shield about her bound.

29

With that there came vnto her chamber dore
　Two Knights, all armed ready for to fight,
　And after them full many other more,
　A raskall rout, with weapons rudely dight.
　Whom soone as *Talus* spide by glims of night,
　He started vp, there where on ground he lay,
　And in his hand his thresher ready keight.
　They seeing that, let driue at him streight way,
And round about him preace in riotous aray.

30

But soone as he began to lay about
　With his rude yron flaile, they gan to flie,
　Both armed Knights, and eke vnarmed rout:
　Yet *Talus* after them apace did plie,
　Where euer in the darke he could them spie;
　That here and there like scattred sheepe they lay.
　Then backe returning, where his Dame did lie,
　He to her told the story of that fray,
And all that treason there intended did bewray.

31

Wherewith though wondrous wroth, and inly burning,
　To be auenged for so fowle a deede,
　Yet being forst to abide the daies returning,
　She there remain'd, but with right wary heede,
　Least any more such practise should proceede.
　Now mote ye know (that which to *Britomart*
　Vnknowen was) whence all this did proceede,
　And for what cause so great mischieuous smart
Was ment to her, that neuer euill ment in hart.

32

The goodman of this house was *Dolon* hight,
　A man of subtill wit and wicked minde,
　That whilome in his youth had bene a Knight,
　And armes had borne, but little good could finde,
　And much lesse honour by that warlike kinde
　Of life: for he was nothing valorous,
　But with slie shiftes and wiles did vnderminde
　All noble Knights, which were aduenturous,
And many brought to shame by treason treacherous.

33

He had three sonnes, all three like fathers sonnes,
　Like treacherous, like full of fraud and guile,
　Of all that on this earthly compasse wonnes:
　The eldest of the which was slaine erewhile
　By *Artegall*, through his owne guilty wile;
　His name was *Guizor*, whose vntimely fate
　For to auenge, full many treasons vile
　His father *Dolon* had deuiz'd of late
With these his wicked sons, and shewd his cankred hate.

34

For sure he weend, that this his present guest
　Was *Artegall*, by many tokens plaine;
　But chiefly by that yron page he ghest,
　Which still was wont with *Artegall* remaine;
　And therefore ment him surely to haue slaine.
　But by Gods grace, and her good heedinesse,
　She was preserued from their traytrous traine.
　Thus she all night wore out in watchfulnesse,
Ne suffred slothfull sleepe her eyelids to oppresse.

Stanza 28
2　treason: as treachery against a guest.
3　doubt: fear.
8　stound: time of trial.

Stanza 29
4　raskall rout: base rabble.　　dight: furnished.
5　glims: glimpse.
7　keight: caught.

Stanza 30
4–6　On this wolf-image, see iv 44.7–9*n*.　　plie: wield his
weapon vigorously; pursue.
9　bewray: reveal.

Stanza 31
5　practise: treachery.

Stanza 32
1　goodman: master; used with irony in this context.
Dolon: named after the spy in Homer, *Iliad* x 314f. Gk δολος,
treachery; Lat. *dolus*, guile, deceit; Eng. 'dole': guile, fraud.
7　vnderminde: undermine.

Stanza 33
1　fathers sonnes: i.e. sons like the father, treacherous.
Proverbial (C. G. Smith, 1970, 243).
3　They were full of all the treachery, etc. to be found on
earth; or they were the most treacherous, etc. of all who live on
earth.
6　Guizor: though apparently a knight, he is the 'groome of
euill guize' (ii 6.6) and servant of Pollente. His name suggests
the disguise of treachery; historically, perhaps, an oblique
allusion to the Dukes of Guise.

Stanza 34
6　On the intervention of **Gods grace**, see II viii 1*n*.
heedinesse: heedfulness.

35

The morrow next, so soone as dawning houre
    Discouered had the light to liuing eye,
    She forth yssew'd out of her loathed bowre,
    With full intent t'auenge that villany,
    On that vilde man, and all his family.
    And comming down to seeke them, where they wond,
    Nor sire, nor sonnes, nor any could she spie:
    Each rowme she sought, but them all empty fond:
They all were fled for feare, but whether, nether kond.

36

She saw it vaine to make there lenger stay,
    But tooke her steede, and thereon mounting light,
    Gan her addresse vnto her former way.
    She had not rid the mountenance of a flight,
    But that she saw there present in her sight,
    Those two false brethren, on that perillous Bridge,
    On which *Pollente* with *Artegall* did fight.
    Streight was the passage like a ploughed ridge,
That if two met, the one mote needes fall ouer the lidge.

37

There they did thinke them selues on her to wreake:
    Who as she nigh vnto them drew, the one
    These vile reproches gan vnto her speake;
    Thou recreant false traytor, that with lone
    Of armes hast knighthood stolne, yet Knight art none,
    No more shall now the darkenesse of the night
    Defend thee from the vengeance of thy fone,
    But with thy bloud thou shalt appease the spright
Of *Guizor*, by thee slaine, and murdred by thy slight.

38

Strange were the words in *Britomartis* eare;
    Yet stayd she not for them, but forward fared,
    Till to the perillous Bridge she came, and there
    Talus desir'd, that he might haue prepared
    The way to her, and those two losels scared.
    But she thereat was wroth, that for despight
    The glauncing sparkles through her beuer glared,
    And from her eies did flash out fiery light,
Like coles, that through a siluer Censer sparkle bright.

39

She stayd not to aduise which way to take;
    But putting spurres vnto her fiery beast,
    Thorough the midst of them she way did make.
    The one of them, which most her wrath increast,
    Vppon her speare she bore before her breast,
    Till to the Bridges further end she past,
    Where falling downe, his challenge he releast:
    The other ouer side the Bridge she cast
Into the riuer, where he drunke his deadly last.

40

As when the flashing Leuin haps to light
    Vppon two stubborne oakes, which stand so neare,
    That way betwixt them none appeares in sight;
    The Engin fiercely flying forth, doth teare
    Th'one from the earth, and through the aire doth beare;
    The other it with force doth ouerthrow,
    Vppon one side, and from his rootes doth reare.
    So did the Championesse those two there strow,
And to their sire their carcasses left to bestow.

Stanza 35
9   **whether, nether kond**: whither, neither she nor Talus
knew.

Stanza 36
2   **light**: nimbly.
4   **the mountenance of a flight**: the distance an arrow
flies; the same distance takes her to the house of Busirane,
III xi 20.8.
8   **Streight**: also narrow, as 9 suggests.
9   **lidge**: ledge.

Stanza 37
4–5   **with lone/Of armes**: for Artegall '*Achilles armes . . .
did win*' (III ii 25.6); or with reference to her own arms,
III iii 58–60.
9   **slight**: sleight, wile.

Stanza 38
5   **losels**: scoundrels; cf. Braggadocchio, iii 20.6   **scared**:
drive off.

Stanza 39
7   **release**: withdrew.

Stanza 40
1   **Leuin**: lightning.
2   **stubborne**: also hard.
4   **Engin**: lightning compared to a battering-ram.
9   **bestow**: stow away.

Cant. VII.

Britomart comes to Isis Church,
Where shee strange visions sees :
She fights with Radigund, her slaies,
And Artegall thence frees.

1

NOught is on earth more sacred or diuine,
 That Gods and men doe equally adore,
Then this same vertue, that doth right define :
For th'heuens themselues, whence mortal men implore
Right in their wrongs, are rul'd by righteous lore
Of highest Ioue, who doth true iustice deale
To his inferiour Gods, and euermore
Therewith containes his heauenly Common-weale :
The skill whereof to Princes hearts he doth reueale.

2

Well therefore did the antique world inuent,
 That Iustice was a God of soueraine grace,
And altars vnto him, and temples lent,
And heauenly honours in the highest place ;
Calling him great *Osyris*, of the race
Of th'old Ægyptian Kings, that whylome were ;
With fayned colours shading a true case :
For that *Osyris*, whilest he liued here,
The iustest man aliue, and truest did appeare.

3

His wife was *Isis*, whom they likewise made
 A Goddesse of great powre and soueraity,
And in her person cunningly did shade
That part of Iustice, which is Equity,
Whereof I haue to treat here presently.
Vnto whose temple when as *Britomart*
Arriued, shee with great humility
Did enter in, ne would that night depart ;
But *Talus* mote not be admitted to her part.

4

There she receiued was in goodly wize
 Of many Priests, which duely did attend
Vppon the rites and daily sacrifize,
All clad in linnen robes with siluer hemd ;
And on their heads with long locks comely kemd,
They wore rich Mitres shaped like the Moone,
To shew that *Isis* doth the Moone portend ;
Like as *Osyris* signifies the Sunne.
For that they both like race in equall iustice runne.

Canto vii

Stanza 1
Cf. Proem 10.

7 **inferiour Gods**: Princes, rather than gods, as at VII vi 24.
8 **Therewith**: i.e. with justice. **containes**: keeps under control.
9 **skill**: art, understanding. See iv 1. 1–2n.

Stanzas 2–4
Derived chiefly from Plutarch, *Of Isis and Osiris*, and Diodorus, *Bibl. Hist.* I xi–xxii. Both note that Osyris was a just king who ruled the Egyptians wisely. Diodorus I xx writes: 'By reason of the magnitude of his benefactions, [he] received the gift of immortality . . . and honour equal to that offered to the gods of heaven.' Isis is said to have ruled with justice and mercy after Osiris's death, and to have caused men to practise justice among themselves. Plutarch 52 records that some assert Osiris to be the Sun and Isis the Moon, and that statues of Isis bear horns in imitation of the crescent moon. Isis is interpreted as Venus by Apuleius, *The Golden Asse* xi 5. Fowler (1964) 213–4 argues that Isis and Osiris are central to the cosmogonic myth that extends through the Book. Following Warton, Roche (1964) 81 notes that the tomb of Osiris is connected with Busiris, the prototype of Busirane. Fowler (1970) 51 suggests that the house of Busirane is an antitype to Isis Church or Temple (stanzas 3 and 5).

Stanza 2
1 **inuent**: feign.
2 **soueraine**: supreme; befitting a sovereign. Osiris becomes a god by grace.
7 **shading**: obscuring; also shadowing forth.

Stanza 3
3 **shade**: shadow forth (cf. 2.7); symbolize; signify (cf. 4.8).
4 Fowler (1964) 45 notes the connection of Isis with Gk ἴσος, equal. At 22.8 her Equity is referred to as 'clemence'.
5 **presently**: now.
7 **with great humility**: allegorized as Humiltá, the porter of the house of Holiness, I x 5.
9 **part**: side.

Stanza 4
4–5 The priests of Isis wore linen robes and were shaven in Plutarch 3; cf. Juvenal, *Satire* vi 533: 'a shaven-pated crew dressed in linen robes'. S.'s change of the one detail would seem deliberate. In Ezek. 44.17, 20, priests are enjoined to wear linen garments and not suffer their locks to grow long. The Geneva gloss adds, 'as did the infideles and heathen'. Since long hair is effeminate, it may indicate service to a goddess. A sign of lust at IV vii 7.3; yet **comely kemd** shows control over desire. The priests may be women, though this is not explicit, as in the Temple of Venus, IV x 38.9. The chief priest is a man, 20.5. Kermode (1971) 55 sees the priests as servants of the imperial equity; their long hair distinguishes them from the tonsured canonists.
7 **portend**: signify.
9 **For that . . . runne**: i.e. because both the moon and the sun are equally just – exact or regular – in their orbits. Fowler (1964) 81 notes two reasons for the equal races: 'because each runs a daily course across the sky from East to West; and because, one being the chief diurnal luminary and the other the chief nocturnal luminary, their annual course eventually accomplishes an *equal sharing* of the total hours of day and night.'

5

The Championesse them greeting, as she could,
    Was thence by them into the Temple led;
    Whose goodly building when she did behould,
    Borne vppon stately pillours, all dispred
    With shining gold, and arched ouer hed,
    She wondred at the workemans passing skill,
    Whose like before she neuer saw nor red;
    And thereuppon long while stood gazing still,
But thought, that she thereon could neuer gaze her fill.

6

Thence forth vnto the Idoll they her brought,
    The which was framed all of siluer fine,
    So well as could with cunning hand be wrought,
    And clothed all in garments made of line,
    Hemd all about with fringe of siluer twine.
    Vppon her head she wore a Crowne of gold,
    To shew that she had powre in things diuine;
    And at her feete a Crocodile was rold,
That with her wreathed taile her middle did enfold.

7

One foote was set vppon the Crocodile,
    And on the ground the other fast did stand,
    So meaning to suppresse both forged guile,
    And open force: and in her other hand
    She stretched forth a long white sclender wand.
    Such was the Goddesse; whom when *Britomart*
    Had long beheld, her selfe vppon the land
    She did prostrate, and with right humble hart,
Vnto her selfe her silent prayers did impart.

8

To which the Idoll as it were inclining,
    Her wand did moue with amiable looke,
    By outward shew her inward sence desining.
    Who well perceiuing, how her wand she shooke,
    It as a token of good fortune tooke.
    By this the day with dampe was ouercast,
    And ioyous light the house of *Ioue* forsooke:
    Which when she saw, her helmet she vnlaste,
And by the altars side her selfe to slumber plaste.

Stanza 5

1   **as she could**: i.e. as she knew how to do.
4   **dispred**: overspread.
7   **red**: imagined.
8–9   Cf. her rapturous gazing into Venus's mirror without comprehension, III ii 22; also her response in the house of Busirane, III xi 49.6–9, 53.1–4, xii 5.1–2.

Stanza 6

1   **Idoll**: image; statue.
4   **line**: linen.
8–9   The iconography of the **Crocodile** is analysed by Aptekar (1969) 90f. She notes precedents for S.'s association of a god standing on a crocodile with justice. Particularly relevant is the association of the virgin goddess Minerva with a dragon: see III xi 48.6–9*n*. For the association of the crocodile with threatening evil, see *Van*. iii. On its relation to lust, see 16*n* below. Cf. Mercilla with the rusty sword at her feet and the chained lion beneath her feet (ix 30, 33).   **her ... taile**: 'his ... taile' sugg. Church (1758). S.'s point may be that the sexes are not distinguished in their union.

Stanza 7

1–4   The relation of **forged guile, / And open force** to the legend of justice is treated by Aptekar (1969) ch. 7. Cf. Mercilla's suppression of forged guile at ix 25.5. The terms relate to Radigund who subdues knights 'by force or guile' (iv 31.1; cf. v Arg.). It is simpler to allow the crocodile to signify both guile and force, as Davidson (1969) 75 claims. The foot on the ground may signify *firmitas*: Donne writes of the foot, 'It is the Emblem that hath figured / Firmness' ('Love's progress' 79–80). Or the foot on the ground may signify suppression of open force, which is seen in the earth's rebellion at stanza 10. Cf. the significance given '*Isis* feete' at 22.6–9. The association of the crocodile with forged guile is traditional, as in the 'harmefull guile' of the 'craftie Crocodile', I v 18.
4   **in her other hand**: i.e. in one of her hands, though surely not the left. Cambina carries the rod of peace in her right hand, IV iii 42.1. The **white ... wand** is the emblem of royal power, specifically, Elizabeth as Equity. See note on the 'white rod' (III iii 49.6–9).   **wand** may imply magical power.
9   **Vnto her selfe**: i.e. to Isis. Lewis (1967) 101 suggests that in praying silently or to herself, she prays to Isis.
impart: communicate.

Stanza 8

2   **amiable looke**: cf. Venus's 'amiable grace' (IV x 56.3) which encourages Scudamour in pursuit of his love.
3   **desining**: indicating by a sign.
6   **dampe**: fog. At vi 21.8, fog and night bring on Dolon's treachery.
8–9   In Dolon's castle, she refuses to doff her arms, sleep, or even lie down, vi 23–26. Fletcher (1971) 267–8 suggests that the unlacing points to the nature of Britomart's experience, her initiation into womanhood. Diodorus I xxv records that Isis appears in sleep to those who seek her aid. Plutarch 80 records that incense in the Temple of Isis brightens the imaginative faculty in dreams and helps sleep cure the soul's ills. A relevant analogue is Brutus's prophetic dream of his progeny when he sleeps before the altar in the temple of Diana, Geoffrey of Monmouth I xi.

9

For other beds the Priests there vsed none,
  But on their mother Earths deare lap did lie,
  And bake their sides vppon the cold hard stone,
  T'enure them selues to sufferaunce thereby
  And proud rebellious flesh to mortify.
  For by the vow of their religion
  They tied were to stedfast chastity,
  And continence of life, that all forgon,
They mote the better tend to their deuotion.

10

Therefore they mote not taste of fleshly food,
  Ne feed on ought, the which doth bloud containe,
  Ne drinke of wine, for wine they say is blood,
  Euen the bloud of Gyants, which were slaine,
  By thundring Ioue in the Phlegrean plaine.
  For which the earth (as they the story tell)
  Wroth with the Gods, which to perpetuall paine
  Had damn'd her sonnes, which gainst them did rebell,
With inward griefe and malice did against them swell.

11

And of their vitall bloud, the which was shed
  Into her pregnant bosome, forth she brought
  The fruitfull vine, whose liquor blouddy red
  Hauing the mindes of men with fury fraught,
  Mote in them stirre vp old rebellious thought,
  To make new warre against the Gods againe:
  Such is the powre of that same fruit, that nought
  The fell contagion may thereof restraine,
Ne within reasons rule, her madding mood containe.

12

There did the warlike Maide her selfe repose,
  Vnder the wings of *Isis* all that night,
  And with sweete rest her heauy eyes did close,
  After that long daies toile and weary plight,
  Where whilest her earthly parts with soft delight
  Of sencelesse sleepe did deeply drowned lie,
  There did appeare vnto her heauenly spright
  A wondrous vision, which did close implie
The course of all her fortune and posteritie.

13

Her seem'd, as she was doing sacrifize
  To *Isis*, deckt with Mitre on her hed,
  And linnen stole after those Priestes guize,
  All sodainely she saw transfigured
  Her linnen stole to robe of scarlet red,
  And Moone-like Mitre to a Crowne of gold,
  That euen she her selfe much wondered
  At such a chaunge, and ioyed to behold
Her selfe, adorn'd with gems and iewels manifold.

Stanza 9

Plutarch 2 mentions the hard services in the temple of Isis and the strict chastity of the priests.

3 **bake**: harden.
4 **sufferaunce**: patient endurance.
5 Cf. Col. 3.5: 'Mortifie therefore your members which are on the earth, fornication, unclennes, the inordinate affection, evil concupiscence.' **mortify**: kill.
8 **all forgon**: all things having been renounced.

Stanzas 10–11

A rare double-stanza. S. follows Plutarch 6 closely.

Stanza 10

1–2 Cf. Gen. 9.4: 'But flesh with the life thereof, I meane, with the blood thereof, shal ye not eat.' Called 'natures first beheast', VI iv 14.9.
4–5 See II vii 41.6*n*.
9 **swell**: behave proudly; also swelling in pregnancy; cf. III vii 47.6–9. Gough (1921) sees an allusion to the rising of volcanic cones in the Phlegrean fields.

Stanza 11

9 **containe**: keep under control.

Stanza 12

1–2 The image is biblical: Ps. 36.7. **all that night**: because prophetic dreams come only before awakening.
7 **heauenly spright**: as Genius 'Who wondrous things concerning our welfare, / And straunge phantomes doth let vs oft forsee' (II xii 47.5–6).
8 **vision**: the *visio* in Macrobius, *In Somn. Scip.* I iii 9, a dream that comes true. **close implie**: secretly express or contain.

Stanzas 13–16

On the general function of a dream, cf. IV v 43.9: 'The things that day most minds, at night doe most appeare.' Britomart's dream releases her repressed desires and fears. It is an allegory of her relationship with Artegall, both past and future. Woodhouse (1949) 216 claims that Britomart's vision is a 'wonderful piece of dream psychology and symbolic art'. For analysis of the dream, see Grellner (1968). Fletcher (1971) 277 notes that the dream and its interpretation are visionary emblems of the coronation ceremony.

Stanza 13

4 **All sodainely**: drawing upon her memory of the masque in the house of Busirane which began 'All suddenly' (III xii 3).
5–6 She sees herself crowned like Isis but wearing instead the royal robe, the monarchial *purpurea*. **scarlet**: a rich cloth associated with royalty.

575

14

And in the midst of her felicity,
  An hideous tempest seemed from below,
  To rise through all the Temple sodainely,
  That from the Altar all about did blow
  The holy fire, and all the embers strow
  Vppon the ground, which kindled priuily,
  Into outragious flames vnwares did grow,
  That all the Temple put in ieopardy
Of flaming, and her selfe in great perplexity.

15

With that the Crocodile, which sleeping lay
  Vnder the Idols feete in fearelesse bowre,
  Seem'd to awake in horrible dismay,
  As being troubled with that stormy stowre;
  And gaping greedy wide, did streight deuoure
  Both flames and tempest: with which growen great,
  And swolne with pride of his owne peerelesse powre,
  He gan to threaten her likewise to eat;
But that the Goddesse with her rod him backe did beat.

16

Tho turning all his pride to humblesse meeke,
  Him selfe before her feete he lowly threw,
  And gan for grace and loue of her to seeke:
  Which she accepting, he so neare her drew,
  That of his game she soone enwombed grew,
  And forth did bring a Lion of great might;
  That shortly did all other beasts subdew.
  With that she waked, full of fearefull fright,
And doubtfully dismayd through that so vncouth sight.

17

So thereupon long while she musing lay,
  With thousand thoughts feeding her fantasie,
  Vntill she spide the lampe of lightsome day,
  Vp-lifted in the porch of heauen hie.
  Then vp she rose fraught with melancholy,
  And forth into the lower parts did pas;
  Whereas the Priestes she found full busily
  About their holy things for morrow Mas:
Whom she saluting faire, faire resaluted was.

18

But by the change of her vnchearefull looke,
  They might perceiue, she was not well in plight;
  Or that some pensiuenesse to heart she tooke.
  Therefore thus one of them, who seem'd in sight
  To be the greatest, and the grauest wight,
  To her bespake; Sir Knight it seemes to me,
  That thorough euill rest of this last night,
  Or ill apayd, or much dismayd ye be,
That by your change of cheare is easie for to see.

19

Certes (sayd she) sith ye so well haue spide
  The troublous passion of my pensiue mind,
  I will not seeke the same from you to hide,
  But will my cares vnfolde, in hope to find
  Your aide, to guide me out of errour blind,
  Say on (quoth he) the secret of your hart:
  For by the holy vow, which me doth bind,
  I am adiur'd, best counsell to impart
To all, that shall require my comfort in their smart.

Stanza 14

1   **her**: refers both to Isis and to Britomart, as the two merge in the dream.
2   **tempest**: recalls the 'stormy whirlwind' in the house of Busirane which heralds the god's entrance and exit (III xii 2–3, 27).
6   **kindled priuily**: refers to the secret flame proper to a celebration of a mystery, as Fletcher (1971) 271 notes; cf. the 'housling fire' kindled at the marriage of Una and the Red Cross Knight, I xii 37.4.
7   **outragious flames**: a common image to describe love's effects, as III vii 16.1–2, and applied to Britomart's love for Artegall at III ii 37.3, 43.4, 52.2–5, iii 1.1–4; cf. the flames at the entrance to Busirane's castle, III xi 21f.
9   **perplexity**: trouble.

Stanza 15

2   The **Crocodile** is **fearelesse** even though the tempest provokes his dismay.
4   **stowre**: tumult.
5–8   In *Van.* iii, S. refers to the 'deuouring hell' of the crocodile's mouth. The beast signifies greed and voracity in Valeriano; noted Aptekar (1969) 95.
5–6   Plutarch 61 notes that the power assigned to the wind is called Osiris.
7   On the dragon as the guardian of chastity, see III xi 48.6–9n.   **swolne with pride** shows that it has become an enemy; cf. the Earth which swells against the gods, 10.9.

Stanza 16

The chief classical analogues to Britomart's dream of a serpent lover are cited by Upton (1758). Alexander the Great, Augustus Caesar, and Scipio were conceived by a dragon or serpent. Svendsen (1956) 169 notes the allegorical interpretation of these stories in Camerarius, *The Living Librarie*: 'The Serpent signifieth allegorically, Lecherie.' More familiar is Ovid's story of how Cadmus, transformed into a serpent, embraced his wife, to the horror of all who watched (*Met.* iv 576–603). Aptekar (1969) 105 notes the crocodile's association with lust. Particularly relevant is the story of Cupid and Psyche: like Psyche, Britomart fears that her lover is a serpent. When she goes to rest, she is called 'the warlike Maide' (12.1; cf. III i 60.4); but since she is seduced in her dream, the address puns on **dismayd** (9), as Fletcher (1971) 271 notes.
1   **humblesse**: humbleness.
5   **game**: amorous play.

Stanza 17

5   **melancholy**: her mood at vi 19.1.
8   **morrow Mas**: the first mass of the day.

Stanza 18

8   **ill apayd**: ill-pleased.

Stanza 19

8   **adiur'd**: bound by oath.

20

Then gan she to declare the whole discourse
  Of all that vision, which to her appeard,
  As well as to her minde it had recourse.
  All which when he vnto the end had heard,
  Like to a weake faint-hearted man he fared,
  Through great astonishment of that strange sight;
  And with long locks vp-standing, stifly stared
  Like one adawed with some dreadfull spright.
So fild with heauenly fury, thus he her behight.

21

Magnificke Virgin, that in queint disguise
  Of British armes doest maske thy royall blood,
  So to pursue a perillous emprize,
  How couldst thou weene, through that disguized hood,
  To hide thy state from being vnderstood?
  Can from th'immortall Gods ought hidden bee?
  They doe thy linage, and thy Lordly brood;
  They doe thy sire, lamenting sore for thee;
They doe thy loue, forlorne in womens thraldome see.

22

The end whereof, and all the long euent,
  They doe to thee in this same dreame discouer.
  For that same Crocodile doth represent
  The righteous Knight, that is thy faithfull louer,
  Like to Osyris in all iust endeuer.
  For that same Crocodile Osyris is,
  That vnder Isis feete doth sleepe for euer:
  To shew that clemence oft in things amis,
Restraines those sterne behests, and cruell doomes of his.

23

That Knight shall all the troublous stormes asswage,
  And raging flames, that many foes shall reare,
  To hinder thee from the iust heritage
  Of thy sires Crowne, and from thy countrey deare.
  Then shalt thou take him to thy loued fere,
  And ioyne in equall portion of thy realme.
  And afterwards a sonne to him shalt beare,
  That Lion-like shall shew his powre extreame.
So blesse thee God, and giue thee ioyance of thy dreame.

24

All which when she vnto the end had heard,
  She much was eased in her troublous thought,
  And on those Priests bestowed rich reward:
  And royall gifts of gold and siluer wrought,
  She for a present to their Goddesse brought.
  Then taking leaue of them, she forward went,
  To seeke her loue, where he was to be sought;
  Ne rested till she came without relent
Vnto the land of Amazons, as she was bent.

25

Whereof when newes to *Radigund* was brought,
  Not with amaze, as women wonted bee,
  She was confused in her troublous thought,
  But fild with courage and with ioyous glee,
  As glad to heare of armes, the which now she
  Had long surceast, she bad to open bold,
  That she the face of her new foe might see.
  But when they of that yron man had told,
Which late her folke had slaine, she bad them forth to hold.

Stanza 20
1 **discourse**: account.
3 **had recourse**: did recur.
5 **fared**: behaved.
8 **adawed**: daunted.
9 **heauenly fury**: prophetic frenzy inspired from above; cf.
Merlin's 'halfe extatick stoure' (III iii 50.5) when he foresees
Elizabeth's reign. **behight**: addressed.

Stanza 21
1 **Magnificke**: renowned. **queint**: strange; cf. Artegall
'In quyent disguise' (IV iv 39.3).
3 **emprize**: enterprise.
4 **hood**: the helmet, which hides her identity, as at IV i 13.1;
or, in a figurative sense, 'covering', 'mask', as at xi 56.7.
7–9 **brood**: parentage. The sense, 'offspring', would
balance **linage**, and in relation to **sire** and **loue**, turn from the
past to the future; yet the future is the subject of the next
stanzas.

Stanza 22
1 **euent**: outcome, implying the course of events.
6 The identification is made by Plutarch 75.

Stanza 23
Cf. Merlin's prophecy of Artegall's aid at III iii 27.6 to 28.4.
Artegall's quest in Book V is to secure for Irena 'the heritage,
which she did clame' (i 3.8).
5 **fere**: husband; with a play on 'fear'.
7–8 See III iii 29–30. Cf. the 'Lion passant' on her shield,
III i 4.9.

Stanza 24
4 **royall**: as she gives them; as she gives them to the
goddess; and as the gifts themselves are royal.
8 **relent**: slackening of speed.

Stanza 25
2–3 **Not with amaze . . .**: i.e. she was not confused with
amazement.
6 **surceast**: abandoned, after she became a lover.
to open: referring to the city gate, as at iv 37.8.
9 **forth to hold**: to defend the city from without; or to keep
them out, referring to Britomart and Talus; or to continue:
even though she knows Talus to be there, she orders her forces
to proceed.

577

26

So there without the gate (as seemed best)
   She caused her Pauilion be pight;
   In which stout *Britomart* her selfe did rest,
   Whiles *Talus* watched at the dore all night.
   All night likewise, they of the towne in fright,
   Vppon their wall good watch and ward did keepe.
   The morrow next, so soone as dawning light
   Bad doe away the dampe of drouzie sleepe,
The warlike Amazon out of her bowre did peepe.

27

And caused streight a Trumpet loud to shrill,
   To warne her foe to battell soone be prest:
   Who long before awoke (for she ful ill
   Could sleepe all night, that in vnquiet brest
   Did closely harbour such a iealous guest)
   Was to the battell whilome ready dight.
   Eftsoones that warriouresse with haughty crest
   Did forth issue, all ready for the fight:
On th'other side her foe appeared soone in sight.

28

But ere they reared hand, the Amazone
   Began the streight conditions to propound,
   With which she vsed still to tye her fone;
   To serue her so, as she the rest had bound.
   Which when the other heard, she sternly frownd
   For high disdaine of such indignity,
   And would no lenger treat, but bad them sound.
   For her no other termes should euer tie
Then what prescribed were by lawes of cheualrie.

29

The Trumpets sound, and they together run
   With greedy rage, and with their faulchins smot;
   Ne either sought the others strokes to ·shun,
   But through great fury both their skill forgot,
   And practicke vse in armes: ne spared not
   Their dainty parts, which nature had created
   So faire and tender, without staine or spot,
   For other vses, then they them translated;
Which they now hackt and hewd, as if such vse they hated,

30

As when a Tygre and a Lionesse
   Are met at spoyling of some hungry pray,
   Both challenge it with equall greedinesse:
   But first the Tygre clawes thereon did lay;
   And therefore loth to loose her right away,
   Doth in defence thereof full stoutly stond:
   To which the Lion strongly doth gainesay,
   That she to hunt the beast first tooke in hond;
And therefore ought it haue, where euer she it fond.

31

Full fiercely layde the Amazon about,
   And dealt her blowes vnmercifully sore:
   Which *Britomart* withstood with courage stout,
   And them repaide againe with double more.
   So long they fought, that all the grassie flore
   Was fild with bloud, which from their sides did flow,
   And gushed through their armes, that all in gore
   They trode, and on the ground their liues did strow,
578 Like fruitles seede, of which vntimely death should grow.

Stanzas 26–27
Cf. iv 46–47: Artegall rests in his pavilion before the day of battle but Radigund cannot rest.

Stanza 26
2   **She**: apparently Radigund who sets up her pavilion for Britomart; more likely, Britomart, for she rejects all parleying. At iv 46.4–5, Artegall sets up his own pavilion before the city gates; cf. v 4.8–9, xii 10.1–2.
8   **dampe**: the dew of sleep and its consequence, a dazed or stupefied condition (*OED* 4).

Stanza 27
2   **prest**: ready.
6   **whilome**: some time before.
7   **haughty**: lofty, both literally and metaphorically.

Stanza 28
2–4   These terms are outlined to Artegall, iv 49.2–5. On Artegall's binding, see v 32.7–33.3, 50.7–8.   **streight**: strict.
5–6   Cf. the affability with which Artegall receives these conditions, iv 51.
8–9   The laws of chivalry do not impose unconditional surrender but allow the victor to exercise compassion, courtesy, and grace, if he wishes.

Stanza 29
2   **faulchins**: falchion, a curved sword; like the 'Cemitare' (v 3.4), it symbolizes the moon.
5   **practicke**: practised, cunning.
5–9   A playful allusion to the etymology of Amazon: Gk α + μαζος, without the breast.

Stanza 30
The **Tygre** is Radigund, a beast noted for its cruelty (e.g. viii 49.7–8) as she is (e.g. v 7.3); the **Lionesse**, as the royal beast, is Britomart. Cirlot (1962) 182 notes that the wild lioness is a symbol of the Magna Mater, Isis. The extended simile represents Artegall's plight as they fight over the right of present possession versus prior ownership. Cf. the quarrel between Una and Duessa over the Red Cross Knight, I xii 27–34.
2   **hungry pray**: prey for which they hunger.
3   **challenge**: claim.
7   **gainesay**: oppose, claim in opposition.

Stanza 31
6   **fild**: also defiled.

32

At last proud *Radigund* with fell despight,
  Hauing by chaunce espide aduantage neare,
  Let driue at her with all her dreadfull might,
  And thus vpbrayding said; This token beare
  Vnto the man, whom thou doest loue so deare;
  And tell him for his sake thy life thou gauest.
  Which spitefull words she sore engrieu'd to heare,
  Thus answer'd; Lewdly thou my loue deprauest,
Who shortly must repent that now so vainely brauest.

33

Nath'lesse that stroke so cruell passage found,
  That glauncing on her shoulder plate, it bit
  Vnto the bone, and made a griesly wound,
  That she her shield through raging smart of it
  Could scarse vphold; yet soone she it requit.
  For hauing force increast through furious paine,
  She her so rudely on the helmet smit,
  That it empierced to the very braine,
And her proud person low prostrated on the plaine.

34

Where being layd, the wrothfull Britonesse
  Stayd not, till she came to her selfe againe,
  But in reuenge both of her loues distresse,
  And her late vile reproch, though vaunted vaine,
  And also of her wound, which sore did paine,
  She with one stroke both head and helmet cleft.
  Which dreadfull sight, when all her warlike traine
  There present saw, each one of sence bereft,
Fled fast into the towne, and her sole victor left.

35

But yet so fast they could not home retrate,
  But that swift *Talus* did the formost win;
  And pressing through the preace vnto the gate,
  Pelmell with them attonce did enter in.
  There then a piteous slaughter did begin:
  For all that euer came within his reach,
  He with his yron flaile did thresh so thin,
  That he no worke at all left for the leach:
Like to an hideous storme, which nothing may empeach.

36

And now by this the noble Conqueresse
  Her selfe came in, her glory to partake;
  Where though reuengefull vow she did professe,
  Yet when she saw the heapes, which he did make,
  Of slaughtred carkasses, her heart did quake
  For very ruth, which did it almost riue,
  That she his fury willed him to slake:
  For else he sure had left not one aliue,
But all in his reuenge of spirite would depriue.

37

Tho when she had his execution stayd,
  She for that yron prison did enquire,
  In which her wretched loue was captiue layd:
  Which breaking open with indignant ire,
  She entred into all the partes entire.
  Where when she saw that lothly vncouth sight,
  Of men disguiz'd in womanishe attire,
  Her heart gan grudge, for very deepe despight
Of so vnmanly maske, in misery misdight.

38

At last when as to her owne Loue she came,
  Whom like disguize no lesse deformed had,
  At sight thereof abasht with secrete shame,
  She turnd her head aside, as nothing glad,
  To haue beheld a spectacle so bad:
  And then too well beleeu'd, that which tofore
  Iealous suspect as true vntruely drad,
  Which vaine conceipt now nourishing no more,
She sought with ruth to salue his sad misfortunes sore.

Stanza 32

4–9 Radigund's boast implies that she has slain Artegall;
cf. Sansjoy's boast at I v 11.1–4 and the reply, 13.1–4.
Britomart charges that she defames her love by her 'vile
reproch' (34.4) that she has slain him or – so Britomart suspects
– has seduced him. Hence **Lewdly**: wickedly; lasciviously, and
deprauest: defame; pervert.   **vainely**: in vain; from vanity.
brauest: boasts.

Stanza 33

1–5 Slander of Artegall almost deprives Britomart of her
shield of faith (in him).

Stanza 34

2 Bieman (1968) 171 notes how verbal ambiguity 'blurs
the demarcation between the figures of the two women'.
4 **vaine**: in vain; vainly; in vanity.

Stanza 35

2 **win**: overtake.
4 **Pelmell**: mingling.
9 **empeach**: hinder, withstand.

Stanza 36

1–2 The rest of the stanza reveals her dilemma: glory may
be expressed only by living subjects, as at ix 32.7, xii 24.9.
Gough (1921) notes that Britomart represents the Equity of
Isis, which tempers the severe justice executed by Talus.
7 **willed**: ordered; cf. xii 8.2.

Stanza 37

1–5 Cf. the 'indignation fell' (I viii 39.6) with which Arthur
rends the iron door of Orgoglio's dungeon.   **partes entire**:
inner parts.
6–9 Deut. 22.5: 'Nether shal a man put on womans raiment;
for all that do so, are abominacion vnto the Lord thy God.'
8 **grudge**: complain.
9 **in misery misdight**: i.e. ill-clad in women's clothes,
which is their misery.

Stanza 38

6–8 The context suggests that now she sees how untrue were
her earlier jealous suspicions (cf. vi 3.2) that Artegall was
unfaithful to her. Yet these lines say the opposite: Artegall's
dress leads her to believe, what before she had only suspected,
that he has been unfaithful. Both readings may stand: her
fears are confirmed at the same moment they are dismissed as
vaine conceipt.
7 **suspect**: suspicion.

39

Not so great wonder and astonishment,
　　Did the most chast *Penelope* possesse,
　　To see her Lord, that was reported drent,
　　And dead long since in dolorous distresse,
　　Come home to her in piteous wretchednesse,
　　After long trauell of full twenty yeares,
　　That she knew not his fauours likelynesse,
　　For many scarres and many hoary heares,
But stood long staring on him, mongst vncertaine feares.

40

Ah my deare Lord, what sight is this (quoth she)
　　What May-game hath misfortune made of you?
　　Where is that dreadfull manly looke? where be
　　Those mighty palmes, the which ye wont t'embrew
　　In bloud of Kings, and great hoastes to subdew?
　　Could ought on earth so wondrous change haue wrought,
　　As to haue robde you of that manly hew?
　　Could so great courage stouped haue to ought?
Then farewell fleshly force; I see thy pride is nought.

41

Thenceforth she streight into a bowre him brought,
　　And causd him those vncomely weedes vndight;
　　And in their steede for other rayment sought,
　　Whereof there was great store, and armors bright,
　　Which had bene reft from many a noble Knight;
　　Whom that proud Amazon subdewed had,
　　Whilest Fortune fauourd her successe in fight,
　　In which when as she him anew had clad,
She was reuiu'd, and ioyd much in his semblance glad.

42

So there a while they afterwards remained,
　　Him to refresh, and her late wounds to heale:
　　During which space she there as Princess rained,
　　And changing all that forme of common weale,
　　The liberty of women did repeale,
　　Which they had long vsurpt; and them restoring
　　To mens subiection, did true Iustice deale:
　　That all they as a Goddesse her adoring,
Her wisedome did admire, and hearkned to her loring.

43

For all those Knights, which long in captiue shade
　　Had shrowded bene, she did from thraldome free;
　　And magistrates of all that city made,
　　And gaue to them great liuing and large fee:
　　And that they should for euer faithfull bee,
　　Made them sweare fealty to *Artegall*.
　　Who when him selfe now well recur'd did see,
　　He purposd to proceed, what so be fall,
Vppon his first aduenture, which him forth did call.

44

Full sad and sorrowfull was *Britomart*
　　For his departure, her new cause of griefe;
　　Yet wisely moderated her owne smart,
　　Seeing his honor, which she tendred chiefe,
　　Consisted much in that aduentures priefe.
　　The care whereof, and hope of his successe
　　Gaue vnto her great comfort and reliefe,
　　That womanish complaints she did represse,
580 And tempred for the time her present heauinesse.

45

There she continu'd for a certaine space,
　　Till through his want her woe did more increase:
　　Then hoping that the change of aire and place
　　Would change her paine, and sorrow somewhat ease,
　　She parted thence, her anguish to appease.
　　Meane while her noble Lord sir *Artegall*
　　Went on his way, ne euer howre did cease,
　　Till he redeemed had that Lady thrall:
That for another Canto will more fitly fall.

Stanza 39
Cf. Homer, *Ody*. xxiii 93–5, 101–2.
3　**drent**: drenched: drowned.
6　**trauell**: also travail.
7　**his fauours likelynesse**: the likeness of his features.

Stanza 40
Cf. Una's lament when she sees her rescued knight: 'this misseeming hew your manly looks doth marre' (I viii 42.9).
2　**May-game**: an object of ridicule. Gough (1921) notes the allusion to the custom of disguising a man in woman's clothes as Maid Marian to take the place of the May Queen. Fletcher (1971) 273 notes the parody of the crocodile's 'game' (16.5).
3–5　Britomart invokes her past vision of him, III ii 24.4; and his prophetic role, III iii 28.1–2 and 23.1–4 above.
mighty palmes: a variation of 'mightie hands' (as iv 1.3), perhaps to stress his justice.　**embrew**: stain.

Stanza 42
Britomart's role in the poem is concluded as she assumes Isis's role and rules with true justice.
5–7　Cf. 1 Tim. 2.12: 'I permit not a woman . . . to usurpe autoritie over the man', and God's curse upon woman: 'Thy desire shal be subject to thine housband, and he shal rule over thee' (Gen. 3.16). Cf. v 25.
9　**loring**: instruction.

Stanza 43
1–2　There is now no Grill to object to his restoration.
4　**liuing**: estates.　**fee**: possessions.
7　**recur'd**: recovered.

Stanza 44
4　**tendred**: cherished.
5　**priefe**: proof.

Stanza 45
2　**his want**: want of him.
5　**parted**: departed.

Cant. VIII.

Prince Arthure and Sir Artegall,
Free Samient from feare:
They slay the Soudan, driue his wife,
Adicia to despaire.

1

NOught vnder heauen so strongly doth allure
The sence of man, and all his minde possesse,
As beauties louely baite, that doth procure
Great warriours oft their rigour to represse,
And mighty hands forget their manlinesse;
Drawne with the powre of an heart-robbing eye,
And wrapt in fetters of a golden tresse,
That can with melting pleasaunce mollifye
Their hardned hearts, enur'd to bloud and cruelty.

2

So whylome learnd that mighty Iewish swaine,
Each of whose lockes did match a man in might,
To lay his spoiles before his lemans traine:
So also did that great Oetean Knight
For his loues sake his Lions skin vndight:
And so did warlike *Antony* neglect
The worlds whole rule for *Cleopatras* sight.
Such wondrous powre hath wemens faire aspect,
To captiue men, and make them all the world reiect.

3

Yet could it not sterne *Artegall* retaine,
Nor hold from suite of his auowed quest,
Which he had vndertane to *Gloriane*;
But left his loue, albe her strong request,
Faire *Britomart* in languor and vnrest,
And rode him selfe vppon his first intent:
Ne day nor night did euer idly rest;
Ne wight but onely *Talus* with him went,
The true guide of his way and vertuous gouernment.

4

So trauelling, he chaunst far off to heed
A Damzell, flying on a palfrey fast
Before two Knights, that after her did speed
With all their powre, and her full fiercely chast
In hope to haue her ouerhent at last:
Yet fled she fast, and both them farre outwent,
Carried with wings of feare, like fowle aghast,
With locks all loose, and rayment all to rent;
And euer as she rode, her eye was backeward bent.

5

Soone after these he saw another Knight,
That after those two former rode apace,
With speare in rest, and prickt with all his might:
So ran they all, as they had bene at bace,
They being chased, that did others chase.
At length he saw the hindmost ouertake
One of those two, and force him turne his face;
How euer loth he were his way to slake,
Yet mote he algates now abide, and answere make.

6

But th'other still pursu'd the fearefull Mayd;
Who still from him as fast away did flie,
Ne once for ought her speedy passage stayd,
Till that at length she did before her spie
Sir *Artegall*, to whom she streight did hie
With gladfull hast, in hope of him to get
Succour against her greedy enimy:
Who seeing her approch gan forward set,
To saue her from her feare, and him from force to let.

Canto viii

Argument

1   Arthur intercedes in the eighth canto as usual to engage
in a number of actions corresponding to the number of the
Book: he frees **Samient** and kills the **Soudan** (viii), captures
Guyle (ix), kills Geryoneo's Seneschal (x), and kills Geryoneo
and his monster (xi).
3   **Soudan**: Souldan or Sultan; see 24.7*n*.

Stanza 1

2   **possesse**: dominate, control absolutely.
3   **procure**: induce, persuade.
7   **wrapt**: also suggesting 'rapt'.

Stanza 2

S. copies the pictures on the gates of Armida's palace (Tasso,
Ger. Lib. xvi 3–7) which portray love's triumph: Hercules
without his lion's skin bearing a distaff, and **Antony** leaving the
battle to follow **Cleopatra**. To Greek and Roman history, he
adds the biblical example of Samson, from Judges 16.17–9.
3   **traine**: snare.
4–5   **that . . . Oetean Knight**: Hercules died on Mount
Oetæus through Iole's love; cf. v 24.

Stanza 3

2   **suite**: pursuit.
5   **languor**: sorrow.
9   Talus's relation to Artegall suggests the Palmer's to
Guyon.   **gouernment**: i.e. instrument of his government, his
executive power; cf. iv 3.9.

Stanza 4

1   **heed**: see.
5   **ouerhent**: overtaken.
8   **all to rent**: entirely torn.

Stanza 5

4–5   **bace**: or prisoners' base, a game in which (as S.
explains) the chasers are chased; it is played at III xi 5.5,
VI x 8.4.
8   **slake**: slacken.
9   **algates**: nevertheless.

Stanza 6

9   **him from force to let**: to prevent him from using force.

7

But he like hound full greedy of his pray,
  Being impatient of impediment,
  Continu'd still his course, and by the way
  Thought with his speare him quight haue ouerwent.
  So both together ylike felly bent,
  Like fiercely met. But *Artegall* was stronger,
  And better skild in Tilt and Turnament,
  And bore him quite out of his saddle, longer   (wronger.
Then two speares length; So mischiefe ouermatcht the

8

And in his fall misfortune him mistooke;
  For on his head vnhappily he pight,
  That his owne waight his necke asunder broke,
  And left there dead. Meane while the other Knight
  Defeated had the other faytour quight,
  And all his bowels in his body brast:
  Whom leauing there in that dispiteous plight,
  He ran still on, thinking to follow fast
His other fellow Pagan, which before him past.

9

In stead of whom finding there ready prest
  Sir *Artegall*, without discretion
  He at him ran, with ready speare in rest:
  Who seeing him come still so fiercely on,
  Against him made againe. So both anon
  Together met, and strongly either strooke
  And broke their speares; yet neither has forgon
  His horses backe, yet to and fro long shooke,
And tottred like two towres, which through a tempest quooke.

10

But when againe they had recouered sence,
  They drew their swords, in mind to make amends
  For what their speares had fayld of their pretence.
  Which when the Damzell, who those deadly ends
  Of both her foes had seene, and now her frends
  For her beginning a more fearefull fray,
  She to them runnes in hast, and her haire rends,
  Crying to them their cruell hands to stay,
Vntill they both doe heare, what she to them will say.

11

They stayd their hands, when she thus gan to speake;
  Ah gentle Knights, what meane ye thus vnwise
  Vpon your selues anothers wrong to wreake?
  I am the wrong'd, whom ye did enterprise
  Both to redresse, and both redrest likewise:
  Witnesse the Paynims both, whom ye may see
  There dead on ground. What doe ye then deuise
  Of more reuenge? if more, then I am shee,
Which was the roote of all, end your reuenge on mee.

12

Whom when they heard so say, they lookt about,
  To weete if it were true, as she had told;
  Where when they saw their foes dead out of doubt,
  Eftsoones they gan their wrothfull hands to hold,
  And Ventailes reare, each other to behold.
  Tho when as *Artegall* did *Arthure* vew,
  So faire a creature, and so wondrous bold,
  He much admired both his heart and hew,
582 And touched with intire affection, nigh him drew.

13

Saying, Sir Knight, of pardon I you pray,
  That all vnweeting haue you wrong'd thus sore,
  Suffring my hand against my heart to stray:
  Which if ye please forgiue, I will therefore
  Yeeld for amends my selfe yours euermore,
  Or what so penaunce shall by you be red.
  To whom the Prince; Certes me needeth more
  To craue the same, whom errour so misled,
As that I did mistake the liuing for the ded.

Stanza 7
4   ouerwent: overcome.
7   Tilt and Turnament: see III i 44.7*n*.
9   mischiefe: misfortune.

Stanza 8
1   mistooke: took wrongfully, i.e. seized disastrously.
5   faytour: miscreant, impostor; suggesting falseness.
7   dispiteous: cruel, deserving only contempt.

Stanza 9
1   prest: at hand.
2   discretion: i.e. discerning who he was.
9   quooke: quaked.

Stanza 10
1-3   The encounter shows their equality: Artegall is
Art-egall, i.e. Arthur's peer; see i 3.2*n* and x 15.2.
pretence: intention.

Stanza 11
4   enterprise: undertake.

Stanza 12
3   out of doubt: without doubt.
5   Ventailes: the movable part of the helmet.
8   hew: appearance.
9   intire: sincere; complete; inner (as the spelling indicates).

Stanza 13
6   red: decided, decreed.
9   This error is the basis of the plot to destroy Adicia; cf.
25.4-5. It relates to Artegall's first appearance dressed in
Achilles's arms (III ii 25.6).

14

But sith ye please, that both our blames shall die,
  Amends may for the trespasse soone be made,
  Since neither is endamadg'd much thereby.
  So can they both them selues full eath perswade
  To faire accordaunce, and both faults to shade,
  Either embracing other louingly,
  And swearing faith to either on his blade,
  Neuer thenceforth to nourish enmity,
But either others cause to maintaine mutually.

15

Then *Artegall* gan of the Prince enquire,
  What were those knights, which there on ground were layd,
  And had receiu'd their follies worthy hire,
  And for what cause they chased so that Mayd.
  Certes I wote not well (the Prince then sayd)
  But by aduenture found them faring so,
  As by the way vnweetingly I strayd,
  And lo the Damzell selfe, whence all did grow,
Of whom we may at will the whole occasion know.

16

Then they that Damzell called to them nie,
  And asked her, what were those two her fone,
  From whom she earst so fast away did flie;
  And what was she her selfe so woe begone,
  And for what cause pursu'd of them attone.
  To whom she thus; Then wote ye well, that I
  Doe serue a Queene, that not far hence doth wone,
  A Princesse of great powre and maiestie,
Famous through all the world, and honor'd far and nie.

17

Her name *Mercilla* most men vse to call;
  That is a mayden Queene of high renowne,
  For her great bounty knowen ouer all,
  And soueraine grace, with which her royall crowne
  She doth support, and strongly beateth downe
  The malice of her foes, which her enuy,
  And at her happinesse do fret and frowne:
  Yet she her selfe the more doth magnify,
And euen to her foes her mercies multiply.

18

Mongst many which maligne her happy state,
  There is a mighty man, which wonnes here by
  That with most fell despight and deadly hate,
  Seekes to subuert her Crowne and dignity,
  And all his powre doth thereunto apply:
  And her good Knights, of which so braue a band
  Serues her, as any Princesse vnder sky,
  He either spoiles, if they against him stand,
Or to his part allures, and bribeth vnder hand.

19

Ne him sufficeth all the wrong and ill,
  Which he vnto her people does each day,
  But that he seekes by traytrous traines to spill
  Her person, and her sacred selfe to slay:
  That O ye heauens defend, and turne away
  From her, vnto the miscreant him selfe,
  That neither hath religion nor fay,
  But makes his God of his vngodly pelfe,
And Idols serues; so let his Idols serue the Elfe.

20

To all which cruell tyranny they say,
  He is prouokt, and stird vp day and night
  By his bad wife, that hight *Adicia*,
  Who counsels him through confidence of might,
  To breake all bonds of law, and rules of right.
  For she her selfe professeth mortall foe
  To Iustice, and against her still doth fight,
  Working to all, that loue her, deadly woe,
And making all her Knights and people to doe so.

Stanza 14
3 **endamadg'd**: injured.
4 **can**: did.
5 **shade**: veil, conceal.

Stanza 15
6 **aduenture**: chance.

Stanza 16
4 **what**: why.   **woe begone**: beset with woe.

Stanza 17
1 **Mercilla**: her name denotes **her mercies** (9).
3 **bounty**: goodness.
8–9 She makes herself greater by showing mercy to her foes.

Stanza 18
1 **maligne**: regard with envy.
8 **spoiles**: destroys.

Stanza 19
3–4 The distinction involves the doctrine of the King's two bodies. In *L.R.* S. explains that Elizabeth 'beareth two persons', one as Queen and the other as a Lady. **traines**: intrigues. **spill**: overthrow.
5 **defend**: avert; forbid.
6 **miscreant**: misbeliever.
7 **religion** should prevent him from seeking to overthrow Mercilla as Queen; **fay** (faith) from seeking to kill her as a private person.
8 **pelfe**: gold which he uses to bribe others and to fashion into the Idol which he worships.
9 **Elfe**: a malignant being; also as he is a knight of fairyland who has rejected the rule of the Faerie Queene and become a **miscreant** (6). Hence the curse, 'Let his Idol preserve him', or 'Let his Idol serve him traitorously as he serves others'.

Stanza 20
3 **Adicia**: Gk Injustice. Cf. 49.8–9.

21

Which my liege Lady seeing, thought it best,
  With that his wife in friendly wise to deale,
  For stint of strife, and stablishment of rest
  Both to her selfe, and to her common weale,
  And all forepast displeasures to repeale.
  So me in message vnto her she sent,
  To treat with her by way of enterdeale,
  Of finall peace and faire attonement,
Which might concluded be by mutuall consent.

22

All times haue wont safe passage to afford
  To messengers, that come for causes iust:
  But this proude Dame disdayning all accord,
  Not onely into bitter termes forth brust,
  Reuiling me, and rayling as she lust,
  But lastly to make proofe of vtmost shame,
  Me like a dog she out of dores did thrust,
  Miscalling me by many a bitter name,
That neuer did her ill, ne once deserued blame.

23

And lastly, that no shame might wanting be,
  When I was gone, soone after me she sent
  These two false Knights, whom there ye lying see,
  To be by them dishonoured and shent:
  But thankt be God, and your good hardiment,
  They haue the price of their owne folly payd.
  So said this Damzell, that hight *Samient*,
  And to those knights, for their so noble ayd,
Her selfe most gratefull shew'd, and heaped thanks repayd.

24

But they now hauing throughly heard, and seene
  Al those great wrongs, the which that mayd complained
  To haue bene done against her Lady Queene,
  By that proud dame, which her so much disdained,
  Were moued much thereat, and twixt them fained,
  With all their force to worke auengement strong
  Vppon the Souldan selfe, which it mayntained,
  And on his Lady, th'author of that wrong,
And vppon all those Knights, that did to her belong.

25

But thinking best by counterfet disguise
  To their deseigne to make the easier way,
  They did this complot twixt them selues deuise,
  First, that sir *Artegall* should him array,
  Like one of those two Knights, which dead there lay.
  And then that Damzell, the sad *Samient*,
  Should as his purchast prize with him conuay
  Vnto the Souldans court, her to present
Vnto his scornefull Lady, that for her had sent.

26

So as they had deuiz'd, sir *Artegall*
  Him clad in th'armour of a Pagan knight,
  And taking with him, as his vanquisht thrall,
  That Damzell, led her to the Souldans right.
  Where soone as his proud wife of her had sight,
  Forth of her window as she looking lay,
  She weened streight, it was her Paynim Knight,
  Which brought that Damzell, as his purchast pray;
And sent to him a Page, that mote direct his way.

27

Who bringing them to their appointed place,
  Offred his seruice to disarme the Knight;
  But he refusing him to let vnlace,
  For doubt to be discouered by his sight,
  Kept himselfe still in his straunge armour dight.
  Soone after whom the Prince arriued there,
  And sending to the Souldan in despight
  A bold defyance, did of him requere
That Damzell, whom he held as wrongfull prisonere.

Stanza 21
5   **repeale**: give up; also in the legal sense, which fits the context.
7   **enterdeale**: mutual dealing.
8   **attonement**: concord.

Stanza 22
5   **lust**: chose.
8   **Miscalling**: reviling.

Stanza 23
1   **And lastly**: a variation on 22.6. She exceeds her own utmost shame in seeking to shame others.
4   **shent**: defiled.
7   **Samient**: bringing together, from 'sam' (I x 57.8), as she was an ambassador who sought 'attonement' (21.8), and as she unites Artegall and Arthur.

Stanza 24
5   **fained**: desired.
7   **Souldan**: or Sultan, the title of a Mohammedan or Egyptian ruler, applied here to a pagan tyrant. Since the term is used only in this episode, it may carry specific political reference.   **it**: i.e. **that wrong**.

Stanza 25
Aptekar (1969) 123 notices the contrast with the earlier books in which Arthur did not need to resort to guile; cf. the guile used to invade Turpine's castle, VI vi 20.
3   **complot**: plot; literally a plot between them; used only here, it stresses their unity.
6   **sad**: as their captive.
7   **purchast**: got by conquest.

Stanza 26
4   **right**: domain, territory.

Stanza 27
4   **doubt**: fear.
5   **straunge**: belonging to another.

28

Wherewith the Souldan all with furie fraught,
  Swearing, and banning most blasphemously,
  Commaunded straight his armour to be brought,
  And mounting straight vpon a charret hye,
  With yron wheeles and hookes arm'd dreadfully,
  And drawne of cruell steedes, which he had fed
  With flesh of men, whom through fell tyranny
  He slaughtred had, and ere they were halfe ded,
Their bodies to his beasts for prouender did spred.

29

So forth he came all in a cote of plate,
  Burnisht with bloudie rust, whiles on the greene
  The Briton Prince him readie did awayte,
  In glistering armes right goodly well beseene,
  That shone as bright, as doth the heauen sheene;
  And by his stirrup *Talus* did attend,
  Playing his pages part, as he had beene
  Before directed by his Lord; to th'end
He should his flaile to finall execution bend.

30

Thus goe they both together to their geare,
  With like fierce minds, but meanings different:
  For the proud Souldan with presumpteous cheare,
  And countenance sublime and insolent,
  Sought onely slaughter and auengement:
  But the braue Prince for honour and for right,
  Gainst tortious powre and lawlesse regiment,
  In the behalfe of wronged weake did fight:
More in his causes truth he trusted then in might.

31

Like to the *Thracian* Tyrant, who they say
  Vnto his horses gaue his guests for meat,
  Till he himselfe was made their greedie pray,
  And torne in peeces by *Alcides* great.
  So thought the Souldan in his follies threat,
  Either the Prince in peeces to haue torne
  With his sharpe wheeles, in his first rages heat,
  Or vnder his fierce horses feet haue borne
And trampled downe in dust his thoughts disdained scorne.

32

But the bold child that perill well espying,
  If he too rashly to his charet drew,
  Gaue way vnto his horses speedie flying,
  And their resistlesse rigour did eschew.
  Yet as he passed by, the Pagan threw
  A shiuering dart with so impetuous force,
  That had he not it shun'd with heedfull vew,
  It had himselfe transfixed, or his horse,
Or made them both one masse withouten more remorse.

Stanzas 28–45
The historical event alluded to is England's defeat of the Spanish Armada in 1588.

Stanza 28
2 **banning**: since the Souldan alludes to Philip II of Spain, the term carries the ecclesiastical sense, 'anathematizing'. As Upton (1758) observes, 'this may be supposed to hint at those many pious cursings and papistical excommunications so liberally thundered out against the Queen and her faithful subjects'. Cf. 39.4.
5–9 Inserted parenthetically. The chariot armed with hooks is a symbol of war, as in Milton's 'hooked chariot' (*Nat. Ode* 56). Cf. 41.6, 42.6. It is classical in origin, as the 'scythed chariots' in Q. Curtius, *History* IV ix 4, but also biblical (2 Macc. 13.2), and contemporary: Camden, *Hist. of Eliz.* (1630) iii 130, records that the Spanish ships were 'headed with yron, and hooked on the sides'. The great height of the Spanish ships is alluded to in hye (4). On yron, see i 12.6n. Graziani (1964b) observes that the *impresa* of Philip II depicted the sun-god driving his chariot across the heavens over land and ocean, with the motto, '*Iam illustrabit omnia*', to indicate his divine mission to spread the light of the true faith to all lands.

Stanza 29
1–5 The Souldan's armour dulled with old blood contrasts with Arthur's brightly shining armour.   **greene** alludes to the sea; cf. 42.9.
6–9 **Talus** need not act because Arthur is aided by the divine power of his shield.   **finall execution** is given to Artegall at 50.

Stanza 30
1 **geare**: business.
3 **cheare**: mien.
4 **sublime**: haughty, proud.
7 **tortious**: illegal. **regiment**: rule.

Stanza 31
1–4 'The nynthe [of Hercules's labours] was the takyng of Diomedes kyng of Thracia, and castyng hym to his horses, who feeding them with mans fleshe, was himselfe of them devoured' (Cooper, 1565). Boccaccio, *Gen. Deor.* xiii 1, notes that the victims were Diomedes's guests; S. adds that Hercules tore the tyrant to pieces. The simile forecasts the Souldan's defeat as it places Arthur in the role of Hercules. For Arthur as Hercules, see II xi 45–46n, V ix 6.2–9n, x 9 –10n. With the guest-eating horses, cf. the guest-eating cows kept by Geryon, x 9.7–9, and the Monster, xi 20.1–4.
9 **his thoughts disdained scorne**: i.e. whom he disdained in his scornful thought.

Stanza 32
1 **child**: applied in the poem only to Arthur: see IV viii 44.8n; cf. 'infant' (41.2).
4 **rigour**: violence.
9 **withouten more remorse**: i.e. without further delay or showing further pity.

585

33

Oft drew the Prince vnto his charret nigh,
　In hope some stroke to fasten on him neare;
　But he was mounted in his seat so high,
　And his wingfooted coursers him did beare
　So fast away, that ere his readie speare
　He could aduance, he farre was gone and past.
　Yet still he him did follow euery where,
　And followed was of him likewise full fast;
So long as in his steedes the flaming breath did last.

34

Againe the Pagan threw another dart,
　Of which he had with him abundant store,
　On euery side of his embatteld cart,
　And of all other weapons lesse or more,
　Which warlike vses had deuiz'd of yore.
　The wicked shaft guyded through th'ayrie wyde,
　By some bad spirit, that it to mischiefe bore,
　Stayd not, till through his curat it did glyde,
And made a griesly wound in his enriuen side.

35

Much was he grieued with that haplesse throe,
　That opened had the welspring of his blood·
　But much the more that to his hatefull foe
　He mote not come, to wreake his wrathfull mood.
　That made him raue, like to a Lyon wood,
　Which being wounded of the huntsmans hand
　Can not come neare him in the couert wood,
　Where he with boughes hath built his shady stand,
And fenst himselfe about with many a flaming brand.

36

Still when he sought t'approch vnto him ny,
　His charret wheeles about him whirled round,
　And made him backe againe as fast to fly;
　And eke his steedes like to an hungry hound,
　That hunting after game hath carrion found,
　So cruelly did him pursew and chace,
　That his good steed, all were he much renound
　For noble courage, and for hardie race,
Durst not endure their sight, but fled from place to place.

37

Thus long they trast, and trauerst to and fro,
　Seeking by euery way to make some breach,
　Yet could the Prince not nigh vnto him goe,
　That one sure stroke he might vnto him reach,
　Whereby his strengthes assay he might him teach.
　At last from his victorious shield he drew
　The vaile, which did his powrefull light empeach;
　And comming full before his horses vew,
As they vpon him prest, it plaine to them did shew.

38

Like lightening flash, that hath the gazer burned,
　So did the sight thereof their sense dismay,
　That backe againe vpon themselues they turned,
　And with their ryder ranne perforce away:
　Ne could the Souldan them from flying stay,
　With raynes, or wonted rule, as well he knew.
　Nought feared they, what he could do, or say,
　But th'onely feare, that was before their vew;
From which like mazed deare, dismayfully they flew.

39

Fast did they fly, as them their feete could beare,
　High ouer hilles, and lowly ouer dales,
　As they were follow'd of their former feare.
　In vaine the Pagan bannes, and sweares, and rayles,
　And backe with both his hands vnto him hayles
　The resty raynes, regarded now no more:
　He to them calles and speakes, yet nought auayles;
　They heare him not, they haue forgot his lore,
But go, which way they list, their guide they haue forlore.

Stanza 33
7–9　They continue the game of prisoners' base, 5.4–5.

Stanza 34
3　embatteld cart: chariot armed for battle.
4　lesse or more: smaller or greater.
6　wyde: used as a substantive.
8　curat: cuirass or breastplate.

Stanza 35
5–9　Noting the lion's traditional fear of fire, e.g. Homer, *Iliad* xi 553, Pliny VIII xix.
5　wood: mad.

Stanza 36
5　carrion: a beast inferior to game, as flesh for hounds.
7–9　The flight of Arthur's horse marks his imminent defeat, as the fearful flight of the Souldan's horses marks his final defeat. The horses are stressed in this encounter because they represent the ships in the historical allegory.

Stanza 37
1　trast, and trauerst: pursued and then turned aside to be pursued; see IV vi 18.1.
5　assay: proof.
6–9　Since the horses are pressing upon Arthur, he draws the veil at the moment of defeat; thus he is saved, as England was saved from the Armada, by divine grace. Cf. I viii 19.1–2 where, through his fall from Orgoglio's blow, 'his shield, that couered was, / Did loose his vele by chaunce, and open flew.' Now he actively cooperates with grace by lifting the veil. See xi 21.5*n*.　empeach: impede.

Stanza 38
1–2　Cf. the effect of Arthur's shield at I viii 21.8–9. As Jove's thunderbolt, it overthrows the Souldan even as it overthrew Phaeton (40).
8　th'onely feare . . . their vew: they feared only what was before them.
9　mazed: terrified.　dismayfully: in dismay; suggested by dismay (2).

Stanza 39
4　bannes: curses; cf. 28.2.
6　resty: resisting control.
8　lore: instruction.
9　forlore: abandoned.

40

As when the firie-mouthed steeds, which drew
  The Sunnes bright wayne to *Phaetons* decay,
  Soone as they did the monstrous Scorpion vew,
  With vgly craples crawling in their way,
  The dreadfull sight did them so sore affray,
  That their well knowen courses they forwent,
  And leading th'euer-burning lampe astray,
This lower world nigh all to ashes brent,
And left their scorched path yet in the firmament.

41

Such was the furie of these head-strong steeds,
  Soone as the infants sunlike shield they saw,
  That all obedience both to words and deeds
  They quite forgot, and scornd all former law;
  Through woods, and rocks, and mountaines they did draw
  The yron charet, and the wheeles did teare,
  And tost the Paynim, without feare or awe;
  From side to side they tost him here and there,
Crying to them in vaine, that nould his crying heare.

42

Yet still the Prince pursew'd him close behind,
  Oft making offer him to smite, but found
  No easie meanes according to his mind.
  At last they haue all ouerthrowne to ground
  Quite topside turuey, and the pagan hound
  Amongst the yron hookes and graples keene,
  Torne all to rags, and rent with many a wound,
  That no whole peece of him was to be seene,
But scattred all about, and strow'd vpon the greene.

43

Like as the cursed sonne of *Theseus*,
  That following his chace in dewy morne,
  To fly his stepdames loues outrageous,
  Of his owne steedes was all to peeces torne,
  And his faire limbs left in the woods forlorne;
  That for his sake *Diana* did lament,
  And all the wooddy Nymphes did wayle and mourne.
So was this Souldan rapt and all to rent,
That of his shape appear'd no litle moniment.

44

Onely his shield and armour, which there lay,
  Though nothing whole, but all to brusd and broken,
  He vp did take, and with him brought away,
  That mote remaine for an eternall token
  To all, mongst whom this storie should be spoken,
  How worthily, by heauens high decree,
  Iustice that day of wrong her selfe had wroken,
  That all men which that spectacle did see,
By like ensample mote for euer warned bee.

45

So on a tree, before the Tyrants dore,
  He caused them be hung in all mens sight,
  To be a moniment for euermore.
  Which when his Ladie from the castles hight
  Beheld, it much appald her troubled spright:
  Yet not, as women wont in dolefull fit,
  She was dismayd, or faynted through affright,
  But gathered vnto her her troubled wit,
And gan eftsoones deuize to be aueng'd for it.

Stanza 40

The story of **Phaeton** is also told at I iv 9 and III xi 38 but in
repetition is wittily varied. Here the horses are the subject:
the details of their fiery mouths and fear of the **Scorpion** may
be drawn directly from Ovid, *Met.* ii 85, 119 and 195–7.
Their terror, not Phaeton's, is S.'s theme. Graziani (1964b)
324 observes that S. turns Philip's *impresa*, Apollo, into
Phaeton. See 41.2*n.*
2   **wayne**: chariot. As applied to the Souldan's chariot, cf.
OED 3: a rendering of Lat. *plaustrum*, a threshing instrument
with wheels, citing Wycliff's trans. of Isaiah 41.15.   **decay**:
downfall.
3–4   **Scorpion**: the constellation Scorpio; also a military
engine for hurling stones; used to destroy the walls of a town.
This latter sense would allude to the English ships attacking
the high Spanish galleons.   **craples**: conflating claws and
'graples' (42.6). Fowler (1964) 202 *n*2 suggests that these denote
the constellation *chelæ scorpionis*, or Libra, 'so that in a sense
the Soldan's horses are terrified by a vision of judgement'.
6   **forwent**: forsook.
9   **their scorched path**: the Milky Way; cf. Chaucer,
House of Fame ii 935–56.

Stanza 41

The extended description seems designed to accommodate an
allusion to the scattering of the Spanish Armada. Camden
(1688) 327 notes that a medal coined in memory of the victory
showed a fleet flying with full sails with the inscription, '*Venit
vidit, fugit*').
2   Arthur may claim the Spanish title, Infant or Prince, by
defeating the Spanish power; cf. II viii 56.1.
9   **nould**: would not.

Stanza 42

5   **topside turuey**: topsyturvy.
6   **graples**: grappling irons.
8–9   Recalls Ovid, *Met.* xv 528–9, suggesting the comparison
to Hippolytus in the next stanza.

Stanza 43

For the story of Hippolytus, see I v 37–40. His steeds caused
his death when they were frightened by two sea-monsters.
The description alludes to his name, 'one torn by horses'.
1   **cursed**: as *Met.* xv 504–5 records.
3   **loues**] loue *1609*.
7   **wooddy**: woodland.
8   'rap and rend' is an alliterative phrase; here **rapt** means
'carried off' or 'pulled down', and **all to rent** means 'entirely
rent'.
9   **no litle moniment**: no trace at all; cf. I v 38.9.

Stanza 44

2   **all to brusd**: entirely battered.
7   **wroken**: wreaked, avenged.

Stanza 45

1–3   Camden (1688) 328 records that after the defeat of the
Armada 'the Banners taken from the Enemy were hung up to
be seen'.
6–7   Cf. Radigund, vii 25.2–4.

46

Streight downe she ranne, like an enraged cow,
　　That is berobbed of her youngling dere,
　　With knife in hand, and fatally did vow,
　　To wreake her on that mayden messengere,
　　Whom she had causd be kept as prisonere,
　　By *Artegall*, misween'd for her owne Knight,
　　That brought her backe. And comming present there,
　　She at her ran with all her force and might,
All flaming with reuenge and furious despight.

47

Like raging *Ino*, when with knife in hand
　　She threw her husbands murdred infant out,
　　Or fell *Medea*, when on *Colchicke* strand
　　Her brothers bones she scattered all about;
　　Or as that madding mother, mongst the rout
　　Of *Bacchus* Priests her owne deare flesh did teare.
　　Yet neither *Ino*, nor *Medea* stout,
　　Nor all the *Mænades* so furious were,
As this bold woman, when she saw that Damzell there.

48

But *Artegall* being thereof aware,
　　Did stay her cruell hand, ere she her raught,
　　And as she did her selfe to strike prepare,
　　Out of her fist the wicked weapon caught:
　　With that like one enfelon'd or distraught,
　　She forth did rome, whether her rage her bore,
　　With franticke passion, and with furie fraught;
　　And breaking forth out at a posterne dore,
Vnto the wyld wood ranne, her dolours to deplore.

49

As a mad bytch, when as the franticke fit
　　Her burning tongue with rage inflamed hath,
　　Doth runne at randon, and with furious bit
　　Snatching at euery thing, doth wreake her wrath
　　On man and beast, that commeth in her path.
　　There they doe say, that she transformed was
　　Into a Tygre, and that Tygres scath
　　In crueltie and outrage she did pas,
To proue her surname true, that she imposed has.

50

Then *Artegall* himselfe discouering plaine,
　　Did issue forth gainst all that warlike rout
　　Of knights and armed men, which did maintaine
　　That Ladies part, and to the Souldan lout:
　　All which he did assault with courage stout,
　　All were they nigh an hundred knights of name,
　　And like wyld Goates them chaced all about,
　　Flying from place to place with cowheard shame,
So that with finall force them all he ouercame.

51

Then caused he the gates be opened wyde,
　　And there the Prince, as victour of that day,
　　With tryumph entertayn'd and glorifyde,
　　Presenting him with all the rich array,
　　And roiall pompe, which there long hidden lay,
　　Purchast through lawlesse powre and tortious wrong
　　Of that proud Souldan, whom he earst did slay.
　　So both for rest there hauing stayd not long,
Marcht with that mayd, fit matter for another song.

Stanza 46
The fearful image of an angry cow running with knife in hand
is not quite prevented by the punctuation.
6　misween'd: mistaken.

Stanza 47
1–2　Cf. the version at IV xi 13.4–6 and see *n*. According to
Ovid, **Ino** threw herself with her son into the sea after her
husband had murdered their other infant. S. may have consulted the several versions in Comes (1616) VIII iv. In the three
examples, he traces the progression from wife-husband to
sister-brother to mother-son; hence Ino's son is called **her
husbands**.
3–4　For **Medea**, see II xii 44–45.
5–6　Pentheus was torn to pieces by his mother and the
Maenades when he spied upon their rites to Bacchus; see Ovid,
Met. iii 701–33.　**madding**: frenzied.

Stanza 48
2　raught: reached; touched.
5　enfelon'd: made furious; suggesting one caught in a
felony.
6　whether: whither.

Stanza 49
S. comments on this metamorphosis at ix. 1. Hecuba was
transformed into a bitch in rage against her son's murderer,
Ovid, *Met*. xiii 567–9. Cooper (1565) writes: 'She finally
waxed madde, and did byte and stryke all men that she mette,
wherfore she was called dogge.' S. describes accurately the
actions of a rabid dog, as Gough (1921) notes. Cf. Geryoneo's
actions at xi 12.1–2.
7　scath: harm; harmfulness.
9　that she imposed has: i.e. that was bestowed on her, viz.
Adicia or Injustice.

Stanza 50
1　discouering: revealing, referring to the display of his
virtue.
4　lout: make obeisance.
6　hundred: an absolute number, as III iv 21.1, etc. He
defeats this number of knights to prove his worth at the
Tournament, iii 11.5.
8　cowheard: the etymological spelling suggests conduct
befitting a cow-herder.
9　with finall force: i.e. with force finally; but suggesting
absolute force.

Stanza 51
6　Purchast: plundered.

Cant. IX.

Arthur and Artegall catch Guyle
whom Talus doth dismay,
They to Mercillaes pallace come,
and see her rich array.

1

WHat Tygre, or what other saluage wight
    Is so exceeding furious and fell,
As wrong, when it hath arm'd it selfe with might?
Not fit mongst men, that doe with reason mell,
But mongst wyld beasts and saluage woods to dwell;
Where still the stronger doth the weake deuoure,
    And they that most in boldnesse doe excell,
    Are dreadded most, and feared for their powre:
Fit for *Adicia*, there to build her wicked bowre.

2

There let her wonne farre from resort of men,
    Where righteous *Artegall* her late exyled;
    There let her euer keepe her damned den,
Where none may be with her lewd parts defyled,
Nor none but beasts may be of her despoyled:
And turne we to the noble Prince, where late
    We did him leaue, after that he had foyled
    The cruell Souldan, and with dreadfull fate
Had vtterly subuerted his vnrighteous state.

3

Where hauing with Sir *Artegall* a space
    Well solast in that Souldans late delight,
They both resoluing now to leaue the place,
Both it and all the wealth therein behight
Vnto that Damzell in her Ladies right,
And so would haue departed on their way.
    But she them woo'd by all the meanes she might,
    And earnestly besought, to wend that day
With her, to see her Ladie thence not farre away.

4

By whose entreatie both they ouercommen,
    Agree to goe with her, and by the way,
    (As often falles) of sundry things did commen.
Mongst which that Damzell did to them bewray
A straunge aduenture, which not farre thence lay;
To weet a wicked villaine, bold and stout,
    Which wonned in a rocke not farre away,
    That robbed all the countrie there about,
And brought the pillage home, whence none could get it out.

5

Thereto both his owne wylie wit, (she sayd)
    And eke the fastnesse of his dwelling place,
    Both vnassaylable, gaue him great ayde:
For he so crafty was to forge and face,
So light of hand, and nymble of his pace,
So smooth of tongue, and subtile in his tale,
    That could deceiue one looking in his face;
    Therefore by name *Malengin* they him call,
Well knowen by his feates, and famous ouer all.

6

Through these his slights he many doth confound,
    And eke the rocke, in which he wonts to dwell,
    Is wondrous strong, and hewen farre vnder ground
A dreadfull depth, how deepe no man can tell;
But some doe say, it goeth downe to hell.
And all within, it full of wyndings is,
    And hidden wayes, that scarse an hound by smell
    Can follow out those false footsteps of his,
Ne none can backe returne, that once are gone amis.

Canto ix

Argument
1   Guyle: i.e. Malengin, 5.8.
2   dismay: defeat.

Stanza 1
4   mell: concern themselves.
5   saluage: wild, uncultivated; hence fierce, ungoverned.

Stanza 2
4   lewd parts: the sexual sense applies to her wicked
conduct at viii 20.4–5.
8   fate: sentence, judgment.

Stanza 3
2   solast: comforted themselves.
4   behight: committed.
5   right: either what had been rightfully Mercilla's or what is
given her now by right of conquest.

Stanza 4
3   commen: commune.
4   bewray: reveal.

Stanza 5
2   fastnesse: security.
4   forge: devise evil; deceive.   face: show a false face.
8   Malengin: deceit, guile; cf. Arg. 1 and III i 53.8. The
etymology, *mal + engin*, is indicated by his 'yron hooke' (11.2).

Stanza 6
1   slights: wiles.
2–9   Upton (1758) compares the den of Cacus in Virgil,
Aen. viii 193–5, and Ovid, *Fasti* i 555–6. Dunseath (1968)
198–204 links the defeat of Malengin to Hercules's defeat of
Cacus, a master of fraud. As a type of Proteus, see 17*n*.

7

Which when those knights had heard, their harts gan earne,
  To vnderstand that villeins dwelling place,
  And greatly it desir'd of her to learne,
  And by which way they towards it should trace.
  Were not (sayd she) that it should let your pace
  Towards my Ladies presence by you ment,
  I would you guyde directly to the place.
  Then let not that (said they) stay your intent;
For neither will one foot, till we that carle haue hent.

8

So forth they past, till they approched ny
  Vnto the rocke, where was the villains won,
  Which when the Damzell neare at hand did spy,
  She warn'd the knights thereof: who thereupon
  Gan to aduize, what best were to be done.
  So both agreed, to send that mayd afore,
  Where she might sit nigh to the den alone,
  Wayling, and raysing pittifull vprore,
As if she did some great calamitie deplore.

9

With noyse whereof when as the caytiue carle
  Should issue forth, in hope to find some spoyle,
  They in awayt would closely him ensnarle,
  Ere to his den he backward could recoyle,
  And so would hope him easily to foyle,
  The Damzell straight went, as she was directed,
  Vnto the rocke, and there vpon the soyle
  Hauing her selfe in wretched wize abiected,
Gan weepe and wayle, as if great griefe had her affected.

10

The cry whereof entring the hollow caue,
  Eftsoones brought forth the villaine, as they ment,
  With hope of her some wishfull boot to haue.
  Full dreadfull wight he was, as euer went
  Vpon the earth, with hollow eyes deepe pent,
  And long curld locks, that downe his shoulders shagged,
  And on his backe an vncouth vestiment
  Made of straunge stuffe, but all to worne and ragged,
And vnderneath his breech was all to torne and iagged.

11

And in his hand an huge long staffe he held,
  Whose top was arm'd with many an yron hooke,
  Fit to catch hold of all that he could weld,
  Or in the compasse of his clouches tooke;
  And euer round about he cast his looke,
  Als at his backe a great wyde net he bore,
  With which he seldome fished at the brooke,
  But vsd to fish for fooles on the dry shore,
Of which he in faire weather wont to take great store.

12

Him when the damzell saw fast by her side,
  So vgly creature, she was nigh dismayd,
  And now for helpe aloud in earnest cride.
  But when the villaine saw her so affrayd,
  He gan with guilefull words her to perswade,
  To banish feare, and with *Sardonian* smyle
  Laughing on her, his false intent to shade,
  Gan forth to lay his bayte her to beguyle,
590 That from her self vnwares he might her steale the whyle.

13

Like as the fouler on his guilefull pype
  Charmes to the birds full many a pleasant lay,
  That they the whiles may take lesse heedie keepe,
  How he his nets doth for their ruine lay:
  So did the villaine to her prate and play,
  And many pleasant trickes before her show,
  To turne her eyes from his intent away:
  For he in slights and iugling feates did flow,
And of legierdemayne the mysteries did know.

Stanza 7
1   **earne**: yearn.
2   **vnderstand**: suggesting 'stand under' in order to comprehend its depths.
4   **trace**: travel.
5   **let**: hinder.
6   **ment**: intended.

Stanza 8
2   **won**: accustomed dwelling-place.
5   **aduize**: consider.

Stanza 9
3   **awayt**: ambush.   **ensnarle**: entangle in a snarl or snare. They plan to capture him with the emblem of guile, the net.
8   **abiected**: cast down; hence literally downcast.

Stanza 10
3   **wishfull boot**: wished-for booty.
4–11.9   As S. notes in *View* 50, the rebel Irish wore 'mantles and long glibs, which is a thick curled bush of hair hanging down over their eyes, and monstrously disguising them'. The description draws on the traditional iconography of guile. Aptekar (1969) 129–31 compares Ripa's *Inganno*: a man with long shaggy hair and strange jagged garments carrying a fishing net in one hand and three fish hooks in the other. Cf. also the wicked in Hab. 1. 14–5 who treat others as fish of the sea: 'Thei take up all with the angle [fish-hook]: thei catche it in their net.' Malengin is the false fisher of men.
6   **shagged**: hung in a shaggy manner.
8   **all to**: entirely.
9   **breech**: rump.

Stanza 11
3   **weld**: wield: prevail over.
4   **compasse**: reach.
5   **cast his looke**: suggests that his glance nets his victims.

Stanza 12
6   **Sardonian**: sardonic; forced laughter which hides bitterness. Proverbial (C. G. Smith, 1970, 676).
7   As Dissemblance 'laught on' Suspect (III xii 15.3) to encourage him.

Stanza 13
2   **Charmes**: plays to fascinate, with a pun on 'charm', the bird-song, which he imitates.
8   **flow**: abound.

14

To which whilest she lent her intentiue mind,
  He suddenly his net vpon her threw,
  That ouersprad her like a puffe of wind;
  And snatching her soone vp, ere well she knew,
  Ran with her fast away vnto his mew,
  Crying for helpe aloud. But when as ny
  He came vnto his caue, and there did vew
  The armed knights stopping his passage by,
He threw his burden downe, and fast away did fly.

15

But *Artegall* him after did pursew,
  The whiles the Prince there kept the entrance still:
  Vp to the rocke he ran, and thereon flew
  Like a wyld Gote, leaping from hill to hill,
  And dauncing on the craggy cliffes at will;
  That deadly daunger seem'd in all mens sight,
  To tempt such steps, where footing was so ill:
  Ne ought auayled for the armed knight,
To thinke to follow him, that was so swift and light.

16

Which when he saw, his yron man he sent,
  To follow him; for he was swift in chace.
  He him pursewd, where euer that he went,
  Both ouer rockes, and hilles, and euery place,
  Where so he fled, he followd him apace:
  So that he shortly forst him to forsake
  The hight, and downe descend vnto the base.
  There he him courst a fresh, and soone did make
To leaue his proper forme, and other shape to take.

17

Into a Foxe himselfe he first did tourne;
  But he him hunted like a Foxe full fast:
  Then to a bush himselfe he did transforme,
  But he the bush did beat, till that at last
  Into a bird it chaung'd, and from him past,
  Flying from tree to tree, from wand to wand:
  But he then stones at it so long did cast,
  That like a stone it fell vpon the land,
But he then tooke it vp, and held fast in his hand.

18

So he it brought with him vnto the knights,
  And to his Lord Sir *Artegall* it lent,
  Warning him hold it fast, for feare of slights.
  Who whilest in hand it gryping hard he hent,
  Into a Hedgehogge all vnwares it went,
  And prickt him so, that he away it threw.
  Then gan it runne away incontient,
  Being returned to his former hew:
But *Talus* soone him ouertooke, and backward drew.

19

But when as he would to a snake againe
  Haue turn'd himselfe, he with his yron flayle
  Gan driue at him, with so huge might and maine,
  That all his bones, as small as sandy grayle
  He broke, and did his bowels disentrayle;
  Crying in vaine for helpe, when helpe was past.
  So did deceipt the selfe deceiuer fayle,
  There they him left a carrion outcast;
For beasts and foules to feede vpon for their repast.

20

Thence forth they passed with that gentle Mayd,
  To see her Ladie, as they did agree.
  To which when she approched, thus she sayd;
  Loe now, right noble knights, arriu'd ye bee
  Nigh to the place, which ye desir'd to see:
  There shall ye see my souerayne Lady Queene
  Most sacred wight, most debonayre and free,
  That euer yet vpon this earth was seene,
Or that with Diademe hath euer crowned beene.

Stanza 14
1 **intentiue**: inwardly attentive.
5 **mew**: den.

Stanza 16
9 **proper**: own.

Stanza 17
The initial transformation declares his crafty guile. The others follow the logic of a childhood rhyme: the fox that hides in the bush becomes a bush, which, when beaten, becomes a bird, etc. Cf. Proteus's transformations at III viii 39–41.
6 **wand**: shrub.

Stanza 18
2 **lent**: gave.
7 **incontinent**: immediately.
8 **hew**: shape.

Stanza 19
1 **againe**: i.e. turn himself again. Transformation into a snake would fully manifest his nature as Guile.
5 **disentrayle**: drag forth from their inner parts; unravel. They undo the 'wyndings' (6.6) of his labyrinthine cave.
7 **the selfe deceiuer**: i.e. the deceiver himself. Polyptoton (using the same word in different cases) is strengthened by the double sense of **fayle**, with its pun on 'deceive' (from Lat. *fallere*; cf. III xi 46.9).

Stanza 20
7 **debonayre**: gracious.   **free**: noble; gracious; magnanimous.

21

The gentle knights reioyced much to heare
　　The prayses of that Prince so manifold,
　　And passing litle further, commen were,
　　Where they a stately pallace did behold,
　　Of pompous show, much more then she had told;
　　With many towres, and tarras mounted hye,
　　And all their tops bright glistering with gold,
　　That seemed to outshine the dimmed skye,
And with their brightnesse daz'd the straunge beholders eye.

22

There they alighting, by that Damzell were
　　Directed in, and shewed all the sight:
　　Whose porch, that most magnificke did appeare,
　　Stood open wyde to all men day and night;
　　Yet warded well by one of mickle might,
　　That sate thereby, with gyantlike resemblance,
　　To keepe out guyle, and malice, and despight,
　　That vnder shew oftimes of fayned semblance,
Are wont in Princes courts to worke great scath and hindrance.

23

His name was *Awe*; by whom they passing in
　　Went vp the hall, that was a large wyde roome,
　　All full of people making troublous din,
　　And wondrous noyse, as if that there were some,
　　Which vnto them was dealing righteous doome.
　　By whom they passing, through the thickest preasse,
　　The marshall of the hall to them did come;
　　His name hight *Order*, who commaunding peace,　(ceasse.
Them guyded through the throng, that did their clamors

24

They ceast their clamors vpon them to gaze;
　　Whom seeing all in armour bright as day,
　　Straunge there to see, it did them much amaze,
　　And with vnwonted terror halfe affray.
　　For neuer saw they there the like array,
　　Ne euer was the name of warre there spoken,
　　But ioyous peace and quietnesse alway,
　　Dealing iust iudgements, that mote not be broken
For any brybes, or threates of any to be wroken.

25

There as they entred at the Scriene, they saw
　　Some one, whose tongue was for his trespasse vyle
　　Nayld to a post, adiudged so by law:
　　For that therewith he falsely did reuyle,
　　And foule blaspheme that Queene for forged guyle,
　　Both with bold speaches, which he blazed had,
　　And with lewd poems, which he did compyle;
　　For the bold title of a Poet bad
He on himselfe had ta'en, and rayling rymes had sprad.

26

Thus there he stood, whylest high ouer his head,
　　There written was the purport of his sin,
　　In cyphers strange, that few could rightly read,
　　BON FONT: but *bon* that once had written bin,
　　Was raced out, and *Mal* was now put in.
　　So now *Malfont* was plainely to be red;
　　Eyther for th'euill, which he did therein,
　　Or that he likened was to a welhed
592 Of euill words, and wicked sclaunders by him shed.

Stanza 21
4–9 Cf. Lucifera's 'stately Pallace' (I iv 4).
5 **pompous**: magnificent; not necessarily derogatory.
6 **tarras**: terraces: galleries; as the 'galleries farre ouer laid' in the house of Pride.

Stanza 22
The entrance resembles that to Hampton Court; see *Var*. v 237–8. Gough (1921) notes that the Queen's porter was said to have been 8 foot 6 inches tall.
3–7 As the gates of Jerusalem 'shal be open continually: nether day nor night shal they be shut' (Isaiah 60. 11). Rev. 21. 27 adds that no unclean thing may enter these open gates 'nether whatsoever worketh abomination or lies'.
7 **guyle** is linked with Malengin (see Arg.), **malice, and despight** with the Souldan and Adicia (cf. viii 17.6, 18.3).
9 **scath**: harm. **hindrance**: injury.

Stanza 23
4 **some**: some one.
8 At VII vii 4.6, Order appears as Nature's 'Sergeant', whose office is to summon persons to appear before the court (*OED* 4).

Stanza 24
3–7 An allusion to the peace during Elizabeth's reign; see 30.6–9n. **amaze**: dazzle, bewilder.
9 **wroken**: wreaked: avenged.

Stanza 25
1 **Scriene**: a room-divider fitted with a door; a place for the execution of justice at x 37.9.
3–5 Cf. Exod. 22.28: 'Thou shalt not raile upon the Judges, nether speake evil of the ruler of thy people'; cited by Paul, Acts 23.5. Mercilla fulfils Isis's role in suppressing 'forged guile' (vii 7.3).
5 **for**: through.
7 **lewd**: wicked. **compyle**: compose.

Stanza 26
4–9 FONT] FONS *1596, 1609*. For the poet as a good fount – the opposite of a welhed / Of euill words – compare S.'s praise of Chaucer as a 'well of English vndefyled' (IV ii 32.8) and the 'pure well head of Poesie' (VII vii 9.4). The poet as maker is suggested by Fr. *font*; here evil maker. Two claimants have been proposed for **Malfont**: Ulpian Fulwell, punning on 'foul well' (Gough) and Richard Verstegan, a printer with a bad font (Neill, *Var.* v 321). **raced**: erased.

27

They passing by, were guyded by degree
  Vnto the presence of that gratious Queene:
  Who sate on high, that she might all men see,
  And might of all men royally be seene,
  Vpon a throne of gold full bright and sheene,
  Adorned all with gemmes of endlesse price,
  As either might for wealth haue gotten bene,
  Or could be fram'd by workmans rare deuice;
And all embost with Lyons and with Flourdelice.

28

All ouer her a cloth of state was spred,
  Not of rich tissew, nor of cloth of gold,
  Nor of ought else, that may be richest red,
  But like a cloud, as likest may be told,
  That her brode spreading wings did wyde vnfold;
  Whose skirts were bordred with bright sunny beams,
  Glistring like gold, amongst the plights enrold,
  And here and there shooting forth siluer streames, (gleames,
Mongst which crept litle Angels through the glittering

29

Seemed those litle Angels did vphold
  The cloth of state, and on their purpled wings
  Did beare the pendants, through their nimblesse bold:
  Besides a thousand more of such, as sings
  Hymnes to high God, and carols heauenly things,
  Encompassed the throne, on which she sate:
  She Angel-like, the heyre of ancient kings
  And mightie Conquerors, in royall state,
Whylest kings and kesars at her feet did them prostrate.

30

Thus she did sit in souerayne Maiestie,
  Holding a Scepter in her royall hand,
  The sacred pledge of peace and clemencie,
  With which high God had blest her happie land,
  Maugre so many foes, which did withstand.
  But at her feet her sword was likewise layde,
  Whose long rest rusted the bright steely brand;
  Yet when as foes enforst, or friends sought ayde,
She could it sternely draw, that all the world dismayde.

Stanza 27
5   **throne of gold**: cf. God's mercy-seat of pure gold which covers the Ark of the Covenant, Exod. 25. 17–8. Its two cherubim, whose wings stretch across the seat, are linked with the angels who vphold the canopy of state in the next stanza. **sheene**: shining.
6   **price**: worth.
9   Mercilla displays the royal arms of England and France. Northrop (1969) 281 claims that Mercilla's court is Parliament, the highest court of justice in the land and the image of sovereignty in England. In Northrop (1973), he notes similarities in the physical descriptions of the setting. Parliament was called on 29 October 1586 to try Mary Queen of Scots; see 38–50n.

Stanzas 28–29
The imagery is scriptural. Cf. Ps. 97.2: 'Cloudes and darkenes are round about him: righteousnes and judgement are the fundation of his throne.' The image of the cloud derives from the cloud of glory in which God appeared to Moses and in which Christ will appear to judge the earth. Aptekar (1969) 72–5 compares Jove's cloud throne. Strong (1963) 41 notes that the symbolism of Elizabeth's state portraits 'is that of the virtue, peace, and justice of an imperial golden age – not just for England alone – but, in the hands of the poets and visionaries, for the whole world'.

Stanza 28
1–4   Over Lucifera's throne 'a cloth of State was spred' (I iv 8.1).   **tissew**: a rich cloth interwoven with gold.   **red**: imagined. The angels declare divine support for Elizabeth.
7   **plights**: pleats.

Stanza 29
3   **pendants**: ornamental fringe. As a technical term in architecture and dress, it applies both to the cloud canopy and to the canopy as a princely garment; noted Bender (1972) 161. **nimblesse**: nimbleness.
4–6   Cf. Rev. 7.11: 'And all the Angels stode rounde about the throne . . . and worshiped God'; also Rev. 14.2–3, Isaiah 6.1–3.
8   **state**: high rank; throne.
9   Cf. Rev. 4.10: 'The foure and twentie elders fell downe before him that sate on the throne.'

Stanza 30
5   **Maugre**: despite.
6–9   Nelson (1965) suggests that Elizabeth kept a rusty sword as a symbol of her peaceful reign and unused strength. The **long rest** (7) had extended from 1569 when the Rising of the North was suppressed. The sword seems to be the sword of justice rather than the curtana, the sword of mercy, with which Elizabeth was invested at her coronation. The latter appears in the Portland portrait, in Strong (1963) plate xi.

Stanzas 31–32
The Litæ, Jove's daughters and Homer's personification of prayer (*Iliad* ix 502–12), are conflated with Hesiod's Horae (*Theog.* 901–2). Lotspeich (1932) notes that Comes relates both the Litæ and the Hours to prayers. S. may recall that the Litæ wander after Ate to undo her mischief; here, in contrast, they surround **Mercilla** when Ate is brought in. Cf. VII vii 45 where the Horae serve as porters of heaven's gate.

31

And round about, before her feet there sate
  A beuie of faire Virgins clad in white,
  That goodly seem'd t'adorne her royall state,
  All louely daughters of high *Ioue*, that hight
  Litæ, by him begot in loues delight,
  Vpon the righteous *Themis*: those they say
  Vpon *Ioues* iudgement seat wayt day and night,
  And when in wrath he threats the worlds decay,
They doe his anger calme, and cruell vengeance stay.

32

They also doe by his diuine permission
  Vpon the thrones of mortall Princes tend,
  And often treat for pardon and remission
  To suppliants, through frayltie which offend.
  Those did vpon *Mercillaes* throne attend:
  Iust *Dice*, wise *Eunomie*, myld *Eirene*,
  And them amongst, her glorie to commend,
  Sate goodly *Temperance* in garments clene,
And sacred *Reuerence*, yborne of heauenly strene.

33

Thus did she sit in royall rich estate,
  Admyr'd of many, honoured of all,
  Whylest vnderneath her feete, there as she sate,
  An huge great Lyon lay, that mote appall
  An hardie courage, like captiued thrall,
  With a strong yron chaine and coller bound,
  That once he could not moue, nor quich at all;
  Yet did he murmure with rebellious sound,
And softly royne, when saluage choler gan redound.

34

So sitting high in dreaded souerayntie,
  Those two strange knights were to her presence brought;
  Who bowing low before her Maiestie,
  Did to her myld obeysance, as they ought,
  And meekest boone, that they imagine mought.
  To whom she eke inclyning her withall,
  As a faire stoupe of her high soaring thought,
  A chearefull countenance on them let fall,
Yet tempred with some maiestie imperiall.

35

As the bright sunne, what time his fierie teme
  Towards the westerne brim begins to draw,
  Gins to abate the brightnesse of his beme,
  And feruour of his flames somewhat adaw:
  So did this mightie Ladie, when she saw
  Those two strange knights such homage to her make,
  Bate somewhat of that Maiestie and awe,
  That whylome wont to doe so many quake,
And with more myld aspect those two to entertake.

36

Now at that instant, as occasion fell,
  When these two stranger knights arriu'd in place,
  She was about affaires of common wele,
  Dealing of Iustice with indifferent grace,
  And hearing pleas of people meane and base.
  Mongst which as then, there was for to be heard
  The tryall of a great and weightie case,
  Which on both sides was then debating hard:
594 But at the sight of these, those were a while debard.

Stanza 32
6 The order is climactic: just judgment upholds good law, which in turn yields peace, the true end of justice: 'And the worke of justice shalbe peace' (Isaiah 32.17). Dunseath (1968) 211 cites Bodin, *Six Bookes of a Commonweal* (1606), who allegorizes the three daughters of Jove and Themis as three kinds of Justice: 'Upright Law, Equitie, and Peace'. **Iust Dice**: the two words merge into 'Justice', and suggest 'just saying' in contrast to Malfont. Aptekar (1969) 19 compares these three daughters of Jove to God's daughters: Justice, Truth or Righteousness, and Peace, with Mercilla, Mercy, making the fourth. On Elizabeth in relation to the imperial virtues, Justitia and Clementia, see Yates (1947) 67–8. Cf. Gloriana's 'faire peace, and mercy' (II ii 40.9).
7–9 **Temperance** ensures that justice is tempered by mercy: see x 4.5 **strene**: strain, lineage.

Stanza 33
3–9 For the iconography of the monarch seated on the lion as mercy restraining force, see Aptekar (1969) 61–9. She reproduces an emblem from Ripa, *Iconologia*, in which the lion may be interpreted as the power of Justice, or force opposed to Justice, and finds a similar ambiguity in S.'s emblem.
8 **rebellious**] rebellions *1596* suggests force that needs to be chained.
7 **quich**: stir; implies rebellious stirring (see *OED* 4c).
9 **royne**: growl. The three quotations cited by *OED* link the term to the lion's roar, prob. after the Fr. *roi*, king. **gan redound**: overflowed.

Stanza 34
2 That Artegall and Arthur are foreign knights is repeatedly emphasized: 21.9, 24.3, 35.6, 36.2, 37.5.
5 **boone**: favour; as the Red Cross Knight 'falling before the Queen of Faries desired a boone (as the manner then was)' (*LR*). Or 'service' (*OED* 6); cf. 'homage' (35.6).
7 **stoupe**: the swoop of a falcon; fig. condescension.

Stanza 35
2 **brim**: edge, horizon; sea.
4 **adaw**: subdue, as its flames are extinguished in the sea.
8 **doe**: make.
9 **entertake**: receive.

Stanza 36
4 Cf. Book of Common Prayer: 'that they may truly and indifferently minister Justice'. **indifferent**: impartial.
9 **these**: the two knights.

37

But after all her princely entertayne,
    To th'hearing of that former cause in hand,
    Her selfe eftsoones she gan conuert againe;
    Which that those knights likewise mote vnderstand,
    And witnesse forth aright in forrain land,
    Taking them vp vnto her stately throne,
    Where they mote heare the matter throughly scand
On either part, she placed th'one on th'one,
The other on the other side, and neare them none.

38

Then was there brought, as prisoner to the barre,
    A Ladie of great countenance and place,
    But that she it with foule abuse did marre;
    Yet did appeare rare beautie in her face,
    But blotted with condition vile and base,
    That all her other honour did obscure,
    And titles of nobilitie deface:
Yet in that wretched semblant, she did sure
The peoples great compassion vnto her allure.

39

Then vp arose a person of deepe reach,
    And rare in-sight, hard matters to reuele;
    That well could charme his tongue, and time his speach
    To all assayes; his name was called Zele:
    He gan that Ladie strongly to appele
    Of many haynous crymes, by her enured,
    And with sharpe reasons rang her such a pele,
    That those, whom she to pitie had allured,
He now t'abhorre and loath her person had procured.

40

First gan he tell, how this that seem'd so faire
    And royally arayd, Duessa hight
    That false Duessa, which had wrought great care,
    And mickle mischiefe vnto many a knight,
    By her beguyled, and confounded quight:
    But not for those she now in question came,
    Though also those mote question'd be aright,
    But for vyld treasons, and outrageous shame,
Which she against the dred Mercilla oft did frame.

41

For she whylome (as ye mote yet right well
    Remember) had her counsels false conspyred,
    With faithlesse Blandamour and Paridell,
    (Both two her paramours, both by her hyred,
    And both with hope of shadowes vaine inspyred,)
    And with them practiz'd, how for to depryue
    Mercilla of her crowne, by her aspyred,
    That she might it vnto her selfe deryue,
And tryumph in their blood, whom she to death did dryue.

Stanza 37
1   **entertayne**: reception.
3   **conuert**: turn; suggests a change of role from Queen to Judge.
5   **witnesse forth aright**: bear witness to the justice of her proceedings; **forth** may belong to the verb or signify 'abroad'.
8–9   She places Arthur on one side of her and Artegall on the other. Their positions on either side of Mercilla suggest Astræa holding the scales of Justice. Fowler (1964) 197 notices that she balances their virtues of Justitia and Clementia; see 32.6n. The Bishops' Bible (1572) shows Elizabeth flanked by Justice and Mercy. Balance is shown when Arthur pities the accused while Artegall remains firm. Only when Arthur withdraws 'from her [Duessa's] partie' (49.3) may judgment be passed.

Stanzas 38–50
James VI complained to Lord Burghley that this episode contained 'some dishonorable effects (as the k. demeth thereof) against himself and his mother [Mary Queen of Scots] deceassed . . . [and] still desyreth that Edward Spencer for his faulte, may be dewly tryed and punished' (cited Carpenter, 1923, 41–2). See Neill (1935). Phillips (1964) 202 concludes that S. offers 'little more than a highly poetic version of officially condoned Protestant literature'. Northrop (1969) shows how S. defends Elizabeth's conduct of the trial.

Stanza 38
2   **countenance**: position, reflected in her bearing.
5   **condition**: behaviour.
8   **semblant**: outward appearance.

Stanza 39
3   **charme his tongue**: tune his tongue to fascinate auditors. Malengin's ability (cf. 13.2) is now used for just purposes.
4   **assayes**: occasions.   Zele expresses Artegall's zeal for justice; cf. his 'zeale of vengeance' at i 14.7. Cf. Milton on Zeal, 'whose substance is ethereal, arming in compleat diamond ascends his fiery Chariot drawn with two blazing Meteors . . . . Thus did the true Prophets of old combat with the false; thus Christ himselfe the fountaine of meeknesse found acrimony anough' (Apology against a pamphlet, Prose Works i 900).
5   **appele**: accuse.
6   **enured**: committed.
9   **procured**: caused.

Stanza 40
3   **care**: trouble, grief.
5   **confounded**: destroyed.
6–9   'The commission by which Mary was tried was not empowered to deal with anything that had occurred before 1585. . . . Mary was charged only with having "conspired the destruction of the Queen of England and the subversion of religion" ' (Gough, 1921).

Stanza 41
1–2   Cf. Duessa in Book I, and her relationship with Blandamour and Paridell beginning at IV i 32.
6   **practiz'd**: schemed.
8   **deryue**: transfer; in the legal sense, 'convey by right of descent', as the political allegory suggests.

42

But through high heauens grace, which fauour not
　　The wicked driftes of trayterous desynes,
　　Gainst loiall Princes, all this cursed plot,
　　Ere proofe it tooke, discouered was betymes,
　　And th'actours won the meede meet for their crymes.
　　Such be the meede of all, that by such mene
　　Vnto the type of kingdomes title clymes.
But false *Duessa* now vntitled Queene,
Was brought to her sad doome, as here was to be seene.

43

Strongly did *Zele* her haynous fact enforce,
　　And many other crimes of foule defame
　　Against her brought, to banish all remorse,
　　And aggrauate the horror of her blame.
　　And with him to make part against her, came
　　Many graue persons, that against her pled;
　　First was a sage old Syre, that had to name
　　The *Kingdomes care*, with a white siluer hed,
That many high regards and reasons gainst her red.

44

Then gan *Authority* her to appose
　　With peremptorie powre, that made all mute;
　　And then the law of *Nations* gainst her rose,
　　And reasons brought, that no man could refute;
　　Next gan *Religion* gainst her to impute
　　High Gods beheast, and powre of holy lawes;
　　Then gan the Peoples cry and Commons sute,
　　Importune care of their owne publicke cause;
And lastly *Iustice* charged her with breach of lawes.

45

But then for her, on the contrarie part,
　　Rose many aduocates for her to plead:
　　First there came *Pittie*, with full tender hart,
　　And with her ioyn'd *Regard* of womanhead;
　　And then came *Daunger* threatning hidden dread,
　　And high alliance vnto forren powre;
　　Then came *Nobilitie* of birth, that bread
　　Great ruth through her misfortunes tragicke stowre;
And lastly *Griefe* did plead, and many teares forth powre.

46

With the neare touch whereof in tender hart
　　The Briton Prince was sore empassionate,
　　And woxe inclined much vnto her part,
　　Through the sad terror of so dreadfull fate,
　　And wretched ruine of so high estate,
　　That for great ruth his courage gan relent.
　　Which when as *Zele* perceiued to abate,
　　He gan his earnest feruour to augment,
And many fearefull obiects to them to present.

47

He gan t'efforce the euidence anew,
　　And new accusements to produce in place:
　　He brought forth that old hag of hellish hew,
　　The cursed *Ate*, brought her face to face,
　　Who priuie was, and partie in the case:
　　She, glad of spoyle and ruinous decay,
　　Did her appeach, and to her more disgrace,
　　The plot of all her practise did display,
And all her traynes, and all her treasons forth did lay.

Stanza 42
2　**driftes**: aims.
3　**loiall**: implies that princes must remain loyal to God's law.
4　**proofe**: effect.
5　**actours**: authors; a sixteenth-century spelling.
6　**mene**: means.
7　**type**: highest point.
8　**vntitled Queene**: in answer to the claim that Mary was a queen and therefore above the law; noted Northrop (1969) 281.

Stanza 43
1　**fact**: crime.
2　**defame**: infamy.
7–9　**Kingdomes care** is separated from the other advocates, supporting Upton's (1758) suggestion that the figure alludes to the aged Burleigh, the Lord Treasurer.　**high regards**: matters of great importance.　**red**: declared.

Stanza 44
Gough (1921) notes the historical matter behind four of these five advocates: **Authority**, the act of 1584, which provided penalties against any attempt upon the Queen's person, gave the authority by which Mary Queen of Scots could be put on trial; **the law of Nations** was transgressed when Mary joined a conspiracy against Elizabeth, the head of a foreign state; **Religion** needed Mary's death to protect the Protestant faith; and the **Commons** twice petitioned Elizabeth to have Mary put to death.
1　**appose**: examine; oppose.
5　**impute**: adduce.
6, 9　The rule against repetition of a rhyme word with the same meaning suggests that **holy lawes** are distinct from **lawes**.

Stanza 45
Dunseath (1968) 217 claims (not quite accurately) that five reasons against Duessa balance five in her favour: '*Kingdomes care*': **Pittie**; '*Authority*': **Regard of womanhead**; 'the law of *Nations*': **Daunger** (of foreign power); the 'Commons': **Nobilitie**. Her defence opens and concludes weakly in an appeal for pity and a show of **Griefe**. The balance suggests that the arguments against her by '*Religion*' cannot be answered.
8　**stowre**: time of distress.

Stanza 46
Arthur is affected by the first two and the last two advocates, 'For pitee renneth soone in gentil herte' (Chaucer, *Knight's Tale* 1761).
1　**neare touch**: deep impression, as Mercilla is 'touched nere' (50.1).

Stanza 47
1　**efforce**: urge more strongly.
2　**accusements**: accusations.
3–9　Cf. IV i 19. Duessa is condemned through evidence brought by the spirit she herself raised from hell.　**hew**: form. **appeach**: accuse.　**practise**: treachery.　**traynes**: plots.

48

Then brought he forth, with griesly grim aspect,
　Abhorred *Murder*, who with bloudie knyfe
　Yet dropping fresh in hand did her detect,
　And there with guiltie bloudshed charged ryfe:
　Then brought he forth *Sedition*, breeding stryfe
　In troublous wits, and mutinous vprore:
　Then brought he forth *Incontinence* of lyfe,
　Euen foule *Adulterie* her face before,
And lewd *Impietie*, that her accused sore.

49

All which when as the Prince had heard and seene,
　His former fancies ruth he gan repent,
　And from her partie eftsoones was drawn cleene.
　But *Artegall* with constant firme intent,
　For zeale of Iustice was against her bent.
　So was she guiltie deemed of them all.
　Then *Zele* began to vrge her punishment,
　And to their Queene for iudgement loudly call,
Vnto *Mercilla* myld for Iustice gainst the thrall.

50

But she, whose Princely breast was touched nere
　With piteous ruth of her so wretched plight,
　Though plaine she saw by all, that she did heare,
　That she of death was guiltie found by right,
　Yet would not let iust vengeance on her light;
　But rather let in stead thereof to fall
　Few perling drops from her faire lampes of light;
　The which she couering with her purple pall
Would haue the passion hid, and vp arose withall.

Cant. X.

*Prince Arthur takes the enterprize
for Belge for to fight.
Gerioneos Seneschall
he slayes in Belges right.*

1

SOme Clarkes doe doubt in their deuicefull art,
　Whether this heauenly thing, whereof I treat,
　To weeten *Mercie*, be of Iustice part,
　Or drawne forth from her by diuine extreate.
　This well I wote, that sure she is as great,
　And meriteth to haue as high a place,
　Sith in th'Almighties euerlasting seat
　She first was bred, and borne of heauenly race;
From thence pour'd down on men, by influence of grace.

2

For if that Vertue be of so great might,
　Which from iust verdict will for nothing start,
　But to preserue inuiolated right,
　Oft spilles the principall, to saue the part;
　So much more then is that of powre and art,
　That seekes to saue the subiect of her skill,
　Yet neuer doth from doome of right depart:
　As it is greater prayse to saue, then spill,
And better to reforme, then to cut off the ill.

3

Who then can thee, *Mercilla*, throughly prayse,
　That herein doest all earthly Princes pas?
　What heauenly Muse shall thy great honour rayse
　Vp to the skies, whence first deriu'd it was,
　And now on earth it selfe enlarged has,
　From th'vtmost brinke of the *Armericke* shore,
　Vnto the margent of the *Molucas*?
　Those Nations farre thy iustice doe adore:
But thine owne people do thy mercy prayse much more.

Stanza 48
An additional five advocates testify against Duessa. Gough (1921) cites Mary's complicity in her husband's murder, her involvement in plots to overthrow the English government, and the charges against her sinful life. Neill (1935) 212 cites the complaint of the Commons against Mary, that she 'hath heaped up together all the Sins of the Licentious sons of *David*, Adulteries, Murders, Conspiracies, Treasons, and Blasphemies against God'.
3   **detect**: expose.

Stanza 50
1–2   As Arthur, 46.1–2.
4   **guiltie**: deserving.
8   **purple pall**: robe of state. Although in her private person she grieves for Mary's death, as Queen she conceals her grief and allows the execution to take place; cf. x 4.5–9. The breaking of this episode by the ending of the canto notes Elizabeth's delay in allowing justice to proceed, the interval of three months being marked by three stanzas.

Canto x

Stanza 1
1–4   Tuve (1966) 67 argues that in the medieval scheme of virtues Misericordia was commonly one of the faces of Justice. On their conflict and reconciliation, see Chew (1947) 35f. As a poet, S. gives short shrift to the philosophical debate and turns to what he knows to be true.   **Clarkes**: scholars. **deuicefull**: cunning.   **extreate**: extraction; from the Lat. *extracta*, as **drawne forth** suggests.
7–9   God's throne is his mercy-seat: Exod. 25.22; cf. Isaiah 16.5: 'And in mercie shal the throne be prepared, and he shal sit upon it in stedfastnes.'
9   As love which the heavens 'pourd into men' (III iii 1.4). **influence**: infusion, literally inflowing.

Stanza 2
2   **start**: swerve.
4   **principall**: chief thing.

Stanza 3
6   **Armericke**: 'Americke' sugg. Todd (1805); not Armoric or Britanny. The sixteenth-century spelling 'America' is noted in *Var*. v 248.
7   **Molucas**: the Moluccas or Spice Islands.

4

Much more it praysed was of those two knights;
  The noble Prince, and righteous *Artegall*,
  When they had seene and heard her doome a rights
Against *Duessa*, damned by them all;
  But by her tempred without griefe or gall,
  Till strong constraint did her thereto enforce.
And yet euen then ruing her wilfull fall,
  With more then needfull naturall remorse,
And yeelding the last honour to her wretched corse.

5

During all which, those knights continu'd there,
  Both doing and receiuing curtesies,
  Of that great Ladie, who with goodly chere
Them entertayn'd, fit for their dignities,
  Approuing dayly to their noble eyes
  Royall examples of her mercies rare,
And worthie paterns of her clemencies;
  Which till this day mongst many liuing are,
Who them to their posterities doe still declare.

6

Amongst the rest, which in that space befell,
  There came two Springals of full tender yeares,
  Farre thence from forrein land, where they did dwell,
To seeke for succour of her and of her Peares,
  With humble prayers and intreatfull teares;
  Sent by their mother, who a widow was,
Wrapt in great dolours and in deadly feares,
  By a strong Tyrant, who inuaded has
Her land, and slaine her children ruefully alas.

7

Her name was *Belge*, who in former age
  A Ladie of great worth and wealth had beene,
  And mother of a frutefull heritage,
Euen seuenteene goodly sonnes; which who had seene
  In their first flowre, before this fatall teene
  Them ouertooke, and their faire blossomes blasted,
More happie mother would her surely weene,
  Then famous *Niobe*, before she tasted
Latonaes childrens wrath, that all her issue wasted.

8

But this fell Tyrant, through his tortious powre,
  Had left her now but fiue of all that brood:
  For twelue of them he did by times deuoure,
And to his Idols sacrifice their blood,
  Whylest he of none was stopped, nor withstood.
  For soothly he was one of matchlesse might,
Of horrible aspect, and dreadfull mood,
  And had three bodies in one wast empight,
And th'armes and legs of three, to succour him in fight.

Stanza 4
3 **a rights**: suggests that they heard Mercilla's judgment aright, and implies their approval of her righteous judgment.
5 **griefe**: anger.
6 **thereto**: i.e. to chop off her head.

Stanza 5
5 **Approuing**: showing for their approval.

Stanza 6
2 **Springals**: youths.
4 **Peares**: referring to her nobility, or to Artegall and Arthur who are her equals in rank.
5 **intreatfull**: full of entreaty.
6 The concept of a desolate city or country as a widow is biblical: cf. Lament. 1.1.
8 **Tyrant**: Geryoneo shares this title in Book V with Grantorto.
9 **ruefully**: in a pitiable fashion.

Stanza 7
1–4 In the historical allegory, **Belge**, from Lat. *Belgae*, refers to the Low Countries, and her seventeen sons to the seventeen provinces suffering under the tyranny of Philip II of Spain. The five unconquered provinces formed the United Provinces. The 'two Springals' are Holland and Zealand which sought England's assistance. Strong and van Dorsten (1964) 2 observe that 'these political realities are transmuted in the language of the renaissance chivalrous epic into those of a universal morality'. Contemporary law allowed that the ruler who possessed the land justly, as Philip did the Netherlands, but ruled as a tyrant might be opposed by a foreign prince though not by his own subjects; see Northrop (1969). Hence English intervention in the Netherlands was justified while, in the Burbon episode (see xi 44–65 and *n*), Spanish intervention in France was not.
5 **teene**: harm, affliction.
7–9 See IV vii 30.5–9*n*. **More happie** than Niobe because she had seventeen sons against Niobe's seven sons and seven daughters.

Stanza 8
1 **tortious**: wrongful.
3 **by times**: from time to time.
4 **Idols**: 'Idol' sugg. Church (1758); cf. 13.8, etc.
8–9 Historically, the three kingdoms of Spain. Cf. the Satanic trinity: Geryoneo, the Seneschal, and the Dragon under the altar; also the three evil knights, 34.1; cf. xi 6.2.
empight: implanted.

Stanzas 9–10
Comes (1616) VII i p. 362 provides most of the information in these stanzas. **Geryon** is evil because he is associated with Spain and Spanish tyranny, because he is an enemy of Hercules who supplies the pattern for the hero's labours in Book V, and perhaps because he is the guardian of the fraudulent in Dante, *Inf.* xvii. Aptekar (1969) 146–9 notes that in the emblem books **Geryon** symbolizes concord and united force. In contrast, Geryoneo (11.1) 'represents a perversion or demonic parody of the power of just concord'.

9

And sooth they say, that he was borne and bred
  Of Gyants race, the sonne of *Geryon*,
He that whylome in Spaine so sore was dred,
  For his huge powre and great oppression,
  Which brought that land to his subiection,
  Through his three bodies powre, in one combynd;
  And eke all strangers in that region
  Arryuing, to his kyne for food assynd;
The fayrest kyne aliue, but of the fiercest kynd.

10

For they were all, they say, of purple hew,
  Kept by a cowheard, hight *Eurytion*,
A cruell carle, the which all strangers slew,
  Ne day nor night did sleepe, t'attend them on,
  But walkt about them euer and anone,
  With his two headed dogge, that *Orthrus* hight;
  Orthrus begotten by great *Typhaon*,
  And foule *Echidna*, in the house of night;
But *Hercules* them all did ouercome in fight.

11

His sonne was this, *Geryoneo* hight,
  Who after that his monstrous father fell
Vnder *Alcides* club, streight tooke his flight
  From that sad land, where he his syre did quell,
  And came to this, where *Belge* then did dwell,
  And flourish in all wealth and happinesse,
  Being then new made widow (as befell)
  After her Noble husbands late decesse;
Which gaue beginning to her woe and wretchednesse.

12

Then this bold Tyrant, of her widowhed
  Taking aduantage, and her yet fresh woes,
Himselfe and seruice to her offered,
  Her to defend against all forrein foes,
  That should their powre against her right oppose.
  Whereof she glad, now needing strong defence,
  Him entertayn'd, and did her champion chose:
  Which long he vsd with carefull diligence,
The better to confirme her fearelesse confidence.

13

By meanes whereof, she did at last commit
  All to his hands, and gaue him soueraine powre
To doe, what euer he thought good or fit.
  Which hauing got, he gan forth from that howre
  To stirre vp strife, and many a Tragicke stowre,
  Giuing her dearest children one by one
  Vnto a dreadfull Monster to deuoure,
  And setting vp an Idole of his owne,
The image of his monstrous parent *Geryone*.

14

So tyrannizing, and oppressing all,
  The woefull widow had no meanes now left,
But vnto gratious great *Mercilla* call
  For ayde, against that cruell Tyrants theft,
  Ere all her children he from her had reft.
  Therefore these two, her eldest sonnes she sent,
  To seeke for succour of this Ladies gieft:
  To whom their sute they humbly did present,
In th'hearing of full many Knights and Ladies gent.

15

Amongst the which then fortuned to bee
  The noble Briton Prince, with his braue Peare;
Who when he none of all those knights did see
  Hastily bent, that enterprise to heare,
  Nor vndertake the same, for cowheard feare,
  He stepped forth with courage bold and great,
  Admyr'd of all the rest in presence there,
  And humbly gan that mightie Queene entreat,
To graunt him that aduenture for his former feat.

16

She gladly graunted it: then he straight way
  Himselfe vnto his iourney gan prepare,
And all his armours readie dight that day,
  That nought the morrow next mote stay his fare.
  The morrow next appear'd, with purple hayre
  Yet dropping fresh out of the *Indian* fount,
  And bringing light into the heauens fayre,
  When he was readie to his steede to mount,
Vnto his way, which now was all his care and count.

Stanza 10
1 purple: crimson, the royal colour, as they belong to the king; also terrifying in appearance.
6–8 Anticipating the Blatant Beast, xii 37.7, also an offspring of **Typhaon** and **Echidna**; cf. VI vi 9.9–12.2.

Stanza 11
1 this: i.e. 'this fell Tyrant' (8.1). **Geryoneo**: suggests 'Geryon-anew'.
6 wealth: well-being.
8 decesse: decease.

Stanza 13
5 stowre: time of distress.

Stanza 14
7 gieft: gift: giving.
9 gent: high-born, gracious.

Stanza 15
2 Peare: companion; equal; see i 3.2n.
5 The pressure of historical allegory may explain this failure to respond; cf. viii 18.6–9.
9 for his former feat: i.e. as a reward for defeating the Souldan; unless former implies 'first'.

Stanza 16
Arthur prepares to fulfil Merlin's prophecy of the time when 'a royall virgin . . . shall / Stretch her white rod ouer the *Belgicke* shore' (III iii 49.6–7).
4 fare: going.
9 count: consideration.

599

17

Then taking humble leaue of that great Queene,
　Who gaue him roiall giftes and riches rare,
　As tokens of her thankefull mind beseene,
　And leauing *Artegall* to his owne care,
　Vpon his voyage forth he gan to fare,
　With those two gentle youthes, which him did guide,
　And all his way before him still prepare.
　Ne after him did *Artegall* abide,
But on his first aduenture forward forth did ride.

18

It was not long, till that the Prince arriued
　Within the land, where dwelt that Ladie sad,
　Whereof that Tyrant had her now depriued,
　And into moores and marshes banisht had,
　Out of the pleasant soyle, and citties glad,
　In which she wont to harbour happily:
　But now his cruelty so sore she drad,
　That to those fennes for fastnesse she did fly,
And there her selfe did hyde from his hard tyranny.

19

There he her found in sorrow and dismay,
　All solitarie without liuing wight;
　For all her other children, through affray,
　Had hid themselues, or taken further flight:
　And eke her selfe through sudden strange affright,
　When one in armes she saw, began to fly;
　But when her owne two sonnes she had in sight,
　She gan take hart, and looke vp ioyfully:
For well she wist this knight came, succour to supply.

20

And running vnto them with greedy ioyes,
　Fell straight about their neckes, as they did kneele,
　And bursting forth in teares; Ah my sweet boyes,
　(Sayd she) yet now I gin new life to feele,
　And feeble spirits, that gan faint and reele,
　Now rise againe, at this your ioyous sight.
　Alreadie seemes that fortunes headlong wheele
　Begins to turne, and sunne to shine more bright,
Then it was wont, through comfort of this noble knight.

21

Then turning vnto him; And you Sir knight
　(Said she) that taken haue this toylesome paine
　For wretched woman, miserable wight,
　May you in heauen immortall guerdon gaine
　For so great trauell, as you doe sustaine:
　For other meede may hope for none of mee,
　To whom nought else, but bare life doth remaine,
　And that so wretched one, as ye do see
Is liker lingring death, then loathed life to bee.

22

Much was he moued with her piteous plight,
　And low dismounting from his loftie steede,
　Gan to recomfort her all that he might,
　Seeking to driue away deepe rooted dreede,
　With hope of helpe in that her greatest neede.
　So thence he wished her with him to wend,
　Vnto some place, where they mote rest and feede,
　And she take comfort, which God now did send:
Good hart in euils doth the euils much amend.

23

Ay me (sayd she) and whether shall I goe?
　Are not all places full of forraine powres?
　My pallaces possessed of my foe,
　My cities sackt, and their sky-threating towres
　Raced, and made smooth fields now full of flowres?
　Onely these marishes, and myrie bogs,
　In which the fearefull ewftes do build their bowres,
　Yeeld me an hostry mongst the croking frogs,
And harbour here in safety from those rauenous dogs.

24

Nathlesse (said he) deare Ladie with me goe,
　Some place shall vs receiue, and harbour yield;
　If not, we will it force, maugre your foe,
　And purchase it to vs with speare and shield:
　And if all fayle, yet farewell open field:
　The earth to all her creatures lodging lends.
　With such his chearefull speaches he doth wield
　Her mind so well, that to his will she bends
And bynding vp her locks and weeds, forth with him wends

Stanza 17
3　beseene: provided; perhaps simply, 'to be seen'.

Stanza 18
8　fastnesse: security.

Stanza 19
3　affray: terror.

Stanza 20
7–8　fortunes headlong wheele . . . : i.e. Fortune's wheel
begins to turn impetuously.

Stanza 21
5　trauell: travail.
6　other meede . . . none of mee: no one may hope for
reward from me.

Stanza 22
3　recomfort: console.
4　Gough (1921) notes that the Dutch regarded the arrival
of the English forces with suspicion.

Stanza 23
5　Raced: razed.
6　marishes: marshes.
7　ewftes: efts or newts.
8　hostry: lodging.

Stanza 24
4　purchase: gain by conquest.
5–6　If we fail in our assault upon the city, we may fare well
in the field of battle; or, welcome the open field. Or, if we fail
in the field of battle, we shall resort to guerilla warfare in the
country.
7　wield: direct, sway.

25

They came vnto a Citie farre vp land,
  The which whylome that Ladies owne had bene;
  But now by force extort out of her hand,
  By her strong foe, who had defaced cleene
  Her stately towres, and buildings sunny sheene;
  Shut vp her hauen, mard her marchants trade,
  Robbed her people, that full rich had beene,
  And in her necke a Castle huge had made,
The which did her commaund, without needing perswade.

26

That Castle was the strength of all that state,
  Vntill that state by strength was pulled downe,
  And that same citie, so now ruinate,
  Had bene the keye of all that kingdomes crowne;
  Both goodly Castle, and both goodly Towne,
  Till that th'offended heauens list to lowre
  Vpon their blisse, and balefull fortune frowne.
  When those gainst states and kingdomes do coniure,
Who then can thinke their hedlong ruine to recure.

27

But he had brought it now in seruile bond,
  And made it beare the yoke of inquisition,
  Stryuing long time in vaine it to withstond;
  Yet glad at last to make most base submission,
  And life enioy for any composition.
  So now he hath new lawes and orders new
  Imposd on it, with many a hard condition,
  And forced it, the honour that is dew
To God, to doe vnto his Idole most vntrew.

28

To him he hath, before this Castle greene,
  Built a faire Chappell, and an Altar framed
  Of costly Iuory, full rich beseene,
  On which that cursed Idole farre proclamed,
  He hath set vp, and him his God hath named,
  Offring to him in sinfull sacrifice
  The flesh of men, to Gods owne likenesse framed,
  And powring forth their bloud in brutishe wize,
That any yron eyes to see it would agrize.

29

And for more horror and more crueltie,
  Vnder that cursed Idols altar stone
  An hideous monster doth in darknesse lie,
  Whose dreadfull shape was neuer seene of none
  That liues on earth; but vnto those alone
  The which vnto him sacrificed bee.
  Those he deuoures, they say, both flesh and bone:
  What else they haue, is all the Tyrants fee;
So that no whit of them remayning one may see.

30

There eke he placed a strong garrisone,
  And set a Seneschall of dreaded might,
  That by his powre oppressed euery one,
  And vanquished all ventrous knights in fight;
  To whom he wont shew all the shame he might,
  After that them in battell he had wonne.
  To which when now they gan approch in sight,
  The Ladie counseld him the place to shonne,
Whereas so many knights had fouly bene fordonne.

31

Her fearefull speaches nought he did regard,
  But ryding streight vnder the Castle wall,
  Called aloud vnto the watchfull ward,
  Which there did wayte, willing them forth to call
  Into the field their Tyrants Seneschall.
  To whom when tydings thereof came, he streight
  Cals for his armes, and arming him withall,
  Eftsoones forth pricked proudly in his might,
And gan with courage fierce addresse him to the fight.

Stanza 25
Gough (1921) notes that the phrasing is determined by historical reference: the **Citie** is Antwerp which lies about fifty miles from the mouth of the Scheldt. Before the war it was the wealthiest city in Europe. It was besieged by the Spanish, its houses burned, and access to it closed. An immense citadel was built on the river by the Duke of Alva in 1567 to keep the city in subjection.
3   **extort**: extorted, literally 'twisted out'.

Stanza 26
1–2   'The citadel of Antwerp was the defence of the country, until the country was ruined by Spanish misrule' (Gough, 1921).
3   **so now**: 'now so' sugg. Church (1758).   **ruinate**: reduced to ruins.
4   **crowne**: dominion.
8   **coniure**: conspire.
9   **recure**: remedy, i.e. prevent.

Stanza 27
2   **inquisition**: specifically, the Papal Inquisition.
5   **composition**: agreement; specifically, terms of surrender.

Stanzas 28–29
The substance is repeated at xi 19–20.

Stanza 28
2–4   The capitals may conceal an anagram or point to specific historical reference, e.g. the **Chappell** to the Roman Catholic worship, and the **Idole** to the Host, as Gough (1921) suggests.
3   **beseene**: adorned.
9   **agrize**: horrify.

Stanza 29
8   **fee**: property.

Stanza 30
2   **Seneschall**: a steward who administers justice; here the Spanish-appointed Regent of the Netherlands.
6   **wonne**: defeated.
9   **fordonne**: ruined; killed.

32

They both encounter in the middle plaine,
  And their sharpe speares doe both together smite
  Amid their shields, with so huge might and maine,
  That seem'd their soules they wold haue ryuen quight
  Out of their breasts, with furious despight.
  Yet could the Seneschals no entrance find
  Into the Princes shield, where it empight;
  So pure the mettall was, and well refynd,
But shiuered all about, and scattered in the wynd.

33

Not so the Princes, but with restlesse force,
  Into his shield it readie passage found,
  Both through his haberieon, and eke his corse:
  Which tombling downe vpon the senselesse ground,
  Gaue leaue vnto his ghost from thraldome bound,
  To wander in the griesly shades of night.
  There did the Prince him leaue in deadly swound,
  And thence vnto the castle marched right,
To see if entrance there as yet obtaine he might.

34

But as he nigher drew, three knights he spyde,
  All arm'd to point, issuing forth a pace,
  Which towards him with all their powre did ryde,
  And meeting him right in the middle race,
  Did all their speares attonce on him enchace.
  As three great Culuerings for battrie bent,
  And leueld all against one certaine place,
  Doe all attonce their thunders rage forth rent,
That makes the wals to stagger with astonishment.

35

So all attonce they on the Prince did thonder;
  Who from his saddle swarued nought asyde,
  Ne to their force gaue way, that was great wonder,
  But like a bulwarke, firmely did abyde,
  Rebutting him, which in the midst did ryde,
  With so huge rigour, that his mortall speare
  Past through his shield, and pierst through either syde,
  That downe he fell vppon his mother deare,
And powred forth his wretched life in deadly dreare.

36

Whom when his other fellowes saw, they fled
  As fast as feete could carry them away;
  And after them the Prince as swiftly sped,
  To be aueng'd of their vnknightly play.
  There whilest they entring, th'one did th'other stay,
  The hindmost in the gate he ouerhent,
  And as he pressed in, him there did slay:
  His carkasse tumbling on the threshold, sent
His groning soule vnto her place of punishment.

37

The other which was entred, laboured fast
  To sperre the gate; but that same lumpe of clay,
  Whose grudging ghost was thereout fled and past,
  Right in the middest of the threshold lay,
  That it the Posterne did from closing stay:
  The whiles the Prince hard preased in betweene,
  And entraunce wonne. Streight th'other fled away,
  And ran into the Hall, where he did weene
Him selfe to saue: but he there slew him at the skreene.

38

Then all the rest which in that Castle were,
  Seeing that sad ensample them before,
  Durst not abide, but fled away for feare,
  And them conuayd out at a Posterne dore.
  Long sought the Prince, but when he found no more
  T'oppose against his powre, he forth issued
  Vnto that Lady, where he her had lore,
  And her gan cheare, with what she there had vewed,
And what she had not seene, within vnto her shewed.

Stanzas 32–33
The striking of the shields represents the conflict of religious faiths.

Stanza 32
7   **where it empight**: where it might infix itself.

Stanza 33
1   **restlesse**: not resting, never ceasing; hence resistless.
4   **vpon the senselesse ground**: i.e. senseless upon the ground.
5   **bound**: emphasizes **thraldome**.

Stanza 34
1–5   On the **three knights**, see 8.8–9*n*. The three strike **attonce** (thrice repeated), i.e. as one.
2   **to point**: completely.   **a pace**: apace, quickly.
4   **in the middle race**: in full career.   **race**: the technical term for chivalric encounter on horseback.
5   **enchace**: enclose; or figuratively, 'set'.
6   **Culuerings**: the culverin, a long cannon.
8   **rent**: burst; describing also the effect of the shot.

Stanza 35
6   **rigour**: violence; referring also to his spear's stiffness.
7   **either syde**: i.e. both sides.
9   **dreare**: sorrow; horror; from 'dreary': bloody (cf. I vi 45.5).

Stanza 36
6   **ouerhent**: overtook.

Stanza 37
2   **sperre**: bolt.
3   **grudging**: complaining.
9   **skreene**: see ix 25.1*n*.

Stanza 38
7   **lore**: left.

39

Who with right humble thankes him goodly greeting,
  For so great prowesse, as he there had proued,
  Much greater then was euer in her weeting,
  With great admiraunce inwardly was moued,
  A̅nd honour him, with all that her behoued,
  Thenceforth into that Castle he her led,
  With her two sonnes, right deare of her beloued,
  Where all that night them selues they cherished,
And from her balefull minde all care he banished.

Cant. XI.

*Prince Arthure ouercomes the great
Gerioneo in fight:
Doth slay the Monster, and restore
Belge vnto her right.*

1

IT often fals in course of common life,
  That right long time is ouerborne of wrong,
  Through auarice, or powre, or guile, or strife,
  That weakens her, and makes her party strong:
  But Iustice, though her dome she doe prolong,
  Yet at the last she will her owne cause right.
  As by sad *Belge* seemes, whose wrongs though long
  She suffred, yet at length she did requight,
And sent redresse thereof by this braue Briton Knight.

2

Whereof when newes was to that Tyrant brought,
  How that the Lady *Belge* now had found
  A Champion, that had with his Champion fought,
  And laid his Seneschall low on the ground,
  And eke him selfe did threaten to confound,
  He gan to burne in rage, and friese in feare,
  Doubting sad end of principle vnsound:
  Yet sith he heard but one, that did appeare,
He did him selfe encourage, and take better cheare.

3

Nathelesse him selfe he armed all in hast,
  And forth he far'd with all his many bad,
  Ne stayed step, till that he came at last
  Vnto the Castle, which they conquerd had.
  There with huge terrour, to be more ydrad,
  He sternely marcht before the Castle gate,
  And with bold vaunts, and ydle threatning bad
  Deliuer him his owne, ere yet too late,
To which they had no right, nor any wrongfull state.

4

The Prince staid not his aunswere to deuize,
  But opening streight the Sparre, forth to him came,
  Full nobly mounted in right warlike wize;
  And asked him, if that he were the same,
  Who all that wrong vnto that wofull Dame
  So long had done, and from her natiue land
  Exiled her, that all the world spake sharne.
  He boldly aunswerd him, he there did stand
That would his doings iustifie with his owne hand.

Stanza 39
1 **greeting**: congratulating.
3 **weeting**: knowledge.
4 **admiraunce**: admiration.
8 **cherished**: cheered.
9 **balefull**: sorrowful.

Canto xi

Argument

The *Burbon* episode, 43.6 to 65, is included in the Argument to
Canto xii; see *n*. It may have been an afterthought, having been
taken from Canto xii and inserted into Canto xi after the Book
had been disposed into Cantos, as J. C. Smith (1909) I xiii
suggests. After stanza 36, the catchword 'Canto' appears in the
1596 text to indicate the beginning of a new canto on the next
page. *Var.* v 372 notes that 36.1 provides a suitable beginning
for a Canto. Its historical basis, the recantation by Henry Burbon
(Henry IV) of his Protestant faith, makes its composition later
than July 1593. The Geryoneo episode occupies almost forty-
three stanzas, the same number as the Grantorto episode in
Canto xii. F. B. Evans (1965) offers bibliographical evidence to
suggest that Artegall's meeting with Sergis (37–43) was inserted
into the poem after some of the copy, originally intended at this
point, had been set in type. According to his argument, Canto
xi consisted originally of Arthur's rescue of Belgae (1–35), with
36 added as transition. It seems clear that S. wanted to expand
his text to offer a comprehensive defence of the justice of
Elizabeth's foreign policy in the Netherlands, France, and
Ireland.

Stanza 1
4 **her party**: i.e. the party opposing her.
5 **prolong**: delay.
9 **redresse**: aid, as i 4.4.

Stanza 2
3 **his Champion**: 'his Champions' sugg. Upton (1758), to
agree with x 34. However, the three knights merge, according to
the image of three-in-one in Geryoneo.
7 **Doubting**: fearing. **principle vnsound**: evil beginning.

Stanza 3
2 **many**: company.
9 **state**: title; claim.

Stanza 4
2 **Sparre**: bolt; cf. the verb, x 37.2.

5

With that so furiously at him he flew,
  As if he would haue ouerrun him streight,
  And with his huge great yron axe gan hew
So hideously vppon his armour bright,
  As he to peeces would haue chopt it quight:
  That the bold Prince was forced foote to giue
  To his first rage, and yeeld to his despight;
  The whilest at him so dreadfully he driue,
That seem'd a marble rocke asunder could haue riue.

6

Thereto a great aduauntage eke he has
  Through his three double hands thrise multiplyde,
  Besides the double strength, which in them was:
For stil when fit occasion did betyde,
  He could his weapon shift from side to syde,
  From hand to hand, and with such nimblesse sly
  Could wield about, that ere it were espide,
  The wicked stroke did wound his enemy,
Behinde, beside, before, as he it list apply.

7

Which vncouth vse when as the Prince perceiued,
  He gan to watch the wielding of his hand,
  Least by such slight he were vnwares deceiued;
And euer ere he saw the stroke to land,
  He would it meete, and warily withstand.
  One time, when he his weapon faynd to shift,
  As he was wont, and chang'd from hand to hand,
  He met him with a counterstroke so swift,
That quite smit off his arme, as he it vp did lift.

8

Therewith, all fraught with fury and disdaine,
  He brayd aloud for very fell despight,
  And sodainely t'auenge him selfe againe,
Gan into one assemble all the might
  Of all his hands, and heaued them on hight,
  Thinking to pay him with that one for all:
  But the sad steele seizd not, where it was hight,
  Vppon the childe, but somewhat short did fall,
And lighting on his horses head, him quite did mall.

9

Downe streight to ground fell his astonisht steed,
  And eke to th'earth his burden with him bare:
  But he him selfe full lightly from him freed,
And gan him selfe to fight on foote prepare.
  Whereof when as the Gyant was aware,
  He wox right blyth, as he had got thereby,
  And laught so loud, that all his teeth wide bare,
  One might haue seene enraung'd disorderly,
Like to a rancke of piles, that pitched are awry.

10

Eftsoones againe his axe he raught on hie,
  Ere he were throughly buckled to his geare,
  And can let driue at him so dreadfullie,
That had he chaunced not his shield to reare,
  Ere that huge stroke arriued on him neare,
  He had him surely clouen quite in twaine,
  But th'Adamantine shield, which he did beare,
  So well was tempred, that for all his maine,
It would no passage yeeld vnto his purpose vaine.

11

Yet was the stroke so forcibly applide,
  That made him stagger with vncertaine sway,
  As if he would haue tottered to one side.
Wherewith full wroth, he fiercely gan assay,
  That curt'sie with like kindnesse to repay;
  And smote at him with so importune might,
  That two more of his armes did fall away,
  Like fruitlesse braunches, which the hatchets slight
Hath pruned from the natiue tree, and cropped quight.

Stanza 5
2   **ouerrun**: trampled down.
8–9   **driue**: either the older form of 'drove', or for 'drives';
hence **riue**: riven.

Stanza 6
2   Cf. x 8.8–9. Geryoneo has **three double hands** or **double
hands thrise multiplyde**: the play on three suggests a parody
of the celestial Hierarchy, the three divisions of angels, each
with three orders.
6   **nimblesse**: nimbleness.
9   **Behinde, beside, before**: i.e. he literally surrounds his
enemies.

Stanza 7
1   **vncouth**: strange.
6   **faynd**: sought; desired.

Stanza 8
5   **hight**: high.
7   **sad**: heavy.   **hight**: directed.
8   **childe**: applied only to Arthur; see IV viii 44.8n.
9   **mall**: knock down.

Stanza 9
1   **astonisht**: stunned.
6   **got**: profited, as IV i 50.8; gained, i.e. gained the victory.

Stanza 10
2   **buckled to his geare**: girded in his arms; ready for the
business at hand.
3   **can**: began to.
7–9   **th'Adamantine shield**: cf. its resistance to the spear
at x 32.7–9; it is described at I vii 33; cf. viii 37.6.   **maine**:
strength.

Stanza 11
5   **kindnesse**: suggesting a stroke of like kind.
6   **importune**: grievous; heavy.
8   **slight**: i.e. skilful stroke.

12

With that all mad and furious he grew,
  Like a fell mastiffe through enraging heat,
  And curst, and band, and blasphemies forth threw,
  Against his Gods, and fire to them did threat,
  And hell vnto him selfe with horrour great.
  Thenceforth he car'd no more, which way he strooke,
  Nor where it light, but gan to chaufe and sweat,
  And gnasht his teeth, and his head at him shooke,
And sternely him beheld with grim and ghastly looke.

13

Nought fear'd the childe his lookes, ne yet his threats,
  But onely wexed now the more aware,
  To saue him selfe from those his furious heats,
  And watch aduauntage, how to worke his care:
  The which good Fortune to him offred faire.
  For as he in his rage him ouerstrooke,
  He ere he could his weapon backe repaire,
  His side all bare and naked ouertooke,
And with his mortal steel quite throgh the body strooke.

14

Through all three bodies he him strooke attonce;
  That all the three attonce fell on the plaine:
  Else should he thrise haue needed, for the nonce
  Them to haue stricken, and thrise to haue slaine.
  So now all three one sencelesse lumpe remaine,
  Enwallow'd in his owne blacke bloudy gore,
  And byting th'earth for very deaths disdaine;
  Who with a cloud of night him couering, bore
Downe to the house of dole, his daies there to deplore.

15

Which when the Lady from the Castle saw,
  Where she with her two sonnes did looking stand,
  She towards him in hast her selfe did draw,
  To greet him the good fortune of his hand:
  And all the people both of towne and land,
  Which there stood gazing from the Cities wall
  Vppon these warriours, greedy t'vnderstand,
  To whether should the victory befall,
Now when they saw it falne, they eke him greeted all.

16

But *Belge* with her sonnes prostrated low
  Before his feete, in all that peoples sight,
  Mongst ioyes mixing some tears, mongst wele, some wo
  Him thus bespake; O most redoubted Knight,
  The which hast me, of all most wretched wight,
  That earst was dead, restor'd to life againe,
  And these weake impes replanted by thy might;
  What guerdon can I giue thee for thy paine,
But euen that which thou sauedst, thine still to remaine?

17

He tooke her vp forby the lilly hand,
  And her recomforted the best he might,
  Saying; Deare Lady, deedes ought not be scand
  By th'authors manhood, nor the doers might,
  But by their trueth and by the causes right:
  That same is it, which fought for you this day.
  What other meed then need me to requight,
  But that which yeeldeth vertues meed alway?
That is the vertue selfe, which her reward doth pay.

18

She humbly thankt him for that wondrous grace,
  And further sayd; Ah Sir, but mote ye please,
  Sith ye thus farre haue tendred my poore case,
  As from my chiefest foe me to release,
  That your victorious arme will not yet cease,
  Till ye haue rooted all the relickes out
  Of that vilde race, and stablished my peace.
  What is there else (sayd he) left of their rout?
Declare it boldly Dame, and doe not stand in dout.

Stanza 12

1–2 Cf. Injustice raging as a rabid dog, viii 49.1–5.
3–4 Cf. the Souldan's cursing, viii 28.2; see also ii 18.7–9, and 20.7–9, 28.1–5 below. **band:** swore.
7 **it:** his blow.

Stanza 13

2 **aware:** vigilant.
4 **worke his care:** cause him trouble.
6 **ouerstrooke:** struck too far.
7 **repaire:** draw.
8 **ouertooke:** reached with a blow.

Stanza 14

3 **for the nonce:** for the purpose, i.e. of slaying him.
6 **Enwallow'd:** lying prostrate.
7 See ii 18.6*n*.
9 **dole:** sorrow; pain.

Stanza 15

4 **greet:** offer congratulations on.
8 **whether:** which.

Stanza 16

7 **impes:** offshoots; scions or descendants.
9 **Belge** (1) offers the sovereignty of the Netherlands to England. Arthur's refusal reflects Elizabeth's.

Stanza 17

1 **forby:** by.
3–5 Cf. viii 30.9. **scand:** judged. The author or doer is judged by the truth of the cause he undertakes, his actions by their rightness.
6 **That same:** i.e. truth and right.
7–9 Proverbial: virtue is its own reward (C. G. Smith, 1970, 818).

Stanza 18

3 **tendred:** taken care of.
6 **relickes:** alluding to objects of Roman Catholic worship.
9 **dout:** fear.

19

Then wote you, Sir, that in this Church hereby,
　　There stands an Idole of great note and name,
　　The which this Gyant reared first on hie,
　　And of his owne vaine fancies thought did frame:
　　To whom for endlesse horrour of his shame,
　　He offred vp for daily sacrifize
　　My children and my people, burnt in flame;
　　With all the tortures, that he could deuize,
The more t'aggrate his God with such his bloudy guize.

20

And vnderneath this Idoll there doth lie
　　An hideous monster, that doth it defend,
　　And feedes on all the carkasses, that die
　　In sacrifize vnto that cursed feend:
　　Whose vgly shape none euer saw, nor kend,
　　That euer scap'd: for of a man they say
　　It has the voice, that speaches forth doth send,
　　Euen blasphemous words, which she doth bray
Out of her poysnous entrails, fraught with dire decay.

21

Which when the Prince heard tell, his heart gan earne
　　For great desire, that Monster to assay,
　　And prayd the place of her abode to learne.
　　Which being shew'd, he gan him selfe streight way
　　Thereto addresse, and his bright shield display.
　　So to the Church he came, where it was told,
　　The Monster vnderneath the Altar lay;
　　There he that Idoll saw of massy gold
Most richly made, but there no Monster did behold.

22

Vpon the Image with his naked blade
　　Three times, as in defiance, there he strooke;
　　And the third time out of an hidden shade,
　　There forth issewd, from vnder th'Altars smooke,
　　A dreadfull feend, with fowle deformed looke,
　　That stretcht it selfe, as it had long lyen still;
　　And her long taile and fethers strongly shooke,
　　That all the Temple did with terrour fill;
Yet him nought terrifide, that feared nothing ill.

23

An huge great Beast it was, when it in length
　　Was stretched forth, that nigh fild all the place,
　　And seem'd to be of infinite great strength;
　　Horrible, hideous, and of hellish race,
　　Borne of the brooding of *Echidna* base,
　　Or other like infernall furies kinde:
　　For of a Mayd she had the outward face,
　　To hide the horrour, which did lurke behinde,
The better to beguile, whom she so fond did finde.

24

Thereto the body of a dog she had,
　　Full of fell rauin and fierce greedinesse;
　　A Lions clawes, with powre and rigour clad,
　　To rend and teare, what so she can oppresse;
　　A Dragons taile, whose sting without redresse
　　Full deadly wounds, where so it is empight;
　　And Eagles wings, for scope and speedinesse,
　　That nothing may escape her reaching might,
Whereto she euer list to make her hardy flight.

606

Stanzas 19–20
Cf. the statement about the Idol and Dragon at x 28–29.

Stanza 19
4　At x 13.8–9, the **Idole** is 'The image of his monstrous
parent *Geryone*'. The phrasing suggests that the Idol is the god
itself rather than an image.
5–9　Cf. Leviticus 18.21: 'Thou shalt not give thy children
to offer them unto Molech.' The gloss reads: 'An idole of the
Ammonites, unto whome they burned and sacrificed their
children.' See also 2 Kings 23.10.　**aggrate**: gratify.　**guize**:
custom.

Stanza 20
9　**decay**: ruin, death.

Stanza 21
1　**earne**: yearn.
2　**assay**: attack; cf. 26.6.
5　For the first time Arthur enters a battle with his shield
already uncovered; cf. 26.2.

Stanzas 23–25
Comes (1616) VII i p. 362 notes that Geryon was attended by a
dragon born of Typhaon and **Echidna**. On Echidna, see VI vi
10. For the interpretation of Echidna as learned error, see Steadman (1961). Lotspeich (1932) 108 compares Comes's description
of the Sphinx (IX xviii), an appropriate archetype for the image
of the Inquisition. Cf. Cooper (1565) on the Sphinx: 'A
monster which had the head and handes of a mayden, the
bodie of a dogge, wynges lyke a byrde, nayles like a lyon, a
tayle like a dragon, the voyce of a man.' A Renaissance symbol
of 'impenetrable mystery of ignorance and of evil' (Rowland,
1973, 148). S. alludes also to his own description of Error
(I i 14); here error of doctrine sought out by the Spanish
Inquisition.

Stanza 23
9　**fond**: foolish.

Stanza 24
4　**oppresse**: take by surprise; overwhelm.
6　**empight**: implanted.

25

Much like in foulnesse and deformity
  Vnto that Monster, whom the Theban Knight,
  The father of that fatall progeny,
  Made kill her selfe for very hearts despight,
  That he had red her Riddle, which no wight
  Could euer loose, but suffred deadly doole.
  So also did this Monster vse like slight
  To many a one, which came vnto her schoole,
Whom she did put to death, deceiued like a foole.

26

She comming forth, when as she first beheld
  The armed Prince, with shield so blazing bright,
  Her ready to assaile, was greatly queld,
  And much dismayd with that dismayfull sight,
  That backe she would haue turnd for great affright.
  But he gan her with courage fierce assay,
  That forst her turne againe in her despight,
  To saue her selfe, least that he did her slay:
And sure he had her slaine, had she not turnd her way.

27

Tho when she saw, that she was forst to fight,
  She flew at him, like to an hellish feend,
  And on his shield tooke hold with all her might,
  As if that it she would in peeces rend,
  Or reaue out of the hand, that did it hend.
  Strongly he stroue out of her greedy gripe
  To loose his shield, and long while did contend:
  But when he could not quite it, with one stripe
Her Lions clawes he from her feete away did wipe.

28

With that aloude she gan to bray and yell,
  And fowle blasphemous speaches forth did cast,
  And bitter curses, horrible to tell,
  That euen the Temple, wherein she was plast,
  Did quake to heare, and nigh asunder brast.
  Tho with her huge long taile she at him strooke,
  That made him stagger, and stand halfe agast
  With trembling ioynts, as he for terrour shooke;
Who nought was terrifide, but greater courage tooke.

29

As when the Mast of some well timbred hulke
  Is with the blast of some outragious storme
  Blowne downe, it shakes the bottome of the bulke,
  And makes her ribs to cracke, as they were torne,
  Whilest still she stands as stonisht and forlorne:
  So was he stound with stroke of her huge taile.
  But ere that it she backe againe had borne,
  He with his sword it strooke, that without faile
He ioynted it, and mard the swinging of her flaile.

30

Then gan she cry much louder then afore,
  That all the people there without it heard,
  And *Belge* selfe was therewith stonied sore,
  As if the onely sound thereof she feard.
  But then the feend her selfe more fiercely reard
  Vppon her wide great wings, and strongly flew
  With all her body at his head and beard,
  That had he not foreseene with heedfull vew,
And thrown his shield atweene, she had him done to rew.

31

But as she prest on him with heauy sway,
  Vnder her wombe his fatall sword he thrust,
  And for her entrailes made an open way,
  To issue forth; the which once being brust,
  Like to a great Mill damb forth fiercely gusht,
  And powred out of her infernall sinke
  Most vgly filth, and poyson therewith rusht,
  That him nigh choked with the deadly stinke:
Such loathly matter were small lust to speake, or thinke.

Stanza 25

3 **that fatall progeny**: Oedipus's children, Eteocles and Polynices, who inherited the curse against the house of Laius.
6 **loose**: undo. By solving the puzzle, Oedipus freed the people from bondage to the Sphinx.   **deadly doole**: the pain (Lat. *dolor*) of death.

Stanzas 26–35

S. imitates the Red Cross Knight's battle against Error, and the victory celebration after he kills the Dragon.

Stanza 27

5 **hend**: hold:
8 **quite**: quit, free. **stripe**: stroke.
9 **wipe**: cut off.

Stanza 29

1 **hulke**: a large, heavy ship.
3 **bulke**: hull or hold.
6 **stound**: stunned.

Stanza 30

4 **the onely sound**: the sound alone.
9 **done to rew**: caused to regret not doing so.

Stanza 31

1 **prest**: may refer in the topical allegory to the torture (cf. 19.8) of pressing. **sway**: force.
5 Cf. I xi 22.6.
6 **sinke**: womb or organs of excretion; cf. I i 22.5.
8 As I i 22.2.
9 **lust**: pleasure.

607

32

Then downe to ground fell that deformed Masse,
  Breathing out clouds of sulphure fowle and blacke,
  In which a puddle of contagion was,
  More loathd then *Lerna*, or then *Stygian* lake,
  That any man would nigh awhaped make.
  Whom when he saw on ground, he was full glad,
  And streight went forth his gladnesse to partake
  With *Belge*, who watcht all this while full sad,
Wayting what end would be of that same daunger drad.

33

Whom when she saw so ioyously come forth,
  She gan reioyce, and shew triumphant chere,
  Lauding and praysing his renowmed worth,
  By all the names that honorable were.
  Then in he brought her, and her shewed there
  The present of his paines, that Monsters spoyle,
  And eke that Idoll deem'd so costly dere;
  Whom he did all to peeces breake and foyle
In filthy durt, and left so in the loathely soyle.

34

Then all the people, which beheld that day,
  Gan shout aloud, that vnto heauen it rong;
  And all the damzels of that towne in ray,
  Came dauncing forth, and ioyous carrols song:
  So him they led through all their streetes along,
  Crowned with girlonds of immortall baies,
  And all the vulgar did about them throng,
  To see the man, whose euerlasting praise
They all were bound to all posterities to raise.

35

There he with *Belge* did a while remaine,
  Making great feast and ioyous merriment,
  Vntill he had her settled in her raine,
  With safe assuraunce and establishment.
  Then to his first emprize his mind he lent,
  Full loath to *Belge*, and to all the rest:
  Of whom yet taking leaue, thenceforth he went
  And to his former iourney him addrest,
On which long way he rode, ne euer day did rest.

36

But turne we now to noble *Artegall*;
  Who hauing left *Mercilla*, streight way went
  On his first quest, the which him forth did call,
  To weet to worke *Irenaes* franchisement,
  And eke *Grantortoes* worthy punishment.
  So forth he fared as his manner was,
  With onely *Talus* wayting diligent,
  Through many perils and much way did pas,
Till nigh vnto the place at length approcht he has.

37

There as he traueld by the way, he met
  An aged wight, wayfaring all alone,
  Who through his yeares long since aside had set
  The vse of armes, and battell quite forgone:
  To whom as he approcht, he knew anone,
  That it was he which whilome did attend
  On faire *Irene* in her affliction,
  When first to Faery court he saw her wend,
Vnto his soueraine Queene her suite for to commend.

38

Whom by his name saluting, thus he gan;
  Haile good Sir *Sergis*, truest Knight aliue,
  Well tride in all thy Ladies troubles than,
  When her that Tyrant did of Crowne depriue;
  What new ocasion doth thee hither driue,
  Whiles she alone is left, and thou here found?
  Or is she thrall, or doth she not suruiue?
  To whom he thus; She liueth sure and sound;
But by that Tyrant is in wretched thraldome bound.

Stanza 32

2 **sulphure**: associated with hell (I v 31.5) and with the Dragon, I xi 13.7.
4 **Lerna**: the marsh inhabited by the Hydra slain by Hercules; see I vii 17.3. **Stygian lake**: **loathd** through name and nature; see II v 22.5–9*n*.
5 **awhaped**: terrified, utterly confounded.

Stanza 33

6 **present**: present occasion. **spoyle**: dead body.
8–9 Cf. Exod. 23.24: 'Thou shalt . . . utterly overthrowe them [the idols], and breake in pieces their images.' **foyle**: tread under foot; defile.

Stanza 34

3 **ray**: array.

Stanza 35

3 **raine**: kingdom.
4 **assuraunce**: suggests also securing her title to rule.
establishment: settled constitution or government.
5 **emprize**: enterprize or quest, his search for Gloriana.
7 **thenceforth**: from that place.

Stanza 36

4 **franchisement**: liberation.
7 **wayting**: attending as a servant.

Stanza 38

2 **Sergis**: from sergeant, one whose office is to summon persons to appear before the court (*OED* 4); hence he summons Artegall. R. M. Smith (1955) 682–3 sees a play on 'service'.
3 **than**: then.

39

For she presuming on th'appointed tyde,
 In which ye promist, as ye were a Knight,
 To meete her at the saluage Ilands syde,
 And then and there for triall of her right
 With her vnrighteous enemy to fight,
 Did thither come, where she afrayd of nought,
 By guilefull treason and by subtill slight
Surprized was, and to *Grantorto* brought,
Who her imprisond hath, and her life often sought.

40

And now he hath to her prefixt a day,
 By which if that no champion doe appeare,
 Which will her cause in battailous array
 Against him iustifie, and proue her cleare
 Of all those crimes, that he gainst her doth reare,
 She death shall by.   Those tidings sad
 Did much abash Sir *Artegall* to heare,
 And grieued sore, that through his fault she had
Fallen into that Tyrants hand and vsage bad.

41

Then thus replide; Now sure and by my life,
 Too much am I to blame for that faire Maide,
 That haue her drawne to all this troublous strife,
 Through promise to afford her timely aide,
 Which by default I haue not yet defraide.
 But witnesse vnto me, ye heauens, that know
 How cleare I am from blame of this vpbraide:
 For ye into like thraldome me did throw,
And kept from complishing the faith, which I did owe.

42

But now aread, Sir *Sergis*, how long space,
 Hath he her lent, a Champion to prouide?
 Ten daies (quoth he) he graunted hath of grace,
 For that he weeneth well, before that tide
 None can haue tidings to assist her side.
 For all the shores, which to the sea accoste,
 He day and night doth ward both far and wide,
 That none can there arriue without an hoste:
So her he deemes already but a damned ghoste.

43

Now turne againe (Sir *Artegall* then sayd)
 For if I liue till those ten daies haue end,
 Assure your selfe, Sir Knight, she shall haue ayd,
 Though I this dearest life for her doe spend:
 So backeward he attone with him did wend.
 Tho as they rode together on their way,
 A rout of people they before them kend,
 Flocking together in confusde array,
As if that there were some tumultuous affray.

44

To which as they approcht, the cause to know,
 They saw a Knight in daungerous distresse
 Of a rude rout him chasing to and fro,
 That sought with lawlesse powre him to oppresse,
 And bring in bondage of their brutishnesse:
 And farre away, amid their rakehell bands,
 They spide a Lady left all succourlesse,
 Crying, and holding vp her wretched hands
To him for aide, who long in vaine their rage withstands.

Stanza 39
1   **presuming**: relying.   **tyde**: time. The usual meaning is suggested by the place of meeting, the shore; cf. 42.5.
3   **saluage**: wild, barbarous, full of savages; cf. S.'s reference to Ireland in the dedicatory sonnet to Ormond: 'saluage soyl . . . With brutish barbarisme . . . ouerspredd'; probably **Ilands** echoes Ireland's.
7   **slight**: treachery.

Stanza 40
1   **prefixt**: appointed.
5   **crimes**: accusations.
6   **by**: suffer. The *1611* edition substituted 'sure aby' to avoid a tetrameter line. Gough (1921) notes that a pause is intended after 'by' to heighten the effect of the tidings.

Stanza 41
5   **default**: neglect of duty; perhaps in the legal sense: failure to attend in a court on the day assigned.   **defraide**: paid, discharged.
6–9   He contradicts his recognition that Irena's imprisonment is 'his fault' (40.8) for which he is **Too much . . . to blame** (2). He offers an excuse that he denied Terpine: 'faulty men . . . lay on heauen the guilt of their owne crimes' (iv 28.1–3).   **vpbraide**: reproach.   **complishing**: accomplishing; fulfilling.

Stanza 42
1   **aread**: declare.
6   **accoste**: provide the coast.
8   **hoste**: army. Either to help him land or prevent him from landing. See xii 4.8–9.

Stanza 43
5   **attone**: together.
7   **kend**: caught sight of.

Stanzas 44–65
The historical reference is to the English intervention in France to support Henry IV against the rebellion of his subjects who were supported by Philip of Spain. As leader of the Huguenots, Henry fought against the Catholic League; later he renounced his faith in order to rule Paris. Since he held sovereignty by natural succession, intervention on his behalf was justified by international law. See x 7.1–4n.

Stanza 44
6   **rakehell**: rascal.

45

Yet still he striues, ne any perill spares,
  To reskue her from their rude violence,
  And like a Lion wood amongst them fares,
  Dealing his dreadfull blowes with large dispence,
  Gainst which the pallid death findes no defence.
  But all in vaine, their numbers are so great,
  That naught may boot to banishe them from thence:
  For soone as he their outrage backe doth beat,
They turne afresh, and oft renew their former threat.

46

And now they doe so sharpely him assay,
  That they his shield in peeces battred haue,
  And forced him to throw it quite away,
  Fro dangers dread his doubtfull life to saue;
  Albe that it most safety to him gaue,
  And much did magnifie his noble name.
  For from the day that he thus did it leaue,
  Amongst all Knights he blotted was with blame,
And counted but a recreant Knight, with endles shame.

47

Whom when they thus distressed did behold,
  They drew vnto his aide; but that rude rout
  Them also gan assaile with outrage bold,
  And forced them, how euer strong and stout
  They were, as well approu'd in many a doubt,
  Backe to recule; vntill that yron man
  With his huge flaile began to lay about,
  From whose sterne presence they diffused ran,
Like scattred chaffe, the which the wind away doth fan.

48

So when that Knight from perill cleare was freed,
  He drawing neare, began to greete them faire,
  And yeeld great thankes for their so goodly deed,
  In sauing him from daungerous despaire
  Of those, which sought his life for to empaire.
  Of whom Sir *Artegall* gan then enquire
  The whole occasion of his late misfare,
  And who he was, and what those villaines were,
The which with mortall malice him pursu'd so nere.

49

To whom he thus; My name is *Burbon* hight,
  Well knowne, and far renowmed heretofore,
  Vntill late mischiefe did vppon me light,
  That all my former praise hath blemisht sore;
  And that faire Lady, which in that vprore
  Ye with those caytiues saw, *Flourdelis* hight,
  Is mine owne loue, though me she haue forlore,
  Whether withheld from me by wrongfull might,
Or with her owne good will, I cannot read aright.

50

But sure to me her faith she first did plight,
  To be my loue, and take me for her Lord,
  Till that a Tyrant, which *Grandtorto* hight,
  With golden giftes and many a guilefull word
  Entyced her, to him for to accord.
  O who may not with gifts and words be tempted?
  Sith which she hath me euer since abhord,
  And to my foe hath guilefully consented:
Ay me, that euer guyle in wemen was inuented.

51

And now he hath this troupe of villains sent,
  By open force to fetch her quite away:
  Gainst whom my selfe I long in vaine haue bent,
  To rescue her, and daily meanes assay,
  Yet rescue her thence by no meanes I may:
  For they doe me with multitude oppresse,
  And with vnequall might doe ouerlay,
  That oft I driuen am to great distresse,
And forced to forgoe th'attempt remedilesse.

Stanza 45
3   **wood**: raging.
4   **large dispence**: lavish liberality.

Stanza 46
When David laments Saul's overthrow, he notes the loss of his
shield: 'There the shield of the mightie is cast downe' (2 Sam.
1.21). Since the Christian is enjoined to 'take the shield of faith'
(Eph. 6.16), to throw it away means to renounce faith. Burbon
is called **recreant** (9) as he is cowardly and as he renounced the
Protestant faith.

Stanza 47
5   **doubt**: peril.
6   **recule**: recoil.
8   **sterne**: merciless.   **diffused**: dispersed.
9   Cf. Isaiah 41.15–6:'[Thou] shalt make the hilles as
chaffe. Thou shalt fanne them, and the winde shal carye them
away.'

Stanza 48
4   **daungerous despaire**: danger which causes him to
despair; cf. 'daungerous dismay' (52.2).
7   **misfare**: misfortune.

Stanza 49
1   **Burbon**: the house of Bourbon of which Henry IV was
head.
6   **Flourdelis**: alluding to France by her royal arms.
7   **forlore**: forsaken.
9   **read**: guess.

Stanza 50
8   **consented**: been in accord.
9   **inuented**: found.

Stanza 51
3   **bent**: applied.
6   **oppresse**: overwhelm.
7   **ouerlay**: crush by force.
9   **remedilesse**: having no hope of rescue.

52

But why haue ye (said *Artegall*) forborne
  Your owne good shield in daungerous dismay?
  That is the greatest shame and foulest scorne,
  Which vnto any knight behappen may
  To loose the badge, that should his deedes display.
  To whom Sir *Burbon*, blushing halfe for shame,
  That shall I vnto you (quoth he) bewray;
  Least ye therefore mote happily me blame,
And deeme it doen of will, that through inforcement came.

53

True is, that I at first was dubbed knight
  By a good knight, the knight of the *Redcrosse*;
  Who when he gaue me armes, in field to fight,
  Gaue me a shield, in which he did endosse
  His deare Redeemers badge vpon the bosse:
  The same longwhile I bore, and therewithall
  Fought many battels without wound or losse;
  Therewith *Grandtorto* selfe I did appall,
And made him oftentimes in field before me fall.

54

But for that many did that shield enuie,
  And cruell enemies increased more;
  To stint all strife and troublous enmitie,
  That bloudie scutchin being battered sore,
  I layd aside, and haue of late forbore,
  Hoping thereby to haue my loue obtayned:
  Yet can I not my loue haue nathemore;
  For she by force is still fro me detayned,
And with corruptfull brybes is to vntruth mis-trayned.

55

To whom thus *Artegall*; Certes Sir knight,
  Hard is the case, the which ye doe complaine;
  Yet not so hard (for nought so hard may light,
  That it to such a streight mote you constraine)
  As to abandon, that which doth containe
  Your honours stile, that is your warlike shield.
  All perill ought be lesse, and lesse all paine
  Then losse of fame in disauentrous field;
Dye rather, then doe ought, that mote dishonour yield.

56

Not so; (quoth he) for yet when time doth serue,
  My former shield I may resume againe:
  To temporize is not from truth to swerue,
  Ne for aduantage terme to entertaine,
  When as necessitie doth it constraine.
  Fie on such forgerie (said *Artegall*)
  Vnder one hood to shadow faces twaine.
  Knights ought be true, and truth is one in all:
Of all things to dissemble fouly may befall.

57

Yet let me you of courtesie request,
  (Said *Burbon*) to assist me now at need
  Against these pesants, which haue me opprest,
  And forced me to so infamous deed,
  That yet my loue may from their hands be freed.
  Sir *Artegall*, albe he earst did wyte
  His wauering mind, yet to his aide agreed,
  And buckling him eftsoones vnto the fight,
Did set vpon those troupes with all his powre and might.

58

Who flocking round about them, as a swarme
  Of flyes vpon a birchen bough doth cluster,
  Did them assault with terrible allarme,
  And ouer all the fields themselues did muster,
  With bils and glayues making a dreadfull luster;
  That forst at first those knights backe to retyre:
  As when the wrathfull *Boreas* doth bluster,
  Nought may abide the tempest of his yre,
Both man and beast doe fly, and succour doe inquyre.

Stanza 52

Yet *Artegall* triumphs over Grantorto when 'loosing soone
his shield, did it forgoe' (xii 22.7). **Burbon**'s account of his
inforcement (9) supports what we see at 46.1–4. See xii
40.3–4*n*.
1   **forborne**: given up.
7   **bewray**: declare.
8   **happily**: haply; perchance.

Stanza 53

4   **endosse**: inscribe.
5   **bosse**: the centre of the shield.

Stanza 54

1   **enuie**: dislike.
4   **scutchin**: the shield with its 'bloudie Crosse' (I i 2.1).
9   **corruptfull**: corrupting; suggests the effect of the bribes,
to make her full of corruption.   **mis-trayned**: led astray; or
simply, trained amiss.

Stanza 55

3   **light**: happen.
6   **honours stile**: title of honour; literally, that upon which
his honour is penned.
8   **disauentrous field**: unsuccessful conflict.

Stanza 56

3–5   Nor is it swerving from truth to accept conditions when
forced by necessity.
6   **forgerie**: deception.
7   Proverbial (C. G. Smith, 1970, 231).
8   Cf. 'truth is one, and right is euer one' (ii 48.6).
9   May shame above all else befall those who dissemble.

Stanza 57

6   **earst**: lately.   **wyte**: blame.

Stanza 58

3   **allarme**: din.
5   **bils and glayues**: Elizabethan infantry weapons with a
blade fastened to a long handle.
8   **yre**: with a pun on 'air'.
9   **inquyre**: try to find.

59

But when as ouerblowen was that brunt,
  Those knights began a fresh them to assayle,
  And all about the fields like Squirrels hunt;
  But chiefly *Talus* with his yron flayle,
  Gainst which no flight nor rescue mote auayle,
  Made cruell hauocke of the baser crew,
  And chaced them both ouer hill and dale:
  The raskall manie soone they ouerthrew,
But the two knights themselues their captains did subdew.

60

At last they came whereas that Ladie bode,
  Whom now her keepers had forsaken quight,
  To saue themselues, and scattered were abrode:
  Her halfe dismayd they found in doubtfull plight,
  As neither glad nor sorie for their sight;
  Yet wondrous faire she was, and richly clad
  In roiall robes, and many Iewels dight,
  But that those villens through their vsage bad
Them fouly rent, and shamefully defaced had.

61

But *Burbon* streight dismounting from his steed,
  Vnto her ran with greedie great desyre,
  And catching her fast by her ragged weed,
  Would haue embraced her with hart entyre.
  But she backstarting with disdainefull yre,
  Bad him auaunt, ne would vnto his lore
  Allured be, for prayer nor for meed.
  Whom when those knights so froward and forlore
Beheld, they her rebuked and vpbrayded sore.

62

Sayd *Artegall*; What foule disgrace is this,
  To so faire Ladie, as ye seeme in sight,
  To blot your beautie, that vnblemisht is,
  With so foule blame, as breach of faith once plight,
  Or change of loue for any worlds delight?
  Is ought on earth so pretious or deare,
  As prayse and honour? Or is ought so bright
  And beautifull, as glories beames appeare,
Whose goodly light then *Phebus* lampe doth shine more cleare?

63

Why then will ye, fond Dame, attempted bee
  Vnto a strangers loue so lightly placed,
  For guiftes of gold, or any worldly glee,
  To leaue the loue, that ye before embraced,
  And let your fame with falshood be defaced?
  Fie on the pelfe, for which good name is sold,
  And honour with indignitie debased;
  Dearer is loue then life, and fame then gold;
But dearer then them both, your faith once plighted hold.

64

Much was the Ladie in her gentle mind
  Abasht at his rebuke, that bit her neare,
  Ne ought to answere thereunto did find;
  But hanging downe her head with heauie cheare,
  Stood long amaz'd, as she amated weare.
  Which *Burbon* seeing, her againe assayd,
  And clasping twixt his armes, her vp did reare
  Vpon his steede, whiles she no whit gainesayd,
612 So bore her quite away, nor well nor ill apayd.

65

Nathlesse the yron man did still pursew
  That raskall many with vnpittied spoyle,
  Ne ceassed not, till all their scattred crew
  Into the sea he droue quite from that soyle,
  The which they troubled had with great turmoyle.
  But *Artegall* seeing his cruell deed,
  Commaunded him from slaughter to recoyle,
  And to his voyage gan againe proceed:
For that the terme approching fast, required speed.

Stanza 59

6   **baser**: most base.
8   **raskall manie**: rabble company.   **they**: 'he', i.e. Talus, sugg. Church (1758).

Stanza 61

4   **entyre**: sincere.
6   **lore**: speech or pleading (sugg. by the context); or 'religion' (*OED* 2 c), as the allegory suggests.
7   **meed**: apparently suggested by the 'a' rhyme; 'hyre', sugg. Church, satisfies the regular rhyme scheme but its implications of bribery (cf. 54.9) may have bothered S.
8   **froward**] forward *1596*. On the relation of these two terms, see II ii 38.5–8*n*.   **forlore**: led astray, morally lost.

Stanza 62

4–5   He echoes Britomart, III i 25.3–6.
6–9   Prepares for the ravages of the Blatant Beast upon **prayse and honour**.

Stanza 63

1   **fond**: foolish.   **attempted**: tempted, seduced.
3   **glee**: glitter.
6–8   Cf. Proverbs 22.1: 'A good name is to be chosen above great riches, and loving favour is above silver and above golde.' **indignitie**: disgraceful action.

Stanza 64

5   **amated**: confounded; perhaps also 'mated', for she recognizes her union with **Burbon**.
9   **apayd**: pleased.

Stanza 65

2   **vnpittied spoyle**: merciless havoc.
7   **recoyle**: draw back.
9   **terme**: i.e. the final date by which a champion of Irena must appear.

Cant. XII.

Artegall doth Sir Burbon aide,
And blames for changing shield:
He with the great Grantorto fights,
And slaieth him in field.

1

O Sacred hunger of ambitious mindes,
And impotent desire of men to raine,
Whom neither dread of God, that deuils bindes,
Nor lawes of men, that common weales containe,
Nor bands of nature, that wilde beastes restraine,
Can keepe from outrage, and from doing wrong,
Where they may hope a kingdome to obtaine.
No faith so firme, no trust can be so strong,
No loue so lasting then, that may enduren long.

2

Witnesse may *Burbon* be, whom all the bands,
Which may a Knight assure, had surely bound,
Vntill the loue of Lordship and of lands
Made him become most faithlesse and vnsound:
And witnesse be *Gerioneo* found,
Who for like cause faire *Belge* did oppresse,
And right and wrong most cruelly confound:
And so be now *Grantorto*, who no lesse
Then all the rest burst out to all outragiousnesse.

3

Gainst whom Sir *Artegall*, long hauing since
Taken in hand th'exploit, being theretoo
Appointed by that mightie Faerie Prince,
Great *Gloriane*, that Tyrant to fordoo,
Through other great aduentures hethertoo
Had it forslackt. But now time drawing ny,
To him assynd, her high beheast to doo,
To the sea shore he gan his way apply,
To weete if shipping readie he mote there descry.

4

Tho when they came to the sea coast, they found
A ship all readie (as good fortune fell)
To put to sea, with whom they did compound,
To passe them ouer, where them list to tell:
The winde and weather serued them so well,
That in one day they with the coast did fall;
Whereas they readie found them to repell,
Great hostes of men in order martiall,
Which them forbad to land, and footing did forstall.

5

But nathemore would they from land refraine,
But when as nigh vnto the shore they drew,
That foot of man might sound the bottome plaine,
Talus into the sea did forth issew,
Though darts from shore and stones they at him threw;
And wading through the waues with stedfast sway,
Maugre the might of all those troupes in vew,
Did win the shore, whence he them chast away,
And made to fly, like doues, whom the Eagle doth affray.

6

The whyles Sir *Artegall*, with that old knight
Did forth descend, there being none them neare,
And forward marched to a towne in sight.
By this came tydings to the Tyrants eare,
By those, which earst did fly away for feare
Of their arriuall: wherewith troubled sore,
He all his forces streight to him did reare,
And forth issuing with his scouts afore,
Meant them to haue incountred, ere they left the shore.

Canto xii

Argument

1–2 See xi Arg. *n.* In Canto xi, which contains this matter, **Burbon** is blamed for abandoning his shield. **changing** reflects more accurately the historical reference: Henry IV was blamed by the English for changing from the Protestant faith to the Church of Rome; see 2.3–4*n.*

Stanza 1

1 **Sacred hunger**: i.e. accursed, as Virgil's *sacra fames* (*Aen.* iii 57).
2 **impotent**: uncontrollable; see II xi 23.8–9*n.*
3 Cf. James 2.19: 'The devils also beleve it [that there is one God] and tremble.'
4 **containe**: confine, keep under control.

Stanza 2

2 **assure**: make secure.
3–4 At xi 54.4–6, **Burbon** admits that he laid his shield aside to obtain his love.

Stanza 3

4 **fordoo**: kill.
6 **forslackt**: neglected.

Stanza 4

3 **compound**: make terms.
6 **they with the coast did fall**: i.e. they reached the coast. Gough (1921) notes that the Irish Sea could be crossed in a day.
9 **forstall**: prevent.

Stanza 5

6 **sway**: force.
9 The traditional opposition between the eagle and dove.

Stanza 6

7 **reare**: gather.

7

But ere he marched farre, he with them met,
　And fiercely charged them with all his force;
　But *Talus* sternely did vpon them set,
　And brusht, and battred them without remorse,
　That on the ground he left full many a corse;
　Ne any able was him to withstand,
　But he them ouerthrew both man and horse,
　That they lay scattred ouer all the land,
As thicke as doth the seede after the sowers hand.

8

Till *Artegall* him seeing so to rage,
　Willd him to stay, and signe of truce did make:
　To which all harkning, did a while asswage
　Their forces furie, and their terror slake;
　Till he an Herauld cald, and to him spake,
　Willing him wend vnto the Tyrant streight,
　And tell him that not for such slaughters sake
　He thether came, but for to trie the right
Of fayre *Irenaes* cause with him in single fight.

9

And willed him for to reclayme with speed
　His scattred people, ere they all were slaine,
　And time and place conuenient to areed,
　In which they two the combat might darraine,
　Which message when *Grantorto* heard, full fayne
　And glad he was the slaughter so to stay,
　And pointed for the combat twixt them twayne
　The morrow next, ne gaue him longer day.
So sounded the retraite, and drew his folke away.

10

That night Sir *Artegall* did cause his tent
　There to be pitched on the open plaine;
　For he had giuen streight commaundement,
　That none should dare him once to entertaine:
　Which none durst breake, though many would right faine
　For fayre *Irena*, whom they loued deare.
　But yet old *Sergis* did so well him paine,
　That from close friends, that dar'd not to appeare,
He all things did puruay, which for them needfull weare.

11

The morrow next, that was the dismall day,
　Appointed for *Irenas* death before,
　So soone as it did to the world display
　His chearefull face, and light to men restore,
　The heauy Mayd, to whom none tydings bore
　Of *Artegalls* arryuall, her to free,
　Lookt vp with eyes full sad and hart full sore;
　Weening her lifes last howre then neare to bee,
Sith no redemption nigh she did nor heare nor see.

12

Then vp she rose, and on her selfe did dight
　Most squalid garments, fit for such a day,
　And with dull countenance, and with doleful spright,
　She forth was brought in sorrowfull dismay,
　For to receiue the doome of her decay.
　But comming to the place, and finding there
　Sir *Artegall*, in battailous array
　Wayting his foe, it did her dead hart cheare,
614 And new life to her lent, in midst of deadly feare.

13

Like as a tender Rose in open plaine,
　That with vntimely drought nigh withered was,
　And hung the head, soone as few drops of raine
　Thereon distill, and deaw her daintie face,
　Gins to looke vp, and with fresh wonted grace
　Dispreds the glorie of her leaues gay;
　Such was *Irenas* countenance, such her case,
　When *Artegall* she saw in that array,
There wayting for the Tyrant, till it was farre day.

Stanza 7

3 **sternely**: cruelly, as Grantorto at 19.6.
4 **brusht**: thrashed.
8–9 Usually **Talus** (3) is seen as the thresher who separates the chaff from the seed (e.g. i 12.8–9); as a sower, the seed he sows is death; cf. Aptekar (1969) 50. The biblical reference may support the historical one: as the seed, which is sown, is not quickened unless it dies (1 Cor. 15.36), the Irish must be slain so that Ireland may be renewed.

Stanza 8

2 **Willd**: ordered; cf. vii 36.7, xi 65.7.

Stanza 9

1 **reclayme**: recall.
3 **conuenient**: fitting. **areed**: appoint.
4 **darraine**: engage.
7 **pointed**: appointed.

Stanza 10

3 **he**: Grantorto. Cf. vii 26.2. **streight**: strict.
8 **close**: secret.
9 **puruay**: provide.

Stanza 11

1 **dismall day**: unlucky or evil day, the day of death.
9 **redemption**: cf. vii 45.8.

Stanza 12

2 **squalid**: see i 13.7n.
5 **doome of her decay**: punishment or judgment of death.

Stanza 13

9 **farre day**: far on in the day.

14

Who came at length, with proud presumpteous gate,
   Into the field, as if he fearelesse were,
   All armed in a cote of yron plate,
   Of great defence to ward the deadly feare,
   And on his head a steele cap he did weare
   Of colour rustie browne, but sure and strong;
   And in his hand an huge Polaxe did beare,
Whose steale was yron studded, but not long,
With which he wont to fight, to iustifie his wrong.

15

Of stature huge and hideous he was,
   Like to a Giant for his monstrous hight,
   And did in strength most sorts of men surpas,
   Ne euer any found his match in might;
   Thereto he had great skill in single fight:
   His face was vgly, and his coūtenance sterne,
   That could haue frayd one with the very sight,
   And gaped like a gulfe, when he did gerne,
That whether man or monster one could scarse discerne.

16

Soone as he did within the listes appeare,
   With dreadfull looke he *Artegall* beheld,
   As if he would haue daunted him with feare,
   And grinning griesly, did against him weld
   His deadly weapon, which in hand he held.
   But th'Elfin swayne, that oft had seene like sight,
   Was with his ghastly count'nance nothing queld,
   But gan him streight to buckle to the fight,
And cast his shield about, to be in readie plight.

17

The trompets sound, and they together goe,
   With dreadfull terror, and with fell intent;
   And their huge strokes full daungerously bestow,
   To doe most dammage, where as most they ment.
   But with such force and furie violent,
   The tyrant thundred his thicke blowes so fast,
   That through the yron walles their way they rent,
   And euen to the vitall parts they past,
Ne ought could them endure, but all they cleft or brast.

18

Which cruell outrage when as *Artegall*
   Did well auize, thenceforth with warie heed
   He shund his strokes, where euer they did fall,
   And way did giue vnto their gracelesse speed:
   As when a skilfull Marriner doth reed
   A storme approching, that doth perill threat,
   He will not bide the daunger of such dread,
   But strikes his sayles, and vereth his mainsheat,
And lends vnto it leaue the emptie ayre to beat.

19

So did the Faerie knight himselfe abeare,
   And stouped oft his head from shame to shield;
   No shame to stoupe, ones head more high to reare,
   And much to gaine, a litle for to yield;
   So stoutest knights doen oftentimes in field.
   But still the tyrant sternely at him layd,
   And did his yron axe so nimbly wield,
   That many wounds into his flesh it made,
And with his burdenous blowes him sore did ouerlade.

20

Yet when as fit aduantage he did spy,
   The whiles the cursed felon high did reare
   His cruell hand, to smite him mortally,
   Vnder his stroke he to him stepping neare,
   Right in the flanke him strooke with deadly dreare,
   That the gore bloud thence gushing grieuously,
   Did vnderneath him like a pond appeare,
   And all his armour did with purple dye;
Thereat he brayed loud, and yelled dreadfully.

Stanza 14

3–9   The Irish foot-soldier was armed 'in a long shirt of mail down to the calf of the leg with a long, broad axe in his hand' (*View* 71). The iron relates him to the tyranny of the iron age. See i 12*n*.   **deadly feare**: i.e. fear of death.   **steale**: handle.

Stanza 15

1   **hideous**: immense.
3   **sorts**: kinds; as multitudes (cf. *OED* 18).
5   **single fight**: alludes to the clash of armies.
8   **gerne**: show the teeth (with open mouth); cf. 16.4. Upton (1758) suggests 'yawn' as AS *geonan*.

Stanza 17

6   **thicke**: rapid.

Stanza 18

2   **auize**: perceive.
4   **gracelesse**: cruel.
5   **reed**: see.
8–9   He shortens the sail and lets it out to hold less wind in order to give the ship less way.

Stanza 19

1   **abeare**: bear, conduct.
2   **from shame**: i.e. from shameful injury.
9   **burdenous**: heavy.   **ouerlade**: press hard.

Stanza 20

2   **felon**: villain; also one who has committed a felony.
5   **deadly dreare**: the pain and sorrow of death.

615

21

Yet the huge stroke, which he before intended,
  Kept on his course, as he did it direct,
  And with such monstrous poise adowne descended,
  That seemed nought could him from death protect:
  But he it well did ward with wise respect,
  And twixt him and the blow his shield did cast,
  Which thereon seizing, tooke no great effect,
  But byting deepe therein did sticke so fast,
That by no meanes it backe againe he forth could wrast.

22

Long while he tug'd and stroue, to get it out,
  And all his powre applyed thereunto,
  That he therewith the knight drew all about:
  Nathlesse, for all that euer he could doe,
  His axe he could not from his shield vndoe.
  Which *Artegall* perceiuing, strooke no more,
  But loosing soone his shield, did it forgoe,
  And whiles he combred was therewith so sore,
He gan at him let driue more fiercely then afore.

23

So well he him pursew'd, that at the last,
  He stroke him with *Chrysaor* on the hed,
  That with the souse thereof full sore aghast,
  He staggered to and fro in doubtfull sted.
  Againe whiles he him saw so ill bested,
  He did him smite with all his might and maine,
  That falling on his mother earth he fed:
  Whom when he saw prostrated on the plaine,
He lightly reft his head, to ease him of his paine.

24

Which when the people round about him saw,
  They shouted all for ioy of his successe,
  Glad to be quit from that proud Tyrants awe,
  Which with strong powre did them long time oppresse;
  And running all with greedie ioyfulnesse
  To faire *Irena*, at her feet did fall,
  And her adored with due humblenesse,
  As their true Liege and Princesse naturall;
And eke her champions glorie sounded ouer all.

25

Who streight her leading with meete maiestie
  Vnto the pallace, where their kings did rayne,
  Did her therein establish peaceablie,
  And to her kingdomes seat restore agayne;
  And all such persons, as did late maintayne
  That Tyrants part, with close or open ayde,
  He sorely punished with heauie payne;
  That in short space, whiles there with her he stayd,
Not one was left, that durst her once haue disobayd.

26

During which time, that he did there remaine,
  His studie was true Iustice how to deale,
  And day and night employ'd his busie paine
  How to reforme that ragged common-weale:
  And that same yron man which could reueale
  All hidden crimes, through all that realme he sent,
  To search out those, that vsd to rob and steale,
  Or did rebell gainst lawfull gouernment;
On whom he did inflict most grieuous punishment.

616

27

But ere he could reforme it thoroughly,
  He through occasion called was away,
  To Faerie Court, that of necessity
  His course of Iustice he was forst to stay,
  And *Talus* to reuoke from the right way,
  In which he was that Realme for to redresse.
  But enuies cloud still dimmeth vertues ray.
  So hauing freed *Irena* from distresse,
He tooke his leaue of her, there left in heauinesse.

Stanza 21
3 **poise**: weight, force.
5 **respect**: care.

Stanza 22
7–8 When Burbon threw away his shield, he was blotted
with endless shame (see xi 46). Artegall's present action may
be justified on the grounds that Church (1758) suggests: he
gives up his shield to gain victory, not peace.   **forgoe**: cf.
'forborne' (xi 52.1) and 'forbore' (xi 54.5).

Stanza 23
1 **pursew'd**: harassed.
3 **souse**: heavy downward blow.
4 **sted**: state.
7 **he fed**: i.e. he bit the dust; see ii 18.6*n*.

Stanza 24
8 **naturall**: legitimate, lawful.

Stanza 25
3 **peaceablie**: according to her name, Irena, Peace.
5–9 Elizabeth complained that Lord Gray 'regarded not the
life of her subjects, no more than dogs, but had wasted and
consumed all, so as now she had almost nothing left but to
reign in their ashes' (*View* 106). **heauie payne**: i.e. torturing
to death.

Stanza 27
Cf. *View* 106: 'In the late government of that good Lord Gray,
when after long travail and many perilous assays, he had
brought things almost to this pass that ye speak of [i.e. total
destruction], that it was even made ready for reformation . . .
complaint was made against him, that he was a bloody man.
. . . the noble Lord eftsoons was blamed.'
5 **reuoke**: recall.
7 **still**: ever.

28

Tho as he backe returned from that land,
  And there arriu'd againe, whence forth he set,
He had not passed farre vpon the strand,
  When as two old ill fauour'd Hags he met,
  By the way side being together set,
Two griesly creatures; and, to that their faces
Most foule and filthie were, their garments yet
Being all rag'd and tatter'd, their disgraces
Did much the more augment, and made most vgly cases.

29

The one of them, that elder did appeare,
  With her dull eyes did seeme to looke askew,
That her mis-shape much helpt; and her foule heare
  Hung loose and loathsomely: Thereto her hew
  Was wan and leane, that all her teeth arew,
And all her bones might through her cheekes be red;
  Her lips were like raw lether, pale and blew,
And as she spake, therewith she slauered;
Yet spake she seldom, but thought more, the lesse she sed.

30

Her hands were foule and durtie, neuer washt
  In all her life, with long nayles ouer raught,
Like puttocks clawes: with th'one of which she scracht
  Her cursed head, although it itched naught;
  The other held a snake with venime fraught,
On which she fed, and gnawed hungrily,
  As if that long she had not eaten ought;
That round about her iawes one might descry
The bloudie gore and poyson dropping lothsomely.

31

Her name was *Enuie*, knowen well thereby;
  Whose nature is to grieue, and grudge at all,
That euer she sees doen prays-worthily,
  Whose sight to her is greatest crosse, may fall,
  And vexeth so, that makes her eat her gall.
For when she wanteth other thing to eat,
  She feedes on her owne maw vnnaturall,
And of her owne foule entrayles makes her meat;
Meat fit for such a monsters monsterous dyeat.

32

And if she hapt of any good to heare,
  That had to any happily betid,
Then would she inly fret, and grieue, and teare
  Her flesh for felnesse, which she inward hid:
  But if she heard of ill, that any did,
Or harme, that any had, then would she make
  Great cheare, like one vnto a banquet bid;
And in anothers losse great pleasure take,
As she had got thereby, and gayned a great stake.

33

The other nothing better was, then shee;
  Agreeing in bad will and cancred kynd,
But in bad maner they did disagree:
  For what so *Enuie* good or bad did fynd,
  She did conceale, and murder her owne mynd;
But this, that euer euill she conceiued,
  Did spred abroad, and throw in th'open wynd,
Yet this in all her words might be perceiued,
That all she sought, was mens good name to haue bereaued.

34

For what soeuer good by any sayd,
  Or doen she heard, she would streightwayes inuent,
How to depraue, or slaunderously vpbrayd,
  Or to misconstrue of a mans intent,
  And turne to ill the thing, that well was ment.
Therefore she vsed often to resort,
  To common haunts, and companies frequent,
To hearke what any one did good report,
To blot the same with blame, or wrest in wicked sort.

Stanza 28
6–7 **to that**: i.e. besides that.   **yet**: in addition.
8 **disgraces**: ill-favouredness.

Stanzas 29–32
On the iconography of Envy, see Chew (1962) 109–11 and
Aptekar (1969) 201–5. Cf. Envy in the House of Pride, I iv
30–32. Dunseath (1968) 232 notes that Hercules's last
opponent, and the only foe whom he did not destroy, was
Invidia. See Aptekar 209–10. See VI xii 32*n*.

Stanza 29
2 Alluding to the etymology of Invidia, Lat. *invidere*, to
look askance upon; see I iv 31.2*n*. Cf. Envy in the *Romance of
the Rose* 291–2: 'she ne lokide but awry / Or overthwart'.
3 **mis-shape**: deformed shape.
4–5 Envy's pallor is stressed by Ovid, *Met.* ii 775.
6 **red**: seen.
9 Proverbial (C. G. Smith, 1970, 471); cf. Tilley (1950)
L 367: 'Though he said little, he thought the more.'

Stanza 31
2 **grudge**: grumble.
7 As I iv 30.5.
9 **monsterous**: because she feeds on a monster.

Stanza 32
2 **happily**: by good chance.
9 **got**: profited.

Stanzas 33–36
On the iconography of **Detraction**, see Chew (1962) 182.

Stanza 33
2 **kynd**: nature.
5 **murder**: torment.

Stanza 34
2 **inuent**: plot.
3 **depraue**: defame; represent as bad; cf. vii 32.8. Ital.
depravare, backbite (Florio, 1611) is relevant to the Blatant
Beast; see 39.9.

35

And if that any ill she heard of any,
　She would it eeke, and make much worse by telling,
　And take great ioy to publish it to many,
　That euery matter worse was for her melling,
　Her name was hight *Detraction*, and her dwelling
　Was neare to *Enuie*, euen her neighbour next;
　A wicked hag, and *Enuy* selfe excelling
　In mischiefe: for her selfe she onely vext;
But this same both her selfe, and others eke perplext.

36

Her face was vgly, and her mouth distort,
　Foming with poyson round about her gils,
　In which her cursed tongue full sharpe and short
　Appear'd like Aspis sting, that closely kils,
　Or cruelly does wound, whom so she wils:
　A distaffe in her other hand she had,
　Vpon the which she litle spinnes, but spils,
　And faynes to weaue false tales and leasings bad,
To throw amongst the good, which others had disprad.

37

These two now had themselues combynd in one,
　And linckt together gainst Sir *Artegall*,
　For whom they wayted as his mortall fone,
　How they might make him into mischiefe fall,
　For freeing from their snares *Irena* thrall,
　Besides vnto themselues they gotten had
　A monster, which the *Blatant beast* men call,
　A dreadfull feend of gods and men ydrad,
Whom they by slights allur'd, and to their purpose lad.

38

Such were these Hags, and so vnhandsome drest:
　Who when they nigh approching, had espyde
　Sir *Artegall* return'd from his late quest,
　They both arose, and at him loudly cryde,
　As it had bene two shepheards curres, had scryde
　A rauenous Wolfe amongst the scattered flockes.
　And *Enuie* first, as she that first him eyde,
　Towardes him runs, and with rude flaring lockes
About her eares, does beat her brest, and forhead knockes.

39

Then from her mouth the gobbet she does take,
　The which whyleare she was so greedily
　Deuouring, euen that halfe-gnawen snake,
　And at him throwes it most despightfully,
　The cursed Serpent, though she hungrily
　Earst chawd thereon, yet was not all so dead,
　But that some life remayned secretly,
　And as he past afore withouten dread,
Bit him behind, that long the marke was to be read.

40

Then th'other comming neare, gan him reuile,
　And fouly rayle, with all she could inuent;
　Saying, that he had with vnmanly guile,
　And foule abusion both his honour blent,
　And that bright sword, the sword of Iustice lent,
　Had stayned with reprochfull crueltie,
　In guiltlesse blood of many an innocent:
　As for *Grandtorto*, him with treacherie
And traynes hauing surpriz'd, he fouly did to die.

Stanza 35
2 eeke: extend; increase. Though her name indicates 'taking away', in her malignancy she adds to evil.
4 melling: meddling.
9 perplext: tormented.

Stanza 36
3–4 Cf. Sclaunder, IV viii 26.8–9. Cf. Ps. 140.3: 'Thei have sharpened their tongues like a serpent: adders poyson is under their lippes.' short: i.e. easily provoked, or speaking angrily. closely: secretly.
6–9 Detraction's distaff, for which there is no iconography (see Aptekar, 1969, 251n4), may be related to the distaff which Artegall bore at v 23 as a token of his effeminacy. Now Detraction mocks him with it. Such detraction was anticipated at vi.1. her other hand: i.e. one of her hands, or her left hand.
7 she litle spinnes, but spils: whatever little she spins, she destroys.
8 faynes: delights. leasings: lies.

Stanza 37
5 Cf. xi 39.7–9.
7 the Blatant Beast: from Lat. *blatero*, 'to bable in vayne' (Cooper, 1565), Engl. 'blatter', to speak or prate volubly, recorded from *c.* 1555, or Lat. *blateratus*, barking. Or from the Gk: J. Wibarne, *The New Age of Old Names* (1609), writes that virtue is assaulted by calumny, 'for actions done by divine instinct have ever found some *Zoylus*, *Momus*, *Mastix*, or tongue of blattant beast, so called of βλαττω, to hurt'; cited Hotson (1958) 36. In *View* 20 S. defends Gray's actions 'however envy list to blatter against him'. Here 'blatter' suggests clamorous noise or bellowing. The source of the Beast is usually taken to be Malory's Glatysaunte (i.e. yelping) Beste: 'That is in Englysh to sey, the questynge beste, for the beste, wheresomever he yode, he quested in the bealy with suche a noyse as hit had bene a thirty couple of howndis' (590). Aptekar (1969) 206 notes that a dog or hydra often accompanies Envy.

Stanza 38
7 first him eyde: because of her nature; see 29.2n.
8 flaring: outspreading.

Stanza 39
1 gobbet: a piece of raw flesh.
8 withouten: used for emphasis.
9 read: seen.

Stanza 40
3–4 Detraction may refer to Artegall's 'loosing soone his shield' (22.7); cf. xi 55.9. abusion: outrage, corrupt practice. blent: corrupted.
5 of: by.
8–9 The lines refer to Lord Gray's massacre of 600 Spaniards at Smerwick: 'Some say that he promised them life, others that at least he did put them in hope thereof' (*View* 107). traynes: wiles.

41

Thereto the Blatant beast by them set on
　At him began aloud to barke and bay,
　With bitter rage and fell contention,
　That all the woods and rockes nigh to that way,
　Began to quake and tremble with dismay;
　And all the aire rebellowed againe.
　So dreadfully his hundred tongues did bray,
　And euermore those hags them selues did paine,
To sharpen him, and their owne cursed tongs did straine.

42

And still among most bitter wordes they spake,
　Most shamefull, most vnrighteous, most vntrew,
　That they the mildest man aliue would make
　Forget his patience, and yeeld vengeaunce dew
　To her, that so false sclaunders at him threw.
　And more to make them pierce and wound more deepe,
　She with the sting, which in her vile tongue grew,
　Did sharpen them, and in fresh poyson steepe:
Yet he past on, and seem'd of them to take no keepe.

43

But *Talus* hearing her so lewdly raile,
　And speake so ill of him, that well deserued,
　Would her haue chastiz'd with his yron flaile,
　If her Sir *Artegall* had not preserued,
　And him forbidden, who his heast obserued.
　So much the more at him still did she scold,
　And stones did cast, yet he for nought would swerue
　From his right course, but still the way did hold
To Faery Court, where what him fell shall else be told.

Stanza 41
6　**rebellowed**: Fletcher (1971) 293–4 notes that the pun associates the Beast with rebellion.
7　**hundred**: as VI xii 33.2, but a thousand at VI i 9.3; cf. VI xii 27.1.
9　**sharpen**: goad.　**straine**: use to the utmost.

Stanzas 42–43
Gray's behaviour towards his detractors resembles David's on his flight from Jerusalem: Shimei cursed him, cast stones, and called him murderer and wicked man because he had brought upon himself all the blood of the house of Saul. Like David, Gray restrains the servant who would have punished the slanderer (2 Sam. 16.5–13); noted Gough (1921). On the other hand, David suffers the curses because they were sent by God for his sin. Cf. Evarchus, in Sidney's *Old Arcadia* 10, who 'could . . . not avoid the assaults of envy – the enemy and yet the honour of virtue'.

Stanza 42
1　**among**: all the while.
7　**She with the sting**: Detraction.

Stanza 43
1　**lewdly**: wickedly.
8　**right**: also direct.
9　**else**: elsewhere; at another time.

Few readers turn from the elaborate mythological and cosmological harmonies of the Temple of Venus and the marriage of Florimell and Marinell at the end of Book IV to the grating discords of the real world that open Book V without the shock of a rude awakening. Few leave Book V for the triumphant opening of Book VI, to rejoice with the poet about 'The waies, through which my weary steps I guyde, / In this delightfull land of Faery', without a sense of relief, relaxation, and a higher awakening. There is a strong sense of escaping from an iron world into a golden one. But do these ways lead to an end that triumphantly crowns the whole work, or to one that shows the impasse of the poet's imaginative powers? For some readers, Book VI relates to the rest of the poem as Shakespeare's final plays to his earlier ones: at last the poet has fulfilled his poetic powers. On the other hand, Lewis (1936) 350, 353 traces the progress of the poem as a descent: 'The sixth [Book] leads us down into the gracious valley of Humiliation. . . . the poem begins with its loftiest and most solemn book and thence, after a gradual descent, sinks away into its loosest and most idyllic.' Berger (1961) finds S. increasingly distracted by the problem of making sense of the world around him as he writes the poem. In Book VI his imaginative quest is defeated: 'the contrivance of the narrative, the inconclusiveness of the adventures, the gradual flawing of the romance world, the failure of chivalric action – these dramatize the claims imposed by actuality on the life of imagination. They also reveal the poet's awareness that the problems of life cannot be solved by poetry, cannot even be adequately represented in the simplified forms of Faerie' (41). Similarly, Neuse (1968) 331 finds that 'the dominant sense of Book VI is one of disillusionment, of the disparity between the poet's ideals and the reality he envisions'. J. Craig (1972) argues that in the course of writing the poem S. found the world an increasing challenge to the certainties necessary for the inspiration and perseverance he needed. Whatever S.'s mood as he writes, the Book itself gives the reader the sense that the poem is drawing to an end. As I have suggested (Hamilton, 1961, 202), 'it is as difficult not to see the poet intruding himself into the poem, as it is not to see Shakespeare in the role of Prospero with the breaking of the pipe, the dissolving of the vision, and our awareness (but surely the poet's too) that his work is being rounded out.' Nowhere else in the poem – and in what other work by any poet? – does the poet himself under his well-known *persona* enter into the fiction to reprimand one of his own characters for his stupid voyeurism as S. does Calidore at x 20, and prophesy unhappiness for him. Frye (1963) 70 refers to the ending of Book VI as 'a summing up and conclusion for the entire poem and for Spenser's poetic career'. Tonkin (1972) 11 finds that 'Book VI sums up and evaluates the driving purpose of the whole poem'.

One problem that literary critics have with Book VI is that they seem redundant. They are reduced to telling the story in prose or commenting on very general background. For no other book does the usual kind of allegorical interpretation seem so entirely inadequate, irrelevant and disposable. Of all the books, Book VI seems closest to romance with its aura of manifold, mysterious meanings conveyed in a 'poetic' context and not at all in any abstract moral, philosophical, or historical argument. In the historical allegory of Book V, the attack of the Blatant Beast on Artegall may be explained by the critic as an allusion to the slanders heaped on Lord Gray for his over-simple method of solving the Irish problem by exterminating the Irish. Presumably such allusion provides the reader with what Kermode (1971) 24 calls the poem's 'presence' or 'application to the human condition'. However, in Book VI if Calidore stands for Sidney, as Jones (1930) 293 claims, this allusion, if it is one, in no way helps us understand the allegory of Book VI. Williams (1966) 190–1 concludes that Book VI 'has a delicacy, and a transparency in its use of mythic figures . . . that makes commentary feel itself absurd. There is nothing to explicate in the legend of Courtesy, little to interpret, no need to demonstrate the fineness of its quality.' Similarly, Hough (1962) 204 notes: 'there is no book in *The Faerie Queene* where historical identifications are of less importance. . . . There is little formal allegory and the few overtly allegorical characters are not prominent.' In the two book-length studies of Book VI, A. Williams (1967) treats only personification-allegory and Tonkin (1972) writes only three concluding pages on the book as 'myth and allegory' in which he concludes that allegory merges into myth. Yet Book VI is part of a whole which is a 'continued Allegory, or darke conceit', and different only in that its complex allegory is especially fine and subtle. Accordingly, interpretation requires more than the usual tact, common sense, and sensitivity.

The problem of interpretation may be illustrated by the Pastorella story. In the course of analysing S.'s treatment of myth in the *Faerie Queene*, I conclude (Hamilton, 1959) that while earlier in the poem S.'s rendering of myth helps us to understand the allegory, in Book VI the myth and its allegory become the same thing because the 'darke conceit' is displayed on the literal surface of the romantic fiction. By intensifying the romance elements in Pastorella's story, for example, S. renders her imprisonment in the pirates' cave as Proserpina's descent into the underworld, as light imprisoned by darkness, and life imprisoned by death. Accordingly, her rescue by Calidore is her resurrection to life, and equally the restoration of beauty, life, and light to the world. Similarly, Williams (1966) 222, noting that Pastorella dies and lives again like Proserpina, concludes that in her story pastoral romance becomes a myth with inexhaustible meanings. Blitch (1973) argues that the key to the allegory of Book VI is Pastorella's resemblance to Proserpina. If one allows that S. creates in the Pastorella story a myth analogous specifically to the Proserpina myth and generally to myths of death and rebirth may one detail such as Calidore's descent to rescue Pastorella be interpreted, as it is by Evans (1970) 224, as an allusion to Christ harrowing Hell? That interpretation may seem blasphemous nonsense but Anderson (1976) 183 cautiously approves: 'The pressures of context make the reality of this allusion more than likely – that is, the pressures from the immediate context of the rescue, from the total context of the poem, and from the still larger context of "antique" descriptions of Christ's breaking open the gates of hell, certainly including Langland's.' Tonkin (1972) 143–50 interprets Calidore's rescue of Pastorella in moral terms: in rescuing the flower of courtesy, he is being trained in his virtue. He sees the myth of Proserpina as a central organizing myth of Book VI, and concludes that S. creates his own mythic patterns.

Courtesy is the culminating virtue of the poem. As it sums up the other virtues, its flowering would 'fashion a gentleman or noble person in vertuous and gentle discipline' within human society. Lewis (1936) 351–2 refers to courtesy as 'the poetry of conduct, an "unbought grace of life" which makes its possessor immediately loveable to all who meet him, and which is the bloom (as Aristotle would say) – the supervenient perfection – on the virtues of charity and humility'. The virtue has been glossed from Aristotle's *Ethics* but more usually from Renaissance moral manuals and courtesy books, such as Elyot's *Governour*, Castiglione's *Courtier*, and Guazzo's *Civile Conversation*. Guazzo's book has particular interest because parts were included in Bryskett's *Discourse of Civill Life* which purports to recount his conversation with S. on moral philosophy, as noted in the General Introduction (p. 2) above. The pertinence of courtesy books to Book VI is suggested by the full title of Bryskett's work: '*A discourse of civill life, containing the ethicke part of morall philosophie: fit to instruct a gentleman in the course of a vertuous life*'. These words could serve as subtitle of the *Faerie Queene*. Bryskett tells Lord Gray that his end is 'to discourse upon the morall vertues, yet not omitting the intellectuall, to the end to frame a gentleman fit for civill conversation, and to set him in the direct way that leadeth him to his civill felicitie' (6). When S. refers to courtesy as the 'roote of ciuill conuersation' (i 1), he means by the term what Guazzo (1581) i 56 calls 'an honest commendable and vertuous kinde of living in the world'.

Yet these courtesy books, as Culp (1971a) notes, do not treat the virtue of courtesy. To treat courtesy as a true moral virtue, S. needed 'to draw together diverse qualities that had been obscured in Renaissance moral treatises by the loose and overlapping definitions of general moral duty, justice, and charity'. Courtesy, for S., is an inclusive and yet a simple, secular virtue, which he may define simply as 'doing gentle deedes with franke delight' (vii 1). Berger (1961) 44 sees it as even more fundamental: 'It is not simply *a* virtue, nor merely an ornamental polish distinguishing gentry from boors, but a technique of survival in a difficult world; courtesy makes virtue and virtuous behavior possible, maintains trust between men, keeps open the lines of civilized communication.'

622   On S.'s structuring of the virtue of courtesy in Book VI, Cheney (1966) argues that the opening cantos

display the conventional aspects of courtesy as civilized behaviour, the central cantos show that 'man must maintain contact with the natural world, with its rigors and its unadorned simplicities, if he is to defend his civilization against the forces for chaos that take nourishment from this same natural world' (195), and the concluding cantos treat Calidore's education in his pastoral sojourn: first, by the vision of concord in the Graces and then by the encounter with the brigands in which 'the poem stresses the necessity of tempering courtesy with strength, to achieve a strategy responsive to the crude demands of this world, which requires the skills of both shepherd and wild man' (237). Culp (1971b) shows how the motif of the chance interruption of a moment of repose, particularly between lovers (see ii 16n), provides the occasion for actions that illustrate courtesy as a virtue. Tonkin (1972) 172–7 argues that S. defines the virtue of Courtesy by offering in the first eight cantos familiar images which the reader would readily allow. As later summarized by Colin, the virtue consists of 'comely carriage, entertainement kynde, / Sweete semblaunt, friendly offices that bynde' (x 23). S. shows also the shortcomings of the virtue thus understood, particularly in Calidore's bumbling interruption of Calepine's love-making which leads to Serena's wounding. At first Calidore is bound to his society; 'only later does he discover a new set of standards outside the chivalric framework, and this set of standards turns out ultimately to be the true courtesy'. In the later cantos, courtesy is redefined as the virtue that orders and harmonizes society. For Tonkin, the vision of the Graces which Calidore sees by abandoning his chivalric quest reveals a conception of courtesy in which harmony and reconciliation are central.

From these summaries of the structure of Book VI, it is clear that the pastoral interlude in Cantos ix–xi is crucial to our understanding of the allegory. The interlude must surprise any reader, not because the knight shamefully abandons his chivalric quest – the Red Cross Knight had done the same – but because he is rewarded for doing so. At the outset of his truancy, it is said explicitly that Calidore would suffer 'daunger, not to be redrest, / If he for slouth forslackt so famous quest' (ix 3). He does just that, only to be rewarded by gaining the love of Pastorella and seeing the Graces. Lewis (1936) 350 claims that 'the greatest mistake that can be made about this book is to suppose that Calidore's long delay among the shepherds is a pastoral truancy of Spenser's from his moral intention. On the contrary, the shepherd's country and Mount Acidale in the midst of it are the core of the book, and the key to Spenser's whole conception of Courtesy.' Williams (1962) 337 concludes that 'the pastoral interlude is not really an interlude at all but a thematic centre which unifies the dispersed adventures preceding it'. As the 'allegorical core' of the Book, the retreat prepares Calidore to fulfil his quest, even as the Red Cross Knight is prepared in the house of Holiness, Guyon in the house of Alma, and Britomart in the Temple of Isis. Cheney (1966) 217 refers to Calidore's sojourn among the shepherds as 'an education in the operation of courtesy', and his views are echoed by Tonkin (1972) 300–6.

Calidore's vision of the Graces during his pastoral retreat is more than the allegorical core of Book VI: it is the allegorical core of the whole poem, its climactic vision, and the moving centre about which the poem turns. As such, it raises central questions about the whole poem, the role of the poet in society, and his art in relation to nature and grace.

THE SIXTE

BOOKE OF THE
FAERIE QVEENE.

Contayning

THE LEGEND OF S. CALIDORE

OR

OF COVRTESIE.

1

The waies, through which my weary steps I guyde,
In this delightfull land of Faery,
Are so exceeding spacious and wyde,
And sprinckled with such sweet variety,
Of all that pleasant is to eare or eye,
That I nigh rauisht with rare thoughts delight,
My tedious trauell doe forget thereby;
And when I gin to feele decay of might,
It strength to me supplies, and chears my dulled spright.

2

Such secret comfort, and such heauenly pleasures,
Ye sacred imps, that on *Parnasso* dwell,
And there the keeping haue of learnings threasures,
Which doe all worldly riches farre excell,
Into the mindes of mortall men doe well,
And goodly fury into them infuse;
Guyde ye my footing, and conduct me well
In these strange waies, where neuer foote did vse,
Ne none can find, but who was taught them by the Muse.

3

Reuele to me the sacred noursery
Of vertue, which with you doth there remaine,
Where it in siluer bowre does hidden ly
From view of men, and wicked worlds disdaine.
Since it at first was by the Gods with paine
Planted in earth, being deriu'd at furst
From heauenly seedes of bounty soueraine,
And by them long with carefull labour nurst,
Till it to ripenesse grew, and forth to honour burst.

4

Amongst them all growes not a fayrer flowre,
Then is the bloosme of comely courtesie,
Which though it on a lowly stalke doe bowre,
Yet brancheth forth in braue nobilitie,
And spreds it selfe through all ciuilitie:
Of which though present age doe plenteous seeme,
Yet being matcht with plaine Antiquitie,
Ye will them all but fayned showes esteeme,
624 Which carry colours faire, that feeble eies misdeeme.

Title

S.: an accepted abbreviation for 'Sir'.

Proem

Stanza 1

7   **trauell**: also travail. In *Amor.* xxxiii, S. refers to the 'tædious toyle' of writing the *Faerie Queene*; in *Amor.* lxxx, he is ready to begin the second six books 'as a steed refreshed after toyle'.

Stanza 2

1   **comfort**: also support, invigoration.
2   **imps**: the Muses.
3–4   Cf. 'wisedome is most riches' (ix 30.7); Prov. 3.13–4.
5   **well**: cause to well up.
6   **fury**: poetic 'rage' (cf. I xi 6.2) or inspiration.
8   Curtius (1953) 85–6 traces the topos: 'I bring things never said before.' Upton (1758) notes that 'nothing is so common as this boast of the poets'; yet S. may claim that none before him has frequented faeryland.

Stanza 3

Cf. the nursery of virtue at III v 52, IV viii 33.
1   **noursery**: nursery garden, as in Cooper (1565), citing Pliny: 'Nutrix, a nourcerie or place where men plante and graffe trees or hearbes . . . afterward to remove them.' Cf. the Garden of Adonis where Amoret 'to perfect ripenesse grew' before being brought into the world (III vi 52.1). Its parody is the Stygian fen in which the Blatant Beast grows 'to perfect ripenesse' (i 8.5) before being sent into the world.
3   **siluer bowre**: the home of the Angels, II viii 2.1; and of Cynthia, VII vi 18.7.
5   **paine**: trouble, care.
6–7   Cf. James 1.17: 'Everie good giving, and everie perfite gift is from above.'

Stanza 4

1–2   A ranking of courtesy found in 1 Peter 3.8: 'Finally, be ye all of one minde: one suffre with another: love as brethren: be pitiful: be courteous.' The final injunction provides a summary and climax, as Spens (1958) 68 notes.
3   **bowre**: lodge.
4   **braue**: splendid.
5   **ciuilitie**: civilization, as med. Lat. *civilitas*, community; courteous behaviour; cf. i 26.6.
9   **misdeeme**: form a wrong judgment of.

5

But in the triall of true curtesie,
  Its now so farre from that, which then it was,
  That it indeed is nought but forgerie,
  Fashion'd to please the eies of them, that pas,
  Which see not perfect things but in a glas:
  Yet is that glasse so gay, that it can blynd
  The wisest sight, to thinke gold that is bras.
  But vertues seat is deepe within the mynd,
And not in outward shows, but inward thoughts defynd.

6

But where shall I in all Antiquity
  So faire a patterne finde, where may be seene
  The goodly praise of Princely curtesie,
  As in your selfe, O soueraine Lady Queene,
  In whose pure minde, as in a mirrour sheene,
  It showes, and with her brightnesse doth inflame
  The eyes of all, which thereon fixed beene;
  But meriteth indeede an higher name:
Yet so from low to high vplifted is your name.

7

Then pardon me, most dreaded Soueraine,
  That from your selfe I doe this vertue bring,
  And to your selfe doe it returne againe:
  So from the Ocean all riuers spring,
  And tribute backe repay as to their King.
  Right so from you all goodly vertues well
  Into the rest, which round about you ring,
  Faire Lords and Ladies, which about you dwell,
And doe adorne your Court, where courtesies excell.

Cant. I.

Calidore saues from Maleffort,
A Damzell osed vylde:
Doth vanquish Crudor, and doth make
Briana wexe more mylde.

1

OF Court it seemes, men Courtesie doe call,
  For that it there most vseth to abound;
  And well beseemeth that in Princes hall
  That vertue should be plentifully found,
  Which of all goodly manners is the ground,
  And roote of ciuill conuersation.
  Right so in Faery court it did redound,
  Where curteous Knights and Ladies most did won
Of all on earth, and made a matchlesse paragon.

Stanza 5

1   **triall**: suggesting legal examination, as does **defynd** (9).
4   **pas**: go by without attending.
5–7   Cf. 1 Cor. 13.12: 'For now we se through a glasse darkely.' Here the glass is a mirror.   **gay** suggests brilliant in its dazzling deception.

Stanza 6

Tonkin (1972) 24 suggests that 'the equivocal formulation of the poet's question leaves doubt whether the court of the **soueraine Lady Queene** is in antiquity or in modern times'.
3   **praise**: that which deserves praise.
5–7   Ellrodt (1960) 34 finds here the one probable instance of a 'technical' use of Platonic imagery in the poem. Yet the mirror image is biblical; cf. 2 Cor. 3.18: 'But we all beholde as in a mirrour the glorie of the Lord with open face, and are changed into the same image, from glorie to glorie, as by the Spirit of the Lord.' Cf. also I Proem 4.2.   **mirrour sheene** opposes the deceiving glass of the previous stanza.
8–9   To avoid the repetition of the rhyme word in the same sense, editors suggest 'fame' for 8 or 9. Church (1758) suggests a homonym: **name** signifies appellation in 8, character in 9.

Stanza 7

2–3   Shakespeare uses this theme in Sonnet 79: 'Yet what of thee thy poet doth invent / He robs thee of, and pays it thee again. / He lends thee virtue, and he stole that word / From thy behaviour.' It is expressed in the dance of the Graces at x 24.8–9. Snare (1974) 3 observes that 'this giving-receiving-returning is . . . a traditional gloss on the nature of grace as well as its exemplar, the Three Graces', and that 'this emblematic description of the court of the Queen is itself a microcosm of the nature of wisdom as a whole, given in stanzas 2 and 3'.
4–5   Eccles. 1.7: 'All the rivers go into the sea . . . whence thei returne, and go'. The gloss adds: 'The sea which compasseth all the earth filleth the veines thereof, the which powre out springs and rivers into the sea againe.' Cf. IV iii 27.
6   **well**: cf. 2.5.

Canto i

Stanza 1

1   The etymology, supported by the spelling, is suggested by the closing line of the Proem. Cf. III vi 1.5–6.
2   **vseth**: implying 'was accustomed'.
6   **ciuill conuersation**: civilized conduct or intercourse. Cf. Guazzo (1581) i 56: 'Civile conversation is an honest commendable and vertuous kinde of living in the world.'
7   **redound**: flourish.
8   **most**: i.e. where the most **curteous Knights**, etc.

2

But mongst them all was none more courteous Knight,
　　Then *Calidore*, beloued ouer all,
　　In whom it seemes, that gentlenesse of spright
　　And manners mylde were planted naturall;
　　To which he adding comely guize withall,
　　And gracious speach, did steale mens hearts away.
　　Nathlesse thereto he was full stout and tall,
　　And well approu'd in batteilous affray,
That him did much renowme, and far his fame display.

3

Ne was there Knight, ne was there Lady found
　　In Faery court, but him did deare embrace,
　　For his faire vsage and conditions sound,
　　The which in all mens liking gayned place,
　　And with the greatest purchast greatest grace:
　　Which he could wisely vse, and well apply,
　　To please the best, and th'euill to embase.
　　For he loathd leasing, and base flattery,
And loued simple truth and stedfast honesty.

4

And now he was in trauell on his way,
　　Vppon an hard aduenture sore bestad,
　　Whenas by chaunce he met vppon a day
　　With *Artegall*, returning yet halfe sad
　　From his late conquest, which he gotten had.
　　Who whenas each of other had a sight,
　　They knew them selues, and both their persons rad:
　　When *Calidore* thus first; Haile noblest Knight
Of all this day on ground, that breathen liuing spright.

5

Now tell, if please you, of the good successe,
　　Which ye haue had in your late enterprize.
　　To whom Sir *Artegall* gan to expresse
　　His whole exploite, and valorous emprize,
　　In order as it did to him arize.
　　Now happy man (sayd then Sir *Calidore*)
　　Which haue so goodly, as ye can deuize,
　　Atchieu'd so hard a quest, as few before;
That shall you most renowmed make for euermore.

6

But where ye ended haue, now I begin
　　To tread an endlesse trace, withouten guyde,
　　Or good direction, how to enter in,
　　Or how to issue forth in waies vntryde,
　　In perils strange, in labours long and wide,
　　In which although good Fortune me befall,
　　Yet shall it not by none be testifyde.
　　What is that quest (quoth then Sir *Artegall*)
That you into such perils presently doth call?

and gift are key terms throughout the book, culminating in the vision – a gift to Calidore – of the Graces who 'to men all gifts of grace do graunt' (x 15.4). His virtue is **naturall** (4), not acquired. Other suggested etymologies: Lat. *calidus*, living (Bennett, 1942, 215); more persuasively, *callidus*, skilful, experienced (Tonkin, 1972, 95 *n*13, citing ii 2, etc.). See III viii 28.8–9*n*. **beloued ouer all**: as courtesy arouses love in others in contrast to prowess which arouses dread; see IV iii 2.6–9.

5　comely guize: pleasing appearance.
6 Cf. ix 18.3–4; cf. also the praise of Sidney: 'That all mens hearts with secret rauishment / He stole away' (*Astrophel* 21–2). Cf. ii 3.2–4.
7–9　Nathlesse indicates that courtesy and prowess are at odds; cf. 41.2. At iii 40.8–9, Calepine maintains that it is seldom 'That curtesie and manhood euer disagree'. The conjunction is found in Britomart (IV i 11.6) and in the three brothers (IV iii 2.6–9). See 26.6–9*n*. **tall**: comely, handsome; brave, valiant. **approu'd**: tested. **batteilous affray**: warlike battle.

Stanza 3
3　For his faire vsage . . . sound: for his pleasing behaviour and good qualities.
5　purchast: gained.
7　embase: degrade; put down.
8–9 As Chaucer's perfect gentle knight 'loved chivalrie, / Trouthe and honour, fredom and curteisie'. **leasing**: lying.

Stanza 4
7　them selues: in knowing the other each knows himself. For the first time eponymous heroes need not be reconciled through conflict. **rad**: knew, recognized.
8　Haile noblest Knight: an address used only to Arthur, II xi 30.7; hence suggesting their kinship; cf. II iii 18.3–4.

Stanza 5
4　emprize: adventure.
7　as ye can deuize: as you know well how to describe; or, as you could wish. The latter reading fittingly praises Artegall for his prowess.

Stanza 6
1–7 Cf. the Palmer's address to the Red Cross Knight on Guyon's quest: 'wretched we, where ye haue left your marke, / Must now anew begin' (II i 32.6–7). **trace**: way. **endlesse**: notes the labyrinth in which Calidore wanders. **Fortune** (6), good and bad, is another key term in the Book: events seem to be governed by chance or fortune rather than by individual will or divine providence. **not by none**: i.e. by no one (the emphatic double negative), an important consideration in a Book that treats the evils of slander. Alone among S.'s knights, Calidore rides unattended (see ii 37.5–8; cf. IV vi 44.6–8, V i 30.8–9) and despairs of the rewards of virtuous action (cf. I ix 2.8–9, III xi 9.8–9). While the Red Cross Knight hopes 'To winne him worship, and her [Gloriana's] grace to haue' (I i 3.4), Calidore shows that good deeds are their own reward, as Arthur upholds (II viii 56, V xi 17.7–9).
8 to 7.1 The first time a questing knight has been so questioned. The question seems framed for its answer: the Blatant or Questing Beast.
9　presently: immediately.

Stanza 2
2　Calidore: Gk καλλι, beautiful, good + δωρον, gift. Beauty

7

The Blattant Beast (quoth he) I doe pursew,
　　And through the world incessantly doe chase,
　　Till I him ouertake, or else subdew:
　　Yet know I not or how, or in what place
　　To find him out, yet still I forward trace.
　　What is that Blattant Beast? (then he replide.)
　　It is a Monster bred of hellishe race,
　　(Then answerd he) which often hath annoyd
Good Knights and Ladies true, and many else destroyd.

8

Of *Cerberus* whilome he was begot,
　　And fell *Chimæra* in her darkesome den,
　　Through fowle commixture of his filthy blot;
　　Where he was fostred long in *Stygian* fen,
　　Till he to perfect ripenesse grew, and then
　　Into this wicked world he forth was sent,
　　To be the plague and scourge of wretched men:
　　Whom with vile tongue and venemous intent
He sore doth wound, and bite, and cruelly torment.

9

Then since the saluage Island I did leaue,
　　Sayd *Artegall*, I such a Beast did see,
　　The which did seeme a thousand tongues to haue,
　　That all in spight and malice did agree,
　　With which he bayd and loudly barkt at mee,
　　As if that he attonce would me deuoure.
　　But I that knew my selfe from perill free,
　　Did nought regard his malice nor his powre,
But he the more his wicked poyson forth did poure.

10

That surely is that Beast (saide *Calidore*)
　　Which I pursue, of whom I am right glad
　　To heare these tidings, which of none afore
　　Through all my weary trauell I haue had:
　　Yet now some hope your words vnto me add.
　　Now God you speed (quoth then Sir *Artegall*)
　　And keepe your body from the daunger drad:
　　For ye haue much adoe to deale withall.
So both tooke goodly leaue, and parted seuerall.

11

Sir *Calidore* thence trauelled not long,
　　When as by chaunce a comely Squire he found,
　　That thorough some more mighty enemies wrong,
　　Both hand and foote vnto a tree was bound:
　　Who seeing him from farre, with piteous sound
　　Of his shrill cries him called to his aide.
　　To whom approching, in that painefull stound
　　When he him saw, for no demaunds he staide,
But first him losde, and afterwards thus to him saide.

12

Vnhappy Squire, what hard mishap thee brought
　　Into this bay of perill and disgrace?
　　What cruell hand thy wretched thraldome wrought,
　　And thee captyued in this shamefull place?
　　To whom he answerd thus; My haplesse case
　　Is not occasiond through my misdesert,
　　But through misfortune, which did me abase
　　Vnto this shame, and my young hope subuert,
Ere that I in her guilefull traines was well expert.

13

Not farre from hence, vppon yond rocky hill,
　　Hard by a streight there stands a castle strong,
　　Which doth obserue a custome lewd and ill,
　　And it hath long mayntaind with mighty wrong:
　　For may no Knight nor Lady passe along
　　That way, (and yet they needs must passe that way,)
　　By reason of the streight, and rocks among,
　　But they that Ladies lockes doe shaue away,
And that knights berd for toll, which they for passage pay.

Stanza 7
1　**Blattant Beast**: see V xii 37.7*n*.
5　**trace**: travel.

Stanza 8
1–5　**Cerberus**: the triple-headed dog guarding the entrance to hell; see I v 34. **Chimæra**: a triple-formed monster guarding its outer gates (Virgil, *Aen*. vi 288). At vi 9.7 to 12.2, Echidna and Typhaon are said to beget the Beast; this pair also begets Cerberus and Chimæra: see Hesiod, *Theog*. 306–24. Chimæra may imply that the dog's slander is a fear-inspiring phantasm without any reality.
3　**commixture**: mingling of his stain with hers through copulation. Cf. 'commixtion' (vi 12.1).
4　**Stygian fen**: associated with discord at II v 22.6–8.
9　The Beast bites and reviles, or bites by reviling. For its etymology, from βλαττω, to hurt, see Hotson (cited V xii 37.7*n*).

Stanza 9
1　**saluage Island**: see V xi 39.3*n*.

Stanza 10
9　**goodly**: courteous. **seuerall**: separately, each going his separate way.

Stanza 11
7　**stound**: plight.
8　**demaunds**: questions.

Stanza 12
2　**Into this bay**: to this extremity, the extremity of the chase at which the quarry must face its pursuers.
6　**misdesert**: ill-deserving.
9　**traines**: wiles.

Stanza 13
On the sources in medieval romance for this disgrace to the knight, see *Var*. vi 365–7. S. adds the parallel disgrace to the knight's lady.
2, 7　**streight**: narrow pass.
3　**lewd**: wicked.
6–7　Church (1758) extends the parenthesis to include both lines.

627

14

A shamefull vse as euer I did heare,
　Sayd *Calidore*, and to be ouerthrowne.
　But by what meanes did they at first it reare,
　And for what cause, tell if thou haue it knowne.
　Sayd then that Squire: The Lady which doth owne
　This Castle, is by name *Briana* hight.
　Then which a prouder Lady liueth none:
　She long time hath deare lou'd a doughty Knight,
And sought to win his loue by all the meanes she might.

15

His name is *Crudor*, who through high disdaine
　And proud despight of his selfe pleasing mynd,
　Refused hath to yeeld her loue againe,
　Vntill a Mantle she for him doe fynd,
　With beards of Knights and locks of Ladies lynd,
　Which to prouide, she hath this Castle dight,
　And therein hath a Seneschall assynd,
　Cald *Maleffort*, a man of mickle might,
Who executes her wicked will, with worse despight.

16

He this same day, as I that way did come
　With a faire Damzell, my beloued deare,
　In execution of her lawlesse doome,
　Did set vppon vs flying both for feare:
　For little bootes against him hand to reare,
　Me first he tooke, vnhable to withstond;
　And whiles he her pursued euery where,
　Till his returne vnto this tree he bond:
Ne wote I surely, whether her he yet haue fond.

17

Thus whiles they spake, they heard a ruefull shrieke
　Of one loud crying, which they streight way ghest,
　That it was she, the which for helpe did seeke.
　Tho looking vp vnto the cry to lest,
　They saw that Carle from farre, with hand vnblest
　Hayling that mayden by the yellow heare,
　That all her garments from her snowy brest,
　And from her head her lockes he nigh did teare,
Ne would he spare for pitty, nor refraine for feare.

18

Which haynous sight when *Calidore* beheld,
　Eftsoones he loosd that Squire, and so him left,
　With hearts dismay and inward dolour queld,
　For to pursue that villaine, which had reft
　That piteous spoile by so iniurious theft,
　Whom ouertaking, loude to him he cryde;
　Leaue faytor quickely that misgotten weft
　To him, that hath it better iustifyde,
And turne thee soone to him, of whom thou art defyde.

19

Who hearkning to that voice, him selfe vpreard,
　And seeing him so fiercely towardes make,
　Against him stoutly ran, as nought afeard,
　But rather more enrag'd for those words sake;
　And with sterne count'naunce thus vnto him spake.
　Art thou the caytiue, that defyest me,
　And for this Mayd, whose party thou doest take,
　Wilt giue thy beard, though it but little bee?
Yet shall it not her lockes for raunsome fro me free.

628

20

With that he fiercely at him flew, and layd
　On hideous strokes with most importune might,
　That oft he made him stagger as vnstayd,
　And oft recuile to shunne his sharpe despight.
　But *Calidore*, that was well skild in fight,
　Him long forbore, and still his spirite spar'd,
　Lying in waite, how him he damadge might.
　But when he felt him shrinke, and come to ward,
He greater grew, and gan to driue at him more hard.

Stanza 14
6　**Briana**: 'shrill voice', the meaning given by Camden
(1605) 74. It befits her outcry against Calidore at 25. She
functions as the Amazon figure of Book VI. Cf. Radigund's
frustrated love, V iv 30. However, Briana is reformed rather
than slain.

Stanza 15
1　**Crudor**: from Lat. *crudus*, raw, bloody, cruel; the sense,
'undeveloped', gives hope of the change which occurs at 43.
3　**againe**: in return.
4-5　The motif is in Malory 54 and Geoffrey of Monmouth
x 3.
6　**dight**: built.
7　**Seneschall**: steward.
8　**Maleffort**: evil endeavour.
9　**with worse despight**: i.e. than Crudor's.

Stanza 16
3　**doome**: decree.

Stanza 17
4　**lest**: list.
5　**vnblest**: wicked.

Stanza 18
2　He had loosed him at 11.9 but then held him by his
questions; cf. iii 23.
5　**spoile**: i.e. the maiden; or her locks which he has taken
as his booty, leaving her distressed.
7　**faytor**: villain.　**weft**: waif; stolen goods abandoned by
a thief upon pursuit.
8　**him . . . better iustifyde**: i.e. one who has better legal
claim. Calidore is acting on behalf of his client, the helpless
youth.

Stanza 19
1　His posture suggests that of the reclining lover.
7　**party**: side.
8　The scorn, apparent from the opprobrious address, is
expressed allegorically in the 'sharpe despight' (20.4) of his
attack. Calidore's youth reflects that of the youth, 12.8-9.

Stanza 20
2　**importune**: grievous, heavy.
3　**vnstayd**: unstable.
6　**his spirite**: i.e. his own strength.
8　**to ward**: into a defensive posture.

21

Like as a water streame, whose swelling sourse
  Shall driue a Mill, within strong bancks is pent,
  And long restrayned of his ready course;
  So soone as passage is vnto him lent,
  Breakes forth, and makes his way more violent.
  Such was the fury of Sir *Calidore*,
  When once he felt his foeman to relent;
  He fiercely him pursu'd, and pressed sore,
Who as he still decayd, so he encreased more.

22

The heauy burden of whose dreadfull might
  When as the Carle no longer could sustaine,
  His heart gan faint, and streight he tooke his flight
  Toward the Castle, where if need constraine,
  His hope of refuge vsed to remaine.
  Whom *Calidore* perceiuing fast to flie,
  He him pursu'd and chaced through the plaine,
  That he for dread of death gan loude to crie
Vnto the ward, to open to him hastilie.

23

They from the wall him seeing so aghast,
  The gate soone opened to receiue him in,
  But *Calidore* did follow him so fast,
  That euen in the Porch he him did win,
  And cleft his head asunder to his chin.
  The carkasse tumbling downe within the dore,
  Did choke the entraunce with a lumpe of sin,
  That it could not be shut, whilest *Calidore*
Did enter in, and slew the Porter on the flore.

24

With that the rest, the which the Castle kept,
  About him flockt, and hard at him did lay;
  But he them all from him full lightly swept,
  As doth a Steare, in heat of sommers day,
  With his long taile the bryzes brush away.
  Thence passing forth, into the hall he came,
  Where of the Lady selfe in sad dismay
  He was ymett, who with vncomely shame
Gan him salute, and fowle vpbrayd with faulty blame.

25

False traytor Knight, (sayd she) no Knight at all,
  But scorne of armes that hast with guilty hand
  Murdred my men, and slaine my Seneschall;
  Now comest thou to rob my house vnmand,
  And spoile my selfe, that can not thee withstand?
  Yet doubt thou not, but that some better Knight
  Then thou, that shall thy treason vnderstand,
  Will it auenge, and pay thee with thy right:
And if none do, yet shame shal thee with shame requight.

26

Much was the Knight abashed at that word;
  Yet answerd thus; Not vnto me the shame,
  But to the shamefull doer it afford.
  Bloud is no blemish; for it is no blame
  To punish those, that doe deserue the same;
  But they that breake bands of ciuilitie,
  And wicked customes make, those doe defame
  Both noble armes and gentle curtesie.
No greater shame to man then inhumanitie.

27

Then doe your selfe, for dread of shame, forgoe
  This euill manner, which ye here maintaine,
  And doe in stead thereof mild curt'sie showe
  To all, that passe. That shall you glory gaine
  More then his loue, which thus ye seeke t'obtaine.
  Wherewith all full of wrath, she thus replyde;
  Vile recreant, know that I doe much disdaine
  Thy courteous lore, that doest my loue deride,
Who scornes thy ydle scoffe, and bids thee be defyde.

Stanza 21
1–5 Imitates Virgil, *Aen.* ii 496–9, but adds specific details,
e.g. **Shall driue a Mill**, and allegorical pointers as **ready** (i.e.
direct, suggesting that Calidore has been restrained from rightful action) and **more violent** (suggesting that evil brings a
stronger countering force). Tonkin (1972) 36 observes that
'an emblem of anarchy in Virgil becomes an emblem of
powerful natural energy in Spenser'.
7 **relent**: slacken.

Stanza 22
9 **ward**: guard.

Stanza 23
Cf. Arthur's slaying of the two knights at the entrance to
Geryoneo's castle, V x 36–37. Even the language corresponds,
e.g. 'lumpe of clay' and **lumpe of sin** (7).
4 **win**: overtake.
9 **on the flore**: on the spot.

Stanza 24
5 **bryzes**: breezes, gadflies.
9 **vpbrayd with faulty blame**: reproach for wrong-doing.

Stanza 25
5 **spoile**: ravish. Her tone, implying 'surely you are going
to', and the declaration that she cannot resist him, reveal her
frustration in love.

Stanza 26
3 **afford**: bestow, attach.
6–9 In his defence of killing, Calidore reveals the dilemma
of the knight of courtesy. For **ciuilitie**, see Proem 4.5 and x 23;
its meanings include social order, civilization and courtesy.
Cf. 'ciuill conuersation' (i.6).   **wicked customes** parallels
the 'wicked customes' (V ii 28.8) which Artegall reforms by
executing justice rather than by offering mercy as does Calidore.
gentle defines courtesy in terms of the end of the poem, 'to
fashion a gentleman or noble person in vertuous and gentle
discipline'.   **inhumanitie** signifies the want of courtesy
proper to civilized men (*OED* 2). Hence, e.g., the praise of the
Salvage Man's 'milde humanity, and perfect gentle mynd'
(v 29.9).

Stanza 27
2 **manner**: custom.
8 **courteous lore**: doctrine of courtesy.

28

To take defiaunce at a Ladies word
(Quoth he) I hold it no indignity;
But were he here, that would it with his sword
Abett, perhaps he mote it deare aby.
Cowherd (quoth she) were not, that thou wouldst fly,
Ere he doe come, he should be soone in place.
If I doe so, (sayd he) then liberty
I leaue to you, for aye me to disgrace
With all those shames, that erst ye spake me to deface.

29

With that a Dwarfe she cald to her in hast,
And taking from her hand a ring of gould,
A priuy token, which betweene them past,
Bad him to flie with all the speed he could,
To *Crudor*, and desire him that he would
Vouchsafe to reskue her against a Knight,
Who through strong powre had now her self in hould,
Hauing late slaine her Seneschall in fight,
And all her people murdred with outragious might.

30

The Dwarfe his way did hast, and went all night;
But *Calidore* did with her there abyde
The comming of that so much threatned Knight,
Where that discourteous Dame with scornfull pryde,
And fowle entreaty him indignifyde,
That yron heart it hardly could sustaine:
Yet he, that could his wrath full wisely guyde,
Did well endure her womanish disdaine,
And did him selfe from fraile impatience refraine.

31

The morrow next, before the lampe of light
Aboue the earth vpreard his flaming head,
The Dwarfe, which bore that message to her knight,
Brought aunswere backe, that ere he tasted bread,
He would her succour, and aliue or dead
Her foe deliuer vp into her hand:
Therefore he wild her doe away all dread;
And that of him she mote assured stand,
He sent to her his basenet, as a faithfull band.

32

Thereof full blyth the Lady streight became,
And gan t'augment her bitternesse much more;
Yet no whit more appalled for the same,
Ne ought dismayed was Sir *Calidore*,
But rather did more chearefull seeme therefore.
And hauing soone his armes about him dight,
Did issue forth, to meete his foe afore;
Where long he stayed not, when as a Knight
He spide come pricking on with al his powre and might.

33

Well weend he streight, that he should be the same,
Which tooke in hand her quarrell to maintaine;
Ne stayd to aske if it were he by name,
But couch his speare, and ran at him amaine.
They bene ymett in middest of the plaine,
With so fell fury, and dispiteous forse,
That neither could the others stroke sustaine,
But rudely rowld to ground both man and horse,
Neither of other taking pitty nor remorse.

34

But *Calidore* vprose againe full light,
Whiles yet his foe lay fast in sencelesse sound,
Yet would he not him hurt, although he might:
For shame he weend a sleeping wight to wound.
But when *Briana* saw that drery stound,
There where she stood vppon the Castle wall,
She deem'd him sure to haue bene dead on ground,
And made such piteous mourning therewithall,
That from the battlements she ready seem'd to fall.

35

Nathlesse at length him selfe he did vpreare
In lustlesse wise, as if against his will,
Ere he had slept his fill, he wakened were,
And gan to stretch his limbs; which feeling ill
Of his late fall, a while he rested still:
But when he saw his foe before in vew,
He shooke off luskishnesse, and courage chill
Kindling a fresh, gan battell ro renew,
To proue if better foote then horsebacke would ensew.

Stanza 28

2 **indignity**: disgraceful act.
4 **Abett**: uphold. **it deare aby**: dearly suffer for it.
9 **deface**: disgrace.

Stanza 29

7 **hould**: custody.

Stanza 30

4 *Var.* vi 191 notes the instances in Book VI of pride as the antithesis of courtesy: the 'despiteous' pride of the knight who abuses his lady (ii 40.6) and of Mirabella (vii 38.7), the 'scornefull' pride of Turpine (iii 47.5), the 'forward' pride of the two knights who sell their services to Turpine (vii 6.5), and the 'ouerweening' pride of Disdain (vii 42.4).
5 **entreaty**: treatment. **indignifyde**: treated with disdain, humiliated.

Stanza 31

9 **He sent ... his basenet**: he sends the helmet as a pledge to protect her. Hence it becomes the means of his defeat, 38.8–9.

Stanza 33

4 **amaine**: with full force; at once.

Stanza 34

2 **sound**: swoon.
3–4 In contrast to Turpine's baseness in seeking to kill the sleeping Arthur, vii 22.6–9.
5 **drery stound**: grievous peril.

Stanza 35

2–3 Suggested by 'sleeping wight' (34.4). **lustlesse**: listless.
7 **luskishnesse**: sluggishness.
9 **To proue if better foote ... would ensew**: i.e. if better (fortune) would follow being on foot.

36

There then began a fearefull cruell fray
   Betwixt them two, for maystery of might.
   For both were wondrous practicke in that play,
   And passing well expert in single fight,
   And both inflam'd with furious despight:
   Which as it still encreast, so still increast
   Their cruell strokes and terrible affright;
Ne once for ruth their rigour they releast,
Ne once to breath a while their angers tempest ceast.

37

Thus long they trac'd and trauerst to and fro,
   And tryde all waies, how each mote entrance make
   Into the life of his malignant foe;
   They hew'd their helmes, and plates asunder brake,
   As they had potshares bene; for nought mote slake
   Their greedy vengeaunces, but goary blood,
   That at the last like to a purple lake
Of bloudy gore congeal'd about them stood,
Which from their riuen sides forth gushed like a flood.

38

At length it chaunst, that both their hands on hie
   At once did heaue, with all their powre and might,
   Thinking the vtmost of their force to trie,
   And proue the finall fortune of the fight:
   But *Calidore*, that was more quicke of sight,
   And nimbler handed, then his enemie,
   Preuented him before his stroke could light,
   And on the helmet smote him formerlie,
That made him stoupe to ground with meeke humilitie.

39

And ere he could recouer foot againe,
   He following that faire aduantage fast,
   His stroke redoubled with such might and maine,
   That him vpon the ground he groueling cast;
   And leaping to him light, would haue vnlast
   His Helme, to make vnto his vengeance way.
   Who seeing, in what daunger he was plast,
   Cryde out, Ah mercie Sir, doe me not slay,
But saue my life, which lot before your foot doth lay.

40

With that his mortall hand a while he stayd,
   And hauing somewhat calm'd his wrathfull heat
   With goodly patience, thus he to him sayd;
   And is the boast of that proud Ladies threat,
   That menaced me from the field to beat,
   Now brought to this? By this now may ye learne,
   Strangers no more so rudely to intreat,
   But put away proud looke, and vsage sterne,
The which shal nought to you but foule dishonor yearne.

41

For nothing is more blamefull to a knight,
   That court'sie doth as well as armes professe,
   How euer strong and fortunate in fight,
   Then the reproch of pride and cruelnesse.
   In vaine he seeketh others to suppresse,
   Who hath not learnd him selfe first to subdew:
   All flesh is frayle, and full of ficklenesse,
   Subiect to fortunes chance, still chaunging new;
What haps to day to me, to morrow may to you.

42

Who will not mercie vnto others shew,
   How can he mercy euer hope to haue?
   To pay each with his owne is right and dew.
   Yet since ye mercie now doe need to craue,
   I will it graunt, your hopelesse life to saue;
   With these conditions, which I will propound:
   First, that ye better shall your selfe behaue
   Vnto all errant knights, whereso on ground;
Next that ye Ladies ayde in euery stead and stound.

Stanza 36
3   **practicke**: experienced.
4   **passing**: surpassing.
7   **affright**: fearsomeness.
8   **releast**: moderated.

Stanza 37
1   **trac'd and trauerst**: a duelling tactic, pursuing and turning aside; see IV vi 18.1.
3   **malignant**: evil; seeking to do evil to him.
5   **potshares**: potsherds, fragments of a broken vessel.

Stanza 38
7   **Preuented**: anticipated.
8   **formerlie**: first.

Stanza 39
9   **lot**: Fortune.

Stanza 40
6 to 41.6   While Crudor himself is not shown guilty of such discourtesy, he is the cause of such discourtesy in Maleffort.
7   **intreat**: treat.
8   **sterne**: cruel.
9   **yearne**: earn.

Stanza 41
5   **suppresse**: subdue.
7   Proverbial (C. G. Smith, 1970, 267).

Stanza 42
1–2   James 2.13: 'For there shalbe judgement merciles to him that sheweth no mercie.'
3   Romans 13.7: 'Give to all men therefore their duetie.'
7   **behaue**: conduct, bear.
9   **in euery stead and stound**: everywhere and at all times.

43

The wretched man, that all this while did dwell
 In dread of death, his heasts did gladly heare,
 And promist to performe his precept well,
 And whatsoeuer else he would requere.
 So suffring him to rise, he made him sweare
 By his owne sword, and by the crosse thereon,
 To take *Briana* for his louing fere,
 Withouten dowre or composition;
But to release his former foule condition.

44

All which accepting, and with faithfull oth
 Bynding himselfe most firmely to obay,
 He vp arose, how euer liefe or loth,
 And swore to him true fealtie for aye.
 Then forth he cald from sorrowfull dismay
 The sad *Briana*, which all this beheld:
 Who comming forth yet full of late affray,
 Sir *Calidore* vpcheard, and to her teld
All this accord, to which he *Crudor* had compeld.

45

Whereof she now more glad, then sory earst,
 All ouercome with infinite affect,
 For his exceeding courtesie, that pearst
 Her stubborne hart with inward deepe effect,
 Before his feet her selfe she did proiect,
 And him adoring as her liues deare Lord,
 With all due thankes, and dutifull respect,
 Her selfe acknowledg'd bound for that accord,
By which he had to her both life and loue restord.

46

So all returning to the Castle glad,
 Most ioyfully she them did entertaine,
 Where goodly glee and feast to them she made,
 To shew her thankefull mind and meaning faine,
 By all the meanes she mote it best explaine:
 And after all, vnto Sir *Calidore*
 She freely gaue that Castle for his paine,
 And her selfe bound to him for euermore;
So wondrously now chaung'd, from that she was afore.

47

But *Calidore* himselfe would not retaine
 Nor land nor fee, for hyre of his good deede,
 But gaue them streight vnto that Squire againe,
 Whom from her Seneschall he lately freed,
 And to his damzell as their rightfull meed,
 For recompence of all their former wrong:
 There he remaind with them right well agreed,
 Till of his wounds he wexed hole and strong,
And then to his first quest he passed forth along.

Cant. II.

Calidore sees young Tristram slay
A proud discourteous knight,
He makes him Squire, and of him learnes
his state and present plight.

1

WHat vertue is so fitting for a knight,
 Or for a Ladie, whom a knight should loue,
 As Curtesie, to beare themselues aright
 To all of each degree, as doth behoue?
 For whether they be placed high aboue,
 Or low beneath, yet ought they well to know
 Their good, that none them rightly may reproue
 Of rudenesse, for not yeelding what they owe:
Great skill it is such duties timely to bestow.

2

Thereto great helpe dame Nature selfe doth lend:
 For some so goodly gratious are by kind,
 That euery action doth them much commend,
 And in the eyes of men great liking find;
 Which others, that haue greater skill in mind,
 Though they enforce themselues, cannot attaine.
 For euerie thing, to which one is inclin'd,
 Doth best become, and greatest grace doth gaine:
Yet praise likewise deserue good thewes, enforst with paine.

Stanza 43

7   **fere**: wife.
8   **composition**: monetary agreement.
9   **release**: revoke.

Stanza 44

3   **liefe or loth**: willing or unwilling.
7   **affray**: fright.
8   **teld**: told (an obsolete form).

Stanza 45

2   **affect**: affection.

Stanza 46

4   **meaning faine**: well-disposed intentions, favourable disposition.
5   **explaine**: display.

Canto ii

Stanza 1

6–7   **know / Their good**: know how to behave with the respect proper to each social class. Not the modern sense of treating everyone the same. The virtue is seen in the Hermit (v 36.8), Reverence (I x 7.5) and Curtesie (IV x 51.4). On courtesy as civility, see x 23.7–9.

Stanza 2

2   **kind**: nature.
5   **skill in mind**: i.e. those who 'know / Their good'.
6   **enforce**: exert.
7–9   Distinguishing between nature and nurture. Those gracious by nature show best and gain greatest grace in contrast to those who seek grace by their own efforts.
9   **thewes**: manners, behaviour.   **enforst with paine**: acquired/exerted with difficulty.

3

That well in courteous *Calidore* appeares,
  Whose euery deed and word, that he did say,
  Was like enchantment, that through both the eyes,
  And both the eares did steale the hart away.
  He now againe is on his former way,
  To follow his first quest, when as he spyde
  A tall young man from thence not farre away,
  Fighting on foot, as well he him descryde,
Against an armed knight, that did on horsebacke ryde.

4

And them beside a Ladie faire he saw,
  Standing alone on foot, in foule array:
  To whom himselfe he hastily did draw,
  To weet the cause of so vncomely fray,
  And to depart them, if so be he may.
  But ere he came in place, that youth had kild
  That armed knight, that low on ground he lay;
  Which when he saw, his hart was inly child
With great amazement, and his thought with wonder fild.

5

Him stedfastly he markt, and saw to bee
  A goodly youth of amiable grace,
  Yet but a slender slip, that scarse did see
  Yet seuenteene yeares, but tall and faire of face
  That sure he deem'd him borne of noble race.
  All in a woodmans iacket he was clad
  Of Lincolne greene, belayd with siluer lace;
  And on his head an hood with aglets sprad,
And by his side his hunters horne he hanging had.

ծ

Buskins he wore of costliest cordwayne,
  Pinckt vpon gold, and paled part per part,
  As then the guize was for each gentle swaine;
  In his right hand he held a trembling dart,
  Whose fellow he before had seen apart;
  And in his left he held a sharpe borespeare,
  With which he wont to launch the saluage hart
  Of many a Lyon, and of many a Beare
That first vnto his hand in chase did happen neare.

7

Whom *Calidore* a while well hauing vewed,
  At length bespake; What meanes this, gentle swaine?
  Why hath thy hand too bold it selfe embrewed
  In blood of knight, the which by thee is slaine,
  By thee no knight; which armes impugneth plaine?
  Certes (said he) loth were I to haue broken
  The law of armes; yet breake it should againe,
  Rather then let my selfe of wight be stroken,
So long as these two armes were able to be wroken.

8

For not I him, as this his Ladie here
  May witnesse well, did offer first to wrong,
  Ne surely thus vnarm'd I likely were;
  But he me first, through pride and puissance strong
  Assayld, not knowing what to armes doth long.
  Perdie great blame, (then said Sir *Calidore*)
  For armed knight a wight vnarm'd to wrong.
  But then aread, thou gentle chyld, wherefore
Betwixt you two began this strife and sterne vprore.

Stanza 3

2–4 **deed and word**] act and deed *1596*. Upton (1758)
defends the 1596 reading although one may be bothered that an
act should **say**. Church (1758) first suggested **act, and word**.
Since the transposition **eyes . . . eares** for 'eares / . . . eyes'
(3–4) is clearly the printer's error, J. C. Smith ii App. 506
suggests that the error in 2 may also be his. Cf. the praise of
Calidore at i 2.3–6.

Stanza 4

2 **foule**: soiled.
5 **depart**: separate.

Stanza 5

4 His seven years in the woods (see 30.9) corresponds to the
more than seven years that Malory's Tristram, in Malory 375,
spent in Brittany to escape his uncle.   **tall**: also handsome.
5 Cf. 24.6.
7 **Lincolne greene**: a bright green material, reputed 'the
best greene of *England*' (gloss to Drayton, *Poly-Olbion* Song
xxv 262) and worn by Robin Hood and his men (Song xxvi
319). **belayd**: ornamented.
8 **aglets**: tags or sequins.

Stanza 6

Tristram appears as a more masculine version of Belphœbe; cf.
II iii 21f, esp. 27, 29.
1 **cordwayne**: cordovan, a Spanish leather, worn by
Belphœbe (II iii 27.3).
2 **Pinckt vpon gold**: ornamented by perforating with a
design to reveal the gold backing. **paled part per part**:
marked with vertical stripes; an heraldic term. The entire
description of Tristram seems heraldic.
3 **guize**: fashion.
4 **trembling**: quivering with the tension of the intended
thrust; 'shivering'.
7 **launch**: pierce.

Stanza 7

5 **which armes impugneth plaine**: i.e. which clearly
violates the law of arms that only a knight may fight a knight.
armes leads to Tristram's pun in 9.
9 **wroken**: avenged.

Stanza 8

5 **long**: belong.
8 **aread**: tell. **gentle chyld**: noble youth, anticipating
his name, 'Chyld *Tristram*' (36.3), and his elevation to Squire.
Cf. 11.9.

9

That shall I sooth (said he) to you declare.
  I whose vnryper yeares are yet vnfit
  For thing of weight, or worke of greater care,
  Doe spend my dayes, and bend my carelesse wit
  To saluage chace, where I thereon may hit
  In all this forrest, and wyld wooddie raine:
  Where, as this day I was enraunging it,
  I chaunst to meete this knight, who there lyes slaine,
Together with this Ladie, passing on the plaine.

10

The knight, as ye did see, on horsebacke was,
  And this his Ladie, (that him ill became,)
  On her faire feet by his horse side did pas
  Through thicke and thin, vnfit for any Dame.
  Yet not content, more to increase his shame,
  When so she lagged, as she needs mote so,
  He with his speare, that was to him great blame,
  Would thumpe her forward, and inforce to goe,
Weeping to him in vaine, and making piteous woe.

11

Which when I saw, as they me passed by,
  Much was I moued in indignant mind,
  And gan to blame him for such cruelty
  Towards a Ladie, whom with vsage kind
  He rather should haue taken vp behind.
  Wherewith he wroth, and full of proud disdaine,
  Tooke in foule scorne, that I such fault did find,
  And me in lieu thereof reuil'd againe,
Threatning to chastize me, as doth t'a chyld pertaine.

12

Which I no lesse disdayning, backe returned
  His scornefull taunts vnto his teeth againe,
  That he streight way with haughtie choler burned,
  And with his speare strooke me one stroke or twaine;
  Which I enforst to beare though to my paine,
  Cast to requite, and with a slender dart,
  Fellow of this I beare, throwne not in vaine,
  Strooke him, as seemeth, vnderneath the hart,
That through the wound his spirit shortly did depart.

13

Much did Sir *Calidore* admyre his speach
  Tempred so well, but more admyr'd the stroke
  That through the mayles had made so strong a breach
  Into his hart, and had so sternely wroke
  His wrath on him, that first occasion broke.
  Yet rested not, but further gan inquire
  Of that same Ladie, whether what he spoke,
  Were soothly so, and that th'vnrighteous ire
Of her owne knight, had giuen him his owne due hire.

14

Of all which, when as she could nought deny,
  But cleard that stripling of th'imputed blame,
  Sayd then Sir *Calidore*; Neither will I
  Him charge with guilt, but rather doe quite clame:
  For what he spake, for you he spake it, Dame:
  And what he did, he did him selfe to saue:
  Against both which that knight wrought knightlesse shame.
  For knights and all men this by nature haue,
Towards all womenkind them kindly to behaue.

15

But sith that he is gone irreuocable,
  Please it you Ladie, to vs to aread,
  What cause could make him so dishonourable,
  To driue you so on foot vnfit to tread,
  And lackey by him, gainst all womanhead?
  Certes Sir knight (sayd she) full loth I were
  To rayse a lyuing blame against the dead:
  But since it me concernes, my selfe to clere,
I will the truth discouer, as it chaunst whylere.

Stanza 9
4 carelesse: carefree.
6 wooddie raine: woodland realm.
7 enraunging it: roaming in it.

Stanza 11
8 in lieu thereof: i.e. in return for reviling him.

Stanza 12
6 Cast: determined.
9 through: meant literally; cf., e.g., IV iii 12.7–9.

Stanza 13
5 first occasion broke: i.e. had first occasioned the combat.

Stanza 14
4 quite clame: i.e. quitclaim, acquit.
7 knightlesse: unknightly.
8–9 'The pun on "kind" [by nature] and kindly serves to underline the connection between natural behaviour and goodness' (Tonkin, 1972, 44).

Stanza 15
2 aread: declare.
5 lackey: run as a footman.
6–7 A common sentiment: e.g. *2 Henry IV* I i 98: 'he doth sin that doth belie the dead.'

16

This day, as he and I together roade
  Vpon our way, to which we weren bent,
  We chaunst to come foreby a couert glade
  Within a wood, whereas a Ladie gent
  Sate with a knight in ioyous iolliment
  Of their franke loues, free from all gealous spyes:
  Faire was the Ladie sure, that mote content
  An hart, not carried with too curious eyes,
And vnto him did shew all louely courtesyes.

17

Whom when my knight did see so louely faire,
  He inly gan her louer to enuy,
  And wish, that he part of his spoyle might share.
  Whereto when as my presence he did spy
  To be a let, he bad me by and by
  For to alight: but when as I was loth,
  My loues owne part to leaue so suddenly,
  He with strong hand down from his steed me throw'th,
And with presumpteous powre against that knight streight go'th.

18

Vnarm'd all was the knight, as then more meete
  For Ladies seruice, and for loues delight,
  Then fearing any foeman there to meete:
  Whereof he taking oddes, streight bids him dight
  Himselfe to yeeld his loue, or else to fight.
  Whereat the other starting vp dismayd,
  Yet boldly answer'd, as he rightly might;
  To leaue his loue he should be ill apayd,
In which he had good right gaynst all, that it gainesayd.

19

Yet since he was not presently in plight
  Her to defend, or his to iustifie,
  He him requested, as he was a knight,
  To lend him day his better right to trie,
  Or stay till he his armes, which were thereby,
  Might lightly fetch. But he was fierce and whot,
  Ne time would giue, nor any termes aby,
  But at him flew, and with his speare him smot;
From which to thinke to saue himselfe, it booted not.

20

Meane while his Ladie, which this outrage saw,
  Whilest they together for the quarrey stroue,
  Into the couert did her selfe withdraw,
  And closely hid her selfe within the groue.
  My knight hers soone, as seemes, to daunger droue
  And left sore wounded: but when her he mist,
  He woxe halfe mad, and in that rage gan roue
  And range through all the wood, where so he wist
She hidden was, and sought her so long, as him list.

21

But when as her he by no meanes could find,
  After long search and chauff, he turned backe
  Vnto the place, where me he left behind:
  There gan he me to curse and ban, for lacke
  Of that faire bootie, and with bitter wracke
  To wreake on me the guilt of his owne wrong.
  Of all which I yet glad to beare the packe,
  Stroue to appease him, and perswaded long:
But still his passion grew more violent and strong.

22

Then as it were t'auenge his wrath on mee,
  When forward we should fare, he flat refused
  To take me vp (as this young man did see)
  Vpon his steed, for no iust cause accused,
  But forst to trot on foot, and foule misused,
  Pounching me with the butt end of his speare,
  In vaine complayning, to be so abused,
  For he regarded neither playnt nor teare,
But more enforst my paine, the more my plaints to heare.

23

So passed we, till this young man vs met,
  And being moou'd with pittie of my plight,
  Spake, as was meet, for ease of my regret:
  Whereof befell, what now is in your sight.
  Now sure (then said Sir *Calidore*) and right
  Me seemes, that him befell by his owne fault:
  Who euer thinkes through confidence of might,
  Or through support of count'nance proud and hault
To wrong the weaker, oft falles in his owne assault.

Stanza 16
A frequently repeated motif: a character is surprised in a moment of diversion. Cf. iii 20–21, 23–24; iv 17; v 10–11, 15; vii 6–7, 18–19; viii 34; x 18, 34, 39. The motif is traced by Berger (1961) 40.
3   **foreby**: i.e. close to, for the wood is a place of passion.
4–6   As the lovers in the Garden of Adonis, III vi 41.5–9, and in the garden surrounding the Temple of Venus, IV x 26.1–2. **gent**: gentle.
7–8   This bitchy remark suggests a jilted lady's **too curious** (i.e. fastidious) eyes.
9   **louely**: loving. **courtesyes**: courteous behaviour.

Stanza 17
5   **let**: hindrance.
7   **part**: side.

Stanza 18
4   **oddes**: advantage. **dight**: prepare.
8   **ill apayd**: ill-pleased.

Stanza 19
1   **plight**: physical condition; state of mind.
2   **his**: i.e. his 'good right' (18.9).
6   **lightly**: quickly.
7   **aby**: abide.

Stanza 21
2   **chauff**: raging; hence 'long raging search'.
4   **ban**: revile.
5   **wracke**: vengeance; violence.
7   **packe**: the burden of his blows.

Stanza 23
3   **regret**: sorrow; obliquely, the pain and grief which she regrets to endure.
7–9   Cf. Ps. 7.16. **confidence**: overboldness. **hault**: haughty.

635

24

Then turning backe vnto that gentle boy,
   Which had himselfe so stoutly well acquit;
   Seeing his face so louely sterne and coy,
   And hearing th'answeres of his pregnant wit,
   He praysd it much, and much admyred it;
   That sure he weend him borne of noble blood,
   With whom those graces did so goodly fit:
   And when he long had him beholding stood,
He burst into these words, as to him seemed good.

25

Faire gentle swayne, and yet as stout as fayre,
   That in these woods amongst the Nymphs dost wonne,
   Which daily may to thy sweete lookes repayre,
   As they are wont vnto *Latonaes* sonne,
   After his chace on woodie *Cynthus* donne:
   Well may I certes such an one thee read,
   As by thy worth thou worthily hast wonne,
   Or surely borne of some Heroicke sead,
That in thy face appeares and gratious goodlyhead.

26

But should it not displease thee it to tell;
   (Vnlesse thou in these woods thy selfe conceale,
   For loue amongst the woodie Gods to dwell;)
   I would thy selfe require thee to reueale,
   For deare affection and vnfayned zeale,
   Which to thy noble personage I beare,
   And wish thee grow in worship and great weale.
   For since the day that armes I first did reare,
I neuer saw in any greater hope appeare.

27

To whom then thus the noble youth; May be
   Sir knight, that by discouering my estate,
   Harme may arise vnweeting vnto me;
   Nathelesse, sith ye so courteous seemed late,
   To you I will not feare it to relate.
   Then wote ye that I am a Briton borne,
   Sonne of a King, how euer thorough fate
   Or fortune I my countrie haue forlorne,
And lost the crowne, which should my head by right adorne.

28

And *Tristram* is my name, the onely heire
   Of good king *Meliogras* which did rayne
   In Cornewale, till that he through liues despeire
   Vntimely dyde, before I did attaine
   Ripe yeares of reason, my right to maintaine.
   After whose death, his brother seeing mee
   An infant, weake a kingdome to sustaine,
   Vpon him tooke the roiall high degree,
And sent me, where him list, instructed for to bee.

29

The widow Queene my mother, which then hight
   Faire *Emiline*, conceiuing then great feare
   Of my fraile safetie, resting in the might
   Of him, that did the kingly Scepter beare,
   Whose gealous dread induring not a peare,
   Is wont to cut off all, that doubt may breed,
   Thought best away me to remoue somewhere
   Into some forrein land, where as no need
636 Of dreaded daunger might his doubtfull humor feed.

Stanza 24
3   **coy**: modest, reserved.
6   Repeating 5.5 to stress the relationship between noble appearance and noble blood.
9   Calidore's own reserve is overwhelmed by his admiration for the boy.

Stanza 25
4–5   **Latonaes sonne**: Apollo.   **Cynthus**: the mountain in Delos where he and Diana were born; cf. II iii 31.1–2. Calidore's outburst shows him open to the vision of the Graces in Canto x.
6   **read**: take to be.
9   **goodlyhead**: excellence; the source of all goodness.

Stanza 26
3   Tactfully expressed: because of some rejected love or love of the woods as a hunter; neither guess proves correct.
5   **zeale**: devotion.
7   **worship**: honour; good and honourable report.   **weale**: well-being.

Stanza 27
2   **estate**: state, rank.
7   **how euer**: although.
8   **forlorne**: left.

Stanzas 28–32
The general source is Malory VIII i. In Malory, Tristram's mother, who dies in childbirth, is called Elizabeth, and her father is Melyodas whose second wife threatens Tristram. S. uses scarcely more than the name, place, and Tristram's education in hunting and hawking, and his fear of his uncle.

Stanza 28
3–4   The sadness of Tristram's birth (Malory 372), which gave him his name, is transferred to his father.

Stanza 29
1   **then**: either 'then conceiving'; or implying that she is dead.
2   **Emiline**: cf. Emmilen, one of the 'women valorous' cited by Glauce, III iii 54.9.
5   **peare**: rival.
6   **doubt**: danger.
9   **doubtfull**: apprehensive, suspicious.

30

So taking counsell of a wise man red,
  She was by him aduiz'd, to send me quight
  Out of the countrie, wherein I was bred,
  The which the fertile *Lionesse* is hight,
  Into the land of *Faerie*, where no wight
  Should weet of me, nor worke me any wrong.
  To whose wise read she hearkning, sent me streight
Into this land, where I haue wond thus long,
Since I was ten yeares old, now growen to stature strong.

31

All which my daies I haue not lewdly spent,
  Nor spilt the blossome of my tender yeares
  In ydlesse, but as was conuenient,
  Haue trayned bene with many noble feres
  In gentle thewes, and such like seemely leres.
  Mongst which my most delight hath alwaies been,
  To hunt the saluage chace amongst my peres,
  Of all that raungeth in the forrest greene;
Of which none is to me vnknowne, that eu'r was seene.

32

Ne is there hauke, which mantleth her on pearch,
  Whether high towring, or accoasting low,
  But I the measure of her flight doe search,
  And all her pray, and all her diet know.
  Such be our ioyes, which in these forrests grow:
  Onely the vse of armes, which most I ioy,
  And fitteth most for noble swayne to know,
  I haue not tasted yet, yet past a boy,
And being now high time these strong ioynts to imploy.

33

Therefore, good Sir, sith now occasion fit
  Doth fall, whose like hereafter seldome may,
  Let me this craue, vnworthy though of it,
  That ye will make me Squire without delay,
  That from henceforth in batteilous array
  I may beare armes, and learne to vse them right;
  The rather since that fortune hath this day
  Giuen to me the spoile of this dead knight,
These goodly gilden armes, which I haue won in fight.

34

All which when well Sir *Calidore* had heard,
  Him much more now, then earst he gan admire,
  For the rare hope which in his yeares appear'd,
  And thus replide; Faire chyld, the high desire
  To loue of armes, which in you doth aspire,
  I may not certes without blame denie;
  But rather wish, that some more noble hire,
  (Though none more noble then is cheualrie,)
I had, you to reward with greater dignitie.

35

There him he causd to kneele, and made to sweare
  Faith to his knight, and truth to Ladies all,
  And neuer to be recreant, for feare
  Of perill, or of ought that might befall:
  So he him dubbed, and his Squire did call.
  Full glad and ioyous then young *Tristram* grew,
  Like as a flowre, whose silken leaues small,
  Long shut vp in the bud from heauens vew,
At length breakes forth, and brode displayes his smyling hew.

36

Thus when they long had treated to and fro,
  And *Calidore* betooke him to depart,
  Chyld *Tristram* prayd, that he with him might goe
  On his aduenture, vowing not to start,
  But wayt on him in euery place and part.
  Whereat Sir *Calidore* did much delight,
  And greatly ioy'd at his so noble hart,
  In hope he sure would proue a doughtie knight:
Yet for the time this answere he to him behight.

Stanza 30
1   **of a wise man red**: of a man esteemed wise.
4   **Lionesse**: the fabled land west of Cornwall, between Land's End and the Scillies.
7   **read**: counsel.

Stanza 31
1   **lewdly**: foolishly.
2   **spilt**: spoiled.
3   **conuenient**: proper.
4   **feres**: companions.
5   **thewes**: manners.   **leres**: lessons.

Stanza 32
1–4   Malory 375 records that Tristram 'began . . . all the tearmys we have yet of hawkynge and huntynge'. The terms here are used in a technical sense.   **mantleth**: the perched bird stretches alternate wings over the corresponding outstretched leg.   **towring**: mounting up in order to swoop down upon a quarry; or 'touring': turning, wheeling. **accoasting**: when a hawk skims the ground.
8   **tasted**: experienced.

Stanza 33
9   **gilden**: gilded; possibly golden: see 39.4.

Stanza 34
4   **Faire chyld**: marks Tristram's transition. Earlier he was addressed contemptuously as a child (11.9); soon he gains the chivalric rank of Child, 36.3.

Stanza 35
7–9   The image fulfils 31.2–3 and shows the flowering of courtesy, Proem 3.9.

Stanza 36
1   **treated**: conversed.
3   **Chyld**: applied to a youth of gentle birth, particularly to a Squire awaiting knighthood.
4   **start**: i.e. desert him.
9   **behight**: addressed.

637

37

Glad would I surely be, thou courteous Squire,
   To haue thy presence in my present quest,
   That mote thy kindled courage set on fire,
   And flame forth honour in thy noble brest:
   But I am bound by vow, which I profest
   To my dread Soueraine, when I it assayd,
   That in atchieuement of her high behest,
   I should no creature ioyne vnto mine ayde,
For thy I may not graunt, that ye so greatly prayde.

38

But since this Ladie is all desolate,
   And needeth safegard now vpon her way,
   Ye may doe well in this her needfull state
   To succour her, from daunger of dismay;
   That thankfull guerdon may to you repay.
   The noble ympe of such new seruice fayne,
   It gladly did accept, as he did say.
   So taking courteous leaue, they parted twayne,
And *Calidore* forth passed to his former payne.

39

But *Tristram* then despoyling that dead knight
   Of all those goodly implements of prayse,
   Long fed his greedie eyes with the faire sight
   Of the bright mettall, shyning like Sunne rayes;
   Handling and turning them a thousand wayes.
   And after hauing them vpon him dight,
   He tooke that Ladie, and her vp did rayse
   Vpon the steed of her owne late dead knight,
So with her marched forth, as she did him behight.

40

There to their fortune leaue we them awhile,
   And turne we backe to good Sir *Calidore*;
   Who ere he thence had traueild many a mile,
   Came to the place, whereas ye heard afore
   This knight, whom *Tristram* slew, had wounded sore
   Another knight in his despiteous pryde;
   There he that knight found lying on the flore,
   With many wounds full perilous and wyde,
That all his garments, and the grasse in vermeill dyde.

41

And there beside him sate vpon the ground
   His wofull Ladie, piteously complayning
   With loud laments that most vnluckie stound,
   And her sad selfe with carefull hand constrayning
   To wype his wounds, and ease their bitter payning.
   Which sorie sight when *Calidore* did vew
   With heauie eyne, from teares vneath refrayning,
   His mightie hart their mournefull case can rew,
And for their better comfort to them nigher drew.

42

Then speaking to the Ladie, thus he sayd:
   Ye dolefull Dame, let not your griefe empeach
   To tell, what cruell hand hath thus arayd
   This knight vnarm'd, with so vnknightly breach
   Of armes, that if I yet him nigh may reach,
   I may auenge him of so foule despight.
   The Ladie hearing his so courteous speach,
   Gan reare her eyes as to the chearefull light,
638 And from her sory hart few heauie words forth sight.

43

In which she shew'd, how that discourteous knight
   (Whom *Tristram* slew) them in that shadow found,
   Ioying together in vnblam'd delight,
   And him vnarm'd, as now he lay on ground,
   Charg'd with his speare and mortally did wound,
   Withouten cause, but onely her to reaue
   From him, to whom she was for euer bound:
   Yet when she fled into that couert greaue,
He her not finding, both them thus nigh dead did leaue.

Stanza 37

Cf. Artegall's rejection of the company of the Squire, V i 30.
6   **assayd**: set out to do.
9   **For thy**: therefore.

Stanza 38

6   **fayne**: glad.

Stanza 39

1–5   The knight had lusted after another's love; Tristram lusts after his arms, and gains both them and his love. In his innocence, he is not aware of the Palmer's injunction: 'To spoile the dead of weed / Is sacrilege, and doth all sinnes exceed' (II viii 16.4–5).
2   **implements of prayse**: as arms are the means to gain praise; cf. II xii 80.1–2.
9   **behight**: command.

Stanza 40

7   **flore**: ground.

Stanza 41

3   **stound**: troublous time.
4   **constrayning**: forcing (cf. her reluctance to bear him at 47.5); more charitably, 'exerting'.
7   **vneath**: with difficulty.
8   **can rew**: did pity.

Stanza 42

2   **empeach**: hinder.
3   **arayd**: afflicted; literally, 'dressed him in his wounds'.
9   **sight**: sighed.

Stanza 43

1   **that discourteous knight**: as Arg. and iii 18.6.
2   **shadow**: shady place.
3   **vnblam'd**: unblamable; neither shameful in them nor deserving shameful attack.
6   **reaue**: take by force.
8   **greaue**: thicket.
9   Her wound is shame; cf. iii 11.6–8.

44

When *Calidore* this ruefull storie had
  Well vnderstood, he gan of her demand,
  What manner wight he was, and how yclad,
  Which had this outrage wrought with wicked hand.
  She then, like as she best could vnderstand,
  Him thus describ'd, to be of stature large,
  Clad all in gilden armes, with azure band
  Quartred athwart, and bearing in his targe
A Ladie on rough waues, row'd in a sommer barge.

45

Then gan Sir *Calidore* to ghesse streight way
  By many signes, which she described had,
  That this was he, whom *Tristram* earst did slay,
  And to her said; Dame be no longer sad:
  For he, that hath your Knight so ill bestad,
  Is now him selfe in much more wretched plight;
  These eyes him saw vpon the cold earth sprad,
  The meede of his desert for that despight,
Which to your selfe he wrought, and to your loued knight.

46

Therefore faire Lady lay aside this griefe,
  Which ye haue gathered to your gentle hart,
  For that displeasure; and thinke what reliefe
  Were best deuise for this your louers smart,
  And how ye may him hence, and to what part
  Conuay to be recur'd. She thankt him deare,
  Both for that newes he did to her impart,
  And for the courteous care, which he did beare
Both to her loue, and to her selfe in that sad dreare.

47

Yet could she not deuise by any wit,
  How thence she might conuay him to some place.
  For him to trouble she it thought vnfit,
  That was a straunger to her wretched case;
  And him to beare, she thought it thing too base.
  Which when as he perceiu'd, he thus bespake;
  Faire Lady let it not you seeme disgrace,
  To beare this burden on your dainty backe;
My selfe will beare a part, coportion of your packe.

48

So off he did his shield, and downeward layd
  Vpon the ground, like to an hollow beare;
  And powring balme, which he had long puruayd,
  Into his wounds, him vp thereon did reare,
  And twixt them both with parted paines did beare,
  Twixt life and death, not knowing what was donne.
  Thence they him carried to a Castle neare,
  In which a worthy auncient Knight did wonne:
Where what ensu'd, shall in next Canto be begonne.

Stanza 44

7–9   A precise heraldic description which suggests the state of his lady, a Phædria come to grief.

9   **barge**: a small row-boat.

Stanza 45

4–9   One might think that Calidore's remark would bring the lady little comfort; yet she thanks him for it (46.6). Justice must be affirmed before courtesy may be exercised.

Stanza 46

3   **displeasure**: offence.
6   **recur'd**: healed.
9   **dreare**: dreary state.

Stanza 47

5   No bawdy sense is intended. There is a witty point: in bearing him she would be base, i.e. lower than he. She is too nice or too high class; cf. Turpine's response to the request that he bear the wounded Serena, iii 31.7–9. Cf. 'Entire affection hateth nicer hands' (I viii 40.3), and 'loue does loath disdainfull nicitee' (II ii 3.3).
9   **coportion**: joint portion.

Stanza 48

3   **long puruayd**: provided long before.
5   **parted paines**: shared labour.

639

Cant. III.

Calidore brings Priscilla home,
Pursues the Blatant Beast:
Saues Serena whilest Calepine
By Turpine is opprest.

1

TRue is, that whilome that good Poet sayd,
  The gentle minde by gentle deeds is knowne.
For a man by nothing is so well bewrayd,
As by his manners, in which plaine is showne
Of what degree and what race he is growne.
For seldome seene, a trotting Stalion get
An ambling Colt, that is his proper owne:
So seldome seene, that one in basenesse set
Doth noble courage shew, with curteous manners met.

2

But euermore contrary hath bene tryde,
  That gentle bloud will gentle manners breed;
As well may be in *Calidore* descryde,
By late ensample of that courteous deed,
Done to that wounded Knight in his great need,
Whom on his backe he bore, till he him brought
Vnto the Castle where they had decreed.
There of the Knight, the which that Castle ought,
To make abode that night he greatly was besought.

3

He was to weete a man of full ripe yeares,
  That in his youth had beene of mickle might,
And borne great sway in armes amongst his peares:
But now weake age had dimd his candle light.
Yet was he courteous still to euery wight,
And loued all that did to armes incline,
And was the father of that wounded Knight,
Whom *Calidore* thus carried on his chine,
And *Aldus* was his name, and his sonnes *Aladine.*

4

Who when he saw his sonne so ill bedight,
  With bleeding wounds, brought home vpon a Beare,
By a faire Lady, and a straunger Knight,
Was inly touched with compassion deare,
And deare affection of so dolefull dreare,
That he these words burst forth; Ah sory boy,
Is this the hope that to my hoary heare
Thou brings? aie me, is this the timely ioy,
Which I expected long, now turnd to sad annoy?

5

Such is the weakenesse of all mortall hope;
  So tickle is the state of earthly things,
That ere they come vnto their aymed scope,
They fall too short of our fraile reckonings,
And bring vs bale and bitter sorrowings,
In stead of comfort, which we should embrace:
This is the state of Keasars and of Kings.
Let none therefore, that is in meaner place,
Too greatly grieue at any his vnlucky case.

Canto iii

Stanzas 1–2
In the Renaissance debate over the relation between breeding
and worth, S.'s position is essentially aristocratic even though
gentle is not to be understood simply in social terms. In Book
VI, courtesy is given by nature or grace rather than achieved by
effort (cf. ii 2). On the relation of nature and art to courtesy,
see Tayler (1964) ch. iv. The argument is continued at vii 1.
See v 1–2*n*. Geller (1975) argues that S. differs from traditional
Renaissance views by asserting the need of high birth to achieve
virtue: his stress on nobility as a prerequisite of courtesy is
'part of his concept of the virtue as a gift of grace, provi-
dentially bestowed on fallen man' (50).

Stanza 1
1–2 **that good Poet**: Chaucer, who writes in the *Wife of
Bath's Tale* that 'he is gentil that dooth gentil dedis' (1170; cf.
1113–24). S. also argues that true, inner nobility will be
revealed whatever man's rank in society.   **whilome**: once
upon a time.
3–4 Cf. Tilley (1950) M 629.
5 **degree**: rank.
6–7 Proverbial (C. G. Smith, 1970, 786).
9 **courage**: heart, nature.   **met**: united.

Stanza 2
1 **tryde**: demonstrated.
7 **decreed**: decided.
8 **ought**: owned.

Stanza 3
8 **chine**: back. Not his shield, as one expects from ii 48.
9 **Aldus**: from 'ald', a form of 'eld'; he is of **full ripe yeares**
and **weake age**. Cf. 'old Knight' (6.1, 9.4). In Tasso, *Ger. Lib.*
i 83, Aladin is aged.   **Aladine**: 'like Aldus', i.e. as Aldus was
in his youth, 'lusty' (7.6) and 'gentle' (8.4).

Stanza 4
4 **deare**: heartfelt; for one dear to him.
5 **affection**: feeling.   **dreare**: sorrow.
6 **sory**: wretched.
8 **timely**: i.e. brought in the fullness of time.

Stanza 5
2 **tickle**: uncertain.
3 **aymed scope**: mark aimed at.

6

So well and wisely did that good old Knight
  Temper his griefe, and turned it to cheare,
  To cheare his guests, whom he had stayd that night,
  And make their welcome to them well appeare:
  That to Sir *Calidore* was easie geare;
  But that faire Lady would be cheard for nought,
  But sigh'd and sorrow'd for her louer deare,
  And inly did afflict her pensiue thought,
With thinking to what case her name should now be brought.

7

For she was daughter to a noble Lord,
  Which dwelt thereby, who sought her to affy
  To a great pere; but she did disaccord,
  Ne could her liking to his loue apply,
  But lou'd this fresh young Knight, who dwelt her ny,
  The lusty *Aladine*, though meaner borne,
  And of lesse liuelood and hability,
  Yet full of valour, the which did adorne
His meanesse much, and make her th'others riches scorne.

8

So hauing both found fit occasion,
  They met together in that luckelesse glade;
  Where that proud Knight in his presumption
  The gentle *Aladine* did earst inuade,
  Being vnarm'd, and set in secret shade.
  Whereof she now bethinking, gan t'aduize,
  How great a hazard she at earst had made
  Of her good fame, and further gan deuize,
How she the blame might salue with coloured disguize.

9

But *Calidore* with all good courtesie
  Fain'd her to frolicke, and to put away
  The pensiue fit of her melancholie;
  And that old Knight by all meanes did assay,
  To make them both as merry as he may.
  So they the euening past, till time of rest,
  When *Calidore* in seemly good array
  Vnto his bowre was brought, and there vndrest,
Did sleepe all night through weary trauell of his quest.

10

But faire *Priscilla* (so that Lady hight)
  Would to no bed, nor take no kindely sleepe,
  But by her wounded loue did watch all night,
  And all the night for bitter anguish weepe,
  And with her teares his wounds did wash and steepe.
  So well she washt them, and so well she wacht him,
  That of the deadly swound, in which full deepe
  He drenched was, she at the length dispacht him,
And droue away the stound, which mortally attacht him.

11

The morrow next, when day gan to vplooke,
  He also gan vplooke with drery eye,
  Like one that out of deadly dreame awooke:
  Where when he saw his faire *Priscilla* by,
  He deeply sigh'd, and groaned inwardly,
  To thinke of this ill state, in which she stood,
  To which she for his sake had weetingly
  Now brought her selfe, and blam'd her noble blood:
For first, next after life, he tendered her good.

12

Which she perceiuing, did with plenteous teares
  His care more then her owne compassionate,
  Forgetfull of her owne, to minde his feares:
  So both conspiring, gan to intimate
  Each others griefe with zeale affectionate,
  And twixt them twaine with equall care to cast,
  How to saue whole her hazarded estate;
  For which the onely helpe now left them last
Seem'd to be *Calidore*: all other helpes were past.

Stanza 6
3 **stayd**: caused to stay.
5 **geare**: matter.

Stanza 7
3 **disaccord**: refuse assent.
6 **lusty**: young; strong; handsome.
7 **liuelood**: livelihood. **hability**: i.e. means.
9 **meanesse**: humble birth.

Stanza 8
Cf. Æmylia who was seized by Lust when she agreed to meet
her lover, IV vii 15–18.
4 **inuade**: attack.
6 **bethinking**: thinking over. **aduize**: reflect.
7 **at earst**: lately.
9 **salue**: smooth over, explain away. **coloured**:
fair-seeming; feigned; cf. 16.9.

Stanza 9
2 **Fain'd**: desired.
7 **array**: referring to the preparations and ceremonies
befitting his state.
9 **trauell**: travail.

Stanza 10
1 **Priscilla**: a diminutive of Lat. *prisca*, 'ancient' (Camden,
1605, 106), linking her to Aldus and Aladine (see 3.9n).
2 **kindely**: natural.
5–9 Her tears are antiseptic. Also, as they express her fear
of shame, they rouse him from his coma.
8 **drenched**: overwhelmed. **dispacht**: relieved.
9 **stound**: state of shock. **attacht**: seized.

Stanza 11
7 **weetingly**: wittingly: knowingly, wilfully.
8 **blam'd**: brought blame upon.
9 **tendered**: cherished.

Stanza 12
2 **care**: i.e. concern for her.
4 **conspiring**: agreeing in feeling. **intimate**: mutually
share (sugg. by the context); or as each makes private grief
known to the other (cf. III ix 30.1–2).
7 **estate**: state; specifically, her reputation.

13

Him they did deeme, as sure to them he seemed,
 A courteous Knight, and full of faithfull trust:
 Therefore to him their cause they best esteemed
 Whole to commit, and to his dealing iust.
 Earely, so soone as *Titans* beames forth brust
 Through the thicke clouds, in which they steeped lay
 All night in darkenesse, duld with yron rust,
 Calidore rising vp as fresh as day,
Gan freshly him addresse vnto his former way.

14

But first him seemed fit, that wounded Knight
 To visite, after this nights per'llous passe,
 And to salute him, if he were in plight,
 And eke that Lady his faire louely lasse.
 There he him found much better then he was,
 And moued speach to him of things of course,
 The anguish of his paine to ouerpasse:
 Mongst which he namely did to him discourse,
Of former daies mishap, his sorrowes wicked sourse.

15

Of which occasion *Aldine* taking hold,
 Gan breake to him the fortunes of his loue,
 And all his disaduentures to vnfold;
 That *Calidore* it dearly deepe did moue.
 In th'end his kyndly courtesie to proue,
 He him by all the bands of loue besought,
 And as it mote a faithfull friend behoue,
 To safeconduct his loue, and not for ought
To leaue, till to her fathers house he had her brought.

16

Sir *Calidore* his faith thereto did plight,
 It to performe: so after little stay,
 That she her selfe had to the iourney dight,
 He passed forth with her in faire array,
 Fearelesse, who ought did thinke, or ought did say,
 Sith his own thought he knew most cleare from wite.
 So as they past together on their way,
 He can deuize this counter-cast of slight,
To giue faire colour to that Ladies cause in sight.

17

Streight to the carkasse of that Knight he went,
 The cause of all this euill, who was slaine
 The day before by iust auengement
 Of noble *Tristram*, where it did remaine:
 There he the necke thereof did cut in twaine,
 And tooke with him the head, the signe of shame.
 So forth he passed thorough that daies paine,
 Till to that Ladies fathers house he came,
Most pensiue man, through feare, what of his childe became.

18

There he arriuing boldly, did present
 The fearefull Lady to her father deare,
 Most perfect pure, and guiltlesse innocent
 Of blame, as he did on his Knighthood sweare,
 Since first he saw her, and did free from feare
 Of a discourteous Knight, who her had reft,
 And by outragious force away did beare:
 Witnesse thereof he shew'd his head there left,
642 And wretched life forlorne for vengement of his theft.

19

Most ioyfull man her sire was her to see,
 And heare th'aduenture of her late mischaunce;
 And thousand thankes to *Calidore* for fee
 Of his large paines in her deiiueraunce
 Did yeeld; Ne lesse the Lady did aduaunce.
 Thus hauing her restored trustily,
 As he had vow'd, some small continuaunce
 He there did make, and then most carefully
Vnto his first exploite he did him selfe apply.

Stanza 14
2   The passing of the night is linked with the passing of the crisis of his illness.
3   **plight**: health.
6   **things of course**: everyday events.
7   **ouerpasse**: pass over by ignoring.
8   **namely**: particularly.

Stanza 15
5   **kyndly**: natural, innate.

Stanza 16
6   **wite**: blame.
8–9   **counter-cast of slight**: a counterplot to suppress part of the truth to justify her honour. On such virtuous duplicity, see A. C. Judson, *Var.* vi 340–1.   **in sight**: i.e. in sight of others.

Stanza 17
6   **signe of shame**: because it shows that the knight suffered a shameful death.
9   **pensiue**: apprehensive.

Stanza 18
Calidore is careful not to swear to her innocence before he saw her, that is, when she enjoyed her love with Aladine. Further, he swears to her innocence, not to the truth of what he says. The 'truth' of his story belongs to the lady reft by Maleffort, whom Calidore slew (i 18, 23).

20

So as he was pursuing of his quest
 He chaunst to come whereas a iolly Knight,
 In couert shade him selfe did safely rest,
 To solace with his Lady in delight:
 His warlike armes he had from him vndight:
 For that him selfe he thought from daunger free,
 And far from enuious eyes that mote him spight.
 And eke the Lady was full faire to see,
And courteous withall, becomming her degree.

21

To whom Sir *Calidore* approaching nye,
 Ere they were well aware of liuing wight,
 Them much abasht, but more him selfe thereby,
 That he so rudely did vppon them light,
 And troubled had their quiet loues delight.
 Yet since it was his fortune, not his fault,
 Him selfe thereof he labour'd to acquite,
 And pardon crau'd for his so rash default,
That he gainst courtesie so fowly did default.

22

With which his gentle words and goodly wit
 He soone allayd that Knights conceiu'd displeasure,
 That he besought him downe by him to sit,
 That they mote treat of things abrode at leasure;
 And of aduentures, which had in his measure
 Of so long waies to him befallen late.
 So downe he sate, and with delightfull pleasure
 His long aduentures gan to him relate,
Which he endured had through daungerous debate.

23

Of which whilest they discoursed both together,
 The faire *Serena* (so his Lady hight)
 Allur'd with myldnesse of the gentle wether,
 And pleasance of the place, the which was dight
 With diuers flowres distinct with rare delight,
 Wandred about the fields, as liking led
 Her wauering lust after her wandring sight,
 To make a garland to adorne her hed,
Without suspect of ill or daungers hidden dred.

24

All sodainely out of the forrest nere
 The Blatant Beast forth rushing vnaware,
 Caught her thus loosely wandring here and there,
 And in his wide great mouth away her bare,
 Crying aloud in vaine, to shew her sad misfare
 Vnto the Knights, and calling oft for ayde,
 Who with the horrour of her haplesse care
 Hastily starting vp, like men dismayde,
Ran after fast to reskue the distressed mayde.

25

The Beast with their pursuit incited more,
 Into the wood was bearing her apace
 For to haue spoyled her, when *Calidore*
 Who was more light of foote and swift in chace,
 Him ouertooke in middest of his race:
 And fiercely charging him with all his might,
 Forst to forgoe his pray there in the place,
 And to betake him selfe to fearefull flight;
For he durst not abide with *Calidore* to fight.

Stanza 20
The setting and situation parallel that in which Aladine and
Priscilla were surprised by the discourteous knight. Cf., e.g.,
couert shade and 'couert glade' (ii 16.3). Although Calidore
displays courtesy, which the other knight lacked, his interruption and the display of his virtue lead to the wounding
of Serena.
1 **So as**: i.e. his pursuit of the Blatant Beast leads to an
occasion for slander.
2 **iolly**: gallant, handsome; 'lusty' (as Aladine, 7.6).

Stanza 21
3–4 In contrast to the earlier test of his courtesy (i 26.1) in
which Briana caused him to be abashed.
6 **not his fault**: cf. the youth bound by Maleffort, i 12.5–9.
8 **default**: fault, error; cf. his apology to Colin Clout
(x 29.6–8) for **approaching nye** (1) where he had no reason to
be. The consequence is Serena's wounding and his first
encounter with the Blatant Beast.

Stanza 22
5 **measure**: suggests the tedium of travel.
7–9 Either Calidore takes **delightfull pleasure** in telling
the frustrated lover his story, or he takes the place of the lady
with whom the lover took 'delight' (20.4). Either way, their
pleasure leaves Serena, left to her pleasure, exposed to attack.
debate: conflict.

Stanza 23
1 Cf. the moment at i 17.1.
2 **Serena**: signifies tranquil (Lat. *serenus*, applied to the
weather), as one who responds to the **gentle wether** (3); or
faire, which is her common epithet (v 9.3, 27.1). Cheney (1966)
200 suggests that her name 'emphasizes her serene trust in her
surroundings . . . her reliance on an apparently friendly natural
environment'. Oakeshott (1960) 98 *n*2 links the name to
Raleigh's Serena, his name for Elizabeth Throckmorton. Their
marriage was an occasion for slander.
Serena] *Crispina 1596* (some copies) signifies smooth, shining,
clear. From this moment, Serena's fortunes belie her name.
4 **pleasaunce**: an ominous term; see I vii 4.2*n*. Only on
Mount Acidale does such pleasantness exist without danger;
see x 5.4*n*. **dight**: adorned.
5 **distinct**: distinguished each from the others.
7 **lust**: desire, inclination; also sexual desire.
9 Cf. Amoret, IV vii 4.1–2. **suspect**: suspicion.

Stanza 24
As Eurydice was stung by a serpent while strolling through the
grass (Ovid, *Met*. x 8–10), and Proserpina was seized by
Pluto. The association of the latter with the temperate air (see
Sandys, 1632, 254) may have suggested Serena's name.
2 **vnaware**: suddenly; as she was unaware.
3 **loosely wandring**: suggesting moral erring.
5 **in vaine**] omitted *1612–13* to avoid the extra foot. The
emphasis given to this parenthetical phrase is justified: in **her
haplesse care** (trouble) she may never be cured from the
wound inflicted by the Blatant Beast. **misfare**: misfortune.

Stanza 25
3 **spoyled**: despoiled, ravished.

643

26

Who nathelesse, when he the Lady saw
  There left on ground, though in full euill plight,
  Yet knowing that her Knight now neare did draw,
  Staide not to succour her in that affright,
  But follow'd fast the Monster in his flight:
  Through woods and hils he follow'd him so fast,
  That he nould let him breath nor gather spright,
  But forst him gape and gaspe, with dread aghast,
As if his lungs and lites were nigh a sunder brast.

27

And now by this Sir *Calepine*, so hight,
  Came to the place, where he his Lady found
  In dolorous dismay and deadly plight,
  All in gore bloud there tumbled on the ground,
  Hauing both sides through grypt with griesly wound.
  His weapons soone from him he threw away,
  And stouping downe to her in drery swound,
  Vprear'd her from the ground whereon she lay,
And in his tender armes her forced vp to stay.

28

So well he did his busie paines apply,
  That the faint sprite he did reuoke againe,
  To her fraile mansion of mortality.
  Then vp he tooke her twixt his armes twaine,
  And setting on his steede, her did sustaine
  With carefull hands soft footing her beside,
  Till to some place of rest they mote attaine,
  Where she in safe assuraunce mote abide,
Till she recured were of those her woundes wide.

29

Now when as *Phœbus* with his fiery waine
  Vnto his Inne began to draw apace;
  Tho wexing weary of that toylesome paine,
  In trauelling on foote so long a space,
  Not wont on foote with heauy armes to trace,
  Downe in a dale forby a riuers syde,
  He chaunst to spie a faire and stately place,
  To which he meant his weary steps to guyde,
In hope there for his loue some succour to prouyde.

30

But comming to the riuers side, he found
  That hardly passable on foote it was:
  Therefore there still he stood as in a stound,
  Ne wist which way he through the foord mote pas.
  Thus whilest he was in this distressed case,
  Deuising what to doe, he nigh espyde
  An armed Knight approaching to the place,
  With a faire Lady lincked by his syde,
The which themselues prepard thorough the foord to ride.

31

Whom *Calepine* saluting (as became)
  Besought of courtesie in that his neede,
  For safe conducting of his sickely Dame,
  Through that same perillous foord with better heede,
  To take him vp behinde vpon his steed.
  To whom that other did this taunt returne,
  Perdy thou peasant Knight, mightst rightly reed
  Me then to be full base and euill borne,
If I would beare behinde a burden of such scorne.

Stanza 26
7 **nould**: would not. **spright**: breath.
9 **lites**: lungs.

Stanza 27
1 **Calepine**: the first syllable of his name links him with
Calidore for whom he functions as surrogate. He is called
'this most courteous knight' (iv 1.6), which is Calidore's title
(i 2.1). The final syllable of his name links him with
Turpine, his adversary (Draper, 1932, 100): their unhappy
history conveys the sense of the English vb 'pine', as Cheney
(1966) 204 suggests, pointing to the word-play in Serena's
story at v 28.6, 8. Parker (1960) 233 suggests 'sweetness of
speech', from καλλι + επος.
5 **grypt**: seized, pierced (cf. 39.3). Cf. Claribell 'whose sides
before with secret wound/Of loue to *Bellamoure* empierced
were' (xii 4.7–8). Her 'mortall wound' of both body and mind
(v 28.3–4) expresses her shame.
6 **weapons . . . threw away**: a natural gesture – he must
put his arms down to pick her up in his arms – but related to
his earlier unarming to make love to her, 20.5. By 29.5 he is
again armed.

Stanza 28
2 **reuoke**: bring back.
9 **recured**: healed.

Stanza 29
2 **Inne**: dwelling-place. This expression may be suggested
by the context: after Serena's soul re-enters 'her fraile mansion
of mortality', she and the sun, both seek 'some place of rest'
(28.3,7).
5 **trace**: travel.

Stanza 30
3 **stound**: state of bewilderment.
9 **thorough**] through *1596*. Emended to repair the metre;
yet the pause before 'through' gives fitting emphasis to the key
word.

Stanza 31
7–9 See ii 47.5*n*. **peasant**: base; a term of abuse. **reed**:
suppose.

32

But as thou hast thy steed forlorne with shame,
  So fare on foote till thou another gayne,
  And let thy Lady likewise doe the same.
  Or beare her on thy backe with pleasing payne,
  And proue thy manhood on the billowes vayne.
  With which rude speach his Lady much displeased,
  Did him reproue, yet could him not restrayne,
  And would on her owne Palfrey him haue eased,
For pitty of his Dame, whom she saw so diseased.

33

Sir *Calepine* her thanckt, yet inly wroth
  Against her Knight, her gentlenesse refused,
  And carelesly into the riuer goth,
  As in despight to be so fowle abused
  Of a rude churle, whom often he accused
  Of fowle discourtesie, vnfit for Knight;
  And strongly wading through the waues vnused,
  With speare in th'one hand, stayd him selfe vpright,
With th'other staide his Lady vp with steddy might.

34

And all the while, that same discourteous Knight,
  Stood on the further bancke beholding him,
  At whose calamity, for more despight
  He laught, and mockt to see him like to swim.
  But when as *Calepine* came to the brim,
  And saw his carriage past that perill well,
  Looking at that same Carle with count'nance grim,
  His heart with vengeaunce inwardly did swell,
And forth at last did breake in speaches sharpe and fell.

35

Vnknightly Knight, the blemish of that name,
  And blot of all that armes vppon them take,
  Which is the badge of honour and of fame,
  Loe I defie thee, and here challenge make,
  That thou for euer doe those armes forsake,
  And be for euer held a recreant Knight,
  Vnlesse thou dare for thy deare Ladies sake,
  And for thine owne defence on foote alight,
To iustifie thy fault gainst me in equall fight.

36

The dastard, that did heare him selfe defyde,
  Seem'd not to weigh his threatfull words at all,
  But laught them out, as if his greater pryde
  Did scorne the challenge of so base a thrall:
  Or had no courage, or else had no gall.
  So much the more was *Calepine* offended,
  That him to no reuenge he forth could call,
  But both his challenge and him selfe contemned,
Ne cared as a coward so to be condemned.

37

But he nought weighing what he sayd or did,
  Turned his steede about another way,
  And with his Lady to the Castle rid,
  Where was his won; ne did the other stay,
  But after went directly as he may,
  For his sicke charge some harbour there to seeke,
  Where he arriuing with the fall of day,
  Drew to the gate, and there with prayers meeke,
And myld entreaty lodging did for her beseeke.

38

But the rude Porter that no manners had,
  Did shut the gate against him in his face,
  And entraunce boldly vnto him forbad,
  Nathelesse the Knight now in so needy case,
  Gan him entreat euen with submission base,
  And humbly praid to let them in that night:
  Who to him aunswer'd, that there was no place
  Of lodging fit for any errant Knight,
Vnlesse that with his Lord he formerly did fight.

Stanza 32
Being on foot, Calepine cannot guide Serena, who is on his horse, across the stream. Turpine assumes that Serena rides her own steed, not recognizing Calepine's generosity in setting her on his (28.5). Turpine refuses to take Calepine on his steed to guide her across, and taunts him that he must take her on his back and swim across. Cf. Priscilla's reluctance to bear her lover, ii 47.5. Rejecting in his huff Blandina's offer to bear him on her steed, Calepine risks crossing on foot. Either he cannot swim (see V ii 16.6–9*n*) or he prefers to wade.
5   **vayne**: in vain; or idle; battling against billows would hardly prove his manhood.
9   **diseased**: afflicted.

Stanza 33
3   **carelesly**: without fear.
7   **vnused**: unfamiliar, for he was unaccustomed to ford on foot.

Stanza 34
1–2   There is a hiatus in the narrative, as *Var.* vi 201 notes: the other knight and his lady have already crossed the river. A. Williams (1967) 7 assumes that they ride by on the other side.   **discourteous Knight**: he inherits this title from the unnamed knight in the Tristram story, ii 43.1.
6   **carriage**: burden.

Stanza 35
3   **Which**] That *1596* University of Washington copy and some others. J. C. Smith (1909) ii App. conjectures that the change was made in other copies at press to avoid repetition.

Stanza 36
2   **weigh**: give importance to.
3   **greater**: too great.
5   **gall**: the source of bitterness of spirit.
8   **contemned**: treated with contempt.

Stanza 37
4   **won**: dwelling.
9   **did for her**] for her did *1596* U. of Washington copy. J. C. Smith (1909) ii App. conjectures that the change was made at press for euphony.   **beseeke**: beseech.

Stanza 38
9   **formerly**: beforehand.

645

39

Full loth am I (quoth he) as now at earst,
  When day is spent, and rest vs needeth most,
  And that this Lady, both whose sides are pearst
With wounds, is ready to forgo the ghost:
  Ne would I gladly combate with mine host,
  That should to me such curtesie afford,
  Vnlesse that I were thereunto enforst.
  But yet aread to me, how hight thy Lord,
That doth thus strongly ward the Castle of the ford.

40

His name (quoth he) if that thou list to learne,
  Is hight Sir *Turpine*, one of mickle might,
  And manhood rare, but terrible and stearne
In all assaies to euery errant Knight,
  Because of one, that wrought him fowle despight.
  Ill seemes (sayd he) if he so valiaunt be,
  That he should be so sterne to stranger wight:
  For seldome yet did liuing creature see,
That curtesie and manhood euer disagree.

41

But go thy waies to him, and fro me say,
  That here is at his gate an errant Knight,
  That house-rome craues, yet would be loth t'assay
The proofe of battell, now in doubtfull night,
  Or curtesie with rudenesse to requite:
  Yet if he needes will fight, craue leaue till morne,
  And tell withall, the lamentable plight,
  In which this Lady languisheth forlorne,
That pitty craues, as he of woman was yborne.

42

The groome went streight way in, and to his Lord
  Declar'd the message, which that Knight did moue;
  Who sitting with his Lady then at bord,
Not onely did not his demaund approue,
  But both himselfe reuil'd, and eke his loue;
  Albe his Lady, that *Blandina* hight,
  Him of vngentle vsage did reproue
  And earnestly entreated that they might
Finde fauour to be lodged there for that same night.

43

Yet would he not perswaded be for ought,
  Ne from his currish will awhit reclame.
  Which answer when the groome returning, brought
To *Calepine*, his heart did inly flame
  With wrathfull fury for so foule a shame,
  That he could not thereof auenged bee:
  But most for pitty of his dearest Dame,
  Whom now in deadly daunger he did see;
Yet had no meanes to comfort, nor procure her glee.

44

But all in vaine; for why, no remedy
  He saw, the present mischiefe to redresse,
  But th'vtmost end perforce for to aby,
Which that nights fortune would for him addresse.
  So downe he tooke his Lady in distresse,
  And layd her vnderneath a bush to sleepe,
  Couer'd with cold, and wrapt in wretchednesse,
  Whiles he him selfe all night did nought but weepe,
And wary watch about her for her safegard keepe.

45

The morrow next, so soone as ioyous day
  Did shew it selfe in sunny beames bedight,
  Serena full of dolorous dismay,
Twixt darkenesse dread, and hope of liuing light,
  Vprear'd her head to see that chearefull sight.
  Then *Calepine*, how euer inly wroth,
  And greedy to auenge that vile despight,
  Yet for the feeble Ladies sake, full loth
To make there lenger stay, forth on his iourney goth.

Stanza 39

1   as . . . earst: just now.
8   aread: tell.

Stanza 40

1–4   Cf. vi 21.3–5. His crime – refusing guests hospitality –
is traditionally one of the greatest.
2   Turpine: from Lat. *turpis*, shameful, as he is shameful and
finally shamed (see vi 33–36); 'fowle, filthie; dishonest,
unhonorable; cruell' (Cooper, 1565). See vi 32.4n. His
reputation is contradicted by his later display of cowardice and
treachery.
3   stearne: cruel.
4   assaies: combats.

Stanza 42

2   moue: make, submit.
4, 7   The rhyme words are transposed in *1596*.
6   Blandina: from Lat. *blandiri*, to flatter; cf. vi 41.3 to 43.6.
Lat. *blandus*, soothing, describes her speech here and links her
with Serena, for whom she functions as surrogate. Later she is
named 'that Ladie myld' (vi 37.2). See vi 41.3–9n. Cf.
Blandamour, IV i 32.4–5n. Nelson (1963) 285 contrasts Calidore's
natural graciousness of speech, i 2.6. De Moss, *Var.* vi 325–6,
relates Blandina and Turpine to the two extremes of the mean
of Courtesy: flattery, obsequiousness and complaisance versus
surliness, disagreeableness, and contentiousness.

Stanza 43

2   reclame: draw back.

Stanza 44

1   for why: because.
3   aby: endure.
4   addresse: prepare.
8–9   Cf. Priscilla weeping and watching over Aladine, 10.3–5:
her actions were restorative, as they took place within the castle
and under the aegis of Calidore.

46

He goth on foote all armed by her side,
  Vpstaying still her selfe vppon her steede,
  Being vnhable else alone to ride;
  So sore her sides, so much her wounds did bleede:
  Till that at length, in his extreamest neede,
  He chaunst far off an armed Knight to spy,
  Pursuing him apace with greedy speede,
That meant to make aduantage of his misery.

47

Wherefore he stayd, till that he nearer drew,
  To weet what issue would thereof betyde,
  Tho whenas he approched nigh in vew,
  By certaine signes he plainely him descryde,
  To be the man, that with such scornefull pryde
  Had him abusde, and shamed yesterday;
  Therefore misdoubting, least he should misguyde
  His former malice to some new assay,
He cast to keepe him selfe so safely as he may.

48

By this the other came in place likewise,
  And couching close his speare and all his powre,
  As bent to some malicious enterprise,
  He bad him stand, t'abide the bitter stoure
  Of his sore vengeaunce, or to make auoure
  Of the lewd words and deedes, which he had done:
  With that ran at him, as he would deuoure
  His life attonce; who nought could do, but shun
The perill of his pride, or else be ouerrun.

49

Yet he him still pursew'd from place to place,
  With full intent him cruelly to kill,
  And like a wilde goate round about did chace,
  Flying the fury of his bloudy will.
  But his best succour and refuge was still
  Behinde his Ladies backe, who to him cryde,
  And called oft with prayers loud and shrill,
  As euer he to Lady was affyde,
To spare her Knight, and rest with reason pacifyde.

50

But he the more thereby enraged was,
  And with more eager felnesse him pursew'd,
  So that at length, after long weary chace,
  Hauing by chaunce a close aduantage vew'd,
  He ouer raught him, hauing long eschew'd
  His violence in vaine, and with his spere
  Strooke through his shoulder, that the blood ensew'd
  In great aboundance, as a well it were,
That forth out of an hill fresh gushing did appere.

51

Yet ceast he not for all that cruell wound,
  But chaste him still, for all his Ladies cry,
  Not satisfyde till on the fatall ground
  He saw his life powrd forth dispiteously:
  The which was certes in great ieopardy,
  Had not a wondrous chaunce his reskue wrought,
  And saued from his cruell villany.
  Such chaunces oft exceed all humaine thought:
That in another Canto shall to end be brought.

Cant. IIII.

*Calepine by a saluage man
from Turpine reskewed is,
And whylest an Infant from a Beare
he saues, his loue doth misse.*

1

Like as a ship with dreadfull storme long tost,
  Hauing spent all her mastes and her ground-hold,
  Now farre from harbour likely to be lost,
  At last some fisher barke doth neare behold,
  That giueth comfort to her courage cold.
  Such was the state of this most courteous knight
  Being oppressed by that faytour bold,
  That he remayned in most perilous plight,
And his sad Ladie left in pitifull affright.

Stanza 47
7 **misdoubting**: fearing.

Stanza 48
4 **stoure**: assault.
5–6 **make auoure/Of**: confess; justify. **words and deedes**: referring to Calepine's challenge, 35; however, **lewd . . . deedes** could refer to his dalliance with Serena which leads to his present plight.
7–8 The characteristic action of the Blatant Beast, i 9.6.
nought could do: because he is on foot.

Stanza 49
Cf. his bold challenge at 35. Calepine's present nightmare is to the masculine world what Cupid's pageant is to the feminine in the house of Busirane. His state of fearing death from one who attacks 'as he would deuoure/His life' corresponds to Serena's when she is attacked by the cannibals in Canto viii.
5 **succour**: shelter, protection.
8 **affyde**: betrothed.

Stanza 50
5 **ouer raught**: overtook. **eschew'd**: avoided.

Canto iv

Stanza 1
2 **spent**: lost. **ground-hold**: i.e. her anchor is slipping.
7 **faytour**: villain.

647

2

Till that by fortune, passing all foresight,
  A saluage man, which in those woods did wonne,
  Drawne with that Ladies loud and piteous shright,
  Toward the same incessantly did ronne,
  To vnderstand what there was to be donne.
  There he this most discourteous crauen found,
  As fiercely yet, as when he first begonne,
  Chasing the gentle *Calepine* around,
Ne sparing him the more for all his grieuous wound.

3

The saluage man, that neuer till this houre
  Did taste of pittie, neither gentlesse knew,
  Seeing his sharpe assault and cruell stoure
  Was much emmoued at his perils vew,
  That euen his ruder hart began to rew,
  And feele compassion of his euill plight,
  Against his foe that did him so pursew:
  From whom he meant to free him, if he might,
And him auenge of that so villenous despight.

4

Yet armes or weapon had he none to fight,
  Ne knew the vse of warlike instruments,
  Saue such as sudden rage him lent to smite,
  But naked without needfull vestiments,
  To clad his corpse with meete habiliments,
  He cared not for dint of sword nor speere,
  No more then for the stroke of strawes or bents:
  For from his mothers wombe, which him did beare,
He was invulnerable made by Magicke leare.

5

He stayed not t'aduize, which way were best
  His foe t'assayle, or how himselfe to gard,
  But with fierce fury and with force infest
  Vpon him ran; who being well prepard,
  His first assault full warily did ward,
  And with the push of his sharp-pointed speare
  Full on the breast him strooke, so strong and hard,
  That forst him backe recoyle, and reele areare;
Yet in his bodie made no wound nor bloud appeare.

6

With that the wyld man more enraged grew,
  Like to a Tygre that hath mist his pray,
  And with mad mood againe vpon him flew,
  Regarding neither speare, that mote him slay,
  Nor his fierce steed, that mote him much dismay,
  The saluage nation doth all dread despize:
  Tho on his shield he griple hold did lay,
  And held the same so hard, that by no wize
He could him force to loose, or leaue his enterprize.

7

Long did he wrest and wring it to and fro,
  And euery way did try, but all in vaine:
  For he would not his greedie grype forgoe,
  But hayld and puld with all his might and maine,
  That from his steed him nigh he drew againe.
  Who hauing now no vse of his long speare,
  So nigh at hand, nor force his shield to straine,
  Both speare and shield, as things that needlesse were,
He quite forsooke, and fled himselfe away for feare.

8

But after him the wyld man ran apace,
  And him pursewed with importune speed,
  (For he was swift as any Bucke in chace)
  And had he not in his extreamest need,
  Bene helped through the swiftnesse of his steed,
  He had him ouertaken in his flight.
  Who euer, as he saw him nigh succeed,
  Gan cry aloud with horrible affright,
And shrieked out, a thing vncomely for a knight.

Stanza 2
2 **saluage**: belonging to the woods. He is the wode-man or woodwose, called 'wyld man' (6.1). See Bernheimer (1952) 7; Osgood, *Var.* vi 202; and Foltinek (1961).
3 **shright**: shriek.
4 **incessantly**: immediately.

Stanza 3
Cf. the salvage nation that befriends Una when moved by 'pitty and vnwonted ruth' (I vi 12.7) at her distress. Although the salvage man is not gentle, by nature he is capable of gentleness.
2 **gentlesse**: gentleness; perhaps suggesting 'gentilesse': courtesy.
5 **ruder**: quite rude.

Stanza 4
6 **dint**: blow.
7 **bents**: reeds or rushes.
9 **leare**: lore.

Stanza 5
1 **aduize**: consider.
3 **infest**: hostile.

Stanza 6
7 **griple**: gripping.

Stanza 7
4 **hayld**: tugged.
7 **straine**: grip.

Stanza 8
2 **importune**: grievous, i.e. exceeding.
7 **succeed**: approach.
9 A. Williams (1967) 117 notes the comedy in this understatement. Revenge is taken for Calepine's degradation as a knight.

9

But when the Saluage saw his labour vaine,
  In following of him, that fled so fast,
  He wearie woxe, and backe return'd againe
  With speede vnto the place, whereas he last
  Had left that couple, nere their vtmost cast.
  There he that knight full sorely bleeding found,
  And eke the Ladie fearefully aghast,
  Both for the perill of the present stound,
And also for the sharpnesse of her rankling wound.

10

For though she were right glad, so rid to bee
  From that vile lozell, which her late offended,
  Yet now no lesse encombrance she did see,
  And perill by this saluage man pretended;
  Gainst whom she saw no meanes to be defended,
  By reason that her knight was wounded sore.
  Therefore her selfe she wholy recommended
  To Gods sole grace, whom she did oft implore,
To send her succour, being of all hope forlore.

11

But the wyld man, contrarie to her feare,
  Came to her creeping like a fawning hound,
  And by rude tokens made to her appeare
  His deepe compassion of her dolefull stound,
  Kissing his hands, and crouching to the ground;
  For other language had he none nor speach,
  But a soft murmure, and confused sound
  Of senselesse words, which nature did him teach,
T'expresse his passions, which his reason did empeach.

12

And comming likewise to the wounded knight,
  When he beheld the streames of purple blood
  Yet flowing fresh, as moued with the sight,
  He made great mone after his saluage mood,
  And running streight into the thickest wood,
  A certaine herbe from thence vnto him brought,
  Whose vertue he by vse well vnderstood:
  The iuyce whereof into his wound he wrought,
And stopt the bleeding straight, ere he it staunched thought.

13

Then taking vp that Recreants shield and speare,
  Which earst he left, he signes vnto them made,
  With him to wend vnto his wonning neare:
  To which he easily did them perswade.
  Farre in the forrest by a hollow glade,
  Couered with mossie shrubs, which spredding brode
  Did vnderneath them make a gloomy shade;
  Where foot of liuing creature neuer trode,
Ne scarse wyld beasts durst come, there was this wights abode.

14

Thether he brought these vnacquainted guests;
  To whom faire semblance, as he could, he shewed
  By signes, by lookes, and all his other gests.
  But the bare ground, with hoarie mosse bestrowed,
  Must be their bed, their pillow was vnsowed,
  And the frutes of the forrest was their feast:
  For their bad Stuard neither plough'd nor sowed,
  Ne fed on flesh, ne euer of wyld beast
Did taste the bloud, obaying natures first beheast.

15

Yet howsoeuer base and meane it were,
  They tooke it well, and thanked God for all,
  Which had them freed from that deadly feare,
  And sau'd from being to that caytiue thrall.
  Here they of force (as fortune now did fall)
  Compelled were themselues a while to rest,
  Glad of that easement, though it were but small;
  That hauing there their wounds awhile redrest,
They mote the abler be to passe vnto the rest.

Stanza 9

5   **nere their vtmost cast**: near death.
8   **stound**: moment of grief.
9   **rankling**: defines the incurable, festering sore inflicted by the Blatant Beast whose bite is rabid, and hence incurable. Cf. original sin, I x 25.4 (see *n*), xi 38.9. Cf. its use at vi 2.9, 5.3, 9.3. At I ix 7.4 the term describes Arthur's love for the Faery Queen. Cf. x 31.3. At v 28.4, Serena calls her wound 'mortall'.

Stanza 10

2   **lozell**: scoundrel.
3   **encombrance**: trouble.
4   **pretended**: held out, presented.
7–9   When the savage shows kindness, she thanks God, 15.2. **sole grace**: grace alone.

Stanza 11

8–9   **which nature . . . passions**: parenthetical, as Church (1758) suggests; otherwise **which** (9) must refer to his **passions** or to his lack of speech which hindered or inhibited his reason.

Stanza 13

1   **Recreant**: by this name he suffers the shame to which he had reduced Calepine; cf. vi 37.2, vii 26.8.

Stanza 14

1   **vnacquainted**: not known to him and his dwelling.
2   **semblance**: demeanour.
3   **gests**: gestures.
5   **vnsowed**: both unsown and growing naturally.
7   **bad**: improvident.
8–9   Cf. Gen. 9.4: 'But flesh with the life thereof, I meane, with the blood thereof, shal ye not eat.' Cf. Isis's priests, V vii 10. 1–2.

Stanza 15

7   **easement**: food and lodging.

16

During which time, that wyld man did apply
　His best endeuour, and his daily paine,
　In seeking all the woods both farre and nye
　For herbes to dresse their wounds; still seeming faine,
　When ought he did, that did their lyking gaine.
　So as ere long he had that knightes wound
　Recured well, and made him whole againe:
　But that same Ladies hurts no herbe he found,
Which could redresse, for it was inwardly vnsound.

17

Now when as *Calepine* was woxen strong,
　Vpon a day he cast abrode to wend,
　To take the ayre, and heare the thrushes song,
　Vnarm'd, as fearing neither foe nor frend,
　And without sword his person to defend.
　There him befell, vnlooked for before,
　An hard aduenture with vnhappie end,
　A cruell Beare, the which an infant bore
Betwixt his bloodie iawes, besprinckled all with gore.

18

The litle babe did loudly scrike and squall,
　And all the woods with piteous plaints did fill,
　As if his cry did meane for helpe to call
　To *Calepine*, whose eares those shrieches shrill
　Percing his hart with pities point did thrill;
　That after him he ran with zealous haste,
　To rescue th'infant, ere he did him kill:
　Whom though he saw now somewhat ouerpast,
Yet by the cry he follow'd, and pursewed fast.

19

Well then him chaunst his heauy armes to want,
　Whose burden mote empeach his needfull speed,
　And hinder him from libertie to pant:
　For hauing long time, as his daily weed,
　Them wont to weare, and wend on foot for need,
　Now wanting them he felt himselfe so light,
　That like an Hauke, which feeling her selfe freed
　From bels and iesses, which did let her flight,
Him seem'd his feet did fly, and in their speed delight.

20

So well he sped him, that the wearie Beare
　Ere long he ouertooke, and forst to stay,
　And without weapon him assayling neare,
　Compeld him soone the spoyle adowne to lay.
　Wherewith the beast enrag'd to loose his pray,
　Vpon him turned, and with greedie force
　And furie, to be crossed in his way,
　Gaping full wyde, did thinke without remorse
To be aueng'd on him, and to deuoure his corse.

21

But the bold knight no whit thereat dismayd,
　But catching vp in hand a ragged stone,
　Which lay thereby (so fortune him did ayde)
　Vpon him ran, and thrust it all attone
　Into his gaping throte, that made him grone
　And gaspe for breath, that he nigh choked was,
　Being vnable to digest that bone;
　Ne could it vpward come, nor downward passe,
Ne could he brooke the coldnesse of the stony masse.

22

Whom when as he thus combred did behold,
　Stryuing in vaine that nigh his bowels brast,
　He with him closd, and laying mightie hold
　Vpon his throte, did gripe his gorge so fast,
　That wanting breath, him downe to ground he cast;
　And then oppressing him with vrgent paine,
　Ere long enforst to breath his vtmost blast,
　Gnashing his cruell teeth at him in vaine,
And threatning his sharpe clawes, now wanting powre to straine.

Stanza 16

4　faine: glad.

Stanza 17

1–5　Cf. Serena who enters the forest 'Allur'd with myldnesse of the gentle wether' (iii 23.3) and Amoret who walks through the wood 'for pleasure, or for need' (IV vii 4.2). Fortune (or Nature), rather than human will, determines events; cf. 21.3, 25.3, 26.3,9, 30.5, and esp. 35.3. The **thrushes song** (3) may have been suggested by **ayre**, in the sense of tune. Cf. the word-play in *Proth.* 1–2. The song contrasts with what he actually hears. Perhaps the **thrushes song** is cited because it heralds spring as a time of birth.

2　cast: determined.

7　vnhappie end: referring to Calidore's separation from Serena.

9　his bloodie iawes: since the babe is unwounded (see 23.9), the blood comes from the bear, or from the babe's recent birth.

Stanza 18

1　scrike: shriek.

Stanza 19

1　Well then him chaunst . . . to want: i.e. it was well for him that he lacked his arms.

2　empeach: impede.

3　pant: run panting; perhaps armour would restrain deep breathing; cf. the bear's 'wanting breath' (22.5).

7–9　bels and iesses: the harness, the weight of which restrains the hawk's flight. Not being encumbered with arms, he overtakes the bear who is encumbered with the child. When the bear is encumbered instead with the stone (see 22.1), Calepine is left 'Much . . . encombred' (25.1) with the child.

Stanza 20

8　without remorse: also immediately.

Stanza 21

9　brooke: digest, continuing the joke in 7; also 'enjoy', 'endure'. There may well be a playful allusion to the myth of Saturn who devoured all his sons except Jove for whom a stone was substituted.

Stanza 22

6　oppressing: pressing down.　vrgent: severe, heavy.

7　vtmost blast: last breath.

9　straine: seize.

23

    Then tooke he vp betwixt his armes twaine
      The litle babe, sweet relickes of his pray;
      Whom pitying to heare so sore complaine,
      From his soft eyes the teares he wypt away,
      And from his face the filth that did it ray,
      And euery litle limbe he searcht around,
      And euery part, that vnder sweathbands lay,
      Least that the beasts sharpe teeth had any wound
Made in his tender flesh, but whole them all he found.

24

    So hauing all his bands againe vptyde,
      He with him thought backe to returne againe:
      But when he lookt about on euery syde,
      To weet which way were best to entertaine,
      To bring him to the place, where he would faine,
      He could no path nor tract of foot descry,
      Ne by inquirie learne, nor ghesse by ayme.
      For nought but woods and forrests farre and nye,
That all about did close the compasse of his eye.

25

    Much was he then encombred, ne could tell
      Which way to take: now West he went a while,
      Then North; then neither, but as fortune fell.
      So vp and downe he wandred many a mile,
      With wearie trauell and vncertaine toile,
      Yet nought the nearer to his iourneys end;
      And euermore his louely litle spoile
      Crying for food, did greatly him offend.
So all that day in wandring vainely he did spend.

26

    At last about the setting of the Sunne,
      Him selfe out of the forest he did wynd,
      And by good fortune the plaine champion wonne:
      Where looking all about, where he mote fynd
      Some place of succour to content his mynd,
      At length he heard vnder the forrests syde
      A voice, that seemed of some woman kynd,
      Which to her selfe lamenting loudly cryde,
And oft complayn'd of fate, and fortune oft defyde.

27

    To whom approching, when as she perceiued
      A stranger wight in place, her plaint she stayd,
      As if she doubted to haue bene deceiued,
      Or loth to let her sorrowes be bewrayd.
      Whom when as *Calepine* saw so dismayd,
      He to her drew, and with faire blandishment
      Her chearing vp, thus gently to her sayd;
      What be you wofull Dame, which thus lament,
And for what cause declare, so mote ye not repent.

28

    To whom she thus, What need me Sir to tell,
      That which your selfe haue earst ared so right?
      A wofull dame ye haue me termed well;
      So much more wofull, as my wofull plight
      Cannot redressed be by liuing wight.
      Nathlesse (quoth he) if need doe not you bynd,
      Doe it disclose, to ease your grieued spright:
      Oftimes it haps, that sorrowes of the mynd
Find remedie vnsought, which seeking cannot fynd.

Stanza 23
5   **ray**: soil.
7   **sweathbands**: swaddling-clothes.
9   Like the Wild Man, the innocent babe is invulnerable;
hence its 'spotlesse spirit' (35.5).

Stanza 24
4   **entertaine**: take.
5   **faine**: wish to be.
7   **inquirie**: seeking.   **ayme**: conjecture.

Stanza 25
5   **vncertaine**: futile.

Stanza 26
2   **wynd**: extricate.
3   **champion**: open country, in contrast to his former
setting 'Farre in the forrest' (13.5); the change of setting
indicates that a resolution may follow his return **vnder the
forrests syde** (6).

Stanza 27
3   **doubted**: feared.
4   **bewrayd**: revealed.
7   **gently**: courteously.

Stanza 28
2   **earst**: just now.   **ared**: discerned.

29

Then thus began the lamentable Dame;
　Sith then ye needs will know the griefe I hoord,
　I am th'vnfortunate *Matilde* by name,
　The wife of bold Sir *Bruin*, who is Lord
　Of all this land, late conquer'd by his sword
　From a great Gyant, called *Cormoraunt*;
　Whom he did ouerthrow by yonder foord,
　And in three battailes did so deadly daunt,
That he dare not returne for all his daily vaunt.

30

So is my Lord now seiz'd of all the land,
　As in his fee, with peaceable estate,
　And quietly doth hold it in his hand,
　Ne any dares with him for it debate.
　But to these happie fortunes, cruell fate
　Hath ioyn'd one euill, which doth ouerthrow
　All these our ioyes, and all our blisse abate;
　And like in time to further ill to grow,
And all this land with endlesse losse to ouerflow.

31

For th'heauens enuying our prosperitie,
　Haue not vouchsaft to graunt vnto vs twaine
　The gladfull blessing of posteritie,
　Which we might see after our selues remaine
　In th'heritage of our vnhappie paine:
　So that for want of heires it to defend,
　All is in time like to returne againe
　To that foule feend, who dayly doth attend
To leape into the same after our liues end.

32

But most my Lord is grieued herewithall,
　And makes exceeding mone, when he does thinke
　That all this land vnto his foe shall fall,
　For which he long in vaine did sweat and swinke,
　That now the same he greatly doth forthinke.
　Yet was it sayd, there should to him a sonne
　Be gotten, not begotten, which should drinke
　And dry vp all the water, which doth ronne
In the next brooke, by whom that feend shold be fordonne.

33

Well hop't he then, when this was propheside,
　That from his sides some noble chyld should rize,
　The which through fame should farre be magnifide,
　And this proud gyant should with braue emprize
　Quite ouerthrow, who now ginnes to despize
　The good Sir *Bruin*, growing farre in yeares;
　Who thinkes from me his sorrow all doth rize.
　Lo this my cause of griefe to you appeares;
For which I thus doe mourne, and poure forth ceaselesse teares.

34

Which when he heard, he inly touched was
　With tender ruth for her vnworthy griefe,
　And when he had deuized of her case,
　He gan in mind conceiue a fit reliefe
　For all her paine, if please her make the priefe.
　And hauing cheared her, thus said; Faire Dame,
　In euils counsell is the comfort chiefe,
　Which though I be not wise enough to frame,
652　Yet as I well it meane, vouchsafe it without blame.

Stanza 29

1　**lamentable**: lamenting.
3　**Matilde**: presumably named after Matilda, in Tasso, *Ger. Lib.* i 59, to whom Rinaldo was given by his mother Sophia to raise as a virtuous warrior; here Calepine gives her the babe to raise 'in goodly thewes' to become 'a famous knight' (38.7–8). The name may have been suggested by Matilda, by whom Merlin was 'wondrously begotten' (III iii 13.3).
4　**Bruin**: brown bear. The association of the wild man with the bear is noted by Bernheimer (1952) 53–5, 198 *n*12. In *View* 64, S. notes that the English-Irish families with the name Macmahon descended from the Fitz-Ursulas, or 'Bear's sons'. Probably there is implicit word-play: he believes that his wife bears the child which in fact she received from a bear.
6　**Cormoraunt**: Crow of the Sea, a traditional symbol of greed (see II xii 8.5*n*). When Edom lies waste, 'the cormorant and the bittern shall possess it' (Isaiah 34.11,KJ). In the allegory, the Giant signifies 'cormorant devouring Time' (Shakespeare, *Love's Labour's Lost* I i 4); see 31.7–9*n*.
7　**yonder foord**: perhaps associated with 'the Castle of the ford' (iii 39.9) held by Turpine.
8　**daunt**: subdue.

Stanza 30

1　**seiz'd**: in legal possession.
2　**fee**: rightful possession.
4　**debate**: contend.
7　**abate**: put an end to.
9　**losse**: ruin.

Stanza 31

5　**In th'heritage . . . paine**: i.e. possessing the land which they laboured to gain; called **vnhappie** because they lack heirs.
7–9　**dayly** (cf. 29.9) and 'time' (30.8) link the **foule feend** with Time itself. **attend**: wait.

Stanza 32

5　**forthinke**: regret.
7–9　This water may be the 'ceaselesse teares' (33.9) which dry up when she receives the babe, 37.8–9. Or the lines may refer to some future battle in which the babe defeats the giant who threatens to 'ouerflow' (30.9) the land.
9　**fordonne**: killed.

Stanza 33

2　**sides**: loins.
3　**magnifide**: extolled.
4　**emprize**: prowess.

Stanza 34

2　**vnworthy**: undeserved.
3　**deuized of**: considered.
5　**priefe**: proof: trial.
7　Proverbial (C. G. Smith, 1970, 123).
9　**vouchsafe**: deign to accept.

35

If that the cause of this your languishment
    Be lacke of children, to supply your place,
    Lo how good fortune doth to you present
    This litle babe, of sweete and louely face,
    And spotlesse spirit, in which ye may enchace
    What euer formes ye list thereto apply,
    Being now soft and fit them to embrace;
    Whether ye list him traine in cheualry,
Or noursle vp in lore of learn'd Philosophy.

36

And certes it hath oftentimes bene seene,
    That of the like, whose linage was vnknowne,
    More braue and noble knights haue raysed beene,
    As their victorious deedes haue often showen,
    Being with fame through many Nations blowen,
    Then those, which haue bene dandled in the lap.
    Therefore some thought, that those braue imps were sowen
    Here by the Gods, and fed with heauenly sap,
That made them grow so high t'all honorable hap.

37

The Ladie hearkning to his sensefull speach,
    Found nothing that he said, vnmeet nor geason,
    Hauing oft seene it tryde, as he did teach.
    Therefore inclyning to his goodly reason,
    Agreeing well both with the place and season,
    She gladly did of that same babe accept,
    As of her owne by liuerey and seisin,
    And hauing ouer it a litle wept,
She bore it thence, and euer as her owne it kept.

38

Right glad was *Calepine* to be so rid
    Of his young charge, whereof he skilled nought:
    Ne she lesse glad; for she so wisely did,
    And with her husband vnder hand so wrought,
    That when that infant vnto him she brought,
    She made him thinke it surely was his owne,
    And it in goodly thewes so well vpbrought,
    That it became a famous knight well knowne
And did right noble deedes, the which elswhere are showne.

39

But *Calepine*, now being left alone
    Vnder the greenewoods side in sorie plight,
    Withouten armes or steede to ride vpon,
    Or house to hide his head from heauens spight,
    Albe that Dame by all the meanes she might,
    Him oft desired home with her to wend,
    And offred him, his courtesie to requite,
    Both horse and armes, and what so else to lend,
Yet he them all refusd, though thankt her as a frend.

40

And for exceeding griefe which inly grew,
    That he his loue so lucklesse now had lost,
    On the cold ground, maugre himselfe he threw,
    For fell despight, to be so sorely crost;
    And there all night himselfe in anguish tost,
    Vowing, that neuer he in bed againe
    His limbes would rest, ne lig in ease embost,
    Till that his Ladies sight he mote attaine,
Or vnderstand, that she in safetie did remaine.

Stanza 35
5   **spotlesse spirit**: proved by the babe's unwounded state, 23.9.
5–9   Nurture may supplement nature by transforming a bear's son into a chivalric knight or philosopher. The belief, which is relevant in this context, that a bear licks its whelps into shape, plays on the etymology, *orsus*, 'perfected after the littering' (Topsell, 1607, i 28).   **enchace**: engrave; used almost in a literal sense.   **noursel vp**: educate. The suggestion that he be trained in **Philosophy** may recall that Rinaldo's mother was Sophia; see 29.3*n*.

Stanza 36
7–9   Cf. Castiglione, *Courtier* 32: 'Truth it is, whether it be through the favor of the Starres or of nature, some there are borne indued with such graces, that they seeme not to have beene borne, but rather fashioned with the verie hand of some God, and abound in all goodnes both of bodie and minde.'

Stanza 37
2   **geason**: strange.
3   **tryde**: proved.
5   The **place** is the forest, a fitting place for fortune to yield a child, and the **season**, spring – see 17.3*n*, a fitting time for the birth of a child.
7   **by liuerey and seisin**: a legal phrase (livery of seisin) for the delivery of property into the corporal possession of a person; hence, by delivery and possession.

Stanza 38
2   **skilled**: understood; i.e. he did not know how to take care of the babe.
3–6   She gains the babe through the Bear though not through Sir Bruin.   **wisely**: because it is a wise father who knows his own child.
7   **thewes**: manners.

Stanza 39
8   **lend**: give.

Stanza 40
3   **maugre himselfe**: in spite of himself, i.e. against his will; or 'to spite himself'.
7   **ne lig in ease embost**: nor lie wrapped in ease.

Cant. V.

*The saluage serues Matilda well
till she Prince Arthure fynd,
Who her together with his Squyre
with th'Hermit leaues behynd.*

1

O What an easie thing is to descry
The gentle bloud, how euer it be wrapt
In sad misfortunes foule deformity,
And wretched sorrowes, which haue often hapt?
For howsoeuer it may grow mis-shapt,
Like this wyld man, being vndisciplynd,
That to all vertue it may seeme vnapt,
Yet will it shew some sparkes of gentle mynd,
And at the last breake forth in his owne proper kynd.

2

That plainely may in this wyld man be red,
Who though he were still in this desert wood,
Mongst saluage beasts, both rudely borne and bred,
Ne euer saw faire guize, ne learned good,
Yet shewd some token of his gentle blood,
By gentle vsage of that wretched Dame.
For certes he was borne of noble blood,
How euer by hard hap he hether came;
As ye may know, when time shall be to tell the same.

3

Who when as now long time he lacked had
The good Sir *Calepine*, that farre was strayd,
Did wexe exceeding sorrowfull and sad,
As he of some misfortune were afrayd:
And leauing there this Ladie all dismayd,
Went forth streightway into the forrest wyde,
To seeke, if he perchance a sleepe were layd,
Or what so else were vnto him betyde:
He sought him farre and neare, yet him no where he spyde.

4

Tho backe returning to that sorie Dame,
He shewed semblant of exceeding mone,
By speaking signes, as he them best could frame;
Now wringing both his wretched hands in one,
Now beating his hard head vpon a stone,
That ruth it was to see him so lament.
By which she well perceiuing, what was done,
Gan teare her hayre, and all her garments rent,
And beat her breast, and piteously her selfe torment.

5

Vpon the ground her selfe she fiercely threw,
Regardlesse of her wounds, yet bleeding rife,
That with their bloud did all the flore imbrew,
As if her breast new launcht with murdrous knife,
Would streight dislodge the wretched wearie life.
There she long groueling, and deepe groning lay,
As if her vitall powers were at strife
With stronger death, and feared their decay,
654 Such were this Ladies pangs and dolorous assay.

6

Whom when the Saluage saw so sore distrest,
He reared her vp from the bloudie ground,
And sought by all the meanes, that he could best
Her to recure out of that stony swound,
And staunch the bleeding of her dreary wound.
Yet nould she be recomforted for nought,
Ne cease her sorrow and impatient stound,
But day and night did vexe her carefull thought,
And euer more and more her owne affliction wrought.

Canto v

Argument

1 **Matilda**] 'Serena' corr. Hughes (1715). Upton (1758) notes that the error was occasioned by iv 29.3. Since Serena is named 'Crispina' *1596* (some copies) at iii 23.2, S. may not have decided the proper name for her.

Stanzas 1–2

It is difficult to reconcile this identification of gentle action and gentle blood with the position expressed by Chaucer, *Wife of Bath's Tale*; see iii 1–2n. Neuse (1968) 341 argues that an over-neat syllogism maintains 'the aristocratic fiction at the expense of a great deal of irony'. The Salvage Man is not a brute who is evolving to the human level but one who degenerated from the human; see Berneimer (1952) 8–9. Perhaps **gentle** may be identified with the prelapsarian state, man's essential nature without nurture.

Stanza 1

6 **vndisciplynd**: uneducated.

Stanza 2

1 **red**: seen.
4 **guize**: behaviour. **good**: good manners.

Stanza 4

2 **semblant**: signs. **mone**: grief.

Stanza 5

3 **flore**: ground. **imbrew**: stain.
4 **launcht**: pierced.
8 **decay**: destruction.
9 **assay**: affliction.

Stanza 6

3 **could**: knew.
4 **recure**: restore.
5 **dreary**: bloody.
7 **impatient**: unendurable. Her 'dolefull stound' (iv 11.4) has now worsened; cf. 28.5.

7

At length, when as no hope of his retourne
 She saw now left, she cast to leaue the place,
 And wend abrode, though feeble and forlorne,
 To seeke some comfort in that sorie case.
 His steede now strong through rest so long a space,
 Well as she could, she got, and did bedight,
 And being thereon mounted, forth did pace,
 Withouten guide, her to conduct aright,
Or gard her to defend from bold oppressors might.

8

Whom when her Host saw readie to depart,
 He would not suffer her alone to fare,
 But gan himselfe addresse to take her part.
 Those warlike armes, which *Calepine* whyleare
 Had left behind, he gan eftsoones prepare,
 And put them all about himselfe vnfit,
 His shield, his helmet, and his curats bare.
 But without sword vpon his thigh to sit:
Sir *Calepine* himselfe away had hidden it.

9

So forth they traueld an vneuen payre,
 That mote to all men seeme an vncouth sight;
 A saluage man matcht with a Ladie fayre,
 That rather seem'd the conquest of his might,
 Gotten by spoyle, then purchaced aright.
 But he did her attend most carefully,
 And faithfully did serue both day and night,
 Withouten thought of shame or villeny,
Ne euer shewed signe of foule disloyalty.

10

Vpon a day as on their way they went,
 It chaunst some furniture about her steed
 To be disordred by some accident:
 Which to redresse, she did th'assistance need
 Of this her groome, which he by signes did reede,
 And streight his combrous armes aside did lay
 Vpon the ground, withouten doubt or dreed,
 And in his homely wize began to assay
T'amend what was amisse, and put in right aray.

11

Bout which whilest he was busied thus hard,
 Lo where a knight together with his squire,
 All arm'd to point came ryding thetherward,
 Which seemed by their portance and attire,
 To be two errant knights, that did inquire
 After aduentures, where they mote them get.
 Those were to weet (if that ye it require)
 Prince *Arthur* and young *Timias*, which met
By straunge occasion, that here needs forth be set.

12

After that *Timias* had againe recured
 The fauour of *Belphebe*, (as ye heard)
 And of her grace did stand againe assured,
 To happie blisse he was full high vprear'd,
 Nether of enuy, nor of chaunge afeard,
 Though many foes did him maligne therefore,
 And with vniust detraction him did beard;
 Yet he himselfe so well and wisely bore,
That in her soueraine lyking he dwelt euermore.

13

But of them all, which did his ruine seeke
 Three mightie enemies did him most despight,
 Three mightie ones, and cruell minded eeke,
 That him not onely sought by open might
 To ouerthrow, but to supplant by slight.
 The first of them by name was cald *Despetto*,
 Exceeding all the rest in powre and hight;
 The second not so strong but wise, *Decetto*;
The third nor strong nor wise, but spightfullest *Defetto*.

Stanza 7
2 **cast**: decided.
4 **comfort**: aid, succour.
6 **bedight**: harness.

Stanza 8
3 **addresse**: make ready.
7 **curats**: cuirasses, breast- and back-plates. **bare**: i.e. he put on.

Stanza 9
1 **vneuen**: unequal, ill-matched.
3 **saluage man . . . Ladie fayre**: a type of Beauty and the Beast.

Stanza 10
2 **furniture**: harness.
4 **redresse**: put in order.
5 **reede**: understand.
7 **doubt**: fear.

Stanza 11
3 **to point**: completely.
4 **portance**: bearing.
5 **inquire**: seek.
7 **require**: ask.

Stanza 12
1–5 Cf. IV iii 17.9 to 18.3. **recured**: recovered.
6 **maligne**: regard with hatred; slander, as it prepares for the attack of the Blatant Beast.

Stanza 13
5 **supplant**: cause to stumble; fall from a position of superiority or virtue. **slight**: wiles, deceit.
6–9 Fowler (1973) 64–5 links the three in opposition to aspects of the three Graces, x 24. **Despetto**: Ital. *despitto*, despite or open malice. *Var*. vi 207 notes that this figure is personified eight times in the poem: it follows in the train of Wrath (I iv 35.4), is the mother of Pyrochles and Cymochles (II iv 41.6), is one of the company that sits by Pluto's gate (II vii 22.2), pursues Malbecco (III x 55.5), is one of the two villains who lead Amoret in the Masque of Cupid (III xii 19.2), lies in ambush behind Daunger (IV x 20.6), and testifies against Mirabella at the court of Cupid (VI vii 34.7). **Decetto**: Deceit or Deception. **Defetto**: Detraction. Ital. *difetto*, 'a fault, a want, an imperfection, a vice' (Florio, 1611); cf. 'vniust detraction' (12.7).

655

14

Oftimes their sundry powres they did employ,
   And seuerall deceipts, but all in vaine:
   For neither they by force could him destroy,
   Ne yet entrap in treasons subtill traine.
   Therefore conspiring all together plaine,
   They did their counsels now in one compound;
   Where singled forces faile, conioynd may gaine.
   The *Blatant Beast* the fittest meanes they found,
To worke his vtter shame, and throughly him confound.

15

Vpon a day as they the time did waite,
   When he did raunge the wood for saluage game,
   They sent that *Blatant Beast* to be a baite,
   To draw him from his deare beloued dame,
   Vnwares into the daunger of defame.
   For well they wist, that Squire to be so bold,
   That no one beast in forrest wylde or tame,
   Met him in chase, but he it challenge would,
And plucke the pray oftimes out of their greedy hould.

16

The hardy boy, as they deuised had,
   Seeing the vgly Monster passing by,
   Vpon him set, of perill nought adrad,
   Ne skilfull of the vncouth ieopardy;
   And charged him so fierce and furiously,
   That his great force vnable to endure,
   He forced was to turne from him and fly:
   Yet ere he fled, he with his tooth impure
Him heedlesse bit, the whiles he was thereof secure.

17

Securely he did after him pursew,
   Thinking by speed to ouertake his flight;
   Who through thicke woods and brakes and briers him drew,
   To weary him the more, and waste his spight,
   So that he now has almost spent his spright.
   Till that at length vnto a woody glade
   He came, whose couert stopt his further sight,
   There his three foes shrowded in guilefull shade,
Out of their ambush broke, and gan him to inuade.

18

Sharpely they all attonce did him assaile,
   Burning with inward rancour and despight,
   And heaped strokes did round about him haile
   With so huge force, that seemed nothing might
   Beare off their blowes, from percing thorough quite.
   Yet he them all so warily did ward,
   That none of them in his soft flesh did bite,
   And all the while his backe for best safegard,
He lent against a tree, that backeward onset bard.

19

Like a wylde Bull, that being at a bay,
   Is bayted of a mastiffe, and a hound,
   And a curre-dog; that doe him sharpe assay
   On euery side, and beat about him round;
   But most that curre barking with bitter sownd,
   And creeping still behinde, doth him incomber,
   That in his chauffe he digs the trampled ground,
   And threats his horns, and bellowes like the thonder,
656 So did that Squire his foes disperse, and driue asonder.

20

Him well behoued so; for his three foes
   Sought to encompasse him on euery side,
   And dangerously did round about enclose.
   But most of all *Defetto* him annoyde,
   Creeping behinde him still to haue destroyde:
   So did *Decetto* eke him circumuent,
   But stout *Despetto* in his greater pryde,
   Did front him face to face against him bent,
Yet he them all withstood, and often made relent.

Stanza 14

Each attempts separately to destroy Timias but in vain. Their combined powers are represented in the Blatant Beast.

2   **seuerall**: different; separate.
4   **traine**: snare.
5   **plaine**: openly.
9   **confound**: destroy.

Stanza 15

5   **defame**: disgrace.

Stanza 16

4   **Ne skilfull . . . ieopardy**: nor mindful of the unknown peril.
9   **secure**: free from care; over-confident.

Stanza 17

1   **Securely**: over-confidently.
5   **spright**: breath.
9   **inuade**: attack.

Stanza 19

Cf. vi 27.4–7, vii 47.1–6. The simile fits the desperate, bestial level to which man is reduced by slander. It is borrowed from II viii 42.

1   **at a bay**: at bay, when it must turn to face its pursuers.
3   **assay**: assail.
6   **incomber**: harass.
7   **chauffe**: rage.
8   **threats**: threatens with.

Stanza 20

1   **so**: i.e. so to defend himself.
9   **relent**: slacken, yield.

21

Till that at length nigh tyrd with former chace,
    And weary now with carefull keeping ward,
    He gan to shrinke, and somewhat to giue place,
    Full like ere long to haue escaped hard;
    When as vnwares he in the forrest heard
    A trampling steede, that with his neighing fast
    Did warne his rider be vppon his gard;
    With noise whereof the Squire now nigh aghast,
Reuiued was, and sad dispaire away did cast.

22

Eftsoones he spide a Knight approching nye,
    Who seeing one in so great daunger set
    Mongst many foes, him selfe did faster hye;
    To reskue him, and his weake part abet,
    For pitty so to see him ouerset;
    Whom soone as his three enemies did vew,
    They fled, and fast into the wood did get:
    Him booted not to thinke them to pursew,
The couert was so thicke, that did no passage shew.

23

Then turning to that swaine, him well he knew
    To be his *Timias*, his owne true Squire,
    Whereof exceeding glad, he to him drew,
    And him embracing twixt his armes entire,
    Him thus bespake; My liefe, my lifes desire,
    Why haue ye me alone thus long yleft?
    Tell me what worlds despight, or heauens yre
    Hath you thus long away from me bereft?
Where haue ye all this while bin wandring, where bene weft?

24

With that he sighed deepe for inward tyne:
    To whom the Squire nought aunswered againe,
    But shedding few soft teares from tender eyne,
    His deare affect with silence did restraine,
    And shut vp all his plaint in priuy paine.
    There they awhile some gracious speaches spent,
    As to them seemed fit time to entertaine.
    After all which vp to their steedes they went,
And forth together rode a comely couplement.

25

So now they be arriued both in sight
    Of this wyld man, whom they full busie found
    About the sad *Serena* things to dight,
    With those braue armours lying on the ground,
    That seem'd the spoile of some right well renownd.
    Which when that Squire beheld, he to them stept,
    Thinking to take them from that hylding hound:
    But he it seeing, lightly to him lept,
And sternely with strong hand it from his handling kept.

26

Gnashing his grinded teeth with griesly looke,
    And sparkling fire out of his furious eyne,
    Him with his fist vnwares on th'head he strooke,
    That made him downe vnto the earth encline;
    Whence soone vpstarting much he gan repine,
    And laying hand vpon his wrathfull blade,
    Thought therewithall forthwith him to haue slaine,
    Who it perceiuing, hand vpon him layd,
And greedily him griping, his auengement stayd.

27

With that aloude the faire *Serena* cryde
    Vnto the Knight, them to dispart in twaine:
    Who to them stepping did them soone diuide,
    And did from further violence restraine,
    Albe the wyld-man hardly would refraine.
    Then gan the Prince, of her for to demand,
    What and from whence she was, and by what traine
    She fell into that saluage villaines hand,
And whether free with him she now were, or in band.

28

To whom she thus; I am, as now ye see,
    The wretchedst Dame, that liue this day on ground,
    Who both in minde, the which most grieueth me,
    And body haue receiu'd a mortall wound,
    That hath me driuen to this drery stound.
    I was erewhile, the loue of *Calepine*,
    Who whether he aliue be to be found,
    Or by some deadly chaunce be done to pine,
Since I him lately lost, vneath is to define.

Stanza 21
4   **hard**: with difficulty.

Stanza 22
4   **part**: side.   **abet**: support.
5   **ouerset**: set upon by superior numbers; oppressed.

Stanza 23
4   **entire**: heartily.
5   **my lifes desire**: as Timias signifies the honour which he seeks; cf. II ix 39.8–9; cf. his 'great desire' on meeting him at viii 27.9.
9   **weft**: wafted, driven upon water, as **wandring** refers to land.

Stanza 24
Timias is silent in shame when Arthur first discovers him (IV vii 44.1–5), and again at VI viii 5.1–7, 27.3.
1   **tyne**: sorrow.
4   **affect**: affection.
6   **spent**: uttered.
9   **couplement**: pair; cf. the Savage Man and Serena, 'an vneuen payre' (9.1).

Stanza 25
3   **dight**: put in order.
5   **some**: someone.
7   **hylding hound**: contemptible or worthless creature.

Stanza 27
7   **traine**: course of events, circumstances.
9   **band**: bond, bondage.

Stanza 28
8   **done to pine**: put to death. For the play on Calepine's name, see iii 27.1*n*.
9   **vneath is to define**: it is difficult to decide.

657

29

In saluage forrest I him lost of late,
  Where I had surely long ere this bene dead,
  Or else remained in most wretched state,
  Had not this wylde man in that wofull stead
  Kept, and deliuered me from deadly dread.
  In such a saluage wight, of brutish kynd,
  Amongst wilde beastes in desert forrests bred,
  It is most straunge and wonderfull to fynd
So milde humanity, and perfect gentle mynd.

30

Let me therefore this fauour for him finde,
  That ye will not your wrath vpon him wreake,
  Sith he cannot expresse his simple minde,
  Ne yours conceiue, ne but by tokens speake:
  Small praise to proue your powre on wight so weake.
  With such faire words she did their heate asswage,
  And the strong course of their displeasure breake,
  That they to pitty turnd their former rage,
And each sought to supply the office of her page.

31

So hauing all things well about her dight,
  She on her way cast forward to proceede,
  And they her forth conducted, where they might
  Finde harbour fit to comfort her great neede.
  For now her wounds corruption gan to breed;
  And eke this Squire, who likewise wounded was
  Of that same Monster late, for lacke of heed,
  Now gan to faint, and further could not pas
Through feeblenesse, which all his limbes oppressed has.

32

So forth they rode together all in troupe,
  To seeke some place, the which mote yeeld some ease
  To these sicke twaine, that now began to droupe,
  And all the way the Prince sought to appease
  The bitter anguish of their sharpe disease,
  By all the courteous meanes he could inuent,
  Somewhile with merry purpose fit to please,
  And otherwhile with good encouragement,
To make them to endure the pains, did them torment.

33

Mongst which, *Serena* did to him relate
  The foule discourt'sies and vnknightly parts,
  Which *Turpine* had vnto her shewed late,
  Without compassion of her cruell smarts,
  Although *Blandina* did with all her arts
  Him otherwise perswade, all that she might;
  Yet he of malice, without her desarts,
  Not onely her excluded late at night,
But also trayterously did wound her weary Knight.

34

Wherewith the Prince sore moued, there auoud,
  That soone as he returned backe againe,
  He would auenge th'abuses of that proud
  And shamefull Knight, of whom she did complaine.
  This wize did they each other entertaine,
  To passe the tedious trauell of the way,
  Till towards night they came vnto a plaine,
  By which a little Hermitage there lay,
Far from all neighbourhood, the which annoy it may.

35

And nigh thereto a little Chappell stoode,
  Which being all with Yuy ouerspred,
  Deckt all the roofe, and shadowing the roode,
  Seem'd like a groue faire braunched ouer hed:
  Therein the Hermite, which his life here led
  In streight obseruaunce of religious vow,
  Was wont his howres and holy things to bed;
  And therein he likewise was praying now,
Whenas these Knights arriu'd, they wist not where nor how

Stanza 29

4   **stead**: place; situation.
5   **deadly dread**: the dread of death, or simply death.
9   **humanity**: civility, good behaviour.

Stanza 30

4   **tokens**: signs, gestures.

Stanza 31

5   **corruption**: putrefaction; cf. the Red Cross Knight's
'Inward corruption, and infected sin' (I x 25.2).

Stanza 32

7   **purpose**: conversation.
9   **the pains . . . torment**: i.e. the pains that did torment
them.

Stanza 33

2   **parts**: acts.
7   **without her desarts**: i.e. without Blandina's good
qualities.

Stanza 34

7–9   Cf. Archimago's hermitage 'Downe in a dale, hard by a
forests side' (I i 34.2).   **neighbourhood**: neighbours.

Stanza 35

3   **roode**: the cross.
6   **streight**: strict.
7   **howres**: prayers at appointed hours.   **holy things**:
devotions.   **bed**: offer.

36

They stayd not there, but streight way in did pas.
  Whom when the Hermite present saw in place,
  From his deuotion streight he troubled was;
  Which breaking off he toward them did pace,
  With stayed steps, and graue beseeming grace:
  For well it seem'd, that whilome he had beene
  Some goodly person, and of gentle race,
  That could his good to all, and well did weene,
How each to entertaine with curt'sie well beseene.

37

And soothly it was sayd by common fame,
  So long as age enabled him thereto,
  That he had bene a man of mickle name,
  Renowmed much in armes and derring doe:
  But being aged now and weary to
  Of warres delight, and worlds contentious toyle,
  The name of knighthood he did disauow,
  And hanging vp his armes and warlike spoyle,
From all this worlds incombraunce did himselfe assoyle.

38

He thence them led into his Hermitage,
  Letting their steedes to graze vpon the greene:
  Small was his house, and like a little cage,
  For his owne turne, yet inly neate and clene,
  Deckt with greene boughes, and flowers gay beseene.
  Therein he them full faire did entertaine
  Not with such forged showes, as fitter beene
  For courting fooles, that curtesies would faine,
But with entire affection and appearaunce plaine.

39

Yet was their fare but homely, such as hee
  Did vse, his feeble body to sustaine;
  The which full gladly they did take in glee,
  Such as it was, ne did of want complaine,
  But being well suffiz'd, them rested faine.
  But faire *Serene* all night could take no rest,
  Ne yet that gentle Squire, for grieuous paine
  Of their late woundes, the which the *Blatant Beast*
Had giuen them, whose griefe through suffraunce sore increast.

40

So all that night they past in great disease,
  Till that the morning, bringing earely light
  To guide mens labours, brought them also ease,
  And some asswagement of their painefull plight.
  Then vp they rose, and gan them selues to dight
  Vnto their iourney; but that Squire and Dame
  So faint and feeble were, that they ne might
  Endure to trauell, nor one foote to frame: (lame.
Their hearts were sicke, their sides were sore, their feete were

41

Therefore the Prince, whom great affaires in mynd
  Would not permit, to make there lenger stay,
  Was forced there to leaue them both behynd,
  In that good Hermits charge, whom he did pray
  To tend them well. So forth he went his way,
  And with him eke the saluage, that whyleare
  Seeing his royall vsage and array,
  Was greatly growne in loue of that braue pere,
Would needes depart, as shall declared be elsewhere.

Stanza 36
3   As Contemplation was distracted from heavenly thoughts,
I x 49.2–3.
5   **stayed**: steady; or supported.
8   **could his good**: knew how to behave; the virtue of
civility: see ii 1.6–7n.
9   **well beseene**: accomplished, referring to his courtesy;
well-provided, referring to his behaviour to his guests;
well-pleasing, referring to his courtesy.

Stanza 37
The substance is repeated at vi 4. S. needs to assure readers
that the Hermit has earned his retirement. Or he may wish to
prepare for Calidore's retiring from the chivalric life in Canto
ix.
1   **fame**: report.
4   **derring doe**: daring deeds; 'manhoode and cheualrie'
(E.K.'s gloss to *S.C.* Oct. 65).
5   **to**: the intensive, 'entirely,' as Todd (1805) suggests.
9   **assoyle**: set free.

Stanza 38
3   **like . . . cage**: expanded at vi 4.9.
4   **turne**: needs.
5   **gay beseene**: of gay appearance; or **beseene** signifies
furnished, adorned, paralleling **Deckt**.
9   **entire**: sincere.

Stanza 39
3   **in glee**] in gree *1609*. The former reading means
heartily; the latter, supported by V vi 21.7, means with
goodwill, in good part.
5   **faine**: gladly.
9   **griefe**: physical pain; or grief to them.   **suffraunce**:
delay in treating, neglect; see 31.7, vi 2.4.

Stanza 40
1   **disease**: discomfort.
8   **frame**: support, direct.
9   'The picturesque and slow broken verse . . . is masterly
contrived' (Upton, 1758).

Cant. VI.

*The Hermite beales both Squire and dame
Of their sore maladies:
He Turpine doth defeate, and shame
For his late villanies.*

1

NO wound, which warlike hand of enemy
Inflicts with dint of sword, so sore doth light,
As doth the poysnous sting, which infamy
Infixeth in the name of noble wight:
For by no art, nor any leaches might
It euer can recured be againe;
Ne all the skill, which that immortall spright
Of *Podalyrius* did in it retaine,
Can remedy such hurts; such hurts are hellish paine.

2

Such were the wounds, the which that *Blatant Beast*
Made in the bodies of that Squire and Dame;
And being such, were now much more increast,
For want of taking heede vnto the same,
That now corrupt and curelesse they became.
Howbe that carefull Hermite did his best,
With many kindes of medicines meete, to tame
The poysnous humour, which did most infest
Their ranckling wounds, and euery day them duely drest.

3

For he right well in Leaches craft was seene,
And through the long experience of his dayes,
Which had in many fortunes tossed beene,
And past through many perillous assayes,
He knew the diuerse went of mortall wayes,
And in the mindes of men had great insight;
Which with sage counsell, when they went astray,
He could enforme, and them reduce aright,
And al the passions heale, which wound the weaker spright.

4

For whylome he had bene a doughty Knight,
As any one, that liued in his daies,
And proued oft in many perillous fight,
Of which he grace and glory wonne alwaies,
And in all battels bore away the baies.
But being now attacht with timely age,
And weary of this worlds vnquiet waies,
He tooke him selfe vnto this Hermitage,
In which he liu'd alone, like carelesse bird in cage.

5

One day, as he was searching of their wounds,
He found that they had festred priuily,
And ranckling inward with vnruly stounds,
The inner parts now gan to putrify,
That quite they seem'd past helpe of surgery,
And rather needed to be disciplinde
With holesome reede of sad sobriety,
To rule the stubborne rage of passion blinde:
660 Giue salues to euery sore, but counsell to the minde.

6

So taking them apart into his cell,
He to that point fit speaches gan to frame,
As he the art of words knew wondrous well,
And eke could doe, as well as say the same,
And thus he to them sayd; Faire daughter Dame,
And you faire sonne, which here thus long now lie
In piteous languor, since ye hither came,
In vaine of me ye hope for remedie,
And I likewise in vaine doe salues to you applie.

Canto vi

Argument
3   **He**: Arthur.

Stanza 1
3   **infamy**: slander (Lat. *infamia*); personified at vii 34.7.
5–6   Since their wound is not physical, it cannot be healed by medicine; only through the Hermit's counsel are they 'throughly heal'd' (15.6). In Shakespeare, *Lucrece* 731, slander is 'the wound that nothing healeth'.   **recured**: healed.
8   **Podalyrius**: 'one of the sonnes of Aesculapius, and a great surgeon' (Cooper, 1565).
9   **hellish**: because eternal.

Stanza 2
6   **Howbe**: howbeit, with the force of 'nevertheless'.
8   **infest**: infect.
9   **ranckling**: see iv 9.9*n*.

Stanza 3
1   **seene**: skilled.
4   **assayes**: trials.
5   **went**: courses.
8   **enforme**: instruct; guide.   **reduce**: lead back.
9   **weaker**: too weak.

Stanza 4
Repeating the substance of v 37 (see *n*).
5   **baies**: the garland of victory.
6   **attacht**: seized.
9   Cf. v 38.3.   **carelesse**: carefree.

Stanza 5
1   **searching**: probing.
3   **vnruly**: violent; literally, not responding to discipline.
stounds: paroxysms of pain.
7   **reede**: counsel.   **sad**: serious.
9   Cf. the proverb, 'There is a salve for every sore' (C. G. Smith, 1970, 672). Cf. II i 44.2–3.

Stanza 6
7   **languor**: illness.

7

For in your selfe your onely helpe doth lie,
    To heale your selues, and must proceed alone
    From your owne will, to cure your maladie.
    Who can him cure, that will be cur'd of none?
    If therefore health ye seeke, obserue this one.
    First learne your outward sences to refraine
    From things, that stirre vp fraile affection;
    Your eies, your eares, your tongue, your talk restraine
From that they most affect, and in due termes containe.

8

For from those outward sences ill affected,
    The seede of all this euill first doth spring,
    Which at the first before it had infected,
    Mote easie be supprest with little thing:
    But being growen strong, it forth doth bring
    Sorrow, and anguish, and impatient paine
    In th'inner parts, and lastly scattering
    Contagious poyson close through euery vaine,
It neuer rests, till it haue wrought his finall bane.

9

For that beastes teeth, which wounded you tofore,
    Are so exceeding venemous and keene,
    Made all of rusty yron, ranckling sore,
    That where they bite, it booteth not to weene
    With salue, or antidote, or other mene
    It euer to amend: ne maruaile ought;
    For that same beast was bred of hellish strene,
    And long in darksome *Stygian* den vpbrought,
Begot of foule *Echidna*, as in bookes is taught.

10

Echidna is a Monster direfull dred,
    Whom Gods doe hate, and heauens abhor to see;
    So hideous is her shape, so huge her hed,
    That euen the hellish fiends affrighted bee
    At sight thereof, and from her presence flee:
    Yet did her face and former parts professe
    A faire young Mayden, full of comely glee;
    But all her hinder parts did plaine expresse
A monstrous Dragon, full of fearefull vglinesse.

11

To her the Gods, for her so dreadfull face,
    In fearefull darkenesse, furthest from the skie,
    And from the earth, appointed haue her place,
    Mongst rocks and caues, where she enrold doth lie
    In hideous horrour and obscurity,
    Wasting the strength of her immortall age.
    There did *Typhaon* with her company,
    Cruell *Typhaon*, whose tempestuous rage
Make th'heauens tremble oft, and him with vowes asswage.

12

Of that commixtion they did then beget
    This hellish Dog, that hight the *Blatant Beast*;
    A wicked Monster, that his tongue doth whet
    Gainst all, both good and bad, both most and least,
    And poures his poysnous gall forth to infest
    The noblest wights with notable defame:
    Ne euer Knight, that bore so lofty creast,
    Ne euer Lady of so honest name,
But he them spotted with reproch, or secrete shame.

Stanza 7
5   **one**: i.e. one rule.
6–9   Cf. 1 Pet. 3.10.   **affection**: passion; **fraile** because it makes man so.   **affect**: are drawn to.   **due termes containe**: retain within proper limits.

Stanza 8
6   **impatient**: unendurable.
8   **close**: secretly.
9   **bane**: death.

Stanza 9
1   **tofore**: earlier.
5   **mene**: means.
7 to 12.2   In Hesiod, *Theog.* 295–332, Echidna appears as 'half a nymph with glancing eyes and fair cheeks, and half again a huge snake, great and awful'. After her birth, the gods thrust her into a cave beneath the earth. With Typhaon, a dread and blustering wind, she gave birth to Orthus (see V x 10.7–9), Geryoneo's monster (see V xi 23.5–6), and the Hydra, with which the Blatant Beast is compared (see xii 32). Cf. Calidore's account of its genealogy at i 8.1–5.
7   **strene**: strain: race.

Stanza 10
3   **hideous**: also immense.
6–9   Cf. Error, I i 14. 7–9.   **former**: front.   **professe**: have the appearance of.   **expresse**: reveal or display her to be.

Stanza 11
1   **face**: general appearance.
4   **enrold**: coiled.
7–9   Typhaon is associated with typhon, or typhoon; hence its **tempestuous rage**. See V x 10.6–8*n*. Cf. Cooper (1565): 'Typhoeus, a great gyaunt, the sonne of Titan. . . . Also a great puissant wynde: a whirlwynde'.   **company**: copulate.

Stanza 12
1   **commixtion**: copulation; literally, mixing of the two. Cf. i 8.3.
4   **most and least**: the highest and lowest in rank.
5   **infest**: infect or assail; cf. 2.8.
6   **notable defame**: notorious infamy.

13

In vaine therefore it were, with medicine
  To goe about to salue such kynd of sore,
  That rather needes wise read and discipline,
  Then outward salues, that may augment it more.
  Aye me (sayd then *Serena* sighing sore)
  What hope of helpe doth then for vs remaine,
  If that no salues may vs to health restore?
  But sith we need good counsell (sayd the swaine)
Aread good sire, some counsell, that may vs sustaine.

14

The best (sayd he) that I can you aduize,
  Is to auoide the occasion of the ill:
  For when the cause, whence euill doth arize,
  Remoued is, th'effect surceaseth still.
  Abstaine from pleasure, and restraine your will,
  Subdue desire, and bridle loose delight,
  Vse scanted diet, and forbeare your fill,
  Shun secresie, and talke in open sight:
So shall you soone repaire your present euill plight.

15

Thus hauing sayd, his sickely patients
  Did gladly hearken to his graue beheast,
  And kept so well his wise commaundements,
  That in short space their malady was ceast,
  And eke the biting of that harmefull Beast
  Was throughly heal'd. Tho when they did perceaue
  Their wounds recur'd, and forces reincreast,
  Of that good Hermite both they tooke their leaue,
And went both on their way, ne ech would other leaue.

16

But each the other vow'd t'accompany,
  The Lady, for that she was much in dred,
  Now left alone in great extremity,
  The Squire, for that he courteous was indeed,
  Would not her leaue alone in her great need.
  So both together traueld, till they met
  With a faire Mayden clad in mourning weed,
  Vpon a mangy iade vnmeetely set,
And a lewd foole her leading thorough dry and wet.

17

But by what meanes that shame to her befell,
  And how thereof her selfe she did acquite,
  I must a while forbeare to you to tell;
  Till that, as comes by course, I doe recite,
  What fortune to the Briton Prince did lite,
  Pursuing that proud Knight, the which whileare
  Wrought to Sir *Calidore* so foule despight;
  And eke his Lady, though she sickely were,
So lewdly had abusde, as ye did lately heare.

18

The Prince according to the former token,
  Which faire *Serene* to him deliuered had,
  Pursu'd him streight, in mynd to bene ywroken
  Of all the vile demeane, and vsage bad,
  With which he had those two so ill bestad:
  Ne wight with him on that aduenture went,
  But that wylde man, whom though he oft forbad,
  Yet for no bidding, nor for being shent,
Would he restrayned be from his attendment.

19

Arriuing there, as did by chaunce befall,
  He found the gate wyde ope, and in he rode,
  Ne stayd, till that he came into the hall:
  Where soft dismounting like a weary lode,
  Vpon the ground with feeble feete he trode,
  As he vnable were for very neede
  To moue one foote, but there must make abode;
  The whiles the saluage man did take his steede,
And in some stable neare did set him vp to feede.

Stanza 13
5–9   Serena and Timias by their 'owne will' (7.3) accept the teaching which he gave at 5.9, 6.8–9.
9   **Aread**: declare, though the play on **read** (3) suggests counsel.

Stanza 14
3–4   Proverbial (C. G. Smith, 1970, 89). However, the Blatant Beast does not need occasion or cause to slander: it attacks the innocent and virtuous as well as the guilty. **surceaseth**: comes to an end.
5   So Medina counsels, II ii 45.4.

Stanza 15
7   **forces**: physical strength; moral strength, virtue.

Stanza 16
4   **indeed**: in deed.
6 to 17.3   A brief introduction to the story of Mirabella which is told at vii 27.7 to 38.9.
8   **iade**: see vii 40.7*n*.
9   **lewd**: ill-mannered; wicked.   **foole**: Scorn's title, which he retains throughout: e.g. vii 27.9, 39.6, 44.5.

Stanza 17
2   **acquite**: free. Since Mirabella chooses not to free herself from her shame, the context suggests 'conduct' (cf. *OED* 13). Cf. viii Arg. 2: Arthur 'Quites Mirabell from dreed'.
5   **lite**: happen.
7   **Calidore**] *Calepine* corr. Hughes (1715). The error may indicate their connection in S.'s mind.
9   **lewdly**: wickedly.

Stanza 18
3   **ywroken**: avenged.
4   **demeane**: behaviour.
8   **shent**: reproved.
9   **his attendement**: attendance on him.

Stanza 19
1   **there**: i.e. at Turpine's castle, although the text provides no hint.

20

Ere long to him a homely groome there came,
    That in rude wise him asked, what he was,
    That durst so boldly, without let or shame,
    Into his Lords forbidden hall to passe.
    To whom the Prince, him fayning to embase,
    Mylde answer made; he was an errant Knight,
    The which was fall'n into this feeble case,
Through many wounds, which lately he in fight
Receiued had, and prayd to pitty his ill plight.

21

But he, the more outrageous and bold,
    Sternely did bid him quickely thence auaunt,
    Or deare aby, for why his Lord of old
    Did hate all errant Knights, which there did haunt,
    Ne lodging would to any of them graunt,
    And therefore lightly bad him packe away,
    Not sparing him with bitter words to taunt;
    And therewithall rude hand on him did lay,
To thrust him out of dore, doing his worst assay.

22

Which when the Saluage comming now in place,
    Beheld, eftsoones he all enraged grew,
    And running streight vpon that villaine base,
    Like a fell Lion at him fiercely flew,
    And with his teeth and nailes, in present vew,
    Him rudely rent, and all to peeces tore:
    So miserably him all helpelesse slew,
    That with the noise, whilest he did loudly rore,
The people of the house rose forth in great vprore.

23

Who when on ground they saw their fellow slaine,
    And that same Knight and Saluage standing by,
    Vpon them two they fell with might and maine,
    And on them layd so huge and horribly,
    As if they would haue slaine them presently.
    But the bold Prince defended him so well,
    And their assault withstood so mightily,
    That maugre all their might, he did repell,
And beat them back, whilest many vnderneath him fell.

24

Yet he them still so sharpely did pursew,
    That few of them he left aliue, which fled,
    Those euill tidings to their Lord to shew.
    Who hearing how his people badly sped,
    Came forth in hast: where when as with the dead
    He saw the ground all strow'd, and that same Knight
    And saluage with their bloud fresh steeming red,
    He woxe nigh mad with wrath and fell despight,
And with reprochfull words him thus bespake on hight.

25

Art thou he, traytor, that with treason vile,
    Hast slaine my men in this vnmanly maner,
    And now triumphest in the piteous spoile
    Of these poore folk, whose soules with black dishonor
    And foule defame doe decke thy bloudy baner?
    The meede whereof shall shortly be thy shame,
    And wretched end, which still attendeth on her.
    With that him selfe to battell he did frame;
So did his forty yeomen, which there with him came.

26

With dreadfull force they all did him assaile,
    And round about with boystrous strokes oppresse,
    That on his shield did rattle like to haile
    In a great tempest; that in such distresse,
    He wist not to which side him to addresse.
    And euermore that crauen cowherd Knight
    Was at his backe with heartlesse heedinesse,
    Wayting if he vnwares him murther might:
For cowardize doth still in villany delight.

27

Whereof whenas the Prince was well aware,
    He to him turnd with furious intent,
    And him against his powre gan to prepare;
    Like a fierce Bull, that being busie bent
    To fight with many foes about him ment,
    Feeling some curre behinde his heeles to bite,
    Turnes him about with fell auengement;
    So likewise turnde the Prince vpon the Knight,
And layd at him amaine with all his will and might.

Stanza 20
5   **fayning to embase**: pretending to humble himself.
6–9   Evidently the 'token' (18.1) which exposes the discourteous knight is his refusal to receive an errant knight: see iii 40.1–4 and 21.3–5 below. Arthur tempts his cowardice, which led him to attack the weakened Calepine.

Stanza 21
3   **aby**: suffer for it.   **for why**: because.
6   **lightly**: quickly.
9   **doing his worst assay**: i.e. in the sense of making his best effort.

Stanza 22
The Salvage Man saves Arthur from having to engage in battle with a groom.

Stanza 24
9   **on hight**: aloud; as loudly as he could.

Stanza 25
1   **traytor**: a slanderous charge; cf. Briana's charge, i 25.1–3.
7   **her**: i.e. Treason.
9   **forty**: used indefinitely to express a large number (Onions).

Stanza 26
2   **boystrous**: violent.   **oppresse**: harass.
6   **cowherd**: the spelling indicates his unknightly nature befitting a herder; cf. 33.4, 34.2, vii 25.7.
7   **heedinesse**: heedfulness.

Stanza 27
4–7   The same simile at v 19 (see *n*) links Defetto or Detraction and Turpine, and shows that Arthur fights the same battle as Timias.   **ment**: joined in battle.

28

Who when he once his dreadfull strokes had tasted,
　Durst not the furie of his force abyde,
　But turn'd abacke, and to retyre him hasted
　Through the thick prease, there thinking him to hyde.
　But when the Prince had once him plainely eyde,
　He foot by foot him followed alway,
　Ne would him suffer once to shrinke asyde
　But ioyning close, huge lode at him did lay:
Who flying still did ward, and warding fly away.

29

But when his foe he still so eger saw,
　Vnto his heeles himselfe he did betake,
　Hoping vnto some refuge to withdraw:
　Ne would the Prince him euer foot forsake,
　Where so he went, but after him did make.
　He fled from roome to roome, from place to place,
　Whylest euery ioynt for dread of death did quake,
　Still looking after him, that did him chace;
That made him euermore increase his speedie pace.

30

At last he vp into the chamber came,
　Whereas his loue was sitting all alone,
　Wayting what tydings of her folke became.
　There did the Prince him ouertake anone,
　Crying in vaine to her, him to bemone;
　And with his sword him on the head did smyte,
　That to the ground he fell in senselesse swone:
　Yet whether thwart or flatly it did lyte,
The tempred steele did not into his braynepan byte.

31

Which when the Ladie saw, with great affright
　She starting vp, began to shrieke aloud,
　And with her garment couering him from sight,
　Seem'd vnder her protection him to shroud;
　And falling lowly at his feet, her bowd
　Vpon her knee, intreating him for grace,
　And often him besought, and prayd, and vowd;
　That with the ruth of her so wretched case,
He stayd his second strooke, and did his hand abase.

32

Her weed she then withdrawing, did him discouer,
　Who now come to himselfe, yet would not rize,
　But still did lie as dead, and quake, and quiuer,
　That euen the Prince his basenesse did despize,
　And eke his Dame him seeing in such guize,
　Gan him recomfort, and from ground to reare.
　Who rising vp at last in ghastly wize,
　Like troubled ghost did dreadfully appeare,
As one that had no life him left through former feare.

33

Whom when the Prince so deadly saw dismayd,
　He for such basenesse shamefully him shent,
　And with sharpe words did bitterly vpbrayd;
　Vile cowheard dogge, now doe I much repent,
　That euer I this life vnto thee lent,
　Whereof thou caytiue so vnworthie art;
　That both thy loue, for lacke of hardiment,
　And eke thy selfe, for want of manly hart,
664 And eke all knights hast shamed with this knightlesse part.

34

Yet further hast thou heaped shame to shame,
　And crime to crime, by this thy cowheard feare.
　For first it was to thee reprochfull blame,
　To erect this wicked custome, which I heare,
　Gainst errant Knights and Ladies thou dost reare;
　Whom when thou mayst, thou dost of arms despoile,
　Or of their vpper garment, which they weare:
　Yet doest thou not with manhood, but with guile
Maintaine this euill vse, thy foes thereby to foile.

Stanza 28
1　**tasted**: felt.
8　**huge lode at him did lay**: i.e. dealt him heavy blows.

Stanza 29
1　**eger**: fierce.

Stanza 30
5　**him to bemone**: to pity him, and therefore plead for him.
8　**thwart**: crosswise.

Stanza 31
3–4　Turpine is reduced to the shameful position to which he brought Calepine, iii 49.5–6.
9　**abase**: lower.

Stanza 32
4　Turpine is reduced almost to a moral abstraction as he lies on the ground in shame: one element of his name is **basenesse**. See iii 40.1–4n; cf. 33.2, 36.5, vii 1.9.
8　**dreadfully**: with terror.

Stanza 33
8　**manly**: repaying Turpine's charge at 25.2.
9　**knightlesse**: unknightly.　**part**: conduct; act.

Stanza 34
4–7　**this wicked custome**: this custom of taking arms from a defeated knight and forcing his lady to go topless is not stated earlier in the poem. Roughly analogous is Pinabello's custom, called *iniquo e fiero*, of taking arms from a defeated knight and stripping his lady (Ariosto, *Orl. Fur*. xxii 47–8).

35
And lastly in approuance of thy wrong,
   To shew such faintnesse and foule cowardize,
   Is greatest shame: for oft it falles, that strong
   And valiant knights doe rashly enterprize,
   Either for fame, or else for exercize,
   A wrongfull quarrell to maintaine by fight;
   Yet haue, through prowesse and their braue emprize,
   Gotten great worship in this worldes sight.
For greater force there needs to maintaine wrong, then right.

36
Yet since thy life vnto this Ladie fayre
   I giuen haue, liue in reproch and scorne;
   Ne euer armes, ne euer knighthood dare
   Hence to professe: for shame is to adorne
   With so braue badges one so basely borne;
   But onely breath sith that I did forgiue.
   So hauing from his crauen bodie torne
   Those goodly armes, he them away did giue
And onely suffred him this wretched life to liue.

37
There whilest he thus was setling things aboue,
   Atwene that Ladie myld and recreant knight,
   To whom his life he graunted for her loue,
   He gan bethinke him, in what perilous plight
   He had behynd him left that saluage wight,
   Amongst so many foes, whom sure he thought
   By this quite slaine in so vnequall fight:
   Therefore descending backe in haste, he sought
If yet he were aliue, or to destruction brought.

38
There he him found enuironed about
   With slaughtred bodies, which his hand had slaine,
   And laying yet a fresh with courage stout
   Vpon the rest, that did aliue remaine;
   Whom he likewise right sorely did constraine,
   Like scattred sheepe, to seeke for safetie,
   After he gotten had with busie paine
   Some of their weapons, which thereby did lie,
With which he layd about, and made them fast to flie.

39
Whom when the Prince so felly saw to rage,
   Approching to him neare, his hand he stayd,
   And sought, by making signes, him to asswage:
   Who them perceiuing, streight to him obayd,
   As to his Lord, and downe his weapons layd,
   As if he long had to his heasts bene trayned.
   Thence he him brought away, and vp conuayd
   Into the chamber, where that Dame remayned
With her vnworthy knight, who ill him entertayned.

40
Whom when the Saluage saw from daunger free,
   Sitting beside his Ladie there at ease,
   He well remembred, that the same was hee,
   Which lately sought his Lord for to displease:
   Tho all in rage, he on him streight did seaze,
   As if he would in peeces him haue rent;
   And were not, that the Prince did him appeaze,
   He had not left one limbe of him vnrent:
But streight he held his hand at his commaundement.

41
Thus hauing all things well in peace ordayned,
   The Prince himselfe there all that night did rest,
   Where him *Blandina* fayrely entertayned,
   With all the courteous glee and goodly feast,
   The which for him she could imagine best.
   For well she knew the wayes to win good will
   Of euery wight, that were not too infest,
   And how to please the minds of good and ill,
Through tempering of her words and lookes by wondrous skill.

42
Yet were her words and lookes but false and fayned,
   To some hid end to make more easie way,
   Or to allure such fondlings, whom she trayned
   Into her trap vnto their owne decay:
   Thereto, when needed, she could weepe and pray,
   And when her listed, she could fawne and flatter;
   Now smyling smoothly, like to sommers day,
   Now glooming sadly, so to cloke her matter;
Yet were her words but wynd, and all her teares but water.

Stanza 35
1   **approuance**: proof.
3–6   Dramatic irony surrounds Arthur's reminder: in the next canto Turpine enlists two valiant knights to kill him.
4   **enterprize**: take in hand.
7   **emprize**: enterprise.
8   **worship**: honour.

Stanza 36
4   **Hence**: henceforth.
5   Since he has borne himself so basely, he must be **basely borne**.
6   **sith . . . forgiue**: since I granted you that, i.e. **breath** or life.

Stanza 38
6   The image of the slaughtering wolf among helpless sheep describes Talus at V iv 44.7–9, vi 30.6.

Stanza 39
9   **who . . . entertayned**: referring to his past or future behaviour.

Stanza 41
1   **ordayned**: set up.
3–9   **Blandina** displays one meaning of her name, from Lat. *blandus*, merry.   **fayrely**: courteously.   **infest**: hostile.

Stanza 42
Like Turpine (see 32.4*n*), Blandina changes from a person to a personification: her name and nature become one in her flattering, deceiving speech. See iii 42.6*n*.
3   **fondlings**: foolish persons.   **trayned**: beguiled.

43

Whether such grace were giuen her by kynd,
　As women wont their guilefull wits to guyde;
　Or learn'd the art to please, I doe not fynd.
　This well I wote, that she so well applyde
　Her pleasing tongue, that soone she pacifyde
　The wrathfull Prince, and wrought her husbands peace.
　Who nathelesse not therewith satisfyde,
　His rancorous despight did not releasse,
Ne secretly from thought of fell reuenge surceasse.

44

For all that night, the whyles the Prince did rest
　In carelesse couch, not weeting what was ment,
　He watcht in close awayt with weapons prest,
　Willing to worke his villenous intent
　On him, that had so shamefully him shent:
　Yet durst he not for very cowardize
　Effect the same, whylest all the night was spent.
　The morrow next the Prince did early rize,
And passed forth, to follow his first enterprize.

```
Cant. VII.

Turpine is baffuld, his two knights
doe gaine their treasons meed,
Fayre Mirabellaes punishment
for loues disdaine decreed.
```

1

Like as the gentle hart it selfe bewrayes,
　In doing gentle deedes with franke delight,
　Euen so the baser mind it selfe displayes,
　In cancred malice and reuengefull spight.
　For to maligne, t'enuie, t'vse shifting slight,
　Be arguments of a vile donghill mind,
　Which what it dare not doe by open might,
　To worke by wicked treason wayes doth find,
By such discourteous deeds discouering his base kind.

2

That well appeares in this discourteous knight,
　The coward *Turpine*, whereof now I treat;
　Who notwithstanding that in former fight
　He of the Prince his life receiued late,
　Yet in his mind malitious and ingrate
　He gan deuize, to be aueng'd anew
　For all that shame, which kindled inward hate.
　Therefore so soone as he was out of vew,
Himselfe in hast he arm'd, and did him fast pursew.

3

Well did he tract his steps, as he did ryde,
　Yet would not neare approch in daungers eye,
　But kept aloofe for dread to be descryde,
　Vntill fit time and place he mote espy,
　Where he mote worke him scath and villeny.
　At last he met two knights to him vnknowne,
　The which were armed both agreeably,
　And both combynd, what euer chaunce were blowne,
Betwixt them to diuide, and each to make his owne.

4

To whom false *Turpine* comming courteously,
　To cloke the mischiefe, which he inly ment,
　Gan to complaine of great discourtesie,
　Which a straunge knight, that neare afore him went,
　Had doen to him, and his deare Ladie shent:
　Which if they would afford him ayde at need
　For to auenge, in time conuenient,
　They should accomplish both a knightly deed,
And for their paines obtaine of him a goodly meed.

Stanza 43
1　**kynd**: nature.
8　**releasse**: moderate.
9　**surceasse**: leave off.

Stanza 44
2　**carelesse**: carefree.
3　**close awayt**: secret ambush.　**prest**: ready.
7　**whylest**: until.

Canto vii

Argument
1　**baffuld**: see 27.3.

Stanza 1
Continues the argument of iii 1.
1　**bewrayes**: reveals.
5　**maligne**: regard with hatred or envy.　**slight**: wiles,
deceit; cf. v 13.5.
6　**arguments**: tokens, evidence.
9　**kind**: nature.

Stanza 2
5　**ingrate**: ungrateful. In his descent into baseness,
Turpine adds ingratitude.

Stanza 3
1　**tract**: trace.
5　**scath**: harm.　**villeny**: shameful injury.
7　**agreeably**: similarly.
8–9　**combynd**: bound together. Each would take up the
other's cause in fighting and share the spoils.

Stanza 4
5　**shent**: disgraced.
7　**conuenient**: due, proper.

5

The knights beleeu'd, that all he sayd, was trew,
And being fresh and full of youthly spright,
Were glad to heare of that aduenture new,
In which they mote make triall of their might,
Which neuer yet they had approu'd in fight;
And eke desirous of the offred meed,
Said then the one of them; Where is that wight,
The which hath doen to thee this wrongfull deed,
That we may it auenge, and punish him with speed?

6

He rides (said *Turpine*) there not farre afore,
With a wyld man soft footing by his syde,
That if ye list to haste a litle more,
Ye may him ouertake in timely tyde.
Eftsoones they pricked forth with forward pryde,
And ere that litle while they ridden had,
The gentle Prince not farre away they spyde,
Ryding a softly pace with portance sad,
Deuizing of his loue more, then of daunger drad.

7

Then one of them aloud vnto him cryde,
Bidding him turne againe, false traytour knight,
Foule womanwronger, for he him defyde.
With that they both at once with equall spight
Did bend their speares, and both with equall might
Against him ran; but th'one did misse his marke,
And being carried with his force forthright,
Glaunst swiftly by; like to that heauenly sparke,
Which glyding through the ayre lights all the heauens darke.

8

But th'other ayming better, did him smite
Full in the shield, with so impetuous powre,
That all his launce in peeces shiuered quite,
And scattered all about, fell on the flowre.
But the stout Prince, with much more steddy stowre
Full on his beuer did him strike so sore,
That the cold steele through piercing, did deuowre
His vitall breath, and to the ground him bore,
Where still he bathed lay in his owne bloody gore.

9

As when a cast of Faulcons make their flight
At an Herneshaw, that lyes aloft on wing,
The whyles they strike at him with heedlesse might,
The warie foule his bill doth backward wring;
On which the first, whose force her first doth bring,
Her selfe quite through the bodie doth engore,
And falleth downe to ground like senselesse thing,
But th'other not so swift, as she before,
Fayles of her souse, and passing by doth hurt no more.

10

By this the other, which was passed by,
Himselfe recouering, was return'd to fight;
Where when he saw his fellow lifelesse ly,
He much was daunted with so dismall sight;
Yet nought abating of his former spight,
Let driue at him with so malitious mynd,
As if he would haue passed through him quight:
But the steele-head no stedfast hold could fynd,
But glauncing by, deceiu'd him of that he desynd.

11

Not so the Prince: for his well learned speare
Tooke surer hould, and from his horses backe
Aboue a launces length him forth did beare,
And gainst the cold hard earth so sore him strake,
That all his bones in peeces nigh he brake.
Where seeing him so lie, he left his steed,
And to him leaping, vengeance thought to take
Of him, for all his former follies meed,
With flaming sword in hand his terror more to breed.

Stanza 5
5   **approu'd**: tested.
6   They err in selling their services (cf. 15.1–3 and Calidore's judgment at i 47.1–2), not in supporting an unjust cause (see vi 35.3–9).

Stanza 6
4   **timely tyde**: fit time.
5   **forward**: bold. Such pride leads them forward.
8   **softly**: easy.   **portance**: demeanour.
9   **Deuizing**: meditating.

Stanza 7
Presumably the one who utters the slander is slain while the other misses Arthur's shield not through lack of skill but because he is courteous (as viii 4.4).
3   **for**: i.e. for which.
5   **bend**: aim, level.

Stanza 8
5   **stowre**: blow, assault.

Stanza 9
1   **cast**: couple; a hawking term.
2   **Herneshaw**: a young heron.
4–7   This defensive ploy is shown in contemporary emblems, e.g. Camerarius, *Symbolorum* (Nuremberg 1590), reprtd in Scoular (1965) pl. iv. See also Harrison (1956) 72–5.
engore: pierce.
9   **souse**: swoop.

Stanza 10
4   **dismall**: causing terror.

Stanza 11
1   **learned**: trained.
8   **meed**: referring to the reward he wanted (4.9, 5.6, 12.7); now seen as the punishment he deserves. Cf. Arg., 13.2.

12

The fearefull swayne beholding death so nie,
Cryde out aloud for mercie him to saue;
In lieu whereof he would to him descrie,
Great treason to him meant, his life to reaue.
The Prince soone hearkned, and his life forgaue.
Then thus said he, There is a straunger knight,
The which for promise of great meed, vs draue
To this attempt, to wreake his hid despight,
For that himselfe thereto did want sufficient might.

13

The Prince much mused at such villenie,
And sayd; Now sure ye well haue earn'd your meed,
For th'one is dead, and th'other soone shall die,
Vnlesse to me thou hether bring with speed
The wretch, that hyr'd you to this wicked deed.
He glad of life, and willing eke to wreake
The guilt on him, which did this mischiefe breed,
Swore by his sword, that neither day nor weeke
He would surceasse, but him, where so he were, would seeke.

14

So vp he rose, and forth streight way he went
Backe to the place, where *Turpine* late he lore;
There he him found in great astonishment,
To see him so bedight with bloodie gore,
And griesly wounds that him appalled sore.
Yet thus at length he said, How now Sir knight?
What meaneth this, which here I see before?
How fortuneth this foule vncomely plight,
So different from that, which earst ye seem'd in sight?

15

Perdie (said he) in euill houre it fell,
That euer I for meed did vndertake
So hard a taske, as life for hyre to sell;
The which I earst aduentur'd for your sake.
Witnesse the wounds, and this wyde bloudie lake,
Which ye may see yet all about my steeme.
Therefore now yeeld, as ye did promise make,
My due reward, the which right well I deeme
I yearned haue, that life so dearely did redeeme.

16

But where then is (quoth he halfe wrothfully)
Where is the bootie, which therefore I bought,
That cursed caytiue, my strong enemy,
That recreant knight, whose hated life I sought?
And where is eke your friend, which halfe it ought?
He lyes (said he) vpon the cold bare ground,
Slayne of that errant knight, with whom he fought;
Whom afterwards my selfe with many a wound
Did slay againe, as ye may see there in the stound.

17

Thereof false *Turpin* was full glad and faine,
And needs with him streight to the place would ryde,
Where he himselfe might see his foeman slaine;
For else his feare could not be satisfyde.
So as they rode, he saw the way all dyde
With streames of bloud; which tracting by the traile,
Ere long they came, whereas in euill tyde
That other swayne, like ashes deadly pale,
668 Lay in the lap of death, rewing his wretched bale.

18

Much did the Crauen seeme to mone his case,
That for his sake his deare life had forgone;
And him bewayling with affection base,
Did counterfeit kind pittie, where was none:
For wheres no courage, theres no ruth nor mone.
Thence passing forth, not farre away he found,
Whereas the Prince himselfe lay all alone,
Loosely displayd vpon the grassie ground,
Possessed of sweete sleepe, that luld him soft in swound.

Stanza 12
3   descrie: reveal.
4   reaue: take away.

Stanza 13
1   mused: wondered.
6–7   Padelford, *Var.* vi 218, notes that 'the success which
attended the Prince in the conflict was *prima facie* evidence that
he had been maligned'.
9   surceasse: desist.

Stanza 14
2   lore: left.

Stanza 15
9   yearned: earned.

Stanza 16
5   ought: owns.
9   againe: in return.   stound: place (cf. 17.2). Its other
sense, 'state of stupefaction' (cf. IV vi 12.1), describes the state
in which Arthur is, in fact, found.

Stanza 17
1   faine: pleased.
6   tracting: tracking (cf. 3.1), continuing the image of the
hunter pursuing his prey.
7   tyde: time.

Stanza 18
1   Crauen: before his final overthrow, Turpine embodies
his moral state; cf. iv 2.6, vi 26.6, 36.7.
4   kind: natural.
5   mone: grief.

19

Wearie of trauell in his former fight,
  He there in shade himselfe had layd to rest,
  Hauing his armes and warlike things vndight,
  Fearelesse of foes that mote his peace molest;
  The whyles his saluage page, that wont be prest,
  Was wandred in the wood another way,
  To doe some thing, that seemed to him best,
The whyles his Lord in siluer slomber lay,
Like to the Euening starre adorn'd with deawy ray.

20

Whom when as *Turpin* saw so loosely layd,
  He weened well, that he in deed was dead,
  Like as that other knight to him had sayd:
  But when he nigh approcht, he mote aread
  Plaine signes in him of life and liuelihead.
  Whereat much grieu'd against that strounger knight,
  That him too light of credence did mislead,
He would haue backe retyred from that sight,
That was to him on earth the deadliest despight.

21

But that same knight would not once let him start,
  But plainely gan to him declare the case
  Of all his mischiefe, and late lucklesse smart;
  How both he and his fellow there in place
  Were vanquished, and put to foule disgrace,
  And how that he in lieu of life him lent,
  Had vow'd vnto the victor, him to trace
And follow through the world, where so he went,
Till that he him deliuered to his punishment.

22

He therewith much abashed and affrayd,
  Began to tremble euery limbe and vaine;
  And softly whispering him, entyrely prayd,
  T'aduize him better, then by such a traine
  Him to betray vnto a strounger swaine:
  Yet rather counseld him contrarywize,
  Sith he likewise did wrong by him sustaine,
To ioyne with him and vengeance to deuize,
Whylest time did offer meanes him sleeping to surprize.

23

Nathelesse for all his speach, the gentle knight
  Would not be tempted to such villenie,
  Regarding more his faith, which he did plight,
  All were it to his mortall enemie,
  Then to entrap him by false treacherie:
  Great shame in lieges blood to be embrew'd.
  Thus whylest they were debating diuerslie,
The Saluage forth out of the wood issew'd
Backe to the place, whereas his Lord he sleeping vew'd.

24

There when he saw those two so neare him stand,
  He doubted much what mote their meaning bee,
  And throwing downe his load out of his hand,
  To weet great store of forrest frute, which hee
  Had for his food late gathered from the tree,
  Himselfe vnto his weapon he betooke,
  That was an oaken plant, which lately hee
Rent by the root; which he so sternely shooke,
That like an hazell wand, it quiuered and quooke.

25

Whereat the Prince awaking, when he spyde
  The traytour *Turpin* with that other knight,
  He started vp, and snatching neare his syde
  His trustie sword, the seruant of his might,
  Like a fell Lyon leaped to him light,
  And his left hand vpon his collar layd.
  Therewith the cowheard deaded with affright,
Fell flat to ground, ne word vnto him sayd,
But holding vp his hands, with silence mercie prayd.

Stanza 19
1   **trauell**: travail.
5   **that wont be prest**: that usually was near at hand.
8–9   **siluer slomber**: cf. 'siluer sleepe' (ix 22.8).
siluer because associated with the moon. Upton (1758) notes
that refined silver is an emblem of purity; hence it suggests
sleep purged of gross vapours.   **deawy ray**: because the star
rises out of the ocean (cf. II xii 65.2), and is therefore associated
with the dew of sleep.

Stanza 20
4   **aread**: perceive.
5   **liuelihead**: life; literally, a source of life.

Stanza 21
1   **start**: escape.
2   **case**: what had happened to him; or in the legal sense.

Stanza 22
See i 34.3–4*n*.
3–9   The repeated use of **him** should confuse the knight as to
who is his enemy.
3   **entyrely**: earnestly.
4   **traine**: trick.

Stanza 23
6   **lieges**: as one to whom he was bound by oath.
embrew'd: stained.

Stanza 24
2   **doubted**: feared.   **meaning**: intention.
7–9   The uprooted tree is the traditional weapon of the wild
man: see IV vii 7*n* and Bernheimer (1952) 1, fig. 47.   **plant**:
young tree.

669

26

But he so full of indignation was,
That to his prayer nought he would incline,
But as he lay vpon the humbled gras,
His foot he set on his vile necke, in signe
Of seruile yoke, that nobler harts repine.
Then letting him arise like abiect thrall,
He gan to him obiect his haynous crime,
And to reuile, and rate, and recreant call,
And lastly to despoyle of knightly bannerall.

27

And after all, for greater infamie,
He by the heeles him hung vpon a tree,
And baffuld so, that all which passed by,
The picture of his punishment might see,
And by the like ensample warned bee,
How euer they through treason doe trespasse.
But turne we now backe to that Ladie free,
Whom late we left ryding vpon an Asse,
Led by a Carle and foole, which by her side did passe.

28

She was a Ladie of great dignitie,
And lifted vp to honorable place,
Famous through all the land of Faerie,
Though of meane parentage and kindred base,
Yet deckt with wondrous giftes of natures grace,
That all men did her person much admire,
And praise the feature of her goodly face,
The beames whereof did kindle louely fire
In th'harts of many a knight, and many a gentle squire.

29

But she thereof grew proud and insolent,
That none she worthie thought to be her fere,
But scornd them all, that loue vnto her ment,
Yet was she lou'd of many a worthy pere,
Vnworthy she to be belou'd so dere,
That could not weigh of worthinesse aright.
For beautie is more glorious bright and clere,
The more it is admir'd of many a wight,
And noblest she, that serued is of noblest knight.

30

But this coy Damzell thought contrariwize,
That such proud looks would make her praysed more;
And that the more she did all loue despize,
The more would wretched louers her adore.
What cared she, who sighed for her sore,
Or who did wayle or watch the wearie night?
Let them that list, their lucklesse lot deplore;
She was borne free, not bound to any wight,
And so would euer liue, and loue her owne delight.

31

Through such her stubborne stifnesse, and hard hart,
Many a wretch, for want of remedie,
Did languish long in lifeconsuming smart,
And at the last through dreary dolour die:
Whylest she, the Ladie of her libertie,
Did boast her beautie had such soueraine might,
That with the onely twinckle of her eye,
She could or saue, or spill, whom she would hight.
What could the Gods doe more, but doe it more aright?

32

But loe the Gods, that mortall follies vew,
Did worthily reuenge this maydens pride;
And nought regarding her so goodly hew,
Did laugh at her, that many did deride,
Whilest she did weepe, of no man mercifide.
For on a day, when *Cupid* kept his court,
As he is wont at each Saint Valentide,
Vnto the which all louers doe resort,
That of their loues successe they there may make report;

Stanza 26

3   **lay vpon the humbled gras**: lay humbled on the grass.
5   **repine**: disdain.
7   **obiect**: reproach.
9   **bannerall**: banderol, a pennant attached to the lance as an emblem of chivalry.

Stanza 27

2   Cf. Gal. 3.13: 'Cursed is everie one that hangeth on tre'.
3   **baffuld so**: disgraced with shame through this action. Braggadocchio is similarly shamed, V iii 37. 5–9.
6   **How euer**: in any way whatever; to whatever extent.
7   **free**: the stock epithet for a lady of noble birth but used here in the particular sense of 30.8, 31.5.
8   **Asse**: a 'mangy iade' at vi 16.8; cf. 40.7 below. Both beasts mark her shame.

Stanzas 28–31

Cf. Mirabella's own version of her beauty and scorn of her lovers, viii 20–21. Her disdain and scorn become her humours which now punish her. Cf. Beatrice in Shakespeare, *Much Ado* III i 51–2: 'Disdain and scorn ride sparkling in her eyes,/ Misprising what they look on.' See Potts (1958) 40–4.

Stanza 28

4   **meane . . . base**: i.e. being of low social rank.
8   **louely fire**: the fire of love.

Stanza 29

1   **insolent**: haughty.
2   **fere**: mate.
6   **weigh**: judge.
7–9   Cf. *H.B.* 176–89. Welsford (1967) 160–1 notes the neo-Platonic doctrine in both passages.   **clere**: glorious.

Stanza 31

7   **the onely**: only the.
8   **spill**: kill.   **hight**: name.

Stanza 32

1–5   **the Gods . . . mercifide**: i.e. the gods scorned her who, having once scorned others, now was pitied by no man.
3   **hew**: appearance.
6–9   The literary tradition of the Court of Cupid is described by E. B. Fowler (1921) 103–6. A. Williams (1967) 108 claims that the legal imagery belongs to an ecclesiastical rather than a civil court. Only the former court tried sexual offences and assigned penances.

33

It fortun'd then, that when the roules were red,
    In which the names of all loues folke were fyled,
    That many there were missing, which were ded,
    Or kept in bands, or from their loues exyled,
    Or by some other violence despoyled.
    Which when as *Cupid* heard, he wexed wroth,
    And doubting to be wronged, or beguyled,
    He bad his eyes to be vnblindfold both,
That he might see his men, and muster them by oth.

34

Then found he many missing of his crew,
    Which wont doe suit and seruice to his might;
    Of whom what was becomen, no man knew.
    Therefore a Iurie was impaneld streight,
    T'enquire of them, whether by force, or sleight,
    Or their owne guilt, they were away conuayd.
    To whom foule *Infamie*, and fell *Despight*
    Gaue euidence, that they were all betrayd,
And murdred cruelly by a rebellious Mayd.

35

Fayre *Mirabella* was her name, whereby
    Of all those crymes she there indited was:
    All which when *Cupid* heard, he by and by
    In great displeasure, wild a *Capias*
    Should issue forth, t'attach that scornefull lasse.
    The warrant straight was made, and therewithall
    A Baylieffe errant forth in post did passe,
    Whom they by name there *Portamore* did call;
He which doth summon louers to loues iudgement hall.

36

The damzell was attacht, and shortly brought
    Vnto the barre, whereas she was arrayned:
    But she thereto nould plead, nor answere ought
    Euen for stubborne pride, which her restrayned.
    So iudgement past, as is by law ordayned
    In cases like, which when at last she saw,
    Her stubborne hart, which loue before disdayned,
    Gan stoupe, and falling downe with humble awe,
Cryde mercie, to abate the extremitie of law.

37

The sonne of *Venus* who is myld by kynd,
    But where he is prouokt with peeuishnesse,
    Vnto her prayers piteously enclynd,
    And did the rigour of his doome represse;
    Yet not so freely, but that nathelesse
    He vnto her a penance did impose,
    Which was, that through this worlds wyde wildernes
    She wander should in companie of those,
Till she had sau'd so many loues, as she did lose.

38

So now she had bene wandring two whole yeares
    Throughout the world, in this vncomely case,
    Wasting her goodly hew in heauie teares,
    And her good dayes in dolorous disgrace:
    Yet had she not in all these two yeares space,
    Saued but two, yet in two yeares before,
    Through her dispiteous pride, whilest loue lackt place,
    She had destroyed two and twenty more.
Aie me, how could her loue make half amends therefore?

39

And now she was vppon the weary way,
    When as the gentle Squire, with faire *Serene*,
    Met her in such misseeming foule array;
    The whiles that mighty man did her demeane
    With all the euill termes and cruell meane,
    That he could make; And eeke that angry foole
    Which follow'd her, with cursed hands vncleane
    Whipping her horse, did with his smarting toole
Oft whip her dainty selfe, and much augment her doole.

Stanza 33

1   **roules**: rolls, records.

3–5   Tonkin (1972) 97 notes that the story deals 'not so much with Mirabella's *sexual* offence as with the *social* consequences of the offence'.

7   **doubting**: fearing.

Stanza 34

2   **suit and seruice**: a feudal term for attendance at court and the personal service owing to the lord.

5   **sleight**: trickery.

7–9   'Merely a figurative way of saying that she has got a bad name (infamy) and incurred the enmity (despite) of many people, who now act to punish her' (A. Williams, 1967, 66). **Infamie**: slander; see vi 1.3*n*.   **Despight**: cf. *Despetto*, v 13.6.

Stanza 35

1   **Mirabella**: Lat. *mira* + *bella*, wondrously beautiful, as she appears at 28. 5–9.

3   **by and by**: straightway.

4–5   He ruled that a writ be issued to have her arrested.

6   **therewithall**: with that.

7   **Baylieffe errant**: an officer of justice who executes writs. **in post**: in haste.

8   **Portamore**: i.e. Messenger of Love.

Stanza 36

3–6   In English law, the failure of the accused to answer charges is interpreted as an acknowledgment of guilt.

6–9   In submitting to Cupid, Mirabella falls in love.

Stanza 37

1   **kynd**: nature.

2   **peeuishnesse**: perverse behaviour (in another).

8   **those**: i.e. the Carl and Fool (27.9) who represent her former disdain and scorn.

9   Cf. the penance imposed on the Squire of Dames, III vii 56.   **lose**: destroy.

Stanza 38

7   **place**: i.e. in her heart.

Stanza 39

4   **demeane**: ill-treat.

5   **meane**: means.

8   Not with the clown's bauble as one might expect, but with a whip.

9   **doole**: grief.

40

Ne ought it mote auaile her to entreat
 The one or th'other, better her to vse:
 For both so wilfull were and obstinate,
 That all her piteous plaint they did refuse,
 And rather did the more her beate and bruse.
 But most the former villaine, which did lead
 Her tyreling iade, was bent her to abuse;
 Who though she were with wearinesse nigh dead,
Yet would not let her lite, nor rest a little stead.

41

For he was sterne, and terrible by nature,
 And eeke of person huge and hideous,
 Exceeding much the measure of mans stature,
 And rather like a Gyant monstruous.
 For sooth he was descended of the hous
 Of those old Gyants, which did warres darraine
 Against the heauen in order battailous,
 And sib to great *Orgolio*, which was slaine
By *Arthure*, when as *Vnas* Knight he did maintaine.

42

His lookes were dreadfull, and his fiery eies
 Like two great Beacons, glared bright and wyde,
 Glauncing askew, as if his enemies
 He scorned in his ouerweening pryde;
 And stalking stately like a Crane, did stryde
 At euery step vppon the tiptoes hie,
 And all the way he went, on euery syde
 He gaz'd about, and stared horriblie,
As if he with his lookes would all men terrifie.

43

He wore no armour, ne for none did care,
 As no whit dreading any liuing wight;
 But in a Iacket quilted richly rare
 Vpon checklaton he was straungely dight,
 And on his head a roll of linnen plight,
 Like to the Mores of Malaber he wore;
 With which his locks, as blacke as pitchy night,
 Were bound about, and voyded from before,
And in his hand a mighty yron club he bore.

44

This was *Disdaine*, who led that Ladies horse
 Through thick and thin, through mountaines and through (plains,
 Compelling her, wher she would not, by force,
 Haling her palfrey by the hempen raines.
 But that same foole, which most increast her paines,
 Was *Scorne*, who hauing in his hand a whip,
 Her therewith yirks, and still when she complaines,
 The more he laughes, and does her closely quip,
To see her sore lament, and bite her tender lip.

45

Whose cruell handling when that Squire beheld,
 And saw those villaines her so vildely vse,
 His gentle heart with indignation sweld,
 And could no lenger beare so great abuse,
 As such a Lady so to beate and bruse;
 But to him stepping, such a stroke him lent,
 That forst him th'halter from his hand to loose,
 And maugre all his might, backe to relent:
672 Else had he surely there bene slaine, or fowly shent.

Stanza 40

6 **former**: foremost, being in front.
7 **tyreling iade**: tired horse (cf. vi 16.8), the lustful
foster's beast (III i 17.4); perhaps also appropriate as a term of
abuse for a woman.
9 **stead**: while.

Stanzas 41–43

The description of *Disdayne* in Mammon's house (II vii 41) is
modified to express Mirabella's state, and also to relate
Disdain to **Orgoglio** in order to prepare for Arthur's entrance.

Stanza 41

1 **sterne**: cruel.
2 **hideous**: immense.
6–7 **those old Gyants** are 'of the *Titans* race' (II vii 41.6),
which makes Disdain sib to Argante (III vii 47.3–5). On the
battle, see II vii 41.6*n*. **darraine**: wage.
9 **maintaine**: conduct himself, or maintain her cause.

Stanza 42

1–4 **fiery eies**: cf. the eyes of the Dragon (I xi 14) and
Corflambo (IV viii 39).
3 **Glauncing askew**: as does Mammon; see II vii 7.5*n*.
5–6 As the Ape, in *Hub.* 663–5, imitates 'some great
Magnifico' when 'Vpon his tiptoes, [he] stalketh stately by'.

Stanza 43

3–4 **a Iacket quilted . . ./Vpon checklaton**: in *View* 70, S.
describes the 'quilted leather jack' worn by the Irish: 'It was
the proper weed of the horseman as ye may read in Chaucer,
where he describeth Sir Thopas's apparel and armour, when he
went to fight against the Geant in his robe of Checklatoun,
which Checklatoun is that kind of gilden leather, with which
they use to embroider their Irish jacks.' (In fact, checklaton is a
thin cloth, and Sir Thopas wears quite different apparel when
he prepares to fight the giant; see *Sir Thopas* 857–68.)
5–8 **a roll of linnen . . .**: Whitney, *Var.* vi 226, cites the
description of the kings of the Moors of Malabar in the *Book of
Duarte Barbosa, etc*: 'They wear their hair tied upon the top of
their heads, and sometimes long hoods like Galician casques.
. . . They go very well attired in rich cloth of gold, silk,
cotton and camlets. They all wear turbans on their heads; these
turbans are long, like Moorish shirts'. More relevant is the ugly
turbaned churl Dangier with his knotted club in the
manuscripts of the *Romance of the Rose*; cited by Tuve (1970)
130 and shown in Fleming (1969) Fig. 11. **plight**: folded.
voyded from before: kept clear from his face.

Stanza 44

7 **yirks**: lashes.
8 **closely quip**: covertly taunt.

Stanza 45

8 **maugre**: in spite of. **relent**: give way.
9 **fowly shent**: shamefully injured.

46

The villaine, wroth for greeting him so sore,
　Gathered him selfe together soone againe,
　And with his yron batton, which he bore,
　Let driue at him so dreadfully amaine,
　That for his safety he did him constraine
　To giue him ground, and shift to euery side,
　Rather then once his burden to sustaine:
For bootelesse thing him seemed, to abide
So mighty blowes, or proue the puissaunce of his pride.

47

Like as a Mastiffe hauing at a bay
　A saluage Bull, whose cruell hornes doe threat
　Desperate daunger, if he them assay,
　Traceth his ground, and round about doth beat,
　To spy where he may some aduauntage get;
　The whiles the beast doth rage and loudly rore:
　So did the Squire, the whiles the Carle did fret,
　And fume in his disdainefull mynd the more,
And oftentimes by Turmagant and Mahound swore.

48

Nathelesse so sharpely still he him pursewd,
　That at aduantage him at last he tooke,
　When his foote slipt (that slip he dearely rewd,)
　And with his yron club to ground him strooke;
　Where still he lay, ne out of swoune awooke,
　Till heauy hand the Carle vpon him layd,
　And bound him fast: Tho when he vp did looke,
　And saw him selfe captiu'd, he was dismayd,
Ne powre had to withstand, ne hope of any ayd.

49

Then vp he made him rise, and forward fare,
　Led in a rope, which both his hands did bynd;
　Ne ought that foole for pitty did him spare,
　But with his whip him following behynd,
　Him often scourg'd, and forst his feete to fynd:
　And other whiles with bitter mockes and mowes
　He would him scorne, that to his gentle mynd
　Was much more grieuous, then the others blowes:
Words sharpely wound, but greatest griefe of scorning growes.

50

The faire *Serena*, when she saw him fall
　Vnder that villaines club, then surely thought
　That slaine he was, or made a wretched thrall,
　And fled away with all the speede she mought,
　To seeke for safety, which long time she sought:
　And past through many perils by the way,
　Ere she againe to *Calepine* was brought;
　The which discourse as now I must delay,
Till *Mirabellaes* fortunes I doe further say.

Cant. VIII.

Prince Arthure ouercomes Disdaine,
Quites Mirabell from dreed:
Serena found of Saluages,
By Calepine is freed.

1

YE gentle Ladies, in whose soueraine powre
　Loue hath the glory of his kingdome left,
　And th'hearts of men, as your eternall dowre,
　In yron chaines, of liberty bereft,
　Deliuered hath into your hands by gift;
　Be well aware, how ye the same doe vse,
　That pride doe not to tyranny you lift;
　Least if men you of cruelty accuse,
He from you take that chiefedome, which ye doe abuse.

2

And as ye soft and tender are by kynde,
　Adornd with goodly gifts of beauties grace,
　So be ye soft and tender eeke in mynde;
　But cruelty and hardnesse from you chace,
　That all your other praises will deface,
　And from you turne the loue of men to hate.
　Ensample take of *Mirabellaes* case,
　Who from the high degree of happy state,
Fell into wretched woes, which she repented late.

Stanza 46

3　**batton**: club.

7　**burden**: bourdon or club; or its weight.

Stanza 47

1–6　Cf. v 19. Now the roles are reversed because Timias is wrong to intervene. Cf. vi 27. 4–9.

3　**assay**: put to the proof.

8　**the more**: greatly.

9　**Turmagant and Mahound**: a Saracen god and Mohammed; see II viii 30.4*n*.

Stanza 49

5　**forst his feete to fynd**: forced him to stand up and keep walking.

6　**mowes**: derisive grimaces.

9　**Words**: 'Swords' sugg. Church (1758), who compares IV iv 4.9. J. C. Smith (1909) ii App. argues that the alliteration favours the text. So does the sense: Scorn attacks with a whip (**Words**) and mocks (**scorning**); cf. 44.6–9. Cf. the proverb, 'Words cut deeper than swords' (C. G. Smith, 1970, 879).

Canto viii

Argument

In this 'regeneration' canto (see I viii Arg. 1–2), Arthur completes the six labours which the number of the Book requires: in Canto v, he saves Timias and succours Serena; in Canto vi, he defeats Turpine; in Canto vii, he defeats Turpine's knights and baffles him; and now he overcomes Disdain to offer Mirabella her freedom.

2　**Quites**: frees; see 29.6–9*n*.

Stanza 2

1　**kynde**: nature.

3

Who after thraldome of the gentle Squire,
　Which she beheld with lamentable eye,
　Was touched with compassion entire,
　And much lamented his calamity,
　That for her sake fell into misery:
　Which booted nought for prayers, nor for threat
　To hope for to release or mollify;
　For aye the more, that she did them entreat,
The more they him misust, and cruelly did beat.

4

So as they forward on their way did pas,
　Him still reuiling and afflicting sore,
　They met Prince *Arthure* with Sir *Enias*,
　(That was that courteous Knight, whom he before
　Hauing subdew'd, yet did to life restore,)
　To whom as they approcht, they gan augment
　Their cruelty, and him to punish more,
　Scourging and haling him more vehement;
As if it them should grieue to see his punishment.

5

The Squire him selfe when as he saw his Lord,
　The witnesse of his wretchednesse, in place,
　Was much asham'd, that with an hempen cord
　He like a dog was led in captiue case,
　And did his head for bashfulnesse abase,
　As loth to see, or to be seene at all:
　Shame would be hid. But whenas *Enias*
　Beheld two such, of two such villaines thrall,
His manly mynde was much emmoued therewithall.

6

And to the Prince thus sayd ; See you Sir Knight,
　The greatest shame that euer eye yet saw?
　Yond Lady and her Squire with foule despight
　Abusde, against all reason and all law,
　Without regard of pitty or of awe.
　See how they doe that Squire beat and reuile;
　See how they doe the Lady hale and draw.
　But if ye please to lend me leaue a while,
I will them soone acquite, and both of blame assoile.

7

The Prince assented, and then he streight way
　Dismounting light, his shield about him threw,
　With which approching, thus he gan to say;
　Abide ye caytiue treachetours vntrew,
　That haue with treason thralled vnto you
　These two, vnworthy of your wretched bands;
　And now your crime with cruelty pursew.
　Abide, and from them lay your loathly hands;
Or else abide the death, that hard before you stands.

8

The villaine stayd not aunswer to inuent,
　But with his yron club preparing way,
　His mindes sad message backe vnto him sent;
　The which descended with such dreadfull sway,
　That seemed nought the course thereof could stay:
　No more then lightening from the lofty sky.
　Ne list the Knight the powre thereof assay,
　Whose doome was death, but lightly slipping by,
Vnwares defrauded his intended destiny.

9

And to requite him with the like againe,
　With his sharpe sword he fiercely at him flew,
　And strooke so strongly, that the Carle with paine
　Saued him selfe, but that he there him slew:
　Yet sau'd not so, but that the bloud it drew,
　And gaue his foe good hope of victory.
　Who therewith flesht, vpon him set anew,
　And with the second stroke, thought certainely
To haue supplyde the first, and paide the vsury.

Stanza 3
The stanza marks Mirabella's partial regeneration: she pities
the lover who becomes her victim. Paradoxically, because she
pities him, she disdains and scorns him all the more, particularly in the company of others as the next stanza shows. Cf.
Astrophel's dilemma in Sidney, *Astrophel and Stella* lx.
2　**lamentable**: lamenting.
3　**entire**: sincere.

Stanza 4
3　**Enias**: the significance of the name is not clear. A.
Williams (1967) 70 suggests as a possibility a variant of Aeneas,
or ἑνια, glossed by Stephanus as halter or bridle, suggesting
restraint. The name may echo Timias because by 11.9 both
share the same plight.

Stanza 5
Cf. his shame at IV vii 44 and VI v 24. Now he is reduced to
'greatest shame' (6.2). Cf. 27.1–3.
3　**hempen cord**: cf. the halter worn by Trevisan (I ix 22.7)
and the cord by which Disdain drags Mirabella (vii 44.4).
5　**bashfulnesse**: mortification through shame.　**abase**:
hang down.
7　As the emblematic posture of shame, cf. II vii 22.9.

Stanza 6
9　**acquite, and . . . assoile**: set free and release from injury
and reproof.

Stanza 7
2　**light**: quickly.
4　**Abide**: stop; repeated in this sense in 8 to play against
the usual sense in 9, await or endure.　**treachetours**:
traitors; see II x 51.3*n*.
6　**vnworthy**: not deserving.

Stanza 8
3　**sad**: heavy, as it refers to the club; punning on the usual
sense for the **message** is death.
4　**sway**: force.

Stanza 9
7　**flesht**: incited; also literally, having thrust his sword into
his enemy's flesh.
9　**supplyde**: reinforced.　**vsury**: interest.

10

But Fortune aunswerd not vnto his call;
   For as his hand was heaued vp on hight,
   The villaine met him in the middle fall,
   And with his club bet backe his brondyron bright
   So forcibly, that with his owne hands might
   Rebeaten backe vpon him selfe againe,
   He driuen was to ground in selfe despight;
   From whence ere he recouery could gaine,
He in his necke had set his foote with fell disdaine.

11

With that the foole, which did that end awayte,
   Came running in, and whilest on ground he lay,
   Laide heauy hands on him, and held so strayte,
   That downe he kept him with his scornefull sway,
   So as he could not weld him any way.
   The whiles that other villaine went about
   Him to haue bound, and thrald without delay;
   The whiles the foole did him reuile and flout,
Threatning to yoke them two and tame their corage stout.

12

As when a sturdy ploughman with his hynde
   By strength haue ouerthrowne a stubborne steare,
   They downe him hold, and fast with cords do bynde,
   Till they him force the buxome yoke to beare:
   So did these two this Knight oft tug and teare.
   Which when the Prince beheld, there standing by,
   He left his lofty steede to aide him neare,
   And buckling soone him selfe, gan fiercely fly
Vppon that Carle, to saue his friend from ieopardy.

13

The villaine leauing him vnto his mate
   To be captiu'd, and handled as he list,
   Himselfe addrest vnto this new debate,
   And with his club him all about so blist,
   That he which way to turne him scarcely wist:
   Sometimes aloft he layd, sometimes alow;
   Now here, now there, and oft him neare he mist;
   So doubtfully, that hardly one could know
Whether more wary were to giue or ward the blow.

14

But yet the Prince so well enured was
   With such huge strokes, approued oft in fight,
   That way to them he gaue forth right to pas.
   Ne would endure the daunger of their might,
   But wayt aduantage, when they downe did light.
   At last the caytiue after long discourse,
   When all his strokes he saw auoyded quite,
   Resolued in one t'assemble all his force,
And make one end of him without ruth or remorse.

15

His dreadfull hand he heaued vp aloft,
   And with his dreadfull instrument of yre,
   Thought sure haue pownded him to powder soft,
   Or deepe emboweld in the earth entyre:
   But Fortune did not with his will conspire.
   For ere his stroke attayned his intent,
   The noble childe preuenting his desire,
   Vnder his club with wary boldnesse went,
And smote him on the knee, that neuer yet was bent.

16

It neuer yet was bent, ne bent it now,
   Albe the stroke so strong and puissant were,
   That seem'd a marble pillour it could bow,
   But all that leg, which did his body beare,
   It crackt throughout, yet did no bloud appeare;
   So as it was vnable to support
   So huge a burden on such broken geare,
But fell to ground, like to a lumpe of durt,
Whence he assayd to rise, but could not for his hurt.

Stanza 10
3   **in the middle fall**: i.e. in the middle of his downward stroke.
4   **brondyron**: sword.
5–7   The gesture indicates that Enias causes his own downfall, overcome by his own disdain. Hence **in selfe despight**: in spite of himself, but also by his own despite.

Stanza 11
3   **strayte**: tightly.
4   **sway**: force.
5   **weld**: wield: manage; hence **weld him**: move himself.

Stanza 12
1   **hynde**: servant.
4   **buxome**: obedient; as adv., bear the yoke obediently.

Stanza 13
3   **debate**: conflict.
4   **blist**: brandished.

Stanza 14
2   **approued**: tested.
4   **daunger**: harm.
5   As in his battle against Orgoglio, I viii 10.
6   **discourse**: running to and fro, from Ital. *discorso* (Florio, 1611); cf. Lat. *discursus*, 'a runnyng hither and thither' (Cooper, 1565).

Stanza 15
S. borrows details from Arthur's battle with Orgoglio; cf. particularly I viii 22.
3   Cf. the power of Orgoglio's blow, I vii 14.3.
4   **entyre**: completely; or as adj., inner.
7   **childe**: applied only to Arthur; see IV viii 44.8n.
preuenting: anticipating.

675

17

Eftsoones the Prince to him full nimbly stept,
 And least he should recouer foote againe,
 His head meant from his shoulders to haue swept.
 Which when the Lady saw, she cryde amaine;
 Stay stay, Sir Knight, for loue of God abstaine,
 From that vnwares ye weetlesse doe intend;
 Slay not that Carle, though worthy to be slaine:
 For more on him doth then him selfe depend;
My life will by his death haue lamentable end.

18

He staide his hand according her desire,
 Yet nathemore him suffred to arize;
 But still suppressing gan of her inquire,
 What meaning mote those vncouth words comprize,
 That in that villaines health her safety lies:
 That, were no might in man, nor heart in Knights,
 Which durst her dreaded reskue enterprize,
 Yet heauens them selues, that fauour feeble rights,
Would for it selfe redresse, and punish such despights.

19

Then bursting forth in teares, which gushed fast
 Like many water streames, a while she stayd;
 Till the sharpe passion being ouerpast,
 Her tongue to her restord, then thus she sayd;
 Nor heauens, nor men can me most wretched mayd
 Deliuer from the doome of my desart,
 The which the God of loue hath on me layd,
 And damned to endure this direfull smart,
For penaunce of my proud and hard rebellious hart.

20

In prime of youthly yeares, when first the flowre
 Of beauty gan to bud, and bloosme delight,
 And nature me endu'd with plenteous dowre,
 Of all her gifts, that pleasde each liuing sight,
 I was belou'd of many a gentle Knight,
 And sude and sought with all the seruice dew:
 Full many a one for me deepe groand and sight,
 And to the dore of death for sorrow drew,
Complayning out on me, that would not on them rew.

21

But let them loue that list, or liue or die;
 Me list not die for any louers doole:
 Ne list me leaue my loued libertie,
 To pitty him that list to play the foole:
 To loue my selfe I learned had in schoole.
 Thus I triumphed long in louers paine,
 And sitting carelesse on the scorners stoole,
 Did laugh at those that did lament and plaine:
But all is now repayd with interest againe.

22

For loe the winged God, that woundeth harts,
 Causde me be called to accompt therefore,
 And for reuengement of those wrongfull smarts,
 Which I to others did inflict afore,
 Addeem'd me to endure this penaunce sore;
 That in this wize, and this vnmeete array,
 With these two lewd companions, and no more,
 Disdaine and *Scorne*, I through the world should stray,
Till I haue sau'd so many, as I earst did slay.

23

Certes (sayd then the Prince) the God is iust,
 That taketh vengeaunce of his peoples spoile.
 For were no law in loue, but all that lust,
 Might them oppresse, and painefully turmoile,
 His kingdome would continue but a while.
 But tell me Lady, wherefore doe you beare
 This bottle thus before you with such toile,
 And eeke this wallet at your backe arreare,
That for these Carles to carry much more comely were?

Stanza 17
1 **nimbly**: swiftly.
4–9 Cf. Amoret's appeal to Britomart not to slay Busirane, III xii 34. Both must be cured by their tormentors. **amaine**: with all her might.
5 The God to whose love she appeals ought to be Cupid, the god of love.

Stanza 18
3 **suppressing**: pressing down.
4 **comprize**: contain.
6 **That**: i.e. her safety.
7 **her dreaded reskue**: i.e. dreaded by others and now by her. **enterprize**: undertake.
8 **feeble rights**: rights of the weak.

Stanzas 20–22
Cf. the earlier account, vii 28–38, especially 20–21 with 28–31.

Stanza 20
1–4 The blossom of her beauty delights others. Her bodily gifts contrast with Belphœbe's heavenly gifts (III vi 2) and Amoret's moral virtues (IV x 49–52).
6 **sude**: attended, offered service.
7 **sight**: sighed.
9 **out on me**: aloud against me; or an interjection of reproach.

Stanza 21
1–4 **list**: the repetition suggests that she believes her lovers are free to love as she is free not to love; but they are subject to love as she is subject to disdain and scorn.
2 **doole**: grief.
7 Cf. Ps. 1.1: 'The man is blest that hath not . . . sat in scorners chayre' (BCP).

Stanza 22
5–9 Cf. vii 37.6–9. **Addeem'd**: adjudged. **lewd**: evil.

Stanza 23
3 Arthur denies the proverb (C. G. Smith, 1970, 488) that there is no law in love. **lust**: chose, following their own will; but not excluding the sexual sense. The Court of Cupid codifies all desire, making men its victims.
4 **turmoile**: torment.
8 **arreare**: behind.

24

Here in this bottle (sayd the sory Mayd)
　I put the teares of my contrition,
　Till to the brim I haue it full defrayd:
　And in this bag which I behinde me don,
　I put repentaunce for things past and gon.
　Yet is the bottle leake, and bag so torne,
　That all which I put in, fals out anon;
　And is behinde me trodden downe of *Scorne*,
Who mocketh all my paine, and laughs the more I mourn.

25

The Infant hearkned wisely to her tale,
　And wondred much at *Cupids* iudg'ment wise,
　That could so meekly make proud hearts auale,
　And wreake him selfe on them, that him despise.
　Then suffred he *Disdaine* vp to arise,
　Who was not able vp him selfe to reare,
　By meanes his leg through his late luckelesse prise,
　Was crackt in twaine, but by his foolish feare
Was holpen vp, who him supported standing neare.

26

But being vp, he lookt againe aloft,
　As if he neuer had receiued fall;
　And with sterne eye-browes stared at him oft,
　As if he would haue daunted him withall:
　And standing on his tiptoes, to seeme tall,
　Downe on his golden feete he often gazed,
　As if such pride the other could apall;
　Who was so far from being ought amazed,
That he his lookes despised, and his boast dispraized.

27

Then turning backe vnto that captiue thrall,
　Who all this while stood there beside them bound,
　Vnwilling to be knowne, or seene at all,
　He from those bands weend him to haue vnwound.
　But when approching neare, he plainely found,
　It was his owne true groome, the gentle Squire,
　He thereat wext exceedingly astound,
　And him did oft embrace, and oft admire,
Ne could with seeing satisfie his great desire.

28

Meane while the Saluage man, when he beheld
　That huge great foole oppressing th'other Knight,
　Whom with his weight vnweldy downe he held,
　He flew vpon him, like a greedy kight
　Vnto some carrion offered to his sight,
　And downe him plucking, with his nayles and teeth
　Gan him to hale, and teare, and scratch, and bite;
　And from him taking his owne whip, therewith
So sore him scourgeth, that the bloud downe followeth.

29

And sure I weene, had not the Ladies cry
　Procur'd the Prince his cruell hand to stay,
　He would with whipping, him haue done to dye:
　But being checkt, he did abstaine streight way,
　And let him rise. Then thus the Prince gan say;
　Now Lady sith your fortunes thus dispose,
　That if ye list haue liberty, ye may,
　Vnto your selfe I freely leaue to chose,
Whether I shall you leaue, or from these villaines lose.

30

Ah nay Sir Knight (sayd she) it may not be,
　But that I needes must by all meanes fulfill
　This penaunce, which enioyned is to me,
　Least vnto me betide a greater ill;
　Yet no lesse thankes to you for your good will.
　So humbly taking leaue, she turnd aside,
　But *Arthure* with the rest, went onward still
　On his first quest, in which did him betide
A great aduenture, which did him from them deuide.

Stanza 24
1–2　This bottle is the lachrymatory vase of the ancients, and of Scripture, e.g. Ps. 56.8.
3　**Till . . . defrayd**: until I have fully discharged my contrition by filling the bottle.

Stanza 25
1　**Infant**: youth of noble birth, from Span. *infante*, Prince. It is Arthur's title at II viii 56.1, etc.　**wisely**: attentively.
3　**auale**: yield.
7　**By meanes**: because.　**prise**: contest.
8　**feare**: companion.　**foolish**: as he is the Fool; see vi 16.9*n*.

Stanza 26
6　**his golden feete**: cf. the golden coat worn by the disdainful Mammon at II vii 4.1–6.
9　**boast**: ostentation, pomp; threatening.

Stanza 27
8　**admire**: gaze at with wonder.

Stanza 28
3　**vnweldy**: unwieldy, unless it means that the knight is unable to move; cf. 11.5.

Stanza 29
2　**Procur'd**: prevailed upon.
6–9　According to the Arg., Arthur '*Quites Mirabell from dreed*': he does not slay Disdain whose death she fears would bring her own (17.9) and he preserves Scorn. Further, he allows her freely to choose a punishment that before had been imposed on her.　**lose**: loose.

Stanza 30
Before, Mirabella was 'the Ladie of her libertie' (vii 31.5); now she chooses bondage.
9　This **great aduenture** divides him from us until his awakening.

677

31

But first it falleth me by course to tell
  Of faire *Serena*, who as earst you heard,
  When first the gentle Squire at variaunce fell
  With those two Carles, fled fast away, afeard
  Of villany to be to her inferd:
  So fresh the image of her former dread,
  Yet dwelling in her eye, to her appeard,
  That euery foote did tremble, which did tread,
And euery body two, and two she foure did read.

32

Through hils and dales, through bushes and through breres
  Long thus she fled, till that at last she thought
  Her selfe now past the perill of her feares.
  Then looking round about, and seeing nought,
  Which doubt of daunger to her offer mought,
  She from her palfrey lighted on the plaine,
  And sitting downe, her selfe a while bethought
  Of her long trauell and turmoyling paine;
And often did of loue, and oft of lucke complaine.

33

And euermore she blamed *Calepine*,
  The good Sir *Calepine*, her owne true Knight,
  As th'onely author of her wofull tine:
  For being of his loue to her so light,
  As her to leaue in such a piteous plight.
  Yet neuer Turtle truer to his make,
  Then he was tride vnto his Lady bright:
  Who all this while endured for her sake,
Great perill of his life, and restlesse paines did take.

34

Tho when as all her plaints she had displayd,
  And well disburdened her engrieued brest,
  Vpon the grasse her selfe adowne she layd;
  Where being tyrde with trauell, and opprest
  With sorrow, she betooke her selfe to rest.
  There whilest in *Morpheus* bosome safe she lay,
  Fearelesse of ought, that mote her peace molest,
  False Fortune did her safety betray,
Vnto a straunge mischaunce, that menac'd her decay.

35

In these wylde deserts, where she now abode,
  There dwelt a saluage nation, which did liue
  Of stealth and spoile, and making nightly rode
  Into their neighbours borders; ne did giue
  Them selues to any trade, as for to driue
  The painefull plough, or cattell for to breed,
  Or by aduentrous marchandize to thriue;
  But on the labours of poore men to feed,
And serue their owne necessities with others need.

36

Thereto they vsde one most accursed order,
  To eate the flesh of men, whom they mote fynde,
  And straungers to deuoure, which on their border
  Were brought by errour, or by wreckfull wynde.
  A monstrous cruelty gainst course of kynde.
  They towards euening wandring euery way,
  To seeke for booty, came by fortune blynde,
  Whereas this Lady, like a sheepe astray,
Now drowned in the depth of sleepe all fearelesse lay.

37

Soone as they spide her, Lord what gladfull glee
  They made amongst them selues; but when her face
  Like the faire yuory shining they did see,
  Each gan his fellow solace and embrace,
  For ioy of such good hap by heauenly grace.
  Then gan they to deuize what course to take:
  Whether to slay her there vpon the place,
  Or suffer her out of her sleepe to wake,
And then her eate attonce; or many meales to make.

Stanzas 31–51
The parallels between the stories of Serena and Amoret are
noted by Cheney (1966) 108–9. Both wander fearlessly in the
forest until captured, the one by a 'saluage man' (IV vii 4f)
and the other by a 'saluage nation', and both are threatened with
being eaten. McNeir (1968) shows S.'s transformation of his
sources in romance, Celtic custom and anthropological rites.

Stanza 31
5 **to her inferd**: inflicted on her; also she fears that she
will be accused of shameful conduct.
9 **read**: take for.

Stanza 32
5 **doubt**: fear.

Stanza 33
3 **tine**: sorrow.
6 **make**: mate.
7 **tride**: proved faithful.
9 **restlesse paines**: cf. Calidore, ix 2.9.

Stanza 34
6 **safe**: used ironically to suggest her over-confidence or to
indicate that she remains secure in the power of Morpheus
while she suffers the ensuing nightmare.
9 **decay**: death.

Stanza 35
3 **stealth**: theft.   **rode**: raid.
7 **marchandize**: trading.

Stanza 36
1 **order**: custom.
4 **errour**: wandering.
5 **kynde**: nature.

38

The best aduizement was of bad, to let her
  Sleepe out her fill, without encomberment:
  For sleepe they sayd would make her battill better.
  Then when she wakt, they all gaue one consent,
  That since by grace of God she there was sent,
  Vnto their God they would her sacrifize,
  Whose share, her guiltlesse bloud they would present,
  But of her dainty flesh they did deuize
To make a common feast, and feed with gurmandize.

39

So round about her they them selues did place
  Vpon the grasse, and diuersely dispose,
  As each thought best to spend the lingring space.
  Some with their eyes the daintest morsels chose;
  Some praise her paps, some praise her lips and nose;
  Some whet their kniues, and strip their elboes bare:
  The Priest him selfe a garland doth compose
  Of finest flowres, and with full busie care
His bloudy vessels wash, and holy fire prepare.

40

The Damzell wakes, then all attonce vpstart,
  And round about her flocke, like many flies,
  Whooping, and hallowing on euery part,
  As if they would haue rent the brasen skies.
  Which when she sees with ghastly griefful eies,
  Her heart does quake, and deadly pallid hew
  Benumbes her cheekes: Then out aloud she cries,
  Where none is nigh to heare, that will her rew,
And rends her golden locks, and snowy brests embrew.

41

But all bootes not: they hands vpon her lay;
  And first they spoile her of her iewels deare,
  And afterwards of all her rich array;
  The which amongst them they in peeces teare,
  And of the pray each one a part doth beare.
  Now being naked, to their sordid eyes
  The goodly threasures of nature appeare:
  Which as they view with lustfull fantasyes,
Each wisheth to him selfe, and to the rest enuyes.

42

Her yuorie necke, her alablaster brest,
  Her paps, which like white silken pillowes were,
  For loue in soft delight thereon to rest;
  Her tender sides, her bellie white and clere,
  Which like an Altar did it selfe vprere,
  To offer sacrifice diuine thereon;
  Her goodly thighes, whose glorie did appeare
  Like a triumphall Arch, and thereupon
The spoiles of Princes hang'd, which were in battel won.

43

Those daintie parts, the dearlings of delight,
  Which mote not be prophan'd of common eyes,
  Those villeins vew'd with loose lasciuious sight,
  And closely tempted with their craftie spyes;
  And some of them gan mongst themselues deuize,
  Thereof by force to take their beastly pleasure,
  But them the Priest rebuking, did aduize
  To dare not to pollute so sacred threasure,
Vow'd to the gods: religion held euen theeues in measure.

44

So being stayd, they her from thence directed
  Vnto a litle groue not farre asyde,
  In which an altar shortly they erected,
  To slay her on. And now the Euentyde
  His brode black wings had through the heauens wyde
  By this dispred, that was the tyme ordayned
  For such a dismall deed, their guilt to hyde:
  Of few greene turfes an altar soone they fayned,
And deckt it all with flowres, which they nigh hand obtayned.

Stanza 38
1 **aduizement**: advice, counsel, plan.   **of bad**: i.e. the worst, as it involves torture.
2 **encomberment**: disturbance.
3 **battill**: grow fat, as do cattle; perhaps with added humour, referring to love's wars.
7 **Whose share, her guiltlesse bloud**: i.e. the god's share in the sacrifice was her blood.
9 **gurmandize**: gluttony.

Stanza 39
Cheney (1966) 106 notes that S.'s wit 'is based on linking the cannibals' confusion of the two appetites of hunger and lust with the language of a love-religion'.

Stanza 40
2 **like many flies**: a common simile for a swarming attack (cf. xi 48); appropriate here for the fly is associated with lechery.
3 **part**: side.
9 **embrew**: moistens with tears, or stains with blood.

Stanza 41
9 **enuyes**: begrudges.

Stanza 42
4 **clere**: bright, shining.
5 Since the episode treats the sexual phantasies of a woman in love, the **Altar** suggests the nuptial bed on which the bride awaits the groom 'Like an appointed lambe, when tenderly/The priest comes on his knees t'embowell her' (Donne, 'Epithalamion made at Lincolnes Inne' 89–90).
7–9 Cf. the imagery at II iii 28.1–4. In the Song of Solomon 4.4, the neck is compared to a tower upon which 'a thousand shields hang . . . and all the targates of the strong men'.

Stanza 43
4 **closely**: secretly.   **tempted**: made trial of.   **spyes**: eyes or glances.
9 **measure**: moderation.

Stanza 44
7 **dismall**: terrible, dreadful.
8 Repeats 3 to stress that the altar is **fayned**, i.e. fashioned and false, being used in an obscene religious ritual.

45

Tho when as all things readie were aright,
  The Damzell was before the altar set,
  Being alreadie dead with fearefull fright.
  To whom the Priest with naked armes full net
  Approching nigh, and murdrous knife well whet,
  Gan mutter close a certaine secret charme,
  With other diuelish ceremonies met:
  Which doen he gan aloft t'aduance his arme,
Whereat they shouted all, and made a loud alarme.

46

Then gan the bagpypes and the hornes to shrill,
  And shrieke aloud, that with the peoples voyce
  Confused, did the ayre with terror fill,
  And made the wood to tremble at the noyce:
  The whyles she wayld, the more they did reioyce.
  Now mote ye vnderstand that to this groue
  Sir *Calepine* by chaunce, more then by choyce,
  The selfe same euening fortune hether droue,
As he to seeke *Serena* through the woods did roue.

47

Long had he sought her, and through many a soyle
  Had traueld still on foot in heauie armes,
  Ne ought was tyred with his endlesse toyles,
  Ne ought was feared of his certaine harmes:
  And now all weetlesse of the wretched stormes,
  In which his loue was lost, he slept full fast,
  Till being waked with these loud alarmes,
  He lightly started vp like one aghast,
And catching vp his arms streight to the noise forth past.

48

There by th'vncertaine glims of starry night,
  And by the twinkling of their sacred fire,
  He mote perceiue a litle dawning sight
  Of all, which there was doing in that quire:
  Mongst whom a woman spoyld of all attire
  He spyde, lamenting her vnluckie strife,
  And groning sore from grieued hart entire,
  Eftsoones he saw one with a naked knife
Readie to launch her brest, and let out loued life.

49

With that he thrusts into the thickest throng,
  And euen as his right hand adowne descends,
  He him preuenting, layes on earth along,
  And sacrifizeth to th'infernall feends.
  Then to the rest his wrathfull hand he bends,
  Of whom he makes such hauocke and such hew,
  That swarmes of damned soules to hell he sends:
  The rest that scape his sword and death eschew,
Fly like a flocke of doues before a Faulcons vew.

50

From them returning to that Ladie backe,
  Whom by the Altar he doth sitting find,
  Yet fearing death, and next to death the lacke
  Of clothes to couer, what they ought by kind,
  He first her hands beginneth to vnbind;
  And then to question of her present woe;
  And afterwards to cheare with speaches kind.
  But she for nought that he could say or doe,
One word durst speake, or answere him a whit thereto.

51

So inward shame of her vncomely case
  She did conceiue, through care of womanhood,
  That though the night did couer her disgrace,
  Yet she in so vnwomanly a mood,
  Would not bewray the state in which she stood.
  So all that night to him vnknowen she past.
  But day, that doth discouer bad and good,
  Ensewing, made her knowen to him at last:
The end whereof Ile keepe vntill another cast.

Stanza 45
4   net: clean or bare, for the purpose of sacrifice.
6   close: covertly.
7   met: meet, fitting; or, as vb, united.

Stanza 46
1–2   The bagpipes announce the lustful satyrs at III x 43.2; as a symbol of gluttony and lechery, see Block (1954).

Stanza 47
4   feared of: alarmed by.

Stanza 48
1   glims: glimpse, glimmering.
2   Either the light of the stars, as **twinkling** suggests; or the light of the 'holy fire' (39.9) under the altar, which is **sacred** because consecrated or accursed.
4   quire: chorus, either as a band or as singers, referring to their yelling.
6   strife: distress.
7   entire: either an adv. 'wholly', or an adj. to describe her unpierced heart.
9   launch: pierce.

Stanza 49
2   On this dramatic intervention, see I ix 51.9*n*.
3–4   *Var.* vi notices the irony of the sacrificer sacrificed.
6   hew: slaughter.
8   eschew: evade.

Stanza 50
4   what they ought by kind: what they are naturally intended to cover.

Stanza 51
Cf. her response to her lover at the beginning of her story, iii 20. The Blatant Beast's wound has been further infected by the Hermit's moralizing (vi 6–14). Staton (1966) compares Italian pastorals in which nymphs scorn their rescuers.
1   case: plight; covering. Only night covers her; her nakedness is her only covering. This vision of woman sitting in shamed silence, withdrawn, ungrateful, and unloving is at the opposite pole to the vision of the hundred naked women dancing in delight in Canto x.
5   bewray: reveal.
8   knowen: the sexual meaning is suggested.
9   cast: throw; or in the fig. sense, 'time'.

Cant. IX.

Calidore hostes with Melibœ
and loues fayre Pastorell;
Coridon enuies him, yet be
for ill rewards him well.

1

NOw turne againe my teme thou iolly swayne,
  Backe to the furrow which I lately left;
I lately left a furrow, one or twayne
Vnplough'd, the which my coulter hath not cleft:
Yet seem'd the soyle both fayre and frutefull eft,
  As I it past, that were too great a shame,
  That so rich frute should be from vs bereft;
Besides the great dishonour and defame,
Which should befall to *Calidores* immortall name.

2

Great trauell hath the gentle *Calidore*
  And toyle endured, sith I left him last
Sewing the *Blatant beast*, which I forbore
To finish then, for other present hast.
Full many pathes and perils he hath past, (plaines
  Through hils, through dales, throgh forests, and throgh
  In that same quest which fortune on him cast,
Which he atchieued to his owne great gaines,
Reaping eternall glorie of his restlesse paines.

3

So sharply he the Monster did pursew,
  That day nor night he suffred him to rest,
Ne rested he himselfe but natures dew,
  For dread of daunger, not to be redrest,
  If he for slouth forslackt so famous quest.
Him first from court he to the cities coursed,
  And from the cities to the townes him prest,
  And from the townes into the countrie forsed,
And from the country back to priuate farmes he scorsed.

4

From thence into the open fields he fled,
  Whereas the Heardes were keeping of their neat,
And shepheards singing to their flockes, that fed,
Layes of sweete loue and youthes delightfull heat:
Him thether eke for all his fearefull threat
  He followed fast, and chaced him so nie,
  That to the folds, where sheepe at night doe seat,
And to the litle cots, where shepherds lie
In winters wrathfull time, he forced him to flie.

5

There on a day as he pursew'd the chace,
  He chaunst to spy a sort of shepheard groomes,
Playing on pypes, and caroling apace,
The whyles their beasts there in the budded broomes
Beside them fed, and nipt the tender bloomes:
  For other worldly wealth they cared nought,
  To whom Sir *Calidore* yet sweating comes,
And them to tell him courteously besought,
If such a beast they saw, which he had thether brought.

6

They answer'd him, that no such beast they saw,
  Nor any wicked feend, that mote offend
Their happie flockes, nor daunger to them draw:
But if that such there were (as none they kend)
They prayd high God him farre from them to send.
  Then one of them him seeing so to sweat,
  After his rusticke wise, that well he weend,
Offred him drinke, to quench his thirstie heat,
And if he hungry were, him offred eke to eat.

Canto ix

Argument

1 **hostes**: lodges.

Stanza 1

The pastoral topos of the poet ploughing with the Muses as his
team is used earlier, III xii 47.3–6 (*1590*), IV v 46.8–9,
and V iii 40. 6–7, but only to announce that he seeks rest.
5 **eft**: also.
8–9 I.e. such would happen if he did not relate Calidore's
story, but said with some irony. **dishonour and defame**
are brought upon Calidore's name through the episode that
follows. Cf. xii 12. Yet the next stanza notes that he does
achieve his quest with glory.

Stanza 2

3 **Sewing**: pursuing.

Stanza 3

3 **but natures dew**: only the sleep due to nature; cf. his
rest in the pastoral retreat.
4 **redrest**: remedied, atoned for.
5 **forslackt**: neglected; cf. xii 12.5.
9 **scorsed**: caused to exchange; or chased, from Ital.
scorsa, 'a running' (Florio, 1611).

Stanza 4

2 **Heardes**: herdsmen. **neat**: cattle.
7 **seat**: lie down.
8 **cots**: cotes or shelters.
9 **time**] 'tine' sugg. Church and Upton (1758), as IV iii 23.7,
xii 34.6.

Stanza 5

2 **sort**: company.
9 **which he had . . . brought**: i.e. which had brought him.

Stanza 6

2 **offend**: attack.
5 In contrast to Calidore's quest for the Beast.
7 **that well he weend**: as he thought best.

7

The knight was nothing nice, where was no need,
  And tooke their gentle offer: so adowne
  They prayd him sit, and gaue him for to feed
  Such homely what, as serues the simple clowne,
  That doth despise the dainties of the towne.
  Tho hauing fed his fill, he there besyde
  Saw a faire damzell, which did weare a crowne
  Of sundry flowres, with silken ribbands tyde,
Yclad in home-made greene that her owne hands had dyde.

8

Vpon a litle hillocke she was placed
  Higher then all the rest, and round about
  Enuiron'd with a girland, goodly graced,
  Of louely lasses, and them all without
  The lustie shepheard swaynes sate in a rout,
  The which did pype and sing her prayses dew,
  And oft reioyce, and oft for wonder shout,
  As if some miracle of heauenly hew
Were downe to them descended in that earthly vew.

9

And soothly sure she was full fayre of face,
  And perfectly well shapt in euery lim,
  Which she did more augment with modest grace,
  And comely carriage of her count'nance trim,
  That all the rest like lesser lamps did dim:
  Who her admiring as some heauenly wight,
  Did for their soueraine goddesse her esteeme,
  And caroling her name both day and night,
The fayrest *Pastorella* her by name did hight.

10

Ne was there heard, ne was there shepheards swayne
  But her did honour, and eke many a one
  Burnt in her loue, and with sweet pleasing payne
  Full many a night for her did sigh and grone:
  But most of all the shepheard *Coridon*
  For her did languish, and his deare life spend;
  Yet neither she for him, nor other none
  Did care a whit, ne any liking lend:
Though meane her lot, yet higher did her mind ascend.

11

Her whyles Sir *Calidore* there vewed well,
  And markt her rare demeanure, which him seemed
  So farre the meane of shepheards to excell,
  As that he in his mind her worthy deemed,
  To be a Princes Paragone esteemed,
  He was vnwares surprisd in subtile bands
  Of the blynd boy, ne thence could be redeemed
  By any skill out of his cruell hands,
Caught like the bird, which gazing still on others stands.

12

So stood he still long gazing thereupon,
  Ne any will had thence to moue away,
  Although his quest were farre afore him gon;
  But after he had fed, yet did he stay,
  And sate there still, vntill the flying day
  Was farre forth spent, discoursing diuersly
  Of sundry things, as fell, to worke delay;
  And euermore his speach he did apply
To th'heards, but meant them to the damzels fantazy.

13

By this the moystie night approching fast,
  Her deawy humour gan on th'earth to shed,
  That warn'd the shepheards to their homes to hast
  Their tender flocks, now being fully fed,
  For feare of wetting them before their bed;
  Then came to them a good old aged syre,
  Whose siluer lockes bedeckt his beard and hed,
  With shepheards hooke in hand, and fit attyre,
That wild the damzell rise; the day did now expyre.

Stanza 7
1   **nothing nice**: not at all fastidious.
4   **what**: thing.   **clowne**: rustic.

Stanza 8
4   **all without**: as the ring of dancing maidens surrounds the Graces and the 'Damzell' (x 12.1).
5   **lustie**: joyful, vigorous; the masculine equivalent of 'lovely'.   **rout**: company.
8   **hew**: form.

Stanza 9
4   **count'nance trim**: beautiful appearance.
5   Extended at x 26.1–4.
9   **Pastorella**: Ital. *pastorella*, 'a prettie Shepheardesse' (Florio, 1611).   **fayrest**: 'fair' is her stock epithet.

Stanza 10
5   **Coridon**: a traditional pastoral name. A. Williams (1967) 72 suggests that it derives from Theocritus, *Idyll* iv, in which he is a cowherd and Virgil, *Ecl.* ii, in which he is the rejected lover.

Stanza 11
3   **meane**: or mien, playing on her 'meane' lot (10.9) and on her **demeanure**; suggesting also the mean or norm; cf. x 27.3.
5   **Paragone**: consort in marriage; companion.
6   **subtile**: thin, fine; crafty.
7   **the blynd boy**: Cupid.
9   **the bird**: the 'darred Larke' (VII vi 47.5); see *n*.

Stanza 12
1   *Var*. vi 237 notes S.'s frequent scenes of astonishment or admiration. The pausing word, **still**, turns back (stood he still) and then ahead (still long gazing).
8   **apply**: address.
9   **fantazy**: fancy.

Stanza 13
2   **humour**: moisture.

14

He was to weet by common voice esteemed
    The father of the fayrest *Pastorell*,
    And of her selfe in very deede so deemed;
    Yet was not so, but as old stories tell
    Found her by fortune, which to him befell,
    In th'open fields an Infant left alone,
    And taking vp brought home, and noursed well
    As his owne chyld; for other he had none,
That she in tract of time accompted was his owne.

15

She at his bidding meekely did arise,
    And streight vnto her litle flocke did fare:
    Then all the rest about her rose likewise,
    And each his sundrie sheepe with seuerall care
    Gathered together, and them homeward bare:
    Whylest euerie one with helping hands did striue
    Amongst themselues, and did their labours share,
    To helpe faire *Pastorella*, home to driue
Her fleecie flocke; but *Coridon* most helpe did giue.

16

But *Melibæe* (so hight that good old man)
    Now seeing *Calidore* left all alone,
    And night arriued hard at hand, began
    Him to inuite vnto his simple home;
    Which though it were a cottage clad with lome,
    And all things therein meane, yet better so
    To lodge, then in the saluage fields to rome.
    The knight full gladly soone agreed thereto,
Being his harts owne wish, and home with him did go.

17

There he was welcom'd of that honest syre,
    And of his aged Beldame homely well;
    Who him besought himselfe to disattyre,
    And rest himselfe, till supper time befell.
    By which home came the fayrest *Pastorell*,
    After her flocke she in their fold had tyde,
    And supper readie dight, they to it fell
    With small adoe, and nature satisfyde,
The which doth litle craue contented to abyde.

18

Tho when they had their hunger slaked well,
    And the fayre mayd the table ta'ne away,
    The gentle knight, as he that did excell
    In courtesie, and well could doe and say,
    For so great kindnesse as he found that day,
    Gan greatly thanke his host and his good wife;
    And drawing thence his speach another way,
    Gan highly to commend the happie life,
Which Shepheards lead, without debate or bitter strife.

19

How much (sayd he) more happie is the state,
    In which ye father here doe dwell at ease,
    Leading a life so free and fortunate,
    From all the tempests of these worldly seas,
    Which tosse the rest in daungerous disease;
    Where warres, and wreckes, and wicked enmitie
    Doe them afflict, which no man can appease,
    That certes I your happinesse enuie,
And wish my lot were plast in such felicitie.

20

Surely my sonne (then answer'd he againe)
    If happie, then it is in this intent,
    That hauing small, yet doe I not complaine
    Of want, ne wish for more it to augment,
    But doe my self, with that I haue, content;
    So taught of nature, which doth litle need
    Of forreine helpes to lifes due nourishment:
    The fields my food, my flocke my rayment breed;
No better doe I weare, no better doe I feed.

Stanza 14
4   **old stories**: these are romances in which a common motif
is the lost princess raised by a shepherd.
9   **tract**: course.

Stanza 15
4   **seuerall**: individual.

Stanza 16
1   **Melibœe**: a traditional pastoral name, used in the *Ruines
of Time* 436; selected here for its etymological meaning, 'honey-
toned' or 'honey-drinker'. 'Thy name is Melibee, this is to
seyn, "a man that drynketh hony"' (Chaucer, *Tale of Melibee*
vii 1410). Cf. 26.2.
5   **lome**: clay.

Stanza 17
2   **homely**: kindly.
3   **disattyre**: unarm.

Stanza 18
2   **table**: food.
4   Calidore's own 'honey-tone' is noted; cf. i 2.6.

Stanza 19
4–5   Cf. 31.4–6.   **rest**: used in a double sense.   **disease**:
distress.

Stanzas 20–25
A close rendering of stock ideas in praise of the pastoral life
expressed by a shepherd in Tasso, *Ger. Lib.* vii 8–13, who, like
Meliboe, once scorned the simple life and chose to live at the
court where he wasted his youth. Finally he returned to his
former peaceful life. Persuaded by his praise of the pastoral life,
Erminia decides to live as a shepherd: like Calidore, she offers
him gold, goes to his cottage where he lives with his aged wife,
and assumes pastoral disguise. Cheney (1966) 219–20 shows
how S. turns Tasso's relatively simple situation into a complex
drama by emphasizing Calidore's manipulation of Meliboe's
remarks to suit his own desire.

Stanza 20
1   **againe**: in return.
2   **intent**: sense.

683

21

Therefore I doe not any one enuy,
    Nor am enuyde of any one therefore;
    They that haue much, feare much to loose thereby,
    And store of cares doth follow riches store.
    The litle that I haue, growes dayly more
    Without my care, but onely to attend it;
    My lambes doe euery yeare increase their score,
    And my flockes father daily doth amend it.
What haue I, but to praise th'Almighty, that doth send it?

22

To them, that list, the worlds gay showes I leaue,
    And to great ones such follies doe forgiue,
    Which oft through pride do their owne perill weaue,
    And through ambition downe themselues doe driue
    To sad decay, that might contented liue.
    Me no such cares nor combrous thoughts offend,
    Ne once my minds vnmoued quiet grieue,
    But all the night in siluer sleepe I spend,
And all the day, to what I list, I doe attend.

23

Sometimes I hunt the Fox, the vowed foe
    Vnto my Lambes, and him dislodge away;
    Sometime the fawne I practise from the Doe,
    Or from the Goat her kidde how to conuay;
    Another while I baytes and nets display,
    The birds to catch, or fishes to beguyle:
    And when I wearie am, I downe doe lay
    My limbes in euery shade, to rest from toyle,
And drinke of euery brooke, when thirst my throte doth boyle.

24

The time was once, in my first prime of yeares,
    When pride of youth forth pricked my desire,
    That I disdain'd amongst mine equall peares
    To follow sheepe, and shepheards base attire:
    For further fortune then I would inquire.
    And leauing home, to roiall court I sought;
    Where I did sell my selfe for yearely hire,
    And in the Princes gardin daily wrought:
There I beheld such vainenesse, as I neuer thought.

25

With sight whereof soone cloyd, and long deluded
    With idle hopes, which them doe entertaine,
    After I had ten yeares my selfe excluded
    From natiue home, and spent my youth in vaine,
    I gan my follies to my selfe to plaine,
    And this sweet peace, whose lacke did then appeare.
    Tho backe returning to my sheepe againe,
    I from thenceforth haue learn'd to loue more deare
This lowly quiet life, which I inherite here.

26

Whylest thus he talkt, the knight with greedy eare
    Hong still vpon his melting mouth attent;
    Whose sensefull words empierst his hart so neare,
    That he was rapt with double rauishment,
    Both of his speach that wrought him great content,
    And also of the obiect of his vew,
    On which his hungry eye was alwayes bent;
    That twixt his pleasing tongue, and her faire hew,
684 He lost himselfe, and like one halfe entraunced grew.

27

Yet to occasion meanes, to worke his mind,
    And to insinuate his harts desire,
    He thus replyde; Now surely syre, I find,
    That all this worlds gay showes, which we admire,
    Be but vaine shadowes to this safe retyre
    Of life, which here in lowlinesse ye lead,
    Fearelesse of foes, or fortunes wrackfull yre,
    Which tosseth states, and vnder foot doth tread
The mightie ones, affrayd of euery chaunges dread.

Stanza 21

6   **attend**: tend.
7   **score**: number.

Stanza 22

2   **forgiue**: give over, grant; the current sense is also present.
5   **decay**: ruin.
6   **combrous**: troublesome.
7   **grieue**: trouble; vex.
8   **siluer sleepe**: see vii 19.8–9n.

Stanza 23

2   **dislodge**: drive out of its lair.
3–4   **practise . . . / . . . to conuay**: scheme how to steal.
8, 9   **euery**: any.

Stanza 24

3   **peares**: companions.
5   **inquire**: seek.
6   **sought**: went.

Stanza 25

2   **them**: i.e. the courtiers.   **entertaine**: engage.
5   **plaine**: lament; deplore.
9   **inherite**: possess. In context it suggests his proper inheritance or lot, in contrast to Calidore's lot, which is the chivalric life.

Stanza 26

2   **melting mouth**: alluding to the etymology of Meliboe: see 16.1n. Cf. 'sweet words, dropping like honny dew' (II v 33.4).   **attent**: attentive.
3   **sensefull**: appealing to his senses rather than his reason. Sight and hearing, the two nobler senses, are overcome.
4   Since he gazes upon Pastorella's 'heauenly hew' (8.8), **rapt** may suggest the biblical sense, 'carried up to heaven'. Certainly he is taken out of himself. He is prepared for his vision at x 17.4.

Stanza 27

1–2   **to occasion meanes . . . / . . . his harts desire**: i.e. to bring about the means to achieve what his mind wants (which is contentment) and to work his way into his heart's desire (which is to gain Pastorella).
5   **to**: compared to.
7   **wrackfull**: destructive.
8   **states**: those of high rank or office.

28

That euen I which daily doe behold
    The glorie of the great, mongst whom I won,
    And now haue prou'd, what happinesse ye hold
    In this small plot of your dominion,
    Now loath great Lordship and ambition;
    And wish the heauens so much had graced mee,
    As graunt me liue in like condition;
    Or that my fortunes might transposed bee
From pitch of higher place, vnto this low degree.

29

In vaine (said then old *Melibæ*) doe men
    The heauens of their fortunes fault accuse,
    Sith they know best, what is the best for them:
    For they to each such fortune doe diffuse,
    As they doe know each can most aptly vse.
    For not that, which men couet most, is best,
    Nor that thing worst, which men do most refuse;
    But fittest is, that all contented rest
With that th y hold: each hath his fortune in his brest.

30

It is the mynd, that maketh good or ill,
    That maketh wretch or happie, rich or poore:
    For some, that hath abundance at his will,
    Hath not enough, but wants in greatest store;
    And other, that hath litle, askes no more,
    But in that litle is both rich and wise.
    For wisedome is most riches; fooles therefore
    They are, which fortunes doe by vowes deuize,
Sith each vnto himselfe his life may fortunize.

31

Since then in each mans self (said *Calidore*)
    It is, to fashion his owne lyfes estate,
    Giue leaue awhyle, good father, in this shore
    To rest my barcke, which hath bene beaten late
    With stormes of fortune and tempestuous fate,
    In seas of troubles and of toylesome paine,
    That whether quite from them for to retrate
    I shall resolue, or backe to turne againe,
I may here with your selfe some small repose obtaine.

32

Not that the burden of so bold a guest
    Shall chargefull be, or chaunge to you at all;
    For your meane food shall be my daily feast,
    And this your cabin both my bowre and hall.
    Besides for recompence hereof, I shall
    You well reward, and golden guerdon giue,
    That may perhaps you better much withall,
    And in this quiet make you safer liue.
So forth he drew much gold, and toward him it driue.

33

But the good man, nought tempted with the offer
    Of his rich mould, did thrust it farre away,
    And thus bespake; Sir knight, your bounteous proffer
    Be farre fro me, to whom ye ill display
    That mucky masse, the cause of mens decay,
    That mote empaire my peace with daungers dread.
    But if ye algates couet to assay
    This simple sort of life, that shepheards lead,
Be it your owne: our rudenesse to your selfe aread.

Stanza 28
3   **prou'd**: experienced.

Stanza 29
1–2   Proverbial (C. G. Smith, 1970, 4); cf. V iv 28.1–3.
3–6   The sentiment is expressed by Juvenal: 'Let the Gods themselves determine what's most appropriate/For mankind, and what best suits our various circumstances. / They'll give us the things we need, not those we want' (*Satire* x 347–9).
    diffuse: send forth.
9   Proverbial (Smith 24).

Stanza 30
1   Cf. *Hamlet* II ii 249–50: 'there is nothing either good or bad, but thinking makes it so'. A commonplace of the age.
2   **wretch**: wretched, so spelled to link with **rich**.
7   Cf. Prov. 3.13–4; C. G. Smith, 1970, 856; Proem 2.3–4.
8   **by vowes deuize**: i.e. scheme to obtain by their earnest desires or will.
9   **fortunize**: control the fortunes of, rendering Boethius, *De Cons. Phil.* IV Prosa vii: 'for it is set in your hand . . . what fortune yow is levest'; noted Lewis (1964) 87. Cf. the conclusion to Juvenal, *Satire x*: 'It is we that make a goddess of thee [Fortune], and place thee in the skies'.

Stanza 31
1–2   Nelson (1964) xxvii notes that Meliboe means that man must be satisfied to accept his station in life 'but Calidore chooses to misunderstand, taking the shepherd's instruction as warrant for electing what "fortune" he wishes'.
3–6   Extending the image from 19.4–5.
7–9   Cf. the Hermit, v 37.5–9, and the Red Cross Knight, I x 63.1–4. By x 2.1–2 he has decided never to turn back.

Stanza 32
In Tasso, *Ger. Lib.* vii 16, Erminia's offer of gems is not refused. Calidore's offer allows S. to introduce the theme of wealth in relation to the simple life. Cf. the Red Cross Knight's offer of 'goodly meed' to Contemplation, I x 68.4–5.
2   **chargefull**: burdensome.
9   **driue**: drove: pushed.

Stanza 33
1   **good man**: a moral description, or his title either as a man of substance or head of the household.
2   **mould**: dirt.
3   **proffer**: offer.
5   **mucky masse**: 'filthy lucre'; cf. 'worldly mucke' (II vii 10.5).
7   **algates**: nevertheless.
9   **aread**: i.e. counsel or advise yourself to take.

685

34

So there that night Sir *Calidore* did dwell,
　And long while after, whilest him list remaine,
　Dayly beholding the faire *Pastorell*,
　And feeding on the bayt of his owne bane.
　During which time he did her entertaine
　With all kind courtesies, he could inuent;
　And euery day, her companie to gaine,
　When to the field she went, he with her went:
So for to quench his fire, he did it more augment.

35

But she that neuer had acquainted beene
　With such queint vsage, fit for Queenes and Kings,
　Ne euer had such knightly seruice seene,
　But being bred vnder base shepheards wings,
　Had euer learn'd to loue the lowly things,
　Did litle whit regard his courteous guize,
　But cared more for *Colins* carolings
　Then all that he could doe, or euer deuize:
His layes, his loues, his lookes she did them all despize.

36

Which *Calidore* perceiuing, thought it best
　To chaunge the manner of his loftie looke;
　And doffing his bright armes, himselfe addrest
　In shepheards weed, and in his hand he tooke,
　In stead of steelehead speare, a shepheards hooke,
　That who had seene him then, would haue bethought
　On *Phrygian Paris* by *Plexippus* brooke,
　When he the loue of fayre *Oenone* sought,
What time the golden apple was vnto him brought.

37

So being clad, vnto the fields he went
　With the faire *Pastorella* euery day,
　And kept her sheepe with diligent attent,
　Watching to driue the rauenous Wolfe away,
　The whylest at pleasure she mote sport and play;
　And euery euening helping them to fold:
　And otherwhiles for need, he did assay
　In his strong hand their rugged teats to hold,
And out of them to presse the milke: loue so much could.

38

Which seeing *Coridon*, who her likewise
　Long time had lou'd, and hop'd her loue to gaine,
　He much was troubled at that straungers guize,
　And many gealous thoughts conceiu'd in vaine,
　That this of all his labour and long paine
　Should reap the haruest, ere it ripened were,
　That made him scoule, and pout, and oft complaine
　Of *Pastorell* to all the shepheards there,
That she did loue a stranger swayne then him more dere.

39

And euer when he came in companie,
　Where *Calidore* was present, he would loure,
　And byte his lip, and euen for gealousie
　Was readie oft his owne hart to deuoure,
　Impatient of any paramoure:
　Who on the other side did seeme so farre
　From malicing, or grudging his good houre,
　That all he could, he graced him with her,
Ne euer shewed signe of rancour or of iarre.

Stanza 34
4　**bayt**: also food.

Stanza 35
2　**queint vsage**: elegant or refined behaviour.
6　**guize**: manner.
7　**Colin**: the traditional pastoral name that S. assumes; see 41.6n, x 16.3–4.

Stanza 36
3　**addrest**: clothed.
6–9　The lines combine two episodes in **Paris**'s pastoral sojourn: his love for **Oenone** (see III ix 36.3–4) and his judgment of the three goddesses in which he presented Venus with the golden apple. His love for Oenone shows why he chose Venus over the others. Like Paris, Calidore is lustful in his present choice; the praise of wisdom at 30.7 points to the correct choice. On the other hand, an irrevocable decision has not yet been made: when presented with his corresponding vision of the three Graces, his correct choice to return to his quest will 'right' history.　**Phrygian**: Trojan. Used since Phrygia is west of Troy, as is Mount Ida; or because Phrygia is associated with Oenone.　**Plexippus**: a difficult crux. Its etymology, 'horse-taming' or 'horse-striking', may be S.'s coinage for the classical Hippocrene, the fountain of the horse on Helicon which first flowed when struck by Pegasus's hooves. Cheney (1966) 223 n8 suggests that S. has conflated Mount Ida with Helicon as a haunt of the Muses.

Stanza 37
3　**attent**: attention.
7　**otherwhiles**: at other times.
9　**loue so much could**: love was capable of so much. The expression is clearer in the Latin, which Upton (1758) quotes: *tantum amor potuit.*

Stanza 38
5　**this**: i.e. Calidore.

Stanza 39
3–4　The state of jealous vexation; see I ii 6.3.
5　**paramoure**: rival lover.
7　**malicing**: regarding with malice.　**good houre**: good luck or fortune.

40

And oft, when *Coridon* vnto her brought
  Or litle sparrowes, stolen from their nest,
  Or wanton squirrels, in the woods farre sought,
  Or other daintie thing for her addrest,
  He would commend his guift, and make the best.
  Yet she no whit his presents did regard,
  Ne him could find to fancie in her brest:
This newcome shepheard had his market mard.
Old loue is litle worth when new is more prefard.

41

One day when as the shepheard swaynes together
  Were met, to make their sports and merrie glee,
  As they are wont in faire sunshynie weather,
  The whiles their flockes in shadowes shrouded bee,
  They fell to daunce: then did they all agree,
  That *Colin Clout* should pipe as one most fit;
  And *Calidore* should lead the ring, as hee
That most in *Pastorellaes* grace did sit.
Thereat frown'd *Coridon*, and his lip closely bit.

42

But *Calidore* of courteous inclination
  Tooke *Coridon*, and set him in his place,
  That he should lead the daunce, as was his fashion;
  For *Coridon* could daunce, and trimly trace.
  And when as *Pastorella*, him to grace,
  Her flowry garlond tooke from her owne head,
  And plast on his, he did it soone displace,
  And did it put on *Coridons* in stead:
Then *Coridon* woxe frollicke, that earst seemed dead.

43

Another time, when as they did dispose
  To practise games, and maisteries to try,
  They for their Iudge did *Pastorella* chose;
  A garland was the meed of victory.
  There *Coridon* forth stepping openly,
  Did chalenge *Calidore* to wrestling game:
  For he through long and perfect industry,
  Therein well practisd was, and in the same   (shame.
Thought sure t'auenge his grudge, and worke his foe great

44

But *Calidore* he greatly did mistake;
  For he was strong and mightily stiffe pight,
  That with one fall his necke he almost brake,
  And had he not vpon him fallen light,
  His dearest ioynt he sure had broken quight.
  Then was the oaken crowne by *Pastorell*
  Giuen to *Calidore*, as his due right;
  But he, that did in courtesie excell,
Gaue it to *Coridon*, and said he wonne it well.

45

Thus did the gentle knight himselfe abeare
  Amongst that rusticke rout in all his deeds,
  That euen they, the which his riuals were,
  Could not maligne him, but commend him needs:
  For courtesie amongst the rudest breeds
  Good will and fauour. So it surely wrought
  With this faire Mayd, and in her mynde the seeds
  Of perfect loue did sow, that last forth brought
The fruite of ioy and blisse, though long time dearely bought.

46

Thus *Calidore* continu'd there long time,
  To winne the loue of the faire *Pastorell*;
  Which hauing got, he vsed without crime
  Or blamefull blot, but menaged so well,
  That he of all the rest, which there did dwell,
  Was fauoured, and to her grace commended.
  But what straunge fortunes vnto him befell,
  Ere he attain'd the point by him intended,
Shall more conueniently in other place be ended.

Stanza 40

2–3   The gifts suggest lechery: the sparrow is notorious for
its lechery, and the squirrel, as one of the animals associated
with Venus's hunt, symbolizes a sexual prize; see Marotti
(1965) 83–4. Cf. III vii 17.   **wanton**: frisky; also the erotic
sense.
4   **addrest**: prepared.

Stanza 41

6   **Colin Clout**: 'Vnder which name this Poete secretly
shadoweth himself, as sometime did Virgil vnder the name of
Tityrus, thinking it much fitter, then such Latine names, for
the great vnlikelyhoode of the language' (E.K.'s gloss to *S.C.*
Jan. 1).

Stanza 42

4   **trimly trace**: neatly step.

Stanza 43

2   **maisteries**: competitions of strength.

Stanza 44

2   **mightily stiffe pight**: very sturdily built; firmly fixed on
his legs.

Stanza 45

1   **abeare**: bear.
4   **needs**: i.e. must needs, of necessity.
7–9   **the seeds/Of perfect loue**: these seeds produce the
harvest which Coridon hopes to enjoy (38.6) but which is
finally enjoyed by Calidore (x 38.5).   **last**: at last.
bought] 'sought' sugg. Church (1758). Yet the text may
stand: Calidore's labours buy the harvest of her love.

Stanza 46

3   **without crime**: without giving occasion for reproach.
4   **menaged**: not simply managed in the sense of conducting
his courtship, but in the sense of putting a horse through its
paces (cf. II iv 2.2), here referring to the handling of his
emotions.
5   **of all**: above all.

Cant. X.

Calidore sees the Graces daunce,
To Colins melody:
The wbiles his Pastorell is led,
Into captiuity.

1

WHo now does follow the foule *Blatant Beast*,
Whilest *Calidore* does follow that faire Mayd,
Vnmyndfull of his vow and high beheast,
Which by the Faery Queene was on him layd,
That he should neuer leaue, nor be delayd
From chacing him, till he had it attchieued?
But now entrapt of loue, which him betrayd,
He mindeth more, how he may be relieued
With grace from her, whose loue his heart hath sore engrieued.

2

That from henceforth he meanes no more to sew
His former quest, so full of toile and paine;
Another quest, another game in vew
He hath, the guerdon of his loue to gaine:
With whom he myndes for euer to remaine,
And set his rest amongst the rusticke sort,
Rather then hunt still after shadowes vaine
Of courtly fauour, fed with light report
Of euery blaste, and sayling alwaies in the port.

3

Ne certes mote he greatly blamed be,
From so high step to stoupe vnto so low.
For who had tasted once (as oft did he)
The happy peace, which there doth ouerflow,
And prou'd the perfect pleasures, which doe grow
Amongst poore hyndes, in hils, in woods, in dales,
Would neuer more delight in painted show
Of such false blisse, as there is set for stales,
T'entrap vnwary fooles in their eternall bales.

4

For what hath all that goodly glorious gaze
Like to one sight, which *Calidore* did vew?
The glaunce whereof their dimmed eies would daze,
That neuer more they should endure the shew
Of that sunne-shine, that makes them looke askew.
Ne ought in all that world of beauties rare,
(Saue onely *Glorianaes* heauenly hew
To which what can compare?) can it compare;
The which as commeth now, by course I will declare.

5

One day as he did raunge the fields abroad,
Whilest his faire *Pastorella* was elsewhere,
He chaunst to come, far from all peoples troad,
Vnto a place, whose pleasaunce did appere
To passe all others, on the earth which were:
For all that euer was by natures skill
Deuized to worke delight, was gathered there,
And there by her were poured forth at fill,
688 As if this to adorne, she all the rest did pill.

Canto x

Argument

3   **The whiles**: since the two events are not concurrent in the narrative, the term may imply that Calidore's vision and its vanishing correspond to Pastorella's seizure by the Brigands.

Stanza 2

1   **sew**: pursue.
3   **game**: the hunted animal, applied to the Beast; sport, amusement, applied to Pastorella. Yet he is the prey at ix 11.9, x 31.
5   **myndes**: intends.
6   **set his rest**: take up permanent abode in contrast to his earlier pursuit of the Beast, ix 3.2. **sort**: company.
7   **shadowes vaine**: Maxwell (1952) 146 notes that it takes an effort '*not* to identify the hunt after **shadowes vaine** with the quest which Calidore abandons'.
9   **in the port**] on the port *1596*, i.e. towards the port without ever arriving. Most editors prefer the *1609* reading 'in the port', which suggests the Lat. proverb *in portu navigare*, 'to be out of daunger' (Cooper, 1565), port-bound; hence being so concerned with the direction of the wind that one never gets under way. Cf. 'gladsome port' (9.4) and the theme of seeking the shore at ix 31.3–9, xi 44.6–9. Since 'in' and 'on' were interchangeable in early usage, and 'port' may be taken as sheltered water, a ship could be said to sail in it or on it.

Stanza 3

2   **stoupe**: a technical term for the swift descent of the falcon upon its prey.
5   **prou'd**: experienced; cf. ix 28.3.
6   **hyndes**: rustics.
8   **there**: in the court, a deliberately oblique reference; cf. the use of 'them' (ix 25.2). **stales**: decoys; snares.
9   **in**: into, to.

Stanza 4

1   **gaze**: that which is gazed at, referring to the 'painted show' (3.7) and obliquely to **that world of beauties rare** (6) in Elizabeth's court.
8   **it compare**: rival it.
9   **by course**: although Calidore gives up his quest, the poet still continues on his course. **declare**: describe.

Stanza 5

3   **troad**: treading.
4   **pleasaunce**: previously associated with Duessa (I ii 30.1), the house of Pride (iv 38.2), the Red Cross Knight's fall (vii 4.2), Phædria (II vi 6.9), the Bower of Bliss (xii 50.3) and Cupid's masque (III xii 18.1). Now almost for the first time used without overt ominous suggestions. Cf. 9.2 and 17.4.
8   **at fill**: at full, fully.
9   **pill**: pillage, plunder.

6

It was an hill plaste in an open plaine,
  That round about was bordered with a wood
  Of matchlesse hight, that seem'd th'earth to disdaine,
  In which all trees of honour stately stood,
  And did all winter as in sommer bud,
  Spredding pauilions for the birds to bowre,
  Which in their lower braunches sung aloud;
  And in their tops the soring hauke did towre,
Sitting like King of fowles in maiesty and powre.

7

And at the foote thereof, a gentle flud
  His siluer waues did softly tumble downe,
  Vnmard with ragged mosse or filthy mud,
  Ne mote wylde beastes, ne mote the ruder clowne
  Thereto approch, ne filth mote therein drowne:
  But Nymphes and Faeries by the bancks did sit,
  In the woods shade, which did the waters crowne,
  Keeping all noysome things away from it,
And to the waters fall tuning their accents fit.

8

And on the top thereof a spacious plaine
  Did spred it selfe, to serue to all delight,
  Either to daunce, when they to daunce would faine,
  Or else to course about their bases light;
  Ne ought there wanted, which for pleasure might
  Desired be, or thence to banish bale:
  So pleasauntly the hill with equall hight,
  Did seeme to ouerlooke the lowly vale;
Therefore it rightly cleeped was mount *Acidale*.

9

They say that *Venus*, when she did dispose
  Her selfe to pleasaunce, vsed to resort
  Vnto this place, and therein to repose
  And rest her selfe, as in a gladsome port,
  Or with the Graces there to play and sport;
  That euen her owne Cytheron, though in it
  She vsed most to keepe her royall court,
  And in her soueraine Maiesty to sit,
She in regard hereof refusde and thought vnfit.

10

Vnto this place when as the Elfin Knight
  Approcht, him seemed that the merry sound
  Of a shrill pipe he playing heard on hight,
  And many feete fast thumping th'hollow ground,
  That through the woods their Eccho did rebound.
  He nigher drew, to weete what mote it be;
  There he a troupe of Ladies dauncing found
  Full merrily, and making gladfull glee,
And in the midst a Shepheard piping he did see.

Stanzas 6–9
Mount Acidale (8.9) recalls the traditional features of the

earthly paradise, particularly Eden which is usually placed on a mountain top walled by trees, and the hill with its wide-extending plain to which Orpheus brings all the trees with their shade (Ovid, *Met*. x 86f). Within the poem Mount Acidale relates to the 'second paradise' which surrounds the Temple of Venus (IV x 21–25), Belphœbe's forest home (III v 39–40), and particularly the home of the Graces (I x 54.6–9). Cf. III vi 43–46 and IV v 5.4–6. For the tradition, see Giamatti (1966) ch. 1.

Stanza 6
4   **all trees of honour**: cf. the garden of Eden with 'everie tre pleasant to the sight, and good for meat' (Gen. 2.9).
6   **bowre**: lodge.
8   **towre**: perch high, rather than mount up; yet the two senses merge.

Stanza 7
Cf. Narcissus's pool with its silver water to which neither shepherds nor beasts dare approach and whose clear surface is never ruffled (Ovid, *Met*. iii 407–10).
1   **flud**: stream.
4   **ruder clowne**: entirely rude rustic.
5   **drowne**: sink.
6   At last true Faeries are seen in faerie land. Hankins (1971) 193–4 notes the association of nymphs or faeries with the dance of the Graces in Horace, *Odes* I iv, xxx, IV vii. See 10.4*n*.

Stanza 8
3   **faine**: desire.
4   The game of prisoners' base: see III xi 5.5*n*; cf. V viii 5.4–5. It is a fairies' dance in Drayton, *Muses Elizium*, 'First Nimphall' 27.   **light**: quickly.
7   **equall**: level.
9   **Acidale**: 'surname of Venus' (Cooper, 1565); cf. Acidalius: 'a wel in Orchomenum, dedicated vnto Venus, and the graces' (Cooper). It may be so named here for its etymology, Gk ακις, a pointed, rising object + δηλος, visible, conspicuous: hence a hill rising from the vale. 8 suggests Lat. *acies*, look + dale: valley-view; cf. VII vi 54.7–9, Renwick (1923) 202 notes that Boccaccio follows Servius in deriving the name from 'akida', which to S. may suggest ακηδης, free from care. Nelson (1963) 293 sees a reference to *accidia*, the sin of sloth, of which Calidore is guilty.

Stanza 9
Cf. IV v 5.4–6.
1   **dispose**: prepare.
6–8   **Cytheron**: cf. '*Cytheron* hill' (III vi 29.4). Church (1758) cites Chaucer, *Knight's Tale* 1936–7: 'al the mount of Citheroun, / Ther Venus hath hir principal dwellynge.' Cf. *Romance of the Rose* 15660f.
9   **in regard hereof**: compared to this place.

Stanza 10
1   **Elfin**: links him with the faeries.
3   **pipe**: the bagpipe; cf. 18.5.   **on hight**: loudly. The context adds 'on the height'.
4   Cf. Horace, *Odes* I iv 5–7: the Cytherean Venus leads the dance with the nymphs and Graces whose beating feet shake the ground.
6   **weete**: referring to his desire to know. He is not content simply to see and hear; cf. 18.9.

11

He durst not enter into th'open greene,
  For dread of them vnwares to be descryde,
  For breaking of their daunce, if he were seene;
  But in the couert of the wood did byde,
  Beholding all, yet of them vnespyde.
  There he did see, that pleased much his sight,
  That euen he him selfe his eyes enuyde,
  An hundred naked maidens lilly white,
All raunged in a ring, and dauncing in delight.

12

All they without were raunged in a ring,
  And daunced round; but in the midst of them
  Three other Ladies did both daunce and sing,
  The whilest the rest them round about did hemme,
  And like a girlond did in compasse stemme:
  And in the middest of those same three, was placed
  Another Damzell, as a precious gemme,
  Amidst a ring most richly well enchaced,
That with her goodly presence all the rest much graced.

13

Looke how the Crowne, which *Ariadne* wore
  Vpon her yuory forehead that same day,
  That *Theseus* her vnto his bridale bore,
  When the bold *Centaures* made that bloudy fray,
  With the fierce *Lapithes*, which did them dismay;
  Being now placed in the firmament,
  Through the bright heauen doth her beams display,
  And is vnto the starres an ornament,
Which round about her moue in order excellent.

14

Such was the beauty of this goodly band,
  Whose sundry parts were here too long to tell:
  But she that in the midst of them did stand,
  Seem'd all the rest in beauty to excell,
  Crownd with a rosie girlond, that right well
  Did her beseeme. And euer, as the crew
  About her daunst, sweet flowres, that far did smell,
  And fragrant odours they vppon her threw;
But most of all, those three did her with gifts endew.

15

Those were the Graces, daughters of delight,
  Handmaides of *Venus*, which are wont to haunt
  Vppon this hill, and daunce there day and night:
  Those three to men all gifts of grace do graunt,
  And all, that *Venus* in her selfe doth vaunt,
  Is borrowed of them. But that faire one,
  That in the midst was placed parauaunt,
  Was she to whom that shepheard pypt alone,
That made him pipe so merrily, as neuer none.

Stanza 11

3 **For breaking**: for dread of breaking.
8 **hundred**: a large number that signifies completeness; cf. the hundred nymphs who attend Cynthia (*Col.* 256) and the hundred Graces (*Amor.* xl 4).

Stanza 12

5 **like a girlond . . . stemme**: i.e. surround them in a circle. **stemme**: encircle, from Lat. *stemma*, garland. More literally, they are the stem to the flower, which is composed of the three Graces and the Damzel. This image is combined with **enchaced** (8): set as a jewel in a ring. Cf. Diana enclosed 'like a girlond' by her nymphs (III vi 19.9), Amoret within the circle of feminine virtues (IV x 52), and Pastorella with her garland of shepherdesses (VI ix 8). In *S.C.* Apr. 109–17, the three Graces dance and sing, and to their number the poet adds his lady as a fourth Grace. See 27n. The **Damzell** (7) is placed as Venus at the centre of her Graces.

Stanza 13

Thomas Watson, *Hekatompathia* (1582), addresses sonnet xxxiii to his mistress of whom he claims that, if she had lived in earlier times, she would have been preferred before the three Graces, and would have been placed by Bacchus in Ariadne's stead in the heavens 'where nowe the Crowne of *Ariadne* called *Corona Gnosia* doth shine continuallie, beinge beautified with greate varietie of lightsome starres'. By associating the battle between the **Centaures** and **Lapithes** (see IV i 23.1–5) with the wedding of **Ariadne** and **Theseus**, rather than that of Pirithous and Hippodamia at which Theseus fought the Centaurs (see Ovid, *Met.* xii 210f), S. conflates the two. When Ariadne was later abandoned by Theseus, she was picked up by Bacchus who placed her bridal crown among the stars as the constellation Corona Borealis (see *Met.* viii 169–82). Berger (1961) 67 observes that 'the comparison unites the heavenly and imaginary dances, the physical and mental orders, the actual zodiac and the zodiac of the poet's wit'. Cheney (1966) 233 suggests that 'such a conflation dramatizes the impermanence of any human attainment of concord'.
1 **Looke how**, in place of the formula, 'Like as . . . / Such was' (as iv 1.1, 6), shows the poet caught up in his vision and makes the reader see. Alpers (1967) 14 notes that what S. makes us see 'is not a fixed image, an emblem in the usual sense, but a transformation of turbulence and fury into order and beauty'.
3 **bridale**: wedding-feast.
5 **dismay**: defeat by sudden onslaught.
9 Hieatt (1970) 148 observes that the Corona Borealis seems to be put in place of the North Star around which the other stars circle.

Stanza 14

8 **odours**: that which gives off a sweet scent, such as flowers (*OED* 2).

Stanza 15

1–2 Traditionally, the **Graces** are handmaids of Venus. **daughters of delight**: as in Comes (1616) IV xv where they signify *hilaritas et laetitia*. For the Renaissance conception of the Graces, see Wind (1967) ch. 2–3, 7, and Geller (1972).
7 **parauaunt**: pre-eminently; suggesting 'be before' (from *par* + *avant*).
9 **pipe . . . as neuer none**: as none had ever piped before.

16

She was to weete that iolly Shepheards lasse,
  Which piped there vnto that merry rout,
  That iolly shepheard, which there piped, was
  Poore *Colin Clout* (who knowes not *Colin Clout?*)
  He pypt apace, whilest they him daunst about.
  Pype iolly shepheard, pype thou now apace
  Vnto thy loue, that made thee low to lout:
  Thy loue is present there with thee in place,
Thy loue is there aduaunst to be another Grace.

17

Much wondred *Calidore* at this straunge sight,
  Whose like before his eye had neuer seene,
  And standing long astonished in spright,
  And rapt with pleasaunce, wist not what to weene;
  Whether it were the traine of beauties Queene,
  Or Nymphes, or Faeries, or enchaunted show,
  With which his eyes mote haue deluded beene.
  Therefore resoluing, what it was, to know,
Out of the wood he rose, and toward them did go.

18

But soone as he appeared to their vew,
  They vanisht all away out of his sight,
  And cleane were gone, which way he neuer knew;
  All saue the shepheard, who for fell despight
  Of that displeasure, broke his bag-pipe quight,
  And made great mone for that vnhappy turne.
  But *Calidore*, though no lesse sory wight,
  For that mishap, yet seeing him to mourne,
Drew neare, that he the truth of all by him mote learne.

19

And first him greeting, thus vnto him spake,
  Haile iolly shepheard, which thy ioyous dayes
  Here leadest in this goodly merry make,
  Frequented of these gentle Nymphes alwayes,
  Which to thee flocke, to heare thy louely layes;
  Tell me, what mote these dainty Damzels be,
  Which here with thee doe make their pleasant playes?
  Right happy thou, that mayst them freely see:
But why when I them saw, fled they away from me?

20

Not I so happy, answerd then that swaine,
  As thou vnhappy, which them thence didst chace,
  Whom by no meanes thou canst recall againe,
  For being gone, none can them bring in place,
  But whom they of them selues list so to grace.
  Right sory I, (saide then Sir *Calidore*,)
  That my ill fortune did them hence displace.
  But since things passed none may now restore,
Tell me, what were they all, whose lacke thee grieues so sore.

21

Tho gan that shepheard thus for to dilate;
  Then wote thou shepheard, whatsoeuer thou bee,
  That all those Ladies, which thou sawest late,
  Are *Venus* Damzels, all within her fee,
  But differing in honour and degree:
  They all are Graces, which on her depend,
  Besides a thousand more, which ready bee
  Her to adorne, when so she forth doth wend:
But those three in the midst, doe chiefe on her attend.

Stanza 16
7　**lout**: stoop in submission.
9　This compliment is paid to 'fayre *Eliza*, Queene of shepheardes all' in *S.C.* Apr. 113–7. Hankins (1971) 194 notes the tradition of a fourth Grace in Comes (1616) IV xv; see 27*n*.

Stanza 17
8　Stress and punctuation emphasize the final phrase: the determination to know, instead of remaining content with the vision itself, causes his unhappiness. The sight of beauty which drives man forward to 'know' provides the poem's central myth, Arthur's quest of the Faerie Queene.

Stanza 18
1–4　S. imitates an episode in Chaucer, *Wife of Bath's Tale*: when the knight sees the dance 'Of ladyes foure and twenty, and yet mo' he draws near 'In hope that som wysdom sholde he lerne. / But certeinly, er he cam fully there, / Vanysshed was this daunce, he nyste where. / No creature saugh he that bar lyf, / Save. . . .' (992–8). Like Chaucer's Knight, Calidore intervenes in order to understand.
6　**turne**: event; also alluding to the breaking of the dance.

Stanza 19
3　**merry make**: merry-making.
5　**louely layes**: lays of love.
9　In his affability, he is less than honest: he knows that they fled because they saw him, 11.3. In reply, Colin Clout exposes his duplicity: they did not flee of themselves but were chased away.

Stanza 20
2　An oblique allusion to the story of Actaeon who was punished for his sight of naked beauty. Cf. Faunus who sees the naked Diana, VII vi 45.3–9.
4　**in place**: back again; cf. 16.8.
5　**grace**: be gracious to.
8–9　At iii 21–22 Calidore consoles another victim of his voyeurism.

Stanza 21
1　**dilate**: relate at length.
2　The poet chooses not to know his own character.
4　**within her fee**: in her service, being her followers.
6　**on her depend**: belong to her, literally surround her as her train.

22

They are the daughters of sky-ruling Ioue,
  By him begot of faire *Eurynome*,
  The Oceans daughter, in this pleasant groue,
  As. he this way comming from feastfull glee,
  Of *Thetis* wedding with *Æacidee*,
  In sommers shade him selfe here rested weary.
  The first of them hight mylde *Euphrosyne*,
  Next faire *Aglaia*, last *Thalia* merry:
Sweete Goddesses all three which me in mirth do cherry.

23

These three on men all gracious gifts bestow,
  Which decke the body or adorne the mynde,
  To make them louely or well fauoured show,
  As comely carriage, entertainement kynde,
  Sweete semblaunt, friendly offices that bynde,
  And all the complements of curtesie:
  They teach vs, how to each degree and kynde
  We should our selues demeane, to low, to hie;
To friends, to foes, which skill men call Ciuility.

24

Therefore they alwaies smoothly seeme to smile,
  That we likewise should mylde and gentle be,
  And also naked are, that without guile
  Or false dissemblaunce all them plaine may see,
  Simple and true from couert malice free:
  And eeke them selues so in their daunce they bore,
  That two of them still froward seem'd to bee,
  But one still towards shew'd her selfe afore;
That good should from vs goe, then come in greater store.

Stanza 22

The ultimate source of this parentage for the Graces is Hesiod, *Theog.* 907–11, and, more immediately, the Renaissance dictionaries which provide this and the alternative parentage given at II viii 6.6. Jove's epithet **sky-ruling** suggests the etymology of **Eurynome**, wide-ruling. Together the two suggest a union of sky and water. As Eurynome ruled with Ophion before both were deposed by Saturn and Ops – who in turn were deposed by Jove (see Apollonius, *Argonautica* i 503–9) – her union with Jove signifies a healing of division and a restoration of original rule. At VII vii 12, S. links the assembly of the gods on Hæmus hill with their previous assembly at the marriage of Peleus and **Thetis**, from whose union Achilles was born. At this marriage, Ate produced the golden apple which led to the fall of Troy; see II vii 55.4–9n.
4   feastfull: festive.
5   Æacidee: Peleus, son of Aeacus; so named to link him with his father who was a son of Jove and so famed for his justice that Pluto made him judge over the dead. Lotspeich (1932) 58 notes that **Thetis and Eurynome** are named together in Homer, *Iliad* xviii 398, which may have suggested to S. her connection and Jove's with Thetis's wedding. The connection is natural enough since Eurynome is the daughter of Ocean, and Thetis's name is used by metonymy for the Ocean.
6   The maid in this posture and place is usually raped by a god.
7–9   Euphrosyne: Cheerfulness.   **Aglaia** is **faire** because her name 'is interpreted brightnesse, cleerenesse, beautie, pleasure, or majestie' (Cooper, 1565).   **Thalia** is **merry** as she is the Muse of Comedy; cf. 'Ioyous *Thalia*' (IV xi 49.2). **cherry**: cheer.

Stanza 23
1   gracious gifts: literally 'all gifts of grace' (15.4).
4–5   carriage: demeanour; behaviour.   **entertainement kynde**: courteous manners in treating others.   **semblaunt**: demeanour shown to others.   **friendly offices that bynde**: acts of kindness which establish bonds of friendship.
6   complements: ceremonies; accomplishments; also that which perfects courtesy, as in Belphœbe chastity and courtesy 'did make in her a perfect complement' (III v 55.9). Starnes and Talbert (1955) 54–5 cite Cooper (1565) as source: 'There were three Graces devised to signifie that men ought to be both bountiful and gracious to other . . . their armes weare painted as it weare linked one within an other, to teach that kyndnesse should bee undissoluble, and one benefite so to provoke an other, as it may make the league of love and frendship sure and perpetual'. On the relation of the three Graces to the three theological virtues, see Goldberg (1966) 207–8.
7–9   Cf. the praise of courtesy as the virtue by which knights and ladies 'beare themselues aright / To all of each degree, as doth behoue' (ii. 1.3–4).

Stanza 24
1–5   Cf. Cooper (1565): 'They were descrived laughing, because pleasures ought to be donne with a chereful and glad minde. . . . They were also painted naked, to dooe men to witte, that pleasures should be done unfeinedly without cloke or dissimulation.'   **That**: teaching us that; also at 9.
malice: wickedness. [*Continued next page.*]

25

Such were those Goddesses, which ye did see;
　But that fourth Mayd, which there amidst them traced,
　Who can aread, what creature mote she bee,
　Whether a creature, or a goddesse graced
　With heauenly gifts from heuen first enraced?
　But what so sure she was, she worthy was,
　To be the fourth with those three other placed:
　Yet was she certes but a countrey lasse,
Yet she all other countrey lasses farre did passe.

26

So farre as doth the daughter of the day,
　All other lesser lights in light excell,
　So farre doth she in beautyfull array,
　Aboue all other lasses beare the bell,
　Ne lesse in vertue that beseemes her well,
　Doth she exceede the rest of all her race,
　For which the Graces that here wont to dwell,
　Haue for more honor brought her to this place,
And graced her so much to be another Grace.

27

Another Grace she well deserues to be,
　In whom so many Graces gathered are,
　Excelling much the meane of her degree;
　Diuine resemblaunce, beauty soueraine rare,
　Firme Chastity, that spight ne blemish dare;
　All which she with such courtesie doth grace,
　That all her peres cannot with her compare,
　But quite are dimmed, when she is in place.
She made me often pipe and now to pipe apace.

28

Sunne of the world, great glory of the sky,
　That all the earth doest lighten with thy rayes,
　Great *Gloriana*, greatest Maiesty,
　Pardon thy shepheard, mongst so many layes,
　As he hath sung of thee in all his dayes,
　To make one minime of thy poore handmayd,
　And vnderneath thy feete to place her prayse,
　That when thy glory shall be farre displayd
To future age of her this mention may be made.

their backs turned, one faces us.　**froward** signifies 'from-ward', going away from us, in opposition to **towards**. (The emendation of 'forward' *1596* to **froward** is supported by Cooper; but 'forward' may stand as signifying 'going forward from us'.) Cf. similar play on 'froward' and 'forward' at II ii 38.5–8, III v 7.4. Geller (1972) 273 cites the order of the Graces in Pico della Mirandola, *Commento*: 'Of the graces, one is painted looking toward us . . . The other two with their faces from us, seeming to return. . . . What comes from God to us, returns from us to God.'

9　This line provides an excellent moral comment on the traditional order of the Graces: if good goes out from us, it will return **in greater store**. The morality agrees with the parable of the talents. S. may have reversed the traditional order to avoid any suspicion of a mercenary motive, so Starnes and Talbert (1955) 55 suggest. Nestrick (1962) 367 argues that S. uses **good** to avoid the suggestion of material benefits present in the Stoic interpretation. Then S.'s moral agrees with the saying of Christ, that it is more blessed to give than to receive. (In the Geneva version: 'It is a blessed thing to give, rather than to receive.') This reading calls for a comma after **come**, and **then** to be read as 'than': i.e. good should go from us in greater store instead of coming to us. Spens (1958) 68 supports this reading from Botticelli's picture: 'The essence of the symbolism is that the Graces are dancing *in a ring*, and the First faces the other two, who, closely linked, are both looking at her. The meaning appears to be that the First gives 'the good' to the Second, who is on her left, and she gives it and her own contribution to the Third, who adds hers and returns the threefold gift to the First. Thus it returns **in greater store**.' Cf. IV iii 27.8–9.

Stanza 25
The past tense is stressed throughout the stanza.
2　**traced**: danced. At 12.6 'placed' suggests that she is standing (cf. 14.3) but she is truly one of the dancing Graces.
3　**aread**: declare; conjecture.
5　**enraced**: implanted; cf. III v 52.1–5.

Stanza 26
1　**the daughter of the day**: Venus, either as the evening or morning star, befitting her exaltation as a fourth Grace and one of '*Venus* Damzels' (21.4); cf. Elizabeth as the sun, 28.1.
9　**another Grace**: as 16.9; a claim repeated in the next line and again at 25.6–7.

Stanza 27
The Renaissance tradition of the fourth grace is described by Snare (1971). In Snare (1974) 4 he describes this 'infolded image at the center' as 'the encyclopedic summation of all Grace' and applies Wind's (1967) concept of Venus 'unfolded' in the three graces. See IV ii 41–43*n*, x 32.4–5*n*.
3　**meane**: average; also playing on 'mien', demeanour, as ix 11.2–3.
4　**Diuine resemblaunce**: appearance resembling the divine.
5–6　On the relationship of chastity and courtesy in Belphœbe, see III v 55.1–5. Either spite does not dare blemish her, or neither spite nor blemish dares confront her.
7　**peres**: companions.

Stanza 28
6　**minime**: a short musical note. Used literally: in his present song of some 4,000 stanzas, the two given her amount to no more than a note.

6–9　**froward**] forward *1596*. Cf. Cooper: 'Wherfore they painte the Graces in this manner, that the ones backe should be towarde us, and hir face fromward, as proceding from us, the other twoo towarde us: noting double thanke to bee due for the benefite we have done'. Such is the traditional order of the three Graces, as in Botticelli's 'Primavera' in which one grace has her back to us, facing the other two who come towards us. Since Cooper is used by E. K. in his gloss to *S.C.* Apr. 109, it is tempting to gain the same order here by inverting **froward** and **towards**; see Hieatt (1970). As the corrected text stands, however, this traditional order is reversed: two Graces have

29

When thus that shepherd ended had his speach,
  Sayd *Calidore*; Now sure it yrketh mee,
  That to thy blisse I made this luckelesse breach,
  As now the author of thy bale to be,
  Thus to bereaue thy loues deare sight from thee:
  But gentle Shepheard pardon thou my shame,
  Who rashly sought that, which I mote not see.
  Thus did the courteous Knight excuse his blame,
And to recomfort him, all comely meanes did frame.

30

In such discourses they together spent
  Long time, as fit occasion forth them led;
  With which the Knight him selfe did much content,
  And with delight his greedy fancy fed,
  Both of his words, which he with reason red;
  And also of the place, whose pleasures rare
  With such regard his sences rauished,
  That thence, he had no will away to fare,
But wisht, that with that shepheard he mote dwelling share.

31

But that enuenimd sting, the which of yore,
  His poysnous point deepe fixed in his hart
  Had left, now gan afresh to rancle sore,
  And to renue the rigour of his smart:
  Which to recure, no skill of Leaches art
  Mote him auaile, but to returne againe
  To his wounds worker, that with louely dart
  Dinting his brest, had bred his restlesse paine,
Like as the wounded Whale to shore flies from the maine.

32

So taking leaue of that same gentle swaine,
  He backe returned to his rusticke wonne,
  Where his faire *Pastorella* did remaine:
  To whome in sort, as he at first begonne,
  He daily did apply him selfe to donne
  All dewfull seruice voide of thoughts impure:
  Ne any paines ne perill did he shonne,
  By which he might her to his loue allure,
And liking in her yet vntamed heart procure.

33

And euermore the shepheard *Coridon*,
  What euer thing he did her to aggrate,
  Did striue to match with strong contention,
  And all his paines did closely emulate;
  Whether it were to caroll, as they sate
  Keeping their sheepe, or games to exercize,
  Or to present her with their labours late;
  Through which if any grace chaunst to arize
To him, the Shepheard streight with iealousie did frize.

34

One day as they all three together went
  To the greene wood, to gather strawberies,
  There chaunst to them a dangerous accident;
  A Tigre forth out of the wood did rise,
  That with fell clawes full of fierce gourmandize,
  And greedy mouth, wide gaping like hell gate,
  Did runne at *Pastorell* her to surprize:
  Whom she beholding, now all desolate
694 Gan cry to them aloud, to helpe her all too late.

35

Which *Coridon* first hearing, ran in hast
  To reskue her, but when he saw the feend,
  Through cowherd feare he fled away as fast,
  Ne durst abide the daunger of the end;
  His life he steemed dearer then his frend.
  But *Calidore* soone comming to her ayde,
  When he the beast saw ready now to rend
  His loues deare spoile, in which his heart was prayde,
He ran at him enraged in stead of being frayde.

Stanza 29
2 **yrketh**: troubles, grieves.

Stanza 30
5 **red**: spoke.
7 **regard**: sight.
8–9 As before, ix 26, pleasures of sight and hearing persuade Calidore to retreat, now to an inner retreat.

Stanza 31
4 **rigour**: violence.
7 **louely dart**: the dart of love.
8 **Dinting**: striking.
9 A startling simile, for the whale goes to its death. Cf. Shakespeare, *2 Henry IV* IV iv 40–1: 'his passions, like a whale on ground, / Confound themselves with working.'

Stanza 32
4 **sort**: manner.
6 **dewfull**: due.

Stanza 33
2 **aggrate**: please.
6 **exercize**: practise.

Stanza 34
2 **strawberies**: the fruit of the golden age (Ovid, *Met.* i 104); however, the outcome of the event suggests its proverbial association with the serpent lurking beneath.
5 **gourmandize**: voraciousness; cf. the cannibals at viii 38.9.
6 Cf. the Dragon's mouth which 'Wide gaped, like the griesly mouth of hell' (I xi 12.8).
7 **surprize**: seize.
9 **all too late**: i.e. before it was too late, though the phrase bears the plain meaning, as the next stanza indicates.

Stanza 35
2 **feend**: as its mouth gapes 'like hell gate' (34.6).
5 Cf. John 15.13. **steemed**: esteemed.
8 **His . . . spoile**: her body, which is the reward or plunder that his love seeks to possess. Clearly two beasts seek her as their spoil. Yet **Calidore** himself becomes the spoil. Through love for her, his own heart is preyed upon: in seeking to spoil her body, the tiger is about to spoil his heart.

36

He had no weapon, but his shepheards hooke,
  To serue the vengeaunce of his wrathfull will,
  With which so sternely he the monster strooke,
  That to the ground astonished he fell;
  Whence ere he could recou'r, he did him quell,
  And hewing off his head, ⟨he⟩ it presented
  Before the feete of the faire *Pastorell*;
  Who scarcely yet from former feare exempted,
A thousand times him thankt, that had her death preuented.

37

From that day forth she gan him to affect,
  And daily more her fauour to augment;
  But *Coridon* for cowherdize reiect,
  Fit to keepe sheepe, vnfit for loues content:
  The gentle heart scornes base disparagement.
  Yet *Calidore* did not despise him quight,
  But vsde him friendly for further intent,
  That by his fellowship, he colour might
Both his estate, and loue from skill of any wight.

38

So well he wood her, and so well he wrought her,
  With humble seruice, and with daily sute,
  That at the last vnto his will he brought her;
  Which he so wisely well did prosecute,
  That of his loue he reapt the timely frute,
  And ioyed long in close felicity:
  Till fortune fraught with malice, blinde, and brute,
  That enuies louers long prosperity,
Blew vp a bitter storme of foule aduersity.

39

It fortuned one day, when *Calidore*
  Was hunting in the woods (as was his trade)
  A lawlesse people, *Brigants* hight of yore,
  That neuer vsde to liue by plough nor spade,
  But fed on spoile and booty, which they made
  Vpon their neighbours, which did nigh them border,
  The dwelling of these shepheards did inuade,
  And spoyld their houses, and them selues did murder;
And droue away their flocks, with other much disorder.

40

Amongst the rest, the which they then did pray,
  They spoyld old *Melibee* of all he had,
  And all his people captiue led away,
  Mongst which this lucklesse mayd away was lad,
  Faire *Pastorella*, sorrowfull and sad,
  Most sorrowfull, most sad, that euer sight,
  Now made the spoile of theeues and *Brigants* bad,
  Which was the conquest of the gentlest Knight,
That euer liu'd, and th'onely glory of his might.

41

With them also was taken *Coridon*,
  And carried captiue by those theeues away;
  Who in the couert of the night, that none
  Mote them descry, nor reskue from their pray,
  Vnto their dwelling did them close conuay.
  Their dwelling in a little Island was,
  Couered with shrubby woods, in which no way
  Appeard for people in nor out to pas,
Nor any footing fynde for ouergrowen gras.

42

For vnderneath the ground their way was made,
  Through hollow caues, that no man mote discouer
  For the thicke shrubs, which did them alwaies shade
  From view of liuing wight, and couered ouer:
  But darkenesse dred and daily night did houer
  Through all the inner parts, wherein they dwelt,
  Ne lightned was with window, nor with louer,
  But with continuall candlelight, which delt
A doubtfull sense of things, not so well seene, as felt.

Stanza 36

4 **astonished**: stunned.
5 **quell**: kill.
6 **head, ⟨he⟩ it**] head, it *1596*. Emendation is necessary unless **head** is disyllabic, as Jortin (1734) suggested, or we read **presented** as a dactyl. The latter alternative is accepted by the *Var.* editors despite the ugly echo.

Stanza 37

1 **affect**: love.
3 **cowherdize**: the spelling suggests base conduct befitting a herder; cf. 35.3.
5 **disparagement**: the disgrace of marriage to one of inferior rank.
6–9 His subterfuge and secrecy are a necessary defence against the Blatant Beast. **colour**: disguise. **estate**: state. **skill**: knowledge.

Stanza 38

5 Coridon had feared that Calidore 'Should reap the haruest, ere it ripened were' (ix 38.6).
7 **brute**: dumb, insensible.

Stanza 39

Cf. the 'saluage nation' that seizes Serena as its spoil (viii 35).
2 **trade**: custom.
3 **Brigants**: Ital. *brigante*, brigand; 'an ancient people in the north part of England' (Cooper, 1565). Blitch (1973) 18 notes that the Italian term meant 'devil'.
8 **spoyld**: plundered.

Stanza 40

6 **sight**: sighed.
9 **th'onely**: the chief or greatest.

Stanza 41

4 **pray**: preying.
5 **close**: secretly.

Stanza 42

1 **For**] 'Far', Upton's (1758) suggested emendation, is supported by the similar description at II i 22.3, IV i 20.4, ii 47.5, and V ix 6.3.
5 **daily night**: night even during the day. Cf. the darkness in which Florimell lived, IV xi 4.2.
7 **louer**: louver or lantern.
9 As the darkness of God's curse upon Egypt, 'even darcknes that may be felt' (Exod. 10.21).

43

Hither those *Brigants* brought their present pray,
    And kept them with continuall watch and ward,
    Meaning so soone, as they conuenient may,
    For slaues to sell them, for no small reward,
    To merchants, which them kept in bondage hard,
    Or sold againe. Now when faire *Pastorell*
    Into this place was brought, and kept with gard
    Of griesly theeues, she thought her self in hell,
Where with such damned fiends she should in darknesse dwell.

44

But for to tell the dolefull dreriment,
    And pittifull complaints, which there she made,
    Where day and night she nought did but lament
    Her wretched life, shut vp in deadly shade,
    And waste her goodly beauty, which did fade
    Like to a flowre, that feeles no heate of sunne,
    Which may her feeble leaues with comfort glade.
    But what befell her in that theeuish wonne,
Will in an other Canto better be begonne.

Cant. XI.

The theeues fall out for Pastorell,
Whilest Melibee is slaine:
Her Calidore from them redeemes,
And bringeth backe againe.

1

THe ioyes of loue, if they should euer last,
    Without affliction or disquietnesse,
    That worldly chaunces doe amongst them cast,
    Would be on earth too great a blessednesse,
    Liker to heauen, then mortall wretchednesse.
    Therefore the winged God, to let men weet,
    That here on earth is no sure happinesse,
    A thousand sowres hath tempred with one sweet,
To make it seeme more deare and dainty, as is meet.

2

Like as is now befalne to this faire Mayd,
    Faire *Pastorell*, of whom is now my song,
    Who being now in dreadfull darknesse layd,
    Amongst those theeues, which her in bondage strong
    Detaynd, yet Fortune not with all this wrong
    Contented, greater mischiefe on her threw,
    And sorrowes heapt on her in greater throng;
    That who so heares her heauinesse, would rew
And pitty her sad plight, so chang'd from pleasaunt hew.

3

Whylest thus she in these hellish dens remayned,
    Wrapped in wretched cares and hearts vnrest,
    It so befell (as Fortune had ordayned)
    That he, which was their Capitaine profest,
    And had the chiefe commaund of all the rest,
    One day as he did all his prisoners vew,
    With lustfull eyes, beheld that louely guest,
    Faire *Pastorella*, whose sad mournefull hew
696 Like the faire Morning clad in misty fog did shew.

4

At sight whereof his barbarous heart was fired,
    And inly burnt with flames most raging whot,
    That her alone he for his part desired
    Of all the other pray, which they had got,
    And her in mynde did to him selfe allot.
    From that day forth he kyndnesse to her showed,
    And sought her loue, by all the meanes he mote;
    With looks, with words, with gifts he oft her wowed;
And mixed threats among, and much vnto her vowed.

5

But all that euer he could doe or say,
    Her constant mynd could not a whit remoue,
    Nor draw vnto the lure of his lewd lay,
    To graunt him fauour, or afford him loue.
    Yet ceast he not to sew and all waies proue,
    By which he mote accomplish his request,
    Saying and doing all that mote behoue;
    Ne day nor night he suffred her to rest,
But her all night did watch, and all the day molest.

Stanza 44

The faulty syntax of this stanza is improved in *1609* by
bracketing 3–7, removing the period after **glade**, and beginning
8 with 'And'.

7   **glade**: gladden.

Canto xi

Stanza 1

3   **worldly chaunces**: mishaps, mischances of life, as in the
Book of Common Prayer: 'All the changes and chances of this
mortal life'.

6–9   The role given Cupid here is given elsewhere to
Fortune, as 2.5. 'That blisse may not abide in state of mortall
men' (I viii 44.9) is one of the commonest lessons in the poem.
The odds against happiness in love have been subject to a
tenfold inflation since IV x 1.   **dainty**: precious.

Stanza 2

8   **heauinesse**: grief.

Stanza 4

3   **part**: share.

Stanza 5

5   **proue**: try.

6

At last when him she so importune saw,
  Fearing least he at length the raines would lend
  Vnto his lust, and make his will his law,
  Sith in his powre she was to foe or frend,
  She thought it best, for shadow to pretend
  Some shew of fauour, by him gracing small,
  That she thereby mote either freely wend,
Or at more ease continue there his thrall:
A little well is lent, that gaineth more withall.

7

So from thenceforth, when loue he to her made,
  With better tearmes she did him entertaine,
  Which gaue him hope, and did him halfe perswade,
  That he in time her ioyaunce should obtaine.
  But when she saw, through that small fauours gaine,
  That further, then she willing was, he prest,
  She found no meanes to barre him, but to faine
A sodaine sickenesse, which her sore .opprest,
And made vnfit to serue his lawlesse mindes behest.

8

By meanes whereof she would not him permit
  Once to approch to her in priuity,
  But onely mongst the rest by her to sit,
  Mourning the rigour of her malady,
  And seeking all things meete for remedy.
  But she resolu'd no remedy to fynde,
  Nor better cheare to shew in misery,
Till Fortune would her captiue bonds vnbynde,
Her sickenesse was not of the body but the mynde.

9

During which space that she thus sicke did lie,
  It chaunst a sort of merchants, which were wount
  To skim those coastes, for bondmen there to buy,
  And by such trafficke after gaines to hunt,
  Arriued in this Isle though bare and blunt,
  T'inquire for slaues; where being readie met
  By some of these same theeues at the instant brunt,
Were brought vnto their Captaine, who was set
By his faire patients side with sorrowfull regret.

10

To whom they shewed, how those marchants were
  Arriu'd in place, their bondslaues for to buy,
  And therefore prayd, that those same captiues there
  Mote to them for their most commodity
  Be sold, and mongst them shared equally.
  This their request the Captaine much appalled;
  Yet could he not their iust demaund deny,
  And willed streight the slaues should forth be called,
And sold for most aduantage not to be forstalled.

11

Then forth the good old *Meliboe* was brought,
  And *Coridon*, with many other moe,
  Whom they before in diuerse spoyles had caught:
  All which he to the marchants sale did showe.
  Till some, which did the sundry prisoners knowe,
  Gan to inquire for that faire shepherdesse,
  Which with the rest they tooke not long agoe,
  And gan her forme and feature to expresse,
The more t'augment her price, through praise of comlinesse.

12

To whom the Captaine in full angry wize
  Made answere, that the Mayd of whom they spake,
  Was his owne purchase and his onely prize,
  With which none had to doe, ne ought partake,
  But he himselfe, which did that conquest make;
  Litle for him to haue one silly lasse:
  Besides through sicknesse now so wan and weake,
That nothing meet in marchandise to passe.
So shew'd them her, to proue how pale and weake she was.

13

The sight of whom, though now decayd and mard,
  And eke but hardly seene by candle-light,
  Yet like a Diamond of rich regard,
  In doubtfull shadow of the darkesome night,
  With starrie beames about her shining bright,
  These marchants fixed eyes did so amaze,
  That what through wonder, and what through delight,
A while on her they greedily did gaze,
And did her greatly like, and did her greatly praize.

Stanza 6
4 **to foe or frend**: i.e. to treat as a foe or to befriend.
5 **for shadow**: in dissimulation.
6 **gracing small**: showing slight favour.
7 **freely wend**: go free.

Stanza 7
4 **her ioyaunce**: enjoyment of her.

Stanza 8
2 **in priuity**: privately.

Stanza 9
2 **sort**: company.
5 **bare**: desolate.   **blunt**: barren.
7 **instant brunt**: very outset.

Stanza 10
4 **most commodity**: greatest profit.
9 **not to be forstalled**: i.e. all the slaves were to be put for sale and none bought beforehand.

Stanza 11
3 **spoyles**: raids.
8 **expresse**: describe.

Stanza 12
3 **purchase**: booty, spoil.   **his onely**: only his.
6 **silly**: simple.
8 **nothing meet . . . to passe**: not fit to be put on the market.

Stanza 13
3 **regard**: value; also 'glance': in their sight she appears rich.
5 Cf. 21.8–9.
6 **amaze**: dazzle, bewilder.

697

14

At last when all the rest them offred were,
  And prises to them placed at their pleasure,
  They all refused in regard of her,
  Ne ought would buy, how euer prisd with measure,
  Withouten her, whose worth aboue all threasure
  They did esteeme, and offred store of gold.
  But then the Captaine fraught with more displeasure,
  Bad them be still, his loue should not be sold:
The rest take if they would, he her to him would hold.

15

Therewith some other of the chiefest theeues
  Boldly him bad such iniurie forbeare;
  For that same mayd, how euer it him greeues,
  Should with the rest be sold before him theare,
  To make the prises of the rest more deare.
  That with great rage he stoutly doth denay;
  And fiercely drawing forth his blade, doth sweare,
  That who so hardie hand on her doth lay,
It dearely shall aby, and death for handsell pay.

16

Thus as they words amongst them multiply,
  They fall to strokes, the frute of too much talke,
  And the mad steele about doth fiercely fly,
  Not sparing wight, ne leauing any balke,
  But making way for death at large to walke:
  Who in the horror of the griesly night,
  In thousand dreadful shapes doth mongst them stalke,
  And makes huge hauocke, whiles the candlelight
Out quenched, leaues no skill nor difference of wight.

17

Like as a sort of hungry dogs ymet
  About some carcase by the common way,
  Doe fall together, stryuing each to get
  The greatest portion of the greedie pray;
  All on confused heapes themselues assay,
  And snatch, and byte, and rend, and tug, and teare;
  That who them sees, would wonder at their fray,
  And who sees not, would be affrayd to heare.
Such was the conflict of those cruell *Brigants* there.

18

But first of all, their captiues they doe kill,
  Least they should ioyne against the weaker side,
  Or rise against the remnant at their will;
  Old *Melibœ* is slaine, and him beside
  His aged wife, with many others wide,
  But *Coridon* escaping craftily,
  Creepes forth of dores, whilst darknes him doth hide,
  And flyes away as fast as he can hye,
Ne stayeth leaue to take, before his friends doe dye.

19

But *Pastorella*, wofull wretched Elfe,
  Was by the Captaine all this while defended,
  Who minding more her safety then himselfe,
  His target alwayes ouer her pretended;
  By meanes whereof, that mote not be amended,
  He at the length was slaine, and layd on ground,
  Yet holding fast twixt both his armes extended
  Fayre *Pastorell*, who with the selfe same wound
Launcht through the arme, fell down with him in drerie swound.

20

There lay she couered with confused preasse
  Of carcases, which dying on her fell.
  Tho when as he was dead, the fray gan ceasse,
  And each to other calling, did compell
  To stay their cruell hands from slaughter fell,
  Sith they that were the cause of all, were gone.
  Thereto they all attonce agreed well,
  And lighting candles new, gan search anone,
How many of their friends were slaine, how many fone.

21

Their Captaine there they cruelly found kild,
  And in his armes the dreary dying mayd,
  Like a sweet Angell twixt two clouds vphild:
  Her louely light was dimmed and decayd,
  With cloud of death vpon her eyes displayd;
  Yet did the cloud make euen that dimmed light
  Seeme much more louely in that darknesse layd,
  And twixt the twinckling of her eye-lids bright,
To sparke out litle beames, like starres in foggie night.

Stanza 14
2 **prises**: prices.
3 **in regard of**: on account of.
4 **prisd with measure**: moderately priced.

Stanza 15
9 **aby**: suffer for. **handsell**: reward; playing on *hand* (8).

Stanza 16
4 **balke**: exception; a figurative sense from the literal, a piece missed in ploughing.
9 **skill**: distinction.

Stanza 17
4 **greedie pray**: prey for which they are greedy.
5 **assay**: assail.

Stanza 18
5 **wide**: round about.
9 Said in scorn of his cowardice though he is allowed to regret his action at 32.

Stanza 19
1 **Elfe**: poor creature.
4 **target**: shield. **pretended**: held, stretched.
9 **Launcht**: pierced. **drerie**: also bloody.

Stanza 21
2 **dreary**: sad; yet cf. 'drerie' (19.9).

22

But when they mou'd the carcases aside,
   They found that life did yet in her remaine:
   Then all their helpes they busily applyde,
   To call the soule backe to her home againe;
   And wrought so well with labour and long paine,
   That they to life recouered her at last.
   Who sighing sore, as if her hart in twaine
   Had riuen bene, and all her hart strings brast,
With drearie drouping eyne lookt vp like one aghast.

23

There she beheld, that sore her grieu'd to see,
   Her father and her friends about her lying,
   Her selfe sole left, a second spoyle to bee
   Of those, that hauing saued her from dying,
   Renew'd her death by timely death denying:
   What now is left her, but to wayle and weepe,
   Wringing her hands, and ruefully loud crying?
   Ne cared she her wound in teares to steepe,
Albe with all their might those *Brigants* her did keepe.

24

But when they saw her now reliu'd againe,
   They left her so, in charge of one the best
   Of many worst, who with vnkind disdaine
   And cruell rigour her did much molest;
   Scarse yeelding her due food, or timely rest,
   And scarsely suffring her infestred wound,
   That sore her payn'd, by any to be drest.
   So leaue we her in wretched thraldome bound,
And turne we backe to *Calidore*, where we him found.

25

Who when he backe returned from the wood,
   And saw his shepheards cottage spoyled quight,
   And his loue reft away, he wexed wood,
   And halfe enraged at that ruefull sight,
   That euen his hart for very fell despight,
   And his owne flesh he readie was to teare,
   He chauft, he grieu'd, he fretted, and he sight,
   And fared like a furious wyld Beare,
Whose whelpes are stolne away, she being otherwhere.

26

Ne wight he found, to whom he might complaine,
   Ne wight he found, of whom he might inquire;
   That more increast the anguish of his paine.
   He sought the woods; but no man could see there:
   He sought the plaines; but could no tydings heare.
   The woods did nought but ecchoes vaine rebound;
   The playnes all waste and emptie did appeare:
   Where wont the shepheards oft their pypes resound,
And feed an hundred flocks, there now not one he found.

27

At last as there he romed vp and downe,
   He chaunst one comming towards him to spy,
   That seem'd to be some sorie simple clowne,
   With ragged weedes, and lockes vpstaring hye,
   As if he did from some late daunger fly,
   And yet his feare did follow him behynd:
   Who as he vnto him approched nye,
   He mote perceiue by signes, which he did fynd,
That *Coridon* it was, the silly shepherds hynd.

28

Tho to him running fast, he did not stay
   To greet him first, but askt where were the rest;
   Where *Pastorell*? who full of fresh dismay,
   And gushing forth in teares, was so opprest,
   That he no word could speake, but smit his brest,
   And vp to heauen his eyes fast streming threw.
   Whereat the knight amaz'd, yet did not rest,
   But askt againe, what ment that rufull hew;
Where was his *Pastorell*? where all the other crew?

29

Ah well away (sayd he then sighing sore)
   That euer I did liue, this day to see,
   This dismall day, and was not dead before,
   Before I saw faire *Pastorella* dye.
   Die? out alas! then *Calidore* did cry:
   How could the death dare euer her to quell?
   But read thou shepheard, read what destiny,
   Or other dyrefull hap from heauen or hell
Hath wrought this wicked deed, doe feare away, and tell.

Stanza 23

8   Ne cared she . . . to steepe: she did not concern herself
that her tears steeped her wound. At iii 10.5–9 tears heal a
wound.

Stanza 24

1   reliu'd: restored again to life.
6   infestred: festered inwardly.

Stanza 25

4   halfe enraged: almost maddened.
5–6   Cf. Joel 2.13.
7–9   Cf. 2 Sam. 17.8: 'They be strong men, and are chafed
in minde as a beare robbed of her whelpes.'   sight: sighed.
fared: acted.

Stanza 27

4   vpstaring: standing on end.
9   hynd: servant.

Stanza 29

3   dismall day: unlucky or evil day.
6   In the sixteenth century, the definite article was used with
death.   quell: kill.
7   read: tell.
9   doe: put.

30

Tho when the shepheard breathed had a whyle,
  He thus began: Where shall I then commence
  This wofull tale? or how those *Brigants* vyle,
  With cruell rage and dreadfull violence
  Spoyld all our cots, and caried vs from hence?
  Or how faire *Pastorell* should haue bene sold
  To marchants, but was sau'd with strong defence?
  Or how those theeues, whilest one sought her to hold,
Fell all at ods, and fought through fury fierce and bold.

31

In that same conflict (woe is me) befell
  This fatall chaunce, this dolefull accident,
  Whose heauy tydings now I haue to tell.
  First all the captiues, which they here had hent,
  Were by them slaine by generall consent;
  Old *Melibœ* and his good wife withall
  These eyes saw die, and dearely did lament:
  But when the lot to *Pastorell* did fall,
Their Captaine long withstood, and did her death forstall.

32

But what could he gainst all them doe alone?
  It could not boot, needs mote she die at last:
  I onely scapt through great confusione
  Of cryes and clamors, which amongst them past,
  In dreadfull darknesse dreadfully aghast;
  That better were with them to haue bene dead,
  Then here to see all desolate and wast,
  Despoyled of those ioyes and iollyhead,
Which with those gentle shepherds here I wont to lead.

33

When *Calidore* these ruefull newes had raught,
  His hart quite deaded was with anguish great,
  And all his wits with doole were nigh distraught,
  That he his face, his head, his brest did beat,
  And death it selfe vnto himselfe did threat;
  Oft cursing th'heauens, that so cruell were
  To her, whose name he often did repeat;
  And wishing oft, that he were present there,
When she was slaine, or had bene to her succour nere.

34

But after griefe awhile had had his course,
  And spent it selfe in mourning, he at last
  Began to mitigate his swelling sourse,
  And in his mind with better reason cast,
  How he might saue her life, if life did last;
  Or if that dead, how he her death might wreake,
  Sith otherwise he could not mend thing past;
  Or if it to reuenge he were too weake,
Then for to die with her, and his liues threed to breake.

35

Tho *Coridon* he prayd, sith he well knew
  The readie way vnto that theeuish wonne,
  To wend with him, and be his conduct trew
  Vnto the place, to see what should be donne.
  But he, whose hart through feare was late fordonne,
  Would not for ought be drawne to former drede,
  But by all meanes the daunger knowne did shonne:
  Yet *Calidore* so well him wrought with meed,
700 And faire bespoke with words, that he at last agreed.

36

So forth they goe together (God before)
  Both clad in shepheards weeds agreeably,
  And both with shepheards hookes: But *Calidore*
  Had vnderneath, him armed priuily.
  Tho to the place when they approched nye,
  They chaunst, vpon an hill not farre away,
  Some flockes of sheepe and shepheards to espy;
  To whom they both agreed to take their way,
In hope there newes to learne, how they mote best assay.

37

There did they find, that which they did not feare,
  The selfe same flocks, the which those theeues had reft
  From *Melibœ* and from themselues whyleare,
  And certaine of the theeues there by them left,
  The which for want of heards themselues then kept.
  Right well knew *Coridon* his owne late sheepe,
  And seeing them, for tender pittie wept:
  But when he saw the theeues, which did them keepe,
His hart gan fayle, albe he saw them all asleepe.

Stanza 30
Upton (1758) observes that the construction is designedly
embarrassed because the words are spoken by a man in a fright
and in a hurry.

Stanza 31
4 **hent**: seized.
9 **forstall**: prevent; here, postpone.

Stanza 32
8 **iollyhead**: merriment.

Stanza 33
1 **raught**: received.

Stanza 34
6 **wreake**: avenge.

Stanza 35
3 **conduct**: guide.
5 **fordonne**: overcome.
8 **meed**: bribes.

Stanza 36
1 **God before**: relates to the theme of fortune in Book VI.
Pastorella is called one 'whom high God did saue' (xii 17.9).
2 **agreeably**: similarly.
9 **assay**: act.

Stanza 37
1 **feare**: expect, anticipate; cf. 41.5.
5 **heards**: herdsmen.

38

But *Calidore* recomforting his griefe,
  Though not his feare; for nought may feare disswade;
  Him hardly forward drew, whereas the thiefe
  Lay sleeping soundly in the bushes shade,
  Whom *Coridon* him counseld to inuade
  Now all vnwares, and take the spoyle away;
  But he, that in his mind had closely made
  A further purpose, would not so them slay,
But gently waking them, gaue them the time of day.

39

Tho sitting downe by them vpon the greene,
  Of sundrie things he purpose gan to faine;
  That he by them might certaine tydings weene
  Of *Pastorell*, were she aliue or slaine.
  Mongst which the theeues them questioned againe,
  What mister men, and eke from whence they were.
  To whom they answer'd, as did appertaine,
  That they were poore heardgroomes, the which whylere
Had from their maisters fled, and now sought hyre elswhere.

40

Whereof right glad they seem'd, and offer made
  To hyre them well, if they their flockes would keepe:
  For they themselues were euill groomes, they sayd,
  Vnwont with heards to watch, or pasture sheepe,
  But to forray the land, or scoure the deepe.
  Thereto they soone agreed, and earnest tooke,
  To keepe their flockes for litle hyre and chepe:
  For they for better hyre did shortly looke,
So there all day they bode, till light the sky forsooke.

41

Tho when as towards darksome night it drew,
  Vnto their hellish dens those theeues them brought,
  Where shortly they in great acquaintance grew,
  And all the secrets of their entrayles sought.
  There did they find, contrarie to their thought,
  That *Pastorell* yet liu'd, but all the rest
  Were dead, right so as *Coridon* had taught:
  Whereof they both full glad and blyth did rest,
But chiefly *Calidore*, whom griefe had most possest.

42

At length when they occasion fittest found,
  In dead of night, when all the theeues did rest
  After a late forray, and slept full sound,
  Sir *Calidore* him arm'd, as he thought best,
  Hauing of late by diligent inquest,
  Prouided him a sword of meanest sort:
  With which he streight went to the Captaines nest.
  But *Coridon* durst not with him consort,
Ne durst abide behind, for dread of worse effort.

43

When to the Caue they came, they found it fast:
  But *Calidore* with huge resistlesse might,
  The dores assayled, and the locks vpbrast.
  With noyse whereof the theefe awaking light,
  Vnto the entrance ran: where the bold knight
  Encountring him with small resistance slew;
  The whiles faire *Pastorell* through great affright
  Was almost dead, misdoubting least of new
Some vprore were like that, which lately she did vew.

44

But when as *Calidore* was comen in,
  And gan aloud for *Pastorell* to call,
  Knowing his voice although not heard long sin,
  She sudden was reuiued therewithall,
  And wondrous ioy felt in her spirits thrall:
  Like him that being long in tempest tost,
  Looking each houre into deathes mouth to fall,
  At length espyes at hand the happie cost,
On which he safety hopes, that earst feard to be lost.

Stanza 38
1 recomforting: consoling.
2 disswade: advise against, and so remove.
3 hardly: forcibly.
5 inuade: attack.
7 closely: secretly.
9 gaue ... day: greeted them. Calidore has a special gift for surprising others in the privacy of love, inspiration or sleep, and then striking up a conversation.

Stanza 39
2 purpose: conversation.
5 againe: in return.
6 mister: sort of.
7 as did appertaine: i.e. as was suitable to their disguises as herdsmen.

Stanza 40
3 euill: unskilful.
6 earnest: pledge.
7 litle hyre and chepe: low wages and small charges.

Stanza 41
2 hellish dens: as 3.1.
4 entrayles: the 'inner parts' (x 42.6) of the cave.

Stanza 42
5 inquest: search.

Stanza 43
4 light: quickly.
8 misdoubting: fearing. of new: anew.

Stanza 44
3 sin: since.
5 thrall: thrilled, pierced; or enthralled.

45

Her gentle hart, that now long season past
  Had neuer ioyance felt, nor chearefull thought,
  Began some smacke of comfort new to tast,
  Like lyfull heat to nummed senses brought,
  And life to feele, that long for death had sought ;
  Ne lesse in hart reioyced *Calidore*,
  When he her found, but like to one distraught
  And robd of reason, towards her him bore,
A thousand times embrast, and kist a thousand more.

46

But now by this, with noyse of late vprore,
  The hue and cry was raysed all about ;
  And all the *Brigants* flocking in great store,
  Vnto the caue gan preasse, nought hauing dout
  Of that was doen, and entred in a rout.
  But *Calidore* in th'entry close did stand,
  And entertayning them with courage stout,
  Still slew the formost, that came first to hand,
So long till all the entry was with bodies mand.

47

Tho when no more could nigh to him approch,
  He breath'd his sword, and rested him till day,
  Which when he spyde vpon the earth t'encroch,
  Through the dead carcases he made his way,
  Mongst which he found a sword of better say,
  With which he forth went into th'open light :
  Where all the rest for him did readie stay,
  And fierce assayling him, with all their might
Gan all vpon him lay : there gan a dreadfull fight.

48

How many flyes in whottest sommers day
  Do seize vpon some beast, whose flesh is bare,
  That all the place with swarmes do ouerlay,
  And with their litle stings right felly fare,
  So many theeues about him swarming are,
  All which do him assayle on euery side,
  And sore oppresse, ne any him doth spare :
  But he doth with his raging brond diuide
Their thickest troups, and round about him scattreth wide.

49

Like as a Lion mongst an heard of dere,
  Disperseth them to catch his choysest pray,
  So did he fly amongst them here and there,
  And all that nere him came, did hew and slay,
  Till he had strowd with bodies all the way ;
  That none his daunger daring to abide,
  Fled from his wrath, and did themselues conuay
  Into their caues, their heads from death to hide,
Ne any left, that victorie to him enuide.

50

Then backe returning to his dearest deare,
  He her gan to recomfort, all he might,
  With gladfull speaches, and with louely cheare,
  And forth her bringing to the ioyous light,
  Whereof she long had lackt the wishfull sight,
  Deuiz'd all goodly meanes, from her to driue
  The sad remembrance of her wretched plight.
  So her vneath at last he did reuiue,
That long had lyen dead, and made againe aliue.

702

51

This doen, into those theeuish dens he went,
  And thence did all the spoyles and threasures take,
  Which they from many long had robd and rent,
  But fortune now the victors meed did make ;
  Of which the best he did his loue betake ;
  And also all those flockes, which they before
  Had reft from *Melibæ* and from his make,
  He did them all to *Coridon* restore.
So droue them all away, and his loue with him bore.

Stanza 45

4 **lyfull**: life-giving, vital.

Stanza 46

7 **entertayning**: encountering.
9 **mand**: piled with men.

Stanza 47

5 **say**: temper.

Stanzas 48–49

An exercise in fitting two contrasting similes to their subjects,
linked by 'fly' (49.3). Upton (1758) compares Homer, *Iliad* ii
469–83 : the Greek troops assembled for battle are compared to
flies, Agamemnon to a bull.

Stanza 49

6 **daunger**: power to inflict injury.
9 **enuide**: refused.

Stanza 50

1 As the lion seeks the choicest deer, 49.1–2.
3 **louely**: loving.
8 **vneath**: with difficulty.
9 The resurrection is rendered as though entirely natural.

Stanza 51

5 **betake**: give to.
7 **make**: mate.

Cant. XII.

Fayre Pastorella by great hap
her parents vnderstands,
Calidore doth the Blatant beast
subdew, and bynd in bands.

1

Like as a ship, that through the Ocean wyde
Directs her course vnto one certaine cost,
Is met of many a counter winde and tyde,
With which her winged speed is let and crost,
And she her selfe in stormie surges tost;
Yet making many a borde, and many a bay,
Still winneth way, ne hath her compasse lost:
Right so it fares with me in this long way,
Whose course is often stayd, yet neuer is astray.

2

For all that hetherto hath long delayd
This gentle knight, from sewing his first quest,
Though out of course, yet hath not bene mis-sayd,
To shew the courtesie by him profest,
Euen vnto the lowest and the least.
But now I come into my course againe,
To his atchieuement of the *Blatant beast*;
Who all this while at will did range and raine,
Whilst none was him to stop, nor none him to restraine.

3

Sir *Calidore* when thus he now had raught
Faire *Pastorella* from those *Brigants* powre,
Vnto the Castle of *Belgard* her brought,
Whereof was Lord the good Sir *Bellamoure*;
Who whylome was in his youthes freshest flowre
A lustie knight, as euer wielded speare,
And had endured many a dreadfull stoure
In bloudy battell for a Ladie deare,
The fayrest Ladie then of all that liuing were.

4

Her name was *Claribell*, whose father hight
The Lord of *Many Ilands*, farre renound
For his great riches and his greater might.
He through the wealth, wherein he did abound,
This daughter thought in wedlocke to haue bound
Vnto the Prince of *Picteland* bordering nere,
But she whose sides before with secret wound
Of loue to *Bellamoure* empierced were,
By all meanes shund to match with any forrein fere.

5

And *Bellamour* againe so well her pleased,
With dayly seruice and attendance dew,
That of her loue he was entyrely seized,
And closely did her wed, but knowne to few.
Which when her father vnderstood, he grew
In so great rage, that them in dongeon deepe
Without compassion cruelly he threw;
Yet did so streightly them a sunder keepe,
That neither could to company of th'other creepe.

Canto xii

Argument
1 **hap**: good fortune.

Stanza 1
Dees (1975) compares this use of the image of a ship in a perilous sea as an analogue for the poetic process to the two earlier uses (I xii 1, 42) to note the poet's change of mood from optimism to pessimism, which 'reflects the felt burden of having sustained an enormous poetic effort to fashion virtuous men, an effort which has increasingly threatened to overcome him' (212).
2 **cost**: coast, apparently suggested by xi 44.8; direction.
4 **let**: hindered.
6 **making many . . . bay**: tacking and turning often before the wind.
7 **compasse**: way; course.

Stanza 2
The poet identifies his course with his knight's.
2 **sewing**: pursuing.

Stanza 3
1 **raught**: taken.
3 **Belgard**: Ital. *bel* + *gard*, goodly attention, a fitting guard for **Pastorella**'s beauty, as before it was a prison for Claribell; or *bel* + *guardo*, loving look, a fit place for its loving lord. Cf. II iii 25.3 and Malory's 'La Beale Regarde', *Works* 642.
4 **Bellamoure**: fair-lover or sweetheart, which he is to his lady. The rhyme with **flowre** suggests the white flower of that name in *Amor*. lxiv 7 and hence the family birthmark on Pastorella at 7.7–9. As *bellum* + *amour*: lover of war, or a knight who is also a lover.
6 **lustie**: vigorous.
7 **stoure**: encounter.

Stanza 4
1 **Claribell**: famous or bright in beauty, Lat. *clara* + *bella*.
6 **Picteland**: Scotland.
9 **fere**: husband.

Stanza 5
1 **againe**: in return.
3 **seized**: possessed.
4 **closely**: secretly.
8 **streightly**: strictly.

6

Nathlesse Sir *Bellamour*, whether through grace
  Or secret guifts so with his keepers wrought,
  That to his loue sometimes he came in place,
  Whereof her wombe vnwist to wight was fraught,
  And in dew time a mayden child forth brought.
  Which she streight way for dread least, if her syre
  Should know thereof, to slay he would haue sought,
  Deliuered to her handmayd, that for hyre
She should it cause be fostred vnder straunge attyre.

7

The trustie damzell bearing it abrode
  Into the emptie fields, where liuing wight
  Mote not bewray the secret of her lode,
  She forth gan lay vnto the open light
  The litle babe, to take thereof a sight.
  Whom whylest she did with watrie eyne behold,
  Vpon the litle brest like christall bright,
  She mote perceiue a litle purple mold,
That like a rose her silken leaues did faire vnfold.

8

Well she it markt, and pittied the more,
  Yet could not remedie her wretched case,
  But closing it againe like as before,
  Bedeaw'd with teares there left it in the place:
  Yet left not quite, but drew a litle space
  Behind the bushes, where she her did hyde,
  To weet what mortall hand, or heauens grace
  Would for the wretched infants helpe prouyde,
For which it loudly cald, and pittifully cryde.

9

At length a Shepheard, which there by did keepe
  His fleecie flocke vpon the playnes around,
  Led with the infants cry, that loud did weepe,
  Came to the place, where when he wrapped found
  Th'abandond spoyle, he softly it vnbound;
  And seeing there, that did him pittie sore,
  He tooke it vp, and in his mantle wound;
  So home vnto his honest wife it bore,
Who as her owne it nurst, and named euermore.

10

Thus long continu'd *Claribell* a thrall,
  And *Bellamour* in bands, till that her syre
  Departed life, and left vnto them all.
  Then all the stormes of fortunes former yre
  Were turnd, and they to freedome did retyre.
  Thenceforth they ioy'd in happinesse together,
  And liued long in peace and loue entyre,
  Without disquiet or dislike of ether,
Till time that *Calidore* brought *Pastorella* thether

11

Both whom they goodly well did entertaine;
  For *Bellamour* knew *Calidore* right well,
  And loued for his prowesse, sith they twaine
  Long since had fought in field. Als *Claribell*
  No lesse did tender the faire *Pastorell*,
  Seeing her weake and wan, through durance long.
  There they a while together thus did dwell
  In much delight, and many ioyes among,
Vntill the damzell gan to wex more sound and strong.

12

Tho gan Sir *Calidore* him to aduize
  Of his first quest, which he had long forlore,
  Asham'd to thinke, how he that enterprize,
  The which the Faery Queene had long afore
  Bequeath'd to him, forslacked had so sore;
  That much he feared, least reprochfull blame
  With foule dishonour him mote blot therefore;
  Besides the losse of so much loos and fame,
As through the world thereby should glorifie his name.

13

Therefore resoluing to returne in hast
  Vnto so great atchieuement, he bethought
  To leaue his loue, now perill being past,
  With *Claribell*, whylest he that monster sought
  Throughout the world, and to destruction brought.
  So taking leaue of his faire *Pastorell*,
  Whom to recomfort, all the meanes he wrought,
  With thanks to *Bellamour* and *Claribell*,
He went forth on his quest, and did, that him befell.

Stanza 6

1 **grace**: favour.
4 **fraught**: burdened.

Stanza 7

3 **bewray**: reveal.
8 **mold**: mole: pattern.

Stanza 8

1 **the more**: greatly.
3 **it**: referring also to the rose whose leaves unfold again
only when Pastorella is restored to her mother, 19.5.
5 **drew**: withdrew.

Stanza 9

6 **pittie**: move to pity.
9 **named**: i.e. called her own.

Stanza 10

5 **retyre**: return.

Stanza 11

5 **tender**: cherish.
6 **durance**: imprisonment.

Stanza 12

1 **aduize**: consider.
2 **forlore**: abandoned.
5 **Bequeath'd**: entrusted.   **forslacked**: neglected.
8 **loos**: renown. The connection with **losse** (8) stresses
Calidore's disgrace.

14

But first, ere I doe his aduentures tell,
  In this exploite, me needeth to declare,
  What did betide to the faire *Pastorell*,
  During his absence left in heauy care,
  Through daily mourning, and nightly misfare:
  Yet did that auncient matrone all she might,
  To cherish her with all things choice and rare;
  And her owne handmayd, that *Melissa* hight,
Appointed to attend her dewly day and night.

15

Who in a morning, when this Mayden faire
  Was dighting her, hauing her snowy brest
  As yet not laced, nor her golden haire
  Into their comely tresses dewly drest,
  Chaunst to espy vpon her yuory chest
  The rosie marke, which she remembred well
  That litle Infant had, which forth she kest,
  The daughter of her Lady *Claribell*,
The which she bore, the whiles in prison she did dwell.

16

Which well auizing, streight she gan to cast
  In her conceiptfull mynd, that this faire Mayd
  Was that same infant, which so long sith past
  She in the open fields had loosely layd
  To fortunes spoile, vnable it to ayd.
  So full of ioy, streight forth she ran in hast
  Vnto her mistresse, being halfe dismayd,
  To tell her, how the heauens had her graste,
To saue her chylde, which in misfortunes mouth was plaste.

17

The sober mother seeing such her mood,
  Yet knowing not, what meant that sodaine thro,
  Askt her, how mote her words be vnderstood,
  And what the matter was, that mou'd her so.
  My liefe (sayd she) ye know, that long ygo,
  Whilest ye in durance dwelt, ye to me gaue
  A little mayde, the which ye chylded tho;
  The same againe if now ye list to haue,
The same is yonder Lady, whom high God did saue.

18

Much was the Lady troubled at that speach,
  And gan to question streight how she it knew,
  Most certaine markes, (sayd she) do me it teach,
  For on her brest I with these eyes did vew
  The litle purple rose, which thereon grew,
  Whereof her name ye then to her did giue.
  Besides her countenaunce, and her likely hew,
  Matched with equall yeares, do surely prieue
That yond same is your daughter sure, which yet doth liue.

19

The matrone stayd no lenger to enquire,
  But forth in hast ran to the straunger Mayd;
  Whom catching greedily for great desire,
  Rent vp her brest, and bosome open layd,
  In which that rose she plainely saw displayd.
  Then her embracing twixt her armes twaine,
  She long so held, and softly weeping sayd;
  And liuest thou my daughter now againe?
And art thou yet aliue, whom dead I long did faine?

20

Tho further asking her of sundry things,
  And times comparing with their accidents,
  She found at last by very certaine signes,
  And speaking markes of passed monuments,
  That this young Mayd, whom chance to her presents
  Is her owne daughter, her owne infant deare.
  Tho wondring long at those so straunge euents,
  A thousand times she her embraced nere,
With many a ioyfull kisse, and many a melting teare.

Stanza 14
4 **care**: grief.
5 **misfare**: sorrow.
8 **Melissa**: Gk bee, to suggest the flower to which she is attracted; or so named as a nurse and goddess of childbirth: 'a woman, who with hir sister *Amalthea* nouryshed Jupiter' (Cooper, 1565).

Stanza 15
2 **dighting**: dressing.

Stanza 16
1 **auizing**: observing.
2 **conceiptfull**: perceptive.
9 **in misfortunes mouth**: cf. fortunes (5) and 'chance' (20.5). Fortune is finally related to God's providence, 17.9.

Stanza 17
2 **thro**: throe, anguish or agony of emotion. The sense, pain of childbirth, is relevant since Pastorella is now 'born' again.
7 **chylded**: gave birth to.   **tho**: then.

Stanza 18
6 The name is not revealed.
7 **likely hew**: similar appearance.
8 **Matched with equall yeares**: i.e. their ages correspond.

Stanza 19
9 **faine**: imagine.

Stanza 20
2 **accidents**: occurrences.
4 **passed monuments**: records of things passed.

21

Who euer is the mother of one chylde,
  Which hauing thought long dead, she fyndes aliue,
  Let her by proofe of that, which she hath fylde
  In her owne breast, this mothers ioy descriue:
  For other none such passion can contriue
  In perfect forme, as this good Lady felt,
  When she so faire a daughter saw suruiue,
  As *Pastorella* was, that nigh she swelt
For passing ioy, which did all into pitty melt.

22

Thence running forth vnto her loued Lord,
  She vnto him recounted, all that fell:
  Who ioyning ioy with her in one accord,
  Acknowledg'd for his owne faire *Pastorell*.
  There leaue we them in ioy, and let vs tell
  Of *Calidore*, who seeking all this while
  That monstrous Beast by finall force to quell,
  Through euery place, with restlesse paine and toile
Him follow'd, by the tract of his outragious spoile.

23

Through all estates he found that he had past,
  In which he many massacres had left,
  And to the Clergy now was come at last;
  In which such spoile, such hauocke, and such theft
  He wrought, that thence all goodnesse he bereft,
  That endlesse were to tell. The Elfin Knight,
  Who now no place besides vnsought had left,
  At length into a Monastere did light,
Where he him found despoyling all with maine and might.

24

Into their cloysters now he broken had,
  Through which the Monckes he chaced here and there,
  And them pursu'd into their dortours sad,
  And searched all their cels and secrets neare;
  In which what filth and ordure did appeare,
  Were yrkesome to report; yet that foule Beast
  Nought sparing them, the more did tosse and teare,
  And ransacke all their dennes from most to least,
Regarding nought religion, nor their holy heast.

25

From thence into the sacred Church he broke,
  And robd the Chancell, and the deskes downe threw,
  And Altars fouled, and blasphemy spoke,
  And th'Images for all their goodly hew,
  Did cast to ground, whilest none was them to rew;
  So all confounded and disordered there.
  But seeing *Calidore*, away he flew,
  Knowing his fatall hand by former feare;
But he him fast pursuing, soone approched neare.

26

Him in a narrow place he ouertooke,
  And fierce assailing forst him turne againe:
  Sternely he turnd againe, when he him strooke
  With his sharpe steele, and ran at him amaine
  With open mouth, that seemed to containe
  A full good pecke within the vtmost brim,
  All set with yron teeth in raunges twaine,
  That terrifide his foes, and armed him,
Appearing like the mouth of *Orcus* griesly grim.

706

Stanza 21
3 **fylde**: felt; or the past tense of 'file': recorded.
4 **descriue**: describe.
5 **contriue**: come to understand; imagine.
6 **perfect forme**: the perfect pattern or idea.
8 **swelt**: swooned.
9 **passing**: surpassing.

Stanza 22
7 **quell**: kill.
9 **tract**: track. **spoile**: plundering.

Stanza 23
1 **all estates**: all sorts of people, or specifically the three estates: Knights, Commons, and Clergy.
8 to 25.9 The possible references to Henry VIII's suppression of the monasteries, Puritan extremism, and the corrupt popish clergy are examined in *Var.* vi 265–8, 382–8. A reference to the Puritans is supported by Jonson's remark: 'By ye Blating beast the Puritans were understood' (*Works* i 137). S. may have in mind the concluding episode of *Piers Plowman*: Holichurch is besieged from without by Antichrist and betrayed from within by false prelates.
8 **Monastere**: the O.F. form of monastery associates the hideout with the monster. Tonkin (1972) 152 sees an allusion to the dangers of religious controversy.

Stanza 24
3 **dortours**: dormitories.
4 **secrets neare**: adjoining secret places.
6 **yrkesome**: loathsome.
9 **heast**: vow.

Stanza 25
1–6 In *View* 163, S. urges that churches be rebuilt: 'For the outward show, assure yourself, doth greatly draw the rude people to the reverencing and frequenting thereof; and whatever some of our late too nice fools say there is nothing in the seemly form and comely order of the church.' **Chancell**: the eastern section where the communion table is placed.
deskes: stalls or choir-seats. **blasphemy**: cf. the many-headed Dragon in Rev. 13.5 'that spake great things and blasphemies'.

Stanza 26
3 **Sternely**: fiercely.
7 Cf. the beast in Daniel's vision, Dan. 7.7. **raunges**: rows.
9 **Orcus**: Pluto, god of the infernal regions; see II xii 41.7. 'It is sometime taken for hell' (Cooper, 1565), as here. Cf. the Tiger with its mouth 'wide gaping like hell gate' (x 34.6), and the brigand's 'hellish dens' (xi 3.1) from both of which Calidore rescued Pastorella. The present battle marks Calidore's third and final defeat over hell.

27

And therein were a thousand tongs empight,
Of sundry kindes, and sundry quality,
Some were of dogs, that barked day and night,
And some of cats, that wrawling still did cry,
And some of Beares, that groynd continually,
And some of Tygres, that did seeme to gren,
And snar at all, that euer passed by:
But most of them were tongues of mortall men,
Which spake reprochfully, not caring where nor when.

28

And them amongst were mingled here and there,
The tongues of Serpents with three forked stings,
That spat out poyson and gore bloudy gere
At all, that came within his rauenings,
And spake licentious words, and hatefull things
Of good and bad alike, of low and hie;
Ne Kesars spared he a whit, nor Kings,
But either blotted them with infamie,
Or bit them with his banefull teeth of iniury.

29

But *Calidore* thereof no whit afrayd,
Rencountred him with so impetuous might,
That th'outrage of his violence he stayd,
And bet abacke, threatning in vaine to bite,
And spitting forth the poyson of his spight,
That fomed all about his bloody iawes.
Tho rearing vp his former feete on hight,
He rampt vpon him with his rauenous pawes,
As if he would haue rent him with his cruell clawes.

30

But he right well aware, his rage to ward,
Did cast his shield atweene, and therewithall
Putting his puissaunce forth, pursu'd so hard,
That backeward he enforced him to fall,
And being downe, ere he new helpe could call,
His shield he on him threw, and fast downe held,
Like as a bullocke, that in bloudy stall
Of butchers balefull hand to ground is feld,
Is forcibly kept downe, till he be throughly queld.

31

Full cruelly the Beast did rage and rore,
To be downe held, and maystred so with might,
That he gan fret and fome out bloudy gore,
Striuing in vaine to rere him selfe vpright.
For still the more he stroue, the more the Knight
Did him suppresse, and forcibly subdew;
That made him almost mad for fell despight.
He grind, hee bit, he scratcht, he venim threw,
And fared like a feend, right horrible in hew.

32

Or like the hell-borne *Hydra*, which they faine
That great *Alcides* whilome ouerthrew,
After that he had labourd long in vaine,
To crop his thousand heads, the which still new
Forth budded, and in greater number grew.
Such was the fury of this hellish Beast,
Whilest *Calidore* him vnder him downe threw;
Who nathemore his heauy load release,
But aye the more he rag'd, the more his powre increast.

33

Tho when the Beast saw, he mote nought auaile,
By force, he gan his hundred tongues apply,
And sharpely at him to reuile and raile,
With bitter termes of shamefull infamy;
Oft interlacing many a forged lie,
Whose like he neuer once did speake, nor heare,
Nor euer thought thing so vnworthily:
Yet did he nought for all that him forbeare,
But strained him so streightly, that he chokt him neare.

Stanza 27

1   **empight**: placed.
4   **wrawling**: caterwauling.   **still**: ceaselessly.
5   **groynd**: growled.
6   **gren**: show their teeth in anger.
7   **snar**: snarl.
9   **reprochfully**: abusively.

Stanza 28

3   **gere**: foul matter.
9   **iniury**: offensive speech, insult, calumny.

Stanza 29

2   **Rencountred**: encountered in return.
3   **outrage**: fury.
7–9   The Beast assumes an heraldic posture.   **former**:
fore.   **on hight**: on high.   **rampt**: reared up on his hind
legs.

Stanza 30

On his use of the shield, see 35.9n.
1   **aware**: wary.

Stanza 31

9   **fared**: acted.

Stanza 32

The Hydra and the Blatant Beast are both offsprings of Typhon
and Echidna. On the Hydra as Invidia or evil speaking whom
only death may slay, see V xii 29–32n. As Tonkin (1972) 270
notes, the comparison 'cast[s] an ominous shadow over
Calidore's struggle against the Beast'. See stanza 35 for a
second comparison to Hercules.
1   **hell-borne**: because she dwells in hell, Virgil, *Aen.*
vi 576–7.
4   **thousand**: S.'s extreme number for its many-headedness.
8   **nathemore**: nevermore.   **release**: removed.

Stanza 33

1   **auaile**: prevail.
8   **forbeare**: spare.
9   **strained**: pressed down.   **streightly**: tightly.

34

At last when as he found his force to shrincke,
　And rage to quaile, he tooke a muzzell strong
Of surest yron, made with many a lincke;
　Therewith he mured vp his mouth along,
　And therein shut vp his blasphemous tong,
For neuer more defaming gentle Knight,
　Or vnto louely Lady doing wrong:
　And thereunto a great long chaine he tight,
With which he drew him forth, euen in his own despight.

35

Like as whylome that strong *Tirynthian* swaine,
　Brought forth with him the dreadfull dog of hell,
Against his will fast bound in yron chaine,
　And roring horribly, did him compell
　To see the hatefull sunne, that he might tell
To griesly *Pluto*, what on earth was donne,
　And to the other damned ghosts, which dwell
　For aye in darkenesse, which day light doth shonne.
So led this Knight his captyue with like conquest wonne.

36

Yet greatly did the Beast repine at those
　Straunge bands, whose like till then he neuer bore,
Ne euer any durst till then impose,
　And chauffed inly, seeing now no more
　Him liberty was left aloud to rore:
Yet durst he not draw backe; nor once withstand
　The proued powre of noble *Calidore*,
　But trembled vnderneath his mighty hand,
And like a fearefull dog him followed through the land.

37

Him through all Faery land he follow'd so,
　As if he learned had obedience long,
That all the people where so he did go,
　Out of their townes did round about him throng,
　To see him leade that Beast in bondage strong,
And seeing it, much wondred at the sight;
　And all such persons, as he earst did wrong,
　Reioyced much to see his captiue plight,
And much admyr'd the Beast, but more admyr'd the Knight.

38

Thus was this Monster by the maystring might
　Of doughty *Calidore*, supprest and tamed,
That neuer more he mote endammadge wight
　With his vile tongue, which many had defamed,
　And many causelesse caused to be blamed:
So did he eeke long after this remaine,
　Vntill that, whether wicked fate so framed,
　Or fault of men, he broke his yron chaine,
And got into the world at liberty againe.

39

Thenceforth more mischiefe and more scath he wrought
　To mortall men, then he had done before;
Ne euer could by any more be brought
　Into like bands, ne maystred any more:
　Albe that long time after *Calidore*,
The good Sir *Pelleas* him tooke in hand,
　And after him Sir *Lamoracke* of yore,
　And all his brethren borne in Britaine land;
708 Yet none of them could euer bring him into band.

40

So now he raungeth through the world againe,
　And rageth sore in each degree and state;
Ne any is, that may him now restraine,
　He growen is so great and strong of late,
　Barking and biting all that him doe bate,
Albe they worthy blame, or cleare of crime:
　Ne spareth he most learned wits to rate,
　Ne spareth he the gentle Poets rime,
But rends without regard of person or of time.

Stanza 34

1　**shrincke**: collapse, fail.
2　**quaile**: lessen, fail.
4　**mured**: closed.　**along**: i.e. along its whole length.
6　To prevent him from evermore, etc.
8　**tight**: tied.
9　**in his own despight**: in defiance of him.

Stanza 35

The **dog of hell** is Cerberus who sired the Blatant Beast, i 8.1–3. Hercules is called the **Tirynthian swaine** because he was born in Tiryns. Chaining Cerberus and dragging him from hell to the upper world was the most difficult of his labours; as such, it is appropriately compared to the last labour of S.'s knight. While Hercules's battle with the Hydra, described in 32, was not an entire victory because only death may slay Invidia, the descent into hell to slay Cerberus was interpreted as a victory over death. Sandys (1632) 343 interprets Cerberus as the grave.
9　**with like conquest**: because Hercules chained Cerberus without force of arms even as Calidore subdues the Blatant Beast with only his shield and an iron muzzle.

Stanza 37

9　**admyr'd**: wondered at.

Stanza 38

3　**endammadge**: injure.
7–9　Cf. Archimago's escape (I xii 36.1–5, II i 1.7–9) and the escape of 'that olde serpent, which is the devil and Satan' (Rev. 20. 1–3).

Stanza 39

Shakespeare, Sonnet lxx 12, speaks of envy as 'evermore enlarg'd'.
1　**scath**: harm.
3　**by any more**: i.e. again.
6–8　Referring to the knights of Arthur's Round Table. **Pelleas** is named 'the good knyght' in Malory 1242. **Lamoracke** encounters Palomydes riding in pursuit of the 'Questynge Beste' (484).

Stanza 40

2　**in each degree**: against every social class.
5　**bate**: bait: attack; beat back.
6　**Albe**: whether.

41
Ne may this homely verse, of many meanest,
  Hope to escape his venemous despite,
  More then my former writs, all were they clearest
  From blamefull blot, and free from all that wite,
  With which some wicked tongues did it backebite,
  And bring into a mighty Peres displeasure,
  That neuer so deserued to endite.
  Therfore do you my rimes keep better measure,
And seeke to please, that now is counted wisemens threasure.

FINIS.

Stanza 41
S. concludes the second section of his poem, as he began it,
with a reference to the blame his writings have received from
one of the Queen's ministers. The **mighty Pere** is generally
taken to be Lord Burghley in the light of S.'s apparent attack
upon him in *Hub*. and *Ruines of Time*.
3   **writs**: writings.   **clearest**] 'cleanest', sugg. Hughes
(1715) for the rhyme.
4   **wite**: blame. Cf. Calidore's aloof response to blame at
iii 16.5–6.
7   **neuer so deserued to endite**: i.e. my former writings
never deserved to be indicted or accused of offence.
9   **seeke . . . threasure**: seek only to please; even wise men
find that is their treasure in a world infected by the Blatant
Beast. Cf. *L.R.* where S. refers scornfully to 'the vse of these
dayes, seeing all things accounted by their showes, and
nothing esteemed of, that is not delightfull and pleasing to
commune sence'.

The Mutabilitie Cantos

The full title of the *Two Cantos of Mutabilitie*, as given below, immediately raises the questions: are they meant to stand as a fragment? are they a fragment of another book of the *Faerie Queene*, perhaps its 'allegorical core'? and how do they relate to the rest of the poem? From vi 37 it would seem clear that the *Cantos* belong to the poem, although this stanza shows a curious reversal: the poet says, in effect, 'if it were not inappropriate for a chivalric poem such as the *Faerie Queene*, I would tell a story about Arlo hill'; and then he proceeds to do just that. Lewis (1936) 353 suggests that we have in the *Cantos* the core of a book about change and permanence without the fringe. However, it is hard to see how any book could contain such a magnificent, two canto-length pageant of the gods, or how it could be incorporated in a poem that treats the virtues and is written in praise of Gloriana. Frye (1963) 71 writes: 'What we can see is that the *Mutabilitie Cantos* are certainly not a fragment: they constitute a single beautifully shaped poem that could not have had a more logical beginning, development, and end.' For him it is impossible 'that in their present form these cantos could have been the "core" of a seventh book. . . . The poem brings us to the poet's "Sabbath's sight" after his six great efforts of creation, and there is nothing which at any point can be properly described as "unperfite".' In contrast, Fowler (1964) 57–9 offers strong numerological reasons for seeing the *Cantos* as part of an unfinished seventh book, noting that seven is the number of the mutable world and also of constancy.

The *Cantos* are usually regarded now as an independent philosophical and cosmological poem that relates time to eternity, change to permanence, and mortality to God's providential scheme. They belong to the poem as its epilogue or coda. Blissett (1964) 26 regards them 'as a detached retrospective commentary on the poem as a whole, forming as they do a satisfactory conclusion to a foreshortened draft, a stopping place at which, after a seriatim reading, can be made a pleasing analysis of all'. More than a coda, then, they are central to the poem, a final and clarifying vision of all that has gone before. Williams (1952) 128 refers to them as 'the culmination of the poem as it now stands, both unifying and illuminating it'. Evans (1970) 237 comments that they 'bring to the surface . . . much of the underlying mythology and meaning of the poem and make the only explicit comment on the theme of the whole'. Holland (1968) argues that the cyclical vision of history expressed in the *Cantos* is central to the form of the whole poem.

Earlier investigation of the sources and philosophical significance of the *Cantos* pointed to classical, medieval and Renaissance works, both learned and popular. Now it is generally allowed that S. draws on no one intellectual tradition but rather upon many. Zitner (1968) 29 concludes rightly that 'it is probably misleading . . . to speak of the "sources" or the "philosophy" of the *Cantos*. Both terms imply a modern particularity and personalism that Spenser would have found dismaying.' Yet study of these traditions helps to establish the particular literary 'presence' of the *Cantos*. S.'s chief literary model is Ovid, as Cumming (1931) and Nelson (1963) 297–304 show in detail. However, it is not that he borrows extensively from the *Metamorphoses* but that he transcends and parodies it. Zitner 32 notes: 'the theme of the *Metamorphoses* is not change, but persistence' while in S. 'Nature's verdict reconciles the alteration of forms with the divine constancy that intends them. This is a truly archaic use of mythology, for it retains myth's earliest function as an emblem of the mysteries.' Holahan (1976) views the Cantos as a brief epic which parodies the Ovidian vision of mutability.

That S.'s art achieves its fullest expression and perfection in the *Cantos* is generally allowed. Lewis (1936) 357 observes that 'all the powers of the poet are more happily united than ever before; the sublime and the ridiculous, the rarified beauties of august mythology and the homely glimpses of daily life in the procession of the months, combine to give us an unsurpassed impression of the harmonious complexity of the world'. All readers learn to appreciate the poet's delight in exercising his craft, his exuberance, and his vitality. The *Cantos* are marked throughout by the energy registered in the earlier line, 'O what an endlesse worke haue I in hand'. If the exhausted reader feels dismay at the length of the poem and the greater length needed to complete it, the poet responds only with joy.

Typically Spenserian is the careful structuring of the narrative. Cheney (1966) 246 notes the triadic narrative pattern – epic, pastoral, and didactic synthesis, which is 'vastly enriched and complicated by a delicately ironic balance of tone within each of these three sections'. Berger (1968) 148 finds a threefold pattern which traces S.'s historical consciousness as it develops 'from pagan through medieval modes of imagination to the lyric (and renaissance) present'. Others have commented on the two narrative movements, the paralleling of the attempt by the foolish God, Faunus, to see Cynthia naked and Mutabilitie's attempt to strip Cynthia and Jove of power: see vi 42.7–9n. There is also a parallel to Calidore's spying on the naked Graces: see vi 46.6–9n. In these narratives, S.'s especial power is his ability to surround his fiction with the most profound implications concerning man's life in time and eternity and yet preserve that fiction in a simple, clear, poetic image.

The argument of the *Cantos* is central within an extended tradition of medieval and Renaissance thought, and the more that tradition is studied, the more central S. is seen to be. Yet his work never seems derivative: it is as fresh and original as though he were the first to write on mutability. This quality of his verse is illustrated in his fashioning of Nature. Each detail may be traced to originals and yet it is as though we see her for the first time, so distinctly is she characterized from the moment when she enters veiled, with flowers blooming before her feet to the final moment when, all open to sight, she delivers her judgment 'with chearefull view' and then mysteriously vanishes 'whither no man whist'.

The pageant of the months and seasons is the symbolic centre of the *Cantos*. Hawkins (1961) notes the markedly symmetrical structure of the two cantos: in each, an abstract debate is followed by a pictorial episode, the Faunus story in the one and the pageant in the other. The former led to the loss of the paradise of Arlo Hill and the latter shows how that paradise is regained by Nature's coming. 'We begin to suspect that Mutabilitie is the victim of a vast dramatic irony. This is, in fact, the case; but Spenser is a poet, not a philosopher: he gives us his essential realities in images, not arguments' (p. 87). These images are presented in the pageants which show Providence at work in the cycle of natural time, and the labour through which man is related to Nature. Since the calendar shows eternal purpose incarnate in time, the evidence presented by Mutabilitie refutes her: 'All things change, but they change according to a providential law, the law of love which guides them to the perfection of their first estate. Thus they undo the fall, the work of Mutabilitie' (p. 98). From his analysis of the images of time in the *F.Q.*, Wilson (1974) 63 concludes that 'the forwardness of time in which the moral dimension of human action unfolds against the judgment of a Providential vision is both the central concept of Spenser's time-sense and the governing concern that links, in a significant unity of thought, the diverse parts of Spenser's work'.

The pageant leads inevitably to Nature's verdict, which it fully supports. The 'deep obscurity' of that verdict is noted by Lewis (1936) 356:

> It is a magnificent instance of Spenser's last-moment withdrawal from dualism. The universe is a battlefield in which Change and Permanence contend. And these are evil and good – the gods, the divine order, stand for Permanence; Change is rebellion and corruption. But behind this endless contention arises the deeper truth – that Change is but the mode in which Permanence expresses itself, that Reality (like Adonis) 'is eterne in mutabilitie', and that the more Mutability succeeds the more she fails.

The verdict is called a Christian paradox by Ellrodt (1960) 70. Fowler (1964) 229 shows how it is mysteriously ambivalent:

> At first she even seems to find for the plaintiff.... Moreover, though Jupiter's power is confirmed, yet it is revealed to be only a temporary and partial jurisdiction, within a larger scheme of things. By one of those fine mythological *peripeteias* which are Spenser's greatest contribution to

our literature, the judgement of Nature discloses that Jupiter's authority, in spite of its supremacy in all that has gone before, is nevertheless neither ultimate nor unqualified.

As a verdict, it is both simple and profound: although judgment is made, there is no rejection but only an affirmation. Jove's order is upheld but so is Mutabilitie's, and beyond both there is the changeless order of Eternity.

Canto viii

While the two final stanzas are named as the two opening stanzas of another canto, it is difficult to regard them other than as a comment on what has gone before, and almost impossible to allow that anything could come after. That an eighth canto should complete the seventh is suggested by Hawkins (1961) 99: 'In the eighth canto, we look beyond creation and its weeks to the sabbath which is both the seventh day of rest and the eighth day of resurrection, the glory of which Gloriana's feast is but a type.'

There have been various and conflicting interpretations of the concluding stanza. Jones (1930) 307 finds 'spiritual affirmation'. Watkins (1950) 72 finds instead 'humble and suppliant prayer, desire rather than affirmation'. If it were prayer, however, the lines would be addressed to God. Berger (1968) 172 finds 'a slow and guarded turning *toward* prayer and faith'. On the other hand, Greene (1963) 322–3 finds a 'terrible pathos': 'If faith is indeed a refuge here, it is a lonely and bitter one.'

It is peculiarly difficult for modern readers not to find in the concluding stanza a retraction or some final farewell to the vanities of the world. For all we know, however, that prayer for rest may mark the rest he seeks in *Amor.* 80, after which he vows to begin again. The moment corresponds to that in Book I when the Red Cross Knight sees the holy Jerusalem: overcome by weariness of the world, he desires to keep that vision. The voice of Contemplation that urges him back to the world might also persuade the poet to resume his labours. There is no evidence in the *Cantos* themselves that the Muses have deserted him.

TWO CANTOS
OF
MVTABILITIE:
Which, both for Forme and Matter, appeare
to be parcell of some following Booke of the
FAERIE QVEENE,
(·∴·)
VNDER THE LEGEND
OF
Constancie.
Neuer before imprinted.

Canto VI.

Proud Change (not pleasd, in mortall things,
beneath the Moone, to raigne)
Pretends, as well of Gods, as Men,
to be the Soueraine.

1

WHat man that sees the euer-whirling wheele
Of *Change,* the which all mortall things doth sway,
But that therby doth find, and plainly feele,
How *MVTABILITY* in them doth play
Her cruell sports, to many mens decay?
Which that to all may better yet appeare,
I will rehearse that whylome I heard say,
How she at first her selfe began to reare,
Gainst all the Gods, and th'empire sought from them to beare.

2

But first, here falleth fittest to vnfold
Her antique race and linage ancient,
As I haue found it registred of old,
In *Faery* Land mongst records permanent:
She was, to weet, a daughter by descent
Of those old *Titans,* that did whylome striue
With *Saturnes* sonne for heauens regiment.
Whom, though high *Ioue* of kingdome did. depriue,
Yet many of their stemme long after did surviue.

3

And many of them, afterwards obtain'd
Great power of *Ioue,* and high authority;
As *Hecaté,* in whose almighty hand,
He plac't all rule and principality,
To be by her disposed diuersly,
To Gods, and men, as she them list diuide:
And drad *Bellona,* that doth sound on hie
Warres and allarums vnto Nations wide,
That makes both heauen and earth to tremble at her pride.

4

So likewise did this *Titanesse* aspire,
Rule and dominion to her selfe to gaine;
That as a Goddesse, men might her admire,
And heauenly honours yield, as to them twaine.
At first, on earth she sought it to obtaine;
Where she such proofe and sad examples shewed
Of her great power, to many ones great paine,
That not men onely (whom she soone subdewed)
714 But eke all other creatures, her bad dooings rewed.

Title
The **Two Cantos of Mutabilitie** first appeared in the *1609*
folio edition published by Matthew Lownes. It is not known
what authority there is for the title, the division and numbering
of the cantos (vi, vii, viii ('vnperfite'), and the running title,
'The Seuenth Booke'. That Constancy should be the subject
of a book seems inevitable. Although the virtue is named only
once before in the poem to describe Guyon's and the Palmer's
state as they prepare to enter the Bower of Bliss, it is implied in
the virtue of each hero. Cf. Elyot, *Governour* III xix:
'That man which in childehode is brought up in sondry vertues,
if eyther by nature, or els by custome, he be nat induced to be
all way constant and stable, so that he meve nat for any affection,
griefe, or displeasure, all his vertues will shortely decaye.' On
seven as the number of Constancy and Mutability, see Fowler
(1964) 58. The number is most appropriate as the seventh day
of the week and the day of rest that rounds out the six days of
labour.

Argument
1   **Change**: Mutabilitie.
2   It was commonly assumed that **beneath the Moone** all
things are mutable while the heaven above remains immutable.
3   **Pretends**: claims.

Stanzas 1–6
Described by Berger (1968) 149–53 as a poem which presents
the themes, attitudes, and problems treated later.

Stanza 1
1–5   The **wheele** is usually Fortune's: see, e.g., V x 20.7.
sway: rule.   **decay**: downfall.
7   **rehearse**: relate.

Stanza 2
5–9   On the war between **Ioue** and the **Titans**, see 27, 33 and
II vii 41.6*n*.   **regiment**: rule; kingdom.   **stemme**: stock.

Stanza 3
3   **Hecaté**: an infernal deity and Titaness by birth whose
power extends over heaven and hell; see I i 43.3*n*. S. follows
Hesiod, *Theog.* 411–52.
7–9   **Bellona**: the Roman goddess of war; see III ix 22.1
(*1590*); for her powers, see 32.4–8 below. Lotspeich (1932) 42
suggests that her role as a Titan is derived from *V.B.* xv in
which Du Bellay's 'la sœur du grand Typhée' is taken to mean
Bellona.

Stanza 4
3   **admire**: wonder at.
4   **twaine**: Hecate and Bellona.

5

For, she the face of earthly things so changed,
  That all which Nature had establisht first
  In good estate, and in meet order ranged,
  She did pervert, and all their statutes burst:
  And all the worlds faire frame (which none yet durst
  Of Gods or men to alter or misguide)
  She alter'd quite, and made them all accurst
That God had blest; and did at first prouide
In that still happy state for euer to abide.

6

Ne shee the lawes of Nature onely brake,
  But eke of Iustice, and of Policie;
  And wrong of right, and bad of good did make,
  And death for life exchanged foolishlie:
  Since which, all liuing wights haue learn'd to die,
  And all this world is woxen daily worse.
  O pittious worke of *MVTABILITIE*!
By which, we all are subiect to that curse,
And death in stead of life haue sucked from our Nurse.

7

And now, when all the earth she thus had brought
  To her behest, and thralled to her might,
  She gan to cast in her ambitious thought,
  T'attempt the empire of the heauens hight,
  And *Ioue* himselfe to shoulder from his right.
  And first, she past the region of the ayre,
  And of the fire, whose substance thin and slight,
  Made no resistance, ne could her contraire,
But ready passage to her pleasure did prepaire.

8

Thence, to the Circle of the Moone she clambe,
  Where *Cynthia* raignes in euerlasting glory,
  To whose bright shining palace straight she came,
  All fairely deckt with heauens goodly story;
  Whose siluer gates (by which there sate an hory
  Old aged Sire, with hower-glasse in hand,
  Hight *Tyme*) she entred, were he liefe or sory:
  Ne staide till she the highest stage had scand,
Where *Cynthia* did sit, that neuer still did stand.

9

Her sitting on an Iuory throne shee found,
  Drawne of two steeds, th'one black, the other white,
  Environd with tenne thousand starres around,
  That duly her attended day and night;
  And by her side, there ran her Page, that hight
  Vesper, whom we the Euening-starre intend:
  That with his Torche, still twinkling like twylight,
  Her lightened all the way where she should wend,
And ioy to weary wandring trauailers did lend:

---

its cause, presumably because change first took place in man and led to his fall. At 11.5 **Mutabilitie** laments man's fall. The idea of Nature here is quite different from that at her triumphant appearance in the next canto. Lewis (1936) 354 writes: 'She [Mutabilitie] is, in fact, Corruption, and since corruption . . . came in with the Fall, Spenser practically identifies his Titaness with sin, or makes her the force behind the sin of Adam.'

Stanza 5
3 **estate**: state.
4 **pervert**: overturn, the etymological sense. **statutes**: decrees.
5 **frame**: applied to the heavens, earth and universe regarded as structures fashioned by God (*OED* 7).
9 **still**: ever, continually.

Stanza 6
2 **Policie**: government; the art of prudent statecraft.
6 As V Proem 1.7–9.
9 **our Nurse**: Nature (5.2); cf. *Daph*. 337: 'Nature nurse of euery liuing thing.'

Stanza 7
3 **cast**: resolve.
4–5 She imitates the Titans who sought 'To scale the skyes, and put *Ioue* from his right' (III vii 47.5). **attempt**: attack, assault.
6–7 **ayre** is the middle region; the region of **fire** above is next under the moon; and beyond is 'the purest sky' (23.7) of the Empyrean which is not open to mortals.
8 **contraire**: oppose.

Stanzas 8–10
S. borrows from Ovid's account of the ascent of the proud Phaeton into the heavens to claim the chariot of the Sun (*Met*. ii 1f): e.g. the shining palace with its decorated gates supported by pillars, the god on his throne surrounded by attendants, and the assembly that discusses the threat to order. See Cumming (1931) 243–5.

Stanza 8
1 **Circle**: sphere.
4 **story**: 'any work of pictorial or sculptural art containing figures' (*OED* sb.[1] 8). The figures may refer to the constellations.
5–7 **Tyme** belongs here because the moon marks the boundary between the temporal and eternal worlds; cf. Arg.1–2.
liefe or sory: willing or unwilling.
8 **stage**: celestial station or 'seat' (12.1). **scand**: climbed.
9 Alluding to the continual increase and decrease of the moon. There is witty paradox in the conjunction of **sit** (enthroned in authority) and **stand** (remain) and in the contradiction of 'never moving–ever moving'.

Stanza 9
2 The black and white steeds refer to aspects of the moon, as in Boccaccio, *Gen. Deor*. IV xvi, and Comes (1616) III xvii (where they appear as an emblem).
6–8 As Milton's Hesperus 'that led / The starry host, rode brightest, till the moon . . . unveiled her peerless light', and her office is 'to bring / Twilight upon the earth' (*P.L.* iv 605–8, ix 49–50). **intend**: call.

Change, which is the consequence of man's fall, is regarded as

10

That when the hardy *Titanesse* beheld
  The goodly building of her Palace bright,
  Made of the heauens substance, and vp-held
  With thousand Crystall pillors of huge hight,
  Shee gan to burne in her ambitious spright,
  And t'envie her that in such glorie raigned.
  Eftsoones she cast by force and tortious might,
  Her to displace; and to her selfe to haue gained
The kingdome of the Night, and waters by her wained.

11

Boldly she bid the Goddesse downe descend,
  And let her selfe into that Ivory throne;
  For, shee her selfe more worthy thereof wend,
  And better able it to guide alone:
  Whether to men, whose fall she did bemone,
  Or vnto Gods, whose state she did maligne,
  Or to th'infernall Powers, her need giue lone
  Of her faire light, and bounty most benigne,
Her selfe of all that rule shee deemed most condigne.

12

But shee that had to her that soueraigne seat
  By highest *Ioue* assign'd, therein to beare
  Nights burning lamp, regarded not her threat,
  Ne yielded ought for fauour or for feare;
  But with sterne countenaunce and disdainfull cheare,
  Bending her horned browes, did put her back:
  And boldly blaming her for comming there,
  Bade her attonce from heauens coast to pack,
Or at her perill bide the wrathfull Thunders wrack.

13

Yet nathemore the *Giantesse* forbare:
  But boldly preacing-on, raught forth her hand
  To pluck her downe perforce from off her chaire;
  And there-with lifting vp her golden wand,
  Threatned to strike her if she did with-stand.
  Where-at the starres, which round about her blazed,
  And eke the Moones bright wagon, still did stand,
  All beeing with so bold attempt amazed,
And on her vncouth habit and sterne looke still gazed.

14

Meane-while, the lower World, which nothing knew
  Of all that chaunced here, was darkned quite;
  And eke the heauens, and all the heauenly crew
  Of happy wights, now vnpurvaide of light,
  Were much afraid, and wondred at that sight;
  Fearing least *Chaos* broken had his chaine,
  And brought againe on them eternall night:
  But chiefely *Mercury*, that next doth raigne,
Ran forth in haste, vnto the king of Gods to plaine.

15

All ran together with a great out-cry,
  To *Ioues* faire Palace, fixt in heauens hight;
  And beating at his gates full earnestly,
  Gan call to him aloud with all their might,
  To know what meant that suddaine lack of light.
  The father of the Gods when this he heard,
  Was troubled much at their so strange affright,
  Doubting least *Typhon* were againe vprear'd,
Or other his old foes, that once him sorely fear'd.

Stanza 10

5 **burne**: cf. 'cast' (7.3).
7 **tortious**: wrongful, illegal.
9 'The moone and the starres . . . governe the night'
(Ps. 136.9).   **wained**: carried along or drawn, suggested by the moon's wain or chariot and referring to the moon's control over the tides; possibly, 'waned' or 'diminished', suggested by the moon's waning.

Stanza 11

3 **wend**: weened: thought.
5–8 Referring to the three roles of the moon: Diana on earth, Luna in heaven, and Hecate in hell.
5 Mutabilitie's hypocrisy is clear from 5–6 above: through her 'we all are subiect to that curse' (6.8), namely death.
6 **maligne**: envy, regard with malice.
7–8 **lone /Of her faire light**: the moon lends her light to the infernal world when invisible on the earth.
9 **condigne**: worthy.

Stanza 12

5 **cheare**: aspect.
6 **horned browes**: playing on the iconographical detail of the moon's horned crescent: the moon bends her brows in anger.
8 **heauens coast**: as the moon marks the boundary of heaven.
9 **Thunders wrack**: the destruction or vengeance of Jupiter Tonans.

Stanza 13

2–3 She declares her Titanic nature, named from τιταινω, because the Titans reached out their hands in violence (Hesiod, *Theog.* 207–10).   **raught**: reached.   **perforce**: forcibly.   **chaire**: the symbol of the possession of power.
4 The white wand is the symbol of royal power; cf. III iii 49.7. Perhaps **golden** because her power derives from Mammon; cf. Philotime's golden chain of ambition, II vii 46.2.
7 **still did stand**: cf. 8.9; cf. Josh. 10.13: 'and the moone stode stil.'

Stanza 14

1–5 In Du Bartas, *Divine Weekes* I iv p. 37, an eclipse of the moon is said to deprive the heaven and earth of light. **vnpurvaide**: unprovided.
6–7 Cf. the 'hatefull darkenesse' of Chaos, III vi 36.7. Mutabilitie is 'great *Chaos* child' (26.6).   **chaine**: cf. the 'inuiolable bands' by which the 'Almightie maker' binds the elements (IV x 35.3–4).
8–9 **Mercury** is the messenger of the gods. He is identified with the planet Mercury which is **next** because its sphere is next beyond the moon's in the Ptolemaic system.   **plaine**: complain.

Stanza 15

8–9 **Doubting**: fearing.   **Typhon**: or Typhoeus, one of the Titans (Cooper, 1565). See III vii 47.3–9. He waged war against the Olympians so effectively that he forced them to change their shapes and flee (cf. Ovid, *Met.* v 325–31). He was imprisoned by Jove under Mount Aetna. Cf. VI vi 11.8–9 and 29.6 below.   **fear'd**: frightened, made afraid.

16

Eftsoones the sonne of *Maia* forth he sent
  Downe to the Circle of the Moone, to knowe
  The cause of this so strange astonishment,
  And why shee did her wonted course forslowe;
  And if that any were on earth belowe
  That did with charmes or Magick her molest,
  Him to attache, and downe to hell to throwe:
  But, if from heauen it were, then to arrest
The Author, and him bring before his presence prest.

17

The wingd-foot God, so fast his plumes did beat,
  That soone he came where-as the *Titanesse*
  Was striuing with faire *Cynthia* for her seat:
  At whose strange sight, and haughty hardinesse,
  He wondred much, and feared her no lesse.
  Yet laying feare aside to doe his charge,
  At last, he bade her (with bold stedfastnesse)
  Ceasse to molest the Moone to walke at large,
Or come before high *Ioue*, her dooings to discharge.

18

And there-with-all, he on her shoulder laid
  His snaky-wreathed Mace, whose awfull power
  Doth make both Gods and hellish fiends affraid:
  Where-at the *Titanesse* did sternely lower,
  And stoutly answer'd, that in euill hower
  He from his *Ioue* such message to her brought,
  To bid her leaue faire *Cynthias* siluer bower;
  Sith shee his *Ioue* and him esteemed nought,
No more then *Cynthia's* selfe; but all their kingdoms sought.

19

The Heauens Herald staid not to reply,
  But past away, his doings to relate
  Vnto his Lord; who now in th'highest sky,
  Was placed in his principall Estate,
  With all the Gods about him congregate:
  To whom when *Hermes* had his message told,
  It did them all exceedingly amate,
  Saue *Ioue*; who, changing nought his count'nance bold,
Did vnto them at length these speeches wise vnfold;

20

Harken to mee awhile yee heauenly Powers;
  Ye may remember since th'Earths cursed seed
  Sought to assaile the heauens eternall towers,
  And to vs all exceeding feare did breed:
  But how we then defeated all their deed,
  Yee all doe knowe, and them destroied quite;
  Yet not so quite, but that there did succeed
  An off-spring of their bloud, which did alite
Vpon the fruitfull earth, which doth vs yet despite.

21

Of that bad seed is this bold woman bred,
  That now with bold presumption doth aspire
  To thrust faire *Phœbe* from her siluer bed,
  And eke our selues from heauens high Empire,
  If that her might were match to her desire:
  Wherefore, it now behoues vs to advise
  What way is best to driue her to retire;
  Whether by open force, or counsell wise,
Areed ye sonnes of God, as best ye can deuise.

22

So hauing said, he ceast; and with his brow
  (His black eye-brow, whose doomefull dreaded beck
  Is wont to wield the world vnto his vow,
  And euen the highest Powers of heauen to check)
  Made signe to them in their degrees to speake:
  Who straight gan cast their counsell graue and wise.
  Meane-while, th'Earths daughter, thogh she nought did reck
  Of *Hermes* message; yet gan now advise,
What course were best to take in this hot bold emprize.

Stanza 16
1   **the sonne of Maia**: Mercury.
4   **forslowe**: delay.
6   Cf. I vii 34.8–9.
7   **attache**: seize.
9   **prest**: promptly.

Stanza 17
4   **hardinesse**: boldness, effrontery.
8   **to walke at large**: i.e. from moving abroad.
9   **discharge**: clear from the charge; justify.

Stanza 18
2–3   **snaky-wreathed Mace**: on the caduceus and its powers, see II xii 41 and IV iii 42.6–7. Mutabilitie's defiance distinguishes her from **Gods** and **hellish fiends**.

Stanza 19
4   **Estate**: his position of state in the assembly or senate of the gods; cf. 'his soueraine throne' (24.7). Greene (1963) 330 observes that 'Jove is partly the god of Homer and Hesiod, partly the planet, partly the principle of order in the celestial universe, and perhaps a little bit the Christian God'.
7   **amate**: confound.

Stanza 20
2   **since**: the time when.   **th'Earths cursed seed**: the Giants, whose assault upon the Olympians is alluded to frequently in the poem (e.g. III xi 22.8–9) and linked with that of the Titans (cf. 2.5–9 above).
7–9   This story of the new race of giants born of the Earth from the blood of the Giants slain by Jove derives from Ovid, *Met.* i 156–62.   **which** (9) may refer to the Earth though Ovid refers to the new race of giants as *contemptrix superum*.

Stanza 21
3   **Phœbe**: the moon as the sister of Phœbus Apollo.
6   **advise**: consider.
9   **Areed**: declare.   The **sonnes of God** now confront the offspring of the Giants.

Stanza 22
2–4   As Homer, *Iliad* i 528–30; cf. 30.6–8.   **beck**: nod of command.   **wield**: direct, sway.   **vow**: desire.
6   **cast**: deliver.
9   **emprize**: enterprise.

717

23

Eftsoones she thus resolv'd; that whil'st the Gods
　　(After returne of *Hermes* Embassie)
　　Were troubled, and amongst themselues at ods,
　　Before they could new counsels re-allie,
　　To set vpon them in that extasie;
　　And take what fortune time and place would lend:
　　So, forth she rose, and through the purest sky
　　To *Ioues* high Palace straight cast to ascend,
To prosecute her plot: Good on-set boads good end.

24

Shee there arriuing, boldly in did pass;
　　Where all the Gods she found in counsell close,
　　All quite vnarm'd, as then their manner was.
　　At sight of her they suddaine all arose,
　　In great amaze, ne wist what way to chose.
　　But *Ioue*, all fearelesse, forc't them to aby;
　　And in his soueraine throne, gan straight dispose
　　Himselfe more full of grace and Maiestie,
That mote encheare his friends, and foes mote terrifie.

25

That, when the haughty *Titanesse* beheld,
　　All were she fraught with pride and impudence,
　　Yet with the sight thereof was almost queld;
　　And inly quaking, seem'd as reft of sense,
　　And voyd of speech in that drad audience;
　　Vntill that *Ioue* himselfe, her selfe bespake:
　　Speake thou fraile woman, speake with confidence,
　　Whence art thou, and what doost thou here now make?
What idle errand hast thou, earths mansion to forsake?

26

Shee, halfe confused with his great commaund,
　　Yet gathering spirit of her natures pride,
　　Him boldly answer'd thus to his demaund:
　　I am a daughter, by the mothers side,
　　Of her that is Grand-mother magnifide
　　Of all the Gods, great *Earth*, great *Chaos* child:
　　But by the fathers (be it not envide)
　　I greater am in bloud (whereon I build)
Then all the Gods, though wrongfully from heauen exil'd.

27

For, *Titan* (as ye all acknowledge must)
　　Was *Saturnes* elder brother by birth-right;
　　Both, sonnes of *Vranus*: but by vniust
　　And guilefull meanes, through *Corybantes* slight,
　　The younger thrust the elder from his right:
　　Since which, thou *Ioue*, iniuriously hast held
　　The Heauens rule from *Titans* sonnes by might;
　　And them to hellish dungeons downe hast feld:
Witnesse ye Heauens the truth of all that I haue teld.

28

Whil'st she thus spake, the Gods that gaue good eare
　　To her bold words, and marked well her grace,
　　Beeing of stature tall as any there
　　Of all the Gods, and beautifull of face,
　　As any of the Goddesses in place,
　　Stood all astonied, like a sort of Steeres;
　　Mongst whom, some beast of strange and forraine race,
　　Vnwares is chaunc't, far straying from his peeres:
So did their ghastly gaze bewray their hidden feares.

Stanza 23
4　　re-allie: rally, form again.
5　　extasie: confused state of astonishment. In line with Mutabilitie's aspirations, it suggests also the etymological sense, 'withdrawn from one's proper place'.
7　　purest sky: the Empyrean and beyond the primum mobile; see Johnson (1937) 56.
9　　Proverbial (C. G. Smith, 1970, 51).

Stanza 24
5　　amaze: bewilderment, panic.
6　　aby: remain.

Stanza 25
5　　audience: with the legal sense, judicial hearing to consider her claims.
8　　make: intend; want.

Stanza 26
5–6　　As Lotspeich (1932) 55 notes, Boccaccio, *Gen. Deor*. I viii, cites Statius's claim, *Theb*. viii 303, that the Earth is the mother of the gods. For earth as the child of Chaos, see, e.g., Golding, Epistle 346–54.　　magnifide: extolled.
7　　envide: begrudged.

Stanza 27
This version of how Saturn gained the throne is found in Comes (1616) VI xx and in Cooper (1565). **Saturn** (Cronos) persuaded his elder brother, **Titan**, to abdicate the throne on the promise that he (Saturn) would devour his own children in order to allow Titan to succeed him. His son, **Ioue**, saved from being devoured, was preserved when his infant cries were drowned by the **Corybantes** beating their shields. Cf. vii 16.5–9.
4　　slight: cunning trick.
5　　The **younger** is Saturn. Through **Corybantes slight**, Jove thrust the elder Saturn from his right; however, Mutabilitie argues the case for the elder Titan against the Saturn–Jove line.
6　　iniuriously: wrongfully.

Stanza 28
3–5　　Her beauty is the beauty of created things which mirrors the divine ideas; see Bennett (1933) 189.　　in place: present.
6　　sort: herd.

29

Till hauing pauz'd awhile, *Ioue* thus bespake;
  Will neuer mortall thoughts ceasse to aspire,
  In this bold sort, to Heauen claime to make,
  And touch celestiall seates with earthly mire?
  I would haue thought, that bold *Procrustes* hire,
  Or *Typhons* fall, or proud *Ixions* paine,
  Or great *Prometheus*, tasting of our ire,
  Would haue suffiz'd, the rest for to restraine;
And warn'd all men by their example to refraine:

30

But now, this off-scum of that cursed fry,
  Dare to renew the like bold enterprize,
  And chalenge th'heritage of this our skie;
  Whom what should hinder, but that we likewise
  Should handle as the rest of her allies,
  And thunder-driue to hell? With that, he shooke
  His Nectar-deawed locks, with which the skyes
  And all the world beneath for terror quooke,
And eft his burning leuin-brond in hand he tooke.

31

But, when he looked on her louely face,
  In which, faire beames of beauty did appeare,
  That could the greatest wrath soone turne to grace
  (Such sway doth beauty euen in Heauen beare)
  He staide his hand: and hauing chang'd his cheare,
  He thus againe in milder wise began;
  But ah! if Gods should striue with flesh yfere,
  Then shortly should the progeny of Man
Be rooted out, if *Ioue* should doe still what he can:

32

But thee faire *Titans* child, I rather weene,
  Through some vaine errour or inducement light,
  To see that mortall eyes haue neuer seene;
  Or through ensample of thy sisters might,
  Bellona; whose great glory thou doost spight,
  Since thou hast seene her dreadfull power belowe,
  Mongst wretched men (dismaide with her affright)
  To bandie Crownes, and Kingdomes to bestowe:
And sure thy worth, no lesse then hers doth seem to showe.

33

But wote thou this, thou hardy *Titanesse*,
  That not the worth of any liuing wight
  May challenge ought in Heauens interesse;
  Much lesse the Title of old *Titans* Right:
  For, we by Conquest of our soueraine might,
  And by eternall doome of Fates decree,
  Haue wonne the Empire of the Heauens bright;
  Which to our selues we hold, and to whom wee
Shall worthy deeme partakers of our blisse to bee.

34

Then ceasse thy idle claime thou foolish gerle,
  And seeke by grace and goodnesse to obtaine
  That place from which by folly *Titan* fell;
  There-to thou maist perhaps, if so thou faine
  Haue *Ioue* thy gratious Lord and Soueraigne.
  So, hauing said, she thus to him replide;
  Ceasse *Saturnes* sonne, to seeke by proffers vaine
  Of idle hopes t'allure mee to thy side,
For to betray my Right, before I haue it tride.

Stanza 29

5–9   **Ioue** (1) cites those whom he punished for rebellion
against his rule. He adds **Procrustes** whom Theseus punished
for fitting his victims to a bed by stretching or lopping off their
limbs. This action and his epithet, **bold**, suggest Mutabilitie's
boldness in seeking 'To thrust faire *Phœbe* from her siluer bed'
(21.3).   **mortall** (2) and **earthly** (4) emphasize Mutabilitie's
connection with the Earth.   **hire**: reward, i.e. punishment.
Typhon: see 15.8–9*n*.   **Ixion**: see I v 35.1–2.
Prometheus: see II x 70.5–9.

Stanza 30

1   Mutabilitie is the **off-scum** or dross; **fry** refers to the
brood of Titans.
3   **chalenge**: lay claim to.
6–9   S. imitates the opening of Ovid, *Metamorphoses*, the
major poem on mutability. Jove assembles the gods when he is
angered by man's evil actions, particularly by the aspirations of
the Giants. In anger he shakes his locks which moves the land,
and threatens to destroy the world with his thunderbolt. See
Nelson (1963) 297–9.   **eft**: afterwards.   **leuin-brond**: bolt
of lightning.

Stanza 31

7–9   Cf. Gen. 6.3: 'The Lord said, My Spirit shal not alway
strive with man, because he is but flesh'; cf. also Ps. 78.39.
with flesh yfere: i.e. against flesh.

Stanza 32

3   The line prepares for Faunus's sight of the forbidden at 46;
see 45.3–5*n*.
5   **Bellona**: see 3.7–9*n*.   **spight**: feel annoyed at; envy.
7   **with her affright**: through fear of her.

Stanza 33

2   Jove's cunning is noted by Ringler (1961) 219:
Mutabilitie's **worth** is not her chief claim.
3   **challenge**: claim.   **interesse**: legal right or title.
5–9   In *View* 9, S. upholds the doctrine, 'all is the
conqueror's', in defending England's right to Ireland for ever.

Stanza 34

1   **gerle**: reminds her of her inferior sex and age.   **foolish**:
links her with Titan's folly.
7   **Saturnes sonne**: asserts her superior claim as Titan's
daughter.

719

35

But thee, O *Ioue*, no equall Iudge I deeme
  Of my desert, or of my dewfull Right;
  That in thine owne behalfe maist partiall seeme:
  But to the highest him, that is behight
  Father of Gods and men by equall might;
  To weet, the God of Nature, I appeale.
  There-at *Ioue* wexed wroth, and in his spright
  Did inly grudge, yet did it well conceale;
And bade *Dan Phœbus* Scribe her Appellation seale.

36

Eftsoones the time and place appointed were,
  Where all, both heauenly Powers, and earthly wights,
  Before great Natures presence should appeare,
  For triall of their Titles and best Rights:
  That was, to weet, vpon the highest hights
  Of *Arlo-hill* (Who knowes not *Arlo-hill?*)
  That is the highest head (in all mens sights)
  Of my old father *Mole*, whom Shepheards quill
Renowmed hath with hymnes fit for a rurall skill.

37

And, were it not ill fitting for this file,
  To sing of hilles and woods, mongst warres and Knights,
  I would abate the sternenesse of my stile,
  Mongst these sterne stounds to mingle soft delights;
  And tell how *Arlo* through *Dianaes* spights
  (Beeing of old the best and fairest Hill
  That was in all this holy-Islands hights)
  Was made the most vnpleasant, and most ill.
Meane while, O *Clio*, lend *Calliope* thy quill.

38

Whylome, when *IRELAND* florished in fame
  Of wealths and goodnesse, far aboue the rest
  Of all that beare the *British* Islands name,
  The Gods then vs'd (for pleasure and for rest)
  Oft to resort there-to, when seem'd them best:
  But none of all there-in more pleasure found,
  Then *Cynthia*; that is soueraine Queene profest
  Of woods and forrests, which therein abound,
Sprinkled with wholsom waters, more then most on ground.

39

But mongst them all, as fittest for her game,
  Either for chace of beasts with hound or boawe,
  Or for to shroude in shade from *Phœbus* flame,
  Or bathe in fountaines that doe freshly flowe,
  Or from high hilles, or from the dales belowe,
  She chose this *Arlo*; where shee did resort
  With all her Nymphes enranged on a rowe,
  With whom the woody Gods did oft consort:
For, with the Nymphes, the Satyres loue to play and sport.

Stanza 35
Fletcher (1971) 219 notes the contradiction. A rebel cannot go to court to defend rebellion: 'She can, in law, only seek to prove she is not a rebel.' Hughes (1926) 555 notes that Mutabilitie echoes 'the whole conscious movement of thought in Spenser's century from Grotius' resort to the idea of natural law in the field of jurisprudence to Hooker's frank dependence upon the same principle in *The Ecclesiastical Polity*'.
1   **equall**: impartial.
4–6   Later **Nature** appears as feminine; however, her higher authority matters, not her sex.   **equall**: i.e. equally over gods and men. R. N. Ringler (1961) 233–6 sees an intended insult in the transfer of Jove's common title, **Father of Gods and men**, to another.
9   **Dan Phœbus Scribe**: i.e. Mercury; on this role, see Seznec (1953) 158–63.

Stanza 36
6–9   The question is meant to be rhetorical, or perhaps witty. **Arlo-hill** is the poet's name for Galtymore, the highest peak of a range of hills near Kilcolman Castle. He transfers to the mountain the name of the valley of Aherlow beneath. Joyce (1911) 95 suggests that by the **Mole** he refers to the whole range, including the Galtys and the Ballahoura Mountains. He notes further (330) that the hill was famous as a resort of gods and goddesses. Presumably readers are expected to know that S. is the shepherd who praises the Mole in *Col.* 104–5 as 'that mountain gray / That walls the Northside of *Armulla* dale'.

Stanza 37
1   **file**: thread (Lat. *filum*) or course of the story, referring to the 'records' of 2.4. The poet imitates Calidore who left wars and knights to live 'in hils, in woods, in dales' (VI x 3.6).
4   **stounds**: conflicts.
5, 8   **Arlo . . . the most vnpleasant**: cf. 'fowle *Arlo*' (*Astrophel* 96).
7   **this holy-Island**: in *View* 92, S. refers to Ireland's ancient name, '*Sacra Insula*, taking *sacra* for *accursed*'.
9   Perhaps deliberately ambiguous: either **Calliope** takes the place held until now by **Clio** to tell the story that follows or she lends Clio her powers so that Clio may tell the story. I prefer the former reading. Cf. the reference to 'thou greater Muse' (vii 1.1). Such ambiguity would prepare for the sudden reversal of intent in the stanza.

Stanza 38
1–3   'It is certain that Ireland hath had the use of letters very anciently, and long before England' (*View* 40).   **wealths**] 'wealth' sugg. Hughes (1715); or the plural may refer to kinds of wealth, or things in which riches or well-being consists.
7   **Cynthia**: as the virgin huntress, Diana is her usual title; but S. wishes to link Faunus's boldness with Mutabilitie's.

Stanza 39
1–6   The syntax is loose but effectively so.   **game** refers in 2 to the hunt, in 3 and 4 to recreation generally. 5 is first taken to belong to the catalogue of **chace, shade, fountaines**; then it applies to **flowe** (fountains that flow either from the hills or dales); and finally it is taken with 6: she chose **Arlo** in place of the high hills or the dales below.
7   Cf. the order at III vi 17.4.

40

Amongst the which, there was a Nymph that hight
   Molanna; daughter of old father *Mole*,
   And sister vnto *Mulla*, faire and bright:
   Vnto whose bed false *Bregog* whylome stole,
   That Shepheard *Colin* dearely did condole,
   And made her lucklesse loues well knowne to be.
   But this *Molanna*, were she not so shole,
   Were no lesse faire and beautifull then shee:
Yet as she is, a fairer flood may no man see.

41

For, first, she springs out of two marble Rocks,
   On which, a groue of Oakes high mounted growes,
   That as a girlond seemes to deck the locks
   Of som faire Bride, brought forth with pompous showes
   Out of her bowre, that many flowers strowes:
   So, through the flowry Dales she tumbling downe,
   Through many woods, and shady coverts flowes
   (That on each side her siluer channell crowne)
Till to the Plaine she come, whose Valleyes shee doth drowne.

42

In her sweet streames, *Diana* vsed oft
   (After her sweatie chace and toilesome play)
   To bathe her selfe; and after, on the soft
   And downy grasse, her dainty limbes to lay
   In couert shade, where none behold her may:
   For, much she hated sight of liuing eye.
   Foolish God *Faunus*, though full many a day
   He saw her clad, yet longed foolishly
To see her naked mongst her Nymphes in priuity.

43

No way he found to compasse his desire,
   But to corrupt *Molanna*, this her maid,
   Her to discouer for some secret hire:
   So, her with flattering words he first assaid;
   And after, pleasing gifts for her puruaid,
   Queene-apples, and red Cherries from the tree,
   With which he her allured and betraid,
   To tell what time he might her Lady see
When she her selfe did bathe, that he might secret bee.

44

There-to hee promist, if shee would him pleasure
   With this small boone, to quit her with a better;
   To weet, that where-as shee had out of measure
   Long lov'd the *Fanchin*, who by nought did set her,
   That he would vndertake, for this to get her
   To be his Loue, and of him liked well:
   Besides all which, he vow'd to be her debter
   For many moe good turnes then he would tell;
The least of which, this little pleasure should excell.

Stanza 40

2   **Molanna**: S.'s name for the Behanna, combining **Mole**
and **Behanna**. Joyce (1911) 99f shows the accuracy of S.'s
topography throughout this episode.
3–6   S. tells the story of **Mulla and Bregog** in *Col.* 104–55.
Mulla is his name for the Awbeg river near Kilcolman, derived
from Kilnemullach, the older name for the vicinity; see Henley,
Var. Minor Poems i 454–5. Cf. IV xi 41.9.   **bed**: a delightful
pun, as 53.6.   **false Bregog**: 'So hight because of this
deceitfull traine, / Which he with *Mulla* wrought to win delight'
(*Col.* 118–9). The Irish name signifies deceitful.   **dearely
did condole**: keenly or lovingly bewailed.
7   **shole**: shallow.

Stanza 41

2   **a groue of Oakes**: as the oak is 'sole king of forrests all'
(I i 8.8), it is associated with Cynthia as 'soueraine Queene
profest / Of woods and forrests' (38.7–8 above); however, a
grove of oaks may, in fact, have crowned the rocks out of which
the Behanna rises, as Joyce (1911) 103 conjectures.
4   **pompous**: magnificent, ceremonious (cf. IV xi 28.4).

Stanzas 42–53

S. adapts three Ovidian stories of metamorphosis: Actaeon's
accidental sight of the naked **Diana** (*Met.* iii 155–252); Diana's
banishment of the pregnant Calisto (*Met.* ii 463–5), though only
punishment for betrayal is common; and the union of the brook
Alpheus with the nymph Aretheusa (*Met.* v 577–641). R. N.
Ringler (1966) adds Ovid's story, *Fasti* ii 267–358, of **Faunus**
who sought to rape Omphale but was discovered and ridiculed.
The influence of Irish folktale is argued by R. M. Smith (1935).
Williams (1966) 227 notes that the episode 'repeats the theme
of sinful presumption on the level of comedy . . . reinforcing the
universal by the particular'.

Stanza 42

1–6   Some details are borrowed from Ovid's description of
Diana's grotto, *Met.* iii 155–64.
7–9   On Faunus, see II ii 7.5–8. Nelson (1963) 300 notes
that **Foolish** supplies the etymology of his name: Servius in his
note to Virgil, *Aen.* vii 47, derives Faunus and Fatuus, the
foolish one, from the same root. Cf. 46.6, 49.2, 9. Cooper
(1565) glosses Fauna: '*idem quod Fatua*'.

Stanza 43

3   **discouer**: reveal.
5   **puruaid**: provided.
6   **Queene-apples, and red Cherries**: the apple is
traditionally associated with temptation; so, too, the cherry.

Stanza 44

2   **quit**: requite.
4   **Fanchin**: S.'s name for the Funsheon, which joins the
Molanna; called the 'Funchin' in *Col.* 301 but changed here to
suggest an etymological connection with Faunus (sugg. J. C.
Smith, 1912, 653).   **set**: esteem.
8   **good turnes**: fancifully referring to delightful bends into
which he would lead the river.

The simple maid did yield to him anone;
 And eft him placed where he close might view
 That neuer any saw, saue onely one;
 Who, for his hire to so foole-hardy dew,
 Was of his hounds devour'd in Hunters hew.
 Tho, as her manner was on sunny day,
 Diana, with her Nymphes about her, drew
 To this sweet spring; where, doffing her array,
She bath'd her louely limbes, for *Ioue* a likely pray.

46

There *Faunus* saw that pleased much his eye,
 And made his hart to tickle in his brest,
 That for great ioy of some-what he did spy,
 He could him not containe in silent rest;
 But breaking forth in laughter, loud profest
 His foolish thought. A foolish *Faune* indeed,
 That couldst not hold thy selfe so hidden blest,
 But wouldest needs thine owne conceit areed.
Babblers vnworthy been of so diuine a meed.

47

The Goddesse, all abashed with that noise,
 In haste forth started from the guilty brooke;
 And running straight where-as she heard his voice,
 Enclos'd the bush about, and there him tooke,
 Like darred Larke; not daring vp to looke
 On her whose sight before so much he sought.
 Thence, forth they drew him by the hornes, and shooke
 Nigh all to peeces, that they left him nought;
And then into the open light they forth him brought.

48

Like as an huswife, that with busie care
 Thinks of her Dairie to make wondrous gaine,
 Finding where-as some wicked beast vnware
 That breakes into her Dayr'house, there doth draine
 Her creaming pannes, and frustrate all her paine;
 Hath in some snare or gin set close behind,
 Entrapped him, and caught into her traine,
 Then thinkes what punishment were best assign'd,
And thousand deathes deuiseth in her vengefull mind:

49

So did *Diana* and her maydens all
 Vse silly *Faunus*, now within their baile:
 They mocke and scorne him, and him foule miscall;
 Some by the nose him pluckt, some by the taile,
 And by his goatish beard some did him haile:
 Yet he (poore soule) with patience all did beare;
 For, nought against their wils might countervaile:
 Ne ought he said what euer he did heare;
But hanging downe his head, did like a Mome appeare.

50

At length, when they had flouted him their fill,
 They gan to cast what penaunce him to giue.
 Some would haue gelt him, but that same would spill
 The Wood-gods breed, which must for euer liue:
 Others would through the riuer him haue driue,
 And ducked deepe: but that seem'd penaunce light;
 But most agreed and did this sentence giue,
 Him in Deares skin to clad; and in that plight,
722 To hunt him with their hounds, him selfe saue how hee might.

Stanza 45

1 **anone**: instantly; soon.
2 **close**: secretly; close-up.
3–5 The **one** is Actaeon; in Ovid he is unlucky, rather than **foole-hardy**. Faunus parallels the 'foolish gerle' (34.1) who sought 'To see that mortall eyes haue neuer seene' (32.3). On the Renaissance interpretation of Actaeon as over-curious, see Starnes and Talbert (1955) 204–7. **hew**: shape. In Ovid, Actaeon is transformed into a stag. S.'s variant version may follow Comes (1616) VI xxiv in which Diana clad him in a deer skin; see 50.8–9. However, the chief point is not metamorphosis but reversal: the hunter becomes the hunted.
9 **likely**: likable, proper; cf. Jove's appearances in the tapestries in the house of Busirane, III xi 30–35. Zitner (1968) 129 notes that the line recalls his susceptibility to Mutabilitie's charms.

Stanza 46

2 **tickle**: be thrilled.
3 **some-what**: some thing, in the bawdy sense.
5 **breaking forth in laughter**: suggesting incontinence.
6–9 Colin Clout still fumes over Calidore's similar failure to contain himself. **conceit**: thought; also personal vanity or pride, since only one before him has seen Diana naked. **areed**: make known.

Stanza 47

2 **guilty brooke**: Molanna, guilty of betraying Diana; cf. 'sweet spring' (45.8).
5 **darred Larke**: dazzled, dazed, referring to the practice of catching larks by paralyzing them with the sight of scarlet cloth or a mirror while the fowler nets them. Gervase Markham, *Hunger's Prevention* (1621) 118, refers to a mirror that gives such a glorious reflection 'that the wanton birds cannot fore-beare but wil play about it with admiration, til they be taken'. Perhaps Faunus is guilty also of self-admiration and pride. The verbal echo in **darred Larke; not daring vp to looke** – one who dared to look now does not dare to look – plays with etymology. The puns here are noted by Harrison (1956) 71; they lead to 'Dairie' and 'Dayr'house' in the next stanza.
8 **nought**: good for nothing.

Stanza 48

7 **traine**: snare.

Stanza 49

2 **baile**: power, custody.
3 **miscall**: revile.
9 **Mome**: dolt, blockhead.

Stanza 50

2 **cast**: consider.
3–4 Cf. 31.7–9. **gelt**: gelded. **spill**: destroy.
5 **driue**: for driven.
8 **plight**: attire; condition, state.
9 **their hounds**: in contrast to Actaeon who was destroyed by his own hounds, allegorized as his uncontrollable passions.

51

But *Cynthia's* selfe, more angry then the rest,
　Thought not enough, to punish him in sport,
　And of her shame to make a gamesome iest;
　But gan examine him in straighter sort,
　Which of her Nymphes, or other close consort,
　Him thither brought, and her to him betraid?
　He, much affeard, to her confessed short,
　That 'twas *Molanna* which her so bewraid.
Then all attonce their hands vpon *Molanna* laid.

52

But him (according as they had decreed)
　With a Deeres-skin they couered, and then chast
　With all their hounds that after him did speed;
　But he more speedy, from them fled more fast
　Then any Deere: so sore him dread aghast.
　They after follow'd all with shrill out-cry,
　Shouting as they the heauens would haue brast:
　That all the woods and dales where he did flie,
Did ring againe, and loud reeccho to the skie.

53

So they him follow'd till they weary were;
　When, back returning to *Molann'* againe,
　They, by commaund'ment of *Diana*, there
　Her whelm'd with stones.　Yet *Faunus* (for her paine)
　Of her beloued *Fanchin* did obtaine,
　That her he would receiue vnto his bed.
　So now her waues passe through a pleasant Plaine,
　Till with the *Fanchin* she her selfe doe wed,
And (both combin'd) themselues in one faire riuer spred.

54

Nath'lesse, *Diana*, full of indignation,
　Thence-forth abandond her delicious brooke;
　In whose sweet streame, before that bad occasion,
　So much delight to bathe her limbes she tooke:
　Ne onely her, but also quite forsooke
　All those faire forrests about *Arlo* hid,
　And all that Mountaine, which doth over-looke
　The richest champian that may else be rid,
And the faire *Shure*, in which are thousand Salmons bred.

55

Them all, and all that she so deare did way,
　Thence-forth she left; and parting from the place,
　There-on an heauy haplesse curse did lay,
　To weet, that Wolues, where she was wont to space,
　Should harbour'd be, and all those Woods deface,
　And Thieues should rob and spoile that Coast around.
　Since which, those Woods, and all that goodly Chase,
　Doth to this day with Wolues and Thieues abound:
Which too-too true that lands in-dwellers since haue found.

Stanza 51
4　**straighter sort**: more strictly.
5　**close consort**: secret confederate.
7　**short**: soon.
8　**bewraid**: betrayed.

Stanza 53
4　**whelm'd**: overwhelmed. The story explains why the river
is 'so shole' (40.7). Joyce (1911) 104 notes that during winter
floods the river brings down vast quantities of stones and gravel
from its mountain source. Similar punishment is given to the
Bregog in *Col.* 149–55. Gottfried (1937) 108 notes S.'s use of
local geographical forms as characters in a myth of locality.
6　**bed**: with a pun on river bed.

Stanza 54
8–9　**champian**: champaign, open country.　**else be rid**:
anywhere be seen.　**the faire Shure**: S. refers to the Vale of
Aherlow in County Tipperary, watered by the river Suir; cf.
'the gentle Shure' (IV xi 43.1).

Stanza 55
While Actaeon is punished by death, Faunus is only chased:
the guilt for his act is attributed to Molanna and from her transferred to Arlo Hill. Edwards (1958) 294 notes that S. wants to
underline the parallel between Faunus and Mutabilitie, making
a curse in the little world reflect that in the greater world. The
connection with Eden is noted by Nelson (1963) 300.
1　**way**: value.
4　**space**: walk.
7　**Chase**: hunting-ground.
8　**Wolues and Thieues abound**: in *Col.* 318–9, S.
laments that wolves and outlaws infect Ireland.

Canto VII.

Pealing, from Ioue, to Natur's Bar,
    bold Alteration pleades
Large Euidence : but Nature soone
    her righteous Doome areads.

1

AH! whither doost thou now thou greater Muse
Me from these woods and pleasing forrests bring?
And my fraile spirit (that dooth oft refuse
This too high flight, vnfit for her weake wing)
Lift vp aloft, to tell of heauens King
(Thy soueraine Sire) his fortunate successe,
And victory, in bigger noates to sing,
Which he obtain'd against that *Titanesse*,
That him of heauens Empire sought to dispossesse.

2

Yet sith I needs must follow thy behest,
Doe thou my weaker wit with skill inspire,
Fit for this turne; and in my feeble brest
Kindle fresh sparks of that immortall fire,
Which learned minds inflameth with desire
Of heauenly things: for, who but thou alone,
That art yborne of heauen and heauenly Sire,
Can tell things doen in heauen so long ygone;
So farre past memory of man that may be knowne.

3

Now, at the time that was before agreed,
The Gods assembled all on *Arlo* hill;
As well those that are sprung of heauenly seed,
As those that all the other world doe fill,
And rule both sea and land vnto their will:
Onely th'infernall Powers might not appeare;
Aswell for horror of their count'naunce ill,
As for th'vnruly fiends which they did feare;
Yet *Pluto* and *Proserpina* were present there.

4

And thither also came all other creatures,
What-euer life or motion doe retaine,
According to their sundry kinds of features;
That *Arlo* scarsly could them all containe;
So full they filled euery hill and Plaine:
And had not *Natures* Sergeant (that is *Order*)
Them well disposed by his busie paine,
And raunged farre abroad in euery border,
They would haue caused much confusion and disorder.

5

Then forth issewed (great goddesse) great dame *Nature*,
With goodly port and gracious Maiesty;
Being far greater and more tall of stature
Then any of the gods or Powers on hie:
Yet certes by her face and physnomy,
Whether she man or woman inly were,
That could not any creature well descry:
For, with a veile that wimpled euery where,
Her head and face was hid, that mote to none appeare.

Canto vii

Argument

1   **Pealing**: appealing.
2   **Alteration**: Mutabilitie; cf. 55.4.
3   **Large**: extensive, copious.   **soone**: cf. 57.1–3, 8.
4   **areads**: declares.

Stanza 1

1   **thou greater Muse**: Calliope, or possibly Clio; see vi 37.9*n*.   **greater**: very great, in contrast to 'weaker' (2.2), too weak. S. may invoke Urania to aid him sing 'Of heauenly things' (2.6). On her role, see *T. M.* 499–534.
5–9   The outcome of the trial is given before it begins, but not Nature's judgment.   **Thy soueraine Sire**: Jove, the father of Apollo, who was father of the Muses; see III iii 4.1–2. **bigger**: louder. In *S.C.* Oct. 46, 'bigger notes' refers to the poet's heroic song.

Stanza 2

3   **turne**: task; or referring to his return to his former Muse. **feeble**] sable *1609*. The emendation, proposed by Hughes (1715), is supported by I xi 6.1.

Stanza 3

The **Gods** appear in order: first, the heavenly; secondly, those of the **other world**, i.e. the Earth, e.g. nymphs, dryads, and Nereids who 'haue the sea in charge to them assinde' (IV xi 52.2); and thirdly, the absent **infernall Powers** represented by **Pluto**, who was once a heavenly god, and by his consort **Proserpina** who is connected with the earth through her mother Ceres. Cf. vi 36.1–5.
8   **they**: i.e. the heavenly and earthly powers.

Stanza 4

In Chaucer, *Parl. Fowls*, birds of every kind assemble, filling all the space, and Nature herself orders her creatures.
6–9   Although all earthly things 'which Nature had establisht first / In good estate, and in meet order ranged' (vi 5.2–3) have been perverted by Mutabilitie, Nature still governs them. Their order is seen in the cycle of the seasons, months, etc.

Stanzas 5–6

Nature resembles a number of earlier descriptions, particularly Chaucer's. S.'s description relates her to Mutabilitie and the earlier goddesses in the poem; e.g. her tall stature (not mentioned by Chaucer) counters Mutabilitie's 'stature tall' (vi 28.3). The ambiguity of her sex relates her to Venus (IV x 41.6–7) who also is covered by a veil. Lewis (1966) 153 cites Cusanus, *Doct. Ignorantia* i 25, who records that Hermes attributed both sexes to God and that the ancients called God, among many other names, Nature. In Macrobius, *In Somn. Scip.* I ii 17, Nature appears veiled.

Stanza 5

5   **physnomy**: countenance.
8   **wimpled**: covered; as Fortune 'couereth and wympleth hir' (Chaucer, *Boece* II Prosa i 59).
9   **that mote to none appeare**: cf. Diana 'That neuer any saw, saue onely one' (vi 45.3); cf. vi 32.3.

6

That some doe say was so by skill deuized,
　To hide the terror of her vncouth hew,
　From mortall eyes that should be sore agrized;
　For that her face did like a Lion shew,
　That eye of wight could not indure to view:
　But others tell that it so beautious was,
　And round about such beames of splendor threw,
　That it the Sunne a thousand times did pass,
Ne could be seene, but like an image in a glass.

7

That well may seemen true: for, well I weene
　That this same day, when she on *Arlo* sat,
　Her garment was so bright and wondrous sheene,
　That my fraile wit cannot deuize to what
　It to compare, nor finde like stuffe to that,
　As those three sacred *Saints*, though else most wise,
　Yet on mount *Thabor* quite their wits forgat,
　When they their glorious Lord in strange disguise
Transfigur'd sawe; his garments so did daze their eyes.

8

In a fayre Plaine vpon an equall Hill,
　She placed was in a pauilion;
　Not such as Craftes-men by their idle skill
　Are wont for Princes states to fashion:
　But th'earth her self of her owne motion,
　Out of her fruitfull bosome made to growe
　Most dainty trees; that, shooting vp anon,
　Did seeme to bow their bloosming heads full lowe,
For homage vnto her, and like a throne did shew.

9

So hard it is for any liuing wight,
　All her array and vestiments to tell,
　That old *Dan Geffrey* (in whose gentle spright
　The pure well head of Poesie did dwell)
　In his *Foules parley* durst not with it mel,
　But it transferd to *Alane*, who he thought
　Had in his *Plaint of kindes* describ'd it well:
　Which who will read set forth so as it ought,
Go seek he out that *Alane* where he may be sought.

10

And all the earth far vnderneath her feete
　Was dight with flowres, that voluntary grew
　Out of the ground, and sent forth odours sweet;
　Tenne thousand mores of sundry sent and hew,
　That might delight the smell, or please the view:
　The which, the Nymphes, from all the brooks thereby
　Had gathered, which they at her foot-stoole threw;
　That richer seem'd then any tapestry,
That Princes bowres adorne with painted imagery.

3　**agrized**: terrified.
4　**her face did like a Lion shew**: in Alanus, *De Planctu Naturae* Prose 1, one of the jewels in Nature's zodiacal diadem bears the image of a lion; noted Greenlaw, *Var.* vi 397. Cf. Una, whose face 'As the great eye of heauen shyned bright' (I iii 4.7), attended by the lion. At their appearance, Abessa flees, for never 'Face of faire Ladie she before did vew, / And that dread Lyons looke her cast in deadly hew' (I iii 11.8–9).
6　**others**: includes Jean de Meun, *Roman de la Rose* 16230–48.
7–8　Cf. Chaucer's description of Nature, *Parl. Fowls* 299–301.
9　Cf. 2 Cor. 3.18: 'But we all beholde as in a mirrour the glorie of the Lord with open face.' Cf. VI Proem 5.5.

Stanza 7

2　**sat**: i.e. sat in judgment.
3　**sheene**: shining.
4–9　**those three sacred Saints**: Peter, James and John who saw on **mount Thabor** (according to the Geneva Bible) the transfigured Jesus: 'his face did shine as the sunne, and his clothes were as white as the light' (Matt. 17.2). For the association of Nature as the revelation of God and Christ as the 'Word made Flesh', see the sources cited by Bennett (1933) 172f. **quite their wits forgat**: cf. Mark 9.6: Peter 'knewe not what he said'.

Stanza 8

Cf. Chaucer, *Parl. Fowls* 302–5: 'And in a launde, upon an hil of floures, / Was set this noble goddesse Nature. / Of braunches were here halles and here boures / Iwrought after here cast and here mesure.'
1　**equall**: level-topped.
4　**states**: the throne of state with its canopy; cf. Jove in his 'principall Estate' (vi 19.4).
5　**her self ... motion**: i.e. spontaneously. Cf. 10.2–3.
7　**anon**: straightway.

Stanza 9

This stanza interrupts the continuity of the argument. Upton (1758) suggests that it properly belongs after 12. Padelford, *Var.* vi 478, suggests that it belongs after 7.
3–6　**Dan Geffrey ... / ... it transferd to Alane**: cf. 'Dan *Chaucer*, well of English vndefyled' (IV ii 32.8).
Poesie: the poet's 'skill, or Crafte of making' (Jonson, *Works* viii 636) rather than poetry.　　**mel**: meddle. Yet Chaucer does not avoid the matter: he simply defers to Alanus (*Parl. Fowls* 316–8).
7　**Plaint of kindes**: Upton suggests that the title should read *Plaint of kinde* and notes that S. may never have read Alanus since his work was available only in manuscript. Hence, perhaps, the tone of exasperation in 9.

Stanza 10

1–3　Spontaneous flowering in honour of the gods is a common classical theme, e.g. Homer, *Iliad* xiv 346–9, Virgil, *Ecl.* iv 23.
4　**mores**: roots. Perhaps used poetically for plant, as *OED* suggests; but in this fertile earth, root and flower are one. **sent**: a nice pun.
8–9　**tapestry / ... with painted imagery**: tapestries often employed a floral motif as background.

Stanza 6

2　**vncouth hew**: strange form.

11

And *Mole* himselfe, to honour her the more,
  Did deck himself in freshest faire attire,
  And his high head, that seemeth alwaies hore
  With hardned frosts of former winters ire,
  He with an Oaken girlond now did tire,
  As if the loue of some new Nymph late seene,
  Had in him kindled youthfull fresh desire,
  And made him change his gray attire to greene;
Ah gentle *Mole*! such ioyance hath thee well beseene.

12

Was neuer so great ioyance since the day,
  That all the gods whylome assembled were,
  On *Hæmus* hill in their diuine array,
  To celebrate the solemne bridall cheare,
  Twixt *Peleus*, and dame *Thetis* pointed there;
  Where *Phœbus* self, that god of Poets hight,
  They say did sing the spousall hymne full cleere,
  That all the gods were rauisht with delight
Of his celestiall song, and Musicks wondrous might.

13

This great Grandmother of all creatures bred
  Great *Nature*, euer young yet full of eld,
  Still moouing, yet vnmoued from her sted;
  Vnseene of any, yet of all beheld;
  Thus sitting in her throne as I haue teld,
  Before her came dame *Mutabilitie*;
  And being lowe before her presence feld,
  With meek obaysance and humilitie,
Thus gan her plaintif Plea, with words to amplifie;

14

To thee O greatest goddesse, onely great,
  An humble suppliant loe, I lowely fly
  Seeking for Right, which I of thee entreat;
  Who Right to all dost deale indifferently,
  Damning all Wrong and tortious Iniurie,
  Which any of thy creatures doe to other
  (Oppressing them with power, vnequally)
  Sith of them all thou art the equall mother,
And knittest each to each, as brother vnto brother.

15

To thee therefore of this same *Ioue* I plaine,
  And of his fellow gods that faine to be,
  That challenge to themselues the whole worlds raign;
  Of which, the greatest part is due to me,
  And heauen it selfe by heritage in Fee:
  For, heauen and earth I both alike do deeme,
  Sith heauen and earth are both alike to thee;
  And, gods no more then men thou doest esteeme:
For, euen the gods to thee, as men to gods do seeme.

Stanza 11

5   Cf. vi 41.2–4.   **tire**: adorn his head.
8   **gray**: as in *Col.* 104.
9   **thee well beseene**: i.e. well becomes you.

Stanza 12

726   At the marriage of **Peleus** and **Thetis**, Ate threw down the

golden apple which incited the quarrel among the three goddesses: see II vii 55.4–9. The present joy contrasts with the succeeding strife; see Hawkins (1961) 87. The importance of this marriage is suggested by its association with the Muses: see VI x 22. Frye (1963) 85–6 argues that the marriage first 'confirm'd [Jove] in his imperiall see' (59.7) by removing the threat to his power from a son of Thetis. Also it led to his reconciliation with Prometheus who was the originator of the elves and fays (II x 70f).
2   **all the gods**: as Homer, *Iliad* xxiv 61–2.
3   **On Hæmus hill**: on Mount Pelion, according to the standard classical sources. Upton (1758) conjectures that S. recalls Ovid's account of Peleus's seduction of Thetis which opens: *Est sinus Haemoniae* (*Met.* xi 229). It is possible that the name suggests 'Hiems', itself suggested by Mole's wintry state (11.3–4). Hæmus was reputed to be 'a great mountain in Thrace, in height vi miles' (Cooper, 1565).
4   **solemne**: sacred, holy.
5   **pointed**: appointed.
6–9   Homer mentions that Apollo attended the wedding with his lyre.

Stanza 13

2–4   The 'Old Woman and Girl' topos is traced by Curtius (1953) 101–5. The combination of youth and age is particularly appropriate to Nature, as Curtius's citations (106–7) reveal. It is found, e.g., in Lydgate, *Reson and Sensuallyte* 334–8.   **Still moouing, yet vnmoued**: applied by Boethius to the God of Nature, 'thow that duellest thiselve ay stedefast and stable, and yevest alle othere thynges to ben meved' (III *Met.* ix 3, trans. Chaucer). Kermode (1965) 226 notes that Nature 'contains in herself the secret answer to Mutability, who is only movement, and does not understand its relation to stillness, or Time's to Eternity'. The third paradox, **Vnseene . . . beheld**, turns from suggestions of God, who is invisible, to Nature as His visible creation. See *H.H.B.* 127–8.
7   **feld**: having fallen.
9   **amplifie**: more than enlarge; Zitner (1968) 135 cites its sense in Renaissance poetic: 'make impressive'.

Stanza 14

1   She also concludes her defence with an address to 'thou greatest goddesse trew' (56.6) to place Nature above Jove; cf. 'greater . . . / Then all the Gods' (vi 26.8–9).
4   **indifferently**: impartially.
7–9   Despite her obeisance to Nature as **onely great** (1), Mutabilitie, like the Giant with the Scales, 'all things would reduce vnto equality' (V ii 32.9). She argues for liberty without order or degree. Hence **vnequally**: unfairly, as though all were not equal.   **equall mother**: in contrast to Jove whom she rejects as 'no equall Iudge' (vi 35.1).

Stanza 15

1   **plaine**: complain.
2–3   Cf. her claim at 26.2.   **faine**: pretend.   **challenge**: claim.
4   It is not clear why she modestly claims only **the greatest part** and not **the whole worlds raign** (3) unless she wishes to exclude the lower world ruled by Pluto and Proserpina.
5   **Fee**: absolute possession.
9   Lewis (1967) 15 concludes that 'Nature is really an image of God himself'.

16

Then weigh, O soueraigne goddesse, by what right
  These gods do claime the worlds whole souerainty;
  And that is onely dew vnto thy might
  Arrogate to themselues ambitiously:
  As for the gods owne principality,
  Which *Ioue* vsurpes vniustly; that to be
  My heritage, *Ioue's* self cannot deny,
From my great Grandsire *Titan*, vnto mee,
Deriv'd by dew descent; as is well knowen to thee.

17

Yet mauger *Ioue*, and all his gods beside,
  I doe possesse the worlds most regiment;
  As, if ye please it into parts diuide,
  And euery parts inholders to conuent,
  Shall to your eyes appeare incontinent.
  And first, the Earth (great mother of vs all)
  That only seems vnmov'd and permanent,
  And vnto *Mutability* not thrall;
Yet is she chang'd in part, and eeke in generall.

18

For, all that from her springs, and is ybredde,
  How-euer fayre it flourish for a time,
  Yet see we soone decay; and, being dead,
  To turne again vnto their earthly slime:
  Yet, out of their decay and mortall crime,
  We daily see new creatures to arize;
  And of their Winter spring another Prime,
  Vnlike in forme, and chang'd by strange disguise:
So turne they still about, and change in restlesse wise.

19

As for her tenants; that is, man and beasts,
  The beasts we daily see massacred dy,
  As thralls and vassalls vnto mens beheasts:
  And men themselues doe change continually,
  From youth to eld, from wealth to pouerty,
  From good to bad, from bad to worst of all.
  Ne doe their bodies only flit and fly:
  But eeke their minds (which they immortall call)
Still change and vary thoughts, as new occasions fall.

20

Ne is the water in more constant case;
  Whether those same on high, or these belowe.
  For, th'Ocean moueth stil, from place to place;
  And euery Riuer still doth ebbe and flowe:
  Ne any Lake, that seems most still and slowe,
  Ne Poole so small, that can his smoothnesse holde,
  When any winde doth vnder heauen blowe;
  With which, the clouds are also tost and roll'd;
Now like great Hills; and, streight, like sluces, them vnfold.

21

So likewise are all watry liuing wights
  Still tost, and turned, with continuall change,
  Neuer abyding in their stedfast plights.
  The fish, still floting, doe at randon range,
  And neuer rest; but euermore exchange
  Their dwelling places, as the streames them carrie:
  Ne haue the watry foules a certaine grange,
  Wherein to rest, ne in one stead do tarry;
But flitting still doe flie, and still their places vary.

Stanza 16
3 **And . . . onely dew**: i.e. And what is due only.
5 **principality**: sovereignty.
8–9 Cf. vi 27.1–5.

Stanza 17
2 **most regiment**: chief rule.
4 **inholders**: inhabitants, with the implication that they 'doe the world in being hold' (27.3).   **conuent**: assemble.
5 **incontinent**: immediately.
6 to 25.9 Mutabilitie lists the four elements in their traditional sequence, which accords with her aspirations. See 26n.
7 **only**: alone; it also modifies **seems**. Mutabilitie may be expected to support the new astronomy.

Stanza 18
Mutabilitie's arguments are paralleled in Ovid, *Met.* xv 237–51, but they are too common to be attributed to any specific source.
1–4 Cf. the Giant's use of this argument (V ii 37.6–7) and Artegall's answer (40.1–5).
5 **mortall crime**: sin of mortality, i.e. death and corruption. Or it may signify judgment or sentence (of death), as Lat. *crimen*.
6 **new creatures to arize**: referring to spontaneous generation, or generally to new life arising from the old.
7 **Prime**: spring.

Stanza 19
1–3 She stresses the fallen nature of the world. Cf. the golden age when herbs and fruit served man for meat (Gen. 1.29).   **tenants**: reminding man that life is only loaned to him, not held in freehold.
8 As *H.L.* 103: 'man, that breathes a more immortall mynd.'

Stanza 20
2 Cf. Gen. 1.7: 'God made the firmament, and parted the waters, which were under the firmament, from the waters which were above the firmament.' The Geneva gloss explains: 'as the sea and rivers, from those waters that are in the cloudes.'
3, 4 **stil**: continually.
9 The balance of the line suggests that the **sluces** are floodgates which open downwards, like inverted hills.

Stanza 21
4 **still floting**: continually swimming.
7 **certaine grange**: fixed dwelling-place.

22

Next is the Ayre: which who feeles not by sense
  (For, of all sense it is the middle meane)
  To flit still? and, with subtill influence
  Of his thin spirit, all creatures to maintaine,
  In state of life?   O weake life! that does leane
  On thing so tickle as th'vnsteady ayre;
  Which euery howre is chang'd, and altred cleane
  With euery blast that bloweth fowle or faire:
The faire doth it prolong; the fowle doth it impaire.

23

Therein the changes infinite beholde,
  Which to her creatures euery minute chaunce;
  Now, boyling hot: streight, friezing deadly cold:
  Now, faire sun-shine, that makes all skip and daunce:
  Streight, bitter storms and balefull countenance,
  That makes them all to shiuer and to shake:
  Rayne, hayle, and snowe do pay them sad penance,
  And dreadfull thunder-claps (that make them quake)
With flames and flashing lights that thousand changes make.

24

Last is the fire: which, though it liue for euer,
  Ne can be quenched quite; yet, euery day,
  Wee see his parts, so soone as they do seuer,
  To lose their heat, and shortly to decay;
  So, makes himself his owne consuming pray.
  Ne any liuing creatures doth he breed:
  But all, that are of others bredd, doth slay;
  And, with their death, his cruell life dooth feed;
Nought leauing, but their barren ashes, without seede.

25

Thus, all these fower (the which the ground-work bee
  Of all the world, and of all liuing wights)
  To thousand sorts of *Change* we subiect see:
  Yet are they chang'd (by other wondrous slights)
  Into themselues, and lose their natiue mights;
  The Fire to Aire, and th'Ayre to Water sheere,
  And Water into Earth: yet Water fights
  With Fire, and Aire with Earth approaching neere:
Yet all are in one body, and as one appeare.

26

So, in them all raignes *Mutabilitie*;
  How-euer these, that Gods themselues do call,
  Of them doe claime the rule and soueranty:
  As, *Vesta*, of the fire æthereall;
  Vulcan, of this, with vs so vsuall;
  Ops, of the earth; and *Iuno* of the Ayre;
  Neptune, of Seas; and Nymphes, of Riuers all.
  For, all those Riuers to me subiect are:
And all the rest, which they vsurp, be all my share.

27

Which to approuen true, as I haue told,
  Vouchsafe, O goddesse, to thy presence call
  The rest which doe the world in being hold:
  As, times and seasons of the yeare that fall:
  Of all the which, demand in generall,
  Or iudge thy selfe, by verdit of thine eye,
  Whether to me they are not subiect all.
  Nature did yeeld thereto; and by-and-by,
728 Bade *Order* call them all, before her Maiesty.

Stanza 22
2   **middle meane**: as the intermediary between the senses and objects perceived. Fowler (1970) 59 *n*1 corrects her claim: air was not considered the means of touch or taste.
6   **tickle**: changeable.

Stanza 23
R. N. Ringler (1961) 394 notes that S. lists the three regions of the air in ascending order: 3–4, the lowest region that is alternately hot and cold; 5–8, the middle region of storms; 9, the highest region, which is next to the region of fire and produces comets or blazing stars. Du Bartas, *Divine Weekes* I ii pp. 12–3, expounds at length the effect of these three regions upon man.
2   **her creatures**: i.e. mankind who belongs to the sublunar vault of the air.
7   **penance**: reminds us that the seasons are punishment for man's sin.

Stanza 24
Mutabilitie holds to the old cosmology according to which the sublunary region of fire is situated above the region of air. Yet her subject is 'vsuall' fire (26.5), i.e. fire as we know it.

Stanza 25
1   **fower**: i.e. the four elements.
4–7   In place of the usual upward movement of the elements, from earth to water to air to fire, Mutabilitie notes their downward movement, which is 'natural' since the Fall. On the transmutation of the elements, see Aristotle, *Meteorologica* I iii 339ᵇ, and Ovid, *Met.* xv 249–51. Comes (1616) VI xx links the change to the revolt of the Titans.   **slights**: devices.
Into themselues: into each other.   **sheere**: bright, clear.
7–9   Cf. the conflict among the elements in *H.L.* 78–91.

Stanza 26
The unusual order – Fire, Earth, Air, and Water – is noted by Fowler (1970) 58–9: Juno is given the central place of sove-reignty. Or the order may be determined by the emphasis upon the rivers through which Mutabilitie claims her power over the other elements.
4–7   **Vesta**: the Roman goddess of the hearth and hence of fire is linked with the sphere of sublunary fire.   **Vulcan** is god of fire as we know it on earth. Du Bartas, *Divine Weekes* I ii p. 17, elaborates the difference between the pureness of the 'Elementall Flame' and the fire 'that for our use we frame'.
Ops: or Rhea, goddess of the earth (Cooper, 1565). Comes (1616) X p. 533 interprets **Iuno** as the air by which, through the influence of Jove, all creatures are born.

Stanza 27
1   **approuen**: prove; suggesting sanction.
3   **in being hold**: as they are 'inholders' (17.4).
6   **verdit**: the spelling suggests the etymology, to speak true.
8   **by-and-by**: immediately; one by one in order (*OED* 1): cf. 'in order went' (32.1).

28

So, forth issew'd the Seasons of the yeare;
  First, lusty *Spring*, all dight in leaues of flowres
  That freshly budded and new bloosmes did beare
  (In which a thousand birds had built their bowres
  That sweetly sung, to call forth Paramours):
  And in his hand a iauelin did beare,
  And on his head (as fit for warlike stoures)
  A guilt engrauen morion he did weare;
That as some did him loue, so others did him feare.

29

Then came the iolly *Sommer*, being dight
  In a thin silken cassock coloured greene,
  That was vnlyned all, to be more light:
  And on his head a girlond well beseene
  He wore, from which as he had chauffed been
  The sweat did drop; and in his hand he bore
  A boawe and shaftes, as he in forrest greene
  Had hunted late the Libbard or the Bore,
And now would bathe his limbes, with labor heated sore.

30

Then came the *Autumne* all in yellow clad,
  As though he ioyed in his plentious store,
  Laden with fruits that made him laugh, full glad
  That he had banist hunger, which to-fore
  Had by the belly oft him pinched sore.
  Vpon his head a wreath that was enrold
  With eares of corne, of euery sort he bore:
  And in his hand a sickle he did holde,
To reape the ripened fruits the which the earth had yold.

31

Lastly, came *Winter* cloathed all in frize,
  Chattering his teeth for cold that did him chill,
  Whil'st on his hoary beard his breath did freese;
  And the dull drops that from his purpled bill
  As from a limbeck did adown distill.
  In his right hand a tipped staffe he held,
  With which his feeble steps he stayed still:
  For, he was faint with cold, and weak with eld;
That scarse his loosed limbes he hable was to weld.

Stanzas 28–46
Mutabilitie's pageant includes the seasons, months, day and
night, the hours, and finally life and death. On the omission
of the planetary week, see 50–53*n*. The irony is noted by
Hawkins (1961): instead of proving the changefulness of
things, the cycle of the seasons and months shows their
permanence in change.

Stanzas 28–31
Mutabilitie begins with the pageant of the seasons because,
when Saturn was overthrown, Jove brought in the four seasons
(Ovid, *Met*. i 113–8). Nature allows Mutabilitie to undo her
case: it is not simply that Nature's Order rather than Mutabilitie governs the change of seasons but that any attempt to
displace Jove would displace the seasons. On the correlation
of the ages of man with the seasons of the year, see Tuve
(1933). S.'s immediate model may be Ovid, *Met*. xv 199–213.
Lewis (1967) 93 notes that the theme of Jocundity receives its
fullest expression in this part of the pageant. The seasons, and
later the months, are extraordinarily joyful.

Stanza 28
This experiment in employing only two rhymes seems designed
to introduce the notion of a cycle; cf. 44.
2 **lusty**: vigorous.
7–9 Spring is the season of both amorous and military
campaigns, as R. N. Ringler (1961) 421 observes, citing
Bartholomaeus (1582) 146. **stoures**: encounters. **guilt**:
gilded. **morion**: a helmet without a beaver; worn by
Bellona, *V.B.* xv 5.

Stanza 29
5 **chauffed**: heated.
8 **Libbard**: leopard.

Stanza 30
7 **corne**: grain.
9 **yold**: yielded.

Stanza 31
1 **frize**: coarse woollen cloth. The pun is reinforced by the
rhyme.
4 **bill**: nose.
5 **limbeck**: alembic, a retort for distilling.
7 **stayed still**: always supported.
9 **loosed**: weakened. **weld**: i.e. wield: move.

Stanzas 32–43
Each month represents the age of man appropriate to its time
of year and in a role appropriate to its agricultural activity.
Each rides, or is associated with, its zodiacal sign, which is the
'house' of the zodiac occupied by the sun during that month.
Cf. the zodiacal signs in V Proem 5.6 to 6.4. Each month is
given a whole stanza, except March, which begins at line 3
because it is the third month, and February which loses the
final line because it is the shortest month. On the iconographical
tradition behind S.'s pageant, see Hawkins (1961) 88f. See also
Ruskin, *Stones of Venice* II vii 52, and the woodcuts to the
months in the *S.C.*

729

32

These, marching softly, thus in order went,
  And after them, the Monthes all riding came;
First, sturdy *March* with brows full sternly bent,
  And armed strongly, rode vpon a Ram,
  The same which ouer *Hellespontus* swam:
Yet in his hand a spade he also hent,
  And in a bag all sorts of seeds ysame,
  Which on the earth he strowed as he went,
And fild her womb with fruitfull hope of nourishment.

33

Next came fresh *Aprill* full of lustyhed,
  And wanton as a Kid whose horne new buds:
Vpon a Bull he rode, the same which led
  Europa floting through th'*Argolick* fluds:
  His hornes were gilden all with golden studs
And garnished with garlonds goodly dight
  Of all the fairest flowres and freshest buds
  Which th'earth brings forth, and wet he seem'd in sight
With waues, through which he waded for his loues delight.

34

Then came faire *May*, the fayrest mayd on ground,
  Deckt all with dainties of her seasons pryde,
And throwing flowres out of her lap around:
  Vpon two brethrens shoulders she did ride,
  The twinnes of *Leda*; which on eyther side
Supported her like to their soueraine Queene.
  Lord! how all creatures laught, when her they spide,
  And leapt and daunc't as they had rauisht beene!
And *Cupid* selfe about her fluttred all in greene.

35

And after her, came iolly *Iune*, arrayd
  All in greene leaues, as he a Player were;
Yet in his time, he wrought as well as playd,
  That by his plough-yrons mote right well appeare:
  Vpon a Crab he rode, that him did beare
With crooked crawling steps an vncouth pase,
  And backward yode, as Bargemen wont to fare
  Bending their force contrary to their face,
Like that vngracious crew which faines demurest grace.

36

Then came hot *Iuly* boyling like to fire,
  That all his garments he had cast away:
Vpon a Lyon raging yet with ire
  He boldly rode and made him to obay:
  It was the beast that whylome did forray
The Nemæan forrest, till th'*Amphytrionide*
  Him slew, and with his hide did him array;
  Behinde his back a sithe, and by his side
Vnder his belt he bore a sickle circling wide.

Argument to the *S.C.* sturdy: stern, surly.
4–5 armed strongly: befitting the month of Mars.
Cf. Spring, 28.7–9. rode vpon a Ram: Jove disguised as a ram bore Helle in flight from her stepmother until she fell into the water that now bears her name (see III xi 30.5 and V Proem 5.6–7); here the zodiacal sign Aries which Boccaccio, *Gen. Deor.* IV lxviii, sees as symbolic of procreation and the fruitfulness of spring (Lotspeich, 1932, 118).
7 ysame: together.

Stanza 33
3–4 Vpon a Bull he rode: Jove, disguised as a bull, carried Europa on his back over the sea; here the zodiacal sign Taurus. The identification is made by Ovid, *Fasti* v 617. See III xi 30.6–9. Argolick: Greek.
5–8 In Ovid, *Met.* ii 856, the bull's horns are more clear than pearls (Golding translates 'More cleare . . . than the Christall stone') and are entwined with garlands of fresh flowers (867–8). golden studs may suggest stars. freshest buds may allude obliquely to the traditional etymology of April, from Lat. *aperire*, to open, as a time when buds open. As Ruskin observes, his wetness refers to April showers.

Stanza 34
1 faire May: the epithet and name prepare for her personification and the play upon her name.
2 pryde: most flourishing state.
4–6 twinnes of Leda: Castor and Pollux; here the zodiacal sign Gemini. They are so named in order to continue Jove's amorous exploits: he seduced Leda by disguising himself as a swan. See III xi 32, V Proem 6.2. R. N. Ringler (1961) 426 notes that May rides on their shoulders because Gemini 'hath mastry in mans body, of the shoulders, armes, and handes' (Bartholomaeus, 1582, 126ʳ).
7–8 Suggesting the festivities of May-day about the may-pole.

Stanza 35
2 greene leaues: the attire of an actor appearing as the wild or savage man.
5–7 Crab: the zodiacal sign Cancer. In this sign the sun begins to move backwards.
9 Like that vngracious crew . . .: i.e. like those who, as they leave, walk backwards and bow with affected politeness. vngracious: devoid of grace, in contrast to the demurest grace which they feign. The opening reference to the actor who appears as the savage man perhaps triggers the reference to the truly 'savage' crew which appears most courtly.

Stanza 36
2 As Summer appears 'naked starke' (Ovid, *Met.* ii 28, trans. Golding).
3–4 Vpon a Lyon raging: Wrath rides upon a lion at I iv 33.2.
5–7 The Nemæan forrest: the Nemean lion was slain by Hercules in the first of his labours (see II v 31.1–5); here the zodiacal sign Leo. Hercules is called th'Amphytrionide because he was the reputed son of Amphitryon; it reminds us that his real father was Jove (see III xi 33.6–9). The associative links are noteworthy: Iuly, who has cast off his garments and appears upon a raging lion, suggests Hercules raging in death when he sought to cast off his burning garment.
8–9 He both reaps and mows, as Ruskin notices.

Stanza 32
1–2 softly: slowly, as do the seasons. S. opens March's stanza with marching. As the months pass more quickly than do the seasons, they ride rather than walk, except for August, September and January.

3 First: because 'the yeare beginneth in March'; see E.K.'s

37

The sixt was *August*, being rich arrayd
　In garment all of gold downe to the ground:
　Yet rode he not, but led a louely Mayd
　Forth by the lilly hand, the which was cround
　With eares of corne, and full her hand was found;
　That was the righteous Virgin, which of old
　Liv'd here on earth, and plenty made abound;
　But, after Wrong was lov'd and Iustice solde,
She left th'vnrighteous world and was to heauen extold.

38

Next him, *September* marched eeke on foote;
　Yet was he heauy laden with the spoyle
　Of haruests riches, which he made his boot,
　And him enricht with bounty of the soyle:
　In his one hand, as fit for haruests toyle,
　He held a knife-hook; and in th'other hand
　A paire of waights, with which he did assoyle
　Both more and lesse, where it in doubt did stand,
And equall gaue to each as Iustice duly scann'd.

39

Then came *October* full of merry glee:
　For, yet his noule was totty of the must,
　Which he was treading in the wine-fats see,
　And of the ioyous oyle, whose gentle gust
　Made him so frollick and so full of lust:
　Vpon a dreadfull Scorpion he did ride,
　The same which by *Dianaes* doom vniust
　Slew great *Orion*: and eeke by his side
He had his ploughing share, and coulter ready tyde.

40

Next was *Nouember*, he full grosse and fat,
　As fed with lard, and that right well might seeme;
　For, he had been a fatting hogs of late,
　That yet his browes with sweat, did reek and steem,
　And yet the season was full sharp and breem;
　In planting eeke he took no small delight:
　Whereon he rode, not easie was to deeme;
　For it a dreadfull *Centaure* was in sight,
The seed of *Saturne*, and faire *Nais*, *Chiron* hight.

41

And after him, came next the chill *December*:
　Yet he through merry feasting which he made,
　And great bonfires, did not the cold remember;
　His Sauiours birth his mind so much did glad:
　Vpon a shaggy-bearded Goat he rode,
　The same wherewith *Dan Ioue* in tender yeares,
　They say, was nourisht by th'*Idæan* mayd;
　And in his hand a broad deepe boawle he beares;
Of which, he freely drinks an health to all his peeres.

42

Then came old *Ianuary*, wrapped well
　In many weeds to keep the cold away;
　Yet did he quake and quiuer like to quell,
　And blowe his nayles to warme them if he may:
　For, they were numbd with holding all the day
　An hatchet keene, with which he felled wood,
　And from the trees did lop the needlesse spray:
　Vpon an huge great Earth-pot steane he stood;
From whose wide mouth, there flowed forth the Romane floud.

Stanza 37

1–2　**August** is given an august appearance, alluding to the Lat. *augustus*, consecrated, venerable.

4–9　**the righteous Virgin**: Astræa, the goddess of Justice, here seen as Virgo, August's zodiacal sign. The association of Astræa with corn is traditional; see Yates (1947) 28. On her flight and stellification, see V i 11.　**extold**: raised.

Stanza 38

1　**September** walks because he bears the scales of the Virgin who also walks, and marks their measured pace.

3　**boot**: booty.

7　**waights**: scales; the zodiacal sign Libra; see V i 11.8–9. **assoyle**: solve or determine.

9　**equall**: what was equitable.　**scann'd**: judged.

Stanza 39

2　**his noule was totty of the must**: his head was always tipsy with the new wine.

3　**wine-fats see**: the sea of liquor in the wine vats.

4　**gust**: taste.

6–8　The **Scorpion** was sent by **Diana** to kill **Orion** when he boasted that he could kill any earthly creature (Comes, 1616, VIII xiii); the zodiacal sign Scorpion. For Stephanus's account, see Starnes and Talbert (1955) 70–1. See II ii 46.1–3.

Stanza 40

5　**breem**: rough, stormy; 'chill, bitter' (E.K.'s gloss to *S.C.* Feb. 43).

7–9　**Nouember's** zodiacal sign is Sagittarius, the Archer who, on earth, was a centaur; here **Chiron**, as in Comes (1616) IV xii.　**Nais**: 'a nymphe of the water' (Cooper, 1565), named '*Philliras*' (Philyra) at III xi 43.7 who was a Naiad. Cf. Apollonius, *Argonautica* ii 1231–41. Fowler (1964) 232 notes that S. conflates two traditions: Chiron as the son of Saturn and Philyra, and as the son of Magnes and Nais; hence who he was **not easie was to deeme**.

Stanza 41

5–7　**December's** zodiacal sign is Capricornus, identified with the **Goat** whose milk fed the infant **Ioue** when he was tended by **th'Idæan mayd**, Amalthea, a nymph on Mount Ida. The connection is made by Comes (1616) VII ii. The birth of Jove implies the renewal of the months which celebrate his later deeds.

Stanza 42

3　**like to quell**: as if he, **Ianuary**, were perishing.

8　**steane**: jar, urn; here the zodiacal sign Aquarius, the water-bearer.

9　The **Romane floud** should be the Tiber though such a reference is puzzling. In *V.B.* ix, a Saturn-like figure leans on a pot from which pours a flood associated with the corruption of Rome. Zitner (1968) 142 suggests that S. recalls the *Ruins of Rome* xiii: the overflowing Tiber washes away Rome's pride. A possible link with **Ianuary** is through the Janiculum, a hill on the right bank of the Tiber, with walls built by Janus (*Aen.* viii 356–8). Of all the months, January alone stands, perhaps with reference to his role of ushering in the year.

43

And lastly, came cold *February*, sitting
   In an old wagon, for he could not ride;
   Drawne of two fishes for the season fitting,
   Which through the flood before did softly slyde
   And swim away: yet had he by his side
   His plough and harnesse fit to till the ground,
   And tooles to prune the trees, before the pride
   Of hasting Prime did make them burgein round:
So past the twelue Months forth, and their dew places found.

44

And after these, there came the *Day*, and *Night*,
   Riding together both with equall pase,
   Th'one on a Palfrey blacke, the other white;
   But *Night* had couered her vncomely face
   With a blacke veile, and held in hand a mace,
   On top whereof the moon and stars were pight,
   And sleep and darknesse round about did trace:
   But *Day* did beare, vpon his scepters hight,
The goodly Sun, encompast all with beames bright.

45

Then came the *Howres*, faire daughters of high *Ioue*,
   And timely *Night*, the which were all endewed
   With wondrous beauty fit to kindle loue;
   But they were Virgins all, and loue eschewed,
   That might forslack the charge to them fore-shewed
   By mighty *Ioue*; who did them Porters make
   Of heauens gate (whence all the gods issued)
   Which they did dayly watch, and nightly wake
By euen turnes, ne euer did their charge forsake.

46

And after all came *Life*, and lastly *Death*;
   Death with most grim and griesly visage seene,
   Yet is he nought but parting of the breath;
   Ne ought to see, but like a shade to weene,
   Vnbodied, vnsoul'd, vnheard, vnseene.
   But *Life* was like a faire young lusty boy,
   Such as they faine *Dan Cupid* to haue beene,
   Full of delightfull health and liuely ioy,
Deckt all with flowres, and wings of gold fit to employ.

47

When these were past, thus gan the *Titanesse*;
   Lo, mighty mother, now be iudge and say,
   Whether in all thy creatures more or lesse
   CHANGE doth not raign and beare the greatest sway:
   For, who sees not, that *Time* on all doth pray?
   But *Times* do change and moue continually.
   So nothing here long standeth in one stay:
   Wherefore, this lower world who can deny
But to be subiect still to *Mutabilitie*?

48

Then thus gan *Ioue*; Right true it is, that these
   And all things else that vnder heauen dwell
   Are chaung'd of *Time*, who doth them all disseise
   Of being: But, who is it (to me tell)
   That *Time* himselfe doth moue and still compell!
   To keepe his course? Is not that namely wee
   Which poure that vertue from our heauenly cell,
   That moues them all, and makes them changed be?
So them we gods doe rule, and in them also thee.

732

Stanza 43

3 The **two fishes** represent the zodiacal sign Pisces, a symbol suitable for the season of Lent, as Renwick (1923) 203 notes.

4–5 This **flood** is the water flowing from Aquarius's urn.

Stanza 44

2 **Day, and Night** ride as a pair to illustrate the seasonal balancing of diurnal and nocturnal hours about the equinoxes. See Fowler (1964) 232. Their balance is illustrated further by the single pair of rhymes in the stanza.

3–5 Cf. Night at I v 20. The **mace** brings sleep, as at I iv 44.6.

7 **trace**: go.

Stanza 45

On S.'s conception of the **Howres**, see Hieatt (1960) 33–8, 111–3.

1–2 **daughters of high Ioue**: traditionally, the Hours are daughters of Jove and Themis. In *Epith.* 98–102, they are daughters of Day and Night. Since Jove rules the heavens, he may be identified with the light, specifically with the sun which Day bears upon his sceptre. See I vii 23.1. **high**: empyrean, eternal, in contrast to **timely**: temporal, belonging to time.

2–3 **beauty fit to kindle loue**: they gain this beauty because they attend Venus together with the Graces. Padelford, *Var.* vi 309, cites the entertainment of the Queen at Elvetham: as Venus, she is greeted by the three Graces and the three Hours 'which by the Poets are fained to be the Guardians of Heaven's gates' (Nichols, 1823, iii 108).

4–6 **loue eschewed**: from the commonplace view that love wastes time. **forslack**: cause the neglect of. **fore-shewed**: showed beforehand, ordained.

6–7 See V ix 31–32*n*.

8–9 Cf. Homer, *Iliad* v 749–51. **wake**: guard. **euen turnes** suggests regular movement in a circle. Fowler (1970) 60 notes that Mutabilitie introduces the notion of Jove as equal distributor: 'The 12 unequal hours can be assigned diurnal and nocturnal watches by *even* turns only because each is as much longer by day at one season as it is longer by night at a season exactly 6 months later.'

Stanza 46

1 **lastly Death**: significantly, however, the celebration of **Life** concludes Time's pageant.

Stanza 47

5 **Time on all doth pray**: cf. 'wicked *Time*' in the Garden of Adonis, III vi 39–41. S.'s phrase stands as a succinct final statement of a theme that haunts the poem; cf. the Latin tag *tempus edax rerum*. Cf. V iv 8.1.

Stanza 48

1–4 Cf. *View* 45: 'time working alteration of all things'. For the proverb, see C. G. Smith (1970) 770. **disseise**: forcibly deprive, usually wrongfully.

5 **still**: always; referring to Mutabilitie's use of the term at 47.9.

6 **namely**: above all, alone.

7 **vertue**: power, influence.

49

To whom, thus *Mutability*: The things
    Which we see not how they are mov'd and swayd,
    Ye may attribute to your selues as Kings,
    And say they by your secret powre are made:
    But what we see not, who shall vs perswade?
    But were they so, as ye them faine to be,
    Mov'd by your might, and ordred by your ayde;
    Yet what if I can proue, that euen yee
Your selues are likewise chang'd, and subiect vnto mee?

50

And first, concerning her that is the first,
    Euen you faire *Cynthia*, whom so much ye make
    Ioues dearest darling, she was bred and nurst
    On *Cynthus* hill, whence she her name did take:
    Then is she mortall borne, how-so ye crake;
    Besides, her face and countenance euery day
    We changed see, and sundry forms partake,
    Now hornd, now round, now bright, now brown and gray:
So that *as changefull as the Moone* men vse to say.

51

Next, *Mercury*, who though he lesse appeare
    To change his hew, and alwayes seeme as one;
    Yet, he his course doth altar euery yeare,
    And is of late far out of order gone:
    So *Venus* eeke, that goodly Paragone,
    Though faire all night, yet is she darke all day;
    And *Phœbus* self, who lightsome is alone,
    Yet is he oft eclipsed by the way,
And fills the darkned world with terror and dismay.

52

Now *Mars* that valiant man is changed most:
    For, he some times so far runs out of square,
    That he his way doth seem quite to haue lost,
    And cleane without his vsuall sphere to fare;
    That euen these Star-gazers stonisht are
    At sight thereof, and damne their lying bookes:
    So likewise, grim Sir *Saturne* oft doth spare
    His sterne aspect, and calme his crabbed lookes:
So many turning cranks these haue, so many crookes.

53

But you *Dan Ioue*, that only constant are,
    And King of all the rest, as ye do clame,
    Are you not subiect eeke to this misfare?
    Then let me aske you this withouten blame,
    Where were ye borne? some say in *Crete* by name,
    Others in *Thebes*, and others other-where;
    But wheresoeuer they comment the same,
    They all consent that ye begotten were,
And borne here in this world, ne other can appeare.

Stanza 49

1–5 Mutabilitie is answered by her allusion to 2 Cor. 4.18: 'The things which are not sene are eternal.'

Stanzas 50–53

The order of the planets follows the Ptolemaic system except that Jove usurps Saturn's role as the last. The planetary week, omitted earlier, is included now in Mutabilitie's review of the seven planets. Fowler (1964) 233 notes: 'It is the consideration of this temporal measure – the most fundamental of the structural series of the poem, but one only now, with Saturn's day, completed – that is Mutabilitie's undoing. For contemplation of the great week of creation leads inevitably to Nature's verdict about time's eternal conclusion.'

Stanza 50

1   **the first**: being closest to the earth.
2   **you**] 'yon' sugg. Birch (1751), for **Cynthia** is not addressed.
3   **Ioues dearest darling**: slanders the virgin Diana; an address without classical warrant.
4   **On Cynthus hill**: see II iii 31.1–2; for her birth, II xii 13.
5   **crake**: boast.
8   **brown**: dark.
9   See C. G. Smith (1970) 98.

Stanzas 51–52

V Proem 8 cites the eccentricity of the sun, Mars and Saturn. Since **Mercury** is difficult to see because of the sun, its eccentricity was difficult to establish. Du Bartas, *Divine Weekes* II iv p. 213, writes that: 'His giddy course seems wandring in disorder; / And yet there's found, in this disorder, order.'

Stanza 51

4   **of late**: this topical allusion has not been clarified.
8   **by the way**: in his course.

Stanza 52

4   **without**: outside. The planets were assumed to be embedded in a sphere whose rolling caused their motion.
7–9   **Saturne**'s baleful influence is modified by conjunction with other planets.   **aspect**: punning on the astrological sense. In 9, Mutabilitie refers to the eccentric circles and the epicycles by which irregularities of the heavenly bodies in the Ptolemaic system were explained.   **cranks**: winding paths. **turning**: alluding to his name.

Stanza 53

3   **misfare**: going astray.
5–9   **Where were ye borne?**: Comes (1616) II i treats the conflicting traditions of Jove's birthplace and concludes that there can be no certainty in the matter.   **comment**: devise.

54

Then are ye mortall borne, and thrall to me,
  Vnlesse the kingdome of the sky yee make
  Immortall, and vnchangeable to bee;
  Besides, that power and vertue which ye spake,
  That ye here worke, doth many changes take,
  And your owne natures change: for, each of you
  That vertue haue, or this, or that to make,
  Is checkt and changed from his nature trew,
By others opposition or obliquid view.

55

Besides, the sundry motions of your Spheares,
  So sundry waies and fashions as clerkes faine,
  Some in short space, and some in longer yeares;
  What is the same but alteration plaine?
  Onely the starrie skie doth still remaine:
  Yet do the Starres and Signes therein still moue,
  And euen it self is mov'd, as wizards saine.
  But all that moueth, doth mutation loue:
Therefore both you and them to me I subiect proue.

56

Then since within this wide great *Vniuerse*
  Nothing doth firme and permanent appeare,
  But all things tost and turned by transuerse:
  What then should let, but I aloft should reare
  My Trophee, and from all, the triumph beare?
  Now iudge then (O thou greatest goddesse trew!)
  According as thy selfe doest see and heare,
  And vnto me addoom that is my dew;
That is the rule of all, all being rul'd by you.

57

So hauing ended, silence long ensewed,
  Ne *Nature* to or fro spake for a space,
  But with firme eyes affixt, the ground still viewed.
  Meane while, all creatures, looking in her face,
  Expecting th'end of this so doubtfull case,
  Did hang in long suspence what would ensew,
  To whether side should fall the soueraigne place:
  At length, she looking vp with chearefull view,
The silence brake, and gaue her doome in speeches few.

58

I well consider all that ye haue sayd,
  And find that all things stedfastnes doe hate
  And changed be: yet being rightly wayd
  They are not changed from their first estate;
  But by their change their being doe dilate:
  And turning to themselues at length againe,
  Doe worke their owne perfection so by fate:
  Then ouer them Change doth not rule and raigne;
But they raigne ouer change, and doe their states maintaine.

Stanza 54
1–6   Mutabilitie's **Vnlesse** destroys her case by invoking a **kingdome** which is **vnchangeable to bee**. Her claim that **your owne natures change** (6) may be applied against her: she will change, for the time will come when 'none no more change shall see' (59.5).
4   **which ye spake**: at 48.7.
6–9   The path and influence (**vertue**) of each planet is modified by its relative position to the other planets, whether opposite (when it is **checkt**) or in an oblique position (when it is **changed**).   **obliquid**: a coinage used only here.

Stanza 55
2   **clerkes**: scholars.
4   **alteration**: which she personifies in the Arg.
5   **the starrie skie**: the crystalline sphere of the fixed stars. Johnson (1937) 195 n81 observes that S. ignores the new star of 1572 which shattered the Aristotelian doctrine of the changeless heavens.   **doth still remaine**: remains constant.   **still** points to the paradox in the next line: they move still, i.e. continually. It is just possible that she means, 'remains to be considered', for she is about to play her trump card.
6–7   **Starres**: the fixed stars.   **Signes**: the zodiacal signs. Mutabilitie refers to the precession of the equinoxes. See V Proem 4.6–9.

Stanza 56
1–3   The emphasis upon turning and change reaches a climax here.   **turned by transuerse**, i.e. turned awry, points to the etymology of **Vniuerse**: one turning. While Mutabilitie proves her point, Nature may reply with the notion of all turning: 'turning to themselues at length againe' (58.6), i.e. turning-to-one.
4–5   She realizes her ambition to rival her sister Bellona in power (vi 32.4–5).   **let**: prevent.
8   Ironically, Mutabilitie invokes judgment against her: she receives her due but not in the way she expects.   **addoom**: judge.

Stanza 57
2   **to or fro**: for or against the question.
4   In effect, Nature's veil is removed by the final clarity of her judgment.
5   **Expecting**: awaiting.
7   **whether**: which.

Stanza 58
3–7   **first estate**: original state of existence.   **dilate**: expand, in the Aristotelian sense of fulfilling the idea, nature, or form. Change is interpreted in Aristotelian terms as a becoming. Yet **first estate** suggests also the Platonic notion: the end of growth is **turning** or returning to original perfection. (The Pauline notion of sowing a natural body to raise a spiritual body, 1 Cor. 15.36–44, is absent because Nature answers Mutabilitie in her own terms.)   **perfection**: implies natural completion, as at III vi 3.9. Heninger (1974) 393 cites the literal sense of the word, from Lat. *perficere*, 'to go through to the end'. This verdict answers at last Despair's claim that 'strong necessitie / . . . holds the world in his still chaunging state' (I ix 42.6–7).

59

Cease therefore daughter further to aspire,
   And thee content thus to be rul'd by me:
   For thy decay thou seekst by thy desire;
   But time shall come that all shall changed bee,
   And from thenceforth, none no more change shall see.
   So was the *Titaness* put downe and whist,
   And *Ioue* confirm'd in his imperiall see.
   Then was that whole assembly quite dismist,
And *Natur's* selfe did vanish, whither no man wist.

The VIII. Canto, vnperfite.

1

WHen I bethinke me on that speech whyleare,
   Of *Mutability*, and well it way:
   Me seemes, that though she all vnworthy were
   Of the Heav'ns Rule; yet very sooth to say,
   In all things else she beares the greatest sway.
   Which makes me loath this state of life so tickle,
   And loue of things so vaine to cast away;
   Whose flowring pride, so fading and so fickle,
Short *Time* shall soon cut down with his consuming sickle.

2

Then gin I thinke on that which Nature sayd,
   Of that same time when no more *Change* shall be,
   But stedfast rest of all things firmely stayd
   Vpon the pillours of Eternity,
   That is contrayr to *Mutabilitie*:
   For, all that moueth, doth in *Change* delight:
   But thence-forth all shall rest eternally
   With Him that is the God of Sabbaoth hight:
O that great Sabbaoth God, graunt me that Sabaoths sight.

Stanza 59

1   **daughter**: Nature claims Mutabilitie as her own. Cf.
Mutabilitie's claim that she is the daughter of Chaos, vi 26.4–6.
further: further than the earth; alternatively, any longer. Both
meanings imply Mutabilitie's exclusion from heaven.
2   **me**: placed emphatically here though Mutabilitie has
always allowed that Nature 'is the rule of all' (56.9).
3   **decay**: downfall. If everything changes, so does Change
itself.
4–5   Upton (1758) cites Paul on the Last Judgment:
'Beholde, I shewe you a secret thing . . . we shal all be changed
. . . when this corruptible hathe put on incorruption, and this
mortal hathe put on immortalitie, then shal be broght to passe
the saying that is written, Death is swallowed up into victorie'
(1 Cor. 15.51, 54).
6   **put downe**: also literally, below the moon.   **whist**:
silenced.
7   **see**: throne.

Canto viii

Title
vnperfite: imperfect.

Stanza 1
5   **else**: yet Mutabilitie has shown that she also rules the
heavens. That her claim is not refuted leads L. J. Owen (1972)
to argue that Nature's verdict does not refute her.
6–7   Berger (1968) 172 finds an added meaning: I am loth
to cast away this state of life and this love of things. He interprets **vaine** in the adverbial sense: 'The state of life and love
of things may be vainly put off if no experience or vision can
attain to what lies beyond the mutable whirl.'
9   **Short**: brief; which makes short; also in the philosophical
sense argued by Hieatt (1960) 56–9: cyclical or planetary time
created by the sun in contrast to the divine time of Eternity.

Stanza 2
5   **contrayr**: the opposite of.
6   Even in this balancing stanza giving Nature's case, S.
recalls Mutabilitie's claim at vii 55.8; but it is one allowed by
Nature herself at 58.2.
7–9   **Sabbaoth God**: Upton (1758) proposed a distinction,
which he thought the text confounded, between 'Sabaoth',
hosts or armies, and 'Sabbath', rest. He emended the text:
'With him, that is the God of Sabaoth hight: / O that great
Sabaoth's God, grant me that Sabbath's sight!', i.e. grant me
sight of that day of rest, that great Sabbath and eternal rest.
However, 'the Lord of Sabaoth' (Rom. 9.29, James 5.4)
appears in the Geneva version as 'Lord of hostes'. Allen (1949)
93–4 argues that 'Sabaoth' *1611* should be kept, and interprets
the final prayer as one for redemption and admission to the
ranks of the saints and not for a state of actionlessness. There is
no reason not to see both meanings present. S. prays for the
sight of the Lord on the last day: both for the sight of the
host, which will be the body of the redeemed, and for the rest
which comes after the six days of history – the six books of his
own history, *The Faerie Queene*.

Appendix 1: A Letter of the Authors

A letter of the Authors expounding his whole intention in the course of this worke: which for that it giueth great light to the Reader, for the better vnderstanding is hereunto annexed.

To the Right noble, and Valorous, Sir Walter Raleigh knight, Lo. Wardein of the Stanneryes, and her Maiesties liefetenaunt of the County of Cornewayll.

Sir knowing how doubtfully all Allegories may be construed, and this booke of mine, which I haue entituled the Faery Queene, being a continued Allegory, or darke conceit, I haue thought good aswell for auoyding of gealous opinions and misconstructions, as also for your better light in reading therof, (being so by you commanded,) to discouer vnto you the general intention and meaning, which in the whole course thereof I haue fashioned, without expressing of any particular purposes or by-accidents therein occasioned. The generall end therefore of all the booke is to fashion a gentleman or noble person in vertuous and gentle discipline: Which for that I conceiued shoulde be most plausible and pleasing, being coloured with an historicall fiction, the which the most part of men delight to read, rather for variety of matter, then for profite of the ensample: I chose the historye of king Arthure, as most fitte for the excellency of his person, being made famous by many mens former workes, and also furthest from the daunger of enuy, and suspition of present time. In which I haue followed all the antique Poets historicall, first Homere, who in the Persons of Agamemnon and Vlysses hath ensampled a good gouernour and a vertuous man, the one in his Ilias, the other in his Odysseis: then Virgil, whose like intention was to doe in the person of Aeneas: after him Ariosto comprised them both in his Orlando: and lately Tasso disseuered them againe, and formed both parts in two persons, namely that part which they in Philosophy call Ethice, or vertues of a priuate man, coloured in his Rinaldo: The other named Politice in his Godfredo. By ensample of which excellente Poets, I labour to pourtraict in Arthure, before he was king, the image of a braue knight, perfected in the twelue priuate morall vertues, as Aristotle hath deuised, the which is the purpose of these first twelue bookes: which if I finde to be well accepted, I may be perhaps encoraged, to frame the other part of pollticke vertues in his person, after that hee came to be king. To some I know this Methode will seeme displeasaunt, which had rather haue good discipline deliuered plainly in way of precepts, or sermoned at large, as they vse, then thus clowdily enwrapped in Allegoricall deuises. But such, me seeme, should be satisfide with the vse of these dayes, seeing all things accounted by their showes, and nothing esteemed of, that is not delightfull and pleasing to commune sence. For this cause is Xenophon preferred before Plato, for that the one in the exquisite depth of his iudgement, formed a Commune welth such as it should be, but the other in the person of Cyrus and the Persians fashioned a gouernement such as might best be: So much more profitable and gratious is doctrine by ensample, then by rule. So haue I laboured to doe in the person of Arthure: whome I conceiue after his long education by Timon, to whom he was by Merlin deliuered to be brought vp, so soone as he was borne of the Lady Igrayne, to haue seene in a dream or vision the Faery Queen, with whose excellent beauty rauished, he awaking resolued to seeke her out, and so being by Merlin armed, and by Timon throughly instructed, he went to seeke her forth in Faerye land. In that Faery Queene I meane glory in my generall intention, but in my particular I conceiue the most excellent and glorious person of our soueraine the Queene, and her kingdome in Faery land. And yet in some places els, I doe otherwise shadow her. For considering she beareth two persons, the one of a most royall Queene or Empresse, the other of a most vertuous and beautifull Lady, this latter part in some places I doe expresse in Belphœbe, fashioning her name according to your owne excellent conceipt of Cynthia, (Phœbe and Cynthia being both names of Diana.) So in the person of Prince Arthure I sette forth magnificence in particular, which vertue for that (according to Aristotle and the rest) it is the perfection of all the rest, and conteineth in it them all, therefore in the whole course I mention the deedes of Arthure applyable to that vertue, which I write of in that booke. But of the xii. other vertues, I make xii. other knights the patrones, for the more variety of the history: Of which these three bookes contayn three, The first of the knight of the Redcrosse, in whome I expresse Holynes: The seconde of Sir Guyon, in whome I sette forth Temperaunce: The third of Britomartis a Lady knight, in whome I picture Chastity. But because the beginning of the whole worke seemeth abrupte and as depending vpon other antecedents, it needs that ye know the occasion of these three knights seuerall aduentures. For the Methode of a Poet historical is not such, as of an Historiographer. For an Historiographer discourseth of affayres orderly as they were donne, accounting as well the times as the actions, but a Poet thrusteth into the middest, euen where it most concerneth him, and there recoursing to the thinges forepaste, and diuining of thinges to come, maketh a pleasing Analysis of all. The beginning therefore of my history, if it were to be told by an Historiographer should be the twelfth booke, which is the last, where I deuise that the Faery Queene kept her Annuall feaste xii. dayes, vppon which xii. seuerall dayes, the occasions of the xii. seuerall aduentures hapned, which being vndertaken by xii. seuerall knights, are in these xii books seuerally handled and discoursed. The first was this. In the beginning of the feast, there presented him selfe a tall clownishe younge man, who falling before the Queen of Faries desired a boone (as the manner then was) which during that feast she might not refuse: which was that hee might haue the atchieuement of any aduenture, which during that feaste should happen, that being graunted, he rested him on the floore, vnfitte through his rusticity for a better place. Soone after entred a faire Ladye in mourning weedes, riding on a white Asse, with a dwarfe behind her leading a warlike steed, that bore the Armes of a knight, and his speare in the dwarfes hand. Shee falling before the Queene of Faeries, com-playned that her father and mother an ancient King and Queene, had bene by an huge dragon many years shut vp in a brasen Castle, who thence suffred them not to yssew: and therefore besought the Faery Queene to assygne her some one of her knights to take on him that exployt. Presently that clownish person vpstarting, desired that aduenture: whereat the Queene much wondering, and the Lady much gainesaying, yet he earnestly importuned his desire. In the end the Lady told him that vnlesse that armour which she brought, would serue him (that is the armour of a Christian man specified by Saint Paul v. Ephes.) that he could not succeed in that enterprise, which being forthwith put vpon him with dewe furnitures thereunto, he seemed the goodliest man in al that company, and was well liked of the Lady. And eftesoones taking on him knighthood, and mounting on that straunge Courser, he went forth with her on that aduenture: where beginneth the first booke, vz.

A gentle knight was pricking on the playne. &c.

The second day ther came in a Palmer bearing an Infant with bloody hands, whose Parents he complained to haue bene slayn by an Enchaunteresse called Acrasia: and therfore craued of the Faery Queene, to appoint him some knight, to performe that aduenture, which being assigned to Sir Guyon, he presently went forth with that same Palmer: which is the beginning of the second booke and the whole subiect thereof. The third day there came in, a Groome who complained before the Faery Queene, that a vile Enchaunter called Busirane had in hand a most faire Lady called Amoretta, whom he kept in most grieuous torment, because she would not yield him the pleasure of her body. Whereupon Sir Scudamour the louer of that Lady presently tooke on him that aduenture. But being vnable to performe it by reason of the hard Enchauntments, after long sorrow, in the end met with Britomartis, who succoured him, and reskewed his loue.

But by occasion hereof, many other aduentures are intermedled, but rather as Accidents, then intend-ments. As the loue of Britomart, the ouerthrow of Marinell, the misery of Florimell, the vertuousnes of Belphœbe, the lasciuiousnes of Hellenora, and many the like.

Thus much Sir, I haue briefly ouerronne to direct your vnderstanding to the wel-head of the History, that from thence gathering the whole intention of the conceit, ye may as in a handfull gripe al the discourse, which otherwise may happily seeme tedious and confused. So humbly crauing the continuaunce of your honorable fauour towards me, and th'eternall establishment of your happines, I humbly take leaue.

23. Ianuary. 1589.

Yours most humbly affectionate.
Ed. Spenser.

A Vision vpon this conceipt of the *Faery Queene*

Me thought I saw the graue, where *Laura* lay,
Within that Temple, where the vestall flame
Was wont to burne, and passing by that way,
To see that buried dust of liuing fame,
Whose tombe faire loue, and fairer vertue kept,
All suddenly I saw the Faery Queene:
At whose approch the soule of *Petrarke* wept,
And from thenceforth those graces were not seene.
For they this Queene attended, in whose steed
Obliuion laid him downe on *Lauras* herse:
Hereat the hardest stones were seene to bleed,
And grones of buried ghostes the heauens did perse.
  Where *Homers* spright did tremble all for griefe,
  And curst th'accesse of that celestiall theife.

Another of the same

The prayse of meaner wits this worke like profit brings,
As doth the Cuckoes song delight when *Philumena* sings.
If thou hast formed right true vertues face herein:
Vertue her selfe can best discerne, to whom they written bin.
If thou hast beautie praysd, let her sole lookes diuine
Iudge if ought therein be amis, and mend it by her cine.
If Chastitie want ought, or Temperance her dew,
Behold her Princely mind aright, and write thy Queene anew.
Meane while she shall perceiue, how farre her vertues sore
Aboue the reach of all that liue, or such as wrote of yore:
And thereby will excuse and fauour thy good will:
Whose vertue can not be exprest, but by an Angels quill.
  Of me no lines are lou'd, nor letters are of price,
  Of all which speake our English tongue, but those of thy deuice.
                                                            W. R.

To the learned Shepheard

Collyn I see by thy new taken taske,
  some sacred fury hath enricht thy braynes,
That leades thy muse in haughtie verse to maske,
  and loath the layes that longs to lowly swaynes.
That lifts thy notes from Shepheardes vnto kings,
So like the liuely Larke that mounting sings.

Thy louely Rosolinde seemes now forlorne,
  and all thy gentle flockes forgotten quight,
Thy chaunged hart now holdes thy pypes in scorne,
  those prety pypes that did thy mates delight.
Those trustie mates, that loued thee so well,
Whom thou gau'st mirth: as they gaue thee the bell.

Yet as thou earst with thy sweete roundelayes,
  didst stirre to glee our laddes in homely bowers:
So moughtst thou now in these refyned layes,
  delight the dainty eares of higher powers.
And so mought they in their deepe skanning skill
Alow and grace our Collyns flowing quill.

And fare befall that *Faerie Queene* of thine,
  in whose faire eyes loue linckt with vertue sits.
Enfusing by those bewties fiers deuyne,
  such high conceites into thy humble wits,
As raised hath poore pastors oaten reede,
From rusticke tunes, to chaunt heroique deedes.

So mought thy *Redcrosse knight* with happy hand
  victorious be in that faire Ilands right:
Which thou doest vaile in Type of Faery land
  Elyzas blessed field, that *Albion* hight.
That shieldes her friends, and warres her mightie foes,
Yet still with people, peace, and plentie flowes.

But (iolly Shepheard) though with pleasing style,
  thou feast the humour of the Courtly traine:
Let not conceipt thy setled sence beguile,
  ne daunted be through enuy or disdaine.
Subiect thy dome to her Empyring spright,
From whence thy Muse, and all the world takes light.
                                                       Hobynoll

Fayre *Thamis* streame, that from *Ludds* stately towne,
Runst paying tribute to the Ocean seas,
Let all thy Nymphes and Syrens of renowne
Be silent, whyle this Bryttane *Orpheus* playes:
Nere thy sweet bankes, there liues that sacred crowne,
Whose hand strowes Palme and neuer-dying bayes,
Let all at once, with thy soft murmuring sowne
Present her with this worthy Poets prayes.
For he hath taught hye drifts in shepeherdes weedes,
And deepe conceites now singes in *Faeries* deedes.
                                                       R. S.

Graue Muses march in triumph and with prayses,
Our Goddesse here hath giuen you leaue to land:
And biddes this rare dispenser of your graces
Bow downe his brow vnto her sacred hand.
Desertes findes dew in that most princely doome,
In whose sweete brest are all the Muses bredde:
So did that great *Augustus* erst in Roome
With leaues of fame adorne his Poets hedde.
Faire be the guerdon of your *Faery Queene*,
Euen of the fairest that the world hath seene.
                                                       H. B.   739

When stout *Achilles* heard of *Helens* rape
And what reuenge the States of Greece deuisd:
Thinking by sleight the fatall warres to scape,
In womans weedes him selfe he then disguisde:
But this deuise *Vlysses* soone did spy,
And brought him forth, the chaunce of warre to try.

When *Spencer* saw the fame was spredd so large,
Through Faery land of their renowned Queene:
Loth that his Muse should take so great a charge,
As in such haughty matter to be seene,
To seeme a shepeheard then he made his choice,
But *Sydney* heard him sing, and knew his voice.

And as *Vlysses* brought faire *Thetis* sonne
From his retyred life to menage armes:
So *Spencer* was by *Sidneys* speaches wonne,
To blaze her fame not fearing future harmes:
For well he knew, his Muse would soone be tyred
In her high praise, that all the world admired.

Yet as *Achilles* in those warlike frayes,
Did win the palme from all the *Grecian* Peeres:
So *Spencer* now to his immortall prayse,
Hath wonne the Laurell quite from all his feres.
What though his taske exceed a humaine witt,
He is excus'd, sith *Sidney* thought it fitt.

                                    W. I.

To looke vpon a worke of rare deuise
The which a workman setteth out to view,
And not to yield it the deserued prise,
That vnto such a workmanship is dew,
    Doth either proue the iudgement to be naught
    Or els doth shew a mind with enuy fraught.

To labour to commend a peece of worke,
Which no man goes about to discommend,
Would raise a iealous doubt that there did lurke,
Some secret doubt, whereto the prayse did tend.
    For when men know the goodnes of the wyne,
    T'is needlesse for the hoast to haue a sygne.

Thus then to shew my iudgement to be such
As can discerne of colours blacke, and white,
As alls to free my minde from enuies tuch,
That neuer giues to any man his right,
    I here pronounce this workmanship is such,
    As that no pen can set it forth too much.

And thus I hang a garland at the dore,
Not for to shew the goodnes of the ware:
But such hath beene the custome heretofore,
And customes very hardly broken are.
    And when your tast shall tell you this is trew,
    Then looke you giue your hoast his vtmost dew.

                                      Ignoto

DEDICATORY SONNETS

To the right honourable Sir Christopher Hatton,
Lord high Chauncelor of England. &c.

Those prudent heads, that with theire counsels wise
   Whylom the Pillours of th'earth did sustaine,
   And taught ambitious *Rome* to tyrannise,
   And in the neck of all the world to rayne,
Oft from those graue affaires were wont abstaine,
   With the sweet Lady Muses for to play:
   So *Ennius* the elder Africane,
   So *Maro* oft did *Cæsars* cares allay.
So you great Lord, that with your counsell sway
   The burdeine of this kingdom mightily,
   With like delightes sometimes may eke delay,
   The rugged brow of carefull Policy:
And to these ydle rymes lend litle space,
   Which for their titles sake may find more grace.

To the right honourable the Lo. Burleigh
Lo. high Threasurer of England.

To you right noble Lord, whose carefull brest
   To menage of most graue affaires is bent,
   And on whose mightie shoulders most doth rest
   The burdein of this kingdomes gouernement,
As the wide compasse of the firmament,
   On *Atlas* mighty shoulders is vpstayd;
   Vnfitly I these ydle rimes present,
   The labor of lost time, and wit vnstayd:
Yet if their deeper sence be inly wayd,
   And the dim vele, with which from comune vew
   Their fairer parts are hid, aside be layd.
   Perhaps not vaine they may appeare to you.
Such as they be, vouchsafe them to receaue,
   And wipe their faults out of your censure graue.

          E. S.

To the right Honourable the Earle of Oxenford,
Lord high Chamberlayne of England. &c.

Receiue most Noble Lord in gentle gree,
   The vnripe fruit of an vnready wit:
   Which by thy countenaunce doth craue to bee
   Defended from foule Enuies poisnous bit.
Which so to doe may thee right well besit,
   Sith th'antique glory of thine auncestry
   Vnder a shady vele is therein writ,
   And eke thine owne long liuing memory,
Succeeding them in true nobility:
   And also for the loue, which thou doest beare
   To th'*Heliconian* ymps, and they to thee,
   They vnto thee, and thou to them most deare:
Deare as thou art vnto thy selfe, so loue
   That loues and honours thee, as doth behoue.

To the right honourable the Earle of Northumberland.

The sacred Muses haue made alwaies clame
   To be the Nourses of nobility,
   And Registres of euerlasting fame,
   To all that armes professe and cheualry.
Then by like right the noble Progeny,
   Which them succeed in fame and worth, are tyde
   T'embrace the seruice of sweete Poetry,
   By whose endeuours they are glorifide,
And eke from all, of whom it is enuide,
   To patronize the authour of their praise,
   Which giues them life, that els would soone haue dide,
   And crownes their ashes with immortall baies.
To thee therefore right noble Lord I send
   This present of my paines, it to defend.

To the right honourable the Earle of Cumberland.

Redoubted Lord, in whose corageous mind
   The flowre of cheualry now bloosming faire,
   Doth promise fruite worthy the noble kind,
   Which of their praises haue left you the haire;
To you this humble present I prepare,
   For loue of vertue and of Martiall praise,
   To which though nobly ye inclined are,
   As goodlie well ye shew'd in late assaies,
Yet braue ensample of long passed daies,
   In which trew honor yee may fashiond see,
   To like desire of honor may ye raise,
   And fill your mind with magnanimitee.
Receiue it Lord therefore as it was ment,
   For honor of your name and high descent.

          E. S.

**To the most honourable and excellent Lo. the Earle of
Essex.** Great Maister of the Horse to her Highnesse, and
knight of the Noble order of the Garter. &c.

Magnificke Lord, whose vertues excellent
   Doe merit a most famous Poets witt,
   To be thy liuing praises instrument,
   Yet doe not sdeigne, to let thy name be writt
In this base Poeme, for thee far vnfitt.
   Nought is thy worth disparaged thereby,
   But when my Muse, whose fethers nothing flitt
   Doe yet but flagg, and lowly learne to fly
With bolder wing shall dare alofte to sty
   To the last praises of this Faery Queene,
   Then shall it make more famous memory
   Of thine Heroicke parts, such as they beene:
Till then vouchsafe thy noble countenaunce,
   To these first labours needed furderaunce.

To the right Honourable the Earle of Ormond and Ossory.

Receiue most noble Lord a simple taste
  Of the wilde fruit, which saluage soyl hath bred,
  Which being through long wars left almost waste,
  With brutish barbarisme is ouerspredd:
And in so faire a land, as may be redd,
  Not one *Parnassus*, nor one *Helicone*
  Left for sweete Muses to be harboured,
  But where thy selfe hast thy braue mansione;
There in deede dwel faire Graces many one.
  And gentle Nymphes, delights of learned wits,
  And in thy person without Paragone
  All goodly bountie and true honour sits,
Such therefore, as that wasted soyl doth yield,
  Receiue dear Lord in worth, the fruit of barren field.

To the most renowmed and valiant Lord, the Lord Grey of Wilton, knight of the Noble order of the Garter, &c.

Most Noble Lord the pillor of my life,
  And Patrone of my Muses pupillage,
  Through whose large bountie poured on me rife,
  In the first season of my feeble age,
I now doe liue, bound yours by vassalage:
  Sith nothing euer may redeeme, nor reaue
  Out of your endlesse debt so sure a gage,
  Vouchsafe in worth this small guift to receaue,
Which in your noble hands for pledge I leaue,
  Of all the rest, that I am tyde t'account:
  Rude rymes, the which a rustick Muse did weaue
  In sauadge soyle, far from Parnasso mount,
And roughly wrought in an vnlearned Loome:
The which vouchsafe dear Lord your fauorable doome.

To the right honourable the Lo. Ch. Howard,
Lo. high Admiral of England, knight of the noble order of the Garter, and one of her Maiesties priuie Counsel. &c.

And ye, braue Lord, whose goodly personage,
  And noble deeds each other garnishing,
  Make you ensample to the present age,
  Of th'old Heroes, whose famous ofspring
The antique Poets wont so much to sing,
  In this same Pageaunt haue a worthy place,
  Sith those huge castles of Castilian king,
  That vainly threatned kingdomes to displace,
Like flying doues ye did before you chace;
  And that proud people woxen insolent
  Through many victories, didst first deface:
  Thy praises euerlasting monument
Is in this verse engrauen semblably,
  That it may liue to all posterity.

To the right honourable the Lord of Buckhurst,
one of her Maiesties priuie Counsell.

  In vain I thinke right honourable Lord,
  By this rude rime to memorize thy name;
  Whose learned Muse hath writ her owne record,
  In golden verse, worthy immortal fame:
Thou much more fit (were leasure to the same)
  Thy gracious Souerains praises to compile.
  And her imperiall Maiestie to frame,
  In loftie numbers and heroicke stile.
But sith thou maist not so, giue leaue a while
  To baser wit his power therein to spend,
  Whose grosse defaults thy daintie pen may file,
  And vnaduised ouersights amend.
But euermore vouchsafe it to maintaine
  Against vile Zoilus backbitings vaine.

To the right honourable the Lord of Hunsdon,
high Chamberlaine to her Maiesty.

Renowmed Lord, that for your worthinesse
  And noble deeds haue your deserued place,
  High in the fauour of that Emperesse,
  The worlds sole glory and her sexes grace,
Here eke of right haue you a worthie place,
  Both for your nearnes to that Faerie Queene,
  And for your owne high merit in like cace,
  Of which, apparaunt proofe was to be seene,
When that tumultuous rage and fearfull deene
  Of Northerne rebels ye did pacify,
  And their disloiall powre defaced clene,
  The record of enduring memory.
Liue Lord for euer in this lasting verse,
  That all posteritie thy honour may reherse.

To the right honourable Sir Fr. Walsingham knight,
principall Secretary to her Maiesty, and of her honourable priuy Counsell.

That Mantuane Poetes incompared spirit,
  Whose girland now is set in highest place,
  Had not *Mecænas* for his worthy merit,
  It first aduaunst to great *Augustus* grace,
Might long perhaps haue lien in silence bace,
  Ne bene so much admir'd of later age.
  This lowly Muse, that learns like steps to trace,
  Flies for like aide vnto your Patronage;
That are the great *Mecenas* of this age,
  As wel to al that ciuil artes professe
  As those that are inspird with Martial rage,
  And craues protection of her feeblenesse:
Which if ye yield, perhaps ye may her rayse
  In bigger tunes to sound your liuing prayse.

E. S.

E. S.

To the right noble Lord and most valiaunt Captaine,
Sir Iohn Norris knight, Lord president of Mounster.

Who euer gaue more honourable prize
  To the sweet Muse, then did the Martiall crew;
  That their braue deeds she might immortalize
  In her shril tromp, and sound their praises dew?
Who then ought more to fauour her, then you
  Moste noble Lord, the honor of this age,
  And Precedent of all that armes ensue?
  Whose warlike prowesse and manly courage,
Tempred with reason and aduizement sage
  Hath fild sad Belgicke with victorious spoile,
  In *Fraunce* and *Ireland* left a famous gage,
  And lately shakt the Lusitanian soile.
Sith then each where thou hast dispredd thy fame,
  Loue him, that hath eternized your name.

                                                E. S.

To the most vertuous, and beautifull Lady, the
Lady Carew.

Ne may I, without blot of endlesse blame,
  You fairest Lady leaue out of this place,
  But with remembraunce of your gracious name,
  Wherewith that courtly garlond most ye grace,
And deck the world, adorne these verses base:
  Not that these few lines can in them comprise
  Those glorious ornaments of heuenly grace,
  Wherewith ye triumph ouer feeble eyes,
And in subdued harts do tyranyse:
  For thereunto doth need a golden quill,
  And siluer leaues, them rightly to deuise,
  But to make humble present of good will:
Which whenas timely meanes it purchase may,
  In ampler wise it selfe will forth display.

                                                E. S.

To the right noble and valorous knight, Sir Walter Raleigh,
Lo. Wardein of the Stanneryes, and lieftenaunt of Cornewaile.

To thee that art the sommers Nightingale,
  Thy soueraine Goddesses most deare delight,
  Why doe I send this rusticke Madrigale,
  That may thy tunefull eare vnseason quite?
Thou onely fit this Argument to write,
  In whose high thoughts Pleasure hath built her bowre,
  And dainty loue learnd sweetly to endite.
  My rimes I know vnsauory and sowre,
To tast the streames, that like a golden showre
  Flow from thy fruitfull head, of thy loues praise,
  Fitter perhaps to thonder Martiall stowre,
  When so thee list thy lofty Muse to raise:
Yet till that thou thy Poeme wilt make knowne,
  Let thy faire Cinthias praises bee thus rudely showne.

                                                E. S.

To the right honourable and most vertuous Lady, the
Countesse of Penbroke.

Remembraunce of that most Heroicke spirit,
  The heuens pride, the glory of our daies,
  Which now triumpheth through immortall merit
  Of his braue vertues, crownd with lasting baies,
Of heuenlie blis and euerlasting praies;
  Who first my Muse did lift out of the flore,
  To sing his sweet delights in lowlie laies;
  Bids me most noble Lady to adore
His goodly image liuing euermore,
  In the diuine resemblaunce of your face;
  Which with your vertues ye embellish more,
  And natiue beauty deck with heuenlie grace:
For his, and for your owne especial sake,
  Vouchsafe from him this token in good worth to take.

                                                E. S.

To all the gratious and beautifull Ladies in the Court.

The Chian Peincter, when he was requirde
  To pourtraict *Venus* in her perfect hew,
  To make his worke more absolute, desird
  Of all the fairest Maides to haue the vew.
Much more me needs to draw the semblant trew,
  Of beauties Queene, the worlds sole wonderment,
  To sharpe my sence with sundry beauties vew,
  And steale from each some part of ornament.
If all the world to seeke I ouerwent,
  A fairer crew yet no where could I see,
  Then that braue court doth to mine eie present,
  That the worlds pride seemes gathered there to bee.
Of each a part I stole by cunning thefte:
  Forgiue it me faire Dames, sith lesse ye haue not lefte.

                                                E. S.

743

Bibliography

AIKIN, J., ed. *Spenser: poetical works*. 1802.

ALCIATI. *Emblemata*. Antwerp 1581.

ALLEN, DON CAMERON. 'Arthur's diamond shield in the *Faerie Queene*', *JEGP* xxxvi (1937) 234–43.

ALLEN, DON C. 'Spenser's Sthenoboea', *MLN* liii (1938) 118–19.

ALLEN, DON C. 'A note on Spenser's orology', *MLN* lxi (1946) 555–6.

ALLEN, DON C. 'On the closing lines of the *Faerie Queene*', *MLN* lxiv (1949) 93–4.

ALLEN, DON C. *Image and Meaning*. Baltimore 1960.

ALLEN, DON C. *The Legend of Noah*. Urbana 1963.
Literature, ed. R. A. Pratt *et al*. Boston 1958.

ALLEN, *Image and Meaning*. Baltimore 1960.

ALLEN. *The Legend of Noah*. Urbana 1963.

ALPERS, PAUL J. *The Poetry of the 'Faerie Queene'*. Princeton 1967.

ALPERS, PAUL J. 'How to read the *Faerie Queene*', *EIC* xviii (1968) 429–43; rptd Hamilton, ed. *Essential Articles, q.v.*

ANDERSON, JUDITH H. 'Redcrosse and the descent into hell', *ELH* xxxvi (1969) 470–92.

ANDERSON, JUDITH H. 'The July eclogue and the house of Holiness: perspective in Spenser', *SEL* x (1970) 17–32. [Cited as 1970a.]

ANDERSON, JUDITH H. '"Nor man it is": the knight of justice in the *Faerie Queene* V'. *PMLA* lxxxv (1970) 65–77; rptd Hamilton, ed. *Essential Articles, q.v.* [Cited as 1b70.]

ANDERSON, JUDITH H. 'Whatever happened to Amoret?: the poet's role in the *Faerie Queene* IV', *Criticism* xiii (1971) 180–200.

ANDERSON, JUDITH H. *The Growth of a Personal Voice: 'Piers Plowman' and the 'Faerie Queene'*. New Haven 1976.

ANDERSON, RUTH LEILA. *Elizabethan Psychology and Shakespeare's Plays*. Univ. Iowa Humanistic Stud. iii, no. 4 1927.

ANGLO, SYDNEY. 'The London pageants for the reception of Katharine of Aragon: November 1501', *JWCI* xxvi (1963) 53–89.

APTEKAR, JANE. *Icons of Justice: iconography and thematic imagery in the 'Faerie Queene' V*. New York 1969.

APULEIUS. *The Golden Asse*, trans. William Adlington (1566). Abbey Classics 1922.

AQUINAS, THOMAS. *Summa Theologica*, trans. Fathers of the English Dominican Province. New York 1921.

ARIOSTO. *Orlando Furioso*. Venice 1619; ed. R. Ceserani, Turin 1962.

ARISTOTLE. *Basic Works*, ed. Richard McKeon. New York 1941.

ARTHOS, JOHN. *On the Poetry of Spenser and the Form of Romances*. 1956.

BACON, FRANCIS. *The Advancement of Learning* (1605). Everyman edn.

BAMBOROUGH, J. B. *The Little World of Man*. 1952.

BARB, A. A. 'The wound in Christ's side', *JWCI* xxxiv (1971) 320–1.

BARCLAY, ALEXANDER. *The Life of St George* (1515), ed. William Nelson. EETS o.s. 230 1955.

BARTHOLOMAEUS, ANGLICUS. *Batman uppon Bartholome his booke 'De proprietatibus rerum'*. 1582.

BAWCUTT, PRISCILLA. 'The lark in Chaucer and some later poets', *Yrbk Eng. Stud.* ii (1972) 5–12.

BAYBAK, MICHAEL, DELANY, PAUL, and HIEATT, A. KENT. 'Placement "in the middest" in the *Faerie Queene*', *PLL* v (1969) 227–34; rptd Hamilton, ed. *Essential Articles, q.v.*

BAYLEY, HAROLD. *The Lost Language of Symbolism*. 1912.

BAYLEY, P. C., ed. *The 'Faerie Queene'*. Book II 1965. Book I 1966.

BELSON, JOEL JAY. 'The names in the *Faerie Queene*', unpublished doctoral dissertation. Columbia University 1964.

BENDER, JOHN B. *Spenser and Literary Pictorialism*. Princeton 1972.

BENNETT, JOSEPHINE WATERS. 'Spenser's Venus and the goddess Nature of the *Mutabilitie Cantos*', *SP* xxx (1933) 160–92.

BENNETT, JOSEPHINE WATERS. *The Evolution of the 'Faerie Queene'*. Chicago 1942.

BENNETT, JOSEPHINE WATERS. 'Genre, milieu, and the "epic-romance"', *Eng. Inst. Essays 1951*, 95–125.

BERGER, HARRY, JR. *The Allegorical Temper: vision and reality in the 'Faerie Queene' II*. New Haven 1957.

BERGER, HARRY, JR. 'A secret discipline: the *Faerie Queene* VI', *Eng. Inst. Essays 1961*, 35–75.

BERGER, HARRY, JR., ed. *Spenser: a collection of critical essays*. Englewood Cliffs 1968.

BERGER, HARRY, JR. 'The Spenserian dynamics', *SEL* viii (1968) 1–18. [Cited as 1968a.]

BERGER, HARRY, JR. 'The *Faerie Queene* III: a general description', *Criticism* xi (1969) 234–61; rptd Hamilton, ed. *Essential Articles, q.v.* [Cited as 1969a.]

BERGER, HARRY, JR. 'Two Spenserian retrospects: the antique Temple of Venus and the primitive marriage of rivers', *TSLL* x (1969) 5–25. [Cited as 1969b.]

BERGER, HARRY, JR. 'The structure of Merlin's chronicle in the *Faerie Queene* III iii', *SEL* ix (1969) 39–51. [Cited as 1969c.]

BERGER, HARRY, JR. 'The discarding of Malbecco: conspicuous allusion and cultural exhaustion in the *Faerie Queene* III ix–x', *SP* lxvi (1969) 135–54. [Cited as 1969d.]

BERGER, HARRY, JR. 'Busirane and the war between the sexes: an interpretation of the *Faerie Queene* III xi–xii', *ELR* i (1971) 99–121.

BERLETH, RICHARD J. '"Heavens favorable and free": Belphoebe's nativity in the *Faerie Queene*', *ELH* xl (1973) 479–500.

BERNHEIMER, RICHARD. *Wild Men in the Middle Ages: a study in art, sentiment, and demonology*. Cambridge, Mass. 1952.

BIBLE. *The Geneva Bible*, 1560. Facsimile ed. Lloyd E. Berry. Madison 1969. [This version is cited in the notes, unless otherwise stated.]

BIBLE. *The Bishops' Bible*, 1572.

BIEMAN, ELIZABETH. 'Britomart in the *Faerie Queene* V', *UTQ* xxxvii (1968) 156–74.

BIRCH, T., ed. *Spenser's 'Faerie Queene'*. 1751.

BLISSETT, WILLIAM. 'Spenser's Mutabilitie', in *Essays in English Literature presented to A. S. P. Woodhouse*, ed. Millar MacLure and F. W. Watt. Toronto 1964, 26–42; rptd Hamilton, ed. *Essential Articles, q.v.*

BLISSETT, WILLIAM. 'Florimell and Marinell', *SEL* v (1965) 87–104.

BLITCH, ALICE FOX. 'Etymon and image in the *Faerie Queene*', unpublished doctoral dissertation. Michigan State University 1965.

BLITCH, ALICE FOX. 'Proserpina preserved: the *Faerie Queene* VI', *SEL* xiii (1973) 15–30.

BLOCK, EDWARD A. 'Chaucer's Millers and their bagpipes', *Speculum* xxix (1954) 239–43.

BLOOMFIELD, MORTON W. *The Seven Deadly Sins*. East Lansing 1952.

BLYTHE, JOAN HEIGES. 'Spenser and the seven deadly sins: the *Faerie Queene* I iv, v', *ELH* xxxix (1972) 342–52.

BOCCACCIO. *De Genealogia Deorum Gentilium* (Venice 1472). Basel 1532.

BOLTON, W. F. *A Short History of Literary English*. 1967.

BOWERS, FREDSON. 'The *Faerie Queene* II: Mordant, Ruddymane, and the nymph's well', in *English Studies in Honor of James Southall Wilson*. Charlottesville 1951, 243–51.

BRADEN, GORDON. 'riverrun: an epic catalogue in the *Faerie Queene*', *ELR* v (1975) 25–48.

BRADNER, LEICESTER. *Edmund Spenser and the 'Faerie Queene'*. Chicago 1948.

BRIDGES, RONALD and WEIGLE, LUTHER A. *The Bible Word Book*. New York 1960.

BRIGGS, K. M. *Pale Hecate's Team*. 1962.

BRIGGS, K. M. 'The folds of folklore', *Shapespeare Survey* xvii (1964) 167–79.

BRILL, LESLEY W. 'Chastity as ideal sexuality in the *Faerie Queene* III', *SEL* xi (1971) 15–26.

BRILL, LESLEY W. ' "Battles that need not be fought": the *Faerie Queene* III i', *ELR* v (1975) 198–211.

BRINK, J. R. 'The Masque of the Nine Muses: Sir John Davies's unpublished "Epithalamion" and the "Belphoebe-Ruby" episode in the *Faerie Queene*', *RES* xxiii (1972) 445–7.

BROOKE, N. S. 'C. S. Lewis and Spenser: nature, art and the Bower of Bliss', *Cambridge Jnl* ii (1949) 420–34; rptd Hamilton, ed. *Essential Articles*, q.v.

BROWNE, SIR THOMAS. *Works*, ed. Geoffrey Keynes. 1928–31.

BRYAN, ROBERT A. 'Apostasy and the fourth bead-man in the *Faerie Queene*', *ELN* v (1968) 87–91.

BRYSKETT, LODOWICK. *A Discourse of Civill Life* (1606), ed. Thomas E. Wright. Northridge, California 1970.

BUCHAN, A. M. 'The political allegory of the *Faerie Queene* IV', *ELH* xi (1944) 237–48.

BULLOUGH, GEOFFREY, ed. *Narrative and Dramatic Sources of Shakespeare*. 1957–75.

BURKHART, R. E. 'History, the epic, and the *Faerie Queene*', *E. Stud.* lvi (1975) 14–9.

BURNET, GILBERT. *An Exposition of the Thirty-nine Articles of the Church of England* (1699); new edn 1850.

BURTON, ROBERT. *The Anatomy of Melancholy* (1621), ed. A. R. Shilleto. 1896.

BUSH, DOUGLAS. *Mythology and the Renaissance Tradition in English Poetry*. Minneapolis 1932; rev. edn, New York 1963.

CAIN, THOMAS H. 'Spenser and the Renaissance Orpheus', *UTQ* xli (1972) 24–47.

CALIN, WILLIAM. *The Epic Quest*. Baltimore 1966.

CALVIN. *Institutes of the Christian Religion*, ed. John T. McNeill, trans. Ford Lewis Battles. Philadelphia 1960.

CAMDEN, WILLIAM. *Britannia* (1586); trans. Philemon Holland 1610.

CAMDEN, WILLIAM. *Remains Concerning Britain* (1605). 1674 edn, ed. John Philipot, Library of Old Authors 1870.

CAMDEN, WILLIAM. *The History of Princess Elizabeth* (1630, 1688), ed. Wallace T. MacCaffrey. Chicago 1970.

CARPENTER, FREDERIC IVES. *A Reference Guide to Edmund Spenser*. Chicago 1923.

CARROLL, WILLIAM MEREDITH. *Animal Conventions in English Renaissance Non-religious Prose (1550–1600)*. New York 1954.

CASTIGLIONE. *The Book of the Courtier*, trans. Sir Thomas Hoby 1561. Everyman edn.

CHAMBERS, A. B. 'The fly in Donne's "Canonization" ', *JEGP* lxv (1966) 252–9.

CHAPMAN, GEORGE. *Poems*, ed. Phyllis Brooks Bartlett. New York 1941.

CHAPMAN, GEORGE. *Works*. 1874–5. Vol iii: Homer's *Iliad* and *Odyssey*, ed. R. H. Shepherd.

CHAUCER, GEOFFREY. *Works*, ed. William Thynne 1532, 1561; ed. Thomas Speght 1598; ed. F. N. Robinson. Boston 1957.

CHENEY, DONALD. *Spenser's Image of Nature: wild man and shepherd in the 'Faerie Queene'*. New Haven 1966.

CHENEY, DONALD. 'Spenser's Hermaphrodite and the 1590 *Faerie Queene*', *PMLA* lxxxvii (1972) 192–200.

CHEW, SAMUEL C. *The Crescent and the Rose*. New York 1937.

CHEW, SAMUEL C. *The Virtues Reconciled: an iconographic study*. Toronto 1947.

CHEW, SAMUEL C. 'The allegorical chariot in English literature of the Renaissance', in Meiss, ed. *Panofsky Essays* (1960) 37–54 q.v.

CHEW, SAMUEL C. *The Pilgrimage of Life*. New Haven 1962.

CHURCH, RALPH, ed. *The 'Faerie Queene'* 1758–9.

CHURCH OF ENGLAND. *Second Book of Homilies* (1563). 1844.

CICERO. *Selected Works*, trans. Michael Grant. Penguin 1960.

CIRILLO, ALBERT R. 'Noon-midnight and the temporal structure of *Paradise Lost*', *ELH* xxix (1962) 372–95.

CIRILLO, ALBERT R. 'The fair hermaphrodite: love-union in the poetry of Donne and Spenser', *SEL* ix (1969) 81–95.

CIRLOT, J. E. *A Dictionary of Symbols*, trans. Jack Sage. New York 1962.

COHN, NORMAN. *The Pursuit of the Millennium*. 1957, 1970.

COLERIDGE, S. T. *Coleridge's Miscellaneous Criticism*, ed. Thomas Middleton Raysor. Cambridge, Mass. 1936.

COLLIER, J. PAYNE. *Spenser: poetical works*. 1862.

COMES, NATALE. *Mythologiae, sive explicationis fabularum, libri decem*. Padua 1616.

COOPER, THOMAS. *Thesaurus Linguae Romanae et Britannicae*. 1565.

CORNELIUS, DAVID K. 'Spenser's *Faerie Queene* I xi 46', *Explicator* xxix (1971) no. 51.

COTGRAVE, RANDLE. *A Dictionarie of the French and English Tongues* (1611); facsimile edn Columbia, S.C. 1950.

COWLEY, ABRAHAM. *English Writings*, ed. A. R. Waller. Cambridge 1905–6.

CRAIG, JOANNE. 'The image of mortality: myth and history in the *Faerie Queene*', *ELH* xxxix (1972) 520–44.

CRAIG, MARTHA. 'The secret wit of Spenser's language', in Paul J. Alpers, ed. *Elizabethan Poetry: modern essays in criticism*. New York 1967, 447–72. Rptd Hamilton, ed. *Essential Articles*, q.v.

CRAMPTON, GEORGIA RONAN. *The Condition of Creatures: suffering and action in Chaucer and Spenser*. New Haven 1974.

CRAWFORD, JOHN W. 'The fire from Spenser's Dragon: the *Faerie Queene* I xi', *South Central Bull.* xxx (1970) 176–8.

CROSSLEY, BRIAN, and EDWARDS, PAUL. 'Spenser's bawdy: a note on the *Faerie Queene* II vi', *PLL* ix (1973) 314–9.

CULLEN, PATRICK. 'Guyon *microchristus*: the Cave of Mammon re-examined'. *ELH* xxxvii (1970) 153–74.

CULLEN, PATRICK. *Infernal Triad: the flesh, the world, and the devil in Spenser and Milton*. Princeton 1974.

CULP, DOROTHY W. 'Courtesy and moral virtue', *SEL* xi (1971) 37–51. [Cited as 1971a.]

CULP, DOROTHY W. 'Courtesy and fortune's chance in the *Faerie Queene* VI', *MP* lxviii (1971) 254–9 [Cited as 1971b.]

CUMMING, WILLIAM P. 'The influence of Ovid's *Metamorphoses* on Spenser's "Mutabilitie Cantos" ', *SP* xxviii (1931) 241–56.

CUMMINGS, R. M. 'A note on the arithmological stanza: the *Faerie Queene* II ix 22', *JWCI* xxx (1967) 410–14.

CUMMINGS, R. M. 'An iconographical puzzle: Spenser's Cupid

at the *Faerie Queene* II viii', *JWCI* xxxiii (1970) 317–21.

CURTIUS, ERNST ROBERT. *European Literature and the Latin Middle Ages*, trans. Willard R. Trask. New York 1953.

CUTTS, JOHN P. 'Spenser's mermaids', *ELN* v (1968) 250–6.

DALLETT, JOSEPH B. 'The *Faerie Queene* IV i–v: a synopsis of discord', *MLN* lxxv (1960) 639–43.

DAVIDSON, CLIFFORD. 'The idol of Isis Church', *SP* lxvi (1969) 70–86.

DAVIS, B. E. C. *Edmund Spenser: a critical study*. Cambridge 1933.

DEES, JEROME S. 'The ship conceit in the *Faerie Queene*: "conspicuous allusion" and poetic structure', *SP* lxxii (1975) 208–25.

DELACY, HUGH. 'Astrology in the poetry of Edmund Spenser', *JEGP* xxxiii (1934) 520–43.

DIDRON, ADOLPHE NAPOLÉON. *Christian Iconography*. 1886.

DIGBY, SIR KENELM, in Wells, ed. *Spenser Allusions*, q.v.

DIXON, JOHN. *The First Commentary on the 'Faerie Queene'* [1597], ed. Graham Hough. Privately printed 1964.

DODGE, R. E. NEIL, ed. *Spenser's Complete Poetical Works*. Boston 1908.

DONNE, JOHN. *Poetical Works*, ed. H. J. C. Grierson. Oxford 1912.

DONNE, JOHN. *Sermons*, ed. George R. Potter and Evelyn M. Simpson. Berkeley 1953–62.

DONNO, ELIZABETH STORY. 'The triumph of Cupid: Spenser's legend of chastity', *Yrbk Eng. Stud.* iv (1974) 37–48.

DOWDEN, EDWARD. 'Spenser, the poet and teacher', 1882; in Grosart, ed. *Spenser*, q.v.

DOYLE, CHARLES CLAY. 'Smoke and fire: Spenser's counter-proverb', *Proverbium* xviii (1972) 683–5.

DRAPER, JOHN W. 'Classical coinage in the *Faerie Queene*', *PMLA* xlvii (1932) 97–108.

DRAYTON, MICHAEL. *Complete Works*, ed. J. W. Hebel. Oxford 1961.

DU BARTAS, GUILLAUME DE SALUSTE. *Divine Weekes and Workes*, trans. Joshua Sylvester. 1633.

DUNSEATH, T. K. *Spenser's Allegory of Justice in the 'Faerie Queene' V*. Princeton 1968.

DURLING, ROBERT M. 'The Bower of Bliss and Armida's palace', *CL* vi (1954) 335–47; rptd Hamilton, ed. *Essential Articles*, q.v.

DURLING, ROBERT M. *The Figure of the Poet in Renaissance Epic*. Cambridge, Mass. 1965.

EDWARDS, CALVIN ROGER. 'Spenser and the Ovidian tradition', unpublished doctoral dissertation. Yale University 1958.

ELIOT, T. S. *Selected Essays 1917–1932*. 1932.

ELLRODT, ROBERT. *Neoplatonism in the Poetry of Spenser*. Geneva 1960.

ELYOT, SIR THOMAS. *The Boke named The Governour* (1531). Everyman edn.

ELYOT, SIR THOMAS. *Of the Knowledge Which Maketh a Wise Man* (?1533), ed. Edwin Johnston Howard. Oxford, Ohio 1946.

ELYOT, SIR THOMAS. *Dictionary* (1538, 1559). Facsimile edn, Menston 1970.

EMPSON, WILLIAM. *Some Versions of Pastoral*. 1935.

Encyclopaedia Britannica. Eleventh edition. Cambridge 1910–11. [Cited as *Enc. Brit.*]

ERASMUS. *Familiar Colloquies*, trans. N. Bailey. 1877.

Essential Articles. See HAMILTON, ed.

EVANS, EDWARD PAYSON. *Animal Symbolism in Ecclesiastical Architecture*. New York 1896.

EVANS, FRANK B. 'The printing of the *Faerie Queene* in 1596', *SB* xviii (1965) 49–67.

EVANS, MAURICE. *Spenser's Anatomy of Heroism: a commentary on the 'Faerie Queene'*. Cambridge 1970.

EVANS, ROBERT O. 'Spenserian humor: the *Faerie Queene* III and IV', *NM* lx (1959) 288–99.

FALCONER, ALEXANDER FREDERICK. *Shakespeare and the Sea*. 1964.

FALLS, MOTHER MARY ROBERT. 'Spenser's Kirkrapine and the Elizabethans', *SP* l (1953) 457–75.

FLEMING, JOHN V. *'The Roman de la Rose': a study in allegory and iconography*. Princeton 1969.

FLETCHER, ANGUS. *Allegory: the theory of a symbolic mode*. Ithaca 1964.

FLETCHER, ANGUS. *The Prophetic Moment: an essay on Spenser*. Chicago 1971.

FLETCHER, GILES, and FLETCHER, PHINEAS. *Poetical Works*, ed. F. S. Boas. Cambridge 1908–9.

FLORIO, JOHN. *Queen Anna's New World of Words*, 1611. Facsimile edn, Menston 1968.

FOLTINEK, HERBERT. 'Die wilden Männer in Spenser's *Faerie Queene*', *NS* x (1961) 493–512.

FOSSO, DOYLE RICHARD. 'Epic simile in the *Faerie Queene*', unpublished doctoral dissertation. Harvard University 1965.

FOWLER, ALASTAIR D. S. 'Six knights at Castle Joyous', *SP* lvi (1959) 583–99.

FOWLER, ALASTAIR D. S. 'The river Guyon', *MLN* lxxv (1960) 289–92. [Cited as 1960a.]

FOWLER, ALASTAIR D. S. 'Emblems of temperance in the *Faerie Queene* II', *RES* xi (1960) 143–9. [Cited as 1960b.]

FOWLER, ALASTAIR D. S. 'Oxford and London marginalia to the *Faerie Queene*', *N&Q* 206 (1961) 416–19. [Cited as 1961a.]

FOWLER, ALASTAIR D. S. 'The image of mortality: the *Faerie Queene* II i–ii', *HLQ* xxiv (1961) 91–110; rptd Hamilton, ed. *Essential Articles*, q.v. [Cited as 1961b.]

FOWLER, ALASTAIR D. S. 'Spenser and Renaissance iconography', *EIC* xi (1961) 235–8. [Cited as 1961c.]

FOWLER, ALASTAIR D. S. *Spenser and the Numbers of Time*. 1964.

FOWLER, ALASTAIR D. S. *Triumphal Forms: structural patterns in Elizabethan poetry*. Cambridge 1970.

FOWLER, ALASTAIR D. S. 'Emanations of glory: neoplatonic order in Spenser's *Faerie Queene*', in Kennedy and Reither, ed. *Theatre* (1973) 53–82 q.v.

FOWLER, EARLE B. *Spenser and the Courts of Love*. Menasha 1921.

FRAUNCE, ABRAHAM. *The Lamentations of Amyntas* (1587), ed. Franklin M. Dickey. Chicago 1967.

FRAUNCE, ABRAHAM. *The Lawiers logike* (1588).

FRAUNCE, ABRAHAM. *The Arcadian Rhetorike* (1588), ed. Ethel Seaton. Luttrell Society 1950.

FRAUNCE, ABRAHAM. *The Third Part of the Countesse of Pembrokes Yvychurch* (1592).

FRECCERO, JOHN. 'Dante's firm foot and the journey without a guide', *Harvard Theol. Rev.* lii (1959) 245–81.

FREEMAN, ROSEMARY. *English Emblem Books*. 1948.

FREEMAN, ROSEMARY. *The 'Faerie Queene': a companion for readers*. 1970.

FRIEDMAN, LIONEL J. 'Gradus amoris', *Romance Philology* xix (1966) 167–77.

FRIEDMANN, ANTHONY E. 'The Diana-Acteon episode in Ovid's *Metamorphoses* and the *Faerie Queene*', *CL* xviii (1966) 289–99.

FRUSHELL, RICHARD C., and VONDERSMITH, BERNARD J., ed. *Contemporary Thought on Edmund Spenser*. Carbondale 1975.

FRYE, NORTHROP. 'The structure of imagery in the *Faerie*

747

Queene', *UTQ* xxx (1961) 109–27; cited from *Fables of Identity*, New York 1963, 69–87; also rptd Hamilton, ed. *Essential Articles*, q.v.

FRYE, NORTHROP. *The Anatomy of Criticism*. Princeton 1957.

FÜGER, WILHELM. 'Ungenutzte Perspektiven der Spenser-Deutung: Dargelegt an *Faerie Queene* I viii 30–34', *Deutsche Vierteljahrsschrift* xlv (1971) 252–301.

GELLER, LILA. 'The Acidalian vision: Spenser's Graces in the *Faerie Queene* VI', *RES* xxiii (1972) 267–77.

GELLER, LILA. 'Spenser's theory of nobility in the *Faerie Queene* VI', *ELR* v (1975) 49–57.

GEOFFREY OF MONMOUTH. *British History*; in J. A. Giles, ed. *Six Old English Chronicles*. 1891.

GIAMATTI, A. BARTLETT. *The Earthly Paradise and the Renaissance Epic*. Princeton 1966.

GIAMATTI, A. BARTLETT. 'Spenser: from magic to miracle', in Herschel Baker, ed. *Four Essays on Romance*, Cambridge, Mass. 1971, 17–31.

GIAMATTI, A. BARTLETT. *Play of Double Senses: Spenser's 'Faerie Queene'*. Englewood Cliffs 1975.

GILBERT, ALLAN H. '"Those two brethren giants": the *Faerie Queene* II xi 15', *MLN* lxx (1955) 93–4.

GILDE, HELEN C. '"The sweet lodge of love and deare delight": the problem of Amoret', *PQ* l (1971) 63–74. [Cited as 1971a.]

GILDE, HELEN C. 'Spenser's Hellenore and some Ovidian associations', *CL* xxiii (1971) 233–9. [Cited as 1971b.]

GOLDBERG, JONATHAN. 'The mothers in the *Faerie Queene* III', *TSLL* xvii (1976) 5–26.

GOLDBERG, VICTORIA L. 'Graces, Muses, and arts: the urns of Henry II and Francis I', *JWCI* xxix (1966) 206–18.

Golden Legend, by Jacobus de Voragine. See *The Lyfe of Saynt George*, app. to Barclay, *The Life of St George*, q.v.

GOLDING, ARTHUR. *Shakespeare's Ovid: Golding's translation of the 'Metamorphoses'* (1567), ed. W. H. D. Rouse. 1904, 1966.

GOMBRICH, E. H. *Symbolic Images*. 1972.

GORDON, BENJAMIN LEE. *Medieval and Renaissance Medicine*. New York 1959.

GOTTFRIED, RUDOLF B. 'Spenser and the Italian myth of locality', *SP* xxxiv (1937) 107–25.

GOTTFRIED, RUDOLF B. 'Spenser expands his text', *Renaissance News* xvi (1963) 9–10.

GOTTFRIED, RUDOLF B. '"Our new poet": archetypal criticism and the *Faerie Queene*', *PMLA* lxxxiii (1968) 1362–77.

GOUGH, A. B., ed. *The 'Faerie Queene' V*. Oxford 1921.

GOWER, JOHN. *Confessio Amantis*, in *Complete Works*, ed. G. C. Macaulay, vol. iii. Oxford 1900–01.

GRAZIANI, RENÉ. 'Elizabeth at Isis Church', *PMLA* lxxix (1964) 376–89. [Cited as 1964a.]

GRAZIANI, RENÉ. 'Philip II's *impresa* and Spenser's Souldan', *JWCI* xxvii (1964) 322–4. [Cited as 1964b.]

GREAVES, MARGARET. *The Blazon of Honour: a study in Renaissance magnanimity*. 1964.

GREENE, THOMAS. *The Descent from Heaven: a study in epic continuity*. New Haven 1963.

GREENLAW, E. *Studies in Spenser's Historical Allegory*. Baltimore 1932.

GREGORY, E. R. 'Spenser's Muse and the Dumaeus Virgil', *S. News* v (1974) 10–11.

GRELLNER, MARY ADELAIDE, S.C.L. 'Britomart's quest for maturity', *SEL* viii (1968) 35–43.

GRIERSON, H. J. C. *Cross Currents in English Literature of the Seventeenth Century*. 1929.

GROSART, A. B., ed. *Spenser: complete works*. Privately printed

1882–4.

GUAZZO, STEFANO. *The Civile Conversation*, trans. George Pettie (1581) and Barth. Young (1586), ed. Edward Sullivan. 1925.

GUILPIN, EVERARD. *Skialetheia* (1598). *Shapespeare Assoc. Facs* ii 1931.

GUREWICH, VLADIMIR. 'Observations on the iconography of the wound in Christ's side, with special reference to its position', *JWCI* xx (1957) 358–62.

GUREWICH, VLADIMIR. 'Rubens and the wound in Christ's side: a postscript', *JWCI* xxvi (1963) 358.

GUTH, HANS P. 'Allegorical implications of artifice in Spenser's *Faerie Queene*', *PMLA* lxxvi (1961) 474–9.

HAKLUYT, RICHARD. *The Principal Navigations*, etc. Glasgow 1903–5.

HALL, JOSEPH. *Poems*, ed. Arnold Davenport. Liverpool 1949.

HAMILTON, A. C. 'Spenser's *Letter to Raleigh*', *MLN* lxxiii (1958) 481–5.

HAMILTON, A. C. 'Spenser and Langland', *SP* lv (1958) 533–48; rev. and expanded in 'The Visions of *Piers Plowman* and the *Faerie Queene*', *Eng. Inst. Essays 1961*, 1–34. [Cited as 1958/61.]

HAMILTON, A. C. '"Like race to runne": the parallel structure of the *Faerie Queene* I and II', *PMLA* lxxiii (1958) 327–34. [Cited as 1958a.]

HAMILTON, A. C. 'A theological reading of the *Faerie Queene* II', *ELH* xxv (1958) 155–62. [Cited as 1958b.]

HAMILTON, A. C. 'Spenser's treatment of myth', *ELH* xxvi (1959) 335–54.

HAMILTON, A. C. *The Structure of Allegory in the 'Faerie Queene'*. Oxford 1961.

HAMILTON, A. C. 'The modern study of Renaissance English literature: a critical survey', *MLQ* xxvi (1965) 150–83.

HAMILTON, A. C. 'Spenser's pastoral', *ELH* xxxiii (1966) 518–31.

HAMILTON, A. C., ed. *Edmund Spenser: selected poetry*. New York 1966.

HAMILTON, A. C. 'Spenser and the common reader', *ELH* xxxv (1968) 618–33.

HAMILTON, A. C. 'The *Faerie Queene*', in Robert M. Lumiansky and Herschel Baker, ed. *Critical Approaches to Six Major English Works*. Philadelphia 1968, 132–66.

HAMILTON, A. C., ed. *Essential Articles for the Study of Edmund Spenser*. Hamden, Conn. 1972.

HAMILTON, A. C. '"Our new poet": Spenser, "well of English undefyld"', in Kennedy and Reither, ed. *Theatre* (1973) 101–23 q.v.; rptd Hamilton, ed. *Essential Articles*, q.v.

HAMILTON, A. C. 'On annotating Spenser's *Faerie Queene*: a new approach to the poem', in Frushell and Vondersmith, ed. *Contemporary Thought* (1975) 41–60, q.v.

HANKINS, JOHN ERSKINE. *Source and Meaning in Spenser's Allegory: a study of the 'Faerie Queene'*. Oxford 1971.

HARINGTON, SIR JOHN. *'Orlando Furioso' in English Heroical Verse*. 1591.

HARPER, CARRIE A. *The Sources of the British Chronicle History in Spenser's 'Faerie Queene'*. Philadelphia 1910.

HARRIS, VICTOR. *All Coherence Gone*. Chicago 1949.

HARRISON, THOMAS P. *They Tell of Birds: Chaucer, Spenser, Milton, Drayton*. Austin 1956.

HARVEY, GABRIEL. *Works*, ed. Alexander B. Grosart. 1884–5.

HARVEY, GABRIEL. *Letter-book*, ed. Edward J. L. Scott. 1884.

HASKER, RICHARD. 'Spenser's "vaine delight"', *MLN* lxii (1947) 334–5.

HAWKINS, HARRIETT. 'Spenser's wanton maidens', *PMLA* lxxxviii (1973) 1185–7.

HAWKINS, SHERMAN. 'Mutabilitie and the cycle of the months', *Eng. Inst. Essays 1961*, 76–102.

HAZLITT, WILLIAM. *Lectures on the English Poets.* 1818.

HENINGER, S. K., JR. 'The Orgoglio episode in the *Faerie Queene*', *ELH* xxvi (1959) 171–87; rptd Hamilton, ed. *Essential Articles*, *q.v.*

HENINGER, S. K., JR. *A Handbook of Renaissance Meteorology.* Durham, N.C. 1960.

HENINGER, S. K., JR. *'Touches of sweet harmony': Pythagorean cosmology and Renaissance poetics.* San Marino 1974.

HERRICK, ROBERT. *Poetical Works*, ed. L. C. Martin. Oxford 1956.

HIEATT, A. KENT. 'Spenser's Atin from *Atine?'* *MLN* lxxii (1957) 249–51.

HIEATT, A. KENT. *Short Time's Endless Monument: the symbolism of the numbers in Spenser's 'Epithalamion'.* New York 1960.

HIEATT, A. KENT. 'Scudamour's practice of "maistrye" upon Amoret', *PMLA* lxxvii (1962) 509–10; rptd Hamilton, ed. *Essential Articles*, *q.v.*

HIEATT, A. KENT. 'Milton's Comus and Spenser's false Genius', *UTQ* xxxviii (1969) 313–18.

HIEATT, A. KENT, and HIEATT, CONSTANCE, ed. *Spenser: selected poetry.* New York 1970.

HIEATT, A. KENT. 'Three fearful symmetries and the meaning of *Faerie Queene* II', in Kennedy and Reither, ed. *Theatre* (1973) 19–52 *q.v.*

HIEATT, A. KENT. *Chaucer, Spenser, Milton: mythopoeic continuities and transformations.* Montreal 1975.

HIEATT, A. KENT. 'A Spenser to structure our myths (Medina, Phaedria, Proserpina, Acrasia, Venus, Isis)', in Frushell and Vondersmith, ed. *Contemporary Thought* (1975) 99–120 *q.v.* [Cited as 1975a.]

HILL, IRIS TILLMAN. 'Britomart and "Be bold, Be not too bold"', *ELH* xxxviii (1971) 173–8.

HOLAHAN, M. N. *'Iamque opus exegi*: Ovid's changes and Spenser's brief epic of mutability', *ELR* vi (1976) 244–70.

HOLINSHED, RAPHAEL. *Chronicles of England, Scotland, and Ireland* (1577, 1587); ed. H. Ellis 1807–8. Volume i contains William Harrison, 'An historicall description of the ilande of Britaine'.

HOLLAND, JOANNE FIELD. 'The Cantos of Mutabilitie and the form of the *Faerie Queene*', *ELH* xxxv (1968) 21–31.

HOLLANDER, JOHN. *The Untuning of the sky: ideas of music in English poetry 1500–1700.* Princeton 1961.

HOLLANDER, JOHN. 'Spenser and the mingled measure', *ELR* i (1971) 226–38.

HONIG, EDWIN. *Dark Conceit: the making of allegory.* Evanston 1959.

HOOKER, RICHARD. *Works*, ed. John Keble. Oxford 1888.

HOTSON, LESLIE. 'The Blatant Beast', in *Studies in honor of T. W. Baldwin.* Urbana 1958, 34–7.

HOUGH, GRAHAM. *A Preface to the 'Faerie Queene'.* 1962.

HOUGH, GRAHAM, ed. Dixon, *The First Commentary*, *q.v.*

HUGHES, J., ed. *Spenser: works.* 1715; rev. edn 1750.

HUGHES, MERRITT Y. 'Burton on Spenser', *PMLA* xli (1926) 545–67.

HUGHES, MERRITT Y. *Virgil and Spenser.* Berkeley 1929.

HUGHES, ROBERT. *Heaven and Hell in Western Art.* 1968.

HUME, KATHRYN. 'Leprosy or syphilis in Henryson's "Testament of Cresseid"', *ELN* vi (1969) 242–5.

JANSON, H. W. *Apes and Ape Lore in the Middle Ages and the Renaissance.* 1952.

JOHNSON, FRANCIS R. *Astronomical Thought in Renaissance England.* Baltimore 1937.

JONES, H. S. V. *A Spenser Handbook.* New York 1930.

JONSON, BEN. *Works*, ed. C. H. Herford, Percy Simpson, and Evelyn Simpson. Oxford 1925–52.

JONSON, BEN. *Conversations with William Drummond* (1619); ed. G. B. Harrison. 1923.

JORTIN, J. *Remarks on Spenser's Poems.* 1734.

JOYCE, P. W. *The Wonders of Ireland.* Dublin 1911.

JUDSON, ALEXANDER C. *Spenser in Southern Ireland.* Bloomington 1933.

JUVENAL. *The Sixteen Satires*, trans. Peter Green. Penguin 1967.

KANTOROWICZ, ERNST. H. *The King's Two Bodies.* Princeton 1957.

KASKE, CAROL V. 'The dragon's spark and sting and the structure of Red Cross's dragon-fight: the *Faerie Queene* I xi–xii', *SP* lxvi (1969) 609–38; rptd Hamilton, ed. *Essential Articles*, *q.v.*

KASKE, CAROL V. 'The Bacchus who wouldn't wash: *Faerie Queene* II i–ii', *Ren. Q* xxix (1976) 195–209.

KEATS, JOHN. *Letters*, ed. Hyder Rollins. Cambridge, Mass. 1958.

KELLOGG, ROBERT, and STEELE, OLIVER, ed. *The 'Faerie Queene' I, II, and the 'Mutabilitie Cantos' and selections from the minor poetry.* New York 1965.

KENDRICK, T. D. *British Antiquity.* 1950.

KENNEDY, JUDITH M., and REITHER, JAMES A., ed. *A Theatre for Spenserians.* Toronto 1973. [Cited as *Theatre*.]

KENNEDY, WILLIAM J. 'Rhetoric, allegory, and dramatic modality in Spenser's Fradubio episode', *ELR* iii (1973) 351–68.

KERMODE, FRANK. 'A Spenser crux: the *Faerie Queene* II v 12.7–9', *N&Q* 197 (1952) 161.

KERMODE, FRANK., ed. *Spenser: selections from the minor poems and the 'Faerie Queene'.* 1965.

KERMODE, FRANK. *The Sense of an Ending: studies in the theory of fiction.* New York 1967.

KERMODE, FRANK. *Shakespeare, Spenser, Donne.* 1971.

KITCHIN, G. W., ed. *The 'Faerie Queene'.* Book I. Oxford 1905; Book II. Oxford 1872.

KLIBANSKY, RAYMOND, PANOFSKY, ERWIN, and SAXL, FRITZ. *Saturn and Melancholy.* 1964.

KNIGHT, W. NICHOLAS. 'The narrative unity of the *Faerie Queene* V: "That part of Justice which is Equity"', *RES* xxi (1970) 267–94.

KOCHER, PAUL H. *Science and Religion in Elizabethan England.* San Marino 1953.

KOSTIĆ, VESELIN. 'Spenser and the Bembian linguistic theory', *Eng. Misc.* (Rome) x (1959) 43–60.

KUNZ, GEORGE FREDERICK. *The Curious Lore of Precious Stones.* Philadelphia 1913.

LANGLAND, WILLIAM. *The Vision of William concerning Piers the Plowman*, ed. W. W. Skeat. Oxford 1869, 1886.

LANHAM, RICHARD A. 'The literal Britomart', *MLQ* xxviii (1967) 426–45.

LA PRIMAUDAYE, PIERRE DE. *The French Academie.* 1618.

LEISHMAN, J. B. *Themes and Variations in Shakespeare's Sonnets.* 1961.

LEVIN, HARRY. *The Myth of the Golden Age in the Renaissance.* Bloomington 1969.

LEWIS, C. S. *The Allegory of Love.* Oxford 1936.

LEWIS, C. S. *English Literature in the Sixteenth Century excluding Drama.* Oxford 1954.

LEWIS, C. S. *The Discarded Image: an introduction to medieval and Renaissance literature.* Cambridge 1964.

LEWIS, C. S. *Studies in Medieval and Renaissance Literature*, ed. W. Hooper. Cambridge 1966.

LEWIS, C. S. *Spenser's Images of Life*, ed. Alastair Fowler. Cambridge 1967.

LINCHE, R. *The Fountaine of Ancient Fiction*. 1599.

LORD, GEORGE DE FOREST. *Homeric Renaissance: the 'Odyssey' of George Chapman*. 1956.

LORRIS, GUILLAUME DE. See *Roman de la Rose*.

LOTSPEICH, HENRY GIBBONS. *Classical Mythology in the Poetry of Edmund Spenser*. Princeton 1932.

LOWELL, JAMES RUSSELL. 'Spenser', *North Amer. Rev.* cxx (1875) 334–94.

LYLY, JOHN. *Works*, ed. R. W. Bond. Oxford 1902.

MACAULAY, G. C. Review of J. C. Smith, ed., *Spenser's 'Faerie Queene'*, *MLR* v (1910) 370–4.

MCELDERRY, BRUCE ROBERT, JR. 'Archaism and innovation in Spenser's poetic diction', *PMLA* xlvii (1932) 144–70.

MACINTYRE, JEAN. 'Spenser's *Faerie Queene* III xi 47–48', *Explicator* xxiv (1966) Item 69.

MACINTYRE, JEAN. 'The *Faerie Queene* I: toward making it more teachable', *College English* xxxi (1970) 473–82.

MACLURE, MILLAR. 'Nature and art in the *Faerie Queene*', *ELH* xxviii (1961) 1–20; rptd Hamilton, ed. *Essential Articles, q.v.*

MCMANAWAY, JAMES G. '"Occasion" in the *Faerie Queene* II iv 4–5', *MLN* xlix (1934) 391–3.

MCNEIR, WALDO F. 'Ariosto's Sospetto, Gascoigne's Suspicion, and Spenser's Malbecco', in *Festschrift für Walther Fischer*, Heidelberg 1959, 34–48.

MCNEIR, WALDO F. 'Trial by combat in Elizabethan literature', *NS* xv (1966) 101–12.

MCNEIR, WALDO F. 'The sacrifice of Serena: the *Faerie Queene* VI viii 31–51', in B. Fabian and U. Suerbaum, ed. *Festschrift für Edgar Mertner*, Munich 1968, 117–56.

MACROBIUS. *Commentary on the Dream of Scipio*, trans. William Harris Stahl. New York 1952.

MACROBIUS. *The Saturnalia*, trans. Percival Vaughan Davies. New York 1969.

MAGILL, A. J. 'Spenser's Guyon and the mediocrity of the Elizabethan settlement', *SP* lxvii (1970) 167–77.

MAJOR, JOHN M. '*Paradise Regained* and Spenser's legend of Holiness', *Ren. Q.* xx (1967) 465–70.

MALORY, SIR THOMAS. *Works*, ed. E. Vinaver. Oxford 1947.

MALYNES, GERARD DE. *Saint George for England, allegorically described*. 1601.

MAPLET, JOHN. *A Greene Forest, or a naturall historie* (1567); ed. W. H. Davies. 1930.

MARLOWE, CHRISTOPHER. *Complete Plays*, ed. Irving Ribner. New York 1963.

MAROTTI, ARTHUR F. 'Animal symbolism in the *Faerie Queene*: tradition and the poetic context', *SEL* v (1965) 69–86.

MAXWELL, J. C. 'The truancy of Calidore', *ELH* xix (1952) 143–9.

MEISS, MILLARD, ed. *De Artibus Opuscula XL: essays in honor of Erwin Panofsky*. Zurich 1960.

MILLER, LEWIS H., JR. 'Phaedria, Mammon, and Sir Guyon's education by error', *JEGP* lxiii (1964) 33–44.

MILLER, LEWIS H., JR. 'A secular reading of the *Faerie Queene* II', *ELH* xxxiii (1966) 154–69; rptd Hamilton, ed. *Essential Articles, q.v.*

MILLER, LEWIS H., JR. 'The ironic mode in the *Faerie Queene* I and II', *PLL* vii (1971) 133–49.

MILLICAN, C. BOWIE. 'Spenser's and Drant's poetic names for Elizabeth: Tanaquil, Gloriana, and Una', *HLQ* ii (1939)

251–63.

MILLS, JERRY LEATH. 'Spenser's Castle of Alma and the number 22: a note on symbolic stanza placement', *N&Q* 212 (1967) 456–7.

MILLS, JERRY LEATH. 'Symbolic tapestry in the *Faerie Queene* II ix 33', *PQ* xlix (1970) 568–9.

MILLS, JERRY LEATH. 'Spenser, Lodowick Bryskett, and the Mortalist controversy: the *Faerie Queene* II ix 22', *PQ* lii *PQ* lv (1976) 281–6.

MILLS, JERRY LEATH. 'Spenser and the numbers of history: a note on the British and Elfin chronicles in the *Faerie Queene*', *PQ* lv (1976) 281–60.

MILLS, LAURENS J. *One Soul in Bodies Twain*. Bloomington 1937.

MILNE, FRED L. 'The doctrine of act and potency: a metaphysical ground for interpretation of Spenser's Garden of Adonis passages', *SP* lxx (1973) 279–87.

MILTON, JOHN. *Complete Prose Works*, ed. Don M. Wolfe *et al.* New Haven 1953–   .

MILTON, JOHN. *Complete Poems and Major Prose*, ed. Merritt Y. Hughes. New York 1957.

MILTON, JOHN. *Poems*, ed. J. Carey and Alastair Fowler. 1968.

MISKIMIN, ALICE S. *The Renaissance Chaucer*. New Haven 1975.

MORE, HENRY. Ψυχωδια *Platonica*. 1642.

MORGAN, KENNETH SCOTT. 'Formal style in the *Faerie Queene*', unpublished doctoral dissertation. Princeton University 1966.

MOUNTS, CHARLES E. 'Spenser's seven bead-men and the corporal works of mercy', *PMLA* liv (1939) 974–80.

MUELLER, WILLIAM R., and ALLEN, DON CAMERON, ed. '*That soueraine light*': *essays in honor of Edmund Spenser, 1552–1952*. Baltimore 1952.

MURRIN, MICHAEL. *The Veil of Allegory: allegorical rhetoric in the English Renaissance*. Chicago 1969.

MURRIN, MICHAEL. 'The rhetoric of fairyland', in Thomas O. Sloan and Raymond B. Waddington, ed. *The Rhetoric of Renaissance Poetry from Wyatt to Milton*. Berkeley 1974, 73–95.

MURTAUGH, DANIEL M. 'The garden and the sea: the topography of the *Faerie Queene* III', *ELH* xl (1973) 325–38.

MUSAEUS. *Hero and Leander*, trans. George Chapman (1616); in *Homer's 'Batrachomyomachina'*, etc., ed. Richard Hooper. 1888.

NASHE, THOMAS. *Works*, ed. Ronald B. McKerrow. Oxford 1904–10.

NEILL, KERBY. 'The *Faerie Queene* and the Mary Stuart controversy', *ELH* ii (1935) 192–214.

NEILL, KERBY. 'The degradation of the Red Cross Knight', *ELH* xix (1952) 173–90.

NELLIST, B. 'The allegory of Guyon's voyage: an interpretation', *ELH* xxx (1963) 89–196; rptd Hamilton, ed. *Essential Articles, q.v.*

NELSON, HERBERT B. 'Amidas v. Bracidas', *MLQ* i (1940) 393–9.

NELSON, WILLIAM. 'A source for Spenser's Malbecco', *MLN* lxviii (1953) 226–9.

NELSON, WILLIAM. *The Poetry of Spenser: a study*. New York 1963.

NELSON, WILLIAM, ed. *Selected Poetry of Spenser*. New York 1964.

NELSON, WILLIAM. 'Queen Elizabeth, Spenser's Mercilla, and a rusty sword', *Ren. News* xviii (1965) 113–17.

NELSON, WILLIAM. 'Spenser *ludens*', in Kennedy and Reither, ed. *Theatre* (1973) 83–100 *q.v.*

NESTRICK, WILLIAM V. 'The virtuous and gentle discipline of

gentlemen and poets', *ELH* xxix (1962) 357–71.

NEUSE, RICHARD. 'Book VI as conclusion to the *Faerie Queene*', *ELH* xxxv (1968) 329–53; rptd Hamilton, ed. *Essential Articles*, *q.v.*

NEVO, RUTH. 'Spenser's "Bower of Bliss" and a key metaphor from Renaissance poetic', in D. A. Fineman, ed. *Studies in Western Literature, Scripta Hierosolymitana* 10, Jerusalem 1962; rptd Hamilton, ed. *Essential Articles*, *q.v.*

NICHOLS, JOHN. *The Progresses and Public Processions of Queen Elizabeth*. 1823.

NICOLSON, MARJORIE H. *A World in the Moon. Smith College Stud.* xvii (1936).

NICOLSON, MARJORIE H. *Mountain Gloom and Mountain Glory*. Ithaca 1959.

NOHRNBERG, JAMES. *The Analogy of the 'Faerie Queene'*. Princeton 1976.

NORTHROP, DOUGLAS A. 'Spenser's defence of Elizabeth', *UTQ* xxxviii (1969) 277–94.

NORTHROP, DOUGLAS A. 'Mercilla's court as Parliament', *HLQ* xxxvi (1973) 153–8.

NOTCUTT, H. CLEMENT. 'The *Faerie Queene* and its critics', *E&S* xii (1926) 63–85.

OAKESHOTT, WALTER. *The Queen and the Poet*. 1960.

OAKESHOTT, WALTER. 'Carew Ralegh's copy of Spenser', *The Library*, 5th ser. xxvi (1971) 1–21.

O'CONNELL, MICHAEL. 'History and the poet's golden world: the epic catalogues in the *Faerie Queene*', *ELR* iv (1974) 241–67.

OKERLUND, ARLENE N. 'Spenser's wanton maidens: reader psychology and the Bower of Bliss', *PMLA* lxxxviii (1973) 62–8.

ONIONS, C. T. *A Shakespeare Glossary*. Oxford 1919.

ORANGE, LINWOOD E. 'Spenser's *Faerie Queene* IV ix 30.5–9', *Explicator* xvii (Dec. 1958) item 22.

ORANGE, LINWOOD E. '"All bent to mirth": Spenser's humorous wordplay', *South Atlantic Quart.* lxxi (1972) 539–47.

ORUCH, JACK B. 'Spenser, Camden, and the poetic marriages of rivers', *SP* lxiv (1967) 606–24.

OSGOOD, CHARLES G. 'Spenser's English rivers', *Trans. Connecticut Acad.* xxiii (1920) 65–108.

OSGOOD, CHARLES G., ed. *Boccaccio on Poetry*. New York 1956.

OWEN, LEWIS J. 'Mutable in eternity: Spenser's despair and the multiple forms of Mutabilitie', *Jnl Med. Ren. Stud.* ii (1972) 49–68.

OWEN, W. J. B. 'The structure of the *Faerie Queene*', *PMLA* lxviii (1953) 1079–1100.

PADELFORD, F. M. *The Political and Ecclesiastical Allegory of the 'Faerie Queene' I*. Boston 1911.

PADELFORD, F. M., and O'CONNOR, MATTHEW. 'Spenser's use of the St George legend', *SP* xxiii (1926) 142–56.

PAINTER, WILLIAM. *The Palace of Pleasure* (1566–67); ed. J. Jacobs 1890.

PANOFSKY, ERWIN. *Studies in Iconology: humanistic themes in the art of the Renaissance*. 1939, 1962.

PANOFSKY, ERWIN. *Meaning in the Visual Arts*. New York 1955.

PARACELSUS. *Selected Writings*, trans. Norbert Guterman; ed. Jolande Jacobi. 1951.

PARKER, MOTHER MARY PAULINE. *The Allegory of the 'Faerie Queene'*. Oxford 1960.

PARTRIDGE, ERIC. *Shakespeare's Bawdy*. 1947; rev. edn 1969.

PERCIVAL, H. M., ed. *The 'Faerie Queene' I*. 1893.

PERRY, T. A. 'Proteus, wry-transformed traveller', *SQ* v (1954) 33–40.

PHILLIPS, JAMES E. 'The background of Spenser's attitude

toward women rulers', *HLQ* v (1942) 5–32.

PHILLIPS, JAMES E. 'The woman ruler in Spenser's *Faerie Queene*', *HLQ* v (1942) 211–34.

PHILLIPS, JAMES E. *Images of a Queen: Mary Stuart in sixteenth-century literature*. Berkeley 1964.

PHILLIPS, JAMES E. 'Spenser's syncretistic religious imagery', *ELH* xxxvi (1969) 110–30.

PHILLIPS, JAMES E. 'Renaissance concepts of justice and the structure of the *Faerie Queene* V', *HLQ* xxxiii (1970) 103–20; rptd Hamilton, ed. *Essential Articles*, *q.v.*

PLATO. *Collected Dialogues*, ed. Edith Hamilton and Huntington Cairns. New York 1961.

POTTS, ABBIE FINDLAY. *Shakespeare and the 'Faerie Queene'*. Ithaca 1958.

PRAZ, MARIO. *Studies in Seventeenth-century Imagery*. 1939–47, 1964.

QUINONES, RICARDO J. *The Renaissance Discovery of Time*. Cambridge, Mass. 1972.

RAGGIO, OLGA. 'The myth of Prometheus', *JWCI* xxi (1958) 44–62.

RALEIGH, SIR WALTER. *Poems*, ed. Agnes M. C. Latham. 1951.

RALEIGH, SIR WALTER. *Selected Prose and Poetry*, ed. Agnes M. C. Latham. 1965.

RALEIGH, WALTER. *Milton*. 1901.

RAMSAY, JUDITH C. 'The Garden of Adonis and the garden of forms', *UTQ* xxxv (1966) 188–206.

RATHBORNE, ISABEL E. *The Meaning of Spenser's Fairyland*. New York 1937.

RENWICK, W., ed. *Spenser Selections*. Oxford 1923.

RENWICK, W. *Edmund Spenser: an essay on Renaissance poetry*. 1925.

RINGLER, RICHARD N. 'Spenser's Mutabilitie Cantos', unpublished doctoral dissertation. Harvard Univ. 1961.

RINGLER, RICHARD N. 'The Faunus episode', *MP* lxiii (1966) 12–19; rptd Hamilton, ed. *Essential Articles*, *q.v.*

RINGLER, WILLIAM. 'Spenser and Thomas Watson', *MLN* lxix (1954) 484–7.

RIPA. *Iconologia* (1603). Hildesheim 1970.

ROBBINS, ROSSELL HOPE, ed. *Secular Lyrics of the XIVth and XVth Centuries*. 1952

ROBERTSON, D. W., JR. *A Preface to Chaucer*. Princeton 1962.

ROBIN, P. ANSELL. *The Old Physiology in English Literature*. 1911.

ROBIN, P. ANSELL. *Animal Lore in English Literature*. 1932.

ROBINSON, FORREST G. *The Shape of Things Known: Sidney's 'Apology' in its philosophical tradition*. Cambridge Mass. 1972.

ROCHE, THOMAS P., JR. *The Kindly Flame: a study of the 'Faerie Queene' III and IV*. Princeton 1964.

ROLLE, RICHARD [?]. *The Pricke of Conscience*, ed. Richard Morris. Berlin 1863.

Roman de la Rose, by Guillaume de Lorris and Jean de Meun, ed. Félix Lecoy. Paris 1965–70; trans. Chaucer: see *Romance of the Rose*, in Chaucer's *Poetical Works*, ed. Robinson.

ROSE, MARK. *Heroic Love: studies in Sidney and Spenser*. Cambridge, Mass. 1968.

ROSE, MARK. *Spenser's Art: a companion to the 'Faerie Queene' I*. Cambridge, Mass. 1975.

ROSENBERG, J. 'On the meaning of a Bosch drawing', in Meiss, ed. *Panofsky Essays* (1960) 422–6 *q.v.*

ROSINGER, LAWRENCE. 'Spenser's Una and Queen Elizabeth', *ELN* vi (1969) 12–17.

ROSSKY, W. 'Imagination in the English Renaissance: psychology and poetic', *S. Ren* v (1958) 49–73.

ROWLAND, BERYL. 'The "seiknes incurabill" in Henryson's *Testament of Cresseid*', *ELN* i (1964) 175–7.

ROWLAND, BERYL. *Animals with Human Faces: a guide to animal symbolism*. Knoxville 1973.

ROWLANDS, R. *A Restitution of Decayed Intelligence*. 1605.

RUSKIN, JOHN. *Works*, ed. E. T. Cook and Alexander Wedderburn. 1903–12.

SACHS, ARIEH. 'Religious despair in mediaeval literature and art', *Medieval Stud.* xxvi (1964) 231–56.

SANDYS, GEORGE. *Ovid's 'Metamorphosis', englished, mythologiz'd and represented in figures* (1632), ed. K. K. Hulley and Stanley T. Vandersall. Lincoln, Nebraska 1970.

SATTERTHWAITE, ALFRED W. *Spenser, Ronsard, and Du Bellay: a Renaissance comparison*. Princeton 1960.

SAUNDERS, J. W. 'The façade of morality', *ELH* xix (1952) 81–114.

SAWTELLE, ALICE E. [RANDALL]. *The Sources of Spenser's Classical Mythology*. Boston 1896.

SCOULAR, KITTY W. *Natural Magic: studies in the presentation of Nature in English poetry from Spenser to Marvell*. Oxford 1965.

SERVIUS. *Servii Grammatici*, ed. G. Thilo and H. Hagen. Lipsiae 1881–7.

SEZNEC, JEAN. *The Survival of the Pagan Gods*, trans. Barbara F. Sessions. Princeton 1953.

SHAKESPEARE, WILLIAM. *Complete Works*, ed. Peter Alexander. 1952.

Shakespeare's England. Oxford 1916–17.

SHROEDER, JOHN W. 'Spenser's erotic drama: the Orgoglio episode', *ELH* xxix (1962) 140–59.

SIDNEY, SIR PHILIP. *Complete Works*, ed. Albert Feuillerat. Cambridge 1912–26.

SIDNEY, SIR PHILIP. *Poems*, ed. William A. Ringler, Jr. Oxford 1962.

SIDNEY, SIR PHILIP. *An apology for poetry* (1595), ed. Geoffrey Shepherd. 1965.

SIDNEY, SIR PHILIP. *The Old Arcadia*, ed. Jean Robertson. Oxford 1973.

SIRLUCK, ERNEST. 'A note on the rhetoric of Spenser's "Despair"', *MP* clvii (1950) 8–11.

SIRLUCK, ERNEST. 'The *Faerie Queene* II and the *Nicomachean Ethics*', *MP* xlix (1952) 73–100.

SMITH, CHARLES G. *Spenser's Theory of Friendship*. Baltimore 1935.

SMITH, CHARLES G. *Spenser's Proverb Lore*. Cambridge, Mass. 1970.

SMITH, G. GREGORY, ed. *Elizabethan Critical Essays*. Oxford 1904.

SMITH, J. C., and SELINCOURT, E. DE, ed. *Spenser's Poetical Works*. Oxford 1909–10; 1 vol. edn with the Spenser–Harvey correspondence. Oxford 1912.

SMITH, ROLAND M. 'Spenser's Irish river stories', *PMLA* l (1935) 1047–56. [Cited as 1935a.]

SMITH, ROLAND M. 'Una and Duessa', *PMLA* l (1935) 917–19; see also *PMLA* lxi (1946) 592–6.

SMITH, ROLAND M. 'Spenser's tale of the two sons of Milesio', *MLQ* iii (1942) 547–57.

SMITH, ROLAND M. 'Spenser's "stony Aubrian"', *MLN* lix (1944) 1–5.

SMITH, ROLAND M. 'Origines Arthurianae: the two crosses of Spenser's Red Cross Knight', *JEGP* liv (1955) 670–83.

SNARE, GERALD. 'Spenser's fourth grace', *JWCI* xxxiv (1971) 350–5.

SNARE, GERALD. 'The poetics of vision: patterns of grace and courtesy in the *Faerie Queene* VI', *Ren. Papers* (1974) 1–8.

SNYDER, SUSAN, 'Guyon the wrestler', *Ren. N* xiv (1961) 249–52.

SONN, CARL ROBINSON. 'Sir Guyon in the Cave of Mammon', *SEL* i (1961) 17–30.

SPENS, JANET. *Spenser's 'Faerie Queene': an interpretation*. 1934.

SPENS, JANET. Review of H. C. Chang, *Allegory and Courtesy in Spenser*, *RES* ix (1958) 66–9.

SPENSER, EDMUND. *Poetical Works*, ed. J. C. Smith, q.v.

SPENSER, EDMUND. *Works: a variorum edition*, ed. E. A. Greenlaw, F. M. Padelford, C. G. Osgood, *et al.* 10 vols. Baltimore 1932–49. [Cited as *Var.*]

SPENSER, EDMUND. *A View of the Present State of Ireland*, ed. W. L. Renwick. Oxford 1970.

Spenser Allusions, see WELLS.

SPINGARN, JOEL E., ed. *Critical Essays of the Seventeenth Century*. Oxford 1908–9.

SPURGEON, PATRICK O'DYER. 'Spenser's Muses', *Ren. Papers* (1969) 15–23.

STARNES, DEWITT T. 'Spenser and the Muses', *TSE* xxii (1942) 31–58.

STARNES, DEWITT T., and TALBERT, ERNEST WILLIAM. *Classical Myth and Legend in Renaissance Dictionaries*. Chapel Hill 1955.

STARNES, DEWITT T. 'The figure Genius in the Renaissance', *S Ren* xi (1964) 234–44.

STATON, WALTER F., JR. 'Ralegh and the Amyas-Aemylia episode', *SEL* v (1965) 105–14.

STATON, WALTER F., JR. 'Italian pastorals and the conclusion of the Serena story', *SEL* vi (1966) 35–42.

STEADMAN, JOHN M. 'Una and the clergy: the ass symbol in the *Faerie Queene*', *JWCI* xxi (1958) 134–7.

STEADMAN, JOHN M. 'Spenser's house of Care: a reinterpretation', *S Ren.* vii (1960) 207–24.

STEADMAN, JOHN M. 'Spenser's *Errour* and the Renaissance allegorical tradition', *NM* lxii (1961) 22–38.

STEADMAN, JOHN M. 'The "inharmonious blacksmith": Spenser and the Pythagoras legend', *PMLA* lxxix (1964) 664–5.

STEADMAN, JOHN M. *Milton's Epic Characters*. Chapel Hill 1968.

STEINBERG, CLARENCE. 'Atin, Pyrochles, and Cymochles: on Irish emblems in the *Faerie Queene*', *NM* lxxii (1971) 749–61.

STEWART, STANLEY. *The Enclosed Garden: the tradition and the image in seventeenth-century poetry*. Madison 1966.

STOW, JOHN. *Annales*. 1598.

STRACHAN, J. *Early Bible Illustrations*. Cambridge 1957.

STRONG, ROY C. 'The popular celebration of the accession day of Queen Elizabeth I', *JWCI* xxi (1958) 86–103.

STRONG, ROY C. *Portraits of Queen Elizabeth*. Oxford 1963.

STRONG, ROY C., and DORSTEN, JAN VAN. *Leicester's Triumph*. Leiden 1964.

SVENDSEN, KESTER. *Milton and Science*. Cambridge, Mass. 1956.

TASSO, TORQUATO. *Gerusalemme Liberata*, in *Opere*, ed. E. Mazzali. Naples 1969; trans. E. Fairfax (1600), ed. R. A. Willmot 1865.

TAYLER, EDWARD W. *Nature and Art in Renaissance Literature*. New York 1964.

TERVARENT, G. DE. *Attributs et symboles dans l'art profane, 1450–1600*. Geneva 1958.

THOMPSON, CLAUD A. 'Spenser's "Many faire pourtraicts, and

many a faire feate"', *SEL* xii (1972) 21–32.

THOMSON, PATRICIA. 'Phantastes and his horoscope', *N&Q* 211 (1966) 372–5.

TILLEY, M. P. *A Dictionary of the Proverbs in England in the Sixteenth and Seventeenth Centuries.* Ann Arbor 1950.

TILLYARD, E. M. W. *The English Epic and Its Background.* 1954.

TODD, H. J., ed. *Spenser: Works.* 1805.

TONKIN, HUMPHREY. *Spenser's Courteous Pastoral: the 'Faerie Queene' VI.* Oxford 1972.

TONKIN, HUMPHREY. 'Discussing Spenser's Cave of Mammon', *SEL* xiii (1973) 1–13. [Cited as 1973a.]

TONKIN, HUMPHREY. 'Spenser's Garden of Adonis and Britomart's quest', *PMLA* lxxxviii (1973) 408–17. [Cited as 1973b.]

TOPSELL, EDWARD. *The History of Four-footed Beasts* (1607), . . . *Serpents* (1608), and . . . *Insects* (1658); facsimile of 1658 edn, 3 vols, New York 1967.

TRAVERSI, DEREK. 'Spenser's *Faerie Queene*', in Boris Ford, ed. *The Age of Chaucer* (Pelican Guide to English Literature). 1954.

TUVE, ROSEMOND. *Seasons and Months.* Paris 1933.

TUVE, ROSEMOND. *Elizabethan and Metaphysical Imagery.* Chicago 1947.

TUVE, ROSEMOND. *Allegorical Imagery: some mediaeval books and their posterity.* Princeton 1966.

TUVE, ROSEMOND. *Essays: Spenser, Herbert, Milton*, ed. Thomas P. Roche, Jr. Princeton 1970.

UPTON, J., ed. *The Faerie Queene.* 1758.

VIVES. *Instruction of a Christian Woman* (1541); in F. Watson, ed. *Vives and the Renascence Education of Women.* 1912.

WALTER, J. H. 'The *Faerie Queene*: alterations and structure', *MLR* xxxvi (1941) 37–58.

WALTON, CHARLES E. '"To maske in myrthe": Spenser's theatrical practices in the *Faerie Queene*', *Emporia State Res. Stud.* ix (1960) 7–45.

WARREN, KATE M., ed. *Spenser's 'Faerie Queene'.* 1897–1900.

WARTON, T. *Observations on the 'Faerie Queene'.* 1762.

WATERS, D. DOUGLAS. *Duessa as Theological Satire.* Columbia, Missouri 1970.

WATKINS, W. B. C. *Shakespeare and Spenser.* Princeton 1950.

WEBB, WILLIAM STANFORD. 'Virgil in Spenser's epic theory', *ELH* iv (1937) 62–84.

WEINER, ANDREW D. '"Fierce warres and faithfull loues": pattern as structure in the *Faerie Queene* I', *HLQ* xxxvii (1974) 33–57.

WELD, J. S. 'The complaint of Britomart [III iv 8–10]: word-play and symbolism', *PMLA* lxvi (1951) 548–51.

WELLS, WILLIAM, ed. *Spenser Allusions in the Sixteenth and Seventeenth Centuries, 1580–1700.* Chapel Hill 1972.

WELSFORD, ENID. *Spenser: 'Fowre Hymnes' and 'Epithalamion': a study of Spenser's doctrine of love.* Oxford 1967.

WEST, MICHAEL. 'Spenser, Everard Digby, and the Renaissance art of swimming', *Ren. Q* xxvi (1973) 11–22.

WEST, R. H. *Milton and the Angels.* Athens, Georgia 1955.

WHITAKER, VIRGIL K. *The Religious Basis of Spenser's Thought.* Stanford 1950.

WHITAKER, VIRGIL K. 'The theological structure of the *Faerie Queene* I', *ELH* xix (1952) 151–64; rptd Hamilton, ed. *Essential Articles*, q.v.

WHITAKER, VIRGIL K. Review of Waters, *Duessa as Theological Satire, Ren Q* xxv (1972) 359–61.

WHITE, T. H., ed. *The Book of Beasts: a translation from a Latin bestiary of the twelfth century.* 1954.

WHITNEY, GEOFFREY. *A Choice of Emblems.* Leiden 1586; facs. edn, Amsterdam 1969.

WICKERT, MAX A. 'Structure and ceremony in Spenser's *Epithalamion*', *ELH* xxxv (1968) 135–57.

WILLIAMS, ARNOLD. *Flower on a Lowly Stalk: the 'Faerie Queene' VI.* East Lansing 1967.

WILLIAMS, KATHLEEN. '"Eterne in mutabilitie": the unified world of the *Faerie Queene*', *ELH* xix (1952) 115–30.

WILLIAMS, KATHLEEN. 'Courtesy and pastoral in the *Faerie Queene* VI', *RES* xiii (1962) 337–46.

WILLIAMS, KATHLEEN. *Spenser's 'Faerie Queene': the world of glass.* 1966.

WILLIAMS, KATHLEEN. 'Spenser: some uses of the sea and the storm-tossed ship', *Res. Opportunities in Ren. Drama* xiii–xiv (1970–71) 135–42.

WILLIAMS, R. D., ed. Virgil, *Aeneid* III. Oxford 1962.

WILSON, ELKIN CALHOUN. *England's Eliza.* Cambridge, Mass. 1939.

WILSON, RAWDON. 'Images and "allegoremes" of time in the poetry of Spenser', *ELR* iv (1974) 56–82.

WILSON, THOMAS. *The Art of Rhetorique* (1560); ed. G. H. Mair. Oxford 1909.

WIND, EDGAR. *Pagan Mysteries in the Renaissance*, rev. edn 1967.

WINSTANLEY, LILIAN, ed. *The 'Faerie Queene' II.* Cambridge 1914; I. Cambridge 1915.

WION, PHILIP KENNEDY. 'The poetic styles of Spenser', unpublished doctoral dissertation. Yale University 1968.

WOODHOUSE, A. S. P. 'Nature and grace in the *Faerie Queene*', *ELH* xvi (1949) 194–228; rptd Hamilton, ed. *Essential Articles*, q.v.

WOODHOUSE, A. S. P. '*Comus* once more', *UTQ* xix (1950) 218–23.

WOODHOUSE, A. S. P. *The Poet and his Faith: religion and poetry in England from Spenser to Eliot and Auden.* Chicago 1965.

WRIGHT, CELESTE TURNER. 'The Amazons in Elizabeth literature', *SP* xxxvii (1940) 433–56.

WRIGHT, LOUIS B., ed. *The Elizabethans' America.* 1965.

YATES, FRANCES A. *Allegorical Portraits of Queen Elizabeth I at Hatfield.* Hatfield House Booklet no. 1.

YATES, FRANCES A. 'Elizabeth as Astraea', *JWCI* x (1947) 27–82.

YATES, FRANCES A. *The Art of Memory.* 1966.

YEATS, W. B., ed. *Selected Poetry of Spenser.* Edinburgh 1906.

YEATS, W. B. *The Cutting of an Agate.* 1912.

ZITNER, S. P., ed. *Spenser: the 'Mutabilitie Cantos'.* 1968.